	1	2
$n = 1$	1 **H** 1.008 $1s^1$	2 **He** 4.003 $1s^2$

p–block

	13 III	14 IV	15 V	16 VI	17 VII	18 VIII
$n = 2$	5 **B** 10.811 $2s^2 2p^1$	6 **C** 12.011 $2s^2 2p^2$	7 **N** 14.007 $2s^2 2p^3$	8 **O** 15.999 $2s^2 2p^4$	9 **F** 18.998 $2s^2 2p^5$	10 **Ne** 20.180 $2s^2 2p^6$
3	13 **Al** 26.982 $3s^2 3p^1$	14 **Si** 28.086 $3s^2 3p^2$	15 **P** 30.974 $3s^2 3p^3$	16 **S** 32.066 $3s^2 3p^4$	17 **Cl** 35.453 $3s^2 3p^5$	18 **Ar** 39.948 $3s^2 3p^6$
4	31 **Ga** 69.723 $4s^2 4p^1$	32 **Ge** 72.61 $4s^2 4p^2$	33 **As** 74.922 $4s^2 4p^3$	34 **Se** 78.96 $4s^2 4p^4$	35 **Br** 79.904 $4s^2 4p^5$	36 **Kr** 83.80 $4s^2 4p^6$
5	49 **In** 114.82 $5s^2 5p^1$	50 **Sn** 118.71 $5s^2 5p^2$	51 **Sb** 121.75 $5s^2 5p^3$	52 **Te** 127.60 $5s^2 5p^4$	53 **I** 126.906 $5s^2 5p^5$	54 **Xe** 131.29 $5s^2 5p^6$
6	81 **Tl** 204.383 $6s^2 6p^1$	82 **Pb** 207.2 $6s^2 6p^2$	83 **Bi** 208.980 $6s^2 6p^3$	84 **Po** (209) $6s^2 6p^4$	85 **At** (210) $6s^2 6p^5$	86 **Rn** (222) $6s^2 6p^6$

d–block

	10	11	12
$n = 3$	28 **Ni** 58.69 $4s^2 3d^8$	29 **Cu** 63.546 $4s^1 3d^{10}$	30 **Zn** 65.39 $4s^2 3d^{10}$
4	46 **Pd** 106.42 $4d^{10}$	47 **Ag** 107.868 $5s^1 4d^{10}$	48 **Cd** 112.411 $5s^2 4d^{10}$
5	78 **Pt** 195.08 $6s^1 5d^9$	79 **Au** 196.967 $6s^1 5d^{10}$	80 **Hg** 200.59 $6s^2 5d^{10}$

f–block

$n = 4$	64 **Gd** 157.25 $6s^2 5d^1 4f^7$	65 **Tb** 158.925 $6s^2 4f^9$	66 **Dy** 162.50 $6s^2 4f^{10}$	67 **Ho** 164.93 $6s^2 4f^{11}$	68 **Er** 167.26 $6s^2 4f^{12}$	69 **Tm** 168.934 $6s^2 4f^{13}$	70 **Yb** 173.04 $6s^2 4f^{14}$
5	96 **Cm** (247) $7s^2 6d^1 5f^7$	97 **Bk** (247) $7s^2 5f^9$	98 **Cf** (251) $7s^2 5f^{10}$	99 **Es** (252) $7s^2 5f^{11}$	100 **Fm** (257) $7s^2 5f^{12}$	101 **Md** (258) $7s^2 5f^{13}$	102 **No** (259) $7s^2 5f^{14}$

PREFACE

You, our audience, are a diverse group because chemistry underlies fields extending from biology and geology, through medicine and pharmacy, to engineering and materials science. Consequently, a textbook must present general chemistry so that whatever your discipline, you can appreciate the elegance of chemistry and master its fundamental concepts. Regardless of where your interests lie, however, the important chemical properties and principles remain the same. These chemical properties and principles are the core of our presentation.

Chemistry is a mature science in the sense that the atomic theory, its primary unifying theme, is nearly 300 years old. Yet it is a surprisingly young science bursting with the excitement of new discoveries such as buckminsterfullerene, taxol, and superconductivity as well as new challenges such as the causes and control of the ozone hole and new drugs to combat AIDS. An introductory chemistry textbook must focus on basic concepts whose validity is well established, and we do this. At the same time, however, the vibrancy and excitement of chemistry centers on what is newly discovered and as yet imperfectly understood. We try to capture this by introducing some of the "cutting edge" developments that chemists were exploring while we were writing this textbook.

ORGANIZATION AND EMPHASES

The title of this book, *Chemistry: The Molecular Science*, reveals our primary unifying theme. This book emphasizes the molecular view of chemical principles because practicing chemists visualize chemical processes at the molecular level. A chemist sees a pot of boiling water and thinks instinctively of water molecules moving from the liquid phase to the gas phase. In every chapter, you will find molecular descriptions and molecular pictures, and you will be asked to visualize how molecules behave and to draw molecular pictures.

Chemistry is molecular, but at the same time it is quantitative. For this reason, a second main thread running through our text is the presentation and use of the quantitative equations of basic chemistry. Qualitative concepts always underlie quantitative equations, however, so our presentation always seeks to buttress quantitative ideas with their conceptual foundations.

The power of quantitative relationships lies in their applications. In presenting equations, therefore, we not only outline their underlying logic, but also illustrate how they are applied to chemical problems. Sample Problems describe these applications and illuminate the conceptual approaches to problem solving and its mechanical aspects. Even though we set them off from the narrative text, we expect you to read the Sample Problems as part of the flow of the chapter.

The various topics within general chemistry present a rich tapestry in which each topic connects with many others. The linear presentation of a textbook cannot show the full richness of these connections, and there is no sequence of topics that avoids cross-references, both forward and backward. Our sequence starts with the molecular composition of matter and a description of chemical reactions and builds an understanding of a variety of chemical topics on those fundamental ideas.

Throughout this development, we describe how substances behave in the context of the concepts presented. This interweaving of concepts and descriptions presents chemistry as chemists understand it, a blend of principles and properties that illumi-

To all those students whose determination to
learn chemistry inspired us to write this book

Dedicated to Publishing Excellence

Editor-in-Chief: James M. Smith
Developmental Editor: John S. Murdzek
Project Manager: Carol Sullivan Wiseman
Senior Production Editor: Pat Joiner
Designer: William A. Seabright
Design Manager: Betty Schulz
Manufacturing Supervisor: John Babrick
Art Developer: John S. Murdzek
Illustrations: ArtScribe, Inc., and J/B Woolsey Associates
Photo Researchers: Patrick Watson, John S. Murdzek
Photographer: Patrick Watson
Cover Design: David Zielinski, Jill Papke

Printed in the United States of America
Composition by Graphic World, Inc.
Printing/binding by Von Hoffmann Press

Mosby–Year Book, Inc.
11830 Westline Industrial Drive
St. Louis, Missouri 63146

Library of Congress Cataloging in Publication Data

Olmsted, John III
Chemistry, the molecular science / John Olmsted III, Gregory M. Williams
p. cm.
Includes index.
ISBN 0-8016-7485-9
1. Chemistry. I. Williams, Gregory M. II. Title.
QD33.046 1994
540—dc20 93-37165
CIP

94 95 96 97 98 / 9 8 7 6 5 4 3 2

Chemistry
THE MOLECULAR SCIENCE

John Olmsted III
CALIFORNIA STATE UNIVERSITY, FULLERTON
FULLERTON, CALIFORNIA

Gregory M. Williams
CALIFORNIA STATE UNIVERSITY, FULLERTON
FULLERTON, CALIFORNIA

with 1033 illustrations, including 920 in color

St. Louis Baltimore Boston Chicago London Madrid Philadelphia Sydney Toronto

Our cover highlights one chemical compound, ascorbic acid (vitamin C), at the macroscopic, microscopic, and molecular levels. Oranges are an important dietary source of this essential vitamin. The ball-and-stick model shows how vitamin C is put together from six carbon atoms (black), six oxygen atoms (red), and eight hydrogen atoms (white). Behind the model is a photograph of microscopic crystals of ascorbic acid.

The photograph shows a photoelectrochemical cell used in research studies on the storage of solar energy in a chemical fuel. Here, hydrogen gas is produced by light shining on the surface of solid silicon immersed in a liquid solution of hydrochloric acid. The three expanded images show the molecular compositions of the three phases, which display distinctively different atomic and molecular structures.

Chemistry
THE MOLECULAR SCIENCE

CONTENTS

CONTENTS IN BRIEF

beauty and readability of the page layout are due entirely to their editing and design skills. Kay Kramer, Jeanne Wolfgeher, and Betty Schulz created a book design that enhances the text without overpowering its purpose, which is to teach you chemistry.

Illustrations can powerfully assist learning, and we hope that the illustrations in this text make it easier for you to grasp chemical concepts. Several talented individuals are responsible for the quality of our illustrations. Patrick Watson took many of the photos and located sources for many of the others. Carolyn Duffy and Greg Holt, who are ArtScribe, Inc., and the artists at J/B Woolsey Associates created elegant four-color artwork from our crude black-and-white sketches.

Our writing has been tempered in the crucible of peer review and criticism. A legion of professors agreed to assist in this role, and they provided us with a wealth of insights that far surpassed our own. All of those listed below contributed to our endeavor, but we wish particularly to thank Allan Burkett, Donald Campbell, John Rund, Paul Hunter, Glenn Kuehn, and Larry Peck. These individuals reviewed our work repeatedly and in detail and always told us explicitly what they thought we were doing wrong while at the same time encouraging us to make things right.

Every student knows that writing is time intensive and that good writing requires focused concentration for blocks of time. In this regard, writing a textbook is no different from other writing. We owe an immense debt to those who permitted us to devote to this project the time required for its completion. Above all, we are indebted to our wives, Eileen and Trudy, who did not realize at the outset how extensive our time commitments would become but who have borne with us understandingly despite several years of long evenings and lost weekends.

Bruce Ault
University of Cincinnati

Caroline Ayers
East Carolina University

George Baldwin
University of Manitoba

Jon M. Bellama
University of Maryland

Allan R. Burkett
Dillard University

Donald Campbell
University of Wisconsin–Eau Claire

John F. Cannon
Brigham Young University

Grover W. Everett
University of Kansas

Michael D. Fryzuk
University of British Columbia

Steven D. Gammon
University of Idaho

Michael F. Golde
University of Pittsburgh

Paul Hunter
Michigan State University

Richard F. Jordan
University of Iowa

Paul J. Karol
Carnegie Mellon University

Robert Kiser
University of Kentucky

Joseph W. Kolis
Clemson University

David Koster
Southern Illinois University at Carbondale

Glenn D. Kuehn
New Mexico State University

Richard S. Lumpkin
University of Alabama

John Luoma
Cleveland State University

Bruce Norcross
SUNY–Binghamton

Henry Offen
University of California, Santa Barbara

M. Larry Peck
Texas A & M University

John V. Rund
University of Arizona

Martha E. Russell
Iowa State University

Sanford Safron
Florida State University

Caesar V. Senoff
University of Guelph

Joanne Stewart
Hope College

Dwight A. Sweigart
Brown University

Wayne Tikkanen
California State University at Los Angeles

Charles Trapp
University of Louisville

D. Rodney Truax
University of Calgary

John Olmsted III
Gregory M. Williams

Section Exercises appear at the end of each section and are designed to give you immediate practice in applying the concepts presented in the section. So that you can know whether or not you are reasoning correctly, we provide the answers to all Section Exercises at the end of each chapter.

At the end of each chapter, we provide material designed to engage you in active learning. For greatest effectiveness, use this material to guide the manner in which you study. A Chapter Summary provides a brief overview of the major themes of the chapter, and a list of Key Terms flags the words with which you must be familiar. Skills to Master reminds you what problem-solving techniques require your attention, whereas the Learning Exercises are qualitative questions designed to help you organize your ideas about the material in the chapter.

Proficiency in using chemical concepts comes only with practice. The chapter Problems are designed to give you the opportunity for such practice. About half of the chapter Problems are identified by the section to which they relate. One of the skills of problem solving, however, is the ability to identify the concepts underlying the problem. For this reason, we have included many problems that are not identified by section. These Additional Problems are not necessarily more difficult than those identified by section; however, by placing them randomly, we give you the opportunity to learn how to recognize problem types.

Two axioms characterize successful students, in our experience. The first is an attitude: **Be an active learner.** *Ask* questions, *seek* help from many sources, *form* study groups, *work* extra problems, and *prepare* chapter outlines. Try a combination of these and additional strategies until you find a set that works best for you. The second is a perspective: **Think molecules.** Every phenomenon in chemistry has an atomic/molecular basis that can make the phenomenon easier to understand. Ask yourself *what* the molecules are doing and *why.* Imagine yourself to be the size of a molecule and ask what you would see. Learn how to draw pictures showing what goes on at the molecular level. When you have mastered this perspective, you will have learned how to think like a chemist and will appreciate the unity of chemistry. You may even decide that you are a chemist.

ACKNOWLEDGMENTS

A textbook in general chemistry does not just happen. It is painstakingly developed over several years. Moreover, it is a team effort that consumes the attention and talents of many individuals. This text has come to fruition over a 5-year span, during which time many individuals have made essential contributions.

Our textbook began with our interactions with several generations of general chemistry students, with whom we have shared the frustrations of imperfect explanations and on whom we have tried out diverse methods of presenting elusive concepts. We have been encouraged time and again by students asking us when this book will appear and lamenting that its appearance follows their completion of the course. We are grateful to them for serving as the educational laboratory in which we improved our instructional skills.

Support and criticism from our talented editors shaped the scope, content, level, and language of our text throughout its development. Jim Smith, our executive editor, has provided unerring guidance as the text moved from a proposal through initial drafts to final product. John Murdzek, our developmental editor, kept our attention on the important details, including accuracy, continuity, and relevance. Carol Sullivan Wiseman, our project manager, and Pat Joiner, our senior production editor, converted our manuscript into the book you now hold in your hands. The nate and reinforce each other. As we present chemical principles, we also describe some of their practical applications. Because instructors differ in their beliefs about the importance of the descriptive aspects of chemistry, your instructor may place greater or lesser emphasis on these descriptive features. We have tried to write the text in a way that supports both a strong emphasis on principles and a strong emphasis on practice.

General chemistry introduces principles and properties common to all facets of the subject. To emphasize this, we use examples from inorganic, organic, industrial, and biological chemistry to illustrate underlying principles. Rather than introduce these branches of chemistry as separate topics, we weave them into our discussion wherever it seems appropriate. We hope that this approach provides insights into the close relationships among all facets of chemistry.

COVERAGE

Although there is a common core to a 1-year course in general chemistry, beyond that core is a number of topics from which each instructor makes a selection. Consequently, we present somewhat more material in this book than is likely to be covered in the usual course. Your instructor will choose to emphasize some topics beyond the core while omitting others. Several chapters contain sections that can be omitted without a loss of continuity. Chapters 10 and 18, in particular, include such optional material. In addition, Chapters 11 and 19 cover topics that, although central to the interface between chemistry and modern society, lie somewhat outside the mainstream of coverage in traditional general chemistry.

In general, our chapters begin with introductions that establish the context for the subject matter to be covered. These are followed by sequential developments of major concepts and techniques, developed using practical examples and illustrated, as much as possible, through molecular pictures. Many chapters end with sections that illustrate some important practical consequences of abstract chemical concepts. Examples are in Chapters 5 (The Earth's Atmosphere), 9 (Band Theory of Solids), 13 (Bioenergetics), 14 (Catalysis), and 17 (Metallurgy).

MASTERING CHEMISTRY

Success in general chemistry requires a blend of ingredients. It requires a clearly presented body of information; we hope you will find that in this textbook. It requires lucid instruction from a committed teacher; we hope that our text facilitates such instruction. Finally, success in chemistry requires commitment and hard work from the student. We have tried to structure the text so that it encourages that commitment and directs the work along productive lines.

Although no single formula is guaranteed to work for every type of student, there are strategies that successful students consistently recommend. Foremost among these is a focus on understanding concepts, because memorization without understanding leads to frustration, not to success. We explain principles using logical underpinnings that can make them easier to understand.

Much of chemistry is concerned with the applications of concepts to practical problems. Our text is laced with Sample Problems, Section Exercises, and chapter Problems designed to help you learn such applications. Each Sample Problem includes a brief explanation of the method, which outlines how the problem should be approached. Following the method is a step-by-step description of the solution.

CHAPTER 1

THE SCIENCE OF CHEMISTRY

1.1 WHAT IS CHEMISTRY?

1.2 THE MOLECULAR NATURE OF CHEMISTRY

1.3 THE PERIODIC TABLE OF THE ELEMENTS

1.4 CHARACTERISTICS OF MATTER

1.5 MEASUREMENTS IN CHEMISTRY

1.6 CALCULATIONS IN CHEMISTRY

1.7 CHEMICAL PROBLEM SOLVING

You are about to study the science of chemistry. Before you begin, ask yourself what chemistry is all about and why students with many different interests need to learn about chemistry. We define chemistry shortly, but a look at some of the questions that chemists are trying to answer may help you understand why this is an important, challenging, and exciting discipline:

- **Can new nontoxic and biodegradable plastics be made?**
- **What can be done to reduce water pollution?**
- **How do cells in green plants convert the energy of sunlight into energy-rich chemicals?**
- **What is the composition of the atmosphere of Jupiter?**
- **Is there a plausible chemical explanation for the formation of biochemical substances in the Earth's early atmosphere?**
- **Can electrical storage batteries be made more compact and longer lived?**
- **What occurs chemically when we see?**
- **How small can a semiconductor chip be?**
- **Are there chemical substances that can cure acquired immunodeficiency syndrome (AIDS)?**

Research chemists in laboratories worldwide are working on answers to questions such as these. These questions interest many other people, from biologists, geologists, and engineers to politicians and concerned citizens. Although we cannot answer such difficult questions in an introductory survey of chemistry, the principles in this text are the basis of advanced chemical research. As you become familiar with these principles, you may come to appreciate the possibilities and limitations of chemistry.

1.1 WHAT IS CHEMISTRY?

Science, in the broadest sense, can be viewed as our continuing attempt to organize and describe the properties of nature. Because this is an infinitely vast subject, science is subdivided into various disciplines, such as chemistry, biology, geology, and physics.

Chemistry is the branch of science that studies the properties and interactions of matter. This definition is very broad, and as Figure 1-1 demonstrates, chemistry is related to many other scientific disciplines. Chemists seek to understand how chemical transformations occur by studying the physical and chemical properties of matter. The interests of chemists often become intertwined with those of physicists, biologists, and geologists. Other scientists also study systems in which chemistry plays an important role. Thus many nonchemists are interested in chemistry. Box 1-1 provides more information about the relationship between chemistry and other disciplines.

All scientific disciplines, including chemistry, share the complementary goals of description and prediction. One major goal of scientists is to develop theories that describe as many different observations as possible. An equally important aim is the extension of those theories to predict properties that have not yet been observed. Scientists also use theories to predict the outcome of experiments that have never been performed.

A theory is a unifying principle that explains a collection of facts.

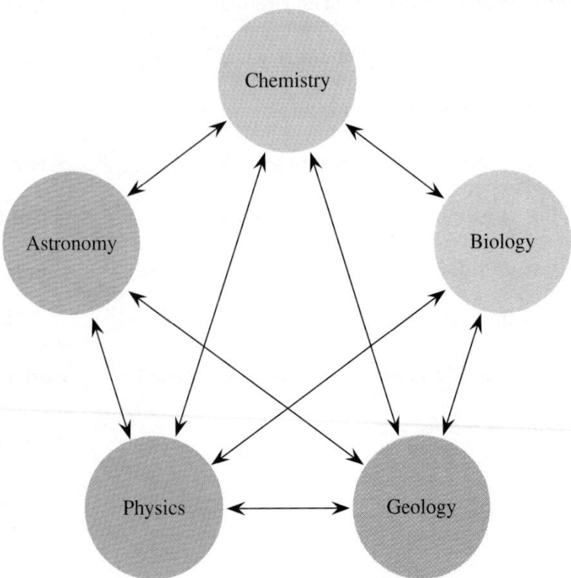

FIGURE 1-1
Schematic representation of the interrelationships among scientific disciplines.

Chemists explore the infinite variety of chemical behavior and use simplifications and generalizations to organize what they find. A common practice is to construct a theory in which a few principles describe how a system behaves. The theory can be used to predict what will happen to the system under different conditions. Chemists design and perform experiments that test whether or not a system behaves as theory predicts. If observations and experiments verify the predicted outcome, chemists become confident that the theories correctly describe how nature behaves.

In Chapter 2, we describe the atomic theory of matter, which underlies our understanding of chemical behavior.

According to the atomic theory, all matter is composed of tiny particles called *atoms.* The atomic theory was developed at the outset of the nineteenth century to explain the observations of early chemists. It was quickly found that new chemical discoveries were consistent with predictions based on the theory. Over the years the atomic theory has been expanded and refined as increasingly sophisticated chemical experiments revealed more detailed information about matter. We describe atomic theory and its applications in more depth in later chapters.

CHEMISTRY IS AN EXPERIMENTAL SCIENCE

This book describes fundamental chemical principles and chemical properties. Chemists learn about these properties and principles by designing and performing experiments that reveal how substances behave.

Chemists also construct theories to explain the results of their experiments. Some of these theories are presented in this book. Every theory is based on experimental observations, and the goal of a theory is to explain some set of experimental results. A useful theory also makes predictions about new phenomena that might be observed, and the test of any theory is whether its predictions match reality. Chemists continually test and refine chemical theories by designing and conducting new experiments.

Sometimes experiments give surprising results. An event deemed impossible by a theory may occur. It can be exciting when experimental observations contradict theoretical predictions, but chemists proceed cautiously when this happens. First,

BOX 1-1

WHY STUDY CHEMISTRY?

Most students who take an introductory course in chemistry are not chemistry majors. Their interests are in engineering, biology, physics, the health professions, geology, or agriculture. Why are you all expected to learn something about chemistry? The answer is that much of what occurs in nature has important chemical aspects. In fact, chemical principles play an important role in everything from weather patterns to brain functions to the operation of a computer. The following paragraphs give some specific examples.

For ages, farmers have known that fertilizers enhance crop yields spectacularly. Fertilizers are chemical substances that stimulate plant growth. From the chemical reactions involved in plant growth, botanists learned that all plants require nitrogen in the form of ammonia or nitrates in the soil. Further studies of plant chemistry have revealed that crops also need calcium, phosphorus, iron, and other chemical species. Gardening supply stores carry a variety of different fertilizers with different chemical compositions. The best fertilizer for a particular situation depends on the chemistry of the soil and the plant.

Oil exploration geologists study rock formations, looking for patterns that indicate where oil is likely to be found. Comparisons of the chemical constituents of rocks and petroleum deposits have revealed that characteristic chemical compounds are often found in the rock formations that surround oil deposits. By analyzing samples of rock for these telltale compounds, geologists can determine where oil is likely to be found in the Earth's crust.

A computer chip is a remarkable feat of electronic engineering. It is an equally remarkable feat of solid-state chemistry. Each chip is made of highly purified elemental silicon that has been chemically modified at the microscopic level. The modifications must be extremely precise in chemical composition and spatial organization. The quest for superminiaturized computer chips requires engineering technology to operate at the microscopic limits of chemistry.

Any disruption of the dynamic balance in an ecosystem may have far-reaching biological consequences. An ecosystem's response to change is governed by fundamental laws of chemical kinetics and thermodynamics. Kinetics describes how fast changes occur and how rates of change vary with the conditions. Thermodynamics, on the other hand, describes what is possible and impossible in any system where changes occur. To understand why an ecosystem responds to changes the way it does, a biologist must be aware of thermodynamic limits and kinetic constraints.

These examples illustrate why people who are not directly interested in chemistry must learn about the subject. The agriculturist who understands soil chemistry, the geologist who knows the chemical composition of petroleum, the engineer who is informed about solid-state chemistry, and the biologist who is knowledgeable about thermodynamics and kinetics are all at a distinct advantage as they try to master their own subjects.

they repeat the experiments to be sure that the original observations are reproducible. If the disagreement between prediction and experiment is verified, the theories must be modified. When theory and experiment disagree, the theory must be wrong. To give you some sense of the excitement that accompanies the ever-expanding field of chemistry, here are three recent developments that have affected how chemists view their subject.

Until the early 1960s the theories of chemical bonding, which describe how atoms can combine with one another, predicted that atoms of the elements known as the *rare gases* were incapable of combining with other atoms. In 1962, however, Neil Bartlett made a compound that contained xenon (one of the rare gases), fluorine, and platinum. Other chemists immediately tested Bartlett's results, and within a year at least 13 different chemical compounds containing xenon had been prepared. As a result, theories of how atoms bind together to make molecules had to be modified to take into account these experimental results.

The phenomenon of superconductivity, in which substances are able to conduct extremely high electrical currents without significant resistance, was discovered in 1911. Until recently, it was believed that superconductivity was possible only at temperatures below −250 °C. In 1986, however, several scientists discovered chemical substances with superconducting properties at temperatures up to about −200 °C. Since then, research has proceeded at a feverish pace as chemists and physicists try to synthesize chemical compounds that display superconductivity at higher and higher temperatures. They hope eventually to develop room-temperature superconductors. These would revolutionize the electrical industry by making it possible to transport electricity over long distances without significant losses caused by resistance. In addition, motors and magnets made with superconductors would be far superior to those that use standard electrical conductors. Figure 1-2 illustrates the remarkable power of superconducting magnets.

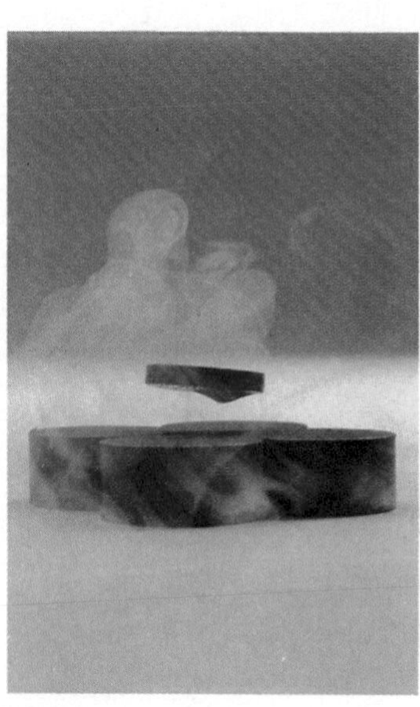

FIGURE 1-2
High-temperature superconductors make it possible to do some surprising things.

Exciting new discoveries sometimes are not verified on further study. In 1988 a pair of respected chemists reported that they had observed "cold fusion," the merging of nuclei of one form of hydrogen to form helium nuclei at room temperature. Because this was an immense departure from the predictions of theory and a potential source of unlimited, inexpensive energy, the entire world took immediate notice. Although cold fusion experiments are not difficult to perform, their results are quite difficult to interpret. Many laboratories tried to duplicate the first reports, with ambiguous and sometimes conflicting results. At publication, there has been no definite confirmation of the original reports. Research into cold fusion continues, but many scientists doubt that the original experiments were interpreted correctly. Cold fusion on a scale that would have practical applications has not been verified.

SECTION EXERCISES

1.1.1 List four ways that chemistry relates to cooking.

1.1.2 Describe how chemistry applies to the automobile industry.

1.1.3 A planetary scientist announces a theory predicting that substances on Venus react differently than they do on Earth. Write a paragraph that describes ways to test whether or not this theory is valid.

1.2 THE MOLECULAR NATURE OF CHEMISTRY

The fundamental unit of a chemical substance is called an **atom.** The word is derived from the Greek *atomos,* meaning "uncuttable." An atom is the smallest possible particle of a substance. Atoms are made up of even smaller particles, which we describe in later chapters. For now, however, you should think of atoms simply as tiny, indivisible spheres of matter.

Atoms are extremely small. Measurements show that the diameter of a single carbon atom is approximately 0.0000000003 m. To give you some idea of just how small that is, a sample of carbon the size of the period at the end of this sentence would contain more atoms than there are stars in the Milky Way. Any sample of matter large enough for us to see, feel, smell, or taste is composed of an unfathomable number of atoms.

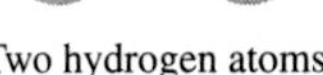

Two hydrogen atoms

One hydrogen molecule

FIGURE 1-3
A hydrogen molecule can be represented by connecting two spheres together, with each sphere representing a hydrogen atom.

MOLECULES

Atoms combine to make all substances in the world around us, but they do so in a very orderly fashion. Most substances that we encounter in our day-to-day lives are made up of small units called *molecules.* A **molecule** is a *combination* of two or more atoms held together in a *specific shape* by attractive forces. The simplest molecules contain just two atoms. For example, a molecule of hydrogen is made up of two hydrogen atoms. A molecule that contains two atoms is classified as a **diatomic molecule.** Figure 1-3 shows a representation of a diatomic hydrogen molecule as two spheres connected together.

We describe how atoms are held together in Chapters 8 and 9.

Because most chemistry deals with the behavior of molecules, this book emphasizes chemistry's molecular foundation. Throughout this book you will see many figures that represent molecules. These molecular pictures are scale models of real molecules in which each atom is represented by a colored sphere. Although 109 different types of atoms exist, only a handful are encountered frequently in our world. Many molecules described in this book are made up of just 10 different types of atoms: hydrogen, carbon, nitrogen, oxygen, phosphorus, sulfur, fluorine, chlorine, bromine, and iodine. Figure 1-4 shows the different color representations that we use for each type of atom. We introduce additional elements as the need arises. Figure 1-5 shows scale models of molecules of some substances, the names of which you may recognize.

Unfortunately the same name, *hydrogen,* is used for both atoms and molecules. To minimize confusion, we refer to *atomic hydrogen* when we mean hydrogen atoms and *molecular hydrogen* when we mean hydrogen molecules. This dual terminology also applies to fluorine, chlorine, bromine, iodine, nitrogen, and oxygen, all of which exist as diatomic molecules under most conditions.

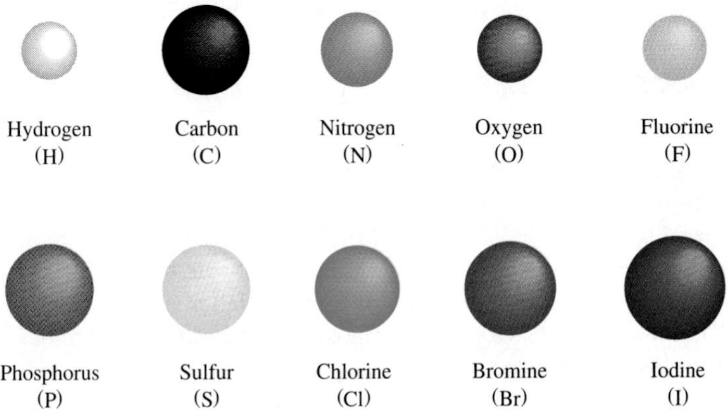

FIGURE 1-4
Scale models of the 10 atoms encountered most frequently in this book.

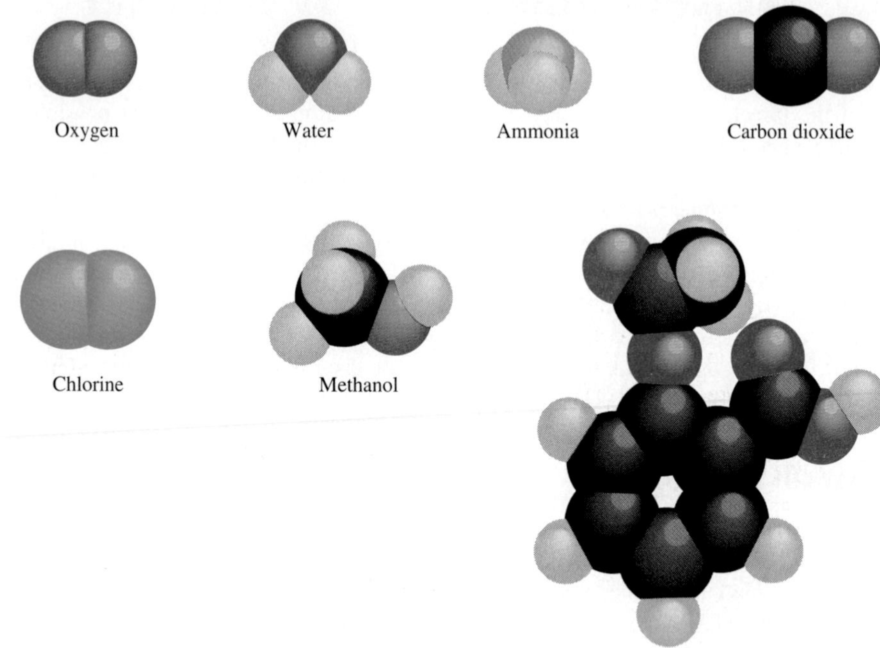

FIGURE 1-5
Scale models of oxygen, water, ammonia, carbon dioxide, chlorine, methanol, and aspirin.

We introduce the properties that give substances color in Chapter 6.

Although substances are colored, individual atoms do not have the colors shown in Figure 1-4. Individual nitrogen atoms are not blue, and oxygen atoms are not red. Elemental sulfur is yellow, but the color is a property of sulfur *molecules* in the sample. We use colored spheres because they provide a convenient way to distinguish different types of atoms in a molecular picture.

With a little practice, you can easily recognize simple molecules, such as carbon dioxide and water, just by looking at their models. The structures of larger molecules, such as aspirin, are too complex to be recognized at a glance. Consequently, chemists have created a shorthand language of symbols, formulas, and equations that convey information about atoms and molecules in a simple, straightforward manner. Symbols are used to designate each different type of atom. These symbols in turn are combined into formulas that describe the compositions of more complicated chemical substances. Formulas can then be used to write chemical equations that describe how molecules are changed in a chemical reaction.

SYMBOLS OF THE ELEMENTS

The artificial elements that have been made in recent years have three-letter symbols, as described in Box 1-2, but we do not deal with these elements.

Each different type of atom is called a **chemical element.** A chemical element is distinguished by the simplicity of its atomic composition. When a sample of a chemical element is broken down into atoms, all the atoms are the same. Each chemical element has a unique name, such as hydrogen, carbon, oxygen, uranium, tantalum, and iron. (See Box 1-2 for an overview of how elements have been named.) Each element can be represented by a unique one- or two-letter symbol. For example, the symbol for hydrogen is H, oxygen's symbol is O, and nitrogen's symbol is N. The first letter of its English name serves as the symbol for nine other elements: B, C, F, I, P, S, U, V, and Y. When more than one element begins with the same English letter, a second letter is added to the symbol. For example, carbon is C, cobalt is Co, and chromium is Cr. To a chemist the symbol for an element is not just a letter or letters. Instead, a chemist sees the symbol Ni and immediately thinks of nickel *atoms*.

BOX 1-2

NAMING ELEMENTS

Until recently the person who discovered an element named it. The name often referred to one of the element's properties. The Romans gave copper its name, *cuprum,* after the island Cyprus, where copper was mined during antiquity. Bromine, first isolated in 1826, received its name from the Greek word *bromos,* meaning "stench." If you ever work with bromine, you will understand the reason for its name.

When scientists began creating artificial elements, the naming process became somewhat more obscure. Technetium, the first element to be created in the laboratory, received its name from the Greek word for artificial, *technitos.* Neptunium and plutonium were named for planets because they were made from uranium, which is named for a planet as well. (It is uncertain why uranium is named for a planet.) The names of americium (element number 95), berkelium (97), and californium (98) honor the country, city, and state where the experiments that first manufactured them were performed. Curium (96), einsteinium (99), fermium (100), mendelevium (101), nobelium (102), and lawrencium (103) all honor famous scientists.

When elements after number 103 were created, a political impasse developed. The creations of some of these elements were reported virtually simultaneously in 1970 by scientists in what was then the Soviet Union and in the United States. Each group proposed different names. Perhaps because of the political antagonism between the two countries at that time, neither group would relinquish its "right" to name the new elements. Finally, the International Union of Pure and Applied Chemistry (IUPAC) decreed a compromise.

The IUPAC decided that the names of elements beyond number 103 should use the Latin words for their numbers: *nil-* for zero, *un-* for one, and so on. Thus element 104 becomes unnilquadium, 106 is unnilhexium, and so forth. The symbols for these elements are three letters derived from their names, so element 104 is symbolized Unq, element 106 is Unh, and so on.

Many scientists view this as an unfortunate compromise. The names are awkward to pronounce, the three-letter symbols break with tradition, and the symbols are easy to confuse because elements 104 to 109 all begin with *Un (unnil-).* Perhaps the very awkwardness of this scheme will encourage scientists to find a way to return to the tradition that gave us colorful, evocative elemental names such as xenon (from the Greek *xenos,* meaning "stranger") and rubidium (from Latin, meaning "dark red").

The elements listed in Table 1-1, most of which are metals, have symbols derived from their names in other languages. These elements were well known from early times, so their symbols reflect the Latin language that was dominant when they were named.

CHEMICAL FORMULAS

A chemical compound is a substance that contains more than one element. However, the relative amounts of each element in a particular compound do not change. Every molecule of a particular chemical substance contains a characteristic number of atoms of its constituent elements. Water molecules, for example, *always* contain two hydrogen atoms and one oxygen atom. To describe this atomic composition, chemists write the chemical formula for water as H_2O.

Not all chemical compounds exist as molecules. Some compounds are made up of chemical species called *ions.* We introduce and describe ions in Chapter 2.

TABLE 1-1 ELEMENTAL SYMBOLS WITH NON-ENGLISH ROOTS

NAME	SYMBOL	ROOT	LANGUAGE
Sodium	Na	Natrium	Latin
Potassium	K	Kalium	Latin
Iron	Fe	Ferrum	Latin
Copper	Cu	Cuprum	Latin
Silver	Ag	Argentum	Latin
Tin	Sn	Stannum	Latin
Antimony	Sb	Stibium	Latin
Tungsten	W	Wolfram	German
Gold	Au	Aurum	Latin
Mercury	Hg	Hydrargyum	Latin
Lead	Pb	Plumbum	Latin

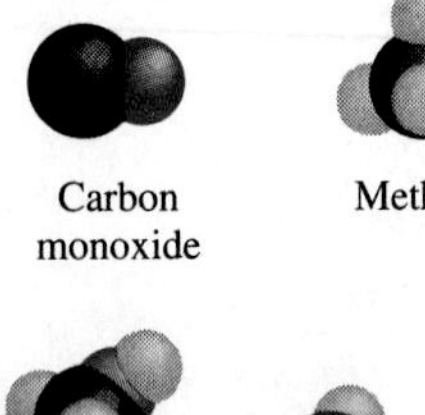

Carbon monoxide   Methane

Sucrose

We explore chemical formulas in greater detail in Chapter 3.

The chemical formula for water illustrates how formulas are constructed. The formula lists the symbols of all elements found in the chemical compound, in this case H (hydrogen) and O (oxygen). A subscript number after the elemental symbol denotes how many atoms of that element are present in the molecule. The subscript 2 in the formula for water indicates that each molecule contains two hydrogen atoms. No subscript is used when only one atom is present, as is the case for the oxygen atom in a water molecule. Molecules always contain whole numbers of atoms because atoms are indivisible. Consequently, the subscripts in chemical formulas are always integers.

Molecules vary considerably in complexity. A carbon monoxide molecule is made of one atom of carbon and one atom of oxygen, so its chemical formula is CO. Methane, the major constituent of natural gas, is somewhat more complicated. Its molecules contain one carbon atom and four hydrogen atoms, so its formula is CH_4. Cane sugar, the chemical name of which is *sucrose,* is a still more complicated combination of carbon, hydrogen, and oxygen; its formula is $C_{12}H_{22}O_{11}$.

SECTION EXERCISES

1.2.1 What are the elemental symbols for cerium, cesium, copper, calcium, and carbon?

1.2.2 What are the names of the elements represented by the following symbols: Zr, Ni, Re, Sn, W, Se, Eu, Be, and Au?

1.2.3 Molecular models of some common molecules are shown here. What are their formulas?

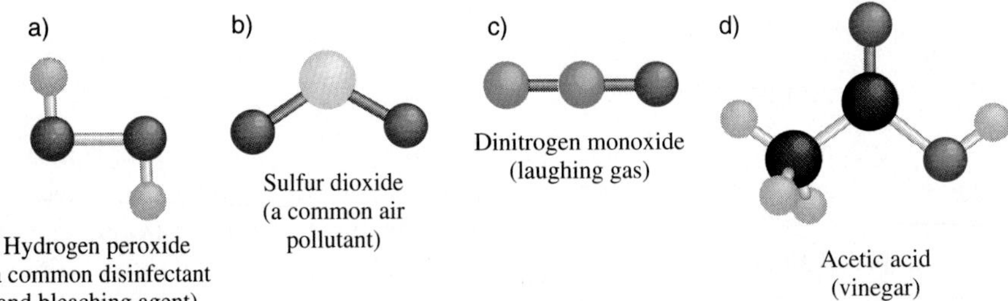

a) Hydrogen peroxide (a common disinfectant and bleaching agent)

b) Sulfur dioxide (a common air pollutant)

c) Dinitrogen monoxide (laughing gas)

d) Acetic acid (vinegar)

1.3 THE PERIODIC TABLE OF THE ELEMENTS

Many more chemical reactions exist than anyone can imagine. Every month's issues of the chemical research journals contain reports of chemical reactions that were previously unknown. Nevertheless, certain patterns of chemical reactivity have been recognized for more than 100 years. They remain valid even though new reactions are discovered constantly. Each chemical element shows a characteristic pattern of chemical reactivity. Moreover, groups of elements called *families* also display similar reaction characteristics. These patterns are the basis for the **periodic table.**

The periodic table lists the elements in order of their mass, starting with the lightest (hydrogen) and proceeding to the most massive (uranium among naturally occurring elements). This table accounts for all the known chemical elements in the universe.

We show in Chapter 2 that the periodic table is based on the structure of atoms rather than on their masses. Elemental masses correlate closely with atomic structure, however, so elemental ordering by mass is almost the same as ordering by structure. Only three exceptions exist among the 109 elements.

ARRANGEMENT

One way to list the elements would be in a long horizontal line. In the periodic table, this line is broken into a series of seven rows. Each row is placed below the previous row so that elements with *similar* chemical properties appear in the *same column* of the table. As we move *across a row* of the periodic table, the elements generally increase in mass and change dramatically in their chemical properties. As we move *down a column* mass also increases, but the elements have similar chemical properties.

A complete periodic table would be arranged as shown in Figure 1-6. Notice that rows 6 and 7 are quite long, which makes the table rather cumbersome. For the sake of convenience, the **lanthanide elements** (row 6) and the **actinide elements** (row 7) are usually separated from the rest of the table and placed beneath the main portion of the table, as shown in Figure 1-7. This is the most common format for the periodic table.

Metals often have a characteristic shiny appearance.

METALS, NONMETALS, AND METALLOIDS

The elements can be divided into three categories: metals, nonmetals, and metalloids. Figure 1-8 displays these categories and shows that most elements are **metals.** Metals display several characteristic properties. For example, they are good conductors of heat and electricity and often have a shiny appearance. Metals also are *malleable,* meaning they can be hammered into thin sheets, and *ductile,* meaning they can be drawn into wires. Except for mercury, which is a liquid, all metals are solids at room temperature.

FIGURE 1-6
Periodic table of the elements with the lanthanides and actinides included in their proper rows.

1																															1 H	2 He
2	3 Li	4 Be																									5 B	6 C	7 N	8 O	9 F	10 Ne
3	11 Na	12 Mg																									13 Al	14 Si	15 P	16 S	17 Cl	18 Ar
4	19 K	20 Ca															21 Sc	22 Ti	23 V	24 Cr	25 Mn	26 Fe	27 Co	28 Ni	29 Cu	30 Zn	31 Ga	32 Ge	33 As	34 Se	35 Br	36 Kr
5	37 Rb	38 Sr															39 Y	40 Zr	41 Nb	42 Mo	43 Tc	44 Ru	45 Rh	46 Pd	47 Ag	48 Cd	49 In	50 Sn	51 Sb	52 Te	53 I	54 Xe
6	55 Cs	56 Ba	57 La	58 Ce	59 Pr	60 Nd	61 Pm	62 Sm	63 Eu	64 Gd	65 Tb	66 Dy	67 Ho	68 Er	69 Tm	70 Yb	71 Lu	72 Hf	73 Ta	74 W	75 Re	76 Os	77 Ir	78 Pt	79 Au	80 Hg	81 Tl	82 Pb	83 Bi	84 Po	85 At	86 Rn
7	87 Fr	88 Ra	89 Ac	90 Th	91 Pa	92 U	93 Np	94 Pu	95 Am	96 Cm	97 Bk	98 Cf	99 Es	100 Fm	101 Md	102 No	103 Lr	104 Unq	105 Unp	106 Unh	107 Uns	108 Uno	109 Une									

FIGURE 1-7
Periodic table of the elements as used in common practice.

																1 H	2 He
3 Li	4 Be											5 B	6 C	7 N	8 O	9 F	10 Ne
11 Na	12 Mg											13 Al	14 Si	15 P	16 S	17 Cl	18 Ar
19 K	20 Ca	21 Sc	22 Ti	23 V	24 Cr	25 Mn	26 Fe	27 Co	28 Ni	29 Cu	30 Zn	31 Ga	32 Ge	33 As	34 Se	35 Br	36 Kr
37 Rb	38 Sr	39 Y	40 Zr	41 Nb	42 Mo	43 Tc	44 Ru	45 Rh	46 Pd	47 Ag	48 Cd	49 In	50 Sn	51 Sb	52 Te	53 I	54 Xe
55 Cs	56 Ba	71 Lu	72 Hf	73 Ta	74 W	75 Re	76 Os	77 Ir	78 Pt	79 Au	80 Hg	81 Tl	82 Pb	83 Bi	84 Po	85 At	86 Rn
87 Fr	88 Ra	103 Lr	104 Unq	105 Unp	106 Unh	107 Uns	108 Uno	109 Une									

57 La	58 Ce	59 Pr	60 Nd	61 Pm	62 Sm	63 Eu	64 Gd	65 Tb	66 Dy	67 Ho	68 Er	69 Tm	70 Yb
89 Ac	90 Th	91 Pa	92 U	93 Np	94 Pu	95 Am	96 Cm	97 Bk	98 Cf	99 Es	100 Fm	101 Md	102 No

Alkali metals
Alkaline earth metals
Transition metals
Main group elements
Hydrogen
Halogens
Rare gases
Lanthanides
Actinides

FIGURE 1-8
The metals (yellow) are found on the left side of the periodic table, and the nonmetals (blue) are in the upper right-hand corner. The metalloids (green) lie diagonally between the metals and the nonmetals.

																1 H	2 He
3 Li	4 Be											5 B	6 C	7 N	8 O	9 F	10 Ne
11 Na	12 Mg											13 Al	14 Si	15 P	16 S	17 Cl	18 Ar
19 K	20 Ca	21 Sc	22 Ti	23 V	24 Cr	25 Mn	26 Fe	27 Co	28 Ni	29 Cu	30 Zn	31 Ga	32 Ge	33 As	34 Se	35 Br	36 Kr
37 Rb	38 Sr	39 Y	40 Zr	41 Nb	42 Mo	43 Tc	44 Ru	45 Rh	46 Pd	47 Ag	48 Cd	49 In	50 Sn	51 Sb	52 Te	53 I	54 Xe
55 Cs	56 Ba	71 Lu	72 Hf	73 Ta	74 W	75 Re	76 Os	77 Ir	78 Pt	79 Au	80 Hg	81 Tl	82 Pb	83 Bi	84 Po	85 At	86 Rn
87 Fr	88 Ra	103 Lr	104 Unq	105 Unp	106 Unh	107 Uns	108 Uno	109 Une									

57 La	58 Ce	59 Pr	60 Nd	61 Pm	62 Sm	63 Eu	64 Gd	65 Tb	66 Dy	67 Ho	68 Er	69 Tm	70 Yb
89 Ac	90 Th	91 Pa	92 U	93 Np	94 Pu	95 Am	96 Cm	97 Bk	98 Cf	99 Es	100 Fm	101 Md	102 No

Metals
Nonmetals
Metalloids

FIGURE 1-9
The metalloids are dull, brittle solids that show some properties of both metals and nonmetals. Shown are silicon *(top)* and germanium *(bottom)*.

The **nonmetals** are found in the upper right-hand corner of the periodic table (Figure 1-8). The physical properties of nonmetals are much more variable than those of metals, but all nonmetals are poor conductors of electricity and heat. The six elements categorized as **metalloids** are dull-appearing, brittle solids, as exemplified by those shown in Figure 1-9. The metalloids are sometimes called *semiconductors,* because they conduct electricity better than nonmetals but not as well as metals. In fact, silicon and germanium are used in the manufacture of semiconductor chips in the electronics industry.

FIGURE 1-10
The alkali metals (left side of each watchglass) are shiny, soft, reactive metals that combine with chlorine to form 1:1 crystalline salts (right side of watchglass).

PERIODIC PROPERTIES

In 1869 the Russian chemist Dmitry Mendeleyev and the German chemist Julius Lothar Meyer independently discovered how to arrange the chemical elements in a table so that elements with similar chemical properties were in the same columns. Their arrangements were based primarily on chemical reactivity patterns and elemental masses. Today's periodic table retains this form, but we can explain the arrangement of elements in the periodic table in terms of atomic structure. We discuss this explanation in later chapters after we describe atoms in more detail.

The first column of the periodic table contains elements that are soft, shiny metals. These are called the **alkali metals** or Group I elements. Each alkali metal combines with fluorine (F), chlorine (Cl), bromine (Br), or iodine (I) in a 1:1 ratio to form a white crystalline solid (Figure 1-10). The general formula of these compounds is MX, where M represents the metal and X represents F, Cl, Br, or I. The Group I elements also react violently with water to liberate hydrogen gas.

The elements in the second column of the table appear very similar to the alkali metals, but they have different properties. For example, each of these metals combines with chlorine in a 1:2 ratio (MCl_2). Each also reacts with atmospheric oxygen, as shown in Figure 1-11, to form a solid with the formula MO. These metals are **alkaline earth metals** or Group II elements.

Fluorine, chlorine, bromine, and iodine appear in the next-to-last column of the periodic table. They are the **halogens** or Group VII elements. These four elements exist in nature as diatomic molecules with the formula X_2. Samples of the halogens are shown in Figure 1-12. As already mentioned, halogens react with Group I metals to form compounds with the formula MX and with Group II metals to form MX_2. Later in this book, we explain why Group VII elements share these and other chemical reactivity patterns.

The last column of the periodic table contains the **rare gas elements** or Group VIII elements, all of which occur in nature as gases. For the most part, these elements do not undergo chemical reactions. As mentioned earlier, however, modern chemists have discovered conditions under which xenon forms chemical compounds. Of all the elements, this group is the most resistant to chemical change.

Elements also can be divided into three broad groups. The set of metals located between columns II and III are known as **transition metals.** The set of metals in rows 6 and 7 that are normally shown below the rest of the table are called the *lanthanides* and *actinides.* All other elements are designated **main group elements.**

The periodic table is a useful way to organize chemical properties. To help you see the patterns, the periodic table on the inside front cover of this book highlights the various groups of elements. As you learn more about chemical structure and behavior, you will discover the principles that account for similarities and differences in the chemical behavior of different elements.

FIGURE 1-11
Magnesium metal burns in air with a bright-white flame and forms a white solid, magnesium oxide.

FIGURE 1-12
Halogens all have elemental formulas X_2, but whereas Cl_2 *(left)* is a gas under normal conditions, Br_2 *(center)* is a liquid and I_2 *(right)* a solid.

SECTION EXERCISES

1.3.1 Predict the formulas of the compounds formed in the reaction between (a) calcium and chlorine; (b) cesium and iodine; (c) barium and oxygen; and (d) magnesium and fluorine.

1.3.2 Boron and fluorine form a compound with the formula BF_3. Based on this, suggest formulas for compounds of aluminum with bromine and gallium with chlorine.

1.3.3 Classify each of the following elements as metals, nonmetals, or metalloids: aluminum, fluorine, gallium, phosphorus, krypton, tellurium, thorium, barium, and strontium. Classify these same elements as alkali metals, alkaline earth metals, halogens, rare gases, main group elements, transition metals, lanthanides, or actinides.

1.4 CHARACTERISTICS OF MATTER

Matter is anything that has mass and occupies space. Matter can be made up of only one substance or any number of different substances. As already described, the building blocks of most substances are molecules, which in turn are composed of atoms. It is convenient to classify samples of matter according to the complexity of their composition, both at the atomic level and at the level that we observe.

The elements are the simplest form of matter. Elements cannot be decomposed into other chemical components because each is composed of only one type of atom. Pure chemical elements are uniform in composition. That is, no matter what part of a sample of a pure element is examined, it always has the same composition. Any sample that has uniform composition is said to be **homogeneous.**

Of the 109 known chemical elements, only a few are found in our world in their pure form. Diamonds, for example, are pure carbon, and nuggets of pure gold can be

FIGURE 1-13
Carbon *(left)*, gold *(center)*, and sulfur *(right)* are examples of pure elements that occur naturally.

found by panning in the right streambed. Sulfur, shown in Figure 1-13, is one of the few elements found in abundance in its elemental form.

When two or more different chemical elements combine, they form a second type of substance called a **chemical compound.** Even though they are made of more than one type of element, pure chemical compounds are uniform in composition. All samples of a particular chemical compound contain the same proportions of each element from which it is formed. For example, ammonia is a chemical compound that contains the elements nitrogen and hydrogen in a 1:3 atomic ratio. A sample of pure NH_3 *always* contains nothing but ammonia molecules made of three hydrogen atoms and one nitrogen atom (Figure 1-14). Pure chemical substances are homogeneous and invariant in composition.

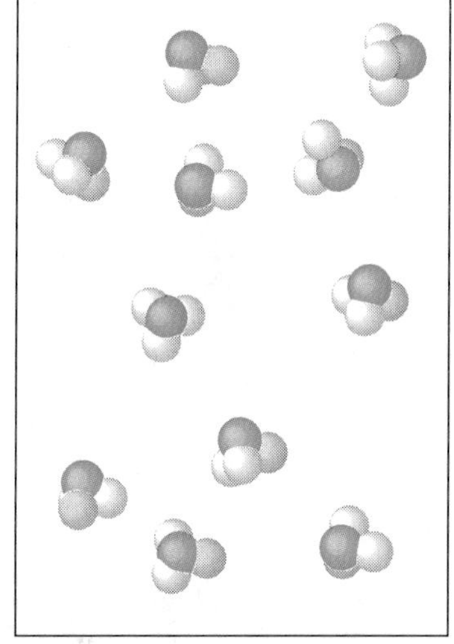

FIGURE 1-14
A sample of pure ammonia contains nothing but molecules made of nitrogen atoms and hydrogen atoms in a 1:3 ratio. The composition of a pure substance is homogeneous and invariant.

A sample is a **mixture** if it contains two or more chemical substances that retain their individual chemical identities. A mixture is homogeneous if it has a uniform composition. A homogeneous mixture is usually called a **solution.** Unlike pure compounds, solutions vary in composition because the proportions of their chemical constituents can change. For example, dissolving table salt in water forms a solution; every portion of the liquid mixture contains salt and water in the same proportions. Adding more water to this solution gives a new solution that is still homogeneous, but the proportions of salt and water are different from those in the original mixture.

The difference between a pure chemical substance and a mixture of substances can be illustrated with hydrogen and chlorine. Under the right conditions, these two elements react in 1:1 atomic ratio to give diatomic molecules of hydrogen chloride, as illustrated in Figure 1-15, *A*. Hydrogen chloride gas is homogeneous and invariant in composition, always containing an equal number of hydrogen atoms and chlorine atoms linked in HCl molecules. Under other conditions, molecular hydrogen and molecular chlorine gases can be mixed without reacting, forming a gaseous solution that is homogeneous but not invariant in composition. As Figure 1-15, *B* and *C*, illustrates, the composition of the mixture can be varied by adding more of either substance.

When different portions of a mixture have different compositions, the mixture is said to be **heterogeneous.** Salad dressing, for example, may appear uniform after thorough mixing, but when allowed to stand, the mixture eventually separates into two distinct liquid layers. Many minerals are heterogeneous mixtures. Quartz is a chemical compound made from silicon and oxygen, and gold is a pure element, but the lump of quartz containing a vein of gold that appears in Figure 1-16 is a heterogeneous mixture because different parts of the lump have different composition.

To classify a sample of matter, we can ask a sequence of questions about its composition. Figure 1-17 is a flowchart that illustrates this procedure.

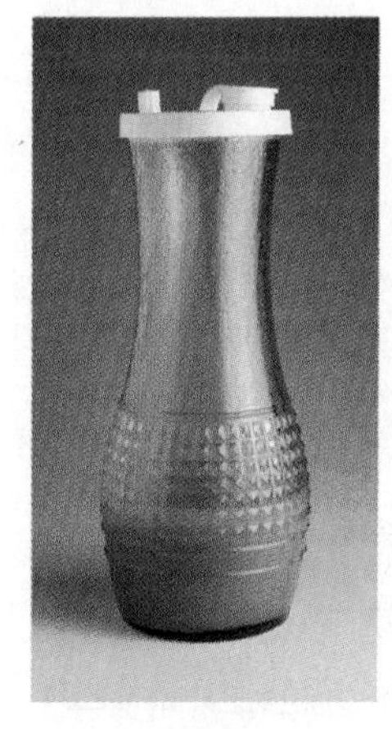

A

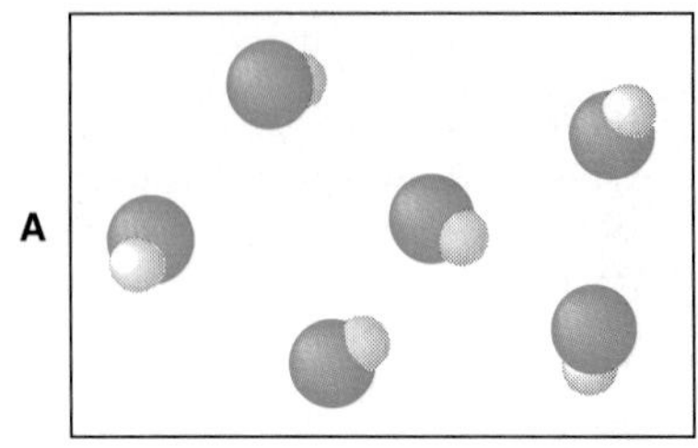

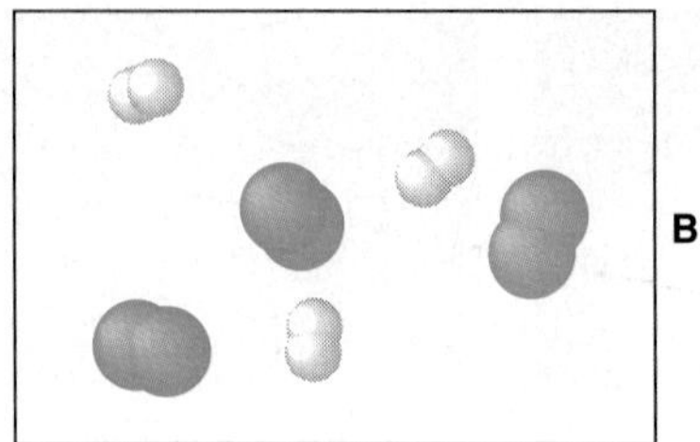

B

C

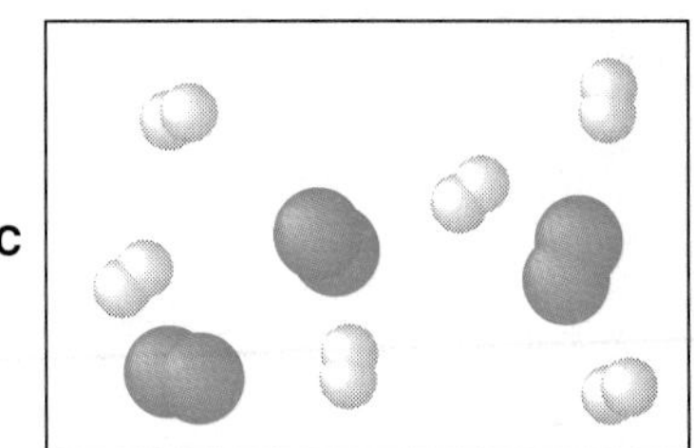

FIGURE 1-15

A sample of hydrogen chloride **(A)** is homogeneous and invariant in composition because atoms of the two elements are always linked in a 1:1 atomic ratio. A mixture of hydrogen gas and chlorine gas is homogeneous but not invariant in composition because the amount of either gas can be varied without changing the amount of the other (**B** and **C**).

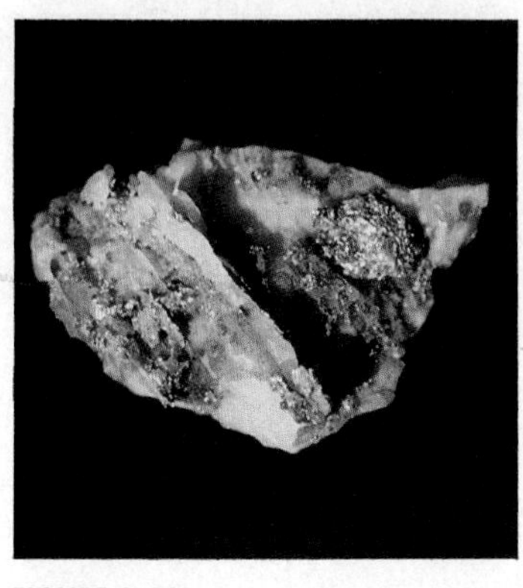

FIGURE 1-16

A sample of quartz containing a vein of gold is a heterogeneous mixture because it contains two distinct chemical compounds that are not uniformly distributed throughout the sample.

A sample of matter

Is it homogeneous (uniform composition)?

or

Is it heterogeneous (different parts differ)?

Homogeneous

Heterogeneous

Example: River water is water mixed with silt.

Is it a single chemical substance?

or

Is it more than one substance?

Single substance

More than one substance: solution

Example: Soda water is carbon dioxide dissolved in water.

Does it contain one chemical element?

or

Does it contain more than one chemical element?

Element

Chemical compound

Example: Oxygen gas

Example: Water is made up of both hydrogen and oxygen.

FIGURE 1-17

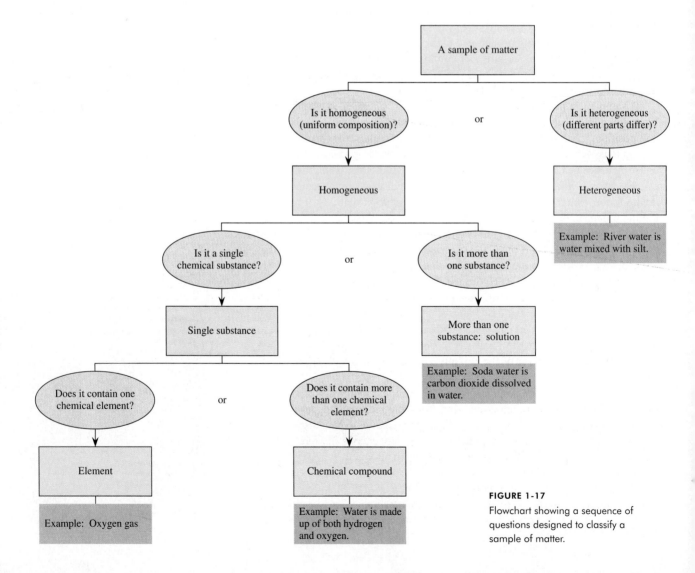

Flowchart showing a sequence of questions designed to classify a sample of matter.

PHASES OF MATTER

Matter can also be categorized according to its shape and volume. Three distinct **phases** can be distinguished: solid, liquid, and gas. An object that is **solid** has a definite shape and volume that cannot be changed easily. Trees, automobiles, and coffee cups are all in the solid phase. Matter that is **liquid** has a definite volume but changes shape quite easily. A liquid flows to take on the shape of its container. Gasoline, water, and cooking oil are examples of common liquids. Solids and liquids are termed *condensed phases* because of their well-defined volumes. A **gas** has neither specific shape nor constant volume. A gas expands or contracts as the container confining it expands or contracts. Helium balloons are filled with helium gas, and the Earth's atmosphere is made up of gas that flows continually from place to place. Figure 1-18 shows three fuels that illustrate the three phases of matter.

The gas of the atmosphere is held in place by gravity, not by the walls of a container.

Although every substance exists in one particular phase under ordinary conditions, every substance can be converted from one phase to another. Water, for instance, changes from its liquid phase into a solid (ice) when the temperature drops below 0 °C, and it changes from a liquid into a gas (steam) when the temperature rises above 100 °C. Similarly, lava is rock that has been heated sufficiently to convert it to the liquid phase, and "dry ice" is carbon dioxide that has been cooled enough to change it from the gas phase to the solid phase. We explore the behaviors of the different phases of matter and the characteristics of phase changes in later chapters.

TRANSFORMATIONS OF MATTER

A transformation is any process that changes the properties of a substance. The conversion of water into ice is an example of a transformation of matter, as is dissolving salt in water to form a solution.

Chemists separate material transformations into physical transformations and chemical transformations. In a **physical transformation,** physical properties change, but the substance's chemical nature remains the same. For example, when water freezes, it undergoes a physical transformation because the chemical makeup

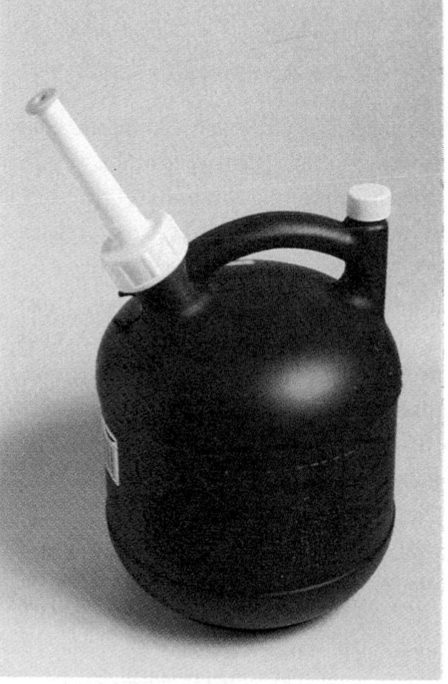

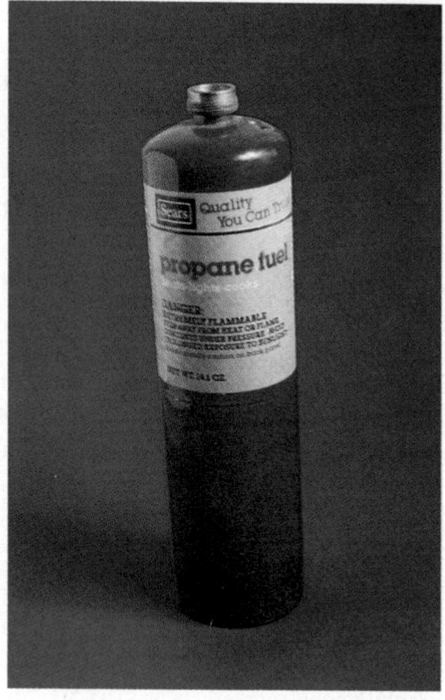

FIGURE 1-18
Matter exists as a solid (piece of coal), a liquid (can of gasoline), or a gas (tank of propane).

of ice is the same as that of liquid water. That is, both ice and water contain molecules made up of two atoms of hydrogen and one atom of oxygen. Another physical transformation is the evaporation of salt water to give water vapor and solid table salt. Although the salt and water are separated from each other in the process, the chemical natures of each substance remain unchanged during the transformation.

A **chemical transformation,** on the other hand, produces new chemical substances. For example, if solid sodium metal is placed in water, it reacts very vigorously to form a solution. Hydrogen gas, H_2, is generated at the same time. When the solution is separated by evaporating the water, the residue is not sodium metal but a new chemical substance, sodium hydroxide, or NaOH. The reaction of sodium metal with water is a chemical transformation that rearranges the chemical elements in sodium and water to give hydrogen gas and sodium hydroxide.

SECTION EXERCISES

1.4.1 Examine Figures 1-9 through 1-11 and make a list of all the pure elements and chemical compounds found in those figures.

1.4.2 Classify each of the following as a pure substance, a solution, or a heterogeneous mixture: a cup of coffee, a lump of sugar, seasoned salt, a silver coin, and sea water.

1.4.3 Classify each of the following as a physical or a chemical transformation: melting snow, burning coal, chopping wood, and digesting food.

FIGURE 1-19
Three different types of laboratory balances.

1.5 MEASUREMENTS IN CHEMISTRY

Chemists are interested in describing, interpreting, and predicting the behavior of chemical compounds. This requires a knowledge of chemical properties, which is gained by making careful experimental measurements. Chemists measure numerous physical properties, including length, area, volume, mass, time, and temperature.

PHYSICAL PROPERTIES

Length, area, and volume measure the spatial extension of an object. Length refers to one dimension, area to two dimensions, and volume to three dimensions of space. Direct measurements of length require a standard measuring device such as a ruler or a tape measure. Area and volume are most often determined indirectly from other properties, as we show later.

The process of determining mass is called *weighing*. Mass and weight are related, but they are not the same property. Mass is a fundamental characteristic of an object, whereas weight results from gravitational force acting on an object's mass. In outer space, objects have mass but no weight because there is no gravitational force. Many mass-measuring instruments on Earth rely on gravity because the Earth's gravitational force generates weights that are directly proportional to masses.

In addition to its volume, every object possesses a certain quantity of matter, called its **mass (*m*).** The more mass an object possesses, the more difficult it is to move. Therefore mass can be determined by measuring resistance to movement. Mass measurements in chemistry are particularly important because chemists often need to know quantities of matter. Consequently, highly accurate mass-measuring machines, called *analytical balances,* are essential instruments in chemistry laboratories. Figure 1-19 shows some examples of analytical balances.

Analytical balances work by comparing masses or forces. The jeweler's balance (Figure 1-20, *A*) is a finely machined lever that is in balance when equal masses are on both ends of the lever. The grocer's scale (Figure 1-20, *B*), on the other hand, compares gravitational force with the restoring force of a spring. Either type of balance must be calibrated using objects of known mass.

A

B

FIGURE 1-20
Masses are determined using balances that compare two masses (**A,** jeweler's balance) or two forces (**B,** grocer's scale).

Chemists measure **time (*t*)** because they want to know how long it takes for chemical transformations to occur. Some chemical reactions, such as the conversion of green plants into petroleum, may take many millions of years. Other chemical processes, such as an explosion of dynamite, are incredibly fast. Most wristwatches and clocks measure time to the nearest second, and Olympic events are timed electronically to the nearest 0.001 second. To measure ultrafast events, chemists have developed instruments that make it possible to study processes that occur in less than 0.00000000001 second.

Most of us associate **temperature (*T*)** with the concepts of hot and cold. More accurately, however, temperature is the property of an object that determines the direction of heat flow. Heat always flows from a warm object to a cool object, from higher temperature to lower temperature. Heat is a form of energy, and because energy changes in chemical systems have important consequences, chemists are interested in temperature changes that occur during chemical transformations.

We discuss energy changes in Chapter 2 and consider temperature and heat flow in detail in Chapters 12 and 13.

Length, mass, time, and temperature are fundamental properties that will arise frequently in your study of chemistry. Two additional basic properties, numbers of atoms or molecules and amount of electric charge, are introduced and defined in Chapter 2. We introduce yet another fundamental property, the intensity of light, when we explore the structure of atoms in Chapter 6.

All experimental sciences rely on quantitative measurements of fundamental properties. Every measurement gives a numerical result that has three aspects: a numerical *magnitude,* a *precision,* and an indicator of scale, called a *unit.* Each aspect is essential, and all three must be reported before a measurement has scientific value.

MAGNITUDE

The magnitudes of experimental values in chemistry range from infinitesimally small to astronomically large. Very small and very large numbers can be unwieldy unless they are expressed in scientific notation. To simplify further the task of manipulating numbers that span such a huge range of magnitudes, scientists also use prefixes that change unit sizes by multiples of 10. The prefixes that you need to know are listed in Table 1-2.

In scientific notation, 0.00000000001 would be written 1×10^{-11}. See Appendix A for a review of scientific notation.

TABLE 1-2 FREQUENTLY USED SCIENTIFIC PREFIXES FOR MAGNITUDES

PREFIX	SYMBOL	NUMBER	EXPONENTIAL NOTATION
giga	G	1,000,000,000	10^9
mega	M	1,000,000	10^6
kilo	k	1000	10^3
—	—	1	10^0
centi	c	0.01	10^{-2}
milli	m	0.001	10^{-3}
micro	μ	0.000001	10^{-6}
nano	n	0.000000001	10^{-9}
pico	p	0.000000000001	10^{-12}

TABLE 1-3 MAGNITUDES OF KNOWN LENGTHS

QUANTITY	LENGTH	COMMON UNITS
Radius of hydrogen nucleus	10^{-15} m	—
Diameter of hydrogen atom	10^{-10} m	1 Å
Length of chlorophyll molecule	10^{-7} m	—
Thickness of blade of grass	10^{-3} m	0.04 inch
Length of football field	10^2 m	100 yards
Distance between Berkeley, Calif, and San Francisco	10^4 m	12 miles
Diameter of Earth	10^7 m	8000 miles
Average distance from Earth to sun	10^{11} m	93 million miles
Distance to nearest neighboring star	10^{17} m	5 light-years
Diameter of known universe	10^{25} m	—

Nonscientists may never deal with lengths less than 1 mm or greater than 1000 km (1 megameter, or Mm), but scientists routinely study objects whose size extends far beyond the narrow range encountered in daily life. Physicists, for example, study atomic nuclei measuring 10^{-15} m across, and astronomers work in a universe that spans about 10^{25} m. Chemists are most often interested in matter on the smaller side of this range. Still, length measurements in the laboratory vary from meters to the atomic size of 10^{-10} m (0.1 nanometer, or nm). Table 1-3 compares the magnitudes of lengths used by humans.

UNITS

The units associated with a numerical value are just as important as the value itself. If the sun were 93,000,000 *feet* away rather than 93,000,000 *miles,* the Earth would not be the hospitable planet that it is. It is *essential* to include units with every experimental value.

A unit of measurement is an agreed-on standard with which other values are compared. Agreement on such standards is not easy to achieve, especially when different standards have been used within the scientific community. For instance, nonscientists in the United States measure length in the English system of inches,

TABLE 1-4 BASE UNITS IN THE SI SYSTEM

QUANTITY	UNIT	SYMBOL
Mass	kilogram	kg
Length	meter	m
Time	second	s
Temperature	kelvin	K
Amount	mole	mol
Electric current	ampere	A
Luminous intensity	candela	cd

feet, yards, and miles. These units are based on various familiar human lengths (the foot is the length of a typical human foot; the yard is the distance from the tip of the nose to the end of an extended finger). Scientists, on the other hand, use the meter, an international standard unit that was originally defined as 10^{-7} times the length of a line from the North Pole to the equator. Volume can be measured in pints, quarts, and gallons, but the scientific standards are the cubic meter and the liter (10^{-3} m^3). Temperature can be measured in degrees Fahrenheit, degrees Celsius, or kelvins.

Since 1960 the international scientific community has attempted to work exclusively with a single set of units, the *Système International* (SI), which expresses each fundamental physical quantity using decimally (power of 10) related units. The seven base units in the SI system are listed in Table 1-4.

Even though volume is a fundamental property, it is not a base unit in the SI system because it can be obtained from the base unit for length. A cube that measures 1 m on a side has a volume of 1 m^3. Chemists most frequently work with volumes smaller than a cubic meter, however, so volumes are often expressed using the liter, which is defined to be exactly 10^{-3} m^3.

Box 1-3 discusses reference standards for calibrating measuring devices.

UNIT CONVERSIONS

It is often desirable to convert measurements from one set of units to another. For example, travelers between the United States and Europe need to be able to convert between miles and kilometers. A unit conversion uses the equivalence between different units for the same quantity. The equivalence may be between SI units and non-SI units: 1 inch = 2.54 cm; between different decimally related units: 1 cm = 10^{-2} m; or between fundamental and derived units: 1 L = 10^3 cm^3.

Each type of equivalence includes a *numerical factor* that links two different *units*. Some of the more common unit equivalences are given on the end pages of this text. Each equivalence can be rearranged to give two conversion ratios:

$$1 = \frac{1 \text{ inch}}{2.54 \text{ cm}} \quad \textit{and} \quad 1 = \frac{2.54 \text{ cm}}{1 \text{ inch}}$$

A numerical value can be multiplied by any ratio that equals 1 without changing the result. However, it is essential to choose a ratio that leads to cancellation of units.

The correct conversion ratio is the one that leads to cancellation of unwanted units.

Sample Problem 1-1 illustrates this procedure.

BOX 1-3

REFERENCE STANDARDS

After defining a reference unit of measurement such as the kilogram or the meter, scientists agree on reference standards that make it possible to calibrate all measuring devices. Otherwise, the measuring devices will not give reliable readings.

Devices that measure temperature are calibrated using the freezing point and the boiling point of water. The kelvin (K) is defined so that the normal freezing point of water is 273.15 K and its normal boiling point is 373.15 K. Thus a thermometer can be calibrated by placing it first in an ice bath and then in boiling water.

The meter was originally defined as 1/10,000,000 times the distance from the equator to the North Pole. This, however, is hardly a length that can be reproduced in the laboratory. In 1960 the length of the meter was redefined as 1.65076373×10^6 times the wavelength of light emitted by a krypton laser (see photo at right). Although this is a cumbersome number, it preserves the length of the meter at its agreed-on value while identifying a reference substance (krypton laser) that laboratory personnel can use to perform their own length calibrations.

The mass standard is the kilogram. It is defined as the mass of a platinum-iridium (Pt-Ir) bar (see photo at right) that is stored at the International Bureau of Weights and Measures in Sevre, France. Pt-Ir was chosen for this standard because it is highly resistant to chemical attack. Thus its mass will not change for an extremely long time.

Pt-Ir bars and krypton lasers are expensive, and comparing lengths and masses to their standard values is tedious and difficult work. In practice, we rely on measuring devices such as meter sticks and analytical balances that have been calibrated by their manufacturers to give correct readings. However, each of these devices was standardized or calibrated against some reference, which ultimately leads back to the laser wavelength or the mass of that Pt-Ir bar in France.

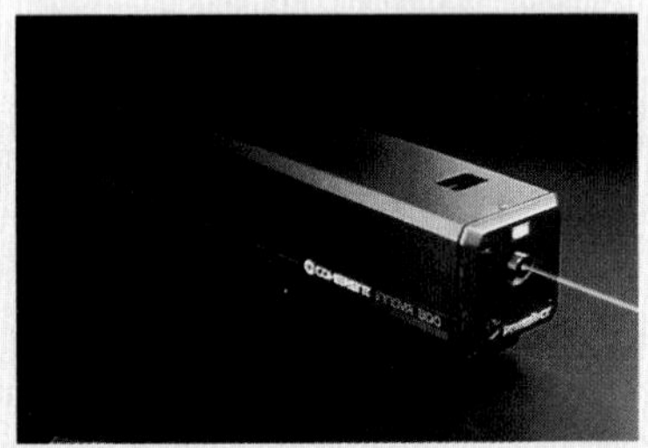

SAMPLE PROBLEM 1-1 UNIT CONVERSIONS

A pair of rock climbers stand at the base of a rock face they estimate to be 155 feet high. Their rope is 65 m long. Is the rope long enough to reach the top of the cliff?

METHOD: The team must compare English measure for the height of the cliff and the SI measure for the length of their rope. Is 65 m more or less than 155 feet? The equivalence between feet and meters can be found on the end pages: 1 m = 3.281 feet. We are given the length of rope in meters. To set up a ratio that converts meters to feet, we must divide both sides of the equivalence by 1 m:

$$\frac{1\text{ m}}{1\text{ m}} = 1 = \frac{3.281\text{ feet}}{1\text{ m}}$$

Now we must multiply the length of the rope by the conversion ratio:

$$(65\ \cancel{m})\left(\frac{3.281\ \text{feet}}{1\ \cancel{m}}\right) = 2.1 \times 10^2\ \text{feet}$$

Thus the two climbers have plenty of rope to climb the rock face.

Notice that we multiply meters by feet/meter, so that meters cancel. Multiplying the height of the cliff by this conversion ratio would have given nonsensical units: (feet) (feet/m) = feet²/m.

Unit conversions can involve many steps. Sample Problem 1-2 is an example.

SAMPLE PROBLEM 1-2 MULTIPLE UNIT CONVERSIONS

The speed limit on most highways in the United States is 55 miles/hr. What is this speed limit in SI units?

METHOD: Again, we are asked to make a unit conversion. The SI unit of length is meters, and the SI unit of time is seconds. We need to convert from miles to meters and from hours to seconds.

Here are the appropriate equivalences: 1 mile = 1.6093 km, 1 km = 10^3 m, 1 hr = 60 min, and 1 min = 60 s. We are given the speed limit in miles per hour. To cancel miles, we must multiply by a ratio that has miles in the denominator. To obtain meters, we must use a ratio that has meters in the numerator. We convert miles to kilometers and then convert kilometers to meters:

$$\left(\frac{55\ \cancel{\text{miles}}}{\text{hr}}\right)\left(\frac{1.6093\ \cancel{\text{km}}}{1\ \cancel{\text{mile}}}\right)\left(\frac{10^3\ \text{m}}{1\ \cancel{\text{km}}}\right) = 8.9 \times 10^4\ \text{m/hr}$$

This completes the conversion into SI units of length. Now we must convert from hours to seconds, following a similar procedure. Because hours appear in the denominator, we must multiply by a ratio that has hours in the numerator:

$$\left(\frac{8.9 \times 10^4\ \text{m}}{\text{hr}}\right)\left(\frac{1\ \text{hr}}{60\ \text{min}}\right)\left(\frac{1\ \text{min}}{60\ \text{s}}\right) = 25\ \text{m/s}$$

Scientists use two units for temperature, the Celsius scale and the kelvin scale. These scales are shown schematically in Figure 1-21. Unlike other scientific units, the *unit size* of the Celsius and kelvin scales is the same, but their *zero points* differ. For both scales, the difference in temperature between the freezing and boiling points of water is defined to be 100 units. However, the temperature at which ice melts to liquid water is 0 °C and 273.15 K.

The conversion between kelvins and degrees Celsius is straightforward because their temperature (T) units are the same size. Thus a temperature change of 1 °C is the same as a temperature change of 1 K. To switch from one scale to the other, we add or subtract 273.15:

$$T\,(\text{K}) = T\,(°\text{C}) + 273.15 \qquad \textbf{(1-1)}$$

$$T\,(°\text{C}) = T\,(\text{K}) - 273.15$$

PRECISION

Precision is the degree of exactness of a measurement. This concept is best explained with an example. Suppose three swimmers are discussing the temperature of a swimming pool. The first dips a finger in the water and proclaims the temperature to be

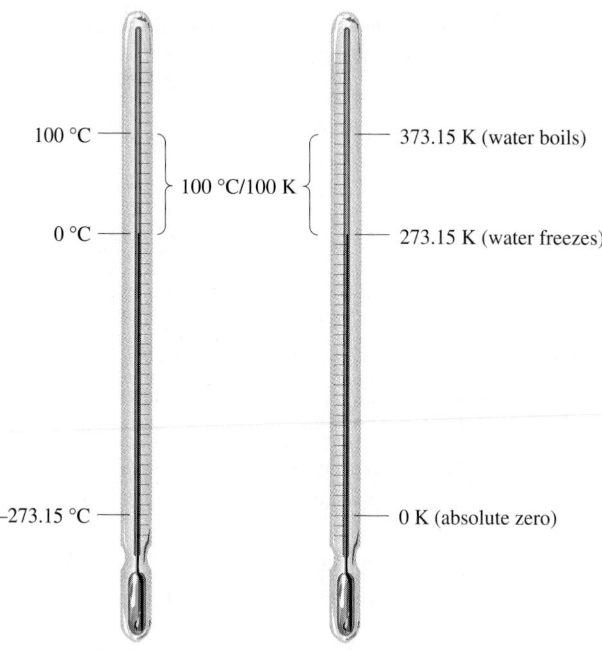

FIGURE 1-21
Celsius and kelvin temperature scales. Kelvins and degrees Celsius have the same unit size but different zero points.

"about 25 °C." The second, not satisfied with this determination, examines an immersed pool thermometer and reports the temperature to be 26 °C. The third swimmer, who has been monitoring daily variations in the pool's temperature, takes out a portable precision digital thermometer, immerses the probe into the water, and reports, "Yesterday at this time the pool temperature was 25.6 °C, but today it is 25.8 °C."

The swimmers have measured the water temperature with three different levels of precision. Each result is correct, within its limits of precision. The "finger test" measurement is subjective, so it is precise only to within perhaps 3 °C. The first swimmer estimates that the temperature is 25 ± 3 °C (read "twenty-five plus or minus three degrees"). The pool thermometer, which probably has degree gradations marked on it, gives a reading that is precise to the nearest degree. A reading of 26 °C means the temperature is more than 25 °C but less than 27 °C, so it is 26 ± 1 °C. The precision thermometer with digital readout reads to the nearest tenth of a degree, so the temperature is 25.8 ± 0.1 °C. Notice that an actual temperature between 25.7 and 25.9 °C falls within the precision ranges of *all three* measurements, so all three are correct to within their stated limits of precision.

The three swimmers who measured the temperature of the pool demonstrated that the precision of a measured value depends on the quality of the measuring device. High-precision devices cost much more than low-precision devices. For example, a few hundred dollars buys a balance that measures mass to three digits, but a balance that can measure masses to eight digits may cost several thousand dollars.

Scientific measurements should always include precision and magnitude. One way to do this is by indicating the precision limits with a plus/minus (±) statement, as in the previous discussion. However, this is a cumbersome way to indicate precision, particularly when many numerical values are being reported at one time. To simplify the reporting of precision, scientists have agreed that a numerical value is precise within an uncertainty of one unit in the last digit. For example, temperature reported as 26 °C is understood to be more than 25 °C but less than 27 °C, or

26 ± 1 °C. A temperature of 25.8 °C is understood to be 25.8 ± 0.1 °C. The number of digits expressed in such numerical values is called the number of **significant figures.** The value 26 has two significant figures, whereas 25.8 has three.

Zeros can present a problem when determining the precision of a numerical value. This is because zeros are needed both to locate the decimal point and to express precision. From the statement that the sun is 93,000,000 miles from the Earth, we cannot tell whether the measurement is precise to eight significant figures or whether the zeros are there only to put the decimal point in the right place. Scientific notation eliminates this ambiguity because a power of 10 locates the decimal point, leaving us free to indicate the precision by the number of digits. For example, a distance of 9.3×10^7 miles means that the number is precise to within $\pm 0.1 \times 10^7$ miles; the number has two significant figures. If this distance is known to a precision of $\pm 0.01 \times 10^7$ miles, it is written as 9.30×10^7 miles, with three significant figures. Zeros trailing the decimal point always indicate increased precision.

To determine how many significant figures there are in a particular numerical value, read the number from left to right and count all the digits, starting with the first digit that is not zero. In this book we always use scientific notation when a trailing zero would be ambiguous. For example, "100" means "100 ± 1" and has three significant figures. To designate 100 ± 10, we write 1.0×10^2. Here are some examples illustrating significant figures:

0.1	1 significant figure
10	2 significant figures
0.010	2 significant figures
101	3 significant figures
1.00	3 significant figures
1.003×10^{-5}	4 significant figures

Writing "0.010" in scientific notation clarifies that is has two significant figures rather than three or four: $0.010 = 1.0 \times 10^{-2}$.

SECTION EXERCISES

1.5.1 Convert to power of 10 notation and express in base SI units: 0.000463 L; 17,935 km; and 260,000 hours (precise to three significant figures).

1.5.2 One light-year is the distance light travels in 1 year. The speed of light is 6.7×10^8 miles/hr. Express the speed of light in SI units.

1.5.3 Convert each of the following measurements to SI units: 155 pounds (mass of a typical person), 120 yards (full length of a football field), 38.5 °C (body temperature of someone with a slight fever), and 365.2422 days (length of 1 year).

1.6 CALCULATIONS IN CHEMISTRY

Chemical experiments are designed to provide information about some chemical system. During an experiment a chemist may measure physical quantities such as mass, length, and temperature. Usually the chemist seeks information that is related to measured quantities but must be found by doing calculations. Much of our presentation in later chapters involves equations that relate measured physical quantities to important chemical properties. Therefore calculations are central to much of general chemistry.

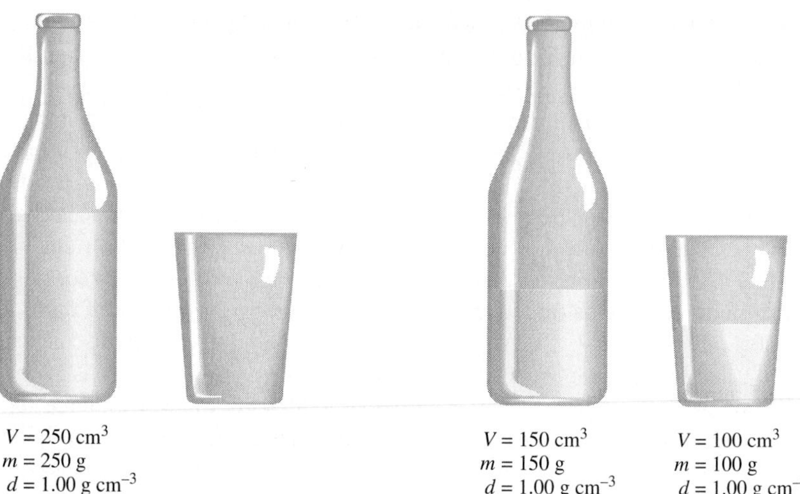

FIGURE 1-22
Volume and mass of the parts are different when a homogeneous object is divided, but density does not change.

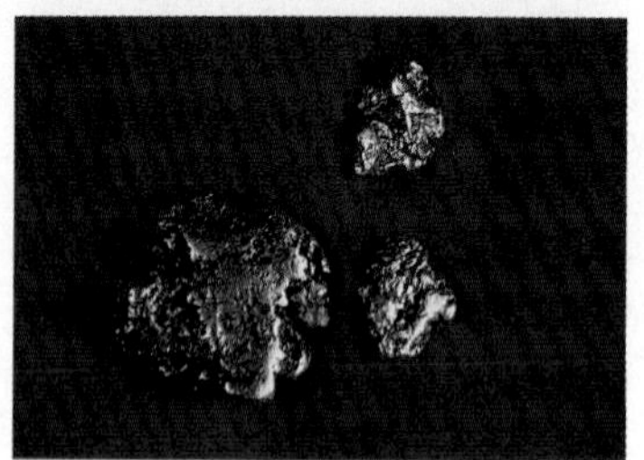

Iron pyrite is also known as *fool's gold* because inexperienced prospectors sometimes mistake it for gold.

When units appear as part of a divisor, they are often written using negative exponents; "cm^{-3}" means "divide by centimeters cubed." 19.3 g cm^{-3} is the same as 19.3 g/cm^3.

DENSITY

As an introduction to chemical calculations, we focus on density, a simple physical property that has several chemical applications. The **density (*d*)** of an object is its mass (*m*) divided by its volume (*V*):

$$\text{Density} = \frac{\text{Mass}}{\text{Volume}}$$

$$d = \frac{m}{V} \tag{1-2}$$

Every pure liquid or solid has a characteristic density that helps distinguish it from other substances. The density of pure gold is 19.3 g cm^{-3}, whether the sample is a nugget in a miner's pan or an ingot in a bank vault. Iron pyrite, a solid that sometimes resembles gold, has a much lower density, 5.0 g cm^{-3}.

Unlike mass and volume, density does not vary with the amount of a substance. Figure 1-22 shows that dividing a sample of liquid into two portions changes the mass and volume of each portion but leaves density unchanged. A property that depends on the amount present is called *extensive.* Mass and volume are two examples of **extensive properties.** A property that is independent of the amount present is called *intensive.* Density is an example of an **intensive property.**

Intensive properties can be tabulated for various substances. Table 1-5 lists the densities of several common substances. Most liquid and solid substances have densities in the range of 0.1 to 20 g cm^{-3}. This 200-fold variation is readily apparent to us and dictates how different materials are used in applications in which density is important. For fishing, floats are made out of cork, but sinkers are made from lead.

Density cannot be measured directly. Instead, it is calculated from measurements of mass and volume, using Equation 1-2. The equation can also be rearranged to find an object's volume or mass. Sample Problem 1-3 illustrates this procedure.

SAMPLE PROBLEM 1-3 USING DENSITY

A diamond is a pure sample of the element carbon. The tabulated density of diamond is 3.51 g cm^{-3}. Jewelers use a unit called a *carat* to describe the mass of a diamond: 1 carat = 0.200 g. What is the volume of the stone in a 2.00 carat diamond engagement ring?

METHOD: Given the diamond's mass and density, we are asked to find its volume. Rearranging the density equation makes this possible:

$$\text{Density} = \frac{\text{Mass}}{\text{Volume}} \qquad so \qquad \text{Volume} = \frac{\text{Mass}}{\text{Density}}$$

A list of the information given in the problem allows us to determine what data will be substituted into the equation:

$$\text{Density}_{\text{diamond}} = 3.51 \text{ g cm}^{-3}$$

$$\text{Mass} = 2.00 \text{ carat}$$

$$1 \text{ carat} = 0.200 \text{ g}$$

In the volume equation, density and mass must have consistent units. Thus mass must be converted from carats to grams:

$$(2.00 \cancel{\text{carat}}) \left(\frac{0.200 \text{ g}}{1 \cancel{\text{carat}}} \right) = 0.400 \text{ g}$$

Now substitute into the equation for volume:

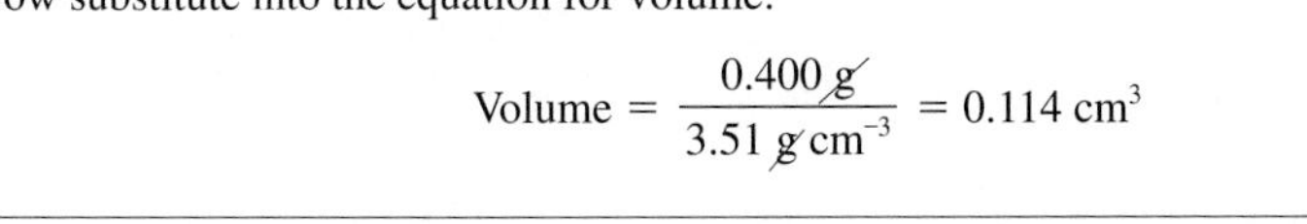

$$\text{Volume} = \frac{0.400 \cancel{\text{g}}}{3.51 \cancel{\text{g}} \text{ cm}^{-3}} = 0.114 \text{ cm}^3$$

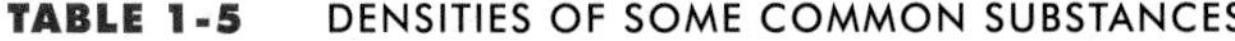

TABLE 1-5 DENSITIES OF SOME COMMON SUBSTANCES

SUBSTANCE	DENSITY (g cm^{-3})
Wood (balsa)	0.12
Cork	0.24
Wood (white pine)	0.35-0.50
Alcohol (ethanol)	0.785
Water	1.00
Quartz	2.65
Aluminum	2.70
Diamond	3.51
Silver	10.50
Lead	11.34
Mercury	13.55
Gold	19.3

PRECISION OF CALCULATIONS

The precision of the measuring instrument determines the precision of a single measurement. However, many scientific investigations require a series of measurements, often involving more than one instrument. Data obtained from multiple measurements are then combined to calculate a quantity of interest. How precise is a value obtained by calculations? As a general rule, the least precise measurement determines the precision of a result. The following example, again using density, illustrates this guideline.

A chemical manufacturer prepares a silicon fluid for possible use as a lubricant. To determine its density, a technician measures 25.0 cm^3 of fluid into a graduated cylinder and determines the mass of the fluid to be 39.086 g. Dividing mass by volume on a calculator, the technician reads the following result: 1.56344. Are all six of these digits significant? What value does the technician report for the fluid's density? A set of measurements is limited by the precision of the least-sensitive instrument used in the experiments. The mass is known to five significant figures, but there are only three significant figures in the volume. Thus only three significant figures are used to report the density of the fluid:

$$d = \frac{39.086\ \text{g}}{25.0\ \text{cm}^3} = 1.56\ \text{g cm}^{-3}$$

Appendix B describes the way precision changes when numbers are combined. Here, we summarize the important result: That two simple guidelines can be used to determine the precision of a sequence of mathematical operations.

1. When *adding* or *subtracting,* the number of *decimal places* in the result is the number of *decimal places* in the number with the fewest places.

0.0120	4 decimal places	3 significant figures
1.6	*1 decimal place*	2 significant figures
8.49026	5 decimal places	6 significant figures
10.1	*1 decimal place*	3 significant figures

The value with the fewest decimal places determines the number of decimal places in a sum.

2. When *multiplying or dividing,* the number of *significant figures* in the result is the same as the quantity with the fewest *significant figures.*

	(0.0120)	(1.6)	(8.49026)	=	(0.16)
Significant figures	3	2	6		2
Decimal place(s)	4	1	5		2

The multiplier with the fewest significant figures determines the number of significant figures in a product.

In a series of computations, it is best not to adjust the results of each step. Instead, wait until the computations are complete, and then express the final value with the appropriate number of significant figures.

When exact numbers are used, their presence has no effect on the significant figures in the result. For example, we can convert 1.855 hours into seconds:

$$1.855\ \text{hr}\left(\frac{60\ \text{min}}{1\ \text{hr}}\right)\left(\frac{60\ \text{s}}{1\ \text{min}}\right) = 6678\ \text{s}$$

How many significant figures should be used? Although the conversion factors contain only two digits, they are exact numbers. There are *exactly* 60 (60.00000...) minutes in an hour and *exactly* 60 (60.00000...) seconds in a minute. Thus the determinant of precision in this product is the time in hours, which is precise to four significant figures. We report the time in seconds to four significant figures as well.

Calculators usually give more significant figures than are justified. For example:

0.0120 + 1.6 + 8.49026 = 10.1*0226* (calculator result)

(0.0120) (1.6) (8.49026) = 0.16*3012992* (calculator result)

In each of these calculations, the calculator displays extra digits that are not significant. (These extra digits are italicized above.) A calculator cannot distinguish the number of significant figures that are appropriate for a calculation. Many calculators can be set so that they display a predetermined number of significant figures; however, these also are not necessarily correct.

Always adjust calculator results to the appropriate number of significant figures, using the two guidelines given earlier.

There are also two guidelines for rounding off numbers that apply when dropping extra digits beyond the precision of the result. If the first digit to be removed is 5 or greater, round the last remaining digit upward by one unit. If the first digit to be removed is smaller than 5, leave the last remaining digit unchanged. Sample Problem 1-4 shows how to apply these guidelines.

To be statistically accurate, we should apply a special rule when the number being dropped is *exactly* 5. This additional rounding rule does not arise very often, and half the time it would give the same result as our simple rules.

SAMPLE PROBLEM 1-4 SIGNIFICANT FIGURES

A farmer owns a rectangular field that fronts along a road. State highway engineers surveyed the frontage and found that it measures 138.3 m in length. The farmer, who wants to build a fence around the field, paces off the field's width and estimates it to be 52 m. How many meters of fence will the farmer have to build? What mass of fertilizer will the farmer need to fertilize the field with 0.0050 kg of fertilizer for each square meter of field?

METHOD: First, we must calculate the field's perimeter to determine the amount of fencing needed. We also need the field's area to find the mass of fertilizer. As part of the calculation, we must also determine the precision of the results:

$$\text{Perimeter} = \text{Length} + \text{Width} + \text{Length} + \text{Width}$$

$$\text{Perimeter} = 138.3\text{ m} + 52\text{ m} + 138.3\text{ m} + 52\text{ m} = 380.6\text{ m}$$

According to the guideline for adding or subtracting, this result must have the same number of *decimal places* as the least precise measurement. In this case, pacing off the width of the field limits the precision of the calculation to the nearest meter. The value should be rounded up because the digit to be dropped is larger than 5. The farmer requires 381 m of fence.

We must calculate the area of the field to determine how much fertilizer it will need:

$$\text{Area} = (\text{Length})(\text{Width}) = (138.3\text{ m})(52\text{ m}) = 7191.6\text{ m}^2$$

This result has too many significant figures, but we should carry the extra digits until the calculation is complete. Each square meter of field requires 0.0050 kg of fertilizer. The amount of fertilizer required is found by multiplying:

$$\text{Mass}_{\text{fertilizer}} = (7191.6\text{ m}^2)(0.0050\text{ kg/m}^2) = 35.958\text{ kg}$$

Now we are ready to round off. In the multiplication steps, we have two numbers that contain only two significant figures. The guideline for multiplying or dividing indicates that our result should also have two significant figures. The farmer requires 36 kg of fertilizer for this field.

Notice that the units work out correctly in this calculation: area multiplied by mass per unit area gives mass.

SECTION EXERCISES

1.6.1 Calculate the mass of a cylindrical cork of radius 1.00 cm and length 4.00 cm. (Volume of a cylinder is $V = \pi r^2 h$.)

1.6.2 A cylindrical jar has an inside diameter of 3.00 cm and a height of 8.00 cm. The empty jar weighs 185.65 g. Filled with gasoline, the same jar weighs 225.40 g. Find the density of gasoline.

1.6.3 Which of the following can be determined exactly, and which must be measured with some degree of uncertainty? (a) mass of a gold nugget, (b) number of seconds in 1 day, (c) time it takes a sprinter to run the 100-m dash, (d) speed of light, (e) number of potatoes in a bushel, and (f) number of centimeters in 1 mile.

1.7 CHEMICAL PROBLEM SOLVING

Many students have difficulty solving chemistry problems, but problem solving is a skill that you can learn and master. To help you, we devote extra attention to ways of setting up and solving problems. Throughout this book the sample problems are accompanied by descriptions of how they should be attacked and solved.

As a general method, we recommend the following steps in working numerical problems in chemistry:

1. Identify the type of problem. In other words, what are you being asked to find?
2. Think molecules. Think about the chemistry, and determine what the molecules are doing. Diagrams and pictures can help you visualize what is occurring.
3. Identify the appropriate equations or relationships that can be applied to the problem.
4. When appropriate, organize the data into a table.
5. Algebraically manipulate the equations to a form that will give the desired quantity.
6. Substitute numerical values and solve. Remember to keep track of units and significant figures.
7. Check the "reasonableness" of the result:
   a. Does it answer the question completely?
   b. Are the units consistent?
   c. Is the magnitude about right?
   d. Does it make chemical sense?

Sample Problem 1-5 illustrates this general method with a practical example.

SAMPLE PROBLEM 1-5 PROBLEM-SOLVING STRATEGY

A quality-control laboratory was asked to check some thin glass tubing that was supposed to have an inside diameter of 1.0 ± 0.2 mm. A technician weighed a piece of the tubing and found the mass to be 0.563 g. Distilled water was sucked into the tubing until it contained a 4.5-cm column of water. Reweighing the tubing plus the water, the technician found the new mass to be 0.590 g. Does the tubing meet its specifications?

METHOD: Apply the seven-step approach.

1. What are you asked to find?
   The question is "does the tubing meet its specifications?" Translate this question into a quantity. The problem specifies that the tubing is "*supposed to have* an inside diameter of 1.0 ± 0.2 mm." Thus you are asked to find the inside diameter of the tubing.

2. What's going on?
   Diameter is a physical property, not a chemical one. Instead of thinking about molecules, draw a physical picture that shows the setup and the information provided in the problem.

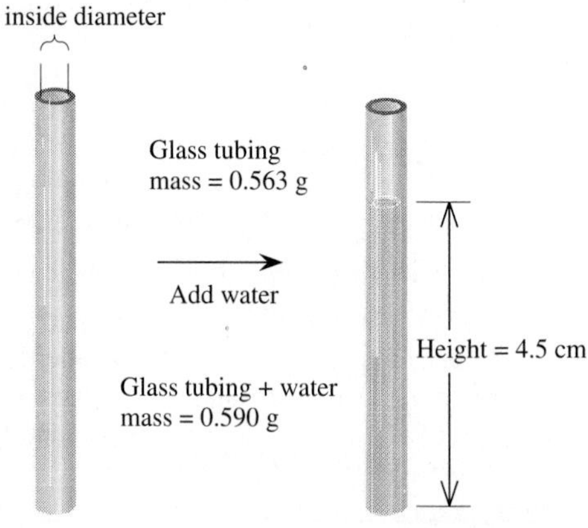

3. What equations are useful?
According to the diagram, adding water to the tubing gives a cylinder of water whose height and mass are known. How are these two quantities related to the tubing's diameter?

a. Mass and volume are related through density:

$$d = \frac{m}{V}$$

b. Volume of a cylinder is determined by its height (h) and radius (r):

$$V_{\text{cylinder}} = \pi r^2 h$$

c. Radius and diameter (D) are directly related:

$$D = 2r$$

4. Tabulate information:
First, what data are given in the problem?

Mass of tubing = 0.563 g

Mass of tubing plus water = 0.590 g

Height of water = 4.5 cm

Second, what information can be found in tables?

π = 3.1416 (probably programmed on your calculator)

Density of water = 1.00 g cm^{-3} (see Table 1-5)

5. Rearrange the equations as needed.
Three equations will be used. You can work through these step by step or combine them into a single equation. Generally the stepwise approach is clearer. Work backward from the equation for diameter:

$$\text{Diameter} = D = 2r$$

To calculate the diameter, we need r, the tubing's internal radius. Rearrange the equation for the volume of a cylinder to solve for r:

$$V = \pi r^2 h \qquad \textit{so} \qquad r^2 = \frac{V}{\pi h} \qquad \textit{and} \qquad r = \sqrt{\frac{V}{\pi h}}$$

To begin the calculations, use the mass and density to calculate the volume:

$$d = \frac{m}{V} \qquad \textit{so} \qquad V = \frac{m}{d}$$

6. Substitute and solve, keeping track of units and significant figures:

m_{water} = (Mass of tubing + Water) − (Mass of tubing)

$m_{\text{water}} = 0.590 \text{ g} - 0.563 \text{ g} = 0.027 \text{ g}$ ← 3 decimal places, 2 significant figures

$V = \frac{0.027 \text{ g}}{1.00 \text{ g cm}^{-3}} = 0.027 \text{ cm}^3$ ← 2 significant figures

$r = \sqrt{\frac{V}{\pi h}} = \sqrt{\frac{0.027 \text{ cm}^3}{\pi \text{ (4.5 cm)}}} = 0.0437 \text{ cm}$ ← (should have 2 significant figures, but do not round off until the end)

$D = 2r = 2(0.0437 \text{ cm}) = 0.0874 \text{ cm}$

Now convert to the units given in the specifications:

$$D = 0.087 \text{ cm} \left(\frac{10 \text{ mm}}{1 \text{ cm}} \right) = 0.87 \text{ mm}$$

Notice that we included units and significant figures in each step.

7. Check "reasonableness" of the result:
   a. Does it answer the question? Not yet. The problem asks if the tubing meets specifications of $D = 1.0 \pm 0.2$ mm. The answer is "yes" because the calculated diameter falls within the acceptable range of 0.8 to 1.2 mm.
   b. Are units consistent? Yes, diameter is a length, and the calculated value has units of millimeters.
   c. Is the magnitude about right? Yes, 0.87 mm is "thin tubing."
   d. Does it make chemical sense? This question is not relevant here because no chemistry is taking place.

SECTION EXERCISES

1.7.1 The standard unit of length in Ferdovia is the frud (2.000 frud = 10^{-2} m). Fast-food restaurants in Ferdovia sell mashed potatoes in rectangular cartons measuring 50.00 by 40.00 by 80.0 fruds. The Frod family left a freshly opened carton on their kitchen table, and their pet ferret (Fred) ate some of the mashed potatoes. Mrs. Frod found the height of the remaining potatoes to be 61 fruds. How many cubic meters of mashed potatoes did Fred eat?

1.7.2 The technician from Sample Problem 1-5 used some of the glass tubing to measure the density of a liquid that the laboratory needed to identify. An empty piece of the tubing weighed 0.785 g. When liquid was drawn into the tubing to a height of 4.0 cm, the tubing and liquid weighed 0.816 g. Find the density of the liquid.

CHAPTER SUMMARY

1. Chemistry deals with the properties and reactions of matter and relates to many other disciplines. All chemistry is based on experiments.
2. The chemical building blocks are atoms and molecules, which are represented by chemical symbols and formulas.
3. The periodic table organizes different types of atoms, called *elements,* into groups with similar properties and into blocks containing metals, nonmetals, and metalloids.
4. Matter can contain a pure substance or a mixture of substances; it can be homogeneous or heterogeneous; and it can be solid, liquid, or gaseous.
5. Measurements of physical properties are important in chemistry. Any measurement has a magnitude, units, and a precision. Precision is expressed using significant figures.
6. Calculations and problem solving play key roles in chemistry.

KEY TERMS

atom
chemical element
chemical compound
diatomic molecule
molecule

periodic table
actinide element
alkali metal
alkaline earth metal
halogen
lanthanide element
main group element
metal
metalloid
nonmetal
rare gas element
transition metal

gas
heterogeneous
homogeneous
liquid
mixture
phase
solid
solution

chemical transformation
extensive property
intensive property
physical transformation

density (d)
mass (m)
significant figure
temperature (T)
time (t)

SKILLS TO MASTER

- Using the periodic table of the elements
- Converting units
- Determining precision and significant figures
- Manipulating equations to calculate properties
- Analyzing and solving problems

LEARNING EXERCISES

1.1 Construct a chapter summary of two pages or less that outlines the important features of Chapter 1. (When you have finished, compare your summary with ours, which appears as Appendix C).

1.2 Make a list of all terms new to you introduced in Chapter 1. Give a one-sentence definition for each. Consult the glossary if you need help.

1.3 "Memory bank" equations are those important enough for you to memorize. Start a list of these equations and learn them. Chapter 1 has only two memory bank equations.

1.4 The following skills are introduced in Chapter 1. Write down a "plan of attack" for accomplishing each: (a) classifying samples of matter; (b) interpreting and drawing simple molecular pictures; (c) working with the density equation; (d) using scientific notation; (e) determining significant figures; (f) converting between different units; and (g) solving chemistry problems.

1.5 Go through the end-of-chapter problems and identify those that require the skills listed in Learning Exercise 1.4. Some problems may require more than one skill, and some require skills that are not listed.

PROBLEMS

WHAT IS CHEMISTRY?

1.1 Describe three political problems for which a knowledge of chemistry would be helpful.

1.2 List three chemical processes used around the home.

1.3 List three reasons why it is important for a pharmacy student to learn about chemistry.

1.4 A chemist says, "My results must be wrong because they don't agree with the theory." Criticize this statement, and make recommendations for what the chemist should do next.

THE MOLECULAR NATURE OF CHEMISTRY

1.5 What are the elemental symbols for each of the following elements? (a) hydrogen; (b) helium; (c) hafnium; (d) nitrogen; (e) neon; and (f) niobium.

1.6 What are the elemental symbols for each of the following elements? (a) potassium; (b) platinum; (c) plutonium; (d) lead; and (e) palladium.

1.7 What are the names of each of the following elements? (a) As; (b) Ar; (c) Al; (d) Am; (e) Ag; (f) Au; (g) At; and (h) Ac.

1.8 What are the names of each of the following elements? (a) Br; (b) Be; (c) B; (d) Bk; (e) Ba; and (f) Bi.

1.9 Write the chemical formula for the compound whose molecules contain four atoms of chlorine and one atom of carbon.

1.10 Write the chemical formula for the compound whose molecules contain 5 carbon atoms and 12 hydrogen atoms.

1.11 Examine the following molecular pictures and determine their molecular formulas.

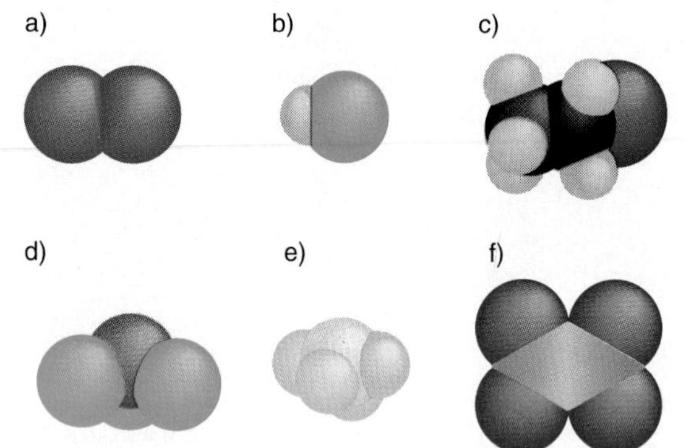

1.12 Examine the following molecular pictures and determine their molecular formulas.

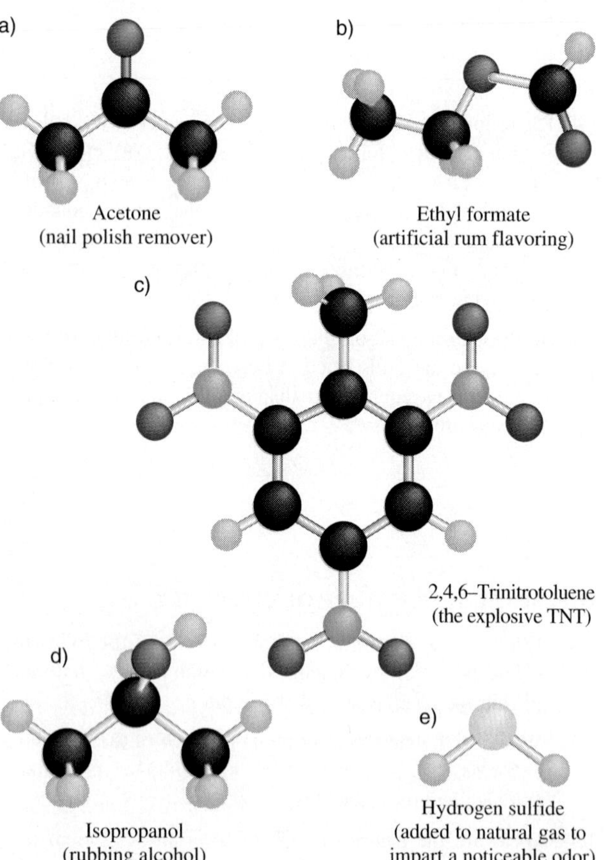

Acetone
(nail polish remover)

Ethyl formate
(artificial rum flavoring)

2,4,6–Trinitrotoluene
(the explosive TNT)

Isopropanol
(rubbing alcohol)

Hydrogen sulfide
(added to natural gas to impart a noticeable odor)

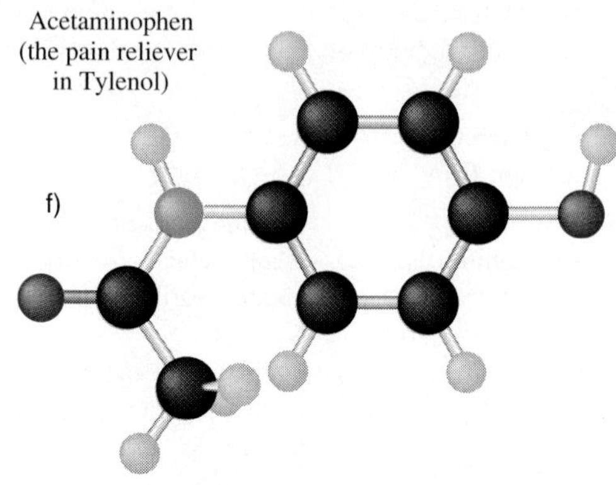

Acetaminophen
(the pain reliever in Tylenol)

THE PERIODIC TABLE OF THE ELEMENTS

1.13 What element immediately follows xenon in the periodic table?

1.14 What element immediately precedes sodium in the periodic table?

1.15 What are the names and chemical symbols of the elements that are vertical and horizontal neighbors of sulfur in the periodic table? Which of these have chemical properties similar to those of sulfur?

1.16 What are the names and chemical symbols of the elements that are vertical and horizontal neighbors of tin in the periodic table? Which of these have chemical properties similar to those of tin?

1.17 (a) Name a metal that reacts with bromine to give *M*Br; and (b) name a metal that reacts with oxygen to give *M*O.

1.18 Write the names and chemical symbols for three examples of each of the following: (a) halogens; (b) alkaline earth metals; (c) actinides; (d) rare gases; (e) transition metals; (f) lanthanides; (g) main group elements; and (h) alkali metals.

1.19 Write the names and symbols of all elements that occupy the same row of the periodic table as nitrogen.

1.20 Write the names and symbols of all elements that occupy the same column of the periodic table as nitrogen.

CHARACTERISTICS OF MATTER

1.21 Classify each of the following as a pure substance, a solution, or a heterogeneous mixture: (a) block of iron; (b) cup of coffee; (c) glass of milk; (d) atmosphere, when dust free; (e) atmosphere, when dusty; and (f) block of wood.

1.22 Classify each of the following as a pure substance, a solution, or a heterogeneous mixture: (a) blood; (b) dry ice; (c) krypton gas; (d) platinum-iridium bar in standard mass measure; (e) table salt; and (f) glass of lemonade.

1.23 Classify each of the following as a solid, liquid, or gas: (a) gasoline; (b) molasses; (c) snow; and (d) chewing gum.

1.24 Classify each of the following as a solid, liquid, or gas: (a) tree sap; (b) ozone; (c) shaving cream; and (d) water vapor.

1.25 Classify each of the following as a chemical or a physical transformation: (a) formation of frost; (b) drying of clothes; and (c) burning of leaves.

1.26 Classify each of the following as a chemical or a physical transformation: (a) water boiling; (b) coffee brewing; and (c) photographic film being developed.

1.27 Classify each of the following as an element, a compound, or a mixture: (a) lake water; (b) distilled water; (c) mud; (d) helium inside a balloon; (e) rubbing alcohol; and (f) paint.

1.28 Classify each of the following as an element, a compound, or a mixture: (a) Earth's atmosphere; (b) beer; (c) iron magnet; (d) ice; (e) liquid bromine, and (f) mercury in a barometer.

MEASUREMENTS IN CHEMISTRY

1.29 Convert to power of 10 notation: (a) 100,000, precise to ± 1; (b) 10,000, precise to 1 part in 100; (c) 0.000400; (d) 0.0003; and (e) 275.3

1.30 Convert to power of 10 notation: (a) 175,906; (b) 0.0000605; (c) $2\frac{1}{2}$ million, precise to $\pm$ 100; and (d) $2\frac{1}{2}$ billion, precise to 1 part in 250.

1.31 Express each of the following in SI base units using power of 10 notation (example: 1.45 mm = 1.45×10^{-3} m): (a) 430 kg; (b) 1.35 μm; (c) 624 ps; (d) 1024 ng; (e) 93,000 km; (f) 1 day; and (g) 0.0426 inch.

1.32 Express each of the following in SI base units using power of 10 notation: (a) 1 week; (b) 15 miles; (c) 4.567 μs; (d) 6.45 mL; and (e) 47 μg.

1.33 The mass unit most often used for precious stones is the carat: 1 carat = 3.168 grains, and 1 g = 15.4 grains. Find the total mass in kilograms (kg) of a ring that contains a 5.0×10^{-1} carat diamond and 7.00 g of gold.

1.34 What is the total mass in grams, expressed in scientific notation with the correct number of significant figures, of a solution containing 10.00 kg of water, 6.5 g of sodium chloride, and 47.546 g of sugar?

CALCULATIONS IN CHEMISTRY

1.35 What is the mass of 1 quart of water (1 L = 1.057 quarts)?

1.36 What is the mass of 1 quart of mercury?

1.37 A solid block of plastic measures 15.5 cm by 4.6 cm by 1.75 cm, and its mass is 98.456 g. Compute the density of the plastic.

1.38 A chemist who prepared a new liquid substance wanted to determine its density. Having only a small sample to work with, the chemist had to use a small container. A tube whose volume was 8.00×10^{-3} cm^3 weighed 0.4763 g when empty and 0.4827 g when filled with the liquid. Compute the density of the liquid in g cm^{-3}.

1.39 Calculate the volume of an aluminum spoon whose mass is 15.4 g.

1.40 Calculate the volume of a quartz crystal of mass 0.246 g.

CHEMICAL PROBLEM SOLVING

1.41 A chemist who wished to verify the density of water constructed a cylindrical container of aluminum whose inside radius measured 0.875 inch and that measured 4.500 inches in height. When empty, the cylinder had a mass of 93.054 g. When filled with water, its mass was 270.064 g. Find the density of water from these data, expressing your result in SI units with the correct precision (cylinder volume, $V = \pi r^2 h$).

1.42 Which possesses more mass, a sphere of mercury with a diameter of 2.00 cm or a cube of lead measuring 2.00 cm on each side (sphere volume, $V = 4\pi r^3/3$)?

ADDITIONAL PROBLEMS

1.43 Perform the following calculations and express the result with the correct number of significant figures: (a) 1.00 kg + 175 kg + 0.0253 kg; (b) 2.54 s − 2.54 ms; (c) 145 miles/2.0 hr; (d) $(\frac{1}{2})$ (175 kg) $(3.25 \text{ m/s})^2$; and (e) (1.75 g) (0.88 J/g K) (295 K − 273.15 K).

1.44 Convert each of the following into SI units: (a) engine displacement of 340 cubic inches; (b) speed of 35 miles/hr; (c) height of 6 feet, 10 inches; (d) mass of 220 pounds; and (e) 32 miles/gallon.

1.45 Light travels at 1.86×10^5 miles/s in a vacuum. Determine how many kilometers a beam of light can travel in 1 year.

1.46 Draw a molecular picture of SO_2, in which each S atom is flanked by two O atoms in a bent arrangement. (SO_2 is a major contributor to acid rain.)

1.47 Elemental sulfur can form rings of S_8 molecules. In these rings, each S atom is connected to two others. Draw a molecular picture showing this arrangement.

1.48 How many elements have symbols beginning with P? Give the name and symbol of each.

1.49 How many elements have symbols beginning with T? Give the name and symbol of each.

1.50 Bromine is one of the two elements that is a liquid at room temperature. (Mercury is the other.) The density of bromine is 3.12 g/mL. What volume of bromine is required if a chemist needs 36.5 g for an experiment?

1.51 Almost all the elements whose symbols come from Latin names are metals. Suggest a chemical reason why these elements were named many years ago.

1.52 What is the name and symbol of the element of lowest mass whose symbol and English names do not match?

1.53 What is the name and symbol of the element of highest mass whose symbol and English names do not match?

1.54 Perform the following calculations, and express the results with the correct number of significant figures: (a) $1.45 + 0.08 + 37.62$; (b) $(1.45)(0.08)(37.62)$; (c) $37.62 - (1.45)(0.08)$; (d) $145 + 0.08 + 37.62$; and (e) $2.457 - 2.43$.

1.55 The day is defined as having exactly 24 hours of 60 minutes, and each minute is exactly 60 seconds. The year is 365.24 days long. How many seconds are there in a century, which is 100 years? Express your answer in scientific notation, with the correct number of significant figures.

1.56 Describe the differences between metals and nonmetals.

1.57 Which elements would you expect to have chemical behavior similar to that of gold?

1.58 A square of aluminum foil measuring 3.00 inches on each side weighs 255 mg. Find the thickness of the aluminum foil in picometers (pm).

1.59 Make a list of all pairs of elements having the same first letter in their chemical symbol that would be expected to show similar chemical properties.

1.60 Some chemists refer to chemistry as the "central" science because of its importance to other sciences. Do you agree? Give your reasons.

1.61 We began this chapter by listing several questions that chemists are interested in answering. List five more.

1.62 The maximum speed limit allowed on U.S. highways is 65 miles/hr. What is the maximum speed in kilometers per hour (km/hr)? What is the maximum speed in meters per second (m/s)?

1.63 Ethylene glycol is used as antifreeze in car radiators. The freezing temperature of ethylene glycol is −11.5 °C. Convert this freezing temperature to kelvins (K).

1.64 (a) The distance between the Earth and the moon is 2.37×10^5 miles. How far is this in kilometers (km)? and (b) The speed of light is 3.00×10^8 m/sec. How long does it take for sunlight reflected off the moon to reach the Earth?

1.65 Perform the following calculations and report your answer with the correct number of significant figures.

(a) $$\frac{(6.531 \times 10^{13})(6.02 \times 10^{23})}{(435)(2.0000)}$$

(b) $$\frac{(4.476) + (3.44)(5.6223) + 5.6666}{(4.3)(7 \times 10^4)}$$

1.66 Examine the following molecular pictures, and determine the molecular formulas of the compounds they represent.

a) b)

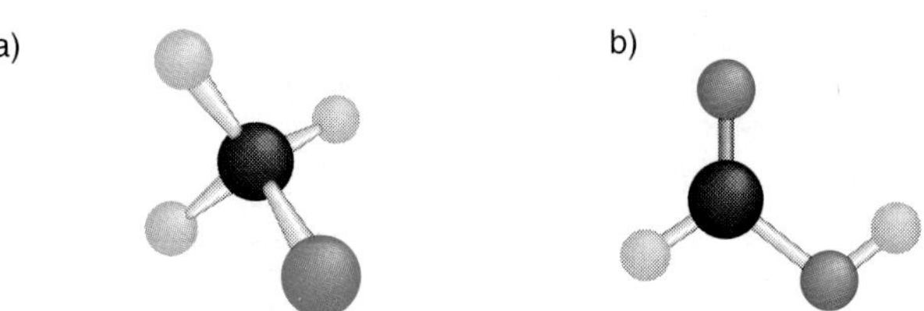

Freon 21 (a refrigerant suspected of damaging the ozone layer in the stratosphere)

Formic acid (the stinging compound in an ant bite)

c) d)

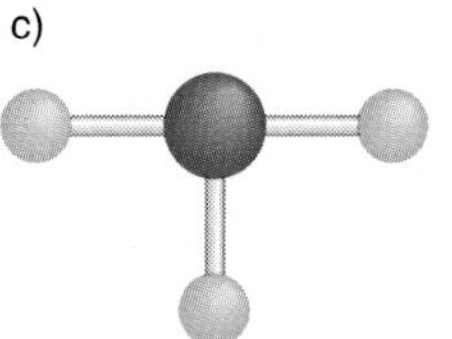

Bromine trifluoride (used in the production of fuel for nuclear reactors)

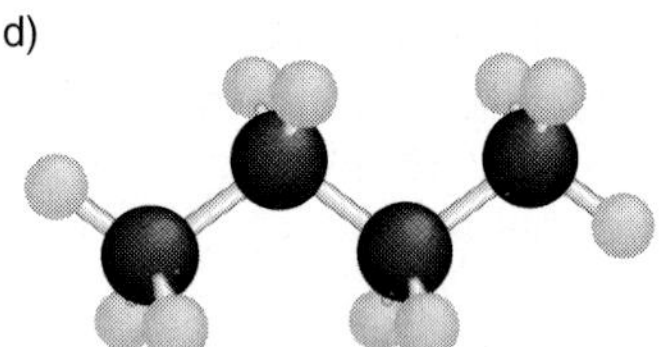

Butane (the fluid in disposable lighters)

1.67 The diameter of metal wire is given by its wire gauge number. For example, 16-gauge wire has a diameter of 0.0508 inch. Calculate the length in meters of a 5.00-pound spool of 16-gauge copper wire. The density of copper is 8.92 g cm^{-3}.

1.68 List three specific examples of each of the following: (a) metalloids; (b) lanthanides; (c) elements that react with fluorine; (d) main group elements; (e) nonmetals; and (f) rare gases.

1.69 An athlete runs the mile in 3 minutes, 57 seconds. At the same speed, how many seconds does it take the same athlete to run 1500 m?

1.70 For each of the following sentences, determine whether the property in italics is extensive or intensive: (a) the *density* of iron is 7.86 g mL^{-1}; (b) liquid oxygen has a *pale-blue color;* (c) the crankcase of an automobile holds *5 quarts* of oil; (d) the *melting point* of gallium metal is 30 °C; and (e) a recipe calls for *100 g* of sugar.

1.71 Carbon monoxide is a common pollutant in urban environments. On one particular day, the air contained 5.5 mg of carbon monoxide per 1.000 m^3 of air. On that day, how many grams of carbon monoxide were present in a room that had the dimensions 12 feet by 9.5 feet by 10.5 feet?

1.72 The diameter of a chlorine atom is 200 pm. How many chlorine atoms lined up end to end would form a line 1.0 inch long?

1.73 The basketball player David Robinson, who played on the U.S. Olympic team in 1992, is 7 feet 1 inch tall, to the nearest 1/4 inch. How tall is Mr. Robinson in millimeters (mm)?

1.74 From the following list of elements—Ne, Cs, Sr, Br, Ge, Co, Pu, In, and O—choose one that fits each of the following descriptions: (a) alkaline earth metal; (b) element whose properties are similar to those of boron; (c) element that reacts with potassium; (d) semiconductor; (e) transition metal; (f) rare gas; and (g) actinide.

1.75 The distance from the Earth to the sun is 9.3×10^7 miles. How long does it take for light from the sun to reach our planet?

1.76 Draw appropriately scaled and colored molecular pictures of each of the following molecules: CH_4, CO_2, CF_4, CCl_4, and CBr_4. Each has a carbon atom in the center.

1.77 Draw an appropriately scaled and colored molecular picture of an HCN molecule, which is linear.

1.78 Using everyday observations, decide which one in the following pairs of substances has the greater density. Explain your reasoning. (a) oil or vinegar; (b) table salt or water; and (c) iron or aluminum.

1.79 Water for irrigation is usually expressed in units of acre-feet. One acre-foot is enough water to cover one acre of land to a depth of 1 foot (1 acre = 43,560 ft^2). A water reservoir has a maximum capacity of 8.97×10^5 acre-feet. What is the lake's volume in (a) liters, (b) cubic feet, and (c) cubic meters?

1.80 The Greek scientist Archimedes was given the task of determining whether his king's crown was pure gold or an alloy of gold and silver. The king specified that no part of the crown could be destroyed. To do this, Archimedes invented volume determination by displacement. First, he determined the crown's mass to be 2.65 kg (they did not use SI units then, but the method does not depend on the units used). Next, he put the crown in a full basin of water and found the amount of overflow to be 145 cm^3. Was the crown pure gold or a gold-silver alloy? Show a calculation that supports your answer.

ANSWERS TO SECTION EXERCISES

1.1.1 (a) Chemistry is involved when sugar dissolves in a glass of iced tea. (b) A chemical process in yeast creates the gas that causes bread to rise. (c) In making candy, "carmelizing" sugar causes a chemical change in the sugar molecules. (d) Marinade tenderizes meats through chemical changes.

1.1.2 Chemistry applies to the automobile industry in many ways. To name just a few, chemistry is involved in the search for new additives that make gasoline more energy efficient and less polluting. Chemistry plays a role in the creation of new plastic materials for automobile interiors and bodies. Ceramics created by chemists and engineers are used to make certain engine parts. New paint formulations give automobiles coatings that inhibit corrosion of metal parts.

1.1.3 Develop a set of chemical reactions that can be performed on Earth and on Venus. Observe the results carefully on both planets. If the results obtained on Venus differ from the results obtained on Earth, the theory may be valid. However if the results are the same, the theory cannot be valid.

1.2.1 Ce, Cs, Cu, Ca, and C

1.2.2 Zirconium, nickel, rhenium, tin, tungsten, selenium, europium, beryllium, and gold

1.2.3 (a) H_2O_2, (b) SO_2, (c) N_2O, and (d) $C_2H_4O_2$ (At this point, the elements in a formula can be listed in any order. In Chapter 3, we describe conventions that chemists follow when they write chemical formulas.)

1.3.1 (a) $CaCl_2$, (b) CsI, (c) BaO; (d) MgF_2

1.3.2 $AlBr_3$ and $GaCl_3$

1.3.3 Metals: aluminum, thorium, barium, and strontium
Nonmetals: fluorine, phosphorus, and krypton
Metalloids: gallium and tellurium
Alkali metals: none
Alkaline earth metals: barium and strontium
Halogens: fluorine
Rare gases: krypton
Main group elements: all but thorium
Transition metals: none
Lanthanides: none
Actinides: thorium

1.4.1 From Figure 11-9, silicon and germanium are pure elements. From Figure 11-10, the alkali metals are pure elements, but the white solids are chemical compounds whose formulas are *M*Cl. From Figure 11-11, magnesium metal is a pure element, but magnesium oxide (MgO) is a chemical compound.

1.4.2 Solution, pure substance, heterogeneous mixture, pure substance, and solution

1.4.3 Physical, chemical, physical, and chemical

1.5.1 4.63×10^{-7} m^3, 1.7935×10^7 m, and 9.36×10^8 s

1.5.2 3.0×10^8 m/s

1.5.3 70.3 kg, 110 m, 311.6 K, and 3.155690×10^7 s

1.6.1 3.0 g

1.6.2 0.703 g

1.6.3 (a) uncertain; (b) exact; (c) uncertain; (d) uncertain; (e) exact; and (f) exact

1.7.1 4.8×10^{-3} m^3

1.7.2 1.3 g/cm^3

CHAPTER 2

THE ATOMIC NATURE OF MATTER

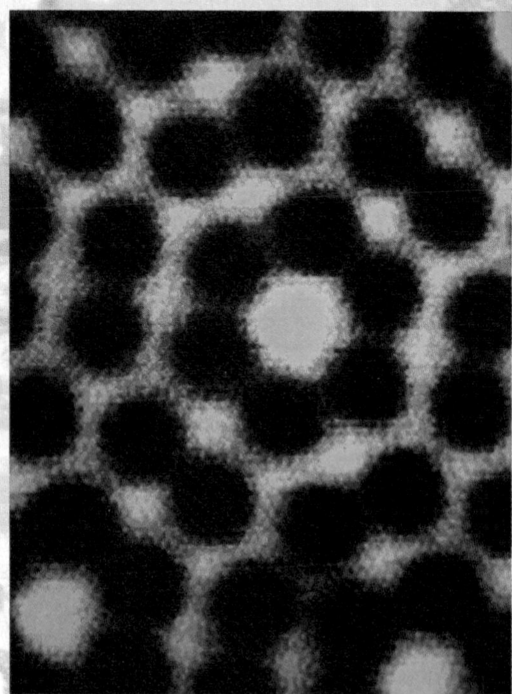

Chemists study how substances combine and rearrange to make new materials. What we see when a chemical reaction occurs are changes in the appearance and properties of the substances involved. For example, when solid potassium metal is added to liquid water, the lustrous metal disappears, and a gas bubbles out of the solution. The reaction is so vigorous that the gas bursts into flame.

The chemical changes we observe at the macroscopic level, including the disappearance of a metal and the formation of a gas, result from interactions among atoms and molecules. At the microscopic level, chemical reactions are described by three layers of organization: subatomic particles organize into atoms, atoms organize into molecules, and molecules organize into gases, liquids, and solids. Each level of organization is governed by the laws that describe how objects interact. To understand chemistry therefore we must become familiar with how matter looks at the atomic level and how atomic-sized objects interact.

The major theme of this chapter is the microscopic picture of matter, as expressed by the atomic theory and the principles of atomic structure. Two important physical ideas, the force exerted between electrically charged objects and the conservation of key physical properties, are indispensable to this picture. These ideas must become integral parts of your thinking if you are to become proficient at chemistry.

2.1 ATOMIC THEORY

Chemists "think atoms." To a chemist, every sample of matter is made up of immense numbers of tiny particles called **atoms.** For example, a chemist views a glass of water as a swarm of tiny water molecules, each composed of two atoms of hydrogen and one atom of oxygen (Figure 2-1). Blocks of steel, the gases of the

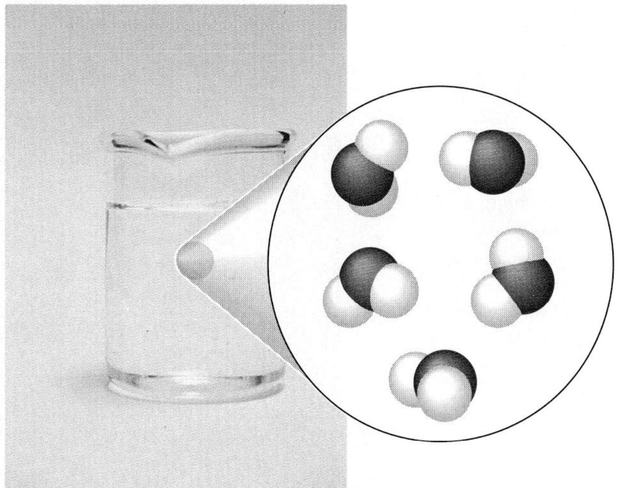

FIGURE 2-1
A chemist views a beaker of water as a collection of molecules, each made of one oxygen atom and two hydrogen atoms.

FIGURE 2-2
An image obtained by scanning tunneling microscopy, showing individual cesium atoms deposited on a solid surface. The underlying material is gallium arsenide.

atmosphere, and human beings also are composed of atoms. Why do we make this assertion with such confidence? The atomic theory of matter was firmly established nearly 200 years ago, and today, with an array of powerful instruments, scientists can actually "see" individual atoms. The example in Figure 2-2 shows silicon atoms on the surface of a silicon chip.

Atomic theory owes its origin to two ancient Greek philosophers, Leucippus (ca. 450 BC) and Democritus (ca. 470-380 BC). They believed that matter contains indivisible parts, *atomos*. Unfortunately, they lacked the necessary scientific evidence to support their assertions, so their ideas were not widely accepted.

Modern atomic theory began with the English chemist John Dalton (1766-1844), who developed and published an atomic description backed by experimental data. Dalton's atomic view was based on experiments showing that elements always combine in fixed proportions. For example, when oxygen and hydrogen combine to make water, the ratio of masses is always 8:1; 8 g of oxygen combine with 1 g of hydrogen to make 9 g of water. This suggests that each element contains discrete, identical atoms and that each atom has a characteristic mass.

Over time, chemists and physicists have refined Dalton's theory as they have learned more about the details of atomic structure. Box 2-1 discusses modern evidence for atomic theory. The essential features of our modern understanding of atoms can be summarized as follows:

1. All matter is composed of tiny particles called *atoms*.
2. All atoms of a given element have identical chemical properties.
3. Atoms of each different element have distinct properties.
4. Atoms form chemical compounds by combining in whole-number ratios. All samples of a pure compound have the same combination of atoms.
5. In chemical reactions, atoms change the ways they are combined, but they are neither created nor destroyed.

The spectacular reaction shown in Figure 2-3 illustrates how chemistry involves changes at the atomic level. A container of hydrogen gas explodes when it is exposed to a flame. Analysis of this reaction reveals that hydrogen combines with oxygen from the atmosphere to produce water. If the reaction is performed using varying amounts of hydrogen and oxygen, the *amount* of water formed changes from one experiment to the next, but the *composition* of water does not. Water *always* contains 1.0 g of hydrogen for every 8.0 g of oxygen.

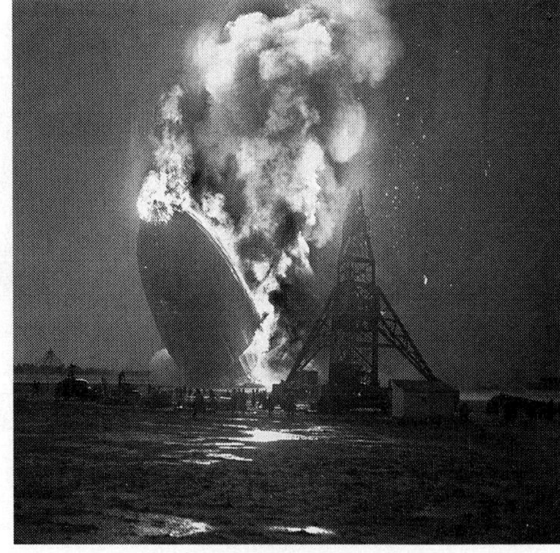

FIGURE 2-3
In May 1939, the Hindenburg, a lighter-than-air dirigible whose balloon was filled with hydrogen gas, exploded and burned in a spectacular and disastrous accident. Modern dirigibles are filled with nonflammable helium gas.

BOX 2-1

MODERN EVIDENCE FOR ATOMIC THEORY

In Dalton's time the primary evidence for atomic theory was the observation that elements always combine to form chemical compounds in fixed, unvarying mass ratios. Although this was enough to convince most scientists, it took almost a century before atomic theory was accepted universally. In recent years, scientists have developed powerful microscopes that can distinguish individual atoms and molecules. Two techniques, transmission electron microscopy (TEM) and scanning tunneling microscopy (STM), generate elegant pictures of atomic layers.

These techniques take advantage of what happens when electron beams pass through thin layers of solids. Just as light lets us see because its characteristics change as it passes through or reflects off an object, the characteristics of an electron beam change as it passes through or reflects off atoms. In essence the beam "takes a picture" of atomic layers that can be magnified billions of times, making it possible to observe individual atoms.

STM reveals the distribution of atoms on the surface of a solid. This technique has been used to view surfaces of silicon, which is used to manufacture computer chips. Examine the STM image of a silicon surface shown in Figure 2-4. The image shows how individual silicon atoms are arranged on the surface. Notice that most of the atoms lie in flat, regular planes, but irregularities can be seen clearly. Several layers, as well as "pits" in the planes, are visible. The figure also shows that silicon atoms are organized into layers, with the atoms in each layer arranged in a hexagonal, "honeycomb" array. Scientists use pictures such as these to learn how atoms combine on a surface.

TEM microscopes have been combined with videotaping to record "movies" that show how reactions proceed at the atomic level. For example, oxygen gas reacts with silicon on a surface such as that shown in Figure 2-4, and the product, SiO, "boils off" of the surface. Videotape images show that this reaction occurs preferentially at a silicon ledge like the one in the center of Figure 2-4. This ledge is "eaten away" by oxygen. The videotapes also reveal that carbon atom impurities in the layer resist attack, forming islands as surrounding silicon atoms combine with oxygen and are removed.

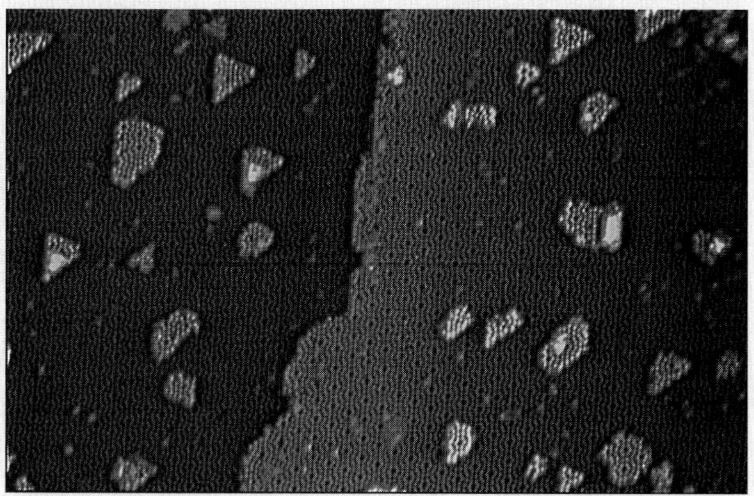

FIGURE 2-4
STM image of silicon atoms on a silicon surface. Individual atoms can be distinguished clearly, and details of the way atoms organize into layers are also visible.

The relationship between electricity and chemistry is explored in Chapter 17.

The *macroscopic level* describes something that is visible to the naked eye.

Molecules that contain just two atoms are called *diatomic*, using the Greek prefix *di-*, meaning "two."

It is also possible to reverse this reaction between hydrogen and oxygen. One way to do this is illustrated in Figure 2-5. An electrical current decomposes water containing a small amount of acid. The electricity causes hydrogen gas and oxygen gas to form. These gases can be captured and their amounts measured as they bubble out of the liquid mixture. It turns out that the gases are always produced in the same mass ratio: Every 9.0 g of water produces 1.0 g of hydrogen and 8.0 g of oxygen.

We have described these two processes at the macroscopic level, in which two gases combine to produce a liquid or a liquid decomposes to produce gases. Chemists, however, think of these processes in terms of atoms, the building blocks of all matter. Figure 2-6 shows how chemists visualize hydrogen gas, oxygen gas, and water. Notice that hydrogen gas contains hydrogen atoms (feature 1 of the atomic theory). Experiments on hydrogen reveal that all its atoms behave identically by combining into diatomic molecules (feature 2). Oxygen gas is made up of diatomic molecules containing oxygen atoms, but these molecules look and act differently than molecules made from hydrogen atoms (feature 3). When molecules of hydrogen and oxygen react to give water, atoms of hydrogen combine with atoms of oxygen in a 2:1 ratio (feature 4). Atoms are rearranged in this chemical process, but the total number of each type of atom remains the same (feature 5 of the atomic theory).

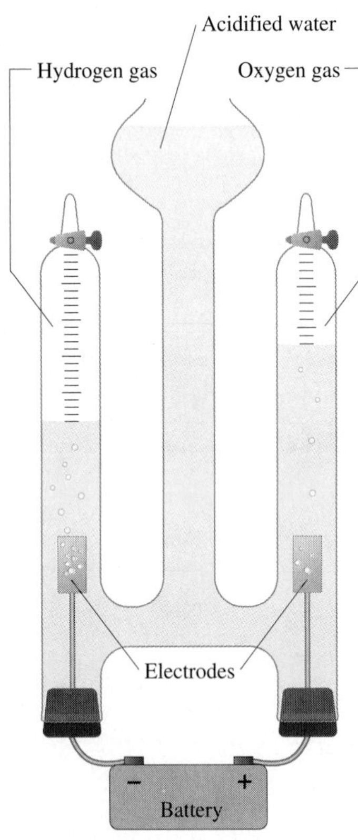

FIGURE 2-5
When electricity passes through acidified water, the liquid decomposes into hydrogen gas and oxygen gas. Every 9.0 g of water that decomposes produces 1.0 g of hydrogen and 8.0 g of oxygen.

Several ways exist to describe the chemical reaction that produces water from hydrogen and oxygen, but the most convenient method uses chemical formulas. Remember from Section 1.2 that a chemical formula is a symbolic representation of the atomic composition of a substance. A chemical equation using chemical formulas is a symbolic representation of how atoms rearrange during a chemical reaction. For the reaction of hydrogen with oxygen to form water, the equation is as follows:

$$2\,H_{2\,(g)} + O_{2\,(g)} \rightarrow 2\,H_2O_{\,(l)}$$

This compact statement contains much information about the chemistry of the system. It identifies hydrogen and oxygen as the **reactants** or **starting materials** by placing them on the left side of the arrow. Water, on the other hand, is on the right side of the arrow because it is the reaction **product.** The *(g)* and *(l)* designations indicate that H_2 and O_2 are gases, whereas H_2O is a liquid. The equation also indicates that elemental oxygen (O_2) and hydrogen (H_2) exist as pairs of atoms combined into diatomic molecules, whereas each molecule of water contains two atoms of hydrogen and one atom of oxygen. The numbers in front of the formulas tell us that two molecules of H_2 react with one molecule of O_2 to make two molecules of H_2O. Finally, the equation verifies that atoms of each element are neither created nor destroyed because there are just as many hydrogen atoms (four) and oxygen atoms (two) in the reactants (before reaction) as in the products (after reaction).

An equation in which atoms of each type are neither created nor destroyed is said to be a **balanced chemical equation.** In accord with feature 5 of atomic theory, all proper chemical equations must be balanced. We describe how to write and balance chemical equations in Chapter 4.

ATOMS COMBINE TO MAKE COMPOUNDS

Common table salt is sodium chloride.

An essential feature of atomic theory is that atoms combine in whole-number ratios to make compounds. Some elements combine in just one way to form a single chemical compound. For example, sodium atoms always combine with chlorine atoms in a 1:1 atomic ratio to form sodium chloride. Most elements, however, can combine with one another in more than one way. Hydrogen and oxygen provide a simple example. Water forms from two hydrogen atoms and *one* atom of oxygen, but two atoms of

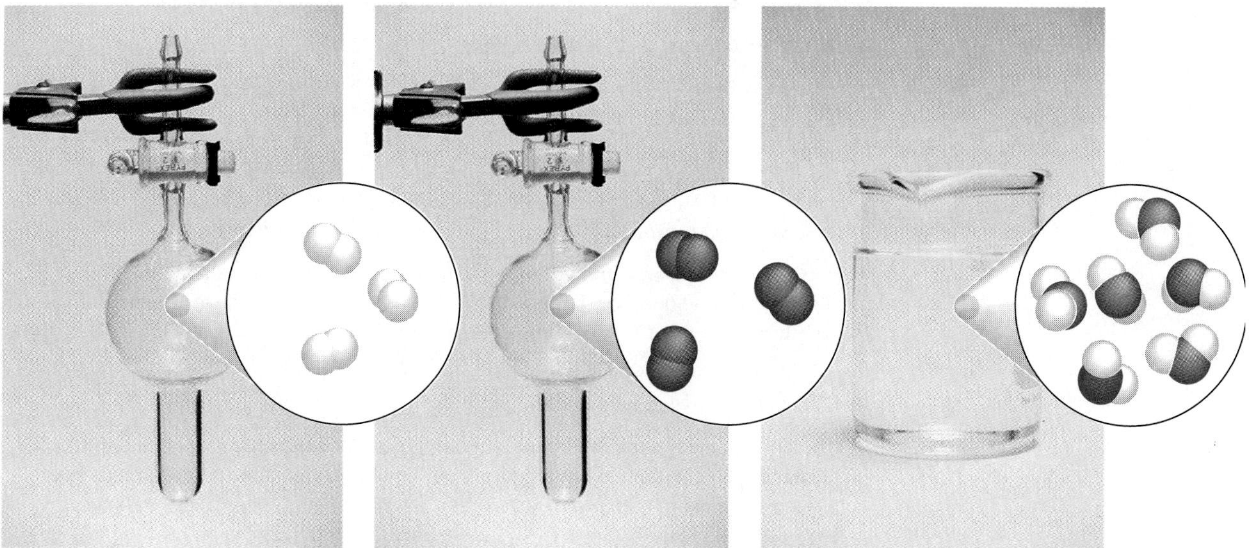

FIGURE 2-6
Hydrogen gas, oxygen gas, and liquid water are all composed of atoms, shown schematically in the "blown-up" windows.

hydrogen can also combine with *two* atoms of oxygen to form a different substance, hydrogen peroxide. Figure 2-7 shows molecular pictures of these reactions.

Although water and hydrogen peroxide are made from the same elements, their chemical properties are very different. Water is stable under most conditions. It is easy to form and difficult to destroy. Hydrogen peroxide, on the other hand, is an extremely reactive molecule. It is not difficult to make under the right conditions, but it can be destroyed in many ways. Water is life sustaining; in fact, life depends completely on water. Hydrogen peroxide is life destroying, even in small quantities. Because it kills microorganisms, hydrogen peroxide is used as a disinfectant. From an understanding of how atoms join together to make molecules, chemists can explain why two compounds that seem so similar have profoundly different reactivity patterns. We describe how atoms link together in Chapters 8 and 9.

Meanwhile, remember that chemists try to visualize chemical reactions at the molecular level. This molecular view is so ingrained that chemists often take it for granted. As you study chemistry, strive to attain this molecular point of view. Sample Problem 2-1 provides an example.

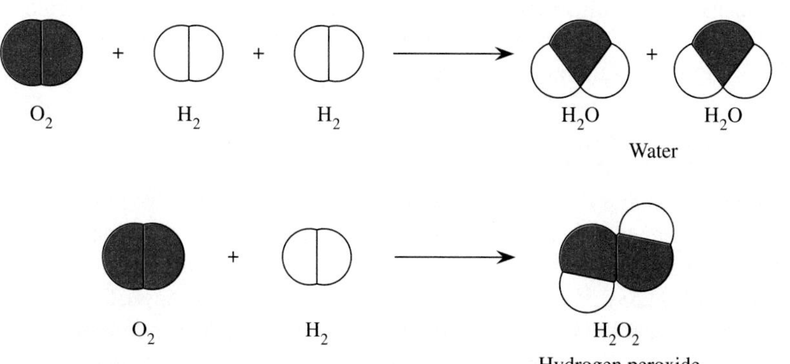

FIGURE 2-7
Molecular pictures of hydrogen reacting with oxygen in two different ways to form two different chemical compounds, water (H_2O) and hydrogen peroxide (H_2O_2).

SAMPLE PROBLEM 2-1 MOLECULAR PICTURES

When charcoal burns in air, carbon atoms combine with oxygen to form carbon dioxide. The chemical equation for this reaction is:

$$C_{(s)} + O_{2\,(g)} \rightarrow CO_{2\,(g)}$$

Experiments on CO_2 show that its molecules are linear, with a carbon atom in the middle. Draw a molecular picture that illustrates this reaction.

METHOD: In molecular pictures, atoms are represented with circles; different colors or shadings are used to distinguish between the elements. The chemical equation provides additional information that can be incorporated into our drawing.

The *(s)* after carbon's symbol tells us it is a solid, so we show it as a cluster of carbon atoms. The formula for oxygen tells us that it exists as diatomic molecules in the gas phase.

We can draw as many atoms and molecules as we choose, but the numbers of atoms of each element must not change during the process. Also, the equation tells us that the reaction between carbon and oxygen occurs in 1:1 ratio. Thus there must be as many carbon atoms and oxygen molecules *consumed* as CO_2 molecules *produced*. Here is how the molecular picture looks if we choose to depict 16 atoms of carbon and eight molecules of oxygen.

In our representation, eight O_2 molecules have been converted to eight CO_2 molecules. This uses up eight carbon atoms from the original supply. The rest of the carbon atoms are left over at the end because no molecules of oxygen remain to carry on the reaction.

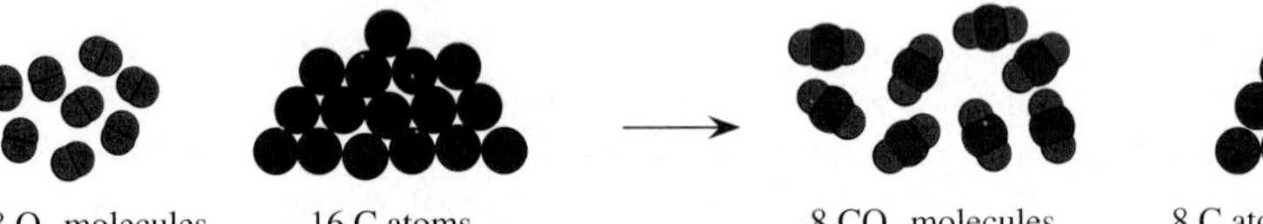

For further practice, draw a molecular picture starting with six carbon atoms that would consume all six of them and leave four oxygen molecules.

ATOMS ARE CONSTANTLY IN MOTION

At the atomic-molecular level, some substances, described as *monatomic*, contain individual atoms that are not bound to any other atoms. An example is argon (Ar). Other substances, such as O_2, H_2, and H_2O, contain groups of atoms bound into molecules. At the atomic-molecular level, the species that move freely about are atoms for monatomic species and molecules for species composed of atomic groups.

Atomic theory states that matter is made up of tiny atoms. STM pictures show that atoms occupy definite locations in solid materials. Liquids and gases, on the other hand, flow easily from one place to another. This fluidity indicates that the atoms or molecules in liquids and gases are free to move about.

Consider a fluid confined in a definite space, such as water in a glass. Are the water molecules moving about, even though the fluid is stationary? The answer is "yes" because in all matter, even substances as solid as granite, individual atoms, and molecules are constantly in motion. In solids, atoms "rattle around," or vibrate, in the cages formed by the atoms that surround them. In liquids, atoms or molecules move past one another continually, much like minnows in a stream endlessly changing positions. In gases, atoms or molecules are free to move over large distances. Figure 2-8 provides a schematic illustration of motion at the atomic-molecular level.

A phenomenon called **brownian motion** provides evidence for the movement of molecules. It was first described in 1828 by a Scottish botanist, Robert Brown, who used a microscope to examine plant spores floating on water. Brown noticed that the spores moved about continuously and underwent irregular changes of direction, as illustrated in Figure 2-9, *A*. They seemed to dance about on the water's surface. A similar irregular dance is observed for other types of small suspended particles, such as fine silt suspended in water and smoke particles in the atmosphere.

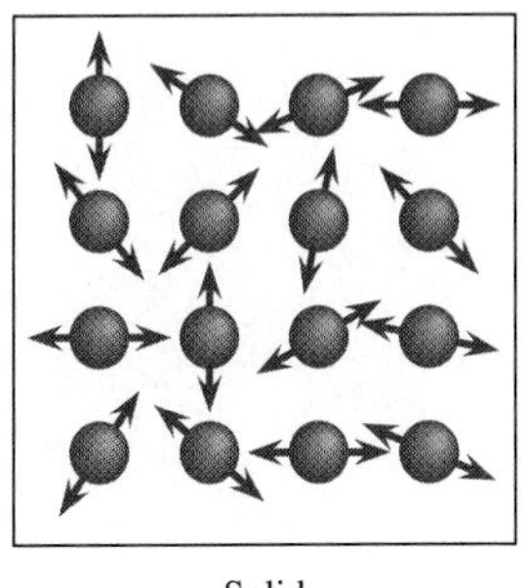

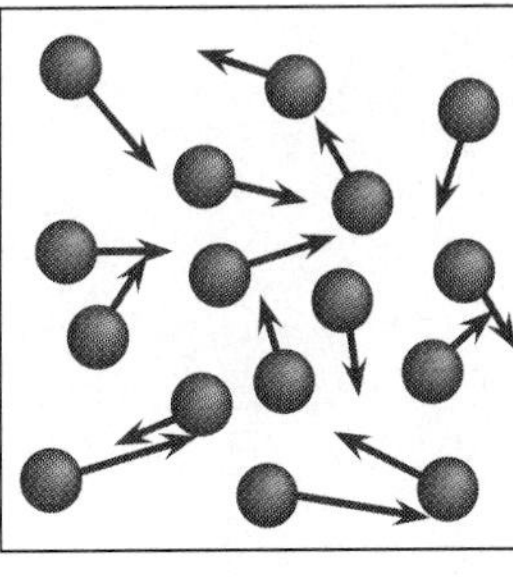

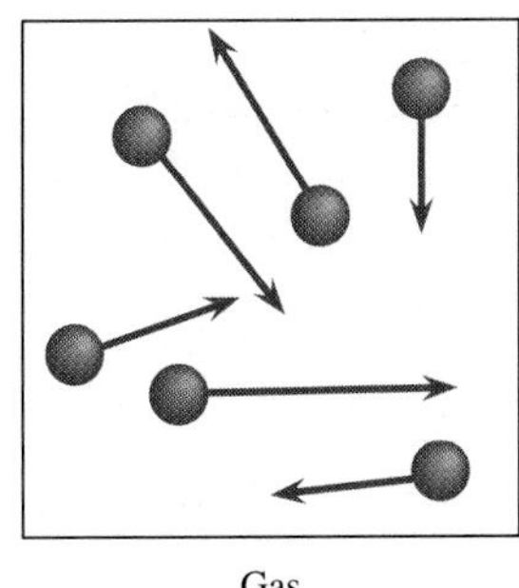

FIGURE 2-8
Atomic pictures of a monatomic solid *(left)*, liquid *(center)*, and gas *(right)*, showing how atoms move about in each phase. Atoms in a monatomic solid vibrate back and forth but seldom move past each other. In a monatomic liquid, atoms collide frequently and move past one another. Gaseous atoms travel relatively far before encountering other atoms.

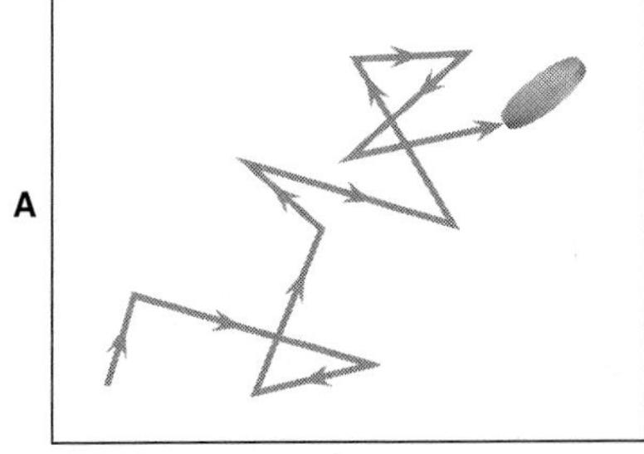

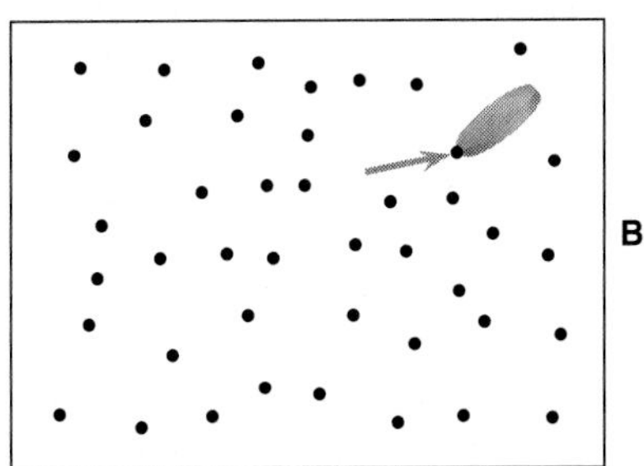

FIGURE 2-9
Brownian motion. **A,** The sketch shows the path of a spore particle when viewed under a microscope. The jagged line indicates the irregular changes in direction that the spore undergoes. **B,** The sketch shows the molecular explanation for the observations. When a molecule *(solid dots)* strikes the spore with high velocity, it causes the spore to "jump" in the direction of the impact. (The sketches are not to scale; individual molecules are many thousands of times smaller than a spore.)

Brownian motion is caused by collisions between the particles and the molecules of the fluid in which they are suspended. Spores move about because they collide constantly with water molecules. Occasionally a collision with a particularly fast-moving water molecule causes the spore to change its direction abruptly (Figure 2-9, *B*). Brown could not see the collisions because individual molecules are much too small to be visible under a botanist's microscope. Instead, he saw the changes in position of the suspended particles that resulted from molecular collisions.

The pressures exerted by gases also demonstrate molecular motion. Gases are composed of molecules, so the pressure exerted by a gas must come from these molecules. Just as the basketball in Figure 2-10 exerts a force when it collides with a backboard, moving gas molecules exert force when they collide with the walls of their container. The collective effect of many molecular collisions generates a pressure.

The **diffusion** of one liquid into another also demonstrates molecular motion. Figure 2-11 shows that if a drop of ink is added to a beaker of colorless, still water, the color slowly but surely spreads throughout the water. The water molecules and the molecules that give ink its color move continuously. As they slide by one another, the ink molecules eventually become distributed uniformly throughout the volume of liquid.

Molecular motion does not stop when the molecules are evenly distributed, even though we see no further change in color. Instead, the molecules move randomly in every direction, always changing position. However, as Figure 2-12 shows, the total number of ink molecules and water molecules in any region of the liquid does not change. As a result, no net change in color occurs.

The diffusion of ink shown in Figure 2-11 demonstrates that the higher the temperature, the faster molecules move. That is, a drop of ink added to a beaker of heated water spreads significantly faster than the same size drop added to a beaker of cold water. Notice the differences between the two right-hand photos in Figure 2-11.

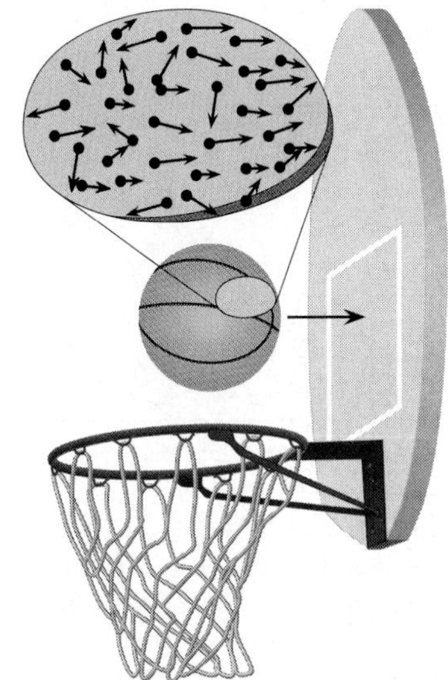

FIGURE 2-10
When a basketball strikes a backboard, it exerts a force against the backboard. The gas molecules inside the basketball *(inset)* also exert force when they strike the walls of the basketball. The net result of many collisions is gas pressure. Pressure is described in Chapter 5.

FIGURE 2-11
The addition of ink to a beaker of water *(left)* is followed by the diffusion of the ink slowly *(center)* until eventually the ink is distributed uniformly *(right)*. Ink diffuses less rapidly at room temperature *(top)* than at elevated temperature *(bottom)*.

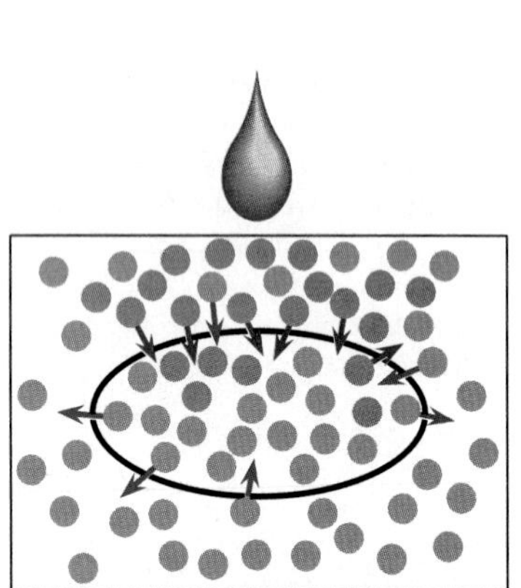

A Shortly after adding a drop of red ink.

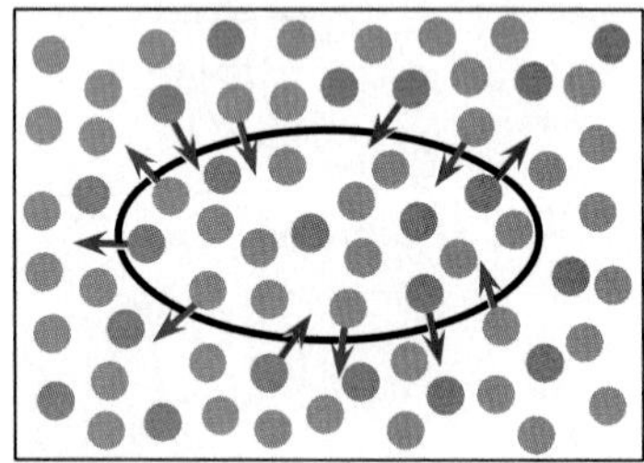

B After complete diffusion.

FIGURE 2-12
A, When ink is added to water, the color slowly diffuses throughout the liquid. **B,** Ink molecules *(red circles)* and water molecules *(blue circles)* continue to move about even after they are distributed evenly throughout the mixture. No net change occurs in the color, however, because the number of ink molecules entering any particular volume of the liquid is balanced by an equal number of ink molecules leaving the same region.

DYNAMIC EQUILIBRIUM

Atoms and molecules are always moving. When a drop of ink is added to water, the ink molecules diffuse through the water until they are distributed uniformly. After that, they continue to diffuse, but our eyes observe no further change because equal numbers of ink molecules move in every direction. This condition of balanced motion is called **dynamic equilibrium.** A system at *equilibrium* shows no change in its observable properties. Our example of ink in water is at equilibrium when the color is uniform and unchanging. A *dynamic* system contains objects that move continuously. Our example is dynamic because even when the color of the liquid is uniform and unchanging, the water and ink molecules move about. Look again at Figure 2-12. In any part of the liquid, ink molecules continue to move, but the number of ink molecules in each region does not change.

Dynamic equilibria occur frequently in chemical systems. All chemical processes reach a state of equilibrium if allowed to continue for a sufficient time, but molecular activity always goes on after equilibrium has been reached. You must become familiar with the dynamic quality of molecular motion. The following example should help you grasp this important idea.

Rain puddles disappear quickly after summer showers, and wet towels hung on a clothesline eventually dry. Why? In the constant motion of molecules in liquid water, some molecules escape from the liquid phase. When a water molecule escapes from the surface of a puddle or a wet towel, the wind sweeps it away into the Earth's atmosphere. A wet towel left in a washing machine, however, stays wet for a long time. This is not because water molecules are no longer escaping from the surface of the towel. Instead, when the lid of the machine is closed, gaseous water molecules seldom escape from the washing chamber. Because water molecules seldom escape from the container, the number of water molecules in the gas phase increases, and some of these molecules are recaptured by the towel when they collide with its surface. The system soon reaches a condition of dynamic equilibrium in which, for every water molecule that leaves the surface of the towel, one water molecule returns from the gas phase to the towel. Under these conditions the towel remains wet indefinitely.

Figure 2-13 illustrates this type of dynamic equilibrium. In a closed container, escaping molecules collect in the gaseous space above the liquid. Some of them collide with the liquid surface and are recaptured. This recapture process occurs more frequently as the number of water molecules in the gas phase increases. Eventually, so many water molecules exist in the gas phase that the number of gas molecules captured by the liquid exactly matches the number of liquid molecules escaping to the gas. The system has reached dynamic equilibrium. Molecules continue to leave the liquid phase for the gas phase, but equal numbers of molecules are captured from the gas by the liquid. The amount of water in each phase remains the same (equilibrium) even though molecules continue to move back and forth between the gas and the liquid (dynamic). As with dye dispersed in water, no *net* change occurs after equilibrium is established.

The examples given here involve physical equilibria, because no chemical reactions occur. We describe chemical equilibria in detail in Chapters 15 and 16.

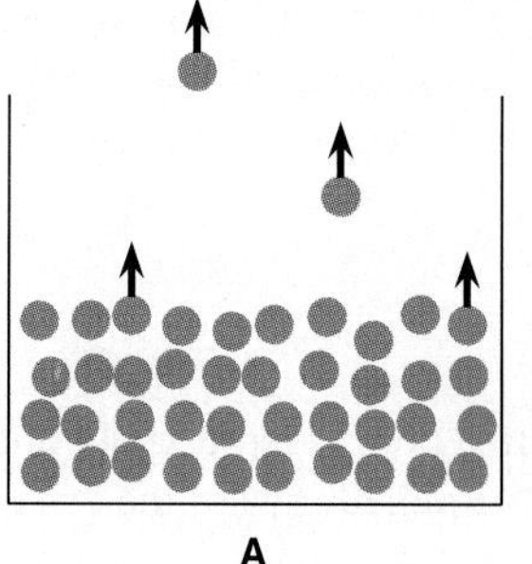

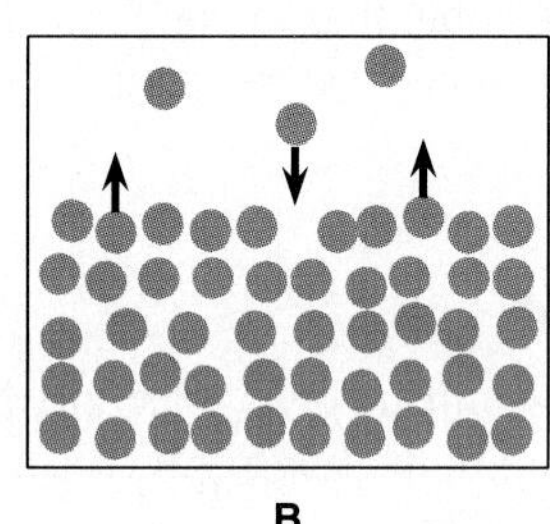

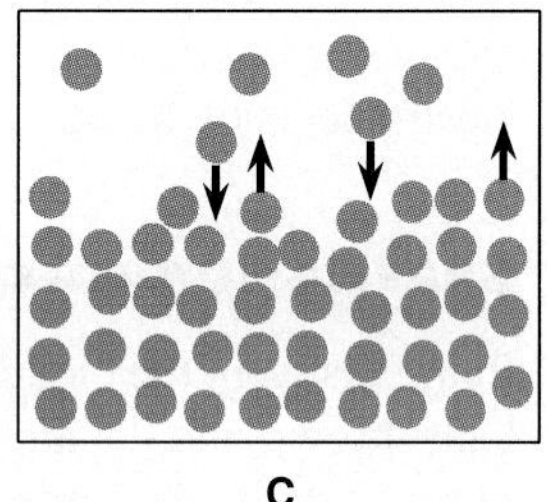

FIGURE 2-13
A, When water evaporates from an open container, molecules escape but are not recaptured. **B,** If the container is closed, water molecules begin to build up in the gas above the liquid, and some are recaptured when they collide with the liquid surface. **C,** Eventually, enough water molecules are present in the gas to make the rate of recapture equal to the rate of escape.

SECTION EXERCISES

2.1.1 Elemental bromine, chlorine, and iodine exist as diatomic molecules. Chlorine is a gas at room temperature, bromine is a liquid, and iodine is a solid. Draw molecular pictures that show how the atoms are arranged in samples of chlorine, bromine, and iodine.

2.1.2 Chlorine and fluorine molecules can react with each other to give several chemical compounds, two of which have formulas ClF and ClF_3. Draw molecular pictures showing six molecules each of F_2 and Cl_2 reacting to give these compounds. A ClF_3 molecule is shaped like a T, with the Cl atom at the center:

$$F_2 + Cl_2 \rightarrow 2\ FCl \qquad Cl_2 + 3\ F_2 \rightarrow 2\ ClF_3$$

2.1.3 When you shower in an enclosed bathroom, the mirrors often become covered with a fog of water droplets, even though no liquid strikes the mirrors. Explain this process in molecular terms.

2.2 ATOMIC ARCHITECTURE: ELECTRONS AND NUCLEI

Atoms are the fundamental building blocks of chemistry. Tiny as they are, atoms nonetheless have internal structures. Furthermore, atoms of a particular chemical element have an internal structure different from that of atoms of every other element. These differences in structure are what make the chemistry of one element different from that of another. Thus the rich diversity of chemical behavior can be traced to the internal structure of atoms.

After atomic theory was established, scientists turned their attention to the following basic questions:

1. Do constituent particles make up the atom, and if so, what are they?
2. How are atoms bound together in chemical compounds?

Both questions ask about what holds matter together. If atoms have parts, something must bind these parts together into atoms. If atoms "stick together" in compounds, something must act as a kind of "molecular glue."

To understand what holds atoms and molecules together, physicists and chemists perform experiments to pull them apart. A series of elegant experiments, designed and performed in the first three decades of the twentieth century, revealed the essential structure of the atom. We outline the main features of the most important experiments here to provide you with an idea of how scientists probe matter at the atomic level. As an introduction, however, we must first present the idea of forces.

Forces hold things together. Physicists have identified four different types of forces: gravitational, electromagnetic, strong nuclear, and weak nuclear. Atomic and molecular structures are determined by electromagnetic forces, but gravitational force is probably the type most familiar to you. To help you understand the characteristics of forces, we describe some features of gravitational force before discussing electromagnetic force.

GRAVITATIONAL FORCE

Rain falls from the clouds, swimmers dive gracefully into a pool (Figure 2-14), and balls thrown into the air return to the Earth. All objects are pulled toward the center of the Earth by the force of gravity.

FIGURE 2-14
Gravitational force pulls objects toward the Earth.

The Earth is not the only body that exerts gravitational force. The sun's gravitational force holds the planets in their regular orbits. In fact, every mass exerts a gravitational attraction on all other masses. The existence of gravitational force between any two bodies is a fundamental law of the universe.

Gravitational force decreases as objects get farther apart. Studies of planetary motion show that this decrease in force depends on the square of the separation between objects. Gravitational force also depends on the masses of the interacting bodies. The following equation describes gravitational force quantitatively:

$$F_{gr} = G\frac{m_1 m_2}{r^2}$$

F_{gr} is the attractive force between the objects, m_1 and m_2 are the masses of the objects, r is the distance between them, and G is a universal proportionality constant.

ELECTRICAL FORCE

Gravitation is the most important force for large objects such as airplanes, humans, and the Earth. For tiny objects such as atoms and molecules, electrical force is most important. Gravitational force always pulls objects together, but electrical force can

FIGURE 2-15
An electroscope demonstrates that like-charged objects repel each other.

pull them together or push them apart. There are two types of electrical charge, positive and negative. Charges of different types attract each other, but charges of the same type repel each other. In other words, electrical forces pull oppositely charged objects toward each other, whereas they push apart particles that have the same charge. Figure 2-15 shows a simple apparatus called an *electroscope,* which contains a metal plate and a metal foil. When the plate and foil are given electrical charges of the same type, they move apart, demonstrating that they repel each other.

Studies show that electrical force increases with the amount of charge on each body and decreases as the square of the distance between them increases. The equation that describes this behavior is similar to the equation for gravitational force:

$$F_{el} = k\,\frac{q_1 q_2}{r^2} \qquad \textbf{(2-1)}$$

In Equation 2-1, F_{el} is the electrical force, q_1 and q_2 are the charges on the two bodies, r is the distance between them, and k is a proportionality constant that makes the units of force consistent with the units of charge. When both charges have the same sign, the force is positive and the charges repel, but when the charges have opposite signs, the force is negative and the charges attract. The French physicist Charles-Augustin de Coulomb discovered these fundamental properties of electricity in the eighteenth century, so Equation 2-1 is called **Coulomb's law.**

Coulomb's law is as important for atoms and molecules as the law of gravitation is for large objects. In later chapters, this law appears as the basis for understanding atomic structure and chemical bonding.

MAGNETISM

Objects with electric charge always act under the influence of Coulomb's law. A charged object *in motion* is also subject to an additional force, called **magnetism.** Objects that generate magnetic force are called *magnets.* Magnets usually have two ends, a north pole and a south pole. As with electrical force, magnetic force attracts and/or repels; opposite poles (north and south) attract, but like poles (north-north or south-south) repel. Figure 2-16 shows that magnetic force can be stronger

The ends of magnets are called *north* and *south poles* because the Earth itself is a large, rather weak magnet whose "ends" are near the North and South Poles.

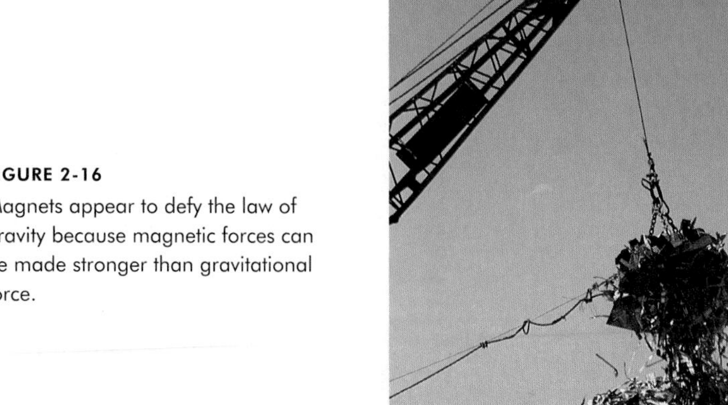

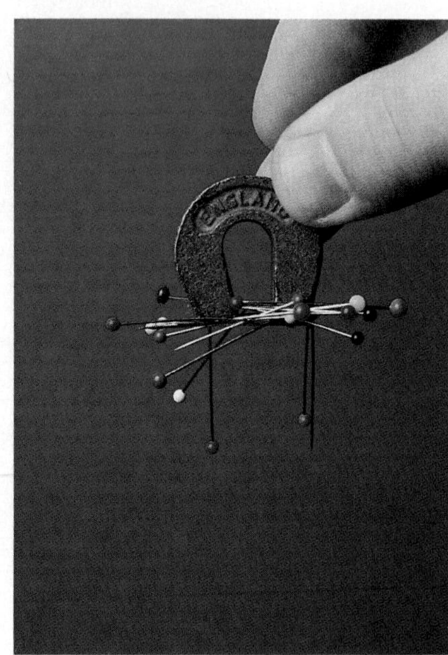

FIGURE 2-16
Magnets appear to defy the law of gravity because magnetic forces can be made stronger than gravitational force.

than the force of gravity. The equation for magnetic force, is beyond the scope of general chemistry.

To understand some early experiments that probed atomic structure, you need to know that a moving electrical charge changes course as it passes between the poles of a magnet. Figure 2-17 illustrates that a magnet causes charged particles to move along a curved path, just as gravitational force causes a moving ball to follow a curved path. Magnetic deflection is used in studies of atomic structure because the curvature of the path reveals information about the properties of moving charges.

ELECTRONS

Important clues about the structure of atoms came from experiments that used electrical force. The simplest of these experiments used two metal plates called *electrodes* sealed inside a glass tube along with a sample of a gas. Figure 2-18 shows a schematic drawing of this type of apparatus. One of the metal plates was given a large positive electrical charge, but the other was given a large negative charge. When the charges became large enough, electrical forces caused an electrical discharge (similar to a lightning bolt) to leap across the space between the plates.

This high-energy discharge caused some of the atoms of the gas to fall apart. The pieces of the broken atoms turned out to be charged particles. Consistent with

FIGURE 2-17
Magnetic force causes a moving charge to travel along a curved path, just as gravitational force causes a moving mass (such as a baseball) to move along a curved path. A moving charged particle changes course when it passes between the poles of a magnet. The amount of bending can be related quantitatively to the charge and mass of the particle.

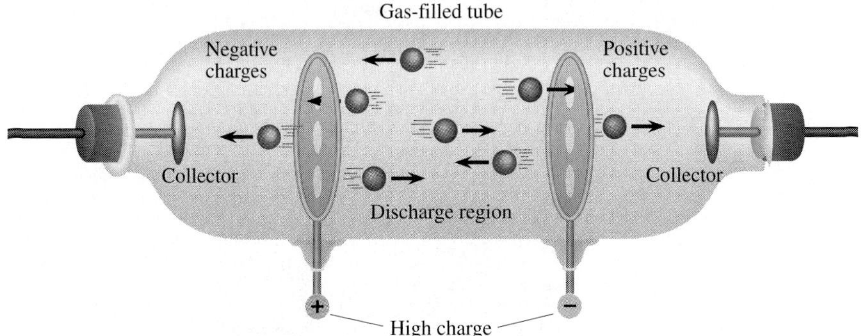

FIGURE 2-18
Schematic drawing of a gas discharge tube in operation. When a very high electrical charge is placed on the two perforated plates, an electrical discharge occurs between them. The positively charged and negatively charged particles that form then move in opposite directions, as described by Coulomb's law.

Coulomb's law, particles with positive charges moved toward the negative electrode, while particles with negative charges moved toward the positive electrode. When the electrodes had holes in them, some of these charged particles passed through the electrodes and were captured by detectors at the ends of the tube.

This experiment showed that atoms are made up of a collection of smaller fragments that possess positive and negative charges. The energy supplied by the discharge between the electrodes was enough to break atoms into these smaller fragments.

To learn more about the nature of these smaller, charged particles, the experiment was repeated using different types of gases. Changing the gas in the tube changed the behavior of the *positively* charged particles, but the *negatively* charged particles always acted the same. These negatively charged fragments are common to all atoms. They are called **electrons.**

The discovery of the electron prompted a series of more sophisticated experiments designed to reveal even more about its nature. J.J. Thomson* performed one such experiment with a device called a *cathode ray tube,* which is illustrated in Figure 2-19. A cathode ray is a beam of electrons generated by an electrical discharge. Because an electron beam is a collection of moving electrical charges, it is affected by electrical and magnetic forces. When either type of force is applied at right angles to the direction of motion of an electron beam, it causes the beam to

* J.J. Thomson (1856-1940) was an English physicist who was awarded the Nobel Prize in physics in 1906 for his work on electrons. He directed the Cavendish Laboratory at Cambridge for 35 years, and seven of his research assistants subsequently won Nobel Prizes.

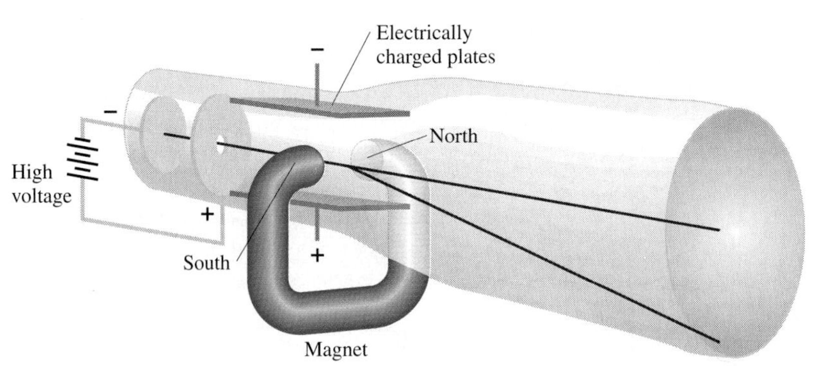

FIGURE 2-19
Schematic drawing of a cathode ray tube (television picture tubes work on this same principle). An electrical discharge generates electrons at the left side of the tube. These negative electrons are pulled through the hole in the positive plate. In the deflection region a pair of charged plates deflects the beam *(bent line)*, but if a magnetic force is also imposed on the deflection region, it is possible to counterbalance the effect of the electric force *(straight line)*.

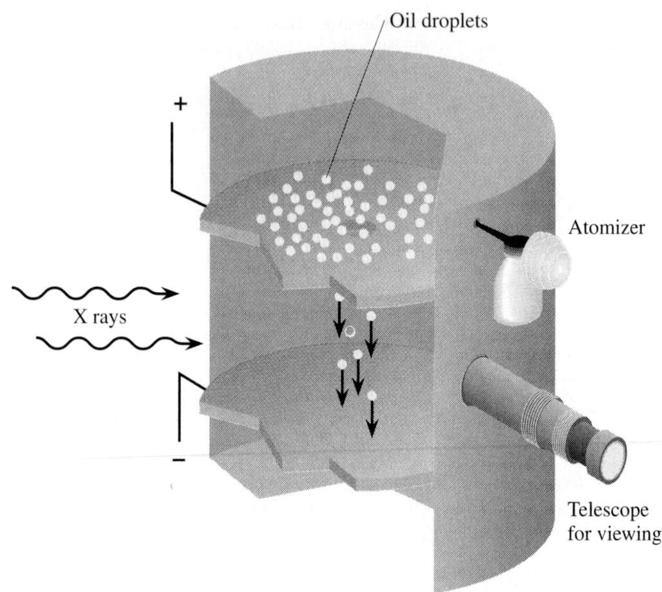

FIGURE 2-20
Schematic view of Millikan's oil drop experiment. Inside the chamber an atomizer generated a fine mist of oil droplets *(yellow circles)*. Bombarding the droplets with x rays gave some of them extra negative charge *(orange circle)*. In the presence of sufficient electrical force, these negatively charged droplets could be suspended in space.

bend. The amount of bending depends on the electrons' velocity, charge, and mass. In Thomson's experiment a cathode ray was subjected simultaneously to electrical and magnetic forces, as indicated in Figure 2-19. By measuring the amount of magnetic force required to exactly counterbalance the deflection of the beam by a known electrical force, Thomson was able to calculate the ratio of the electron's charge to its mass:

The fundamental unit of electrical charge is the *coulomb* (C), defined as the quantity of electricity transferred by a current of 1 ampere in 1 second.

$$\frac{\text{Charge}}{\text{Mass}} = \frac{e}{m} = 1.76 \times 10^{11}\ \text{C/kg}$$

Thomson's experiment showed that 1 kg of electrons has a charge of -1.76×10^{11} C, but he was unable to find out how much charge resides on a single electron. An American physicist, Robert A. Millikan, was able to determine this using a different experiment. In Millikan's experiment, electric plates were set up to oppose the Earth's gravitational force, as shown in Figure 2-20. A fine mist of oil droplets was sprayed into the chamber. Using a telescope, Millikan could watch the motion of the droplets as they drifted slowly downward under the force of gravity. Millikan then changed the behavior of the droplets in two ways. First, he irradiated the droplets with x rays. This irradiation generated extra electrical charges on some droplets. By themselves, these excess electrical charges had no effect on the motion of the droplets. However, the chamber also contained two metal plates that could act as electrodes. Adding charge to the plates generated an upward force on any droplets that carried extra electrons. By adjusting the amount of electrical force on the plates, Millikan could stop the downward drift of these negatively charged particles. With just the right amount of electrical force, the downward-acting gravitational force on a droplet was exactly counterbalanced by the upward-acting electrical force, so the droplet's motion ceased.

Gravitational force acted on the masses of the oil droplets. Millikan determined the mass of a droplet by observing its behavior when it moved under the force of gravity only. Electrical force acted on the negative charges on the oil droplets.

Millikan measured the amounts of electrical force required to suspend the motion of many different droplets and calculated the charges on the droplets. He found several different values, but the charge on a droplet was always equal to $n(-1.6 \times 10^{-19}$ C), where n was an integer (1, 2, 3...).

Millikan concluded that oil droplets carried from one to several extra electrons. Thus n is the number of extra electrons on the droplet, and the charge of an individual electron is -1.6×10^{-19} C. Combining this value with Thomson's measurement of charge/mass ratio, Millikan computed the mass of a single electron:

$$m_{\text{electron}} = \frac{e}{(e/m)} = \frac{-1.6 \times 10^{-19}\ \text{C}}{-1.76 \times 10^{11}\ \text{C/kg}} = 9.1 \times 10^{-31}\ \text{kg}$$

Today our understanding of the electron goes well beyond the description presented here. In Chapter 6 we return to the electron and explore its nature in greater detail.

THE NUCLEUS

By the early twentieth century, scientists had discovered that atoms contain electrons and positively charged particles. The nature of electrons had been elucidated by the experiments of Thomson and Millikan, but the nature of the positive particles was entirely unknown. Also, it was not known how the particles fit together to make an atom.

The definitive experiment that showed how charges and masses are distributed in an atom was carried out in 1909 by Ernest Rutherford. At the time, scientists hypothesized that the atom was similar to a chocolate chip cookie, with negative electrons (the "chips") embedded in the positive "dough" of the atom in a way that balanced repulsion between like charges and attraction between unlike charges. Rutherford tested this model of the atom using subatomic projectiles to bombard a target of atoms. The projectiles, called *alpha particles,* had been discovered during research on radioactivity. Alpha particles are high-energy, positively charged fragments of helium atoms emitted during radioactive decay of unstable elements such as uranium.

Rutherford, who was from New Zealand, used plum pudding with raisins as his analogy.

We describe the details of radioactive decay in Chapter 19.

In Rutherford's experiment, alpha particles were directed at a thin film of gold metal. According to the "cookie model," the mass of each gold atom in the foil should have been spread evenly over the entire atom. Rutherford knew that alpha particles had enough energy to pass directly through such a uniform distribution of mass. He expected the particles to slow down and change direction only by a small amount as they passed through the foil.

The results of the experiment were quite unexpected. Most alpha particles passed directly through the gold film, and some were deflected slightly. To Rutherford's astonishment, however, a few particles bounced back in the direction from which they came. Rutherford said it was similar to shooting an artillery shell at a piece of tissue paper and having it bounce back at him. Somewhere within the atom there had to be a positively charged mass capable of deflecting high-energy, positively charged alpha particles. The cookie model of the atom crumbled.

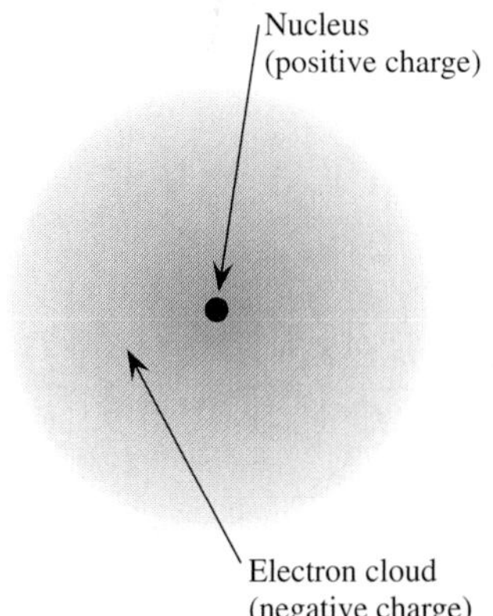

FIGURE 2-21
Schematic drawing of an atom, showing a central, positive nucleus surrounded by a cloud of electrons. This form of atom is consistent with the results of Rutherford's scattering experiments.

To explain his experiment, Rutherford proposed a new theory for atomic structure. He suggested that every atom contains a tiny central core where all the positive charge and most of the mass is concentrated. This central core, called the **nucleus,** is surrounded by the electrons, as shown schematically in Figure 2-21.

Rutherford's experiment and its interpretation are represented in Figure 2-22. Electrons occupy a volume that is huge compared with the size of the nucleus, but

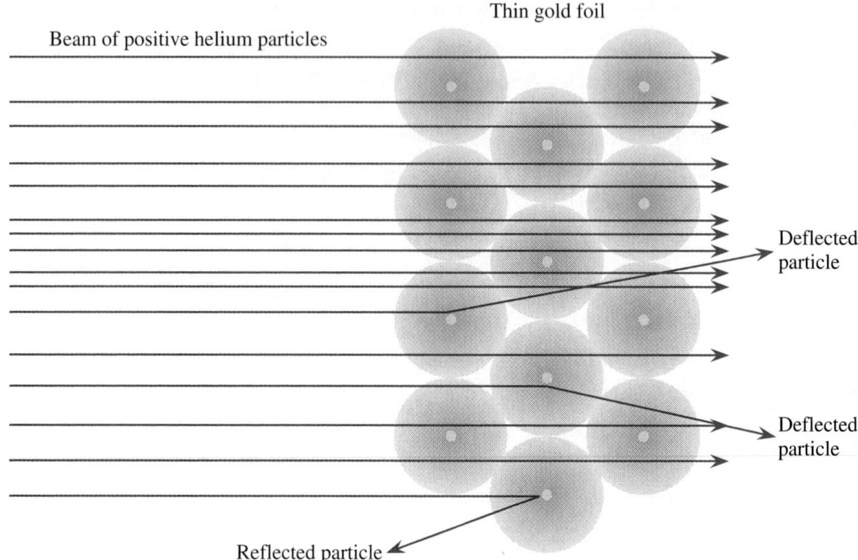

FIGURE 2-22
Schematic view of Rutherford's scattering experiment. When a beam of positively charged helium particles was "shot" at a thin gold foil, most of them passed through without much effect. Some, however, were reflected backward.

each electron has such a small mass that this volume appears as empty space to an alpha particle. As they passed through the gold atoms in the foil, the relatively heavy alpha particles were almost unaffected by interactions with electrons. An alpha particle was deflected only when it passed very near a nucleus. Because most of an atom's volume contains only electrons, most projectiles passed through the foil without being affected.

From the number of particles deflected and the pattern of deflection, Rutherford calculated the fraction of the atomic volume occupied by the positive nucleus. That fraction is 1 part in 10^{14}. To give you an idea of what that means, an atom the size of a baseball stadium would have a nucleus the size of a pea. The mass of the nucleus is concentrated in such a small volume that a nucleus the size of a pea would have a mass greater than 250 million tons.

Box 2-2 describes how Rutherford's experiment is representative of scientific methods and models.

Experiments on nuclei showed that the nucleus itself contains two types of subatomic fragments called **protons** and **neutrons.** Protons account for the positive charges of nuclei, whereas neutrons contribute mass but are electrically neutral. A proton's positive *charge* is equal in magnitude to the negative *charge* of an electron. The *mass* of a proton, on the other hand, is almost 2000 times greater than the *mass* of an electron. The mass of a neutron is almost the same as the mass of a proton.

In Chapter 19, we return to the nucleus to examine some of its special chemistry.

According to Coulomb's law, a nucleus that contains more than one proton should fly apart because the protons strongly repel one another. The third type of fundamental force, called the *strong nuclear force,* acts within nuclei and generates enough attraction among nuclear particles to hold nuclei together despite their multiple positive charges.

The experiments leading to the discovery of protons and neutrons were as important as the experiments leading to the discovery of the electron. Our interest is in chemistry, however, and as we show in later chapters, the chemistry of atoms and molecules stems mainly from their electrons. For this reason, we do not discuss the discovery or the details of nuclear structure.

Our picture of atomic architecture is now complete. Three particles—electrons, protons, and neutrons—combine in various numbers to make the different atoms of all the elements of the periodic table. Table 2-1 summarizes the characteristics of these three atomic building blocks.

BOX 2-2

SCIENTIFIC METHODS

The "cookie" model of the atom and Rutherford's experiment to test it represent an elegant example of one method by which science progresses. All science begins with experiments and observations. After collecting enough data, scientists suggest a theory that explains their observations. A good scientific theory does more than explain known facts; it also predicts results of new experiments. Scientists return to the laboratory to test the predictions made by theory. If the tests match the predictions of the theory, confidence in the theory increases. However, if the test gives results that do not agree, the theory must be discarded, or at least revised so that it agrees with the new results as well as the previous ones.

Experiments that showed the electrical nature of the atom led to the "cookie" model, which was developed to explain the presence of positively and negatively charged particles within the atom. The model predicted that projectiles such as alpha particles should pass directly through a thin foil of atoms. Rutherford's experiment was designed to test this prediction. In this case the theory failed spectacularly.

However, in the failure of one model are the seeds of a more successful one. The new model had to retain positive and negative parts of the atom because experiments showed clearly that atoms contain such parts. A new model, which proposed that the atom has a positively charged core called the *nucleus*, is what finally emerged. This nuclear model of the atom explained both the positive and negative parts of the atom and Rutherford's scattering results.

The nuclear model has been developed in quantitative detail and leads to many additional predictions about how atoms and nuclei behave. Physicists have performed many experiments that test these predictions, and they have all been verified. Consequently the nuclear model is firmly established as a correct view of atomic architecture.

TABLE 2-1 ATOMIC BUILDING BLOCKS

NAME	SYMBOL	CHARGE	MASS
Electron	e	-1.6022×10^{-19} C	9.1094×10^{-31} kg
Proton	p	$+1.6022 \times 10^{-19}$ C	1.6726×10^{-27} kg
Neutron	n	0	1.6749×10^{-27} kg

SECTION EXERCISES

2.2.1 Draw a sketch (include appropriate signs for the electric plates) for a tube in which *positive* ions are accelerated into a deflection region. Use Figure 2-19 as a guide.

2.2.2 In a Millikan type of experiment, an oil droplet with a mass of 1.2 μg and carrying three extra electrons is held motionless by an electrical force, $F_{el.}$
(a) In which direction is a droplet of mass 1.2 μg and carrying four electrons moving? (Refer to Figure 2-20.)
(b) In which direction is a droplet of mass 2.0 μg and carrying three extra electrons moving?

2.2.3 (a) How many electrons are required to give a total mass of 1.0 mg?
(b) What is the mass of the same number of neutrons?

2.3 ATOMIC DIVERSITY: THE ELEMENTS

Each element has distinct physical and chemical properties. According to atomic theory, differences among elements are caused by differences among atoms. All atoms are composed of electrons, protons, and neutrons, so ultimately, elements differ from one another because their atoms contain different numbers of these three subatomic particles.

Table 2-1 shows that the electrical charge of a proton is equal in magnitude but opposite in sign to an electron's electrical charge. When an atom has the same number of electrons as protons in its nucleus, the total negative charge of the electrons exactly balances the total positive charge of the nucleus. Such an atom has a net charge of zero. It is a neutral atom. Because of the attraction between opposite charges, charged atoms or molecules tend to gain or lose electrons until they become neutral, so most matter is electrically neutral.

Atoms subjected to strong electrical forces may lose or gain electrons. When this occurs, the charge on the nucleus remains constant. For example, a neutral hydrogen atom has one electron and a nucleus that consists of a single proton. In an electrical discharge a hydrogen atom may lose its electron, but the nucleus is still a hydrogen nucleus with a charge of 1.602×10^{-19} C. If a neutral hydrogen atom gains a second electron, the two-electron system still contains a hydrogen nucleus.

We see later that electrons are shifted about during chemical reactions. Again, however, each nucleus retains its characteristic charge. The defining feature of an element, therefore is the charge carried by its nucleus.

An element is identified by the charge of its nucleus because nuclei retain their characteristic electrical charges when electrons are lost or gained.

We mentioned in Chapter 1 that the periodic table lists elements in order of increasing masses, with a few exceptions. Now we see that nuclear charge is the organizing feature. However, as nuclear charge increases, so also does nuclear mass (with few exceptions), so these two characteristics of elements are closely related.

The charge of a nucleus depends on its protons. All atoms of a particular element have the same nuclear charge and the same number of protons. In turn, every different element has its own unique nuclear charge and a specific and unchanging number of protons. The number of protons in the nucleus is called the **atomic number** and is symbolized Z. Thus all atoms with the same value of Z belong to the same element. For example, all hydrogen atoms have Z of 1, all helium atoms have Z of 2, and all uranium atoms have Z of 92. The periodic table lists the elements in order of increasing atomic number. Each element has a unique name, symbol, and atomic number. The symbol H represents hydrogen ($Z = 1$), He represents helium ($Z = 2$), and U represents uranium ($Z = 92$).

ISOTOPES

Recall from Table 2-1 that the mass of an electron is almost 2000 times smaller than the mass of a proton or a neutron. Consequently the mass of an atom is almost entirely determined by the mass of its nucleus.

The *identity* of an atom is determined by its nuclear charge, but its *mass* is the sum of the contributions from all its atomic building blocks. Thus the mass of an atom depends on the number of protons *and neutrons* in its nucleus. Two atoms with the same number of protons but different numbers of neutrons are called **isotopes.** For example, every uranium atom has 92 protons in its nucleus, but whereas most uranium nuclei contain 146 neutrons, some contain only 143 neutrons. Naturally occurring uranium contains both isotopes, so any sample of pure uranium is a homogeneous mixture of uranium atoms with two slightly different masses.

An isotope is usually specified by giving its **mass number.** Mass number is the *total* number of *protons and neutrons* contained in a nucleus. Every isotope of a chemical element can be represented completely by writing its chemical symbol *(X)* preceded by a superscript giving its mass number *(A)* and a subscript giving its atomic number *(Z)*:

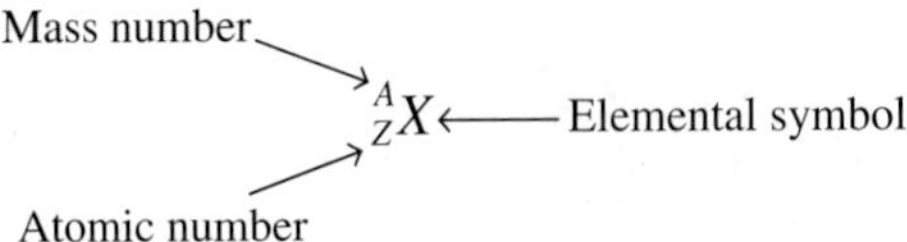

The subscript *Z* is redundant because each chemical symbol already defines a unique atomic number. The subscripts are nevertheless useful for isotopic bookkeeping.

Another way to describe an isotope is to cite its elemental name and mass number. The isotopes of uranium are ^{238}U, or uranium-238, and ^{235}U, or uranium-235. Sample Problem 2-2 provides practice in determining the composition of atoms.

SAMPLE PROBLEM 2-2 DETERMINING THE COMPOSITION OF ATOMS

Determine the number of protons, neutrons, and electrons in the following species: (a) $^{19}_{9}F$; (b) ^{54}Cr; and (c) lead-207.

METHOD: The number of subatomic particles is determined from the atomic number *(Z)* and the mass number *(A)*.

a. F is the symbol for fluorine. The subscript 9 is *Z*, which is the number of protons in the nucleus. The superscript 19 is *A*. The number of neutrons is found by subtracting *Z* from *A*: $A - Z = 19 - 9 = 10$ neutrons. Because this is a neutral atom, the number of electrons must equal the number of protons. Fluorine has 9 protons, 10 neutrons, and 9 electrons.

b. Cr is the symbol for chromium. *A* is 54, but *Z* is not given. The value of Z can be found in the periodic table. Chromium has *Z* of 24, which tells us the nucleus of this isotope contains 24 protons. Subtracting *Z* from *A*, we find that there are 30 neutrons. Finally, because this is a neutral atom, 24 electrons are present.

c. Lead has *Z* of 82. A neutral atom of lead-207 has 82 protons, 82 electrons, and $207 - 82 = 125$ neutrons.

Some elements, such as fluorine and phosphorus, occur naturally with just one isotope. More often, naturally occurring samples are mixture of isotopes. For example, element number 22 is titanium (Ti), a light and strong metal used in jet engines. Five naturally occurring Ti isotopes exist. Each has 22 protons in its nuclei, but the number of neutrons varies from 24 to 28.

Titanium dioxide (TiO_2) is a white substance used to make white paint.

In a chemical reaction, all isotopes of an element behave the same way. This means that the isotopic composition of an element does not change. The titanium in TiO_2, for example, has the same Ti isotopes in the same percentages as pure Ti metal in a jet engine.

Because isotopic composition is the same for every sample of an element, we can tabulate the isotopic percentages of the elements. Table 2-2 summarizes the isotopic composition of Ti. Any natural sample of Ti will have this distribution of isotopes. Figure 2-23 illustrates the range of isotopic compositions by showing the isotopic abundances of four additional elements that have from 2 to 10 stable isotopes.

The chemistry of titanium can be described without distinguishing among its five isotopes. When a chemist speaks of titanium, other chemists know this means a mixture of the five isotopes with the percentages given in Table 2-2. Only when we need to distinguish among the isotopes do we emphasize the different mass numbers of different isotopes.

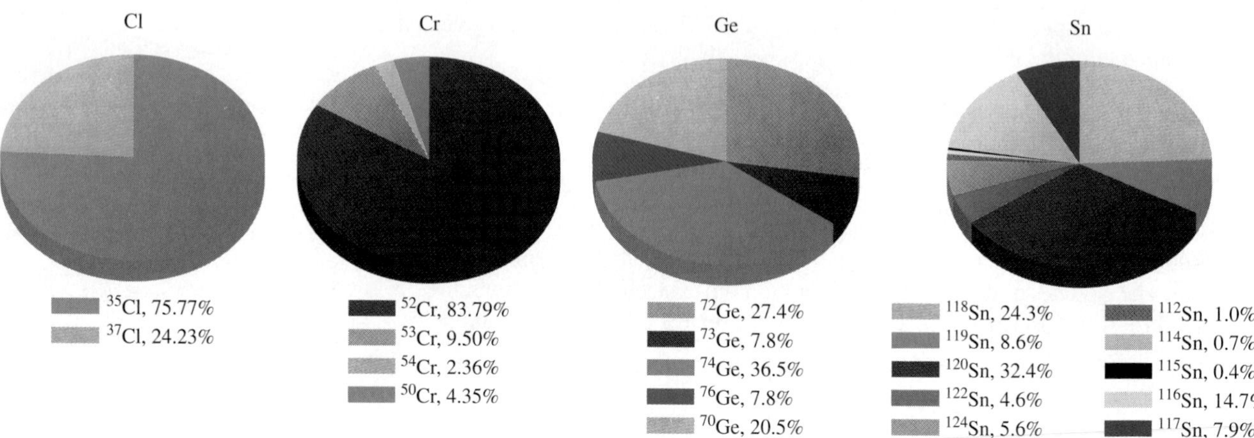

FIGURE 2-23
The natural abundances of the isotopes of four elements (Cl, Cr, Ge, and Sn), illustrating the diversity of isotopic distributions. The mass number and percent abundance of each isotope are indicated.

TABLE 2-2 ISOTOPIC COMPOSITION OF TITANIUM (Ti)

MASS NO.	PROTONS	NEUTRONS	ABUNDANCE (%)
46	22	24	8.2
47	22	25	7.4
48	22	26	73.8
49	22	27	5.4
50	22	28	5.2

Hydrogen, the simplest of all chemical elements, has two naturally occurring isotopes. Its most common isotope contains a single electron and a single proton, and 99.98% of the hydrogen atoms in the universe have this composition. The second isotope of hydrogen has an extra neutron. The addition of this neutron doubles the mass of the atom. Doubling the mass is enough to make its chemistry somewhat different, so the chemical behavior of ^2H differs somewhat from the chemistry of ^1H. Thus the element hydrogen is an exception to our generalization about the common chemical properties of isotopes. This effect is so important that chemists give the "heavy" isotope its own name and symbol: **deuterium** (D). In naturally occurring substances the abundance of deuterium is so low that the subtle differences in its chemistry are rarely observed. It is possible to prepare samples enriched in deuterium, however, and this allows chemists to take advantage of its special properties. The most common compound of deuterium is "heavy" water, D_2O, which is available from chemical supply houses at a price of about $50 for 100 g.

Chemists have found ways to make different isotopes of elements other than hydrogen react selectively, but this can be achieved only under very special conditions.

A third isotope of hydrogen, called **tritium,** has a nucleus that contains two neutrons and one proton. Tritium is not found in naturally occurring hydrogen because its nuclei are unstable. Unstable nuclei, which are said to be **radioactive,** decompose spontaneously into other nuclei. In most cases, all the isotopes making up the natural abundances of an element are stable. For instance, none of the five isotopes of titanium listed in Table 2-2 is radioactive. However, all isotopes of the elements beyond Z of 83 are radioactive, and radioactive isotopes of every element can be prepared in the laboratory.

In Chapter 19 we describe the production and properties of radioactive isotopes.

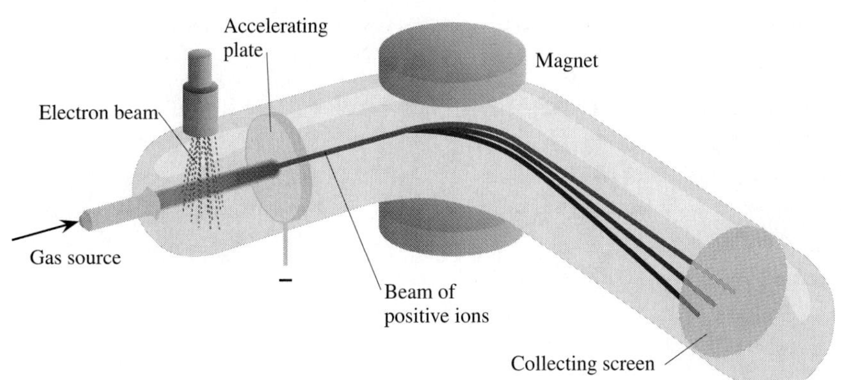

FIGURE 2-24
Schematic representation of one type of mass spectrometer. The electron beam fragments gas molecules into positively charged particles. The positive particles are accelerated and then deflected by a magnet. Each fragment follows a trajectory that depends on its mass, with more massive particles being deflected by smaller amounts than less massive particles. After deflection the charged particles are captured and counted at a collecting screen.

MASS SPECTROMETRY

The existence of isotopes is demonstrated dramatically by research done with an instrument known as a **mass spectrometer.** This instrument separates positively charged atomic and molecular fragments according to their masses and produces a graph of their abundance as a function of mass. Figure 2-24 provides a schematic representation of one type of mass spectrometer. In a mass spectrometry experiment an electrical discharge is used to remove electrons from the atoms or molecules in a sample. The resulting positively charged fragments are shaped into a beam by electrical force. The beam then passes between the poles of a magnet that deflects the paths of the particles according to their masses. Particles with large masses are deflected less than particles with small masses.

Figure 2-25 shows the mass spectrum of the element neon. The three peaks in the mass spectrum come from three different isotopes of neon, and the peak heights are proportional to the natural abundances of these isotopes. The most common form of neon has a mass number of 20, with 10 protons and 10 neutrons in its nucleus, whereas its two minor isotopes have 11 and 12 neutrons. Sample Problem 2-3 illustrates how to read and interpret an atomic mass spectrum, and Box 2-3 outlines various applications of the mass spectrometer.

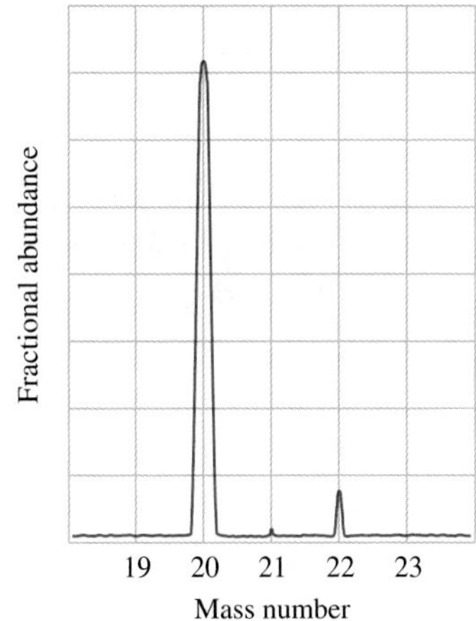

FIGURE 2-25
Mass spectrum of neon.

SAMPLE PROBLEM 2-3 MASS SPECTRA

A sample of lead atoms is analyzed by mass spectrometry. The results are shown as a bar graph in the following figure. Use information from the graph to write the elemental symbol that represents each Pb isotope. List the number of protons and neutrons in each. Determine the isotopes' natural abundances.

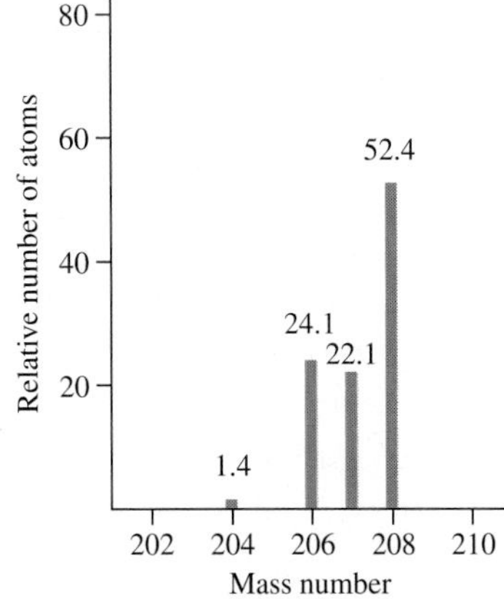

METHOD: Each peak in a mass spectrum corresponds to an ion with a different mass. The height of each peak is proportional to the abundance of fragments of that particular mass. From the mass numbers of these peaks, we can determine the isotopic symbols and obtain a count of the protons and the neutrons. From peak heights, we can also determine abundances.

The four peaks in the mass spectrum represent four Pb isotopes. Their *A* values are 204, 206, 207, and 208. Consulting the periodic table, we find that *Z* of lead is 82. Thus the elemental symbols are as follows:

$$^{204}_{82}Pb \quad ^{206}_{82}Pb \quad ^{207}_{82}Pb \quad ^{208}_{82}Pb$$

BOX 2-3

APPLICATION OF THE MASS SPECTROMETER

Mass spectrometers were first used to observe that atoms have different masses. Since then, scientists have developed the mass spectrometer into an analytical instrument found in virtually every modern chemistry laboratory. Mass spectrometers are used to measure atomic masses, determine molecular structures, and identify chemical substances.

Masses and abundances of atomic ions. Mass spectrometric analyses have been made on all chemical elements. By measuring the amount of deflection caused by known electrical and magnetic forces, scientists determine atomic masses with high accuracy. The atomic mass of fluorine is known to eight significant figures as a result of mass spectrometric measurements.

Molecular formulas. When a chemical compound is subjected to mass spectrometry, individual molecules lose electrons to form positively charged fragments. The mass spectrometer measures the masses of these positively charged species. Accurate mass measurements, coupled with the natural abundances of atomic isotopes, make it possible to determine the molecular formulas of new and unknown chemical compounds. As an example, consider the molecular formulas: C_7H_{14}, $C_6H_{10}O$, and $C_5H_{10}N_2$. At an accuracy of four significant figures, one molecule of each of the three has a mass of 1.629×10^{-22} g/molecule. However, at an accuracy of six significant figures, each has a unique mass:

C_7H_{14}	1.62917×10^{-22} g/molecule
$C_6H_{10}O$	1.62856×10^{-22} g/molecule
$C_5H_{10}N_2$	1.62875×10^{-22} g/molecule

With enough significant figures, every chemical formula has its own characteristic mass. The best mass spectrometers can measure masses to eight or more significant figures, making it possible to identify the molecular formulas of unknown compounds.

Chemical analysis. The most widespread modern use of mass spectrometers is in identifying chemical substances. Not only can the mass spectrum provide the molecular formula of a molecule, it also gives a chemical "fingerprint," providing information about exactly how the atoms in a molecule are connected together. The "parent" fragment, formed by stripping one electron away from a molecule, usually falls apart into a collection of smaller pieces, many of which are also positively charged. For example, the mass spectrum of ethane shows positive molecular fragments containing one or two carbon atoms and from one to six hydrogen atoms (Figure 2-26). The peak heights correspond to the relative amounts of various fragments. Each chemical substance has its own distinct mass spectral pattern that can be used to help verify the presence of a particular compound in a mixture. In crime investigation laboratories,

The atomic number (Z) gives the number of protons in the nucleus, so all four isotopes have 82 protons. On the other hand, A gives the sum of the number of protons and neutrons. Subtracting 82 from each A yields the number of neutrons in the nucleus of each isotope. Finally, the natural abundances of the isotopes are given by the heights of the peaks in the mass spectrum. These values are given on the spectrum. To summarize:

^{204}Pb	82 protons	122 neutrons	1.4% abundant
^{206}Pb	82 protons	124 neutrons	24.1% abundant
^{207}Pb	82 protons	125 neutrons	22.1% abundant
^{208}Pb	82 protons	126 neutrons	52.4% abundant

forensic chemists use the mass spectrometers to identify illegal drugs by comparing the mass spectrum of a confiscated sample with the known fragmentation pattern of a particular substance. Mass spectrometry is also used in analyzing urine samples for evidence of substance abuse. Figure 2-27 shows the characteristic mass spectral fragmentation patterns for cocaine and heroin.

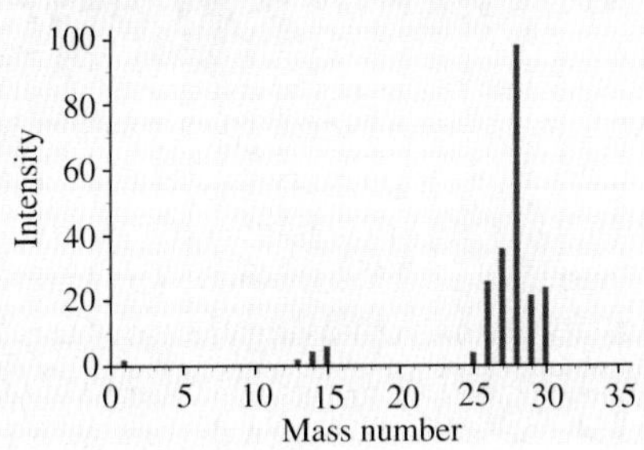

FIGURE 2-26
Mass spectrum of ethane, C_2H_6. This spectrum shows prominent peaks corresponding to $C_2H_6^+$, $C_2H_5^+$, $C_2H_4^+$, and $C_2H_3^+$ ions, with less abundant peaks for other ions, including CH_3^+, CH_2^+, and H^+.

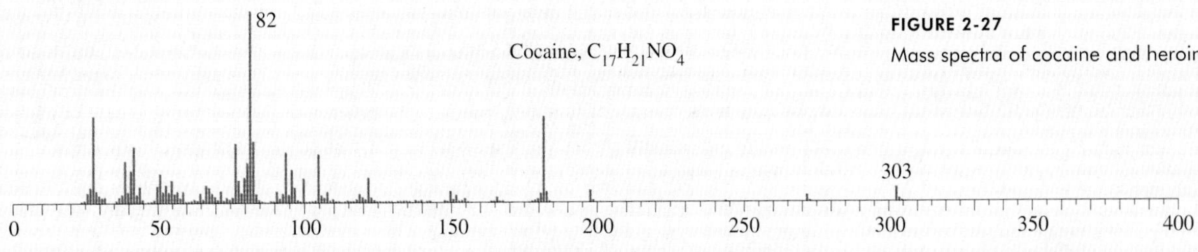

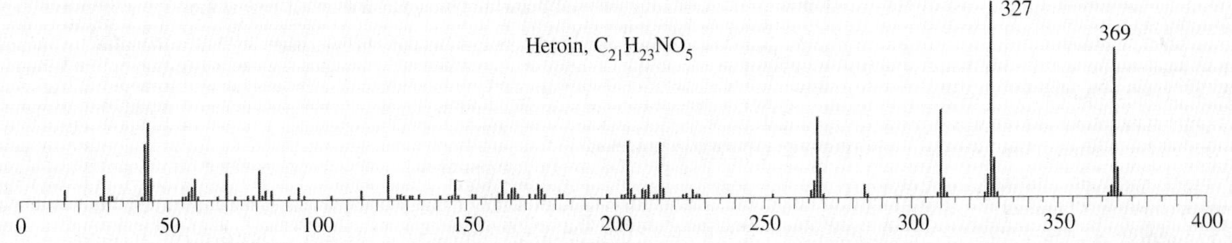

FIGURE 2-27
Mass spectra of cocaine and heroin.

SECTION EXERCISES

2.3.1 Use a periodic table to fill in the missing information:

Name	Symbol	Z
Carbon	C	6
	Au	
Iron		
		33

2.3.2 Write isotopic symbols for (a) a cobalt atom with 30 neutrons; (b) the element with $Z = 3$ and $A = 7$; and (c) potassium with one more neutron than protons.

2.3.3 Naturally occurring chromium (Cr) is a mixture of the following four isotopes:

A	Abundance (%)
50	4.35
52	83.79
53	9.50
54	2.36

Draw a bar graph that shows the mass spectrum of Cr.

2.4 CHARGED ATOMS: IONS

Experiments using mass spectrometers and electric discharge tubes show that electrons can be stripped away from neutral atoms and molecules. An atom is neutral when it has the same number of electrons as its nuclear charge. Likewise, a molecule is neutral when it has the same number of electrons as the sum of the nuclear charges of all its atoms. Removing electrons from neutral atoms and molecules leaves behind fragments that have positive electrical charges. Charged atomic or molecular particles are called **ions.** When the charge is positive, the particles are **cations.** Electrons are not classified as ions, but if extra electrons become attached to neutral atoms or molecules, the resulting negative particles are called **anions**.

Ion is pronounced "eye'-un," cation "cat'-eye-un," and anion "an'-eye-un."

Because like electrical charges repel each other, a collection of cations or anions is highly unstable. Even in a mass spectrometer, the cations in the beam capture electrons and are neutralized as soon as they strike the collector. Therefore although chemical stockrooms may stock pieces of sodium metal and tanks of chlorine gas, they never have containers of just sodium cations or just anions of chlorine.

Whereas like charges repel, opposite charges attract each other. This makes it possible for a collection containing both cations and anions to be stable, even though collections of either type alone are not. To be stable, a collection of cations and anions must be electrically neutral overall. That is, the amount of positive charge carried by its cations must be balanced exactly by the amount of negative charge carried by its anions. Two types of ion collections, ionic compounds and ionic solutions, occur frequently.

When an element gains an electron to become a negative ion, its name is modified by changing the suffix to *-ide*. In this example, chlorine becomes chloride. Chemical nomenclature is presented in Chapter 3.

IONIC COMPOUNDS

The simplest collection of oppositely charged ions is a regular array of cations alternating with anions. Such an array, known as an **ionic compound,** contains cations and anions in fixed whole-number ratios described by a chemical formula.

Sodium chloride, commonly known as table salt, is a simple example of an ionic compound. Studies show that sodium chloride crystals contain equal numbers of Na^+ cations and Cl^- anions packed together in an alternating cubic array called a **lattice.** A portion of a sodium chloride lattice is illustrated in Figure 2-28. The cations and anions are held in the lattice by electrical forces. According to Coulomb's law, each Na^+ cation is attracted to all the nearby Cl^- anions. Likewise, each Cl^- anion is attracted to all its Na^+ neighbors. Positive cations and negative anions group together in equal numbers in the solid lattice to make the entire collection neutral.

Sodium chloride can form through the chemical reaction of elemental sodium and elemental chlorine. Sodium is a soft, silver-colored metal composed of Na atoms. Chlorine is a pale-yellow toxic gas made up of diatomic, neutral Cl_2 molecules. These two elements react to form NaCl, which is white and crystalline:

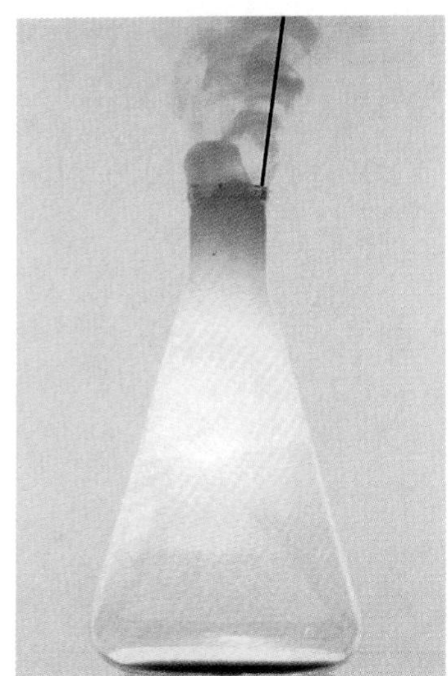

Solid sodium metal reacts with chlorine gas to produce white crystalline sodium chloride.

$$2\ Na_{(s)} + Cl_{2\ (g)} \rightarrow 2\ NaCl_{(s)}$$

In the course of this reaction, electrons are transferred from sodium atoms to chlorine atoms to generate atomic ions. Each Na atom loses one electron and ends up with a positive charge. Each Na^+ has one *less* electron than the number of protons in its nucleus. The sodium atom has lost an electron whose electrical charge is -1.6×10^{-19} C, so the cation (Na^+) possesses this much excess positive charge. Ionic charges are conventionally measured in electron charge units because excess charge always is some integral multiple of the charge of an electron. The sodium cation therefore has a charge of +1 unit, designated by a superscript plus ($^+$):

$$Na \rightarrow Na^+ + e^-$$

Electrons are often symbolized as an "e" with a superscript minus sign: e^-.

The electron lost by a sodium atom becomes attached to a chlorine atom. As a result, each Cl now has a net electric charge of -1.60×10^{-19} C, or −1 charge unit. We designate the negative charge by showing chlorine's elemental symbol with a superscript minus ($^-$):

$$Cl + e^- \rightarrow Cl^-$$

FIGURE 2-28

Photographs and molecular pictures of sodium metal **(A),** chlorine gas **(B),** and crystalline sodium chloride **(C).** In the crystal, Na^+ cations and Cl^- anions alternate in a closely packed array that is electrically neutral overall.

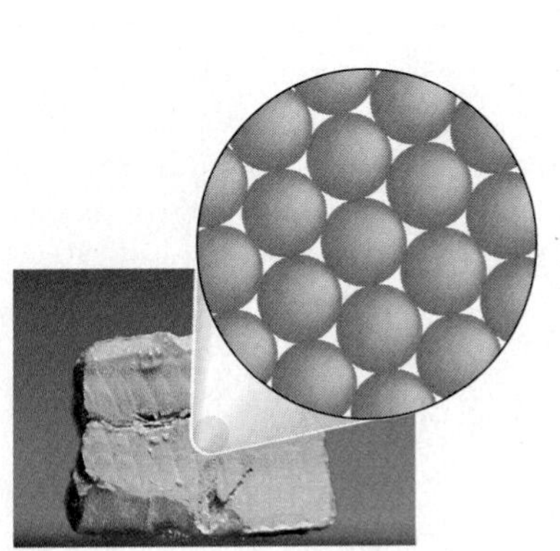

A Sodium metal

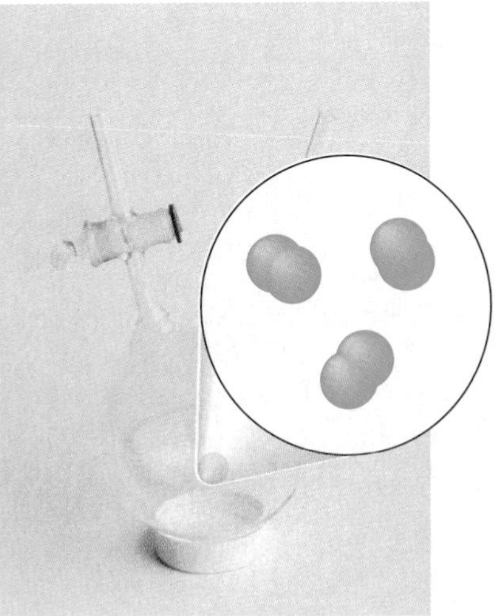

B Chlorine gas

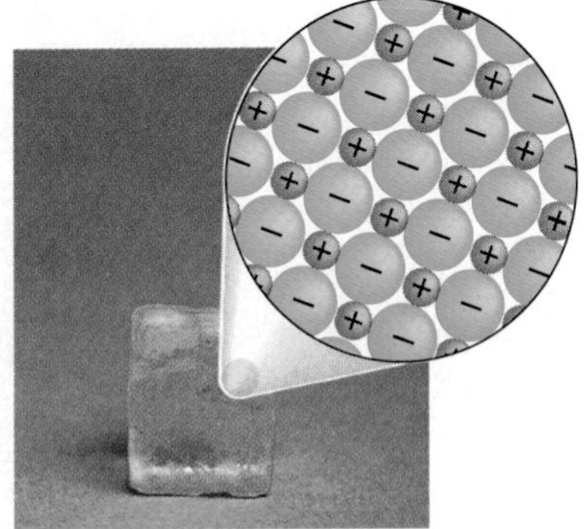

C A crystal of sodium chloride

Several elements have a strong tendency to form compounds containing atomic ions. All the alkali metals, such as sodium, form stable ionic compounds containing atomic cations with +1 charges. All the Group VII elements, such as chlorine, form stable ionic compounds containing atomic anions with −1 charges. The metals in Group II form ionic compounds containing atomic cations that have lost two electrons. Magnesium chloride, for example, contains Mg^{2+} cations and Cl^- anions. To maintain electrical neutrality, this compound has a 1:2 ratio of cations to anions, giving it the chemical formula $MgCl_2$. Oxygen and sulfur form ionic compounds containing atomic anions that have gained two electrons. Examples are calcium oxide (CaO), which contains Ca^{2+} cations and O^{2-} anions in a 1:1 ratio, and potassium sulfide, (K_2S), which contains K^+ cations and S^{2-} anions in a 2:1 ratio. Ionic compounds such as these are known collectively as **salts.** The formulas of salts are dictated by the fact that cations and anions always group together in simple ratios that maintain overall charge neutrality. We develop additional ideas about ionic compounds in Chapters 3 and 7.

Atomic ions have very different chemical properties than the neutral atoms from which they form. Sodium metal reacts violently with water, and chlorine gas is poisonous and highly corrosive. In contrast, sodium chloride simply dissolves in water and is a substance that most people use to season their food. Ions and atoms of the same element behave differently. For example, Mg and Mg^{2+} are different species with different properties, as are O_2 and O^{2-}.

IONIC SOLUTIONS

Unlike pure water, tap water conducts electricity because it is a solution containing small amounts of cations and anions. In Chapter 15 we find that even pure water contains some cations and anions, but not enough to make it a conductor.

Solid sodium chloride dissolves in water. The resulting liquid solution looks the same as water, but it behaves very differently. One striking difference is the ability of these liquids to conduct electricity. Figure 2-29 shows that pure water does not conduct electricity, whereas a solution of NaCl does.

When NaCl dissolves in water, its ions enter the solution. Each ion becomes surrounded by a sheath of water molecules, as shown in Figure 2-30. The ions move

FIGURE 2-29

Pure water *(left)* does not conduct electricity because it contains virtually no charged species. A salt solution *(right)*, on the other hand, is a good conductor because it contains mobile cations and anions.

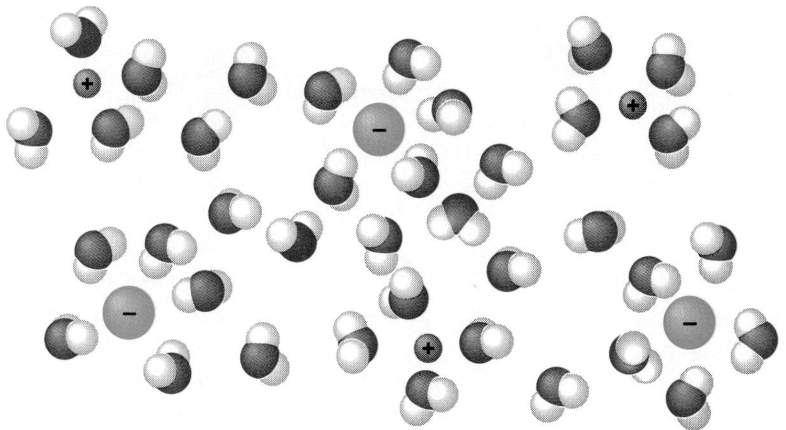

FIGURE 2-30
Molecular picture of a solution of sodium chloride. All the molecules and ions move freely about, but overall electrical neutrality is maintained because the total amount of anionic charge equals the total amount of cationic charge.

freely among the water molecules. After a solution has been well mixed, Na^+ and Cl^- ions are distributed uniformly throughout the entire solution.

The presence of ions in solution is what gives an NaCl solution the ability to conduct electricity. If positively and negatively charged wires are dipped into the solution, the ions in the solution respond to the charges on the wires as described by Coulomb's law. Chloride anions move toward the positive wire, and sodium cations move toward the negative wire. This directed movement of ions in solution is a flow of electric current. Pure water, which has no dissolved ions, does not conduct electricity. Any aqueous solution formed by dissolving an ionic solid in water conducts electricity.

We mentioned previously that "molecular" pictures may contain atoms and molecules. They may also contain ions. A molecular picture is a schematic view of how matter appears at the molecular-atomic-ionic level.

Ionic compounds and ionic solutions may contain molecular and atomic ions. We introduce the most common molecular ions in Chapter 3 after describing the basic features of molecular composition.

SECTION EXERCISES

2.4.1 Draw a molecular picture that shows a portion of a solution of calcium chloride ($CaCl_2$) in water that is electrically neutral overall. (Omit the water molecules.)

2.4.2 When magnesium reacts with oxygen, each magnesium atom loses two electrons, and each oxygen atom gains two electrons.
- (a) What are the symbols that describe the resulting ions?
- (b) What is the chemical formula of the ionic compound formed from magnesium and oxygen?
- (c) Draw a molecular picture that shows the reaction between Mg metal and O_2 gas.

2.4.3 What is the total number of protons in a Mg^{2+}? What is the total number of electrons?

2.5 CONSERVATION LAWS

One of the cornerstones of atomic theory is that atoms are neither created nor destroyed. In other words, the number of atoms of each type is constant and unchanging. When a quantity does not change, regardless of what process occurs, that quantity is said to be conserved. Atoms are conserved in chemical and physical processes.

In Chapter 19 we describe nuclear reactions that convert atoms of one element into atoms of other elements. Atoms are not conserved in nuclear processes.

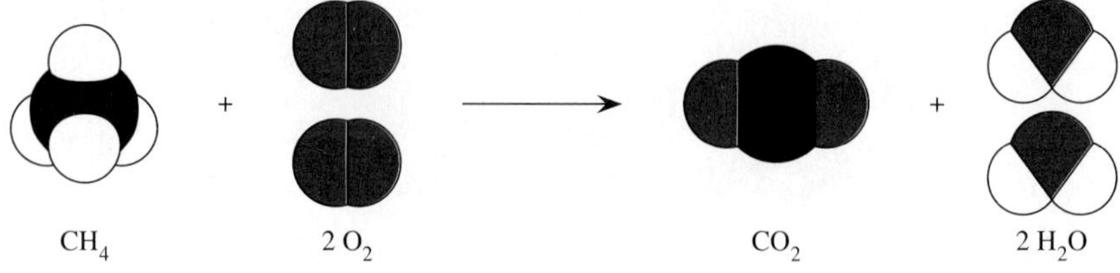

FIGURE 2-31
Schematic molecular picture of the reaction of methane (CH_4) with oxygen (O_2) to produce carbon dioxide (CO_2) and water (H_2O). Atoms of each element are conserved. Four atoms of hydrogen from CH_4 become four atoms of hydrogen in two H_2O molecules. The single atom of carbon in CH_4 appears in a CO_2 molecule, and the two oxygen molecules supply the four oxygen atoms needed for a CO_2 molecule and two H_2O molecules.

A statement that some quantity is conserved is called a **conservation law.** Conservation laws are among the most important unifying principles of science because we can always account for conserved quantities. In this section we introduce conservation of atoms, electrons, mass, and energy. All four of these conserved quantities are central to an understanding of chemistry.

CONSERVATION OF ATOMS

All chemical reactions are regulated by the requirement that the number of atoms of each chemical element be conserved. When methane is burned to produce heat for our homes, for example, the carbon atom from each molecule of methane ends up in a molecule of carbon dioxide. This chemical reaction can be represented by the molecular sketch shown in Figure 2-31. Counting the atoms, we see that there are four oxygen atoms (red), four hydrogen atoms (white), and one carbon atom (black) before and after the reaction. The atoms have rearranged and recombined during the course of the reaction, but the numbers of each type of atom do not change.

Atoms are also conserved in physical transformations. When a block of ice melts, water molecules are transformed from the solid state to the liquid state, but the *number* of water molecules remains the same. Because each water molecule is made up of two hydrogen atoms and one oxygen atom, the total numbers of hydrogen atoms and oxygen atoms remain the same as the ice melts.

CONSERVATION OF ELECTRONS

Positive ions are created in an electric discharge, and sodium cations and chloride anions are created in the reaction of sodium metal with chlorine to form sodium chloride. Many other processes also generate positively or negatively charged species. Experiments show that all such processes involve *movement* of electrons from one location to another but that electrons are neither created nor destroyed. As with atoms, electrons are conserved.

We keep track of atoms by writing chemical equations using elemental symbols. Accounting for electrons is somewhat more difficult because the presence of electrons in neutral atoms is not explicitly recorded. For example, the loss of an electron by a neutral sodium atom is written in a way that makes it appear that an electron has been created: $Na \rightarrow Na^+ + e^-$. However, a neutral sodium atom has 11 electrons, but a sodium cation has only 10 electrons. Thus 11 electrons are present both before and after the ionization.

The key to keeping track of electrons is *net* charge. Moving electrons around may generate positive charges in one location and negative charges in another location, but the net charge of the entire system remains unchanged. The ionization of sodium atoms provides an illustration. The net charge of a sodium cation plus an electron is zero, the same as the net charge of one sodium atom.

Net electrical charge is always conserved.

Because opposite charges attract, matter is always most stable when it contains equal numbers of positive and negative charges. Therefore conservation of charge usually means zero net charge before and after a process occurs. However, the net charge need not be zero, as long as it does not change. Sample Problem 2-4 illustrates the application of conservation laws to a chemical process in which the net charge is not zero.

SAMPLE PROBLEM 2-4 CONSERVATION LAWS

When ethane is placed in a mass spectrometer, an electron is first stripped off to generate $C_2H_6^+$. This ion subsequently decomposes to give various other fragments, including CH_2^+:

$$C_2H_6^+ \rightarrow CH_2^+ + X$$

Identify *X*, the other product that results from this decomposition.

METHOD: Atoms and electrons are conserved in any process. We can identify the chemical formula of *X* by making sure that each element is conserved, and we can identify the charge on *X* by making sure that net charge is conserved.

Before fragmentation, two C atoms and six H atoms are present. The CH_2^+ ion contains one C atom and two H atoms, so *X* must contain one C atom and four H atoms: $X = CH_4$. The net charge before fragmentation is +1, so the sum of the charges after fragmentation must also be +1. Because CH_2^+ has +1 charge, CH_4 must be neutral.

CONSERVATION OF MASS

On the atomic level, we keep track of individual atoms and electrons. In the laboratory, however, we measure mass. Neither the numbers nor the masses of atoms and electrons change during chemical and physical transformations, so mass is also conserved.

> ***Mass is neither created nor destroyed during physical and chemical transformations.***

The law of conservation of mass is an approximation. As Albert Einstein discovered in 1905, mass can be converted into energy and energy into mass. However, in chemical and physical transformations, the amount of mass lost or gained is always too small to measure.

Mass is converted into energy in measurable quantities during the nuclear reactions that we consider in Chapter 19.

Within the limits of our measurements, the total mass of all components of a chemical system remains constant during any transformation. For instance, when a block of ice is weighed and allowed to melt and the resulting water is reweighed, the mass of the liquid water is the same as the mass of the original ice.

Chemical transformations occur in which it *appears* that mass is not conserved. After iron rusts, the mass of the sample is greater than the initial mass of iron. After wood burns, the mass of the ash is much less than the mass of the original wood, as the photos in Figure 2-32 illustrate. On closer inspection, however, these processes are found to obey the law of conservation of mass. When iron rusts, oxygen from the atmosphere reacts with the metal to form rust:

$$4\ Fe_{(s)} + 3\ O_{2\,(g)} \rightarrow 2\ Fe_2O_{3\,(s)}$$

The gain in mass of the solid results from the oxygen atoms that have been transferred from the atmosphere to combine with iron atoms. The combined mass of this

FIGURE 2-32
It appears that mass is lost when wood burns, but the mass lost by the wood is transferred to the atmosphere as molecules of carbon dioxide and water, as well as particulate matter that we see as smoke.

atmospheric oxygen and the iron metal with which it reacts is equal to the mass of the rust. Mass and atoms are conserved when iron rusts. Similarly, when wood burns, the carbon, hydrogen, and oxygen atoms that make up most of the wood are converted into carbon dioxide and water vapor, which escape into the atmosphere. Careful experiments in which all the products are captured and weighed show that the total mass of the entire system remains unchanged.

The conservation of atoms, electrons, and mass is the fundamental principle of **stoichiometry,** which is the determination of how amounts of different chemical substances change during a chemical reaction. By applying these conservation laws to chemical reactions, we can calculate information about the production and consumption of chemical substances during chemical transformations. We explore stoichiometry in detail in Chapters 3 and 4.

CONSERVATION OF ENERGY

In addition to mass and charge, atoms and molecules also possess energy. Unlike mass and charge, the energy of any particular type of atom or molecule varies greatly as conditions change. For example, when water is heated to boiling, the energies of its molecules increase substantially. Nonetheless, energy is also a conserved quantity. To increase the energies of water molecules, we must provide a heat source that loses energy. The law of conservation of energy states:

> ***Energy is neither created nor destroyed in any process, although it may be transferred from one body to another or converted from one form into another.***

In other words, when an increase occurs in the energy of one body, a compensating decrease must occur in the energy of some other body.

Chemical and physical transformations are accompanied by energy transfers that *must* conform to the law of conservation of energy. The law requires that energy is conserved when a green plant absorbs sunlight and manufactures carbohydrates and when polymeric plastics are manufactured in a chemical plant. Even such commonplace processes as using ice cubes to cool soft drinks are governed by the law of conservation of energy.

At the molecular level, conservation of energy is an equally valuable concept that helps us interpret not only molecular behavior but also the very nature of atoms and molecules. In later chapters, energy diagrams are used to illustrate energy relationships among atoms and molecules. Such diagrams are constructed from energy measurements and from the knowledge that energy must be conserved. The law of conservation of energy is applied to chemical processes and interactions throughout this book.

Chapters 12 and 13 focus particularly on the subject of energy in chemical systems.

FORMS OF ENERGY

The analysis of energy flow and conservation is complicated because energy takes on several different forms. Kinetic, potential, thermal, and radiant energy all play important roles in chemistry. Working with energy at the molecular level requires a molecular perspective and an understanding of energy flow. Here we introduce types of energy using examples that do not require molecular thinking.

Any moving object possesses energy of motion, which is called **kinetic energy.** Kinetic energy varies with the mass of the body and the velocity at which it is moving. The exact relationship that links kinetic energy *(kE)* to mass *(m)* and velocity *(u)* is given by Equation 2-2:

$$kE = \tfrac{1}{2} mu^2 \tag{2-2}$$

Equation 2-2, which can be derived from the basic notions of physics, is a quantitative definition of kinetic energy.

Equation 2-2 requires that the units for energy be (mass)(distance)^2(time)$^{-2}$, so the SI unit for kinetic energy is (kg) (m)^2 (s)$^{-2}$. No matter what form energy takes, it always has these same dimensions and units. Because energy is such a fundamental property, this unit is given a special name. It is called the *joule (J),* in honor of James Joule, a nineteenth century English physicist who did pioneering experiments on the nature of different forms of energy:

$$\text{Energy} = \frac{(\text{Mass})\,(\text{Distance})^2}{(\text{Time})^2} = \frac{(\text{kg})(\text{m})^2}{(\text{s})^2} = \text{Joules (J)}$$

In doing energy calculations, we work exclusively with joules in this book. Sample Problem 2-5 provides an example from everyday life.

SAMPLE PROBLEM 2-5 KINETIC ENERGY

A hard-throwing baseball pitcher can throw a 115 g baseball 95.5 mi/hr. How much kinetic energy does this baseball possess?

METHOD: We follow the seven-step approach introduced in Chapter 1:

1. Type of problem? This is an energy calculation ("how much kinetic energy").
2. Molecular view? This particular problem does not involve molecular thinking, so we can skip this step.

3. Equations?

$$kE = \tfrac{1}{2}\, mu^2$$

4. Data? We are given mass and velocity, but we need unit conversion factors that express the result in SI units: mass = 115 g, velocity = 95.5 miles/hr, 1000 g = 1 kg (exact), 1 hour = 60 minutes (exact), 1 minute = 60 seconds (exact), 1 km = 0.6215 miles, and 1 km = 10^3 m (exact).

5. Rearrange? No rearrangement is needed, because the equation gives kinetic energy directly.

6. Substitute and solve. In this case, it is convenient to convert each quantity into SI units before substituting in the energy equation:

$$\text{Mass conversion:} \qquad (115\ \text{g})\left(\frac{1\ \text{kg}}{1000\ \text{g}}\right) = 0.115\ \text{kg}$$

$$\text{Velocity conversion:} \left(\frac{95.5\ \text{mi}}{\text{hr}}\right)\left(\frac{1\ \text{hr}}{60\ \text{min}}\right)\left(\frac{1\ \text{min}}{60\ \text{s}}\right) = 0.0265\ \frac{\text{mi}}{\text{s}}$$

We carry one extra digit in the velocity until we round the final answer to the appropriate number of significant figures.

$$\left(0.0265\ \frac{\text{mi}}{\text{s}}\right)\left(\frac{1\ \text{km}}{0.6215\ \text{mi}}\right)\left(\frac{1000\ \text{m}}{\text{km}}\right) = 42.64\ \frac{\text{m}}{\text{s}}$$

Now we can use the equation for kinetic energy to complete the problem:

$$kE = \tfrac{1}{2}\, mu^2 = \tfrac{1}{2}\,(0.115\ \text{kg})\left(\frac{42.64\ \text{m}}{\text{s}}\right)^2 = 104.5\ \frac{\text{kg m}^2}{\text{s}^2} = 1.05 \times 10^2\ \text{J}$$

7. Check for reasonableness. The result yields energy units, kg m^2/s^2, or J. Not knowing how large a joule is, you cannot assess whether or not 1.05×10^2 J is a "reasonable" value for the energy of a baseball. As you work many chemical problems, however, you should develop a better sense for the magnitudes of numerical results.

Neither a baseball pitcher standing on the mound nor the baseball has any kinetic energy. In flight, however, a 95.5-mi/hr fastball has 105 J of kinetic energy. Because energy is conserved, this kinetic energy must have come from somewhere, but where? To answer this question, we must introduce **potential energy.**

Potential energy is stored energy. For instance, a rock teetering high on a ledge is about to release stored gravitational energy, a cloud on the verge of "hurling" a thunderbolt earthward is about to release stored electrical energy, and gasoline in the cylinder of an automobile engine is about to release stored **chemical energy.** In each case, the stored energy is called *potential energy.*

A baseball that has been popped up has kinetic energy. The baseball slows, however, until it reaches its highest point. At that point, it has no velocity, so it has no kinetic energy. What has happened to its initial kinetic energy? During its climb, the baseball slows down because gravitational force acts to convert its kinetic energy into potential energy. When the ball reaches its highest point, all the kinetic energy of its initial upward motion has been stored as gravitational potential energy. If the ball were to be trapped at this point (for example, if it landed on top of the screen behind home plate), the energy would remain stored until the ball fell back to the playing field. Then the stored energy would be released again as kinetic energy.

Gravitational potential energy is familiar to us, but two other types of potential energy are particularly important in the study of chemistry. Electrical potential energy is the result of electrical forces between charged bodies, and chemical potential energy is the result of the attractive forces between atoms that are bound in molecules. We describe the roles of these types of potential energy in later chapters.

A pitcher is very tired after throwing fastballs for nine innings. That tired feeling is the body's signal that much stored chemical energy was consumed in throwing all those pitches. Each time your body moves, it does so at the expense of chemical energy. The body releases this stored energy by breaking down complex molecules such as carbohydrates into carbon dioxide and water. To replenish our supply of stored chemical energy, we must eat.

When a catcher catches a 95-mi/hr fastball, the ball loses the kinetic energy it had while it was in flight because the ball is now at rest in the catcher's glove. This energy has not been transformed into gravitational potential energy because the ball is no higher above the Earth than before the pitch. It seems that energy has not been conserved. However, careful measurements of the temperature of the ball and of the glove would reveal that as the ball came to rest, the temperature of both objects increased slightly. After an inning of catching fastballs, a catcher's glove becomes quite warm.

When these temperature measurements are performed, the result is always the same. Temperature rises whenever a body loses kinetic energy without gaining potential energy. When a catcher catches a fastball, the kinetic energy lost by the ball shows up as **thermal energy** of the glove and the ball. The transfer of energy results in a temperature change. If a system gains thermal energy, its temperature increases; if a system loses thermal energy, its temperature decreases.

Another form of energy also plays a fundamental role in chemistry. The temperature of an object increases when it is placed in direct sunlight, because light possesses energy. This energy is called **radiant energy.** The radiant energy absorbed by an object is converted to thermal energy, thus the increase in temperature. Radiant energy is not restricted to light from the sun. Heat lamps, for example, give off infrared radiation, and microwave ovens cook food using the radiant energy of microwave radiation.

In Chapter 6 we examine radiation and radiant energy more closely.

SECTION EXERCISES

2.5.1 Describe an experiment that would allow you to find out whether or not mass is conserved when 1.00 L of liquid water is heated on a stove until all of it has boiled away.

2.5.2 In a mass spectrometer, a molecule of methane (CH_4) loses an electron. The resulting ion subsequently decomposes to produce a molecule of H_2. What is the chemical formula and charge on the remaining fragment? Write equations for the loss of an electron and the decomposition reaction.

2.5.3 Humans replenish their supply of stored chemical energy by eating foods, which come from plants or other animals. Where do plants obtain their supply of energy?

CHAPTER SUMMARY

1. All matter is composed of atoms, and atoms combine to form molecules.
2. Atoms and molecules are in constant motion, even in a chemical system that undergoes no net change. Such a system is at dynamic equilibrium.
3. Atoms contain tiny, relatively massive nuclei containing positive protons and neutral neutrons. Most of an atom's volume is occupied by its electrons. Neutral atoms have as many electrons as protons in their nuclei.
4. Every atom of a particular element has the same number of protons, but different isotopes have different numbers of neutrons. Isotopes of an element all show the same chemical behavior.
5. Neutral atoms can lose or gain electrons to become electrically charged ions, which can form ionic compounds or solutions.
6. Atoms, electrons, charge, and mass are conserved in chemical and physical transformations. Energy, which can take on several forms, is also conserved.

KEY TERMS

balanced chemical equation
product
reactant
starting material
stoichiometry

brownian motion
diffusion
dynamic equilibrium

atom
Coulomb's law
electron
magnetism
nucleus
neutron
proton

anion
cation
ion
ionic compound
lattice
salt

atomic number
deuterium
isotope
mass number
mass spectrometer
radioactive
tritium

chemical energy
conservation law
kinetic energy
potential energy
radiant energy
thermal energy

SKILLS TO MASTER

· Drawing molecular pictures
· Writing and interpreting atomic symbols
· Reading mass spectra
· Applying conservation laws to chemical processes

LEARNING EXERCISES

2.1 List the conservation laws that appear in this chapter. Describe each one in your own words.

2.2 Write a two-page chapter summary that outlines the important features of this chapter.

2.3 Describe what atoms "look like," what they are composed of, and how they behave.

2.4 List all terms new to you that appear in this chapter. Use your own words to write a one-sentence definition of each. Consult the glossary if you need help.

2.5 Continue your list of "memory bank" equations, adding those from Chapter 2 that you need to memorize.

2.6 List the new skills that were presented in this chapter. Go through the end-of-chapter problems and identify those that require skills from your list.

PROBLEMS

ATOMIC THEORY

2.1 Draw molecular pictures that show part of a sample of (a) helium, a monatomic gas; (b) tungsten, an atomic solid; and (c) mercury, an atomic liquid.

2.2 The element iodine exists as diatomic molecules and is a solid under normal conditions. Draw a molecular picture of elemental iodine.

2.3 The following is a molecular picture of carbon reacting with oxygen to form carbon monoxide, a deadly poisonous gas.

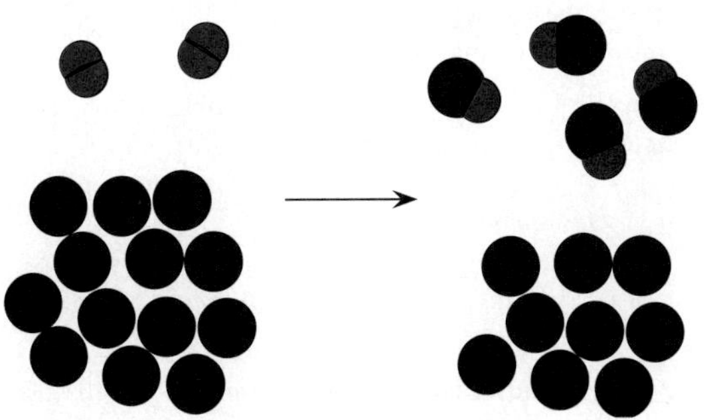

Describe how this picture illustrates each of the five features of atomic theory.

2.4 In lightning strikes, N_2 sometimes reacts with O_2 to generate NO. Draw a molecular picture that illustrates this reaction.

2.5 The reaction of carbon with hydrogen to form methane is as follows:

$$C_{(s)} + 2\,H_{2\,(g)} \rightarrow CH_{4\,(g)}$$

Consider a reaction in which 25 atoms of C are consumed.
(a) How many molecules of CH_4 are formed?
(b) How many molecules of H_2 are consumed?
(c) How many atoms of hydrogen are involved?

2.6 Given the following molecular picture of methane, draw a molecular picture that illustrates the production of three molecules of methane in the reaction of Problem 2.5.

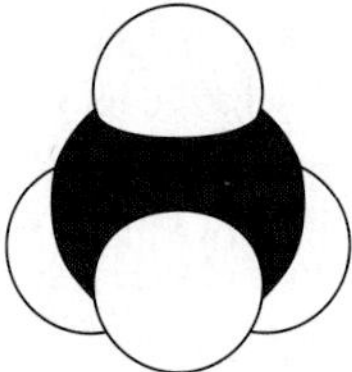

2.7 When we smell the odor of a rose, our olfactory nerves are sensing molecules of the scent. Explain how smelling a rose demonstrates that molecules are always moving.

2.8 A covered beaker that contains a highly concentrated salt solution with many small salt crystals on the bottom is allowed to stand for a long time. Some crystals become smaller, whereas others grow even though the total mass of crystals is constant. Explain what is happening at the molecular level in terms of a dynamic equilibrium.

ATOMIC ARCHITECTURE: ELECTRONS AND NUCLEI

2.9 By what factor does electric force between two charged bodies change when the following changes occur?
(a) One charge is increased by a factor of three.
(b) Both charges are increased by a factor of three.
(c) Distance between the charges is doubled.

2.10 Figure 2-15 shows an electroscope. Assume that the plate and foil are positively charged. Describe qualitatively how the foil will respond to each of the following changes:
(a) Some electrons are removed from the foil.
(b) Enough electrons are added to the foil to make it negatively charged.
(c) Sufficient electrons are added to the plate and foil to make their charges negative by the amount that they were previously positive.

2.11 In Millikan's oil-drop experiment, some droplets have negative charges, so others must have positive charges. Suppose the upper electric plate in Figure 2-20 is made negative and the lower plate positive. Describe the results that would be obtained under these conditions.

2.12 Describe the scattering pattern that would have been observed in Rutherford's experiment if atoms were like chocolate chip cookies.

2.13 What mass of electrons has a net charge of -1.00×10^{-6} C?

2.14 What is the net charge on 5.26×10^{14} protons?

2.15 A helium atom is electrically neutral, with two protons and two neutrons in its nucleus.
(a) How many electrons does it have?
(b) What fraction of a helium atom's mass comes from its electrons?

ATOMIC DIVERSITY: THE ELEMENTS

2.16 What are the symbols and atomic numbers for each of the following elements: sodium, silicon, sulfur, silver, samarium, strontium, scandium, and selenium?

2.17 What are the names and atomic numbers of the following elements: Mg, Mn, Cu, Co, P, and Pb?

2.18 What are the names and symbols of the elements with the following atomic numbers: 26, 7, 18, 80, 50, and 19?

2.19 Write the symbols of the following isotopes: (a) Z of 26 with 30 neutrons; (b) argon with two more neutrons than protons; (c) U-236; and (d) an atom with 9 protons, 10 neutrons, and 9 electrons.

2.20 Write the isotopic symbols for the following nuclei: (a) helium with one neutron; (b) zinc with A of 66; (c) element number 54 with 78 neutrons; and (d) nitrogen with the same number of protons and neutrons.

2.21 Elemental boron is 20.0% boron-10 and 80.0% boron-11. Sketch the mass spectrum of this element.

2.22 Platinum has five stable isotopes whose mass numbers and percentages are 192, 0.8%; 194, 32.9%; 195, 33.8%; 196, 25.3%; and 198, 7.2%. Construct a pie chart illustrating these isotopic abundances.

2.23 Elemental chlorine is a mixture of two isotopes: ^{35}Cl, 75.77%, and ^{37}Cl, 24.23%. The mass spectrum of chlorine gas contains several peaks because of Cl_2^+ ions. How many different peaks exist? Which one is most intense? Which is least intense?

2.24 Elemental bromine is a mixture of two isotopes: ^{79}Br, 50.51%, and ^{81}Br, 49.49%. The mass spectrum of bromine contains several peaks because of Br_2^+ ions. How many different peaks exist? Which one is most intense? Which is least intense?

CHARGED ATOMS: IONS

2.25 Group the following species into cations, anions, and neutral species: C, Cl^-, CCl_4, Cl_2^+, CO_2, CO^+, $Cr_2O_7^{2-}$, and Cr^{3+}.

2.26 Write the chemical formula for the species resulting from each of the following processes:
(a) An argon atom loses an electron.
(b) A water molecule loses H^+.
(c) An oxygen molecule gains an electron.
(d) A water molecule gains H^+.

2.27 Write the chemical formula for the species resulting from each of the following processes:
(a) A hydroxide ion gains H^+.
(b) A sodium atom loses an electron.
(c) A HCl molecule loses H^+.
(d) An oxygen atom gains two electrons.

2.28 Draw a molecular picture that illustrates a solution of $MgCl_2$ in water. Make sure your picture is electrically neutral.

2.29 Aluminum is one of the few elements that forms cations with +3 charges. What is the chemical formula of aluminum oxide, which is electrically neutral?

2.30 Based on their position in the periodic table, decide what ion each of the following elements is likely to form (a) cesium, (b) strontium, and (c) iodine.

2.31 Write the chemical formulas of all ionic compounds that can form between the elements listed in Problem 2.30.

CONSERVATION LAWS

2.32 Write the conservation law for each conserved property introduced in this chapter.

2.33 Explain how each of the following observations is consistent with conservation laws:
(a) A marathon runner loses mass ("weight") while running.
(b) An apple gains kinetic energy as it falls from a tree.
(c) When that apple hits the ground, it loses its kinetic energy.

2.34 Compute *kE* for an electron moving at 4.55×10^5 m/s.

2.35 Compute the speed of a helium atom whose kinetic energy is 3.75×10^{-23} J.

2.36 The mass spectrum of methane (CH_4) shows a peak corresponding to a CH^+ fragment.
(a) Write the reaction that converts methane to its molecular ion.
(b) Assuming that the molecular ion loses atoms to generate CH^+, write the reaction for this process.

2.37 In each of the following processes, energy is transformed from one type to another. Identify what type of energy is consumed and what type of energy is produced.
(a) Sunlight heats the roof of a house.
(b) Packed snow breaks loose in an avalanche.
(c) Wax burns in a candle flame.

ADDITIONAL PROBLEMS

2.38 Compute the kinetic energy of a neutron whose velocity is 7.44×10^3 km/hr.

2.39 Write the symbols of the elements that form ionic compounds whose chemical formulas are XF_2.

2.40 Give the names of the elements that form ionic compounds whose chemical formulas are Na*X*.

2.41 Table salt, which has the formula NaCl, is made up of Na^+ and Cl^- ions arranged in a cubic crystal. When heated to a very high temperature, salt crystals melt to give a liquid that still contains these ions. Draw molecular pictures of table salt crystals and of liquid NaCl.

2.42 A scientist wants to prepare a sample of chlorine gas that is isotopically pure. Which scientific apparatus described in this chapter could be used to test the chlorine's purity? Explain.

2.43 Air is mostly diatomic molecules of nitrogen and oxygen. What positive and negative ions might form when a lightning bolt, which is an immense electrical discharge, passes through the atmosphere? (*Hint*: recall the experiments that revealed the existence of electrons.)

2.44 Write the appropriate isotopic symbols for a hydrogen atom (1-proton nucleus), a deuterium atom (1 proton, 1 neutron), and a fluorine atom (9 protons, 10 neutrons).

2.45 How many protons, neutrons, and electrons are contained in each of the following atoms or ions? (a) $^{16}_{8}O^{2-}$, (b) $^{15}_{7}N$, (c) $^{55}_{25}Mn^{3+}$, (d) $^{35}_{17}Cl^-$, and (e) $^{37}_{17}Cl^+$.

2.46 Naturally occurring magnesium has three isotopes whose masses and percent abundances are 3.984×10^{-26} kg, 78.6%; 4.150×10^{-26} kg, 10.1%; and 4.315×10^{-26} kg, 11.3%. Sketch the mass spectrum of Mg^+.

2.47 Determine the number of protons and neutrons of each of the following isotopes: (a) Co-60, used in radiation treatments of cancer patients; (b) C-14, used in radiocarbon dating; (c) U-235, used in atomic bombs; and (d) U-238, used in "breeder" reactors.

2.48 List the ways in which electrons, protons, and neutrons differ from one another.

2.49 The ratio of neutrons to protons in stable nuclei varies from 1:1 to about 1.5:1. Write the isotopic symbols for all isotopes that contain 14 nuclear particles and have ratios in this range.

2.50 Use the law of conservation of charge to determine the number of electrons that must be removed in each of the following processes:
(a) H_2O molecule decomposes into an H^+ ion and an OH^- ion.
(b) P_4 molecule decomposes into four P^{3+} ions.
(c) Oxalate ion, $C_2O_4^{2-}$, decomposes into two CO_2 molecules.

2.51 The following pie chart shows the isotopic abundances for germanium. Sketch this element's mass spectrum.

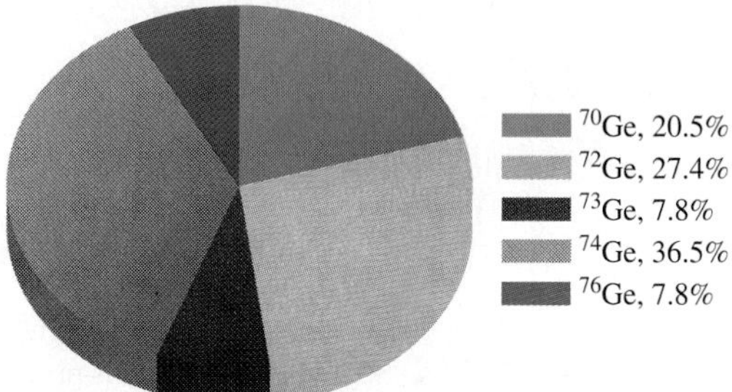

2.52 Ethylene is a compound of carbon and hydrogen with the molecular formula C_2H_4. Assume the mass of hydrogen is 1 "unit" and the mass of carbon is 12 "units." List the possible positive ions found in the mass spectrum of ethylene and give their masses in "units."

2.53 What is the kinetic energy (in J) of a 2250-pound automobile traveling at 57.5 mi/ hr?

2.54 Air is mostly diatomic molecules of nitrogen and oxygen, in a molecular ratio of 4:1. Draw a molecular picture of a sample of air containing a total of 10 molecules.

2.55 Nuclei with the same A value but different Z values are called *isobars.* Argon, potassium, and calcium each has a nucleus with A of 40. Write correct elemental symbols for these isobars.

2.56 Except for beryllium, each of the elements with Z values from 1 to 8 has a stable isotope with the same number of protons as neutrons. Write the correct atomic symbols for each of these isotopes.

2.57 The process in which a solid is converted directly to a gas is called *sublimation.* Solid carbon dioxide (CO_2), which is known as dry ice, is one common substance that sublimes. Draw a series of molecular pictures that shows how a piece of dry ice in a closed container at low temperature illustrates the principle of dynamic equilibrium.

2.58 What mass of protons has a net charge of $+1.00\times10^{-6}$ C? What mass of electrons has this same charge?

2.59 The combination of nitrogen with hydrogen to form ammonia is an important industrial reaction:

$$N_2 + 3\,H_2 \rightarrow 2\,NH_3$$

Consider a reaction that consumes 10 molecules of nitrogen.
(a) How many hydrogen molecules are consumed?
(b) How many ammonia molecules are formed?
(c) How many atoms of nitrogen and of hydrogen are involved?

2.60 Given the following molecular picture of ammonia, draw a molecular sketch that illustrates the reaction in Problem 2.59 when two molecules of N_2 are consumed.

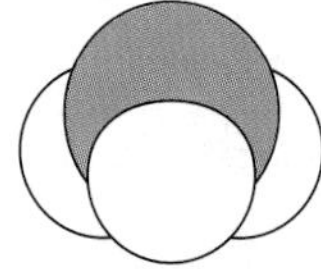

2.61 Draw a molecular picture that shows what happens when the salt KBr dissolves in water.

2.62 Water molecules (H_2O) contain hydrogen atoms of mass 1.67×10^{-27} kg and oxygen atoms with 16 times this mass. In a mass spectrometer, gaseous H_2O is broken down into positive ions of various masses. Write the formulas and masses of all the possible ions resulting from H_2O.

2.63 Several elements of the periodic table do not occur naturally, but chemists and physicists have created them in the laboratory. The first such synthetic element was technetium (Tc). (The name comes from the Greek word for "artificial.") There are two isotopes of technetium: ^{98}Tc and ^{99}Tc. List the number of protons, neutrons, and electrons in one neutral atom of each of these isotopes.

2.64 Give the atomic symbols for all the isotopes of elements between $Z = 20$ and $Z = 40$ that have exactly 1.25 times as many neutrons as protons (HINT: Z must be divisible by 4.)

2.65 Fluorine has just one stable isotope. How many peaks will be present in the mass spectrum of F_2? Give the chemical formula corresponding to each peak.

2.66 Liquid mercury metal can be obtained from a mercury ore called *cinnabar* simply by heating the ore in air. There is a significant loss of mass when this process occurs. How can this loss of mass be reconciled with the law of conservation of mass?

2.67 How fast is a proton moving if its kinetic energy is the same as that of an electron moving 1.55×10^{6} m/s?

2.68 How many protons and electrons are present in the following ions? (a) Al^{3+}, (b) Se^{2-}, (c) K^+, and (d) Ca^{2+}.

2.69 When a strip of magnesium metal burns in air, the mass of the resulting residue is greater than the mass of the original metal strip. Explain this observation in terms of conservation of mass.

ANSWERS TO SECTION EXERCISES

2.1.1, 2.1.2

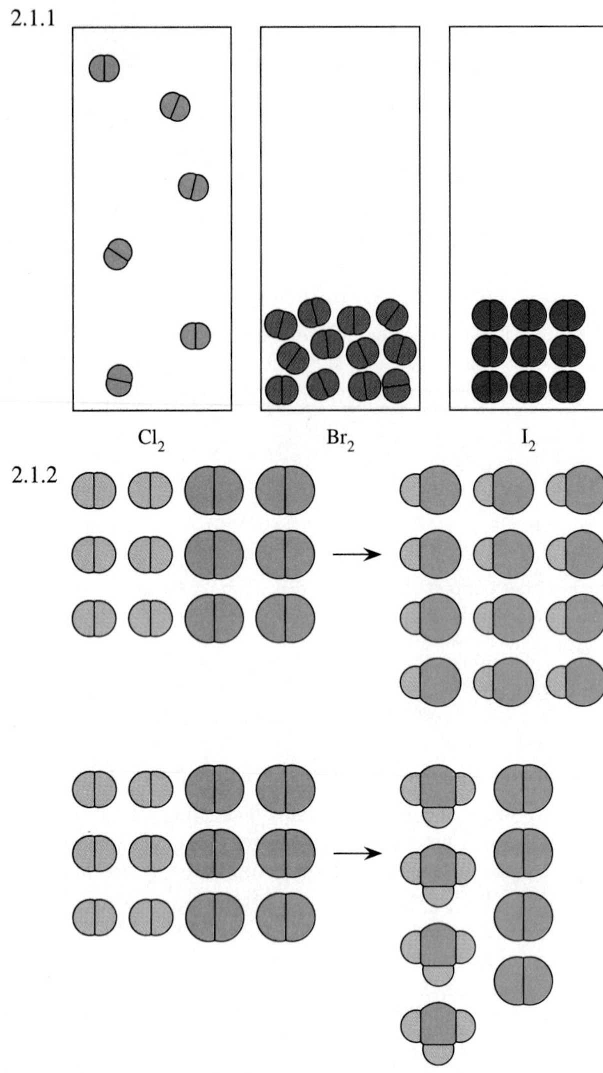

2.1.3 Some of the molecules in the warm shower water move from the liquid phase to the gas phase. These molecules move through the air until they collide with the cool glass surface of the bathroom mirror, where they condense from the gas phase to the liquid phase.

2.2.1

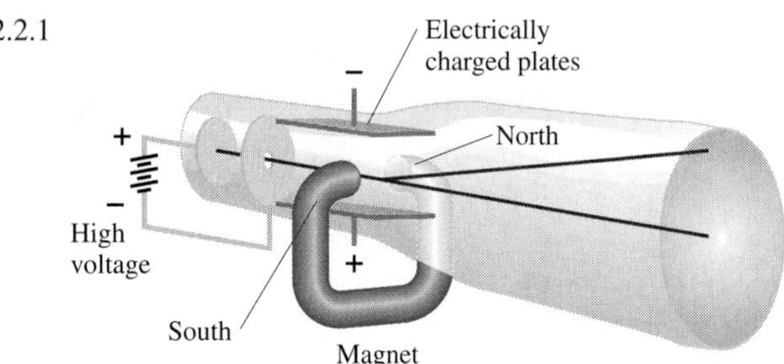

2.2.2 (a) Upward, toward the positively charged plate. (b) Downward, pulled by the force of gravity.

2.2.3 (a) 1.1×10^{24} electrons; (b) 1.8 g

2.3.1

gold	Au	79
iron	Fe	26
arsenic	As	33

2.3.2 (a) ^{57}Co; (b) ^{7}Li; (c) ^{39}K

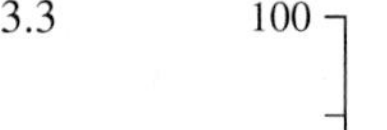

2.3.3

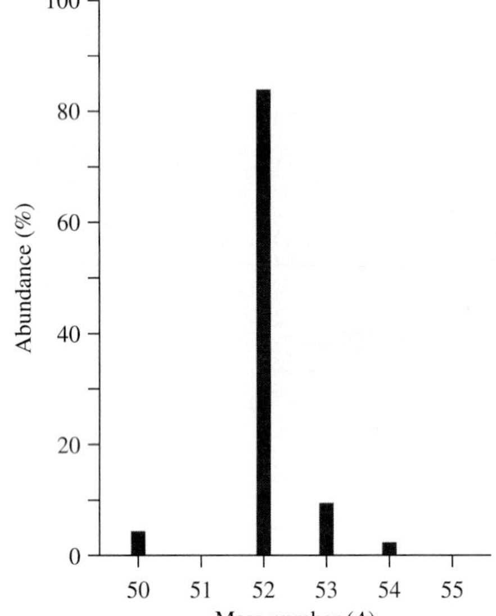

2.4.1

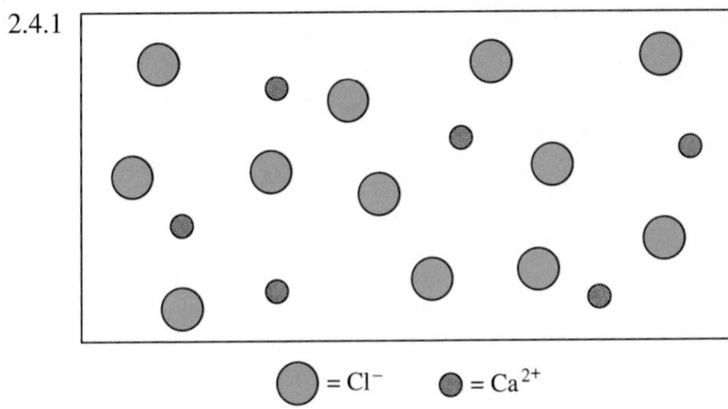

2.4.2 (a) Mg^{2+} and O^{2-}; (b) MgO; (c)

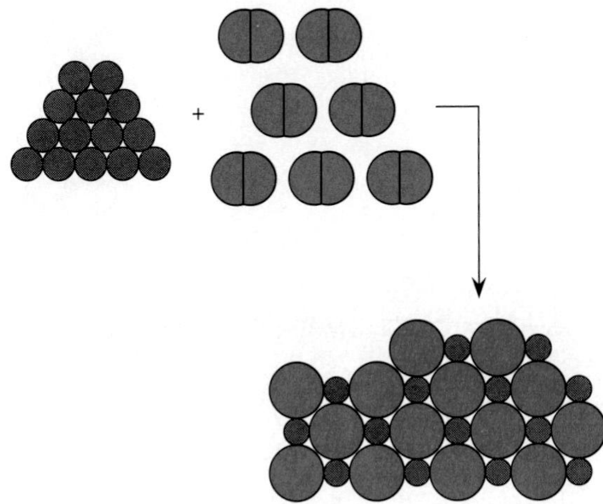

2.4.3 12 protons and 10 electrons

2.5.1 You would have to design an apparatus to collect the steam as it boils away, condense the steam to the liquid phase, and weigh the recovered water. If mass is conserved, the water will retain its original mass of 1000 g. (The density of water is 1.00 g/mL.)

2.5.2 The fragment is CH_2^+; $CH_4 \rightarrow CH_4^+ + e^-$; $CH_4^+ \rightarrow CH_2^+ + H_2$

2.5.3 Plants absorb radiant energy from sunlight and convert it into chemical energy through photosynthesis.

CHAPTER 3

THE COMPOSITION OF MOLECULES

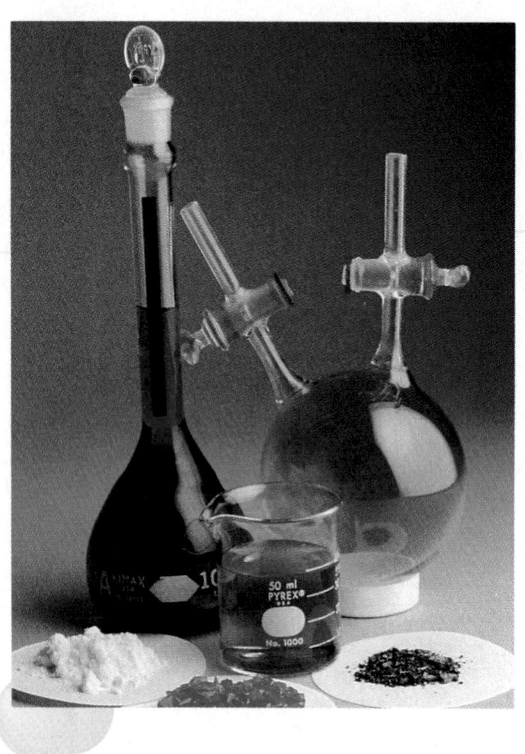

Chemistry is a qualitative and a quantitative science. In other words, when chemists work with substances, they want to know "What is it?" and "How much is there?" Chemists aren't the only ones who ask such questions. Most of us ask them every day. However, in answering both kinds of questions, chemists emphasize the molecular view of chemistry, whereas laypersons are unlikely to give answers in molecular terms. It may take some time to get used to the chemist's perspective.

"What is it?" The answer often takes the form of a name, such as "It's a bird! It's a plane! It's Superman!" The name of a chemical substance is usually designed systematically to contain information about its molecular composition. The naming of chemical compounds is called *chemical nomenclature*. Answers to "What is it?" may also take the form of a picture (Figure 3-1). Pictures are especially important in chemistry because they focus attention on the structures of molecules. Atomic and molecular pictures were introduced in Chapter 1, but in this chapter we describe in more detail how to construct and interpret them.

"How much is there?" When we ask this question in everyday life, we usually mean "How much mass or volume?" For example, how many milligrams of vitamin C do I need each day to stay healthy? How many gallons of gasoline does my car need to get me from home to work? How many pounds of fertilizer should be applied to my garden?

In contrast, when chemists ask, "How much?" they usually mean "How many atoms or molecules?" This is because the foundation of chemistry is atomic theory, and substances are composed of atoms and molecules. However, chemists seldom count atoms and molecules directly. Instead, they measure mass or volume, just as everyone else does. The "tools" of chemistry, analytical balances and volumetric glassware, make it easy and convenient to measure mass and volume with a high degree of accuracy. Nevertheless, chemistry has to do with atoms and molecules, so chemists have to be able to convert between masses and volumes and atoms and molecules.

FIGURE 3-1
Answers to the question "What is it?" may take the form of pictures or drawings.

3.1 REPRESENTING MOLECULES

Chemists use chemical formulas, chemical names, and various types of molecular pictures to describe molecules. We use four different types of molecular pictures throughout this text. They are structural formulas, ball-and-stick models, space-filling models, and line structures. Such pictures accompany our descriptions of chemical substances and their behavior. These molecular representations should help you improve your ability to "think molecules."

CHEMICAL FORMULAS

The fundamental aspects of chemical formulas were introduced in Section 1.2. Recall that atoms of each element are represented by a letter or pair of letters and that the number of atoms of each type is given by a subscripted number. Seven of the elements form diatomic molecules, so their chemical formulas take the form X_2. Figure 3-2 gives the formulas and molecular pictures of these diatomic elements.

Recall that diatomic means "two atoms."

It is extremely important to use correct molecular compositions for chemical substances, because substances containing the same elements in different arrangements can have quite different chemical properties. Oxygen, one of the elements that exists as a diatomic molecule under normal conditions, illustrates this. There is a second form of elemental oxygen called *ozone* whose molecules contain three oxygen atoms arranged in a bent chain. The formula for ozone is O_3. The chemical properties of ozone and diatomic oxygen are dramatically different, as illustrated by the fact that we must breathe O_2 to live, whereas O_3 seriously damages the lungs even in very small quantities.

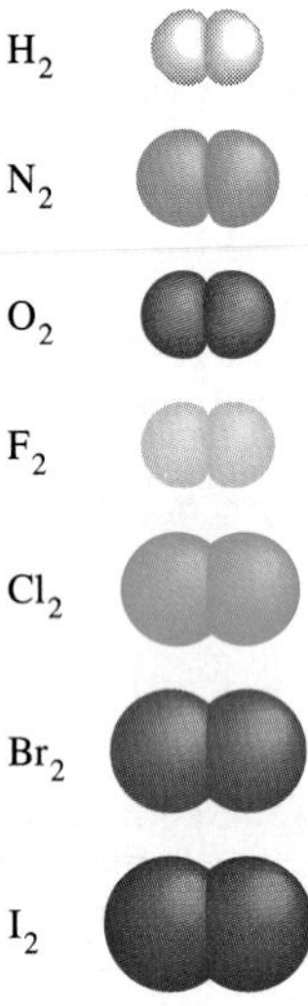

FIGURE 3-2
The seven chemical elements that normally exist as diatomic molecules are iodine, bromine, chlorine, fluorine, oxygen, nitrogen, and hydrogen. A mnemonic for these seven diatomic molecules is *I Bring Clay For Our New House.*

A chemical compound is a combination of atoms of different elements. Because a compound contains more than one element, there is more than one way to write its formula. For example, hydrogen chloride is a diatomic molecule with one atom each of hydrogen and chlorine. Thus its chemical formula might be written as HCl or ClH. To avoid possible confusion, chemists have adopted a standard order for writing chemical formulas. For binary compounds—those containing only two elements—the following rules apply:

1. Except for hydrogen, the element farther to the left in the periodic table appears first: KCl, PCl_3, Al_2S_3, and Fe_3O_4.
2. If hydrogen is present, it appears last except when the other element is from column VI or VII of the periodic table: LiH, NH_3, B_2H_6, and CH_4 but H_2O_2, H_2S, HCl, and HI.
3. If both elements are from the same column of the periodic table, the lower one appears first: SiC, and BrF_3.

Sample Problem 3-1 shows how to use these rules.

SAMPLE PROBLEM 3-1 WRITING CHEMICAL FORMULAS

Write the correct chemical formulas for the compounds containing sulfur whose molecular pictures follow:

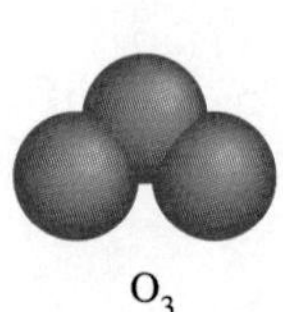

Ozone at ground level is a major component of smog and can be damaging to living beings. On the other hand, ozone in the upper atmosphere is life-protecting, as we describe in later chapters. In fact, scientists are concerned about the "ozone hole" resulting from depletion of ozone in the upper atmosphere.

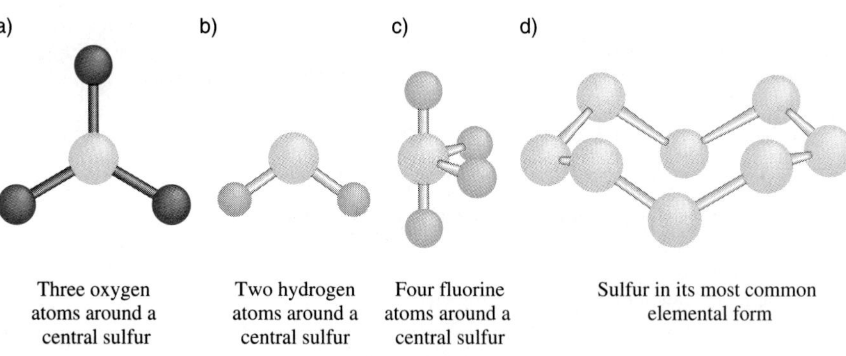

METHOD: Chemical formulas follow specified guidelines. We must use the correct symbols and subscripts and place the symbols in the correct order.

a. Oxygen and sulfur are in the same column of the periodic table. According to the third guideline, the lower element appears first. Thus the correct formula is SO_3.

b. This compound contains hydrogen and sulfur, an element from column VI of the periodic table. According to the second guideline, hydrogen appears before elements from this column. Thus the correct formula is H_2S.

c. The elements in this compound fall in two different columns of the periodic table. According to the first guideline, the element farther to the left appears first. Thus the correct formula is SF_4.

d. Only one element is present in this compound, whose molecules contain eight atoms. Thus the correct formula is S_8.

When three or more different elements occur in a compound, the order depends on whether or not the compound contains ions. Ionic compounds will be described in the next section. Multiple-element compounds that do not contain ions usually contain carbon. The formulas of carbon-containing compounds start with carbon, followed by hydrogen. After that, any other elements appear in alphabetical order, as illustrated by the following examples: C_2H_6O, C_4H_9BrO, CH_3Cl, and $C_8H_{10}N_4O_2$.

Among compounds that contain carbon and hydrogen, there are many examples of structurally distinct molecules that have identical chemical formulas. For example, C_2H_6O describes dimethyl ether and ethanol. For this reason, chemists often depart from the strict elemental sequence to provide additional information about the molecule. Instead of lumping all atoms of a given element together, structural subunits can be listed separately. Figure 3-3 shows that one of the two different compounds with the chemical formula C_2H_6O has a C—O—C linkage, whereas the other contains C—O—H. To distinguish between these two different substances, chemists write the formula of one as $(CH_3)_2O$ and the formula of the other as C_2H_5OH. In the first case the parentheses indicate that the molecule has two CH_3 subunits linked to an oxygen atom. The second formula tells us that there is a C_2H_5 subunit attached to an OH group. Molecules that have the same molecular formula but a different arrangement of atoms are called **isomers.**

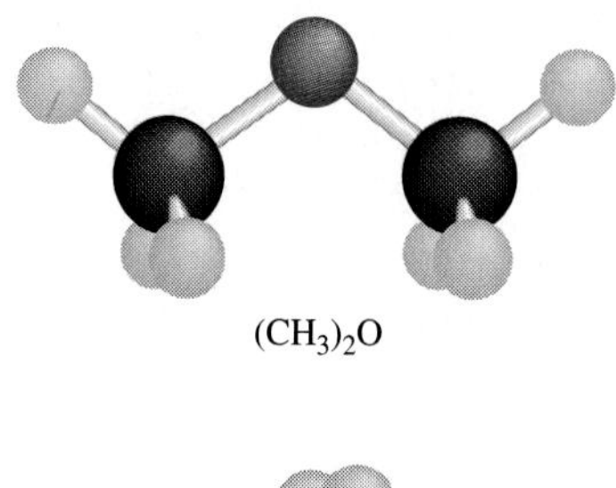

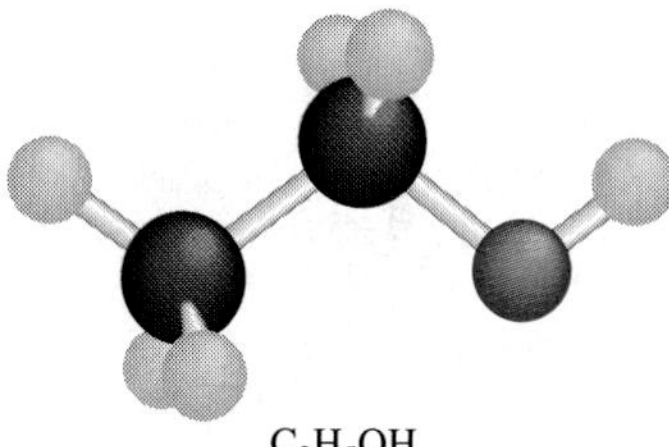

FIGURE 3-3
There are two distinct chemical compounds with the formula C_2H_6O. These isomers can be distinguished by writing their chemical formulas using subunits that indicate how the atoms are linked together.

STRUCTURAL FORMULAS

The chemical formula of a molecule gives only the number of atoms of each element present in one of its molecules. A **structural formula,** on the other hand, not only gives the number of atoms but also shows how the atoms are connected to one another.

The atoms in molecules have specific arrangements because they are held together by attractive forces called **bonds.** In brief, a bond is the result of coulombic attraction between positively charged nuclei and negatively charged electrons. In Chapters 8 and 9 we will explore chemical bonding in detail. For now, it is sufficient to know that a pair of electrons shared between two atoms generates a chemical bond.

In a structural formula the bonds between atoms are represented by lines connecting the elemental symbols. For example, the major component of bottled cooking gas is propane. Each molecule of propane contains three carbon atoms and eight hydrogen atoms, so its chemical formula is C_3H_8. The three carbon atoms of a propane molecule bond together to form a chain. Each outer carbon is bonded to three hydrogens, and the inner carbon is bonded to two hydrogens. This arrangement results in the structural formula of propane that is shown in Figure 3-4, *A*. Notice that the structural formula of propane contains the same information about the number of atoms as the chemical formula: three C atoms and eight H atoms. However, the structural formula also shows how the atoms are connected.

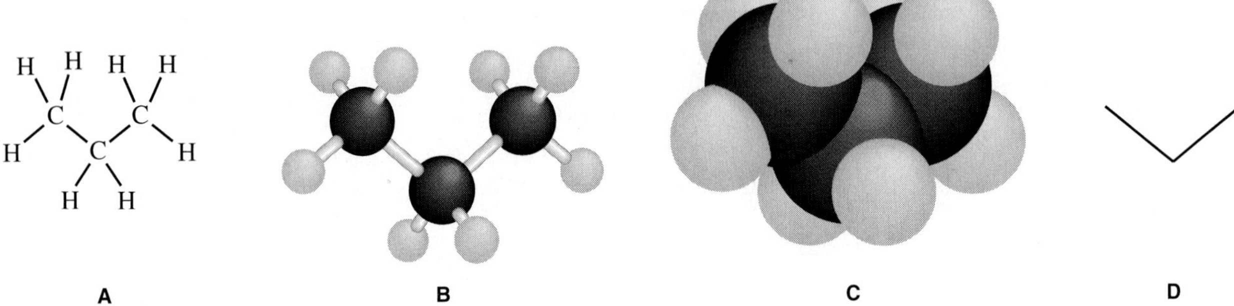

FIGURE 3-4
Structural **(A)**, ball-and-stick **(B)**, space-filling **(C)**, and line **(D)** models for propane, C_3H_8.

Ethane	Ethylene	Acetylene
$H_3C{-}CH_3$	$H_2C{=}CH_2$	$H{-}C{\equiv}C{-}H$
C_2H_6	C_2H_4	C_2H_2
C—C single bond	C=C double bond	C≡C triple bond

FIGURE 3-5
Structural formulas of the three different chemical compounds formed from two carbon atoms and a varying number of hydrogen atoms. Ethane, which is a component of natural gas, contains a C—C single bond. Ethylene, which is the third-ranked industrial chemical because it is widely used to make plastics, contains a C=C double bond. Acetylene, which is used as a fuel for welding torches, contains a C≡C triple bond.

Each line in a structural formula represents one pair of shared electrons, but atoms may share more than one pair of electrons. When two atoms share one pair of electrons, the bond is called a single bond, and the structural formula shows a single line. All atoms in a propane molecule are held together by single bonds. When two atoms share four electrons, the bond is called a double bond, and the structural formula shows two lines between the atoms. Similarly, when two atoms share six electrons, the bond is a triple bond, and the structural formula shows three lines between the atoms.

Two carbon atoms can bond to each other through any of these three kinds of bonds. Figure 3-5, for example, shows the structural formulas of three different compounds that contain two carbon atoms and a variable number of hydrogen atoms. Each compound contains a different type of carbon-carbon bond, resulting in significantly different chemical properties.

THREE-DIMENSIONAL MODELS

A molecule is a three-dimensional array of atoms. In fact, many of a molecule's most important properties, such as its odor and chemical reactivity, depend on its three-dimensional shape. Although molecular and structural formulas provide information about the composition of a molecule, they do not represent the molecule's shape. To provide information about shapes, chemists frequently use ball-and-stick models or space-filling models. Because molecules are three dimensional, accurate models of these types must be constructed from wood or plastic, but two-dimensional drawings can also indicate the essential features of molecular shapes.

In a **ball-and-stick model,** balls represent atoms, and sticks represent chemical bonds. To distinguish among different elements, the balls are labeled with elemental symbols or different colors (that is, each atom is a different color). Figure 3-4, *B*, shows a ball-and-stick model for propane.

The color code used for atoms in this book is shown in Figure 1-4.

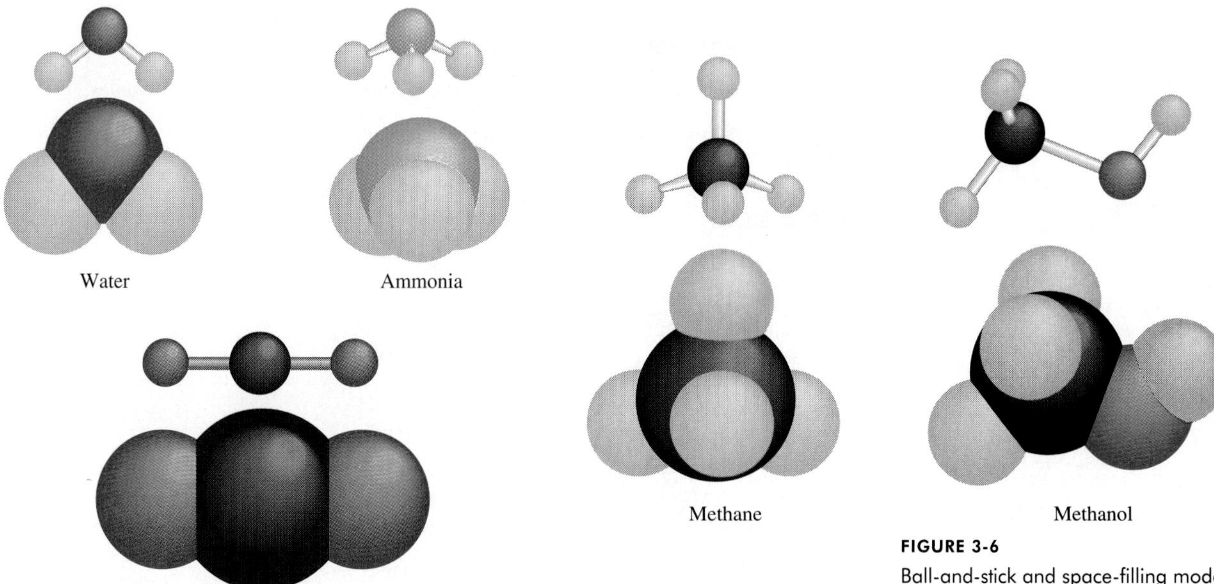

FIGURE 3-6
Ball-and-stick and space-filling models of water, ammonia, carbon dioxide, methane, and methanol.

A **space-filling model** recognizes that a molecule is defined by the space occupied by its electrons. Recall from Rutherford's experiment that electrons make up nearly the entire volume of any atom. Therefore each atom in a space-filling model is shown as a distorted sphere representing its electrons. These spheres merge into one another to build up the entire molecule. We have already shown you a number of space-filling models, such as the ones in Figure 3-2. Figure 3-4, *C* also shows a space-filling model of propane. Notice that these models do not show the individual atomic nuclei, but they give a much better picture of how the molecule appears to another molecule or to an atomic-sized observer. Figure 3-6 shows ball-and-stick and space-filling models for several chemical compounds common in everyday life.

LINE STRUCTURES

The chemistry of living processes is complex, and many carbon-based molecules found in living beings, such as cholesterol or deoxyribonucleic acid (DNA), have extremely complicated structures. Describing and understanding carbon chemistry require the ability to visualize three-dimensional molecular structure, but writing complete structural formulas becomes very tedious for all but the simplest molecules. Because of this, chemists have developed **line structures,** which are compact representations of the structural formulas of carbon compounds. Line structures are constructed according to the following guidelines:

1. All bonds except C—H bonds are shown as lines.
2. C—H bonds are not shown in the line structure.
3. Single bonds are shown as a single line; double bonds are shown as two lines; triple bonds are shown as three lines.
4. Carbon atoms are not labeled.
5. All atoms except carbon and hydrogen are labeled with their elemental symbols.
6. Hydrogen atoms are labeled when they are attached to any atom other than carbon.

Sample Problem 3-2 illustrates these guidelines for three simple molecules.

SAMPLE PROBLEM 3-2 DRAWING LINE STRUCTURES

Construct line structures for the compounds with the following structural formulas.

METHOD: A line structure is built using information about how atoms are connected in the molecule. When a structural formula is known, it forms the basis for the line structure. We apply the guidelines to convert the structural formula representation into a line-structure representation.

$C_5H_{12}O$
MTBE
(a key antiknock ingredient in gasoline)

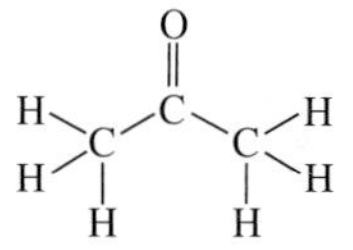

C_3H_6O
Acetone
(a common solvent, and a principal ingredient in nail polish remover)

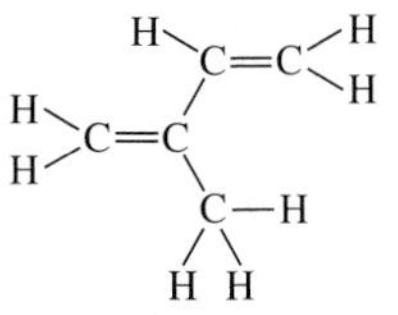

C_5H_8
Isoprene
(the building block of natural rubber)

The first two guidelines tell us that bonds are represented by lines and that all C—H bonds are ignored. Thus we remove the C—H bonds from the structural formula, leaving a bond framework. According to the third guideline, the double bonds remain as two lines.

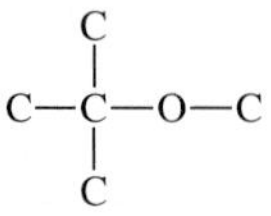

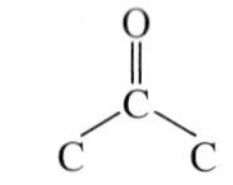

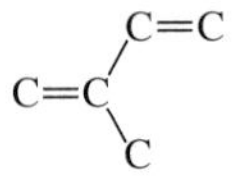

According to the fourth guideline, carbon atoms are not labeled, so we remove the *C*s.

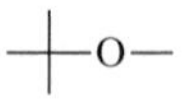

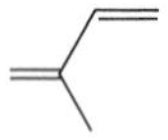

These are the line structures for the three molecules.

Although line structures are a convenient, shorthand version of structural formulas, a chemist must be able to convert them back into chemical formulas. The reconstruction of a complete formula from a line structure relies on the most important general feature of carbon chemistry: In all neutral molecules containing carbon, each carbon atom has *four* chemical bonds. If you look back at the examples we have presented and count the bonds around each carbon atom, you find that the total is always four. For example, each carbon atom in acetylene (Figure 3-5) has three bonds to the other carbon atom and one C—H bond. Another example is the middle carbon atom of acetone, which has one bond to each of its neighboring carbon atoms and two bonds to the oxygen atom. Finally, either of the end carbons of propane (Figure 3-4) has one bond to the middle carbon and three bonds to hydrogen atoms.

Carbon monoxide (CO), which has three bonds to carbon, is the only exception to the generalization that neutral carbon compounds have four bonds to carbon.

Keep in mind that carbon atoms are not shown in a line structure, so the first step in constructing a structural formula from a line structure is to place a C at every line intersection and at the end of every line. We then add singly bonded hydrogen atoms (—H) until every carbon atom has four bonds. Sample Problem 3-3 illustrates this procedure.

SAMPLE PROBLEM 3-3 CONVERTING LINE STRUCTURES

Construct the structural formulas and determine the chemical formulas from the following line drawings:

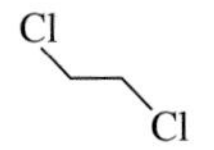

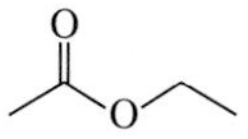

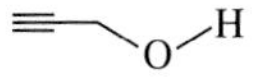

METHOD: Line drawings show all structural features except carbon atoms and C—H bonds. Thus structural formulas are constructed in two steps. First, place a C at any unlabeled line end and line intersection. Second, add C—H bonds until each carbon atom has a total of four bonds. The chemical formula is then obtained by counting the atoms of each element.

In step 1 we place a C at each intersection and line end:

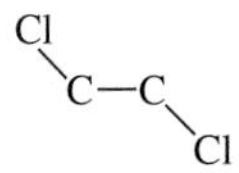

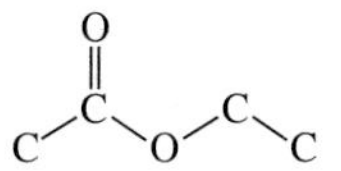

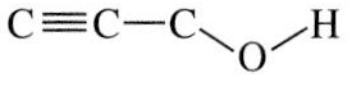

Step 2 requires the addition of C—H bonds to these incomplete structures until each carbon atom has a total of four bonds. We will treat the compounds in sequence.

Each carbon atom in the first structure has two bonds, so each carbon needs two C—H bonds to complete the structural formula:

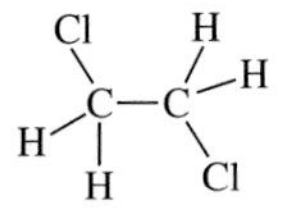

The second structure has four carbon atoms. The two end carbons have just one bond, so each needs three C—H bonds. The carbon with the double bond to oxygen already has its complete set of four bonds. The fourth carbon atom has a bond to C and a bond to O, so it needs two C—H bonds.

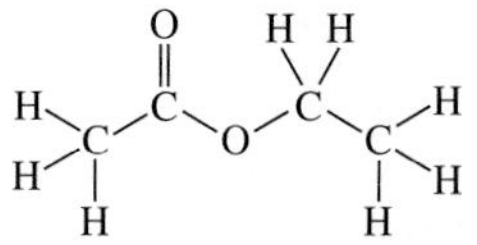

The third structure contains a triple bond. The end carbon needs one C—H bond, but the other carbon atom of the triple bond already has four bonds. The next carbon has two bonds, one to the triple bond and one to the oxygen. Two C—H bonds are needed to give this atom its usual set of four bonds.

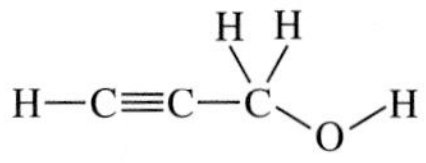

These are the correct structural formulas. Now it is a simple matter to count the number of atoms of each element and write the chemical formulas of the compounds: $C_2H_4Cl_2$, $C_4H_8O_2$, and C_3H_4O.

FIGURE 3-7
Line drawings of caffeine, the stimulant found in coffee, cola, and tea, and cholesterol, a substance that is one cause of heart disease. For comparison, the structural formula of caffeine is also shown. If you still are not convinced that line structures are an efficient way to represent molecules, try drawing the complete structural formula of cholesterol.

Caffeine, $C_8H_{10}N_4O_2$

Cholesterol, $C_{27}H_{46}O$

The structural formulas of the examples we have used are not immensely complicated; yet their line structures are clearer than other representations. As carbon-containing compounds become ever larger, the simplification provided by line drawings makes them increasingly attractive. Line structures are easier not only to draw, but also to interpret because they are not cluttered by all the C—H bonds. Figure 3-7 shows the line drawings of two biologically important molecules that may be familiar to you.

SECTION EXERCISES

3.1.1 Write correct chemical formulas for each of the following substances: (a) stearic acid, whose molecules contain 36 hydrogen atoms, 18 carbon atoms, and 2 oxygen atoms; (b) silicon tetrachloride, whose molecules contain one silicon atom and four chlorine atoms; and (c) freon-113, whose molecules contain three atoms each of fluorine and chlorine and two atoms of carbon.

3.1.2 A ball-and-stick model of cyclohexane follows. Determine its molecular formula, structural formula, and line structure.

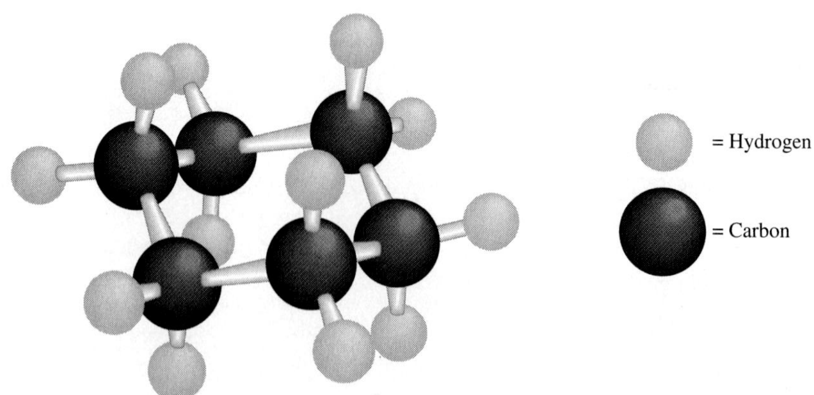

3.1.3 The line structure for methyl methacrylate follows. Draw its structural formula and give its chemical formula. Methyl methacrylate is used to make poly(methylmethacrylate), or PMMA. PMMA is a transparent plastic used in objects such as window panes and contact lenses.

Methyl methacrylate

3.2 NAMING CHEMICAL COMPOUNDS

The naming of cats is a difficult matter,
It isn't just one of your holiday games;
You may think at first I'm as mad as a hatter
When I tell you, a cat must have THREE DIFFERENT NAMES.

T. S. Eliot, *Old Possum's Book of Practical Cats*

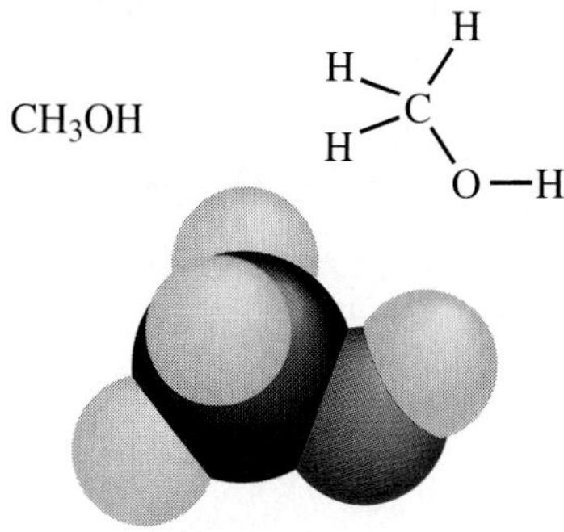

Each chemical substance has a unique structure, but as with cats, the same molecule can have several different names. Consider, for example, the chemical substance whose formula is CH_4O. Its formula is usually written CH_3OH to emphasize that it has an O—H linkage. This substance is commonly known as *wood alcohol* because it was first isolated by burning wood under carefully controlled conditions. It is also called *methyl alcohol.* Its third name, which is the one that chemists have agreed to use, is *methanol.*

The three names for CH_3OH represent three different approaches to chemical nomenclature. *Wood alcohol* is a common name, the name that nonchemists are likely to use. *Methyl alcohol* and *methanol* are names that have been systematically constructed by chemists using two different sets of guidelines. The International Union of Pure and Applied Chemistry (IUPAC) has agreed that *methanol* is the preferred name of CH_3OH. In most cases we use IUPAC names, which are constructed from structural formulas following very specific guidelines. However, you must know about common names because many of them are still in use. The same is true for some systematic names that are different from IUPAC-approved names.

A system for naming is called *nomenclature,* from two Latin words: *nomen* means "name" and *calare* means "call."

COMMON NAMES

In the early days of chemistry the list of known compounds was short, so chemists could memorize the names of all of them. New compounds were often named for their place of origin, physical appearance, or properties (for example, wood alcohol, grain alcohol, rubbing alcohol, milk of magnesia, caustic soda, limestone, baking soda, and laughing gas). As the science of chemistry grew, the number of known compounds quickly became too large for anyone to be able to keep track of all of the common names. Today, over 10 million different compounds are known, and thousands of new ones are discovered or created each year. Consequently, chemists had to develop systematic procedures for naming chemical compounds, and common names, including those listed previously, are being replaced by their IUPAC-approved counterparts (for example, methanol, ethanol, 2-propanol, magnesium hydroxide, sodium hydroxide, calcium carbonate, sodium hydrogencarbonate, and dinitrogen monoxide). Systematic names are less colorful than common names, but they make chemistry much less hectic because it is much easier to learn a few systematic guidelines than to memorize the names of thousands of individual compounds.

There are different guidelines for different types of chemical substances. We focus on naming substances that are most commonly encountered in general chemistry: binary compounds of metals and nonmetals and compounds containing ions. Because many useful and interesting chemical compounds are carbon based, we will also describe a few principles for naming this rich array of substances. In this section we describe guidelines for compounds that do not contain metallic elements. The naming of compounds containing metals is described in Section 3.3.

NAMING BINARY COMPOUNDS

The guidelines presented in Section 3.1 for writing the chemical formulas of binary compounds include one for determining the order in which the elements appear. This order also determines how the compound is named. Some additional guidelines for naming binary compounds follow:

1. The element that appears first retains its elemental name.
2. The second element bears a root derived from its elemental name and ends with the suffix *-ide*. Some common roots are listed in Table 3-1.
3. When there is more than one atom of a given element in the formula, the name of the element usually contains a prefix that specifies the number of atoms present. If the numerical prefix ends with the letter *o* or *a and* the name of the element begins with a vowel, the last letter of the prefix is dropped. For example, use *monoxide* instead of *monooxide* and *tetroxide* instead of *tetraoxide*. Common prefixes are given in Table 3-2.

Numerical prefixes are essential in naming one of a series of similar binary compounds. For example, nitrogen and oxygen form six different molecules: NO, nitrogen monoxide; NO_2, nitrogen dioxide; N_2O, dinitrogen monoxide; N_2O_3, dinitrogen trioxide; N_2O_4, dinitrogen tetroxide; and N_2O_5, dinitrogen pentoxide. Sample Problem 3-4 shows some additional examples.

TABLE 3-1 COMMON ROOTS FOR NAMING COMPOUNDS

ELEMENT	ROOT
As	Arsen-
Br	Brom-
C	Carb-
Cl	Chlor-
F	Fluor-
H	Hydr-
I	Iod-
N	Nitr-
O	Ox-
P	Phosph-
S	Sulf-
Se	Selen-

SAMPLE PROBLEM 3-4 NAMING BINARY COMPOUNDS

Name the following binary compounds: SO_2, CS_2, BCl_3, and BrF_5

METHOD: None of these compounds contains a metallic element, so we apply the guidelines for binary compound nomenclature. Name the first element, use a root plus *-ide* for the second, and indicate the number of atoms with prefixes.

Here are the correct names: sulfur dioxide, carbon disulfide, boron trichloride, and bromine pentafluoride.

BINARY COMPOUNDS OF HYDROGEN

Hydrogen requires special consideration because it may appear first or second in the formula and name of a compound. With elements from Groups I and VII, hydrogen forms diatomic molecules named according to our guidelines. For example, LiH is lithium hydride, and HF is hydrogen fluoride. With elements from Groups II and VI,

TABLE 3-2 NUMBER PREFIXES FOR CHEMICAL NAMES

NUMBER	PREFIX	EXAMPLE	NAME
1	Mon(o)-	CO	Carbon monoxide
2	Di-	SiO_2	Silicon dioxide
3	Tri-	NI_3	Nitrogen triiodide
4	Tetr(a)-	CCl_4	Carbon tetrachloride
5	Pent(a)-	PCl_5	Phosphorus pentachloride
6	Hex(a)-	SF_6	Sulfur hexafluoride
7	Hept(a)-	IF_7	Iodine heptafluoride

hydrogen forms compounds containing two atoms of hydrogen. Except for oxygen, there is only one known binary compound for each element, so the prefix *di-* is omitted. Examples are H_2S, hydrogen sulfide, and CaH_2, calcium hydride. Oxygen forms two binary compounds with hydrogen, and each is known by its common name. One is water, H_2O, and the other is hydrogen peroxide, H_2O_2.

The structural formula of hydrogen peroxide is H—O—O—H.

The systematic approach to chemical nomenclature is abandoned for binary compounds of hydrogen with the elements from Groups III, IV, and V. The IUPAC-approved name for NH_3 is ammonia, not nitrogen trihydride. Similarly, the molecules PH_3 and AsH_3 are called *phosphine* and *arsine,* respectively. Carbon, boron, and silicon form many different binary compounds with hydrogen. Binary compounds of silicon and hydrogen are called *silanes* because the simplest member of the group, SiH_4, is silane. Similarly, the binary compounds of boron and hydrogen are called *boranes* because the simplest member of this group, BH_3, is borane. We will not delve any further into the naming of these compounds.

CARBON-BASED COMPOUNDS

The chemistry of carbon and its compounds is called *organic chemistry.* Biology and biochemistry build on the foundations of organic chemistry because the world of living matter is composed largely of carbon-based compounds. Because the principles of general chemistry apply to all kinds of compounds, we present examples of organic molecules throughout this book. Hence, we need to present *some* of the guidelines for naming organic compounds. However, the details of organic nomenclature are beyond the scope of our coverage.

Carbon forms a huge number of binary compounds with hydrogen. Binary C—H compounds can be divided into three categories: alkanes, alkenes, and alkynes. An alkane has only single bonds between carbon atoms. The four simplest alkanes, which are shown in Figure 3-8, are methane, ethane, propane, and butane. An alkene, on the other hand, is a binary C—H compound with one or more double bonds between carbons, and an alkyne has one or more triple bonds between carbon atoms. Ethylene is the simplest alkene, and acetylene is the simplest alkyne. Their structures appear in Figure 3-5.

The IUPAC names for ethylene and acetylene are *ethene* and *ethyne*, respectively, but chemists generally prefer the common names for these substances.

A major organizing principle in organic chemistry is the presence of special atomic groups, called functional groups, that convey particular chemical properties.

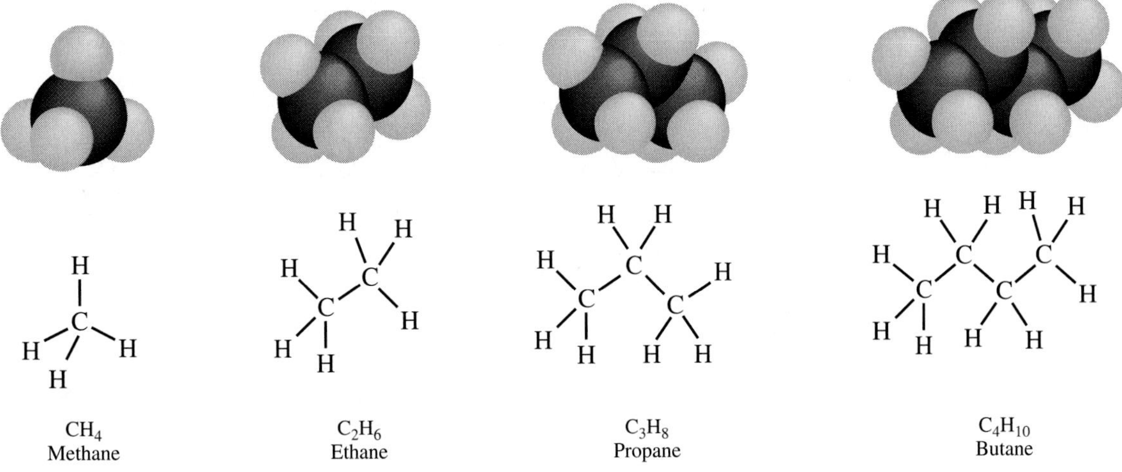

FIGURE 3-8
The four simplest alkanes are methane, ethane, propane, and butane.

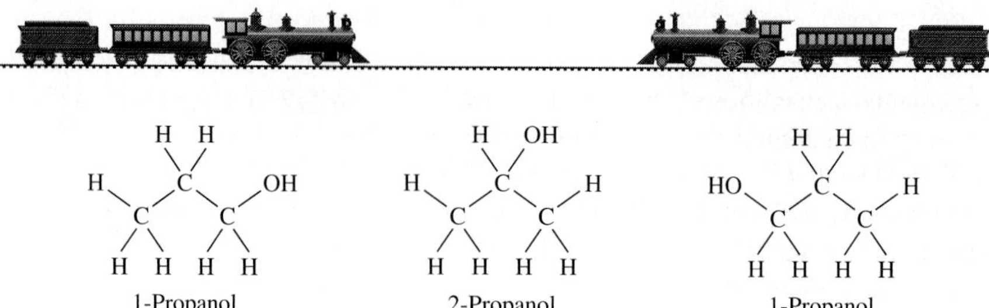

FIGURE 3-9
Structural formulas of 1-propanol and 2-propanol. When the —OH group is attached to an end carbon atom, the compound is 1-propanol. The molecule is the same whether we view it from left to right or from right to left, just as a train has its engine as its first car whether the train is moving from left to right or from right to left.

For example, substances that contain an —OH group are called alcohols. Methanol, ethanol, and 2-propanol, which we mentioned at the beginning of this section, are all alcohols because all contain —OH groups. The systematic name of an alcohol is obtained from the name of the alkane with the same carbon framework by adding the suffix *—ol.* Thus CH_3OH has the carbon framework of methane and is named *methanol,* whereas C_2H_5OH has the carbon framework of ethane and is named *ethanol.*

Two different alcohols, shown in Figure 3-9, are derivatives of propane. If one of the hydrogens on either of the *end* carbons is replaced with OH, the alcohol is called *1-propanol.* If OH replaces one of the hydrogens on the *central* carbon, the alcohol is called *2-propanol.* The numerical prefix specifies the carbon that bears the functional group. Notice that there is no such molecule as 3-propanol. The two end carbons of propane are identical, so replacing a hydrogen on either of them gives the same molecule. This situation is analogous to the train shown in Figure 3-9. We identify the engine as the first car of the train whether the train travels from left to right or from right to left.

Many different families of organic molecules will be introduced as we proceed through the chapters of this book. Names will be introduced as we need them.

SECTION EXERCISES

3.2.1 Write chemical formulas for the following compounds: chlorine monofluoride, xenon trioxide, hydrogen bromide, silicon tetrachloride, sulfur dioxide, and hydrogen peroxide.

3.2.2 Name the following compounds: ClF_3, H_2Se, ClO_2, $SbCl_3$, PCl_5, N_2O_5, N_2Cl_4, and NH_3.

3.2.3 Draw structural formulas of the following molecules: butane, 2-butanol, 1-butanol, and 1-bromobutane.

3.3 IONIC COMPOUNDS

Recall from Chapter 2 that some substances exist as collections of cations and anions, arranged so that the positive and negative charges are balanced. Any stable sample of matter is electrically neutral. This principle helps determine how ionic compounds are organized.

ATOMIC CATIONS AND ANIONS

Many ionic compounds contain atomic ions. The elements classified as metals have a strong tendency to lose electrons and form atomic cations. Almost every compound whose formula contains a metallic element from Group I or Group II is ionic. The transition metals often form ionic species, but these elements also form numerous compounds by sharing electrons. The metals aluminum, tin, and lead also tend to form atomic cations.

In Chapter 2 we describe how an atomic ion forms when a neutral atom gains or loses one or more electrons.

The metals in column I form cations with a +1 charge only (Li^+, Na^+, K^+, and Cs^+), whereas the cations of column II metals always have +2 charge (Mg^{2+}, Ca^{2+}, Sr^{2+}, and Ba^{2+}). The only stable cation of aluminum is Al^{3+}. Most transition metals, on the other hand, can exist in more than one cationic form. Iron, for example, forms both +2 and +3 cations, and copper may be either Cu^+ or Cu^{2+}. Three transition metals have only one stable cation (Ag^+, Cd^{2+}, and Zn^{2+}).

Although many elements form stable atomic cations, only six form stable atomic anions. The four elements in Group VII form atomic anions, always with a −1 charge (F^-, Cl^-, Br^-, and I^-), and oxygen and sulfur form atomic anions, always with a −2 charge (O^{2-} and S^{2-}).

POLYATOMIC IONS

In addition to atomic ions such as Na^+ and Cl^-, ionic compounds often contain clusters of atoms with a net electrical charge. Sodium nitrate is an example of an ionic substance that contains such a cluster. The formula of sodium nitrate is $NaNO_3$. This compound has Na^+ atomic cations, but all of the rest of the atoms of sodium nitrate are grouped together in one structure, NO_3^-, which carries a −1 charge (Figure 3-10). This anion is a molecular ion called the *nitrate ion.* The nitrate ion displays some properties of ions and some properties of molecules. It has a negative electrical charge, but it also contains chemical bonds. Molecular ions are also called **polyatomic ions** to distinguish them from neutral molecules and atomic ions.

We encounter only two important polyatomic *cations* in introductory chemistry. These are the ammonium ion, NH_4^+, and the hydronium ion, H_3O^+, both of which are shown in Figure 3-11. These cations always have a +1 charge.

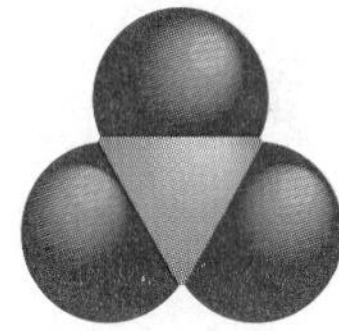

FIGURE 3-10
The nitrate anion is a group of four atoms held together by chemical bonds. The entire unit bears −1 electrical charges.

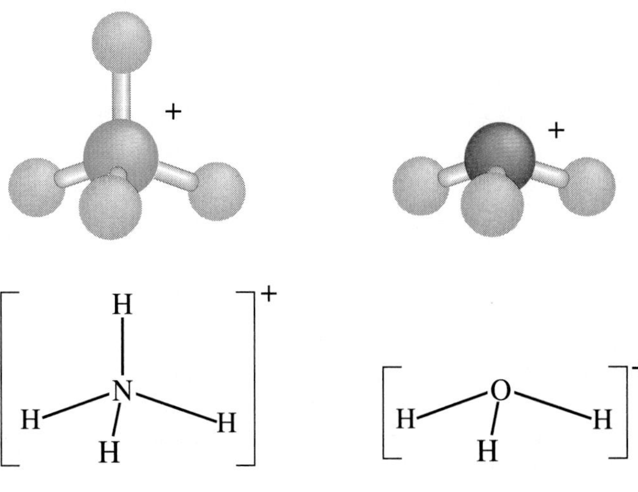

FIGURE 3-11
Structures of the ammonium and hydronium cations. Both always bear +1 charge.

TABLE 3-3 COMMON POLYATOMIC IONS

FORMULA	NAME	FORMULA	NAME
Cations		**Oxyanions**	
NH_4^+	Ammonium	SO_4^{2-}	Sulfate
H_3O^+	Hydronium	SO_3^{2-}	Sulfite
Diatomic Anions		NO_3^-	Nitrate
OH^-	Hydroxide	NO_2^-	Nitrite
CN^-	Cyanide	PO_4^{3-}	Phosphate
Anions With Carbon		MnO_4^-	Permanganate
CO_3^{2-}	Carbonate	CrO_4^-	Chromate
$CH_3CO_2^-$	Acetate	$Cr_2O_7^{2-}$	Dichromate
$C_2O_4^{2-}$	Oxalate	ClO_4^-	Perchlorate
		ClO_3^-	Chlorate
		ClO_2^-	Chlorite
		ClO^-	Hypochlorite

There are many different polyatomic anions, including several that are abundant in nature. Each is a stable species that maintains its structure in crystals and in aqueous solution. Polyatomic anions are treated as distinct units in writing chemical formulas, naming compounds, and drawing molecular pictures. The names, formulas, and charges of the more common polyatomic anions are listed in Table 3-3. You should memorize the common polyatomic ions because they appear regularly throughout this textbook.

Most polyatomic anions, called oxyanions, contain a central atom surrounded by one to four oxygen atoms. The following standard guidelines are used to name oxyanions:

1. The name has a root taken from the name of the central atom (for example, carbonate, CO_3^{2-}, and nitrite, NO_2^-).
2. When an element forms two different oxyanions, the one with fewer oxygen atoms ends in *-ite,* and the other ends in *-ate* (for example, SO_3^{2-}, sulfite, and SO_4^{2-}, sulfate).
3. Chlorine, bromine, and iodine each form four different oxyanions that are distinguished by prefixes and suffixes. The nomenclature of these ions is illustrated for bromine, but it applies to the other halogens as well: BrO^-, hypobromite; BrO_2^-, bromite; BrO_3^-, bromate; and BrO_4^-, perbromate.
4. Polyatomic anions with a charge more negative than −1 may add a hydrogen ion (H^+) to give another anion. These anions are named from the parent anion by adding hydrogen. For example, HCO_3^- is hydrogencarbonate, HPO_4^{2-} is hydrogenphosphate, and $H_2PO_4^-$ is dihydrogenphosphate.

The HCO_3^- anion is also commonly called *bicarbonate*.

IONIC COMPOUNDS

Every ionic compound contains discrete ionic units with specific charges. In addition, ionic compounds must always contain equal amounts of positive and negative charge. These requirements dictate the ratio of cations to anions in an ionic substance. The chemical formula of an ionic compound identifies its ionic units and the cation-to-anion ratio. The following guidelines ensure uniformity in writing these formulas:

1. The cation is always listed before the anion.
2. The formula of any polyatomic ion is written as a unit.
3. Polyatomic ions are placed in parentheses with a following subscript to indicate ratios different from 1:1.

Here are some specific examples illustrating chemical formulas of ionic compounds:

Ammonium cations are always charged +1, and nitrate anions are always −1, so these ions combine in 1:1 ratio. The cation is listed before the anion: NH_4NO_3. Notice that we do not lump together the two nitrogen atoms, because of the structural integrity of the ammonium and nitrate ions.

Sodium cations always carry +1 charges, and carbonate anions are always −2, so their compound must contain two Na^+ ions for every CO_3^{2-}: Na_2CO_3.

Calcium metal forms +2 cations, whereas phosphate carries a charge of −3. There must be three cations (total charge +6) for every two anions (total charge −6) for a chemical formula of $Ca_3(PO_4)_2$.

Ionic compounds are named by using the same guidelines used for naming binary molecules; however, cations are named before anions. Thus NH_4NO_3 is ammonium nitrate, Na_2CO_3 is sodium carbonate, and $Ca_3(PO_4)_2$ is calcium phosphate. The subscripts do not need to be specified in these names because the fixed ionic charges determine the cation-anion ratios unambiguously. Sample Problem 3-5 reinforces these guidelines by showing how to construct chemical formulas from chemical names.

SAMPLE PROBLEM 3-5 FORMULAS OF IONIC COMPOUNDS

Determine the chemical formulas of calcium chloride, magnesium nitrate, and potassium dihydrogenphosphate.

METHOD: The names of the cations and anions identify the chemical formulas, including the *charges* of each ion. The charges, in turn, dictate the ion ratio that must appear in the chemical formulas.

Calcium chloride contains Ca^{2+} (Group II) and Cl^- (Group VII), so there must be two anions for every cation: $CaCl_2$.

Magnesium nitrate contains Mg^{2+} (Group II) and the polyatomic anion NO_3^-. Again, there must be two anions for every cation: $Mg(NO_3)_2$.

Potassium dihydrogenphosphate requires an extra step in reasoning. Potassium (Group I) is K^+, and phosphate is PO_4^{3-}. However, *dihydrogen* means that two hydrogen +1 cations are attached to phosphate, reducing its charge to −1. The dihydrogen phosphate ion, $H_2PO_4^-$, is a single structural unit, so the two ions are present in a 1:1 ratio: KH_2PO_4.

CATIONS OF VARIABLE CHARGE

By convention the chemical formulas of many ionic compounds do not explicitly state the charges of the ions. It is not necessary to do so because the charges can be deduced from a knowledge of the various ions. However, most metals form more than one stable cation. For example, iron forms two different ionic compounds with sulfate: $FeSO_4$ and $Fe_2(SO_4)_3$. The sulfate ion has a −2 charge, so for the compound to be neutral the iron cation in the first species must bear a +2 charge. In the second case the three sulfate anions contribute a total charge of −6, which must be balanced by a +3 charge on each of the two iron cations: Fe^{3+}.

Without an additional guideline for nomenclature, each of these ionic compounds would be called *iron sulfate.* These are different compounds, however, so we must introduce a way to distinguish between them. For any metal that forms *more than one* stable cation, the charge is specified by using a Roman numeral in parentheses after the name of the metal.

According to this guideline, $FeSO_4$ is iron(II) sulfate, and $Fe_2(SO_4)_3$ is iron(III) sulfate. Sample Problem 3-6 combines the guidelines that we have developed thus far.

SAMPLE PROBLEM 3-6 REVIEW OF BINARY NOMENCLATURE

Name the chlorine compounds that have the following chemical formulas: $MgCl_2$, $CoCl_3$, PCl_3, $SnCl_2$, $SnCl_4$, and $GeCl_4$.

METHOD: We name compounds by applying the guidelines. Binary compounds containing metals obey different guidelines from those with no metal. Unless a metal forms only one stable atomic cation, its charge must be specified with Roman numerals in parentheses. Metals that form just one stable cation are those in Groups I and II, Al, Cd, Zn, and Ag.

$MgCl_2$: Magnesium is a metal that always forms a +2 ion. This ionic compound is named without Roman numerals or prefixes: magnesium chloride.

$CoCl_3$: Cobalt, a transition metal, forms more than one stable cation: cobalt(III) chloride.

PCl_3: Phosphorus is not a metal, so we use the guidelines for binary compounds: phosphorus trichloride.

$SnCl_2$: Tin is not one of the metals that forms a single cation: tin(II) chloride.

$SnCl_4$: Same as in tin(II) chloride: tin(IV) chloride.

$GeCl_4$: Germanium is a metalloid, so the standard binary guidelines apply: germanium tetrachloride.

Many ionic compounds can have water molecules incorporated into their crystalline structures. Such compounds are called **hydrates.** To emphasize the presence of discrete water molecules in the chemical structure, the chemical formula of any hydrate shows the waters of hydration separated from the rest of the chemical formula by a dot. A coefficient before H_2O indicates the number of water molecules in the formula. Nickel(II) sulfate hexahydrate is a good example. Its chemical formula is $NiSO_4 \cdot 6H_2O$, indicating that six water molecules are associated with each $NiSO_4$ unit. Aluminum nitrate nonahydrate is another example. The chemical formula of this compound is $Al(NO_3)_3 \cdot 9H_2O$. The compound contains nine water molecules for every one Al^{3+} cation and three NO_3^- anions.

Unfortunately, the nature of cations and anions cannot be used to determine how many waters of hydration will be included when the ions form solid crystals. The number of water molecules, which can range from 0 to as high as 18, must be determined by doing experiments. In fact, some ionic substances exist in several different forms with different numbers of water molecules.

Sample Problems 3-7 and 3-8 integrate the procedures used to convert between names and chemical formulas.

SAMPLE PROBLEM 3-7 NAMING CHEMICAL COMPOUNDS

Name the following compounds: CrO_3, ClF_3, Ag_2SO_4, NH_4HSO_4, $AlCl_3$, and Cu_2O.

METHOD: Apply the guidelines for naming compounds.

CrO_3: As a transition metal, chromium forms more than one stable cation. Name the metal first, using a Roman numeral to designate chromium's charge. Each of the three oxide anions has a −2 charge. To maintain net charge neutrality, Cr must be +6: chromium(VI) oxide.

Studies of the structure of CrO_3 reveal that electrons are shared between the oxygen atoms and the chromium atoms, so oxygen is not present as O^{2-} anions, and chromium does not have an actual charge of +6. The compound is nevertheless named *chromium(VI) oxide* as if O^{2-} anions were present.

ClF_3: This compound contains two elements from column VII of the periodic table. Chlorine is named first, and we add a prefix that specifies the number of fluorine atoms: chlorine trifluoride.

Ag_2SO_4: The polyatomic sulfate ion indicates that this is an ionic compound. Silver is always +1, so no Roman numeral is needed: silver sulfate.

NH_4HSO_4: The polyatomic ammonium cation is combined with a hydrogen-containing anion: ammonium hydrogensulfate.

$AlCl_3$: Aluminum is a metal that has just one stable atomic cation. No Roman numeral is required: aluminum chloride.

Cu_2O: Copper is a transition metal, so we use a Roman numeral to designate the charge on copper. Oxygen forms a −2 oxide anion. To achieve charge neutrality, each copper must be +1: copper(I) oxide.

SAMPLE PROBLEM 3-8 CHEMICAL FORMULAS

Determine the correct chemical formulas of potassium permanganate, dinitrogen tetroxide, lead(IV) nitrate, sodium hydrogenphosphate, and iron(III) oxide.

METHOD: In this problem we work from name to formula, using our knowledge of polyatomic ions and being careful to build a formula that is electrically neutral.

Potassium permanganate: Permanganate is MnO_4^- (Table 3-3), and potassium always has a +1 charge (Group I). The formula is $KMnO_4$.

Dinitrogen tetroxide: The prefixes tell us the formula: N_2O_4.

Lead(IV) nitrate: Lead(IV) is Pb^{4+}, and nitrate is NO_3^-. To achieve electrical neutrality, the formula must be $Pb(NO_3)_4$.

Sodium hydrogenphosphate: One hydrogen (H^+) attached to phosphate (PO_4^{3-}) leaves two negative charges, which requires two sodium ions for neutrality: Na_2HPO_4.

Iron(III) oxide: Iron(III) is Fe^{3+}, and oxide is O^{2-}. To be a neutral compound, there must be two Fe^{3+} ions (total charge = +6) for every three oxide ions (total charge = −6): Fe_2O_3.

RECOGNIZING IONIC COMPOUNDS

Ionic substances show distinctive chemical behavior, so it is important to recognize which substances are classified as ionic. There is no single method that identifies ionic compounds unambiguously under all circumstances, but the following guideline encompasses most ionic compounds encountered in general chemistry.

> ***A compound is ionic if it contains a metal from Group I or Group II or one of the polyatomic ions.***

Sample Problem 3-9 makes use of this guideline.

SAMPLE PROBLEM 3-9 RECOGNIZING IONIC COMPOUNDS

Determine which of the following substances are ionic: CCl_4, $SrCl_2$, Li, $Co(NO_3)_3$, KCN, $TiCl_4$, and KH_2PO_4.

METHOD: To identify an ionic compound, look for a Group I or Group II metal or one of the polyatomic ions.

CCl_4: Chlorine can exist as a −1 anion, but there is no cation in carbon tetrachloride, so the compound cannot be ionic.

$SrCl_2$: The presence of strontium, a Group II metal, indicates that strontium chloride is an ionic compound.

Li: Lithium is a Group I metal, but there is no other element present to neutralize the charge that would accompany Li^+ ions in an ionic compound. This is lithium in its elemental, nonionic state.

$Co(NO_3)_3$: The nitrate ion tells us that cobalt(III) nitrate is an ionic compound. This is an example of an ionic compound containing a transition metal cation.

KCN: This compound contains a Group I cation and a polyatomic anion, so it is ionic.

$TiCl_4$: Titanium tetrachloride does not meet either guideline for ionic compounds. This is an example of a transition metal compound that is not considered ionic.

KH_2PO_4: Potassium dihydrogenphosphate contains a Group I metal and a common polyatomic anion, so it is ionic.

The guideline identifies most common ionic substances. However, transition and main group metals form ionic compounds that are not covered by the guidelines. For instance, some metal halides and metal oxides are ionic, whereas others are not. In Chapter 8, after we develop ideas about chemical bonding, we present further guidelines for identifying ionic compounds.

SECTION EXERCISES

3.3.1 Name the following compounds: SCl_2, $CaCl_2$, $PbCl_2$, $NaNO_3$, MnO_2, $ZrCl_4$, NaH, and $NaIO_3$.

3.3.2 Write correct molecular formulas for aluminum oxide, lead(II) nitrate, dinitrogen pentoxide, sodium sulfate, iodine pentafluoride, manganese(II) acetate, potassium dichromate, and sodium hypochlorite.

3.3.3 Name the following compounds:

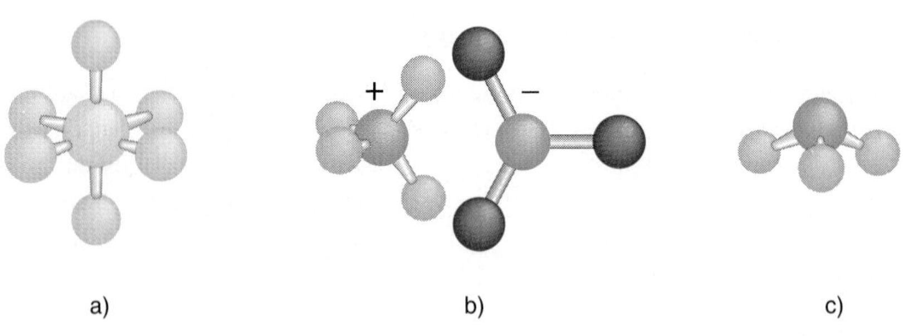

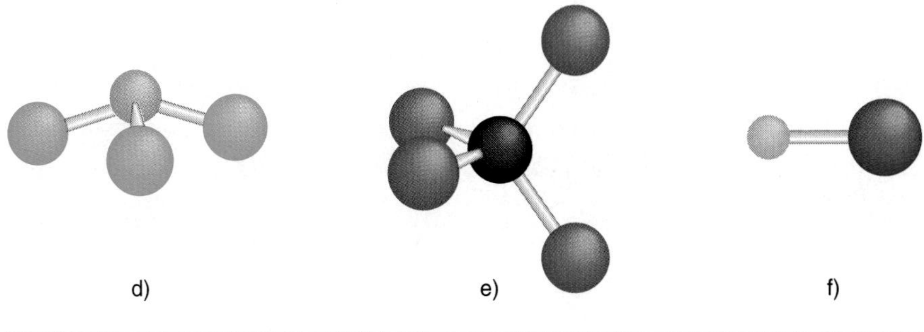

3.4 THE MOLE

Sections 3.1 through 3.3 described qualitative aspects of atoms, molecules and ions, which answer questions about "What is it?" Equally important, we need ways to describe the quantitative aspects of chemistry. In molecular terms the question, "How much is there?" translates into "How many atoms, molecules, and/or ions are present?" Chemists must be able to keep track of numbers of atoms and molecules.

It is very difficult to *count* atoms and molecules, but we can *weigh* substances routinely. Then, from the mass of a sample, we can calculate the number of molecules it contains if we know the mass of an individual molecule. Modern laboratories have instruments such as mass spectrometers that measure the mass of an individual atom or molecule. The problem with this way of handling mass-to-number conversions is that there is an enormous difference between the mass of one molecule and the masses that we measure in the laboratory. For example, a routine laboratory balance measures mass values from about 10^{-4} to 10^{3} g. A typical atom, on the other hand, has a mass between 10^{-23} and 10^{-21} g. Even the smallest mass that we can measure contains approximately 10^{18} or 1,000,000,000,000,000,000 molecules.

THE MOLE AND AVOGADRO'S NUMBER

To avoid having to work with unimaginably large numbers, chemists use a convenient unit called the **mole (mol),** which is the number of atoms in a reference sample having a convenient mass:

> ***One mole is the number of atoms in exactly 12 g of the pure isotope carbon-12.***

Using mass spectrometers, scientists have determined that the mass of a ^{12}C atom is $m_{^{12}C} = 1.992648 \times 10^{-23}$ g/atom. Combining this experimental mass with the definition of the mole gives the number of atoms in one mole:

Every atom of carbon-12 has six electrons, six protons, and six neutrons.

$$\frac{12\text{ g }^{12}\text{C/mol}}{1.992648 \times 10^{-23}\text{ g }^{12}\text{C/atom}} = 6.022137 \times 10^{23}\text{ atoms/mol}$$

The experimental value for the mass of a ^{12}C atom is known to seven significant figures, and 12 g of ^{12}C/mol is an exact number by definition. Thus the number of atoms in 1 mol is known to seven significant figures.

The mole must be defined in terms of the mass of a particular isotope because atoms of different isotopes have different masses. Thus an atom of ^{12}C has a different mass than an atom of ^{13}C. Similarly, equal masses of different *elements* contain different numbers of atoms; so 12 g of ^{12}C and 12 g of ^{13}C contain different numbers of atoms. For the mole to be a specific number of objects, it must be related to the mass of one particular isotope of one particular element. Box 3-1 describes the history of the mole.

BOX 3-1

HISTORY OF THE MOLE

The size of the mole—6.022×10^{23} items—and the choice of the molar mass standard—1 mol of carbon-12 has a mass of 12 g—may seem peculiar and arbitrary. They are indeed arbitrary, but they were chosen for a combination of historic and logical reasons.

The units of mass were established well before the concept of atomic mass was developed. In fact, the scientific community had already agreed to use the gram as the fundamental mass unit when atomic theory became accepted. Thus when nineteenth-century chemists determined the mass ratios of the elements in common chemical substances, their measurements were made in grams. The mole was introduced to relate mass ratios to numbers of atoms at a time when the mass of an individual atom could not be directly measured.

Oxygen was a natural choice on which to base mass ratios of the elements because oxygen forms compounds with most of the other elements. As chemists carried out measurements on oxygen-containing materials, they noticed that if 16 g of oxygen were used as a common amount, the masses of other elements were often very close to whole numbers. For example, 2 g of hydrogen combines with 16 g of oxygen, 14 g of nitrogen combines with 16 g of oxygen, 137 g of barium combines with 16 g of oxygen, and so on. Thus the mole was originally defined to be exactly 16 g of oxygen, making the molar masses of many other elements close to integers.

After the size of the molar mass unit had been assigned, it fixed the number of atoms in the mole. If 16 g of oxygen make 1 mol, then 1 mol contains however many oxygen atoms it takes to give 16 g; that number is Avogadro's number, 6.022×10^{23} atoms/mol.

While chemists were working with combining masses of oxygen, physicists were busy determining the physical properties of atoms. For reasons of their own, physicists based their molar mass scale on carbon rather than oxygen. They chose to define 12 g of naturally occurring carbon to be 1 mol.

The combining mass ratio of oxygen to carbon is not exactly 16:12, so the physicists' scale gave slightly different values for molar masses. Oxygen, for example, has a molar mass of 15.98 g/mol rather than 16.00 g/mol. This difference is very small—only a little over 0.1%—but as mass measurements became more and more accurate, the discrepancy between the scales became unacceptable.

Neither the chemists nor the physicists wanted to give up their scale, but after a great deal of negotiation, they finally agreed to select ^{12}C as the basis for everyone's molar mass unit. The choice of ^{12}C rather than naturally occurring carbon (which is a mixture of isotopes) had two advantages. The most accurate mass measurements are made with mass spectrometers, which measure a single isotope rather than a natural mixture, so it made more sense to base the scale on a particular isotope. The choice of ^{12}C made the new scale nearly identical with the old chemists' scale. Naturally occurring oxygen now has an atomic molar mass of 15.999 rather than exactly 16, a difference of less than 0.01%. Thus a scale based on ^{12}C is not only very precise but also very close to one of the old standards.

The number of items in 1 mol is important enough to have its own name and symbol. It is known as **Avogadro's number,** commonly symbolized N, N_o, or N_A.* In this text we use N_A for Avogadro's Number. Although this quantity is known with seven-figure accuracy, four figures are enough for most calculations: $N_A = 6.022 \times 10^{23}$ items/mol.

The mole is a convenient unit for chemical amounts because a typical laboratory mass contains about 1 mol of atoms or molecules. For example, 1.20 g of ^{12}C contains 6.02×10^{22} atoms of carbon, which is 0.100 mol. The convenience of using a larger unit to describe many small items is not limited to atoms and molecules. Pencils are sold by the dozen, and paper is sold by the ream. Stationers sell paper by the ream; chemists "sell" atoms and molecules by the mole. There are 500 sheets of paper in a ream, and 6.022×10^{23} atoms in a mole of atoms (Figures 3-12 and 3-13).

FIGURE 3-12
Different units are useful for measuring different-sized items. Pencils are sold by the dozen, paper is sold by the ream, and atoms are measured by the mole. Twenty-four pennies contain 1 mol of copper atoms.

How large is a mole? One mole of marbles would cover the Earth with a layer 3 miles thick. If one mole of U.S. pennies were divided equally among all the people in the United States, one individual could pay off our national debt and have a few trillion dollars left over for incidental expenses. Obviously, the mole is not a useful measure for things much larger than atoms. On the other hand, one mole of copper atoms is enough to make 24 pennies. The mole is very useful as a measure for things that are atomic sized. One mole is Avogadro's number of atoms, molecules, ions, nuclei, or electrons.

FIGURE 3-13
One-mole samples of nickel *(upper left)*, tin *(upper right)*, carbon *(lower left)*, copper *(lower right)*, and sulfur *(center)*.

MOLAR MASS

We learned in Chapter 2 that each isotope has a unique mass, so we must conclude that the mass of one mole of any isotope will have some unique value. One mole of the ^{12}C isotope has a mass of exactly 12 g. The characteristic mass of 1 mol of any other isotope can be found by multiplying the mass of one atom of that isotope by Avogadro's number. For example, the mass of 1 mol of carbon-13 atoms is:

$$\left(\frac{2.15928 \times 10^{-23}\ \text{g}}{\cancel{\text{atom of }^{13}\text{C}}}\right)\left(\frac{6.022137 \times 10^{23}\ \cancel{\text{atoms of }^{13}\text{C}}}{\text{mol}}\right) = 13.0035\ \text{g/mol}$$

A sample of a chemical element is usually a mixture of all of its stable isotopes. Any terrestrial sample of elemental hydrogen contains 99.985% ^{1}H and 0.015% ^{2}H; elemental titanium is a mixture of 5 stable isotopes, and tin has 10 isotopes, each with its own particular mass.

Despite their small mass differences, all isotopes of the same element otherwise have the same physical and chemical properties. For instance, as titanium (Ti) metal is extracted from its ores, mixed with other metals to make alloys, and then fashioned into turbine blades for a jet engine, the same five isotopes are always present in the same proportions: 8.2% ^{46}Ti, 7.4% ^{47}Ti, 73.8% ^{48}Ti, 5.4%, ^{49}Ti, and 5.2% ^{50}Ti. The mass of 1 mol of naturally occurring titanium is the sum of the masses contributed by each isotope. Table 3-4 summarizes the contribution of each isotope to the mass of 1 mol of titanium.

The mass of 1 mol of any naturally occurring element is the sum of the contributions from each of its isotopes:

$$\text{Elemental molar mass} = \sum \text{(fractional abundance)(isotopic molar mass)} \qquad \textbf{(3-1)}$$

The symbol Σ is the Greek letter sigma. It means "Take the sum of the following quantities."

* Avogadro's number is named in honor of Amedeo Avogadro, a nineteenth-century Italian scientist who was an early champion of atomic theory.

TABLE 3-4 THE COMPOSITION OF 1 MOL OF TITANIUM

ISOTOPE	ISOTOPIC MOLAR MASS (g/mol)	FRACTIONAL ABUNDANCE	TOTAL MASS (g)
46	45.95263	0.082	3.768
47	46.9518	0.074	3.474
48	47.948	0.738	35.386
49	48.94787	0.054	2.643
50	49.9448	0.052	2.597
Naturally occurring Ti		1.000	47.868

For purposes of chemical bookkeeping, it is unnecessary to know isotopic molar masses and isotopic compositions of the elements. Instead, we need to know the mass of 1 mol of an element containing its natural composition of isotopes (e.g., the mass of 1 mol of naturally occurring elemental titanium is 47.868 g). These molar masses are usually included in the periodic table, and they appear on the endpapers of this textbook.

We will refer to the mass of 1 mol of any substance as its **molar mass (*MM*).** Elsewhere, however, you may find this same quantity called by other names such as *atomic mass* and *atomic weight*. These names are misleading because *atomic* implies a single atom, but individual atoms do not have average masses. Instead, each atom has a mass characteristic of one isotope. To avoid possible confusion, we will use *atomic mass* to denote the mass (in grams) of a single atom and *molar mass* to denote the mass (in grams) of 1 mol of substance. Furthermore, we will use *isotopic molar mass* for the mass of 1 mol of an individual isotope and *elemental molar mass* for the mass of 1 mol of an element containing its isotopes in their naturally occurring abundances. Sample Problem 3-10 illustrates the use of isotopic molar masses and natural abundances to calculate the elemental molar mass of iron.

SAMPLE PROBLEM 3-10 CALCULATING AN ELEMENTAL MOLAR MASS

The mass spectral analysis of an iron sample gives the following data. Calculate the elemental molar mass of iron (Fe).

Isotope	Isotopic Molar Mass (g/mol)	Abundance
^{54}Fe	53.940	5.82%
^{56}Fe	55.935	91.66%
^{57}Fe	56.935	2.19%
^{58}Fe	57.933	0.33%

METHOD: The molar mass is given by the weighted average of the individual isotopes (Equation 3-1). First, the percentages must be converted to fractions by dividing by 100. Then we multiply these fractional abundances by the isotopic masses and add the results:

$$MM = (0.0582)\,(53.940\text{ g/mol }^{54}\text{Fe}) + (0.9166)\,(55.935\text{ g/mol }^{56}\text{Fe}) + (0.0219)\,(56.935\text{ g/mol }^{57}\text{Fe}) + (0.0033)\,(57.933\text{ g/mol }^{58}\text{Fe})$$

$$MM = (3.14\text{ g/mol }^{54}\text{Fe}) + (51.27\text{ g/mol }^{56}\text{Fe}) + (1.25\text{ g/mol }^{57}\text{Fe}) + (0.19\text{ g/mol }^{58}\text{Fe})$$

$$MM = 55.85\text{ g/mol of natural Fe}$$

MASS-MOLE-ATOM CONVERSIONS

Elemental molar masses can be thought of as conversion factors between masses in grams and number of moles. To determine the amount of an elemental sample, we can measure its mass and convert to moles by dividing by the molar mass of that element. Similarly, if we wish to know the mass of a particular number of moles of an element, we can multiply that number of moles by the elemental molar mass.

Suppose, for example, that a bracelet contains 168 g of silver (Ag). To determine the number of moles of silver in the bracelet, we divide mass by molar mass:

$$\frac{168 \not{g}\ \text{Ag}}{107.868 \not{g}/\text{mol}} = 1.56 \text{ mol Ag}$$

Similarly, if a chemical reaction calls for 0.250 mol of Ag, we multiply moles by molar mass to determine the mass of Ag that should be used:

$$(0.250 \not{\text{mol}}\ \text{Ag})\ (107.868\ \text{g}/\not{\text{mol}}) = 27.0 \text{ g Ag}$$

Avogadro's number is the conversion factor between number of moles and number of individual particles. To determine the number of atoms in a sample of an element, we multiply the number of moles by Avogadro's number. Similarly, if we know that a sample contains a certain number of atoms of an element, we can calculate the number of moles it contains by dividing by Avogadro's number.

The number of silver atoms in the bracelet that contains 1.56 mol of Ag is found by multiplying by Avogadro's number:

$$(1.56 \not{\text{mol}}\ \text{Ag})\ (6.022 \times 10^{23}\ \text{atoms}/\not{\text{mol}}) = 9.39 \times 10^{23} \text{ atoms Ag}$$

As an example of the opposite conversion, if a radioactivity detector counts 175 decays of ^{14}C nuclei in 1 hour, dividing by Avogadro's number converts to moles:

$$\frac{175\ \not{\text{nuclei}}\ ^{14}\text{C}}{6.022 \times 10^{23}\ \not{\text{nuclei}}/\text{mol}} = 2.91 \times 10^{-22} \text{ mol } ^{14}\text{C}$$

Avogadro's number and atomic mass allow us to move readily back and forth between the mass of a substance, the number of moles, and the number of atoms. These interconversions among mass, moles, and atoms can be represented schematically in the flowchart shown in Figure 3-14.

The mole is the currency of chemistry. In Figure 3-14, moles occupy the central position because the mole is the unit we use to move through almost all chemical calculations. When solving chemical problems, we must first interpret the question on the molecular level. After we visualize what the molecules are doing, a second part of chemical problem solving often requires quantitative calculations, which usually require that we work with *moles.*

All chemical calculations are built around the mole.

Sample Problem 3-11 provides a practical application of these ideas.

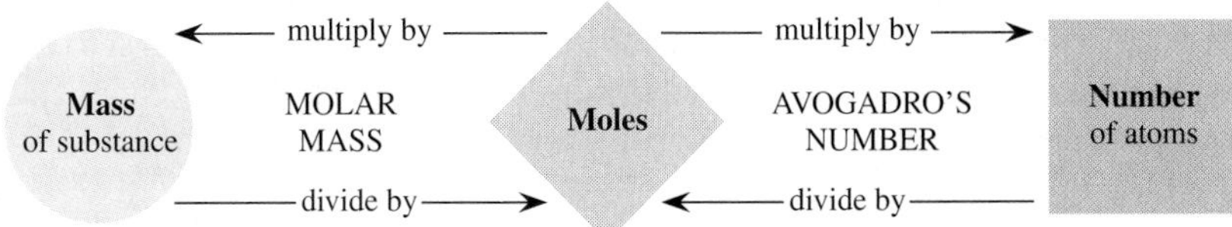

FIGURE 3-14
This flowchart shows how the number of moles is connected to the mass of an element and the number of atoms or molecules.

SAMPLE PROBLEM 3-11 MASS-MOLE-ATOM CONVERSIONS

The eruption of Mount St. Helens on May 18, 1980, provided geologists with a unique opportunity to study the action of volcanos. Gas samples from the plume were collected and analyzed for toxic heavy metals. To collect mercury (Hg) from the plume, unfiltered gas samples were passed over a piece of gold metal, which binds Hg atoms very tightly. The mass of the metal increased as it absorbed Hg from the plume. From a plume-gas sample containing 200 g of ash, 3.60 μg of Hg was deposited on the gold. How many moles of mercury were present in the gas sample? How many atoms is this?

METHOD: This problem contains several pieces of information, not all of which are needed to answer the questions. The seven-step approach described in Chapter 1 is particularly useful for extracting the essential features from such a problem.

1. What are you asked to find? The problem explicitly asks you to calculate the number of moles and atoms of Hg present in the plume sample.
2. What are the molecules/atoms doing? Mercury atoms from the gas plume "stick" to the gold metal, causing an increase in mass. Thus the increase in mass of the piece of gold equals the mass of Hg in the plume sample.
3. What equations apply? The mass of mercury is given. Conversion from mass to number of moles and number of atoms requires equations developed in this section: mol $= m/MM$ and Atoms $= (\text{mol})(N_A)$.
4. What data are available? The data available include what is given in the problem and what can be looked up in tables:

Given in the problem:	3.60 μg of Hg deposited
From tables:	μg $= 10^{-6}$ g
	MM of Hg $= 200.6$ g/mol
	$N_A = 6.022 \times 10^{23}$ atoms/mol

5. If necessary, manipulate the equations. Moles and atoms of mercury are the goal of the calculation. The equations listed in Step 3 do not require manipulation.
6. Substitute and solve, being careful about units:

Carry one extra digit and round to the correct number of significant figures after the final calculation.

$$\text{Moles Hg} = \frac{(3.60\ \mu\text{g Hg})}{(200.6\ \text{g mol}^{-1})(10^6\ \mu\text{g g}^{-1})} = 1.795 \times 10^{-8}\ \text{mol Hg}$$

$$\text{Atoms Hg} = (1.795 \times 10^{-8}\ \text{mol})(6.022 \times 10^{23}\ \text{atoms mol}^{-1}) = 1.08 \times 10^{16}\ \text{atoms}$$

7. Are the results reasonable? First of all, the units cancel to give moles and atoms, which are the units for which the problem asked. Further, the mass of Hg is quite small, so we expect the number of moles to be small also. The number of atoms, 1.08×10^{16}, is large but much smaller than Avogadro's number.

This may not seem like much mercury, but consider that the initial eruption blanketed the Yakima Valley with 35 metric tons of volcanic ash per acre. Given that a metric ton is 1000 kg, determine for yourself how many grams, moles, and atoms of Hg the volcano deposited on every acre of the Yakima Valley.

CHEMICAL COMPOUNDS

Just as each element has a characteristic molar mass, so does every chemical compound. Chemical compounds are composed of atoms bound together into molecules or ions clustered together in electrically neutral aggregates. In either case a chemical formula describes the atomic composition of a compound.

One mole of any chemical compound is 1 mol of its chemical formula unit.

Here are some examples:

1. One mole of O_2 is 1 mol of diatomic O_2 molecules. Each molecule contains two oxygen atoms, so 1 mol of O_2 contains *2* mol of oxygen *atoms.*
2. One mole of methane (CH_4) is 1 mol of CH_4 molecules, so it contains *1* mol of carbon atoms and *4* mol of hydrogen atoms.
3. One mole of sodium chloride (NaCl) contains 1 mol each of Na^+ cations and Cl^- anions.
4. One mole of magnesium chloride ($MgCl_2$) contains 1 mol of Mg^{2+} and 2 mol of Cl^-.

When atoms combine to form molecules, they retain their atomic identities and characteristic molar masses. The mass of an ion differs slightly from the mass of its parent atom because the ion has more or fewer electrons. However, the mass of an electron is so much smaller than the mass of a nucleus that the differences can be neglected. Consequently, the molar mass of a compound is found by adding together the molar mass of each element, taking into account the number of moles of each element present.

One mole of O_2 molecules contains 2 mol of O_2 atoms, so the molar mass of molecular O_2 is calculated as follows:

$$\left(\frac{2\ \cancel{\text{mol O}}}{1\ \text{mol O}_2}\right)\left(\frac{16.00\ \text{g}}{\cancel{\text{mol O}}}\right) = 32.00\ \text{g/mol O}_2$$

$$MM \text{ of O}_2 = 32.00\ \text{g/mol}$$

Verify for yourself that the molar masses of CH_4, NaCl, and $MgCl_2$ are 16.04 g/mol, 58.44 g/mol, and 95.21 g/mol, respectively.

As chemical formulas become more complicated, the calculation of molar mass requires more steps, but the principles remain the same. Sample Problems 3-12 and 3-13 illustrate some of these more elaborate calculations.

SAMPLE PROBLEM 3-12 MOLAR MASSES OF IONIC COMPOUNDS

Sodium carbonate, ammonium nitrate, and ammonium sulfate are ionic substances that rank among the 30 most important industrial chemicals. Determine the molar mass of each compound.

METHOD: To calculate the molar mass of a compound, we must first ascertain its chemical formula. This tells us the number of moles of each element present in 1 mol of the compound. This knowledge is combined with elemental molar masses to compute the molar mass of the compound.

The formula of sodium carbonate is Na_2CO_3. Every mole of the salt contains 2 mol of Na^+ cations and 1 mol of CO_3^{2-} anions. Carbonate is a single structural unit made up of one carbon atom and three oxygen atoms. Here is the molar mass calculation:

$$MM\ \text{Na}_2\text{CO}_3 =$$

$$\left[\frac{2\ \text{mol Na}}{1\ \text{mol Na}_2\text{CO}_3}(22.99\ \text{g/mol Na})\right] + \left[\frac{1\ \text{mol C}}{1\ \text{mol Na}_2\text{CO}_3}(12.01\ \text{g/mol C})\right]$$

$$+\left[\frac{3\ \text{mol O}}{1\ \text{mol Na}_2\text{CO}_3}(16.00\ \text{g/mol O})\right] = 105.99\ \text{g/mol Na}_2\text{CO}_3$$

$$MM\ \text{Na}_2\text{CO}_3 = 105.99\ \text{g/mol}$$

Ammonium nitrate is NH_4NO_3. This salt contains one NH_4^+ cation for every NO_3^- anion. Thus in every mole of NH_4NO_3 there are 2 mol of N, 4 mol of H, and 3 mol of O.

3.5 MASS-MOLE-NUMBER CONVERSIONS

Just as Avogadro's number serves as a conversion factor between moles of an element and the number of atoms, it also allows conversions between moles of a compound and the number of molecules. This is because 1 mol of any substance contains Avogadro's number of its constituent particles. Similarly, the molar mass links the mass of a sample with the number of moles that the sample contains.

The flowchart in Figure 3-15 shows the connections among mass, moles, and number of atoms or molecules. Notice that moles are at the center of the scheme. As we have already mentioned, *calculations of chemical amounts center on the mole.* Sample Problems 3-14 and 3-15 illustrate mass-mole-number interconversions.

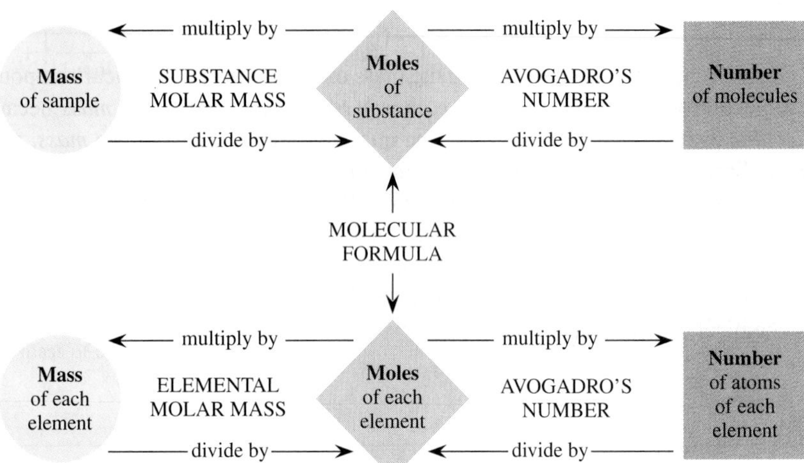

FIGURE 3-15
This flowchart illustrates the mass-mole-number relationships for a compound.

SAMPLE PROBLEM 3-14 ELEMENTAL CONTENT

Ammonium nitrate (NH_4NO_3) is used as fertilizer because it is a good source of nitrogen atoms. It is such a good source, in fact, that 15.3 billion pounds of it were produced in the United States in 1992, which made it the fifteenth ranked industrial chemical in that year. How many moles of nitrogen atoms are present in a 1.00-pound bag of NH_4NO_3 fertilizer? How many atoms is this? (1 pound = 454 g.)

METHOD: First, think about the chemistry of the problem, and then construct a mathematical solution. Use the seven-step procedure.

1. The problem asks for the number of moles and atoms of nitrogen in a 1.00-pound sample of NH_4NO_3.
2. Start by visualizing NH_4NO_3. (Always think atoms and molecules.) Ammonium and nitrate are common polyatomic ions whose chemical formulas you must remember.
3. The equations linking mass, moles, and atoms are: mol = m/mm and atoms = $(\text{mol})(N_A)$.
4. The equations indicate that we need masses and molar masses: mass of sample = 1.00 pound = 454 g NH_4NO_3 and molar mass of NH_4NO_3 = 80.05 g/mol (calculated in Sample Problem 3-12).
5. Often, it helps to draw a flowchart that organizes the steps necessary to analyze and solve a problem. The following is a flowchart for this particular problem:

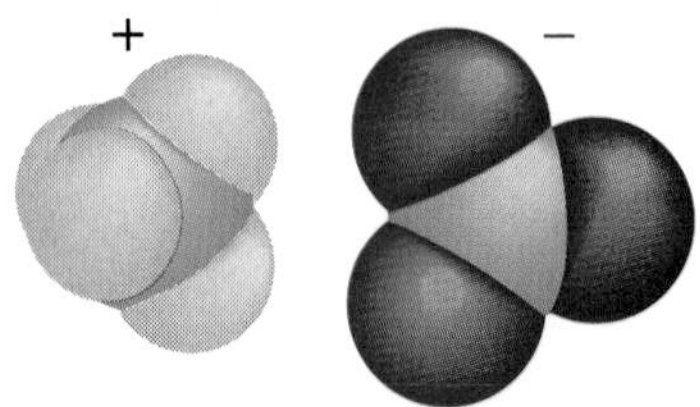

Ammonium nitrate is good fertilizer because both ions provide nitrogen atoms.

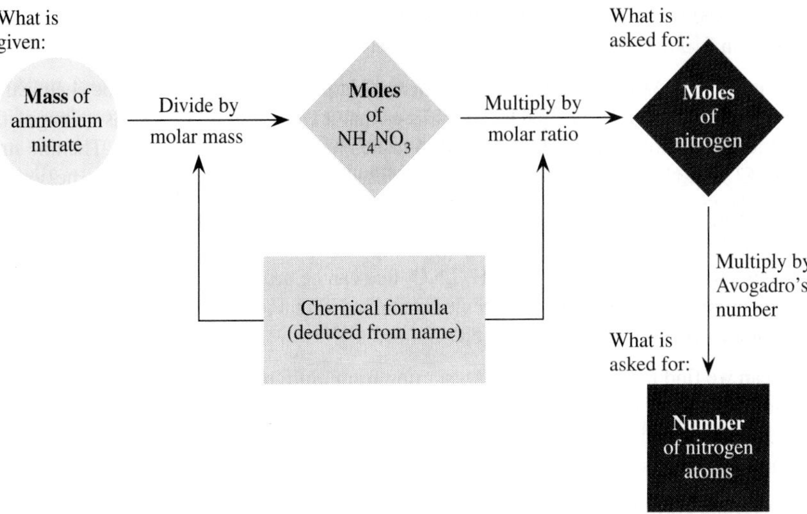

6. Now we are ready to work through the mathematics of the solution. Begin by dividing the sample mass by the molar mass to determine moles of NH_4NO_3:

$$\frac{454 \text{ g } NH_4NO_3}{80.05 \text{ g/mol}} = 5.671 \text{ mol } NH_4NO_3$$

The chemical formula reveals that every mole of NH_4NO_3 contains 2 mol of nitrogen atoms:

$$(5.671 \text{ mol } NH_4NO_3)\left(\frac{2 \text{ mol N atoms}}{1 \text{ mol } NH_4NO_3}\right) = 11.34 \text{ mol N atoms}$$

Finish the problem by using Avogadro's number to convert from the number of moles to the number of atoms:

$$(11.34 \text{ mol N})(6.022 \times 10^{23} \text{ atoms/mol}) = 6.83 \times 10^{24} \text{ N atoms}$$

SAMPLE PROBLEM 3-15 MASS-MOLE-NUMBER CONVERSIONS

The thyroid gland produces hormones that help regulate body temperature, metabolic rate, reproduction, growth, the synthesis of blood cells, and more. Iodine must be present in the diet for these thyroid hormones to be produced. Iodine deficiency leads to sluggishness and weight gain and can cause severe problems in the development of fetuses.

One thyroid hormone is thyroxine, whose chemical formula is $C_{15}H_{11}I_4NO_4$. A typical 180-pound adult consumes 210 mg of iodine/day. How many milligrams of $C_{15}H_{11}I_4NO_4$ can be produced from 210 mg of iodine atoms? How many molecules of $C_{15}H_{11}I_4NO_4$ is this?

HO–(structure)–O–(structure) with I, I, I, I, H_2N, O, OH

Thyroxine
$C_{15}H_{11}I_4NO_4$

METHOD: At first glance this problem might seem more challenging than Sample Problem 3-14. The formula of thyroxine, $C_{15}H_{11}I_4NO_4$, is much more complicated than NH_4NO_3 and the line structure seems to add complexity to the problem. Also, it asks about one substance (thyroxine), but the data concern another (iodine). However, by using the standard approach, you will find that these two problems are similar.

BOX 3-2

USING CHEMISTRY TO FEED THE WORLD

Ammonium nitrate and other fertilizers are immensely important to humanity. Primitive people raised crops on a plot of land until the nutrients in the soil were exhausted. Then they would move on to new ground, where they would burn all of the natural vegetation and begin farming again. This slash-and-burn method of growing food is still used extensively in South America, where farmers are destroying vast tracts of rain forest.

Fertilization using animal products has been practiced since ancient times. Animal manure returns nutrients to the soil, replenishing elements that were depleted as crops were grown and harvested. It is likely that the use of such fertilization followed quickly on the heels of the domestication of animals such as goats, sheep, and cattle. According to legend, the first European settlers in the United States were taught by the Native Americans to use fish as a fertilizer for corn.

Crop yields can rise dramatically with the use of commercial fertilizers. For example, in 1800 an acre of land in the United States produced about 25 bushels of corn. In the 1980s the same acre of land produced 110 bushels. Worldwide, approximately 4 billion acres of land are used to grow food crops. This would probably be enough land to feed the world's population if the entire acreage could be commercially fertilized. It has been estimated that world crop production would increase by about 50% if about \$40 per acre were spent to apply modern chemical fertilizers. However, it would cost about \$160 trillion dollars to produce this additional food. Furthermore, the use of chemical fertilizers can lead to the contamination of rivers and bays with phosphates and nitrates.

Agriculture requires fertilizers because as plants grow, they remove various chemical elements from the soil. In a fully contained ecosystem, decaying organic matter replenishes these elements, but the material in crops that are harvested and shipped elsewhere is not recycled. Thus intensive agriculture inevitably depletes the soil of essential elements, which must be replaced by fertilization.

Many elements are required by growing plants. Those required in the greatest amounts are nitrogen, phosphorus, and potassium, but plants also need trace amounts of calcium, copper, iron, zinc, and other elements. By far the most substantial need is for nitrogen. The Earth's atmosphere is 80% molecular nitrogen, but N_2 cannot be used by most plants. Instead, most plants absorb nitrogen from the soil in the form of nitrate ions.

The production of nitrogen fertilizers is one of the primary activities of the chemical industry. Every year, the top 15 chemicals in industrial production in the United States include five nitrogen-containing compounds whose major use is in fertilizers. Molecular nitrogen, which serves as the primary source of nitrogen for chemical production, ranks second perennially. Ammonia, which is synthesized from N_2 and H_2, ranked fifth in 1992. Ammonia is injected directly into the ground, where it dissolves in moisture in the soil. In slightly acidic soil, ammonia is converted to ammonium ions and eventually into nitrate ions. Ammonia is also an intermediate for the production of other fertilizers. Nitric acid, which reacts with ammonia to produce ammonium nitrate, was in thirteenth place. Urea and ammonium nitrate, both of which are primarily used as fertilizers, ranked twelfth and fifteenth.

The production of fertilizers from molecular nitrogen is very energy intensive. In the United States alone, hundreds of millions of barrels of oil are used every year to produce fertilizers. As world supplies of petroleum are depleted, and as the Earth's population steadily increases, society will be forced to develop more efficient ways to make fertilizer. Genetic engineering offers a promising solution. There is a remarkable bacterium that lives in the roots of leguminous plants such as soybeans, peas, and peanuts. This organism can convert molecular nitrogen into ammonia. The plant and the bacterium have a symbiotic relationship. Ammonia produced by the bacterium nourishes the plant, and the plant provides other nutrients to the bacterium. Exactly how the bacterium converts nitrogen to ammonia is the subject of vigorous research. Scientists hope eventually to transfer the bacterial gene responsible for the conversion of nitrogen to ammonia into the cells of nonleguminous plants.

Each mole of NH_4NO_3 has a total mass of 80.05 g. Of this total, 28.02 g is nitrogen. The ratio of these is the mass fraction of nitrogen, and the percent nitrogen by mass is the mass fraction multiplied by 100:

$$\frac{28.02 \text{ g}}{80.05 \text{ g}} = 0.3500 \text{ (mass fraction of nitrogen in } NH_4NO_3\text{)}$$

$$(0.3500)(100\%) = 35.00\% \text{ (mass percent of nitrogen in } NH_4NO_3\text{)}$$

The symbol % means "percent," from Latin meaning "out of 100."

In other words, 35.00% of the mass of NH_4NO_3 comes from the element nitrogen. This means that every 100 g of NH_4NO_3 contains 35.00 g of nitrogen. The mass percents of hydrogen and oxygen can be found in the same fashion:

$$\left(\frac{4.032 \text{ g}}{80.05 \text{ g}}\right)(100\%) = 5.037\% \text{ H} \qquad \left(\frac{48.00 \text{ g}}{80.05 \text{ g}}\right)(100\%) = 59.96\% \text{ O}$$

If the calculations have been done properly, the sum of the percent compositions of the individual elements will be 100%.

$$\begin{array}{r} 35.00\% \text{ N} \\ 5.037\% \text{ H} \\ 59.96\% \text{ O} \\ \hline 99.997\%, \text{ rounds to } 100.00\% \end{array}$$

This example shows how to compute mass percentages from a chemical formula. When the formula of a compound is unknown, chemists must work in the opposite direction. First, they do experiments to find the mass percentage of each element, and then they deduce what chemical formula matches those percentages.

Elemental analysis of a compound is usually performed by a laboratory that specializes in this technique. A chemist who has prepared a new compound sends a sample to the laboratory for analysis. The laboratory charges a fee that depends on the type and number of elements analyzed. The results are mailed back to the chemist as a listing of mass percent composition. The chemist must then figure out which chemical formula matches this composition.

Sometimes, the chemist may have an expected chemical formula. A specific compound may be the target of a synthesis, or other information may suggest what the compound might be. If the chemist has an expected formula, the observed percentages can be matched against the calculated percentages for the expected formula. This process is illustrated in Sample Problem 3-16.

SAMPLE PROBLEM 3-16 FORMULA FROM ELEMENTAL ANALYSIS

A sample thought to be caffeine, the stimulant found in coffee, tea, and cola beverages, was sent out for elemental analysis. The results of testing were:

$$\left.\begin{array}{r} 49.5\% \text{ C} \\ 5.2\% \text{ H} \\ 28.8\% \text{ N} \\ 16.5\% \text{ O} \end{array}\right\} \text{Elemental analysis of sample}$$

$$\begin{array}{r} \hline 100.0\% \end{array}$$

Does this elemental analysis agree with the chemical formula of caffeine, which is $C_8H_{10}N_4O_2$?

METHOD: To compare an elemental analysis with a chemical formula, we must convert mass percentages to mole amounts or convert the formula to mass percentages. It is easier to compute mass percentages and compare them with the measured values. Begin by calculating the mass of one mole of caffeine:

$$(8 \text{ mol C})(12.01 \text{ g/mol}) = 96.08 \text{ g C}$$

$$(10 \text{ mol H})(1.008 \text{ g/mol}) = 10.08 \text{ g H}$$

$$(4 \text{ mol N})(14.01 \text{ g/mol}) = 56.04 \text{ g N}$$

$$(2 \text{ mol O})(16.00 \text{ g/mol}) = \underline{32.00 \text{ g O}}$$

$$\text{TOTAL} = 194.20 \text{ g}$$

Divide the mass of each element by 194.20 g to obtain its mass fraction. Next multiply by 100% to convert mass fractions to mass percentages:

Element	Expected for $C_8H_{10}N_4O_2$	Found
C	49.47	49.5
H	5.19	5.2
N	28.86	28.8
O	16.48	16.5

Within the accuracy of the measured elemental analysis, the experimental percentages are the same as those expected for $C_8H_{10}N_4O_2$. Thus the data are consistent with $C_8H_{10}N_4O_2$.

Caffeine

Molecular formula: $C_8H_{10}N_4O_2$
Molar mass: 194.2 g/mol

Elemental analysis is a powerful tool for confirming molecular formulas, but it has its limitations. Consider caffeine again. Its chemical formula is $C_8H_{10}N_4O_2$, which means that the four elements are present in molar ratios 8:10:4:2. Dividing this set of numbers by 2 does not change the relative molar amounts, so a compound whose formula is $C_4H_5N_2O$ has exactly the same elemental analysis as caffeine. A compound whose formula is $C_{12}H_{15}N_6O_3$ has the same elemental analysis, too. Elemental analysis cannot distinguish among these three possibilities. For that, we need to know the molar mass of the substance. Mass spectrometry, described in Chapter 2, is one way of measuring molar mass. If the mass spectrum of the substance shows that the molar mass is 194.2 g/mol, the formula is $C_8H_{10}N_4O_2$. On the other hand, a molar mass of 291.3 g/mol would correspond to $C_{12}H_{15}N_6O_3$. Other techniques for determining molar mass are described in later chapters.

If the molar mass of the compound is not known, the best we can do is to find the *simplest* formula that agrees with the elemental analysis. This simplest formula is called the **empirical formula.** It is the formula with the smallest set of whole numbers that match the elemental analysis. The empirical formula of caffeine is $C_4H_5N_2O$.

Sometimes chemists have to analyze substances about which they know very little. Petroleum, for example, is a complex mixture of compounds that contain carbon and hydrogen. One particular compound that has been isolated from a sample of petroleum might have any number of formulas. As another example, a chemist may isolate an interesting molecule from a natural source, such as a plant or an insect. Under these conditions the chemical formula must be deduced from only mass percentage data, without the help of an "expected" formula. The procedure for doing this depends on mass-mole conversions using molar masses of the elements. The following is a set of guidelines for solving elemental analysis problems:

1. Because mass percentage gives the number of grams of each element in 100 g of compound, it is convenient to base the formula determination on a 100-g sample. Divide each mass percentage by the molar mass of the element to obtain the number of moles of the element in a 100-g sample.
2. Chemical formulas must contain whole numbers of each element, so it is necessary to convert the data from Step 1 into simple integers. Divide each molar amount by whichever amount is the smallest. This maintains the mole ratios from Step 1 but references them to one mole of the least abundant element.
3. If some results from Step 2 are far from integers, multiply through by a common factor that converts all molar amounts to integers or near-integers.
4. Round off each molar number to the nearest integer.

Sample Problem 3-17 shows how to apply these guidelines.

SAMPLE PROBLEM 3-17 CHEMICAL FORMULA FROM COMPOSITION

Analysis of ibuprofen, the active ingredient in Advil, shows that it contains 75.7% carbon, 8.8% hydrogen, and 15.5% oxygen. The mass spectrum of ibuprofen shows that it has a molar mass of about 200 g/mol. Determine the chemical formula of this compound.

METHOD: First, apply the procedure to convert the mass percentages into the empirical formula. Then compare the empirical formula with the molar mass information to find the true formula. Follow the four-step process for finding the empirical formula.

1. 100 g of this compound contain

$$(75.7 \text{ g C})\left(\frac{1 \text{ mol C}}{12.01 \text{ g}}\right) = 6.30 \text{ mol C in the 100-g sample}$$

$$(8.8 \text{ g H})\left(\frac{1 \text{ mol H}}{1.008 \text{ g}}\right) = 8.7 \text{ mol H in the 100-g sample}$$

$$(15.5 \text{ g O})\left(\frac{1 \text{ mol O}}{16.00 \text{ g}}\right) = 0.969 \text{ mol O in the 100-g sample}$$

2. Dividing each molar number by the smallest gives

$$6.30 \text{ mol C}/0.969 \text{ mol O} = 6.50 \text{ mol C/mol O}$$

$$8.7 \text{ mol H}/0.969 \text{ mol O} = 9.0 \text{ mol H/mol O}$$

$$0.969 \text{ mol O}/0.969 \text{ mol O} = 1.00 \text{ mol O/mol O}$$

3. The value for carbon is not an integer, but if we multiply all values by 2, we obtain integers: 13.0 mol C, 18.0 mol H, and 2.00 mol O.

4. The empirical formula of ibuprofen is $C_{13}H_{18}O_2$.

The mass spectrum of the compound indicates that its molar mass is around 200 g/mol. The molar mass calculated from the emprical formula is 206.27 g/mol. This tells us that the chemical formula of ibuprofen is the same as its empirical formula.

Moving from molar numbers to a chemical formula may require qualitative decisions. A petroleum component that contains 84.3% carbon and 15.7% hydrogen, for example, contains 2.22 mol of hydrogen for every 1.00 mol of carbon. We might round off to give CH_2 as the empirical formula, or we might multiply each value by

5 to give 5.00 mol of C and 11.10 mol of H, which rounds off to C_5H_{11}. A third possibility would be to multiply by 9, giving 9.00 mol of C and 19.98 mol of H, which rounds off to C_9H_{20}. A chemist would look for other information before making this decision. In particular, the accuracy of the analysis provides important information. If the measurements have an uncertainty of 1%, 2.22 should not be rounded to 2, as 2.22 is more than 1% larger than 2. At 1% accuracy, C_5H_{11} is a reasonable choice, because 11.10 differs from 11 by only 1%. If the measurements are accurate to 0.2%, C_9H_{20} is probably the correct empirical formula.

The three possible formulas just mentioned look very different, but keep in mind that elemental analysis gives only empirical formulas, not actual formulas. When elemental analysis gives the formula CH_2, that means that the chemical formula contains carbon and hydrogen in 1:2 mol ratio. The compound may be C_2H_4, C_3H_6, C_4H_8, and so on. Knowing this, we see that the three results of rounding in the last paragraph are not so different: CH_2 could be $C_{10}H_{20}$, and C_5H_{11} could be $C_{10}H_{22}$, both of which are rather close to C_9H_{20}.

We have shown how to convert mass percentages to formulas, but we have not yet shown how mass percentages are determined. Somehow we must analyze a compound of unknown formula for the masses of each element. This involves converting the unknown compound into known compounds and measuring the masses of the product compounds.

ANALYSIS BY DECOMPOSITION

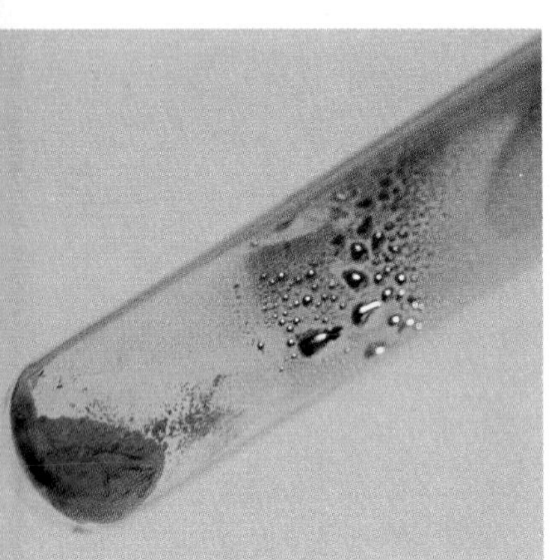

FIGURE 3-16
When mercury (II) oxide is heated, it decomposes into liquid mercury, driving off oxygen gas in the process.

Elemental analysis is relatively straightforward for a compound that can be decomposed into pure elements. Figure 3-16, for example, shows that an orange-red solid compound of mercury decomposes on heating to yield elemental mercury, which is a silver-colored liquid. A colorless gas is also produced. To exploit this decomposition reaction for elemental analysis, we must carefully measure the masses. Suppose we start with 5.00 g of the compound and collect the gas that is driven off on heating. Weighing the gas gives its mass as 0.37 g, and mass spectroscopy identifies the gas as oxygen. The liquid mercury has a mass of 4.63 g. The sum of the masses of oxygen and mercury totals the original mass of the compound: 4.63 g + 0.37 g = 5.00 g. Because mass is always conserved and the entire 5.00 g has been accounted for, this tells us that the compound contains only mercury and oxygen.

Because each chemical element is conserved, the masses of the products are equal to the masses of the elements contained in the original compound. This lets us complete the elemental analysis of the original compound. The 5.00-g sample contained 4.63 g mercury (Hg) and 0.37 g O. The percent composition is found by dividing each elemental mass by total mass and multiplying by 100:

$$\left(\frac{4.63 \text{ g Hg}}{5.00 \text{ g}}\right)(100\%) = 92.6\% \text{ Hg} \qquad \left(\frac{0.37 \text{ g O}}{5.00 \text{ g}}\right)(100\%) = 7.4\% \text{ O}$$

To get from elemental analysis to a chemical formula, we begin by dividing each mass percentage by the appropriate molar mass:

$$\frac{92.6 \text{ g Hg}}{200.6 \text{ g/mol}} = 0.462 \text{ mol Hg} \qquad \frac{7.4 \text{ g O}}{16.0 \text{ g/mol}} = 0.46 \text{ mol O}$$

Both amounts are the same to within the accuracy of the measurements, so we conclude that the compound contains mercury and oxygen in 1:1 molar ratio. The empirical formula is HgO.

Mercury(II) oxide is one of the very few compounds that decomposes cleanly into chemical elements. In fact, very few oxides decompose to give molecular oxygen. To carry out elemental analyses on most compounds, it is necessary to convert them into simple, known chemical *compounds* rather than into pure elements. Then an elemental analysis can be calculated from the masses of product compounds and their known chemical formulas.

COMBUSTION ANALYSIS

Combustion analysis is one of the most widely used methods for determining the empirical formula of an unknown compound. It is particularly useful for carbon-containing compounds. In combustion analysis an accurately known mass of a compound is burned in a stream of oxygen gas. Under carefully controlled conditions, all the products of this burning process are simple oxides with known chemical formulas.

In a combustion reaction, all of the carbon in the sample is converted to carbon dioxide, and all of the hydrogen is converted to water. Certain other elements present in the sample are also converted to their oxides. Figure 3-17 shows a schematic view of an apparatus for combustion analysis. The stream of oxygen used to burn the substance carries the combustion products out of the reaction chamber and through a series of traps. Each trap is designed to collect just one combustion product. The mass of each trap is measured before and after combustion, and the difference is the mass of that particular product that formed during combustion.

The flowchart in Figure 3-18 schematically shows ways to analyze the data from a combustion analysis. The most important feature in this analysis is that atoms of each element involved in the reaction are conserved. Every *carbon* atom in the original sample ends up in a CO_2 molecule, and every *hydrogen* atom in the original sample ends up in a molecule of H_2O. Mass is also conserved in a combustion reaction, so the mass of carbon contained in the carbon dioxide (CO_2) is the same as the mass of carbon in the original sample, and the mass of hydrogen in water (H_2O) is the same as the mass of hydrogen in the original sample. After the masses of CO_2 and H_2O produced in the combustion reaction have been determined, the mass percentages of carbon and hydrogen in these products can be used to calculate the masses of carbon and hydrogen present in the original sample. This leads to an elemental analysis of the unknown compound from which we can deduce the empirical formula.

The products of a combustion reaction contain oxygen, carbon, and hydrogen. Did the oxygen in these products come from the original sample or from the oxygen used in the combustion process? To answer this question, we note that *all the mass of the original sample must be accounted for* because mass is never destroyed in a chemical reaction. The masses of CO_2 and H_2O tell us how much carbon and hydrogen was present in the original sample. Subtracting the combined masses of carbon and hydrogen from the mass of the original sample gives the total mass of any other elements that were present in the original sample. If the unknown compound contained only carbon and hydrogen, this difference in mass will be zero. If the mass difference is not zero, then other elements must have been present in the original

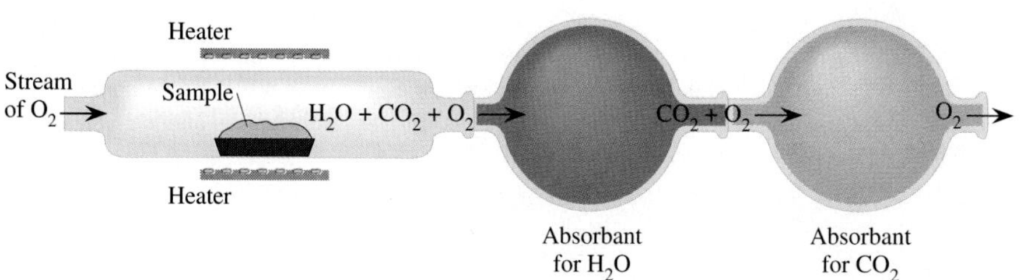

FIGURE 3-17
In combustion analysis a hot stream of oxygen gas reacts with a compound to form CO_2, H_2O, and other products if elements other than carbon and hydrogen are present in the compound. The product gases are trapped, and their masses are determined by the gain in mass of each trap.

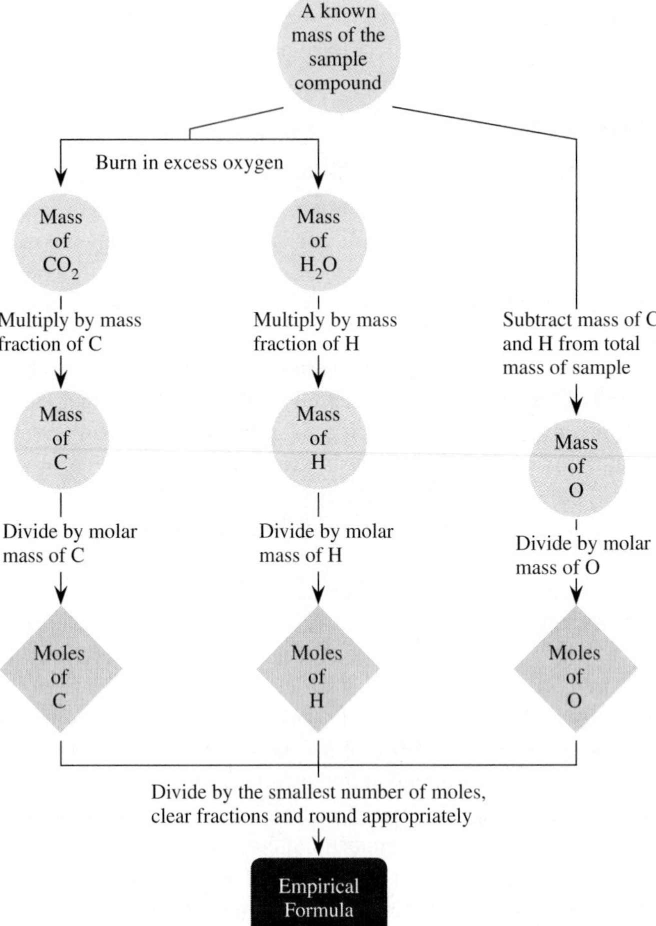

FIGURE 3-18
This flowchart summarizes the method for determining the empirical formula of a compound from combustion analysis data.

sample. If a compound contains only carbon, hydrogen, and oxygen, then the mass difference is the mass of oxygen in the original sample.

Sample Problem 3-18 demonstrates how to use combustion analysis to determine the formula of a compound.

SAMPLE PROBLEM 3-18 COMBUSTION ANALYSIS

A petroleum chemist isolated a major component of gasoline and found its molar mass to be 114.2 g/mol. When 1.55 g of this compound were completely burned in excess oxygen, 2.21 g of H_2O and 4.80 g CO_2 were produced. Find the empirical and molecular formulas of the compound.

METHOD: The flowchart in Figure 3-18 outlines the process. From masses of products we determine masses of elements. Then convert masses of elements to moles of elements. From moles of the elements we find the empirical formula. Finally, information about the molar mass reveals the molecular formula.

Begin by computing masses and moles of carbon and hydrogen for the combustion products:

$$\text{C: } (4.80 \text{ g } CO_2)\left[\frac{12.01 \text{ g/mol C}}{44.01 \text{ g/mol } CO_2}\right] = 1.31 \text{ g C} \qquad \frac{1.31 \text{ g C}}{12.01 \text{ g/mol}} = 0.109 \text{ mol C}$$

$$\text{H: } (2.21 \text{ g } H_2O)\left[\frac{(2)(1.008 \text{ g/mol H})}{18.02 \text{ g/mol } H_2O}\right] = 0.247 \text{ g H} \qquad \frac{0.247 \text{ g H}}{1.008 \text{ g/mol}} = 0.245 \text{ mol H}$$

Next compare the masses of carbon and hydrogen with the mass of the original sample to see whether the sample contained oxygen:

$$1.31 \text{ g C} + 0.247 \text{ g H} = 1.56 \text{ g} \qquad \text{Sample mass} = 1.55 \text{ g}$$

These are virtually the same, so carbon and hydrogen account for all of the mass in the original sample. Thus there is no oxygen or other elements in the unknown compound.

We now have a molar relationship between hydrogen and carbon in the original compound: 0.245 mol H to 0.109 mol C. Divide each by the smaller value:

$$\frac{0.245 \text{ mol H}}{0.109 \text{ mol C}} = 2.25 \frac{\text{mol H}}{\text{mol C}} \qquad \frac{0.109 \text{ mol C}}{0.109 \text{ mol C}} = 1.00 \frac{\text{mol C}}{\text{mol C}}$$

The mole ratio for hydrogen is not close to an integer, so we must multiply each ratio by a common integer that will make the value for hydrogen an integer or near-integer. In this case, 4 is the smallest integer that accomplishes this (2.25) (4) = 9 and (1.00) (4) = 4. This means that the empirical formula is C_4H_9.

Now, what is the chemical formula of the unknown? We must compare the empirical molar mass with the molar mass. The molar mass given is 114.2 g. Compute the empirical mass from the empirical formula and elemental molar masses:

$$\text{Empirical mass} = 4 \text{ (C) } (12.01 \text{ g/mol}) + 9 \text{ (H) } (1.008 \text{ g/mol}) = 48.04 \text{ g/mol} + 9.072 \text{ g/mol} = 57.11 \text{ g/mol}$$

$$\frac{MM}{\text{Empirical mass}} = \frac{114.2 \text{ g/mol}}{57.11 \text{ g/mol}} = 2$$

The molecular formula of this hydrocarbon, known as *octane,* is twice its empirical formula: C_8H_{18}.

Because the final calculations will give integers, it is not necessary to carry an extra significant figure in this problem.

In determining the mass fraction of hydrogen in water, do not forget that there are two hydrogen atoms in each molecule of water.

Several decimals are readily converted to integers by multiplying by a *small whole number*. When you see any of these, think about multiplying rather than rounding: (0.20) (5) = 1, (0.25) (4) = 1, (0.33) (3) = 1, (0.40) (5) = 2, (0.50) (2) = 1, (0.60) (5) = 3, (0.67) (3) = 2, (0.75) (4) = 3, and (0.80) (5) = 4.

Sample Problem 3-18 is relatively straightforward because the unknown compound contained only carbon and hydrogen. Sample Problem 3-19 shows how combustion analysis is conducted when the compound contains oxygen.

SAMPLE PROBLEM 3-19 EMPIRICAL FORMULA

Butyric acid, a component of rancid butter, has a vile stench. Burning 0.440 g of butyric acid in excess oxygen yields 0.882 g of CO_2 and 0.360 g of H_2O as the only products. What is the empirical formula of butyric acid?

METHOD: Proceed exactly as in Sample Problem 3-18. Start by determining how much carbon was present in the sample of butyric acid:

$$(0.882 \text{ g } CO_2)\left[\frac{12.01 \text{ g/mol C}}{44.01 \text{ g/mol } CO_2}\right] = 0.241 \text{ g C}$$

And for hydrogen:

$$(0.360 \text{ g } H_2O)\left[\frac{(2)(1.008 \text{ g/mol H})}{18.02 \text{ g/mol } H_2O}\right] = 0.0403 \text{ g H}$$

$$\frac{20.5 \text{ g sugar}}{342 \text{ g/mol}} = 5.994 \times 10^{-2} \text{ mol sugar}$$

Now convert the volume of the solution from milliliters to liters:

$$(250 \text{ mL})(10^{-3} \text{ L/mL}) = 2.50 \times 10^{-1} \text{ L}$$

Finally, divide moles of sugar by volume in liters to obtain molarity:

$$\frac{5.994 \times 10^{-2} \text{ mol}}{2.50 \times 10^{-1} \text{ L}} = 2.40 \times 10^{-1} \text{ M}$$

Concentrations are used so frequently in chemistry that a shorthand notation for concentration is almost essential. Chemists represent the concentration of a species by enclosing its formula in brackets. For the sugar solution, $[C_{12}H_{22}O_{11}] = 0.240$ M.

IONIC SOLUTIONS

To understand the chemical behavior of solutions, we must "think molecules." Before working any problem involving solutions, begin with the question, "What chemical species are present in the solution?"

Aqueous solutions of molecular substances such as sugar ($C_{12}H_{22}O_{11}$) or ethanol (C_2H_5OH) contain individual molecules dissolved in a "sea" of water molecules. How do we know that these solutes dissolve as molecular units? Recall from Chapter 2 that ions in solution allow a flow of current between a pair of electrically charged plates dipped into the solution. The electrical current results from the motion of charged particles. Because solutions of sugar or ethanol do not conduct electricity, we can conclude that these solutions contain no mobile charged particles. Sugar and ethanol dissolve as neutral molecules.

An aqueous solution of sodium chloride conducts electricity. When NaCl or any other salt dissolves in water, the ions represent mobile charges that promote an electrical current. Any time an *ionic solid* dissolves in water, the salt breaks apart to give a solution of *cations* and *anions.* A solution of sodium chloride is best viewed as a solution containing three species: Na^+, Cl^-, and H_2O.

All salts dissolve according to their stoichiometric ratio of cations and anions. Thus a salt that contains an equal number of cations and anions gives a solution in which the molarities of the cation and the anion are equal. A 1.0 M solution of sodium chloride is 1.0 M each in Na^+ and Cl^-. One formula unit of NaCl breaks up into one Na^+ cation and one Cl^- anion. On the other hand, $ZnCl_2$, one of the ionic metal halides, contains 2 mol of Cl^- anions for every 1 mol of Zn^{2+} cations. This ratio is maintained when zinc chloride dissolves in water; a 1.0 M solution of $ZnCl_2$ is 1.0 M in Zn^{2+} and 2.0 M in Cl^-. Notice that preserving the cation-anion ratio ensures that the solution is electrically neutral overall. The total positive charge carried by 1 mol of Zn^{2+} equals the total negative charge carried by 2 mol of Cl^-:

$$\underset{\substack{\uparrow \\ 1 \text{ mol}}}{ZnCl_{2\,(s)}} \xrightarrow{H_2O} \underset{\substack{\uparrow \\ 1 \text{ mol}}}{Zn^{2+}_{(aq)}} + \underbrace{Cl^-_{(aq)} + Cl^-_{(aq)}}_{\substack{\uparrow \\ 2 \text{ mol}}}$$

In later chapters, we encounter situations in which species in solution transfer protons among themselves. For example, NH_4^+ can lose a proton to neutral H_2O, creating neutral NH_3 and cationic H_3O^+.

When a salt containing polyatomic ions dissolves in water, cations separate from anions, but *each polyatomic ion remains intact*. For example, ammonium nitrate is composed of NH_4^+ polyatomic cations and NO_3^- polyatomic anions. Ammonium

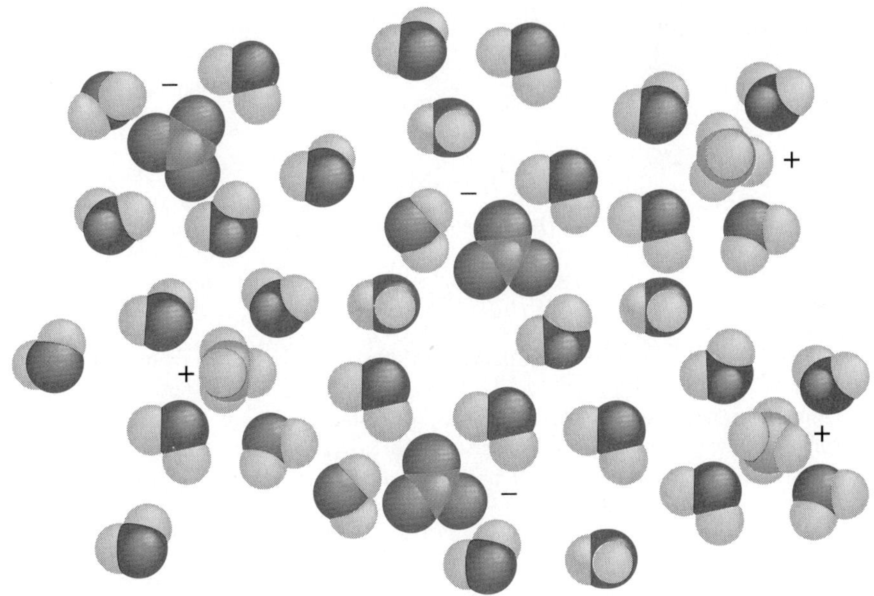

FIGURE 3-20
Molecular view of an aqueous solution of ammonium nitrate. Ammonium cations dissociate from nitrate anions, but neither of these polyatomic species breaks down into smaller pieces. Instead, they retain their identities as polyatomic clusters.

nitrate dissolves in water to give a solution containing NH_4^+ cations and NO_3^- anions. Figure 3-20 shows a molecular picture of an ammonium nitrate solution, and Sample Problems 3-20 and 3-21 concern aqueous solutions that contain polyatomic ions.

SAMPLE PROBLEM 3-20 MOLARITY OF IONS IN SOLUTION

Find the molarities of the ionic species present in 250 mL of an aqueous solution containing 1.75 g of ammonium sulfate, $(NH_4)_2SO_4$.

METHOD: The chemical formula tells us what ions will be present in the final solution and how many moles of each ion are contained in 1 mol of the salt. Use mass, molar mass, and volume to calculate molarity.

Looking at the formula, we recognize the ammonium cation, NH_4^+, and the sulfate anion, SO_4^{2-}. When this salt dissolves in water, it dissociates into its component polyatomic ions. Each mole of salt will produce a total of *3* mol of ions: 2 mol of NH_4^+ and 1 mol of SO_4^{2-}.

After identifying what species are present in solution, we can calculate molarities. Begin with the molar mass of the salt:

$$\begin{aligned}
(2 \text{ mol N})(14.01 \text{ g/mol}) &= 28.02 \text{ g N} \\
(8 \text{ mol H})(1.008 \text{ g/mol}) &= 8.064 \text{ g H} \\
(1 \text{ mol S})(32.06 \text{ g/mol}) &= 32.06 \text{ g S} \\
(4 \text{ mol O})(16.00 \text{ g/mol}) &= 64.00 \text{ g O} \\
\hline
1 \text{ mol } (NH_4)_2SO_4 &= 132.14 \text{ g}
\end{aligned}$$

The molar mass is used to determine the number of moles of salt and, in turn, the number of moles of each ion. Notice that even though we are aiming for molarities of ionic species, we determine moles of the salt. We have the mass *of the salt,* which we must divide by the molar mass *of the salt:*

$$\text{Mol} = \frac{m}{MM} \qquad \frac{1.75 \text{ g}}{132.14 \text{ g/mol}} = 1.324 \times 10^{-2} \text{ mol } (NH_4)_2SO_4$$

Remember to carry an extra significant figure until the final calculation.

From the moles of salt we can calculate the moles of each ion:

$$(0.01324 \text{ mol } (NH_4)_2SO_4)\left[\frac{2 \text{ mol } NH_4^+}{1 \text{ mol } (NH_4)_2SO_4}\right] = 0.02649 \text{ mol } NH_4^+$$

$$(0.01324 \text{ mol } (NH_4)_2SO_4)\left[\frac{1 \text{ mol } SO_4^{2-}}{1 \text{ mol } (NH_4)_2SO_4}\right] = 0.01324 \text{ mol } SO_4^{2-}$$

Now we can find the molarities of the individual ions:

$$(250 \text{ mL})\left[\frac{10^{-3} \text{ L}}{\text{mL}}\right] = 0.250 \text{ L}$$

$$[NH_4^+] = \frac{0.02649 \text{ mol}}{0.250 \text{ L}} = 0.106 \text{ M} \qquad [SO_4^{2-}] = \frac{0.01324 \text{ mol}}{0.250 \text{ L}} = 0.0530 \text{ M}$$

This solution is described as 0.0530 M in $(NH_4)_2SO_4$, stating moles of salt divided by liters of solution. However, it is critical to understand that in saying this, we are describing a solution that actually contains *a mixture of ions, each with its own molarity.*

General chemistry students often make mistakes in unit conversions. This Sample Problem requires a conversion from milliliters to liters. In haste, a student might multiply by "10^3" meaning 10^3 mL/L. This is a correct conversion factor, but it would be applied in the wrong order. Here we need to multiply by 10^{-3} L/mL. Careful attention to unit cancellation will eliminate this pitfall.

SAMPLE PROBLEM 3-21 PREPARING A SOLUTION

How many grams of the blue crystalline solid, copper(II) sulfate pentahydrate, are required to prepare 750 mL of aqueous solution whose concentration is 0.255 M?

METHOD: As with all calculations of chemical amounts, we must work with moles. We begin with the chemical formula of copper(II) sulfate pentahydrate. The presence of a polyatomic ion indicates that the compound is ionic. The formula also tells us that the salt contains five water molecules for each unit of copper sulfate. Thus each formula unit of the salt contains one Cu^{2+} cation, one SO_4^{2-} anion, and five water molecules: $CuSO_4 \cdot 5H_2O$.

To determine the mass of $CuSO_4 \cdot 5H_2O$ required to prepare the solution, first calculate the number of moles of the salt required, and then use the molar mass to determine the number of grams:

$$\left(\frac{0.255 \text{ mol}}{\cancel{\text{L}}}\right)(750 \cancel{\text{mL}})\left(\frac{10^{-3} \cancel{\text{L}}}{\cancel{\text{mL}}}\right) = 0.1913 \text{ mol } CuSO_4 \cdot 5H_2O$$

We need the molar mass of $CuSO_4 \cdot 5H_2O$ to convert moles to mass. By now, molar mass calculations should be routine. The molar mass of copper sulfate pentahydrate is 249.68 g/mol.

$$(0.1913 \text{ mol } CuSO_4 \cdot 5H_2O)\left(\frac{249.68 \text{ g}}{\text{mol } CuSO_4 \cdot 5H_2O}\right) = 47.8 \text{ g}$$

To prepare the desired solution of copper(II) sulfate, we would add enough water to 47.8 g of the pentahydrate to bring the total volume to 750 mL.

In the laboratory, solutions of known concentration are often prepared in a piece of glassware called a *volumetric flask.* A picture of one is shown in Figure 3-21. Notice the thin upper neck on which a line has been etched. When the container is filled with liquid to the etched line, the volume of solution in the container is the exact amount specified for that volumetric flask.

Aqueous solution chemistry dominates the chemistry of the Earth and the biosphere. The oceans, for instance, are a rich broth of various cations and anions, sodium and chloride being the most abundant. Another example is blood, an aqueous

FIGURE 3-21
Solutions of known concentration are prepared by using a volumetric flask.

system that contains many ionic species, most notably carbonate, sodium, and potassium. Because aqueous solutions play a central role in the world around us, the chemistry of aqueous solutions is discussed in depth in several chapters of this book. To understand the chemistry of aqueous solutions, *it is essential that you learn to recognize the common ions at a glance.* This is especially true of the polyatomic ions. Chemistry takes place among *molecules* and *ions,* so you must learn to think in *molecular-ionic* terms.

DILUTIONS

A solution of high molarity is diluted by adding more solvent. In a **dilution** the *quantities of solutes* remain the same, but the *volume of solution* increases. When the volume of a solution is increased without increasing the amounts of solutes, the result is a solution of lower molarity.

A chemist's workbench often includes a collection of aqueous solutions that are used frequently in the laboratory. One example is a solution of hydrochloric acid, HCl. Pure HCl is a corrosive gas that is difficult to store and transport. As a solution, it is still corrosive and must be handled with care, but it is easier to use. Thus HCl is usually sold as an aqueous solution whose concentration is 12.0 M (Figure 3-22). This solution is commonly referred to as *concentrated HCl.*

Laboratory applications usually require solutions that are less than 12.0 M. For example, a chemist may need to use 1.50 M HCl for a number of different applications. Rather than prepare small amounts of dilute acid for each use, it is more efficient to prepare a large volume of the solution to store in a reagent bottle.

To prepare 1.00 L of 1.50 M HCl, the correct volume of concentrated acid must be measured out and then diluted to 1.00 L. The key is to measure the proper number of moles of HCl because the addition of extra water does not change the number of moles of solute. In 1.00 L of 1.50 M HCl, there are

$$(1.00\text{ L})\left(\frac{1.50\text{ mol HCl}}{1.00\text{ L solution}}\right) = 1.50\text{ mol HCl}$$

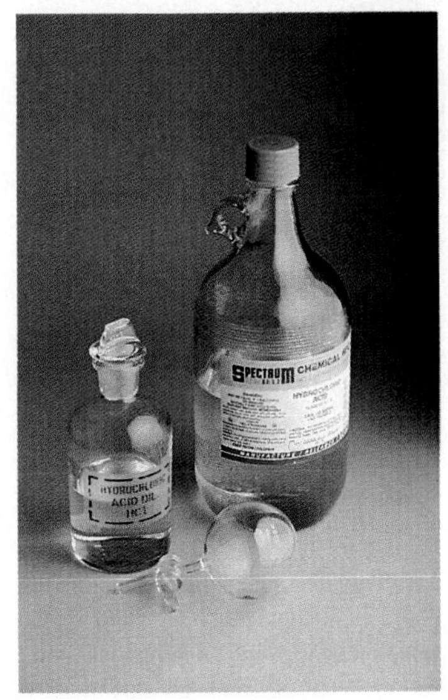

FIGURE 3-22
Approximately 6 billion pounds of hydrochloric acid, used in the manufacture of chemicals and metals, are produced annually.

What volume of concentrated HCl contains 1.50 mol of HCl? One liter of concentrated acid contains 12.0 mol of HCl, so we need the appropriate fraction of a liter:

Water should *never* be added directly to concentrated acid; this causes a vigorous reaction that may lead to a dangerous acid splash. Instead, concentrated acid is *always* added to water. Additional water can then be added safely to the less concentrated solution that results.

$$(1.50 \text{ mol HCl})\,(1.00 \text{ L concentrated solution}/12.0 \text{ mol HCl}) = 0.125 \text{ L concentrated acid}$$

To prepare the solution, 125 mL of concentrated HCl must be measured out by using an appropriate volumetric device. One such device is a graduated cylinder, which is shown in Figure 3-23. After adding about 500 mL of distilled water to a 1.00-L volumetric flask, the concentrated acid is added from the graduated cylinder. The volumetric flask is then filled to the mark by adding distilled water. After thorough mixing, the solution is transferred to a stoppered, properly labeled reagent bottle.

The most important feature of a dilution is the fact that *the number of moles of solute does not change during the dilution.* If we add a concentrated solution containing 1.5 mol of potassium chloride (KCl) to a volumetric flask and then dilute to the mark by adding more water, the number of moles of KCl does *not* change. There are still 1.5 mol of KCl in the dilute solution, as shown in Figure 3-24. Both beakers contain the same *number* of K^+ and Cl^- ions, but the *concentrations* of the two solutions are different.

The quantitative aspects of dilutions can be summarized by remembering that moles of solute do not change during dilution. Thus

$$\text{Moles}_{\text{solute,initial}} = \text{Moles}_{\text{solute,final}}$$

Because Moles = (Molarity)(Volume), this leads to a simple equation:

$$M_i V_i = M_f V_f \qquad \textbf{(3-3)}$$

Equation 3-3 is very convenient for dilution calculations because if we know any three of the quantities, we can calculate the fourth. Sample Problem 3-22 shows how to do this.

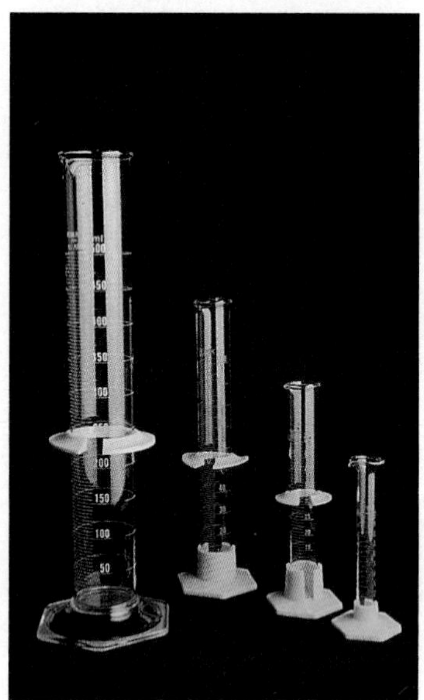

FIGURE 3-23
Graduated cylinders are cylindrical containers whose sides are marked with various volume measurements.

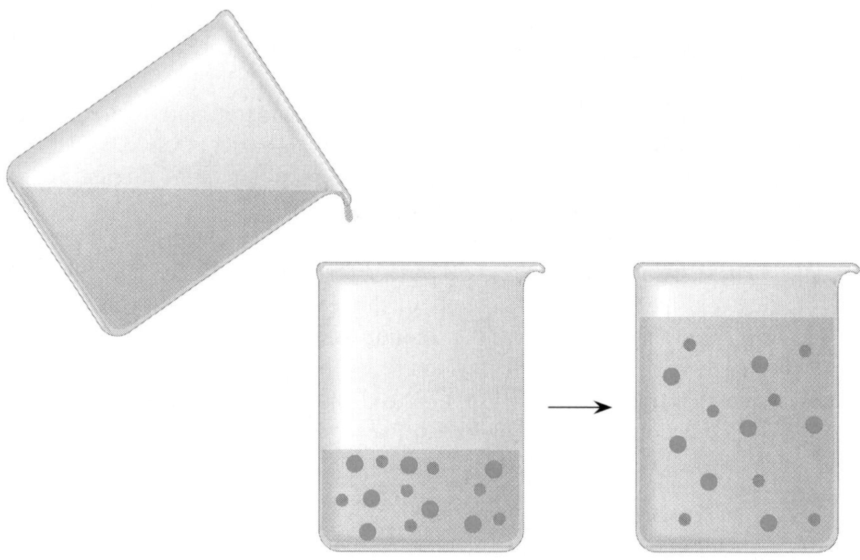

FIGURE 3-24
When a concentrated solution of KCl (left) is diluted by adding more solvent, the resulting solution (right) contains the same number of K^+ and Cl^- ions. The solution is more dilute, however, because the ions are spread around in a larger volume of solvent. Individual water molecules have been omitted for clarity.

BOX 3-3

ISOTONIC SOLUTIONS

When a person suffers from severe dehydration or is unable to take food or drink by mouth, it is often necessary to supply fluids by slow injection into the bloodstream. Such intravenous infusions have become a near-routine procedure in hospitals all over the world.

To avoid disrupting the body's cells, it is essential that the solutions used for infusions be prepared with the right concentration of solutes. For now, you need to know only that the ability of water molecules to pass freely through cell membranes depends on solution concentration. In Chapter 10, we explain in molecular terms why this is so. The total molarities of solutes in blood plasma is normally very close to 0.31 M. When infusions are administered therefore, they should be aqueous solutions whose total concentration of solutes is 0.31 M. Such a solution is called *isotonic.*

The two most common solutions that are used for infusions are sugar and saline. Sugar solutions are administered when the body requires an energy source (sugar is one of the body's main fuel sources), and saline (NaCl) solutions are given when the body is dehydrated. Sugar solutions must be 0.31 M because sugar dissolves in water as molecular units. Saline solutions, on the other hand, must be 0.155 M NaCl, because sodium chloride dissolves as individual ions, yielding one Na^+ cation and one Cl^- anion for every molecular unit of NaCl. The total solute concentration in a solution of NaCl is twice the molarity of NaCl.

SAMPLE PROBLEM 3-22 PREPARING SOLUTIONS BY DILUTION

When aqueous solutions are used for intravenous infusions, it is essential that the molarity of the solution match the molarity of blood (see Box 3-3). Blood is approximately 0.31 M, so a solution of sodium chloride for infusion, called *saline,* must have a concentration of 0.155 M. Calculate the mass of NaCl that should be used to prepare 5.00 L of a 1.00 M stock solution, and then calculate how many milliliters of the resulting stock solution must be diluted to give 455 mL of 0.155 M solution for infusion.

METHOD: Two solutions must be prepared in this problem. The first is a stock reagent solution that is rather concentrated, and the second is prepared by dilution of the first. We break the calculations into two parts, but both parts must be done with moles in mind.

Part I: Calculate the required mass of solute.

The preparation of 5.00 L of 1.00 M NaCl requires

$$(5.00 \text{ L})\left(\frac{1.00 \text{ mol}}{\text{L}}\right) = 5.00 \text{ mol NaCl}$$

We get from moles to mass in the usual way:

$$(5.00 \text{ mol NaCl})\left(\frac{58.44 \text{ g}}{\text{mol}}\right) = 292 \text{ g NaCl}$$

The 292 g of NaCl would be measured on a balance, placed in a volumetric flask, and dissolved in enough distilled water to give exactly 5.00 L of solution.

Part II: Calculate the volume required for the dilution.

First, we need to find out how many moles of NaCl will be present in the final solution:

$$\text{Moles} = (\text{Volume})(\text{Molarity}) = (0.455\ \text{L})(0.155\ \text{M}) = 7.05 \times 10^{-2}\ \text{mol}$$

Now we must determine what volume of the stock solution provides this number of moles of NaCl. The molarity of the stock solution provides the key:

$$\text{Moles} = (\text{Volume})(\text{Molarity}) \qquad \textit{so} \qquad \text{Volume} = \frac{\text{Moles}}{\text{Molarity}}$$

$$\text{Volume} = \frac{7.05 \times 10^{-2}\ \text{mol}}{1.00\ \text{mol/L}} = 7.05 \times 10^{-2}\ \text{L}$$

After you become proficient at the reasoning involved in these calculations, you can set them up in a more compact form:

$$M_{\text{saline}}V_{\text{saline}} = M_{\text{stock}}V_{\text{stock}}$$

$$V_{\text{stock}} = \frac{M_{\text{saline}}V_{\text{saline}}}{M_{\text{stock}}} = \frac{(0.155\ \text{M})(0.455\ \text{L})}{1.0\ \text{M}} = 70.5 \times 10^{-2}\ \text{L} = 70.5\ \text{mL}$$

To prepare the dilute solution, 70.5 mL of the stock solution is placed in a 500-mL graduated cylinder, and then distilled water is added until the total volume is 455 mL. The procedure described in this problem is typical of actual solution preparations in the laboratory.

PRECIPITATION ANALYSIS

Silver nitrate dissolves readily in water to give a solution that contains Ag^+ cations and NO_3^- anions. Sodium chloride also dissolves readily in water to give a solution that contains Na^+ cations and Cl^- anions. In both cases the dissolved cations and anions move freely through their respective solutions. If these two solutions are mixed together, an incompatible combination arises because silver chloride is not very soluble in water. Silver cations and chloride anions combine to give solid silver chloride, which separates from the solution as a white solid in a process called **precipitation.** Figure 3-25 illustrates the precipitation of AgCl at the molecular level, and Figure 3-26 shows what it looks like in the laboratory.

Precipitation makes it possible to do elemental analysis on elements, such as chlorine, that cannot easily be determined by combustion. If a compound that

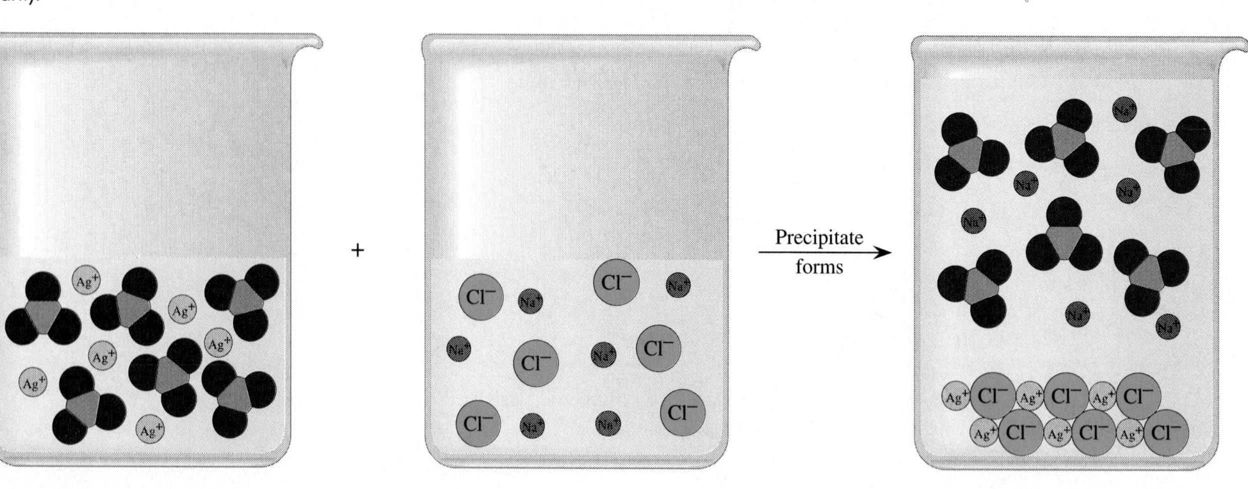

FIGURE 3-25
A molecular view of the precipitation of silver chloride, which occurs when solutions of silver nitrate and sodium chloride are mixed. The solutions contain hundreds of water molecules for every ion present, so water molecules have been omitted for clarity.

contains C, H, O, and Cl is burned, the chlorine does not give a single product whose mass can be measured. Thus to complete the elemental analysis, a separate sample of the compound is treated to convert all the chlorine atoms in the molecules into chloride ions that dissolve in water. Then an excess amount of silver nitrate solution is added, which causes all the Cl^- to precipitate as solid AgCl. This process is illustrated in Figure 3-27. The chloride content in the original sample can be calculated from the mass of the AgCl precipitate. The key feature of the analysis is that the number of moles of chloride in the AgCl equals the number of moles in the original sample. Sample Problem 3-23 shows how the combination of precipitation analysis, mass spectroscopy, and combustion analysis can be used to determine the molecular formula of a compound.

FIGURE 3-26
Silver chloride, a white insoluble salt, precipitates when a solution of sodium chloride is poured into a solution of silver nitrate.

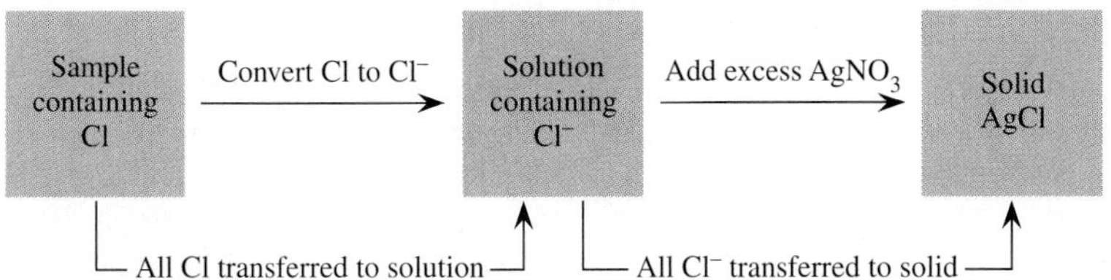

FIGURE 3-27
This flowchart illustrates how precipitation can be used in elemental analysis. The chlorine in a sample is transferred quantitatively, in two steps, to make AgCl.

SAMPLE PROBLEM 3-23 ANALYZING A COMPOUND

An environmental waste-disposal company received a drum of a liquid from a cleaning firm. The firm reported that the liquid was a pure substance, but its label had been destroyed, making its identity uncertain. The disposal company analyzed the liquid using mass spectroscopy, combustion analysis, and precipitation analysis. The mass spectrum showed that the compound had a molar mass of 131.4 g/mol and that it contained chlorine. Combustion of a 1.75-g sample gave 0.121 g of H_2O and 1.17 g of CO_2. The chlorine in a separate 0.655-g sample was converted into chloride ions and precipitated by treatment with aqueous silver nitrate. The mass of AgCl was 2.16 g. Determine the molecular formula of the compound.

METHOD: This is a relatively complicated chemical process, but it can be clarified with a flow chart.

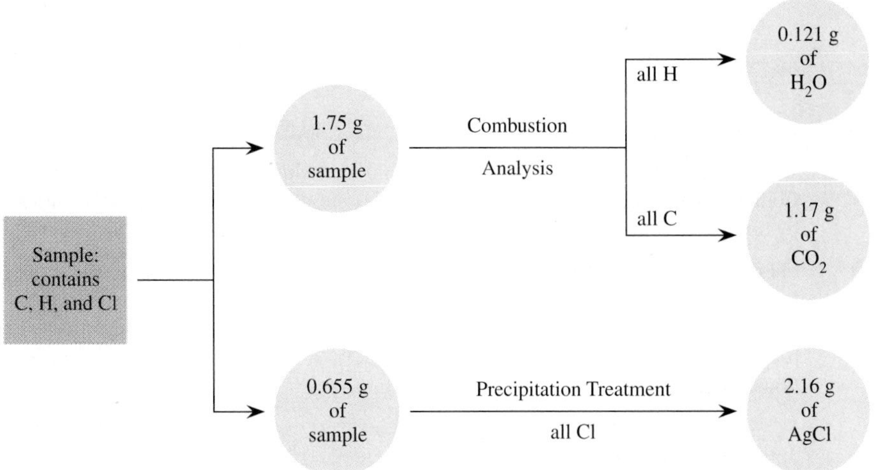

Results of the combustion analysis provide the carbon and hydrogen content of the unknown, and the precipitation results give the compound's chlorine content. These two experiments lead to the empirical formula, which can be combined with the molar mass to determine the molecular formula of the unknown. It is best to analyze each experiment individually.

First, use the data from the combustion analysis to determine the mass percent of C and H:

$$(0.121 \text{ g } H_2O)\left(\frac{2.016 \text{ g H}}{18.02 \text{ g } H_2O}\right) = 1.35 \times 10^{-2} \text{ g H}$$

$$\left(\frac{1.35 \times 10^{-2} \text{ g H}}{1.75 \text{ g sample}}\right)(100\%) = 0.771\% \text{ H}$$

$$(1.17 \text{ g } CO_2)\left(\frac{12.01 \text{ g C}}{44.01 \text{ g } CO_2}\right) = 3.19 \times 10^{-1} \text{ g C}$$

$$\left(\frac{3.19 \times 10^{-1} \text{ g C}}{1.75 \text{ g sample}}\right)(100\%) = 18.2\% \text{ C}$$

Use the same procedure to determine the mass percent of chlorine, but remember that the precipitation is a separate experiment. The mass of sample used for the chloride precipitation is different from the mass of sample used for the combustion analysis.

$$(2.16 \text{ g AgCl})\left(\frac{35.45 \text{ g Cl}}{143.3 \text{ g AgCl}}\right) = 5.34 \times 10^{-1} \text{ g Cl}$$

$$\left(\frac{5.34 \times 10^{-1} \text{ g Cl}}{0.655 \text{ g sample}}\right)(100\%) = 81.5\% \text{ Cl}$$

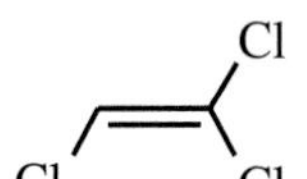

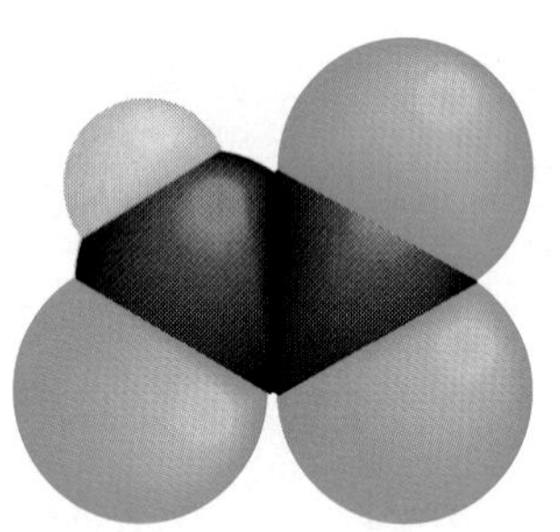

Next, add the percentages to see whether all the elements in the compound are accounted for: 81.5% + 18.2% + 0.77% = 100.5%. The result is 100% within the experimental accuracies of the measurements. This tells us that the compound contains no additional elements.

Now convert elemental percentages into moles per 100 g sample:

$$\frac{0.77 \text{ g H}}{1.008 \text{ g/mol}} = 0.768 \text{ mol H} \qquad \frac{18.2 \text{ g C}}{12.0 \text{ g/mol}} = 1.52 \text{ mol C} \qquad \frac{81.5 \text{ g Cl}}{35.5 \text{ g/mol}} = 2.30 \text{ mol Cl}$$

Divide each by the smallest value, which is 0.76 mol H:

$$\frac{0.76 \text{ mol H}}{0.76 \text{ mol H}} = 1.00 \frac{\text{mol H}}{\text{mol H}} \qquad \frac{1.52 \text{ mol C}}{0.76 \text{ mol H}} = 2.00 \frac{\text{mol C}}{\text{mol H}} \qquad \frac{2.30 \text{ mol Cl}}{0.76 \text{ mol H}} = 3.03 \frac{\text{mol Cl}}{\text{mol H}}$$

The empirical formula of the liquid is C_2HCl_3. The mass that corresponds to this formula is 131.4 g/mol. This is an exact match of the molar mass determined by mass spectroscopy. The compound is trichlorethylene, which is used widely as a cleaning solvent.

SECTION EXERCISES

3.7.1 An urban gardener buys a 1.0-kg bag of ammonium nitrate to fertilize house plants. Compute the concentrations of the ionic species present in a stock solution prepared by dissolving 7.5 g of the salt in 300 mL of water.

3.7.2 Plants can be badly damaged by solutions that are highly concentrated. A biochemist friend of the urban gardener recommends against using fertilizer solutions that are greater than 1.0 mM (1.0×10^{-3} M) in total nitrogen. If the urban gardener wants to prepare 750 mL of 1.0 mM fertilizer solution, how many milliliters of the stock solution will be needed to make the desired solution?

3.7.3 Draw a molecular picture of a portion of the solution described in Section Exercise 3.7.2. Make sure the solution is electrically neutral.

CHAPTER SUMMARY

1. Chemical compounds are identified by names, chemical formulas, structural formulas, and molecular models. Each class of compounds, such as binary, carbon-containing, and ionic, is named according to systematic guidelines.
2. Ionic compounds usually contain Group I or II metals or polyatomic ions.
3. Amounts of atoms and molecules are measured by using the mole, which is 6.022×10^{23} objects. The molar mass of a substance is the mass in grams of 1 mol of its atoms or molecules. Amount calculations in chemistry center around the mole and molar masses.
4. Chemical formulas are determined from mass percentages, which in turn are determined by careful measurements of the masses of known compounds produced when a substance undergoes decomposition, combustion, or precipitation reactions.
5. An aqueous solution contains varying amounts of solutes, which are expressed as moles of solute per liter of solution, or molarity. Solution concentrations can be varied by dilution, which is the addition of solvent to a solution.

KEY TERMS

ball-and-stick model
bond
line structure
space-filling model
structural formula

Avogadro's number
molar mass *(MM)*
mole (mol)

hydrate
isomer
polyatomic ion

combustion analysis
elemental analysis
empirical formula
mass percent composition

aqueous
concentration
dilution
molarity (*M*)
precipitation
solute
solvent

SKILLS TO MASTER

- Drawing various types of chemical structures
- Naming binary and ionic compounds
- Drawing molecular pictures
- Recognizing ionic compounds
- Converting among mass, moles, and number of molecules
- Calculating molar masses
- Converting between mass percentages and chemical formulas
- Determining empirical formulas
- Calculating molarities

LEARNING EXERCISES

3.1 Construct a chapter summary of two pages or less outlining the important features of Chapter 3.

3.2 List the different ways of representing molecules. Describe how they differ from each other.

3.3 Explain how to determine whether a chemical compound is ionic or whether it shares electrons.

3.4 Diagram the process for converting from the mass of a compound of known chemical formula to the number of atoms of one of its constituent elements. Include all necessary equations and conversion factors.

3.5 Explain in words the reasoning used to deduce an empirical formula from combustion analysis of a compound containing C, H, and O.

3.6 Describe what a solution of magnesium nitrate looks like to a molecular-sized observer.

3.7 Update your list of "memory bank" equations.

3.8 List all the terms in Chapter 3 that are new to you. Using your own words, write a one-sentence definition of each. Consult the glossary if you need help.

PROBLEMS

REPRESENTING MOLECULES

3.1 Write chemical formulas for the compounds whose ball-and-stick models follow:

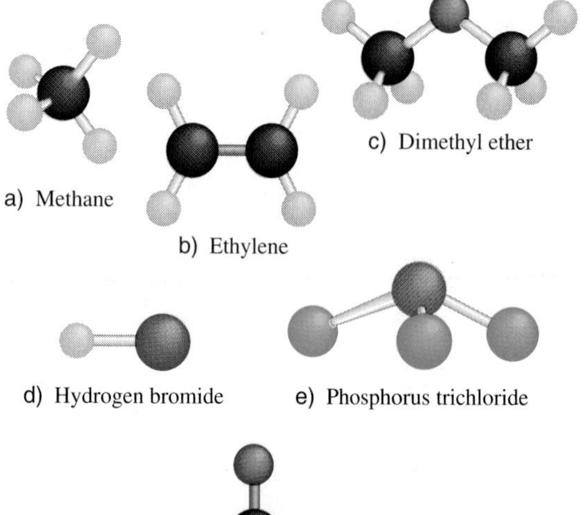

a) Methane b) Ethylene c) Dimethyl ether d) Hydrogen bromide e) Phosphorus trichloride

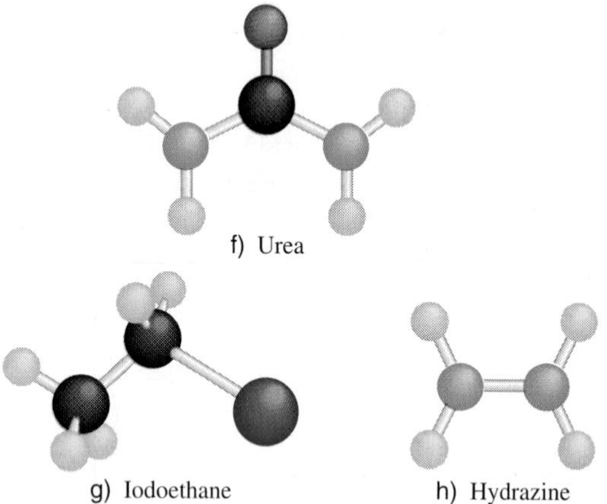

f) Urea g) Iodoethane h) Hydrazine

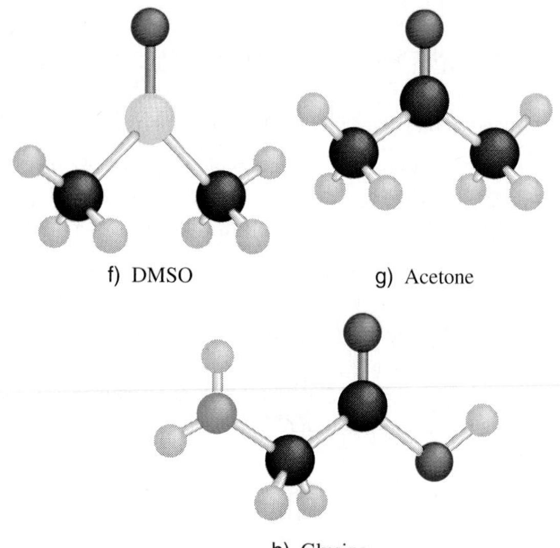

f) DMSO g) Acetone h) Glycine

3.2 Write chemical formulas for the compounds whose ball-and-stick models follow:

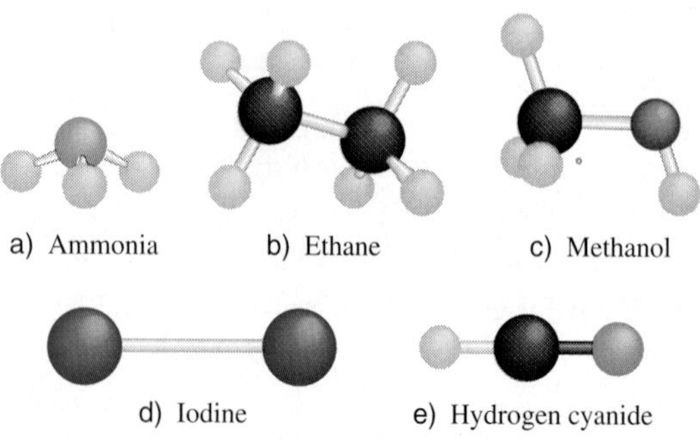

a) Ammonia b) Ethane c) Methanol d) Iodine e) Hydrogen cyanide

3.3 Write structural formulas for the compounds shown in Problem 3.1.

3.4 Write structural formulas for the compounds shown in Problem 3.2.

3.5 Convert the following line structures into structural formulas:

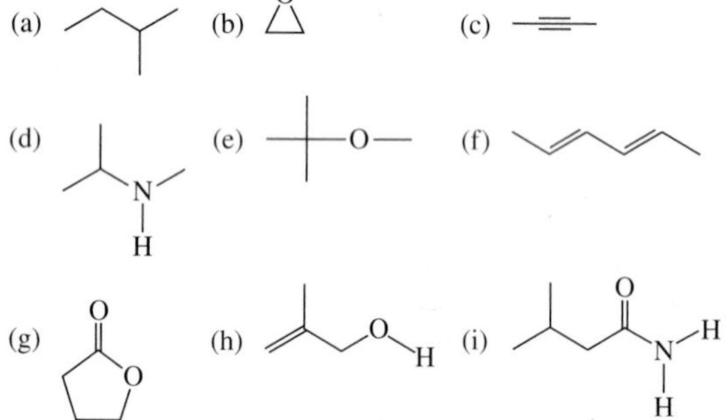

3.6 Convert the following structural formulas into line structures:

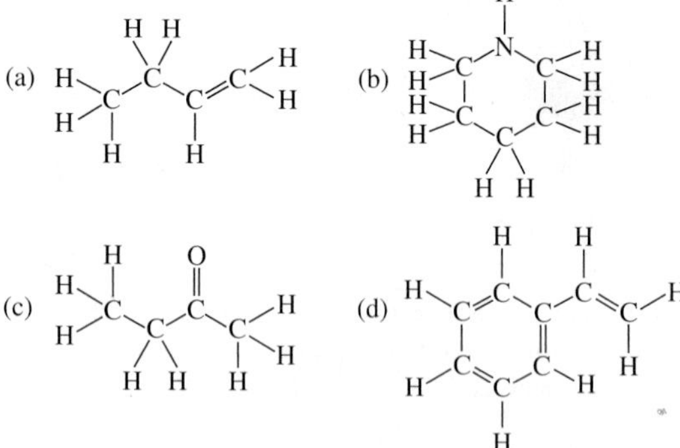

3.7 Draw structural formulas for the following compounds:

3.8 Convert each of the following representations into a line structure:

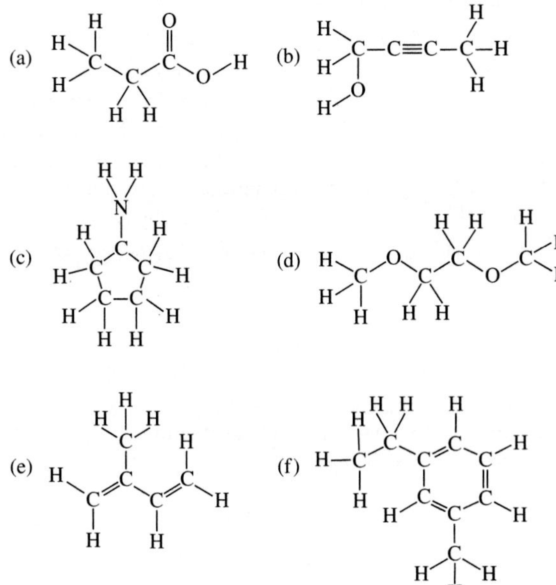

NAMING CHEMICAL COMPOUNDS

3.9 Write chemical formulas and names for the compounds whose space-filling models follow:

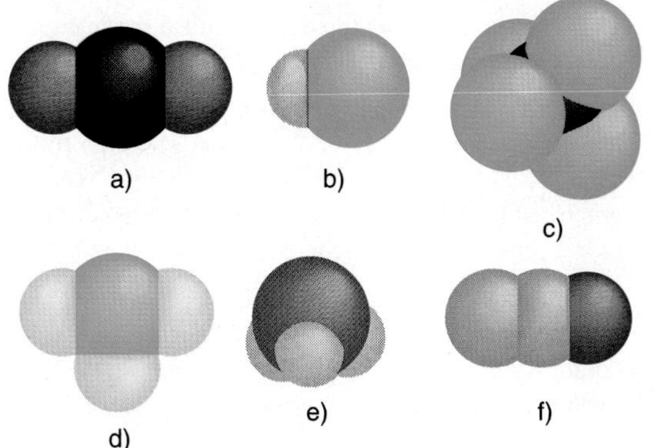

3.10 Write chemical formulas and names for the compounds whose ball-and-stick models follow:

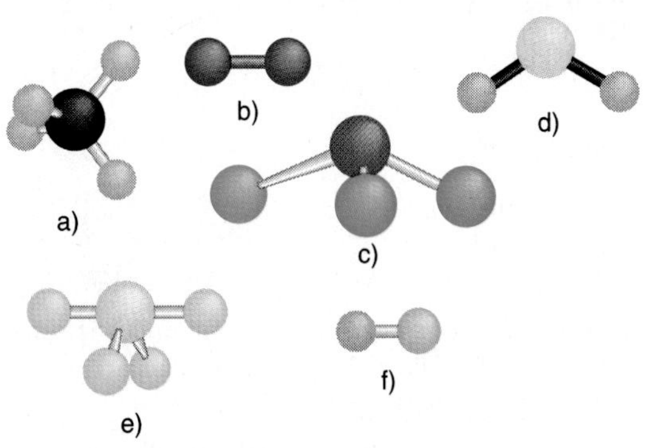

3.11 Write chemical formulas for the following compounds: (a) methane; (b) hydrogen fluoride; (c) calcium hydride; (d) phosphorus trichloride; (e) dinitrogen pentoxide; (f) sulfur hexafluoride; (g) boron trifluoride; and (h) 3-pentanol.

3.12 Write chemical formulas for the following compounds: (a) ammonia; (b) hydrogen sulfide; (c) 2-chloropropane; (d) silicon dioxide; (e.) nitrogen; (f) acetylene; (g) xenon tetrafluoride; and (h) bromine pentafluoride.

3.13 Name the following compounds: (a) S_2Cl_2; (b) IF_7; (c) HBr; (d) N_2O_3; (e) SiC; and (f) CH_3OH.

3.14 Name the following compounds: (a) XeF_2; (b) $GeCl_4$; (c) N_2F_4; (d) LiH; (e) SeO_2; and (f) CH_3CH_2OH.

IONIC COMPOUNDS

3.15 Which of the following compounds are ionic? Write the formula of each. (a) hydrogen fluoride; (b) calcium fluoride; (c) aluminum sulfate; (d) ammonium sulfide; (e) sulfur dioxide; and (f) carbon tetrachloride.

3.16 Which of the following species are ionic? Write the formula of each. (a) manganese(II) acetate; (b) sodium hypochlorite; (c) silicon tetrachloride; (d) lithium periodate; (e) magnesium bromide; and (f) hydrogen selenide.

3.17 Which of the following compounds are ionic? (a) CH_2Cl_2; (b) CO_2; (c) CaO; (d) K_2CO_3; (e) PBr_3; (f) HF; and (g) Na_2HPO_4.

3.18 Write chemical formulas for the following compounds: (a) potassium chlorate; (b) ammonium hydrogencarbonate; (c) iron(II) phosphate; (d) copper(II) nitrate hexahydrate; (e) aluminum chloride; (f) cadmium(II) chloride; (g) potassium oxide; (h) sodium bicarbonate; and (i) lithium perbromate.

3.19 Name the following compounds: (a) $CaCl_2 \cdot 6H_2O$; (b) $Fe(NH_4)_2(SO_4)_2$; (c) K_2CO_3; (d) $SnCl_2 \cdot 2H_2O$; (e) NaClO; (f) Ag_2SO_4; (g) $CuSO_4$; (h) KH_2PO_4; (i) $NaNO_3$; (j) $CaSO_3$; and (k) $KMnO_4$.

3.20 Name the following compounds: (a) $K_2Cr_2O_7$; (b) $NaNO_2$; (c) $Mg_3(PO_4)_2$; (d) $CrCl_3$; (e) V_2O_3; (f) $KHSO_4$; (g) CsBr; (h) $In(NO_3)_3 \cdot 5H_2O$; (i) $Al(ClO_4)_3$; (j) $SnCl_4$; (k) $TaCl_5$.

THE MOLE

3.21 Calculate the number of moles in the following masses: (a) 7.85 g of Fe; (b) 6.55×10^{13} atoms of ^{14}C; (c) 4.68 μg of Si; and (d) 1.46 metric tons of Al (1 metric ton = 10^3 kg).

3.22 Calculate the number of moles in the following masses: (a) 3.67 kg of titanium; (b) 7.9 mg of calcium; (c) 1.56 g of ruthenium; and (d) 9.63 pg of technetium.

3.23 Use the data in the following table to calculate the molar mass of naturally occurring argon:

Isotope	Isotopic Molar Mass	Abundance
^{36}Ar	35.96755 g/mol	0.337%
^{38}Ar	37.96272 g/mol	0.063%
^{40}Ar	39.9624 g/mol	99.600%

3.24 Calculate the molar mass of each of the following compounds: (a) CCl_4 (dry cleaning fluid); (b) N_2O (laughing gas); (c) O_3 (ozone); (d) NH_3 (ammonia); (e) GaAs (semiconductor); and (f) C_4H_{10} (butane).

3.25 Calculate the molar mass of each of each of the following ionic compounds: (a) ammonium carbonate; (b) potassium sulfide; (c) calcium carbonate; (d) lithium bromide; (e) sodium sulfate; and (f) silver nitrate.

3.26 The following four molecules are B vitamins. For each, determine the molecular formula and calculate the molar mass.

(a) Biotin

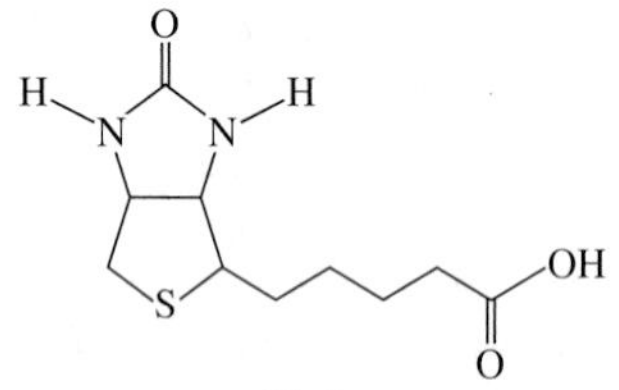

(b) Nicotinamide

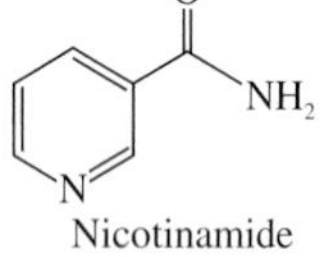

(c) Pyridoxamine

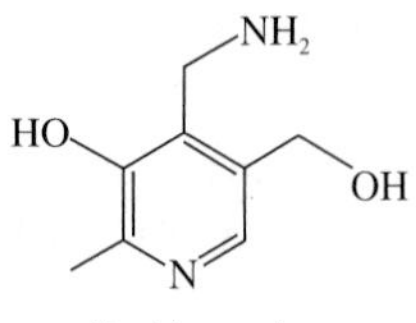

(d) Pantothenic acid

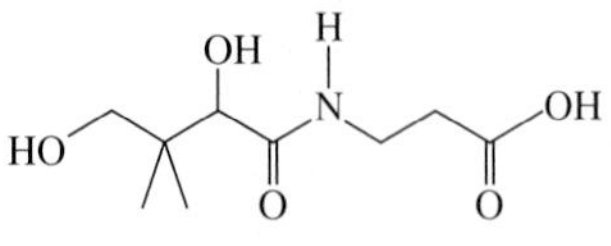

MASS-MOLE-NUMBER CONVERSIONS

3.27 Calculate the number of atoms present in 5.86 μg of each of the following elements: (a) beryllium; (b) phosphorus; (c) zirconium; and (d) uranium.

3.28 Calculate the mass of each of the following: (a) 5000 molecules of cholesterol, $C_{27}H_{46}O$; (b) 10^{15} molecules of ozone; and (c) one molecule of vitamin B_{12}, $C_{63}H_{88}CoN_{14}O_{14}P$.

3.29 Calculate the mass of each of the following: (a) 375,000 molecules of methane; (b) 2.5×10^9 molecules of adrenaline, $C_9H_{13}O_3N$; and (c) one molecule of chlorophyll, $C_{55}H_{72}O_5MgN_4$.

3.30 The U.S. recommended daily allowances (RDAs) of several vitamins follow. In each case, calculate how many molecules of each are in the U.S. RDA. (a) 60 mg vitamin C, $C_6H_8O_6$; (b) 400 μg folic acid, $C_{19}H_{19}N_7O_6$; (c) 1.5 mg vitamin A, $C_{20}H_{30}O$; and (d) 1.70 mg vitamin B_2 (riboflavin), $C_{17}H_{20}N_4O_6$.

3.31 The seventh-ranked industrial chemical in U.S. production is phosphoric acid, whose chemical formula is H_3PO_4. One method of manufacture starts with elemental phosphorus, which is burned in air and then reacted with water to give the final product. In 1992 the United States manufactured 2.47×10^8 pounds of phosphoric acid. How many moles is this? If 35% of this material was made by burning elemental phosphorus, how many moles and how many kilograms of phosphorus were consumed?

3.32 A particular oral contraceptive contains 0.035 mg ethinyl estradiol in each pill. The formula of this compound is $C_{20}H_{24}O_2$. How many moles of ethinyl estradiol are there in one pill? How many molecules is this? How many carbon atoms are in a 0.035-mg sample of ethinyl estradiol? What mass of carbon is this?

DETERMINING CHEMICAL FORMULAS

3.33 Portland cement is a mixture of CaO, SiO_2, Al_2O_3, and Fe_2O_3. Calculate the mass percent composition of each ingredient.

3.34 Small amounts of the following compounds are added to glass to give it color: CaF_2 (milky white), MnO_2 (violet), CoO (blue), and Cu_2O (green). Calculate the mass percent composition of each additive.

3.35 Nicotine is an extremely toxic compound found in tobacco leaves. Elemental analysis of nicotine gives the following data: C, 74.0%; H, 8.65%; and N, 17.35%. What is the empirical formula of nicotine? The molar mass of nicotine is 162 g/mol. What is the molecular formula of nicotine?

3.36 Tooth enamel is composed largely of the mineral hydroxyapatite, which has the following mass percent composition: O, 41.41%; P, 18.50%; H, 0.20%; and Ca, 39.89%. Calculate the empirical formula of hydroxyapatite.

3.37 Police officers confiscate a packet of white powder, which they believe contains heroin. Purification by a forensic chemist gave a 38.7-mg sample for combustion analysis. This sample gave 97.46 mg CO_2 and 20.81 mg H_2O. A second sample was analyzed for its nitrogen content, which was 3.8%. Show by calculations whether or not these data are consistent with the formula for heroin, $C_{21}H_{23}O_5N$.

3.38 Quinine is the bitter-tasting compound in tonic water. Quinine is also used to prevent malaria. Burning a 0.137-g sample of quinine in excess oxygen gave 0.372 g CO_2 and 0.0910 g H_2O. In a second experiment a 0.183-g sample of quinine was found to contain 0.0158 g of nitrogen. The molar mass of quinine is 324 g/mol. Determine the chemical formula of quinine.

AQUEOUS SOLUTIONS

3.39 A student prepares a solution by dissolving 4.75 g of solid KOH in enough water to make 275 mL of solution. Calculate the molarities of the major ionic species present.

3.40 A 25.00-mL sample of the solution described in Problem 3.39 is added to a 100-mL volumetric flask, and water is added to the mark. Calculate the molarity of this KOH solution.

3.41 Draw molecular pictures of portions of the solutions in Problems 3.39 and 3.40, showing how they differ.

3.42 A chemist places 3.25 g of sodium carbonate in a 250-mL volumetric flask and fills it to the mark with water. Calculate the molarity of the sample.

3.43 Draw a molecular picture that shows a portion of the sodium carbonate solution described in Problem 3.42. Make sure the portion is electrically neutral.

3.44 A student discovered an old bottle labeled "copper sulfate, hydrated" on a laboratory shelf. When the student heated 0.500 g of this compound in an oven for 1 hour, it lost its waters of hydration. The resulting residue had a mass of 0.320 g. When the student dissolved 0.300 g of the compound in water and added excess $BaCl_2$ solution, 0.280 g of solid $BaSO_4$ was produced. Find the empirical formula of the hydrated copper sulfate.

3.45 A pure substance was known to contain only C, H, and Cl. When a 4.00-g sample was burned, 4.34 g of CO_2 was produced. In a separate experiment, the chlorine contained in 0.125 g of the compound was converted to 0.334 g of AgCl. Determine the empirical formula of the compound.

ADDITIONAL PROBLEMS

3.46 A dollar bill is 0.1 mm thick. How high would a stack of 1 mol of dollar bills be?

3.47 Name the following compounds: (a) NH_4Cl; (b) XeF_4; (c) Fe_2O_3; (d) SO_2; (e) $KClO_4$; (f) $KClO_3$; (g) $KClO_2$; (h) KClO; (i) KCl; and (j) Na_2HPO_4.

3.48 Calculate the mass percentage of all of the elements in the following semiprecious minerals: (a) lapis lazuli: $Na_4Al_3Si_3O_{12}Cl$; (b) turquoise: $CuAl_6(PO_4)_4(OH)_8{\cdot}4H_2O$; (c) garnet: $Mg_3Al_2(SiO_4)_3$; (d) jade: $Ca_2Mg_5Si_8O_{22}F_2$.

3.49 Heart disease causes 37% of the deaths in the United States. However, the death rate from heart disease has dropped significantly in recent years, partly because of the development of new drugs for heart therapy. These new compounds are developed by chemists working in the pharmaceutical industry. One of these new heart drugs is verapamil. This compound is used for the treatment of arrhythmia, angina, and hypertension. Verapamil inhibits accumulation of excess calcium in the muscle tissue of the heart by blocking transport channels for the Ca^{2+} ion. Calcium is essential for muscle contraction, but if concentrations are too high, proper relaxation of the muscle is inhibited. The structure of verapamil follows. A tablet contains 120.0 mg of verapamil. Determine the following quantities: (a) the molar mass of verapamil, (b) the number of moles of verapamil in one tablet, and (c) the number of nitrogen atoms in one tablet.

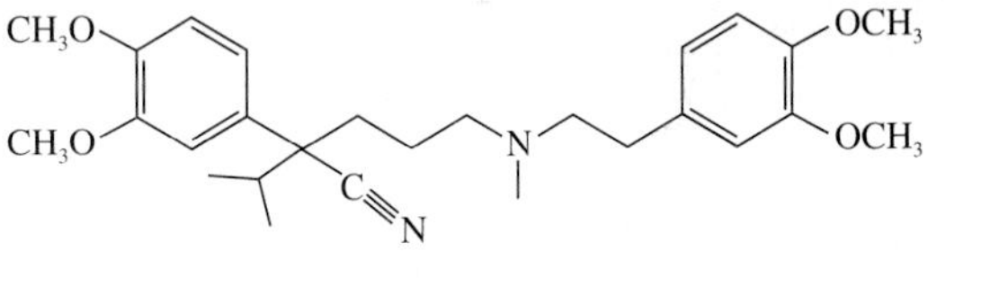

Verapamil
$C_{27}H_{38}O_4N_2$

3.50 Write correct molecular formulas for the following compounds: (a) calcium bromide; (b) sodium bromate; (c) sodium bromite; (d) sodium hydrogencarbonate; (e) aluminum oxide; (f) phosphorus pentafluoride; (g) ammonium sulfate; and (h) cobalt(II) chloride.

3.51 A sample of a component of petroleum was subjected to combustion analysis. An empty vial of mass 2.7534 g was filled with the sample, after which vial plus sample had a mass of 2.8954 g. The sample was burned in a combustion train whose CO_2 trap had a mass of 54.4375 g and whose H_2O trap had a mass of 47.8845 g. At the end of the analysis, the CO_2 trap had a new mass of 54.9140 g, and the H_2O trap had a new mass of 47.9961 g. Determine the empirical formula of this component of petroleum.

3.52 Describe how the results of the analysis in Problem 3.51 would be affected by the following errors in operation of the apparatus. Which measurements would change, and in what direction? How would that affect the calculation of the empirical formula?
  (a) A limited supply of oxygen was provided, rather than excess oxygen.
  (b) Some of the H_2O leaked through the H_2O trap but was collected in the CO_2 trap.
  (c) The H_2O trap functioned properly, but some of the CO_2 leaked through the CO_2 trap.

3.53 The following pairs of substances are quite different despite having similar names. Write correct formulas for each. (a) sodium nitrite and sodium nitrate; (b) potassium carbonate and potassium hydrogencarbonate; (c) iron(II) oxide and iron(III) oxide; and (d) iodine and iodide ion.

3.54 Compute the molar masses of each of the following: (a) Fe_3O_4; (b) C_2H_6O; (c) $C_3H_5(OH)_3$; (d) $Al_2(SO_4)_3$; and (e) $NiSO_4{\cdot}6H_2O$.

3.55 How many moles are contained in 25.0 g of each of the compounds in Problem 3.54?

3.56 Find the percent composition of each of the compounds in Problem 3.54.

3.57 What mass of each of the compounds in Problem 3.54 contains 1.00 moles of O?

3.58 The line structures of three different plant growth hormones are given below. In each case, write the chemical formula for the compound.

(a)

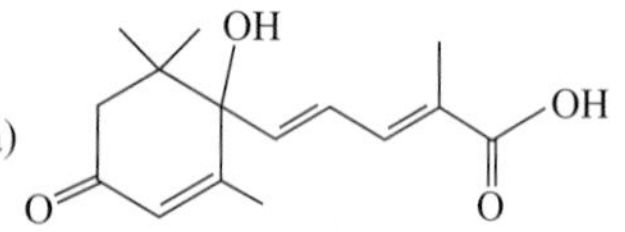

Abscisic acid
(inhibits germination)

(b)

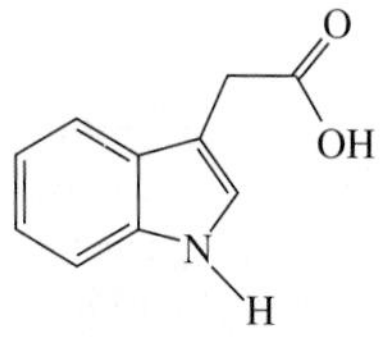

Indole acetic acid
(promotes growing shoots)

(c)

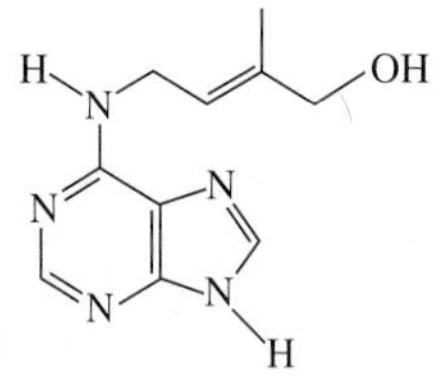

Zeatin
(promotes root growth)

3.59 The waters of the oceans contain many elements in trace amounts. Rubidium, for example, is present at the level of 2.2 nM (1 nM = 10^{-9} M). How many molecules of rubidium are present in 1 L of seawater? How many liters would have to be processed to recover 1 kg of rubidium, assuming that the recovery process was 100% efficient?

3.60 Draw a molecular picture that illustrates a solution of $MgCl_2$ in water. Be sure your picture is electrically neutral.

3.61 Without looking back at the text, write chemical formulas for each of the following ions: (a) iodate; (b) periodate; (c) phosphate; (d) perchlorate; (e) sulfate; (f) acetate; (g) hydrogencarbonate; and (h) nitrate.

3.62 A crystal of $CuSO_4{\cdot}5\,H_2O$ has a mass of 4.59 grams.
  (a) What is its molar mass?
  (b) How many atoms of sulfur does the crystal contain?
  (c) How many moles of oxygen does the crystal contain?
  (d) How many grams of hydrogen does the crystal contain?

3.63 What fraction of the mass of propane (C_3H_8) is carbon?

3.64 Disodium aurothiomalate ($Na_2C_4H_3O_4SAu$) has the trade name Myochrysine and is used to treat arthritis.
  (a) A stock solution is prepared by dissolving 0.25 g of Myochrysine in 10.0 mL of water. The drug is diluted by adding 2.00 mL of the stock solution to a 10.00-mL volumetric flask and filling to the mark with water. Patients receive 0.40 mL of the dilute Myochrysine solution by intramuscular injection. Calculate the number of grams of Myochrysine that are administered in each injection.
  (b) During the treatment the concentration of gold can be as high as 30.0 μg of gold per 10.0 mL of serum. How many atoms of gold will there be in a 5.0-mL sample of serum?

3.65 Four commonly used fertilizers are ammonium nitrate (NH_4NO_3), ammonium sulfate [$(NH_4)_2SO_4$], urea [$(NH_2)_2CO$], and ammonium hydrogenphosphate [$(NH_4)_2HPO_4$]. How many kilograms of each of these would be required to provide 1 kg of nitrogen?

3.66 How many grams of oxygen are contained in 1.80×10^2 g of H_2SO_4?

3.67 When an unknown compound is burned completely in O_2, 1.23 g of CO_2 and 1.02 g of H_2O are recovered. What additional information is needed before the molecular formula of the unknown compound can be determined?

3.68 A major copper-containing ore contains chalcopyrite, $CuFeS_2$. How many kilograms of chalcopyrite would have to be processed to produce 1.00 metric ton (1000 kg) of pure copper?

3.69 Seawater at 25 °C contains 8.3 mg/L of molecular oxygen. What molarity is this?

3.70 A 1.45-g sample of a compound containing C, H, and O was burned completely in excess oxygen. It yielded 1.56 g of H_2O and 3.83 g of CO_2. Find its empirical formula.

3.71 Penicillin was discovered in 1928 by Alexander Fleming, who was a bacteriologist at the University of London. This molecule was originally isolated from a mold that contaminated some of Fleming's experiments. Penicillin destroys bacterial cells without harming animal cells, so it has been used as an antibiotic and has saved countless lives. The molecular formula of penicillin G is $C_{16}H_{18}N_2O_4S$. (a) Calculate the molar mass of penicillin G. (b) How many moles of penicillin G are in a 50.0-mg sample? (c) How many carbon atoms are in a 50.0-mg sample? (d) What is the mass of sulfur in a 75.0-mg sample?

Penicillin G
$C_{16}H_{18}N_2O_4S$

3.72 One molecule of sucrose has a mass of 5.69×10^{-22} g. What is the molar mass of sucrose?

3.73. A chemical compound was found to contain only Fe, C, and H. When 5.00 g of this compound was completely burned in O_2, 9.1 g of CO_2 and 1.80 g of H_2O were produced. Find the percentage by mass of each element in the original compound and its empirical formula.

3.74 What mass of silver chloride will be recovered if excess sodium chloride solution is added to 595 mL of an aqueous solution containing 1.75×10^{-2} M Ag^+?

3.75 A compound was analyzed and found to contain C, H, N, O, and Cl. When a 0.150-g sample of this compound was burned, it produced 0.138 g of CO_2 and 0.0566 g of H_2O. All of the nitrogen in another sample of mass 0.200 g was converted to 0.0238 of NH_3. Finally, the chlorine in a 0.500-g sample of the compound was converted to Cl^- and precipitated as AgCl. The AgCl precipitate had a mass of 1.004 g. Find the empirical formula of the compound.

3.76 Calculate the mass of lithium that has the same number of atoms as 5.75 g of platinum.

3.77 Cinnabar is an ore of mercury known to contain Hg and S. When a 0.350-g sample of cinnabar is heated in oxygen, the ore decomposes to 0.302 g of pure Hg metal and 0.0964 g of SO_2 gas. Find the empirical formula of cinnabar.

3.78 In Sample Problem 3-13 we calculated the molar masses of two widely used insecticides, malathion and sevin. Answer the following questions about these two compounds:

(a) How many moles of carbon atoms are there in 8.3 g of sevin?

(b) How many sulfur atoms are there in 6.5 g of malathion?

(c) How many grams of oxygen atoms are there in 17.8 g of malathion?

(d) The label on a 75-mL bottle of garden insecticide states that the solution contains 0.01% sevin and 99.99% inert ingredients. How many moles and how many molecules of sevin are in the bottle? (Assume that the density of the solution is 1.00 g/mL.)

(e) The instructions for the bottle of insecticide from part (d) say to dilute the insecticide by adding 1.0 mL of the solution to 1.0 gallons of water. If you spray 15 gallons of the diluted insecticide mixture on your rose garden, how many moles of sevin are dispersed?

3.79 In 1987 a molecule called FK-506 was isolated from the bacterium *Streptomyces tsukubaensis*. FK-506 was found to be an extremely potent immunosuppressant. Immunosuppressant compounds are used in transplant surgery to inhibit the body's tendency to reject a new organ. In this regard FK-506 is an exciting molecule because it works considerably better than common surgical immunosuppressing agents. Early in 1989 a group of chemists published the first synthesis of FK-506.

FK-506
$C_{44}H_{69}O_{12}N$

(a) Calculate the molar mass of FK-506.

(b) How many moles of FK-506 are there in a 5.0-mg sample?

(c) How many oxygen atoms are present in a 5.0-mg sample of FK-506?

3.80 The medicinal properties of garlic have been known for many centuries. These properties, as well as garlic's obvious odor, can be attributed to a variety of sulfur-containing molecules. One such molecule is allicin, a potent antibacterial agent that is effective in the treatment of typhus. Allicin's clinical use has been abandoned, however, because of its potent odor. From 4.0 kg of garlic a chemist isolates 6.0 g of allicin. Combustion analysis of allicin yields the following data:

$$\begin{array}{lcccc} \text{Allicin} & \longrightarrow & CO_2 & + \; SO_2 & + \; H_2O \\ 5.00\text{ mg} & & 8.13\text{ mg} & 3.95\text{ mg} & 2.76\text{ mg} \end{array}$$

In a separate experiment the molar mass of allicin was found to be about 160 g/mol. Determine the molecular formula of allicin.

3.81 The density of water is 1.0 g/mL. Calculate the number of moles of water present in a swimming pool containing 8.50×10^4 L of water.

3.82 Hemlock is a poisonous herb of the carrot family. The ancient Greeks used hemlock extracts for state executions. Socrates was killed in this way. You decide to study hemlock to discover the compound that makes it poisonous. From several pounds of the plant, you isolate a small quantity of a colorless liquid that seems to be very effective at killing rats and, presumably, people. In a combustion experiment, 50.50 mg of the colorless liquid are burned in excess oxygen. The products are 139.9 mg CO_2 and 60.91 mg H_2O. In a second experiment, 75.62 mg of the compound was found to contain 8.35 mg of nitrogen. Being just a novice chemist, you haven't yet learned how to determine the molar mass of the compound, but being an intuitive sort, you suspect that the molar mass must be less than 200 g/mol. Determine the molecular formula of the poisonous compound found in hemlock.

3.83 In everyday life we encounter chemicals with unsystematic names. What is the name a chemist would use for each of the following substances? (a) dry ice (CO_2); (b) saltpeter (KNO_3); (c) salt (NaCl); (d) baking soda ($NaHCO_3$); (e) soda ash (Na_2CO_3); (f) lye (NaOH); (g) lime (CaO); and (h) milk of magnesia ($Mg(OH)_2$).

3.84 Draw as many different line structures as you can think of for the formula C_6H_{14}. Remember that carbon always forms a total of four bonds. Draw the structural formula for each of your line structures.

3.85 Vitamin B_{12} is a large molecule called *cobalamin*. There is one atom of cobalt in each molecule of B_{12}. The mass percent of cobalt in vitamin B_{12} is 4.34%. Calculate the molar mass of cobalamin.

3.86 The following molecules are known for their characteristic fragrances. For each one, convert the line structure into a complete structural formula, and calculate its molar mass.

(a) Benzaldehyde (cherry)

(b) Methylbutyl acetate (banana)

(c) Jasmone (jasmine)

(d) Limonene (lemon)

(e) Vanillin (vanilla)

3.87 Just as the molecules in Problem 3.86 are known for their pleasant odors, the ones shown below are recognized for their vile stenches. Convert each structural formula into a line structure.

(a) 3-Methylbutane thiol (excreted by skunks)

(b) Trimethyl amine (present in rotting fish)

(c) Cadaverine (found in rotting meat)

(d) Pyridine (a nonaqueous solvent)

3.88 A mineral is a chemical compound found in the Earth's crust. What are the chemical names of the following minerals? (a) TiO_2 (rutile); (b) PbS (galena); (c) Al_2O_3 (bauxite); (d) $CaCO_3$ (limestone); (e) $BaSO_4$ (barite); (f) $Mg(OH)_2$ (brucite); (g) HgS (cinnabar); (h) Sb_2S_3 (stibnite).

3.89 The federal government regulates the amounts of pollutants that industry emits. Emissions in excess of allotted levels are taxed. As an incentive to clean up emissions, companies that emit less than their allotted amounts are allowed to sell their unused portions (so-called emission credits) to other companies. Recently the Tennessee Valley Authority (TVA), which operates 11 coal-fired electricity plants, purchased emission credits from Wisconsin Power and Light, one of cleanest energy producing companies in the nation. The TVA bought "pollution rights" for the emission of 10,000 tons of sulfur dioxide per year at a price of \$275 per ton. How much will it cost TVA to emit 1 mol of SO_2? How many molecules can be emitted for \$1.00?

3.90 What species are present in solution when the following compounds are dissolved in water? (a) ammonium sulfate; (b) carbon dioxide; (c) sodium fluoride; (d) potassium carbonate; (e) sodium hydrogensulfate; (f) molecular chlorine; (g) sodium dichromate; (h) copper(II) chloride; and (i) barium hydroxide.

3.91 The alkane with six carbons in a single chain is called *hexane*. Alcohols with six carbons are called *hexanols*. Draw structural formulas, and name all the possible hexanols.

3.92 In modern microanalysis for toxic materials, it is possible to detect parts per billion levels of contamination (1 billion = 10^9). One liter of water contains 55.5 mol of water. At 1 part per billion, how many moles of a contaminant are present in 1.00 L of water? How many molecules of contaminant is that?

ANSWERS TO SECTION EXERCISES

3.1.1 (a) $C_{36}H_{18}O_2$; (b) $SiCl_4$; and (c) $C_2Cl_3F_3$

3.1.2

C_6H_{12}

Molecular formula | Structural formula | Line structure

3.1.3 $C_5H_8O_2$

3.2.1 ClF, XeO_3, HBr, $SiCl_4$, and H_2O_2

3.2.2 Chlorine trifluoride, dihydrogen selenide, chlorine dioxide, antimony trichloride, phosphorus pentachloride, dinitrogen pentoxide, dinitrogen tetrachloride, ammonia.

3.2.3

```
   H  H  H  H
   |  |  |  |
H—C—C—C—C—H
   |  |  |  |
   H  H  H  H
     Butane

         H
         |
   H  O  H  H
   |  |  |  |
H—C—C—C—C—H
   |  |  |  |
   H  H  H  H
    2-Butanol

      H  H  H  H
      |  |  |  |
H—O—C—C—C—C—H
      |  |  |  |
      H  H  H  H
       1-Butanol

    H  H  H  H
    |  |  |  |
Br—C—C—C—C—H
    |  |  |  |
    H  H  H  H
   1-Bromobutane
```

3.3.1 Sulfur dichloride, calcium chloride, lead (II) chloride, sodium nitrate, manganese (IV) dioxide, zirconium (IV) chloride, sodium hydride, and sodium iodate

3.3.2 Al_2O_3, $Pb(NO_3)_2$, N_2O_5, Na_2SO_4, IF_5, $Mn(CH_3CO_2)_2$, $K_2Cr_2O_7$, and NaClO

3.3.3 Sulfur hexafluoride, ammonium nitrate, ammonia, nitrogen trichloride, carbon tetrabromide, and hydrogen iodide

3.4.1 4.0×10^{-16} mol and 2.4×10^8 atoms

3.4.2 (a) 129.91 g/mol; (b) 184.04 g/mol; (c) 142.98 g/mol; (d) 261.34 g/mol; and (e) 504.83 g/mol

3.4.3 (a) 155.16 g/mol, (b) 121.16 g/mol, and (c) 132.12 g/mol

3.5.1 (a) 2.21×10^{23} atoms; (b) 3.2×10^{22} atoms; and (c) 7.8×10^{21} atoms

3.5.2 (a) 9.86×10^{-5} mol (b) 5.94×10^{19} molecules; (c) 1.78×10^{20} atoms; (d) 2.97×10^{20} atoms; (e) 20.5 mg; and (f) 2.79×10^{21} atoms

3.5.3 0.783 mol and 196 g

3.6.1 C, 23.68%; H, 3.18%; N, 13.81%; O, 41.01%; and P, 18.32%

3.6.2 Cu_2S

3.6.3 $C_6H_8O_6$

3.7.1 $[NH_4^+] = 0.31$ M $[NO_3^-] = 0.31$ M

3.7.2 1.2 mL

3.7.3

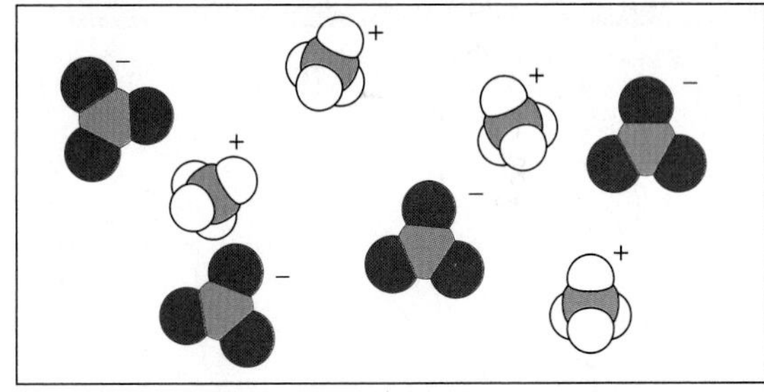

CHAPTER 4

CHEMICAL REACTIONS AND STOICHIOMETRY

Chemical reactions take place all around us. Indeed, life itself is a highly organized sequence of chemical reactions. The materials that make up skin, bone, blood, and flesh are assembled through a vast interlinked network of chemical reactions. Furthermore, the energy required to drive muscle movement comes from chemical reactions involving oxygen from the atmosphere and the food that we consume. Green plants grow by assembling carbon dioxide and water into larger molecules such as starch and cellulose. Fire is a series of chemical reactions, and so is the formation of rust and tarnish.

Much of the activity of industrial society depends on chemical reactions. For example, aluminum, iron, and other metals are extracted from their ores by using chemical reactions. The world of plastics, from food wrap to carpets to molded objects, is created through chemical reactions. Medicines that keep us healthy are produced in the laboratory by chemical reactions. The refining of petroleum into oil and gasoline is a chemical process, too.

All chemical reactions take place according to a set of general principles that relate the amounts of materials consumed in a reaction to the amounts of products formed. As described in this chapter, we can use these principles to calculate how much material is needed to make a desired amount of product.

INTRODUCTION: SYNTHESIS IN CHEMISTRY

For thousands of years, people have taken advantage of the medicinal effects of plants. These beneficial properties come from complex molecules that some plants produce. Unfortunately, nature frequently produces these substances in very small amounts. After these molecules have been identified, chemists try to devise sequences of reactions to produce them in the laboratory. When they are successful, the cost is usually reduced and availability is greatly improved. Quinine, an important antimalarial drug, is one example. For many years, quinine could be isolated only in small amounts from the bark of cinchona, a tropical tree that grows only in special environments (Figure 4-1). Today, chemical synthesis has made quinine readily available at low cost. A similar effort is currently underway to produce a substance found in the bark of yew trees. This substance, called *taxol*, shows great promise as an anticancer drug.

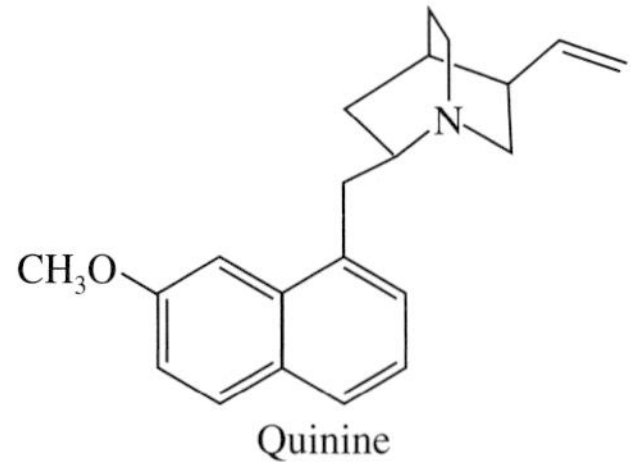

FIGURE 4-1
Quinine is a molecule found in the bark of the cinchona tree. The substance is an effective treatment for malaria. In fact, it saved thousands of lives during construction of the Panama Canal. Quinine is responsible for the bitter flavor of tonic water.

As we understand more about the biochemistry of diseases, we improve our ability to design new drugs for effective treatment. Today, many new medicines are designed by chemists rather than by plants and animals. Chemical synthesis plays a central role in finding substances that can be used to treat illnesses such as cancer, heart disease, and AIDS.

SYNTHESIS OF PROSTAGLANDINS

The importance of chemical synthesis is exemplified by the story of prostaglandins, which are hormones produced in the tissues of most mammals. Prostaglandins have potent and widespread physiological activity from blood clotting to the production of allergic and inflammatory responses. They also affect blood pressure, heart rate, fertility, and conception. Even though these hormones play key roles in the biochemistry of our bodies, our cells produce them in only minute amounts, just 10 to 100 ng/g of tissue. Furthermore, prostaglandins are unstable. They decompose in minutes under physiological conditions. There are dozens of different prostaglandins, and each has a slightly different chemical formula. Consequently, the isolation and structural determinations of prostaglandins were remarkable accomplishments.

One nanogram (ng) is equal to 10^{-9} g.

Medical applications of prostaglandins are developing very rapidly because chemists have learned to synthesize these important compounds in the laboratory. Figure 4-2 shows the line structure of prostaglandin $PGF_{2\alpha}$, which can now be made synthetically. The starting material is a simple, inexpensive molecule, cyclopentadiene, but 16 individual chemical reactions are required for the synthesis.

Designing a chemical synthesis is a challenging task that requires creativity and a thorough understanding of molecular structure and reactivity. Despite their complexities, however, all chemical syntheses are built on the principles and concepts of general chemistry.

"FIXED" NITROGEN

The synthesis of a prostaglandin or quinine is much too complicated to be used to introduce the fundamental principles of chemical reactions. Instead, we will use the Haber process, which is used industrially for the chemical synthesis of ammonia. Ammonia can be made by a single chemical reaction involving simple molecules. Although it is simple, this synthesis has immense industrial importance. The United States produces over 30 billion pounds of ammonia every year, and virtually all of it is made by the Haber process.

Ammonia is such an important industrial chemical because the nitrogen that it contains is essential to all life on the Earth. Nitrogen is a vital component of proteins

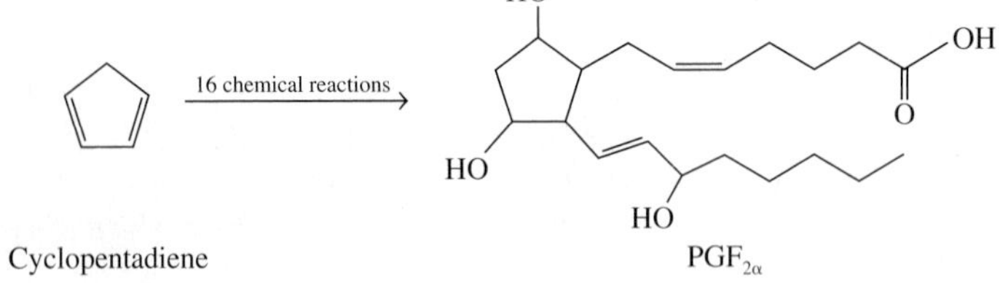

16 chemical reactions

Cyclopentadiene

HO
OH
O
HO
HO
$PGF_{2\alpha}$

FIGURE 4-2
One of the prostaglandins, $PGF_{2\alpha}$, can be made from the simple organic molecule cyclopentadiene.

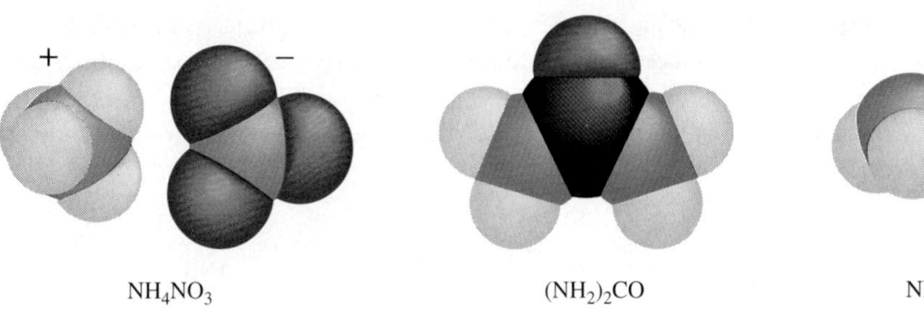

FIGURE 4-3
Formulas and molecular models of ammonium nitrate, urea, and ammonia, which are used as fertilizers.

and nucleic acids. Although the Earth's atmosphere is 79% N_2, molecular nitrogen is not readily available to plants and animals because diatomic nitrogen molecules are extremely stable and highly resistant to chemical attack. Consequently, molecular nitrogen must be converted into a biologically useful form such as ammonia molecules or nitrate anions. This conversion, called *nitrogen fixation,* is carried out in nature by blue-green algae, by chemical reactions that occur during lightning strikes, and by special bacteria that live in nodules on the roots of certain plants such as soybeans and alfalfa. Most plants, including almost all of our food crops, lack these essential bacteria, so "fixed" nitrogen must be supplied from an outside source. Farmers add additional fixed nitrogen to the soil in the form of ammonium nitrate, urea $[(NH_2)_2CO]$, or ammonia. The formulas and molecular models of these three fertilizers are shown in Figure 4-3.

Before World War I, most commercial nitrogen fertilizer came from natural deposits of sodium and potassium nitrate or from the excrement of bats and sea birds (guano). In the early 1900s, Germany was concerned that a naval blockade would cut off natural sources of fixed nitrogen. The concern was not for fertilizer, but for the other major product of nitrogen chemistry, explosives. By the time World War I broke out in 1914, a German chemist named Fritz Haber* had developed a process for the conversion of molecular nitrogen into ammonia. Haber was awarded the 1918 Nobel Prize for chemistry for his studies of ammonia synthesis. Ammonia is an essential industrial chemical, and the Haber synthesis is the process by which it is manufactured. The quantitative description of this and other chemical reactions will be the focus of this chapter.

4.1 WRITING CHEMICAL EQUATIONS

BALANCED EQUATIONS

All chemical reactions obey one inviolate law: *The amounts of each element are always conserved.* This is the law of conservation of matter that Dalton recognized as one postulate of atomic theory. An equation that represents a reaction while conserving amounts of all elements is called a **balanced chemical equation.** A

* Fritz Haber (1868-1934) obtained a doctorate in chemistry after discovering that his father's business did not interest him. In addition to discovering the principles of the Haber process, he invented the glass electrode, which is still used as a simple, rapid, and accurate device for measuring acidity.

balanced equation provides a list of ingredients for the reaction, and it shows what species the reaction produces. It also tells us the relative amounts of each species involved in the reaction.

As an example, consider the balanced chemical equation for the Haber synthesis of ammonia:

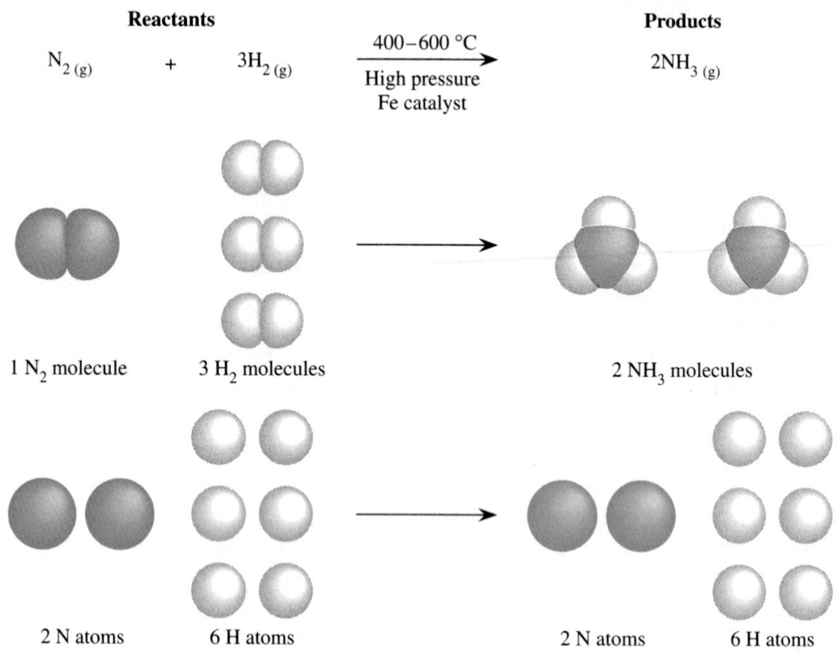

Notice these essential features of the equation:

1. The **reactants** appear on the left, and the **products** appear on the right. The arrow joining them indicates the direction of reaction.
2. An integer is associated with each substance. These numbers are known as **stoichiometric coefficients.** When no number appears, we understand that it is 1. The stoichiometric coefficient for N_2 in this equation is 1.
3. *Stoichiometric coefficients* refer to the relative number of molecules involved in the reaction. Because the number of molecules of any substance divided by Avogadro's number gives the number of moles of the substance, the coefficients also describe the relative numbers of moles involved in the reaction.
4. The stoichiometric coefficients in any chemical equation are the set of smallest integers that gives a balanced equation.

A balanced chemical equation can be interpreted in two ways. The equation for the ammonia synthesis, for example, tells us that:

a. One *molecule* of nitrogen reacts with three *molecules* of hydrogen to give two *molecules* of ammonia.
b. One *mole* of nitrogen reacts with 3 *mol* of hydrogen to give 2 *mol* of ammonia.

Keep in mind that the key feature of balanced chemical equations is the conservation law:

The number of atoms of each element is conserved in any chemical reaction.

The term *reagent* refers to any substance participating in a reaction. A reagent may be a reactant or product.

A balanced chemical equation often includes information about the conditions for the reaction. For example, the physical states of the **reagents** involved in a reaction may be indicated in parentheses: (s) for solid, (l) for liquid, (g) for gas, and (aq) for aqueous, meaning dissolved in water. In the Haber process, N_2, H_2, and NH_3 all exist as gases under the conditions of the synthesis.

Additional information about the reaction conditions can be provided above and below the arrow. The equation for the Haber synthesis indicates that the reaction requires high temperature and pressure and that an iron catalyst is required to help the reaction along. Although this additional information is often useful, it is not needed for the equation to be properly balanced.

A catalyst is an agent that causes a chemical reaction to go faster. How catalysts work will be described in Chapter 14.

BALANCING EQUATIONS

The integers in a balanced chemical equation must be chosen so that the atoms of each element are conserved. For now, we will balance chemical equations *by inspection.* "Balancing by inspection" means changing coefficients until the number of atoms of each element is the same on each side of the arrow. Usually, we can tell what changes need to be made by looking closely at the reaction and matching the numbers of atoms of each element on both sides of the equation. Consider the following example.

Propane, which is used as a fuel for gas barbecues, burns according to the following *unbalanced* equation:

C_3H_8	+	O_2	$\rightarrow$	CO_2	+	H_2O
Propane	plus	oxygen	yields	carbon dioxide	plus	water

To balance this equation, begin with a list of the elements and numbers of atoms on each side:

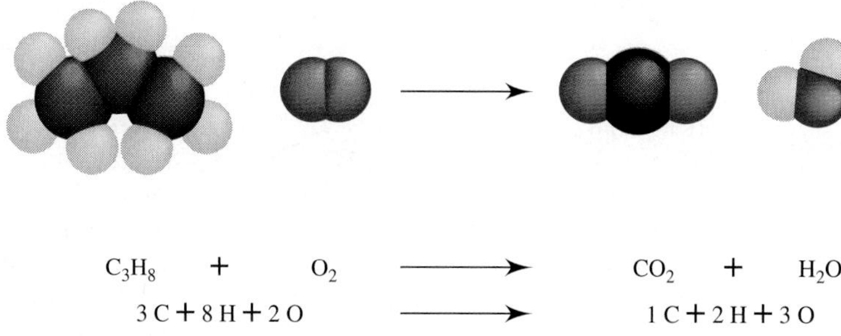

As written, there are too many carbon and hydrogen atoms on the left and too many oxygen atoms on the right. To achieve balance, change the numbers of molecules by changing stoichiometric coefficients until the numbers of atoms of each element are equal. It is easiest to balance a chemical equation one element at a time, starting with the elements that appear in only one substance on each side. Notice that all of the carbon atoms in propane end up in carbon dioxide molecules and all of propane's hydrogen atoms appear in water molecules. This feature, which is true of all combustion reactions, allows us to balance carbon and hydrogen easily.

To take care of the three carbon atoms per propane molecule, we need three molecules of CO_2. Thus the carbon atoms are balanced by changing the stoichiometric coefficient of CO_2 from 1 to 3. In this combustion reaction the **stoichiometric ratio** of CO_2 to propane is 3:1. Similarly, we need four molecules of water for the eight hydrogen atoms in one molecule of propane, so the stoichiometric ratio of propane to water is 1:4. With this updated information the equation can be rewritten as follows:

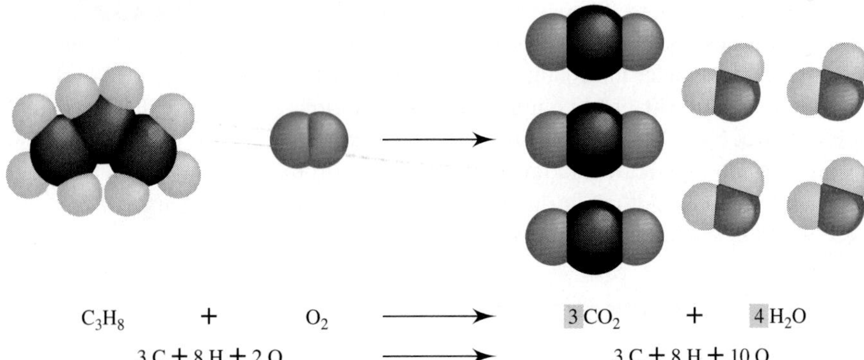

The situation is looking better because atoms of carbon and hydrogen are now conserved. However, the equation still is not balanced because there are too few oxygen atoms on the left side. To balance oxygen, we must give O_2 a stoichiometric coefficient of 5:

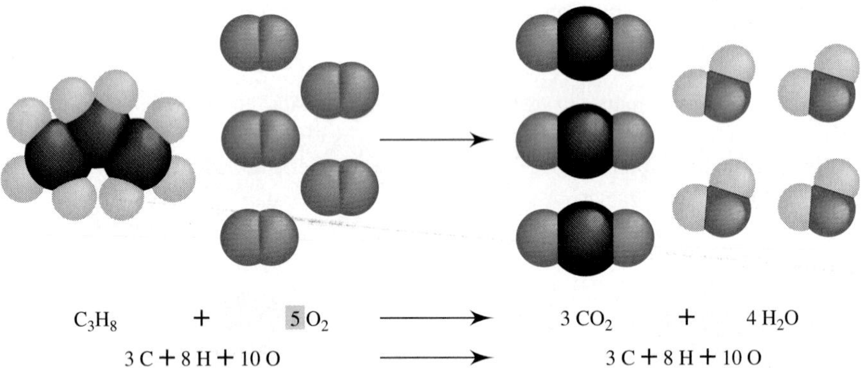

Now the equation is balanced. Combustion of *one* molecule of propane produces *three* molecules of CO_2 and *four* molecules of H_2O and consumes *five* molecules of O_2. Alternatively, combustion of 1 *mol* of propane produces 3 *mol* of CO_2 and 4 *mol* of H_2O and consumes 5 *mol* of O_2. Sample Problem 4-1 shows how to balance another reaction.

SAMPLE PROBLEM 4-1 BALANCING CHEMICAL EQUATIONS

Ammonium nitrate, a colorless ionic solid used as a fertilizer, explodes when it is heated above 300 °C. The products are three gases: molecular nitrogen, molecular oxygen, and steam (water vapor). Write a balanced equation for the explosion of ammonium nitrate.

METHOD: The description in the problem tells us what happens to be the starting material: NH_4NO_3 breaks apart into molecules of N_2, O_2, and H_2O. From this description, we can write an unbalanced form of the equation. Then we must balance each element in turn by inspection.

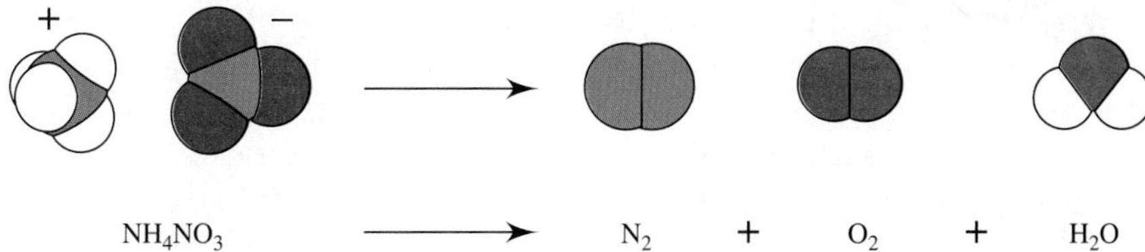

$$NH_4NO_3 \longrightarrow N_2 + O_2 + H_2O$$

First, count all atoms of each type on both sides of the equation to see whether the elements are in balance:

$$2\,N \quad 4\,H \quad 3\,O \longrightarrow 2\,N \quad 2\,H \quad 3\,O$$

Focus first on the elements that appear in only one reactant and product, nitrogen and hydrogen in this case. Nitrogen is already balanced. To balance the hydrogen atoms, we must change the stoichiometric coefficient of water from 1 to 2:

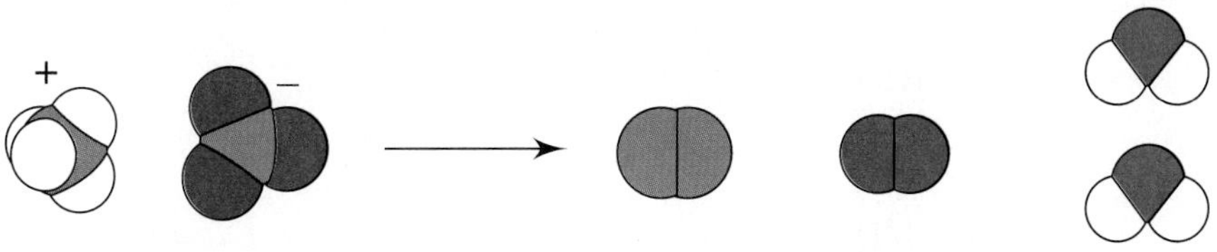

$$NH_4NO_3 \longrightarrow N_2 + O_2 + 2\,H_2O$$

$$2\,N + 4\,H + 3\,O \longrightarrow 2\,N + 4\,H + 4\,O$$

This step balances nitrogen and hydrogen, but oxygen is not yet conserved. We must balance oxygen *without changing* the 1:1 ratio of NH_4NO_3 to N_2 and the 1:2 ratio of NH_4NO_3 to H_2O, which must be retained to keep hydrogen and nitrogen in balance. Thus the only coefficient that can be adjusted to balance the oxygen atoms is that of O_2. Numerically, we can take care of oxygen by making the coefficient of O_2 $\frac{1}{2}$:

$$NH_4NO_3 \longrightarrow N_2 + \boxed{\tfrac{1}{2}}\,O_2 + 2H_2O$$

$$2\,N \quad 4\,H \quad 3\,O \longrightarrow 2\,N \quad 4\,H \quad 3\,O$$

This balances the equation, but it is molecularly unrealistic because there is no such thing as half a molecule. To get rid of the $\frac{1}{2}$ without unbalancing the reaction, we multiply *all* the coefficients by 2:

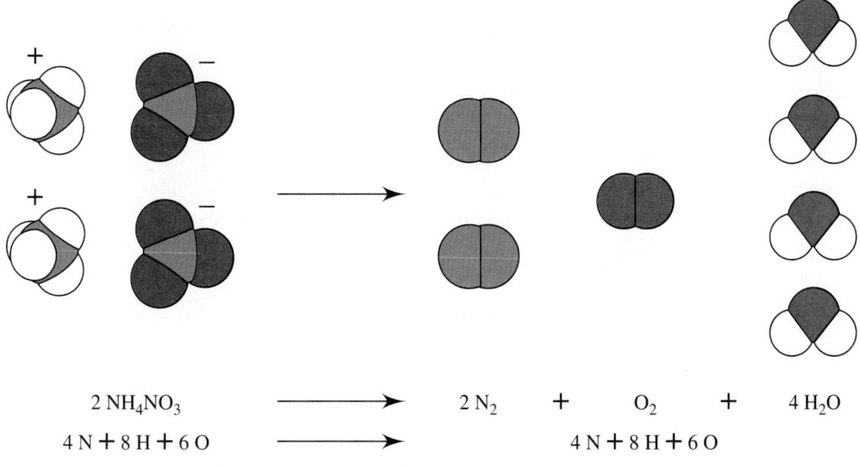

$$2\,NH_4NO_3 \longrightarrow 2\,N_2 + O_2 + 4\,H_2O$$

$$4\,N + 8\,H + 6\,O \longrightarrow 4\,N + 8\,H + 6\,O$$

Now the reaction is balanced and molecularly reasonable.

Later, we show that it can be convenient to use noninteger coefficients such as $\frac{1}{2}$. When this is the case, the coefficient refers to $\frac{1}{2}$ mol, not $\frac{1}{2}$ molecule.

SECTION EXERCISES

4.1.1 The burning of fossil fuels releases millions of tons of carbon dioxide into the Earth's atmosphere each year. Although gasoline is a complex mixture of molecules, we can represent the chemical reaction that takes place in an automobile engine by using the molecule octane, C_8H_{18}. Write a balanced equation for the combustion of octane.

4.1.2 Additional reactions accompany the combustion of octane. For example, molecular nitrogen reacts with molecular oxygen in an automobile cylinder to give nitrogen monoxide. After leaving the engine, nitrogen monoxide reacts with atmospheric oxygen to give nitrogen dioxide, the red-brown gas seen in the air over many urban areas. Write balanced equations for these two reactions.

4.1.3 Acrylonitrile is used to make synthetic fibers such as Orlon. Approximately 2 billion pounds of acrylonitrile are produced each year. Balance the following chemical equation, which shows how acrylonitrile is made from ammonia, propene, and oxygen.

$$C_3H_6 + NH_3 + O_2 \longrightarrow C_3H_3N + H_2O$$

Propene

$H_2C{=}C(H)CH_3$

Acrylonitrile

$H_2C{=}C(H)C{\equiv}N$

4.2 THE STOICHIOMETRY OF CHEMICAL REACTIONS

Stoichiometry **is pronounced "stoy-ke-om'-etry." It combines two Greek words, *stoicheion* ("element") and *metron* ("measure").**

One metric ton = 1000 kg.

In Chapter 3 we showed how the relationships among atoms, moles, and masses allow us to answer "how much" questions about individual molecules. Combining these ideas with the concept of a balanced chemical equation lets us answer "how much" questions about chemical reactions. The study of the amounts of materials consumed and produced in a chemical reaction is called **stoichiometry.**

How much molecular hydrogen is required to produce 2.0 metric tons of ammonia by the Haber process? It would be a mistake to mix random amounts of N_2 and H_2 and hope for the best. In making a cake, a baker must mix the right proportions of flour, sugar, water, and eggs, or the product will be inedible. As in cooking, a chemical synthesis requires the proper mix of starting materials for a successful outcome. In cooking, a recipe provides the proper proportions of ingredients. In chemistry, a balanced chemical equation gives the appropriate *molar* stoichiometric ratios for amounts of starting materials.

To find out how much hydrogen is needed to make 2.0 tons of ammonia, we begin with the balanced chemical equation for the Haber process:

$$N_2 + 3\,H_2 \longrightarrow 2\,NH_3$$

The synthesis of 2.0 mol of ammonia requires 3.0 mol of hydrogen and 1.0 mol of nitrogen. Note, however, that the balanced equation does not give us any direct information about the *masses* involved in the synthesis. One ton of N_2 plus 3 tons of H_2 does *not* make 2 tons of NH_3. Remember the most important lesson from Chapter 3:

Calculations in chemistry are centered around the mole.

In other words, a chemical recipe for making ammonia requires amounts in moles, not masses. Thus to prepare 2.0 metric tons of ammonia, we need to know the number of moles of ammonia in 2.0 tons. To do that, we must first convert tons to grams:

$$(2.0 \text{ tons NH}_3)\left(\frac{1000 \text{ kg}}{\text{ton}}\right)\left(\frac{1000 \text{ g}}{\text{kg}}\right) = 2.0 \times 10^6 \text{ g NH}_3$$

Next, divide the mass of ammonia by the molar mass of ammonia to convert grams to moles:

$$\frac{2.0 \times 10^6 \text{ g NH}_3}{17.03 \text{ g NH}_3\text{/mol}} = 1.17 \times 10^5 \text{ mol NH}_3$$

We have carried one additional significant figure during the intermediate steps of this calculation, rounding off to three figures only at the end of the chain of steps.

How many moles of N_2 and H_2 are needed to make 1.17×10^5 moles of NH_3? According to the balanced equation, 2 mol of NH_3 require 1 mol of N_2 and 3 mol of H_2. Apply these mole ratios to the desired amount of NH_3:

$$(1.17 \times 10^5 \text{ mol NH}_3)\left(\frac{3 \text{ mol H}_2}{2 \text{ mol NH}_3}\right) = 1.76 \times 10^5 \text{ mol H}_2$$

↑

Stoichiometric ratio

Notice that the mole ratio makes the units the same on both sides of the equation: *mol* NH_3 cancels on the left, leaving *mol* H_2 on the left and the right.

All that remains is to convert from moles of H_2 to mass:

$$(1.76 \times 10^5 \text{ mol H}_2)\left(\frac{2.016 \text{ g H}_2}{\text{mol H}_2}\right) = 3.55 \times 10^5 \text{ g H}_2$$

$$(3.55 \times 10^5 \text{ g H}_2)\left(\frac{10^{-3} \text{ kg}}{\text{g}}\right)\left(\frac{10^{-3} \text{ ton}}{\text{kg}}\right) = 0.36 \text{ tons H}_2$$ required to produce 2.0 metric tons of ammonia

Exactly the same procedure can be used to show that 2.0 tons of ammonia require 1.6 tons of nitrogen gas.

The procedure for relating amounts of different chemicals can be summarized as follows:

To convert from moles of one reagent to moles of any other reagent, multiply by the mole ratio given by the stoichiometric coefficients in the balanced equation.

Balanced equation: $n_A \text{ A} \longrightarrow n_B \text{ B}$

Conversion: $$\text{Moles B} = \frac{n_B}{n_A}(\text{Moles A}) \quad \textbf{(4-1)}$$

Sample Problems 4-2 and 4-3 illustrate the use of the mole ratio.

SAMPLE PROBLEM 4-2 HOW MUCH PRODUCT CAN BE MADE?

Geranyl formate is used as a synthetic rose essence in cosmetics. The compound is prepared from formic acid and geraniol:

$$\underset{\text{Formic acid}}{HCO_2H} + \underset{\text{Geraniol}}{C_{10}H_{18}O} \longrightarrow \underset{\text{Geranyl formate}}{C_{11}H_{18}O_2} + H_2O$$

A chemist needs to make some geranyl formate for a batch of perfume. How many grams of geranyl formate can a chemist make from 375 g of geraniol?

METHOD: There are some exotic chemical names and line structures here, but they should not distract you from the basic principles of reaction stoichiometry. The chemical formulas and balanced chemical equation, which are required to calculate the masses of geraniol and geranyl formate, are provided in the problem. The stoichiometric coefficients state that 1 mol of each reactant will produce 1 mol of each product.

The following flowchart summarizes the steps involved in converting the mass of geraniol into the mass of geranyl formate.

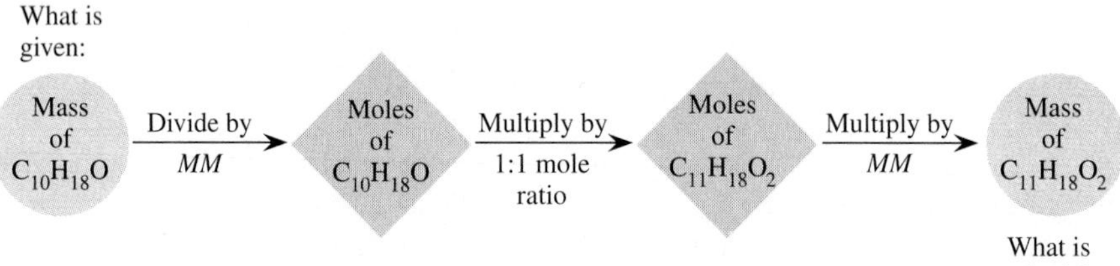

If you are not yet proficient at calculating molar mass, return to Chapter 3 for a review.

First, convert the mass of geraniol into moles by dividing by the molar mass:

$$\frac{375 \text{ g geraniol}}{154.2 \text{ g/mol}} = 2.432 \text{ mol geraniol}$$

The mole ratio relates moles of geraniol to moles of geranyl formate. In this case the stoichiometric ratio is 1:1, or 1 mol of geraniol to 1 mol of geranyl formate. If the chemist starts the reaction with 2.43 mol of geraniol, the synthesis can produce 2.43 mol of geranyl formate. To finish the problem, multiply by the molar mass of geranyl formate to determine the mass of geranyl formate produced in the reaction:

$$(2.432 \text{ mol geranyl formate})\left(\frac{182.3 \text{ g geranyl formate}}{\text{mol geranyl formate}}\right) = 443 \text{ g geranyl formate}$$

The result has three significant figures, just like the initial mass of geraniol.

SAMPLE PROBLEM 4-3 AMOUNTS OF REACTANTS AND PRODUCTS

The poisonous gas hydrogen cyanide is an important industrial chemical. It is produced from methane (CH_4), ammonia, and molecular oxygen. The reaction also produces water. An industrial manufacturer wants to convert 175 kg of methane into HCN. How much hydrogen cyanide can be produced in the reaction? What masses of ammonia and oxygen will be required?

METHOD: This problem looks complicated, but actually it is very similar to the two examples discussed previously in this section. Knowing the mass of one reagent, we are asked to find the masses of others. Starting with a balanced chemical equation, we need to determine molar amounts and then convert to kilograms.

Begin by writing the unbalanced form of the equation from the information given, namely methane, ammonia, and molecular oxygen react to yield hydrogen cyanide and water:

$$CH_4 + NH_3 + O_2 \rightarrow HCN + H_2O$$

Then balance the equation by inspection, one element at a time.

Carbon and nitrogen are in balance when there are equal numbers of molecules of CH_4, NH_3, and HCN. Hydrogen and oxygen, however, are not in balance. There are seven hydrogen atoms on the left but only three on the right. The coefficient for HCN cannot be changed without unbalancing C and N. To balance H, we must multiply the coefficient for H_2O by 3:

$$CH_4 + NH_3 + O_2 \rightarrow HCN + 3\ H_2O$$

This gives three oxygen atoms on the right, which corresponds to $1\frac{1}{2}$ O_2 molecules among the starting materials. To avoid the impossible $\frac{1}{2}$ molecule, we multiply all of the stoichiometric coefficients by 2. This gives a balanced equation:

$$2\ CH_4 + 2\ NH_3 + 3\ O_2 \rightarrow 2\ HCN + 6\ H_2O$$

The calculations require two equations for interconversion of moles and mass:

$$\text{mol} = \frac{m}{MM} \qquad \textit{and} \qquad \text{mol B} = \frac{n_B}{n_A}(\text{mol A})$$

A flowchart for the stoichiometry of the problem can be written as follows:

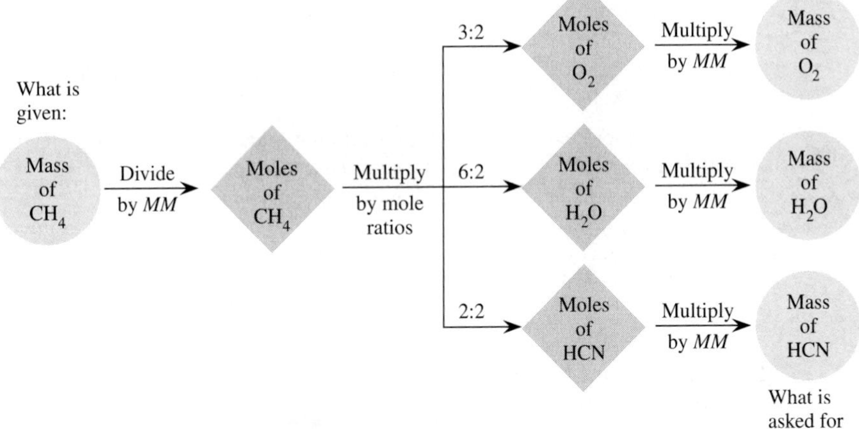

Begin by converting mass of methane to moles:

$$(175\ \text{kg}\ CH_4)\left(\frac{10^3\ \text{g}}{\text{kg}}\right) = 1.75 \times 10^5\ \text{g}\ CH_4$$

$$\frac{1.75 \times 10^5\ \text{g}\ CH_4}{16.04\ \text{g/mol}} = 1.091 \times 10^4\ \text{mol}\ CH_4$$

Next use the mole ratio to find the number of moles of O_2 required for the synthesis:

$$(1.091 \times 10^4\ \text{mol}\ CH_4)\left(\frac{3\ \text{mol}\ O_2}{2\ \text{mol}\ CH_4}\right) = 1.636 \times 10^4\ \text{mol}\ O_2$$

Finally, use the molar mass of O_2 to convert from moles back to mass:

$$(1.636 \times 10^4\ \text{mol}\ O_2)\left(\frac{32.00\ \text{g}\ O_2}{\text{mol}\ O_2}\right)\left(\frac{10^{-3}\ \text{kg}}{\text{g}}\right) = 524\ \text{kg}\ O_2 \text{ required for synthesis}$$

Notice that we keep careful track of the units in each step of the calculations. In the first conversion, *g* and *kg* cancel, leaving *mol*. In the second conversion, canceling *mol* CH_4 leaves *mol* O_2. In the third conversion, *mol* and *g* cancel, leaving *kg*. The final unit, *kg*, indicates that the calculations are all in order because the question asked for the *mass* of oxygen. The mass is also reasonable. The mass of O_2 required for the synthesis, 524 kg, is a large quantity, but it is reasonable because the reaction also involves a large quantity of methane (175 kg).

Similar calculations for ammonia, hydrogen cyanide, and water show that 186 kg of NH_3 are required as a starting material and that the reaction produces 295 kg of HCN and 589 kg H_2O. You should carry out the appropriate calculations to confirm these values.

SECTION EXERCISES

4.2.1 Phosphorus trichloride is produced from the reaction of solid phosphorus and chlorine gas:

$$P_{4\,(s)} + 6\,Cl_{2\,(g)} \longrightarrow 4\,PCl_{3\,(l)}$$

(a) What mass of phosphorus trichloride can be prepared from 75.0 g of phosphorus?
(b) How many grams of chlorine will be consumed in the reaction?

4.2.2 Tooth enamel consists, in part, of a compound known as hydroxyapatite, $Ca_5(PO_4)_3(OH)$. Tin(II) fluoride (toothpaste labels call it *stannous fluoride*) is commonly added to toothpaste because it reacts with hydroxyapatite to give a more decay-resistant compound called *fluoroapatite*, $Ca_5(PO_4)_3F$. In addition to fluoroapatite, this reaction produces tin(II) oxide and water. What mass of hydroxyapatite can be converted to fluoroapatite by reaction with 0.115 g of tin(II) fluoride?

4.2.3 Combustion reactions require significant quantities of molecular oxygen. In an automobile the fuel-injection system must be adjusted to provide the right "mix" of gasoline and air. Compute the number of grams of oxygen required to react completely with 1.00 L of octane (C_8H_{18}, density = 0.80 g/mL). How many grams of water and carbon dioxide are produced in this reaction? (HINT: Recall from Chapter 1 how to convert from volume to mass using density.)

4.3 YIELDS OF CHEMICAL REACTIONS

When chemical reactions are performed under practical conditions, the amounts of products obtained are almost always less than the amounts predicted by stoichiometric analysis. There are at least four important reasons why amounts of products fall short of expectations.

1. The reaction may stop before it reaches completion. For example, solid sodium metal reacts with oxygen gas to give sodium peroxide (Na_2O_2). For this reaction to occur, gaseous oxygen molecules must collide with sodium atoms at the metal surface. As the reaction proceeds, a solid crust may build up on the surface of the metal, as shown in Figure 4-4. This crust prevents the reactants from encountering one another, and the reaction stops even though oxygen and sodium metal are still present.

2. Competing reagents may consume some of the starting materials. Sodium metal also reacts very rapidly with water vapor to produce sodium hydroxide. If a sample of oxygen is contaminated with water, some sodium atoms react with water rather than with oxygen. The more H_2O present in the gas mixture, the less Na_2O_2 produced in the desired reaction.

3. The starting materials may form more than one product. For example, pure elemental carbon in the form of graphite reacts with molecular oxygen to produce carbon dioxide. However, carbon also reacts with molecular oxygen to form carbon monoxide, and unless the reaction conditions are carefully controlled, mixtures of CO and CO_2 are obtained. Chemists try to design reaction conditions that favor the desired product. By controlling the proportions of oxygen and carbon, it is possible to make carbon dioxide or carbon monoxide selectively from molecular oxygen and graphitic carbon.

4. When the product of a reaction is purified and isolated, some of it is inevitably lost during the collection process. Liquids adhere to glass surfaces, making it impossible to transfer every drop of a liquid product. Likewise, it is impossible to scrape every trace of a solid material from a reaction vessel.

We describe amounts obtained from a reaction in terms of the reaction **yield.** The quantity of product *predicted* by stoichiometry is called the **theoretical yield,** whereas the amount *actually* obtained is called the **actual yield.** Usually, a reaction yield is reported as a **percent yield,** which is the percentage of the theoretical amount:

$$\text{Percent yield} = \left(\frac{\text{Actual yield}}{\text{Theoretical yield}}\right)(100\%) \quad \textbf{(4-2)}$$

Sample Problem 4-4 shows how to use Equation 4-2.

FIGURE 4-4
The reaction of sodium metal with oxygen produces a crust of sodium peroxide (*top*) that hinders further reaction even though sodium metal is still present (*bottom*).

SAMPLE PROBLEM 4-4 CALCULATING PERCENT YIELD

In Sample Problem 4-2 a chemist set out to make 443 g of geranyl formate for a batch of perfume. If 417 g of the desired product is collected, what is the percent yield of the synthesis?

METHOD: The theoretical yield of geranyl formate is 443 g. This is the amount of product that would result from complete conversion of geraniol into geranyl formate. The actual yield, 417 g, is the quantity of the desired product that the chemist collects. The percent yield is their ratio multiplied by 100%.

$$\text{Percent yield} = \left(\frac{417\text{ g}}{443\text{ g}}\right)(100\%) = 94.1\%$$

You may wonder why we did not convert from mass to moles to find theoretical and actual yields in this problem. A *percent yield* is obtained by taking the *ratio* of these two amounts. *A ratio is dimensionless.* As long as both amounts are given in the same units, we will obtain a correct result.

Yield calculations are also done in reverse. If the percent yield of a reaction is known from previous experiments, we can calculate the amount of starting material needed to make a specific amount of product. Sample Problem 4-5 shows how this is done.

SAMPLE PROBLEM 4-5 CALCULATING REACTANT MASS FROM YIELD

The industrial production of hydrogen cyanide was described in Sample Problem 4-3. If the yield of this synthesis is 97.5%, how many kilograms of methane and how many of ammonia should be used to produce 1.50×10^5 kg of HCN?

METHOD: This is a two-stage problem that requires a yield calculation and an interconversion among molar amounts of products and reactants. This is typical of yield calculations. Use the percent yield to determine the theoretical amount and then the mole ratios to calculate masses of starting materials. The following flowchart summarizes the calculations:

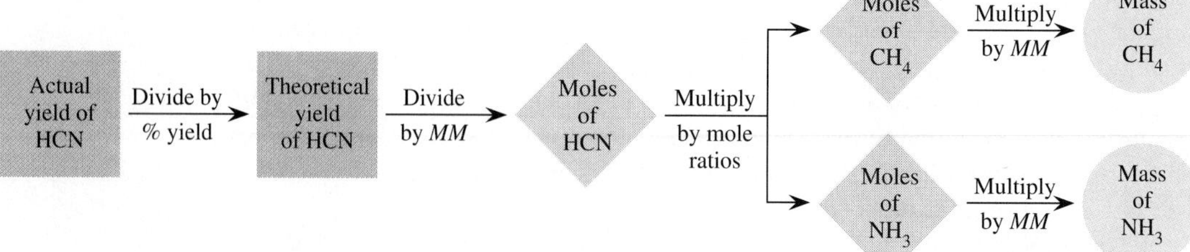

First, rearrange the equation for percent yield to find the theoretical yield that will give an actual yield of 1.50×10^5 kg:

$$\frac{\text{Actual yield}}{\text{Theoretical yield}} = \frac{97.5\%}{100\%} = 0.975$$

$$\text{Theoretical yield} = \frac{\text{Actual yield}}{0.975} = \frac{1.50 \times 10^5 \text{ kg}}{0.975} = 1.538 \times 10^5 \text{ kg HCN}$$

Next, convert this mass to moles, apply the mole ratio, and multiply by the molar mass of methane:

$$(1.538 \times 10^5 \text{ kg HCN})(10^3 \text{ g/kg}) = 1.538 \times 10^8 \text{ g HCN}$$

$$\frac{1.538 \times 10^8 \text{ g HCN}}{27.03 \text{ g/mol}} = 5.690 \times 10^6 \text{ mol HCN}$$

$$(5.690 \times 10^6 \text{ mol HCN})\left(\frac{2 \text{ mol } CH_4}{2 \text{ mol HCN}}\right) = 5.690 \times 10^6 \text{ mol } CH_4$$

$$(5.690 \times 10^6 \text{ mol } CH_4)(16.04 \text{ g/mol})(10^{-3} \text{ kg/g}) = 9.13 \times 10^4 \text{ kg } CH_4$$

A similar calculation will show that the synthesis also requires 9.69×10^4 kg of NH_3.

Suppose a chemical reaction gives a 50% yield. Is that a good yield or a poor yield? The answer depends on the circumstances. Many valuable chemicals are manufactured in processes that require several steps. The more chemical reactions there are in the process, the higher the yield of every step needs to be to ensure that sufficient amounts of the final product can be prepared at an acceptable price.

The synthesis of sulfanilamide, the simplest member of a group of antibacterial compounds called *sulfa drugs,* illustrates this point. These compounds attack bacteria by inhibiting their production of folic acid, a vitamin essential for cell growth. Our bodies need folic acid too, but we produce it by different biochemical pathways than bacteria. Sulfa drugs do not interrupt these processes, so they are safe for humans but toxic for bacteria. Sulfanilamide can be synthesized in a six-step procedure starting from chlorobenzene. The reaction scheme for the synthesis and a set of representative yields is outlined next.

Cl

Chlorobenzene $\xrightarrow[79\%]{\text{Step 1}}$ Product A $\xrightarrow[94\%]{\text{Step 2}}$ Product B $\xrightarrow[68\%]{\text{Step 3}}$ Product C $\xrightarrow[78\%]{\text{Step 4}}$ Product D $\xrightarrow[74\%]{\text{Step 5}}$ Product E $\xrightarrow[92\%]{\text{Step 6}}$ Sulfanilamide

NH_2

O=S=O

NH_2

Suppose we started a synthesis with 1.0 mol of chlorobenzene. After the first reaction we would have (1.0 mol) (0.79) = 0.79 mol of Product A, after step 2 we would have (0.79 moles) (0.94) = 0.74 mol of Product B, and so on. The overall yield of the synthesis is the product of all of the individual fractional yields.

$$(1.0 \text{ mol chlorobenzene}) \overbrace{\underbrace{(0.79)(0.94)(0.68)(0.78)(0.74)(0.92)}_{\text{Overall fractional yield} = 0.27}}^{\text{Fractional yields of the individual reactions}} = 0.27 \text{ mol sulfanilamide}$$

In other words, sulfanilamide can be made from chlorobenzene in an overall yield of 27%, which is considerably lower than the yield of any individual step in the synthesis. To produce 1.0 mol of sulfanilamide, we would need 3.7 mol of chlorobenzene.

The more steps there are in a synthesis, the more important the yields of the individual reactions become. The synthesis of prostaglandin $PGF_{2\alpha}$ mentioned earlier requires 16 individual chemical reactions. At an average yield per step of 95% the overall yield of the synthesis would be 44%, but at an average yield of 75% the overall yield of the prostaglandin synthesis falls to 1.0%!

The yield of product must be taken into consideration in the design of a synthesis. A 50% yield can be acceptable if the reaction comes very early in the sequence when dozens of grams of inexpensive reagents are used in the individual reaction. On the other hand, a 50% yield might be a disaster 15 steps into the synthesis of a prostaglandin, when the chemist has already invested much time and expense and may be working with just a few milligrams of compound.

Many-step reactions that have only moderate yields at each step are wasteful and expensive. For this reason, industrial chemists spend a great deal of time, effort, and ingenuity to devise reaction sequences and conditions that result in high yields. Our most important industrial chemicals are produced in billion-pound quantities on an annual basis. Here, improving the synthesis yield by even a few tenths of a percent can save a company millions of dollars each year.

SECTION EXERCISES

4.3.1 When heated, potassium chlorate decomposes to potassium chloride and oxygen:

$$2\ KClO_{3\,(s)} \rightarrow 2\ KCl_{\,(s)} + 3\ O_{2\,(g)}$$

What is the theoretical yield of oxygen in the decomposition of 5.00 g of potassium chlorate? Calculate the percent yield if a 5.00-g sample gives 1.84 g O_2 on decomposition. Suggest a reason why the actual yield may be less than the theoretical yield.

4.3.2 Sulfuric acid is made from pure elemental sulfur in a highly efficient three-step industrial process. How many tons of sulfur are required to produce 10 tons of H_2SO_4 if the three steps have yields of 94%, 92.5%, and 97%?

4.3.3 Aspirin is produced from two carbon-containing compounds, salicylic acid and acetic anhydride:

$$2\ C_7H_6O_3 + C_4H_6O_3 \rightarrow 2\ C_9H_8O_4 + H_2O$$

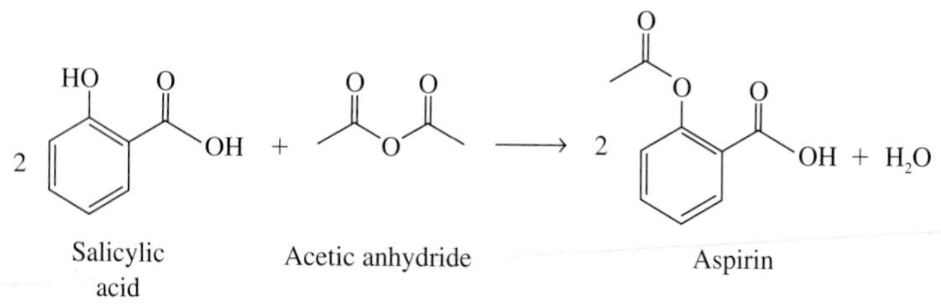

2 [Salicylic acid: HO, O, OH] + [Acetic anhydride: O, O, O] ⟶ 2 [Aspirin: O, O, O, OH] + H_2O

Salicylic acid Acetic anhydride Aspirin

If the synthesis goes in 87% yield, how many grams of salicylic acid and acetic anhydride will be required to produce 75 g of aspirin?

4.4 THE LIMITING REAGENT

The reactions encountered so far in this chapter were set up so that all the starting materials were used up at the same time. In other words, there were no "leftovers" at the end of the reaction. Chemists often run reactions in which the starting materials are measured in exactly the proper amounts as determined by the stoichiometric ratios. Just as often, however, chemical reactions are run with an *excess* of one or more starting materials. This means that one reactant will "run out" before the others. The reactant that runs out is called the **limiting reagent** because it limits how much product can be made.

We illustrate the limiting reagent concept with the bicycle analogy shown in Figure 4-5. Suppose a bicycle shop has the following parts in inventory: wheels, 8; frames, 5; handlebars, 6; and chains, 5. How many bicycles can be built with these parts? It takes two wheels, a frame, a set of handlebars, and a chain to build a bicycle. There are enough frames, handlebars, and chains to make *five* bicycles, but there are only enough wheels to make *four*. It takes two wheels to build a bicycle, so we can build four bicycles using eight wheels. Even though there are more wheels around the shop than any of the other parts, we will run out of wheels first. After four bicycles are built, the shop inventory will be bicycles, 4; wheels, 0; frames, 1; handlebars, 2; and chains, 1. There aren't enough parts left to make a fifth bicycle because we are short by two wheels. In this bicycle shop, wheels are the limiting reagent.

Chemical reactions must be analyzed in this same way. Instead of comparing numbers of bicycle parts, we compare the number of moles of each starting material on hand with the number of moles required to make the desired product. Consider, for example, the reaction of graphitic carbon with molecular oxygen to give carbon dioxide:

$$C_{(s)} + O_{2\,(g)} \rightarrow CO_{2\,(g)}$$

How much CO_2 can be made from 96.1 g of carbon and 192 g of oxygen gas? Moles are the currency of chemistry, so first we must convert masses of starting materials into moles:

Parts Inventory:

Finished Products:

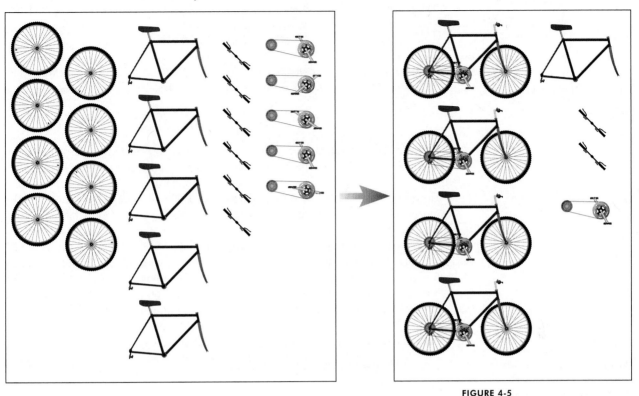

FIGURE 4-5
The number of bicycles that can be assembled is limited by whichever part runs out first. In the inventory shown in this figure, wheels are the part that runs out first.

$$\frac{96.1 \text{ g C}}{12.01 \text{ g/mol}} = 8.00 \text{ mol C} \qquad \frac{192 \text{ g } O_2}{32.00 \text{ g/mol}} = 6.00 \text{ mol } O_2$$

According to the balanced chemical equation, 1 mol of molecular oxygen and 1 mol of carbon are required for each mole of CO_2. We have 8.00 mol of carbon but only 6.00 mol of oxygen, so there is only enough oxygen to make 6.00 mol of CO_2. Thus there is not enough oxygen to consume all the carbon. When the 6.00 mol of oxygen have been consumed, 2.00 mol of carbon will be left. Although the mass of oxygen is greater than the mass of carbon, O_2 is the limiting reagent. This shows that *masses* do not indicate which of the starting materials is the limiting reagent.

Six moles of carbon dioxide is 264 g, and the 2.00 mol of unreacted carbon represent 24 g of material. Hence the total mass is 288 g, which is what we started with (96 + 192 = 264 + 24 g). In other words, mass is conserved in the reaction. Figure 4-6 illustrates this reaction at the molecular level.

Masses cannot be used to determine the "limiting reagent" in bicycle manufacture either. Five chains have less mass than eight wheels, but the wheels are used up before the chains are.

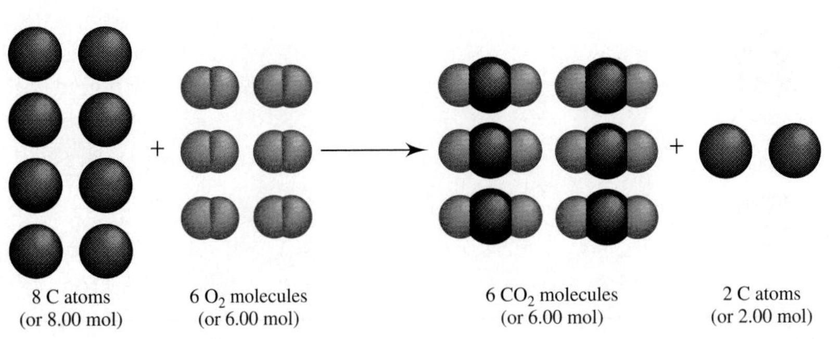

FIGURE 4-6
When eight atoms (or moles) of carbon react with six molecules (or moles) of oxygen, six molecules (or moles) of carbon dioxide are formed, and two atoms (or moles) of carbon are left over. Oxygen is the limiting reagent.

As a second example, consider the preparation of carbon tetrachloride from chlorine gas and graphitic carbon:

$$C_{(s)} + 2\,Cl_{2\,(g)} \longrightarrow CCl_{4\,(l)}$$

How many grams of carbon tetrachloride can be prepared from 36.0 g of carbon and 284 g of chlorine? First, convert from masses to moles:

$$\frac{36.0 \text{ g C}}{12.01 \text{ g/mol}} = 3.00 \text{ mol C} \qquad \frac{284 \text{ g } Cl_2}{70.91 \text{ g/mol}} = 4.00 \text{ mol } Cl_2$$

In this reaction, two chlorine molecules combine with one atom of carbon to form one molecule of CCl_4, so the mole ratio of carbon to molecular chlorine is 1:2.

There are 3.00 mol of carbon, which is enough to prepare 3.00 mol of CCl_4. However, it would take 6.00 mol of Cl_2 to make 3.00 mol of CCl_4. Because only 4.00 mol of Cl_2 are provided, chlorine will be used up before carbon. Chlorine is the limiting reagent.

Now analyze the process starting with chlorine molecules. Four molecules of Cl_2 are enough to make two molecules of CCl_4. According to the stoichiometric ratio, four molecules of chlorine react with two atoms of carbon. On the molar scale, 4.00 mol of Cl_2 combine with 2.00 mol of C to generate 2.00 mol of CCl_4. When all the chlorine has been incorporated into CCl_4, 1.00 mol of carbon will remain unreacted (Figure 4-7). Even though we started with more chlorine than carbon in terms of both mass and moles, chlorine is the limiting reagent in this example.

Number ratios cannot be used to determine the "limiting reagent" in bicycle manufacture either. Even though five chains are fewer than eight wheels, the wheels are used up before the chains because bicycle manufacture requires twice as many wheels as chains.

The limiting reagent cannot be identified by comparing masses or moles.

The limiting reagent must be identified by comparing *stoichiometric ratios* with the *numbers of moles* of starting materials.

TABLES OF AMOUNTS

A table of amounts is a convenient way to recognize the limiting reagent in a chemical reaction because it organizes the data and summarizes the calculations. A table of amounts also shows how much product will form during the reaction and how much of the excess reagent will be left over. The following is a table of amounts for the carbon tetrachloride example:

We use *amt* as an abbreviation for *amount*.

Reaction:	C	+	$2\,Cl_2$	→	CCl_4
Starting amt	3.00 mol		4.00 mol		0 mol
Change in amt	−2.00 mol		−4.00 mol		+2.00 mol
Final amt	1.00 mol		0 mol		2.00 mol

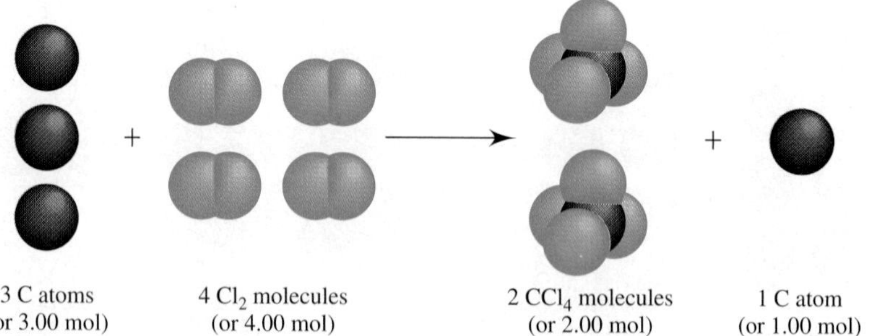

FIGURE 4-7
When three atoms (or 3.00 mol) of C react with 4 molecules (or 4.00 mol) of Cl_2, two atoms (or 2.00 mol) of C are consumed and one atom (or 1.00 mol) is left over.

The table has one column for each substance involved in the reaction. The balanced chemical equation at the top of the table identifies the substances and their stoichiometric coefficients. The first row lists the *starting* amounts for all the substances. The second row shows the *changes* that occur during the reaction, and the last row lists the amounts present *at the end* of the reaction. A table of amounts has the following three key features:

1. *All changes are related by stoichiometry.* In other words, each ratio of changes in amount must equal the mole ratio in the balanced equation. In the example above, the changes in amount for Cl_2 and C are in the ratio 2:1, the same as the mole ratio for the coefficients of Cl_2 and C in the balanced equation.
2. *Changes are negative for reactants and positive for products.* This is because the amounts of reactants *decrease* during the reaction and the amounts of products *increase* during the reaction.
3. *Each entry in the final amount row of the table is the sum of the previous entries in the same column;* that is, the starting amount plus the change in amount gives the final amount.

These three key features can be used to construct a data table for any reaction.

When a reaction goes to completion, the limiting reagent is consumed completely, so its final amount must be zero. Two facts help identify the limiting reagent. First, final amounts can never be negative. If a negative amount appears in the bottom row of the table, a mistake has been made in identifying the limiting reagent. Second, the limiting reagent is always the one whose ratio of moles to stoichiometric coefficient is smallest. In our example, dividing moles by stoichiometric coefficient for chlorine gives 2.00 for Cl_2 and 3.00 for carbon:

$$\frac{4.00 \text{ mol } Cl_2}{2 \text{ mol } Cl_2} = 2.00 \qquad \frac{3.00 \text{ mol C}}{1 \text{ mol C}} = 3.00$$

The smallest ratio indicates the limiting reagent, which is Cl_2 in this case. Thus dividing starting amounts by coefficients is a quick way to identify the limiting reagent. Sample Problems 4-6 and 4-7 illustrate the features of limiting reagents and tables of amounts.

SAMPLE PROBLEM 4-6 SIMPLE LIMITING REAGENT CALCULATION

Esters are pleasant-smelling substances responsible for the flavor and fragrance of many fruits and flowers. For example, an ester called *banana oil* gives bananas their characteristic odor. Banana oil can be prepared by the following reaction:

***Banana oil* is the common name of this ester. Like T. S. Eliot's cats, it has other names. Its unsystematic chemical name is *isopentyl acetate*. The IUPAC-approved name is *3-methylbutyl acetate*.**

OH + O H → O + H_2O
O O

Methylbutanol $C_5H_{12}O$ + Acetic acid $C_2H_4O_2$ → Banana oil $C_7H_{14}O_2$ + H_2O

How many grams of banana oil can a chemist prepare from 38 g of 3-methylbutanol and 32 g of acetic acid? Which starting material will be present in excess, and how much of it will be left over after the reaction is complete?

METHOD: The line structures summarize the chemistry: Two molecules combine to generate an ester molecule and one molecule of water. The structures may appear complicated, but the balanced chemical equation is simple because all coefficients are 1. We know the amounts of both starting materials, so the limiting reagent can be identified using moles and the stoichiometric ratio. A table of amounts simplifies the problem.

Converting the masses to moles requires the molar masses of the starting materials, which are calculated in the usual way: $C_5H_{12}O$ = 88.1 g/mol and $C_2H_4O_2$ = 60.1 g/mol.

$$\frac{38 \text{ g 3-methylbutanol}}{88.1 \text{ g/mol}} = \begin{matrix}0.431 \text{ mol}\\ \text{3-methylbutanol}\end{matrix} \qquad \frac{32 \text{ g acetic acid}}{60.1 \text{ g/mol}} = \begin{matrix}0.532 \text{ mol}\\ \text{acetic acid}\end{matrix}$$

Next we identify the limiting reagent. Because both stoichiometric coefficients are 1, the ratio of moles to coefficient is simply the number of moles of starting material. As banana oil is produced, both starting materials are consumed in equimolar amounts, so when 0.43 mol of the product has formed, all the 3-methylbutanol will be gone. The alcohol is the limiting reactant.

A table of amounts organizes all of the data.

Reaction:	$C_5H_{12}O$	+	$C_2H_4O_2$	→	$C_7H_{14}O_2$	+	H_2O
Starting amt	0.431 mol		0.532 mol		0 mol		0 mol
Change in amt	−0.431 mol		−0.431 mol		+0.431 mol		+0.431 mol
Final amt	0 mol		0.101 mol		0.431 mol		0.431 mol

Notice that the table incorporates all of the features mentioned above: The amounts in the change row all correspond to the stoichiometric coefficients, the changes are negative for starting materials and positive for products, the last entry in each column is the sum of the first two, and the final amount of the limiting reagent is zero.

Finish the problem by multiplying final amounts by the appropriate molar masses:

(0.431 mol banana oil) (130.2 g/mol) = 56 g banana oil produced

(0.101 mol acetic acid) (60.1 g/mol) = 6.1 g acetic acid left over

---

SAMPLE PROBLEM 4-7 LIMITING REAGENT CALCULATIONS

Phosphoric acid is among the top 10 U.S. industrial chemicals. Approximately 20 billion pounds of it are produced annually for fertilizers, detergents, and agents for water treatment. Phosphoric acid can be prepared by treating the mineral fluoroapatite with sulfuric acid in the presence of excess water:

$$Ca_5(PO_4)_3F + 5\,H_2SO_4 + 10\,H_2O \rightarrow 3\,H_3PO_4 + 5\,CaSO_4{\cdot}2H_2O + HF$$

Fluoroapatite — Sulfuric acid — Phosphoric acid — Gypsum — Hydrogen fluoride

If a chemical manufacturer has 2.00 metric tons of fluoroapatite and 1.50 metric tons of sulfuric acid, how much phosphoric acid can be produced? How much of the excess reactant will be left over?

METHOD: This problem can be solved using the same procedure developed in Sample Problem 4-6. The balanced chemical equation is provided, but the limiting reagent must be identified by using moles and mole ratios. As usual, we begin by converting masses into moles: 1 metric ton = 1000 kg, *MM* fluoroapatite = 504 g/mol, *MM* phosphoric acid = 98.0 g/mol, and *MM* sulfuric acid = 98.1 g/mol.

$$(1.5 \text{ tons } H_2SO_4)\left(\frac{10^3 \text{ kg}}{\text{ton}}\right)\left(\frac{10^3 \text{ g}}{\text{kg}}\right) = 1.5 \times 10^6 \text{ g } H_2SO_4$$

$$\frac{1.5 \times 10^6 \text{ g } H_2SO_4}{98.1 \text{ g/mol}} = 1.53 \times 10^4 \text{ mol } H_2SO_4$$

$$2.0 \text{ tons } Ca_5(PO_4)_3F = 2.0 \times 10^6 \text{ g } Ca_5(PO_4)_3F$$

$$\frac{2.0 \times 10^6 \text{ g } Ca_5(PO_4)_3F}{504 \text{ g/mol}} = 3.97 \times 10^3 \text{ mol } Ca_5(PO_4)_3F$$

We identify the limiting reagent by dividing the starting amount of each reagent by its stoichiometric coefficient:

$$\frac{3.97 \times 10^3 \text{ mol } Ca_5(PO_4)_3F}{1 \text{ mol } Ca_5(PO_4)_3F} = 3.97 \times 10^3$$

$$\frac{1.53 \times 10^4 \text{ mol } H_2SO_4}{5 \text{ mol } H_2SO_4} = 3.06 \times 10^3$$

Sulfuric acid has the smaller ratio, so H_2SO_4 is the limiting reagent. There are more moles of sulfuric acid than fluoroapatite, but the reaction consumes 5 times as much H_2SO_4 as $Ca_5(PO_4)_3F$.

We need to construct a table of amounts to summarize the numerical information. The problem states that water is present in excess, and it asks only for the mass of phosphoric acid. Therefore water, calcium sulfate, and hydrogen fluoride are of no concern and can be omitted from the table.

The key feature in constructing the table of amounts is the use of mole ratios in the change row. Five moles of sulfuric acid are used up for each mole of fluoroapatite. This same 5:1 ratio must also be maintained in the change row. Use the mole ratio to calculate how much fluoroapatite is consumed:

$$(1.53 \times 10^4 \text{ mol } H_2SO_4)\left(\frac{1 \text{ mol } Ca_5(PO_4)_3F}{5 \text{ mol } H_2SO_4}\right) = 3.06 \times 10^3 \text{ mol } Ca_5(PO_4)_3F \text{ consumed}$$

A similar calculation shows how much phosphoric acid is produced:

$$(1.53 \times 10^4 \text{ mol } H_2SO_4)\left(\frac{3 \text{ mol } H_3PO_4}{5 \text{ mol } H_2SO_4}\right) = 9.18 \times 10^3 \text{ mol } H_3PO_4 \text{ produced}$$

Adding these amounts to the change row allows us to complete the table. Remember to subtract the amounts of consumed reactants and to add the amount of product formed.

Reaction:	$Ca_5(PO_4)_3F$ +	$5\ H_2SO_4$ +	$10\ H_2O$ →	$3\ H_3PO_4$ +	$5\ CaSO_4{\cdot}2H_2O$ +	HF
Starting amt (10^3 mol)	3.97	15.3		0		
Change in amt	−3.06	−15.3		+9.18		
Final amt	0.91	0		9.18		

You should verify that if fluoroapatite is selected as the limiting reagent, there will be a negative amount of sulfuric acid at the end of the reaction. A negative final amount is impossible.

Completing the table tells us that the theoretical yield of phosphoric acid is 9.18×10^3 moles, which is converted to mass as follows:

$$(9.18 \times 10^3 \text{ mol } H_3PO_4)\left(\frac{98.0 \text{ g}}{\text{mol g}}\right)\left(\frac{10^{-6} \text{ ton}}{\text{g}}\right) = 0.90 \text{ tons } H_3PO_4$$

Finally, the problem asks how much fluoroapatite will be left at the end of the reaction. The table of amounts provides the number of moles, which is converted to mass as follows:

$$(9.1 \times 10^2 \text{ mol } Ca_5(PO_4)_3F)\left(\frac{504 \text{ g}}{\text{mol}}\right)\left(\frac{10^{-6} \text{ tons}}{\text{g}}\right) = 0.46 \text{ tons } Ca_5(PO_4)_3F \text{ left}$$

SECTION EXERCISES

4.4.1 Suppose that the industrial synthesis of HCN described in Sample Problem 4-3 is carried out by using 500 kg each of ammonia and methane in excess oxygen. What is the maximum mass of HCN that could be produced, and how much of which reactant would be left over?

4.4.2 Lithium metal is one of the few substances that reacts directly with molecular nitrogen:

$$6\,Li_{(s)} + N_{2\,(g)} \rightarrow 2\,Li_3N_{(s)}$$

How many grams of the product, lithium nitride, can be prepared from 4.5 g of lithium metal and 9.5 g of molecular nitrogen?

4.4.3 If 150 g of carbon reacts with 250 g of Cl_2 and the reaction goes in 87% yield, how many grams of CCl_4 are produced?

4.5 PRECIPITATION REACTIONS

The diversity of chemical reactions is immense. If we are to have any hope of making sense out of the vast expanse of chemistry, we need a system for grouping chemical reactions into categories. Within each category the reactions should share some characteristic or follow a common theme. There is no single way of grouping chemical reactions that accounts for every possible situation, but the following categories encompass much interesting and important chemistry.

1. In a **precipitation reaction,** ions in solution combine to form a solid salt.
2. In an **acid-base reaction,** a hydrogen cation is transferred from one chemical species to another.
3. In a **reduction-oxidation (redox) reaction,** electrons are transferred between chemical species.

In the final sections of this chapter, we describe these three classes of reactions, beginning with precipitation reactions.

SPECIES IN SOLUTION

Recall from Section 3.7 that a chemical reaction in which a solid forms from solution is a precipitation reaction, and the solid is called a **precipitate.** For instance, mixing colorless solutions of lead(II) nitrate and potassium iodide causes a brilliant yellow solid to precipitate from the mixture (Figure 4-8). To identify this yellow solid, we must examine the chemical species present in the solutions.

Lead(II) nitrate and potassium iodide are ionic solids. We described in Chapter 2 how ionic solids dissolve in water to form solutions containing cations and anions. A solution of lead(II) nitrate contains Pb^{2+} cations and NO_3^- anions, whereas a potassium iodide solution contains K^+ and I^-. The drawings in Figure 4-9 depict these solutions at the molecular level. Mixing the solutions gives a new solution that contains all four types of ions. A precipitate forms if any possible combination of the

FIGURE 4-8

Mixing aqueous solutions of potassium iodide and lead(II) nitrate results in the formation of a yellow precipitate. The precipitate is lead(II) iodide.

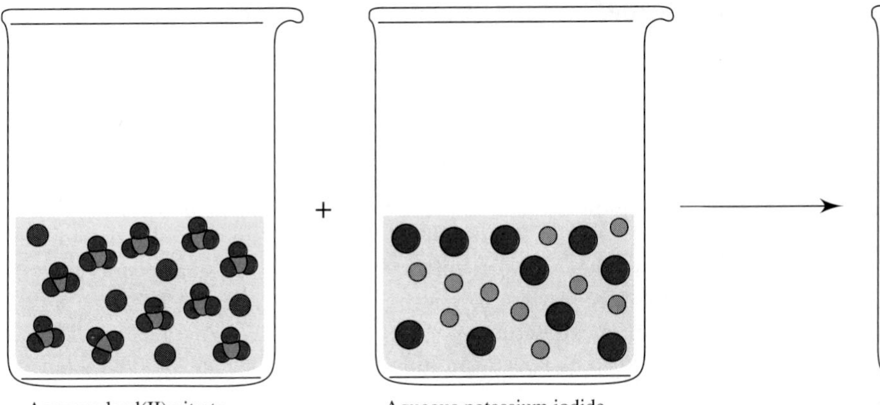

FIGURE 4-9
Molecular pictures of aqueous solutions of lead(II) nitrate, potassium iodide, and a mixture of the two solutions before any precipitation has occurred. Water molecules are present in abundance, but they have been omitted for reasons of clarity.

ions forms a salt that is **insoluble** in water. The ions in our example solution might combine in four different ways: KI, KNO_3, PbI_2 and $Pb(NO_3)_2$:

$$K^+_{(aq)} + I^-_{(aq)} \rightarrow KI_{(s)}$$

$$K^+_{(aq)} + NO_3^-{}_{(aq)} \rightarrow KNO_{3\,(s)}$$

$$Pb^{2+}_{(aq)} + 2\ NO_3^-{}_{(aq)} \rightarrow Pb(NO_3)_{2\,(s)}$$

$$Pb^{2+}_{(aq)} + 2\ I^-_{(aq)} \rightarrow PbI_{2\,(s)}$$

Two of the possibilities, KI and $Pb(NO_3)_2$, can be eliminated immediately because these two salts were contained in the starting solutions. Thus the precipitate is either lead(II) iodide or potassium nitrate. When solutions of KCl and $NaNO_3$ are mixed, no precipitate forms. This demonstrates that K^+ and NO_3^- ions do not form a solid precipitate, so the bright yellow precipitate must be lead(II) iodide, PbI_2.

As the two salt solutions mix, Pb^{2+} cations and I^- anions combine to produce lead(II) iodide, which precipitates from the solution. On standing, the yellow precipitate settles to the bottom of the beaker, leaving a colorless solution that contains potassium cations and nitrate anions (Figure 4-10).

Actually, tiny amounts of Pb^{2+} and I^- ions remain in the aqueous solution, but the concentrations are so small that we consider PbI_2 to be an insoluble salt. One liter of water dissolves just 4.1×10^{-6} moles of PbI_2 at 25 °C. In comparison, 3.5 mol of potassium nitrate dissolves in 1 L of water at 25 °C.

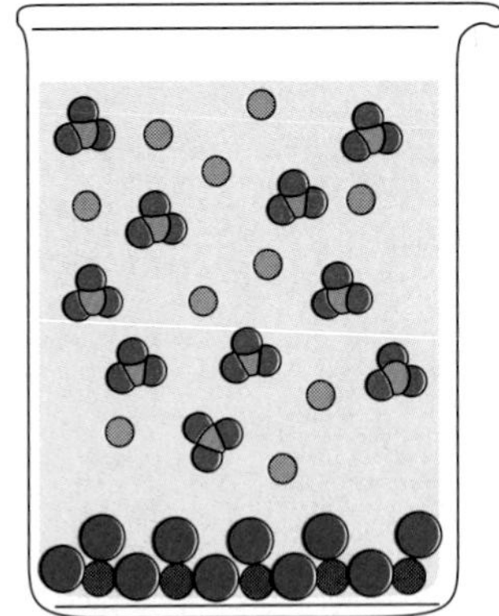

FIGURE 4-10
As soon as the solutions are mixed, solid lead(II) iodide precipitates, leaving potassium cations and nitrate anions in the solution.

NET IONIC REACTIONS

Aqueous solutions contain ions that may combine to form neutral solids, as the lead(II) iodide example illustrates. The balanced chemical equation for such a reaction has *ions* as the reactants and a *neutral ionic solid* as the product. Although one reactant carries positive charge and the other carries negative charge, the sum of all charges on the reactant side is the same as the sum of all charges on the product side. In a precipitation reaction, charges on both sides total zero. To give another example, suppose that we mix aqueous solutions of potassium hydroxide (KOH) and iron(III) chloride ($FeCl_3$) to form a mixed solution that contains K^+ and Fe^{3+} cations, Cl^- and OH^- anions. A precipitate forms, which analysis shows to be iron(III) hydroxide. Iron(III) cations combine with hydroxide anions to form neutral $Fe(OH)_3$ solid. This precipitation reaction can be expressed with a chemical equation. Iron(III) cations have +3 charges, so the neutral solid must contain three OH^- anions for every iron(III) cation. This balanced chemical equation is called the **net ionic equation:**

$$Fe^{3+}_{(aq)} + 3\ OH^-_{(aq)} \longrightarrow Fe(OH)_{3\ (s)}$$

A net ionic equation contain all species that participate in a chemical reaction. Notice that neither K^+ nor Cl^- appears in the equation for the precipitation of $Fe(OH)_3$. Although they are present in the solution, these two ions undergo no change during the precipitation reaction. Similarly, neither K^+ nor NO_3^- appears in the equation for the precipitation of PbI_2. Ions that are not involved in the chemical change are referred to as **spectator ions.** Spectator ions are omitted from the net ionic equation.

SOLUBILITY GUIDELINES

Why is lead(II) nitrate soluble in water, but lead(II) iodide is insoluble? Why is iron(III) hydroxide insoluble, but potassium hydroxide is soluble? Detailed explanations are beyond our scope at this point because solubility depends on an interplay of several chemical properties. Nevertheless, through many years of experience and research, chemists have discovered regularities in the solubilities of ionic substances. These patterns can be summarized in the following set of guidelines that identify ionic substances soluble in water.

Memorize the following:
1. The list of cations that confer solubility
2. The list of anions that confer solubility
3. The six exceptions to guideline 2
4. The four soluble salts not covered by the guidelines

1. Salts that contain the following *cations* are soluble: NH_4^+ and Group I metal cations.
2. Salts that contain the following *anions* are soluble: nitrate, chloride, bromide, iodide, sulfate, hydrogensulfate, acetate, and perchlorate.
3. Any salt not covered by guidelines 1 or 2 is insoluble.
4. There are several exceptions to guideline 2: AgX, PbX_2, Hg_2X_2 (where X = Cl, Br, or I), Ag_2SO_4, $BaSO_4$, and $PbSO_4$ are insoluble.
5. A few compounds not covered by guidelines 1 and 2 are nevertheless soluble: $Ba(OH)_2$, MgS, CaS, and BaS are soluble.

Solubilities actually cover a large and continuous range from virtually insoluble to highly soluble. Some compounds fall in between soluble and insoluble and must be categorized as slightly soluble or moderately soluble. Including these intermediate categories would needlessly complicate the guidelines.

Our guidelines predict whether a salt is soluble or insoluble. For example, will $Fe(OH)_2$ dissolve in water? According to the guidelines, Fe^{2+} is not a cation that confers solubility (guideline 1), and OH^- is not an anion that confers solubility (guideline 2). Because $Fe(OH)_2$ does not appear among the exceptions (guideline 5), it must be insoluble (guideline 3). Sample Problem 4-8 further illustrates the solubility guidelines and net ionic equations.

SAMPLE PROBLEM 4-8 SALT SOLUBILITY

Will a precipitate form when solutions of magnesium sulfate and barium chloride are mixed? If so, write the net ionic equation for the reaction.

METHOD: After mixing, the solution will contain all the ions of the original solutions. First list these ions and then apply the solubility guidelines to find out whether any combination of cations and anions gives an insoluble salt. Then write the net ionic equation that gives a neutral salt.

The ions present are Mg^{2+}, SO_4^{2-}, Ba^{2+}, and Cl^-, so the possible combinations are $MgSO_4$, $MgCl_2$, $BaCl_2$, and $BaSO_4$.

Guideline 2 predicts that salts of chloride and sulfate are soluble. Therefore no precipitate will form unless one of the combinations is included among the five exceptions listed in guideline 4. Barium sulfate is one of these exceptions, so it is an insoluble salt.

Solid barium sulfate will be formed when the two solutions are combined. Each ion carries two units of charge, so they combine in 1:1 stoichiometric ratio:

$$Ba^{2+}_{(aq)} + SO_4^{2-}{}_{(aq)} \rightarrow BaSO_{4\,(s)}$$

PRECIPITATION STOICHIOMETRY

Precipitation reactions can be treated quantitatively. For example, how much $Fe(OH)_3$ will form when 50.0 mL of 1.50 M NaOH is mixed with 35.0 mL of 1.00 M $FeCl_3$ solution? A mixture of the two solutions contains Fe^{3+} and Na^+ cations and OH^- and Cl^- anions. Sodium and chloride ions are not involved in the precipitation, so we can ignore these spectator ions in our calculations. First we calculate the number of moles of Fe^{3+} and OH^-.

$$(35.0\text{ mL})\left(\frac{10^{-3}\text{ L}}{\text{mL}}\right)\left(\frac{1.00\text{ mol FeCl}_3}{1.00\text{ L}}\right)\left(\frac{1\text{ mol Fe}^{3+}}{1\text{ mol FeCl}_3}\right) = 0.0350\text{ mol Fe}^{3+}$$

If the conversion from molarity to moles is unclear to you, you should review Section 3.7.

$$(50.0\text{ mL})\left(\frac{10^{-3}\text{ L}}{\text{mL}}\right)\left(\frac{1.50\text{ mol NaOH}}{1.00\text{ L}}\right)\left(\frac{1\text{ mol OH}^-}{1\text{ mol NaOH}}\right) = 0.0750\text{ mol OH}^-$$

Because there are fixed amounts of Fe^{3+} and OH^-, this is a limiting reagent situation: Whichever ion is consumed first determines how much $Fe(OH)_3$ precipitates. Dividing the numbers of moles by the stoichiometric coefficients identifies the limiting reagent:

$$\frac{0.0350\text{ mol Fe}^{3+}}{1\text{ mol Fe}^{3+}} = 0.0350 \qquad \frac{0.0750\text{ mol OH}^-}{3\text{ mol OH}^-} = 0.0250$$

Hydroxide has the smaller ratio, so it is the limiting reagent. A table of amounts helps determine the number of moles of $Fe(OH)_3$ that precipitates from solution.

Reaction:	Fe^{3+}	+	$3\ OH^-$	→	$Fe(OH)_3$
Starting amt	0.0350 mol		0.0750 mol		0
Change in amt	−0.0250 mol		−0.0750 mol		+0.0250 mol
Final amt	0.0100 mol		0		0.0250 mol

Mixing the two solutions will produce 0.025 mol of $Fe(OH)_3$ precipitate. Notice that this precipitation reaction is treated just like other limiting reagent problems. Sample Problems 4-9 and 4-10 further illustrate the application of general stoichiometric principles to precipitation reactions.

SAMPLE PROBLEM 4-9 PERCENT YIELD OF PRECIPITATION

Silver bromide is a major component of photographic films and paper. When a film manufacturer mixed 75.0 L of a 1.25 M solution of silver nitrate with 90.0 L of a 1.50 M potassium bromide solution, 17.0 kg of silver bromide solid was obtained. What was the percent yield of this precipitation reaction?

METHOD: The problem asks for a percent yield, so we need to compare the actual yield, 17.0 kg, with the theoretical yield. The presence of two solutions of known concentration signals a limiting reagent situation.

First, identify all species present in solution and write a balanced net ionic equation. The two solutions contain four different ions: K^+, Br^-, Ag^+, NO_3^-. The identified precipitate, AgBr, is the only insoluble salt among the various combinations. The net ionic equation is:

$$Ag^+_{(aq)} + Br^-_{(aq)} \longrightarrow AgBr_{(s)}$$

The 1:1 stoichiometric ratio between Ag^+ and Br^- makes it easy to identify the limiting reagent.

$$\text{mol } Ag^+ = MV = (1.25 \text{ mol/L})(75.0 \text{ L}) = 93.8 \text{ mol}$$

$$\text{mol } Br^- = MV = (1.50 \text{ mol/L})(90.0 \text{ L}) = 135 \text{ mol}$$

Clearly, Ag^+ is limiting, so the precipitation reaction can produce no more than 93.8 mol of AgBr. The theoretical yield of the salt in kilograms is calculated using the molar mass:

$$\text{Theoretical yield} = (\text{mol AgBr})\ (MM \text{ AgBr})$$

$$\text{Theoretical yield} = (93.8 \text{ mol})(187.8 \text{ g/mol})(10^{-3} \text{ kg/g}) = 17.6 \text{ kg}$$

Now we can compute the percent yield:

$$\text{Percent yield} = \left(\frac{\text{Actual yield}}{\text{Theoretical yield}}\right)(100\%) = \left(\frac{17.0 \text{ kg}}{17.6 \text{ kg}}\right)(100\%) = 96.6\%$$

Silver is an expensive substance, so it is important to maximize the yield of AgBr based on silver. Consequently, silver ion is always made the limiting reagent in this preparation. In other words, the precipitation is always carried out with a small excess of bromide ions to ensure that as much Ag^+ precipitates as possible.

SAMPLE PROBLEM 4-10 PRECIPITATION STOICHIOMETRY

A white precipitate forms when 200 mL of 0.200 M potassium phosphate solution is mixed with 300 mL of 0.250 M calcium chloride solution. Write the net ionic equation that describes this process. Calculate the mass of the precipitate that forms, and identify the ions remaining in solution.

METHOD: As always, begin this kind of problem by determining what species are present in the reaction mixture. Next, use the solubility guidelines to identify the precipitate. After writing the balanced net ionic reaction, use solution stoichiometry and a table of amounts to find the required quantities.

The combined solutions contain four different ions: Ca^{2+}, K^+, Cl^-, and PO_4^{3-}. According to the solubility guidelines, potassium salts and chloride salts are soluble, so the white precipitate must be calcium phosphate. To balance the charges, three Ca^{2+} ions must combine with two PO_4^{3-} ions. Potassium and chloride are spectator ions.

If you had trouble writing the balanced equation, you should review Section 4.1.

$$3\ Ca^{2+}_{(aq)} + 2\ PO_4^{3-}{}_{(aq)} \longrightarrow Ca_3(PO_4)_{2\,(s)}$$

To calculate the mass of the precipitate, we need to know the number of moles of Ca^{2+} and PO_4^{3-}:

$$(200 \text{ mL})\left(\frac{10^{-3} \text{ L}}{\text{L}}\right)\left(\frac{0.200 \text{ mol } K_3PO_4}{\text{L}}\right)\left(\frac{1 \text{ mol } PO_4^{3-}}{1 \text{ mol } K_3PO_4}\right) = 0.0400 \text{ mol } PO_4^{3-}$$

$$(300 \text{ mL})\left(\frac{10^{-3} \text{ L}}{\text{mL}}\right)\left(\frac{0.250 \text{ mol } CaCl_2}{\text{L}}\right)\left(\frac{1 \text{ mol } Ca^{2+}}{1 \text{ mol } CaCl_2}\right) = 0.0750 \text{ mol } Ca^{2+}$$

Identify the limiting reagent by dividing the numbers of moles by the stoichiometric coefficients:

$$\frac{0.0750 \text{ mol } Ca^{2+}}{3 \text{ mol } Ca^{2+}} = 0.0250 \qquad \frac{0.0400 \text{ mol } PO_4^{3-}}{2 \text{ mol } PO_4^{3-}} = 0.0200$$

The smaller value identifies phosphate as the limiting reagent, so its final amount will be zero. Using this information, construct a table of amounts such that all of the PO_4^{3-} is converted to calcium phosphate:

Reaction:	$3\ Ca^{2+}$	+	$2\ PO_4^{3-}$	→	$Ca_3(PO_4)_2$
Starting amt	0.0750 mol		0.0400 mol		0 mol
Change in amt	−0.0600 mol		−0.0400 mol		+0.0200 mol
Final amt	0.0150 mol		0 mol		0.0200 mol

If we tried to make calcium the limiting reagent, precipitation would require 0.0500 mol of phosphate, leaving a negative value for the final amount of phosphate. Final amounts can never be negative.

The table of amounts shows that 0.0200 mol of calcium phosphate will precipitate. We can now compute the mass of product:

$$(0.0200 \text{ mol } Ca_3(PO_4)_2)\ (310.2 \text{ g/mol}) = 6.20 \text{ g } Ca_3(PO_4)_2$$

The second part of the problem asks us to identify the ions remaining in solution. There are two spectator ions in the mixture: K^+ and Cl^-. In addition, the table of amounts reveals that some of the Ca^{2+} remains in solution after the precipitation reaction.

The ions remaining in solution are K^+, Cl^-, and excess Ca^{2+}.

SYNTHESIS VIA PRECIPITATION

The solubility guidelines can be used to design ways of making salts. Suppose that we want to prepare barium sulfate, $BaSO_4$. This substance is opaque to x rays, so it is often used to visualize the intestinal tract. Patients are given a "barium cocktail," and then the areas of interest are irradiated. Barium sulfate absorbs the x rays to give a "picture" of the intestines, as shown in Figure 4-11. Soluble barium salts are poisonous, but $BaSO_4$ is insoluble in water, so it can be administered safely. (Only 1.0×10^{-5} mol dissolves in 1 L of water at 25 °C.)

A source of soluble Ba^{2+} cations is required for the synthesis of barium sulfate. That is to say, we can use any barium salt that is soluble, such as barium nitrate, barium acetate, and barium chloride. A soluble source of sulfate ions is also needed, such as Na_2SO_4 or $(NH_4)_2SO_4$. Because Ba^{2+} ions are toxic, it is important to precipitate all of the barium, so the two salts are measured out in quantities that will ensure that barium is the limiting reagent. Each salt is dissolved separately in water, and then the two solutions are mixed. After precipitation the $BaSO_4$ is collected by filtration. Finally the mass of the product is measured, and the yield of the reaction is calculated. It is important to know the yield of the reaction because any toxic barium ions left in the solution will have to be disposed of properly. Sample Problem 4-11 shows how to apply these principles to the synthesis of $Ni(OH)_2$.

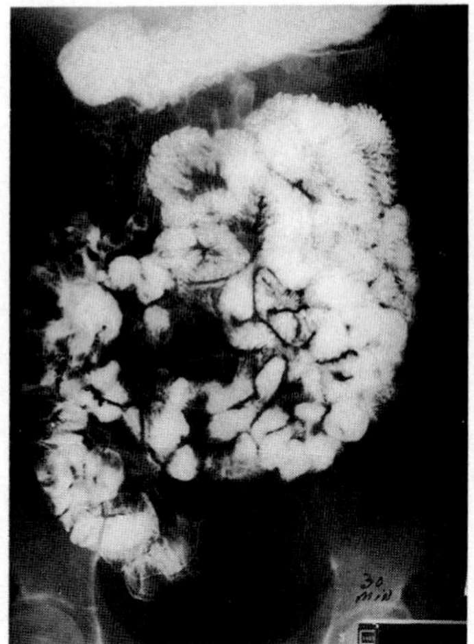

FIGURE 4-11
Because barium sulfate does not transmit x rays, an intestinal tract containing barium sulfate shows up clearly on an x-ray photograph.

SAMPLE PROBLEM 4-11 SYNTHESIS VIA PRECIPITATION

Design a synthesis of 1.0 g of $Ni(OH)_2$.

METHOD: The synthesis of nickel hydroxide requires soluble sources of Ni^{2+} ions and OH^- ions. We can choose any pair of appropriate salts that happen to be available in the laboratory. Common cations that confer solubility are Na^+ and K^+, so the hydroxide of either would be an appropriate choice. As a source of Ni^{2+}, choose a salt containing an anion that confers solubility, such as Cl^-, NO_3^-, or SO_4^{2-}. Two compounds that are inexpensive and found in many laboratories are NaOH and $NiSO_4{\cdot}6H_2O$ (nickel(II) sulfate hexahydrate).

To calculate the masses that should be used, begin by writing the net ionic equation for the synthesis:

$$Ni^{2+}_{(aq)} + 2\ OH^-_{(aq)} \rightarrow Ni(OH)_{2\ (s)}$$

By now, the conversion of 1.0 g of $Ni(OH)_2$ to 0.011 mol should be straightforward. This means that we need 0.011 mol of Ni^{2+} and 0.022 mol of hydroxide, which can be provided by 0.011 mol of $NiSO_4{\cdot}6H_2O$ and 0.022 mol of NaOH. Use molar masses to determine the masses of the two starting materials:

$$(0.011\ \text{mol}\ NiSO_4{\cdot}6H_2O)\left(\frac{262.8\ \text{g}}{\text{mol}}\right) = 2.9\ \text{g}\ NiSO_4{\cdot}6H_2O$$

$$(0.022\ \text{mol NaOH})\left(\frac{40.00\ \text{g}}{\text{mol}}\right) = 0.88\ \text{g NaOH}$$

The proper amount of nickel sulfate is measured out on an analytical balance and dissolved in water. Because nickel ions are toxic, we should use an excess of sodium hydroxide. It does not matter exactly how much NaOH is used, as long as the mass is greater than 0.88 g. The appropriate amount of sodium hydroxide is dissolved in water, and then this solution is added to the nickel solution. The desired product forms a precipitate, which is isolated by filtration. One of the attractive features of this synthesis is that the ions left in the solution, Na^+, SO_4^{2-}, and excess OH^-, are nontoxic.

SECTION EXERCISES

4.5.1 Decide whether the following salts are soluble or insoluble: (a) sodium acetate; (b) silver nitrate; (c) barium hydroxide; (d) calcium oxide; (e) lead(II) sulfate; (f) zinc chloride; and (g) manganese(II) sulfide.

4.5.2 Design a synthesis of 1.5 g of silver sulfate.

4.5.3 Cadmium ions are environmental pollutants found in mining waste, metal plating, water pipes, and industrial discharge. Cadmium ions replace zinc ions in biochemistry and cause kidney damage, high blood pressure, and brittle bones. Dissolved Cd^{2+} impurities can be removed from a water sample by precipitation with sulfide ions. What is the minimum mass of ammonium sulfide required to precipitate all the Cd^{2+} from 5.0×10^3 L of water contaminated with 0.087 M cadmium ions? Even though Cd^{2+} is a pollutant, cadmium sulfide is a brilliant orange solid that has often been used as a pigment for highway signs.

4.6 ACID-BASE REACTIONS

One of the most fundamental and important chemical reactions is the combination of a hydroxide ion and a hydronium ion to produce two molecules of water:

$$OH^-_{(aq)} + H_3O^+_{(aq)} \rightarrow 2\ H_2O_{\ (l)}$$

A molecular view of this reaction shows that each hydroxide anion accepts one hydrogen atom from the hydronium cation (Figure 4-12). To be more specific, it is a hydrogen *cation* that is transferred. The reaction takes place by way of a collision between H_3O^+ and OH^- ions. The hydroxide anion accepts a hydrogen cation from the hydronium cation to give two neutral water molecules.

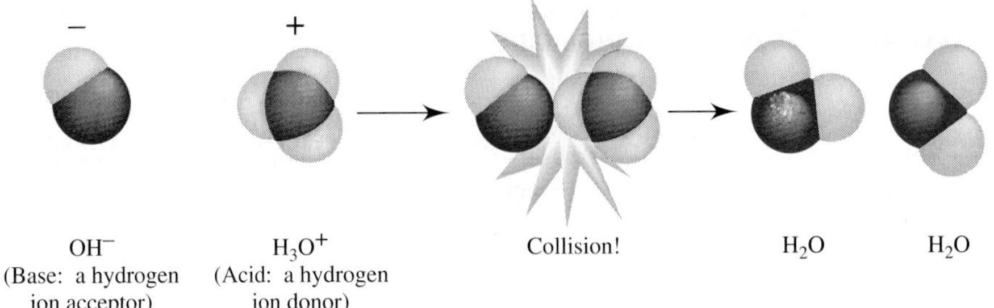

FIGURE 4-12
Proton transfer between H_3O^+ and OH^-.

PROTON TRANSFER

A hydrogen cation is a hydrogen atom that has lost its single electron. Removing the electron leaves a hydrogen nucleus, which is just a proton, so a hydrogen cation is the same thing as a proton. Thus any reaction in which H^+ moves from one species to another is called a **proton transfer reaction.** Protons are unstable by themselves. In aqueous solution, they associate with water molecules to form hydronium ions.

In many books you will see the hydronium ion abbreviated as $H^+_{(aq)}$ or just H^+. We prefer H_3O^+ because it serves as a reminder of the molecular structure of the hydronium ion.

The production of water from hydroxide and hydronium ions is the most fundamental example of an acid-base reaction. Any reaction in which a *proton is transferred* from one substance to another is an acid-base reaction. In an acid-base reaction an acid molecule donates a proton, and a base molecule accepts the proton.

Acid: ***A substance that donates protons.***

Base: ***A substance that accepts protons.***

Defining acids and bases in terms of proton transfer is known as the Brønsted-Lowry definition of acids and bases. In Chapter 18, we introduce a second definition of acids and bases, the Lewis definition, which focuses attention on electron movement rather than proton movement. Until then, acid-base always means "proton transfer."

In Figure 4-12 the hydronium ion acts as an acid because it donates a proton to a base. The hydroxide anion acts as a base because it accepts a proton from an acid. Because a proton carries a charge of $+1$, the -1 charge of the hydroxide ion is neutralized in this reaction. Likewise the single positive charge on a hydronium cation is neutralized when it donates a proton to a base. Thus this reaction of an acid and a base is also called a **neutralization reaction.** Not all acid-base reactions are neutralization reactions, as we shall see shortly.

Acids and bases are abundant in chemistry. Any species that can give up a proton to another substance is classified as an acid, and any substance that can accept a proton from another substance is classified as a base. Of the top 12 industrial chemicals, three are acids—sulfuric acid, phosphoric acid, and nitric acid—and three are bases—ammonia, calcium oxide (also called *lime*), and sodium hydroxide. A fourth acid, hydrogen chloride (HCl), is in the top 30 industrial chemicals.

The top 50 industrial chemicals in industrial production in the United States are listed in Appendix J.

A solution of hydrochloric acid is produced when hydrogen chloride dissolves in water. Hydrogen chloride is a colorless gas with a pungent, irritating odor. In water, hydrogen chloride acts as an acid because it donates a proton to a water molecule, giving a hydronium ion and a chloride ion. In this reaction, which is shown in Figure 4-13, water acts as a base, accepting a proton from an acid (hydrogen chloride). Notice that proton transfer always involves an acid and base.

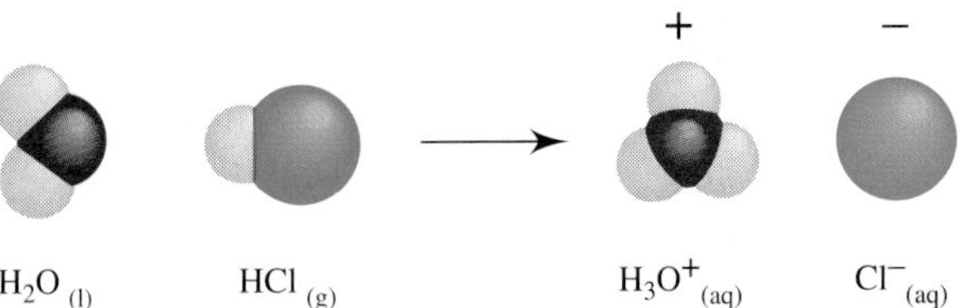

FIGURE 4-13
Proton transfer between HCl and H_2O.

SAMPLE PROBLEM 4-13 WEAK ACID REACTION WITH OH^- IONS

Write the balanced net ionic equation for the reaction of phosphoric acid with an excess of aqueous potassium hydroxide.

METHOD: When an acid and a base react, the acid transfers a proton to the base. We must identify each and determine the number of protons that can be transferred.

An aqueous solution of potassium hydroxide contains potassium ions and hydroxide ions. Hydroxide is a powerful base that removes all acidic hydrogen atoms from strong and weak acids. An excess of potassium hydroxide solution means that we have enough hydroxide to remove all three acidic hydrogen atoms from phosphoric acid. Each proton combines with a hydroxide anion to make a water molecule. Because phosphoric acid has three acidic hydrogen atoms, it produces three molecules of water in the presence of excess hydroxide:

$$H_3PO_{4\,(aq)} + 3\,OH^-_{(aq)} \rightarrow PO_4^{3-}{}_{(aq)} + 3\,H_2O_{\,(l)}$$

ACID NOMENCLATURE

The conventions for naming acids are summarized as follows:

1. Halogen acids are named by using the prefix *hydro-* and the suffix *-ic*. In aqueous solution, HCl is hydrochloric acid.
2. An acid that contains a polyatomic anion whose name ends in *-ate* has a name ending in *-ic*. For example, H_2CO_3 contains the carbonate polyatomic anion, so H_2CO_3 is carbonic acid. Likewise $HClO_4$ is perchloric acid.
3. An acid that contains a polyatomic anion whose name ends in *-ite* has a name ending in *-ous*. For example, HNO_2 contains nitrite and is nitrous acid, and H_2SO_3 is sulfurous acid.
4. In the chemical formulas of acids that are not carbon based, acidic hydrogen atoms are listed first: H_2SO_4, HCl, and so on.
5. The names of acids containing CO_2H all end in *-ic*, and their corresponding anions end in *-ate*. The chemical formulas of these acids usually contain the CO_2H group at the end of the formula: CH_3CO_2H is acetic acid, and $C_6H_5CO_2H$ is benzoic acid.

Acetate is an anion that confers solubility, and sodium benzoate is a common food preservative.

$$\underset{\text{Acetic acid}}{CH_3CO_2H} + OH^- \rightarrow \underset{\text{Acetate anion}}{CH_3CO_2^-} + H_2O$$

$$\underset{\text{Benzoic acid}}{C_6H_5CO_2H} + OH^- \longrightarrow \underset{\text{Benzoate anion}}{C_6H_5CO_2^-} + H_2O$$

BASES

We noted earlier that three top industrial chemicals are bases: ammonia, calcium oxide, and sodium hydroxide. Sodium hydroxide and calcium oxide are examples of **strong bases** because they dissolve readily in water, giving stoichiometric quantities of hydroxide ions:

$$NaOH_{(s)} \longrightarrow Na^+_{(aq)} + OH^-_{(aq)}$$

$$CaO_{(s)} + H_2O_{(l)} \longrightarrow Ca^{2+}_{(aq)} + 2\ OH^-_{(aq)}$$

Solutions of strong bases react readily with strong or weak acids because hydroxide anions are very good proton acceptors.

Ammonia, on the other hand, is an example of a **weak base.** A weak base does *not* readily accept protons from water molecules, but it does accept protons from hydronium ions. Ammonia reacts quantitatively with hydronium ions to generate ammonium ions:

$$NH_{3\ (aq)} + H_3O^+_{(aq)} \longrightarrow NH_4^+{}_{(aq)} + H_2O_{(l)}$$

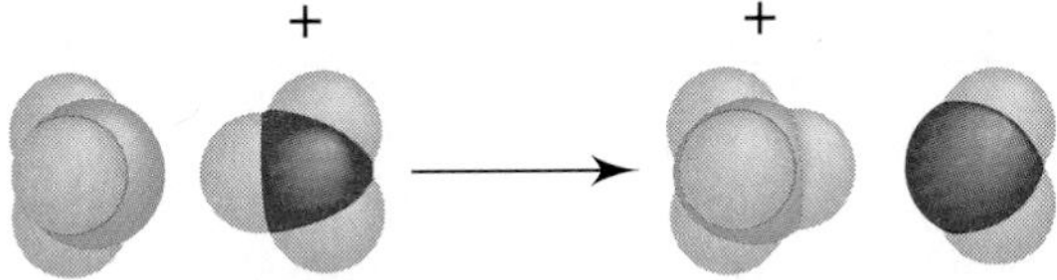

ACID-BASE STOICHIOMETRY

The quantitative aspects of acid-base chemistry depend on the same principles that were introduced earlier in this chapter. Sample Problem 4-14 uses a reaction of the hydroxide ion to illustrate the essential features of aqueous acid-base stoichiometry.

SAMPLE PROBLEM 4-14 ACID-BASE STOICHIOMETRY

What volume of 0.050 M nitric acid solution is needed to neutralize 0.075 L of 0.065 M $Ba(OH)_2$?

METHOD: As always, the first step is to think about the molecules and ions present in solution and the reactions that might occur among them. Then we can set up the appropriate molar equalities and work toward a quantitative solution.

Nitric acid is one of the six strong acids, so an aqueous solution of nitric acid contains hydronium ions and nitrate ions. A solution of $Ba(OH)_2$ contains Ba^{2+} and OH^- ions.

The two solutions that are mixed together contain four different ions and neutral water: NO_3^-, Ba^{2+}, H_3O^+, OH^-, and H_2O. Among these four ions, we must consider the possibility of precipitate formation and proton transfer.

We recognize hydronium ions as strongly acidic and hydroxide ions as strongly basic, so acid-base neutralization will take place almost instantaneously. In fact, by the time the solutions have mixed thoroughly, the proton transfer reaction will be complete:

$$H_3O^+_{(aq)} + OH^-_{(aq)} \longrightarrow 2\ H_2O_{(l)}$$

According to the solubility guidelines, all nitrate salts are soluble, so a precipitation reaction will not occur.

After sorting out the chemistry that will occur, we begin working toward the quantitative solution to the problem by thinking about moles. First determine how many moles of hydroxide must be neutralized.

$$\text{Mol} = MV$$

$$(0.075 \text{ L solution})\left(\frac{0.065 \text{ mol Ba(OH)}_2}{\text{L solution}}\right)\left(\frac{2 \text{ mol OH}^-}{1 \text{ mol Ba(OH)}_2}\right) = 9.75 \times 10^{-3} \text{ mol OH}^-$$

Neutralization requires one hydronium ion for every hydroxide ion, so we need 9.75×10^{-3} mol of hydronium ion.

$$\frac{9.75 \times 10^{-3} \text{ mol H}_3\text{O}^+}{0.050 \text{ mol H}_3\text{O}^+/\text{L}} = 2.0 \times 10^{-1} \text{ L solution}$$

The hydroxide ions are neutralized by 0.20 L of the acid solution. This is a bit more than twice the volume of the base solution. The answer is reasonable because each mole of $Ba(OH)_2$ contains 2 mol of hydroxide, but each mole of HNO_3 supplies just 1 mol of H_3O^+. Furthermore, the molarity of the base solution is larger than the molarity of the acid solution.

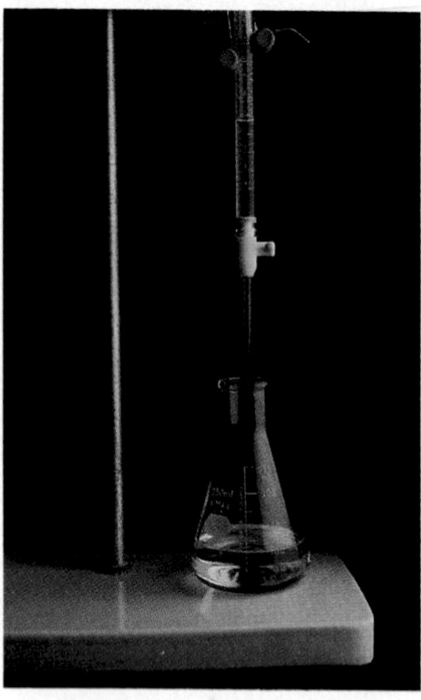

FIGURE 4-15

A buret set up to titrate an acidic solution with a basic solution. When phenolphthalein is used as the indicator, the solution turns pink, as shown, at the stoichiometric point.

TITRATION

Analysis of acids and bases is often carried out by adding one to the other until the amount of acid exactly matches the amount of base. The solution to be analyzed is placed in a beaker or flask. Then the other solution, called the **titrant,** is added slowly by means of a calibrated measuring vessel called a **buret.** This process is called **titration.** Figure 4-15 shows a buret set up to carry out a titration. In one type of titration a solution of a strong base, such as sodium hydroxide, is added slowly to a solution that contains an unknown amount of acid. The hydroxide solution is added slowly to the unknown solution in the beaker. Each ion of hydroxide added to the acid solution accepts one proton from a molecule of acid. As the titration proceeds, fewer and fewer acid molecules remain in the beaker, but the solution is nevertheless acidic. At the **stoichiometric point,** just enough hydroxide ions have been added to react with every transferrable proton present in the beaker before the titration was started. The hydroxide ions in the next drop of titrant do not react because acid molecules are no longer present in the solution. Before the stoichiometric point, the solution contains excess acid. After passing the stoichiometric point, the solution contains excess OH^-.

At the stoichiometric point, the amount of base added exactly matches the amount of acid originally present. Therefore the concentration of the unknown acid solution can be calculated from the volume of titrant required to reach the stoichiometric point.

The phrase *moles of acidic hydrogen* refers to the total moles of acidic protons. Thus 1 mol of H_3PO_4 contains 3 mol of acidic hydrogen.

$$\text{Stoichiometric point:} \quad \text{mol OH}^- \text{ added} = \text{mol acidic hydrogen present} \qquad \textbf{(4-3)}$$

Knowing the molarity and volume of the titrant, we can compute the number of moles of hydroxide required to react with all the acid.

How do we know when the stoichiometric point of a titration has been reached? Because we cannot "see" the hydroxide ions directly, we place a tiny amount of a substance called an **indicator** in the solution to be titrated. An indicator is a molecule whose color depends on the concentration of hydroxide ions. A properly chosen indicator shows a distinct color change when the solution changes from excess acid to excess hydroxide at the stoichiometric point. This color change signals an end to the titration. As soon as we see the color change, we stop adding base and measure the volume that has been delivered from the buret. Sample Problem 4-15 illustrates how to calculate concentration from a titration volume.

SAMPLE PROBLEM 4-15 ACID-BASE TITRATION

Vinegar is acidic because it is a solution of acetic acid in water. A 5.000-mL sample of vinegar is diluted to 150.0 mL with water and titrated with 0.1250 M sodium hydroxide. It takes 38.65 mL to reach the stoichiometric point. What is the molarity of acetic acid in the vinegar?

METHOD: In any acid-base titration, at the stoichiometric point the moles of base added equal the moles of acidic hydrogen originally present. We need a balanced equation describing the proton-transfer reaction. Acetic acid, whose formula is CH_3CO_2H, donates the proton that becomes attached to the oxygen atom of a hydroxide ion:

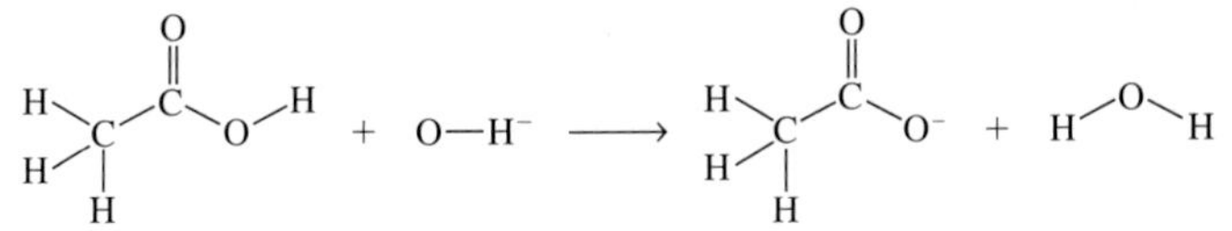

$$CH_3CO_2H + OH^- \longrightarrow CH_3CO_2^- + H_2O$$

Equation 4-3 can be used to calculate the moles of acidic hydrogen present, which equals the number of moles of acetic acid:

$$\text{mol OH}^- \text{ added} = \text{mol acidic hydrogen present}$$

$$\text{mol OH}^- \text{ added} = MV$$

$$\text{mol OH}^- \text{ added} = (0.1250 \text{ mol/L})(38.65 \text{ mL})(10^{-3} \text{ L/mL}) = 4.8313 \times 10^{-3} \text{ mol}$$

This is also the number of moles of acetic acid in the original sample. Because the original sample was 5.000 mL of vinegar, its molarity is

$$M = \frac{\text{mol}}{V} = \frac{4.8313 \times 10^{-3} \text{ mol}}{(5.000 \text{ mL})(10^{-3} \text{ L/mL})} = 0.9663 \text{ mol/L}$$

Notice that the dilution factor in this procedure has nothing to do with the calculations because the addition of water to the sample does not change the number of moles of acid present. We are interested in the molarity of the vinegar *before the titration,* not at the stoichiometric point.

Titrations require a titrant whose concentration is known. In Sample Problem 4-15 the NaOH solution used as the titrant was known to be 0.1250 M. The concentration of the titrant is determined by a titration called **standardization.** An excellent acid for standardization is potassium hydrogenphthalate, $KHC_8H_4O_4$, commonly abbreviated as KHP.

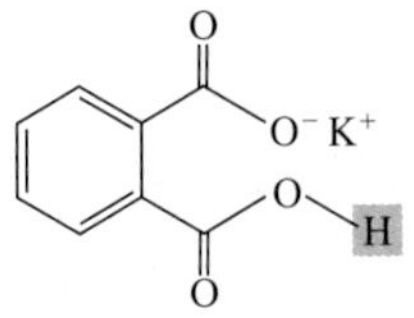

In the abbreviation KHP, the *P* stands for phthalate, whose full chemical formula is $C_8H_4O_4^{2-}$.

One molecule of KHP contains one acidic hydrogen atom, and the compound is easily obtained as a highly pure solid. A known number of moles of KHP can be weighed on an analytical balance, dissolved in pure water, and then titrated with the base solution that we wish to standardize. Sample Problem 4-16 illustrates the standardization procedure, and Box 4-1 discusses standards for chemical analysis.

BOX 4-1

STANDARDS FOR CHEMICAL ANALYSIS

Potassium hydrogenphthalate is frequently used when a chemist needs to prepare a solution containing an accurately known number of moles of acid. It is referred to as a *standard substance* because it is used as a standard against which amounts of base are compared. Why do we need standard substances, and what characteristics must they have?

Standard substances are required because many compounds change chemical composition in storage. A good example is sodium hydroxide, which is sold as waxy white pellets. Solid NaOH readily absorbs water vapor from the atmosphere. This process is so rapid that on a humid day the mass of NaOH pellets may increase measurably while they are on the balance pan. The mass of pellets of sodium hydroxide is partly NaOH and partly H_2O. Because the water content of these pellets is variable, it is impossible to know how much of the total mass is NaOH. Thus we cannot determine moles of NaOH by mass measurement. Before we can be confident of the molarity of any solution of NaOH, it must be standardized by titrating a sample of KHP.

Why not use HCl as a standard? Hydrogen chloride is a gas whose mass is not easy to measure. Furthermore, the molarity of HCl in water can vary widely, and the molarity of a solution may change as HCl vapor escapes. If you remove the cap from a bottle of concentrated HCl (under a hood, because HCl fumes are caustic), you are likely to see signs that HCl vapor is escaping. Hydrogen chloride is not a reliable standard because it is not easy to measure directly the number of moles of acid present.

The properties of potassium hydrogenphthalate are characteristic of a good standard. It is easily prepared as a white, crystalline solid of high purity. Although it slowly absorbs water on exposure to humid air, this water can be driven off by heating the solid in an oven at about 110 °C. A heat-dried sample of this acid can be relied on to be 100% potassium hydrogenphthalate. Thus an accurately determined mass of KHP contains an accurately known number of moles of acid.

Strong acids can be standardized by titrating solutions of sodium carbonate. Like KHP, oven-dried Na_2CO_3 has a stable composition. In solution it generates carbonate anions, which are good proton acceptors. The titration reaction involves capture of two protons by each carbonate anion:

$$CO_3^{2-} + 2\,H_3O^+ \rightarrow H_2CO_3 + 2\,H_2O$$

Thus the molar equality describing this standardization reaction follows:

$$\text{mol } Na_2CO_3 = 2(\text{mol } H_3O^+)$$

Acid solutions can also be standardized with KHP but in an indirect way. For example, to standardize a solution of HCl, a chemist might first standardize a solution of NaOH by titrating a sample of KHP. The molarity of the hydrochloric acid solution could then be determined by titrating a sample with the standardized NaOH.

SAMPLE PROBLEM 4-16 STANDARDIZATIONS

A biological chemist needed to standardize a solution of KOH. A sample of potassium hydrogenphthalate weighing 0.6745 g was dissolved in 100.0 mL of water. A drop of indicator was added to the KHP solution, which was then titrated with the KOH solution. The titration required 41.75 mL of base to reach the stoichiometric point. Find the molarity of the KOH solution.

METHOD: First we must identify the chemistry. This is an acid-base titration in which KHP (the acid) reacts with OH^- (the base). We use the molar equality of acid and base at the stoichiometric point, together with the equations that link moles with mass and volume.

The net reaction shows there is a 1:1 molar ratio between KHP and hydroxide:

$$HC_8H_4O_4^- + OH^- \rightarrow C_8H_4O_4^{2-} + H_2O$$

$$\text{mol KHP} = \frac{0.6745 \text{ g}}{204.2 \text{ g/mol}} = 3.3031 \times 10^{-3} \text{ mol}$$

At the stoichiometric point of the titration, the moles of hydroxide added from the buret equal the moles of KHP:

$$\text{mol base added} = 3.3031 \times 10^{-3} \text{ mol}$$

$$\text{Volume added} = 41.75 \text{ mL} = 41.75 \times 10^{-3} \text{ L}$$

$$M = \text{mol} \div V = \frac{3.3031 \times 10^{-3} \text{ mol}}{41.75 \times 10^{-3} \text{ L}} = 7.912 \times 10^{-2} \text{ mol/L}$$

TITRATION OF BASES

The technique of titration was described for the titration of an unknown acid by a base of known concentration. The same principles also apply to the titration of an unknown base by a solution of strong acid. The calculations proceed exactly as described previously. For the titration of a base, the stoichiometric point is reached when the number of moles of added acid in the titrant equals the number of moles of base in the unknown solution.

$$\text{Stoichiometric point:} \quad \text{mol } H_3O^+ \text{ added} = \text{mol base present} \qquad \textbf{(4-4)}$$

SECTION EXERCISES

4.6.1 When a solution of ammonia is mixed with a solution of hydrochloric acid, proton transfer occurs, giving an ammonium chloride solution. Write the net ionic reaction and draw a molecular picture of the process.

4.6.2 Vitamin C (also called *ascorbic acid*) is a weak organic acid whose formula is $HC_6H_7O_6$. Just one of the hydrogens is acidic. A pharmacist suspects that the vitamin C tablets received in a recent shipment are not pure. When a single 500.0-mg tablet is dissolved in 200.0 mL of water and titrated with a standard base that is 0.1045 M, it takes 24.45 mL to reach the stoichiometric point. Are the tablets pure? If not, what is the mass percentage of impurities?

4.6.3 While cleaning a laboratory, a technician discovers a large bottle containing a colorless solution. The bottle is labeled "$Ba(OH)_2$," but the molarity of the solution is not given. Concerned because of the toxicity of Ba^{2+} ions, the technician titrates with a solution of hydrochloric acid standardized at 0.1374 M. A 25.00-mL sample of the barium hydroxide solution requires 36.72 mL of the HCl solution to reach the stoichiometric point. What is the concentration of Ba^{2+} in the solution?

4.7 REDUCTION-OXIDATION REACTIONS

A third general class of chemical reactions are reduction-oxidation reactions. They occur when electrons from one chemical substance is transferred to another. Reduction-oxidation reactions, or *redox reactions* for short, include the rusting of iron, the bleaching of hair, and the burning of gasoline. All metals used in the chem-

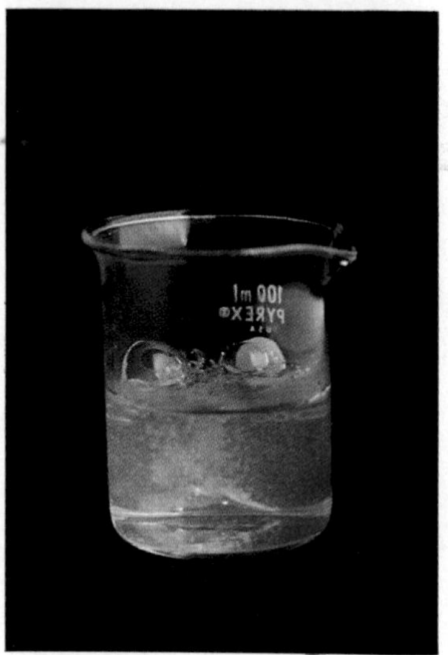

FIGURE 4-16
Magnesium metal reacts with a strong aqueous acid, generating hydrogen gas and a solution containing Mg^{2+} cations.

ical industry and manufacturing are extracted and purified by using redox chemistry, and many biochemical pathways involve the transfer of electrons from one substance to another.

The reaction of magnesium metal with aqueous strong acid, which is shown in Figure 4-16, illustrates the fundamental principles of redox chemistry. When a piece of magnesium is dropped into 6 M HCl solution, a vigorous reaction starts almost immediately. The metal dissolves, and a gas bubbles from the solution. Analysis of the gas shows that it is H_2, and analysis of the solution reveals the presence of Mg^{2+} ions. A list of chemical species before and after reaction indicates what has taken place:

Before reaction	After reaction
$Mg_{(s)}$	$Mg^{2+}_{(aq)}$
$H_3O^+_{(aq)}$	$H_{2\,(g)}$
$Cl^-_{(aq)}$	$Cl^-_{(aq)}$
$H_2O_{(l)}$	$H_2O_{(l)}$
	$H_3O^+_{(aq)}$(excess reagent)

Solid magnesium has been transformed into Mg^{2+} ions, and hydronium ions have decomposed to give H_2 gas. Quantitative measurements reveal that for every mole of Mg consumed, 1 mol of H_2 is produced and 2 mol of H_3O^+ are consumed. The reaction can be summed up in the following balanced chemical equation:

$$Mg_{(s)} + 2\,H_3O^+_{(aq)} \longrightarrow Mg^{2+}_{(aq)} + H_{2\,(g)} + 2\,H_2O_{(l)}$$

$$\overbrace{Mg_{(s)}}^{-2\,e^-\ \rightarrow\ Mg^{2+}} + \underbrace{2\,H_3O^+_{(aq)}}_{+2\,e^-\ \rightarrow\ H_2} \longrightarrow Mg^{2+}_{(aq)} + H_{2\,(g)} + 2\,H_2O_{(l)}$$

The loss of electrons by magnesium atoms to form Mg^{2+} cations indicates that this reaction between magnesium metal and hydronium ions is a redox process. An atom of magnesium forms a Mg^{2+} cation by losing two electrons. Because electrons must be conserved in every chemical process, the electrons lost by magnesium must be gained by some other species. In this example the electrons lost by Mg are gained by H_3O^+ to form H_2 and H_2O:

Conservation of electrons is the basis of oxidation and reduction. Gains and losses of electrons *always* occur together.

Oxidation ***is the loss of electrons from a substance.***

Reduction ***is the gain of electrons by a substance.***

When magnesium reacts with acid, magnesium atoms are oxidized, and hydronium ions are reduced. We can also describe magnesium as a **reducing agent,** because a reducing agent donates electrons to the species that is being reduced. An **oxidizing agent,** in turn, accepts electrons from a reducing agent. A reducing agent causes reduction and is oxidized in the process. An oxidizing agent gets reduced as it causes oxidation.

Redox reactions are more complicated than proton transfer reactions or precipitation reactions because the electrons transferred in redox chemistry do not appear in the balanced chemical equation. Instead, they are "hidden" among the starting materials and products. However, we can keep track of electrons by writing two **half-reactions** that describe the oxidation and the reduction separately. A half-reaction is a balanced chemical equation that describes either the oxidation or reduction but not both. Thus a half-reaction describes half of the redox reaction. Here are the half-reactions for the oxidation of magnesium by acid:

$$\begin{array}{lcll} Mg & \longrightarrow & Mg^{2+} + \cancel{2e^-} & \text{oxidation} \\ 2\,H_3O^+ + \cancel{2e^-} & \longrightarrow & H_2 + 2\,H_2O & \text{reduction} \\ \hline 2\,H_3O^+ + Mg & \longrightarrow & Mg^{2+} + H_2 + 2\,H_2O & \end{array}$$

Separating the oxidation from the reduction makes it possible to verify that electrons are conserved in a chemical transformation. Note that the electrons produced in the oxidation of magnesium are consumed in the reduction of hydronium ions. It is important to understand that this separation of half-reactions is only a thought process. Oxidations and reductions never occur alone; they always take place together. This is because electrons are conserved; they can move from species to species and from place to place, but they cannot be created or destroyed. Thus the electrons required for a reduction must come from an oxidation.

A detailed discussion of redox reactions must wait until Chapter 17, after we have explored the nature of the atom, periodic properties of the elements, and thermodynamics. For now, we will focus on only a few types of redox reactions that are common and relatively simple.

METAL DISPLACEMENT

In a metal displacement reaction, one metal ion in solution is replaced by another. For example, if zinc metal is added to a blue solution of copper(II) sulfate, the color slowly fades, and gray zinc metal is replaced by red-orange copper metal (Figure 4-17). Copper ions in the solution are reduced to copper metal, whereas zinc atoms are oxidized to Zn^{2+} cations. In this redox reaction, zinc displaces copper from the solution.

FIGURE 4-17
Zinc metal displaces copper ions from aqueous solution. The blue color signals the presence of copper ions. The color fades and copper metal appears as the reaction proceeds.

$$\text{Oxidation:}\quad Zn_{(s)} \longrightarrow Zn^{2+}_{(aq)} + 2\,e^- \qquad \text{Reduction:}\quad Cu^{2+}_{(aq)} + 2\,e^- \longrightarrow Cu_{(s)}$$

$$\text{Redox:}\quad Zn_{(s)} + Cu^{2+}_{(aq)} \longrightarrow Zn^{2+}_{(aq)} + Cu_{(s)}$$

Many metal displacement reactions can be visualized, but not all of them actually occur. For example, zinc displaces copper ions from aqueous solutions, but zinc will not displace Mg^{2+} ions. Copper ions are displaced by aluminum but not by silver. The relative abilities of metals to displace one another are summarized in a listing called an **activity series,** shown in Table 4-2. Neutral metals high on the list transfer electrons to metal cations lower on the list. The greater the separation between the species, the more vigorous the reaction.

The activity series is divided into three groups. At the top of the list are metals that are oxidized by water. These metals react vigorously with water to generate hydrogen gas and hydroxide ions, as illustrated by the reaction of sodium with water:

$$2\,Na_{(s)} + 2\,H_2O_{(l)} \longrightarrow 2\,Na^+_{(aq)} + H_{2\,(g)} + 2\,OH^-_{(aq)}$$

In the middle of the list are metals like magnesium that react readily with aqueous hydronium ions but do not react readily with water. Metals at the bottom of the list do not react with water or hydronium ions. These metals are quite resistant to oxidation. Sample Problem 4-17 shows how to use the activity series.

TABLE 4-2 ACTIVITY SERIES OF THE METALS

	ION	NEUTRAL	
Ions difficult to displace	K^+	K	Metals that react with water
	Ca^{2+}	Ca	
	Na^+	Na	
	Mg^{2+}	Mg	
	Al^{3+}	Al	
	Zn^{2+}	Zn	Metals that react with acid
	Fe^{2+}	Fe	
	Ni^{2+}	Ni	
	Pb^{2+}	Pb	
	H_3O^+	H_2	
Easily displaced cations	Cu^{2+}	Cu	Metals that are highly unreactive
	Ag^+	Ag	
	Au^{3+}	Au	

SAMPLE PROBLEM 4-17 THE ACTIVITY SERIES

Predict whether a reaction will occur in the following instances. Explain your conclusions.

(a) A copper wire is dipped in 6 M HCl.

(b) A strip of aluminum foil is dipped in aqueous silver nitrate.

(c) Iron pellets are added to a solution of magnesium chloride.

(d) A small piece of calcium is added to a beaker of water.

METHOD: A reaction will occur if a metal high in the activity series is added to a solution containing a cation lower on the list. For each case, we need to identify the species present in the mixture and make an evaluation based on the activity series.

(a) Solid copper metal is dipped in a solution that contains H_3O^+ and Cl^-. Copper metal is below H_3O^+ on the list, so no reaction will take place.

(b) Solid aluminum metal is dipped in a solution that contains Ag^+ ions and NO_3^- anions. Aluminum is in the middle of the neutral metals, and Ag^+ is near the bottom of the ions. Thus aluminum displaces Ag^+.

$$\text{Reduction: } 3\,(Ag^+_{(aq)} + e^- \rightarrow Ag_{(s)}) \qquad \text{Oxidation: } Al_{(s)} \rightarrow Al^{3+}_{(aq)} + 3\,e^-$$

$$\text{Redox: } 3\,Ag^+_{(aq)} + Al_{(s)} \rightarrow 3\,Ag_{(s)} + Al^{3+}_{(aq)}$$

(c) Solid iron metal is added to a solution that contains Mg^{2+} and Cl^-. Iron is below Mg^{2+} in the activity series, so no reaction will occur.

(d) Solid calcium metal is added to water. According to the activity series, calcium is one of the metals that reacts with water.

$$\text{Reduction: } 2\,H_2O_{(l)} + 2\,e^- \rightarrow H_{2\,(g)} + 2\,OH^-_{(aq)} \qquad \text{Oxidation: } Ca_{(s)} \rightarrow Ca^{2+}_{(aq)} + 2\,e^-$$

$$\text{Redox: } 2\,H_2O_{(l)} + Ca_{(s)} \rightarrow Ca^{2+}_{(aq)} + H_{2\,(g)} + 2\,OH^-_{(aq)}$$

OXIDATION BY OXYGEN

Almost all elements will combine with molecular oxygen to form oxides. In fact, loss of electrons is called *oxidation* because elements lose electrons when they combine with oxygen. Most metals react with atmospheric oxygen to form oxides. Only those low on the activity series, such as silver and gold, do not.

Moving up the activity series, metals become progressively easier to oxidize. Objects made from iron must be protected from oxygen, or they will react to form iron(III) oxide, better known as *rust.* Objects made of aluminum also react readily with O_2, but the product of this redox reaction, Al_2O_3, forms an impervious film on the metal surface that prevents O_2 from reaching the underlying metal.

The stoichiometry of metal oxides is determined by the most stable cationic species of the metal. In metal oxides, oxygen atoms have captured two electrons to form O^{2-} anions. For every oxygen anion a counterbalancing cationic charge of +2 is required. Remember that Group I metals form stable cations with +1 charge, Group II metals form stable cations with +2 charge, and Al forms Al^{3+}. Here is an example from each category:

$$4\,Li + O_2 \rightarrow 2\,Li_2O \qquad 2\,Ca + O_2 \rightarrow 2\,CaO \qquad 4\,Al + 3\,O_2 \rightarrow 2\,Al_2O_3$$

Other metals, such as iron, have more than one possible stable cation. In these cases the cationic charge must be specified before a balanced redox equation can be written. Sample Problem 4-18 demonstrates this point.

SAMPLE PROBLEM 4-18 METAL OXIDES

Iron commonly forms cations with +2 or +3 charges. One major source of iron for steel production is ore rich in hematite, an oxide of iron containing Fe^{3+} ions. Write a balanced equation showing the oxidation of iron atoms to hematite.

METHOD: First, the chemical formula of hematite must be determined from the principle of charge neutrality. Then chemical equation can be balanced by inspection:

Hematite contains Fe^{3+} ions. As an oxide, it also contains O^{2-} ions. To be electrically neutral, every two Fe^{3+} cations require three O^{2-} anions. Thus the chemical formula of hematite is Fe_2O_3.

Unbalanced: $Fe_{(s)} + O_{2\,(g)} \rightarrow Fe_2O_{3\,(s)}$

Balance O: $Fe_{(s)} + 3\,O_{2\,(g)} \rightarrow 2\,Fe_2O_{3\,(s)}$

Balance Fe: $4\,Fe_{(s)} + 3\,O_{2\,(g)} \rightarrow 2\,Fe_2O_{3\,(s)}$

Almost all metals are found in the Earth's crust as cations combined with oxide or sulfide (S^{2-}) in the form of minerals. Metallurgical processes combine chemistry and engineering to reduce metals in minerals to their elemental forms.

Reactions with oxygen do not necessarily generate cations and anions. The combustion of organic compounds was discussed in Chapter 3. In a combustion reaction oxygen combines with carbon and hydrogen to give CO_2 and H_2O. Even though neither product contains ions, combustion reactions nonetheless are redox reactions. In a combustion reaction, carbon atoms lose electrons, and oxygen atoms gain electrons.

Metallurgy and redox reactions that do not involve metal ions are discussed in Chapter 17.

SECTION EXERCISES

4.7.1 Although aluminum cans are not attacked by water, strong acid oxidizes Al to Al^{3+} cations, liberating hydrogen gas in the process. How many moles of H_2 gas will be liberated if a 2.43-g sample of pure Al metal reacts completely with an excess of 3.00 M sulfuric acid solution?

4.7.2 Metallic titanium is produced from rutile ore (TiO_2) by a direct replacement reaction with magnesium that frees titanium metal and produces MgO.
 (a) Write the balanced redox reaction for this process, and identify the reducing agent and the oxidizing agent.
 (b) How many kilograms of magnesium are required to manufacture 100 kg of titanium metal, assuming that the reaction goes in 100% yield?

4.7.3 Predict whether or not a reaction will occur in the following instances. If a reaction does take place, write the half-reactions and the balanced redox reaction.
 (a) A strip of nickel wire is dipped in 6.0 M HCl.
 (b) Aluminum foil is dipped in aqueous calcium chloride.
 (c) A lead rod is dipped in a beaker of water.
 (d) An iron wire is immersed in a solution of silver nitrate.

CHAPTER SUMMARY

1. Chemical reactions, such as those used to synthesize useful chemical compounds, are described by chemical equations that identify the reactants, the products, and the molar proportions in which they react.
2. In a properly balanced chemical equation the number of atoms of each element is conserved. Many chemical equations can be balanced by inspection.
3. Calculations of the amounts of reagents that participate in a reaction use the stoichiometric ratios expressed in the balanced chemical equation.
4. The products of a reaction are seldom formed quantitatively; instead, every reaction has a fractional yield expressed as the amount actually obtained divided by the amount predicted by stoichiometric ratios.
5. When supplies of two or more reactants are limited, a limiting reagent is consumed first. Limiting reagent problems are solved conveniently by using amount tables, which summarize the amounts consumed and produced.
6. In aqueous solutions, ionic salts, strong acids, and strong bases generate ionic species, and reactions among ions are best described by using net ionic equations.
7. Solution reactions are divided conveniently into three categories. Precipitation reactions involve ions combining to form neutral solids; acid-base reactions involve transfer of protons (H^+) from acids to bases; and redox reactions involve transfer of electrons (e^-) between species.
8. Solution stoichiometry is treated by using molarity-volume-mole conversions, and acid-base analyses can be carried out by using titrations.
9. Oxidation, which is the loss of electrons, and reduction, which is the gain of electrons, always occur together. Metals have characteristic susceptibilities to being oxidized, and molecular oxygen is a particularly effective oxidizing agent.

KEY TERMS

balanced chemical equation
limiting reagent
net ionic equation
product
reactant
reagent
spectator ion
stoichiometric coefficient
stoichiometric ratio
stoichiometry

actual yield
percent yield
theoretical yield
yield

insoluble
precipitate
precipitation reaction

acid
acid-base reaction
base
neutralization reaction
proton transfer reaction
strong acid
strong base
weak acid
weak base

buret
indicator
standardization

stoichiometric point
titrant
titration

activity series
half-reaction
oxidation
oxidizing agent
reducing agent
reduction
reduction-oxidation (redox) reaction

SKILLS TO MASTER

- Balancing chemical equations by inspection
- Using molar ratios
- Determining and using reaction yields
- Identifying the limiting reagent
- Constructing amount tables
- Identifying species in aqueous solution
- Writing net ionic equations
- Identifying soluble salts, acids, and bases
- Analyzing by titration
- Recognizing redox reactions

LEARNING EXERCISES

4.1 Write a chapter summary of two pages or less that outlines the important features of this chapter.

4.2 Several examples of chemical reasoning were introduced in this chapter. Write out the reasoning steps that you will follow in: (a) balancing a chemical equation; (b) identifying the limiting reagent; (c) determining whether a precipitate forms; and (d) computing a reaction yield.

4.3 List features that can be used to distinguish each of the three types of reactions introduced in this chapter.

4.4 Draw one specific molecular picture that illustrates each of the reaction types introduced in this chapter.

4.5 Define each of these terms: (a) percent yield; (b) limiting reagent; (c) spectator ion; (d) precipitate; (e) titration; and (f) oxidation.

4.6 Update your list of memory bank equations. For each equation, add a phrase that describes what kinds of chemical problems the equation is used for.

4.7 List all terms new to you that appear in Chapter 4. In your own words, give a one-sentence definition of each. Consult the glossary if you need help.

PROBLEMS

WRITING CHEMICAL EQUATIONS

4.1 The gases leaving an automobile cylinder after combustion include CO_2, CO (from incomplete combustion), NO, H_2O, H_2, N_2, O_2, and unburned hydrocarbons. After leaving the engine, these exhaust gases are passed through a catalytic converter whose purpose is to change pollutants into less harmful substances. Many reactions occur in a catalytic converter, including those shown below. Write a balanced chemical equation for each.
(a) $H_2 + NO \rightarrow NH_3 + H_2O$
(b) $CO + NO \rightarrow N_2 + CO_2$
(c) $NH_3 + O_2 \rightarrow N_2O + H_2O$
(d) Nitrogen monoxide and ammonia react to give nitrogen and water.

4.2 Balance the following chemical equations:
(a) $NH_4NO_3 \rightarrow N_2O + H_2O$
(b) $P_4O_{10} + H_2O \rightarrow H_3PO_4$
(c) $HIO_3 \rightarrow I_2O_5 + H_2O$
(d) $As + Cl_2 \rightarrow AsCl_5$
(e) $Mg_3N_2 + H_2O \rightarrow Mg(OH)_2 + NH_3$

4.3 Balance the following chemical equations:
(a) $N_2O_{5\,(g)} + H_2O_{(l)} \longrightarrow HNO_{3\,(aq)}$
(b) $KClO_{3\,(s)} \longrightarrow KCl_{(s)} + O_{2\,(g)}$
(c) $Fe_{(s)} + O_{2\,(g)} + H_2O_{(l)} \longrightarrow Fe(OH)_{2\,(s)}$
(d) $Au_2S_{3\,(s)} + H_{2\,(g)} \longrightarrow H_2S_{(g)} + Au_{(s)}$

4.4 Balance the chemical equations for the following important industrial processes:
(a) Molecular nitrogen and hydrogen combine to give ammonia.
(b) Molecular hydrogen and carbon monoxide react to form methanol (CH_3OH).
(c) Calcium oxide and carbon react to form carbon monoxide and CaC_2.
(d) $C_2H_4 + O_2 + HCl \longrightarrow C_2H_4Cl_2 + H_2O$

4.5 The following reactions play a role in the manufacture of nitric acid. Write a balanced equation for each.
(a) $NH_3 + O_2 \longrightarrow NO + H_2O$
(b) $NO + O_2 \longrightarrow NO_2$
(c) $NO_2 + H_2O \longrightarrow HNO_3 + NO$
(d) $NH_3 + O_2 \longrightarrow N_2 + H_2O$
(e) $NH_3 + NO \longrightarrow N_2 + H_2O$

4.6 Draw a molecular picture illustrating the reaction in Problem 4.4a.

4.7 Draw a molecular picture illustrating the reaction in Problem 4.5d.

4.8 Magnesium metal burns with a bright flame in oxygen gas, and the product is solid white magnesium oxide. Draw a molecular picture showing six magnesium atoms and four oxygen molecules. Then draw another molecular picture of this same system after reaction occurs.

THE STOICHIOMETRY OF CHEMICAL REACTIONS

4.9 For each reaction given in Problem 4.1, calculate the mass of the second reactant that is required to react completely with 5.00 g of the first material.

4.10 For each reaction in Problem 4.4, calculate the mass of the first reactant that would react completely with 875 kg of the second reactant.

4.11 The use of freons is being phased out because of the damage these compounds do to the stratospheric ozone layer. One of the freons, CCl_2F_2, is manufactured by reacting carbon tetrachloride with hydrogen fluoride. The other reaction product is hydrogen chloride. If a manufacturer wishes to convert 175 kg of carbon tetrachloride into CCl_2F_2, what is the minimum mass of hydrogen fluoride required? What masses of the two products will be obtained if this reaction is 100% efficient?

4.12 Iodine can be prepared by bubbling chlorine gas through an aqueous solution of sodium iodide:

$$2\ NaI_{(aq)} + Cl_{2\,(g)} \longrightarrow I_{2\,(s)} + 2\ NaCl_{(aq)}$$

How many grams of sodium iodide are required to produce 150 g of iodine?

4.13 The fertilizer ammonium sulfate is prepared by the reaction between ammonia and sulfuric acid:

$$2\ NH_{3\,(g)} + H_2SO_{4\,(aq)} \longrightarrow (NH_4)_2SO_{4\,(aq)}$$

How many kilograms of NH_3 are needed to make 3.50 metric tons of ammonium sulfate?

4.14 The fermentation of sugar to produce ethanol occurs by the following reaction:

$$C_6H_{12}O_6 \xrightarrow{\text{Yeast}} 2\ C_2H_5OH_{(l)} + 2\ CO_{2\,(g)}$$

How much ethanol can be made from 1.00 kg of sugar?

4.15 Ethanol is sometimes used as a fuel. It reacts quantitatively with molecular oxygen, forming carbon dioxide and water as products. What mass of each product will result from the complete combustion of 5.75 g of ethyl alcohol?

4.16 Write the balanced equation, and determine the number of moles of water produced when 2.95 mL of pyridine (C_5H_5N, density = 0.982 g/mL) reacts with excess O_2 to produce water, carbon dioxide, and molecular nitrogen.

YIELDS OF CHEMICAL REACTIONS

4.17 An industrial plant is synthesizing phosphoric acid from fluoroapatite (see Sample Problem 4-7). If every kilogram of apatite yields 400 g of phosphoric acid, what is the yield based on the fluoroapatite consumed?

4.18 When HgO is heated, it decomposes into elemental mercury and diatomic oxygen gas. If 60 g of Hg is obtained from 80 g of the oxide, what is the percent yield of the reaction?

4.19 Phenobarbitone is a sleep-inducing drug whose chemical formula is $C_{12}H_{12}N_2O_3$. It is manufactured in an eight-step process starting from toluene, C_7H_8. Theoretically, each molecule of toluene yields one molecule of phenobarbitone. If each of the steps has a yield of 90%, what mass of toluene is needed to manufacture 25 kg of phenobarbitone?

4.20 What is the yield of the reaction described in Problem 4.11 if the manufacturer obtains 105 kg of CCl_2F_2 from 175 kg of CCl_4? Given this reaction yield, what masses of CCl_4 and hydrogen fluoride should be used to make 155 kg of CCl_2F_2?

4.21 If the fermentation reaction described in Problem 4.14 is 76.5% efficient, what mass of glucose is required to produce 3.50 kg of ethanol?

THE LIMITING REAGENT

4.22 A fast-food restaurant makes double cheeseburgers using one hamburger roll, two quarter-pound patties of beef, one slice of cheese, a fourth of a tomato, and 15 g of shredded lettuce. At the start of the day a store manager finds the following inventory: 12 dozen rolls, 40 lb of beef patties, 2 packages of sliced cheese containing 65 slices each, 40 tomatoes, and 1 kg of lettuce. Which ingredient will run out first, and how many cheeseburgers can be made?

4.23 A hardware store sells a "handyman assortment" of wood screws containing the following:

Type	Number of screws	Mass per screw (g)
#8, ½"	10	12.0
#8, 1"	8	21.5
#10, ½"	8	14.5
#10, 1 ½"	6	31.0
#12, 2"	4	45.0

The store buys these screws in 1-pound boxes. From one box of each type of screws, how many "handyman assortments" can the store prepare?

4.24 For each of the reactions given in Problem 4.1, consider starting with 7.50 g of each reactant. Determine the limiting reagent and the masses of all substances when the limiting reagent is consumed.

4.25 For each of the reactions given in Problem 4.4, consider an industrial process that starts with 740 kg of each reactant. Compute the maximum mass of each product that could be produced.

4.26 Silicon carbide, commonly known as *carborundum,* is a very hard and abrasive substance. The compound is prepared by heating silicon dioxide in the presence of graphitic carbon:

$$SiO_{2\,(s)} + 2\,C_{\,(s)} \rightarrow SiC_{\,(s)} + CO_{2\,(g)}$$

How many grams of silicon carbide can be formed from 50.0 g of graphite and 50.0 g of silicon dioxide?

4.27 Elemental phosphorus, P_4, reacts vigorously with oxygen to give P_4O_{10}. How much P_4O_{10} can be prepared from 3.75 g of P_4 and 6.55 g O_2? How much of the excess reagent will remain at the end of the reaction?

4.28 Acrylonitrile is an important building block for synthetic fibers and plastics. Over 2 billion pounds of acrylonitrile are produced in the United States each year. The compound is synthesized from propene in the following reaction:

$$2\,C_3H_{6\,(g)} + 2\,NH_{3\,(g)} + 3\,O_{2\,(g)} \rightarrow 2\,C_3H_3N_{\,(l)} + 6\,H_2O_{\,(l)}$$

Propene   Acrylonitrile

How many kilograms of acrylonitrile can be prepared from 1.50×10^3 kg of propene, 6.8×10^2 kg of ammonia, and 1.92×10^3 kg of oxygen?

4.29 Silicon tetrachloride is used in the electronics industry to make elemental silicon for computer chips. Silicon tetrachloride is prepared from silicon dioxide, graphitic carbon, and chlorine gas:

$$SiO_{2\,(s)} + 2\,C_{\,(s)} + 2\,Cl_{2\,(g)} \rightarrow SiCl_{4\,(l)} + 2\,CO_{\,(g)}$$

If the reaction goes in 95.7% yield, how much silicon tetrachloride can be prepared from 75.0 g of each starting material?

4.30 A scientist studying the reaction between decaborane and oxygen mixed 1.00×10^2 g of $B_{10}H_{18}$ with 2.75×10^2 g of O_2. Compute the masses of all substances present after the reaction went to completion, generating B_2O_3 and H_2O as the only products.

PRECIPITATION REACTIONS

4.31 What are the major species present in aqueous solutions of each of the following? (a) NH_4Cl; (b) $Fe(ClO_4)_2$; (c) Na_2SO_4; and (d) KBr.

4.32 What are the major species present in aqueous solutions of each of the following? (a) potassium hydrogenphosphate; (b) acetic acid; (c) sodium hypochlorite; (d) ammonia; and (e) magnesium chloride.

4.33 Consider the addition of each of the following solutions to each solution described in Problem 4.31. In each case, decide whether a precipitate will form. If so, identify the precipitate. (a) $AgNO_3$; (b) Na_2CO_3; and (c) $Ba(OH)_2$.

4.34 Write the appropriate net ionic equation that describes these processes:
(a) Aqueous $AgNO_3$ mixed with aqueous K_2SO_4 gives $Ag_2SO_{4\,(s)}$.
(b) Aqueous $Fe(ClO_4)_3$ mixed with aqueous $(NH_4)_2C_2O_4$ gives $Fe_2(C_2O_4)_{3\,(s)}$.
(c) Aqueous $Pb(NO_3)_2$ mixed with aqueous NaBr gives $PbBr_{2\,(s)}$.

4.35 Write the appropriate net ionic equation that describes these processes:
(a) Aqueous $AlCl_3$ mixed with aqueous KOH gives $Al(OH)_{3\,(s)}$.
(b) Aqueous $MgSO_4$ mixed with aqueous Na_3PO_4 gives $Mg_3(PO_4)_{2\,(s)}$.
(c) Aqueous $Ba(OH)_2$ mixed with aqueous Na_2SO_4 gives $BaSO_{4\,(s)}$.

4.36 If 55.0 mL of a 5.00×10^{-2} M solution of $AgNO_3$ is mixed with 95.0 mL of 3.50×10^{-2} M K_2CO_3, what mass of solid forms, and what ions remain in solution?

4.37 If 75.0 mL of a 0.750 M solution of lead(II) nitrate is mixed with 125 mL of 0.855 M ammonium chloride, what mass of solid forms, and what ions remain in solution?

4.38 Draw a molecular picture to illustrate the solutions described in Problem 4.37, showing how they appear before mixing and after the reaction is complete.

ACID-BASE REACTIONS

4.39 Write the net ionic reaction and draw a molecular picture that shows what happens when 50 mL of a 0.010 M HNO_3 solution is mixed with 50 mL of a 0.0050 M $Ba(OH)_2$ solution.

4.40 Classify each of the following as a strong acid, strong base, weak acid, weak base, or none of these: (a) H_2CO_3; (b) CH_4; (c) LiOH; (d) ammonia; and (e) C_2H_5OH (ethanol).

4.41 Calculate the molarities of all ions present in a solution made by mixing 1.50×10^2 mL of a 2.00×10^{-2} M $Ba(OH)_2$ solution with 1.00×10^2 mL of a 5.00×10^{-2} M HCl solution.

4.42 Calculate the molarities of all ions present in solution when 1.53 g of $NaOH_{(s)}$ is added to 215 mL of 0.150 M acetic acid.

4.43 A student prepared 1.00 L of a solution of NaOH for use in titrations. The solution was standardized by titrating a sample of potassium hydrogenphthalate whose mass was 0.7996 g. Before titration the buret reading was 0.15 mL. When the solution changed color, the buret reading was 43.75 mL. Calculate the molarity of the NaOH solution.

REDUCTION-OXIDATION REACTIONS

4.44 Some of the following react when added together, but others do not. For those that do, write a balanced net ionic redox equation. (a) Cu + $HCl_{(aq)}$; (b) Cu + $MgCl_{2\,(aq)}$; (c) Cu + $AgNO_{3\,(aq)}$; and (d) K + H_2O.

4.45 Some of the following react when added together, but others do not. For those that do, write a balanced net ionic redox equation. (a) Al + $HCl_{(aq)}$; (b) Zn + $Au^{3+}_{(aq)}$; (c) Ni + $MgCl_{2\,(aq)}$; and (d) Na + H_2O.

4.46 Identify the half-reactions for each example in Problems 4.44 and 4.45 that undergoes a reaction.

4.47 Write the balanced redox reactions for the formation of each of the following oxides from the reaction of molecular oxygen with pure metal: (a) strontium oxide; (b) chromium(III) oxide; (c) tin(IV) oxide.

4.48 Aluminum metal generates H_2 gas when dropped into 6 M HCl. Calculate the mass of H_2 that will form from the complete reaction of 0.355 g Al with 8.00 mL of 6.00 M HCl.

ADDITIONAL PROBLEMS

4.49 The reaction of atom X with atom Y is represented in the following diagram. Which of the equations best describes the balanced equation?

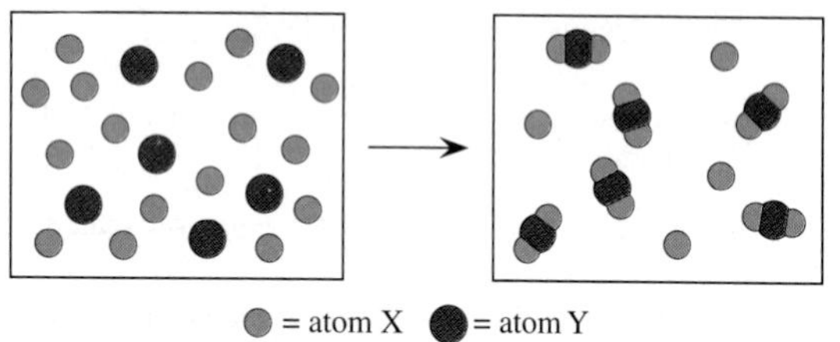

a $16X + 6Y \rightarrow 6YX_2 + 4X$
b $12X + 6Y \rightarrow Y_6X_{12} + 4X$
c $X + 2Y \rightarrow XY_2$
d $2X + Y \rightarrow YX_2$

4.50 The reaction of atom X with atom Y is represented in the following diagram. Which of the equations best describes the balanced chemical equation?

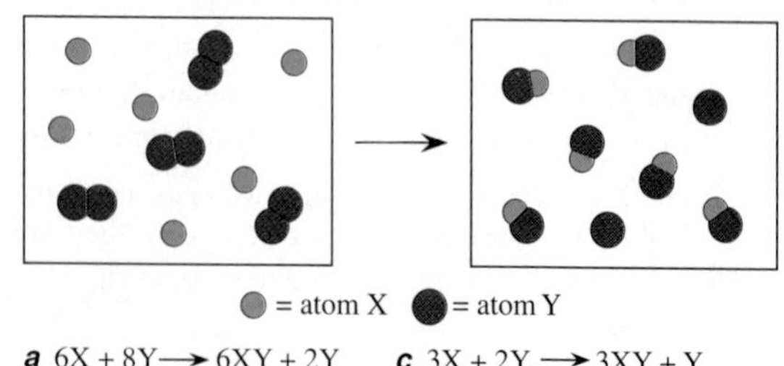

a $6X + 8Y \rightarrow 6XY + 2Y$
b $2X + Y_2 \rightarrow 2XY$
c $3X + 2Y_2 \rightarrow 3XY + Y$
d $X + Y \rightarrow XY$

4.51 Superphosphate, a water-soluble fertilizer, is a mixture of $Ca(H_2PO_4)_2$ and $CaSO_4$ in a 1:2 mole ratio. It is formed by the following reaction:

$$Ca_3(PO_4)_2 + 2\,H_2SO_4 \rightarrow Ca(H_2PO_4)_2 + 2\,CaSO_4$$

If 255 g of $Ca_3(PO_4)_2$ are treated with 151 g of H_2SO_4, how many grams of superphosphate could be formed?

4.52 The Solvay process is a commercial method for producing sodium carbonate. In one step of this process, sodium hydrogencarbonate is precipitated by mixing aqueous solutions of sodium chloride and ammonium hydrogencarbonate:

$$NH_4HCO_{3\,(aq)} + NaCl_{(aq)} \rightarrow NaHCO_{3\,(s)} + NH_4Cl_{(aq)}$$

(a) Write the net ionic reaction for this step of the Solvay process.
(b) What are the spectator ions?
(c) In a typical procedure, 5.00×10^2 L of 1.50 M NH_4HCO_3 is treated with 5.00×10^2 L of 6.00 M NaCl, and 61.7 kg of $NaHCO_3$ are produced. What is the percent yield of the process?

4.53 A 4.6-g sample of C_2H_5OH is burned completely in air.
(a) How many moles of H_2O are formed?
(b) How many molecules?
(c) How many grams?

4.54 If 1.00×10^2 g of P_4O_{10} are dissolved in excess water, how many grams of H_3PO_4 (the only product) will be produced?

4.55 The following diagram represents a reaction vessel that contains the starting materials for the Haber synthesis of ammonia.

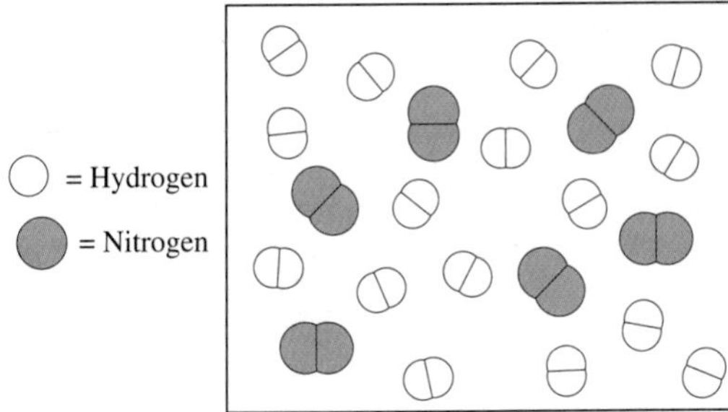

(a) Draw a picture that shows what the vessel will look like when the reaction is complete.
(b) What is the limiting reagent in this reaction?
(c) If each picture of a molecule represents 1 mol of compound, how many grams of ammonia will the system produce, and how many grams of the excess reagent will be left behind?

4.56 Even though xenon is a rare gas, it reacts with fluorine and oxygen. When xenon gas reacts with F_2 gas at high temperatures, XeF_4 is one of the products. If 5.00 g of xenon reacts with excess fluorine and generates 4.00 g of XeF_4, what is the percent yield?

4.57 Decaborane, $B_{10}H_{18}$, was used as a fuel for the Redstone rockets of the 1950s. Decaborane reacts violently with oxygen according to the following equation:

$$B_{10}H_{18} + 12\ O_2 \rightarrow 5\ B_2O_3 + 9\ H_2O$$

The two starting materials are stored in separate containers. When mixed, they ignite spontaneously, releasing large amounts of energy. If one fuel tank of a rocket contains 1.3×10^5 g of decaborane and the second tank contains 6.5×10^4 g of liquid oxygen, which tank will empty first, and how much of the second reactant will be left over?

4.58 The best design for rockets is one in which both fuel materials run out at the same time because this minimizes the excess mass that the rocket must carry. If the total mass of both components in Problem 4.57 is to be 12.0×10^5 g, what mass of liquid oxygen and what mass of decaborane should be used?

4.59 The element titanium is commonly found as the ore ilmenite, $FeTiO_3$. Much of the world reserves of titanium is found in Canada. At a particular mine, a sample of earth was found to contain 15% ilmenite by mass. What mass of pure titanium metal can be isolated from 1.00 metric ton of earth if the extraction process is 95% efficient?

4.60 Most of the ammonia produced by the Haber process is used as fertilizer. A second important use of NH_3 is in the production of nitric acid, a top-15 industrial chemical (15 billion pounds in 1991). Nitric acid is produced by a three-step synthesis called the *Ostwald process:*

$$4\ NH_3 + 5\ O_2 \rightarrow 4\ NO + 6\ H_2O$$

$$2\ NO + O_2 \rightarrow 2\ NO_2$$

$$3\ NO_2 + H_2O \rightarrow 2\ HNO_3 + NO$$

Starting with 750 kg of ammonia, what mass of nitric acid can be produced if each step is 94.5% efficient?

4.61 Carbon dioxide, which is used to carbonate beverages and as a coolant (dry ice), is produced from methane and water vapor:

$$CH_{4\,(g)} + H_2O_{\,(g)} \rightarrow CO_{2\,(g)} + H_{2\,(g)} \text{ (unbalanced)}$$

Use the following symbols to write a balanced form of the equation. (The hydrogen produced in this reaction is separated from the carbon dioxide and used in the Haber synthesis.)

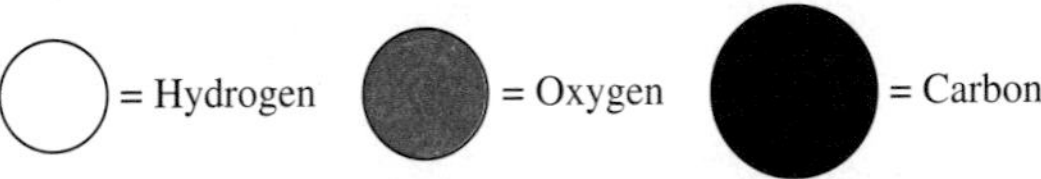

4.62 The following unbalanced reaction is called the *thermite reaction.* It releases tremendous amounts of energy and is sometimes used to generate heat for welding.

$$Al + Fe_3O_4 \rightarrow Fe + Al_2O_3 \quad \text{(unbalanced)}$$

Compute the masses of all substances present at the end of the reaction if 2.00×10^2 g of Al and 7.00×10^2 g of Fe_3O_4 react to completion.

4.63 Elemental arsenic, a poison that kills humans and animal pests, may be obtained by reacting As_2O_3 with carbon, giving As and CO. Compute the masses of As and CO formed if 49.5 g of As_2O_3 reacts completely with 7.20 g of C.

4.64 In the Haber synthesis of ammonia, N_2 and H_2 react at high temperature, but they never react completely. In a typical reaction, 24.0 kg of H_2 and 84 kg of N_2 react to produce 68 kg of NH_3. Find the theoretical yield, the percent yield, and the masses of H_2 and N_2 that remain unreacted, assuming that no other products form.

4.65 A white precipitate forms when 100.0 mL of 1.50 M aqueous calcium nitrate is mixed with 75.0 mL of 3.00 M aqueous ammonium sulfate. Identify the precipitate, and write the net ionic equation for the precipitation reaction. Calculate the mass of the precipitate, and calculate the concentrations of all dissolved ions at the end of the reaction.

4.66 Write net ionic reactions for each of the following. Assume that all occur when two aqueous solutions are mixed. (a) $HgCl_2$ + MgS; (b) $BaCl_2$ + K_2SO_4; (c) NaOH + CH_3CO_2H; (d) KOH + $FeCl_3$; and (e) $BaCl_2$ + $NaBrO_3$.

4.67 Methyl *t*-butyl ether (MTBE) is a carbon-based compound that has replaced lead-containing materials as the principal antiknock ingredient in gasoline. Today's gasoline is about 7% MTBE by mass. MTBE is produced from isobutene by the following reaction:

$$H_3C{-}O{-}H + (H_3C)_2C{=}CH_2 \xrightarrow{H_2SO_4} H_3C{-}C(CH_3)(O{-}CH_3){-}CH_3$$

Methanol	Isobutene	MTBE
CH_4O	C_4H_8	$C_5H_{12}O$

Approximately 2 billion pounds of MTBE are produced each year at a cost of about 10¢ per pound. Assume that you are a chemist working for a company that sold 750 million pounds of MTBE last year.

(a) If the synthesis had a reaction yield of 86%, how much isobutene was used to produce the MTBE?

(b) You have improved the synthesis of MTBE so that the yield of the reaction increases from 86% to 93%. If the company uses the same mass of isobutene for next year's production, how many pounds of MTBE will the company sell if it uses your new process?

(c) Assuming that the price of MTBE does not change, how much more money will the company make next year because of your work?

4.68 Propylene oxide is a highly reactive, toxic substance that is a suspected carcinogen. Nevertheless, approximately 2.5 billion pounds of this compound are produced annually. Propylene oxide is primarily used in the synthesis of poly(propylene glycol), a polymer used in the manufacture of automobile seats, bedding, and carpets. Propylene oxide is produced by the following reaction:

2 *t*-Butyl hydroperoxide + Propene ⟶ Propylene oxide + *t*-Butanol

t-Butyl hydroperoxide	Propene	Propylene oxide	*t*-Butanol
$C_4H_{10}O_2$	C_3H_6	C_3H_6O	$C_4H_{10}O$

(a) How many kilograms of propylene oxide can be prepared from 75 kg of *t*-butyl hydroperoxide?

(b) What mass of propene will be required for the synthesis? (The *t*-butanol formed as a byproduct in this reaction is used as a starting material in an alternative to the synthesis of MTBE shown in Problem 4.67.)

4.69 What species (ions, compounds) would you expect to find in aqueous solutions of the following? Write appropriate net ionic reactions describing what reaction occurs, if any, on mixing equimolar portions of the two solutions. (a) NaCl and HNO_3; (b) $CaCl_2$ and Na_2SO_4; (c) KOH and HCl; and (d) NH_3 and HCl.

4.70 Draw a molecular picture of a very dilute aqueous solution of $Ca(NO_3)_2$.

4.71 Devise a synthesis, write the net ionic reaction, and compute masses of each starting material needed to make 2.50 kg of each of the following solid ionic compounds: (a) $FePO_4$, (b) $Zn(OH)_2$; and (c) $NiCO_3$.

4.72 As a final examination in the general chemistry laboratory, a student was asked to determine the mass of $Ca(OH)_2$ that dissolves in 1.0 L of water. Following a published procedure, the student did the following:

(a) Approximately 1.5 mL of concentrated HCl (12 M) was added to 750 mL of distilled water.

(b) A solution of KOH was prepared by adding approximately 1.37 g KOH to 1.0 L of distilled water.

(c) A sample of KHP (185.9 mg) was dissolved in 100 mL of distilled water. Titration with the KOH solution required 25.67 mL to reach the equivalence point.

(d) A 50.00-mL sample of the HCl solution prepared in step (a) was titrated with the KOH solution. The titration required 34.02 mL of titrant to reach the equivalence point.

(e) The student was given a 25.00-mL sample of a saturated solution of $Ca(OH)_2$ for analysis. Titration with the HCl solution required 29.28 mL to reach the equivalence point.

How many grams of calcium hydroxide dissolve in 1.00 L of water?

4.73 A student was asked to determine the amount of inert impurities in a contaminated sample of oxalic acid ($H_2C_2O_4{\cdot}2H_2O$; two acidic hydrogens). The student prepared a standard solution of NaOH by diluting 50.00 mL of a 1.632 M solution to 1.000 L in a volumetric flask. This solution was used to titrate a 0.2500-g sample of the contaminated oxalic acid dissolved in 75 mL of water. The titration required 40.00 mL of base to reach the stoichiometric point. Find the percent purity of the oxalic acid sample.

4.74 Magnesium metal reacts with HCl solution, liberating H_2 gas and generating Mg^{2+} cations in solution. A 1.215-g sample of Mg metal is added to 100.0 mL of a 4.00 M HCl solution, and the reaction goes to completion.

(a) What mass of H_2 is formed?

(b) What are the concentrations of ions in the solution?

4.75 Predict the products and write the net ionic reaction when a solution of HCl reacts with each of the following (a) $Mg_{(s)}$; (b) $KOH_{(aq)}$; and (c) $BaCl_{2\,(aq)}$.

4.76 Surface deposits of elemental sulfur around hot springs and volcanoes are believed to come from a two-step redox process. In the first reaction the combustion of hydrogen sulfide (H_2S) produces sulfur dioxide and water. In the second step, sulfur dioxide reacts with more hydrogen sulfide to give elemental sulfur and water. Write balanced chemical equations for these two reactions.

4.77 What is the minimum mass of hydrogen sulfide that a volcano must emit to deposit 1.25 kg of sulfur? (Refer to Problem 4.76.)

4.78 The largest single use of sulfuric acid is for the production of phosphate fertilizers. The acid reacts with calcium phosphate to give calcium sulfate and calcium dihydrogenphosphate. The mixture is crushed and spread on fields, where the salts dissolve in rainwater. Calcium phosphate, commonly found in phosphate rock, is too insoluble to be a direct source of phosphate for plants.

(a) Write a balanced equation for the reaction of sulfuric acid with calcium phosphate.
(b) How many kilograms each of sulfuric acid and calcium phosphate are required to produce 50.0 kg of the phosphoric acid–calcium sulfate mixture?
(c) In this mixture, how many moles of phosphate ion will be available to the plants?

4.79 Predict the product(s) of the following reactions by writing balanced equations. When the reaction involves ions, write a net ionic equation. Identify each reaction as precipitation, acid-base, or redox. If no reaction occurs, write *nr*. (Some of these transformations may involve more than one type of reaction.)

(a) $H_3PO_{4\,(aq)} + KOH_{(aq)} \rightarrow$
(b) $Sr_{(s)} + O_{2\,(g)} \rightarrow$
(c) $C_4H_8O_{(l)} + O_{2\,(g)} \rightarrow$
(d) $Mg_{(s)} + HBr_{(aq)} \rightarrow$
(e) $Pb(NO_3)_{2\,(aq)} + (NH_4)_2S_{(aq)} \rightarrow$
(f) $Ag_{(s)} + HCl_{(aq)} \rightarrow$
(g) $Ni_{(s)} + HCl_{(aq)} \rightarrow$
(h) $AgNO_{3\,(aq)} + KCH_3CO_{2\,(aq)} \rightarrow$

4.80 Vinyl chloride, one of the top 20 industrial compounds, is used primarily for the production of the polymer poly(vinyl chloride), better known as PVC. This versatile polymer is used to make piping, siding, gutters, floor tile, clothing, and toys. Vinyl chloride is made by oxychlorination of ethylene (C_2H_4). The overall balanced equation is

$$2\ H_2C{=}CH_2 + 2\ HCl + O_2 \rightarrow 2\ H_2C{=}CHCl + 2\ H_2O$$

Ethylene Vinyl chloride

Annual production of vinyl chloride is about 8 billion pounds. What minimum masses of ethylene and hydrochloric acid are required to produce this much vinyl chloride?

4.81 Iron reacts with HCl solution to give H_2 gas and Fe^{2+} ions. Suppose that 5.8 g of iron are to be dissolved in 1.5 M HCl. What is the minimum volume of the acid solution required to react with all of the iron?

4.82 Iron pyrite (FeS_2) reacts with molecular oxygen to give iron(III) oxide and SO_2. What masses of products will be formed in the complete processing of 175 metric tons of iron pyrite with excess oxygen?

4.83 One common component of antacids is $Al(OH)_3$. If an upset stomach contains 155 mL of 0.175 M HCl, how many grams of $Al(OH)_3$ would be required to completely neutralize the acid?

4.84 The "plop-plop-fizz-fizz" of an Alka Seltzer tablet is due to the acid-base reaction between citric acid and sodium hydrogencarbonate:

$$3\ HCO_3^-{}_{(aq)} + H_3C_6H_5O_{7\,(aq)} \rightarrow 3\ CO_{2\,(g)} + 3\ H_2O_{(l)} + C_6H_5O_7^{3-}{}_{(aq)}$$

One Alka Seltzer tablet contains 1.916 g of sodium hydrogencarbonate and 1.00 g of citric acid. What mass of CO_2 gas will fizz out when one tablet is plopped into water?

4.85 One of the starting materials for the preparation of nylon is adipic acid. Adipic acid is produced from the oxidation of cyclohexane:

$$2\ C_6H_{12} + 5\ O_2 \rightarrow 2\ HO_2C(CH_2)_4CO_2H + 2\ H_2O$$

Cyclohexane C_6H_{12} Adipic acid $C_6H_{10}O_4$

If 375 kg of cyclohexane reacts with an unlimited supply of oxygen, how much adipic acid can be formed?

4.86 Chromic acid is a powerful oxidizing solution used to clean laboratory glassware. This solution is a syrupy, dark orange-black liquid that is extremely corrosive. (Chromic acid is rarely used nowadays because the form of chromium in chromic acid is carcinogenic.) A recipe for chromic acid calls for adding 8.0×10^2 mL of concentrated sulfuric acid slowly and with stirring to a mixture of 92 g of sodium dichromate ($Na_2Cr_2O_7{\cdot}2H_2O$) in 460 mL of water. Calculate the concentrations of all species present in the resulting chromic acid solution. Assume that sulfuric acid forms only one hydronium ion per molecule. From Table 4-1, concentrated H_2SO_4 = 18 M.

4.87 Calcium carbonate (limestone) reacts with hydrochloric acid to generate water and carbon dioxide gas. In a certain experiment, 5.0 g of $CaCO_3$ was added to 0.50 L of 0.10 M HCl. Write a balanced equation for this reaction, and calculate the concentrations of all species present in solution at the end of the reaction.

4.88 Several important industrial acids and bases were described in Section 4.6. List each of them and their uses.

4.89 Give four reasons why the yield of a chemical synthesis may be less than 100%.

4.90 Lithopone is a mixture of two insoluble ionic solids, ZnS and $BaSO_4$. Lithopone is a white pigment used in paints, paper, and white rubber products. Suggest how 1.0 kg of lithopone could be prepared by a precipitation reaction.

4.91 Phosphorus is essential for plant growth, and it is often the limiting nutrient in aqueous ecosystems. However, too much phosphorus can cause algae to grow at an explosive rate. This process, known as *eutrophication,* robs the rest of the ecosystem of essential oxygen, often destroying all other aquatic life. One source of aquatic phosphorus pollution is the HPO_4^{2-} used in detergents in sewage plants. The simplest way to remove HPO_4^{2-} is to treat the contaminated water with lime, CaO, which generates Ca^{2+} and OH^- ions in water. The phosphorus precipitates as $Ca_5(PO_4)_3OH$.

(a) Write the balanced equation for CaO dissolving in water.
(b) Write the balanced equation for the precipitation reaction. (HINT: Proton transfer and solid formation occurs.)
(c) How many kilograms of lime are required to remove all the phosphorus from a 1.00×10^4 L holding tank filled with contaminated water that is 0.0156 M in HPO_4^{2-}?

4.92 Analysis of a sample of natural gas gives the following results: 74% (by mass) methane (CH_4), 18% ethane (C_2H_6), and 8% propane (C_3H_8). How many moles of CO_2 would be produced in the combustion of 750 g of this gas?

4.93 Brass is an alloy of copper and zinc. When a 5.73-g sample of brass was dissolved in excess aqueous HCl, 21.3 mg of H_2 bubbled out of the solution. What was the percentage by mass composition of the brass? (HINT: Consult the activity series shown in Table 4-2.)

4.94 Silver jewelry is usually made from silver and copper alloys. The amount of copper in an alloy can vary considerably. The finest-quality alloy is sterling silver, which is 92.5% by mass silver. To determine the composition of a silver-copper alloy, a jeweler dissolved 0.135 g of metal shavings in 50.0 mL of concentrated nitric acid and then added 1.00 M KCl solution until no more precipitate formed. Filtration and drying yielded 0.156 g of AgCl precipitate. What was the mass composition of the silver alloy?

4.95 What reaction, if any, occurs when the following aqueous solutions are mixed? (a) Na_2CO_3 and $Fe(NO_3)_3$; (b) $HClO_4$ and KOH; (c) NaCl and $Ba(OH)_2$.

4.96 What are the main species present when each of the following is dissolved in water? (a) nitric acid; (b) ammonium sulfate; (c) potassium hydrogencarbonate; and (d) carbon dioxide.

4.97 Although H_2SO_4 has two acidic hydrogen atoms, only one of them is classified as strong. The second one is weak. Thus an aqueous solution of sulfuric acid contains water molecules, hydronium cations, and hydrogensulfate anions. The following drawing represents one part of an aqueous solution of sulfuric acid. (The solvent water molecules have been omitted for clarity.)

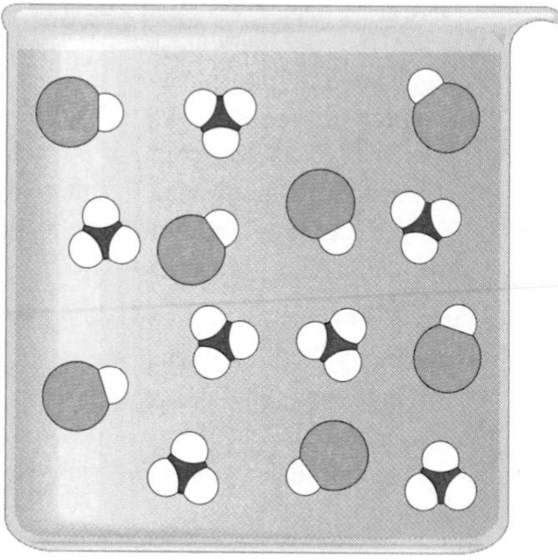

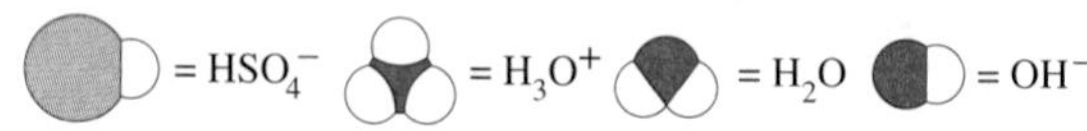

For each of the following situations, draw a new picture that shows what the solution looks like after the reaction is complete. Be sure to show any water molecules produced in the reaction. (HINT: Hydroxide ions react with hydronium ions in preference to HSO_4^-.)
(a) Six OH^- ions are added to the solution
(b) Twelve OH^- ions are added to the solution.
(c) Eighteen OH^- ions are added to the solution.

4.98 The CO_2 exhaled by astronauts must be "scrubbed" (removed) from the spacecraft atmosphere. One way to do this is with solid LiOH:

$$CO_{2\,(g)} + 2\,LiOH_{(s)} \rightarrow Li_2CO_{3\,(s)} + H_2O_{(l)}$$

The CO_2 output of an astronaut is about 1.0 kg/day. What is the minimum mass of LiOH required for a 6-day space shuttle flight involving five astronauts?

4.99 Potassium hydroxide is considerably cheaper than lithium hydroxide and undergoes the analogous reaction with CO_2. Repeat the calculation of Problem 4.98 for KOH. Your answer should suggest a reason why the more expensive substance is used on the space shuttle.

4.100 One set of reactants for rocket fuel is hydrazine and hydrogen peroxide, which react vigorously when mixed:

$$N_2H_{4\,(l)} + H_2O_{2\,(l)} \rightarrow N_{2\,(g)} + H_2O_{(g)} \quad \text{(unbalanced)}$$

The density of liquid hydrazine is 1.44 g/mL, and that of hydrogen peroxide is 1.01 g/mL. What volume ratio of these two liquids should be used if both fuels are to be used up at the same time?

4.101 Sulfur dioxide is an atmospheric pollutant that is converted to sulfuric acid when it reacts with water vapor. This is one source of acid rain, one of our most pressing environmental problems. The sulfur dioxide content of an air sample can be determined as follows. A sample of air is bubbled through an aqueous solution of hydrogen peroxide to convert all of the SO_2 to H_2SO_4:

$$H_2O_2 + SO_2 \longrightarrow H_2SO_4$$

Titration of the resulting solution completes the analysis. In one such case, analysis of 1550 L of Los Angeles air gave a solution that required 5.70 mL of 5.96×10^{-3} M NaOH to complete the titration. Determine the number of grams of SO_2 present in the air sample.

4.102 Balance the following reaction for the decomposition of nitroglycerine, a violent explosive:

$$C_3H_5N_3O_9 \longrightarrow N_2 + CO_2 + H_2O + O_2$$

4.103 Recall that combustion is a reaction with O_2. Write balanced chemical equations for the combustion reactions of the following organic substances. Assume that the only products are H_2O and CO_2: (a) C_4H_{10} (butane, the substance used in lighter fluid); (b) C_6H_6 (benzene, a carcinogenic solvent); (c) C_2H_6O (ethanol, the intoxicant in alcoholic beverages); (d) C_5H_{12} (pentane, a highly volatile hydrocarbon liquid; and (e) $C_6H_{12}O$ (cyclohexanol, a useful organic solvent).

4.104 For each of the reactions in Problem 4.103, determine how many grams of carbon dioxide and how many grams of water will be produced when 1.50 g of the organic compound burns completely.

4.105 When an organic compound with the molecular formula $C_9H_{14}O_3$ is burned completely in air, oxygen is consumed and CO_2 and H_2O are produced. If 3.00 g of this compound is burned completely, how many grams of O_2 are consumed and how many grams of H_2O are produced?

ANSWERS TO SECTION EXERCISES

4.1.1 $2\,C_8H_{18} + 25\,O_2 \longrightarrow 16\,CO_2 + 18\,H_2O$

4.1.2 $N_2 + O_2 \longrightarrow 2\,NO$ $\quad 2\,NO + O_2 \longrightarrow 2\,NO_2$

4.1.3 $2\,C_3H_6 + 2\,NH_3 + 3\,O_2 \longrightarrow 2\,C_3H_3N + 6\,H_2O$

4.2.1 333 g PCl_3 can be prepared; 258 g Cl_2 are consumed.

4.2.2 0.762 g

4.2.3 2.80×10^3 g O_2 is required; 2.27×10^3 g H_2O and 2.47×10^3 g CO_2 are produced.

4.3.1 Theoretical yield is 1.96 g, and percent yield is 94.0%. Possible reason is that not all the $KClO_3$ decomposes or that some O_2 escapes and is not collected.

4.3.2 Start with 3.9 tons of sulfur.

4.3.3 66 g salicylic acid and 24 g acetic anhydride are required.

4.4.1 The maximum mass is 793 kg HCN, and 28.7 kg CH_4 are left.

4.4.2 7.5 g

4.4.3 236 g

4.5.1 d, e, and g are insoluble; a, b, c, and f are soluble.

4.5.2 Mix solutions of a soluble silver salt and a soluble bromide salt (for example, $AgNO_3$ and KBr). To make 1.5 g of product requires 0.86 g Ag and 0.64 g Br, 1.35 g $AgNO_3$ and 0.95 g KBr.

4.5.3 34 kg

4.6.1 Net reaction: $NH_{3\,(aq)} + H_3O^+_{(aq)} \longrightarrow NH_4{}^+_{(aq)} + H_2O_{(l)}$

Molecular picture:

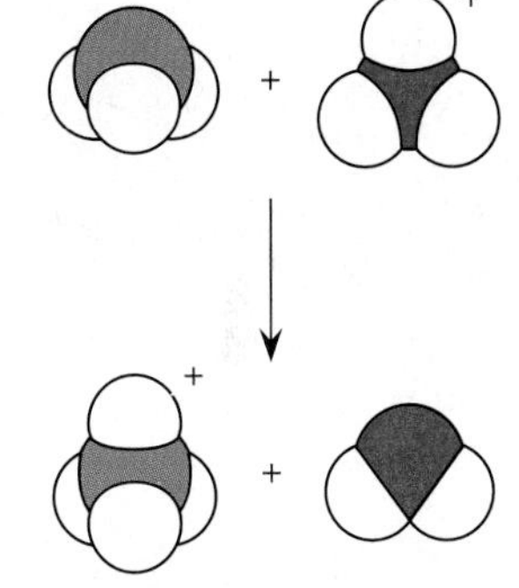

4.6.2 The tablets are impure, containing 10% impurities.

4.6.3 0.1009 M

4.7.1 135 mol

4.7.2 (a) $2\,Mg + TiO_2 \longrightarrow Ti + 2\,MgO$. Mg is the reducing agent and TiO_2 is the oxidizing agent. (b) 102 kg

4.7.3 (a) $Ni_{(s)} + 2\,H_3O^+_{(aq)} \longrightarrow Ni^{2+}_{(aq)} + H_{2\,(g)} + 2\,H_2O_{(l)}$
(b) and (c) No reaction
(d) $Fe_{(s)} + 2\,Ag^+_{(aq)} \longrightarrow Fe^{2+}_{(aq)} + 2\,Ag_{(s)}$

CHAPTER 5

THE BEHAVIOR OF GASES

Atoms and molecules can exist in three physical phases: solid, liquid, or gas. Solids and liquids are easy to handle because their atoms and molecules adhere to one another. For example, water can be poured into a glass and carried from one place to another. In contrast, molecules in the gas phase do not adhere to one another. Consequently a specific quantity of air cannot be moved from one place to another unless the sample is captured in a closed container such as a balloon.

Everyday experience brings us in contact with gases. The atmosphere is a gaseous mixture containing nitrogen and oxygen molecules as its two major components. Helium is used to fill "lighter-than-air" balloons. The bubbles escaping from a carbonated beverage are carbon dioxide. Natural gas, the major component of which is methane, is used to heat homes and cook food.

Chemists need to learn how gases behave because many important chemical processes involve gases. For example, 6 of the top 10 industrial chemicals are gases: nitrogen, ethylene, oxygen, ammonia, chlorine, and propene. Additionally, other chemicals in the top 50 are produced by processes that include gases as reactants or byproducts. Furthermore, the Earth's atmosphere is an immense system of gases where many chemical reactions occur. For example, plants extract carbon dioxide gas from the atmosphere and use it in photosynthesis to produce carbohydrates. Another example is the combustion of gasoline, which requires gaseous oxygen. A gaseous reaction with potentially disastrous consequences occurs in the upper atmosphere, where chlorofluorocarbon gases destroy ozone.

To begin this chapter, we develop a molecular description that explains features common to all gases. Next, the principles of stoichiometry are expanded to include gas-phase chemical reactions. The chapter concludes with a description of two special cases of gases, the Earth's atmosphere and vacuum systems.

5.1 MOLECULES IN MOTION

Gases differ from liquids and solids because their molecules move freely about to fill any volume. The substances that exist as gases under normal conditions (Table 5-1) are almost all small molecules of low molar mass. Later in this book, when we describe the forces that act between molecules, we show why large molecules are likely to form liquids and solids, whereas small molecules are likely to be able to move freely about and therefore exist as gases.

Because gas molecules move about freely, the molecules in a sample of gas move about until the gas has the same shape and volume as its container. Also, this freedom of motion allows gas molecules to move very easily from one place to another and makes gases highly fluid. Wind is an example of a gas flowing from place to place.

The atoms and molecules that make up a gas are in constant motion. Evidence for this comes from molecular **diffusion,** which is the movement of molecules of one substance through space occupied by another. For example, when a vase full of freshly cut roses is placed on a table, the fragrance of the flowers soon fills the room.

TABLE 5-1 SUBSTANCES THAT ARE GASES UNDER NORMAL CONDITIONS

SUBSTANCE	FORMULA	MM (g/mol)
Helium	He	4.0
Neon	Ne	20.2
Argon	Ar	39.9
Hydrogen	H_2	2.0
Carbon monoxide	CO	28.0
Nitrogen	N_2	28.0
Nitrogen monoxide	NO	30.0
Oxygen	O_2	32.0
Hydrogen chloride	HCl	36.5
Fluorine	F_2	38.0
Chlorine	Cl_2	71.0
Hydrogen sulfide	H_2S	34.1
Carbon dioxide	CO_2	44.0
Nitrogen dioxide	NO_2	46.0
Ozone	O_3	48.0
Ammonia	NH_3	17.0
Acetylene	C_2H_2	26.0
Methane	CH_4	16.0
Ethylene	C_2H_4	28.0
Ethane	C_2H_6	30.0
Propene	C_3H_6	42.0
Ethylene oxide	C_2H_4O	44.0

MM, Molar mass (grams per mole).

The volatile molecules that give roses their odor move easily from the liquid phase on the surface of the flower to the gas phase. These fragrant gas molecules then diffuse throughout the room's entire volume. In this example, gas molecules from the rose make their way through the gas molecules of the room's atmosphere.

In Chapter 2 we introduced the diffusion of ink in water as evidence that molecules in a liquid are in constant motion. The ability to smell a rose (or a skunk) from some distance is evidence that molecules in a gas are in constant motion.

The rate of diffusion depends on the speed at which the molecules are moving. How fast do gas molecules move? Molecular velocities can be measured using a molecular beam apparatus, which is shown schematically in Figure 5-1. Gas molecules escape from an oven through a small hole into a vacuum chamber, where a set of slits blocks the passage of all molecules except those moving in the forward direction. The result is a beam of molecules, all moving in the same direction. A movable shutter that blocks the beam path is opened briefly, allowing a small packet of molecules to pass through. Each molecule moves down the beam axis at its own velocity, and the faster a molecule moves, the less time it takes to travel the length of the beam. A detector at the end of the vacuum chamber measures the number of molecules arriving as a function of time, giving a profile of velocities.

When the velocity profile of a gas is measured in this way, it always shows a distribution of values, as illustrated by Figure 5-2. If all molecules had the same velocity, the molecules would reach the detector in a single clump. Instead, faster molecules move ahead of the main packet, and slower molecules fall behind. This experiment demonstrates that molecules in a gas have a distribution of velocities.

A police officer parked 1 block from a traffic light makes the same type of measurements on automobile velocities. After a light turns green, fast-moving autos come abreast of the officer sooner than those moving slowly.

A pattern emerges when this molecular beam experiment is repeated for various gases at a common temperature. Each gas shows a distribution of molecular velocities, but molecules with small mass move faster than molecules with large mass. Figure 5-3 illustrates this feature for H_2, CH_4, and CO_2. Of these, H_2 has the smallest mass and CO_2 the largest. The vertical lines drawn for each gas show the

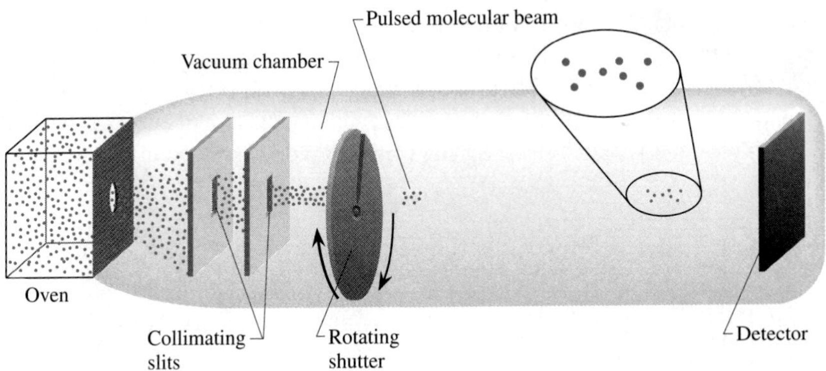

FIGURE 5-1
Schematic diagram of a molecular beam apparatus designed to measure the velocity distribution of gas molecules.

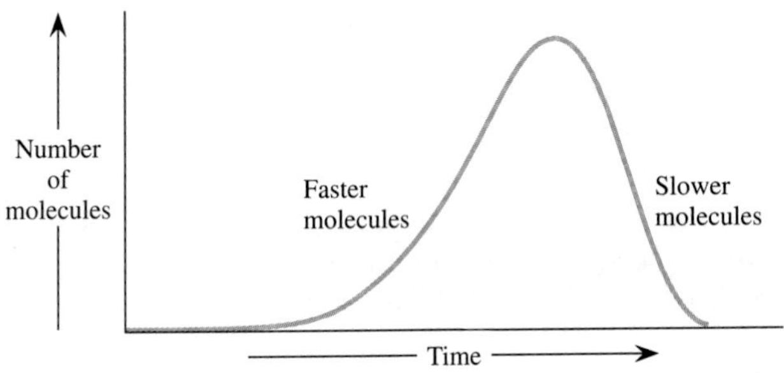

FIGURE 5-2
Distribution of molecules observed by the detector of a molecular beam apparatus (see Figure 5-1) as a function of time after opening the shutter. Slow molecules take longer to reach the detector than fast molecules.

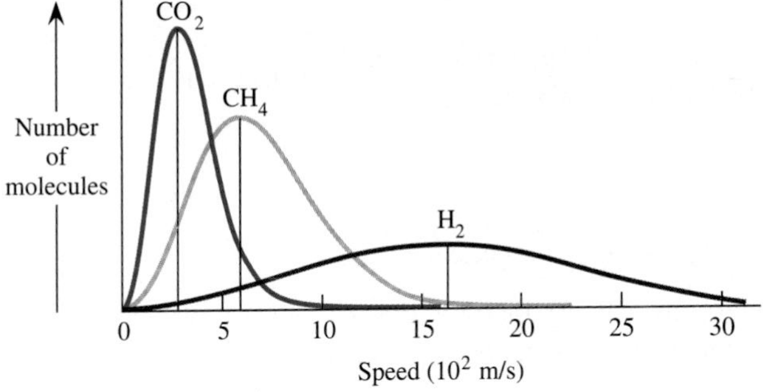

FIGURE 5-3
Molecular velocity distributions for H_2, CH_4, and CO_2 at a temperature of 300 K.

velocity at which each distribution reaches its maximum height. More molecules have this velocity than any other, so this is the most probable velocity for molecules of that gas. The most probable velocity for a molecule of hydrogen at 300 K is 1.57×10^3 m/s, which is 3.51×10^3 mi/hr.

VELOCITY AND ENERGY

Recall from Chapter 2 that any moving object has kinetic energy (*kE*), as defined by Equation 2-2:

$$kE = \tfrac{1}{2} mu^2$$

where *m* is the object's mass and *u* its velocity.

The most probable velocity of hydrogen molecules at 300 K is 1.57×10^3 m/s, but we need the mass of one H_2 molecule before we can calculate its most probable kinetic energy. We compute this from the molar mass (MM), Avogadro's number (N_A), and the appropriate unit conversion. The fundamental unit of energy is the joule (J). One joule equals 1 kg m^2 s^{-2}, so mass (m) should be expressed in kilograms:

$$m\ (\text{kg}) = \frac{MM}{N_A}\left(\frac{10^{-3}\ \text{kg}}{\text{g}}\right)$$

$$m = \left(\frac{2.016\ \text{g}}{1\ \text{mol}}\right)\left(\frac{1\ \text{mol}}{6.022 \times 10^{23}\ \text{molecules}}\right)\left(\frac{10^{-3}\ \text{kg}}{\text{g}}\right) = 3.348 \times 10^{-27}\ \text{kg/H}_2\ \text{molecule}$$

Now apply Equation 2-2:

$$kE = \tfrac{1}{2}\,(3.348 \times 10^{-27}\ \text{kg molecule}^{-1})(1.57 \times 10^{3}\ \text{m sec}^{-1})^2$$

$$= 4.13 \times 10^{-21}\ \text{kg m}^2\ \text{sec}^{-2}\ \text{molecule}^{-1}$$

$$kE_{\text{most probable}} = 4.13 \times 10^{-21}\ \text{J/molecule}$$

Because molecular velocities vary over a range of values, molecules have a wide distribution of kinetic energies. The most probable kinetic energy for H_2 molecules at 300 K is 4.13×10^{-21} J, but about half have more energy, and about half have less energy.

The most probable velocities of methane and carbon dioxide are slower than the most probable velocity of hydrogen, but CH_4 and CO_2 are more massive than H_2. When kinetic energy calculations are repeated for these gases, they show that the most probable kinetic energy is the same for all three gases. For CH_4:

$$\frac{(16.04\ \text{g/mol})(10^{-3}\ \text{kg/g})(5.57 \times 10^{2}\ \text{m/s})^2}{2(6.022 \times 10^{23}\ \text{molecules/mol})} = 4.13 \times 10^{-21}\ \text{J/CH}_4\ \text{molecule}$$

For CO_2:

$$\frac{(44.01\ \text{g/mol})(10^{-3}\ \text{kg/g})(3.37 \times 10^{2}\ \text{m/s})^2}{2(6.022 \times 10^{23}\ \text{molecules/mol})} = 4.13 \times 10^{-21}\ \text{J/CO}_2\ \text{molecule}$$

Even though the *velocity* distributions for these three gases peak at different values, the *kinetic energy* distributions are identical.

At a given temperature, all gases have the same molecular kinetic energy distribution.

Molecular beam experiments also show that molecules move faster as temperature increases. A packet of molecules released through the shutter at 900 K takes less time to reach the detector than a packet of molecules released at 300 K. Velocity and kinetic energy increase with temperature. Figure 5-4 shows kinetic energy distributions at 300 and 900 K. Because all gases have the same kinetic energy distribution at any temperature, the distributions shown in Figure 5-4 apply to any gas.

AVERAGE KINETIC ENERGY

More molecules have the most probable kinetic energy than any other value. By proportion, however, very few molecules actually have the *most probable* kinetic energy. This is because any sample of gas contains many molecules that move with many different kinetic energies. The *average* kinetic energy (kE_{avg}) per molecule can

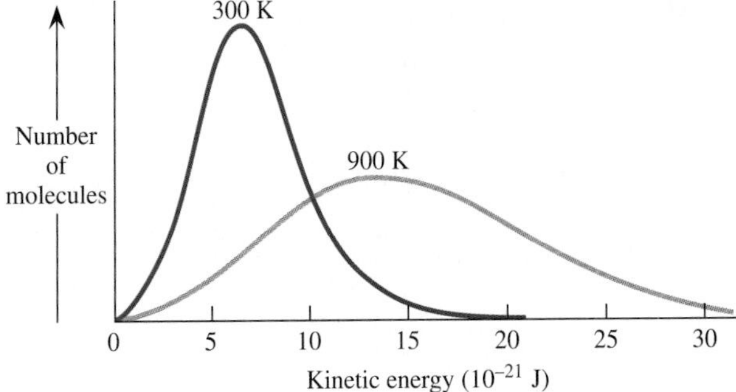

FIGURE 5-4
Distribution in molecular energies for a gas at 300 and 900 K.

be found by adding all the individual molecular energies and dividing by the total number of molecules. As shown in Equation 5-1, the result depends on the temperature of the gas:

$$kE_{avg} = \frac{3RT}{2N_A} \tag{5-1}$$

where T is the temperature in kelvins, N_A is Avogadro's number, and $\boldsymbol{R}$ is a new quantity called the **gas constant.** The value of R is determined experimentally, and its units are those required to give kinetic energy in joules per molecule:

$$R = 8.314 \text{ J mol}^{-1}\text{ K}^{-1}$$

T is in kelvins, and N_A has units of molecules per mole. Therefore, to give kinetic energy in J/molecule, R must have units of J/mol K.

The average kinetic energy expressed by Equation 5-1 is kinetic energy *per molecule.* The total kinetic energy (kE_{total}) of 1 mol of gas molecules is obtained by multiplying Equation 5-1 by Avogadro's number:

$$kE_{total} = (\text{No. of molecules})(kE_{avg}) = (N_A)\left(\frac{3RT}{2N_A}\right) = \tfrac{3}{2}RT$$

Thus 1 mol of *any* gas has a total molecular kinetic energy of $\frac{3}{2}RT$. Sample Problem 5-1 applies these equations to sulfur hexafluoride.

SAMPLE PROBLEM 5-1 MOLECULAR KINETIC ENERGIES

Sulfur hexafluoride (SF_6) has a relatively large molar mass of 146 g/mol, but it is still a gas under normal conditions. Compute the average molecular kinetic energy and molar kinetic energy of SF_6 at 150 °C.

METHOD: The problem asks for a calculation of kinetic energies and provides a chemical formula, molar mass, and a temperature.

We have two equations for the kinetic energy of a gas:

$$kE_{avg} = \frac{3RT}{2N_A} \qquad kE_{molar} = \tfrac{3}{2}RT$$

To carry out the calculations, we need the constants R and N_A as well as T in kelvins. The constants are found in standard reference tables, but both are used so frequently in chemical calculations that it is wise to memorize them:

$$R = 8.314 \text{ J/mol K} \qquad N_A = 6.022 \times 10^{23} \text{ molecules/mol}$$

Convert the temperature from °C to K by adding 273:

$$T = 150\ °C + 273 = 423\ K$$

Now substitute and perform the calculations:

$$kE_{avg} = \frac{3(8.314\ J/mol\ K)(423\ K)}{2(6.022 \times 10^{23}\ molecules/mol)} = 8.76 \times 10^{-21}\ J/molecule$$

$$kE_{molar} = \frac{3(8.314\ J/mol\ K)(423\ K)}{2} = 5.28 \times 10^{3}\ J/mol$$

Does it bother you to find that neither the chemical formula nor the molar mass is needed for these calculations? Remember that not all data are necessarily required for doing any particular calculation. Because average kinetic energy depends on temperature but not on molecular mass, we do not need mass information to do this problem.

RATES OF DIFFUSION

Equation 5-1 provides a basis for relating the average velocity (u_{avg}) of molecules to their molar mass and temperature. Because Equations 2-2 and 5-1 both describe kinetic energy, we can set them equal to one another:

$$\tfrac{1}{2}\, m u^2_{avg} = \frac{3RT}{2N_A}$$

Now solve this equality for u:

$$u^2_{avg} = \frac{3RT}{mN_A} = \frac{3RT}{MM}$$

$$u_{avg} = \left(\frac{3RT}{MM}\right)^{1/2} \qquad \textbf{(5-2)}$$

According to Equation 5-2, the average velocity of gas molecules is directly proportional to the square root of the temperature and is inversely proportional to the square root of the molar mass.

Gas molecules move from one place to another by diffusion or effusion. As mentioned earlier, diffusion is the movement of one type of molecule through molecules of another type. For example, molecules of rose fragrance spread through a room by diffusing through the oxygen and nitrogen molecules that make up the atmosphere. **Effusion** is the movement of molecules as they escape from a container into a vacuum. Effusion is exemplified by the escape of molecules from the oven of Figure 5-1. Both types of motion are governed by Equation 5-2. Rates of diffusion and effusion are directly proportional to molecular velocities, so we can compare the rates for two different substances, A and B, moving under similar conditions.

$$\frac{Rate_A}{Rate_B} = \frac{u_{avg\ A}}{u_{avg\ B}} = \frac{\left(\dfrac{3RT}{2MM_A}\right)^{1/2}}{\left(\dfrac{3RT}{2MM_B}\right)^{1/2}} = \left(\frac{\dfrac{3RT}{2MM_A}}{\dfrac{3RT}{2MM_B}}\right)^{1/2}$$

The factor $3RT$ is the same for both substances, so the ratio of the average velocities depends only on the molar masses:

$$\frac{Rate_A}{Rate_B} = \left(\frac{MM_B}{MM_A}\right)^{1/2} \qquad \textbf{(5-3)}$$

Equation 5-3 is known as *Graham's law.*

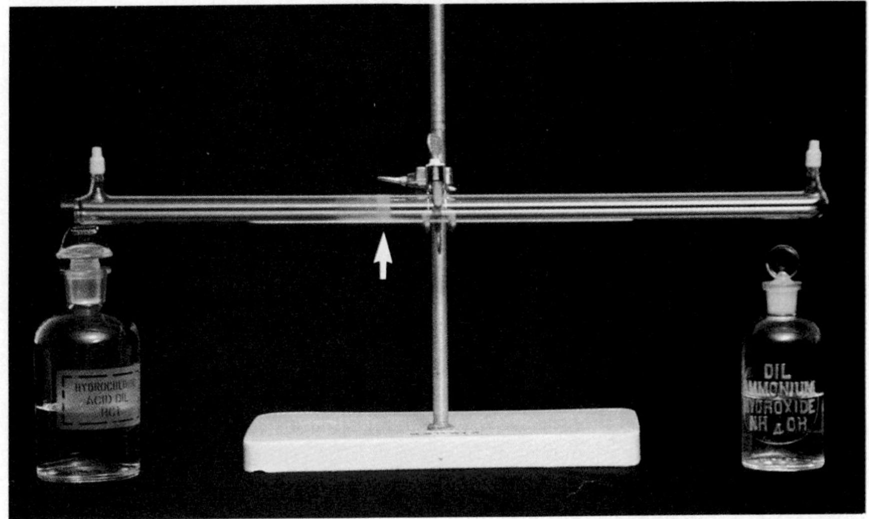

FIGURE 5-5
Because of its lower molar mass, NH_3 diffuses through a glass tube faster than HCl. The deposition of ammonium chloride (NH_4Cl), which appears as a white band *(arrow)*, occurs closer to the bottle of aqueous HCl.

The diffusion rates expressed by Graham's law are illustrated in Figure 5-5, which shows solutions of aqueous hydrochloric acid and aqueous ammonia (NH_3) at opposite ends of a glass tube. Molecules of hydrogen chloride gas and NH_3 gas escape from the solutions and diffuse through the air in the tube. When the two gases meet, they undergo a proton transfer reaction to make ammonium chloride, a white solid salt:

$$HCl_{(g)} + NH_{3\,(g)} \rightarrow NH_4Cl_{(s)}$$

The salt can be seen in Figure 5-5 as a white solid on the wall of the tube. The salt is deposited closer to the bottle of hydrochloric acid because the lighter NH_3 molecules diffuse faster than the heavier HCl molecules. Substituting molar masses into Equation 5-3 gives the relative rates of diffusion:

$$\frac{\text{Rate}_{NH_3}}{\text{Rate}_{HCl}} = \left(\frac{MM_{HCl}}{MM_{NH_3}}\right)^{1/2} = \left(\frac{36.46 \text{ g/mol}}{17.03 \text{ g/mol}}\right)^{1/2} = 1.463$$

The calculation verifies our observations; NH_3 diffuses 1.463 times faster than HCl.

SECTION EXERCISES

5.1.1 A molecular beam experiment of the type illustrated in Figure 5-1 is performed using an equimolar mixture of He and CO_2. Sketch the appearance of a graph of the number of molecules reaching the detector as a function of time.

5.1.2 Calculate each of the following energies: (a) total kinetic energy of 1.00 mol of He atoms at −100 °C; (b) total kinetic energy of 1.00 g of N_2 molecules at 0 °C; and (c) kinetic energy of a single molecule of SF_6 that has twice as much energy as the average molecular energy at 200 °C.

5.1.3 According to Graham's law, isotopes of an element can be separated from one another because lighter isotopes effuse faster than heavier ones. Calculate the ratio of effusion rates for H_2O and D_2O escaping from an oven at $T = 500$ °C.

5.2 THE IDEAL GAS EQUATION

A gas can be described by its macroscopic properties. It contains some number of *moles* of atoms or molecules, has a *mass,* occupies a *volume,* and is at some *temperature.* This section develops the link between the molecular description of a gas and its macroscopic properties.

When an object strikes a surface, it exerts a force against that surface. For instance, a basketball exerts force when it strikes a backboard. A wave breaking on the beach is a liquid exerting force on the sand. A billiard ball exerts force when it caroms off a cushion on the pool table. Gases also exert forces. For example, the wind moves a sailboat through the water as a result of the force it exerts on the sail, and the gas inside a balloon exerts forces on the walls of the balloon that prevent it from collapsing. When we view a gas at the molecular level, we find that its molecules exert forces through their never-ending collisions with the walls of their container, as shown schematically in Figure 5-6. The collision of a liquid or solid with a surface also is a set of molecular collisions, each of which results in a force. Force is exerted when one collection of molecules undergoes a set of collisions with another set of molecules.

The collective effect of molecular collisions is measured by **pressure,** which is the force exerted per unit area. Pressure is caused by molecular collisions, but it is a macroscopic property. The pressure exerted by a gas is caused by the combined effects of all collisions. To move from our molecular view of collisions to a description of the pressure exerted by a gas, we must examine more closely the nature of collisions.

THE IDEAL GAS

Our approach to the properties of gases is to consider the effect of each gas molecule and then add up the effects of all the molecules. This approach works as long as each gas molecule behaves independently. That is, adding or removing molecules from the container does not cause any change in the way an individual molecule behaves.

The macroscopic properties of a gas suggest that gas molecules really do behave independently. For example, gases are easy to compress, indicating that much of the volume of a gas is empty space. In other words, the distance between gas molecules is very large compared to the size of the molecules. Consequently, each molecule moves in a volume that is unlikely to contain other molecules. Also, gases expand rapidly through any opening, indicating an absence of strongly attractive forces holding gas molecules together.

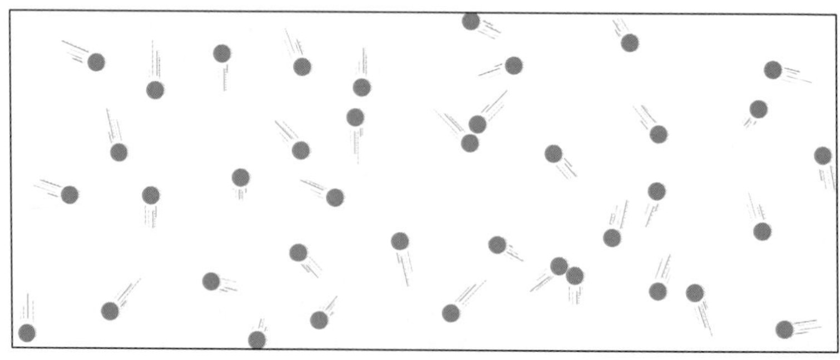

FIGURE 5-6
Atomic picture of helium gas. Most of the volume is empty space. Atoms are constantly in motion, colliding with the walls and each other.

The volume occupied by the molecules of a gas is insignificant compared with the volume of their container.

The forces between gas molecules are small.

The properties of a gas indicate that molecular volumes and forces are small. When they are *negligibly small*, each molecule is completely independent of every other molecule, and the gas is said to be *ideal*. This gives us a way of defining an **ideal gas** in terms of molecular parameters:

An ideal gas is defined as one for which both the volume of molecules and the forces between the molecules are so small that they have no effect on the behavior of the gas.

In an ideal gas, each molecule travels freely through space until it strikes a wall of the container. When a molecule strikes a wall, it exerts a force and gives the wall an impulse. During each second, many collisions impart many impulses. The pressure exerted by the gas is the sum of all impulses occurring per second. We first analyze the impulse imparted by each molecule, and then see how they are added together.

The size of the impulse given to the wall depends on the mass and velocity of the molecule. A molecule with a small mass imparts a smaller impulse than a massive molecule. Similarly, a molecule with a lower velocity imparts a smaller impulse than the same molecule with higher velocity. In terms of everyday objects, which would you rather have hit you, a fast-moving Ping-Pong ball, a slow-moving golf ball, or a fast-moving golf ball? The Ping-Pong ball will not cause any damage because of its small mass (small mass means small impulse), nor will the slow-moving golf ball because of its small velocity (small velocity means small impulse). However, a fast-moving golf ball can exert a large, damaging impulse. Consequently, prudent golf spectators stay out of the way. Impulse is proportional to *mass* and *velocity.*

More precisely, impulse is proportional to mass and the change in velocity. A golf ball that glances off does much less damage than one that hits directly. Although this distinction is important in calculating impulses exactly, we do not need to consider it in our qualitative development of pressure.

A single molecule exerts a total effect that also depends on how often it strikes the walls of its container. This collision frequency depends on molecular velocity. For example, a molecule with velocity $2u$ moves across a container in half the time it takes a molecule moving with velocity u. Therefore fast-moving molecules hit the walls more often than slow-moving molecules.

Individual impulses are proportional to mass and velocity, and number of impulses per second is proportional to velocity. Thus the total effect of a single molecule on the pressure of a gas is proportional to the mass of the molecules multiplied by the square of its velocity. Recall that kinetic energy is also proportional to mass multiplied by the square of velocity, so we can conclude that the effect of each molecule is proportional to its kinetic energy. Furthermore, Equation 5-1 shows that the average molecular kinetic energy is proportional to temperature. This lets us link the average effect per molecule to the temperature of the gas. The average contribution of each molecule to the pressure *(P)* of a gas is proportional to the temperature *(T):*

$$P_{\text{per molecule}} \propto T$$

The symbol $\propto$ should be read as "is proportional to." It means that when the property on the right is multiplied by some factor, the property on the left is multiplied by the same factor.

At this point, we might expect that simply multiplying the average effect per molecule by number of molecules would give the total pressure, but we must consider another feature. In any unit of time, only the molecules in the space near a wall are able to reach the wall. Thus the number of collisions per second depends on the number of molecules *per unit volume,* not on the total number of molecules in the

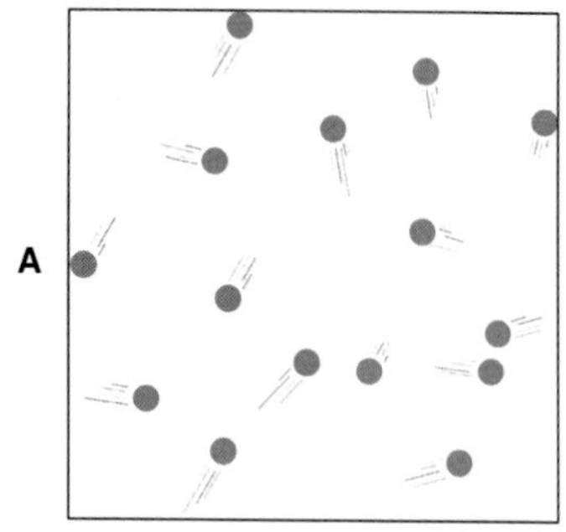

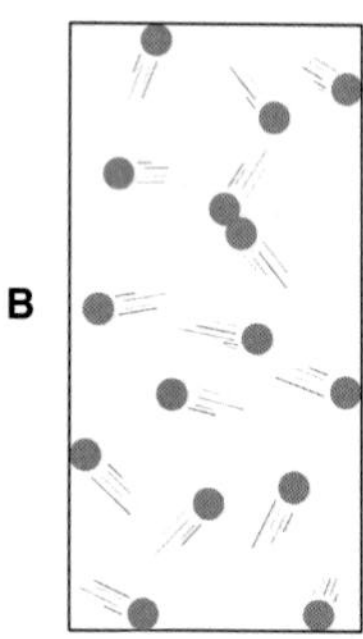

FIGURE 5-7
Schematic view of the effect of compressing a fixed quantity of gas into a smaller volume. Container *B* has the same number of molecules as *A* but half its volume. Consequently the molecular density is twice as great in *B*, with twice as many collisions per second with the walls.

container. The number of molecules per unit volume is the *molecular density.* To relate pressure to other macroscopic properties, we must explore how macroscopic properties depend on molecular density.

First, consider what happens when a gas is compressed to half its original volume. The volume decreases, but the total number of molecules remains the same. Thus cutting the volume in half doubles the molecular density because there are twice as many molecules in any given space. This results in twice as many wall collisions, as shown in Figure 5-7.

Second, doubling the *amount* of gas in a fixed volume also doubles the molecular density, and doubling the molecular density doubles the number of collisions. This is shown in Figure 5-8.

An increase in the molecular density of a gas gives a proportionate increase in number of collisions per second, which in turn increases the pressure of the gas. This proportionality can be expressed in terms of the molar density (n/V, where n is the number of moles and V is the volume):

$$P \propto \frac{n}{V}$$

We now have two proportional relationships that describe gas behavior at the molecular level:

$$P_{\text{per molecule}} \propto T \qquad\qquad P \propto \frac{n}{V}$$

The molecular density of a gas is independent of its temperature. In other words, changing the temperature of the gas changes neither n nor V. Because they are independent, these two expressions can be combined into a single proportionality that gives the dependence of pressure on amount, volume, and temperature:

$$P \propto \frac{nT}{V}$$

A proportional relationship is converted to an equation by introducing a constant:

$$P = (\text{constant})\ \frac{nT}{V}$$

Scientists have evaluated the constant in this equation experimentally by measuring the pressure exerted by gases when n, T, and V are known. It turns out to be the gas constant R, which we introduced in Section 5.1:

$$P = R\ \frac{nT}{V}$$

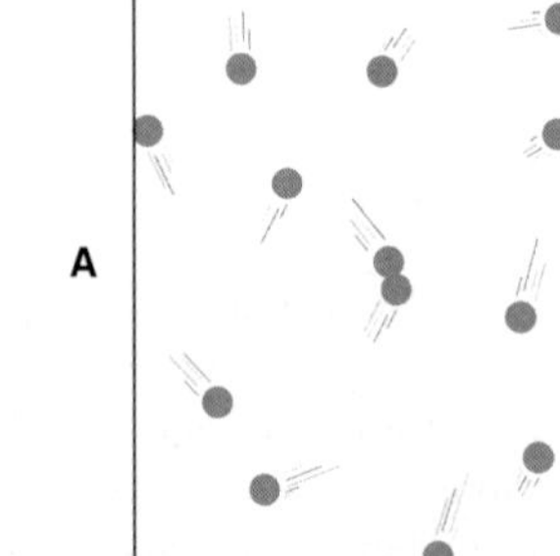

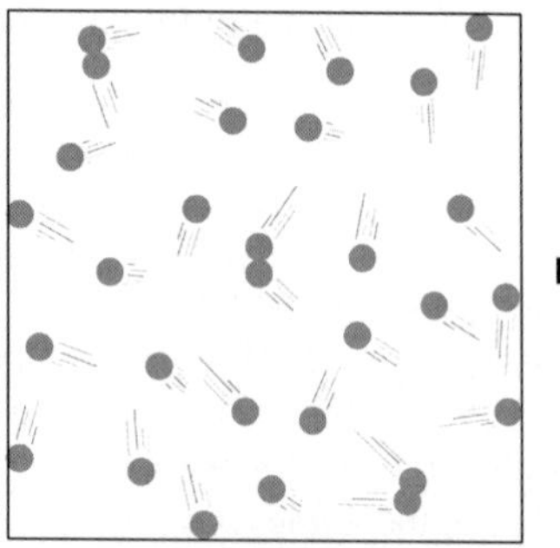

FIGURE 5-8
Schematic view of the effect of doubling the number of gas molecules in a fixed volume. Container *B* has twice as many molecules as *A*. Consequently the molecular density is twice as large in *B*, with twice as many collisions per second with the walls.

This equality describes the macroscopic behavior of an ideal gas. Multiplying both sides by V puts it into the form that is known as the **ideal gas equation:**

$$PV = nRT \quad \textbf{(5-4)}$$

The ideal gas equation predicts that every gas behaves identically. The constant R has the same value for all gases, so the equation makes no reference to any particular molecular property, such as size or mass. The only restrictions on the applicability of the ideal gas equation are those needed for molecules to behave independently. Molecular sizes must be negligible compared to container volume, and forces between molecules must be negligible. These restrictions may appear to be drastic, but many gases show near-ideal behavior under normal conditions.

SECTION EXERCISES

5.2.1 According to the ideal gas equation, what will happen to the pressure of a gas if we make each of the following changes, holding all other conditions constant? (a) double the temperature (in kelvins); (b) reduce the container's volume by a factor of two; (c) triple the amount of gas in the container; and (d) replace the gas with an equal number of moles of another gas whose molar mass is twice as great.

5.2.2 The following molecular picture represents a small portion of an ideal gas exerting a pressure P. Redraw the figure in two ways, each of which gives a new pressure that is half as great.

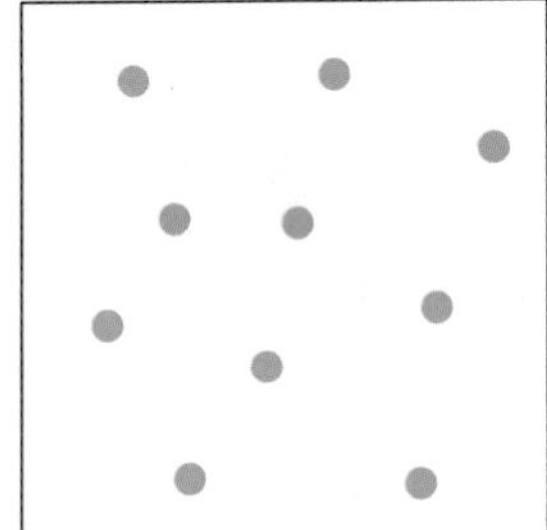

5.2.3 Is a gas more likely to behave ideally at low molecular density or at high molecular density? Explain your answer in terms of the two assumptions made for ideal gases.

5.3 PRESSURE

ATMOSPHERIC PRESSURE

The air around us is a huge reservoir of gas whose atoms and molecules exert pressure on the Earth's surface. This pressure exerted by the atmosphere can be measured with an instrument called a **barometer.** A simple mercury barometer is shown schematically in Figure 5-9. A glass tube, closed at one end, is filled with liquid mercury. The filled tube is carefully inverted into a dish that is partially filled with more mercury. The force of gravity pulls downward on the mercury in the tube. With no opposing force, the mercury would all run out of the tube and mix with the mercury in the dish. The mercury does fall if the tube is long enough, but the flow stops at a fixed height. The column of mercury stops falling because the atmosphere

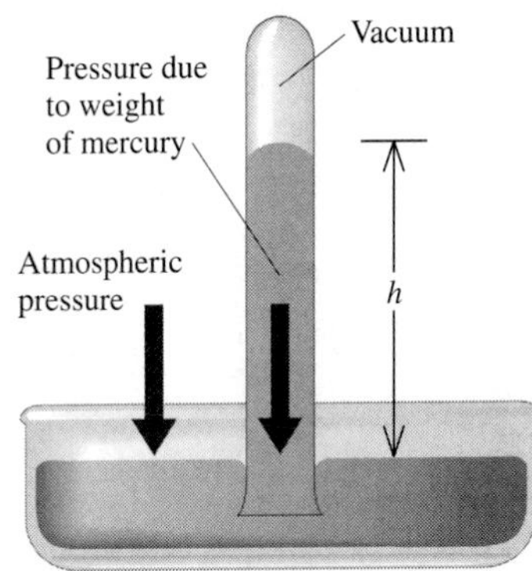

FIGURE 5-9
Schematic diagram of a mercury barometer. Air pressure exerted on the pool of liquid mercury forces the column of liquid up into the evacuated tubing. At the same time, the force of gravity pulls the column of mercury downward. The column's equilibrium height is reached when the two opposing forces are balanced.

exerts a pressure on the mercury in the dish, exerting a force that pushes it *up* the tube. The column is in balance where the force of the atmosphere on the mercury in the dish exactly balances the downward force of gravity on the mercury column.

At sea level, atmospheric pressure supports a mercury column approximately 760 mm in height. Changes in the weather cause minor variations in the density of air, leading to fluctuations in atmospheric pressure. Nevertheless, the height of the column seldom varies by more than 10 mm. Only under extreme conditions, such as in the eye of a hurricane, does the mercury in a barometer fall below 740 mm.

UNITS OF PRESSURE

Traditionally, chemists define the units associated with pressure in terms of the Earth's atmosphere and the mercury barometer. The standard **atmosphere** (atm) is the normal pressure exerted by the Earth's atmosphere that will support a column of mercury 760 mm in height.

The torr is named for the seventeenth-century Italian physicist Evangelista Torricelli, who invented the barometer.

A second common pressure unit, the **torr,** is also based on the mercury barometer. One torr is the pressure exerted by a column of mercury 1 mm in height. Often, units in torr are expressed simply as "millimeters." Because the standard atmosphere supports a 760 mm column of mercury, the relationship between the atmosphere and the torr is: 1 atm = 760 torr = 760 mm Hg.

Although atmospheres, torr, and millimeters are used by chemists in their day-to-day routine, the accepted SI unit for pressure is the **pascal** (Pa).* Recall that pressure is force per unit area, so the pascal can be expressed using the SI units for force and area. The SI unit of force is the newton (N), and area is measured in square meters (m^2). Thus the pascal is 1 N/m^2. Expressed in pascals, the numerical value of atmospheric pressure is quite large. By international agreement, 1 atm is defined exactly in terms of pascals: 1 atm = 1.01325×10^5 Pa. The pressures encountered most frequently by humans are in the range of hundreds of kilopascals (kPa). For this reason, chemists find it more convenient to use torr, millimeters, or atmospheres to measure pressure. Because so few chemists use the pascal, we use torr, millimeters, or atmospheres in this text, even though they are not part of the SI system.

1 Pa = 1 N m^{-2}, and 1 N = 1 kg m s^{-2}. Thus, as with the joule, the pascal is a collection of fundamental SI units: 1 Pa = 1 kg m^{-1} s^{-2}.

PRESSURE AND THE IDEAL GAS EQUATION

With a set of units for pressure, we can begin quantitative applications of the ideal gas equation. However, using atmospheres rather than pascals as the unit of pressure means that we need a different value for the gas constant. The value of R introduced earlier, 8.314 J/mol K, is appropriate only when SI units are used exclusively. This means that R = 8.314 J/mol K can be used only when pressure is expressed in pascals. When the pressure of a gas is expressed in atmospheres and volume is expressed in liters, the gas constant becomes: $R = 0.08206 \text{ L atm mol}^{-1} \text{ K}^{-1}$. Sample Problem 5-2 shows how to calculate pressure using the ideal gas equation. Box 5-1 discusses the manometer and measuring pressure.

* Blaise Pascal was a French scientist who lived only 39 years, from 1623 to 1662. Despite his short life, he made prodigious contributions to both mathematics and science. Pascal studied the properties of pressures exerted by fluids, studying both liquids and the atmosphere. He discovered the principle of the hydraulic press and performed experiments proving that atmospheric pressure decreases with altitude. At age 16, Pascal published a book that contained new insights into geometry, and 3 years later he invented a calculating machine that was the forerunner of cash registers. In collaboration with another mathematician, Pascal founded the modern theory of probability, which 200 years later was instrumental in the description of molecular motion.

BOX 5-1

MEASURING PRESSURE

"The barometer is at 29.72 inches and falling." "Your blood pressure is 120/80 (torr, or mm Hg), which is normal." "Check your tires before leaving on a trip. Underinflation or overinflation can cause excessive tire wear." Pressure measurements are very much a part of our everyday lives, but how are pressures measured?

The easiest way to measure the pressure exerted by the atmosphere is to compare the force it exerts with the gravitational force exerted by the Earth on a column of liquid mercury. The Earth's atmosphere exerts enough pressure to support a column of mercury to a height of 760 mm (29.92 inches). Because this is a convenient height to measure, mercury barometers are typically used to measure atmospheric pressure. A barometer is a closed glass tube that has been filled with mercury and then inverted (see Figure 5-9). As gravity pulls some of the mercury out of the tube's bottom, a vacuum is created in the tube's closed end. Gas pressure is exerted on the outside surface of the mercury but not on the surface of the mercury inside the tube.

A manometer is similar to a barometer, but in a manometer, gases exert pressure on *both* liquid surfaces. Consequently a manometer measures the *difference* in pressures exerted by two gases. A simple manometer, shown in Figure 5-10, is a U-shaped glass tube containing mercury. One side of the tube is exposed to the atmosphere and the other to a gas whose pressure we want to measure. The difference in heights of mercury on the two sides of the U tube equals the difference in the pressures exerted by the two gases.

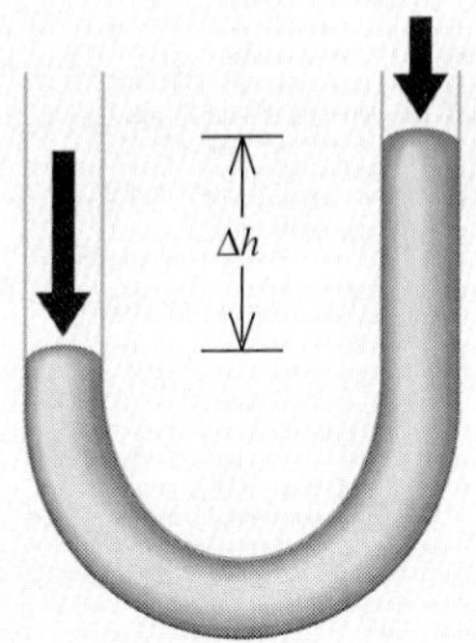

FIGURE 5-10
A manometer is an open U tube containing mercury. When the gas pressures on the two arms are different, the mercury column is higher in the arm exposed to the lower pressure. The difference in height (Δh) is the difference between the two pressures.

Many tire pressure gauges compare the force exerted by a gas to the restoring force of a spring. The pressure of gas inside the tire exerts a force on the gauge, which compresses a spring. The spring "pushes back" with an opposing force that becomes greater as the spring is compressed. The point of balance is reached when the restoring force of the spring balances the force exerted by the gas. This gives a measure of the gas pressure.

Blood pressure measurements result from two different comparisons of pressure. First, the air pressure inside a tourniquet applied to the arm is increased until its pressure is sufficient to prevent the flow of blood in the arteries. The tourniquet pressure equals the pressure that the blood exerts inside the arteries. Second, this tourniquet pressure is measured by a pressure gauge that may be a mercury manometer or a spring-type gauge. Blood pressure readings have two components: the pressure exerted by the heart as it contracts (higher value) and the "resting" pressure between contractions (lower value).

SAMPLE PROBLEM 5-2 PRESSURE AND THE IDEAL GAS EQUATION

A 265-gallon steel storage tank contains 88.5 kg of methane (CH_4). If the temperature is 25 °C, what is the pressure inside the tank?

METHOD: Pressure is calculated using the ideal gas equation, but we need to make sure all the variables are expressed in their proper units. Temperature must be in kelvins, amount of methane in moles, and volume in liters. Each conversion is straightforward:

$$V = (265 \text{ gallons})\left(\frac{3.7854 \text{ L}}{\text{gallon}}\right) = 1.003 \times 10^3 \text{ L} \qquad T = 25 + 273.15 = 298 \text{ K}$$

$$n = (88.5 \text{ kg})\left(\frac{10^3 \text{ g}}{\text{kg}}\right)\left(\frac{1 \text{ mol}}{16.04 \text{ g}}\right) = 5.517 \times 10^3 \text{ mol CH}_4$$

Next, rearrange the ideal gas equation so that pressure is isolated on the left:

$$PV = nRT \qquad so \qquad P = \frac{nRT}{V}$$

Before we substitute the known values and solve for pressure, it is essential to choose the proper value of the gas constant. In common usage, pressure is expressed in atmospheres, so we must use $R = 0.08206$ L atm mol^{-1} K^{-1}.

$$P = \frac{(5.517 \times 10^3 \text{ mol})(0.08206 \text{ L atm mol}^{-1} \text{ K}^{-1})(298 \text{ K})}{1.003 \times 10^3 \text{ L}} = 1.35 \times 10^2 \text{ atm}$$

SECTION EXERCISES

5.3.1 In the eye of a severe hurricane, the height of a mercury barometer may drop as low as 700 mm. Express this pressure in torr and atmospheres. What percentage change from standard atmospheric pressure is this?

5.3.2 Oxygen gas is sold in large pressurized tanks. Calculate the pressure in atmospheres inside a tank that has a volume of 7.45 L, contains 0.500 kg of O_2, and has a temperature of 20 °C. Convert the result into pascals.

5.3.3 What pressure is exerted on the left side of the manometer shown in Figure 5-10 when $\Delta h = 4.75$ cm, the right side is open to the atmosphere, and barometric pressure is 752.8 torr? Express your result in torr, atmospheres, and kilopascals.

5.4 APPLYING THE IDEAL GAS EQUATION

The ideal gas model was developed from the molecular properties of gases with two key assumptions. If these assumptions are valid, we should be able to apply the ideal gas equation to any change of conditions on any system of gases. To begin this section, we consider pressure-volume variations and temperature-volume variations, which were important in the historical development of the ideal gas model.

PRESSURE-VOLUME VARIATIONS

Quantitative measurements on gases were made as early as 1662 by Robert Boyle, who carried out many experiments on gases confined to J-shaped glass tubes that were closed at one end, as shown schematically in Figure 5-11. A fixed quantity of

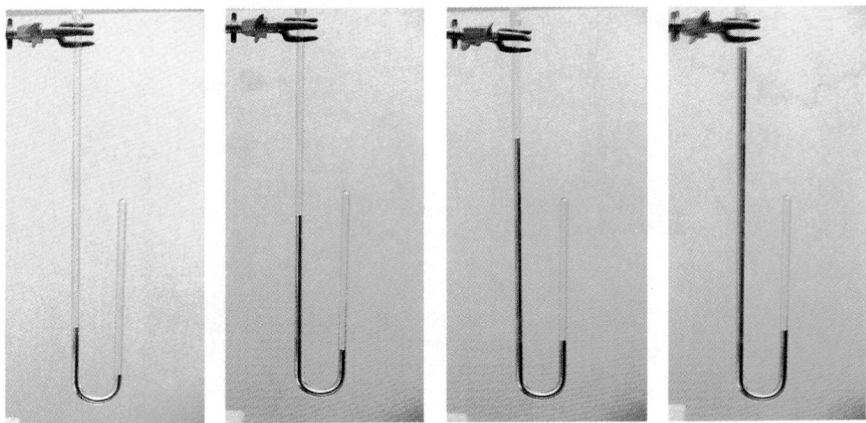

FIGURE 5-11
As the pressure on the air trapped in the tube increases, the volume of gas in the closed end decreases. The pressure is increased by adding more mercury to the open end of the tube. Thus pressure increases as the height of the column of mercury increases.

air was trapped inside the tube by adding a known amount of liquid mercury. As the figure shows, adding additional mercury to the open end of the tube changed the pressure on the trapped air. The mass of the additional mercury compressed the trapped gas to a smaller volume. Boyle found that the volume occupied by the trapped air was inversely proportional to the total pressure applied by the mercury plus the atmosphere. In other words, doubling the total pressure on the trapped air reduced its volume by a factor of two. The pressure-volume product, PV, always remained the same. Boyle concluded that the product of pressure and volume is a constant for a fixed quantity of gas at constant temperature.

This behavior is exactly what the ideal gas equation predicts. Boyle worked with a fixed amount of air trapped inside the tube, so the number of moles of gas was always the same during his experiments. In other words, n was held constant. Furthermore, Boyle worked at only one temperature ("room" temperature), so T was held constant. As a result, in Boyle's experiments the product nRT was a set of constants. Thus the ideal gas equation agrees with Boyle's observations: $PV = nRT =$ constant when T and n are fixed. Sample Problem 5-3 applies the ideal gas equation to a pressure-volume variation.

SAMPLE PROBLEM 5-3 PRESSURE-VOLUME VARIATIONS

A sample of helium gas is held at constant temperature inside a cylinder whose volume is 0.80 L when a piston exerts a pressure of 1.5 atm. If the external pressure on the piston is increased to 2.1 atm, what will be the new volume?

METHOD: Think about atoms and molecules, and make molecular sketches of the system before and after the change of state. Initially the system is in balance, with just enough pressure exerted by the He atoms inside the cylinder to counteract the pressure exerted by the piston and the external atmosphere.

The system is disturbed by increasing the total pressure exerted by the piston to 2.1 atm. Greater force is applied to the gas inside the cylinder, and the piston compresses the gas, moving He atoms closer together until the internal pressure balances the total external pressure of 2.1 atm. Increasing the external pressure causes a decrease in gas volume. As the volume decreases, the molecular density increases; thus collision frequency and internal pressure rise until the interval pressure equals the external pressure. A molecular picture summarizes what happens:

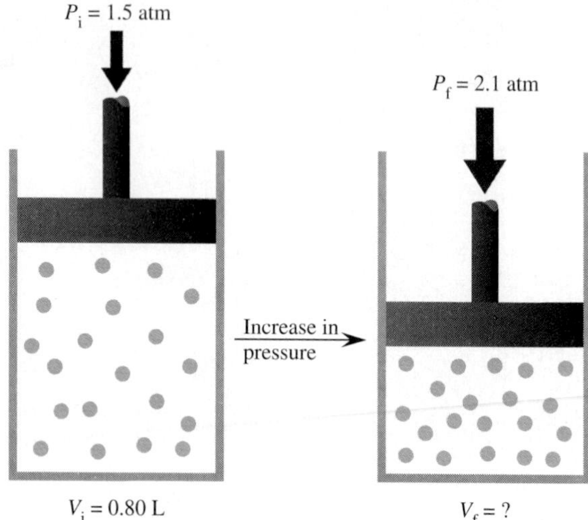

We are asked to compute the new volume. The quantitative solution is found using $PV = nRT$. However, rearranging the gas equation to solve for V will not help much because we know neither n, the number of moles of He present in the system, nor T, the temperature of the gas. We do know that neither variable changes as the pressure increases.

To determine the final volume of the helium gas, we must work with two different sets of conditions called the *initial* (i) and *final* (f) states of the system. The ideal gas equation can be applied to each set of conditions:

$$P_iV_i = n_iRT_i \qquad \textit{and} \qquad P_fV_f = n_fRT_f$$

When dealing with two sets of conditions, calculations often can be simplified by dividing one equality by the other to give ratios:

$$\frac{P_iV_i}{P_fV_f} = \frac{n_iRT_i}{n_fRT_f}$$

In this problem, the quantity of He inside the cylinder and the temperature of the gas are constant:

$$n_i = n_f \qquad \textit{and} \qquad T_i = T_f \qquad \textit{so} \qquad n_iRT_i = n_fRT_f \qquad \textit{and} \qquad \frac{n_iRT_i}{n_fRT_f} = 1$$

Therefore:

$$\frac{P_iV_i}{P_fV_f} = 1 \qquad \textit{and} \qquad P_iV_i = P_fV_f \text{ (constant } T \text{ and } n\text{)}$$

Notice that this equality can be solved for V_f without a knowledge of the values for n and T. The data are: $P_i = 1.5$ atm, $P_f = 2.1$ atm, $V_i = 0.80$ L, and $V_f = ?$. Now solve for the final volume:

$$V_f = \frac{P_iV_i}{P_f} = \frac{(1.5 \text{ atm})\ (0.80 \text{ L})}{2.1 \text{ atm}} = 0.57 \text{ L}$$

This answer is reasonable because a pressure increase has caused a volume decrease.

TEMPERATURE-VOLUME VARIATIONS

Boyle also observed that heating a gas causes it to expand in volume, but over a century passed before Jacques-Alexandre-César Charles reported the first *quantitative* studies of gas volume as a function of temperature.* Charles found that gas volume increases linearly with temperature as long as the pressure and number of moles are held constant. In other words, a graph of volume vs. temperature gives a straight line, as shown in Figure 5-12.

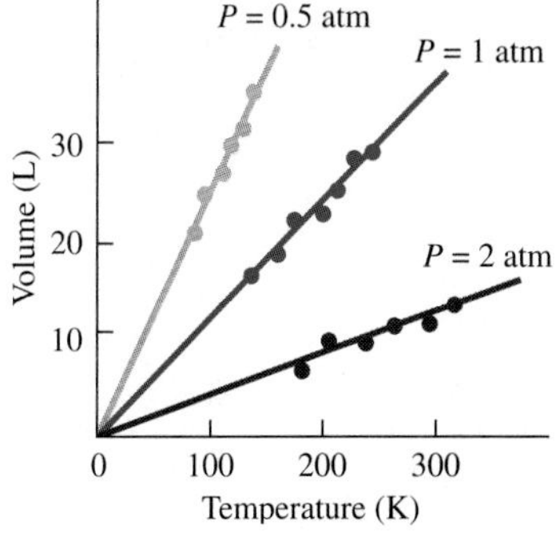

FIGURE 5-12
Plots of volume vs. temperature for 1 mol of air at three constant pressures.

These data are consistent with the ideal gas model. To see this, rearrange the ideal gas equation to isolate volume:

$$PV = nRT \qquad \text{so} \qquad V = \frac{nRT}{P} = \left(\frac{nR}{P}\right) T$$

Grouping *n, R,* and *P* shows the direct relationship between temperature (T) and volume (V) when amount (n) and pressure (P) are constant. The value of the constant nR/P can be evaluated from the slopes of the individual plots.

Notice in Figure 5-12 that the volume of the gas always extrapolates to zero at 0 K. Experiments performed on a series of different gases all give this result. Does this make sense? The ideal gas model assumes that the volume occupied by the atoms and molecules is negligible when compared with the *total* volume of the gas. As long as the fractional volume is negligible, the compression data fall on a straight line. However, as a gas is cooled, the volume of the *gas* decreases but the volume of its *molecules* remains fixed. For an *ideal* gas, volume would indeed shrink to zero at 0 K, but for any *real* gas, the fractional volume occupied by the molecules becomes significant when the gas volume becomes very small. Because all molecules are made up of matter, and because all matter occupies space, molecular volume can never be *completely* negligible. Nonetheless, all the gases listed in Table 5-1 behave ideally at "normal" temperatures and pressures of about 298 K and 1 atm, respectively. Under these conditions, the fractional volume occupied by the molecules is insignificant.

In Chapter 10 we show that every gas condenses to a liquid when temperature is lowered sufficiently. Near its condensation temperature, a gas no longer obeys the ideal gas equation unless its pressure is substantially less than 1 atm.

The direct proportionality between T and V applies only when T is expressed in kelvins. Recall Equation 5-1, which relates temperature in kelvins to kinetic energy. Because kinetic energy is always positive, temperature in kelvins is also always positive. The minimum value for T is 0 K. This is known as **absolute zero temperature,** and the Kelvin scale is an absolute temperature scale. *Any calculation that uses the gas constant must involve temperatures in kelvins.* Sample Problem 5-4 illustrates this point.

The Celsius temperature scale (°C) is *defined* around an *arbitrary* zero point, so negative Celsius temperatures exist (see Section 1.5).

SAMPLE PROBLEM 5-4 TEMPERATURE-VOLUME VARIATIONS

A 1.54-L gas bulb in a chemistry laboratory contains oxygen gas at 21 °C and 758 torr (see the figure). The air conditioning in the laboratory breaks down, and the temperature rises to 31 °C. What pressure does the gauge show now?

---

* Jacques-Alexandre-César Charles was a French physicist who pioneered the use of hydrogen in lighter-than-air balloons. He performed experiments on volume changes with temperature in about 1787 but never published his results. Another Frenchman, Joseph-Louis Gay-Lussac, repeated the experiments and published them in 1802.

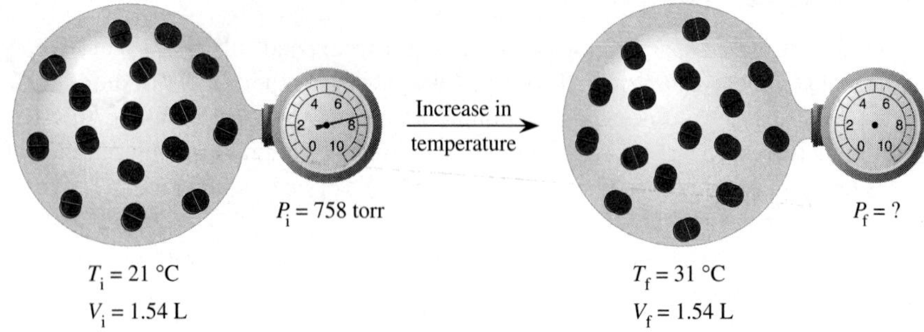

METHOD: Once again, think molecules. Neither the number of gas molecules nor the volume of the flask changes as the temperature rises. Instead, the molecules inside the flask move faster, and the faster a molecule travels, the more pressure it exerts when it strikes a wall. Thus the gas exerts a higher pressure as the temperature rises. The ideal gas equation allows us to calculate the amount of the increase, but the temperature must be expressed in kelvins.

As in Sample Problem 5-3, it is useful to organize the data into two sets, one for the initial conditions and one for the final conditions:

$$P_i = 758 \text{ torr} \qquad P_f = ?$$
$$n_i = ? \qquad n_f = n_i$$
$$T_i = 21\ °\text{C} = 294 \text{ K} \qquad T_f = 31\ °\text{C} = 304 \text{ K}$$
$$V_i = 1.54 \text{ L} \qquad V_f = 1.54 \text{ L}$$

The ideal gas equation applies to both sets of conditions with n and V constant. Rearrange the equation so that all the constants are grouped together:

$$PV = nRT \qquad so \qquad \frac{P}{T} = \frac{nR}{V} = \text{constant}$$

This relationship applies to both sets of conditions, giving the following ratio:

$$\frac{P_i}{T_i} = \frac{P_f}{T_f} \quad (\text{constant } n \text{ and } V)$$

Now rearrange the expression and solve for the final pressure:

$$P_f = T_f\left(\frac{P_i}{T_i}\right) = 304 \text{ K}\left(\frac{758 \text{ torr}}{294 \text{ K}}\right) = 784 \text{ torr}$$

Notice that temperature must be in kelvins (always true for gas calculations) and that the final pressure is in the same units as the initial pressure. Is the result reasonable? Temperature increased by a small fraction (294 to 304 K), and our calculated pressure is larger than the original pressure by a small fraction, so the answer seems reasonable.

VARIATIONS ON THE GAS EQUATION

Pressure-volume studies and temperature-volume studies verify that gases obey the ideal gas equation, $PV = nRT$. Now we can use this equation with confidence to calculate gas properties under various circumstances. During chemical and physical processes, any of the four variables in the ideal gas equation (P, V, n, T) may be fixed, and any of them may change. Consequently a good strategy for organizing gas calculations is to determine which variables do not change and rearrange the gas equation to group them all on the right. Here are some examples:

For a fixed amount at constant temperature, $PV = nRT =$ constant

For a fixed amount at constant volume, $\frac{P}{T} = \frac{nR}{V} =$ constant

For a fixed amount at constant pressure, $\frac{V}{T} = \frac{nR}{P} =$ constant

For a fixed volume and temperature, $\frac{P}{n} = \frac{RT}{V} =$ constant

Each calculation of gas properties proceeds from the ideal gas equation. Rather than memorize a variety of versions of this equation, we strongly recommend that you learn how to analyze gas problems. Sample Problems 5-5 and 5-6 provide two examples, and Box 5-2 discusses the gas equation in relation to tire pressure.

SAMPLE PROBLEM 5-5 CHANGING GAS CONDITIONS

A sample of carbon dioxide in a 10.0 L gas cylinder at 25 °C and 1.00 atm pressure is compressed and heated. The final temperature and volume are 50 °C and 5.00 L. Compute the final pressure.

METHOD: Again, we begin by analyzing this change at the molecular level. As the sample is heated, CO_2 molecules absorb energy and move faster. This leads to more frequent collisions, hence an increase in pressure. At the same time, the gas is compressed into a smaller volume, so the molecular density of CO_2 rises accordingly. Higher molecular density also means more frequent collisions and higher pressure. Thus we expect to find that the pressure has increased. The amount of increase is computed using the ideal gas equation.

Start the quantitative part of the problem by collecting and organizing the numerical data:

Initial	Final
$P_i = 1.00$ atm	$P_f = ?$
$V_i = 10.0$ L	$V_f = 5.00$ L
$T_i = 298$ K	$T_f = 323$ K

$$n_i = n_f$$

The data tell us that P, V, and T all change. The number of moles of CO_2 is not mentioned directly, but the physical transformation performed on the gas does not affect the number of molecules, so we can conclude that $n_i = n_f$. Grouping the constants, we find:

$$\frac{P_i V_i}{T_i} = nR = \frac{P_f V_f}{T_f}$$

Rearrange the expression to solve for the final pressure, insert the known information, and perform the calculations:

$$P_f = \left(\frac{P_i V_i}{T_i}\right)\left(\frac{T_f}{V_f}\right) = \left(\frac{(1.00 \text{ atm})(10.0 \text{ L})}{298 \text{ K}}\right)\left(\frac{323 \text{ K}}{5.00 \text{ L}}\right) = 2.17 \text{ atm}$$

The final pressure is 2.17 atm. The numerical answer agrees with our qualitative analysis at the molecular level.

BOX 5-2

THE GAS EQUATION IN ACTION

Why do automobile manufacturers recommend that tire pressure be measured before driving very far? The gas equation provides the answer. Tires have almost fixed volumes, and unless they leak or are being filled, they contain a fixed amount (n) of air. Under these conditions, pressure is directly proportional to temperature. As a car is driven, road friction causes the tires to heat up, which causes tire pressure to be higher after prolonged driving. The pressure value recommended by the manufacturer refers to pressure exerted by air in a cold tire, not a hot one.

Tire gauges in the United States typically read pressures in pounds per square inch (psi); 1 atm = 14.7 psi. Tire pressures are always measured as the difference in pressure between the gas inside the tire and the atmosphere, so when a pressure gauge reads 28 psi, the actual pressure exerted by the air inside the tire is 14.7 + 28 = 43 psi.

We can estimate the pressure difference between cold and hot conditions. Suppose, for example, that the tires are 60 °C after prolonged driving, compared with their "normal" temperature of 25 °C. In kelvins, this is 333 K compared with 298 K, which is an increase of about 12%. If the tire pressure when cold is 28 psi, then the pressure when hot will be about 12% higher, or 31 psi.

What happens when air is added or removed? As air is pumped into the tire or allowed to escape, volume and temperature are almost constant, so pressure is directly proportional to the amount of air in the tire. To increase tire pressure, pump more air into the tire; to reduce tire pressure, allow some air to escape.

Why do cars have inflatable tires rather than hard rubber tires, as do tricycles? The air in inflatable tires provides a cushion of gas between the passengers and the road. When a tire strikes a rough spot in the road, it experiences a brief but sharp increase in pressure. Without the cushion of gas, that pressure increase would be transmitted directly to the automobile (and the passengers) as a sharp jolt. The gas equation tells us that air in a tire is compressible: at constant temperature and amount, volume is inversely proportional to pressure. With the cushion of air in the tire, the pressure increase is largely absorbed as a volume decrease, which reduces the effect of the rough spot and smooths the ride.

Tires are not the only ride-smoothing devices in an automobile. Springs and shock absorbers also play essential roles in making the ride comfortable. Many shock absorbers also depend on the compressibility of gases.

SAMPLE PROBLEM 5-6 GAS LAW CALCULATIONS

Two natural gas storage tanks, with volumes of 1.5×10^4 and 2.2×10^4 L, are connected by pipes that equalize their pressures. What fraction of the stored natural gas is in the larger tank?

METHOD: Think about the molecules. When the pipe between the two tanks is open, the molecules can move freely back and forth. Every *unit* of volume contains the same number of molecules. In other words, the molecular density, n/V, is the same in the two tanks. Pressure and temperature are also the same in each tank. Rearrange the gas equation to group the constants:

$$PV = nRT \qquad \frac{n}{V} = \frac{P}{RT} \quad \text{(constant)}$$

There are not many data to summarize: $V_1 = 1.5 \times 10^4$ L and $V_2 = 2.2 \times 10^4$ L. We are asked to find the *fraction* of gas in the larger tank. This fraction is the *ratio* of the moles in the *larger* tank to the total moles in *both* tanks. Because *P* and *T* are constant, we can write:

$$\frac{n_{\text{large tank}}}{V_{\text{large tank}}} = \frac{n_{\text{total}}}{V_{\text{total}}}$$

Now solve for the fraction of gas in the larger container:

$$\frac{n_{\text{large tank}}}{n_{\text{total}}} = \frac{V_{\text{large tank}}}{V_{\text{total}}} = \frac{2.2 \times 10^4\ \text{L}}{1.5 \times 10^4\ \text{L} + 2.2 \times 10^4\ \text{L}} = 0.59$$

A fraction of 0.59, or 59% of the total gas is in the larger tank. This seems reasonable because more than half the gas has to be in the larger tank.

Here is a recap of the strategy used to solve gas problems:

1. Analyze and define the problem by thinking about what is occurring at the molecular level. (This is the most important step of the strategy.)
2. Collect and organize all the numerical data.
3. Decide what equations apply.
4. Manipulate the equations until the "unknown" variable is isolated from the known variables.
5. Substitute the numerical values and solve.
6. Keep track of units and check to make sure the numerical answer is consistent with the molecular interpretation.

DETERMINATION OF MOLAR MASS

The ideal gas equation can be combined with the mole-mass relation to find the molar mass of an unknown gas:

$$PV = nRT \quad \text{(ideal gas equation)} \qquad \textit{and} \qquad n = \frac{m}{MM} \quad \text{(mole-mass relation)}$$

Remember that *m* is mass and *MM* is molar mass.

First, solve the ideal gas equation for n:

$$n = \frac{PV}{RT}$$

Now, set the two expressions for n equal to each other:

$$\frac{m}{MM} = \frac{PV}{RT}$$

Finally, rearrange this equation to obtain an equation for molar mass:

$$MM = \frac{mRT}{PV}$$

Sample Problem 5-7 demonstrates how to use the properties of a gas to determine its molar mass.

SAMPLE PROBLEM 5-7 MOLAR MASS DETERMINATION

Calcium carbide (CaC_2) is a hard, gray-black solid with a melting point of 2000 °C. This compound reacts vigorously with water to produce a gas. A 12.8 g sample of CaC_2 was treated with excess water. The resulting gas was collected in an evacuated 5.00 L glass bulb with a mass of 254.49 g. The filled bulb had a mass of 259.70 g and a pressure of 0.988 atm when its temperature was 26.8 °C. Identify the gas and determine the balanced chemical equation for the reaction.

METHOD: The process involves a gas reaction and a chemical reaction, so we must make a connection between gas measurements and the chemistry taking place. We begin by analyzing the chemistry, then use the gas data to determine the number of moles of gas.

Because the reactants are known, we can write a partial equation that describes the chemical reaction:

$$CaC_{2\,(s)} + H_2O_{(l)} \rightarrow \text{Gas} + ?$$

In any chemical reaction, atoms must be conserved, so the gas molecules can contain only H, O, C, and Ca atoms. The problem asks us to identify the gas from its properties.

Now we summarize what is known about this gas. The following data relate to the gas:

$$V_{bulb} = V_{gas} = 5.00 \text{ L} \qquad T = 26.8\ °\text{C} = 300.0 \text{ K} \qquad P = 0.988 \text{ atm}$$

$$m_{bulb+gas} = 259.70 \text{ g} \qquad m_{bulb} = 254.49 \text{ g}$$

$$m_{gas} = m_{bulb+gas} - m_{bulb} = 5.21 \text{ g}$$

We use *V, T, P,* and the ideal gas equation to find the number of moles of gas. Then, with the mass of the gas sample, we can determine the molar mass:

$$\frac{PV}{RT} = n_{gas} = \frac{m_{gas}}{MM}$$

We could determine *n* and then solve for *MM*, but we can also solve the equality for *MM* and then substitute the data directly:

$$MM = \frac{RT\,m_{gas}}{PV}$$

$$MM = \frac{(0.08206 \text{ L atm mol}^{-1} \text{ K}^{-1})(300.0 \text{ K})(5.21 \text{ g})}{(0.988 \text{ atm})(5.00 \text{ L})} = 26.0 \text{ g/mol}$$

To identify the gas, we examine the formulas and molar masses of known compounds that contain H, O, C, and Ca:

Formula	MM	Comment
Ca	40	A gas with *MM* of 26 g/mol cannot contain Ca.
CO	28	This is close, but too high.
O_2	32	This is also too high, as is H_2O_2.
H_2O	18	$H_{10}O$ would have *MM* of 26, but this compound does not exist.
CH_4	16	CH_{14}, *MM* of 26, does not exist.
C_2H_2	26	This substance has the observed molar mass.

Acetylene is a high-energy molecule used as a fuel for oxyacetylene welding.

A little trial and error leads to the molecular formula: C_2H_2, commonly known as *acetylene*. Now we can balance the equation for the gas-forming reaction:

$$CaC_{2\,(s)} + 2\,H_2O_{(l)} \rightarrow Ca(OH)_{2\,(s)} + C_2H_{2\,(g)}$$

Box 5-3 discusses chemical characteristics of CaC_2.

BOX 5-3

CALCIUM CARBIDE CHEMISTRY

Calcium carbide (CaC_2) is an unusual substance that contains a carbon anion, C_2^{2-}. The reaction with water described in Sample Problem 5-7 involves several steps that occur in rapid succession.

CaC_2 is a salt (notice that its name is similar to sodium chloride). When a salt dissolves in water, ions leave the crystal lattice and enter the aqueous (aq) solution:

$$CaC_{2\,(s)} \xrightarrow{H_2O} Ca^{2+}_{(aq)} + C_2^{2-}{}_{(aq)}$$

In solution the carbide dianion is extremely reactive. It is a strong base that rapidly captures protons (H^+ ions) from water molecules:

$$C_2^{2-}{}_{(aq)} + H_2O_{(l)} \rightarrow C_2H^-_{(aq)} + OH^-_{(aq)}$$

$$C_2H^-_{(aq)} + H_2O_{(l)} \rightarrow C_2H_{2\,(g)} + OH^-_{(aq)}$$

Besides acetylene (C_2H_2), the products of these three steps are Ca^{2+} cations and OH^- anions. Most of these ions do not remain in solution because calcium hydroxide is a sparingly soluble salt. Thus aqueous cations and anions combine to form a precipitate:

$$Ca^{2+}_{(aq)} + 2\,OH^-_{(aq)} \rightarrow Ca(OH)_{2\,(s)}$$

The sum of these four sequential reactions is the net equation of Sample Problem 5-7:

$$CaC_{2\,(s)} + 2\,H_2O_{(l)} \rightarrow Ca(OH)_{2\,(s)} + C_2H_{2\,(g)}$$

CaC_2 is prepared at high temperature from limestone and charcoal:

$$\underset{\text{(limestone)}}{CaCO_{3\,(s)}} \xrightarrow{800\ °C} CaO_{(s)} + CO_{2\,(g)}$$

$$CaO_{(s)} + 3\,C_{(s)} \xrightarrow{2000\ °C} CaC_{2\,(s)} + CO_{(g)}$$

Because of the energy costs of these processes, commercial acetylene production using CaC_2 is more costly than obtaining it from the decomposition reaction of natural gas (methane) under controlled conditions. However, CaC_2 is industrially important in the manufacture of plastics. At elevated temperatures, it reacts directly with nitrogen gas:

$$CaC_{2\,(s)} + N_{2\,(g)} \xrightarrow{1000\ °C} CaCN_{2\,(s)} + C_{(s)}$$

The product of this reaction is called *calcium cyanamide*. This compound is one of the starting materials in a four-step industrial synthesis of melamine polymers, which are used to make lightweight, heat-resistant tableware.

SECTION EXERCISES

5.4.1 On a summer day the temperature inside a house rises to 37 °C (99 °F). In the evening the house may cool to 21 °C (68 °F). Does air enter or leave the house as it cools? If the volume of the house is 9.50×10^5 L and the barometric pressure has held steady at 768 mm Hg, what mass of air is transferred (average molar mass of air is 28.8 g/mol)?

5.4.2 Draw molecular pictures that show the behavior of a gas whose temperature is doubled at constant pressure.

5.4.3 A 2.96-g sample of a compound of mercury and chlorine is vaporized in a 1000-mL bulb at 307 °C, and the final pressure is found to be 394 torr. What is the molar mass and chemical formula of the compound?

5.5 GAS MIXTURES

Before we can apply the ideal gas model to chemical reactions, we must consider how mixtures of gases behave. So far, we have considered only gases that are composed of just one chemical substance. Many gaseous systems are mixtures of two or more compounds. For example, consider the synthesis of methanol, a simple alcohol used as a solvent and as a fuel additive. More than a billion gallons of methanol are produced annually, much of it by the following gas phase reaction:

Under normal conditions, methanol is a liquid. However, the synthesis is carried out at high temperature, at which methanol exists as a gas.

$$CO_{(g)} + 2\,H_{2\,(g)} \rightarrow CH_3OH_{(g)}$$

To run this reaction, CO and H_2 gases must first be mixed together. How do we treat this mixture of gases? The ideal gas model provides useful guidance.

In an ideal gas, all molecules act independently, so in an ideal gas mixture, molecules of each gas act independently. Gas behavior depends on the *number* of gas molecules but not on the *identity* of gas molecules. The ideal gas equation applies to each gas in the mixture, as well as to the entire collection of molecules.

Suppose we have a glass bulb that contains 0.40 mol of hydrogen. If we pump in another 0.40 mol of H_2, the bulb will contain 0.80 mol of gas. The pressure inside the bulb is given by the ideal gas equation, with $n = 0.40 + 0.40 = 0.80$ mol. Now suppose that we pump in 0.40 mol of carbon monoxide. At this point the bulb contains a total of 1.20 mol of gas. The total pressure is given by the ideal gas equation, with $n = 0.80 + 0.40 = 1.20$ mol. According to the ideal gas model, it does not matter whether we add the same gas or a different gas. Because all molecules in a sample of an ideal gas behave exactly the same way, the pressure increases in proportion to the increase in the total moles of gas.

How does a 1:2 mixture of CO and H_2 appear on the molecular level? As CO is added to the bulb, its molecules move throughout the volume and become distributed uniformly. Diffusion quickly causes gas mixtures to become homogeneous. This is shown in Figure 5-13.

DALTON'S LAW OF PARTIAL PRESSURES

The pressure exerted by an ideal gas mixture is determined by the total number of moles:

$$P = \frac{n_{\text{total}}RT}{V}$$

However, total moles can be written as the sum of the amounts of each gas present. For the CO and H_2 mixture:

$$n_{\text{total}} = n_{\text{CO}} + n_{\text{H}_2}$$

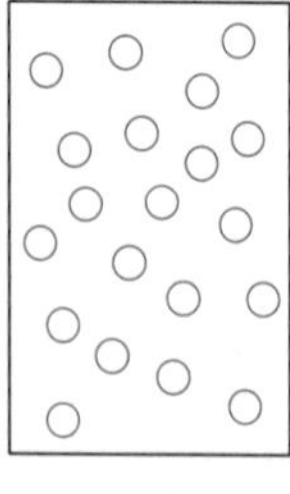

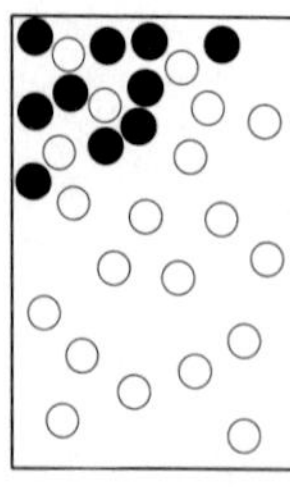

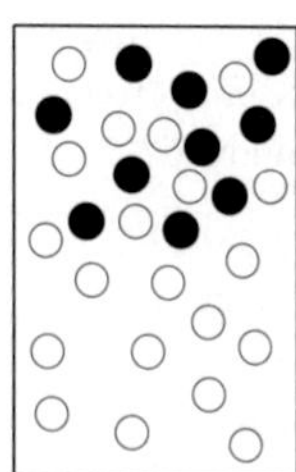

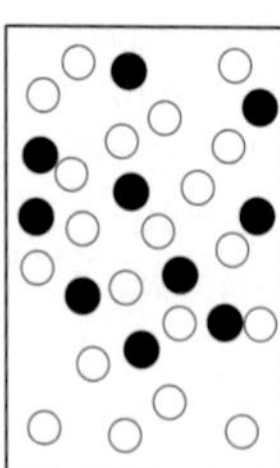

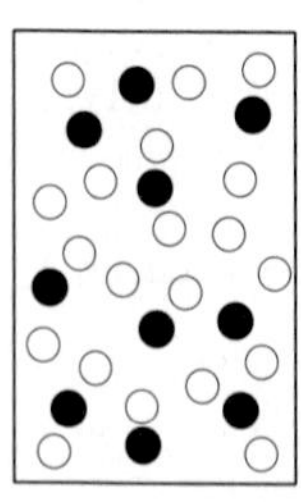

FIGURE 5-13
Diffusion causes gases to mix uniformly throughout their container. **A,** Originally the bulb contains only H_2 gas (*open circles*). **B,** Immediately after adding CO, the CO molecules (*dark circles*) are clustered near the entry point. **C** and **D,** Molecules move about independently, and this causes the gases to mix. **E,** Eventually, H_2 and CO are distributed uniformly through the bulb.

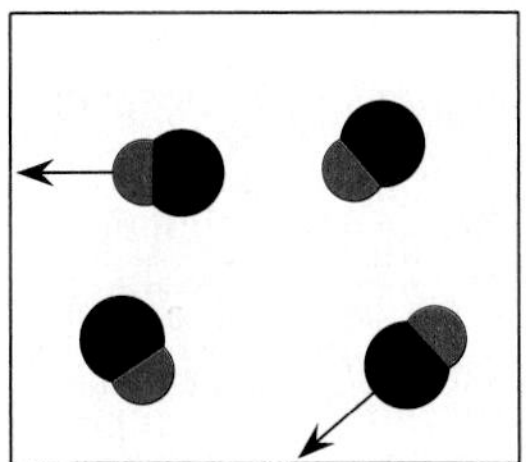

3.0 L at 273 K
0.40 mol CO
P_{CO} = 3.0 atm

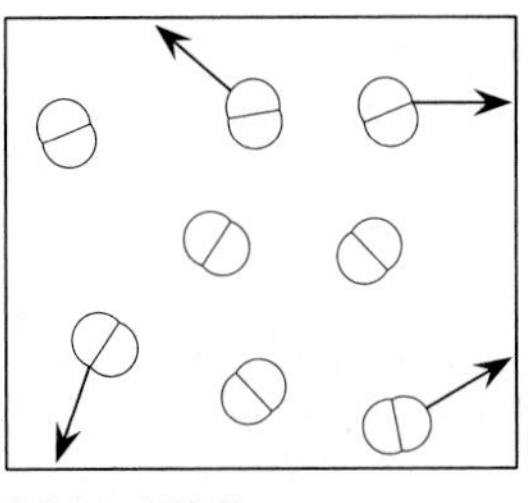

3.0 L at 273 K
0.80 mol H_2
P_{H_2} = 6.0 atm

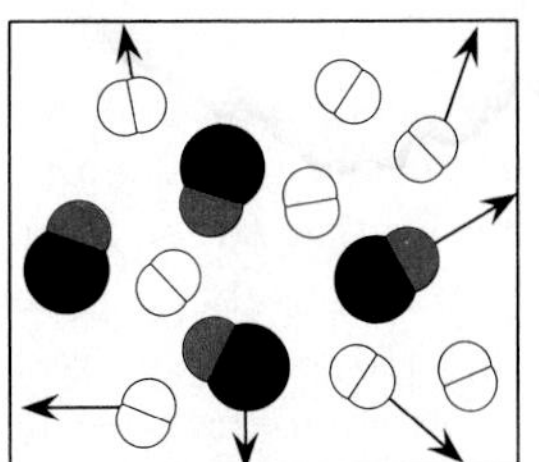

3.0 L at 273 K
1.20 mol of gas
p_{CO} = 3.0 atm
p_{H_2} = 6.0 atm
P_{total} = 9.0 atm

FIGURE 5-14
Molecular pictures of a sample of CO, a sample of H_2, and a mixture of the two gases. Both components are dispersed uniformly throughout the gas volume. Each gas behaves the same, whether it is pure or part of a mixture.

Substitution gives a two-term equation for the total pressure:

$$P = \frac{(n_{CO} + n_{H_2})RT}{V} = \frac{n_{CO}RT}{V} + \frac{n_{H_2}RT}{V}$$

Notice that each term on the right resembles the ideal gas equation rearranged to express pressure. Each term therefore represents the **partial pressure** (p) of one of the gases. As Figure 5-14 illustrates, partial pressure is the pressure that would be present in a gas bulb if one gas were present by itself:

$$p_{CO} = \frac{n_{CO}RT}{V} \qquad p_{H_2} = \frac{n_{H_2}RT}{V}$$

The partial pressure of each gas is designated with a lower-case *p* to distinguish it from the total pressure of the mixture, *P*.

The total pressure in the bulb is the sum of the partial pressures:

$$P_{total} = p_{CO} + p_{H_2}$$

We have used CO and H_2 to illustrate the behavior of a mixture of ideal gases, but the same result is obtained regardless of the number and identity of the gases.

In a mixture of gases, each gas contributes to the total pressure the amount that it would exert if the gas were present in the container by itself.

This is **Dalton's law of partial pressures.** To obtain a total pressure, simply add the contributions from all gases present:

John Dalton was the first to describe gas mixtures in this way as an application of his atomic theory.

$$P_{total} = p_1 + p_2 + p_3 + \dots p_i$$

When doing calculations on a mixture of gases, we can apply the ideal gas equation to each component to find its partial pressure (p_i). Alternatively, we can treat the entire gas as a unit, using the total number of moles to determine the total pressure of the mixture (P).

DESCRIBING GAS MIXTURES

There are several ways to describe the chemical composition of a mixture of gases. The simplest method is merely to list each component with its partial pressure or number of moles. Two other descriptions, parts per million and mole fractions, are also used frequently.

When referring to very minor components of a gas mixture, scientists typically use **parts per million (ppm)** to designate the relative number of molecules of a substance present in a sample of the gas mixture. Concentrations of atmospheric pollutants, for example, often are given in ppm. A pollutant concentration of 1 ppm means that out of 1 million molecules, there is one molecule of the pollutant. In molar terms, 1 ppm means that there is 10^{-6} mol of pollutant in every mole of air. The city of Los Angeles issues a first-stage smog alert when the concentration of ozone in its atmosphere reaches 0.5 ppm. This means that in every mole of air, there is 0.5×10^{-6} mol of ozone. This may not seem like much, but ozone is a very toxic substance that is particularly damaging to soft tissue such as the lungs. Even rarer components of a gas mixture are expressed in **parts per billion (ppb):**

$$1 \text{ ppm} = 1 \text{ molecule out of every } 10^6 \text{ molecules}$$

$$1 \text{ ppb} = 1 \text{ molecule out of every } 10^9 \text{ molecules}$$

Chemists often express chemical composition in fractional terms, expressing the moles of a substance as a fraction of the number of moles of all substances. This way of stating composition is the **mole fraction (X):**

$$\text{Mole fraction of } A = X_A = \frac{n_A}{n_{\text{total}}}$$

Mole fractions provide a simple way to relate the partial pressure of one component to the total pressure of the gas mixture:

$$p_A = \frac{n_A RT}{V} \qquad P_{\text{total}} = \frac{n_{\text{total}} RT}{V}$$

Dividing p_A by P_{total} gives:

$$\frac{p_A}{P_{\text{total}}} = \frac{n_A RT/V}{n_{\text{total}} RT/V} = \frac{n_A}{n_{\text{total}}} = X_A$$

or:

$$p_A = X_A P_{\text{total}} \tag{5-5}$$

The partial pressure of any component in a gas mixture is the its mole fraction times the total pressure. Sample Problem 5-8 illustrates calculations with gas mixtures.

SAMPLE PROBLEM 5-8 GAS MIXTURES

To study the details of methanol synthesis, a chemist placed 0.160 g of H_2 and 1.12 g of CO in a 3.00-L reaction vessel at 298 K. Determine the total pressure of the mixture, and find the partial pressures and mole fractions of the two gases.

METHOD: We have a mixture of two gases in a container whose volume and temperature are known. The problem asks for pressures and mole fractions. Each gas can be treated independently using the ideal gas equation. As usual, we need molar amounts for the calculations.

Begin with the data provided:

$$V = 3.00 \text{ L} \qquad T = 298 \text{ K} \qquad m_{H_2} = 0.160 \text{ g} \qquad m_{CO} = 1.12 \text{ g}$$

Convert the mass of each gas into the number of moles:

$$n = m/MM \qquad n_{H_2} = 7.94 \times 10^{-2} \text{ mol} \qquad n_{CO} = 4.00 \times 10^{-2} \text{ mol}$$

Next, use the ideal gas equation to compute the partial pressure of each gas:

$$p_{CO} = \frac{(4.00 \times 10^{-2}\ \text{mol})(8.206 \times 10^{-2}\ \text{L atm mol}^{-1}\ \text{K}^{-1})\ (298\ \text{K})}{3.00\ \text{L}} = 0.326\ \text{atm}$$

The same calculation for H_2 gives $p_{H_2} = 0.648$ atm.

The total pressure is the sum of the partial pressures:

$$P_{total} = p_{CO} + p_{H_2} = (0.326\ \text{atm}) + (0.648\ \text{atm}) = 0.974\ \text{atm}$$

Mole fractions can be calculated from moles or partial pressures:

$$X_{CO} = \frac{n_{CO}}{n_{total}} = \frac{4.00 \times 10^{-2}\ \text{mol}}{11.94 \times 10^{-2}\ \text{mol}} = 0.335 \qquad X_{H_2} = \frac{p_{H_2}}{P_{total}} = \frac{0.648\ \text{atm}}{0.974\ \text{atm}} = 0.6652$$

The description presented in this section applies to a gas mixture that is not undergoing chemical reactions. As long as reactions do not occur, the number of moles of each gas is determined by the amount of that substance initially present. When reactions occur, the numbers of moles of reactants and products change in conformity with stoichiometric principles. Changes in composition must be taken into account before the properties of the gas mixture can be computed. Gas stoichiometry is described in the next section.

SECTION EXERCISES

5.5.1 Find the partial pressures and mole fractions of a gas mixture that contains 1.00 g each of H_2 and N_2, if the total pressure exerted by this mixture is 2.30 atm.

5.5.2 Draw a molecular picture that shows how a sample of the gas mixture in Section Exercise 5.5.1 appears at the molecular level.

5.5.3 An atmospheric chemist reported that the air in an urban area contained CO at a concentration of 35 ppm. The temperature of the air was 29 °C, and the atmospheric pressure was 745 torr. (a) What was the mole fraction of CO? (b) What was the partial pressure of CO? (c) How many molecules of CO were in 1000 L of this air?

5.6 GAS STOICHIOMETRY

The principles of stoichiometry apply equally to solids, liquids, and gases. No matter what phase substances are in, their chemical behavior can be described in molecular terms, and their transformations must be visualized and balanced using molecules and moles.

The ideal gas equation does not describe the chemical properties of a gas, but it does relate measurable gas properties to the number of moles of gas. When a chemical reaction involves a gas, the ideal gas equation provides the link between *P-V-T* data and molar amounts.

$$n = \frac{PV}{RT}$$

Stoichiometric calculations on gases require amounts in moles, which are usually obtained using the ideal gas equation. Sample Problem 5-9 provides an example.

SAMPLE PROBLEM 5-9 GAS STOICHIOMETRY

In Sample Problem 5-7 we described the synthesis of acetylene (C_2H_2) from calcium carbide (CaC_2). Modern production of acetylene, however, is based on the decomposition of methane (CH_4) under carefully controlled conditions. At temperatures greater than 1600 K, two methane molecules rearrange to give three molecules of hydrogen and one molecule of acetylene. This process is called *cracking*:

$$2\ CH_{4\ (g)} \xrightarrow{1600\ K} C_2H_{2\ (g)} + 3\ H_{2\ (g)}$$

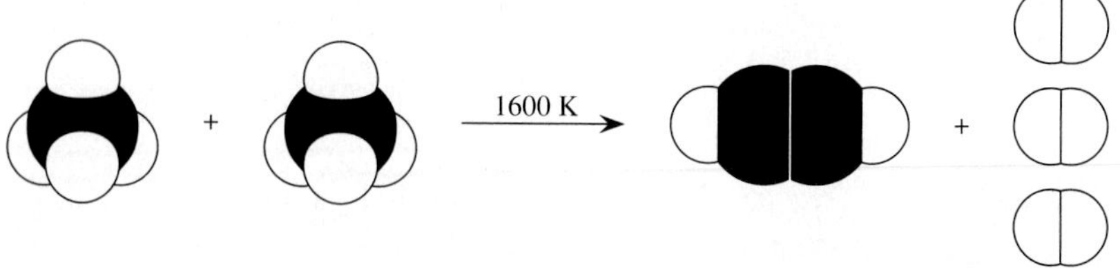

A 50.0-L steel vessel was filled with CH_4 to a pressure of 10.0 atm at 298 K. The gas was heated to 1600 K to crack CH_4 and produce C_2H_2. If this process went in 100% yield, what mass of C_2H_2 would be produced? What pressure would the reactor reach at 1600 K?

METHOD: The amount of C_2H_2 produced in the synthesis can be found from the 1 : 2 mole ratio between C_2H_2 and CH_4. We use the ideal gas equation to convert *P-V-T* data to molar amounts. Then, standard mole ratio calculations give amounts of products. Another application of the ideal gas equation gives the final pressure. Begin with a data summary:

$$T_1 = 298\ K \quad T_2 = 1600\ K$$
$$V = 50.0\ L \quad P_1 = 10.0\ atm$$

Use these data to determine the number of moles of CH_4 that were placed in the steel vessel:

$$n = \frac{PV}{RT} = \frac{(10.0\ atm)(50.0\ L)}{(0.08206\ L\ atm\ mol^{-1}\ K^{-1})(298\ K)} = 20.45\ mol\ CH_4$$

(We carry one additional significant figure to avoid errors caused by premature rounding).

Next, work out the stoichiometry of the problem. The stoichiometric ratio tells us that 2 mol of CH_4 produce 1 mol of C_2H_2. Use the molar mass of C_2H_2 to convert moles to mass:

$$20.45\ mol\ CH_4\left(\frac{1\ mol\ C_2H_2}{2\ mol\ CH_4}\right)\left(\frac{26.04\ g\ C_2H_2}{mol}\right) = 266\ g\ acetylene$$

(This result is rounded off to three significant figures to match the precision of the data.)

To calculate the pressure inside the reactor, we must determine the total number of moles of gas produced in this reaction. Two moles of CH_4 give 1 mol of C_2H_2 and 3 mol of H_2, so 20.45 mol of CH_4 will produce a *total* of 40.90 mol of gas:

$$20.45\ mol\ CH_4 \rightarrow 10.22\ mol\ C_2H_2 + 30.67\ mol\ H_2 = 40.89\ mol\ of\ gas$$

Now the ideal gas equation can be used to calculate the pressure developed in the steel vessel:

Rearrange $PV = nRT$ *to* $P = \dfrac{nRT}{V}$

$$P = \frac{(40.89\ mol\ gas)\ (0.08206\ L\ atm\ mol^{-1}\ K^{-1})\ (1600\ K)}{50.0\ L} = 107\ atm$$

Any of the types of problems discussed in Chapters 3 and 4 can involve gases. The strategy for doing stoichiometric calculations is the same whether the species involved are solids, liquids, or gases. In this chapter, we add the ideal gas equation to our set of equations for converting measured quantities into moles. Sample Problem 5-10 is a limiting-reagent problem that involves a gas.

SAMPLE PROBLEM 5-10 LIMITING REAGENTS WITH A GAS

Margarine can be made from natural oils such as coconut oil by hydrogenation:

$$\underset{\text{Oil}}{C_{57}H_{104}O_{6\ (l)}} + 3\ H_{2\ (g)} \xrightarrow[\text{Ni catalyst}]{200\ °C,\ 7\ \text{atm}} \underset{\text{Margarine}}{C_{57}H_{110}O_{6\ (s)}}$$

If an industrial hydrogenator with a volume of 250 L is charged with 12.0 kg of oil and 7.00 atm of hydrogen (H_2) at 200 °C and the reaction goes to completion, how many kilograms of margarine will be produced?

METHOD: We are given data about the amounts of both starting materials, so this is a limiting-reagent problem. With the chemical equation in hand, the first step in a limiting-reagent problem is to determine the number of moles of each starting material present at the beginning of the reaction. Next compute ratios of moles to coefficient to identify the limiting reagent. After that, a table of amounts summarizes the stoichiometry.

The ideal gas equation is used for any starting materials that are gases:

$$\text{mol } H_2 = \frac{PV}{RT} = \frac{(7.00 \text{ atm})(250 \text{ L})}{(0.08206 \text{ L atm mol}^{-1}\text{ K}^{-1})(473 \text{ K})} = 45.09 \text{ mol}$$

$$\text{mol oil} = \frac{m}{MM} = \frac{1.20 \times 10^4 \text{ g}}{885.4 \text{ g mol}^{-1}} = 13.55 \text{ mol}$$

Now divide each number of moles by the stoichiometric coefficient to identify the limiting reagent.

$$\frac{45.09 \text{ mol } H_2}{3 \text{ mol } H_2} = 15.03 \qquad \frac{13.55 \text{ mol oil}}{1 \text{ mol oil}} = 13.55$$

Oil is the limiting reagent because its ratio is smaller.

The table of amounts follows:

Reaction:	$3\ H_2$	+	$C_{57}H_{104}O_6$	→	$C_{57}H_{110}O_6$
Initial amt	45.09		13.55		0
Change in amt	−40.65		−13.55		+13.55
Final amt	4.4		0		13.6

(The final amounts have been rounded off correctly.)

Now calculate the mass of margarine:

$$\text{mol margarine} = 13.6 \text{ mol} \times \frac{891.5 \text{ g}}{\text{mol}} = 1.21 \times 10^4 \text{ g} = 12.1 \text{ kg}$$

You should be able to show that the pressure of H_2 remaining in the reactor after reaction is 0.685 atm. In this example, oil is the limiting reagent. Hydrogen is less expensive than natural oils, so margarine manufacturers make the oil the limiting reagent to ensure complete conversion of oil into margarine. The excess H_2 gas is recovered and used again in a subsequent reaction.

SUMMARY OF MOLE CONVERSIONS

Because moles are the currency of chemistry, all stoichiometric computations require amounts in moles. In the real world, we measure mass, volume, temperature, and pressure. With the ideal gas equation, our catalog of relationships for mole conversion is complete. Table 5-2 lists the three equations; each applies to a particular category of chemical substances.

All three of these equations should be firmly embedded in your memory, *along with the conditions under which they apply.* Using $PV = nRT$ on an aqueous solution gives impossible results. Sample Problem 5-11 uses all three relationships.

TABLE 5-2 SUMMARY OF MOLE RELATIONSHIPS

SUBSTANCE	RELATIONSHIP	EQUATION
Pure liquid or solid	$\text{Moles} = \dfrac{\text{Mass}}{\text{Molar mass}}$	$n = \dfrac{m}{MM}$
Liquid solution	Moles = (Molarity)(Volume)	$n = MV$
Gas	$\text{Moles} = \dfrac{\text{(Pressure)(Volume)}}{R\text{(Temperature)}}$	$n = \dfrac{PV}{RT}$

R, Gas constant.

SAMPLE PROBLEM 5-11 GENERAL STOICHIOMETRY

Redox reactions of metals with acids were introduced in Chapter 4. Recall that oxidation of the metal generates hydrogen gas and an aqueous solution of ions. Suppose 3.50 g of magnesium metal is dropped into 150 mL of 6.00 M HCl in a 5.00-L sealed cylinder at 25.0 °C under an initial pressure of 1.00 atm air. Find the final partial pressure of hydrogen, the total pressure in the container, and the concentrations of all ions in solution.

METHOD: This is another limiting-reagent problem, so we must balance the chemical equation and then work with a table of molar amounts.

Begin by analyzing the chemistry, listing all major species present in the system before reaction: $Mg_{(s)}$, $H_3O^+_{(aq)}$, $Cl^-_{(aq)}$, and $H_2O_{(l)}$.

Magnesium, a Group II metal, reacts with acids to generate +2 cations:

$$Mg_{(s)} + H_3O^+_{(aq)} \rightarrow Mg^{2+}_{(aq)} + H_{2\,(g)} \text{ (unbalanced)}$$

This reaction can be balanced by inspection. Charge balance requires that the +2 charge on the Mg^{2+} be matched by two hydronium ions among the starting materials. Two oxygen atoms on the left must then be balanced by two water molecules on the right:

$$Mg_{(s)} + 2\,H_3O^+_{(aq)} \rightarrow Mg^{2+}_{(aq)} + H_{2\,(g)} + 2\,H_2O_{(l)}$$

The problem asks for pressures and ion concentrations. The final pressure can be determined from *P-V-T* data and n_{H_2}. Moles of hydrogen can be found using the mass of magnesium, the stoichiometric ratio, and a table of amounts. Begin with a summary of the data:

$V_{container} = 5.00\text{ L}$	$T = 298\text{ K}$	$m_{Mg} = 3.50\text{ g}$
$V_{solution} = 0.150\text{ L}$	$p_{N_2} = 1.00\text{ atm}$	$[H_3O^+] = [Cl^-] = 6.00\text{ M}$

Next analyze the stoichiometry of the reaction. The starting amounts of H_3O^+ and Mg are given, but the data must be converted to moles before we can construct a table of amounts:

$$\text{mol Mg} = n_{mg} = \frac{m}{MM} = \frac{3.50 \text{ g Mg}}{24.31 \text{ g mol}^{-1}} = 0.1439 \text{ mol Mg}$$

$$\text{mol } H_3O^+ = n_{H_3O^+} = MV = (6.00 \text{ mol/L})(0.150 \text{ L}) = 0.900 \text{ mol } H_3O^+$$

You should be able to use the number of moles and the stoichiometric ratio to show that magnesium is the limiting reagent. The table of amounts follows:

Reaction	Mg	+	$2\ H_3O^+$	→	Mg^{2+}	+	H_2	+	$2\ H_2O$
Initial amt (mol)	0.1439		0.900		0		0		
Change in amt	−0.1439		−0.2878		+0.1439		+0.1439		
Final amt	0		0.6122		0.1439		0.1439		

Now that we know the final number of moles, the final concentrations can be calculated:

$$[Mg^{2+}] = \frac{0.1439 \text{ mol}}{0.150 \text{ L}} = 0.959 \text{ M} \qquad [H_3O^+] = \frac{0.6122 \text{ mol}}{0.150 \text{ L}} = 4.08 \text{ M} \qquad [Cl^-] = 6.00 \text{ M}$$

Remember, chloride is a spectator ion so its concentration does not change.

Before calculating the pressures, we must visualize the reaction vessel. The container's *total* volume is 5.00 L, but 0.150 L is occupied by the aqueous solution. This leaves 4.85 L for the gas mixture. The partial pressure of hydrogen is calculated by using the ideal gas equation and assuming that none of the H_2 remains in solution; this is a good assumption because hydrogen gas is not very soluble in water:

$$P_{H_2} = \frac{nRT}{V} = \frac{(0.1439 \text{ mol})(0.08206 \text{ L atm mol}^{-1} \text{ K}^{-1})(298 \text{ K})}{4.85 \text{ L}} = 0.726 \text{ atm}$$

The amount of air does not change in the reaction, so its partial pressure remains constant at 1.00 atm. The final total pressure is the sum of the partial pressures:

$$P_{total} = p_{H_2} + p_{N_2} = 0.726 \text{ atm } H_2 + 1.00 \text{ atm air} = 1.73 \text{ atm}$$

Viewed as a whole, Sample Problem 5-11 may seem quite complicated. After breaking it into separate parts, however, we find that each part is based on simple chemical and stoichiometric principles. Complicated problems are often simplified considerably by looking at them one piece at a time.

SECTION EXERCISES

5.6.1 In an oxyacetylene torch, acetylene (C_2H_2) burns in a stream of oxygen. This combustion reaction produces a flame with a temperature exceeding 3000 K. In a 30 °C welding shop with an air volume of 1.50×10^5 L, what mass of C_2H_2 must be burned to raise the CO_2 partial pressure to 0.10 atm? Assume that the shop is poorly ventilated and that a negligible amount of the CO_2 escapes the building before all the C_2H_2 has been burned. What mass of water will be produced during the burn?

5.6.2 A reaction vessel contains H_2 gas at 2.40 atm. If just enough O_2 is added to react completely with the H_2 to form H_2O, what will the total pressure in the vessel be before any reaction occurs? (H_2 and O_2 can also be used as a torch. The flame produced in an oxyhydrogen torch is about 4000 K.)

5.6.3 When ammonium nitrate (NH_4NO_3) explodes, all the products are gases:

$$2\ NH_4NO_{3\ (s)} \rightarrow 4\ H_2O_{\ (g)} + O_{2\ (g)} + 2\ N_{2\ (g)}$$

If 5.00 g of NH_4NO_3 explodes in a closed 2.00-L container that originally contains air at $P = 1.00$ atm, $T = 25$ °C, and if the temperature rises to 200 °C, what total pressure develops?

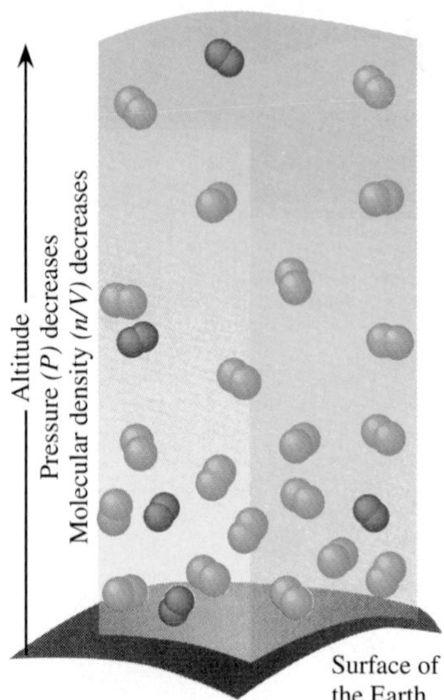

FIGURE 5-15
Molecular profile of the Earth's atmosphere, showing a column above some point on the Earth's surface. As altitude increases, both pressure *(P)* and molecular density *(n/V)* decrease.

TABLE 5-3 COMPOSITION OF DRY AIR AT SEA LEVEL

SUBSTANCE	MOLE FRACTION
Major Components	
N_2	0.7808
O_2	0.2095
Minor Components	
Ar	9.34×10^{-3}
CO_2	3.25×10^{-4}
H_2O	Variable
Trace Components	
Ne	1.82×10^{-5}
He	5.24×10^{-6}
CH_4	1.4×10^{-6}
Kr	1.14×10^{-6}
H_2	5.0×10^{-7}
NO	5.0×10^{-7}
N_2O	2.5×10^{-7}
CO	8.0×10^{-8}
O_3	2.5×10^{-8}
NH_3	6×10^{-9}
NO_2	4×10^{-9}
SO_2	2×10^{-10}

Intermolecular forces are discussed in detail in Chapter 10.

5.7 THE EARTH'S ATMOSPHERE

The ideal gas equation provides a framework for examining the behavior of the Earth's atmosphere. The blanket of air that cloaks our planet behaves as an ideal gas, but the atmosphere is bound to the Earth by gravitational attraction, not by confining walls. The pressure exerted by the atmosphere can be thought of as the pressure of a column of air, just as the pressure exerted by mercury in a barometer is the pressure of the column of mercury. As altitude increases, the amount of air above that altitude decreases, as does the pressure. Lower pressure means lower molecular density, as indicated by the ideal gas equation:

$$\frac{n}{V} = \frac{P}{RT}$$

Figure 5-15 shows a molecular profile of a column of atmospheric air.

Pressure also varies with atmospheric conditions. For example, molecules in the atmosphere move with greater velocity when they are heated by the sun. This in turn causes an increase in pressure that is described by the ideal gas equation:

$$P = \frac{nRT}{V}$$

Molecules in high-pressure areas flow into regions of lower pressure, generating winds. This continual interplay of temperature and pressure creates our planet's weather.

COMPOSITION OF THE LOWER ATMOSPHERE

The atmosphere is a complex, dynamic mixture of gases. The composition and chemical reactivity patterns of the atmosphere change significantly as altitude above the surface of the Earth increases, as we explore in Chapter 6. Here, we focus on the layer closest to the surface, called the **troposphere.** The troposphere is a mixture of many chemical substances, but nitrogen and oxygen make up more than 99% of its composition. Only three others, H_2O, Ar, and CO_2, are present in amounts greater than 0.01%. Of the five principal constituents, all but water are present in nearly constant proportions. Because water can condense and evaporate readily, the water content of the atmosphere changes from day to day, depending on temperature and geography. The composition of dry air at sea level, expressed in mole fractions, is shown in Table 5-3.

VAPOR PRESSURE

After a rainfall, puddles of water slowly disappear. The higher the temperature, the faster the puddles disappear. Puddles disappear because water molecules move from the liquid phase to the gas phase in a process called **evaporation.** Evaporation is common to all substances in the condensed phases, not just water. We use the term **vapor** to describe a gaseous substance that arises by evaporation. The Earth's atmosphere always contains some water vapor.

Evaporation can be understood by examining the kinetic energies of molecules. All molecules—solid, liquid, and gas—have some kinetic energy of motion, and any sample of molecules has a distribution of kinetic energies determined by its temperature (see Figure 5-4). Attractive forces between the molecules confine liquids and solids to a fixed volume, but some molecules at the surface of that volume have enough kinetic energy to overcome the forces holding them in the condensed phase.

Molecules that evaporate from a liquid or solid move into the vapor phase. The rate of evaporation increases with temperature because the fraction of molecules with sufficient energy to escape into the vapor phase increases as the sample warms up.

The water vapor that evaporates from a puddle is swept away into the atmosphere. This process continues until the puddle has vaporized completely. The situation is quite different when a substance is confined to an enclosed space. If the vaporized molecules cannot escape, their numbers increase, and they exert pressure on the walls of the closed container. As evaporation proceeds, more and more molecules enter the vapor phase, and the partial pressure of the vapor rises accordingly. Figure 5-16 shows that as this happens, some gas molecules are recaptured when they collide with the surface of the liquid. Eventually, the partial pressure of the substance in the vapor phase reaches a level at which the number of molecules being recaptured in any period equals the number of molecules escaping from the surface.

When the rate of evaporation equals the rate of condensation, the system is said to have reached a state of **dynamic equilibrium.** The system is dynamic because molecular transfers continue, and it has reached equilibrium because no further *net* change occurs. The pressure of the vapor at dynamic equilibrium is called the **vapor pressure (*vp*)** of the substance. Table 5-4 lists the vapor pressures for water at temperatures in the vicinity of room temperature. Vapor pressures increase rapidly with temperature because the kinetic energies of the molecules increase as the temperature rises. This is true for any substance, not only water.

A vapor pressure is the pressure exerted by a gas at equilibrium with its condensed phase. When this equilibrium has been reached, we say that the gas is **saturated** with that particular vapor. Notice in Table 5-4 that at 25 °C the atmosphere is saturated with water vapor when the partial pressure of H_2O is 23.756 torr. At this pressure the density of water molecules is sufficient to make the rate of condensation equal to the rate of evaporation from the liquid. Any attempt to add more water molecules to the gas phase would result in condensation, and the partial pressure of H_2O would remain fixed at 23.756 torr.

In most cases the atmosphere contains less water vapor than the maximum amount it can hold; That is, $p_{H_2O} < vp_{H_2O}$. The amount of water vapor actually present in the atmosphere can be described by the **relative humidity,** which is the partial pressure of water present in the atmosphere, divided by the vapor pressure of water at that temperature and multiplied by 100% to convert to percentage:

$$\text{Relative humidity} = \left(\frac{p_{H_2O}}{vp_{H_2O}}\right)(100\%) \qquad \textbf{(5-6)}$$

TABLE 5-4 VAPOR PRESSURES (*vp*) OF WATER AT VARIOUS TEMPERATURES (*T*)

T (°C)	*vp* (torr)
−20	0.776*
−15	1.241*
−10	1.950*
−5	3.013*
0	4.579
5	6.543
10	9.209
15	12.788
20	17.535
25	23.756
30	31.824
35	42.175
40	55.324
45	71.88
50	92.51
55	118.04
60	149.38
65	187.54
70	233.7
75	289.1
80	355.1
85	433.6
90	525.76
95	633.90
100	760.00
105	906.07
110	1074.56
115	1267.98
120	1489.14

* Vapor pressures above solid H_2O (ice).

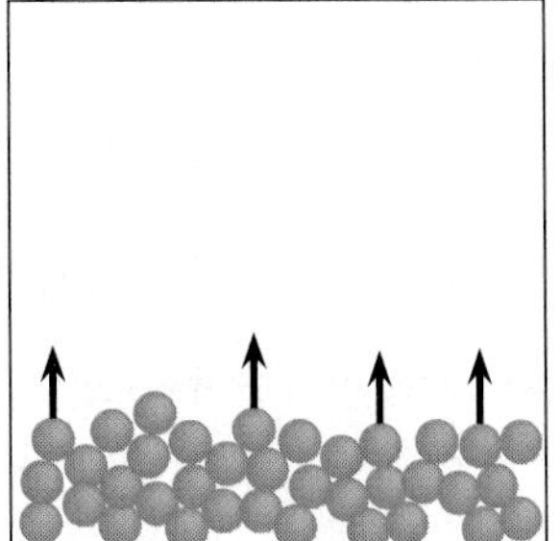

A No vapor present: escapes >> captures

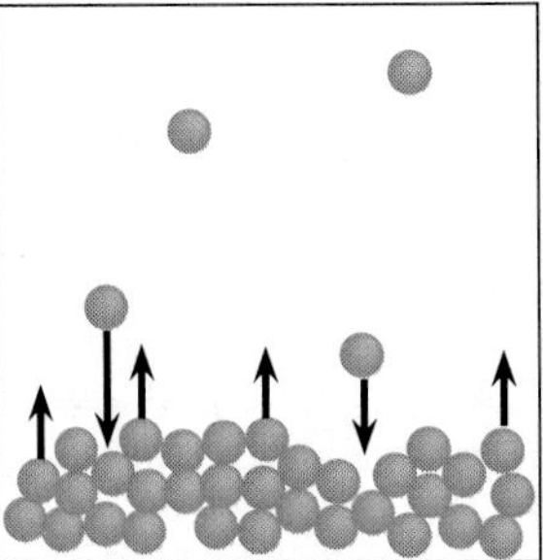

B Small amount of vapor present: escapes > captures

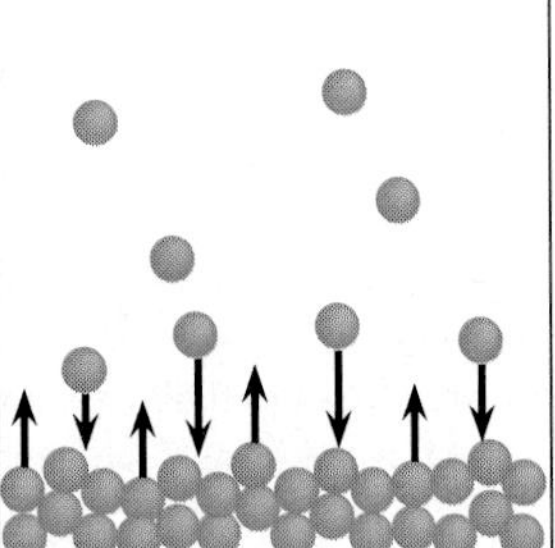

C Equilibrium: escapes = captures

FIGURE 5-16
Schematic view of the dynamics of evaporation and condensation in a closed system. **A,** Before vapor is present, evaporation occurs without condensation. **B,** As vapor builds, condensation begins to occur with evaporation. **C,** When the pressure equals the vapor pressure, the rates of evaporation and condensation are equal.

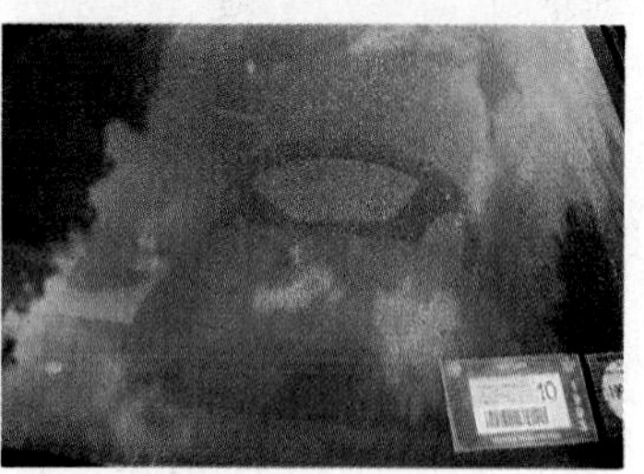

FIGURE 5-17
Dew and fog form when water vapor condenses from the atmosphere.

Relative humidity describes how close the atmosphere is to being saturated with water vapor.

Because the vapor pressure of water varies with temperature, a given amount of water in the atmosphere represents a higher relative humidity as the temperature falls. For example, a partial pressure of H_2O of 6.54 torr at 15 °C corresponds to a relative humidity of about 50% (12.788 torr from Table 5-4):

$$\left(\frac{6.54 \text{ torr}}{12.788 \text{ torr}}\right)(100\%) = 51.1\%$$

At 5 °C, however, this same partial pressure is 100% relative humidity.

The formation of dew and fog are consequences of this variation in relative humidity (Figure 5-17). Warm air at high relative humidity may cool below the temperature at which its partial pressure of H_2O equals the vapor pressure. When air temperature falls below this temperature, called the *dew point,* some H_2O must condense from the atmosphere. Sample Problem 5-12 shows how to work with vapor pressure variations with temperature, and Box 5-4 provides additional details about weather patterns.

SAMPLE PROBLEM 5-12 WATER VAPOR PRESSURE

Fog forms when humid warm air moves inland from a body of water and cools. What is the highest temperature at which fog could form from air that is at 65% relative humidity when its temperature is 27.5 °C?

METHOD: This problem addresses the partial pressure of water vapor in the atmosphere. Fog can form when that partial pressure exceeds the vapor pressure. Partial pressures are not given among the data, but relative humidity describes how close the partial pressure of water vapor is to its vapor pressure. Because vapor pressure varies strongly with temperature, we must use the information given in Table 5-4.

To convert relative humidity at 27.5 °C into a partial pressure, we need the vapor pressure of water at that temperature. Table 5-4 lists vapor pressures in 5 °C increments, so we must interpolate to find the correct value. At 27.5 °C, the vapor pressure is about halfway between its values at 25 °C and 30 °C:

T (°C)	25	30	27.5
vp (torr)	23.756	31.824	$\frac{1}{2}(23.756 + 31.824) = 27.790$

Next, we find the partial pressure from a rearranged version of Equation 5-6:

$$p_{H_2O} = \frac{(\text{Relative humidity})(vp_{H_2O})}{100\%}$$

$$p_{H_2O} = \frac{(65\%)(27.790 \text{ torr})}{100\%} = 18 \text{ torr}$$

This partial pressure remains constant as the temperature drops, so fog can form below the temperature at which the vapor pressure of water is 18 torr. Examining Table 5-4, we find that the first listed temperature at which $vp_{H_2O} < 18$ torr is $T = 20$ °C, $vp_{H_2O} = 17.535$ torr. Thus fog can form if the temperature drops below 20 °C.

BOX 5-4

THE WEATHER

The ever-changing conditions of the gases in the Earth's atmosphere constitute the weather. The three variables that most influence the weather are the temperature, pressure, and water content of air. Each varies widely, and their intricate interplay, energized by sunlight, creates weather patterns.

Energy from the sun is the driving force behind the weather. When sunlight is absorbed by the Earth, it heats the atmosphere near the Earth's surface. Atmospheric heating is not uniform for several reasons, the most important being the difference between the oceans and the continents. The oceans circulate constantly, so the heat absorbed from the sun is distributed over a huge volume. In addition, some energy of sunlight causes evaporation rather than a temperature increase. Sunlight shining on land masses is concentrated on the surface. Without circulation and evaporation, the same amount of sunlight raises the land temperature more than the ocean temperature. When the surface temperature is high, the air above that surface is heated more than when the surface temperature is low. As a result, temperature differences arise between different portions of the atmosphere.

When air is heated, it expands and flows outward from the higher-temperature region toward colder regions. In addition to this lateral movement, warm air moves upward in the atmosphere, which lowers the pressure near the planet's surface. Conversely, cool air moves downward in the atmosphere, which increases pressure near the surface. Thus pressure differences are created by uneven heating. The atmosphere adjusts to these pressure differences by more airflows; in other words, the wind blows.

Energy absorbed from the sun causes water to evaporate, increasing the amount of water vapor in the atmosphere. As this humid air cools, it eventually reaches the temperature at which the partial pressure of water exceeds the vapor pressure. Below this temperature, water condenses from the gas phase as liquid droplets, which can appear as clouds, fog, or dew. If a cloud becomes dense enough, its water droplets coalesce into rain. If the temperature falls below 0 °C, dense clouds lose water in the form of ice or snow. Photos of snowflakes appear below.

These meteorological processes can be described in terms of the ideal gas law, but weather dynamics are so complex that accurate predictions of what will happen next remain beyond our abilities. An exact understanding of the weather and the ability to predict weather over long periods remain major scientific challenges.

CHEMISTRY IN THE TROPOSPHERE

Every year humanity releases millions of tons of gaseous and particulate pollutants into the Earth's atmosphere. The main source of atmospheric pollution is the burning of fossil fuels. For example, combustion of diesel fuel and gasoline provides energy for automobiles, trucks, and buses, but burning these mixtures also produces vast quantities of CO_2 and lesser amounts of CO. Carbon monoxide is highly toxic, and carbon dioxide is a principal agent in global warming, as discussed in Chapter 6. In addition, internal combustion engines are notoriously inefficient, so significant amounts of unburned hydrocarbons are emitted in exhaust gases. Combustion also generates nitrogen oxide and sulfur oxides, both of which undergo reactions in the atmosphere that contribute to pollution, including acid rain.

OXIDES OF NITROGEN

Normally, N_2 is a very stable, unreactive molecule, as noted in Chapter 4. However, under the extreme conditions found in an automobile cylinder, nitrogen molecules may react with oxygen molecules to produce nitrogen monoxide:

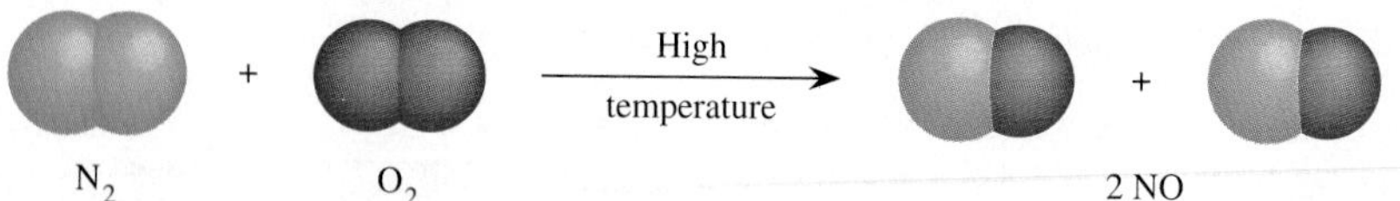

Nitrogen monoxide reacts in the atmosphere with O_2 to form nitrogen dioxide:

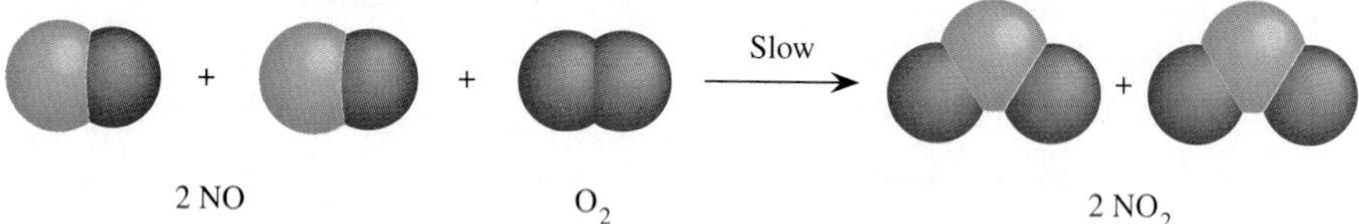

This compound is a red-brown gas that can be seen in the atmosphere over many large cities, where levels of NO_2 often reach 0.9 ppm. Tolerable limits for this toxic, irritating gas are around 3 to 5 ppm.

Nitrogen dioxide absorbs energy from sunlight and decomposes into NO molecules and oxygen atoms. Remember that oxygen is one of the elements that exists as a diatomic molecule in its natural state, so oxygen *atoms* are very reactive. Molecular nitrogen is too stable to react with oxygen atoms, but molecules of oxygen react with oxygen atoms to produce ozone (O_3), a toxic and highly reactive molecule:

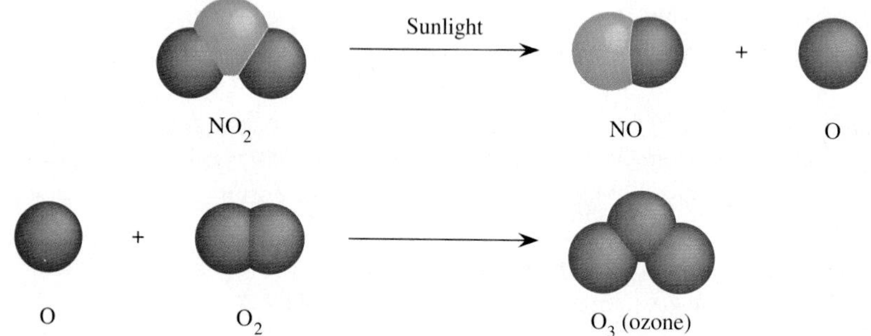

Both ozone and oxygen atoms react with unburned hydrocarbons to produce many different compounds that are harmful to the respiratory system.

The mixture of all these pollutants is sometimes called **photochemical smog.** To control photochemical smog, governments have set limits on the levels of NO and unburned hydrocarbons allowed in automobile exhaust. Today, chemists and engineers are researching cleaner-burning fuels and more efficient engines. Catalytic converters remove much of the NO and NO_2 from exhaust gases before they are released into the atmosphere. These have helped alleviate pollution from nitrogen oxides at only a small additional cost. We could control pollution emissions much better, but consumers and manufacturers have been reluctant to pay the higher costs required to develop and produce cleaner fuels and engines.

FIGURE 5-18
Coal lacks a regular, patterned structure. Instead, it is an extended network of carbon atoms containing randomly distributed atoms of H, O, N, and S. The figure shows a representative portion of coal structure.

OXIDES OF SULFUR

About half the electricity produced in the United States comes from burning coal. Like petroleum, coal was formed millions of years ago from decaying plants under conditions of high temperature and pressure. Coal is a network of carbon atoms in a variety of complex forms, as shown by the structure in Figure 5-18. Coal always contains small amounts of other elements, including hydrogen, oxygen, nitrogen, and sulfur.

When coal burns, its sulfur combines with O_2 to produce sulfur dioxide:

$$S_{(s,\ \text{from coal})} + O_{2\ (g)} \rightarrow SO_{2\ (g)}$$

In the presence of dust particles or ultraviolet (UV) light, atmospheric SO_2 reacts further with O_2 to form SO_3:

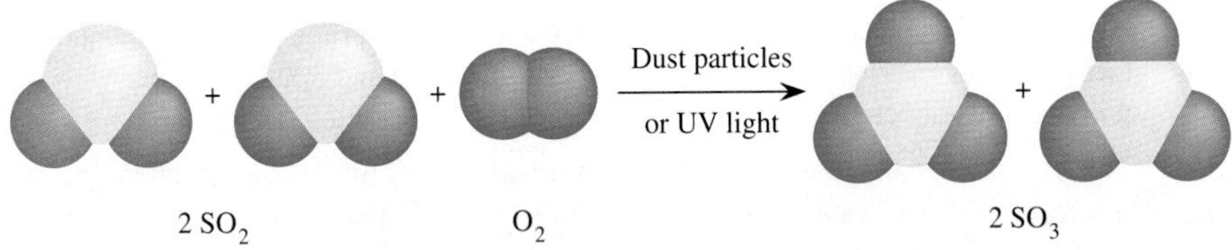

The sulfur impurities in coal are particularly damaging to the environment. In humans, prolonged exposure to sulfur dioxide diminishes lung capacity and aggravates respiratory problems such as asthma, bronchitis, and emphysema. Concentrations as low as 0.15 ppm can incapacitate persons with these diseases, and at about 5 ppm, everyone experiences severe breathing difficulties. In 1952 a particularly serious episode of SO_2 pollution in London caused approximately 4000 deaths over several days.

One particularly troubling aspect of SO_2 and SO_3 pollution is **acid rain,** which occurs when these gases combine with water to produce acid mists:

$$SO_{2\ (g)} + H_2O_{\ (g)} \rightarrow H_2SO_{3\ (\text{sulfurous acid mist})}$$

$$SO_{3\ (g)} + H_2O_{\ (g)} \rightarrow H_2SO_{4\ (\text{sulfuric acid mist})}$$

Raindrops passing through such mists become acidic. These two acids can cause up to a 1000-fold increase in the acidity of rainwater. Acid rain is common in the heavily industrialized areas of the United States, Canada, and Europe. In areas where acid rain is particularly acute, lakes are becoming so acidic that fish can no longer survive. In addition to the devastating effect on aquatic life, acid rain accelerates the leaching of nutrients from the soil, damages important building materials such as limestone and marble, alters the metabolism of organisms in the soil, and accelerates the corrosion of metals.

Sulfur dioxide can be removed from power plant exhaust gas using a so-called scrubber system. One common method involves the reaction of SO_2 with calcium oxide (lime) to form calcium sulfite:

$$SO_{2\,(g)} + CaO_{(s)} \rightarrow CaSO_{3\,(s)}$$

Unfortunately, scrubber systems are expensive to operate, and the solid $CaSO_3$ is generated in large enough quantities to create significant disposal problems.

Sulfur pollution may become increasingly significant in the United States, where it has been estimated that 30% of energy production will come from coal-fired plants within a decade. Because different deposits of coal have different sulfur levels, the amount of pollution will depend on the type of coal used. The oldest coal, anthracite, is 90% carbon and has a sulfur content lower than 1%, whereas bituminous coal can contain as much as 5% sulfur by mass. Unfortunately, much of the vast reserve of coal in North America is high-sulfur bituminous coal. Thus increased dependence on coal as a source of energy will come with a high cost to society. Until society can turn away from fossil fuels entirely, we will have to spend more money to develop efficient, less expensive scrubber systems or face disastrous consequences for our environment.

Later in the text we discuss the greenhouse effect (Chapter 6) and ozone depletion (Chapters 6 and 14).

SECTION EXERCISES

5.7.1 What are the concentrations in parts per million of the three most abundant trace atmospheric constituents listed in Table 5-3?

5.7.2 Argon gas can be recovered from the atmosphere by appropriate cooling and liquefaction processes. How many liters of dry air at 1.00 atm and 300 K must be processed to collect 10.0 mol of Ar?

5.7.3 The frost point is the temperature at which ice condenses from the atmosphere. A weather forecast gives the current temperature at +5 °C and sets the frost point at −5 °C. Using data from Table 5-4, determine the partial pressure of water vapor in the atmosphere and calculate the relative humidity.

5.8 VACUUM AND ITS USES

Anywhere near the surface of the Earth, we are immersed in a sea of gas molecules that exerts a pressure of about 1 atm. On the other hand, when a spacecraft leaves the atmosphere, it moves into outer space, a region where the molecular density is extremely low. A volume that contains very few atoms or molecules is called a **vacuum.** At 150 km above the Earth, the pressure is only 10^{-10} atm. Spacecraft reach this altitude and more; the Landsat satellites, which have photographed much of the globe, travel 700 km above the Earth's surface.

Long before space exploration, scientists were creating vacuums on Earth by removing air from enclosed containers. As early as 1650 a German named Otto von Guericke used an air pump of his own invention to create a vacuum inside a pair of hemispheres that were in contact with each other. He demonstrated the force exerted by atmospheric pressure by showing that two teams of horses pulling on the hemispheres in opposite directions could not pull them apart until the vacuum was broken by letting air in through a valve.

Vacuums have many uses in modern society. For instance, a thermos flask is a container with double walls separated by a vacuum. A thermos flask keeps liquids hot or cold because a vacuum, being mostly empty space, is a poor conductor of heat.

Vacuums are used in scientific instruments when molecular collisions must be reduced or eliminated. As a system is evacuated, pressure falls and molecular density is reduced, meaning that there are fewer molecules per unit volume. As the number of molecules is reduced, each molecule travels a longer distance before colliding with another molecule, as depicted in Figure 5-19. When the average distance between collisions is greater than the dimensions of the container, molecules travel from one end to the other without colliding.

This feature is essential to the operation of instruments that have "beams" of particles. The molecular velocity experiment depicted in Figure 5-1 would not work at high pressure because the molecules would be scattered out of the beam by collisions. The mass spectrometer, described in Chapter 2, requires collision-free conditions because the separation of molecular ions according to their masses is effective only when the ions travel through the spectrometer without being deflected by molecular collisions. Mass spectrometers are equipped with pumps that create the vacuum necessary to allow ions to move without many collisions.

Some unusual substances that chemists have learned to make are easily destroyed by atmospheric oxygen, so chemists use vacuum systems to remove oxygen from the apparatus in which the reactions are carried out. A good vacuum system allows near-complete removal of oxygen, which can then be replaced with a nonreactive gas such as nitrogen or argon.

The term *vacuum* describes a gaseous system whose pressure is less than 1 atm, but how much less? Even outer space is not a *total* vacuum because a few molecules per cubic centimeter exist even in interstellar regions. In the Earth's atmosphere, it is impossible to reduce molecular concentrations to that level. Ultimately, how "high" a vacuum we achieve (that is, how low a pressure) depends on how quickly gas leaks back into the system. In space, molecules leak into the interstellar regions from the stars. Even solids such as glass and stainless steel release atoms and molecules into the gas phase at very low pressure. The highest vacuums that scientists have attained are limited by these release rates and by the leakage of atmospheric gases through joints and valves in the vacuum apparatus.

Vacuum is measured by the residual pressure of the system. A rough vacuum may range from about 0.1 atm down to 10^{-3} torr (760 torr = 1 atm). High vacuum extends down to about 10^{-7} torr. This is almost 10 orders of magnitude below atmospheric pressure; yet at this pressure there are still more than 10^9 molecules per cubic centimeter. Ultrahigh vacuum can extend to as low as 10^{-10} torr.

High vacuums require special types of pumps. The most common high-vacuum pump is the diffusion pump, illustrated schematically in Figure 5-20. A diffusion pump works at the molecular level. A "jet" of heavy molecules is created by heating a liquid until it vaporizes. The stream of vapor molecules travels in the direction of pumping toward a cool surface, where they condense to the liquid phase and flow back to the bottom of the pump. The result is a "jet stream" in which "pumping molecules" traverse a circular path by cycling back and forth between the vapor phase and the liquid phase. Meanwhile, gas molecules in the system diffuse into the pumping region. Collisions with the pumping molecules force the gas molecules to travel in the direction of the jet. These collisions push the gas molecules to one end of the diffusion pump, where they are removed from the system by a mechanical pump. The pumping molecules condense back to the liquid phase before they can be captured by the mechanical pump. Most diffusion pumps use silicon-containing oils that have high molar masses and are not easily attacked by oxygen.

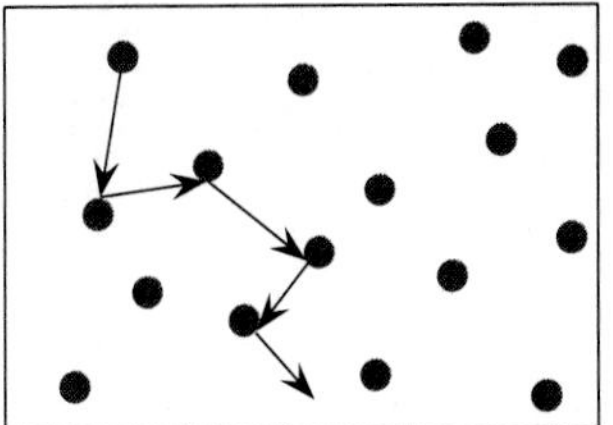

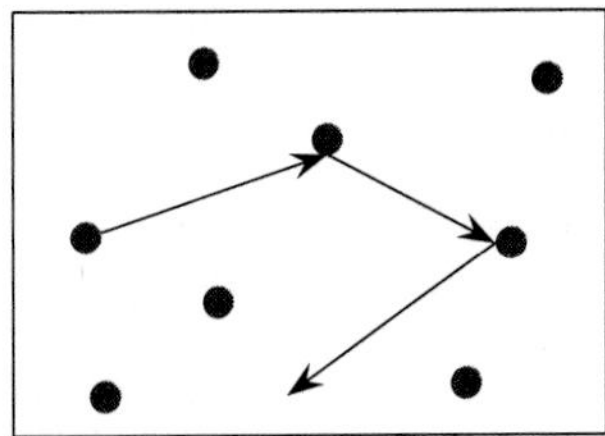

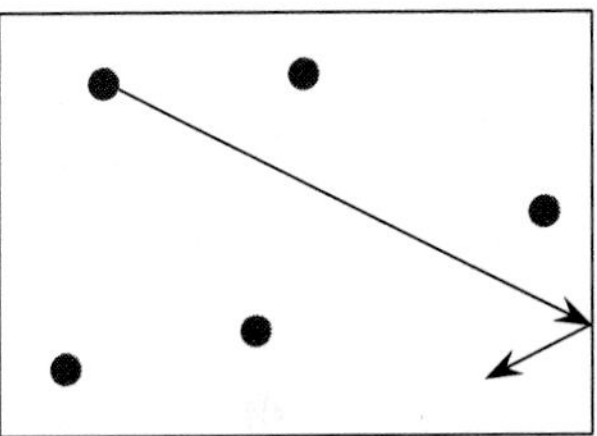

FIGURE 5-19
When pressure is reduced, the molecular density (number of molecules per unit volume) is reduced proportionally. As a result, the average distance traveled between molecular collisions increases. At sufficiently low pressure, molecules travel the length of their container without striking another molecule.

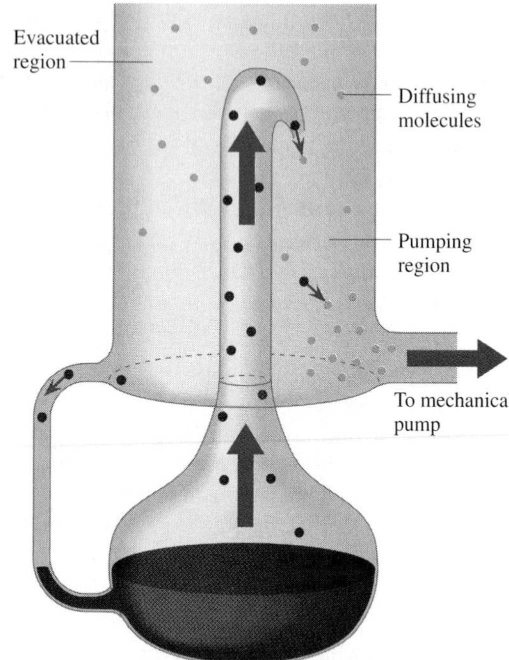

FIGURE 5-20
Diffusion pump and diagram of its operation. Gas molecules *(yellow circles)* diffuse from the evacuated region into the pumping region. There they are struck by molecules from the jet *(purple circles)*, driving them to the bottom of the pump, where they are removed by the mechanical pump.

SECTION EXERCISES

5.8.1 At 1 atm pressure, the average distance a molecule travels between collisions is about 10^{-8} m. How high a vacuum (in torr) is required for a mass spectrometer 0.5 m in length to function without significant numbers of collisions? (Assume that the average distance between collision must be 4 times the spectrometer's length to meet this requirement, and consult Figure 5-19 for a molecular picture.)

5.8.2 A liquid used in a diffusion pump must have a relatively high molar mass, boil at a moderate temperature, and have a low vapor pressure at 298 K. Explain why each of these features is desired.

CHAPTER SUMMARY

1. Gases contain molecules moving independently with a distribution of molecular energies. The average kinetic energy depends on temperature but is the same for all gases.
2. When molecules move completely independently of one another, the gas is ideal and obeys the ideal gas law, $PV = nRT$. The ideal gas law can be used to calculate several gas properties, including molar mass.
3. Pressure, the force per unit area exerted by a gas, can be measured using barometers and manometers.
4. In a gas mixture, each component exerts a partial pressure that is given by the ideal gas law. The composition of gaseous mixtures can be specified by partial pressures or by mole fractions. Stoichiometric calculations use the ideal gas equation to find moles of gases.
5. The Earth's atmosphere is a complex mixture of gases in which many chemical reactions occur.
6. Scientists use vacuum systems to study collision-free processes and synthesize oxygen-sensitive compounds. The low molecular density of a vacuum is generated by gas pumps.

KEY TERMS

diffusion
effusion
evaporation
partial pressure
pressure
vacuum
vapor

atmosphere
barometer
pascal
torr

absolute zero temperature
Dalton's law of partial pressures
dynamic equlibrium
ideal gas
ideal gas equation ($PV = nRT$)

acid rain
photochemical smog
relative humidity
saturated
troposphere

gas constant *(R)*
mole fraction *(X)*
parts per billion (ppb)
parts per million (ppm)
vapor pressure *(vp)*

SKILLS TO MASTER

- Visualizing molecular motion in gases
- Calculating gas properties using the ideal gas equation
- Relating final conditions to initial conditions
- Determining partial pressures
- Solving stoichiometry problems that include gaseous reagents
- Working with vapor pressures

LEARNING EXERCISES

5.1 Write a chapter summary of two pages or less that outlines the important features of this chapter.

5.2 List the macroscopic properties and the microscopic properties of gases.

5.3 Update and reorganize your list of memory bank equations so that all equations that involve moles are grouped together.

5.4 Summarize the strategy for calculating final pressures of gases in a limiting-reagent problem.

5.5 Define partial pressure, vapor pressure, and relative humidity. Explain how they are related.

5.6 List all terms new to you that appear in Chapter 5. Write a one-sentence definition of each in your own words. Consult the glossary if you need help.

PROBLEMS

MOLECULES IN MOTION

5.1 Redraw Figure 5-3 to show how the distribution of molecules would vary if the temperature of the oven was raised from 300 to 600 K.

5.2 Draw a single graph that shows the *velocity* distributions of the following: N_2 at 200 K, N_2 at 300 K, and He at 300 K.

5.3 Redraw the graph in Problem 5.2 to make it a graph of energy distributions for the three gases.

5.4 Calculate the most probable speed for each of the following (refer to Figure 5-4 for most probable kinetic energies): (a) He at 900 K; (b) O_2 at 300 K; and (c) SF_6 at 900 K.

5.5 Calculate the average kinetic energy per mole for each gas in Problem 5.4.

5.6 To make atomic bombs from uranium, naturally occurring uranium must be enriched in its lighter isotope, ^{235}U. This was first accomplished using gaseous diffusion of UF_6. Gas molecules containing ^{235}U diffuse slightly faster than those containing ^{238}U. Calculate the ratio of rates of diffusion of the two forms of UF_6.

THE IDEAL GAS EQUATION

5.7 Which of the following exerts a higher force when it collides with a wall, and why? (a) neon atom at 2000 K or xenon atom at 2000 K; (b) methane molecule at 390 K or methane molecule at 700 K; and (c) H_2 molecule traveling 10^5 m/s or F_2 molecule traveling at the same speed.

5.8 Explain in molecular terms why each of the following statements is true:
   (a) At very high pressure, no gas behaves ideally.
   (b) At very low temperature, no gas behaves ideally.

5.9 The following figure represents an ideal gas in a container with a movable piston.

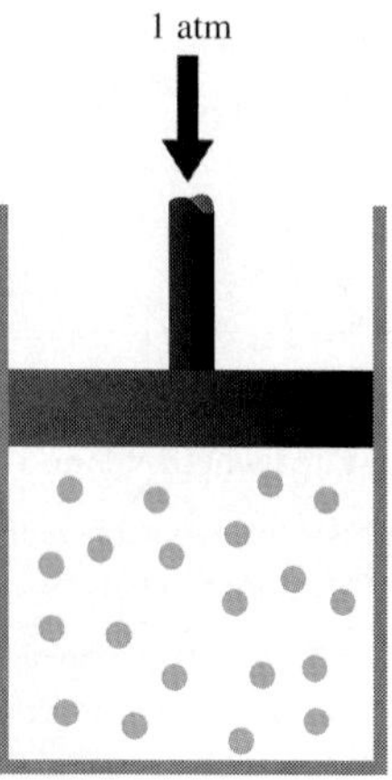

   (a) The external pressure on the piston exerted by the atmosphere is 1 atm. What is the pressure inside the container? Explain in terms of molecular collisions.
   (b) Redraw the sketch to show what would happen if the temperature of the gas inside the container is doubled. Explain in terms of molecular collisions.

5.10 A cylinder with a movable piston contains a sample of gas. Describe in molecular terms the effect on pressure exerted by the gas for each of the following changes:
   (a) The piston is pushed in.
   (b) Some gas is removed while the piston is held in place.
   (c) The gas is heated while the piston is held in place.

PRESSURE

5.11 Describe what would happen to the barometer shown in Figure 5-9 if the tube holding the mercury had a small pinhole at its top.

5.12 Manometers can use liquids other than mercury to measure small pressure differences. On a day when the barometric pressure is 764.4 torr, a water manometer connected between the atmosphere and a glass bulb containing a sample of helium gas has a height difference of 18.4 cm. The water level is higher in the arm connected to the bulb. Compute the pressure in the bulb in torr, atmospheres (atm), and kilopascals (kPa).

5.13 Express the following in SI units: (a) 455 torr; (b) 2.45 atm; (c) 0.46 torr; and (d) 1.33×10^{-3} atm.

5.14 Convert the following to torr: (a) 1.00 Pa; (b) 125.6 kPa; (c) 75.0 atm; and (d) 4.55×10^{-10} atm.

5.15 A sample of air was compressed to a volume of 20.0 L. The temperature was 298 K, and the pressure was 5.00 atm. How many moles of gas were in the sample? If the sample had been collected from air at $P = 1$ atm, what was the original volume of the gas?

APPLYING THE IDEAL GAS EQUATION

5.16 Rearrange the ideal gas equation to give the following expressions: (a) $n = ?$; (b) $V = ?$; and (c) $n/V = ?$.

5.17 Rearrange the ideal gas equation to give the following expressions: (a) an equation that relates P_i, T_i, P_f, and T_f when n and V are constant; (b) an equation that relates V_i, n_i, V_f, and n_f when P and T are constant; and (c) an equation that relates P_i, V_i, P_f, and V_f when n and T are constant.

5.18 A pressurized can of whipped cream has an internal pressure of 1.075 atm at 25 °C. If it is placed in a freezer at −10 °C, what is the new value for its internal pressure?

5.19 It requires 0.255 L of air to fill a metal foil balloon to 1.000 atm pressure at 25 °C. The balloon is tied off and placed in a freezer at −10 °C. What is the new volume of air in the balloon?

5.20 Describe the molecular changes that account for the result in Problem 5.18.

5.21 When a sealed bulb containing a gas is immersed in an ice bath, it has a gas pressure of 345 torr. When the same bulb is placed in an oven, the pressure of the gas rises to 745 torr. Calculate the oven's temperature in degrees Celsius.

5.22 Under which of the following conditions could you *not* use the equation, $P_1V_1/T_1 = P_2V_2/T_2$?
(a) P is expressed in torr.
(b) T is expressed in °C.
(c) V is changing.
(d) n is changing.

5.23 Freons are compounds that contain carbon, chlorine, and fluorine in various proportions. They are used as foaming agents, propellants, and refrigeration fluids. Freons are controversial because of the damage they do to the ozone layer in the stratosphere. A 2.55-g sample of a particular freon in a 1.50-L bulb at 25 °C has a pressure of 262 torr. What is the molar mass and formula of the compound?

GAS MIXTURES

5.24 Find the partial pressures, total pressure, and mole fractions of a gas mixture in a 4.00 L container at 375 °C if it contains 1.25 g each of Ar, CO, and CH_4.

5.25 In a smoggy atmosphere the amount of NO_2 in the air is 0.78 ppm. If the barometric pressure is 758.4 torr, compute the partial pressure of NO_2 in atmospheres.

5.26 The following figures represent very small portions of three gas mixtures, all at the same volume and temperature.

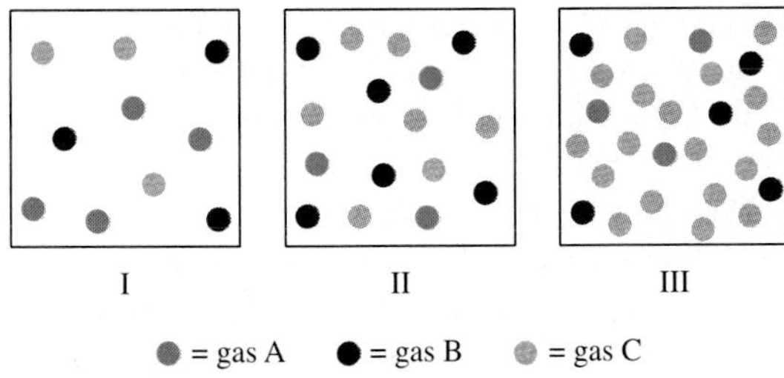

(a) Which sample has the highest partial pressure of gas A?
(b) Which sample has the highest mole fraction of gas B?
(c) In sample III, what is the concentration of gas A in ppm?

5.27 In dry atmospheric air, the four most abundant components are N_2, $X = 0.7808$; O_2, $X = 0.2095$; Ar, $X = 9.34 \times 10^{-5}$; and CO_2, $X = 3.25 \times 10^{-4}$. Calculate the partial pressures of these four gases, in torr, under standard atmospheric conditions.

5.28 California's automobile emission standards require that exhaust gases contain less than 220 ppm hydrocarbons and less than 1.2% CO (these values are in moles per mole of air). What are the partial pressures, in torr and in atmospheres, that correspond to these values?

5.29 The natural gas in a storage tank is analyzed. A 2.00-g sample of the gas contains 1.57 g CH_4, 0.41 g C_2H_6, and 0.020 g C_3H_8. Calculate the partial pressure of each gas in the storage tank if it is under a total pressure of 2.35 atm.

GAS STOICHIOMETRY

5.30 Oxygen gas can be generated by heating $KClO_3$ in the presence of some MnO_2.

$$2\ KClO_3 \rightarrow 2\ KCl + 3\ O_2$$

If all the $KClO_3$ in a mixture containing 1.57 g $KClO_3$ and 0.25 g MnO_2 is decomposed, what volume of O_2 gas will be generated at $T = 20$ °C and $P = 765.1$ torr?

5.31 Humans consume glucose to produce energy. The products of glucose consumption are CO_2 and H_2O:

$$C_6H_{12}O_{6\,(s)} + O_{2\,(g)} \rightarrow CO_{2\,(g)} + H_2O_{(l)} \quad \text{(unbalanced)}$$

What volume of CO_2 is produced under body conditions (37 °C, 1.00 atm) during the consumption of 4.65 g of glucose?

5.32 Carbon monoxide and oxygen react to form carbon dioxide. A 50.0-L reactor at 25.0 °C, is charged with 1.00 atm of CO. The gas is then pressurized with O_2 to give a total pressure of 3.56 atm. The reactor is sealed, heated to 300 °C to drive the reaction to completion, and cooled back to 25.0 °C. Compute the final partial pressures of each gas.

5.33 Solid sodium metal reacts with chlorine gas to form sodium chloride. A closed container of volume 3.00×10^3 mL is filled with chlorine gas at 27 °C and 1.25×10^3 torr. If 6.90 g of sodium is introduced and the reaction goes to completion, what will the final pressure be if the temperature rises to 47 °C?

5.34 Ethylene oxide is produced industrially from the reaction of ethylene with oxygen at atmospheric pressure and 280 °C, in the presence of a silver catalyst:

$$C_2H_{4\,(g)} + O_{2\,(g)} \rightarrow C_2H_4O_{(g)} \quad \text{(unbalanced)}$$

Assuming a 100% yield, how many kilograms of ethylene oxide would be produced from 5.00×10^4 L of a mixture containing ethylene and oxygen in 1:1 mole ratio?

5.35 In actual practice, the ethylene oxide reaction of Problem 5.34 gives only a 65% yield under optimum conditions. Repeat the calculation assuming a 65% yield.

THE EARTH'S ATMOSPHERE

5.36 How much does the partial pressure of nitrogen gas in the atmosphere change at 30 °C and 1.00 atm as the relative humidity varies from 0% to 100%?

5.37 Find the dew point for relative humidity 78% at 25 °C?

5.38 What mass of krypton does 1.0 km^3 of dry air contain, assuming an atmospheric pressure of 1.0 atm. (See Table 5-3.)

5.39 In the tropics, water condenses in human lungs when the temperature and relative humidity are too high. Using Table 5-4, estimate the vapor pressure of water at body temperature of 37 °C. If atmospheric temperature is 40 °C, at what relative humidity does this life-threatening process occur?

5.40 If 1.00 metric ton of soft coal containing 4.55% (by mass) sulfur is burned, what volume of SO_2 is produced at 50 °C and 1.00 atm? What mass of CaO is required to "scrub" this SO_2? What mass of $CaSO_3$ must be disposed of?

VACUUM AND ITS USES

5.41 Explain why a vacuum system is likely to be used in each of the following experiments: (a) determination of molar masses using mass spectrometry; (b) studies of the suitability of materials for use in outer space; and (c) studies of ultraclean metal surfaces.

5.42 Molecular clouds composed mostly of hydrogen molecules have been detected in interstellar space. The molecular density in these clouds is about 10^{10} molecules m^{-3}, and their temperature is around 25 K. What is the pressure in such a cloud?

ADDITIONAL PROBLEMS

5.43 How many grams of krypton are present in a 600-mL container at 1000 °C in which the pressure of krypton is 10.0 atm? How many atoms is this?

5.44 A 96.0-g sample of O_2 gas at 0 °C and 380 torr is compressed and heated until the volume is 3.00 L and the temperature is 27 °C. What is the final pressure in torr?

5.45 Describe a gas experiment that would show that the element oxygen exists naturally as diatomic molecules.

5.46 The air in a bicycle tire of volume 2.00×10^2 in^3 is allowed to escape and is collected at atmospheric pressure. The volume collected is 0.35 ft^3. What was the pressure inside the bicycle tire in torr?

5.47 A mixture of cyclopropane gas (C_3H_6) and oxygen (O_2) in a 1:4 mole ratio is used as an anesthetic. What mass of each of these gases is present in a 2.00-L bulb at 23 °C if the total pressure is 1.00 atm?

5.48 Two chambers are connected by a valve. One chamber has a volume of 10 L and contains N_2 gas at a pressure of 2.0 atm. The other has a volume of 1.0 L and contains O_2 gas at 3.0 atm. The valve is opened, and the two gases are allowed to mix thoroughly. The temperature is constant at 300 K throughout this process.

(a) How many moles each of N_2 and O_2 are present?
(b) What are the final pressures of N_2 and O_2, and what is the total pressure?
(c) What fraction of the O_2 is in the smaller chamber after mixing?

5.49 A 3.00-g sample of an ideal gas occupies 0.963 L at 22 °C and 0.969 atm. What will be its volume at 0 °C and 1 atm?

5.50 Liquid helium at 4.2 K has a density of 0.147 g/mL. Suppose that a 2.00-L metal bottle at 90 K contains air at 1.0 atm pressure. If we introduce 100 mL of liquid helium, seal the bottle, and allow the entire system to warm to room temperature (25 °C), what is the pressure inside the bottle?

5.51 A mouse is placed in a sealed chamber filled with air at 760 torr and equipped with enough solid KOH to absorb any CO_2 and H_2O produced. The gas volume in the chamber is 2.05 L, and its temperature is held at 300 K. After 2 hours, the pressure inside the chamber has fallen to 720 torr. What mass of oxygen has the mouse consumed?

5.52 When heated to 150 °C, copper sulfate pentahydrate ($CuSO_4 \cdot 5\,H_2O$) loses its water of hydration as gaseous H_2O. A 2.50-g sample of the compound is placed in a sealed 4.00-L steel vessel containing dry air at 1.00 atm and 27 °C, and the vessel is then heated to 227 °C. What is the final partial pressure of H_2O and the final total pressure?

5.53 The methanation reaction, $3\,H_2 + CO \rightarrow CH_4 + H_2O$, is used commercially to prepare methane. A gas reactor with a volume of 100 L is pressurized at 600 K with 20.0 atm H_2 gas and 10.0 atm CO gas; 150 g of CH_4 is produced. What is the percent yield of the synthesis?

5.54 A sample of warm air saturated with H_2O is collected in a container at $P = 756$ torr and $T = 30$ °C. Find the new pressure after a drying agent is added to remove the water vapor and the mole fraction and concentration in grams per liter of water vapor in the original air sample.

5.55 A 0.1054 g mixture of $KClO_3$ and MnO_2 was placed in a quartz tube and heated vigorously to decompose $KClO_3$ into KCl and O_2. The O_2 was collected at 25 °C and a pressure of 759.2 torr. The volume of gas collected was 22.96 mL.

(a) How many moles of oxygen were produced?
(b) How many moles of $KClO_3$ were in the original mixture?
(c) What was the mass percentage of $KClO_3$ in the original mixture?

5.56 Find the partial pressures in atmospheres of the eight most abundant atmospheric components in Table 5-3 at 25 °C, 50% relative humidity, and $P = 765$ torr.

5.57 Calculate the density of (a) dry air at 1 atm and 300 K and (b) air of 100% relative humidity at 1 atm and 300 K.

5.58 Liquid oxygen, used in some large rockets, is produced by cooling dry air to 90 K. How many liters of dry air at 25 °C and 750 torr would have to be processed to produce 100 L of liquid oxygen (density = 1.14 g/mL)?

5.59 The dew point is the temperature at which water vapor begins to condense from moist air as it is cooled. Use data from Table 5-4 to estimate the dew point for air that has (a) relative humidity of 80% at 35 °C; (b) relative humidity of 50% at 15 °C; and (c) relative humidity of 30% at 25 °C.

5.60 On a smoggy day the ozone content of air over Los Angeles reaches 0.50 ppm. Compute the partial pressure of ozone and the number of molecules of ozone per cubic centimeter if the total atmospheric pressure is 762 torr and the temperature is 28 °C.

5.61 Elemental analysis of an organic liquid with a fishy odor gives the following elemental mass percentages: H, 14.94; C, 71.22; and N, 13.84. Vaporization of 250 mg of the compound in a 150-mL bulb at 150 °C gives a pressure of 435 torr. What is the molecular formula of the compound?

5.62 Humanity releases huge amounts of CO_2 into the Earth's atmosphere. Scientists suspect that increasing concentrations of CO_2 in the atmosphere are causing the Earth's temperature to increase. According to a government report, in 1989 global CO_2 emissions reached "6000 million metric tons of carbon." What mass of CO_2 is this? How many moles?

5.63 The following figure shows three chambers with equal volumes connected by valves. Each chamber contains gaseous helium, with amounts proportional to the number of atoms shown. Answer each of the following questions, briefly stating your reasoning.

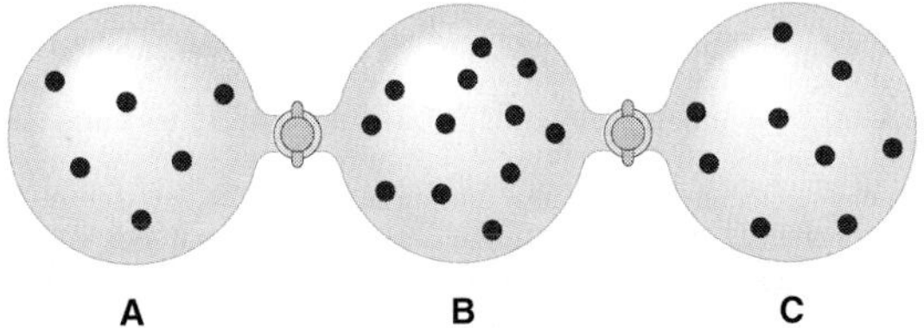

(a) Which of the three has the highest pressure?
(b) If the pressure of B is 1.0 atm, what is the pressure of A?
(c) If the pressure of A starts at 1.0 atm and then all the atoms from B and C are added to container A, what will be the new pressure?
(d) If the pressure in B is 0.50 atm, what will the pressure be after the valves are opened?

5.64 Nitrogen gas is available commercially in pressurized 9.50-L steel cylinders. If a tank has a pressure of 150 atm at 298 K, how many moles of N_2 are in the tank? What is the mass of N_2?

5.65 You are on vacation in Hawaii, where the temperature is 27 °C. You wish to go for a scuba dive. Your tank, with a volume of 12.5 L, is filled with air to a pressure of 2500 psi (170 atm). If your body requires you to consume 14.0 g O_2/min, how long can you dive at a depth of 70 feet if you must allow 6.0 minutes to return to the surface? Assume that the mole fraction of O_2 in air is 0.20.

5.66 At an altitude of 40 km above the Earth's surface the temperature is about −25 °C, and the pressure is about 3.0 torr. Calculate the average molecular velocity of ozone (O_3) at this altitude.

5.67 A gas cylinder of volume 5.00 L contains 1.00 g of Ar and 0.050 g of Ne. The temperature is 275 K. Find the partial pressures, total pressure, and mole fractions.

5.68 The following figure shows two tanks connected by a valve. Each tank contains a different gas, both at 0 °C.

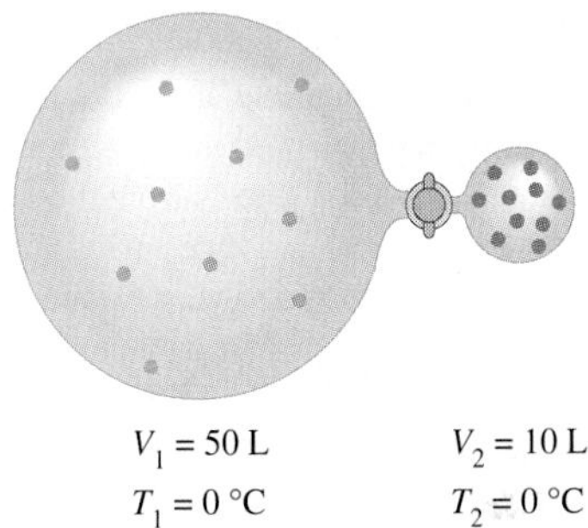

(a) Redraw the system to show how it appears after the valve has been opened.
(b) If each "picture molecule" in the diagram represents 1 mol of real molecules, what is the system's total pressure after the valve is opened? (Assume that the valve has negligible volume.)
(c) If all the gas is pumped into the smaller tank, what are the partial pressures of the two gases?

5.69 Explain in your own words how sulfur impurities in coal lead to acid rain. Use balanced equations when appropriate.

5.70 The average kinetic energy of a 1.55-g sample of argon gas in a 5.00-L bulb is 1.02×10^{-22} J/atom. What is the pressure of the gas? What is the average velocity of the argon atoms under these conditions?

5.71 Molecular beam experiments on ammonia at 400 K give the following velocity distribution.

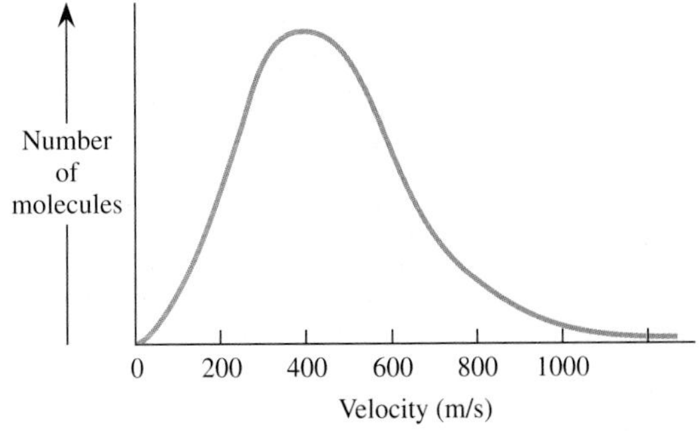

(a) What is the most probable velocity?
(b) What is the most probable kinetic energy?

5.72 Benzaldehyde is a fragrant molecule used in artificial cherry flavoring. Combustion of 125 mg of benzaldehyde gives 363 mg CO_2 and 63.7 mg of H_2O. In a separate experiment a 110-mg sample is vaporized at 150 °C in a 0.100-L bulb. The vapor gives a pressure of 274 torr. Determine the molecular formula of benzaldehyde.

5.73 A balloon filled with helium gas at 1.0 atm and 25 °C is to lift a 300-kg payload. What is the minimum volume required for the balloon? Assume dry air at the same pressure and temperature make up the atmosphere. (HINT: the total mass of payload plus He must be less than the mass of air displaced by the balloon.)

5.74 Suppose that the balloon in Problem 5.73 is going to use hot air instead of helium. What temperature must the air be?

5.75 In an explosion, a compound that is a solid or a liquid decomposes very rapidly, producing large volumes of gas. The force of the explosion results from the rapid expansion of the hot gases. For example, trinitrotoluene (TNT) explodes according to the following balanced equation:

$$2\ C_7H_5(NO_2)_{3\ (s)} \rightarrow 12\ CO_{\ (g)} + 2\ C_{\ (s)} + 5\ H_{2\ (g)} + 3\ N_{2\ (g)}$$

NO_2

O_2N NO_2

TNT
$C_7H_5(NO_2)_3$

(a) How many moles of gas are produced in the explosion of 1.0 kg of TNT? (b) What volume will these gases occupy if they expand to a total pressure of 1.0 atm at 25 °C? (c) At a total pressure of 1 atm, what would be the partial pressure of each gas?

5.76 In 1990, CO_2 levels at the South Pole reached 351.5 ppm by volume. What is the partial pressure of CO_2 at the South Pole? At this level, how many CO_2 molecules are there in 1.0 L of dry air at −50 °C? (By comparison, the 1958 reading was 314.6 ppm by volume.)

5.77 The gas SF_6 is used to trace air flows because it is nontoxic and can be detected selectively in air at a concentration of 1 ppb. What partial pressure is this? At this concentration, how many molecules of SF_6 are contained in 1.00 cm^3 of air at T = 21 °C?

5.78 Many of the transition metals form complexes with CO; these complexes are called *metal carbonyls* and have the general formula $M(CO)_x$. A 0.500-g sample of gaseous nickel carbonyl in a 0.100-L bulb generates a pressure of 552 torr at 30 °C. What is the formula of nickel carbonyl?

5.79 Construct the following graphs for an ideal gas at T = 298 K: (a) V vs. P; (b) PV vs. P; and (c) $1/V$ vs. P. Describe in words the shape of each of these graphs.

5.80 Describe how gas measurements can be used to obtain the molar mass of an unknown gas.

5.81 The Haber synthesis of ammonia is a gas phase reaction conducted at high temperature (400 to 500 °C) and pressure (100 to 300 atm). The starting materials for the Haber synthesis are placed inside a container in proportions shown in the following figure. Assuming 100% yield, draw a sketch that illustrates the system at the end of the reaction.

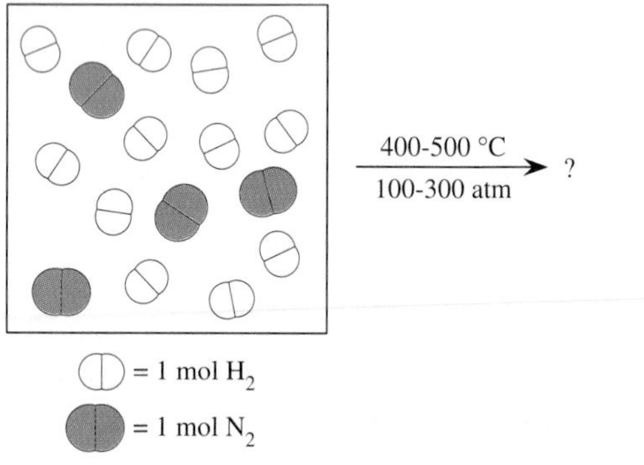

5.82 A sample of gas is found to exert a pressure of 500 torr when it is in a 3.00-L flask at 0.0 °C. Compute (a) the new volume if P becomes 750 torr and T is unchanged; (b) the new pressure if V becomes 2.00 L and T is unchanged; (c) the new pressure if the temperature is raised to 50.0 °C and V is unchanged; (d) the new pressure if the volume is reduced to 1.50 L and T becomes −50.0 °C; and (e) the new pressure if half the gas is removed but V and T remain the same.

5.83 A 15.00-g piece of dry ice (solid CO_2) is dropped into a bottle with a volume of 0.750 L, and the air is pumped out. The bottle is sealed and the CO_2 allowed to evaporate. What is the final pressure in the bottle if the final temperature is 0.0 °C?

5.84 Compute the density (g/L) of H_2 gas at 380 torr and −23 °C.

5.85 Compute the density (g/L) of SF_6 gas at 755 torr and 27 °C.

5.86 Determine whether each of the following statements is true or false. If false, rewrite the statement so that it is true.

(a) At constant T and V, P is inversely proportional to the number of moles of gas, n.
(b) At constant V, the pressure of a fixed amount of gas is directly proportional to T.
(c) When gas is added to a chamber at fixed V and T, the pressure increases as n^2.
(d) At fixed n and P, V is independent of T.
(e) At fixed n and T, the product of P and V is constant.

5.87 Write a series of balanced chemical equations that show how nitrogen dioxide is formed in the atmosphere.

5.88 Consider two gas bulbs of equal volume, one filled with H_2 gas at 0 °C and 2 atm, the other containing O_2 gas at 25 °C and 1 atm. Which of the bulbs has (a) more molecules; (b) more mass; (c) higher average kinetic energy of molecules; and (d) higher average molecular velocity?

ANSWERS TO SECTION EXERCISES

5.1.1

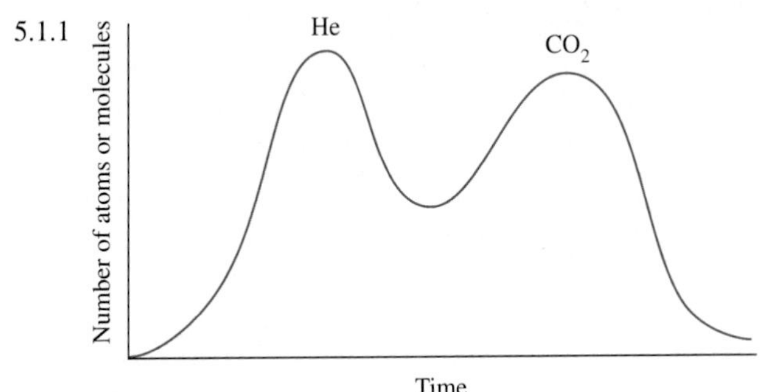

5.1.2 (a) 2.16×10^3 J; (b) 122 J, and (c) 1.96×10^{-20} J

5.1.3 Ratio of rates is 1.05.

5.2.1 (a) and (b) pressure doubles; (c) pressure triples; (d) no change.

5.2.2

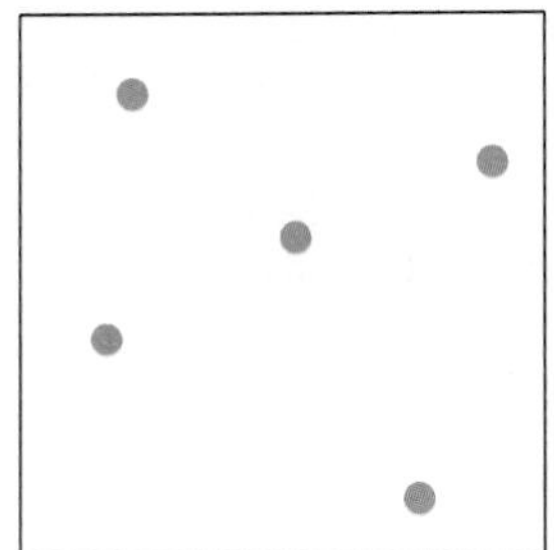

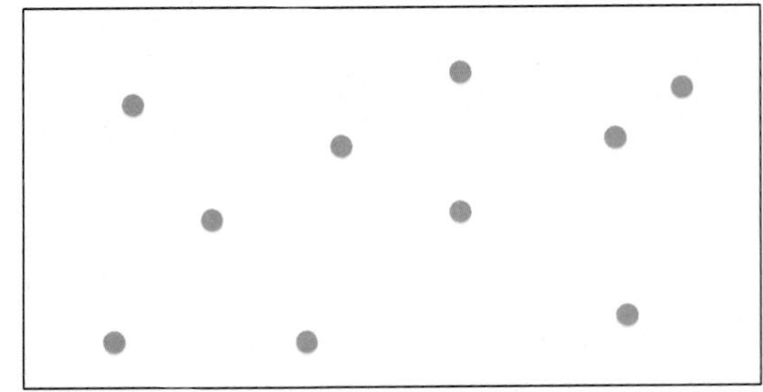

5.2.3 Low molecular density because there are fewer molecular interactions

5.3.1 700 torr, 0.921 atm, and 7.9% change

5.3.2 50.4 atm and 5.11×10^6 Pa

5.3.3 800.3 torr, 1.053 atm, and 1.067×10^2 kPa

5.4.1 59.1 kg of air enters as the house cools.

5.4.2

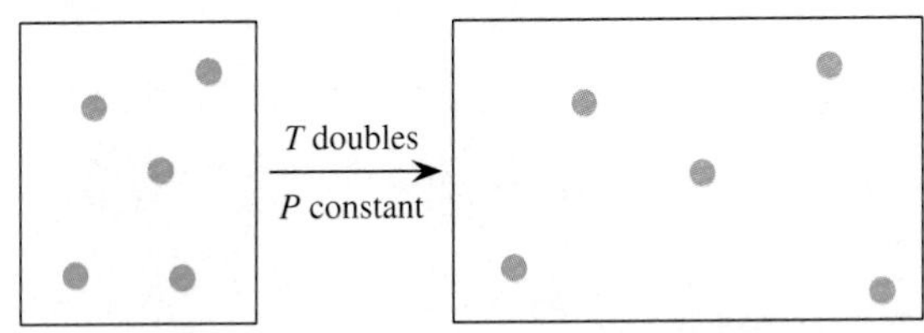

5.4.3 272 g/mol, $HgCl_2$

5.5.1 H_2: $X = 0.933$ and $p = 2.15$ atm;
N_2: $X = 0.067$, $p = 0.15$ atm

5.5.2

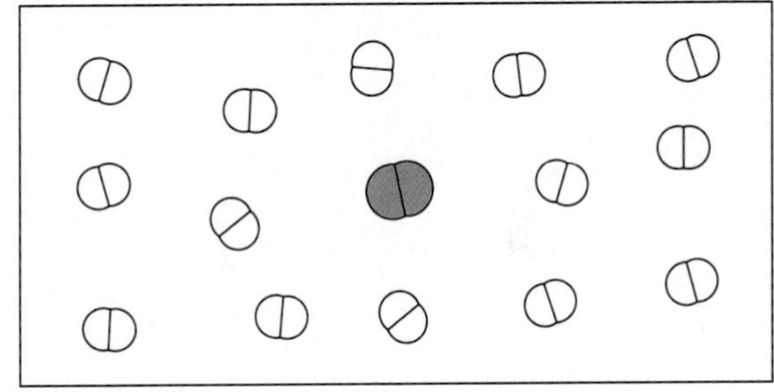

5.5.3 (a) 3.5×10^{-5}; (b) 2.6×10^{-2} torr; and (c) 8.3×10^{20} molecules

5.6.1 7.8 kg C_2H_2 and 5.4 kg H_2O

5.6.2 3.60 atm

5.6.3 5.83 atm (remember to calculate the new partial pressure of air at the higher temperature)

5.7.1 Ne, 18.2 ppm; He, 5.24 ppm; and CH_4, 1.4 ppm

5.7.2 2.64×10^3 L

5.7.3 $vp = 3.013$ torr, 46% relative humidity

5.8.1 3.8×10^{-6} torr

5.8.2 High molar mass, so it transfers a lot of momentum per collision; boil at moderate temperature so it can be vaporized using moderate heating; low *vp* at 298 K so it does not contaminate the vacuum.

CHAPTER 6

ATOMS AND LIGHT

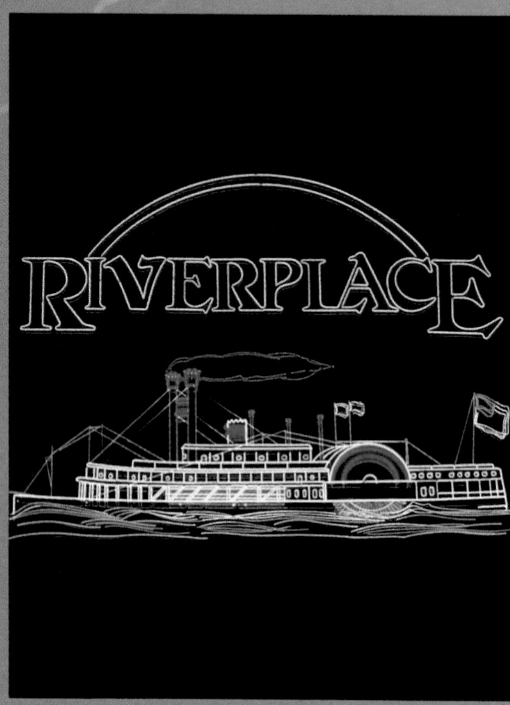

The showy display from a neon light is caused by photons emitted as excited-state neon atoms relax back to their ground states.

Elegant experiments carried out in the late nineteenth and early twentieth centuries showed that atoms consist of positively charged nuclei and negatively charged electrons. We described J.J. Thomson's cathode ray tube experiments, Robert Millikan's oil drop experiment, and Ernest Rutherford's scattering experiment in Chapter 2. In the first five chapters of this book, however, atoms have been treated as though they were not much more than the building blocks of matter. Now it is time to examine the detailed structure of atoms more closely. Differences in atomic structure distinguish the elements from one another and generate the rich array of chemical behavior exhibited by different types of atoms.

We begin with the nuclear model. Recall from Chapter 2 that the nucleus contains most of the mass of the atom, but it is confined to a very small volume. Electrons, on the other hand, contain very little mass but are spread out through space. Therefore a collision between two atoms is a collision of their electron clouds. The electron clouds repel each other but are attracted by the nuclei. Chemists describe molecular structure, properties of materials, and chemical reactions in terms of how electrons respond to these coulombic forces. In describing atoms, therefore, our main focus must be on the behavior of electrons.

Chemists are confident that the description of atoms presented in this chapter is correct. First, the description is consistent with the imaginative experiments that established the nuclear model of the atom. Second, this description explains chemical behavior. Third, chemists can use the description to make accurate predictions about new types of chemical behavior. Finally, the most powerful of modern microscopes allow chemists to "see" individual atoms.

Our presentation reveals the structure of atoms in several stages. First, we summarize the properties of atoms. Then we examine light, which is a powerful tool for studying atomic properties. Next, we describe the energy changes that accompany interactions between electrons and light. Finally, we describe the properties of atomic electrons and construct a picture of atomic electron structure. In succeeding chapters, this structure will help you understand why atoms combine to form molecules.

6.1 CHARACTERISTICS OF ATOMS

How would atoms appear to an atomic-sized observer? We introduced the fundamental characteristics of atoms earlier. Here is a summary.

Atoms possess mass. Matter possesses mass, and matter is made up of atoms, so atoms possess mass. This property was already recognized in the time of John Dalton, who made it one of the postulates of his atomic theory.

Atoms contain positive nuclei. Recall from Chapter 2 what Rutherford's scattering experiment demonstrated. Every atom contains a tiny central core where all the positive charge and most of the mass are concentrated. Subsequent experiments have shown that the mass of the positive nucleus is about 2000 times larger than the mass of the electron. Thus 99.95% of the mass of an atom is contained in its nucleus.

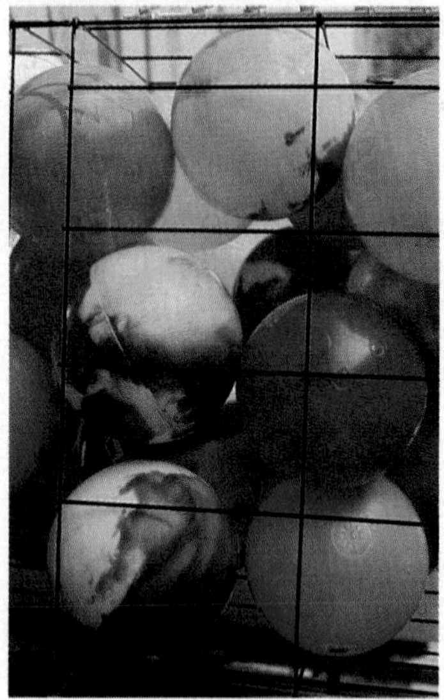

FIGURE 6-1
When a bin is full of balls, no more balls can be squeezed inside. Atoms, like balls, occupy volume. When a volume has been filled completely with atoms, no more can be squeezed inside.

Atoms contain electrons. Each element has a characteristic positive charge associated with its nucleus, ranging from +1 for hydrogen to greater than +100 for the heaviest elements. For an atom to be neutral, however, it must contain just as many electrons as the positive charge on its nucleus.

Atoms occupy volume. Matter occupies space, and matter is made up of atoms, so atoms occupy space. Why is it almost impossible to compress a solid substance such as copper? The electron cloud of each copper atom occupies some volume that no other atom is able to penetrate because of electron-electron repulsion. The atoms in a block of copper can be visualized as a set of atomic spheres nestled together like balls in a bin. Figure 6-1 shows that when the bin is full, no more balls can be added because each ball occupies a specific volume.

The volume of an atom can be determined from the density of a sample, the molar mass of the substance, and Avogadro's number. Sample Problem 6-1 shows how this is done.

SAMPLE PROBLEM 6-1 ATOMIC VOLUMES

The density of lithium, the lightest metal, is 0.534 g cm^{-3}. Calculate the volume occupied by a single atom in solid Li.

METHOD: It is convenient to work with 1 mol of lithium, which contains Avogadro's number (N_A) of atoms. The molar mass *(MM)* of Li tells us the mass of 1 mol of lithium, and we can use its density to find the volume of 1 mol of Li. Dividing by N_A then gives the volume per atom:

$$MM \text{ of Li} = 6.941 \text{ g/mol} \qquad \text{Density of Li} = 0.534 \text{ g cm}^{-3} = 5.34 \times 10^5 \text{ g m}^{-3}$$

$$V_{molar} = \frac{MM}{\text{Density}} = \frac{6.941 \text{ g/mol}}{5.34 \times 10^5 \text{ g m}^{-3}} = 1.300 \times 10^{-5} \text{ m}^3\text{/mol}$$

$$V_{atom} = \frac{V_{molar}}{\text{Atoms/mol}} = \frac{1.300 \times 10^{-5} \text{ m}^3\text{/mol}}{6.022 \times 10^{23} \text{ atoms/mol}} = 2.16 \times 10^{-29} \text{ m}^3\text{/atom}$$

This is much too small a volume to visualize, but we can obtain a better sense of its magnitude by computing the radius *(r)* of a Li atom, using the equation for the volume of a sphere:

$$V_{sphere} = \tfrac{4}{3}\pi r^3 \qquad \text{so} \qquad r = \left(\frac{3}{4\pi}V_{sphere}\right)^{1/3}$$

$$r = \left(\frac{(3)(2.16 \times 10^{-29} \text{ m}^3)}{(4)(3.1416)}\right)^{1/3} = 1.73 \times 10^{-10} \text{ m}$$

The radius of a lithium atom is slightly more than 10^{-10} m.

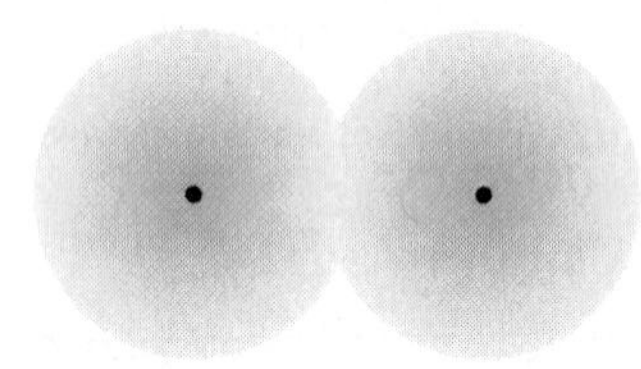

FIGURE 6-2
Depiction of two atoms colliding, with their electron clouds (*shaded*) in contact. Closer approach is prevented by strong coulombic electron-electron repulsions.

If an atom were the size of a sports stadium, its nucleus would be the size of a pea.

The volume of an atom is determined by its electron cloud. Sample Problem 6-1 demonstrates that the radius of an atom is about 10^{-10} m (0.1 nanometer, nm), whereas Rutherford's experiments showed that the radius of the nucleus is only about 10^{-15} m (1 femtometer, fm). This is 100,000 times smaller than the radius of an atom, so the nucleus is "buried" deep within the electron cloud. Figure 6-2 shows a schematic view of two atoms with their electron clouds in contact with each other.

Atoms have various properties. The periodic table is a catalog of all the known different elements; each has unique properties. The properties of an element arise from the properties of its atoms. Each atom has characteristic physical properties (mass, volume, attractive forces, and so on) and chemical properties (the types of atoms with which it will combine and in what proportions). As described later, all these differences in properties can be attributed to differences in the number of electrons.

Atoms attract one another. Every gaseous substance can be changed into a liquid if the pressure is high enough and the temperature is low enough. Liquids "stick together" in a finite volume rather than expanding, as gases do, to fill all available space. Liquids have a finite volume because their atoms and molecules attract one another. What "stick together" in a liquid are the atoms and molecules. This cohesiveness comes from coulombic attractions between the negative electron cloud of each atom and the positive nuclei of other atoms.

The forces that hold atoms and molecules together in the liquid and solid phases are discussed in Chapter 10.

Atoms can combine with one another. Atoms combine with one or more other atoms to form molecules with distinct properties. This is another of the fundamental observations of the atomic theory.

In Chapters 8 and 9 we describe how electron clouds interact as atoms combine to make molecules.

Our catalog of atomic characteristics emphasizes *electrons* because electrons determine most chemical properties of atoms. For the same reason, the next several chapters are devoted to electrons and the way they influence chemical properties. First, however, we must describe *light* and its interaction with atoms because light is an essential tool for probing properties of electrons.

SECTION EXERCISES

6.1.1 The density of gold metal is 18.9 g/cm^3.
(a) What is the volume of one gold atom?
(b) If a gold nucleus is 1/100,000 times as large as a gold atom, what is the volume of one gold nucleus?
(c) How many layers of gold atoms are there in a strip of gold foil that is 1 μm thick (1 μm = 10^{-6} m)? Assume that gold atoms stack in a line.

6.1.2 Atoms attract one another when they are far apart, but they strongly repel one another when they get too close together. Draw two atomic pictures similar to Figure 6-2. In one, show two atoms at a separation distance where they attract one another. In the other, show the same two atoms at a separation distance where they repel one another.

6.2 CHARACTERISTICS OF LIGHT

By far the most useful tool for studying the structure of atoms is **electromagnetic radiation.** What we call **light** is one form of this radiation. To understand what electromagnetic radiation reveals about atomic structure, we must first describe the properties of radiation.

Light behaves like a wave. In many respects, light behaves in ways that are best understood using waves. A wave is a regular oscillation in some particular property, such as the up-and-down variation in position of the water in a water wave. The height of a water wave differs from one place to another; that is, water waves *vary in space.* Light waves vary in space as well, in a manner illustrated in Figure 6-3. This variation in space is characterized by the **wavelength (λ),** which is the distance between successive wave crests. Wavelengths are measured in units of distance, such as meters or nanometers. Water waves also *vary in time.* A surfer waiting for a "big one" bobs up and down as "small ones" pass by. Light waves vary in time, as well. This variation in time is characterized by the wave's **frequency (ν),** which is the number of wave crests passing a point in space in 1 second. The frequency unit is s^{-1}, also known as Hertz (Hz).

Wavelength is usually designated by the Greek letter lambda, λ.

Frequency is usually designated by the Greek letter nu, ν.

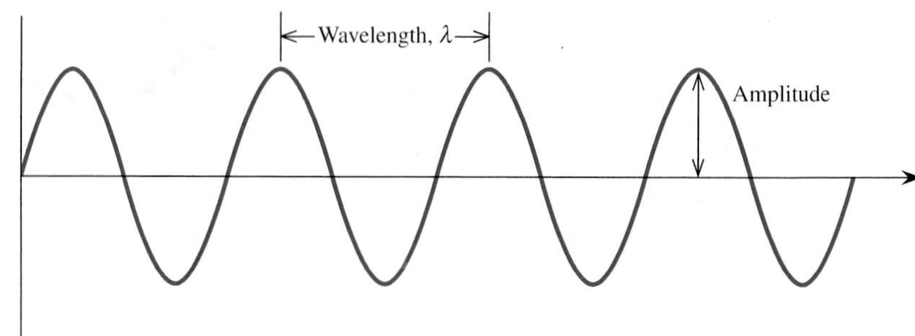

FIGURE 6-3
A wave possesses a characteristic wavelength and amplitude.

The value of c can be rounded to 2.998×10^8 m s^{-1} for most calculations.

Wavelength and frequency are related through the wave's velocity. The wavelength (in units of m) times the frequency (s^{-1}) equals the velocity (m s^{-1}). Light waves always move through empty space at a constant velocity of 2.997925×10^8 m s^{-1}. The velocity of light, denoted by the symbol *c*, is a fundamental constant:

$$\lambda\nu = c \tag{6-1}$$

Sample Problem 6-2 provides an example of how Equation 6-1 is used.

SAMPLE PROBLEM 6-2 WAVELENGTH-FREQUENCY CONVERSION

What is the frequency of blue light with a wavelength of 430 nm?

METHOD: The link between wavelength (λ) and frequency (ν) is given by Equation 6-1.

Rearrange $\nu\lambda = c$ *to* $\nu = c/\lambda$

$c = 2.998 \times 10^8$ m/s $\quad \lambda = 430$ nm $= 430 \times 10^{-9}$ m

$$\nu = \frac{2.998 \times 10^8 \text{ m s}^{-1}}{430 \times 10^{-9} \text{ m}} = 6.97 \times 10^{14} \text{ s}^{-1}$$

The wavelengths and frequencies of electromagnetic radiation span an immense range. What we call light is only the tiny part of the spectrum that can be detected by the human eye. Figure 6-4 shows that the visible spectrum of light covers the wave-

FIGURE 6-4
The electromagnetic spectrum, showing its various regions and the wavelengths and frequencies associated with each.

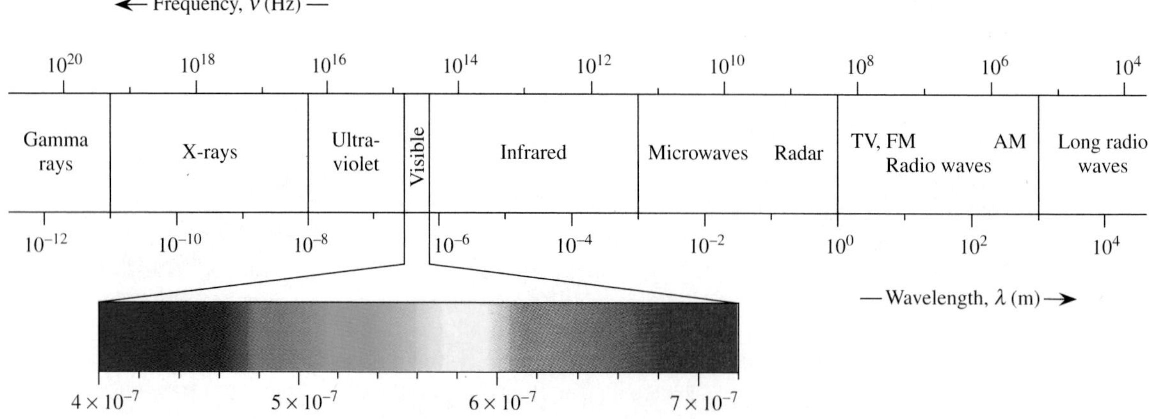

length range from about 400 nm (violet) to 700 nm (red). The center of this range is yellow light, with a wavelength around 550 nm and a frequency of $5.5 \times 10^{14}\ s^{-1}$. Although visible light is extremely important to living creatures for seeing, the gamma ray, x-ray, ultraviolet and infrared, microwave, and radio frequency portions of the electromagnetic spectrum have diverse applications in our lives. We return to these portions of the electromagnetic spectrum later in the chapter. Here, we concentrate on visible and ultraviolet light because they are particularly useful for probing the structure of atoms.

What we perceive as white light actually contains a variety of wavelengths. Figure 6-5 shows that these wavelengths are revealed when the light passes through a prism. The prism bends different wavelengths of light through different angles, so the light emerging from the prism is spread out in space, with each wavelength appearing at its own characteristic angle. The rainbow in Figure 6-5 is another manifestation of this effect. In this case, raindrops act as prisms, bending sunlight of different wavelengths by different amounts and spreading out the various colors.

Light possesses energy. Light carries energy. When our bodies absorb sunlight, for example, we feel hot because the energy of the sunlight has been transferred to our skin. Moreover, the total energy of a beam of light depends on its brightness, which is also called **intensity.** Sunlight from the midday sun is more intense than the rays of the setting sun, which are reduced in intensity as they pass through the dust-laden atmosphere. Similarly, the intense lights that illuminate a theater stage generate more heat than normal room lights.

FIGURE 6-5
When white light passes through a prism, each wavelength is bent through a different angle, generating the color pattern of a rainbow.

THE PHOTOELECTRIC EFFECT

A phenomenon known as the *photoelectric effect* shows how the energy of light depends on its frequency and intensity. An apparatus for studying the photoelectric effect is illustrated schematically in Figure 6-6. In a photoelectric experiment, a beam of light strikes the surface of a metal. Under the right conditions, the light ejects electrons from the metal's surface. These electrons strike a detector that measures the number of electrons and their kinetic energy. A detailed study of the photoelectric effect reveals how the behavior of the electrons relates to the characteristics of the light:

1. Below a characteristic threshold frequency ν_0, no electrons are observed, regardless of the light's intensity.
2. Above the threshold frequency, the kinetic energy of the ejected electrons increases in proportion to the frequency of the light, as shown in Figure 6-7. However, the kinetic energy does *not* depend on the light's intensity.

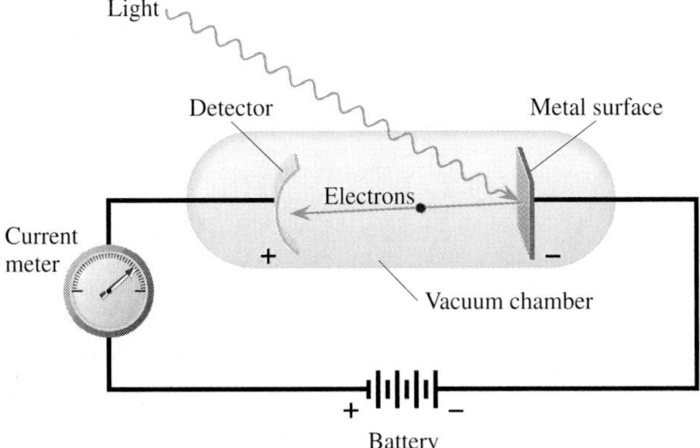

FIGURE 6-6
An apparatus for studying the photoelectric effect. Light of a particular frequency strikes a clean metal surface inside a vacuum chamber. Electrons are ejected from the metal and are counted by a detector that measures their kinetic energy.

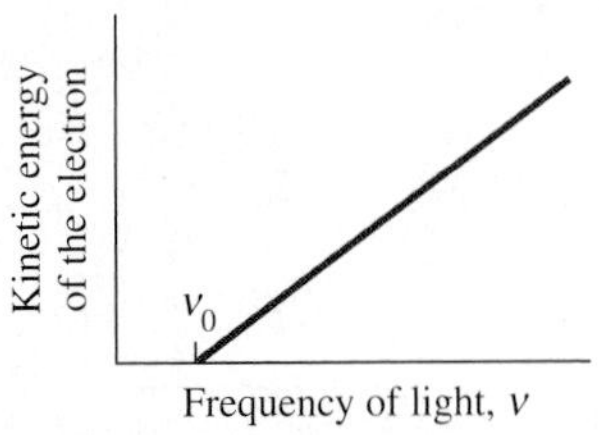

FIGURE 6-7
Variation in the kinetic energy of electrons ejected from a metal surface by light of various frequencies.

Planck's constant (*h*) is named in honor of Max Planck, who first introduced this constant in 1900 to explain another phenomenon of light.

3. Above the threshold frequency, the *number* of emitted electrons increases with the light's intensity.
4. All metals exhibit the same pattern, but each metal has a different threshold frequency.

In 1905 Albert Einstein provided an elegant explanation of the photoelectric effect.* Using the principle of conservation of energy, Einstein postulated that light comes in packets or bundles, called **photons;** each photon has an energy that is directly proportional to the frequency:

$$E_{\text{photon}} = h\nu_{\text{photon}} \qquad \textbf{(6-2)}$$

In this equation, E is the energy of light and ν is its frequency. The proportionality constant between energy and frequency is known as **Planck's constant *(h)*** and has a value of $6.6260755 \times 10^{-34}$ J sec. Sample Problem 6-3 illustrates the use of Equation 6-2.

SAMPLE PROBLEM 6-3 THE ENERGY OF LIGHT

What is the energy of a photon of red light of wavelength 650 nm?

METHOD: Equations 6-1 and 6-2 relate the energy of a photon to its frequency and wavelength. Combining these qualities we find that the energy of a photon is *inversely* proportional to its wavelength:

$$E = h\nu \qquad \textit{and} \qquad \nu\lambda = c \qquad \textit{so} \qquad E = \frac{hc}{\lambda}$$

$$h = 6.626 \times 10^{-34}\ \text{J s} \qquad \lambda = 650\ \text{nm} = 650 \times 10^{-9}\ \text{m} \qquad c = 2.998 \times 10^{8}\ \text{m s}^{-1}$$

$$E_{\text{photon}} = \frac{(6.626 \times 10^{-34}\ \text{J s})(2.998 \times 10^{8}\ \text{m s}^{-1})}{(650 \times 10^{-9}\ \text{m})} = 3.06 \times 10^{-19}\ \text{J}$$

Einstein further asserted that when a metal surface absorbs a photon, the photon's energy is transferred to an electron:

$$\Delta E_{\text{photon}} = \Delta E_{\text{electron}}$$

Some of this energy is used to overcome the forces that bind the electron to the metal, whereas the remainder shows up as kinetic energy of the ejected electron. Energy is conserved in this partitioning of energy, as shown diagrammatically in Figure 6-8.

* Albert Einstein was the greatest physicist of the twentieth century. He was born in Germany in 1879 and died in Princeton, NJ, in 1955. Einstein's performance as a student was unspectacular because he had little interest for any subject except theoretical physics. In 1905 he published five papers in a prestigious German physics journal. These papers dealt with three different problems in physics and established Einstein as a leading theoretician. The 1905 papers explained the photoelectric effect and gave a mathematical explanation for brownian motion. They also described Einstein's famous theory of relativity, which replaced Newton's theory as the unifying principle of motion. Einstein went on to develop the more comprehensive general theory of relativity in 1915.

The threshold frequency (ν_0) corresponds to the binding energy of the electron. In other words, the energy of a photon at the threshold frequency equals the minimum energy needed to overcome the forces that bind the electron to the metal. Putting these ideas together, Einstein obtained a simple linear equation that matched the graph in Figure 6-7:

Photon energy = Binding energy + Electron kinetic energy

$$h\nu = h\nu_0 + kE_{\text{electron}} \tag{6-3}$$

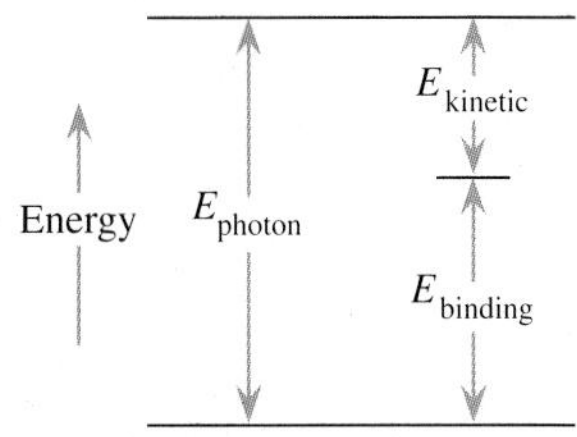

FIGURE 6-8
Diagram of energy balance for the photon and electron in the photoelectric effect. When a metal surface absorbs a photon, the energy of the photon is partly used to overcome the binding energy, whereas the remainder appears as kinetic energy *(kE)* of the electron.

Einstein's explanation accounts for all four properties of the photoelectric effect. First, when the energy of the photon is less than $h\nu_0$ (low-frequency light), not enough energy per photon exists to overcome the electron's binding energy, so no electrons can escape from the metal surface, no matter how intense the light. Second, after the energy of the photon exceeds the threshold value ($h\nu > h\nu_0$), electrons are ejected. The "extra" energy is transferred to the ejected electron as kinetic energy, and this extra kinetic energy increases linearly with ν. Third, the intensity of a light beam is a measure of the number of photons it contains, not the amount of energy each photon possesses. Higher intensity means more photons but not more energy *per photon.* More photons striking the metal result in more electrons being emitted, but the energy of each photon and each electron is unchanged. Finally, each metal has its own characteristic threshold frequency because electrons are bound more tightly to some metals than to others. Sample Problem 6-4 shows how to apply Einstein's analysis of the photoelectric effect.

SAMPLE PROBLEM 6-4 THE PHOTOELECTRIC EFFECT

The minimum energy needed to remove an electron from potassium metal is 3.7×10^{-19} J. Will photons of frequencies 4.3×10^{14} s^{-1} (red light) and 7.5×10^{14} s^{-1} (blue light) trigger the photoelectric effect? If so, how fast will the ejected electrons move?

METHOD: We must analyze the energy requirements for ejection of an electron. Recall that no electrons will be ejected unless the energy of the photons exceeds some threshold energy characteristic of the metal. If the photon energy exceeds this threshold energy, the electrons will be ejected with kinetic energy given by Equation 6-3.

The threshold energy of potassium metal, 3.7×10^{-19} J, is given in the problem. To determine whether the red and blue photons will eject electrons, we must convert the frequencies of these photons to their corresponding energies:

$$E_{\text{red photon}} = h\nu = (6.626 \times 10^{-34}\ \text{J s})(4.3 \times 10^{14}\ \text{s}^{-1}) = 2.8 \times 10^{-19}\ \text{J}$$

$$E_{\text{blue photon}} = h\nu = (6.626 \times 10^{-34}\ \text{J s})(7.5 \times 10^{14}\ \text{s}^{-1}) = 5.0 \times 10^{-19}\ \text{J}$$

According to these calculations, a photon of red light does not have enough energy to overcome the forces that bind the electrons to the metal. A blue photon, however, will eject an electron from the surface of potassium metal because its energy exceeds the threshold value.

What happens to the "extra" energy of a blue photon? Equation 6-3 indicates that it is transferred to the electron as kinetic energy:

$$h\nu = h\nu_0 + kE_{\text{electron}} \qquad \text{so} \qquad kE_{\text{electron}} = h\nu - h\nu_0$$

$$kE_{\text{electron}} = 5.0 \times 10^{-19}\ \text{J} - 3.7 \times 10^{-19}\ \text{J} = 1.3 \times 10^{-19}\ \text{J}$$

From this value, we can calculate the velocity (u) of the electron as it leaves the surface of the metal (m, mass; m, meter):

$$kE = \frac{m_{\text{electron}}u^2}{2} \qquad so \qquad u^2 = \frac{2kE}{m_{\text{electron}}}$$

$$m_{\text{electron}} = 9.109 \times 10^{-31}\ \text{kg}$$

$$u = \left[\frac{2KE}{m}\right]^{1/2} = \left[\frac{2(1.3 \times 10^{-19}\ \text{J})}{9.109 \times 10^{-31}\ \text{kg}}\right]^{1/2} = \left[\frac{2(1.3 \times 10^{-19}\ \text{kg m}^2\ \text{s}^{-2})}{9.109 \times 10^{-31}\ \text{kg}}\right]^{1/2}$$

$$u = 5.3 \times 10^5\ \text{m s}^{-1}$$

Sample Problem 6-4 illustrates an important difference between photon energy and electron energy. *Photon energy* is related to its *frequency* (Greek ν): $E_{\text{photon}} = h\nu$. *Electron kinetic energy* is related to its *velocity* (English u): $E_{\text{electron}} = mu^2/2$.

LIGHT BEHAVES LIKE PARTICLES

Before 1905 the properties of light had been explained using a wave picture. If light behaved only like a wave, however, its energy would depend on light's intensity but not on its frequency. If this were true, an intensity threshold would exist for the ejection of electrons, not a frequency threshold. Also, the energy of a wave is directly proportional to its intensity, so the kinetic energy of emitted electrons would increase with the intensity of the light. Einstein's explanation of the photoelectric effect was simple but revolutionary. Light contains photons, each of which is a "bullet" with the discrete energy $E = h\nu$. Thus light can be described as discrete "particles" of energy, and a complete description of light includes wavelike and particle-like properties.

Neither the particle nor the wave view of light is "wrong" or "right." Light has some properties of waves and some properties of particles. When light interacts with a relatively large body such as a raindrop or a prism, its wave properties dominate the interaction. On the other hand, when light interacts with a small body such as an atom or an electron, particle properties dominate the interaction. Thus each view provides different information about the properties of light, and when we think about light, we must think of "wave-particles" that combine both types of features.

LIGHT AND ATOMS

When a photon is absorbed, its energy is transferred to whatever absorbs the photon. In the photoelectric effect, this energy is transferred to an electron at the metal's surface. In addition to revealing the particle nature of light, photoelectric experiments can be used to determine the binding energies of electrons to *metal surfaces*. On the other hand, when light interacts with *free* atoms, rather than atoms bound to a metal, the interaction reveals information about electrons bound to *individual atoms*.

When an atom absorbs a photon, it gains the energy of that photon, so the atom is transformed to a higher energy state, called an **excited state.** Atoms in excited states subsequently give up their excess energy to return to their lowest-energy, most stable state, called the **ground state.** These transformations can be represented using diagrams such as the one shown in Figure 6-9. In such an **energy level diagram,** energy increases along the Y axis. Each energy state of the atom is represented by a horizontal line. Absorption of a photon, shown by an upward vertical arrow, causes a transition from the ground state to one of the excited states. Excited states may lose some or all of their excess energy by emitting photons, shown by downward vertical arrows. We develop the ideas of energy level diagrams in more detail in Section 6.3.

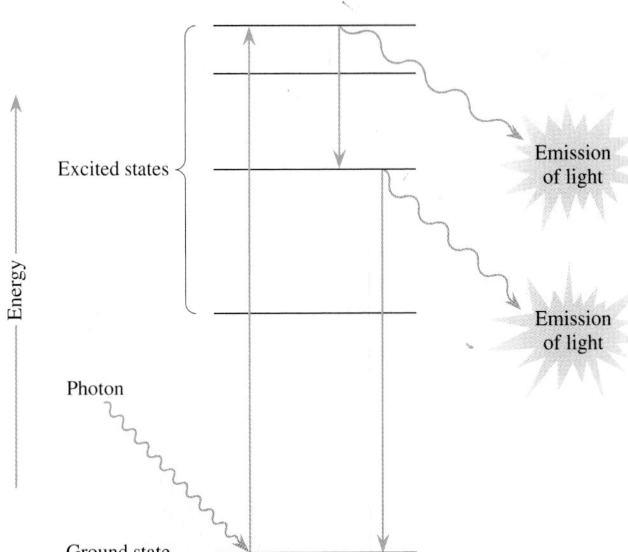

FIGURE 6-9
When an atom in its ground state absorbs a photon, the atom's energy increases, so the atom is converted to an excited state. Later, when the atom loses this extra energy, it may do so in more than one step, emitting one or more photons with lower energies in the process.

The key feature in the exchange of energy between atoms and light is that the change in energy of the atom *exactly* equals the energy of the photon, as required by the principle of conservation of energy:

$$\Delta E_{\text{atom}} = h\nu_{\text{photon}} \qquad \textbf{(6-4)}$$

When an atom absorbs a photon, the atom gains the photon's energy. When an atom emits a photon, the atom loses the photon's energy. As an atom returns from an excited state to the ground state, it must lose exactly the amount of energy that it originally gained. However, an excited atom may lose its excess energy in several steps involving small energy changes, so the frequencies of emitted photons may be lower than those of absorbed photons. Sample Problem 6-5 provides an example of energy changes associated with emission of light.

SAMPLE PROBLEM 6-5 EMISSION ENERGIES

A sodium vapor street lamp emits bright-yellow light at wavelength $\lambda = 589$ nm. What is the energy change for a sodium atom involved in this emission? How much energy is emitted per mole of sodium atoms?

METHOD: This problem begins with sodium atoms in an excited state. These atoms return to a lower energy level by emitting photons of light. One of these emissions has a wavelength of 589 nm. We can use Equations 6-1 and 6-2 to relate the energy of one of these photons to its wavelength and frequency:

$$E_{\text{photon}} = h\nu = hc/\lambda$$

Energy is conserved, so the energy of the emitted photon must exactly equal the energy change of the relaxing atom:

$$\Delta E_{\text{atomic electron}} = E_{\text{photon}} = hc/\lambda$$

To calculate the energy of a photon, we need the following data:

$$h = 6.626 \times 10^{-34}\ \text{J s} \qquad c = 2.998 \times 10^{8}\ \text{m/s} \qquad \lambda = 589\ \text{nm} = 589 \times 10^{-9}\ \text{m}$$

$$\Delta E_{\text{atom}} = E_{\text{photon}} = \frac{(6.626 \times 10^{-34}\ \text{J s})\,(2.998 \times 10^{8}\ \text{m s}^{-1})}{589 \times 10^{-9}\ \text{m}} = 3.37 \times 10^{-19}\ \text{J}$$

This result is the energy change for *one* sodium atom emitting *one* photon. We can use Avogadro's number to convert from energy per atom to energy *per mole* of atoms that undergo this transition:

$$\Delta E_{\text{mol}} = (\Delta E_{\text{atom}})\,(N_{\text{A}}) = (3.37 \times 10^{-19}\ \text{J})(6.022 \times 10^{23}\ \text{mol}^{-1}) = 2.03 \times 10^{5}\ \text{J/mol}$$

$$\Delta E_{\text{mol}} = 2.03 \times 10^{2}\ \text{kJ/mol}$$

When light is absorbed, as in the photoelectric effect, photons are destroyed, and the decrease in energy of the light beam is matched by an increase in energy of the system that absorbed the light. Einstein's analysis of the photoelectric effect is an example of this energy balance. Conversely, when light is emitted, as in a light bulb, the energy of the photons must be matched by a decrease in energy of the system that generated the light. We describe in subsequent sections of this chapter how the energy changes that accompany these transitions between energy levels provide valuable information about the structures of atoms and molecules.

SECTION EXERCISES

6.2.1 A compact disc player uses light with a frequency of $3.85 \times 10^{14}\ \text{s}^{-1}$. (a) What is this light's wavelength? (b) In what portion of the electromagnetic spectrum does this wavelength fall (visible, ultraviolet, and so on)? (c) What is the energy of 1 mol of photons at this frequency?

6.2.2 The light reaching us from distant stars is extremely dim. Consequently, astronomers must use instruments capable of detecting a small number of photons. An infrared photon detector registers a signal at 1250 nm from Alpha Centauri with a total energy of 1.20×10^{-16} J. How many photons were detected?

6.2.3 Light energy of 6.00×10^{-19} J is absorbed by a metal in a photoelectric effect experiment, and the kinetic energy of the ejected electrons is 2.00×10^{-19} J. Calculate the frequency of the light and the binding energy in joules per electron, and convert this energy into kilojoules per mole.

6.3 ABSORPTION AND EMISSION SPECTRA

When a beam of light containing a wide range of frequencies passes through an atomic gas, atoms absorb photons of particular frequencies. As a result, the emerging beam of light is less intense at those frequencies. The intensity pattern of the emerging beam of light is characteristic of the atoms in the sample. An apparatus that measures these intensity patterns is shown schematically in Figure 6-10. A light beam passes through a tube containing an atomic gas. The atoms absorb specific and characteristic frequencies of the light, so the beam emerging from the sample tube contains fewer photons at these frequencies. Next, the light passes through a prism, which deflects different frequencies through different angles and separates the

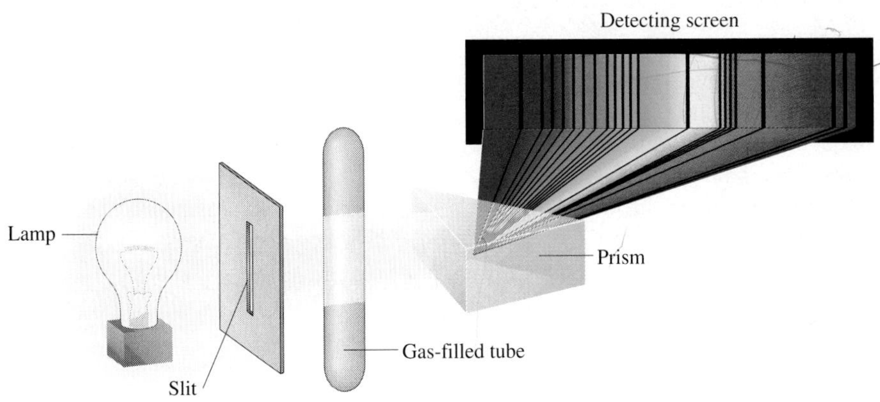

FIGURE 6-10
Schematic representation of an apparatus that measures an absorption spectrum of a gaseous element. The gas in the tube absorbs light at specific wavelengths, called *lines,* so the intensity of transmitted light is reduced at these particular wavelengths.

frequencies from one another. After leaving the prism, the beam strikes a screen, where it shows several "gaps" or dark bands. These gaps, or "missing" frequencies, are the frequencies of light absorbed by the atoms in the sample tube. The resulting pattern is called an **absorption spectrum.** It can be presented as a plot of the fraction of light absorbed as a function of frequency or wavelength, shown schematically in Figure 6-10. This plot shows sharp absorption "lines" at the frequencies absorbed by the atoms.

Spectra can be plotted as a function of photon frequency or photon wavelength. The order of the sequence of lines is reversed on a wavelength plot because of the inverse relationship between frequency (ν) and wavelength (λ; c = speed of light): $\nu = c/\lambda$.

An absorption spectrum measures the energies of the photons that an element *absorbs.* A similar experiment can be performed to measure the energies of the photons *emitted* by atoms in excited states. An apparatus that measures these emitted photons is shown schematically in Figure 6-11. An electrical discharge supplies energy to excite a collection of atoms from their ground state into excited states. These excited atoms lose all or part of their excess energy by emitting photons. This emitted light can be analyzed by passing it through a prism. The result is a plot of the intensity of light emitted as a function of frequency, called an **emission spectrum.** The emission spectrum for hydrogen atoms is shown in Figure 6-11. Notice that this spectrum shows sharp emission "lines" of *increased* intensity at frequencies that hydrogen atoms emit as they relax. This contrasts with absorption spectra, which show *decreased* intensity at the frequencies that atoms absorb.

Each element has unique absorption and emission spectra, consisting of many different lines. That is, each has its own set of characteristic wavelengths and frequencies of light that it can absorb or emit. Each frequency can be converted into an energy, which can be used to determine information about atomic structure.

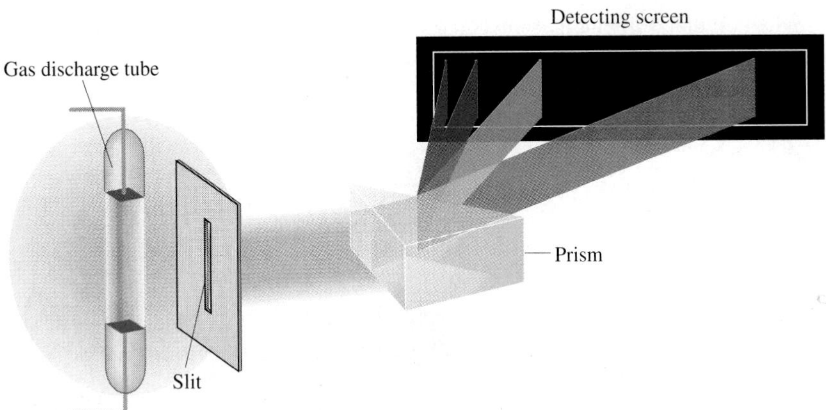

FIGURE 6-11
Schematic representation of an apparatus that measures the emission spectrum of a gaseous element. The emission lines appear as increased intensities. The spectrum shown is the emission spectrum for hydrogen atoms.

QUANTIZATION OF ENERGY

When an atom absorbs light of frequency ν, the light beam loses energy $h\nu$. As described by Equation 6-4, the atom gains that amount of energy.

What happens to the energy that the atom gains? A clue is that when the frequency of the bombarding light is high enough, it produces cations and free electrons. This indicates that the energy lost by a photon is gained by one of the atomic electrons, and when the photon energy is large enough, it imparts enough energy to remove an electron from the atom. Consequently, the energy change for the atom equals the energy change for one of its *electrons:*

$$\Delta E_{\text{atom}} = \Delta E_{\text{atomic electron}} = h\nu$$

Most atomic spectra show little regularity, but the emission spectrum of a hydrogen atom can be described by a single formula:

$$\nu_{\text{emission}} = (3.29 \times 10^{15}\ \text{s}^{-1})\left(\frac{1}{n_1^2} - \frac{1}{n_2^2}\right)$$

Both n_1 and n_2 are integers (1, 2, 3, and so on). This formula was discovered in 1885 by a Swiss mathematician and physicist, Johann Balmer, before the link between frequency and energy was known. In 1913, Niels Bohr used the discovery that $E = h\nu$ to interpret Balmer's observations.* Bohr realized that the restricted values of emission frequencies arise because the electron in a hydrogen atom is restricted to energies described by an equation containing an integer n:

The constants in Bohr's equation and Balmer's equation are related through $E = h\nu$: $(6.626 \times 10^{-34}\ \text{J s})(3.29 \times 10^{15}\ \text{s}^{-1}) = 2.18 \times 10^{-18}\ \text{J}$.

$$E_n = -\frac{2.18 \times 10^{-18}\ \text{J}}{n^2} \qquad \textbf{(6-5)}$$

Bohr's idea of restricted energy levels was revolutionary because at the time it was thought that there were no restrictions on the amount of energy that a system could have. Scientists believed that the electron in a hydrogen atom could have any energy, not just the ones described by Equation 6-5. In contrast, Bohr's interpretation of the hydrogen line spectrum showed that atomic electrons are not free to take on all energies. Instead, they are restricted to certain specific values. When a property is restricted to certain specific values, that property is said to be **quantized.** Thus the atomic energy levels of hydrogen (or any other element) are quantized. In Equation 6-5, each different integral value of n describes one of the allowed energy levels of the hydrogen atom. For example, the energy of an electron in hydrogen's fourth level is:

The negative sign arises because a free electron, removed from the hydrogen atom, is *defined* to have zero energy. Binding an electron to a hydrogen atom releases energy, so any bound electron has lower (negative) energy relative to this zero point.

$$E_4 = -\frac{2.18 \times 10^{-18}\ \text{J}}{4^2} = -1.36 \times 10^{-19}\ \text{J}$$

When an electron changes energy levels, we refer to an electronic transition between quantum levels. When a hydrogen atom absorbs or emits a photon, its electron changes from one energy level to another. Thus the change in energy of the atom is the difference between the two levels:

$$\Delta E_{\text{atom}} = E_2 - E_1 = \left(-\frac{2.18 \times 10^{-18}\ \text{J}}{n_2^2}\right) - \left(-\frac{2.18 \times 10^{-18}\ \text{J}}{n_1^2}\right)$$

* Niels Bohr (1885-1962) was a Danish physicist whose discovery of the quantization of atomic energy levels won him a Nobel Prize in 1922. Bohr headed a world-renowned institute for atomic studies in Copenhagen in the 1920s and 1930s. Bohr made major contributions to our understanding of quantization, the structure of atomic energy levels, and wave-particle duality.

$$\Delta E_{\text{atom}} = (2.18 \times 10^{-18}\ \text{J})\left(\frac{1}{n_1^2} - \frac{1}{n_2^2}\right)$$

In Sample Problem 6-6, we show how to apply Equation 6-5 to determine energy changes for a hydrogen atom.

SAMPLE PROBLEM 6-6 HYDROGEN ENERGY LEVELS

How much energy does a hydrogen atom lose when its electron changes from the fourth energy state to the second energy state? What is the wavelength of the photon emitted?

METHOD: When a hydrogen atom emits a photon, its electron moves from a high-energy state to a lower one. In this case the electron moves from the fourth energy level to the second. The gap in energy between these two states is given by the *difference* between their energy levels:

$$\Delta E_{\text{atom}} = E_{\text{final}} - E_{\text{initial}} = (E_2 - E_4)$$

We have already determined that the fourth level has an energy of -1.36×10^{-19} J. An identical calculation for the second energy level gives a value of -5.45×10^{-19} J. This lower energy level has a more negative energy. The energy gap between these two levels can now be calculated:

$$\Delta E = E_{\text{final}} - E_{\text{initial}} = (-5.45 \times 10^{-19}\ \text{J}) - (-1.36 \times 10^{-19}\ \text{J}) = -4.09 \times 10^{-19}\ \text{J}$$

This energy change is negative because the atom *loses* energy. This lost energy appears as a photon with $E_{\text{photon}} = 4.09 \times 10^{-19}$ J. To determine the wavelength of the photon, we use Equations 6-1 and 6-2:

$$E_{\text{photon}} = h\nu = hc/\lambda$$

$$\lambda_{\text{photon}} = \frac{hc}{\Delta E_{\text{atom}}} = \frac{(6.626 \times 10^{-34}\ \text{J s})(2.998 \times 10^{8}\ \text{m s}^{-1})}{4.09 \times 10^{-19}\ \text{J}}$$

$$\lambda_{\text{photon}} = (4.86 \times 10^{-7}\ \text{m})\ (10^{9}\ \text{nm/m}) = 486\ \text{nm}$$

According to Figure 6-4, a photon with a wavelength of 486 nm is blue-green in color.

Photons always have positive energies, but an energy *change* (ΔE) can be either positive or negative. When absorption occurs, an atom gains energy, ΔE for the atom is positive, and a photon disappears:

$$E_{\text{absorbed photon}} = \Delta E_{\text{atom}}$$

When emission occurs, an atom loses energy, ΔE for the atom is negative, and a photon appears:

$$E_{\text{emitted photon}} = -\Delta E_{\text{atom}}$$

ENERGY LEVEL DIAGRAMS

The quantum levels of an atomic electron are crudely analogous to the potential energies available to a ball on a staircase. As illustrated in Figure 6-12, a ball may sit on any of the steps, with potential energy given by the gravitational potential of that particular step. For example, a ball on step 2 has energy $E_2 = mgh_2$. To move a ball from the bottom of the staircase to step 2 requires this specific amount of energy. If too little energy is supplied, the ball cannot reach this step. Conversely, if a ball

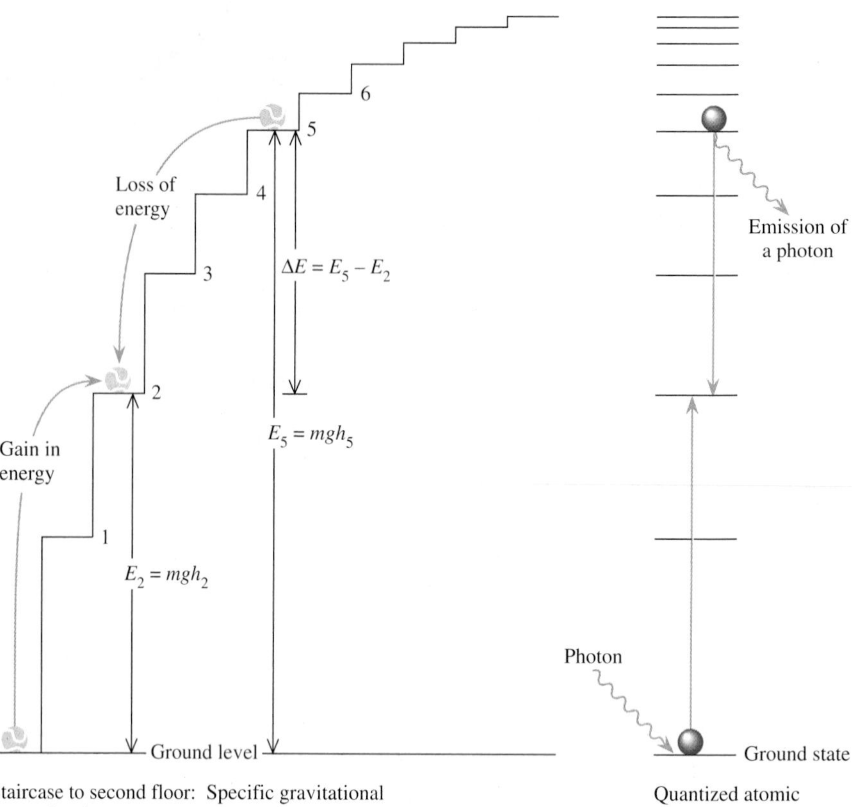

FIGURE 6-12
A ball on a staircase shows some properties of quantized energy states.

moves down the staircase, it releases specific amounts of energy. If a ball moves from step 5, with energy $E_5 = mgh_5$, to step 2, it loses energy $\Delta E = E_5 - E_2$. Although a ball may rest squarely on any step, it cannot be suspended at some position between the stairsteps. Electrons in atoms, like balls on steps, cannot exist "between steps" but must occupy one of the specific, quantized energy levels. (Remember that this is an analogy; atomic energy levels are not at all similar to staircases except in being quantized.)

According to Equation 6-5, hydrogen atoms have a regular progression of quantized energy levels. Figure 6-13 is an energy level diagram for hydrogen atoms; some of the absorption and emission transitions are represented by arrows.

Elements other than hydrogen also have quantized energy levels, but they lack the regular spacing described by Equation 6-5. To construct an energy level diagram for all other elements, the energies of observed absorption and emission lines are used to calculate the allowed energy levels. As an example, Figure 6-14 shows the energy level diagram for mercury. The absorption spectrum of mercury shows two dominant lines (upward arrows). Its emission spectrum, which can be generated by an electrical discharge, contains light of many different wavelengths (downward arrows).

The diagram for mercury in Figure 6-14 is typical of atomic energy level diagrams. No simple relationship describes the differences in energy between its many energy levels. Nevertheless, energy level diagrams summarize the energy relationships among the quantized levels of an atom that are deduced from light measurements and energy conservation. Sample Problem 6-7 shows another example of this type of reasoning.

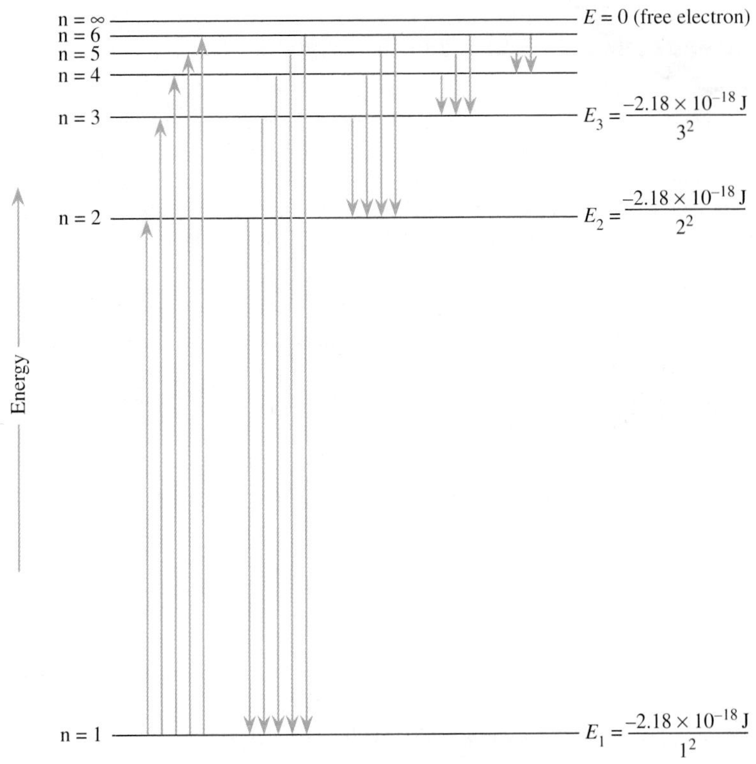

FIGURE 6-13
Allowed energy levels for the hydrogen atom, and some of the transitions that occur between them. Upward arrows represent absorption transitions, whereas downward arrows represent emissions. Some of the atomic energy level values are also shown.

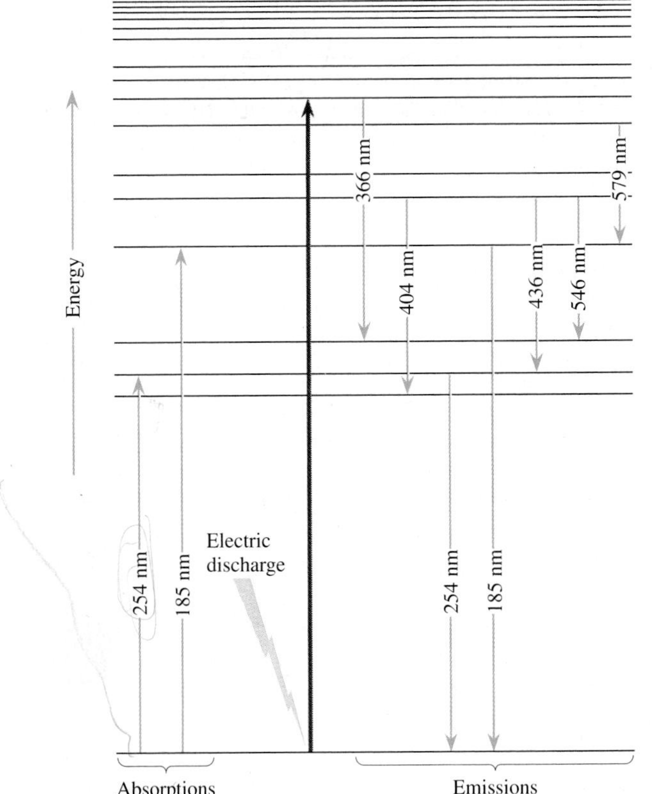

FIGURE 6-14
Energy level diagram for mercury (Hg) atoms showing the most prominent absorption and emission lines. Absorption occurs at two wavelengths in the ultraviolet spectral region. Emission can be observed after excitation by an electrical discharge. Emission may occur among many of the different energy levels as the atoms cascade back to the ground state. The numbers accompanying the arrows are the wavelengths in nanometers (nm) of the photons associated with these transitions.

SAMPLE PROBLEM 6-7 ENERGY LEVEL DIAGRAMS

Ruby lasers use crystals of Al_2O_3 that contain small amounts of Cr^{3+} ions. When visible light shines on these crystals, the Cr^{3+} ions strongly absorb light between 400 and 560 nm. Excited Cr^{3+} ions lose a portion of their energy as heat. Then they emit red light of wavelength 694.3 nm as they return to their ground state. Calculate (a) the molar energy of the 500 nm radiation used to excite the Cr^{3+} ions, (b) the molar energy of the emitted light, and (c) the fraction of the excitation energy emitted as red photons and the fraction lost as heat. (d) Draw an electronic energy level diagram, in kilojoules per mole, that summarizes these processes.

METHOD: When a photon is absorbed or emitted, the change in energy of the atom or ion is equal to the energy of the photon. We can determine photon energy using Equations 6-1 and 6-2 and then convert to molar energies using Avogadro's number. After we have determined the energies of the transitions, we can draw an energy level diagram that shows how the levels are related.

Parts *a* and *b* are solved in the same manner, using equations that were introduced earlier:

$$\Delta E = h\nu = hc/\lambda$$

$$\Delta E_{\text{absorbed}} = \frac{(6.626 \times 10^{-34}\text{ J s})(2.998 \times 10^{8}\text{ m/s})}{(500\text{ nm})(10^{-9}\text{ m/nm})} = 3.97 \times 10^{-19}\text{ J}$$

$$\Delta E_{\text{emitted}} = \frac{(6.626 \times 10^{-34}\text{ J s})(2.998 \times 10^{8}\text{ m/s})}{(694.3\text{ nm})(10^{-9}\text{ m/nm})} = 2.861 \times 10^{-19}\text{ J}$$

These are energy changes *per atom.* To calculate the changes *per mole,* we multiply by Avogadro's number, $N_A = 6.022 \times 10^{23}$ atoms/mol, and convert from joules to kilojoules:

$$\Delta E_{\text{absorbed}} = (3.97 \times 10^{-19}\text{ J})(6.022 \times 10^{23}\text{ atoms/mol})(10^{-3}\text{ kJ/J})$$

$$\Delta E_{\text{absorbed}} = 239\text{ kJ/mol}$$

$$\Delta E_{\text{emitted}} = (2.861 \times 10^{-19}\text{ J})(6.022 \times 10^{23}\text{ atoms/mol})(10^{-3}\text{ kJ/J})$$

$$\Delta E_{\text{emitted}} = 172.3\text{ kJ/mol}$$

To solve part *c*, we must calculate the fractions of the total energy that appear as emitted light and as heat. If 239 kJ/mol is absorbed and 172.3 kJ/mol emitted, the fraction of the excitation energy reemitted is 172.3/239 = 0.721. The fraction converted to heat is the difference between this value and 1.000, 0.279. In other words, 72.1% of the energy absorbed by the chromium ion is emitted as red light, and the other 27.9% is lost as heat.

Part *d* asks for an energy level diagram for this process. The electron starts in the ground state. On absorption of a photon, the electron moves to an energy level that is higher by 239 kJ/mol. The chromium ion loses 27.9% of its excited state energy as heat as the electron moves to a different level that is 172.3 kJ/mol above the ground state. Finally, emission of the red photon returns Cr^{3+} ions to the ground state configuration. The numerical values allow us to construct an accurate diagram (see right):

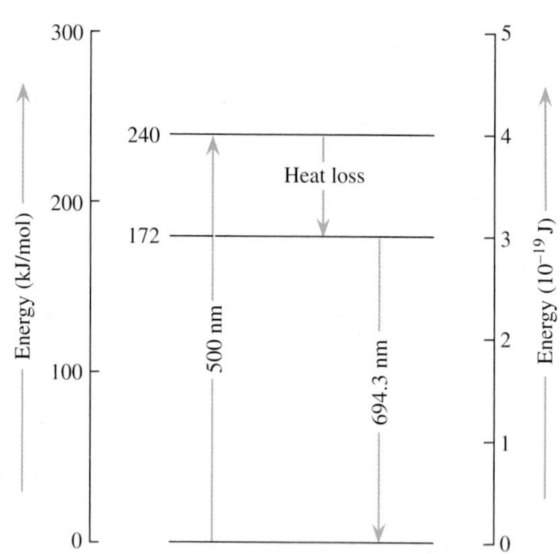

Are these results reasonable? Yes. When the Cr^{3+} ions absorb light, they are "pumped" to an energy level higher than the energy that they later emit. If calculations had shown that the emitted light had a higher energy than the absorbed light, the result would have been unreasonable because the system would violate the law of conservation of energy.

Photons emitted as an atom relaxes from an excited state may themselves excite electrons in other atoms. A mercury vapor "black light" is a common example of this phenomenon. Mercury atoms in the lamp are excited by an electrical discharge. As they return to the ground state, the atoms emit a variety of high-energy photons, most of which cannot be seen because they are in the ultraviolet (UV) region of the spectrum. These high-energy UV photons can be absorbed by nearby atoms and molecules. The electrons excited by this UV absorption often lose energy by emitting visible light. Thus mercury black lights can generate showy colors when they illuminate the right substances. Figure 6-15 shows an example of this phenomenon. Box 6-1 discusses how spectroscopic observations led to the discovery of helium.

Our eyes cannot detect ultraviolet (UV) light, but it is nevertheless absorbed by tissue. UV light has sufficient energy contant to damage cells. Mercury lights are used as germicidal lamps because their UV radiation kills germs, but UV light can also damage vision and cause skin cancers.

BOX 6-1

PUTTING SPECTROSCOPY TO USE: THE DISCOVERY OF HELIUM

By the mid-nineteenth century, scientists had studied the spectra of all the known elements and had catalogued their characteristic "signatures" of emission and absorption wavelengths. In 1868, astronomers making spectroscopic observations of the sun during a solar eclipse found emission lines that did not match those of any known element. The English astronomer Joseph Lockyer attributed these lines to a new element that he named *helium,* from *helios,* the Greek word for the sun. For 25 years the only evidence for helium was these solar spectral lines, so chemists showed little interest in this proposed new element.

Interest grew in 1894, when Scottish chemist William Ramsay discovered that dry air contains an element in addition to nitrogen and oxygen. By removing nitrogen and oxygen through chemical reactions, Ramsay isolated near-pure argon, the first rare gas to be discovered and characterized. Argon is chemically inert because it cannot easily gain or lose electrons, so Ramsay placed it in the periodic table between the halogens (which easily gain one electron) and the alkali metals (which easily lose one electron). The molar mass of argon is 39.95 g/mol, so Ramsay assigned it atomic number 18 and placed it between chlorine ($Z = 17$, $MM = 35.45$ g/mol) and potassium ($Z = 19$, $MM = 39.10$ g/mol).

From the structure of the periodic table, Ramsay concluded that other elements with similar properties must exist. This led him on a search for other inert gases. Having isolated argon from air, he focused his attention on other gas samples.

A year after discovering argon, Ramsay obtained an unreactive gas from uranium-containing mineral samples. The gas was believed to be nitrogen, but spectroscopic analysis revealed lines that belonged to neither nitrogen nor argon. Instead, the gas exhibited the same spectral lines that had been observed in the solar eclipse of 1868. After this new element was shown to exist on Earth, it was studied and characterized. Honoring the original discovery, Ramsay retained the name "helium," which is appropriate for an element that is quite rare on Earth but extremely abundant in the sun. After his discovery of argon and helium, Ramsay went on to discover neon ("new"), krypton ("hidden"), and xenon ("stranger") by cooling air until it became a liquid, then slowly boiling it and collecting the gases that boiled off first.

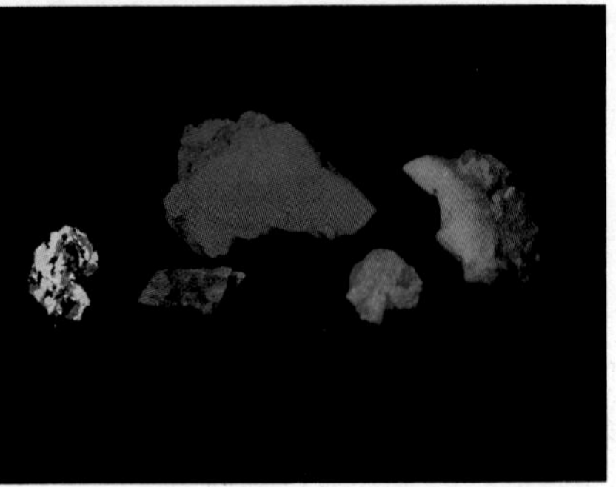

FIGURE 6-15
When certain minerals are irradiated with ultraviolet (UV) light, metal ions contained in the mineral absorb invisible UV photons. The excited metals ions return to the ground state by losing energy as a combination of heat and photons in the visible region of the spectrum.

THE ELECTROMAGNETIC SPECTRUM

As summarized in Table 6-1, the electromagnetic spectrum contains many different spectral regions. Photons from each region interact with matter in particular ways. The energies of photons in the visible and UV regions of the spectrum match the possible energy changes for many atomic and molecular electrons. For example, retinal, a molecular pigment in the eye, absorbs a photon of visible light in the first step of the process that allows us to see. This "match" between photon energies and *electron* energies occurs only in the visible and UV regions.

Photons whose energies fall in other regions of the electromagnetic spectrum also interact with matter, but they have too much or too little energy to move electrons into excited states. Photons in the x-ray and gamma-ray regions have energies high enough to generate ions by completely removing electrons from atoms and molecules. These ions are highly reactive and can cause serious damage to the material that absorbed the photons. However, under closely controlled conditions, x rays are used in medical imaging, and gamma rays are used to treat cancer.

At the low-energy end of the spectrum are the infrared, microwave, and radio frequencies. Photons from these regions have insufficient energy to pump electrons to higher energy levels, but they are energetic enough to cause *molecular* energy changes. Infrared photons, for example, can cause molecules to *vibrate* at higher energies, so infrared spectra reveal information about the way that molecules vibrate. Microwave photons, which are lower in energy than infrared photons, can cause molecules to *rotate* at higher energies, so microwave spectra reveal information about the way that molecules rotate. Finally, radio frequency photons cause even smaller, subtler changes in molecular energies. Consequently, chemists use every region of the electromagnetic spectrum in their studies of the way that molecules are put together and behave.

TABLE 6-1 REGIONS OF THE ELECTROMAGNETIC SPECTRUM

FREQUENCY (ν, in s^{-1})	WAVELENGTH (λ, in m)	ENERGY	NAME	USES
10^{20} to 10^{21}	10^{-12}	Nuclear	Gamma rays	Cancer treatment
10^{17} to 10^{19}	10^{-10}	Electronic	x rays	Medical "pictures," materials testing
10^{15} to 10^{16}	10^{-7}	Electronic	Ultraviolet	"Black lights," germicidal lamps
10^{13} to 10^{14}	10^{-6}	Electronic	Visible	Illumination
10^{12} to 10^{13}	10^{-4}	Vibrational	Infrared	Heating
10^{9} to 10^{11}	10^{-2}	Rotational	Microwave	Cooking
10^{5} to 10^{8}	10^{2}	—	Radio frequency	Signal transmission

SECTION EXERCISES

6.3.1 When minerals absorb "black light" from a mercury lamp, they emit visible light of a longer wavelength, converting the remaining energy into heat. How much energy per mole is converted to heat by a mineral that absorbs ultraviolet light at 366 nm and emits green light at 540 nm?

6.3.2 Gaseous helium atoms absorb x rays of wavelength 53.7 nm. After absorbing an x ray of this wavelength, a helium atom may emit light of wavelength 501.6 nm. What is the net energy change for a helium atom that has gone through this absorption-emission sequence? Draw an energy level diagram that shows the sequence.

6.3.3 Calculate all the wavelengths emitted by hydrogen atoms in their fifth energy level.

6.4 SUNLIGHT AND THE EARTH

The Earth processes solar energy through the interactions of light and matter, as introduced in Section 6.3. Light from the sun bathes the Earth in a continual flux of light. This light interacts with atoms and molecules in the atmosphere according to the principles developed in the previous section. When solar photons are absorbed, their energy is transferred to whatever absorbs them. As one result, the Earth is warmed up. Warm objects give off energy as radiation, so the Earth continually radiates energy. Thus the Earth simultaneously absorbs light energy from the sun and emits light energy into space.

As the temperature of a body rises, the energy of its emitted light undergoes two changes: The emission spectrum *shifts* to shorter wavelengths, and the *amount* of emission increases. The sun, which is at a very high temperature, emits tremendous amounts of light in the visible and UV regions of the spectrum. The Earth, which is at a much lower temperature, emits modest amounts of low-energy infrared light. As the Earth's surface absorbs solar energy, it warms slightly and emits larger amounts of infrared light.

In Chapter 19 we describe the processes that fuel the sun by converting gravitational energy into radiation.

The surface of the Earth exposed to sunlight absorbs more energy than it emits, so during the daytime, it tends to warm up. The surface that is in darkness continues to emit energy and tends to cool down. On average, however, the temperature on Earth has a value that puts the planet in a state of energy balance. That is, the total amount of energy emitted by the Earth is equal to the total amount of energy that it absorbs. This energy balance is affected by conditions in the Earth's atmosphere, which absorbs a significant portion of the light from the sun. Atmospheric interactions with light affect the properties of the atmosphere and the conditions at the Earth's surface.

ATMOSPHERIC TEMPERATURE VARIATIONS

Figure 6-16 shows the temperature profile of the atmosphere as a function of altitude. The figure shows that the atmosphere can be divided into regions of decreasing and increasing temperature that blend into one another without distinct boundaries. Molecules in the thermosphere and in the upper stratosphere absorb sunlight. Consequently, the air at these altitudes is higher in temperature than air in the lower stratosphere and the upper mesosphere, where very little sunlight is absorbed. Sunlight is also absorbed at the Earth's surface, warming the lower reaches of the troposphere.

In the **thermosphere,** the outermost part of the atmosphere, molecules of nitrogen and oxygen absorb high-frequency (low-wavelength) solar light. These photons have enough energy to ionize molecules and to break chemical bonds:

$$N_2 + h\nu \rightarrow N_2^+ + e^- \qquad O_2 + h\nu \rightarrow O + O$$

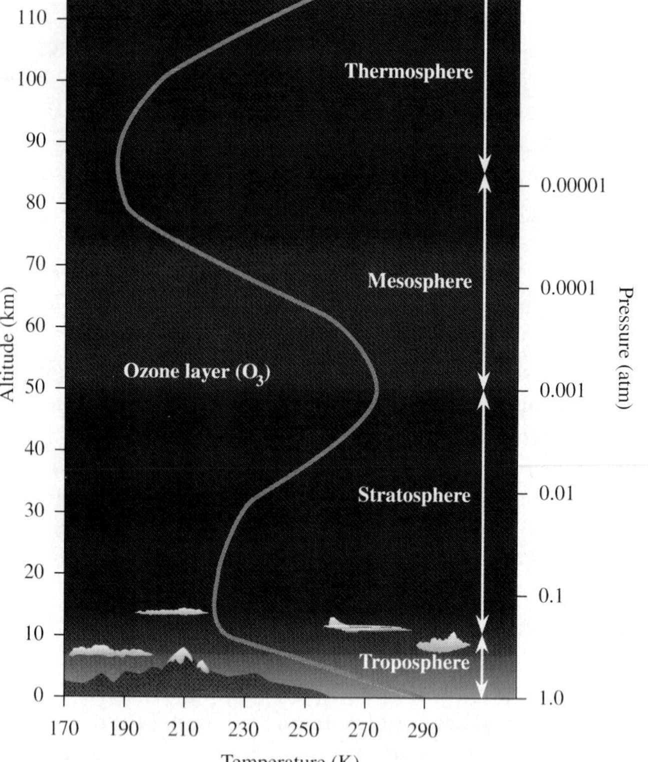

FIGURE 6-16

Variation in temperature (*graph*) and pressure (*right*) with altitude. Note that the scale for pressure is logarithmic.

The products of these reactions are unstable, however, so they eventually recombine, releasing energy and heating this region of the atmosphere:

$$N_2^+ + e^- \rightarrow N_2 + \text{Heat} \qquad O + O \rightarrow O_2 + \text{Heat}$$

Although the atomic and ionic species in the thermosphere are unstable, they are produced continuously by sunlight. Consequently, the thermosphere is a complex mixture of atomic and molecular species, including a high mole fraction of ions and oxygen atoms. At the same time, however, the pressure is less than 10^{-7} atm, which means that the density of atoms and molecules in the thermosphere is quite low.

As solar light passes through the thermosphere, its highest-energy photons are removed progressively through absorption by atoms and molecules. Thus the intensity of high-energy light decreases as sunlight moves down through the atmosphere toward the Earth's surface. Lower-intensity light means fewer photons, so less energy is deposited in the atmosphere. Consequently, the temperature of the thermosphere decreases as altitude decreases. At the bottom of the thermosphere, which is about 85 km above the Earth's surface, all the ionizing radiation has been absorbed, and its heating effect reaches a minimum. This marks the boundary between the thermosphere and the mesosphere. Sunlight not absorbed in the thermosphere passes through the **mesosphere,** which is about 35 km thick; little absorption occurs here.

THE OZONE LAYER

The top of the **stratosphere,** about 50 km above the Earth's surface, is the second region where atmospheric temperature is high. The stratosphere contains a thin layer of ozone (O_3) molecules, which are formed in a two-step process:

$$O_2 + h\nu_{(\lambda \sim 200\ nm)} \rightarrow O + O$$

$$O_2 + O \rightarrow O_3 + \text{Heat}$$

In the first step, an O_2 molecule absorbs a photon in the wavelength region between 180 and 240 nm and fragments into two atoms of oxygen. Ozone is generated in the second step when an oxygen molecule captures one of these oxygen atoms. For the stratosphere, the most apparent consequence of the ozone layer is increased temperature. The sunlight that is absorbed by ozone is eventually converted to heat through the reaction between oxygen molecules and oxygen atoms. This heat is sufficient to increase the temperature of the atmosphere at altitudes of 20 to 50 km.

The production of ozone requires a source of oxygen atoms and frequent collisions between the atoms and the molecules that make up the atmosphere. Above 35 km, many oxygen atoms exist, but not enough collisions occur to form ozone in significant amounts. This is because pressure, molecular density, and the rate of molecular collisions decrease as altitude increases. Below 20 km, on the other hand, all the light that splits oxygen molecules into oxygen atoms has already been absorbed. Consequently, below this altitude insufficient oxygen atoms are present to generate ozone. Therefore the ozone layer lies between 20 and 35 km above the Earth's surface.

The **ozone layer** is responsible for heating the stratosphere, but it also has important consequences for life on Earth. Figure 6-17 shows that although molecular oxygen absorbs light of very short wavelengths, it is transparent to photons with wavelengths longer than about 240 nm. Ozone, on the other hand, strongly absorbs UV light in the 200 to 340 nm region. The energies of these photons are high enough to break ozone apart into O_2 molecules and oxygen atoms:

$$O_3 + h\nu_{(\lambda = 200\text{-}340\ nm)} \rightarrow O + O_2$$

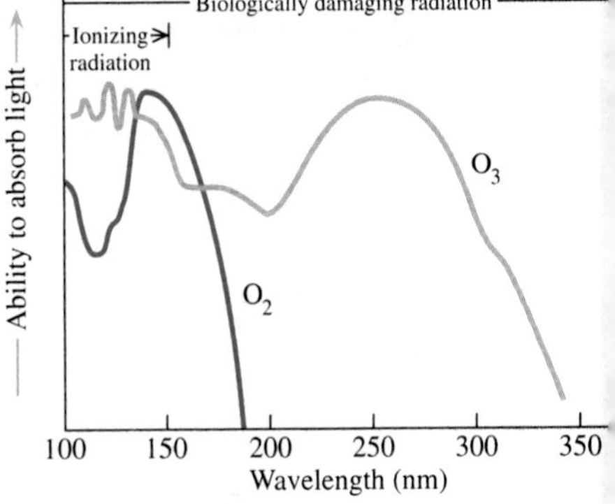

FIGURE 6-17
A graph of light absorption as a function of wavelength for O_2 (*blue line*) and O_3 (*yellow line*). Note that ozone strongly absorbs light between 200 and 340 nm, where diatomic oxygen does not.

The absorption of UV light by ozone molecules is essential for life on Earth. If this radiation reached the Earth's surface, it would cause severe biological damage because light of wavelengths around 300 nm has enough energy to break biological molecules apart. If we were continually bathed in such light, death rates would increase dramatically for almost all species.

The interactions of molecules and light in the ozone layer result in a delicate balance that holds ozone concentration at a relatively constant value. This balance is maintained by the three reactions already mentioned: (1) photons with wavelengths in the 180 to 240 nm range break apart O_2 molecules, (2) photons with wavelengths in the 200 to 340 nm range break apart O_3 molecules, and (3) oxygen atoms combine with O_2 molecules to produce O_3 molecules. In Chapter 14 we examine the ozone layer in more detail and discuss ways that its delicate balance has been endangered by human activities.

Figure 6-18 shows that by the time sunlight reaches the Earth's surface, most of the high-energy light less than 350 nm has been filtered out. What is left is sunlight in the visible, infrared, and near-ultraviolet regions. The Earth's surface reflects some of this sunlight, but most is absorbed by the planet and its inhabitants. This absorption process is critical for life because it heats the surface to comfortable temperatures, evaporates water from the oceans that later falls as rain or snow, and drives photosynthesis, the chemical engine of life.

Warm bodies emit radiation, and the Earth is no exception. The radiation emitted by the Earth has its maximum intensity at the far-infrared wavelengths, at much

The de Broglie equation predicts that every particle has wave characteristics. The wave natures of subatomic particles such as electrons and neutrons play important roles in their behavior, but in our everyday experience we never see any wavelike behavior for the matter around us. The reason is the scale of the waves. For all except subatomic particles, the wavelengths involved are so short that we are unable to detect the wave properties. This is illustrated in Sample Problem 6-9.

SAMPLE PROBLEM 6-9 MATTER WAVES

What wavelengths are associated with (a) an electron traveling at 1.00×10^5 m/s and (b) a Ping-Pong ball of mass 11 g traveling at 2.5 m/s?

METHOD: This problem deals with particle-waves that have mass. Equation 6-6 relates an object's wavelength (λ) to its velocity (u), mass (m), and Planck's constant (h):

$$\lambda_{\text{electron}} = \frac{h}{mu} = \frac{6.626 \times 10^{-34}\ \text{kg m}^2\ \text{s}^{-1}}{(9.109 \times 10^{-31}\ \text{kg})(1.00 \times 10^5\ \text{m s}^{-1})} = 7.27 \times 10^{-9}\ \text{m}$$

$$\lambda_{\text{ball}} = \frac{h}{mu} = \frac{6.626 \times 10^{-34}\ \text{kg m}^2\ \text{s}^{-1}}{(11 \times 10^{-3}\ \text{kg})(2.5\ \text{m s}^{-1})} = 2.4 \times 10^{-32}\ \text{m}$$

The wavelength of the ball is shorter than the radius of a single nucleus, but the wavelength of the electron is the same size as atomic radii. Thus Ping-Pong ball wavelengths are inconsequential, but electron wavelengths have a significant effect on electron-atom interactions.

HEISENBERG'S UNCERTAINTY PRINCIPLE

Whereas a particle occupies a particular spot, a wave has no exact position. Instead, it extends over some region of space. Because of their wave properties, electrons are always spread out rather than located in one particular place.

The position of an electron cannot be defined. Each electron is spread out over some region of space, just as a wave spreads over some region of the ocean. Electrons are **delocalized** because their waves are spread out rather than pinpointed.

Most of us think of objects as being located in some precise position, such as a book on a shelf or a car parked in a garage. Even for tiny objects such as electrons, we are used to thinking in terms of precise locations because that is how the universe was described before it was recognized that all things are particle-waves. Isaac Newton introduced the idea of a "clockwork" universe, in which everything can be measured exactly. According to Newton's ideas, after we measure the positions and rates of motion of any set of bodies in a clockwork universe, we can describe perfectly, forever after, where those bodies will go and how they will behave. The movement of planets through the solar system is an example.

Viewing electrons and other particle-waves as delocalized, however, changes the way we view the universe. Instead of things being exactly specified in space, they are distributed over some volume. Werner Heisenberg, a German physicist, showed in the 1920s that this distribution could be described mathematically. According to Heisenberg, particle-waves have the curious property that their velocity and position cannot be simultaneously "pinned down." Thus if a particular particle-wave can be pinpointed in a specific location, its velocity must be unknown. Conversely, if the velocity of a particle-wave is known precisely, its location must be unknown. Heisenberg summarized this uncertainty in what has become known as the **uncertainty principle:** The more accurately we know position, the more uncertain we are about velocity, and vice versa.

Heisenberg's uncertainty principle forced everybody to change their thinking about how to describe the universe. In a universe subject to uncertainty, many things cannot be measured exactly, and it is never possible to predict with certainty exactly what will occur next.

The philosophical and scientific profoundness of Heisenberg's principle was immediately obvious to scientists. Many of them spent tremendous effort on theoretical and experimental efforts to disprove it, but the idea has withstood every test. In fact, many esoteric phenomena of the subatomic world can be interpreted only using the uncertainty principle. Thus uncertainty has become accepted as a fundamental feature of the universe at the scale of electrons, protons, and neutrons.

PROPERTIES OF BOUND ELECTRONS

The properties of electrons described so far (mass, charge, spin, and wave nature) apply to all electrons. Electrons traveling freely in space, electrons moving in a copper wire, and electrons bound to atoms all have these characteristics. Electrons bound to atoms have two additional characteristics: They are described by delocalized waves, and their energies are quantized. These two fundamental properties determine the chemical behavior of atoms and molecules.

Bound electrons are described by delocalized waves. Recall that although most of the mass of an atom is concentrated in its nucleus, most of its volume comes from its electrons. Thus the volume of an atom is "filled" with wave-particle electrons. To picture how an electron occupies the volume around the nucleus, we must try to visualize a "three-dimensional wave." Scientists have coined a name for these three-dimensional waves that characterize electrons; they are called **orbitals.** The word comes from *orbit,* which describes the path that a planet follows when it moves about the sun. An orbit, however, is two-dimensional (circle, ellipse, and so on), whereas an *orbital* is a three-dimensional volume (sphere, hourglass, and so on). The shape of a particular orbital shows how an atomic or molecular electron fills three-dimensional space.

The wave characteristics of electrons mean that they are "smeared out" rather than located at an exact position in space. Orbitals are a consequence of this delocalization. Each atomic electron, rather than being a point charge, is a three-dimensional particle-wave that is distributed throughout space in an orbital. We will find that as an electron undergoes a transition from one energy level to another, the size and shape of its distribution in space changes, as well.

Each atomic energy level can be associated with a specific three-dimensional atomic orbital.

An atom that contains many electrons can be described by superimposing orbitals for each of its electrons, and the overall size and shape of an atom is determined by this superposition of all the orbitals that describe its electrons.

Energies of bound electrons are quantized. Quantization of the energy of an atomic electron is described in Section 6.3 (see Figures 6-13 to 6-14). Recall that each element has a set of unique quantized electronic energy levels. When an atom undergoes a transition from one energy level to another, the energies of electrons change, but the amounts of change are restricted.

Quantization of energy is a property of *bound* electrons. A bound electron is one held in a specific region in space by coulombic attraction for a nucleus in an atom or a molecule. The absorption and emission spectra of atoms consist of discrete energies because electrons undergo transitions from one bound state to another. In contrast, when an atom or molecule absorbs enough energy to remove an electron completely, the free electron can take on any amount of kinetic energy. Above this ionization threshold, the system absorbs photons of all energies. *Bound* electrons have quantized energy states; *free* electrons have continuous energy states.

In summary, the important properties of electrons are as follows:

1. Every electron has charge $e = 1.6 \times 10^{-19}$ C and mass $m_e = 9.1 \times 10^{-31}$ kg.
2. Every electron behaves like a tiny magnet pointing in one of two directions.
3. Every electron behaves somewhat like a particle and somewhat like a wave.
5. Atomic electrons are described by three-dimensional waves called *orbitals*.
6. Atomic electrons have specific, quantized energy values.

We explore the details of the properties of atomic electrons in Chapter 7.

SECTION EXERCISES

6.5.1 Calculate the wavelength associated with a photon of energy 1.00×10^{-19} J and the wavelength associated with an electron having a kinetic energy of 1.00×10^{-19} J.

6.5.2 The smallest distance that can be resolved by a microscope is typically $d = 1.25\lambda$, where λ is the wavelength of light or electrons used. The microscope can be greatly improved if a beam of electrons is used instead of a beam of light. If an electron microscope is to successfully resolve objects 0.600 nm apart, what velocity must the electrons have?

6.5.3 Describe the differences between the properties of a free electron and those of a Ping-Pong ball.

6.6 THE SCHRÖDINGER EQUATION

The first three decades of the twentieth century were a time of great turmoil and excitement in the world of physical science. The particle properties of light and the quantization of energy levels revealed serious flaws in the classical newtonian views of matter. It became apparent that wave phenomena played a role in the behavior of atoms and molecules, so a new description of matter was needed that would account for quantization and incorporate wave characteristics.

De Broglie's postulate that electrons have wave properties provided the key to finding this new description of matter. In 1926 and 1927 the Austrian physicist Erwin Schrödinger modified classical mechanics by introducing a wave function. This was the basis for the **quantum theory** that underlies our current understanding of atomic and molecular structure. The mathematics of quantum theory is complicated, and we do not yet know how to solve the equations exactly except for very simple systems such as the hydrogen atom. Nevertheless, by making various approximations in the equations, it is possible to describe the quantum features of atoms and molecules. These features agree with the observations of experimental chemistry and physics. Because the theory describes experimental observations accurately, quantum mechanics is firmly established as a reasonable description of matter at the atomic and molecular level. The details of how the equations of quantum theory are set up and solved are too complicated for our purposes. However, a brief description of the method used helps to show how some properties of matter that were incomprehensible within the framework of classical mechanics are a natural consequence of the new theory.

"ACTUALLY I STARTED OUT IN QUANTUM MECHANICS, BUT SOMEWHERE ALONG THE WAY I TOOK A WRONG TURN."

The theory begins by expressing the classical coulombic forces between charged particles in terms of how the system's total energy *(E)* is divided between kinetic energy and potential energy. This gives an expression for the total energy called the *hamiltonian* ($\mathcal{H}$). The next step is to convert the hamiltonian into a new form that incorporates wave aspects. The resulting equation contains a new function, the wave function (Ψ). The final equation, which is the basis for all quantum mechanical calculations, looks deceptively simple: $(\mathcal{H} - E)\Psi = 0$. In reality, however, this equation is quite complicated because the hamiltonian contains terms for the kinetic and potential energies of all the particle-waves in the atom or molecule.

Ψ is the Greek capital letter psi.

PROPERTIES OF THE SCHRÖDINGER EQUATION

The **Schrödinger equation** is mathematically sophisticated, but it has four important features that you can appreciate without understanding its mathematical properties.

First, the hamiltonian is different for every different atom, ion, or molecule. A hydrogen atom has one particular $\mathcal{H}$, a helium atom a different one, an oxygen molecule yet another, and so on. Using the method outlined in the previous section, physicists and chemists can always determine the correct Schrödinger equation for any physical system. Because each different system has a different equation, each system also has a different description.

Second, the wave function (Ψ) has wave properties and is generally a function of all the spatial variables: $\Psi = \Psi(x,y,z)$. Each wave function satisfies the equation $(\mathcal{H} - E)\Psi = 0$. Every atom, ion, or molecule has a different $\mathcal{H}$, so Ψ also differs for every system. The physical meaning of the wave function is that its square, Ψ^2, describes where we are likely to find electrons. A graph of Ψ^2 vs. location in space tells us the distribution of the electrons in space. For example, if the system is the electron of a hydrogen atom, the squared wave function describes how likely we are to find the electron at different distances from the hydrogen nucleus.

Third, the Schrödinger equation has solutions only for specific values of *E*. This is a quantum condition: The system possesses discrete, fixed (quantized) energies. Other physical properties such as spin also have specific quantized values.

Finally, the Schrödinger equation for any atom or molecule has an infinite number of solutions. According to quantum theory, every atom, ion, or molecule has an infinite number of discrete energies, E_n, and for each of them there is a corresponding wave function, Ψ_n. The system may jump from one of these states to another, absorbing or emitting light and/or heat in the process. For the hydrogen atom, these transitions between different energy states are described by Equation 6-5, which can be derived from the Schrödinger equation for hydrogen atoms.

To summarize, when the wave-particle duality of subatomic matter is incorporated into the mathematics that describes the energy of an atom, ion, or molecule, many mysterious features of the subatomic world appear as natural mathematical consequences of the Schrödinger equation. We can use this new, powerful tool to describe atoms, ions, and molecules.

SECTION EXERCISE

6.6.1 The hamiltonian contains one energy term for each coulombic interaction among charged particles. Identify these interactions for a helium atom, which contains two electrons and one nucleus.

CHAPTER SUMMARY

1. The mass of an atom is concentrated in its nucleus, but its volume is made up almost entirely of electrons, which are responsible for atomic interactions.
2. Light is composed of photons, with $E = h\nu = hc/\lambda$. When light interacts with atoms, photons may be absorbed, and electrons gain the energy lost by the photons. Atoms can also emit photons, losing energy in the process.
3. The energy levels of atoms are quantized; this quantization is displayed conveniently using energy level diagrams. The quantized energies of the hydrogen atom show a regular pattern.
4. In the Earth's atmosphere, sunlight of various wavelengths is absorbed by different species at various altitudes, leading to variations in temperature and chemical composition.
5. All electrons have the same mass, charge, and spin and behave like wave-particles, with wavelength $\lambda = h/mu$. Bound electrons have quantized energies and are described by delocalized orbitals. Wave-particles are subject to the uncertainty principle.
6. The fundamental equation describing electrons is the Schrödinger equation, which mathematically describes electron waves.

KEY TERMS

electromagnetic radiation
frequency (ν)
intensity
light
photon
Planck's constant (h)
wavelength (λ)

absorption spectrum
emission spectrum
energy level diagram
excited state
ground state
quantized

mesosphere
ozone layer
stratosphere
thermosphere

delocalized
orbital
spin

de Broglie equation
quantum theory
Schrödinger equation
uncertainty principle

SKILLS TO MASTER

- Calculating photon energies, wavelengths and frequencies
- Sketching and interpreting energy level diagrams
- Calculating energies of hydrogen atoms
- Analyzing the photoelectric effect
- Understanding how sunlight interacts with the Earth
- Using the de Broglie equation
- Visualizing wave-particles

LEARNING EXERCISES

6.1 Write a chapter summary of two pages or less that outlines the important features of this chapter.

6.2 List the properties of electrons and of photons, including the equations used to describe each.

6.3 Write a short description of (a) photoelectric effect; (b) wave-particle duality; (c) electron spin; (d) uncertainty principle; and (e) Schrödinger equation.

6.4 Describe an atomic energy level diagram and the information it incorporates.

6.5 Update your list of memory bank equations. For each new equation, specify the conditions under which it can be used.

6.6 Make a list of all terms new to you that were introduced in this chapter. Write a one-sentence definition of each in your own words. Consult the glossary if you need help.

PROBLEMS

CHARACTERISTICS OF ATOMS

6.1 The density of aluminum metal is 2.70 g/cm^3, the density of mercury metal is 13.55 g/cm^3, and the density of lead is 11.34 g/cm^3. Of these three elements, which has the largest atoms? Which has the smallest?

6.2 Calculate the thicknesses of film containing 6.5×10^6 layers of atoms of each of the metals in Problem 6.1.

6.3 List all the evidence you can think of that indicates that atoms have mass and volume.

6.4 The radius of a typical atom is 10^{-10} m, and the radius of a typical nucleus is 10^{-15} m. Compute typical atomic and nuclear volumes.

6.5 Draw an atomic picture of a layer of aluminum metal.

CHARACTERISTICS OF LIGHT

6.6 Calculate the energy in joules of one photon of (a) blue-green light with a wavelength of 490 nm; (b) red light, $\lambda = 665$ nm; (c) x rays, $\lambda = 25.5$ nm; and (d) infrared radiation, $\lambda = 1250$ nm.

6.7 Calculate the energies in kilojoules of 1 mol of the photons in Problem 6.6.

6.8 Calculate λ for a photon with $E = 2.00 \times 10^{-15}$ J.

6.9 What is λ photons with a molar energy of 745 kJ?

6.10 A phototube delivers an electrical current when a beam of light strikes a metal surface inside the tube. Phototubes do not respond to ultraviolet photons because this light of the spectrum is absorbed by the tube's windows. Phototubes also do not respond to infrared photons, even though infrared light passes through the glass and strikes the metal. Explain why phototubes do not respond to infrared light.

6.11 When light of frequency 1.30×10^{15} s^{-1} shines on the surface of cesium metal, electrons are ejected with a maximum kinetic energy of 5.2×10^{-19} J. Calculate (a) the wavelength of this light; (b) the binding energy of electrons to cesium metal; and (c) the longest wavelength of light that will eject electrons.

6.12 The binding energy of electrons to chromium metal is 7.21×10^{-19} J. What is the longest wavelength of light that will eject electrons from chromium metal?

6.13 Draw energy level diagrams that illustrate the difference in binding energy between cesium metal and chromium metal. Refer to Problems 6.11 and 6.12.

ABSORPTION AND EMISSION SPECTRA

6.14 The bright-red color of highway safety flares comes from strontium ions in salts such as $Sr(NO_3)_2$ and $SrCO_3$. Burning a flare produces strontium ions in excited states, which then emit red photons at 606 nm and several wavelengths between 636 and 688 nm. Calculate the frequency and energy (kilojoules per mole) of the 606-nm emission.

6.15 From Figure 6-14, calculate the energy difference in kilojoules per mole between the excited state of mercury that emits 404-nm light and the ground state.

6.16 From Figure 6-14, determine the wavelength of light needed to excite an electron from the ground state to the lowest excited state of the mercury atom.

6.17 Determine the wavelengths that hydrogen atoms absorb to reach the $n = 8$ and $n = 9$ states. In what region of the electromagnetic spectrum do these photons lie?

6.18 It takes 486 kJ/mol to remove electrons completely from sodium atoms. Sodium atoms absorb and emit light of wavelengths 589.6 and 590.0 nm.

(a) Calculate the energies of these two wavelengths in kilojoules per mole.

(b) Draw an energy level diagram for sodium atoms that shows the levels involved in these transitions.

(c) If a sodium atom has already absorbed a 590.0 nm photon, what is the wavelength of the second photon a sodium atom must absorb to remove an electron?

SUNLIGHT AND THE EARTH

6.19 When molecules of nitrogen and oxygen in the thermosphere absorb short-wavelength light, the N_2 molecules ionize and the O_2 molecules break into atoms. Draw molecular pictures that illustrate these processes.

6.20 It requires 496 kJ/mol to break O_2 molecules into atoms and 945 kJ/mol to break N_2 molecules into atoms. Calculate the maximum wavelengths of light that can break these molecules apart. What part of the electromagnetic spectrum contains these photons?

6.21 List atmospheric gases that absorb light in each of the following spectral ranges (for one region, no atmospheric gas absorbs light effectively): (a) less than 200 nm; (b) 200 to 240 nm; (c) 240 to 310 nm; (d) 310 to 700 nm; and (e) 700 to 2000 nm.

6.22 List the region of the atmosphere where most light is absorbed for each spectral range listed in Problem 6.21.

6.23 A high-altitude balloon equipped with a transmitter and temperature sensor reports an air temperature of −30 °C. Is this sufficient information to determine the balloon's approximate altitude (see Figure 6-16)? If so, what is the altitude? If not, list all the possibilities.

6.24 If the balloon in Problem 6.23 is above the troposphere and cannot rise above the altitude where $P = 1$ torr, is there enough data to determine its approximate altitude? If so, what is it? If not, what other data are needed?

PROPERTIES OF ELECTRONS

6.25 What is the mass of 1 mol of electrons?

6.26 What is the charge of 1 mol of electrons?

6.27 What is the wavelength of an electron, $u = 4.8 \times 10^5$ m/s?

6.28 Although a helium atom has two electrons, each with spin and a magnetic moment, it has no net magnetic moment, because the two magnets point in opposite directions and cancel. Which of the following must have magnetism, and which might have no net magnetism because of cancellation? (a) Be; (b) K; (c) I; and (d) Kr.

THE SCHRÖDINGER EQUATION

6.29 Three terms are used in the Schrödinger equation. Explain what each term represents.

6.30 The Schrödinger equation can be solved exactly for an electron trapped inside a box. For a cubical box, the quantized energies are given by the equation: $E_n = n^2h^2/8ma^2$, where a is the length of the box, m is the mass of the electron, n is any nonzero integer, and h is Planck's constant. For an electron in the lowest energy state inside a cube of length 0.80 nm (about the size of molecular dimensions), calculate (a) its energy; (b) its wavelength; and (c) the wavelength of light needed to change it to the next higher energy state.

ADDITIONAL PROBLEMS

6.31 Using Figure 6-13, explain why more lines appear in emission spectra than in absorption spectra.

6.32 Calculate the following for a photon ($\lambda = 500$ nm) emitted by the sun: (a) its frequency; (b) its energy; and (c) the time it takes to reach the Earth, which is 93 million miles from the sun.

6.33 The argon-ion laser has two major emission lines, at 488 and at 514 nm. These emissions leave the Ar^+ ion in an energy level that is 2.76×10^{-18} J above the ground state.
(a) Draw an energy level diagram (in joules per atom) that illustrates these facts.
(b) What frequency and wavelength radiation is emitted when the Ar^+ ion returns to its lowest energy level?

6.34 The human eye can detect as little as 2.35×10^{-18} J of green light of wavelength 510 nm. Calculate the minimum number of photons that can be detected by the human eye.

6.35 Gaseous Ca^+ cations absorb light at 422.7, 272.2, and 239.9 nm. After the 272.2-nm absorption, an emission at 671.8 nm is observed. Absorption of light at 239.9 nm is followed by emission at 504.2 nm. Construct an energy level diagram for Ca^+ ions and answer the following questions:
(a) After the 504.2-nm emission, what wavelength would have to be emitted to return to the lowest energy state?
(b) What wavelength of light corresponds to the energy difference between the state reached using 422.7-nm light and that reached using 272.2-nm light?
(c) Do any sequences described by the data lead to a common energy level? If so, which ones?

6.36 It requires 364 kJ/mol to break the chemical bond in HBr molecules. What is the maximum wavelength (nm) of light that has enough energy to break this bond?

6.37 A hydrogen atom undergoes an electronic transition from the $n = 4$ to the $n = 2$ state. In the process the H atom emits a photon, which then strikes a cesium metal surface and ejects an electron. It takes 3.2×10^{-19} J to remove an electron from Cs metal. Calculate (a) the energy of the $n = 4$ state of the H atom; (b) the wavelength of the emitted photon; (c) the energy of the ejected electron; and (d) the wavelength of the ejected electron.

6.38 One of the hydrogen emission lines has a wavelength of 486 nm. Identify the values for n_{final} and $n_{initial}$ for the transition giving rise to this line.

6.39 A nitrogen laser emits a pulse containing 10 mJ of energy at a wavelength of 337.1 nm. How many photons is this?

6.40 The sun's atmosphere contains vast quantities of He^+ cations. These ions absorb some of the sun's thermal energy, promoting electrons from the He^+ ground state to various excited states. A He^+ ion in the fifth energy level may return to the ground state by emitting three successive photons. It emits an infrared photon, ($\lambda = 1014$ nm), a green photon, ($\lambda = 469$ nm) and an x ray, ($\lambda = 26$ nm). Calculate the excitation energies of each level occupied by the He^+ ion as it returns to the ground state.

6.41 Neutrons, like electrons and photons, are particle-waves whose diffraction patterns can be used to determine the structures of molecules. Calculate (a) the velocity of a neutron λ with a wavelength of 75 pm and (b) λ of a neutron moving at 1.25% of the velocity of light.

6.42 Small helium-neon lasers emit 1 mJ/s of light at 634 nm. How many photons does such a laser emit in 1 minute?

6.43 The temperature drops more on clear nights than on cloudy nights. What feature of clouds accounts for this?

6.44 Give three examples of things that are "quantized" in the macroscopic world.

6.45 It takes 216.4 kJ/mol to remove an electron from a potassium metal surface. What is the longest wavelength that can do this?

6.46 If UV light at 250 nm strikes a potassium metal surface, what is the maximum velocity of the ejected electrons? Refer to Problem 6.45 for the threshold energy.

6.47 Describe what happens to temperature and pressure in moving upward through Earth's atmosphere.

6.48 Gaseous lithium atoms absorb light of wavelength 323 nm. After absorbing this light, lithium atoms return to the ground state by emitting two photons with $\lambda = 812.7$ and 670.8 nm.

Draw an energy level diagram that shows this process. What fraction of the energy of the absorbed photon is lost in collisions?

6.49 In a typical photoelectric effect experiment, light of energy 6.00×10^{-19} J is absorbed by a metal, and the ejected electrons have a maximum kinetic energy of 2.70×10^{-19} J.
(a) What is the binding energy of electrons in the metal?
(b) What is the wavelength of the light?
(c) What is the wavelength of the electrons?

6.50 The minimum frequency needed to eject electrons from a metal is $7.5 \times 10^{14}\ s^{-1}$. Suppose that a 366-nm photon strikes the metal. Calculate (a) the binding energy of the electrons in the metal, (b) the maximum kinetic energy of the ejected electron, and (c) the wavelength and velocity of that electron.

6.51 Calculate the wavelengths associated with an electron and a proton traveling at 5% the velocity of light.

6.52 It takes 242.7 kJ/mol to fragment Cl_2 molecules into Cl atoms. What is the longest wavelength of sunlight that could accomplish this? Will Cl_2 molecules in the troposphere be fragmented into atoms?

6.53 The emission lines that result from excited hydrogen atoms undergoing transitions to the $n = 3$ level are called the "Paschen series." Draw an energy level diagram that shows this series of transitions.

6.54 The photoelectric effect for magnesium metal has a threshold frequency of $8.95 \times 10^{14}\ s^{-1}$. Can this metal be used in photoelectric devices that sense visible light?

6.55 One frequency of a CB radio is 27.3 MHz. Calculate the wavelength and energy of photons at this frequency.

6.56 Energetic free electrons can transfer their energy to bound electrons in atoms. In 1913, electrons were passed through mercury vapor at low pressure to determine the minimum kinetic energy required to produce the excited state that emits UV light at 253.7 nm. What is that minimum kinetic energy? What electron velocity was required?

6.57 Barium salts are added to fireworks to impart a yellow-green color. Barium ions emit light with $\lambda = 487, 514, 543, 553$, and 578 nm. Convert these wavelengths into frequencies and into energies in kJ/mol.

ANSWERS TO SECTION EXERCISES

6.1.1 (a) $1.70 \times 10^{-28}\ m^3$; (b) $1.70 \times 10^{-33}\ m^3$; and (c) 2.91×10^3

6.1.2

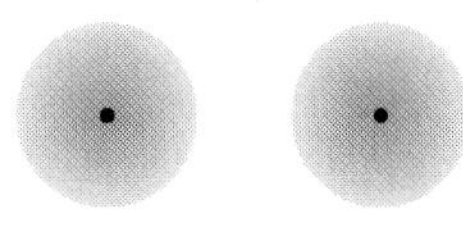

Attraction

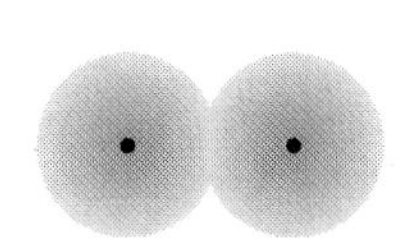

Repulsion

6.2.1 (a) 779 nm; (b) visible; and (c) 154 kJ

6.2.2 754 photons

6.2.3 $\nu = 9.04 \times 10^{14}\ s^{-1}$; BE $= 4.00 \times 10^{-19}$ J $= 241$ kJ/mol

6.3.1 106 kJ/mol

6.3.2 3.31×10^{-18} J

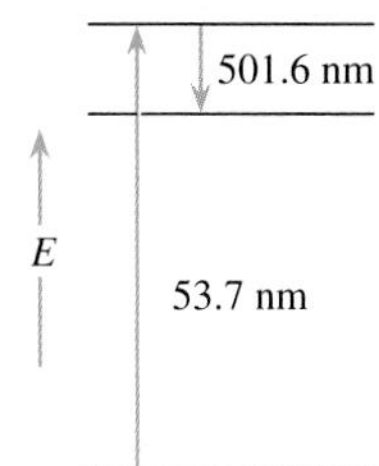

6.3.3 4054 nm, 1304 nm, 434 nm, and 95 nm

6.4.1

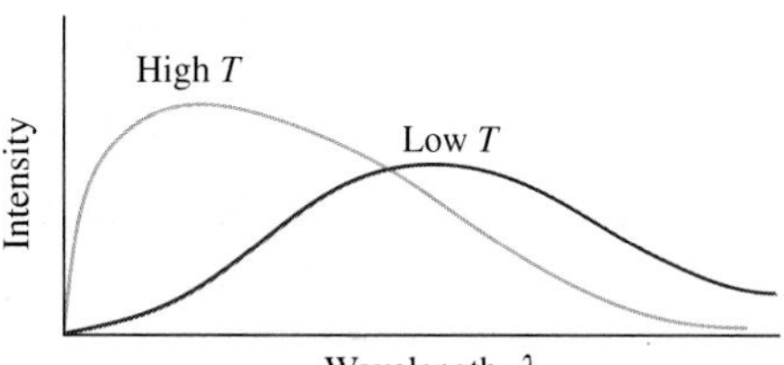

6.4.2 Decreases the temperature

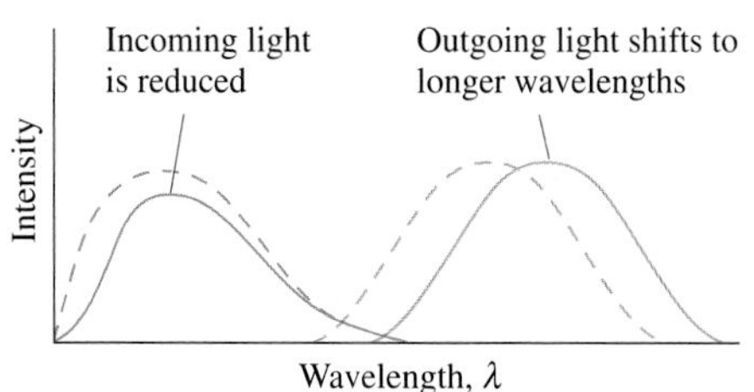

6.5.1 Photon: 1990 nm; electron: 1.56 nm

6.5.2 $1.52 \times 10^6\ m\ s^{-1}$

6.5.3 Their masses are very different. A free electron carries electrical charge, is a small magnet, and sometimes displays wave behavior; a Ping-Pong ball is electrically neutral and nonmagnetic and displays particle behavior.

6.6.1 Electron-electron repulsion and two electron-nucleus attractions

CHAPTER 7

ATOMIC STRUCTURE AND PERIODICITY

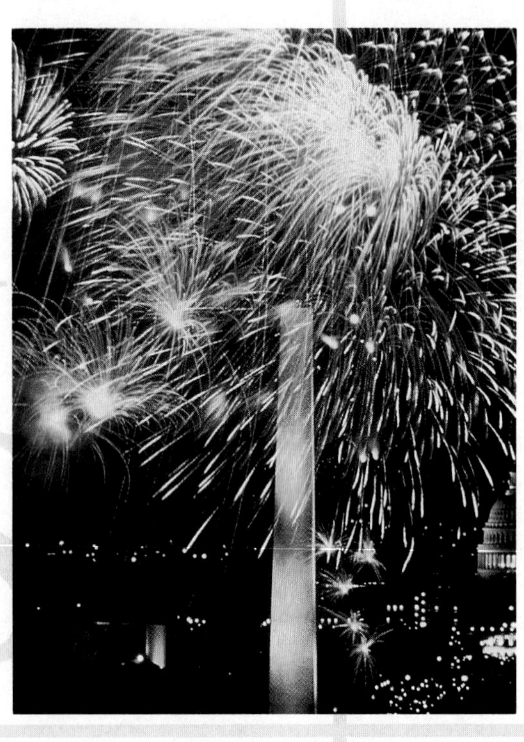

The chemical properties of the over 100 known elements vary systematically with the number of electrons in their neutral atoms. Even though each element is chemically unique, the periodic table is organized into groups of elements with similar chemical properties. The variations from group to group can be striking. For example, fluorine (9 electrons), chlorine (17 electrons), and bromine (35 electrons) form stable diatomic molecules that react with a variety of other elements, including hydrogen, oxygen, and carbon. In contrast, the elements with the next higher atomic numbers, neon (10 electrons), argon (18 electrons), and krypton (36 electrons), are chemically nonreactive monatomic gases. A further increase of one electron leads to sodium (11 electrons), potassium (19 electrons), and rubidium (37 electrons), all of which are difficult to obtain in pure form because they react so readily with oxygen. These metallic elements are most stable as positively charged cations in salts such as sodium chloride or potassium nitrate.

Why does an atom with 18 electrons resist chemical reactions, but one with 17 electrons readily forms a diatomic molecule with another of its kind? Why does an atom with 37 electrons form compounds as a positively charged ion, whereas an atom with 36 electrons resists chemical reactions? To answer these questions, we must describe the properties of atomic electrons in more detail. Descriptions of atomic electrons are based on quantum theory and the Schrödinger equation, which we introduced at the end of Chapter 6.

In this chapter we develop the qualitative features of quantum theory. Our goals are to describe the properties of atomic electrons, to show how to construct a composite picture of a multielectron atom, and to relate such pictures to patterns of chemical behavior.

7.1 QUANTUM NUMBERS

Recall from Chapter 6 that every electron has the same charge, the same mass, and the same spin. Electrons in atoms display four other characteristic properties, each of which has more than one possible value. These properties are energy, orbital shape, orbital orientation, and spin orientation. As discussed in Chapter 6, the properties of an atom are quantized, which means that each of these properties is restricted to certain specific values.

One way to describe an atom is to list the properties of all its electrons. Unfortunately, this kind of list is very tedious to construct. Another way to describe an atom is to solve the Schrödinger equation and determine the wave function (Ψ) for each of its electrons. Unfortunately, these wave equations are too abstract to be useful to most chemists. Instead, chemists use sets of integers and half-integers called **quantum numbers** to specify the values of the electron's quantized properties. Each electron in an atom has a set of four quantum numbers, one for each of its four variable properties, energy, orbital shape, orbital orientation and spin orientation. Thus to describe an atomic electron completely, we need only to specify a value for each of its four quantum numbers.

ENERGY QUANTUM NUMBER

Equation 6-5 is:

$$E_n = \frac{-2.18 \times 10^{-18}\text{J}}{n^2}$$

It was originally determined from experiments, but it can also be derived from the Schrödinger equation.

The most important property of an atomic electron is its energy. Absorption and emission spectra reveal that this energy is quantized. The quantum number for energy is called the **principal quantum number *(n)*.** The energy levels for the hydrogen atom, which were described in Chapter 6, are reproduced in Figure 7-1. According to Equation 6-5, the energy of the electron in a hydrogen atom can be calculated if we provide the value of the integer, ***n*,** which is the principal quantum number.

There is no equation that provides the exact energies of an atom with more than one electron. Nonetheless, each electron in an atom can be assigned a principal quantum number, ***n*,** that correlates with its energy. The most stable energy for an atomic electron corresponds to $n = 1$, and each successively higher value of n describes a less stable energy state.

Remember that free electrons have zero energy, so an electron bound to an atom always has negative energy. *Most stable* therefore corresponds to *most negative*.

The principal quantum number must be a positive integer.

$$n = 1, 2, 3, \ldots 8, 9, \text{etc.}$$

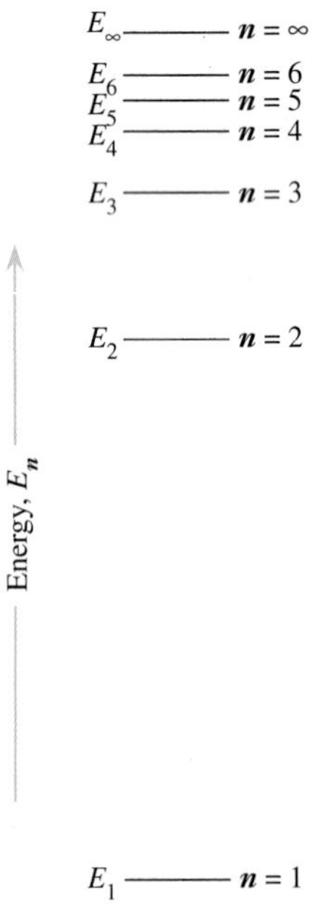

Values such as $n = 0$, $n = -3$, and $n = 5/2$ are unacceptable because they do not represent a solution to the Schrödinger equation.

The principal quantum number also tells us something about an atomic *orbital* because the energy of an electron is correlated with its distribution in space. In keeping with Coulomb's law, the negatively charged electron is attracted to the positively charged nucleus. However, its energy of motion spreads the electron over some volume in space around the nucleus. The more energy the electron has, the more it is spread out in space. As illustrated by Figure 7-2, this situation is roughly analogous to a bouncing tennis ball: The more kinetic energy we give the ball, the higher it bounces and the greater its average distance above the court. Similarly, the higher the principal quantum number, the more energy the electron has and the greater is its average distance from the nucleus.

Summarizing, the principal quantum number ***(n)*** can have any positive integral value. It indexes the energy of the electron and is correlated with orbital size. As n increases, the energy of the electron increases, its orbital gets bigger, and it becomes less stable.

E_∞ — $n = \infty$
E_6 — $n = 6$
E_5 — $n = 5$
E_4 — $n = 4$
E_3 — $n = 3$
E_2 — $n = 2$
E_1 — $n = 1$
Energy, E_n

FIGURE 7-1
The energy level diagram for a hydrogen atom. Specific energy values are indexed by the principal quantum number (n), which is a positive integer. See Section 6.3 for a detailed discussion of the quantization of energy levels.

AZIMUTHAL QUANTUM NUMBER

In addition to size, an atomic orbital also has a specific shape. The orbitals shown in Figure 7-2 are spherical, but the solutions for the Schrödinger equation and experimental evidence show that not all orbitals are spheres. A second quantum number indexes the shapes of atomic orbitals. This quantum number is called the **azimuthal quantum number *(l)*.**

Shapes of objects, such as the beach ball, football, and tire iron illustrated in Figure 7-3, can be categorized according to their preferred axes. A beach ball has no preferred axis because its mass is distributed equally in all directions about its center. A football has one preferred axis, with more mass along this axis than in any other direction. A tire iron has two preferred axes, at right angles to each other. In analogous fashion, electron density in any orbital is concentrated along preferred axes.

The value of l identifies the number of preferred axes in a particular orbital and thereby identifies the orbital's shape. According to quantum theory, orbital shapes are highly restricted. These restrictions are linked to energy, so the possible values of l are limited by the value of the principal quantum number, n. The smaller n is, the more compact the orbital and the more restricted its possible shapes.

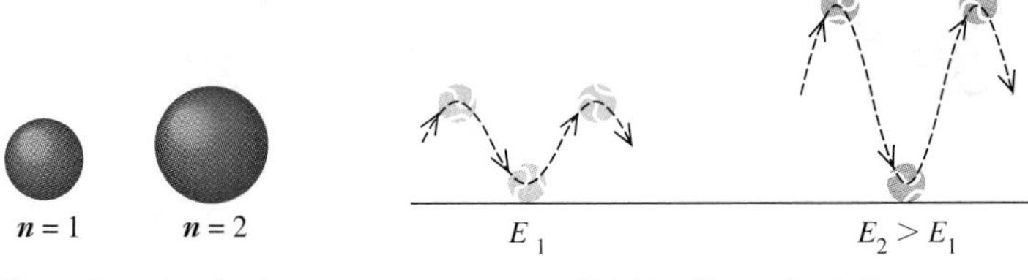

FIGURE 7-2
The orbital size of an atomic electron is correlated with its orbital energy (*left*), just as the bounce height of a tennis ball is correlated with its kinetic energy (*right*).

The azimuthal quantum number (l) can be any positive integer smaller than n.

When the Schrödinger equation for a one-electron atom is solved mathematically, the restrictions on *n* and *l* emerge as quantization conditions that correlate with energy and the shape of the wave function.

$$l = 0, 1, 2, \ldots (\boldsymbol{n} - 1)$$

Historically, orbital shapes have been identified with letters rather than numbers. These letter designations correspond to the values of $\boldsymbol{l}$ as follows:

Value of $\boldsymbol{l}$	0	1	2	3	4
Orbital letter	*s*	*p*	*d*	*f*	*g*

An orbital is named by listing the numerical value for $\boldsymbol{n}$, followed by the letter that corresponds to the numerical value for $\boldsymbol{l}$. Thus an electron with quantum numbers $\boldsymbol{n} = 3, \boldsymbol{l} = 0$ is described as a 3*s* orbital. A 5*f* orbital has $\boldsymbol{n} = 5, \boldsymbol{l} = 3$. Notice that the restrictions on $\boldsymbol{l}$ mean that many orbital names do not correspond to actual orbitals. For example, when $\boldsymbol{n} = 1$, $\boldsymbol{l}$ can only be zero. Thus 1*s* orbitals exist, but there are no 1*p*, 1*d*, or 1*f* orbitals. Similarly, there are 2*s* and 2*p* orbitals but no 2*d*, 2*f*, or 2*g* orbitals. Remember that $\boldsymbol{n}$ restricts $\boldsymbol{l}$ but $\boldsymbol{l}$ does not restrict $\boldsymbol{n}$. Thus a 10*d* orbital ($\boldsymbol{n} = 10, \boldsymbol{l} = 2$) is rather unstable but perfectly legitimate, whereas there is no orbital with $\boldsymbol{n} = 2, \boldsymbol{l} = 10$.

FIGURE 7-3
Some everyday objects have their masses concentrated along preferred axes. Beach balls have no such axes, but footballs have one, and tire irons have two.

MAGNETIC QUANTUM NUMBER

A sphere has no preferred axis, so it has no directionality in space. When there is a preferred axis, as for a football, Figure 7-4 shows that the axis can point in many different directions relative to an x, y, and z coordinate system. Thus objects with preferred axes, such as footballs, have directionality as well as shape.

Among atomic orbitals, *s* orbitals are spherical and have no directionality. All other orbitals are nonspherical, so in addition to having shape, they point in some direction. Like energy and orbital shape, orbital direction is quantized. That is, *p, d,* and *f* orbitals have restricted orientations, unlike footballs, which are free to point in any direction. These restrictions are indexed by a third quantum number called the **magnetic quantum number** (m_l).

The magnetic quantum number derives its name from the fact that different orbital orientations generate different behaviors in the presence of magnetic fields.

Just as the orbital size **(*n*)** limits the maximum value for the *number* of preferred axes **(*l*)**, the number of preferred axes **(*l*)** restricts the *orientations* of the preferred

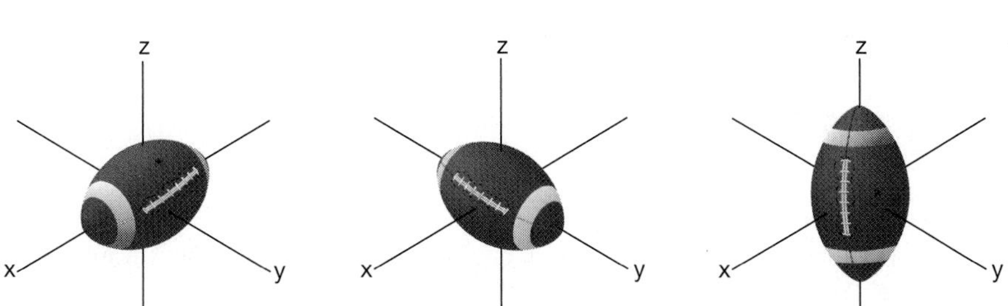

FIGURE 7-4
A football has directionality and shape. The figure shows three of the many ways in which a football can be oriented relative to a set of x, y, and z axes.

axes (m_l). When $l = 0$, there is no preferred axis and there is no orientation, so $m_l = 0$. One preferred axis ($l = 1$) can orient in any of three directions, giving three possible values for m_l: +1, 0, and −1. Each time l increases in value by one unit, two additional values of m_l become possible.

> ***The magnetic quantum number (m_l) can have any positive or negative integral value between 0 and l.***

$$m_l = 0, \pm 1, \pm 2, \ldots, \pm l$$

SPIN QUANTUM NUMBER

In Section 6-5 we pointed out that an electron has magnetism associated with a property called "spin." Magnetism is directional, so the spin of an electron is directional, too. Recall that electron spin must be oriented in one of two ways, labeled "up" or "down." Thus spin orientation is quantized. The quantum number describing this is called the **spin orientation quantum number** ***(m_s)***. The two possible values of m_s are $+\frac{1}{2}$ (up) and $-\frac{1}{2}$ (down).

A complete description of an atomic electron requires a set of four quantum numbers, n, l, m_l, and m_s, which must meet all the restrictions summarized in Table 7-1. Any set of quantum numbers that does not obey these restrictions does not correspond to an orbital and cannot describe an electron.

An atomic orbital is designated by its n and l values, such as 1*s*, 4*p*, 3*d*, and so on. For each type of orbital the two orientation quantum numbers, m_l and m_s, can have several different values. Thus there is more than one set of quantum numbers for each orbital designation. The 3*s* orbital, for example, has two valid sets of quantum numbers:

$$n = 3, \quad l = 0, \quad m_l = 0, \quad m_s = +\tfrac{1}{2} \qquad\qquad n = 3, \quad l = 0, \quad m_l = 0, \quad m_s = -\tfrac{1}{2}$$

As n increases, so does the number of valid sets of quantum numbers. Sample Problem 7-1 gives an example. Box 7-1 discusses quantum restrictions.

TABLE 7-1 RESTRICTIONS ON QUANTUM NUMBERS FOR ATOMS

QUANTUM NO.	RESTRICTIONS	RANGE
n	Positive integers	$1, 2, \ldots, \infty$
l	Positive integers less than n	$0, 1, \ldots, (n-1)$
m_l	Integers between l and $-l$	$-l, -(l-1) \ldots 0 \ldots +l$
m_s	Half-integers, $+\frac{1}{2}$ or $-\frac{1}{2}$	$-\frac{1}{2}, +\frac{1}{2}$

SAMPLE PROBLEM 7-1 VALID QUANTUM NUMBERS

How many valid sets of quantum numbers are there for 4*d* orbitals? Give two examples.

METHOD: We are looking for the sets of quantum numbers that have $n = 4$ and $l = 2$. Each set must meet all the restrictions listed in Table 7-1. The easiest way to see how many valid sets there are is to list all the valid quantum numbers.

Because this is a $4d$ orbital, n and l are specified and cannot vary. The other two quantum numbers, however, have several acceptable values. For each value of m_l, either value of m_s is acceptable, so the total number of possibilities is the product of the number of possible values for each quantum number.

Quantum number	n	l	m_l	m_s
Possible values	4	2	2, 1, 0, −1, −2	$+\frac{1}{2}, -\frac{1}{2}$
No. of possible values	1	1	5	2

Possible values for a $4d$ electron: (1)(1)(5)(2) = 10

There are ten sets of quantum numbers that describe a $4d$ orbital. Here are two of them, chosen randomly:

$$n=4,\ l=2,\ m_l = 1,\quad m_s = +\tfrac{1}{2}$$

$$n=4,\ l=2,\ m_l = -2,\ m_s = -\tfrac{1}{2}$$

You should be able to list the other eight sets.

BOX 7-1

JUSTIFICATION OF QUANTUM RESTRICTIONS

The restrictions on quantum numbers are rules, but where do they come from? What does it mean to require that n be an integer, l have an upper limit of $n - 1$, m_l vary between $+l$ and $-l$, and m_s only be $+\frac{1}{2}$ or $-\frac{1}{2}$? These rules may appear arbitrary, but they are as valid a part of our physical world as $E = \frac{1}{2}mu^2$ because they come from a rigorous mathematical derivation and describe our universe accurately.

The mathematical derivation of quantum numbers starts with the Schrödinger equation for a hydrogen atom. Solving it leads to wave functions for the various orbitals. Each such solution to the Schrödinger equation carries with it a set of quantum restrictions, which match the conditions given in Table 7-1 for the values of n, l, and m_l.

Restrictions on quantum numbers are a bit like restrictions on a quadratic equation. For a given set of constants a, b, and c, only certain values of x allow the quadratic equation to have a value of zero. Some values of x satisfy the equation, but others do not.

$$ax^2 + bx + c = 0$$

Quadratic equation

$$x = \frac{-b \pm \sqrt{b^2 - 4ac}}{2a}$$

Restrictions on x

Quantum restrictions are a direct consequence of a mathematical framework that describes the hydrogen atom. But is that mathematical framework correct? All the experimental evidence, such as discrete atomic energy levels and quantized magnetism of atoms, indicates that it is. These two features, which were presented in Chapter 6, show the validity of energy quantization (n) and spin quantization (m_s). Moreover, energy and spin are quantized with experimental values that match those predicted by the mathematics. The other quantization restrictions have also been verified by many observations on atomic systems. No known experimental data are inconsistent with the restrictions given in Table 7-1.

The form of the periodic table of the elements provides additional strong chemical evidence in support of quantum restrictions. Later in this chapter, we show how details of periodicity can be explained based on orbital restrictions. The world of chemistry is constructed the way it is as a consequence of these mysterious but fundamental quantum restrictions.

SECTION EXERCISES

7.1.1 List all the valid sets of quantum numbers for $n = 3$. Give each its proper orbital name (for example, the orbital with $n = 1, l = 0$ is 1*s*).

7.1.2 Which of the following sets of quantum numbers describe actual orbitals, and which are nonexistent? For each one that is nonexistent, list the restriction that makes it forbidden.

	n	l	m_l	m_s
(a)	4	1	1	0
(b)	4	4	1	$\frac{1}{2}$
(c)	4	0	1	$\frac{1}{2}$
(d)	4	2	2	$-\frac{1}{2}$

7.1.3 Determine the number of different allowable sets of quantum numbers that have $n = 4$.

7.2 SHAPES OF ATOMIC ORBITALS

The chemical properties of atoms are determined by the behavior of their electrons. Because atomic electrons are described by orbitals, these electron interactions can be described in terms of **orbital interactions.** The two characteristics of orbitals that determine how electrons interact are orbital shapes and energies. Orbital *shapes,* the subject of this section, describe the distribution of electrons in three-dimensional space. Orbital *energies,* which are discussed in Section 7.3, tell us how easily electrons can be moved about.

The size and shape of an orbital are determined by the quantum numbers n and l. As n increases, the size of the orbital increases, and as l increases, the shape of the orbital becomes more elaborate.

ORBITAL DEPICTIONS

Recall from Chapter 6 that an electron is a particle-wave delocalized in three-dimensional space in a way described by a wave function (Ψ). An orbital depiction gives a spatial view of the wave function and provides a "map" of how the electron wave is distributed in space.

There are several ways to draw representations of these three-dimensional maps. Each drawing shows some important orbital features, but none shows all of them. We use four different representations: plots of the wave function (Ψ) vs. distance from the nucleus (r), plots of the square of the wave function (Ψ^2) vs. r, pictures of electron density, and pictures of electron contour surfaces.

A plot of Ψ vs. r is the most mathematically direct way of depicting a wave function. A plot of the 2*s* orbital is shown in Figure 7-5, *A*. This type of plot has the advantage of emphasizing the wavelike properties of the electron. Note in Figure 7-5, *A*, for example, that the wave function has a positive value at some distances and a negative value at other distances, much like the amplitude of a sine wave. However, although a plot of Ψ vs. r shows a wave function, it does not map the most important feature of orbital shape, how the electron is spread out in space.

The distribution of the electron in space depends on Ψ^2, the *square* of the wave function. Thus a plot of Ψ^2 vs. r provides more information about electron distributions. The plot of Ψ^2 vs. r for the 2*s* orbital, shown in Figure 7-5, *B*, describes how electron density varies with distance from the nucleus.

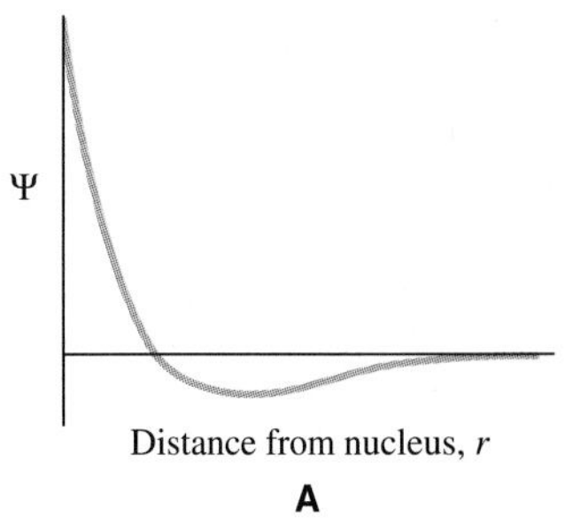

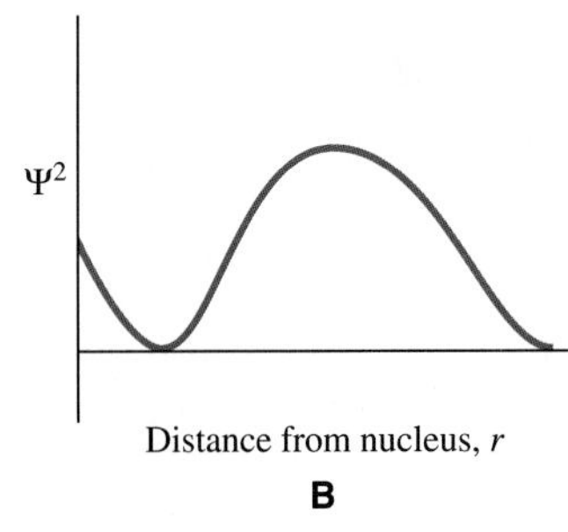

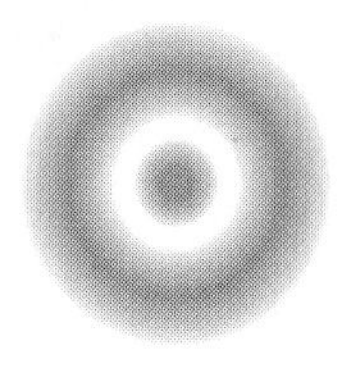

FIGURE 7-5
Different depictions of the $2s$ orbital. **A,** A plot of Ψ vs. r. **B,** A plot of Ψ^2 vs. r. **C,** An orbital density picture. **D,** An electron contour picture.

Orbital pictures have an advantage over plots in that they can indicate the three-dimensional nature of orbitals. One type of orbital picture is a two-dimensional dot pattern in which the density of dots represents electron density. Such an **orbital density picture** of the $2s$ orbital is shown in Figure 7-5, *C*. Note that this two dimensional pattern of dots shows a cross-sectional slice through the middle of the orbital.

Orbital density pictures are probably the most comprehensive views we can draw, but they require much time and care. A simplified orbital picture is provided by an **electron contour drawing.** In this representation, we draw a contour surface that encloses almost all the electron density. Commonly, "almost all" means 90%. Thus the electron density is high inside the contour surface but very low outside the surface. Figure 7-5, *D,* shows the contour surface depiction of the $2s$ orbital.

A useful analogy for understanding the value of contour surfaces is a swarm of bees around a hive. At any one time some bees will be off foraging for nectar, so a contour surface drawn around *all* the bees might cover several acres. This would not be a very useful map of bee density. A contour surface containing 90% of the bees, on the other hand, would be just a bit bigger than the hive itself. This would be a very useful map of bee density because anyone inside that contour surface would surely interact with bees.

The drawback of contour surfaces is that all details of electron density *inside* the surface are lost. Thus if we want to convey maximum information about orbitals, we must use combinations of the various types of depictions.

ORBITAL SIZE

How large are orbitals? Experiments designed to measure the radius of an atom give us information about the size of an orbital. Theory, moreover, provides wave functions that can be examined to see how an orbital changes with distance from the nucleus, r. When these sources of information are combined, they reveal several regular features about orbital size.

In any particular atom, orbitals get larger as the value of $\boldsymbol{n}$ *increases.* In fact, orbital radii grow approximately with $\boldsymbol{n}^2$. For any particular atom the $\boldsymbol{n} = 2$ orbitals are about four times larger than the $1s$ orbital, the $\boldsymbol{n} = 3$ orbitals are about nine times larger, and so on. The electron density plots in Figure 7-6 show this trend for the first three s orbitals of the hydrogen atom.

In any atom, all orbitals with the same principal quantum number are similar in size. For example, Figure 7-7 shows that the $\boldsymbol{n} = 3$ orbitals of the hydrogen atom have their maximum electron densities at about the same distance from the nucleus. The same regularity holds for all other atoms. Quantum numbers other than $\boldsymbol{n}$ affect orbital size only slightly. We describe these small effects in the context of orbital energy in Section 7.3.

The nuclear charge, Z, is the total positive charge of the nucleus and is equal to the number of protons contained in the nucleus. Thus the number of protons in the nucleus is given by the atomic number of the element. See Section 2.4.

Each orbital becomes smaller as nuclear charge increases. Nuclear-electron interactions are dominated by Coulomb's law. Thus as the positive charge of the

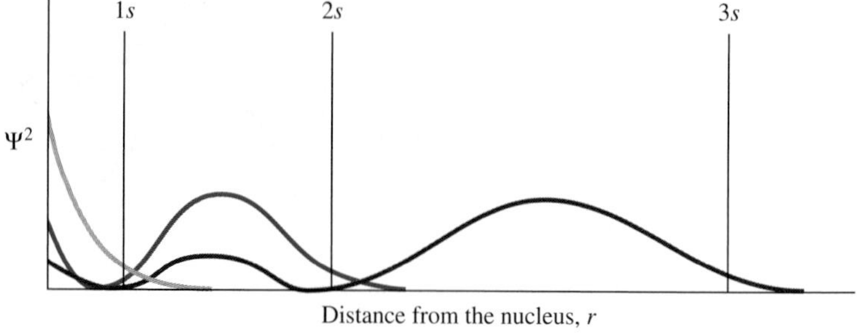

FIGURE 7-6
Electron density plots for the 1*s*, 2*s*, and 3*s* atomic orbitals of the hydrogen atom. The vertical lines indicate the value of *r* where the 90% contour surface would be located. Notice that this value is about four times as large for 2*s* as for 1*s* and about nine times as large for 3*s* as for 1*s*.

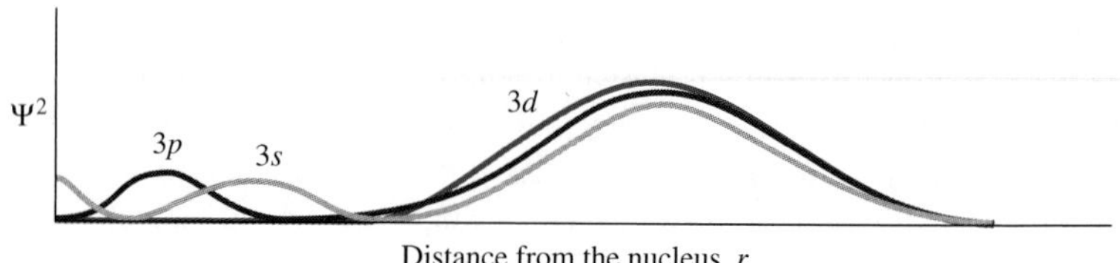

FIGURE 7-7
Electron density plots for the 3*s*, 3*p*, and 3*d* orbitals for the hydrogen atom. For all three orbitals, maximum electron density occurs at about the same distance from the nucleus. In other words, all three orbitals are about the same size.

nucleus increases, it binds the negatively charged electrons more tightly. This, in turn, contracts the radius of the orbital. As a result, each orbital shrinks in size as atomic number increases. For example, the 2*s* orbital steadily decreases in size across the second row of the periodic table from Li ($Z = 3$) to Ne ($Z = 10$).

DETAILS OF ORBITAL SHAPES

The shapes of orbitals strongly influence chemical interactions. Hence we need to have detailed pictures of orbital shapes to understand the chemistry of the elements. What follows is a catalog of how various orbitals appear.

The quantum number $l = 0$ corresponds to an *s* orbital. According to the restrictions on quantum numbers, there is only one *s* orbital for each value of the principal quantum number. We have already pointed out that all *s* orbitals are spherical, with radii that increase as n increases.

The quantum number $l = 1$ corresponds to a *p* orbital. Because a *p* electron can have any of three values for m_l, there are three similarly shaped *p* orbitals for each value of n. All *p* orbitals are nonspherical, with one preferred axis. Figure 7-8 shows contour diagrams of the three 2*p* orbitals. Notice that each has its electron density concentrated along its preferred axis on both sides of the nucleus. Each *p* orbital is oriented along one cartesian axis, perpendicular to the other two, with the nucleus at the center of the system. To recognize these orientations, we can subscript the orbitals accordingly: p_x, p_y, and p_z.

As n increases, the shapes of the *p* orbitals become more complicated, but their outermost features do not change. Each *p* orbital is perpendicular to the other two in its set, and each *p* orbital has a lobe along its preferred axis, where electron density is high. To an approaching atom, therefore, an electron in a 3*p* orbital presents the same orbital characteristics as one in a 2*p* orbital, except that the 3*p* orbital is bigger. Consequently, the shapes and relative orientations of the 2*p* orbitals in Figure 7-8 represent the prominent spatial features of all *p* orbitals.

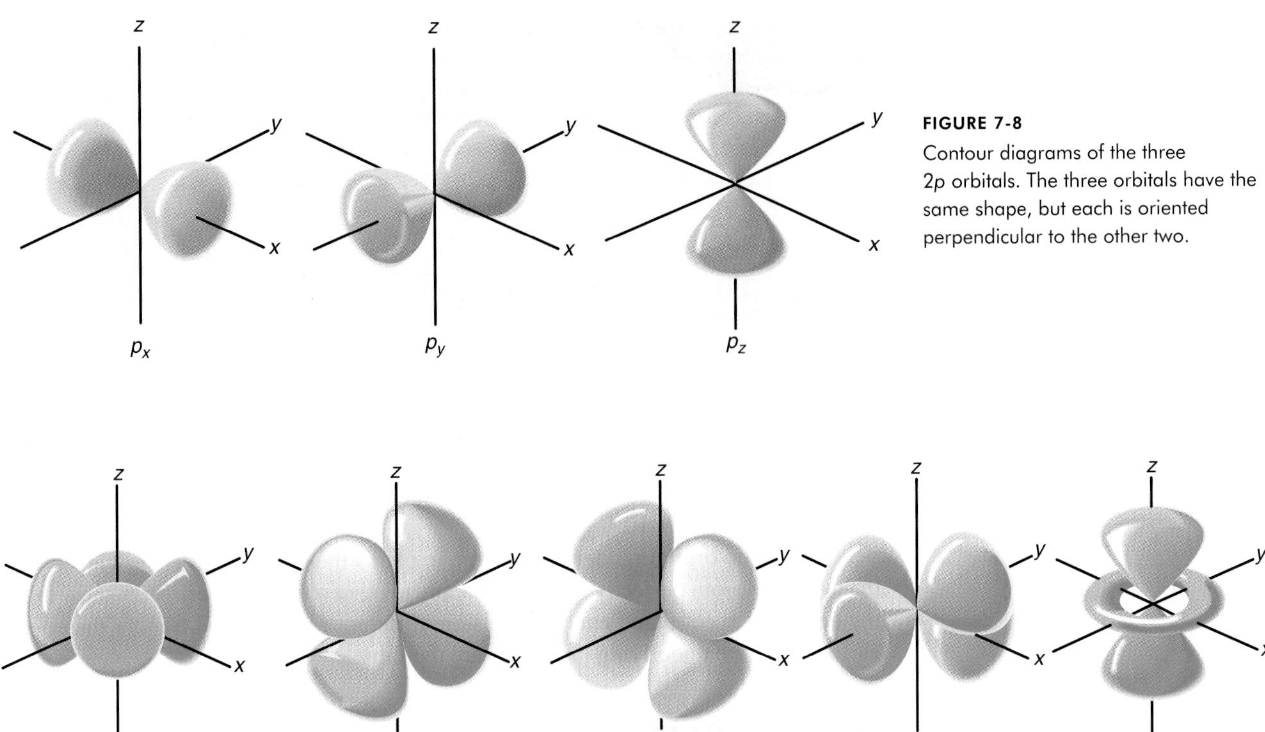

FIGURE 7-8
Contour diagrams of the three 2*p* orbitals. The three orbitals have the same shape, but each is oriented perpendicular to the other two.

FIGURE 7-9
Contour drawings of the d orbitals. Each has two preferred axes. Four of the *d* orbitals have similar shapes, possessing four lobes at right angles to each other. Each of the four points is in a different direction in space. The fifth *d* orbital has one pair of lobes pointing along the z axis and a "doughnut" of electron density in the xy plane.

The quantum number $\boldsymbol{l} = 2$ corresponds to a *d* orbital. A *d* electron can have any of five values for $\boldsymbol{m_l}$ (−2, −1, 0, +1, and +2), so there are five different orbitals in each set. The shapes of the *d* orbitals are more complicated than their *s* and *p* counterparts. As shown by the contour drawings in Figure 7-9, three of them look like three-dimensional "cloverleafs" lying in a cartesian plane with their lobes pointed between the axes. A subscript is used to identify the plane in which they lie: d_{xy}, d_{xz}, and d_{yz}. A fourth orbital is also a clover-leaf in the xy plane, but its lobes point along the x and y axes. This orbital is designated $d_{x^2-y^2}$. The fifth orbital looks quite different. Its major lobes point along the z axis, but there is also a "doughnut" of electron density in the xy plane. This orbital is designated d_{z^2}.

The fifth d orbital has only one preferred axis, but it also has a "preferred ring" of significant electron density in the xy plane.

The chemistry of all the common elements can be described completely by using *s, p,* and *d* orbitals, so we need not extend our catalog of orbital shapes to the *f* orbitals and beyond.

SECTION EXERCISES

7.2.1 Draw *s, p,* and *d* orbitals until you can sketch them quickly and with confidence. Be sure to include coordinate axes.

7.2.2 Draw orbital pictures that show a 2*p* orbital on one atom interacting with a 2*p* orbital on a different atom: (a) end-on (preferred axes pointing toward each other); (b) side-by-side (preferred axes parallel to each other); (c) crossed (preferred axes at right angles to each other).

A given orbital is less stable in a multielectron atom than it is in the single-electron ion with the same nuclear charge. For instance, Table 7-2 shows that it takes more than twice as much energy to remove the electron from He^+ (one electron) as it does to remove one of the electrons from a neutral He atom (two electrons). This demonstrates that the 1*s* orbital in He^+ is more than twice as stable as the 1*s* orbital in neutral He. Because the nuclear charge of both species is +2, the lower ionization energy for He must result from the presence of the second electron. A negatively charged electron in a multielectron atom is *attracted* to the positively charged nucleus, but it is *repelled* by the other negatively charged electrons. This electron-electron repulsion accounts for the lower ionization energy of the helium atom.

SCREENING

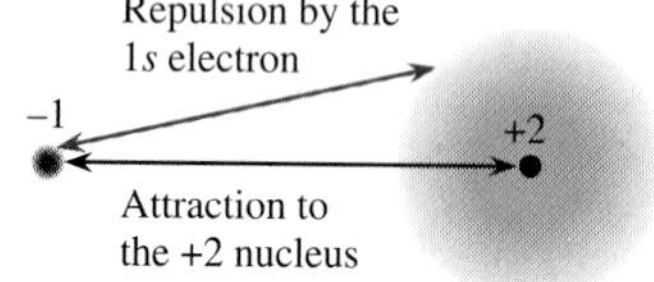

FIGURE 7-13
When a free electron approaches a He^+ cation, it is attracted to the +2 charge on the nucleus but repelled by the −1 charge on the 1*s* electron. When it is far from the cation, the electron experiences a net charge of +1.

Figure 7-13 shows a free electron approaching a helium cation. The incoming electron is attracted to the +2 charge of the nucleus, but it is also repelled by the 1*s* electron that is already present. This electron-electron repulsion nullifies a portion of the attraction between the nucleus and any given electron. Chemists call this partial cancellation **screening.**

The 1*s* electron in the He^+ ion contributes a −1 charge that counteracts part of the +2 nuclear charge. In other words, the 1*s* electron *screens* part of the total nuclear charge. As a result, an approaching electron feels a net attraction resulting from some **effective nuclear charge** (**Z_{eff}**) less than *Z*. With its −1 charge, each electron could reduce Z_{eff} by a maximum of one unit. When it is far enough away from a He^+ ion, an approaching electron experiences $Z_{eff} = +1$, the net charge of the ion.

Screening between electrons is never complete because electrons are delocalized over three-dimensional space. The portion of the electron density close to the nucleus is very effective at screening the nuclear charge. However, electron density relatively far from the nucleus is not effective at canceling the attraction resulting from the nucleus. Incomplete screening can be seen in the ionization energies of hydrogen atoms, helium atoms, and helium ions (Table 7-2). Without *any* screening, the ionization energy of a helium atom would be 8.72×10^{-18} J, the same as that of a helium ion. With *complete* screening, one helium electron would compensate for one of the protons in the nucleus, making $Z_{eff} = +1$. The energy required to remove an electron from a helium atom would then be 2.18×10^{-18} J, the same as the energy required to remove an electron from a hydrogen atom. The actual ionization energy of a helium atom is 3.94×10^{-18} J, which is approximately halfway between the fully screened and totally unscreened values. Screening is incomplete because both helium electrons occupy the same region of space, so neither is completely effective at "blanketing" the other from the +2 charge of the nucleus.

Electrons in compact orbitals are closer to the nucleus, so they are more effective at screening nuclear charge than electrons in large, diffuse orbitals. Because the size of an orbital increases with $\boldsymbol{n}^2$, an electron's ability to screen decreases as ***n*** gets larger. In a multielectron atom, lower-***n*** electrons are concentrated between the nucleus and higher-***n*** electrons. The negative charge of these inner electrons counteracts much of the positive charge of the nucleus. The efficient screening by electrons with low values of ***n*** can be appreciated by comparing the ionization energies of the screened and unscreened 2*p* orbitals listed in Table 7-2. Notice that it takes 2.18×10^{-18} J to ionize an excited He^+ ion with its lone electron in a 2*p* orbital. This is almost four times as much energy as it takes to remove the 2*p* electron from an excited-state helium *atom* that has one electron in the 1*s* orbital and its second electron in a 2*p* orbital (IE = 0.585×10^{-18} J). In the excited He atom the electron in the 1*s* orbital is very effective at screening the electron in the 2*p* orbital from the full

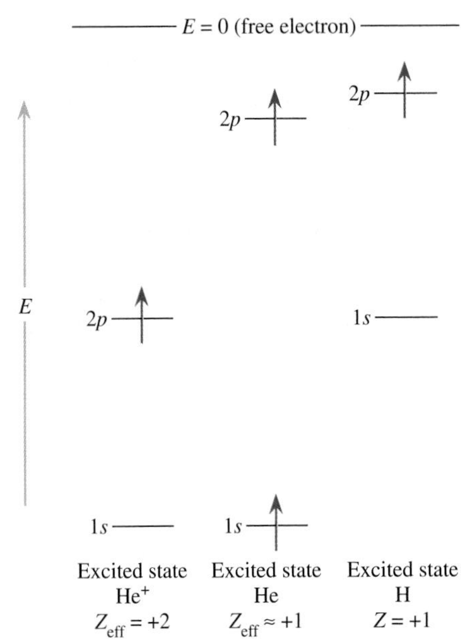

FIGURE 7-14
Inner electrons screen outer electrons very effectively. A 2*p* electron in an excited state He atom is almost completely screened by the electron in the smaller 1*s* orbital. The lower effective nuclear charge makes the ionization energy of a He 2*p* electron nearly the same as that of a 2*p* electron in an excited-state H atom. (The 1*s* energy level for He is actually much lower in energy, as shown in Figure 7-12.)

FIGURE 7-15
Cutaway view of the first three *s* orbitals. The 1*s* orbital lies closest to the nucleus, so it effectively screens the 2*s* and 3*s* orbitals. The 2*s* orbital lies between the 1*s* and 3*s* orbitals, so it is well screened by the 1*s*, but it screens the 3*s* orbital. Finally, the 3*s* orbital is well screened by the 1*s* and 2*s* orbitals.

+2 charge of the nucleus. In fact, the ionization energy of this excited He atom is almost the same as that of an excited hydrogen atom with its lone electron in a 2*p* orbital. The data indicate that Z_{eff} is very close to +1 for the 2*p* orbital of an excited helium atom. The energy level diagrams in Figure 7-14 summarize the stabilities of the 2*p* orbital.

In multielectron atoms, electrons with any given value of ***n*** provide effective screening for any orbital with a larger value of ***n***. For example, ***n*** = 1 electrons screen the ***n*** = 2, ***n*** = 3, and larger orbitals. The ***n*** = 2 electrons provide little screening for the ***n*** = 1 orbital, but they do provide effective screening for the ***n*** = 3, ***n*** = 4, and larger orbitals. Figure 7-15 shows this for the 1*s*, 2*s*, and 3*s* orbitals.

The amount of screening also depends on the shape of the orbital. The smaller 1*s* orbital screens the 2*s* and the 2*p* orbitals. However, Figure 7-16 shows that the 1*s* orbital screens the 2*p* orbital more effectively than the 2*s* orbital, even though both ***n*** = 2 orbitals are about the same size. This is because the 2*s* orbital has a region of significant electron density, shown shaded in Figure 7-16, near the nucleus. The 2*p* orbital lacks this inner layer, so virtually all of its electron density lies outside the region occupied by the 1*s* orbital. The result is that a 2*s* electron feels a larger effective nuclear charge than a 2*p* electron. This stronger coulombic attraction makes the 2*s* orbital slightly lower in energy than the 2*p* orbitals. In multielectron atoms the 2*p* orbitals are always less stable (higher in energy) than the 2*s* orbital.

The screening differences experienced by the 2*s* and 2*p* orbitals also extend to higher values of ***n***. The 3*s* orbital is lower in energy than the 3*p* orbital, the 4*s* is lower than the 4*p*, and so on. Similar effects are observed for orbitals with higher ***l*** values. The 3*d* orbitals are always less stable than the 3*p* orbitals, and the 4*d* orbitals are less stable than the 4*p* orbitals. These effects can be summarized in a single general statement:

The higher the value of the l quantum number, the more that orbital is screened by electrons in smaller, more stable orbitals.

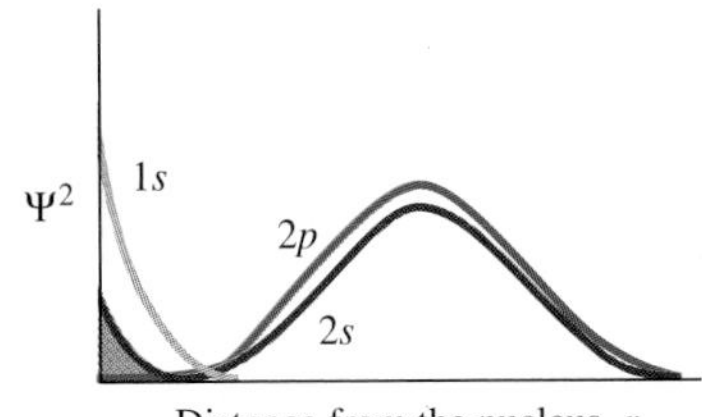

FIGURE 7-16
Electron density plots for the 1*s*, 2*s*, and 2*p* orbitals. The 2*s* orbital has significant electron density very near the nucleus *(shaded region)*. Consequently, the 1*s* electrons are more effective at screening the 2*p* orbital than the 2*s* orbital.

In a one-electron system (H, He^+, Li^{2+}, and so on) the stability of the orbitals depends only on Z and $\boldsymbol{n}$. In multielectron systems, orbital stability depends primarily on Z and $\boldsymbol{n}$ but it also depends significantly on $\boldsymbol{l}$. In a sense, $\boldsymbol{l}$ "fine tunes" orbital energies.

Electrons with the same $\boldsymbol{n}$ value do not screen one another effectively. For example, when electrons are placed in different *p* orbitals, the amount of mutual screening is slight. This is because screening is effective only when much of the electron density of one orbital lies between the nucleus and the electron density of another. As shown in Figure 7-8, however, the *p* orbitals are all perpendicular to one another, in distinctly different regions of space. Thus the electron density of the $2p_x$ orbital, for example, does not lie between the $2p_y$ orbital and the nucleus, resulting in little screening. The *d* orbitals and *f* orbitals are also oriented in distinctly different regions of space from one another, so mutual screening among electrons in these orbitals is also small.

These ideas about screening and Z_{eff} can be used to construct a general orbital energy level diagram for multielectron atoms and ions as shown in Figure 7-17. You should understand the features of this diagram, for we use it extensively in Section 7.4. Box 7-2 describes photoelectron spectroscopy, an experimental technique that verifies screening effects on atomic orbitals.

SECTION EXERCISES

7.3.1 Electron density plots of $\boldsymbol{n} = 1$, $\boldsymbol{n} = 2$, and $\boldsymbol{n} = 3$ orbitals are shown in Figures 7-6, 7-16, and 7-7 respectively. Redraw all the plots on one master figure that shows all of the orbitals to scale. Use different colors to keep the figure as clear as possible. Shade the regions of the 3*s* and 3*p* plots where screening is ineffective.

7.3.2 The outer layers of the sun contain He atoms in various excited states, one of which contains one 1*s* electron and one 3*p* electron. Based on the effectiveness of screening, estimate the ionization energy of the 3*p* electron in this excited atom.

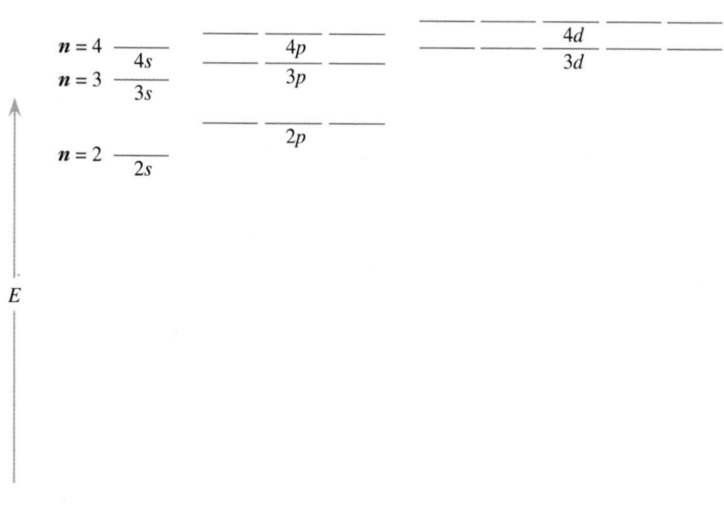

FIGURE 7-17
The general orbital energy level diagram for multielectron atoms from $\boldsymbol{n} = 1$ to $\boldsymbol{n} = 4$ and from $\boldsymbol{l} = 0$ to $\boldsymbol{l} = 2$.

BOX 7-2

PHOTOELECTRON SPECTROSCOPY: MAPPING ORBITAL ENERGIES

The absorption and emission spectra of atoms and ions yield information about the difference in energy *between* orbitals, but they do not give an orbital's *absolute* energy. The most direct measurements of orbital energies come from a technique called *photoelectron spectroscopy.*

Photoelectron spectroscopy is very similar to the photoelectric effect described in Chapter 6. Light shines on a sample of matter, a photon is absorbed by the sample, and the photon's energy is transferred to an electron. If the photon energy is high enough, the electron is ejected from the sample with a kinetic energy equal to the difference between the photon energy and the binding energy (ionization energy) of the electron.

In a photoelectron spectrometer, gaseous atoms or molecules are irradiated with very high energy photons. Typically, photons of 2104 kJ/mol (emitted by excited He^+ ions) or 11,900 kJ/mol (emitted by excited Mg atoms) are used. These energies are much greater than the energy required to knock an electron out of an atom or molecule of the sample. Excess photon energy appears as kinetic energy of the departing electron. The kinetic energies of the ejected electrons can be determined accurately by measuring their velocities. Knowing the photon energy and the electron's kinetic energy, we can find the energy of the orbital from which the electron came:

$$\text{Orbital energy} = E_{\text{photon}} - kE_{\text{electron}}$$

The photoelectron spectrum of a monatomic gas is a series of "peaks" at different kinetic energies; each represents the energy of a particular atomic orbital. A simple example is the spectrum of neon shown in Figure 7-18. Notice the two peaks that correspond to orbital energies of 2080 and 4680 kJ/mol. The lower value is the ionization energy of the 2*p* orbital, whereas the higher value is the ionization energy of the 2*s* orbital. The ionization energies of neon's 1*s* electrons are more than 12,000 kJ/mol, so they cannot be ejected by the photons used in these experiments. The ionization energy of an electron measures its stability when the electron is bound to the atom. In other words, a 2*p* electron of a neon atom is 2080 kJ/mol more stable than a free electron floating in a vacuum.

Photoelectron spectroscopy measures orbital energies directly. It shows conclusively that real atoms have the energetic features of atomic orbitals that we have presented in this section.

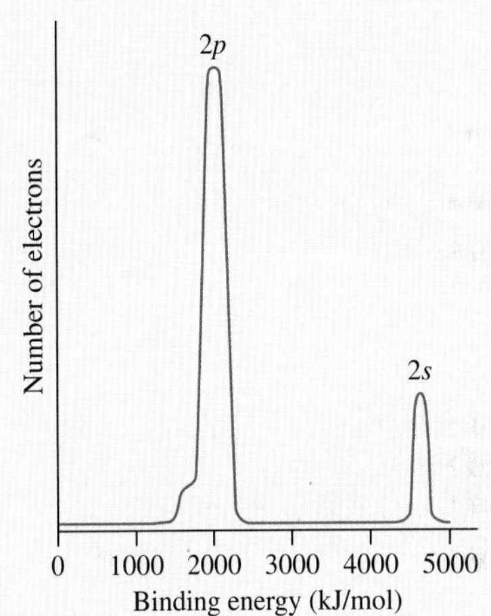

FIGURE 7-18
Photoelectron spectrum of Ne atoms. The peak at 2080 kJ/mol corresponds to the ionization energy of the 2*p* electrons, whereas the peak at 4680 kJ/mol corresponds to the ionization energy of the 2*s* electrons.

7.4 ELECTRON CONFIGURATIONS

Each atomic electron can be described by a set of four quantum numbers, and a description of all electrons in an atom is an **electron configuration.** There is an infinite number of acceptable sets of quantum numbers, but only one set describes an atom in its most stable form. This set is the **ground-state configuration.** The principles for determining ground-state configurations are the focus of this section.

THE PAULI EXCLUSION PRINCIPLE

Each electron in an atom must have a unique set of quantum numbers. All electron configurations must obey this fundamental law of quantum mechanics, which is known as the **Pauli exclusion principle.** Named for the Austrian physicist Wolfgang Pauli,* this principle can be derived from the mathematics of quantum mechanics, but it cannot be rationalized in a simple manner. Nevertheless, all experimental evidence upholds the idea. After an electron in an atom has a particular set of quantum numbers, all other electrons in the atom are excluded from that set. There are no exceptions to the Pauli exclusion principle.

THE AUFBAU PRINCIPLE

Aufbau is a German word meaning "construction."

The ground-state configuration of an atom is, by definition, the most stable arrangement of its electrons. *Most stable* means that the electrons occupy the lowest energy orbitals available. To construct the ground-state configuration of an atom, we use the general atomic energy level diagram shown in Figure 7-17. Electrons are placed in the orbitals starting with the lowest in energy and moving progressively upward. The building of a ground-state configuration proceeds according to the **Aufbau principle.** This principle states that each successive electron is placed in the *most stable orbital* whose quantum numbers *have not already been assigned* to another electron. In applying the principle, remember that a full description of an electron requires four quantum numbers: $\boldsymbol{n}$, $\boldsymbol{l}$, $\boldsymbol{m_l}$, and $\boldsymbol{m_s}$.

Each combination of the quantum numbers $\boldsymbol{n}$ and $\boldsymbol{l}$ describes one quantized energy level, and each level is made up of a set of orbitals with different values of $\boldsymbol{m_l}$. In addition, different values of the magnetic quantum number, $\boldsymbol{m_s}$, describe different spin orientations of electrons in otherwise identical orbitals. Within a set, all orbitals with the same value of $\boldsymbol{l}$ have the same energy. Orbitals with identical energy are called **degenerate orbitals.** For example, the $2p$ energy level ($\boldsymbol{n} = 2$, $\boldsymbol{l} = 1$) is triply degenerate. There are three distinct p orbitals ($\boldsymbol{m_l} = -1$, 0, and $+1$) with the same energy. When the two possible values of $\boldsymbol{m_s}$ are taken into account, we find that *six* different sets of quantum numbers can be used to describe an electron in a $2p$ energy level:

$$
\begin{array}{llll}
n = 2 & l = 1 & m_l = +1 & m_s = +\tfrac{1}{2} \\
n = 2 & l = 1 & m_l = +1 & m_s = -\tfrac{1}{2} \\
n = 2 & l = 1 & m_l = 0 & m_s = +\tfrac{1}{2} \\
n = 2 & l = 1 & m_l = 0 & m_s = -\tfrac{1}{2} \\
n = 2 & l = 1 & m_l = -1 & m_s = +\tfrac{1}{2} \\
n = 2 & l = 1 & m_l = -1 & m_s = -\tfrac{1}{2}
\end{array}
$$

In other words, the $2p$ energy level can hold as many as six electrons without violating the Pauli exclusion principle.

There are three common ways to represent electron configurations. First, we can list the values of all quantum numbers for every one of the atom's electrons. This

---

* Pauli was an outstanding theoretician but a notoriously clumsy experimenter. When anything went wrong in the physics laboratories where he worked, the other scientists blamed it on him. Physics lore has it that on one occasion a train carrying Pauli stopped for 5 minutes in the city of Göttingen, and at that very time a physics laboratory at the University exploded. However, Pauli didn't need to do experiments. Working with the observations of others, he "invented" electron spin and formulated the exclusion principle, for which he received the Nobel Prize in Physics in 1945. He also postulated the existence of a massless and uncharged subatomic particle, the neutrino. Neutrinos were detected experimentally in 1956, 25 years after Pauli's description. Born in 1900, Pauli lived only until 1958 and made his most famous discoveries when he was only 25.

presents no difficulty for the single electron in a hydrogen atom: $n = 1$, $l = 0$, $m_l = 0$, and $m_s = +\frac{1}{2}$ or $n = 1$, $l = 0$, $m_l = 0$, and $m_s = -\frac{1}{2}$. The choice is entirely arbitrary because both spin orientations have the same energy unless a strong magnet is present.

For an iron atom with 26 electrons, a complete listing of quantum numbers is very tedious. To save time and space, chemists have devised a shorthand notation to write electron configurations in a compact way. The orbital symbols (1*s*, 2*p*, 4*d*, etc.) are followed by superscripts designating how many electrons are in each set of orbitals. Thus the compact configuration for a hydrogen atom is $1s^1$, indicating one electron in the 1*s* orbital.

Figure 6-20 showed that in the presence of a strong magnetic field, atoms whose electrons have $m_s = +\frac{1}{2}$ behave differently from atoms whose electrons have $m_s = -\frac{1}{2}$. A large collection of atoms has half its atoms described by one configuration and half described by the other configuration.

The third way to represent an atomic configuration is to place the electrons in an energy level diagram like the one shown in Figure 7-17. Each electron is represented by an arrow. The direction of the arrow indicates the value of the spin orientation quantum number. For $m_s = +\frac{1}{2}$, the arrow points upward, and for $m_s = -\frac{1}{2}$, it points downward. The configuration of hydrogen can be represented as

$$1s\ \uparrow$$

Remember that it would be equally valid to show the arrow pointing in the other direction because the two sets of allowed quantum numbers for the 1s orbital are equal in energy.

The simplest case of a multielectron atom is neutral helium, which has two electrons. To write the ground state electron configuration of helium, we must apply the Aufbau principle. Thus we assign one set of unique quantum numbers to each electron, moving from the lowest possible energy upward until all the electrons have been assigned. The lowest energy orbital is always 1*s* ($n = 1$, $l = 0$, $m_l = 0$). Both helium electrons can occupy the 1*s* orbital, provided that one has spin quantum number $m_s = +\frac{1}{2}$ and the other has $m_s = -\frac{1}{2}$. The three representations of helium's ground state electron configuration follow:

$n = 1$	$l = 0$	$m_l = 0$	$m_s = +\frac{1}{2}$	$1s^2$	$\uparrow\downarrow$ 1*s*
$n = 1$	$l = 0$	$m_l = 0$	$m_s = -\frac{1}{2}$		

The two electrons in this configuration are said to be **paired electrons,** meaning that they are in the same energy level, with opposing spins. Opposing spins cancel, so paired electrons have zero net spin.

A lithium atom has three electrons. The first two electrons fill lithium's lowest possible energy level, the 1*s* orbital. The third electron cannot be placed in the 1*s* level because we have used all possible combinations of quantum numbers for $n = 1$. Adding a third electron to the 1*s* orbital would violate the Pauli exclusion principle. According to the Aufbau principle, lithium's third electron must be placed in the next most stable available energy level. Because of the screening influence of the 1*s* electrons, the 2*s* orbital is somewhat more stable than the set of 2*p* orbitals, so the third electron occupies the 2*s* orbital. The three representations for the ground state electron configuration of a lithium atom are as follows:

					$\uparrow$ 2*s*
$n = 1$	$l = 0$	$m_l = 0$	$m_s = +\frac{1}{2}$	$1s^2\,2s^1$	
$n = 1$	$l = 0$	$m_l = 0$	$m_s = -\frac{1}{2}$		
$n = 2$	$l = 0$	$m_l = 0$	$m_s = -\frac{1}{2}$		$\uparrow\downarrow$ 1*s*

The set $n = 2$, $l = 0$, $m_l = 0$, $m_s = +\frac{1}{2}$ is equally valid for the third electron.

The next atoms of the periodic table are beryllium and boron. You should be able to write the three different representations for the ground-state configurations of these elements. The filling principles remain the same as we move to higher atomic numbers. Sample Problem 7-2 shows how these principles are applied to aluminum.

SAMPLE PROBLEM 7-2 APPLYING THE AUFBAU PRINCIPLE

Construct an energy level diagram and the shorthand representation of the ground-state configuration of aluminum. Provide one set of valid quantum numbers for the highest-energy electron.

METHOD: First we must consult the periodic table to determine the number of electrons in a neutral aluminum atom. The electron configuration is then constructed by using the Aufbau and Pauli principles and the general energy level diagram shown in Figure 7-17.

The atomic number of aluminum is 13, so a neutral atom of Al has 13 electrons. The 13 electrons are placed sequentially, using arrows, into the most stable orbitals available:

3p — ↑ —

3s ↑↓

2p ↑↓ ↑↓ ↑↓

2s ↑↓

1s ↑↓

Placing the last electron in the "middle" 3*p* orbital is an arbitrary choice because these three orbitals are degenerate. Likewise the final electron could be given either spin orientation.

The shorthand configuration is $1s^2\ 2s^2\ 2p^6\ 3s^2\ 3p^1$.

The highest energy-electron is in a 3*p* orbital, meaning $\boldsymbol{n} = 3$ and $\boldsymbol{l} = 1$. The value of $\boldsymbol{m_l}$ can be any of three values: $+1, -1$, or 0. The spin quantum number, $\boldsymbol{m_s}$, can be $+\frac{1}{2}$ or $-\frac{1}{2}$. One valid set of quantum numbers is $\boldsymbol{n} = 3, \boldsymbol{l} = 1, \boldsymbol{m_l} = 1$, and $\boldsymbol{m_s} = +\frac{1}{2}$.

You should be able to write the other five possible sets.

Electron configurations become more elaborate as the number of electrons increases. To make the writing of a configuration even more compact, chemists often condense the symbols for all electrons except those in the highest-***n*** orbitals. Compare the configurations of neon and aluminum:

Ne (10 electrons)	$1s^2\ 2s^2\ 2p^6$
Al (13 electrons)	$1s^2\ 2s^2\ 2p^6\ 3s^2\ 3p^1$

The configuration of aluminum for orbitals with $\boldsymbol{n} = 1$ and $\boldsymbol{n} = 2$ is identical to that of neon, so we can represent that portion as [Ne]. When we use this notation, the configuration of Al becomes [Ne] $3s^2\ 3p^1$. The element at the end of each row of the periodic table is said to have a **filled shell configuration** that can be written in the following shorthand notation:

He (2 electrons)	$1s^2$ = [He]
Ne (10 electrons)	[He] $2s^2\ 2p^6$ = [Ne]
Ar (18 electrons)	[Ne] $3s^2\ 3p^6$ = [Ar]
Kr (36 electrons)	[Ar] $4s^2\ 3d^{10}\ 4p^6$ = [Kr]
Xe (54 electrons)	[Kr] $5s^2\ 4d^{10}\ 5p^6$ = [Xe]
Rn (86 electrons)	[Xe] $6s^2\ 5d^{10}\ 4f^{14}\ 6p^6$ = [Rn]

ELECTRON-ELECTRON REPULSION

The Aufbau principle allows us to assign quantum numbers to aluminum's 13 electrons without ambiguity. The first 12 electrons fill the 1*s*, 2*s*, 2*p*, and 3*s* energy levels, and the last electron can occupy any 3*p* orbital with either spin orientation. But what happens when more than one electron must be placed in a *p* energy level? Carbon atoms, for example, have six electrons. The first four fill the 1*s* and 2*s* energy levels, but how are the final two electrons arranged in the 2*p* orbitals? Three different arrangements of these electrons appear to be consistent with the Aufbau principle:

1. The electrons could be paired in the same 2*p* orbital (same m_l value but different m_s values):

2. The electrons could be placed in different 2*p* orbitals with the same spin orientation (different m_l values but the same m_s value):

3. The electrons could be placed in different 2*p* orbitals with opposite spin orientations (different m_l values and different m_s values):

These three arrangements have different energies because when electrons are close together, they repel one another more than when they are far apart. Thus given a choice between otherwise equal-energy orbitals, an electron will occupy the orbital that keeps it farthest from other electrons in the system. Placing two electrons in different *p* orbitals keeps them relatively far apart, so an atom is more stable with the two electrons in different *p* orbitals. Thus arrangements 2 and 3 are more stable than arrangement 1.

Arrangements 2 and 3 look spatially equivalent, but theory and experiment show that a configuration that gives unpaired electrons the same spin orientation is always more stable than one that gives them opposite orientations. This fundamental feature of ground-state configurations is called **Hund's rule.**

Remember that spin has magnitude and direction. Electrons with different values for m_s have the same spin *magnitude*, but the spins point in opposite *directions*.

For an atom in its ground-state configuration, all unpaired electrons have the same spin orientation.

According to Hund's rule, the ground-state configuration for carbon atoms is arrangement 2. Sample Problem 7-3 provides another example of the application of Hund's rule.

SAMPLE PROBLEM 7-3 APPLYING HUND'S RULE

Draw the ground-state orbital energy level diagram and write the shorthand electron configuration for the electrons in a sulfur atom.

METHOD: From the periodic table, we see that sulfur has 16 electrons. To build its ground-state configuration, we must use the Aufbau and Pauli principles and Figure 7-17, and then apply Hund's rule if needed.

The first 12 electrons fill the four lowest energy orbitals: $1s^2\ 2s^2\ 2p^6\ 3s^2$.

Sulfur's remaining four electrons must occupy the most stable available orbitals, which are the three 3*p* orbitals. To minimize electron-electron repulsion, put three of these electrons in different *p* orbitals and then pair one of them with the fourth electron. According to Hund's rule, all electrons that are not paired are given the same value of m_s, so the two unpaired electrons must be given the same spin orientation. Here is the complete energy level diagram:

3*p* ↑↓ ↑ ↑

3*s* ↑↓

2*p* ↑↓ ↑↓ ↑↓

2*s* ↑↓

1*s* ↑↓

The complete configuration is $1s^2\ 2s^2\ 2p^6\ 3s^2\ 3p^4$, or [Ne] $3s^2\ 3p^4$.

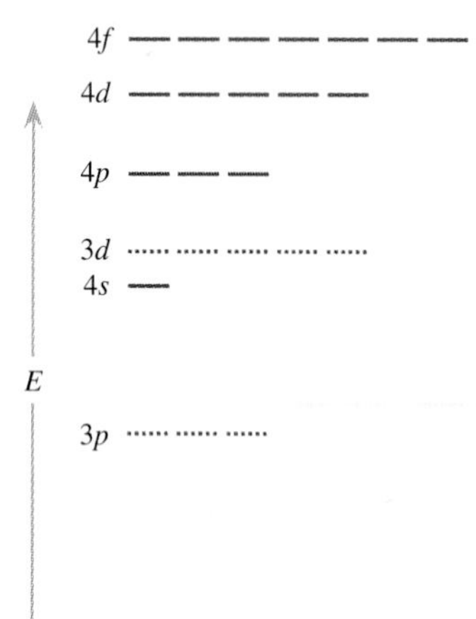

FIGURE 7-19

The energy level diagram for $n = 3$ and $n = 4$ atomic orbitals for Z ≅ 25. All other orbitals have been omitted for clarity.

ORDER OF ORBITAL STABILITY

The energy spacing between sets of orbitals gets smaller as the principal quantum number increases. For instance, the energy gap between the $n = 1$ and $n = 2$ orbitals is greater than the gap between the $n = 2$ and $n = 3$ orbitals (see Figure 7-1). At the same time, orbital splitting between different l values increases as nuclear charge increases. The energy difference between the 3*s* and 3*p* orbitals, for example, is greater than the energy difference between the 2*s* and 2*p* orbitals. This is because screening becomes increasingly important for large nuclear charges. As Z increases, the stability of the *s* orbitals increases more rapidly than the stability of the *d* orbitals.

As a consequence of these two trends in energy spacing, the 4*s* and 3*d* orbitals of the elements from Z = 19 to Z = 30 have nearly the same energy. Figure 7-19 shows the order of orbital stability for the $n = 3$ and $n = 4$ orbitals for these elements. Notice that the most stable $n = 4$ orbital (4*s*) is *more stable* than the least stable $n = 3$ orbitals (3*d*). Experiments confirm that potassium (Z = 19) has the ground-state configuration [Ar] $4s^1$ rather than [Ar] $3d^1$. In potassium and other neutral atoms in this row of the periodic table, the 4*s* orbital is slightly more stable than the 3*d* orbitals. In calcium (Z = 20) the 4*s* orbital is filled. Now the 3*d* set fills, starting with scandium (Z = 21) and finishing with zinc (Z = 30).

This pattern repeats for the 5*s* and 4*d* pair of orbitals for neutral atoms between Z = 37 and Z = 48. Here, the 5*s* orbital is more stable than the 4*d* orbital. Furthermore the 4*f* orbital is very effectively screened by $n = 3$ electrons, so this orbital does not fill until after the 5*s*, 4*d*, 5*p*, and 6*s* orbitals. Thus Rb has the configuration [Kr] $5s^1$, and Sr has the configuration [Kr] $5s^2$. The $(n)s$ orbital is always more stable than its $(n - 1)d$ counterpart for elements in columns I and II of the periodic table. Radium, for example, has the configuration [Rn] $7s^2$.

The diagram shown in Figure 7-20 summarizes the sequence of orbital filling without referring to an energy level diagram. The orbitals are listed in a table in which all orbitals with the same principal quantum number n lie in the same row and all orbitals with the same azimuthal quantum number l values lie in the same column. The order of orbital filling follows the 45-degree diagonal lines that move down and across the table from right to left. In constructing a configuration this way, we must remember the capacity of each set of orbitals. This is shown at the bottom of the columns. Using this mnemonic, we can quickly write the ground-state configuration of elements with many electrons, as Sample Problem 7-4 illustrates for bismuth.

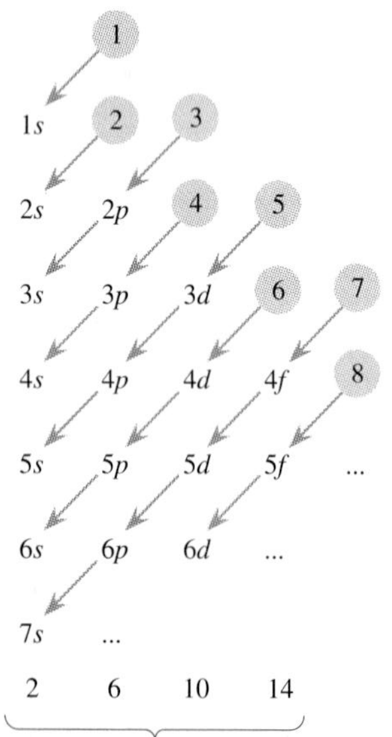

FIGURE 7-20

A diagram of the atomic orbitals that shows how the correct order of filling can be determined without referring to the orbital energy level diagram.

SAMPLE PROBLEM 7-4 GROUND-STATE CONFIGURATIONS

What is the ground-state configuration of bismuth, $Z = 83$? Specify quantum numbers of any unpaired electrons.

METHOD: For the 83 electrons of the bismuth atom, use the mnemonic diagram shown in Figure 7-20. Then apply Hund's rule to any electrons in partially filled sets of orbitals.

We assign electrons to orbitals following the diagonal arrows in Figure 7-20. It is convenient to keep a running total of electrons by listing the number beneath each set of orbitals:

Config.:	$1s^2$	$2s^2$	$2p^6$	$3s^2$	$3p^6$	$4s^2$	$3d^{10}$	$4p^6$	$5s^2$	$4d^{10}$	$5p^6$	$6s^2$	$4f^{14}$	$5d^{10}$	$6p^3$
Tot. e^-:	2	4	10	12	18	20	30	36	38	48	54	56	70	80	83

[Xe] (comprising $1s^2$ through $5p^6$)

The shorthand configuration is [Xe] $6s^2\ 4f^{14}\ 5d^{10}\ 6p^3$.

The final three electrons are placed in the three degenerate $6p$ orbitals. To minimize electron-electron repulsion, each electron occupies a different p orbital (different m_l values). Hund's rule requires that we distribute the electrons to give the same value of m_s to as many of them as possible. One valid set of quantum numbers follows:

Electron no.	Orbital designation	n	l	m_l	m_s
81	$6p$	6	1	+1	$-\frac{1}{2}$
82	$6p$	6	1	0	$-\frac{1}{2}$
83	$6p$	6	1	−1	$-\frac{1}{2}$

You should be able to write a second, equally valid set of quantum numbers for these three electrons.

NEAR-DEGENERATE ORBITALS

The filling order described by the mnemonic diagram in Figure 7-20 is valid as long as orbital energies are well separated. However, Figure 7-19 shows that the $4s$ and $3d$ orbitals have nearly the same energy for elements between $Z = 19$ and $Z = 30$. Orbitals with nearly the same energy are **near-degenerate orbitals.** When these orbitals are partially filled, electron-electron repulsion leads to some exceptions to the normal filling sequence. Table 7-3 lists the near-degenerate orbitals and the atomic numbers where abnormal filling sequences are found. In particular, an s orbital may contain only one electron rather than two. Five abnormal ground-state configurations have a common pattern and are easy to remember: Cr and Mo are $s^1\ d^5$, and Cu, Ag, and Au are $s^1\ d^{10}$. The other exceptional cases follow no recognizable pattern, because they are generated by subtle interactions among all the electrons.

TABLE 7-3 NEAR-DEGENERATE ATOMIC ORBITALS

ORBITALS	ATOMIC NUMBERS AFFECTED	EXAMPLE
$4s$, $3d$	24, 29	Cr [Ar] $4s^1\ 3d^5$
$5s$, $4d$	41-47	Ru [Kr] $5s^1\ 4d^7$
$6s$, $5d$, $4f$	57, 58, 64, 78, 79	Au [Xe] $6s^1\ 4f^{14}\ 5d^{10}$
$6d$, $5f$	89, 91-93, 96	U [Rn] $7s^2\ 5f^3\ 6d^1$

IONIC CONFIGURATIONS

See Section 2-4 for a discussion of ions.

An atomic cation is formed by removing one or more electrons from its parent atom. Addition of one or more electrons to the neutral atom generates an atomic anion. We can write electron configurations of atomic ions using the same procedures as for neutral atoms, as long as we take into account the number of electrons added or removed. For an anion, *add* one electron for each unit of *negative* charge. For a cation, *remove* one electron for each unit of *positive* charge.

For most atomic ions, the filling order of orbitals is the same as that of neutral atoms. For example, Na^+, Ne, and F^- all contain 10 electrons, and each has the configuration $1s^2\,2s^2\,2p^6$. Atoms and ions that have the same number of electrons are said to be **isoelectronic.**

The near-degeneracy of $(\boldsymbol{n})$s and $(\boldsymbol{n}-1)d$ orbitals causes some cation configurations to differ from the configurations generated by using Figure 7-20. This feature is particularly important for the transition metals. Experiments show that *$(\boldsymbol{n})s$ electrons are always removed before $(\boldsymbol{n}-1)d$ electrons*. For example, the electron configuration of a neutral iron atom is [Ar] $4s^2\,3d^6$. However, when iron loses three electrons to form Fe^{3+} cations, the first two electrons come from the 4*s* orbital, and the third comes from the 3*d* set. Thus the configuration of an Fe^{3+} cation is [Ar] $3d^5$.

Removal of electrons to form a cation is oxidation. Iron and many other metals oxidize readily because of the ease with which their s electrons can be removed. In fact, both Fe^{2+} [Ar] $3d^6$ and Fe^{3+} [Ar] $3d^5$ are relatively stable cations.

Vanadium atoms ([Ar] $4s^2\,3d^3$) and Fe^{3+} cations ([Ar] $3d^5$) have different configurations, even though each has 23 electrons. The different configurations arise because the 4*s* and 3*d* orbitals, which are nearly degenerate, are affected differently by the increase in nuclear charge in going from vanadium to iron. These differences follow a regular pattern. In *neutral* transition metal atoms the $(\boldsymbol{n}-1)d$ and $(\boldsymbol{n})s$ orbitals are nearly degenerate, with $(\boldsymbol{n})s$ slightly more stable. For transition metal *cations,* however, the $(\boldsymbol{n}-1)d$ orbitals are *always* more stable than the $(\boldsymbol{n})s$ orbital. Consequently the configuration of a transition metal cation must be obtained from the configuration of the neutral atom by removing the appropriate number of electrons. Sample Problem 7-5 shows how this is done.

SAMPLE PROBLEM 7-5 CONFIGURATION OF A CATION

What is the ground-state electron configuration of Cr^{3+} cations?

METHOD: Follow the usual filling procedure for the neutral atom, but bear in mind the irregularities cited in Table 7-3 for some of the transition metals with near-degenerate orbitals. Then remove electrons to obtain the cation, remembering that *s* electrons are always removed before *d* electrons.

First, we need the configuration of neutral chromium, which has 24 electrons.

By now you should recognize that the first 18 electrons are in the same configuration as an argon atom:

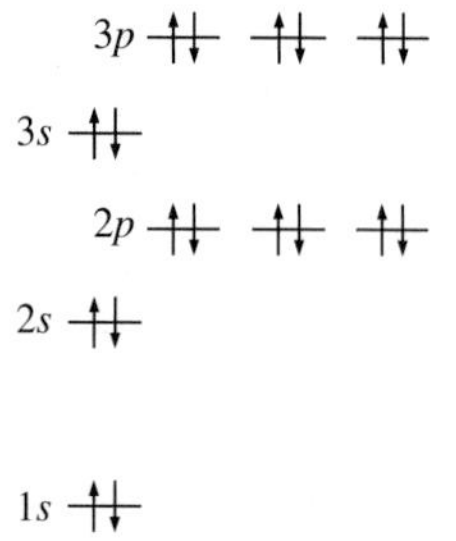

3p ⥮ ⥮ ⥮
3s ⥮
2p ⥮ ⥮ ⥮
2s ⥮
1s ⥮

$1s^2\,2s^2\,2p^6\,3s^2\,3p^6$ = [Ar]

The remaining six electrons go into the $4s$ and $3d$ orbitals, and the normal filling sequence predicts $4s^2\ 3d^4$. However, chromium is one of the exceptions caused by $4s$-$3d$ near-degeneracy. The actual ground-state configuration is:

$4s$ ↑ $3d$ ↑ ↑ ↑ ↑ ↑ $\qquad 4s^1\ 3d^5$

To generate Cr^{3+}, remove an s electron and two d electrons from this configuration:

$4s$ —

$3d$ — — ↑ ↑ ↑ $\qquad 3d^3$

[Ar]

The correct ground-state configuration of Cr^{3+} is [Ar] $3d^3$. In the cation the empty $4s$ orbital is slightly higher in energy than the partially filled $3d$ orbital. Notice that this is the same ground-state configuration as the isoelectronic cation V^{2+}, but differs from the isoelectronic neutral atom, scandium, whose configuration is [Ar] $4s^2\ 3d^1$.

EXCITED STATES

A ground-state configuration is the *most stable* arrangement of electrons, so an atom or ion will usually have this configuration. However, when an atom absorbs light or is bombarded by energetic electrons, it can gain energy to reach an excited state with a new electronic configuration. For example, all atoms in a sample of sodium gas normally have the ground-state configuration [Ne] $3s^1$, but an electric discharge can induce transitions that transfer the $3s$ electron to some higher-energy orbital, such as $3p$ or $4s$. Excited atoms are unstable and will spontaneously return to the ground-state configuration, giving up their excess energy in the process. This is the principle behind sodium vapor lamps, which are commonly used for street lighting. The light from a sodium vapor lamp comes from photons emitted as excited sodium atoms return to their ground state.

Excited-state configurations are perfectly valid as long as they meet the restrictions given in Table 7-1. In the electric discharge of a sodium vapor lamp, for instance, we find some sodium atoms in excited states, with configurations like $1s^2\ 2s^2\ 2p^6\ 3p^1$ or $1s^2\ 2s^2\ 2p^5\ 3s^2$. These configurations use valid orbitals and are in accord with the Pauli principle, but they describe atoms that are less stable than those in the ground state. Each atom or ion has only one state that is most stable, and that is the ground state.

Sodium is a gas at low pressure and high temperature in a sodium vapor lamp, whose yellow light comes from excited atoms returning to the ground state.

Excited states play important roles in chemistry. Recall from Chapter 6 that the properties of atoms can be studied by observing excited states. In fact, the characteristics of excited states are used extensively in chemistry and physics to probe the structure and reactivity of atoms, ions, and molecules. Excited states also serve less theoretical purposes. For example, lamps use the emissions from excited sodium atoms, the dazzling colors of a fireworks display come from photons emitted by metal ions in excited states, and the red light in highway flares often comes from excited Sr^{2+} ions.

ATOMIC MAGNETISM

An Fe^{3+} ion in its ground state has the configuration, [Ar] $3d^5$. We can divide its electrons into two categories with different spin characteristics. In the filled orbitals, all the electrons are "paired." Each electron with spin orientation $+\frac{1}{2}$ has a "partner" with spin orientation $-\frac{1}{2}$. The spins of these electrons cancel each other, because one spin exactly opposes the other, giving a net spin of zero. In contrast, spins do not cancel in half-filled orbitals. In Fe^{3+}, Hund's rule dictates that the five d electrons all have the same spin orientation. For these five electrons the spins all act together, giving a net spin of $(\frac{1}{2}) + (\frac{1}{2}) + (\frac{1}{2}) + (\frac{1}{2}) + (\frac{1}{2}) = \frac{5}{2}$.

Remember from Chapter 6 that spin gives rise to magnetism. Consequently, any atom or ion with unpaired electrons has nonzero net spin and has magnetism. Moreover, the amount of magnetism is proportional to the number of unpaired spins. Thus magnetic properties of atoms and ions reveal the number of unpaired electrons in a given species. An atom or ion with unpaired electrons is said to be **paramagnetic.** The Fe^{3+} cation is paramagnetic, with a net spin of $\frac{5}{2}$. If all electrons are paired to give zero net spin (for example in the Al^{3+} cation, whose configuration is [Ne]) the species is said to be **diamagnetic.** Sample Problem 7-6 shows how to determine whether an atom or ion is diamagnetic or paramagnetic.

SAMPLE PROBLEM 7-6 UNPAIRED ELECTRONS

Which of these species are paramagnetic: F^-, Zn^{2+}, and Ti?

METHOD: Paramagnetism results from unpaired spins, which can exist only in partially filled sets of orbitals. We need to build the configurations and look for any orbitals that are partially filled.

F^-: A fluorine atom has nine electrons, so F^- has 10 electrons. The configuration is $1s^2\ 2s^2\ 2p^6$. There are no partially filled orbitals, so this ion is diamagnetic.

Zn^{2+}: The parent atom has 30 electrons in the configuration [Ar] $4s^2\ 3d^{10}$. Two electrons must be removed to generate the cation, and the *s* electrons are removed first, so the configuration for Zn^{2+} is [Ar] $3d^{10}$. Again, there are no partially filled orbitals, so this ion is also diamagnetic.

Ti: A neutral titanium atom has 22 electrons. Use the diagram from Figure 7-20 to generate its ground-state configuration: [Ar] $4s^2\ 3d^2$. The *d* orbitals are partially filled, with two unpaired electrons. This ion is paramagnetic, with spin = 1.

The ground-state configurations of most neutral atoms and many ions contain unpaired electrons, so we might expect most materials to be paramagnetic. On the contrary, most substances are diamagnetic. This is because free atoms are seldom found in stable substances. Instead, atoms are bonded together in molecules, and as we show in Chapter 8, bonding results in the pairing of electrons and the cancellation of spin. As a result, paramagnetism is observed primarily among salts of the transition and rare-earth metals, whose cations have partially filled *d* and *f* orbitals.

SECTION EXERCISES

7.4.1 Determine the ground-state electronic configurations, and predict the net spin of (a) Au^+; (b) the neutral element with $Z = 118$; and (c) S^{2-}.

7.4.2 The ground-state configuration of Np^+ is [Rn] $7s^2\ 5f^4\ 6d^1$. Draw an energy level diagram that shows how the 7*s*, 5*f*, and 6*d* orbitals are related. Include arrows representing the seven electrons that occupy these orbitals.

7.4.3 Determine the ground-state configurations of Mo, I, and Hg^+.

7.5 THE PERIODIC TABLE

The periodicity of chemical properties, which is summarized in the periodic table, is one of the most useful organizing principles in chemistry. The ground-state configurations of the elements form the basis for periodicity of their chemical properties. The regularities of configurations also explain why periodicity takes the particular form summarized in the periodic table.

The periodic table is constructed by listing all the elements in order of increasing atomic number. This "ribbon" of elements is "cut" at regular intervals to generate strips that are placed in rows. The rows are positioned so that elements with similar chemical properties fall in the same column. Figure 7-21 illustrates how the first 20 elements of the ribbon are cut and relocated in block form. Notice that the first cut comes just before lithium, which is the first element with an $n = 2$ electron in its ground-state configuration; the second cut comes just before sodium, which is the first element with an $n = 3$ electron in its ground-state configuration; and the third cut comes just before potassium, which is the first element with an $n = 4$ electron in its ground-state configuration.

Figure 7-22 shows the complete periodic table, which lists the elements so that Z increases one unit at a time from left to right across a row. At the end of each row we move down one row and return to the left side to find the next higher Z value. Inspection of Figure 7-22 reveals that the ribbon is cut after elements 2, 10, 18, 36, 54, and 86. Thus as the atomic number increases, the length of ribbon between "cuts" increases, too. The first segment contains only hydrogen and helium. Then there are two 8-element segments, followed by two 18-element segments, and finally two 32-element pieces. The last segment stops before reaching its full length, however, because these elements have not been discovered in nature, nor have they been prepared in the laboratory.

Recall that a one-unit increase in Z means that one proton has been added to the nucleus.

Elements with very high Z are very unstable, as we show in Chapter 19.

In Figure 7-22 the rows and columns have been labeled to highlight the linkage between periodicity and electron configuration. Each *row* is labeled with the *principal quantum number* of the least stable occupied orbital. For example, elements of the third row (Na → Ar) have their least stable electrons in $n = 3$ orbitals. Each *column* is labeled with the *number of electrons in the least stable set of orbitals.* Germanium, in the fourteenth column of the fourth row ($n = 4$), is labeled p^2 (two p electrons). Thus germanium's two least stable electrons are in the degenerate set of $4p$ orbitals. All other members of this column (C, Si, Sn, and Pb) also have their two highest-energy electrons in the $(n)p$ orbitals. In general, elements in the same column of the periodic table have the same outermost configurations.

Recall from Table 7-2 that some elements in the *d* block have exceptional configurations, generally with an extra *d* electron and only one *s* electron. Some elements in the *f* block also have exceptional configurations, generally with an extra *d* electron and one less *f* electron.

First cut — Second cut — Third cut

1 H	2 He	3 Li	4 Be	5 B	6 C	7 N	8 O	9 F	10 Ne	11 Na	12 Mg	13 Al	14 Si	15 P	16 S	17 Cl	18 Ar	19 K	20 Ca

						1 H	2 He
3 Li	4 Be	5 B	6 C	7 N	8 O	9 F	10 Ne
11 Na	12 Mg	13 Al	14 Si	15 P	16 S	17 Cl	18 Ar
19 K	20 Ca						

FIGURE 7-21
The first 20 elements organized in a linear "ribbon" of increasing atomic number. To generate the periodic table, the ribbon is "cut," and the segments are placed in rows so that elements with similar chemical properties fall in the same column. For example, Li, Na, and K all are highly reactive metals.

UNDERLYING PATTERNS

Two fundamental features of orbitals form the basis of periodicity:

1. ***As Z increases, atomic orbitals become smaller and more stable.***

2. ***As n increases, atomic orbitals become larger and less stable.***

Moving from left to right across a *row* of the periodic table, *Z* increases, but the ***n*** value of the least stable occupied orbital remains the same. A larger nuclear charge exerts a stronger coulombic attraction for the electron cloud, and this stronger attraction results in smaller orbitals. Furthermore, electrons closer to the nucleus are lower in energy. Moving from *left to right* across a row, orbitals become *smaller and more stable.*

Proceeding down a *column* of the periodic table, ***n*** and *Z* increase. As ***n*** increases, orbitals become larger and less stable, but as *Z* increases, orbitals become smaller and more stable. Which trend dominates here? Moving down a column, the number of core electrons increases. Sodium ($Z = 11$), for example, has 1 valence electron and 10 core electrons. Potassium ($Z = 19$) also has just 1 valence electron, but it has 18 core electrons. The screening of potassium's additional eight core electrons largely cancels the effect of the additional eight protons in its nucleus. When moving down a column, therefore, higher *Z* is offset by increased screening. As a consequence, ***n*** is the most important factor in determining orbital size and stability within a column. From *top to bottom* of a column, orbitals become *larger and less stable.* These essential features are summarized on the periodic table in Figure 7-23.

ATOMIC RADII

Because most of the volume of an atom is occupied by its electron cloud, the size of an atom is determined by the size of its orbitals. Atomic size is mapped by the radius of the atom:

Atomic radii decrease moving from left to right across a row of the periodic table.

Atomic radii increase moving from top to bottom down a column of the periodic table.

																H	He
Li	Be											B	C	N	O	F	Ne
Na	Mg											Al	Si	P	S	Cl	Ar
K	Ca	Sc	Ti	V	Cr	Mn	Fe	Co	Ni	Cu	Zn	Ga	Ge	As	Se	Br	Kr
Rb	Sr	Y	Zr	Nb	Mo	Tc	Ru	Rh	Pd	Ag	Cd	In	Sn	Sb	Te	I	Xe
Cs	Ba	Lu	Hf	Ta	W	Re	Os	Ir	Pt	Au	Hg	Tl	Pb	Bi	Po	At	Rn
Fr	Ra	Lr	Unq	Unp	Unh	Uns	Uno	Une									

n **increases but** Z_{eff} **is fixed**
Consequences: Orbitals expand
Stability decreases

Z increases but *n* is fixed
Consequences: Orbitals shrink
Stability increases

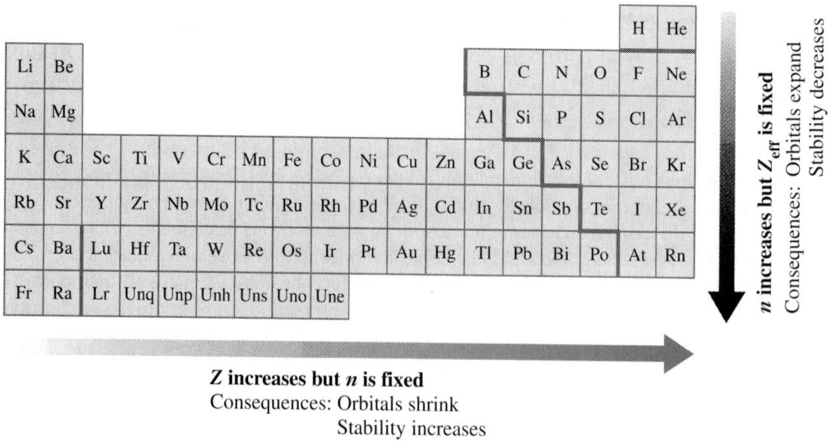

FIGURE 7-23
Underlying features of the periodic table. In moving across a row the dominant factor is the increasing coulombic attraction caused by increasing Z. In moving down a column the dominant factor is the change in size and stability as *n* increases.

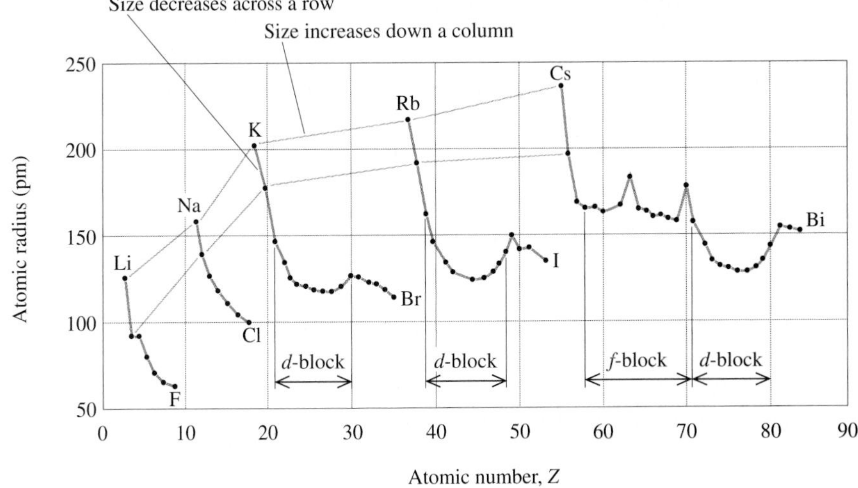

FIGURE 7-24
Variations in the radii of gaseous atoms with atomic number. In moving across any main group *(blue lines)* the radius decreases. In moving down any column *(yellow lines)* the radius increases.

Figure 7-24 shows that atomic radius decreases smoothly across Row 4, from 203 pm for potassium to 114 pm for bromine. Atomic radius increases smoothly down column I, from 125 pm for lithium to 235 pm for cesium. Notice, however, that the atomic radius changes very little across the *d* and *f* blocks of the table. This is due to screening. For these elements the *largest* orbital is the filled $(\boldsymbol{n})s$ orbital. From left to right across a row, *Z* increases and electrons are added to the smaller $(\boldsymbol{n} - 1)d$ or $(\boldsymbol{n} - 2)f$ orbitals. Each increase in *Z* by one unit is matched by the addition of one screening electron. From the perspective of the outlying *s* orbital, the increases in *Z* are counteracted by increased screening from the added *d* or *f* electrons. Thus the electron in the outermost occupied orbital, $(\boldsymbol{n})s$, feels an effective nuclear charge that changes very little across these blocks. As a consequence, atomic size remains nearly constant. Sample Problem 7-7 reinforces these trends with a few examples.

SAMPLE PROBLEM 7-7 TRENDS IN ATOMIC RADII

For each of the following pairs, predict which atom is larger: Si or Cl, S or Se, and Mo or Ag.

METHOD: Qualitative predictions about atomic size can be made by using relative positions of the elements in the periodic table and the trends described in this section.

Silicon lies to the left of chlorine in the same *row* of the periodic table. Size decreases from left to right as *Z* increases, and $\boldsymbol{n}$ stays the same. Thus silicon is *larger* than chlorine.

Sulfur is above selenium in the same *column* of the periodic table. Size increases from top to bottom as $\boldsymbol{n}$ increases, whereas increasing *Z* is compensated by increased screening. Thus sulfur is *smaller* than selenium.

Molybdenum and silver are neighbors in the *d block* of the periodic table. In this region, screening offsets increasing Z, so molybdenum and silver are *nearly the same* size.

It is important to be familiar with periodic trends in physical and chemical properties, but it is just as important to understand the principles that give rise to these trends. Therefore let us take another look at this problem, this time from the perspective of electron configurations and nuclear charge.

Both silicon and chlorine are in the third row of the periodic table. Their configurations are:

$$Si = [Ne]\ 3s^2\ 3p^2 \qquad Cl = [Ne]\ 3s^2\ 3p^5$$

Chlorine's nuclear charge (17) is larger than silicon's (14), so chlorine's nucleus exerts a stronger pull on its electron cloud. Chlorine also has four more electrons than silicon, which raises the possibility that screening effects could counter the extra nuclear charge. Remember, however, that electrons in the same type of orbital do a poor job of screening one another from the nuclear charge. For Si and Cl, screening comes mainly from the [Ne] $3s^2$ set of electrons, not from the electrons in the $3p$ orbitals. Because screening effects are similar for these elements, nuclear charge determines which of the two is larger. Therefore we conclude that chlorine, with its greater nuclear attraction for the electron cloud, is the smaller atom.

Both sulfur and selenium are in Column VI of the periodic table. Their configurations are as follows:

$$\mathrm{S} = [\mathrm{Ne}]\ 3s^2\ 3p^4 \qquad \mathrm{Se} = [\mathrm{Ar}]\ 4s^2\ 4p^4$$

Although they have the same valence configurations ($s^2\ p^4$), selenium's least stable electrons are in orbitals with a larger $\boldsymbol{n}$ value. Orbital size increases with $\boldsymbol{n}$. Selenium also has a greater nuclear charge than sulfur, which raises the possibility that nuclear attraction could offset increased $\boldsymbol{n}$. Remember, however, that much of this extra nuclear charge is offset by the screening influence of the core electrons. Selenium has 18 core electrons, and sulfur has 10. Thus we conclude that selenium, with its larger $\boldsymbol{n}$ value, is larger than sulfur.

Finally, molybdenum and silver have the following configurations:

$$\mathrm{Mo} = [\mathrm{Kr}]\ 5s^1\ 4d^5 \qquad \mathrm{Ag} = [\mathrm{Kr}]\ 5s^1\ 4d^{10}$$

In each case, $5s$ is the largest occupied orbital. The volume of the $4d$ orbitals is mostly inside the $5s$ orbital. Consequently, $4d$ is effective at screening $5s$. The nuclear charge of silver is four units higher than that of molybdenum, but silver also has four extra screening electrons. These offset the extra nuclear charge, making Mo and Ag nearly the same size.

IONIZATION ENERGY

An atom can absorb light, causing an electron to be promoted to a higher-energy orbital. As orbitals become higher in energy, their electrons have smaller coulombic attraction for the nucleus. Thus moving the electron to ever-higher energy orbitals weakens the hold of the nucleus on the electron. If the photon has sufficient energy, an electron can be ejected from the atom. Recall that the photoelectric effect and photoelectron spectroscopy are two examples of this phenomenon. Data for the ionization energies of hydrogen and helium atoms were presented in Table 7-2.

The minimum amount of energy needed to remove an electron from a neutral atom is called the first ionization energy. Variations in ionization energy mirror variations in orbital stability because an electron in a less stable orbital is easier to remove than one in a more stable orbital.

First ionization energy increases from left to right across a row of the periodic table.

First ionization energy decreases from top to bottom down a column of the periodic table.

Figure 7-25 shows how the first ionization energy of gaseous atoms varies with atomic number. Notice how ionization energy increases smoothly across row 3, from 496 kJ/mol for sodium to 1520 kJ/mol for argon. It decreases smoothly down Column VIII, from 2372 kJ/mol for helium to 1037 kJ/mol for radon. As with atomic radius, ionization energy is fairly constant for elements in the d and f blocks because increases in Z are offset by increased screening from the d and f orbitals.

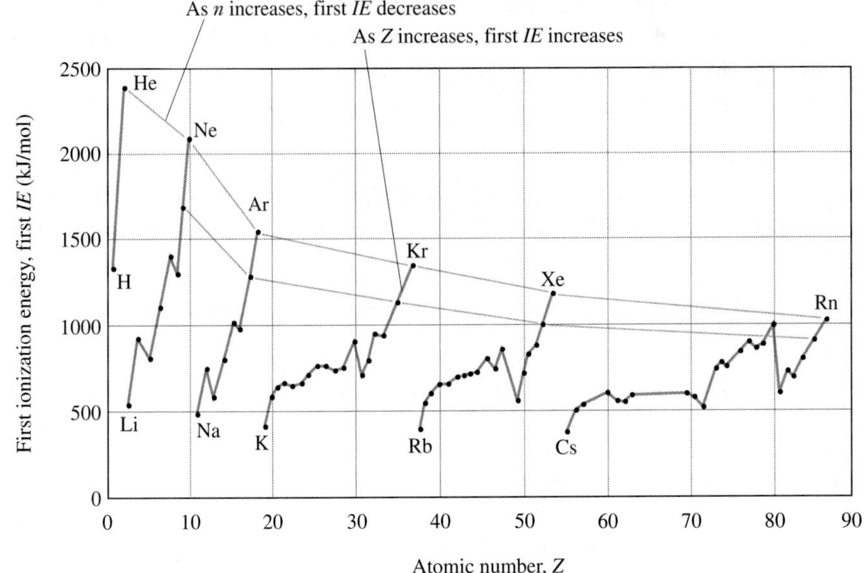

FIGURE 7-25
Variations in the first ionization energy with atomic number. In moving across any main group *(blue lines)* the ionization energy increases. In moving down any column *(yellow lines)* the ionization energy decreases. As the *d* and *f* blocks fill, ionization energy is relatively constant.

HIGHER IONIZATIONS

A multielectron atom can lose more than one electron, but ionization becomes more difficult as cationic charge increases. For example, the first three ionization energies for a magnesium atom in the gas phase follow:

Appendix D gives the first three ionization energies for the first 36 elements.

$Mg_{(g)} \rightarrow Mg^{+}_{(g)} + e^{-}$	$[Ne]\ 3s^2 \rightarrow [Ne]\ 3s^1$	0.738×10^3 kJ/mol
$Mg^{+}_{(g)} \rightarrow Mg^{2+}_{(g)} + e^{-}$	$[Ne]\ 3s^1 \rightarrow [Ne]$	1.45×10^3 kJ/mol
$Mg^{2+}_{(g)} \rightarrow Mg^{3+}_{(g)} + e^{-}$	$[Ne] \rightarrow [He]\ 2s^2\ 2p^5$	7.73×10^3 kJ/mol

Notice that the second ionization energy is almost twice as large as the first, even though both electrons are removed from the 3*s* orbital. This is because Z_{eff} increases as the number of electrons decreases. That is, the positive charge on the magnesium nucleus remains the same throughout the ionization process, but the *net charge* of the electron cloud decreases with each successive ionization. As the number of electrons decreases, each electron feels a greater coulombic attraction to the nucleus, resulting in a larger ionization energy.

The third ionization energy of magnesium is huge in comparison to the first two. In addition to the larger positive charge of the cation, the electron that is removed is a core electron having a lower principal quantum number (2*p* rather than 3*s*). Removing core electrons from any atom requires much more energy than removing valence electrons.

ELECTRON AFFINITY

A neutral atom can be converted to a positive ion by removing an electron. Neutral atoms also can be converted into *negative* ions by *adding* electrons. The energy required to remove an electron from a negative ion is called the **electron affinity.** Ionization energy (IE) and electron affinity (EA) measure the stability of a bound electron. Here, for example, are the values for fluorine:

$$F \rightarrow F^{+} + e^{-} \qquad IE_1 = 1.68 \times 10^3 \text{ kJ/mol}$$
$$F^{-} \rightarrow F + e^{-} \qquad EA = 0.322 \times 10^3 \text{ kJ/mol}$$

By convention, electron affinities refer to the process of removing an electron, just as ionization energies refer to the process of removing an electron. The energy associated with adding an electron to a neutral atom has the opposite sign. Thus for the process, $F + e^{-} \rightarrow F^{-}$, $\Delta E = -322$ kJ/mol.

Energy is required to strip an electron away from a fluoride ion. In other words, fluoride ions are more stable than fluorine atoms. The element fluorine has an affinity for electrons.

The Aufbau principle must be obeyed when an electron is added to a neutral atom, so the electron goes into the most stable orbital available. Hence we expect trends in electron affinity to parallel trends in orbital stability. However, because the roles of electron-electron repulsion and screening are more important for negative ions than for neutral atoms, there is no clear trend in electron affinities as n increases. Thus there is only one general pattern:

> ***Electron affinity tends to increase from left to right across a row of the periodic table.***

The plot in Figure 7-26 shows how electron affinity varies with atomic number. Notice the upward trends in electron affinity, which are indicated by the colored lines, across each row of the periodic table. These upward trends are due to increasing effective nuclear charge, which binds the extra electron more tightly to the nucleus. Notice also that, in contrast to the pattern for ionization energies, values for electron affinities remain nearly constant among elements occupying the same column of the periodic table.

IRREGULARITIES IN ORBITAL STABILITY

Ionization energies and electron affinities deviate somewhat from smooth periodic behavior. These deviations can be attributed to screening effects and electron-electron repulsion. Aluminum, for example, has a lower ionization energy than either of its neighbors in row 3:

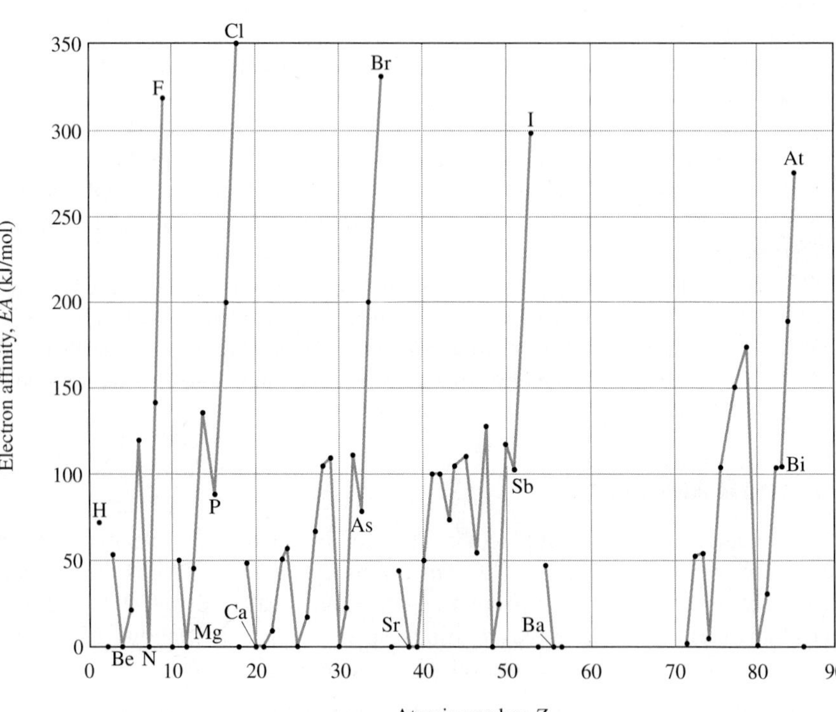

FIGURE 7-26
Variations in electron affinity with atomic number. In moving across any main group *(blue lines)* the electron affinity increases, but this is the only clear trend. Electron affinities vary less regularly than the analogous variations in first ionization energy shown in Figure 7-25.

Element	Z	Atom config.	IE_1(kJ/mol)	Cation config.
Mg	12	[Ne] $3s^2$	735	[Ne] $3s^1$
Al	13	[Ne] $3s^2\ 3p^1$	577	[Ne] $3s^2$
Si	14	[Ne] $3s^2\ 3p^2$	787	[Ne] $3s^2\ 3p^1$

The configurations of these elements show that a 3*s* electron must be removed to ionize magnesium, whereas a 3*p* electron must be removed to ionize aluminum or silicon. Screening makes the 3*s* orbital significantly more stable than a 3*p* orbital, and this difference in stability more than offsets the increase in nuclear charge in going from magnesium to aluminum.

As another example, nitrogen has a lower electron affinity than either of its neighbors in row 2:

2*p*
2*s*
N
2*p*
2*s*
N^-

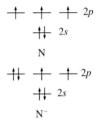

Element	Z	Atom config.	EA (kJ/mol)	Anion config.
C	6	$1s^2\ 2s^2\ 2p^2$	122	$1s^2\ 2s^2\ 2p^3$
N	7	$1s^2\ 2s^2\ 2p^3$	< 0	$1s^2\ 2s^2\ 2p^4$
O	8	$1s^2\ 2s^2\ 2p^4$	141	$1s^2\ 2s^2\ 2p^5$

Electron affinity generally increases across a row because progressively higher nuclear charge makes the orbitals more stable. Making an anion out of a nitrogen atom, however, requires pairing two electrons in one of the *p* orbitals. The increased nuclear charge on moving from carbon to nitrogen is not enough to overcome the coulombic repulsion generated by confining two electrons in one *p* orbital. Consequently, neutral nitrogen atoms are more stable than N^- anions.

Forming an anion from an oxygen atom also requires pairing electrons in a *p* orbital, but for oxygen the destabilization caused by electron-electron repulsion is offset by the progressive increase in nuclear charge. In other words, increasing nuclear charge from 6 to 7 (C $\rightarrow$ N) is not enough to overcome electron-electron repulsion, but increasing *Z* from 6 to 8 (C $\rightarrow$ O) does provide enough orbital stabilization to make electron pairing favorable. Keep in mind, as well, that screening does not increase as we add electrons to the *p* orbitals.

ISOELECTRONIC SERIES

In Section 7-4, we pointed out that the neon atom, the F^- anion, and the Na^+ cation are isoelectronic, each with 10 electrons in the configuration [He] $2s^2\ 2p^6$. Properties change regularly with *Z* across an isoelectronic series, reflecting changes in *Z* without corresponding changes in the number of electrons. Table 7-4 shows, for example, that the ionic radius shows a regular decrease and the difficulty of removing an electron shows a regular increase with *Z* for the 10-electron isoelectronic series.

TABLE 7-4 TRENDS IN AN ISOELECTRONIC SERIES

SPECIES	O^{2-}	F^-	Ne	Na^+	Mg^{2+}
Z	8	9	10	11	12
Radius (pm)	140	136	*	95	65
Energy (kJ/mol)	< 0 (EA_2)	322 (EA)	2100 (IE_1)	4560 (IE_2)	7730 (IE_3)

* Radii of neutral atoms cannot be measured by the same methods used for ionic species.

SECTION EXERCISES

7.6.1 Explain the following observations, using variations in Z, Z_{eff}, and $\boldsymbol{n}$:
- (a) Chlorine has a higher ionization energy than aluminum.
- (b) Chlorine has a higher ionization energy than bromine.
- (c) Strontium is larger than magnesium.
- (d) Cl^- is larger than K^+.
- (e) The first electron affinity of oxygen is positive, but the second is negative.

7.6.2 Use periodic properties to explain the following observations:
- (a) Niobium and indium have nearly the same atomic size.
- (b) The first ionization energy of gallium is significantly lower than that of zinc.
- (c) Manganese has a negative electron affinity.

7.6.3 Explain why ionization energy decreases substantially as the configuration changes from $(\boldsymbol{n})p^6$ to $(\boldsymbol{n})p^6(\boldsymbol{n} + 1)s^1$.

7.7 ENERGETICS OF IONIC COMPOUNDS

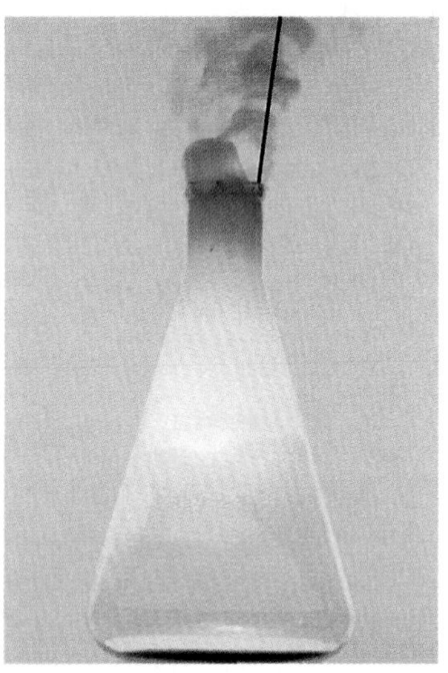

FIGURE 7-27
Sodium and chlorine react vigorously and spontaneously to form sodium chloride. The salt can be seen as the white cloud rising from the flask.

The trends in ionization energies shown in Figure 7-25 and the trends in electron affinities shown in Figure 7-26 indicate that some elements form ions more easily than others. Moreover, we know that ions with opposite charges are attracted to each other. Thus we can visualize some combinations of cations and anions that might be energetically stable. In this section, we perform energy analyses to show which chemical compounds can contain ions.

According to Figure 7-25, column I of the periodic table contains the elements with the lowest ionization energies; and according to Figure 7-26, column VII of the periodic table contains the elements with the highest electron affinities. In other words, it requires less energy to remove an electron from an element from column I than from most other elements, and attaching an electron to an element from column VII releases more energy than attaching an electron to most other elements. Thus reactions between one element from each of these columns are most likely to involve electron transfer.

One example of such a reaction is illustrated in Figure 7-27. It shows that soft, lustrous sodium metal reacts vigorously with yellow-green chlorine gas to form sodium chloride, a white crystalline solid used as common table salt. Sodium chloride contains sodium and chlorine in a 1 : 1 elemental ratio, so its chemical formula is NaCl. We can visualize a crystal of sodium chloride as being made up of equal numbers of Na^+ and Cl^- ions organized in a regular alternating array. Using features of ionization energy, electron affinity, and Coulomb's law, we can analyze the energetics of this reaction to see whether ion formation is favorable.

Remember that the electron affinity is the energy required to *remove* an electron from the negative ion. Attaching an electron to a neutral atom is the reverse of removing that electron from the negative ion. Thus the energy released when an electron becomes *attached* to a neutral atom has the opposite sign as the electron affinity.

Consider a collection of sodium atoms and chlorine atoms in the gas phase. To convert the atoms into ions, each sodium atom must transfer its valence electron to a chlorine atom. Ionizing sodium atoms requires an input of energy:

$$Na_{(g)} \rightarrow Na^+_{(g)} + e^- \qquad \Delta E = IE = 495.5 \text{ kJ/mol}$$

A smaller amount of energy is released when electrons become attached to chlorine atoms:

$$Cl_{(g)} + e^- \rightarrow Cl^-_{(g)} \qquad \Delta E = -EA = -348.5 \text{ kJ/mol}$$

The sum of these two energies shows that free sodium cations and chloride anions are less stable by 147.0 kJ/mol than free neutral gaseous atoms:

$$Na_{(g)} + Cl_{(g)} \rightarrow Na^+_{(g)} + Cl^-_{(g)}$$

$$\Delta E = [495.5 \text{ kJ} + (-348.5 \text{ kJ})] = 147.0 \text{ kJ}$$

We know, however, that oppositely charged species attract one another. Using Coulomb's law, we can calculate the energy released when sodium and chloride ions combine to form $Na^+ - Cl^-$ ion pairs. Recall that coulombic energy depends on the charges on the ions and the distance between them, as shown in Equation 7-1:

$$E_{coulomb} = \frac{(1.389 \times 10^5 \text{ kJ pm mol}^{-1})(q^+)(q^-)}{d} \quad \textbf{(7-1)}$$

According to Coulomb's law, the force between two charged species is $F = kq_1q_2/r^2$ (Equation 2-2). When two oppositely charged ions approach each other, this force results in the energy of attraction given by Equation 7-1. The numerical value of the constant k depends on the units used for the charges and distance.

In Equation 7-1, q^+ and q^- are the charges on the cation and anion, and d is the distance in picometers between their nuclei. For the sodium chloride ion pair, $q^+ = +1$ and $q^- = -1$. To complete the calculation, we need to know how closely the ions approach each other before their mutual attraction is balanced by electron cloud repulsion. This distance of closest approach is found by measuring the ion-ion distance in the sodium chloride crystal, which turns out to be 283 pm. Using this value for d, we can calculate the energy released in the reaction:

$$Na^+_{(g)} + Cl^-_{(g)} \rightarrow NaCl_{(g)}$$

$$E_{coulomb} = \frac{(1.389 \times 10^5 \text{ kJ pm/mol})(+1)(-1)}{(283 \text{ pm})} = -491 \text{ kJ/mol}$$

Combining all three energy terms shows that the formation of NaCl ion pairs from neutral atoms releases 344 kJ/mol of energy:

$$Na_{(g)} + Cl_{(g)} \rightarrow NaCl_{(g, \text{ ion pair})}$$

$$\Delta E = 495.5 \text{ kJ/mol} + (-348.5 \text{ kJ/mol}) + (-491 \text{ kJ/mol}) = -344 \text{ kJ/mol}$$

↑	↑	↑
IE of Na	EA of Cl	Energy released in forming ion pairs

The actual reaction of sodium metal with diatomic chlorine gas to give crystalline sodium chloride involves three additional energy terms. First, energy must be supplied to vaporize metallic sodium. Second, energy must also be supplied to break chlorine molecules into atoms. Third, considerable energy is released when NaCl pairs cluster in a three-dimensional solid array of ions. The energy released in forming the solid exceeds the energy required in the other two steps, so the total energy released in this reaction, 411 kJ/mol, is somewhat larger than that given by our calculations:

$$Na_{(s)} + \tfrac{1}{2} Cl_{2(g)} \rightarrow NaCl_{(s)} \qquad \Delta E = -411 \text{ kJ/mol}$$

Nevertheless, our simplified energy analysis reveals that the main feature of this energy-releasing reaction is the coulombic attraction between ions.

WHY NOT $Na^{2+}Cl^{2-}$?

The coulombic attraction between doubly charged ions is significantly greater than the attraction between singly charged ions because q^+ and q^- are larger. This suggests that the transfer of a second electron might give an even more stable crystal composed of Na^{2+} and Cl^{2-} ions. We can extend our calculation to see if this is true.

According to Equation 7-1, the energy of attraction between Na^{2+} and Cl^{2-} ions in a $Na^{2+}Cl^{2-}$ ion pair would be about 4 times that for a Na^+Cl^- pair, or about 2000 kJ/mol. However, to collect this energy, we must pay the price of forming the doubly charged ions. To form Cl^{2-} from Cl^- requires an energy input because the second electron affinity of chlorine is less than zero. Appendix D provides the first two ionization energies for sodium:

$$Na \rightarrow Na^+ + e^- \qquad 1s^2\,2s^2\,2p^6\,3s^1 \rightarrow 1s^2\,2s^2\,2p^6 \qquad IE_1 = 495.5 \text{ kJ/mol}$$

$$Na^+ \rightarrow Na^{2+} + e^- \qquad 1s^2\,2s^2\,2p^6 \rightarrow 1s^2\,2s^2\,2p^5 \qquad IE_2 = 4.56 \times 10^3 \text{ kJ/mol}$$

Thus forming Na^{2+} and Cl^{2-} from Na^+ and Cl^- requires over 4000 kJ/mol, much more energy than the 2000 kJ/mol released in bringing together a $Na^{2+}Cl^{2-}$ pair.

The second ionization energy of Na is much larger than its first ionization energy because whereas a *valence* 3*s* electron is removed to create Na^+ from Na, a *core* 2*p* electron must be removed to create Na^{2+} from Na^+. Removal of a core electron always requires a great deal of energy, so it is a general feature of ionic systems that ions formed by removing core electrons are not found in stable ionic compounds.

CATION STABILITY

Ionization energies determine which cations will be stable. For example, our comparison of ionization energies with coulombic energies shows that Na^+ ions can be stable, but Na^{2+} ions cannot. Tables of ionization energies such as the one in Appendix D provide exact values for quantitative calculations, but a knowledge of ground-state configurations is all that we need to make qualitative predictions about cation stability. Knowing that the energy cost of removing core electrons is always excessive, we can predict where the ionization process will stop.

All elements in column I of the periodic table have a single valence electron. These elements are most stable in ionic compounds containing M^+ cations. Examples are KCl and Na_2CO_3. All elements in column II of the periodic table have two valence electrons and are most stable in ionic compounds containing M^{2+} cations. Examples are $CaCO_3$ and $MgCl_2$.

Beyond these two columns the removal of all valence electrons is usually not energetically feasible, and actual values of ionization energies must be consulted. For example, iron has eight valence electrons but forms only two stable cations, Fe^{2+} and Fe^{3+}. Although the third ionization energy of iron (2.96×10^3 kJ/mol) is much greater than its second ionization energy (1.56×10^3 kJ/mol), it is considerably less than the energy required to remove the first core electron of sodium (4.56×10^3 kJ/mol). Consequently, Fe^{2+} and Fe^{3+} ions can be stable in ionic compounds. Compounds of iron containing both these ions are abundant in the Earth's crust. Iron(II) sulfide (FeS) and iron(II) carbonate ($FeCO_3$, or siderite) are examples of Fe^{2+} salts. Iron(III) oxide (Fe_2O_3, or hematite) contains Fe^{3+} ions. One of the most abundant iron ores, magnetite, has the chemical formula Fe_3O_4 and contains a 2:1 ratio of Fe^{3+} and Fe^{2+} cations. The formula of magnetite can also be written as $FeO{\cdot}Fe_2O_3$ to emphasize the presence of two different cations.

Other metallic elements form ionic compounds that contain cations with charges ranging from +1 to +3. Aluminum oxide (Al_2O_3), the ore from which aluminum metal is extracted, can be viewed as a lattice made up of Al^{3+} cations and O^{2-} anions. Silver(I) nitrate ($AgNO_3$), which contains Ag^+ cations, is a soluble silver salt that can be used in silver plating.

ANION STABILITY

Halogens, the elements in column VII of the periodic table, have the largest electron affinities of all the elements, so halogen atoms ($s^2\,p^5$) readily accept electrons to give halide anions ($s^2\,p^6$). As a result, fluoride, chloride, bromide, and iodide anions are all found commonly in ionic crystals.

Gaseous atomic anions with negative charges greater than −1 are always unstable, but oxide (O^{2-}, [He] $2s^2\,2p^6$ configuration) and sulfide (S^{2-}, [Ne] $3s^2\,3p^6$ configuration) are found in many ionic solids, including CaO and FeS. In these crystals the dianions are stabilized because they are surrounded by cations in a three-dimensional solid array.

The ionic model works well for metal halides, oxides, and sulfides, but it does not adequately describe most other chemical substances. Whereas compounds such as CaO, NaCl, and MgF_2 behave like simple cations and anions held together by coulombic attraction, compounds such as CO, Cl_2, and HF do not. In a crystal of CaO, electrons have been *transferred* from calcium atoms to oxygen atoms, but the stability of CO molecules arises from the *sharing* of electrons between carbon atoms and oxygen atoms. Electron sharing, which is central to molecular stability, is described in Chapters 8 and 9.

SECTION EXERCISES

7.7.1 CaO has a crystal spacing of 238 pm, and the second electron affinity for O is estimated to be −780 kJ/mol. Use these values and data from Appendix D to calculate the energy released in forming $Ca^{2+}O^{2-}_{(g)}$ from gaseous atoms of the elements.

7.7.2 Use the table of ionization energies in Appendix D to predict which transition metal elements other than iron are likely to form stable cations with charges greater than +2.

7.7.3 From the location of each element in the periodic table, predict which ion of each of the following elements will be found in ionic compounds: Ca, Cs, Al, and Br.

7.8 IONS AND CHEMICAL PERIODICITY

In Section 7.7 we explored the formation of ionic salts. The elements that form ionic salts are found in specific places in the periodic table. Atomic anions in compounds are restricted to the halogens and their close neighbors on the right side of the table, oxygen and sulfur. Atomic cations in compounds, on the other hand, can form from all elements in the *s, d,* and *f* blocks.

Ion formation is only one pattern of chemical behavior. Although we must wait until we have presented more information about chemical bonding to explain other periodic properties, all chemical trends can be traced ultimately to valence electron configurations. Meanwhile, we can describe some patterns in chemical behavior that can be attributed directly to the formation of ions.

Aluminum, copper, and iron are typical metals.

METALS AND NONMETALS

Figure 7-28 shows how the periodic table can be divided into three classes of elements based on their chemical behavior. All of the elements in the *s, d,* and *f* blocks, plus a few from the *p* block, can be classified as **metals.** Most elements in the *p* block show quite different chemical properties and are classified as **nonmetals.** A diagonal region at the boundary between these two classes contains the elements called **metalloids,** which behave in a manner intermediate between the behaviors of metals and nonmetals.

In their pure elemental form, metals such as aluminum, iron, and copper are shiny solids that are good conductors of heat and electricity. They can be formed into a variety of shapes by melting and casting, hammering, and rolling. Metals are not very reactive toward other metals, but they form many compounds with nonmetals. These compounds are often ionic salts that may contain polyatomic anions. Examples are CuS (copper(II) sulfide), NaOH (sodium hydroxide), Al_2O_3 (aluminum oxide), $MgSO_4{\cdot}7H_2O$ (magnesium sulfate heptahydrate, commonly known as *Epsom salts*), and KNO_3 (potassium nitrate).

Nonmetals such as bromine, iodine, sulfur, and phosphorus have different characteristic appearances from the metals.

In their elemental forms, nonmetals display a range of properties, but none act like metals. The nonmetals in column VIII of the periodic table, called the **rare gases,** are monatomic gases that resist chemical attack. Other nonmetallic elements—fluorine, chlorine, oxygen, nitrogen, and hydrogen—exist normally as diatomic gases, whereas bromine is a diatomic liquid and iodine is a diatomic solid under normal conditions. Sulfur and phosphorus are solids, but they lack the characteristics of metallic solids. They are not shiny, for instance, and they do not conduct electricity.

Unlike metals, nonmetals are reactive toward one another, forming both binary compounds and polyatomic species that are not ionic in nature. A few examples are CO_2 (carbon dioxide), NH_3 (ammonia), H_2SO_4 (sulfuric acid), CCl_4 (carbon tetrachloride), CH_3CO_2H (acetic acid, found in vinegar), and C_8H_{18} (octane, a component of gasoline).

The metalloids are a group of elements with properties intermediate between those of metals and nonmetals. These elements—B, Si, Ge, As, Sb, and Te—lie between the metals and the nonmetals in the periodic table. One of the most striking

The metalloids do not look like metals, but they have properties that are intermediate between those of metals and nonmetals.

																1 H	2 He
3 Li	4 Be											5 B	6 C	7 N	8 O	9 F	10 Ne
11 Na	12 Mg											13 Al	14 Si	15 P	16 S	17 Cl	18 Ar
19 K	20 Ca	21 Sc	22 Ti	23 V	24 Cr	25 Mn	26 Fe	27 Co	28 Ni	29 Cu	30 Zn	31 Ga	32 Ge	33 As	34 Se	35 Br	36 Kr
37 Rb	38 Sr	39 Y	40 Zr	41 Nb	42 Mo	43 Tc	44 Ru	45 Rh	46 Pd	47 Ag	48 Cd	49 In	50 Sn	51 Sb	52 Te	53 I	54 Xe
55 Cs	56 Ba	71 Lu	72 Hf	73 Ta	74 W	75 Re	76 Os	77 Ir	78 Pt	79 Au	80 Hg	81 Tl	82 Pb	83 Bi	84 Po	85 At	86 Rn
87 Fr	88 Ra	103 Lr	104 Unq	105 Unp	106 Unh	107 Uns	108 Uno	109 Une									

57 La	58 Ce	59 Pr	60 Nd	61 Pm	62 Sm	63 Eu	64 Gd	65 Tb	66 Dy	67 Ho	68 Er	69 Tm	70 Yb
89 Ac	90 Th	91 Pa	92 U	93 Np	94 Pu	95 Am	96 Cm	97 Bk	98 Cf	99 Es	100 Fm	101 Md	102 No

Metals Nonmetals Metalloids

FIGURE 7-28

The periodic table can be divided into three regions: the metals, the nonmetals, and the boundary region of metalloids.

features of the metalloids is their electrical conductivity. Whereas metals are good conductors of electricity and nonmetals are normally nonconductors, metalloids can be switched from nonconductors to conductors by slight changes in conditions. For this reason the metalloids are also called *semiconductors.* We explore semiconductors in more detail in Chapter 9.

Polonium (Po) and astatine (At) are unstable elements whose chemical properties have not been fully characterized. Although their positions in the periodic table indicate that they may behave as metalloids, polonium forms a metallic lattice, whereas astatine is predicted to resemble iodine in its properties. Thus we classify Po as a metal and At as a nonmetal.

One reason that all the metals have similar properties is that all have outlying *s* electrons that are relatively easy to ionize. The elements in the *s* block all have s^1 or s^2 valence configurations. In the *d* block, all elements except palladium also have one or two *s* electrons, with varying numbers of *d* electrons. For example, the valence configuration of titanium is $4s^2\ 3d^2$, and that of silver is $5s^1\ 4d^{10}$. Elements in the *f* block have two *s* electrons and a number of *f* electrons of lower principal quantum number. For example, the valence configuration of samarium is $6s^2\ 4f^6$. In pure metals, as we describe later, these *s* electrons are shared readily among all atoms, whereas in ionic salts, *s, d,* and/or *f* electrons have been removed from the metal atoms to form cations.

Elemental properties vary widely within the *p* block. Elements toward the left and/or bottom of the *p* block have metallic properties because they can lose electrons easily. Examples are aluminum ($3s^2\ 3p^1$), tin ($5s^2\ 5p^2$), and bismuth ($6s^2\ 6p^3$). In contrast, the elements toward the right, for example, the halogens and noble gases, are distinctly nonmetallic. Within the *p* block, elements with the same valence configuration can have very different chemical properties. Carbon, silicon, germanium, and tin all have s^2p^2 valence configurations; yet carbon is a nonmetal, silicon and germanium are metalloids, and tin is a metal.

Qualitatively, we can understand this variation by recalling that as the principal quantum number increases, the valence orbitals become less stable. In tin the four $n = 5$ valence electrons are bound loosely to the atom, resulting in the metallic properties associated with electrons that are easily removed. In carbon the four $n = 2$ valence electrons are much more tightly bound to the atom, resulting in nonmetallic behavior. Silicon ($n = 3$) and germanium ($n = 4$) fall in between these two extremes. Sample Problem 7-8 describes the elements with five valence electrons.

SAMPLE PROBLEM 7-8 CLASSIFYING ELEMENTS

Nitrogen is a colorless diatomic gas. Phosphorus has several different elemental forms, but the most common is a red solid that is used for matches. Arsenic and antimony are grey solids, and bismuth is a lustrous solid. Classify these elements of Column V as metals, nonmetals, or metalloids.

METHOD: We know that all elements except those in the *p* block are metals. Group V, however, falls in the *p* block, with the $s^2\ p^3$ valence configuration. We must examine its position relative to the diagonal arrangement of the metalloids.

III	IV	V	VI	VII	VIII
		N		Non-metals	
		P			
		As			
		Sb			
Metals		Bi			

We see that this column cuts across all three classes of elements. The elements with lowest Z values, nitrogen and phosphorus, are nonmetals. The element with highest Z value, bismuth, is a metal, and the two elements with intermediate Z values, arsenic and antimony, are metalloids.

s-BLOCK ELEMENTS

The electronic configuration of any element in columns I and II of the periodic table contains a core of tightly bound electrons and one or two *s* electrons that are rather loosely bound. These are the **alkali metals** (column I, s^1 configuration) and the **alkaline earth metals** (column II, s^2 configuration). These elements form very stable ionic salts because their valence electrons are easily removed. Nearly all salts of alkali metals and many salts of alkaline earth metals dissolve readily in water, so naturally occurring sources of water frequently contain these ions.

Beryllium behaves differently from the other *s*-block elements. Because its first ionization energy of 899 kJ/mol is comparable with those of nonmetals, beryllium does not form compounds that are clearly ionic.

The four most abundant *s*-block elements in the Earth's crust are sodium, potassium, magnesium, and calcium, whose occurrence is summarized in Table 7-5. These elements are found in nature as salts such as NaCl, KNO_3, $MgCl_2$, $MgCO_3$ and $CaCO_3$. Portions of these solid salts dissolve in rainwater as it percolates through the Earth's crust. The resulting solution of anions and cations eventually finds its way to the oceans. When water evaporates from the oceans, the ions are left behind. Over many eons the continual influx of fresh water containing these ions has built up the substantial salt levels found in the Earth's oceans.

Table 7-5 shows that each of the four common *s*-block ions are found in body fluids, too. There they play essential biochemical roles. Sodium is the most abundant cation in blood and other fluids that are outside of cells, and proper functioning of body cells requires that sodium concentrations be maintained within a very narrow range. One of the main functions of the kidneys is to control the excretion of sodium. Whereas sodium cations are abundant in the fluids *outside* of cells, potassium cations are the most abundant ions in the fluids *inside* cells. The difference in ion concentration across cell walls is responsible for the generation of nerve impulses that drive muscle contraction. If the difference in potassium ion concentration across cell walls deteriorates, muscular activity, including the regular muscle contractions of the heart, can be seriously disrupted.

The cations Mg^{2+} and Ca^{2+} are major components of bones. Although the structural form of magnesium in bones is not fully understood, calcium is known to occur as hydroxyapatite, a complicated ionic substance whose chemical formula is $Ca_5(PO_4)_3(OH)$. In addition to being essential ingredients of bone, these two divalent

TABLE 7-5 ABUNDANCE OF *s*-BLOCK ELEMENTS

ELEMENT	CRUSTAL ABUNDANCE (% by mass)	ABUNDANCE IN SEAWATER (mol/L)	ABUNDANCE IN PLASMA (mol/L)
Na	2.27	0.462	0.142
K	1.84	0.097	0.005
Mg	2.76	0.053	0.003
Ca	4.66	0.100	0.005

TABLE 7-6 INDUSTRIAL CHEMICALS AMONG THE TOP 50 THAT CONTAIN *s*-BLOCK ELEMENTS

NAME	FORMULA	RANK (1992)	PRODUCTION (BILLION KG)	USES
Lime	CaO	6	15.8	Cement, fertilizer, paper
Sodium hydroxide	$NaOH$	8	10.9	Industrial chemicals, detergents
Sodium carbonate	Na_2CO_3	11	9.50	Glass, industrial chemicals
Potash	K_2CO_3	33	1.71	Fertilizer
Sodium silicate	Na_2SiO_3	45	0.82	Detergents
Calcium chloride	$CaCl_2$	47	0.63	Various
Sodium sulfate	Na_2SO_4	49	0.61	Detergents

cations also play key roles in various biochemical reactions, including the transmission of nerve impulses, photosynthesis, and the formation of blood clots.

Table 7-6 shows that compounds of the *s*-block elements are important industrial chemicals, too. For example, almost 4 billion pounds of potash (K_2CO_3) are produced in the United States each year. This compound, which is obtained from mineral deposits, is the most common source of potassium for fertilizers. Fertilization with potassium is necessary because this element is essential for healthy plant growth. Moreover, potassium salts are highly soluble in water, so potassium quickly becomes depleted from the soil. Consequently, agricultural land requires frequent addition of potassium fertilizers.

Three other compounds of *s*-block elements—lime (CaO), sodium hydroxide ($NaOH$), and sodium carbonate (Na_2CO_3)—are among the top 15 industrial chemicals in annual production. Lime, in fact, is perennially in the top 10 because it is the key ingredient in construction materials such as concrete, cement, mortar, and plaster.

Many industrial processes make use of chemically useful anions such as hydroxide (OH^-), carbonate (CO_3^{2-}), and chlorate (ClO_3^-). These anions must be supplied as chemical compounds that include a cation. Sodium is most frequently used as this "spectator" cation because it is abundant, inexpensive, and nontoxic. Sodium hydroxide is used to manufacture other chemicals, textiles, paper, soaps, and detergents. Hydroxide ion is industrially important because it is a strong base. Sodium carbonate and sand are the major starting materials in the manufacture of glass. Glass contains sodium and other cations embedded in a matrix of silicate (SiO_3^{2-}) anions. About half the sodium carbonate produced in the world is used in glass making.

SECTION EXERCISES

7.8.1 Consult the table of first ionization energies in Appendix D and calculate the average values for the nonmetals, metalloids, and *s*-block elements. How does the trend in these averages relate to the ionic chemistry of these elements?

7.8.2 Classify each of the following elements as a metal, nonmetal, or metalloid: S, Si, Sr, Se, Sc, and Sn.

CHAPTER SUMMARY

1. The energy, orbital shape, spatial orientation, and spin orientation of electrons in atoms are quantized, and quantum numbers $\boldsymbol{n}$, $\boldsymbol{l}$, $\boldsymbol{m_l}$, and $\boldsymbol{m_s}$ are used to designate the allowed values of these properties. Each quantum number can take on a restricted set of values.
2. Orbital shapes are depicted by plots, electron density maps, and contour diagrams.
3. Orbital size depends on $\boldsymbol{n}$, whereas shape depends on $\boldsymbol{l}$. Orbital energies depend on $\boldsymbol{n}$, Z, and, through screening generated by the presence of other electrons, $\boldsymbol{l}$.
4. According to the Aufbau principle, electrons fill the most stable orbitals available. The Pauli exclusion principle states that no two electrons have the same quantum numbers, and Hund's rule requires that electron spin is maximized for partly filled orbitals.
5. Chemical behavior is determined by the outermost, valence electrons. Elements in the same column of the periodic table share chemical properties because they have the same number of valence electrons. Atomic size, ionization energy, and electron affinity all show systematic periodic variations with $\boldsymbol{n}$ and Z.
6. Ionic compounds form between metals and halogens, oxygen, or sulfur.
7. The elements can be classified as metals, nonmetals, and metalloids.

KEY TERMS

azimuthal quantum number ($\boldsymbol{l}$)
electron contour drawing
magnetic quantum number ($\boldsymbol{m_l}$)
orbital density picture
principal quantum number ($\boldsymbol{n}$)
quantum number
spin orientation quantum number ($\boldsymbol{m_s}$)

electron affinity
effective nuclear charge (Z_{eff})
ionization energy (IE)
orbital interaction
photoelectron spectroscopy
screening

Aufbau principle
core electron
degenerate orbital
diamagnetic

electron configuration
filled shell configuration
ground-state configuration
Hund's rule
isoelectronic
near-degenerate orbital
paired electrons
paramagnetic
Pauli exclusion principle
valence electron

alkali metal
alkaline earth metal
metalloid
metal
nonmetal
rare gas

SKILLS TO MASTER

- Determining sets of quantum numbers
- Drawing shapes of *s*, *p*, and *d* orbitals
- Arranging orbitals in order of energy
- Writing electron configurations for atoms and ions
- Recognizing the effects of near-degenerate orbitals
- Correlating configurations with periodicity
- Counting valence electrons
- Predicting periodic variations in properties
- Calculating ionic stabilities

LEARNING EXERCISES

7.1 Write a chapter summary of two pages or less that outlines the important features of this chapter.

7.2 Draw appropriately scaled pictures of each of the occupied orbitals in a krypton atom.

7.3 Provide brief explanations of (a) screening; (b) Pauli exclusion principle; (c) Aufbau principle; (d) Hund's rule; (e) degeneracy; and (f) valence electrons.

7.4 Construct an orbital energy level diagram for all orbitals with $\boldsymbol{n} < 8$ and $\boldsymbol{l} < 4$. Use the mnemonic filling order to help determine the correct order of the energy levels.

7.5 Describe patterns in periodic properties; explain how they affect ionization energy and electron affinity.

7.6 List all the elements classified as nonmetals. Your list should contain 18 elements. Give the name, symbol, and atomic number for each.

7.7 Update your list of "memory bank" equations by adding "memory bank" principles for atomic configurations.

7.8 List all terms new to you that appear in Chapter 7. Write a one-sentence definition of each, using your own words. Consult the glossary if you need help.

PROBLEMS

QUANTUM NUMBERS

7.1 List all the valid sets of quantum numbers for a $6p$ electron.

7.2 List all the valid sets of quantum numbers for a $4f$ electron.

7.3 If an electron has $\boldsymbol{n} = 3$, list the restrictions on its other quantum numbers.

7.4 If an electron has $\boldsymbol{m}_l = -2$, list the restrictions on its other quantum numbers.

7.5 For the following sets of quantum numbers, determine which describe actual orbitals and which are nonexistent. For each one that is nonexistent, list the restriction that forbids it:

	n	l	m_l	m_s
(a)	5	3	−2	−1
(b)	5	3	−3	$\frac{1}{2}$
(c)	3	3	−3	$\frac{1}{2}$
(d)	3	0	0	$-\frac{1}{2}$

7.6 For the following sets of quantum numbers, determine which describe actual orbitals and which are nonexistent. For each one that is nonexistent, list the restriction that forbids it:

	n	l	m_l	m_s
(a)	3	−1	−1	$\frac{1}{2}$
(b)	3	1	−1	$-\frac{1}{2}$
(c)	3	1	2	$\frac{1}{2}$
(d)	3	2	2	$\frac{3}{2}$

SHAPES OF ATOMIC ORBITALS

7.7 Draw an electron contour surface of an orbital that corresponds to each of the following sets of quantum numbers. Be sure to include coordinate axes and indicate areas of the orbital where the wave equation has opposite signs. (a) $\boldsymbol{n} = 2$, $\boldsymbol{l} = 1$, $\boldsymbol{m}_l = -1$, $\boldsymbol{m}_s = +\frac{1}{2}$; (b) $\boldsymbol{n} = 2$, $\boldsymbol{l} = 0$, $\boldsymbol{m}_l = 0$, $\boldsymbol{m}_s = -\frac{1}{2}$; (c) $\boldsymbol{n} = 3$, $\boldsymbol{l} = 0$, $\boldsymbol{m}_l = 0$, $\boldsymbol{m}_s = +\frac{1}{2}$; (d) $\boldsymbol{n} = 3$, $\boldsymbol{l} = 2$, $\boldsymbol{m}_l = -2$, $\boldsymbol{m}_s = -\frac{1}{2}$.

7.8 Identify each of the following orbitals, and give a valid set of quantum numbers for each. (HINT: Use the size of the $3s$ orbital to identify the other three.)

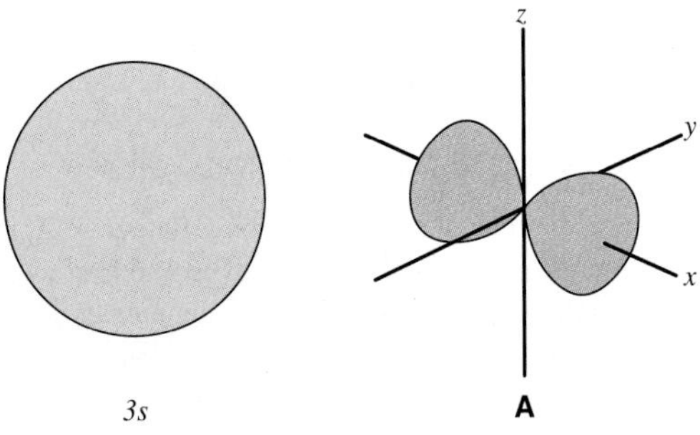

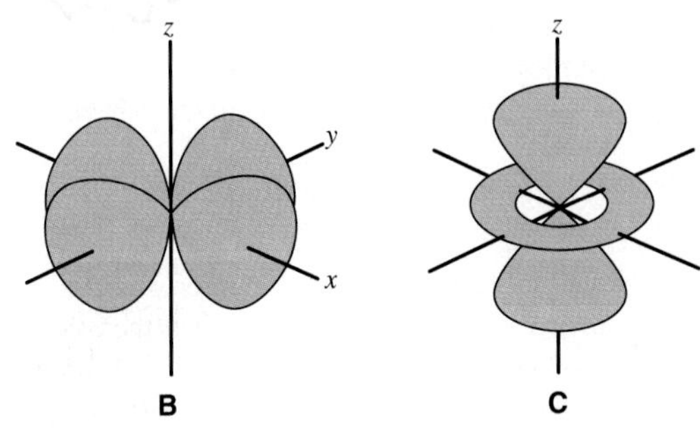

7.9 Shown below are orbital density plots and Ψ^2 vs. r plots for the $1s$, $2s$, $2p$, and $3p$ orbitals. Assign the various depictions to their respective orbitals.

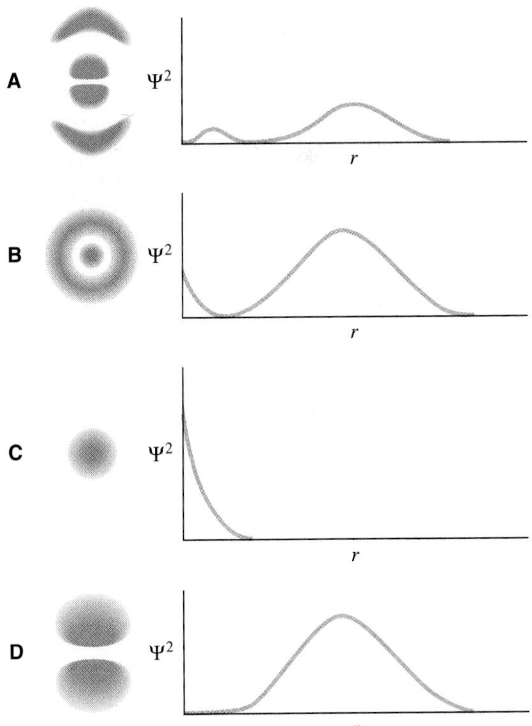

7.10 The conventional method of showing the three-dimensional shape of an orbital is an electron contour surface. What are the limitations of this representation?

7.11 Redraw the plots in Figure 7-7 as Ψ vs. r plots. (Concentrate on qualitative, not quantitative, features.)

7.12 Draw contour plots for the orbitals graphed in Figure 7-7.

ORBITAL ENERGIES

7.13 For each pair of orbitals, choose which is more stable and explain why: (a) He $1s$ and He $2s$; (b) Kr $5p$ and Kr $6p$; (c) He $2s$ and He^+ $2s$; and (d) Ar $4s$ and Ar $4p$.

7.14 Write a one-sentence explanation for each of the following:
(a) In a hydrogen atom the 2*s* and 2*p* orbitals have identical energy.
(b) In a helium atom the 2*s* and 2*p* orbitals have different energies.
(c) All three 2*p* orbitals of a helium atom have identical energy.
(d) The 2*p* orbital in He has nearly the same energy as the 2*p* orbital in H.

7.15 In a hydrogen atom the 3*s*, 3*p*, and 3*d* orbitals all have the same energy. In a helium atom, however, the 3*s* orbital is lower in energy than the 3*p* orbital, which, in turn, is lower in energy than the 3*d* orbital. Explain why the energy rankings of hydrogen and helium are different.

7.16 Refer to Table 7-2 to answer the following questions. In each case, provide a one-sentence explanation.
(a) Which ionization energies show that an electron in a 1*s* orbital provides nearly complete screening of an electron in a 2*p* orbital?
(b) Which ionization energies show that the stability of $n = 2$ orbitals increases with Z^2?
(c) Which ionization energies show that an electron in a 1*s* orbital incompletely screens another electron in the same orbital?

ELECTRON CONFIGURATIONS

7.17 List a set of values of the quantum numbers for electrons in the ground-state configurations of Be, O, Ne, and P.

7.18 For the atoms in Problem 7.17 for which there is more than one set of quantum numbers, list all other possibilities.

7.19 The following are hypothetical configurations for a Be atom. Which use nonexistent orbitals, which are Pauli forbidden, which are excited states, and which is the ground-state configuration: (a) $1s^3\,2s^1$; (b) $1s^1\,2s^3$; (c) $1s^1\,2p^3$; (d) $1s^2\,2s^1\,2p^1$; (e) $1s^2\,2s^2$; (f) $1s^2\,1p^2$; and (g) $1s^2\,2s^1\,2d^1$.

7.20 None of the following hypothetical configurations describes the ground state of an F atom. For each, state the reason why it is not correct: (a) $1s^2\,2s^2\,2p^4$; (b) $1s^2\,2s^1\,2p^6$; (c) $1s^3\,2s^2\,2p^4$; and (d) $1s^2\,2s^2\,1p^5$.

7.21 In their ground states, Mo has higher spin than Tc. Construct energy level diagrams for the valence electrons showing how electron configurations account for this.

7.22 Use the periodic table to find and list (a) all elements whose ground-state configurations indicate near-degeneracy of the 5*s* and 4*d* orbitals; (b) two adjacent elements whose configurations indicate near-degeneracy of the 6*s*, 5*d*, and 4*f* orbitals; and (c) three elements in the same column that have different valence configurations.

7.23 Which of the atoms of Problem 7.17 are paramagnetic? Draw orbital energy level diagrams to support your answer.

7.24 For fluorine, how many excited-state configurations are there in which no electron has $n > 2$? Write all of them.

7.25 For nitrogen, how many excited-state configurations are there in which no electron has $n > 2$? Write all of them.

THE PERIODIC TABLE

7.26 Draw the periodic table in block form, and outline and label each of the following sets: (a) elements having $n = 1$; (b) elements for which the 5*f* orbitals are filling; (c) elements with $s^2\,p^4$ configurations; and (d) elements with filled *s* orbitals but empty *p* orbitals.

7.27 Draw the periodic table in block form, and outline and label each of the following sets: (a) elements one electron short of filled *p* orbitals; (b) elements for which $n = 3$ orbitals are filling; (c) elements with half-filled *d* orbitals; and (d) the first element that contains a 5*s* electron.

7.28 Determine the atomic number and valence configuration of the element below francium in the periodic table.

7.29 Predict the ground-state configuration of element 111.

PERIODICITY OF ATOMIC PROPERTIES

7.30 Arrange the following atoms in order of increasing size (largest last): Cl, F, P, and S.

7.31 Arrange the following atoms in order of decreasing first ionization energy (smallest last): Ar, Cl, Cs, and K.

7.32 One element has the following ionization energies and electron affinity (all in kJ/mol): $IE_1 = 502.8$, $IE_2 = 965$, $IE_3 = 3.60 \times 10^3$, $EA = -46$. In what column of the periodic table is this element found? Give your reasoning.

7.33 According to Appendix D, each of the following elements has a negative electron affinity. For each one, construct its valence orbital energy level diagram and use it to explain why its anion is unstable: Be, N, Mg, Ar, and Zn.

7.34 Use electron-electron repulsion and orbital energies to explain these irregularities in first ionization energies:
(a) Boron has a lower ionization energy than beryllium.
(b) Sulfur has a lower ionization energy than phosphorus.

7.35 List the species that are isoelectronic with Br^- and have net charges (absolute values) that are less than 4 units. Arrange these in order of increasing size.

ENERGETICS OF IONIC COMPOUNDS

7.36 Use periodic trends and the electron affinities in Appendix D to list the elements you would expect to find as atomic anions with −1 or −2 charge in ionic compounds.

7.37 Given the following data, estimate the energy released when $K^+I^-_{(g)}$ forms from gaseous atoms:

Element	EA (kJ/mol)	IE_1 (kJ/mol)	IE_2 (kJ/mol)	Radius (pm)
K	48.4	418.8	3051	133 (cation)
I	295.3	1008.4	1845.9	220 (anion)

7.38 Repeat the calculation in Problem 7.37 for $K^{2+}I^{2-}_{(g)}$, using −500 kJ/mol as the second electron affinity of iodine and assuming no change in distance of closest approach.

7.39 From the following list, select the elements that would form ionic compounds: Ca, C, Cu, Cs, Cl, and Cr. Indicate whether the element forms a stable cation or a stable anion.

7.40 Which form ionic compounds: B, Ba, Be, Bi, and Br? Indicate whether each forms a stable cation or anion.

IONS AND CHEMICAL PERIODICITY

7.41 Use the underlying patterns of periodicity to explain why elements on the left lower edges of the *p* block show metallic character.

7.42 We list polonium as a metal, but some chemists classify it as a metalloid. List other metals that might be expected to show properties in between those of metals and metalloids.

7.43 Classify each of the elements from column VI of the periodic table as a metal, a nonmetal, or a metalloid.

7.44 Classify each of the elements listed in Problem 7.39 as a metal, a nonmetal, or a metalloid.

ADDITIONAL PROBLEMS

7.45 How many sets of quantum number values are there for a 4*p* electron?

7.46 Write the correct electron configuration for the Fe^{3+} ground state, and give a correct set of quantum numbers for all electrons in the least stable occupied orbital.

7.47 List all sets of quantum number values for a 4*d* electron.

7.48 Arrange the following in order of increasing ionization energy: N, O, Ne, Na, and Na^+.

7.49 What would be the next two orbitals to fill after 7*p*?

7.50 How many valence electrons does each of the following atoms have? H, Cs, Ca, Ge, Br, and Xe.

7.51 Which has the most unpaired electrons, S^+, S, or S^-? Use electron configurations to support your answer.

7.52 Make a Ψ^2 vs. *r* sketch that shows how the 3*s* and 3*p* orbitals are screened effectively by the 2*p* orbitals. Provide a brief explanation of your plot.

7.53 Explain why the oceans are "salty" but rivers and lakes are "fresh."

7.54 Which has a larger radius, Rb or Br? What about Rb^+ and Br^-? Explain your answers using electron configurations and *Z* values.

7.55 Make a table of the symbols for the quantum numbers, the property associated with each of them, and the restrictions on their possible values.

7.56 Write correct ground-state electron configurations for the neutral atoms with atomic numbers 9, 20, 26, and 33.

7.57 Write correct ground-state electron configurations for the doubly positive ions of the atoms in Problem 7.56.

7.58 For the $3d_{xy}$ orbital, draw graphs of Ψ^2 vs. *r*: (a) for *r* lying along the z axis; (b) for *r* lying along the x axis; and (c) for *r* pointing halfway between the x and y axes in the xy plane. (HINT: See Figure 7-9 for where the wave function has a large value and where its value is small or zero.)

7.59 Draw the contour diagrams for a 1*s* and a $2p_z$ orbital for the same atom, shown to scale.

7.60 Draw energy level diagrams that show the ground-state valence electron configuration for Cu^+, Mn^{2+}, and Au^{3+}.

7.61 Predict the total electron spins for P, Br^-, Cu^+, Gd, and Sr.

For problems 7.62 to 7.64, explain your ranking in terms of quantum numbers and coulombic interactions.

7.62 Arrange the following species in order of decreasing ionization energy: Ne, Ar, Ar^+, and Cl.

7.63 Arrange the following in order of decreasing size (radius): Cl^-, K^+, Ca, and Br.

7.64 Arrange the following in order of increasing size (radius): K, K^+, Ne, Na, and Ar.

7.65 From its location in the periodic table, predict some of the physical and chemical properties of francium. What element does it most closely resemble?

7.66 Name the metals that have s^2p^1 configurations.

7.67 What is the maximum number of valence *p* electrons possessed by a metallic element? Which metal(s) have this configuration?

7.68 Which has the lower-energy 2*s* orbital, a lithium atom or a Li^{2+} cation? Explain your reasoning.

7.69 Make a Ψ^2 vs. *r* plot that shows why the $n = 3$ orbitals have the energy ranking: $3s < 3p < 3d$. Briefly explain your plot.

7.70 Use the data in Appendix D to explain why the rare gases seldom take part in chemical reactions.

7.71 What m_l values can a 5*d* electron and a 4*f* electron have?

7.72 Write the electron configuration for the lowest-energy *excited* state of the following: O^{2+}, O^{2-}, Br^-, Ca^+, and Sb^{3+}. For each, sketch the orbital that holds the excited electron.

7.73 Are the ground-state configurations of the isoelectronic ions Ce^{3+}, La^{2+}, and Ba^+ the same? What features of orbital energies account for this?

7.74 Consider the following three atomic orbitals. They are drawn to scale, and orbital A has $n = 2$.

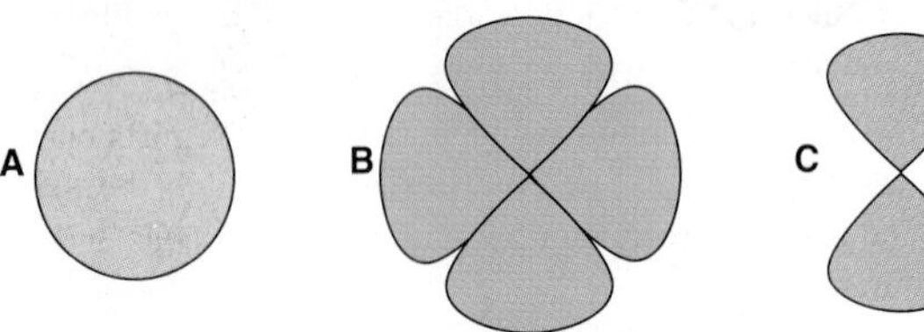

(a) How many electrons can be placed in orbital B?
(b) Provide three sets of quantum numbers that describe orbital C.
(c) Arrange these orbitals in order of increasing stability.
(d) In a lithium atom, how many other orbitals have exactly the same energy as orbital B?
(e) Give the name of an element that has orbital A filled but orbitals B and C empty.
(f) Give the name of an element that has both an empty and a partially filled orbital C.
(g) Give the name of a common anion that has two electrons in orbital C.

7.75 The ionization energy of lithium atoms in the gas phase is about half as large as the ionization energy of beryllium atoms in the gas phase. In contrast, the ionization energy of Li^+ is about 4 times larger than the ionization energy of Be^+. Explain the difference between the atoms and the ions.

7.76 Consider the three atomic orbitals shown below. They are drawn to scale, and orbital C has $n = 3$.

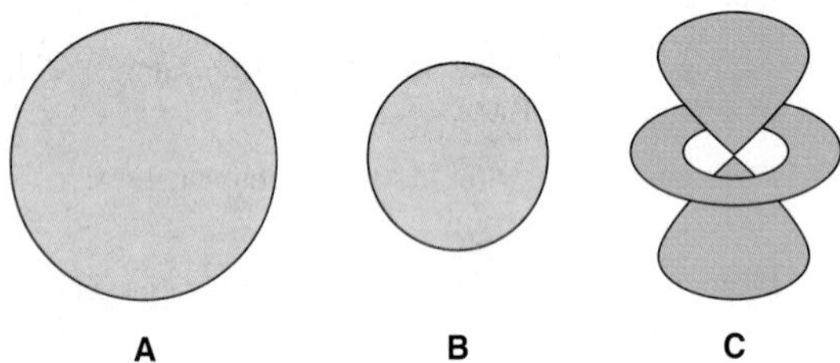

(a) Rank the orbitals in order of stability for a multi-electron atom.
(b) Provide two sets of quantum numbers for orbital A.
(c) Give the atomic number of an element that has two electrons in orbital A but no electrons in orbital C.
(d) Give the name of a cation that has one electron in orbital C.
(e) What is the maximum number of orbitals that can have the same principal quantum number as orbital C?
(f) An element has its two least stable electrons in orbital B. If an atom of that element loses one electron, what happens to the size of orbital B?

7.77 The first ionization energy of sodium is 496.5 kJ/mol. The $3s \longrightarrow 3p$ transition is promoted by a photon whose wavelength is 589 nm. What is the ionization energy of this excited atom?

7.78 Draw energy level diagrams for the $n = 1$, 2, and 3 sets of orbitals for Li^+ and Li^{2+}. Why are they different?

7.79 No elements have ground-state configurations with electrons in g ($l = 4$) orbitals, but some excited states have electrons in g orbitals.
(a) How many different g orbitals are there?
(b) What are the possible values of m_l?
(c) What is the lowest principal quantum number for which there are g orbitals?
(d) Which orbitals may be near-degenerate with the lowest energy g orbitals?
(e) Include the first set of g orbitals in Figure 7-17. What is the atomic number of the first element that has a g electron in its ground-state configuration?

7.80 Element X has an electron affinity of 295.3 kJ/mol and the following ionization energies (kJ/mol): $IE_1 = 1.008 \times 10^3$, $IE_2 = 1.846 \times 10^3$, $IE_3 = 3.20 \times 10^3$. In which column of the periodic table is this element located? Explain.

7.81 Which of the following are nonexistent wave functions? 5*s*, 4*g*, 2*d*, 3*d*, 4*d*, and 6*g*.

7.82 Write the correct ground-state electron configurations for C, Cr, Sb, Br, and Xe.

7.83 In the galaxy Topsumturvum, all of the rules for atomic configurations are the same as ours except that orbital stability *increases* slightly as l increases. A 3*s* orbital is more stable than a 4*d* orbital, but a 4*f* orbital is slightly *more stable* than a 3*s* orbital.
(a) Draw an orbital energy ladder for Topsumturvum.
(b) Determine the ground-state configuration for the Topsumturvum atom containing 27 electrons.
(c) Draw a diagram showing the first 50 elements in the periodic table for the galaxy Topsumturvum.

In the universe Morspin, electrons have three spins ($m_s = +\frac{1}{2}, -\frac{1}{2}, 0$) rather than the two spins ($m_s = +\frac{1}{2}, -\frac{1}{2}$) in our universe. The periodic table of Morspin follows:

1	2											3
4	5	6		7	8	9	10	11	12	13	14	15
16	17	18		19	20	21	22	23	24	25	26	27
28	29	30	31–45	46	47	48	49	50	51	52	53	54
55	56	57	58–72	73	74	75	76	77	78	79	80	81

Assuming that all other physical laws in the two universes are the same, answer problems 7.84 through 7.87 about the periodic table for Morspin.

7.84 (a) The electron configuration of Morspin element 6 is $1s^3 2s^3$. What is the electron configuration of element 19?
(b) How many unpaired electrons would there be in Morspin element 28? Explain.
(c) What would be the highest positive charge of cations found in ionic salts that could form from Morspin element 30? Explain.

7.85 (a) Which would have the larger first ionization energy, Morspin element 18 or Morspin element 30? Explain.
(b) Which would have the larger radius, Morspin element 15 or cation 17^{2+}? Explain.
(c) Which would have the larger electron affinity, Morspin element 47 or 48? Explain.

7.86 (a) What would be the electron configuration of Morspin cation 38^{3+}?
(b) Sketch the d_{xy} orbital as it would appear in this alternative universe. Be sure to include the coordinate axes.
(c) What would be the correct ground-state configurations for Morspin atoms of atomic numbers 3 and 14?

7.87 (a) How many electrons would the first three noble gases in Morspin have?
(b) Write acceptable sets of quantum numbers for Morspin elements 4, 14, 16, and 18.
(c) Which would screen a 4*s* electron more effectively, the $n = 3$ electrons of Morspin or the $n = 3$ electrons of our own universe? Explain.

ANSWERS TO SECTION EXERCISES

7.1.1

n	l	m_l	m_s	
$n = 3$	$l = 0$	$m_l = 0$	$m_s = +\frac{1}{2}$	3*s*
$n = 3$	$l = 0$	$m_l = 0$	$m_s = -\frac{1}{2}$	3*s*
$n = 3$	$l = 1$	$m_l = 0$	$m_s = +\frac{1}{2}$	3*p*
$n = 3$	$l = 1$	$m_l = 0$	$m_s = -\frac{1}{2}$	3*p*
$n = 3$	$l = 1$	$m_l = +1$	$m_s = +\frac{1}{2}$	3*p*
$n = 3$	$l = 1$	$m_l = +1$	$m_s = -\frac{1}{2}$	3*p*
$n = 3$	$l = 1$	$m_l = -1$	$m_s = +\frac{1}{2}$	3*p*
$n = 3$	$l = 1$	$m_l = -1$	$m_s = -\frac{1}{2}$	3*p*
$n = 3$	$l = 2$	$m_l = 0$	$m_s = +\frac{1}{2}$	3*d*
$n = 3$	$l = 2$	$m_l = 0$	$m_s = -\frac{1}{2}$	3*d*
$n = 3$	$l = 2$	$m_l = +2$	$m_s = +\frac{1}{2}$	3*d*
$n = 3$	$l = 2$	$m_l = +2$	$m_s = -\frac{1}{2}$	3*d*
$n = 3$	$l = 2$	$m_l = -2$	$m_s = +\frac{1}{2}$	3*d*
$n = 3$	$l = 2$	$m_l = -2$	$m_s = -\frac{1}{2}$	3*d*
$n = 3$	$l = 2$	$m_l = +1$	$m_s = +\frac{1}{2}$	3*d*
$n = 3$	$l = 2$	$m_l = +1$	$m_s = -\frac{1}{2}$	3*d*
$n = 3$	$l = 2$	$m_l = -1$	$m_s = +\frac{1}{2}$	3*d*
$n = 3$	$l = 2$	$m_l = -1$	$m_s = -\frac{1}{2}$	3*d*

7.1.2 (a) Nonexistent, m_s must be $+\frac{1}{2}$ or $-\frac{1}{2}$; (b) nonexistent, l must be less than n; (c) nonexistent, m_l cannot exceed l; and (d) actual

7.1.3 32

7.2.1 Refer to Figures 7-8 and 7-9.

7.2.2

7.2.3

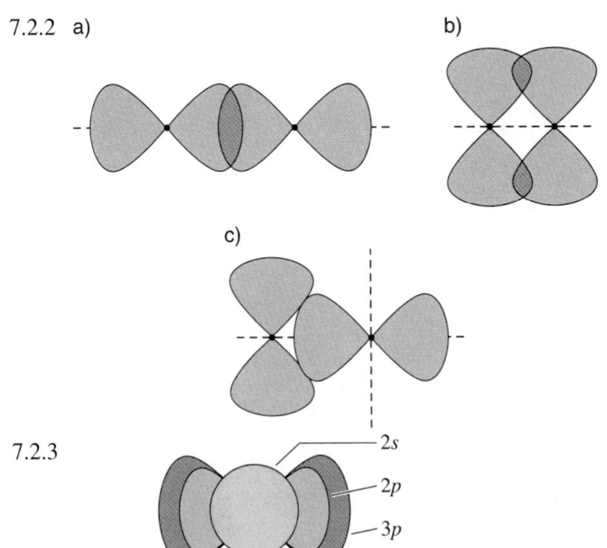

The $n = 2$ orbitals are not important when $3p_x$ is occupied.

7.3.1

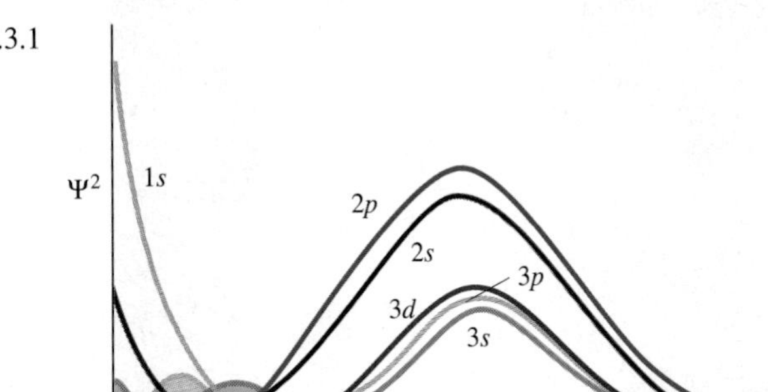

Distance from the nucleus, *r*

7.3.2 2.4×10^{-19} J

7.4.1 (a) [Xe] $4f^{14}\,5d^{10}$, zero spin; (b) [Rn] $7s^2\,5f^{14}\,6d^{10}\,7p^6$, zero spin; and (c) [Ar], zero spin

7.4.2 ⇅ 7*s*; 6*d*: — ↑; 5*f*: — — — ↑ ↑ ↑ ↑

7.4.3 Mo, [Kr] $5s^1$ $4d^5$; I, [Kr] $5s^2$ $4d^{10}$ $5p^5$; and Hg^+, [Xe] $6s^1\,5d^{10}\,4f^{14}$

7.5.1 117

7.5.2 C, 4; Br, 7; Cr, 6; and Ta, 5

7.5.3 Be, Mg, Ca, Sr, Ba, Ra, Zn, Cd, and Hg; all have s^2.

7.6.1 (a) Cl has larger Z; (b) has lower n; (c) Sr has higher n; (d) Cl^- has smaller Z; and (e) O^- has larger Z_{eff}.

7.6.2 (a) Between Nb and In, a *d* block fills, so Z_{eff} remains nearly constant; (b) Ga loses a 4*p* electron, which is easier to remove than the 4*s* electrons of Zn; and (c) Mn has d^5 valence configuration, so the next electron must pair with an existing electron.

7.6.3 Stability decreases markedly with n.

7.7.1 Energy is required: +39.3 kJ/mol.

7.7.2 Sc, Ti, V, and Cr

7.7.3 Ca^{2+}, Cs^+, Al^{3+}, and Br^-

7.8.1 Nonmetals, 1390; metalloids, 824; *s*-block, 610; low ionization energy leads to formation of ions.

7.8.2 S, nonmetal; Si, metalloid; Sr, metal; Se, metalloid; Sc, metal; and Sn, metal

FUNDAMENTALS OF CHEMICAL BONDING

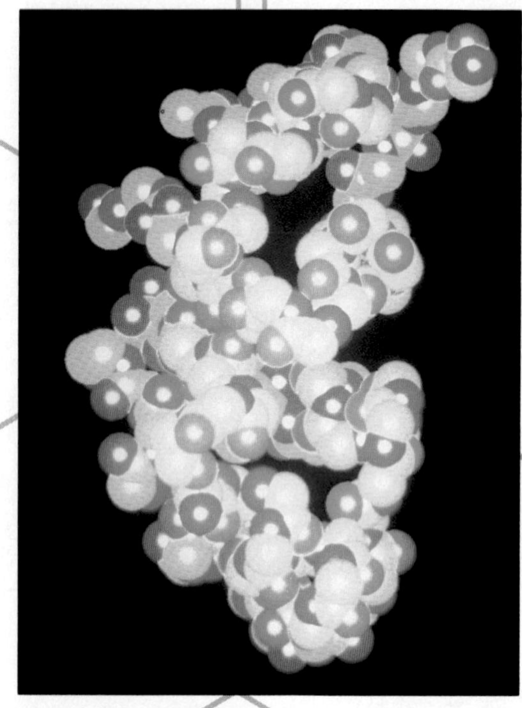

Every molecule, from diatomic hydrogen to the most complex protein, is held together by the "glue" of shared electrons.

In Chapters 6 and 7, we developed a description of the atom that explains many properties of the chemical elements. Now we are ready to explore how atoms join together to form the stable molecules that are the basic units of most substances. For example, the first chemical element, hydrogen, readily combines with other atoms to form molecules. Two hydrogen atoms combine to form an H_2 molecule; an atom of hydrogen combines with one of chlorine to form an HCl molecule; and four atoms of hydrogen and one atom of carbon combine to make a molecule of methane, CH_4.

When atoms combine to make molecules, they form chemical bonds in which electrons are shared between atoms. Chemical bonds are the "glue" of every molecule, from diatomic hydrogen to the proteins contained in our bodies. Although the basic principles of bond formation are always the same, chemical bonds show a variety of forms and strengths. Moreover, different elements have different bond-forming abilities. For instance, hydrogen atoms always form chemical bonds, but helium atoms never do. Our goal in Chapters 8 and 9 is to present the principles of chemical bonding that explain these variations. In this chapter we explore fundamental principles of bond formation. In Chapter 9 we describe a more extensive model for the elaborate chemical bonds that play important roles in materials as diverse as deoxyribonucleic acid (DNA) and transistors.

8.1 OVERVIEW OF BONDING

Bonds form because the resulting molecule is more stable than the separated atoms. Any collection of nuclei and electrons arranges itself in a manner that gives the greatest stability. In Chapter 7, we described the ground states of isolated atoms, in which electrons occupy the most stable orbitals. Another example of energy minimization is the formation of ionic compounds, as described in Section 7.7. Metals with low ionization energy lose electrons to nonmetals with high electron affinity, forming crystalline arrays of ions as a result of the coulombic attraction between oppositely charged ions. A crystalline ionic array is the most stable arrangement under these conditions.

Atoms achieve maximum stability when their electrons occupy the atomic orbitals of the lowest possible energies, and ions achieve maximum stability when they cluster in ionic solids. Molecules, on the other hand, achieve maximum stability when electrons are shared between nuclei. Electron sharing is called *covalent bonding*. A **covalent bond** consists of electrons shared between nuclei.

All charged species are subject to Coulomb's law:

$$E_{\text{coulomb}} = (2.31 \times 10^{-16} \text{ J pm})\frac{q_1 q_2}{r} \quad \textbf{(8-1)}$$

In Equation 7-1 we were interested in molar energies, so we expressed coulombic energy in kilojoules per mole. In Equation 8-1, however, we are interested in a single molecule, so we express the energy in terms of one pair of charges.

Here, q_1 and q_2 are the magnitudes of the charges, and r is the distance between them in picometers (pm). For an electron, $q = -1$, and for a nucleus, $q = +Z$. Equation 8-1 describes the energy of one pair of charges, such as one electron attracted to one nucleus, but molecules contain two or more nuclei and two or more electrons. To obtain the total coulombic energy of a molecule, Equation 8-1 must be applied to every possible pair of charged species. These pair-wise interactions are of three types. First, electrons and nuclei are oppositely charged, so electron-nucleus interactions generate negative energies and stabilize a molecule. Second, electrons repel each other, so electron-electron interactions give positive energies and destabilize a molecule. Third, nuclei repel each other, so nucleus-nucleus interactions also destabilize a molecule.

In a stable molecule, electrons and nuclei are arranged to give maximum stability. A covalent bond is an arrangement of electrons that maximizes electron-nuclear attraction and promotes molecular stability. In any covalent bond, the energy of attraction between nuclei and electrons exceeds the energy of repulsion arising from nuclear-nuclear and electron-electron interactions.

THE HYDROGEN MOLECULE

We can use hydrogen molecules, which contain just two nuclei and two electrons, to illustrate how coulombic interactions generate covalent bonds. Begin by thinking about what happens as two hydrogen atoms approach each other. In each atom the electron and proton attract each other strongly, but as two atoms come together, each electron is also attracted by the opposite nucleus. In addition, the two protons repel each other, and the two electrons repel each other. The repulsive interactions tend to drive the two atoms apart, whereas the attractive interactions pull them together. For H_2 to be a stable molecule, the sum of the electron-nucleus attractive energies must exceed the sum of electron-electron and nucleus-nucleus repulsive energies.

In Figure 8-1 the electrons and protons are arranged so that the electron-nuclear attractions are larger than the electron-electron and nuclear-nuclear repulsions. Notice that the two electrons occupy the region between the two nuclei, where they can strongly interact with both nuclei at once. When this occurs, the electrons are shared between the atoms.

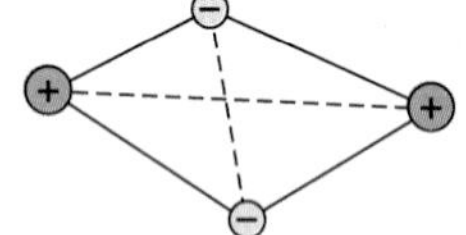

FIGURE 8-1
Schematic illustration of two electrons and two protons arranged so that attractive coulombic interactions *(four solid lines)* are greater than repulsive coulombic interactions *(two dotted lines)*.

ORBITAL OVERLAP

Figure 8-1 emphasizes the coulombic attraction between electrons and nuclei, but it is not an accurate representation of a hydrogen molecule. Recall from Chapter 6 that electrons are not point charges. Instead, electrons are "smeared out" in space in ways that are represented by orbitals. In a hydrogen molecule, electrons are smeared out throughout the molecule in a manner that concentrates electron density between the two nuclei. To understand chemical bonding, we must develop new orbital pictures that show this delocalization of electrons between nuclei.

Determining the exact orbitals of even a simple molecule such as H_2 is an extremely difficult mathematical task that still occupies the attention of theoreticians. Fortunately, we can closely approximate the orbital description of H_2 using the atomic orbitals of each atom. The atomic orbital that describes the electron in a hydrogen atom is the spherical $1s$ orbital. This orbital changes when two hydrogen atoms come together to form a molecule.

As two hydrogen atoms approach each other, the orbitals that describe their electrons must be modified to account for the coulombic forces between the two atoms. These modifications can be made by superimposing the wave functions. When two *waves* are superimposed, they interact to generate a new wave. When two *orbitals*

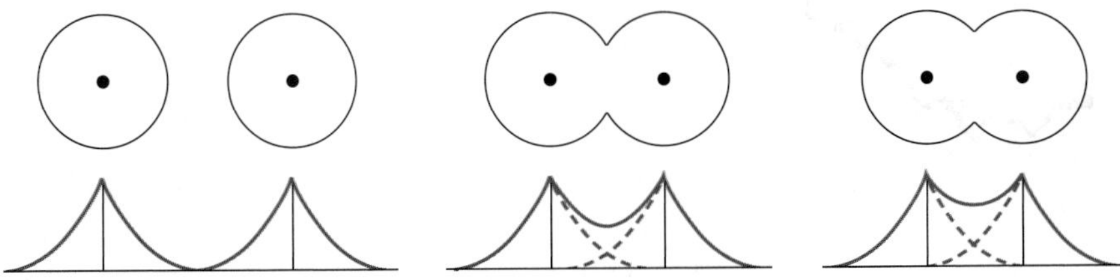

FIGURE 8-2
As two hydrogen atoms approach each other, their 1*s* atomic orbitals overlap to a greater and greater extent. Constructive interference generates a new orbital with high electron density between the nuclei.

are superimposed, their interaction is called *orbital overlap.* Orbital overlap can be described very simply: The amplitude of the new wave function at any point is the sum of the amplitudes of the overlapping wave functions. As illustrated in Figure 8-2, the orbital overlap of the 1*s* wave functions of two hydrogen atoms gives a new wave function with electron density concentrated between the nuclei. The new orbital replaces the atomic orbitals as the description of the electrons in a hydrogen molecule.

BOND LENGTH AND BOND ENERGY

As two hydrogen atoms come together, the molecule is stabilized by attractive forces between the nuclei and the electrons. The amount of stabilization varies with the separation between the nuclei, as shown in Figure 8-3. At distances greater than 300 pm, there is almost no interaction between the atoms, orbital overlap is nearly zero, and the energy of the two atoms is just the sum of their atomic energies. At closer distances the attraction between the electrons and the nuclei increases, orbital overlap becomes substantial, and energy is released. Moving the nuclei closer together generates greater stability until they are 74 pm apart. At distances closer than 74 pm, however, the nucleus-nucleus repulsion increases more rapidly than the electron-nucleus attraction. Thus at a separation distance of 74 pm, the molecule is at the bottom of an "energy well," where it is most stable. The atoms are combined in a molecule, sharing two electrons in a covalent bond.

1 picometer = 1 pm = 10^{-12} m

Because the energy of the separated atoms is defined to be zero, potential energy takes on a negative value as the system releases energy.

Figure 8-3 shows two characteristic features of chemical bonds. The separation distance where the molecule is most stable is known as the **bond length,** and the amount of stability at this separation distance is known as the **bond energy** or

Experimental studies of molecular motions reveal that nuclei are in continual vibrational motion, oscillating about their optimum separation distance like two balls attached to opposite ends of a spring.

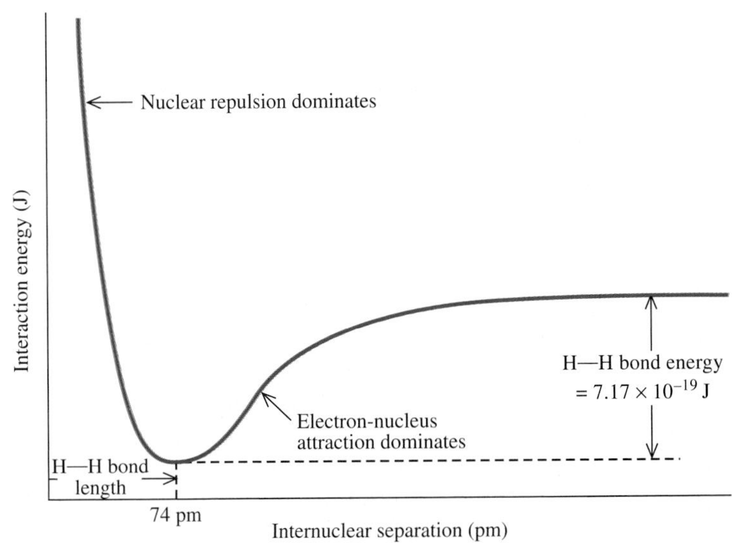

FIGURE 8-3
A graph shows how the interaction energy of a pair of hydrogen atoms varies with internuclear separation. At distances greater than 74 pm, attraction resulting from orbital overlap dominates, and energy is released as the atoms move closer. At distances less than 74 pm, nuclear-nuclear repulsion dominates, and energy must be absorbed if the two atoms are to move closer together.

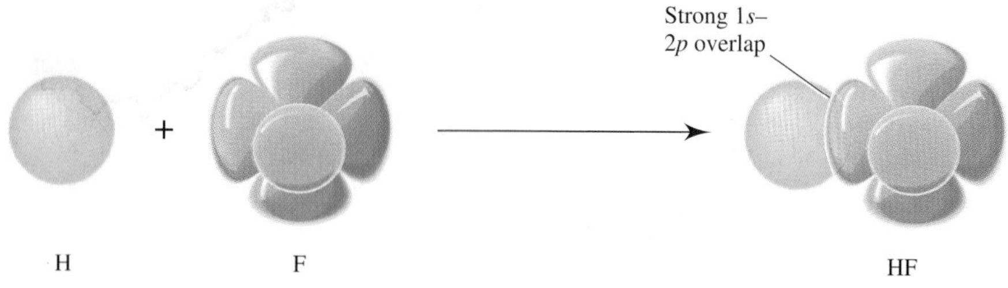

FIGURE 8-4
Bond formation in HF can be represented by the overlap between a hydrogen 1*s* atomic orbital and the fluorine 2*p* atomic orbital that points toward the approaching hydrogen atom.

strength of the bond. Bond lengths and strengths are important properties of bonds that are used frequently as we develop the concepts of chemical bonding.

It has been found experimentally that the bond energy of a hydrogen molecule is 7.17×10^{-19} J. Multiplying this value by Avogadro's number (6.022×10^{23} /mol) gives 432 kJ/mol as the bond energy of 1 mol of hydrogen. This means that 1 mol of H_2 is more stable than 2 mol of H atoms by 432 kJ. We can think of this bond energy as the price that must be paid to tear H_2 molecules apart into individual H atoms.

OTHER DIATOMIC MOLECULES: HF AND F_2

Bond formation in H_2 is relatively easy to describe because we must account for the orbital interactions of just two orbitals and the placement of just two electrons. Bond formation in other molecules, however, involves interactions among many orbitals and configurations that contain many electrons. Nevertheless, simple orbital overlap can be used to describe bond formation in various diatomic molecules, such as HF and F_2.

As hydrogen and fluorine atoms approach each other, their electron clouds interact. Figure 8-4 indicates that although fluorine has five occupied atomic orbitals, the fluorine 2*p* orbital that points directly at the approaching hydrogen atom is the only one with significant orbital overlap. The fluorine 2*s* orbital is less effectively screened from the nuclear charge than the 2*p* orbitals, so it is more compact than the 2*p* orbitals. The fluorine 1*s* orbital has a lower principal quantum number and is very compact. The other two 2*p* orbitals point in the wrong directions to overlap effectively. Thus bonding in HF can be described by one covalent bond that results from overlap between the hydrogen 1*s* orbital and the fluorine 2*p* orbital that points along the bond axis.

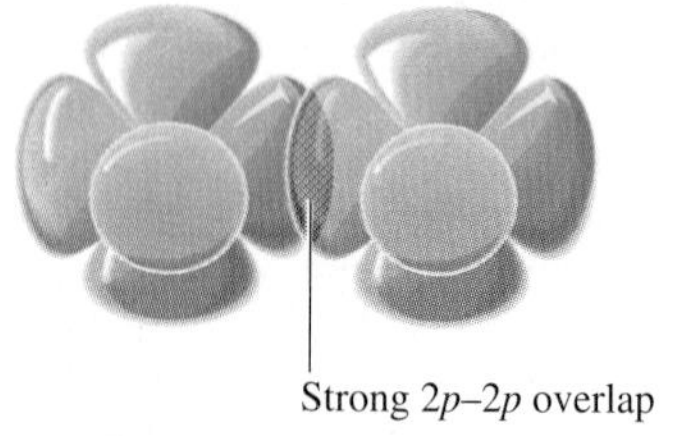

FIGURE 8-5
Bond formation in F_2 can be represented by the overlap between the two fluorine 2*p* atomic orbitals that point along the internuclear axis.

A similar situation, shown in Figure 8-5, arises when two fluorine atoms approach each other. The first valence atomic orbitals to overlap are the 2*p* orbitals pointing along the axis that joins the atoms. Bond formation in fluorine is the result of the strong overlap of these two 2*p* atomic orbitals.

APPROACHES TO BONDING

A single orbital can describe both electrons of the bond in a diatomic molecule of H_2, HF, or F_2 because any orbital can hold two electrons with opposite spins without violating the Pauli exclusion principle. The complete descriptions of other molecules, however, require entire sets of orbitals that describe how all the electrons are "packaged" amid the framework of nuclei. Although these descriptions provide the maximum information about the molecule, they are too complicated to be very useful. Consequently, chemists resort to various approximations that simplify the description of how electrons are distributed in a molecule.

In this chapter and in Chapter 9, we describe two different ways to think about chemical bonds: localized orbitals and delocalized orbitals. These two approaches to bonding differ in the approximations they make about the set of orbitals that describe a molecule, but they share the following features:

1. Each electron is described by a wave function. In other words, each electron in a molecule is assigned to a specific orbital.
2. No two electrons in a molecule can ever have identical wave functions because the Pauli exclusion principle applies to electrons in molecules as well as in atoms.
3. In the description of a stable molecule, all electrons have wave functions with the lowest possible energies because the Aufbau principle applies to molecules as well as atoms.
4. Every atom has an unlimited number of atomic orbitals, but the valence orbitals are all that are needed to describe bonding.

Bonding results almost exclusively from interactions among the valence orbitals because they have the appropriate sizes and stabilities to interact strongly. Consider, for example, the orbital interactions between F atoms combined to form a fluorine molecule. Each atom has the energy level diagram shown schematically in Figure 8-6. Recall that the sizes of the orbitals increase substantially as the principal quantum number ($\boldsymbol{n}$) increases. As a result, the core 1*s* orbitals are much smaller than any of the $\boldsymbol{n} = 2$ orbitals and do not participate effectively in orbital overlap. On the other hand, orbitals with $\boldsymbol{n} > 2$ lie at considerably higher energy than the $\boldsymbol{n} = 2$ orbitals and are too unstable to form stable covalent bonds. The only orbitals of fluorine atoms that combine high stability with appropriate size to form chemical bonds are the valence orbitals, those with $\boldsymbol{n} = 2$.

The orbital features illustrated by molecular fluorine apply to all molecules. That is, core orbitals are too compact to overlap significantly, so they do not participate in bond formation, and all orbitals beyond the valence shell are too high in energy to give bonding orbitals that will be occupied by electrons. Only the valence orbitals are large enough to overlap strongly and stable enough to generate new orbitals that are more stable than the occupied atomic orbitals.

In this chapter we discuss the **localized orbital model** of covalent bonding. In this approach, bonding electrons are localized between two atoms. Valence electrons not involved in chemical bonds are said to be **nonbonding electrons** and remain in atomic orbitals. Orbitals are either purely atomic or the result of overlap of one orbital from each of two atoms.

The localized orbital model using valence atomic orbitals is often called the *valence bond theory.*

The localized orbital model is easy to apply, even to very complex molecules, and it does an excellent job of explaining much chemical behavior. In many

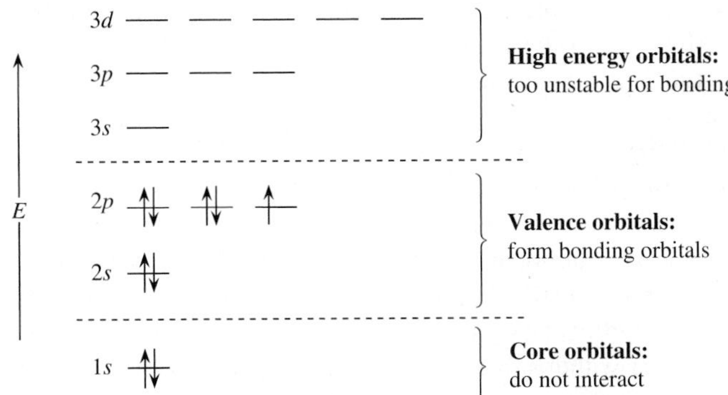

FIGURE 8-6
The energy level diagram for a fluorine atom ($1s^2\ 2s^2\ 2p^5$). Only the $n = 2$ orbitals (the valence orbitals) have the right sizes and energies to form bonding orbitals.

Delocalized orbitals are also called *molecular orbitals,* and this approach is often called *molecular orbital theory.*

instances, however, localized bonds are insufficient to explain molecular properties and chemical reactivity. In Chapter 9 we show how to construct delocalized orbitals, which spread over several atoms. Delocalized orbitals explain chemical properties that localized orbitals cannot, but delocalized orbitals require more complicated analysis than localized orbitals.

These two approaches to bonding are complementary because each describes some features of how a molecule is put together. Remember that the underlying molecule is the reality, and that the molecule does not change when we modify the way we *describe* its bonding. Bonding has many features, and each approach is well suited to describe some of them but less well suited for others. Thus a comprehensive understanding of bonding requires more than one approach.

SECTION EXERCISES

8.1.1 Draw a figure similar to Figure 8-2 that shows changes in the wave functions as a hydrogen atom approaches a fluorine atom and forms an H—F bond.

8.1.2 Describe bond formation between H atoms and Cl atoms to form HCl molecules.

8.1.3 Which orbitals of selenium atoms are used to form covalent bonds? Which orbitals are used by phosphorus?

8.2 UNEQUAL ELECTRON SHARING

In a hydrogen molecule, each nucleus has a unit charge of +1. Consequently, electrons are attracted equally to each nucleus. The result is a symmetrical orbital in which the electron density near one nucleus is the same as the density near the other nucleus. In fluorine molecules the coulombic description is more complicated but still symmetrical. Each nucleus has a charge of +9 units and is screened from the bonding orbital by an electron cloud that contains eight electrons. The bonding electrons experience the same net force toward each nucleus. In both H_2 and F_2 therefore, bonding electrons are shared equally between the two nuclei.

The bonding electrons in hydrogen fluoride molecules, on the other hand, experience *unsymmetrical* attractive forces. The bonding electrons are attracted in one direction by the +1 charge on the hydrogen nucleus. In the other direction, the same electrons are attracted by the +9 charge of the fluorine nucleus, screened by electrons in 1*s*, 2*s*, and 2*p* orbitals. Although the 1*s* and 2*s* electrons provide highly effective shielding, the 2*p* orbitals point in the wrong directions to screen the fluorine nucleus effectively from the bonding electrons. As a result, the effective nuclear charge of the fluorine atom is greater than +1.

Unsymmetrical attractive forces lead in turn to an unsymmetrical electron distribution, with electron density concentrated closer to the larger effective nuclear charge than to the smaller effective nuclear charge. The HF molecule reaches maximum stability when the electron density of its bonding pair is concentrated closer to the fluorine atom than the hydrogen atom. This is an example of unequal sharing of electrons. The H—F bonding orbital has greater electron density near fluorine than near hydrogen. Although two electrons are shared between the nuclei, bond formation has withdrawn electron density from the vicinity of the hydrogen nucleus and added electron density in the vicinity of the fluorine nucleus. As a result, the hydrogen end of the molecule bears a partial positive charge, and the fluorine

	s^1	s^2
2	Li 1.0	Be 1.5
3	Na 0.9	Mg 1.2
4	K 0.8	Ca 1.0
5	Rb 0.8	Sr 1.0
6	Cs 0.7	Ba 0.9

	d^1	d^2	d^3	d^4	d^5	d^6	d^7	d^8	d^9	d^{10}
3	Sc 1.3	Ti 1.5	V 1.6	Cr 1.6	Mn 1.5	Fe 1.8	Co 1.9	Ni 1.9	Cu 1.9	Zn 1.6
4	Y 1.2	Zr 1.4	Nb 1.6	Mo 1.8	Tc 1.9	Ru 2.2	Rh 2.2	Pd 2.2	Ag 1.9	Cd 1.7
5	Lu 1.2	Hf 1.3	Ta 1.5	W 1.7	Re 1.9	Os 2.2	Ir 2.2	Pt 2.2	Au 2.4	Hg 1.9

	s^1	s^2
1	H 2.1	He

	p^1	p^2	p^3	p^4	p^5	p^6
2	B 2.0	C 2.5	N 3.0	O 3.5	F 4.0	Ne
3	Al 1.5	Si 1.8	P 2.1	S 2.5	Cl 3.0	Ar
4	Ga 1.6	Ge 1.8	As 2.0	Se 2.4	Br 2.8	Kr
5	In 1.7	Sn 1.8	Sb 1.9	Te 2.1	I 2.5	Xe
6	Tl 1.8	Pb 1.9	Bi 1.9	Po 2.0	At 2.2	Rn

Electronegativity (EN) < 2.0	EN > 2.4
EN 2.0-2.4	EN unknown

FIGURE 8-7
Pauling values for the average electronegativities of the elements. Elements with electronegativities less than 2.0 are shaded pink, those with electronegativities greater than 2.4 are shaded yellow, and those with intermediate values are shaded blue.

atom bears a partial negative charge of equal magnitude. We describe this by saying that there is **polarized electron density** toward the fluorine atom and that HF has a polar covalent bond.

ELECTRONEGATIVITY

Any covalent bond between two different atoms is polar to some extent because no two elements have identical effective nuclear charges and attract bonding electrons by exactly the same amount. The extent to which an element attracts bonding electrons is called its **electronegativity** and is symbolized by the Greek letter chi (χ). When two atoms have different electronegativities, the bond between them is polar, and the greater the difference, the more polar the bond.

Chi is pronounced *kai* (rhymes with eye).

Electronegativity is related to electron affinity and ionization energy. Electronegativity measures the attraction of a *bound* electron to an atom to make a polar bond. In contrast, electron affinity measures the attraction of a *free* electron to a neutral atom to make an atomic anion, and ionization energy measures the attraction between a free electron and an atomic cation.

An element's electronegativity cannot be measured directly because experiments that measure the electron density distribution of a chemical bond have not been devised. Instead, electronegativities are estimated using combinations of properties that depend on effective charge, including ionization energy, electron affinity, and bond energy. The most widely used estimates of electronegativity were developed by the American chemist Linus Pauling.* These values, which are dimensionless, are presented in the periodic table shown in Figure 8-7.

Notice in Figure 8-7 that electronegativities increase from the lower left to the upper right of the periodic table. Thus cesium ($\chi = 0.70$) has the lowest value and fluorine ($\chi = 4.0$) the highest value. Notice also that electronegativities decrease down most columns and increase from left to right across the *s* and *p* blocks. These trends parallel the periodic trends in ionization energies and electron affinities.

* Linus Pauling was awarded the Nobel Prize in chemistry in 1954 for his pioneering ideas about chemical bonds. Pauling was the first to propose that giant organic molecules such as proteins can have helical structures, an idea that led Watson and Crick to propose a double helix for the structure of DNA. Throughout the 1950s, Pauling was also a leader in the movement to limit the proliferation of nuclear weapons, for which he was awarded the Nobel Prize for peace in 1963.

Metals generally have low electronegativities. Metals in the *s* block have $\chi \leq 1$, except for magnesium ($\chi = 1.3$) and beryllium ($\chi = 1.6$). Those in the *f* block have $\chi = 1.3 \pm 0.2$. Transition metals and posttransition metals have more variable values, but most have $\chi < 2$.

Nonmetals have high electronegativities, which range from phosphorus and hydrogen ($\chi = 2.1$) to fluorine. As shown in Figure 8-7, all nonmetals except phosphorus and hydrogen have $\chi > 2.5$, whereas the electronegativities of metalloids vary between 1.9 for silicon and 2.2 for arsenic.

NaF is a crystalline solid that is used for fluoridation of water and toothpastes.

Electronegativity differences ($\Delta\chi$) provide a measure of where any particular bond lies on the continuum of bond polarities. The two extremes in polarities are represented by F_2 and NaF. The chemical bond in F_2 ($\Delta\chi = 0$) is nonpolar because electrons are shared equally between the two fluorine atoms. In contrast, NaF ($\Delta\chi = 3.1$) is an ionic compound in which electrons have been fully transferred to give Na^+ cations and F^- anions. Between these extremes are many polar bonds between atoms whose electronegativity differences are small but not zero. Sample Problem 8-1 illustrates the periodicity of electronegativity and bond polarity variations.

SAMPLE PROBLEM 8-1 ELECTRONEGATIVITIES

Without looking up electronegativity values, rank the following bonds from least polar to most polar: (a) P—Cl, As—Cl, N—Cl and (b) C—S, C—O, C—F.

METHOD: The larger the difference in electronegativity, the more polar the bond. Therefore we can use the *trends* in electronegativity to arrange these bonds in order of polarity. First, locate the elements in the periodic table, and then use periodic trends to determine relative electronegativity differences and rank the bond polarities.

(a) Each of these three bonds contains chlorine, so the trend in bond polarity matches the trend in the electronegativities of P, As, and N. These three elements are in the same column of the periodic table (column V), and electronegativity *decreases* from top to bottom of a column. Chlorine, in column VII, has a higher electronegativity than the elements in column V, so the electronegativity *difference* increases from nitrogen to phosphorus to arsenic. Thus the least polar bond is N—Cl, and the most polar is As—Cl:

$$\text{N—Cl} < \text{P—Cl} < \text{As—Cl}$$

(b) Each of these bonds contains carbon, so the trend in bond polarities depends on the trend in electronegativities for S, O, and F. Sulfur is beneath oxygen in column VI of the periodic table, so sulfur is less electronegative than oxygen. Oxygen and fluorine are in the same row, so fluorine is more electronegative than oxygen because electronegativity *increases* across a row. All three have larger electronegativities than carbon, so the electronegativity difference and bond polarity increases as electronegativity increases:

$$\text{C—S} < \text{C—O} < \text{C—F}$$

You can use actual electronegativity values to verify that these rankings are correct.

Although bond polarities vary continuously from zero to fully ionic, it is convenient to classify substances as ionic or polar. Table 8-1 indicates that when $\Delta\chi < 1.6$, the compound is classified as *polar,* and when $\Delta\chi > 2.0$, the compound is classified as *ionic.* When electronegativity differences are 1.6 to 2.0, however, the classification depends on whether or not the compound contains a metal. Metal-containing compounds in this range, such as $MgCl_2$ and KI, are classified as ionic. Nonmetallic compounds, such as HF and SiO_2, are classified as polar despite the large differences in their electronegativities.

TABLE 8-1 REPRESENTATIVE ELECTRONEGATIVITY DIFFERENCES ($\Delta\chi$)

POLAR COMPOUND	$\Delta\chi$	IONIC COMPOUND	$\Delta\chi$
NO	0.5	LiF	3.0
CO	1.0	CaO	2.5
SO_2	1.0	NaCl	2.1
SiO_2	1.7	KI	1.7
HF	1.9	$MgCl_2$	1.8

SECTION EXERCISES

8.2.1 For each of the following pairs, identify which element tends to attract electron density from the other in a covalent bond: (a) Si and O; (b) C and H; (c) As and Cl; and (d) Cl and Sn.

8.2.2 List the bonds of Exercise 8.2.1 from least polar to most polar.

8.2.3 Using electronegativity differences, determine which of the following compounds are clearly ionic and which should be considered to have some covalent bond character: LiCl, $CeCl_3$, AgCl, Al_2O_3, Fe_2O_3, Na_2S, and ZnS.

8.3 LEWIS STRUCTURES

According to the localized orbital model of bonding, two types of valence electrons exist: (1) bonding electrons, which are shared between two nuclei, and (2) nonbonding electrons, which are localized on individual atoms. In this section we develop a process for constructing schematic drawings of molecules called **Lewis structures.** A Lewis structure shows the atoms that are bonded together and the locations within the molecule of all bonding and nonbonding valence electrons. In a sense, these are molecular blueprints that show how molecules are laid out. Thus writing a suitable Lewis structure is the first step in developing an orbital description of a molecule.*

THE CONVENTIONS

Lewis structures are constructed using the following conventions:

1. *Only the valence electrons appear in a Lewis structure.* The core electrons occupy compact atomic orbitals that are not involved in bonding.

* Lewis structures were developed by the American chemist Gilbert N. Lewis (1875-1946). In addition to introducing many important ideas about chemical bonding, Lewis made fundamental contributions to thermodynamics (see Chapters 12 and 13) and introduced a general model of acid-base chemistry (see Chapter 18). Lewis was also a dedicated, inspiring teacher. In fact, he conceived the idea of the Lewis structure while teaching general chemistry in 1902. He was head of the chemistry department at the University of California at Berkeley for many years.

2. *A line joining two atoms represents a pair of electrons shared between two atoms.* Two atoms may share up to three pairs of electrons in **single bonds** (two shared electrons, one line), **double bonds** (four shared electrons, two lines), or **triple bonds** (six shared electrons, three lines).
3. *Dots placed next to an atom represent nonbonding electrons.* Nonbonding electrons are usually found in pairs because orbitals usually contain two electrons with opposing spins.

These conventions divide molecular electrons into three groups. Core electrons are purely atomic in nature and are not shown in the Lewis structure. Bonding valence electrons are shared between atoms and are shown as lines. Nonbonding valence electrons are localized on atoms and are shown as dots.

WRITING LEWIS STRUCTURES

The Lewis structure for a molecule can be constructed in the following step-by-step procedure:

1. Treat ions separately.
2. Count the valence electrons.
3. Assemble the bonding framework, with two electrons per bond.
4. Place three pairs of nonbonding electrons on each outer atom, except H.
5. Assign the remaining valence electrons to inner atoms.
6. Calculate the formal charge on each atom.
7. Minimize formal charges by shifting electrons to make double bonds and triple bonds.

We describe each guideline in detail and apply them to explicit examples.

1. Treat ions separately. Ions do not share electrons with other ions. Thus, each ion is an individual chemical species with its own Lewis structure. An ionic compound has two Lewis structures, one for its cation and one for its anion. Consequently, you must identify ionic compounds from their elemental makeup. The first indication that a compound is ionic is the presence of a metal or an ammonium cation. The second indication is the presence of a polyatomic anion or atoms from columns VI and VII of the periodic table. Because ionic compounds must contain cations and anions, both indications must be present in an ionic compound. (See Table 3-3 for the common polyatomic ions.) Sample Problem 8-2 provides examples of recognizing ionic compounds.

SAMPLE PROBLEM 8-2 RECOGNIZING IONIC COMPOUNDS

Which of the following common fertilizers are ionic: NH_3 (ammonia), $(NH_4)_2SO_4$ (ammonium sulfate), $(NH_2)_2CO$ (urea), and KNO_3 (potassium nitrate)?

METHOD: To determine whether a compound is ionic, look for a metal atom or ammonium ions *and* a Group VI or VII atom or one of the common polyatomic ions in its formula.

Ammonia and urea lack either a metal or a common polyatomic ion, so neither is ionic.

From the presence of the NH_4^+ cation and the SO_4^{2-} anion, we recognize that ammonium sulfate is ionic.

Potassium nitrate is also ionic because it contains a metal cation, K^+, and a polyatomic anion, NO_3^-.

Notice that parentheses in a formula are not an indicator of whether or not the compound is ionic. For ionic $(NH_4)_2SO_4$, the parentheses group together the atoms of the ammonium ion.

The 2 subscript tells us that two ammonium ions (+1 charge each) are present for each sulfate anion (−2 charge). On the other hand, the parentheses around the NH_2 group in the formula of urea indicate that two NH_2 fragments are covalently bound to the carbon atom. The formulas for these two compounds demonstrate that groups of atoms enclosed in parentheses may or may not be ions, so it is important that you learn to recognize the common polyatomic ions.

---

2. *Count the valence electrons.* A count of valence electrons is essential because a Lewis structure shows *all* valence electrons and *only* valence electrons. Recall from Section 7.5 that the number of valence electrons of an atom can be found from its position in the periodic table. For example, each atom from column V has five valence electrons (s^2p^3 configuration), whereas each atom from column IV has four (s^2p^2). Add the contributions from all atoms to obtain a total count of valence electrons. Finally, if the compound is a polyatomic anion, *add* one electron for each negative charge. If the compound is a polyatomic cation, *subtract* one electron for each positive charge. Sample Problem 8-3 shows examples of how to count valence electrons.

Anions have excess negative charge because they have gained negatively charged electrons. Cations have excess positive charge because they have lost electrons.

SAMPLE PROBLEM 8-3 COUNTING VALENCE ELECTRONS

How many valence electrons are in each of the fertilizers listed in Sample Problem 8-2?

METHOD: Refer to the periodic table to determine the number of valence electrons contributed by each atom. Treat ions separately. Sum all the valence electrons, and take net charges into account.

NH_3: Nitrogen (column V) has five valence electrons ($2s^2\,2p^3$), and each of the three hydrogen atoms contributes one valence electron ($1s^1$), for a total of eight valence electrons.

$(NH_4)_2SO_4$: Ammonium sulfate is an ionic compound, so we must perform separate counts for the cation and the anion. Sulfur and oxygen (column VI) have six valence electrons (s^2p^4). One electron must be subtracted from the count for the ammonium cation to account for its +1 charge, and two electrons must be added to the count for the sulfate anion to account for its −2 charge.

For NH_4^+		For SO_4^{2-}	
$1\ N = (1)(5\ e^-) =$	$5\ e^-$	$1\ S = (1)(6\ e^-) =$	$6\ e^-$
$4\ H = (4)(1\ e^-) =$	$4\ e^-$	$4\ O = (4)(6\ e^-) =$	$24\ e^-$
$+1$ ion $=$	$-1\ e^-$	-2 ion $=$	$2\ e^-$
Total valence e^- =	8	Total valence e^- =	32

$(NH_2)_2CO$: Urea is a covalent compound. The only element whose valence electrons were not previously counted is carbon (column IV), which has four.

$$
\begin{aligned}
(2\ N)(5\ e^-) &= 10\ e^- \\
(4\ H)(1\ e^-) &= 4\ e^- \\
(1\ C)(4\ e^-) &= 4\ e^- \\
(1\ O)(6\ e^-) &= 6\ e^- \\
\hline
\text{Total valence } e^- &= 24
\end{aligned}
$$

KNO_3: The two ions must be treated separately. A potassium *atom* has one valence electron, but in forming a cation, the atom loses its single 4*s* valence electron, so K^+ has zero valence electrons. Verify for yourself that the nitrate anion has 24 valence electrons.

---

3. Assemble the bonding framework. Put the molecule together by placing a bonding pair of electrons between each pair of bonded atoms. A line between atoms indicates a bonding pair. Subtract the number of bonding electrons from the total number of valence electrons to determine the number of electrons that remain to be placed in the structure.

No foolproof method exists for putting the atoms together in the correct arrangement. However, the following guidelines, which distinguish between **outer atoms** (atoms that bond to one other atom) and **inner atoms** (atoms that bond to more than one other atom), are helpful.

a. In the compounds that we consider in this text, hydrogen atoms are *always* outer because hydrogen can form just one localized bond. This means, for example, that CH_4 must contain a carbon atom bonded to four outer hydrogen atoms:

```
    H
    |
H—C—H
    |
    H
```

b. Except for hydrogen, outer atoms are usually those with the highest electronegativities. Here are some examples. In carbon dioxide (CO_2) an inner carbon atom ($\chi = 2.5$) bonds to two outer oxygens ($\chi = 3.5$). In dinitrogen monoxide (N_2O) the more electronegative oxygen atom is an outer atom, so the two nitrogen atoms ($\chi = 3.0$) must be bonded to each other: N—N—O. Phosphoric acid (H_3PO_4) has its less electronegative phosphorus atom ($\chi = 2.1$) surrounded by four more electronegative oxygen atoms. The hydrogen atoms, in turn, are outer atoms attached to the oxygen atoms. In potassium chlorate ($KClO_3$), an ionic compound, the chlorate anion has three outer oxygen atoms bonded to a central chlorine atom ($\chi = 3.0$). In chlorine trifluoride (ClF_3), chlorine bonds to three outer fluorine atoms ($\chi = 4.0$).

```
          O                        O   -              F
          |                        |                  |
H—O—P—O—H             K+          Cl                 Cl
          |                       /  \               /  \
          O                      O    O             F    F
          |
          H
       H3PO4                    KClO3               ClF3
```

The guidelines for outer atoms do not always give an unambiguous structure, but additional information may come from the way the chemical formula is written.

c. The order in which atoms are listed in the formula often indicates the bonding pattern. For example, in HCN the framework is H—C—N; the atoms in the OCN^- anion are in the order O—C—N; and CH_3NH_2 has the framework shown here:

```
    H
    |      H
H—C—N<
    |      H
    H
```

d. Atoms enclosed in parentheses are bonded together, and the entire group can be bound to the preceding or following atom. Both conventions are widespread, and sometimes it takes experience and practice to sort it all out.

These guidelines will lead you from the chemical formula to the correct arrangement of atoms *in many cases.* Other molecules are so complex, however, that the framework of atoms must be provided before the Lewis structure can be assembled. Sample Problem 8-4 provides some examples of how to determine bonding frameworks.

SAMPLE PROBLEM 8-4 BONDING FRAMEWORKS

Determine the bonding frameworks of the fertilizers in Sample Problem 8-2.

METHOD: Use the chemical formulas to determine the appropriate frameworks. To keep track of the number of valence electrons needed for the bonding framework, remember that every chemical bond contains two electrons.

NH_3: The three hydrogens must be outer atoms, so they must be bonded to an inner nitrogen atom:

```
    H
    |
    N
  /   \
 H     H
```

Each bond uses two of ammonia's eight valence electrons, leaving two still to be placed.

$(NH_4)_2SO_4$: Treat each ion separately because no covalent bonds exist between ions. The ammonium ion has four outer hydrogens surrounding the nitrogen atom. Sulfate has four outer oxygen atoms ($\chi = 3.5$) bonded to the less electronegative sulfur atom ($\chi = 2.5$):

```
                          H  +            O  2−
                          |               |
                       H—N—H           O—S—O
                          |               |
                          H               O
Remaining electrons:   8 − 8 = 0      32 − 8 = 24
```

These frameworks raise an important point about Lewis structures. Although Lewis structures frequently can be drawn to show approximate molecular shapes, a Lewis structure does not necessarily represent the three-dimensional shape of a molecule. In fact, neither ammonium nor sulfate is a flat "square" molecule. We discuss the shapes of molecules later.

$(NH_2)_2CO$: Here, the parentheses help us work out the framework. There are two NH_2 groups, each bonded to the carbon atom. Oxygen, which is an outer atom, is also bonded to carbon, giving the following framework:

```
     H       H
     |       |
     N       N
   /   \   /   \
  H      C      H
         |
         O
```

Remaining electrons: 24 − 14 = 10

KNO_3: Potassium is listed separately because it is a metal cation. The NO_3^- ion has an inner nitrogen atom and three outer oxygen atoms:

```
            O  −
            |
 K+         N
          /   \
         O     O
```

Remaining electrons: 24 − 6 = 18

---

4. *Place three nonbonding pairs of electrons on each outer atom except H.* An atom with four pairs of valence electrons uses all four of its *s* and *p* valence orbitals. Three nonbonding electron pairs, also called *lone pairs,* plus one pair in a bond, give each outer atom four electron pairs. A set of four pairs of electrons surrounding an atom is often referred to an *octet.* Other than hydrogen, outer atoms are most stable when associated with an octet of electrons. Hydrogen uses only the 1*s* orbital for bonding, so a hydrogen atom can accommodate no more than two electrons.

In diatomic molecules, there may not be enough "leftover" valence electrons to place three nonbonding pairs on each atom. Assign three pairs to the more electronegative atom, then place the remaining electrons on the other atom. Sample Problem 8-5 continues our treatment of the Lewis structures of fertilizers.

Homonuclear diatomic molecules such as N_2 and O_2 are treated by assigning three pairs of electrons to one atom and the remaining electrons to the other atom.

SAMPLE PROBLEM 8-5 ASSIGNING ELECTRONS TO OUTER ATOMS

Complete the outer atom valence shells of the fertilizers in Sample Problem 8-2.

METHOD: This sample problem builds on the work done in Sample Problems 8-3 and 8-4, where we counted valence electrons and constructed the bonding frameworks. Valence shells are then completed by adding three nonbonding pairs to each outer atom except hydrogen. Each pair is shown as two dots placed next to the atomic symbol. We maintain valence electron bookkeeping by subtracting the number of nonbonding electrons from our running totals. Here are the results:

NH_3: No outer atoms other than H. Remaining electrons: $8 - 6 - 0 = 2$

NH_4^+: No outer atoms other than H. Remaining electrons: $8 - 8 - 0 = 0$

SO_4^{2-}: Four outer oxygen atoms, each of which takes three pairs of electrons:

```
      ..
     :O:  2-
      |
  ..  |   ..
 :O — S — O:
  ''  |   ''
      |
     :O:
      ''
```

Remaining electrons: $32 - 8 - (6)(4) = 0$

$(NH_2)_2CO$: Four outer hydrogen atoms and one outer oxygen atom that takes three pairs of electrons:

```
     H       H
     |       |
   / N \   / N \
  H      C       H
         |
        :O:
         ''
```

Remaining electrons: $24 - 14 - 6 = 4$

NO_3^-: Three outer oxygen atoms, each of which takes three pairs of electrons:

```
      ..
     :O:  –
      |
  ..  N   ..
 :O /   \ O:
  ''      ''
```

Remaining electrons: $24 - 6 - (3)(6) = 0$

5. *Assign the remaining valence electrons to inner atoms.* This step is straightforward if only one inner atom exists. If the molecule has more than one inner atom, place nonbonding pairs around the most electronegative atom until its number of bonds plus nonbonding pairs totals four. If there are still unassigned electrons, do the same for the next most electronegative atom. Continue in this manner until all valence electrons have been assigned. At this point, we have built a **provisional Lewis structure.** Sample Problem 8-6 completes the provisional Lewis structures for our fertilizer examples.

SAMPLE PROBLEM 8-6 PROVISIONAL LEWIS STRUCTURES

Complete the provisional Lewis structures of the fertilizers in Sample Problem 8-2.

METHOD: Again, this problem builds on Sample Problems 8-2 through 8-5. A provisional Lewis structure must contain all the valence electrons. The electrons left over after outer atoms have been assigned octets are placed on inner atoms, beginning with the most electronegative one.

The structures of the ammonium cation, sulfate anion, and nitrate anion shown in Problem 8-5 have no additional valence electrons to be placed, so they are already provisional Lewis structures.

To complete the provisional structure of NH_3, place the two remaining electrons on the inner nitrogen atom:

H–N(:)(–H)–H   Remaining electrons: 8 − 6 − 0 − 2 = 0

Urea has three inner atoms. Among the three, nitrogen is more electronegative than carbon, so add electrons to the nitrogen atoms first. Each nitrogen atom already has three bonds, so adding one lone pair gives a total of four bonds plus lone pairs. When two electrons have been added to each nitrogen atom, all the valence electrons are assigned. No additional electrons are available to place on the carbon atom:

H₂N(:)–C(–:Ö:)–N(:)H₂   Remaining electrons: 24 − 14 − 6 − 2(2) = 0

If valence electrons are left over after each inner atom has a total of four nonbonding pairs and bonds, place any remaining electrons on any inner atom that has $n > 2$. This occurs *only* when an inner atom has a valence shell with a principal quantum number *greater than* 2. Valence shells beyond $n = 2$ include d orbitals and can accommodate more than eight electrons. For example, phosphorus, sulfur, and bromine have nine valence orbitals (3s, 3p, and 3d), so they can accommodate as many as 18 valence electrons. Many transition metals (see Chapter 18) form compounds with 18-electron configurations, but for p block elements, either 8 or 12 electrons are encountered most often. None of the fertilizers from our earlier examples requires this treatment, but Sample Problem 8-7 provides an example.

SAMPLE PROBLEM 8-7 LEWIS STRUCTURE OF ClF_3

Chlorine trifluoride is used to recover uranium from nuclear fuel rods in a high-temperature reaction that produces gaseous uranium hexafluoride:

$$2\ ClF_{3\,(g)} + U_{(s)} \rightarrow UF_{6\,(g)} + Cl_{2\,(g)}$$

Determine the provisional Lewis structure of ClF_3.

METHOD: We apply the five-step procedure for building a provisional structure.

1. ClF_3 contains no metals, and no common polyatomic ions are present. Therefore the molecule is covalent and should be treated as a single unit.

2. Determine the total valence electron count. Chlorine and fluorine both occupy column VII, so each has seven valence electrons (s^2p^5).

$$\begin{aligned} (1\ Cl)\,(7\ e^-) &= 7\ e^- \\ (3\ F)\,(7\ e^-) &= 21\ e^- \\ \hline \text{Total valence } e^- &= 28\ e^- \end{aligned}$$

3. Build the framework. Chlorine, with lower electronegativity, is the inner atom. Make a single bond to each of the three fluorine atoms:

```
    F
    |
F—Cl—F
```

Remaining electrons: 28 − 6 = 22

4. Add three nonbonding pairs of electrons to each outer atom:

```
    :F̤̈:
     |
:F̤̈—Cl—F̤̈:
```

Remaining electrons: 28 − 6 − 3(6) = 4

5. Four electrons are yet to be assigned. They must be placed on the inner chlorine atom, giving it three bonds and two nonbonding pairs. This puts 10 electrons around chlorine, but chlorine has *d* orbitals available to accept valence electrons, so this is a legitimate provisional Lewis structure:

```
     :F̤̈:
      |
:F̤̈—:C̤l:—F̤̈:
```

FORMAL CHARGE

A provisional Lewis structure contains the correct bonding framework and the correct number of valence electrons. However, the *distribution* of valence electrons in the provisional structure may not be the one that gives maximum stability. To determine the most stable arrangement of electrons, we must examine how charge is distributed in the provisional Lewis structure. A charge imbalance indicates that a more stable configuration can be reached by shifting some valence electrons to a new location. The two remaining guidelines provide a method for estimating charge distribution and making appropriate adjustments.

6. Calculate the formal charge on each atom. To assess charge distribution, we assume that all nonbonding electrons are localized on the atoms to which they are assigned and that one electron of each bonding pair is associated with each bonded atom. These assumptions allow us to calculate the **formal charge (FC)** on every atom in a Lewis structure. Each atom has a formal charge, which is the difference between the number of valence electrons in the free atom and the number of electrons located on that atom in the Lewis structure.

Formal charge calculations can be simplified by remembering that hydrogen always has a formal charge of zero.

$$\text{Formal charge} = (\text{Valence electrons of free atom}) - (\text{Valence electrons assigned in Lewis structure}) \quad \textbf{(8-2)}$$

In Equation 8-2 the number of valence electrons in the *free atom* is the same number used in guideline 2. The number of valence electrons *assigned in the Lewis structure* is found from the Lewis structure by counting the electrons around each atom. A quick way to determine electrons assigned to an atom is by counting dots and lines around that atom. Each dot is a nonbonding electron, and each line is a bonding pair, *one* of whose electrons is assigned to the atom. Sample Problem 8-8 applies this counting procedure to the set of fertilizers with provisional Lewis structures as determined in Sample Problem 8-6. Box 8-1 discusses formal charge and bond polarity.

BOX 8-1

FORMAL CHARGE AND BOND POLARITY

Formal charge calculations do not indicate how charge is *actually* distributed in molecules. Remember that most bonds are polar, meaning that the electrons in a bond are skewed toward the more electronegative atom. Formal charges, however, are found by *assuming* that all bonding electrons are shared equally. As a result, formal charge calculations are extremely useful for assessing whether a valence electron distribution is reasonable, but they do not reliably indicate bond polarity or the distribution of charge. Some of the previous examples illustrate this point.

In chlorine trifluoride, all formal charges are zero. Based on electronegativities, however, each F—Cl bond is significantly polar. The electronegativity of F is 4.0, whereas that of Cl is 3.0, indicating that a fluorine atom attracts electrons more strongly than a chlorine atom. In a ClF_3 molecule, each F atom has a small net negative charge (less than one unit), and the Cl atom has a net positive charge of 3 times this amount (also less than one unit). These partial charges are symbolized δ^+ or δ^- as shown in the figure, above right.

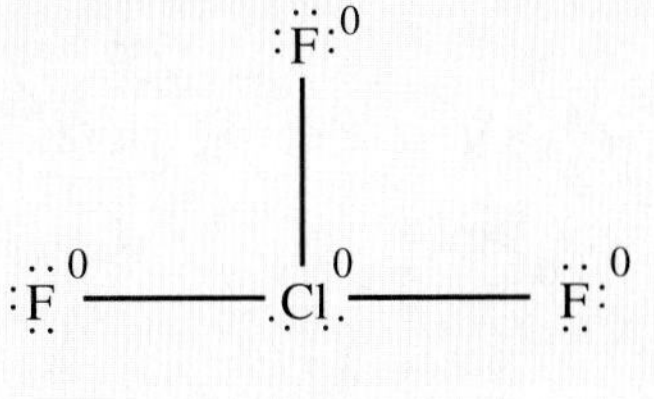

Formal charges

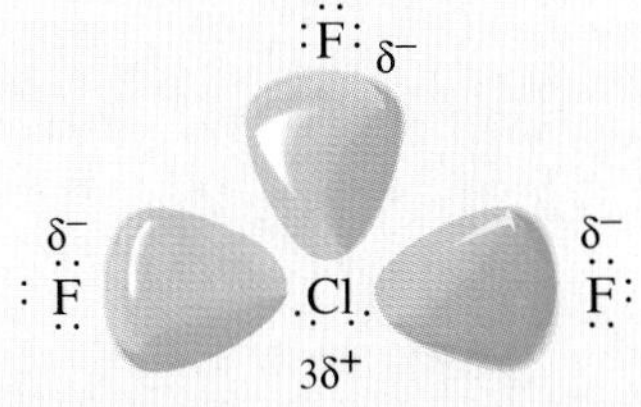

Actual charges

The ammonium cation illustrates the difference between formal charge and actual charge even more dramatically. The + 1 formal charge of NH_4^+ is assigned to the nitrogen atom, but we find from electronegativity values that N attracts electrons more strongly than H ($\chi_N = 3.0$, $\chi_H = 2.1$). Thus the actual electron distribution in an N—H bond is skewed toward nitrogen, leaving each H atom with a partial positive charge and the N atom with a partial negative charge as shown in the figure, above right.

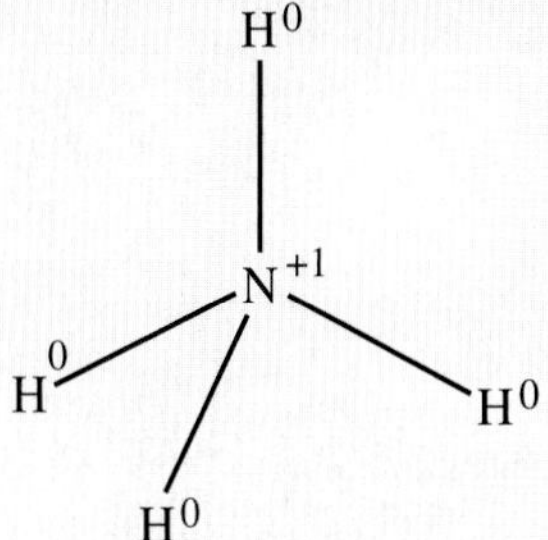

Formal charges

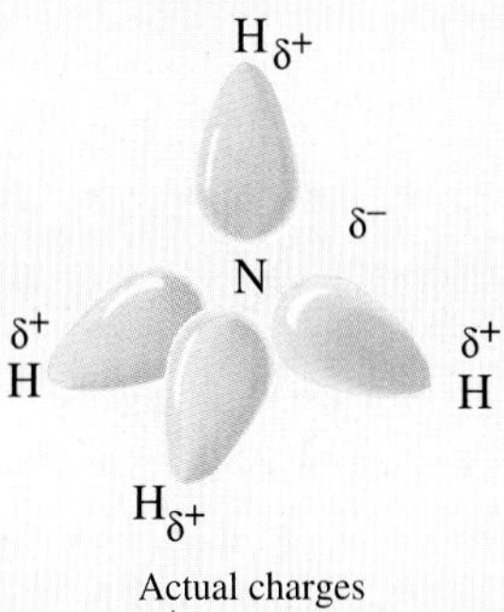

Actual charges
($4\delta^+ - \delta = +1$)

The positively charged environment of the hydrogen atoms in NH_4^+ is reflected in its chemical behavior. This ion readily gives up a hydrogen *cation* to a hydroxide *anion:*

$$NH_4^+ + OH^- \rightarrow NH_3 + H_2O$$

Remember that *formal charges are not actual charges.* Instead, formal charges are simply a device that helps us determine the most stable distribution of a molecule's valence electrons. Formal charges are determined by a formula that oversimplifies the way electrons are distributed in chemical bonds.

SAMPLE PROBLEM 8-8 DETERMINING FORMAL CHARGES

Determine the formal charges of all atoms with provisional Lewis structures as determined in Sample Problem 8-6.

METHOD: To determine the formal charges associated with provisional Lewis structures, apply Equation 8-2 to each atom in each provisional Lewis structure.

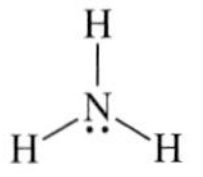

H: Valence electrons = 1
Assigned electrons = 1 (1 bond, 0 lone pairs)
$FC_H = 1 - 1 = 0$

N: Valence electrons = 5
Assigned electrons = 5 (3 bonds + 1 lone pair)
$FC_N = 5 - 5 = 0$

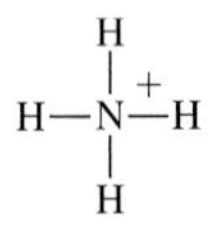

H: Calculation is the same as for NH_3.
$FC_H = 1 - 1 = 0$

N: Valence electrons = 5
Assigned electrons = 4 (4 bonds + 0 lone pairs)
$FC_N = 5 - 4 = +1$

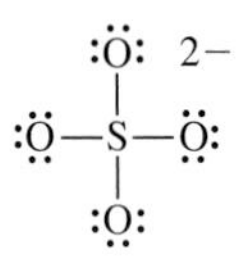

O: Valence electrons = 6
Assigned electrons = 7 (1 bond + 3 lone pairs)
$FC_O = 6 - 7 = -1$

S: Valence electrons = 6
Assigned electrons = 4 (4 bonds + 0 lone pairs)
$FC_S = 6 - 4 = +2$

Sum of FC = 4(−1) + 1(+2) = −2

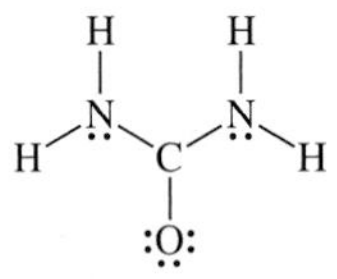

H: $FC_H = 1 - 1 = 0$

O: Valence electrons = 6
Assigned electrons = 7 (1 bond + 3 lone pairs)
$FC_O = 6 - 7 = -1$

N: Valence electrons = 5
Assigned electrons = 5 (3 bonds + 1 lone pairs)
$FC_N = 5 - 5 = 0$

C: Valence electrons = 4
Assigned electrons = 3 (3 bonds + 0 lone pairs)
$FC_C = 4 - 3 = +1$

Sum of FC = 4(0) + 1(−1) + 2(0) + 1(+1) = 0

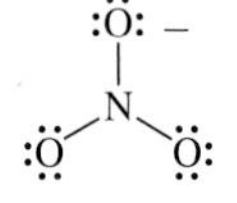

$FC_O = 6 - 7 = -1$
$FC_N = 5 - 3 = +2$

Sum of FC = 3(−1) + 1(+2) = −1

You should be able to verify that all formal charges are zero for the provisional Lewis structure of ClF_3, which is determined in Sample Problem 8-7.

These calculations demonstrate an important requirement:

> ***The sum of the formal charges on all atoms must add up to the charge of the species.***

For a neutral molecule, formal charges sum to zero, and for any polyatomic ion, the formal charges sum to the ion's charge. This provides a useful check on formal charge calculations.

7. Minimize formal charges by shifting electrons to make double and triple bonds. A positive formal charge on an atom indicates that the provisional Lewis structure does not allocate as many electrons to that atom as it can accommodate. Thus a more stable structure will result if electrons can be transferred to atoms with positive formal charges without generating positive formal charges on other atoms. This can be achieved by transferring nonbonding electrons from atoms with negative formal charges to make additional bonds to atoms with positive formal charges.

Minimizing formal charge in this way creates double bonds (four shared electrons) or triple bonds (six shared electrons) between atoms. An atom with negative formal charge retains the same number of occupied valence orbitals because it loses a nonbonding pair as it gains a bond. An atom with positive formal charge gains valence electrons, which can occur only if that atom has a valence orbital available for bond formation. Second-row elements (B, C, N, and O) have only four orbitals in the valence shell (2*s* and 2*p*). Elements beyond the second row (for example, P, S, Cl, and Br) have up to nine valence orbitals (*s*, *p*, and *d*). As a result, second-row atoms must be treated differently than all others:

a. Transfer electrons to a *second-row* atom until it has four occupied valence orbitals.
b. Transfer enough electrons to *any other* atom to reduce its formal charge to zero.

Sample Problem 8-9 applies these principles to our fertilizer examples.

SAMPLE PROBLEM 8-9 MINIMIZING FORMAL CHARGE

Complete the Lewis structures for the fertilizers first introduced in Sample Problem 8-2.

METHOD: To complete a Lewis structure, the provisional Lewis structure must be modified to minimize formal charges, if possible. Modifications can be made when positive and negative formal charges are present in the provisional Lewis structure.

Of the five provisional Lewis structures determined in Sample Problems 8-6 and 8-8, two need no modification. The provisional structures of NH_3 and NH_4^+ contain no atoms with negative formal charges, so these structures are the correct, complete Lewis structures.

Because of the requirement that the sum of all formal charges equal the charge of the species, cations such as NH_4^+ must have atoms that bear positive formal charge.

Each of the other provisional structures contains positive and negative formal charges and may therefore be improved by shifting electron pairs.

For urea, the provisional Lewis structure contains an atom with a positive formal charge and one with a negative formal charge; thus this is *not* the correct representation of the molecule:

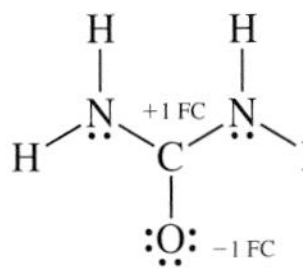

H H
N +1 FC N
H C H
:O: −1 FC

The atoms with nonzero formal charges are carbon (+1) and oxygen (−1).

The formal charges in urea can be eliminated by transferring two nonbonding electrons from the oxygen atom to form a second C—O bond. As a result, the correct Lewis structure of urea shows that four electrons are shared in a double bond between carbon and oxygen:

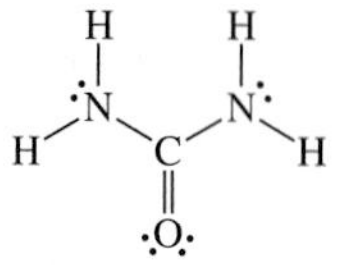

Correct Lewis structure of urea

$$FC_C = 4 \text{ valence } e^- - 4 \text{ assigned electrons (4 bonds + 0 lone pairs)} = 0$$

$$FC_O = 6 \text{ valence } e^- - 6 \text{ assigned electrons (2 bonds + 2 lone pairs)} = 0$$

In the sulfate anion, we also find both positive and negative formal charges, so we can improve the Lewis structure by shifting electron pairs:

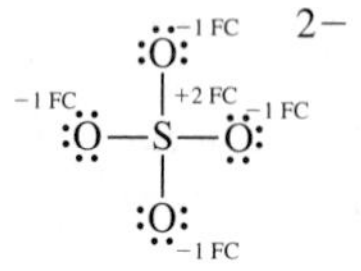

The sulfur atom has a formal charge of +2, and each oxygen atom has a formal charge of −1.

The overall charge on the sulfate anion is 2−.

Sulfur is a third-row element, so we must apply guideline 7b and transfer two electron pairs to reduce its formal charge to zero. We can choose to move electrons from any two of the four oxygen atoms because they are all equivalent. Here are two of the possible structures:

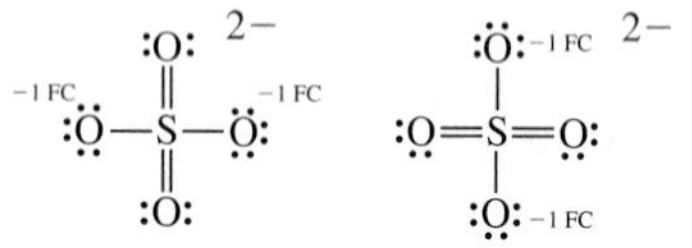

The provisional structure of the nitrate anion also contains positive and negative formal charges:

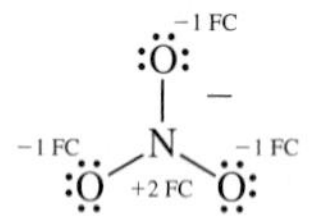

The nitrogen atom has a formal charge of +2, and each oxygen atom has a formal charge of −1.

Nitrogen is a second-row element, so we must apply guideline 7a and transfer electrons until it has four occupied valence orbitals. Only one pair can be transferred, leaving nitrogen with a formal charge of +1 and two oxygen atoms with formal charges of −1. The three oxygen atoms are equivalent, so we can transfer electrons from any one of them:

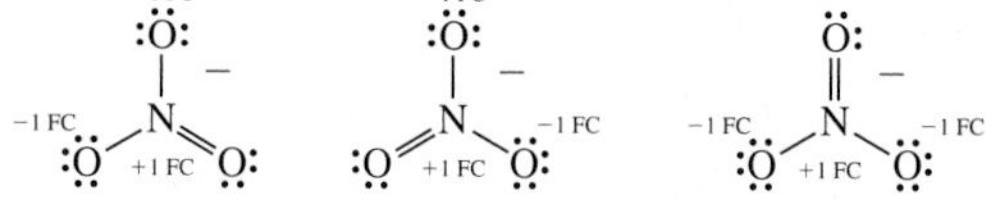

EQUIVALENT LEWIS STRUCTURES

No individual Lewis structure for the sulfate anion or the nitrate anion describes its bonding adequately. Any single Lewis structure of SO_4^{2-} shows the anion with two S=O double bonds and two S—O single bonds. In Chapter 9 we show that single bonds and double bonds have very different chemical properties. In contrast, experiments show that all four oxygen atoms in the sulfate anion are identical. Likewise, the nitrate anion has three equivalent N—O bonds, but any single Lewis structure shows one N=O double bond and two N—O single bonds. To convey that the oxygen atoms in sulfate and nitrate are all alike, we must use a composite of equivalent Lewis structures. Three equivalent Lewis structures exist for the nitrate anion, so the most appropriate Lewis depiction of the bonding in NO_3^- is a composite of all three structures.

Equivalent Lewis structures are traditionally called **resonance structures.** Resonance structures are connected by double-headed arrows to emphasize that a complete depiction includes all of them:

The sulfate anion has six resonance structures, two of which appear in Sample Problem 8-9. You should be able to draw the other four.

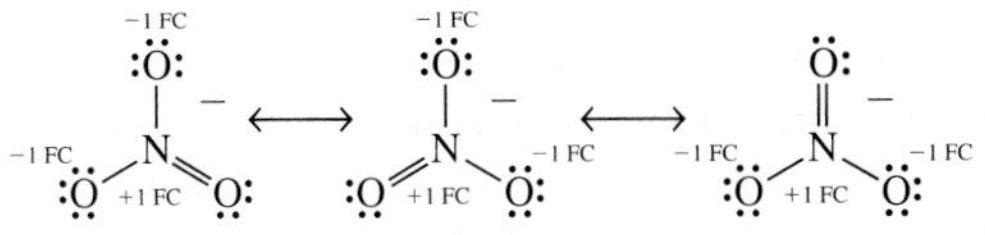

−1 FC :Ö: | N (−1 FC :Ö:, +1 FC, =Ö:) − ⟷ −1 FC :Ö: | N (:O=, +1 FC, :Ö: −1 FC) − ⟷ Ö: ‖ N (−1 FC :Ö:, +1 FC, :Ö: −1 FC) −

It is essential to realize that electrons in the nitrate anion *do not* "flip" back and forth between the three bonds as implied by the resonance structures. The true character of the anion is a composite of the three, with all three oxygen atoms equivalent. The need to show several equivalent structures for these and similar species reflects the fact that Lewis structures are molecular representations. They reveal much about how electrons are distributed in a molecule or ion, but they are imperfect instruments that cannot describe the entire story of chemical bonding. In Chapter 9 we show how these resonance structures can be interpreted from an orbital perspective.

Resonance usually arises from the presence of identical atoms, but many examples of resonance structures exist for similar, but not equivalent, atoms. Sample Problem 8-10 shows an example of nonequivalent resonance structures.

SAMPLE PROBLEM 8-10 LEWIS STRUCTURE OF N_2O

Determine the Lewis structure of dinitrogen oxide, a gas used as an anesthetic, a foaming agent, and a propellant for whipped cream.

METHOD: Lewis structures are determined by the stepwise procedure outlined in this section:

1. Treat ions separately.
2. Count the valence electrons.
3. Assemble the bonding framework, with two electrons per bond.
4. Place six nonbonding electrons on each outer atom except hydrogen.
5. Assign the remaining valence electrons to inner atoms.
6. Calculate the formal charge on each atom.
7. Minimize formal charges by shifting electrons to make double bonds and triple bonds.

1. Neither a metal nor an ammonium cation is present, so N_2O should be treated as a molecular unit.

2. Each nitrogen atom contributes five valence electrons, and the oxygen atom contributes six valence electrons, for a total of 16.

3. Guidelines for structures indicate that the more electronegative oxygen should be an outer atom, giving the framework N—N—O. The two bonds require four valence electrons, leaving 12 to be placed.

4. Each outer atom is assigned three pairs of nonbonding electrons. This uses the 12 remaining valence electrons.

$$:\ddot{\underset{..}{N}}—N—\ddot{\underset{..}{O}}:$$

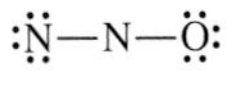

$FC_{C_a} = 4 \text{ valence } e^- - (0 + 4) = 0$ $FC_{O_a} = 6 \text{ valence } e^- - (6 + 1) = -1$

$FC_{C_b} = 4 \text{ valence } e^- - (0 + 3) = +1$ $FC_{O_b} = 6 \text{ valence } e^- - (4 + 2) = 0$

7. Shifting one pair of nonbonding electrons from O_a to make a double bond eliminates the formal charges of +1 on C_b and −1 on O_a. This gives C_b four occupied valence orbitals and reduces all formal charges in the molecule to zero:

```
     H  :O:
     |   ||    ..
  H—C—C—O—H
     |         ..
     H
```

SAMPLE PROBLEM 8-13 LEWIS STRUCTURE OF A BORON COMPOUND

Determine the Lewis structure of boron trifluoride (BF_3).

METHOD: As always, we follow the stepwise procedure, but in a more compact form.

This covalent compound has 24 valence electrons. The boron atom is in the middle, and each fluorine has three lone pairs. No electrons are left to place on the central boron. Here is the provisional structure:

```
       ..
      :F:
       |
       B
  ..  / \  ..
 :F:      :F:
  ..       ..
```

Now calculate formal charges:

$$FC_F = 7 \text{ valence } e^- - (6 + 1) = 0$$

$$FC_B = 3 \text{ valence } e^- - (0 + 3) = 0$$

All formal charges are zero, so the provisional structure is the correct Lewis structure.

The boron atom in BF_3 has four valence orbitals, but only three of its orbitals are occupied in its Lewis structure. The unused valence orbital on the boron atom makes BF_3 highly reactive. We return to BF_3 when we develop a more detailed picture of bonding in Section 8.6.

The Lewis structure of a molecule shows where its valence electrons are distributed. These structures present simple yet information-filled views of the bonding in chemical species. In the remaining sections of this chapter and in Chapter 9, we build on Lewis structures to develop views of orbital overlap.

SECTION EXERCISES

8.3.1 Determine Lewis structures for the following molecules, showing any nonzero formal charges: (a) Br_2; (b) SO_2; (c) SF_4; and (d) $CaCO_3$.

8.3.2 Determine Lewis structures for the following molecules: (a) CF_2Cl_2 (Freon 12, used in air conditioners; both Cl and both F atoms are bonded to C); (b) HCCH (acetylene, used in welding torches); and (c) $(H_3C)_2CO$ (acetone, an organic solvent).

8.3.3 One of the products of the reaction described in Sample Problem 8-7 is gaseous UF_6. Determine the Lewis structure of this substance.

8.4 TETRAHEDRAL MOLECULES: CARBON

The Lewis structure of a molecule shows how the valence electrons are distributed among the atoms. This gives a useful qualitative picture, but a more thorough understanding of chemistry requires a more detailed description of molecular bonding and molecular shapes. In particular, Lewis structures do not directly show the *three-dimensional* arrangements of atoms in a molecule, which play a key role in determining chemical reactivity. In the next few sections, we develop an orbital overlap picture of localized bonding that includes molecular shapes.

THE SHAPE OF METHANE

The Lewis structure of methane (CH_4) shows that the molecule contains four C—H single covalent bonds. How are these bonds arranged in three-dimensional space? Based on its chemical behavior, chemists concluded more than a century ago that the methane molecule has a highly symmetrical shape. Modern spectroscopic measurements show that the carbon atom is at the center of the molecule, with the four hydrogen atoms located at the four corners of a regular **tetrahedron.**

A regular tetrahedron has four identical faces and four identical corners. Each face is an equilateral triangle. Although methane is the simplest molecule with a tetrahedral shape, many molecules contain atoms with tetrahedral geometry, so it is very important to be able to visualize the shape of a tetrahedron.

In a methane molecule, one hydrogen atom is at each of the four corners of a tetrahedron. Each H—C—H set makes a **bond angle** of 109.5 degrees, and all C—H bond lengths are 109 pm. This three-dimensional structure cannot be depicted accurately on a two-dimensional surface, but Figure 8-8 shows some two-dimensional approximate representations of methane. Neither the chemical formula (Figure 8-8, *A*) nor the Lewis structure (Figure 8-8, *B*) indicates the shape of methane. To convey shape, we must use more elaborate representations, such as ball-and-stick (Figure 8-8, *C*) or space-filling (Figure 8-8, *D*) models.

Chemists use a variation on the ball-and-stick model to depict more clearly the three-dimensional character of molecules. Such a modified ball-and-stick model for methane is shown in Figure 8-9. The central carbon atom is placed in the plane of the paper. In these models, *solid lines* represent bonds lying in the plane of the paper, *wedges* represent bonds that protrude outward from the plane of the paper, and *dashed lines* represent bonds extending backward, behind the plane.

WHY A TETRAHEDRON?

The most stable shape for any molecule maximizes electron-nuclear attractive interactions while minimizing nuclear-nuclear and electron-electron repulsions. The distribution of electron density in each individual chemical bond is the result of

The idea of minimizing electron-electron repulsion is called *valence shell electron pair repulsion,* often abbreviated VSEPR.

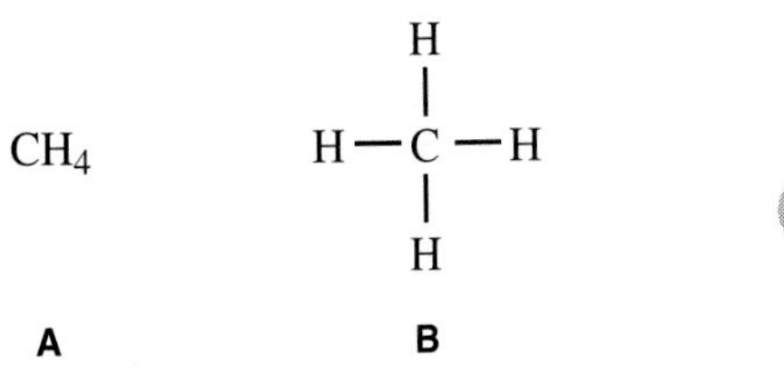

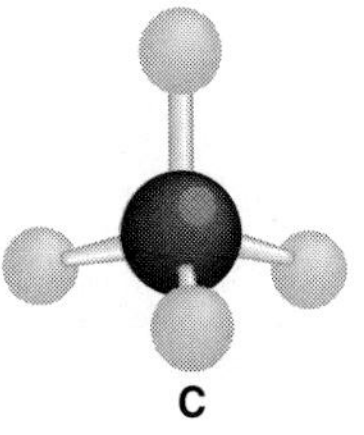

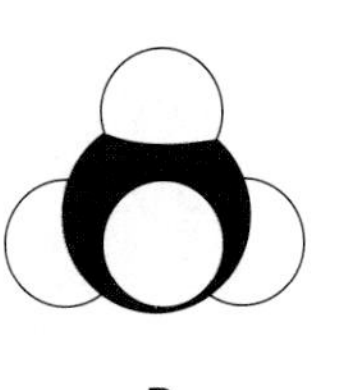

FIGURE 8-8
Four ways of representing a methane molecule on a two-dimensional surface. **A,** Chemical formula. **B,** Lewis structure. **C,** Ball-and-stick model. **D,** Space-filling model.

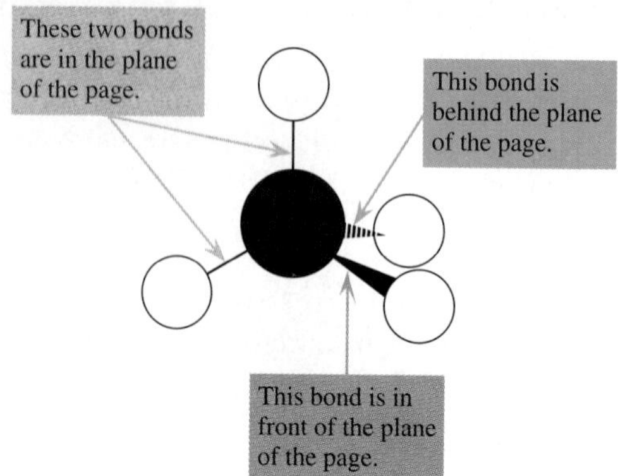

FIGURE 8-9
Three dimensional ball-and-stick model of methane. Lines represent bonds that lie in the plane of the page, a wedge represents the bond that protrudes outward from the page, and a dashed line represents the bond that extends backward from the plane.

attractions between the electrons and the nuclei. The distribution of chemical bonds relative to one another, on the other hand, is dictated by coulombic repulsion between electrons in different bonds. The spatial arrangement of bonds must minimize electron-electron repulsion. This is accomplished by keeping chemical bonds as far apart as possible.

Methane contains four pairs of valence electrons; each is shared in a chemical bond between the carbon atom and one of the four hydrogen atoms. In any one bond, most electron density must be localized between the two nuclei. At the same time, these four pairs of electrons all repel one another, and electron-electron repulsion is minimized by keeping the four C—H bonds as far apart as possible. Consider constructing the molecule by sequential addition of hydrogen atoms, as shown schematically in Figure 8-10. The first atom can approach from any direction. To stay as far away from the first as possible, the second hydrogen atom approaches

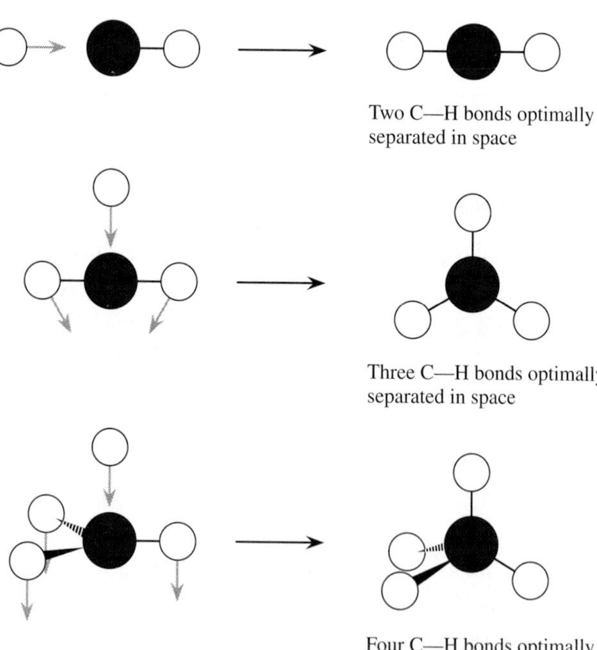

FIGURE 8-10
The methane tetrahedron can be visualized as built up from sequential additions of C—H bonds, always keeping the bonds separated as far as possible. The result is a tetrahedral shape for the molecule.

from the opposite side of the carbon atom, generating a linear array. The third hydrogen approaches this structure from one side and repels the two existing C—H bonds to make a triangular array. The fourth hydrogen approaches from above or below the plane of the existing bonds and repels the three existing C—H bonds. This converts the triangular array into the tetrahedral shape of methane.

HYBRIDIZATION: *sp*³ ORBITALS

We cannot generate a tetrahedron by simple overlap of atomic orbitals because atomic orbitals do not point toward the corners of a tetrahedron. The valence 2*s* orbital is shaped like a sphere, so it has no directionality. Moreover, the 2*p* orbitals point at right angles to one another, so simple overlap of carbon 2*p* orbitals with hydrogen 1*s* orbitals would give 90-degree H—C—H bond angles, not the 109.5-degree angles found in tetrahedral methane.

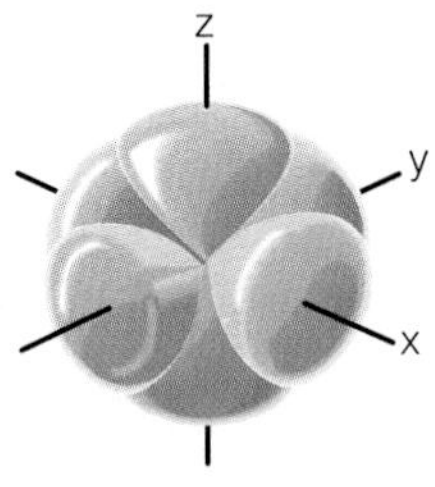

The 2*p* orbitals point at right angles to one another, so 1*s*-2*p* overlap would lead to bond angles of 90 degrees.

The most convenient way to visualize tetrahedral geometry for a carbon atom is to imagine the four valence orbitals of the carbon atom mixing together to generate a set of four new orbitals. This can be done in such a way that each new orbital points toward a different corner of a tetrahedron. Combining an atom's atomic orbitals to form a special set of directional orbitals is referred to as **hybridization.** Bond formation in methane can then be viewed as the overlap of each hydrogen 1*s* orbital with one of these hybrid orbitals of the carbon atom.

Any hybrid orbital is named from the atomic valence orbitals from which it is constructed. In this case the hybrids are called ***sp*³ hybrid orbitals** because the set of four is made up by combining one *s* orbital and three *p* orbitals.

All hybrid orbitals are directional, with a lobe of high electron density pointing in one specific direction. This is indicated by the orbital picture in Figure 8-11. All four sp^3 hybrids have the same shape, but each points to one corner of a regular tetrahedron. This gives each orbital a strongly favored direction for overlap with an orbital from an approaching atom. Overlap of each hybrid orbital with the atomic 1*s* orbital of a hydrogen atom generates a new orbital that can hold two electrons. Four such interactions generate four localized bonds that use all the valence electrons of the five atoms involved. Figure 8-11 illustrates this orbital picture for the methane molecule.

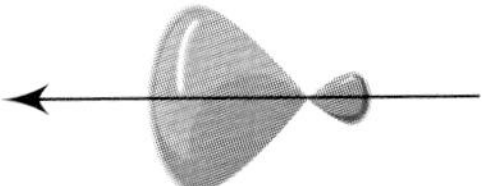

An sp^3 hybrid orbital

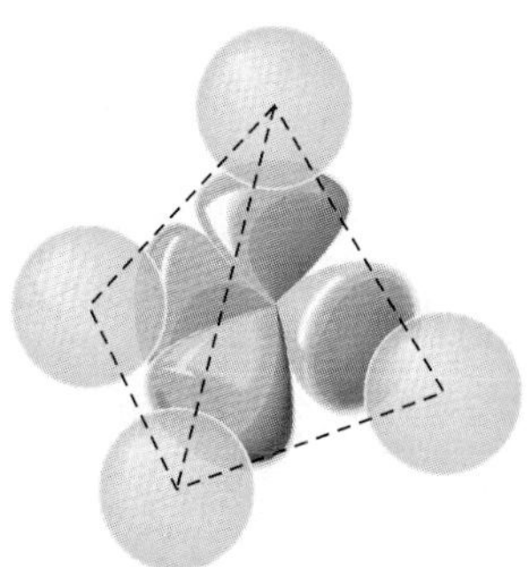

Methane, CH_4

FIGURE 8-11
Drawings of an sp^3 hybrid orbital *(top)*, and the four hybrids interacting with hydrogen 1*s* orbitals to generate the four bonds of methane *(bottom)*. Each bond is represented by the overlap between one sp^3 hybrid and one 1*s* orbital. The "tails" of the sp^3 hybrids have been omitted for clarity, and two faces of the tetrahedron have been outlined with dashed lines.

OUTER ATOMS

All the outer atoms in methane are hydrogen atoms, which use 1*s* orbitals to form bonds to the carbon atom. To visualize how other outer atoms form bonds, consider the carbon-chlorine bonds in CCl_4. Chlorine has four valence orbitals that can participate in bonding. Which one is used to form a C—Cl bond? Remember that overlap is strongest when orbitals point in the appropriate direction in space. For an outer atom, all we need is one orbital pointing toward its bonding partner. One 3*p* orbital of chlorine meets this requirement, so the four C—Cl bonds can be visualized to form from overlap between a carbon sp^3 hybrid and a chlorine 3*p* atomic orbital:

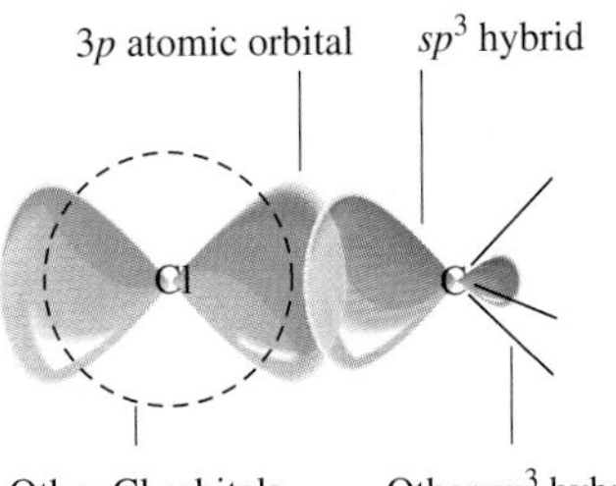

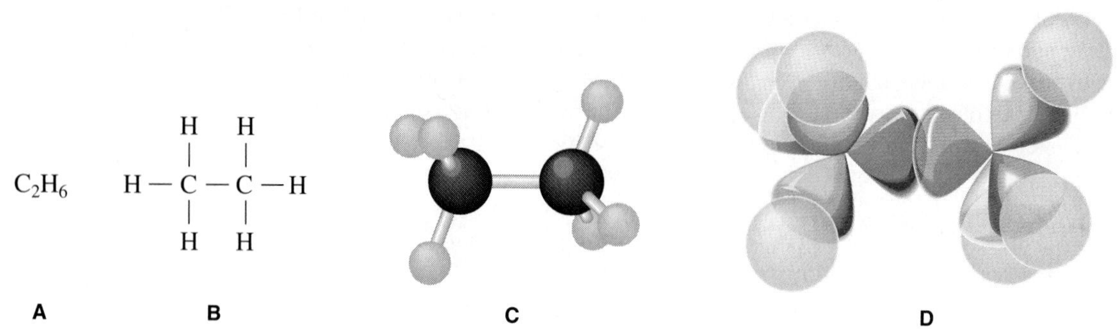

C_2H_6

```
   H   H
   |   |
H— C — C —H
   |   |
   H   H
```

A B C D

FIGURE 8-12
The chemical formula **(A)**, Lewis structure **(B)**, ball-and-stick model **(C)**, and orbital overlap picture **(D)** for ethane.

Hybridization is a useful way to describe orbital interactions for *inner* atoms because inner atoms must form bonds in directions that minimize electron-electron repulsion. Outer atoms bond in only one direction, however, so bond formation can always be represented adequately using valence *p* orbitals. Consequently, it is *never* necessary to invoke hybridization for *outer* atoms. Instead, hydrogen atoms use atomic 1*s* orbitals to form bonds, and bonding for all other outer atoms can be described using atomic *p* orbitals.

ALKANES

Methane is the first member of a huge class of compounds called **hydrocarbons,** which contain only carbon and hydrogen. Hydrocarbons in which each carbon atom is bonded to four other atoms are called **alkanes.** Alkanes contain chains of carbon atoms held together by covalent single bonds, all of which can be visualized as forming from sp^3 hybrid orbitals.

The bonding of alkanes is illustrated by ethane (C_2H_6), which is shown in Figure 8-12. We can think of ethane as a methane molecule with one hydrogen atom replaced by a CH_3 group. The Lewis structure of ethane shows each carbon atom surrounded by four pairs of bonding electrons. The bonds around each carbon are arranged in a tetrahedron to keep the four bonding pairs as far apart as possible. Each of the six C—H bonds can be viewed as resulting from the overlap of a 1*s* hydrogen orbital with one carbon sp^3 hybrid, and the carbon-carbon bond forms from sp^3-sp^3 overlap.

Most alkanes have the general formula C_nH_{2n+2}, where *n* is an integer. The structures of alkanes that contain two and three carbon atoms are unambiguous because the carbon atoms can be placed only in a row. Figure 8-13 demonstrates, however, that there are two possible carbon backbones when $n = 4$. Starting from propane, we can replace a hydrogen atom on a *terminal* carbon with a methyl group and form

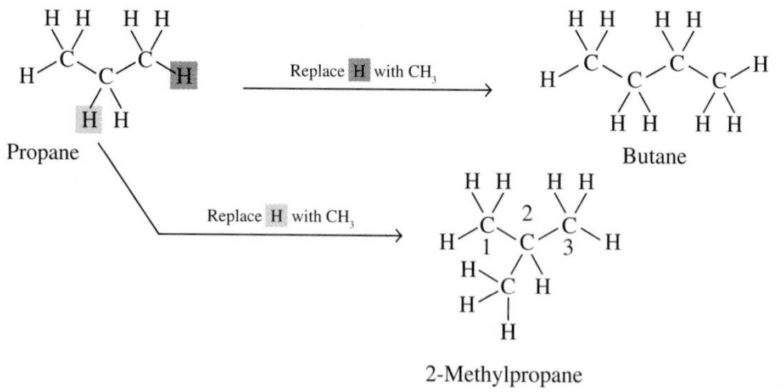

Propane
Replace H with CH_3
Butane
Replace H with CH_3
1 2 3
2-Methylpropane

FIGURE 8-13
Structural representations of alkanes with formulas of C_4H_{10}. These are examples of structural isomers. They have the same chemical formula but different bonding arrangements, giving them distinct chemical properties.

butane, an alkane with four carbon atoms in a row. The 109.5-degree bond angles about each carbon give the molecular backbone a zigzag shape. Alternatively, we can replace either hydrogen atom on the *inner* carbon of propane to give a different compound, 2-methylpropane. In this compound, three carbon atoms are in a row, but the fourth carbon atom is off to one side.

When two or more compounds have the same molecular formula but different arrangements of atoms, they are called **structural isomers.** Butane and 2-methylpropane are structural isomers with the formula C_4H_{10}. As the number of carbon atoms in the alkane increases, so does the number of possible structural isomers. Thousands of different alkanes exist because there are no limits on the length of the carbon chain.

The CH_3 group is called *methyl* because it can be viewed as a derivative of methane, and 2-methylpropane is the systematic name for this compound. A brief introduction to organic nomenclature is given in Section 3.2, but we do not present detailed guidelines for systematic names of organic compounds. We name individual compounds as the need arises.

Petroleum, a complex mixture of many different hydrocarbons, is the main source of alkanes. Petroleum can be processed into various fractions; each contains alkanes with a relatively narrow range of molar masses. Table 8-2 lists these major fractions and some of their uses. As the table shows, these compounds are the principal source of energy in our society.

TABLE 8-2 MAJOR FRACTIONS OF PETROLEUM AND THEIR USES

FRACTION	FORMULAS	BOILING POINT RANGE (°C)	USES
Natural gas	CH_4 to C_4H_{10}	−160 to +20	Fuel, cooking gas
Petroleum ether	C_5H_{12} to C_6H_{14}	30 to 60	Solvent for organic compounds
Gasoline	C_6H_{14} to $C_{12}H_{26}$	60 to 180	Fuel, solvent
Kerosene	$C_{12}H_{26}$ to $C_{16}H_{34}$	170 to 275	Rocket and jet engine fuel, domestic heating
Heating oil	$C_{15}H_{32}$ to $C_{18}H_{38}$	250 to 350	Industrial heating, fuel for electricity production
Lubricating oil	$C_{16}H_{34}$ to $C_{24}H_{50}$	300 to 370	Lubricants for automobiles and machines
Residue	$C_{20}H_{42}$ and up	Over 350	Asphalt, paraffin

SECTION EXERCISES

8.4.1 Freons have been much in the news recently because these compounds are implicated in the reduction of the ozone layer. One Freon has the formula CF_2Cl_2, the Lewis structure of which was the subject of Section Exercise 8.3.2. Describe the bonding of this molecule in terms of hybrids and atomic valence orbitals. Draw a ball-and-stick model that shows the shape of this molecule.

8.4.2 Consider the alkane that results when each of the hydrogen atoms of a CH_4 molecule is replaced by a methyl group (CH_3). Determine the molecular formula and Lewis structure of this molecule, which is 2,2-dimethylpropane. Draw a ball-and-stick figure of the molecule. Describe the bonding and geometry around the carbon atoms.

8.4.3 Draw ball-and-stick models of the three structural isomers with a chemical formula of C_5H_{12}. Then determine the number of structural isomers for molecules whose chemical formula is $C_5H_{11}Cl$.

8.5 OTHER TETRAHEDRAL MOLECULES

Tetrahedral geometry is common among molecules formed from the nonmetallic elements. In particular, many important compounds of nitrogen, oxygen, and silicon contain atoms with bonding that can be described using sp^3 hybrid orbitals.

TETRAHEDRAL NITROGEN AND OXYGEN

The Lewis structure of NH_4^+ shows the cation with four N—H single covalent bonds, so the ammonium ion, with its four pairs of bonding electrons spaced as far apart as possible, is a structural analog of methane. The cation can be viewed as an sp^3 hybridized nitrogen atom with tetrahedral molecular geometry.

Proton-transfer reactions were defined and described in Section 4.6.

The ammonium ion can be formed by proton transfer from a hydronium ion (H_3O^+) to ammonia (NH_3). The Lewis structures of the substances involved in this reaction follow:

$$\mathrm{H{-}\ddot{N}(H){-}H} + \mathrm{H{-}\overset{+}{\ddot{O}}(H){-}H} \longrightarrow \mathrm{H{-}\overset{+}{N}(H)(H){-}H} + \mathrm{H{-}\ddot{\underset{..}{O}}{-}H}$$

Notice that the inner atoms in these four structures are bonded to different numbers of outer atoms. These differences are described by the atom's **coordination number,** which is the number of other atoms to which the atom is bonded in a molecule. In the ammonium ion, nitrogen has a coordination number of four because it is bonded to four hydrogen atoms, whereas the coordination number of nitrogen in ammonia is three. The oxygen atom in water has a coordination number of two, but the oxygen atom in a hydronium ion has a coordination number of three. These species also have different numbers of lone pairs: H_2O has two, NH_3 and H_3O^+ each have one, and NH_4^+ has none. We define the **steric number** of an inner atom to be the sum of its coordination number and the number of its lone pairs. Each species involved in this proton-transfer reaction has a steric number of four.

The steric number measures the number of electron pairs that must be widely separated in space, so it also determines orbital geometry. In ammonia, for example, the nitrogen atom bonds to three hydrogen atoms and has one lone pair of electrons. How are the three hydrogen atoms and the lone pair oriented in space? Just as in methane and the ammonium ion, the four groups of electrons are positioned as far apart as possible to minimize electron-electron repulsion. Electrons repel one another regardless of whether they are bonding pairs or lone pairs, so the orientation of orbitals is determined by the sum of bonding electron pairs plus lone pairs.

An atom has tetrahedral orbital geometry and can be described using sp^3 hybrid orbitals when its steric number is four.

Three-dimensional drawings of the four species involved in the protonation of ammonia are shown in Figure 8-14. Notice that, although all have tetrahedral orbital orientation, the four molecules have different shapes. The steric number dictates orbital geometry because it describes the number of electron pairs that must be arranged to minimize electron-electron repulsion. The *shape* of a molecule, on the other hand, describes how *atomic nuclei,* not orbitals, are arranged in space. Lone pairs do not appear in a molecular shape. Nonetheless, the shape of any molecule can be derived from its orbital geometry.

Molecular shapes can be found from orbital geometry by ignoring the orbitals that contain lone pairs. For example, the shape of ammonia is found by ignoring the

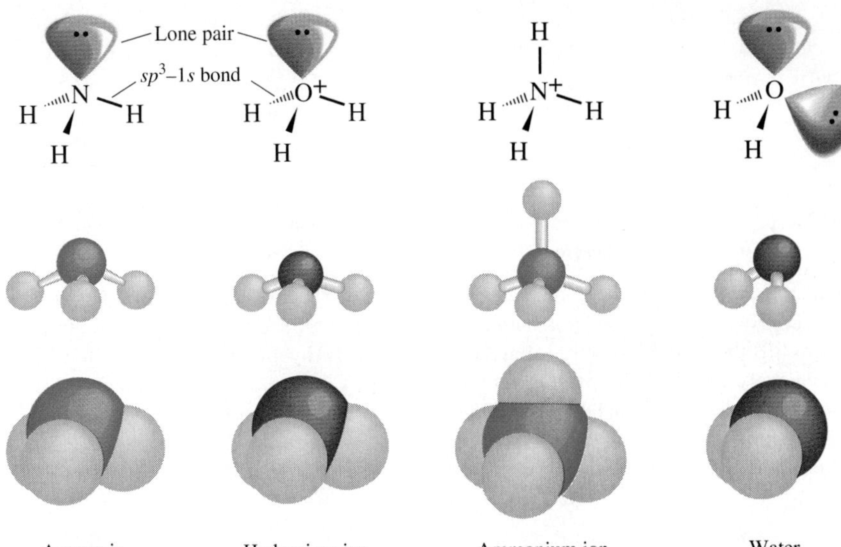

FIGURE 8-14
Representations of an ammonia molecule, a hydronium ion, an ammonium ion, and a water molecule, showing how their molecular shapes are related to orbital geometries.

tetrahedral arm occupied by the lone pair. What remains is a nitrogen atom atop three N—H legs. This shape is called a **trigonal pyramid.** Nitrogen is at the apex of the pyramid, and the three hydrogen atoms make up the triangular base of the pyramid. To find the shape of a water molecule, we ignore the tetrahedral arms that contain lone pairs. This leaves a planar atomic system with a nonlinear geometry, or **bent geometry,** for H—O—H. Sample Problem 8-14 shows another example, and Table 8-3 summarizes the characteristics of steric number four.

TABLE 8-3 CHARACTERISTICS OF STERIC NUMBER FOUR

Hybridization: sp^3
Tetrahedral orbital orientation with angles of 109.5 degrees

COORDINATION NUMBER	LONE PAIRS	MOLECULAR SHAPE	EXAMPLE	PICTURE
4	0	Tetrahedron	CH_4, NH_4^+	
3	1	Trigonal pyramid	NH_3, H_3O^+	
2	2	Bent	H_2O	

SAMPLE PROBLEM 8-14 SHAPE OF HYDRONIUM IONS

Describe the bonding and shape of the hydronium ion (H_3O^+).

METHOD: Begin with the Lewis structure. Use this structure to determine the steric number, which indicates the orbital geometry. From the orbital geometry, deduce the molecular shape and hybridization.

First, determine the Lewis structure. A hydronium ion has eight valence electrons. Six are used to make three O—H single bonds, and two are placed as a lone pair on the oxygen atom:

$$\text{H}-\overset{\overset{\text{H}}{|}+}{\underset{\cdot\cdot}{\text{O}}}-\text{H}$$

The formal charge on the oxygen atom is +1, but no atom has a negative formal charge, so this is the correct Lewis structure.

From the Lewis structure, determine the steric number of the inner atom. The sum of the lone pairs (1) and the coordination number (3) indicates a steric number of 4. This in turn dictates that the orbital geometry is tetrahedral and that sp^3 hybrids are appropriate for the oxygen atom. Three orbitals overlap with hydrogen 1*s* atomic orbitals to form bonds. The fourth sp^3 hybrid contains a lone pair of electrons. The tetrahedral arm containing the lone pair is ignored in visualizing the shape of the hydronium ion, which, as with ammonia, is a trigonal pyramid. The following orbital overlap sketch completes the description:

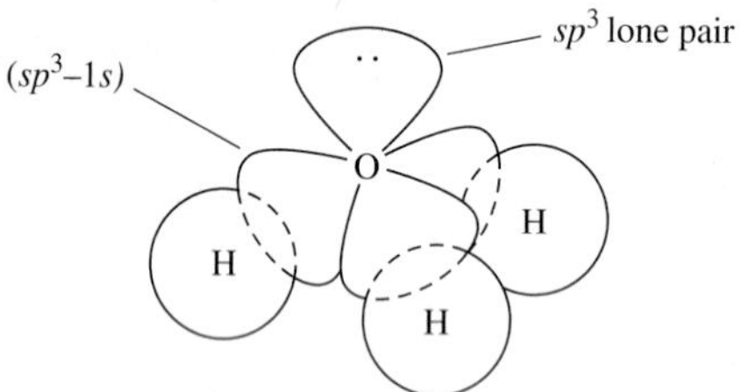

Silicon tetrachloride is treated with magnesium to prepare ultrapure elemental silicon for the semiconductor industry:

$2\,Mg + SiCl_4 \rightarrow 2\,MgCl_2 + Si$

Semiconductors are discussed in Chapter 9.

Methanol and dichloromethane are common nonaqueous solvents that rank among the top 100 industrial chemicals in terms of production. Dichloromethane is often called methylene chloride.

Many other chemical substances also have shapes based on tetrahedral, sp^3 orbital arrangements. Figure 8-15 shows three additional examples. Silicon tetrachloride ($SiCl_4$) is a regular tetrahedron like methane. Dichloromethane (CH_2Cl_2) and methanol (CH_3OH) have tetrahedral shapes, as well, but they are asymmetrical, with different atoms at different corners. The oxygen atom in methanol also has a tetrahedral orbital arrangement, but two lone pairs give it a bent shape. Consequently, methanol can be visualized as (1) methane with one H atom replaced by an OH group or (2) water with one H atom replaced by a CH_3 group.

SILICON

One class of silicon compounds are the **silanes,** structural analogs of alkanes that contain only Si and H. Much less structural diversity exists among silanes than among alkanes because chain lengths seldom exceed eight silicon atoms. Unlike alkanes, silanes are extremely reactive and ignite or explode spontaneously in air. The differences between the properties of silanes and alkanes result from the different sizes of the valence orbitals of silicon and carbon. The 3*s* and 3*p* orbitals of

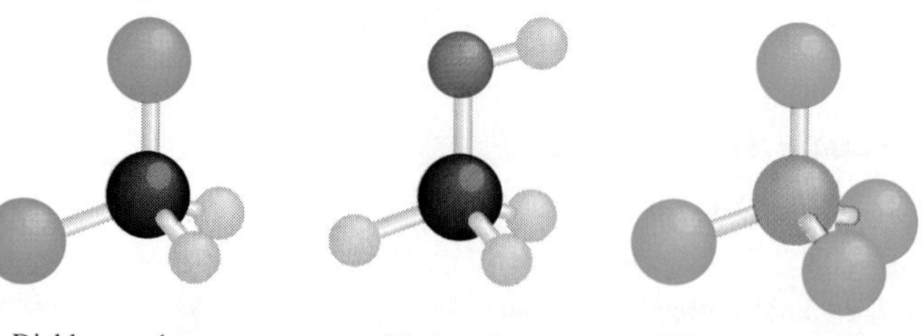

FIGURE 8-15
Three-dimensional ball-and-stick models of CH_2Cl_2, CH_3OH, and $SiCl_4$. All are molecules containing inner atoms that possess tetrahedral geometry.

a silicon atom are much more diffuse (that is, spread out in space) than the 2*s* and 2*p* orbitals of a carbon atom. Consequently, Si—Si bonds are significantly longer and weaker than C—C bonds. Long, weak bonds are more reactive than short, strong bonds.

Compounds of silicon with oxygen are prevalent in the Earth's crust. About 95% of crustal rock and its various decomposition products (sand, clay, soil) are composed of silicon oxides. These abundant silicon oxides account for oxygen being the most abundant element in the Earth's crust (45% by mass) and silicon being second (27%). Near Earth's surface, four of every five atoms is silicon or oxygen.

The principal oxide of silicon is called *silica.* Although the empirical formula of silica is SiO_2, silica consists of a continuous network of Si—O bonds rather than individual SiO_2 molecules. Figure 8-16 shows part of this network. Each silicon atom is at the center of a regular tetrahedron, bonded to four oxygen atoms. As in water molecules, each oxygen atom has two bonding and two nonbonding pairs. The valence orbitals of both elements can be described by sp^3 hybridization.

More than 20 different forms of silica exist, because the bonds and lone pairs around the oxygen atoms can be arranged in various ways; each arrangement creates a different structural form for the silica network. Quartz, the most common form of silica, is found in granite, sandstone, and beach sand.

Pure quartz is a colorless silica crystal. Granite, sandstone, and other forms of igneous rock contain quartz mixed with aluminosilicates, in which some silicon atoms are replaced by aluminum atoms. These materials can also contain oxides of iron and other metals, some of which are responsible for their coloration.

Closely related to silica are the silicate minerals, all of which contain polyatomic anions made of silicon and oxygen. The simplest silicates, called *orthosilicates,* contain SiO_4^{4-} anions. The SiO_4^{4-} anion, which is illustrated in Figure 8-17, has a central silicon atom bonded to four outer oxygen atoms. The silicon atom has tetrahedral geometry and is described using sp^3 hybridization, as is the carbon atom in methane. The Si—O bonds are described using overlap of an atomic 2*p* orbital from oxygen with one of silicon's sp^3 hybrids.

Different minerals contain different metal cations to balance the −4 charge on the orthosilicate ion. Examples include calcium silicate (Ca_2SiO_4), an important ingredient in cement, and zircon ($ZrSiO_4$), which is often sold as "artificial diamond." One of the most prevalent minerals in the Earth's mantle is olivine, $M_2(SiO_4)$, in which M is one or two of the abundant metal cations, Fe^{2+}, Mg^{2+}, and Mn^{2+}.

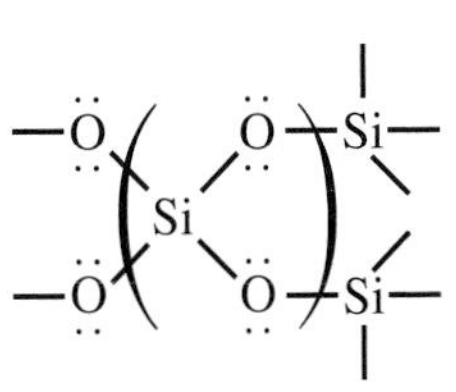

Network Lewis structure

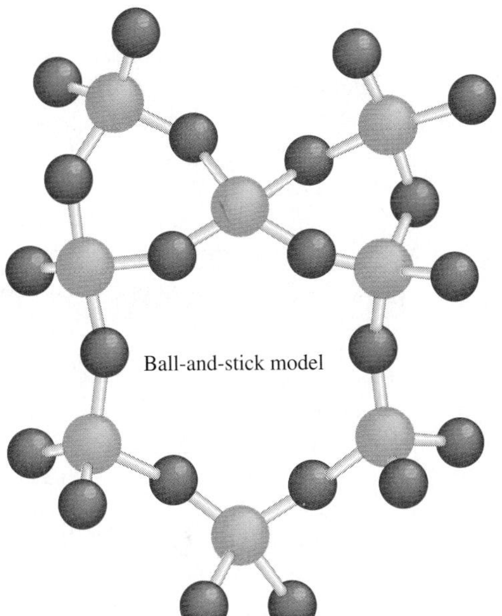

Ball-and-stick model

FIGURE 8-16

The network Lewis structure of silica and a ball-and-stick representation of part of the silica network that shows its tetrahedral arrangement.

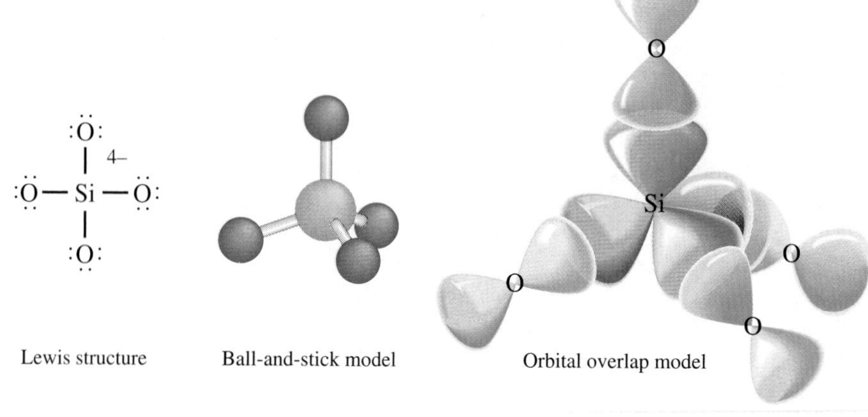

FIGURE 8-17
Several views of the orthosilicate ion, including Lewis structure, ball-and-stick model, and orbital overlap model.

The orthosilicates have different Lewis structures than silica. In orthosilicates, every oxygen atom is an outer atom with a formal charge of −1. There are discrete SiO_4^{4-} ionic units and a 4 : 1 ratio of oxygen atoms to silicon atoms. In silica, on the other hand, all oxygen atoms are inner atoms bonded to two silicon atoms. Silica has no ionic units and a 2 : 1 ratio of oxygen atoms to silicon atoms.

Many other silicate minerals contain inner *and* outer oxygen atoms. In *metasilicates,* for example, two oxygen atoms bonded to each silicon atom are inner and two are outer. As the models in Figure 8-18 show, the ratio of silicon to oxygen in a metasilicate is 3 : 1. Notice also that metasilicates consist of large networks of Si—O—Si linkages bearing negative charges that must be counterbalanced by metal cations. Metasilicate networks can be linear chains or ring systems. Jade, $NaAlSi_2O_6$, has a linear chain structure. Beryl, $Be_3Al_2Si_6O_{18}$, the principal commercial source of beryllium metal, has six silicon tetrahedra linked in a ring. Pure beryl is colorless, but if 2% of the Al^{3+} ions in beryl are replaced by Cr^{3+} ions, the mineral becomes a brilliant green emerald. Figure 8-19 shows these colorful silicate minerals.

Silicates also exist with three oxygen atoms around each silicon bonded to another silicon atom. The result is a linked network of $Si_2O_5^{2-}$ anions arranged in a planar, sheetlike structure. In many minerals, some silicon atoms are replaced by aluminum atoms to give aluminosilicates. The minerals called *micas*—one has the chemical formula $KMg_3(AlSi_3O_{10})(OH)_2$—contain sheets in which every fourth

FIGURE 8-18
Ball-and-stick representations of two forms of metasilicates, the six-Si ring of beryl *(left)* and a portion of the linear chain of jade *(right)*.

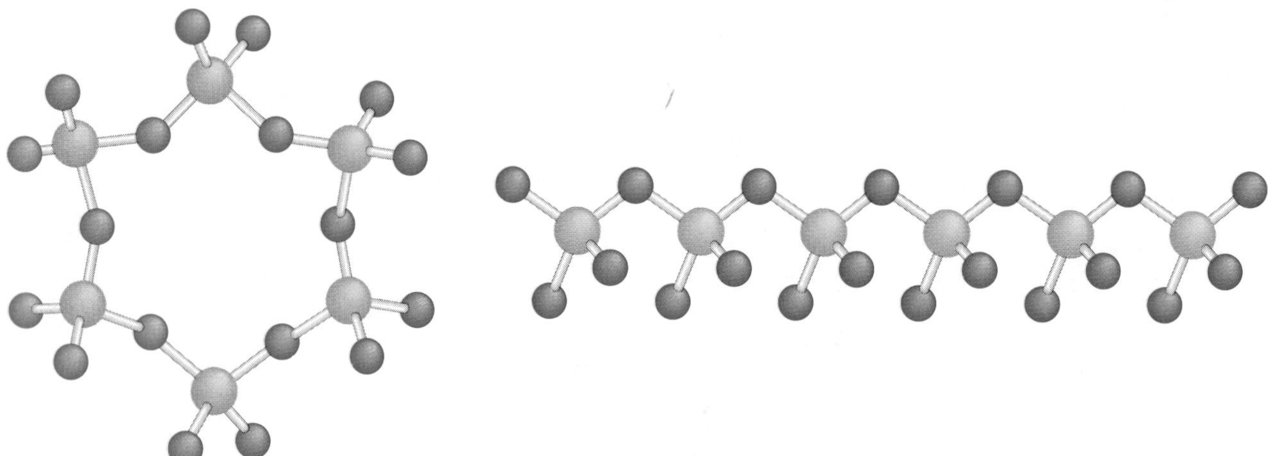

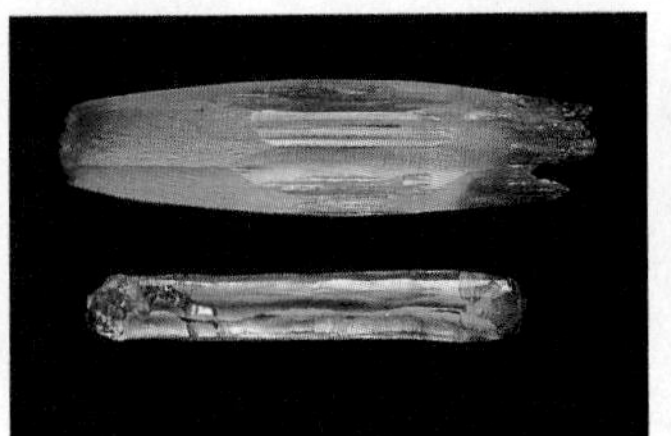

FIGURE 8-19
Mica, asbestos, beryl, and emerald all are silicates. The silicates take on many forms, depending on the detailed structure of the Si—O bonding network.

silicon atom is replaced by an aluminum atom. Because of the planar arrangement of its aluminosilicate network, mica is easily broken into flakes. Figure 8-19 includes a photograph of mica.

Even more complicated chemical formulas result when some silicon atoms have one outer oxygen atom, whereas others in the same mineral have two outer oxygen atoms. The asbestos minerals—one is crocidolite, $Na_2Fe_5(OH)_2(Si_4O_{11})_2$—have this type of structure. The empirical formula unit of the silicate is ($Si_4O_{11}^{6-}$), but the materials are composed of long fibrous chains, as shown in the photograph in Figure 8-19.

Despite the structural diversity exhibited by the silicates, their silicon atoms always have tetrahedral geometry that can be represented by sp^3 hybridization. Moreover, those oxygen atoms that link two silicon atoms can be viewed as sp^3 hybridized, whereas atomic $2p$ orbitals are sufficient to describe the bonding for oxygen atoms that occupy outer positions.

When asbestos is handled, microscopic fibers become suspended in the atmosphere and are breathed into the lungs. There, they lodge in lung tissue, where they remain for many years, causing irritation that eventually leads to loss of lung function. Asbestos, which was once used extensively as insulation, is now recognized as a significant health hazard.

SECTION EXERCISES

8.5.1 Tin compounds are used to stabilize certain plastics against thermal breakdown. They are also important agricultural pesticides because their toxic action is selective for microorganisms, allowing for control of pests at minimum risk for higher life forms. Tin tetrachloride ($SnCl_4$) is an important starting material for the preparation of a variety of tin compounds. Write a Lewis structure for $SnCl_4$, and give a complete description of its bonding, including a sketch of the orbital overlap model.

8.5.2 Hydrazine, occasionally used as a rocket fuel, has the chemical formula N_2H_4. Write the Lewis structure of hydrazine, describe its bonding, and draw a picture that shows the shape of the molecule.

8.5.3 Draw a ball-and-stick model of the $Si_2O_5^{2-}$ unit found in mica. Your sketch should show that it connects to four other $Si_2O_5^{2-}$ units to form an interlocking sheet.

8.6 OTHER HYBRIDIZATIONS

THE SHAPE OF BORON TRIFLUORIDE: *sp*² HYBRIDIZATION

Millions of pounds of boron trifluoride are used each year in the chemical industry because it is *very* reactive and because it makes some reactions occur more rapidly. It is so reactive, in fact, that it makes some reactions occur that would not occur in its

Top view:

F
120 degrees
B
F F

Side view:

F
B—F
F

FIGURE 8-20
Top and side views of boron trifluoride, a molecule with trigonal planar geometry.

absence. Boron trifluoride is particularly important in the production of organic molecules. The structure and bonding of BF_3 indicate why it is reactive.

We determined the Lewis structure of BF_3 in Sample Problem 8-13. Recall that each boron atom has three pairs of bonding electrons and no lone pairs, for a steric number of three. The three pairs of bonding electrons must be as far apart as possible to minimize electron-electron repulsion.

***The optimum orbital arrangement for a steric number of three is a* trigonal plane.**

As Figure 8-20 shows, bond angles in a regular trigonal planar molecule such as BF_3 are 120 degrees.

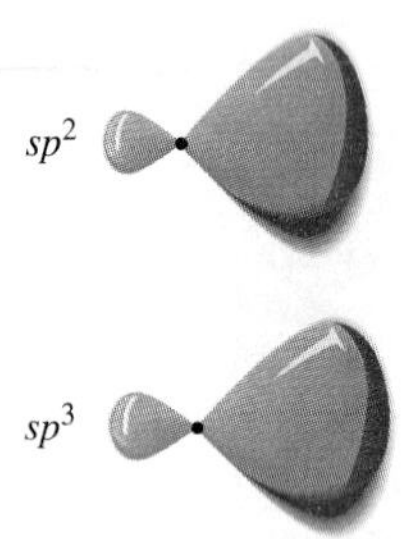

The sp^2 hybrid orbitals look much like sp^3 hybrids.

The valence orbitals of the boron atom have the wrong geometry to form a trigonal plane. Also, a set of sp^3 hybrids is not appropriate because these would give F—B—F bond angles of 109.5 degrees rather than 120 degrees. The trigonal planar geometry atom is best represented using a different set of hybrid orbitals. Proper mixing of the $2s$ orbital and *two* of the $2p$ orbitals gives a set of three new orbitals, called **sp^2 hybrid orbitals,** that have the correct orbital geometry. An sp^2 hybrid orbital looks very much like its sp^3 counterpart, with high electron density along one direction of one axis. These hybrid orbitals differ from the sp^3 set in their orientations. As Figure 8-21 shows, the three sp^2 hybrid orbitals point to the three corners of an equilateral triangle, giving the trigonal planar shape possessed by the BF_3 molecule.

Three sp^2 hybrid orbitals require three of boron's atomic valence orbitals. One valence $2p$ orbital, oriented perpendicular to the plane containing the three hybrids, remains unchanged. This orbital is not needed to describe the bonding in BF_3. The arrangement of orbitals around an sp^2 hybridized atom is illustrated in Figure 8-21. Each B—F bond of BF_3 can be visualized as resulting from the overlap of a boron sp^2 hybrid with an atomic $2p$ orbital of the outer fluorine atom.

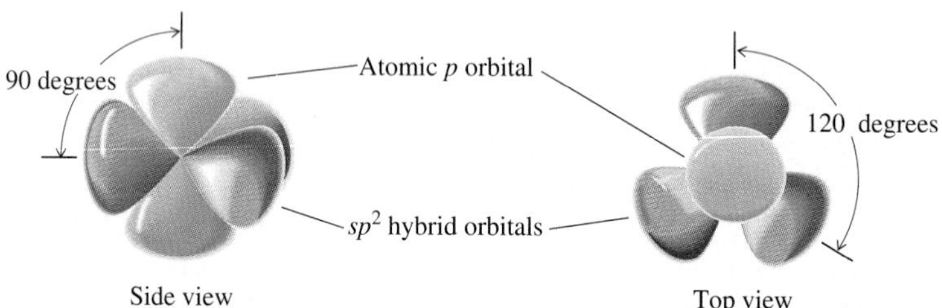

FIGURE 8-21
An sp^2 hybridized atom has three co-planar hybrid orbitals separated by 120-degree angles. One p orbital is left unchanged, oriented perpendicular to the plane of the hybrids.

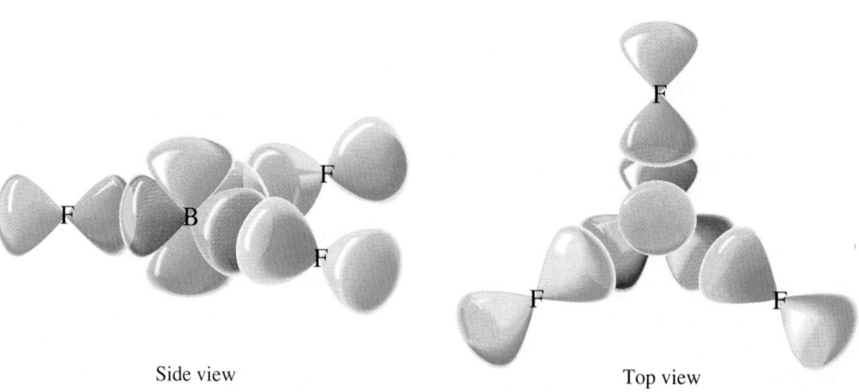

FIGURE 8-22
An orbital overlap picture of boron trifluoride, showing its three equivalent bonds and the unused $2p$ valence orbital.

Figure 8-22 shows this bonding representation, with three equivalent B—F bonds and an unused *p* orbital on the boron atom. The three lone pairs on each fluorine atom, which are not shown in the figure, are nonbonding electrons in the 2*s* orbital and the two 2*p* orbitals not used to form the bonds.

Boron trifluoride is highly reactive because of the unused valence 2*p* orbital on the boron atom. Because energy is released when a bond is formed, atoms that form covalent bonds tend to use all their valence *s* and *p* orbitals to make as many bonds as possible. Thus we expect that boron can form a bond to a fourth atom by way of boron's unused 2*p* orbital. The strength of B—F bonds is more than 600 kJ/mol, so substantial energy is released when boron uses all its valence orbitals and forms a fourth bond. Boron, however, has only three valence electrons to share with bonding partners (B $= 1s^2\ 2s^2\ 2p^1$). Therefore if boron is to form a fourth bond, the fourth bonding partner must supply *both* the electrons. Boron trifluoride reacts with almost any chemical species that can donate two electrons to form a covalent bond. For example, fluoride ions can supply a pair of electrons, so BF_3 will react with fluoride ions to make the tetrafluoroborate anion (BF_4^-). Sample Problem 8-15 addresses the bonding and geometry of this species.

SAMPLE PROBLEM 8-15 BONDING CHANGES DURING A REACTION

Describe the bonding changes that occur when boron trifluoride reacts with fluoride to form the tetrafluoroborate ion: $BF_3 + F^- \rightarrow BF_4^-$.

METHOD: When analyzing the bonding changes that occur in a chemical reaction, we first must write Lewis structures for all species that undergo chemical change. The Lewis structures allow us to determine steric numbers and analyze for variations from one compound to another.

We have already determined the Lewis structure of BF_3 in Sample Problem 8-13. The Lewis structure for BF_4^- follows:

```
     ..
    :F:   -
     |
 ..  |   ..
:F—B—F:
 ''  |   ''
     |
    :F:
     ''
```

(4 F) (7 valence e^-) = 28 e^-
(1 B) (3 valence e^-) = 3 e^-
−1 charge = 1 e^-

Total valence e^- = 32

The central boron atom has a steric number of 4. Therefore boron must adopt tetrahedral geometry to minimize electron-electron repulsion, and its bonding can be represented using sp^3 hybrid orbitals.

In BF_3, boron has trigonal planar orbital geometry, which is well represented using sp^2 hybrid orbitals. Fluoride ion attacks BF_3, allowing boron to use its unused 2*p* orbital to form a new bond. As a fourth bond forms, the geometry about the boron atom changes in a way that positions the four electron pairs as far apart as possible. In orbital terms, the best representation of the bonds changes from one using sp^2 hybrid orbitals to one using sp^3 hybrid orbitals.

Boron trifluoride, with three pairs of bonding electrons, is a trigonal planar molecule with bonding that can be represented using sp^2 hybrid orbitals. Because any molecule with an unused valence *p* orbital is very reactive, few molecules exist with structural features identical to BF_3. Nevertheless, molecules that contain atoms with trigonal planar geometry are very important in chemistry, as we show in Chapter 9.

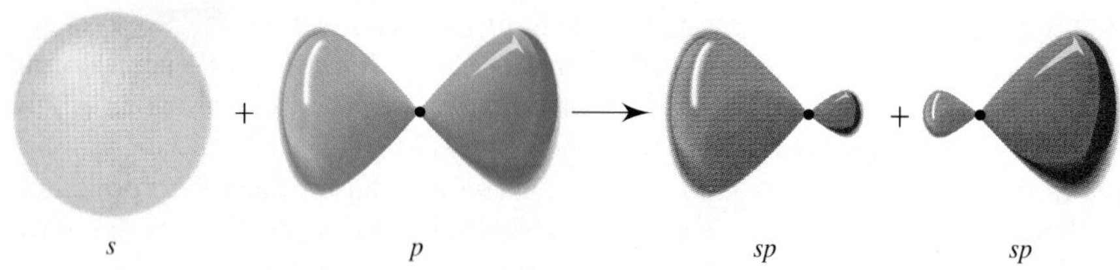

FIGURE 8-23
A pair of *sp* hybrid orbitals that point in opposite directions is formed by mixing together an *s* atomic orbital and one *p* atomic orbital.

THE SHAPE OF DIMETHYL MERCURY: sp HYBRIDIZATION

Mercury forms a variety of ionic and covalent compounds. Dimethyl mercury, $Hg(CH_3)_2$, a highly toxic substance that has two Hg—C bonds, is an example of a covalent compound. Dimethyl mercury can be prepared by reacting a solution of sodium in mercury with methyl chloride:

Solutions of other metals in liquid mercury are called *amalgams*. In a sodium/mercury amalgam, mercury is the solvent and sodium the solute.

$$Hg_{(l)} + 2\,Na_{(amalgam)} + 2\,CH_3Cl_{(g)} \rightarrow Hg(CH_3)_{2\,(l)} + 2\,NaCl_{(s)}$$

Because we know that the compound contains two Hg—C bonds, we can readily determine the Lewis structure of dimethyl mercury. Mercury has a filled valence *d* shell, so it has only two valence electrons. Thus there are 16 valence electrons, all of which are used in the bonding framework:

Hg = [Xe] $6s^2\ 4f^{14}\ 5d^{10}$

$H_3C—Hg—CH_3$ (Lewis structure)

(1 Hg) (2 valence e^-) = 2 e^-
(2 C) (4 valence e^-) = 8 e^-
(6 H) (1 valence e^-) = 6 e^-
Total valence e^- = 16

This Lewis structure shows two pairs of bonding electrons and no lone pairs on the mercury atom, so it has a steric number of two. Two pairs of electrons are kept farthest apart when they are arranged along a line. Thus the C—Hg—C bond angle is 180 degrees, and **linear geometry** exists about the mercury atom.

Methyl mercury compounds are synthesized by bacteria from industrial waste containing mercury. These toxic molecules accumulate in tissues of fish and are concentrated as they move up the food chain. Methyl mercury poisoning caused the deaths of more than 200 people living around Minamata Bay, Japan, when they ate large quantities of fish contaminated with these mercury compounds.

To describe a linear geometry, we need a hybridization scheme that generates two orbitals pointing in opposite directions. This new scheme is a pair of ***sp* hybrid orbitals,** which form from the *s* orbital and *one* of the *p* orbitals. Figure 8-23 shows the shape, orientation, and energy of *sp* hybrids.

Each carbon-mercury bond in dimethyl mercury can be described as a localized orbital resulting from the overlap of an sp^3 hybrid on the carbon atom and an *sp* hybrid on the mercury atom. The mercury atom in dimethyl mercury is unusual because its bonding description includes vacant *p* orbitals as well as *sp* hybrids. In Chapter 9, however, we encounter further examples of molecules with bonding that can be represented using *sp* hybrid orbitals.

PARTICIPATION OF *d* ORBITALS: TRIGONAL BIPYRAMIDAL GEOMETRY

The elements beyond row 2 of the periodic table have valence *d* orbitals that can participate in bonding, giving rise to steric numbers greater than four. Recall from Sample Problem 8-7 that the chlorine atom in ClF_3 has three pairs of bonding electrons and two lone pairs. This gives the chlorine atom a steric number of five and requires five valence orbitals, one of which is a *d* orbital.

The Lewis structure of PCl_5 is:

(Lewis structure: P bonded to five :Cl: atoms)

Phosphorus pentachloride exemplifies the orbital geometry associated with a steric number of five. The Lewis structure of PCl_5 shows that this molecule has five P—Cl single bonds. The five pairs of bonding electrons must be localized in areas

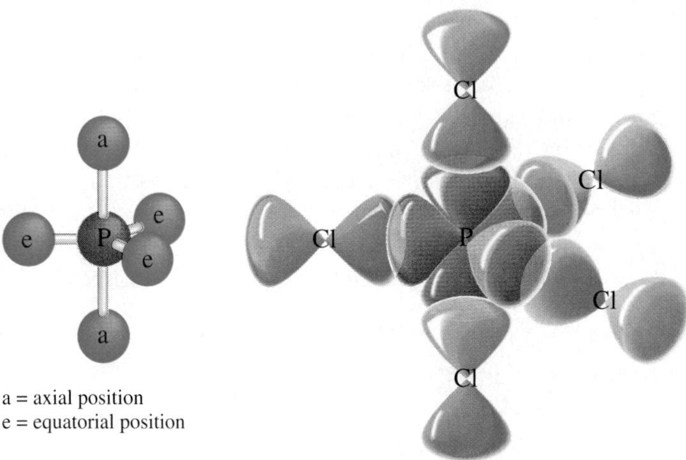

FIGURE 8-24
A ball-and-stick model of phosphorus pentachloride and an orbital representation illustrating its trigonal bipyramidal geometry.

that keep the chlorine atoms as far apart as possible. The arrangement that accomplishes this combines a triangular plane of three well-separated bonds with a linear arrangement of two well-separated bonds. This gives a triangular plane with the fourth bond protruding above the plane and the fifth extended below the plane. The resulting shape, which is shown in Figure 8-24, is called a **trigonal bipyramid.**

***Trigonal* refers to the triangle formed by the three atoms in the plane. Each additional atom forms a pyramid with this triangle, giving a *bipyramid*.**

How does phosphorus form five bonds? Four valence 3*s* and 3*p* orbitals can form no more than four covalent bonds, but the phosphorus atom also has a set of 3*d* orbitals in its valence shell. These five atomic orbitals are also available for bonding. We can combine the 3*s* orbital, the set of 3*p* orbitals, and one 3*d* orbital to form a set of five ***sp*³*d* hybrid orbitals.** Then, each P—Cl bond can be visualized as resulting from overlap between a chlorine 3*p* orbital and an sp^3d hybrid on the phosphorus atom.

> ***An atom adopts trigonal bipyramidal orbital geometry, and its bonding can be represented using sp³d hybrid orbitals when its steric number is five.***

Unlike the geometries for other steric numbers, the five positions in a trigonal bipyramid are *not* all equivalent. Three positions lie at the corners of an equilateral triangle around the phosphorus atom, separated by 120-degree bond angles. Atoms in these positions are said to occupy **equatorial positions.** The other two positions lie along an axis above and below the equatorial plane, separated from equatorial positions by 90-degree bond angles. Atoms in these positions are said to occupy **axial positions.**

The Lewis structure of SF_4 is:

:F̤: S :F̤: (four S—F bonds, one lone pair on S)

The inequivalency of equatorial and axial positions plays a role in determining the arrangement of bonding pairs and lone pairs around an atom with a steric number of five. An example is provided by sulfur tetrafluoride, a colorless gas that has industrial uses as a potent fluorinating agent. The Lewis structure of SF_4 shows four S—F bonds and one lone pair of electrons localized on the sulfur atom. These five pairs of electrons are distributed in a trigonal bipyramid around the sulfur atom, whose bonding can be represented using sp^3d hybrid orbitals.

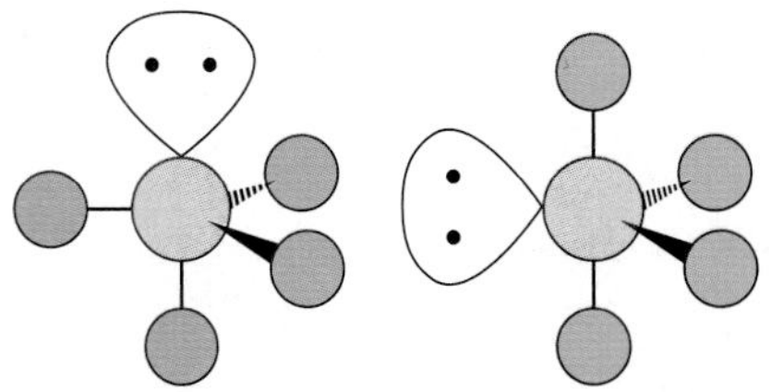

Trigonal pyramid "Seesaw"

FIGURE 8-25
Sulfur tetrafluoride has two possible molecular geometries because the axial and equatorial positions are not equivalent. To minimize electron-electron repulsions, the molecule adopts the seesaw shape.

Because equatorial and axial positions differ, two molecular geometries are possible for SF_4. As Figure 8-25 shows, placing the lone pair in an axial position gives a trigonal pyramid, whereas placing the lone pair in an equatorial position gives a **"seesaw" shape.**

Experiments show that SF_4 has the "seesaw" geometry, which means that this shape is more stable than the trigonal pyramid. Lone pairs occupy more space than electrons in bonds because they are attracted to just one nucleus instead of two. Consequently, stability is maximized when lone pairs are placed as far as possible from bonding pairs. The greater stability resulting from placing the lone pair in an equatorial position indicates that less net electron-electron repulsion is associated with this arrangement. Studies of the geometries about other atoms with steric number five show that lone pairs *always* occupy equatorial positions.

The trigonal bipyramid (PCl_5) and the seesaw (SF_4) are two of the four geometries for an atom with steric number five. Sample Problem 8-16 introduces a third.

SAMPLE PROBLEM 8-16 GEOMETRY OF ClF_3

The Lewis structure of chlorine trifluoride is treated in Sample Problem 8-7. Determine the molecular geometry, draw a three-dimensional picture of the molecule, and describe the bonding using an appropriate set of hybrid orbitals.

METHOD: Use the Lewis structure of ClF_3 to determine the steric number of the chlorine atom. The molecular geometry is obtained from the orbital geometry after placing lone pairs in appropriate positions. Use the steric number to select appropriate hybrid orbitals.

:F̤̈—C̤̈l(—F̤̈:)(—F̤̈:)

The steric number for Cl is five, leading to a trigonal bipyramidal orbital geometry.

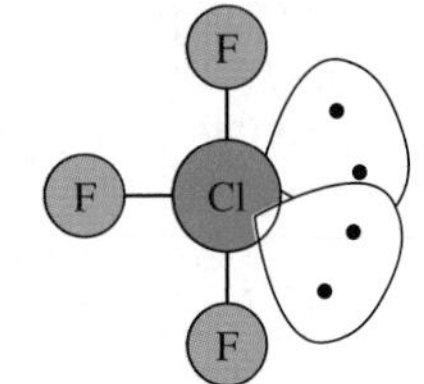

When the steric number is five, there are two distinct positions, equatorial and axial. Placing lone pairs in equatorial positions always leads to the greatest stability. Thus, ClF_3 is a **T-shaped molecule** with two equatorial lone pairs.

The fourth molecular geometry arising from a steric number of five is represented by the polyatomic anion I_3^-. You should be able to show that this anion has linear molecular geometry, with three lone pairs in the equatorial positions. Table 8-4 summarizes the characteristics of atoms with steric number five.

TABLE 8-4 CHARACTERISTICS OF STERIC NUMBER FIVE

Hybridization: sp^3d
Trigonal bipyramidal orbital orientation with 120-degree and 90-degree angles

COORDINATION NUMBER	LONE PAIRS	MOLECULAR SHAPE	EXAMPLE	PICTURE
5	0	Trigonal bipyramid	PCl_5	
4	1	Seesaw	SF_4	
3	2	T-shape	ClF_3	
2	3	Linear	I_3^-	—•—

OCTAHEDRAL GEOMETRY

Sulfur hexafluoride is a colorless, odorless, unreactive, tasteless, nontoxic, nonflammable gas. It is prepared commercially by burning sulfur in the presence of excess fluorine or can be made by treating SF_4 with F_2 at high temperature. Because of its unusual stability, SF_6 is used as an insulating gas for high-voltage electrical devices.

The Lewis structure of SF_6, shown in Figure 8-26, indicates that the molecule has six S—F bonds and no lone pairs. The molecular geometry that keeps the six fluorine atoms as far apart as possible is an **octahedron,** which is also shown in Figure 8-26. All six positions around an octahedron are equivalent, as can be shown by replacing one fluorine atom in SF_6 with a chlorine atom to give SF_5Cl. Figure 8-27 shows that no matter which fluorine is replaced, the SF_5Cl molecule has four fluorine atoms in a square, with the fifth fluorine and the chlorine atom on opposite sides, at right angles to the plane of the square.

Octahedral refers to eight faces associated with this shape. Each face of an octahedron is a triangle, just as each face of a tetrahedron or trigonal bipyramid is a triangle.

To form six bonds, the sulfur atom must use six valence orbitals. Six equivalent orbitals can be constructed by combining the 3*s* orbital, the three 3*p* orbitals, and two of the five 3*d* orbitals to form a set of six sp^3d^2 **hybrid orbitals.** One hybrid orbital points toward each of the octahedron's six corners. We can visualize each S—F bond forming from the overlap of one of these sulfur sp^3d^2 hybrid orbitals with a fluorine 2*p* atomic orbital.

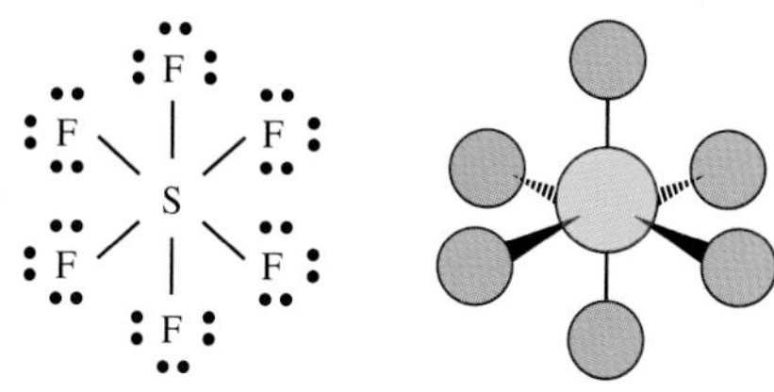

FIGURE 8-26
Sulfur hexafluoride, the Lewis structure of which is shown on the left, is an example of an octahedral molecule. All six positions in the octahedron are equivalent. Notice that each fluorine atom is separated from four others by 90-degree bond angles.

An atom adopts octahedral orbital geometry, and its bonding can be represented using sp^3d^2 hybrid orbitals when its steric number is six.

Three common molecular geometries are associated with an octahedral set of sp^3d^2 hybrids. Most often an inner atom with a steric number of six has octahedral molecular geometry with no lone pairs. Sample Problem 8-17 shows a second common molecular geometry, **square planar.**

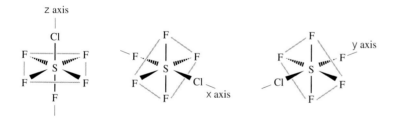

FIGURE 8-27
Replacing any of the six fluorine atoms of sulfur hexafluoride with a chlorine atom gives a molecule with a square of fluorines capped by one fluorine and one chlorine. This shows that all six positions in an octahedron are equivalent.

SAMPLE PROBLEM 8-17 STRUCTURE AND BONDING OF XeF_4

Write a Lewis structure and describe the geometry and bonding in xenon tetrafluoride.

METHOD: By now you should be very familiar with the procedure:
Lewis structure → steric number → orbital arrangement → molecular geometry.

The xenon atom contributes eight valence electrons to the molecule ($5s^2\,5p^6$). Four fluorine atoms add 28 more for a total of 36 valence electrons. Eight electrons are used to make the four Xe-F bonds, and 24 more fill the valence shells of the fluorine atoms. We are left with four electrons that must be placed as lone pairs on the xenon atom:

Lewis structure

8 e^- used to make Xe—F bonds
24 e^- used to fill the F valence shells
4 e^- used in two Xe lone pairs
36 total valence electrons

The model predicts that ClF_3 is a T-shaped molecule, with F—Cl—F bond angles of 90 degrees. However, two of the three equatorial positions contain lone pairs, which extend over more space than bonding pairs. To reduce overall electron-electron repulsion, the two axial fluorine atoms move slightly away from the lone pairs and toward the equatorial fluorine. This explains why the observed bond angle is slightly less than 90 degrees.

The triatomic molecules, water, ozone, and beryllium difluoride, provide particularly strong experimental evidence that our bonding model is accurate:

H—O—H (104 degrees) | O=O—O ⟷ O—O=O (117 degrees) | F—Be—F (180 degrees)

As discussed earlier, the H—O—H bond angle in water is distorted slightly from its tetrahedral value to minimize repulsion between the lone pairs on the oxygen atom. The inner oxygen atom of ozone has just one lone pair and a steric number of three, giving a predicted bond angle of 120 degrees. The bond angle in ozone is reduced by 3 degrees to minimize electron-electron repulsion between the lone pair and the two bonding pairs. In contrast, the beryllium atom in BeF_2 has no lone pairs and a steric number of two. In agreement with the observed bond angle of 180 degrees, the model predicts that the two Be—F bonds point in opposite directions along a line.

DIPOLE MOMENTS

As described in Section 8.2, most chemical *bonds* are polar, meaning that one end is slightly negative and the other is slightly positive. Bond polarities in turn tend to give a *molecule* a negative end and a positive end. A molecule with this type of asymmetrical distribution of electrons is said to have a **dipole moment.**

Some molecules contain polar bonds but have no dipole moment. In these molecules, symmetrical geometry causes polar bonds to cancel one another. A linear triatomic molecule such as BeF_2 is a simple example. Both bonds in BeF_2 are polar, but they point in opposite directions along a line, as shown in Figure 8-28. A polar bond is shown using an arrow with a crosshatch at one end. The arrow points to the negative end of the polar bond, and the "+ " end of the arrow points toward the positive end. For BeF_2 the two arrows point is opposite directions, and the effect of one polar bond exactly cancels the effect of the other. In H_2O, on the other hand, the effects of the two polar bonds do not cancel. Water has a partial negative charge on its oxygen atom and partial positive charges on its hydrogen atoms. The resulting dipole moment of the molecule is shown by the colored arrow.

Molecular dipole moments can be measured experimentally because a molecule with an asymmetrical charge distribution is attracted to an electrically charged plate. Figure 8-29 illustrates this phenomenon. A charged rod deflects a liquid that contains molecules with dipole moments, such as chloroform ($CHCl_3$), whereas there is no deflection for a liquid such as carbon tetrachloride (CCl_4), the molecules of which have no dipole moment.

In a symmetrical octahedral system such as SF_6, each polar S—F bond has a counterpart pointing in the opposite direction. The bond polarities cancel in pairs, leaving this molecule without a dipole moment. Sample Problem 8-19 examines molecular variations on octahedral geometry.

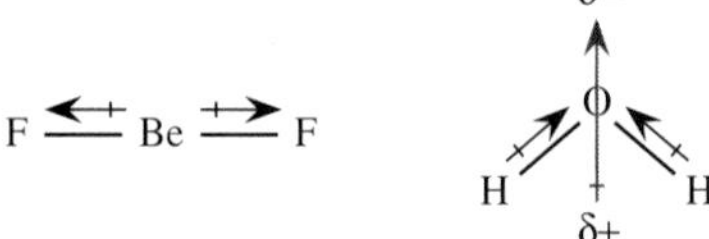

Opposing polar bonds cancel

δ−
H
H
δ+

Polar bonds that are not exactly opposed do not cancel

FIGURE 8-28
When identical polar bonds point in opposite directions, the effects of their polarities cancel, giving no net dipole moment. When they do not point in opposite directions, there is a net effect and a net molecular dipole moment.

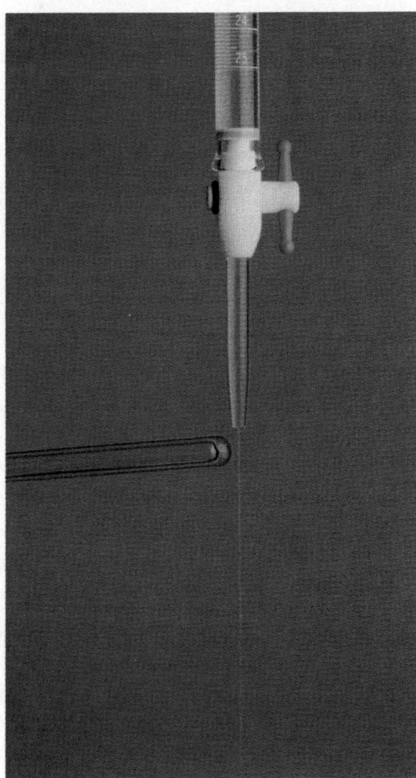

FIGURE 8-29
An electrically charged rod attracts a stream of chloroform because its molecules have dipole moments, but there is no effect on a stream of carbon tetrachloride because its molecules have no dipole moments.

SAMPLE PROBLEM 8-19 PREDICTING DIPOLE MOMENTS

Which molecule has a dipole moment, ClF_5 or XeF_4?

METHOD: Molecules have dipole moments unless their symmetries are sufficient to cancel their bond polarities. Therefore we must examine the structure and layout of bonds in each molecule.

Both chlorine pentafluoride and xenon tetrafluoride are listed in Table 8-5. Each has an inner atom with a steric number of six, but their octahedral molecular arrangement includes lone pairs. As a result, ClF_5 has a square pyramidal geometry, whereas XeF_4 has a square planar geometry. Pictures can help us determine whether or not the bond polarities cancel.

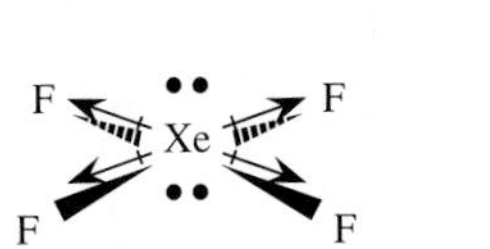

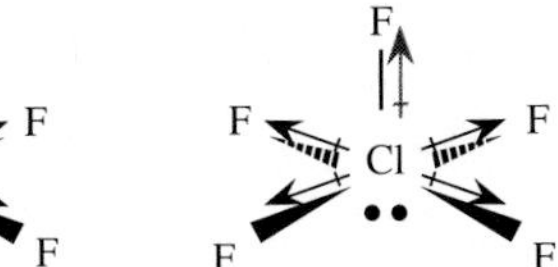

Each molecule has four fluorine atoms at the corners of a square. The Xe—F bond polarities cancel in pairs, leaving XeF_4 with no dipole moment. Four bond polarities also cancel in ClF_5, but the fifth Cl—F bond has no counterpart in the opposing direction, so ClF_5 has a dipole moment that points along the axis containing the lone pair.

No dipole moment exists for any fully symmetrical molecule. Boron trifluoride, for example, has no dipole moment. Although three B—F bonds arranged in a trigonal plane have no counterparts pointing in opposite directions, trigonometric analysis shows that three identical bonds in a trigonal plane cancel exactly. Likewise, four identical bonds arranged in a tetrahedron have polarities directed so that their effects cancel exactly, so neither CH_4 nor CCl_4 has a dipole moment. The trigonal bipyramid of PCl_5 can be analyzed as a combination of a trigonal plane and a line. The two axial P—Cl bonds cancel, and the three identical equatorial bonds also cancel, so PCl_5 has no dipole moment.

The perfect symmetry of these geometric forms is disrupted when a lone pair replaces a bond, and the result is a molecule with a dipole moment. Examples are SF_4 (seesaw), ClF_3 (T shape), NH_3 (trigonal pyramid), and H_2O (bent), all of which have dipole moments. Replacing one or more bonds with a bond to a different atom has the same effect. Chloroform ($CHCl_3$), for example, with three C—Cl bonds and a C—H bond, has a dipole moment, whereas CCl_4 does not. The carbon atom of chloroform forms four bonds in a near-regular tetrahedron, but the four bonds are not identical. The C—Cl bonds are more polar than the C—H bond, so the polarities of the four bonds do not cancel.

SUMMARY OF GEOMETRIES AND HYBRIDIZATION

The relationships among steric number, hybridization, orbital orientation, and shapes are summarized in Table 8-6. If you remember the orbital orientation and hybridization scheme associated with each steric number, you can deduce molecular shapes, bond angles, and existence of dipole moments.

TABLE 8-6 FEATURES OF MOLECULAR GEOMETRIES

STERIC NUMBER	ORBITAL ORIENTATION	HYBRIDIZATION	LONE PAIRS	MOLECULAR SHAPE	BOND ANGLES*
2	Linear	sp	0	Linear	180
3	Trigonal plane	sp^2	0	Trigonal plane	120
			1	Bent	< 120
4	Tetrahedron	sp^3	0	Tetrahedron	109.5
			1	Trigonal pyramid	< 109.5
			2	Bent	< 109.5
5	Trigonal bipyramid	sp^3d	0	Trigonal bipyramid	120, 90
			1	Seesaw	< 120, < 90
			2	T shape	< 90
			3	Linear	180
6	Octahedron	sp^3d^2	0	Octahedron	90
			1	Square pyramid	< 90
			2	Square plane	90

* In degrees.

We have shown that a relatively small catalog of molecular geometries accounts for the shapes of a remarkable number of molecules. Even complicated molecules such as proteins and other polymers have shapes that can be traced back to these relatively simple templates. The overall shape of a large molecule results from the geometry around each of its inner atoms. To obtain a view of this shape, we construct a Lewis structure, which provides the steric number of each inner atom. The steric number unambiguously establishes an orbital orientation and a hybridization. Finally, ignoring the lone pairs reveals the shape about the inner atom.

SECTION EXERCISES

8.7.1 Predict the bond angles for BCl_3, SF_4, and $SnCl_4$.

8.7.2 Determine whether or not BCl_3, PCl_3, and $SnCl_4$ have dipole moments.

8.7.3 Experimental evidence shows that PF_3Cl_2 has a dipole moment, whereas PCl_3F_2 does not. Determine the structures of these two compounds and explain how the structures minimize repulsions.

CHAPTER SUMMARY

1. Chemical bonds form as a result of the sharing of electrons between atoms. Electron density is distributed between the nuclei to maximize electron-nucleus attractions. Bonds can be represented by constructing bonding orbitals from overlapping atomic orbitals. Each bond reaches its maximum stability, called its *bond strength,* at an internuclear separation called the *bond length.*
2. In bonds between atoms of different elements, differences in effective nuclear charge lead to unequal sharing of electrons and polar bonds. Electronegativity indexes the ability of an atom to attract electrons in a bond.
3. The Lewis structure of a molecule is a compact representation of the distribution of its valence electrons. The Lewis structure allows the determination of the steric number for each atom, from which orbital geometry and molecular geometry can be deduced.
4. There are 11 basic molecular shapes: linear, bent, trigonal plane, trigonal pyramid, tetrahedron, trigonal bipyramid, seesaw, T shape, square plane, square pyramid, and octahedron. Many molecules containing carbon, nitrogen, and silicon have shapes derived from the tetrahedron.
5. Orbital overlap to form bonds can be represented using sets of hybrid orbitals (sp, sp^2, sp^3, sp^3d, and sp^3d^2) for inner atoms and atomic valence orbitals ($1s$ for H and p for other elements) for outer atoms. The geometries predicted by this bonding model match the experimental evidence from bond angles and molecular dipole moments.

KEY TERMS

bond angle
bond energy
bond length
covalent bond
dipole moment
electronegativity
polarized electron density

alkane
hydrocarbon
silane

double bond
formal charge (FC)
inner atom
Lewis structure
localized orbital model
nonbonding electron
outer atom
provisional Lewis structure
resonance structures
single bond
triple bond

coordination number
hybridization
steric number
sp hybrid orbital
sp^2 hybrid orbital
sp^3 hybrid orbital
sp^3d hybrid orbital
sp^3d^2 hybrid orbital

axial position
bent geometry
equatorial position
linear geometry
octahedron
"seesaw" shape
square plane
square pyramid
structural isomer
tetrahedron
trigonal bipyramid
trigonal plane
trigonal pyramid
T-shape

SKILLS TO MASTER

- Drawing sketches that show orbital overlap
- Assessing bond polarity using electronegativities
- Writing Lewis structures
- Determining steric number, orbital arrangements, and hybridization
- Predicting and depicting molecular shapes
- Predicting and explaining bond angles
- Identifying which molecules have dipole moments

LEARNING EXERCISES

8.1 Write a chapter summary of two pages or less that outlines the important features of this chapter.

8.2 Design a flow chart that shows how to determine the Lewis structure of a molecule.

8.3 Design a flow chart that shows how to determine the shape of a molecule.

8.4 Describe the role that Coulomb's law plays in determining each of the following properties: (a) bond length; (b) bond polarity; (c) bond angle; and (d) molecular geometry.

8.5 Write a paragraph that explains why formal charges do not match actual charges.

8.6 Draw as many different pictures as you can that illustrate geometric shapes of molecules that have no dipole moments.

8.7 Explain in your own words the meaning of each of the following terms: (a) orbital overlap; (b) electronegativity; (c) bonding framework; (d) inner atom; (e) multiple bond; (f) hybridization; and (g) alkane.

8.8 In your own words, write a one-sentence definition of each term in Chapter 8 that is new to you. Consult the glossary if you need help.

PROBLEMS

OVERVIEW OF BONDING

8.1 What is the electron configuration of a beryllium atom? Which of its electrons will be involved in bond formation?

8.2 Hydrogen forms diatomic molecules with elements from column I of the periodic table. Describe the bonding in LiH, and include a picture of the overlapping orbitals.

8.3 It is possible to synthesize Na_2 molecules in the gas phase at low pressure. Describe the bonding in Na_2, and include a picture of the overlapping orbitals.

8.4 Which orbitals participate in bond formation for carbon, sulfur, mercury, and xenon?

8.5 Describe bond formation between two bromine atoms to form a Br_2 molecule.

UNEQUAL ELECTRON SHARING

8.6 Based on the Pauling electronegativity values in Figure 8-7, compile a list of pairs of elements from the *p* block whose electronegativities do not obey the normal periodic trends.

8.7 Classify the following diatomic molecules as nonpolar, polar, or ionic: F_2, NaF, HF, NaH, and CaO.

8.8 For each of the following pairs, identify which element tends to attract electron density from the other in a covalent bond: (a) C and O; (b) O and H; (c) Hg and C; and (d) Si and Cl.

8.9 List the following X—H bonds from smallest electronegativity difference to largest electronegativity difference: C—H, F—H, N—H, O—H, and Si—H.

8.10 Arrange the following bonds in order of increasing polarity: H—F, Al—Cl, C—Br, Se—H, and Cl—Cl.

8.11 Arrange the following molecules in order of increasing bond polarity: H_2O, NH_3, PH_3, and H_2S.

LEWIS STRUCTURES

8.12 Classify each of the following substances as ionic or covalent: HBr, KBr, NH_4Br, CBr_4, and Br_2.

8.13 How many valence electrons are contained in each of the compounds in Problem 8.12? (For ionic substances, determine valence electrons of each ion.)

8.14 Classify each of the following molecules as ionic or covalent: Na_2SO_3, SO_3, $AlCl_3$, PCl_3, PCl_5, and NH_4PCl_6.

8.15 How many valence electrons are contained in each of the compounds in Problem 8.14? (For ionic substances, determine valence electrons of each ion.)

8.16 Classify each of the following substances as ionic or covalent: NH_3, NH_4NO_3, HNO_3, KNO_2, and NO_2.

8.17 How many valence electrons are contained in each of the compounds in Problem 8.16? (For ionic substances, determine valence electrons of each ion.)

8.18 Identify the polyatomic ions present in each of the following ionic substances: $NH_4(HSO_4)$, $NaClO_3$, $LiNO_3$, $(NH_4)_2CO_3$, KPF_6, and $KMnO_4$.

8.19 Identify the polyatomic ions present in each of the following ionic substances: LiOH, KH_2PO_4, $NaBF_4$, $LiIO_4$, NaCN, and $(NH_4)_2Cr_2O_7$.

8.20 How many valence electrons are in each of the following molecules: N_2O (laughing gas); O_3 (ozone); CCl_4 (used as a dry-cleaning fluid); H_2S (vile-smelling molecule mixed in small amounts with natural gas to serve as a leak indicator); and PH_3 (gas that burns spontaneously in air)?

8.21 How many valence electrons are contained in each of the polyatomic ions in Problem 8.18?

8.22 Determine the bonding frameworks of the polyatomic ions in Problem 8.18.

8.23 Determine the bonding frameworks of the compounds in Problem 8.20.

8.24 Determine the provisional Lewis structures and formal charges of the ions in Problem 8.18.

8.25 Determine the provisional Lewis structures and formal charges of the compounds in Problem 8.20.

8.26 Adjust the provisional Lewis structures of the ions in Problem 8.18 as required to minimize formal charges.

8.27 Adjust the provisional Lewis structures of the ions in Problem 8.20 as required to minimize formal charges.

8.28 Determine the Lewis structures of H_3PO_4, $HClO_3$, and H_2SO_3, in each of which all hydrogen atoms are bonded to oxygen atoms.

TETRAHEDRAL MOLECULES: CARBON

8.29 Describe the bonding and geometry of dichloromethane, CH_2Cl_2.

8.30 Describe the bonding and geometry of ethyl bromide, C_2H_5Br.

8.31 Cyclohexane has the chemical formula C_6H_{12} and contains a ring of six carbon atoms. Determine the Lewis structure and draw a ball-and-stick model of this compound.

8.32 Draw all possible structural isomers for hexane, the alkane with the formula C_6H_{14}.

8.33 Match the formulas of the following compounds with their uses:

Compounds: C_8H_{18}, C_3H_8, $C_{30}H_{62}$, $C_{18}H_{38}$, and $C_{15}H_{32}$

Uses: jet fuel, cooking gas, lubricant, automobile fuel, and asphalt

OTHER TETRAHEDRAL MOLECULES

8.34 Write the Lewis structure of dimethyl ether, $(CH_3)_2O$. Determine its geometry and hybridization. Draw a ball-and-stick model of this molecule, showing it as a water molecule with each hydrogen atom replaced by a CH_3 group.

8.35 Write the Lewis structure of ethyl alcohol, C_2H_5OH. Determine its geometry and hybridization. Draw a ball-and-stick model of this molecule, showing it as a methane molecule with one hydrogen atom replaced by a CH_3 group and another hydrogen atom replaced by an OH group.

8.36 The second simplest silicate is the disilicate anion, $Si_2O_7^{6-}$, in which one oxygen bridges between the two silicon atoms. Determine the Lewis structure of this anion and draw a ball-and-stick model that shows its geometry.

8.37 Silicon forms a tetramethyl compound with the formula $(CH_3)_4Si$. Determine the Lewis structure, geometry, and hybridizations about each inner atom of this substance, then draw a ball-and-stick model of the compound.

OTHER HYBRIDIZATIONS

8.38 When PCl_5 solidifies, it ionizes according to the following equation: $2\ PCl_5 \rightarrow PCl_4^+ + PCl_6^-$. Determine the molecular geometry and hybridization of the phosphorus atom in each of these ions.

8.39 Determine the Lewis structure, molecular geometry, and hybridization of $XeOF_4$. (Xe is the only inner atom.)

8.40 Iodine forms three compounds with chlorine: ICl, ICl_3, and ICl_5. Determine Lewis structures, molecular shapes, and hybridizations of these three compounds.

8.41 Determine the Lewis structures, geometries, and hybridizations of GeF_4, SeF_4, and XeF_4.

CONFIRMATION OF MOLECULAR SHAPES

8.42 Predict the bond angles for the compounds given in Problem 8.40.

8.43 Predict the bond angles for the compounds given in Problem 8.41.

8.44 Which of the following compounds have dipole moments: CH_4, $CHCl_3$, CH_3Cl, CH_2Cl_2, and CCl_4?

8.45 Determine the Lewis structures of the following compounds, and determine which ones have dipole moments: (a) CF_4; (b) H_2S; (c) XeF_2; and (d) NF_3.

ADDITIONAL PROBLEMS

8.46 Among the halogens, only one known molecule has the formula XY_7. It has pentagonal bipyramidal geometry, with five Y atoms in a pentagon around the central atom X. The other two Y atoms are in axial positions. Based on our discussion of electron-electron repulsion and atomic size, determine the identities of atoms X and Y. Explain your reasoning. (Astatine is not involved. This element is radioactive and highly unstable.)

8.47 Draw Lewis structures and three-dimensional ball-and-stick structures for the following molecules: (a) Cl_2O, dichlorine oxide (used for bleaching wood pulp and water treatment; about 10^5 tons produced each year); (b) C_6H_6, benzene, which contains a ring of six carbon atoms (one of the top 20 industrial chemicals, used in production of polymers); and (c) C_2H_4O, ethylene oxide, which contains a C—C—O triangular ring (one of the top 50 industrial chemicals, used in polymer production).

8.48 Recall from Section 4.6 that H_3O^+ transfers a hydrogen ion to the base in an acid-base reaction. A lone pair of electrons on the base is used to form the new bond to the hydrogen atom. Draw orbital overlap pictures that illustrate the bonding changes that occur when a hydronium ion reacts with a hydroxide ion to produce water.

8.49 Write Lewis structures for the following molecules: $OPCl_3$, HN_3 (contains four atoms in a row), $(CH_3)_2O$, $SeCl_6$, and $H_2S_2O_6$ (has an S—S bond).

8.50 In the following reactions, phosphorus forms a bond to a row 2 element. In one reaction, phosphorus donates two electrons to make the fourth bond, but in the other reaction, phosphorus accepts two electrons to make the fourth bond. Use Lewis structures of starting materials and products to determine in which reaction phosphorus is a donor and in which it acts as an acceptor:

$$PCl_3 + N(CH_3)_3 \rightarrow Cl_3PN(CH_3)_3$$

$$PCl_3 + BBr_3 \rightarrow Cl_3PBBr_3$$

8.51 Both PF_3 and PF_5 are known compounds. NF_3 also exists, but NF_5 does not. Show that these facts are consistent with this chapter's orbital model.

8.52 Identify which of the four octahedral molecules shown here are equivalent:

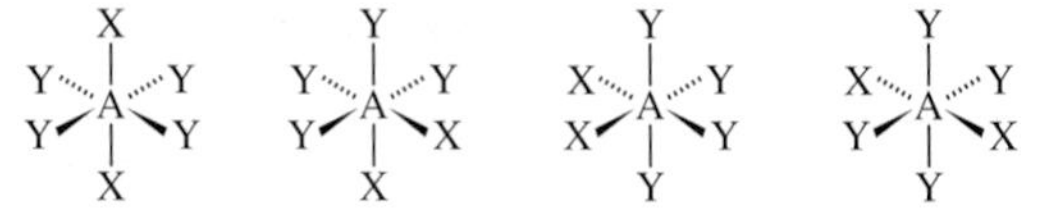

a *b* *c* *d*

8.53 How many different structural isomers are there for octahedral molecules with the general formula AX_3Y_3? Draw three-dimensional structures of each.

8.54 Write the Lewis structure and describe the bonding of borazine, $B_3N_3H_6$. The molecule contains a planar ring of alternating boron and nitrogen atoms, with a hydrogen atom attached to each ring atom.

8.55 In the gas phase, aluminum trichloride exists as individual $AlCl_3$ molecules. Describe the bonding in gaseous $AlCl_3$.

8.56 The methylene fragment, CH_2, has been identified as a reactive species in some gas-phase chemical reactions. Determine its Lewis structure, describe its bonding, and predict the H—C—H bond angle.

8.57 Tellurium compounds, which are toxic and have a hideous stench, must be handled with extreme care. Predict the formulas of the tellurium-fluorine molecules (or ions) with the following molecular geometries: (a) bent; (b) T shape; (c) square pyramid; (d) trigonal bipyramid; (e) octahedron; and (f) seesaw.

8.58 Arrange the following molecules in order of increasing bond angles (smallest first): H_2O, BeH_2, XeF_4, and CH_4.

8.59 With one exception, sulfur forms compounds with all steric numbers. Find an example of each, and identify which steric number is not found.

8.60 Predict all the bond angles in the glycine molecule, $H_2NCH_2CO_2H$, one of the simplest amino acids.

8.61 Determine the Lewis structures of the following compounds: (a) NO_2, nitrogen dioxide (red-brown gas that pollutes the air over many cities); (b) CH_3NCO, methyl isocyanate (toxic compound responsible for thousands of deaths in Bhopal, India, in 1984); (c) ClO_2, chlorine dioxide (highly explosive gas used as an industrial bleach); and (d) N_2F_4, tetrafluorohydrazine (colorless liquid used as rocket fuel).

8.62 Predict the structures of the following ions: ClF_2^-, BF_4^-, and PF_4^+.

8.63 Use formal charge calculations to determine the net charges on the following polyatomic ions:

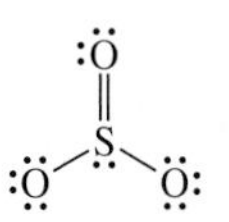

Sulfite, a preservative in wine

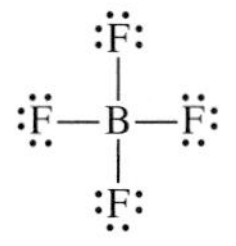

Tetrafluoroborate, a relatively inert anion

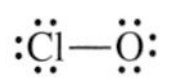

Hypochlorite, a bleaching agent

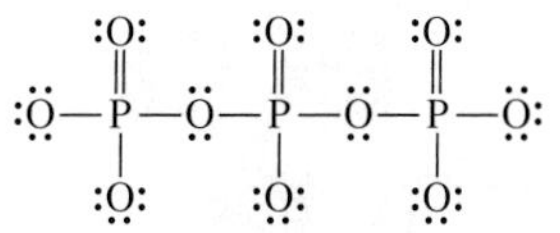

Tripolyphosphate, an important component of detergents

8.64 a. Consider a hypothetical square planar molecule, XY_2Z_2, in which X is the central atom and Z is more electronegative than Y. Two distinct structural isomers are possible. Draw them.

b. Suppose you have samples of both isomers, but you do not know which is which. Explain how measuring the dipole moments of each isomer would distinguish them.

8.65 Draw ball-and-stick models of the orthosilicate and metasilicate anions.

8.66 Antimony trichloride, a soft colorless solid, is used widely as a flame retardant. Describe in detail the bonding in a molecule of antimony trichloride.

8.67 Match each mineral in the left column with the appropriate silicon bonding form in the right column:

Quartz	Metasilicate
Mica	Silica
Zircon	Silicate fibers
Asbestos	Orthosilicate
Jade	Silicate sheets

8.68 Indium triiodide exists in the gas phase as individual InI_3 molecules. In the liquid phase, on the other hand, two InI_3 molecules combine to give In_2I_6. In In_2I_6 two iodine atoms bridge between indium atoms, and four outer iodine atoms exist. Describe in detail the bonding in InI_3 and In_2I_6. Draw a ball-and-stick model of In_2I_6.

8.69 Write Lewis structures and calculate formal charges for the following atoms: (a) bromate, (b) cyanide, (c) nitrate, (d) nitrite, (e) phosphate, and (f) hydrogen carbonate.

8.70 What is the distinction between electronegativity and electron affinity?

8.71 Determine the molecular geometries of the following species: $SiCl_4$, SeF_4, CI_4, $CdCl_4^{2-}$, XeF_4, and $BeCl_4^{2-}$.

8.72 Cyclopropane, C_3H_6, which has three carbon atoms in a ring, is much more reactive than other alkanes. Determine the Lewis structure of this molecule and the hybridization of the carbon atoms. Suggest a reason for the reactivity of C_3H_6. (HINT: What is the bond angle between the carbon atoms?)

8.73 The bond angles in NH_3 are 107.3 degrees, in PCl_3 100.3 degrees, and in PH_3 93.3 degrees. Explain these variations in bond angles using orbital sizes and electron-electron repulsion arguments.

8.74 Draw an orbital overlap picture that depicts the bonding in carbon tetrachloride, CCl_4.

8.75 Amines are organic substances derived from ammonia. The simplest amine is methyl amine, H_3CNH_2. Determine its Lewis structure and draw a ball-and-stick model of it.

8.76 Determine the geometry and hybridization of each inner atom in acetone, $(CH_3)_2CO$.

8.77 About 90% of the matter in our galaxy is present in the stars. Much of the remaining 10% is concentrated in interstellar clouds. These clouds consist mostly of molecular hydrogen, but many other small molecules are present, as well. The molecules listed next are known to exist in interstellar clouds; draw a Lewis structure for each: (a) H_2O (water); (b) C_2H_2 (acetylene); (c) HCN (hydrogen cyanide); (d) CH_2O (formaldehyde); (e) H_2S (hydrogen sulfide); (f) H_3CCN (acetonitrile); and (g) NH_3 (ammonia).

8.78 Carbocations are unstable high-energy compounds that contain positively charged carbon atoms. Carbocations form during the course of a reaction but are usually consumed rapidly. Describe the bonding of the carbocation $(CH_3)_3C^+$.

8.79 Sulfur and fluorine form seven different molecules: SF_2, SSF_2, FSSF, F_3SSF, SF_4, F_5SSF_5, and SF_6. Draw the Lewis structure of each molecule.

8.80 For each compound in Problem 8.79, determine the molecular geometry and hybridization associated with each sulfur atom.

8.81 Explain the difference between silica, silicate minerals, and metasilicate minerals.

8.82 Expand each of the following line structures to include all atoms and lone pairs. For each atom, identify the atomic or hybrid orbitals used for bonding:

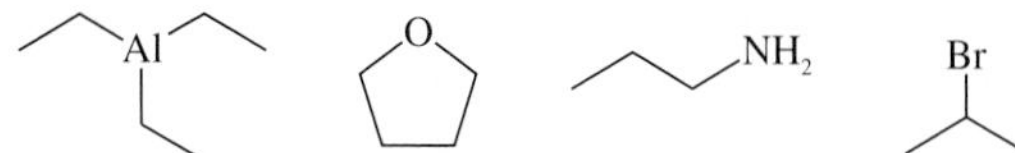

8.83 The H—O—H bond angle in a water molecule is 104.5 degrees. However, in the isoelectronic analog hydrogen sulfide, the H—S—H bond angle is only 92.2 degrees.

Draw orbital overlap pictures that illustrate the bonding in both molecules, and identify the type of bonding orbitals used by the central atom in each case. Use Coulomb's law and atomic size arguments to explain why oxygen and sulfur use different orbitals and have different bonding patterns in these two molecules.

8.84 Carbon, nitrogen, and oxygen form two different polyatomic ions: the cyanate ion, NCO^-, and the isocyanate ion, CNO^-. Write Lewis structures for each of the anions, including near-equivalent resonance structures.

ANSWERS TO SECTION EXERCISES

8.1.1

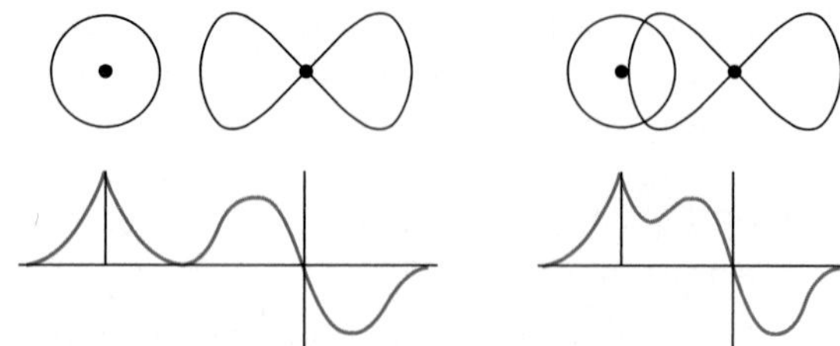

8.1.2 The 1*s* orbital of H overlaps with the 3*p* orbital of Cl pointing along the bond axis. Two electrons occupy this orbital.

8.1.3 Se, 4*s*, 4*p*; and P, 3*s*, 3*p*

8.2.1 (a) O; (b) C; (c) Cl; and (d) Cl

8.2.2 C—H < As—Cl < Sn—Cl < Si—O

8.2.3 Ionic: LiCl, Al_2O_3, Fe_2O_3, Na_2S; and covalent: $FeCl_3$, AgCl, ZnS

8.3.1

(a) :Br—Br: (b) O=S=O (c) SF_4 (S bonded to four F)

(d) Ca^{2+} [CO_3^{2-} resonance structures: O—C(=O)—O ⟷ O=C(—O)—O ⟷ O—C(—O)=O; each singly bonded O labelled –1 FC]

8.3.2

(a) CF_2Cl_2 (C bonded to two F and two Cl) (b) H—C≡C—H (c) H_3C—C(=O)—CH_3

8.3.3

UF_6 (U bonded to six F)

8.4.1 The carbon atom uses sp^3 hybrids and each halogen atom uses a *p* orbital.

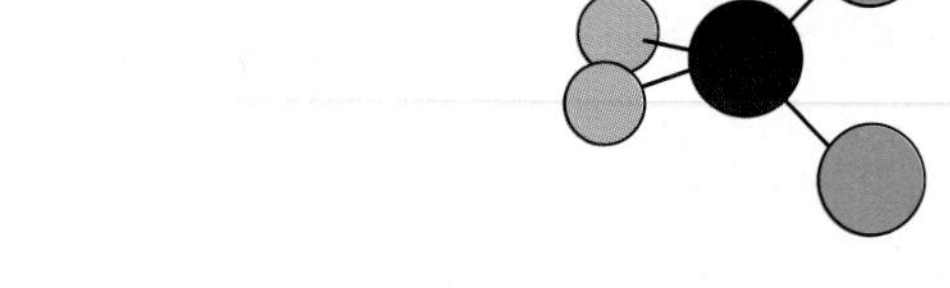

8.4.2 Molecular formula is C_5H_{12}.

C(CH₃)₄: central C bonded to four C atoms, each bonded to three H

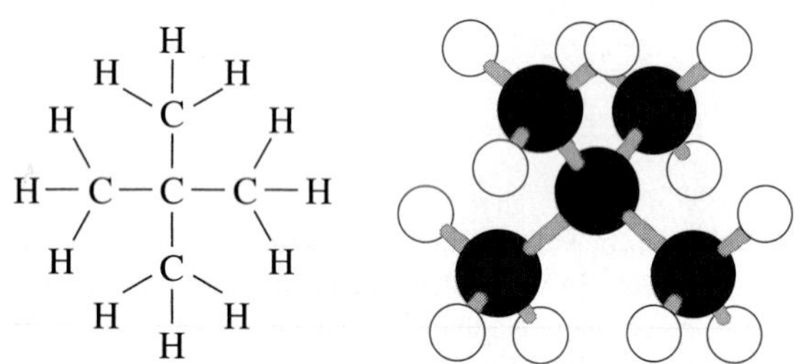

Each carbon atom uses sp^3 hybrids and has tetrahedral geometry.

8.4.3

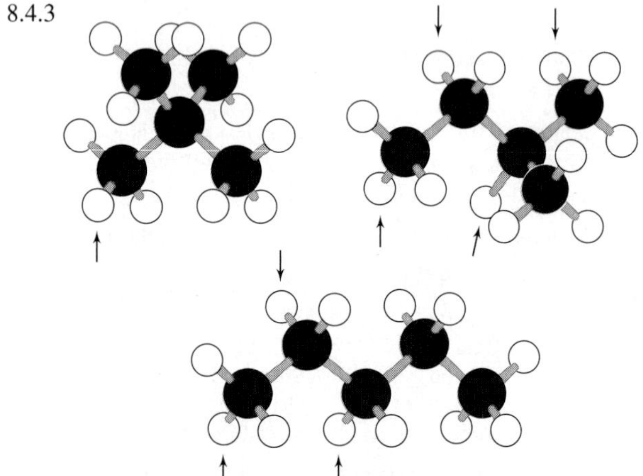

The arrows indicate different types of H atoms. There are eight structural isomers with the chemical formula $C_5H_{11}Cl$.

8.5.1

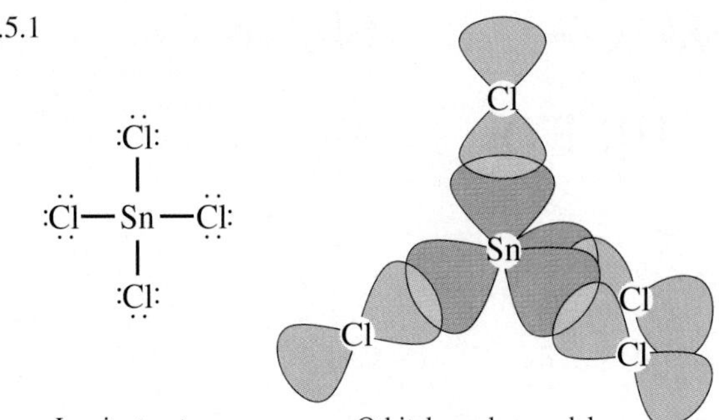

Lewis structure Orbital overlap model

Each bond forms from an sp^3 hybrid from Sn and a $3p$ atomic orbital from Cl.

8.5.2

H H N — N H H

Each N atom uses sp^3 hybrids to form an N—N bond and two N—H bonds. There is a lone pair in the remaining hybrid, and the shape around each N atom is a trigonal pyramid.

8.5.3 The atoms inside the circle make up one $Si_2O_5^{2-}$ unit:

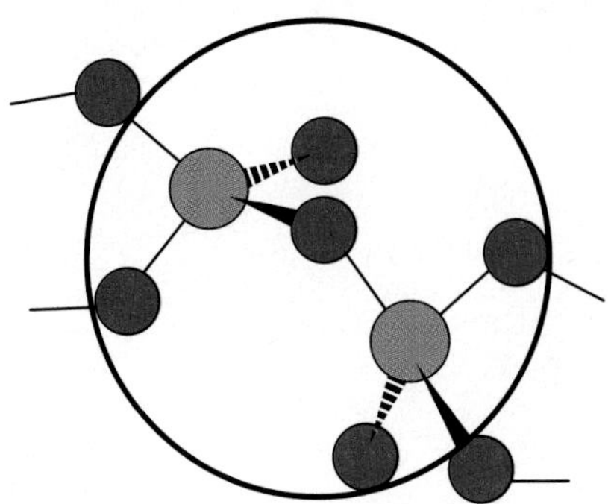

8.6.1

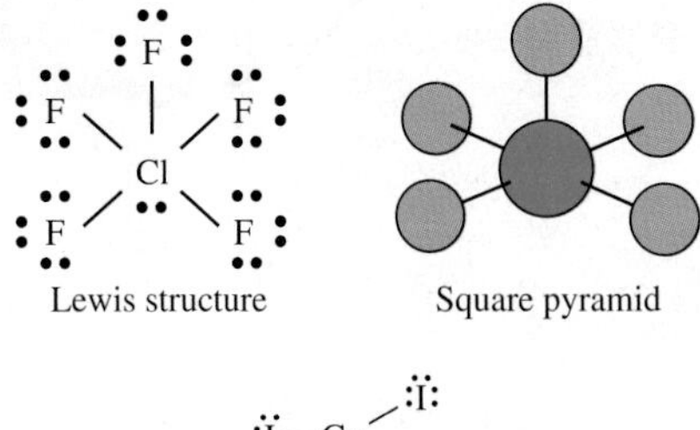

Lewis structure Square pyramid

8.6.2

I—Ga I I

The bonding is similar to that in BF_3. Gallium uses sp^2 hybrid orbitals to overlap with p atomic orbitals of iodine. The molecule is trigonal planar in shape.

8.6.3

Cl As Cl Cl Cl

The bonding is similar to that in SF_4. Arsenic uses sp^3d hybrids to overlap with p atomic orbitals of chlorine. The fifth hybrid holds a lone pair. The ion has seesaw shape.

8.7.1 BCl_3, 120 degrees; SF_4, < 90 degrees and < 120 degrees; and $SnCl_4$, 109.5 degrees

8.7.2 Only PCl_3 has a dipole moment.

8.7.3

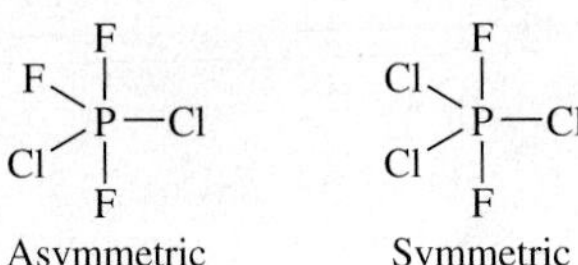

Asymmetric Symmetric

The chlorine atoms, being larger than fluorine atoms, occupy the equatorial positions because this minimizes atom-atom repulsion.

CHAPTER 9

CHEMICAL BONDING: MULTIPLE BONDS

The green color of plants comes from chlorophyll, a molecule with an extended delocalized π bonding system. In the fall, as leaves die and fall from the trees, chlorophyll molecules break down into smaller pieces that are also colored because they contain extended π bonding systems.

Chapter 8 addresses the basic features of chemical bonding, which can be summarized as follows. Electrons are shared to maximize nucleus-electron attractions and minimize electron-electron and nucleus-nucleus repulsions. The starting point for this model is the Lewis structure, which shows a molecule's bonding framework and the distribution of its valence electrons. Then, orbital overlap between suitable hybrid and/or atomic orbitals from adjacent atoms provides representations of bond formation and molecular geometry.

The success of the orbital overlap model in describing all sorts of molecules that contain *single* bonds indicates that its basic features are correct. The form of the model presented in Chapter 8, however, does not account for *multiple* bonds. This makes the model incomplete because Lewis structures indicate that many molecules contain double bonds and/or triple bonds, and experimental data on bond properties confirm their existence. The orbital overlap model must therefore be expanded to include double and triple bonds.

We begin Chapter 9 with an orbital description of multiple bonds in carbon-containing molecules. Next, we examine how bond lengths and bond strengths correlate with the model. Then we present additional orbital characteristics that apply to bonding in diatomic molecules and molecules that contain extended systems of multiple bonds. Finally, we describe how the bonding model accounts for properties of metals and semiconductors.

9.1 MULTIPLE BONDS IN CARBON COMPOUNDS

In Section 8.3, we constructed the Lewis structures of urea and acetic acid. According to the Lewis structures, each of these molecules contains a double bond between a carbon atom and an oxygen atom. Other simple organic substances, such as ethylene and acetylene, contain carbon-carbon multiple bonds. In many complex molecules, including biochemical compounds such as chlorophyll and deoxyribonucleic acid (DNA), extended systems of multiple bonds involve carbon, nitrogen, and oxygen atoms. All these bonds can be described by orbital overlap. We begin with ethylene, a simple hydrocarbon with the chemical formula C_2H_4.

BONDING IN ETHYLENE

Every description of bonding, including that of ethylene, starts with its Lewis structure. Ethylene has 12 valence electrons; 10 are used to construct the framework of the molecule, which has 1 C—C bond and 4 C—H bonds. The final two electrons are placed as a lone pair on one of the carbon atoms. In this provisional structure, the carbon with the lone pair has a −1 formal charge (FC), and the carbon with no lone pair has a +1 FC. Making a double bond between the carbon atoms reduces both FCs to zero and completes the Lewis structure:

```
   H     H                                  H     H
    \   /                  Lewis             \   /
−1 FC :C—C +1 FC           structure          C=C
    /   \           (formal charges = 0)     /   \
   H     H                                  H     H
  Provisional
   structure
```

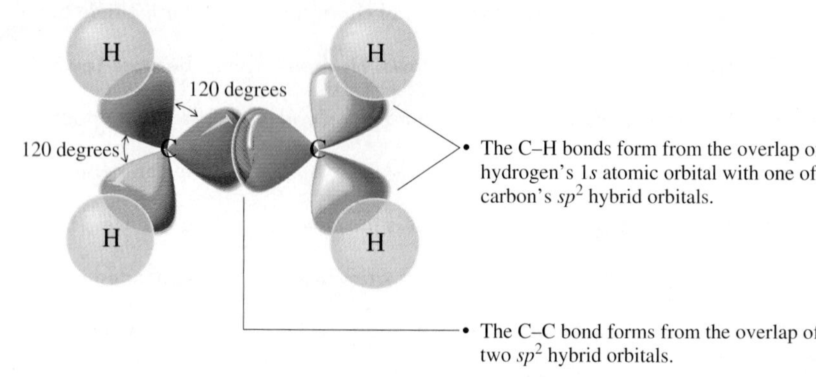
H
H
120 degrees
120 degrees
C
C
H
H
• The C–H bonds form from the overlap of hydrogen's 1s atomic orbital with one of carbon's sp^2 hybrid orbitals.
• The C–C bond forms from the overlap of two sp^2 hybrid orbitals.

FIGURE 9-1
Schematic drawing of the bonding framework of ethylene. The orbitals of each carbon atom can be represented using sp^2 hybrids, so the C—H bonds form from overlapping 1*s* atomic orbitals from hydrogen and sp^2 hybrids from carbon. The C—C bond forms from the overlap of two sp^2 hybrid orbitals.

What orbital picture best describes ethylene? First, experiments show that C_2H_4 is a planar molecule with 120-degree bond angles. Second, the Lewis structure shows that each carbon atom forms bonds to three other atoms, and neither has a lone pair, giving each carbon atom a steric number of three. Both these features are consistent with sp^2 hybridization, so a bonding framework can be constructed using carbon hybrid orbitals and hydrogen 1*s* orbitals. According to this model, each C—H bond involves overlap of a carbon sp^2 hybrid with a hydrogen 1*s* atomic orbital, and a C—C bond forms from the overlap of sp^2 hybrid orbitals. Figure 9-1 shows the bonding framework for ethylene.

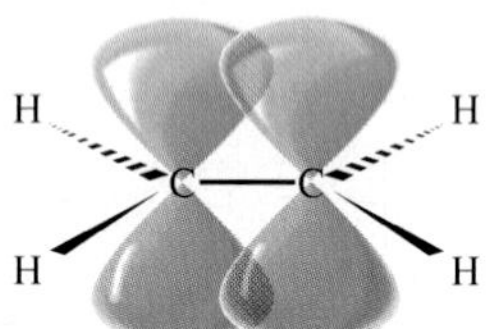
H
H
C
C
H
H

FIGURE 9-2
Formation of an sp^2 hybrid set leaves one unused valence *p* orbital. In ethylene, these orbitals can overlap to form a second bond between the carbon atoms.

Figure 9-1 shows one bond joining the carbon atoms in ethylene, but the Lewis structure shows that a *double* bond exists between the carbon atoms. By examining the full set of valence orbitals of the carbon atoms, we can see how to construct a second bond between the carbon atoms of ethylene. The sp^2 hybrid set requires three valence orbitals, leaving one valence *p* orbital that is not part of the hybrid set. The electron density of this *p* orbital is concentrated above and below the sp^2 plane. As shown in Figure 9-2, these "leftover" *p* orbitals on adjacent carbon atoms can overlap in a side-by-side fashion.

σ BONDS AND π BONDS

In the bond framework shown in Figure 9-1, all the bonds form as a result of end-on overlap of orbitals directed toward each other. As illustrated by the three examples in Figure 9-3, this type of overlap gives high electron density distributed symmetrically *along* the internuclear axis. A bond of this type is called a **sigma (σ) bond,** and an orbital that describes a σ bond is a σ orbital.

The symbol σ is the Greek letter corresponding to the English letter s. This designation is used because the cross-sectional profiles of s and σ orbitals both are circles.

Sigma bonds have high electron density distributed symmetrically along the bond axis.

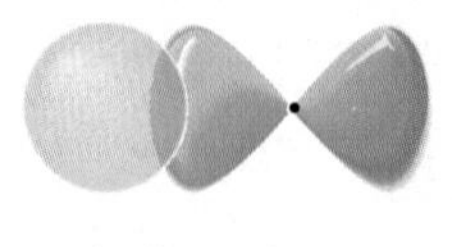

1*s*–2*p* overlap in HF

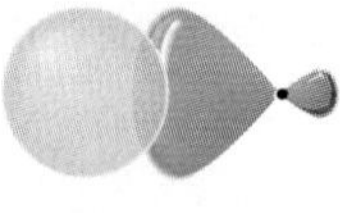

1*s*–sp^2 overlap in C_2H_4

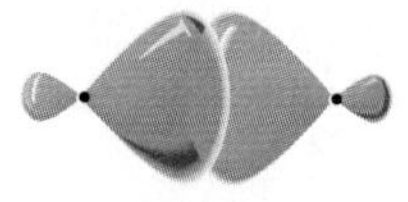

sp^2–sp^2 overlap in C_2H_4

Cross-sectional end view of all three orbitals

FIGURE 9-3
Schematic views of the σ bonds in HF and C_2H_4. All have high electron density concentrated along the internuclear axis and axial symmetry, so their end-on profiles are circles.

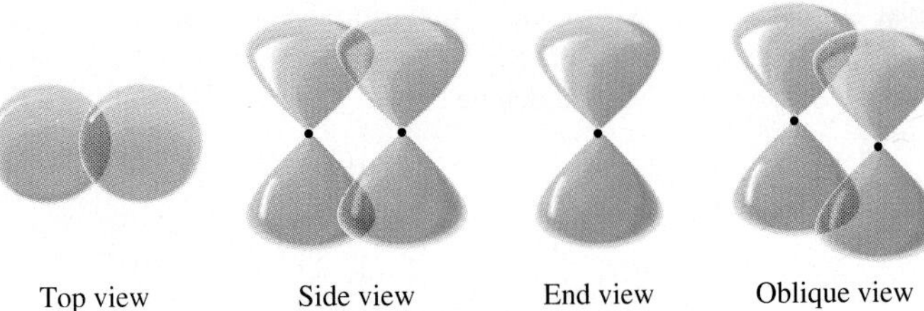

FIGURE 9-4
Four views of a π bond. Viewed from above, it resembles a σ bond. The end view, however, has an hourglass profile, whereas the side view and oblique view emphasize that electron density is concentrated in two lobes between the bonded atoms, one above and one below the bond axis.

Bonds that form from the side-by-side overlap of atomic *p* orbitals have different electron density profiles than σ orbitals. A *p* orbital has zero amplitude in a plane passing through the nucleus, so bonds that form from side-by-side overlap have no electron density directly along the bond axis. High electron density exists between the bonded atoms, but it is concentrated *above and below* the bond axis. A bond of this type is called a **pi (π) bond,** and an orbital that describes a π bond is a π orbital. Figure 9-4 shows a π bond from four different perspectives.

The symbol π is the Greek letter corresponding to the English letter *p*. This designation is used because end-view profiles of *p* and π orbitals both resemble hourglasses.

Pi bonds have high electron density above and below the bond axis.

The double bond in ethylene combines a σ bond and a π bond. The σ bond forms from the end-on overlap of two hybrid orbitals, whereas the π bond forms from the side-by-side overlap of two atomic *p* orbitals. Figure 9-5 illustrates the complete orbital picture of the bonding in ethylene. The alkenes, which are the subject of Box 9-1, all display similar orbital pictures.

The availability of a leftover valence *p* orbital to form π bonds is characteristic of sp^2 hybridization and is not restricted to carbon atoms. Sample Problem 9-1 shows how the same bonding picture applies to a compound that has a carbon-nitrogen double bond.

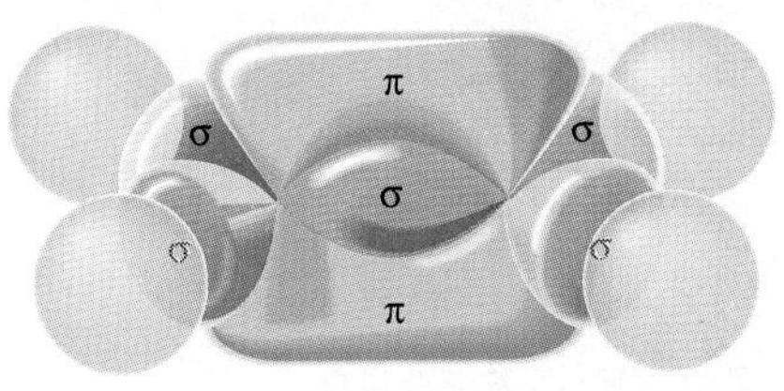

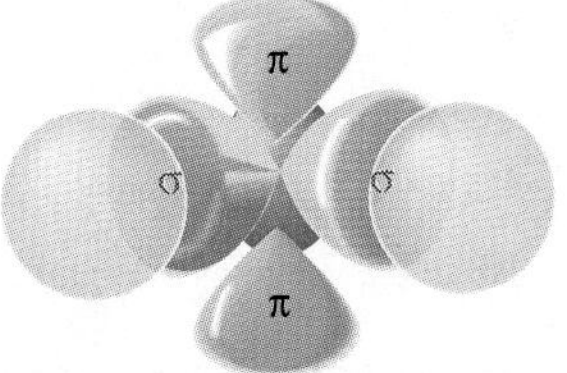

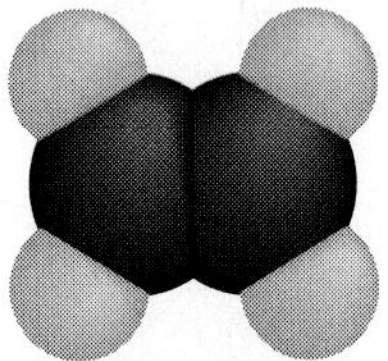

FIGURE 9-5
An orbital picture of the bonding in ethylene, viewed from the side and from one end. Notice that the electron density in the π bond is distributed above and below the plane containing the six nuclei, whereas the electron densities of the σ bonds are concentrated along the internuclear axes.

SAMPLE PROBLEM 9-1 ORBITAL OVERLAP IN DOUBLE BONDS

An imine is a molecule with a carbon-nitrogen double bond. Describe the bonding of the simplest possible imine, H_2CNH, by sketching the σ and π bonding systems.

METHOD: Begin by writing the Lewis structure for the molecule. From the Lewis structure, deduce the appropriate hybridization. Then draw sketches of the various orbitals involved in the bonding.

Each molecule of H_2CNH has 12 valence electrons. Eight are used to construct the σ bonds, leaving four electrons. These are placed on the more electronegative inner atom, which is nitrogen, to give a provisional Lewis structure. In this provisional structure, the carbon atom has a +1 FC, and nitrogen has a −1 FC. The FCs can be reduced to zero by transferring one of nitrogen's lone pairs to make a C═N double bond:

$H_2C^{+1\,FC}$—$\ddot{\underset{..}{N}}$:$^{-1\,FC}$—H
Provisional structure

H_2C═$\ddot{N}$—H
Lewis structure (formal charges = 0)

The carbon and nitrogen atoms both have steric numbers of three, so their bonding frameworks can be represented using sp^2 hybrid orbitals. Now we can sketch the σ bonding system of imine:

H
sp^2 lone pair
sp^2–1s σ bond
C
N
sp^2–1s σ bond
H
sp^2–sp^2 σ bond
H

The carbon and nitrogen atoms have a p orbital left over after construction of the sp^2 hybrids. These two p orbitals are perpendicular to the plane that contains the five nuclei. Side-by-side overlap of the p orbitals gives a π bond that completes the bonding description of this molecule:

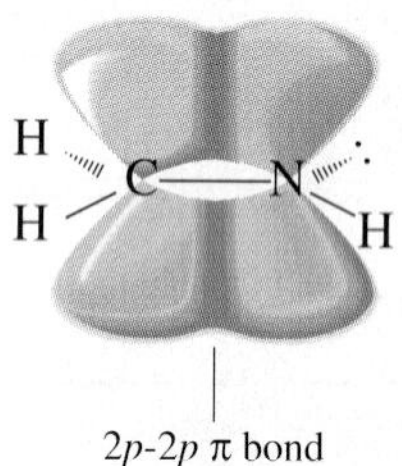

ACETYLENE: FORMATION OF A TRIPLE BOND

The Lewis structure of acetylene (C_2H_2) shows that a triple bond exists between the carbon atoms:

H—C≡C—H

Thus each carbon atom has two valence electrons shared in a C—H σ bond and six shared in a C≡C triple bond. Acetylene is found to be a linear molecule, and because both carbon atoms have a steric number of two, sp hybrid orbitals can be used to construct the orbital framework. The σ bonding system of acetylene is shown in Figure 9-6, A.

The sp hybrid set requires just one of the valence p orbitals. The remaining two p orbitals are oriented at right angles to the axis of the acetylene molecule and at right angles to each other, as shown in Figure 9-6, B. Each p orbital can overlap with its counterpart on the other carbon atom, just as in ethylene. Thus two π bonds of acetylene form from the side-by-side overlap of the two p orbitals on each carbon atom.

BOX 9-1

ALKENES

An alkene is a hydrocarbon that contains one or more carbon-carbon double bonds. Ethylene, whose bonding is described at the beginning of this section, is the simplest alkene. It is a colorless, flammable gas with a boiling point of −104 °C. More than 18 billion kg of ethylene are produced annually in the United States, making it one of the top five industrial chemicals. The manufacture of plastics (polyethylene is the most common example) consumes 75% of this output, and much of the rest is used to make antifreeze. Ethylene is also a plant growth hormone. It stimulates the breakdown of cell walls, making fruit soften during the ripening process. Thus ethylene is used commercially to hasten the ripening of fruit, particularly bananas.

Alkenes occur widely in nature, and often the structures of these molecules are complex. The orange pigment of carrots, for example, is carotene, an alkene. Vitamin A, which is essential for vision, forms when carotene breaks down. The line structures of these alkenes appear to the right.

Insects communicate by excreting minute amounts of pheromones. Pheromones have a wide variety of chemical structures, but many of them are alkenes. Some pheromones attract members of a common species, and others repel predators, mark trails, or signal alarm. The trail marker used by termites is neocembrene, an alkene that contains four carbon-carbon double bonds.

Plants produce a vast array of alkenes that belong to a class of molecules called *terpenes*. Terpenes are important in the flavor and fragrance industry. One example is limonene, the principal component of lemon oil. Many other terpenes have important medicinal properties.

Neocembrene ($C_{20}H_{35}$)
(a termite trail marker)

Limonene ($C_{10}H_{16}$)
(the principal component of lemon oil)

Carotene ($C_{40}H_{56}$)
(an orange plant pigment, and the precursor to Vitamin A)

Vitamin A ($C_{20}H_{30}O$)

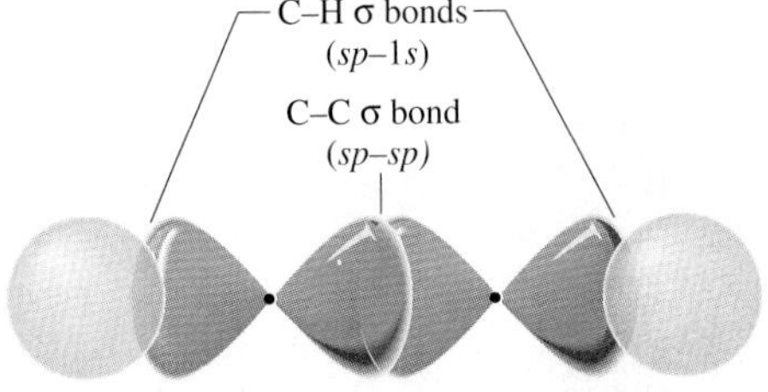

A Side view

B End view

FIGURE 9-6
The bond framework for acetylene. The side view **(A)** shows the σ-bonding system, whereas the end view **(B)** calls attention to the unused valence *p* orbitals that lie at right angles to the molecular skeleton.

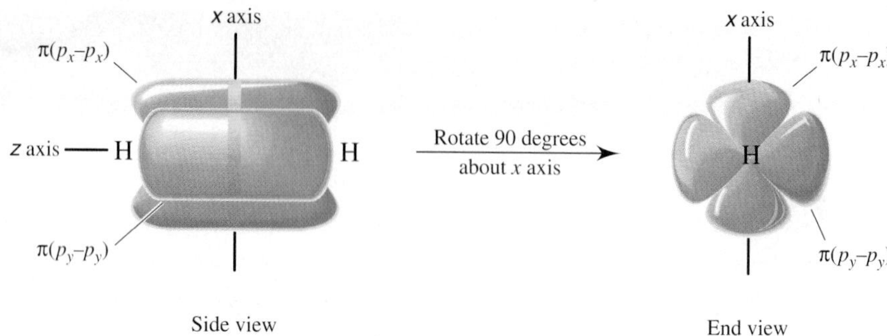

FIGURE 9-7
Two views of the π bonding in acetylene. *Left,* Molecule viewed from the side. *Right,* Molecule viewed from one end. Notice that the π bonds are perpendicular to each other and have electron density off the internuclear axis.

This is illustrated in Figure 9-7. According to this description, a triple bond is made up of one σ bond and two π bonds. Figure 9-8, which is a superimposition of the views shown in Figures 9-6 and 9-7, depicts all the bonds in the acetylene molecule.

Sample Problem 9-2 provides another example of a molecule with bonding that can be described by *sp* hybrid orbitals.

FIGURE 9-8
Composite view of the σ and π bonds in the acetylene molecule. The C—C σ bond is shown in red, the C—C π bonds are shown in blue, and the C—H bonds are shown in orange.

SAMPLE PROBLEM 9-2 ORBITAL OVERLAP IN TRIPLE BONDS

Hydrogen cyanide (HCN) is an extremely poisonous gas with an odor resembling that of almonds. Approximately 1 billion pounds of HCN are produced each year, most of which are used to prepare starting materials for polymer manufacture. Construct a complete bonding picture for HCN.

METHOD: Begin with the Lewis structure for the molecule, and then construct the appropriate hybrids and bonding orbitals.

The provisional structure and the final Lewis structure follow:

H—C—N̈: (−2 FC on N, +2 FC on C)
Provisional structure

H—C≡N:
Lewis structure
(formal charges = 0)

Hydrogen and nitrogen are outer atoms, so they use atomic orbitals to form covalent bonds. The carbon atom has a steric number of two, so it can be described in terms of *sp* hybrids. With this information, we can construct the σ bonding network for HCN:

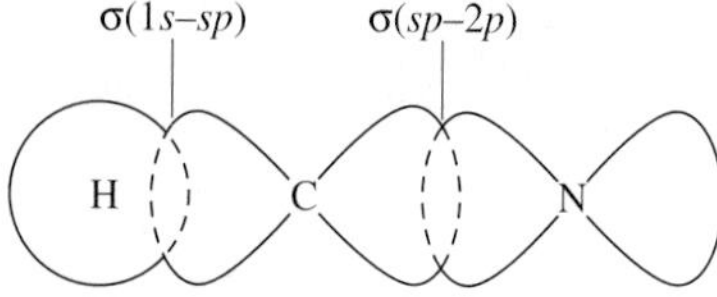

The triple bond includes two π bonds formed by the pairwise overlap of the two *p* orbitals that remain on the carbon and nitrogen atoms:

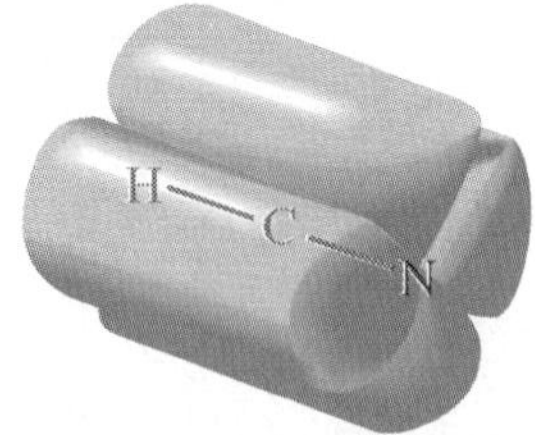

The nonbonding pair on the nitrogen atom occupies the $2s$ orbital, which is the only valence orbital of this atom not used for bonding.

The σ and π bonding networks are shown separately for clarity. Keep in mind, however, that the molecule is a *composite* of both networks, so visualize the HCN molecule as both bonding networks superimposed.

SECTION EXERCISES

9.1.1 Determine the Lewis structure and describe the bonding completely (including an orbital sketch) for the formaldehyde molecule (H_2CO). Formaldehyde is a pungent, colorless gas that is a highly toxic, suspected carcinogen. Aqueous solutions of it are used to preserve biological specimens.

9.1.2 Propene is the three-carbon alkene, and propyne is the three-carbon hydrocarbon that contains a triple bond.

Determine the chemical formulas and Lewis structures of these two substances. Describe their bonding completely, including the geometry and hybridization for each carbon atom.

9.1.3 Convert the line structure of limonene into a Lewis structure. Determine how many of its carbon atoms participate in π bonding, and draw orbital sketches for a π bond, a C—C σ bond, and a C—H σ bond in this molecule. (See Box 9-1 for the line structure of limonene.)

9.2 BOND LENGTHS AND ENERGIES

Our coverage of bonding has already touched on three important properties of chemical bonds. First, a bond has maximum stability at a characteristic separation distance called the **bond length.** Second, a bond has maximum stability when electrons are distributed between the atoms in a characteristic pattern that generates **bond polarity.** Third, the stability of a chemical bond is measured by its **bond energy.** In this section we describe trends in bond length and examine bond energy in detail.

Section 8.2 presents the relationship between bond polarity and electronegativity.

BOND LENGTH

The H—H bond length in molecular hydrogen is 74 picometers (pm) because at this distance, attractive interactions are maximized relative to repulsive interactions (see Figure 8-3). This is the shortest possible chemical bond because it results from overlap between the smallest atomic orbitals, two $1s$ orbitals. Bond length increases as the atomic valence orbitals become larger. For example, the H—F bond forms by overlap of a hydrogen $1s$ orbital with a fluorine $2p$ orbital (see Figure 8-4). The $2p$ orbitals are larger than the $1s$ orbitals, giving this bond a length of 92 pm. The F—F bond, which forms by overlap of two $2p$ orbitals, has a length of 128 pm. These three bond lengths demonstrate a general trend: the principal quantum number (n) of the valence orbitals strongly influences bond length. Because size increases with ***n***, length varies predictably with the principal quantum number of the valence orbitals.

Table 9-1 lists average bond lengths for the most common chemical bonds. Bonds generated using valence orbitals with the same value of ***n*** are grouped together to emphasize the connection between bond length and the principal quantum number of the valence electrons.

Within any valence shell, nuclear charge also affects bond length. Recall from Section 7.6 that atomic size decreases from left to right across a row of the periodic table. Larger orbitals form longer bonds, so Si—Si bonds are longer than P—P bonds, and P—P bonds are longer than Cl—Cl bonds. Bond polarity contributes a small additional effect to bond length, too, because partial charges generate coulombic attraction that pulls the atoms closer together. Notice in Table 9-1, for example, that C—O bonds are slightly shorter than O—O bonds. This is a result of the polarity of the C—O bond.

The bond lengths in Table 9-1 show one final feature: multiple bonds are shorter than the corresponding single bonds. This is because placing additional electrons between atoms increases coulombic attraction and shrinks the distance between the atoms. Thus triple bonds are the shortest of all bonds among second-row elements.

To summarize, several factors influence bond lengths:

1. The smaller the principal quantum numbers of the valence orbitals, the shorter the bond.

TABLE 9-1 AVERAGE BOND LENGTHS*

H—X bonds

n_a	n_b								
1	1	H—H	74						
1	2	H—C	109	H—N	101	H—O	96	H—F	92
1	3	H—Si	148	H—P	144	H—S	134	H—Cl	127
1	4							H—Br	141

Second-Row Elements

n_a	n_b								
2	2	C—C	154	C—N	147	C—O	143	C—F	135
2	2			N—N	145	O—O	148	F—F	142
2	3	C—Si	185	C—P	184	C—S	182	C—Cl	177
2	3			O—P	163	O—Si	166	F—Si	157
2	3					F—S	156	N—Cl	175
2	4, 5			F—Xe	190	C—Br	194	C—I	214

Larger Elements

n_a	n_b								
3	3	Si—Si	235	P—P	221			Cl—Cl	199
3	3	Si—Cl	202	P—Cl	203				
4, 5					Br—Br 228		I—I	267	

Multiple Bonds

C=C	133	C=N	138	C=O	120	O=O	121
C≡C	120	C≡N	116	C≡O	113	P=O	150

*All values in (pm); 1 pm = 10^{-12} m.

2. The higher the bond multiplicity, the shorter the bond.
3. The higher the effective nuclear charges of the bonded atoms, the shorter the bond.
4. The larger the electronegativity difference of the bonded atoms, the shorter the bond.

Sample Problem 9-3 provides practice in the use of these factors.

SAMPLE PROBLEM 9-3 BOND LENGTHS

What factor accounts for each of the following differences in bond length?

(a) I_2 has a longer bond than Br_2.

(b) C—O bonds are shorter than C—C bonds.

(c) H—C bonds are shorter than the C≡O bond.

(d) The carbon-oxygen bond in formaldehyde, H_2C=O, is longer than the bond in carbon monoxide.

METHOD: Bond lengths are controlled by four factors, some of which are more influential than others. To explain a difference in bond length, we need to determine how the factors are balanced.

(a) Iodine and bromine are in different rows of the periodic table, with $n = 5$ for the valence orbitals of iodine and $n = 4$ for the valence orbitals of bromine. Thus iodine has larger valence orbitals, and the I_2 bond is longer than the Br_2 bond.

(b) Carbon and oxygen are second-row elements, so $n = 2$ for both. Oxygen has a higher nuclear charge than carbon, however, so its valence orbitals are somewhat smaller than carbon's valence orbitals. This makes C—O bonds shorter than C—C bonds. In addition, a C—O bond is polar, which contributes to the shortening of the C—O bond.

(c) Here, we are comparing bonds in which the principal quantum number and the amount of multiple bonding influence bond length. Because H—C bonds are shorter than the triple C≡O bond, the compactness of the $n = 1$ valence orbital of hydrogen is a more important factor than the presence of multiple bonding.

(d) Both bonds are between carbon and oxygen, so n, atomic number (Z), and electronegativity difference ($\Delta\chi$) are the same. However, carbon monoxide contains a triple bond, whereas formaldehyde has a double bond. The triple bond in CO is shorter than the double bond in H_2CO because more shared electrons means a shorter bond.

TO π BOND OR NOT TO π BOND: CARBON VS. SILICON

The single bond between silicon and oxygen in the silicate minerals can be described using sp^3 hybrid orbitals. In fact, silicon forms single bonds with tetrahedral geometry in almost all its compounds. This is because the $3p$ valence orbitals of silicon atoms form much more stable σ bonds than π bonds. In contrast, the $2p$ valence orbitals of carbon form stable π and σ bonds, and carbon atoms display linear, trigonal planar, and tetrahedral geometries. This versatility in bonding gives rise to the vast, intricate worlds of organic chemistry and biochemistry.

Why does silicon not form π bonds as readily as its column IV neighbor? The answer can be found by examining the sizes of the valence orbitals of silicon and carbon. Figure 9-9 compares side-by-side p orbital overlap for carbon atoms and

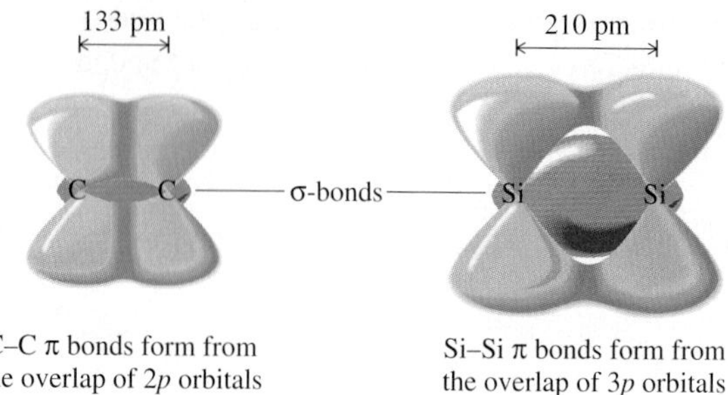
133 pm
210 pm
C
C
σ-bonds
Si
Si
C–C π bonds form from the overlap of 2p orbitals
Si–Si π bonds form from the overlap of 3p orbitals

FIGURE 9-9
Comparison of π bonding between two carbon atoms and two silicon atoms. The 3*p* orbitals of silicon do not approach each other very closely because the σ bond formed from $n = 3$ orbitals is considerably longer than the σ bond formed from $n = 2$ orbitals. This leads to poor side-by-side overlap and a very weak π bond.

silicon atoms. Notice that for the larger silicon atom, the 3*p* orbitals are too far apart for strong side-by-side overlap. The result is a very weak π bond. Consequently, silicon makes more effective use of its valence orbitals to form four σ bonds, which can be described using sp^3 hybrid orbitals.

In general, σ bond lengths are such that π bonding requires the presence of a second-row element. Carbon, nitrogen, and oxygen readily form π bonds with one another. Oxygen also readily forms π bonds with third-row and fourth-row elements. Phosphate (PO_4^{3-}), sulfate (SO_4^{2-}), perchlorate (ClO_4^-), and other similar anions contain O—X π bonds, which we describe in Section 9.5. Many other examples of π bonding exist, but we confine our descriptions to bonds between second-row elements and in oxyanions.

BOND ENERGY

Energy must be supplied to break a chemical bond because a chemical bond represents a stable arrangement of electrons shared between the bonded atoms. Energy is released, on the other hand, when a bond forms. As described in Section 8.1, 1 mol of hydrogen molecules has a total bond energy *(BE)* of 432 kJ. In other words, the formation of 1 mol of H_2 from 2 mol of hydrogen atoms releases 432 kJ of energy:

$$H_{(g)} + H_{(g)} \rightarrow H_{2\,(g)} \qquad \Delta E = -432 \text{ kJ/mol}$$

Molar bond energies are tabulated as positive quantities because a bond energy is the amount of energy required to *break* 1 mol of chemical bonds:

$$H_{2\,(g)} \rightarrow H_{(g)} + H_{(g)} \qquad \Delta E = BE = +432 \text{ kJ/mol}$$

The idea of a bond energy is relatively easy to grasp. Think about holding onto both ends of a molecule and "pulling it apart" at one particular junction between atoms. The bond energy is the energy needed to accomplish this on an entire mole of molecules. Bond energies differ from substance to substance, as the following examples illustrate:

$$HCl_{(g)} \rightarrow H_{(g)} + Cl_{(g)} \qquad BE = 428 \text{ kJ/mol}$$

$$Br_{2\,(g)} \rightarrow Br_{(g)} + Br_{(g)} \qquad BE = 190 \text{ kJ/mol}$$

$$N_{2\,(g)} \rightarrow N_{(g)} + N_{(g)} \qquad BE = 942 \text{ kJ/mol}$$

In polyatomic molecules, there are usually several different types of bonds, each with its own energy. Ethanol, for example, has five different chemical bonds:

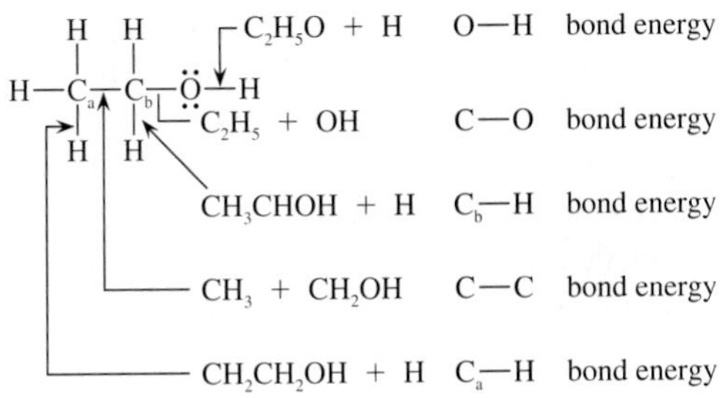

$$H-\underset{H}{\overset{H}{C_a}}-\underset{H}{\overset{H}{C_b}}-\ddot{\underset{..}{O}}-H$$

Products	Bond broken	
C_2H_5O + H	O—H	bond energy
C_2H_5 + OH	C—O	bond energy
CH_3CHOH + H	C_b—H	bond energy
CH_3 + CH_2OH	C—C	bond energy
CH_2CH_2OH + H	C_a—H	bond energy

Bond energy depends not only on the types of atoms in the bond, but also on the rest of the molecular structure. Thus it requires 410 kJ/mol to break the C_a—H bonds in C_2H_5OH, but only 393 kJ/mol to break the C_b—H bonds. Although bond energy depends on the entire molecular environment, many bonds between specific atoms have energies that cluster around an average value. Table 9-2 gives *average* bond energies for a variety of chemical bonds. Notice that both C—H bond energies for ethanol are close to the average value of 415 kJ/mol, but neither matches exactly. The bond energies for the diatomic molecules listed in Table 9-2, on the other hand, are specific measured values for those molecules.

Bond energies are difficult to measure accurately. Most molecules are similar to ethanol in that they contain many different bonds. Consequently, measuring one specific bond energy in a molecule is never easy. Furthermore, the fragments that result when molecules are torn apart are unstable. They recombine quickly, releasing energy as the new chemical bonds form. In short, it is difficult to keep track of every energy change that occurs when we experiment with molecules.

TABLE 9-2 AVERAGE BOND ENERGIES*

Diatomic Molecules (Specific Values)

Bond	Energy	Bond	Energy	Bond	Energy
H—H	432.0	F—F	154.8	O=O	493.6
H—F	565	Cl—Cl	239.7	N=O	607
H—Cl	428.0	Br—Br	190.0	N≡N	942.7
H—Br	362.3	I—I	149.0	C≡O	1071
H—I	294.6				

Single Covalent Bonds (Average Values)

Bond	Energy	Bond	Energy	Bond	Energy	Bond	Energy	Bond	Energy
H—C	415	C—C	345	Si—Si	220	N—N	165	O—O	145
H—N	390	C—N	305	Si—F	565	N—O	200	O—Si	450
H—O	460	C—O	360	Si—Cl	380	N—F	285	O—P	335
H—Si	315	C—Si	290	Si—Br	310	N—Cl	315	O—F	190
H—P	320	C—P	265	Si—N	320	P—P	200	O—Cl	220
H—S	365	C—S	270	Sn—Sn	145	P—F	490	O—Br	200
H—Te	240	C—F	485	Sn—Cl	325	P—Cl	325	S—S	250
		C—Cl	325			P—Br	265	S—F	285
		C—Br	285			P—I	185	S—Cl	255
		C—I	215			As—Cl	320	Se—Se	170

Multiple Covalent Bonds (Average Values)

Bond	Energy		Bond	Energy	Bond	Energy
C=C	615		N=N	420	C≡C	835
C=N	615		N=O	605	C≡N	890
C=O	750	805†	O=P	545		
C=S	575		O=S	515		

* All values in kilojoules per mole (kJ/mol).

† C=O bond energy in CO_2.

Because direct measurements of bond energies are very difficult to accomplish, chemists have developed clever experiments to measure bond energies *indirectly.* Still, the uncertainties in these techniques lead to ambiguities in bond energy values. Consequently, bond energies are not considered reliable unless they have been verified by independent measurements using different techniques. The bond energy of H_2, for example, has been determined in two different ways, giving values that agree within 0.5%. The values in Table 9-2 represent our best knowledge of bond energies based on all the methods in the chemist's arsenal.

FACTORS AFFECTING BOND ENERGY

Bond energies, like bond lengths, vary in ways that can be traced to atomic properties. The following three factors that cause shortening of chemical bonds also strengthen them:

1. *Bonds become stronger as more electrons are shared between the atoms.* Shared electrons are the "glue" of chemical bonding, so sharing more electrons strengthens the bond. Carbon-carbon bonds clearly demonstrate this trend:

C—C	Single bond	BE = 345 kJ/mol
C═C	Double bond	BE = 615 kJ/mol
C≡C	Triple bond	BE = 835 kJ/mol

Notice that a double bond is less than twice as strong as a single bond. This is because side-by-side overlap is not as effective as end-on overlap and because electrons in a π bond are farther from the nuclei than electrons in a σ bond. Consequently, π electrons stabilize a molecule less than σ electrons.

2. *The greater the electronegativity difference ($\Delta\chi$) between bonded atoms, the stronger the bond.* Polar bonds gain additional stability from the coulombic attraction between the negative and positive fractional charges around the bonded atoms. This trend is exemplified by bonds between oxygen and other second-row elements:

O—O	$\Delta\chi = 0.0$	BE = 145 kJ/mol
O—N	$\Delta\chi = 0.5$	BE = 220 kJ/mol
O—C	$\Delta\chi = 1.0$	BE = 360 kJ/mol

3. *The smaller the principal quantum number, the stronger the bond.* As n becomes larger, the valence orbitals become more diffuse. This spreads the electron density of a bond over a wider region, reducing the amount of overlap along the bond axis and decreasing the net coulombic attraction. The following bond energies illustrate this effect:

H—H	$n = 1$	BE = 432 kJ/mol
C—C	$n = 2$	BE = 345 kJ/mol
Si—Si	$n = 3$	BE = 220 kJ/mol

The fourth factor that shortens chemical bonds, effective nuclear charge, has an unpredictable effect on bond strength. As Z_{eff} increases, the valence orbitals become more compact. Although this gives a shorter bond, it also means that greater repulsion occurs between the nuclei and among the core electrons, which can weaken the bond. Single-bond strengths for second-row elements illustrate that no clear trend exists:

Bond	Bond length (pm)	Bond strength (kJ/mol)
C—C	154	345
N—N	145	165
O—O	148	145
F—F	128	154.8

The magnitudes of the effects from these four factors are about the same, which leads to many subtle variations in bond energy. Notice, for example, that four very different types of bonds have values close to 425 kJ/mol:

H—H $BE = 432$ kJ/mol

H—Cl $BE = 428$ kJ/mol

H—C $BE = 415$ kJ/mol

N=N $BE = 420$ kJ/mol

Although it is possible to *explain* many differences in bond energy, it is not possible to *predict* differences with confidence. Sample Problem 9-4 provides practice in explaining the different energies of several types of bonds.

SAMPLE PROBLEM 9-4 COMPARISONS OF BOND ENERGIES

Account for the observation that H—H, H—Cl, H—C, and N=N bonds have almost the same energy.

METHOD: Values for bond energy correlate with the four factors that contribute to bond stability. To determine which factors play important roles among bonds of almost the same energy, we choose one bond as a starting point and compare the factors influencing its strength with those influencing the strengths of the other bonds.

We choose the H—C bond as the basis for comparison. This is a bond between $n = 1$ and $n = 2$ atoms. Its strength primarily results from low n values, with some contribution from bond polarity and the relatively low Z value for carbon.

Compared with H—C, the H—H bond is strengthened by the lower value of n but weakened by the absence of bond polarity. The near equality of the two bond energies indicates that these two effects counterbalance each other.

Compared with H—C, the H—Cl bond is strengthened by considerably higher polarity but weakened by Cl's $n = 3$ valence orbitals. Once again, the equal strengths of the bonds show that these opposing trends cancel.

Compared with H—C, the N=N double bond is strengthened by sharing four electrons rather than two. However, the N—N single bond is quite weak because of its compact orbitals and the absence of any bond polarity. The near equality of these bond strengths shows that the extra electrons just compensate for these intrinsic weaknesses.

REACTION ENERGY

In chemical reactions, some chemical bonds break and other chemical bonds form. Breaking a bond *always* requires an input of energy, whereas forming a bond *always* results in a release of energy. Therefore chemical reactions are accompanied by changes in energy. The balance between the energy absorbed in bond breakage and the energy released in bond formation determines whether the reaction absorbs or releases energy overall.

Bond energies play a major role in determining the outcome of a chemical reaction. Products with stronger bonds are usually favored over products with weaker bonds. Thus a large bond energy is an asset in a chemical product. By the same reasoning, strong bonds are a liability in chemical reactants. The stronger a bond, the more difficult it is to break, and thus the less likely it is to participate in a chemical reaction.

Exo is Greek for "outward," *endo* is Greek for "within," and *therm* is Greek for "heat."

The energy change accompanying a chemical reaction requires that energy be transferred between the chemicals and their surroundings. A reaction that transfers energy to the surroundings is called **exothermic.** A reaction that cannot occur without absorbing energy from the surroundings is called **endothermic.**

The reaction of molecular hydrogen with molecular oxygen to produce gaseous water illustrates how energy changes accompany a chemical reaction. Starting from the balanced equation, imagine this reaction occurring in two steps. In the first step, two hydrogen molecules and one molecule of oxygen break apart to give four free gaseous atoms of hydrogen and two free gaseous atoms of oxygen. In the second step, these atoms recombine to produce two molecules of water:

$$2\,H_{2\,(g)} + O_{2\,(g)} \rightarrow 2\,H_2O_{(g)}$$

O=O, H—H, H—H —Breaking bonds→ H· H· :O: H· H· :O: —Making bonds→ H—O—H, H—O—H

Remember that the Greek symbol Δ means "change in." Thus, Δ*E* = change in energy = $E_{final} - E_{initial}$.

The energy change in the first step, $\Delta E_{\text{bond breaking}}$, is the sum of all the bond energies of reactant molecules:

$$\Delta E_{\text{bond breaking}} = (2\text{ mol } H_2)(BE\ H_2) + (1\text{ mol } O_2)(BE\ O_2)$$

$$\Delta E_{\text{bond breaking}} = (2\text{ mol } H_2)\left(\frac{432\text{ kJ}}{\text{mol } H_2}\right) + (1\text{ mol } O_2)\left(\frac{493.6\text{ kJ}}{\text{mol } O_2}\right) = 1358\text{ kJ}$$

↑ Energy required to break all bonds of starting materials

This energy change is *positive* because the chemical system *gains* the energy required to break the chemical bonds.

The energy change in the second step, $\Delta E_{\text{bond formation}}$, is the sum of all the energies released during bond formation of the products. The reaction produces 2 mol of water and forms 4 mol of O—H bonds. Bond formation always releases energy, so the chemical system loses energy to the surroundings. Consequently, the energy change is negative:

$$\Delta E_{\text{bond formation}} = -(4\text{ mol O—H bonds})\left(\frac{460\text{ kJ}}{\text{mol O—H bonds}}\right) = -1840\text{ kJ}$$

↑ Energy released during formation of bonds of products

The overall energy change for the reaction is the sum of these two terms:

$$\Delta E_{\text{reaction}} = \Delta E_{\text{bond breaking}} + \Delta E_{\text{bond formation}} = (1358 \text{ kJ}) + (-1840 \text{ kJ}) = -482 \text{ kJ}$$

The reaction of hydrogen with oxygen to form water is exothermic. That is, during the reaction the chemicals give off energy to their surroundings. To understand why, examine the bonds broken and formed. Three bonds break among the reactants, two H—H bonds and one O═O double bond. Four O—H bonds form in making the products. The H—H bond (432 kJ/mol) and the OH bond (460 kJ/mol) have similar energies, but the bond strength *per electron pair* of O═O is only 493.6/2 = 246.8 kJ/mol. Thus replacing an O═O bond with two O—H bonds yields a large amount of energy. Many reactions of molecular oxygen are exothermic because the O═O double bond is relatively weak compared with two O—X single bonds formed with most other elements.

The energy released in the reaction between H_2 and O_2 is used to drive the main engines of the space shuttle.

For any chemical reaction, the energy change is the sum of all bond energies of the reactants minus the sum of all bond energies of the products:

$$\Delta E_{\text{reaction}} = \Sigma\, BE_{\text{reactants}} - \Sigma\, BE_{\text{products}} \qquad \textbf{(9-1)}$$

The Greek letter Σ means "the sum of." Thus Σ *BE* means "the sum of all the bond energies."

As a second example, consider the energy changes during the combustion reaction of propane with oxygen. Propane (C_3H_8) contains only C—H and C—C single bonds. As shown in Table 9-2, C—H and C—C are among the strongest single bonds. Remember that strong bonds are a liability in starting materials because they are difficult to break. As a result, propane is not particularly reactive at low temperature. At high temperature, however, propane reacts with oxygen in a combustion reaction that produces carbon dioxide and water. We have just seen that reactions of O_2 often release energy because of the relative weakness of the O═O bond. In addition, many reactions that generate CO_2 are exothermic because each electron pair in a C═O bond contributes more stability than the same pair in a C—X or O—Y bond. Each C═O bond in CO_2 has a strength of 805 kJ/mol, for a strength per electron pair of 402.5 kJ/mol, whereas a C—C bond, for example, has a strength of 345 kJ/mol.

The stoichiometry of combustion reactions appears in Chapters 3 and 4.

Lewis structures show bond changes that occur during the combustion of propane:

```
  H  H  H       :O=O: :O=O:         :O=C=O:      H–O–H  H–O–H
  |  |  |
H–C––C––C–H  +      :O=O:     ───→  :O=C=O:  +
  |  |  |
  H  H  H       :O=O: :O=O:         :O=C=O:      H–O–H  H–O–H
```

C_3H_8 $\qquad$ $5\,O_2$ $\qquad$ $3\,CO_2$ $\qquad$ $4\,H_2O$

To estimate the amount of energy absorbed or released in this reaction, we must compile an inventory of all the bonds that break and all the bonds that form. Eight C—H bonds and two C—C bonds break in each propane molecule, and one O═O bond breaks in each oxygen molecule. Two C═O bonds form in each CO_2 molecule, and two O—H bonds form in each H_2O molecule. In summary:

$$C_3H_8 + 5\,O_2 \longrightarrow 3\,CO_2 + 4\,H_2O$$

Bonds broken	Bonds formed
2 C—C single bonds	6 C═O double bonds
8 C—H single bonds	8 O—H single bonds
5 O═O double bonds	

Now we can apply Equation 9-1, using the average bond energy values from Table 9-2:

$$\Delta E_{\text{reaction}} = \Sigma\, BE_{\text{(bonds broken)}} - \Sigma\, BE_{\text{(bonds formed)}}$$

$$\Delta E_{\text{reaction}} = \left[(2 \text{ mol C—C})\left(\frac{345 \text{ kJ}}{\text{mol C—C}}\right) + (8 \text{ mol C—H})\left(\frac{415 \text{ kJ}}{\text{mol C—H}}\right) + (5 \text{ mol O=O})\left(\frac{493.6 \text{ kJ}}{\text{mol O=O}}\right)\right] - \left[(6 \text{ mol C=O})\left(\frac{805 \text{ kJ}}{\text{mol C=O}}\right) + (8 \text{ mol O—H})\left(\frac{460 \text{ kJ}}{\text{mol O—H}}\right)\right]$$

$$\Delta E_{\text{reaction}} = 6478 \text{ kJ} - 8510 \text{ kJ} = -2032 \text{ kJ}$$

At the outset of this example, we noted that propane will not react with oxygen unless energy is added to break the strong C—H and C—C bonds of the starting materials. This added energy is required to initiate the reaction. *Once underway*, the reaction produces more energy than it consumes. This behavior is a consequence of the kinetics of combustion. Kinetics, which is the study of how fast reactions occur, is discussed in Chapter 14.

This energy analysis shows that burning 1 mol of propane releases 2032 kJ of energy. In general, burning a compound that contains carbon and hydrogen releases a great amount of energy that can be used to heat homes, cook food, power vehicles, or produce electricity. In fact, most of our society is driven by the energy released during the combustion of hydrocarbons derived from petroleum.

Energy analyses can be extended to reactions other than combustion, as shown in Sample Problem 9-5.

SAMPLE PROBLEM 9-5 REACTION ENERGIES

Approximately 10 billion pounds of vinyl chloride are produced in the United States each year. Most is converted to the polymer poly(vinyl chloride) (PVC), which is used to make piping, siding, gutters, floor tiles, clothing, and toys. Vinyl chloride is made in a two-step process. The balanced overall equation is as follows:

$$2\ \text{H}_2\text{C=CH}_2 + 2\ \text{H—Cl} + \text{O=O} \longrightarrow 2\ \text{H}_2\text{C=CHCl} + 2\ \text{H—O—H}$$

Ethylene ... Vinyl chloride

What energy change accompanies the formation of 1 mol of vinyl chloride? Is the synthesis exothermic or endothermic?

METHOD: First, we use the balanced equation to construct a "bond inventory" for the synthesis. To do so, we need the Lewis structures of all species involved in the reaction. In this case the structures are given in the equation. Here is the inventory:

Starting materials		Products
8 C—H single bonds	⟶	6 C—H single bonds
2 C=C double bonds		2 C—Cl single bonds
2 H—Cl single bonds		2 C=C double bonds
1 O=O double bond		4 O—H single bonds

Bond energies from Table 9-2 are needed to calculate the energy change:

C—H = 415 kJ/mol C=C = 615 kJ/mol H—Cl = 428.0 kJ/mol

O=O = 493.6 kJ/mol C—Cl = 325 kJ/mol O—H = 460 kJ/mol

Now use Equation 9-1:

$$\Delta E_{\text{reaction}} = \Sigma\, BE_{\text{reactants}} - \Sigma\, BE_{\text{products}}$$

Sum the bond energies for reactants and products, and subtract the latter from the former:

Reactants	Products
$(8 \text{ mol C—H})\left(\dfrac{415 \text{ kJ}}{\text{mol C—H}}\right)$	$(6 \text{ mol C—H})\left(\dfrac{415 \text{ kJ}}{\text{mol C—H}}\right)$
$(2 \text{ mol C=C})\left(\dfrac{615 \text{ kJ}}{\text{mol C=C}}\right)$	$(2 \text{ mol C—Cl})\left(\dfrac{325 \text{ kJ}}{\text{mol C—Cl}}\right)$
$(2 \text{ mol H—Cl})\left(\dfrac{428.0 \text{ kJ}}{\text{mol H—Cl}}\right)$	$(2 \text{ mol C=C})\left(\dfrac{615 \text{ kJ}}{\text{mol C=C}}\right)$
$(1 \text{ mol O=O})\left(\dfrac{493.6 \text{ kJ}}{\text{mol O=O}}\right)$	$(4 \text{ mol O—H})\left(\dfrac{460 \text{ kJ}}{\text{mol O—H}}\right)$

$$\Delta E_{\text{reaction}} = [5900 \text{ kJ}] - [6210 \text{ kJ}] = -310 \text{ kJ}$$

Our calculation is based on the balanced chemical equation and shows that 310 kJ of energy is released for every *2 mol* of vinyl chloride. However, the problem asks for the energy change associated with *1 mol* of product, so we divide by two to obtain a value of 155 kJ of energy released per mole of vinyl chloride. The negative sign for $\Delta E_{\text{reaction}}$ indicates that the chemicals release energy to the surroundings. In other words, this is an exothermic reaction.

A calculation based on average bond energies provides only an *estimate* of the energy change of a chemical reaction because the values listed in Table 9-2 are *averages* taken from measurements on many different substances containing each particular type of bond. The actual bond energies in any given molecule usually differ somewhat from the average values. For example, the energy released when propane burns has been measured accurately to be −2044 kJ/mol of propane. Our calculated estimate, −2032 kJ/mol of propane, is off by only 12 kJ/mol, an error of about 0.6%. This discrepancy arises because C—H and C—C bond energies vary somewhat from their average values. Estimates of reaction energies from average bond energies are accurate enough to predict the amount of energy that a particular reaction will release to the surroundings or absorb from the surroundings.

As another example of this type of analysis, consider the differences in energy and reactivity among carbon-carbon single, double, and triple bonds. Double bonds are stronger but more reactive than single bonds. Triple bonds, in turn, are stronger but more reactive than double bonds or single bonds. We can illustrate this trend with hydrogenation, a reaction of vital importance in the chemical industry. During hydrogenation, molecular hydrogen adds to a molecule with multiple bonds. Ethylene and acetylene, for example, react with hydrogen under appropriate conditions to produce ethane:

$$\text{H—C}\equiv\text{C—H} + 2\,\text{H}_2 \longrightarrow \text{H}_3\text{C—CH}_3$$

$$\text{H}_2\text{C=CH}_2 + \text{H}_2 \longrightarrow \text{H}_3\text{C—CH}_3$$

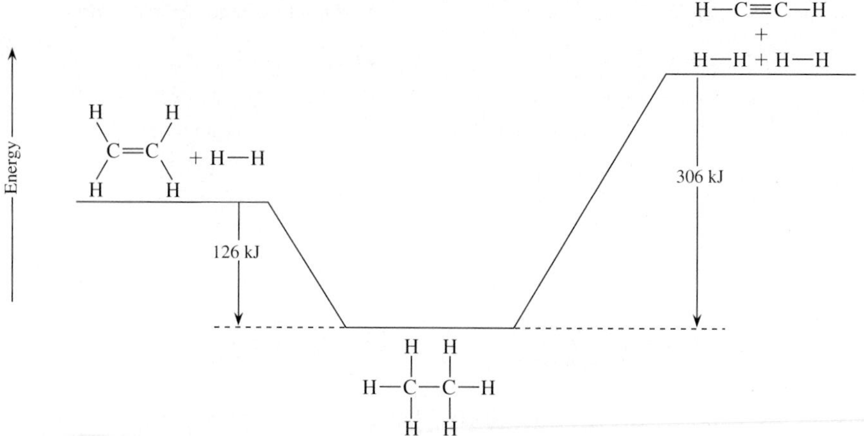

FIGURE 9-10
An energy level diagram for the hydrogenation of acetylene and ethylene. Conversion of C—C multiple bonds into C—H single bonds is always an exothermic process.

The energy changes that accompany hydrogenation can be estimated from average bond energies. According to the balanced equation, hydrogenation of ethylene creates two new C—H bonds at the expense of one H—H bond and converts a C=C double bond into a C—C single bond. The remaining C—H bonds are unchanged and can be left out of the calculation:

$$\Delta E_{\text{reaction}} = \left[(1 \text{ mol } H_2)\left(\frac{432 \text{ kJ}}{\text{mol } H_2}\right) + (1 \text{ mol C=C})\left(\frac{615 \text{ kJ}}{\text{mol C=C}}\right)\right]$$
$$- \left[(2 \text{ mol C—H})\left(\frac{415 \text{ kJ}}{\text{mol C—H}}\right) + (1 \text{ mol C—C})\left(\frac{345 \text{ kJ}}{\text{mol C—C}}\right)\right] = -128 \text{ kJ}$$

A similar calculation for acetylene gives a hydrogenation energy of -306 kJ/mol of C_2H_2.

These two reactions give the same product, ethane. Thus the difference in hydrogenation energy must be caused by the difference in energy between the starting materials. Because more energy was released from the hydrogenation of acetylene, the system, acetylene + 2 H_2, is higher in energy than the system, ethylene + H_2. The energy level diagram in Figure 9-10 summarizes these energy relationships.

SECTION EXERCISES

9.2.1 Arrange the following bonds in order of increasing length (shortest first). State the factors responsible for the position of each bond in your sequence: C—C, C=O, C=C, C—H, and C—Cl.

9.2.2 Methanol (CH_3OH) is sometimes mixed with gasoline to give gasohol, an alternative fuel for automobiles. Estimate how much energy is released when 1 mol of methanol is burned in air.

9.2.3 Methyl chloride (CH_3Cl) can be produced from methane in either of two reactions:

$$CH_{4\,(g)} + HCl_{(g)} \rightarrow CH_3Cl_{(g)} + H_{2\,(g)}$$
$$CH_{4\,(g)} + Cl_{2\,(g)} \rightarrow CH_3Cl_{(g)} + HCl_{(g)}$$

(a) Draw the Lewis structures of all substances, and create a bond inventory.
(b) Estimate the energy changes that accompany each of these reactions. Based on the values that you calculate, which reaction is more suitable for industrial production of methyl chloride? Explain.

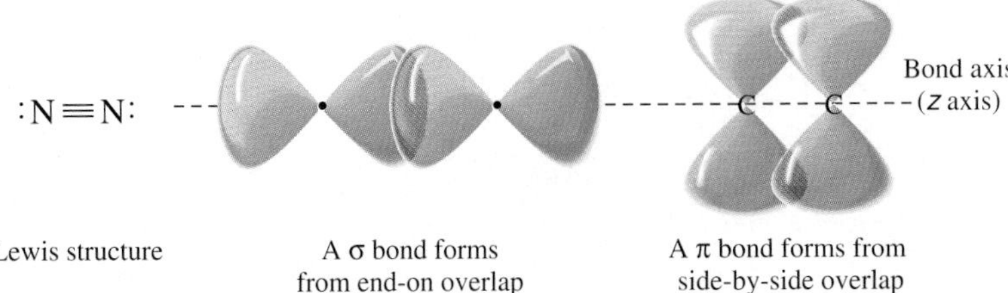
:N≡N:
Bond axis
(z axis)
Lewis structure
A σ bond forms
from end-on overlap
A π bond forms from
side-by-side overlap

FIGURE 9-11
Orbital sketches show how the overlap of $2p$ valence orbitals forms bonds. End-on overlap gives a σ bond with electron density along the bond axis, whereas side-by-side overlap gives a π bond with electron density above and below the bond axis.

9.3 SECOND-ROW DIATOMIC MOLECULES

Several common gases are diatomic molecules made of elements from the second row of the periodic table. Two of them, N_2 and O_2, dominate the Earth's atmosphere. Other examples include carbon monoxide, a poisonous byproduct of combustion reactions, and nitrogen monoxide, one of the important components of photochemical smog. These second-row diatomic molecules all have double or triple bonds. In this section we use molecular nitrogen to develop an orbital overlap picture that applies to the bonding of all these diatomic molecules.

BONDING IN N_2

The Lewis structure of molecular nitrogen appears in Sample Problem 8-11.

In the Lewis structure of molecular nitrogen, the two atoms are connected by a triple bond, and there is a nonbonding electron pair on each nitrogen atom. Both atoms in N_2 are outer atoms, so no need exists for hybridization. Atomic valence $2p$ orbitals can be used to construct the three bonds.

By convention, the orbital overlap model of a diatomic molecule is constructed with the nuclei on the cartesian z axis.

The sketches in Figure 9-11 show how one of the three bonds can be constructed from the overlap of the two $2p_z$ atomic orbitals that point along the bond axis. This gives a new orbital that concentrates electron density between the two nitrogen nuclei.

The two remaining $2p$ orbitals on each atom, which point at right angles to the bond axis, overlap side by side to form the second and third bonds between nitrogen atoms. The pair of $2p_y$ orbitals overlap side by side, as shown in Figure 9-11. The $2p_x$ atomic orbitals overlap in the same side-by-side manner as the $2p_y$ atomic orbitals, but the bonding orbital formed by $2p_x$-$2p_x$ overlap is perpendicular to the one formed from the two $2p_y$ orbitals. Figure 9-12 shows the bonding orbitals formed from the $2p_x$ and $2p_y$ orbitals from three different perspectives. Notice that the π orbitals of N_2 closely resemble those of acetylene.

Side view

End view

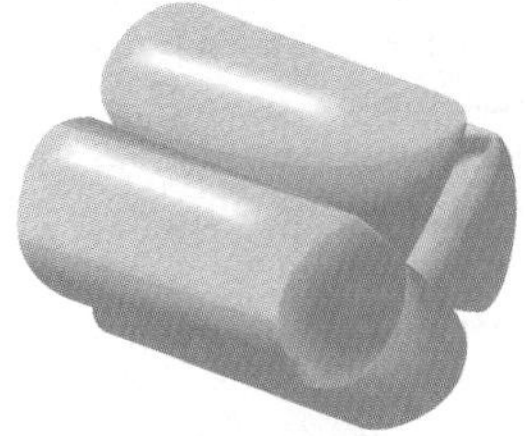
Oblique view

FIGURE 9-12
Three views of the two side-by-side π bonds of N_2.

ANTIBONDING ORBITALS

The bonding picture for nitrogen molecules can be completed by considering the valence $2s$ orbitals. To provide a full treatment of the interactions of the $2s$ orbitals, we must first return to the wavelike behavior of electrons.

Waves interact by addition of their amplitudes, allowing orbital overlap to be described by adding contributions from each individual orbital. Two waves that occupy the same region of space become superimposed, generating a new wave that is a composite of the original waves. If the wave amplitudes add, the new wave is larger than either original wave; this is *constructive interference.* If one wave amplitude is subtracted from the other, the new wave is smaller than either original wave; this is *destructive interference.* These features are shown in Figure 9-13 for two simple sine waves, which exist in one dimension along a line. The orbitals that describe electrons must be viewed as three-dimensional waves, but the principles of

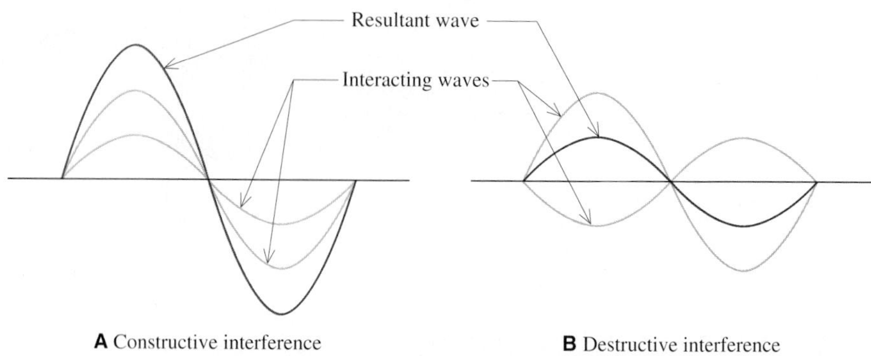

FIGURE 9-13
A, When two sine waves have amplitudes with the same sign, constructive interference produces a new wave with larger amplitude. **B,** When wave amplitudes have opposing signs, destructive interference produces a new wave with smaller amplitude.

wave interference apply equally to both one-dimensional sine waves and three-dimensional electron waves.

All the orbital interactions described so far have been constructive. That is, the wave amplitudes add in the overlap region, generating a new wave function with larger magnitude between the nuclei. A complete mathematical treatment requires, however, that when *two* wave functions interact, they *must* generate *two* new wave functions. One interaction is additive, leading to constructive interference and producing what is called a **bonding orbital.** The other is subtractive, leading to *destructive* interference and producing what is called an **antibonding orbital.** These two types of orbital have distinctly different properties, so an antibonding orbital is distinguished from a bonding orbital by a superscript asterisk (*).

Waves destroy each other in the overlap region of an antibonding orbital. Whereas bonding orbitals concentrate electron density *between* the two nuclei, antibonding orbitals concentrate electron density *outside* the internuclear region. Figure 9-14 shows the bonding and antibonding orbitals that result from the interaction of the $2s$ orbitals in N_2.

Although we have not previously shown it, the twin patterns of constructive and destructive overlap also apply to overlap of p orbitals. Figure 9-11 shows only the bonding orbitals for N_2. Figure 9-15 shows the antibonding orbitals generated from destructive overlap of $2p$ orbitals. The $2p_z$ orbitals overlap along the bond axis, generating a σ^* orbital, whereas the $2p_x$ orbitals and the $2p_y$ orbitals generate two π^* orbitals.

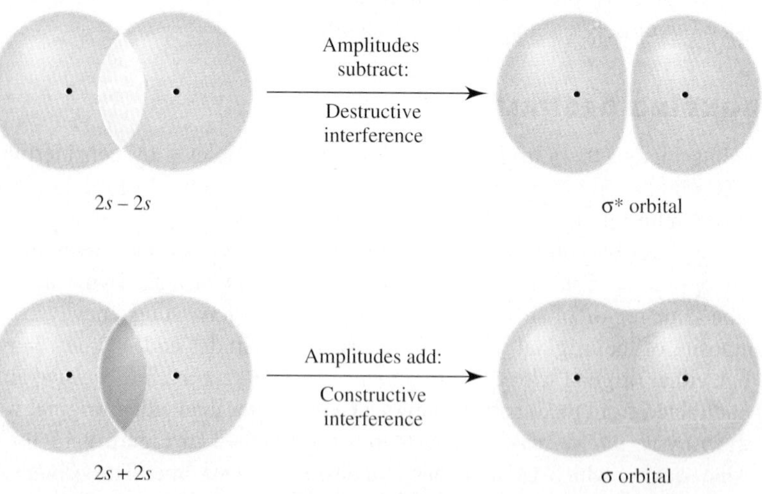

FIGURE 9-14
When two atomic orbitals interact, they generate two new orbitals. One is characterized by constructive interference and is a bonding orbital. The other is characterized by destructive interference and is an antibonding (*) orbital.

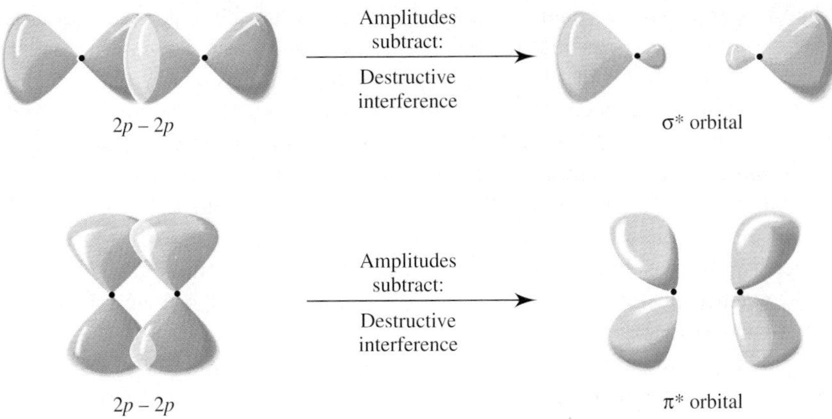

FIGURE 9-15
Overlap between 2p orbitals results in antibonding (*) orbitals when the two interacting wave functions have opposite signs in the overlap region, leading to destructive interference.

When destructive overlap is taken into consideration, eight orbitals can be constructed from the eight atomic valence orbitals of a diatomic molecule. The 2*s* orbitals generate one bonding and one antibonding orbital, and the 2*p* orbitals generate three bonding orbitals and three antibonding orbitals. The energy ranking of the orbitals is based on the following features:

1. Because atomic 2*s* orbitals are lower in energy than atomic 2*p* orbitals, the bonding and antibonding orbitals formed from the atomic 2*s* orbitals are lower in energy than any of the six orbitals derived from the atomic 2*p* orbitals.
2. Energy ranking of the *p*-based orbitals depends on the extent of orbital overlap. End-on overlap is generally greater than side-by-side overlap, as shown in Figure 9-11. This makes the σ orbital more stable than the π orbitals.
3. End-on overlap also leads to greater destructive interference than side-by-side overlap, so the σ* orbital is more unstable than the π* orbitals.
4. The two π bonding orbitals have identical energies because the atomic orbitals from which they were constructed had identical energies. Likewise, the two π* orbitals have identical energies.

Following these considerations, the eight orbitals can be arranged in the energy level diagram shown in Figure 9-16. This diagram also shows how the valence electrons of N_2 are placed in accordance with the Pauli and Aufbau principles. This arrangement of valence electrons can also be described by writing a valence configuration for the ground state of N_2 using appropriate symbols for each orbital:

$$(\sigma_s)^2\,(\sigma_s{}^*)^2\,(\sigma_p)^2\,(\pi_x)^2\,(\pi_y)^2$$

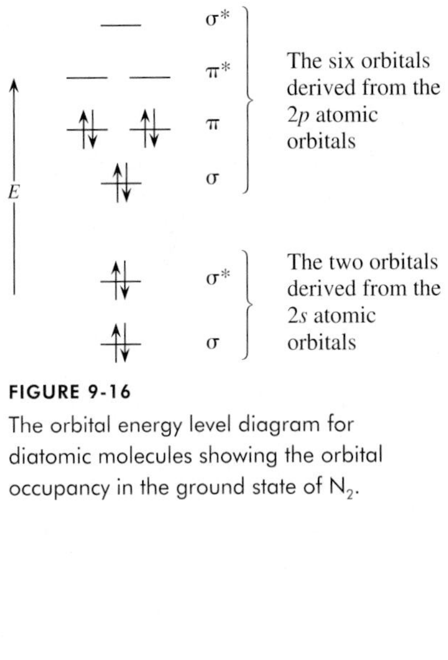

E

σ*
π*
π
σ
The six orbitals derived from the 2*p* atomic orbitals

σ*
σ
The two orbitals derived from the 2*s* atomic orbitals

FIGURE 9-16
The orbital energy level diagram for diatomic molecules showing the orbital occupancy in the ground state of N_2.

BOND ORDER

The Lewis structure of nitrogen contains a triple bond, but its orbital configuration shows four pairs of bonding electrons and one antibonding pair. This apparent discrepancy can be reconciled by noting that the destabilizing effect of antibonding electrons cancels the stabilizing effect of bonding electrons. Thus the two antibonding electrons of N_2 cancel the contributions of two bonding electrons. This leaves *net* resulting from three pairs of electrons, which is a triple bond. The net amount of bonding between two atoms is called the **bond order.** It is defined by Equation 9-2:

$$\text{Bond order} = \frac{(\text{No. of bonding electrons}) - (\text{No. of antibonding electrons})}{2} \qquad \textbf{(9-2)}$$

When a configuration contains no antibonding electrons, the bond order equals the number of bonding pairs. Thus the bond order also can be found from the number of lines joining two atoms in a Lewis structure. Nitrogen, with eight bonding electrons and two antibonding electrons, has a bond order of three (a triple bond). Note that the Lewis structure of N_2 (see Figure 9-11), which contains three lines joining the two atoms, accurately predicts the bond order of nitrogen, even though a more detailed bonding description reveals that N_2 contains antibonding electrons.

Lewis structure of O_2:

:Ö=Ö:

The orbital picture developed for nitrogen can also be applied to molecular oxygen. We have exactly the same set of valence orbitals in both molecules, but O_2 has 12 valence electrons, whereas N_2 has 10. According to the Aufbau principle, the first 10 valence electrons of O_2 are placed in the same orbitals as in N_2: 4 in the σ and σ^* orbitals generated by the atomic 2*s* orbitals, 2 in the σ orbital, and 4 in the two π orbitals generated by the atomic 2*p* orbitals. The remaining two electrons must be placed in the degenerate pair of π^* orbitals. According to Hund's rule, one electron goes in each orbital, and both electrons have the same spin. We can write the orbital configuration of O_2, showing the symbols for the various orbitals and the number of electrons that occupy each:

Energy level diagram for O_2:

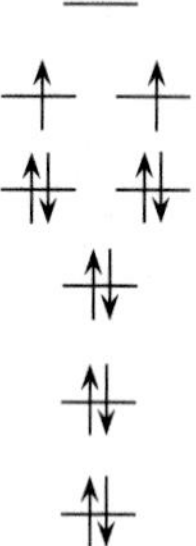

$$(\sigma_s)^2 (\sigma_s^*)^2 (\sigma_p)^2 (\pi_x)^2 (\pi_y)^2 (\pi^*_x)^1 (\pi^*_y)^1$$

This configuration states that there are two pairs of electrons in orbitals formed from the 2*s* atomic orbitals, two electrons in a σ orbital, four electrons in a pair of π orbitals, and one electron in each of the two antibonding π^* orbitals. The bond order calculated from Equation 9-2 is two, in agreement with the two lines shown in the Lewis structure. Unlike the Lewis structure, however, the more detailed description predicts that O_2 has two unpaired π^* electrons. Experiments verify that this is the case.

Sample Problem 9-6 addresses fluorine, the next diatomic molecule in this sequence.

SAMPLE PROBLEM 9-6 BONDING IN FLUORINE MOLECULES

In Chapter 8 the bonding in molecular fluorine was described in terms of two overlapping 2*p* orbitals. Determine the configuration of F_2 using antibonding orbitals. Do the two treatments predict different bond properties?

METHOD: To obtain a complete orbital view, we must allow all the valence orbitals to interact and generate a set of bonding and antibonding orbitals. Then we can construct an energy level diagram and place the valence electrons according to the Aufbau and Pauli principles. The energy level diagram of F_2 is qualitatively the same as for N_2:

E

σ^*

π^*

π

σ

Orbitals generated by 2*p* atomic orbitals

σ^*

σ

Orbitals generated by 2*s* atomic orbitals

Fluorine has 14 valence electrons that fill the seven most stable orbitals. Only the highest-energy σ^* orbital is empty, and the configuration is:

$$(\sigma_s)^2 (\sigma_s^*)^2 (\sigma_p)^2 (\pi_x)^2 (\pi_y)^2 (\pi^*_x)^2 (\pi^*_y)^2$$

According to this treatment, F_2 has a bond order of one because its six antibonding electrons nullify the bonding effect of six bonding electrons, leaving net bonding from two electrons. The simple approach of Chapter 8 gives the same result.

HETERONUCLEAR DIATOMIC MOLECULES

The bonding in single-bonded heteronuclear molecules such as HF is described in Chapter 8.

There are two stable second-row heteronuclear diatomic molecules, carbon monoxide and nitrogen monoxide. Because the qualitative features of orbital overlap do not depend on the identity of the atoms, the bonding in CO and NO can be described using the same sets of orbitals that describe the bonding in N_2 and O_2 and the appropriate numbers of valence electrons.

Carbon monoxide has 10 valence electrons, so its orbital configuration is identical with that of N_2, giving CO a bond order of 3. On the other hand, NO is one of the few stable molecules that contains an odd number of valence electrons. It has 11 valence electrons, which is 1 more than N_2 and 1 less than O_2. The last valence electron of NO must be placed in an antibonding π^* orbital, as shown in Figure 9-17. Consequently, the bond order of NO is 2.5, which is intermediate between the double bond of O_2 and the triple bond of N_2.

***Stable* is a relative term. Diatomic molecules such as CN, C_2, and NF are stable relative to their separated atoms, and these species can be observed in gas discharge tubes and interstellar space. Under normal conditions, however, these heteronuclear diatomic molecules are rapidly destroyed by chemical reactions. Carbon monoxide and nitrogen monoxide are the only two heteronuclear second-row diatomic molecules that are stable in the Earth's atmosphere.**

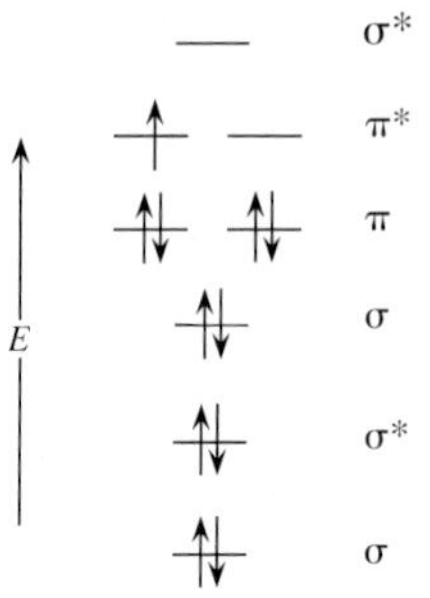

σ*
π*
π
σ
E
σ*
σ

:N̈=Ö:
Lewis structure

$(\sigma_s)^2 (\sigma_s^*)^2 (\sigma_p)^2 (\pi)^4 (\pi^*)^1$
Configuration

Bond order: $\frac{8-3}{2} = 2.5$

FIGURE 9-17
The Lewis structure, orbital occupancy diagram, configuration, and bond order of nitrogen monoxide, which has an odd number of valence electrons.

Nitrogen monoxide, which has one electron in a partially-filled antibonding orbital, is one of the few molecules whose bond order is not predicted accurately by its Lewis structure.

SECTION EXERCISES

9.3.1 The cyanide ion (CN^-), is a diatomic anion found in ionic compounds such as potassium cyanide. Determine the Lewis structure and describe the bonding in this ion, including its electron configuration and bond order.

9.3.2 Draw orbital sketches of each of the occupied valence orbitals for the CN^- ion.

9.3.3 The first ionization energy of NO is 891 kJ/mol, whereas the first ionization energy of N_2 is 1500 kJ/mol and that of CO is 1350 kJ/mol. Use electron configurations to explain why NO ionizes so much more easily than N_2 or CO.

9.4 DELOCALIZED π ORBITALS

We have described π orbitals localized between two atoms. Section 9.1 addresses the π orbitals for carbon-containing molecules such as ethylene and hydrogen cyanide, whereas Section 9.3 describes the multiple bonds in diatomic molecules of the second-row elements. In these molecules, a *p* orbital from one atom overlaps side by side with a *p* orbital from a second atom to give a bonding and an antibonding π orbital. The π orbitals are not always localized between pairs of atoms. More extended orbitals can form when a set of *p* orbitals overlaps in the appropriate geometry. We introduce extended orbitals by describing the bonding in a simple hydrocarbon molecule, 1,3-butadiene. Then we examine triatomic molecules composed of second-row elements.

π BONDING IN 1,3-BUTADIENE

The role of butadiene in the rubber industry is described in Chapter 11.

1,3-Butadiene, industrially important as the primary starting material in the manufacture of synthetic rubbers, is a hydrocarbon with the chemical formula C_4H_6. Its Lewis structure shows two double bonds separated by a single bond:

```
      H       H
      |       |
H    C      C      H
   /    \\  /   \\  /
         C       C
         |       |
         H       H
```

The chemistry of 1,3-butadiene, including its ability to form rubber, can be traced to the special properties of its π system.

All four carbon atoms of 1,3-butadiene have a steric number of three and can be described in terms of sp^2 hybridization. The Lewis structure shows no lone pairs, so all the hybrid orbitals are used to form σ bonds. There are three C—C σ bonds (sp^2-sp^2) and six C—H σ bonds (sp^2-1s). These bonds use 18 of the 22 valence electrons in the molecule, leaving 4 for the π system.

As Figure 9-18 shows, all the atoms in butadiene lie in a common plane defined by the sp^2 hybrids. The four leftover *p* orbitals all point perpendicular to this common plane, perfectly oriented for side-by-side overlap to form π orbitals. The simplest picture would show two localized π orbitals, giving π bonds between each end carbon atom and its immediate neighbor. Figure 9-18 shows, however, that each *p* orbital on an inner carbon atom overlaps with *p* orbitals from *both* its neighbors. All four orbitals interact, producing new orbitals with electron density spread over all four carbon atoms. These are **delocalized π orbitals.** A delocalized orbital spreads electron density over *more than two atoms.*

We have seen that when two *p* orbitals overlap side by side, they generate a bonding π orbital and an antibonding π* orbital. It is a general feature of orbital interactions that when *p* orbitals overlap side by side, the resulting number of delocalized bonding π orbitals equals the number of delocalized antibonding π* orbitals. Thus butadiene, with four overlapping atomic orbitals, has two π orbitals and two π* orbitals. According to the Pauli and Aufbau principles, the four valence electrons that are not in σ orbitals occupy the two π bonding orbitals. A schematic view of the valence orbital energy levels for butadiene is shown in Figure 9-19.

The diatomic molecules discussed in Section 9.3 are the only ones that we describe that have electrons in antibonding orbitals.

Figure 9-19 illustrates three important features of most stable molecules that contain π electrons. First, σ orbitals are more stable than π orbitals because end-on overlap is more extensive than side-by-side overlap. Second, all the bonding orbitals are filled, maximizing molecular stability. Third, no electrons exist in destabilizing π* orbitals, a consequence of the Aufbau principle.

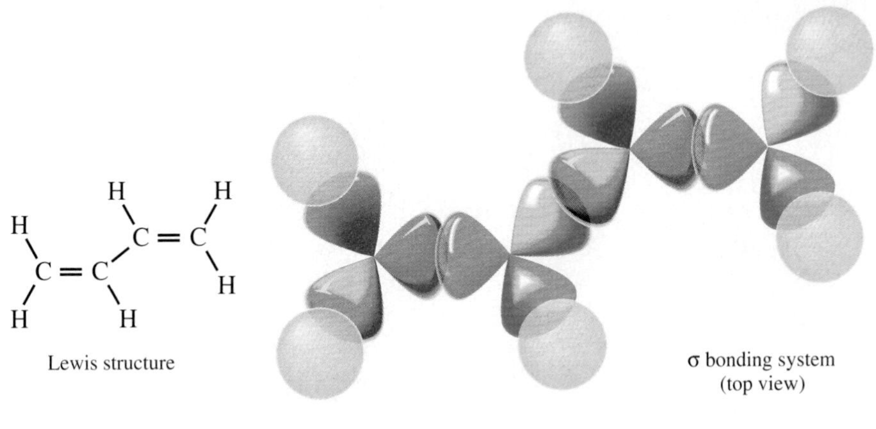

π bonding system
(side view)

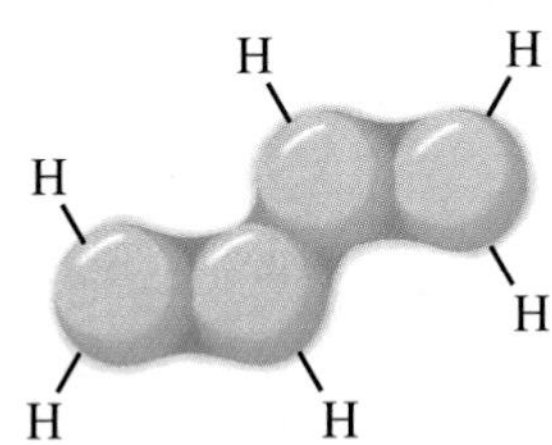

π bonding system
(top view)

FIGURE 9-18
The atoms of butadiene all lie in a common plane that contains the sp^2 hybrid orbitals on the carbon atoms. Each carbon atom has a leftover *p* orbital pointing perpendicular to the molecular plane, and the four orbitals overlap to form continuous, delocalized orbitals extending over the entire carbon skeleton.

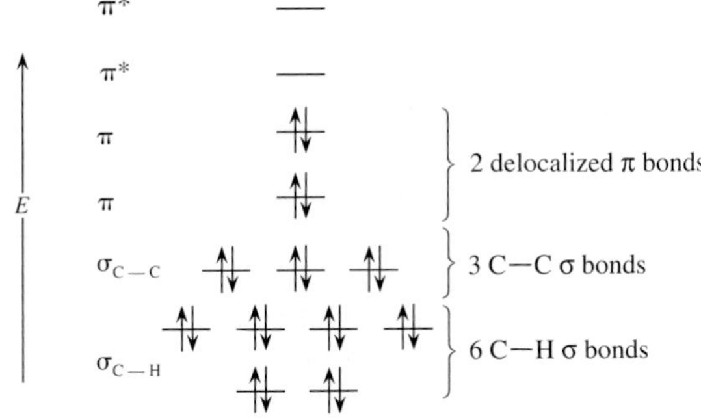

FIGURE 9-19
Schematic energy level diagram for the valence orbitals of butadiene. There are 11 pairs of electrons in bonding orbitals, which matches the 11 bonds shown in the Lewis structure. Butadiene also has vacant σ* orbitals, but these are even less stable than the π* orbitals.

CONJUGATED π SYSTEMS

When the Lewis structure of a molecule shows double or triple bonds alternating with single bonds, the orbital description includes delocalized π orbitals. Instead of alternating single and double bonds, delocalized orbitals spread the π electrons over the entire carbon skeleton. Molecules that have alternating single and multiple bonds are said to have **conjugated π systems,** which are stabilized by numerous side-by-side orbital overlaps.

Experimental measurements of reaction energies verify that conjugated π systems are more stable than localized π systems. For example, Figure 9-20 shows the Lewis structures of 1,3-pentadiene and 1,4-pentadiene. The π system of 1,3-pentadiene is conjugated. As in butadiene, all four *p* orbitals overlap to form a set of delocalized π orbitals. The π system of 1,4-pentadiene, on the other hand, has a

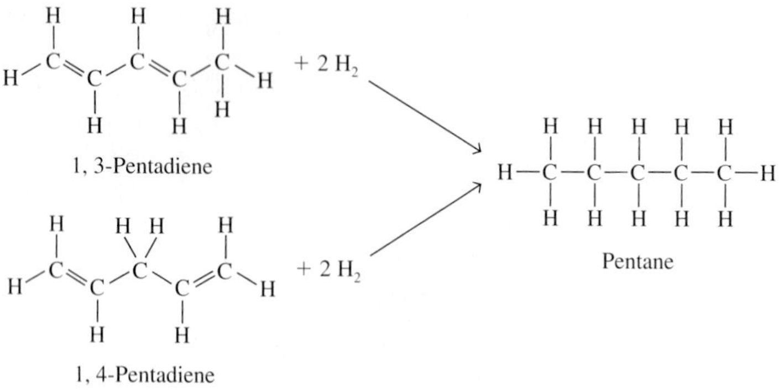

FIGURE 9-20
The Lewis structure of 1,3-pentadiene shows two conjugated double bonds between carbon atoms 1 and 2 and 3 and 4. The Lewis structure of 1,4-pentadiene shows two localized double bonds between carbon atoms 1 and 2 and 4 and 5. The hydrogenation of these two compounds leads to the same product, pentane.

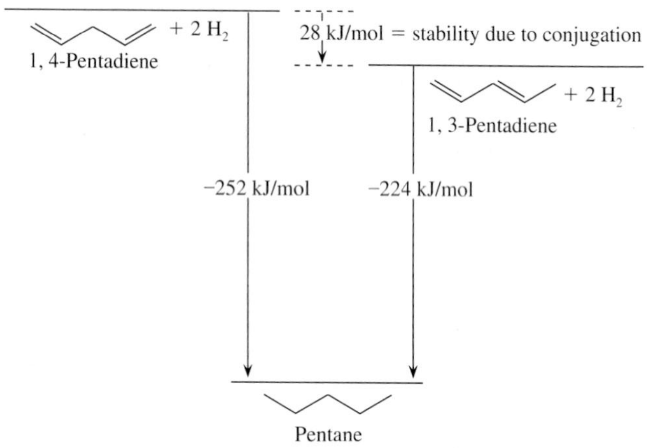

FIGURE 9-21
Schematic energy level diagram for the hydrogenation reactions of 1,4-pentadiene and 1,3-pentadiene. The difference in these energies, 28 kJ/mol, represents the additional stability that 1,3-pentadiene gains from delocalization of the electrons in its conjugated π system.

Remember that a negative value for an energy change means that the chemicals transfer energy to their surroundings. The more negative the energy change, the more energy released by the chemical reaction.

CH_2 group acting as a "spacer" to separate the double bonds. The carbon atom of this group is sp^3 hybridized, so it has no p orbitals for π bonding. As a result, the two π orbitals of 1,4-pentadiene are localized.

Figure 9-20 also shows that the hydrogenation of these two compounds leads to the same product, pentane. Thus a comparison of experimental energies of hydrogenation allows us to determine the relative stabilities of two conjugated π bonds and two localized π bonds. The hydrogenation of 1,4-pentadiene releases 252 kJ/mol as the π bonds are converted into C—H bonds, whereas the hydrogenation of 1,3-pentadiene releases only 224 kJ/mol. As Figure 9-21 demonstrates, these hydrogenation energies show that 1,3-pentadiene, with two conjugated double bonds, is *more stable* than 1,4-pentadiene, with two localized double bonds. Because the bonding in these two molecules is otherwise the same (eight C—H bonds, two C—C bonds, and two C═C bonds), we can conclude that delocalization of the four π electrons gives 1,3-pentadiene 28 kJ/mol of extra stability.

Many biological molecules have large conjugated π systems. Carotene, for example, is an alkene that gives plants such as carrots and tomatoes their color. It has a π system made up of 11 conjugated double bonds extending over 22 carbon atoms (see the figure in Box 9-1). Carotene is the precursor to retinal, a key molecule in the chemistry of vision. The π orbital system of a molecule as complex as carotene is complicated, but the guidelines presented earlier still apply. There are 11 delocalized bonding π orbitals, each occupied by a pair of electrons. This conjugated system is more stable than would be the case for 11 isolated π bonds.

Carbon is not the only element whose p orbitals can participate in the formation of delocalized π orbitals. Many biological molecules contain π-bonded nitrogen and oxygen atoms that are part of conjugated systems. Sample Problem 9-7 describes an organic molecule with an oxygen atom involved in delocalized π bonds.

SAMPLE PROBLEM 9-7 DELOCALIZED ORBITALS

Describe the geometry and bonding of methyl methacrylate, the line structure of which follows. This compound is an important industrial chemical, ranking in the second 50 in annual production. It is used mainly to make plastics such as poly(methyl methacrylate) (PMMA).

Plastics such as PMMA are described in Chapter 11.

Methyl methacrylate
$C_5H_8O_2$

METHOD: First, translate the line drawing into a Lewis structure. The Lewis structure allows us to determine the steric number, hybridization, and geometry of each inner atom. Then we can determine which atoms have leftover p orbitals that can interact to form delocalized π orbitals.

The Lewis structure is shown here with the steric numbers for each inner atom. The atoms with p orbitals that can overlap side by side have been highlighted in blue.

Each atom with steric number four can be described by sp^3 hybridization. The sp^3 hybrid orbitals on the carbon atoms form four σ bonds each, and the sp^3 hybrid orbitals on the inner oxygen atom form two σ bonds and hold two lone pairs. The three adjacent carbon atoms with steric number three can be described by sp^2 hybrid orbitals that form σ bonds. Each of these atoms has a leftover p orbital that can form π bonds. These three p orbitals plus one p orbital on the outer oxygen atom are oriented in the same way as the p orbitals in butadiene. They form a set of four delocalized orbitals, two bonding and two antibonding. Each π bonding orbital contains a pair of electrons.

The energy level diagram for the π orbitals of methyl methacrylate is similar to the one for butadiene:

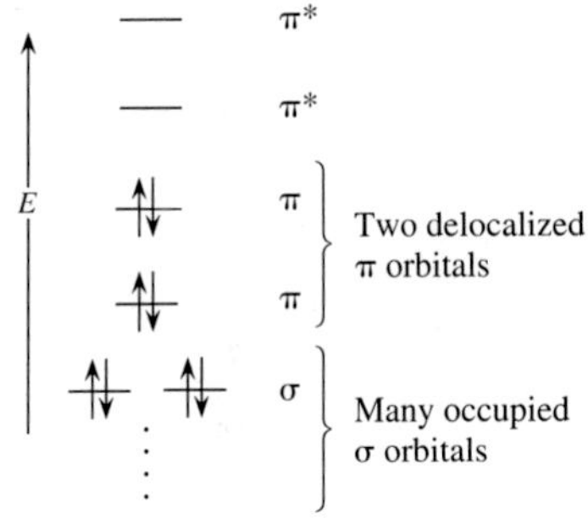

OZONE

Although elemental oxygen normally exists as a diatomic molecule, a triatomic molecule of oxygen called *ozone* is also stable. As described in Chapter 6, ozone in the upper stratosphere absorbs ultraviolet light from the solar spectrum, thus protecting plants and animals on the Earth's surface from this hazardous radiation. Ozone, whose Lewis structure is shown in Figure 9-22, is a bent triatomic molecule with 18 valence electrons.

FIGURE 9-22
The Lewis structure and the σ bonding framework of the ozone molecule. Two resonance structures exist.

Provisional Lewis structure

Lewis structure

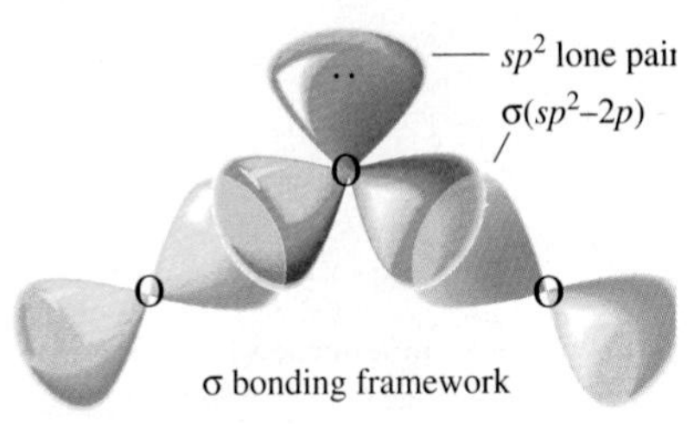

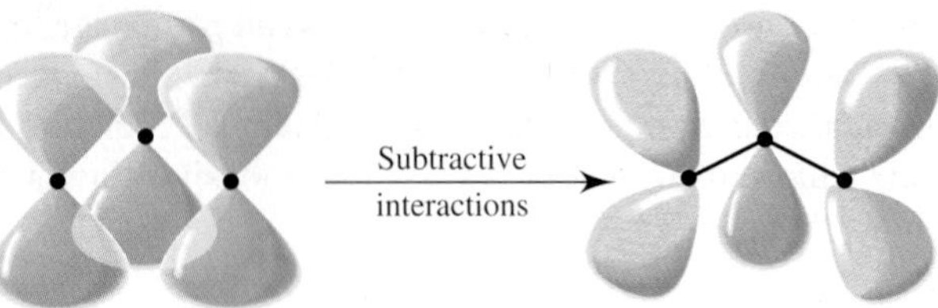

FIGURE 9-23
The three π orbitals that result from overlap of $2p$ atomic orbitals from the three oxygen atoms in ozone. The most stable orbital is bonding, the least stable orbital is antibonding, and the third orbital, intermediate in stability, is nonbonding.

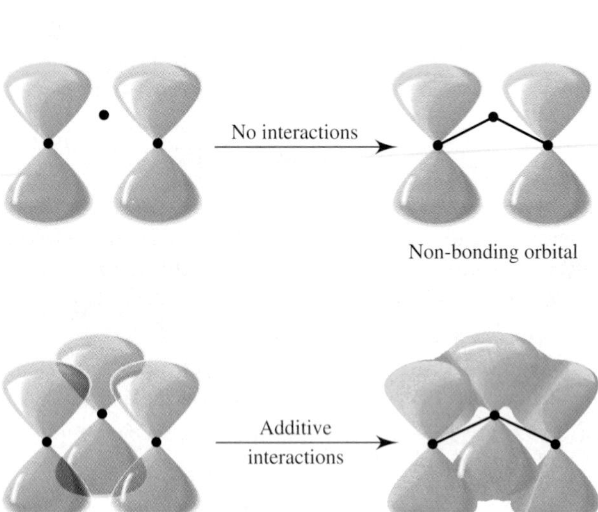

The bond framework of ozone can be described by the localized σ bonds shown in Figure 9-22. The inner oxygen atom, with a steric number of three, can be described using sp^2 hybrid orbitals. Two of these orbitals form σ bonds with $2p$ orbitals from the outer oxygen atoms, and the third contains a lone pair of electrons. The inner oxygen atom has one remaining $2p$ orbital, which is oriented perpendicular to the molecular plane. This orbital is perfectly positioned for side-by-side overlap with similarly oriented $2p$ orbitals on each of the outer atoms. As Figure 9-23 indicates, the p orbital on the inner atom overlaps simultaneously with orbitals on both outer atoms, generating a set of three delocalized orbitals.

The three delocalized orbitals include one that is a new type. A bonding orbital has high electron density between the bonded atoms. An antibonding orbital has low electron density between the bonded atoms. The third orbital is delocalized over the two *outer* atoms but has no electron density on the *central* atom. This type of π orbital is neither stabilizing nor destabilizing, so it is called a π **nonbonding orbital** and is symbolized π_n.

The bonding picture for ozone can be completed using the Pauli and Aufbau principles. The σ bonding framework accounts for 6 of ozone's 18 valence electrons because there are 2 σ bonds and a localized nonbonding sp^2 lone pair on the central oxygen atom. Of the remaining 12 electrons, 4 are in the stable $2s$ orbitals on the outer oxygen atoms, and 4 more occupy the outer-atom p orbitals that lie in the molecular plane. This leaves four electrons to be placed in the delocalized π orbitals. Two electrons occupy the bonding orbital because it is the most stable of the three, and two occupy the delocalized nonbonding orbital because it is second in stability. The antibonding orbital is highly unstable and remains empty.

The valence configuration for ozone can be written as $(2s_{oxygen})^4\,(\sigma)^4\,(\pi)^2\,(sp^2_{lone\ pair})^2\,(2p_{oxygen})^4\,(\pi_n)^2$.

The bond lengths in ozone provide evidence that the π electrons extend over the entire molecule rather than being localized between two atoms. Both bond lengths are 128 pm, intermediate between the length of the localized double bond in O_2 (120.7 pm) and the length of the single O—O bond in H_2O_2 (148 pm).

CARBON DIOXIDE

Recall from Chapter 6 that the increasing concentration of CO_2 in the Earth's atmosphere may lead to global warming. Carbon dioxide is also a crucial molecule in biochemistry because plants use the carbon atoms of CO_2 for the synthesis of biomolecules. Furthermore, animals and plants use fats and carbohydrates for energy production, and eliminate the carbon atoms from these molecules as CO_2.

Carbon dioxide has 16 valence electrons. Its Lewis structure shows that the molecule has two double bonds. The molecule is linear, a geometry predicted by the steric number of two for the carbon atom. Figure 9-24 shows the two σ bonds formed by end-on overlap of *sp* hybrids on the carbon atom and $2p_z$ atomic orbitals of oxygen.

Lewis structure of CO_2:

:Ö=C=Ö:

The $2p_x$ and $2p_y$ orbitals of the carbon atom are not used in forming the hybrid set. Each of these orbitals is oriented perfectly to overlap side by side with *p* orbitals of each oxygen neighbor. Similar to ozone, this gives the three delocalized π orbitals shown schematically in Figure 9-25. One of these orbitals is bonding, one is antibonding, and the third is nonbonding. The $2p_x$ atomic orbitals combine in exactly the same way, except that the resulting three orbitals point at right angles to the π_y set.

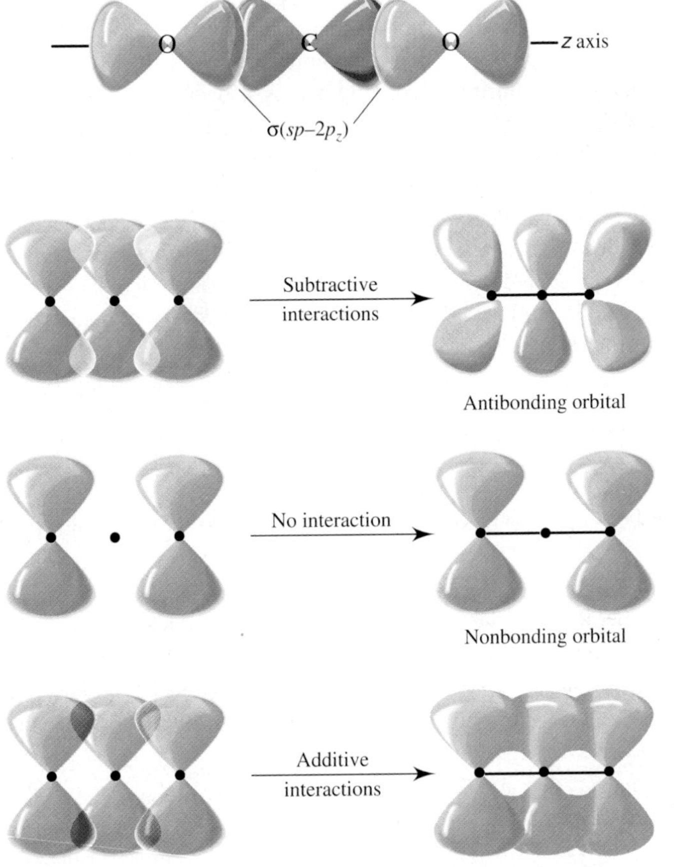

FIGURE 9-24
The σ bonding system of CO_2. Two σ bonds form from the overlap of carbon *sp* hybrids with oxygen $2p_z$ atomic orbitals. All other valence orbitals have been omitted for clarity.

FIGURE 9-25
One of the sets of delocalized π orbitals of CO_2. Except for their linear geometry, these orbitals closely resemble those of ozone.

π^*_y — — π^*_x

E π_{ny} ⇅ ⇅ π_{nx}

π_y ⇅ ⇅ π_x

FIGURE 9-26

The energy level diagram for the delocalized π orbitals of CO_2. In accordance with the Pauli and Aufbau principles, the four most stable orbitals contain pairs of electrons. The valence configuration for CO_2 can be written as $(2s_{oxygen})^4\ (\sigma)^4\ (\pi)^4\ (\pi_n)^4$.

These two sets of delocalized π orbitals have exactly the same energy. In other words, the π_x and π_y bonding orbitals are degenerate, as are the other two pairs. Figure 9-26 shows the energies of all six orbitals on an energy level diagram. Of the 16 valence electrons in the CO_2 molecule, four are in σ bonds and four more occupy the $2s$ atomic orbitals on the outer oxygen atoms. This leaves eight electrons to be placed in the six π orbitals. As indicated in Figure 9-26, four electrons occupy the two π bonding orbitals, and the remaining four are in the two π_n nonbonding orbitals. This completes the valence configuration, leaving the π^* antibonding orbitals vacant.

OTHER TRIATOMIC MOLECULES

The bonding description of a triatomic molecule is determined by the number of its valence electrons. For example, a count of the electrons for dinitrogen monoxide reveals that it has 16 valence electrons and is isoelectronic with CO_2. As a consequence, N_2O has the identical orbital configuration as CO_2. The N_2O molecule is linear, and its inner nitrogen atom, like the carbon atom in CO_2, has a steric number of two. The bonding framework of N_2O can be represented using *sp* hybrid orbitals. This leaves the inner atom with two unused *p* orbitals, each of which can overlap with *p* orbitals from both outer atoms. As in CO_2, therefore, eight electrons occupy four delocalized *p* orbitals, two that are bonding and two that are nonbonding. The resonance structures of N_2O, described in Sample Problem 8-10, reflect this delocalization.

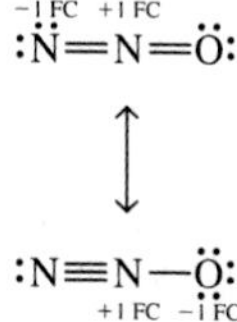

Triatomic molecules can be bent or linear, depending on their electron count. Ozone, which has 18 valence electrons, exemplifies bent molecules. The principles of orbital overlap do not depend on the identity of the atoms involved, so the bonding scheme of ozone applies to other triatomic species with 18 valence electrons. One such example is nitrite (NO_2^-), which is a bent anion. Its bonding can be represented using sp^2 hybrid orbitals for the inner nitrogen atom and one set of delocalized π orbitals. Carbon dioxide, with 16 valence electrons, is representative of linear molecules. The bonding scheme of CO_2 and N_2O applies to other triatomic molecules with 16 valence electrons. Examples include the azide ion (N_3^-) and carbon disulfide (CS_2). These are linear species that have inner atoms with bonding that can be represented using *sp* hybrid orbitals and two sets of delocalized π orbitals. Sample Problem 9-8 describes nitrogen dioxide, a rare example of a 17-electron molecule.

Nitrite salts, whose breakdown products may be carcinogenic, are used as preservatives for processed meats. Azide ion is a powerful reducing agent that forms explosive compounds. Carbon disulfide is used in the production of rayon and cellophane.

SAMPLE PROBLEM 9-8 BONDING IN NITROGEN DIOXIDE

Describe the bonding and geometry of nitrogen dioxide, a red-brown gas that is a common pollutant in urban atmospheres.

METHOD: Begin by counting valence electrons and writing the Lewis structure. The Lewis structure provides the steric number of the inner atom, from which the bonding framework and details can be determined.

Nitrogen dioxide contains 17 valence electrons, 5 from the nitrogen atom and 6 from each oxygen atom. Following the usual procedure, we can determine the provisional Lewis structure:

+2 FC, −1 FC, −1 FC

4 electrons are in the two σ bonds.
12 electrons form six lone pairs on the O atoms.
1 electron is placed on the central N atom.

The formal charges indicate that a structure with double bonds is more stable. Making two double bonds to nitrogen would reduce all formal charges to zero, but this requires five valence orbitals on the nitrogen atom, one more than it has. One double bond is all that can be made using the four valence orbitals of the nitrogen atom. Because the two oxygen atoms are equivalent, there are two resonance structures:

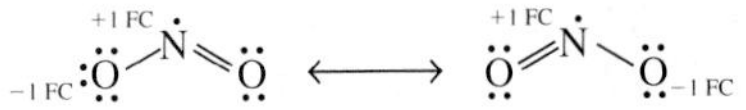

$$\overset{+1\ \text{FC}}{} \; {}_{-1\ \text{FC}}\ddot{\underset{..}{\text{O}}}{:}-\dot{\text{N}}=\ddot{\text{O}} \longleftrightarrow \ddot{\text{O}}=\dot{\text{N}}-\ddot{\underset{..}{\text{O}}}{:}_{-1\ \text{FC}} \qquad \text{Lewis structure}$$

The existence of resonance structures indicates that there are delocalized orbitals in this molecule.

To determine the steric number, we must first decide how to treat the lone electron on the nitrogen. Experiments show that NO_2, like O_3, is bent. This indicates that the lone electron behaves like a lone pair. Thus we conclude that the steric number of nitrogen is three, and we can represent the bonding framework using sp^2 hybrid orbitals.

Consequently, the bonding in NO_2 is described exactly like the bonding in ozone, except that the nonbonding sp^2 orbital on the inner nitrogen atom holds only one electron. Review the description of ozone, and construct orbital sketches of all the occupied orbitals in NO_2.

PROCEDURE TO DESCRIBE BONDING

Delocalized orbitals become progressively more complex as the number of atoms increases, but the bonding in even the most complex biochemical molecules can be described using a combination of localized σ bonds and delocalized π bonds. From the Lewis structure of a molecule, we can determine the steric number and hybridization for all the inner atoms. This information allows us to construct localized orbitals for the σ bonding framework. When multiple bonds are present, we must determine which valence orbitals participate in side-by-side overlap. If necessary, conjugated π bonding is described using delocalized orbitals. The overall procedure can be summarized in the following steps.

1. Count the valence electrons and determine the Lewis structure of the molecule. Work from provisional to final structure, and include any resonance forms. The Lewis structure provides essential information about the features of the σ and π systems.
2. Use localized orbitals to construct the σ bonding framework. Determine the steric number and hybridization of each inner atom from the Lewis structure. (Remember that outer atoms are not hybridized.) Each σ bond holds two valence electrons. Any hybrid orbitals not used for σ bonds are filled with lone pairs (or occasionally single electrons).
3. If the molecule contains multiple bonds, construct the π bonding system using the *p* orbitals left over after hybridization. Watch for resonance structures, which signal the presence of delocalized orbitals. All appropriately oriented atomic *p* orbitals on adjacent atoms form π orbitals through side-by-side overlap.
4. Place a pair of valence electrons in each atomic orbital that has not been used in hybridization or delocalized orbital formation. Each outer atom (except H) always has two atomic *s* electrons and may or may not have atomic *p* electrons.
5. To complete the configuration, use the Pauli and Aufbau principles to place all remaining electron pairs in π orbitals. This results in a configuration that has occupied π orbitals and may have occupied nonbonding, π_n orbitals.

Sample Problem 9-9 illustrates how to apply this five-step procedure.

SAMPLE PROBLEM 9-9 DESCRIBING BONDING

Determine the valence electron configuration of the acetate anion ($CH_3CO_2^-$). This polyatomic anion forms when acetic acid, the acid present in vinegar, is treated with hydroxide ion:

$$CH_3CO_2H + OH^- \rightarrow CH_3CO_2^- + H_2O$$

METHOD: Because acetate is a polyatomic species, we apply the five-step procedure to build its valence configuration.

Step 1. Count valence electrons and determine the Lewis structure.

Atom	C	O	H
Valence electrons	4	6	1
Number of atoms	2	2	3
TOTAL	8	12	3 + 1 (negative charge) = 24

Provisional structure

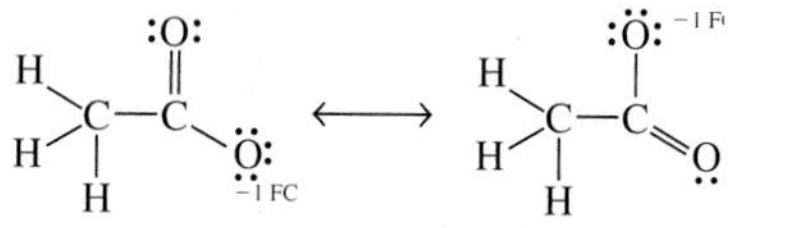

Lewis structures, including resonance

Step 2. Use localized electrons to construct the σ bonding system. The Lewis structure shows that the CH_3 carbon has a steric number of four, so we describe it using sp^3 hybrid orbitals. The other carbon has a steric number of three, so we describe it using sp^2 hybrid orbitals. Three of the sp^3 hybrid orbitals form σ bonds by overlap with 1*s* orbitals on the hydrogen atoms. The fourth sp^3 hybrid forms a σ bond with an sp^2 hybrid from the neighboring carbon atom. The two remaining sp^2 hybrids bond to 2*p* orbitals from the outer oxygen atoms. This gives a total of six σ bonds and uses 12 of the 24 valence electrons.

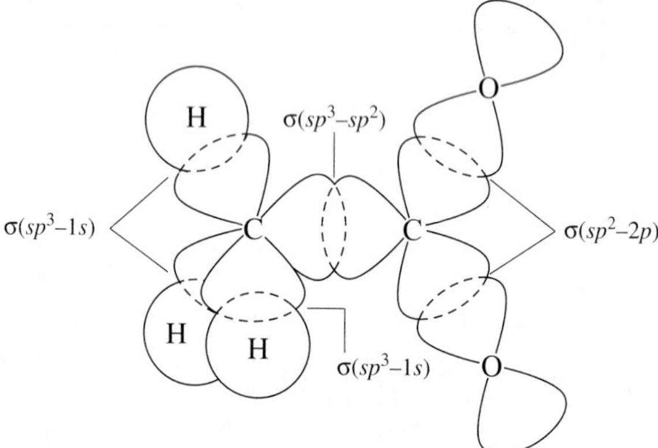

Step 3. The Lewis structure shows the presence of multiple bonds, so the next task is to construct the π orbitals. The existence of resonance structures indicates that the π orbitals are delocalized. The sp^2 hybridized carbon atom has a 2*p* orbital available for side-by-side overlap, and each of the outer oxygen atoms has a 2*p* orbital oriented for proper side-by-side overlap. These three orbitals form a set of three delocalized π orbitals like those of the ozone molecule: π, π_n, and π*.

Step 4. Now we survey the valence atomic orbitals to determine which have not been used for hybridization, σ bond formation, or π orbitals. The hydrogen 1*s* orbitals were used for bond formation. All carbon valence orbitals went into hybrids or the delocalized π orbitals. Each oxygen atom used one 2*p* orbital to form a σ bond and another for the delocalized π orbitals. This leaves a 2*s* orbital and one 2*p* orbital on each oxygen; these four orbitals are filled with eight more valence electrons.

Step 5. Assign any remaining valence electrons to the appropriate delocalized orbitals. The valence electron count is:

$$24 \text{ valence} - 12\ \sigma \text{ bonding} - 8 \text{ atomic} = 4 \text{ delocalized electrons}$$

The four remaining electrons are placed in the π and π_n orbitals. The π system for acetate has the same orbital assignments as the π system for ozone. The occupied orbitals are shown below:

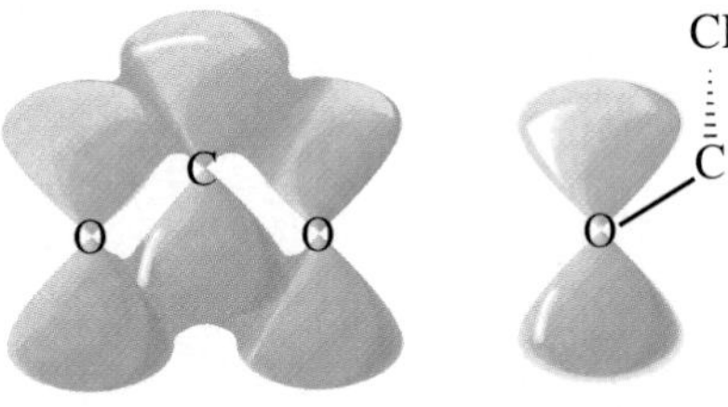

Bonding orbital Non-bonding orbital

We can summarize the orbital assignments in acetate and match them with the Lewis structure as follows:

- Six filled localized σ orbitals, matching six single bonds in the provisional Lewis structure (step 2). This gives the bonding framework shown.
- Four filled atomic orbitals, matching four localized lone pairs in the resonance Lewis structures (step 4)
- Two filled delocalized orbitals, matching the two pairs of electrons that occupy different locations in the resonance structures (step 5)

The valence electron configuration for the acetate anion can be written as $(\sigma)^{12}\ (\pi)^2\ (2s_O)^4\ (2p_O)^4\ (\pi_n)^2$.

SECTION EXERCISES

9.4.1 Construct the bonding description (Lewis structure, hybridization, geometry, and orbital assignments and shapes) for the azide anion (N_3^-). Explain why this anion has a different bonding description from nitrogen dioxide.

9.4.2 Explain the difference between a localized orbital and a delocalized orbital.

9.4.3 The line structure of hydrocarbon follows. Azulene is a deep purple, almost black solid. How many delocalized π and π^* orbitals are in an azulene molecule? How many of these orbitals are occupied?

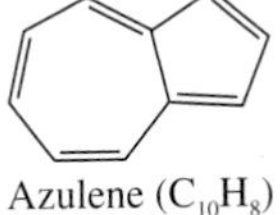

Azulene ($C_{10}H_8$)

9.5 π BONDING IN POLYATOMIC ANIONS

In this section we describe the π bonding of common polyatomic anions such as nitrate, sulfate, carbonate, and phosphate. First we consider nitrate and carbonate, whose inner atoms fall in the second row of the periodic table. Then we examine anions with inner atoms from the third row.

See Table 3-3 for a list of the common polyatomic ions.

NITRATE AND CARBONATE ANIONS

These anions have identical Lewis structures even though their inner atoms have different formal charges in the provisional structure because second-row elements are limited to four pairs of electrons.

As part of Sample Problems 8-2 through 8-9, we determined the Lewis structure of the nitrate anion. The carbonate anion, which is isoelectronic with NO_3^-, has the same Lewis structure except that the formal charge on the inner atom is different:

Carbonate anion (CO_3^{2-})

Nitrate anion (NO_3^-)

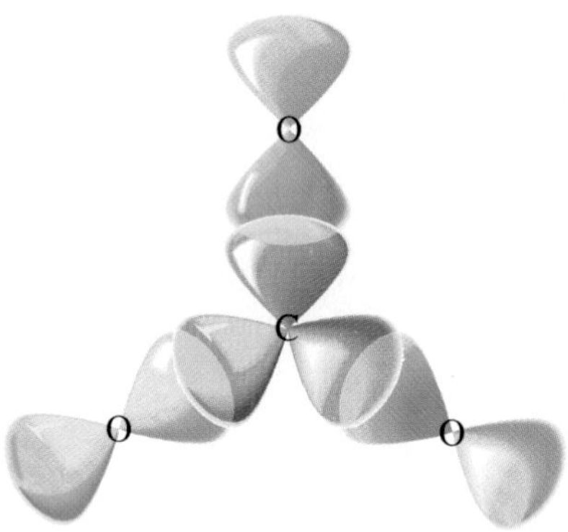

A σ bonding framework in CO_3^{2-} (top view)

B Delocalized π bonding framework (side view)

FIGURE 9-27

A, The σ bonding framework of the carbonate anion forms from sp^2 hybrids on the carbon atom overlapping with 2*p* orbitals on the oxygen atoms. **B,** The leftover *p* orbital on the inner atom of the carbonate anion overlaps simultaneously with *p* orbitals from all three outer oxygen atoms, giving delocalized π orbitals.

The existence of resonance structures indicates that a complete description of these ions requires delocalized electrons. In each case the inner atom has a steric number of three, which indicates that sp^2 hybrid orbitals can be used for the bonding framework. As Figure 9-27 shows, all three oxygen atoms have *p* orbitals oriented properly for side-by-side overlap with the leftover *p* orbital on the inner atom. This gives π orbitals delocalized over the entire anion and best represented by a set of three equivalent resonance structures.

The σ bonding framework for CO_3^{2-} can be described by localized orbitals. The carbon atom forms σ bonds in the molecular plane using sp^2 hybrid orbitals that overlap with 2*p* orbitals of the three oxygen atoms, as shown in Figure 9-27, *A*. This arrangement leaves carbon with an unused 2*p* orbital perpendicular to the molecular plane. Each oxygen atom has a similarly oriented 2*p* orbital, as shown in Figure 9-27, *B*. These four *p* orbitals overlap to form a set of four delocalized π orbitals. These π orbitals are different from the set for butadiene, however, because the four atoms in the carbonate anion are not aligned in a row. Instead, the oxygen atoms form a triangular array around the central carbon atom. Figure 9-28, *A*, shows that the most stable π orbital resulting from this geometry has a "propeller" shape when viewed from above.

The energy arrangement of the carbonate π orbitals is also different from that of butadiene (see Section 9.4). Instead of two bonding and two antibonding orbitals, carbonate has one bonding orbital, one antibonding orbital, and a degenerate pair of nonbonding orbitals. These nonbonding orbitals place electron density only on the outer oxygen atoms, not on the inner atom, analogous to the delocalized nonbonding orbital in ozone.

To determine which of the delocalized orbitals are occupied in carbonate and nitrate anions, we need a count of valence electrons and a list of available orbitals. There are 24 valence electrons, 6 of which are involved in σ bonds. All four valence

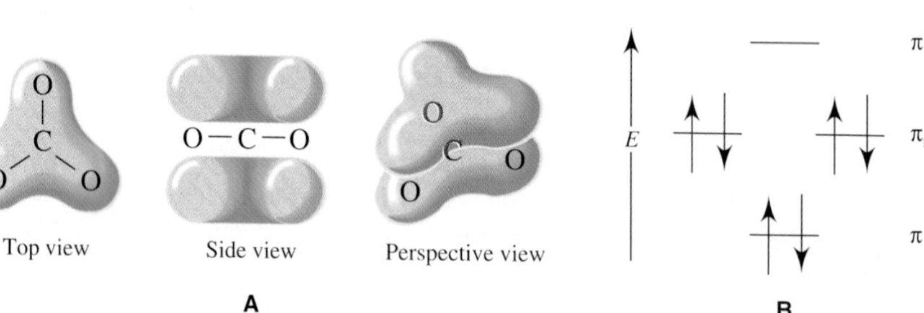

FIGURE 9-28

A, Three views of the most stable, delocalized bonding π orbital of carbonate. **B,** Energy level diagram for the delocalized orbitals of carbonate.

orbitals of the inner atom have been used, three to form sp^2 hybrids and one for the delocalized orbitals. Each oxygen atom also has four valence orbitals; one has been contributed to the delocalized set, and another has been used for σ bonding. The 2*s* orbital and the third 2*p* orbital are still available, and these hold 4 electrons per atom, for a total of 12. The remaining six electrons occupy the π orbital and the two π_n orbitals, as shown in Figure 9-28, *B*.

The valence electron configuration for the carbonate and nitrate anions can be written as $(\sigma)^6 (\pi)^2 (2s_O)^6 (2p_O)^6 (\pi_n)^4$.

INNER OXYGEN ATOMS

The bonding in nitrate and carbonate anions illustrates the ease with which outer oxygen atoms contribute to π bonding. In fact, outer oxygen atoms always have some π character in their bonding. Inner oxygen atoms, on the other hand, do not participate in π bonding. Any inner oxygen atom has a steric number of four and can be described appropriately using sp^3 hybrid orbitals. This difference is illustrated by the hydrogencarbonate anion (HCO_3^-), the subject of Sample Problem 9-10.

Ozone, discussed in Section 9.4, is the only exception to this generalization about inner oxygen atoms. The inner oxygen atom of ozone has a steric number of three and contributes an atomic *p* orbital to the delocalized π system.

SAMPLE PROBLEM 9-10 BONDING IN HYDROGENCARBONATE

Develop a bonding description for the hydrogencarbonate anion.

METHOD: Use the same procedure we developed for other bonding descriptions. The following flowchart illustrates this procedure:

1. Determine the Lewis structure, including resonance forms.

↓

2. Construct the σ bonding framework, using an appropriate set of hybrid orbitals, as determined by the steric numbers.

↓

3. Build delocalized π orbitals from *p* orbitals having the appropriate spatial orientations.

↓

4. Allocate the valence electrons to the orbitals with the greatest stability.

1. The HCO_3^- ion contains 24 valence electrons. Its bonding framework is deduced from the framework for carbonate, recognizing that hydrogen usually bonds to oxygen:

O
|
O–C–O–H

This bonding framework requires 8 electrons, leaving 16 still to be distributed. Six are assigned to each outer oxygen atom, leaving four to be placed on inner atoms. Of the two inner atoms, oxygen is more electronegative, so it is assigned the last four electrons. What follows is the provisional Lewis structure, including formal charges:

:Ö: −1 FC
|
:Ö(−1 FC)–C(+1 FC)–Ö–H

We can make one double bond to minimize formal charge. Either of the outer oxygen atoms can supply the electron pair, so two equivalent resonance structures exist:

2. The steric number of the carbon atom is three, indicating that sp^2 hybrid orbitals are appropriate. For the inner oxygen atom, a steric number of four indicates that sp^3 hybrid orbitals can be used. The σ bonding framework is completed using the appropriate atomic orbitals from the outer atoms:

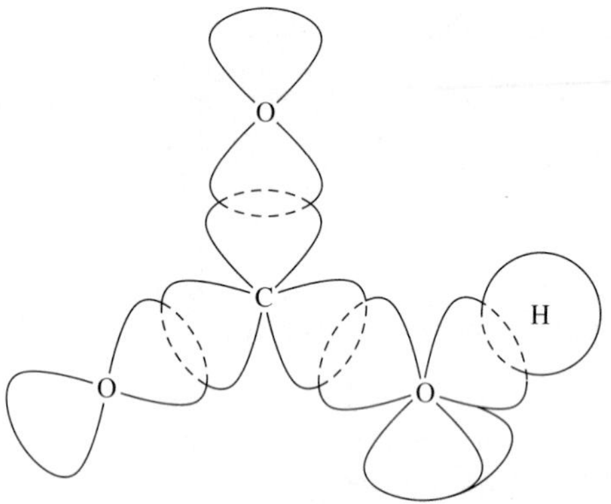

3. The two outer oxygen atoms and the carbon atom have atomic p orbitals oriented for side-by-side overlap. This generates an ozonelike arrangement of three orbitals: π, π_n, and π^*.

4. Of the 24 valence electrons, 8 are in σ bonds and 4 are in sp^3 lone pair orbitals on the inner oxygen atom. Four more are in 2s orbitals on the two outer oxygen atoms, and an additional four are in the 2p atomic orbitals lying in the O—C—O plane but oriented perpendicular to the bond axes. This accounts for 20 electrons, leaving 4 to be placed in the π and π_n delocalized orbitals.

Notice that the delocalized orbitals do not extend over the inner oxygen atom. This is because the inner oxygen atom uses all its valence orbitals to form two σ bonds and to accommodate two lone pairs.

π BONDING BEYOND THE SECOND ROW

Several common polyatomic anions, including sulfate, perchlorate, and phosphate, have inner atoms from the third row of the periodic table. In these anions, valence

FIGURE 9-29

All four oxygen atoms are equivalent, so six resonance structures are needed to represent the π bonding of the sulfate anion. These structures indicate that delocalized orbitals span the entire anion.

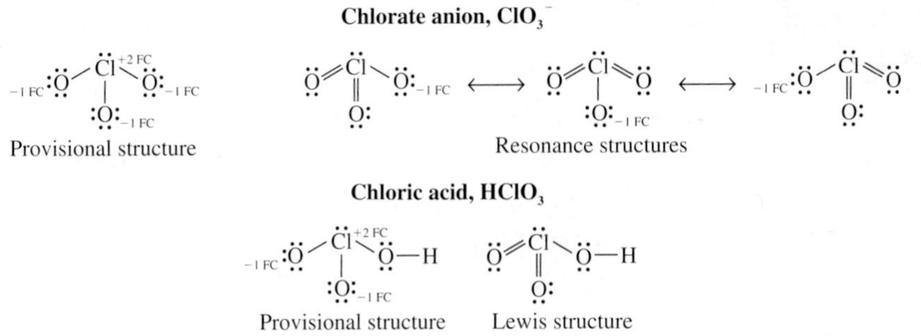

Chlorate anion, ClO_3^-

Provisional structure

Resonance structures

Chloric acid, $HClO_3$

Provisional structure

Lewis structure

FIGURE 9-30
Lewis structures of the chlorate anion and chloric acid, which contain chlorine atoms in tetrahedral geometry with *p*-*d* π bonding.

d orbitals are available to participate in bonding. We use the sulfate anion as an example; its Lewis structure is determined in Sample Problems 8-2 through 8-9. According to our procedures for determining Lewis structures, two pairs of electrons are shifted to minimize formal charge. The four equivalent oxygen atoms give rise to six resonance structures, as shown in Figure 9-29.

Another example is provided by the chlorate anion (ClO_3^-), whose Lewis structure, shown in Figure 9-30, indicates that the inner chlorine atom has a lone pair as well as π bonds to oxygen atoms.

The oxygen atoms of anions such as sulfate and chlorate can form bonds to protons, as in hydrogencarbonate. This generates acids that contain polar O—H bonds. Protonated chlorate anion is chloric acid ($HClO_3$), whose Lewis structure is also shown in Figure 9-30.

The steric number of the sulfur atom in SO_4^{2-}, HSO_4^-, and H_2SO_4 is four and so is the steric number of the chlorine atom in ClO_3^- and $HClO_3$. This indicates that sp^3 hybrid orbitals can be used to describe the bonding framework of these species. Consequently, all three valence 3*p* orbitals of the S and Cl atoms participate in the formation of σ bonds. Notice from the Lewis structures, however, that these atoms are associated with *six* electron pairs. This signals the participation of valence *d* orbitals in the bonding scheme. Sulfur and chlorine can form π bonds to oxygen through side-by-side overlap of 3*d* orbitals with 2*p* orbitals on oxygen atoms. Figure 9-31 shows how a *localized* π orbital can form through this type of orbital overlap. The details of the *delocalized* π orbitals of sulfate, chlorate, and other tetrahedral anions are beyond our scope. You need only recognize that they include bonding and nonbonding π orbitals formed through the side-by-side overlap of *d* orbitals and *p* orbitals.

Box 9-2 provides experimental evidence for delocalized and antibonding orbitals.

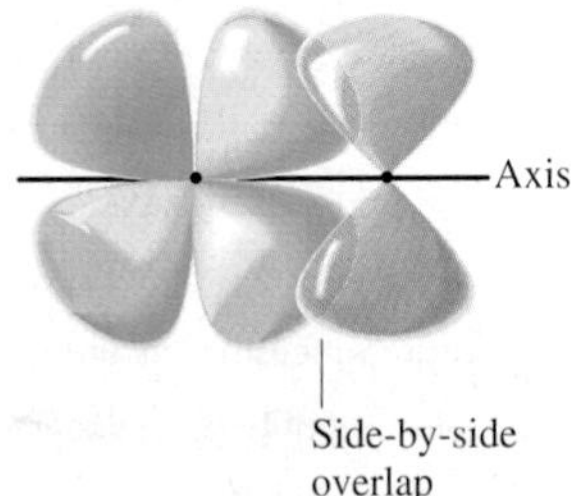

FIGURE 9-31
A localized π bond can form through side-by-side overlap between a *d* orbital and a *p* orbital. As with other π bonds, electron density is concentrated between the nuclei, above and below the internuclear axis.

SECTION EXERCISES

9.5.1 Describe the bonding in the hydrogenphosphate anion (HPO_4^{2-}).

9.5.2 The chromate ion (CrO_4^{2-}) has the same number of valence electrons as the sulfate anion. Describe the bonding in CrO_4^{2-}.

9.5.3 In some compounds of the transition metals, π bonds are formed by overlap between a *pair* of *d* orbitals. Draw a sketch that shows how two d_{xy} orbitals can overlap to form a π bond. (HINT: Examine Figure 9-31 for clues on how to draw this sketch.)

BOX 9-2

EVIDENCE FOR DELOCALIZED AND ANTIBONDING ORBITALS

The orbital descriptions developed in this chapter are more elaborate than those used to describe bond frameworks in Chapter 8, but are more complicated pictures needed to give a good picture of chemical bonding? Much experimental evidence, some of which cannot be explained using only the bond framework model of Chapter 8, supports the picture of π bonding outlined in this chapter. The following examples use molecules whose bonding we have already described.

The photographs below show that liquid oxygen adheres to the poles of a strong magnet, whereas liquid nitrogen does not. This is evidence that nitrogen molecules are not paramagnetic but oxygen molecules are paramagnetic because attraction to the poles of a magnet is a sign of paramagnetism. Recall from Chapter 7 that paramagnetism arises when a ground-state configuration includes unpaired electrons. The Lewis structure of oxygen does not reveal the presence of unpaired electrons, but our detailed orbital picture does. The least stable occupied orbital is the degenerate pair of π^* orbitals, each of which contains one electron.

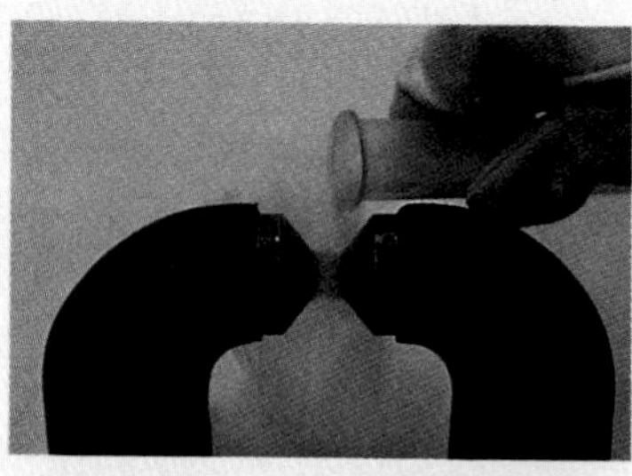

Bond length and bond strength measurements on oxygen and its cation also indicate that the highest occupied orbital is a destabilizing, antibonding orbital. Removing an electron from a bonding orbital increases the bond length and decreases its strength, but when an electron is removed from O_2 to form O_2^+, the bond length *decreases* and the bond strength *increases:*

Species	Bond length (pm)	Bond energy (kJ/mol)	Configuration
O_2	121	496	$\pi^4\ (\pi^*)^2$
O_2^+	112	643	$\pi^4\ (\pi^*)^1$

Because the least stable occupied orbital of O_2 is antibonding in character, removal of an electron reduces the amount of *antibonding* in the molecule and strengthens the bond.

Bond energies provide evidence for the delocalization of π electrons. The difference in the hydrogenation energies of pentadienes can be attributed to the delocalization of π electrons in the 1,3-isomer. The bond strength in CO_2 also demonstrate the presence of delocalized orbitals. The measured bond energy of CO_2 is 805 kJ/mol, 55 kJ/mol stronger than the average C=O energy of 750 kJ/mol (see Table 9-2). The π electrons are delocalized over the entire molecule rather than restricted between pairs of atoms, generating additional stability from side-by-side overlap between the 2p orbitals on *both* sides of the inner carbon atom.

	N_2	O_2
σ^*	—	—
π^*	— —	↑ ↑
π	↑↓ ↑↓	↑↓ ↑↓
σ	↑↓	↑↓

Our bonding picture for sulfate anions includes π orbitals delocalized over all four oxygen atoms. In sulfuric acid (H_2SO_4), on the other hand, the two oxygen atoms bonded to hydrogen atoms are inner, with no delocalized orbitals. The S—O bond lengths in these species support this bonding description:

Bond	HO—S (H_2SO_4)	O—S (SO_4^{2-})	O=S (H_2SO_4)
Length (pm)	157	149	142

Sulfuric acid has two relatively long (157 pm) S—O bonds between the sulfur atom and the oxygen atoms bonded to hydrogen atoms. Sulfuric acid also has two short (142 pm) S=O bonds, with four π electrons delocalized across them. Removing two protons from sulfuric acid yields the sulfate anion, which has four bonds of the same length (149 pm), between the lengths of the S—O and S=O bonds. Delocalization of the π electrons over all four bonds makes the bonds shorter than the S—O bonds but longer than the two highly stabilized S=O bonds in sulfuric acid.

9.6 BAND THEORY OF SOLIDS

Copper, iron, and aluminum are three of the most common metals in modern society. Copper wires, for example, carry the electricity that powers most of our appliances, including the lamp by which you may be reading. The chair in which you are sitting may have an iron frame, and you may be sipping a soft drink from an aluminum can. The properties of metals that allow them to be used for such a wide range of products can be traced to their bonding and electronic structure.

Iron and other metals have tremendous mechanical strength, which suggests that the bonds between their atoms must be strong. At the same time, most metals are malleable, which means they can be shaped into thin sheets to make objects such as aluminum cans. Metals are also ductile, which means they can be drawn into wires. The properties of malleability and ductility suggest that atoms in metals can be moved about without weakening the bonding. Finally, metals conduct electricity, which suggests that the electrons in metals are free to move throughout the solid.

All these properties of metals are consistent with a bonding description that places the valence electrons in delocalized orbitals. In this section we describe the bonding in metals and many other solids using **band theory of solids,** an extension of the delocalized orbital ideas that are the theme of this chapter. Band theory accounts for the properties of metals, and it also explains the properties of metalloids such as silicon.

DELOCALIZED ORBITALS IN LITHIUM METAL

Lithium, the lightest metal, can be used to develop the principles of band theory. Solid lithium contains atoms held together in a three-dimensional crystal lattice. Bonding interactions among these atoms can be described by orbital overlap. To see how this occurs, consider building an array of lithium atoms one at a time.

The bonding in Li_2 can be described using overlapping valence orbitals. The valence $2s$ orbitals of two lithium atoms interact to form a σ bonding orbital and a σ^* antibonding orbital. The bonding orbital is filled, and the antibonding orbital is empty. The single bond in Li_2 is relatively weak, 105 kJ/mol, because compact $2s$ orbitals do not overlap strongly.

Although Li_2 molecules are unstable relative to metallic lithium, the Li—Li bond is strong enough that these diatomic molecules can exist as long as they are isolated in the gas phase.

We can envision an Li_3 molecule bonded together by three $2s$ orbitals that have interacted to give three delocalized orbitals. Likewise, Li_6 would have 6 orbitals, Li_{10} would have 10 orbitals, and so on. As with delocalized π orbitals, these interactions generate equal numbers of bonding and antibonding orbitals. In 1 cm^3 of Li metal there are approximately 4×10^{22} atoms with interacting $2s$ atomic orbitals that generate approximately 4×10^{22} delocalized orbitals. This is a huge number of bonding orbitals and an equally huge number of antibonding orbitals, and yet they all obey the principles developed in this chapter. Most important, each orbital is delocalized over the entire lattice of atoms.

Clusters of lithium atoms such as Li_6 and Li_{18} can be generated in the gas phase by bombarding a piece of lithium metal with gaseous metal atoms in a chamber at very low pressure.

Figure 9-32 illustrates that as the number of delocalized orbitals increases, the energy spacing between them decreases. For a huge number of atoms, such as 4×10^{22}, the orbitals are spaced so closely that they behave as if they were merged together into an energy band. Because energy bands are a feature of this bonding model, it is called *band theory.*

To keep our picture simple, we have included only the $2s$ orbitals in Figure 9-32. For most metals, however, a comprehensive picture of the bonding includes interactions among all valence *s, p, d,* and even *f* orbitals. Each group of orbitals interacts to generate an energy band. Interactions among bands is complex, and often the bands overlap. Despite this complexity, however, the fundamental features illustrated in Figure 9-32 remain valid.

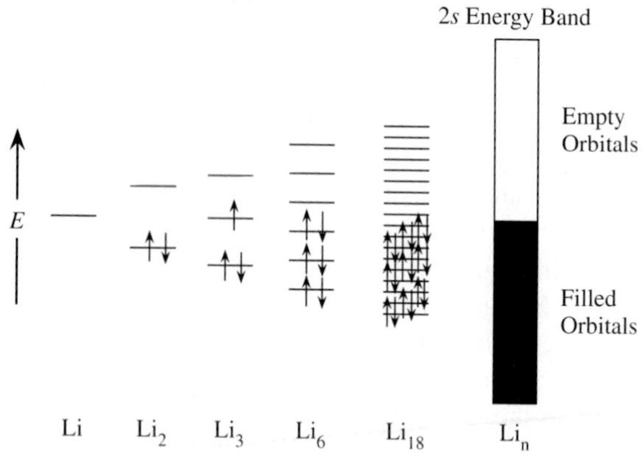

FIGURE 9-32
Schematic view of the energies of delocalized orbitals made from the 2s orbitals of lithium atoms. A metal sample containing *n* atoms of lithium has a continuous band of filled bonding and empty antibonding orbitals.

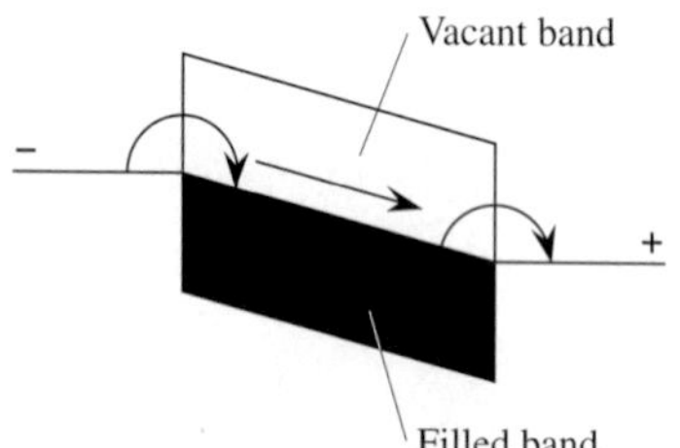

FIGURE 9-33
An electrical potential shifts the energy levels in the substance to which it is applied. When that substance is a metal, the presence of vacant orbitals allows electrons to move easily from the negative end toward the positive end. The arrows show the direction of electron flow.

PROPERTIES OF METALS

A metal has energy bands that consist of an immense number of delocalized orbitals. The valence electrons of the metal atoms occupy these orbitals according to the Aufbau and Pauli principles. Many properties of metals can be explained in terms of how valence electrons populate these energy bands.

The most important feature of metallic bonding is the energy bands that arise because of the close spacing between orbital energies. The countless orbitals within the band are separated by infinitesimally small energy gaps. This means that the highest-energy occupied orbitals are so close in energy to the unoccupied orbitals of lowest energy that it requires very little energy to transfer an electron from an occupied orbital to an unoccupied orbital.

When an electrical potential is applied to a metal, the negative pole repels electrons, whereas the positive pole attracts them. In energy terms the occupied orbitals near the negative pole are pushed higher in energy than unoccupied orbitals near the positive pole. This "tilts" the energy levels, as shown in Figure 9-33, and electrons can move "downhill" out of filled orbitals into empty orbitals. As a result, electrons flow through the metal from the negative end to the positive end, generating an electrical current.

Delocalized electrons also explain the ductility and malleability of metals. When a piece of metal is hammered into a new shape, the atoms change position. Changes in atomic position always change orbital energies, but the *total* energy of the filled delocalized orbitals does not change as atoms shift. This is because as any one orbital becomes less stable, electrons move to some other orbital that is more stable. Thus metals can be forced into many shapes, including sheets and wires, without destroying the bonding nature of their band of filled, delocalized orbitals.

Sodium is so soft that it can be cut with a knife.

Among the metals, a range of properties is encountered. Sodium and potassium, for example, are quite soft compared with iron and nickel. Copper and silver are much better electrical conductors than chromium. Tungsten has very low ductility. All these differences result from variations in band structure and numbers of electrons. For example, the alkali metals are soft and have low melting points because they contain only one valence electron per atom. Consequently, only one bonding electron can exist for every atom in the metal lattice. On the other hand, a transition metal such as vanadium or chromium possesses five or six valence electrons per atom; all occupy bonding orbitals in the metal lattice. As a result, attractive forces among the metal atoms are strong, and vanadium and chromium are strong and hard. Beyond the middle of the transition metal series, the additional valence electrons occupy antibonding orbitals, which reduces the net bonding.

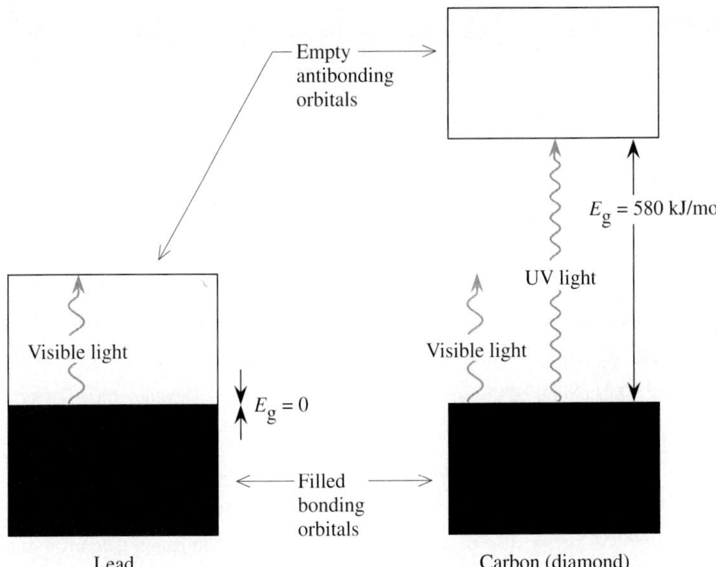

FIGURE 9-34
Carbon and lead have different properties because the energy differences between their filled bonding orbitals and their empty antibonding orbitals are different. The band gap (E_g) for carbon is 580 kJ/mole, whereas E_g for lead is zero.

INSULATORS AND CONDUCTORS: CARBON VS. LEAD

Metallic lead is soft, dark, malleable, and an electrical conductor. Diamond, the most valuable form of carbon, is hard, transparent, and brittle and is an electrical insulator. Although their physical properties are very different, lead and carbon fall in column IV of the periodic table and have the same valence configuration, s^2p^2. Why, then, are diamonds transparent insulators, whereas lead is a dark-colored conductor?

C = [He] $2s^2$ $2p^2$; Pb = [Xe] $4d^{10}$ $6s^2$ $6p^2$.

Both diamond and lead have delocalized orbitals and energy bands, but as Figure 9-34 shows, the energy distributions of the bands are quite different. Lead is metallic because the energy separation between its filled and vacant orbitals is infinitesimally small. One continuous band of orbitals results in highly mobile electrons and electrical conductivity. The valence orbitals of carbon, on the other hand, form two distinct bands. The filled bonding orbitals are well separated in energy from the empty, antibonding orbitals. The energy difference between these two bands is called the **band gap** and is symbolized E_g. For diamond, E_g = 580 kJ/mol.

Graphite, the most common form of elemental carbon, has quite different properties than diamonds. Box 9-3 discusses the fact that carbon exists in different elemental forms with different bonding and energy band characteristics.

Lead and diamonds have distinctly different band structures for two reasons. First, the smaller size of diamond's valence orbitals results in stronger overlap. This results in a large stabilization energy and a large band gap. Second, lead has valence *d* and *f* orbitals that are involved in band formation. These bands overlap the *s* and *p* bands, contributing to the continuous distribution of orbital energies that gives lead its metallic properties.

Carbon in the form of diamond is an electrical insulator because of its huge band gap. In fact, its 580 kJ/mol E_g exceeds the C—C bond energy of 345 kJ/mol. In other words, it requires much more energy to promote an electron from band to band in diamond than to break a covalent bond. Lead, in contrast, is a metallic conductor because it has E_g = 0.

The differences in their band structures also explain why diamonds are transparent and lead is dark. Recall from Chapter 6 that substances can absorb only photons whose energies match differences between energy levels. A colored substance absorbs photons in the visible portion of the electromagnetic spectrum,

BOX 9-3

FORMS OF ELEMENTAL CARBON

Several elements exist in more than one form. Diatomic oxygen and ozone, for example, are quite different molecules, even though both are composed entirely of oxygen atoms. Three elemental forms of carbon with strikingly different appearances and properties are diamond (transparent), graphite (black), and fullerene (red-violet).

A diamond contains a three-dimensional lattice of carbon atoms in which every atom bonds to four others. Geometrically, each atom is at the center of a regular tetrahedron, and we can view the bonding as completely localized. The bonding can be represented using sp^3 hybrid orbitals, with four σ bonds around each carbon atom. From the perspective of band theory, the diamond array has a set of filled bonding orbitals that are separated from vacant antibonding orbitals by a large energy gap. From either perspective, the bonding in diamond makes it strong, hard, transparent, and insulating.

The most common form of carbon is graphite, which is a black, soft solid. Although graphite is brittle, it has the metallic property of electrical conductivity. In graphite, each carbon atom is bonded to *three* neighbors in the same plane. This gives a σ bond framework of planar hexagons that can be described using sp^2 hybrid orbitals. Each atom also has one $2p$ orbital available to form delocalized π orbitals extending throughout the atomic lattice. These orbitals generate an energy band that is only half filled, giving graphite its metallic properties.

The properties of graphite differ from those of typical metals because the graphite lattice is arranged in planar layers rather than a three-dimensional array. Electrons move readily about in any single layer, but they cannot easily move from one layer to the next. Thus

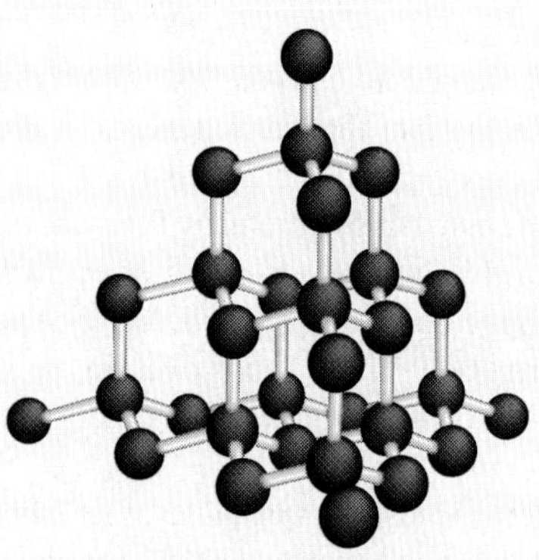

Ball-and-stick model of diamond

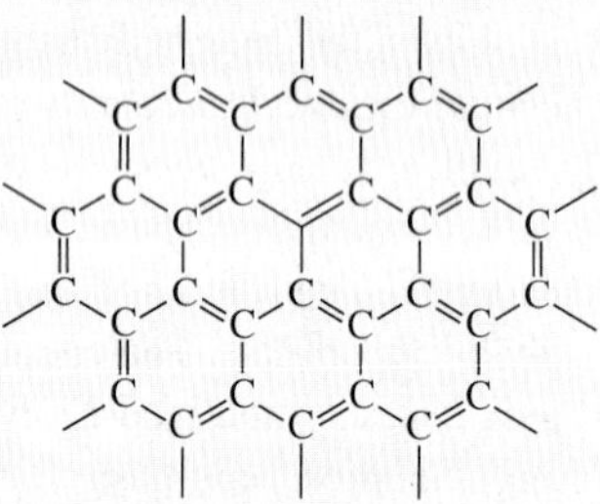

Lewis structure of graphite

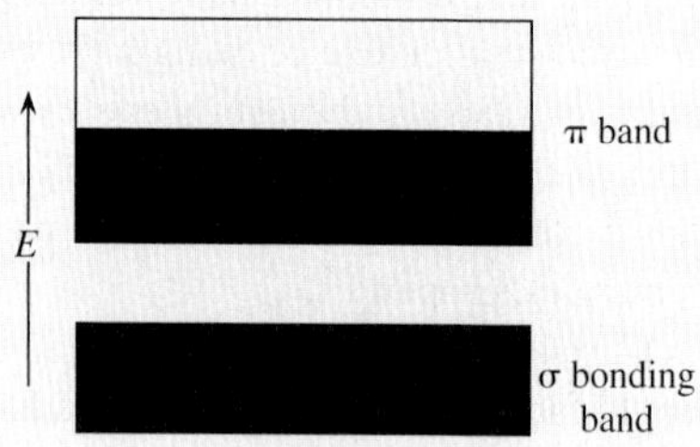

Energy bands of graphite

a perfect crystal of graphite conducts electricity in two dimensions but not in the third. Although each layer of atoms is tightly bound to the layers above and below, no covalent bonds exist between layers. This allows adjacent layers to slide past each other, giving graphite useful lubricating properties. It also accounts for the brittleness of graphite compared with the strength and hardness of diamond. Graphite fractures along layer lines without breaking chemical bonds, whereas bonds must be broken to fracture diamond.

The third form of carbon, fullerene, was not even imagined before 1985, when it was first proposed to explain some unusual mass spectrometry observations. When samples of fullerene were isolated in 1990, many research chemists began studying its properties.

Whereas diamond and graphite are extended lattices of interconnected carbon atoms, fullerenes are made up of molecules with the formula C_n. Several different values exist for *n,* but the most common is C_{60}. The 60 carbon atoms are arranged in a regular structure that resembles a soccer ball or a geodesic dome. The C_{60} molecule has been named *buckminsterfullerene,* in honor of Buckminster Fuller, the architect who championed the use of geodesic dome structures.

In buckminsterfullerene, five carbon atoms bond together in a pentagonal ring. Each side of the pentagonal ring is also a side of a hexagonal ring. These clusters of rings join to form a ball of 60 carbon atoms in which each carbon atom is at a corner of one pentagon and two hexagons. Every atom bonds to two others in a distorted arrangement that, although not quite planar, can nevertheless be described using σ bonds formed from sp^2 hybrid orbitals. The remaining p orbitals generate a set of 60 delocalized π orbitals. Because the molecular surface wraps around on itself, these orbitals are not delocalized throughout the crystal. As a result, buckminsterfullerene crystals are colored but nonconducting.

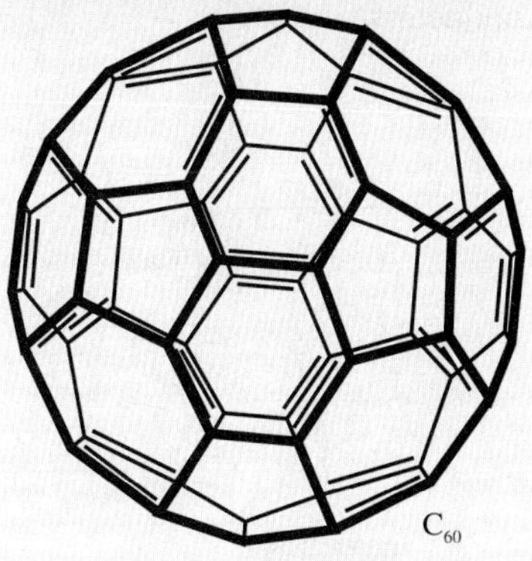

C_{60}

Although C_{60} molecules are very rare under natural conditions, they are easy to synthesize. When graphite is heated intensely in the absence of oxygen, for example, it vaporizes and recondenses largely as C_{60}. The chemical properties of this form of carbon are being studied intensively. The chances are very good that some properties of fullerenes will have been newly discovered and reported in the chemical research journals while you are enrolled in introductory chemistry. We do not know what these properties will be, but they will generate much excitement in the chemistry community.

where energies are 180 to 330 kJ/mol. For diamond, the energy difference between the top of the filled band and the bottom of the empty band is 580 kJ/mol, so diamond cannot absorb visible light. Lead, on the other hand, has vacant orbitals into which visible photons can promote electrons. Thus lead can absorb all visible wavelengths, making it gray in color.

METALLOIDS

The stabilization of bonding orbitals and the destabilization of antibonding orbitals among elements in group IV of the periodic table are determined largely by the amount of spatial overlap. Because atomic orbitals become increasingly diffuse (spread out in space) as their n value (principal quantum number) increases, the spatial overlap of the valence orbitals decreases as the valence shell n value increases (see Figure 9-9). Thus the band gap shrinks as we move down the column from carbon to lead. Carbon ($n = 2$) has a very large band gap and is a nonmetal, but tin ($n = 5$) and lead ($n = 6$) have $E_g = 0$ and are metals. Silicon and germanium, on the other hand, have intermediate band gap values, which cause them to behave as **metalloids.** Metalloids have useful and intriguing properties.

Like carbon, Si and Ge have low energy bands of bonding orbitals that are completely filled with electrons. The higher energy bands of Si and Ge are empty antibonding orbitals. For silicon, E_g = 105 kJ/mol, whereas E_g = 64 kJ/mol for germanium. Electrons cannot make the transition between these bands unless sufficient energy is supplied. Thus Si and Ge are nonconductors in the absence of an energy source. However, electrons can move between the bands at higher temperatures or in the presence of photons with energy that matches E_g. When electrons are transferred into the high-energy band, they can move freely among the many vacant near-degenerate orbitals. In addition, electron transfer creates vacancies (holes) among the bonding orbitals in the low-energy band. The combination of holes and high-energy electrons allows electricity to flow. Thus silicon and germanium become conductors in the presence of an energy source. These elements are called **semiconductors** to indicate their ability to conduct electricity under special conditions. Figure 9-35 uses band gap diagrams to summarize a semiconductor's behavior.

Transfer of electrons from one band to another requires energy equal to the band gap. This energy can be provided by heating (exploited in thermistors) or by absorption of light (used in photoconductors). Sample Problem 9-11 deals with photoconductors.

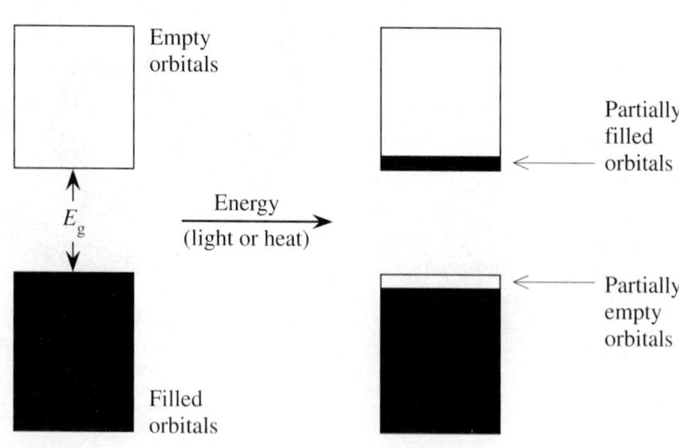

FIGURE 9-35
When a semiconductor absorbs heat or light, electrons are excited from the filled band to the empty band. As a result, partially filled and partially empty bands allow electrons to move freely. Under these conditions, the semiconductor conducts electricity.

SAMPLE PROBLEM 9-11 PROPERTIES OF PHOTOCONDUCTORS

"Electric eye" door openers operate using photoconductors and infrared light with a wavelength (λ) of 1500 nm. Which semiconductor material is suitable for photoconductors operating at this wavelength, germanium (E_g = 64 kJ/mol) or silicon (E_g = 105 kJ/mol)?

METHOD: To conduct electricity, a semiconductor must be provided with energy that is *at least* equal to its band gap. In a photoconductor, this energy must come from photons. Recall from Chapter 6 that photon energy is related to wavelength.

First, calculate the energy of 1500 nm light (see Equations 6-1 and 6-2):

$$E_{\text{photon}} = h\nu = \frac{hc}{\lambda}$$

$$E_{\text{photon}} = \frac{hc}{\lambda} = \frac{(6.627 \times 10^{-34}\text{ J sec})(2.998 \times 10^{8}\text{ m sec}^{-1})}{(1500\text{ nm})(10^{-9}\text{ m nm}^{-1})} = 1.3245 \times 10^{-19}\text{ J}$$

Multiply by Avogadro's number to convert photon energy into the energy of 1 mol of photons in kilojoules per mole:

$$(1.3245 \times 10^{-19}\text{ J/photon})(6.022 \times 10^{23}\text{ photons/mol})(10^{-3}\text{ kJ/J}) = 79.76\text{ kJ/mol}$$

This energy is insufficient to overcome the band gap of silicon, so silicon could not be used for an infrared photoconductor. Germanium, however, with its smaller band gap (E_g = 64 kJ/mol), becomes an electrical conductor when illuminated by infrared light with λ = 1500 nm.

DOPED SEMICONDUCTORS

The relatively large band gaps of silicon and germanium limit their usefulness in electrical devices. Fortunately, however, the conductive properties of these solid elements can be altered by adding tiny amounts of elements that have different valence electron configurations. When a specific impurity is deliberately added to a pure substance, the resulting material is said to be *doped.* A **doped semiconductor** has almost the same band structure as the pure material, but it has different electron populations in its bands.

In pure silicon, all orbitals of the low-energy band are filled, and all orbitals of the high-energy band are empty. When pure silicon is doped with arsenic atoms, the As atoms replace some of the Si atoms in the crystal lattice. Each arsenic atom contributes five valence electrons instead of the four contributed by a silicon atom. The fifth valence electron cannot enter the low-energy band of the solid because that band is already filled. The fifth valence electron from each As atom must therefore occupy the higher-lying energy band. Silicon or germanium doped with atoms from group V is called an **n-type semiconductor** because extra negative charges exist in its high-energy band. These few electrons in a partially occupied band make the doped material an electrical conductor.

Si = [Ne] $3s^2\ 3p^2$
As = [Ar] $3d^{10}\ 4s^2\ 4p^3$
Arsenic has one more valence electron than silicon.

Silicon can also be doped with gallium, a group III element. Gallium has three valence electrons, so each Ga atom in the Si lattice has one less electron than the atom that the Ga replaces. In Ga-doped silicon, there are not quite enough electrons to fill all the bonding orbitals. Silicon and germanium doped with atoms from group III are known as **p-type semiconductors** because their low-energy bands have positive vacancies. Electrons move through the crystal by flowing from filled orbitals into these vacant ones.

Si = [Ne] $3s^2\ 3p^2$
Ga = [Ar] $3d^{10}\ 4s^2\ 4p^1$
Gallium has one less valence electron than silicon.

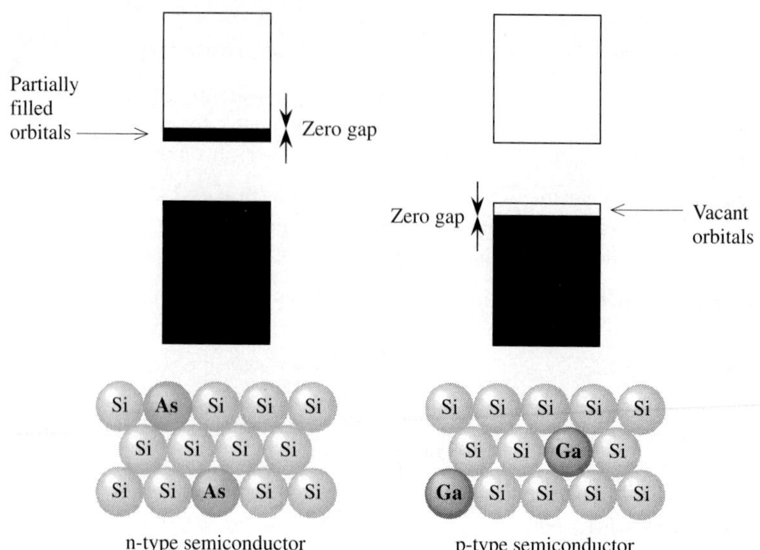

FIGURE 9-36
Schematic views of an n-type and a p-type semiconductor. Each arsenic (As) atom contributes five valence electrons instead of four, which forces an electron to occupy the higher-energy band. Each gallium (Ga) atom contributes three valence electrons instead of four, which leaves a vacancy in the lower-energy band.

Semiconductors such as silicon are extremely sensitive to impurities. Replacing just 0.00001% of the Si atoms with a dopant can cause as much as a 100,000-fold increase in electrical conductivity.

Figure 9-36 shows band gap diagrams of n-type and p-type semiconductors. Current flows in a doped semiconductor the same way as current flows in a metal (see Figure 9-33). Essentially zero energy difference exists between the top of the filled band and the next available orbital, so the slightest applied potential tilts the bands enough to allow electrons to move and current to flow.

Not all semiconductors are made from Si or Ge. Compounds made from equimolar amounts of group III and group V elements are also semiconductors. Gallium arsenide (GaAs) is a typical example. One Ga atom and one As atom have eight valence electrons, so GaAs is isoelectronic with Ge. Gallium arsenide can be doped with zinc atoms to make a p-type semiconductor or with tellurium atoms to make an n-type semiconductor. Other semiconductors contain equimolar compositions of an element such as zinc that has two valence electrons and a group VI element (S, Se, Te) with six valence electrons. Zinc sulfide is an example.

SECTION EXERCISES

9.6.1 The following energies measure the strength of bonding in sodium, magnesium, and aluminum metals:

$$Na_{(s)} \rightarrow Na_{(g)} \qquad \Delta E = 99 \text{ kJ/mol}$$

$$Mg_{(s)} \rightarrow Mg_{(g)} \qquad \Delta E = 127 \text{ kJ/mol}$$

$$Al_{(s)} \rightarrow Al_{(g)} \qquad \Delta E = 291 \text{ kJ/mol}$$

Use band theory to explain these data.

9.6.2 Draw a band gap diagram that illustrates a semiconductor made of gallium arsenide doped with zinc atoms.

9.6.3 Cadmium sulfide is a semiconductor being studied for use in solar cells. This yellow solid absorbs blue light at 470 nm. Calculate its band gap in kilojoules per mole.

CHAPTER SUMMARY

1. Multiple bonds include σ bonds formed from end-on overlap of *s, p,* and *d* hybrid orbitals and π bonds formed from side-by-side overlap of atomic *p* or *d* orbitals on adjacent atoms. Whereas σ bonds have high electron density along the bond axis, π bonds have high electron density above and below the bond axis.
2. The characteristic bond properties of length and energy depend on the n values of the valence orbitals, bond polarity, bond multiplicity, and effective nuclear charge.
3. The greater length of bonds between atoms with $n > 2$ restricts π bond formation to second-row elements and oxyanions.
4. Average bond energies can be used to estimate the energy changes accompanying chemical reactions.
5. A detailed description of bonding in diatomic molecules requires antibonding orbitals generated by subtractive orbital interactions and bonding orbitals generated by additive orbital interactions. When bonding and antibonding electrons are present, bond stability is given by the bond order, which is the number of bonding pairs minus the number of antibonding pairs.
6. Many polyatomic species contain electrons that occupy delocalized π orbitals extending over more than two atoms. Such delocalized orbitals, which are signaled by the existence of resonance structures, can be bonding, antibonding, or nonbonding.
7. Delocalized π systems gain stability as a result of multiple side-by-side interactions. Polyatomic oxyanions and the acids derived from them contain delocalized π orbitals. When the inner atom is from row 2 of the periodic table, the species are planar. When the inner atom is from the third row or beyond, however, the species are tetrahedral and *d* orbitals contribute to the π bonds.
8. Delocalized orbitals give rise to energy bands that explain the properties of metals and metalloids (semiconductors). Metals have partially filled orbital bands, among which electrons can move freely.
9. Doped semiconductors contain deliberately added impurities that add electrons to otherwise empty bands or remove electrons from otherwise filled bands, generating partially filled bands and leading to charge mobility.

KEY TERMS

bond energy
bond length
bond order
bond polarity
endothermic
exothermic

antibonding orbital
bonding orbital
conjugated π system
delocalized π orbital
nonbonding orbital
pi (π) bond
sigma (σ) bond

band gap
band theory of solids
doped semiconductor
metalloid
n-type semiconductor
p-type semiconductor
semiconductor

SKILLS TO MASTER

- Describing side-by-side orbital overlap
- Explaining trends in bond lengths and energies
- Estimating reaction energies from average bond energies
- Describing bonding in diatomic molecules
- Recognizing and sketching delocalized π orbitals
- Describing energy bands in metals and semiconductors

LEARNING EXERCISES

9.1 Write a chapter summary of two pages or less that outlines the important features of this chapter.

9.2 Design a detailed flow chart that shows how to describe the bonding of a second-row diatomic molecule.

9.3 Design a detailed flow chart that shows how to describe the bonding of a polyatomic species that has multiple bonds.

9.4 Prepare a table of the four factors that affect bond lengths and strengths, contrasting the importance of each for the two bond properties.

9.5 Prepare a list of molecules and ions that contain electrons in delocalized orbitals. Organize your list by the number of atoms over which delocalization occurs: three, four, and so on.

9.6 Describe in your own words your understanding of each of the following terms: (a) σ bond; (b) π bond; (c) antibonding orbital; (d) nonbonding electrons; (e) bond order; and (f) delocalized orbital.

9.7 Prepare a table that lists the properties of solid nonmetallic elements, metals, and metalloids.

9.8 Summarize the types of experimental evidence that support the idea of delocalized orbitals.

9.9 Prepare a list of all terms new to you that appear in Chapter 9. Write a one-sentence definition of each. Consult the glossary if you need help.

PROBLEMS

MULTIPLE BONDS IN CARBON COMPOUNDS

9.1 Describe the bonding in the common solvent acetone, $(CH_3)_2CO$. Include sketches of all the bonding orbitals.

9.2 Determine the steric number, geometry, and hybridization about each of the atoms of capsaicin, the molecule responsible for the "hot" spiciness of chili peppers.

Capsaicin
$(C_{18}H_{27}O_3N)$

9.3 Predict the bond angles for the imine molecule with the Lewis structure determined in Sample Problem 9-2.

9.4 The four-carbon compounds butane, 2-butene, and 2-butyne differ in the bonding between the second and third carbon atoms in the chain. For butane, all atoms are linked through single bonds. In 2-butene, a double bond exists between the second and third carbon atom, and 2-butyne has a triple bond in this position.

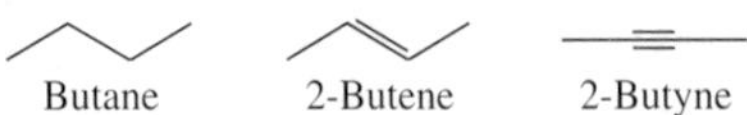
Butane 2-Butene 2-Butyne

Use steric numbers and hybridization to develop bonding pictures of these three molecules.

BOND LENGTHS AND ENERGIES

9.5 Arrange the following bonds in order of increasing length (shortest first). List the factors responsible for each placement: H—N, N—N, Cl—N, N≡N, and C≡N.

9.6 Arrange the following bonds in order of increasing length (shortest first). List the factors responsible for each placement: Cl—Cl, Br—Br, F—Cl, Cl—O, and H—F.

9.7 Using Table 9-2, arrange the bonds in Problem 9.5 in order of increasing bond *strength.* List the most important factor for each successive increase in strength.

9.8 Carbon monoxide has the strongest known chemical bond, 1070 kJ/mol. Explain why this bond is stronger than any other.

9.9 Use average bond energies to estimate the energy change for the reaction of N_2 and O_2 to give N_2O_4.

9.10 Estimate the energy change for each of the four reactions, $2\,HX_{(g)} \rightarrow H_{2\,(g)} + X_{2\,(g)}$, where X is a halogen.

9.11 Acrylonitrile is an important starting material for the manufacture of plastics and synthetic rubber. The compound is made from propene:

$$2\,C_3H_6 + 2\,NH_3 + 3\,O_2 \rightarrow 2\,H_2C{=}CH{-}C{\equiv}N + 6\,H_2O$$

Determine the energy change for the acrylonitrile synthesis.

SECOND-ROW DIATOMIC MOLECULES

9.12 Use an orbital energy ladder to show that the Ne_2 molecule is unstable.

9.13 Use an orbital energy ladder to show that the Na_2 molecule is stable.

9.14 In each of the following pairs, which has the stronger bond? Use orbital configurations to justify your selections: (a) O_2 or O_2^+; (b) N_2 or N_2^+; (c) F_2 or F_2^+; and (d) CN^- or CN.

9.15 The active ingredient in commercial laundry bleach is sodium hypochlorite (NaClO). Describe the bonding in the hypochlorite anion. (HINT: In this ion, chlorine's valence orbitals behave like $n = 2$ orbitals.)

9.16 Draw orbital sketches that show the shapes of each of the bonding and antibonding orbitals of O_2.

9.17 Write the electron configuration and determine the bond order of NO, NO^+, and NO^-. Which ones display magnetism?

DELOCALIZED π ORBITALS

9.18 Describe the bonding of carbon disulfide, in terms of orbital overlap and delocalized electrons. How many valence electrons occupy delocalized *p* orbitals in this molecule?

9.19 The two common oxides of carbon are CO and CO_2, which are linear. A third oxide of carbon, which is rare, is carbon suboxide, OCCCO. Draw a Lewis structure for carbon suboxide. Determine its geometry and identify all orbitals involved in delocalized π orbitals. Make separate sketches of the σ and π bonding systems.

9.20 Describe the bonding in NO_2^+ and NO_2^-. Include sketches of the σ bonding systems, and be sure to include any lone pairs on the nitrogen atoms. Explain why these two ions have different geometries.

9.21 Hydrazoic acid has the formula HN_3, with the three nitrogen atoms in a row. Determine the Lewis structure, hybridization, and bond angles of this compound. Describe its π bonding network.

9.22 Explosive charges containing TNT (trinitrotoluene) do not explode when subjected to mechanical shock, but they do explode violently when detonated properly. The most common type of detonator is a "blasting cap" containing mercury fulminate, $Hg(CNO)_2$, which explodes when struck. Write a Lewis structure for the CNO^- anion and describe its bonding, including any delocalized orbitals.

9.23 Acrolein has the following line structure. Determine its Lewis structure and describe its bonding, including geometry, hybridization, and extent of delocalization.

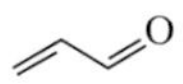

O

9.24 Which of the following molecules are stabilized by conjugation? For those that are, identify the atoms over which delocalization extends.

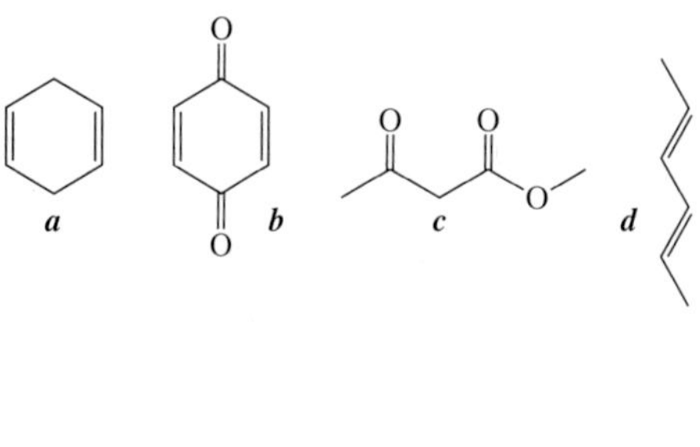

O O O O O

a *b* *c* *d*

9.25 Vitamin C has the following structure:

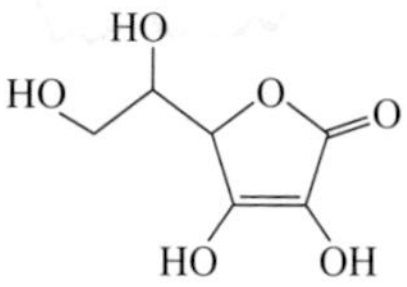

HO HO O O HO OH

Vitamin C ($C_6H_8O_6$)

(a) Identify the hybridization of each carbon and oxygen atom.

(b) How many delocalized electrons are in vitamin C?

9.26 Carvone, whose line structure follows, is the principal flavor and fragrance ingredient in spearmint. Identify the hybridization of all the carbon atoms in carvone. How many π bonds are present in the molecule? How many σ bonds?

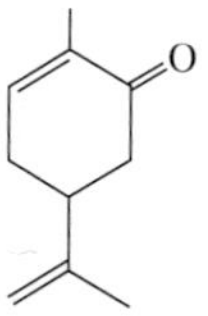

O

Carvone ($C_{14}H_{14}O$)

π BONDING IN POLYATOMIC ANIONS

9.27 Sulfur forms two stable oxides, SO_2 and SO_3. Describe the bonding and geometry of these compounds.

9.28 Draw a Lewis structure of the hydrogen phosphate anion (HPO_4^{2-}). Include all resonance structures. Which orbitals does the phosphorus atom use to form σ bonds? Which orbitals are used for the π bonds?

9.29 The oxalate anion ($C_2O_4^{2-}$) has a C—C bond and two outer oxygen atoms bonded to each carbon atom. Determine the Lewis structure of this anion, including all resonance structures. How many atoms contribute *p* orbitals to the delocalized π system?

9.30 When oxalate anions add two protons to form oxalic acid, two C—O bonds become longer and two become shorter than the bonds in oxalate anions. Which bonds become longer and which shorter? Use bonding principles to explain these changes.

9.31 The permanganate ion (MnO_4^-) gives potassium permanganate solutions a rich burgundy color. Determine the Lewis structure and describe the bonding in these ions.

BAND THEORY OF SOLIDS

9.32 Which are p-type, n-type, and undoped semiconductors: (a) GaP; (b) InSb doped with Te; (c) CdSe; (d) Ge; (e) Ge doped with P; and (f) AlAs doped with Zn?

9.33 Draw a band gap diagram of silicon doped with antimony.

9.34 You have been asked to develop a p-type semiconductor using Al, Si, and/or P. Which two elements would you choose, and what role would each element play in the semiconductor? Draw a band gap diagram that illustrates how the semiconductor would function.

ADDITIONAL PROBLEMS

9.35 Use the principles of orbital overlap to explain why two different isomers of 1,2-dichloroethylene exist, but only one isomer of 1,2-dichloroethane.

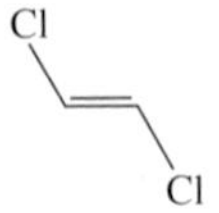

Trans-1,2-dichloroethylene  *Cis*-1,2-dichloroethylene

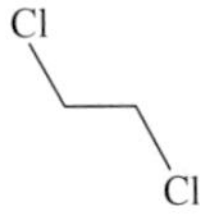

1,2-Dichloroethane

(HINT: Consider what must happen to the π bond to convert the *trans* isomer to the *cis* isomer.) Use bond strength arguments to estimate the amount of energy required to interconvert the *cis* and *trans* isomers.

9.36 What is the relationship among bond length, bond energy, and bond order. Which of the three can be measured?

9.37 Buckminsterfullerene contains 60 carbon atoms, each of which uses sp^2 hybrid orbitals and contributes one $2p$ orbital to make delocalized molecular orbitals. How many π orbitals does this molecule have and how many π bonding electrons does this molecule have?

9.38 Shorter bonds are usually stronger bonds, but this is not always true. Review Tables 9-1 and 9-2 and prepare a list of bonds to fluorine that are both longer and stronger than F—F bonds.

9.39 What type of semiconductor is each of the following: (a) Ge doped with Sb; (b) As doped with Si; and (c) Si doped with In?

9.40 Allyl alcohol and acetone have the same empirical formula, C_3H_6O. Use average bond energies to compare the stabilities of allyl alcohol, CH_2CHCH_2OH, and acetone, $(CH_3)_2CO$.

9.41 Use orbital energy diagrams to decide which of NO, CO, CN, and NF would be stabilized by adding one electron to make the corresponding anion. Which would be stabilized by removing an electron to form the corresponding cation?

9.42 Silicon carbide (Carborundum), is a very hard crystalline material similar to diamond. It is widely used for cutting tools. Describe the bonding in silicon carbide, whose empirical formula is SiC. Draw an energy band picture showing how you expect the band gap for SiC to compare with those of diamond and silicon.

9.43 The molecule CN is not stable in our atmosphere, but it has been detected in interstellar regions. Describe its bonding, and sketch its least stable occupied molecular orbital.

9.44 Describe the bonding in ketene, (H_2CCO). Make separate sketches of the σ and π bonding systems.

9.45 The following partial structure is that of azodicarbonamide. When heated, azodicarbonamide breaks apart into gaseous carbon monoxide, nitrogen, and ammonia. Azodicarbonamide is used as a foaming agent in the polymer industry. Foamed polystyrene, for example, which is used to make one type of fast-food container, is produced by adding azodicarbonamide to the molten plastic. As the foaming agent decomposes, the bubbles of gas are trapped in the polymer, resembling a frozen head of beer. Add nonbonding electron pairs and multiple bonds as required to complete the structure of this molecule, and then determine the geometry and hybridization about each inner atom.

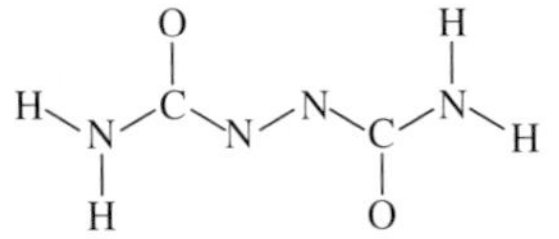

Bonding framework of azodicarbonamide

9.46 Saxitoxin is a fatally toxic natural product produced by certain marine organisms. The molecule occasionally accumulates in clams and mussels during conditions of red tide.

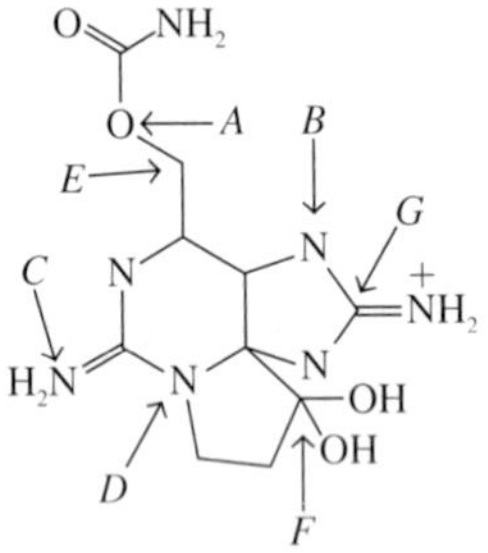

Saxitoxin

(a) What hybrid orbitals are appropriate for atoms *A* to *D*?

(b) What are the bond angles about atoms *E* to *G*?

(c) Three planes of four atoms exist in saxitoxin. Redraw the structure and circle these three planes.

(d) How many π bonds are in saxitoxin?

9.47 Both ethanol, C_2H_5OH, and dimethyl ether, $(CH_3)_2O$, have the empirical formula C_2H_6O. Using average bond energies, predict which is the more stable compound.

9.48 Determine what type of orbitals (atomic, sp^3, or sp^2) are used by each atom in the following molecules:

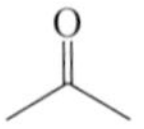

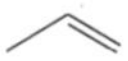

N_2H_4 H_3CNH_2

9.49 The concept of threshold energy was introduced in Chapter 6 as part of our discussion of the photoelectric effect. What feature of band theory is associated with the threshold energy? Consider electrons ejected by photons with a frequency significantly higher than the threshold frequency. With what you know about bands, do you expect these electrons all to have the same kinetic energy? Explain.

9.50 Use average bond energies (Table 9-2) to compare the combustion energies of ethane, ethylene, and acetylene. Calculate which of these hydrocarbons releases more energy per gram.

9.51 The following four molecules have been detected in interstellar space. Describe the bonding in each molecule, identify the hybrid orbitals used to make σ bonds, and determine the extent of delocalization for the π systems: (a) CCCO; (b) HNCO; (c) OCS; and (d) HCCCCH.

9.52 Use band theory to explain why iron is harder and melts at a higher temperature than potassium.

9.53 Why is the bond strength listed in Table 9-2 for an H—Cl bond more precise (4 significant figures) than the bond strength listed for an H—C bond (3 significant figures).

9.54 Elements in the same column of the periodic table usually have similar chemical properties. Nitrogen and oxygen are unique among elements in their columns, however, because they are stable as diatomic molecules. Phosphorus and sulfur, the next two members of these columns, are stable as long-chain molecules. Use the properties of orbitals to account for these striking differences in chemical behavior.

9.55 Metal carbonyls are compounds in which several molecules of carbon monoxide form covalent bonds to transition metals. Examples include $Cr(CO)_6$, $Fe(CO)_5$, and $Ni(CO)_4$.
(a) The principal bonding interaction in a metal carbonyl is a σ bond formed between the carbon atom of CO and one of the valence d orbitals of the metal. Use the $d_z{}^2$ orbital to make an orbital overlap sketch of the M—CO σ bond.
(b) Metal carbonyl bonding also involves delocalized electrons. A π bond can be formed from overlap of the π^* orbital of CO with one of the metal d orbitals. Use the d_{xz} orbital to make an orbital overlap sketch of the π bond in a metal carbonyl. (HINT: The π^* orbital of CO appears in Figure 9-5.)

9.56 Isooctane (C_8H_{18}) is the basis of the octane rating system because it burns smoothly, with a minimum of engine "knocking." Pure isooctane is assigned a value of 100. Octane ratings are assigned to gasoline mixtures based on their ability to prevent knocking relative to isooctane. Estimate the energy released during the combustion of 1 mol of pure isooctane.

```
            H
            |
         H—C—H
    H       |          H      H  H
    |       |          |      |  |
 H—C——————C——————————C——————C—C—H
    |       |          |      |  |
    H       |          |      H  H
         H—C—H    H—C—H
            |          |
            H          H
```

Isooctane (C_8H_{18})

9.57 Consider the bond lengths of the following molecules: N_2, 110 pm; O_2, 121 pm; and F_2, 143 pm. Explain the variation in length in terms of the orbital descriptions of these molecules.

9.58 Imagine making an O_4 molecule by attaching an oxygen atom to the nonbonding pair of electrons on the central oxygen of ozone (O_3). Describe the bonding in O_4, which is isoelectronic with the nitrate and carbonate anions. Compare the expected stability of the O_4 molecule with that of two O_2 molecules. Does our simple picture of bonding explain why trigonal O_4 does not exist?

9.59 The bond strength of diatomic Cl—F is 249 kJ/mol, and that of Br—Cl is 216 kJ/mol. List these, along with F—F, Cl—Cl, and Br—Br bonds, in order of increasing bond strength. State the factors that account for the ordering of bonds in this list.

9.60 Chlorine forms several oxyanions, including $ClO_4{}^-$ (perchlorate), $ClO_3{}^-$ (chlorate), and $ClO_2{}^-$ (chlorite). Determine Lewis structures and describe the bonding for each of these anions, including delocalization.

9.61 In addition to the anions described in Problem 9.60, chlorine also forms a neutral oxide, ClO_2. Describe the bonding in this unusual compound. Explain why it is considered unusual.

9.62 Phosgene (Cl_2CO) is a highly toxic gas used for chemical warfare during World War I. Using the bond energies in Table 9-2, estimate the energy change that occurs when carbon monoxide and chlorine combine to make phosgene:

$$CO_{(g)} + Cl_{2\,(g)} \rightarrow Cl_2CO_{(g)}$$

9.63 Four different bonds are found in H_2O, CO_2, and HCN. Which is the shortest? Which is the longest? What factors are responsible for each?

9.64 Arrange the four different bonds in Problem 9.63 in order of increasing bond strength; give the reasons for your placements.

9.65 Use average bond energies (see Table 9-2) to estimate the net energy change per mole of silicon for the conversion of a silicon chain into an Si—O—Si chain. Repeat this calculation per mole of carbon for the conversion of a carbon chain into to a C—O—C chain.

9.66 Oxygen forms three different ionic compounds with potassium: Potassium oxide (K_2O), potassium superoxide (KO_2), and potassium peroxide (K_2O_2). Write electron configurations for the superoxide and peroxide anions. Compare these configurations with the configuration of the oxygen molecule. Rank the three species in order of increasing bond order, bond energy, and bond length. Which of the three are magnetic? Which has the largest magnetism?

9.67 Based on periodic trends, arrange the following in order of increasing band gap and classify them as insulators, semiconductors, or conductors: As, Bi, and P.

9.68 Use orbital sketches to illustrate the bonding of allene (H_2CCCH_2). Identify all orbitals in the bonding scheme. Make sure your sketches show the three-dimensional arrangement of the hydrogen atoms. Make separate sketches of the σ and π bonding systems.

9.69 In the lower atmosphere, NO_2 participates in a series of reactions in air that is also contaminated with unburned hydrocarbons. One product of these reactions is peroxyacetyl nitrate (PAN). The skeletal arrangement of the atoms in PAN follows.

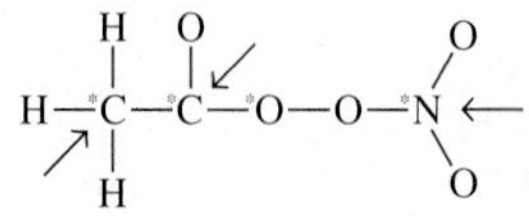

(a) Complete the Lewis structure of this compound. (HINT: Start by determining the number of valence electrons present.)
(b) Determine the hybridization for the atoms marked with asterisks.
(c) Give the approximate values of the bond angles indicated with arrows.
(d) If delocalized orbitals exist, describe them.

9.70 Use tabulated bond energies to estimate the energy change when HCl adds to ethylene (C_2H_4) to produce C_2H_5Cl and when Cl_2 adds to ethylene to produce $C_2H_4Cl_2$.

9.71 In the stratosphere, chlorofluorocarbons (Freons) absorb high-energy ultraviolet light, breaking C—Cl bonds. The chlorine atom then enters a reaction cycle that converts ozone to molecular oxygen. What is the minimum frequency of the photons that can break a C—Cl bond? (Refer to Table 9-2 and Chapter 6 for help.)

9.72 Explain how a C≡C triple bond can be stronger but more reactive than a C=C double bond.

9.73 Explain how the following bond lengths (in picometers) support the existence of delocalized electrons in the carbonate ion: C—O (avg.), 143; C=O (avg.), 122; CO_3^{2-}, 129.

9.74 The ionization energy of molecular oxygen is smaller than the ionization energy of atomic oxygen (1314 kJ/mol vs. 1503 kJ/mol). In contrast, the ionization energy for molecular nitrogen is larger than the ionization energy of atomic nitrogen (1503 kJ/mol vs. 1402 kJ/mol). Explain these data using the electron configurations of the diatomic molecules.

9.75 One compound used to treat acquired immunodeficiency syndrome (AIDS) is azidothymidine (AZT). The line structure of AZT is:

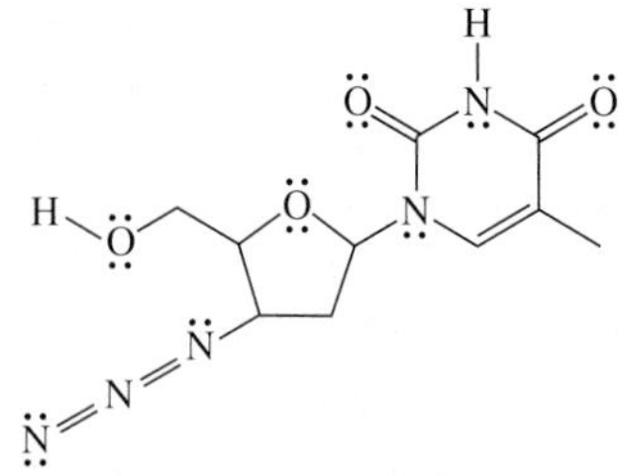

(a) Identify the type of orbitals used for bonding by each of the nitrogen atoms.
(b) What is the bond angle around the oxygen atom in the five-membered ring?
(c) How many carbon atoms can be described using sp^3 hybrid orbitals?
(d) How many σ bonds are there?
(e) How many π bonds are there?

9.76 Nitrogen molecules can absorb photons to generate excited-state molecules. Construct an energy level diagram and place the valence electrons so that it describes the most stable *excited* state of an N_2 molecule. Is the N-N bond in this excited-state N_2 molecule stronger or weaker than the N-N bond in ground-state nitrogen? Explain your answer.

9.77 The pentadienyl cation ($C_5H_7^+$) is a high-energy species that can be generated in the laboratory under carefully controlled conditions.

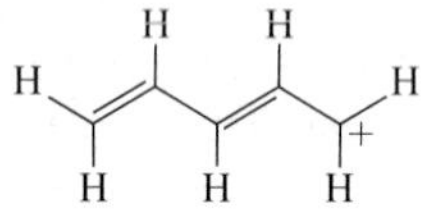

(a) Describe the bonding orbitals used by each of the carbon atoms.
(b) How many p orbitals contribute to the π bonding system? How many molecular orbitals do they form?
(c) How many delocalized electrons are in $C_5H_7^+$?
(d) Make an energy level diagram of the π system for $C_5H_7^+$, including the delocalized electrons. Label the *bonding*, *nonbonding*, and *antibonding* π orbitals.

ANSWERS TO SECTION EXERCISES

9.1.1

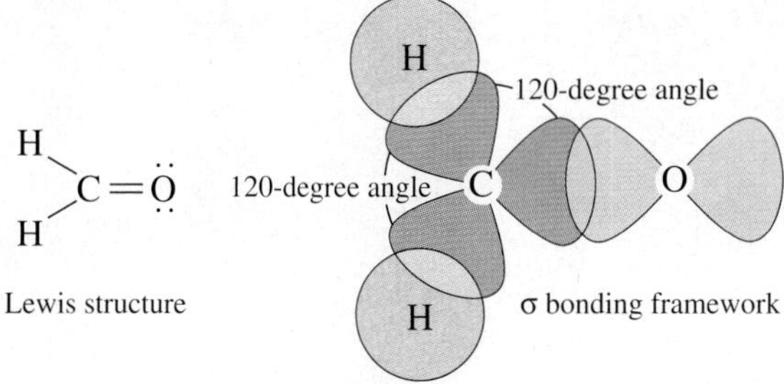

Lewis structure σ bonding framework

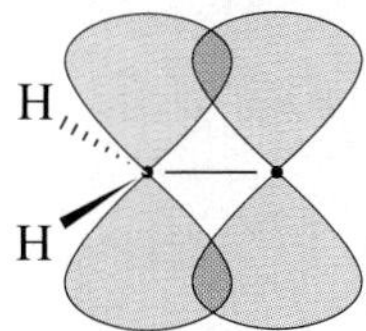

π bonding framework

The carbon atom uses sp^2 hybrids to form three sigma bonds. Its unused *p* orbital overlaps with an oxygen *p* orbital to form a π bond.

9.1.2

H—C—C≡C—H

Propene (C_3H_6) Propyne (C_3H_4)

The CH_3 carbon in each compound uses sp^3 hybrids and has tetrahedral geometry. In propene, the other two carbon atoms have trigonal planar geometry, use sp^2 hybrids for three σ bonds, and have a π bond between them. In propyne, the other two carbon atoms have linear geometry, use *sp* hybrids for two σ bonds, and have two π bonds between them.

9.1.3

Four carbon atoms participate in π bonding. For appropriate orbital sketches, see Figures 9-3 and 9-4.

9.2.1 C—H (1*s*) < C=O (double, polar) < C=C (double) < C—C (single) < C—Cl (3*p*)

9.2.2 −645 kJ

9.2.3 (a) H—C—H H—Cl: H—C—Cl: H—H :Cl—Cl:

CH_4, 4 C—H bonds; CH_3Cl, 3 C—H bonds, 1 C—Cl bond; others have 1 bond each. (b) First reaction is endothermic by 86 kJ; second reaction is exothermic by 98 kJ. The second reaction is used in industry because it does not require an energy input.

9.3.1 CN^- has 10 valence electrons, isoelectronic with N_2. Its bonding is identical to that of N_2.

9.3.2 See Figures 9-11 and 9-12.

9.3.3 The electron that is removed to ionize NO comes from a π* orbital, which is less stable than the π orbitals from which electrons must be removed to ionize N_2 or CO.

9.4.1 With 16 valence electrons, N_3^- is isoelectronic with CO_2. Its bonding is identical with that of CO_2, and it is linear, with the inner atom having a steric number of 2.

9.4.2 In a localized orbital, electron density is spread over a single atom or a pair of atoms. In a delocalized orbital, electron density is spread over more than two atoms.

9.4.3 Azulene has five π orbitals and five π* orbitals. All five π orbitals are occupied but none of the π* orbitals are.

9.5.1

:Ö:
H—Ö—P=Ö +2 resonance structures
:Ö:

The oxygen atom bonded to H as a steric number of 4, sp^3 hybrids, and bent geometry. The phosphorus atom has a steric number of 4 and sp^3 hybrids. It has tetrahedral geometry but forms a delocalized π bond with the three outer oxygen atoms through *p-d* π bonding.

9.5.2 Lewis structure and bonding are the same as in the sulfate anion. The ion is tetrahedral. The Cr atom uses sp^3 hybrids to form four σ bonds and uses *d* orbitals to form two delocalized π bonds with the O atom.

9.5.3

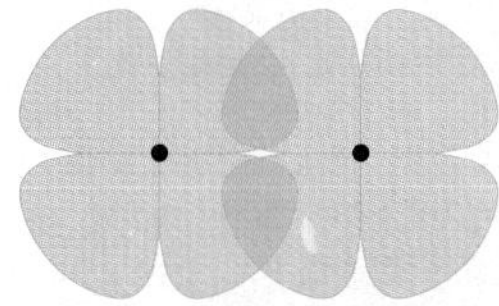

9.6.1 From Na to Mg to Al, the number of valence electrons increases. Thus the number of bonding electrons also increases, increasing the bond strength of the metal.

9.6.2 This is a p-type semiconductor, because Zn has one fewer valance elecrons than Ga.

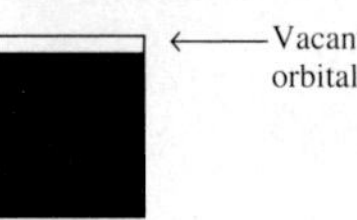

9.6.3 255 kJ/mol

CHAPTER 10

EFFECTS OF INTERMOLECULAR FORCES

The properties of ice crystals, icebergs, and liquid water are consequences of intermolecular forces.

As we have developed ideas about chemistry, we have emphasized the forces that bind atoms together into molecules. In Chapters 8 and 9, for example, we described the bonding forces that exist *within molecules.* These are called **intramolecular forces.** In Chapter 5, on the other hand, we described the properties of a gas using the ideal gas model, which assumes that the forces acting *between molecules* of a gas are negligible. In reality, there are indeed forces between molecules. These forces are called **intermolecular forces.** They affect the properties of gases and explain the existence and properties of liquids and solids.

Intermolecular forces are considerably weaker than intramolecular forces. In a liquid, for example, intermolecular forces are weak enough to allow individual molecules to move about relatively freely. On the other hand, intramolecular forces are strong enough to prevent atoms from breaking away from the molecules to which they are bonded.

Our discussion of bonding ignored relatively weak intermolecular interactions, but to understand the properties of liquids and solids, we must take these interactions into account. Intermolecular forces "lock" molecules into the fixed positions that characterize a solid and prevent vaporization of molecules in the liquid phase. This chapter is devoted to describing intermolecular forces and their role in the world of chemistry.

10.1 THE NATURE OF INTERMOLECULAR FORCES

We can begin an exploration of intermolecular forces by considering the properties of the elements. At room temperature and pressure, all but 13 of the elements are solids. Two others, mercury and bromine, are liquids, leaving only 11 elements that are gases. Only for these 11 gases are intermolecular forces small enough to neglect at room temperature. More commonly, intermolecular forces are strong enough to lock molecules in place in the solid state.

FIGURE 10-1
Under ambient conditions, chlorine is a pale yellow-green gas, bromine is a dark red liquid, and iodine is a purple crystalline solid.

THE HALOGENS

The halogens, the elements from column VII of the periodic table, provide a good introduction to intermolecular forces. The halogens are most stable as diatomic molecules: F_2, Cl_2, Br_2, I_2, and At_2. At room temperature and pressure, fluorine and chlorine are gases, bromine is a liquid, and iodine is a solid. Figure 10-1 shows the strikingly different physical appearances of these elements.

The heaviest halogen, astatine, is a highly unstable radioactive element. Astatine is extremely rare and has no chemical applications.

The bonding patterns of the four halogens are identical. Each molecule contains two atoms held together by a single covalent bond that can be described by the overlap of valence *p* orbitals. In contrast to this common bonding pattern, bromine and iodine differ from chlorine and fluorine in their macroscopic physical appearance and in their molecular behavior, as Figure 10-2 illustrates.

A bonding description of F_2 is given in Chapters 8 and 9. The other diatomic molecules form bonds in an analogous manner, using valence p orbitals.

Fluorine and chlorine molecules move freely throughout their gaseous volume, traveling many molecular diameters before colliding with one another or with the

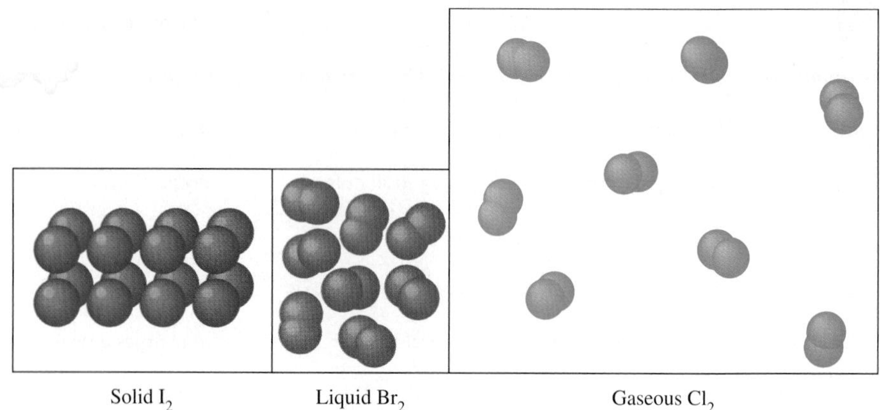

FIGURE 10-2
Molecular representations of solid I_2, liquid Br_2, and gaseous Cl_2 demonstrate why gases, liquids, and solids behave differently. A gas is mostly empty space, so the molecules are free to move about the entire volume of their container. Molecules in a liquid, on the other hand, are packed closely together but can still move past one another. A crystalline solid contains a regular array of molecules that vibrate about favored positions but cannot move freely by one another.

walls of their container. Because much of the volume of a gas is empty space, samples of gaseous F_2 and Cl_2 readily expand or contract in response to changes in pressure. This freedom of motion indicates that the intermolecular forces between these molecules are quite small.

Molecules of liquid bromine also move about relatively freely, but there is not much empty space between molecules. A liquid cannot be compressed significantly by increasing the pressure because molecules are already in close contact with one another. Also, a liquid does not expand significantly if the pressure above it is reduced. This is because intermolecular forces in a liquid are large enough to prevent the molecules from breaking away from one another.

Solid iodine has even less empty space between molecules than liquid bromine. Furthermore, the molecules in this solid do not move freely past one another. A sample of solid iodine contains highly regular crystals in which I_2 molecules are arranged in ordered arrays. Each molecule vibrates back and forth about a single lowest-energy position, but it cannot slide easily past its neighbors. Like liquids, solids do not expand or contract significantly when pressure decreases or increases.

Bromine does not exist as a gas at room temperature and iodine molecules cannot move freely because intermolecular forces between these molecules are relatively strong. Attractive intermolecular forces pull molecules toward one another, and energy is released as they get closer together. Molecules in a gas remain separated from one another because they have sufficient kinetic energy to overcome these attractive forces. Molecules in a liquid or solid remain close to one another because they lack sufficient kinetic energy to overcome these attractive forces. Hence whether a substance is a gas, liquid, or solid depends on the balance between the energy of motion of its molecules and the stabilization energy generated by its intermolecular forces.

The graph in Figure 10-3 shows that the intermolecular stabilization energy is substantially greater for Br_2 than for F_2. At room temperature, fluorine molecules have more kinetic energy of motion than the stabilization energy of F_2-F_2 interactions, whereas bromine molecules have enough kinetic energy to move freely about but insufficient energy of motion to overcome the intermolecular forces that hold them together in the liquid phase. At room temperature, iodine molecules are locked in position in the solid state because the stabilization energy between I_2 molecules is even larger than that between Br_2 molecules. To summarize, whether a substance is a gas, a liquid, or a solid depends on the balance between its intermolecular stabilization energy and its average molecular energy of motion.

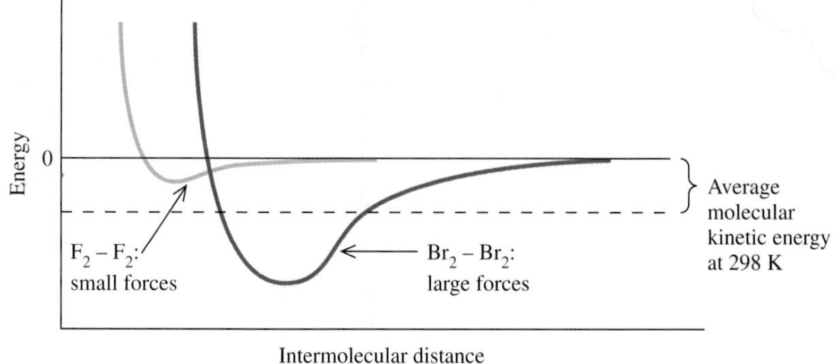

FIGURE 10-3
Intermolecular attractive forces stabilize molecules that are close to one another. The plot shows that there are larger attractive energies between bromine molecules than between fluorine molecules. This is the reason that at room temperature, fluorine is more stable as a gas, but bromine is more stable as a liquid.

Because the energy of motion depends on temperature, changing the temperature changes the balance between interaction energy and energy of motion and eventually changes the stable form of matter. For example, liquid bromine boils when it is heated to 59 °C at atmospheric pressure, forming gaseous bromine. Similarly, gaseous chlorine condenses when it is cooled to −34 °C at atmospheric pressure, forming liquid chlorine. At −101 °C, moreover, liquid chlorine becomes a solid. Fluorine liquefies at −188 °C and solidifies at −220 °C.

The link between kinetic energy and temperature is described in Chapter 5.

REAL GASES

Fluorine and chlorine are gases under ambient conditions. Yet both gases can be liquefied by lowering the temperature sufficiently. This shows the existence of attractive forces sufficient to hold molecules in the confined volume of the liquid phase at low temperature. Therefore the assumption of the ideal gas model—that intermolecular forces in a gas can be neglected—cannot be correct under conditions that cause a gas to liquefy. In other words, neither Cl_2 nor F_2 behaves ideally under all conditions.

The ideal gas model also assumes that molecular sizes can be neglected; yet no substance can be compressed indefinitely. When the distance between molecules gets small enough, repulsive forces among their electron clouds strongly resist further reduction of the volume. This is shown by the steeply rising plots of Figure 10-3. Thus finite molecular sizes also lead to deviations from ideal gas behavior.

What effect do intermolecular forces and molecular volumes have on real gases? In other words, how close do real gases come to ideal behavior? To see how far real gases stray from the ideal gas model, we can compare experimental values of real gas properties with those computed from the ideal gas equation. A convenient way to make these comparisons is to examine the experimental ratio, PV/nRT. For an ideal gas, this ratio, which is called the *compressibility,* must equal 1.

Figure 10-4 shows how compressibility varies with pressure for chlorine gas at room temperature. If chlorine were ideal, the compressibility would always be 1, as shown by the red line on the graph. Notice in the inset of Figure 10-4 that chlorine behaves very nearly ideally at pressures around 1 atmosphere (atm). In fact, its compressibility deviates from 1.0 by less than 4% at pressures below 4 atm. As the pressure increases, however, the deviations become increasingly significant. At 100 atm, chlorine is far from ideal because chlorine molecules are close enough together for attractive forces to play a significant role. Figure 10-4 also indicates that up to about 375 atm pressure, the compressibility of Cl_2 is *smaller* than 1, which means that intermolecular attractions hold chlorine molecules somewhat closer

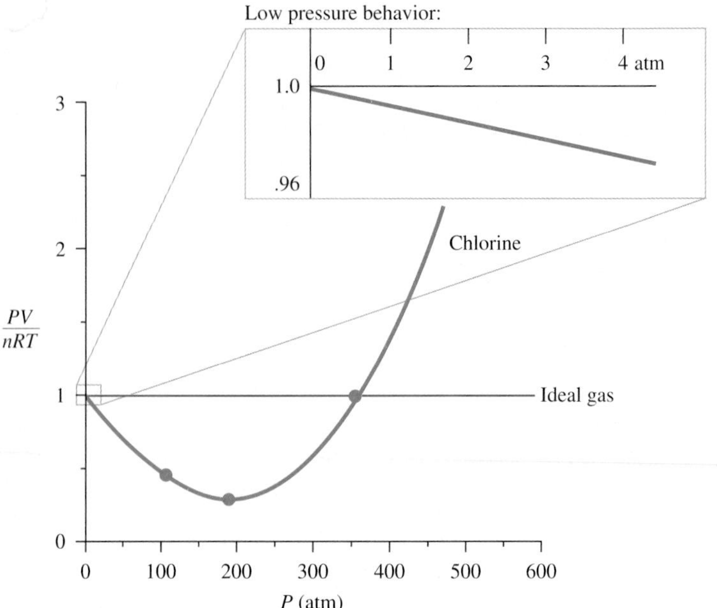

FIGURE 10-4
Variation in PV/nRT with pressure for chlorine gas at room temperature. The inset at the upper right shows the low-pressure region on an expanded scale.

together, on average, than would be the case for an ideal gas. At pressures greater than 375 atm, the compressibility becomes *larger* than 1. This is the effect of finite molecular size. At high enough pressure, molecules are so close together that repulsive interactions outweigh attractive ones.

Every gas deviates from ideal behavior. Given this fact, does it make sense to use the ideal gas model to discuss the properties of real gases? The answer is "yes," as long as conditions do not become too extreme. The gases that chemists usually work with, such as chlorine, helium, and nitrogen, are nearly ideal at and above room temperature at pressures below about 10 atm.

At high pressure, every gas shows deviations from ideal behavior. Figure 10-5 shows compressibilities of He, F_2, CH_4, and N_2, which are gases at room temperature. Notice that the compressibility of helium increases steadily as pressure increases. Interatomic forces are too small to reduce the compressibility below 1, but the finite size of helium atoms generates deviations from ideality that become significant at pressures above 100 atm.

Deviations from ideal behavior always decrease as temperature increases. Figure 10-6 shows compressibility plots for fluorine at several temperatures. Notice that

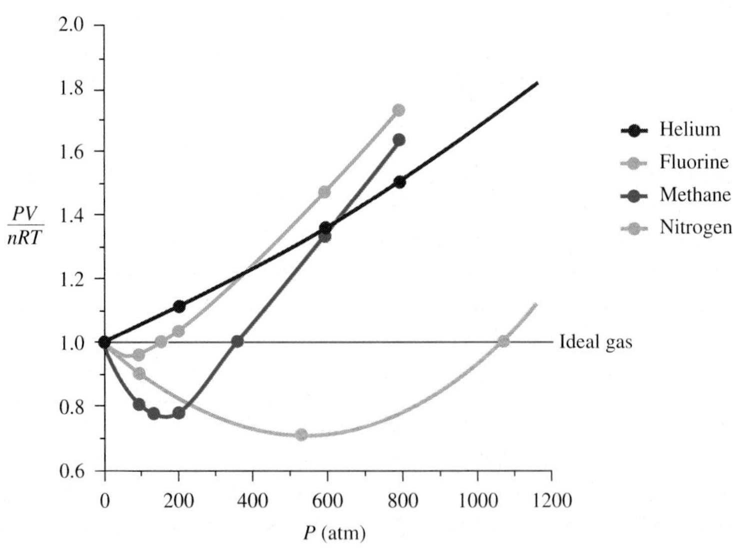

FIGURE 10-5
Compressibilities of He, F_2, CH_4, and N_2 at 300 K. Even substances that we normally think of as gases are not completely ideal.

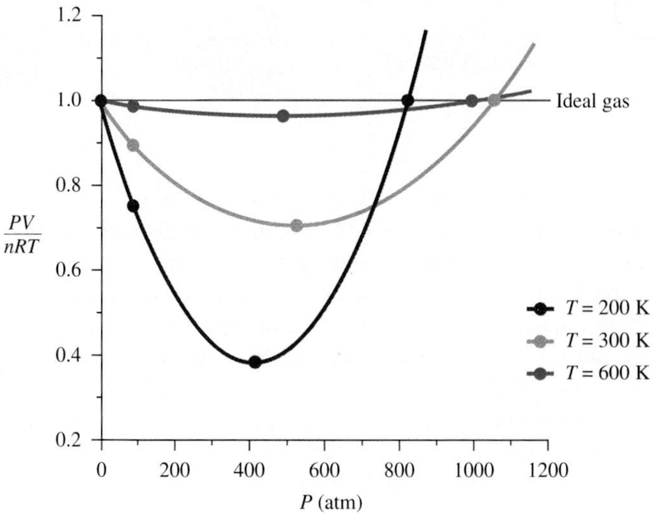

FIGURE 10-6

Variation in PV/nRT with pressure for fluorine gas at several temperatures. As temperature increases, the behavior of all gases becomes more nearly ideal.

fluorine deviates considerably from ideal behavior at 200 K and high pressure but that it is nearly ideal at 600 K, even at 1000 atm. High temperature means high average kinetic energy, and molecules with high energy have more than enough energy to overcome intermolecular forces of attraction.

DISPERSION FORCES

The strength of intermolecular interactions in a liquid determines its normal boiling point, which is the temperature at which liquid converts to vapor at a pressure of 1.00 atm. A liquid boils when the average kinetic energy of its molecules becomes larger than the stabilization energy between molecules. Thus a low boiling point signifies small intermolecular forces, whereas a high boiling point signifies large intermolecular forces. Among the halogens, fluorine boils at −188 °C, chlorine at −34 °C, bromine at 59 °C, and iodine at 185 °C. These boiling points indicate that intermolecular forces between halogen molecules increase with atomic number.

To explain this trend in forces, we can examine what happens when two halogen molecules approach each other. Each molecule contains positive nuclei surrounded by a cloud of negative electrons. As two molecules approach each other, the nucleus of one molecule attracts the electron cloud of the other. At the same time the two electron clouds repel each other. Because electrons are highly mobile, however, their orbitals can change shape to minimize electron-electron repulsion, as shown in Figure 10-7. This distortion of the electron cloud creates a temporary charge imbalance, giving the molecule a slight positive charge at one end and a slight negative charge at the other. The net attractive forces generated by all these temporary charge imbalances are called **dispersion forces.**

δ− δ+ δ− δ+ δ− δ+

← Distortion — ← Distortion — ← Distortion —

FIGURE 10-7

Schematic view of how dispersion forces arise. As the molecule in the center approaches the one on the left, its electron cloud distorts slightly in response to coulombic attraction to the nuclei of the other molecule. This creates a small, temporary positive charge at the right end of the center molecule, which in turn distorts the electron cloud of the molecule on the right.

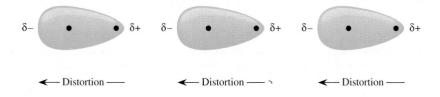

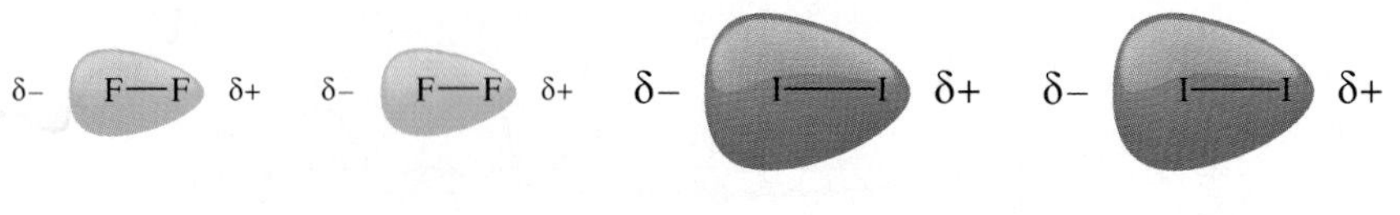

FIGURE 10-8
Iodine's electron cloud is much larger and much more polarizable than fluorine's. Iodine therefore has stronger dispersion forces than fluorine, which is why F_2 is a gas and I_2 is a solid at room temperature.

The magnitude of dispersion forces depends on how easy it is to distort the electron cloud of the molecule. The ease of distortion is called molecular **polarizability** because distortion of an electron cloud generates a temporary polarity within the molecule. As Figure 10-8 illustrates, the large electron cloud of an I_2 molecule distorts more readily than the small electron cloud of F_2. Both F_2 and I_2 contain 14 valence electrons, but those of F_2 are in relatively compact $n = 2$ orbitals, whereas those of I_2 occupy highly diffuse $n = 5$ orbitals. As a result, the valence orbitals of I_2 distort much more readily than those of F_2, generating large dispersion forces that make I_2 a solid at room temperature. This reasoning is extended to include the elemental rare gases in Sample Problem 10-1.

SAMPLE PROBLEM 10-1 BOILING POINT TRENDS

At room temperature, neon and xenon are gases, but both become liquids if the temperature is low enough. Draw a molecular picture showing the relative sizes and polarizabilities of atoms of neon and xenon, and use the picture to determine which substance has a lower boiling point.

METHOD: The boiling point of a substance depends on the magnitude of its intermolecular forces, which in turn depend on the polarizability of its electron cloud. Monatomic gases contain atoms rather than molecules, so we must assess *interatomic* forces for these substances.

The only force acting between atoms of rare gases is due to the polarizability of their electron clouds. The valence electrons of neon are in small, $n = 2$ atomic orbitals that have low polarizability, whereas those of xenon are in relatively large, polarizable $n = 5$ orbitals. The smaller electron cloud of neon distorts less than the larger electron cloud of xenon when two atoms approach each other, as a molecular picture illustrates.

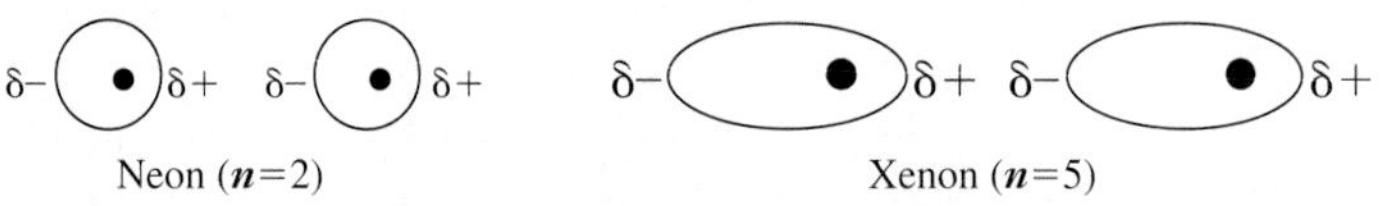

Neon (n=2) Xenon (n=5)

Less polarizability means smaller partial charges and weaker intermolecular forces. Thus neon has the lower boiling point.

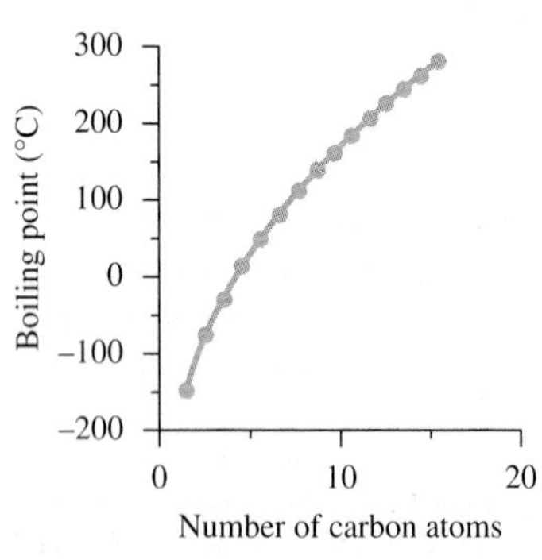

FIGURE 10-9
The boiling points of alkanes increase with the length of their carbon chains.

It is easier to distort the electron cloud of a large molecule than of a small molecule. Thus size also affects polarizability. Figure 10-9 shows how the boiling points of alkanes change as the carbon chain gets longer. As alkanes get longer, their electron clouds become larger and more polarizable, making dispersion forces larger and raising the boiling point. For example, at room temperature methane (CH_4) is a gas, pentane (C_5H_{12}) is a liquid, and eicosane ($C_{20}H_{42}$) is a waxy solid. Figure 10-10 compares the polarizabilities of pentane and decane.

Among otherwise similar substances, more extended molecules have higher polarizabilities than more compact molecules. This trend is illustrated by the boiling points of the three isomers with the formula C_5H_{12}. Figure 10-11 shows that the

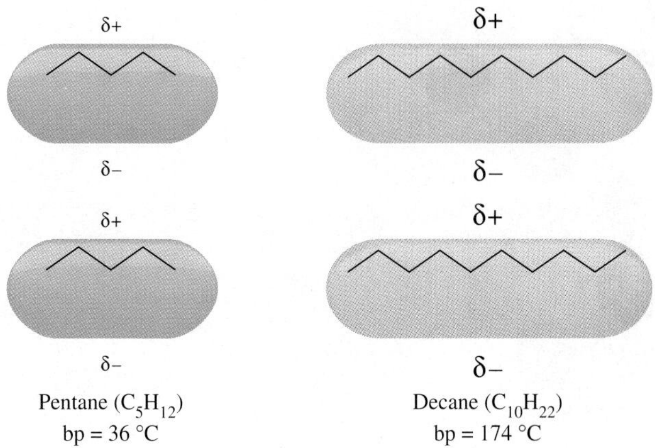

FIGURE 10-10
Large alkanes have higher boiling points than small alkanes. Their dispersion forces are larger because of the increased polarizability of their larger electron clouds.

highest-boiling isomer, pentane, is most extended and the lowest-boiling isomer, 2,2-dimethylpropane, is most compact, with 2-methylbutane in between in compactness and boiling point.

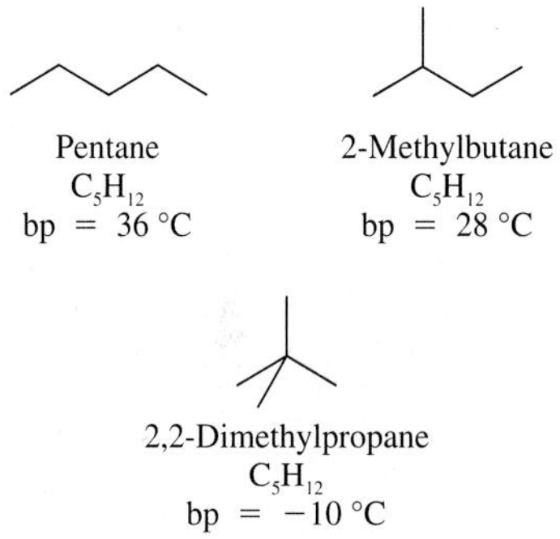

Pentane
C_5H_{12}
bp = 36 °C

2-Methylbutane
C_5H_{12}
bp = 28 °C

2,2-Dimethylpropane
C_5H_{12}
bp = −10 °C

FIGURE 10-11
The three isomers with chemical formula C_5H_{12} have somewhat different boiling points because polarizability increases as molecules become more extended.

DIPOLAR FORCES

Dispersion forces exist between all molecules, but some substances remain liquid at much higher temperatures than can be accounted for by dispersion forces alone. As examples, consider 2-methylpropane and acetone, whose structures are shown in Figure 10-12. These two molecules have the same molar mass, similar shape, and nearly the same number of valence electrons (34 vs. 32). They are so similar that we might expect the two compounds to have similar boiling points, but acetone is a liquid at room temperature, whereas 2-methylpropane is a gas. Acetone boils at 56 °C, whereas 2-methylpropane boils at −12 °C. Why does acetone remain a liquid at temperatures well above the boiling point of 2-methylpropane? The cause is charge asymmetry in the molecular structure of acetone.

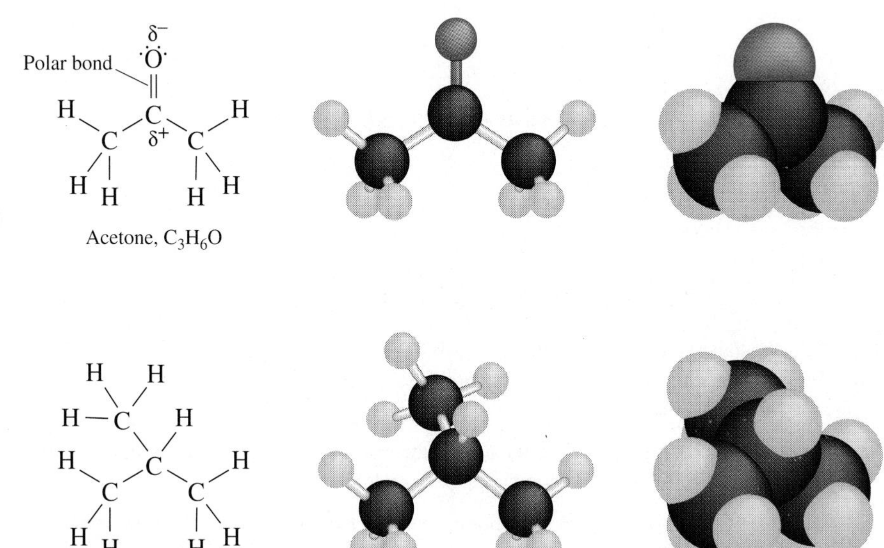

FIGURE 10-12
Models and Lewis structures of 2-methylpropane and acetone show that they have similar molecular shapes. The important difference between them is the polar bond in acetone.

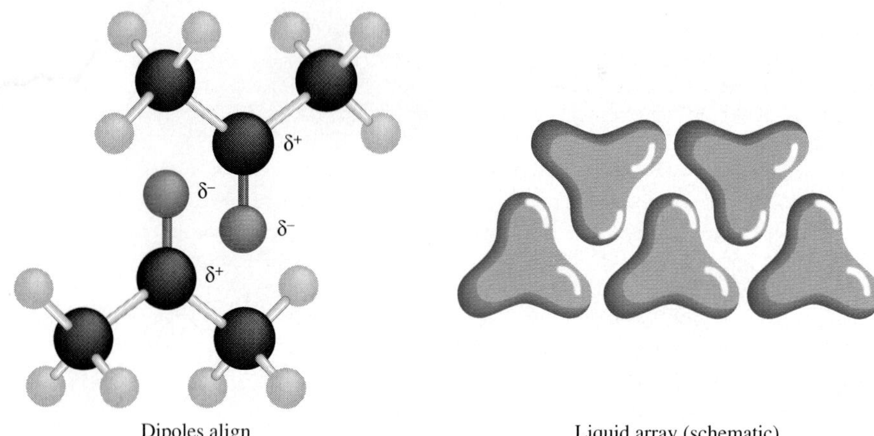

FIGURE 10-13
In liquid acetone the permanent dipoles tend to align with positive ends nearer negative ones and negative ends nearer positive ones.

Remember from the bonding picture presented in Chapter 8 that chemical bonds are polarized toward the more electronegative atom. Whereas carbon ($\chi = 2.5$) and hydrogen ($\chi = 2.2$) have nearly equal electronegativity, the electronegativity of oxygen is considerably larger ($\chi = 3.4$). Thus a C—O bond is highly polarized, with a partial negative charge on the oxygen atom and a partial positive charge on the carbon atom.

Electronegativity and polarized bonds were introduced in Section 8.2.

When two polar acetone molecules approach each other, they align with the positive end of one molecule close to the negative end of the other. In a liquid array, this repeating pattern of head-to-tail alignment gives rise to significant net attractive **dipolar forces** among the molecules. Figure 10-13 illustrates this schematically.

The dispersion forces in acetone are about the same as those in 2-methylpropane, but the addition of dipolar forces makes the total amount of intermolecular attraction between acetone molecules substantially greater than that between molecules of 2-methylpropane. Consequently, acetone boils at a considerably higher temperature than 2-methylpropane. Sample Problem 10-2 provides some additional comparisons of dispersion forces and dipole forces.

SAMPLE PROBLEM 10-2 BOILING POINTS AND STRUCTURE

The line structures of butane, methyl ethyl ether, and acetone are as follows. Explain the trend in boiling points: butane (0 °C), methyl ethyl ether (8 °C), and acetone (56 °C).

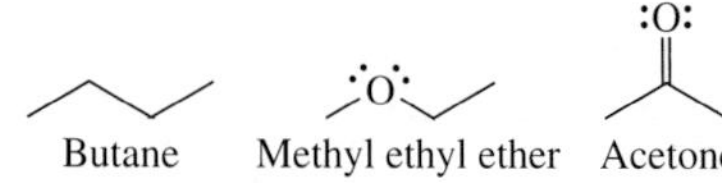

METHOD: We can explain these boiling points in terms of dispersion forces and dipolar forces. First, assess the magnitudes of dispersion forces, which are present in all substances, and then look for molecular polarity.

Dispersion forces depend primarily on the size of the electron cloud and secondarily on the shape of the molecule. A table helps organize the available information.

Substance	Boiling point	Electrons	Shape
Butane	0 °C	34	Elongated
Methyl ethyl ether	8 °C	34	Elongated
Acetone	56 °C	32	Compact

The table shows that dispersion forces alone cannot account for the range in boiling temperatures. Methyl ethyl ether and butane have the same number of electrons and similar shapes; yet their boiling points are different. Acetone, which has fewer electrons and a more compact shape than the other compounds, has smaller dispersion forces; yet it boils at a higher temperature. The order of boiling points indicates that acetone is a more polar molecule than methyl ethyl ether, which in turn is more polar than butane.

We expect butane to have a low polarity because of the small electronegativity difference between carbon and hydrogen. Acetone and methyl ethyl ether, on the other hand, contain polar C—O bonds. The molecular geometry about the polar C—O bonds reveals why acetone is more polar than methyl ethyl ether. The full Lewis structures of these molecules show that the oxygen atom in the ether has a steric number of four and bent geometry. Arrows show the charge displacement for each polar bond.

Methyl ethyl ether

Acetone

Notice that the two C—O bond dipoles in methyl ethyl ether partially cancel each other, leaving a relatively small polarity, whereas the polar C—O bond in acetone is unopposed. Thus acetone is more polar than methyl ethyl ether.

SECTION EXERCISES

10.1.1 On the basis of the behavior of the other elements of Group VII, predict whether At_2 will be a gas, liquid, or solid at room temperature. Sketch its intermolecular stabilization energy curve relative to that of F_2.

10.1.2 From the compressibility curves shown in Figure 10-5, determine which of the four gases has the largest intermolecular forces and which has the smallest. State your reasoning.

10.1.3 Explain the following differences in normal boiling points:
(a) Kr boils at −152 °C, and propane boils at −42 °C.
(b) $C(CH_3)_4$ boils at 10 °C, and CCl_4 boils at 77 °C.
(c) N_2 boils at −196 °C, and CO boils at −91.5 °C.

10.2 HYDROGEN BONDING

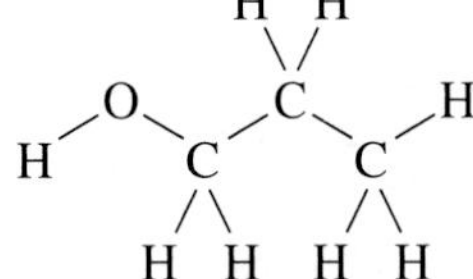

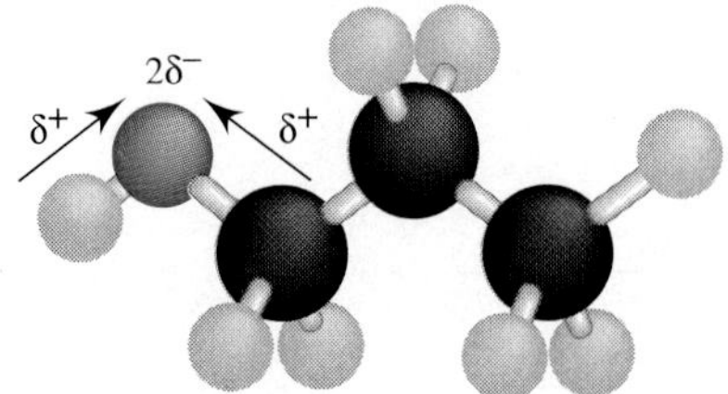

FIGURE 10-14
The Lewis structure and ball-and-stick model of 1-propanol. Polar bonds to the oxygen atom have been highlighted in the ball-and-stick model.

Methyl ethyl ether is a gas at room temperature (boiling point, or bp, = 8 °C), whereas 1-propanol, whose structure is shown in Figure 10-14, is a liquid (bp = 97 °C). Both compounds have the same molecular formula, C_3H_8O, and both have chains of four atoms, C—O—C—C and O—C—C—C. Consequently, the electron clouds of these two molecules are about the same size, and their dispersion forces are comparable. Each molecule has an sp^3-hybridized oxygen atom with two polar single bonds, so their dipolar forces should be similar. The very different boiling points of 1-propanol and methyl ethyl ether make it clear that dispersion and dipolar forces do not reveal the entire story of intermolecular attractions.

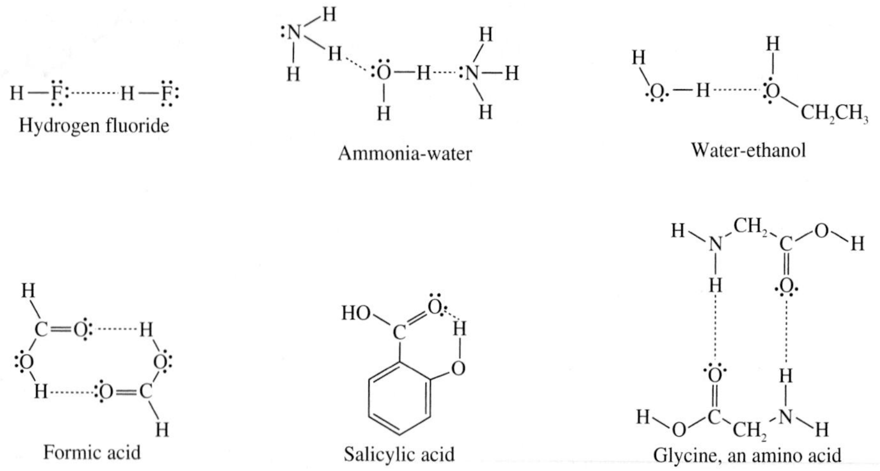

FIGURE 10-15
Examples of hydrogen bonding among some small molecules.

The forces of attraction between 1-propanol molecules are stronger than those between methyl ethyl ether molecules because of a special intermolecular interaction called a **hydrogen bond.** A hydrogen bond occurs when electrons from a highly electronegative atom are partially shared with a positively polarized hydrogen atom. Hydrogen bonds are only 5% to 10% as strong as covalent bonds, but they are comparable to and sometimes stronger than dipolar and dispersion interactions.

There are two requirements for hydrogen bond formation. The covalent bond to hydrogen must be highly polar, and there must be nonbonding electrons on a highly electronegative atom. These requirements restrict hydrogen bond formation to molecules that have hydrogen atoms bonded to fluorine, oxygen, and nitrogen. The presence of any of these elements signals that hydrogen bonding may occur. Figure 10-15 shows representative examples of hydrogen bonding. Dashed lines designate hydrogen bonds to indicate the partially bonding nature of these interactions.

Chlorine and sulfur atoms are also sufficiently electronegative to participate in hydrogen bonding, and there is some evidence for such bonding in HCl. However, the nonbonding electrons on these atoms are in diffuse 3*p* orbitals that do not interact as strongly with a hydrogen atom as electrons in more compact 2*p* orbitals.

Notice from the examples shown in Figure 10-15 that hydrogen bonds can form between *different* molecules (for example NH_3····H_2O) and *identical* molecules (for example, HF····HF). Also notice that molecules can form more than one hydrogen bond (for example, glycine) and that hydrogen bonds can form within a molecule (for example, salicylic acid) and between molecules. Sample Problem 10-3 explores the possibilities for hydrogen bond formation.

SAMPLE PROBLEM 10-3 FORMATION OF HYDROGEN BONDS

In which of the following systems will hydrogen bonding play an important role: CH_3F, $(CH_3)_2CO$ (acetone), CH_3OH, and NH_3 dissolved in $(CH_3)_2CO$?

METHOD: Hydrogen bonds occur when both polar H—X bonds and electronegative atoms with nonbonding pairs of electrons are present. Lewis structures provide the best starting point in determining whether these requirements are met:

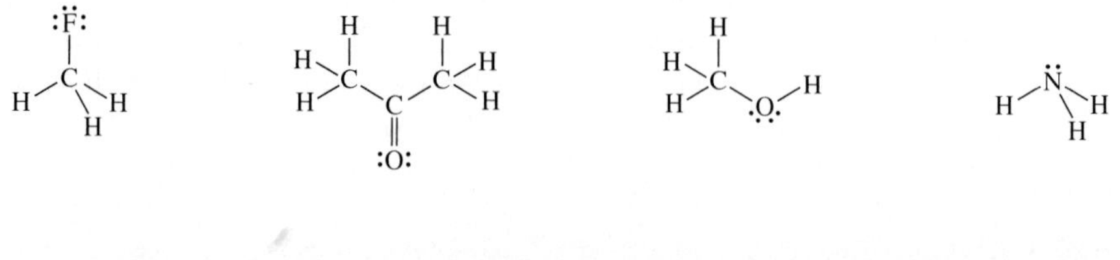

Acetone and CH_3F each has an electronegative atom with nonbonding pairs, but neither has highly polar H—X bonds. Thus there is no hydrogen bonding between molecules of these substances.

Its O—H bond gives CH_3OH an electronegative atom with nonbonding pairs and a polar O—H bond. Hydrogen bonding occurs between the O—H hydrogen atom on one molecule and the oxygen atom of a neighboring molecule:

```
 H                    H
  \                  /
H—C                 C—H
  / \  ..          /   \
 H   O:·········H—O:    H
     |           ..
     H
```

For a solution of ammonia in acetone, we must examine both components. Acetone has an electronegative oxygen atom with nonbonding pairs, whereas NH_3 has a polar N—H bond. Consequently, a mixture of these two compounds will display hydrogen bonding between ammonia's hydrogen atoms and acetone's oxygen atoms:

```
    H
 H  |
H—C                H
    \               \
     C=O:····H—N:
    / ..            /
H—C               H
 H  |
    H
```

For extra practice, draw a similar picture that shows the hydrogen bonding in a solution of acetone in water.

BINARY HYDROGEN COMPOUNDS

The graph in Figure 10-16 shows that there are regular periodic trends in the boiling points of the binary hydrogen compounds. For each column of the periodic table the boiling points of the binary hydrogen compounds increase from top to bottom of the column. This trend can be attributed to increasing dispersion forces: The more electrons the molecule has, the stronger the dispersion forces and the higher the boiling

Many elements in the *p* block of the periodic table have electronegativities close to that of hydrogen. This means that the H-X bonds have low bond polarity, so dispersion forces dominate the intermolecular interactions.

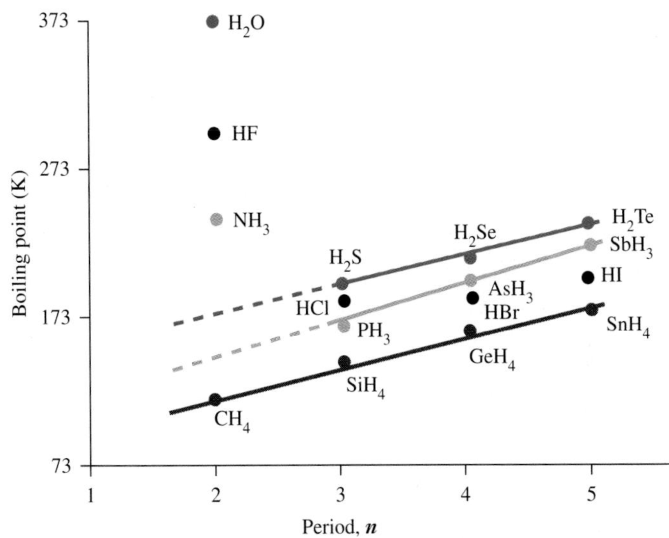

FIGURE 10-16
Periodic trends in the boiling points of binary hydrogen compounds. Notice that H_2O, HF, and NH_3 are exceptions to the trends.

point. For example, H_2S (18 electrons) boils at −60 °C, whereas H_2Se (36 electrons) and H_2Te (54 electrons) boil at −41 °C and −4 °C, respectively.

Ammonia, water, and hydrogen fluoride depart dramatically from the periodic behavior illustrated in Figure 10-16. This is because their molecules experience particularly large intermolecular forces resulting from hydrogen bonding. In hydrogen fluoride, for instance, partial donation of an electron pair from the highly electronegative fluorine atom of one HF molecule to the electron-deficient hydrogen atom of another HF molecule creates a hydrogen bond. Similar interactions among many HF molecules result in a network of hydrogen bonds that gives HF a boiling point much higher than those of HCl, HBr, and HI.

Water has a substantially higher boiling point than hydrogen fluoride, which indicates that the overall strength of hydrogen bonding in H_2O is greater than that in HF. Fluorine has the highest electronegativity, however, so the strongest *individual* hydrogen bonds are those in HF. The higher boiling point of water reflects the fact that it forms more hydrogen bonds *per molecule* than hydrogen fluoride.

Every hydrogen atom in liquid HF is involved in a hydrogen bond, but there is only one polar hydrogen atom per molecule. Thus each HF molecule participates in two hydrogen bonds with two other HF partners. There is one hydrogen bond involving the partially positive hydrogen atom and a second involving the partially negative fluorine atom. In contrast, a water molecule has *two* hydrogen atoms that can form hydrogen bonds and *two* nonbonding electron pairs on each oxygen atom. This permits every water molecule to form *four* hydrogen bonds.

Hydrogen bonding in liquid water and, even more strikingly, in solid ice creates a three-dimensional network that puts each oxygen atom at the center of a distorted tetrahedron. Figure 10-17 shows that two arms of the tetrahedron are regular covalent O—H bonds, whereas the other two arms of the tetrahedron are hydrogen bonds to two different water molecules.

HYDROGEN BONDING IN BIOMOLECULES

Hydrogen bonding is particularly important in biochemical systems because biomolecules contain many oxygen and nitrogen atoms that participate in hydrogen bonding. For example, the amino acids from which proteins are made contain NH_2

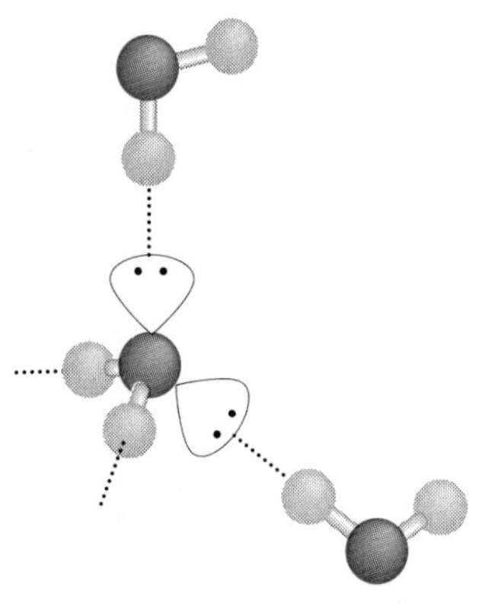

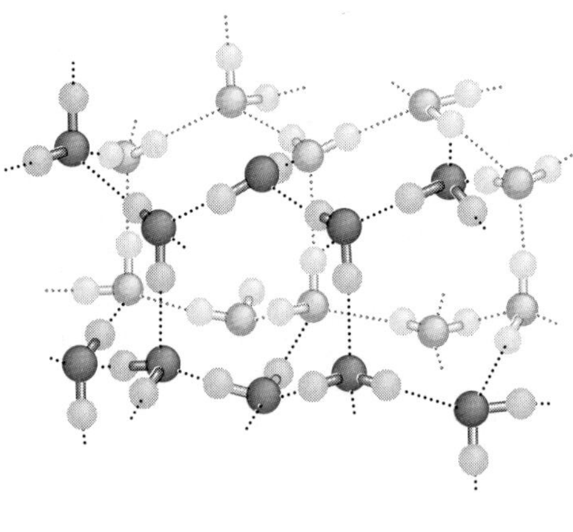

FIGURE 10-17
The structure of ice. **A,** Each oxygen atom is at the center of a distorted tetrahedron of hydrogen atoms. The tetrahedron is composed of two short covalent O••••H bonds and two long H—O hydrogen bonds. **B,** Water molecules are held in a network of these tetrahedra.

(amino) and CO_2H (carboxylic acid) groups. Four different types of hydrogen bonds exist in these systems: O—H····N, N—H····O, O—H····O and N—H····N. Hydrogen bonding between glycine molecules is shown in Figure 10-15, and Sample Problem 10-4 provides further illustrations. We examine more details of hydrogen bonding in biomolecules in Chapter 11.

SAMPLE PROBLEM 10-4 HYDROGEN BONDING IN AMINO ACIDS

In aqueous solution, amino acids undergo intramolecular proton transfer to form ions. The line structures of two amino acid ions, serine and glutamine, follow. For each molecule, identify the hydrogen atoms that can form hydrogen bonds and the electronegative atoms to which hydrogen bonds can form.

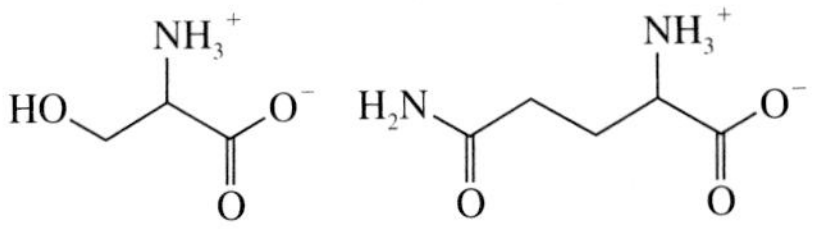

Serine
$C_3H_7NO_3$

Glutamine
$C_5H_{10}N_2O_3$

METHOD: Hydrogen atoms in polar H—X bonds can form hydrogen bonds with lone pairs on other nitrogen, oxygen, or fluorine atoms. To identify hydrogen bonding possibilities, we need Lewis structures to determine the locations of nonbonding pairs of electrons. Carbon atoms are never involved in hydrogen bonds, so we can ignore the carbon framework of the molecules. The following partial Lewis structures show the nonbonding pairs of electrons and the polar H—X bonds:

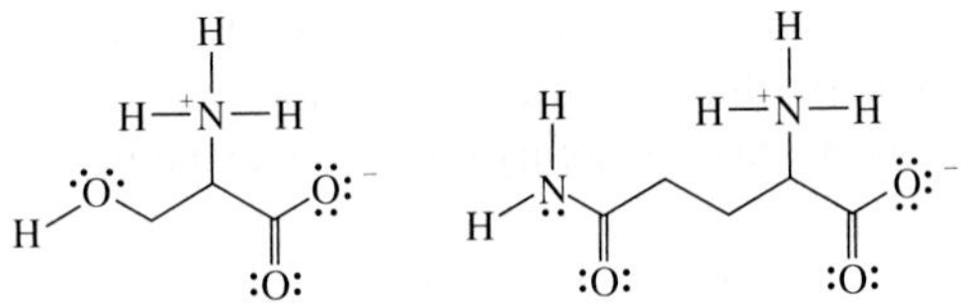

Any N—H or O—H hydrogen atom in these molecules can participate in hydrogen bonding. These are highlighted in blue in the following structures. The N atoms and O atoms with lone pairs of electrons can also participate in hydrogen bonding. These atoms are highlighted in yellow.

Serine

Glutamine

Dispersion forces, dipole interactions, and hydrogen bonds are all much weaker than covalent intramolecular bonds. For example, the average C—C bond energy is 345 kJ/mol, whereas dispersion forces are just 0.1 to 5 kJ/mol for small alkanes such as propane. Moreover, dipolar interactions between polar molecules such as acetone range from 5 to 20 kJ/mol, and hydrogen bonds vary from 5 to 50 kJ/mol.

Recall from Chapter 9 that bond energy is the amount of energy required to break 1 mol of a particular bond. Table 9-2 lists bond energies.

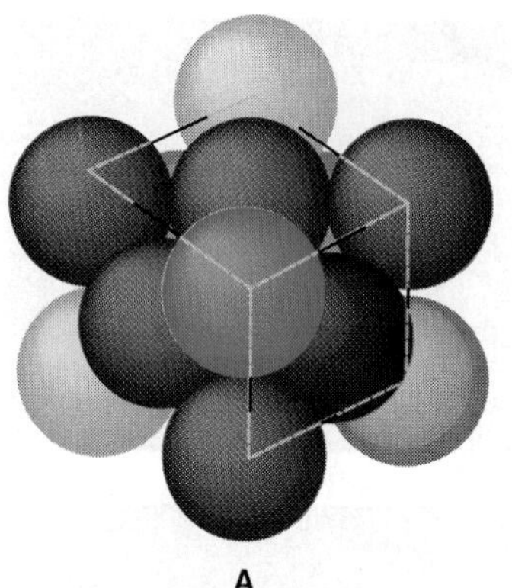

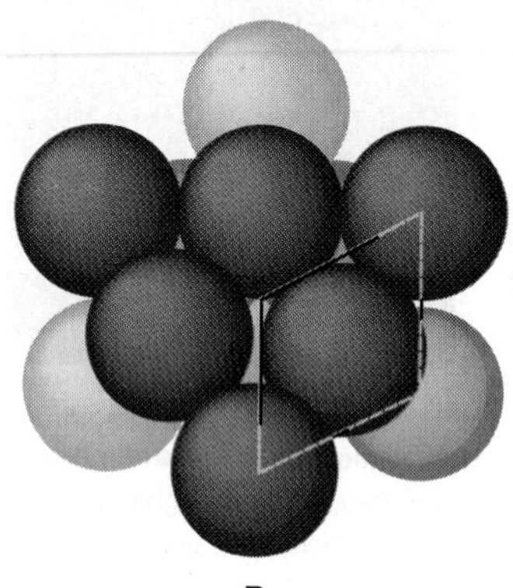

FIGURE 10-23
A cubic close-packed array viewed at an angle to reveal its cubic structure. **A,** Two faces of the cube have been outlined. A sphere sits in the center of each face. **B,** One corner sphere has been removed to show more clearly the underlying hexagonal plane of spheres.

To see the cubes in a cubic close-packed structure, we need to rotate the array so that the hexagonal planes tilt upward at a 45-degree angle, as shown in Figure 10-23, *A*. Notice that we have rotated the entire array but have not changed the relative positions of the spheres. From this perspective, three spheres from one hexagonal plane lie along a diagonal of a square, with one sphere from each adjacent plane forming the other two corners of the square. At right angles to this first square are other sets of squares that form cubes. Figure 10-23, *B* shows one such cube with one corner sphere removed to reveal the original hexagonal planar array.

The exploded views in Figure 10-24 show yet another way of looking at the hexagonal close-packed and cubic close-packed crystal types. In the hexagonal close-packed structure, notice that the *third* layer lies directly above the first, the fourth above the second, and so on. Thus we can label the layers ABAB, and so on. In the cubic close-packed structure, the third layer is offset from the other two, but the *fourth* layer is directly above the first. Thus this arrangement can be labelled ABCABC, and so on.

Atoms and molecules with spherical symmetry often form crystals with hexagonal close-packed or cubic close-packed geometry. For instance, magnesium and zinc crystallize with their atoms in a hexagonal close-packed array. Silver, aluminum, and gold, on the other hand, crystallize in the cubic close-packed arrangement. Argon solidifies at low temperature as a cubic close-packed crystal, and neon can solidify in either form.

The packing in ionic crystals requires that ions of opposite charges alternate with one another to maximize interionic attraction. For many 1:1 ionic crystals such as NaCl, the most stable arrangement is two interlocking face-centered cubic arrays, as is illustrated in Figure 10-25.

Another type of arrangement, which is shown in Figure 10-26, *A*, is a **body-centered cubic structure.** A body-centered cube can be constructed by assembling a set of spheres in a *square* planar array, as shown in Figure 10-26, *B*, and then nesting a second set of spheres in the dimples of the first set, as shown in Figure

FIGURE 10-24
Side and expanded views of the hexagonal close-packed and cubic close-packed crystal types. In the hexagonal close-packed structure, spheres on both sides of any plane are in the same positions, and the third layer is directly above the first. In the cubic close-packed structure, layers take up three different positions, and the fourth layer is directly above the first.

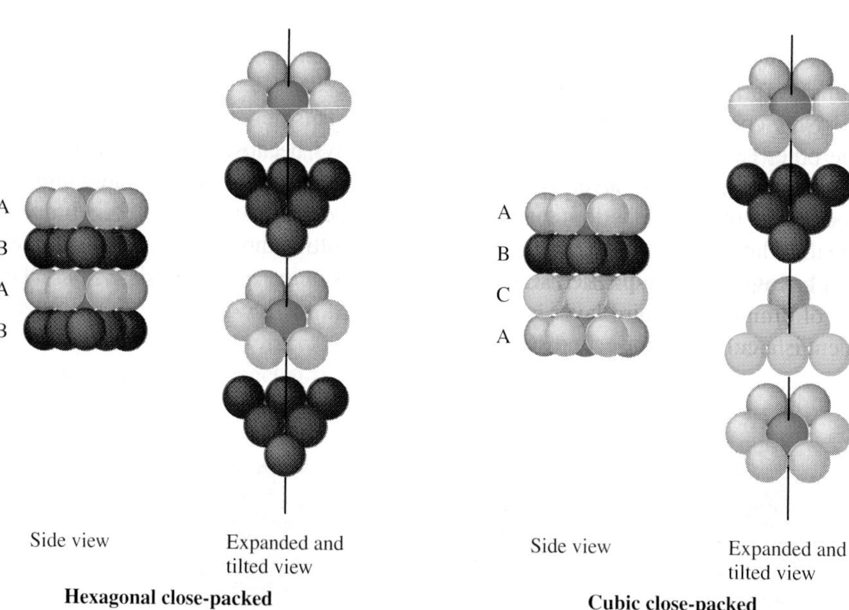

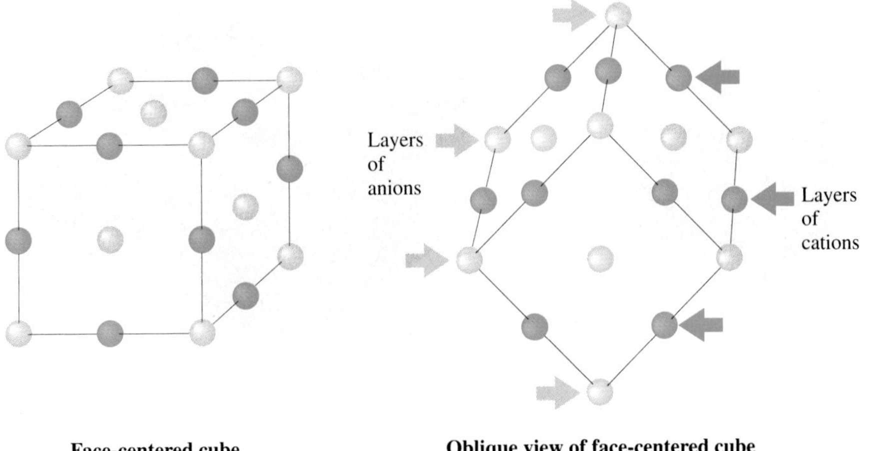

FIGURE 10-25
Ionic crystals such as NaCl contain face-centered cubic arrangements of each ion. In this view a cube is drawn with the cations, shown as yellow spheres, at its corners and in the centers of the faces. The anions, shown as blue spheres, occupy positions at the center of each edge of the cube. A view from an oblique angle reveals that this structure contains alternating hexagonal planar arrays of cations and anions.

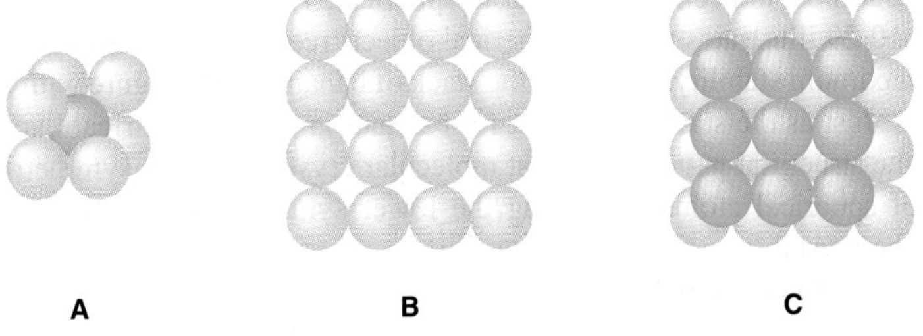

FIGURE 10-26
A body-centered cubic array is made up of layers of spheres arranged in a square pattern. The basic pattern **(A)** has one corner sphere removed to reveal the sphere nested in the center of the cube. The array can be constructed by laying down a square layer of spheres **(B),** and then placing a second square layer in the dimples between the spheres **(C).** A third layer directly above the first completes the cubes.

10-26, *C*. This arrangement gives a second square array, on which yet another set can be nested.

UNIT CELLS

Any crystal is a near-infinite array of atoms, molecules, or ions arranged in some regular repeating pattern. Because of this repeating pattern, every crystal has one smallest unit from which the entire pattern can be assembled. This minimum unit is called a **unit cell.** The idea of the unit cell is illustrated in two dimensions by the art of M.C. Escher, as shown in Figure 10-27. Escher often used symmetrical patterns aligned together to create an overall design. The repeating units can be visualized as "tiles" placed edge to edge. A unit cell in a crystal is a three-dimensional fragment stacked together like a set of blocks.

The body-centered cubic crystal provides a good illustration of three-dimensional unit cells. A drawing of the unit cell of this crystal is shown in Figure 10-28, *A*. Notice that it is a cube defined by the centers of eight iron atoms that surround a central iron atom. This cube contains a central Fe atom and portions of additional Fe atoms. The body-centered cubic crystal is built up by stacking together many unit cells, as shown in Figure 10-28, *B*. It takes eight unit cells stacked together to complete one of the corner atoms, so each unit cell contains one eighth of an atom at each of its corners. The cell has eight such corners, so each unit cell contains two complete iron atoms.

FIGURE 10-27
M.C. Escher used repeating patterns to create works of art with exquisite symmetry. The repeating patterns in Escher's work are two-dimensional analogs of the unit cells that define the symmetry of a crystalline solid.

SAMPLE PROBLEM 10-7 SOLUBILITY TRENDS

Give a molecular explanation for the following trend in alcohol solubilities in water:

Propanol	$CH_3CH_2CH_2OH$	Completely miscible
Butanol	$CH_3CH_2CH_2CH_2OH$	1.1 M
Pentanol	$CH_3CH_2CH_2CH_2CH_2OH$	0.30 M
Hexanol	$CH_3CH_2CH_2CH_2CH_2CH_2OH$	0.056 M

METHOD: Solubility limits depend on the relative magnitude of the destabilization that occurs when solvent bonding networks and solute bonding networks are disrupted, compared with the stabilization generated by solute-solvent interactions. This problem refers to a series of aqueous solutions, which are dominated by hydrogen bonding interactions.

When any alcohol dissolves in water, the hydrogen-bonding network of water is disrupted by the nonpolar hydrocarbon part of the alcohol. Counterbalancing these disruptions, hydrogen-bonding interactions are generated in the solution between the OH groups of the alcohol and water molecules.

As the nonpolar region of an alcohol grows longer, more and more hydrogen bonds are disrupted by each solute molecule. At the same time, each alcohol listed has only one OH group, so the amount of compensating solute-solvent hydrogen bonding is the same for all the alcohols.

This explains why longer-chain alcohols are progressively less soluble in water. As the hydrocarbon chain gets longer, more destabilization is involved in inserting the alcohol into the water matrix, so the alcohol gets increasingly less soluble as the chain grows.

Zinc methyl reacts with aqueous acids.

SOLUBILITY OF SOLIDS

Like dissolves like also describes the solubility properties of solids. There are four different kinds of solids: covalent, ionic, molecular, and metallic. Each is held together by a different kind of interaction, and each has its own solubility characteristics.

Covalent solids such as diamond, graphite, or silica cannot dissolve without breaking covalent chemical bonds. Because intermolecular forces of attraction are always much weaker than covalent bonds, solvent-solute interactions are never strong enough to offset the energy cost of breaking bonds. Covalent solids are insoluble in all solvents, but they may be chemically attacked by some liquids or vapors.

The network bonding of metals was discussed in Section 9.6.

Metals are the next most difficult solids to dissolve because they contain extensive delocalized bonding networks that must be disrupted before the metal can dissolve.

Recall from Section 4.6 that strong acids generate hydronium ions in aqueous solution.

When an alkali metal contacts water or when other metals such as Ca, Zn, or Fe are treated with aqueous acid, the metal *reacts* with the solution, producing hydrogen gas and a solution of the metal cation (for example, Na^+ and Ca^{2+}). A chemical reaction has occurred, so the aqueous medium has *not* dissolved the metal. Zinc metal, for example, reacts with hydrochloric acid to generate H_2 gas and displace Zn^{2+} cations in solution:

$$Zn_{(s)} + 2\,H_3O^+_{(aq)} \rightarrow Zn^{2+}_{(aq)} + H_{2(g)} + 2\,H_2O_{(l)}$$

The solution produced when zinc reacts with hydrochloric acid is an aqueous solution of zinc ions from the chemical reaction and chloride ions from HCl, not a solution of zinc metal in water. If this solution is boiled to dryness, the remaining solid is $ZnCl_2$, not zinc metal.

A few metals *react* with water, and several *react* with aqueous acids, but no metals will simply *dissolve* in water. Likewise, metals do not dissolve in nonpolar liquid solvents.

Metals are insoluble in common liquid solvents but can dissolve in each other (like dissolves like). A mixture of substances with metallic properties is called an **alloy.** Some alloys are solutions, and others are heterogeneous mixtures. Brass, for instance, is a homogeneous solution of copper (20% to 97%) and zinc (80% to 3%), but common plumber's solder is a heterogeneous alloy of lead (67%) and tin (33%). When solder is examined under a microscope, separate regions of solid lead and solid tin can be seen. When brass is examined, no such regions can be seen.

Mercury, the only metal that is a liquid at room temperature, dissolves a number of metals to give liquid solutions. Any solution of another metal in mercury is called an **amalgam.** Metals close to mercury in the periodic table, such as silver, gold, zinc, and tin, are particularly soluble in mercury. An amalgam of silver, tin, and mercury has been widely used to make dental fillings. When the intermetallic compound Ag_3Sn is ground with mercury, it forms a semisolid amalgam that can be shaped to fill a cavity. On standing, mercury reacts with the other metals to form a hard solid mixture of Ag_5Hg_8 and Sn_7H_8. The mixture expands slightly during reaction, forming a tight fit within the cavity.

The mercury atoms in dental fillings are chemically bound and do not dissolve, so they are safe for the wearer, despite the fact that mercury is highly toxic. Dentists who mix the amalgams, however, may be at risk of mercury poisoning.

As described in Section 7.7, *ionic solids* contain cations and anions held in a three-dimensional ionic lattice by strong coulombic attractions. Thus ionic solids do not dissolve unless considerable solvent-ion interactions exist to counterbalance the energy cost of breaking the ions free from the lattice. There are no ionic liquids at room temperature, so at first we might think there are no solvents suitable for ionic solids. Some ionic solids dissolve in water, however, because water is a *highly polar* liquid in which strong ion-dipole interactions exist between water molecules and ions in aqueous solution. Figure 10-33 illustrates the solvation of Na^+ and Cl^- ions as NaCl dissolves in water.

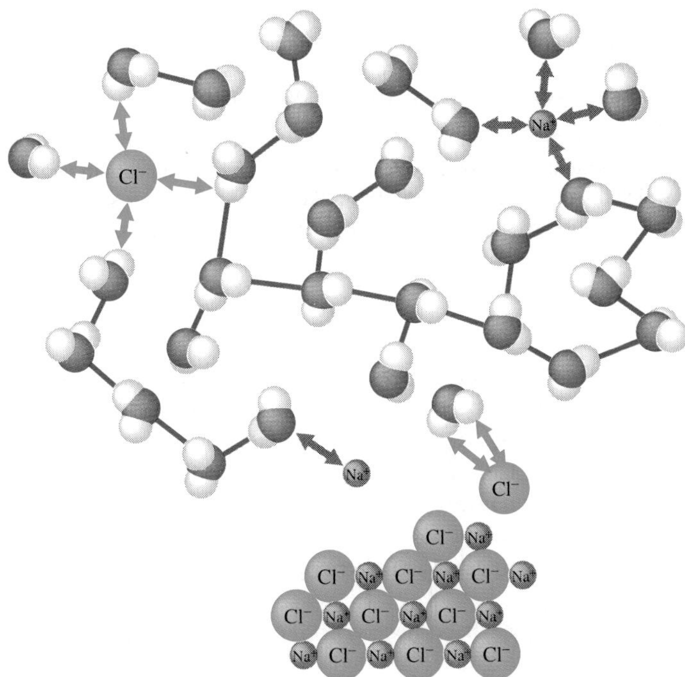

FIGURE 10-33
A molecular picture showing the ion-dipole interactions that help a solid ionic crystal dissolve in water. Arrows indicate ion-dipole interactions.

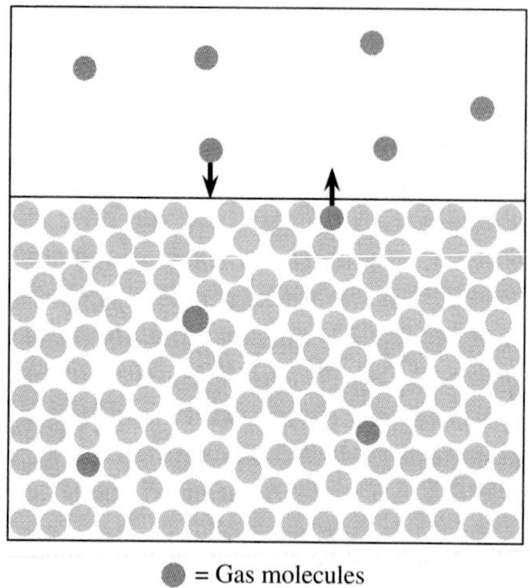

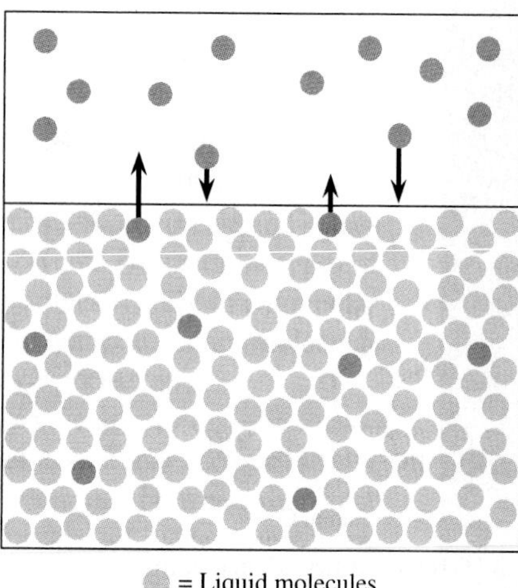

FIGURE 10-35
When the partial pressure of a gas above a solution increases *(right)*, the capture rate goes up, so the concentration of gas in the solution increases.

This is because when HCl gas dissolves in water, proton transfer occurs to generate H_3O^+ ions:

$$HCl_{(g)} + H_2O_{(l)} \rightarrow Cl^-_{(aq)} + H_3O^+_{(aq)}$$

Although this is a chemical reaction, we say that HCl dissolves in water rather than reacts with water because boiling the solution regenerates HCl and H_2O vapors.

Ammonia is another gas that is very soluble in water, giving solutions as concentrated as 14.8 M. Ammonia dissolves because it forms hydrogen bonds with water molecules. When an ammonia molecule displaces a water molecule, one hydrogen-bonding interaction is exchanged for another.

Gas solubility increases with the partial pressure of the gas in contact with the solution. The molecular view of a solution in Figure 10-35 shows the reasons. Gas molecules that collide with a liquid surface can be captured into solution, and as the partial pressure increases, the number of collisions between gas molecules and the solution surface also increases. This, in turn, causes more gas molecules to be captured by the solution and increases the concentration of dissolved gas.

At the same time that gas molecules are being captured at the liquid surface, dissolved gas molecules escape from the liquid if their motion brings them to the surface. As more and more gas molecules enter the solution, the escape rate of molecules returning to the gas phase increases accordingly. At any given partial pressure, the concentration of gas dissolved in the liquid changes until the number of gas molecules that leave the solution matches the number of molecules that enter the solution. The gas-liquid system is then in a condition of dynamic equilibrium, in which molecules are continually transferred between phases without any net change in concentrations.

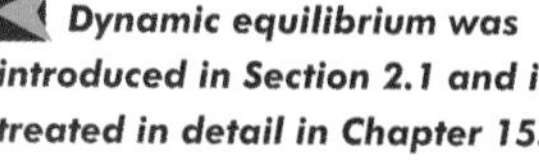
Dynamic equilibrium was introduced in Section 2.1 and is treated in detail in Chapter 15.

The rate of capture from the gas phase is directly proportional to pressure, and the rate of escape from the solution is directly proportional to the concentration of dissolved gas molecules. The solubility of a gas is the concentration at which these two rates exactly balance. Thus gas solubility is directly proportional to partial pressure. **Henry's law** expresses this quantitatively:

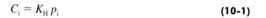

$$C_i = K_H p_i \qquad \textbf{(10-1)}$$

TABLE 10-2 HENRY'S LAW CONSTANTS

GAS	K_H (10^{-3} M/atm) 0 °C	25 °C	30 °C
N_2	1.1	0.67	0.40
O_2	2.5	1.3	0.89
CO	1.6	0.96	0.44
Ar	2.5	1.5	1.0
He	0.41	0.38	0.40
CO_2	78	34	16

*Aqueous solutions.

We usually express dissolved gas concentration in molarity and gas pressure in atmospheres, so K_H has units of molarity/atmosphere.

Here, C_i is the concentration of gas in the solution, and p_i is the partial pressure of the same gas in the vapor phase above the solution. These two variables are linked by the Henry's law constant (K_H). The value of K_H depends on the identity of the gas, the solvent, and on the temperature of the system. Table 10-2 lists values for the Henry's law constants for several gases dissolving in water. Sample Problem 10-9 makes use of Henry's law to determine the concentrations of atmospheric gases that dissolve in water, and Box 10-1 discusses how Henry's law applies to deep-sea diving.

SAMPLE PROBLEM 10-9 SOLUBILITIES OF ATMOSPHERIC GASES

The Earth's atmosphere is 78% N_2, 21% O_2, and minor amounts of other gases, including CO_2 (0.31%). Find the concentration of N_2, O_2, and CO_2 in water at equilibrium with the Earth's atmosphere at 25 °C.

METHOD: Each gas establishes its own dynamic equilibrium with water. The concentration depends on the partial pressure of the gas in the atmosphere and on the value of the Henry's law constant at 25 °C.

Recall from Chapter 5 that the partial pressure of any gas in a mixture is given by the mole fraction (X_i) multiplied by total pressure. Using 1.0 atmosphere (atm) for the total pressure:

$$p_{O_2} = X_{O_2}P = \left(\frac{21\%\ O_2}{100\%}\right) \times (1.0\ \text{atm}) = 0.21\ \text{atm}\ O_2$$

Likewise, the partial pressure of N_2 is 0.78 atm and that of CO_2 is 3.1×10^{-3} atm.

Now we can use Henry's law to calculate the concentrations of dissolved gas:

$$C_{N_2} = \left(6.7 \times 10^{-4}\ \frac{\text{M}}{\text{atm}}\right)(0.78\ \text{atm}) = 5.2 \times 10^{-4}\ \text{M}\ N_2$$

$$C_{O_2} = \left(1.3 \times 10^{-3}\ \frac{\text{M}}{\text{atm}}\right)(0.21\ \text{atm}) = 2.7 \times 10^{-4}\ \text{M}\ O_2$$

$$C_{CO_2} = \left(3.4 \times 10^{-2}\ \frac{\text{M}}{\text{atm}}\right)(3.1 \times 10^{-3}\ \text{atm}) = 1.1 \times 10^{-4}\ \text{M}\ CO_2$$

BOX 10-1

HENRY'S LAW AND THE BENDS

According to Henry's law, gases become more soluble as pressure increases. Normally, this variation has few consequences because atmospheric pressure varies slowly with changing altitude or weather. However, very large pressure changes are routine in deep-sea diving. As a result, divers returning from the depths to the surface must take special precautions to allow their bodies to adjust to changes in the solubility of the gases in their blood.

Carbonated beverages illustrate what happens when a gas dissolved in a liquid experiences a rapid drop in pressure. Soft drinks, soda water, champagne, and beer are all bottled under several atmospheres' pressure of carbon dioxide. When a bottle is uncapped, the total pressure quickly falls to 1 atm, and the partial pressure of CO_2 drops to 0.003 atm. At this lower pressure, the concentration of CO_2 in the solution is much higher than its solubility, so the excess CO_2 forms gas bubbles and escapes from the liquid.

Deep-sea divers experience pressure changes similar to those of bottled drinks. For every 30 feet a diver descends, the pressure increases by 1 atmosphere. As a result, the amount of nitrogen gas dissolved in the diver's blood increases significantly as the diver descends. If a diver returns to the surface too quickly after a deep dive, gas dissolved in the blood may form bubbles in the same way as the CO_2 in a freshly opened carbonated drink. These bubbles interfere with the transmission of nerve impulses and restrict the flow of blood. This condition, known as *the bends*, is extremely painful and can cause paralysis or death.

Divers avoid the bends by returning to the surface slowly, taking short "decompression stops" at intermediate depths to allow excess gas to escape from the blood without forming bubbles. Another way of preventing the bends is by using helium-oxygen gas mixtures instead of air in divers' breathing apparatus. Helium is only half as soluble as nitrogen in blood, so less extra gas dissolves in blood.

SECTION EXERCISES

10.5.1 List the types of intermolecular interactions that stabilize a solution of acetone in methanol, and draw molecular pictures that illustrate any dipole-dipole and hydrogen-bonding interactions that exist between molecules of these substances.

10.5.2 Gases can be collected by bubbling them through water into an evacuated container. If 0.18 mol of CO_2 at $P = 0.98$ atm is bubbled through 450 mL of water into an empty glass vessel at 298 K, what fraction of the gas dissolves in the water?

10.5.3 On the basis of their molecular structures, predict which of the following silicon-containing materials are water soluble: elemental Si, SiO_2, Na_2SiO_3, and $SiCl_4$.

10.6 DUAL-NATURE MOLECULES: SURFACTANTS AND BIOLOGICAL MEMBRANES

Now that we have described intermolecular forces, solutions, and solubility properties, we can apply these concepts to examples of solute-solvent interactions of key importance in the chemical industry and in biology.

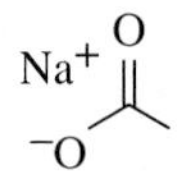

Sodium acetate
$NaCH_3CO_2$

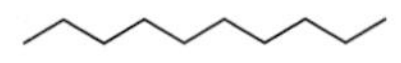

Decane
$C_{10}H_{22}$

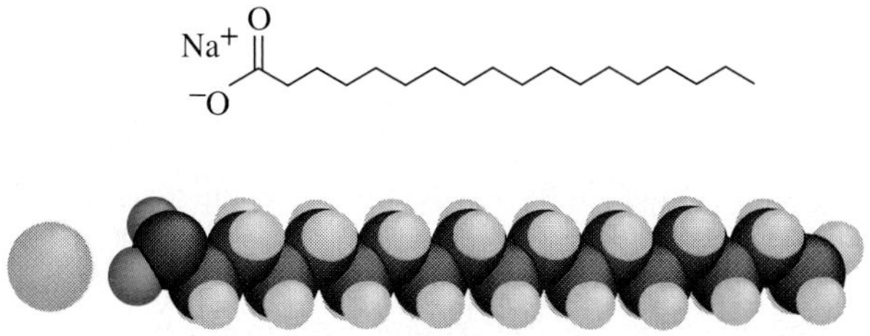

Sodium stearate
$NaC_{17}H_{35}CO_2$

FIGURE 10-36
Sodium stearate is a typical dual-nature molecule. It has a hydrophilic polar head that resembles sodium acetate and a hydrophobic nonpolar tail that is a hydrocarbon similar to decane.

Substances that do not dissolve in water, such as organic fats and oils, are called **hydrophobic.** Substances that are miscible with water, such as the organic but hydrogen-bonding molecules methanol and acetone, are called **hydrophilic.** Some molecules contain both hydrophilic and hydrophobic regions. Such dual-nature molecules may have a polar or ionic "head" that is compatible with water and a long hydrocarbon "tail" that is incompatible with water. Sodium stearate, whose structure is shown in Figure 10-36, is a dual-nature molecule. The head of the stearate anion resembles the water soluble acetate anion, and the tail is a hydrocarbon chain containing 17 carbon atoms.

Figure 10-37 shows three different structures that dual-nature molecules such as sodium stearate can form when they are placed in water. They may form a molecular **monolayer** on the surface, in which the polar head groups are immersed in the water while the nonpolar tails are aggregated together on the surface. Agitating the solution may cause the molecules to arrange into spherical aggregates called **micelles,** in which the hydrophobic tails point inward and the polar heads lie on the outside of the structure, where they interact with the aqueous solvent. Dual-nature molecules may also form enclosed **bilayers,** called **vesicles,** which have two parallel rows of molecules oriented so that their hydrocarbon tails are clustered together.

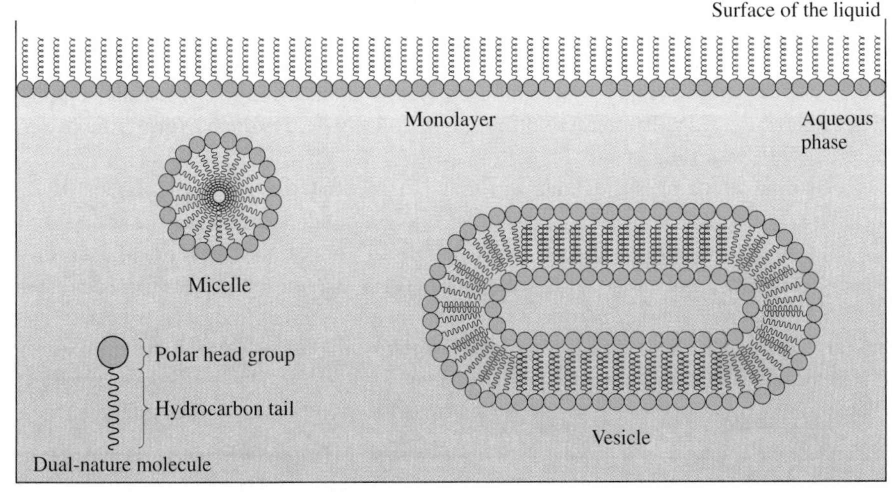

FIGURE 10-37
Cross-sectional molecular views of the structures that can form when dual-nature molecules are placed in water. The molecules may form a monolayer at the surface, spherical clusters called *micelles,* or bilayer structures called *vesicles.* In all three structures the hydrocarbon tails cluster together to minimize their interactions with water molecules, and the polar head groups are positioned to maximize their interactions with water molecules.

All these arrangements obey the principle of like dissolving like. The hydrocarbon tails aggregate through dispersion forces because they are incompatible with the aqueous medium. The hydrogen-bonding network of the solvent would be disrupted by incorporating these tails into the solution. The polar heads, on the other hand, interact strongly with water to maximize hydrogen bonding and ion-dipole interactions.

SURFACTANTS

Dual-nature molecules are widely used in industrial chemistry to modify the behavior of aqueous solutions. In this context they are called **surfactants.** Common surfactant head groups include carboxylate ($—CO_2^-$), sulfonate ($—SO_3^-$), sulfate ($—OSO_3^-$), and ammonium ($—NH_3^+$). Sodium is the most common counter-ion for anionic surfactants and chloride for cationic surfactants because these ions are nontoxic and their salts are highly soluble.

Surfactants are widely used as soaps and detergents. Clothing becomes soiled by a wide variety of substances; some are water soluble, and others are not. Surfactants remove water-insoluble grease (for example, butter, fat, and oil) from solid surfaces. Dispersion forces stabilize grease particles in the hydrocarbon tails of surfactant aggregates. Agitation removes these aggregates from the fabric, suspending them in solution as a large number of tiny micelles with grease particles trapped inside. The micelles do not redeposit on the fabric because their hydrophilic heads hold them in solution. When water is drained from the washing machine, the grease-containing micelles are swept away, leaving clean clothes behind.

Soap made by boiling animal fat in an alkaline solution obtained from ashes has been known since the time of the ancient Sumerians, 2500 BC.

Soaps are carboxylate surfactants derived from natural sources such as animal fats that contain stearic acid and other long-chain organic acids. These carboxylate surfactants form insoluble salts with Ca^{2+} and Mg^{2+}. In regions where water is "hard," these soaps precipitate calcium and magnesium stearate as a "scum" that inhibits cleansing action and is responsible for bathtub rings. Detergents, on the other hand, contain sulfonate and sulfate surfactants that are "synthetic" compounds, originally prepared in the laboratory. Detergents such as sodium lauryl sulfate do not form precipitates with divalent cations, but they have a tendency to lather and foam. Foaming is a disadvantage in washing machines but is considered to be an advantage in hair shampoos. The cleaning action of soaps and detergents is similar, but detergents have largely replaced soaps because of their superior behavior in hard water.

O—S(=O)(=O)—O⁻ Na⁺

Sodium lauryl sulfate
(common ingredient in shampoo)

Surfactants are used in such a wide variety of ways that billions of dollars are spent on them every year. They appear in many household products, including cleansing agents and shampoos. Some surfactants are used as emulsifiers in processed foods such as bottled salad dressing. An emulsifier causes normally incompatible liquids such as the oil and water in salad dressing to disperse in each other. Surfactants emulsify by forming molecular connections between the liquids. Their hydrophobic tails interact with oil molecules, whereas their hydrophilic heads interact with water molecules.

Gasoline contains surfactants designed to prevent the accumulation of high-boiling compounds on the surfaces of fuel injectors and carburetors. These deposits interfere with the flow of air and cause rough idling and poor gas mileage. In this case the hydrophilic polar ends interact strongly with the solid surface, and the hydrophobic ends are compatible with liquid gasoline. The polar ends adhere to the metal walls of the injection system, whereas their tails extend into the fuel mixture. This creates a thin nonpolar film that protects the surface from gummy deposits. These same films help prevent the formation of rust by screening the metal surface from water molecules.

Figure 10-38 illustrates that surfactants also decrease the surface tension of water. In the figure, the drop of water that contains a surfactant is flattened and deformed, giving it a larger surface area than the drop of water that contains no surfactant. Surfactant molecules reduce surface tension by forming a monolayer on the aqueous surface. Unlike water molecules at the surface, this monolayer does not experience an attractive force drawing molecules back into the bulk of the liquid.

A surfactant also causes water to form a film coating on any surface it contacts. In this sense, surfactants make water "wetter." Because of its improved ability to coat surfaces, surfactant-treated water is used occasionally to fight fires.

Chemists and engineers in the petroleum industry are studying ways to use surfactants to increase the amount of oil that can be recovered from wells. The goal is to develop inexpensive, environmentally safe surfactants that can be mixed with water and injected into existing oil wells. The surfactant will promote formation of an oil-water emulsion that has a lower viscosity than oil and should be easier to extract from the well.

FIGURE 10-38
Surfactants reduce surface tension by forming a monolayer at the water-air interface. The water droplet on the left contains a surfactant, making its surface tension lower and causing it to flatten and spread out.

Approximately half of the surfactants produced in the United States are used in household and industrial cleaning products, but the remaining half are used in a wide range of industries. In agriculture, surfactants are used as wetting agents that assist in the uniform application of sprayed pesticides. They also are used to prevent caking of fertilizers. Surfactants used in agricultural products must not interfere with the active agents and must be biodegradable and environmentally benign. In the food industry, different surfactants are used as emulsifiers, cleaners, foaming agents, and antifoaming agents. Paints are dispersions of dyes, binding agents, and fillers. Most paints contain surfactants that convey improved flow and mixing properties. Surfactants are used widely in the plastics industry as foaming agents to assist in the production of plastic foams and to improve moldability and extrudability of specially shaped products. In the manufacture of textiles, surfactants are used to clean natural fibers, as lubricants that reduce friction during the spinning and weaving processes, emulsifiers that improve the application of dyes and finishes, and antistatic agents.

This is just a sampling of the industrial applications of these versatile materials. A host of other industries also uses surfactants in significant amounts. Examples include pharmaceuticals, paper, mining, petroleum, tanning, photography, electroplating, and adhesives.

CELL MEMBRANES

It may seem like a huge conceptual leap from industrial surfactants to biological cell membranes, but the same principles apply to both sets of substances.

Every biological cell is surrounded by a thin membrane only a few molecules thick. Among the major components of membranes are molecules called *phospholipids,* which are dual-nature molecules. Although their chemical structures are much more complex than simple surfactants such as sodium stearate, phospholipids nevertheless have hydrophilic heads and hydrophobic tails. Figure 10-39 shows the structure of lecithin, which is a common membrane phospholipid. The hydrophilic end of lecithin has a cationic $N(CH_3)_3^+$ group and eight oxygen atoms with nonbonding pairs of electrons, all of which form hydrogen bonds with water molecules. The hydrophobic portion of lecithin consists of two hydrocarbon tails.

Phospholipids form bilayers in aqueous media. The molecules form two approximately parallel rows with tails aligned and heads in contact with the solution. This arrangement, shown in Figure 10-40, is analogous to the vesicles in Figure 10-37. The bilayer forms a closed sac that contains the aqueous cytoplasm and all the cellular components. Thus a cell can be viewed as a large and complex vesicle.

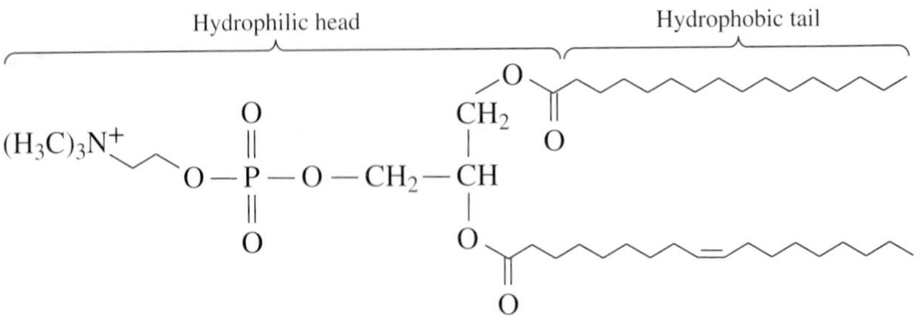

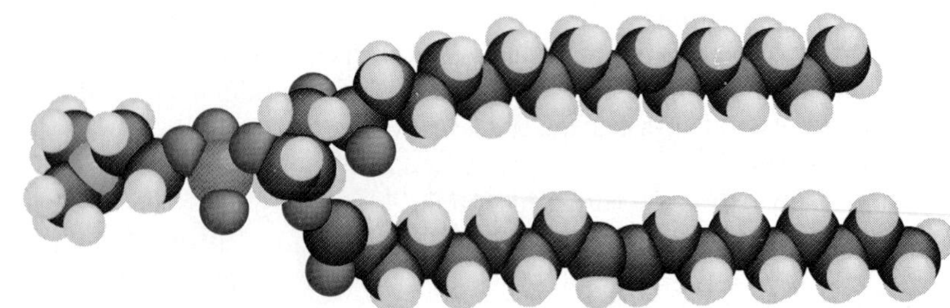

FIGURE 10-39
The chemical structure of lecithin. Lecithin is one of the most common phospholipids used for the construction of cell membranes. It is also used as a "natural" emulsifier in beauty products.

FIGURE 10-40
A lipid bilayer contains two layers of dual-nature molecules arranged tail to tail. The polar head groups face outward and are stabilized by dipolar and hydrogen-bonding interactions with water molecules.

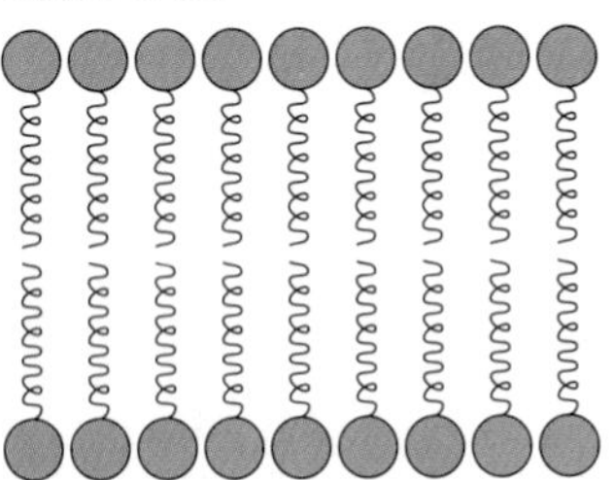

A Schematic of a lipid bilayer

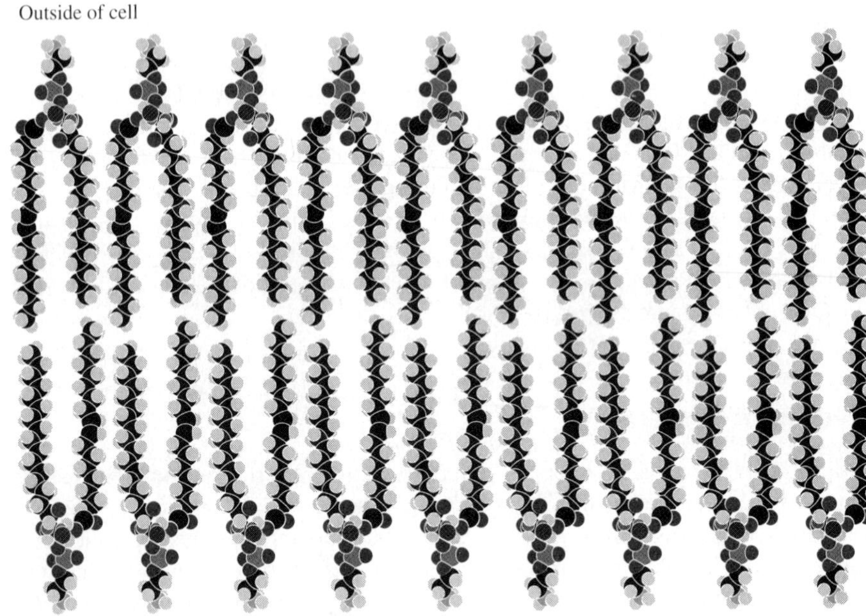

B Space-filling model of a lipid bilayer

One purpose of a cellular lipid bilayer is to control which molecules pass into and out of the cell. Uncharged small molecules such as water, ammonia, and oxygen can diffuse through the membrane. Hydrophobic molecules such as hydrocarbons can also pass through because they are soluble in the overlapping tails that make up the interior of the bilayer. Ions and water-soluble polar molecules such as glucose and urea, on the other hand, cannot get through the membrane.

For cells to carry out their functions, glucose and other nutrients must be brought in, and urea and other waste products must be expelled. This would be an impossible task if cell membranes were composed only of phospholipids. Specific large biomolecules act as molecular "gates" through the membranes. These proteins are embedded in the bilayers but protrude into the surrounding water and/or into the cell interiors.

The structures of proteins are described in Chapter 11.

SECTION EXERCISES

10.6.1 Line drawings of some molecules follow. Identify the hydrophilic and hydrophobic regions of each, and determine which are surfactants.

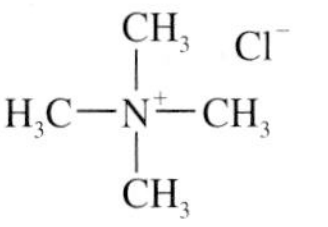

$(CH_3)_4N^+\ Cl^-$ Tetramethylammonium chloride

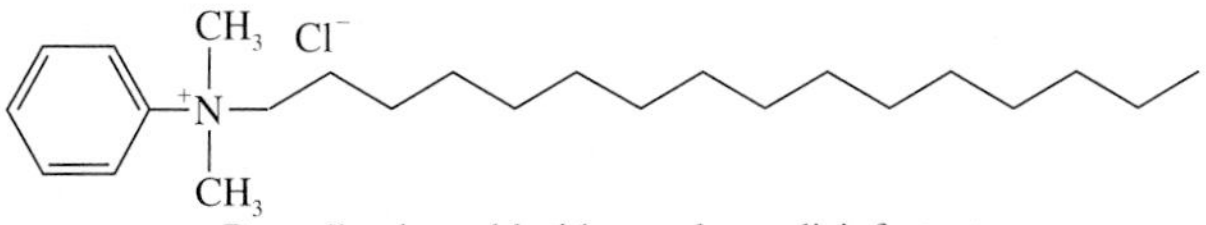

Benzalkonium chloride, used as a disinfectant

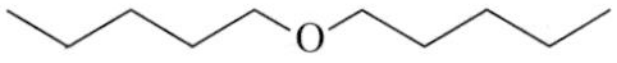

Dipentyl ether

10.6.2 Explain why glucose and other large, water-soluble molecules cannot pass through a lipid bilayer. (The structure of glucose is shown in Figure 10-34.)

10.7 PROPERTIES OF AQUEOUS SOLUTIONS

Solute molecules alter many properties of a liquid. For instance, adding salt to water gives a solution that boils at a higher temperature than pure water, and adding ethylene glycol to the water in an automobile radiator gives a solution that protects against freezing because the solution freezes at a lower temperature than pure water. Changes such as these in the behavior of liquids can be understood from a molecular perspective if we first describe phase changes from a molecular viewpoint and then examine the effect of added solute molecules. We consider aqueous solutions specifically because they are by far the most important in general chemistry, biology, and geology.

PHASE EQUILIBRIA

If pure water at 0 °C is cooled, it freezes, and if ice at 0 °C is warmed, it melts. The temperature at which this transformation between the liquid and solid forms of H_2O occurs is the freezing point of water. At exactly 0 °C, solid ice and liquid water are equally stable, so in a thoroughly insulated container, ice and water could coexist at 0 °C indefinitely.

The temperature 0 °C can also be characterized as the melting point of ice.

The molecular view shown in Figure 10-41, *A,* reveals that two processes occur in a mixture of ice and water at 0 °C. First, water molecules in the liquid that collide

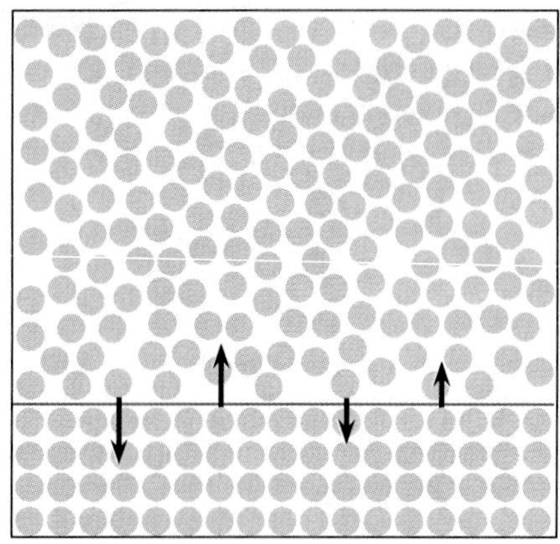

A Solid–pure liquid equilibrium

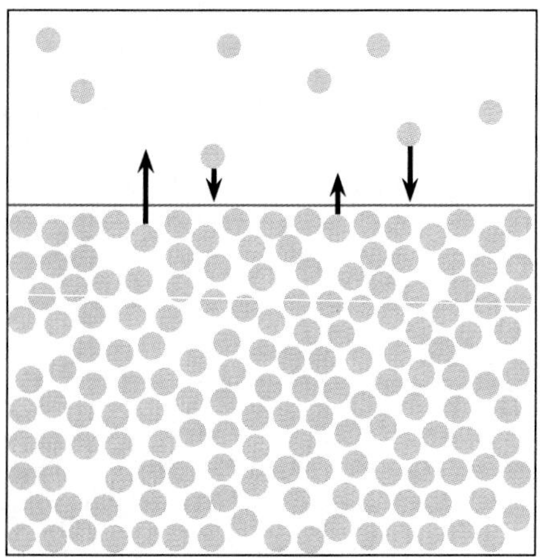
B Pure liquid–gas equilibrium

FIGURE 10-41
Molecular views of the dynamic equilibria between pure phases. **A,** The equilibrium between liquid and solid. **B,** The equilibrium between liquid and gas. At the equilibrium temperature, exactly the same number of molecules escape from the liquid phase as are captured by the liquid phase. Remember that all molecules are constantly in motion; for clarity, however, the motions of molecules confined within a phase have not been shown.

Dynamic equilibrium is consistent with the kinetic theory of molecular motion. One proof of molecular transfer between phases comes from radioactivity studies. If radioactive ice is placed in nonradioactive water at 0 °C, the water slowly becomes radioactive because of molecular transfer of radioactive water molecules between phases.

When water boils in an open container, the steam diffuses into the surrounding atmosphere, leading to a continual escape of molecules. Consequently, the liquid-vapor equilibrium can be observed only when the gas is confined to a closed space.

with the crystals are sometimes captured and added to the solid phase. Second, molecules on the surface of the ice crystals sometimes become detached and enter the surrounding liquid. The mixture reaches a state of dynamic equilibrium when equal numbers of molecules move in each direction in any given time. When the pressure exerted on the mixture is 1 atm, this ice-water equilibrium exists only at 0 °C because any change of temperature throws the rates out of balance. Lowering the temperature decreases the rate at which molecules escape from the surface of the ice, whereas raising the temperature increases the rate of escape.

A dynamic equilibrium also exists between liquid water and steam when the pressure exerted on the liquid is 1 atm and the temperature is 100 °C (Figure 10-41, *B*). Some molecules at the liquid surface have sufficient energy to escape into the gas phase, and some molecules in the gas phase are captured when they strike the liquid surface. Under conditions of dynamic equilibrium, equal numbers of molecules move in each direction in any given time. At a pressure of 1 atm, this equilibrium exists only at 100 °C because lowering the temperature reduces the rate at which molecules escape from the liquid phase and condensation occurs. Raising the temperature, on the other hand, increases the rate of escape from the liquid phase, and the liquid boils.

These two equilibria provide the basis for precise definitions of the normal freezing point and the normal boiling point. The **normal freezing point *(fp)*** of a substance is the temperature at which solid and liquid coexist at equilibrium under a pressure of 1 atm. The **normal boiling point *(bp)*** of a liquid is the temperature at which liquid and vapor coexist at equilibrium under a pressure of 1 atm.

EFFECT OF SOLUTES

Four common properties of solutions are modified by the presence of solute molecules. These properties are freezing point, boiling point, vapor pressure, and osmotic pressure. They are called the *colligative properties*.

The molecular view of freezing and boiling provides a basis for determining the influence of dissolved substances on melting and boiling points. In a solution, solute molecules displace some of the solvent molecules, so a given volume of a solution contains a smaller number of solvent molecules than the same volume of pure solvent. Consequently, the presence of solute molecules reduces the rate at which solvent molecules leave the liquid phase. Figure 10-42 shows that changing one rate without changing the other rate throws the dynamic equilibrium out of balance.

The addition of solutes *decreases* the freezing point of a solution because collisions between solvent molecules and crystals of solid solvent occur less frequently

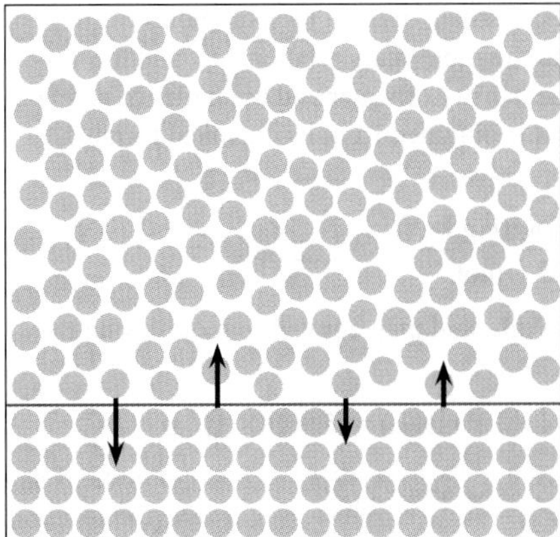

Dynamic equilibrium:
Two solid molecules escape,
two liquid molecules are captured

Solute disrupts equilibrium:
Two solid molecules escape,
one liquid molecule is captured

FIGURE 10-42
Molecular views of the rates of solid-liquid phase transfer of a pure liquid and a solution at the normal freezing point. The addition of solute does not change the rate of escape from the solid, but it decreases the rate at which the solid captures solvent molecules from the solution. This disrupts the dynamic equilibrium between escape and capture.

than in the pure solvent. Consequently, fewer molecules are captured by the solid phase than escape from the solid to the liquid. Cooling the solution restores dynamic equilibrium because it simultaneously reduces the number of molecules that have sufficient energy to break away from the surface of the solid and increases the number of molecules in the liquid with low enough kinetic energy to be captured by the solid.

Experiments show that at low solute concentration the change in freezing point of a solution, ΔT_f, obeys a simple equation:

$$\Delta T_f = K_f X_{solute} \tag{10-2}$$

Equation 10-2 can be derived from our simple molecular picture and principles of kinetic molecular theory. The derivation is independent of the nature of solute and solvent, so Equation 10-2 is valid for other solvents besides water, except that K_f has a different value for each solvent.

where X_{solute} is the total mole fraction of solutes and K_f is a constant, called the **freezing point depression constant.** The constant is different for different *solvents* but does not depend on the identity of the *solutes*. For water, K_f is 105.0 °C. Sample Problem 10-10 illustrates the use of Equation 10-2.

SAMPLE PROBLEM 10-10 FREEZING POINT DEPRESSION

Ethylene glycol (1,2-ethanediol) is added to automobile radiators to prevent cooling water from freezing. What is the freezing point of radiator coolant that contains 2.00 kg of ethylene glycol and 5.00 L of water?

H–Ö–C(H)(H)–C(H)(H)–Ö–H Ethylene glycol

METHOD: The question asks for the freezing point of a solution. The phrase *to prevent the water from freezing* reveals that we are dealing with the depression of the freezing point of water. Equation 10-2 describes this process quantitatively: $\Delta T_f = K_f X_{solute}$.

The freezing point depression constant for water is known from experiments and can be found in tables: $K_f = 105.0$ °C. To calculate the freezing point, we must first determine the mole fraction of the solute in this solution.

OSMOSIS

Water molecules can pass through cell membranes, but most solutes cannot. This is a **semipermeable membrane,** and the movement of water through it is **osmosis.**

If a semipermeable membrane separates two identical solutions, solvent molecules move in both directions at the same rate, and there is no net osmosis. The two sides of the membrane are at dynamic equilibrium. The situation changes when the solution on the two sides of the membrane are different. Consider the membrane in Figure 10-43, which has pure water on one side and a solution of sugar in water on the other. The sugar molecules in the solution reduce the concentration of solvent molecules in the solution. Consequently, more solvent molecules pass through the membrane from the solvent side to the solution side than from the solution side to the solvent side. Now water flows from the solvent side to the solution side, and there is a net rate of osmosis.

What can be done to increase the rate of solvent flow from the solution side of the membrane? An increase in pressure on the solution side accomplishes this, because as pressure increases, the flow rate of any liquid also increases. An increase in pressure on the solution side of the membrane increases the rate of transfer of water molecules from the solution side to the solvent side.

Figure 10-44 shows that when the pressure is increased until the rate of solvent transfer is equal in both directions, dynamic equilibrium has been reestablished and net osmosis falls to zero. The pressure increase needed to equalize the transfer rates is called the **osmotic pressure** (Π). Osmotic pressure is a pressure *difference.* Both sides of a semipermeable membrane have some pressure exerted on them, and Π is the *extra pressure* that must be exerted on the solution to maintain dynamic equilibrium.

Like freezing point depression and boiling point elevation, osmotic pressure is proportional to the concentration of solute molecules. Osmotic pressure does not involve a temperature change, however, so there is no disadvantage in using the usual measure of solution concentration, molarity. Experiments also show that osmotic pressure increases as temperature increases:

The osmotic pressure equation seems very simple, but its derivation requires the molecular model, differential calculus, and detailed principles of physical chemistry that are beyond the scope of this book.

$$\Pi = MRT \tag{10-4}$$

In Equation 10-4, M is the total molarity of all solutes, T is the temperature in kelvins, and R is the gas constant. If osmotic pressure is expressed in atmospheres, the fact that molarity is in moles per liter requires us to use $R = 0.08206$ L atm/mol K.

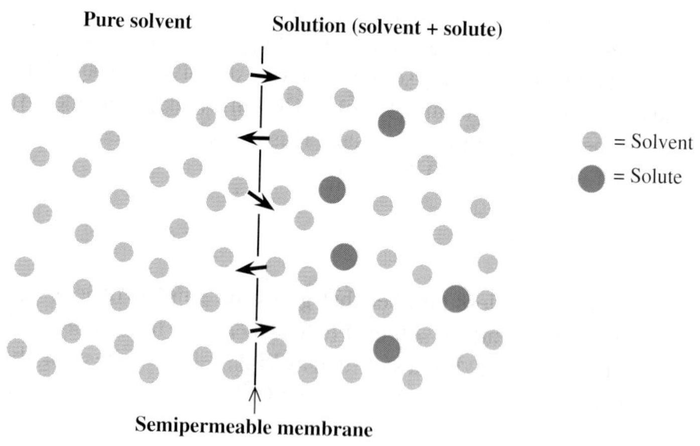

FIGURE 10-43
Small solvent molecules can pass back and forth freely through the pores of a semipermeable membrane, but solute molecules cannot. The presence of solute molecules in a solution reduces the concentration of solvent molecules, and this in turn reduces the rate at which solvent molecules pass out of the solution. There is an imbalance in transfer rates, which leads to osmosis.

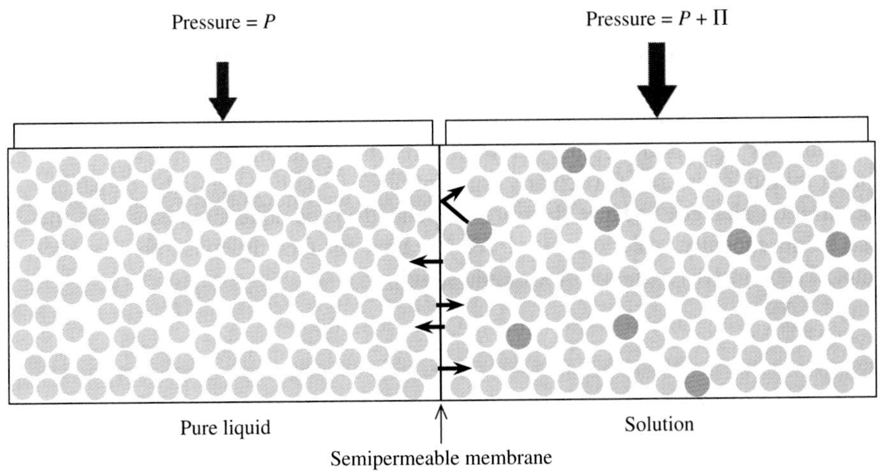

FIGURE 10-44
To equalize the rates of transfer of solvent molecules from a solution and from pure solvent, an additional pressure Π (osmotic pressure) must be exerted on the solution.

Osmotic pressure effects can be substantial. For example, the waters of the oceans contain dissolved salts at a total ionic molarity of about 1.13 M. We can calculate the osmotic pressure of ocean water:

$$\Pi = MRT = (1.13 \text{ mol/L})(0.08206 \text{ L atm/mol K})(298 \text{ K}) = 27.6 \text{ atm}$$

Thus the osmotic pressure of ocean water is *more than 25 times atmospheric pressure.* By comparison the freezing point of ocean water is depressed by only about 1% from the freezing point of pure water, from 273 K to about 271 K (−2 °C).

Osmotic pressure plays a key role in biological chemistry because the cells of the human body are encased in semipermeable membranes and bathed in body fluids. Under normal physiological conditions the body fluid outside the cells has the same total solute molarity as the fluid inside the cells, and there is no *net* osmosis across cell membranes. Solutions with the same solute molarity are isotonic solutions.

The situation changes if a molarity imbalance is created. Figure 10-45 shows red blood cells immersed in solutions of different molarities. When the fluid outside the cell is at *higher* solute molarity, transport of water across the membrane into the cell slows. The result is that water leaves the cell, causing it to shrink. When the fluid

FIGURE 10-45
When bathed in isotonic solution *(left)*, red blood cells retain their normal shape because there is no net osmosis across their membranes. In a solution at higher concentration *(center)*, the net osmotic flow removes water from the cell interior, causing cells to shrink and wrinkle. In a solution at lower concentration *(right)*, the net osmotic flow pumps water into cells, expanding them until they may rupture.

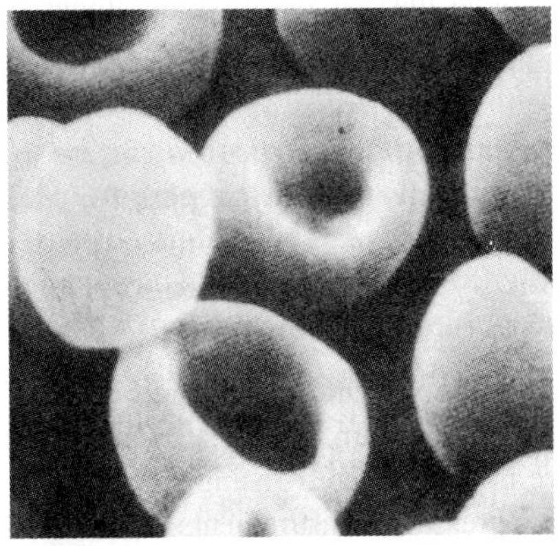

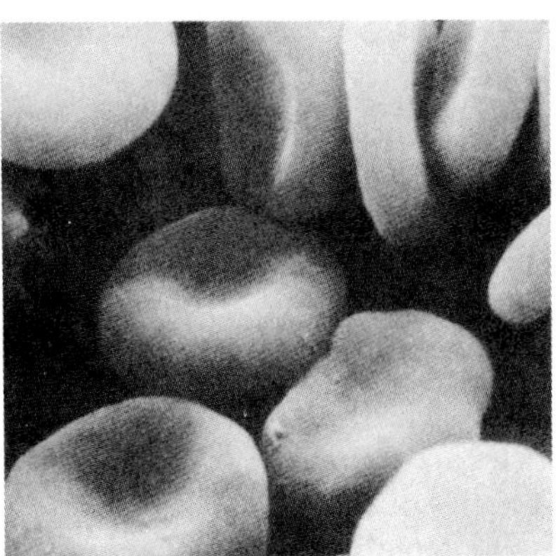

RECRYSTALLIZATION

Most laboratory syntheses are carried out in liquid solution. If the product is a solid, it may spontaneously precipitate from the reaction solvent, or it may be isolated by boiling off the solvent. In either case the solid product almost always contains impurities. Recrystallization is the classic way of removing impurities from a crude solid.

Recrystallization takes advantage of the way in which the solubilities of solids vary with temperature. Most solid solutes are more soluble in hot than in cold solvent because fast-moving, high-energy molecules are less likely to be captured by the solid phase than slow-moving ones, and solute molecules move faster in hot than in cold solutions.

If a solid substance is dissolved in a minimum volume of hot solvent that is then allowed to cool, the solubility of the solid is exceeded, and it crystallizes from the solution. In favorable cases the impurities remain dissolved in the cold solvent, and the solid has been purified. Purification by recrystallization works best when the crude solid contains a low percentage of impurities. If a large amount of an impurity is present, the impurity is likely to crystallize with the desired substance. The example in Sample Problem 10-14 illustrates this feature.

SAMPLE PROBLEM 10-14 PURIFICATION BY RECRYSTALLIZATION

A chemist has synthesized 10.0 g of crude organic solid that contains an estimated 10% impurities. The desired product is less soluble in cold ethanol (5.0 g/100 mL) than in hot ethanol (15 g/100 mL). The chemist estimates that the impurity is similar to the product and therefore has the same solubility properties. Can the compound be purified by recrystallization from ethanol?

METHOD: If the sample is dissolved in the minimum amount of hot ethanol, chilling the solution will cause the solid to precipitate. This will purify the compound if none of the impurity precipitates at the same time. We need to determine the minimum volume of hot solvent needed to dissolve the entire sample and then find out whether the impurity precipitates when that volume of solvent is chilled.

Because 10% of the crude sample is impurity, the 10.0-g sample contains 9.00 g of the desired compound. From the solubility of 15 g/100 mL in hot ethanol, we can calculate the minimum volume of solvent that will dissolve the entire sample:

$$(9.0\text{ g})\left(\frac{100\text{ mL}}{15\text{ g}}\right) = 60\text{ mL}$$

There is an estimated 1.0 g of impurities in the sample. If the impurities have solubility properties similar to those of the desired product, 60 mL of hot ethanol will dissolve 9.0 g of impurities, too, so both the desired product and the impurities will dissolve completely in 60 mL of hot ethanol.

When the ethanol is cooled, the mass of solid that it can hold can be calculated from the solubility in cold ethanol:

$$(60\text{ mL})\left(\frac{5\text{ g}}{100\text{ mL}}\right) = 3.0\text{ g}$$

The cold solution can contain 3.0 g each of the desired solid and its impurity.

Of the 9.0 g of the desired substance, 6.0 g will recrystallize on cooling. All of the 1.0 g of impurity will remain dissolved. A single recrystallization of the contaminated sample will give 6.0 g of pure compound.

Chemists frequently recover a "second crop" of substance by boiling off some of the solvent and then rechilling the solution. You should be able to determine how much additional pure substance could be recovered from this solution before the impurity begins to precipitate.

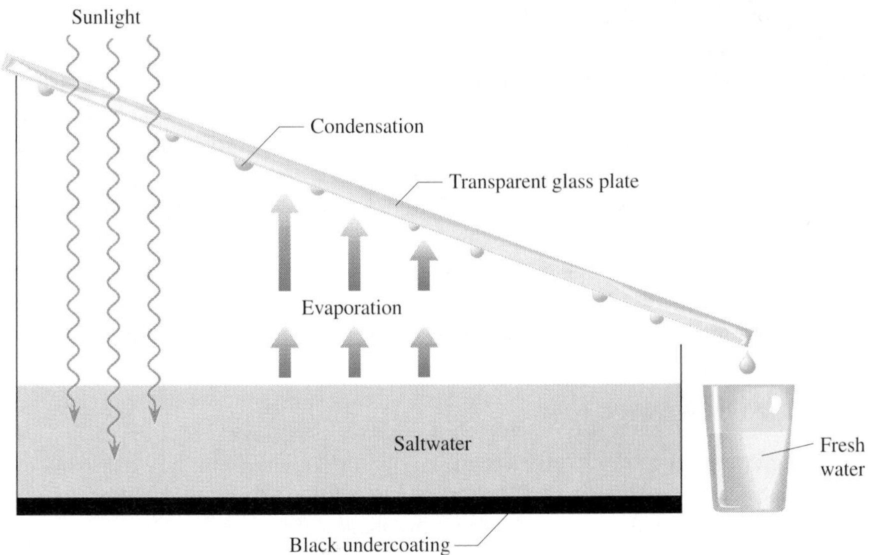

FIGURE 10-47
A simple solar saltwater still. Stills designed along these lines find commercial use in areas where sunlight and saltwater are plentiful and natural supplies of fresh water are scarce.

As Sample Problem 10-14 shows, some product is always lost during recrystallization. In the single recrystallization described, 3.0 g of the original material remains in solution. Thus the yield of the one-step process is 67%. By taking a second crop, an additional 2.0 g can be recovered, increasing the yield to 89%, but the remaining 1.0 g remains mixed with 1.0 g of impurity and cannot be recovered by further recrystallization. Chemical syntheses seldom give 100% yields, in part because the process of purifying the product always results in some losses.

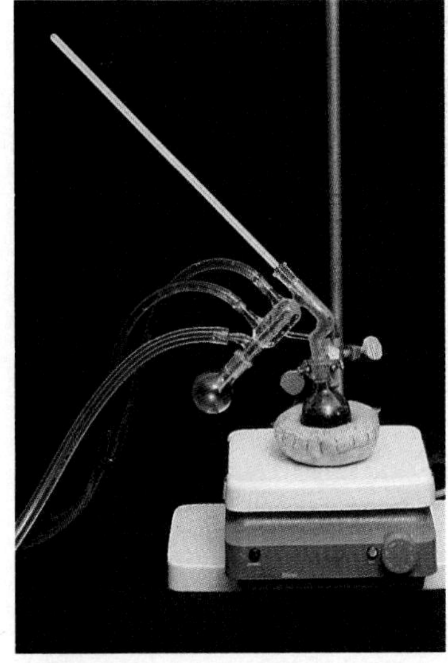

FIGURE 10-48
Liquids susceptible to oxidation or thermal decomposition can be purified by distilling them under reduced pressure.

DISTILLATION

The most common method for purifying liquids is **distillation,** which is based on a liquid-vapor phase change. A liquid solution is heated until it boils, and if the solutes remain nonvolatile, pure solvent boils off. This pure solvent vapor is captured by condensing it on a chilled surface.

Fresh water can be obtained by distilling saltwater. Figure 10-47 shows a simple solar still, in which the energy needed to vaporize the water comes from sunlight absorbed by the black coating on the bottom of the still. As the solution is heated, water evaporates, leaving the nonvolatile salt behind. The water vapor comes into contact with the underside of the glass plate, which is cooled by natural air flow. Fresh water condenses on the cool plate and trickles down to a collection vessel at the bottom of the still.

Obtaining high-purity liquids in the laboratory often requires a more elaborate procedure because many liquids decompose or react with oxygen at high temperature. For this reason, high-boiling liquids are often distilled under reduced pressure to lower the boiling temperature. Figure 10-48 shows a common laboratory apparatus used for reduced-pressure distillation.

The effect of pressure on boiling points is considered in Chapter 13. Qualitatively, reducing the pressure reduces the rate of capture of molecules from the gas phase, and this lowers the temperature at which liquid-vapor equilibrium exists.

When a liquid is contaminated with volatile impurities, simple boiling gives a mixture of compounds rather than a pure solvent. In these cases, chemical treatment of the solution can be used to convert the volatile impurity into a nonvolatile solid. For example, small amounts of water are removed from organic solvents such as cyclohexane and diethyl ether by placing a piece of sodium metal in the distilling flask. Water in the solution reacts with sodium to give sodium hydroxide, which is nonvolatile, and hydrogen gas, which does not recondense. Air is excluded from the still, moreover, to prevent immediate contamination of the distilled solvent with

$2\ Na + 2\ H_2O \rightarrow 2\ NaOH + H_2$. Dry solvents are needed for reactions that give undesirable side products when water is present.

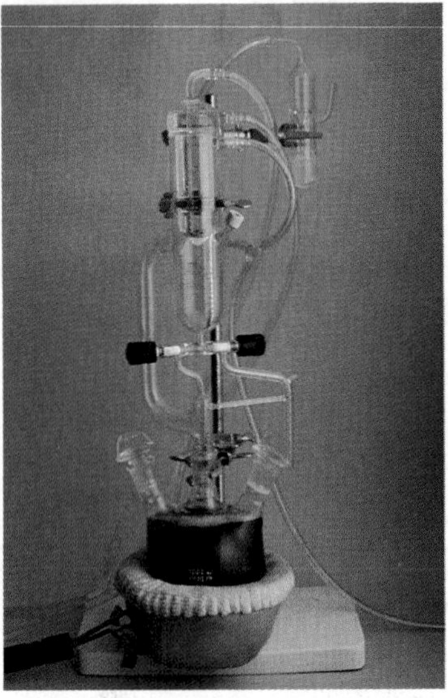

FIGURE 10-49
To produce scrupulously dry solvents, the solvent must be treated with a chemical purifying agent and then distilled under an atmosphere of a dry inert gas. The blue color in the distillation flask is due to the drying agent. Diethyl ether, which is colorless, is collected by condensing the solvent into a bulb above the boiling solvent.

water vapor from the atmosphere. Figure 10-49 shows a laboratory still for producing scrupulously dry diethyl ether.

Distillations in the chemical industry are performed on an enormous scale. Distillation is an essential step in the refining of petroleum, for example. Crude oil is a complex mixture of hydrocarbons without a single well-defined boiling point. Instead, crude oil boils over a broad range of temperatures as the lighter, more volatile hydrocarbons boil off first. As the temperature increases gradually, heavier and heavier components of the oil distill out of the mixture. The end product is asphalt, a gooey black tar. In the first step of petroleum refining, crude oil is separated into several fractions according to specific ranges of boiling point. Figure 10-50 shows the huge distillation towers used for these kinds of separations.

CHROMATOGRAPHY

There are many types of **chromatography,** but all are based on the same essential principles. A *mobile phase* carries the compounds to be separated, and a *stationary phase* binds these compounds through intermolecular forces.

Figure 10-51 shows how chromatography separates compounds. The mobile phase dissolves the compounds of interest and carries them over the stationary phase. The rate of movement of compounds depends on how strongly they interact with the stationary phase. Because solutes move only when in the mobile phase, molecules that have a very low affinity for the stationary phase move quickly, whereas those that bind tightly to the stationary phase lag behind. After the materials have traveled a sufficient distance, they become separated into distinct "bands"; each band may contain one pure material. As the mobile phase comes off the lower end of the column, it can be collected in small volumes called *fractions* or *cuts.* When the separations are complete, the various components of the original mixture are found in different fractions.

Chromatography is extremely versatile because the stationary phase and the mobile phase can be varied to match the types of compounds that need to be separated. For example, some stationary phases separate solutes according to their polarity. Polar groups on the stationary phase bind solutes through dipole-dipole or hydrogen-bonding interactions. The binding is reversible, and eventually the solvent washes the solutes off the stationary phase. The more polar the solute, the tighter it binds to the stationary phase. Thus the faster the solutes move through the column, the lower their polarity.

FIGURE 10-50
Oil refineries use immense distillation towers to separate crude oil into its various useful fractions.

The different fractions of hydrocarbons that can be obtained from petroleum are listed in Table 8-2.

In other cases the stationary phase binds solutes according to their size. Here, the stationary phase is made up of particles that are perforated with holes or channels, much like a sponge or a Wiffle ball (Figure 10-52). Small molecules can pass through the holes into the interior of the particle. Eventually these molecules make their way back out of the stationary phase. The smallest molecules move into and out of particles many times as they travel along the column. Larger molecules enter fewer times because they do not fit inside the pores as easily. The more particles a solute molecule enters, the more time it spends bound to the stationary phase, and the more slowly it moves along the column. Thus the largest solute molecules emerge from the chromatography column first, and the smallest molecules emerge last. Pore size in these stationary phases can be controlled to accommodate an enormous range of molecular sizes, from mixtures of small gas molecules to huge biomolecules with molar masses in excess of 100,000 g/mol.

METHODS OF CHROMATOGRAPHY

Chromatographic techniques are classified according to the nature of their mobile and stationary phases. Gas chromatography (GC) is used to separate mixtures of

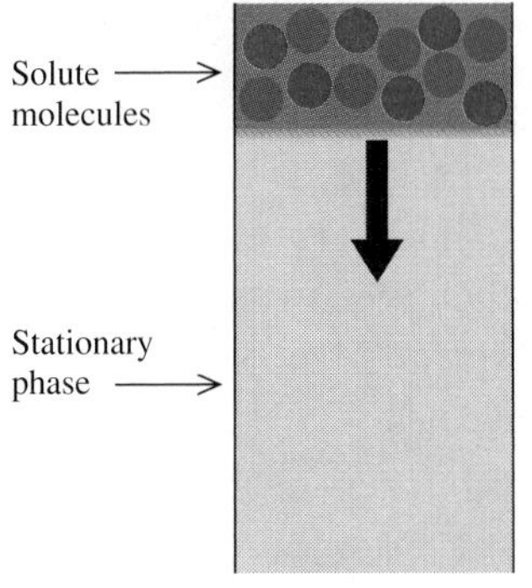

Start: Solute molecules are dissolved in the mobile phase (the solvent) and deposited on the stationary phase

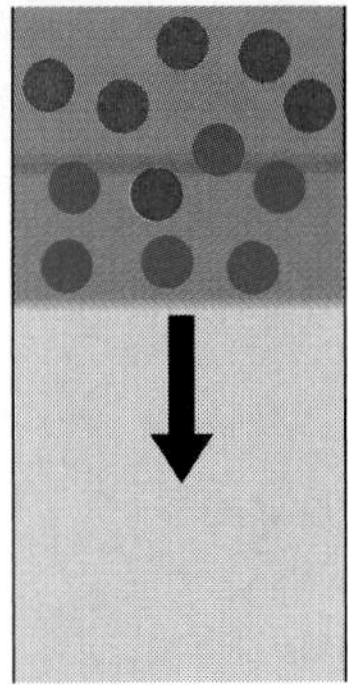

Partial separation

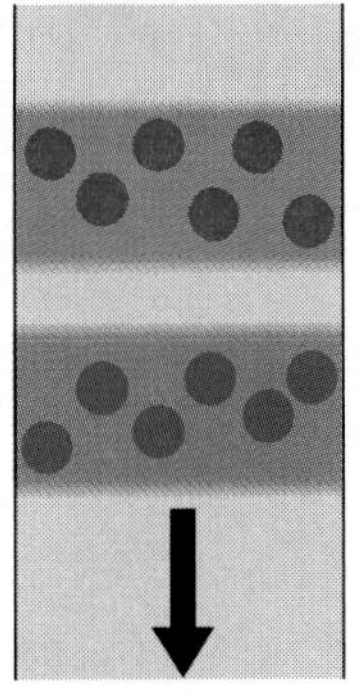

Complete separation

FIGURE 10-51
Diagrammatic view of how column chromatography works. Solute molecules that bind strongly to the stationary phase *(red circles)* move down the column more slowly than those that bind only weakly *(blue circles)*. For clarity, solvent molecules and the detailed structure of the stationary phase are not shown.

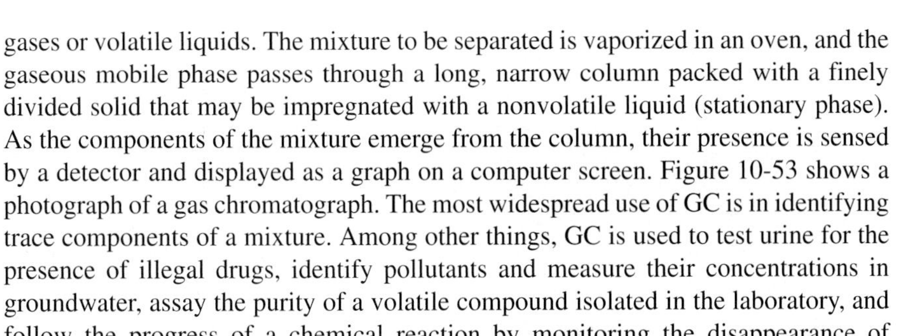

gases or volatile liquids. The mixture to be separated is vaporized in an oven, and the gaseous mobile phase passes through a long, narrow column packed with a finely divided solid that may be impregnated with a nonvolatile liquid (stationary phase). As the components of the mixture emerge from the column, their presence is sensed by a detector and displayed as a graph on a computer screen. Figure 10-53 shows a photograph of a gas chromatograph. The most widespread use of GC is in identifying trace components of a mixture. Among other things, GC is used to test urine for the presence of illegal drugs, identify pollutants and measure their concentrations in groundwater, assay the purity of a volatile compound isolated in the laboratory, and follow the progress of a chemical reaction by monitoring the disappearance of starting materials or the appearance of products.

Liquid chromatography (LC) uses a liquid mobile phase that passes down the stationary phase of a finely divided solid. An LC apparatus is shown in Figure 10-54. This technique is widely used to purify chemical substances on a multigram scale.

In thin-layer chromatography (TLC) a minute amount of a mixture is placed as a small spot at the bottom of a plate coated with a thin layer of a solid stationary phase, usually SiO_2 or Al_2O_3. The plate is placed "spotted" end down in a chamber containing a small amount of a suitable liquid solvent that acts as the mobile phase. Capillary action carries the solvent and the mixture up the plate, and the dissolved

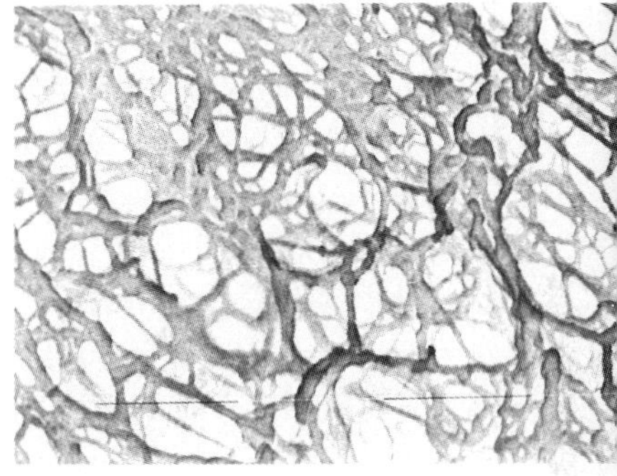

FIGURE 10-52
Chromatographic columns that separate substances according to molecular sizes have stationary phases made up of many tiny porous beads. This image was magnified 50,000 times.

FIGURE 10-53
A gas chromatograph separates a small sample of a mixture into its individual components. The printout shown here highlights the large number of compounds used to make perfume.

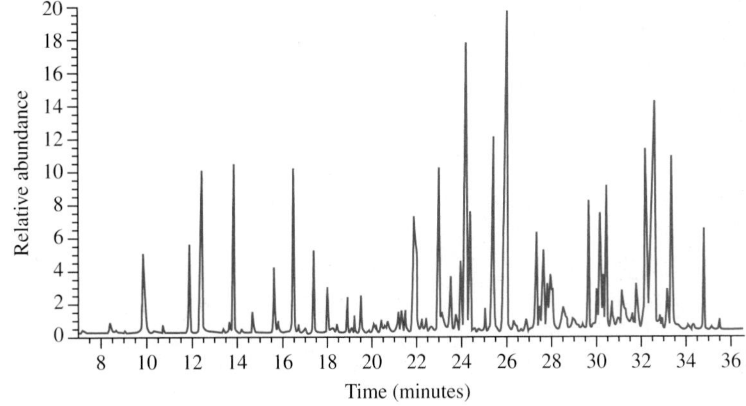

BOX 10-2

ION-EXCHANGE CHROMATOGRAPHY

The cations or anions in solutions of ionic compounds can be exchanged for other cations or anions by using the technique of **ion-exchange chromatography**. The stationary phases used in ion-exchange columns are large polymer molecules with charged functional groups. In an **anion-exchange column** the polymer is linked covalently to a positively charged group. Negative counter-ions are loosely associated with the polymer through ion-ion attractions. In a **cation-exchange column** the polymer contains covalently bound substituents with a negative charge, and the positive counter-ions are loosely associated through ion-ion attractions.

Before an ion exchange column can be used, the stationary phase must first be *charged*. In the charging process a highly concentrated solution of a specific cation or anion is passed through the column. All the mobile ions associated with the resin are replaced by the specific cation or anion. For example, to charge a cation-exchange resin with sodium ions, the column is treated with concentrated aqueous sodium chloride. After the column is charged, an aqueous solution containing other cations (for example, calcium cations) can be passed through the column, and the column will attract these cations, releasing sodium ions to enter the solution. Cations have exchanged places between solution and polymer, hence the term **ion exchange.**

As this description suggests, ion-exchange chromatography does not *remove* ions from a solution. Instead, it *replaces* them with other ions. Nonetheless, this method is used widely in the water treatment industry to soften and deionize water.

"Hard" water has high concentrations of divalent Mg^{2+} and Ca^{2+} cations. We explained earlier that the large molecules that make up soaps contain negatively charged groups that form precipitates with these divalent metal cations. The sodium salts of soaps, on the other hand, do not precipitate from solution. The function of a water softener is to exchange the "hard" Ca^{2+} and Mg^{2+} cations for the "soft" Na^+ cation. Thus even though soft water is no more pure than hard water, it dissolves soaps better. This makes soft water a better medium than hard water for household and industrial cleaning.

Deionization, shown below, removes ions from solution. An aqueous salt solution passes in sequence through a cation-exchange column charged with hydronium ions and an anion-exchange column charged with hydroxide ions. In the first column H_3O^+ replaces metal cations in the solution. In the second column OH^- replaces the anions present in the original salt solution. Hydroxide ions and hydronium ions immediately combine to give water:

$$H_3O^+_{(aq)} + OH^-_{(aq)} \rightarrow 2\,H_2O_{(l)}$$

Although ion exchange is a cost-effective way to produce ion-free water for laboratory and home use, it cannot be applied economically to the desalinization of seawater. After a short period of use, the columns become depleted of H_3O^+ and OH^- ions and must be recharged by passing aqueous HCl through the cation exchanger and aqueous NaOH through the anion exchanger. Because seawater is much higher in total ion content than fresh water, the cost of the chemicals for recharging quickly becomes prohibitive.

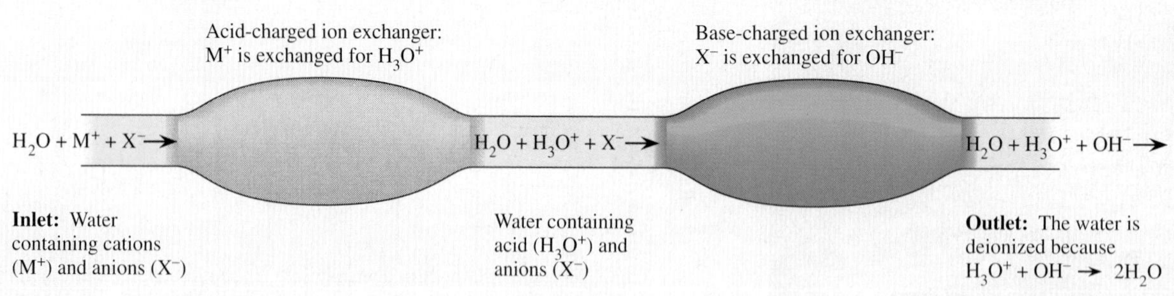

solutes spread out according to their polarity. The plate is removed from the chamber when the solvent nears the top. The plate dries as the solvent evaporates, leaving the nonvolatile components of the mixture as spots located at different positions on the plate. The TLC in Figure 10-55 shows that common blue ink is a mixture of several different colored compounds. TLC is often used to monitor the progress of chemical reactions. It is also used to determine the optimum separation conditions for larger-scale chromatographic techniques such as LC. Box 10-2 explains another chromatographic technique, ion-exchange chromatography.

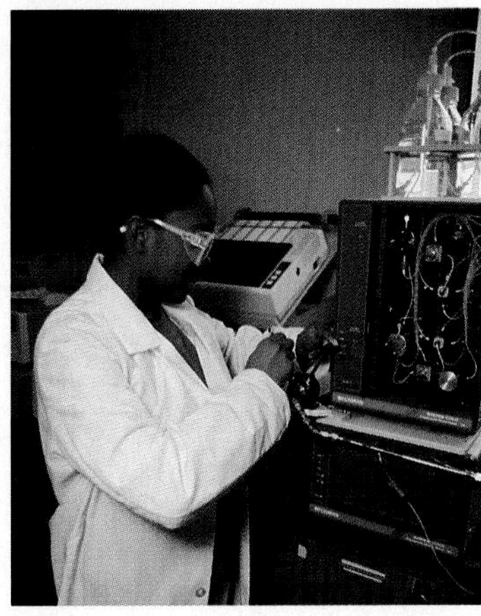

FIGURE 10-54
A liquid chromatograph involves the same principles as GC but on a larger scale.

SECTION EXERCISES

Explain in molecular terms the following features of purification techniques.

10.8.1 When a precipitate forms too quickly, it is likely to be less pure than if it is allowed to crystallize slowly from the same solution.

10.8.2 Distillation of an organic liquid that contains a volatile impurity always gives a distilled liquid that still contains some of the impurity.

10.8.3 If your home water softener runs out of salt, your water soon feels hard again.

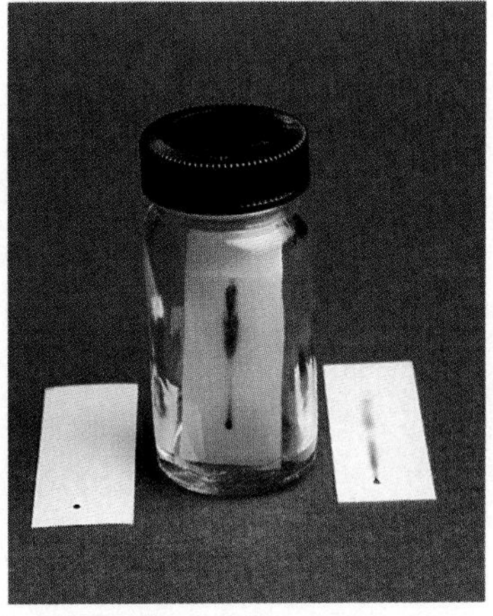

FIGURE 10-55
In thin-layer chromatography a solvent moves along a plate by capillary action, carrying different components with it at different rates. The photograph shows the separation of a blue ink into its component pigments.

CHAPTER SUMMARY

1. Attractive forces between molecules cause most substances to be liquids or solids under normal conditions, as well as leading to nonideal behavior of gases at high pressure and low temperature. These forces include dispersion forces, dipole-dipole interactions, and hydrogen bonding.
2. Hydrogen bonds, which are particularly important in aqueous environments, involve partial sharing of electrons between a fluorine, oxygen, or nitrogen atom and a hydrogen atom in a highly polar bond.
3. The molecules in liquids cohere but move freely. Liquid properties include surface tension, capillary action, and viscosity. Solids, on the other hand, are held in fixed structures by ionic, metallic, covalent, or intermolecular interactions.
4. Amorphous solids lack a regular structure, but any crystalline solid is composed of a repeating pattern whose smallest complete part is a unit cell. The simplest of these repeat patterns, adopted by many atomic and metallic solids, are hexagonal close-packed, face-centered cubic, and body-centered cubic structures.
5. A solution is a homogeneous mixture of varying amounts of solutes contained in a solvent. Substances that are subject to similar intermolecular forces tend to dissolve in each other, leading to the generalization, like dissolves like.
6. Gaseous solutions have unrestricted composition ranges, but most liquid solutions have an upper limit on the amount of solute they can hold. The solubility of a gas in a liquid depends not only on the natures of solvent and solute, but also on the partial pressure of solute in the gas phase.
7. Surfactants, which are molecules that contain water-compatible and water-incompatible structures, form monolayers, micelles, and vesicles in aqueous media.
8. Solutes depress the freezing point, raise the boiling point, and generate an osmotic pressure of a solution. The magnitudes of these colligative properties are concentration-dependent.
9. Transfers between phases form the basis for separation and purification techniques, including recrystallization, distillation, and chromatography.

KEY TERMS

adhesive forces
cohesive forces
dipolar forces
dispersion forces
hydrogen bond
intermolecular forces
intramolecular forces
polarizability

capillary action
surface tension
viscosity

amorphous
body-centered cubic structure
close-packed structure
crystalline
cubic close-packed structure
hexagonal close-packed structure
unit cell

alloy
amalgam
Henry's law
miscible
saturated solution
solubility
solute
solution
solvent

bilayer
hydrophilic
hydrophobic
micelle
monolayer
surfactant
vesicle

boiling point elevation constant
freezing point depression constant
normal boiling point (bp)
normal freezing point (fp)
osmosis
osmotic pressure (Π)
semipermeable membrane

chromatography
distillation
ion exchange

SKILLS TO MASTER

- Explaining variations in boiling points
- Identifying hydrogen bonds
- Describing surface tension, capillary action, and viscosity
- Recognizing types of solids
- Depicting simple crystal types
- Predicting solubility patterns
- Calculating gas solubilities
- Describing surfactant properties
- Calculating colligative properties
- Drawing molecular pictures of solutions
- Describing separation techniques

LEARNING EXERCISES

10.1 Write a chapter summary of two pages or less that summarizes the important ideas and concepts presented in this chapter.

10.2 List all the types of interactions that can act to hold a solid together. Organize the list from strongest to weakest.

10.3 Draw molecular pictures that show every type of hydrogen bond that exists in a solution containing methanol, water, and ammonia.

10.4 Write a paragraph that describes the factors that make glycerol highly viscous and explains why its viscosity falls as temperature rises.

10.5 Define and give an example of each of the following: (a) close-packed structure; (b) unit cell; (c) molecular solid; (d) covalent solid; (e) amorphous solid; and (f) surfactant.

10.6 Update your list of memory-bank equations. Be sure to mention how the equations in this chapter are used.

10.7 Write a paragraph that describes the types of substances that form monolayers, micelles, and vesicles in water. Explain the differences among these structures.

10.8 Describe how each of the following separation processes works: recrystallization, distillation, and chromatography.

10.9 Prepare a list of the terms in Chapter 10 that are new to you. Write a one-sentence definition for each, using your own words. If you need help, consult the glossary.

PROBLEMS

THE NATURE OF INTERMOLECULAR FORCES

10.1 Methane condenses at 121 K, but carbon tetrachloride boils at 350 K. Sketch an energy-distance plot similar to that of Figure 10-3 that shows the behavior of both of these substances.

10.2 Draw pictures showing the atomic arrangements in samples of $Ag_{(s)}$, $Ar_{(g)}$, and $Hg_{(l)}$.

10.3 Predict whether intermolecular attractions become more or less significant when the following changes are imposed:

(a) A gas is expanded to a larger volume at constant temperature.

(b) More gas is forced into the same volume at constant temperature.

(c) The temperature of the gas is lowered at constant volume.

10.4 Predict whether molecular volume becomes more or less significant when each of the changes in Problem 10.3 is imposed.

10.5 From the following experimental data, calculate the percent deviation from ideal behavior for each gas:

(a) 1.00 mol CO_2 in a 1.20-L container at 40.0 °C exerts 19.7 atm pressure.

(b) 3.00 g H_2 at 0.00 °C and 200 atm occupies a volume of 189.18 cm^3.

10.6 Arrange the following in order of increasing boiling point: Ar, He, Ne, and Xe. Explain your ranking.

10.7 Arrange the following in order of ease of liquefaction: CCl_4, CH_4, and CF_4. Explain your ranking.

10.8 Benzene (C_6H_6), naphthalene ($C_{10}H_8$), and anthracene ($C_{14}H_{10}$) are three ring compounds with similar molecular structures. One is a liquid, another is a relatively volatile solid, and the third is a less volatile solid. Which is which? Explain your assignments.

Benzene
C_6H_6

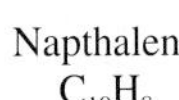

Napthalene
$C_{10}H_8$

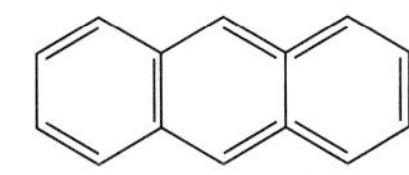

Anthracene
$C_{14}H_{10}$

10.9 Which of the following ions have the stronger interaction with water molecules in an aqueous solution? Explain your choices. (a) Na^+ or Mg^{2+}; (b) Na^+ or K^+; and (c) SO_4^{2-} or SO_3^{2-}.

HYDROGEN BONDING

10.10 Draw Lewis structures that show the hydrogen bonding interactions for each of the following: (a) two NH_3 molecules; (b) two CH_3OH molecules; and (c) an HF molecule and an acetone molecule [$(CH_3)_2C{=}O$].

10.11 List ethanol (C_2H_5OH), propane (C_3H_8), and *n*-pentane (C_5H_{12}) in order of increasing boiling point, and explain what features determine this order.

10.12 How many hydrogen bonds can be formed by one glycerol molecule ($HOCH_2CHOHCH_2OH$)? Draw Lewis structures that show the hydrogen bonding of a glycerol molecule dissolved in water.

10.13 Which of the following will hydrogen bond? (a) CH_2Cl_2; (b) H_2SO_4; (c) H_3COCH_3; and (d) $H_2NCH_2CO_2H$.

PROPERTIES OF LIQUIDS

10.14 Given that a lubricant must flow easily to perform its function, which grade of motor oil is preferred for winter use: high or low viscosity? Why?

10.15 Pentane is a C_5 hydrocarbon, gasoline contains mostly C_8 hydrocarbons, and fuel oil contains hydrocarbons in the C_{12} range. List these three hydrocarbons in order of increasing viscosity, and explain what molecular feature accounts for the variation.

10.16 Water in a glass tube takes on a concave shape, whereas mercury in a glass tube takes on a convex shape. Explain why the two liquids display different shapes.

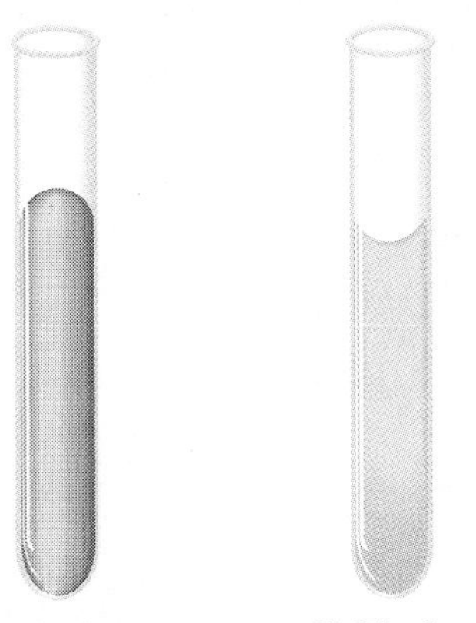

Hg in glass H_2O in glass

10.17 To make a good solder joint, the liquid metal solder must adhere well to the metal surfaces being joined. "Flux" is used to clean the metal surfaces. What types of substances must flux remove?

10.18 A pipet is considered to be "dirty" when water forms beads on its walls rather than forming a thin film that drains well. Which of the following on the surface of a pipet wall will make it dirty? In each case, explain the intermolecular forces underlying your classification. (a) grease; (b) Mg^{2+} ions; (c) acetone; and (d) SiO_2.

PROPERTIES OF SOLIDS

10.19 Classify each of the following as ionic, covalent, molecular, or metallic solids: Sn, S_8, Se, SiO_2, and Na_2SO_4.

10.20 Amorphous silica has a density of around 2.3 g/cm^3, whereas crystalline quartz has a density of 2.65 g/cm^3. Why do these two forms of the same substance have different densities?

10.21 Construct part of the Lewis structure of carborundum, the diamondlike compound of empirical formula SiC.

10.22 The unit cell of a compound of xenon and fluorine follows. What is the formula of the compound?

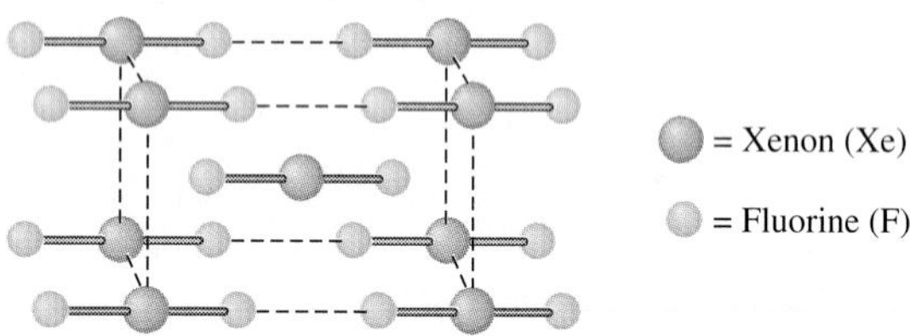

10.23 Recently, a new group of solids was prepared that can act as superconductors at temperatures near the boiling point of liquid nitrogen. (A superconductor is a material whose electrical resistance is zero.) The unit cell of one of these new superconductors is shown here. Identify the formula of the compound.

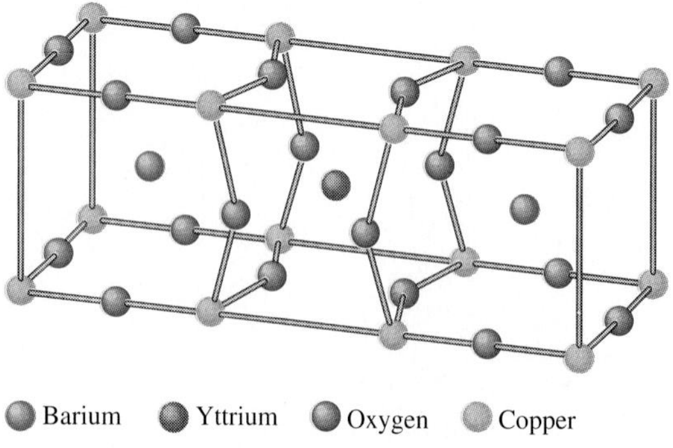

10.24 Draw the unit cell of the NaCl crystal and determine the number of nearest neighbors of opposite charge for each ion in these unit cells.

THE NATURE OF SOLUTIONS

10.25 Do you expect gasoline to dissolve in water? Knowing that gasoline is less dense than water, would you use water to fight a gasoline fire? Explain.

10.26 Acetone, $(CH_3)_2CO$, is miscible with both water and cyclohexane (C_6H_{12}), but water and cyclohexane are nearly insoluble in each other. Explain.

10.27 Ammonia can be condensed to a liquid at low temperature. What kinds of solids would you expect to be soluble in liquid ammonia?

10.28 One of the detrimental effects of the "thermal pollution" of water supplies is that a rise in temperature reduces the amount of dissolved oxygen available for fish. Using the information in Table 10-2, calculate the number of liters of water a fish requires at 30 °C to obtain the same amount of oxygen that it could obtain from 1 L of water at 25 °C.

10.29 Using the information in Table 10-2, calculate the number of grams of CO_2 that can be dissolved in 250 mL of a carbonated beverage at 1.10 atm pressure and 25 °C.

10.30 If a bottle of the carbonated beverage in Problem 10.29 is stored in an ice chest at 0 °C, what is the partial pressure of CO_2 in the gas space above the liquid?

DUAL-NATURE MOLECULES: SURFACTANTS AND BIOLOGICAL MEMBRANES

10.31 Dichlorodiphenyltrichloroethane (DDT) has the following structure:

Is this compound hydrophilic or hydrophobic? Is it readily excreted by animals, or will it concentrate in fatty tissues? Does your answer explain why DDT has been banned as a pesticide?

10.32 Of the following compounds, which will be the best and which will be the worst surfactant? Support your choices with molecular pictures. (a) propionic acid, $H_3CCH_2CO_2H$; (b) lauryl alcohol, $H_3C(CH_2)_{11}OH$; and (c) sodium lauryl sulfate $H_3C(CH_2)_{11}OSO_3^-Na^+$.

10.33 Some surfactants form membranes that span small holes between two aqueous solutions. These membranes are liquid bilayers two molecules thick. Draw a molecular picture of one of these membranes.

10.34 Stearic acid forms a monolayer on the surface of gasoline. Draw a molecular picture that shows how stearic acid molecules are arranged in this monolayer.

PROPERTIES OF AQUEOUS SOLUTIONS

10.35 Compute the freezing point of a wine that is 12% ethanol by mass. (Ignore all other solutes.)

10.36 Do you have enough information to calculate the boiling point of the wine in Problem 10.35? If so, calculate it. If not, explain what feature of wine prevents you from doing this calculation.

10.37 An aqueous solution contains 1.00 g/L of a derivative of the detergent lauryl alcohol. The osmotic pressure of this solution at 25 °C is 17.8 torr.
(a) What is the molar mass of the detergent?
(b) The hydrocarbon portion of the molecule is an 11-carbon chain. What is the molar mass of the polar portion?

10.38 Calculate the boiling point of a solution that contains 2.50 g NaCl in 155 mL of water.

SEPARATION PROCESSES

10.39 Describe how you would purify diethyl ether, $(C_2H_5)_2O$, which is contaminated with a small amount of water.

10.40 You have prepared a new, highly colored solid compound and want to determine whether your product is pure or contains several components. What technique would provide this information most conveniently? Describe how the technique works.

10.41 The solubility of $HgCl_2$ in water is 380 g/L at 100 °C and 30 g/L at 0 °C. What is the minimum volume of water needed to recrystallize a crude sample of this compound whose mass is 250 g? What fraction of the crude sample will be recovered? (For calculation purposes, assume that the crude sample is 95% $HgCl_2$ and that the impurity is more soluble than $HgCl_2$.)

10.42 You have prepared a sample of polymer and have performed liquid chromatography using molecular sieves to determine its molecular size. The chromatogram follows:

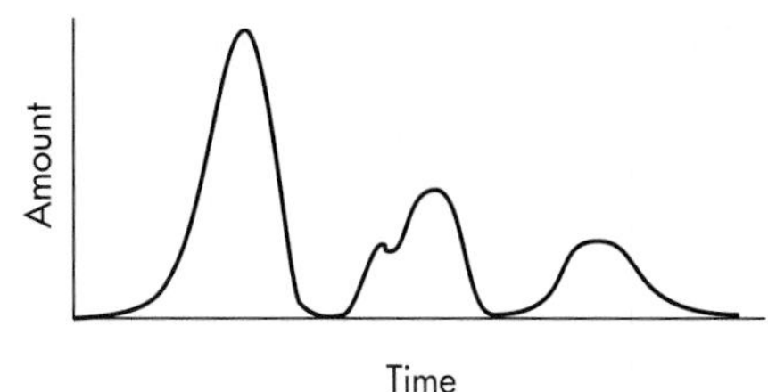

(a) How many components does your sample contain?
(b) Is there a larger amount of long-, medium-, or short-chain polymer molecules in the sample? Explain.

10.43 A sample for gas chromatography contains the following compounds:

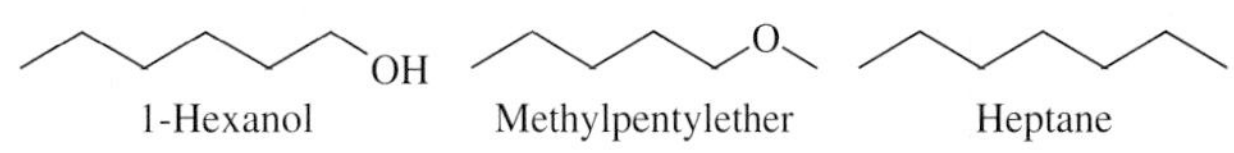

If the GC column separates molecules according to their polarity, in what order will the compounds come off the column? Explain.

ADDITIONAL PROBLEMS

10.44 Will water, ethanol, or acetone rise the highest in a glass capillary tube? Which will rise the least? Explain why in terms of intermolecular forces.

10.45 An aqueous solution containing 1.00 g of a sugar in 100 mL of solution has an osmotic pressure of 1.36 atm at 25 °C. What is the molar mass of this sugar?

10.46 Classify each of the following solids as covalent, metallic, ionic, or molecular: (a) a solid that conducts electricity; (b) a solid that does not conduct electricity but dissolves in water to give a conducting solution; and (c) a solid that does not conduct electricity and melts below 100 °C to give a nonconducting liquid.

10.47 Rank the following substances in order of increasing solubility in water, and state the reasons for your rankings: C_6H_6 (benzene), $HOCH_2CH(OH)CH(OH)CH_2OH$ (erythritol), and $C_5H_{11}OH$ (pentanol).

10.48 What mole fraction of ethanol is required to protect the water in an automobile cooling system from freezing at −20 °C?

10.49 Aqueous solutions of 0.5 M acetic acid and 0.5 M $MgSO_4$ each have freezing points higher than the freezing point of 1 M glucose but lower than the freezing point of 0.5 M glucose. Explain these observations.

10.50 The osmotic pressure of a 0.10 M solution of H_3PO_4 at 300 K is 3.03 atm. What is the *total* molarity of the solutes under these conditions? On the basis of this result, would you call H_3PO_4 a strong acid?

10.51 The solubility of NaCl is 26 g/100 mL at 0 °C and 28 g/100 mL at 100 °C. Is it practical to purify NaCl by recrystallization from water? Explain your answer.

10.52 Why is the boiling point of H_2S lower than the boiling point of H_2O? Why is it also lower than the boiling point of H_2Te?

10.53 List the following liquids in order of increasing viscosity at room temperature, and explain the order of your list: (a) butanol, C_4H_9OH; (b) pentane, C_5H_{12}; and (c) propane-1,3-diol, $HOCH_2CH_2CH_2OH$.

10.54 Rank the following substances in order of increasing solubility in cyclohexane (C_6H_{12}) and explain the order of your list: KCl, C_2H_5OH, and C_3H_8.

10.55 Approximately what value of *total* solute molarity would you expect to find for 0.1 M aqueous solutions of each of the following: (a) citric acid (a weak organic acid); (b) $FeCl_3$; (c) NaOH; and (d) $(NH_4)_2CO_3$.

10.56 Brackish water, with a salt content around 0.5% by mass, is found in semiarid regions such as the American Southwest. Assuming that brackish water contains only sodium chloride, estimate the osmotic pressure of brackish water.

10.57 The freezing point of 0.050 M $KHSO_3$ is −0.19 °C. Which of the following equations best represents what happens when this compound dissolves in water? Explain your choice.

(a) $KHSO_{3\,(s)} \rightarrow KHSO_{3\,(aq)}$
(b) $KHSO_{3\,(s)} \rightarrow K^+{}_{(aq)} + HSO_3^-{}_{(aq)}$
(c) $KHSO_{3\,(s)} + H_2O \rightarrow K^+{}_{(aq)} + H_3O^+{}_{(aq)} + SO_3^{2-}{}_{(aq)}$

10.58 Butylated hydroxytoluene (BHT) is used as a food preservative. It has the following molecular structure:

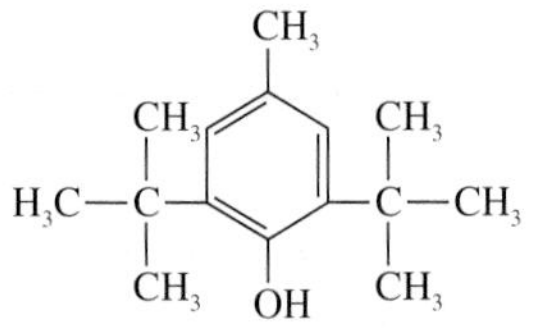

Would you expect to find this compound in urine or stored in body fat? BHT is nontoxic to humans.

10.59 Water and carbon tetrachloride are not miscible. When mixed, they form two layers, like water and oil. If an aqueous solution of I_2 is shaken with CCl_4, the iodine is "extracted" into the CCl_4 layer. Explain this behavior on the basis of your knowledge of intermolecular forces.

10.60 Some chemists interpret the boiling point of HCl as evidence for hydrogen bonding in this compound. How does the location of HCl on the graph in Figure 10-16 suggest that it may form hydrogen bonds? Draw a molecular picture that shows the possible hydrogen bonds between HCl molecules.

10.61 List the following aqueous solutions in order of increasing osmotic pressure, and explain your rankings: (a) 3.0×10^{-3} M KBr; (b) 3.0×10^{-3} M glucose; and (c) 4.0×10^{-3} M glucose.

10.62 Identify two elements that form molecular crystals, two that form metallic crystals, and two that form covalent crystals. Identify regions of the periodic table where elements of these three kinds are located.

10.63 One of the earliest methods of preserving fish was by salting. Explain what happens when fish is placed in a strong salt solution.

10.64 Would water dissolve salts as well as it does if it had a linear structure (such as CO_2) instead of a bent one? Explain.

10.65 List all the intermolecular forces that stabilize the liquid phase of each of the following compounds: (a) NH_3; (b) Xe; (c) SF_4; (d) CF_4; and (e) CH_3CO_2H (acetic acid).

10.66 Fish have blood that is isotonic with seawater, which freezes at −2.30 °C. What is the osmotic pressure of fish blood at 15 °C?

10.67 Homemade ice cream is frozen by churning it in a bucket suspended in an ice-water-salt mixture. A typical mix calls for 1.1 kg of rock salt (NaCl) and 7.25 kg of ice. Compute the mole fraction of NaCl in this mixture after all the ice melts, and estimate its freezing point.

10.68 Compute the molar mass of vitamin C if a solution containing 22.0 g in 100 g of water freezes at −2.33 °C.

10.69 For each of the following pairs, identify which has the higher boiling point, and identify the type of force that is responsible: (a) CH_3OCH_3 and CH_3OH; (b) SO_2 and SiO_2; (c) HF and HCl; and (d) Br_2 and I_2.

10.70 When an aqueous solution is cooled to a low temperature, part of the water freezes as pure ice. What happens to the freezing point of the remaining solution when this occurs? A glass of wine placed in a freezer at −10 °C for a very long time forms some ice crystals but does not completely freeze. Compute the mole fraction of ethanol in the remaining liquid phase.

10.71 Molecular hydrogen and atomic helium have two electrons, but He boils at 4.2 K, whereas H_2 boils at 20 K. Neon boils at 27.1 K, whereas methane, which has the same number of electrons, boils at 114 K. Explain why molecular substances boil at a higher temperature than atomic substances with the same number of electrons.

10.72 Arrange the following liquids in order of increasing viscosity, and state the factors that determine the ranking: 1-butanol, $CH_3CH_2CH_2CH_2OH$; *n*-pentane, $CH_3CH_2CH_2CH_2CH_3$; 2,2-dimethylpropane, $(CH_3)_4C$; and propane-1,3-diol, $HOCH_2CH_2CH_2OH$.

10.73 The structures and boiling points of *n*-pentane and 2,2-dimethylpropane follow:

Pentane	2,2-Dimethylpropane
C_5H_{12}	C_5H_{12}
bp = 36 °C	bp = −10 °C

Use the boiling point data and molecular drawings to explain how shape affects the magnitude of dispersion forces. (See Figures 10-10 and 10-11.)

10.74 Describe the similarities and the differences between hexagonal close-packed and body-centered cubic structures.

10.75 The thin-layer chromatograph of black ink follows. Rank the colored dyes in the ink from most polar to least polar.

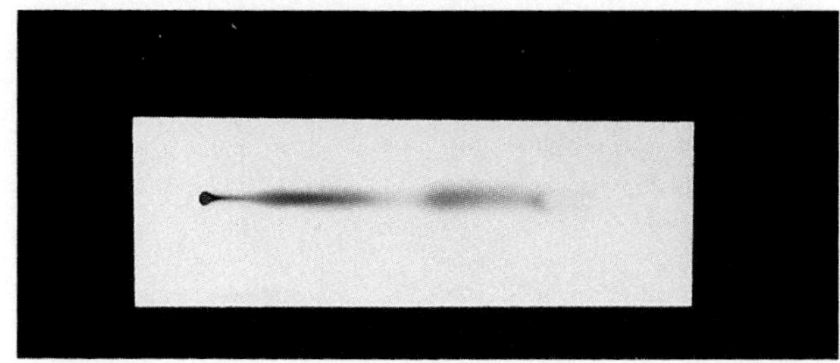

10.76 Quartz and glass are forms of silicon dioxide. A piece of quartz breaks into a collection of smaller regular crystals with smooth faces. A piece of glass breaks into irregular shards. Use molecular structures to explain why the two solids break so differently.

10.77 For each of the following pairs of gases, which one will deviate more from ideal *PV/nRT* behavior: (a) F_2 and Cl_2; and (b) CH_4 and SnH_4.

10.78 Drinking too much seawater can be dangerous because seawater is more concentrated than a person's body fluids. Discuss the consequences of drinking too much seawater from the cellular perspective and at the molecular level.

10.79 The unit cell of the mineral perscovite follows. What is the formula of perscovite?

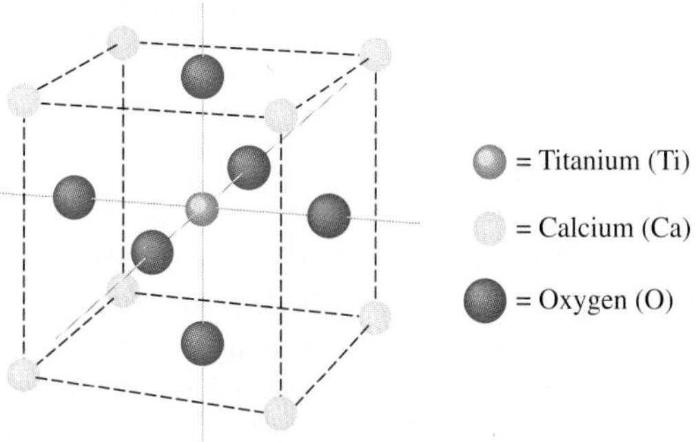

10.80 Why do the two isomers shown have very different melting points?

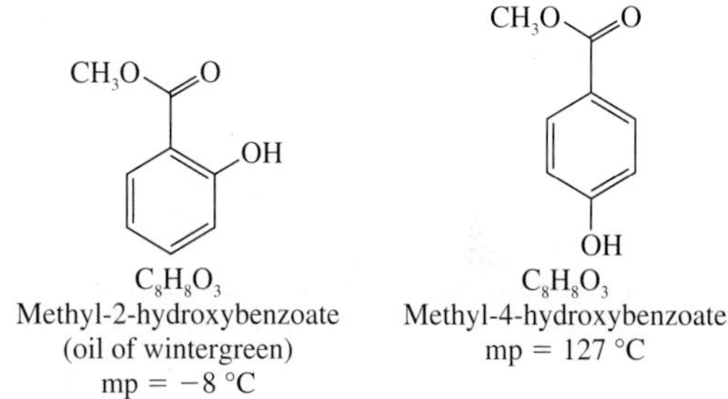

10.81 There are two geometric isomers of 1,2-dichloroethylene (ClCHCHCl). One isomer boils at 47 °C, the other at 60 °C. Draw Lewis structures of the two isomers. Use dipole moments and symmetry arguments to assign the boiling points to the isomers.

10.82 Which can form hydrogen bonds with water: (a) CH_4; (b) I_2; (c) HF; (d) $CH_3—O—CH_3$; and (e) $(CH_3)_3COH$.

10.83 List all of the different kinds of forces that must be overcome to convert each of the following from a liquid to a gas: (a) NH_3; (b) $CHCl_3$; (c) CCl_4; and (d) CO_2.

10.84 Indicate what type of crystal (ionic, covalent, metallic, or molecular/atomic) each forms on solidification: (a) HCl; (b) KCl; (c) NH_4NO_3; (d) Mn; and (e) Si.

ANSWERS TO SECTION EXERCISES

10.1.1 At_2 is a solid. Its curve looks like the Br_2-Br_2 curve in Figure 10-3 but with an even deeper well at a somewhat larger intermolecular distance.

10.1.2 Intermolecular forces cause pV/nRT to be smaller than 1.0. Fluorine reaches the smallest value, so it has the largest intermolecular forces. Helium never dips below 1.0, indicating very small intermolecular forces.

10.1.3 (a) Propane has larger polarizability because its electrons are spread over a larger volume than those in krypton; (b) CCl_4 has a larger polarizability because it has more electrons than $C(CH_3)_4$; and (c) CO has a dipole moment, generating dipole-dipole attractions that are not present in N_2.

10.2.1 The higher boiling compound is CH_3OH because of hydrogen bonding. See the drawing of hydrogen bonding in Sample Problem 10-3.

10.2.2 Acetone has dispersion forces and dipole-dipole forces. Methanol has dispersion forces, dipole-dipole forces, and hydrogen bonding forces. Their boiling points are similar because the dipolar and dispersion forces in acetone are larger than the analogous forces in methanol, counterbalancing the hydrogen bonding in methanol.

10.2.3

O—H---N: H_3N:---H—O(H):

O—H---F: H—F:---H—O:—H

F—H---F: H—F:---H—F:

F—H---N: :F:—H---:NH_3

F—H---O: :F:—H---:OH_2

N—H---F: :NH_2—H---:F:—H

N—H---N: :NH_2—H---:NH_3

N—H---O: :NH_2—H---:OH_2

H—O:—H---:OH_2

10.3.1 There are strong attractive forces between water molecules and clean glass and weak attractive forces between water molecules and dirty glass.

10.3.2 Polyethylene straw: Weak adhesive forces

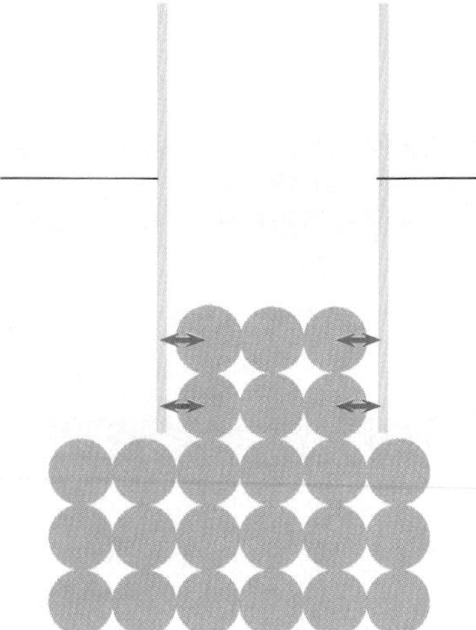

Cohesive forces (between H_2O molecules) are stronger than adhesive forces (between H_2O and polyethylene)

10.3.3 Octadecane molecules are long and thin, like strands of spaghetti. They get tangled in one another.

10.4.1 All these are examples of molecular solids. All have only dispersion forces holding the molecules in the solid array.

10.4.2 All angles in a hexagonal crystal are multiples of 60 degrees, so we expect angles of 60 degrees, 120 degrees, and so on. A cubic close-packed crystal also has right angles, so we expect 90-degree angles as well.

10.4.3

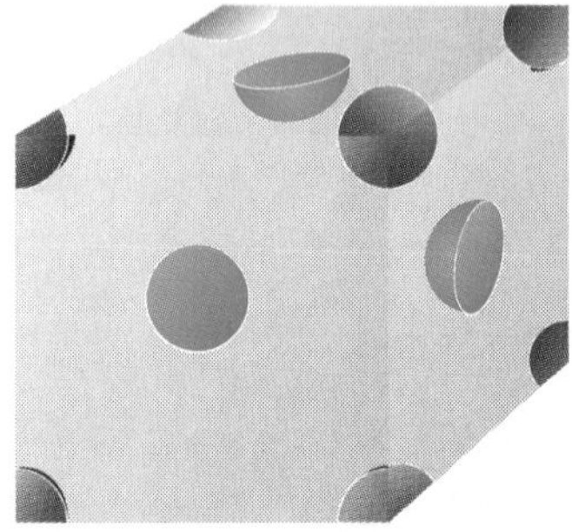

An eighth of each corner atom and half of each face atom is in the unit cell.

10.5.1 Intermolecular interactions are dispersion, dipole-dipole, and hydrogen bonding.

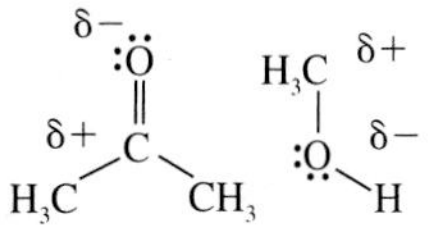

Dipole-dipole

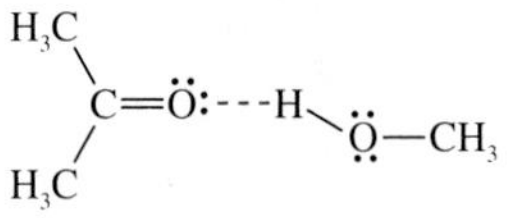

Hydrogen bonding

10.5.2 The fraction that dissolves is 8.3×10^{-3}.

10.5.3 Only Na_2SiO_3, which is an ionic solid, is water soluble.

10.6.1

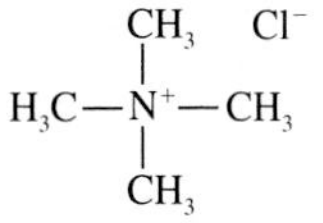

All hydrophilic (ions)

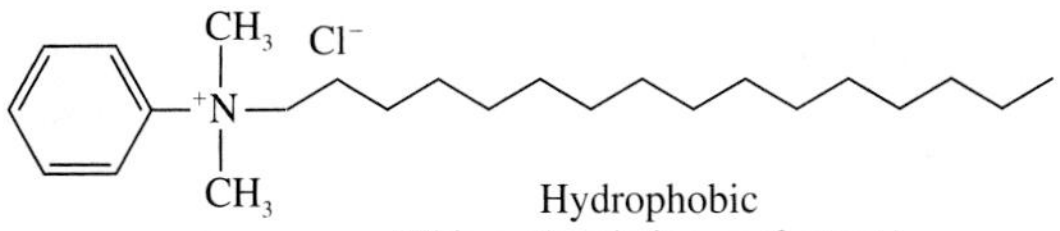

Hydrophilic

Hydrophobic
(This molecule is a surfactant.)

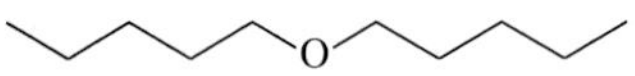

All hydrophobic

10.6.2 Large, water-soluble molecules are hydrophilic and large. Because they are large, they cannot slip easily between the molecules of a lipid bilayer membrane. Because they are hydrophilic, they do not dissolve in the bilayer.

10.7.1 Freezing point depression = 1.44×10^{-3} °C; boiling point elevation = 3.96×10^{-4} °C; and osmotic pressure = 1.87×10^{-2} atm = 14.2 torr

10.7.2 The figure should look the same, except there should be more arrows moving from right to left than from left to right.

10.7.3 Your description should include the features shown in your figure for 10.7.2 and the prevention of ion passage through the pores of the semipermeable membrane.

10.8.1 During rapid precipitation, the solid may trap some molecules of impurities.

10.8.2 During distillation, molecules of all volatile substances vaporize, so volatile impurities vaporize and recondense with the distilled substance.

10.8.3 When all the sodium ions in the ion exchange column have been exchanged, the "hard" ions in the water that passes through the water softner are no longer replaced with "soft" sodium ions.

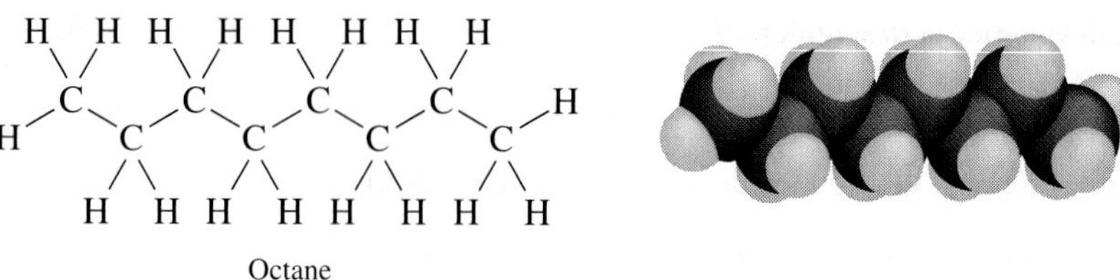

Octane

FIGURE 11-1
Alkanes are the simplest molecules with repeat units. Polyethylene is an alkane polymer with 500 or more repeating CH_2 units.

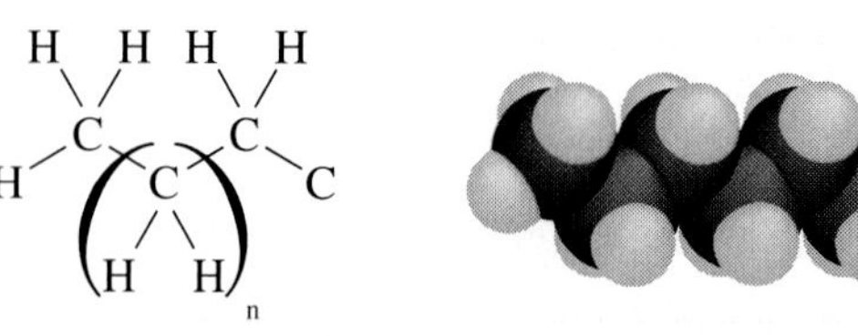

n = 6 Octane
n = 48 Pentacontane
n > 500 Polyethylene

polyethylene with thousands of atoms would be very time consuming and tedious. Fortunately, we can show the entire structure of a polyethylene molecule just by specifying its repeat unit, as shown in Figure 11-1.

SYNTHESIS OF POLYETHYLENE

Polymers do not just happen; they must be manufactured. Polymer synthesis starts with **monomers,** which are the molecular building blocks that create the repeat structure of the macromolecule. Polyethylene is made by polymerizing ethylene, C_2H_4. Remember from Chapter 9 that ethylene has a C=C bond made up of one σ bond plus one π bond. The reactivity patterns of ethylene are dominated by the chemistry of its π electrons because the electrons in the π bond are not as stable as the σ electrons. Thus the π electrons are responsible for the polymerization of ethylene.

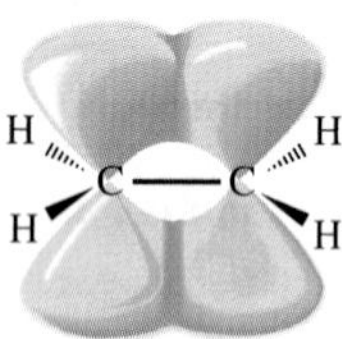

Ethylene does not polymerize spontaneously. Although π bonds are available for chemical reactions, they are stable enough not to break without some appropriate stimulus. That stimulus comes from a chemical substance called an **initiator.** After π bond breakage has been initiated, the polymerization reaction continues in a sequence of **propagation** steps. Each propagation step lengthens the growing polymer chain by adding on one monomer unit. Eventually, a third type of reaction **terminates** the synthesis. Initiation, propagation, and termination are important steps in the synthesis of many polymers.

The average O—O σ bond energy is only 145 kJ/mol, so single bonds between oxygen atoms are among the easiest covalent bonds to break. Molecules with O—O bonds are peroxides.

The polymerization of ethylene starts with the thermal decomposition of an initiator molecule into two fragments. Benzoyl peroxide is a common initiator that decomposes into two fragments containing oxygen atoms with single unpaired electrons:

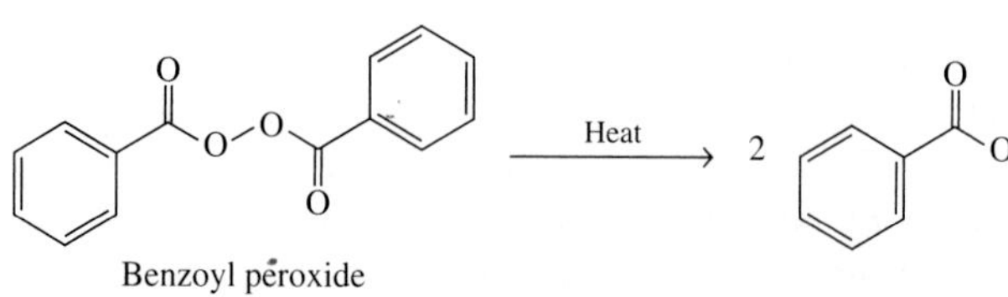

Molecules that have unpaired electrons are highly reactive and are called **free radicals.** A free radical produced in the decomposition of benzoyl peroxide attacks the π bond of an ethylene molecule:

$$C_6H_5C(=O)O\cdot + H_2C{=}CH_2 \longrightarrow C_6H_5C(=O)O{-}CH_2{-}\dot{C}H_2$$

In this reaction, one π electron of the ethylene molecule pairs up with the single electron on the oxygen atom of the free radical. Together, these two electrons create a new C—O σ bond. The second electron from the ethylene π bond ends up as an unpaired electron on the outermost carbon atom of the product.

The carbon atom with the unpaired electron is highly reactive, so now the stage is set for propagation. The carbon atom attacks the π bond of another molecule of ethylene, making a new C—C σ bond and leaving another carbon atom with an unpaired electron:

$$C_6H_5C(=O)O{-}CH_2{-}\dot{C}H_2 + H_2C{=}CH_2 \longrightarrow C_6H_5C(=O)O{-}CH_2{-}CH_2{-}CH_2{-}\dot{C}H_2$$

This addition reaction can be repeated over and over again in the propagation process, and each step adds two CH_2 groups to the growing polymer chain. The propagation can be written in the following general form:

In this representation of polyethylene the repeat unit is considered to be (CH_2CH_2), the monomer from which the polymer is constructed, rather than (CH_2), the simplest possible repeat unit.

$$C_6H_5C(=O)O{-}(CH_2{-}CH_2)_n{-}CH_2{-}\dot{C}H_2 + C_2H_4 \longrightarrow C_6H_5C(=O)O{-}(CH_2{-}CH_2)_{n+1}{-}CH_2{-}\dot{C}H_2$$

The chain does not grow indefinitely, because when two free radicals collide, they react in a way that terminates the polymerization. For example, another initiator fragment can react with the carbon atom at the end of the chain:

$$C_6H_5C(=O)O{-}(CH_2{-}CH_2)_n{-}CH_2{-}\dot{C}H_2 + \cdot O{-}C(=O)C_6H_5 \longrightarrow C_6H_5C(=O)O{-}(CH_2{-}CH_2)_{n+1}{-}O{-}C(=O)C_6H_5$$

Because chain growth involves free radicals, this type of polymerization is called **free radical polymerization.**

The product of the last reaction may not look like polyethylene, but remember that *n* is a large number, around 500 or more. Thus the benzoyl ends of the macromolecule are insignificant compared to the many —CH_2— repeat units that make up the bulk of the polymer.

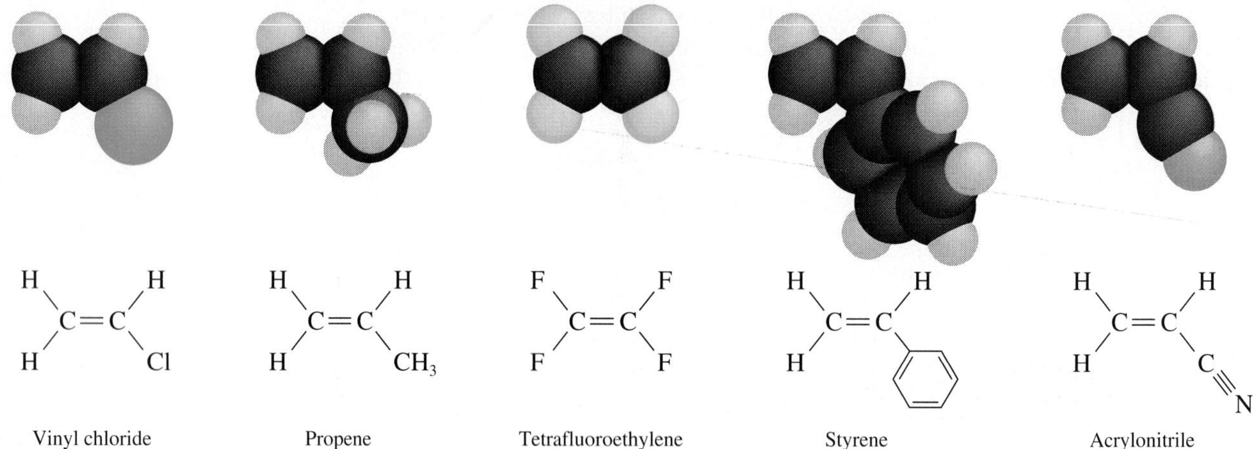

FIGURE 11-2
Structures of alkene monomers used in the manufacture of important polymers.

TABLE 11-1 IMPORTANT POLYMERS MADE FROM ALKENES

MONOMER	POLYMER	USES	PRODUCTION (10^9 kg)*
Ethylene	Polyethylene	Piping, bottles, toys	9.9
Vinyl chloride	Polyvinylchloride (PVC)	Piping, floor tile, clothing	4.5
Propene	Polypropylene	Carpets, labware, toys	3.8
Styrene	Polystyrene (Styrofoam)	Containers, heat insulators	2.3
Acrylonitrile	Polyacrylonitrile (PAN)	Carpets, knitware	0.2
Tetrafluoroethylene	Teflon (PTFE)	Cookware, bearings, electrical insulators	<0.05

*1992 figures.

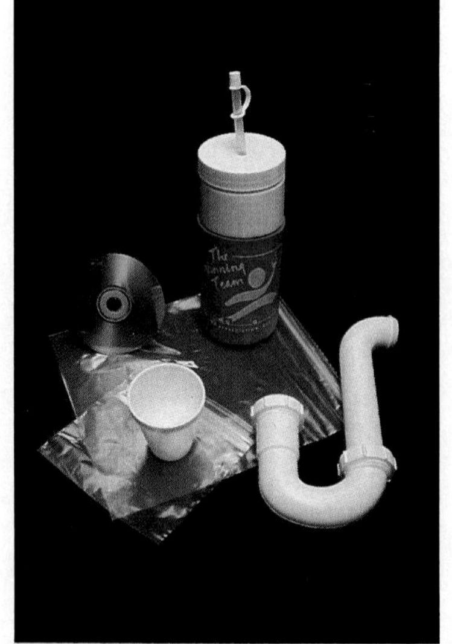

Polyalkenes created in the laboratory are used to make many of the items that we use in our everyday lives.

OTHER POLYALKENES

Polyethylene is only one of many plastics generated from alkenes. A variety of different polymers can be made by using derivatives of ethylene in which one or more of the hydrogen atoms is replaced with other atoms or combinations of atoms. These variations in the structure of the monomer make it possible to "tune" the properties of the polymer. Table 11-1 lists several important alkene monomers and their corresponding polymers. You may recognize some of their common names. Figure 11-2 shows the molecular structures of these monomers. Notice the variety of groups that can replace hydrogen atoms: CH_3, Cl, F, CN, and C_6H_5. Sample Problem 11-1 shows how to write the structure of a polyethylene derivative.

SAMPLE PROBLEM 11-1 DRAWING THE STRUCTURE OF A POLYMER

Polyacrylonitrile, known commercially as *Orlon,* is used to make fibers for carpeting and clothing. Draw the Lewis structure of polyacrylonitrile, showing at least three repeat units.

METHOD: Polyalkenes form by linking together carbon atoms in a free radical polymerization. We construct the polymer structure by connecting monomer units. The structure of the monomer, acrylonitrile, is shown in Figure 11-2:

```
H     H
 \   /
  C=C
 /   \
H     C
       \\\
        N:
```

Acrylonitrile polymerizes in the same way as ethylene. A free radical initiator attacks the π electrons of the C=C bond. The chain grows through propagation steps until a termination reaction occurs. As with polyethylene, propagation creates a long chain of C—C σ bonds. In polyacrylonitrile the CN groups "dangle" from the chain. Here is the structure, showing three repeat units:

```
  H H     H H     H H
   \ /     \ /     \ /
 [-C       C       C      ]
    \    /   \    /  \    /
     C          C       C
    / \        / \     / \
   H   C      H   C   H   C
       |||        |||     |||
       N:         N:      N:
```

Notice that this polymer has the same structure as polyethylene, with the exception that a CN group is attached to every second carbon atom. A line structure of polyacrylonitrile eliminates the "clutter" caused by the hydrogen atoms. A space-filling model of the same polymer segment is included for comparison.

See Section 3.1 for a review of line structures.

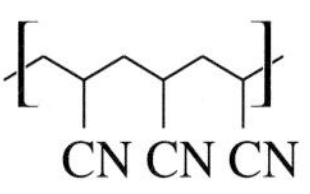

RUBBER

The first alkene-type polymer to be used in society was polyisoprene, a natural product extracted from the sap of rubber trees, as shown in Figure 11-3. The monomer from which this polymer is constructed is isoprene, an alkene with *two* double bonds. The line structure of isoprene and the repeat unit of polyisoprene are shown in Figure 11-4. When isoprene polymerizes, attack on one π bond causes the second π bond to shift, giving a macromolecule containing a four-carbon repeat

One of the first uses of natural rubber was for erasers, called *rubbers* by the British. Eventually, this name came to mean any substance made of polymerized dienes.

FIGURE 11-3
Natural rubber is produced from the milky white sap of trees found in tropical rain forests. The sap, called *latex,* is a suspension of polyisoprene particles in water.

Butadiene Isoprene Polyisoprene (natural rubber)

FIGURE 11-4
The structures of isoprene and butadiene, two dienes that form rubberlike polymers. The repeat unit of natural rubber is also shown.

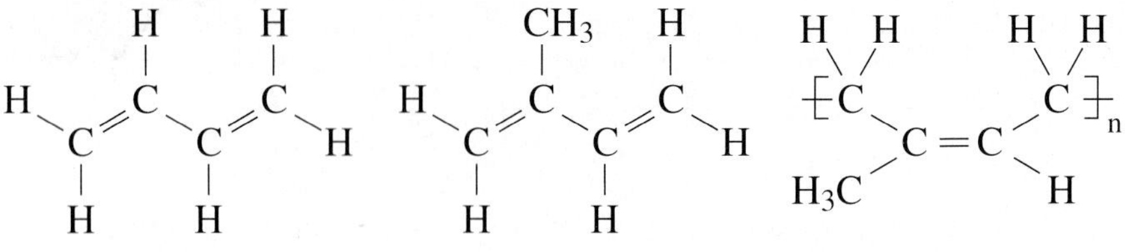

Polyisoprene

FIGURE 11-5
The line structure of a portion of the butadiene-styrene copolymer prepared from a 3 : 1 ratio of monomers. The incorporation of styrene and butadiene into the polymer is completely random, but the probabilities are determined by the monomer ratio. There is a 75% probability of adding a butadiene unit and a 25% probability of adding a styrene unit.

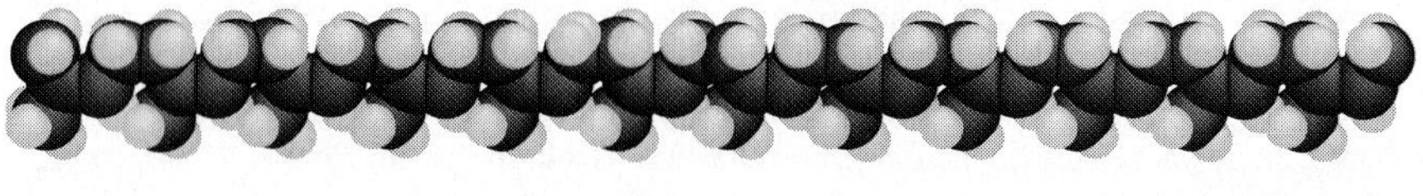

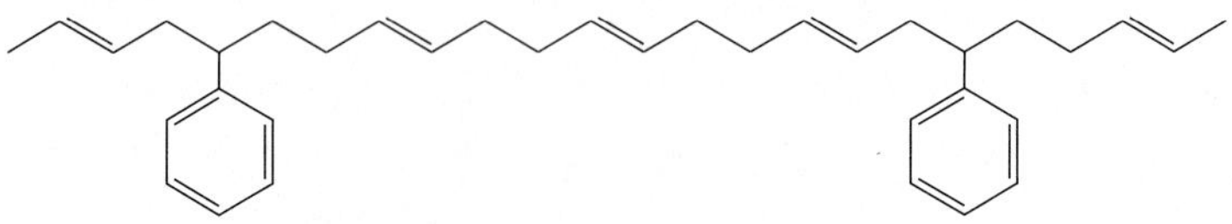

The bonding of butadiene was discussed in Section 9.4.

unit with a double bond in its center. Butadiene, whose structure is also shown in Figure 11-4, polymerizes in the same fashion as isoprene to give a synthetic rubber.

Natural rubber and polybutadiene together account for just over half of the 2.7×10^9 kg of rubber produced in the United States each year. The rest are **copolymers,** made by polymerizing mixtures of two different monomers. The largest production, accounting for 10^9 kg of total rubber production, is a mixed polymer of butadiene and styrene. A ratio of butadiene to styrene of about 3:1 gives optimum polymer properties. During polymerization of butadiene and styrene the chain grows by adding whichever monomer happens to collide with the chain end. The propagation process is therefore random, but the resulting polymer contains three butadiene units for every styrene unit. Figure 11-5 shows the line structure of a representative portion of such a polymer, but the exact sequence cannot be specified. At any point in the chain, there is a 75% probability of finding a butadiene unit and a 25% probability of finding a styrene unit.

The long-chain molecules that we have described so far are used for flexible items such as rubber bands, but they do not convey the durability and strength that we associate with rubber products such as automobile tires. To achieve these properties, rubber must be treated chemically to create chemical bonds between long-chain molecules. This process is called **cross-linking** because links are formed *across* the chains in addition to bonds *along* the chains. Vulcanization, the formation of cross-links in rubber, was discovered by Charles Goodyear, founder of the first U.S. rubber company, in 1839. Box 11-1 discusses the history of the rubber industry.

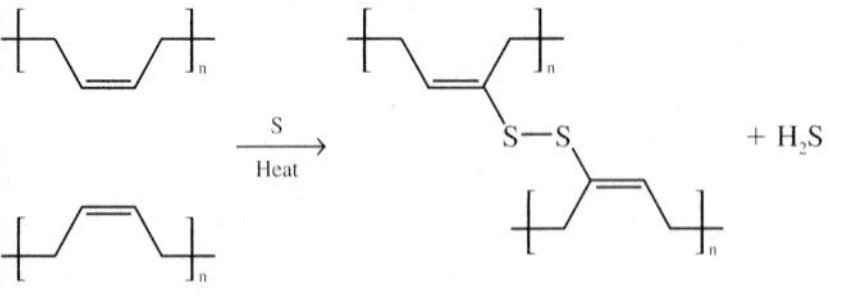

FIGURE 11-6
Schematic view of the vulcanization of polybutadiene. When heated in the presence of sulfur, rubber forms cross-links between polymer chains. A few of the C—H bonds are replaced by C—S bonds, and S—S bonds form the cross-link.

Vulcanization is a complicated chemical process, and the details are still not fully understood. However, the starting materials and end product are well characterized. Figure 11-6 shows the overall scheme as it is applied to polybutadiene. Sulfur is added to the polymer, and the mixture is heated under controlled conditions. Some of the polymer C—H bonds break and are replaced by C—S bonds. The cross-links consist of C—(S_n)—C chains, with n being two or more. Vulcanization increases the tensile strength of rubber by a factor of 10, but it also increases its rigidity. Above about 10% by mass sulfur content, vulcanized rubber becomes hard and brittle. Thus the amount of cross-linking must be controlled to optimize tensile strength.

Sulfur cross-links also play an important role in determining the structures of proteins, as is discussed in Section 11.5.

BOX 11-1

THE NATURAL RUBBER INDUSTRY

The rubber industry has a long and colorful history. Natural rubber is produced from latex, a milky fluid found in cells that lie between the bark and the wood of many plants. You may have seen latex flow from the broken stalks of milkweed plants, but the source of commercial rubber is the Hevea tree, a native of Brazil. Before Columbus came to the new world, the indigenous people of the Amazon jungle made bouncing balls, shoes, and water jars out of rubber. Later, Portuguese explorers sent waterproof boots and a rubber-coated coat back to their king. The first commercial exports included a few hundred pairs of rubber shoes shipped to Boston in 1823.

Commercial growth of the rubber industry started slowly. Entrepreneurs in Europe and the United States experimented with rubber hats, coats, erasers, life preservers, and a number of other products. However, through the first half of the nineteenth century, rubber items were more novel than practical because natural rubber becomes sticky in hot weather and brittle in cold weather. In 1830 the world consumed just 156 tons of rubber, all of it from Brazil. Nine years later, Charles Goodyear discovered vulcanization, and rubber quickly became an essential part of the world economy.

Goodyear's discovery set off a rubber boom that rivaled the famous California gold rush. Adventurers swarmed to the steamy jungles to amass huge fortunes as the price of rubber soared. The Amazon people were captured and forced to work at harvesting the precious latex fluid. Many of them died under the harsh and unfamiliar conditions. New towns sprang to life along the river as paddle-wheel steamers carried all manner of luxury goods to rubber barons, who built grand mansions up the tributaries of the Amazon. The pinnacle of the rubber boom was the town of Manaus, which is located a thousand miles up the Amazon system on the Negro river. At the height of the boom, Manaus teemed with mansions, cafes, and fine hotels. It had a streetcar system and even an enormous ornate opera house.

For all its wealth and glory, the Amazon rubber industry collapsed almost overnight. In 1876 an English botanist named Henry Wickham shipped 70,000 Hevea seeds to the Royal Botanic Gardens in London. New strains of Hevea were developed that produced 3 to 4 times as much rubber and were much more disease-resistant that their wild Amazonian cousins. Soon, seedlings were sent to Malaya, Sumatra, Java, and other islands of the East Indies. Thirty-five years later, rubber plantations like the one in the figure took control of the industry.

In 1910 the price of rubber was $2.88 a pound, world production was 94,000 tons, and wild rubber from Brazil accounted for 83,000 tons. In 1912 the price collapsed, and by 1932 a pound of rubber cost 2.5¢. In 1937 the world bought more than 1.1 million tons of rubber, less than 2% of which came from Brazil. The rubber cities of the Amazon became near ghost towns as the wild rubber market vanished. The opulent opera house in Manaus had barely opened its doors when the curtain came down on the Brazilian rubber economy.

The rubber industry changed again when the Japanese captured the East Indian rubber plantations during World War II. The resulting shortage of rubber prompted an intensive research program to produce synthetic rubber. Today, more than 2 million tons of various synthetic rubbers are produced each year in the United States. Natural rubber is still produced in tropical regions, but its importance pales in comparison to the glory days of the Malaysian rubber plantations.

THE CARBONYL GROUP

The carbon-oxygen double bond, generally referred to as *carbonyl,* is one of the most important groups in organic chemistry. The C=O linkage occurs in several functional groups. **Aldehydes, ketones,** and **carboxylic acids** are organic compounds of the following forms:

The O atom in the C=O linkage has two nonbonding pairs of valence electrons, but chemists frequently omit them from drawings of molecular structures.

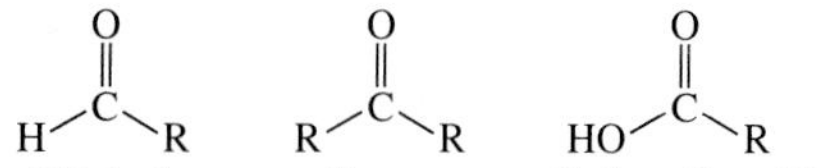

$$\underset{\text{Aldehyde}}{\text{H}-\overset{\overset{\text{O}}{\|}}{\text{C}}-\text{R}} \qquad \underset{\text{Ketone}}{\text{R}-\overset{\overset{\text{O}}{\|}}{\text{C}}-\text{R}} \qquad \underset{\text{Carboxylic acid}}{\text{HO}-\overset{\overset{\text{O}}{\|}}{\text{C}}-\text{R}}$$

The R groups in these structures can be almost any organic fragment as long as the atom bonded directly to the carbonyl is a carbon. It can be as simple as a methyl group (CH_3) or a phenyl ring (C_6H_5), or it can represent an organic fragment composed of dozens of atoms. The symbol R is used extensively in organic chemistry to represent any unspecified organic group.

The chemistry of aldehydes and ketones is dominated by the polarity of the carbonyl group. The difference in electronegativity (EN) between carbon and oxygen polarizes the double bond, creating a partial positive charge on the carbon and a partial negative charge on the oxygen.

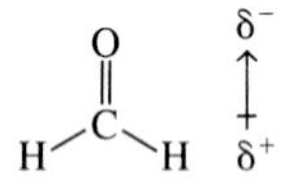

$$\underset{\text{Formaldehyde}}{\text{H}-\overset{\overset{\text{O}}{\|}}{\text{C}}-\text{H}} \quad \delta^- \uparrow \delta^+ \qquad \text{EN}_\text{O} = 3.5 \quad \text{EN}_\text{C} = 2.5$$

Aldehydes are more important than ketones in polymerization reactions, but both groups are important in all aspects of chemistry. The simplest aldehyde, formaldehyde, is a top 50 industrial chemical that plays a major role in polymer synthesis.

Carboxylic acids, which can be represented as RCO_2H, appear again and again in organic chemistry and biochemistry. A carboxylic acid is highly polar and can give up a hydrogen cation to form a carboxylate anion, RCO_2^-. The carboxyl group also readily forms hydrogen bonds. These properties enhance the solubility of carboxylic acids in water, a property particularly important for biochemical macromolecules. Like aldehydes and ketones, carboxylic acids react in many different ways, but breakage of the C—OH bond is the only reaction that is important in polymer formation.

To summarize from the perspective of polymer formation, the most important role of functional groups in polymerization is to provide bonds that are relatively easy to break. Because C—H and C—C σ bonds are relatively strong and do not break easily, condensation polymerization requires monomers that contain two functional groups. To form polymers, bonds in these groups must break, and new bonds must form that link monomers together into macromolecules.

Functional groups that form during condensation reactions are referred to as **linkage groups.** The three linkage groups listed in Table 11-3 are particularly important in polymerization reactions.

ESTERS

An **ester** is an organic compound formed from the condensation reaction of a carboxylic acid and an alcohol. A water molecule is eliminated as the oxygen atom of the alcohol bonds to the carbon atom of the carbonyl group. For example, ethanol reacts with acetic acid to give ethyl acetate:

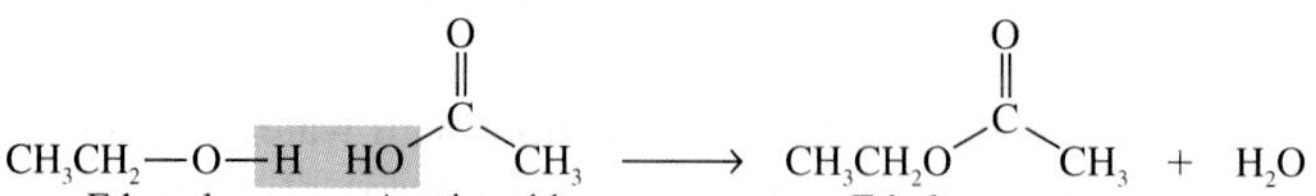

$$\underset{\substack{\text{Ethanol}\\ \text{(an alcohol)}}}{CH_3CH_2-O-H} \quad \underset{\substack{\text{Acetic acid}\\ \text{(a carboxylic acid)}}}{HO-\overset{\overset{O}{\|}}{C}-CH_3} \longrightarrow \underset{\substack{\text{Ethyl acetate}\\ \text{(an ester)}}}{CH_3CH_2O-\overset{\overset{O}{\|}}{C}-CH_3} + H_2O$$

TABLE 11-3 IMPORTANT POLYMER LINKAGE GROUPS

LINKAGE	NAME	PRECURSORS	POLYMER TYPE
C(=O)–O	Ester	Acid + alcohol	Polyesters
C(=O)–N(H)	Amide	Acid + amine	Polyamides, proteins
C—O—C	Ether	Alcohol + alcohol	Cellulose, starch

Many esters have pleasant smells and tastes and are important components of flavorings and fragrances. To name a few, isopentyl acetate gives bananas their characteristic odor, methyl salicylate has the fragrance of wintergreen, and ethyl butyrate occurs in pineapples.

$CH_3C(=O)OCH_2CH_2CH(CH_3)CH_3$

Isopentyl acetate

Methyl salicylate

$CH_3CH_2CH_2C(=O)OCH_2CH_3$

Ethyl butyrate

AMIDES

Carboxylic acids react with amines to form amides. Water is eliminated as the new N—C bond forms:

$C_6H_5CO_2H$ (a carboxylic acid) + $H_2NC_2H_5$ (an amine) ⟶ (an amide) + H_2O

The amide linkage occurs in nature in proteins, biological macromolecules with amazing structural and functional diversity. In a protein, small molecules called **amino acids** are strung together through a series of condensation reactions that give amide linkages.

Proteins are discussed in Section 11.5.

ETHERS

The reaction of two alcohol molecules to eliminate water and form a C—O—C linkage is yet another condensation reaction. A molecule that contains a C—O—C linkage is called an **ether:**

C_3H_7OH (an alcohol) + C_3H_7OH (an alcohol) $\xrightarrow[\text{Heat}]{\text{Conc. } H_2SO_4}$ $(C_3H_7)_2O$ (an ether) + H_2O

This direct condensation of alcohols has limited utility because many alcohols undergo other reactions under the conditions required for condensation. The most important polymers containing ether linkages are starch and cellulose, which are biochemical macromolecules. Nature forges ether linkages in a more roundabout way than by directly eliminating water.

SECTION EXERCISES

11.2.1 Molecular pictures of several molecules follow. Identify the functional groups present in each of them. (Some contain more than one functional group.)

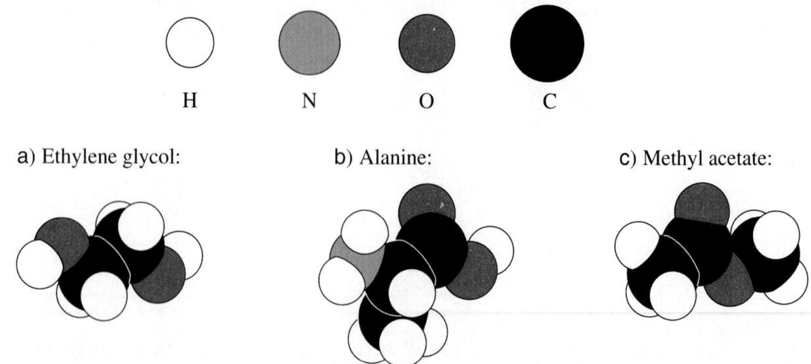

11.2.2 Amino acids are the molecular building blocks of proteins. Any two amino acids can condense in two ways; each creates an amide linkage. Draw the structures of the two condensation products that link these two amino acids:

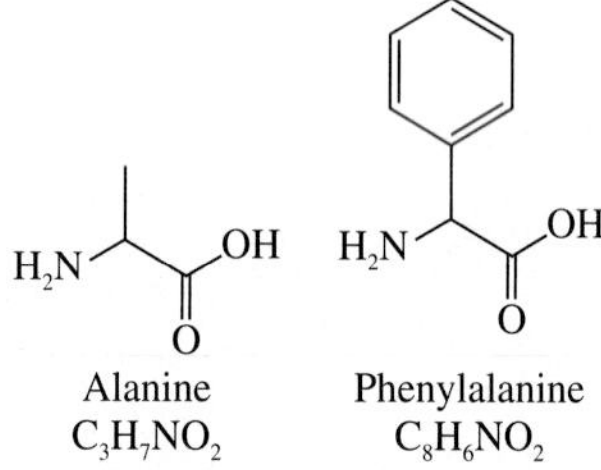

Alanine
$C_3H_7NO_2$

Phenylalanine
$C_8H_6NO_2$

11.2.3 Draw one complete specific structure for (a) an amine with the formula $C_6H_{15}N$; (b) an ester with at least seven carbon atoms; (c) an alcohol with a molar mass of 74 g/mol; and (d) a molecule with at least 10 carbons that contains an aldehyde and a phenyl group.

11.3 CONDENSATION POLYMERS

In a condensation reaction, two molecules link together by forging bonds between their functional groups. If no additional functional groups are present, that is as far as the linkage process goes. Polymer formation via condensation requires that each monomer contain *two* linkage-forming functional groups. After the two molecules link together, there are still two functional groups that can link to two more monomers, allowing the chain to grow into a polymer.

There are two arrangements of functional groups that make polymerization possible. In the first, a single compound contains two *different* functional groups capable of linking together. Amino acids belong to this category. As its name implies, an amino acid contains an amine and a carboxylic acid group. Amino acids join together through amide linkages:

H_2N–…–C(=O)OH + H_2N–…–C(=O)OH ⟶ H_2N–…–C(=O)–N(H)–…–C(=O)OH + H_2O

The product still has an amine group at one end and a carboxylic acid group at its other. As a result, each end can form another amide linkage, extending the chain.

Condensation polymers can also form from different monomers; each contains two of the *same* functional group. For example, a monomer with two carboxylic acid groups links to a monomer with two hydroxyl groups to give an ester:

The product is a bifunctional molecule with a carboxylic acid group at one end and a hydroxyl group at the other. Chain growth can continue through repeated condensation reactions at both ends of the molecule.

Most polymers in production today are made from two different monomers because experience has shown that this synthetic route offers advantages over the use of bifunctional monomers. First, monomers that contain two identical functional groups are easier and less expensive to produce than monomers with two different groups. Second, the properties of the polymer can be varied simply by changing the structure of one of the monomers. Finally, bifunctional monomers tend to link into cyclical structures rather than make the long chains needed for polymers.

POLYAMIDES

Any polymer that contains amide linkage groups is called a **polyamide.** Proteins, the biological macromolecules that contain this linkage, are described in Section 11.5. In this section, we focus on three commercially important polyamides: Nylon 66, Nylon 6, and Kevlar.

Nylon 66 was the first polyamide to be produced commercially. Developed by Wallace Carothers at the Du Pont Chemical Company in 1935, it still leads the

Both adipic acid and hexamethylenediamine have six carbons, hence the name *Nylon 66*.

Adipic acid

Hexamethylenediamine

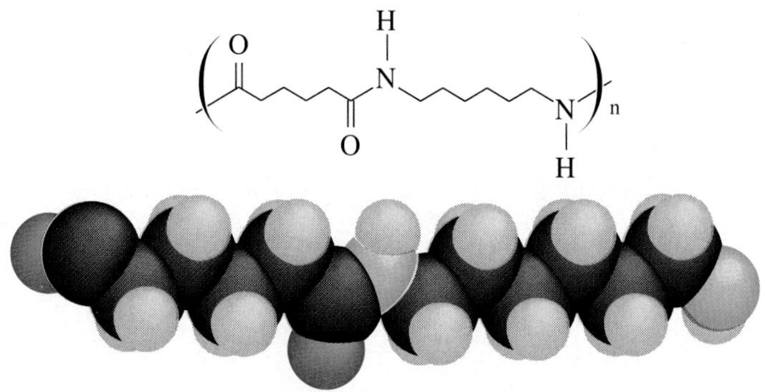

Nylon 66

FIGURE 11-8

The polymerization of adipic acid with hexamethylenediamine to form Nylon 66 is a condensation reaction in which carboxylic acid groups and amine groups combine to give amide linkages. Water molecules are eliminated in the process.

FIGURE 11-9
Nylon 66 can be drawn from a beaker containing the two starting materials. The bottom layer is an aqueous solution of hexamethylenediamine, and the top layer is adipoyl chloride (a more reactive derivative of adipic acid) dissolved in hexane. Nylon 66 forms at the interface between the two liquids.

polymer industry in annual production. Nylon 66 is made from adipic acid, a top 50 industrial chemical, and hexamethylenediamine. The line structures of Nylon 66 and its monomers appear in Figure 11-8. Nylon 66 is so easy to make that it is often used for a classroom demonstration, as shown in Figure 11-9.

Nylon 66 is the leading example of polyamides made by condensing a diacid with a diamine, but many other useful polymers can be made by using different diamines and diacids. Kevlar, for example, is a polyamide made by condensing terephthalic acid with phenylenediamine:

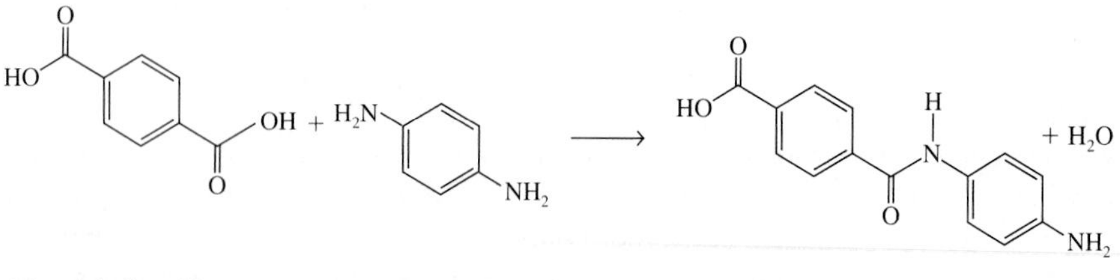

HO, O, OH + H_2N, NH_2 ⟶ HO, O, H, N, O, NH_2 + H_2O

Terephthalic acid Phenylenediamine

Figure 11-10 shows a portion of the structure of Kevlar, which is so strong it is used to make bulletproof vests.

The tremendous strength of Kevlar comes from a combination of intermolecular and intramolecular forces. Intramolecularly, the stiff phenyl rings make each polymer chain strong and rigid. Intermolecularly, the chains are held together by hydrogen bonds. Interchain hydrogen bonds enhance the strength and durability of all polyamides, but Kevlar has a particularly large number of hydrogen bonds per unit volume because of its compact, highly regular molecular structure.

Sample Problem 11-2 shows another example of a polyamide.

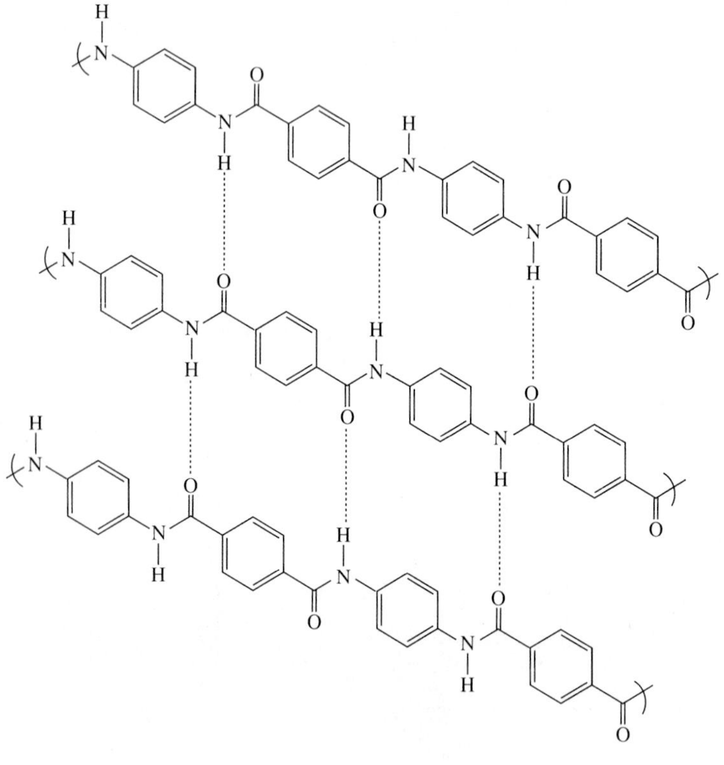

FIGURE 11-10
A portion of the structure of Kevlar, a nylon made from terephthalic acid and phenylenediamine. Pound for pound, this polymer is stronger than steel. The great strength of Kevlar is due to its phenyl rings and the high degree of hydrogen bonding between chains (*dotted lines*).

SAMPLE PROBLEM 11-2 THE STRUCTURE OF A POLYAMIDE

Qiana, a polyamide that feels much like silk, has the following structure:

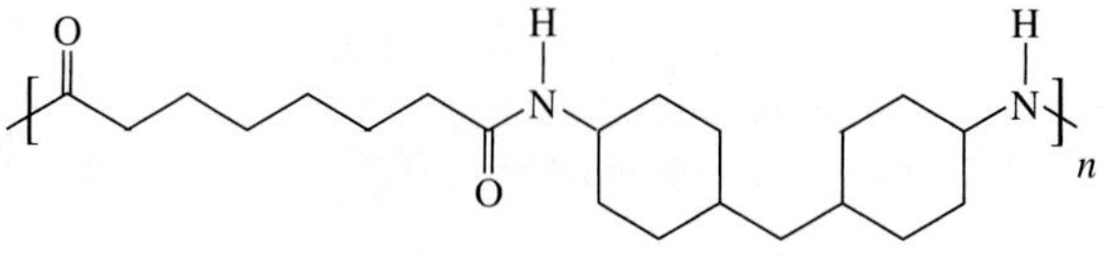

Identify the monomers used to make Qiana.

METHOD: A polyamide is made from the condensation reaction of a diamine and a dicarboxylic acid. To identify the monomers, we separate the amide linkage group and add water across the C—N bond:

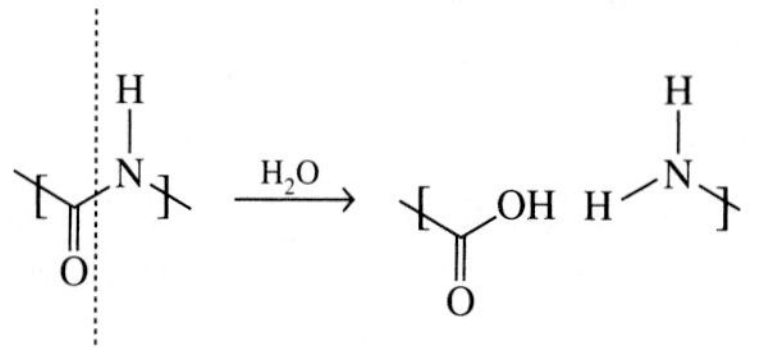

Now we can construct the monomers:

Not all polyamides are made from diamines and diacids. For example, the reaction scheme illustrated in Figure 11-11 shows that Nylon 6 is produced from caprolactam, a monomer that is derived from an amino acid. Caprolactam is a cyclic amide that easily converts into a linear amino acid. Under most conditions, nearly all of the molecules are in the cyclic form. However, when the caprolactam is heated in the presence of water, some of it converts to the amino acid. If the concentration of the amino acid is high enough, the monomer polymerizes.

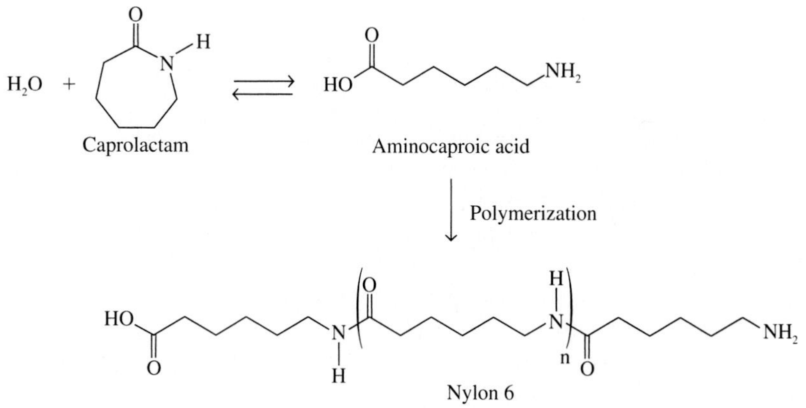

Caprolactam

Aminocaproic acid

Polymerization

Nylon 6

FIGURE 11-11
Caprolactam is a cyclic amide formed by intramolecular condensation of aminocaproic acid. When caprolactam is heated in water, the ring opens, and the amino acid polymerizes to form Nylon 6.

POLYESTERS

Nylon was the first commercial polymer to make a substantial impact on the textile industry, but **polyesters** now comprise the largest segment of the market for synthetic fibers. In fact, polyesters account for approximately 40% of the over 4 billion kg of synthetic fibers produced in the United States each year. The leading polyester, by far, is poly(ethylene terephthalate), or PET. This polymer is made from terephthalic acid and ethylene glycol in an acid-alcohol condensation reaction:

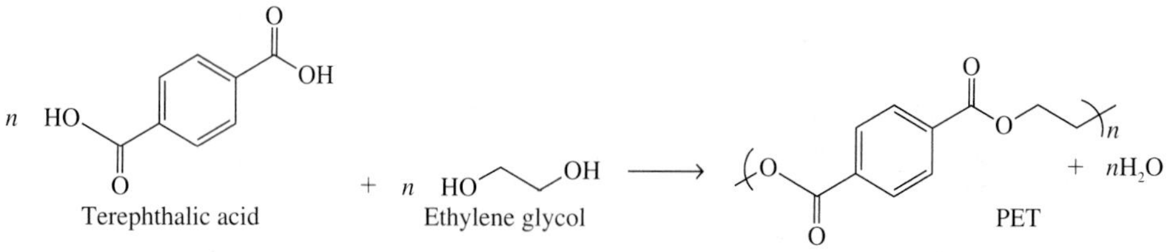

n Terephthalic acid + n Ethylene glycol ⟶ PET + $n H_2O$

A typical polyester molecule has 50 to 100 repeat units and a molar mass between 10,000 and 20,000 g/mol. PET can be formed into fibers (such as Dacron) or films (such as Mylar). Mylar films, which can be rolled into sheets 30 times thinner than a human hair, are used to make magnetic recording tape and packaging for frozen food. Dacron and other polyester fibers are best known for their use in clothing, but they also have many other applications. For example, tubes of Dacron are used as synthetic blood vessels in heart bypass operations because they are inert, nonallergenic, and noninflammatory. Over 2 billion kg of PET are produced in the United States each year. This polymer is used to make tire cord, beverage bottles, home furnishings, small appliances, and many other common items.

FORMALDEHYDE POLYMERS

Formaldehyde ($H_2C{=}O$) forms several condensation polymers; all are characterized by a high degree of cross-linking. Polymerizations that involve formaldehyde proceed by way of alcohol intermediates.

Bakelite, a copolymer of phenol and formaldehyde, was first synthesized by Leo Baekeland in 1907. In the first step, a molecule of formaldehyde adds to a molecule of phenol. A C—H bond and the C=O double bond break, and a C—C and O—H bond form, producing a phenolic alcohol:

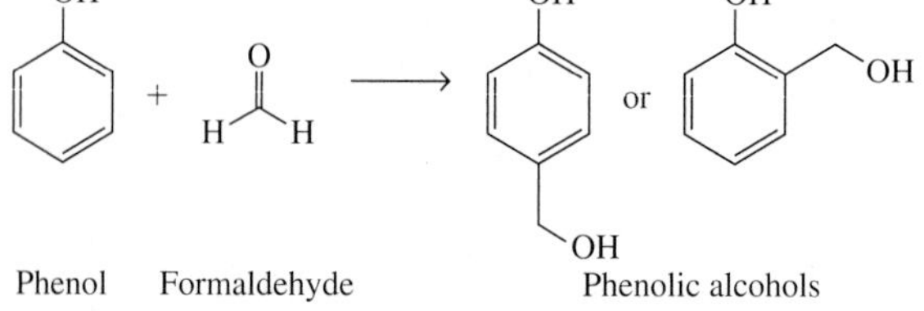

Phenol + Formaldehyde ⟶ Phenolic alcohols

Each of these products has hydrogen atoms attached to its ring that can condense with a hydroxyl group to eliminate water. Figure 11-12 provides a structural view of the process, which leads to a network of bonds in which every phenol molecule can form as many as three $—CH_2—$ links to its neighbors. The reaction occurs readily, as shown in Figure 11-13.

Because of its rigid phenyl rings and the high degree of cross-linking, Bakelite is a very strong and very stiff polymer that does not melt when heated. At the same time, it is very light. The polymer is molded into a variety of products, including distributor caps, radios, and buttons.

$+ \; 3\,H_2O$

FIGURE 11-12
A structural view of the synthesis of Bakelite. Each molecule of the phenolic alcohol, which forms from the addition of formaldehyde to phenol, is capable of forming three —CH_2— links to other molecules. The result is a highly cross-linked polymer.

FIGURE 11-13
Preparation of phenol-formaldehyde polymer.

Other condensation polymers form from the reactions of formaldehyde with amines. For example, polymers useful as binders and coatings are made from formaldehyde and urea. As with phenol, the first step is an addition reaction to give an alcohol:

Urea

When the concentration of formaldehyde is low, only one NH_2 group of urea reacts, but both groups react if the concentration of formaldehyde is high. Polymerization follows this first step because every N—H hydrogen can undergo a condensation reaction with a hydroxyl group to give a chain of alternating carbon and nitrogen atoms:

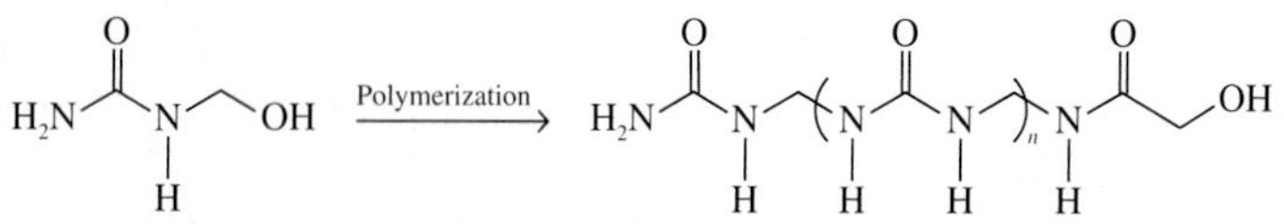

Urea and formaldehyde react in another fashion to form a strong, lightweight, and heat-resistant polymer. To prepare the polymer, urea is first condensed to give melamine, a cyclic compound:

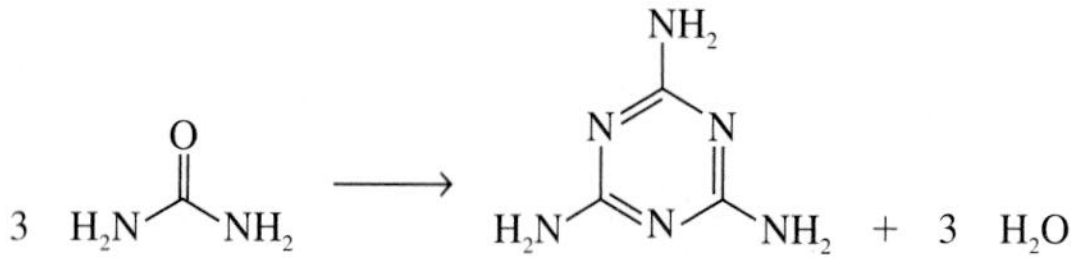

Melamine

Each molecule of melamine then reacts with three molecules of formaldehyde:

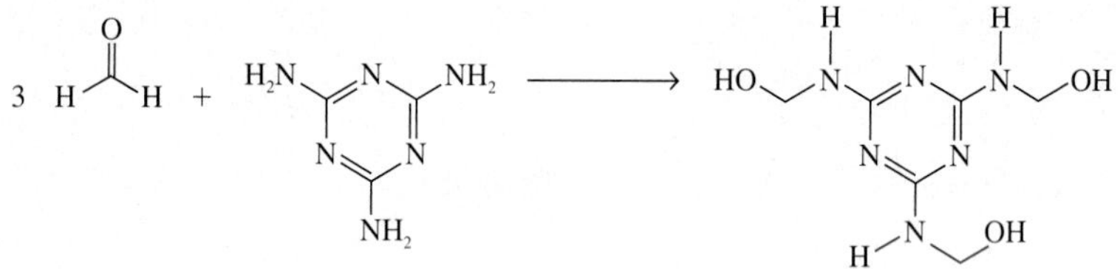

Finally, alcohol-amine condensation gives a polymer with a regular array of cross-links, as shown in Figure 11-14. Melmac dinnerware and Formica countertops contain this polymer. Box 11-2 discusses the use of petroleum as the raw material for polymeric materials.

SILICONES

Polymers called **silicones** have backbones that consist of alternating silicon and oxygen atoms. The synthesis of silicone polymers begins with an organic chloride and an alloy of silicon and copper:

$$2\ CH_3Cl + Si(Cu) \longrightarrow (CH_3)_2SiCl_2 + Cu$$

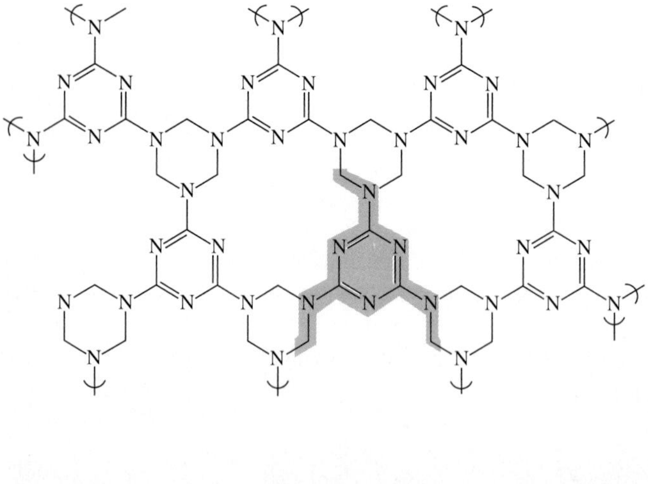

FIGURE 11-14
A portion of the structure of the polymer made from melamine and formaldehyde with one of the monomer units highlighted. This material is used to make Formica countertops because it is strong, lightweight, and heat resistant.

The resulting chlorosilanes are treated with water to replace the chlorine atoms with hydroxyl groups:

$$(CH_3)_2SiCl_2 \;+\; 2\;H_2O \longrightarrow (CH_3)_2Si(OH)_2 \;+\; 2\;HCl$$

Finally, these dihydroxysilanes eliminate water in a condensation reaction to give a polymer with an Si—O—Si linkage.

H_3C CH_3 H_3C CH_3 H_3C CH_3 H_3C CH_3

—O—Si—O—Si—O—Si—O—Si—O—

The properties of the silicone polymer depend on the identity of the organic fragment bonded to the silicon atom. With methyl groups the polymer is a silicone oil that has greater thermal stability and less tendency to thicken at low temperature than hydrocarbon oils. The stability of silicone oils comes from the strong Si—O bonds that make up the backbone of the polymer.

Average bond energies:
Si—O = 450 kJ/mol; C—C = 345 kJ/mol.

Silicone rubbers, polymers with extensive Si—O—Si cross-linking and high molar masses, can be purchased as long single chains that cross-link at room temperature. These polymers "cure" by reaction with water in the atmosphere. Figure 11-15 shows this process. The curing process releases acetic acid, which accounts for the odor of these materials.

Approximately 70,000 tons of silicone polymers are produced each year in the United States. Silicones are used as greases, waxes, caulking, gaskets, biomedical devices, cosmetics, surfactants, antifoaming agents, hydraulic fluids, and water repellents.

$$-Si(CH_3)_2-O-Si(CH_3)(OCOCH_3)-O-Si(CH_3)_2-O- \;+\; H_2O \longrightarrow -Si(CH_3)_2-O-Si(CH_3)(OH)-O-Si(CH_3)_2-O- \;+\; CH_3COOH$$

$$2\; -Si(CH_3)_2-O-Si(CH_3)(OH)-O-Si(CH_3)_2-O- \longrightarrow \begin{array}{c} -Si(CH_3)_2-O-Si(CH_3)-O-Si(CH_3)_2-O- \\ | \\ O \\ | \\ -Si(CH_3)_2-O-Si(CH_3)-O-Si(CH_3)_2-O- \end{array} \;+\; H_2O$$

FIGURE 11-15
A self-curing silicone rubber cross-links by reacting with water. A weakly bound CH_3CO_2 group reacts with water to generate a hydroxysilane, which then undergoes a condensation reaction to cross-link the polymer chains.

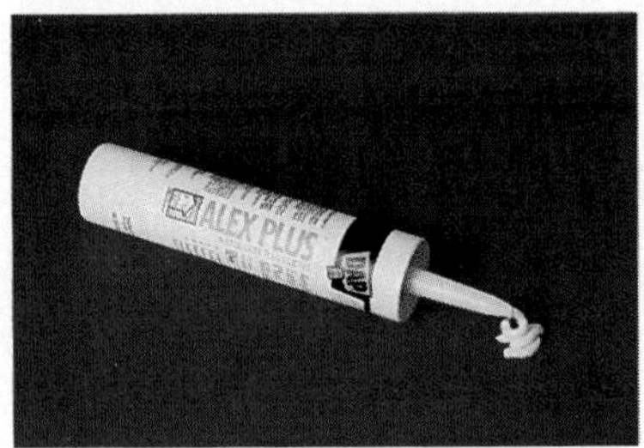

BOX 11-2

RAW MATERIALS FOR POLYMERS

Every polymer is built from monomer units. Except for natural rubber, the monomer building blocks for industrially important polymers must themselves be manufactured from appropriate starting materials. More than half of the top 50 industrial chemicals owe their positions to their use as monomers in the polymer industry. Ethylene, for example, is the monomer for polyethylene, but it is also used to make several other monomers, including ethylene glycol, styrene, and vinyl chloride. Ethylene is the third leading industrial chemical, and ethylene glycol, styrene, and vinyl chloride are also among the top 50.

Ethylene C_2H_4 $\xrightarrow{O_2}$ Ethylene oxide C_2H_4O $\xrightarrow{H_2O}$ Ethylene glycol $C_2H_6O_2$ (PET)

Ethylene C_2H_4 + Benzene C_6H_6 ⟶ Ethylbenzene C_8H_{10} $\xrightarrow{-H_2}$ Styrene C_8H_8 (polystyrene)

Ethylene C_2H_4 + Cl_2 ⟶ Dichlorethane $C_2H_4Cl_2$ $\xrightarrow{-HCl}$ Vinyl chloride C_2H_3Cl (PVC)

In addition to being the monomer from which polypropylene is synthesized, propene is converted into other important monomers, including acrylonitrile and phenol:

Propene C_3H_6 $\xrightarrow[-H_2O]{O_2}$ Acrolein C_3H_4O $\xrightarrow[-H_2O]{NH_3, O_2}$ Acrylonitrile C_3H_3N (polyacrylonitrile)

Propene C_3H_6 + Benzene C_6H_6 $\xrightarrow{O_2}$ Acetone C_3H_6O (industrial solvent) + Phenol C_6H_6O (Bakelite and others)

Neither ethylene nor propene is found in abundance in nature. Both are produced by the controlled decomposition of petroleum.

Urea is a starting material for urea-formaldehyde and melamine-formaldehyde polymers and is important as a fertilizer. It is manufactured from carbon dioxide and ammonia:

$$CO_2 + 2\,NH_3 \longrightarrow H_2N{-}C(=O){-}NH_2 + H_2O$$

Ammonia, in turn, is made from molecular nitrogen and hydrogen via the Haber process. Petroleum is the primary source for hydrogen and carbon dioxide.

Benzene reacts with ethylene and propene to produce styrene and phenol. Benzene is also converted into cyclohexane, which is a starting material for the synthesis of nylon monomers. Several derivatives of benzene are also important monomer precursors. Ethyl benzene, styrene, terephthalic acid, and the xylenes are precursors of polyester fibers and plastics:

Terephthalic acid (CO_2H, CO_2H) p-Xylene (CH_3, CH_3) o-Xylene (CH_3, CH_3)

Benzene and its derivatives can be produced from coal, but petroleum is by far the main source of these chemicals.

Formaldehyde is produced from carbon monoxide and hydrogen, which are first combined into methanol:

$$CO + 2\,H_2 \rightarrow CH_3OH$$

Methanol is then decomposed directly or in a controlled reaction with oxygen:

$$CH_3OH \rightarrow H_2CO + H_2$$

$$2\,CH_3OH + O_2 \rightarrow 2\,H_2CO + 2\,H_2O$$

Here again, the starting materials come from petroleum.

You may have noticed that *every important polymer starting material comes from petroleum.* Therefore without a copious, relatively inexpensive supply of petroleum, the present polymer industry would not exist. World petroleum reserves are a finite resource, and at present 90% of U.S. petroleum consumption is for fuel. As a result, our society is rapidly burning the raw material on which the current plastics industry is based. As petroleum supplies eventually dwindle, our society will be forced to make difficult choices between using petroleum for energy or for polymeric materials.

SECTION EXERCISES

11.3.1 The following monomers can be used to synthesize polymers:

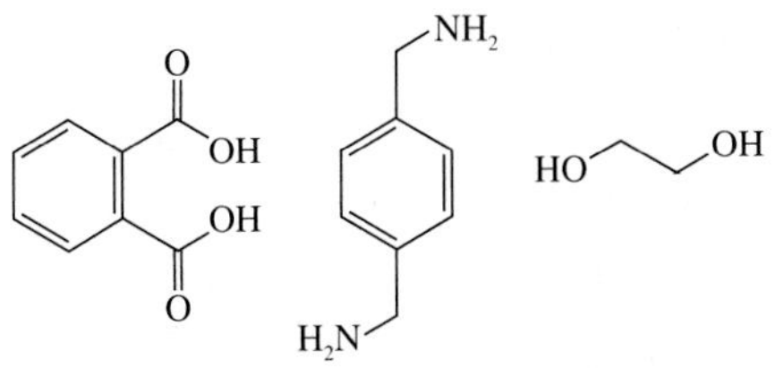

Draw structures that show the repeat units of the polyamide and the polyester arising from these monomers.

11.3.2 Polycarbonates are colorless polymers nearly as tough as steel. One of the most common polycarbonates, Lexan, is used in "bulletproof" windows and as face plates in the helmets worn by astronauts. Lexan is made by condensing phosgene with a diphenol, with the elimination of HCl:

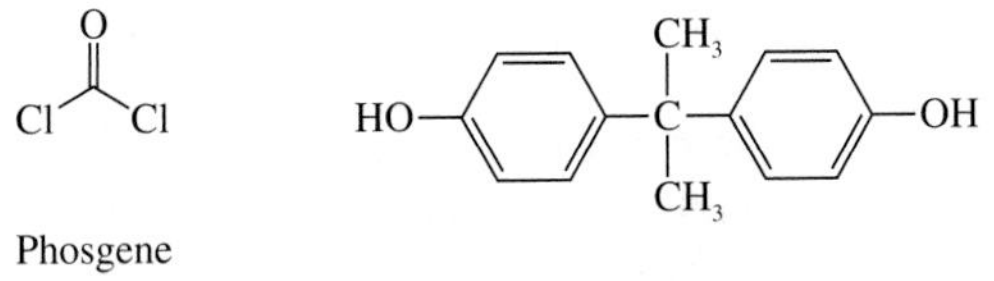

Phosgene

Write the structure of Lexan. Show at least two complete repeat units of the polymer.

11.3.3 The following polymer is used to make carpets because its fibers have a single most stable three-dimensional structure. Footprints quickly disappear from a carpet made of these fibers because compressed fibers quickly return to their most stable orientation. Identify the monomer used to make the polymer, and write a balanced equation that shows the condensation of two of these monomers.

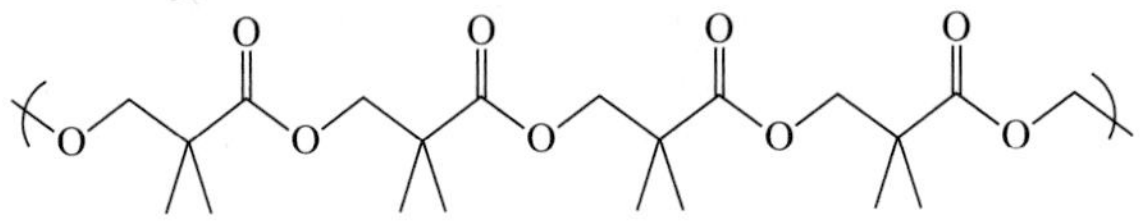

11.4 POLYMER PROPERTIES

To a chemist, a polymer is described by its chemical structure. To a manufacturer or a consumer, on the other hand, the important features of a polymer are its macroscopic properties. A tire manufacturer needs a flexible, tough, and durable polymer. A shirtmaker wants to spin a polymer into fibers that wear well, hold dyes, and are wrinkle-free. Makers of lenses look for transparent polymers that can be molded into precise shapes. Each of these polymer applications has somewhat different requirements.

Although they have an endless variety of properties, polymers can be divided into three categories based on their general physical properties, especially their resistance to stretching. These are **plastics, fibers,** and **elastomers.** Plastics exist as

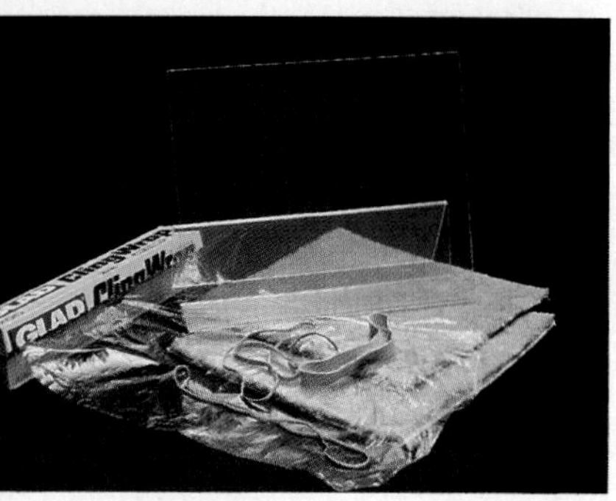

FIGURE 11-16
Common objects that exemplify the three categories of polymers are a plastic book holder, swatches of nylon carpet, some plastic wrap, and several large rubber bands.

blocks or sheets, whereas fibers have been drawn into long threads. Both are inflexible, but elastomers can be stretched without breaking. Formica tabletops and polyethylene packaging films are examples of plastics, Orlon carpets are made from polymer fibers, and rubber bands are elastomers (Figure 11-16). Some polymers, such as nylon, can be formed into both plastics and fibers.

PLASTICS

To the general public the term *plastic* has become synonymous with *polymer.* Actually, a plastic is a polymeric material that hardens on cooling or on evaporation of solvent, allowing it to be molded or extruded into specific shapes or spread into thin films.

Plastics fall into two groups based on their response to heating. Polymers that melt or deform on heating are classed as **thermoplastic** materials, whereas those that retain their structural integrity are said to be **thermosetting.** The degree of cross-linking in a polymer determines whether it is thermoplastic or thermosetting: the more a polymer is cross-linked, the less it deforms on heating. For example, polyethylene consists of huge alkane molecules held together only by dispersion forces between the chains. This is a thermoplastic polymer because when it is heated, individual molecules acquire enough kinetic energy to overcome the dispersion forces, and the solid melts. On the other hand, Bakelite (see Figure 11-12) is so extensively cross-linked that it can be viewed as an immense single molecule. To melt Bakelite would require the breakage of covalent bonds. This is a thermosetting polymer, which may decompose irreversibly if it is heated to a high enough temperature but will not reversibly melt or deform.

Polyethylene, the best known plastic, exists in two general forms. High-density polyethylene is a rigid, strong polymer that is used to make bottlecaps, toys, pipes, and cabinets for electronic devices such as computers and televisions. Low-density polyethylene is a soft, semirigid material with a low melting point that is used to make plastic bags, squeeze bottles, food packaging films, and other common items. Both kinds of polyethylene have the same repeat unit, CH_2, but different structures of individual polyethylene molecules, as shown in Figure 11-17. High-density polyethylene forms under conditions that produce polymers made of straight chains of CH_2 units. These linear molecules maximize dispersion forces by "lining up" in rows that create crystalline regions within the polymer. Maximizing the dispersion forces

FIGURE 11-17
High-density polyethylene has long, straight chains of CH_2 units. The chains form a parallel array that maximizes dispersion forces between molecules, giving a tough, rigid polymer with a high melting point. In low-density polyethylene, branches along the main polymer chain prevent the molecules from moving close together. This reduces dispersion forces, giving a soft polymer with a low melting point.

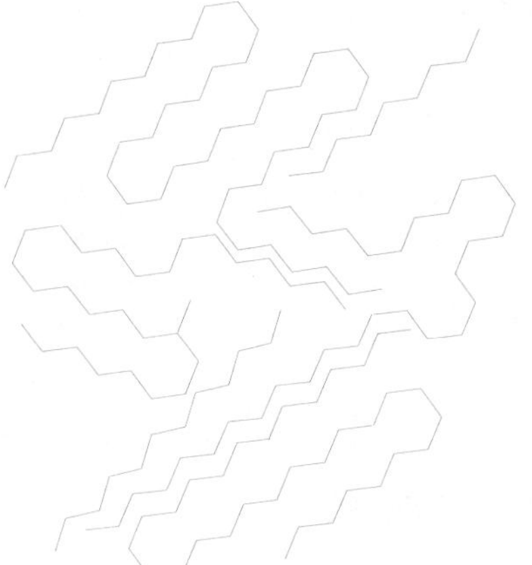

High-density polyethylene

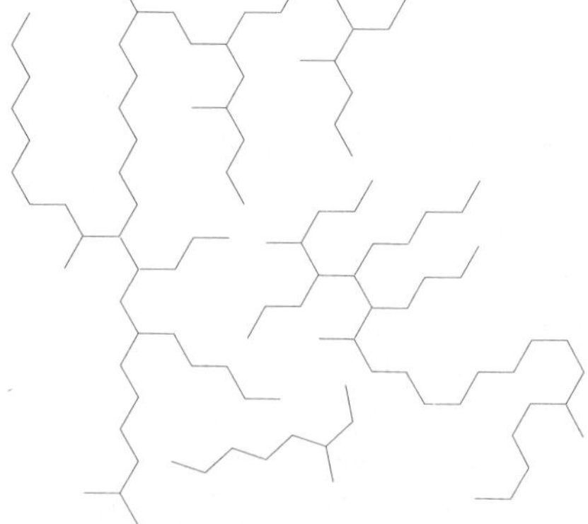

Low-density polyethylene

between the chains imparts strength and rigidity to the polymer. On the other hand, low-density polyethylene has chains of CH_2 groups that branch off the main backbone of the polymer. These branches prohibit the polymer molecules from packing closely together, thus decreasing dispersion forces and weakening the attraction between the chains. The result is an amorphous polymer that is flexible and melts at relatively low temperature.

The flexibility of some plastics can be improved by the addition of small molecules called **plasticizers.** For example, pure polyvinylchloride (PVC) turns brittle and cracks too easily to make useful flexible plastic products. With an added plasticizer, however, PVC can be used to make seat covers for automobiles, raincoats, garden hoses, and other flexible plastic objects. Plasticizers must be liquids that mix readily with the polymer. In addition, they must have low volatility so that they do not escape rapidly from the plastic. Many plasticizers are esters derived from phthalic acid; several are shown in Figure 11-18. The annual U.S. production of dioctylphthalate, the leading plasticizer, is approximately 350 million pounds.

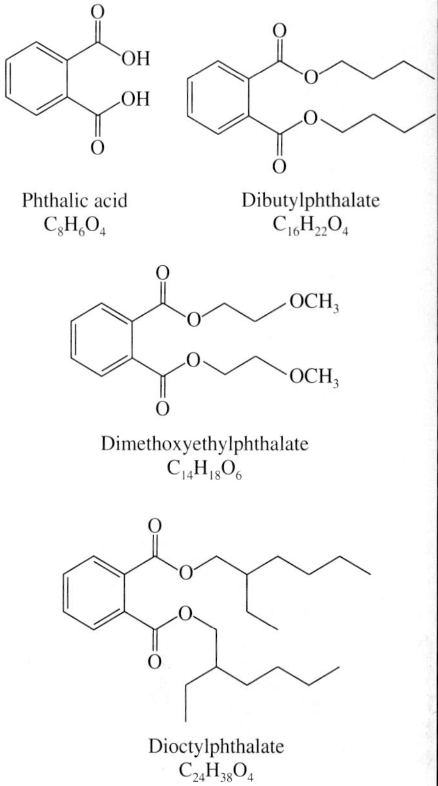

Phthalic acid $C_8H_6O_4$

Dibutylphthalate $C_{16}H_{22}O_4$

Dimethoxyethylphthalate $C_{14}H_{18}O_6$

Dioctylphthalate $C_{24}H_{38}O_4$

FIGURE 11-18
Molecular structures of phthalic acid and three common plasticizers that are esters derived from this acid.

FIBERS

For centuries, humans have woven and spun cotton, wool, and silk into fabrics for clothing and other purposes. These natural fibers are described later in this chapter. Today, synthetic fibers are also important components of the fabrics industry.

Fibers are thin threads of polymer made by forcing a fluid thermoplastic material through a set of tiny pores, as shown in Figure 11-19. This process requires that the polymer be in the liquid phase, so a fiber-forming polymer must melt at low temperature or dissolve in a convenient volatile solvent. Most synthetic fibers are polyesters, polyamides, or polyacrylonitrile. The polar functional groups in these polymers produce strong intermolecular forces that add significant tensile strength to the material.

ELASTOMERS

An elastomer is a polymer that is flexible, allowing it to be distorted from one shape to another. Polyisoprene (natural rubber), polybutadiene, and butadiene-styrene copolymer are the most important commercial elastomers. All contain some C=C bonds, and their bulk properties are affected by the varying geometries about the carbon atoms that make up the polymer backbone.

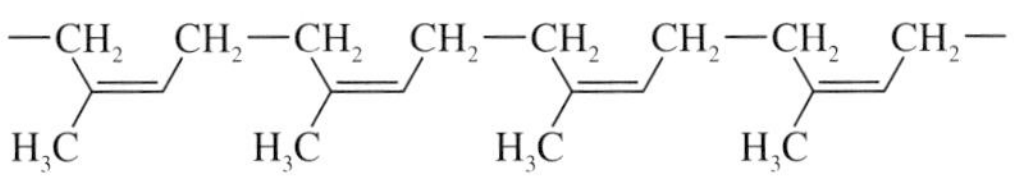

$$-CH_2\ \ CH_2-CH_2\ \ CH_2-CH_2\ \ CH_2-CH_2\ \ CH_2-$$
$$H_3C\qquad H_3C\qquad H_3C\qquad H_3C$$

The geometry about the carbon atoms of the CH_2 groups is tetrahedral, whereas the geometry about those carbon atoms involved in double bonds is trigonal. Because of these varied shapes, the molecules lack the structural regularity required to form a polymer with crystalline properties. Consequently, elastomers such as polyisoprene are amorphous solids with individual polymer strands tangled together. This lack of structural regularity keeps the molecules from approaching too closely, thus minimizing dispersion forces. This in turn allows individual polymer molecules to slide past one another and makes the polymer flexible.

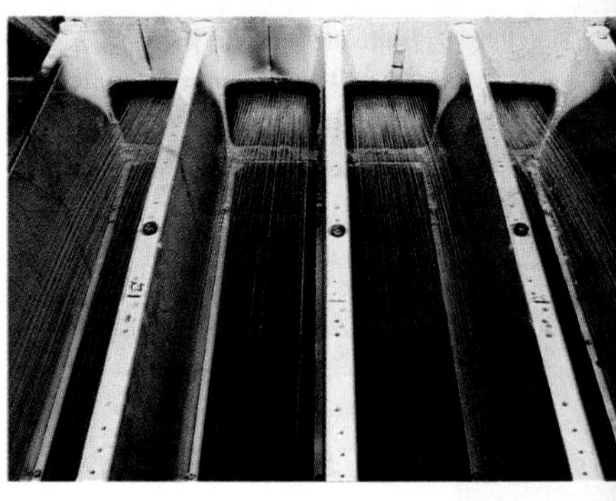

FIGURE 11-19
Fibers form when a fluid thermoplastic polymer is forced through tiny pores into long, thin threads, which solidify as they cool or as solvent evaporates.

The π bonds in polyisoprene introduce further structural variations that influence the properties of the elastomer. A molecule cannot readily undergo rotation about a double bond because of the directional character of π bonding. Consequently, there are two distinct geometries about the double bonds in polyisoprene, as shown in

remaining sections of this chapter, we survey some essential features of these three groups.

Life is organized around the cell, the smallest functioning unit of an organism. The most important components of cells, including enzymes, antibodies, hormones, transport molecules, and the structural materials that make up the cell itself, are all proteins. Proteins protect us from disease, extract energy from the food we eat, move essential cellular components from place to place, and are responsible for vision, taste, and smell. Proteins even synthesize the genetic material contained in all cells. In other words, proteins are the molecular machinery of the cell. The major structural materials in most animals—hair, skin, muscle, tendons, cartilage, claws, nails, horns, hooves, and feathers—are also made of proteins. How can this single group of molecules play so many different roles in the chemistry of life? To answer that question, we need to look at the structure of proteins.

AMINO ACIDS

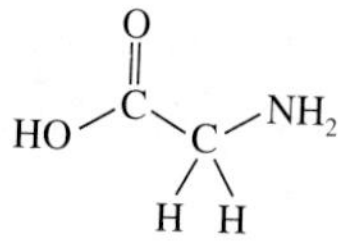

All proteins are polyamides made from the condensation reactions of amino acids. As the name implies, an amino acid is a bifunctional molecule with a carboxylic acid group at one end and an amino group at the other. The simplest amino acid, glycine, has a CH_2 spacer separating the two functional groups. Glycine and 19 other amino acids are used to build proteins in biological cells.

In each of the 19 amino acids other than glycine, a C—C bond replaces one C—H bond of the CH_2 spacer group. In alanine, for example, the added carbon atom bonds to three hydrogen atoms to give a CH_3 fragment. The other 18 amino acids, shown in Figures 11-21 and 11-22, contain more elaborate fragments.

Among the common amino acids, the nine shown in Figure 11-21 have nonpolar hydrophobic side chains containing mostly carbon and hydrogen atoms. These amino acids are often tucked into the *inside* of a protein, away from the aqueous environment of the cell.

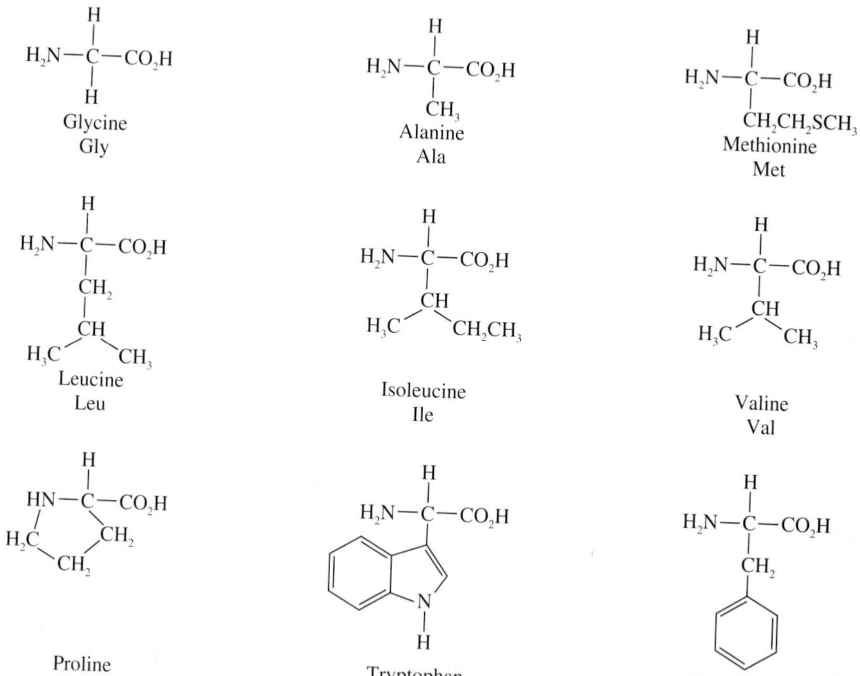

HO—C(=O)—CH₂—NH₂ Glycine

HO—C(=O)—CH(CH₃)—NH₂ Alanine

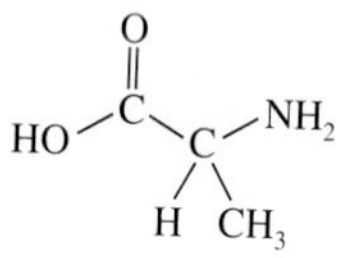

The hydrophilic and hydrophobic properties of molecules are discussed in Chapter 10.

$H_2N—CH(H)—CO_2H$ Glycine Gly

$H_2N—CH(CH_3)—CO_2H$ Alanine Ala

$H_2N—CH(CH_2CH_2SCH_3)—CO_2H$ Methionine Met

$H_2N—CH(CH_2CH(CH_3)_2)—CO_2H$ Leucine Leu

$H_2N—CH(CH(CH_3)CH_2CH_3)—CO_2H$ Isoleucine Ile

$H_2N—CH(CH(CH_3)_2)—CO_2H$ Valine Val

Proline Pro

Tryptophan Trp

Phenylalanine Phe

FIGURE 11-21
Of the 20 amino acids used to build proteins, 9 have nonpolar side chains made mostly of carbon and hydrogen. Under the name of each amino acid is its three-letter abbreviation.

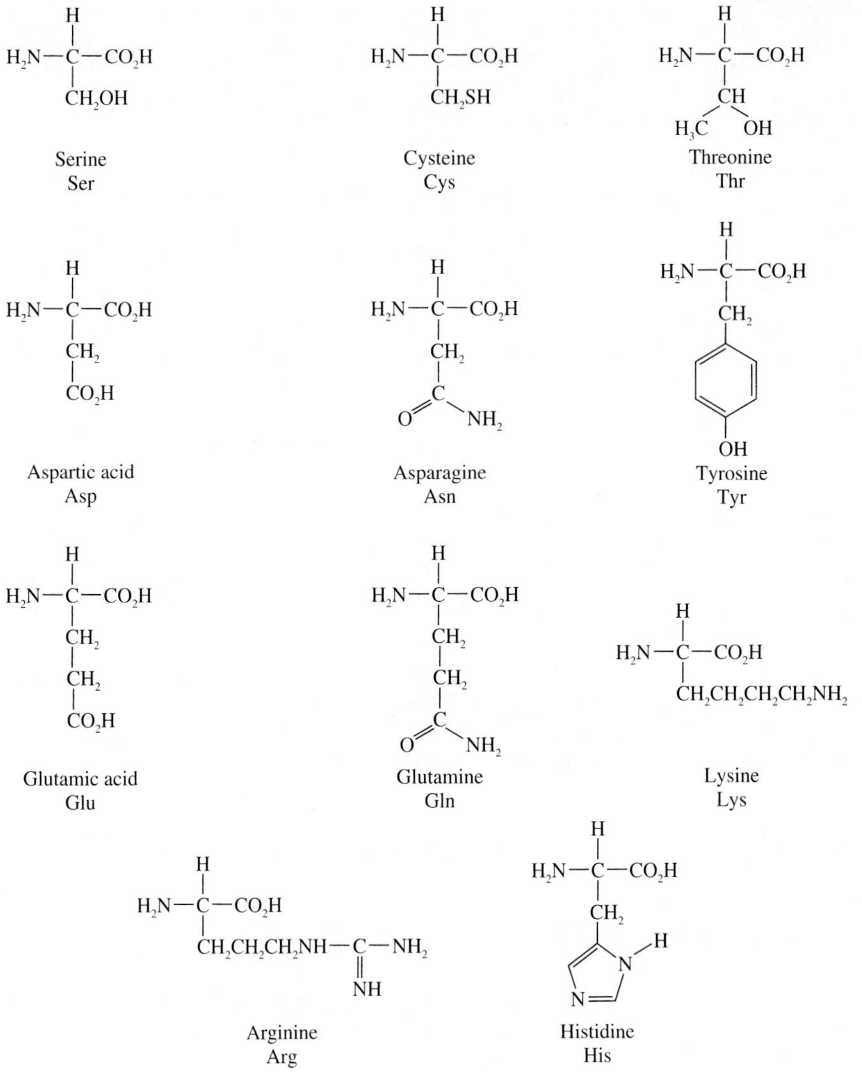

Serine
Ser

Cysteine
Cys

Threonine
Thr

Aspartic acid
Asp

Asparagine
Asn

Tyrosine
Tyr

Glutamic acid
Glu

Glutamine
Gln

Lysine
Lys

Arginine
Arg

Histidine
His

FIGURE 11-22
Of the 20 amino acids used to build proteins, 11 have side chains with highly polar functional groups. Under the name of each amino acid is its three-letter abbreviation.

The 11 amino acids shown in Figure 11-22 have side chains that contain polar functional groups such as hydroxyl, amino, or carboxylic acid. These hydrophilic amino acids are commonly found on the *outside* of a protein, where their interactions with water molecules increase the solubility of the protein.

Biochemists represent each amino acid with a three-letter abbreviation. These abbreviations appear under the names of the amino acids in Figures 11-21 and 11-22. For example, the abbreviation for glycine is *Gly.*

POLYPEPTIDES

Proteins form in a sequence of condensation reactions in which the amino end of one amino acid combines with the carboxylic acid end of another, eliminating a molecule of water to create an amide linkage. The amide group that connects two amino acids is called a **peptide linkage.** When two amino acids are linked, the product is a dipeptide. For example, alanine and glycine can form the dipeptide shown in Figure 11-23.

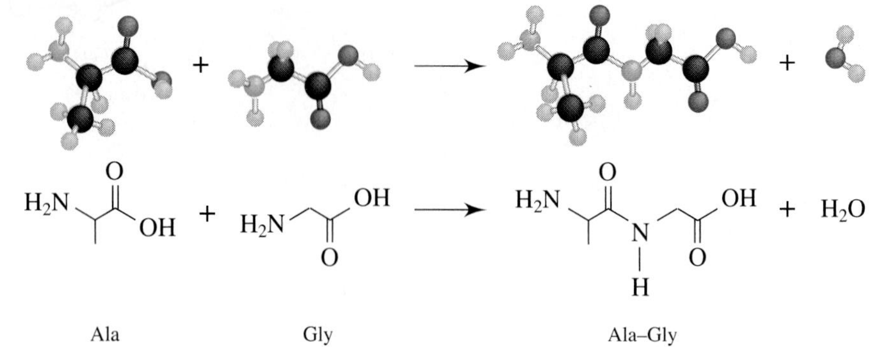

FIGURE 11-23
Ball-and-stick models of glycine (Gly) and alanine (Ala) and of the condensation reaction between them to form a dipeptide.

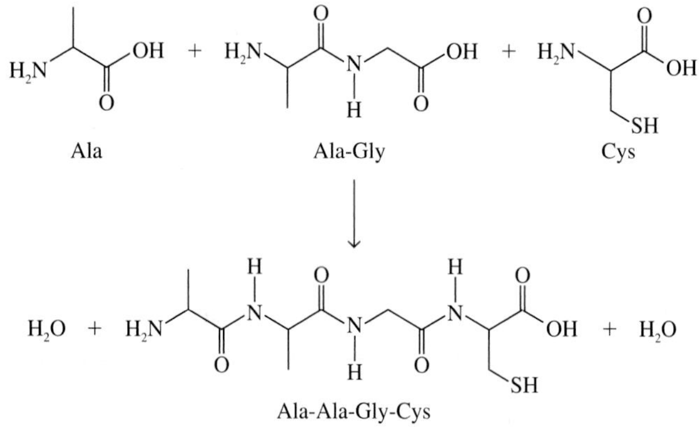

FIGURE 11-24
Additional condensation reactions can take place at either end of a dipeptide. In either case, the product is another amino acid that can continue to grow into a polypeptide or a protein. The figure illustrates alanine (Ala) and cysteine (Cys) adding to opposite ends of the Aly-Gly dipeptide.

Cells synthesize proteins by adding one amino acid unit at a time, always adding the next unit to the carboxylic acid end of the growing polypeptide chain.

Notice that this dipeptide is also an amino acid because one component retains its amino group, whereas the other retains its acid group. Consequently, additional amino acids can add to either end of a dipeptide to form a new peptide with an amino terminal group at one end and a carboxylic acid terminal group at its other end. Figure 11-24 shows the peptide that results from addition of another alanine molecule at the amino end and a cysteine molecule at the carboxyl end of the Ala-Gly dipeptide.

Additional condensation reactions lengthen the chain, eventually leading to a macromolecule called a **polypeptide.** All proteins are macromolecular polypeptides. A small protein may consist of a chain of 50 to 100 amino acids, larger proteins contain hundreds of them, and myosin, a very large muscle protein, has approximately 1750 amino acid units.

The sequence of amino acids in a polypeptide is called its **primary structure.** It is customary to write the primary structure of a polypeptide using the three-letter abbreviation for each amino acid. By convention the structure is written so that the amino acid on the left bears the terminal amino group of the polypeptide and the amino acid on the right bears the terminal carboxylic acid group. Figure 11-25 shows the two dipeptides that can be made from glycine and serine. Although they contain the same amino acids, they are different molecules with many different chemical and physical properties. Sample Problem 11-3 shows how to draw the structure of a peptide.

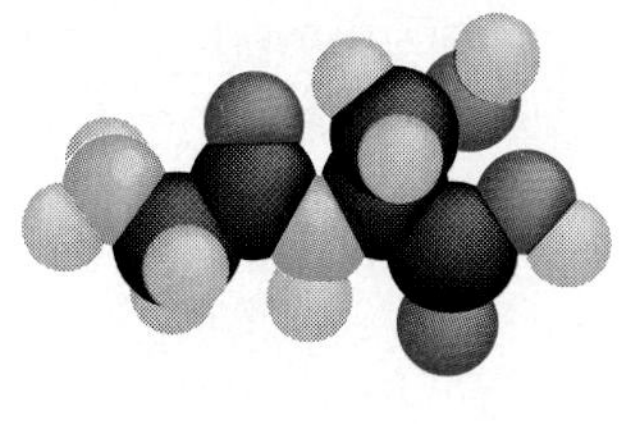

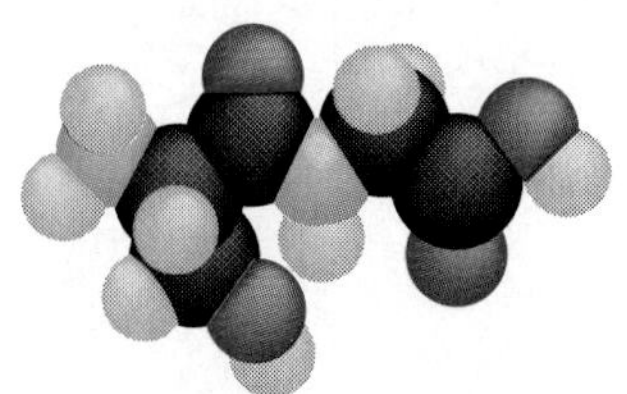

Glycine–Serine
Gly–Ser

Serine–Glycine
Ser–Gly

FIGURE 11-25 Glycine and serine form two dipeptides, Gly-Ser and Ser-Gly.

SAMPLE PROBLEM 11-3 WRITING THE STRUCTURE OF A PEPTIDE

Write the line structure of the peptide Asp-Met-Val-Tyr.

METHOD: We are asked to translate a shorthand designation into a line drawing that represents the molecule. First, construct a backbone containing four amide linkages, putting the terminal NH_2 group on the left end and the terminal CO_2H group on the right end of the peptide. Then attach the appropriate side groups, as determined from the molecular structures of the amino acids in Figures 11-21 and 11-22.

These four amino acids are joined with peptide linkages in the order given. We put the backbone in place as a line structure. Remember, however, that carbon atoms are not shown in line structures and hydrogens are included only for atoms other than carbon.

Next, add the four side chains in the positions marked R_1, R_2, R_3, and R_4 to give the final structure of the peptide. The leftmost amino acid, aspartic acid, is at the amino end. Aspartic acid is followed by methionine, valine, and tyrosine. Tyrosine is at the carboxylic acid end. Here are the individual amino acids, with their R groups highlighted:

Aspartic acid Asp	Methionine Met	Valine Val	Tyrosine Tyr
$H_2N-CH(CO_2H)-$ with R_1 = CH_2CO_2H	R_2 = $CH_2CH_2SCH_3$	R_3 = $CH(CH_3)_2$	R_4 = $CH_2C_6H_4OH$

To finish the structure, we replace the R groups on the peptide backbone with their appropriate line structures.

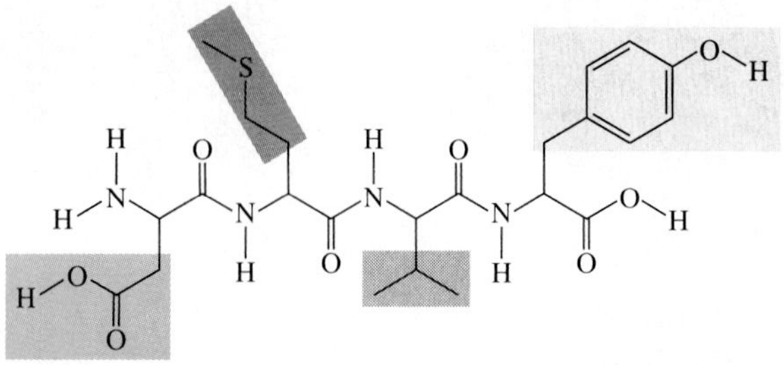

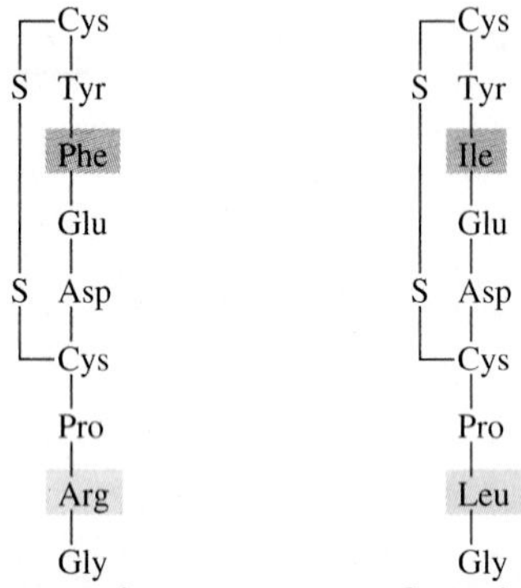

Cys–Tyr–Phe–Glu–Asp–Cys–Pro–Arg–Gly (S–S link between Cys residues)
Vasopressin

Cys–Tyr–Ile–Glu–Asp–Cys–Pro–Leu–Gly (S–S link between Cys residues)
Oxytocin

FIGURE 11-26

The primary structures of the pituitary hormones vasopressin and oxytocin differ by just two amino acids. (There are sulfur cross-links between the cysteine residues, known as *disulfide linkages,* that are described later in this section.)

Proteins with very similar primary structures can serve very different functions. For example, Figure 11-26 shows the primary structures of two pituitary hormones, oxytocin and vasopressin. These structures differ by just two amino acids (those highlighted in color), but changing these two amino acids has a profound effect on the biochemistry of these molecules. Vasopressin regulates the rate at which water is reabsorbed by the kidneys and intestine. Alcohol suppresses the release of vasopressin, which is why consumption of alcoholic beverages leads to excessive urine production and dehydration. Oxytocin, on the other hand, induces contractions of the uterus during childbirth, and it triggers the release of milk by contracting muscles around the ducts that come from the mammary glands.

The enormous diversity of protein structure and function comes from the many ways in which 20 amino acids can combine into polypeptide chains. Consider the four peptide chains that can be made from just two amino acids, for example, cysteine and aspartic acid:

Cys-Cys-Cys-Cys	Cys-Cys-Cys-Asp	Cys-Cys-Asp-Cys	Cys-Cys-Asp-Asp
Cys-Asp-Cys-Cys	Cys-Asp-Cys-Asp	Cys-Asp-Asp-Cys	Cys-Asp-Asp-Asp
Asp-Cys-Cys-Cys	Asp-Cys-Cys-Asp	Asp-Cys-Asp-Cys	Asp-Cys-Asp-Asp
Asp-Asp-Cys-Cys	Asp-Asp-Cys-Asp	Asp-Asp-Asp-Cys	Asp-Asp-Asp-Asp

In all, there are $2^4 = 16$ different ways to combine two amino acids in chains of four. The 20 common amino acids combine to give 20^4 tetrapeptides, which is 1.6×10^5 different molecules. Each time the chain adds an amino acid, the number of possibilities is multiplied by 20, so a set of n amino acids can form 20^n different polypeptides. Because proteins contain hundreds of amino acids, each of which can be any of the 20 common structures, the number of possible structures becomes immense. In fact, 20^{100}, the number of ways to construct a protein of 100 units, is greater than the known number of atoms in the universe.

SECONDARY PROTEIN STRUCTURE

So far, we have described polypeptides as simple linear strings of amino acids. Actually, within long polypeptides, certain sections fold into sheets or twist into coils. These regions with specific structural characteristics make up the **secondary structure** of the protein.

The secondary structure of a protein is determined by hydrogen bonding between C=O and N—H groups of the peptide linkages that make up the backbone of the protein. Hydrogen bonds can exist within the same protein chain or between different chains. Hydrogen bonding within a single protein chain gives a spiral structure known as the **α-helix,** shown in Figure 11-27. Notice that the α-helix is held together by hydrogen bonds between the carbonyl oxygen on one amino acid and a hydrogen

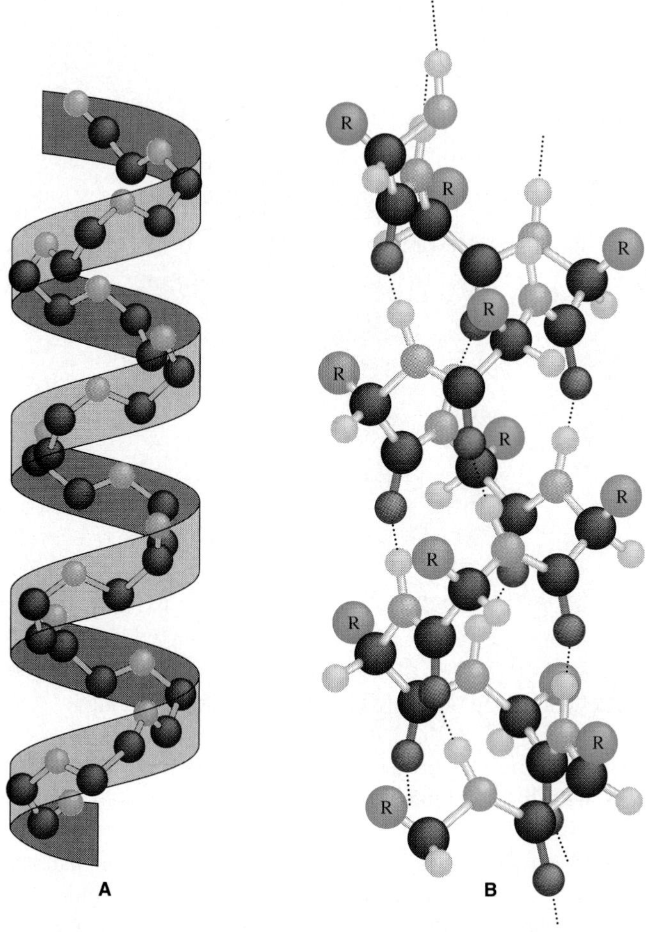

FIGURE 11-27
Two views of the α-helix. **A,** The peptide backbone with side chains and H and O atoms omitted to emphasize the shape of the helix. If you hold your right hand so that the thumb points up the axis of the helix, your fingers will curl in the same direction as the spiral of the helix. The alpha designation refers to this right-handed spiral. **B,** A ball-and-stick model of the α-helix with R groups representing the side chains. Notice the hydrogen bonding between N—H and C=O groups.

atom from an amide nitrogen three amino acids away. One complete turn of the helix contains 3.6 amino acids.

Another common form of secondary protein structure is the **pleated sheet,** illustrated in Figure 11-28. In a sheet the chains are fully extended rather than coiled, and hydrogen bonds exist between different protein chains, with one chain bonded to another. In pleated regions the carbonyl oxygen and the amide hydrogen protrude at 90-degree angles to the axis of the extended protein backbone. This allows row upon row of polypeptides to form hydrogen bonds and make a sheet of protein. The pleats in the sheet are caused by the bond angles of the peptide linkages.

Several other secondary protein structures have roles in determining the shapes of proteins, but they are far less common than the α-helix and pleated sheet. A discussion of these less common secondary structures is beyond our scope.

TERTIARY PROTEIN STRUCTURE

Each protein has a unique three-dimensional shape called its **tertiary structure.** The tertiary structure is the result of the bends and folds that a polypeptide chain adopts to achieve the lowest possible energy. As an analogy, consider the cord in Figure 11-29 that connects the computer to its keyboard. The cord can be pulled out so that it is long and straight; this corresponds to its primary structure. Normally, the cord

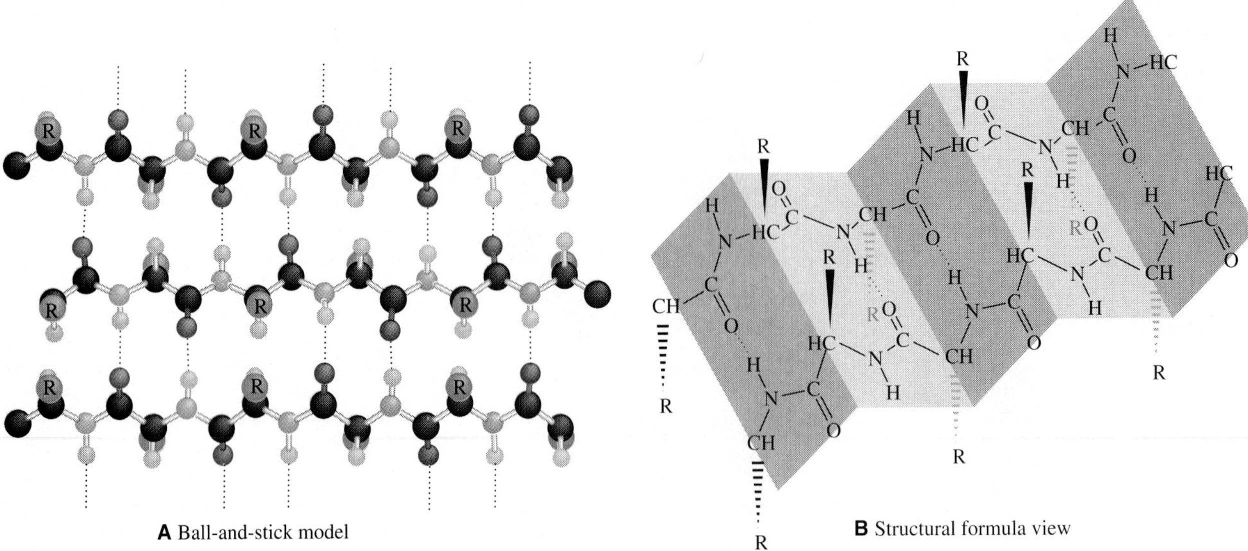

FIGURE 11-28
Two views of the pleated sheet. **A,** The three-dimensional ball-and-stick view emphasizes the hydrogen bonding in the pleated sheet. **B,** The structural formula view emphasizes the sheets.

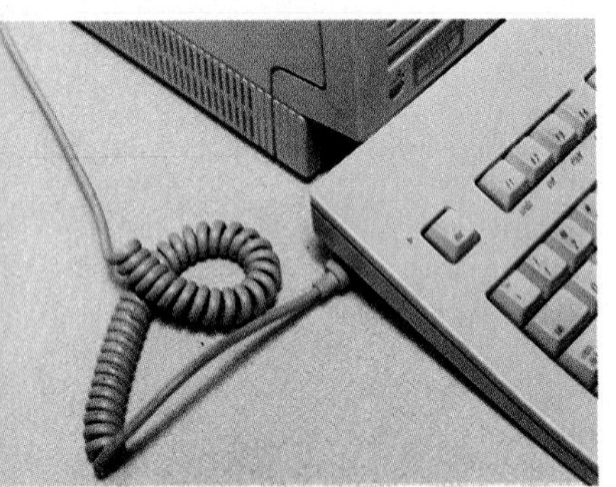

FIGURE 11-29
The cord that connects this computer to its keyboard illustrates the primary, secondary, and tertiary levels of protein structure.

has a helical region in its center; this is its secondary structure. In addition, the helix is twisted and folded on top of itself. This three-dimensional character of the cord is its tertiary structure.

The tertiary structure of a protein is determined primarily by the way in which water interacts with the functional groups on the amino acids in the polypeptide chain. The polar interactions with water molecules are maximized and the system made most stable when the polypeptide folds into a three-dimensional shape that places its hydrophobic regions inside the overall structure. The folding of the protein is further directed and strengthened by a large number of hydrogen bonds. Water forms hydrogen bonds with the protein backbone and with hydrophilic side chains such as serine, lysine, and tyrosine. These same hydrophilic side chains form hydrogen bonds among themselves and with the protein backbone. Sample Problem 11-4 shows how water forms hydrogen bonds with a peptide.

SAMPLE PROBLEM 11-4 HYDROGEN BONDING IN PEPTIDES

Draw a line structure that shows the various ways that water molecules form hydrogen bonds with a protein backbone.

METHOD: Remember from Chapter 10 that the partial positive charges on water's hydrogen atoms lead to hydrogen bonding with electronegative oxygen and nitrogen atoms, whereas the partial negative charge on the oxygen atom of a water molecule forms hydrogen bonds with highly polar N—H and O—H bonds.

Begin by drawing a section of protein backbone. Because the side chains are not involved in this problem, they may be designated simply as R.

Now add water molecules to illustrate the hydrogen bonding interactions. Each hydrogen bond is shown as a dotted line. Because the problem does not ask that all hydrogen bonds be shown, it is sufficient to show one or two examples of each type.

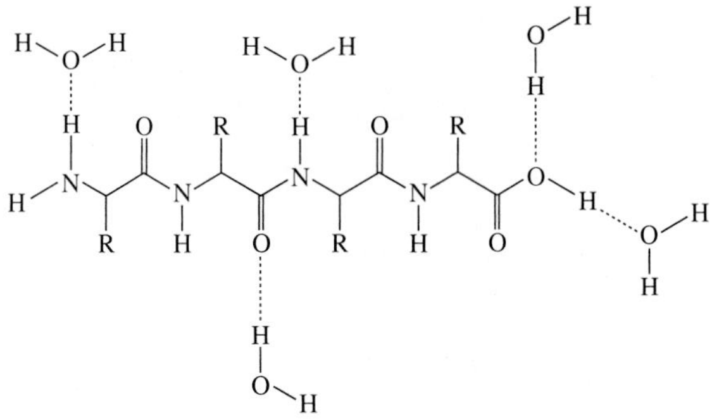

The amino acid cysteine plays an important role in tertiary protein structure. The —SH groups of two cysteine side chains can cross-link through an S—S bond called a **disulfide bridge.** The formation of this bridge is shown in Figure 11-30.

Recall from Figure 11-26 that the primary structures of oxytocin and vasopressin have two cysteine residues connected by a disulfide bridge. The three-dimensional structure of the oxytocin backbone is shown in Figure 11-31. Notice that the disulfide bridge locks the peptide chain into a compact cyclic structure.

GLOBULAR PROTEINS

A huge and diverse group of molecules called **globular proteins** carries out most of the work done by cells, including synthesis, transport, and energy production. Globular proteins have compact, roughly spherical tertiary structures containing folds and grooves. **Enzymes** are globular proteins that speed up biochemical reactions. The reactions of metabolism proceed too slowly to be of use to living organisms unless enzymes make them go faster. Antibodies, the agents that protect us from disease, are also globular proteins. Other globular proteins transport smaller molecules through the blood. Hemoglobin, the macromolecule that carries oxygen in the blood, is the best-known example of a transport protein. Globular proteins, including oxytocin and vasopressin, also act as hormones. Others are bound in cell membranes, facilitating passage of nutrients and ions into and out of the cell. Many globular proteins have hydrophilic side chains over the outer surface of their tertiary structures, making them soluble in the aqueous environment of the cell.

A species that speeds up a reaction is called a catalyst. Catalysts are covered in Chapter 14.

Transport of oxygen by hemoglobin is discussed in Chapter 18.

Not all hormones are proteins. Steroids and prostaglandins, for example, are powerful hormones, but they are not proteins.

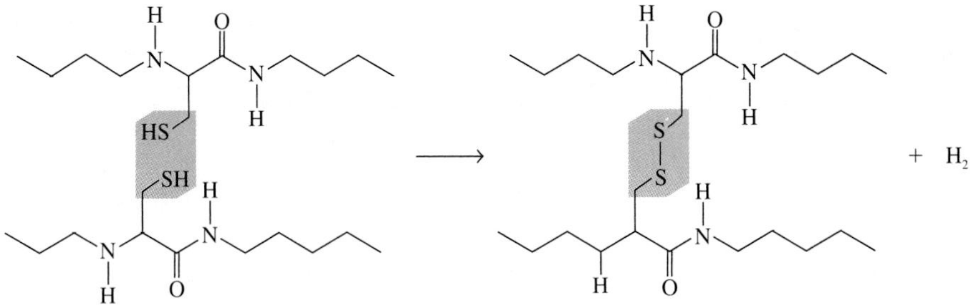

$+ \; H_2$

FIGURE 11-30
Schematic view of cross-linking via formation of a disulfide bridge.

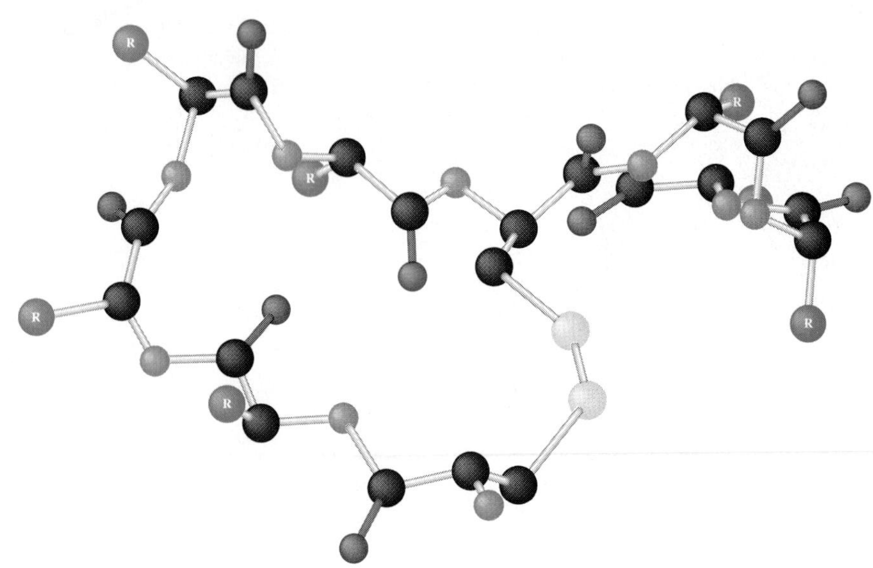

FIGURE 11-31
The three-dimensional structure of oxytocin. The sulfur atoms of the disulfide bridge are in yellow. The R groups have been simplified as green spheres to emphasize the shape of the polypeptide chain.

The secondary structures of globular proteins include α-helices and pleated sheets in varying proportions. For example, myoglobin, the protein that stores oxygen in muscle tissue, is composed of about 70% α-helix. The polypeptide chain contains eight helical strands connected by sharp kinks that produce the globular tertiary structure of the protein. The tertiary structure of myoglobin is shown in Figure 11-32.

FIGURE 11-32
The tertiary structure of myoglobin, showing the carbon and nitrogen atoms of the protein chain (*left*). and the structure as a continuous "ribbon" (*right*). The α-helical regions are highlighted in red.

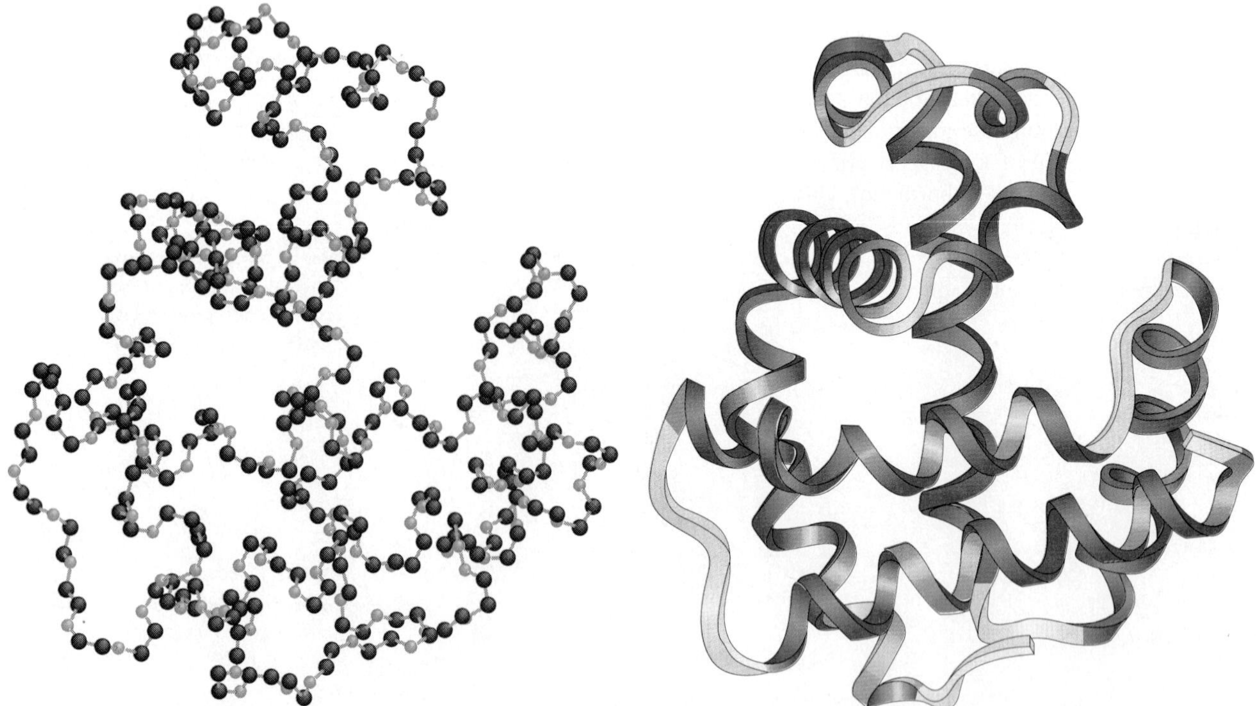

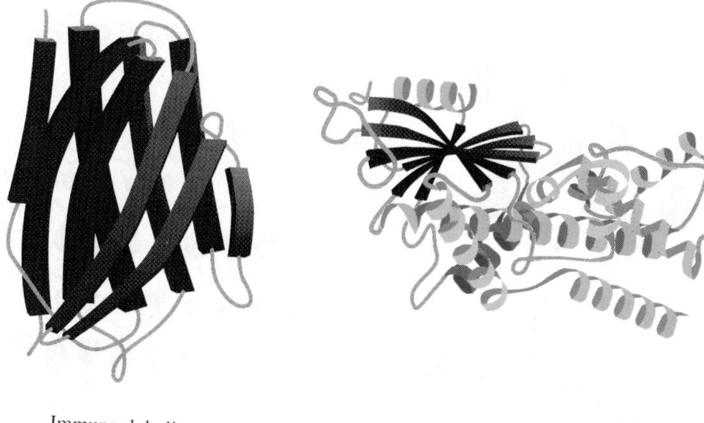

Immunoglobulin

Hexokinase

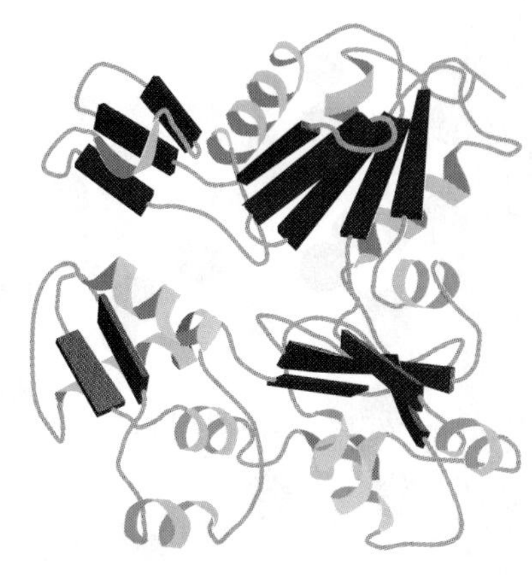

G-actin

FIGURE 11-33
Ribbon views of proteins with varying amounts of α-helices and pleated sheets. Immunoglobulin, an antibody, is made up of almost entirely pleated sheets (purple). Hexokinase, an enzyme, contains many α-helices (blue) and one region dominated by pleated sheets. G-actin, a component of muscle protein fibers, is a complex mixture of helices and sheets. Regions with no specific secondary structure are shown in orange.

The unique primary structure of each globular protein leads to a unique distribution of secondary structures and to a specific tertiary structure. The stylized "ribbon" views of globular proteins in Figure 11-33 illustrate the diversity and beauty of these molecules. Regions of α-helix are shown in blue, regions of pleated sheet are purple, and sections that have no specific secondary structure are orange.

FIBROUS PROTEINS

Structural components of cells and tissue are made of proteins that form fibers. These **fibrous proteins** are the cables, girders, bricks, and mortar of organisms.

The α-helix is the prevalent secondary structure in keratins, which include wool, hair, skin, fingernails, and fur. These molecules are long strands of helical protein that lie with their axes parallel to the axis of the fiber. In hair, individual keratin molecules are wound together like the strands of a rope. The arrangement of keratin molecules in hair is shown in Figure 11-34.

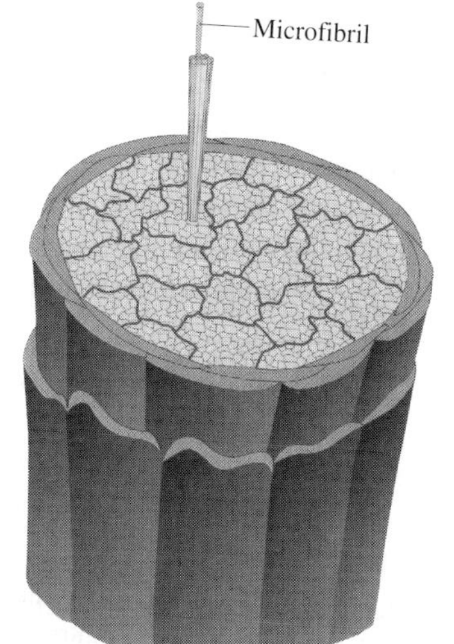

A single human hair

Microfibril: Made up of strands of protofibrils

Protofibril: Made up of individual α-helices

α-Helix

FIGURE 11-34
Hair is made up of thousands of α-helical keratin molecules wound together like strands in a rope.

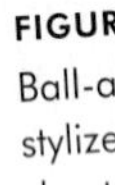

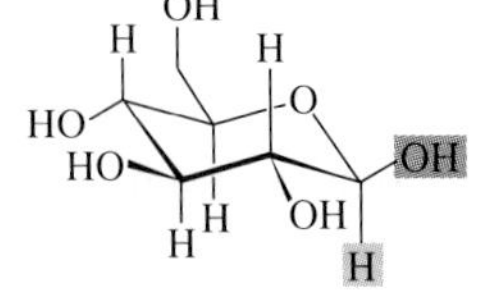

FIGURE 11-37

The structures of β- and α-glucose, with the symbols for the C atoms omitted for clarity. The structures are identical except for the placement of the C—H and C—OH bonds around the carbon atom immediately next to the ring oxygen atom. The orientation of this hydroxyl group plays a crucial role in the chemistry of polysaccharides produced from glucose monomers.

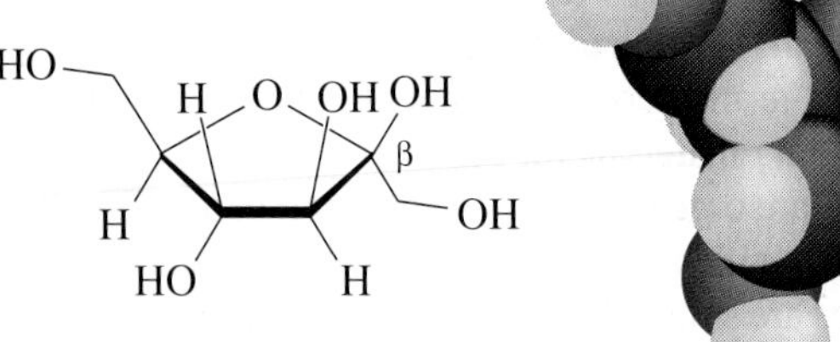

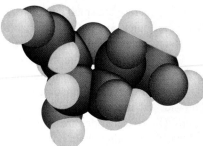

FIGURE 11-38

Fructose is a hexose monosaccharide that forms a five-membered ring structure.

In subsequent figures, we omit the symbols for carbon atoms and CH_2 groups to show more clearly the ring structures and placement of hydroxyl groups in carbohydrate molecules.

Fructose and glucose are present in fruit juice and honey. Fructose is sometimes called *levulose.*

less stable form, α-glucose, the OH group on the carbon atom next to the ring oxygen atom is in the perpendicular position.

Hexose monosaccharides can form five- and six-membered rings. In most cases, the six-membered ring structure is more stable, but fructose is more stable as a five-membered ring. The line structure of fructose is shown in Figure 11-38. Notice that there are —CH_2OH fragments bonded to two positions of this five-membered ring. Sample Problems 11-5 and 11-6 explore the structures of monosaccharides in more detail.

SAMPLE PROBLEM 11-5 MONOSACCHARIDE STRUCTURES

Describe the differences in the structures of ribose and fructose.

METHOD: Monosaccharides can differ in their empirical formulas, their ring sizes, and the spatial orientations of their hydroxyl groups. To analyze the differences between two monosaccharides, we must begin with structural drawings of the molecules. Then we can examine the structures to locate differences in constituents and bond orientations.

Ribose is shown in Figure 11-36, and fructose appears in Figure 11-38, but their line structures are reproduced at left for convenience.

Ribose
$C_5H_{10}O_5$

β-Fructose
$C_6H_{12}O_6$

Although the chemical formulas tell us that ribose is a pentose and fructose is a hexose, the ring structures are identical. Proceeding clockwise around the rings from the oxygen atom, we see that the structures differ only at the first two positions. In the first position, ribose has a C—H bond, and β-fructose has a C—CH_2OH linkage. In the second position the two saccharides have the same two bonds but in different orientations. The OH group points "up" in β-fructose and "down" in ribose.

SAMPLE PROBLEM 11-6 DRAWING MONOSACCHARIDES

Galactose is a six-carbon sugar that is identical to glucose except at the carbon atom next to the one bonded to the —CH_2OH fragment, where the orientations are different. Draw the molecular structure of α-galactose.

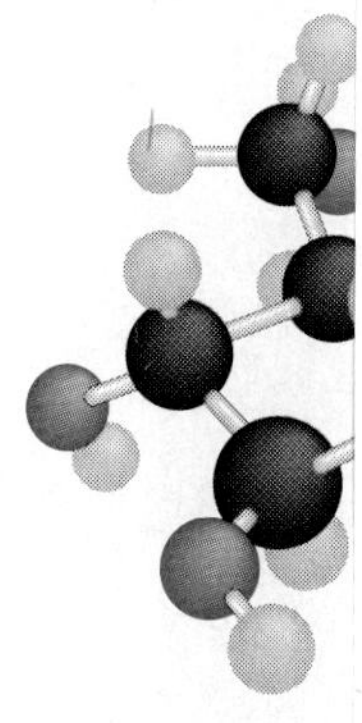

METHOD: When drawing a carbohydrate with a six-membered ring, it is best to start with the ring itself. Next, use α-glucose (see Figure 11-37) as a convenient template to obtain the proper orientations for the groups that galactose and glucose have in common. Finally, switch positions of groups as needed to obtain the correct final structure for galactose.

Begin with the six-membered ring in "lawn chair" shape:

Next, look up the structure of α-glucose to get the appropriate template:

α-Glucose:

The problem states that α-galactose differs from glucose in the position of the hydroxyl groups on the carbon adjacent to the one bonded to the —CH_2OH fragment. This position is highlighted in the structure. Starting from glucose, we move the hydroxyl group into a perpendicular orientation:

α-Galactose:

Many other organic molecules besides carbohydrates adopt the chair-shaped six-membered ring structure. One key to success in organic chemistry is the ability to draw structures such as these quickly and clearly.

OLIGOSACCHARIDES

Monosaccharides can combine by way of a condensation reaction between two hydroxyl groups in which water is eliminated, leaving an oxygen atom linking two saccharide rings. The C—O—C linkage between the two sugars is a glycosidic bond. Monosaccharides contain several hydroxyl groups, so many glycosidic linkages are possible. Nevertheless, in all natural glycosidic bonds one sugar forms a linkage through a hydroxyl group adjacent to a ring oxygen atom. The second sugar can link to the first through any of its hydroxyl groups. For example, maltose forms from two molecules of α-glucose. The glycosidic bond occurs at different positions on the two sugars, as shown in Figure 11-39. Maltose is formed from starch by the action of enzymes found in malt, saliva, and yeast and decomposes in the presence of yeast, first to give glucose and then ethanol and water.

$R{-}O{-}H + H{-}O{-}R' \longrightarrow R{-}O{-}R' + H_2O$

α-Glucose $C_6H_{12}O_6$ α-Glucose $C_6H_{12}O_6$ → Maltose $C_{12}H_{22}O_{11}$ + H_2O

The structures in Figure 11-39 are line drawings. Recall that carbon atoms and all C—H bonds are omitted from line drawings to show underlying structural features more clearly.

FIGURE 11-39
Line drawings showing the structure of maltose. The glycosidic bond links different ring carbon atoms of α-glucose and β-glucose.

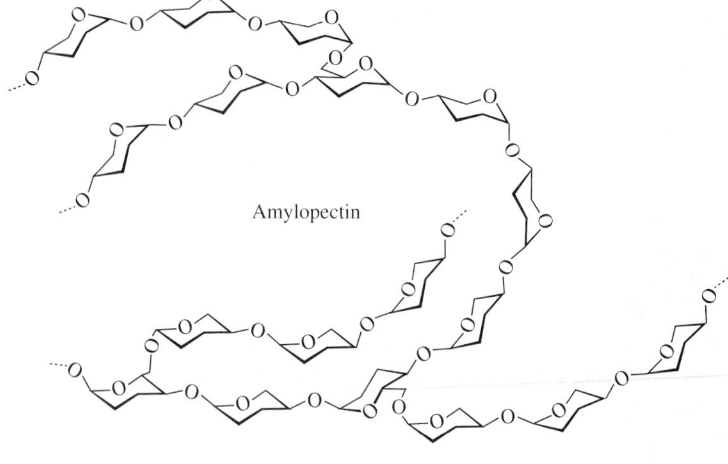

FIGURE 11-41
The structure of amylopectin. Long chains of glucose molecules are linked via glycosidic bonds. Branching occurs through additional linkages at some glucose rings. The hydroxyl groups that are not involved in linkages have been omitted for clarity.

We have streamlined our line drawings of polysaccharides by omitting all OH groups. Remember that glucose rings always contain OH groups in the orientations shown in Figure 11-36.

FIGURE 11-42
Starch collects in granules in plant cells and in animal livers.

fragments into maltose. Finally, maltose is cleaved into glucose molecules, which are metabolized for energy production. Humans as well as other animals and plants have the enzymes necessary to digest plant starch.

Animals store glucose in the form of glycogen. The structure of glycogen is similar to that of amylopectin, except that glycogen has more frequent, shorter branches than amylopectin. As shown in Figure 11-42, glycogen is synthesized and stored as granules in the liver. Glycogen deposits are also found in muscle tissue, where the sugar is readily available for rapid energy production. The liver has a limited capacity to store glycogen. When that capacity is exceeded, the body activates alternative biochemical pathways that convert sugar into fat.

The most abundant organic molecule in the biosphere is **cellulose,** a polysaccharide that is the principal building material for plants. Like amylose, cellulose is a linear polymer of glucose. Unlike amylose, however, the glucose monomers in cellulose are in the β-configuration. Figure 11-43 shows the structure of cellobiose, which is two β-glucose molecules linked head to tail.

Cellobiose

FIGURE 11-43
Cellobiose is two glucose units connected by a β-linkage. When the chain is continued by connecting many cellobiose units together, the result is cellulose, a polymer made of β-glucose units.

Cellobiose and maltose are made from very similar monomers, but they have distinctly different shapes. In maltose (Figure 11-39), whose repeat unit is one molecule of α-glucose and one molecule of β-glucose, the glycosidic linkage imparts a distinct kink to the structure. As a result, a chain of maltose units can coil upon itself, resulting in the granular shape of starch deposits. In contrast, cellobiose, which is made entirely from β-glucose, has a nearly flat structure. Linking a series of

530

FIGURE 11-40
Sucrose is a su
glucose and a
linked. The nun
the fructose mo
that you can ke
individual ring
molecule is flip

FIGURE 11-44
Line structure showing the planar arrangement of cellulose. The glycosidic linkage makes cellobiose a nearly flat molecule. This, in turn, leads to long, flat ribbons of cellulose. Hydrogen bonding between the chains gives an arrangement of macromolecules similar to the pleated sheet structure found in many proteins.

cellobiose units together to make cellulose gives a long ribbonlike chain of sugar units. The planar arrangement of cellulose makes it possible for hydrogen bonds to form between polysaccharide chains, as shown in Figure 11-44. This generates extended packages of cellulose ribbons that are similar to the pleated sheet structure of silk.

A typical cellulose molecule contains 2000 to 3000 glucose units in an unbranched linear chain. Individual chains group together through hydrogen bonds in bundles. The cell walls of plants are made up of these bundles laid down in a cross-hatched pattern that gives cellulose strength in all directions. This cross-hatched structure is shown in Figure 11-45.

The enzymes used to cleave α-glucose units from starches cannot attack the β-glucose linkages of cellulose because the geometry of the glycosidic linkage is different. As a result, cows and other ruminants must rely on bacteria in their digestive tracts to break down cellulose. These microorganisms, which are also present in termites, use a different group of enzymes to cleave β-glucose units.

Cellulose is the most abundant structural polysaccharide, but it is by no means the only one. Plants and animals use a variety of polysaccharides for a wide range of structural applications. Some polysaccharides contain sugars other than glucose, whereas others are derivatives of cellulose in which some of the hydroxyl groups on the ring have been converted into other functional groups. One important example is chitin, a derivative of cellulose present in many animals. Chitin makes up the exoskeletons of crustaceans, spiders, insects, and other arthropods. The structure of chitin, which is shown in Figure 11-46, is similar to that of cellulose, except that one hydroxyl group is replaced by an amide group.

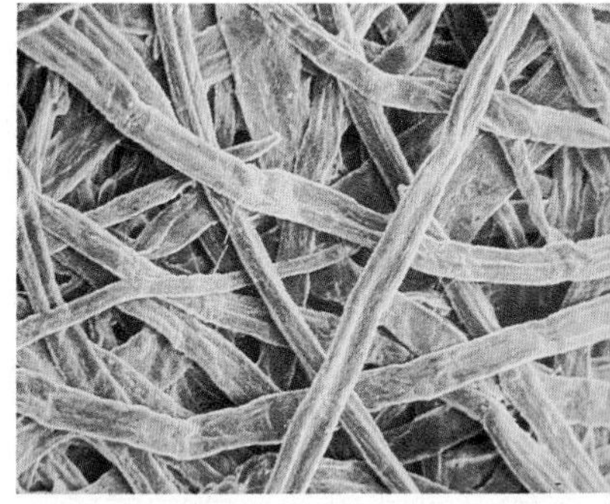

FIGURE 11-45
Plant cell walls are made of bundles of cellulose chains laid down in a cross-hatched pattern that gives cellulose strength in all directions.

Termites contain symbiotic microorganisms that break cellulose into glucose.

The exoskeletons of crabs and other arthropods are made of chitin.

Chitin

FIGURE 11-46
Chitin is a structural polysaccharide found in arthropods. The macromolecule is a derivative of cellulose in which one of the hydroxyl groups has been replaced by an amide.

SECTION EXERCISES

11.6.1 Gulose is a six-carbon sugar that differs from glucose in two positions. In gulose the hydroxyl groups marked with an asterisk in the following figure are perpendicular to the molecular plane rather than in the plane. Draw the chairlike structures of α- and β-gulose.

11.6.2 Approximately 5% of milk is lactose, which is made from β-galactose and β-glucose. The hydroxyl group adjacent to the ring oxygen atom in galactose links to the hydroxyl group in glucose that is adjacent to the ring carbon bearing the —CH_2OH fragment. Draw a picture of the structure of lactose. (The structure of galactose appears in Sample Problem 11-6.)

11.6.3 Many adults suffer from lactose intolerance. They cannot digest lactose because they are missing the enzyme that cleaves lactose into two monosaccharides. Examine the structures of lactose and sucrose (Figure 11-40). Point out the differences in their shapes that make it necessary to have different enzymes to break down these disaccharides.

11.7 NUCLEIC ACIDS

All biological organisms have the ability to reproduce themselves. The instructions for self-replication are stored and transmitted by macromolecules called **nucleic acids.** There are two types of nucleic acid, one to store genetic information and the other to transmit the information. Genetic information is *stored* in molecules of **deoxyribonucleic acid (DNA),** which are found in the nucleus of the cell. These huge molecules have molar masses as large as 1 trillion g/mol. The information stored in DNA is *transmitted* by **ribonucleic acid (RNA).** Almost all RNA is found outside the nucleus in the cytoplasm of the cell. There are several kinds of RNA; each has its own role in the operation of a cell. Molecules of RNA have molar masses of 20,000 to 40,000 g/mol, so they are much smaller than their DNA counterparts. In this section we examine the structures of nucleic acids and survey their biochemical functions.

THE BUILDING BLOCKS

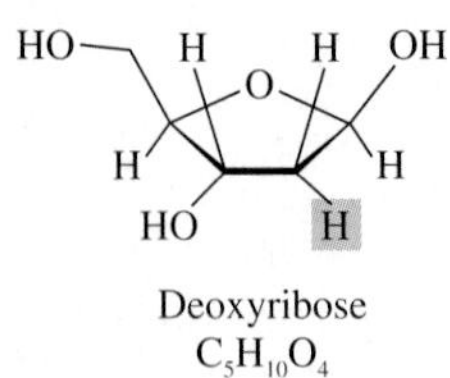

Replacing one hydroxyl group of ribose with a hydrogen atom (outlined in color) gives deoxyribose.

Nucleic acids are macromolecules made of three component parts:

1. A pentose sugar. In RNA the sugar is ribose (see Figure 11-36), and in DNA the sugar is deoxyribose, a ribose in which one hydroxyl group has been replaced with a hydrogen atom.
2. A nitrogen-containing organic base. There are five of these: **adenine, guanine, thymine, cytosine,** and **uracil.** Their structures are shown in Figure 11-47.
3. A phosphate linkage derived from phosphoric acid.

These three parts are linked through condensation reactions. The sugar is joined to the base when the hydroxyl group adjacent to the oxygen atom in the ribose ring

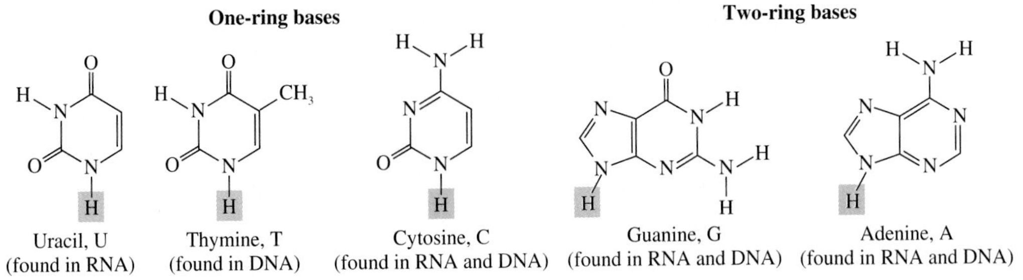

One-ring bases

Two-ring bases

Uracil, U (found in RNA)

Thymine, T (found in DNA)

Cytosine, C (found in RNA and DNA)

Guanine, G (found in RNA and DNA)

Adenine, A (found in RNA and DNA)

FIGURE 11-47
The organic bases found in DNA and RNA are divided into two groups, one with single rings and one with two rings. Uracil, thymine, and cytosine contain a single ring, whereas guanine and adenine have two rings. The hydrogen atoms that are eliminated during condensation have been highlighted.

combines with an N—H hydrogen from the base, thus connecting the rings with a C—N bond. This is shown for adenine in Figure 11-48. The combination of a base and a sugar is named for its base: cytidine, uridine, thymidine, guanosine, and adenosine. Phosphoric acid condenses with the CH_2OH hydroxyl group of the sugar to complete the linkage and form a **nucleotide.** Adenosine monophosphate (AMP), the nucleotide that contains adenine, is shown in Figure 11-49. Sample Problem 11-8 shows the formation of another nucleotide.

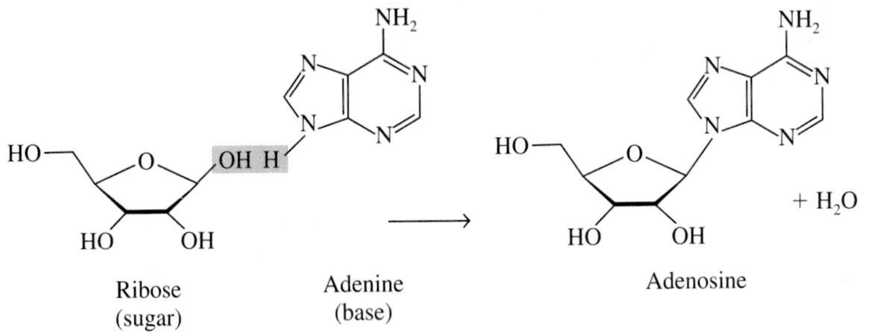

Ribose (sugar)

Adenine (base)

Adenosine

$+ H_2O$

FIGURE 11-48
Line structures showing the formation of adenosine from adenine and ribose.

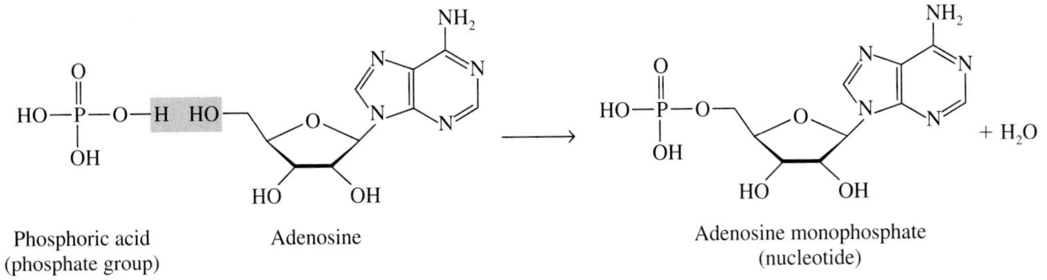

Phosphoric acid (phosphate group)

Adenosine

Adenosine monophosphate (nucleotide)

$+ H_2O$

FIGURE 11-49
The formation of adenosine monophosphate (AMP) from adenosine and phosphoric acid. The three linked units form the nucleotide building block required for nucleic acid synthesis.

SAMPLE PROBLEM 11-8 DRAWING NUCLEOTIDES

Draw the structure of uridine monophosphate (UMP).

METHOD: In constructing molecules made from component parts, a good approach is to draw each piece separately and then combine them in the proper order. The pieces are linked together by condensation reactions. Uridine monophosphate contains ribose, uracil, and one phosphate group. The structure of uracil and the hydrogen eliminated during the condensation is given in Figure 11-47.

Here are the component parts, drawn in position to eliminate water molecules and link together:

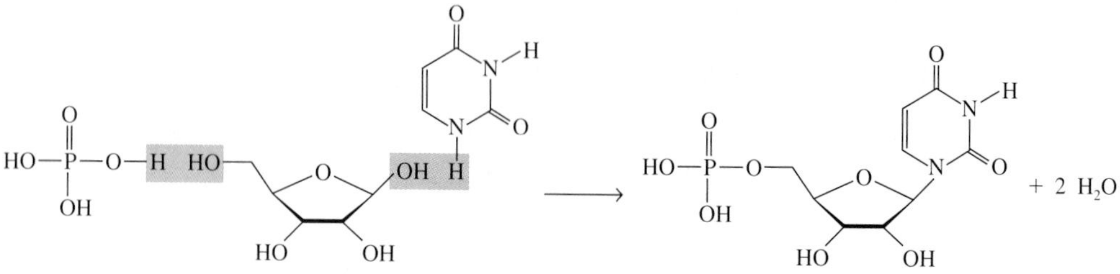

Phosphoric acid Ribose Uracil Uridine monophosphate

After we have placed the components next to one another, drawing the final structure is just a matter of removing the H_2O units. Uridine monophosphate has three components. From right to left in the drawing, they are: uracil, a single-ring base; ribose, the sugar; and one phosphate group.

THE PRIMARY STRUCTURE OF NUCLEIC ACIDS

A nucleic acid polymer contains chains of nucleotides, in which the phosphate group of one nucleotide links to the ribose ring of a second. The resulting backbone is an alternating sequence of sugars and phosphates, as shown in Figure 11-50.

Each position along a nucleic acid sequence is identical except for the identity of its base. Consequently, the sequence of bases defines the primary structure of a polynucleotide chain. Primary structure can be described simply by listing the order of bases in the nucleic acid. By convention the listing always begins with the nucleotide that has the terminal phosphate group, and it continues to the opposite end of the chain, where the sugar has an unreacted hydroxyl group in the linkage position. The nucleotides are listed as their one-letter abbreviations, A, C, G, and T or U. For example, ACGT stands for the following sequence:

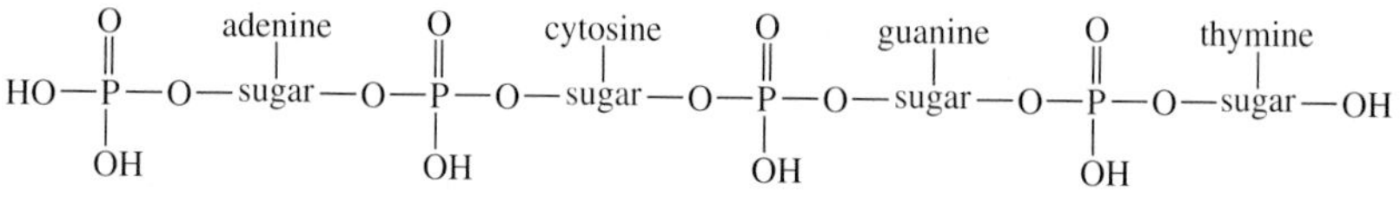

HO—P(=O)(OH)—O—sugar(adenine)—O—P(=O)(OH)—O—sugar(cytosine)—O—P(=O)(OH)—O—sugar(guanine)—O—P(=O)(OH)—O—sugar(thymine)—OH

SECONDARY STRUCTURE OF DNA: THE DOUBLE HELIX

Although DNA was first isolated in 1868, the nature of nucleic acids remained a mystery for more than 50 years thereafter. Not until the 1920s were the structures of

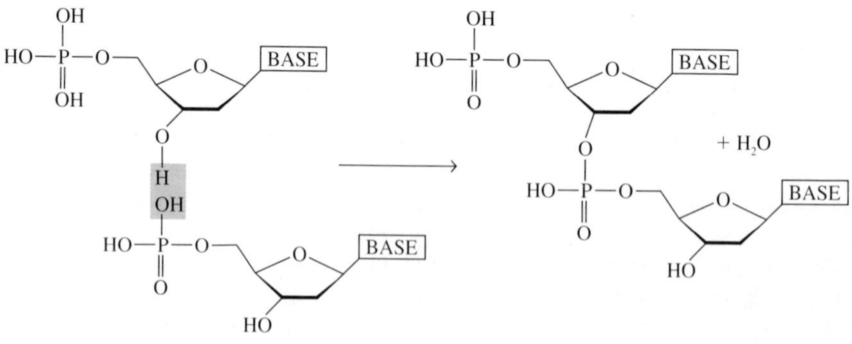

BASE BASE + H_2O BASE BASE

FIGURE 11-50

The backbone of a nucleic acid is formed by condensation reactions between nucleotides. The backbone of DNA is shown.

nucleotides determined. By then, many scientists suspected that DNA was the genetic material, but no one could fathom how sequences of just four different nucleotides could store immense quantities of genetic information. During the 1940s the British chemist Alexander Todd performed research on nucleic acids that eventually won him a Nobel Prize. Todd discovered the basic composition of the polynucleotide chain, with sugars, phosphates, and bases linked together as shown in Figure 11-50. Another crucial step was made early in the 1950s by Edwin Chargaff at Columbia University, who studied the composition of DNA from a variety of plants and animals. Chargaff found that the relative amounts of different bases changed from one species to another. In every species that he examined, however, the molar ratio of guanine to cytosine and adenine to thymine was always very close to 1.0. Chargaff concluded that these constant ratios could not be coincidence. Somehow, adenine and thymine are paired in DNA, and so are guanine and cytosine.

By now the stage was set for the discovery of the three-dimensional structure of DNA, so some of the best minds in science were working on the problem, driven in part by the expectation of winning a Nobel Prize. In 1953 James D. Watson and Francis Crick of Cambridge University announced that they had discovered the structure of DNA. Watson and Crick relied on X-ray diffraction patterns of DNA taken from the thymus gland of a calf. The diffraction photographs, among the best obtained at that time, were taken by Rosalind Franklin, a researcher in the laboratory of Maurice Wilkins at King's College in London. Combining Franklin's data with the earlier insights of Chargaff, Todd, and many others, Watson and Crick concluded that DNA must consist of two helices wound one around another in a **double helix.** In the double helix, shown in Figure 11-51, the hydrophilic sugars and the phosphate groups lie on the outside of the molecule, with the hydrophobic bases tucked inside the structure. For their brilliant insight, Watson, Crick, and Wilkins shared the 1963 Nobel Prize in medicine and physiology.

According to the Watson-Crick model, hydrogen bonding holds the double helix together. The bases of one strand of DNA form hydrogen bonds to the bases of the second strand. Because of their matching structures, adenine pairs with thymine through two hydrogen bonds, and guanine pairs with cytosine through three hydrogen bonds. These sets are said to be **complementary base pairs.** As shown in

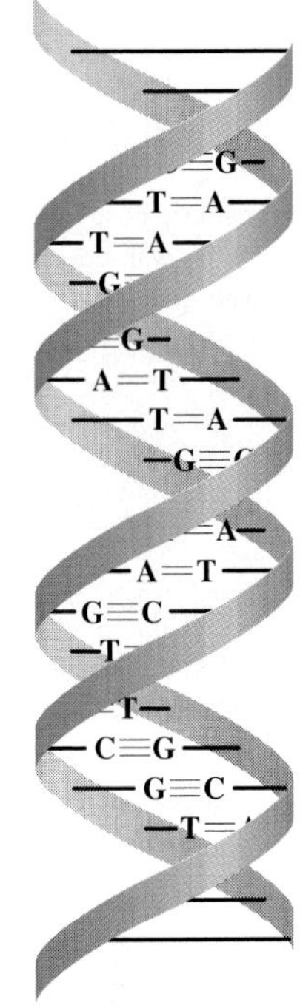

FIGURE 11-51
DNA consists of two strands wound one around the other in a double helix. The two helices are connected by hydrogen bonds between bases that pair within the molecule.

The structure of DNA was discovered by Francis Crick, James Watson, Maurice Wilkins, and Rosalind Franklin.

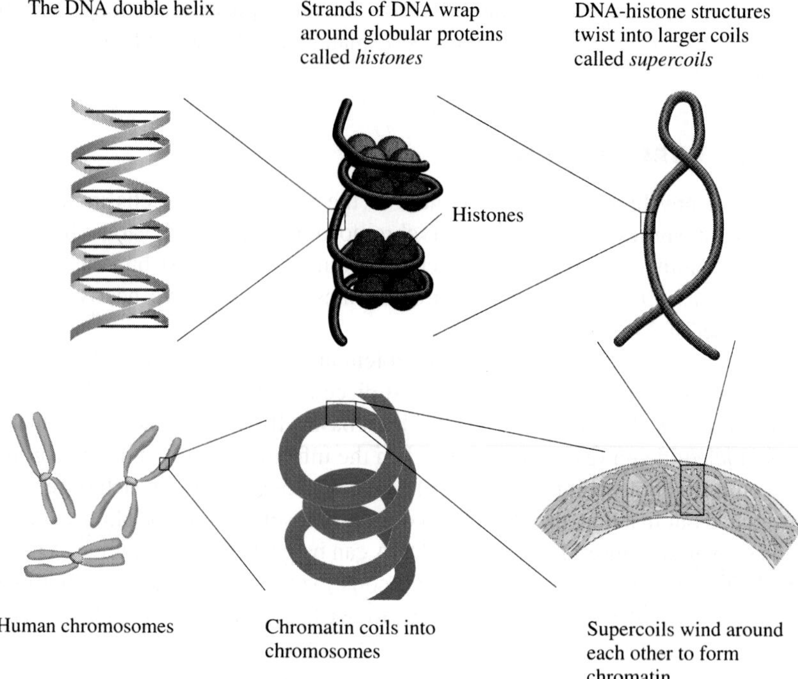

FIGURE 11-56
Levels of DNA organization within a chromosome.

Although RNA is usually single stranded, an RNA molecule often has distinct double-stranded regions. Intramolecular base pairing between guanine and cytosine and between adenine and uracil creates loops and kinks in the RNA molecule. The structure of one kind of RNA molecule is shown in Figure 11-57.

Whereas DNA is the storehouse of genetic information, RNA plays a much more varied role in the operation of a cell. There are several different types of RNA; each has its own function. The principal job of RNA is to synthesize proteins. Protein synthesis requires several steps, each assisted by RNA. One type of RNA copies the genetic information from DNA. This RNA carries the "blueprint" for protein

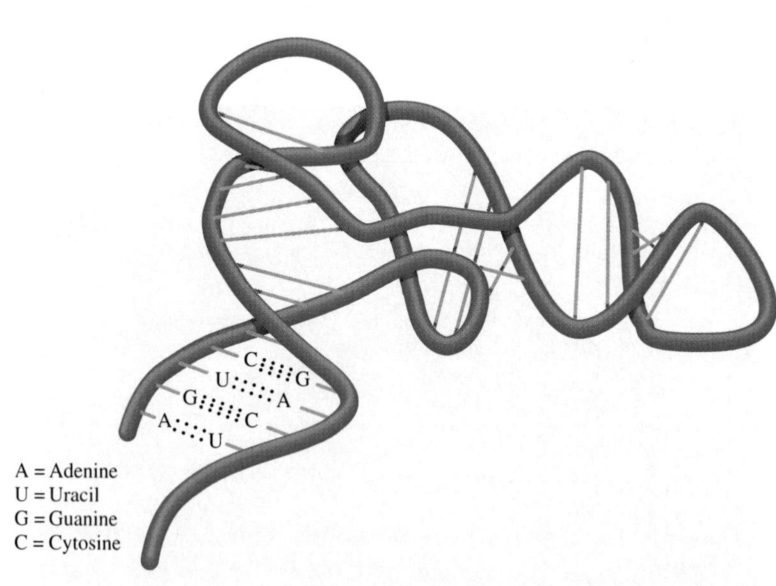

FIGURE 11-57
The structure of an RNA molecule. Notice the folding caused by the intrastrand base pairing.

LEARNING EXERCISES

11.1 Write a chapter summary of two pages or less that outlines the important features of this chapter.

11.2 Prepare a list of the types of polymer linkage reactions described in this chapter. List at least one important polymer that forms from each type of reaction.

11.3 Define *primary, secondary,* and *tertiary structure.* Give examples of each type of structure for a protein and for DNA.

11.4 Draw molecular pictures that illustrate the linkages in each of the following polymer types: polyethylene, polyester, polyamide, polyether, and silicone.

11.5 Draw pictures that illustrat α-helix, the pleated structur

11.6 Write a paragraph that de bonding in the structures of

11.7 List all terms new to you th one-sentence definition of Consult the index and gloss

PROBLEMS

POLYMERIZATION OF ALKENES

11.1 Saran is a copolymer made from vinyl chloride and vinylidene chloride ($H_2C{=}CCl_2$). Draw the structure of Saran showing at least four monomer units in the polymer.

11.2 Nitrile rubber, whose structure follows, is a copolymer made from two monomers. The polymer is used to make automotive hoses and gaskets. Draw the structures of the monomers and name them.

CN CN

11.3 Use the polymerization of acrylonitrile to describe each of the three steps of free radical polymerization. Write structures that illustrate the steps.

11.4 Draw a section of the polymer chain showing at least four repeat units for each of the following polymers: (a) Teflon; (b) PVC; and (c) Styrofoam.

11.5 Identify the monomers used to make the following polymers.

(a) $-\!\!\!+\!CH_2CH(NO_2){-}CH_2CH(NO_2)\!+\!\!\!-$

(b) $-\!\!\!+\!CFCl{-}CF_2{-}CFCl{-}CF_2\!+\!\!\!-$

FUNCTIONAL GROUPS

11.6 Draw structural formulas and circle and identify the functional groups in the following molecules:

(a) O OH (b) NH_2 O

(c) 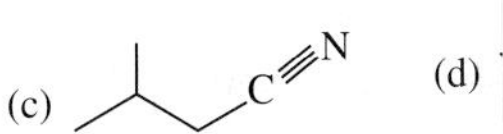

(d)

(e) (f)

11.7 Identify the functional grou

a)
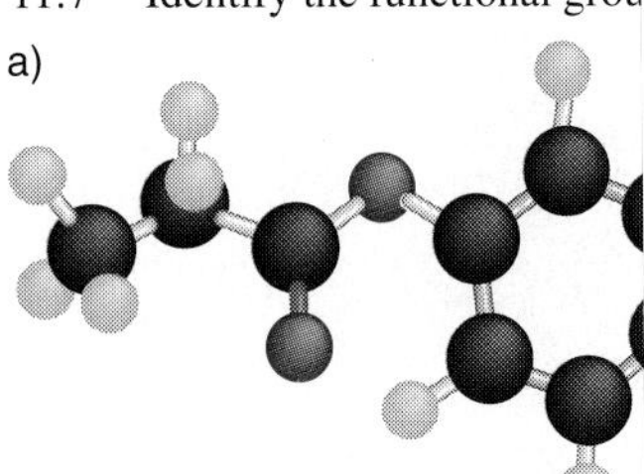

b)
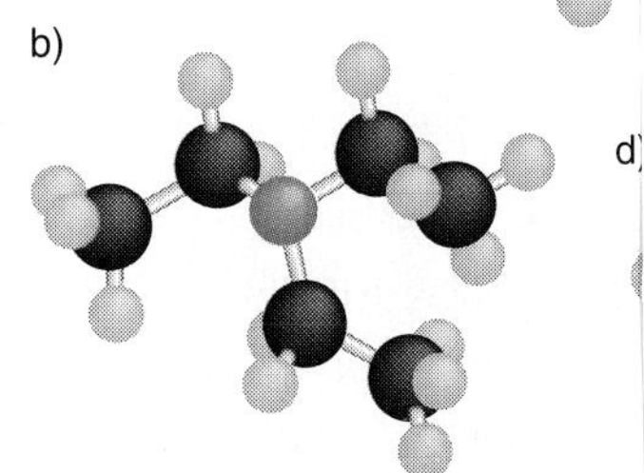

d)

e)
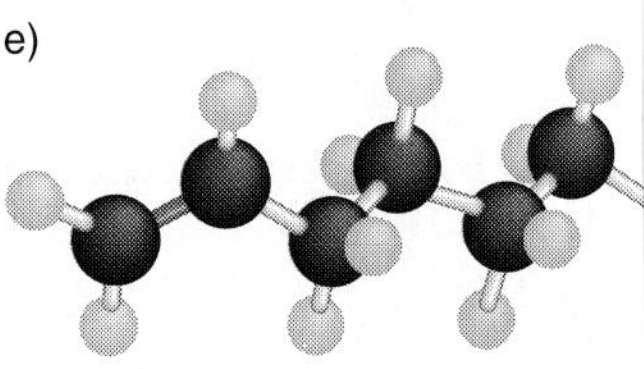

11.8 Draw one example of (a) $C_4H_{10}O$; (b) a carboxylic aci 60 g/mol; (c) a thiol with amide that also contains a carbons.

synthesis out of the cell nucleus and into the cytoplasm, where construction of the protein takes place. The protein is assembled on the surface of a ribosome, a cell component that contains both a protein and a second type of RNA. The protein is constructed by sequential addition of amino acids in the order specified by the DNA. The individual amino acids are carried to the growing protein chain by yet a third type of RNA. The details of protein synthesis are well understood, but the process is much too complex to be described in an introductory course in chemistry.

SECTION EXERCISES

11.7.1 Draw the structure of the RNA nucleotide that contains guanine.

11.7.2 Part of a DNA sequence is G-C-C-A-T-A-G-G-T. What is its complementary sequence?

11.7.3 Nucleotides can contain more than one phosphate group. For example, adenosine triphosphate (ATP) is an energy storage molecule discussed in Chapter 13. An ATP molecule is formed in two sequential condensation reactions between phosphoric acid and the phosphate group of AMP:

$$AMP + 2\,H_3PO_4 \rightarrow ATP + 2\,H_2O$$

Draw the structure of ATP.

CHAPTER SUMMARY

1. A polymer is a macromolecule constructed from monomers.
2. Polyethylene is a long-chain hydrocarbon polymer made from ethylene monomers. Polyethylene forms in a free-radical chain process that begins when an initiator breaks into fragments and ends when two polymer fragments combine. Substituted derivatives of ethylene can also polymerize.
3. Rubbers are polymers formed from dienes or copolymers of dienes and alkenes, such as butadiene and styrene. Rubbers are strengthened by introducing sulfur-sulfur cross-links.
4. Many polymers form from the condensation reactions between monomers containing functional groups. Alcohols, carboxylic acids, and amines are the functional groups that participate most frequently in condensation polymerization. They link together via ester, amide, and ether linkages. Silicone polymers contain Si—O—Si chains and hydrocarbon side groups.
5. Polymers are classed as plastics, fibers, or elastomers. Thermoplastic polymers are flexible and melt on heating, whereas thermosetting polymers are rigid and heat-resistant. Fibers can be drawn from a melt or solution but harden into durable filaments. Elastomers are flexible yet resilient.
6. Biological macromolecules, though more complex than synthetic macromolecules, also form from monomeric building blocks by condensation reactions.
7. Proteins are polypeptides built from combinations of 20 different amino acids; some are hydrophilic, and others are hydrophobic. The primary structure of a protein is its amino acid sequence, its secondary structure is the geometric organization of neighboring peptide units, and its tertiary structure is the bends and folds in the polypeptide chain. Protein secondary structure includes coiled α-helices and planar pleated sheets. Many proteins are globular in overall shape, whereas others are fibrous.

8. Carbohydrates are compounds of carbon, hydrogen, an[d] Monosaccharides are carbohydrates constructed around Monosaccharides link into polysaccharides such as star[ch] drates differ from one another only in the orientations o[f] these differences lead to different shapes and biological
9. DNA and RNA contain three types of building blocks: [...] containing organic bases, and phosphate linkages. The [...] is its sequence of bases. Each organic base forms hydro[gen] base, and DNA is organized into a double-helical "stair[case] hydrogen-bonded bases. RNA has a less regular second[ary]

KEY TERMS

copolymer	alcohol	amino acid
free radical	aldehyde	disulfide bridge
free radical polymerization	amine	enzyme
initiator	carboxylic acid	fibrous protein
monomer	condensation reaction	globular protein
polyamide	ester	α-helix
polyester	ether	peptide linkage
polyethylene	functional group	pleated sheet
polymer	hydroxyl group	polypeptide
propagation	ketone	primary structure
silicone	linkage group	secondary structure
termination	thiol	tertiary structure
	cross-linking	carbohydrate
	elastomer	cellulose
	fiber	monosaccharide
	plasticizer	polysaccharide
	plastic	starch
	thermoplastic	
	thermosetting	

SKILLS TO MASTER

- Describing free radical polymerization
- Drawing structures of polyalkenes and rubbers
- Identifying alkene monomers
- Recognizing functional groups
- Recognizing linkage groups
- Describing condensation polymerization
- Drawing structures of condensation polymers
- Describing primary, secondar[y]
- Recognizing hydrophilic and
- Describing hydrogen bonding
- Drawing structures of saccha[rides]
- Visualizing geometries of pol[...]
- Drawing DNA and RNA stru[ctures]
- Determining complementary

11.9 Draw one example of (a) an amine with the formula $C_5H_{13}N$; (b) an ester with eight carbon atoms; (c) an aldehyde whose molar mass is at least 80 g/mol; and (d) an ether that contains a phenyl group.

11.10 Write balanced equations that show how the following molecules are produced in condensation reactions.

(a) 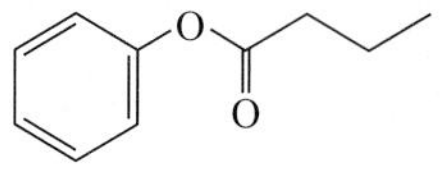 [structure]

(b) 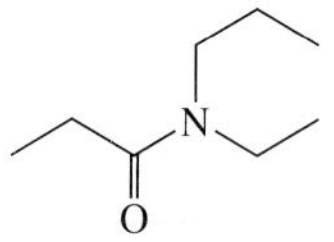 [structure] (c) 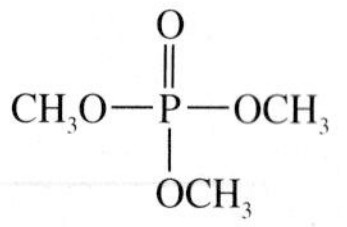 $CH_3O-P(=O)(OCH_3)-OCH_3$

11.11 Write balanced equations that show how the following molecules are produced in condensation reactions.

(a) 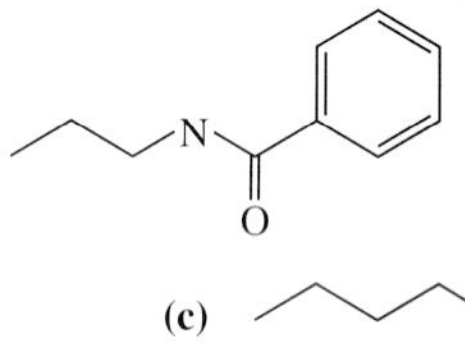 [structure] (b) 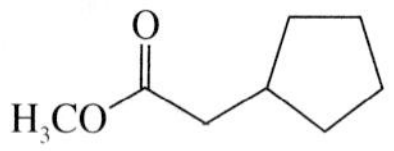 [structure, H_3CO] (c) 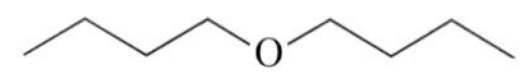 [structure]

11.12 Draw the structures of the condensation products of the following reactions:

(a) 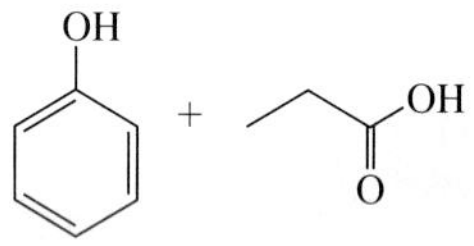 [phenol] + [propanoic acid]

(b) 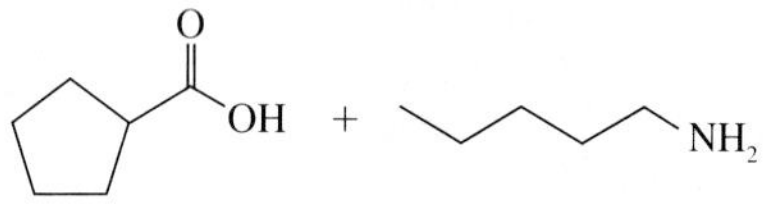 [cyclopentyl acetic acid] + [pentylamine, NH_2]

CONDENSATION POLYMERS

11.13 The structure of Nylon 11 is shown below. Draw line structures of the monomer(s) used to make this polymer.

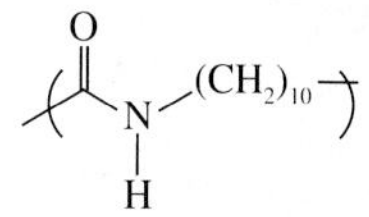

[structure: $-(C(=O)-NH-(CH_2)_{10})-$]

11.14 Kodel is a polyester fiber made from terephthalic acid and cyclohexanedimethanol. Draw a segment of Kodel that contains at least four repeat units.

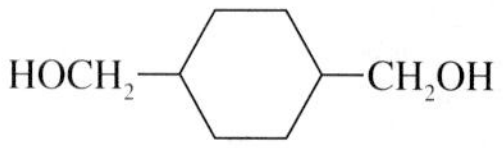

$HOCH_2-C_6H_{10}-CH_2OH$ Cyclohexanedimethanol

11.15 Ethylene oxide forms a polyether by ring opening followed by chain formation. Draw the structure of this polymer.

Ethylene oxide

11.16 Draw two strands of Nylon 6, each with four repeat units. Show the two strands connected by hydrogen bonds.

POLYMER PROPERTIES

11.17 Which is more cross-linked, the rubber in an automobile tire or the rubber in a pair of surgical gloves? Explain.

11.18 Plastic wrap can be stretched slightly to fit snugly over a food container. Is plastic wrap a thermoplastic or a thermosetting polymer? Explain.

11.19 What category of polymer would you use to make each of the following items: (a) balloon; (b) rope; and (c) camera case.

11.20 Describe the changes in polymer properties that occur on cross-linking.

11.21 Describe the changes in polymer properties that occur on adding dioctylphthalate to the reaction mixture.

PROTEINS

11.22 Draw the structures of the following amino acids: (a) Tyr; (b) Phe; (c) Glu; (d) His; (e) Leu; and (f) Pro.

11.23 Assign each amino acid in Problem 11-22 as possessing hydrophobic or hydrophilic side chains. Explain each assignment.

11.24 Identify the following amino acids and characterize them as possessing hydrophilic or hydrophobic side chains:

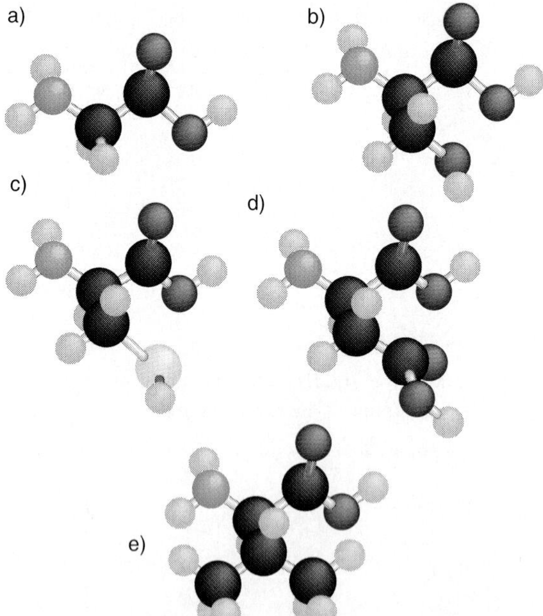

11.25 Draw the line structures of all possible dipeptides that can form in condensation reactions between alanine, glutamic acid, and methionine.

11.26 Draw the line structures of all possible dipeptides that can be formed from Cys, Gly, and Asn.

11.27 Suppose a polypeptide is constructed with alanine as the only monomer. What is the empirical formula of this polypeptide? If the polypeptide has a molar mass of 1.20×10^3 g/mol, how many amino acids does it contain?

11.28 The artificial sweetener aspartame (Nutra-Sweet) is the methyl ester of the following dipeptide:

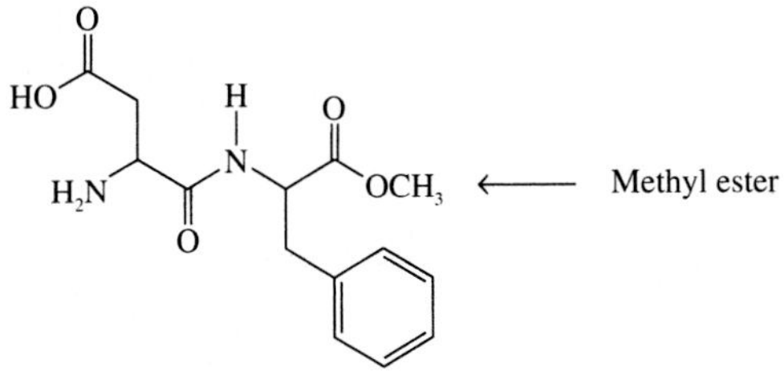

HO, O, H, N, O, H_2N, OCH_3 ⟵ Methyl ester, O

What two amino acids are used to make aspartame?

CARBOHYDRATES

11.29 Cyclohexanediol is a six-membered ring composed of four CH_2 groups and two CHOH groups at opposite ends of the ring. Draw this molecule in its "chair" form, with the OH groups projecting parallel to the plane defined by the bonds in the ring.

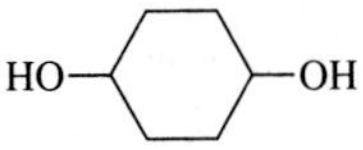

HO—⬡—OH Cyclohexanediol

11.30 Gentobiose is a disaccharide found bonded to a number of biological molecules. Gentobiose contains two linked β-glucose molecules. One molecule links through the hydroxyl group adjacent to the ring oxygen, whereas the other links through the CH_2OH hydroxyl group. Draw the structure of gentobiose.

11.31 The six-carbon sugar talose differs from glucose in the orientations of the hydroxyl groups at the positions that are indicated with asterisks in the following structure. Draw the structures of α- and β-talose.

11.32 Glycogen and cellulose are polymers of glucose. Explain why humans can use glycogen as an energy source but not cellulose. Why can cows digest cellulose, but humans cannot?

11.33 Glycogen is a glucose polymer that collects in granules in the liver. Cellulose is also a polymer of glucose, but cellulose forms sheetlike arrangements that are used in the cell walls of plants. What are the distinguishing structural features that allow glycogen to form granules while cellulose forms sheets? Illustrate your answer.

NUCLEIC ACIDS

11.34 Complete the following table:

	RNA	DNA
Sugar		
One-ring bases		
Two-ring bases		

11.35 Part of a DNA sequence is A-A-T-G-C-A-C-T-G. What is its complementary sequence?

11.36 Draw the complete structure of the following segment of RNA: G-U-A-C.

11.37 Draw the complete structure of the following segment of DNA: A-T-C-G.

11.38 Although RNA is a single-stranded molecule, it can have extensive regions of double-stranded structure resulting from intramolecular hydrogen bonding between guanine and cytosine and between adenine and uracil. Draw the hydrogen bonding interaction between adenine and uracil.

11.39 One strand of DNA contains the base sequence A-T-C. What is the base sequence of the complementary strand? Draw a structure of this section of DNA that shows the hydrogen bonding between the base pairs.

ADDITIONAL PROBLEMS

11.40 Condensation polymers are usually made from two different monomers; each has two of the same functional group. Give three reasons that this strategy is used so often in polymer synthesis.

11.41 What is the hybridization of the nitrogen atom in a peptide linkage? (HINT: The nitrogen has trigonal planar geometry.) Explain why nitrogen adopts this form of hybridization.

11.42 Hair spray is a solution of a polymer in a volatile solvent. When the solvent evaporates, a thin film of polymer is left behind that holds the hair in place. Many hair sprays contain a copolymer made of the following monomers.

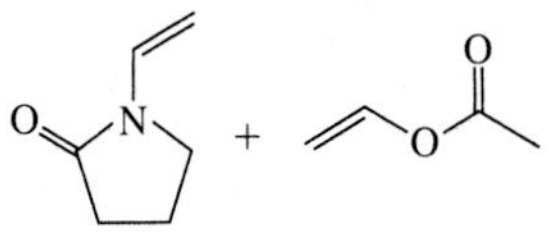

O, N, +, O, O

(a) Assume that the polymer is made from a 1 : 1 mixture of the two monomers. Will the two monomers alternate in the polymer, or will the arrangement be random? Explain.
(b) Draw a section of the copolymer containing at least six repeat units.
(c) What structural features of the copolymer allow it hold hair in place?

11.43 The development of biomaterials, artificial substances compatible with human tissue, is an important area of research. The use of PET polymers as permanent replacements for blood vessels is one example of a biomaterial in current use. Another example is a polymer of lactic acid, used to make body implants that are necessary for only a short time. The body absorbs the polymer and leaves no permanent residue. Over time, the polymer is hydrolyzed back to lactic acid, which is metabolized to CO_2 and water in the same manner as natural lactic acid. What is the structure of the polymer made from lactic acid?

Lactic acid

11.44 Automobiles and major appliances such as refrigerators and washing machines require very tough, long-lasting paints that are baked onto the surface of the object. One group of such paints is known as *alkyds,* which stands for *al*cohol and ac*id.* These polyesters have extensive cross-linking that characterizes a tough coating material. One of the simplest alkyds is formed from phthalic acid and glycerol. Heating at 130 °C for about an hour maximizes the amount of cross-linking. Draw the structure of the condensation polymer that forms from these two monomers:

$2n$ Glycerol + $3n$ Phthalic acid ⟶ Alkyd polymer

11.45 Compute the molar mass of a polystyrene molecule that has 452 monomer units.

11.46 The smallest proteins contain 50 or so amino acids. How many different 50-amino-acid proteins can be formed from the 20 common amino acids? (Express your answer in power of ten notation.)

11.47 Identify all the molecular building block units in one nucleotide and its hydrogen-bonded partner of double-stranded DNA. Draw a molecular picture of one of these units.

11.48 Almost 1000 g of α-glucose will dissolve in 1 L of water. Draw the structure of α-glucose and include enough hydrogen-bonded water molecules to account for its tremendous solubility.

11.49 For a cell to synthesize a particular protein, the information about that protein, which is stored in the nucleus in DNA, must be transmitted to the cytoplasm where protein synthesis takes place. This "shuttling" of genetic information is accomplished by a type of RNA called messenger RNA (mRNA). The DNA is used as a template to make the mRNA, so the bases of mRNA must be complementary to DNA. Assuming that mRNA is made from strand A of the DNA shown below, identify bases 1, 2, 3, and 4 in the mRNA.

Strand A		Strand B		mRNA
S—G	······	C—S		S—1
S—A	······	T—S		S—2
S—T	······	A—S	⟶	S—3
S—C	······	G—S		S—4

S, Sugar; *P*, phosphate.

11.50 Identify the monomers used to make the following polymers: (a) Nylon 6; (b) PET; (c) Dacron; (d) PVC; and (e) Styrofoam.

11.51 Proteins are synthesized in the cell by adding one amino acid at a time to the growing polypeptide chain. Each amino acid is carried to the protein in a form in which the amino acid is linked to adenosine monophosphate. The amino acid is joined to AMP by a condensation of its carboxylic acid with the phosphate group. Draw the structure of Ala-AMP.

11.52 The names of most enzymes end in *-ase*. In many cases the prefix refers to the type of molecules on which the enzymes act. Match each enzyme with its reaction.

1. Peptidase	a. Removes carboxyl groups from organic compounds
2. Transmethylase	b. Catalyzes the formation of esters
3. Carboxylase	c. Hydrolyzes peptide linkages
4. Esterase	d. Moves a CH_3 group from one position in a molecule to another

11.53 Fungal lactase is an enzyme found in fungi that live on rotting wood. The enzyme is blue in color and contains 0.40% by mass copper. The molar mass of the enzyme is approximately 64,000 g/mol. How many copper atoms are there in one molecule of fungal lactase?

11.54 How do interactions with solvents affect the tertiary structure of a protein?

11.55 The first step of glucose metabolism is an enzyme-catalyzed condensation reaction between phosphoric acid and the CH_2OH hydroxyl on glucose. Draw the structure of this glucose phosphate.

11.56 Use cytosine, ribose, and a phosphate group to draw the structure of a nucleotide.

11.57 Explain the gross differences between fibrous proteins and globular proteins. What role does each type of protein play in biological organisms?

11.58 The melting point of DNA, which is the temperature at which the double helix "unwinds," increases as the amount of guanine and cytosine increases and the amount of adenine and thymine decreases. Explain this observation.

11.59 According to Table 11-2, amines can form polymers by reacting with alcohols. The polymerization reaction is condensation with elimination of water. Draw the structure of the repeat unit of the polymer that forms from ethylene glycol and *p*-phenylenediamine.

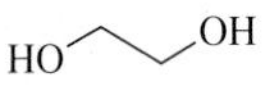

HO OH H_2N NH_2

Ethylene glycol  *p*-Phenylenediamine

11.60 What features do nylon and proteins have in common? In what ways are they distinctly different?

11.61 One of the problems encountered in the polymerization of monomers that contain two different functional groups is that the molecules tend to cyclize rather than polymerize. Draw the structure of the cyclized product that would be produced from the following monomer.

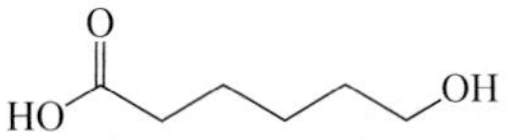

O HO OH

11.62 Chewing gum is mostly *polyvinylacetate*. The monomer used to make chewing gum is vinyl acetate.

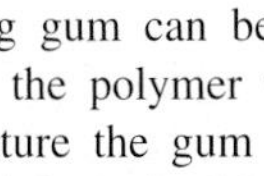

O O Vinyl acetate $C_4H_6O_2$

(a) Draw a portion of the polyvinylacetate polymer. Show at least three repeat units.
(b) Is polyvinylacetate a plastic, a fiber, or an elastomer? Use the behavior of chewing gum to justify your choice.
(c) Chewing gum can be removed from clothing by cooling the polymer with a piece of ice. At low temperature the gum crumbles easily and can be removed from the fabric. Explain this procedure at the molecular level.

11.63 High-density polyethylene has more CH_2 groups per unit volume than does low-density polyethylene. Explain why this is so in terms of the structures of the two forms of the polymer.

11.64 In the synthesis of glycogen an enzyme catalyzes the transfer of a glucose molecule from glucose-UDP to the growing end of a glycogen polysaccharide. Glucose-UDP is a uridine diphosphate molecule linked to the hydroxyl group on the carbon adjacent to the ring oxygen atom of α-glucose. The glucose is at the end of UDP's phosphate chain. Draw the structure of glucose-UDP.

11.65 Draw the structures of polyethylene and the copolymer of butadiene and styrene, showing at least four repeat units for each polymer. On the basis of their molecular structures, explain why polyethylene is more rigid than butadienestyrene copolymer.

11.66 In the 1950s Edwin Chargaff of Columbia University studied the composition of DNA from a variety of plants and animals. He found that the relative amounts of different bases changed from one species to another. However, in every species Chargaff studied, the molar ratio of guanine to cytosine and adenine to thymine was found to be very close to 1.0. Explain Chargaff's observations in terms of the Watson-Crick model of DNA structure.

11.67 Copolymerization of styrene with a small amount of divinylbenzene gives a cross-linked polymer that is hard and insoluble. Draw a picture of this polymer that shows at least two cross-links. (HINT: The cross-linking starts when divinylbenzene is incorporated into the growing polystyrene chain.)

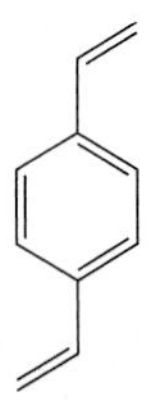

Divinylbenzene

11.68 Glyptal is a highly cross-linked polymer made by heating glycerol and phthalic anhydride. Show the structure of glyptal. (HINT: The highlighted section of phthalic anhydride reacts with water in a "reverse condensation reaction" to give the monomer that polymerizes with glycerol.)

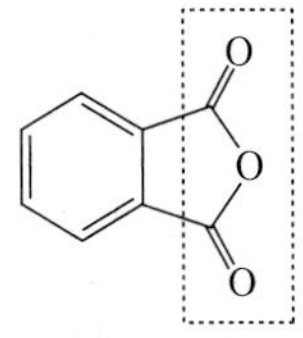

O O O Phthalic anhydride

11.69 Globular proteins adopt three-dimensional structures that place some of the amino acids on the inside of the molecule, out of contact with the aqueous environment, and others on the outer surface of the molecule. Which of the following amino acids would be most likely to be found on the inside of a globular protein? Explain your choices. (a) Arg; (b) Val; (c) Met; (d) Thr; and (e) Asp.

ANSWERS TO SECTION EXERCISES

11.1.1

(a) F F F n (b) n

(c) O O O H_3CO H_3CO H_3CO n

11.1.2

Ph Ph

11.1.3

Cl

11.2.1 (a) Hydroxyl; (b) amine and carboxyl; and (c) ester

11.2.2

NH_2 H N O OH O NH_2 H N O OH O

11.2.3 (In each case there are several correct answers.)

(a) N (b) O O

(c) OH (d) H—C(=O)—

11.3.1

11.3.2

11.3.3

HO OH + HO OH ⟶ HO O OH + H_2O

11.4.1 In Kevlar, hydrogen bonding between the amide linkage groups holds the polymer chains in a sheetlike arrangement. This gives the benzene rings a specific ordered orientation and makes the polymer highly crystalline. On the other hand, polystyrene chains are held together by weaker dispersion forces. The polymer is less ordered and more flexible than Kevlar.

11.4.2 Polyethylene and isoprene are both made from alkenes by free radical polymerization. Polyethylene has long chains of CH_2 groups; in some applications there are branches off the main chain of the polymer. The chains of CH_2 groups can "line up" in rows that create regions of crystallinity within the polymer. The degree of crystallinity, which depends on the amount of branching, determines whether polyethylene is a thermosetting or thermoplastic polymer. In contrast, polyisoprene is made by polymerizing a diene, so the repeat unit of the polymer retains one C=C double bond. Because of the specific geometry of the double bonds, polyisoprene lacks the structural regularity required to form a crystalline polymer. Instead, polyisoprene chains are tangled together in no specific arrangement. As a consequence, the polymer is an elastomer.

11.4.3

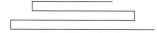

Crystallinity comes from dispersion forces that are easily overcome by stretching the polymer.

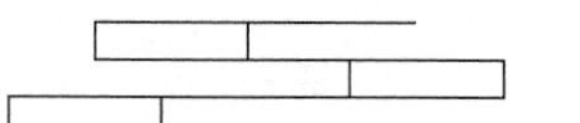

In this case, the ordered structure of the polymer comes from strong covalent cross-links that prohibit stretching of the chain.

11.5.1 Ala-Thr-Val-Gly-His

11.5.2 (Lone pairs shown only on hydrogen-bonded atoms.)

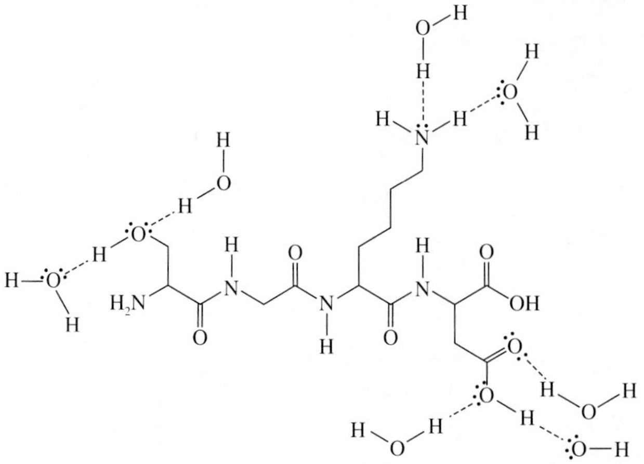

11.5.3 The primary structure of a protein is the linear sequence of amino acids, which are held together by covalent bonds. "Secondary structure" refers to regions of the protein chain that twist into coils or fold into sheets. Hydrogen bonding between the amide residues of the protein backbone accounts for secondary structure. The overall shape of a protein is its tertiary structure. Dispersion forces, hydrogen bonding, and covalent cross-links between cysteine side-chains contribute to the tertiary structure.

11.6.1

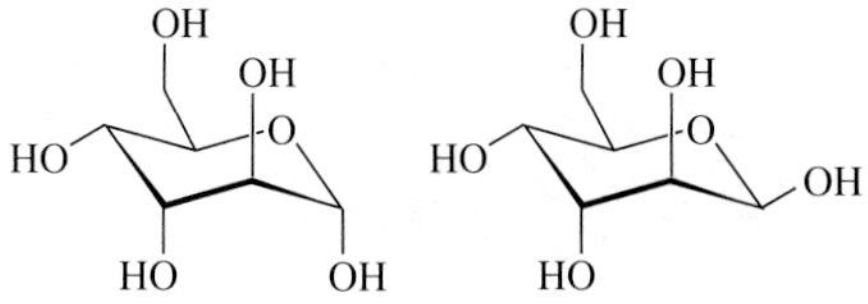

α–Gulose β–Gulose

11.6.2

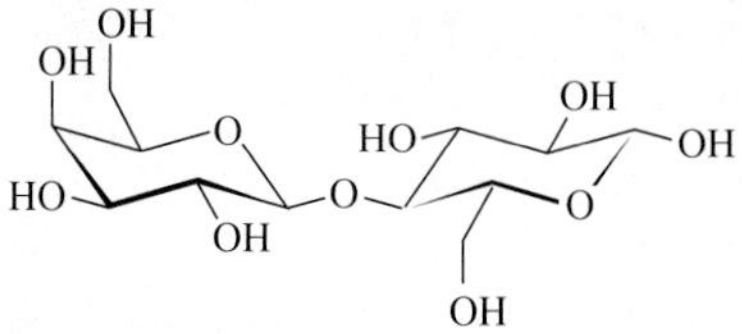

11.6.3 Sucrose is fructose linked to α-glucose. Lactose is galactose linked to β-glucose. The different glycosidic linkages give different shapes; lactose is nearly flat, whereas sucrose is, to some extent, bent around the glycosidic linkage. Different-shaped sugars require different-shaped enzymes for the cleavage reaction.

11.7.1

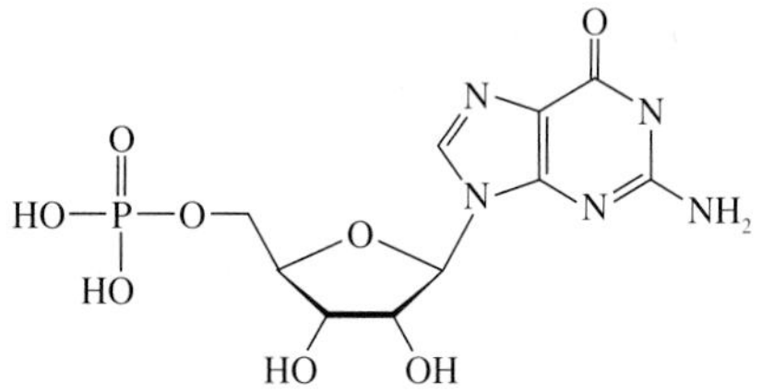

11.7.2 C-G-G-T-A-T-C-C-A

11.7.3

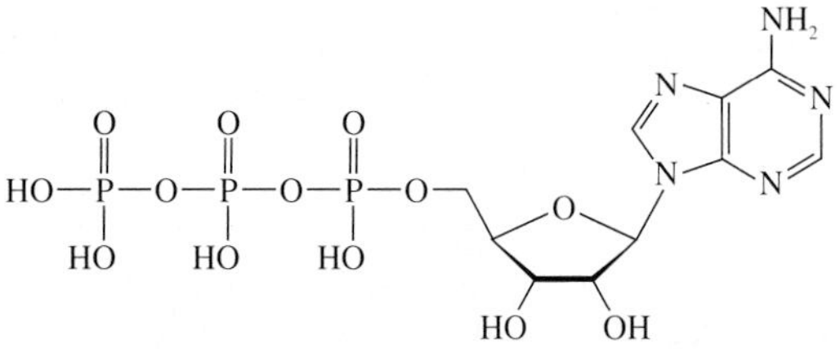

CHAPTER 12 CHEMICAL ENERGETICS

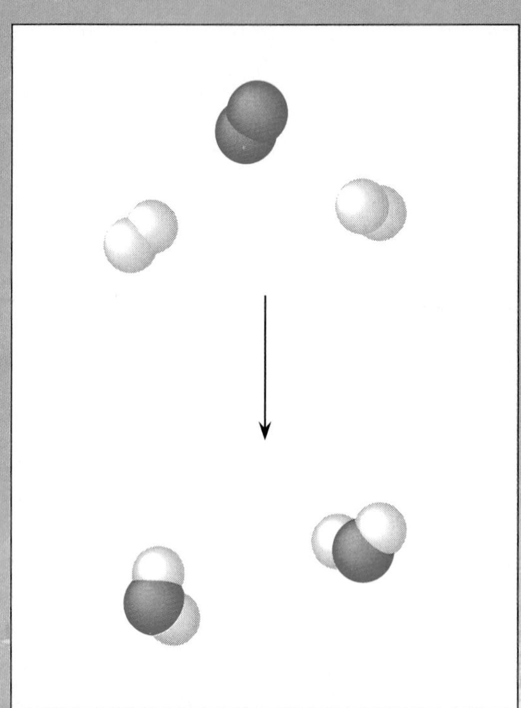

The enormous amount of energy needed to lift the space shuttle into orbit is supplied by the chemical reaction of hydrogen with oxygen to produce water.

The energy released by burning fuels is indispensable for modern society. One example is the chemical energy stored in petroleum, which we use to propel automobiles and airplanes and to generate electricity. Moreover, the chemical energy stored in natural gas is exploited to heat our homes, and the energy stored in dynamite is used to build roads and tunnels.

Energy changes also dominate many important industrial processes. For example, the production of iron and aluminum from their ores, which we explore in Chapter 17, requires immense amounts of energy. The synthesis of ammonia, a top 50 industrial chemical that is crucial for the fertilizer industry, also consumes huge quantities of energy. Energy production and consumption play key roles in every part of the chemical industry, from plastics to metals and from foodstuffs to drugs.

Every chemical process, from the burning of natural gas to the decomposition of aluminum oxide into aluminum metal, has an energy balance determined by the strengths of the chemical bonds in the reactants and the products. Other chemical properties, such as whether a substance is a gas, liquid, or solid, depend on the energies of atoms and molecules. Moreover, the energy released during the formation of chemical bonds determines the stability of a chemical compound. See Chapters 8 to 10 for more details.

It is a fundamental law of nature that energy can be transformed from one form to another, but it cannot be created or destroyed. This law of conservation of energy lets us account accurately for the energy changes that accompany chemical and physical transformations of matter. Thermodynamics, which we introduce in this chapter and Chapter 13, describes in detail the principles that govern energy changes. Our major focus in this chapter is the balance and flow of energy. In Chapter 13 we examine how the direction of chemical change is related to changes in energy.

12.1 THERMODYNAMIC DEFINITIONS

Thermodynamics is a precise, quantitative subject whose concepts must be defined carefully. One fundamental notion is the **state of a system.** In thermodynamic analyses, we often describe the state of a system or changes in the state of a system, but what do we mean by system and state?

SYSTEM

A thermodynamic **system** is any part of the universe that we want to describe and study by itself. Figure 12-1 shows several examples of thermodynamic systems: a light bulb, a dog, an automobile engine, an automobile, a thundercloud, and the Earth. After we have selected a particular thing to be a system, the rest of the universe is defined to be the **surroundings:**

$$\text{System} + \text{Surroundings} = \text{Universe}$$

FIGURE 12-1
Some examples of thermodynamic systems. Note that an automobile can be defined as a system, but its component parts, such as its engine, can, too.

The choice of what to include in the system and what to leave as part of the surroundings depends on our particular interests. One design engineer might regard an entire automobile as the system. A second might focus on the engine as the system, and a third might define an individual cylinder and piston as the system. A chemist, on the other hand, would be inclined to define the chemicals in the cylinder as the system. Each of these would be an acceptable and useful choice for a system, but each of these four people would have to describe their choices clearly before they could have a sensible discussion about the different systems.

A system may be open, closed, or isolated, depending on its interactions with the surroundings. An open system exchanges matter and energy with its surroundings. A closed system exchanges energy but not matter, and an isolated system exchanges neither matter nor energy with the surroundings. Figure 12-2 shows the same system, a soft drink, in each of these three situations.

Almost all real systems are open. Automobiles, for example, take in gasoline and air and expel exhaust gases and heat. Open systems are very difficult to describe quantitatively, however, so much of our discussion of thermodynamics concerns closed and isolated systems. Isolated systems represent an ideal situation that can be approached but never actually attained in the real world. For example, no matter how good we make the insulation for the thermos flask shown in Figure 12-2, *C,* it will slowly exchange energy (heat) with its surroundings.

FIGURE 12-2
Examples of systems involving a soft drink. *Left,* A glass of a soft drink is an open system. *Center,* An unopened can of a soft drink is a closed system. *Right,* A stoppered thermos of a soft drink approximates an isolated system.

STATE AND CHANGES OF STATE

The conditions that describe a system are collectively called its *state.* When these conditions change, we speak of a **change of state.** Conditions that must be specified to establish the state of a system are called **state variables.** For chemical systems, state variables are often familiar quantities: pressure *(P)*, volume *(V)*, temperature *(T)*, and amounts of substances *(n)*. Frequently, state variables are related in some way. A mathematical equation that describes such a relationship is an **equation of state.** If the system is an ideal gas, for example, the equation of state is the familiar $PV = nRT$. Other, more complicated systems have more complicated equations of state.

Changes of state occur during most interesting processes in thermodynamics. For instance, a gas initially described by conditions P_i, V_i, T_i, and n_i may undergo a transformation to a different set of final conditions P_f, V_f, T_f, and n_f. It is not necessary for *all* the conditions to change during a change of state. If 1 mol of helium atoms expands at constant temperature, as shown in Figure 12-3, its volume increases and its pressure decreases, but the temperature and the number of moles remain constant. Any process in which *at least one* state variable changes its value is a change of state.

A subscript *i* denotes initial conditions, and a subscript *f* denotes final conditions.

CHEMICAL CHANGES OF STATE

The expansion of helium gas illustrated in Figure 12-3 is a *physical* change of state. The atoms are distributed over a larger volume after expansion, but the atoms themselves do not change during the expansion. Thus no chemical change occurs in the system as the gas expands. For chemists, however, most applications of thermodynamics deal with *chemical* changes of state. In a chemical change of state, the amounts of reactants and products change as well as their physical variables. To describe a chemical change of state, we must specify not only the changes in the physical variables (*P, V,* and *T*) but also changes in the identities and the amounts of starting materials and products. This requires a chemical equation and information about the number of moles of each species.

A simple example of a system undergoing a chemical change of state is the decomposition of calcium carbonate (limestone) at high temperature to form calcium oxide (quicklime) and carbon dioxide:

$$CaCO_{3\,(s)} \xrightarrow{\text{Heat}} CaO_{(s)} + CO_{2\,(g)}$$

To specify this system and its change of state completely, we must describe the number of moles of $CaCO_3$ that decompose, as well as the temperature and pressure changes that accompany the reaction.

In a chemical reaction, some bonds break, and other bonds form. Bond breakage and formation are always accompanied by a change in energy. In the limestone example, energy in the form of heat must be added to drive the reaction. In other cases, chemical reactions release energy to the surroundings. Thermodynamics helps us understand the flow of energy in a chemical process.

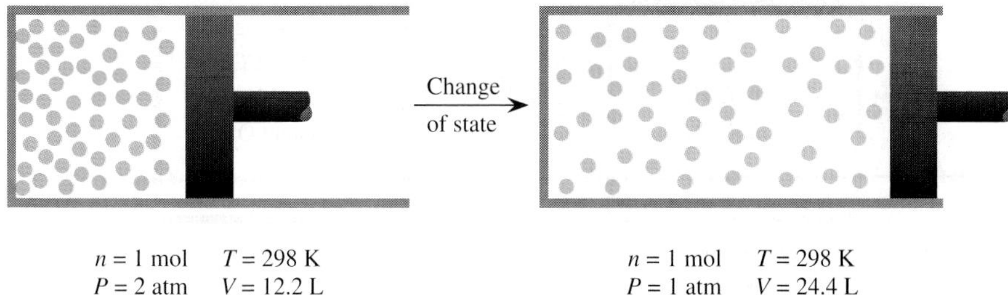

FIGURE 12-3
A schematic example of a change of state. When 1 mol of helium gas expands at constant temperature, its volume and pressure change but not its temperature or amount:

2. As a result, state changes can be computed using the most convenient path available. The airline distance on a direct San Francisco–Denver flight probably provides the most convenient path for figuring the distance between the two cities. Other means, such as satellite mapping, can provide extremely accurate determinations of the distance.
3. A change in a state function is independent of path. No matter how a change of state is accomplished, a change in any state function has only one value. This means that state function values can be tabulated and looked up when needed. The distance from San Francisco to Denver can be found in an atlas of the United States.

These three properties of state functions are more important for scientists than for cross-country travelers such as the Daltons. Chemists determine values of state functions by doing careful experiments using some convenient path. These values are collected in tables, just as distances between cities are collected in an atlas. Energy, for example, is a state function, and chemists use tabulated energy values to analyze chemical processes from a thermodynamic point of view. For instance, recall from Chapter 9 that tabulated bond strengths can be used to estimate the energy changes that accompany a chemical reaction.

SECTION EXERCISES

12.1.1 Define an appropriate choice of the system for studying each of the following transformations:
(a) 100 g of water is heated in an open container.
(b) A mixture of H_2 and O_2 is detonated in a closed container.
(c) A balloon filled with air is placed in a freezer.

12.1.2 Which of the variables (*P, V, T,* and *n*) change during the transformations described in Exercise 12.1.1?

12.1.3 Which of the following is a change in a state function: (a) the change in energy when 1 gallon of gasoline is burned completely; and (b) the miles traveled in an automobile when 1 gallon of gasoline is burned completely?

12.2 ENERGY

Energy ***(E)*** is the foundation of thermodynamics. Energy can be transferred among objects and converted from one form to another, but it is always conserved. In this chapter we consider energy transfers and conversions that accompany chemical reactions. In particular, we examine how chemical energy can be converted into other forms.

EXOTHERMIC AND ENDOTHERMIC REACTIONS

Recall from Chapter 9 that bond breaking always consumes energy and that bond making always releases energy. The balance between these two processes results in two classes of reactions, which are illustrated in Figure 12-6. When the energy released by bond forming is greater than the energy consumed by bond breaking, there is a net release of chemical energy by the system. Energy-releasing reactions

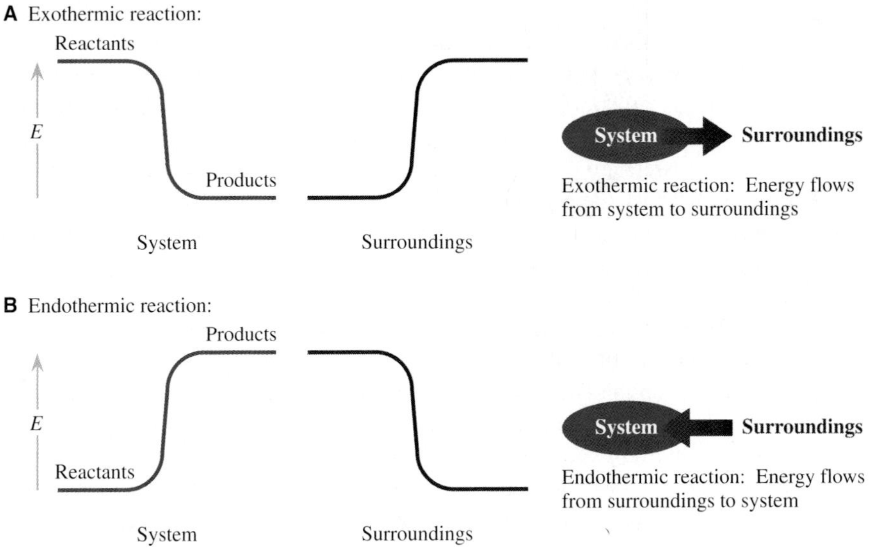

A Exothermic reaction:

Reactants

E

Products

System

Surroundings

System → Surroundings

Exothermic reaction: Energy flows from system to surroundings

B Endothermic reaction:

Products

E

Reactants

System

Surroundings

System ← Surroundings

Endothermic reaction: Energy flows from surroundings to system

FIGURE 12-6

Energy diagrams showing exothermic and endothermic reactions. **A,** When a reaction releases energy, the surroundings gain energy. For exothermic reactions, change in energy (ΔE) is negative for the system and positive for the surroundings. **B,** When the reaction absorbs energy, the surroundings lose energy. For endothermic reactions, ΔE is positive for the system and negative for the surroundings.

are said to be **exothermic** (Figure 12-6, *A*). In an exothermic reaction the chemical system transfers energy to the surroundings as reactants are converted to products. The reactions of fuels with oxygen gas are all highly exothermic, and the energy released can be used to heat a home or to drive an engine.

Exo is Greek for "out," *endo* is Greek for "within," and *therm* is Greek for "heat."

When the energy of bond breaking is greater than the energy of bond forming, the chemical reaction must be driven by energy absorbed from the surroundings. Energy-absorbing reactions are said to be **endothermic** (Figure 12-6, *B*). In an endothermic reaction the surroundings transfer energy to the chemical system as reactants are converted to products.

If a reaction is exothermic when going in one direction, it will be endothermic in the opposite direction. Reversing the *direction* of a reaction changes the *sign* of its energy change. This applies not only to changes in energy, but to all other state functions, as well. If a change is "uphill" going in one direction, it must be "downhill" in the other direction.

The reaction of two molecules of NO_2 to form a molecule of N_2O_4 provides a simple example of this. When two NO_2 molecules collide, they may form a chemical bond in an exothermic reaction:

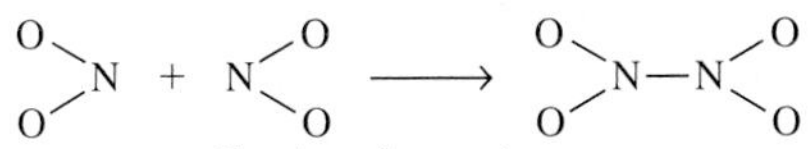

$$NO_2 + NO_2 \longrightarrow O_2N{-}NO_2$$

Exothermic reaction

The energy profile for NO_2 reacting to form N_2O_4 resembles Figure 12-6, *A*. When N_2O_4 is heated, on the other hand, it can decompose into NO_2 molecules:

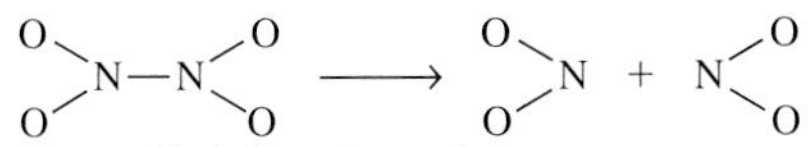

$$O_2N{-}NO_2 \longrightarrow NO_2 + NO_2$$

Endothermic reaction

The decomposition reaction is endothermic, with an energy profile similar to Figure 12-6, *B*.

ENERGY AND HEAT

As described in Chapter 2, several forms of energy are important in chemistry, including kinetic energy, potential energy, and radiant energy. In chemistry, one of the most important forms of energy is thermal motion. A change in thermal motion of a system requires a flow of energy, and a transfer of thermal energy is known as **heat (*q*)**. Heat transfers are changes in energy, so they are measured in joules (J).

A flow of heat frequently causes a temperature change. Temperature is not energy, but it is related to energy. Experiments show that a change in an object's temperature (ΔT) depends on three factors:

1. ΔT depends on q, the amount of heat that has been transferred. That is, the transfer of 50 J of heat to an object causes an increase in temperature that is twice as large as the increase caused by 25 J of heat.
2. ΔT depends on the amount of material. That is, the transfer of 50 J of heat to 1 mol of a substance causes a temperature increase that is twice as large as the increase caused by the transfer of 50 J of heat to 2 mol of the same substance.
3. ΔT depends on the identity of the material. For instance, 50 J of heat increases the temperature of 1 mol of gold more than it increases the temperature of 1 mol of water.

This sensitivity to heat is expressed by a quantity called the **molar heat capacity (C_p)**. Molar heat capacity is the heat needed to raise the temperature of 1 mol of substance by one kelvin (1 K). Putting these three factors together gives an expression for the temperature change that accompanies a heat transfer:

$$\Delta T = T_{\text{final}} - T_{\text{initial}} = \frac{q}{n\,C_p}$$

In this equation, q is the heat transferred, n is the number of moles of material involved, and C_p is the molar heat capacity of the substance. Neither temperature nor temperature change can be equated directly to the energy flow q. We can relate q to ΔT only if we know the identity and amount of the material that undergoes a change of state.

The molar heat capacities of several chemical substances are listed in Tables 12-1 and 12-2. A more extensive collection of heat capacities appears in Appendix E.

Rearranging the heat capacity equation yields Equation 12-1, which is very useful for determining heat flows:

$$q = nC_p\Delta T \qquad \textbf{(12-1)}$$

Relating q and ΔT in this manner demonstrates that any change of temperature is accompanied by a heat transfer. We can use Equation 12-1 to compute the amount of heat transferred in a change of state that involves a temperature change. Sample Problem 12-1 provides an example.

TABLE 12-1 MOLAR HEAT CAPACITIES (C_p) OF SEVERAL GASES AT 25 °C

SUBSTANCE	C_p (J/mol K)
Ar	20.786
He	20.786
H_2	28.824
HCl	29.12
N_2	29.125
CO	29.142
O_2	29.355
NO	29.844
Cl_2	33.907
H_2S	34.23
NH_3	35.06
CO_2	37.11

Although temperatures in Celsius and Kelvin differ, temperature *changes* have the same magnitude in the two scales because the size of the temperature unit is the same. Thus, heat capacities have the same values whether expressed in J/mol K or J/mol °C.

TABLE 12-2 MOLAR HEAT CAPACITIES (C_p) OF LIQUIDS (l) AND SOLIDS (s) AT 25 °C

SUBSTANCE	PHASE	C_p (J/mol K)
$C_{(graphite)}$	s	8.527
Si	s	20.00
S	s	22.64
Al	s	24.35
Cu	s	24.435
Fe	s	25.10
Ag	s	25.351
Ni	s	26.07
Hg	l	27.983
Na	s	28.24
KCl	s	51.30
NaOH	s	59.54
H_2O	l	75.291
$BaCl_2$	s	75.14
Al_2O_3	s	79.04
$CaCO_3$	s	81.88
NH_4Cl	s	84.1
$MgSO_4$	s	96.48
$FeCl_3$	s	96.65
CCl_4	l	131.75
$K_2Cr_2O_7$	s	219.24

SAMPLE PROBLEM 12-1 HEAT TRANSFER AND TEMPERATURE CHANGE

An aluminum frying pan that weighs 745 g is heated on a stove from 25 °C to 205 °C. What is q for the frying pan?

METHOD: A temperature change signals a heat flow. Equation 12-1 lets us calculate how much heat flows, provided we know n, C_p, and ΔT.

The mass of the frying pan and the molar mass of aluminum are used to calculate n:

$$n = \frac{m}{MM} = \frac{745 \text{ g Al}}{26.98 \text{ g mol}^{-1}} = 27.61 \text{ mol Al}$$

Molar heat capacities are tabulated in Table 12-2:

$$C_{p\,(\text{aluminum})} = 24.35 \text{ J/mol K}$$

Temperatures are given in the problem:

$$T_i = 25\ °C = 298 \text{ K} \qquad T_f = 205\ °C = 478 \text{ K}$$

$$\Delta T = T_f - T_i = 478 \text{ K} - 298 \text{ K} = 180 \text{ K}$$

Now we substitute and compute, converting to the more convenient unit of kilojoules to avoid very large numbers:

$$(27.61 \text{ mol})(24.35 \text{ J/mol K})(180 \text{ K})(10^{-3} \text{ kJ/J}) = 121 \text{ kJ}$$

FIGURE 12-7
Whether at work or at play, human activities involve doing thermodynamic work, which the body supplies from the chemical energy stored in foods.

WORK AND ENERGY

Some of the energy released when gasoline burns in an automobile engine is converted to heat that must be dissipated by the engine's cooling system. The rest of the energy released by burning gasoline is what moves an automobile from one place to another. Energy used to move an object against an opposing force is called **work (w).** To move an automobile, work must overcome the forces of friction and gravity. The amount of work depends on the magnitude of the force that must be overcome and the amount of movement or displacement. The equation that connects work, force (F), and displacement (d) is:

$$w = Fd \qquad \textbf{(12-2)}$$

The SI unit of force is the newton (N), which can be expressed as a product of fundamental units:

$$1 \text{ N} = 1 \text{ kg m s}^{-2}$$

The fundamental units for the newton can be obtained by analyzing the units associated with Newton's second law of motion, $f = ma$. Mass (m) is in kilograms, and acceleration (a) is meters per second per second.

Displacements are measured in meters, so the product of force times displacement has units of N m. Work, however, is energy transferred between objects, so it is measured in joules. Thus the joule and the N m must be equivalent:

$$1 \text{ J} = 1 \text{ N m} = 1 \text{ kg m}^2 \text{ s}^{-2}$$

As we will see, this equivalence is useful as a conversion factor in some calculations of work.

Humans convert chemical energy into work in a variety of activities. We have already given the example of automobile engines, which accomplish the work of movement by burning gasoline. Many other machines also rely on chemical energy to accomplish work. In addition, humans themselves require chemical energy to fuel their activities, many of which entail thermodynamic work (Figure 12-7). Whether "at work" or "at play," a person expends energy to accomplish movement, and this energy comes from the chemical energy stored in food.

EXPANSION WORK

When a system expands, its container undergoes a displacement against the external force exerted by the container walls. The work done in moving the walls of the container must be taken into account when we analyze the energy balance for any change of state that includes a volume change. Work can always be analyzed using forces and displacements, but expansion work is more conveniently determined using pressure and volume.

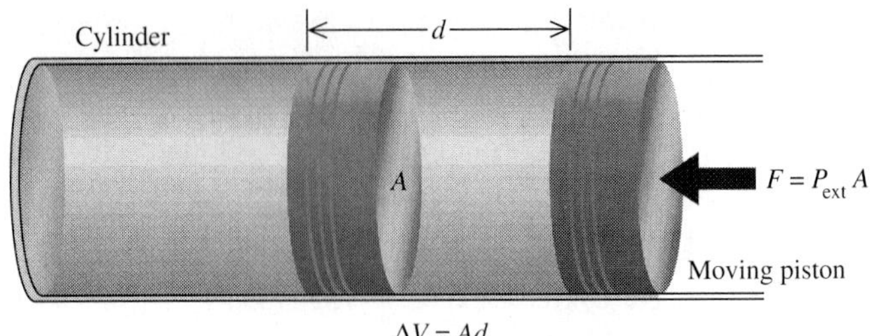

FIGURE 12-8
Schematic drawing of an automobile cylinder and piston. When the gas inside a cylinder expands, the piston undergoes a displacement. In this displacement, work is done against the force exerted on the area of the piston by the external pressure.

Expansion work can be illustrated using an automobile cylinder and piston. Figure 12-8 shows the displacement of a piston. The expanding gas inside the cylinder pushes the piston through a displacement (d). The opposing force is related to the *external* pressure, which, as described in Chapter 5, is force per unit area:

$$\text{Pressure} = \frac{\text{Force}}{\text{Area}} = \frac{F}{A} \quad or \quad F = PA$$

Substituting this expression into Equation 12-2, we see how the work done on the surroundings (w_{surr}) is related to external pressure (P_{ext}):

$$w_{surr} = P_{ext} Ad$$

During expansion, the gas changes its volume. As Figure 12-8 illustrates, this volume change is the product of area multiplied by displacement:

$$\Delta V = Ad$$

This lets us write the expression for expansion work transferred to the surroundings in terms of the opposing pressure and the change of volume:

$$w_{surr} = P_{ext}\, \Delta V$$

The units of pressure times volume are the same as the units of force times displacement:

Units of PV: $(\text{N m}^{-2})(\text{m}^3) = \text{N m} = \text{J}$
Units of Fd: $\text{N m} = \text{J}$

In keeping track of energy transfers, we must pay careful attention to the *direction* of energy flow. When a system does work on the surroundings, the energy of the *surroundings* increases (the crankshaft turns faster, so the automobile speeds up). Chemical thermodynamics, however, always focuses on the *system.* Because energy is conserved, the energy of the *system* must decrease by an equal amount. Viewed from the molecular perspective, the energy required to move the piston in the expansion shown in Figure 12-8 is supplied through countless collisions between gas molecules and the head of the piston. The molecules that make up the system lose energy in each collision. Thus ΔE_{sys} has a negative sign in an expansion, and because this energy change involves a transfer of work, work must also have a negative sign for a system undergoing expansion. The volume of the system (V_{sys}) increases in an expansion, however, so a negative sign is required to give work for the system (w_{sys}) the proper sign:

$$w_{sys} = -P_{ext}\Delta V_{sys} \qquad \textbf{(12-3)}$$

Equation 12-3 is used to calculate the amount of work done during the expansion of any system.

To recapitulate, an expanding system does work on its surroundings. This represents a loss of energy by the system, so w for the system is negative for an expansion, as expressed by Equation 12-3. In an expansion, P_{ext} and ΔV_{sys} are positive, so the negative sign in the equation is required to make w_{sys} negative. In a contraction, on the other hand, the pressure is still positive, but ΔV_{sys} is negative; thus Equation 12-3 gives a positive w_{sys} for a contraction. Sample Problem 12-2 shows how to apply Equation 12-3.

SAMPLE PROBLEM 12-2 CALCULATING WORK

An automobile piston of diameter 5.00 cm is displaced 8.00 cm when the cylinder fires. If the gas expands against an external pressure of 3.50 atm, how much work is done in each stroke of the piston?

METHOD: When the cylinder fires, the hot gas molecules push the piston back against the external pressure. As a result, the volume of the system increases, and the system does work on the surroundings. We expect the sign of w to be negative. Equation 12-3 is used to calculate expansion work:

$$w_{sys} = -P_{ext}\Delta V_{sys}$$

The external pressure, 3.50 atm, is given in the problem, but the volume change must be calculated from the dimensions of the cylinder and the displacement of the piston:

$$\text{Volume} = (\text{Area})(\text{Displacement}) = Ad$$

$$A = \pi r^2 = (3.1416)(2.50\text{ cm})^2 = 19.64\text{ cm}^2$$

$$\Delta V_{sys} = Ad = (19.64\text{ cm}^2)(8.00\text{ cm}) = 157.1\text{ cm}^3$$

$$\text{Work} = w_{sys} = -P_{ext}\Delta V_{sys} = -(3.50\text{ atm})(157.1\text{ cm}^3) = -550\text{ cm}^3\text{ atm}$$

These units look wrong. How do units of "cm³ atm" relate to energy? Recall from Chapter 5 that the SI measure of pressure is the pascal (Pa). To find the proper energy units, we must make the appropriate substitutions:

$$1\text{ atm} = 1.013 \times 10^5\text{ Pa} = 1.013 \times 10^5\text{ kg m}^{-1}\text{ s}^{-2}$$

$$\text{Work} = (-550\text{ cm}^3\text{ atm})\left(\frac{1\text{ m}}{10^2\text{ cm}}\right)^3\left(\frac{1.013 \times 10^5\text{ kg m}^{-1}\text{ s}^{-2}}{\text{atm}}\right) = -55.7\text{ kg m}^2\text{ s}^{-2}$$

As noted earlier, $1\text{ J} = 1\text{ kg m}^2\text{ s}^{-2}$, so the work for the system is −55.7 J.

FIRST LAW OF THERMODYNAMICS

We have described two distinct ways that a system can exchange energy with its surroundings: Energy can be transferred as heat or work. Heat and work can be transferred into or out of a system. During a chemical reaction, changes in chemical energy may cause heat transfer (for example, a gas flame heats an aluminum frying pan) and/or work transfer (for example, burning gasoline drives an automobile piston). Because energy must be conserved, the energy change of the system is linked to the flow of heat and work:

$$\Delta E_{sys} = q_{sys} + w_{sys} \qquad \textbf{(12-4)}$$

Scientists have found that heat and work transfers are sufficient to account for the energy change that accompanies any process. Therefore Equation 12-4 is a general law called the **first law of thermodynamics.**

The subscripts on the terms in Equation 12-4 are reminders that energy transfer is directional. That is, when heat or work is transferred from a system to its surround-

grouped into general types, each of which has a characteristic energy content. Three of these—fats, carbohydrates, and proteins—are the main sources of energy for the body. As shown in Table 12-3, the energy contents (in kilojoules per gram) of these substances differ substantially.

People in the United States usually measure food masses in ounces (oz) and food energies in nutritional calories (Cal). To convert kilojoules to calories, divide by 4.184 kJ/Cal. To convert grams to ounces, divide by 28.35 g/oz.

Different types of foods contain different proportions of these constituents. Vegetables and fruits contain much water but very little fat, so their energy content per gram is low. Margarine, on the other hand, is mostly fat, so its energy content per gram is extremely high. Table 12-4 lists the average energy content (in kilojoules per gram) for some representative foods.

Table 12-4 shows that *what* we eat is at least as important as *how much* we eat. For example, 10 g of margarine provide the same energy content as 250 g of green vegetables. A 100 g serving of low-fat yogurt, moreover, contains less than half the energy of a 100 g serving of regular yogurt. The easiest way to reduce our energy intake is by eliminating fats and greasy foods such as hamburgers and pizza.

Energy intake is only half the equation. We can also adjust our energy balance through amount and type of exercise. Table 12-5 shows average energy outputs (in kilojoules per hour) of various forms of exercise. Exercise involves doing thermodynamic work, and the amount of work depends on the amount of mass being displaced. To demonstrate this dependence, Table 12-5 lists values for three different body weights.

People in the United States usually measure weight in pounds (lb). To convert to pounds, multiply kilograms by 2.205 lb/kg.

TABLE 12-3 ENERGY CONTENT OF FOOD CONSTITUENTS

CONSTITUENT	ENERGY CONTENT (kJ/g)
Fat	39
Protein	17
Carbohydrate	16
Water	0
Minerals	0

TABLE 12-4 ENERGY CONTENT OF TYPICAL FOODS

TYPE OF FOOD	ENERGY CONTENT (kJ/g)	TYPE OF FOOD	ENERGY CONTENT (kJ/g)
Green vegetables	1.2	Broiled steak	12
Beer	2.0	Bread, cheese	12
Fruits	2.5	Ground beef	16
Low-fat yogurt	4.5	Sugar	16
Broiled chicken	6.0	Margarine	30
Regular yogurt	10		

TABLE 12-5 ENERGY REQUIRED FOR VARIOUS ACTIVITIES

		ENERGY CONSUMED (kJ/hr)		
ACTIVITY	BODY WEIGHT	55 KG	70 KG	85 KG
Resting		290	335	380
Driving an automobile		440	500	560
Doing housework		650	750	850
Walking at 4 km/hr		770	880	990
Walking at 6 km/hr		1090	1250	1410
Bicycling at 9 km/hr		775	880	985
Bicycling at 20 km/hr		2400	2760	3120
Playing tennis or volleyball		1380	1590	1800
Skiing at 16 km/hr		2175	2510	2825
Running at 16 km/hr		3285	3770	4245

A simple example illustrates the relative importance of diet and exercise in weight control. Most soft drinks contain about 9% sugar. Virtually all the remaining contents is water, which has no energy content. Therefore, a 340 g can of a soft drink contains about 31 g of sugar. Sugar provides 16 kJ/g, so the total energy content of a can of soft drink is 490 kJ. To expend 490 kJ of energy, a 70 kg person must walk at 6 km/hr for 23 minutes, play tennis or volleyball for 18 minutes, run at 16 km/hr for 8 minutes, or rest and watch television for 1½ hours. A 100 g (about a quarter-pound) hamburger on a bun, moreover, contains 1600 kJ of energy. Thus you would have to play volleyball continuously for 2 hours to burn off the energy contained in a hamburger and soft drink.

This comparison demonstrates that it is much easier to control our energy balance through diet than by exercise. One additional comparison should reinforce this point. Our bodies store excess energy in fatty tissues. When half a kilogram of this fatty tissue is consumed, it releases 20,000 kJ of energy, which is enough to fuel about 9 hours of tennis, 6 hours of skiing, or 4 hours of strenuous running.

SECTION EXERCISES

12.2.1 How much heat is required to raise the temperature of 25.0 g of water from 25 °C to 65 °C on an octane-burning stove?

12.2.2 In a steam engine, water vapor drives a piston to accomplish work. What is work in joules, if 25.0 g of water at 100 °C is vaporized to steam, pushing a piston against 1.00-atm external pressure? (HINT: Use the ideal gas equation to find the volume change when liquid water becomes water vapor.)

12.2.3 Assuming that the average speed is 20 km/hr and the riders are on the road an average of 6 hr/day, how much ground beef must a 55 kg bicyclist in the Tour de France consume daily to *not* lose weight? If the cyclist ate fruit rather than ground beef, how much fruit would be required?

12.3 HEAT MEASUREMENTS: CALORIMETRY

In a chemical reaction such as the combustion of octane, it is not possible to make direct measurements of the changes in chemical bond energies. Instead, chemists measure the transfers of heat (q) and work (w) to determine the energy change that accompanies a chemical change of state. In this section we focus on the measurement of heat.

Early scientists believed that heat was a substance called *caloric*. Thus a device to measure heat was called a calorimeter. This word stem also occurs in the nutritional calorie, a non-SI unit of energy.

CALORIMETERS

A device that measures heat flow is called a **calorimeter.** The basic features of a calorimeter are shown in Figure 12-12. A calorimeter includes a water bath, a container, and a thermometer, all of which are thermally insulated from the surroundings. In a calorimetry experiment, a set of chemicals undergoing a change in energy is enclosed in the water bath. The calorimeter and the chemicals that it contains act as an isolated system because the insulation blocks the flow of heat between system and surroundings:

Treating the calorimeter and the chemicals as an isolated system is an approximation that is valid *within the time scale of a calorimetry experiment.* After undergoing a temperature change, the calorimeter must exchange energy with its surroundings until the temperature of the calorimeter returns to room temperature. However, insulating the calorimeter ensures that the calorimetry experiment can be completed before this temperature equilibration occurs.

$$q_{surr} = q_{sys} = 0$$

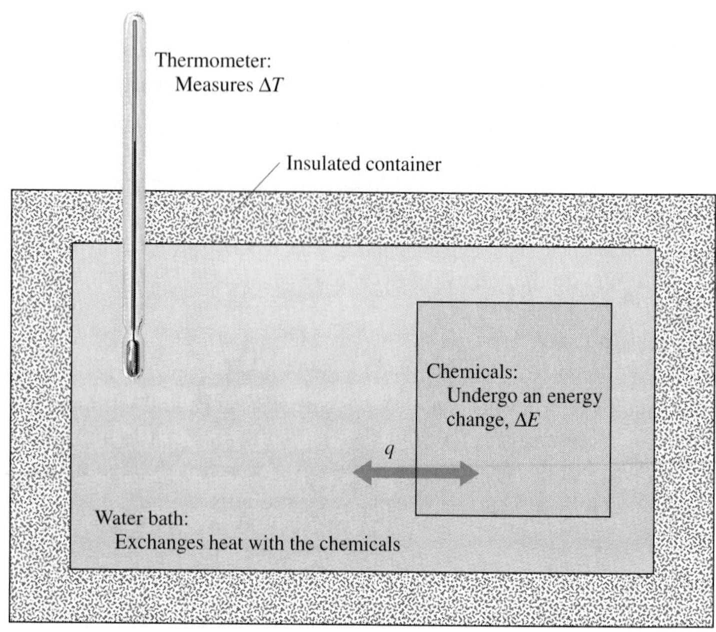

FIGURE 12-12
Block diagram of a calorimeter. In its simplest form, a calorimeter is composed of a water bath, an insulated container, and a thermometer. When a set of chemicals placed in the calorimeter undergoes an energy change, the heat flow results in a temperature change, which is measured by the thermometer.

When the chemicals react, their energy change causes heat to flow *within* the system, but none of the energy is *transferred* to the surroundings. The flow of energy within the system causes a temperature change in the water bath that can be linked to the amount of heat transferred. For example, in an exothermic reaction, the chemicals release energy in the form of heat, and this heat raises the temperature of the calorimeter. The law of conservation of energy allows us to account for all the heat flow within the isolated system:

$$q_{sys} = q_{calorimeter} + q_{chemicals} = 0$$

Thus the amount of heat released or absorbed in a chemical process can be determined by measuring $q_{calorimeter}$:

$$q_{chemicals} = -q_{calorimeter}$$

We can determine $q_{calorimeter}$ from its temperature change using an equation similar to Equation 12-1:

$$q_{calorimeter} = C_{cal}\,\Delta T \quad \textbf{(12-5)}$$

A total heat capacity is the amount of heat that an entire object must absorb to increase its temperature by 1 K. A total heat capacity has units of J/K, whereas a molar heat capacity has units of J/mol K. If we have *n* moles of a pure substance, its total heat capacity is $C_{total} = nC_{molar}$.

Here, C_{cal} is the *total* heat capacity of the calorimeter. C_{cal} of a calorimeter usually is determined by measuring the temperature change that accompanies the transfer of a known amount of heat. For example, an electrical heater can supply heat ($q_{electric}$) that can be measured very accurately by way of current, voltage, and time. Then, $q_{electric}$ and the measured temperature increase are used in Equation 12-5 to calculate C_{cal}:

$$C_{cal} = \frac{q_{electric}}{\Delta T_{electric}}$$

Calculated from electrical measurements ($q_{electric}$)
Measured directly ($\Delta T_{electric}$)

Sample Problem 12-3 illustrates this technique.

SAMPLE PROBLEM 12-3 DETERMINING TOTAL HEAT CAPACITY

A calorimeter is calibrated using an electrical heater. Before turning on the heater, the calorimeter temperature is 23.55 °C. The addition of 10.00 kJ of electrical energy raises the temperature to 24.67 °C. Determine the total heat capacity of this calorimeter.

METHOD: The electrical heater produces energy that flows into the calorimeter and raises the temperature of the water bath. We determine C_{cal} from the heat and temperature data. Equation 12-5 provides the needed link:

$$q = C_{cal}\,\Delta T \qquad or \qquad C_{cal} = \frac{q_{electric}}{\Delta T_{electric}}$$

$$q_{electric} = 10.00\text{ kJ} \qquad \Delta T_{electric} = T_f - T_i = (24.67 - 23.55\ °\text{C}) = 1.12\ °\text{C}$$

Now, substitute and evaluate:

$$C_{cal} = (10.00\text{ kJ})/(1.12\ °\text{C}) = 8.93\text{ kJ/°C} = 8.93\text{ kJ/K}$$

Remember that temperature *difference* (ΔT) has the same magnitude in °C and K.

When a chemical reaction occurs in a calorimeter, the temperature of the bath rises or falls, depending on whether the reaction is exothermic or endothermic. An exothermic reaction releases energy, so the temperature of the calorimeter *rises* during an exothermic reaction. An endothermic reaction absorbs energy, so the temperature of the calorimeter *falls* during an endothermic reaction.

TYPES OF CALORIMETERS

Volume, pressure, temperature, and amounts of substances may change during a chemical reaction. When scientists make experimental measurements, however, they prefer to control volume, pressure, or both, to simplify the interpretation of their results. In general, it is possible to hold volume or pressure constant, but not both, because volume and pressure usually are related through equations of state.

In constant-volume calorimetry, the volume of the system is fixed. In constant-pressure calorimetry, the pressure of the system is fixed. Whichever type of calorimetry is used, temperature changes are used to calculate q.

To perform constant-pressure calorimetry, all we need is a thermally insulated container and a thermometer. A simple, inexpensive constant-pressure calorimeter can be made from two nested Styrofoam cups with a cover, stirrer, and thermometer. An example of a coffee-cup calorimeter, is shown in Figure 12-13. The inner cup holds the water bath and the starting materials involved in the reaction. The outer cup provides extra thermal insulation. The thermometer and stirrer can be inserted through the cover.

To use the calorimeter, aqueous solutions containing the reactants are mixed in the cup, and the resulting temperature change is measured with the thermometer. The heat capacity of the calorimeter must be determined independently. One way to do this would be through electrical heating, as described in Sample Problem 12-3. However, satisfactory accuracy is often obtained by assuming that the heat capacity of the calorimeter is the same as the heat capacity of the water that the calorimeter contains. This neglects the contribution from the nested cups and the thermometer, which may be only about 1% of C_{cal}. Sample Problem 12-4 illustrates constant-pressure calorimetry.

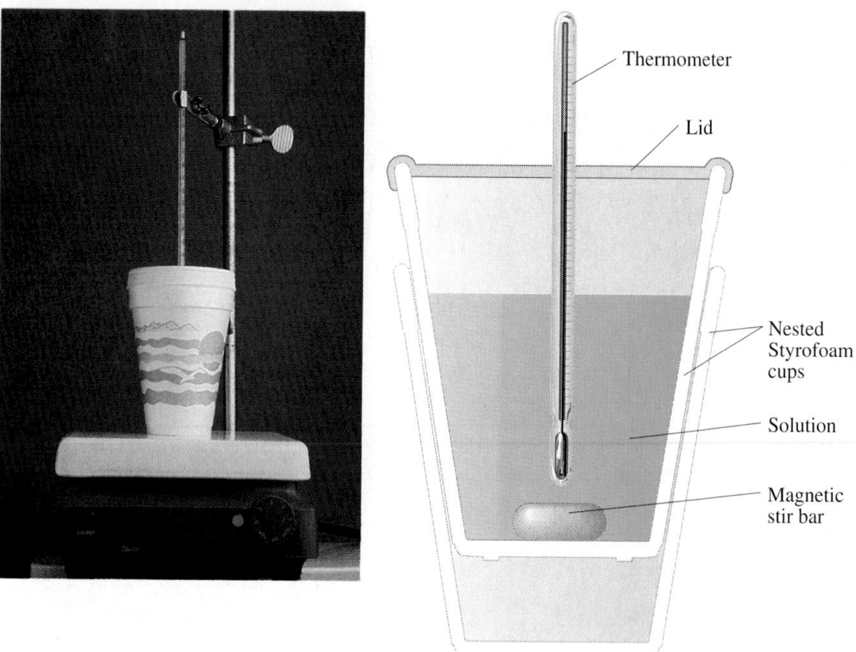

FIGURE 12-13
A constant-pressure calorimeter can be constructed from two Styrofoam cups, a cover, a stirrer, and a thermometer.

SAMPLE PROBLEM 12-4 CONSTANT-PRESSURE CALORIMETRY

Ammonium nitrate (NH_4NO_3, MM = 80.05 g/mol) is a salt used in cold packs for "icing" injuries. When 20.0 g of this salt dissolves in 125 g of water in a coffee-cup calorimeter, the temperature falls from 23.5 °C to 13.4 °C.

a. Is the chemical process exothermic or endothermic?

b. Determine q for the calorimeter.

METHOD: The temperature of the calorimeter changes in response to a heat flow, and Equation 12-5 lets us determine q after heat capacity and temperature change are known. We must use data given in the problem to find these two quantities.

a. This is a qualitative question. The temperature of the calorimeter *falls* during the process, which means that heat is transferred from the calorimeter to the reactants. In other words, the water in the calorimeter loses heat as the ammonium nitrate dissolves. The salt gains energy, so the dissolving process is *endothermic*.

b. To find q use Equation 12-5 to relate heat, temperature change, and heat capacity:

$$q = C_{\text{cal}}\, \Delta T$$

$$\Delta T = T_{\text{f}} - T_{\text{i}} = (13.4 + 273.15)\text{ K} - (23.5 + 273.15)\text{ K} = -10.1\text{ K}$$

Given no additional information, we must approximate C_{cal} as the heat capacity of its water content:

$$C_{\text{cal}} \cong C_{\text{water}} = n_{\text{water}}\, C_{\text{p,water}}$$

$$n = \frac{\text{Mass}}{\text{Molar mass}} = \frac{125\text{ g}}{18.016\text{ g/mol}} = 6.938\text{ mol}$$

$$C_{\text{water}} = (6.938\text{ mol})(75.291\text{ J/mol K}) = 522.4\text{ J/K}$$

$$q = (522.4\text{ J/K})(-10.1\text{ K}) = -5276\text{ J} = -5.28\text{ kJ}$$

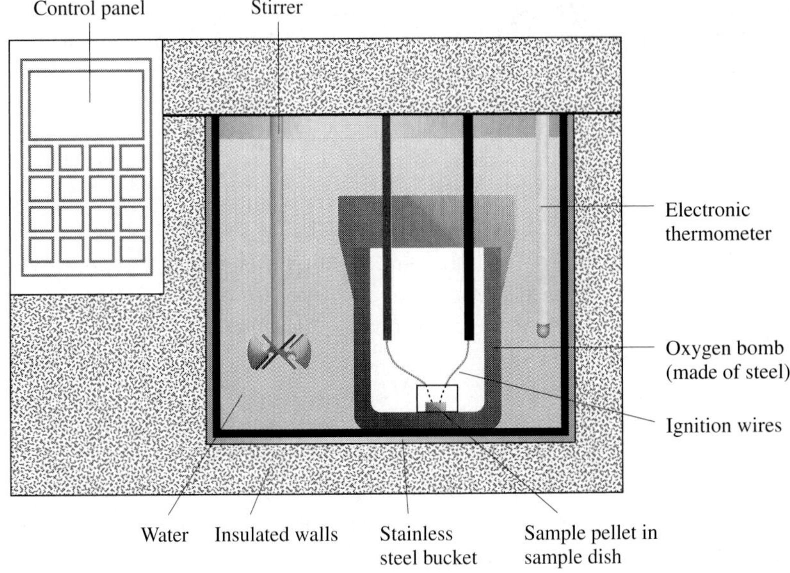

FIGURE 12-14
A commercially produced device for constant-volume calorimetry.

Figure 12-14 illustrates a constant-volume calorimeter, which is often used to measure q for combustion reactions. A sample of the substance to be burned is placed inside the sealed calorimeter in the presence of excess oxygen gas. When the sample burns, energy flows from the chemicals to the calorimeter. The temperature change of the calorimeter, with the calorimeter's heat capacity, gives the amount of heat released in the reaction. Sample Problem 12-5 provides an example.

SAMPLE PROBLEM 12-5 CONSTANT-VOLUME CALORIMETRY

A 1.250-g sample of octane (C_8H_{18}, MM = 114.2 g/mol) is burned in excess O_2 in the constant-volume calorimeter described in Sample Problem 12-3. The temperature of the calorimeter rises from 21.05 °C to 27.78 °C. Find the heat transferred to the calorimeter during the combustion of the octane.

METHOD: Assume that the calorimeter and the chemicals are an isolated system. Thus the heat given off in the combustion reaction is absorbed by the calorimeter. To find $q_{\text{calorimeter}}$, we need to know the temperature change and the total heat capacity of the calorimeter. The value of C_{cal} is calculated in Sample Problem 12-3, and ΔT can be found from the data:

$$C_{\text{cal}} = 8.93 \text{ kJ/°C} \quad \textit{and} \quad \Delta T_{\text{reaction}} = (27.78 - 21.05) \text{ °C} = 6.73 \text{ °C}$$

Now we can use C_{cal} and $\Delta T_{\text{reaction}}$ to find q_{reaction}:

$$q = C_{\text{cal}}\Delta T = (8.93 \text{ kJ/°C})(6.73 \text{ °C}) = 60.1 \text{ kJ}$$

This is the amount of heat that the calorimeter absorbs during the combustion reaction.

ENERGY CHANGES AND CALORIMETRY

In a calorimetry experiment, the heat flow resulting from a chemical reaction is determined by measuring the temperature change of the calorimeter. Then q can be related to energy change through the first law of thermodynamics (Equation 12-4):

$$\Delta E = q + w$$

Because heat and work are path functions, however, we must specify the conditions of the experiment. When the experiment is performed at constant volume, we use a subscript "v." When the experiment is performed at constant pressure, we use a subscript "p." This gives two different expressions for the two types of calorimeters:

$$\Delta E = q_v + w_v \qquad \textit{and} \qquad \Delta E = q_p + w_p$$

To go from measured values of q to the state function change ΔE, we must evaluate w. Calorimeters are designed so that only expansion work occurs. Recall that Equation 12-3 describes work done by expansion:

$$w = -P_{ext}\Delta V_{sys}$$

For a constant-*volume* calorimeter $\Delta V_{sys} = 0$, so $w_v = 0$. Thus:

$$\Delta E = q_v \qquad \text{Constant-volume calorimeter}$$

For a constant-*pressure* calorimeter, the volume of the system may change, so $w_p \neq 0$ and Equation 12-3 must be evaluated. We return to this evaluation shortly.

MOLAR ENERGY CHANGE

Energy change is an extensive quantity, which means that the amount of energy released or absorbed depends on the amount of substances that react. For example, as more octane burns, more energy is released. Thus when we report an energy change, we must also report the amounts of the chemical substances that generate the energy change. For tabulation purposes, all changes in thermodynamic functions such as ΔE are given in molar terms, just as heat capacities are conveniently tabulated as molar values. Here we use ΔE_{molar} for the energy change that accompanies reaction of 1 mol of a particular substance. The molar energy change can be found from an experimental energy change by dividing by the number of moles that reacted:

$$\Delta E_{molar} = \Delta E/n \qquad \textbf{(12-6)}$$

Calorimetry measurements usually involve amounts different from 1 mol. Equation 12-6 is used to convert from ΔE for the actual amount used in the reaction to the molar quantity, ΔE_{molar}. Sample Problem 12-6 shows how to evaluate ΔE_{molar} for the combustion of octane.

SAMPLE PROBLEM 12-6 MOLAR ENERGY CHANGE

What is ΔE_{molar} for the combustion of octane described in Sample Problem 12-5?

METHOD: In the combustion reaction, 1.250 g of octane are burned, and energy is released as heat. In Sample Problem 12-5, we evaluated $q_{calorimeter}$, which is actually $q_{v,calorimeter}$ because the experiment was performed in a constant-volume calorimeter. Because the calorimeter and its contents are an isolated system, none of the energy released in the combustion reaction escapes to the surroundings. Thus all the energy released in the reaction is absorbed by the calorimeter:

$$q_{system} = q_{reaction} + q_{v,calorimeter} = 0 \qquad \textit{so} \qquad q_{reaction} = -q_{v,calorimeter}$$

We calculated q for the calorimeter, which was positive. This means that heat energy flowed out of the chemicals and into the calorimeter, so q and ΔE for the reaction are both *negative.* From Sample Problem 12-5, $q_{v,calorimeter} = 60.1$ kJ. This is the amount of heat the calorimeter absorbed during the combustion of 1.250 g of octane. Thus for 1.250 g of octane, $\Delta E = -60.1$ kJ. To obtain the molar energy change, we need to use Equation 12-6. First, convert from grams to moles using molar mass:

$$n = \frac{m}{MM} = \frac{1.250 \text{ g}}{114.2 \text{ g/mol}} = 0.010946 \text{ mol}$$

$$\Delta E_{molar} = \frac{-60.1 \text{ kJ}}{0.010946 \text{ mol}} = -5.49 \times 10^3 \text{ kJ/mol octane}$$

SECTION EXERCISES

12.3.1 In a constant-pressure calorimeter, 1.530×10^3 J of electrical energy changes the water temperature from 20.50 °C to 21.85 °C. When 1.75 g of a solid salt is dissolved in the water, the temperature falls from 21.85 °C to 21.44 °C. Find the value of q_p for the solution process.

12.3.2 In a constant-volume calorimeter, 3.56 g of solid sulfur is burned in excess oxygen gas:

$$S_{(s)} + O_{2\,(g)} \rightarrow SO_{2\,(g)}$$

The calorimeter has a total heat capacity of 4.32 kJ/ °C. The combustion reaction causes the temperature of the calorimeter to increase from 25.93 °C to 33.56 °C. Calculate the heat evolved per mole of sulfur burned.

12.3.3 Imagine a calorimeter with a sliding piston that makes it possible to perform constant-pressure calorimetry experiments on a mixture of liquids and gases. Imagine also that 1.250 g of octane is burned in this calorimeter, which initially is at 25 °C.

(a) Will the calorimeter temperature rise or fall?

(b) Use the ideal gas equation to determine whether the volume of the system will increase or decrease. (HINT: The temperature change is almost the same as in Sample Problem 12-5.)

(c) Is the work positive, negative, or zero?

(d) Will ΔE be the same, more negative, or more positive than ΔE calculated in Sample Problem 12-6?

12.4 ENTHALPY

In the world around us, most chemical processes occur in contact with the Earth's atmosphere, at a constant pressure of 1 atm. For example, plants convert carbon dioxide and water into carbohydrates; animals metabolize food; gas water heaters and stoves burn fuel; and running water dissolves minerals from the soil. All these processes involve energy changes at constant pressure. Virtually all aqueous-solution chemistry also occurs at constant pressure. Thus constant-pressure calorimetry closely approximates many real-world processes.

Unlike the constant-volume situation, reactions that occur at constant pressure involve both heat and work, as we have already seen:

$$\Delta E = q_p + w_p$$

Heat flow can be measured directly using a calorimeter, but to determine the energy change, we must also measure work.

In a typical constant-pressure calorimeter, the work done is caused by expansion against the constant external pressure, and the pressure exerted by the system equals this constant external pressure:

$$w_p = -P_{ext}\Delta V_{sys} = -P\Delta V$$

We omit the subscripts because all quantities now refer to the chemical system. Making this substitution into the energy equation, we have:

$$\Delta E = q_p - P\Delta V$$

Of the quantities in this equation, q_p is the easiest to measure, so it is useful to solve this equation for q_p:

$$q_p = \Delta E + P\Delta V$$

The $P\Delta V$ term can be regrouped using $\Delta V = V_f - V_i$:

$$P\Delta V = P(V_f - V_i) = PV_f - PV_i = \Delta(PV) \quad \textit{so} \quad q_p = \Delta E + \Delta(PV)$$

Furthermore, because $\Delta A + \Delta B = \Delta(A + B)$:

$$q_p = \Delta(E + PV)$$

This analysis indicates that $(E + PV)$ is directly related to heat flow under constant-pressure conditions. This sum is called **enthalpy (*H*)**. By definition:

$$H = E + PV \qquad \textbf{(12-7)}$$

Because it is composed entirely of state functions, enthalpy is also a state function.

According to our derivation, enthalpy change is equal to the heat flow in a constant-pressure process:

$$\Delta H = \Delta(E + PV) \qquad \textit{and} \qquad q_p = \Delta(E + PV)$$

$$\Delta H = q_p \qquad \textbf{(12-8)}$$

Consequently, enthalpy changes can be measured very conveniently using a coffee-cup calorimeter.

The units of enthalpy are the same as those of energy, joules or kilojoules. Enthalpy, like energy, is an extensive quantity, but for tabulation purposes, chemists work with molar enthalpies. Molar enthalpies are expressed in kilojoules per mole.

Energy is a *fundamental* thermodynamic property. On the other hand, enthalpy is a *defined* thermodynamic property that is very convenient when working at constant pressure. Enthalpy changes and energy changes are related through the PV product:

$$\Delta H = \Delta E + \Delta(PV)$$

For solids and liquids, volume changes during chemical reactions are very small:

$$\Delta(PV)_{\text{(condensed phases)}} \cong 0$$

Thus enthalpy changes and energy changes are essentially equal for processes that involve only liquids and solids. An example of such a process is the dissolving of ammonium nitrate in water to produce aqueous ions:

$$NH_4NO_{3\,(s)} \rightarrow NH_4{}^+{}_{(aq)} + NO_3{}^-{}_{(aq)}$$

In Sample Problem 12-4, we determined that 20.0 g of this salt absorbs 5.28 kJ of energy when it dissolves in a constant-pressure calorimeter. From this information, we can calculate the molar enthalpy of solution:

$$\Delta H = q_p = 5.28 \text{ kJ} \qquad n = \frac{20.0 \text{ g}}{80.05 \text{ g/mol}} = 0.2498 \text{ mol}$$

$$\Delta H_{molar} = \Delta H/n = \frac{5.28 \text{ kJ}}{0.2498 \text{ mol}} = 21.1 \text{ kJ/mol}$$

For this process, none of the reactants or products is a gas, so the energy and enthalpy changes are essentially equal:

$$\Delta E_{molar} \cong 21.1 \text{ kJ/mol}$$

The total volume can change significantly if gases are produced or consumed during a reaction. When gases are involved in chemical reactions, either as starting materials or as products, the enthalpy change differs from the energy change. To determine the difference between them, the change in volume must be evaluated using the ideal gas equation:

$$PV_{(gas)} = nRT \quad \text{so} \quad \Delta(PV)_{(gas)} = \Delta(nRT)$$

Combining the equations for $\Delta(PV)$, we find that the enthalpy and energy changes for any chemical reaction are related according to Equation 12-9:

$$\Delta H_{rxn} = \Delta E_{rxn} + \Delta(PV)_{rxn} \cong \Delta E_{rxn} + \Delta(PV)_{(gases)}$$

$$\Delta H_{rxn} \cong \Delta E_{rxn} + \Delta(nRT)_{(gases)} \qquad \textbf{(12-9)}$$

The subscript "rxn" designates that a thermodynamic quantity refers to a chemical reaction.

Sample Problem 12-7 demonstrates how large this difference can be.

SAMPLE PROBLEM 12-7 ENTHALPY AND ENERGY CHANGES IN COMBUSTION

Find the difference between ΔH and ΔE for the combustion of 1 mol of octane at 298 K.

METHOD: The molar enthalpy change and the molar energy change are related by Equation 12-9:

$$\Delta H_{molar} = \Delta E_{molar} + \Delta(nRT)_{(gases)}$$

We need information about the $\Delta(nRT)$ term to calculate the difference between ΔH_{molar} and ΔE_{molar}. This term can be expanded as follows:

$$\Delta(nRT)_{(gases)} = n_f RT_f - n_i RT_i$$

Here, n_f and n_i are the number of moles of gaseous products and gaseous reactants in the balanced chemical equation. To determine these, we must write the balanced chemical equation for 1 mol of octane burning at 298 K:

$$C_8H_{18\,(l)} + 25/2\ O_{2\,(g)} \rightarrow 8\ CO_{2\,(g)} + 9\ H_2O_{\,(l)}$$

Over the years, scientists have measured standard enthalpies of formation of many chemical substances. The values are tabulated in chemical reference books, such as the *CRC Handbook of Chemistry and Physics*. Values for many common substances are listed in Appendix E of this text.

ENTHALPY CHANGES FOR CHEMICAL REACTIONS

Standard enthalpies of formation are particularly useful because they can be used to find the enthalpy change for *any* reaction that occurs under standard conditions. We show how this is done for nitrogen dioxide reacting to form N_2O_4:

$$2\ NO_{2\,(g)} \rightarrow N_2O_{4\,(g)}$$

Imagine the reaction following a two-step pathway. In the first step, 2 mol of NO_2 molecules decompose into nitrogen molecules and oxygen molecules:

$$2\ NO_{2\,(g)} \rightarrow N_{2\,(g)} + 2\ O_{2\,(g)}$$

In the second step, nitrogen and oxygen molecules react to produce N_2O_4:

$$N_{2\,(g)} + 2\ O_{2\,(g)} \rightarrow N_2O_{4\,(g)}$$

A molecular picture of this two-step process is shown in Figure 12-15.

The pathway shown in Figure 12-15 is not how the reaction actually occurs. This does not matter, however, because enthalpy is a state function, and the change of any state function is independent of the path of the reaction. Thus the enthalpy change for the overall reaction is equal to the sum of the enthalpy changes of the two steps:

$$\Delta H^\circ_{rxn} = \Delta H^\circ_{decomposition} + \Delta H^\circ_{formation}$$

$$\begin{array}{rcll} 2\ NO_{2\,(g)} & \longrightarrow & N_{2\,(g)} + 2\ O_{2\,(g)} & \Delta H^\circ_{decomposition} \\ N_{2\,(g)} + 2\ O_{2\,(g)} & \longrightarrow & N_2O_{4\,(g)} & \Delta H^\circ_{formation} \\ \hline 2\ NO_{2\,(g)} & \longrightarrow & N_2O_{4\,(g)} & \Delta H^\circ_{rxn} \end{array}$$

The decomposition reaction can be related to the formation reaction of NO_2. First, notice that the decomposition reaction is the formation reaction of NO_2 running in the reverse direction. The enthalpy change of a decomposition reaction has the same magnitude but the opposite sign as the corresponding formation reaction.

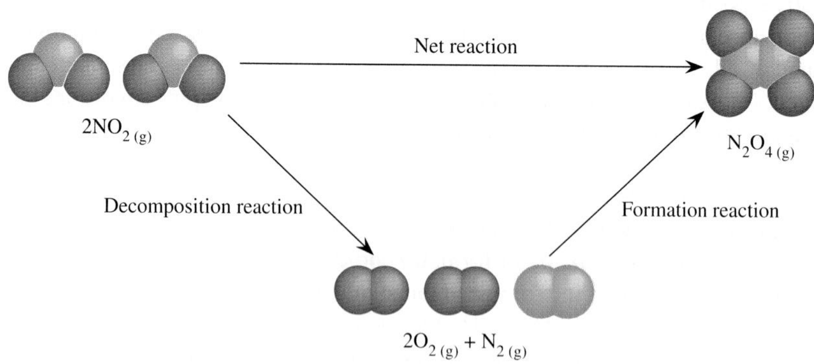

FIGURE 12-15
The enthalpy change for the reaction of nitrogen dioxide to produce N_2O_4 can be determined using a two-step path. In the first step, NO_2 decomposes to N_2 and O_2. In the second step, the elements react to form N_2O_4. Enthalpy is a state function, so ΔH for the overall reaction is the sum of the enthalpy changes for the two steps.

Second, the stoichiometric coefficients of the decomposition reaction are multiplied by 2. Decomposition of 2 mol of NO_2 involves twice the enthalpy change of the decomposition of 1 mol. Using both these factors, we can express the enthalpy change of the decomposition reaction in terms of the standard enthalpy of formation of NO_2:

$$\Delta H^\circ_{\text{decomposition}} = -2\,\Delta H^\circ_f\,(NO_2)$$

The enthalpy change of the formation reaction is just ΔH°_f of N_2O_4. Thus the molar enthalpy change of the overall reaction can be expressed entirely in terms of standard formation reactions:

$$\Delta H^\circ_{\text{rxn}} = \Delta H^\circ_f\,(N_2O_4) - 2\,\Delta H^\circ_f\,(NO_2)$$

The enthalpy change of the overall reaction is the sum of the formation enthalpies of the products minus the sum of the formation enthalpies of the reactants.

Using standard enthalpies of formation from Appendix E, we can calculate the enthalpy change for the overall reaction:

$$\Delta H^\circ_{\text{rxn}} = (1 \text{ mol } N_2O_4)\left(\frac{9.16 \text{ kJ}}{\text{mol } N_2O_4}\right) - (2 \text{ mol } NO_2)\left(\frac{33.18 \text{ kJ}}{\text{mol } NO_2}\right) = -57.2 \text{ kJ}$$

The negative value for the enthalpy change indicates that this reaction is exothermic. Qualitatively, this is logical because during the reaction a new bond forms between the nitrogen atoms, but none of the bonds of the starting materials breaks.

The enthalpy change of −57.2 kJ is for 2 mol of NO_2 reacting to form 1 mol of N_2O_4. These amounts constitute one **reaction unit** for this reaction. A reaction unit of any reagent is the same number of moles as appear in the balanced chemical equation. In this case, one reaction unit refers to 2 mol of NO_2 consumed and 1 mol of N_2O_4 produced, and the enthalpy change can be thought of as −57.2 kJ/reaction unit. Because there are 2 mol of NO_2 in the reaction unit, the enthalpy change per mole of NO_2 is:

$$\left(\frac{-57.2 \text{ kJ}}{\text{Reaction unit}}\right)\left(\frac{\text{Reaction unit}}{2 \text{ mol } NO_2}\right) = -28.6 \text{ kJ/mol } NO_2$$

The reaction unit is rarely included in thermodynamic calculations. Instead, chemists recognize that ΔH_{rxn} refers to the balanced chemical equation. To find the molar enthalpy change for any component of the reaction, simply divide ΔH_{rxn} by the appropriate stoichiometric coefficient.

Our analysis of the reaction of nitrogen dioxide molecules is not unique. In fact, the same type of path can be visualized for any chemical reaction. Thus the reaction enthalpy for any chemical reaction can be found by summing the standard enthalpies of formation for all products and then subtracting the sum of the standard enthalpies of formation for all reactants. This procedure is summarized in Equation 12-10:

$$\Delta H^\circ_{\text{rxn}} = \sum \text{coeff}_p\, \Delta H^\circ_f(\text{products}) - \sum \text{coeff}_r\, \Delta H^\circ_f(\text{reactants}) \qquad \textbf{(12-10)}$$

Remember that Σ means "the sum of"; coeff_p refers to the stoichiometric coefficients of the products in the balanced equation and coeff_r to those of the reactants.

Multiply each standard enthalpy of formation by the appropriate stoichiometric coefficient and then add the values for the products and subtract the values for the reactants. To illustrate the use of Equation 12-10, we calculate the enthalpy of combustion of methane, the principal component of natural gas. We must begin with the balanced chemical equation:

$$CH_{4\,(g)} + 2\,O_{2\,(g)} \rightarrow CO_{2\,(g)} + 2\,H_2O_{\,(l)}$$

The enthalpy change that accompanies this reaction could be evaluated step by step by first decomposing methane into its elemental constituents and then recombining the elements into carbon dioxide and liquid water. There is no need to do this in detail, however, because the outcome of this set of processes is summarized by Equation 12-10, which we can apply directly. The products are 1 mol of CO_2 and 2 mol of H_2O, whereas the reactants are 1 mol of CH_4 and 2 mol of O_2:

$$\Delta H^\circ_{\text{combustion}} = [\Delta H^\circ_f(CO_2) + 2\,\Delta H^\circ_f(H_2O)] - [\Delta H^\circ_f(CH_4) + 2\,\Delta H^\circ_f(O_2)]$$

We make use of data from Appendix E, bearing in mind that O_2 is an element in its standard state:

$$\Delta H^\circ_{\text{combustion}} = \left[(1 \text{ mol } CO_2)\left(\frac{-393.5 \text{ kJ}}{\text{mol } CO_2}\right) + (2 \text{ mol } H_2O)\left(\frac{-285.8 \text{ kJ}}{\text{mol } H_2O}\right)\right]$$

$$- \left[(1 \text{ mol } CH_4)\left(\frac{-74.81 \text{ kJ}}{\text{mol } CH_4}\right) + (2 \text{ mol } O_2)\left(\frac{0 \text{ kJ}}{\text{mol } O_2}\right)\right] = -890.3 \text{ kJ}$$

The enthalpy change for a chemical reaction can often be determined by calorimetric measurements. Then Equation 12-10 can be used to find an unknown standard enthalpy of formation. Sample Problem 12-8 shows an example of this application.

SAMPLE PROBLEM 12-8 STANDARD ENTHALPY OF FORMATION

Recall from Sample Problem 12-7 that the enthalpy of combustion of octane (C_8H_{18}) is -5.50×10^3 kJ/mol. Using tabulated standard enthalpies of formation in Appendix E, compute the enthalpy of formation of octane.

METHOD: We are asked to find an enthalpy of formation. Because enthalpy is a state function, we can use the fact that ΔH for a reaction is independent of the reaction path. We begin by writing the balanced chemical equation for octane combustion. Then we use Equation 12-10, which links enthalpies of formation with the enthalpy of a reaction.

The balanced combustion equation must be written for 1 mol of octane because the enthalpy of combustion refers to 1 mol:

$$C_8H_{18} + 25/2\ O_2 \rightarrow 8\ CO_2 + 9\ H_2O$$

Now we can use Equation 12-10 to set the heat of combustion, $\Delta H^\circ_{\text{molar}}$, equal to the sum of the enthalpies of formation and solve for the value for octane.

$$\Delta H^\circ_{\text{molar}} = \Sigma\ \text{coeff}_p\ \Delta H^\circ_f(\text{products}) - \Sigma\ \text{coeff}_r\ \Delta H^\circ_f(\text{reactants})$$

$$-5.50 \times 10^3 \text{ kJ} = 8\ \Delta H^\circ_f(CO_2) + 9\ \Delta H^\circ_f(H_2O) - \Delta H^\circ_f(\text{octane}) - (25/2)\ \Delta H^\circ_f(O_2)$$

$$\Delta H^\circ_f(\text{octane}) = 8\ \Delta H^\circ_f(CO_2) + 9\ \Delta H^\circ_f(H_2O) - (25/2)\ \Delta H^\circ_f(O_2) + 5.50 \times 10^3 \text{ kJ}$$

Substitute heats of formation from Appendix E:

$$\Delta H^\circ_f(\text{octane}) = (8 \text{ mol } CO_2)(-393.5 \text{ kJ/mol}) + (9 \text{ mol } H_2O)(-285.8 \text{ kJ/mol})$$

$$- (25/2 \text{ mol } O_2)(0 \text{ kJ/mol}) + 5.50 \times 10^3 \text{ kJ/mol}$$

$$\Delta H^\circ_f(\text{octane}) = -220 \text{ kJ/mol}$$

The formation enthalpies found in tables are values for "standard" conditions: $T = 298$ K and $P = 1$ atm. What if a reaction occurs under nonstandard conditions? Energies and enthalpies of substances change as temperature and pressure change, so we must expect that ΔH for a reaction depends on temperature and pressure, as well. These dependencies can be calculated, but such calculations are beyond the scope of our present coverage. Fortunately, for the vast majority of chemical reactions, ΔH changes *very slowly* with temperature or pressure. Therefore, calculations of reaction enthalpies using standard enthalpies of formation provide reasonable results, even when the temperature and pressure depart somewhat from standard conditions. Sample Problem 12-9 provides another example of the use of tabulated enthalpies.

Box 12-2 discusses requirements for a "good" chemical fuel.

SAMPLE PROBLEM 12-9 MOLAR ENTHALPY CHANGE

Nitric acid (HNO_3), which is produced from ammonia in the gas phase at elevated temperature and pressure, is an important chemical in the fertilizer industry because it can be converted into ammonium nitrate. The industrial reaction takes two steps, but the overall chemical equation for the conversion of ammonia into nitric acid is:

$$12\ NH_{3\,(g)} + 21\ O_{2\,(g)} \rightarrow 8\ HNO_{3\,(g)} + 4\ NO_{(g)} + 14\ H_2O_{(g)}$$

Determine whether this industrial process is exothermic or endothermic, and estimate the energy change per mole of HNO_3 formed.

METHOD: The first question asks whether this reaction releases energy (exothermic) or absorbs energy (endothermic). The second question asks us to estimate the molar energy change for the reaction. Even though the reaction conditions differ from standard conditions, we expect ΔH to vary slowly with temperature and pressure, so we can use Equation 12-10 and tabulated standard enthalpies of formation to estimate the reaction enthalpy. Because reaction enthalpy is almost the same as reaction energy, this calculation will give a satisfactory estimate of the reaction energy. Appendix E lists the following standard heats of formation, all in kJ/mol: $NH_{3\,(g)}$, −46.1; $H_2O_{(g)}$, −242; $HNO_{3\,(g)}$, −135; and $NO_{(g)}$, +90.2.

In Sample Problem 12-8 we used −285.8 kJ/mol, the standard formation enthalpy for *liquid* water. However, $H_2O_{(g)}$ is a different species, so it has a different heat of formation than $H_2O_{(l)}$. This demonstrates how important it is to keep track of the phase of each species.

Now we substitute these values into Equation 12-10 and use the stoichiometric coefficients from the balanced chemical equation:

$$\Delta H_{rxn} = [(8\text{ mol})(-135\text{ kJ/mol}) + (4\text{ mol})(90.2\text{ kJ/mol}) + (14\text{ mol})(-242\text{ kJ/mol})]$$
$$- [(12\text{ mol})(-46.1\text{ kJ/mol}) - (21\text{ mol})(0\text{ kJ/mol})]$$
$$= [-1080\text{ kJ} + 361\text{ kJ} - 3388\text{ kJ}] - [-553\text{ kJ} + 0\text{ kJ}] = [-4107\text{ kJ}] - [-553\text{ kJ}]$$
$$\Delta H_{rxn} = -3554\text{ kJ} = -3.55 \times 10^3\text{ kJ}$$

It is important to pay careful attention to the signs, which we have done by carrying out the calculations in sequence. First, multiply each standard enthalpy, including its sign, by the appropriate coefficient. Then combine values for reactants and values for products, adding or subtracting according to the sign of each enthalpy. Finally, subtract the sum for reactants from the sum for products to obtain the final result.

The negative sign for ΔH_{rxn} indicates that this reaction is *exothermic*. This is the value per *reaction unit*, which generates 8 mol of $HNO_{3\,(g)}$. Therefore the value *per mole* of nitric acid produced is:

$$\Delta H_{molar} = \frac{-3.55 \times 10^3\text{ kJ}}{8\text{ mol } HNO_3} = -444\text{ kJ/mol } HNO_3$$

BOX 12-2

WHAT MAKES A GOOD FUEL?

Energy expenditure is so closely linked with industrial activity that the energy consumption per capita can be used as a measure of a nation's level of development. For uses as diverse as automobiles, airplanes, and plastics manufacture, technological societies consume huge amounts of fuel. Although an abundant supply of fuel is essential for the operation of modern society, the *number* of chemical fuels is surprisingly small. To see why this is, we examine the characteristics of "good" chemical fuels.

Modern industrial society relies heavily on chemical fuels such as gasoline to keep it "humming."

The first requirement of a chemical fuel is that it reacts with a readily available substance to release a large amount of energy. In other words, a fuel is a chemical substance in a high-energy state from which there is a "downhill" reaction path. The most common fuels react with oxygen and generate carbon dioxide and water:

Natural gas: $CH_4 + 2\ O_2 \rightarrow CO_2 + 2\ H_2O$

$\Delta H_{rxn} = -810$ kJ/mol

Gasoline: $C_8H_{18} + 25/2\ O_2 \rightarrow$

$8\ CO_2 + 9\ H_2O$

$\Delta H_{rxn} = -5500$ kJ/mol

Space shuttle fuel: $2\ H_2 + O_2 \rightarrow 2\ H_2O$

$\Delta H_{rxn} = -484$ kJ/mol

It is no accident that the common chemical fuels employ reactions with gaseous oxygen. This is the only substance that has relatively weak chemical bonds and that is present everywhere on the Earth's surface. Compare the energies of the bonds that break and the bonds that form in the combustion of natural gas, gasoline, and molecular hydrogen:

Bond	Bond energy	Energy/bond
C—H	415	415
H—H	432	432
C—C	345	345
O=O	494	247
O—H	460	460
C=O (in CO_2)	805	402

From this list, we see that combustion releases energy because C=O and O—H bonds are considerably more stable than the O=O bond. The conversion of O=O bonds into C=O bonds and O—H bonds is accompanied by the release of over 300 kJ/mol of energy.

Another requirement of a fuel is that it must be possible to control the reaction. This involves a delicate balance. A fuel that is too reactive cannot be stored safely, but if it is not reactive enough, it releases too little energy to be a good fuel. Even with the best of fuels, combustion can get out of control, with disastrous results. Here are some examples: leaking natural gas forms a mixture in air that can explode and burn intensely; oil

SECTION EXERCISES

12.4.1 Which of the following substances have zero values for their standard enthalpy of formation: (a) ozone, $O_{3(g)}$; (b) solid mercury, $Hg_{(s)}$; (c) liquid bromine, $Br_{2(l)}$; (d) graphite, $C_{(s)}$; (e) atomic fluorine, $F_{(g)}$; and (f) solid sulfur, $S_{8(s)}$?

12.4.2 Hydrogen gas is prepared industrially from methane and steam:

$$CH_{4(g)} + H_2O_{(g)} \rightarrow CO_{(g)} + 3\ H_{2(g)}$$

well fires can be extremely difficult to extinguish; a leaking fuel gasket led to the hydrogen-oxygen explosion that destroyed the space shuttle Challenger; and fires in coal mines may burn out of control for years.

For special uses such as travel in space, materials other than O_2 may be used to react with a fuel. The lunar landers, for example, used a mixture of dimethylhydrazine and dinitrogen tetroxide (N_2O_4). The enthalpy change for this reaction is −1772 kJ:

$$H_2NN(CH_3)_{2\,(l)} + 2\,N_2O_{4\,(l)} \rightarrow 3\,N_{2\,(g)} + 2\,CO_{2\,(g)} + 4\,H_2O_{(g)}$$

Dimethylhydrazine also reacts with O_2, but N_2O_4 offers two advantages over O_2 for operation in space. First, the reaction occurs instantaneously when the starting materials are mixed. In contrast, the reaction of dimethylhydrazine with O_2 requires an ignition device. Second, N_2O_4 is liquefied more easily than O_2, so it is easier to store aboard a spacecraft.

The fuels of the biosphere are carbohydrates such as glucose and sucrose. Green plants absorb solar energy and use it to drive the highly endothermic formation of carbohydrates from CO_2 and H_2O:

$$6\,CO_2 + 6\,H_2O \xrightarrow{\text{Sunlight}} C_6H_{12}O_6 + 6\,O_2$$

Carbohydrates react with O_2, releasing 2820 kJ/mol of energy:

$$C_6H_{12}O_6 + 6\,O_2 \rightarrow 6\,CO_2 + 6\,H_2O \quad \Delta H_{rxn} = -2820 \text{ kJ/mol}$$

This reaction, operating under carefully controlled conditions, is used by both plants and animals as their chemical source of energy.

Our major chemical fuels, natural gas, petroleum products, and coal, are "fossil" fuels, formed from the decomposition of plants over many millions of years. At the rate that the world is consuming these fuels, it is estimated that natural gas and petroleum will be depleted within 50 years, and even the much more abundant deposits of coal may be consumed within 2 to 3 centuries. Once we deplete this reservoir of chemical energy, we will have to turn to nonchemical energy sources, such as nuclear, solar, and maybe even gravitational energy. Unfortunately, none of these forms of energy has the attractive features of good chemical fuels: controllability, high intensity, and transportability. Developing fuel sources to replace nonrenewable fossil fuels is a major long-term challenge for our technological society.

A burning oil well reminds us that fuels unleash large quantities of energy when they react and that a fuel burning out of control poses a serious threat to human life and the environment.

Use standard enthalpies of formation to determine ΔH_{rxn} and ΔE_{rxn} for this process.

12.4.3 In the smelting of iron ore, iron oxides are decomposed in the presence of carbon. The process involves several steps, but the overall stoichiometry can be summarized in a single chemical equation:

$$Fe_2O_{3\,(s)} + C_{(graphite)} \rightarrow Fe_{(s)} + CO_{2\,(g)} \qquad \text{(Unbalanced)}$$

Compute the standard enthalpy change for the balanced equation.

12.5 ENTHALPY AND INTERMOLECULAR FORCES

So far in this chapter, most of our attention has been focused on the energy changes that accompany chemical reactions. These energy changes largely result from making and breaking chemical bonds. In this section we consider the energy released or absorbed because of changes in intermolecular forces. Specifically, we discuss phase changes and the formation of solutions.

HEAT OF SOLUTION

Recall from Chapter 10 what happens when an ionic salt dissolves in water. Strong attractive forces among the ions must be overcome to break ions loose from the solid lattice, and strong ion-dipole attractive forces bind the ions to water molecules in the solution. The molar **heat of solution** (ΔH_{soln}) measures the net energy flow that occurs as a substance dissolves.

Because of the large attractive forces in both solids and solutions, heats of solution vary from significantly exothermic to significantly endothermic. If the crystal binds ions more tightly than the solution, the salt must absorb energy as it dissolves, and we have an endothermic solution process with positive enthalpy change. When this ΔH_{soln} is large, the salt is unlikely to be soluble. One soluble salt with a relatively large positive ΔH_{soln} is ammonium nitrate (NH_4NO_3, ΔH_{soln} = 21.1 kJ/mol). On the other hand, if the solution binds ions more tightly than the crystal, energy is released as the salt dissolves, and we have an exothermic process with negative ΔH_{soln}. Many salts, including calcium chloride ($CaCl_2$, ΔH_{soln} = −83 kJ/mol) and magnesium sulfate ($MgSO_4$, ΔH_{soln}= −91.2 kJ/mol), release large amounts of energy when they dissolve in water.

FIGURE 12-16
Instant hot and cold packs rely on heats of solution to generate instant heating or cooling for the treatment of minor injuries such as pulled muscles and sprains.

Heats of solution are the basis for "instant cold packs" and "instant hot packs" used for the first-aid treatment of minor sprains and pulled muscles. These packs contain two separate compartments. One contains water, and the other contains a salt: NH_4NO_3 for cold packs and $MgSO_4$ or $CaCl_2$ for hot packs. Kneading the pack breaks the wall between the compartments, allowing the salt to mix with water. As the salt dissolves to form an aqueous solution, the temperature of the pack changes. Heat is absorbed or released only as the salt dissolves, however, so after all the salt has dissolved, the pack gradually returns to room temperature. Further manipulation of the pack has no effect. Figure 12-16 shows these packs, and Sample Problem 12-10 addresses their enthalpy changes.

SAMPLE PROBLEM 12-10 ENTHALPIES OF SOLUTION

If an instant cold pack contains 75 g of ammonium nitrate and 250 g of water, how much will the temperature of the bag decrease when the chemicals are mixed? Assume that all the energy absorbed during the solution process is provided by the water.

METHOD: This process involves a heat transfer. The energy required to break up the NH_4 NO_3 lattice is supplied by the water in the form of heat. The energy lost by the water causes a drop in temperature. Because energy is conserved, the sum of the energy needed to dissolve the salt and the energy lost by the water is zero. A block diagram of the process helps clarify the relationships:

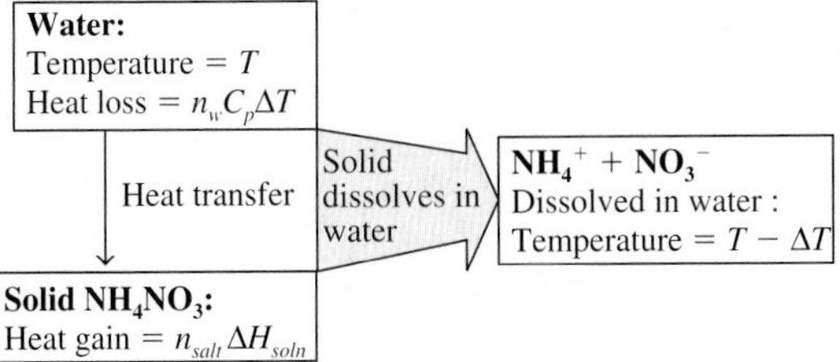

The total amount of heat absorbed by the salt is the number of moles of salt multiplied by the molar heat of solution:

$$q_{\text{salt}} = n_{\text{salt}} \, \Delta H_{\text{soln}}$$

This heat comes from the water, so the water cools as it gives up heat:

$$q_{\text{water}} = n_{\text{water}} \, C_{\text{p,water}} \, \Delta T$$

Energy is conserved, so the sum of these two heats is zero:

$$q_{\text{water}} + q_{\text{salt}} = 0$$

Combining these equalities gives a single equation:

$$n_{\text{salt}} \, \Delta H_{\text{soln}} + n_{\text{water}} \, C_{\text{p,water}} \, \Delta T = 0$$

This equation can be solved to give an expression for ΔT:

$$\Delta T = \frac{-n_{\text{salt}} \, \Delta H_{\text{soln}}}{n_{\text{water}} \, C_{\text{p,water}}}$$

Now we can tabulate the data and carry out the calculation: ΔH_{soln} for ammonium nitrate = 21.1 kJ/mol and, from Table 12-2, $C_{\text{p,water}}$ = 75.3 J/mol K:

$$n_{\text{salt}} = \frac{m}{MM} = \frac{75 \text{ g}}{80.05 \text{ g/mol}} = 0.937 \text{ mol } NH_4NO_3$$

$$n_{\text{water}} = \frac{m}{MM} = \frac{250 \text{ g}}{18.02 \text{ g/mol}} = 13.87 \text{ mol } H_2O$$

$$\Delta T_{\text{water}} = \frac{-n_{\text{salt}} \, \Delta H_{\text{soln}}}{n_{\text{water}} \, C_{\text{p,water}}} = \frac{-(0.937 \text{ mol})(21.1 \text{ kJ/mol})(1000 \text{ J/kJ})}{(13.87 \text{ mol})(75.3 \text{ J/mol K})}$$

$$\Delta T_{\text{water}} = -19 \text{ K}$$

The temperature change in °C is numerically equal to the temperature change in K. Thus if the cold pack was initially at ambient temperature (around 25 °C), its temperature would fall to about 6 °C.

Complete solvation of ions involves two to eight water molecules per ion. In highly concentrated aqueous solutions, there are not enough water molecules to fully solvate all the ions. Because of this, the addition of water to a concentrated solution may increase ion-solvent interaction energies. This releases energy and leads to a temperature increase when a concentrated solution is diluted by adding water. The molar change in interaction energies when the concentration of a solution changes is called the **heat of dilution.**

Aqueous strong acids often have large heats of dilution because proton transfer from a strong acid to water is highly exothermic. This can lead to problems when a concentrated acid is diluted with water. At the point where water contacts the solution, much energy is released. This energy can heat the solution locally beyond its boiling point. If this occurs, droplets of the surrounding acid can splatter from the solution. Hot acid is a caustic material that rapidly burns the skin and attacks many other materials, including clothing. Sulfuric acid is particularly likely to "spatter" because H_2SO_4 has a high viscosity and does not mix readily with added water. Therefore acids should always be diluted by slowly adding the concentrated *acid* to *water*. In this way the transformation of concentrated acid into a more dilute solution occurs relatively slowly, and no local "hot spots" of high temperature can develop.

PHASE CHANGES

Phase changes are accompanied by enthalpy changes, even though a phase change involves neither a chemical reaction nor a temperature change. Consider a teakettle filled with water that has been heated to 100 °C. To transfer molecules of water from the liquid phase into the gas phase, we must add energy to the kettle. The temperature remains constant as the water boils away. Steam escapes into the atmosphere as the stove (surroundings) transfers heat to the water molecules (system).

When a substance undergoes a phase change, its temperature normally remains fixed, even though heat is being added or withdrawn. Thus mixtures of two phases, such as ice-water baths, serve as convenient constant-temperature devices.

We can see why energy must be supplied to boil water by examining this process from a molecular perspective. Liquid water is held together by hydrogen bonds between water molecules (see Chapter 10). These forces stabilize liquid water by about 40 kJ/mol. A molecule cannot escape the liquid phase unless it has enough energy of motion to overcome these attractive forces. Heat must be supplied to increase the molecular energy of motion.

Normally, phase changes occur at constant pressure, so the heat needed to cause a phase change is equal to an enthalpy change: $q_p = \Delta H$. Thus an enthalpy change accompanies any change of phase. The magnitude of the enthalpy change depends on the strength of intermolecular forces acting on the substance undergoing the phase change. For example, the many intermolecular hydrogen bonds among water molecules, shown in Figure 12-17, generate large intermolecular forces that hold water molecules in the liquid phase. For an organic liquid such as acetone, on the other hand, intermolecular forces are significantly smaller. Thus it requires less heat to vaporize 1 mol of acetone than it does to vaporize 1 mol of water. The amount of heat

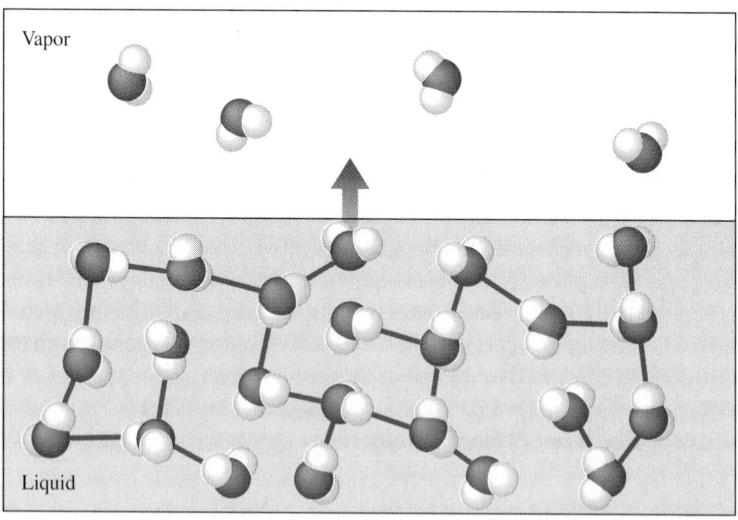

FIGURE 12-17
When molecules of water leave the liquid phase to enter the vapor phase (*shaded arrow*), they must absorb energy to overcome intermolecular hydrogen bonding in the liquid phase (*solid lines*).

TABLE 12-6 MOLAR HEATS OF PHASE CHANGE

SUBSTANCE	FORMULA	T_{fus} (K)	ΔH_{fus} (kJ/mol)	T_{vap} (K)	ΔH_{vap} (kJ/mol)
Argon	Ar	83	1.3	87	6.3
Oxygen	O_2	54	0.45	90	9.8
Methane	CH_4	90	0.84	112	9.2
Ethane	C_2H_6	90	2.85	184	15.5
Diethyl ether	$(C_2H_5)_2O$	157	6.90	308	26.0
Ethanol	C_2H_5OH	156	7.61	351	39.3
Benzene	C_6H_6	278.5	10.9	353	31.0
Water	H_2O	273	6.01	373	40.79
Mercury	Hg	234	23.4	630	59.0

Vaporization is designated by the subscript "vap," fusion is designated by the subscript "fus," and sublimation is designated by the subscript "subl."

required also depends on the amount of substance being vaporized. Twice as much energy is required to overcome all the intermolecular forces in 2 mol of water than in 1 mol. We call the heat needed to vaporize 1 mol of a substance at its normal boiling point the **molar heat of vaporization (ΔH_{vap})**.

Energy must also be provided to melt a substance. This energy is used to overcome the intermolecular forces that hold the molecules or ions in fixed positions in the solid phase. Thus melting also has characteristic enthalpy changes. The heat needed to melt 1 mol of a substance at its normal melting point is called the **molar heat of fusion (ΔH_{fus})**.

Table 12-6 lists values of ΔH_{fus} and ΔH_{vap} for different chemical substances, and Sample Problem 12-11 provides practice in using these quantities.

SAMPLE PROBLEM 12-11 HEAT OF PHASE CHANGE

A swimmer emerging from a pool is covered with a film containing about 75 g of water. How much heat must be supplied to evaporate this water?

METHOD: Energy in the form of heat is required to evaporate the water from the swimmer's skin. The energy needed to vaporize the water can be found using the molar heat of vaporization and the number of moles of water. The process can be shown with a simple block diagram:

$$\boxed{\begin{array}{c}75\text{ g }H_2O\\\text{liquid}\end{array}} \xrightarrow{n_{H_2O}\,\Delta H_{vap}} \boxed{\begin{array}{c}75\text{ g }H_2O\\\text{vapor}\end{array}}$$

The ΔH_{vap} of water (see Table 12-6) is 40.79 kJ/mol. The molar mass of water is 18.02 g/mol, so 75 g of water is 4.16 mol.

Therefore the heat that must be supplied is:

$$q_p = n\,\Delta H_{vap} = (4.16\text{ mol})(40.79\text{ kJ/mol}) = 1.7 \text{ x } 10^2\text{ kJ}$$

If the swimmer's body must supply all this heat, a substantial chilling effect occurs. Thus swimmers usually towel off (to reduce the amount of water that must be evaporated) or lie in the sun (to let the sun provide most of the heat required).

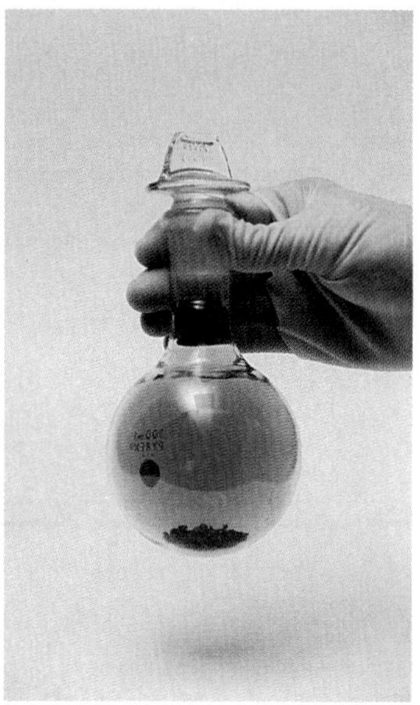

FIGURE 12-18
The red-violet color in the gas phase above iodine crystals in this sealed flask provides visual evidence that this substance sublimes at room temperature.

Table 12-6 lists enthalpy changes for fusion and vaporization, which are the most common phase changes. Less common is **sublimation,** in which a solid is transformed directly to a vapor without passing through the liquid phase. "Dry ice" (solid CO_2) sublimes at 195 K with $\Delta H_{subl} = 25.2$ kJ/mol. Mothballs contain naphthalene ($C_{10}H_8$, $\Delta H_{subl} = 73$ kJ/mol), a crystalline white solid that slowly sublimes to produce vapor whose odor repels moths. The red-violet color of the gas phase above the iodine crystals shown in Figure 12-18 is visible evidence that this solid also sublimes at room temperature.

Under the right conditions, phase changes can go in either direction. When steam is cooled, it condenses; when liquid water is cooled, it freezes. Each of these is an *exothermic* process because each is the reverse of an endothermic phase change. That is, heat is released as a gas condenses to a liquid and as a liquid freezes to a solid. To make ice cubes, for instance, you place water in the freezer compartment of your refrigerator, where the refrigerator absorbs the heat that is released as ice forms. A phase change that is exothermic has a negative enthalpy change:

$$\Delta H_{\text{solidification}} = -\Delta H_{\text{fus}} \quad \textit{and} \quad \Delta H_{\text{condensation}} = -\Delta H_{\text{vap}}$$

By convention, tabulated values of heats of phase changes are always specified in the endothermic direction:

Solid → Liquid	ΔH_{fus}
Liquid → Vapor	ΔH_{vap}
Solid → Vapor	ΔH_{subl}

A solid must absorb heat to melt. This makes ice a good substance to use for cooling. As ice melts, it absorbs heat from its surroundings, lowering the temperature. Because energy is conserved, the amount of heat given up by the surroundings is equal to the amount of heat absorbed by melting ice. This concept is illustrated by Sample Problem 12-12.

SAMPLE PROBLEM 12-12 PHASE AND TEMPERATURE CHANGES

A thirsty marathon runner pours 200 mL of Gatorade from a can at 25 °C. What is the minimum mass of ice that must be added to cool the drink to 0 °C?

METHOD: This problem involves an energy balance. The Gatorade must be cooled by removing energy, so some ice must melt to absorb that energy. The heat released in cooling the Gatorade must equal the heat absorbed to melt some amount of ice. A block diagram helps us visualize the computational path:

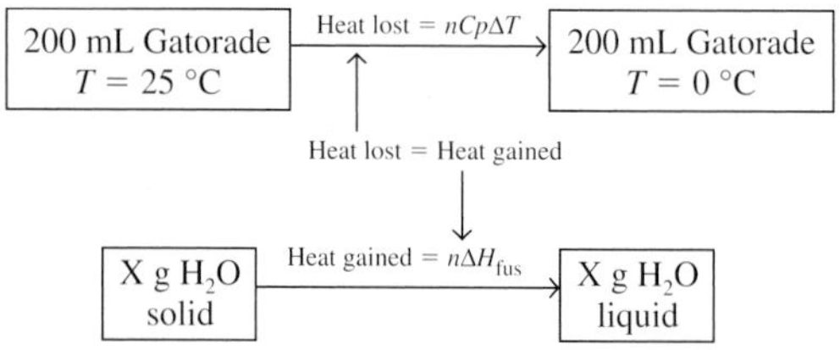

The minimum mass of ice needed is represented by X, the mass that, on melting, will gain as much heat as the Gatorade gives up as it cools to 0 °C. First, we compute the heat loss; then we use it to find the mass of ice needed:

$$\Delta H_{\text{Gatorade}} = q_p = nC_p\Delta T$$

Assuming that Gatorade is essentially water (a reasonable thermodynamic assumption), we use the heat capacity of water from Table 12-2:

$$C_p = 75.29 \text{ J/mol K}$$

$$\Delta T = (0\ °\text{C} - 25\ °\text{C}) = -25\ °\text{C} = 25 \text{ K}$$

We are given the volume of Gatorade, which must be converted to moles using the density and molar mass of water:

$$n_{\text{Gatorade}} = \frac{(200 \text{ mL})(1.00 \text{ g/mL})}{(18.02 \text{ g/mol})} = 11.10 \text{ mol}$$

$$q_{\text{Gatorade}} = (11.10 \text{ mol})(75.29 \text{ J/mol K})(-25 \text{ K})(10^{-3} \text{ kJ/J}) = -20.9 \text{ kJ}$$

Energy is conserved, so 20.9 kJ of heat must be absorbed by the ice:

$$q_{\text{Gatorade}} + q_{\text{ice}} = 0 \quad \textit{so} \quad q_{\text{ice}} = -q_{\text{Gatorade}} = 20.9 \text{ kJ}$$

The heat absorbed by the ice causes it to melt:

$$q_{\text{ice}} = \Delta H_{\text{ice}} = n_{\text{ice}}\, \Delta H_{\text{fus}} = 20.9 \text{ kJ}$$

The molar heat of fusion of ice (see Table 12-6) is 6.01 kJ/mol:

$$n_{\text{ice}} = \frac{20.9 \text{ kJ}}{6.01 \text{ kJ/mol}} = 3.478 \text{ mol}$$

$$m_{\text{ice}} = (n)(MM) = (3.478 \text{ mol})(18.02 \text{ g/mol}) = 62.7 \text{ g ice required}$$

ENERGIES OF PHASE TRANSFER

Phase changes normally occur at constant pressure, so the heat absorbed or released is directly related to their molar enthalpies. For solids and liquids, the volume change that accompanies a phase transition is very small, so the amount of work done is negligible. Thus energy changes (ΔE) are almost identical to enthalpy changes (ΔH) for phase transitions between liquids and solids. However, if the phase change involves a gas, the process includes a significant work component, and the difference between ΔH and ΔE cannot be ignored.

Remember that ΔH and ΔE are related by PV: $\Delta H = \Delta E + \Delta(PV)$. The change in volume for a transformation from a condensed phase to the gas phase is almost equal to the volume of the resulting gas. For example, consider boiling water. According to the ideal gas equation, the molar volume of water vapor at 373 K is 30.6 L/mol:

$$\frac{V}{n} = \frac{RT}{P} = \frac{(0.08206 \text{ L atm/mol K})(373 \text{ K})}{(1.00 \text{ atm})} = 30.6 \text{ L/mol}$$

Liquid water at 373 K has a molar volume of only about 18 mL, which is 0.018 L. This small molar volume of the liquid can be neglected compared with the large molar volume of the gas. Thus for any vaporization process:

$$\Delta(PV) = P\,\Delta V \simeq PV_{\text{gas}} = nRT_{\text{vap}}$$

because we are dealing with molar quantities, moreover, $n = 1$. This gives us a general equation that relates the energy of vaporization or sublimation to the corresponding enthalpy:

For thermodynamic calculations, we express R in units that include an energy: $R = 8.314 \times 10^{-3}$ kJ/mol K.

$$\Delta E_{\text{vap}} = \Delta H_{\text{vap}} - RT_{\text{vap}}$$

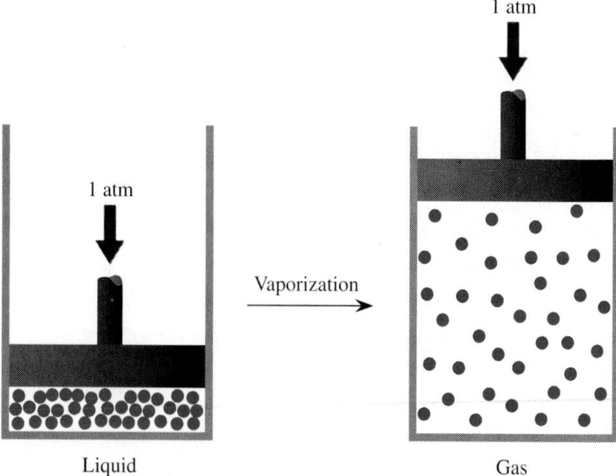

FIGURE 12-19
This schematic view of vaporization illustrates that work accompanies vaporization at constant pressure. As liquid molecules escape to the gas phase, they exert pressure on the piston, moving it back against a constant external pressure exerted by the atmosphere.

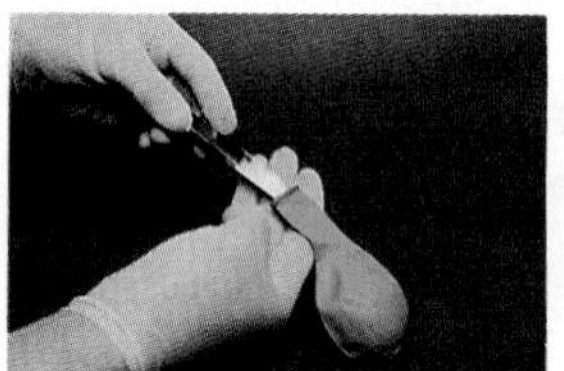

FIGURE 12-20
Sublimation of dry ice trapped inside a balloon generates gas molecules that "blow up" the balloon as they expand.

Vaporization and sublimation energies are typically about 10% less than their corresponding enthalpies. Using water as an example, $\Delta H_{vap} = 40.79$ kJ/mol and $RT_{vap} = 3.10$ kJ/mol, giving $\Delta E_{vap} = 37.69$ kJ/mol. This difference arises because vaporization at constant pressure accomplishes work against the surroundings, as well as overcoming intermolecular forces in the condensed phase. The escaping vapor accomplishes work by expanding against the constant external pressure of the atmosphere. Figures 12-19 and 12-20 illustrate this concept.

SECTION EXERCISES

12.5.1 The heat of fusion of sodium chloride is 27.2 kJ/mol, but its heat of solution in water is only 3 kJ/mol. Use intermolecular forces to explain the difference between these two molar enthalpies.

12.5.2 To make iced tea, 100.0 g of ice at 273 K is added to 500.0 mL of tea at 298 K in an insulated glass. What is the temperature after all the ice melts? Assume that the heat capacity of tea is the same as that of water.

12.5.3 If dry ice is heated under a pressure greater than 10 atm, it melts instead of subliming. If the pressure is then reduced to 1 atm, the liquid boils to give gaseous CO_2. Is the enthalpy change for this two-step process larger than, smaller than, or the same as the enthalpy of sublimation for CO_2? Give reasoning to support your answer.

CHAPTER SUMMARY

1. Thermodynamics plays a central role in chemistry because energy is at the heart of chemistry. Chemical energy is stored in chemical bonds and is released or absorbed during chemical reactions. The phase behavior of substances also highly depends on energy.
2. Substances such as petroleum store large quantities of chemical energy and provide the energy needed to drive many processes in technological societies.
3. Processes release stored chemical energy *(E)* as heat *(q)* and/or work *(w)*, and these are linked through the first law of thermodynamics, $\Delta E = q + w$.
4. A heat transfer causes a temperature change whose magnitude depends on the molar heat capacity (C_p) of the substance: $q = nC_p\Delta T$. This relationship between heat flow and temperature change is the working equation for calorimetric measurements.
5. Work results when a force generates a displacement. Expansion work against a constant external pressure is given by $w = -P_{ext}\Delta V_{sys}$.
6. When the volume of a system remains fixed, no expansion work occurs. Under these conditions, heat and energy change are equal: $\Delta E = q_v$.
7. In many everyday chemical processes, pressure is constant but volume is not. For these processes, a useful function is enthalpy, defined by $H = E + PV$. At constant pressure, the change in enthalpy can be found directly from the heat flow: $\Delta H = q_p$.
8. For many chemical reactions, enthalpy change and energy change differ by so little that one can be substituted for the other.
9. Changes of phase such as melting, vaporization, and solution formation usually occur at constant pressure and can be characterized by their enthalpy changes.
10. The heats of fusion, vaporization, and sublimation are always positive. Solution enthalpies, which involve a balance between solid-phase attractions and solute-solvent attractions, may be positive or negative.

KEY TERMS

change of state
equation of state
path function
state function
state of a system
state variables
surroundings
system

calorimeter
endothermic
energy *(E)*
enthalpy *(H)*
exothermic
first law of thermodynamics
heat *(q)*
molar heat capacity (C_p)
work *(w)*

formation reaction
heat of dilution
heat of solution
molar heat of fusion (ΔH_{fus})
molar heat of vaporization (ΔH_{vap})
reaction unit
standard enthalpy of formation (ΔH°_f)
sublimation

SKILLS TO MASTER

- Defining system and surroundings
- Calculating *q* and *w*
- Working with standard enthalpies of formation
- Relating energy and enthalpy changes
- Making calorimetric calculations
- Calculating enthalpies of phase changes and solution

LEARNING EXERCISES

12.1 Write a chapter summary of two pages or less that summarizes the important ideas and concepts presented in this chapter.

12.2 List all the properties that may change as a chemical reaction occurs in a closed system. Draw a "before-and-after" block diagram that schematically represents such a process.

12.3 Write a paragraph that explains the relationships among energy, heat, work, and temperature.

12.4 Describe in your own words what enthalpy is and why it is preferred to energy in describing the thermodynamics of many chemical processes.

12.5 Energy accounting on open systems is much more difficult than on closed systems. Explain the feature of an open system that creates difficulties, and describe how you would set up an energy balance for an open system.

12.6 Update your list of memory bank equations. Write a sentence that describes the restrictions on each equation (for example, $H = E + PV$ is a definition that has no restrictions).

12.7 Prepare a list of the terms in Chapter 12 that are new to you. Write a one-sentence definition for each, using your own words. If you need help, consult the glossary.

PROBLEMS

THERMODYNAMIC DEFINITIONS

12.1 Which of the following are open systems, closed systems, and (almost) isolated systems: (a) human being; (b) coffee in a thermos flask; (c) ice-cube tray filled with water; and (d) helium-filled balloon.

12.2 Categorize each of the following as open, closed, or (almost) isolated systems from the thermodynamic perspective. Explain your reasoning in each case: (a) can of tomato soup; (b) freezer chest full of ice; (c) the Earth; and (d) a satellite in orbit.

12.3 Which of the following properties of a sodium chloride solution are state variables: (a) temperature at which it was prepared; (b) its current temperature; (c) mass of NaCl used in its preparation; and (d) when it was prepared.

12.4 Which of the following are state functions: (a) height of a mountain; (b) distance traveled in climbing that mountain; (c) energy consumed in climbing the mountain; and (d) gravitational potential energy of a climber on top of the mountain.

12.5 Consider driving an automobile. Define as many different systems as you can that might be used to discuss thermodynamic properties that involve you and the automobile.

12.6 Consider the human body. Define as many different systems as you can that might be used to discuss the thermodynamics of human life.

ENERGY

12.7 An electrical heater is used to supply 25.0 J of energy to each of the following samples. Compute the final temperature in each case: (a) 10.0 g block of Al originally at 15.0 °C; (b) 25.0 g block of Al originally at 295 K; (c) 25.0 g block of Ag originally at 295 K; and (d) 25.0 g sample of H_2O originally at 22.0 °C.

12.8 A piece of silver with mass of 15.0 g is immersed in 25.0 g of water. This system is heated electrically from 24.0 to 37.6 °C. How many joules of energy are absorbed by the silver, and how many by the water?

12.9 A silver coin weighing 27.4 g is heated to 100.0 °C in boiling water. It is then dropped into 37.5 g of water at 20.5 °C. Find the final temperature of coin + water.

12.10 A dish containing 145 g of water at 54.0 °C is put in a refrigerator to cool. It is removed when its temperature is 5.50 °C. What is q for the water?

12.11 How much work is done in blowing up a balloon from zero volume to a volume of 2.5 L, assuming that no work is required to stretch the rubber? (In reality, the work that goes into stretching the rubber is substantial.)

12.12 A helium-filled balloon is at 320 K, contains 0.10 g He, and has a volume of 1.31 L. It is placed in a deep freeze (T = 250 K), and its volume decreases to 1.01 L. Find ΔE for the gas. (C_p of He = 20.8 J/mol K.)

12.13 State the first law of thermodynamics (a) as a conservation statement; (b) in terms of energy of the universe; and (c) in terms of heat and work.

12.14 Only one of the following expressions describes the heat of a chemical reaction under all possible conditions. Which is it? For each of the others, give an example for which the expression gives the wrong value for the heat: (a) ΔE; (b) ΔH; (c) q_v; (d) q_p; or (e) $\Delta E - w$.

HEAT MEASUREMENTS: CALORIMETRY

12.15 Constant-volume calorimeters are sometimes calibrated by running a combustion reaction of known ΔE and measuring the change in temperature. For example, the combustion energy of glucose is 15.57 kJ/g. When a 1.7500-g sample of glucose burns in a constant-volume calorimeter, the calorimeter temperature increases from 21.45 to 23.34 °C. Find the total heat capacity of the calorimeter.

12.16 An electrical heater is used to add 19.75 kJ of heat to a constant-volume calorimeter. The temperature of the calorimeter increases by 4.22 °C. When 1.75 g of methanol is burned in the same calorimeter, the temperature increases by 8.47 °C. Calculate the molar heat of combustion for methanol.

12.17 When a 4.75-g sample of $CaCl_2$ dissolves in 110.0 g of water in a coffee-cup calorimeter, the temperature rises from 22.0 to 29.7 °C. How much heat does this solution process release? Express your answer in joules per mole of salt.

12.18 A 1.35 g sample of caffeine ($C_8H_{10}N_4O_2$) burns in a constant-volume calorimeter that has a heat capacity of 7.85 kJ/K. The temperature increases from 297.65 K to 302.04 K. Determine the amount of heat released and the molar heat of combustion of caffeine.

12.19 When 1.350 g of benzoic acid ($C_7H_6O_2$) burns completely in excess O_2 gas at constant volume and 298 K, it releases 35.61 kJ of energy.
(a) What is the balanced chemical equation for this reaction?
(b) What is the molar energy of combustion of benzoic acid?
(c) What is the energy released per mole of O_2 consumed?

12.20 Suppose 100 mL of 1.00 M HCl and 100 mL of 1.00 M NaOH, both initially at 25.0 °C, are mixed in a thermos flask. When the reaction is complete, the temperature is 31.8 °C. Assuming that the solutions have the same heat capacity as pure water, compute the heat released. Use this value to evaluate the molar heat of the neutralization reaction:

$$H_3O^+_{(aq)} + OH^-_{(aq)} \rightarrow 2\,H_2O_{(l)}$$

ENTHALPY

12.21 Determine ΔH°_{rxn} for each of the following reactions:
(a) $C_2H_{4\,(g)} + 3\,O_{2\,(g)} \rightarrow 2\,CO_{2\,(g)} + 2\,H_2O_{(l)}$
(b) $2\,NH_{3\,(g)} \rightarrow N_{2\,(g)} + 3\,H_{2\,(g)}$
(c) $5\,PbO_{2\,(s)} + 4\,P_{(s,white)} \rightarrow P_4O_{10\,(s)} + 5\,Pb_{(s)}$
(d) $SiCl_{4\,(l)} + 2\,H_2O_{(l)} \rightarrow SiO_{2\,(s)} + 4\,HCl_{(g)}$

12.22 Determine ΔH°_{rxn} for each of the following reactions:
(a) $2\,NH_{3\,(g)} + 3\,O_{2\,(g)} + 2\,CH_{4\,(g)} \rightarrow 2\,HCN_{(g)} + 6\,H_2O_{(g)}$
(b) $2\,Al_{(s)} + 3\,Cl_{2\,(g)} \rightarrow 2\,AlCl_{3\,(s)}$
(c) $3\,NO_{2\,(g)} + H_2O_{(l)} \rightarrow 2\,HNO_{3\,(aq)} + NO_{(g)}$
(d) $2\,C_2H_{2\,(g)} + 5\,O_{2\,(g)} \rightarrow 4\,CO_{2\,(g)} + 2\,H_2O_{(l)}$

12.23 Find ΔE°_{rxn} for each of the reactions in Problem 12.21.

12.24 Find ΔE°_{rxn} for each of the reactions in Problem 12.22.

12.25 For each of the reactions listed, estimate the difference between ΔH°_{rxn} and ΔE°_{rxn}:
(a) $Ni^{2+}_{(aq)} + Cu_{(s)} \rightarrow Ni_{(s)} + Cu^{2+}_{(aq)}$
(b) $C_{(graphite)} + H_2O_{(l)} \rightarrow CO_{(g)} + H_{2\,(g)}$
(c) Complete combustion of butanol (C_4H_9OH) in excess $O_{2\,(g)}$

12.26 Write the balanced equation for the formation reaction of each of the following substances: (a) butanol, $C_4H_9OH_{(l)}$; (b) $Na_2CO_{3\,(s)}$; (c) ozone, $O_{3\,(g)}$; and (d) rust, $Fe_3O_{4\,(s)}$.

12.27 Write a balanced equation for the formation reaction of the following: (a) $K_3PO_{4\,(s)}$; (b) acetic acid, $CH_3CO_2H_{(l)}$; (c) trimethylamine, $(CH_3)_3N_{(g)}$; and (d) bauxite, $Al_2O_{3\,(s)}$.

12.28 Solid urea, $(NH_2)_2CO$, burns to give CO_2, N_2, and liquid H_2O. Its heat of combustion is −632.2 kJ/mol.
(a) Write the balanced combustion equation.
(b) Calculate the heat generated per mole of H_2O formed.
(c) Using this heat of formation and the appropriate thermodynamic data, determine the heat of formation of urea.

12.29 Using standard heats of formation, determine the heats of the following reactions:
(a) $4\,NH_{3\,(g)} + 5\,O_{2\,(g)} \rightarrow 4\,NO_{(g)} + 6\,H_2O_{(l)}$
(b) $4\,NH_{3\,(g)} + 3\,O_{2\,(g)} \rightarrow 2\,N_{2\,(g)} + 6\,H_2O_{(l)}$

ENTHALPY AND INTERMOLECULAR FORCES

12.30 When 1.00 g of $KClO_3$ dissolves in 50.0 g of water in a coffee-cup calorimeter, the temperature drops from 298.00 K to 296.36 K. Calculate the molar heat of solution of $KClO_3$.

12.31 For the reaction, $Mg^{2+}_{(aq)} + SO_4^{2-}{}_{(aq)} \rightarrow MgSO_{4\,(s)}$ $\Delta H = 91.2$ kJ/mol.
(a) When $MgSO_4$ dissolves in water, is heat absorbed or released by the water?
(b) Calculate q_{water} for 2.55 g of solid $MgSO_4$ dissolving in 500 mL of water.
(c) Calculate ΔT for the process in (b), assuming that the container is completely insulated.

12.32 Explain, based on interionic and intermolecular forces, why the reaction in Problem 12.31 has a positive enthalpy change.

12.33 Referring to Table 12-6, explain the following:
(a) Methane has a lower heat of vaporization than ethane.
(b) Ethanol has a significantly higher heat of vaporization than diethyl ether.
(c) Argon has a higher heat of fusion than methane.

12.34 Determine ΔE_{vap} for argon, ethane, and mercury. Which of these substances has the largest percentage difference between ΔE_{vap} and ΔH_{vap}?

12.35 Steam causes more severe burns than boiling water. To show why, calculate the following: (a) energy released when 2.50 g of boiling water is cooled to body temperature (37.5 °C) and (b) energy released when 2.50 g of steam at 100 °C is condensed and cooled to body temperature.

ADDITIONAL PROBLEMS

12.36 Does more heat have to be removed from an automobile engine when it burns 1 g of gasoline while idling in a traffic jam or when it burns 1 g of gasoline while accelerating? Explain in terms of ΔE, q, and w.

12.37 The amount of heat produced in an "ice calorimeter" is determined from the quantity of ice that melts. Suppose that a 12.7 g copper block at 200 °C is dropped into an ice calorimeter. How many grams of ice will melt?

12.38 For each of the following, make an appropriate choice for the system, and define it completely. State whether the system absorbs or releases heat.
(a) Water on your skin evaporates after you shower.
(b) Methane burns in a Bunsen burner, heating a beaker of water.
(c) Strong acid and strong base solutions are mixed in a thermos flask. The temperature of the resulting solution increases.

12.39 In Chapter 9, we described three different forms of carbon, graphite, diamond, and buckminsterfullerene (C_{60}). Of these, the standard state of carbon is graphite. The heat of combustion of graphite at 298 K and 1 atm pressure is −393.51 kJ/mol (gaseous CO_2 is the only product). Does buckminsterfullerene have a more or less negative molar heat of combustion than graphite? Does it have more or less heat of combustion per gram?

12.40 The five different stable oxides of nitrogen are NO, NO_2, N_2O, N_2O_4, and N_2O_5. Balance each of the following oxidation reactions, and then use standard formation enthalpies to calculate the heats of reaction per mole of *atomic* nitrogen for each reaction.
(a) $N_2 + O_2 \rightarrow NO$
(b) $N_2O + O_2 \rightarrow NO$
(c) $NO + O_2 \rightarrow NO_2$
(d) $NO_2 + O_2 \rightarrow N_2O_5$

12.41 Explain what will happen to any living organism if we try to make it an isolated thermodynamic system.

12.42 Two equations have been used in this chapter to relate q to T: $q = nC_p\Delta T$ and $q = C_{cal}\Delta T$.
(a) What are the units associated with each type of heat capacity?
(b) If a coffee-cup calorimeter contains 115 mL of water, what is the heat capacity of the calorimeter, assuming negligible contributions from the cup and the thermometer?

12.43 Some chemists classify sodium chloride dissolving in water as a chemical change that is described by the equation: $NaCl_{(s)} \rightarrow Na^+_{(aq)} + Cl^-_{(aq)}$. Others classify this as a physical change because NaCl is an ionic solid whose species are unchanged when it dissolves. Which classification do you prefer? Defend your choice using your understanding of "chemical" and "physical."

12.44 A 9.50-g copper block, initially at 200 °C, is dropped into a thermos flask containing 200 mL of water initially at 5.00 °C. What is the final temperature of the system?

12.45 The human body "burns" glucose ($C_6H_{12}O_6$) for energy. Burning 1.00 g of glucose produces 15.7 kJ of heat.
(a) Write the balanced equation for the combustion (burning) of glucose.
(b) Determine the molar heat of combustion of glucose.
(c) Using appropriate thermodynamic data, determine the heat of formation of glucose.

12.46 A 70-kg person uses 220 kJ of energy to walk a kilometer. This energy comes from "burning" glucose, but only about 30% of the heat of combustion of glucose can be used for propulsion. The rest is used for other body functions or is "wasted" as heat. Assuming that a "sugar-coated" cereal contains 35% sugar (which can be considered glucose) and no other energy source, calculate how many grams of cereal provide enough energy to walk 1 km.

12.47 A student studying the properties of gaseous $C_2Cl_2F_2$, a chlorofluorocarbon refrigerant, cooled a 1.25-g sample, at a constant atmospheric pressure of 1 atm, from 50 to 20 °C. During the cooling, the sample volume decreased from 274 to 248 mL. The heat capacity of $C_2Cl_2F_2$ is 80.7 J/mol K. Calculate ΔH and ΔE for the chlorofluorocarbon for this process.

12.48 Recall from Chapter 6 that light is radiant energy. Solar hot-water heaters use the radiant energy of sunlight. How many moles of photons from the middle of the solar spectrum (500 nm) would be required to heat 40 L of water from 25 °C to 50 °C, assuming 80% efficiency of heating?

12.49 One way to cool a hot beverage is with a cold spoon. A silver spoon weighing 99 g is placed in a Styrofoam cup containing 200 mL of hot coffee at 350 K. Find the final temperature of the coffee, assuming that the initial temperature of the spoon is 280 K and that the coffee has the same heat capacity as water. Would an aluminum spoon of the same mass cool the coffee more or less effectively?

12.50 A room in a home measures 3.0 m by 5.0 m by 4.0 m. Assuming no heat losses, how many grams of natural gas (methane, CH_4) must be burned to heat the air in this room from 15 to 25 °C? Assume that air is 78% N_2 and 22% O_2, and use data from Table 12-1 and Appendix E.

12.51 An ideal gas is initially at $T = 300$ K, $P = 2.00$ atm, and $V = 30.0$ L. The gas is compressed at constant temperature by a constant external pressure of 4.00 atm until its volume is 20.0 L. Compute q, w, and ΔE for the gas.

12.52 According to Table 12-1, molar heat capacities of monatomic gases (He and Ar) are significantly smaller than those of diatomic gases (N_2, O_2, and H_2). Explain in molecular terms why more heat must be supplied to raise the temperature of 1 mol of diatomic gas by 1 K than to raise the temperature of 1 mol of monatomic gas by 1 K.

12.53 Use standard enthalpies of formation to determine ΔH_{rxn} for the following reactions:
(a) $2\ SO_{2(g)} + O_{2(g)} \rightarrow 2\ SO_{3(g)}$
(b) $2\ NO_{2(g)} \rightarrow N_2O_{4(g)}$
(c) $Fe_2O_{3(s)} + 2\ Al_{(s)} \rightarrow Al_2O_{3(s)} + 2\ Fe_{(s)}$

12.54 A coin dealer, offered a rare silver coin, suspected that it might be a counterfeit nickel copy. The dealer heated the coin, which weighed 15.5 g, to 100.0 °C in boiling water and then dropped the hot coin into 21.5 g of water at T = 15.5 °C in a coffee-cup calorimeter. The temperature of the water rose to 21.5 °C. Was the coin made of silver or nickel?

12.55 In metric terms, a typical automobile averages about 6.0 km/L of gasoline burned. Gasoline has a heat of combustion of about 48 kJ/g and a density of 0.68 g/mL. How much energy is consumed to drive an automobile 1 km?

12.56 One way to vaporize a liquid is to inject a droplet into a high vacuum. If this is done, is the heat absorbed by the droplet equal to ΔE or ΔH for the phase change? (HINT: Think about whether or not work is done in the vaporization.)

12.57 Using standard enthalpies of formation, calculate ΔH_{rxn} for the following reactions:

(a) $2\,NH_{3(g)} + 3\,O_{2(g)} + 2\,CH_{4(g)} \rightarrow 2\,HCN_{(g)} + 6\,H_2O_{(g)}$
(b) $2\,C_2H_{2(g)} + 5\,O_{2(g)} \rightarrow 4\,CO_{2(g)} + 2\,H_2O_{(g)}$
(c) $C_2H_{4(g)} + O_{3(g)} \rightarrow CH_3CHO_{(g)} + O_{2(g)}$

12.58 A home swimming pool contains 155 m^3 of water. At the beginning of swimming season, the water must be heated from 20 to 30 °C.

(a) How much heat energy must be supplied?
(b) If this energy is supplied by a natural gas heater with an 80% heat transfer efficiency, how many grams of methane must be burned? The heat of combustion of methane is −803 kJ/mol.

12.59 Calculate how many grams of methane must be burned to convert 250 g of water at 25 °C into steam at 100 °C.

12.60 Chlorine trifluoride reacts readily with ammonia:

$$2\,ClF_{3(g)} + 2\,NH_{3(g)} \rightarrow N_{2(g)} + 6\,HF_{(g)} + Cl_{2(g)}$$
$$\Delta H_{rxn} = -1196 \text{ kJ}$$

Using standard heats of formation, determine ΔH°_f for $ClF_{3(g)}$.

12.61 Using standard heats of formation, determine ΔH_{rxn} for the following phase change:

$$H_2O_{(l,\,298\,K)} \rightarrow H_2O_{(g,\,298\,K)}$$

Compare your result with ΔH_{vap} for H_2O. What differences in conditions account for the difference in values?

12.62 Write the balanced chemical equation associated with each of the following enthalpy changes: (a) heat of sublimation of elemental iodine; (b) heat of formation of gaseous atomic iodine; (c) heat of formation of $C_2H_3Cl_{(g)}$; and (d) heat of solution of sodium sulfate.

12.63 It requires 100.0 J of heat to raise the temperature of 52.5 g of lead from 280.0 K to 299.6 K. What is the molar heat capacity of lead?

12.64 For spacecraft fuels, the energy content *per gram* of fuel should be as large as possible. Which of the following has the largest energy content per gram, and which has the smallest? (a) dimethylhydrazine, $(CH_3)_2NNH_2$, $\Delta H_{combustion} = -1694$ kJ/mol; (b) methanol, CH_3OH, $\Delta H_{combustion} = -726$ kJ/mol; or (c) octane, C_8H_{18}, $\Delta H_{combustion} = -5500$ kJ/mol.

12.65 "Strike anywhere" matches contain P_4S_3, a compound that ignites when heated by friction. It reacts vigorously with oxygen, as follows:

$$P_4S_{3\,(s)} + 8\,O_{2\,(g)} \rightarrow P_4O_{10\,(s)} + 3\,SO_{2\,(g)} \qquad \Delta H_{rxn} = -3677 \text{ kJ}$$

Use data from Appendix E to determine ΔH°_f for $P_4S_{3\,(s)}$.

12.66 What energy transformations occur when a moving automobile brakes and skids to a stop?

12.67 For the following process, give the sign (+, −, or 0) for each of the specified thermodynamic functions. In each case, give a brief account of your reasoning: (a) ΔH_{sys}; (b) ΔE_{surr}; and (c) $\Delta E_{universe}$.

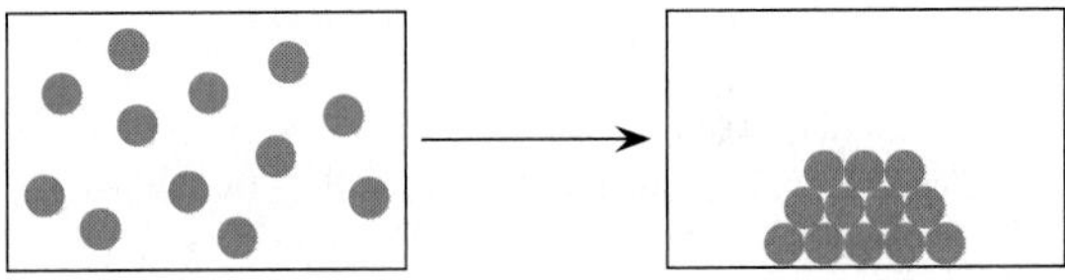

12.68 For the following process, give the sign (+, −, or 0) for each of the specified thermodynamic functions. In each case, give a brief account of your reasoning: (a) w_{sys}; (b) q_{sys}; and (c) ΔE_{surr}.

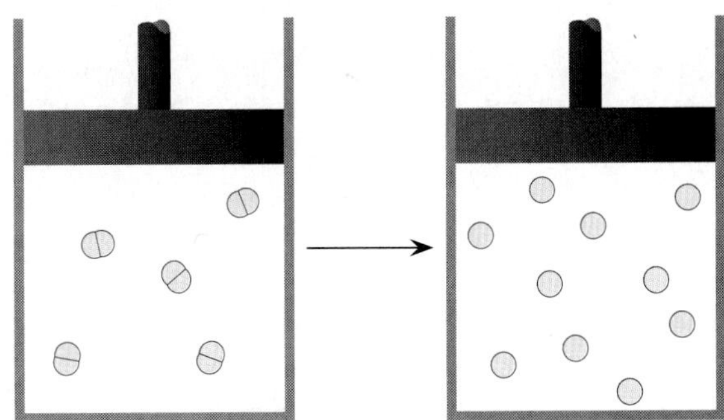

12.69 For the following constant-temperature process, give the sign (+, −, or 0) for each of the specified thermodynamic functions. In each case, give a brief account of your reasoning: (a) w_{sys}; (b) ΔE_{surr}; and (c) q_{sys}.

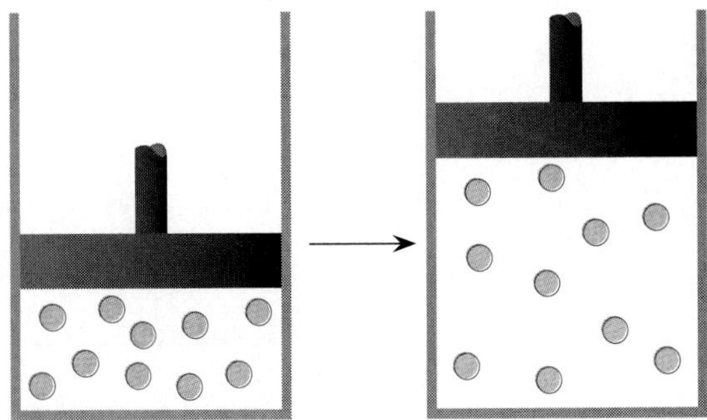

12.70 When a corpse decomposes, much of the phosphorus in the body is converted to phosphine (PH_3), a colorless gas with the odor of rotting fish. Phosphine is a highly reactive molecule that ignites spontaneously in air. In a graveyard, phosphine that escapes from the ground ignites in air, giving small flashes of flame. These flashes are sometimes attributed to supernatural causes, such as a will-o'-the-wisp. Determine ΔH_{rxn} for the combustion of phosphine.

$$PH_{3\,(g)} + O_{2\,(g)} \rightarrow P_4O_{10\,(s)} + H_2O_{\,(g)} \text{ (unbalanced)}$$

12.71 The heat required to sustain animals that hibernate comes from the biochemical combustion of fatty acids, one of which is arachidonic acid ($\Delta H^\circ_f = -636$ kJ/mol):

$$C_{20}H_{32}O_{2\,(s)} + 27\ O_{2\,(g)} \rightarrow 20\ CO_{2\,(g)} + 16\ H_2O_{\,(l)}$$

Arachidonic acid ($C_{20}H_{32}O_2$)

Calculate the mass of arachidonic acid needed to warm a 500 kg bear from 5 to 25 °C. Assume that the average heat capacity of bear flesh is 4.18 J/g K.

12.72 In liquid-fuel rockets, such as the lunar lander module of the Apollo moon missions, the fuels are liquid hydrazine (N_2H_4) and dinitrogentetroxide gas (N_2O_4). The two chemicals ignite on contact to release very large amounts of energy:

$$2\ N_2H_{4\,(l)} + N_2O_{4\,(g)} \rightarrow 3\ N_{2\,(g)} + 4\ H_2O_{\,(g)}$$

(a) Calculate the enthalpy change that occurs when 1 mol of hydrazine is burned in a lunar lander.
(b) If O_2 was used in the lander instead of N_2O_4, would the reaction give off more heat per mole of hydrazine or less heat per mole of hydrazine? Explain.

12.73 The following figure represents a piston and cylinder containing a collection of gas molecules. The piston can move in either direction.

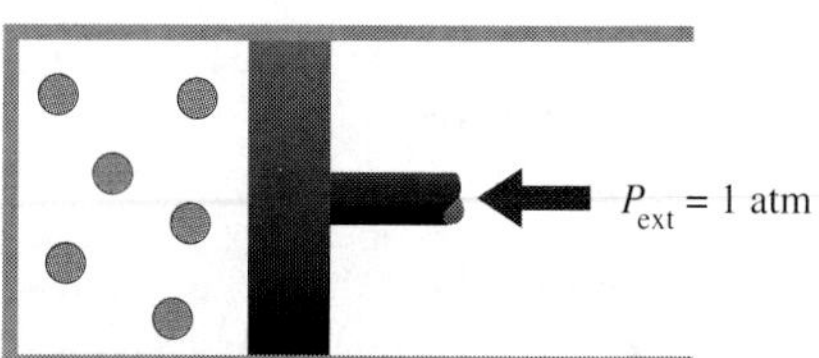

Assume the gas molecules are the system.
(a) Redraw the figure to show what happens when some work is done on the system.
(b) Redraw the figure to show what happens when some heat is added to the system.

12.74 A 44.0-g sample of an unknown metal at 100.0 °C is placed in a constant-pressure calorimeter containing 80.0 g of water at 24.8 °C. Assume the heat capacity of the calorimeter is negligible. The final temperature is 28.4 °C. Calculate the heat capacity of the metal and use the result to identify the metal: Al = 0.903 J/g K; Cr = 0.616 J/g K; Co = 0.421 J/g K; or Cu = 0.385 J/g K.

ANSWERS TO SECTION EXERCISES

12.1.1 (a) The water in the container; (b) the H_2-O_2 mixture; and (c) the air in the balloon

12.1.2 (a) *V, T,* and *n;* (b) *P, V, T,* and *n;* and (c) *V* and *T*

12.1.3 (a) State function change and (b) not a state function change

12.2.1 $q_{sys} = 4.2 \times 10^3$ J

12.2.2 $w_{sys} = -4.30 \times 10^3$ J

12.2.3 900 g of ground beef or 5.76 kg of fruit

12.3.1 $q_p = +4.6 \times 10^2$ J

12.3.2 297 kJ/mol

12.3.3 (a) Temperature will rise; (b) volume will decrease because although the temperature rises slightly, the number of moles of gas decreases; (c) work is positive; and (d) *E* is a state function, so ΔE is the same.

12.4.1 c, d, and f

12.4.2 $\Delta H_{rxn} = +206.1$ kJ and $\Delta E_{rxn} = +201.1$ kJ

12.4.3 Balanced chemical equation is:

$$2\ Fe_2O_{3\ (s)} + 3\ C_{(graphite)} \longrightarrow 4\ Fe_{\ (s)} + 3\ CO_{2\ (g)}$$

$$\Delta H_{rxn} = +467.9 \text{ kJ}$$

12.5.1 In both cases, interionic forces must be overcome to break apart the crystals, but when NaCl dissolves in water, energy is released through ion-dipole interactions.

12.5.2 Melting all the ice yields 100 mL of water at 0 °C and cools the tea to 9.07 °C. When these mix and equilibrate, the resulting temperature is 7.55 °C.

12.5.3 The same because enthalpy is a state function, so its change is independent of path.

CHAPTER 13

SPONTANEITY OF CHEMICAL PROCESSES

Plants use sunlight to construct carbohydrate molecules from CO_2 and H_2O, but a spontaneous reaction with oxygen can rapidly return carbohydrate molecules to CO_2 and H_2O.

Most processes have one preferred direction. As a commonplace example, sugar dissolves in hot coffee to give a sweet beverage. Left to stand, the solution never reverts to unsweetened coffee and sugar granules. Gasoline reacts with oxygen to produce carbon dioxide, water, and heat, but CO_2 and H_2O do not combine to produce gasoline, even when heated.

Other familiar processes go in one direction under some conditions but in the opposite direction under other conditions. Everyone knows that liquid water freezes if the temperature drops below 0 °C, but ice melts if the temperature rises above 0 °C. The preferred direction for this conversion depends on the temperature. The preferred direction for another familiar conversion depends on the pressure. Carbonated beverages are produced by dissolving CO_2 gas in water under high pressure. When a bottle of a carbonated beverage is opened, the pressure drops, and CO_2 gas "fizzes" out of the solution.

The preferred direction of many chemical reactions depends on the conditions. For instance, fires destroy carbohydrates, breaking them down into CO_2 and H_2O. On the other hand, plants use CO_2, H_2O, and sunlight to synthesize the carbohydrates that make up their cell walls. In the presence of sunlight, a leaf can assemble carbohydrate molecules from CO_2 and H_2O, whereas in the presence of oxygen, these molecules can decompose into CO_2 and H_2O.

It is important for chemists to know in advance if a particular product will form when a set of reactants is mixed. Furthermore, if a chemical reaction does not proceed under one set of conditions, chemists need to know whether or not it will proceed under some other set of conditions. This chapter describes the factors that determine the preferred direction of a chemical process. As we will see, energy and enthalpy changes by themselves do not determine this preferred direction. To predict the outcome of a chemical reaction, it is necessary to know about two additional thermodynamic properties, entropy and free energy.

13.1 SPONTANEITY

Every process has a preferred direction called its **spontaneous direction.** A process follows its spontaneous direction unless acted on by some external agent. For example, water runs downhill unless it is forced uphill by a pump. The spontaneous direction for water movement is from higher altitude to lower altitude. A process may not occur, however, even though it is spontaneous. Water can be stored behind a dam indefinitely, even though its movement downhill is a spontaneous process. As another example, redwood planks in a fence remain unchanged for a very long time, even though decomposition of wood into CO_2 and H_2O is a spontaneous process.

Thermodynamic spontaneity has a somewhat different meaning than ordinary spontaneity. In thermodynamic terms, a process may be spontaneous even though it does not occur. That is, spontaneous processes may proceed extremely slowly.

A process that does not occur may be nonspontaneous, or it may be spontaneous but very slow. An example of a process that is nonspontaneous under normal conditions is the decomposition of water into molecules of hydrogen and oxygen. Water will not decompose, even if it is heated or poured on a fire.

$$\text{Nonspontaneous:} \quad 2\ H_2O_{(l)} \rightarrow 2\ H_{2\ (g)} + O_{2\ (g)}$$

The spontaneous process is for hydrogen and oxygen to combine into water molecules:

$$\text{Spontaneous:} \quad 2\ H_{2\ (g)} + O_{2\ (g)} \rightarrow 2\ H_2O_{(l)}$$

The factors that determine how fast a chemical reaction goes are discussed in Chapter 14.

Even though this reaction is spontaneous, it occurs at an immeasurably slow pace when the two gases are mixed. Nonetheless, a mixture of hydrogen and oxygen must be handled very carefully because the slightest spark triggers a violent reaction that generates water and releases a huge amount of stored chemical energy. Box 13-1 discusses the processes involved in another spontaneous reaction.

BOX 13-1

SPONTANEOUS COMBUSTION

Many home fires are caused by "spontaneous combustion." In one common scenario, a pile of oil-soaked rags has been left carelessly in some out-of-the-way corner. Almost imperceptibly at first, the rags begin to heat up by absorbing sunlight or through the slow exothermic reaction of the oil with atmospheric oxygen. As the rags warm, the combustible materials react faster and faster, until eventually a threshold temperature is reached. At this point the pile of rags bursts into flame, which, if not quickly detected and extinguished, leads to a disastrous fire.

The combustion of oil-soaked rags is thermodynamically spontaneous whether we have one oil-soaked rag used by an amateur car enthusiast or an entire pile of rags in a corner of an automobile shop. The combustion of a wood-frame house is also thermodynamically spontaneous, whether or not a source of flame is supplied to start a fire. Fortunately, the combustion of a house or an oil-soaked rag is immeasurably slow unless some triggering event starts the fire.

These and other examples show us that thermodynamically spontaneous processes do not occur automatically. Water runs downhill spontaneously, but the water in a bathtub remains there indefinitely unless someone "pulls the plug," thus providing a pathway for the downhill process. Alternatively, an energetic child in the tub might splash most of the water out of the tub onto the bathroom floor. Even if a process is thermodynamically spontaneous, it needs a low-energy path or some extra impetus before it can proceed.

In Chapter 14, we explore how to "pull the plug" or "splash the bath water" at the molecular level. Even without a detailed knowledge of these processes, however, we can appreciate that oil-soaked rags and wood-frame houses are the chemical equivalent of water in a bathtub. A chemical "plug" operates at the molecular level to keep the spontaneous combustion reaction from occurring.

Chemical manufacturers design elaborate, expensive plants to produce valuable chemical products spontaneously from starting materials. The blast furnaces in a steel mill, for example, mix many chemicals under carefully controlled conditions to convert iron ore into steel. Because of the expense involved in designing and building a chemical plant, a manufacturer must be able to determine in advance the conditions required to make a reaction spontaneous. Fortunately, this can be done using thermodynamics.

ENERGY AND SPONTANEITY

One of the characteristics of a chemical process is its energy change. As described in Chapter 12, an exothermic process releases energy to the surroundings (a "downhill" process for the system), whereas an endothermic process absorbs energy from the surroundings (an "uphill" process for the system).

Knowing that a reaction is energetically downhill or uphill is not enough to determine whether it is spontaneous. Consider what happens to a glass that contains a mixture of liquid water and ice at 0 °C. As shown in Figure 13-1, liquid water freezes spontaneously if the ice and water mixture is placed in a freezer at −15 °C:

$$H_2O_{(l,\,0\,°C)} \xrightarrow{\text{Freezer, }-15\text{ °C}} H_2O_{(s,\,0\,°C)}$$

Suppose that this mixture is left in the freezer until 2 mol of water has frozen. The enthalpy change can be calculated from the heat of fusion of ice:

$$\Delta H = -n\Delta H_{\text{fus}} = -(2 \text{ mol})(6.01 \text{ kJ/mol}) = -12.0 \text{ kJ}$$

The energy change is also −12.0 kJ because $\Delta E \cong \Delta H$ for processes that occur in condensed phases. The negative values for ΔE and ΔH tell us that this spontaneous process is exothermic.

Now suppose that the same glass is removed from the freezer and placed on a table. In contact with the atmosphere at 25 °C, ice melts spontaneously:

$$H_2O_{(s,\,0\,°C)} \xrightarrow{\text{Table, }+25\text{ °C}} H_2O_{(l,\,0\,°C)}$$

The enthalpy and energy changes for melting 2 mol of ice can be found using its heat of fusion:

$$\Delta E \cong \Delta H = n\Delta H_{\text{fus}} = (2 \text{ mol})(6.01 \text{ kJ/mol}) = 12.0 \text{ kJ}$$

The positive signs for ΔH and ΔE tell us that this spontaneous process is endothermic.

Both these everyday processes are spontaneous, but one is exothermic and the other endothermic. This example demonstrates that knowing ΔE or ΔH is not enough

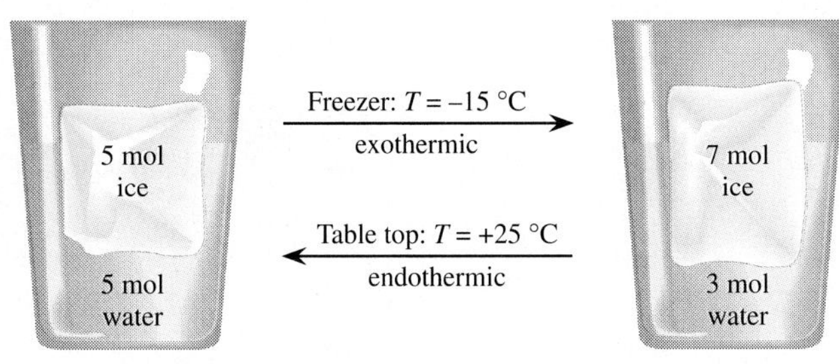

FIGURE 13-1
Schematic view of the spontaneous processes for a water and ice mixture in a freezer and on a tabletop. Depending on the conditions, either the exothermic or the endothermic process can be spontaneous.

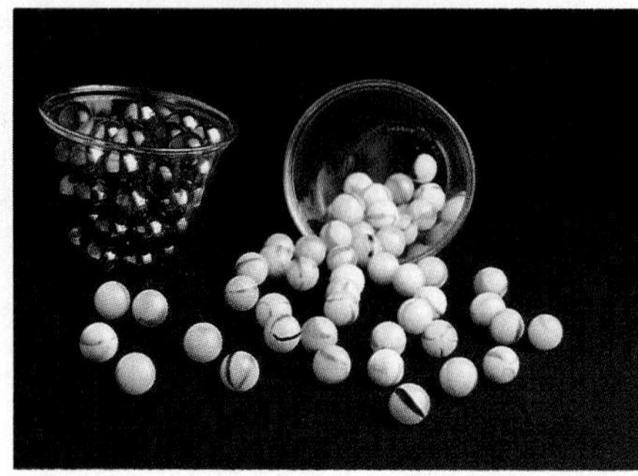

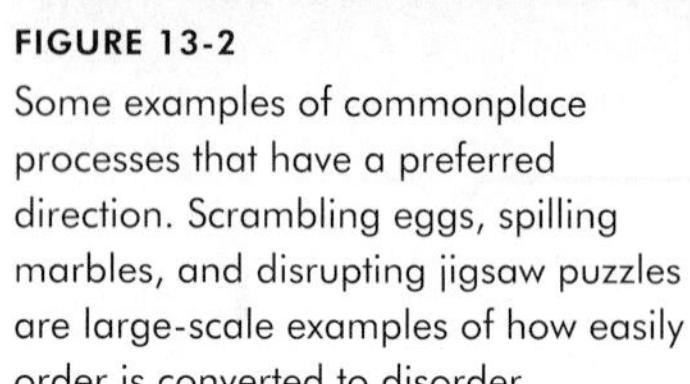

FIGURE 13-2
Some examples of commonplace processes that have a preferred direction. Scrambling eggs, spilling marbles, and disrupting jigsaw puzzles are large-scale examples of how easily order is converted to disorder.

to predict whether a process will occur spontaneously. If we plan to use thermodynamics to determine when a process will be spontaneous, we need another state function besides energy and enthalpy.

MOLECULAR DISORDER

To understand spontaneity, we need to examine what occurs at the molecular level during spontaneous chemical processes. Before looking at molecular processes, however, consider some common large-scale events that go in one particular direction:

1. It is easy to scramble an egg but impossible to unscramble one.
2. If you drop a handful of marbles on the floor, they will scatter everywhere. They will not spontaneously roll back into your hand.
3. A completed jigsaw puzzle can be disassembled by a sweep of the hand. Unworked jigsaw puzzles never assemble themselves by random events.

Each of these processes (Figure 13-2) has a spontaneous direction, from an **ordered** (organized) structure to a **disordered** (disorganized) structure. Our experience with these events can be summarized in a commonsense law:

Things tend to become disorganized.

***Disorder* and *randomness* are synonyms for *disorganization*. We use these terms interchangeably.**

Now let us see if this commonsense law also applies to events at the molecular level. Consider the two glass bulbs shown in Figure 13-3. One of the bulbs contains nitrogen dioxide, a red-brown gas, but the second bulb is empty. When the valve

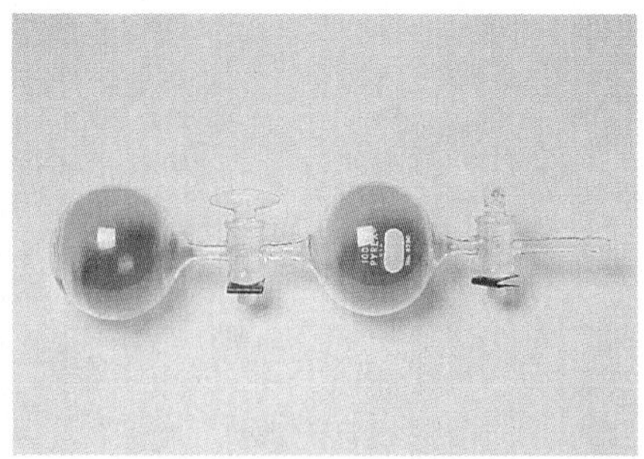

FIGURE 13-3
When the valve is opened between two bulbs, one of which is empty and the other filled with nitrogen dioxide gas, NO_2 expands spontaneously from the filled bulb into the empty bulb.

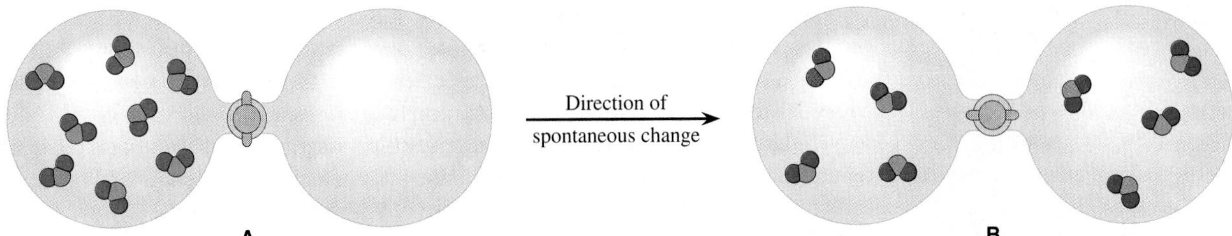

FIGURE 13-4
When the valve in system **A** is opened, the gas molecules redistribute randomly throughout the total system, as shown in **B**. The reverse process never occurs.

that connects the bulbs is opened, the red-brown gas expands to fill both bulbs. The opposite process never occurs. That is, if both bulbs contain NO_2 at the same pressure, opening the valve never causes the pressure to rise in one bulb and fall in the other.

The molecular view of what happens in the two bulbs is shown in Figure 13-4. The NO_2 molecules in the filled bulb are in constant motion, continually colliding with themselves and with the walls of their container. When the valve between the two bulbs is opened, this molecular motion drives the molecules into the empty bulb until equal numbers of molecules exist in each bulb. Eventually, the gas molecules reach a state of dynamic equilibrium. Molecules still move back and forth between the two bulbs, but the number of molecules in each bulb remains the same.

See Chapter 5 for a description of the molecular motion of gas molecules, and see Section 2.1 for an introduction to dynamic equilibrium.

The gas in Figure 13-4 is the molecular equivalent of a handful of marbles. That is, gas molecules are more organized when they are confined to a small volume than when spread throughout a large volume. Our commonsense law applies to this molecular example.

For a second example, consider Figure 13-5, which shows sugar dissolving in coffee from a molecular perspective. Before the solid sugar dissolves, all the sugar molecules are organized in a crystal. As they dissolve, the molecules distribute themselves randomly and uniformly throughout the liquid coffee. The opposite process never occurs. That is, sugar cubes do not form from sweet coffee. Once again, the direction of spontaneous change at the molecular level conforms to our commonsense law, because sugar molecules are distributed more randomly when they are dissolved in coffee than when they are part of a solid crystal. A dissolved sugar cube is the molecular equivalent of the scrambled egg. The well-organized molecules in a sugar cube become "scrambled" as they dissolve in coffee.

Ice contains water molecules held in a highly structured three-dimensional lattice, whereas liquid water contains molecules that are free to move about through their entire volume. In a sense, water molecules in the liquid phase are "scrambled." When ice melts, the water molecules become *more* disordered. Conversely, water

FIGURE 13-5
Sugar dissolving in coffee is a disordering process. Sugar molecules are distributed more randomly in solution than they are in the solid crystal.

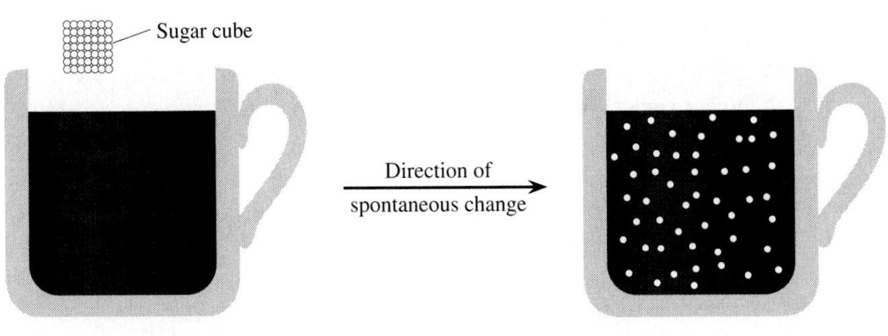

molecules become *less* disordered when liquid water freezes. Nevertheless, this conversion can go in either direction: from water to ice at low temperature and from ice to water at high temperature. The conversion from water to ice leads to less disorder for the system and appears to violate our commonsense law.

To understand how water can freeze, we must recognize that this phase change is accompanied by a flow of heat between the system and the surroundings. Freezing is an exothermic process, so as the liquid freezes, heat flows out of the water sample and into the surroundings. How does this heat affect the surroundings? Macroscopically, heat increases the temperature. Microscopically, it increases the thermal energy of the molecules that make up the surroundings. In other words, the molecules move faster, and the faster the molecules move, the more disordered they become.

As an analogy, consider the dancers shown in Figure 13-6. The first pair is dancing slowly, so their positions are somewhat ordered. The second pair is much more disorganized. The dancers expend more energy as they move rapidly from place to place. In this analogy, molecules are similar to dancers. At high energy, molecules move faster and are more disordered than they are at low energy, when they move more slowly.

FIGURE 13-6
Dancers illustrate that disorder increases when rate of motion increases.

Now let us return to the water sample. When water freezes, the molecules become more ordered as heat flows from the system to the surroundings. At the same time, the surroundings absorb the heat and become more disordered. Consequently, the commonsense law that things tend to become disorganized is still obeyed, provided that the increased order of the system is smaller than the decreased order of the surroundings. The situation is reversed when ice melts. In this case the system becomes more disordered, but heat is withdrawn from the surroundings, which become more ordered as its molecules move more slowly. Again, the commonsense law is obeyed, provided that the loss of order in the system is greater than the gain in order of the surroundings.

In most chemical processes, such as water freezing or ice melting, heat flows change the amount of disorder in the system and surroundings. Chemists and physicists have measured the changes in disorder for many spontaneous processes. They always obtain the same result, which is the **second law of thermodynamics:**

Total disorder increases in any spontaneous process.

Written in this way, this result may not seem to be a law of thermodynamics. After all, how is disorder related to energy? Qualitatively, our earlier observation that adding heat increases molecular motion shows that a link exists between energy and disorder. In Section 13.2, we examine the quantitative link between heat flow and disorder.

SECTION EXERCISES

13.1.1 Explain the following observations in terms of organization and disorganization:
- (a) Untended fences eventually fall down.
- (b) A glass is easy to break but very difficult to mend.
- (c) A wine cooler does not spontaneously separate into alcohol, water, and fruit juice.

13.1.2 Solid sugar can be recovered from coffee by boiling off the water. (Coffee candy can be made in this way.) Sugar molecules become more organized in this process. What else must occur in order for total disorder to increase?

13.1.3 Draw molecular pictures of liquid water and water vapor that show what happens to the amount of order among H_2O molecules when water evaporates.

13.2 ENTROPY, THE MEASURE OF DISORDER

Increasing disorder is a qualitative criterion for the preferred direction of a chemical process. Measuring disorder quantitatively allows us to make accurate predictions about the spontaneity of reactions. Scientists can measure disorder in two ways. One of them involves counting the amount of disorder. We describe this method briefly, but its application is beyond the scope of general chemistry. The second way links the change in disorder with the flow of heat between a system and its surroundings.

ENTROPY

Regardless of how disorder is measured, we need a state function whose value is related to the amount of disorder. That state function is called **entropy** and symbolized ***S***. Qualitatively, entropy is a measure of the *disorder* in a substance or system. Therefore we can restate the second law of thermodynamics in terms of entropy:

The total entropy of the universe increases in spontaneous processes.

Quantitatively, entropy is defined by the Boltzmann equation,* $S = k \ln W$. According to this equation, entropy is equal to a constant multiplied by the natural logarithm of the number of ways (W) the system can be described. Although it is simple, the Boltzmann equation is challenging to work with because it is always difficult to determine the value of W.

A more direct way to measure disorder involves the flow of heat. According to the second law of thermodynamics, the entropy of the universe always increases in a spontaneous process. Therefore we can focus our attention on the *change* in entropy (ΔS) rather than on the total entropy of the system and the surroundings. As we will see, a change in entropy can be computed from the flow of heat.

It is possible to compute the entropy change for a process that is not at constant temperature, but the techniques require the use of calculus and are beyond the scope of this text.

Our treatment of entropy changes is restricted to situations in which a flow of heat occurs without a temperature change. Heat flow at constant temperature may seem paradoxical because usually we associate a flow of heat with a change in temperature. However, three types of chemical processes occur in which heat flows without a temperature change:

1. A substance, such as water, can change phase at a constant temperature, absorbing or releasing heat in the process.
2. A chemical reaction may occur under conditions in which temperature is held constant, such as in the human body or a thermostated automobile engine. Although the temperature is constant, the exothermicity or endothermicity of the reaction generates a heat flow.
3. The surroundings may be so large that they can absorb or release significant amounts of heat before the temperature changes by a measurable amount. Experiments performed in a constant-temperature water bath are a common example of this category.

When heat flows at constant temperature, the entropy change is equal to the heat transferred (q_T) divided by the temperature (T) in kelvins:

$$\Delta S = \frac{q_T}{T} \qquad \textbf{(13-1)}$$

* Ludwig Boltzmann was a brilliant mathematical physicist. Born in 1844, he committed suicide in 1906 after bouts of severe depression. In addition to clarifying the nature of entropy, Boltzmann contributed to the kinetic theory of gases and the laws of radiant energy. By his request, "his" equation, $S = k \ln W$, is inscribed on his tombstone.

The subscript "T" in Equation 13-1 is a reminder that this equation is restricted to processes that occur at constant temperature. Because q is an energy term, the units of ΔS are energy/temperature, or J/K. The presence of q is consistent with our earlier observation that adding heat to a substance increases its disorder. Heat is divided by temperature because temperature is a measure of how much thermal disorder is already present in a substance. At low temperature, there is little disorder, so the addition of a given amount of heat increases the disorder significantly. At high temperature, however, there is considerable disorder, so the same amount of additional heat increases total disorder by a smaller amount.

The ice and water example in Section 13.1 provides a good test of whether or not Equation 13-1 is consistent with the second law of thermodynamics. Sample Problem 13-1 applies the entropy equation to water freezing in a freezer.

SAMPLE PROBLEM 13-1 ENTROPY CHANGE DURING FREEZING

What is the total entropy change when 2.00 mol of liquid water at 0 °C freezes in a freezer compartment whose temperature is −15 °C? (ΔH_{fus} = 6.01 kJ/mol for H_2O.)

METHOD: The problem asks for the *total* entropy change, which includes ΔS of the water and ΔS of the surroundings. When the water freezes, heat flows from the system into the surroundings. Thus we expect the entropy of the water to decrease, whereas the entropy of the surroundings increases. Entropy changes can be computed using Equation 13-1, provided the temperature remains constant. Here, the system remains at a constant temperature of 0 °C while the phase change occurs. (In this example, we consider only the freezing of water to ice at 0 °C, ignoring the subsequent cooling of the ice from 0 °C to −15 °C.) The refrigerator holds the immediate surroundings at constant temperature of −15 °C, so we can use the equation for system and surroundings.

The amount of heat lost by the water can be calculated from the heat of fusion:

$$q_{H_2O} = -n\ \Delta H_{fus}$$

Remember that in thermodynamic calculations, the temperature must *always* be in kelvins.

Remember that ΔH_{fus}, which is positive, refers to ice melting. Heat flows out of the system as the water freezes, so q_{H_2O} has a negative value. The problem tells us that n = 2.00 mol and $\Delta H_{fus} = 6.01 \times 10^3$ J/mol. Thus for the formation of 2 mol of ice we have:

$$q_{H_2O} = -(2.00\ \text{mol})(6.01 \times 10^3\ \text{J/mol}) = -1.202 \times 10^4\ \text{J}$$

$$\Delta S_{H_2O} = \frac{q_{H_2O}}{T_{H_2O}} = \frac{-1.202 \times 10^4\ \text{J}}{273.15\ \text{K}} = -44.0\ \text{J/K}$$

The negative sign is consistent with our qualitative picture of greater disorder in a liquid than in a solid.

The freezer absorbs the heat released by the water, but it does so at *its* temperature, −15 °C = 258 K. Because the freezer absorbs heat, q has a positive sign. Thus for the freezer we have:

$$q_{freezer} = -q_{H_2O} = +1.202 \times 10^4\ \text{J}$$

$$\Delta S_{freezer} = \frac{q_{freezer}}{T_{freezer}} = +\frac{1.202 \times 10^4\ \text{J}}{258\ \text{K}} = 46.6\ \text{J/K}$$

The total entropy change is the sum of these changes:

$$\Delta S_{total} = \Delta S_{H_2O} + \Delta S_{freezer} = (-44.0\ \text{J/K}) + (46.6\ \text{J/K}) = +2.6\ \text{J/K}$$

A positive value for the net entropy change is a reasonable result because the formation of ice in a freezer is spontaneous and the second law of thermodynamics tells us that total entropy must increase in a spontaneous process.

Equation 13-1 gives a positive value for the entropy change for the spontaneous freezing of water in a freezer. We can analyze the total entropy change for 2.00 mol of ice melting on a table in a room at 25 °C in exactly the same manner. The heat required to melt the ice has the same magnitude but the opposite sign as the heat used to freeze the water in Sample Problem 13-1: 1.202×10^4 J/mol. Ice melts at the same temperature as water freezes, 0 °C, so the entropy change for the water is also equal in magnitude but opposite in sign: 44.0 J/K. The entropy change of the surroundings, on the other hand, must be calculated using the temperature of the surroundings, 25 °C = 298 K. The heat required to melt the ice comes from the surroundings, but the amount of heat is so small and the surroundings are so large that the temperature remains constant.

$$\Delta S_{\text{surroundings}} = \frac{-1.202 \times 10^3 \text{ J}}{298 \text{ K}} = -40.3 \text{ J/K}$$

$$\Delta S_{\text{total}} = 44.0 - 40.3 = +3.7 \text{ J/K}$$

For both these spontaneous processes, we see that the overall change in entropy is a positive quantity, even though one process is exothermic and the other endothermic. This is in agreement with the second law of thermodynamics. In other words, this new state function of entropy provides a thermodynamic criterion for spontaneity.

The ice and water example illustrates potential pitfalls in evaluating entropy changes. First, we must be very careful about the sign of q. The sign is different for the system and the surroundings and depends on whether the process is endothermic or exothermic. Table 13-1 summarizes the signs for our example. Second, we must always use the temperature of the component whose entropy change we are evaluating. In our example the freezer, room, and water and ice mixture each has a different temperature. Third, *total* entropy change must be found by summing the entropy changes of the system and the surroundings. This gives the total entropy change, which is more generally known as the *entropy change of the universe:*

$$\Delta S_{\text{universe}} = \Delta S_{\text{system}} + \Delta S_{\text{surroundings}} \quad \textbf{(13-2)}$$

We can state both the first and the second laws of thermodynamics in terms of the universe:

First law: $\Delta E_{\text{universe}} = 0$ (always)

Second law: $\Delta S_{\text{universe}} > 0$ (always)

Sample Problem 13-2 is another example of entropy calculations, and Box 13-2 describes how entropy is linked with time and life.

TABLE 13-1 SIGNS ASSOCIATED WITH HEAT TRANSFERRED (q)

PROCESS	ICE AND WATER SYSTEM	SURROUNDINGS
Exothermic (freezing)	−	+
Endothermic (melting)	+	−

BOX 13-2

ENTROPY, TIME, AND LIFE

According to the second law of thermodynamics, events go only in the direction that increases the entropy of the universe. Time, like entropy, is unidirectional. Despite the time machines invented by novelists, time always marches on. You are older as you read this sentence than you were when you started reading the chapter.

Entropy and time are two unidirectional parameters that have been connected by philosophers. Some have characterized entropy as "time's arrow." The idea is that entropy changes can be used to determine which of two states is "before" and which is "after," even if no clock is present. For example, the following figure shows two views of a chamber at two different times. The chamber contains two different gases. On the left the two gases are separated, whereas on the right they are mixed uniformly. If the chamber is isolated so that the surroundings cannot contribute to the entropy changes, the spontaneous change is from left to right because the arrangement on the right is less ordered than the arrangement on the left. Using entropy as time's arrow, we conclude that the arrangement on the right must be at a later time than the one on the left. If this were not the case, we would have a violation of the second law of thermodynamics.

Although living things cannot escape the unidirectional aspect of time, it may seem at times that they successfully reduce entropy. As an example, ask yourself which of the two views of the same house is "before" and which is "after." Left to itself, any structure degenerates into disorder, but with human intervention, structures can be made "as good as new."

To analyze the spontaneous direction of events that are influenced by living beings, we must consider the surroundings as well as the system.

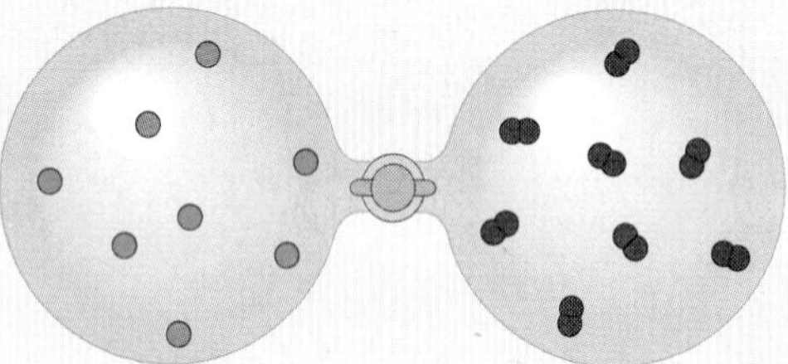

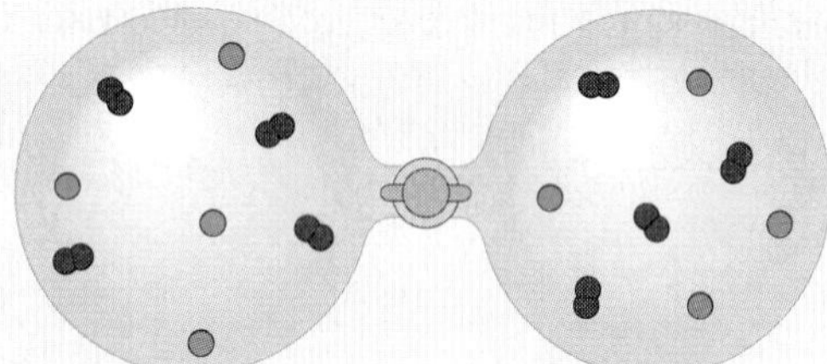

SAMPLE PROBLEM 13-2 ENTROPY CHANGE OF A REFRIGERANT

In a refrigerator a liquid refrigerant absorbs heat from the material being cooled. This heat vaporizes the refrigerant, which is later recondensed to a liquid using a mechanical pump. One common refrigerant is Freon-22, $CHClF_2$ (MM = 86.5 g/mol). Freon-22 boils at 41 °C with a heat of vaporization of 17.6 kJ/mol. Calculate the entropy change of the universe when 1.50×10^2 g of Freon-22 evaporates at −41 °C, holding the temperature of food in a refrigerator constant at 5 °C.

METHOD: The problem describes a relatively complicated process, but our only interest is in the thermodynamic changes of state. Freon-22 evaporates at constant temperature (T_{Freon}), absorbing heat from the contents of the refrigerator at their temperature (T_{refrig}). A block diagram is a useful way to summarize the thermodynamics:

The house on the left is obviously more disordered than the one on the right. If this house has been left alone, the right picture is "before" and the left is "after." On the other hand, if the house on the right is the house on the left after repainting, calculating the total entropy change of house *plus the painter* shows that the painter generated disorder in the surroundings to make this house more ordered. Then the picture of the less ordered house may predate the picture of the more ordered house.

If humans ever travel to distant galaxies, how will they recognize the presence of new life forms? One likely way is to look for ordered structures whose construction appears to violate the second law of thermodynamics. If a visitor from outer space were to land in California's Mojave Desert, with no one in sight, and find a fence running in a straight line across the landscape, that visitor would surely infer the existence of intelligent life from the improbable order of the fence.

Even without leaving our planet, we search for signs of extraterrestrial life by looking for improbable patterns of order. Our planet is bombarded incessantly by electromagnetic radiation of many wavelengths, coming to us across the far reaches of space from elsewhere in the universe. If intelligent beings are trying to make their presence known, they may be transmitting some highly ordered pattern of electromagnetic signals that other intelligent life could recognize as too ordered to occur except by design.

150 g Freon-22 $T = 232$ K Liquid	$\xrightarrow{n\,\Delta H_{vap}}$ ($\uparrow q_T$ from Food, $T = 278$ K)	150 g Freon-22 $T = 232$ K Vapor

After reducing this problem to its thermodynamic essentials, we see that Equation 13-1 and the given data let us find the entropy changes for the food and Freon-22. For Freon-22 boiling at −41 °C and 1 atm pressure, $q = n\Delta H_{vap}$. From the mass of Freon and its molar mass, we find n:

$$n_{Freon} = \frac{1.50 \times 10^2 \text{ g}}{86.5 \text{ g/mol}} = 1.734 \text{ mol}$$

$$q_{Freon} = (1.734 \text{ mol})(17.6 \text{ kJ/mol})(10^3 \text{ J/kJ}) = 3.052 \times 10^4 \text{ J}$$

$$\Delta S_{Freon} = \frac{q_{Freon}}{T_{Freon}} = \frac{3.052 \times 10^4 \text{ J}}{232 \text{ K}} = 132 \text{ J/K}$$

This is the entropy change of the Freon. The refrigerator contents give up heat equal to the heat absorbed by the Freon:

$$q_{\text{refrig}} = -q_{\text{Freon}}$$

$$\Delta S_{\text{refrig}} = \frac{-q_{\text{Freon}}}{T_{\text{refrig}}} = \frac{-3.05 \times 10^4 \text{ J}}{278 \text{ K}} = -110 \text{ J/K}$$

The overall entropy change is calculated using Equation 13-2:

$$\Delta S_{\text{universe}} = \underset{\substack{\uparrow \\ \text{System}}}{\Delta S_{\text{Freon}}} + \underset{\substack{\uparrow \\ \text{Surroundings}}}{\Delta S_{\text{refrig}}} = 132 - 110 = 22 \text{ J/K}$$

DIRECTION OF HEAT FLOW

Equation 13-1 states that an entropy change is heat flow divided by temperature, and according to the second law of thermodynamics, the total entropy change is always positive. Taken together, these two requirements dictate that spontaneous heat flow between two bodies at different temperatures always goes from the warmer body to the colder body. For example, when a kettle of boiling water sits on the heating element of a stove, heat always flows from the hot burner to the relatively cooler boiling water.

To understand why this must occur, consider the entropy changes that would accompany heat transfer in the *opposite* direction. Suppose the burner is at 450 K and the water is at 373 K. We can calculate the entropy change that would occur if 1.00 J of heat flowed from the water to the burner. In this scenario, q for the burner is positive, so it gains entropy. For the water, q is negative, so it loses entropy:

$$\Delta S_{\text{burner}} = 1.00 \text{ J}/450 \text{ K} = 0.00222 \text{ J/K} \qquad \Delta S_{\text{water}} = -1.00 \text{ J}/373 \text{ K} = -0.00268 \text{ J/K}$$

$$\Delta S_{\text{universe}} = \Delta S_{\text{burner}} + \Delta S_{\text{water}} = 0.00222 - 0.00268 = -4.6 \times 10^{-4} \text{ J/K}$$

A spontaneous "uphill" flow of heat, from the cooler water to the hotter burner, would result in a *decrease* in the entropy of the universe, which is forbidden by the second law of thermodynamics. According to all observations, which are summarized in the second law, heat never flows spontaneously from a cold body to a hot one.

SECTION EXERCISES

13.2.1 Benzene (C_6H_6) has a freezing point of 5.5 °C with $\Delta H_{\text{fusion}} = 10.9$ kJ/mol, whereas water freezes at 0 °C with $\Delta H_{\text{fusion}} = 6.01$ kJ/mol. Suppose that an ice and water mixture at 0 °C is put into thermal contact with a benzene solid and liquid mixture at 5.5 °C. What will happen?

13.2.2 Compute $\Delta S_{\text{universe}}$ for 10.0 g of benzene changing phase, as described in Section Exercise 13.2.1.

13.2.3 Suppose that an ice and water mixture is placed in a refrigerator that is at exactly 0 °C. Calculate ΔS for the ice and water mixture, for the refrigerator and for the universe when 5.00 g of ice forms. Is this process spontaneous? Is the reverse process spontaneous?

13.3 ENTROPIES OF SUBSTANCES

Chapter 12 describes how to determine changes in enthalpy or energy, but as noted there, no practical method exists to determine the *absolute* enthalpy or energy of a substance. Unlike energy and enthalpy, entropy has a well-defined zero point, where disorder is at a minimum. Having a zero point for molecular disorder makes it possible to determine the **absolute entropy** of any substance.

DISORDER AND TEMPERATURE

According to the discussion in Section 13.2, removing heat from any substance decreases its disorder. We can explore that relationship in more detail using 1 mol of argon initially at 300 K and 1 atm pressure. Under these conditions, argon is a near-ideal gas that occupies a volume of 24.4 L. The argon atoms exhibit substantial disorder because they are distributed randomly throughout the entire volume, moving in all directions with a wide range of molecular velocities.

Now consider what happens to this sample of argon gas when the temperature is lowered to 90 K. Heat flows from the system to the surroundings, reducing the entropy of the argon. Because the temperature of the argon changes from 300 to 90 K, we cannot use Equation 13-1 to calculate ΔS. However, we can describe the entropy change qualitatively. As shown in Figure 13-7, the gas volume decreases to 7.3 L, reducing disorder by confining the atoms to a smaller space. The atoms also move more slowly at the lower temperature, which makes an additional contribution to the decrease in disorder.

The entropy change for this cooling process can be determined using calculus.

As the temperature is lowered further, the volume of the gas decreases, the atoms move ever more slowly, and the amount of disorder drops steadily. When the temperature reaches 87.3 K, the argon gas condenses to the liquid phase, as illustrated in

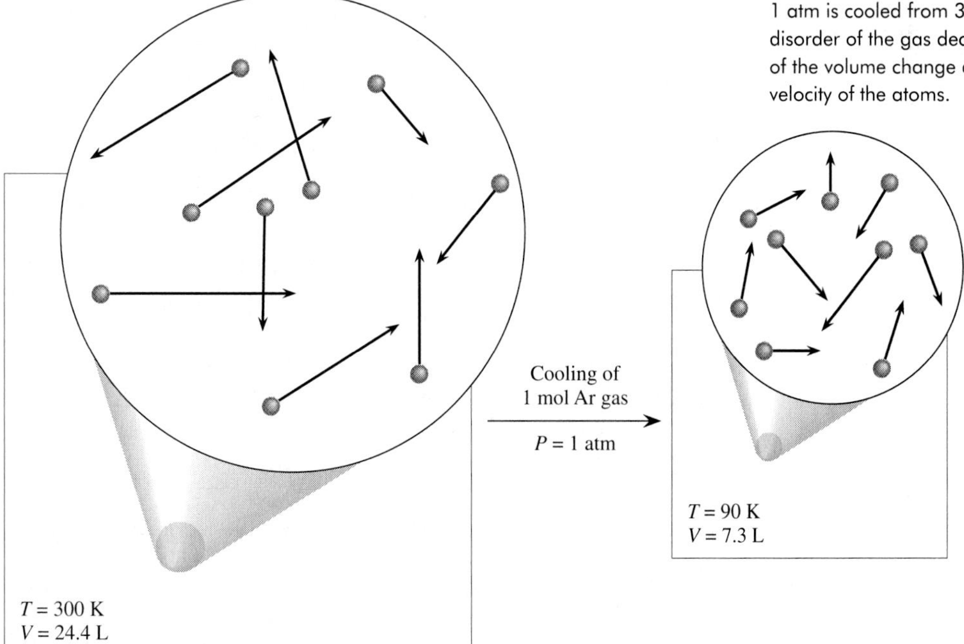

FIGURE 13-7
A molecular view of the changes that occur when a sample of argon gas at 1 atm is cooled from 300 to 90 K. The disorder of the gas decreases because of the volume change and the lower velocity of the atoms.

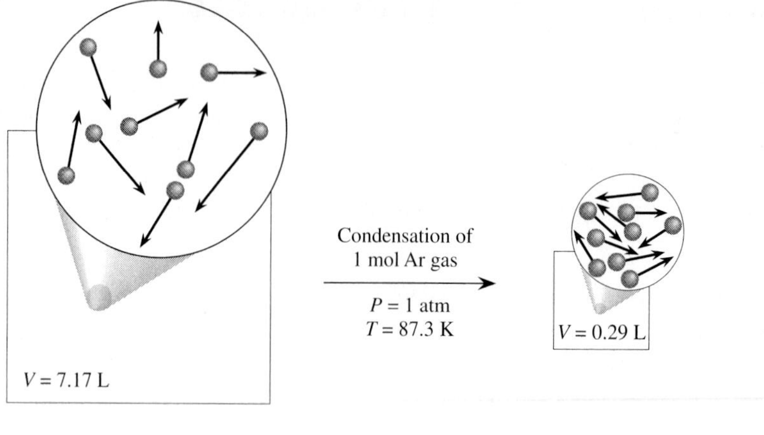

FIGURE 13-8
A molecular view of the changes that accompany the condensation of argon from a gas to a liquid at 87.3 K. The atoms are confined to a much smaller space, causing a large reduction in entropy.

Figure 13-8. This phase change occurs at constant temperature and is accompanied by a large reduction in entropy, which we can calculate using Equation 13-1 and the molar enthalpy of vaporization of argon:

$$q_{Ar} = -n\,\Delta H_{vap} = -(1.00\text{ mol})(6.53\text{ kJ/mol})(10^3\text{ J/kJ}) = -6.53 \times 10^3\text{ J}$$

$$\Delta S_{condensation} = \frac{q_{Ar}}{T_{condensation}} = \frac{-6.53 \times 10^3\text{ J}}{87.3\text{ K}} = -74.8\text{ J/K}$$

This decrease in entropy is caused primarily by the decrease in volume that accompanies the condensation. At 87.3 K the molar volume of argon gas is 7.17 L, but as a liquid the same amount of argon occupies just 29 mL.

When the temperature reaches 83.8 K, argon freezes to form a regular cubic crystal. Again, we can use Equation 13-1 to calculate ΔS for this phase change at constant temperature, this time using the molar enthalpy of fusion:

$$q_{Ar} = -n\,\Delta H_{fus} = -(1.00\text{ mol})(1.21\text{ kJ/mol})(10^3\text{ J/kJ}) = -1.21 \times 10^3\text{ J}$$

$$\Delta S_{solidification} = \frac{q_{Ar}}{T_{solidification}} = \frac{-1.21 \times 10^3\text{ J}}{83.8\text{ K}} = -14.4\text{ J/K}$$

As shown in Figure 13-9, atoms in the solid state are organized in a highly ordered, regular crystalline array, whereas atoms in the liquid move freely about, forming less-ordered patterns.

Even as a solid, argon is still significantly disordered. As shown in Figure 13-10, argon atoms vibrate back and forth within the crystal, so there is still some random-

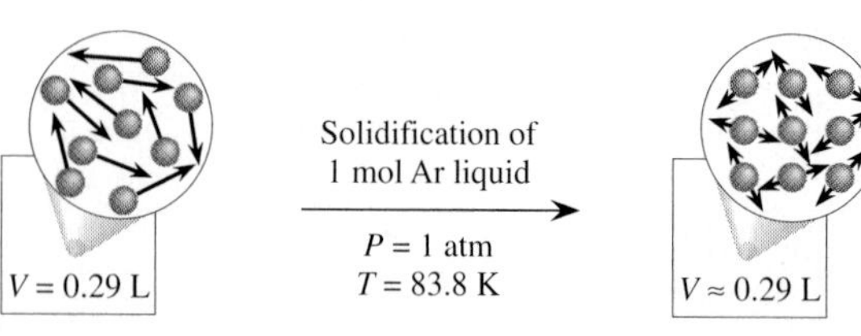

FIGURE 13-9
A molecular view of the changes that occur when argon freezes. From liquid to solid, disorder decreases because of the high degree of regularity in the solid phase.

ness in their individual positions. However, as the solid is cooled to even lower temperatures, the vibrational motion of the atoms continues to diminish. Eventually, the solid reaches a temperature at which the atoms have minimal thermal energy, and each atom is locked in place in the crystal. That temperature is 0 K. The entropy of the system is now at a minimum, provided there are no impurities in the sample or imperfections in the solid crystal. Impurities are a source of disorder because impure molecules are distributed randomly throughout the crystal. Imperfections in a crystal are a source of disorder because atoms are out of place. A crystal that contains impurities or imperfections contains some residual entropy.

When the disorder in the sample is at a minimum, we specify that the entropy of the sample is zero. The **third law of thermodynamics** states that a pure, perfect crystal at 0 K has no entropy. In equation form the third law is:

$$S_{(\text{pure, perfect crystal; T = 0 K})} = 0 \quad \textbf{(13-3)}$$

Our development of the third law is based on a logical analysis of how disorder decreases as the temperature drops. The law has also been tested experimentally by comparing measured entropy changes with calculated values based on $S = 0$ J/mol at $T = 0$ K. The results confirm our qualitative analysis.

The third law of thermodynamics establishes a "starting point" for entropies. At 0 K, any pure perfect crystal is completely ordered and has $S = 0$ J/mol. At any higher temperature, that substance is disordered, so it has a positive entropy. The amount of entropy in a sample depends on the conditions. Thermodynamicists have measured the molar entropies of many pure substances under standard thermodynamic conditions of 1 atm and 298 K. These absolute molar entropies, designated $S°$, are found in the same thermodynamic tables that list heats of formation. A few values of $S°$ are listed in Table 13-2 to give you an idea of the magnitudes of absolute entropies. A more extensive list can be found in Appendix E.

The representative values of $S°$ listed in Table 13-2 reveal the following general trends in absolute entropies:

1. Unlike enthalpies of formation, $S°$ values are *never* zero. Absolute entropies are zero only at 0 K, and $S°$ values refer to substances at 298 K.

High temperature:

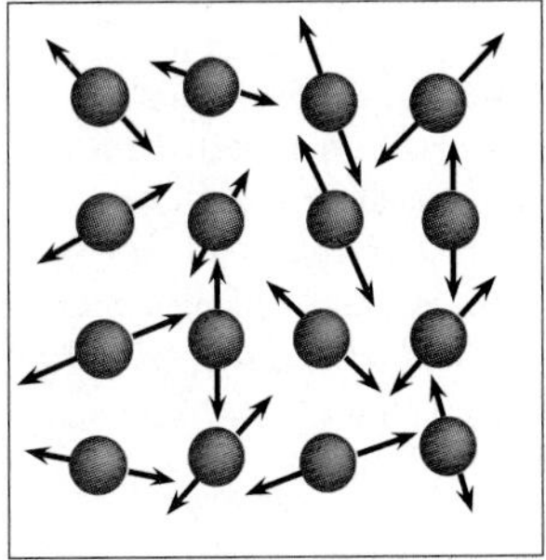

Lower temperature:

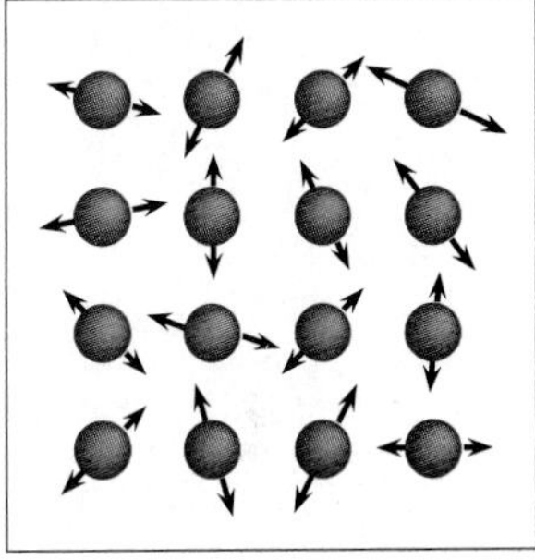

FIGURE 13-10
The vibrational motion in a solid crystal creates some randomness in the positions of the atoms. As the temperature is reduced, the magnitude of vibrational motions decreases, as does the disorder of the sample.

The superscript "o" for absolute entropies always designates standard thermodynamic conditions, meaning 1 atm pressure and 298 K.

TABLE 13-2 ABSOLUTE MOLAR ENTROPIES (S°) OF SELECTED SUBSTANCES*

Substance	Phase	S° (J/mol K)	Substance	Phase	S° (J/mol K)
C	Diamond	2.43	He	Gas	126
C	Graphite	5.67	H_2	Gas	131
Si	Solid	18.9	Ar	Gas	155
Al	Metal	28	Xe	Gas	170
Cu	Metal	33	C_2H_2	Gas	201
SiO_2	Crystal	41	F_2	Gas	203
Ag	Metal	43	CO_2	Gas	213.7
H_2O	Liquid	70	C_2H_4	Gas	220
NaCl	Crystal	72	Cl_2	Gas	223
Hg	Liquid	76	C_2H_6	Gas	230
I_2	Solid	116	Br_2	Gas	245
Br_2	Liquid	152	I_2	Gas	261
			$SiCl_4$	Gas	331

*$T = 298$ K, $P = 1$ atm.

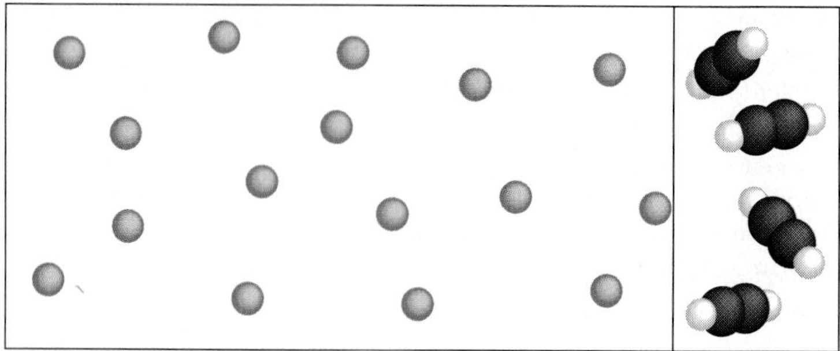

FIGURE 13-11
When both are at the same temperature, a 4-mol sample of gaseous He (*left*) is much more disordered than a 1-mol sample of C_2H_2 (*right*), even though the two samples contain the same number of atoms. Binding atoms together into molecules reduces their disorder substantially.

2. The absolute entropy of a substance depends on its phase. For example, compare liquid bromine with gaseous bromine and solid iodine with iodine gas.

$Br_{2\,(l)}$	$S^\circ = 152$ J/mol K	$I_{2\,(s)}$	$S^\circ = 116$ J/mol K
$Br_{2\,(g)}$	$S^\circ = 245$ J/mol K	$I_{2\,(g)}$	$S^\circ = 261$ J/mol K

In each case the more restricted phase has the lower entropy. For a given substance: $S_{solid} < S_{liquid} < S_{gas}$.

3. Among substances of otherwise similar structure, S° values tend to increase with molar mass. For example:

He	$MM = 4$ g/mol	$S^\circ = 126$ J/mol K
Ar	$MM = 40$ g/mol	$S^\circ = 155$ J/mol K
Cu	$MM = 63.5$ g/mol	$S^\circ = 33$ J/mol K
Ag	$MM = 108$ g/mol	$S^\circ = 43$ J/mol K

4. Molar entropies also increase as the size of the molecule increases. A molecule with many atoms has many more ways of arranging its atoms in space than a molecule with only a few atoms. Thus larger molecules have a greater amount of intramolecular disorder. Compare, for example, the standard molar entropies of acetylene, ethylene, and ethane:

Acetylene	C_2H_2	$S^\circ = 201$ J/mol K
Ethylene	C_2H_4	$S^\circ = 220$ J/mol K
Ethane	C_2H_6	$S^\circ = 230$ J/mol K

Notice, however, that 4 mol of gaseous helium have considerably more total entropy than 1 mol of gaseous C_2H_2, even though 4 mol contain the same number of atoms as 1 mol of acetylene. Binding atoms together into molecules always reduces the amount of disorder, even though atoms within a molecule retain some disorder because of vibrations and rotations within the molecule. Figure 13-11 illustrates this feature. Sample Problem 13-3 provides additional examples of how absolute entropies vary with molecular properties.

SAMPLE PROBLEM 13-3 ABSOLUTE ENTROPIES

For each of the following pairs of substances, predict which has the larger standard entropy and give a reason why: (a) 1 mol each of Hg and Au; (b) 1 mol each of NO and NO_2; (c) 2 mol of NO_2 and 1 mol of N_2O_4; and (d) 1 mol each of Xe and Kr.

METHOD: Keep in mind that several features affect molecular disorder and entropy, including phase, number of atoms or molecules, amount of bonding, and molar mass.

(a) At 298 K, mercury is a liquid metal, but gold is a solid metal. In general, a liquid has more disorder than a solid. The two elements have almost the same molar mass, so we predict that Hg has a larger S° value than Au. The values from Appendix E confirm our prediction: Hg, 76 J/mol K, and Au, 47 J/mol K.

(b) Both nitrogen monoxide and nitrogen dioxide are gases under standard conditions, but each molecule of NO_2 has three atoms, and each molecule of NO has two atoms. Thus NO_2 should have a higher standard molar entropy than NO, and experimental values confirm this: NO_2, 240 J/mol K, and NO, 211 J/mol K.

(c) Two moles of NO_2 contain the same number of atoms as 1 mol of N_2O_4. In N_2O_4, however, pairs of NO_2 units are "tied together" by a bond that reduces their randomness. Therefore 2 mol of NO_2 should have more entropy than 1 mol of N_2O_4:
NO_2, (240 J/mol K)(2 mol) = 480 J/K, and N_2O_4, (304 J/ mol K)(1 mol) = 304 J/K.

(d) Both xenon and krypton are monatomic gases from Group VIII of the periodic table. Xe has a higher molar mass than Kr, so we expect Xe to have greater entropy: Xe, 170 J/mol K, and Kr, 164 J/mol K.

ENTROPY AND CONCENTRATION

The entropy of 1 mol of gas is larger than the entropy of 1 mol of the same substance in a condensed phase because molecules are more disordered in a dispersed sample than in a compact sample. This link between dispersion and disorder also means that entropy depends on concentration. Consider, for example, a gas expanding, as shown in Figure 13-12. As the gas expands, its molecules become more randomly distributed in space, increasing the amount of disorder and entropy. In expanding, the gas also becomes less concentrated. According to the ideal gas equation (Equation 5-4), the pressure exerted by a gas is directly proportional to its concentration (c):

$$c = \frac{n}{V} = \frac{P}{RT}$$

Thus the entropy of a gas increases as its pressure decreases.

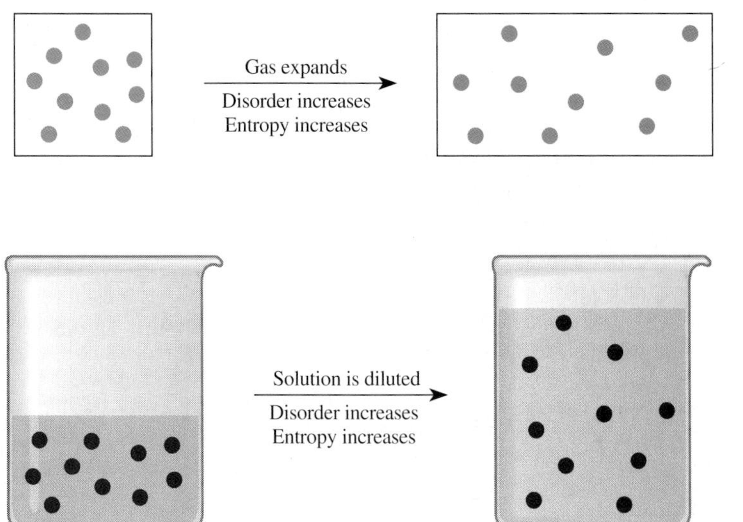

FIGURE 13-12
When a gas expands, its disorder and entropy increase. When a solution is diluted by a factor of 2, the increase in disorder of the solute is the same as when the pressure of a gas is reduced by a factor of 2.

Figure 13-12 illustrates that the dilution of a *solution* from higher molarity to lower molarity has the same disordering effect as the expansion of a *gas* from higher pressure to lower pressure. After each concentration change, the same number of molecules is distributed throughout a larger volume. The less concentrated the sample, the more random its molecular distribution and the greater its disorder. Entropy increases as concentration decreases.

The mathematical machinery of thermodynamics allows this qualitative statement to be expressed quantitatively. The derivation requires the use of calculus, so we give only the result: The molar entropy of a gas or solute varies logarithmically with concentration:

$$S_{(c \neq 1)} = S^{\circ} - R \ln c \quad \text{(1 mol, nonstandard concentration)} \qquad \textbf{(13-4)}$$

The logarithmic term in Equation 13-4 actually contains the ratio of concentration to standard concentration. Standard concentrations are 1 M for solutes and 1 atm for gases, however, so we can omit the standard concentration, remembering that, to ensure unit cancellation, pressures must be in atmospheres and solution concentrations in moles per liter.

Here, c is expressed in atmospheres for gases and molarity for solutes. Notice that Equation 13-4 refers to molar quantities. To obtain the total entropy of a sample of a gas or solute, its molar entropy must be multiplied by n, the number of moles that it contains. Sample Problem 13-4 illustrates the calculation of ΔS for a change in concentration.

SAMPLE PROBLEM 13-4 ENTROPY CHANGE ON EXPANSION

Oxygen gas is used in many practical applications, from welders' torches to respirators. The gas is sold commercially in pressurized steel tanks. Suppose that a tank contains O_2 at $P = 6.50$ atm and $T = 298$ K. Using standard thermodynamic data, compute the molar entropy of the gas in the tank at 6.50 atm and the change in entropy of a 0.155-mol sample of gas withdrawn from the tank at 1.10 atm and constant temperature.

METHOD: In the pressurized tank, O_2 is under nonstandard concentration conditions. Equation 13-4 describes molar entropy for pressures other than 1.00 atm. To complete the calculation, we require the standard molar entropy, which is found in Appendix E. Begin by summarizing all the information given in the problem:

Initial conditions: O_2 gas, $T = 298$ K, $P = 6.50$ atm

Final conditions: O_2 gas, $T = 298$ K, $P = 1.10$ atm, $n = 0.155$ mol

From Appendix E: $S^{\circ}(O_{2,\,g}) = 205$ J/mol K

To calculate the molar entropy of the gas in the tank, apply Equation 13-4:

$$S_{(P = 6.50\text{ atm})} = S^{\circ} - R \ln P = 205 \text{ J/mol K} - (8.314 \text{ J/mol K}) \ln(6.50)$$

$$S_{(P = 6.50\text{ atm})} = 205 \text{ J/mol K} - 15.562 \text{ J/mol K} = 189 \text{ J/mol K}$$

As the gas expands, its entropy increases. To calculate ΔS for the expansion, Equation 13-4 must be applied to the initial and final pressures.

$$S_{(P = 1.10\text{ atm})} = S^{\circ} - R \ln P = 205 \text{ J/mol K} - (8.314 \text{ J/mol K}) \ln(1.10)$$

$$S_{(P = 1.10\text{ atm})} = 205 \text{ J/mol K} - 0.7924 \text{ J/mol K} = 204 \text{ J/mol K}$$

To calculate the entropy change for the expansion, take the difference in molar entropies between initial and final conditions and multiply by the number of moles undergoing the expansion:

$$\Delta S = n(S_{\text{final}} - S_{\text{initial}}) = (0.155 \text{ mol})(204 \text{ J/mol K} - 189 \text{ J/mol K}) = 2.33 \text{ J/K}$$

The positive value for this entropy change reflects the fact that the expansion is a spontaneous process.

STANDARD REACTION ENTROPIES

Entropy changes are important in every process that occurs in the universe. However, chemists are interested primarily in the effects of entropy on chemical reactions. If a reaction occurs under standard conditions, its entropy change can be calculated from absolute entropies in exactly the same way as reaction enthalpies can be calculated from standard heats of formation.

To determine the standard entropy change for a chemical reaction, we multiply each standard molar entropy by the stoichiometric coefficient in the balanced chemical equation and subtract values for reactants from values for products:

$$\Delta S^{o}_{\text{reaction}} = \Sigma \text{coeff}_p S^{o}_{\text{(products)}} - \Sigma \text{coeff}_r S^{o}_{\text{(reactants)}} \quad \textbf{(13-5)}$$

Notice how similar Equation 13-5 is to Equation 12-11, which is used to calculate reaction *enthalpies*. As Sample Problem 13-5 shows, the application of these equations follows parallel paths.

SAMPLE PROBLEM 13-5 ENTROPY AND ENTHALPY CHANGES

Acrylonitrile is an essential monomer in the polymer industry because it is used to make polyacrylonitrile for synthetic fibers:

$$\left[-CH_2-\underset{\displaystyle CN}{\underset{|}{CH}}- \right]_n \quad \text{Polyacrylonitrile}$$

Acrylonitrile is made from propene by the ammoxidation process:

$$2\ \text{Propene } (C_3H_6) + 2\ NH_3 + 3\ O_2 \longrightarrow 2\ \text{Acrylonitrile } (CH_2CHCN) + 6\ H_2O$$

Calculate ΔH^{o}_{rxn} and ΔS^{o}_{rxn} for ammoxidation from standard thermodynamic data. (All three starting materials are gases, and both products are liquids.)

METHOD: When we want to find standard thermodynamic changes for a reaction, we should immediately recall Equations 12-10 and 13-5:

$$\Delta H^{o}_{rxn} = \Sigma\ \text{coeff}_p \Delta H^{o}_f\text{(products)} - \Sigma\ \text{coeff}_r \Delta H^{o}_f\text{(reactants)}$$

$$\Delta S^{o}_{rxn} = \Sigma\ \text{coeff}_p S^{o}\text{(products)} - \Sigma\ \text{coeff}_r S^{o}\text{(reactants)}$$

Standard heats of formation and standard entropies are tabulated in Appendix E. Here are the values for the substances involved in this reaction:

Substance	$C_3H_{6\,(g)}$	$NH_{3\,(g)}$	$O_{2\,(g)}$	$C_3H_3N_{\,(l)}$	$H_2O_{\,(l)}$
ΔH^{o}_f (kJ/mol)	20.41	−46.11	0	172.9	−285.83
S^{o} (J/mol K)	226.9	192.45	205.14	188	69.91
Coefficient	2	2	3	2	6

We leave it to you to "plug in" the numbers and calculate the answers. The results are as follows:

$$\Delta H^{o}_{rxn} = -1.318 \times 10^3\ \text{kJ} \qquad \Delta S^{o}_{rxn} = -659\ \text{J/K}$$

According to these values, ammoxidation is exothermic, but the system becomes more ordered as it reacts. Because liquids are formed from gases, this increase in order is a reasonable result.

SECTION EXERCISES

13.3.1 Of the following pairs, which has the greater entropy? Explain why in each case: (a) 1 g of dew or 1 g of frost; (b) 1 mol of gaseous hydrogen atoms or 0.5 mol of gaseous hydrogen molecules; (c) "Perfect" diamond or flawed diamond, each $^1/_4$ carat; (d) 5 mL of liquid ethanol at 0 °C or 5 mL of liquid ethanol at 50 °C.

13.3.2 Explain the following differences in entropies in molecular terms (substances are at standard conditions unless otherwise noted):
(a) 1 mol of O_2 has less entropy than 1 mol of O_3.
(b) 3 mol of O_2 has more entropy than 2 mol of O_3.
(c) 1 mol of I_2 has less entropy than 1 mol of O_2.
(d) 1 mol of $HCl_{(aq)}$ in concentrated solution (12 M) has less entropy than 1 mol of $HCl_{(aq)}$ in dilute solution (0.100 M).

13.3.3 Draw molecular pictures to illustrate your answers to part b of Section Exercise 13.3.1 and part b of Section Exercise 13.3.2.

13.3.4 Compute the standard entropy change for the following reaction:

$$12\ NH_{3\,(g)} + 21\ O_{2\,(g)} \rightarrow 8\ HNO_{3\,(g)} + 4\ NO_{(g)} + 12\ H_2O_{(l)}$$

13.4 SPONTANEITY AND FREE ENERGY

The second law of thermodynamics states that the entropy of the universe must increase during a spontaneous process. Consequently, the sign of $\Delta S_{universe}$ must be positive for any chemical process to be spontaneous. To determine whether a particular chemical process is spontaneous, we must calculate the value of $\Delta S_{universe}$ that accompanies the process. Unfortunately, this is not practical for most processes. It is usually possible to calculate the entropy change for a *system,* but the *surroundings* may undergo complicated changes of state for which ΔS cannot be determined easily. The surroundings include virtually all the universe, and keeping track of changes in the universe is a tricky matter. It would be much more convenient if we had some way to determine the direction of spontaneous change using *just the system,* not the surroundings.

No such criterion can be applied to *all* processes. If we restrict the conditions sufficiently, however, there is a state function whose change for the *system* predicts spontaneity. This new state function is called **free energy *(G)*** and is defined by Equation 13-6:

$$\text{Free energy} = G = H - TS \qquad \textbf{(13-6)}$$

where H is enthalpy, T is temperature, and S is entropy.*

* The American J. Willard Gibbs introduced free energy into chemical thermodynamics. A professor of mathematical physics at Yale University from 1871 until his death in 1903, Gibbs was the first to show how the laws of thermodynamics apply to chemical processes. Because Gibbs published in a little-known American journal at a time when most scientific work was being done in Europe, his outstanding contributions to chemical thermodynamics were not recognized until 13 years after they were first published. In the 1890s, however, his 400 pages of elegant mathematical development of this subject were translated into French and German, and European scientists quickly recognized the greatness of his work. To commemorate Gibbs, free energy is symbolized G and is sometimes called *Gibbs free energy*.

The definition of free energy gives us an equation that relates the change in free energy for any system to other thermodynamic changes:

$$\Delta G_{sys} = \Delta H_{sys} - \Delta(TS)_{sys}$$

To use ΔG_{sys} to predict spontaneity, we must relate this equation to the total entropy change of the universe. This cannot be done unless some restrictions are placed on the conditions. First, the process must occur at *constant temperature.* This lets us relate $\Delta(TS)_{sys}$ to ΔS_{sys}:

$$\Delta(TS) = (TS)_{final} - (TS)_{initial} = T(S_f - S_i) = T\Delta S_{sys}$$

$$\Delta G_{sys} = \Delta H_{sys} - T\Delta S_{sys} \qquad \text{(constant } T\text{)} \qquad \textbf{(13-7)}$$

Next, the *enthalpy* change for the system can be related to the *entropy* change for the surroundings by restricting the conditions to *constant pressure.* Recall that ΔH equals q when P is constant:

$$\Delta H_{sys} = q_{sys} \qquad \text{(constant } P\text{)}$$

Remember also that the heat flow for a system is always equal in magnitude but opposite in sign to the heat flow of the surroundings:

$$q_{sys} = -q_{surr} \quad \textit{and} \quad \Delta H_{sys} = -q_{surr}$$

Furthermore, we have already restricted the process to constant temperature, so the heat flow of the surroundings measures the entropy change of the surroundings. That is:

$$\frac{q_{surr}}{T} = \Delta S_{surr} \quad \textit{and} \quad q_{surr} = T\Delta S_{surr}$$

Combining these equalities gives an equation that relates ΔH_{sys} and ΔS_{surr}:

$$\Delta H_{sys} = -T\Delta S_{surr} \text{ (constant } P \text{ and } T\text{)}$$

Now we substitute this result into Equation 13-7:

$$\Delta G_{sys} = -T\Delta S_{surr} - T\Delta S_{sys} = -T(\Delta S_{surr} + \Delta S_{sys})$$

Finally, because $\Delta S_{surr} + \Delta S_{sys} = \Delta S_{universe}$:

$$\Delta G_{sys} = -T\Delta S_{universe} \qquad \text{(constant } T \text{ and } P\text{)}$$

This a powerful result because it states that the free energy of the *system* changes in a way that mirrors the entropy change of the *universe* in any process that occurs at constant T and P. By defining a new function and imposing some restrictions, we have found a way to use properties of a system to determine whether a process is spontaneous. Because T is always positive, and $\Delta S_{universe}$ is positive for any spontaneous process, ΔG_{sys} is *negative* for spontaneous processes under constant T and P conditions. Although the restrictions of constant T and P are stringent, they are met by many important chemical processes. For example, the human body has a constant T of 37 °C. Any biochemical reaction that occurs in the body occurs under conditions in which the immediate surroundings are at constant T and P.

Because free energy is a state function, its values can be tabulated for use in chemical calculations. As with standard heats of formation, the **standard molar free energy of formation (ΔG°_f)** for any substance is defined to be the change of free energy when 1 mol of that substance is formed from elements in their standard states. Following the same reasoning we used for enthalpy changes, we obtain an equation for calculating the free energy change for any chemical reaction:

$$\Delta G^\circ_{\text{reaction}} = \Sigma\, \text{coeff}_p\, \Delta G^\circ_f(\text{products}) - \Sigma\, \text{coeff}_r\, \Delta G^\circ_f(\text{reactants}) \tag{13-8}$$

The form of Equation 13-8 should be familiar because it is analogous to Equation 12-11 for reaction enthalpies and Equation 13-5 for reaction entropies.

The standard free energy change for a reaction can also be calculated from ΔH° and ΔS° for the reaction by making use of Equation 13-7 under standard conditions:

$$\Delta G^\circ = \Delta H^\circ - T\Delta S^\circ \tag{13-9}$$

Either of these equations can be used to find standard free energy changes. Which equation we use depends on the available data. Sample Problem 13-6 illustrates both types of calculations.

SAMPLE PROBLEM 13-6 FREE ENERGY OF REACTION

Find the standard free energy change for the acrylonitrile synthesis discussed in Sample Problem 13-5.

METHOD: There are two ways to calculate ΔG°_{rxn}. The first method uses standard free energies of formation and Equation 13-8. The second method uses Equation 13-9 and the values of ΔH° and ΔS° calculated earlier. We perform both calculations to show they give the same result. First, recall the balanced equation for the acrylonitrile synthesis:

$$2\,C_3H_{6\,(g)} + 2\,NH_{3\,(g)} + 3\,O_{2\,(g)} \rightarrow 2\,C_3H_3N_{\,(l)} + 6\,H_2O_{\,(l)}$$

(a) Using ΔG°_f values from Appendix E:

$$\Delta G^\circ_{rxn} = [(6\text{ mol})(-237.13\text{ kJ/mol}) + (2\text{ mol})(208.6\text{ kJ/mol})] -$$

$$[(3\text{ mol})(0\text{ kJ/mol}) + (2\text{ mol})(-16.45\text{ kJ/mol}) + (2\text{ mol})(74.62\text{ kJ/mol})]$$

$$\Delta G^\circ_{rxn} = -1122\text{ kJ}$$

(b) Using the results of Sample Problem 13-5:

$$\Delta G^\circ_{rxn} = \Delta H^\circ - T\Delta S^\circ$$

$$\Delta G^\circ_{rxn} = [-1318\text{ kJ}] - [(298\text{ K})(-659\text{ J/K})(10^{-3}\text{ kJ/J})] = -1122\text{ kJ}$$

The large negative ΔG°_{rxn} found in this problem indicates that the production of acrylonitrile is highly spontaneous under standard conditions.

Pay close attention to units when using Equation 13-9. The values of ΔH° and ΔG° are usually given in kJ or kJ/mol, but entropies are usually expressed in J/K or J/mol K. Thus entropies must be multiplied by 10^{-3} kJ/J before adding the two terms.

CHANGE IN FREE ENERGY UNDER NONSTANDARD CONDITIONS

Standard conditions refer to unit concentrations and 298 K, but chemical reactions occur at many different concentrations and temperatures. To use ΔG as a measure of spontaneity under nonstandard conditions, we must understand how free energy depends on temperature and concentration. First, Equation 13-9 is valid at *any* temperature as long as the temperature is *constant*. However, to apply the equation to a temperature different from 298 K, we must have the appropriate values for ΔH_{rxn} and ΔS_{rxn}.

Chemical substances become more disordered as temperature increases. These changes in entropy as a function of temperature can be calculated, but the techniques require calculus. Fortunately, temperature affects the entropies of reactants and products in the same way. In other words, changes in the disorder of the reactants are often almost the same as changes in the disorder of the products. As a result, the temperature effect on the *net* entropy change of a reaction is usually small. In fact, in most cases we can assume that ΔS_{rxn} is independent of temperature.

Recall that ΔH_{rxn} also does not change rapidly with temperature. As a result, we can estimate free energy changes at temperatures other than 298 K by assuming that standard enthalpies and entropies at 298 K also apply at any other temperature:

The temperature variation of the change in entropy during a reaction (ΔS_{rxn}) can often be neglected, but temperature variations in *absolute* entropies of individual substances (S_{molar}) are *never* negligible.

$$\Delta G^{\circ}_{rxn,\,T} \cong \Delta H^{\circ}_{rxn,\,298} - T\Delta S^{\circ}_{rxn,\,298} \qquad \textbf{(13-10)}$$

In Equation 13-10 we use the superscript "o" to denote standard *concentrations* (1 atm, 1 M) of all reagents, even though *temperature* is nonstandard ($T \neq$ 298 K). When the temperature is not specified, "o" means 298 K and standard concentrations. Therefore ΔG° means "free energy change at 298 K, all reagents at unit concentration," whereas ΔG°_{500} means "free energy change at 500 K, all reagents at unit concentration."

An immediate consequence of Equation 13-10 is that any reaction with a large ΔS° is very sensitive to temperature. Sample Problem 13-7 shows a simple example.

SAMPLE PROBLEM 13-7 TEMPERATURE AND SPONTANEITY

Dinitrogen tetroxide can decompose into two molecules of nitrogen dioxide:

$$N_2O_{4\,(g)} \rightarrow 2\ NO_{2\,(g)}$$

(a) Show that this reaction is not spontaneous under standard conditions.
(b) Find the temperature at which the reaction becomes spontaneous at standard pressures.

METHOD: The key word here is *spontaneous,* which suggests that we need to work with free energies to solve this problem. Recall that the criterion for spontaneity is $\Delta G_{rxn} < 0$. We must find this free energy change at standard temperature. Then, using Equation 13-10, we can calculate the temperature that makes $\Delta G_{rxn} < 0$.

(a) Use Equation 13-8 and values for ΔG°_{f} from Appendix E to show that the decomposition reaction is not spontaneous under standard conditions:

$$\Delta G^{\circ} = (2\ \text{mol})(51.31\ \text{kJ/mol}) - (1\ \text{mol})(97.89\ \text{kJ/mol}) = 4.73\ \text{kJ}$$

The positive value for ΔG° indicates that this reaction is *not* spontaneous under standard conditions. In fact, the calculation tells us that the reaction will be spontaneous in the opposite direction. Under standard conditions, NO_2 reacts to form N_2O_4:

$$2\ NO_{2\,(g)} \rightarrow N_2O_{4\,(g)} \qquad \Delta G^{\circ} = -4.73\ \text{kJ}$$

(b) Use Equation 13-10 to find the temperature at which N_2O_4 decomposition becomes spontaneous when the partial pressures of both gases are 1 atm:

$$\Delta G^{\circ}_{rxn,\,T} \cong \Delta H^{\circ}_{rxn,\,298} - T\Delta S^{\circ}_{rxn,\,298}$$

As temperature changes, ΔG must become zero before it becomes negative. We must find the temperature at which $\Delta G = 0$. Begin by calculating ΔH° and ΔS° using tabulated data:

$$\Delta H^{\circ} = (2\ \text{mol})(33.18\ \text{kJ/mol}) - (1\ \text{mol})(9.16\ \text{kJ/mol}) = 57.2\ \text{kJ}$$

$$\Delta S^{\circ} = (2\ \text{mol})(240.1\ \text{J/mol K}) - (1\ \text{mol})(304.3\ \text{J/mol K}) = 175.9\ \text{J/K}$$

$$\Delta S^{\circ} = 0.1759\ \text{kJ/K} \qquad \Delta H^{\circ} = 57.2\ \text{kJ}$$

Set ΔG equal to zero and rearrange the equation to solve for temperature:

$$\Delta G = \Delta H^{\circ} - T\Delta S^{\circ} = 0 \quad or \quad T\Delta S^{\circ} = \Delta H^{\circ}$$

$$T = \frac{\Delta H^{\circ}}{\Delta S^{\circ}} = \frac{57.2\ \text{kJ}}{0.1759\ \text{kJ/K}} = 325\ \text{K}$$

At 325 K, $\Delta G^{\circ} = 0$. Therefore at all temperatures greater than 325 K, ΔG° is negative, and decomposition of N_2O_4 is spontaneous at 1 atm partial pressures.

CHANGING CONCENTRATION

The substances participating in a chemical reaction typically are at concentrations different from 1 M or pressures different from 1 atm. For example, a biochemist who wants to know what processes are spontaneous under physiological conditions will find that the substances dissolved in biological fluids are rarely at 1 M concentration. How does change in free energy vary with changes in molarity and pressure? Recall that enthalpy is virtually independent of concentration but that entropy obeys Equation 13-4.

To see how entropy affects ΔG, consider the synthesis of ammonia carried out in a pressurized reactor containing N_2, H_2, and NH_3 at partial pressures *(p)* different from 1 atm:

$$N_{2\,(g)} + 3\,H_{2\,(g)} \rightarrow 2\,NH_{3\,(g)}$$

Equation 13-4 gives the molar entropy of each gas as a function of its partial pressure:

$$S = S^{\circ} - R\,ln\,c = S^{\circ} - R\,ln\,p$$

$$\textit{For example, } S(N_2) = S^{\circ}(N_2) - R\,ln\{p(N_2)\}$$

The entropy change for the reaction is the difference in entropy between products and reactants, obtained by multiplying each corrected entropy by the appropriate stoichiometric coefficient:

$$\Delta S_{rxn} = 2\,S(NH_3) - 3\,S(H_2) - S(N_2)$$

Now we substitute each of the corrected entropies:

$$\Delta S_{rxn} = 2[S^{\circ}(NH_3) - R\,ln\{p(NH_3)\}] - 3[S^{\circ}(H_2) - R\,ln\{p(H_2)\}] - [S^{\circ}(N_2) - R\,ln\{p(N_2)\}]$$

Next, rearrange the equation so that all the logarithmic terms are together:

$$\Delta S_{rxn} = 2\,S^{\circ}(NH_3) - 3\,S^{\circ}(H_2) - S^{\circ}(N_2) - 2\,R\,ln\{p(NH_3)\} + 3\,R\,ln\{p(H_2)\} + R\,ln\{p(N_2)\}$$

The first three terms are the standard entropy change for the reaction, allowing us to simplify:

$$\Delta S_{rxn} = \Delta S^{\circ}_{rxn} - 2\,R\,ln\{p(NH_3)\} + 3\,R\,ln\{p(H_2)\} + R\,ln\{p(N_2)\}$$

The properties of logarithms can be used to combine the *ln* terms. First, $x\,ln\,y = ln\,y^x$, giving:

$$2\,R\,ln\{p(NH_3)\} = R\,ln\{p^2(NH_3)\} \quad \text{and} \quad 3\,R\,ln\{p(H_2)\} = R\,ln\{p^3(H_2)\}$$

With these changes, the equation becomes:

$$\Delta S_{rxn} = \Delta S^{\circ}_{rxn} - R\,[ln\{p^2(NH_3)\} - ln\{p^3(H_2)\} - ln\{p(NH_3)\}]$$

A second logarithmic property, $(ln\,x - ln\,y) = ln(x/y)$, lets us put all the logarithmic terms into a single ratio:

$$\Delta S_{rxn} = \Delta S^\circ_{rxn} - R\,ln\left[\frac{p^2(NH_3)}{p(N_2)\,p^3(H_2)}\right]$$

Note that the pressure ratio has product concentrations raised to their stoichiometric coefficients in the numerator and reactant concentrations raised to their stoichiometric coefficients in the denominator. The form of this equation applies to all reactions, not just the synthesis of ammonia. Thus for the general reaction,

$$aA + bB \rightarrow cC + dD$$

the entropy change is:

$$\Delta S_{rxn} = \Delta S^\circ_{rxn} - R\,ln\left[\frac{[C]^c[D]^d}{[A]^a[B]^b}\right]$$

The ratio in the logarithmic term is called the **concentration quotient *(Q)*:**

$$\frac{[C]^c[D]^d}{[A]^a[B]^b} = Q \qquad \textbf{(13-11)}$$

A concentration quotient always contains the concentrations that are variable, that is, those of gases and solutes. The concentrations must be expressed relative to standard conditions, so gas concentrations are in atm, whereas solute concentrations are in mol/L.

The entropy change for a reaction under nonstandard concentrations can be expressed in terms of the standard entropy change and Q:

$$\Delta S_{rxn} = \Delta S^\circ_{rxn} - R\,ln\,Q$$

This allows us to write an equation for the free energy change when concentrations are nonstandard:

$$\Delta G_{rxn} = \Delta H^\circ_{rxn} - T(\Delta S^\circ_{rxn} - R\,ln\,Q)$$

Notice that $\Delta H^\circ - T\Delta S^\circ$ is just ΔG°, so this equation reduces to Equation 13-12:

$$\Delta G_{rxn} = \Delta G^\circ_{rxn} + RT\,ln\,Q \qquad \textbf{(13-12)}$$

An immediate consequence of Equation 13-12 is that the direction of spontaneity in a reaction depends heavily on the concentrations of reactants and products. Product concentrations appear in the numerator of Q, so when the concentration of a product increases, $ln\,Q$ increases, as well. Increasing the $ln\,Q$ term makes ΔG less negative, so a reaction becomes less spontaneous as product concentrations increase. Conversely, reactant concentrations appear in the denominator of Q, so increasing the concentration of a reactant also increases $ln\,Q$, which in turn makes ΔG more negative. Thus a reaction becomes more spontaneous as reactant concentrations increase.

If we have a reaction that is not spontaneous at unit concentrations, we can try to force it to go forward by increasing the concentrations of reactants or by removing products as quickly as they form. If a reaction has a very positive ΔG°_{rxn}, however, it may not be possible to change the value of Q sufficiently to make $\Delta G_{rxn} < 0$. Remember that the term $ln\,Q$ changes much more slowly than Q itself. A 10-fold change in Q, for instance, only changes $ln\,Q$ by a factor of 2.3. Nonetheless, reactions that are almost spontaneous under standard conditions can be driven forward by making appropriate changes in concentration. Sample Problem 13-8 shows how this is done.

SAMPLE PROBLEM 13-8 EFFECT OF CONCENTRATION ON SPONTANEITY

The decomposition of dinitrogen tetroxide follows:

$$N_2O_{4\,(g)} \rightarrow 2\ NO_{2\,(g)}$$

(a) Find the minimum partial pressure of N_2O_4 at which the reaction is spontaneous if $p(NO_2) = 1$ atm and $T = 298$ K.

(b) Find the maximum partial pressure of NO_2 at which the reaction is spontaneous if $p(N_2O_4) = 1$ atm and $T = 298$ K.

METHOD: This is a two-part problem, so each part should be solved independently. Both parts require us to relate change in free energy to concentrations, so we must use Equation 13-12:

$$\Delta G = \Delta G^{\circ} + RT\ ln\ Q = \Delta G^{\circ} + RT\ ln\left[\frac{p^2(NO_2)}{p(N_2O_4)}\right]$$

The mol unit in the value of ΔG° refers to "per mole of reaction" and comes from the concept of the *reaction unit.* The mol unit in ΔG° is included in the calculation to cancel the mol unit in *R*. For a review of the reaction unit, see Section 12.4.

(a) We are asked to find the partial pressure of N_2O_4 that will make the decomposition spontaneous when $T = 298$ K and p of $NO_2 = 1$ atm. The value of ΔG must be zero before it can become negative. Therefore to find the threshold pressure of N_2O_4 that makes the decomposition spontaneous, we set $\Delta G = 0$ and $p(NO_2) = 1$ atm, and then rearrange to solve for the partial pressure of N_2O_4:

$$0 = \Delta G^{\circ} + RT\ ln\left[\frac{(1\ \text{atm})^2}{p(N_2O_4)}\right]$$

$$ln\left[\frac{(1\ \text{atm})^2}{p(N_2O_4)}\right] = -\frac{\Delta G^{\circ}}{RT} = \frac{4.73 \times 10^3\ \text{J/mol}}{(8.314\ \text{J/mol K})(298\ \text{K})} = -1.909$$

Recall that when y = *ln*x, x = e^y, where e is the basis for natural logarithms.

$$\frac{(1\ \text{atm})^2}{p(N_2O_4)} = e^{-1.909} = 0.1482 \quad \textit{and} \quad p(N_2O_4) = 1/0.1482 = 6.75\ \text{atm}$$

This decomposition is spontaneous as long as the pressure of N_2O_4 is greater than 6.75 atm. As always, we have to be careful about units. Standard free energy was converted to joules to use the appropriate value of the gas constant *(R)* in J/mol K. Our final number is an antilogarithm, which has no dimensions, but the pressure must have the same units as the standard state for gases, which is atmospheres.

(b) We are asked to find the maximum partial pressure of NO_2 below which the decomposition is spontaneous when $T = 298$ K and p of $N_2O_4 = 1$ atm. The procedure is analogous to the one we just developed. You should be able to show that the desired pressure is 0.385 atm.

This problem shows that a reaction with a small positive ΔG° can be made spontaneous by relatively small changes in concentrations.

If neither temperature nor concentrations are at their standard values, free energy calculations must be done in two steps. First, correct for temperature to obtain ΔG°_T using Equation 13-10. Second, use that result in Equation 13-12 to complete the calculation of ΔG.

INFLUENCING SPONTANEITY

Suppose we want to design a particular chemical synthesis, but we find that the reaction has a positive value for ΔG°. The thermodynamic calculation indicates that the reaction is spontaneous in the wrong direction under *standard* conditions, but this does not prevent it from occurring under *all* conditions. What can we do to make the reaction go in the desired direction?

Sample Problem 13-8 illustrates that changing the concentration quotient changes the entropy change of the system. In particular, reducing the pressure of NO_2 below 0.386 atm or increasing the pressure of N_2O_4 above 6.71 atm would cause spontaneous decomposition of N_2O_4, even though this reaction is not spontaneous under standard conditions. As with this gas-phase reaction, a reaction in liquid solution may be induced to proceed spontaneously by increasing the concentrations of reactants or by reducing the concentrations of products.

Changing the temperature of the system is another way to influence the spontaneity of a reaction. The equation for ΔG has two parts, ΔH and $T\Delta S$, which can work together or in opposition:

$$\Delta G^\circ_T = \Delta H^\circ - T\Delta S^\circ$$

A *positive* ΔS° promotes spontaneity because it makes ΔG° more negative. This reflects the fact that a positive ΔS° means the system becomes more disordered during the reaction. A *negative* ΔH° promotes spontaneity, as well, because it also makes ΔG° more negative. This reflects the fact that the surroundings become more disordered when a reaction releases energy. Thus a reaction that has a positive ΔS° and a negative ΔH° is spontaneous at any T.

The combustion of propane is an example of a reaction that is spontaneous at all temperatures:

$$C_3H_{8\,(g)} + 5\,O_{2\,(g)} \rightarrow 3\,CO_{2\,(g)} + 4\,H_2O_{\,(g)}$$

$$\Delta H^\circ = -897\text{ kJ} \qquad \Delta S^\circ = +145\text{ J/K}$$

The products of this reaction are more disordered than the reactants, and the reaction releases energy. Consequently, ΔG° is negative at all T, so the reverse reaction cannot be made spontaneous by altering T.

By the same reasoning, a *negative* ΔS° and a *positive* ΔH° oppose spontaneity, so a reaction that meets these criteria is nonspontaneous regardless of T. The system and its surroundings would experience decreases in entropy if such a process were to occur, and this would violate the second law of thermodynamics.

A reaction that has the same sign for ΔS° and ΔH° will be spontaneous at some temperatures but nonspontaneous at others. At low temperature, ΔS° is multiplied by a small value for T, so at sufficiently low temperature, ΔH° contributes more to ΔG° than $T\Delta S^\circ$. At high temperature, ΔS° is multiplied by a large value for T, so at sufficiently high temperature, ΔS° contributes more to ΔG° than ΔH°.

Reactions with positive ΔH° and positive ΔS° are favored by entropy but disfavored by enthalpy. Such reactions are spontaneous at high T, where the $T\Delta S^\circ$ term dominates ΔG°. The reactions are nonspontaneous at low T, where the ΔH° term dominates ΔG°. These reactions are spontaneous at high temperature by virtue of the increased disorder in the system.

The opposite situation holds for reactions that have negative values for ΔH° and ΔS°. These reactions are spontaneous at low T by virtue of the increased disorder in the surroundings. The favorable ΔH° dominates ΔG° as long as T does not become too large. At high T, however, the unfavorable ΔS° dominates ΔG°, and the reaction is no longer spontaneous. The effects of temperature on spontaneity are summarized in Table 13-3.

TABLE 13-3 THE INFLUENCE OF TEMPERATURE ON SPONTANEITY

ΔH°	ΔS°	ΔG° (HIGH T)	ΔG° (LOW T)	SPONTANEOUS
−	+	−	−	All T
+	−	+	+	No T
+	+	−	+	High T
−	−	+	−	Low T

ΔH°, Standard enthalpy change; ΔS°, standard entropy change; ΔG°, standard change in free energy.

Calcium sulfate, the solid used to absorb water in desiccators, provides an example of this sensitivity to temperature. Anhydrous calcium sulfate absorbs water vapor from the atmosphere to give the hydrated salt. The reaction has a negative ΔS° because the system becomes more ordered when gaseous water molecules move into the solid state. The reaction also has a negative ΔH° because of the coulombic forces of attraction between the ions of the salt and the polar water molecules.

$$CaSO_{4\,(s)} + 2\,H_2O_{\,(g)} \rightarrow CaSO_4{\cdot}2H_2O_{\,(s)}$$

$$\Delta H^\circ = -104.9\text{ kJ} \qquad \Delta S^\circ = -290.2\text{ J/K}$$

At 300 K, the favorable ΔH° contributes more to ΔG° than the unfavorable ΔS°:

$$\Delta G^\circ_{300\text{ K}} = (-104.9\text{ kJ}) - (300\text{ K})(-290.2\text{ J/K})(10^{-3}\text{ kJ/J}) = -17.8\text{ kJ}$$

Thus at room temperature, anhydrous calcium sulfate acts as a "chemical sponge," trapping water vapor spontaneously to form calcium sulfate dihydrate.

The calcium sulfate in a desiccator is effective at removing water vapor only as long as some anhydrous salt remains. When all the anhydrous salt has been converted to the dihydrate, the desiccator can no longer maintain a dry atmosphere. Fortunately, the thermodynamics of this reaction makes it possible to regenerate the drying agent. At 450 K, ΔS° contributes more to ΔG° than does ΔH°:

$$\Delta G^\circ_{450\text{ K}} = (-104.9\text{ kJ}) - (450\text{ K})(-290.2\text{ J/K})(10^{-3}\text{ kJ/J}) = +25.7\text{ kJ}$$

At this T, the reverse reaction is spontaneous. Calcium sulfate dihydrate can be converted to anhydrous calcium sulfate by placing it in a drying oven at 450 K. Then it can be cooled and returned to a desiccator, ready once more to act as a chemical sponge for water.

SECTION EXERCISES

13.4.1 Estimate ΔG° for the formation of gaseous water at $T = 373$ K.

13.4.2 Using Sample Problem 13-8, find the minimum partial pressure of N_2O_4 at which decomposition of N_2O_4 occurs, if T is 400 K and p of $NO_2 = 0.50$ atm.

13.4.3 Does a temperature exist at which the water formation reaction becomes nonspontaneous under standard pressure? If so, compute this T. If not, explain why in molecular terms.

13.5 SOME APPLICATIONS OF THERMODYNAMICS

NITROGEN FIXATION

The distribution of nitrogen between the Earth's crust and the atmosphere is very uneven. In the crust, nitrogen is present at the level of 19 parts per million (ppm) by mass, four orders of magnitude less than oxygen (4.55×10^5 ppm) and silicon (2.72×10^5 ppm). In contrast, 80% of the atmosphere is molecular nitrogen. Paradoxically, nitrogen is absolutely essential for all life, but the sea of atmospheric nitrogen is virtually inaccessible to higher life forms. Most biochemical systems lack the ability to break the strong triple bond between the nitrogen atoms in N_2. Molecular nitrogen must be converted to some other form, usually ammonia (NH_3) or nitrate (NO_3^-), before most life forms can incorporate nitrogen atoms into their biochemical molecules. This process, known as **nitrogen fixation,** is accomplished by various algae and bacteria, including a special group of bacteria that live in the roots of certain leguminous plants.

:N≡N:
Bond energy = 940 kJ/mol

The thermodynamics of nitrogen chemistry helps explain why nitrogen is so abundant in our atmosphere and yet remains inaccessible to most life forms. Table 13-4 shows that most of the abundant elements react with molecular oxygen under standard conditions. This is why many of the elements are encountered in the Earth's crust as their oxides. Nitrogen, however, is resistant to oxidation, as shown by the positive ΔG°_f for NO_2.

Because of their resistance to chemical attack, nitrogen atoms are not "locked up" in any solid or liquid substances as are other elements, such as Si, Al, Fe, and H. On the Earth the most stable form of the element nitrogen is a gaseous diatomic molecule. Therefore the element nitrogen is concentrated in the Earth's gaseous atmosphere even though it is only a trace element in overall abundance.

Every breath of air we take is 80% nitrogen, but our bodies must rely on the nitrogen found in the proteins we eat to supply the elemental nitrogen required for biosynthesis. In the plant kingdom, the most important sources of nitrogen are NH_3 and the ammonium cation (NH_4^+).

TABLE 13-4 SURFACE-ABUNDANT ELEMENTS AND THEIR OXIDES

ELEMENT	% BY MASS	OXIDE	ΔG°_f (kJ/mol)
O	49.1	O_2	0
Si	26.1	SiO_2	−856
Al	7.5	Al_2O_3	−1376
Fe	4.7	Fe_3O_4	−1013
Ca	3.4	CaO	−604
Na	2.6	Na_2O	−377
K	2.4	KO_2	−239
Mg	1.9	MgO	−570
H	0.88	H_2O	−237
Ti	0.58	TiO_2	−885
Cl	0.19	Cl_2O	+98
C	0.09	CO_2	−394
N	**<0.1**	**NO_2***	**+51**

* Several other oxides of nitrogen exist. All have even more positive free energies of formation than NO_2.

According to Table 13-4, chlorine (Cl) is also resistant to oxidation. Unlike nitrogen, however, chlorine reacts spontaneously with metals to generate such salts as NaCl and $MgCl_2$. Thus among abundant elements on Earth, nitrogen is uniquely stable in its elemental form.

Why is the nitrogen atom in NH_3 accessible to living organisms? Consider an organism synthesizing the amino acid glycine from its nitrogen-deficient precursor, acetic acid. In elemental terms, the net reaction is:

$$CH_3CO_2H + N + H \rightarrow H_2NCH_2CO_2H$$

Neither nitrogen nor hydrogen exists as free atoms, so the synthesis of glycine from acetic acid requires molecular sources of nitrogen and hydrogen. Atmospheric nitrogen and water are the most abundant sources of these two elements, but the production of glycine from N_2 and H_2O is significantly nonspontaneous under standard conditions:

$$CH_3CO_2H + \tfrac{1}{2} N_2 + \tfrac{1}{2} H_2O \rightarrow H_2NCH_2CO_2H + \tfrac{1}{4} O_2$$

$$\Delta G^\circ_{rxn} = (0.25 \text{ mol})(0 \text{ kJ/mol}) + (1 \text{ mol})(-367 \text{ kJ/mol}) - (1 \text{ mol})(-389 \text{ kJ/mol}) -$$

$$(0.5 \text{ mol})(-237 \text{ kJ/mol}) - (0.5 \text{ mol})(0 \text{ kJ/mol}) = +141 \text{ kJ}$$

On the other hand, NH_3 can provide nitrogen and hydrogen atoms. Each NH_3 molecule also contains two extra hydrogen atoms that can be "burned" to produce water:

$$CH_3CO_2H + NH_3 + O_2 \rightarrow H_2NCH_2CO_2H + H_2O$$

$$\Delta G^\circ_{rxn} = (1 \text{ mol})(-237 \text{ kJ/mol}) + (1 \text{ mol})(-367 \text{ kJ/mol}) - (1 \text{ mol})(-389 \text{ kJ/mol}) -$$

$$(1 \text{ mol})(-17 \text{ kJ/mol}) - (1 \text{ mol})(0 \text{ kJ/mol}) = -198 \text{ kJ}$$

This reaction is significantly spontaneous under standard conditions because it "couples" the production of water with the formation of the N—C bond in glycine.

The intensive agriculture that is characteristic of industrialized countries requires much more fixed nitrogen than is readily available from natural sources. Consequently, one of the major products of the chemical industry is nitrogen-containing fertilizers. Among the top 50 industrial chemicals, nitrogen gas (separated from air by cooling and liquefaction) perennially ranks number 2, with ammonia, nitric acid (HNO_3), urea [$(NH_2)_2CO$], and ammonium nitrate (NH_4NO_3) all in the top 13. All these chemicals are produced in huge amounts because of their roles in the fertilizer industry as feedstocks (nitrogen gas and nitric acid), as fertilizers (urea and ammonium nitrate), or as both (ammonia).

Free energies of formation suggest that ammonia and ammonium nitrate could be produced spontaneously in nature:

$$\tfrac{1}{2} N_{2(g)} + \tfrac{3}{2} H_{2(g)} \rightarrow NH_{3(g)} \qquad \Delta G^\circ_f = -16.45 \text{ kJ/mol}$$

$$N_{2(g)} + \tfrac{3}{2} O_{2(g)} + 2\, H_{2(g)} \rightarrow NH_4NO_{3(s)} \qquad \Delta G^\circ_f = -183.87 \text{ kJ/mol}$$

These reactions might occur in an atmosphere containing significant amounts of molecular hydrogen, but on Earth the only readily available source of hydrogen is water. The free energies of the reactions that yield NH_3 and NH_4NO_3 from gaseous nitrogen and water are highly unfavorable:

$$N_2 + 3\, H_2O \rightarrow 2\, NH_3 + \tfrac{3}{2} O_2 \qquad \Delta G^\circ_{rxn} = +655 \text{ kJ}$$

$$N_2 + 2\, H_2O + \tfrac{1}{2} O_2 \rightarrow NH_4NO_3 \qquad \Delta G^\circ_{rxn} = +274 \text{ kJ}$$

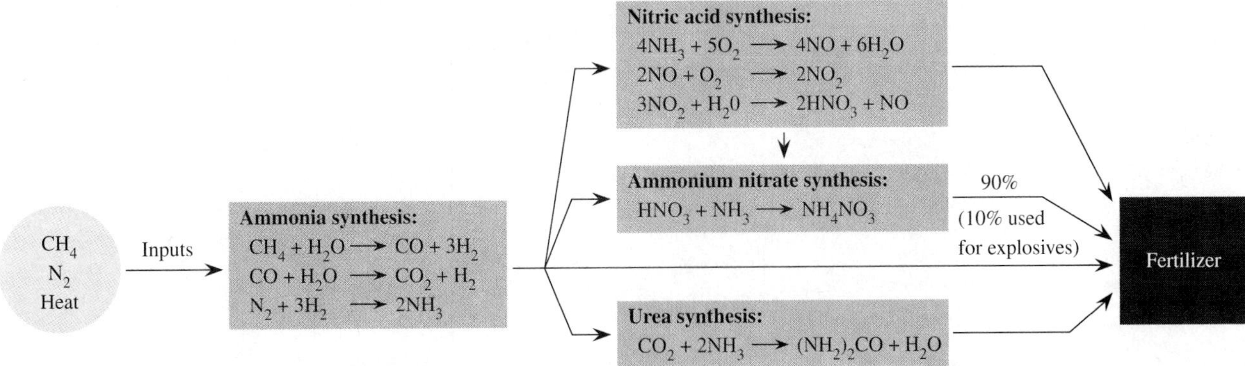

FIGURE 13-13
Block diagram of the industrial routes from nitrogen gas to fertilizers. Methane and energy in the form of heat are key ingredients in the first step.

Thus large energy costs are involved in generating fixed nitrogen.

The strategy used in fertilizer production is to synthesize molecular hydrogen from methane:

$$CH_4 + H_2O \rightarrow CO + 3\ H_2$$

$$\Delta G^\circ = +122.7 \text{ kJ} \qquad \Delta H^\circ = +206.5 \text{ kJ} \qquad \Delta S^\circ = +213.6 \text{ J/K}$$

Although this reaction is not spontaneous at room temperature, it becomes thermodynamically favorable at a temperature of 1000 K:

$$\Delta G^\circ_{1000\text{ K}} = +206.5 \text{ kJ} - (1000 \text{ K})(213.6 \text{ J/K})(10^{-3} \text{ kJ/J}) = -7.1 \text{ kJ}$$

To keep the temperature from falling while the endothermic reaction proceeds, heat energy must be supplied continuously. Otherwise, the temperature would quickly fall below the minimum value at which H_2 synthesis is spontaneous. For this reason, the production of H_2 (and ultimately of fertilizer) requires considerable amounts of energy. The energy cost is even greater if we consider that methane is obtained from nonrenewable reservoirs of natural gas, created over countless eons through the photosynthetic storage of solar energy.

With an ample supply of hydrogen, production of ammonia from N_2 becomes feasible:

$$N_2 + 3\ H_2 \rightarrow 2\ NH_3 \qquad \Delta G^\circ_{rxn} = -34 \text{ kJ}$$

Figure 13-13 shows sequences of other spontaneous reactions that lead from ammonia to nitric acid, urea, and ammonium nitrate.

PHASE DIAGRAMS

All phase changes display similar thermodynamic characteristics. In any change from a more ordered phase to a less ordered phase, the enthalpy and entropy of a substance increase. Enthalpy increases because the molecules of the substance must gain energy to overcome the intermolecular forces that hold them in the more ordered phase. Entropy increases because the molecules are more randomly distributed in the less ordered phase. Thus as illustrated in Figure 13-14, when a solid melts or sublimes or a liquid vaporizes, ΔH and ΔS are positive.

As shown in Section 13.4, the spontaneous direction of a process depends on the temperature when ΔH and ΔS have the same sign. At low T, enthalpy dominates ΔG,

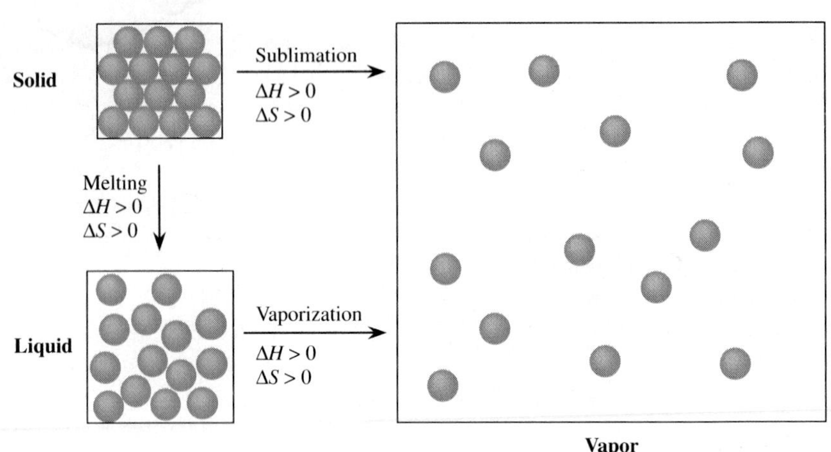

FIGURE 13-14
Schematic view of the three phase changes leading from more-ordered to less-ordered phases. Each is accompanied by positive enthalpy and entropy changes for the substance.

and the exothermic direction is spontaneous. At high T, entropy dominates ΔG, and the direction that increases system disorder is spontaneous. At one characteristic T, $\Delta G = 0$ and the phase change can proceed in either direction.

The spontaneous direction of a phase change also depends on pressure, primarily because the molar entropy of a gas exhibits a strong P dependence:

$$S_{gas} = S^{\circ} - R\ ln\ P_{gas}$$

$$\Delta G_{vap} = \Delta H_{vap} - T\Delta S_{vap} = \Delta H_{vap} - T\Delta S^{\circ}_{vap} + RT\ ln\ P_{gas}$$

Vapor pressure was first introduced in Chapter 5. The vapor pressure of water at various temperatures appears in Table 5-4.

At any temperature, a pressure exists at which $\Delta G_{vap} = 0$. This P is the vapor pressure (vp) of the substance at that temperature. At the normal boiling point of a substance, $vp_{gas} = 1.00$ atm. At lower temperatures, $vp_{gas} < 1.00$ atm. For example, the vapor pressure of water at 25 °C is 23.756 torr.

The variations of phase stability with temperature and pressure can be described succinctly using graphs called **phase diagrams.** A phase diagram is a P-T graph that shows the domains in which each phase is stable. Figure 13-15 shows the phase diagram for water.

A phase diagram consists of areas in which each phase is stable, separated by boundary lines that indicate the conditions under which phase changes occur. Anywhere along a boundary line, the phases on either side of that line can coexist. For example, Figure 13-15 shows that liquid and solid water can coexist at

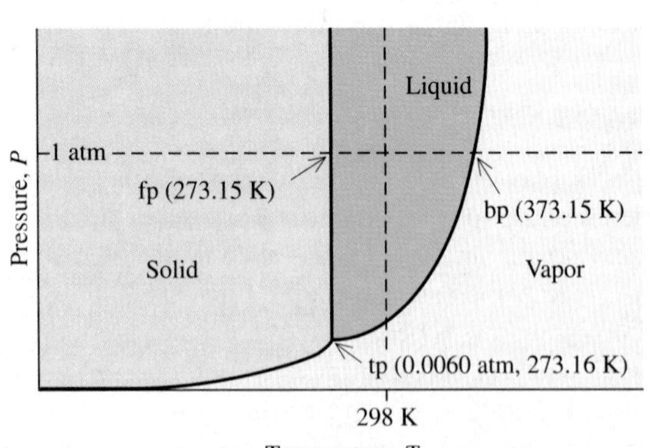

FIGURE 13-15
The phase diagram for water, showing the conditions under which each of the three phases is stable. Arrows indicate the triple point (*tp*), normal freezing point (*fp*), and normal boiling point (*bp*).

$T = 273.15$ K and $P = 1.00$ atm. By convention, phase diagrams are constructed with P plotted on the Y axis and T on the X axis. Thus a horizontal line across a phase diagram represents a change of temperature at constant pressure, and a vertical line represents a change of pressure at constant temperature.

A phase diagram is a map of the pressure-temperature world that depicts much information about the phase behavior of a substance. Features that can be read from the phase diagram for water in Figure 13-15 include the following:

1. As water is cooled from 400 K at constant $P = 1.00$ atm (dashed horizontal line in Figure 13-15), it remains in the gas phase until $T = 373.15$ K, when it condenses to a liquid. Water then remains liquid until $T = 273.15$ K, when it freezes to a solid.
2. As pressure on water at 298 K is reduced below 1.00 atm (dashed vertical line in Figure 13-15), water remains a liquid until pressure falls below 0.03 atm, at which point it vaporizes. The pressure at which the phase change occurs is the vapor pressure of water at 298 K.
3. The three boundary lines meet in a single point at $T = 273.16$ K and $P = 0.006$ atm. At this unique point, called the **triple point,** all three phases are stable simultaneously. Notice that, although *two* phases are stable under any of the conditions specified by the boundary lines, *three* phases can be stable simultaneously only at the triple point.
4. When P is lower than 0.006 atm, there is no temperature at which water is stable as a liquid. At low pressure, ice sublimes but does not melt.
5. The solid-vapor boundary line extrapolates to $P = 0$, and $T = 0$. This is a consequence of the direct link between temperature and molecular energy. At $T = 0$ K, molecules have no thermal energy, so they cannot escape from the solid lattice. At 0 K, the vapor pressure of every substance would be 0 atm.
6. The temperature at which vapor condenses depends strongly on pressure. Increasing the pressure on a gas decreases its entropy, which in turn results in a decrease in ΔS_{phase}. Along the boundary lines, $\Delta G_{\text{phase}} = 0$. Thus a decrease in ΔS_{phase} must be accompanied by an increase in temperature to maintain the condition, $\Delta G_{\text{phase}} = 0 = \Delta H_{\text{phase}} - T\Delta S_{\text{phase}}$.
7. The temperature at which melting occurs is almost independent of pressure because neither ΔH_{phase} nor ΔS_{phase} shows a significant P dependence for transformations between condensed phases. Thus ΔG_{phase} is almost independent of *P; the* boundary line between solid and liquid is nearly vertical.

All phase diagrams share these common features, but the detailed appearance changes from substance to substance according to the strength of intermolecular interactions. Figure 13-16 shows two additional examples, the phase diagrams for carbon dioxide and molecular nitrogen. Both these substances are gases under normal conditions. Unlike H_2O, whose triple point lies close to 298 K, both CO_2 and N_2 have triple points well below room temperature. Although both are gases at room temperature and pressure, they behave differently when cooled at $P = 1$ atm. Molecular nitrogen liquefies at 77 K and then solidifies at 63 K, whereas carbon dioxide condenses directly to the solid phase at 195 K. This difference in behavior arises because the triple point of CO_2, unlike those of H_2O and N_2, occurs at a P greater than 1 atm. The phase diagram of CO_2 shows that at a pressure of 1 atm, no T exists at which the liquid phase is stable.

Accurate phase diagrams are determined from measured temperatures and pressures at which phase changes occur, reinforced by thermodynamic calculations of temperatures and pressures at which $\Delta G_{\text{phase}} = 0$. Approximate phase diagrams such as those shown in Figures 13-15 and 13-16 can be constructed from the triple point, normal melting point, and normal boiling point of a substance. Sample Problem 13-9 illustrates this procedure.

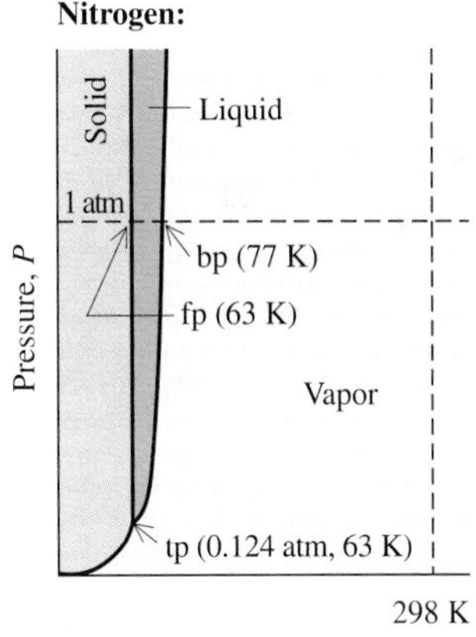

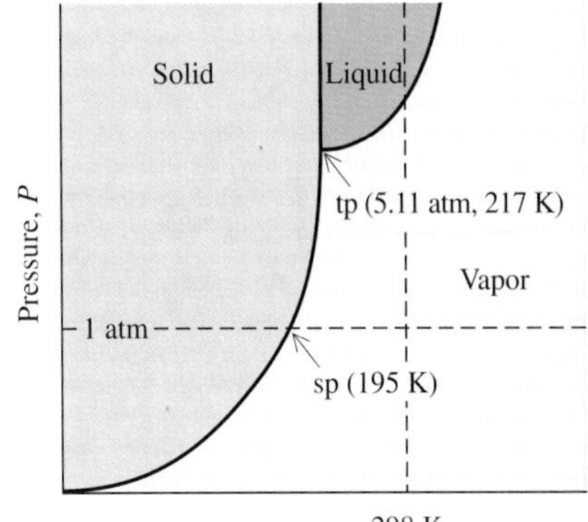

FIGURE 13-16
Phase diagrams for nitrogen and carbon dioxide, two substances that are gases at room temperature and pressure. Arrows indicate the triple point (*tp*), normal freezing point (*fp*), normal boiling point (*bp*), and normal sublimation point (*sp*).

BOX 13-3

WOULD YOU BUY THIS MACHINE?

Every so often, advertisements appear for some fantastic machine that generates useful work continuously without requiring any fuel. If such a machine really worked, it would indeed be fantastic because it would violate the second law of thermodynamics. To show this, we must analyze the entropy changes that accompany work.

Any machine that runs continuously must go through a *cycle*. The machine does useful work in one part of its cycle, but it must then be returned to its starting point in the rest of the cycle. If the machine does not return to its starting point, it cannot operate continuously because eventually it will "run down," reaching some final state from which it cannot go any further. The machine, which we define to be the *system*, must return to the same state at the start of each cycle. Because entropy is a state function, S of the machine at the end of a cycle must be the same as it was at the start of the cycle. In other words, the machine undergoes no net change in entropy as it goes through a cycle: $\Delta S_{\text{machine, cycle}} = 0$.

A machine that does useful work drives some part of the surroundings in a nonspontaneous direction. It may compress a gas, pump water uphill, generate electricity, and so on. In doing useful work, a system creates order in the surroundings, so in the part of the cycle where the machine accomplishes useful work, $\Delta S_{\text{surroundings}}$ is negative. Because $\Delta S_{\text{machine}} = 0$ for each cycle, $\Delta S_{\text{universe}}$ would be negative for the entire cycle unless there is a large positive ΔS for the surroundings in the part of the cycle that does not accomplish useful work. Otherwise, the machine would violate the second law of thermodynamics, which requires that $\Delta S_{\text{universe}}$ always be positive.

How do cyclical machines work, given that they must have $\Delta S_{\text{machine, cycle}} = 0$ but produce order in their surroundings? As the diagram indicates, they accomplish useful work by producing heat, which generates disorder in some other part of the surroundings. The gasoline engine is an excellent example. To power an automobile, pump water, or generate electricity, the gasoline engine burns fuel, releasing much energy. Some of this energy does work that decreases S of one part of the surroundings, but much of the energy goes into heat that increases S of other parts of the surroundings. Any cyclical machine must release enough heat to the surroundings to offset the decrease in S caused by doing useful work. Although you might think that an optimally efficient engine would not produce heat, the second law requires that at least enough heat be generated to ensure that S_{universe} increases.

To generate order (work) in one part of the universe, any machine must simultaneously produce more disorder in another part of the universe. Usually, this is accomplished by dissipating energy as heat. If the machine is going to operate continuously, it must consume fuel as its source of this energy. Thus, something called a *perpetual motion machine* cannot exist.

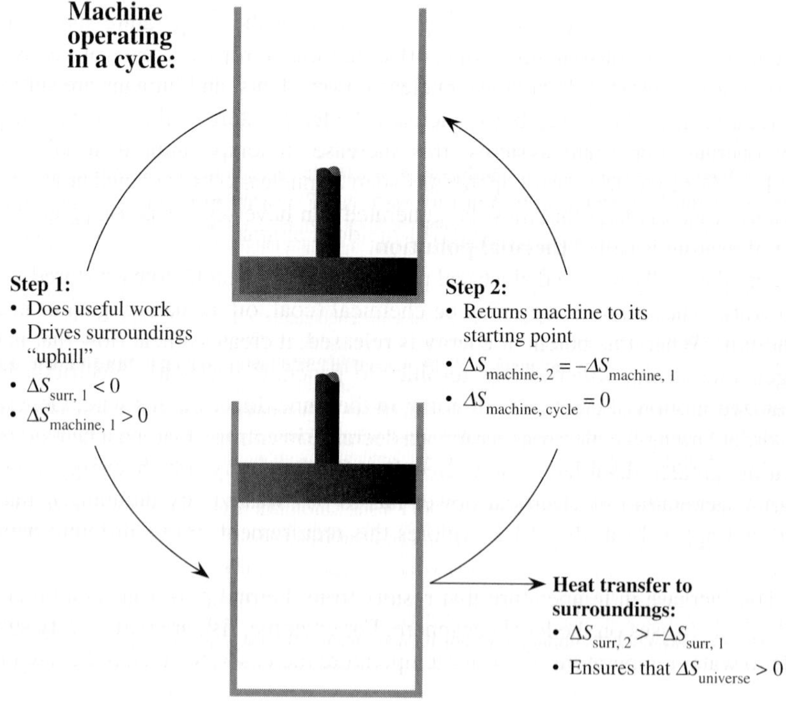

Machine operating in a cycle:
Step 1:
• Does useful work
• Drives surroundings "uphill"
• $\Delta S_{\text{surr, 1}} < 0$
• $\Delta S_{\text{machine, 1}} > 0$
Step 2:
• Returns machine to its starting point
• $\Delta S_{\text{machine, 2}} = -\Delta S_{\text{machine, 1}}$
• $\Delta S_{\text{machine, cycle}} = 0$
Heat transfer to surroundings:
• $\Delta S_{\text{surr, 2}} > -\Delta S_{\text{surr, 1}}$
• Ensures that $\Delta S_{\text{universe}} > 0$

increases. At the same time, however, the amount of oxygen available to supply metabolic demands of fish decreases because oxygen is less soluble in warm water than in cold water. Species such as trout, which thrive in cold water, die if water temperature rises by more than a few degrees. The ecology of lower aquatic life forms is also highly sensitive to temperature. Plankton that provide the food base for many aquatic ecosystems thrive at temperatures in the 14 to 24 °C range. When water temperatures exceed 24 °C, blue-green algae crowd out these essential plankton, leading to serious disruption of the ecological balance.

Hydroelectric generation of electricity need not lead to thermal pollution because gravitational energy can drive turbines with minimum generation of heat. Unfortunately, there are other detrimental ecological consequences of hydroelectric power plants, such as the flooding of vast natural habitats, disruption of rivers and streams, and changes in local weather patterns caused by the creation of a huge body of water. Although these effects are perhaps less destructive than thermal pollution, no truly "clean" power source seems to exist. The second law of thermodynamics states that a price must always be paid for generating order. Inevitably, human existence generates order, so we pay this price continually. Conservation measures minimize the thermodynamic costs, but these costs can never be eliminated completely.

SECTION EXERCISES

13.5.1 Atmospheric nitrogen can be transformed to ammonia by various nitrogen-fixing bacteria. The overall process is complicated, but the net reaction can be written as:

$$N_2 + 3\,H_2O \rightarrow 2\,NH_3 + \tfrac{3}{2}\,O_2$$

Assuming standard conditions (not quite true, but close enough for approximations), how much free energy must the bacteria consume to fix 1 mol of N atoms?

13.5.2 Refer to the phase diagrams in this chapter to answer the following questions:

a. What is the maximum pressure at which solid N_2 can sublime?

b. What happens if the pressure above ice at −10 °C is reduced to 0.5 atm, to 0.05 atm, and finally to 0.005 atm?

c. What occurs if "dry ice" (solid CO_2) is heated from 180 K to room temperature in a container held at constant pressure of 7.0 atm?

13.5.3 All automobile engines operate at relatively high temperature and require continual cooling. Using our description of thermal pollution, explain how the second law of thermodynamics requires automobile engines to "dump" heat to their surroundings.

13.6 BIOENERGETICS

Life creates order out of chaos, but our exploration of thermodynamics has shown that any spontaneous process must increase the total amount of disorder in the universe. To generate order in a system, it is necessary to release stored energy as heat, which increases the disorder of the surroundings. Consequently, living things must use large amounts of energy to survive. The plant kingdom extracts energy from sunlight to fuel its organizational processes. The animal kingdom, on the other hand, uses the chemical energy stored in plants or other animals to drive its organizational efforts. In this section we describe a few of the energy cycles that operate in plants and animals.

BIOCHEMICAL ENERGY PRODUCTION

Living organisms use carbohydrates as their source of energy. Plants make their own carbohydrates through photosynthesis. Animals, on the other hand, obtain carbohydrates by eating plants or other animals. Plants and animals transform carbohydrates into fats, which also can be used as sources of energy. The extraction of chemical energy from these compounds is called **metabolism.**

Metabolism involves highly spontaneous oxidation reactions, as illustrated by glucose (a carbohydrate) and palmitic acid (a fat):

Glucose and other important carbohydrates are discussed in Section 11.6.

$$\text{Glucose: } C_6H_{12}O_6 + 6\,O_2 \rightarrow 6\,CO_2 + 6\,H_2O \qquad \Delta G^\circ = -2870 \text{ kJ}$$

$$\text{Palmitic acid: } C_{15}H_{31}CO_2H + 23\,O_2 \rightarrow 16\,CO_2 + 16\,H_2O \qquad \Delta G^\circ = -9790 \text{ kJ}$$

Palmitic acid:

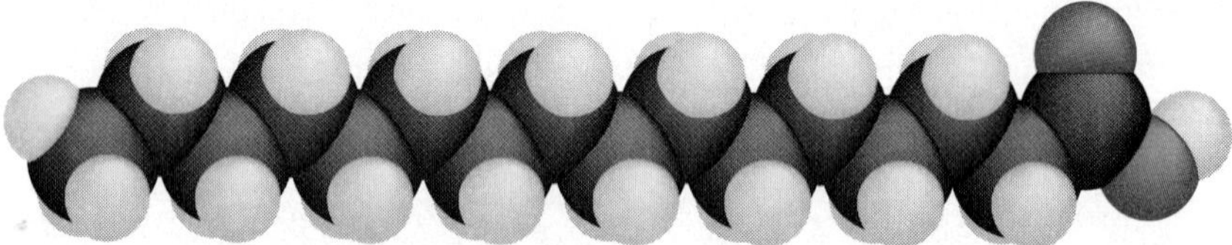

The negative standard free energy changes of these reactions arise because the relatively weak O=O bond in molecular oxygen is converted into stronger O—H and C=O bonds in H_2O and CO_2. Entropy also favors these reactions because gaseous oxygen converts a solid into gaseous CO_2 and liquid H_2O. Not only are the products in more disordered phases, but there are also more molecules on the product side of the equation than on the side of the starting materials.

The large amount of energy stored in molecules such as glucose and palmitic acid means that a little fat or carbohydrate goes a long way as a fuel for life processes. However, a living cell would be destroyed quickly if all the energy stored in these molecules were released in a single reaction. To utilize energy-rich molecules without being destroyed, cells use elaborate chains of sequential reactions that allow this stored energy to be harvested a little at a time. Part of this energy is released as heat that maintains our constant body temperature as it is dissipated to the surroundings. Another portion of the energy is stored in other high-energy molecules that the body uses as "power sources" for the many reactions that occur within cells. In addition to storing the energy produced in metabolism, these high-energy species serve as energy transport molecules, moving to different regions of the cell where energy is required for cell functions.

The most important of these energy transport molecules is **adenosine triphosphate (ATP).** Some of the energy released during the oxidation of glucose is used to drive a condensation reaction in which adenosine diphosphate (ADP) and phosphoric acid link together and eliminate water. This reaction stores chemical energy, as indicated by its positive standard free energy change:

$$\text{ADP} + H_3PO_4 \rightarrow \text{ATP} + H_2O \qquad \Delta G^\circ = +30.6 \text{ kJ}$$

The molecular details of this reaction are illustrated in Figure 13-17. Although ATP is a complex molecule, notice that the adenosine portion does not change as this reaction occurs. The condensation reaction merely adds an additional phosphate group to the end of an existing chain.

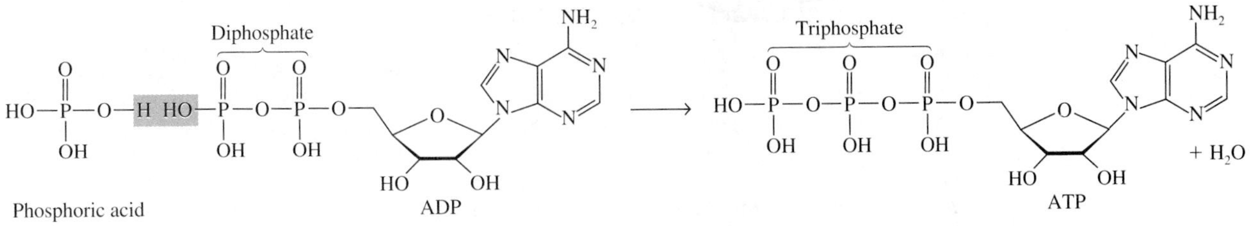

Diphosphate
Phosphoric acid
ADP
Triphosphate
ATP
$+ H_2O$

FIGURE 13-17
Phosphoric acid reacts with ADP to produce water and ATP. Because a P—O—P linkage is weaker than a P—O—H linkage, this reaction is endothermic by about 30 kJ/mol. Notice that the adenosine portion of the molecule remains intact during this reaction.

The exact processes by which carbohydrates and fats are converted to CO_2 and H_2O depend on the conditions and the particular needs of the cell. Each possible route involves a complex series of chemical reactions, many of which are accompanied by the conversion of ADP to ATP. Glucose, for example, can convert as many as 36 ADP molecules into ATP molecules as it is oxidized to CO_2 and H_2O:

$$C_6H_{12}O_6 + 6\ O_2 + 36\ ADP + 36\ H_3PO_4 \rightarrow 6\ CO_2 + 36\ ATP + 42\ H_2O$$

The right-hand portion of the ATP molecule is adenosine. It contains adenine, an important biochemical building block introduced in Section 11.7.

COUPLED REACTIONS

Cells use the energy stored in ATP molecules to drive reactions that would otherwise be nonspontaneous under physiological conditions. This is accomplished by coupling the nonspontaneous reaction with the conversion of ATP back to ADP and phosphoric acid:

$$ATP + H_2O \rightarrow ADP + H_3PO_4 \qquad \Delta G^o = -30.6\ kJ$$

Coupled reactions share a common intermediate that transfers energy from one reaction to the other. For example, the amino acid glutamine is synthesized in cells by reacting ammonia with another amino acid, glutamic acid.

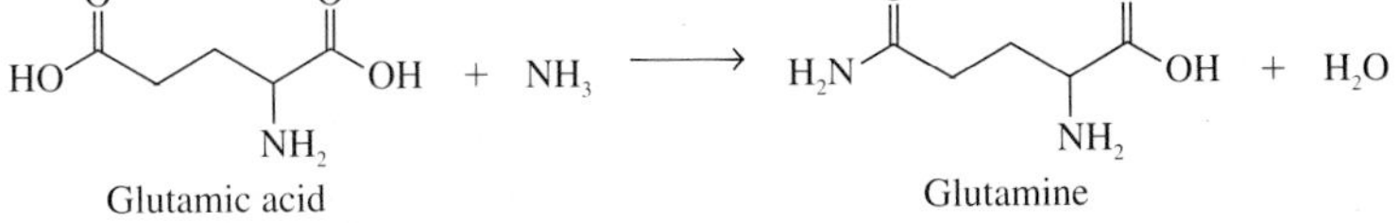

Glutamic acid $+ NH_3 \longrightarrow$ Glutamine $+ H_2O$

This reaction is thermodynamically unfavorable, $\Delta G^o = +14$ kJ. The reaction is driven by coupling it with the conversion of ATP into ADP.

$$\text{Glutamic acid} + NH_3 \rightarrow \text{Glutamine} + H_2O$$

$$ATP + H_2O \rightarrow ADP + H_3PO_4$$

$$\textit{Net:}\quad \text{Glutamic acid} + ATP + NH_3 \rightarrow \text{Glutamine} + ADP + H_3PO_4$$

The net energy change for the coupled process is the sum of the ΔG^o values for the individual reactions:

$$\Delta G^o_{rxn} = \Delta G^o_{glutamine} + \Delta G^o_{ATP} = 14\ kJ + (-30.6\ kJ) = -17\ kJ$$

The negative value of ΔG^o_{rxn} shows that the free energy released in the ATP reaction is more than enough to drive the conversion of glutamic acid into glutamine.

Although the coupled reactions can be represented by the net reaction, this process actually occurs in steps. In the first step of the coupled reaction, a phosphate group is transferred from ATP to glutamic acid:

$$HO{-}P(=O)(OH){-}O{-}ADP + HO_2C{-}CH_2CH_2CH(NH_2){-}CO_2H \longrightarrow HO{-}P(=O)(OH){-}O{-}C(=O)CH_2CH_2CH(NH_2){-}CO_2H + ADP$$

Glutamic acid

Next, an ammonia molecule reacts with the phosphorylated form of glutamic acid, producing phosphoric acid and glutamine:

$$NH_3 + HO{-}P(=O)(OH){-}O{-}C(=O)CH_2CH_2CH(NH_2){-}CO_2H \longrightarrow H_3PO_4 + H_2N{-}C(=O)CH_2CH_2CH(NH_2){-}CO_2H$$

Phosphorylated glutamic acid

Overall, one molecule of ATP is converted to ADP and phosphoric acid for each molecule of glutamine produced from glutamic acid.

Coupled biochemical reactions occur on the surface of an enzyme. As we describe in Chapter 11, enzymes are huge proteins that catalyze an immense variety of biochemical reactions. The surface area of an enzyme has a particular shape that accommodates the various molecules that must react in a coupled reaction.

A catalyst is a chemical species that makes a reaction go faster than it would in the absence of a catalyst. Enzymes and other catalysts are discussed in Chapter 14.

Coupled reactions are also involved in the synthesis of ATP. Sample Problem 13-11 illustrates one of these energy-storing reactions.

SAMPLE PROBLEM 13-11 ATP-FORMING REACTIONS

One of the biochemical reactions that produces ATP involves the conversion of acetyl phosphate to acetic acid and phosphoric acid:

$$CH_3C(=O){-}O{-}P(=O)(OH){-}OH + H_2O \longrightarrow CH_3C(=O)OH + H_3PO_4 \qquad \Delta G^\circ = -46.9\ \text{kJ/mol}$$

Acetyl phosphate — Acetic acid

Write the overall balanced equation, and show that the coupled reaction is spontaneous.

Although the standard free energy change of the ADP/ATP reaction is 30.6 kJ/mol under *standard* conditions, the concentrations of the phosphate species in cells are far from 1 M. This causes the free energy to vary from its standard value. Typically, the conversion of ATP to ADP *in a living cell* releases around 50 kJ/mol of energy.

METHOD: A coupled process links a spontaneous reaction with a nonspontaneous one. In this case the energy released in the acetyl phosphate reaction provides the energy needed to drive the conversion of ADP to ATP.

Combining the two reactions gives the overall balanced equation:

$$\begin{array}{c} \text{Acetyl phosphate} \qquad\qquad \text{Acetic acid} \\ CH_3CO_2PO_3H_2 + \cancel{H_2O} \rightarrow CH_3CO_2H + \cancel{H_3PO_4} \\ ADP + \cancel{H_3PO_4} \rightarrow ATP + \cancel{H_2O} \\ \hline \textit{Net}: CH_3CO_2PO_3H_2 + ADP \rightarrow CH_3CO_2H + ATP \end{array}$$

The net energy change for the coupled process is the sum of the ΔG° values for the individual reactions:

$$\Delta G^\circ_{rxn} = \Delta G^\circ_{\text{acetyl phosphate}} + \Delta G^\circ_{ATP} = -46.9\ \text{kJ} + 30.6\ \text{kJ} = -16.3\ \text{kJ}$$

The negative value of ΔG°_{rxn} shows that the free energy released in the acetyl phosphate reaction is more than enough to drive the conversion of ADP to ATP.

ENERGY EFFICIENCY

Cells store the energy that is released during the oxidation of glucose by converting ADP into ATP. The storage process cannot be perfectly efficient, however, because each step in the reaction sequence must have a negative free energy change. In practical terms, this requires that some energy be released to the surroundings as heat.

The complete balanced equation for glucose oxidation coupled with ATP production under normal physiological conditions is:

$$C_6H_{12}O_6 + 6\ O_2 + 36\ ADP + 36\ H_3PO_4 \rightarrow 6\ CO_2 + 42\ H_2O + 36\ ATP$$

According to this equation, the oxidation of 1 mol glucose yields 36 mol ATP. We can determine the overall free energy change for this process from the values for its uncoupled parts:

$$C_6H_{12}O_6 + 6\ O_2 \rightarrow 6\ CO_2 + 6\ H_2O \qquad \Delta G^\circ = -2870\ \text{kJ}$$

$$36\ (ADP + H_3PO_4 \rightarrow ATP + H_2O) \qquad \Delta G^\circ = (36\ \text{mol})(-30.6\ \text{kJ/mol}) = +1100\ \text{kJ}$$

$$\Delta G_{\text{overall}} = -2870\ \text{kJ} + 1100\ \text{kJ} = -1770\ \text{kJ}$$

Although 1100 kJ of energy is stored in this coupled process, 1770 kJ of energy is "wasted." Thus cells harness 38% of the chemical energy stored in glucose to drive the biochemical machinery of metabolism. The remaining 62% is dissipated as heat, raising the entropy of the surroundings as the living cell organizes itself and its immediate environment.

Fats such as palmitic acid are metabolized through pathways similar to the ones used for the oxidation of glucose. The complete oxidation of 1 mol of palmitic acid molecule liberates 9790 kJ of free energy and produces 130 ATP molecules. You should be able to verify that this metabolic process has about the same efficiency as the oxidation of glucose.

One mole of glucose releases 2870 kJ of free energy, whereas one mole of palmitic acid releases much more free energy, 9790 kJ. Although some of this extra energy results from its larger molecular size, palmitic acid also releases more energy per atom of carbon than glucose. Glucose oxidation releases about 480 kJ/mol of carbon atoms, whereas palmitic acid releases about 610 kJ/mol of carbon atoms. Organisms convert carbohydrates into fats because fats store more energy per unit mass.

SECTION EXERCISES

13.6.1 Nitrogen-fixing bacteria react N_2 with H_2O to produce NH_3 and O_2 using ATP as their energy source. Approximately 24 molecules of ATP are consumed per molecule of N_2 fixed. What percentage of the free energy derived from ATP is stored in NH_3?

13.6.2 The hydrolysis of ATP to ADP has $\Delta H^\circ = -21.0$ kJ/mol, whereas $\Delta G^\circ = -30.6$ kJ/mol at 298 K. Calculate ΔS° for this reaction. What happens to the spontaneity of this reaction as the temperature is increased to 37 °C?

13.6.3 In running a mile, an average person consumes about 500 kJ of energy.

a. How many moles of ATP does this represent?

b. Assuming 38% conversion efficiency, how many grams of glucose must be "burned"?

CHAPTER SUMMARY

1. In thermodynamics, *spontaneous* refers to the preferred direction of a process. Spontaneous processes may be exothermic or endothermic, but the amount of disorder in the universe increases in every spontaneous process.
2. Entropy is a measure of the amount of disorder, and the second law of thermodynamics states that the total entropy of the universe always increases.
3. The entropy change accompanying a constant-temperature process equals the heat flow divided by the temperature. Heat always flows from warmer objects to cooler objects.
4. The entropy of an object increases as its temperature increases. Entropies also vary with the logarithm of concentration.
5. At 0 K, pure, perfect crystals are perfectly ordered and have no entropy. Based on this zero point, it is possible to determine absolute entropies for pure substances at any temperature. Absolute entropies are always positive.
6. Standard molar entropies can be used to calculate the entropy change that accompanies a chemical reaction.
7. Free energy is defined by $G = H - TS$. The free energy change for a system at constant temperature and pressure is always negative.
8. Free energy changes for chemical reactions depend strongly on the value of the concentration quotient (Q), which is the ratio of product concentrations to reactant concentrations, all raised to powers equal to their stoichiometric coefficients.
9. The formation of nitrogen compounds from molecular nitrogen is nonspontaneous unless it is coupled with other highly spontaneous processes.
10. Phase diagrams summarize the thermodynamics of phase behavior.
11. Large-scale conversion of fuel into electricity inevitably results in thermal pollution around the power plant.
12. Many biological processes lead to increased order and are nonspontaneous unless coupled to energy-releasing, disordering reactions. Living organisms utilize energy-rich substances, including fats, carbohydrates, and adenosine triphosphate (ATP).

KEY TERMS

disorder
order
spontaneous direction

absolute entropy
concentration quotient (Q)
entropy (S)
free energy (G)
second law of thermodynamics
standard molar free energy of formation ($\Delta G^o{}_f$)
third law of thermodynamics

nitrogen fixation
phase diagram
thermal pollution
triple point

adenosine triphosphate (ATP)
coupled reactions
metabolism

SKILLS TO MASTER

- Assessing molecular disorder and entropy
- Calculating entropy changes at constant temperature
- Calculating entropy changes with concentration
- Calculating reaction entropies
- Determining spontaneity from change in free energy (ΔG)
- Estimating changes in ΔG with temperature
- Calculating changes in ΔG with concentration
- Drawing and interpreting phase diagrams
- Estimating energy efficiencies of biological reactions

LEARNING EXERCISES

13.1 Prepare a summary of two pages or less that describes all the important features of this chapter.

13.2 Describe the thermodynamic criteria for spontaneity.

13.3 Describe in your own words what entropy is and why it is not a conserved quantity.

13.4 Make a list of everyday processes that illustrate that disorder always increases.

13.5 Write a paragraph that explains why living creatures must convert some stored energy into heat in the course of their activities.

13.6 Update your list of memory bank equations. Write a sentence that describes the restrictions on each equation.

13.7 Make a list of all terms new to you that appear in Chapter 13. Using your own words, write a one-sentence definition for each. Consult the Glossary if you need help.

PROBLEMS

SPONTANEITY

13.1 Describe the order-disorder qualities of the following processes:
(a) Ocean waves wash away a sand castle.
(b) A secretary "straightens up" the boss' desk.
(c) A bundle of the child's game "pick up sticks" is dropped to the floor.
(d) A skilled mechanic reassembles a torn-down engine.

13.2 Describe the order-disorder aspects of the following chemical processes:
(a) Water and acetone, two liquids, mix to form a liquid solution.
(b) Wood burns, producing CO_2 and H_2O vapors.
(c) I_2 crystals form as a hot solution of I_2 in CCl_4 cools.

13.3 The following figures shows what happens when a drop of ink is added to a beaker of water. Using ideas of organization and disorganization, explain what is occurring.

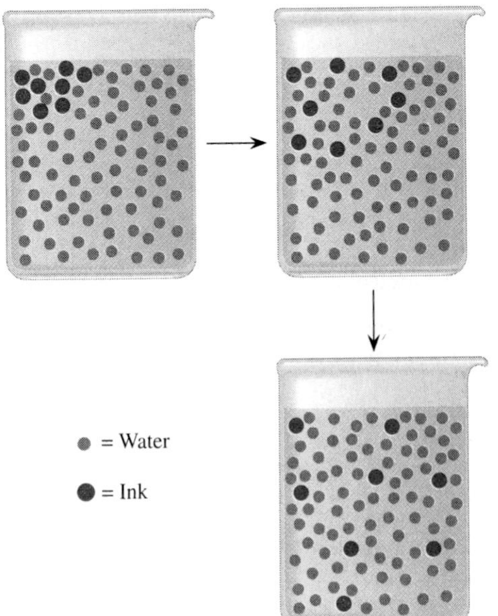

13.4 "All the king's horses and all the king's men couldn't put Humpty together again." Describe Humpty-Dumpty's fate using ideas of organization and disorganization.

13.5 Explain each of the following observations from the order-disorder perspective:
(a) A puncture causes a tire to deflate.
(b) An open bottle of perfume on a table eventually fills the room with the fragrance of the perfume.

ENTROPY, THE MEASURE OF DISORDER

13.6 Solid CO_2 (dry ice) sublimes at 195 K with ΔH_{subl} = 25.2 kJ/mol. A block of dry ice with a mass of 27.5 g sublimes in a room whose temperature is 26.5 °C.
(a) What is the entropy change (ΔS) of the CO_2?
(b) What is the ΔS of the room?
(c) What is the overall ΔS?

13.7 A piece of dry ice at T = 195 K is dropped into a beaker containing water at T = 273.15 K. You may assume that all resulting CO_2 vapor escapes into the atmosphere.
(a) Describe the process that occurs.
(b) Calculate the overall entropy change if 12.5 g of dry ice undergoes this process.

13.8 What are the signs of ΔS for the system and for the surroundings in each of the following processes:
(a) Ice forms on the surface of a birdbath in winter.
(b) A hot cup of coffee cools when left to stand.
(c) A popsicle melts when left on a table.

13.9 Calculate the entropy change of 15.5 g of steam that condenses to liquid water at 373.15 K. Without doing additional calculations, what can you say about the entropy change of the surroundings?

13.10 Molar heats of vaporization of several substances can be found in Table 12-6. Calculate the molar entropy of vaporization at the normal boiling point for (a) oxygen; (b) ethane; (c) benzene; and (d) mercury.

ENTROPIES OF SUBSTANCES

13.11 Determine the sign of ΔS for the system for each of the following changes:
(a) A soft drink is chilled in an ice chest.
(b) The air in a bicycle pump is compressed.
(c) A carton of juice concentrate is mixed with water.

13.12 For each of the following pairs of substances, determine which has the larger molar entropy at 298 K, and state the main reason for the difference: (a) Br_2 and Cl_2; (b) Ni and Pt; (c) C_5H_{12} (pentane, liquid) and C_8H_{18} (octane, liquid); and (d) SiH_4 and CH_4 (both gases).

13.13 For each of the following pairs of substances, determine which has the larger molar entropy at 298 K, and state the main reason for the difference: (a) $HgO_{(s)}$ and $HgS_{(s)}$; (b) $NaCl_{(aq)}$ and $MgCl_{2\,(aq)}$; and (c) $Br_{2\,(l)}$ and $I_{2\,(s)}$.

13.14 Mercury, water, and bromine are all liquids at standard temperature. Their molar entropies are in the sequence $H_2O < Hg < Br_2$. Using molecular properties, explain why bromine is more disordered than mercury but water is the most highly ordered of these three.

13.15 Using tabulated values of $S°$, calculate the standard entropy per mole of *atoms* for He, H_2, CH_4, and C_3H_8. Explain the trend that you find in terms of what bond formation does to atomic order.

13.16 Compute the standard entropy change for the following reactions:
(a) $2\,H_{2\,(g)} + O_{2\,(g)} \rightarrow 2\,H_2O_{(l)}$
(b) $C_{(s)} + 2\,H_{2\,(g)} \rightarrow CH_{4\,(g)}$
(c) $C_2H_5OH_{(l)} + 3\,O_{2\,(g)} \rightarrow 2\,CO_{2\,(g)} + 3\,H_2O_{(l)}$
(d) $Fe_2O_{3\,(s)} + 2\,Al_{(s)} \rightarrow Al_2O_{3\,(s)} + 2\,Fe_{(s)}$

13.17 Compute the standard entropy change for the following reactions:
(a) $N_{2\,(g)} + 3\,H_{2\,(g)} \rightarrow 2\,NH_{3\,(g)}$
(b) $3\,O_{2\,(g)} \rightarrow 2\,O_{3\,(g)}$
(c) $PbO_{2\,(s)} + 2\,Ni_{(s)} \rightarrow Pb_{(s)} + 2\,NiO_{(s)}$
(d) $C_2H_{4\,(g)} + 3\,O_{2\,(g)} \rightarrow 2\,CO_{2\,(g)} + 2\,H_2O_{(l)}$

13.18 For each reaction in Problem 13.16, explain what features of the disorder of reactants and products account for the magnitude and sign of $\Delta S°$.

13.19 For each reaction in Problem 13.17, explain what features of the disorder of reactants and products account for the magnitude and sign of $\Delta S°$.

13.20 Compute the absolute entropy of (a) 1.00 mol of molecular hydrogen gas at $p = 5.0$ atm; (b) 0.25 mol of propane gas at $p = 0.10$ atm; and (c) 1.00 mol of a mixture of N_2 ($p = 125$ atm) and H_2 ($p = 375$ atm).

13.21 The diagram represents two flasks connected by a valve. Each flask contains a different gas.
(a) If the valve is opened, the two gases can move back and forth between the two flasks. Redraw the figure to show the system at maximum entropy.
(b) Redraw the figure in a way that shows the state of the system at its lowest possible entropy (the substances need not remain gaseous).

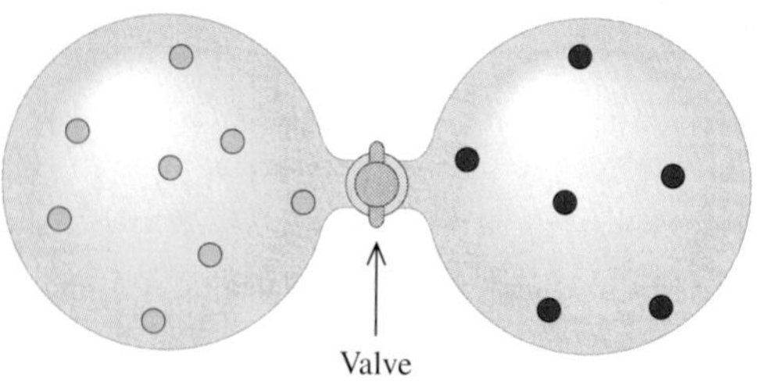

SPONTANEITY AND FREE ENERGY

13.22 Each of the following statements is false. Rewrite them so that each makes a correct statement about free energy.
(a) In any process at constant T and P, the free energy of the universe decreases.
(b) When T changes during a process, the free energy of a system always decreases.
(c) $\Delta G_{sys} > 0$ for any spontaneous process.
(d) $\Delta G = \Delta H + \Delta S$.

13.23 Compute the standard free energy change for each reaction in Problem 13.16.

13.24 Compute the standard free energy change for each reaction in Problem 13.17.

13.25 Estimate $\Delta G°_{425}$ for each reaction in Problem 13.17. (Assume no phase changes occur.)

13.26 Calculate ΔG_{rxn} at 298 K for each reaction in Problem 13.17 if each gaseous substance is present at $p = 0.25$ atm.

SOME APPLICATIONS OF THERMODYNAMICS

13.27 Compute $\Delta H°$, $\Delta S°$, and $\Delta G°$ for the production of NH_4NO_3 from ammonia and oxygen:

$$2\,NH_{3\,(g)} + 2\,O_{2\,(g)} \rightarrow NH_4NO_{3\,(s)} + H_2O_{(l)}$$

(This reaction is not feasible industrially because NH_3 combustion cannot be controlled to give NH_4NO_3 as a product.)

13.28 Compute $\Delta H°$, $\Delta S°$, and $\Delta G°$ for the production of urea from ammonia (see Figure 13-13).

13.29 Even though ammonia can be used directly as a fertilizer, much of it is converted to urea or ammonium nitrate before being applied in the field. Considering the physical properties of these substances, suggest why ammonia is not preferred as a fertilizer.

13.30 Oxygen has a normal melting point of 55 K and a normal boiling point of 90 K; its triple point is at $p = 0.0015$ atm and $T = 54$ K. Sketch the phase diagram for oxygen as accurately as you can and label the axes and the areas where each phase is stable.

13.31 Refer to Figure 13-16. Describe in detail what occurs when each of the following is carried out:
(a) A sample of CO_2 is compressed from 1.00 to 50.0 atm at a constant T of 298 K.
(b) A sample of N_2 is compressed from 1.00 to 50.0 atm at a constant T of 298 K.

(c) A sample of N_2 is cooled at a constant P of 1.00 atm from 298 to 50 K.

(d) A sample of CO_2 is cooled at a constant P of 1.00 atm from 298 to 50 K.

13.32 Heat pumps extract heat from a cold reservoir (usually the ground) and use it to maintain the temperature of a warmer reservoir (for example, a home). Explain why heat pumps cannot operate without converting some energy into heat.

BIOENERGETICS

13.33 The standard free energy change of the ATP → ADP reaction is −30.6 kJ/mol. Under cellular conditions, this reaction releases more than 50 kJ/mol. List the ways in which cellular conditions differ from standard conditions.

13.34 A pair of weights and a pulley can be used as an analogy for a coupled reaction. Use the following figure to describe a coupled process. Be sure to identify spontaneous and nonspontaneous portions of the process.

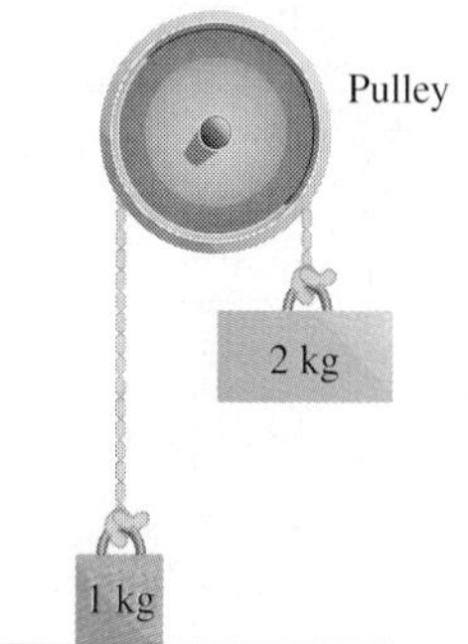

13.35 Although the ATP/ADP reaction is the principal energy shuttle in metabolic pathways, many other examples of coupled reactions exist. For example, the glutamic acid–glutamine reaction discussed in the text can couple with the following:

$H_3C-C(=O)-OH + H_3PO_4$

Acetic acid

$\Delta G^\circ = 41.8$ kJ (↓) $\Delta G^\circ = -41.8$ kJ (↑)

$H_3C-C(=O)-O-P(=O)(=O)-OH + H_2O$

Acetyl phosphate

Write the balanced equation for the coupled reaction operating in the direction of overall spontaneity, and calculate ΔG° for the overall process.

13.36 ATP and ADP have been referred to as the *energy currency* of the cell. Explain this analogy.

ADDITIONAL PROBLEMS

13.37 On a hot day, one of your friends suggests opening the door of your refrigerator to cool your kitchen. Will this work? Explain your answer using thermodynamic principles.

13.38 Two moles of HCl gas has more standard entropy, 374 J/mol K, than 1 mol each of H_2 gas and Cl_2 gas, 354 J/mol K. What feature of the molecular structures of these substances accounts for this difference?

13.39 A teaspoon stored in a freezer is placed in a glass of water, and the two equilibrate to the same temperature. In this process, what can you deduce about each of the following: (a) $\Delta E_{universe}$; (b) $\Delta E_{teaspoon}$; (c) $\Delta S_{universe}$; (d) ΔS_{water}; and (e) $q_{teaspoon}$.

13.40 A pie is removed from a hot oven, placed on a hot pad, and allowed to cool to room temperature. In this process, what can you deduce about the changes in each of the following: (a) $\Delta E_{universe}$; (b) ΔE_{pie}; (c) $\Delta S_{universe}$; (d) ΔS_{pie}; and (e) q_{pie}.

13.41 Arrange the following in order of increasing entropy, from smallest to largest value: 1.0 mol H_2O (liquid, 373 K); 0.50 mol H_2O (liquid, 298 K); 1.0 mol H_2O (liquid, 298 K); 1.0 mol H_2O (gas, 373 K, 1 atm) and 1.0 mol H_2O (gas, 373 K, 0.1 atm).

13.42 Arrange the following in order of increasing entropy, from smallest to largest value: 1.00 g Br_2 (gas, 331.9 K, 0.10 atm); 1.00 g Br_2 (gas, 331.9 K, 1.00 atm); 1.00 g Br_2 (liquid, 331.9 K, 1.00 atm); and 1.00 g Br atoms (gas, 331.9 K, 0.10 atm).

13.43 An ice-cube tray containing 150 g of H_2O at 0 °C is placed in a freezer whose temperature is −20 °C. As soon as all the H_2O has frozen, the tray is removed from the freezer.

(a) Find ΔS for the H_2O.

(b) Find ΔS for the universe.

(c) If the tray were left in the freezer until its temperature reached −20 °C, would an additional entropy change occur for the universe? Explain.

13.44 The most important commercial process for generating hydrogen gas is the water-gas shift reaction:

$$CH_{4\,(g)} + H_2O_{\,(g)} \rightarrow CO_{\,(g)} + 3\ H_{2\,(g)}$$

Use tabulated thermodynamic data to find (a) ΔG^o and (b) ΔG^o_{1300}.

13.45 For the chemical reaction:

$$Al_2O_{3\,(s)} + 3\ H_{2\,(g,\,p\,=\,1\,atm)} \rightarrow 2\ Al_{\,(s)} + 3\ H_2O_{\,(l)}$$

at T = 298 K, answer each of the following by doing a quantitative calculation of the appropriate thermodynamic function:

(a) Is this a spontaneous reaction?
(b) Does the reaction absorb or release heat?
(c) Are the products more or less ordered than the reactants?

13.46 For the chemical reaction:

$$3\ Fe_{(s)} + 4\ H_2O_{\,(l)} \rightarrow Fe_3O_{4\,(s)} + 4\ H_{2\,(g,\,p\,=\,1\,atm)}$$

at T = 298 K, answer each of the following by doing a quantitative calculation of the appropriate thermodynamic function:

(a) Is this a spontaneous reaction?
(b) Does the reaction absorb or release heat?
(c) Are the products more or less ordered than the reactants?

13.47 What is the efficiency of the metabolic conversion of palmitic acid to ATP?

13.48 Using the result of Problem 13.47, compute the number of grams of palmitic acid that would have to be metabolized to provide the heat to warm a swimmer from whose skin 75 g of water evaporates.

13.49 Lightning in the atmosphere causes the following reaction:

$$N_2 + O_2 + \text{Lightning} \rightarrow 2\ NO$$

A firefly produces light by converting the compound luciferin to dehydroluciferin:

$$\text{Luciferin} \rightarrow \text{Dehydroluciferin} + \text{Light}$$

For each of these processes, decide whether ΔG is negative or positive. Explain your reasoning.

13.50 Humans perspire as a way of keeping their bodies from overheating during strenuous exercise. The evaporation of perspiration transfers heat from the body to the surrounding atmosphere. Calculate ΔS of the universe for the evaporation of 1 g of water if the skin is at 37.5 °C and air temperature is 23.5 °C. Use ΔH_{vap} of water to find q. (HINT: Be careful about your choice for the system.)

13.51 Use data from Appendix E to compute ΔS^o for each of the following reactions:

(a) $2\ ClO_{2^-(aq)} + O_{2\,(g)} \rightarrow 2\ ClO_{3^-(aq)}$
(b) $4\ FeCl_{3\,(s)} + 3\ O_{2\,(g)} \rightarrow 2\ Fe_2O_{3\,(s)} + 6\ Cl_{2\,(g)}$
(c) $3\ N_2H_{4\,(l)} + 4\ O_{3\,(g)} \rightarrow 6\ NO_{\,(g)} + 6\ H_2O_{\,(l)}$

13.52 Use data from Appendix E to compute ΔG^o for each reaction in Problem 13.51.

13.53 Use data from Appendix E to compute ΔG^o_{350} for each reaction in Problem 13.51.

13.54 For the following process, give the sign (+, −, or 0) for each of the specified thermodynamic functions. In each case, give a brief account of your reasoning: (a) q_{sys}; (b) ΔS_{sys}; and (c) $\Delta E_{universe}$.

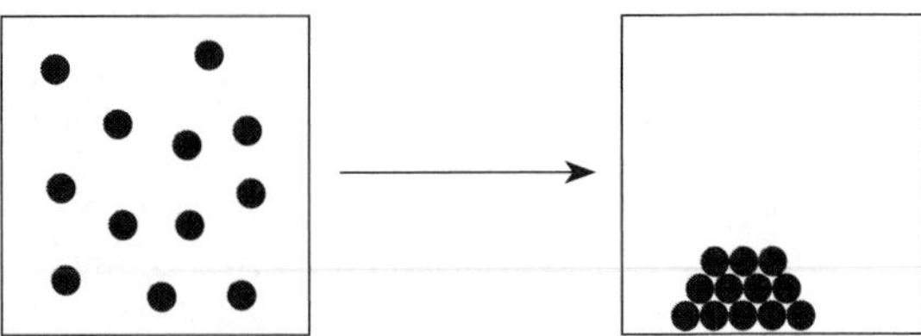

13.55 For the following process, give the sign (+, −, or 0) for each of the specified thermodynamic functions. In each case, give a brief account of your reasoning: (a) w_{sys}; (b) q_{sys}; and (c) ΔS_{surr}.

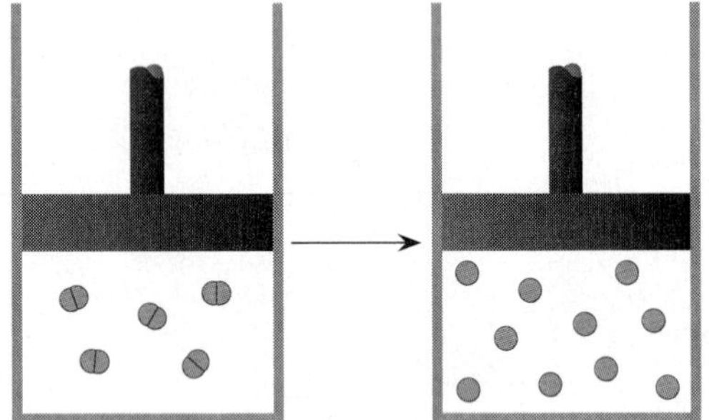

13.56 What are the four most important nitrogen-containing chemicals, and for what are they used?

13.57 Phosphorus forms white crystals made of P_4 molecules. The two forms of white crystalline phosphorus are called α and β. The difference between $P_{4\alpha}$ and $P_{4\beta}$ relates to the way the P_4 molecules pack together in the crystal lattice. The α form is always obtained when liquid phosphorus freezes. However, at temperatures below −77 °C, the $P_{4\alpha}$ crystals change spontaneously to $P_{4\beta}$:

$$P_{4\alpha} \xrightarrow{-77\ ^\circ C} P_{4\beta}$$

(a) Which form of phosphorus has a more ordered crystalline structure?
(b) Predict the signs of ΔH and ΔS for this process. Explain.

13.58 Plants and a few bacteria use sunlight as an energy source to produce glucose from CO_2 and H_2O. Other bacteria that live very deep in the sea, where there is no sunlight, use hydrogen sulfide to generate the free energy required to drive glucose synthesis:

$$2\ H_2S_{\,(g)} + O_{2\,(g)} \rightarrow 2\ H_2O_{\,(l)} + 2\ S_{\,(s)}$$

Write a balanced equation for the coupled process, and perform a calculation that shows the process is spontaneous under standard conditions.

13.59 Without doing any calculations, predict the signs (+, −, or 0) of ΔH and ΔG for the following processes, all occurring at constant T and P. Explain your predictions.
(a) $2\ NO_{2\,(g)} \rightarrow N_2O_{4\,(g)}$
(b) A 10 g block of gold is melted in a jeweler's crucible.
(c) $CH_{4\,(g)} + 2\ O_{2\,(g)} \rightarrow CO_{2\,(g)} + 2\ H_2O_{(g)}$

13.60 A sample of liquid bromine (0.08 mol) at 273 K and 1 atm is placed in a cylinder equipped with a piston. (Assume the liquid bromine has negligible volume.) The cylinder is placed inside a constant-temperature bath at 332 K, the boiling point of bromine. The system undergoes a constant-temperature expansion to a final volume of 2.2 L. The following sketch illustrates the apparatus immediately after the cylinder is placed in the bath (C_p, Molar heat capacity).

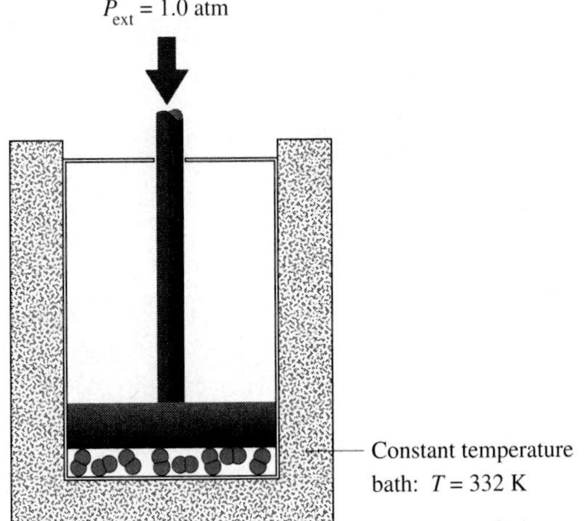

For $Br_{2\,(l)}$:
melting point = 226 K
boiling point = 332 K
C_p = 75.7 J/mol K

For $Br_{2\,(g)}$:
C_p = 36.0 J/mol K

(a) Draw a sketch that shows how system appears when it reaches its final state.
(b) Use the data in Appendix E to calculate q, w, ΔE, ΔH, and ΔS for the process.

13.61 Few of the elements are found in the Earth in their pure form. Most elements exist as oxides or sulfides. Explain why this is so, and explain why nitrogen does exist as a pure element.

13.62 The molar enthalpy of fusion and the molar entropy of fusion of ammonia follow:

$$NH_{3\,(s)} \rightarrow NH_{3\,(l)}$$

$$\Delta H^\circ = 5.65\text{ kJ/mol} \qquad \Delta S^\circ = 28.9\text{ J/mol K}$$

(a) Calculate ΔG° for the melting of 1.00 mol of ammonia.
(b) What is the freezing point of ammonia?

13.63 Crystalline KCl has S° = 83 J/mol K, whereas crystalline CaO has S° = 55 J/mol K. What accounts for the larger disorder of KCl crystals?

13.64 In the upper atmosphere, ozone is produced from oxygen:

$$3\ O_{2\,(g)} \rightarrow 2\ O_{3\,(g)}$$

(a) Compute ΔH°, ΔS°, and ΔG° for this reaction.
(b) Is there a temperature at which this reaction becomes spontaneous at 1 atm pressure? If so, find it. If not, explain why one does not exist.
(c) Assume an atmosphere with $p(O_2)$ = 0.20 atm and T = 298 K. Below what pressure of O_3 is O_3 production spontaneous?
(d) In view of your answers to parts a to c, how can the ozone layer form? (You may need to review Section 6.4.)

13.65 The idea of thermodynamic coupling of a nonspontaneous process with a spontaneous process is not restricted to chemical reactions. Identify the spontaneous and nonspontaneous portions of the following coupled processes:
(a) Water behind a dam passes through a turbine and generates electricity.
(b) A gasoline engine pumps water from a valley to the top of a hill.

13.66 Calculate ΔH°, ΔS°, and ΔG° at 200 °C for each of the following reactions, which are important in the chemistry of coal (assume that coal has the same thermodynamic properties as graphite):
(a) $C_{(s,\,coal)} + H_2O_{(g)} \rightarrow CO_{(g)} + H_{2\,(g)}$
(b) $C_{(s,\,coal)} + O_{2\,(g)} \rightarrow CO_{2\,(g)}$
(c) $C_{(s,\,coal)} + \frac{1}{2}O_{2\,(g)} \rightarrow CO_{(g)}$
(d) $CO_{(g)} + H_2O_{(g)} \rightarrow CO_{2\,(g)} + H_{2\,(g)}$

13.67 One possible source of acid rain is the reaction between nitrogen dioxide, a pollutant from automobile exhausts, and water:

$$3\ NO_{2\,(g)} + H_2O_{(l)} \rightarrow 2\ HNO_{3\,(g)} + NO_{(g)}$$

Determine whether this is thermodynamically feasible (a) under standard conditions and (b) at 298 K, with each gas present at $p = 1.00 \times 10^{-6}$ atm.

13.68 Sketch the phase diagram for Br_2 from the following information: normal melting point = 265.9 K, normal boiling point = 331.9 K, triple point T = 265.7 K, and $P = 5.79 \times 10^{-2}$ atm.

13.69 Using the phase diagram of Problem 13.68, describe what happens to a sample of Br_2 as the following processes occur. Draw lines on the phase diagram showing each process.
(a) A sample at T = 400 K is cooled to 250 K at constant P = 1.00 atm.
(b) A sample is compressed at constant T = 265.8 K from $P = 1.00 \times 10^{-3}$ atm to $P = 1.00 \times 10^{3}$ atm.
(c) A sample is heated at constant $P = 2.00 \times 10^{-2}$ atm from 250 to 400 K.

13.70 Determine the free energy content per gram of palmitic acid and of glucose. On a per-gram basis, which is the better energy source?

13.71 Methane gas has a lower S° (186.3 J/mol K) than gaseous ammonia (S° = 192.4 J/mol K), whereas S° of gaseous H_2O is 188.8 J/mol K. Does this surprise you? Why or why not? Suggest a reason why methane has a lower absolute entropy.

13.72 Find ΔS for system, surroundings, and universe when 25.0 g of liquid H_2O is evaporated at 100 °C, if the heat required is provided by a hot plate with T = 300 °C.

13.73 Both CCl_4 (carbon tetrachloride) and CS_2 (carbon disulfide) are liquids used as solvents in special industrial applications. Using data from Appendix E, calculate ΔH° and ΔG° for combustion of these liquids:

$$CCl_{4\,(l)} + 5\,O_{2\,(g)} \rightarrow CO_{2\,(g)} + 4\,ClO_{2\,(g)}$$

$$CS_{2\,(l)} + 3\,O_{2\,(g)} \rightarrow CO_{2\,(g)} + 2\,SO_{2\,(g)}$$

Based on your results, would you recommend special precautions against fires for industrial plants using either solvent? Explain your recommendations.

13.74 The molar entropy of graphite is 3 times larger than the molar entropy of diamond. Explain why this is so. (You may need to review the structures and properties of graphite and diamond in Chapter 9.) The newest form of elemental carbon, fullerene, is a solid that consists of individual molecules of the formula C_{60}. Is the molar entropy of fullerene larger or smaller than that of graphite? Explain.

13.75 In a system operating without any restrictions, heat is not a state function. However, heat flow becomes a state function under certain restricted conditions. For each of the following conditions, identify the state function that corresponds to heat flow: (a) q_v; (b) q_p; and (c) q_T.

13.76 Explain why a nuclear power plant contributes thermal pollution to the environment.

13.77 Use data from Appendix E to answer quantitatively the following questions about the dissolving of table salt in water under standard conditions:

$$NaCl_{(s)} \rightarrow Na^{+}_{(aq)} + Cl^{-}_{(aq)}$$

(a) Is this a spontaneous reaction?
(b) Does this reaction release energy?
(c) Does the amount of order in the chemical system increase?

13.78 Repeat the calculations of Problem 13.77 for silver chloride (AgCl) dissolving in water. What do the results reveal about the difference in solubility of these two salts and the reasons for the difference?

ANSWERS TO SECTION EXERCISES

13.1.1 (a) A fence represents order; when it falls down, it becomes disordered; (b) a glass has a relatively ordered structure, whereas a broken glass is highly disordered; and (c) any solution of several substances is disordered compared to the separate components.

13.1.2 Increased organization in one place (formation of sugar crystals) must be accompanied by even greater disorganization elsewhere. In this example, the water molecules that boil away are much more disordered than water molecules in the liquid.

13.1.3

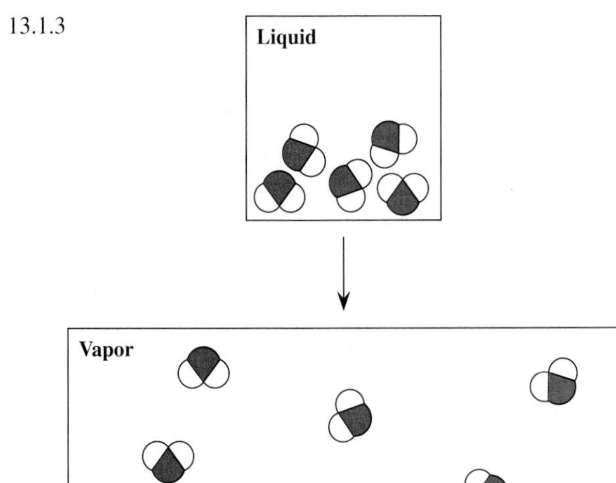

13.2.1 Heat will flow from the warmer mixture to the cooler mixture, so benzene will freeze and ice will melt.

13.2.2 0.10 J/K

13.2.3 $\Delta S_{\text{mixture}} = -6.11$ J/K, $\Delta S_{\text{refrigerator}} = 6.11$ J/K, $\Delta S_{\text{universe}} = 0$; neither this process nor the reverse process is spontaneous.

13.3.1 (a) 1 g of dew because liquids are more disordered than solids of the same material; (b) 1 mol of gaseous hydrogen atoms because although both samples contain the same number of atoms, binding atoms into molecules reduces the amount of disorder; (c) the flawed diamond because flaws represent disorder; and (d) the sample at 50 °C because increasing the temperature of a sample increases its molecular motion and disorder.

13.3.2 (a) There are more atoms in the sample of O_3, so there are more opportunities for randomness in the molecular arrangement; (b) both samples have the same number of atoms, but there are more molecules in 3 mol of O_2, so there is more randomness in its molecular arrangement; (c) I_2 is a solid under standard conditions, so it is more ordered than gaseous O_2; and (d) diluting a solution spreads its solute particles (ions in this case) over a larger region, giving it greater disorder.

13.3.3

Hydrogen atoms Hydrogen molecules

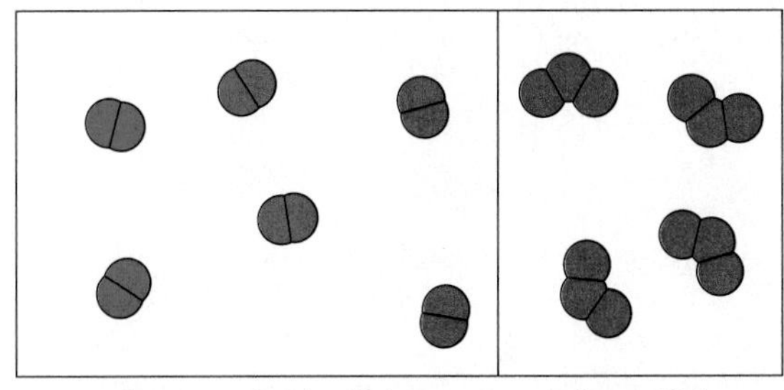

Oxygen molecules (O_2) Ozone (O_3)

13.3.4 −2804.29 J/mol K

13.4.1 −225.2 kJ/mol

13.4.2 4.8×10^{-3} atm

13.4.3 yes, $T = 5.44 \times 10^3$ K

13.5.1 339.2 kJ

13.5.2 (a) 0.124 atm; (b) ice remains solid until the pressure drops to about 0.005 atm, when it sublimes; and (c) at 7.0 atm, dry ice melts at around 217 K and is liquid at room temperature.

13.5.3 When an automobile engine moves an automobile, it does work and generates order (all parts of the automobile move together in the same direction). To do this without violating the second law of thermodynamics, enough heat must be transferred to the surroundings to generate an amount of disorder greater than the amount of order accompanying the work.

13.6.1 92%

13.6.2 +32.2 J/mol K; the spontaneity increases as temperature increases.

13.6.3 (a) 16.3 mol of ATP; and (b) 82.5 g of glucose

CHAPTER 14

MECHANISMS OF CHEMICAL REACTIONS

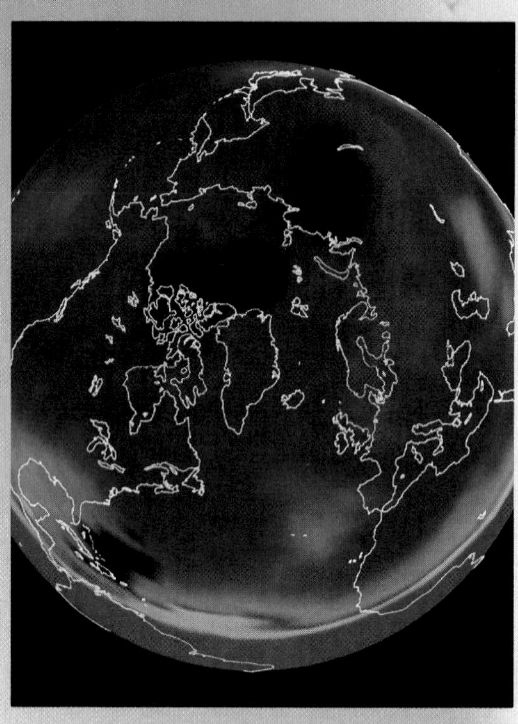

In recent years the concentration of ozone in the upper atmosphere has been reduced by chemical reactions with Freons. The mechanisms of these reactions are being studied intensively.

What happens at the molecular level during a chemical reaction? We have emphasized that a chemical reaction involves breaking some chemical bonds and forming others. Which bonds break easily, how fast they break, what the sequence of bond rearrangements is, and what factors influence these changes all play important roles in determining the course of a chemical reaction.

Chemists have always been interested in the details of chemical reactions at the molecular level. Synthetic chemists use information about how reactions occur to design and synthesize useful new compounds. Industrial chemists explore how reaction conditions can be modified to minimize the cost of producing industrial chemicals. Atmospheric chemists study the ways that pollutants interact with the naturally occurring components of the Earth's atmosphere. Thus the molecular details of chemical reactions have immense practical importance in many fields.

This chapter provides an introduction to how chemical reactions occur at the molecular level. We show how to describe a reaction from the molecular perspective, introduce the basic principles that govern these processes, and describe some experimental methods used to study chemical reactions.

INTRODUCTION: THE OZONE PROBLEM

Early in this century, when refrigeration systems were just being developed, refrigerators contained toxic gases such as ammonia and sulfur dioxide. In 1928 two scientists at General Motors developed a new refrigerant, CF_2Cl_2, that was nontoxic and nonflammable. Recognizing that this new compound would greatly improve the safety of refrigerators, General Motors began a joint venture with the Du Pont Chemical Company to produce CF_2Cl_2 and other similar compounds called *chlorofluorocarbons (CFCs).*

The CFCs, or Freons as they are known commercially, were a tremendous success. In addition to being nontoxic and nonflammable, Freons were found to be odorless, tasteless, noncorrosive, and chemically stable. Furthermore, their thermodynamic properties turned out to be ideal for refrigeration. Industrial applications of CFCs mushroomed. By the late 1980s CFCs were being used as refrigerants, foaming agents for the manufacture of plastics, cleaning solutions for electrical components, and propellants in aerosol cans. Worldwide consumption of CFCs in 1988 was more than 1 million tons.

Unfortunately, the chemical stability that made Freons such a commercial success may lead eventually to environmental disaster. CFCs do not react with substances in the troposphere. Instead, CFCs diffuse slowly through the atmosphere, rising until they reach the ozone layer in the stratosphere. In the mid-1970s chemists discovered that ultraviolet light, which is abundant in the stratosphere, causes CFCs to react with ozone. These studies predicted that continued release of CFCs would eventually lead to significant depletion of ozone in the stratosphere. Atmospheric data collected between 1978 and 1985 showed that stratospheric ozone concentrations over populated regions of the world decreased by about 2.5%. Since then, studies of the polar atmospheres have shown alarming annual ozone decreases of

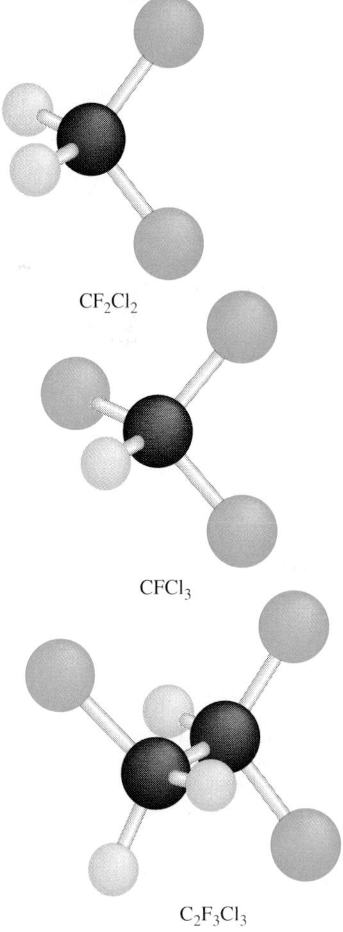

CF_2Cl_2 is Freon-12. Other CFCs include $CFCl_3$ (Freon–11) and $C_2F_3Cl_3$ (Freon–113).

more than 50% above Antarctica, and data from 1991 and 1992 indicate smaller but nevertheless substantial decreases in the ozone over the Arctic regions.

As discussed in Chapter 6, life on Earth would be imperiled without ozone in the stratosphere to filter the high-energy ultraviolet radiation coming from the sun. It has been estimated that every 1% loss of ozone in the stratosphere allows an additional 2% of the sun's ultraviolet light to reach the Earth's surface. As long as ozone depletion remained confined to polar atmospheres, increased exposure to ultraviolet radiation had no direct consequences for human populations. In 1989, however, it was found that the thinning of the ozone layer had spread from Antarctica to regions over southern Australia, where schoolchildren are now required by law to wear hats and neck scarves to and from school. In addition, recent data indicate that increased exposure to ultraviolet radiation is damaging the ecosystem of southern Chile.

The laboratory evidence showing that CFCs can cause ozone decomposition under conditions found in the stratosphere, with documented decreases in stratospheric ozone concentrations, might lead a prudent society to abandon these potentially dangerous compounds. However, consider the consequences of an outright ban on CFCs. In the United States, for example, CFC-related goods and services contributed more than $28 billion per year to the national economy and accounted for more than 700,000 jobs in 1990. Given these statistics, government officials and business leaders have been reluctant to eliminate CFCs. Some have suggested that periodic variations in stratospheric ozone concentrations, including the dramatic changes above Antarctica, are part of the natural fluctuations in the dynamic behavior of the atmosphere.

It is an important task for scientists to determine the facts about the controversial (and highly politicized) assertions made regarding this problem. World leaders cannot make rational decisions concerning what role CFCs will play in future society unless scientists learn in detail how CFCs interact with ozone. Today, meteorologists, physicists, and chemists are studying the mechanism of CFC reactions with ozone. They want to determine the *molecular processes* by which these reactions occur, *how fast* these reactions proceed, and *what factors* control them in hopes of slowing or preventing further damage to the ozone layer.

14.1 WHAT IS A MECHANISM?

We have emphasized that atoms, ions, and molecules rearrange and recombine during chemical reactions. The sequence of molecular events by which a chemical reaction occurs is called its **reaction mechanism.** The reaction mechanism is the *exact molecular pathway* that starting materials follow on their way to becoming products.

Much is now known about how CFCs destroy ozone, but the molecular processes that occur are too complicated to be used as an introduction to the fundamental principles of mechanisms. We introduce the principles of mechanisms with a set of simpler chemical reactions and return to the ozone problem later in this chapter.

EXAMPLE OF A MECHANISM: FORMATION OF N_2O_4

Even though nitrogen dioxide, a red-brown gas, is stable, under the right conditions it readily undergoes a reaction in which two NO_2 molecules combine to form colorless N_2O_4 gas. Figure 14-1 shows that N_2O_4 is more stable at low temperatures, whereas NO_2 predominates at room temperature.

FIGURE 14-1
When a flask containing orange NO_2 gas at room temperature (*left*) is cooled in a low-temperature bath, NO_2 molecules combine to form colorless N_2O_4 molecules (*right*).

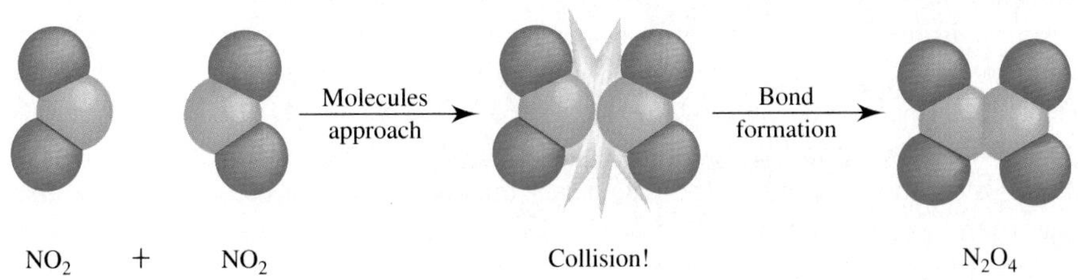

FIGURE 14-2
A molecule of N_2O_4 forms when a pair of NO_2 molecules collide in the right orientation to form a bond between the nitrogen atoms. This is a molecular view of the mechanism for the reaction.

The mechanism of this reaction describes what occurs at the molecular level. As illustrated in Figure 14-2, an N_2O_4 molecule forms when two NO_2 molecules collide and stick together by forming a bond between the two nitrogen atoms.

The formation of N_2O_4 requires more than a simple collision between two NO_2 molecules. The product molecule contains a bond between the nitrogen atoms, so the collision must bring the two nitrogen atoms into contact. As Figure 14-3 shows, a collision between the nitrogen atom of one NO_2 molecule and an oxygen atom of a second cannot lead to N_2O_4. The product can form only from a collision that brings together the nitrogen atoms of two NO_2 molecules. Collisions that have the appropriate orientation and lead to bond formation are termed *effective collisions,* whereas those that do not lead to bond formation are termed *ineffective collisions.*

The Lewis structure of NO_2 indicates that the nitrogen atom has an unpaired electron. Two NO_2 molecules combine by using their unpaired electrons to form an N—N bond:

NO_2 $\longleftrightarrow$

N_2O_4

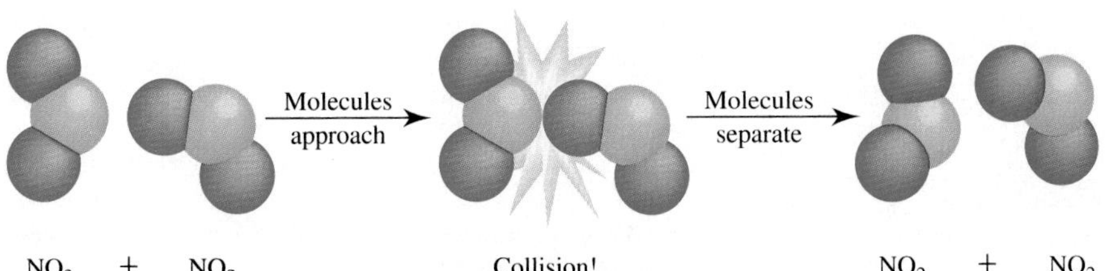

FIGURE 14-3
This molecular view shows a collision between NO_2 molecules that is ineffective for formation of N_2O_4. An N—N bond cannot form when an oxygen atom from either molecule strikes the other molecule.

ELEMENTARY REACTIONS

A mechanism is a sequence of simple molecular processes; just one or two reactant molecules or atoms participates in each process. Each step in such a sequence is called an **elementary reaction.** The formation of N_2O_4 from NO_2 can be described by a single elementary reaction, but in most cases, mechanisms consist of sequences of more than one elementary reaction. Thus an *overall* chemical reaction usually is not an *elementary reaction.* Although an overall reaction describes the starting materials and final products, it does not represent the individual steps by which the reaction occurs.

Elementary reactions can be bimolecular, unimolecular, or termolecular. A **bimolecular reaction** is an elementary reaction that results from the collision of two molecules, atoms, or ions. The collision of two NO_2 molecules to give N_2O_4 is a bimolecular reaction. Three additional examples follow:

$$H_3O^+ + OH^- \rightarrow H_2O + H_2O$$

$$O_2 + O \rightarrow O_3$$

$$NO_2 + NO_2 \rightarrow NO_3 + NO$$

Notice that the characteristic feature of a bimolecular elementary reaction is a collision between two species that results in a rearrangement of chemical bonds. The two reaction partners stick together by forming a new bond or form two new species by transferring one or more atoms from one partner to another.

In a **unimolecular reaction,** a single molecule fragments into two pieces or rearranges to a new isomer. A simple example of a unimolecular reaction is the decomposition of N_2O_4 into two molecules of NO_2. The N—N bond cleaves in this reaction, as shown in Figure 14-4. A vibration of the molecule stretches the N—N bond. If the molecule has sufficient energy, the bond breaks, much like a spring that has been stretched too far. A stable molecule such as N_2O_4 does not decompose unless it first acquires the energy needed to break one of its bonds. This energy can come from molecular collisions that transfer energy from one molecule to another.

Any collection of gas molecules has a distribution of kinetic energies. For a review, see Section 5.1 and Figure 5-4.

***Isomers,* which appear several times in this book, are two molecules that have the same molecular formula but different arrangements of atoms. Isomers have different chemical and physical properties.**

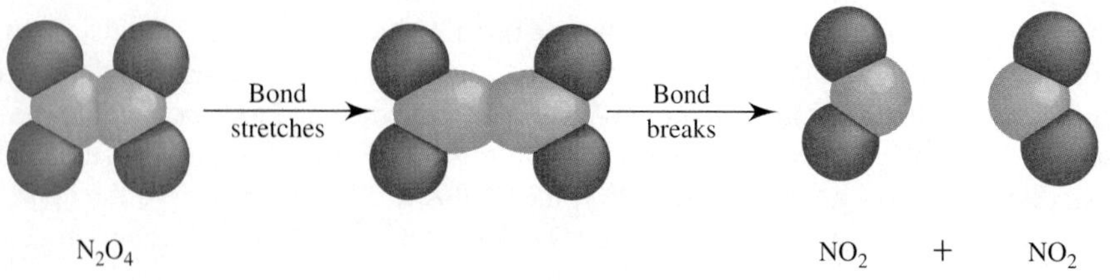

Figure 14-5 shows another unimolecular reaction, the conversion of *cis*-azobenzene to its isomer, *trans*-azobenzene. This reaction occurs after collisions transfer to

Bond stretches → Bond breaks →

N_2O_4 → NO_2 + NO_2

FIGURE 14-4
A unimolecular elementary reaction may involve bond breakage. A high-energy N_2O_4 molecule undergoes a vibration that stretches the N—N bond. If the molecule possesses enough energy, the vibration can break the N—N bond to produce two NO_2 molecules.

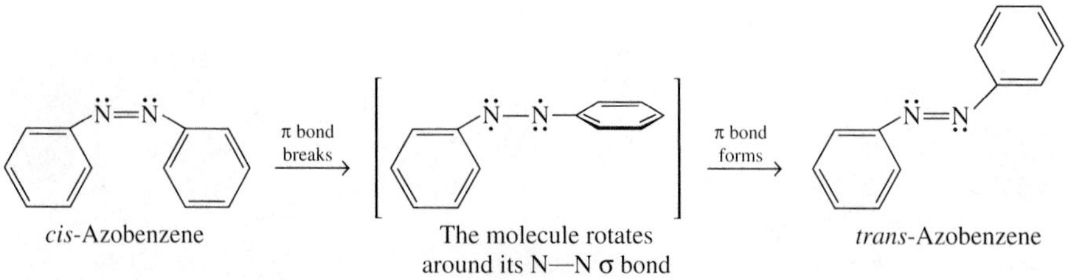

cis-Azobenzene → π bond breaks → [The molecule rotates around its N—N σ bond] → π bond forms → *trans*-Azobenzene

FIGURE 14-5
A unimolecular elementary reaction may lead to molecular isomerization. An azobenzene molecule can rearrange if collisions give the molecule sufficient extra energy to break its π bond and rotate from one form to another.

a *cis*-azobenzene molecule enough energy to break its N—N π bond. When the π bond is broken, the two $N(C_6H_5)$ fragments can rotate independently about the N—N σ bond. Then the π bond may form again, with the two C_6H_5 groups now on opposite sides of the double bond.

In a **termolecular reaction,** three chemical species collide simultaneously. Termolecular reactions are rare because they require a collision of three particles at the *same time* and in *exactly the right orientation* to form products. The odds against such a three-body collision are high. Most chemical reactions, including all those introduced in this book, can be described at the molecular level as a sequence of bimolecular and unimolecular elementary reactions. Together, bimolecular collisions and/or unimolecular rearrangements convert starting materials into products.

DECOMPOSITION OF NO_2

Very few chemical reactions are as simple as the low-temperature reaction of NO_2 to form N_2O_4. For example, at high temperature NO_2 decomposes into nitrogen monoxide and molecular oxygen:

$$2\ NO_2 \rightarrow 2\ NO + O_2$$

Later, we explore *why* NO_2 molecules can react in two different ways. We are now interested only in *how* these reactions occur.

One possible sequence that explains the decomposition of NO_2 molecules starts with a fragmentation. At high temperature, collisions may transfer enough energy to some NO_2 molecules to allow them to break apart. That is, an N—O bond in NO_2 may break to produce a molecule of NO and an oxygen atom. Because oxygen atoms are highly reactive, a subsequent bimolecular collision between an oxygen atom and an NO_2 molecule would then generate NO and O_2. This reasoning can be summarized as Mechanism I for NO_2 decomposition:

$NO_2 \rightarrow NO + O$	Step I-1	
$O + NO_2 \rightarrow O_2 + NO$	Step I-2	(Mechanism I)
$2\ NO_2 \rightarrow 2\ NO + O_2$	Overall reaction	

Figure 14-6 illustrates Mechanism I using molecular pictures.

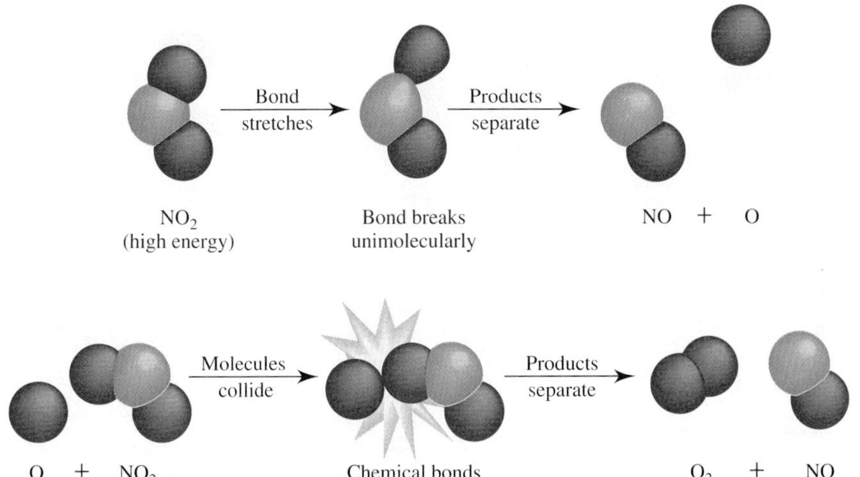

FIGURE 14-6
In Mechanism I for NO_2 decomposition, an energetic NO_2 molecule first fragments into an NO molecule and an O atom. The reactive O atom then collides with another NO_2 molecule and removes one of its O atoms, producing an O_2 molecule and a second NO molecule.

Mechanism I illustrates an important requirement for reaction mechanisms. Because a mechanism is a summary of actual events at the molecular level, a mechanism *must* lead to the correct stoichiometry if it is to be an accurate description of the chemical reaction. The sum of the steps of a mechanism must give the balanced stoichiometric equation for the chemical reaction. In Mechanism I the net result of two sequential elementary reactions is the observed reaction stoichiometry.

A second possible molecular sequence for NO_2 decomposition starts with a bimolecular reaction. When two fast-moving NO_2 molecules collide, an oxygen atom may be transferred between them to form molecules of NO_3 and NO. Like oxygen atoms, NO_3 molecules are unstable; they decompose spontaneously into NO and O_2. This reasoning can be summarized as Mechanism II for NO_2 decomposition:

The reactivity of NO_3 is suggested by its Lewis structure. Not only does the molecule contain an odd number of electrons, but it also has too few electrons to fill the valence shells of all its atoms:

$$\ddot{\text{O}}{=}\text{N}(\text{—}\ddot{\text{O}}\text{:})(\text{—}\ddot{\text{O}}\cdot)$$

$NO_2 + NO_2 \longrightarrow NO_3 + NO$	Step II-1	
$NO_3 \longrightarrow O_2 + NO$	Step II-2	(Mechanism II)
$2\ NO_2 \longrightarrow 2\ NO + O_2$	Overall reaction	

Mechanism II gives the observed overall stoichiometry because the NO_3 molecule produced in the first step is consumed in the second step. Figure 14-7 illustrates Mechanism II using molecular pictures.

We have described two different molecular mechanisms that might account for the decomposition of NO_2. Each contains a unimolecular step and a bimolecular step, each generates an unstable species that reacts further, and each accounts for the observed reaction stoichiometry. Does either mechanism describe what really happens at the molecular level? Before describing how to test whether or not a mechanism is realistic, we must introduce some additional features of mechanisms.

INTERMEDIATES

Both proposed mechanisms for NO_2 decomposition contain chemical species produced in the first step and consumed in the second. This is the defining characteristic of an **intermediate.** An intermediate is a chemical species *produced* in an early step of a mechanism and *consumed* in a later step. Intermediates never appear in the overall chemical equation. Notice that neither the oxygen atoms of Mechanism I nor the NO_3 molecules of Mechanism II appear in the balanced chemical equation for NO_2 decomposition.

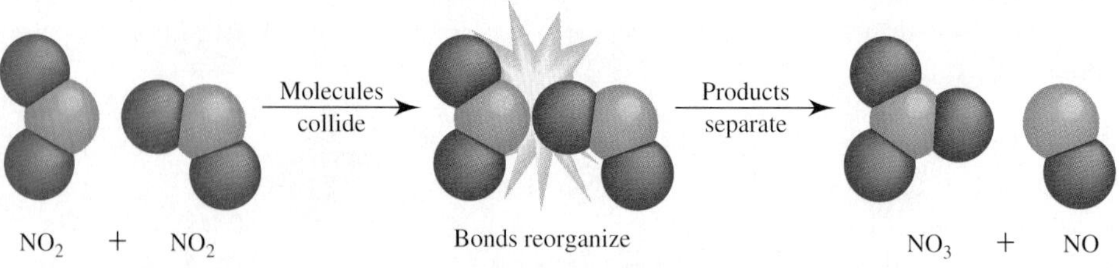

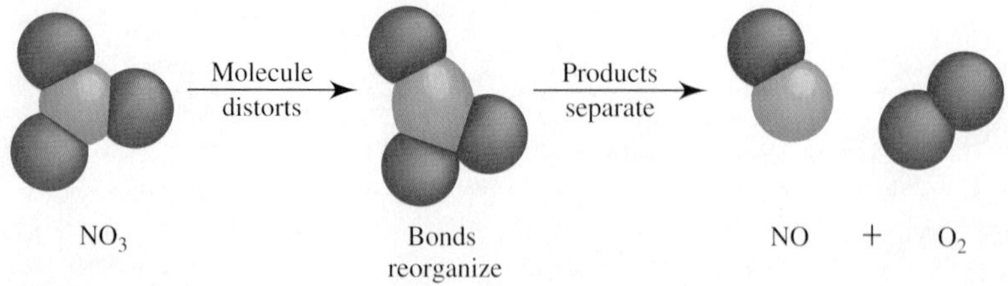

FIGURE 14-7
In Mechanism II for NO_2 decomposition, a collision between energetic NO_2 molecules in the correct orientation produces NO_3 and NO molecules. One product, NO_3, is an unstable molecule that spontaneously decomposes into molecules of O_2 and NO.

Intermediates are reactive chemical species that usually exist only briefly. They are consumed rapidly by bimolecular collisions with other chemical species or by spontaneous unimolecular decomposition. The intermediate in Mechanism I is an unstable oxygen atom that reacts rapidly with NO_2 molecules. The intermediate in Mechanism II is an unstable NO_3 molecule that decomposes spontaneously.

The most direct way to test the validity of a mechanism is to determine what intermediates are present during the reaction. If we could detect the presence of oxygen atoms, we would know that Mechanism I is a reasonable description of NO_2 decomposition. If we could detect the presence of NO_3 molecules, we would know that Mechanism II is reasonable. In practice, the detection of intermediates is quite difficult because intermediates are usually reactive enough to be consumed as rapidly as they are produced. As a result, the concentration of an intermediate in a reaction mixture is very low. Highly sensitive measuring techniques are required for the direct detection of chemical intermediates.

THE RATE-DETERMINING STEP

Every unimolecular and bimolecular elementary reaction has a characteristic rate. Some reactions are so fast that they are complete in the smallest measurable fraction of a second, whereas others are so slow that they require almost an eternity to reach completion. The observed rate of an *overall* chemical reaction is determined by the rates of the elementary reactions that make up the mechanism.

We rarely find that two elementary reactions in a mechanism occur at exactly the same rate. Each step has a unique rate, and every mechanism has one elementary reaction that is slower than all the others. The slowest elementary step in a mechanism is called the **rate-determining step.** The rate-determining step governs the rate of the overall chemical reaction because no net chemical reaction can go faster than its slowest step. The idea of the rate-determining step is central to the study of reaction mechanisms.

Anyone who has flown on a commercial airline is familiar with the consequences of rate-determining steps, as illustrated by Figure 14-8. At a busy airport, for example, an airplane must await clearance from the control tower before taking off. After the plane has permission to take off, it becomes airborne very quickly. Therefore the time required to be cleared for takeoff determines how much time passes between leaving the gate and taking off. That is, the rate-determining step for airplane takeoff is clearance from the control tower. Baggage claim is the rate-determining step at the end of a flight. No matter how quickly the passengers leap from their seats, push through the aisle, and race through the terminal, no one can leave the airport any faster than the baggage is delivered.

FIGURE 14-8
The slowest step in any sequential process is rate-determining. Airplanes take off at the rate they are cleared by the control tower, and arriving passengers leave the terminal at the rate their baggage is delivered.

We can often use chemical knowledge to assess which step of a mechanism is likely to be rate determining. For example, in both proposed mechanisms for the decomposition of NO_2, chemical knowledge leads us to expect that the first step is much slower than the second step. In Mechanism I an oxygen atom is produced in the first step. We know that oxygen atoms are unstable, so we predict that this intermediate reacts rapidly with NO_2 molecules. Thus the second step of this mechanism is expected to be fast, and the step that forms oxygen atoms is slow and rate determining. Similarly, the Lewis structure of NO_3 indicates that this species is unstable and will decompose in the second step of Mechanism II almost as fast as it forms. Again, the second step of this mechanism is expected to be fast, so the step that forms the reactive intermediate is slow and rate determining. Later in this chapter we discuss experiments that make it possible to distinguish between Mechanisms I and II.

Box 14-1 applies the ideas of this section to the formation of ozone.

BOX 14-1

HOW OZONE IS FORMED

Ozone is formed in the stratosphere by the action of ultraviolet light on oxygen molecules:

$$3\,O_2 \xrightarrow{h\nu} 2\,O_3$$

Experimental evidence suggests that this reaction proceeds in a two-step mechanism:

$$O_2 \xrightarrow{h\nu} 2\,O \qquad \text{Step 1}$$

$$O + O_2 \longrightarrow O_3 \qquad \text{Step 2}$$

In the first step an oxygen molecule absorbs a photon ($h\nu$) of high-energy ultraviolet light (λ <280 nm). The energy of the photon breaks the bond of the O_2 molecule, which fragments into two oxygen atoms. Oxygen atoms are reactive species that can add to O_2 molecules to produce ozone. The ozone molecule formed in this step contains excess energy, and unless that energy is transferred to some other species, the ozone molecule breaks apart to regenerate O_2 and an oxygen atom. In the stratosphere, however, high-energy ozone molecules usually collide with nitrogen molecules and give up their excess energy before they can break apart.

As written, steps 1 and 2 do not add together to give the balanced chemical equation. However, a valid mechanism *must* lead to the correct reaction stoichiometry. In the ozone process, two oxygen atoms react with two O_2 molecules to give two ozone molecules. In the complete mechanism, the second step occurs *twice* each time the first step occurs:

$$O + O_2 \rightarrow O_3 \quad O + O_2 \rightarrow O_3$$

Chemists find it convenient to write this elementary process just once, but they understand that step 2 must occur twice to consume both the oxygen atoms produced in step 1. Writing out all three steps shows that the mechanism does lead to the correct stoichiometry:

$$O_2 \xrightarrow{h\nu} 2\,O$$
$$O + O_2 \longrightarrow O_3$$
$$O + O_2 \longrightarrow O_3$$
$$\overline{3\,O_2 \xrightarrow{h\nu} 2\,O_3}$$

The oxygen atoms produced in the initial fragmentation step are extremely reactive, so as soon as an oxygen atom forms, it is "snapped up" by the nearest available O_2 molecule. Consequently, the cleavage of an O_2 molecule by a photon is the rate-determining step in the formation of ozone.

SECTION EXERCISES

14.1.1 Nitrogen dioxide in polluted air forms from NO and CO_2 by a single bimolecular reaction. Identify the second molecular product of this reaction, and draw a molecular picture similar to the ones in this section that shows how this chemical reaction occurs.

14.1.2 The following mechanism has been proposed for the reaction of NO with H_2:

$$2\,NO \longrightarrow N_2O_2$$
$$N_2O_2 + H_2 \longrightarrow H_2O + N_2O$$
$$N_2O + H_2 \longrightarrow N_2 + H_2O$$

Determine the balanced chemical equation for the reaction that occurs by this mechanism and identify any chemical intermediates.

14.1.3 One common analogy for the rate-determining step involves a tollbooth. In your own words, explain rate-determining steps using the tollbooth analogy.

14.2 RATES OF CHEMICAL REACTIONS

Some of the most important information about a mechanism comes from experiments that determine how fast a chemical reaction occurs under various conditions. We describe how fast a process occurs by giving its **rate.** Rate is the number of events per unit time. For example, the rate of airplane takeoffs at an airport may be four takeoffs/min. Chemical reaction rates can be measured in molecules/second, mol/min, or any other units that express concentration/time. The study of the rates of chemical reactions is called **kinetics.** Kinetic studies cover many types of reactions, some with mechanisms that are very simple and others that are extremely complex. Such studies are important in many areas of science, including biochemistry, synthetic chemistry, biology, environmental science, engineering, and geology. Despite its many complexities, the fundamentals of chemical kinetics can be understood by exploring the differences in rate behavior of unimolecular and bimolecular elementary reactions.

RATES OF CHEMICAL REACTIONS: A MOLECULAR VIEW

For a molecular perspective of reaction rates, we examine the unimolecular isomerization of *cis*-azobenzene, which was shown in Figure 14-5. Figure 14-9 illustrates schematically how this reaction progresses with time. If we focus our attention on a volume that contains 12 *cis*-azobenzene molecules, we find that six of these molecules isomerize during the first minute. Thus the average rate is six molecules/min for this period. As the reaction proceeds, however, the rate of reaction decreases. During the second minute, only three molecules isomerize, giving an average rate for that period of three molecules/min.

Why does the rate become slower as this reaction proceeds? The answer is revealed if we divide the number of *cis*- molecules that react by the total number of *cis*- molecules present at the beginning of the interval:

First minute: $\dfrac{6\ \textit{cis}\text{- molecules react}}{12\ \textit{cis}\text{- molecules present}} = 0.5$ Second minute: $\dfrac{3\ \textit{cis}\text{- molecules react}}{6\ \textit{cis}\text{- molecules present}} = 0.5$

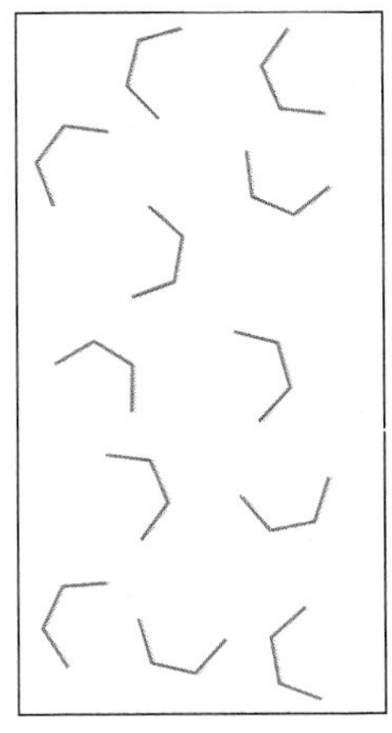

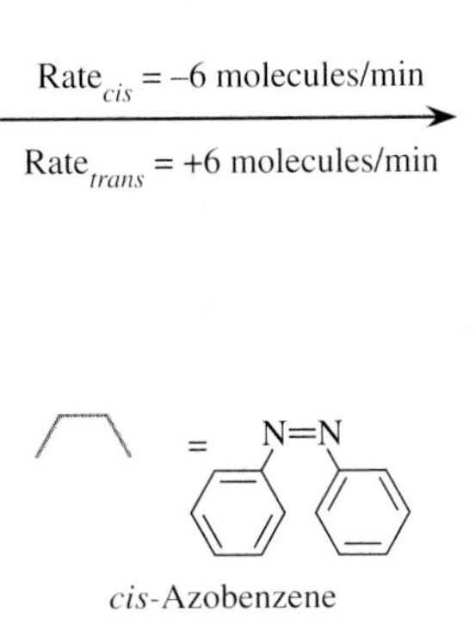

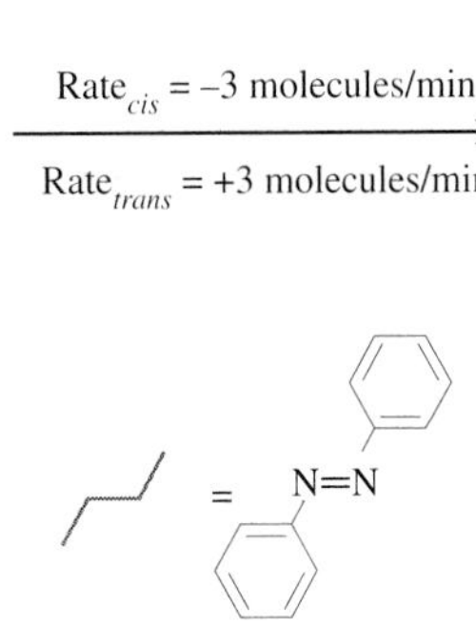

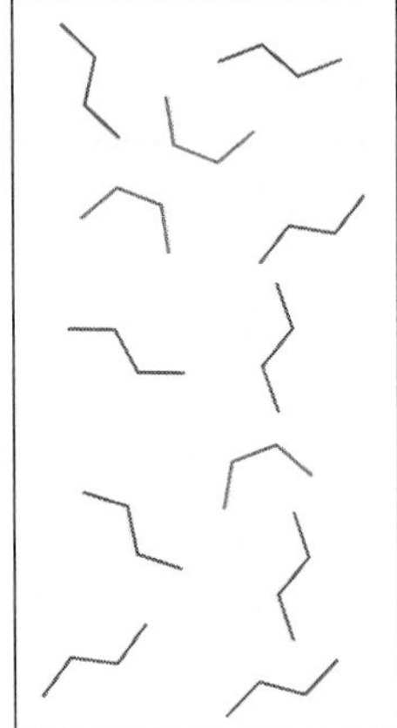

FIGURE 14-9
A molecular view of the isomerization of *cis*-azobenzene illustrates that the rate of isomerization decreases as the number of *cis*-azobenzene molecules decreases.

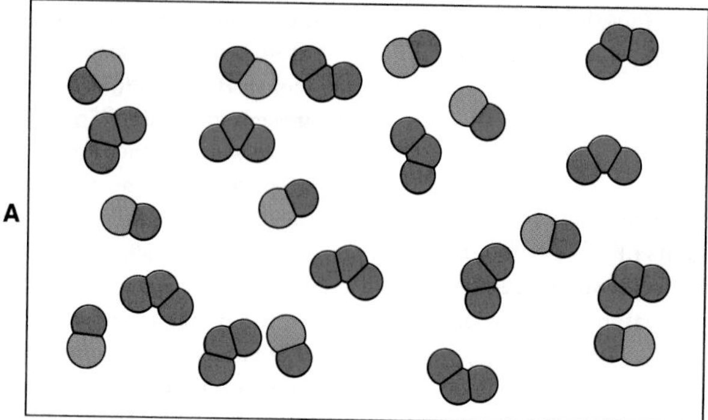

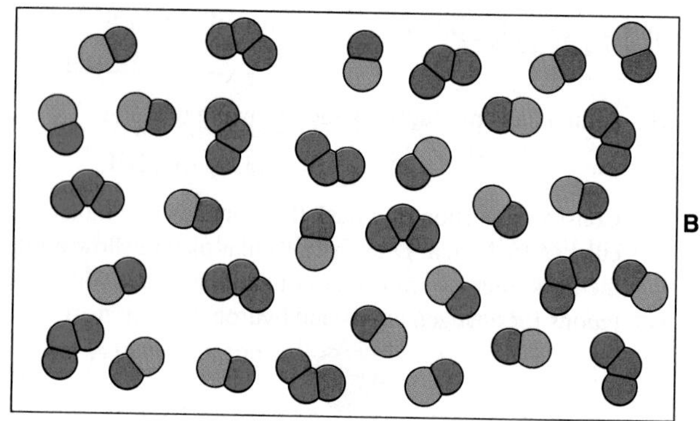

FIGURE 14-13
A schematic illustration of two flasks of equal volume containing different amounts of ozone and nitrogen monoxide. The flask in **B** has the same amount of O_3 but twice as much NO as the flask in **A**. With twice as many NO molecules, twice as many NO—O_3 collisions occur, so the reaction in **B** proceeds twice as fast as the reaction in **A**.

To understand the effect of changing concentrations on the rate of a chemical reaction, it helps to visualize the reaction at the molecular level. Figure 14-13 is a molecular view of two flasks of equal volume, each containing NO and O_3. The flask in Figure 14-13, *B*, contains the same number of O_3 molecules but twice as many NO molecules as the flask in Figure 14-13, *A*. We can analyze the collision rates in these two flasks to determine the relative rates of reaction.

In this one-step bimolecular reaction, a single collision in the proper orientation leads to transfer of an oxygen atom from O_3 to NO. As we saw for the formation of N_2O_4, the rate of a bimolecular reaction is proportional to the number of collisions: the more collisions, the more often the reaction occurs. The flask in Figure 14-13, *B*, contains twice as many NO molecules as the flask in Figure 14-13, *A*, so an O_3 molecule in *B* has twice as many opportunities to collide with an NO molecule. We conclude that the rate of reaction in the flask in *B* is twice as fast as the rate in the flask in *A*. Sample Problem 14-2 extends this reasoning to O_3 molecules.

SAMPLE PROBLEM 14-2 RATES AND NUMBER OF MOLECULES

The flask shown here is filled with ozone and nitrogen monoxide. Compared with the flask in Figure 14-13, *A*, how fast will the reaction proceed?

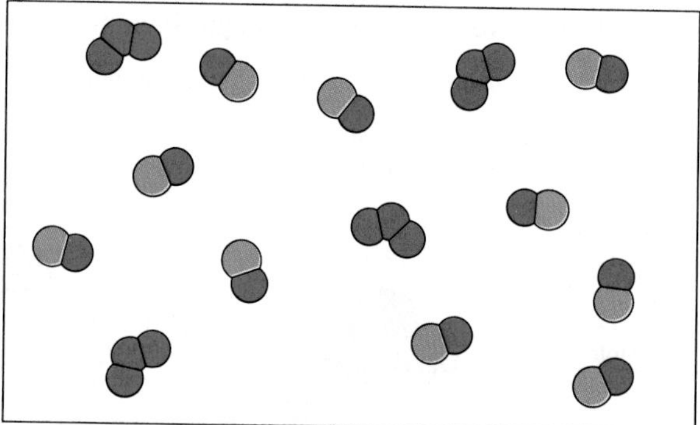

METHOD: We know the mechanism of this reaction requires a collision between an NO molecule and an O_3 molecule, as shown in Figure 14-12. The rate of the reaction therefore depends on the number of collisions that occur, and the collision frequency is proportional to the number of molecules.

In Figure 14-13, *A*, there are 12 molecules of O_3 and 10 of NO. In the new flask we find 10 molecules of NO and 4 molecules of O_3. The concentration of O_3 is only one third as great, so any one molecule of NO will encounter an O_3 molecule 3 times less often than it would in the flask in Figure 14-13, *A*. We conclude that this new mixture will react one third as fast than the one in Figure 14-13, *A*.

RATE LAWS

The effect of concentration on the rate of some particular chemical reaction can be summarized in an algebraic expression known as a **rate law.** The rate law for a reaction links the rate of a reaction with the concentrations of the reactants. We have seen that the rate of the reaction between NO and O_3 is directly proportional to the concentration of NO when the concentration of O_3 is fixed:

$$\text{Rate} \propto [\text{NO}] \qquad \{[O_3] = \text{Constant}\}$$

Furthermore, the rate of this reaction is directly proportional to the concentration of O_3 when the concentration of NO is fixed:

$$\text{Rate} \propto [O_3] \qquad \{[\text{NO}] = \text{Constant}\}$$

These two proportionalities can be combined into a single proportionality that describes both variations:

$$\text{Rate} \propto [O_3][\text{NO}]$$

Introducing a proportionality constant (k) gives an equality that is the rate law for the NO + O_3 reaction:

$$\text{Rate} = k[O_3][\text{NO}]$$

This rate law is fully consistent with the molecular view of the mechanism. If the concentration of either O_3 or NO is doubled, the rate of reaction also doubles. If the concentrations of *both* starting materials are doubled, the collision rate and the reaction rate increase by a factor of four.

RATE LAWS AND MECHANISMS

Now that we have established some of the characteristics of mechanisms, we can study the experimental behavior for the decomposition of NO_2 and compare it with behavior predicted by each of the mechanisms that we have proposed. We suggested the following two mechanisms for this reaction:

$NO_2 \rightarrow NO + O$	Step I-1 (rate determining)	(Mechanism I)
$O + NO_2 \rightarrow O_2 + NO$	Step I-2 (fast)	
$2\ NO_2 \rightarrow NO_3 + NO$	Step II-1 (rate determining)	(Mechanism II)
$NO_3 \rightarrow NO + O_2$	Step II-2 (fast)	

The two mechanisms predict two different variations in the rate of reaction with NO_2 concentration. Remember that the overall rate of a reaction is determined by the

We see that this graph is not linear, so we conclude that the decomposition of NO_2 does not follow first-order kinetics. Consequently, Mechanism I, which predicts first-order behavior, cannot be correct.

Data must be collected over a relatively long period before we can see clearly whether or not a first-order plot is linear. Notice that the first six points on the plot in Sample Problem 14-4 fall reasonably on the dashed straight line. Only after more than 50% of the reactant has been consumed does this plot deviate substantially from linearity.

Another characteristic of first-order reactions is that the time it takes for half the reactant to disappear is the same, no matter what the concentration. This time is called the **half-life ($t_{1/2}$).** We can obtain an equation for $t_{1/2}$ by manipulating Equation 14-3. First, rearrange the equation to isolate time:

$$ln[A] = ln[A]_o - kt \qquad so \qquad kt = ln[A]_o - ln[A]$$

Next, use a property of logarithms, $ln\,x - ln\,y = ln\,(x/y)$, to group the two logarithmic terms:

$$kt = ln\,([A]_o/[A])$$

Finally, apply this equation to a time interval equal to the half-life. When half the original concentration has been consumed, $[A] = 0.5[A_o]$:

$$kt_{1/2} = ln\left(\frac{[A]_o}{0.5\,[A]_o}\right) = ln\,2$$

After canceling the $[A]_o$ terms, rearrange to give an equation for $t_{1/2}$:

$$t_{1/2} = \frac{ln\,2}{k} \qquad \textbf{(14-4)}$$

Equation 14-4 does not contain the concentration of A, so the half-life of a first-order reaction is a constant that is independent of how much A is present. Sample Problem 14-5 deals with half-lives.

SAMPLE PROBLEM 14-5 HALF-LIVES

Carbon-14 (^{14}C) is a radioactive isotope with a half-life of 5.73×10^3 years. The amount of ^{14}C present in an object can be used to determine its age. Calculate the rate constant for decay of ^{14}C and determine how long it requires for 90% of the ^{14}C in a sample to decompose.

METHOD: The half-life of a first-order process is related to the rate constant through Equation 14-4. After we find the rate constant, Equation 14-3 can be used to determine the time required to reach a certain concentration.

First, rearrange Equation 14-4 to obtain an equation for the rate constant (k):

$$t_{1/2} = \frac{ln\,2}{k} \qquad so \qquad k = \frac{ln\,2}{t_{1/2}}$$

Next, substitute and calculate k:

$$k = \frac{0.6931}{5.73 \times 10^3\ \text{yr}} = 1.21 \times 10^{-4}\ \text{yr}^{-1}$$

Finally, use k and Equation 14-3 to calculate the time required for 90% of a sample to decay. When 90% has decayed, 10% remains, or $0.10[A]_o$:

$$\ln[A] = \ln[A]_o - kt \qquad so \qquad kt = \ln\frac{[A]_o}{[A]} = \ln\frac{[A]_o}{0.10[A]_o} = \ln 10$$

$$t = \frac{\ln 10}{k} = \frac{2.303}{1.21 \times 10^{-4}\ \text{yr}} = 1.90 \times 10^{4}\ \text{yr}$$

It requires 19,000 years for 90% of a sample of ^{14}C to decompose.

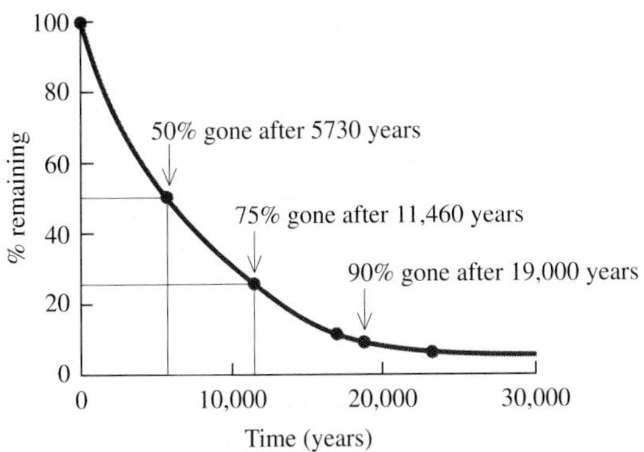

The use of radioactive isotopes and their half-lives to determine the age of an object is discussed in detail in Chapter 19.

SECOND-ORDER INTEGRATED RATE LAW

Mechanism II for the decomposition of NO_2 predicts that the reaction should have a second-order rate law:

$$\text{Rate} = \frac{-\Delta[NO_2]}{\Delta t} = k[NO_2]^2$$

The general form of a second-order rate expression is:

$$\text{Rate} = k[A]^2$$

Mathematical treatment converts this general form into an integrated rate law that shows that the reciprocal of concentration varies linearly with time:

$$\frac{1}{[A]} = kt + \frac{1}{[A]_o} \qquad \textbf{(14-5)}$$

Appendix F describes the mathematical conversion between the second-order rate law and its integrated form.

In this expression, $[A]$ is the concentration of reactant A at time t, and $[A]_o$ is the concentration of reactant A at the beginning of the reaction ($t = 0$).

Equation 14-5, the second-order integrated rate law, is a linear function. That is, for a second-order reaction, a plot of $1/[A]$ along the Y axis vs. t along the X axis gives a straight line. The slope of the line is equal to the rate constant (k), and the intercept is $1/[A]_o$. Figure 14-15 shows the decomposition data of Figure 14-11 plotted in this way. The graph is linear, showing that the reaction is second-order in NO_2. Thus the kinetic behavior of the decomposition of NO_2 matches the predicted rate law for Mechanism II (see earlier discussion). Chemists have accepted Mechanism II as the correct mechanism for this decomposition because it predicts the correct rate law and consists of plausible molecular processes.

Sample Problem 14-6 provides another example of the analysis of rate data.

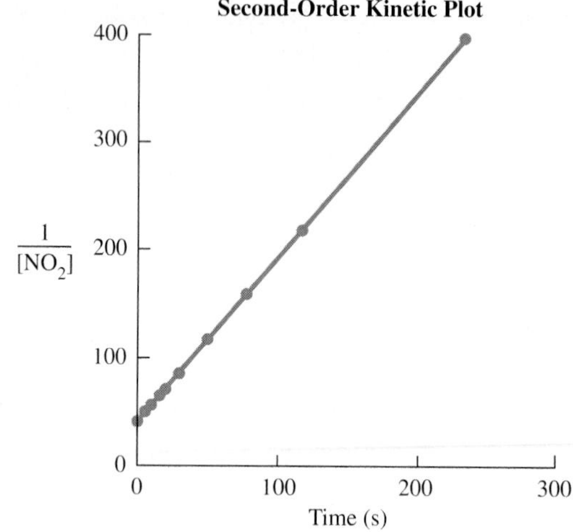

FIGURE 14-15
The decomposition data for NO_2 plotted as the reciprocal of concentration vs. time. This graph is linear, with a slope equal to the second-order rate constant.

SAMPLE PROBLEM 14-6 ANALYSIS OF RATE DATA

Otto Diels and Kurt Alder were awarded the Nobel Prize in chemistry in 1950 for showing the synthetic usefulness of this reaction.

The Diels-Alder reaction, in which two alkenes combine to give a new product, is one of the most frequently used reactions for the synthesis of organic compounds, with thousands of examples found in the chemical literature. The reaction of butadiene is a simple example:

C_8H_{12}

$2\ C_4H_6$
(butadiene)

Use the data in the table to determine the rate law and the rate constant for the Diels-Alder reaction of butadiene:

Time (min)	$[C_4H_6]$ (M)
0	0.130
4.0	0.0872
8.0	0.0650
12.0	0.0535
16.0	0.0453
20.0	0.0370
30.0	0.0281

METHOD: To find the rate law for this reaction, we need to determine the order with respect to butadiene:

$$\text{Rate} = k[C_4H_6]^x$$

The data provided in the problem allow us to test graphically whether the reaction is first order or second order. If the reaction is first order, a plot of $ln[C_4H_6]$ vs. t is linear. If the reaction is second order, a plot of $1/[C_4H_6]$ vs. t is linear. If neither plot is a straight line, the dimerization is something other than first or second order.

First, we calculate the values for the logarithms and the reciprocals of the concentrations:

Time (min)	$ln\ [C_4H_6]$	$1/[C_4H_6]$
0	−2.04	7.69
4	−2.44	11.5
8	−2.73	15.4
12	−2.93	18.7
16	−3.09	22.1
20	−3.30	27.0
30	−3.57	35.6

Next, we prepare first-order and second-order plots to see whether either gives a straight line:

First-Order Plot

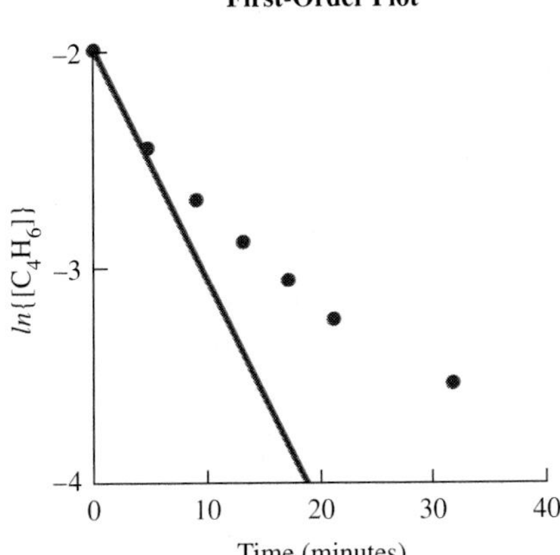

Second-Order Plot

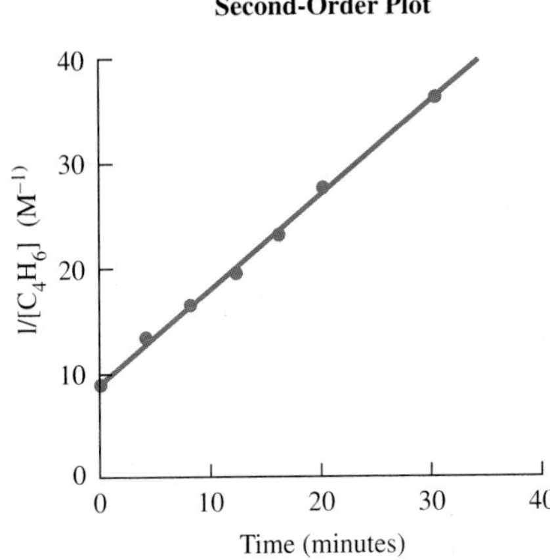

The first-order plot is not linear, so the reaction cannot be first order. The straight line in the $1/[C_4H_6]$ vs. t plot shows that the reaction is second order in butadiene. The rate law for this Diels-Alder reaction is:

$$\text{Rate} = -\frac{\Delta[C_4H_6]}{\Delta t} = k[C_4H_6]^2$$

Two points on the best-fit line are required to evaluate the rate constant. We choose two convenient times along the X axis and read the appropriate values of $1/[C_4H_6]$ from the best-fit line through the data points:

$$k = \text{Slope} = \frac{\Delta y}{\Delta x} = \frac{35.9\ M^{-1} - 7.98\ M^{-1}}{30\ \text{min} - 0\ \text{min}} = 0.93\ M^{-1}\ \text{min}^{-1}$$

"ISOLATION" EXPERIMENTS

The first-order and second-order integrated rate laws presented earlier describe the change in concentration of a *single* reactant. However, most reactions involve concentration changes for more than one reactant. Although it is possible to develop integrated rate laws for such reactions, they are more complicated and more difficult to interpret than rate laws that involve just one chemical species. Fortunately, it is often possible to simplify the experimental behavior of a reaction.

One way to simplify the behavior of a reaction is to adjust the conditions so that the initial concentration of one starting material is much smaller than the initial concentrations of the others. This establishes experimental conditions under which the concentration of only one of the starting materials changes significantly during the reaction. This concentration is then said to be *isolated.* We illustrate the **isolation method** in detail using another reaction that is important in atmospheric chemistry.

Trees and shrubs contain a group of fragrant compounds called *terpenes.* The simplest terpene is isoprene. All other terpenes are built around carbon skeletons constructed from one or more isoprene units. Plants emit terpenes into the atmosphere, where they react with ozone. The possible effect of terpenes on the concentration of ozone in the troposphere has been the subject of much debate and has led to careful measurements of rates of reaction with ozone.

Recall from Chapter 11 that natural rubber is a polymer of isoprene:

The familiar odors of pine forests and eucalyptus groves are caused by terpenes.

The reactions of terpenes with ozone lead to a complicated array of products, but the rate behavior for ozone reacting with a terpene can be studied by measuring the concentration of the terpene as a function of time:

$$O_3 + \text{Terpene} \longrightarrow \text{Products} \qquad \text{Rate} = k[O_3]^y[\text{Terpene}]^z$$

Because the reaction rate depends on two concentrations rather than one, we cannot determine y or z from integrated rate laws unless we isolate one of the concentrations. Isolation is achieved by making the initial concentration of one reactant much smaller than the initial concentration of the other. Data collected under these conditions can then be analyzed using integrated rate laws (see Equations 14-3 and 14-4).

For example, an experiment could be performed on the reaction of ozone with isoprene with the following initial concentrations:

$$[O_3]_o = 5.40 \times 10^{-4}\ \text{M} \qquad [\text{Isoprene}]_o = 2.5 \times 10^{-6}\ \text{M}$$

Notice that the initial concentration of ozone is more than 200 times larger than the initial concentration of isoprene. The reaction stoichiometry shows that one molecule of isoprene reacts with one molecule of ozone, so when all the isoprene has been consumed, the ozone concentration will have changed by less than 0.5%:

$$\underset{\substack{\text{Initial ozone}\\ \text{concentration}}}{(5.40 \times 10^{-4}\text{M})} - \underset{\substack{\text{Concentration}\\ \text{decrease}\\ \text{because of}\\ \text{reaction with}\\ \text{isoprene}}}{(2.5 \times 10^{-6}\text{M})} = \underset{\substack{\text{Final ozone}\\ \text{concentration}}}{5.37 \times 10^{-4}\text{M}}$$

In other words, the reaction is "flooded" with a large excess of ozone. Because the concentration of ozone does not change appreciably, we can group the near-constant concentration of ozone with the rate constant:

$$\text{Rate} = \underbrace{k[O_3]^y}[\text{isoprene}]^z$$

This quantity remains constant over the course of the reaction because $[O_3] >> [\text{isoprene}]$.

Therefore let:

$$k[O_3]^y = k_{obs}$$

The term k_{obs} is short for "observed rate constant."

Now the rate law simplifies to: rate $= k_{obs}[\text{isoprene}]^z$. In this case, $k_{obs} = k[O_3]^y$. It is important to remember that k_{obs} is an *experimental rate constant,* but it is *not* the *true rate constant* (k) that appears in the general rate law.

By isolating isoprene as the only reactant whose concentration changes significantly, we have simplified the general rate law to a form that can be tested against the integrated rate laws:

$$\text{First-order case:} \quad ln[\text{isoprene}] = ln[\text{isoprene}]_o - k_{obs}t$$

$$\text{Second-order case:} \quad \frac{1}{[\text{isoprene}]} = \frac{1}{[\text{isoprene}]_o} + k_{obs}t$$

Experimental data collected under these conditions are plotted in Figure 14-16. Notice that the *ln*[isoprene] plot is linear, but the 1/[isoprene] plot is not, demonstrating that the reaction is first order in isoprene. The slope of the first-order plot gives the observed rate constant:

$$k_{obs} = -\text{Slope} = k[O_3]^y = 4.4\ s^{-1}$$

Time (s)	[isoprene] (10^{-6} M)	*ln*[isoprene]	1/[isoprene] ($10^6\ M^{-1}$)
0.000	2.500	−12.899	0.400
0.215	1.110	−13.711	0.901
0.495	0.305	−15.003	3.28
0.955	0.037	−17.11	27

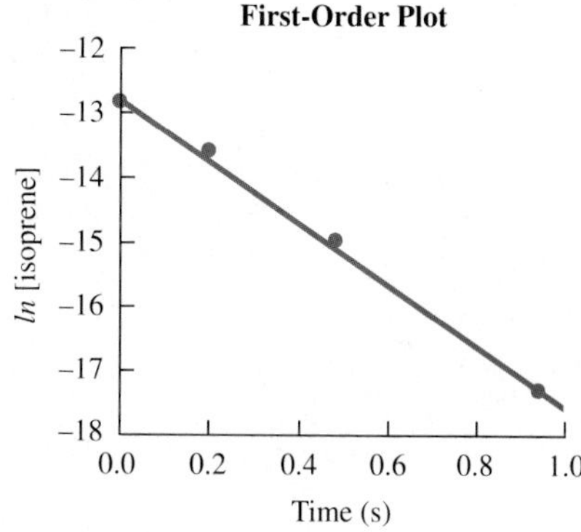

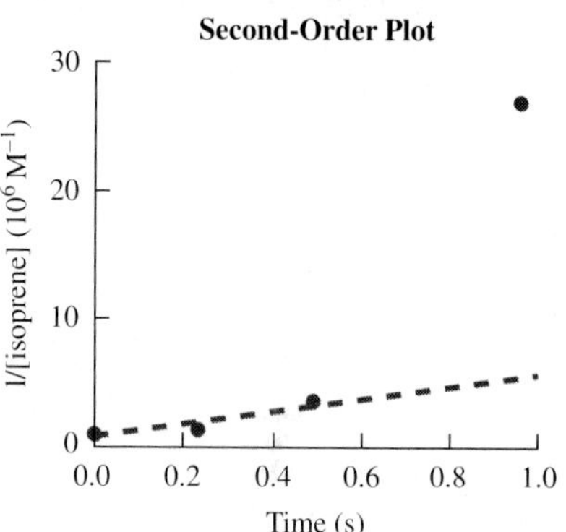

FIGURE 14-16
Data for the reaction of isoprene with ozone under conditions when the concentration of isoprene is isolated. The experimental behavior is first order under these conditions.

The true rate constant (k) cannot be computed unless we determine y, the order with respect to ozone. One way to do this is to repeat the isolation experiment with a different initial concentration of ozone. For example, we could repeat the experiment with an initial ozone concentration of 2.70×10^{-4} M, half as large as the concentration in the first experiment. When all the isoprene has been consumed, the ozone concentration is 2.68×10^{-4} M, a decrease of less than 1%. In this second experiment, we would find $k_{obs} = 2.2\ s^{-1}$, half as large as k_{obs} in the first experiment. To determine the value of y, we take the ratio of the observed rate constants:

$$\frac{k_{obs,\,I}}{k_{obs,\,II}} = \frac{k[O_3]_I^{\,y}}{k[O_3]_{II}^{\,y}} = \frac{4.4\ s^{-1}}{2.2\ s^{-1}} = 2.0$$

Now group the exponential terms, cancel the true rate constant, and substitute for ozone concentration:

$$\frac{k[O_3]_I^{\,y}}{k[O_3]_{II}^{\,y}} = \left(\frac{k[O_3]_I}{k[O_3]_{II}}\right)^y = \left(\frac{5.4 \times 10^{-4}\ M}{2.7 \times 10^{-4}\ M}\right)^y = (2.0)^y$$

The experimental rate constant ratio must equal this expression: $2.0 = (2.0)^y$. By inspection, it can be seen that $y = 1$, so the reaction is first order in ozone. Thus the complete experimental rate law for the reaction is: rate $= k[O_3]$[isoprene]. Finally, the true rate constant can be calculated from k_{obs} using the data from either experiment:

$$k_{obs} = k[O_3] \quad so \quad k = \frac{k_{obs}}{[O_3]} = \frac{4.4\ s^{-1}}{5.4 \times 10^{-4}\ M} = 8.1 \times 10^3\ M^{-1}\ s^{-1}$$

In this example, after we took the ratio of observed rate constants, the order of reaction could be determined by inspection. Sample Problem 14-7 shows what to do when the order of reaction is not obvious.

SAMPLE PROBLEM 14-7 RATE LAW FROM ISOLATION EXPERIMENTS

The reaction between hydrogen and bromine produces hydrogen bromide, a caustic gas:

$$H_{2\,(g)} + Br_{2\,(g)} \rightarrow 2\ HBr_{(g)}$$

To determine the rate law for this reaction, a chemist performed two isolation experiments using different initial concentrations. Both experiments gave linear *ln* $[H_2]$ vs. t plots but with different slopes. Here are the details:

$[Br_2]_o$	$[H_2]_o$	Slope of plot
3.50×10^{-5} M	2.50×10^{-7} M	$-8.87 \times 10^{-4}\ s^{-1}$
2.00×10^{-5} M	2.50×10^{-7} M	$-6.71 \times 10^{-4}\ s^{-1}$

Determine the rate law and the rate constant for the reaction.

METHOD: We begin with the general expression for the rate law of the reaction, which may contain the concentrations of both reactants raised to powers that we must determine:

$$\text{Rate} = k[H_2]^x[Br_2]^y$$

Since the rate law contains more than one species, isolation experiments are required to determine the orders of reaction. In these experiments, the system is "flooded" with Br_2, so the Br_2 concentration remains essentially constant over the course of the reaction. This allows us to rewrite the rate law with $[Br_2]$ included as part of the observed rate constant.

$$\text{Rate} = k_{obs}[H_2]^x \quad \textit{where} \quad k_{obs} = k[Br_2]^y$$

In each experiment, a plot of $ln[H_2]$ vs. time is a straight line, which tells us the reaction is first order in hydrogen. The values of k_{obs} are found from the slopes of the lines:

$$k_{obs,\,I} = -\text{Slope}_I = 8.87 \times 10^{-4}\ s^{-1} \quad \textit{and} \quad k_{obs,\,II} = -\text{Slope}_{II} = 6.71 \times 10^{-4}\ s^{-1}$$

To find the order of reaction with respect to bromine, take the ratio of the observed rate constants:

$$\frac{k_{obs,\,I}}{k_{obs,\,II}} = \frac{k[Br_2]_I{}^y}{k[Br_2]_{II}{}^y} = \frac{8.87 \times 10^{-4}\ M}{6.71 \times 10^{-4}\ M} = 1.32$$

Now substitute the appropriate bromine concentrations, cancel the true rate constant, and group the exponential terms:

$$\frac{\cancel{k}[3.50 \times 10^{-5}\ M]^y}{\cancel{k}[2.00 \times 10^{-5}\ M]^y} = (1.75)^y = 1.32$$

The value of y cannot be determined by inspection, but we can isolate the exponent by taking the logarithm of both sides:

$$ln\,(1.75)^y = ln\,(1.32) \quad \textit{and} \quad ln\,(1.75)^y = y\,ln\,(1.75)$$

$$y\,(0.560) = 0.278 \quad \textit{from which} \quad y = 0.496$$

Reaction orders must be integers or simple fractions, so we round off to 0.5. The reaction is half order in bromine, and the rate law is:

$$\text{Rate} = k[H_2][Br_2]^{1/2}$$

Finally, solve for the true rate constant using the data from either of the two experiments.

$$k_{obs} = k[Br_2]^{1/2} \quad \textit{so} \quad k = \frac{k_{obs}}{[Br_2]^{1/2}}$$

$$k = \frac{8.87 \times 10^{-4}\ s^{-1}}{(3.50 \times 10^{-5}\ M)^{1/2}} = \frac{8.87 \times 10^{-4}\ s^{-1}}{5.92 \times 10^{-3}\ M^{1/2}} = 0.150\ M^{-1/2}\ s^{-1}$$

We explain the half-order dependence on bromine concentration in Section 14.5.

SECTION EXERCISES

14.4.1 The reaction of N_2O_5 with gaseous H_2O is a potentially important reaction in the chemistry of acid rain:

$$N_2O_{5\,(g)} + H_2O_{\,(g)} \rightarrow 2\ HNO_{3\,(g)}$$

It is possible to monitor the concentration of N_2O_5 with time. Describe a set of isolation experiments from which the rate law and rate constant for this reaction could be determined.

14.4.2 In addition to reacting with water vapor, N_2O_5 can decompose to nitrogen dioxide and oxygen:

$$2\ N_2O_{5\,(g)} \rightarrow 4\ NO_{2\,(g)} + O_{2\,(g)}$$

Here are some data for this decomposition reaction:

Time (min)	0	20	40	60	80
$[N_2O_5]$ (10^{-2} M)	0.92	0.50	0.28	0.15	0.08

Determine the order and the rate constant by constructing appropriate graphs using these data.

14.4.3 Nitrogen dioxide reacts with carbon monoxide at elevated temperature:

$$NO_{2\,(g)} + CO_{(g)} \longrightarrow NO_{(g)} + CO_{2\,(g)}$$

Use the following information to determine the rate law.

(a) When an experiment is performed with $[CO]_o = 0.15$ M and $[NO_2]_o = 1.75 \times 10^{-3}$ M, a plot of $1/[NO_2]$ vs. t gives a straight line.

(b) When this experiment is repeated with $[CO]_o = 0.25$ M and $[NO_2]_o = 1.75 \times 10^{-3}$ M, the slope of the $1/[NO_2]$ vs. t plot is identical to the slope of the plot for experiment a.

14.5 LINKING MECHANISMS AND RATE LAWS

The mechanism of any chemical reaction has the following characteristics:

1. The mechanism is a sequence of one or more bimolecular and unimolecular elementary reactions that describes how the chemical process may occur.
2. The sum of the individual steps in the mechanism must give the overall balanced chemical equation.
3. The reaction mechanism must be consistent with the experimental rate law.

Termolecular reactions are rare. Furthermore, any termolecular reaction can be written as a pair of bimolecular reactions.

Sometimes the balance is achieved by allowing an individual step to occur two or more times.

A proposed mechanism stands or falls on the third requirement. In this section we show that every mechanism predicts a rate law. If the rate law predicted by a proposed mechanism matches the experimental rate law, the mechanism is a possible description of how the reaction proceeds. On the other hand, if the rate law predicted by the proposed mechanism does not match the experimental rate law, the proposed mechanism must be wrong.

Remember that an *elementary* reaction represents a single event at the molecular level. That is, a bimolecular reaction is a collision between two molecules with a rate expression that contains the concentrations of both reactants:

$$A + B \longrightarrow \text{Products} \qquad \text{Elementary rate} = k[A][B]$$

Also, a unimolecular reaction is the fragmentation or rearrangement of a single chemical species with a rate expression that contains the concentration of that species:

$$C \longrightarrow \text{Products} \qquad \text{Elementary rate} = k[C]$$

The relationship between the rate expressions for *elementary steps* and the experimental rate law for the *overall reaction* depends on whether the first step or some later step in the mechanism is rate determining.

RATE-DETERMINING FIRST STEP

Each example we have used to introduce the concepts of chemical mechanisms has a first step that is rate determining. These mechanisms and their rate laws are summarized in Table 14-1.

TABLE 14-1 SOME MECHANISMS AND RATE LAWS*

STOICHIOMETRY	MECHANISM	RATE LAW
$2\ NO_2 \rightarrow N_2O_4$	$NO_2 + NO_2 \rightarrow N_2O_4$	Rate = $k[NO_2]^2$
$2\ NO_2 \rightarrow 2\ NO + O_2$	$2\ NO_2 \rightarrow NO_3 + NO$ (slow) $NO_3 \rightarrow NO + O_2$	Rate = $k[NO_2]^2$
$NO + O_3 \rightarrow NO_2 + O_2$	$NO + O_3 \rightarrow NO_2 + O_2$	Rate = $k[NO][O_3]$
Cis-azobenzene → *Trans*-azobenzene	*Cis*-azobenzene → *Trans*-azobenzene	Rate = k[*cis*-azobenzene]
$C_5H_{11}Br + H_2O \rightarrow C_5H_{10} + H_3O^+ + Br^-$	$C_5H_{11}Br \rightarrow C_5H_{11}^+ + Br^-$ (slow) $C_5H_{11}^+ + H_2O \rightarrow C_5H_{10} + H_3O^+$	Rate = $k[C_5H_{11}Br]$

*Examples from Sections 14.1 through 14.4.

In each of these mechanisms, the *first* elementary reaction is the rate-determining step. Because the overall reaction can go no faster than its rate-determining step, no elementary reaction that occurs *after* the rate-determining step has an effect on the overall rate of reaction. Therefore:

> ***When the first step of a mechanism is rate determining, the predicted rate law for the overall reaction is the rate expression for that first step.***

The predicted rate law is first order for a reaction whose first step is unimolecular and rate determining. The predicted rate law is second order overall for a reaction whose first step is bimolecular and rate determining. For example, the first step of the mechanism for the $C_5H_{11}Br$ elimination reaction is unimolecular and slow, so the rate law predicted by this mechanism is first order: Rate = $k[C_5H_{11}Br]$. Sample Problem 14-8 gives another example of rate laws when the first step is rate determining.

SAMPLE PROBLEM 14-8 PREDICTED RATE LAWS

At elevated temperature, nitrogen dioxide reacts with carbon monoxide to produce carbon dioxide and nitrogen monoxide:

$$NO_2 + CO \rightarrow CO_2 + NO$$

Two simple mechanisms can be envisioned for this reaction. In one mechanism, products form directly in a one-step bimolecular process that transfers an oxygen atom from NO_2 to CO. In another mechanism, a pair of NO_2 molecules collide in the rate-determining step to form NO and NO_3, and then the highly reactive NO_3 intermediate transfers an oxygen atom to CO in a fast bimolecular collision. What is the predicted rate law for each of these mechanisms?

METHOD: It is best to work with each mechanism separately. When the first step is rate determining, the predicted rate law matches the rate expression for that first elementary step. First, analyze the one-step mechanism:

$$NO_2 + CO \rightarrow CO_2 + NO$$

This process is analogous to the reaction of NO and O_3 discussed in Section 14.3. In a simple one-step atom transfer, the reaction is first order in each of the starting materials and second order overall:

$$\text{One-step mechanism:} \quad \text{Rate} = k[NO_2][CO]$$

The second mechanism occurs in two steps:

$$2\ NO_2 \longrightarrow NO + NO_3 \text{ (slow)}$$

$$NO_3 + CO \longrightarrow NO_2 + CO_2 \text{ (fast)}$$

In this mechanism the first step is slow and rate determining. Because the collision partners are identical, this reaction is second order in NO_2 and second order overall:

$$\text{Two-step mechanism:} \quad \text{Rate} = k[NO_2]^2$$

Carbon monoxide does not appear in this rate law because it participates in the mechanism *after* the rate-determining step. Remember, any reaction that occurs after the rate-determining step does not affect the overall rate of reaction.

Experiments show that this reaction is second order in NO_2, as predicted by the second proposed mechanism. We can rule out the one-step mechanism because it is not consistent with the experimental rate law. Agreement with the rate law *does not prove* the second mechanism to be the correct one, however, because other mechanisms may predict the same rate law. It is only one strong piece of evidence that supports this particular two-step process.

RATE-DETERMINING LATER STEP

The rate-determining step in many chemical mechanisms occurs after one or more faster steps. In such cases the reactants in the early steps may or may not appear in the rate law. Furthermore, the rate law is likely to depart from simple first-order or second-order behavior. Sample Problem 14-7 reveals the experimental rate law for the reaction of H_2 gas with Br_2 gas. Although the reaction follows simple 1:1 stoichiometry, its experimental rate law cannot be explained by a simple mechanism. The reaction rate depends on the square root of the Br_2 concentration as well as being first order in H_2:

$$H_2 + Br_2 \longrightarrow 2\ HBr \qquad\qquad \text{Rate} = k[H_2][Br_2]^{1/2}$$

The first step of the mechanism for this reaction cannot be rate determining because no elementary step has a rate expression that contains a square root. Instead, some later step in the mechanism must be rate determining.

The accepted mechanism for this reaction is illustrated with molecular pictures in Figure 14-17. The reaction begins with the dissociation of Br_2 molecules into Br atoms:

Typically, elementary reactions in a mechanism are written with their rate constants above or below the reaction arrow.

$$Br_2 \xrightarrow{k_1} 2\ Br$$

Almost all the Br atoms produced in the first step simply recombine to regenerate Br_2 molecules:

$$2\ Br \xrightarrow{k_{-1}} Br_2$$

This is an example of a **reversible reaction,** one that occurs rapidly in both directions. For simplicity, we combine these two elementary reactions in a single expression:

The recombination reaction is the reverse of this first step, so its rate constant is labeled k_{-1}. We explore chemical reversibility in detail in Chapters 15 and 16.

$$Br_2 \underset{k_{-1}}{\overset{k_1}{\rightleftarrows}} 2\ Br \quad \text{(fast, reversible)}$$

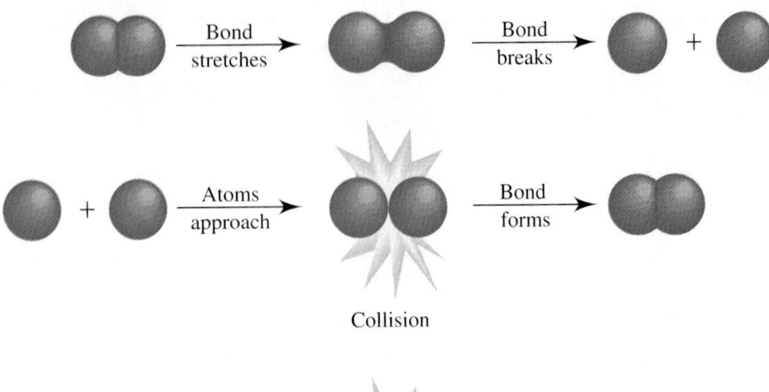

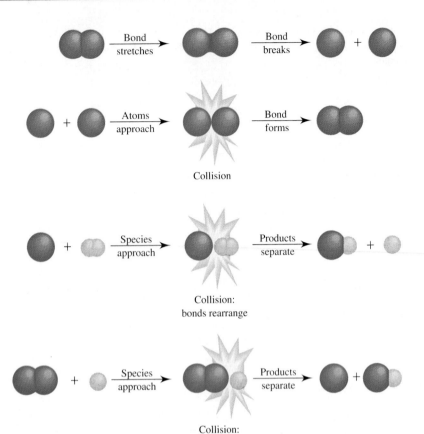

FIGURE 14-17
A molecular view of the accepted mechanism for the reaction of H_2 and Br_2 to produce 2 HBr.

Although most Br atoms produced in the first step recombine, occasionally a Br atom reacts with a molecule of H_2 to form one molecule of HBr and a hydrogen atom. This step is slow and rate determining:

$$\text{Br} + \text{H}_2 \xrightarrow{k_2} \text{HBr} + \text{H} \quad \text{(slow, rate determining)}$$

Finally, the hydrogen atom produced in the rate-determining step undergoes a third elementary reaction, a bimolecular collision with a Br_2 molecule. The H atom rapidly forms a bond with one Br atom to form one molecule of HBr and a Br atom:

$$\text{H} + \text{Br}_2 \xrightarrow{k_3} \text{HBr} + \text{Br} \quad \text{(fast)}$$

The second step in this mechanism is rate determining, so the overall rate of the reaction is governed by the rate of this step:

$$\text{Rate} = k_2[\text{Br}][\text{H}_2]$$

This rate law describes the rate behavior predicted by the proposed mechanism accurately, but it cannot be tested against experiments because it contains the concentration of Br atoms, which are intermediates in the reaction. As we indicated earlier, an intermediate has a short lifetime and is difficult to detect, so measuring its concentration is difficult, if not impossible. Furthermore, we cannot adjust the experimental conditions to change the concentration of an intermediate by a known amount. Therefore if we are to test this rate law against experimental behavior, we must somehow express the concentration of the intermediate in terms of reactants and products.

EQUALITY OF RATES

Our proposed mechanism begins with the decomposition of Br_2 molecules into Br atoms that recombine rapidly to give Br_2 molecules. At first, Br_2 molecules decompose faster than Br atoms recombine, but before long the Br atom concentration becomes large enough for recombination to occur at the same rate as decomposition. When the two rates are equal, so are their rate expressions:

$$k_1[Br_2] = k_{-1}[Br]^2$$

This equality lets us determine the concentration of the intermediate in terms of concentrations of the reactants. We isolate [Br] by rearranging the rate expressions and taking the square root of both sides:

$$[Br]^2 = \frac{k_1}{k_{-1}}[Br_2] \qquad \textit{and} \qquad [Br] = \left(\frac{k_1}{k_{-1}}\right)^{1/2}[Br_2]^{1/2}$$

Now substitute this expression for [Br] into the rate expression for the rate-determining step:

$$\text{Rate} = k_2[H_2][Br] = k_2\left(\frac{k_1}{k_{-1}}\right)^{1/2}[H_2][Br_2]^{1/2} = k[H_2][Br_2]^{1/2}$$

In this expression, *k,* the rate constant for the overall reaction, is related to the elementary rate constants:

$$k = k_2\left(\frac{k_1}{k_{-1}}\right)^{1/2}$$

The predicted rate law is first order in hydrogen and one-half order in bromine, in agreement with the experimental rate law determined in Sample Problem 14-7. In Sample Problem 14-9, we show that this mechanism also meets the other criteria for a satisfactory mechanism.

SAMPLE PROBLEM 14-9 THE H_2-Br_2 MECHANISM

The proposed mechanism for the reaction between H_2 and Br_2 predicts the experimental rate law. Does it meet the other criteria for a satisfactory mechanism?

METHOD: A satisfactory mechanism must be made up entirely of elementary steps, must give the correct stoichiometry of the reaction, and must predict the experimental rate law. We have shown that the proposed mechanism predicts the rate law. To see whether the mechanism meets the other criteria, we must examine the individual steps.

This mechanism has four steps. The first step is the unimolecular decomposition of Br_2. The remaining steps all are simple bimolecular collisions. Because all the reactions are unimolecular or bimolecular, the mechanism meets the first criterion.

We can most easily determine whether the steps lead to the correct stoichiometry by writing all four reactions in the same direction. We can then cancel those species that appear on the left and on the right:

$$Br_2 \rightarrow 2\,Br$$
$$2\,Br \rightarrow Br_2$$
$$Br + H_2 \rightarrow HBr + H$$
$$H + Br_2 \rightarrow HBr + Br$$
$$\text{Net reaction: } H_2 + Br_2 \rightarrow 2\,HBr$$

Combining the steps of the mechanism leads to the balanced equation for the overall reaction, so the second criterion also is satisfied. The proposed mechanism satisfies the three requirements, so we conclude that the mechanism is acceptable.

BOX 14-3

MECHANISMS OF REACTIONS IN THE STRATOSPHERE

Chemistry in the stratosphere is initiated by ultraviolet light. Oxygen molecules absorb light with wavelengths of less than 240 nanometers (nm). The energy of these photons causes O_2 to decompose into oxygen atoms:

$$O_2 + h\nu_{\,(<240\text{ nm})} \rightarrow O + O$$

Many of the oxygen atoms recombine to give O_2 molecules. However, a collision between an oxygen atom and an O_2 molecule produces ozone:

$$O + O_2 \rightarrow O_3$$

The O_3 molecules possess high energy, so they decompose back to O_2 and O unless an O_3 molecule collides with an N_2 molecule before decomposing. A collision stabilizes the O_3 molecule by transferring its extra energy to the N_2 molecule. The net result is a buildup of ozone:

$$\text{Net}_{\,(\text{2nd step occurs twice})}: 3\,O_2 + h\nu_{\,(<240\text{ nm})} \rightarrow 2\,O_3$$

The formation of ozone goes on continuously, but ozone is also decomposed by ultraviolet light between 240 and 340 nm:

$$O_3 + h\nu_{\,(240\text{-}340\text{ nm})} \rightarrow O_2 + O$$

The oxygen atom produced in the decomposition can react with a second molecule of ozone:

$$O + O_3 \rightarrow 2\,O_2$$

The net result of this pair of reactions is a reduction in the amount of ozone:

$$\text{Net: } 2\,O_3 + h\nu_{\,(240\text{-}340\text{ nm})} \rightarrow 3\,O_2$$

Ultraviolet light in the short UV wavelength region decomposes O_2, leading to the formation of O_3, whereas ultraviolet light of longer UV wavelengths decomposes O_3, regenerating O_2. The two sets of reactions form a delicate balance in which the rate of O_3 decomposition matches the rate of O_3 production. The resulting ozone layer absorbs nearly all the solar photons in the 240- to 340-nm range. Photons in this wavelength range have enough energy to damage and even destroy living cells, so the ozone layer protects life on Earth.

As long as these are the only reactions that occur, the ozone layer prevents lethal ultraviolet light from reaching Earth's surface. Unfortunately, other chemical species produced by humans, including NO and CFCs, can alter the balance of rates in ways that reduce the O_3 concentration.

For example, NO alters the oxygen balance through the following reactions:

$$NO + O_3 \rightarrow NO_2 + O_2$$
$$NO_2 + h\nu_{\,(<400\text{ nm})} \rightarrow NO + O$$
$$NO_2 + O \rightarrow NO + O_2$$

The net result is that NO in the stratosphere increases the rate of O_3 decomposition, and this in turn reduces the O_3 concentration:

$$\text{Net}_{\,(\text{1st step occurs twice})}: 2\,O_3 + h\nu_{\,(<400\text{ nm})} \rightarrow 3\,O_2$$

As mentioned in the introduction to this chapter, CFCs also have potentially devastating effects on the ozone layer. In Section 14.7 we describe how CFCs destroy stratospheric ozone.

As the mechanism for the reaction between H_2 and Br_2 illustrates, the observation of an order other than first or second indicates that some step beyond the first one in the mechanism is rate determining. The one-half order rate dependence for Br_2 comes about because of the initial rapid cleavage reaction into a *pair* of Br atoms. Fractional, negative, and overall orders greater than two are all signals that a fast first step is followed by a slow subsequent step.

To conclude our introduction to the connection between mechanisms and rate laws, Sample Problem 14-10 incorporates the various principles that we have introduced, and Box 14-3 discusses reactions in the stratosphere.

SAMPLE PROBLEM 14-10 REACTION BETWEEN NO AND O_3

Nitrogen monoxide converts ozone into molecular oxygen:

$$O_3 + NO \rightarrow O_2 + NO_2$$

The experimental rate law is: rate $= k[O_3][NO]$. Which of the following mechanisms are consistent with the experimental rate law?

Mechanism I

$$O_3 + NO \xrightarrow{k_1} O + NO_3 \text{ (slow)}$$
$$O + O_3 \xrightarrow{k_2} 2\ O_2 \quad \text{(fast)}$$
$$NO_3 + NO \xrightarrow{k_3} 2\ NO_2 \quad \text{(fast)}$$

Mechanism II

$$O_3 \underset{k_{-1}}{\overset{k_1}{\rightleftharpoons}} O + O_2 \text{ (fast, reversible)}$$
$$NO + O \xrightarrow{k_2} NO_2 \quad \text{(slow)}$$

Mechanism III

$$O_3 + NO \xrightarrow{k_{1'}} O_2 + NO_2$$

METHOD: In each case we must determine if the rate law predicted by the mechanism matches the experimental rate law.

Mechanism I is a three-step process in which the first step is rate determining. When the first step of a mechanism is rate determining, the predicted rate law is the same as the rate expression for that first step. In this case the rate-determining step is a bimolecular collision. The rate expression for a bimolecular collision is first order in each collision partner:

$$\text{Rate} = k_1[O_3][NO]$$

Mechanism I is consistent with the experimental rate law.

Mechanism II begins with a fast reversible ozone cleavage followed by a rate-determining bimolecular collision of an oxygen atom with a molecule of NO. The rate of the slow step is:

$$\text{Rate} = k_2[NO][O]$$

This rate expression contains the concentration of oxygen atoms, which are intermediates. To convert the rate expression into a form that can be compared with the experimental rate law, we assume that the rate of the first step is equal to the rate of its reverse process. Then we solve the equality for the concentration of the intermediate:

$$k_1[O_3] = k_{-1}\,[O][O_2] \qquad \textit{from which} \qquad [O] = \frac{k_1[O_3]}{k_{-1}[O_2]}$$

$$\text{Rate} = \frac{k_1k_2[O_3][NO]}{k_{-1}[O_2]} = k[O_3][NO][O_2]^{-1}$$

Mechanism II is inconsistent with the experimental rate law. Notice that this mechanism predicts a negative order with respect to molecular oxygen.

Mechanism III is a simple one-step bimolecular collision. Its predicted rate law is:

$$\text{Rate} = k_1[O_3][NO]$$

Mechanism III is consistent with the experimental rate law.

Therefore the O_3 + NO reaction might go by Mechanism I or Mechanism III, but not by Mechanism II.

SECTION EXERCISES

14.5.1 A student proposes the following mechanism for the decomposition of dinitrogen pentoxide:

Step 1: $N_2O_{5\,(g)} \longrightarrow N_2O_{4\,(g)} + O_{(g)}$

Step 2: $O + N_2O_{5\,(g)} \longrightarrow N_2O_{4\,(g)} + O_{2\,(g)}$

Overall reaction: $2\ N_2O_{5\,(g)} \longrightarrow 4\ NO_{2\,(g)} + O_{2\,(g)}$

(a) Propose a third step to complete this mechanism.
(b) Experiments show that this decomposition reaction is first order. Which step in the mechanism must be rate determining?

14.5.2 What order for N_2O_5 does the mechanism in Section Exercise 14.5.1 predict if its first step is fast and reversible and its second step is rate determining?

14.5.3 The oxidation of NO by O_2 is an example of a third-order reaction:

$$2\ NO_{(g)} + O_{2\,(g)} \longrightarrow 2\ NO_{2\,(g)} \qquad \text{Rate} = k[NO]^2[O_2]$$

Although a single elementary termolecular mechanism is consistent with the rate law, three-body collisions are rare in the gas phase. It is more likely that the reaction begins with bimolecular production of an intermediate:

$$NO + NO \underset{k_{-1}}{\overset{k_1}{\rightleftharpoons}} N_2O_2 \quad \text{(very fast)}$$

(a) Propose a slow second step to complete this mechanism.
(b) Show that this mechanism is consistent with the observed rate law.

14.6 REACTION RATES AND TEMPERATURE

Earlier in this chapter, we stated that the rate of a reaction depends on concentrations and on temperature. In the last few sections we have used a molecular perspective to examine how *concentrations* affect rates. In this section we see how *temperature* affects the rate of a reaction.

From a macroscopic perspective, common experience tells us that chemical reactions proceed faster at higher temperature. Food is stored in refrigerators because food spoils more slowly at low temperature than at high temperature. Wood does not burn at room temperature, but it burns vigorously at high temperature. How does temperature affect the rate of a reaction at the molecular level? Because temperature is a measure of the energy of motion of molecules, we need to explore the relationship between reaction rates and molecular energy to answer this question.

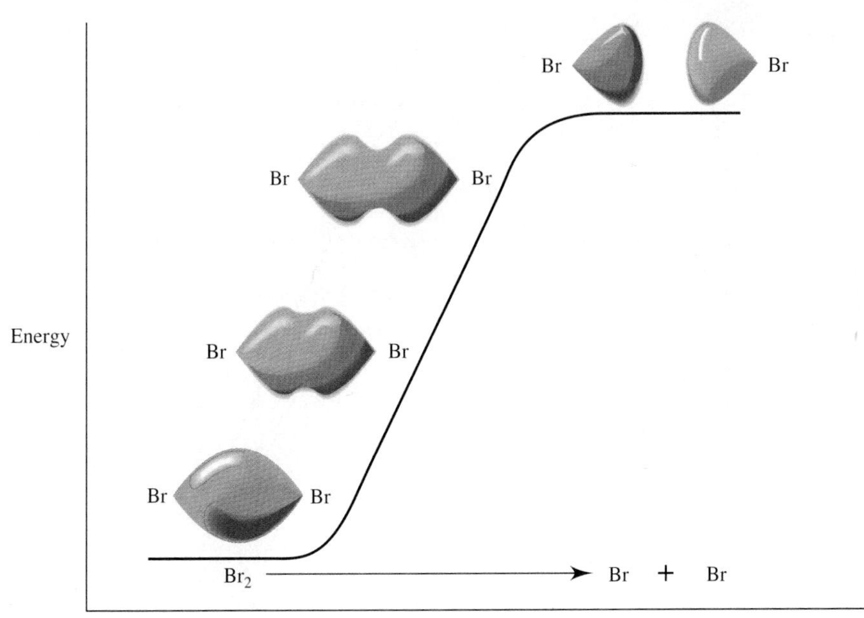

FIGURE 14-18
The energy profile for the unimolecular decomposition of bromine molecules. As the bromine atoms in a bromine molecule move apart, orbital overlap decreases and the Br—Br σ bond weakens and breaks.

ENERGY CHANGES IN A UNIMOLECULAR REACTION

In a unimolecular reaction, a molecule fragments into two pieces or rearranges to a different isomer. In either case, a chemical bond breaks. For example, in the fragmentation of bromine molecules, breaking a σ bond gives a pair of bromine atoms:

$$Br_2 \longrightarrow 2\ Br$$

Recall that this unimolecular process is the first step of the reaction between hydrogen and bromine to give HBr.

Figure 14-18 shows the energy changes that occur during the fragmentation of a bromine molecule. The reaction begins with a stretch of the Br—Br bond. As the bond becomes longer, the system moves to higher energy. This decreased stability results from the loss of orbital overlap as the bromine atoms move apart. If the bond is stretched far enough, the molecule fragments into two bromine atoms.

As discussed in Chapter 9, bond breaking always requires energy. Thus the reaction is endothermic, and the two bromine atoms are less stable than the original Br_2 molecule.

ENERGY CHANGES DURING BIMOLECULAR REACTIONS

In a bimolecular reaction, some bonds break and other bonds form. For example, in the reaction between nitrogen monoxide and ozone, an oxygen atom is transferred from O_3 to NO:

$$O_3 + NO \longrightarrow O_2 + NO_2$$

In the collision process the ozone molecule distorts as the O—O bond stretches and weakens. Nitrogen monoxide must also undergo distortion as it bonds with the incoming oxygen atom from ozone. Distorting a molecule from its most favored configuration always requires energy. Thus at the outset of the reaction, the system is destabilized by the molecular distortions required for atom transfer. At the end of the process, on the other hand, the system becomes stabilized as the products adopt their lowest-energy configuration. Figure 14-19 shows the energy profile for this reaction.

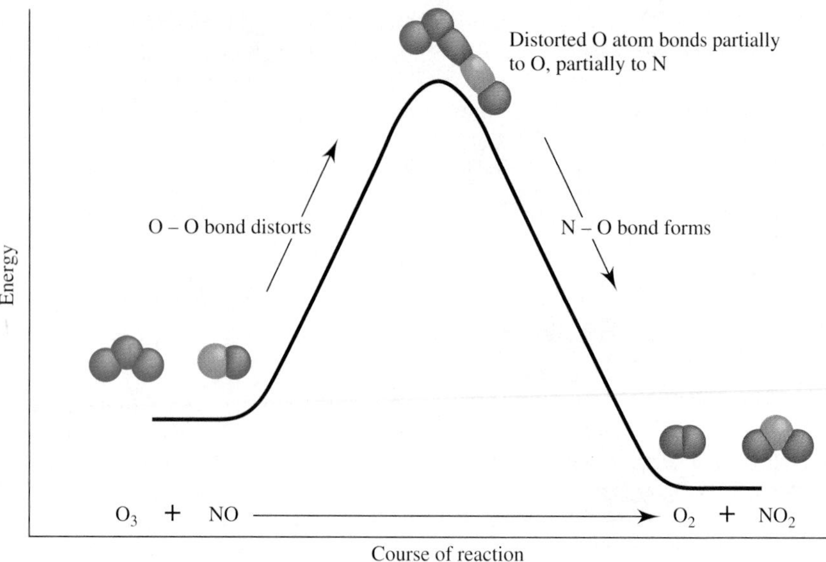

FIGURE 14-19
The energy profile for the bimolecular reaction between ozone and nitrogen monoxide molecules. In the collision, energy must be supplied to distort the electron clouds of the two reactants.

ACTIVATION ENERGY

The energy profiles for these two elementary reactions share several common features, but one is particularly important for our discussion of reaction rates. In both examples the system moves "uphill" from the energy of reactants to an energy maximum. In almost all chemical reactions, the molecules must overcome an energy barrier before starting materials can become products. This energy barrier is called the **activation energy (E_a)** of the chemical reaction. Activation energies arise because chemical bonds in reactant molecules must distort or break before new bonds can be formed in product molecules. The activation energy for any reaction mechanism is independent of both reactant *concentrations* and *temperature.*

In unimolecular isomerization reactions, such as the conversion of *cis*-azobenzene into *trans*-azobenzene, a bond breaks and another bond forms within the same molecule. The activation energy profile for such a reaction appears qualitatively similar to the one in Figure 14-19.

Figures 14-18 and 14-19 are **activation energy diagrams** for elementary reactions. They are plots of the change in energy as reactants are transformed into products. Figure 14-20 shows a generalized activation energy diagram labeled with its various characteristics.

The X axis represents the course of the reaction as starting materials are transformed into products. Because these transformations may involve complicated combinations of rotations, vibrations, and atom transfers, accepted practice is to label this axis as the **reaction coordinate** without specifying further details about what changes occur.

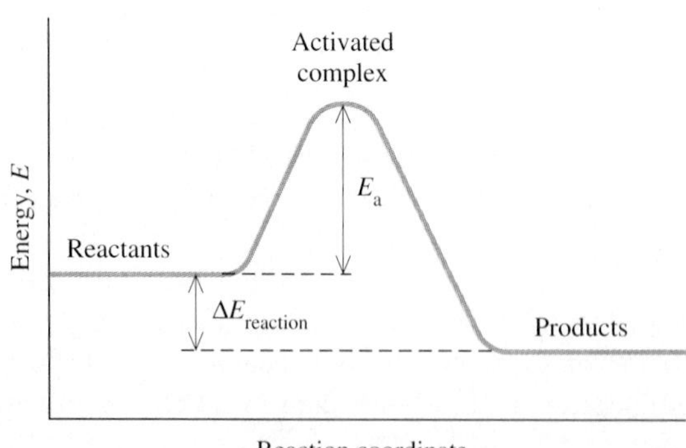

FIGURE 14-20
A generalized activation energy diagram for an elementary reaction. The energy of the starting materials appears on the left, and the energy of the products appears on the right. The highest point in energy along the reaction coordinate represents the activated complex. The figure shows a reaction with a negative overall energy change (ΔE). This is an exothermic reaction, in which energy is released.

The Y axis of an activation energy diagram is the energy of the molecular system. The graph shows how chemical energy, also called *potential energy* or *total bond energy,* changes during the course of the reaction. Low values of energy represent high molecular stability, and high values represent low molecular stability. In the exothermic reaction shown in the activation energy diagram in Figure 14-20, the energy of the products is lower than the energy of the reactants, reflecting the fact that energy has been released during the reaction. For an endothermic reaction, on the other hand, the activation energy diagram shows the energy of the products to be higher than the energy of the reactants.

The molecular arrangement at the point of highest energy along the diagram is known as the **activated complex.** The difference in energy between the reactants and this activated complex is the activation energy and is generally labeled E_a. An activated complex is *not* an intermediate. An intermediate is stable for a short time, perhaps milliseconds, and may be observed with highly sensitive instruments. An activated complex, on the other hand, forms and disappears in the time required for a molecular collision, which is about 10^{-13} second. In other words, the activated complex represents the configuration of atoms at the moment of collision.

The activated complex is also shown as the "transition state."

The magnitude of an activation energy depends on the details of the bonding changes that occur during the formation of the activated complex. Although a good estimate of energy change (ΔE) for a reaction can be obtained from average bond energies, E_a is not so easily estimated. Theoreticians attempt to calculate E_a values using bonding theory, but reliable activation energies can be obtained only by measuring how rate constants vary with temperature.

ACTIVATION ENERGY AND THE RATE CONSTANT

A chemical reaction cannot occur unless the starting materials have enough energy to overcome the activation energy barrier. Where do molecules obtain this energy? In addition to its chemical potential energy, every molecule has kinetic energy that causes the molecule to translate, rotate, and vibrate. During a chemical reaction, some of this kinetic energy is transformed into chemical energy as a molecule distorts or as two molecules collide.

A collection of molecules always contains molecules with many different kinetic energies. Some molecules have much energy, but others have very little. This distribution of molecular energies is called the **Boltzmann distribution.** The specific shape of the Boltzmann distribution depends on the temperature of the sample, as shown in Figure 14-21. Adding thermal energy to the molecules gives them more kinetic energy. Thus as the temperature increases, the Boltzmann distribution broadens and shifts toward higher energy.

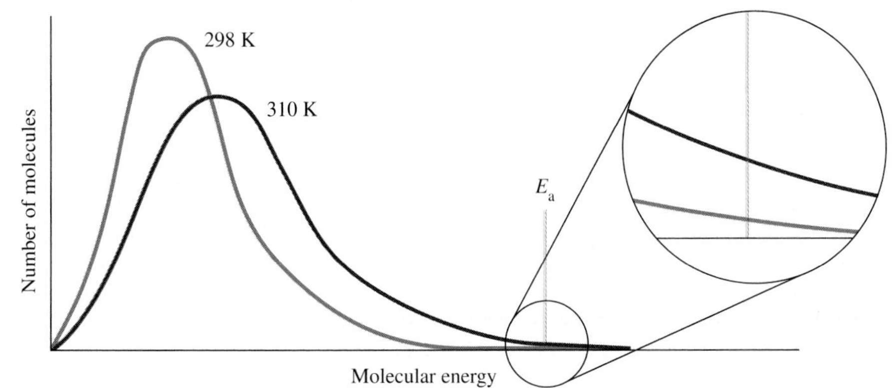

FIGURE 14-21
The Boltzmann distribution of molecular energies. As temperature increases, the distribution broadens and shifts to higher energy. As shown in the inset, this shift gives a greater fraction of molecules enough energy to overcome the activation energy for a chemical reaction. Notice that E_a does not shift as temperature changes.

The Boltzmann distribution indicates that only a fraction of all molecules in any reaction system has energy greater than that required for reaction. How large a fraction this is depends on E_a and temperature:

1. At any T, a larger fraction of molecules can react if E_a is small than if E_a is large.
2. For any reaction, a larger fraction of molecules can react if T is high than if T is low.

The rate of a reaction increases with temperature.

THE ARRHENIUS EQUATION

The value of the rate constant for a particular reaction depends on several factors, including temperature, the activation energy for the reaction, and any geometric requirements that must be met before the reaction can occur. All these factors can be summarized in a single equation, called the **Arrhenius equation:**

$$k = Ae^{-E_a/RT} \qquad \textbf{(14-6)}$$

According to the Arrhenius* equation, rate constants depend exponentially on temperature (T, in K), the activation energy (E_a, in J/mol) and the gas constant (R, in J/mol K). The preexponential term (A) is the value that the rate constant would have if all molecules had sufficient energy to react. For bimolecular reactions, A is the frequency at which molecules collide multiplied by the probability that the collision occurs in an orientation that allows the reaction to occur. For unimolecular reactions, A is the frequency of molecular vibration multiplied by an orientation factor.

Equation 14-6 can be used to calculate a rate constant after E_a, A, and T are known. However, E_a and A must be determined by doing rate experiments that provide the value of k, so in practice, the Arrhenius equation is used to determine E_a and A. For this purpose, we take the natural logarithm of both sides:

This equation is obtained from Equation 14-6 using two properties of logarithms: *ln xy* = *ln x*+ *ln y* and *ln* (e^{-x}) = −x.

$$\ln k = \ln A - \frac{E_a}{RT} \qquad \textbf{(14-7)}$$

Equation 14-7 has the familiar linear form $y = b + mx$, so a graph of $\ln k$ along the Y axis vs. $1/T$ along the X axis will be a straight line with a slope of $-(E_a/R)$ and an intercept of $\ln A$. Thus we can evaluate A and E_a from measurements of k at a series of different temperatures.

When rate constants have been measured at several temperatures, graphing is the most accurate method to find the value of E_a. However, a good estimate of E_a can also be calculated from rate constants measured at just two temperatures:

$$\ln k_1 = \ln A - \frac{E_a}{RT_1} \qquad \text{and} \qquad \ln k_2 = \ln A - \frac{E_a}{RT_2}$$

* Svante Arrhenius was a brilliant Swedish chemist (1859-1927) who not only discovered activation energy, but also developed the theory of the ionic nature of salts and aqueous solutions. He was awarded the Nobel Prize in chemistry in 1903. The Arrhenius equation can be derived using calculus and the mathematical formula for the Boltzmann distribution.

The activation energy is independent of T, and A changes slowly enough with T that A usually can be treated as a constant for temperature changes of 50 K or less. Thus the A term is eliminated if one equation is subtracted from the other:

$$ln\, k_2 - ln\, k_1 = \left(ln\, A - \frac{E_a}{RT_2}\right) - \left(ln\, A - \frac{E_a}{RT_1}\right) = \frac{E_a}{R}\left(\frac{1}{T_1} - \frac{1}{T_2}\right)$$

We now combine the logarithmic terms and then isolate E_a on the left side of the equation:

$$E_a = \frac{R\, ln\left(\frac{k_2}{k_1}\right)}{\left(\frac{1}{T_1} - \frac{1}{T_2}\right)} \qquad \textbf{(14-8)}$$

Sample Problem 14-11 shows how to use Equation 14-8.

SAMPLE PROBLEM 14-11 CALCULATING AN ACTIVATION ENERGY

The reactions of NO_2 have been studied as a function of temperature. For the decomposition reaction:

$$2\, NO_2 \longrightarrow 2\, NO + O_2$$

the rate constant is measured to be $2.7 \times 10^{-2}\, M^{-1}\, s^{-1}$ at 227 °C and $2.4 \times 10^{-1}\, M^{-1}\, s^{-1}$ at 277 °C.

Experimental studies of the conversion of NO_2 to N_2O_4:

$$2\, NO_2 \longrightarrow N_2O_4$$

give $k = 5.2 \times 10^8\, M^{-1}\, s^{-1}$ at both 298 and 350 K.

Calculate the activation energies of these two reactions.

METHOD: The graphical treatment of the variation of rate constants with temperature is appropriate when a set of values is available. When only two values of the rate constant are available, E_a is calculated using Equation 14-8. Remember that the units must be consistent: T must be in K and R in J/mol K:

$$E_a = \frac{R\, ln\left(\frac{k_2}{k_1}\right)}{\left(\frac{1}{T_1} - \frac{1}{T_2}\right)}$$

For the decomposition of NO_2:

$$E_a = \frac{(8.314\text{ J mol}^{-1}\text{ K}^{-1})\left[ln\left(\frac{2.4 \times 10^{-1}\text{ M}^{-1}\text{ s}^{-1}}{2.7 \times 10^{-2}\text{ M}^{-1}\text{ s}^{-1}}\right)\right]}{\left(\frac{1}{500\text{ K}} - \frac{1}{550\text{ K}}\right)}$$

$$E_a = \frac{(8.314\text{ J mol}^{-1}\text{ K}^{-1})\,(ln\, 8.89)}{(2.000 \times 10^{-3}\text{ K}^{-1}) - (1.818 \times 10^{-3}\text{ K}^{-1})} = \frac{(8.314\text{ J mol}^{-1}\text{ K}^{-1})(2.18)}{1.82 \times 10^{-4}\text{ K}^{-1}}$$

As usual, we carry one additional significant figure until we round the final answer to two significant figures:

$$E_a = 9.96 \times 10^4\text{ J/mol} = 10\text{ kJ/mol}$$

For the formation of N_2O_4:

$$k_2 = k_1, \quad so \quad ln\,(k_2/k_1) = ln\,1 = 0$$

$$Thus\ E_a = 0 \text{ kJ/mol}$$

An activation energy of 0 kJ/mol indicates that no bonds need to be distorted or broken in this reaction. We discuss this in more detail shortly.

After the activation energy of a reaction has been determined, the Arrhenius equation can be used to estimate values of the rate constant for the reaction at temperatures where experiments have not been carried out. This is particularly useful for temperatures at which a reaction is too slow or too fast to be studied conveniently. Sample Problem 14-12 illustrates this application.

SAMPLE PROBLEM 14-12 COMPARING RELATIVE REACTION RATES

When two NO_2 molecules collide and react, they can form a bond or exchange an oxygen atom. Use the results of Sample Problem 14-11 to estimate whether or not oxygen exchange is fast enough at room temperature to compete with bond formation.

METHOD: The competition between two modes of reaction depends on their rate constants. We have a rate constant at 298 K for bond formation to produce N_2O_4, but our values for the oxygen exchange reaction that leads to O_2 and NO are at 500 K and 550 K. We must use the Arrhenius equation to calculate the rate constant at 298 K. Equation 14-8 can be rearranged to give an equation that can be solved for the rate constant at a given temperature:

$$ln\left(\frac{k_2}{k_1}\right) = \frac{E_a}{R}\left(\frac{1}{T_1} - \frac{1}{T_2}\right)$$

From Sample Problem 14-11, we have the activation energy for decomposition as well as the rate constants at two temperatures:

$$E_a = 1.0 \times 10^2 \text{ kJ/mol}$$

$$227\ °C: \quad k = 2.7 \times 10^{-2} \text{ M}^{-1} \text{ s}^{-1}$$

$$277\ °C: \quad k = 2.4 \times 10^{-1} \text{ M}^{-1} \text{ s}^{-1}$$

Either of the rate constants can be used to calculate k at 298 K. Arbitrarily, we choose the rate constant at 227 °C.

$$k_1 = 2.7 \times 10^{-2} \text{ M}^{-1} \text{ sec}^{-1} \qquad T_1 = 227\ °C = 500 \text{ K} \qquad T_2 = 298 \text{ K}$$

Next, substitute these values into the rearranged form of Equation 14-8 and solve for k_2, the rate constant of the decomposition reaction at 298 K:

$$ln\left(\frac{k_2}{2.7 \times 10^{-2} \text{ M}^{-1} \text{ s}^{-1}}\right) = \frac{(1.0 \times 10^2 \text{ kJ/mol})(10^3 \text{ J/kJ})}{(8.314 \text{ J/mol K})}\left(\frac{1}{500 \text{ K}} - \frac{1}{298 \text{ K}}\right)$$

$$ln\left(\frac{k_2}{2.7 \times 10^{-2} \text{ M}^{-1} \text{ s}^{-1}}\right) = -16.3$$

$$\frac{k_2}{2.7 \times 10^{-2} \text{ M}^{-1} \text{ s}^{-1}} = e^{-16.3} = 8.3 \times 10^{-8}$$

$$k_2 = (8.3 \times 10^{-8})(2.7 \times 10^{-2} \text{ M}^{-1} \text{ s}^{-1}) = 2.2 \times 10^{-9} \text{ M}^{-1} \text{ s}^{-1}$$

At 298 K, the rate constant for decomposition is 10^{17} times smaller than the rate constant for dimerization. Thus at room temperature the rate of exchange of oxygen atoms is negligible compared with the rate of bond formation. This is a reasonable result because exchange of atoms requires breakage of an N—O bond, whereas bond formation does not.

VALUES OF ACTIVATION ENERGY

Reactions between stable molecules typically have activation energies of 100 kJ/mol or greater, even when the overall reaction is exothermic. As an example, consider the reaction of hydrogen and oxygen:

$$2\,H_{2\,(g)} + O_{2\,(g)} \rightarrow 2\,H_2O_{\,(g)}$$

$$\Delta H^{o} = -484 \text{ kJ mol}^{-1} \qquad \Delta G^{o} = -457 \text{ kJ mol}^{-1}$$

Recall that ΔH^{o} is the standard enthalpy change and ΔG^{o} is the standard free energy change.

This combustion reaction is so spontaneous and exothermic that it is used to drive the main engines of the space shuttle. Nevertheless, mixtures of hydrogen and oxygen are stable indefinitely at room temperature. This reaction does not occur at room temperature because strong bonds must be broken to transform H_2 and O_2 into water molecules. In other words, the bonds in the reactant molecules generate a large activation energy for the reaction. However, Figure 14-22 shows that a violent explosion occurs when a spark is applied to a mixture of H_2 and O_2. The spark gives some of the molecules enough energy to overcome the activation barrier, and after the reaction starts, the formation of water molecules releases enough energy to drive the reaction to completion very quickly.

Bond strengths: H—H = 434 kJ/mol and O=O = 496 kJ/mol.

The combustion of hydrocarbons such as natural gas and gasoline, which also release large amounts of energy, results in negligible rates at room temperature because a C—H bond breaks in their rate-determining steps. The bond energies for typical C—H bonds are 415 kJ/mol, and activation energies for combustion reactions are typically about half this value, 150 to 220 kJ/mol.

Even elementary reactions can have large activation energies. For example, the isomerization of *cis*-butene to *trans*-butene is a unimolecular rotation with activation energy of 285 kJ/mol. This high value arises because the C=C π bond must be broken during the course of the isomerization:

H, CH_3, H_3C, H —(π bond breakage)→ H, H, H_3C, CH_3 —(π bond formation)→ H, H, H_3C, CH_3

Sample Problem 14-11 shows that no energy barrier exists for the combination of two NO_2 molecules to form N_2O_4. The activation energy for this reaction is zero because NO_2 is an odd-electron molecule with a lone electron readily available for bond formation:

$$O_2N\cdot + \cdot NO_2 \longrightarrow O_2N{-}NO_2$$

The recombination of two bromine atoms to form a Br_2 molecule has zero activation energy for the same reason.

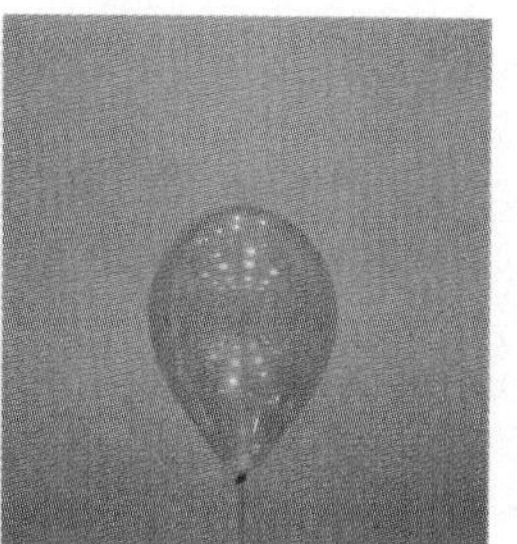

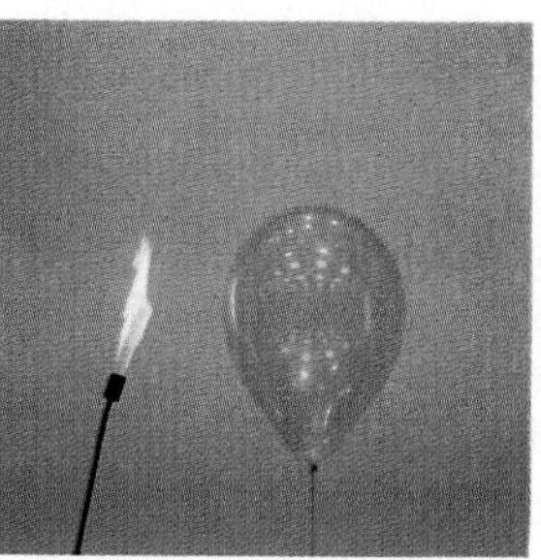

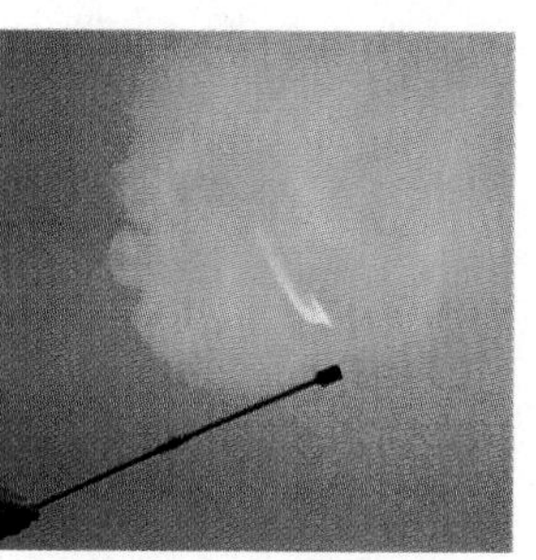

FIGURE 14-22
A balloon filled with a mixture of hydrogen and oxygen is stable until a source of energy is supplied to initiate the reaction. After the reaction begins, the energy released as water forms is enough to cause an explosion.

SECTION EXERCISES

14.6.1 Use bonding arguments to predict whether the ammonia synthesis reaction:

$$N_{2\,(g)} + 3\,H_{2\,(g)} \longrightarrow 2\,NH_{3\,(g)} \qquad \Delta H = -93 \text{ kJ}$$

has a high or a low activation energy, E_a.

14.6.2 The reaction of H_2 with Br_2 discussed in Section 14.5 has been studied extensively as a function of temperature. Here are some experimental results:

T (K)	498	524	550	574
k ($L^{1/2}\,mol^{-1/2}\,s^{-1}$)	8.08×10^{-7}	6.48×10^{-6}	3.97×10^{-5}	2.13×10^{-4}

(a) Determine E_a and A by graphical analysis.
(b) Estimate k at 300 K.

14.6.3 For the reaction of CO with NO_2 to give CO_2 and NO, E_a = 133 kJ. Using standard thermodynamic data to determine ΔE for the reaction, construct the activation energy diagram for the CO + NO_2 reaction. (HINT: No $\Delta(PV)$ exists for this reaction, so enthalpies and energies can be used interchangeably.)

14.7 CATALYSIS

In Section 14.6 we showed that one way to make a reaction go faster is to run it at higher temperature. Many industrial reactions are carried out at high temperature to maximize the amount of product that can be synthesized in a given time. Greater rates of production mean more income for the company, but the extra energy required to run a reaction at higher temperature adds to production costs. Furthermore, high-temperature reactions introduce safety concerns, and many chemical species are not stable at high temperature. Thus a different method for increasing the rates of chemical reactions would be useful.

Another way to make a reaction go faster is to change its mechanism in a manner that lowers the activation energy of the rate-determining step. The mechanism of a reaction can be changed by introducing a catalyst. A **catalyst** is a substance that changes the mechanism of a reaction to make the reaction go faster *without participating* in the overall reaction stoichiometry.

Catalysts are vital in the chemical industry. The market for catalysts in the United States in 1992 was about \$2.0 billion, including over \$600 million for petroleum refining and more than \$750 million for chemical production. Although these are large sums of money, the products made available by catalysts are much more valuable than the catalysts themselves. For example, the total value of fuels and chemicals produced by catalysts in 1992 was about \$900 *billion,* approximately 18% of the gross national product.

CATALYSIS AND THE OZONE PROBLEM

Catalysts are immensely beneficial in industry, but accidental catalysis in the atmosphere can be highly detrimental. Recall from Section 14.5 that the chemistry of ozone in the stratosphere involves a delicate balance of reactions that maintain a stable concentration of O_3. CFCs shift that balance by acting as catalysts for the destruction of O_3 molecules.

One of the properties that make CFCs attractive for industrial applications—their resistance to chemical attack—makes them very stable in the lower atmosphere, where they can exist for up to 100 years. This stability gives CFCs time to diffuse up

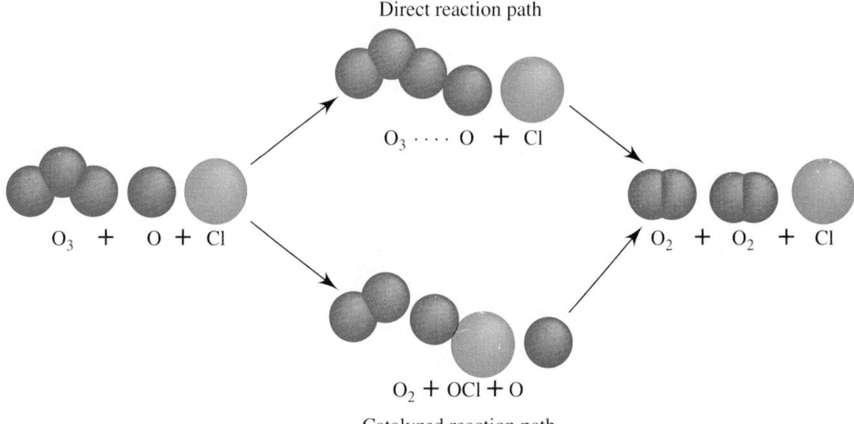

FIGURE 14-23
Chlorine atoms catalyze the reaction of ozone with oxygen atoms by forming a Cl—O_3 activated complex that readily decomposes into ClO and O_2. Chlorine monoxide readily transfers an oxygen atom to a second oxygen atom, forming another O_2 molecule and regenerating a Cl atom. Thus a different molecular path exists for the catalyzed and uncatalyzed reactions.

through the troposphere and into the stratosphere. There, CFCs absorb short-wavelength ultraviolet light from the sun that breaks carbon-chlorine bonds and produces chlorine atoms.

Chlorine atoms react with O_3 molecules to produce O_2 and ClO, as shown by the molecular pictures in Figure 14-23. One chlorine atom has a multiplying effect, however, because chlorine monoxide reacts with an oxygen atom to produce a second O_2 molecule and *regenerate the chlorine atom:*

$$O_3 + Cl \longrightarrow O_2 + ClO$$
$$O + ClO \longrightarrow O_2 + Cl$$
$$\text{Net: } O_3 + O \xrightarrow{Cl} 2\,O_2$$

Because a catalyst does not appear in the overall stoichiometry of a reaction, its presence is noted by writing the formula of the catalyst above or below the reaction arrow.

The net reaction for this two-step mechanism is the conversion of an O_3 molecule and an oxygen atom into two O_2 molecules. In this mechanism, chlorine atoms are a catalyst for ozone decomposition. They participate in the mechanism, but they do not appear in the overall stoichiometry. Chlorine atoms are consumed in the first step, but they are regenerated in the second. Because of the cyclical nature of this process, each chlorine atom can catalyze the destruction of many O_3 molecules. It has been estimated that several million tons of CFCs are present in the atmosphere and that each chlorine atom destroys about 100,000 molecules of ozone before it is removed by other reactions.

Figure 14-24 illustrates the activation energy diagram for the ozone-oxygen atom reaction. It shows that the direct reaction between O_3 and O has a substantially higher activation energy than the chlorine-catalyzed reaction sequence. In other words, the activated complex between chlorine atoms and O_3 molecules lies at a lower energy than the activated complex between oxygen atoms and O_3 molecules, making chlorine atoms much more effective than oxygen atoms at destroying O_3 molecules. At the temperature of the ozone layer, 220 K, the rate data for the two pathways are:

$O_3 + O \longrightarrow 2\,O_2$	$E_a = 17.1$ kJ/mol	$k = 4.1 \times 10^5$ L M^{-1} s^{-1}
$O_3 + Cl \longrightarrow ClO + O_2$	$E_{a1} = 2.1$ kJ/mol	$k_1 = 5.2 \times 10^9$ L M^{-1} s^{-1}
$ClO + O \longrightarrow Cl + O_2$	$E_{a2} = 0.4$ kJ/mol	$k_2 = 2.2 \times 10^{10}$ L M^{-1} s^{-1}

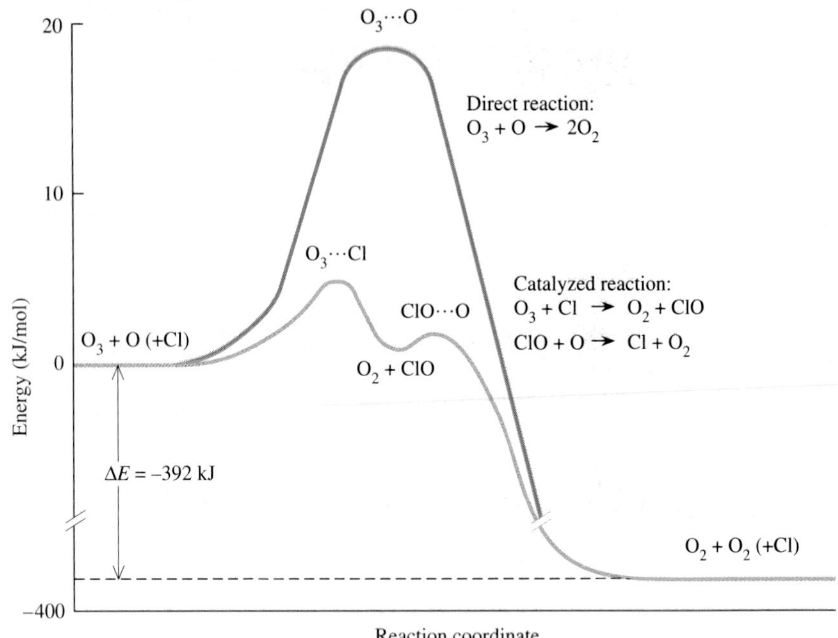

FIGURE 14-24
The activation energy diagram for the reaction between O_3 and O. The direct reaction has a much higher activation energy than the chlorine–catalyzed reaction, so Cl atoms are effective catalysts for this reaction. Notice that a break occurs in the vertical scale; the overall reaction is exothermic by almost 400 kJ.

Notice that both steps of the chlorine-catalyzed reaction appear on the activation energy diagram. Each step of a mechanism has its own activation energy, so the diagram has two activation barriers. Experimental data indicate that the first barrier is higher than the second. Because the direct reaction involves just one step, it has only one activation barrier.

The activation energy diagram in Figure 14-24 provides a clear picture of the role of a catalyst. Chlorine atoms provide an alternative mechanism for the reaction of ozone with oxygen atoms. This lower-energy pathway breaks down ozone in the stratosphere at a significantly faster rate than in the absence of the catalyst. As a result, the delicate balance between ozone, oxygen atoms, and oxygen molecules is being changed in a way that poses a serious threat to the life-protecting ozone layer.

HOMOGENEOUS AND HETEROGENEOUS CATALYSTS

The catalysis of ozone decomposition by chlorine atoms occurs entirely in the gas phase. We classify chlorine as a **homogeneous catalyst** because the catalyst and the reactants are present in the *same phase,* in this case the gas phase. A **heterogeneous catalyst,** on the other hand, is in a *different phase* than the one where the reaction occurs. A heterogeneous catalyst is usually a solid, and the reactants are gases or are dissolved in a liquid solvent. Heterogeneous catalysts often contain transition metals as the pure metal, a metal halide, or a metal oxide. Figure 14-25 shows photographs of several important heterogeneous catalysts.

Heterogeneous catalysts are used in many industrial processes. Three examples follow: (1) the gas-phase reaction of ethylene, hydrogen chloride, and oxygen to produce vinyl chloride is carried out using solid copper(II) chloride as a heterogeneous catalyst; (2) methanol is synthesized from hydrogen and carbon monoxide using a catalyst of zinc oxide and aluminum oxide; and (3) the Haber synthesis for ammonia is catalyzed by iron(III) oxide containing small amounts of aluminum oxide and potassium oxide:

The development of the ozone hole over Antarctica is believed to have been accelerated by heterogeneous catalysis on microcrystals of ice. These microcrystals form in abundance in the Antarctic spring, which is when the ozone hole appears. Ice microcrystals are much less common in the Arctic atmosphere, so ozone depletion has not been as extensive in the northern hemisphere. However, recent data suggest that an Arctic ozone hole may develop within the next few years.

$$\textbf{(1)}\ 2\ C_2H_4 + 2\ HCl + O_2 \xrightarrow{CuCl_2} 2\ \text{CH}_2\text{=CHCl} + 2\ H_2O$$

$$\textbf{(2)}\ CO + 2\ H_2 \xrightarrow{ZnO/Al_2O_3} CH_3OH$$

$$\textbf{(3)}\ N_2 + 3\ H_2 \xrightarrow{Fe_2O_3/Al_2O_3/K_2O} 2\ NH_3$$

Heterogeneous reactions are complicated because the reacting species must be transferred from one phase to another before the reaction can occur. Despite much research, chemists still have incomplete knowledge about the mechanisms of reactions that involve heterogeneous catalysts. However, it is known that heterogeneous catalysis generally proceeds in four general steps, as illustrated in Figure 14-26 for the conversion of nitrogen monoxide into N_2 and O_2. This reaction, which is catalyzed by platinum metal, occurs in automobile catalytic converters (Box 14-4).

1. The starting materials bind to the surface of the catalyst. This process is known as **adsorption.** When a substance is adsorbed, its internal bonds are weakened or broken in favor of bonds to the catalyst.
2. Bound materials migrate over the surface of the catalyst.
3. Bound substances react to form products.
4. Products escape from the surface of the catalyst. This step is called **desorption.**

FIGURE 14-25
Most heterogeneous catalysts are solid metal halides, metal oxides, or pure metals.

CATALYSIS IN INDUSTRY

The business of the chemical industry is to transform inexpensive molecules into more valuable ones. In many cases, catalysts play important roles in these processes. In this section we describe the roles of catalysts in some important industrial reactions. Other catalyzed industrial reactions are considered in Chapter 15 when we describe properties of chemical equilibria.

Petroleum refining. Petroleum is the source of carbon compounds used for synthesis in the chemical industry. Crude petroleum is a complex mixture containing thousands of different compounds, most of which are alkanes, alkenes, and derivatives of benzene. Petroleum refining begins with distillation, which separates the various components into fractions with different boiling point ranges. Large, high-boiling hydrocarbons are less versatile than smaller ones, so a further step in refining is the catalytic cracking of large hydrocarbons into smaller ones. Cracking is

For more information about petroleum, see Sections 8.4 and Box 11-2.

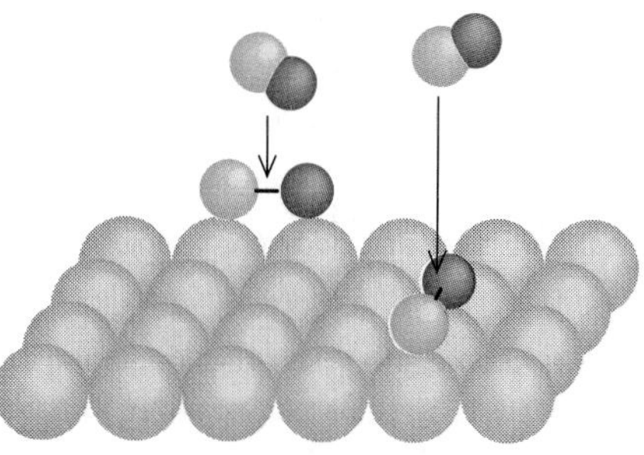

Step 1: Adsorption and bond weakening

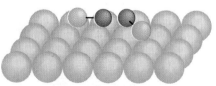

Step 2: Migration

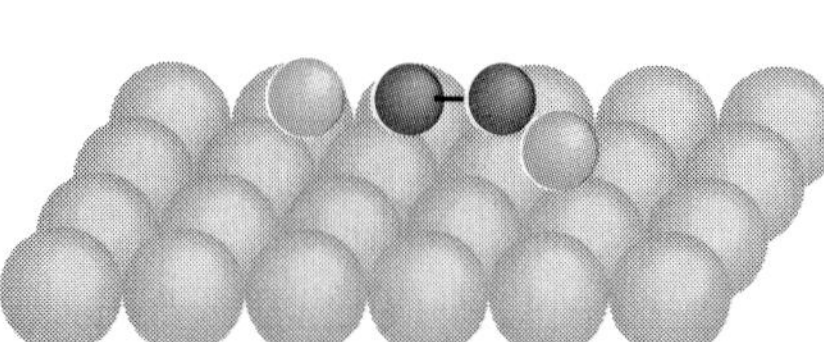

Step 3: Bond reorganization

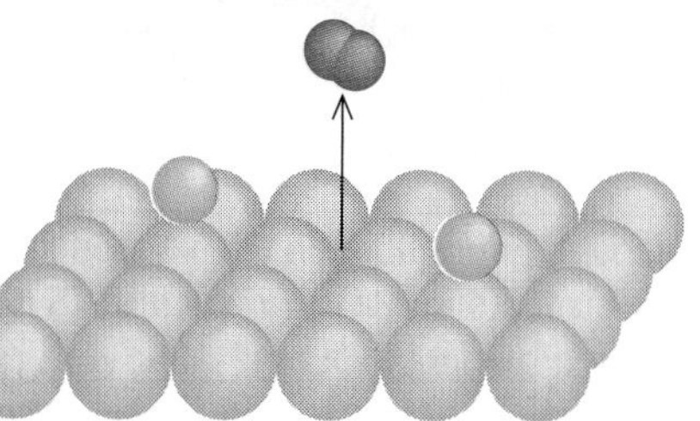

Step 4: Desorption

FIGURE 14-26
Molecular pictures of the four steps for the conversion of nitrogen monoxide to N_2 and O_2 on a platinum metal surface.

the problem is the high cost of gasification, both in energy and in capital investment. Perhaps a breakthrough in catalysis will eventually solve this problem.

We have summarized just three examples of important catalytic reactions, but many others exist. Catalyst research is one of the most active areas of chemistry and chemical engineering.

ENZYMES

Living organisms carry out an astonishing array of chemical processes. For example, they can use small molecules to assemble complex biopolymers such as deoxyribonucleic acid (DNA) and proteins. Organisms can produce molecules that combat bacterial invaders. Organisms can break down large, energy-rich molecules in many steps to extract chemical energy in small portions to drive their many activities. Organisms can even break chemical bonds selectively without resorting to high temperature.

Protein structure is discussed in Section 11.5.

Most of these reactions are regulated by biochemical catalysts called **enzymes.** An enzyme is a specialized protein that catalyzes a specific biochemical reaction. Some enzymes are found in extracellular fluids such as saliva and gastric juices, but most are found inside cells. Each type of cell has a different array of enzymes that act together to determine what role the cell plays in the overall biochemistry of the organism.

Enzymes have elaborate molecular structures, many of which have not yet been completely deciphered. Despite the wide diversity of structures, however, most enzyme activity follows one general mechanism that contains several reversible steps.

In the first step, a reactant molecule binds to a specific location on the enzyme called the **active site,** which is usually in a groove or a pocket on the surface of the protein:

$$\underset{\text{Enzyme}}{E} + \underset{\text{Reactant}}{R} \rightleftarrows \underset{\text{Enzyme-reactant complex}}{E\text{-}R}$$

The reactant binds to the active site through intermolecular interactions similar to those described in Chapter 10. Hydrogen bonding plays a key role in enzyme-reactant binding. Binding causes subtle changes in the structure of the enzyme, which in turn distorts the reactant, weakening specific bonds:

$$\underset{\text{Enzyme-reactant complex}}{E\text{-}R} \rightleftarrows \underset{\text{Distorted complex}}{[E\text{-}R]_D}$$

This allows a product species to form:

$$\underset{\text{Distorted complex}}{[E\text{-}R]_D} \rightleftarrows \underset{\text{Enzyme-product complex}}{E\text{-}P}$$

After the product forms, it no longer binds strongly to the enzyme, so the product is released. As required in a catalytic process, the enzyme is regenerated at the end of the sequence:

$$\underset{\text{Enzyme-product complex}}{E\text{-}P} \longrightarrow \underset{\text{Enzyme}}{E} + \underset{\text{Product}}{P}$$

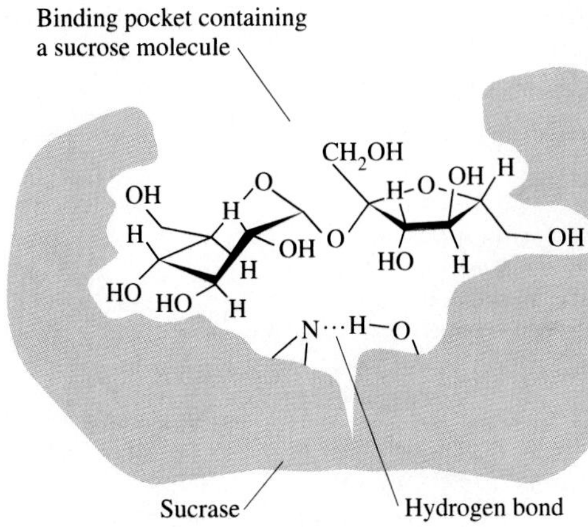

Binding pocket containing a sucrose molecule

Sucrase

Hydrogen bond

FIGURE 14-27
Schematic view of sucrase binding a sucrose molecule. The enzyme has a binding "pocket" that matches the shape of sucrose.

The schematic illustrations of sucrase shown in Figures 14-27 to 14-29 do not represent the actual shape or size of the enzyme molecule. Compared with sucrose, sucrase is an immense molecule. The enzyme is a globular protein.

Note that the steps in this enzyme-catalyzed biochemical mechanism are similar to the steps in nonbiochemical heterogeneous catalysis: binding with bond weakening, reaction at the bound site, and release of products.

A specific illustration of enzymatic catalysis is the breakdown of sucrose into glucose and fructose. This the first step in a long sequence of reactions that the body uses to harness the chemical energy of sucrose. Organisms use the enzyme sucrase to catalyze this reaction.

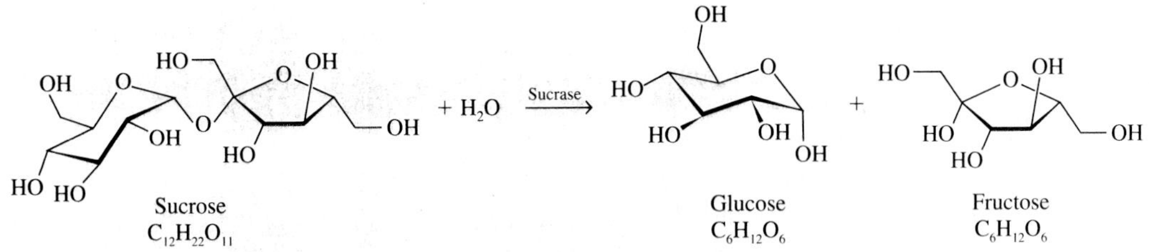

$$\underset{\substack{\text{Sucrose} \\ C_{12}H_{22}O_{11}}}{} + H_2O \xrightarrow{\text{Sucrase}} \underset{\substack{\text{Glucose} \\ C_6H_{12}O_6}}{} + \underset{\substack{\text{Fructose} \\ C_6H_{12}O_6}}{}$$

The first step is binding of sucrose by the enzyme. Figure 14-27 shows a representation of the active site of sucrase as a pocket into which the sucrose molecule fits. During binding, the enzyme may modify its shape somewhat to bind the sucrose molecule more tightly. This cooperative binding process is termed an **induced fit.**

When sucrose binds to sucrase, chemical interactions between the two molecules induce a modification in the structure of the sugar. Figure 14-28 shows, for example,

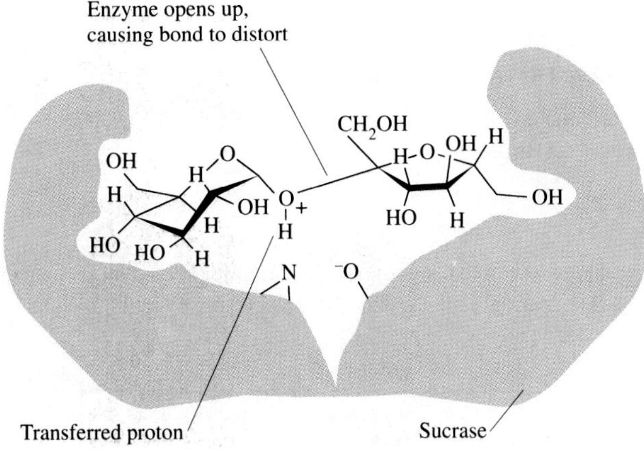

FIGURE 14-28
After binding, proton transfer from sucrase to the bridging oxygen atom of sucrose may "open up" the enzyme conformation and distort and weaken a C—O bond in sucrose.

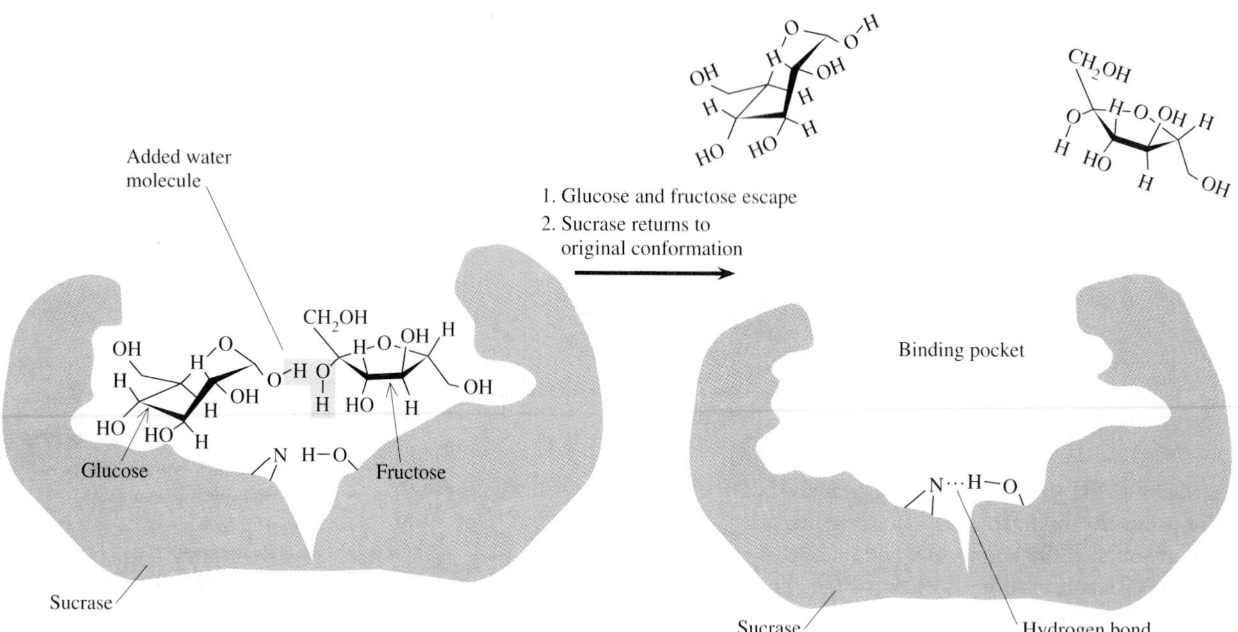

FIGURE 14-29
The weakened sucrose molecule is vulnerable to the addition of a water molecule to produce glucose and fructose. These molecules, being smaller than sucrose, escape from the pocket. Then the enzyme closes up again, ready to capture the next sucrose molecule that comes along.

the transfer of a proton from an acidic amino acid side chain of sucrase to the bridging oxygen atom of sucrose. This may destroy a hydrogen-bonding interaction within the enzyme and allow sucrase to open wider and "pull" one end of the sucrose molecule away from its other end.

In its distorted form, sucrose is highly vulnerable to C—O bond breakage and attack by water. Figure 14-29 shows that after this reaction, glucose and fructose have been formed and the proton is transferred back to its original location on the enzyme. The product molecules, being smaller than sucrose, are not held as tightly to the active site, so they can migrate out of the pocket. The enzyme now is free to return to its original conformation, ready to accommodate another sucrose molecule.

Although the molecular details of enzyme mechanisms are complex, the kinetic behavior of many enzymatic processes is first order in both reactant and enzyme. Sample Problem 14-13 shows that the mechanism just outlined is consistent with this kinetic behavior.

SAMPLE PROBLEM 14-13 ENZYME KINETICS

Derive the predicted rate law for the general mechanism for enzyme catalysis, assuming that the distortion step is rate determining:

$$E + R \underset{k_{-1}}{\overset{k_1}{\rightleftarrows}} E\text{-}R \overset{k_2,\text{ slow}}{\rightleftarrows} [E\text{-}R]_D \rightleftarrows E\text{-}P \longrightarrow E + P$$

METHOD: The rate law predicted by a mechanism can be derived by recognizing that the overall rate of reaction is equal to the rate of the slowest step. We assume that any earlier steps have equal forward and reverse rates.

Here, step 2 is assumed to be rate determining, so the rate expression is:

$$\text{Rate} = k_2[\text{E-R}]$$

Because this rate equation contains the concentration of an intermediate, we use the forward and reverse rates of the first step to derive an expression for [E-R] in terms of [E] and [R]:

$$k_1[\text{E}][\text{R}] = k_{-1}[\text{E-R}] \quad \textit{so} \quad [\text{E-R}] = \frac{k_1}{k_{-1}}[\text{E}][\text{R}]$$

Now substitute into the original rate expression:

$$\text{Rate} = \frac{k_1 k_2}{k_{-1}}[\text{E}][\text{R}] = k[\text{E}][\text{R}] \quad \text{where} \quad k = \frac{k_1 k_2}{k_{-1}}$$

Enzyme reactions are almost always first order in enzyme, as one would expect for a reaction in which one molecule of enzyme participates in the rate-determining step. The rate dependence on reactant concentration generally shows two distinct regions of kinetic behavior. At low reactant concentration, the binding step is rate determining, and the reaction is first order in reactant. However, when reactant concentration is high, all the enzyme molecules are bound to reactant or to product. Under these conditions, some other step of the mechanism is rate determining, and the reaction is now zero order in reactant. At this point, the enzyme is catalyzing the reaction as fast as it can, and adding more substrate cannot make the enzyme work any faster.

This has been a brief overview of a rich, varied field of study. Details of enzyme structure and catalytic activity are being studied in biochemical laboratories worldwide. Moreover, genetic engineering makes it possible to "manufacture" key enzymes in large quantities, so we can look forward to the use of enzymes as industrial catalysts, accomplishing reactions rapidly and selectively.

SECTION EXERCISES

14.7.1 When metals such as platinum, palladium, and rhodium are used as catalysts, they are usually deposited as thin layers over a highly porous material such as charcoal. Explain why these materials are less expensive and more effective catalysts than pieces of pure metal.

14.7.2 Which of the following statements are true? Correct the untrue statements so that they are true.

(a) The concentration of a homogeneous catalyst appears in the rate law.
(b) A catalyst changes an endothermic reaction into an exothermic reaction.
(c) A catalyst lowers the activation energy of the rate-determining step.
(d) A catalyst is consumed in an early step of a mechanism and regenerated in a later step.

14.7.3 Why would it be advantageous to develop a catalyst for the following reaction?

$$4\,CO + 2\,NO_2 \rightarrow N_2 + 4\,CO_2$$

CHAPTER SUMMARY

1. A chemical reaction occurs in a sequence of elementary molecular reactions. These include bimolecular collisions, unimolecular fragmentations, and unimolecular rearrangements.
2. A mechanism is a sequence of elementary steps that describes a reaction. The rate of a reaction is determined by the slowest, rate-determining step in its mechanism.
3. The rates of change of concentrations of reactants and products are related through the stoichiometric coefficients of the balanced chemical equation. A rate law expresses how the reaction rate depends on concentrations.
4. Every mechanism has a predicted rate law given by the rate expression for its rate-determining step. When a step beyond the first is rate determining, the concentrations of intermediates may appear in the rate expression. These must be eliminated from the rate law before it can be compared with experimental data. A technique for doing this equates the forward and reverse rates for early fast steps.
5. Rate laws have the general form, Rate $= k[A]^x[B]^y$, where k is the rate constant. Most often the exponents have values of 1 (first order) or 2 (second order). The specific form of a rate law must be determined by experimental measurements of how concentrations vary with time. For a first-order reaction, $ln\ c$ varies linearly with time, whereas for a second-order reaction, $1/c$ varies linearly with time.
6. A reaction displaying elaborate rate behavior can often be made to display first-order or second-order behavior by isolating one reactant concentration so that it is much smaller than all other reactant concentrations.
7. A satisfactory mechanism must be a set of elementary steps that adds up to the correct overall stoichiometry and predicts the experimentally observed rate law.
8. An elementary reaction usually requires an energy input to drive the rearrangements of chemical bonds. This activation energy (E_a) of the reaction results in a dependence of the rate constant on temperature. The change of k with T depends on E_a. The Arrhenius equation expresses this dependence and allows E_a to be calculated from measurements of rate constants at different temperatures.
9. Reaction rates are also altered by catalysts, which change the mechanisms of reactions, thereby reducing their activation energies. Homogeneous catalysts act in the same phase where the reaction normally occurs, whereas heterogeneous catalysts, which are usually solids, provide sites where reactants can be deposited, react, and then be released.

KEY TERMS

bimolecular reaction
elementary reaction
intermediate
kinetics
rate
rate-determining step
reaction mechanism
termolecular reaction
unimolecular reaction

first order
half-life ($t_{1/2}$)
integrated rate law
isolation method
overall order of reaction
rate constant (k)
rate law
reversible reaction
second order

active site
adsorption
catalyst
desorption
enzyme
heterogeneous catalyst
homogeneous catalyst
induced fit

activated complex
activation energy (E_a)
activation energy diagram
Arrhenius equation
Boltzmann distribution
reaction coordinate

SKILLS TO MASTER

- Visualizing elementary reactions
- Completing reaction mechanisms
- Predicting rate laws from mechanisms
- Determining reaction orders from concentration/time data
- Evaluating rate constants from experimental data
- Testing the consistency of a mechanism
- Applying the Arrhenius equation
- Interpreting activation energy diagrams
- Explaining the action of catalysts

LEARNING EXERCISES

14.1 Write a chapter summary of two pages or less that summarizes the main points of this chapter.

14.2 List the requirements of a satisfactory mechanism, and describe the characteristics of the steps of a mechanism.

14.3 Write one-sentence explanations for the following kinetic terms: (a) first order; (b) second order; (c) isolation; (d) elementary step; (e) catalyst; (f) intermediate; and (g) enzyme.

14.4 Describe the differences among the rate, the rate law, and the rate constant for a chemical reaction.

14.5 Write a paragraph that describes what the activation energy is and how it affects the kinetic behavior of a reaction.

14.6 Update your list of memory bank equations. Include information about how to apply each new equation.

14.7 Make a list of terms new to you that appear in Chapter 14. In your own words, write a one-sentence definition of each. Consult the Glossary if you need help.

PROBLEMS

WHAT IS A MECHANISM?

14.1 What is the rate-determining step in each of the following processes?
(a) A line of people gets coffee from a large coffee urn.
(b) You go through the express line (10 items or less, no checks) at a supermarket.
(c) You leave a pay-as-you-exit parking lot.
(d) A squad of parachutists makes a "jump" from an airplane cargo door.

14.2 The reaction of NO with Cl_2 is $2\ NO + Cl_2 \longrightarrow 2\ NOCl$. Use reactant molecules to write appropriate elementary reactions that satisfy the following criteria: (a) a unimolecular decomposition that generates Cl; (b) a bimolecular collision in which a Cl atom is transferred between reactants; and (c) a termolecular collision leading to the observed products.

14.3 Draw molecular pictures that illustrate each process in Problem 14.2.

14.4 Write three different satisfactory mechanisms for the reaction in Problem 14.2, one having your elementary reaction (a) as its first step, one having elementary reaction (b) as its first step, and one having elementary reaction (c) as its first step.

14.5 Identify any intermediates in the decomposition of ozone, as described in Box 14-1.

14.6 Draw molecular pictures illustrating both steps in the mechanism for the decomposition of ozone.

RATES OF CHEMICAL REACTIONS

14.7 Consider the reaction $2\ NO + Cl_2 \longrightarrow 2\ NOCl$.
(a) Express the rate in terms of the disappearance of Cl_2.
(b) Relate the rate of NOCl formation to the rate of Cl_2 disappearance.
(c) If Cl_2 reacts at a rate of 47 M s^{-1}, how fast does NOCl form?

14.8 Do the following for the ozone decomposition mechanism:
(a) List three sets of units that would be appropriate for expressing the rate.
(b) Express the rate in terms of O_2 formation.
(c) Relate the rate of O_3 consumption with the rate of O_2 production.

14.9 Consider the $2\ NO + Cl_2 \longrightarrow 2\ NOCl$ reaction again.
(a) Draw a molecular picture showing a sample that contains 12 NO molecules and 5 Cl_2 molecules.
(b) Redraw the picture after four molecules of NO have reacted.
(c) Redraw it again when one reactant has been consumed completely.

14.10 Calcium oxide (CaO), an important ingredient in cement, is produced by decomposing calcium carbonate ($CaCO_3$) at high temperature:

$$CaCO_{3\,(s)} \rightarrow CaO_{(s)} + CO_{2\,(g)}$$

In one particular reaction, 35 g of $CaCO_3$ is heated at 550 °C in a 5.0 L vessel. The pressure of CO_2 is 0.15 atm after 5.0 minutes.

(a) What is the average rate of CO_2 production in moles per minute during the 5-minute interval?

(b) How many moles of $CaCO_3$ decompose in the 5-minute interval?

14.11 At high temperature, cyclopropane isomerizes to propene:

Cyclopropane (C_3H_6) ⟶ Propene (C_3H_6)

In a small sample containing 10 molecules of cyclopropane, the reaction proceeds at an average rate of 0.25 molecule/min for 20 minutes.

(a) Use line drawings to illustrate the small sample before the reaction begins.

(b) Redraw the picture after 20 minutes of reaction.

14.12 An industrial chemist is studying the rate of the Haber synthesis: $N_2 + 3\ H_2 \rightarrow 2\ NH_3$. Starting with a closed reactor containing 1.25 mol/L of N_2 and 0.50 mol/L of H_2, the chemist finds that the H_2 concentration has fallen to 0.25 mol/L after 30 seconds.

(a) What is the average rate of reaction of H_2 over this time?

(b) What is the average rate of NH_3 production?

(c) What is the N_2 concentration after 30 seconds?

14.13 Explain using molecular arguments why the Haber synthesis cannot proceed in a single-step elementary reaction.

CONCENTRATION AND REACTION RATES

14.14 Popcorn kernels "pop" independently (that is, "unimolecularly"). At constant temperature, 6 kernels pop in 5 seconds when 150 kernels are present.

(a) After 50 kernels have popped, how many kernels pop in 5 seconds?

(b) Has the average "popping time" per kernel changed? If so, by how much?

(c) Explain the relationship between your answers to (a) and (b).

14.15 Red and white Ping-Pong balls with small Velcro patches are placed in an air-blowing machine similiar to the ones used to scramble numbered balls in lottery drawings on TV. If red and white balls collide at the Velcro points, they stick together. When 20 red and 10 white balls are put in the machine, 4 pairs form after 2 minutes of blowing.

(a) If 10 balls of each color had been placed in the machine, how many pairs would form under the same conditions?

(b) What if there were 20 red and 15 white balls?

(c) What if there were 10 red and 20 white balls?

(d) What if the machine had been crammed with 40 red and 20 white balls?

(e) Explain why the rates change with the number of balls.

14.16 For the net reaction $2\ AB + 2\ C \rightarrow A_2 + 2\ BC$, the following slow first steps have been proposed. What rate law is predicted by each of these steps?

(a) $2\ C + AB \rightarrow AC + BC$

(b) $2\ AB \rightarrow A_2 + 2\ B$

(c) $C + AB \rightarrow BC + A$

(d) $AB \rightarrow A + B$

14.17 Determine the units of the rate constant for each rate law in Problem 14.16.

14.18 For each first step in Problem 14.16, write additional steps that complete the mechanism.

14.19 What happens to the rate of a reaction involving hydrogen if the concentration of H_2 is tripled and the reaction is (a) second order in H_2; (b) zero order in H_2; and (c) 3/2 order in H_2?

14.20 The two pictures shown here represent starting conditions for the following reaction:

$$O_2 + NO_2 \rightarrow O_3 + NO \qquad \text{Rate} = k[O_2][NO_2]$$

Will flask B react faster, slower, or at the same rate as flask A, and by how much? Explain your reasoning in terms of molecular collisions.

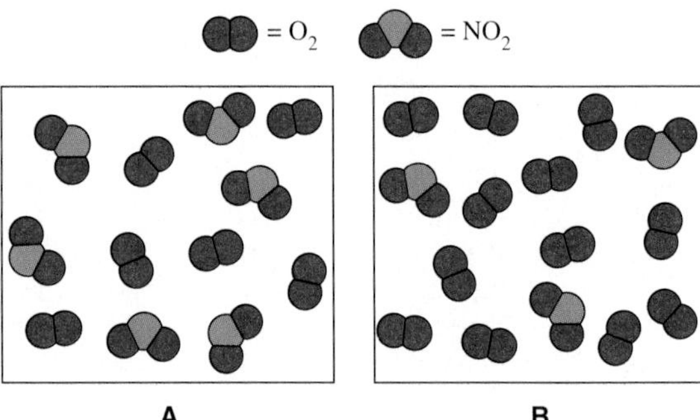

EXPERIMENTAL KINETICS

14.21 The following data are obtained for the decomposition of N_2O_5 at 45 °C:

$$2\ N_2O_{5\,(g)} \rightarrow 4\ NO_{2\,(g)} + O_{2\,(g)}$$

Time (s)	0	200	400	600	800
$[N_2O_5]$ (atm)	2.50	2.22	1.96	1.73	1.53

Find the order and the rate constant for the decomposition reaction.

4.22 Radioactive iodine (^{131}I) is used frequently in biological studies. A radiation biologist studies the rate of decomposition of this substance and obtains the following data:

Time (days)	0	4.0	8.0	12.0	16.0
Mass ^{131}I (μg)	12.0	8.48	6.0	4.24	3.0

(a) Use these data to determine the order of the decomposition process. Show your reasoning.
(b) Determine the rate constant, including appropriate units.
(c) How many micrograms will remain after 32 days?
(d) How many days will it require for the sample size to decrease to 1.2 μg?

14.23 The decomposition reaction of NOBr is second order in NOBr, with a rate constant at 20 °C of 25 L/mol-min. If the initial concentration of NOBr is 0.025 M, find (a) the time at which the concentration will be 0.010 M and (b) the concentration after 100 minutes of reaction.

14.24 A chemist interested in a reaction having overall stoichiometry $3A + 2B \longrightarrow$ Products carries out two sets of experiments, both at 25 °C. In an experiment in which $[B]$ is 1.00 M and $[A]$ is 0.050 M at the start of the reaction, the chemist obtains these data:

Time (s)	0	10	20	30	40	50
$[A]$ (M)	0.050	0.040	0.032	0.025	0.020	0.016

Then the chemist performs another experiment with $[B] =$ 1.50 M and $[A] = 0.050$ M. Again, it requires 30 seconds for the concentration of A to fall to 0.025 M.
(a) What is the rate law of the reaction? Show your reasoning.
(b) Calculate the rate constant.

14.25 Azomethane decomposes into nitrogen and ethane at elevated temperature:

$$H_3C—N{=}N—CH_3 \longrightarrow N_2 + C_2H_6$$

A chemist studying this reaction at 300 °C obtains the following data:

Time (s)	0	100	150	200	250	300
[Azomethane] (mM)	7.94	6.15	5.40	4.75	4.20	3.69

Prepare first-order and second-order graphical plots of these data, determine the order of the reaction, and calculate its rate constant.

14.26 Gas A decomposes according to the reaction $3\,A \longrightarrow B + C$ at 45 °C, and its concentration changes as follows:

Time (s)	0	200	400	600	800
$[A]$ (M)	2.50	2.22	1.96	1.73	1.53

Find the rate law and determine the rate constant.

LINKING MECHANISMS AND RATE LAWS

14.27 Can the assumption that the forward and reverse rates are equal ever be exact for a reacting system? Explain your answer.

14.28 The reaction of CO with Cl_2 gives phosgene ($COCl_2$), a nerve gas used in World War I. Even though the stoichiometry is simple, the mechanism has several steps:

$$Cl_2 \rightleftarrows 2\,Cl \qquad \text{(fast, reversible)}$$

$$Cl + CO \longrightarrow COCl \qquad \text{(slow, rate determining)}$$

$$COCl + Cl_2 \longrightarrow COCl_2 + Cl \qquad \text{(fast)}$$

(a) Show that this mechanism gives the correct overall stoichiometry.
(b) What rate law does this mechanism predict?
(c) Identify any reactive intermediates in the mechanism.

14.29 A student proposes the following mechanism for the atmospheric decomposition of ozone to molecular oxygen:

$$O_3 + O_2 \rightleftarrows O_5 \qquad \text{(fast, reversible)}$$

$$O_5 \longrightarrow 2\,O_2 + O \qquad \text{(slow, rate determining)}$$

(a) Propose a third step that completes this mechanism.
(b) Determine the rate law predicted by this mechanism.
(c) Atmospheric chemists would consider this mechanism to be molecularly unreasonable. Explain why.

14.30 The reaction of NO with O_2 to give NO_2 is an important process in the formation of Los Angeles smog:

$$2\,NO + O_2 \longrightarrow 2\,NO_2$$

Experiments show that this reaction is third order overall. The following mechanism has been proposed:

$$NO + NO \rightleftarrows N_2O_2 \quad (k_1, k_{-1})$$

$$N_2O_2 + O_2 \longrightarrow NO_2 + NO_2 \quad (k_2)$$

(a) If the second step is rate determining, what is the rate law?
(b) Is this rate law consistent with the overall third-order behavior? Explain.
(c) Draw molecular pictures that show different ways the intermediate species might bind together, and identify the one that is most reasonable with respect to the second step of the mechanism.

14.31 In Problem 14.4 you are asked to suggest mechanisms for the reaction of NO with Cl_2. For parts (a) and (b) of that problem, assume the first step in your mechanism is fast and reversible and the second step is rate determining. Derive the rate laws under these assumptions.

14.32 In Problem 14.18 you are asked to complete mechanisms for the hypothetical reaction of AB with C. For parts (b), (c), and (d) of that problem, assume that the second step is rate determining and that the first step is reversible. Derive the rate laws under these assumptions.

REACTION RATES AND TEMPERATURE

14.33 If a reaction has an activation energy of zero, how will its rate constant change with temperature? Explain in molecular terms what $E_a = 0$ means.

14.34 If a reaction has an activation energy of zero, how is ΔE for the forward reaction related to E_a for the reverse reaction? Draw an activation energy diagram illustrating your answer.

14.35 For the reaction coordinate diagram shown, which of the following statements is true?

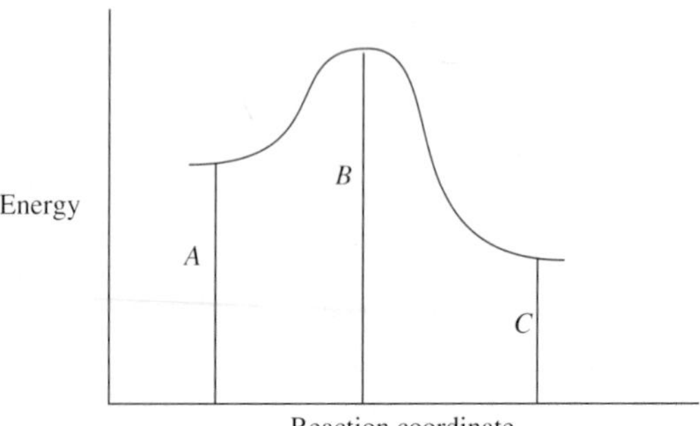

(a) $\Delta E_{rxn} = A - C$
(b) $\Delta E_{rxn} = B - C$
(c) E_a(forward) = E_a (reverse)
(d) A represents the energy of the starting materials.
(e) E_a(forward) = $B - C$
(f) E_a of the forward reaction is less than E_a of the reverse reaction.

14.36 Nitrogen dioxide in smog can combine in an elementary reaction to form N_2O_4 molecules (containing an N—N bond). The combination reaction is exothermic by 57 kJ/mol. For the reverse reaction, the dissociation of N_2O_4, E_a = 70 kJ.
(a) Draw a molecular picture of NO_2 combining to form N_2O_4.
(b) Draw an activation energy diagram that shows the energy relationships as quantitatively as possible. Be sure to label the diagram completely.

14.37 At high temperature, cyclopropane isomerizes to propene (see Problem 14.11). This reaction is exothermic by 33 kJ/mol, and E_a = 60 kJ/mol. Draw the activation energy diagram for the reaction, and label it completely.

14.38 The rate at which tree crickets chirp is 1.9×10^2/min at 28 °C but only 39.6/min at 5 °C. From these data, calculate the "energy of activation" for the chirping process. (HINT: the ratio of rates is equal to the ratio of rate constants.)

CATALYSIS

14.39 How can you identify intermediates and catalysts in a proposed mechanism for a reaction?

14.40 The addition of molecular hydrogen to ethylene is extremely slow unless palladium metal is present. In the presence of the metal, however, H_2 is adsorbed on the metal surface as H atoms, which then add to C_2H_4 when it strikes the surface:

$$\mathrm{H{-}H} + \mathrm{H_2C{=}CH_2} \xrightarrow{\text{Pd}} \mathrm{H{-}CH_2{-}CH_2{-}H}$$

(a) Is Pd metal a reactant, product, intermediate, homogeneous catalyst, or heterogeneous catalyst in this reaction?
(b) Draw a molecular picture that illustrates how this addition occurs.

14.41 Bromide ions catalyze the decomposition of aqueous H_2O_2:

$$2\ H_2O_{2\,(aq)} \longrightarrow 2\ H_2O_{\,(l)} + O_{2\,(g)}$$

by abstracting an oxygen atom to form BrO^-:

$$H_2O_{2\,(aq)} + Br^-_{\,(aq)} \longrightarrow H_2O_{\,(l)} + BrO^-_{\,(aq)}$$

The BrO^- ion then quickly reacts with another H_2O_2 molecule:

$$BrO^-_{\,(aq)} + H_2O_{2\,(aq)} \longrightarrow H_2O_{\,(l)} + A + B$$

(a) Identify A and B.
(b) Construct an activation energy diagram for this reaction. Consult thermodynamic tables to obtain an estimate of ΔE. Clearly show the effect of bromide ion catalysis, and locate on your diagram the energy of the BrO^- intermediate.

14.42 If chlorofluorocarbons catalyze ozone decomposition, they must also catalyze O_3 production from O_2. Using the energies shown in Figure 14-24, explain why catalysis results in net O_3 destruction even though reactions in both directions have been accelerated.

14.43 In your own words, describe the induced-fit model of enzyme specificity. Illustrate with diagrams using a hypothetical enzyme that catalyzes the decomposition of a square but cannot catalyze the decomposition of a triangle:

14.44 Cellulose and starch are long chains constructed of glucose units, but they are connected in different ways:

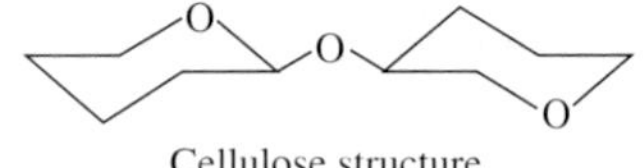

Cellulose structure

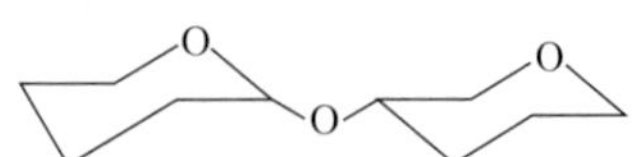

Starch structure

Humans can digest starches because they have an enzyme that catalyzes C—O bond breakage in this structure. Humans are unable to digest cellulose, which passes through the body as "roughage." Draw a cartoon picture of how the starch enzyme must be shaped to act as a catalyst for starches but be unable to catalyze the breakdown of cellulose.

ADDITIONAL PROBLEMS

14.45 The experimental rate law for the reaction between CO and NO_2 is Rate = $k[CO][NO_2]$:

$$NO_2 + CO \rightarrow NO + CO_2$$

Which of the following sets of conditions will give the fastest rate? Explain your choice. (a) 0.5 mol of NO_2 and 0.5 mol of CO in a 2.0-L vessel; (b) 0.5 mol of NO_2 and 0.5 mol of CO in a 1.0-L vessel; and (c) 2.0 mol of NO_2 and 0.1 mol of CO in a 1.0-L vessel.

14.46 Oxygen reacts with CO to form CO_2. Here is a proposed first step of the mechanism:

$$O_2 + CO \rightarrow CO_2 + O$$

(a) What second step is required to complete a satisfactory mechanism?
(b) Draw molecular pictures that illustrate both steps.

14.47 With appropriate catalysts, it is possible to make benzene from acetylene. The reaction has simple overall stoichiometry and can be studied in kinetics experiments:

$$3\,C_2H_{2\,(g)} \rightarrow C_6H_{6\,(g)}$$

(a) Write the rate *expression* (not the rate law) for this reaction in terms of the disappearance of C_2H_2 and in terms of the appearance of C_6H_6.
(b) If enough information is given to find the rate law, find it. If not, describe the data that you would need and how you would analyze the data to determine the rate law.

14.48 For each of the following reactions, what is the order with respect to each starting material, and what is the overall order of the reaction?

(a) $2\,N_2O_5 \rightarrow 4\,NO_2 + O_2$ Rate = $k[N_2O_5]$
(b) $2\,NO + 2\,H_2 \rightarrow N_2 + 2\,H_2O$ Rate = $k[NO]^2[H_2]$
(c) $CHCl_3 + Cl_2 \rightarrow CCl_4 + HCl$ Rate = $k[CHCl_3][Cl_2]^{1/2}$
(d) $N_2 + 3\,H_2 \xrightarrow{\text{Catalyst}} 2\,NH_3$ Rate = k
(e) Glucose + ATP $\xrightarrow{\text{Enzyme}}$ Glucose-phosphate + ADP Rate = k[enzyme]

14.49 Molecule *A* decomposes to give *B* and *C*. The following figures represent two experiments conducted to study this decomposition reaction. Flask 2 is found to react 4 times faster than flask 1. What is the rate law for the decomposition of *A*? Explain your reasoning in terms of molecular collisions.

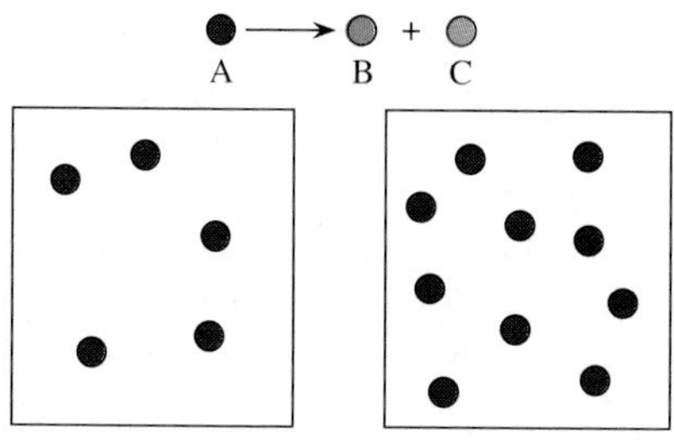

14.50 The first step in the Ostwald process for the synthesis of nitric acid is the combustion of ammonia:

$$4\,NH_3 + 5\,O_2 \xrightarrow{\text{Pt gauze}} 4\,NO + 6\,H_2O$$

In a catalytic experiment, the rate of reaction is found to be:

$$\text{Rate} = \frac{\Delta[NO]}{\Delta t} = 1.5 \times 10^{-3}\ \text{mol L}^{-1}\ \text{s}^{-1}$$

What is the rate of reaction expressed in terms of NH_3, O_2, and H_2O?

14.51 Given the following data for a chemical reaction, determine whether it is zero, first, or second order:

Time (s)	0	10.0	20.0	30.0
Concentration (M)	0.64	0.52	0.40	0.28

14.52 According to our model of enzyme activity, binding a reactant to the enzyme causes a distortion in the conformation of the reactant itself. This distortion decreases the activation energy of the catalyzed reaction. For the hypothetical unimolecular reaction $A \rightarrow B + C$, draw a reaction coordinate diagram for the uncatalyzed reaction and for the same reaction catalyzed by an enzyme. Explain the differences in the two diagrams using the enzyme model. (HINT: Think about the effect of conformational distortion on the stability of the reactant.)

14.53 The enzyme urease catalyzes the hydrolysis of urea to ammonia and carbon dioxide:

$$H_2N\text{–}C(=O)\text{–}NH_2 + H_2O \xrightarrow{\text{Urease}} CO_2 + 2\,NH_3$$

The uncatalyzed reaction has an activation energy of 125 kJ/mol. The enzyme catalyzes a mechanism that has an activation energy of 46 kJ/mol. By what factor does urease increase the rate of urea hydrolysis at 21 °C? (HINT: Use the Arrhenius equation.)

14.54 Write the balanced equations for the reactions that maintain the balance between O_3, O_2, and O in the stratosphere.

14.55 Use molecular arguments to explain why each of the following factors speeds up a chemical reaction: (a) a catalyst; (b) an increase in temperature; and (c) an increase in concentration.

14.56 What is the difference between speed and spontaneity of a chemical reaction?

14.57 Ammonium cyanate (NH_4NCO) rearranges in water to urea (NH_2CONH_2). The following data are obtained at 50 °C.

Time (hr)	0	2	3	5	7	9
Concentration (M)	0.500	0.300	0.250	0.188	0.150	0.125

At 25 °C, the concentration falls from 0.500 M to 0.300 M in 6 hours.

(a) Determine the rate law.
(b) Determine the rate constant at 50 °C.
(c) Determine the activation energy.

14.58 The Haber reaction for the manufacture of ammonia is $N_2 + 3\ H_2 \rightarrow 2\ NH_3$. Without doing any experiments, which of the following can you say *must* be true?
(a) Reaction rate = $-\Delta[N_2]/\Delta t$.
(b) The reaction is first order in N_2.
(c) Rate of disappearance of H_2 = 3 (rate of disappearance of N_2).
(d) Rate of disappearance of N_2 = 3 (rate of disappearance of H_2).
(e) $\Delta[H_2]/\Delta t$ will have a positive value.
(f) The reaction is not an elementary reaction.
(g) The activation energy is positive.

14.59 Phosphine (PH_3) decomposes into phosphorus and molecular hydrogen:

$$4\ PH_{3\,(g)} \rightarrow P_{4\,(g)} + 6\ H_{2\,(g)}$$

Experiments show that this a first-order reaction, with a rate constant of $1.73 \times 10^{-2}\ s^{-1}$ at 650 °C. Which of the following statements are true?
(a) The overall reaction is elementary.
(b) The data given allow the activation energy to be evaluated.
(c) The rate constant would be smaller than $1.73 \times 10^{-2}\ s^{-1}$ at 500 °C.
(d) The reaction $PH_3 \rightarrow PH_2 + H$ might be the first, rate-determining step in the mechanism of this reaction.

14.60 Calculate the time required for 90% of the PH_3 of Problem 14.59 to decompose at 650 °C.

14.61 The reaction of ethylene (C_2H_4) with H_2 to form ethane (C_2H_6) (see Problem 14.40) is exothermic by 137 kJ/mol, has E_a = 200 kJ/mol, and is catalyzed by Pd metal, which reduces E_a by 60 kJ/mol. Draw an activation energy diagram for this reaction, using H—H distance/C—H distance as the reaction coordinate. Be sure all the facts given are illustrated in the diagram, and label it clearly.

14.62 A chemical reaction is thought to proceed by the following mechanism:

$$A + B \underset{k_{-1}}{\overset{k_1}{\rightleftharpoons}} C$$

$$C + D \xrightarrow{k_2} A + E$$

$$E + B \xrightarrow{k_3} 2\ F$$

(a) What is the net stoichiometry of the reaction?
(b) If the second step is rate determining, what is the rate law?
(c) Identify any catalysts and intermediates.

14.63 The reaction between ozone and nitrogen dioxide is:

$$2\ NO_{2\,(g)} + O_{3\,(g)} \rightarrow N_2O_{5\,(g)} + O_{2\,(g)} \qquad \Delta H^\circ = -200\ kJ$$

The reaction proceeds according to the experimental rate law, Rate = $k[NO_2][O_3]$, and NO_3 has been identified as an intermediate in the reaction. The reaction has an activation energy of 50 kJ/mol.
(a) Devise a two-step mechanism for the reaction that is consistent with the experimental observations. Identify the rate-determining step.
(b) Draw a molecular picture that illustrates what happens in your rate-determining step.
(c) Sketch the activation energy diagram for this reaction, and label it as completely as you can.

14.64 An atmospheric scientist interested in how NO is converted to NO_2 in urban atmospheres performs two experiments to measure the rate of this reaction. The data are tabulated. Find the rate law and rate constant for this reaction.

Experiment A: $[NO]_o = 9.63 \times 10^{-3}$ M; $[O_2]_o = 4.1 \times 10^{-4}$ M

Time (s)	0	3.0	6.0	9.0	12.0
$[O_2]$ (10^{-4} M)	4.1	2.05	1.02	0.51	0.25

Experiment B: $[NO]_o = 4.1 \times 10^{-4}$ M; $[O_2]_o = 9.75 \times 10^{-3}$ M

Time (s)	0	100	200	300	400
[NO] (10^{-4} M)	4.1	2.05	1.43	1.02	0.82

14.65 Use the following information to construct an accurate activation energy diagram for the reaction:

$$S_{(s)} + O_{2\,(g)} \rightarrow SO_{2\,(g)}$$

$$\Delta H^\circ_f\,(SO_2) = -296.1\ \text{kJ/mol} \qquad E_a = 150\ \text{kJ/mol}$$

$$O_2 \text{ bond strength} = 498\ \text{kJ/mol}$$

14.66 In the preparation of cobalt complexes, one reaction involves displacement of H_2O by Cl^-:

$$[Co(NH_3)_5H_2O]^{3+} + Cl^- \rightarrow [Co(NH_3)_5Cl]^{2+} + H_2O$$

A proposed mechanism for this displacement starts with rapid reversible dissociation of water:

$$[Co(NH_3)_5H_2O]^{3+} \rightleftharpoons [Co(NH_3)_5]^{3+} + H_2O$$

(a) Propose a slow second step that completes the mechanism and gives the correct overall stoichiometry.
(b) Derive the rate law that this mechanism predicts.
(c) When the rate is studied in 1 M aqueous HCl solution that is 1 mM in $[Co(NH_3)_5H_2O]^{3+}$, first-order experimental kinetics is observed. Is this observation consistent with the proposed mechanism? State your reasoning clearly and in detail.

14.67 Cyclopropane decomposes to propene by first-order kinetics with a rate constant at 500 °C of $5.5 \times 10^{-4}\ s^{-1}$. Calculate how long it requires for 10% of a sample to decompose, for 50% to decompose, and for 99.9% to decompose.

14.68 The reaction of Cl_2 with H_2S in aqueous solution is second order overall, with a rate constant $k = 3.5 \times 10^{-2}\ M^{-1}\ s^{-1}$ at 28 °C. A solution has $[Cl_2]$ = 0.035 M and $[H_2S]$ = 5.0×10^{-5} M.

(a) Find the H_2S concentration after 200 seconds of reaction.
(b) Find the time at which the H_2S concentration has fallen to 1.0×10^{-5} M.

14.69 At least four possible reaction mechanisms exist for the reaction of hydrogen with halogens, $H_2 + X_2 \rightarrow 2\,HX$. Determine the rate law predicted by each of them:

(a)	$H_2 + X_2 \rightarrow 2\,HX$	(bimolecular, direct)
(b)	$X_2 \rightarrow X + X$	(slow dissociation)
	$X + H_2 \rightarrow HX + H$	(fast)
	$H + X \rightarrow HX$	(fast)
(c)	$X_2 \rightleftarrows X + X$	(fast dissociation)
	$X + H_2 \rightarrow HX + H$	(slow)
	$H + X \rightarrow HX$	(fast)
(d)	$X_2 + X_2 \rightleftarrows X_3 + X$	(fast disproportionation)
	$X + H_2 \rightarrow HX + H$	(slow)
	$H + X_3 \rightarrow HX + X_2$	(fast)

14.70 Gaseous N_2O_5 decomposes according to the following equation:

$$2\,N_2O_5 \rightarrow 4\,NO_2 + O_2$$

Much evidence suggests that the mechanism is:

$N_2O_5 \rightleftarrows NO_2 + NO_3$	(fast decomposition)
$NO_2 + NO_3 \longrightarrow NO + NO_2 + O_2$	(slow)
$NO + NO_3 \longrightarrow 2\,NO_2$	(fast)

(a) Show that this mechanism gives the correct overall stoichiometry.
(b) Determine the rate law predicted by this mechanism.
(c) This decomposition is first order experimentally. Does this information prove that step 2, rather than step 1, is rate determining? Explain your answer.

14.71 Photographers use the "rule of thumb," that development time is cut in half for a 10 °C temperature rise, to determine how to modify film development time as the temperature varies.
(a) Calculate the activation energy for the chemistry of film developing, assuming that "normal" temperature is 20 °C.
(b) If a certain film requires 10 minutes to develop at 20 °C, how long will it require at 25 °C? (HINT: The answer is *not* 7.5 minutes.)

14.72 Explain the purpose and function of an automobile catalytic converter.

14.73 For most enzymes, a plot of rate of product formation vs. concentration of reactant has the following general appearance:

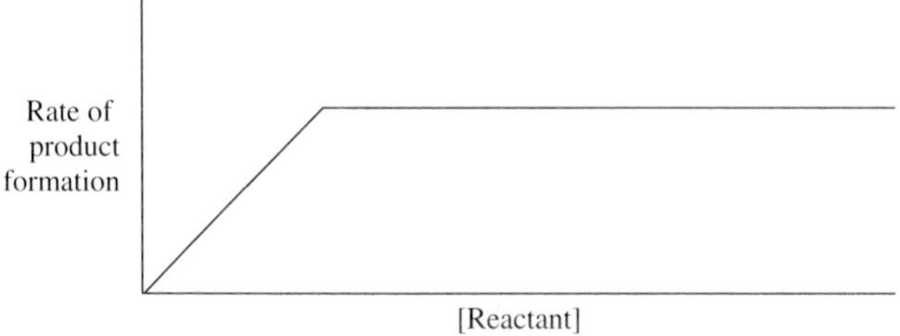

Explain the shape of the plot.

14.74 One possible mechanism for the reaction between hydrogen and nitrogen monoxide follows:

$2\,NO \rightleftarrows N_2O_2$	(fast)
$N_2O_2 + H_2 \longrightarrow N_2O + H_2O$	(slow)
$N_2O + H_2 \longrightarrow N_2 + H_2O$	(fast)

(a) What is the overall stoichiometry of this reaction?
(b) What rate law is predicted by this mechanism?

14.75 Write balanced equations that show how CF_2Cl_2 contributes to the destruction of ozone in the stratosphere.

14.76 Acetaldehyde decomposes to methane and carbon monoxide according to the following balanced equation:

$$\mathrm{H_3C{-}C({=}O){-}H \longrightarrow CH_4 + CO}$$

Kinetics data for the decomposition of acetaldehyde are:

Time (s)	0	1000	2000	3000	4000
$[CH_3CHO]$ (mol L^{-1})	0.250	0.118	0.0770	0.0572	0.0455

(a) Determine the rate law for the decomposition of acetaldehyde.
(b) What is the value of the rate constant?
(c) How long does 75% of the acetaldehyde require to decompose?

14.77 Consider the following hypothetical reaction, which is 1/2 order in

and 3/2 order overall:

The following figure represents one set of initial conditions for the reaction. Draw a similar figure that represents a set of initial conditions that would be twice as fast as the first case.

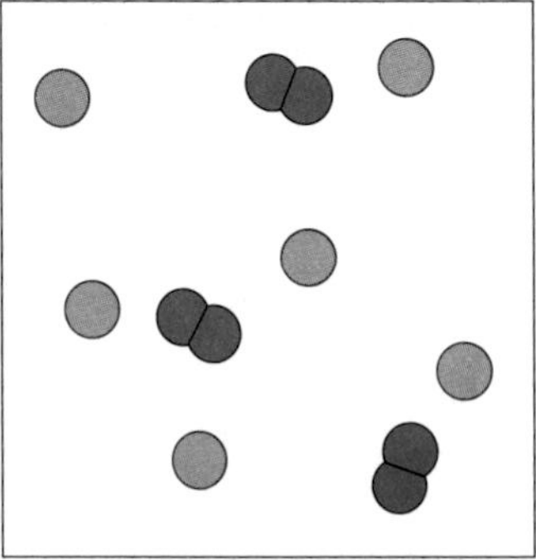

14.78 The following mechanism has been proposed for the gas-phase reaction of chloroform ($CHCl_3$) and chlorine:

$$Cl_2 \underset{k_{-1}}{\overset{k_1}{\rightleftharpoons}} 2\,Cl \qquad \text{(fast, reversible)}$$

$$Cl + CHCl_3 \xrightarrow{k_2} HCl + CCl_3 \qquad \text{(slow)}$$

$$CCl_3 + Cl \xrightarrow{k_3} CCl_4 \qquad \text{(fast)}$$

(a) Write the net balanced equation.
(b) What are the intermediates in the reaction?
(c) What rate law is predicted by this mechanism?

14.79 The element phosphorus has a radioactive isotope called ^{32}P. The decomposition of ^{32}P is a unimolecular first-order process. The following figures represent two flasks containing six atoms of ^{32}P. Will the time required for the six atoms in flask 2 to decompose to three atoms be faster, slower or the same as in flask 1, and by how much? Explain.

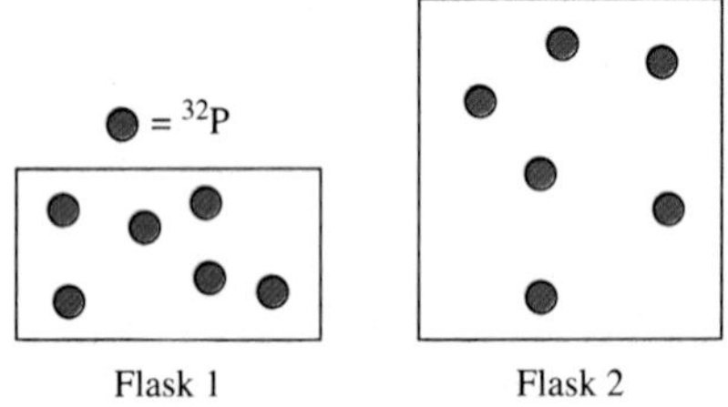

14.80 Nitrogen monoxide is an atmospheric pollutant that destroys ozone in the stratosphere. Here is the accepted mechanism:

$$O_3 + NO \rightarrow NO_2 + O_2 \qquad \text{(slow)}$$

$$NO_2 + O \rightarrow NO + O_2 \qquad \text{(fast)}$$

$$O_3 + O \rightarrow 2\,O_2$$

(a) Draw an activation energy diagram for this mechanism. Include as many details as possible.
(b) Identify any catalysts or intermediates that participate in the mechanism. Explain.
(c) The activation energy for decomposition of ozone promoted by NO is 11.9 kJ/mol. The activation energy for decomposition of ozone promoted by Cl is 2.1 kJ/mol. Which pollutant is a more serious threat to the ozone layer, Cl or NO? Explain.

14.81 The hypothetical reaction: $X_2 + 2\,Y \rightarrow 2\,XY$ goes by the following mechanism:

$$X_2 \rightarrow 2\,X \qquad \text{(slow)}$$

$$X + Y \rightarrow XY \qquad \text{(fast)}$$

In each case shown in the accompanying molecular pictures, what would the rate of reaction be for flask B compared with flask A? Explain.

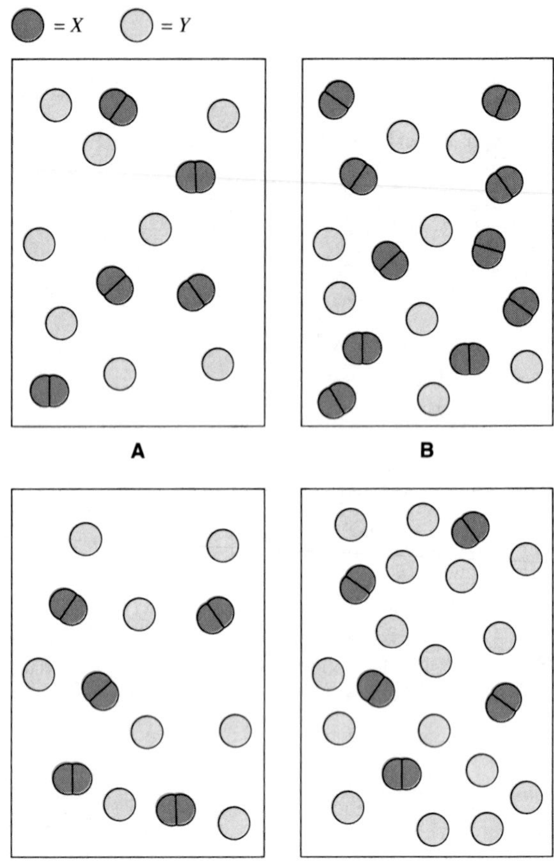

ANSWERS TO SECTION EXERCISES

14.1.1 Second product is CO: $NO + CO_2 \rightarrow NO_2 + CO$.

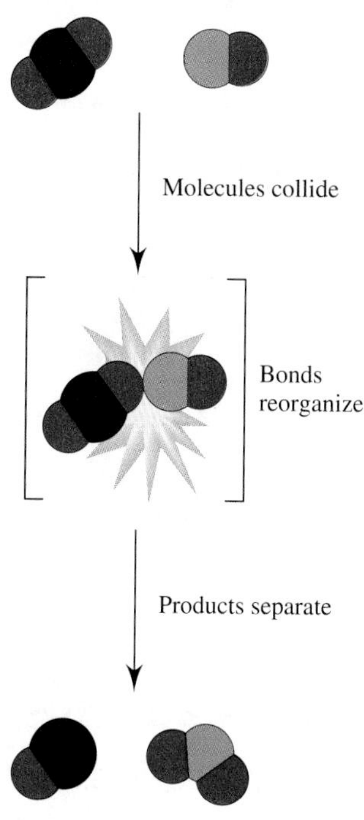

14.1.2 Chemical equation is $2\ NO + 2\ H_2 \rightarrow 2\ H_2O + N_2$, and the intermediates are N_2O_2 and N_2O.

14.1.3 Your description should include highway speeds and the rate at which toll-takers take tolls.

14.2.1

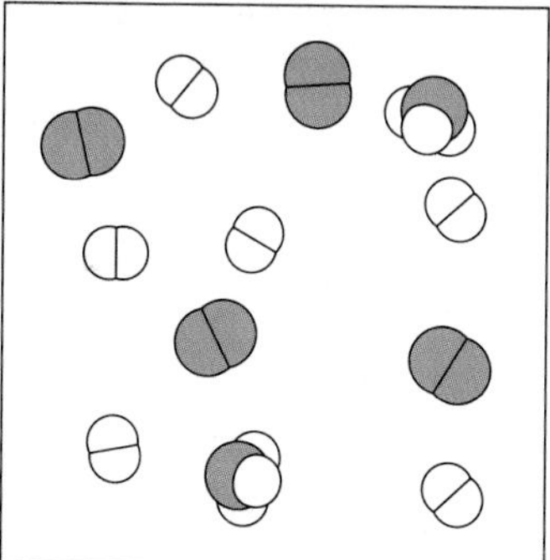

14.2.2 Hydrogen

14.2.3 Relative rate $= -\dfrac{\Delta[N_2]}{\Delta t} = -\dfrac{1}{3}\dfrac{\Delta[H_2]}{\Delta t} = \dfrac{1}{2}\dfrac{\Delta[NH_3]}{\Delta t}$

14.3.1

14.3.2 The rate law is rate = k[AB], and the rate constant has units of $time^{-1}$.

14.3.3 The rate law is rate $= k[H_2][Br_2]^{1/2}$, the overall order is $3/2$, and the rate constant has units of $M^{-1/2}$, $time^{-1}$.

14.4.1 Do two experiments; in each $[H_2O]_0 > 100\ [N_2O_5]_0$ but with two different values for $[H_2O]_0$. Plot $ln[N_2O_5]$ and $1/[N_2O_5]$ vs. t to determine order with respect to N_2O_5, and use the ratio of slope values and H_2O concentrations to determine order with respect to H_2O.

14.4.2 ln c vs. t plot is linear, so the reaction is first order. $k = 3.05 \times 10^{-2}\ min^{-1}$.

14.4.3 The rate law is rate $= k[NO_2]^2$. The fact that the rate does not change when the initial concentration of CO changes shows that the rate law does not depend on [CO].

14.5.1 (a) $N_2O_4 \rightarrow 2\ NO_2$ (occurs twice); and (b) the first step must be rate determining.

14.5.2 If the second step is rate-determining, the law is second order in N_2O_5.

14.5.3 (a) $N_2O_2 + O_2 \rightarrow 2\ NO_2$; and (b) rate $= k_2[N_2O_2][O_2]$, but using equality of rates, $[N_2O_2] = k_1[NO]^2/k_{-1}$, so rate $= k[NO]^2[O_2]$.

14.6.1 The N_2 triple bond is extremely stong. The H_2 bond, 432 kJ/mol, is a strong single bond. From these bond strengths, we predict a high activation energy for the reaction.

14.6.2 (a) $E_a = 20.8$ kJ/mol, $A = 1.2 \times 10^{12}\ s^{-1}$; and (b) $8.3 \times 10^{-19}\ s^{-1}$.

14.6.3

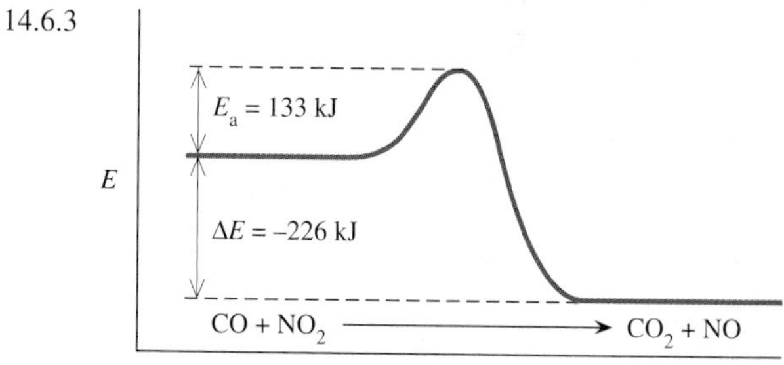

14.7.1 They are less expensive because only a thin layer of the expensive metal is required, rather than solid pieces. They are more effective because a layer on porous charcoal has a much larger surface area (where the catalyzed reaction occurs) than the relatively smooth surface of a pure piece of metal.

14.7.2 (a) True; (b) a catalyst does not change the overall energy change of a reaction; (c) a catalyst lowers the activation energy of an overall reaction by changing its mechanism; and (d) true.

14.7.3 The reaction converts pollutants (CO and NO_2) into benign constituents of the atmosphere (CO_2 and N_2), so catalyzing this reaction could reduce atmospheric pollution levels.

This process, introduced in Chapter 4, provided a plentiful and relatively inexpensive industrial source of fixed nitrogen that thoroughly dominates the modern fertilizer industry.

The Haber process does not proceed appreciably at room temperature. It must be carried out at high temperature and pressure in the presence of a catalyst:

$$N_2 + 3\ H_2 \xrightarrow[450\ °C,\ 270\ atm]{\text{Fe powder doped with } K_2O \text{ and } Al_2O_3} 2\ NH_3$$

Even under these optimum conditions, the ammonia synthesis does not go to completion. Instead, it reaches chemical equilibrium when substantial amounts of N_2 and H_2 are still present. Despite intensive efforts, the optimum yield of the ammonia synthesis in industrial reactors is only about 13%.

We show in Box 15-1 that the overall yield of the Haber synthesis is increased considerably by repeatedly removing the products and recycling the unreacted gases.

Currently, the annual production of ammonia in the United States, all of which uses the Haber process, is more than 17 million tons, of which almost 85% is used to manufacture fertilizer. Other major uses include the production of nylon fibers and explosives. As an indispensable source of fertilizer, the ammonia formation reaction is one of the most important chemical equilibria in industrial chemistry.

In this chapter, we present basic features of chemical equilibria that explain why the Haber process and other reactions cannot go to completion. We also show why increasing the temperature and using catalysts can accelerate the rate of this reaction but cannot shift its equilibrium position in favor of ammonia.

15.1 DYNAMIC EQUILIBRIUM

The detailed chemistry of the ammonia synthesis is relatively complex, so we introduce the principles of equilibrium using nitrogen dioxide chemistry, which we described in Chapter 14. In a sample of nitrogen dioxide, NO_2 molecules collide continuously with one another. At room temperature, a reaction occurs that forms N_2O_4 molecules:

$$2\ NO_2 \rightarrow N_2O_4$$

In a vessel that contains only NO_2 molecules, this is the only reaction that occurs. After N_2O_4 molecules are present, however, an N_2O_4 molecule can fragment after collisions give it sufficient energy to break its N—N bond. Such fragmentations regenerate NO_2:

$$N_2O_4 \rightarrow 2\ NO_2$$

Figure 15-1 depicts these two processes from the molecular perspective.

EQUILIBRIUM

Collisions between NO_2 molecules produce N_2O_4 and consume NO_2. On the other hand, fragmentation of N_2O_4 produces NO_2 and consumes N_2O_4. In a sample whose concentration of N_2O_4 is very low, the first process occurs much more frequently than the second. Consequently, the NO_2 concentration decreases and the N_2O_4 concentration increases. Eventually, the concentrations of the two species reach values at which the rate of production of N_2O_4 equals its rate of decomposition. Even though

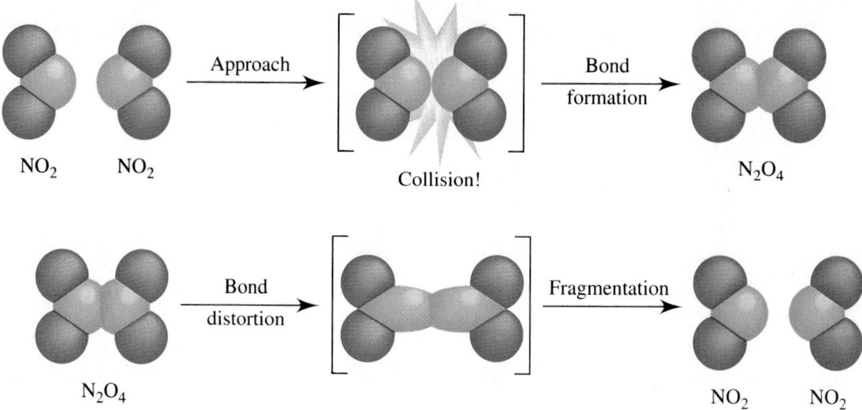

FIGURE 15-1
When two NO_2 molecules collide in the proper orientation, an N—N bond forms to produce a molecule of N_2O_4. When a molecule of N_2O_4 acquires sufficient energy through molecular collisions, its N—N bond distorts and eventually fragments to produce two molecules of NO_2.

individual molecules continue to combine and decompose, the rate of one process is exactly balanced by the rate of the other. This is a **dynamic equilibrium.** At dynamic equilibrium, the rates of the forward and reverse reactions are equal. The system is *dynamic* because individual molecules react continuously. It is *at equilibrium* because no *net* change occurs.

EXPERIMENTAL CONFIRMATION

The molecular processes that occur in a mixture of NO_2 and N_2O_4 lead to changes in the concentrations of the species that can be observed by monitoring changes in partial pressures. The partial pressure of NO_2 can be determined experimentally, since NO_2 is orange and N_2O_4 is colorless. Thus the color intensity of the gas mixture is proportional to the partial pressure of NO_2.

Measurements show that whether there is a high initial concentration of NO_2 or of N_2O_4, the reaction does not go to completion. Even after a very long time, the gas still has an orange hue. Figure 15-2 summarizes the results of quantitative experiments on the NO_2/N_2O_4 system. The data show that the partial pressures of both gases level off to constant nonzero values as the reaction reaches equilibrium.

If the reaction to form N_2O_4 shown in Figure 15-2, *A*, had gone to completion, the final pressure of N_2O_4 would have been 0.500 atm. If the reaction to decompose N_2O_4 shown in Figure 15-2, *B*, had gone to completion, the final pressure of NO_2 would have been 1.00 atm. Instead, these reactions reach equilibrium when substantial amounts of both gases are present.

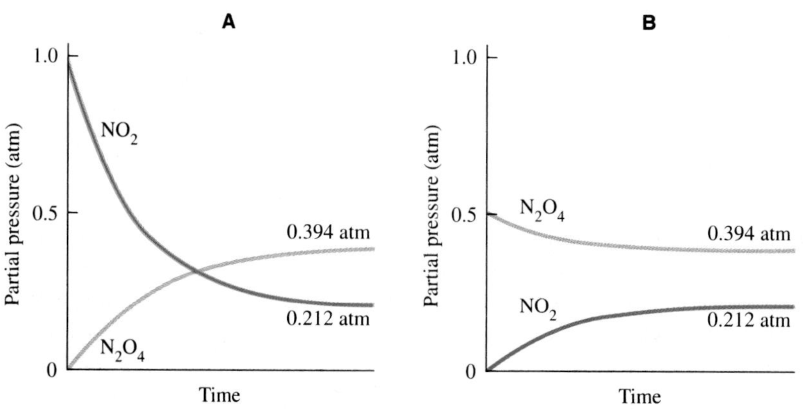

FIGURE 15-2
Variations with time of the partial pressures of NO_2 and N_2O_4.
A, Starting with pure NO_2 at 1.00 atm pressure. **B,** Starting with pure N_2O_4 at 0.50 atm pressure. Each system reaches equilibrium before either reactant is fully consumed.

THE EQUILIBRIUM CONSTANT

The equilibrium condition for the NO_2/N_2O_4 system is described by formation and decomposition of N_2O_4 occurring at the same time:

The subscripts on the rate constants refer to formation and decomposition.

Formation $\quad NO_2 + NO_2 \xrightarrow{k_f} N_2O_4$

Decomposition $\quad N_2O_4 \xrightarrow{k_d} NO_2 + NO_2$

Each of these reactions is the reverse of the other, so instead of writing two separate elementary reactions, we can combine them and use double arrows to show that the reaction proceeds in both directions:

Equilibrium mechanism $\quad NO_2 + NO_2 \underset{k_d}{\overset{k_f}{\rightleftharpoons}} N_2O_4$

At equilibrium, the reactions continue, even though the pressures of both NO_2 and N_2O_4 are constant. That is, the rate of formation of N_2O_4 is exactly counterbalanced by the rate of its decomposition, so no *net* change occurs. We can express the rates of these elementary reactions as shown in Chapter 14:

$$\text{Rate of formation of } N_2O_4 = k_f[NO_2]^2$$

$$\text{Rate of decomposition of } N_2O_4 = k_d[N_2O_4]$$

At equilibrium, the rate of disappearance equals the rate of appearance:

We designate a concentration at equilibrium with a subscript "eq."

$$k_f[NO_2]^2_{eq} = k_d[N_2O_4]_{eq}$$

This equality can be rearranged to group the concentrations on one side and the rate constants on the other:

$$\frac{k_f}{k_d} = \frac{[N_2O_4]_{eq}}{[NO_2]^2_{eq}}$$

The ratio of concentrations is called the **equilibrium constant (K_{eq})**:

$$K_{eq} = \frac{[N_2O_4]_{eq}}{[NO_2]^2_{eq}}$$

The equilibrium constant describes the equilibrium concentrations of reactants and products.

Notice that this analysis of the NO_2-N_2O_4 equilibrium follows the same logic as the assumption for equality of rates introduced in Chapter 14.

REVERSIBILITY

The mechanism describing the NO_2/N_2O_4 system is an example of the **reversibility** of elementary molecular reactions. If molecules of NO_2 combine to give N_2O_4 molecules, N_2O_4 molecules *must* decompose to give NO_2 molecules. The concept of reversibility emerged from our analysis of the NO_2/N_2O_4 mechanism, but it is a general principle that applies to all molecular processes. Whenever we write an elementary step in a chemical *mechanism,* we can give it a double arrow that describes what happens at chemical *equilibrium.* Every *elementary* reaction is a molecular rearrangement that goes both in the forward and in the reverse direction.

To illustrate the generality of reversibility and the equilibrium expression, we extend our kinetic analysis to an equilibrium with a two-step mechanism. The mechanism for the decomposition reaction of nitrogen dioxide appears in Chapter 14:

$$NO_2 + NO_2 \underset{k_{-1}}{\overset{k_1}{\rightleftharpoons}} NO + NO_3 \quad \text{(slow)}$$

$$NO_3 \xrightarrow{k_2} NO + O_2 \quad \text{(fast)}$$

Recall that if the rate constant for a forward reaction is k_1, the rate constant for its reverse reaction is k_{-1}.

Just as the decomposition of N_2O_4 is reversible, the decomposition of NO_3 is also reversible. That is, if an O_2 molecule and an NO molecule collide in the proper orientation, they can "stick together" to form NO_3:

$$NO + O_2 \xrightarrow{k_{-2}} NO_3$$

This reaction plays a negligible role early in the decomposition of NO_2 because the concentrations of O_2 and NO are too small for collisions between these products to occur frequently. As the products accumulate, however, the reaction becomes more and more likely. Eventually, product concentrations become large enough that the rate of the reverse reaction matches the rate of the forward reaction. After this time, the system has reached equilibrium, and each step in the mechanism has a forward rate that equals its reverse rate:

$$NO_2 + NO_2 \underset{k_{-1}}{\overset{k_1}{\rightleftharpoons}} NO + NO_3$$

$$NO_3 \underset{k_{-2}}{\overset{k_2}{\rightleftharpoons}} NO + O_2$$

$$k_1[NO_2]^2_{eq} = k_{-1}[NO]_{eq}[NO_3]_{eq} \quad \textit{and} \quad k_2[NO_3]_{eq} = k_{-2}[NO]_{eq}[O_2]_{eq}$$

We can rearrange each of these rate equalities to give an equilibrium expression for each step of the mechanism:

$$\frac{k_1}{k_{-1}} = \frac{[NO]_{eq}[NO_3]_{eq}}{[NO_2]^2_{eq}} \quad \textit{and} \quad \frac{k_2}{k_{-2}} = \frac{[NO]_{eq}[O_2]_{eq}}{[NO_3]_{eq}}$$

Each of these equilibrium expressions contains the equilibrium concentration of the intermediate, $[NO_3]_{eq}$. Solving the second expression for $[NO_3]_{eq}$ and substituting into the first, we obtain an equilibrium expression in terms of concentrations of reactants and products:

$$[NO_3]_{eq} = \frac{k_{-2}}{k_2}[NO]_{eq}[O_2]_{eq} \quad \textit{so} \quad \frac{k_1}{k_{-1}} = \frac{[NO]_{eq}}{[NO_2]^2_{eq}}\left(\frac{k_{-2}}{k_2}[NO]_{eq}[O_2]_{eq}\right)$$

$$\frac{k_1 k_2}{k_{-1}k_{-2}} = \frac{[NO]^2_{eq}[O_2]_{eq}}{[NO_2]^2_{eq}}$$

The right-hand side of this expression is a ratio of equilibrium concentrations that we identify as the equilibrium constant for this reaction:

$$K_{eq} = \frac{[NO]^2_{eq}[O_2]_{eq}}{[NO_2]^2_{eq}}$$

Both equilibrium expressions described so far contain concentrations of products in the numerator and concentrations of reactants in the denominator. Moreover, each concentration is raised to a power equal to its stoichiometric coefficient in the balanced equation for the overall reaction:

$$2\,NO_2 \rightleftharpoons 2\,NO + O_2 \qquad\qquad 2\,NO_2 \rightleftharpoons N_2O_4$$

$$K_{eq} = \frac{[NO]^2_{eq}[O_2]_{eq}}{[NO_2]^2_{eq}} \qquad\qquad K_{eq} = \frac{[N_2O_4]_{eq}}{[NO_2]^2_{eq}}$$

It is always possible to carry out this type of kinetic analysis, whether a mechanism is simple or elaborate. That is, we can always derive an equilibrium expression by applying reversibility and setting forward and reverse rates equal to one another at equilibrium. However, it is impractical to go through the mechanism for every chemical equilibrium. We have done it for two examples to demonstrate that inspection of the overall stoichiometry *always* gives the correct expression for the equilibrium constant. That is, a reaction of the form:

$$aA + bB \rightleftarrows cC + dD$$

has an equilibrium constant expression given by Equation 15-1:

$$K_{eq} = \frac{[C]^c_{eq}\,[D]^d_{eq}}{[A]^a_{eq}\,[B]^b_{eq}} \tag{15-1}$$

Thus the equilibrium expression for any reaction can be written from its overall stoichiometry. In Sample Problem 15-1, Equation 15-1 is applied to the Haber process.

SAMPLE PROBLEM 15-1 EQUILIBRIUM CONSTANT EXPRESSION

What is the equilibrium expression for the Haber synthesis of ammonia?

$$N_{2\,(g)} + 3\,H_{2\,(g)} \rightleftarrows 2\,NH_{3\,(g)}$$

METHOD: If we knew the mechanism for this equilibrium, we could derive the equilibrium expression using the principle of reversibility. However, Equation 15-1 allows us to write the expression directly.

The product concentration, raised to a power equal to its stoichiometric coefficient, appears in the numerator. The concentrations of starting materials, each raised to a power equal to its stoichiometric coefficient, appear in the denominator:

$$K_{eq} = \frac{[NH_3]^2_{eq}}{[N_2]_{eq}\,[H_2]^3_{eq}}$$

Three features of Equation 15-1 are especially important:

1. K_{eq} *applies only at equilibrium.* As the subscripts indicate, the concentrations of reactants and products used in the ratio must be equilibrium concentrations.
2. K_{eq} *is independent of initial conditions.* At a given temperature, the equilibrium constant has only one value. Whether we start with pure reactants, pure products, or any composition in between, the system reaches a state of *equilibrium,* as determined by the value of K_{eq}.
3. K_{eq} *is related to the stoichiometry of the balanced net reaction.* The numerator contains only concentrations of products, whereas the denominator contains only concentrations of reactants. Each concentration is raised to a power equal to its stoichiometric coefficient.

It is important to recognize the difference between the *rate law* and the *equilibrium constant* of a reaction. Although each expression contains concentrations raised to powers, each describes a fundamentally different aspect of a chemical reaction. The rate law describes how the rate of a reaction changes with concentration; the equilibrium expression describes the concentrations of reactants and products when the net rate of the reaction is zero:

$$K_{eq} = \frac{[NO]^2_{eq}\,[O_2]_{eq}}{[NO_2]^2_{eq}}$$

$2\ NO_2 \rightarrow 2\ NO + O_2$ $\qquad$ Rate $= k[NO_2]^2$

SECTION EXERCISES

15.1.1 One simple possible mechanism for the O_2/O_3 equilibrium in the stratosphere is:

$$O_3 \underset{k_{-2}}{\overset{k_1}{\rightleftarrows}} O_2 + O$$

$$O + O_3 \underset{k_{-2}}{\overset{k_2}{\rightleftarrows}} 2\ O_2$$

Use this mechanism to derive an expression for the equilibrium constant.

15.1.2 Draw molecular pictures like the ones shown in Figure 15.1 to illustrate all the reactions that occur when the O_3/O_2 system is at equilibrium.

15.1.3 Write the equilibrium expression for the combustion of NH_3 during the Ostwald synthesis of nitric acid:

$$4\ NH_{3\ (g)} + 5\ O_{2\ (g)} \rightleftarrows 4\ NO_{\ (g)} + 6\ H_2O_{\ (g)}$$

15.2 PROPERTIES OF EQUILIBRIUM CONSTANTS

According to Equation 15-1, the equilibrium constant expression is a ratio of product and reactant concentrations, raised to appropriate powers. However, concentrations can be expressed in several ways, and as a matter of convenience, we choose to use different concentration units for different phases of matter. We show in Section 15.5 that equilibrium constants can be related to thermodynamic properties, so the most convenient concentration units are the ones that are used to specify the standard conditions in thermodynamics:

1. Pure liquid or solid: mole fraction (X)
2. Gas: partial pressure (p_i)
3. Solutes: molarity (M)
4. Solvent: mole fraction (X)

These units allow us to simplify the equilibrium constant expressions for reactions in which pure liquids, pure solids, or the solvent are among the reactants and products.

The mole fraction of any pure substance is always 1.00, so we do not need to include it explicitly in the ratio of concentrations. In other words, for a general reaction:

$$A + B \rightarrow C + S$$

where S is a pure solid or liquid, the concentration of S is $X = 1.00$ and can be left out of the concentration ratio without altering the value of K_{eq}:

$$K_{eq} = \frac{[C]_{eq}}{[A]_{eq}\,[B]_{eq}}$$

The mole fraction of a *solvent* is not quite 1.00 because solutes dilute the solvent. In most solutions, however, the concentration of the solvent is much greater than that of any solute, so the mole fraction of solvent differs negligibly from 1.00. As an example, consider a 1.0 M solution of glucose in water. The concentration of pure water is 55.5 M, so the mole fraction of water in the glucose solution is:

$$X_{H_2O} = \frac{55.5 \text{ M water}}{1.0 \text{ M glucose} + 55.5 \text{ M water}} = \frac{55.5}{56.5} = 0.98$$

Although aqueous solutions are usually dilute enough to ignore changes in solvent mole fraction, nonaqueous liquid mixtures are likely to have substantial concentrations of both components. In such solutions, it is usually convenient to express the concentrations of *all* components as molarities.

The sugar molecules in the solution dilute the solvent by only 2%. Equilibrium calculations are seldom accurate to better than 5%, so this small deviation from 1.00 can be neglected, and we need not include the concentration of the solvent in the concentration ratio.

UNITS AND THE EQUILIBRIUM CONSTANT

Every concentration that appears in an equilibrium expression must be given in the appropriate units. Concentrations of solvents, pure liquids, and pure solids are expressed in mole fractions, which are unitless. We use molarities for the concentrations of solutes in aqueous solutions and partial pressures in atmospheres for the concentrations of gases. These choices make it possible to relate equilibrium constant values directly to standard thermodynamic quantities, which are defined for partial pressures equal to 1.00 atm and solute concentrations equal to 1.00 M.

The numerical value of any equilibrium constant for a reaction depends on the units used to express concentrations, so it is essential to express all concentrations in the appropriate units. For example, all components of the NO_2/N_2O_4 system described at the beginning of this chapter are gases:

$$2\ NO_{2\ (g)} \rightleftharpoons N_2O_{4\ (g)}$$

We choose to express gas concentrations as partial pressures, so the equilibrium constant expression for this reaction is as follows:

$$K_{eq} = \frac{(p_{N_2O_4})_{eq}}{(p_{NO_2})^2_{eq}}$$

From the data shown in Figure 15-2, we can calculate the value of K_{eq}:

$$K_{eq} = \frac{(0.394 \text{ atm})}{(0.212 \text{ atm})^2} = 8.77 \text{ atm}^{-1}$$

In our treatment of equilibria, we *always* use molarities for substances in aqueous solution, atmospheres for substances in the gas phase, and mole fractions for pure substances and solvents. In other books, however, you may encounter equilibrium constants that are expressed in other units. The concentrations of reactants and products that are used in carrying out equilibrium calculations must always be consistent with the units used for the equilibrium constant. In Sample Problem 15-2, we apply these ideas to some aqueous equilibria for carbon dioxide.

SAMPLE PROBLEM 15-2 CO_2 AQUEOUS EQUILIBRIA

Carbon dioxide enters the aqueous biosphere by dissolving in water to give carbonic acid:

$$CO_{2\ (g)} + H_2O_{\ (l)} \rightleftharpoons \underset{\text{Carbonic acid}}{H_2CO_{3\ (aq)}}$$

In aqueous solution, carbonic acid is at equilibrium with hydrogencarbonate anions:

$$H_2CO_{3\,(aq)} + H_2O_{(l)} \rightleftarrows HCO_3^-{}_{(aq)} + H_3O^+{}_{(aq)}$$

In regions where the soil contains calcium ions, carbonate precipitates as limestone, $CaCO_3$:

$$Ca^{2+}{}_{(aq)} + H_2O_{(l)} + HCO_3^-{}_{(aq)} \rightleftarrows H_3O^+{}_{(aq)} + CaCO_{3\,(s)}$$

For each of these reactions, write the expression for the equilibrium constant, and indicate the appropriate units.

METHOD: Equation 15-1 can be used to write the equilibrium expression, but we must be careful to express each species in the proper units. The expression can be simplified by omitting the concentrations of species whose mole fractions are one. The units associated with the equilibrium constant can be deduced from the units of the concentrations.

In the first reaction, water is the solvent, so we can set its mole fraction equal to 1:

$$K_{eq} = \frac{[H_2CO_3]_{eq}}{(p_{CO_2})_{eq}(X_{H_2O})_{eq}} = \frac{[H_2CO_3]_{eq}}{(p_{CO_2})_{eq}}$$

The units associated with this equilibrium constant are those of the concentration ratio, M/atm.

In the second reaction, water again is the solvent, so its mole fraction is 1 and can be omitted from the concentration ratio:

$$K_{eq} = \frac{[HCO_3^-]_{eq}[H_3O^+]_{eq}}{[H_2CO_3]_{eq}}$$

All concentrations are expressed in molarities, so the units associated with this equilibrium constant are $M^2/M = M$.

In the third reaction, water is again the solvent, and calcium carbonate is a pure solid with $X = 1.00$. The equilibrium expression reduces to:

$$K_{eq} = \frac{[H_3O^+]_{eq}}{[Ca^{2+}]_{eq}[HCO_3^-]_{eq}}$$

Again, all concentrations are expressed as molarities, so the units associated with this equilibrium constant are $M/M^2 = M^{-1}$.

DIRECTION OF AN EQUILIBRIUM REACTION

For a reaction at equilibrium, the rate of the forward reaction is balanced exactly by the rate of the reverse reaction. For this reason, we can write the equilibrium reaction in either direction. The equilibrium constant for the Haber synthesis of ammonia, for example, can be expressed in two ways:

$$N_{2\,(g)} + 3\,H_{2\,(g)} \rightleftarrows 2\,NH_{3\,(g)} \qquad K_{eq} = \frac{(p_{NH_3})^2_{eq}}{(p_{N_2})_{eq}(p_{H_2})^3_{eq}}$$

$$2\,NH_{3\,(g)} \rightleftarrows N_{2\,(g)} + 3\,H_{2\,(g)} \qquad K_{eq}' = \frac{(p_{N_2})_{eq}(p_{H_2})^3_{eq}}{(p_{NH_3})^2_{eq}}$$

The two equilibrium constants are reciprocals of each other:

$$K_{eq} = \frac{1}{K_{eq}'} \qquad \textbf{(15-2)}$$

Equilibrium constant for forward reaction (K_{eq}) — Equilibrium constant for reverse reaction (K_{eq}')

The direction that we choose for the equilibrium reaction is determined by our particular interests. Haber wanted to produce ammonia from N_2 and H_2, so he would have used K_{eq}. On the other hand, a chemist studying the decomposition of ammonia on a metal surface would use K_{eq}'. Either choice works, as long as *products* of the net reaction appear in the *numerator* of the equilibrium constant expression and *reactants* appear in the *denominator.*

MAGNITUDES OF EQUILIBRIUM CONSTANTS

The magnitudes of equilibrium constants vary over a tremendous range and depend on the nature of the reaction and on the temperature of the system in ways that we describe later in this chapter. Many reactions have very large equilibrium constants. For example, the reaction between H_2 and Br_2 to form HBr, whose mechanism we described in Chapter 14, has a huge equilibrium constant:

$$H_{2\,(g)} + Br_{2\,(g)} \rightleftarrows 2\,HBr_{(g)} \qquad K_{eq} = \frac{(p_{HBr})^2_{eq}}{(p_{H_2})_{eq}(p_{Br_2})_{eq}} = 5.4 \times 10^{18}$$

The large value for this equilibrium constant indicates that the reaction goes virtually to completion. If we start with 1 atm each for H_2 and Br_2, 2 atm of HBr will exist when the system reaches equilibrium. The partial pressures of the reactant gases at equilibrium will be 10^{-9} atm, which is negligible compared with the initial pressures.

Other reactions have extremely small equilibrium constants. For example, elemental fluorine, a diatomic molecule under standard conditions, is nevertheless at equilibrium with fluorine atoms:

$$F_{2\,(g)} \rightleftarrows 2\,F_{(g)} \qquad K_{eq} = \frac{(p_F)^2_{eq}}{(p_{F_2})_{eq}} = 2.1 \times 10^{-22}\ \text{atm}$$

The tiny value of this equilibrium constant indicates that a sample of fluorine at 25 °C consists almost entirely of F_2 molecules. If the partial pressure of F_2 is 1.00 atm, the partial pressure of fluorine atoms is 10^{-11} atm, which is negligible compared with 1.00 atm. Nevertheless, the equilibrium constant is not zero, so some fluorine atoms are present in the gas.

Other equilibrium constants are neither large nor small. We calculated earlier that the dimerization of NO_2 has a moderate equilibrium constant at 25 °C.

$$2\,NO_{2\,(g)} \rightleftarrows N_2O_{4\,(g)} \qquad K_{eq} = \frac{(p_{N_2O_4})_{eq}}{(p_{NO_2})^2_{eq}} = 8.77\ \text{atm}^{-1}$$

An equilibrium mixture of NO_2 and N_2O_4 at 25 °C contains enough of each molecule for readily measured partial pressures of both to exist. Equilibrium calculations are essential to the description of chemical composition and behavior when the equilibrium constant of a reaction falls in the range where the equilibrium concentrations of reactants and products both can be measured readily.

SECTION EXERCISES

15.2.1 Write expressions for the equilibrium constants for the following reactions:

(a) $PCl_{5\,(s)} \rightleftarrows PCl_{3\,(l)} + Cl_{2\,(g)}$
(b) $CaCO_{3\,(s)} \rightleftarrows CaO_{(s)} + CO_{2\,(g)}$
(c) $Ca_3(PO_4)_{2\,(s)} \rightleftarrows 3\,Ca^{2+}_{(aq)} + 2\,PO_4^{3-}{}_{(aq)}$
(d) $HCN_{(g)} + H_2O_{(l)} \rightleftarrows H_3O^+_{(aq)} + CN^-_{(aq)}$
(e) $H_3O^+_{(aq)} + CN^-_{(aq)} \rightleftarrows HCN_{(g)} + H_2O_{(l)}$

15.2.2 What are the units associated with the equilibrium constant for each of the equilibria in Exercise 15.2.1?

15.2.3 Proton transfer reactions can be written in two ways:

$$HA_{(aq)} \rightleftharpoons H^+_{(aq)} + A^-_{(aq)}$$

$$HA_{(aq)} + H_2O_{(l)} \rightleftharpoons H_3O^+_{(aq)} + A^-_{(aq)}$$

Write the equilibrium expressions for each of these. Do the two equilibrium constants have the same numerical value? Explain.

FIGURE 15-3
The "fogging" of bathroom mirrors is a consequence of the liquid-vapor equilibrium of water. When air that is saturated with water vapor comes into contact with a surface at lower temperature, molecules of water condense to form liquid droplets.

15.3 TYPES OF EQUILIBRIA

Several general types of equilibria appear repeatedly in chemistry. These equilibria have been given special names, and it is helpful to learn to recognize them. Keep in mind, however, that the principles described in the two previous sections apply to all chemical equilibria. Chemists categorize equilibria for convenience, but they treat all equilibria the same way.

VAPORIZATION EQUILIBRIA

The phase change of a pure substance between a condensed phase and the gas phase leads to equilibrium. The vaporization equilibrium of water is an example whose consequences appear in everyday life. The "fogging" of bathroom mirrors, shown in Figure 15-3, occurs when the water vapor in warm air comes into contact with the cooler surface of the mirror, causing vapor to condense:

Phase changes of pure substances are described in detail in Chapters 10 and 13, and the vapor pressure of water in the Earth's atmosphere is presented in Chapter 5.

$$H_2O_{(l)} \rightleftharpoons H_2O_{(g)} \qquad K_{eq} = (p_{H_2O})_{eq} = \text{Vapor pressure}$$

Solids also have vaporization equilibria. The sublimation of solid carbon dioxide (dry ice) is a common example:

$$CO_{2\,(s)} \rightleftharpoons CO_{2\,(g)} \qquad K_{eq} = (p_{CO_2})_{eq} = \text{Vapor pressure}$$

In every case of vaporization equilibrium, K_{eq} at any particular temperature is equal to the **vapor pressure** of the substance in the gas phase. The condensed phase is a pure liquid or a pure solid, so its concentration is expressed by its mole fraction and is equal to 1.00.

The color of bromine shows that molecules are present in the gas phase at equilibrium with the liquid.

GAS SOLUBILITY

The solubility of gases in liquids and solids is presented in Chapter 10. As Figure 15-4 illustrates, equilibrium is established when the rate at which gas molecules dissolve in the solution equals the rate at which gas molecules escape from the solution. We have already seen this equilibrium expression in another form. Recall from Chapter 10 that Henry's law describes the solubility of gases. The Henry's law constant, K_H, is the equilibrium constant for gas solubility. The equilibrium expression for gas solubility contains both the concentration of gas dissolved in the solution and the partial pressure of the gas above the solution. One critical example is the solubility of molecular oxygen in aqueous solutions. Fish and other aquatic plants

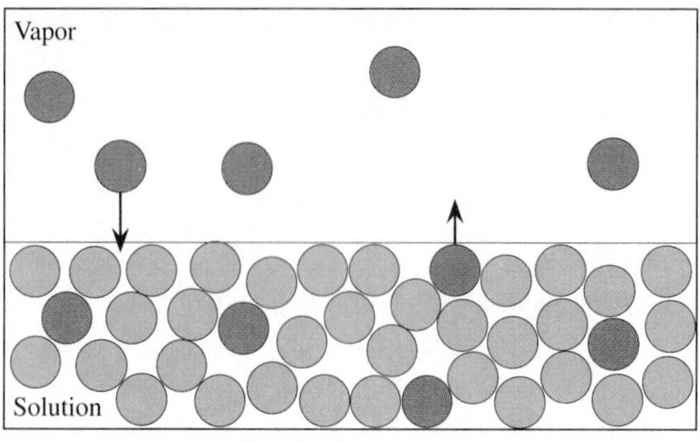

FIGURE 15-4
Schematic molecular view of gas-solution equilibrium. At equilibrium, the concentration of gas dissolved in the solution is sufficient to make the rate of escape of gas molecules from the solution equal to the rate of capture of gas molecules by the solution, and the concentration of dissolved gas remains constant.

Plants and fish depend on the equilibrium between oxygen in the atmosphere and oxygen dissolved in water. Home aquariums must have air bubblers to replenish the oxygen consumed by fish and plants.

and animals would die if O_2 gas in the atmosphere were not at equilibrium with O_2 dissolved in water:

$$O_{2\,(g)} \rightleftarrows O_{2\,(aq)} \qquad K_{eq} = \frac{[O_{2\,(aq)}]_{eq}}{(p_{O_2})_{eq}} = K_H$$

SOLUBILITY OF SALTS

A vast amount of interesting and important chemistry occurs in aqueous solution, and many substances that participate in aqueous reactions are salts. These crystalline solids dissolve in water to give solutions of cations and anions. For almost all salts, there is an upper limit to the amount that will dissolve in water. A salt solution that has reached this upper limit of solubility is said to be **saturated.** Any additional salt added to a saturated solution remains undissolved at the bottom of the vessel. When excess solid salt and a saturated solution are present, a solubility equilibrium exists. At equilibrium, ions dissolve continually, but other ions precipitate out at exactly the same rate. This equilibrium is illustrated for sodium chloride by the molecular picture in Figure 15-5.

Conventionally, a solubility equilibrium is written in the direction of a solid dissolving to give aqueous ions, and the equilibrium constant for this reaction is

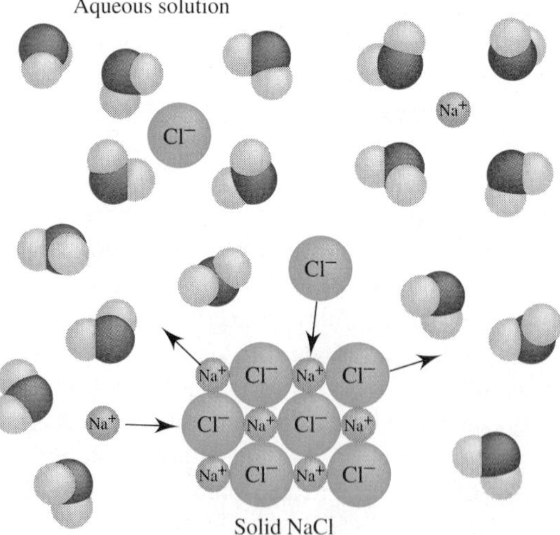

FIGURE 15-5
Molecular view of the solubility equilibrium for sodium chloride in water. At equilibrium, ions dissolve from the crystal surface at the same rate they are captured, so the concentration of ions in the solution remains constant.

called the **solubility product (K_{sp}).** The reaction describing the solubility equilibrium of sodium chloride, for example, is:

$$NaCl_{(s)} \rightleftharpoons Na^+_{(aq)} + Cl^-_{(aq)} \qquad K_{eq} = [Na^+]_{eq}[Cl^-]_{eq} = K_{sp}$$

Tabulated values of K_{sp} always refer to the equilibrium constant for the salt dissolving in water.

The evaporation of water from a saturated solution leaves a solution in which the ion concentrations exceed the solubility limit. To return to equilibrium, the salt must precipitate from the solution. Evaporation is used to "mine" sodium chloride as well as other salts from the highly salty waters of the Great Salt Lake in Utah, as shown in Figure 15-6.

The blue color of a copper sulfate solution shows that copper cations are present in the aqueous phase at equilibrium with the solid salt.

FORMATION OF COMPLEX IONS

Metal cations in aqueous solution often form chemical bonds to anions or neutral molecules that have lone pairs of electrons. A silver ion, for example, can associate with two ammonia molecules to form $Ag(NH_3)_2^+$:

$$H_3N{:} + Ag^+ + {:}NH_3 \rightleftharpoons H_3N{-}Ag^+{-}NH_3$$

The resulting species is called a **complex ion.** The equilibrium constant for the formation of a complex ion is called the **formation constant (K_f).** Tabulated values of formation constants always refer to the formation of a complex ion from its constituent species:

$$Ag^+_{(aq)} + 2\,NH_{3\,(aq)} \rightleftharpoons [Ag(NH_3)_2]^+_{(aq)} \qquad K_{eq} = \frac{[Ag(NH_3)_2]^+_{eq}}{[Ag^+]_{eq}[NH_3]^2_{eq}} = K_f$$

FIGURE 15-6
The water in land-locked seas such as the Great Salt Lake in Utah is a highly concentrated solution containing various cations and anions. When the water is evaporated, solid salts precipitate.

ACID-BASE EQUILIBRIA

One of the most important reactions that occur in aqueous solution is the transfer of a proton from an acid to a base. In aqueous solutions, water can act as an acid or a base. In the presence of an acid HA, water acts as a base by accepting a proton. The equilibrium constant for this transfer of a proton from an acid to a water molecule is called the **acid ionization constant (K_a).**

Recall from Section 4.6 that proton donors are called *acids* and proton acceptors are called *bases.*

$$HA_{(aq)} + H_2O_{(l)} \rightleftharpoons A^-_{(aq)} + H_3O^+_{(aq)} \qquad K_{eq} = \frac{[A^-]_{eq}[H_3O^+]_{eq}}{[HA]_{eq}} = K_a$$

For instance, when acetic acid, an example of a weak acid, dissolves in water, some acetic acid molecules transfer protons to water to produce acetate anions and hydronium ions:

The addition of a colorless ammonia solution to a green solution of Ni^{2+} cations results in the formation of the deep-blue complex ion $[Ni(NH_3)_4]^{2+}$.

Vinegar is an aqueous solution of acetic acid.

$$\underset{\text{Acetic acid}}{H_3C-C(=O)-OH} + H-O-H \rightleftharpoons \underset{\text{Acetate}}{H_3C-C(=O)-O^-} + H-O^+(H)-H$$

$$K_a = \frac{[CH_3CO_2^-]_{eq}\,[H_3O^+]_{eq}}{[CH_3CO_2H]_{eq}}$$

In the presence of a base B, water acts as an acid by donating a proton, and the equilibrium constant for the transfer of a proton from water to a base is called the **base ionization constant (K_b):**

$$H_2O_{(l)} + B_{(aq)} \rightleftharpoons BH^+_{(aq)} + OH^-_{(aq)} \qquad K_{eq} = \frac{[BH^+]_{eq}\,[OH^-]_{eq}}{[B]_{eq}} = K_b$$

When ammonia, an example of a weak base, dissolves in water, some ammonia molecules accept protons from water to produce ammonium cations and hydroxide ions:

An aqueous solution of ammonia is a common household cleanser.

$$NH_{3\,(aq)} + H_2O_{(l)} \rightleftharpoons NH_4^+{}_{(aq)} + OH^-_{(aq)} \qquad K_b = \frac{[NH_4^+]_{eq}\,[OH^-]_{eq}}{[NH_3]_{eq}}$$

WATER EQUILIBRIUM

In Chapter 4, we introduced the reaction of hydronium ions and hydroxide ions to produce water:

$$H_3O^+_{(aq)} + OH^-_{(aq)} \longrightarrow 2\,H_2O_{(l)}$$

Although we wrote this reaction as though it goes to completion, it actually reaches a balance, with small concentrations of the ions remaining in solution. In other words, the reaction leads to an equilibrium among the hydronium ions, the hydroxide ions, and the water molecules. Normally, this equilibrium is written in the opposite direction to emphasize that two water molecules participate in a proton transfer reaction:

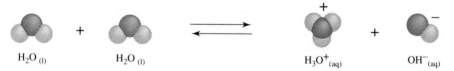

$$H_2O_{(l)} + H_2O_{(l)} \rightleftharpoons H_3O^+_{(aq)} + OH^-_{(aq)}$$

The equilibrium constant for this proton transfer reaction, the **water equilibrium constant,** is designated K_w**.** It has the value of 1.00×10^{-14} M^2 at 25 °C. That is, the concentrations of hydronium ions and hydroxide ions in pure water at 25 °C are 1.00×10^{-7} M:

$$K_{eq} = [H_3O^+]_{eq}\,[OH^-]_{eq} = K_w = 1.00 \times 10^{-14}\ M^2 \qquad \text{(At 25 °C)}$$

$$[H_3O^+]_{eq} = [OH^-]_{eq} = 1.00 \times 10^{-7}\ M \qquad \text{(Pure water at 25 °C)}$$

Several general types of equilibria that we have just described play very important roles in aqueous chemistry. The interplay among these types of equilibria are explored in detail in Chapter 16. It is important to be able to recognize examples of each type. Sample Problem 15-3 provides some practice in such recognition.

SAMPLE PROBLEM 15-3 TYPES OF AQUEOUS EQUILIBRIA

Write expressions for the equilibrium constants, and decide which general category applies to each of these equilibria:

(a) $H_2CO_{3\,(aq)} + H_2O_{(l)} \rightleftarrows HCO_3{}^-{}_{(aq)} + H_3O^+{}_{(aq)}$

(b) $Fe^{3+}{}_{(aq)} + 6\,CN^-{}_{(aq)} \rightleftarrows Fe(CN)_6{}^{3-}{}_{(aq)}$

(c) $NH_4{}^+{}_{(aq)} + OH^-{}_{(aq)} \rightleftarrows NH_{3\,(aq)} + H_2O_{(l)}$

METHOD: Examine each reaction closely, and look for the characteristic features of the general equilibria. The equilibrium constant expression can be written by inspecting the overall stoichiometry.

(a) In this reaction, water accepts a proton from H_2CO_3. The equilibrium constant for a proton transfer reaction that consumes H_2O and produces H_3O^+ is called K_a:

$$\frac{[H_3O^+]_{eq}\,[HCO_3{}^-]_{eq}}{[H_2CO_3]_{eq}} = K_a$$

(b) In this reaction, a metal cation forms a complex ion with six cyanide anions; this is a formation reaction whose equilibrium constant is called K_f:

$$\frac{[Fe(CN)_6{}^{3-}]_{eq}}{[Fe^{3+}]_{eq}\,[CN^-]^6_{eq}} = K_f$$

(c) At first glance, this equilibrium does not seem to belong to any of the categories. However, it is important to remember that at equilibrium, a reaction goes in *both* directions at equal rates. This is a proton transfer reaction. In the *forward* direction, a hydroxide ion removes a proton from an ammonium ion. In the *reverse* direction, a proton is transferred from water to ammonia. This reverse reaction is included among the general categories. It is the transfer of a proton from a water molecule to a base, so its equilibrium constant is K_b. According to Equation 15-2, the equilibrium constant must be $1/K_b$ for the reaction in the direction written:

$$\frac{[NH_3]_{eq}}{[NH_4{}^+]_{eq}\,[OH^-]_{eq}} = \frac{1}{K_b}$$

The values of equilibrium constants are different for different chemical substances. Many K_a, K_b, and K_{sp} values appear in Appendix G. More extensive tables can be found in *The Handbook of Chemistry and Physics.*

GAS EQUILIBRIA

We introduced equilibrium using the gas-phase reactions of NO_2 because it is easy to visualize these reactions at the molecular level. Although the equilibrium constants for gas-phase equilibria do not have specific designations such as K_a or K_f, many gaseous reaction equilibria play key roles in the manufacture of industrial chemicals. Some of these important equilibria are described next.

Production of Sulfuric Acid. In 1992, 40 billion kg of sulfuric acid (H_2SO_4) were produced in the United States. A total of 60% of the production of this leading industrial chemical is used to make fertilizers, but H_2SO_4 is also used in the manufacture of inorganic salts and acids, detergents, pigments, drugs, dyes, explosives, and paper.

Sulfuric acid is manufactured in a series of steps known as the *contact process.* First, elemental sulfur is burned in air to give sulfur dioxide, a reaction that goes virtually to completion:

$$S_{(s)} + O_{2\,(g)} \rightarrow SO_{2\,(g)}$$

BOX 15-2

THE CARBON CYCLE

Carbon is only the twelfth most abundant element in the Earth's crust, accounting for just 0.08% of the mass. Nevertheless, all life on Earth is based on the chemistry of carbon. Living organisms take in carbon, process it through biochemical reactions, and expel it as waste. Carbon dioxide is especially important in the exchange of carbon between the biosphere and its environment.

Green plants store energy from sunlight by converting carbon dioxide and water into carbohydrates. As discussed in Chapter 11, most carbohydrates have the general formula $(CH_2O)_n$:

$$n\,CO_2 + n\,H_2O \xrightarrow{h\nu} (CH_2O)_n + n\,O_2$$

Plants and animals use the chemical energy stored in carbohydrates to power the many processes that characterize life. That is, enzymes catalyze the conversion of carbohydrates back to CO_2 and H_2O, a process that releases chemical energy:

$$(CH_2O)_n + n\,O_2 \xrightarrow{\text{Enzymes}} n\,CO_2 + n\,H_2O + \text{Energy}$$

These two processes cycle carbon between the atmosphere, where it is found primarily as CO_2, and the biosphere, where it is found primarily as carbohydrates. However, the cycle is complicated by several equilibria that involve CO_2. These equilibria transfer carbon between the atmosphere and the hydrosphere (Earth's surface waters) and between the hydrosphere and the lithosphere (Earth's crustal solids). Together, the carbohydrate-CO_2 cycle and the interlocking aqueous equilibria of CO_2 result in a relatively stable distribution of carbon among the different terrestrial spheres. The processes that move carbon from one sphere to another are illustrated schematically in Figure 15-11.

Almost all the Earth's carbon is found in the lithosphere as calcium carbonate and other carbonate sediments and rocks. Carbon is transferred continuously into the lithosphere as carbonate sediments precipitate from the oceans and accumulate on the sea floor. The shells of aquatic animals also contribute calcium carbonate to the lithosphere. Carbon enters the biosphere and the atmosphere as carbonate minerals dissolve in water percolating through the Earth's crust. This is a slow process limited by the solubility product for

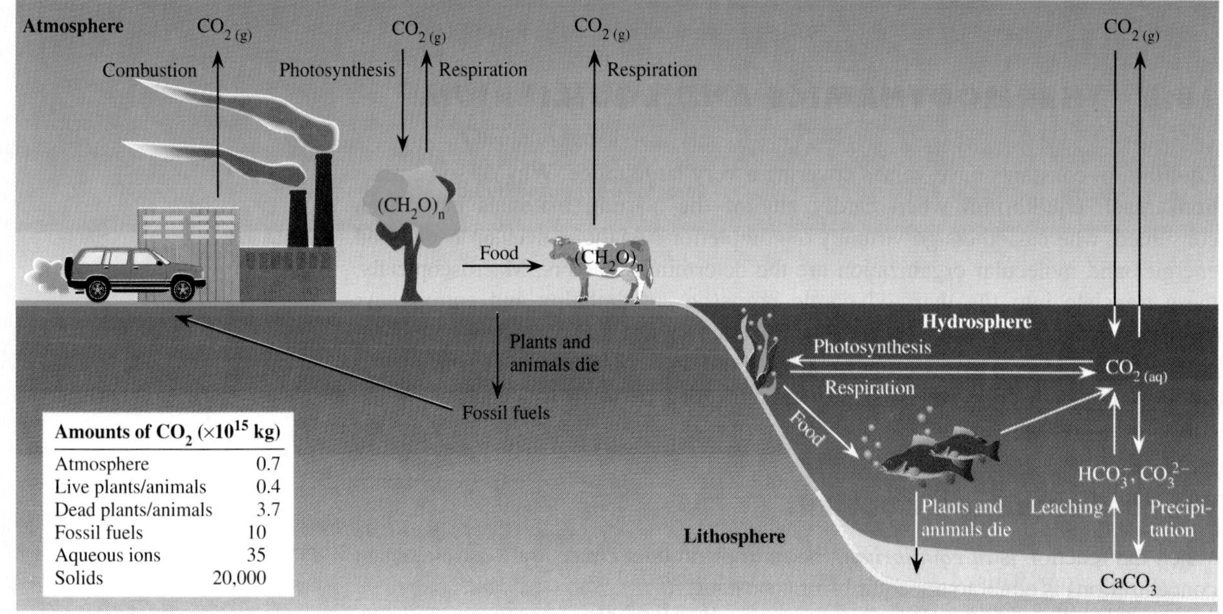

FIGURE 15-11 Carbon cycles in and out of the biosphere through a variety of chemical processes, several of which involve equilibria.

carbonate salts, so lithospheric carbonates represent a relatively inaccessible storehouse of carbon.

Dissolved carbon dioxide is a significant source of atmospheric CO_2, even though it accounts for much less of the total carbon inventory than do carbonates. The significance of carbon exchange between the hydrosphere and the atmosphere arises from the immense capacity of the oceans to absorb CO_2. Not only is there a large surface between the gaseous atmosphere and the liquid hydrosphere across which CO_2 exchange can occur, but also there is a large volume of ocean water that circulates continually between the ocean surface and its depths.

The carbon locked in fossil fuels was a relatively insignificant source of atmospheric carbon until the advent of the industrial age. Since then, human consumption of fossil fuels has increased dramatically. When fossil fuels are burned, carbon is transferred into the atmosphere as CO_2. This is one of the few rapidly changing features of the overall carbon cycle. The clearing of tropical rain forests also disrupts the atmospheric carbon balance because cutting and burning a forest destroys a significant part of the Earth's photosynthetic apparatus.

Over the last quarter century, the atmospheric concentration of CO_2 has increased by more than 10%, and many scientists attribute this change to human activities such as deforestation and the burning of fossil fuels. Unless these activities are modified, the atmospheric concentration of CO_2 may continue to rise.

What the increase in atmospheric CO_2 portends for the future of our planet is a matter of intense debate. One of the uncertainties is the amount of CO_2 that can be absorbed by the oceans. Several equilibria operate in the hydrosphere, and it is difficult to predict the eventual result of a change of one concentration. We know that increased atmospheric concentration of CO_2 leads to more CO_2 dissolved in the oceans:

$$CO_{2\,(g)} \rightleftharpoons CO_{2\,(aq)}$$

This in turn generates a higher concentration of hydrogencarbonate and carbonate ions.

$$CO_{2\,(aq)} + H_2O_{\,(l)} \rightleftharpoons H_2CO_{3\,(aq)}$$

$$H_2CO_{3\,(aq)} + H_2O_{\,(l)} \rightleftharpoons H_3O^+_{\,(aq)} + HCO_3^-{}_{(aq)}$$

$$HCO_3^-{}_{(aq)} + H_2O_{\,(l)} \rightleftharpoons H_3O^+_{\,(aq)} + CO_3^{2-}{}_{(aq)}$$

When a higher concentration of these anions exists, more carbonate salts such as $CaCO_3$ precipitate, transferring carbon to the lithosphere:

$$CO_3^{2-}{}_{(aq)} + Ca^{2+}{}_{(aq)} \rightleftharpoons CaCO_{3\,(s)}$$

Some scientists believe that this string of equilibria has the capacity to offset the buildup of atmospheric CO_2, after the hydrosphere has time to respond to the change in CO_2 pressure. This is far from certain, however, because much depends on the *rates* of all these reactions. Even assuming that atmospheric CO_2 equilibrates quickly with aqueous CO_2 at the atmosphere-ocean interface, the transfer of substantial quantities of CO_2 requires the thorough mixing of both atmosphere and oceans. Such mixing may be too slow to respond to rate at which the burning of fossil fuels pumps CO_2 into the atmosphere.

You may wonder why we should be concerned about an increase in atmospheric CO_2. After all, its concentration in air is only 350 parts per million, so even a doubling of its concentration still leaves it well below 0.1% of the atmosphere. Despite its low concentration, however, CO_2 exerts a major effect on the average temperature of Earth's surface. Recall from Chapter 6 that CO_2 is a "greenhouse" gas that traps outgoing radiation. By acting as a one-way energy window, CO_2 in the atmosphere may contribute to global warming that could have catastrophic consequences. In a warmer climate, for example, much of the polar ice caps would melt, and the oceans would expand as their temperatures increased. This could raise sea level by up to 15 meters and inundate many of the world's most populous regions, such as Bangladesh and the East and Gulf Coasts of the United States. Additionally, even small temperature fluctuations may alter global weather patterns and perhaps lead to serious droughts.

Our planet is such a complicated, dynamic set of interconnected systems that we simply do not know the possible result of a "simple" change such as doubling the concentration of atmospheric CO_2. Many scientists are studying aspects of the carbon cycle in hopes of learning what lies ahead for our planet.

When a chemical system is *not at equilibrium,* the ratio of concentrations is called the **concentration quotient, (Q).** The concentration quotient has the same form as the equilibrium concentration ratio, but the concentrations *are not equilibrium values:* Consequently, Q can have *any* value.

$$K_{eq} = \frac{[C]^c_{eq}\,[D]^d_{eq}}{[A]^a_{eq}\,[B]^b_{eq}} \qquad Q = \frac{[C]^c[D]^d}{[A]^a[B]^b}$$

The subscript "eq" indicates that these are equilibrium concentrations.

These are **not** equilibrium concentrations.

The NO_2/N_2O_4 system can be used to show how Q is related to K_{eq}. We have seen that NO_2 gas reacts to produce N_2O_4 until an equilibrium is established between the two gases. If a sample contained only NO_2, the partial pressure of N_2O_4 would be zero and $Q = 0$. This system would react to form N_2O_4 and consume NO_2, and the value of Q would increase until $Q = K_{eq}$. At these concentrations, the system would be at equilibrium. If, on the other hand, a sample contained only N_2O_4 but no NO_2, the partial pressure of NO_2 would be zero and $Q = \infty$. Under these conditions, the system would react to form NO_2 and consume N_2O_4, and the value of Q would decrease, again until $Q = K_{eq}$. Thus we see that the direction in which a reaction proceeds depends on the relationship between Q and K_{eq}:

$Q < K_{eq}$ *reaction goes to the right to make products.*

$Q > K_{eq}$ *reaction goes to the left to make reactants.*

Notice that if the concentration of any *product* is zero, $Q = 0$, and the reaction must go to the *right,* toward products. If any *reactant* concentration is zero, $Q = \infty$, and the reaction must go to the *left,* toward reactants.

The relationship between Q and K_{eq} signals the direction of a chemical reaction. The free energy change, ΔG (introduced in Chapter 13), also signals the direction of a chemical reaction. These two criteria can be compared:

Reaction goes right when	Equilibrium when	Reaction goes left when
$Q < K_{eq}$ $\Delta G_{rxn} < 0$	$Q = K_{eq}$ $\Delta G_{rxn} = 0$	$Q > K_{eq}$ $\Delta G_{rxn} > 0$

The similarities suggest a link among Q, K_{eq}, and ΔG. This link can be found from the equations of thermodynamics. The concentration quotient appears in Equation 13-12 as a link between the standard free energy change for a reaction and its free energy change under nonstandard conditions:

$$\Delta G = \Delta G^o + RT \ln Q \qquad \textbf{(13-12)}$$

At equilibrium, $\Delta G = 0$ and $Q = K_{eq}$. Substituting these equalities into Equation 13-12, we obtain:

$$0 = \Delta G^o + RT \ln K_{eq}$$

This rearranges to:

$$\Delta G^o = -RT \ln K_{eq} \qquad \textbf{(15-5)}$$

Equation 15-5 is an extremely important relationship, because it links thermodynamic data with equilibrium constants. Because many values of ΔG°_f appear in tables, K_{eq} can be calculated from Equation 15-5 for many reactions. This equation is applied to the Haber process in Sample Problem 15-9.

SAMPLE PROBLEM 15-9 THERMODYNAMICS AND K_{eq}

Using standard thermodynamic data, find the value of K_{eq} at 298 K for the Haber reaction:

$$N_{2\,(g)} + 3\,H_{2\,(g)} \rightleftharpoons 2\,NH_{3\,(g)}$$

METHOD: Equation 15-5 provides the link between thermodynamic data and K_{eq}. We must first calculate ΔG°_{rxn} from tabulated standard free energies of formation.

Remember that ΔG_f° for any element in its standard state is zero.

$$\Delta G^\circ_{rxn} = \Sigma\,(\text{coeff})\,\Delta G^\circ_f\,(\text{products}) - \Sigma\,(\text{coeff})\,\Delta G^\circ_f\,(\text{reactants})$$

Appendix E contains the appropriate values:

$$\Delta G^\circ_f\ (\text{kJ/mol}):\ N_{2\,(g)},\ 0;\ H_{2\,(g)},\ 0;\ NH_{3\,(g)},\ -16.4\ \text{kJ/mol}$$

$$\Delta G^\circ = (2\ \text{mol NH}_3)(-16.4\ \text{kJ/mol NH}_3) - 3(0) - 1(0) = -32.8\ \text{kJ}$$

To determine the equilibrium constant, Equation 15-5 must be rearranged to isolate $ln\ K_{eq}$.

$$ln\ K_{eq} = -\frac{\Delta G^\circ}{RT} = \frac{-(-32.8\ \text{kJ})(10^3\ \text{J/kJ})}{(8.314\ \text{J/K})(298\ \text{K})} = 13.24$$

$$K_{eq} = e^{13.4} = 5.6 \times 10^5\ \text{atm}^{-2}$$

The exponential gives a dimensionless number, since e^x is always a pure number. However, we assign units to K_{eq} as required by the concentration quotient. Remember that the superscript "o" in ΔG° refers to standard conditions that include concentrations of 1 M for solutes and 1 atm partial pressure for gases.

EQUILIBRIUM CONSTANTS AND TEMPERATURE

Studies of the effect of temperature on equilibria reveal a consistent pattern. The equilibrium constant of an *exothermic* reaction *decreases* with increasing temperature, whereas the equilibrium constant of an *endothermic* reaction *increases* with increasing temperature. Equation 15-5 provides a thermodynamic explanation for this behavior. Recall that free energy is related to enthalpy and entropy through Equation 13-9:

$$\Delta G^\circ = \Delta H^\circ - T\Delta S^\circ \qquad \textbf{(13-9)}$$

This equality can be substituted into Equation 15-5 to show how $ln\ K_{eq}$ depends on ΔH°, ΔS°, and T:

$$\Delta H^\circ - T\Delta S^\circ = -RT\ ln\ K_{eq}$$

which rearranges to give:

$$ln\ K_{eq} = -\frac{\Delta H^\circ}{RT} + \frac{\Delta S^\circ}{R} \qquad \textbf{(15-6)}$$

An exothermic reaction has a negative ΔH°, making the first term on the right of Equation 15-6 positive. As T increases, this term *decreases,* causing K_{eq} to decrease. An endothermic reaction, in contrast, has a positive ΔH°, making the first term on the right of Equation 15-6 negative. As T increases, this term becomes less negative, causing K_{eq} to increase. These variations in K_{eq} with temperature, which can be substantial, can be estimated using Equation 15-6 and standard thermodynamic functions. Sample Problem 15-10 applies Equation 15-6 to the Haber synthesis.

SAMPLE PROBLEM 15-10 K_{eq} AND TEMPERATURE

Use tabulated thermodynamic data to estimate K_{eq} for the Haber reaction at 500 °C.

METHOD: Values for ΔH° and ΔS° can be calculated using tabulated thermodynamic values. Then Equation 15-6 can be applied to determine the value of the equilibrium constant at 500 °C. First, we need ΔH°_{rxn} and ΔS°_{rxn}:

$$\Delta H^\circ_{rxn} = \Sigma \text{ (coeff) } \Delta H^\circ_f \text{ (products)} - \Sigma \text{ (coeff) } \Delta H^\circ_f \text{ (reactants)}$$

$$\Delta S^\circ_{rxn} = \Sigma \text{ (coeff) } S^\circ \text{ (products)} - \Sigma \text{ (coeff) } S^\circ \text{ (reactants)}$$

Appendix E contains the appropriate values:

ΔH°_f (kJ/mol)	$N_{2\,(g)}$: 0	$H_{2\,(g)}$: 0	$NH_{3\,(g)}$: −46
S° (J/mol K)	$N_{2\,(g)}$: 191.6	$H_{2\,(g)}$: 130.7	$NH_{3\,(g)}$: 192.45

$$\Delta H^\circ_{rxn} = (2)(-46 \text{ kJ/mol}) - 3(0) - 0 = -92 \text{ kJ/mol}$$

$$\Delta S^\circ_{rxn} = (2)(192.45 \text{ J/mol K}) - (3)(130.7 \text{ J/mol K}) - 191.6 \text{ J/mol K}$$

$$\Delta S^\circ_{rxn} = -198.8 \text{ J/mol K}$$

Now calculate K_{eq} at 500 °C using Equation 15-6:

$$ln\ K_{eq} = \frac{\Delta H^\circ}{RT} + \frac{\Delta S^\circ}{R}$$

$$ln\ K_{eq} = -\frac{(-92 \text{ kJ/mol})(10^3 \text{ J/kJ})}{(8.314 \text{ J/mol K})(500 + 273 \text{ K})} + \frac{(-198.8 \text{ J/mol K})}{(8.314 \text{ J/mol K})}$$

$$ln\ K_{eq} = 14.3 - 23.9 = -9.6$$

Taking the anti*ln*, or e^x, of −9.6 gives the estimated equilibrium constant at 500 °C:

$$K_{eq} = 6.7 \times 10^{-5} \text{ atm}^{-2}$$

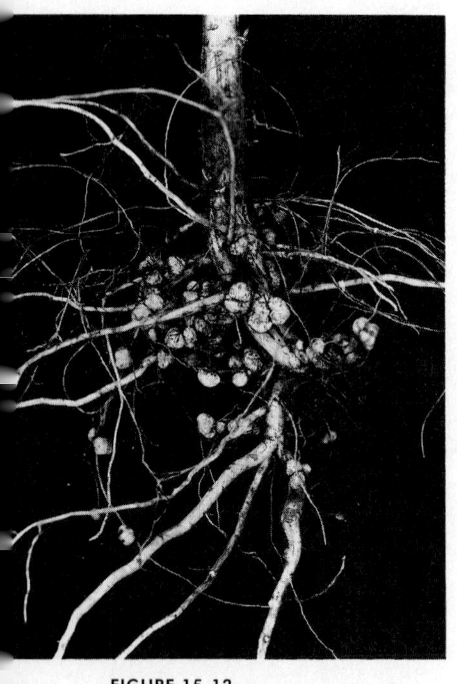

FIGURE 15-12
Rhizobium bacteria, which form colonies in nodules on the roots of leguminous plants, have an enzyme that allows them to manufacture ammonia from molecular nitrogen at ambient temperature.

Sample Problems 15-9 and 15-10 underscore the dilemma faced by industrial chemists and engineers. At 298 K, the equilibrium position of the Haber reaction strongly favors the formation of ammonia. Why, then, is the Haber synthesis not carried out at 298 K, where equilibrium strongly favors the desired product? The reason is that even with a catalyst, the reaction is much too slow to be useful at this temperature. At low temperature, thermodynamics favors ammonia, but kinetics prohibits the reaction from occurring at a discernible rate. To make the reaction proceed at a practical rate, the temperature must be increased. Unfortunately, the equilibrium constant falls dramatically as temperature increases. At 773 K, a realistic temperature for the Haber reaction, the equilibrium position does not favor NH_3:

$$N_2 + 3\,H_2 \rightleftarrows 2\,NH_3$$

$$K_{eq,\,298\,K} = 5.6 \times 10^5 \text{ atm}^{-2} \qquad K_{eq,\,773\,K} = 6.7 \times 10^{-5} \text{ atm}^{-2}$$

Nature has solved this problem with the enzyme nitrogenase. This enzyme is found in bacteria that live in nodules among the roots of leguminous plants such as soybeans and clover (Figure 15-12). Nitrogenase catalyzes the formation of ammonia from atmospheric nitrogen. Chemists are studying the mechanism of nitrogenase, but its chemistry is so complicated that we still have incomplete knowledge of how the enzyme converts nitrogen to ammonia. Perhaps further research will uncover its secret and make it possible to design new commercial catalysts for nitrogen fixation that operate at 298 K.

The Haber reaction is a practical example of the effect of temperature on an exothermic reaction. A practical example of an endothermic reaction is the use of methane and steam to produce the molecular hydrogen needed for the Haber reaction. This reaction is highly endothermic, so it is carried out at temperatures much greater than 1000 K to force the equilibrium toward the products:

$$CH_{4\,(g)} + H_2O_{(g)} \rightleftarrows CO_{(g)} + 3\,H_{2\,(g)} \qquad \Delta H^\circ = +206\text{ kJ}$$

$$K_{eq,\,298\text{ K}} = 1.2 \times 10^{-25}\text{ atm}^{-2} \qquad K_{eq,\,1500\text{ K}} = 1.1 \times 10^{4}\text{ atm}^{-2}$$

SECTION EXERCISES

15.5.1 Use thermodynamic data to determine K_{eq} for the oxidation of NO at 298 K:

$$2\,NO_{(g)} + O_{2\,(g)} \rightleftarrows 2\,NO_{2\,(g)}$$

15.5.2 Does K_{eq} for the reaction described in 15.5.1 increase or decrease when the temperature is raised above room temperature? Give your reasoning.

15.5.3 Use thermodynamic data to estimate K_{eq} at 1000 °C for the reaction in 15.5.1.

15.6 SHIFTS IN EQUILIBRIUM

We call K_{eq} the equilibrium *constant* because it has the *same value* regardless of the amounts of reactants and products that we put into the system. In other words, K_{eq} is independent of initial concentrations. No matter what value Q has before the reaction occurs, equilibrium will be reached when concentrations have changed so that $Q = K_{eq}$.

LE CHÂTELIER'S PRINCIPLE

What happens if we change the conditions on a system that is already at equilibrium? Suppose we vary the amounts or concentrations of one or more substances, or change the temperature of the system. How does a system that is at equilibrium respond to these changes? Although the equations that describe equilibrium provide quantitative answers to these questions, a simple principle can be applied to obtain a quick qualitative indication. This principle, which was first formulated by Henri-Louis Le Châtelier, a French industrial chemist of the early twentieth century, states:

When a change is imposed on a system at equilibrium, the system will react, if possible, in the direction that reduces the amount of change.

According to **Le Châtelier's principle,** if we introduce more of one reactant, the reaction will proceed in the direction that consumes this reactant. If we reduce the temperature, thereby removing heat from the system, the reaction will proceed in the exothermic direction, producing some heat.

Le Châtelier's principle is a compact summary of how several possible factors can influence equilibrium. It contains no information that we have not already considered, and it is entirely qualitative. Nevertheless, it is quite useful for obtaining a sense of how any given system at equilibrium will respond to changes in conditions.

CHANGES IN AMOUNTS

A change in the amount of any substance whose concentration appears in the concentration quotient will displace the system from its equilibrium position. Consider, for example, an industrial reactor containing an equilibrium mixture of methane, hydrogen, steam, and carbon monoxide:

$$CH_{4\,(g)} + H_2O_{(g)} \rightleftarrows CO_{(g)} + 3\,H_{2\,(g)} \qquad Q = \frac{(p_{H_2})^3\,(p_{CO})}{(p_{CH_4})(p_{H_2O})}$$

How will this system respond if more steam is injected into the reactor? Adding one of the starting materials decreases the value of Q, making $Q < K_{eq}$. Because the system will respond in a way that restores equilibrium, adding more steam will cause the reaction to proceed to the right, consuming CH_4 and H_2O while producing CO and H_2 until equilibrium is restored.

Removing a product from a system at equilibrium also makes $Q < K_{eq}$ and leads to the formation of additional products. This behavior can be used to advantage in chemical synthesis. For example, calcium oxide, an important material in the construction industry, is made by heating calcium carbonate to about 1100 K:

$$CaCO_{3\,(s)} \rightleftarrows CaO_{(s)} + CO_{2\,(g)} \qquad K_{eq} = (p_{CO_2})_{eq} = 1.00 \text{ atm at } 1100 \text{ K}$$

If the pressure of CO_2 in a limestone kiln were allowed to reach 1.00 atm, the system would be at equilibrium, and no additional products would form. To drive the reaction to completion, the CO_2 is allowed to escape from the reactor as it is formed. This constant removal of a product maintains Q at a smaller value than K_{eq}, and the reaction continues until all the $CaCO_3$ has been converted to CaO.

A change in amounts that has no impact on the reaction quotient will not disturb a chemical equilibrium. Thus adding or removing air has no effect on the equilibrium conditions of the $CaO/CaCO_3/CO_2$ system, since the equilibrium constant depends only on the partial pressure of CO_2, not on the total pressure of gas in the system. Likewise, adding more $CaCO_3$ to a limestone reactor at equilibrium does not result in more products, since $CaCO_3$, a pure solid, does not appear in the equilibrium constant expression.

The effects of changes in amounts on a system at equilibrium can be summarized in accordance with Le Châtelier's principle:

1. Any change in conditions that *increases* the value of the reaction quotient causes the reaction to consume products and produce reactants until equilibrium is reestablished.
2. Any change in conditions that *decreases* the value of Q causes the reaction to form products and consume reactants until equilibrium is reestablished.
3. Any change in amounts that has no effect on the value of Q also has no effect on the equilibrium position.

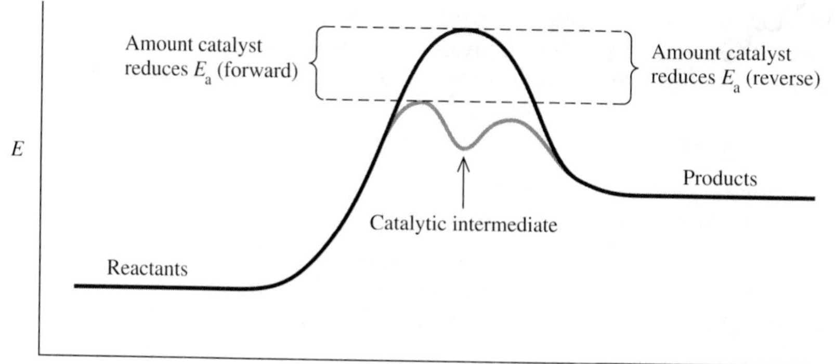

FIGURE 15-13
A catalyst changes the mechanism and lowers the net activation energy barrier for the reaction in either direction. This increases the rates of forward and reverse reactions, but it does not affect the nature of the reactants or the products, so it has no effect on the overall free energy change for the reaction.

EFFECT OF CATALYSTS

Catalysts *do not* affect the equilibrium constant. Figure 15-13 provides a reminder that a catalyst changes the mechanism of the reaction in a way that reduces the net activation energy barrier, but it does not alter the thermodynamic changes that accompany the reaction. In other words, both the forward activation energy and the reverse activation energy are reduced by a catalyst, so the rates of both reactions are increased. The natures of reactants and products are not affected, however, so the free energy change, ΔG°, does not change, and neither does K_{eq}. A catalyst allows a reaction to reach equilibrium *more rapidly,* but it does not alter the equilibrium *position.*

EFFECT OF TEMPERATURE

In Section 15.5, we showed that K_{eq} varies with temperature in a way that can be understood using the principles of thermodynamics. Temperature is the *only* variable that causes a change in the value of K_{eq}. The way that temperature affects K_{eq} depends on the enthalpy change, ΔH, of the reaction. An *increase* in temperature always shifts the equilibrium position in the *endothermic* direction, and a *decrease* in temperature always shifts the equilibrium position in the *exothermic* direction.

Sample Problem 15-11 provides additional examples of changes that may lead to shifts in equilibrium.

SAMPLE PROBLEM 15-11 SHIFTS IN EQUILIBRIUM

Consider a saturated solution of $CaCl_2$ at equilibrium with excess $CaCl_{2\,(s)}$. The solubility reaction is:

$$CaCl_{2\,(s)} \rightleftharpoons Ca^{2+}{}_{(aq)} + 2\,Cl^{-}{}_{(aq)} \qquad \Delta H^\circ_{rxn} = +585\text{ kJ}$$

How do the following changes affect the amount of dissolved $CaCl_2$?

(a) More $CaCl_{2\,(s)}$ is added.
(b) Some NaCl is dissolved in the solution.
(c) Some $NaNO_3$ is dissolved in the solution.
(d) Some pure water is added.
(e) The solution is heated.

METHOD: According to Le Châtelier's principle, the system will respond in the direction that reduces the amount of change. It will only do so, however, if an appropriate response exists. Changes in quantities of substances must be analyzed for their effect, if any, on the value of Q. If Q becomes smaller, the reaction will proceed to the right, and more $CaCl_2$ will dissolve. If Q becomes larger, the reaction must proceed to the left, and $CaCl_2$ will precipitate.

(a) More $CaCl_{2\,(s)}$ is added. Because $Q = [Ca^{2+}][Cl^-]^2$, adding $CaCl_{2\,(s)}$ does *not* change Q. The system remains at equilibrium. There is no effect on the amount of dissolved $CaCl_2$.

(b) Some NaCl is dissolved in the solution. This change increases $[Cl^-]$, making $Q > K_{eq}$. The reaction must proceed to the left, and some $CaCl_2$ will precipitate.

(c) Some $NaNO_3$ is dissolved in the solution. There is no effect on Q, so there is no effect on the amount of dissolved $CaCl_2$.

(d) Some pure water is added. Adding water dilutes the solution and lowers $[Ca^{2+}]$ and $[Cl^-]$. Because Q is now less than K_{eq}, the reaction proceeds to the right. More $CaCl_2$ will dissolve.

(e) The solution is heated. Because the solubility reaction is endothermic (ΔH° is positive), K_{eq} increases as T increases. More $CaCl_2$ will dissolve.

SECTION EXERCISES

15.6.1 The following solubility reaction is exothermic by about 70 kJ/mol:

$$Ba(OH)_{2\,(s)} \rightleftharpoons Ba^{2+}{}_{(aq)} + 2\,OH^-{}_{(aq)}$$

Will more $Ba(OH)_2$ dissolve, or will some precipitate, or will no change occur, when each of the following changes are made on a saturated solution of $Ba(OH)_2$?

(a) More $Ba(OH)_{2\,(s)}$ is added to the solution.
(b) More water is added to the solution.
(c) Some HCl is added to the solution.
(d) The solution is cooled on an ice bath.

15.6.2 Refer to Sample Problems 15-10 and 15-11. List four changes in conditions that might be used to increase the yield of ammonia in the Haber process.

15.6.3 Chemists are optimistic that one day a catalyst will be found for the production of ammonia from hydrogen and nitrogen under standard conditions. In contrast, no hope exists of developing a catalyst for the production of hydrogen from methane and steam under standard conditions. Explain.

CHAPTER SUMMARY

1. Chemical equilibrium is a dynamic state in which all steps in the mechanism of the reaction proceed with equal rates in both directions. Consequently, a chemical reaction can approach equilibrium from either direction.
2. The equilibrium constant expression describes the relationship among concentrations of reactants and products at equilibrium. It contains a constant on the left-hand side and the ratio of equilibrium concentrations, raised to powers equal to their stoichiometric coefficients, on the right-hand side.
3. By convention, the concentrations of solutes are expressed as molarities, the concentrations of gases are expressed as partial pressures in atmospheres, and the concentrations of pure liquids, pure solids, and solvents are expressed as mole fractions, which equal 1.
4. The chemical equation for a reaction at equilibrium can be written in either direction, and the equilibrium constant in one direction is the inverse of the equilibrium constant in the other direction.
5. Chemical equilibria can be organized into several categories. Each category of aqueous equilibria is identified by a characteristic subscript: K_{sp}, K_f, K_a, K_b, K_w.
6. Calculations of equilibrium concentrations are best done using the step-by-step procedure of identifying the chemistry, determining the equilibrium that exists, writing its equilibrium constant expression, completing a concentration table, and then substituting equilibrium concentrations into the equilibrium constant expression.
7. Equilibrium calculations can often be simplified by making appropriate approximations about equilibrium concentrations.
8. When a reaction has a very large equilibrium constant, equilibrium concentrations are most conveniently found from the difference between concentrations at completion and concentrations at equilibrium.
9. Equilibrium constants are directly related to standard free energies of reaction, so K_{eq} can be calculated from standard thermodynamic properties. Thermodynamics also explains the variations in K_{eq} with temperature.
10. When a system is at equilibrium, a change in conditions may disturb the equilibrium. When this occurs, the system reacts in the direction that re-establishes equilibrium.

KEY TERMS

chemical equilibrium
dynamic equilibrium
equilibrium constant (K_{eq})
reversibility

complex ion
fixed nitrogen
Le Châtelier's principle
saturated
vapor pressure

acid ionization constant (K_a)
base ionization constant (K_b)
formation constant (K_f)
solubility product (K_{sp})
water equilibrium constant (K_w)

concentration quotient (Q)
concentration table
initial concentration

SKILLS TO MASTER

- Visualizing molecular processes at dynamic equilibrium
- Writing equilibrium constant expressions
- Using correct units in equilibrium constant expressions
- Recognizing types of equilibria
- Relating equilibrium constant expressions to tabulated values
- Determining the chemistry of equilibria
- Completing concentration tables
- Calculating K_{eq} from equilibrium concentrations
- Calculating equilibrium concentrations
- Using approximations in equilibrium calculations
- Calculating K_{eq} from thermodynamic properties
- Predicting changes in K_{eq} with temperature
- Predicting the effects of changes in conditions on equilibrium

LEARNING EXERCISES

15.1 Write a chapter summary of two pages or less that outlines the important features of this chapter.

15.2 List the types of chemical equilibrium introduced in this chapter and give a specific example of each.

15.3 Draw a molecular picture that illustrates each of the examples that you gave in Exercise 15.2.

15.4 Describe in your own words how to set up and solve a problem that asks for concentrations at equilibrium.

15.5 Describe how to calculate K_{eq} from equilibrium concentrations and from thermodynamic functions.

15.6 Write a paragraph that describes the logic, process, and justification for using approximations in solving equilibrium problems.

15.7 Use your own words to define (a) initial concentrations, (b) change to equilibrium, (c) change to completion, and (d) equilibrium concentrations.

15.8 Summarize in writing the connections between equilibrium constants and thermodynamic functions.

15.9 Update your list of memory bank equations and procedures.

15.10 List all terms new to you that appear in Chapter 15. Write a one-sentence definition for each in your own words. Consult the glossary if you need help.

PROBLEMS

DYNAMIC EQUILIBRIUM

15.1 The alkene called 2-butene has two isomers, *cis*-butene and *trans*-butene, which interconvert at high temperature or in the presence of a catalyst:

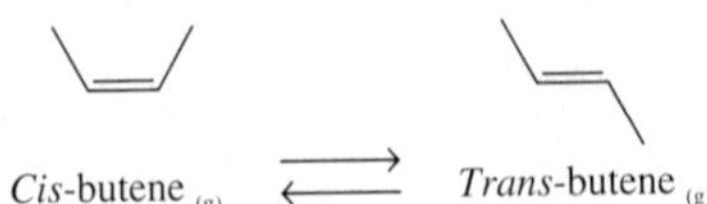

Cis-butene $_{(g)}$ $\rightleftarrows$ *Trans*-butene $_{(g)}$

Suppose that the equilibrium constant for this reaction is 3.0. Draw a qualitative graph that shows how the pressures of the two gases change with time if the system initially contains pure *cis*-butene at a pressure of 1.0 atm.

15.2 Redraw the graph for the reaction in Problem 15.1 showing what happens if the system initially contains pure *trans*-butene at a pressure of 1.0 atm.

15.3 Aqueous solutions of sodium hypochlorite undergo decomposition according to this two-step mechanism:

$$ClO^-_{(aq)} + ClO^-_{(aq)} \xrightarrow{k_1} Cl^-_{(aq)} + ClO_2{}^-_{(aq)}$$
$$ClO^-_{(aq)} + ClO_2{}^-_{(aq)} \xrightarrow{k_2} Cl^-_{(aq)} + ClO_3{}^-_{(aq)}$$

(a) What additional reactions will be important as the reaction approaches equilibrium?
(b) What is the equilibrium constant expression for the overall reaction?
(c) Express the equilibrium constant in terms of the rate constants of the elementary reactions.

15.4 The reaction of H_2 gas with CO gas has been described by the following mechanism (all species in the gas phase):

$$H_2 \underset{k_{-1}}{\overset{k_1}{\rightleftarrows}} 2H$$
$$H + CO \xrightarrow{k_2} HCO$$
$$HCO + H \xrightarrow{k_3} HCOH$$

(a) What reactions describe the decomposition of HCOH under these same conditions?
(b) What is the equilibrium constant expression for this reaction?
(c) Express the equilibrium constant in terms of rate constants for the elementary reactions.

15.5 Draw molecular pictures that illustrate the reversibility of the reactions involved in the hypochlorite decomposition given in Problem 15.3. (See Figure 15-1 for examples.)

15.6 Draw molecular pictures that illustrate the reversibility of the reactions involved in the reaction of H_2 with CO to form HCHO.

15.7 Describe experiments that could be done to demonstrate that the decomposition reaction of ClO^- ions (Problem 15.3) is reversible.

15.8 Describe experiments that could be done to demonstrate that the reaction of H_2 with CO (Problem 15.4) is reversible.

PROPERTIES OF EQUILIBRIUM CONSTANTS

15.9 Write equilibrium constant expressions for each of the following reactions. Indicate the units associated with each equilibrium constant.
(a) $Cl_{2\,(g)} + PCl_{3\,(g)} \rightleftharpoons PCl_{5\,(g)}$
(b) $P_{4\,(s)} + 5\,O_{2\,(g)} \rightleftharpoons P_4O_{10\,(s)}$
(c) $BaCO_{3\,(s)} + C_{(s)} \rightleftharpoons BaO_{(s)} + 2\,CO_{(g)}$
(d) $CO_{(g)} + 2\,H_{2\,(g)} \rightleftharpoons CH_3OH_{(l)}$
(e) $H_3PO_{4\,(aq)} + 3\,H_2O_{(l)} \rightleftharpoons PO_4{}^{3-}{}_{(aq)} + 3\,H_3O^+{}_{(aq)}$

15.10 Write equilibrium constant expressions for each of the following reactions. Indicate the units associated with each equilibrium constant.
(a) $2\,H_2S_{(g)} + 3\,O_{2\,(g)} \rightleftharpoons 2\,H_2O_{(l)} + 2\,SO_{2\,(g)}$
(b) $Fe_2O_{3\,(s)} + 3\,CO_{(g)} \rightleftharpoons 2\,Fe_{(s)} + 3\,CO_{2\,(g)}$
(c) $Fe^{3+}{}_{(aq)} + 3\,C_2O_4{}^{2-}{}_{(aq)} \rightleftharpoons Fe(C_2O_4)_3{}^{3-}{}_{(aq)}$
(d) $NH_{3\,(g)} + H_3O^+{}_{(aq)} \rightleftharpoons NH_4{}^+{}_{(aq)} + H_2O_{(l)}$
(e) $SnO_{2\,(s)} + 2\,H_{2\,(g)} \rightleftharpoons Sn_{(s)} + 2\,H_2O_{(l)}$

15.11 Write equilibrium constant expressions for each of the following reactions. Indicate the units associated with each equilibrium constant.
(a) $P_4O_{10\,(s)} \rightleftharpoons P_{4\,(s)} + 5\,O_{2\,(g)}$
(b) $BaO_{(s)} + 2\,CO_{(g)} \rightleftharpoons BaCO_{3\,(s)} + C_{(s)}$
(c) $PO_4{}^{3-}{}_{(aq)} + 3\,H_3O^+{}_{(aq)} \rightleftharpoons H_3PO_{4\,(aq)} + 3\,H_2O_{(l)}$

15.12 Write each chemical reaction of Problem 15.10 in the opposite direction, and determine the equilibrium constant expressions for these reactions.

TYPES OF EQUILIBRIA

15.13 For each of the following reactions, write the equilibrium constant expression and relate K_{eq} to one of the standard equilibrium types.
(a) $I_{2\,(g)} \rightleftharpoons I_{2\,(s)}$
(b) $I_{2\,(g)} \rightleftharpoons I_{2\,(solution)}$
(c) $Pb^{2+}{}_{(aq)} + 2\,I^-{}_{(aq)} \rightleftharpoons PbI_{2\,(s)}$
(d) $HCN_{(aq)} + H_2O_{(l)} \rightleftharpoons CN^-{}_{(aq)} + H_3O^+{}_{(aq)}$
(e) $PtCl_4{}^{2-}{}_{(aq)} \rightleftharpoons Pt^{2+}{}_{(aq)} + 4\,Cl^-{}_{(aq)}$

15.14 For each of the following reactions, write the equilibrium constant expression and relate K_{eq} to one of the standard equilibrium types.
(a) $C_2H_5OH_{(l)} \rightleftharpoons C_2H_5OH_{(g)}$
(b) $Ru^{2+}{}_{(aq)} + 6\,NH_{3\,(aq)} \rightleftharpoons Ru(NH_3)_6{}^{2+}{}_{(aq)}$
(c) $NH_{3\,(aq)} \rightleftharpoons NH_{3\,(g)}$
(d) $NH_4{}^+{}_{(aq)} + Cl^-{}_{(aq)} \rightleftharpoons NH_4Cl_{(s)}$
(e) $C_5H_5NH_{(aq)} + H_2O_{(l)} \rightleftharpoons C_5H_5NH_2{}^+{}_{(aq)} + OH^-{}_{(aq)}$

15.15 Draw a molecular picture, like the one in Figure 15-4, that shows how reducing the pressure of O_2 above a body of water leads to a reduced concentration of dissolved O_2.

15.16 A student mixes sodium chloride and water until the solid and the aqueous solution are at equilibrium. If more solid sodium chloride is added to this mixture, does the concentration of solid in the aqueous solution change? Explain your answer in molecular terms.

WORKING WITH EQUILIBRIA

15.17 An industrial chemist puts 1.00 mol each of $H_{2\,(g)}$ and $CO_{2\,(g)}$ in a 1.00-L container at 800 °C. When equilibrium is reached, 0.49 mol of $CO_{(g)}$ is in the container. Find K_{eq} at 800 °C for the following reaction:

$$H_{2\,(g)} + CO_{2\,(g)} \rightleftharpoons H_2O_{(g)} + CO_{(g)}$$

15.18 At high temperature, HCl and O_2 react to give Cl_2 gas:

$$4\,HCl_{(g)} + O_{2\,(g)} \rightleftharpoons 2\,Cl_{2\,(g)} + 2\,H_2O_{(g)}$$

If HCl at 2.3 atm and O_2 at 1.0 atm are reacted at 750 K, the equilibrium pressure of Cl_2 is measured to be 0.93 atm. Determine the value of K_{eq} at 750 K.

15.19 When 0.050 mol of propionic acid ($C_2H_5CO_2H$) is dissolved in 500 mL of water, the equilibrium concentration of H_3O^+ ions is measured to be 1.15×10^{-3} M. What is K_a for this acid?

15.20 Cyanic acid, HCNO, is a weak acid. In 0.20 M aqueous solution of HCNO, the concentration of H_3O^+ cations is 6.5×10^{-3} M. What is K_a for HCNO?

15.21 When PbF_2 is dissolved in water at 25 °C, the equilibrium concentration of Pb^{2+} cations is 1.9×10^{-3} M. What is K_{sp} for this salt?

15.22 The solubility of calcium arsenate, $Ca_3(AsO_4)_2$, in water is 0.036 g/L. What is K_{sp} for this salt?

15.23 The equilibrium constant for the following reaction is 1.6×10^5 at 1024 K:

$$H_{2\,(g)} + Br_{2\,(g)} \rightleftharpoons 2\,HBr_{(g)}$$

Find the equilibrium pressures of all gases if 10.0 atm of HBr is introduced into a sealed container at 1024 K.

15.24 At 1000 °C, $K_{eq} = 0.403$ for the following reaction:

$$FeO_{(s)} + CO_{(g)} \rightleftarrows Fe_{(s)} + CO_{2\,(g)}$$

If CO gas at 5.0 atm is injected into a container at 1000 °C that contains excess FeO, what are the partial pressures of all gases present at equilibrium?

15.25 At 100 °C, $K_{eq} = 1.5 \times 10^8\ atm^{-1}$ for the following reaction:

$$CO_{(g)} + Cl_{2\,(g)} \rightleftarrows COCl_{2\,(g)}$$

Using appropriate approximations, calculate the partial pressure of CO at 100 °C at equilibrium in a chamber that initially contains $COCl_2$ at a pressure of 0.250 atm.

15.26 The equilibrium constant for the dissociation of Cl_2 into atomic chlorine at 1200 K is 2.5×10^{-5} atm. If 5.0 g of Cl_2 gas are placed in a 3.0-L container and heated to 1200 K, what is the equilibrium pressure of Cl atoms? Use appropriate approximations.

THERMODYNAMICS AND EQUILIBRIUM

15.27 The solubility product for $PbCl_2$ is $2 \times 10^{-5}\ M^3$. If 0.50 g of solid $PbCl_2$ is added to 300 mL of water, will all the solid dissolve? (HINT: Calculate Q if all the solid dissolves.)

15.28 If 200 mL of 2.50×10^{-2} M NaCl solution is mixed with 300 mL of 4.00×10^{-2} M $Pb(NO_3)_2$ solution, will solid $PbCl_2$ form ($K_{sp} = 2 \times 10^{-5}\ M^3$)?

15.29 Using standard thermodynamic data from Appendix E, calculate equilibrium constants at 298 K for each of the following chemical equilibria:
(a) $2\ SO_{2\,(g)} + O_{2\,(g)} \rightleftarrows 2\ SO_{3\,(g)}$
(b) $2\ CO_{(g)} + O_{2\,(g)} \rightleftarrows 2\ CO_{2\,(g)}$
(c) $BaCO_{3\,(s)} + C_{(s)} \rightleftarrows BaO_{(s)} + 2\ CO_{(g)}$

15.30 Using standard thermodynamic data from Appendix E, calculate equilibrium constants at 298 K for each of the following chemical equilibria:
(a) $CO_{(g)} + H_2O_{(l)} \rightleftarrows CO_{2\,(g)} + H_{2\,(g)}$
(b) $CH_{4\,(g)} + H_2O_{(l)} \rightleftarrows CO_{(g)} + 3\ H_{2\,(g)}$
(c) $SnO_{2\,(s)} + 2\ H_{2\,(g)} \rightleftarrows Sn_{(s)} + 2\ H_2O_{(l)}$
(d) $4\ NH_{3\,(g)} + 5\ O_{2\,(g)} \rightleftarrows 4\ NO_{(g)} + 6\ H_2O_{(l)}$
(e) $3\ Fe_{(s)} + 4\ H_2O_{(l)} \rightleftarrows Fe_3O_{4\,(s)} + 4\ H_{2\,(g)}$

15.31 Determine K_{eq} for each equilibrium in Problem 15.30 if H_2O is present as a gas rather than as a liquid.

15.32 Determine K_{eq} for each equilibrium in Problem 15.29 at 500 K.

15.33 Determine K_{eq} for each equilibrium in Problem 15.31 at 700 K.

15.34 Use thermodynamic data to determine K_{eq} for the water-gas shift reaction at 298 K and at 1200 K:

$$CO_{(g)} + H_2O_{(g)} \rightleftarrows CO_{2\,(g)} + H_{2\,(g)}$$

SHIFTS IN EQUILIBRIUM

15.35 For each equilibrium in Problem 15.29, predict the effect of injecting additional $CO_{(g)}$ into the system.

15.36 For each equilibrium in Problem 15.31, predict the effect of injecting additional $H_2O_{(g)}$ into the system.

15.37 Consider the following reaction at equilibrium in water:

$$PbCl_{2\,(s)} \rightleftarrows Pb^{2+}_{(aq)} + 2\ Cl^-_{(aq)}$$

Will $PbCl_2$ dissolve or precipitate, or will neither occur after each of the following changes?
(a) More $PbCl_{2\,(s)}$ is added.
(b) More H_2O is added.
(c) Solid NaCl is added.
(d) Solid KNO_3 is added.

15.38 The following exothermic gas phase reaction is at equilibrium:

$$2\ SO_{2\,(g)} + O_{2\,(g)} \rightleftarrows 2\ SO_{3\,(g)}$$

What happens to the amount of SO_3 in the system when each of the following changes is made?
(a) The temperature is raised.
(b) More O_2 is added.
(c) Some Ar gas is introduced.

15.39 Consider the following gas-phase reaction:

$$SO_{2\,(g)} + Cl_{2\,(g)} \rightleftarrows SO_2Cl_{2\,(g)} + \text{Heat}$$

Describe four changes that would drive the equilibrium to the left.

15.40 Consider the following gas-phase reaction:

$$PCl_{5\,(g)} + \text{Heat} \rightleftarrows PCl_{3\,(g)} + Cl_{2\,(g)}$$

List four changes that would drive the equilibrium to the left.

ADDITIONAL PROBLEMS

15.41 The following figure represents a system coming to equilibrium:

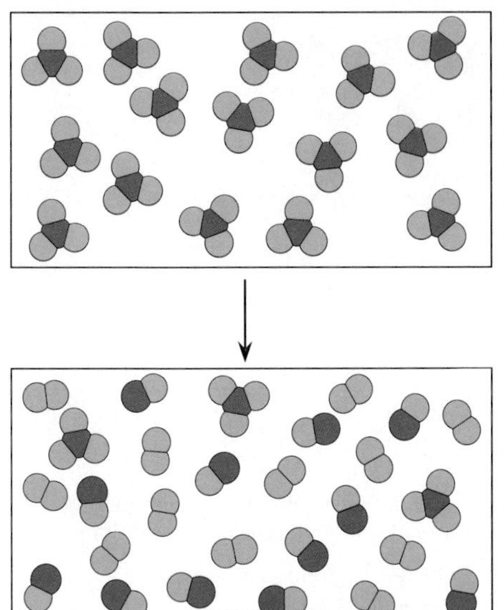

(a) Use molecular pictures to write a balanced equation for the equilibrium reaction.
(b) What is K_{eq} for the reaction?

15.42 Write the equilibrium reaction and equilibrium constant expression for the acid dissociation reaction of HClO in water.

15.43 Hydrogen fluoride is a highly reactive gas. It has many industrial uses, but the most familiar property of HF is its ability to react with glass. As a result, although HF is used to etch glass and "frost" the inner surfaces of light bulbs, it cannot be stored in glass containers. Hydrogen fluoride gas must be stored in stainless steel containers, and aqueous solutions must be stored in plastic bottles. Hydrogen fluoride can be produced from H_2 and F_2:

$$H_{2\,(g)} + F_{2\,(g)} \rightleftarrows 2\,HF_{(g)} \qquad K_{eq} = 115$$

In a particular experiment, 3.00 atm each of H_2 and F_2 are added to a 1.50-L flask. Calculate the equilibrium partial pressures of all species.

15.44 Write the equilibrium constant expression for the oxidation reaction used to convert ammonia to nitric oxide in the preparation of nitric acid:

$$4\,NH_{3\,(g)} + 5\,O_{2\,(g)} \rightleftarrows 4\,NO_{(g)} + 6\,H_2O_{(l)}$$

15.45 Using tabulated standard thermodynamic data from Appendix E, calculate K_{eq} for the reaction of NO_2 to form N_2O_4 at 298 K and at 500 K:

$$2\,NO_{2\,(g)} \rightleftarrows N_2O_{4\,(g)}$$

15.46 Predict the effect of each of the following changes on the equilibrium position of the reaction in problem 15.45:
(a) The partial pressure of NO_2 is cut in half.
(b) The temperature of the system is cut in half.
(c) 10.0 atm of Ar gas is added to the system.

15.47 Describe the appropriate concentration units for each substance, and write the equilibrium constant expression using those units for the reaction:

$$Ca^{2+}_{(aq)} + 3\,H_2O_{(l)} + CO_{2\,(g)} \rightleftarrows CaCO_{3\,(s)} + 2\,H_3O^{+}_{(aq)}$$

15.48 How many grams of BaF_2 will dissolve in 500 ml of 1.00×10^{-1} M NaF solution?

15.49 The figure shown here represents a set of initial conditions for the following reaction:

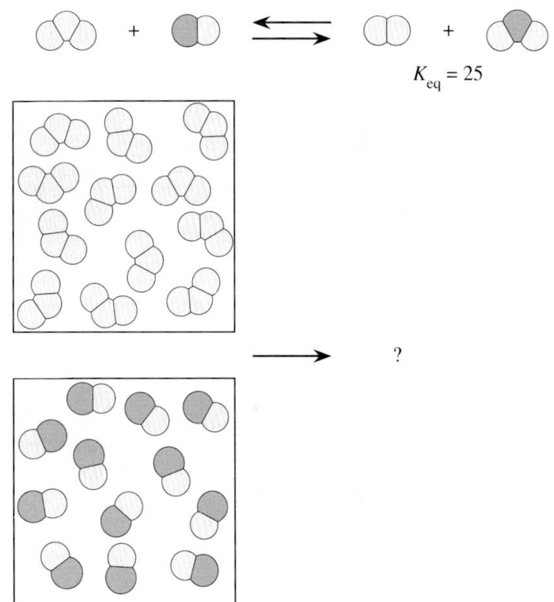

Draw a molecular picture that shows what the system looks like when it reaches equilibrium.

15.50 A container contains CO_2 at $p = 0.464$ atm. When graphite is added to the container, some CO_2 is converted to CO, and at equilibrium, the total pressure is 0.746 atm. Compute K_{eq} for the following reaction:

$$CO_{2\,(g)} + C_{(s)} \rightleftarrows 2\,CO_{(g)}$$

15.51 The equilibrium constant for the Haber reaction is 2.81×10^{-5} atm^{-2} at 472 °C. If a reaction starts with 3.0 atm of H_2 and 5.0 atm of N_2 at 472 °C, what is the equilibrium pressure of NH_3?

15.52 At 1000 °C, K_{eq} for the conversion of $CO_{2\,(g)}$ to $CO_{(g)}$ by solid graphite, $C_{(s)}$, is 167.5 atm. A 1-L, high-pressure chamber containing excess graphite powder is charged with 0.500 mol each of CO_2 and CO and then is heated to 1000 °C. What is the equilibrium total pressure?

15.53 $K_{eq} = 1.07 \times 10^{-33}\ atm^{-1}$ for the following reaction at 298 K:

$$Sn_{(s)} + 2\,H_{2\,(g)} \rightleftarrows SnH_{4\,(g)}$$

Find the equilibrium pressure of $SnH_{4\,(g)}$ in a 10-L container at 298 K containing 10 g of $Sn_{(s)}$ and 2.00×10^2 atm of H_2. How many molecules of SnH_4 are present?

15.54 At elevated temperature, carbon tetrachloride decomposes to its elements:

$$CCl_{4\,(g)} \rightleftarrows C_{(s)} + 2\,Cl_{2\,(g)}$$

At 700 K, if the initial pressure of CCl_4 is 1 atm, the total pressure at equilibrium is 1.35 atm. Use these pressures to calculate K_{eq} at 700 K.

15.55 Suppose that the equilibrium system described in Problem 15.54 is expanded to twice its initial volume. Find the new equilibrium pressure.

15.56 Benzene can be sulfonated by concentrated sulfuric acid according to the following net reaction:

$$C_6H_6 + H_2SO_4 \rightarrow C_6H_5SO_3^- + H_3O^+$$

This reaction occurs by the following three-step mechanism:

$$H_2SO_4 \rightarrow SO_3 + H_2O$$

$$SO_3 + C_6H_6 \rightarrow C_6H_6SO_3$$

$$C_6H_6SO_3 + H_2O \rightarrow C_6H_5SO_3^- + H_3O^+$$

Determine the relationship between the equilibrium constant for the net reaction and the rate constants for the various elementary steps.

15.57 Write equilibrium constant expressions and determine the units associated with the equilibrium constant for the following reactions:

(a) $BeO_{(s)} + H_2O_{(l)} \rightleftarrows Be^{2+}_{(aq)} + 2\,OH^-_{(aq)}$
(b) $CO_{2\,(g)} + 2\,H_2O_{(l)} \rightleftarrows HCO_3^-{}_{(aq)} + H_3O^+_{(aq)}$
(c) $NH_{3\,(aq)} + CH_3CO_2H_{(aq)} \rightleftarrows NH_4^+{}_{(aq)} + CH_3CO_2^-{}_{(aq)}$
(d) $3\,H_2S_{(g)} + 6\,H_2O_{(l)} + 2\,Fe^{3+}_{(aq)} \rightleftarrows Fe_2S_{3\,(s)} + 6\,H_3O^+_{(aq)}$

15.58 When 1 mol of gaseous HI is sealed in a 1.00-L flask at 225 °C, it decomposes until the equilibrium amount of I_2 present is 0.182 mol:

$$2\,HI_{(g)} \rightleftarrows H_{2\,(g)} + I_{2\,(g)}$$

(a) Use these data to calculate K_{eq} for this reaction at 225 °C.
(b) Using standard thermodynamic data from Appendix E, estimate K_{eq} at 600 °C.

15.59 In a saturated aqueous solution of MgF_2, the concentration of Mg^{2+} ions is 1.14×10^{-3} M. Write the equilibrium reaction and the equilibrium constant expression, and compute K_{sp} for MgF_2.

15.60 The figure represents a set of initial conditions for the following reaction:

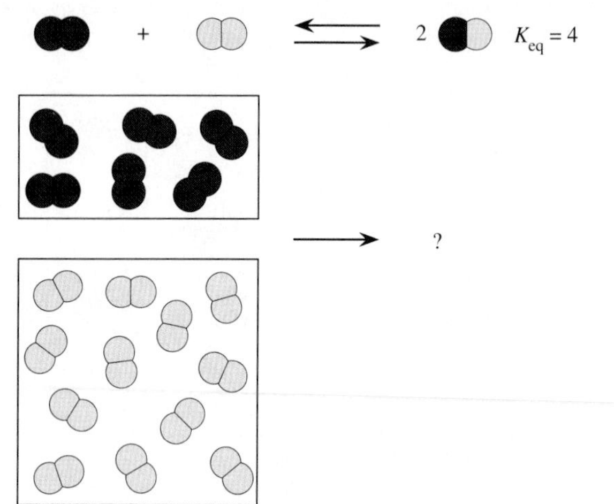

Draw a molecular picture that shows what the system looks like when it reaches equilibrium.

15.61 Consider the following reaction:

$$CO_{2\,(g)} + 2\,OH^-_{(aq)} \rightleftarrows CO_3^{2-}{}_{(aq)} + H_2O_{(l)}$$

(a) Write the equilibrium constant expression for this reaction.
(b) What will happen to the pressure of CO_2 in this equilibrium system if some Na_2CO_3 solid is dissolved in the solution?
(c) What will happen to the pressure of CO_2 in this equilibrium system if some HCl gas is bubbled through the solution?

15.62 For the following reaction, K_{eq} is 2.24×10^{-2} M at 500 K and 33.3 at 760 K:

$$PCl_{5\,(g)} \rightleftarrows PCl_{3\,(g)} + Cl_{2\,(g)}$$

(a) If 2.00 g of PCl_5 is placed in a 3.00-L bulb at 500 K, what is the equilibrium pressure of Cl_2?
(b) If the temperature is raised to 760 K, what is the new equilibrium pressure of Cl_2?
(c) Use the equilibrium constants to calculate the enthalpy change for this reaction.

15.63 Using tabulated thermodynamic data from Appendix E, compute (a) K_{eq} at 298 K; (b) the temperature at which the equilibrium pressure is 1.00 atm; and (c) K_{eq} at 1000 K for the following reaction:.

$$Hg_{(g)} + HgCl_{2\,(s)} \rightleftarrows Hg_2Cl_{2\,(s)}$$

15.64 Coal (solid carbon plus a collection of impurities) can be converted to a mixture of carbon dioxide and hydrogen gas by the following process:

$$C_{(s)} + 2\,H_2O_{(g)} \rightleftarrows CO_{2\,(g)} + 2\,H_{2\,(g)} \quad K_{eq} = 0.38 \text{ atm at 1300 K}$$

At an industrial plant, a mixture of coal and water is placed inside a steel reaction vessel. When the mixture is heated to 1300 K, the equilibrium partial pressure of water is 280 atm. Calculate the partial pressures of H_2 and CO_2.

15.65 A company wants to use the reaction in Problem 15.64 to generate H_2 for use as a fuel, but the K_{eq} does not favor the products. A chemist proposes research to develop a new catalyst that will increase K_{eq} at 1300 K. Explain why this research cannot succeed.

15.66 In today's chemical industry, carbon-containing starting materials for synthesis come from petroleum. As worldwide oil deposits are used up, alternative sources of carbon-containing starting materials will have to be developed. One promising future source of carbon is "synthesis gas," a mixture of carbon monoxide and hydrogen generated by heating coal and steam under high pressure. Commercial applications of synthesis gas are under development. Use thermodynamic data from Appendix E to calculate K_{eq} at 500 K for each of the following reactions of synthesis gas at 500 K. All species are gases at 500 K.
(a) $CO + H_2 \rightarrow HCHO$ (formaldehyde)
(b) $2\,CO + 3\,H_2 \rightarrow H_2O + CH_3CHO$ (acetaldehyde)
(c) $3\,CO + 6\,H_2 \rightarrow 3\,H_2O + C_3H_6$ (propene)

15.67 The Haber synthesis is perhaps the most important chemical reaction in the world economy. Explain why this is so.

15.68 For the water-gas shift reaction (Problem 15.34), K_{eq} is less than one at low temperature and greater than 1 at high temperature. Calculate the temperature at which $K_{eq} = 1$.

15.69 Write out the sequence of reactions used in each of the following industrial processes: (a) Haber synthesis of ammonia, including the two reactions used to make hydrogen; (b) Ostwald process for nitric acid production; and (c) Contact process for sulfuric acid production.

15.70 Strontium iodate, $Sr(IO_3)_2$, is considerably more soluble in hot than in cold water. At 25 °C, 0.030 g of this compound dissolves in 100 mL of water, but 0.80 g dissolves at 100 °C. Calculate K_{sp} and ΔG° at each temperature.

15.71 At 350 K, K_{eq} for the following reaction is 322:

$$Br_{2\,(g)} + I_{2\,(g)} \rightarrow 2\,IBr_{(g)}$$

Suppose that the equilibrium partial pressure of bromine is 0.512 atm and that of iodine is 0.327 atm. What is the pressure of IBr?

15.72 Limestone caverns are formed by the reaction of H_2O and CO_2 with natural deposits of calcium carbonate:

$$CaCO_{3\,(s)} + CO_{2\,(g)} + H_2O_{(l)} \rightleftharpoons Ca^{+2}_{(aq)} + 2\,HCO_3^-{}_{(aq)}$$

$$K_{eq} = 1.56 \times 10^{-8}\ M^3\ atm^{-1}$$

The partial pressure of CO_2 in the Earth's atmosphere is 3.2×10^{-4} atm. What is the equilibrium concentration of calcium ions in ground water?

Problems 15.73 to 15.75 refer to the combustion of sulfur dioxide, one of the steps in the synthesis of sulfuric acid:

$$2\,SO_2 + O_2 \rightleftharpoons 2\,SO_3$$

The following diagram represents an equilibrium mixture of SO_2, O_2, and SO_3 at 1100 K.

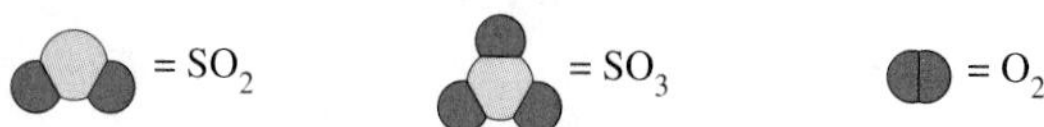

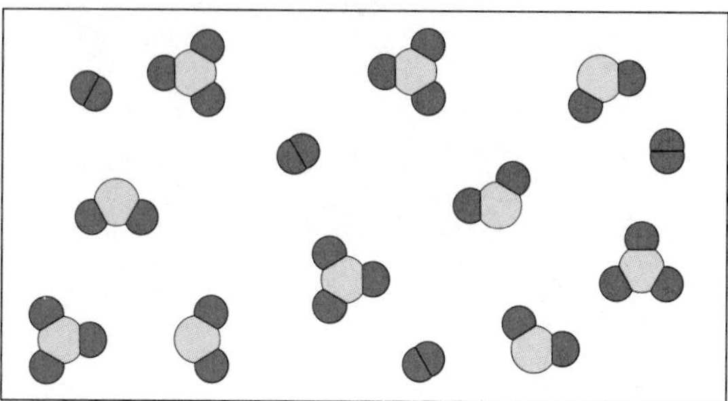

15.73 The original equilibrium mixture is changed to the following configuration. What happens to the position of the equilibrium? Explain.

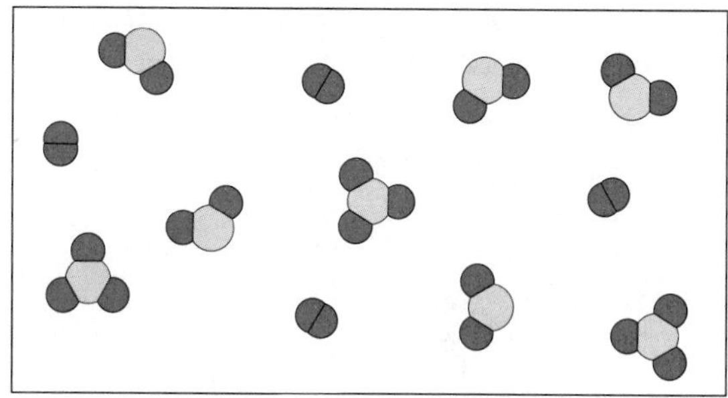

15.74 When the temperature of the system is increased to 1300 K, the equilibrium shifts to the following configuration:

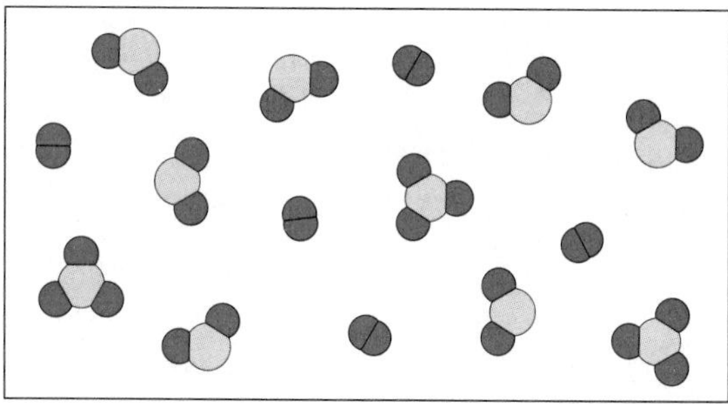

Is the reaction exothermic or endothermic? Use equilibrium arguments to explain your answer.

15.75 The original equilibrium mixture is changed to the following configuration:

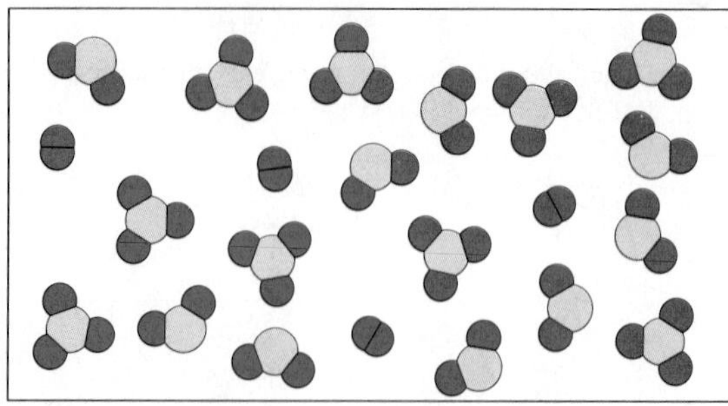

What happens to the position of the equilibrium? Explain.

15.76 Butyric acid is a vile-smelling compound present in rancid butter:

O

OH $K_a = 1.52 \times 10^{-5}$ M

Butyric acid

($C_4H_8O_2$)

$MM = 88.0$ g/mol

A solution of butyric acid is formed by dissolving 1.75 g of the compound in 0.125 L of water. Calculate the equilibrium concentration of hydronium ions.

15.77 In the gas phase, acetic acid is in equilibrium with a dimer that is held together by a pair of hydrogen bonds:

$$2\ CH_3COOH \rightleftarrows \text{Dimer} \qquad K_{eq} = 3.72\ \text{atm}^{-1} \text{ at } 100\ °\text{C}$$

Dimer

(a) If the total pressure of acetic acid gas in a glass bulb is 0.75 atm, what is the partial pressure of the dimer?

(b) Is the equilibrium constant for this reaction higher or lower at 200 °C? (HINT: Hydrogen bonds must be broken for the dimer to decompose to acetic acid molecules.)

15.78 Sodium sulfate is more soluble in water at low temperature than at high temperature. If this salt is dissolved in water in a thermos flask, will the temperature increase or decrease? Explain your answer.

15.79 A chemist claims to have discovered a new gaseous element, effluvium (Ef), which reacts with atmospheric nitrogen to form effluvium nitride:

$$2\ Ef_{(g)} + 3\ N_{2\ (g)} \rightleftarrows 2\ EfN_{3\ (g)}$$

In a container initially containing N_2 at 1.00 atm. pressure and Ef gas at 0.75 atm, the total gas pressure at equilibrium, according to the chemist's measurements, is 0.85 atm. Compute K_{eq} for this reaction.

15.80 Calculate the mass of the precipitate that will form and the concentration of Ag^+ remaining in solution after 250 mL of 0.200 M $AgNO_3$ solution is mixed with 350 mL of 0.300 M Na_2CO_3 solution. K_{sp} for Ag_2CO_3 is 8.2×10^{-12} M^3.

ANSWERS TO SECTION EXERCISES

15.1.1 $K_{eq} = \dfrac{[O_2]^3}{[O_3]^2}$

15.1.2

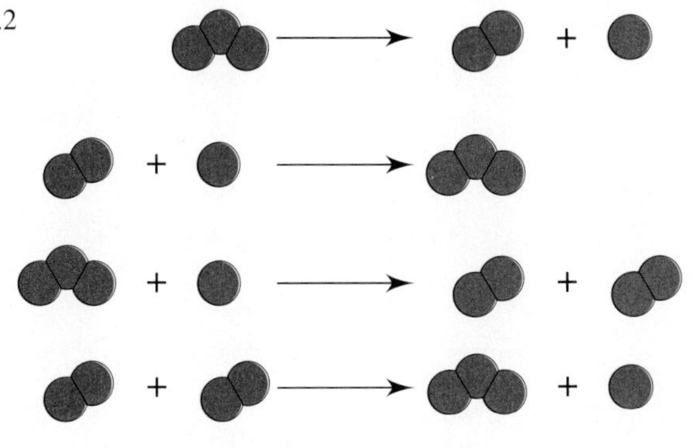

15.1.3 $K_{eq} = \dfrac{[H_2O]^6[NO]^4}{[NH_3]^4[O_2]^5}$

15.2.1 (a) $K_{eq} = (p_{Cl_2})_{eq}$
(b) $K_{eq} = (p_{CO_2})_{eq}$
(c) $K_{eq} = [PO_4^{3-}]^2_{eq}\,[Ca^{2+}]^3_{eq}$
(d) $K_{eq} = \dfrac{[H_3O^+]_{eq}\,[CN^-]_{eq}}{(p_{HCN})_{eq}}$
(e) $K_{eq} = \dfrac{(p_{HCN})_{eq}}{[H_3O^+]_{eq}\,[CN^-]_{eq}}$

15.2.2 (a) atm; (b) atm; (c) M^5; (d) $M^2\ atm^{-1}$; and (e) atm M^{-2}

15.2.3 $K_{eq} = \dfrac{[H^+_{(aq)}]_{eq}\,[A^-]_{eq}}{[HA]_{eq}}$ *and* $K_{eq} = \dfrac{[H_3O^+]_{eq}\,[A^+]_{eq}}{[HA]_{eq}}$

They have the same value, since $[H^+_{(aq)}]_{eq} = [H_3O^+]_{eq}$.

15.3.1 (a) $1/K_w$; (b) K_f; (c) K_a; and (d) $1/K_b$

15.3.2 (a) M^{-2}; (b) M^{-4}; (c) M; and (d) M^{-1}

15.3.3

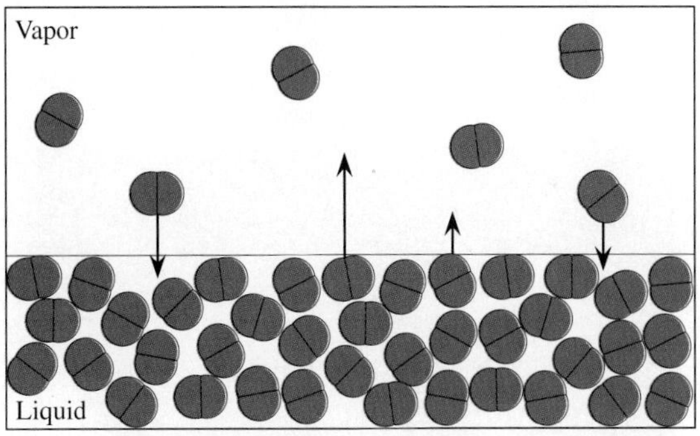

Vapor

Liquid

15.4.1 $K_{sp} = 1.10 \times 10^{-10}\ M^2$

15.4.2 $[CH_3CO_2^-]_{eq} = [H_3O^+]_{eq} = 6.7 \times 10^{-3}$ M and $[CH_3CO_2H]_{eq} = 2.5$ M

15.4.3 $(p_{SO_3})_{eq} = 0.348$ atm; $(p_{SO_2})_{eq} = 1.93 \times 10^{-3}$ atm and $(p_{O_2})_{eq} = 0.588$ atm

15.5.1 $2.26 \times 10^{12}\ atm^{-1}$

15.5.2 Decreases because the reaction is exothermic

15.5.3 $9.39 \times 10^2\ atm^{-1}$

15.6.1 (a) No change in Q, thus, no change; (b), (c), and (d) more $Ba(OH)_2$ dissolves

15.6.2 Lower T, remove NH_3, and increase pressures of H_2 and/or N_2

15.6.3 The H_2-N_2 reaction has a large K_{eq} at room temperature, whereas the CH_4-H_2O reaction has a small K_{eq} at room temperature.

CHAPTER 16

AQUEOUS EQUILIBRIA

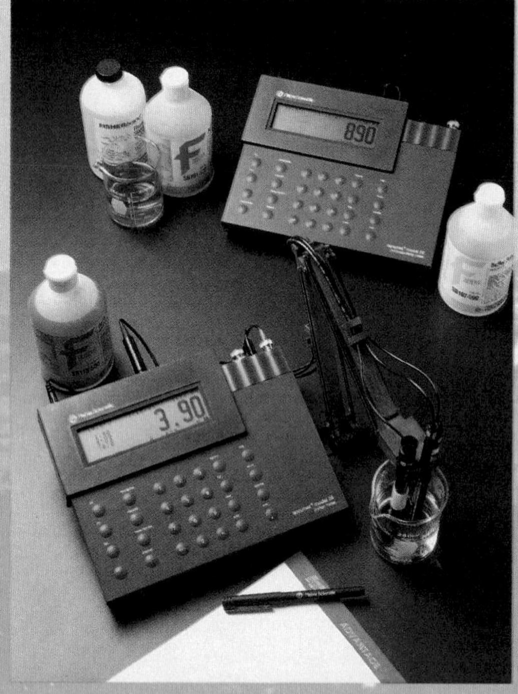

Water is the Earth's most important chemical substance. The oceans and seas cover nearly three quarters of the planet's surface. Water shapes and carves the features of the Earth's crust. Many natural processes are influenced by the aqueous equilibria that exist in seas, lakes, and rivers. All life forms have water-based biochemistry that involve equilibria. Without water, life would not exist on Earth.

Ultrapure water, free of solutes, is a useful liquid for laboratory chemists, but all bodies of water found in nature contain dissolved material. Even the most pristine freshwater lakes and rivers contain dissolved ions, principally Na^+, K^+, Ca^{2+}, and Mg^{2+} cations and Cl^-, SO_4^{2-}, and HCO_3^- anions. The concentrations of these ions vary from place to place, but an average sample of fresh water has a total ion concentration of about 2.4 mM. Sea water contains the same ions but at a total concentration of 1.1 M. Natural waters also contain a 0.1- to 0.5-mM concentration of dissolved gases, primarily N_2, O_2, and CO_2. Chemical equilibria among these ions and other species in solution play key roles in determining the properties of aqueous solutions. From rainwater to blood, the aqueous solutions of our environment have properties that must be interpreted using the principles of chemical equilibria.

All equilibrium reactions that occur in aqueous solutions conform to the principles presented in Chapter 15. In this chapter, we describe in more detail two major categories of aqueous equilibria, solubility reactions and acid-base reactions.

INTRODUCTION: AQUEOUS CHEMISTRY OF CALCIUM

Calcium is the fifth most abundant element in the Earth's crust. Only oxygen, silicon, aluminum, and iron are more abundant. In animals, only carbon, oxygen, nitrogen, and hydrogen are more abundant than calcium. Both in the Earth's crust and in our bodies, aqueous equilibria play important roles in the distribution of calcium.

In the primordial Earth, it is likely that calcium was present primarily in silicate minerals such as anorthite, $CaAl_2Si_2O_8$. Although the solubility products of these minerals are very small, they release calcium ions into solution when they react with hydronium ions. Atmospheric carbon dioxide makes rainwater weakly acidic:

Silicate minerals are discussed in Chapter 8.

$$CO_{2\,(aq)} + 2\,H_2O_{\,(l)} \rightleftarrows HCO_3^{-}{}_{(aq)} + H_3O^{+}{}_{(aq)}$$

Consequently, water passing over calcium-containing silicates gradually accumulates calcium ions:

$$CaAl_2Si_2O_{8\,(s)} + 2\,H_3O^{+}{}_{(aq)} \rightleftarrows Ca^{2+}{}_{(aq)} + Al_2Si_2O_5(OH)_{4\,(s)} + H_2O_{\,(l)}$$

Thus aqueous equilibria involving CO_2 lead indirectly to the transfer of calcium from landmasses to sea water.

The concentration of Ca^{2+} ions in sea water is only about 1 mM, which is nearly 500 times less than the concentration of Na^+ ions. The Ca^{2+} concentration is so low because corals, mollusks, and other marine organisms incorporate calcium ions into solid calcium carbonate that makes up their shells and skeletons. This process takes advantage of the low solubility product ($K_{sp} = 7.1 \times 10^{-9}$ M^2) of calcium carbonate.

When sea creatures die, their remains accumulate on the ocean floor. Over many eons, the shells and skeletons are compressed into rock, whose origin is indicated by the presence of fossils. Limestone, calcite, chalk, and marble are forms of calcium carbonate that often contain fossils of sea creatures. Although insoluble in water, calcium carbonate rock dissolves in weakly acidic water. The acidity of aqueous carbon dioxide is sufficient to promote solubility:

$$CO_{2\,(g)} + 2\,H_2O_{\,(l)} \rightleftharpoons HCO_3^-{}_{(aq)} + H_3O^+{}_{(aq)}$$

$$CaCO_{3\,(s)} + H_3O^+{}_{(aq)} \rightleftharpoons Ca^{2+}{}_{(aq)} + HCO_3^-{}_{(aq)} + H_2O_{\,(l)}$$

$$\text{Net: } CaCO_{3\,(s)} + CO_{2\,(g)} + H_2O_{\,(l)} \rightleftharpoons Ca^{2+}{}_{(aq)} + 2\,HCO_3^-{}_{(aq)}$$

Through this reaction, nature recovers deposited calcium, which eventually returns to the sea to be reassembled into the shells and skeletons of marine creatures.

Carlsbad Caverns (Figure 16-1) formed as a direct result of the action of water on underground limestone deposits. The stalactites and stalagmites in the figure attest to the action of aqueous equilibria in the formation of the cavern. These vertical growths of calcium carbonate have precipitated from water dripping from the roof of the cave. Water that percolates through limestone becomes saturated with carbon dioxide and calcium hydrogencarbonate. When the solution reaches the cavern and comes into contact with air, some dissolved CO_2 escapes into the gas phase. In accordance with Le Châtelier's principle, the equilibrium shifts to the left, and solid calcium carbonate precipitates:

FIGURE 16-1
Stalactites and stalagmites are produced by shifts in the aqueous equilibrium between calcium carbonate and dissolved carbon dioxide, operating over many years.

$$CaCO_{3\,(s)} + \underset{\uparrow \text{Escapes}}{CO_{2\,(g)}} + H_2O_{\,(l)} \xleftarrow[\text{to left}]{\text{Shifts}} Ca^{2+}{}_{(aq)} + 2\,HCO_3^-{}_{(aq)}$$

These deposits grow downward from the cave ceiling and upward from its floor and may eventually merge to form columns.

The bones and the teeth of mammals are composed of hydroxyapatite, $3Ca_3(PO_4)_2 \cdot Ca(OH)_2$, a mixed crystal of calcium phosphate and calcium hydroxide. More than 95% of the calcium in the human body is hydroxyapatite. The rest participates in aqueous equilibria that regulate nerve activity and muscle contractions. The body stores the calcium required for nerve activity as solid calcium phosphate. Although crystalline hydroxyapatite is semipermanently incorporated into bone, amorphous calcium phosphate is in contact with extracellular fluids. A small amount of it dissolves at equilibrium:

$$Ca_3(PO_4)_{2\,(s)} \rightleftharpoons 3\,Ca^{2+}{}_{(aq)} + 2\,PO_4^{3-}{}_{(aq)} \qquad K_{sp} = 1.0 \times 10^{-29}\ M^5$$

In blood and other extracellular fluids, calcium is present in three forms. Almost half is free Ca^{2+} cations, which are the agents responsible for nerve impulses and muscle contractions. An equal amount is complexed to proteins, and about 6% is bound to small organic molecules. The concentration of free Ca^{2+} ions in extracellular fluids is regulated very tightly by a series of aqueous equilibria. Although the intricacies of such multiple equilibria are beyond our scope here, they are based on the fundamental features described in this chapter.

16.1 THE COMPOSITION OF AQUEOUS SOLUTIONS

The chemistry of calcium illustrates that the solutes in an aqueous solution may participate in more than one equilibrium. The natures of these equilibria depend on the identity of the solutes. Consequently, the properties of a solution cannot be understood without first determining the chemical species present in a solution.

MAJOR SPECIES IN SOLUTION

The species present in an aqueous solution can be categorized broadly into two groups. We designate those present in relatively high concentrations as **major species.** We designate those present in relatively low concentrations as **minor species.** The major species in aqueous solutions are water and the solute species present in highest concentration.

An analysis of any aqueous system must be based on the major species and their equilibria. Consequently, the first step in analyzing an aqueous equilibrium is to identify the major species. Pure water contains H_2O molecules at a concentration of 55.5 M. Thus water contains H_2O as a major species. As described in Chapter 15, water molecules undergo a proton transfer reaction that generates low but measurable concentrations of hydronium ions and hydroxide ions:

$$H_2O_{(l)} + H_2O_{(l)} \rightleftarrows H_3O^+_{(aq)} + OH^-_{(aq)} \qquad K_w = 1.00 \times 10^{-14}\ M^2$$

In pure water at 25 °C, the concentration of each ion is 1.00×10^{-7} M. Thus hydronium and hydroxide ions are minor species in pure water.

In addition to water, the solute species present at highest concentration are major species. Salts and strong bases dissociate into ions when they dissolve in water, so solutions of these substances contain *ions* as major species. Strong acids undergo quantitative proton transfer when they dissolve in water, so solutions of strong acids also contain *ions* as major species. All other solutes dissolve as molecules, so their solutions contain *molecules* as major species.

Minor solute species in aqueous solutions generally have concentrations at least three orders of magnitude lower than the concentrations of major solute species.

IONIC SOLUTIONS

When a salt such as copper(II) sulfate pentahydrate, $CuSO_4{\cdot}5H_2O$, dissolves in pure water, the waters of hydration become part of the solvent, and $Cu^{2+}_{(aq)}$ and $SO_4{}^{2-}_{(aq)}$ ions form. As a result, the major species in this solution are $Cu^{2+}_{(aq)}$ and $SO_4{}^{2-}_{(aq)}$ in addition to H_2O. In any aqueous salt solution, the major species are *water molecules*, and the *cations* and *anions* generated by the salt.

A strong acid is a substance that is a better proton donor than a hydronium ion. Any acid that is a better proton donor than hydronium ions reacts quantitatively with water to produce hydronium ions. For example, HCl is a strong acid. When hydrogen chloride gas dissolves in water, the HCl molecules react with water to produce hydronium ions:

$$H_2O + HCl \rightarrow H_3O^+_{(aq)} + Cl^-_{(aq)}$$

Nitric acid (HNO_3) and sulfuric acid (H_2SO_4) are two other examples of strong acids:

$$H_2O + HNO_3 \rightarrow H_3O^+_{(aq)} + NO_3{}^-_{(aq)}$$

$$H_2O + H_2SO_4 \rightarrow H_3O^+_{(aq)} + HSO_4{}^-_{(aq)}$$

Many ionic compounds, including copper(II) sulfate, form "hydrated salts" *(left)* by crystallizing with a specific number of water molecules in the crystal lattice. The anhydrous salt *(right)* can usually be formed by heating the compound in the solid state.

Strong acids and bases are first described in Chapter 4.

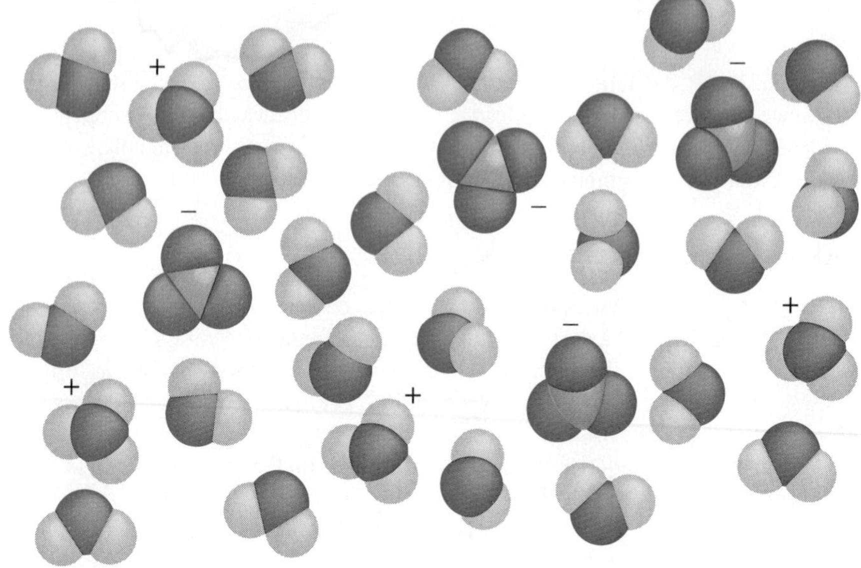

FIGURE 16-2
The major species present in an aqueous solution of nitric acid are water molecules, hydronium ions, and nitrate anions, but there is a negligible concentration of HNO_3 molecules.

These reactions are written with single arrows to designate that they go virtually to completion. In equilibrium terms, the equilibrium constants for these proton transfer reactions are so large that the concentration of unreacted acid is negligible. This situation is illustrated in Figure 16-2, which shows a molecular picture of aqueous nitric acid. The major species in an aqueous solution of any *strong acid* are H_2O, H_3O^+, and the *anion* produced by removing a proton from the acid.

Pure sulfuric acid is a liquid that mixes with water in all proportions. Thus solutions of water and sulfuric acid can contain more H_2SO_4 molecules than H_2O molecules. In such highly concentrated H_2SO_4, the major species are H_2SO_4 and H_3O^+ but not H_2O. Concentrated H_2SO_4 is extremely caustic because, in addition to being a strong acid, it extracts water from water-containing materials.

Notice that, although some acids are stronger than hydronium ions, these acids cannot exist in aqueous solution. Any acid that is stronger than H_3O^+ produces H_3O^+ when it dissolves in water.

Whereas a strong acid generates hydronium ions when it dissolves in water, a strong base generates hydroxide ions when it dissolves in water. The primary examples of strong bases are soluble metal hydroxides like NaOH and KOH. These ionic substances produce ions when they dissolve in water:

$$KOH_{(s)} \rightarrow K^+_{(aq)} + OH^-_{(aq)}$$

Sodium amide ($NaNH_2$), methyl lithium ($LiCH_3$), and sodium ethoxide ($NaOCH_2CH_3$) are also strong bases because each undergoes proton transfer with water to generate hydroxide ions as it dissolves:

$$NaNH_{2\,(s)} + H_2O_{(l)} \rightarrow Na^+_{(aq)} + OH^-_{(aq)} + NH_{3\,(aq)}$$

$$LiCH_{3\,(s)} + H_2O_{(l)} \rightarrow Li^+_{(aq)} + OH^-_{(aq)} + CH_{4\,(g)}$$

$$NaOCH_2CH_{3\,(s)} + H_2O_{(l)} \rightarrow Na^+_{(aq)} + OH^-_{(aq)} + CH_3CH_2OH_{(aq)}$$

Very strong bases such as sodium amide, methyl lithium, and sodium ethoxide are important bases in organic chemistry. Their applications require the use of a water-free environment.

These three compounds are salts that contain better proton acceptors than the hydroxide ion, so each is a stronger base than the hydroxide ion. Any base stronger than hydroxide reacts instantaneously with water to produce hydroxide ions. Thus the hydroxide ion is the strongest base that can exist in aqueous solution. The major species in any aqueous solution of a *strong base* are H_2O, OH^-, and the *cation* generated by the base. A base stronger than hydroxide ions also generates a neutral

TABLE 16-1 COMMON STRONG ACIDS AND BASES

Acids of Industrial Importance		Bases of Industrial Importance	
H_2SO_4	Sulfuric acid	NaOH	Sodium hydroxide
HNO_3	Nitric acid	$Ca(OH)_2$	Calcium hydroxide
HCl	Hydrochloric acid	KOH	Potassium hydroxide
Acids with Laboratory Applications		**Bases with Laboratory Applications**	
$HClO_4$	Perchloric acid	LiOH	Lithium hydroxide
HBr	Hydrobromic acid	$Ba(OH)_2$	Barium hydroxide

molecule as a major species. For example, sodium amide forms an ammonia molecule in addition to OH^- and Na^+ ions.

The common strong acids and bases are listed in Table 16-1. These compounds are used so widely both in industry and in chemical laboratories that you should memorize their names and formulas.

MOLECULAR SOLUTIONS

Many substances besides salts, strong acids, and strong bases dissolve in water. Vinegar, for example, is an aqueous solution of acetic acid (CH_3CO_2H) and various minor components. The major species present in vinegar are H_2O and CH_3CO_2H. Similarly, beer is a dilute aqueous solution of ethanol (C_2H_5OH) and various minor components. The major species present in beer are H_2O and C_2H_5OH. Figure 16-3 shows a molecular picture of the major species in a vinegar solution.

To identify the major species in any aqueous solution, first categorize the solutes. An insoluble substance remains undissolved. A soluble salt, strong acid, or strong

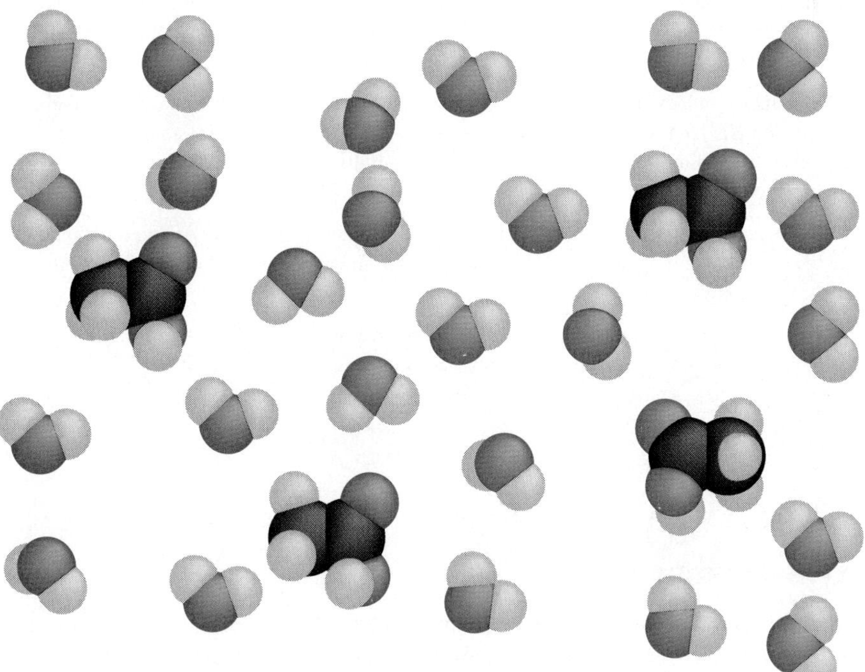

FIGURE 16-3
A molecular view of the major species present in a solution of acetic acid (vinegar).

base generates the appropriate cations and anions as major species. Any other solute generates its molecular species in solution. In addition, H_2O is *always* a major species in aqueous solutions. Sample Problem 16-1 shows some additional examples of the major species in solution.

SAMPLE PROBLEM 16-1 MAJOR SPECIES IN SOLUTION

Identify the major species in each of the following aqueous solutions: (a) $NaCH_3CO_2$ (sodium acetate); (b) $HClO_4$ (perchloric acid); (c) $C_6H_{12}O_6$ (glucose, used for intravenous feeding); and (d) NH_3 (ammonia, used for household cleaning).

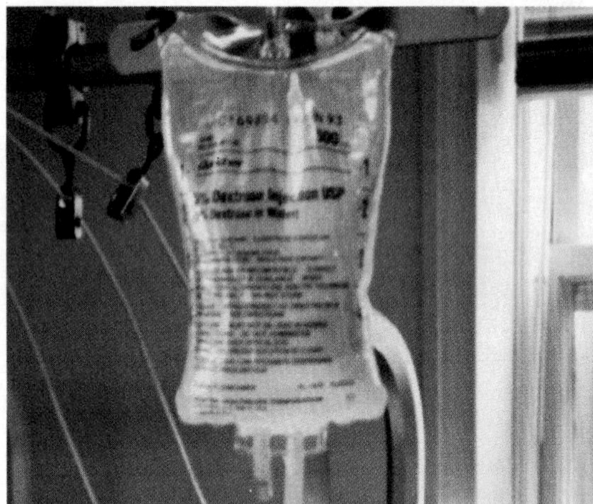

If you have forgotten how to recognize a salt, review Section 8.3.

METHOD: We must identify the nature of each solute. If it is a salt, strong acid, or strong base, it generates ions in aqueous solution. All other solutes give aqueous solutions that contain molecules as the major species.

(a) From its formula, you should recognize that $NaCH_3CO_2$ is a salt. It contains the alkali metal cation Na^+ and the polyatomic acetate anion, $CH_3CO_2^-$. According to the solubility guidelines, all sodium salts are soluble. Thus this salt dissolves, generating an aqueous solution in which the major species are H_2O, Na^+, and $CH_3CO_2^-$.

Glucose ($C_6H_{12}O_6$)

(b) $HClO_4$ is a strong acid, so it transfers a proton to water quantitatively. (You must memorize the important strong acids listed in Table 16-1.) The major species in aqueous perchloric acid are H_2O, H_3O^+, and ClO_4^-.

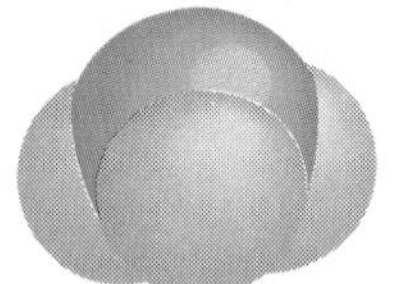

Ammonia

(c) Glucose is not a strong acid, a strong base, or a salt. It dissolves in water without reacting, so the major species in intravenous feeding solutions are molecules of $C_6H_{12}O_6$ and H_2O.

(d) NH_3 is not a strong acid, a strong base, or a salt. The major species in household ammonia are molecules of NH_3 and H_2O.

TYPES OF EQUILIBRIA

After the major species in an aqueous solution have been identified, our next task is to determine their equilibria. Recall from Chapter 15 that the major categories of aqueous equilibria are acid-base (proton transfer), solubility, and complex formation. Each of these may be approached from either direction, giving six different types of equilibria in which major species may participate:

1. An acid may donate a proton to water or some other base.
2. A base may accept a proton from water or some other acid.
3. A salt or a gas may dissolve in water.
4. Cations and anions in a solution may react to form a solid or a gas.
5. A metal cation may form a complex with anions or molecules.
6. A complex ion may dissociate into a metal cation and anions or molecules.

Each major species present in the solution must be examined in light of these six general equilibria. Are any of the major species weak acids or weak bases? Are there ions present that combine to form an insoluble salt? Does the solution contain anions or molecules that can form a complex with a metal cation? Do any of the major species participate in more than one equilibrium? In this chapter, we consider solubility and acid-base reactions in detail, deferring further consideration of complexation equilibrium until Chapter 18.

SPECTATOR IONS

With all the possible equilibria in aqueous systems, most species can be expected to participate in one or more equilibria. Nonetheless, in many solutions some ionic species undergo no significant reactions. These species are classed as **spectator ions.**

In Section 4.5 we described what happens when a solution of potassium iodide is mixed with a solution of lead(II) nitrate. The major species present are $K^+_{(aq)}$, $I^-_{(aq)}$, $Pb^{2+}_{(aq)}$, $NO_3{}^-_{(aq)}$, and H_2O. As shown in Figure 16-4, PbI_2 is only slightly soluble in water, so when the two salt solutions are combined, a bright-yellow solid precipitates from the mixture. The Pb^{2+} and I^- ions that remain in solution establish a solubility equilibrium with the precipitate:

$$PbI_{2\,(s)} \rightleftarrows Pb^{2+}_{(aq)} + 2\,I^-_{(aq)} \qquad K_{sp} = 7.1 \times 10^{-9}\ M^3$$

FIGURE 16-4
Mixing aqueous solutions of potassium iodide and lead(II) nitrate results in the formation of a yellow precipitate. The precipitate is lead(II) iodide.

Notice that two of the major species are not involved in the solubility equilibrium. Potassium ions and nitrate ions are spectator ions in this system. Sample Problem 16-2 provides another example of spectator ions.

SAMPLE PROBLEM 16-2 SPECTATOR IONS

When a 0.100 M solution of sodium bromide is mixed with an equal volume of a 0.100 M solution of silver nitrate, a white solid precipitates from the solution. Identify the precipitate, write the net ionic reaction for the solubility equilibrium, and identify any spectator ions.

METHOD: Analyze the problem from the molecular perspective. Begin by identifying the major species present. Then identify the equilibria in which these ions participate.

Sodium bromide and silver nitrate are both salts, so the major species are Na^+, Ag^+, Br^-, $NO_3{}^-$, and water molecules.

The solubility guidelines presented in Section 4.5 identify the precipitate as silver bromide:

$$AgBr_{(s)} \rightleftarrows Ag^+_{(aq)} + Br^-_{(aq)} \qquad K_{sp} = 5.0 \times 10^{-13}\ M^2$$

Major ionic species that do not participate in aqueous equilibria are classified as spectator ions. In this case the spectator ions are sodium cations and nitrate anions.

The waste water contains Pb^{2+}, so an anion must be present in the solution to balance the charge of the lead ions, and other species may exist as well. We are asked only about the lead in the waste water, however, so we can assume that any other ions are spectators. The sodium hydroxide solution contains Na^+ and OH^-, so the major species in the treated waste water are H_2O, Pb^{2+}, OH^-, and Na^+.

The equilibrium constant for the precipitation reaction is the inverse of K_{sp} for $Pb(OH)_2$:

$$Pb^{2+}_{(aq)} + 2\,OH^-_{(aq)} \rightleftarrows Pb(OH)_{2\,(s)}$$

$$K_{eq} = \frac{1}{[Pb^{2+}]_{eq}\,[OH^-]^2_{eq}} = \frac{1}{K_{sp}} = \frac{1}{1.1 \times 10^{-20}\ M^3} = 9.1 \times 10^{19}\ M^{-3}$$

The problem asks for the residual concentration of lead ions. In other words, we need to determine the Pb^{2+} ion concentration in a saturated solution of lead(II) hydroxide. Before the concentration table can be completed, we must determine initial ion concentrations. The total volume of the mixed solutions is 1501.5 L, negligibly different from 1500 L. This means the initial lead concentration is 2.9×10^{-3} M. We must calculate the concentration of hydroxide ions in the mixed solution:

$$M_2 = \frac{M_1V_1}{V_2} = \frac{(6.0\ M)(1.5\ L)}{1500\ L} = 6.0 \times 10^{-3}\ M = [OH^-]_{initial}$$

For a review of the technique for dealing with large equilibrium constants, see Sample Problem 15-8.

Now we set up the concentration table. The equilibrium constant for precipitation is very large, so we envision the precipitation in two steps. First, take the reaction to completion. Then "switch on" the solubility equilibrium.

Species (reaction)	$Pb^{2+}_{(aq)}$	+	$2\,OH^-_{(aq)} \rightleftarrows Pb(OH)_{2\,(s)}$
Initial concentration, M	2.9×10^{-3}		6.0×10^{-3}
Change to completion, M	-2.9×10^{-3}		-5.8×10^{-3}
Completion concentration, M	0		0.2×10^{-3}
Change to equilibrium, M	y		$2y$
Equilibrium concentration, M	y		$0.2 \times 10^{-3} + 2y$

A tiny amount of $Pb(OH)_2$ *dissolves* in this approach to equilibrium, so we can use the solubility equilibrium and K_{sp}:

$$K_{sp} = [Pb^{2+}]_{eq}\,[OH^-]^2_{eq} = 1.1 \times 10^{-20}\ M^3$$

The variable y represents the change to equilibrium in a reaction with a small equilibrium constant, so we can assume that y will be small compared with 0.2×10^{-3} M:

$$K_{sp} = (y)\,(0.2 \times 10^{-3} + 2y)^2 \cong (y)(0.2 \times 10^{-3})^2 = 1.1 \times 10^{-20}\ M^3$$

$$y = \frac{(1.1 \times 10^{-20}\ M^3)}{(0.2 \times 10^{-3}\ M)^2} = 2.8 \times 10^{-13}\ M \qquad [Pb^{2+}]_{eq} = 3 \times 10^{-13}\ M$$

This final value is rounded to one significant figure because the equilibrium concentration of OH^-, being a difference between two numbers, is precise only to one significant figure.

The problem also asks for the mass of $Pb(OH)_2$ that precipitates. The moles of precipitate equal the number of moles of Pb^{2+} ions removed by hydroxide treatment. The necessary information is contained in the concentration table in the row that gives the completion conditions. The precipitation equilibrium constant is so large ($\sim 10^{20}$) that we can neglect equilibrium considerations for this calculation:

$$\text{mol } Pb(OH)_2 = \text{mol } Pb^{2+} = MV = (2.9 \times 10^{-3}\ M)(1500\ L) = 4.35\ \text{mol}$$

$$\text{Mass } Pb(OH)_2 = (\text{mol})(MM) = (4.35\ \text{mol})(241\ \text{g/mol}) = 1048\ \text{g} = 1.0\ \text{kg}$$

SECTION EXERCISES

16.2.1 What is the concentration of Mg^{2+} in a saturated aqueous solution of $Mg(OH)_2$?

16.2.2 Sea water is approximately 0.5 M each in Na^+ and Cl^- ions. By evaporation, NaCl can be precipitated from this solution. If we start with 100 L of sea water and begin evaporation, at what volume will the first solid NaCl appear? ($K_{sp} = 0.4\ M^2$.)

16.2.3 Determine the concentration of Mg^{2+} ions remaining in solution after 150 mL of 0.125 M $MgCl_2$ solution is treated with 100 mL of 0.65 M NaOH solution. Does NaCl also precipitate from this solution?

16.3 PROTON-TRANSFER EQUILIBRIA

In any acid-base reaction, a proton (H^+) is transferred from one chemical species to another. A species that donates a proton is an acid, and a species that accepts a proton is a base. This identification of acids and bases with proton transfer is the Brønsted-Lowry definition of acid-base reactions.

A major advantage of this definition is its simplicity. From this perspective, *every* acid-base reaction has two reactants, an acid and a base. Every acid-base reaction also has two products formed when the acid transfers H^+ to the base:

ACID	BASE		
$HCl_{(g)}$	$+ H_2O_{(l)}$	$\rightarrow Cl^-_{(aq)}$	$+ H_3O^+_{(aq)}$
$H_2O_{(l)}$	$+ PO_4^{3-}{}_{(aq)}$	$\rightarrow OH^-_{(aq)}$	$+ HPO_4^{2-}{}_{(aq)}$
$CH_3CO_2H_{(aq)}$	$+ OH^-_{(aq)}$	$\rightarrow CH_3CO_2^-{}_{(aq)}$	$+ H_2O_{(l)}$
$H_3O^+_{(aq)}$	$+ OH^-_{(aq)}$	$\rightarrow H_2O_{(l)}$	$+ H_2O_{(l)}$

Although these reactions may look different, they all represent the *same* chemical process. In each case an acid molecule collides with a base molecule and transfers H^+. Figure 16-5 illustrates this process at the molecular level.

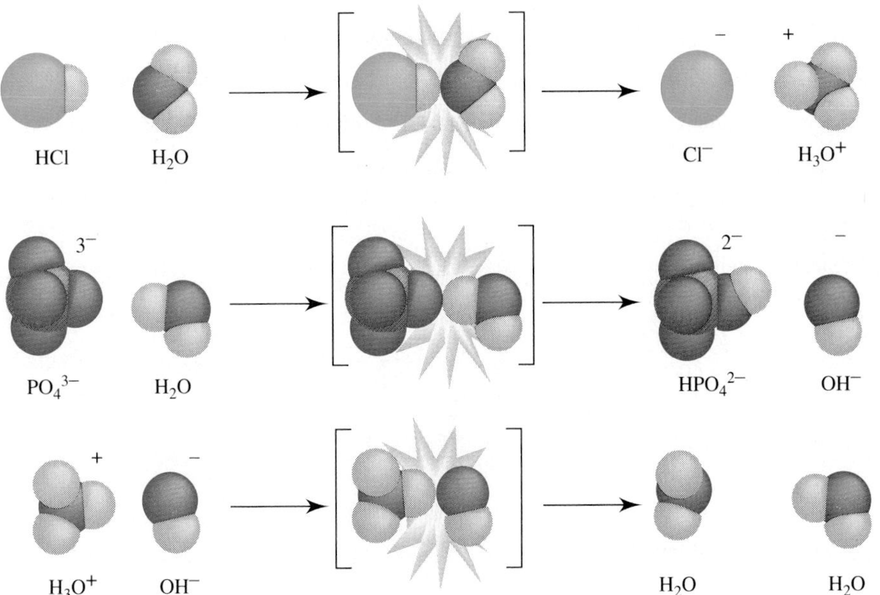

FIGURE 16-5
Acid-base reactions involve transfers of protons from an acid to a base.

A chemical species that can act as either an acid or a base is said to be *amphiprotic*. Water is an amphiprotic molecule.

Notice that a water molecule participates in each of these examples. Aqueous acid-base chemistry usually includes water as either a starting material or a product. Notice also that water can be either an acid or a base. As an acid, water donates a proton to a base and becomes a hydroxide anion. As a base, water accepts a proton from an acid and becomes a hydronium cation.

THE RANGE OF H_3O^+ CONCENTRATION

In a solution of strong acid, the concentration of hydronium ions is equal to the molarity of the acid. For example, in 6.0 M aqueous HCl, the concentration of H_3O^+ is 6.0 M. The proton-transfer equilibrium constant for HCl is so large that the amount of residual hydrogen chloride is negligible.

$$HCl_{(aq)} \rightarrow H_3O^+_{(aq)} + Cl^-_{(aq)} \qquad K_a >> 1$$

In other aqueous solutions, the concentration of hydronium ions may be quite small. For example, the hydronium ion concentration in pure water is determined by its proton-transfer equilibrium:

$$H_2O_{(l)} + H_2O_{(l)} \rightleftarrows H_3O^+_{(aq)} + OH^-_{(aq)}$$

$$K_w = [H_3O^+]_{eq}[OH^-]_{eq} = 1.00 \times 10^{-14} \text{ M}^2 \text{ (at 25 °C)}$$

In any solution of an acid, the total hydronium ion concentration includes the 10^{-7} M contribution from the water reaction. This contribution is negligible except in highly dilute solutions, which we do not discuss in this text.

Hydronium and hydroxide ions have concentrations of 10^{-7} M in pure water.

The concentrations of H_3O^+ and OH^- in *any* aqueous solution are linked by the water equilibrium. That is, the product of these two concentrations is *always* 1.00×10^{-14} M^2 at 25 °C. If one concentration increases, the other concentration must decrease so that their product remains fixed.

In a solution of a strong base, the hydroxide ion concentration is determined by the molarity of the base. In a 0.25 M NaOH solution, for example, the OH^- concentration is 0.25 M. In this solution the hydronium ion concentration is determined by the water equilibrium, as illustrated in Sample Problem 16-6.

SAMPLE PROBLEM 16-6 HYDRONIUM ION CONCENTRATION

What is the hydronium ion concentration in a 0.25 M solution of NaOH at 25 °C?

METHOD: Sodium hydroxide dissolves in water to generate Na^+ cations and OH^- anions. To determine the hydronium ion concentration, we must work with the appropriate equilibrium.

The major species in this solution are Na^+, OH^-, and H_2O, and the only equilibrium reaction among these species is the water equilibrium:

$$H_2O_{(l)} + H_2O_{(l)} \rightleftarrows H_3O^+_{(aq)} + OH^-_{(aq)} \qquad K_w = 1.00 \times 10^{-14} \text{ M}^2 = [H_3O^+]_{eq}[OH^-]_{eq}$$

Set up a concentration table, defining the change in hydronium ion concentration as x:

Species (reaction)	$H_2O_{(l)} + H_2O_{(l)} \rightleftarrows$ $H_3O^+_{(aq)}$	$+ OH^-_{(aq)}$
Initial concentration, M	0	0.25
Change in concentration, M	$+x$	$+x$
Equilibrium concentration, M	x	$0.25 + x$

The equilibrium constant is much smaller than 0.25, so we expect that $x << 0.25$ and make the approximation, $0.25 + x \cong 0.25$. Solving for x gives the equilibrium concentration of hydronium ions.

$$K_w = 1.00 \times 10^{-14}\ \text{M}^2 = x\,(0.25 + x) \cong 0.25\,x$$

$$x \cong \frac{1.00 \times 10^{-14}\ \text{M}^2}{0.25\ \text{M}} = 4.0 \times 10^{-14}\ \text{M} = [\text{H}_3\text{O}^+]_{\text{eq}}$$

Note that x is indeed much smaller than 0.25. The addition of OH^- ions to water causes the water equilibrium to shift to the left, reducing the hydronium ion concentration.

pH: A CONVENIENT MEASURE OF ACIDITY

We have just shown that in acid-base systems, the hydronium ion concentration covers more than 14 orders of magnitude, from greater than 1 M in solutions of strong acids, to 10^{-7} M in pure water, to less than 10^{-14} M in solutions of strong bases. To express this immense range of concentrations conveniently, chemists have defined a logarithmic scale of acid concentration called the **pH**:

$$\text{pH} = -\log\,[\text{H}_3\text{O}^+] \qquad \textbf{(16-1)}$$

Log refers to powers of 10, whereas _ln_ refers to powers of e. The pH scale is defined using powers of 10 because of the easy conversion of power of 10 notation into logarithmic notation: if $[H_3O^+] = 10^{-8}$ M, pH = 8.

The pH of a solution is obtained by taking the logarithm of the hydronium ion concentration and then changing the sign. For example, the pH of pure water is:

$$\text{pH} = -\log\,[\text{H}_3\text{O}^+] = -\log\,(1.00 \times 10^{-7}) = -(-7.00) = 7.00$$

The logarithmic scale for concentration values is useful not only for hydronium ion concentrations, but also for expressing hydroxide ion concentrations and equilibrium constants. That is, the pH definition can be generalized to other quantities:

$$\text{pOH} = -\log\,[\text{OH}^-] \qquad \text{p}K_a = -\log K_a \qquad \text{p}K_b = -\log K_b$$

Using these definitions, we can take advantage of the properties of logarithms to restate the water equilibrium in terms of pH:

$$K_w = [\text{H}_3\text{O}^+][\text{OH}^-] = 1.00 \times 10^{-14}$$

$$\log\,[\text{H}_3\text{O}^+] + \log\,[\text{OH}^-] = \log\,(1.00 \times 10^{-14}) = -14.00$$

$$-\log\,[\text{H}_3\text{O}^+] - \log\,[\text{OH}^-] = 14.00$$

$$\text{pH} + \text{pOH} = 14.00 \qquad \textbf{(16-2)}$$

Equation 16-2 connects pH and pOH for any aqueous solution. Sample Problem 16-7 demonstrates the usefulness of this equation.

SAMPLE PROBLEM 16-7 pH AND pOH

What is the pH of a 0.25 M solution of NaOH?

METHOD: To find pH of a solution, we first compute either $[H_3O^+]$ or $[OH^-]$ and then apply Equation 16-1 or 16-2.

In this solution of strong base, $[OH^-]$ is equal to the concentration of sodium hydroxide:

$$[OH^-] = 0.25\ M$$

$$pOH = -\log(0.25) = -(-0.60) = 0.60$$

$$pH = 14.00 - pOH = 14.00 - 0.60 = 13.40$$

Notice how much easier this calculation is than the analysis in Sample Problem 16-6. The detailed reasoning of the concentration table, K_w, and an approximation have been compressed into two steps.

We can verify that this result is the same as the one obtained in Sample Problem 16-6 by converting from pH to $[H_3O^+]$:

$$13.40 = pH = -\log[H_3O^+] \quad \log[H_3O^+] = -13.40 \quad [H_3O^+] = 10^{-13.40} = 4.0 \times 10^{-14}\ M$$

A logarithm has two parts. The numbers preceding the decimal point determine the power of 10. The numbers following the decimal point determine the numerical value. When two digits follow the decimal place of the logarithm, therefore, the corresponding numerical value has two significant figures.

PROTON TRANSFER TO WATER

In a 0.25 M solution of HCl, the concentration of hydronium ions is 0.25 M and pH = 0.60. For a 0.25 M solution of HF, however, experiments show that the concentration of hydronium ions at equilibrium is only 9.4×10^{-3} M, pH = 2.03. In other words, when HF dissolves in water, equilibrium is established when only a fraction of the HF molecules have transferred protons to water molecules:

$$H_2O_{(l)} + HF_{(aq)} \rightleftarrows H_3O^+_{(aq)} + F^-_{(aq)}$$

This is an example of a proton-transfer reaction that does not go to completion. An acid that reaches equilibrium when only a small fraction of its molecules has transferred protons to water is called a **weak acid.**

The strength of a weak acid is measured by its acid equilibrium constant, K_a. This equilibrium constant can be calculated from the measured pH of the solution, as illustrated in Sample Problem 16-8.

As shown in Chapter 15, equilibrium constants vary with temperature. In this chapter, all values are at 25 °C unless otherwise stated.

SAMPLE PROBLEM 16-8 CALCULATING K_a

The pH of a 0.25 M aqueous HF solution is 2.04. Calculate K_a for this weak acid.

METHOD: First identify species in solution. Then identify the equilibria involving these species as reactants. After identifying the chemistry, set up and complete the appropriate concentration table and solve for the desired quantity, in this case K_a.

Hydrogen fluoride is neither a strong acid nor a salt, so the major species in solution are H_2O and HF molecules. The problem states that hydrogen fluoride is a weak acid, which tells us that in aqueous solution, HF transfers protons to H_2O:

$$H_2O_{(l)} + HF_{(aq)} \rightleftarrows H_3O^+_{(aq)} + F^-_{(aq)}$$

$$K_a = \frac{[H_3O^+]_{eq}[F^-]_{eq}}{[HF]_{eq}}$$

From the pH, we determine the concentration of hydronium ions at equilibrium:

$$[H_3O^+] = 10^{-pH} = 10^{-2.04} = 9.1 \times 10^{-3}\ M$$

Now construct the concentration table. The key is to use the initial and equilibrium concentrations of H_3O^+ to complete the "change" row. We use colored type to show the concentrations that provide the starting points for completing this table.

Species (reaction):	H_2O + HF $\rightleftarrows$	H_3O^+	+ F^-
Initial conc., M:	0.25	0	0
Change in conc., M:	-9.1×10^{-3}	$+9.1 \times 10^{-3}$	$+9.1 \times 10^{-3}$
Equilibrium conc., M:	0.24	9.1×10^{-3}	9.1×10^{-3}

The problem identified this solution as "0.25 M HF," but at equilibrium, [HF] = 0.24 M. Conventionally, a solution's concentration is stated as its initial concentration, even though the correct equilibrium concentrations may differ slightly from this initial concentration.

Now substitute and solve for K_a:

$$K_a = \frac{(9.1 \times 10^{-3}\ M)^2}{(0.24\ M)} = 3.5 \times 10^{-4}\ M$$

Sample Problem 16-8 shows that hydrogen fluoride is a weak acid, but although it is not strongly reactive as an *acid*, HF has other unique reactive properties. It is one of the few common substances that reacts with glass. For this reason, artists use aqueous solutions of HF to etch glass, and it is used industrially to "frost" light bulbs. Because it destroys glass bottles, aqueous HF must be stored in plastic containers. Besides attacking glass, HF has a devastating effect on human nerve tissues. It is readily absorbed through the skin, so people who work with HF must always wear strong plastic gloves.

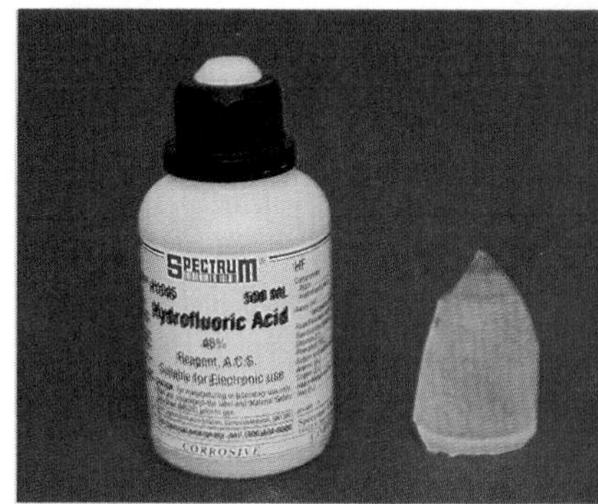

Solutions of hydrogen fluoride (left) are used to etch glass (right).

PROTON TRANSFER FROM WATER

When a weak acid such as HF dissolves in water, proton transfer generates a solution in which the hydronium ion concentration is greater than that in pure water. Consequently, the pH of an acidic solution is always *less* than 7.00. On the other hand, when ammonia dissolves in water, the resulting solution has a pH *greater* than 7.00, indicating that the equilibrium concentration of hydronium ions is less than that in pure water. Thus according to Equation 16-1, aqueous ammonia must have a hydroxide ion concentration that is greater than that of pure water. Ammonia molecules *accept* protons from water molecules, generating ammonium cations and hydroxide anions:

$$NH_{3\,(aq)} + H_2O_{(l)} \rightleftarrows NH_4^{+}{}_{(aq)} + OH^{-}{}_{(aq)}$$

Ammonia is an example of a **weak base.** A weak base reaches equilibrium when only a fraction of its molecules have accepted protons from water. The equilibrium constant for this type of equilibrium is designated K_b.

$$K_b = \frac{[NH_4^{+}]_{eq}\,[OH^{-}]_{eq}}{[NH_3]_{eq}}$$

Sample Problem 16-9 explores the ammonia equilibrium in more detail.

SAMPLE PROBLEM 16-9 pH OF A WEAK BASE

What is the pH of 0.25 M aqueous ammonia ($K_b = 1.6 \times 10^{-5}$ M)?

METHOD: To calculate the pH of the solution, we need the equilibrium concentration of either H_3O^+ or OH^-. The procedure developed in Chapter 15 for solving equilibrium problems leads us to these equilibrium concentrations.

(c) Add H^+ to HSO_4^- to obtain its conjugate acid, H_2SO_4:

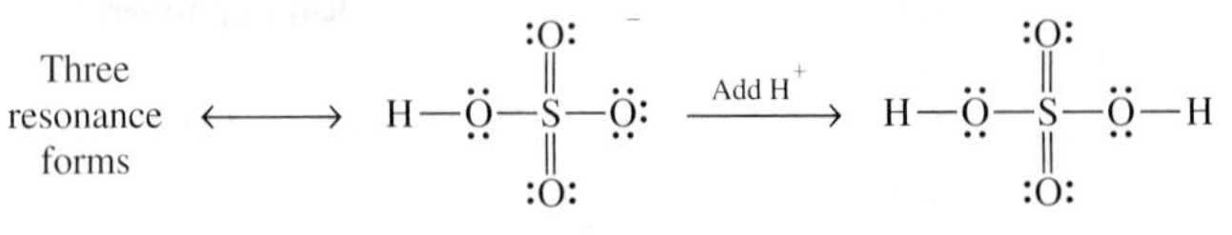

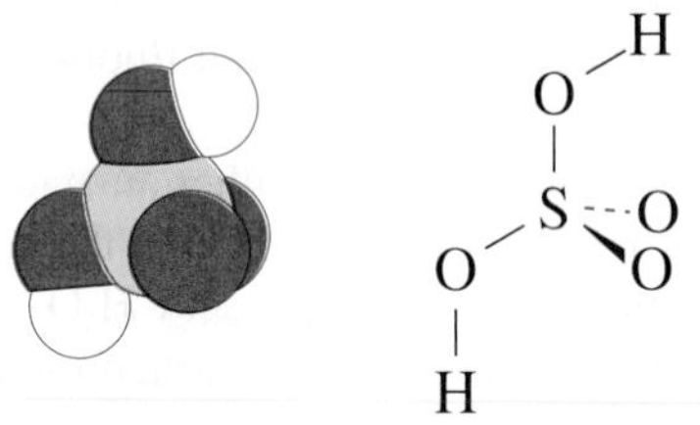

Three resonance forms ⟷ H—Ö—S(=O)(=O)—Ö: —Add H^+→ H—Ö—S(=O)(=O)—Ö—H

HSO_4^-, like H_2O, is amphiprotic, so it has both a conjugate base (SO_4^{2-}) and a conjugate acid (H_2SO_4).

When sodium fluoride dissolves in water, the major species present are Na^+, F^-, and H_2O. A water molecule can be either a proton donor or a proton acceptor, and according to the analysis that we just completed, F^- is a base. Thus in a solution of sodium fluoride, F^- is in equilibrium with its conjugate acid, HF:

$$H_2O_{(l)} + F^-_{(aq)} \rightleftarrows HF_{(aq)} + OH^-_{(aq)}$$

This reaction generates hydroxide anions, so the solution is basic. We have defined the equilibrium constant for this type of reaction as K_b. In this case, it is K_b for the F^- anion, which is a weak base.

The fluoride ion equilibrium is linked to two other proton-transfer equilibria. The relationship is revealed by combining the proton-transfer equilibrium for HF with the proton-transfer equilibrium for F^-:

$$\begin{array}{ll} \cancel{HF} + H_2O \rightleftarrows \cancel{F^-} + H_3O^+ & K_a \\ \cancel{F^-} + H_2O \rightleftarrows \cancel{HF} + OH^- & K_b \\ \hline 2\,H_2O \rightleftarrows H_3O^+ + OH^- & K_w \end{array}$$

When we combine these two equilibria, HF and F^- cancel, so the sum of the two is the water equilibrium. The three equilibrium constants are related in an equation obtained by multiplying the concentration quotients for K_a and K_b:

$$\underbrace{\frac{[H_3O^+]_{eq}\cancel{[F^-]_{eq}}}{\cancel{[HF]_{eq}}}}_{K_a}\ \underbrace{\frac{[OH^-]_{eq}\cancel{[HF]_{eq}}}{\cancel{[F^-]_{eq}}}}_{K_b} = \underbrace{[H_3O^+]_{eq}[OH^-]_{eq}}_{K_w}$$

When two or more equilibria are combined, the equilibrium constant for the net reaction is the product of the individual equilibrium constants of the summed reactions.

$$K_aK_b = K_w \qquad \textbf{(16-3)}$$

Equation 16-3 applies to any acid and its conjugate base. The equation can also be expressed in logarithmic form using pK notation and the numerical value, $pK_w = -\log(1.00 \times 10^{-14}) = 14.00$:

$$pK_a + pK_b = 14.00 \qquad \textbf{(16-4)}$$

Knowing K_a and K_w, we can use Equation 16-3 to determine K_b for fluoride anions. From Sample Problem 16–5, $K_a = 3.6 \times 10^{-4}$ M for HF, and as always, $K_w = 1.00 \times 10^{-14}\ M^2$. Thus:

$$K_b = \frac{K_w}{K_a} = \frac{1.00 \times 10^{-14}\ M^2}{3.6 \times 10^{-4}\ M} = 2.8 \times 10^{-11}\ M$$

Because of the extremely small value of K_w, both K_a and K_b are much smaller than 1.00, so HF is a weak acid, and F^- is a weak base. Unless K_a is smaller than about 10^{-12} M, the conjugate base of a weak acid is also weak, and unless K_b is smaller than about 10^{-12} M, the conjugate acid of a weak base is also weak.

The interrelated equilibria among an acid, its conjugate base, and water allow us to express K_{eq} for three additional equilibria once K_a is known.

1. A salt of a weak acid, for example NaA, generates A^- anions in aqueous solution. The A^- anion is a weak base with a proton transfer equilibrium described by K_b:

$$A^- + H_2O \rightleftarrows HA + OH^- \qquad K_b = \frac{K_w}{K_a}$$

2. When a solution of a strong base is added to a solution of a weak acid, hydroxide ions accept protons from HA:

$$OH^- + HA \rightleftarrows H_2O + A^- \qquad K_{eq} = \frac{1}{K_b} = \frac{K_a}{K_w} >> 1$$

Because $K_b >> 1$, the equilibrium constant for this reaction is much larger than one, and this reaction goes nearly to completion.

3. When a solution of a strong acid is added to a salt solution, hydronium ions transfer protons to A^- anions:

$$H_3O^+ + A^- \rightleftarrows H_2O + HA \qquad K_{eq} = \frac{1}{K_a} >> 1$$

Because $K_a >> 1$, the equilibrium constant for this reaction is much larger than one, and this reaction also goes nearly to completion.

SECTION EXERCISES

16.3.1 A 4.8×10^{-2} M aqueous solution of hypochlorous acid (HClO) has pH = 4.42. Compute K_a for this acid.

16.3.2 Draw a molecular picture showing the proton-transfer equilibrium established in an aqueous solution of HClO. Identify the conjugate base of HClO.

16.3.3 Calculate pK_b for hypochlorite anions.

16.4 ACIDS AND BASES

Why is H_2CO_3 a weak acid, H_2O both a weak acid and a weak base, and OH^- a strong base? Electron configurations determine whether a chemical substance is a proton donor, a proton acceptor, or neither. Proton donors must contain polar H—X bonds, whereas proton acceptors must contain lone pairs of electrons that can form H—X bonds.

ACIDS

A proton donor must contain at least one hydrogen atom. Moreover, because an acid donates hydrogen as an H^+ ion, it must have a *polar* H—*X* bond. Both a water molecule and a hydronium ion have a polar O—H bond, so both are acids. Of the many other compounds that have polar H—*X* bonds, most fall into one of three categories:

1. **Binary acids** contain hydrogen atoms and Group VI or Group VII elements. The strong acids HCl and HBr are of this type, and HF, H_2O, H_2S, and H_2Se are examples of weak binary acids.
2. **Oxy acids** contain inner atoms bonded to OH groups and O atoms. The inner atom is usually but not always a nonmetal. Strong oxy acids include H_2SO_4 and HNO_3, and HNO_2, H_3PO_4, and H_2CO_3 are weak oxy acids.
3. **Carboxylic acids** contain the carboxyl group, $-CO_2H$. All carboxylic acids are weak. Examples include CH_3CO_2H (acetic acid), $C_6H_5CO_2H$ (benzoic acid), and HCO_2H (formic acid). As Box 16-1 on pp. 780-781 describes, carboxylic acids are present in many foods.

Figure 16-6 highlights the common features of these three types of acidic molecules, and Table 16-2 is a representative list of weak acids and their equilibrium constants. A more comprehensive table appears in Appendix G.

POLYPROTIC ACIDS

A molecule that has two acidic hydrogen atoms is diprotic, whereas one that has three acidic hydrogen atoms is triprotic.

An acid that contains more than one acidic hydrogen atom is called a **polyprotic acid.** Sulfuric acid (H_2SO_4) and oxalic acid ($H_2C_2O_4$) are two common examples; each has two acidic hydrogens. The formulas and structures of these acids are shown in Figure 16-7. Table 16-3 lists other examples of polyprotic acids.

TABLE 16-2 REPRESENTATIVE WEAK ACIDS

pK_a	FORMULA	NAME	TYPE*	BASE	pK_b
3.35	HNO_2	Nitrous acid	O	NO_2^-	10.65
3.45	HF	Hydrofluoric acid	B	F^-	10.55
3.74	HCO_2H	Formic acid	C	HCO_2^-	10.26
4.19	$C_6H_5CO_2H$	Benzoic acid	C	$C_6H_5CO_2^-$	9.81
4.75	CH_3CO_2H	Acetic acid	C	$CH_3CO_2^-$	9.25
7.05	H_2S	Hydrosulfuric acid	B	HS^-	6.95
7.52	HClO	Hypochlorous acid	O	ClO^-	6.48
9.14	H_3BO_3	Boric acid	O	$H_2BO_3^-$	4.86
9.31	HCN	Hydrocyanic acid	—	CN^-	4.69

*B, Binary acid; C, carboxylic acid; O, oxy acid.

TABLE 16-3 K_a VALUES OF REPRESENTATIVE POLYPROTIC ACIDS

NAME	FORMULA	K_{a1} (M)	K_{a2} (M)
Sulfuric acid	H_2SO_4	Strong	1.2×10^{-2}
Oxalic acid	$(CO_2H)_2$	5.9×10^{-2}	6.4×10^{-5}
Sulfurous acid	H_2SO_3	1.7×10^{-2}	6.2×10^{-8}
Phosphoric acid	H_3PO_4	7.5×10^{-3}	6.2×10^{-8}
(Triprotic: $K_{a3} = 4.8 \times 10^{-13}$ M)			
Phthalic acid	$C_6H_4(CO_2H)_2$	1.3×10^{-3}	3.9×10^{-6}
Carbonic acid	H_2CO_3	4.3×10^{-7}	5.6×10^{-11}

Binary acids:

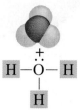

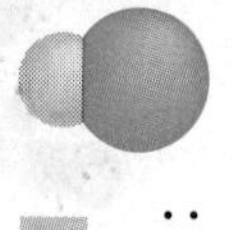

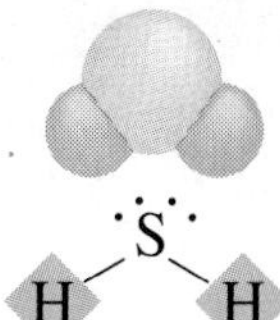

Oxy acids:

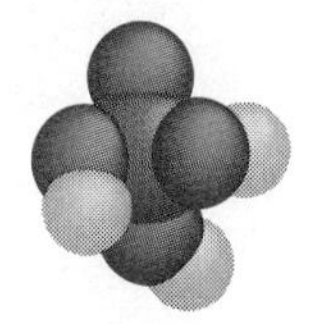

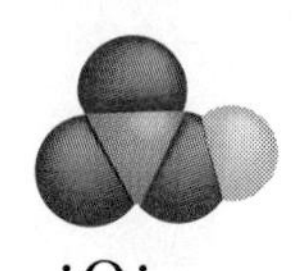

FIGURE 16-6

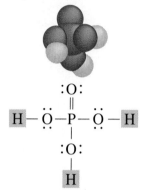

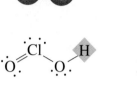

Lewis structures and space-filling models of some examples of the three main classes of acids. Acidic hydrogens are highlighted. Notice that hydrogen atoms bonded to carbon are *not* acidic. Carbon-hydrogen bonds are not polar enough for proton transfer to occur easily.

Carboxylic acids:

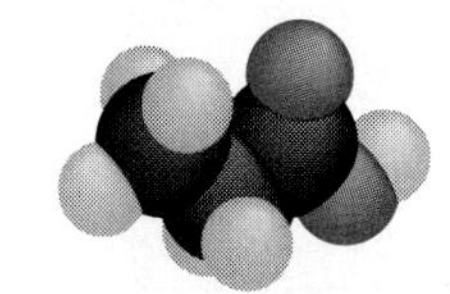

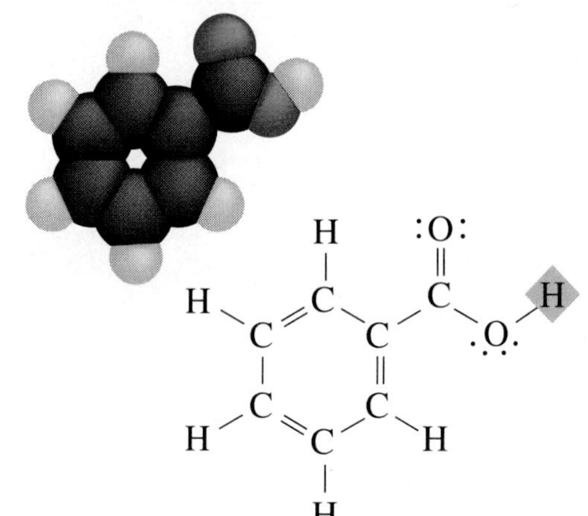

FIGURE 16-7

Lewis structures and space-filling models of sulfuric acid and oxalic acid, two representative examples of polyprotic acids, and their conjugate base species.

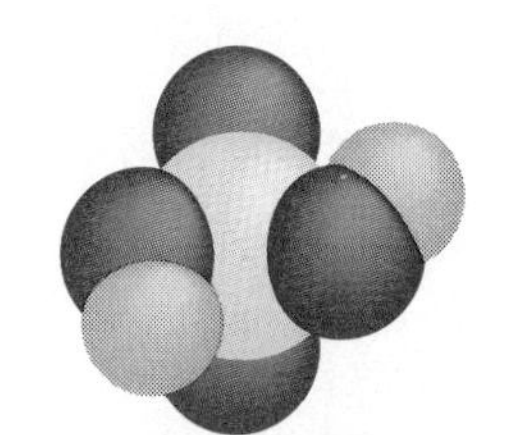

Sulfuric acid
H_2SO_4

Hydrogen sulfate anion
HSO_4^-

Sulfate anion
SO_4^{2-}

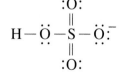

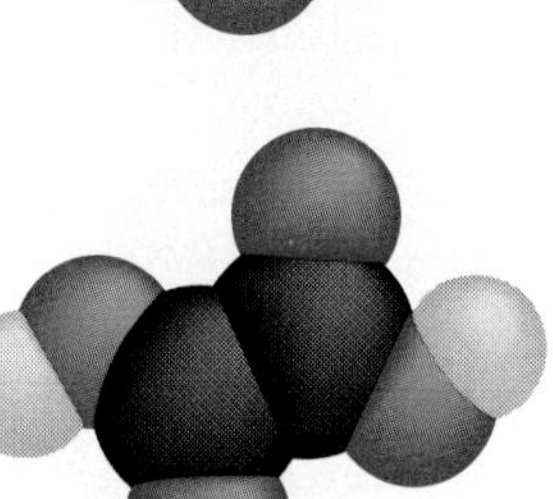

Oxalic acid
HO_2CCO_2H

Hydrogenoxalate anion
$HO_2CCO_2^-$

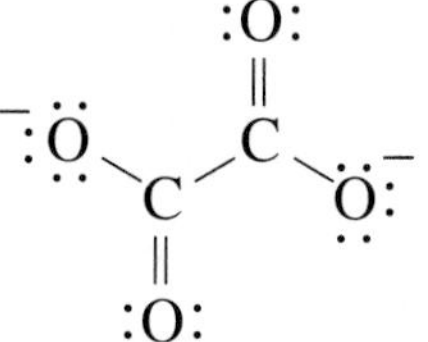

Oxalate anion
$^-O_2CCO_2^-$

BOX 16-1

CARBOXYLIC ACIDS IN FOODS

We can write the chemical formula for a general carboxylic acid as RCO_2H, where "R" represents a carbon atom bonded to a collection of atoms. Two examples appear in Figure 16-6. Propionic acid, $CH_3CH_2CO_2H$, has $R = CH_3CH_2—$, whereas the other carboxylic acid shown in the figure, benzoic acid, has a more elaborate R group whose chemical formula is C_6H_5. Regardless of the size and shape of R, the CO_2H fragment etains its character as a weak acid. Carboxylic acids are important in many biochemical processes and are found in many foods.

Acidic substances taste sour, perhaps because they donate protons to carboxylate anions ($—CO_2^-$) in the proteins of the taste buds. Whatever the exact mechanism, the sour taste of vinegar and lemon juice and the tartness of Granny Smith apples arise from carboxylic acids.

Vinegar is a solution of acetic acid (CH_3CO_2H) in water, typically containing about 5% by mass of the acid and a pH of 2.4. It can be produced from sugar-containing foods by a combination of fermentation and oxidation, which breaks down glucose molecules into ethanol and then converts ethanol to acetic acid. Thus wine vinegar, cider vinegar, and rice vinegar all are sour but with slightly different flavors because of different trace ingredients. The word *vinegar* comes from the French term for "sour wine"; indeed, poor or spoiled wine tastes sour because some of its ethanol has become acetic acid.

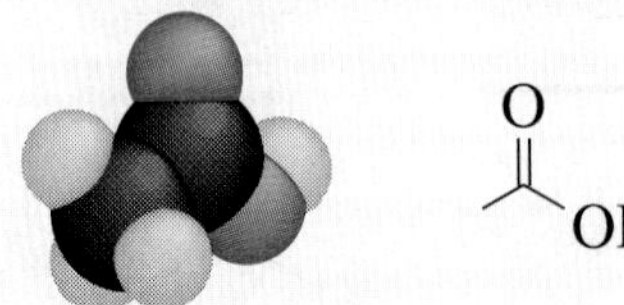

Lemons, whose juice has a pH of 2.0, probably is the most acidic food. The acidity of lemons is caused by citric acid, a polyprotic acid with three carboxylic acid groups. Lemons can contain as much as 3% by mass citric acid. Citric acid is prevalent in all citrus fruits, berries, pineapples, pears, and tomatoes.

Citric acid

Other fruits have a milder tartness that comes from malic acid. This diprotic carboxylic acid occurs in apples, cherries, apricots, and bananas. Peaches contain roughly equal amounts of malic and citric acid, and most fruits contain some amounts of both acids.

Malic acid

Grapes contain tartaric acid, whose structure and chemical formula differ from malic acid only by the presence of one additional oxygen atom. When grapes are fermented to make wine, their sugar is largely converted into ethanol. Tartaric acid remains unchanged, however, and small amounts of more complex acids such as galactouronic acid add to the tartness of the wine. A wine is "sweet" if its residual sugar content masks the sour taste of these residual acids and "dry" if its residual sugar content is less than about 1%.

Galactouronic acid

Tartaric acid

Vegetables also contain carboxylic acids that contribute to their flavors. For example, oxalic acid is prevalent in spinach and rhubarb. Raw rhubarb is poisonous, and folklore holds that its toxicity is caused by oxalic acid; however, raw spinach can be safely eaten despite its equally high content of this acid.

Oxalic acid

Asparagus contains several carboxylic acids. Its unmistakable odor is caused by the compound that forms from a sulfur-containing carboxylic acid, asparagusic acid, as asparagus is cooked.

CO_2H — Degrades to →

S—S S—S

Asparagusic acid

When milk sours, bacteria have fed on its lactose (milk sugar) and produced lactic acid. Under more carefully controlled conditions, this process produces yogurt. The proper combination of yeast and bacteria acts on flour to form just enough lactic acid and acetic acid to give sourdough bread its distinctive tang.

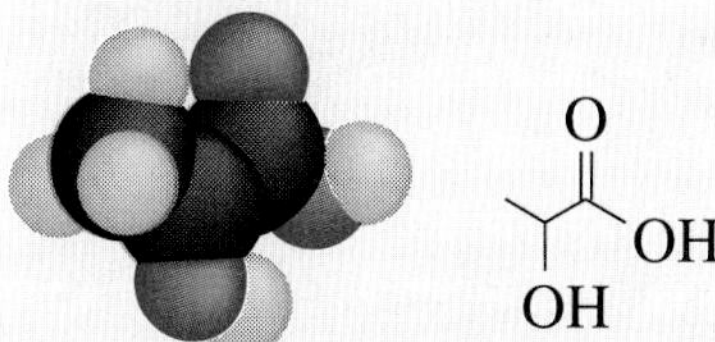

Our list of carboxylic acids in foods has thus far focused on acids that contain six or fewer carbon atoms. These are the acids responsible for sour taste. Carboxylic acids containing chains of 16 or more carbon atoms are equally important components of foods. These long-chain acids are the fatty acids, which are responsible for much of the energy content of nuts, seeds, vegetable oils, and animal fats.

The simplest structure for a fatty acid is a long chain of singly-bonded carbon atoms with a carboxyl group at one end. Stearic acid ($C_{17}H_{35}CO_2H$) is one of the most prevalent fatty acids of this type. It is a major constituent of almost all animal and vegetable fats. When a fatty acid contains one or more carbon-carbon double bonds, it is said to be *unsaturated* because it contains fewer hydrogen atoms than the saturated compound with the same number of carbon atoms. Unsaturated fatty acids are considered to be more healthful than their saturated cousins. Oleic acid ($C_{17}H_{33}CO_2H$) has the structure of stearic acid except for one carbon-carbon double bond. This acid is the principal fatty acid in olive oil and is also found in pork, lamb, and poultry fat. Linoleic acid ($C_{17}H_{31}CO_2H$), which contains two double bonds, is the principal fatty acid in corn oil (see below).

Many other carboxylic acids occur in foods. In addition, carboxylic acids are produced and consumed during the metabolic processes by which the body extracts chemical energy from carbohydrates. Our survey has highlighted just a few of these essential biochemical materials.

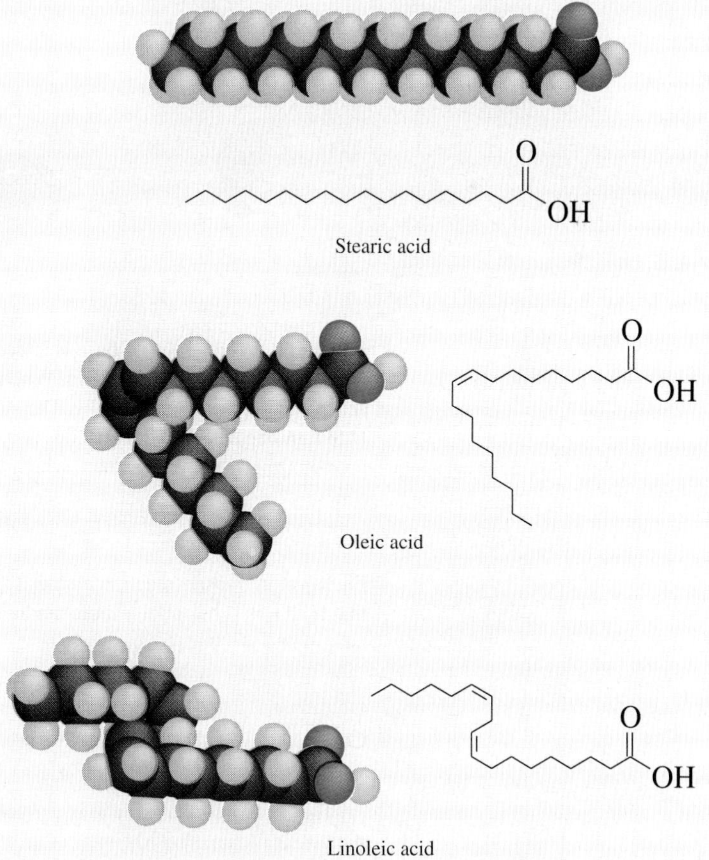

When a proton is removed from a neutral polyprotic acid molecule, the remainder of the molecule carries a negative charge that exerts a coulombic attraction on the remaining protons. Thus the K_a value for the second proton transfer is smaller than K_a for the first. For small polyprotic acids such as the ones listed in Table 16-3, K_a decreases by three to five orders of magnitude for each successive proton transfer. The practical outcome of this decreasing acidity is that when a base is added to a solution that contains both a neutral polyprotic acid and its anion, the base accepts acidic protons preferentially from the neutral acid. Only after the neutral acid has been consumed does the anionic species participate significantly in proton transfer. Sample Problem 16-11 provides a molecular illustration of this feature.

SAMPLE PROBLEM 16-11 MOLECULAR VIEW OF A POLYPROTIC ACID

The following drawing shows a molecular view of a very small region of an aqueous solution of sulfurous acid. For clarity, water molecules are not shown. Redraw this molecular picture to show the solution (a) after four hydroxide ions enter the region and (b) after eight hydroxide ions enter the region. (Omit water molecules and spectator ions to keep the picture simple.)

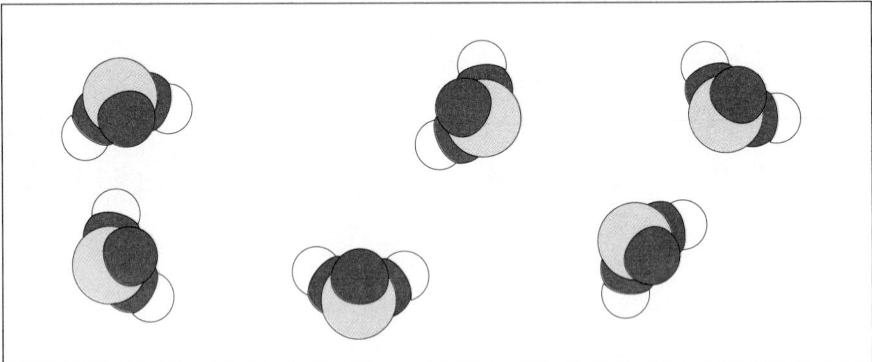

METHOD: When a strong base is added to a weak acid, hydroxide ions remove protons from the molecules of weak acid. When more than one acidic species is present, the stronger acid loses protons preferentially. The sulfurous acid solution contains water molecules and H_2SO_3 molecules as major species. Any hydroxide ions that enter the solution remove protons from the strongest acid, which is H_2SO_3:

$$H_2SO_{3\,(aq)} + OH^-_{(aq)} \rightleftarrows HSO_3^-{}_{(aq)} + H_2O_{(l)}$$

Each proton transfer reaction creates HSO_3^-, which is itself a weak acid. The K_a values show that H_2SO_3 is substantially more acidic than HSO_3^-:

H_2SO_3	HSO_3^-
$K_a = 1.7 \times 10^{-2}$ M	$K_a = 6.2 \times 10^{-8}$ M

Consequently, hydroxide ions react preferentially with H_2SO_3. Any added OH^- ions react with H_2SO_3 until all the sulfurous acid molecules have been consumed.

(a) The first four hydroxide ions convert four H_2SO_3 molecules into HSO_3^- ions. Thus the molecular picture should contain four HSO_3^- anions and two H_2SO_3 molecules.

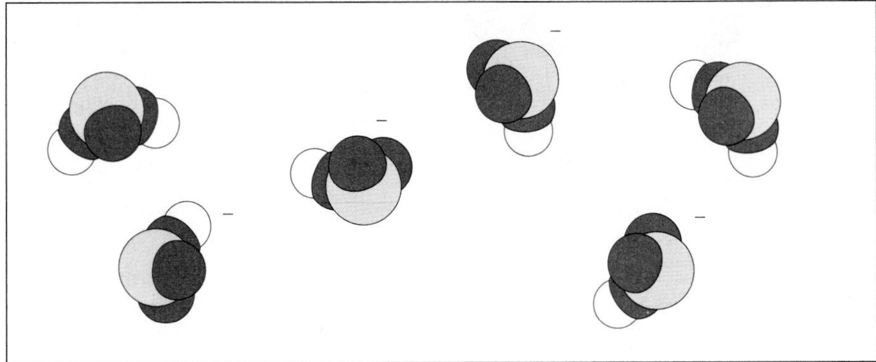

(b) When eight OH^- ions are added, the first six consume all the H_2SO_3 molecules. The remaining two OH^- ions react with the weaker acid, HSO_3^-:

$$HSO_3^-{}_{(aq)} + OH^-{}_{(aq)} \rightleftarrows SO_3^{2-}{}_{(aq)} + H_2O_{(l)}$$

This reaction goes virtually to completion, so at equilibrium, this system contains four HSO_3^- and two SO_3^{2-}.

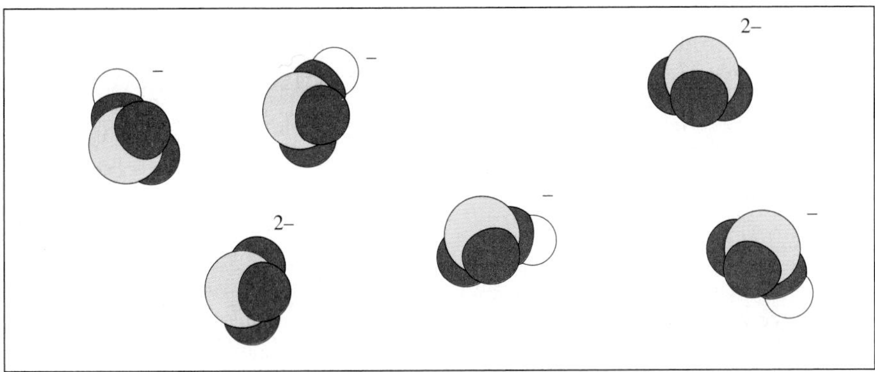

Although we have left them out for the sake of clarity, keep in mind that each proton-transfer reaction also produces a water molecule, which joins the immense pool of water molecules already present.

BASES

A base is a proton acceptor, so it must contain at least one lone pair of electrons that can bond with a proton. We can group bases into three main categories:

1. Water and the hydroxide ion contain an oxygen atom with lone pairs of electrons that can bond to protons.
2. Ammonia and the amines contain a nitrogen atom with a lone pair of electrons that can bond to a proton.
3. The conjugate base of any weak acid contains a lone pair of electrons that can bond to a proton.

Except for water, all the common neutral bases are amines. Representative examples are listed in Table 16-4, and representative structures appear in Figure 16-8.

Amines, introduced in Chapter 11, are derivatives of ammonia in which one or more hydrogen atoms have been replaced by some other group of atoms.

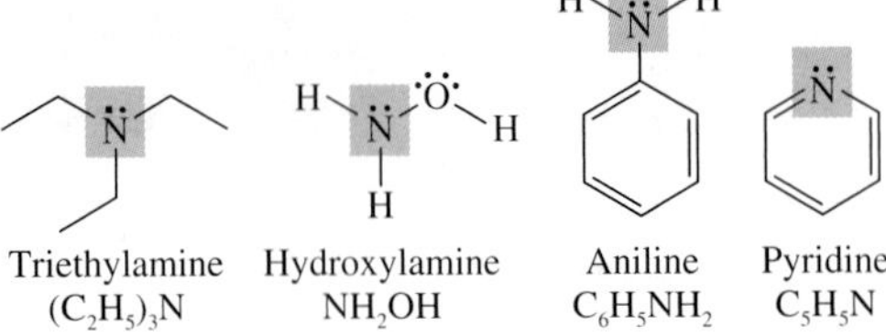

FIGURE 16-8
Line structures of some nitrogen-containing bases. Note the presence of nitrogen atoms with lone pairs of electrons.

Table 16-4 introduces a fourth general category of weak *acids*, the conjugate acids of amines. All these acids are cations rather than neutral molecules.

TABLE 16-4 REPRESENTATIVE WEAK BASES

pK_b	FORMULA	NAME	CONJUGATE ACID	pK_a
3.27	$(CH_3)_2NH$	Dimethylamine	$(CH_3)_2NH_2^+$	10.73
3.43	CH_3NH_2	Methylamine	$CH_3NH_3^+$	10.57
4.19	$(CH_3)_3N$	Trimethylamine	$(CH_3)_3NH^+$	9.81
4.75	NH_3	Ammonia	NH_4^+	9.25
7.96	NH_2OH	Hydroxylamine	NH_3OH^+	6.04
8.74	C_5H_5N	Pyridine	$C_5H_5NH^+$	5.26
9.37	$C_6H_5NH_2$	Aniline	$C_6H_5NH_3^+$	4.63

We can determine the acid-base properties of a molecule from its structure and a knowledge of the categories of acids and bases. Sample Problem 16-12 provides an example, and Box 16-2 describes the features of some naturally occurring weak bases.

SAMPLE PROBLEM 16-12 RECOGNIZING ACIDS AND BASES

Glycine has the formula $H_2NCH_2CO_2H$. Determine the acid-base characteristics of this compound.

METHOD: The Lewis structure of glycine reveals any functional groups that result in acidic and/or basic properties.

Use the principles developed in Chapter 8 to construct the Lewis structure from the molecular formula:

H :O:
H–N–C–C–O–H
H H

Glycine contains a carboxyl group, CO_2H, at one end and an amino group, NH_2, at the other. Consequently, the molecule has the properties of both acids and bases. Glycine is one of the amino acids used in the construction of proteins.

BOX 16-2

ALKALOIDS

For thousands of years, humans have used plants to make medicines and drugs. Many of the biologically active ingredients in plant extracts are alkaloids. All alkaloids contain at least one nitrogen atom with a lone pair of electrons, so they are weak bases.

Alkaloids can have profound physiological properties. For example, Socrates was put to death with an extract of hemlock, whose principal toxin is an alkaloid, coniine.

Although coniine is a deadly poison, other alkaloids are notorious narcotics. Morphine, which occurs naturally in poppies, was first isolated in pure form in 1805 and was the first alkaloid to be characterized. This substance is responsible for the narcotic effects of opium and is also the starting material for the synthesis of codeine and heroin. Three other well-known narcotic alkaloids are nicotine, mescaline, and cocaine.

Many alkaloids, including morphine, are important in modern medicine. Other examples are quinine, used to treat malaria, and atropine, used to treat Parkinson's disease and in eye drops to dilate the pupils.

Because of their basic properties, alkaloids were among the first natural substances that early chemists extracted and purified. When treated with aqueous strong acid, alkaloids accept protons to produce their positively charged conjugate acids. Even though the alkaloids are weak bases, the acid strength of hydronium ions drives this reaction nearly to completion. The cations are water soluble, so they enter the aqueous medium while the rest of the plant materials remain insoluble.

$$\text{Alkaloid}_{(s)} + H_3O^+_{(aq)} \rightarrow \text{Alkaloid H}^+_{(aq)} + H_2O_{(l)}$$

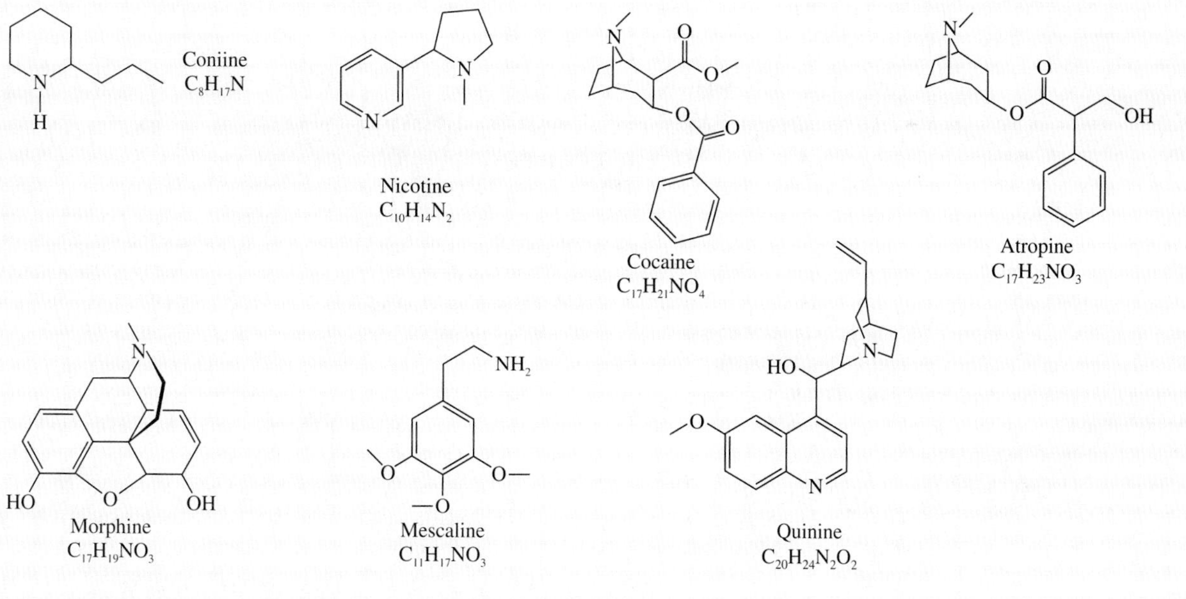

Coniine $C_8H_{17}N$

Nicotine $C_{10}H_{14}N_2$

Cocaine $C_{17}H_{21}NO_4$

Atropine $C_{17}H_{23}NO_3$

Morphine $C_{17}H_{19}NO_3$

Mescaline $C_{11}H_{17}NO_3$

Quinine $C_{20}H_{24}N_2O_2$

BASIC AND ACIDIC SALTS

We have shown that any neutral weak acid has an anion that is a weak base. In the solid state, these anions associate with various metal cations to form salts. Thus a salt of a weak acid dissolves in water to produce a basic solution. Sample Problem 16-13 shows how to deal quantitatively with the resulting equilibrium.

SAMPLE PROBLEM 16-13 SALT OF A WEAK ACID

Sodium hypochlorite (NaOCl) is the active ingredient in commercial laundry bleach. Typically, bleach contains 5% of this salt by mass, which is a 0.67 M solution. Determine the concentrations of all species and compute the pH of laundry bleach.

METHOD: First, determine what major species are present in the solution and then identify their acid-base properties. After that, set up a concentration table and solve the equilibrium constant expression to find the desired concentrations.

Sodium hypochlorite is a salt, so its aqueous solution contains the ionic species Na^+ and OCl^-. Thus the major species in solution are Na^+, OCl^-, and H_2O.

Water is both a proton donor and a proton acceptor. The sodium ion is neither an acid nor a base, so it is a spectator ion in this solution. Knowing that HOCl is a weak oxy acid, we recognize that OCl^- is its conjugate base. The hypochlorite ion accepts a proton from a water molecule:

$$H_2O + OCl^- \rightleftharpoons HOCl + OH^- \qquad K_{eq} = K_b$$

We can determine K_b for OCl^- from the information given in Table 16-2:

$$pK_b\,(OCl^-) = 6.48 \qquad K_b = 10^{-pK_b} = 3.3 \times 10^{-7}\text{ M}$$

This is the starting point for the calculations. The next step is to set up a concentration table for the equilibrium. The initial concentration of OCl^- is stated in the problem, and we let $\boldsymbol{x}$ represent the change in concentration of HOCl.

Species (reaction)	$H_2O + OCl^-$ $\rightleftharpoons$	$HOCl$ +	OH^-
Initial concentration, M	0.67	0	0
Change in concentration, M	$-x$	x	x
Equilibrium concentration, M	$0.67 - x$	x	x

Substitute into the equilibrium constant expression and solve:

$$K_b = \frac{[HOCl]_{eq}}{[OCl^-]_{eq}} = \frac{(x)\,(x)}{(0.67 - x)} = 3.3 \times 10^{-7}\text{ M}$$

This equality could be solved using the quadratic equation, but because the initial concentration of OCl^- is very large compared with K_b, an approximation can simplify the calculation. The variable $\boldsymbol{x}$ represents the concentration of a product in a reaction with an equilibrium constant that is small relative to the initial concentration, so we expect the value of $\boldsymbol{x}$ to be much smaller than 0.67:

$$0.67 - x \cong 0.67 \qquad 3.3 \times 10^{-7}\text{ M} \cong \frac{x^2}{0.67}$$

$$x^2 \cong 2.21 \times 10^{-7}\text{ M}^2 \qquad \textit{from which} \qquad x \cong 4.7 \times 10^{-4}\text{ M}$$

This value of $\boldsymbol{x}$ is three orders of magnitude smaller than 0.67 M, so the approximation is valid. The value of $\boldsymbol{x}$ provides three of the concentrations we need:

$$[OCl^-] = 0.67 - x = 0.67\text{ M} - 4.7 \times 10^{-4}\text{ M} = 0.67\text{ M}$$

$$[HOCl] = x = 4.7 \times 10^{-4}\text{ M}$$

$$[OH^-] = x = 4.7 \times 10^{-4}\text{ M}$$

The sodium ion concentration is simply equal to the initial concentration of the salt: $[Na^+] = 0.67$ M.

To find $[H_3O^+]$, we invoke the water equilibrium and use the expression for K_w:

$$[H_3O^+] = \frac{K_w}{[OH^-]} = \frac{1.00 \times 10^{-14}\text{ M}^2}{4.7 \times 10^{-4}\text{ M}} = 2.1 \times 10^{-11}\text{ M}$$

Finally, use $[H_3O^+]$ to determine the pH of the bleach solution:

$$pH = -\log [H_3O^+] = -\log (2.1 \times 10^{-11}) = 10.68$$

The ammonium cation is the conjugate *acid* of ammonia. It combines with various anions to form salts. When ammonium salts dissolve in water, NH_4^+ ions transfer protons to H_2O molecules, generating H_3O^+ and making the solution slightly acidic:

$$NH_4^+{}_{(aq)} + H_2O_{(l)} \rightleftarrows NH_{3\,(aq)} + H_3O^+{}_{(aq)}$$

The conjugate acids of amines also form acidic salts. Pyridinium chloride, which has important pharmaceutical uses, is the subject of Sample Problem 16-14.

SAMPLE PROBLEM 16-14 SALT OF A WEAK BASE

What are the important acid-base equilibria in an aqueous solution of pyridinium chloride, (C_5H_5NHCl)? What are the values of their equilibrium constants?

METHOD: The method is the same as always. Identify the major species and then list the equilibria in which they participate. Values for equilibrium constants can be found in tables in this chapter and Appendix G.

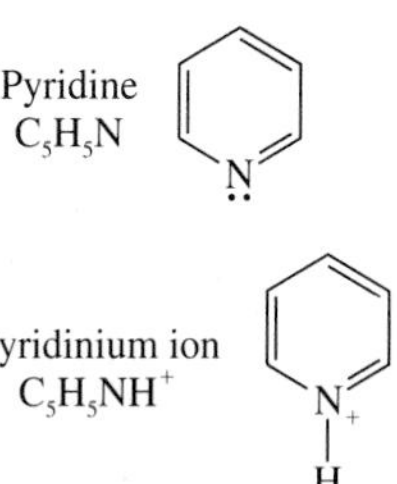

Pyridinium chloride is a salt that generates ions in solution. The major species are the pyridinium cation ($C_5H_5NH^+$), chloride anion, and water. From the formula, we recognize the pyridinium cation as the conjugate acid of the weak base, pyridine.

The chloride anion is the conjugate base of a strong acid, so we can consider Cl^- as a spectator ion. There are two acid-base equilibria with major species as reactants:

$$H_2O + C_5H_5NH^+ \rightleftarrows H_3O^+ + C_5H_5N \qquad K_a$$

$$H_2O + H_2O \rightleftarrows H_3O^+ + OH^- \qquad K_w = 1.00 \times 10^{-14}\ M^2$$

The pK_a of pyridinium cation, listed in Table 16-4, allows us to calculate K_a:

$$pK_a\ (C_5H_5NH^+) = 5.26 \qquad K_a = 10^{-pK_a} = 10^{-5.26} = 5.5 \times 10^{-6}\ M$$

This value is much greater than the value of K_w, so the pH of a pyridinium chloride solution is determined by the weak acid.

SECTION EXERCISES

16.4.1 Classify each of the following substances as a weak acid, strong acid, weak base, strong base, both a weak acid and a weak base, or neither an acid nor a base: (a) $HClO_4$; (b) $NaClO_4$; (c) NaOH; (d) CH_3OH; (e) $C_3H_7CO_2H$; and (f) $HSCH_2CH(NH_2)CO_2H$.

16.4.2 Determine the concentrations of all species present in a 0.35 M solution of KCN. (Potassium cyanide is a deadly poison.)

16.4.3 Ammonium acetate ($NH_4CH_3CO_2$) forms nearly neutral aqueous solutions. Determine the proton-transfer equilibria present in these solutions. What feature of these equilibria accounts for the nearly neutral pH of the solutions?

16.5 BUFFER SOLUTIONS

Blood contains a variety of acids and bases that maintain the pH very close to 7.4 at all times. Close control of blood pH is necessary because death results if the pH of human blood drops below 7.0 or rises above 7.8. This narrow pH range corresponds to only a fivefold change in the concentration of hydronium ion. Chemical equilibria work in the blood to hold the pH within this narrow window. Close control of pH is achieved by the presence of both an acid and its conjugate base as major species. A solution that contains an acid and its conjugate base as major species is called a **buffer solution** because it protects, or buffers, the solution against pH variations.

THE NATURE OF BUFFER SOLUTIONS

In an aqueous solution of a weak acid, water and the acid are the only major species. A solution of acetic acid contains many molecules of CH_3CO_2H but relatively few acetate anions. Likewise, in a solution of a weak base, water and the base are major species, but the conjugate acid is not. Thus a solution of sodium acetate contains the acetate anion as a major species but minor amounts of acetic acid. However, mixing a solution of acetic acid with a solution of sodium acetate produces a solution in which *both* acetic acid and acetate anions are major species.

A buffer solution is an aqueous solution that contains both members of an acid-base conjugate pair as major species.

Sample Problem 16-15 describes one common buffer solution.

SAMPLE PROBLEM 16-15 CONCENTRATIONS IN A BUFFER SOLUTION

A solution contains 0.125 mol of solid sodium acetate dissolved in 1.00 L of 0.250 M acetic acid. Determine the concentrations of hydronium ions, acetate ions, and acetic acid.

METHOD: Work this equilibrium problem following the standard procedure: Determine the species, identify equilibria, set up a concentration table, and calculate the results.

When a salt dissolves in a solution, the new solution contains the major species present in the original solution plus those generated by the salt. The original solution contains water and acetic acid molecules. Sodium acetate dissolves to produce sodium ions and acetate ions. Thus the buffer solution has four major species: H_2O, Na^+, $CH_3CO_2^-$, and CH_3CO_2H.

Acetic acid is a weak acid, acetate anion is a weak base, water can act as either an acid or a base, and Na^+ is a spectator ion. These species are reactants in three acid-base equilibria:

$$CH_3CO_2H_{(aq)} + H_2O_{(l)} \rightleftarrows CH_3CO^-_{(aq)} + H_3O^+_{(aq)} \qquad K_a = 1.8 \times 10^{-5}\ M$$

$$CH_3CO_2^-{}_{(aq)} + H_2O_{(l)} \rightleftarrows CH_3CO_2H_{(aq)} + OH^-_{(aq)} \qquad K_b = \frac{K_w}{K_a} = 5.6 \times 10^{-10}\ M$$

$$H_2O_{(l)} + H_2O_{(l)} \rightleftarrows H_3O^+_{(aq)} + OH^-_{(aq)} \qquad K_w = 1.00 \times 10^{-14}\ M^2$$

Among these equilibria, the first has the largest K_{eq}, so it will generate the largest changes from initial concentrations. We can set up a concentration table for this equilibrium.

Species (reaction)	$H_2O + CH_3CO_2H \rightleftarrows$	$CH_3CO_2^- +$	H_3O^+
Initial concentration, M	0.250	0.125	0
Change in concentration, M	$-x$	$+x$	$+x$
Concentration at completion, M	$0.250 - x$	$0.125 + x$	x

Because the initial concentrations are much larger than K_{eq}, we make the approximation that x is negligible compared with the initial concentrations:

$$0.250 - x \cong 0.250 \qquad 0.125 + x \cong 0.125$$

To determine the concentration of hydronium ions, rearrange the expression for K_a and substitute these concentrations:

$$\frac{[H_3O^+]_{eq}[CH_3CO_2^-]_{eq}}{[CH_3CO_2H]_{eq}} = K_a \qquad [H_3O^+]_{eq} = \frac{K_a[CH_3CO_2H]_{eq}}{[CH_3CO_2^-]_{eq}}$$

$$[H_3O^+]_{eq} = x = \frac{(1.8 \times 10^{-5}\ M)(0.250\ M)}{0.125\ M} = 3.6 \times 10^{-5}\ M$$

Notice that this concentration is much smaller than those of acetic acid and acetate, verifying our approximation:

$$[CH_3CO_2H]_{eq} = 0.250\ M \qquad [CH_3CO_2^-]_{eq} = 0.125\ M$$

The analysis carried out in Sample Problem 16-15 reveals one of the key features of buffer solutions: the *equilibrium* concentrations of the weak acid *and* its conjugate base are essentially the same as their *initial* concentrations.

THE MOLECULAR VIEW OF A BUFFER SOLUTION

The purpose of a buffer solution is to maintain the pH within a very narrow range. To see how this is accomplished, we must examine the reactions that occur when H_3O^+ or OH^- is added to a buffer solution. Consider what happens when a small amount of hydroxide ion is added to the acetic acid–acetate buffer solution described in Sample Problem 16-15. The hydroxide ion is the strongest aqueous base and acetic acid is a weak acid, so proton transfer from CH_3CO_2H to OH^- goes essentially to completion:

OH⁻ HA Collision and proton transfer H_2O A^-

$$OH^- + CH_3CO_2H \rightleftharpoons H_2O + CH_3CO_2^- \qquad K_{eq} = \frac{1}{K_b} = 1.8 \times 10^9\ M^{-1}$$

As long as the buffer solution contains both acetic acid and acetate as major species, a small amount of hydroxide ion added to the solution reacts virtually completely. Sample Problem 16-16 illustrates this point at the molecular level.

SAMPLE PROBLEM 16-16 MOLECULAR PICTURE OF A BUFFER SOLUTION

The following drawing represents a portion of the buffer solution described in Sample Problem 16-15. (Water molecules of the solvent and sodium spectator ions have been omitted for clarity.)

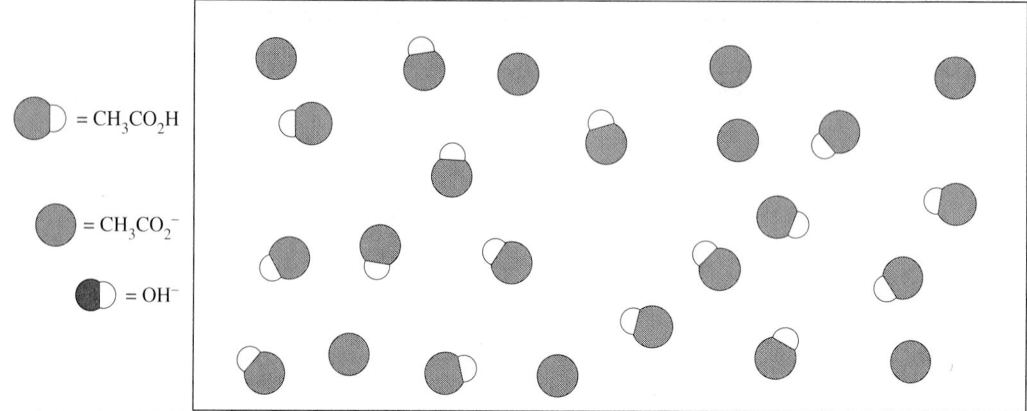

Suppose that added base contributes two hydroxide ions to this picture. Redraw the figure as it would appear at equilibrium.

METHOD: Acetic acid molecules in the buffer solution react with hydroxide ions to make acetate anions and water:

$$OH^- + CH_3CO_2H \rightleftharpoons H_2O + CH_3CO_2^- \qquad K_{eq} = \frac{1}{K_b} = 1.8 \times 10^9\ M^{-1}$$

Provided that more acetic acid molecules exist in the solution than the amount of added hydroxide, the proton-transfer reaction goes virtually to completion. Acetic acid molecules change into acetate anions as they "mop up" added hydroxide.

We can analyze this system by taking an inventory of the species present under initial conditions and completing a concentration table. For most calculations, water is omitted from the concentration table, but in this case, we include the H_2O molecules formed in the proton-transfer reactions so that our final drawing can include all species involved in the buffer chemistry.

Species	OH^-	+ CH_3CO_2H	$\rightarrow H_2O$	+ $CH_3CO_2^-$
Initial number	2	16	Many	8
Change in number	−2	−2	+2	+2
Number at completion	0	14	Many + 2	10

Finally, we redraw the molecular picture, showing the proper number of acetic acid molecules, newly formed water molecules, and acetate ions. Once again, only the two water molecules formed in the proton-transfer reaction are included in the figure. You should keep in mind, however, that since water is solvent, it is by far the most abundant component of the solution.

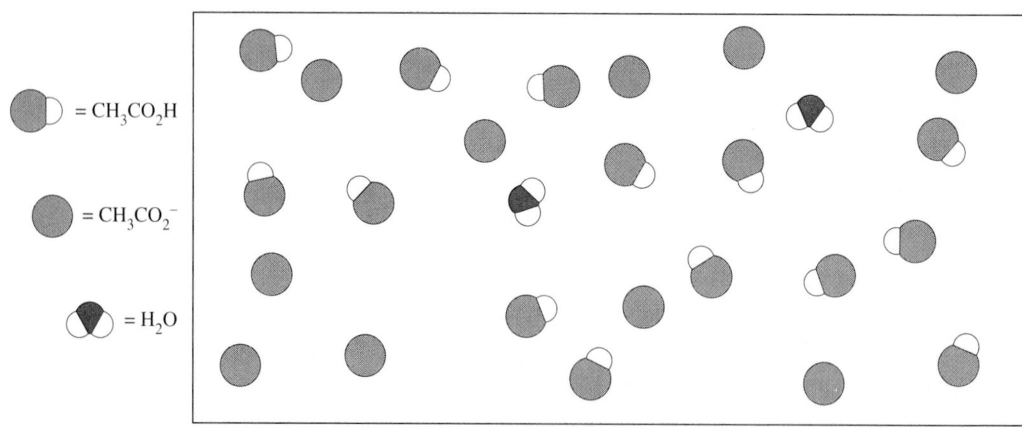

As before, this proton-transfer reaction has a large equilibrium constant, so the neutralization reaction goes almost to completion. The buffer system "mops up" small amounts of hydroxide ions, but the acid and its conjugate base remain major species.

The same molecular reasoning shows that a buffer solution can absorb added hydronium ions. Because the hydronium ion is the strongest aqueous acid and acetate is a weak base, we expect the proton-transfer reaction to go essentially to completion, and the equilibrium constant for the reaction verifies this expectation:

$$H_3O^+ + CH_3CO_2^- \rightleftharpoons H_2O + CH_3CO_2H \qquad K_{eq} = \frac{1}{K_a} = 5.6 \times 10^4\ M^{-1}$$

THE BUFFER EQUATION

In a buffer solution, both members of a conjugate acid-base pair are present as major species. This feature simplifies calculations in the analysis of a buffer solution. To show this, we begin by expressing the equilibrium constant expression in logarithmic form:

$$K_a = \frac{[H_3O^+]_{eq}[A^-]_{eq}}{[HA]_{eq}} \qquad so \qquad \log K_a = \log\left\{\frac{[H_3O^+]_{eq}[A^-]_{eq}}{[HA]_{eq}}\right\}$$

$\log(xy) = \log x + \log y$.

$$\log K_a = \log [H_3O^+]_{eq} + \log\left\{\frac{[A^-]_{eq}}{[HA]_{eq}}\right\}$$

Multiplying both sides of the equation by −1 lets us use pK_a and pH instead of $\log K_a$ and $\log [H_3O^+]$:

$$-\log K_a = -\log [H_3O^+] - \log\left\{\frac{[A^-]_{eq}}{[HA]_{eq}}\right\} \qquad and \qquad pK_a = pH - \log\left\{\frac{[A^-]_{eq}}{[HA]_{eq}}\right\}$$

Now we rearrange this equation to solve for pH:

$$pH = pK_a + \log\left\{\frac{[A^-]_{eq}}{[HA]_{eq}}\right\}$$

In a buffer solution, the *equilibrium* concentrations of both the weak acid and its conjugate base are virtually the same as their *initial* concentrations. Thus instead of using equilibrium concentrations in this equation, we can substitute the initial concentrations to give the **buffer equation:**

$$[A^-]_{eq} \cong [A^-]_{initial} \qquad [HA]_{eq} \cong [HA]_{initial}$$

$$pH = pK_a + \log\left\{\frac{[A^-]_{initial}}{[HA]_{initial}}\right\} \qquad \textbf{(16-5)}$$

The buffer equation is used to calculate the *equilibrium* pH of a buffer solution directly from *initial* concentrations. The approximation is valid as long as the difference between initial concentrations and equilibrium concentrations is negligibly small. As a rule of thumb, the buffer equation can be applied when initial concentrations of HA and A^- differ by less than a factor of 10. Sample Problem 16-17 provides an illustration of the use of the buffer equation.

In honor of the two scientists who first derived it, the buffer equation is often called the Henderson-Hasselbach equation.

SAMPLE PROBLEM 16-17 THE BUFFER EQUATION

Buffer solutions with a pH of about 10 are prepared using sodium carbonate (Na_2CO_3) and sodium hydrogencarbonate ($NaHCO_3$). What is the pH of a solution prepared by dissolving 10.0 g each of these two salts in enough water to make 0.250 L of solution?

METHOD: Our first task is to identify species in solution. Then we must analyze the equilibria that give the solution its buffer properties. Knowing that this solution is a buffer solution, we can use initial concentrations and the buffer equation to calculate the pH.

Both compounds are salts that dissolve in water to give their constituent ions, so the major species in this buffer solution are H_2O, Na^+, HCO_3^-, and CO_3^{2-}.

A buffer solution must contain both a weak acid and its conjugate base. In this solution, HCO_3^- is the weak acid, and CO_3^{2-} is the conjugate base:

$$H_2O_{(l)} + HCO_3^-{}_{(aq)} \rightleftharpoons CO_3^{2-}{}_{(aq)} + H_3O^+{}_{(aq)}$$

In this proton-transfer reaction, the *second* proton of carbonic acid is transferred, so the appropriate equilibrium constant is K_{a2}, which is found in Table 16-3: $K_{a2} = 5.6 \times 10^{-11}$ M, $pK_{a2} = 10.25$.

The initial concentrations are found from the masses and molar masses of the salts and the volume of the solution:

$$[HCO_3^-]_{initial} = \frac{m}{(MM)\ V} = \frac{(10.0\text{ g})}{(84.01\text{ g/mol})(0.250\text{ L})} = 0.476\text{ M}$$

$$[CO_3^{2-}]_{initial} = \frac{m}{(MM)\ V} = \frac{(10.0\text{ g})}{(106.0\text{ g/mol})(0.250\text{ L})} = 0.377\text{ M}$$

Because the initial concentrations of both anions are close in concentration, we can apply the buffer equation:

$$pH = pK_a + \log\left\{\frac{[CO_3^{2-}]_{initial}}{[HCO_3^-]_{initial}}\right\} = 10.25 + \log\left\{\frac{(0.377\text{ M})}{(0.476\text{ M})}\right\}$$

$$pH = 10.25 + (-0.10) = 10.15$$

BUFFER CAPACITY

When small amounts of hydronium or hydroxide ions are added to a buffer solution, pH changes are very small. There is a limit, however, to the amount of protection that a buffer solution can provide. After the buffering agents are consumed, the solution loses its ability to maintain near-constant pH. The **buffer capacity** of a solution is the quantity of added H_3O^+ or OH^- the buffer solution can tolerate without exceeding a specified pH range.

Buffer capacity depends on the concentration of the buffer, the volume of the buffer, and the pH variation that the system can tolerate. A 0.500 M buffer solution has a greater capacity than an equal volume of 0.100 M buffer solution. A liter of 0.100 M buffer solution has a greater capacity than 0.5 L of the same buffer solution. If pH must be controlled to ± 0.05 units, the buffer capacity of a given solution is smaller than if deviations of ± 0.20 units are permissible.

If added hydroxide or hydronium ions exceed the buffer capacity of a solution, the buffer is no longer effective. Sample Problem 16-18 shows a calculation involving buffer capacity.

SAMPLE PROBLEM 16-18 BUFFER CAPACITY

Biochemists and molecular biologists use phosphate buffers because they mimic physiological conditions. A buffer solution that contains $H_2PO_4^-$ as the weak acid and HPO_4^{2-} as the weak base has a pH value very close to 7.0. A biochemist uses 250 mL of a buffer solution that contains 0.225 M HPO_4^{2-} and 0.330 M $H_2PO_4^-$ to isolate an enzyme that is stable in solution only if the pH is held between 6.90 and 7.15. Is this an appropriate buffer? If 0.40 g of solid NaOH is added to this solution, will the enzyme decompose?

METHOD: The enzyme decomposes if the added hydroxide ions raise the pH of the solution above 7.15. We need to analyze the chemistry of the buffer and then calculate the pH of the solution before and after adding NaOH.

The buffering action of this solution is created by its weak acid ($H_2PO_4^-$) and conjugate base (HPO_4^{2-}). The proton that is transferred is the second proton of H_3PO_4, so the appropriate K_{eq} is K_{a2}:

$$H_2PO_4^-{}_{(aq)} + H_2O_{(l)} \rightleftharpoons HPO_4^{2-}{}_{(aq)} + H_3O^+{}_{(aq)} \qquad pK_{a2} = 7.21$$

We can use the buffer equation and the initial concentrations to determine the pH of the buffer solution:

$$pH = pK_a + \log\left\{\frac{[HPO_4^{2-}]_{initial}}{[H_2PO_4^-]_{initial}}\right\} = 7.21 + \log\left\{\frac{(0.225\ M)}{(0.330\ M)}\right\} = 7.04$$

The calculation shows that this is an appropriate buffer solution for an enzyme that is stable between pH = 6.90 and pH = 7.15.

The problem asks whether 0.40 g of NaOH can be added without destroying the enzyme. We need to calculate the pH after addition of the hydroxide ion. As solid NaOH is added, each hydroxide ion that enters the buffer solution consumes one $H_2PO_4^-$ and produces one ion of HPO_4^{2-} and one water molecule:

$$OH^-{}_{(aq)} + H_2PO_4^-{}_{(aq)} \rightarrow H_2O_{(l)} + HPO_4^{2-}{}_{(aq)} \qquad K_{eq} = \frac{K_a}{K_w} >> 1$$

As long as the amount of added hydroxide ions is less than the amount of $H_2PO_4^-$ initially present, this reaction consumes virtually all the added hydroxide ions, and the pH changes by a small amount. To determine the final pH, we must first determine the changes in concentration generated by the added hydroxide ions:

$$\text{Mol } OH^- \text{ added} = m/MM = 0.59\ g/40.00\ g/mol = 0.010\ mol$$

When this amount of OH^- is added to 250 mL of buffer solution, it generates an initial hydroxide ion molarity:

$$[OH^-]_{initial} = mol/V = (0.010\ mol)/(0.250\ L) = 0.040\ M$$

The buffer solution consumes this added hydroxide ion, causing a change in concentrations of the buffer species:

$$[HPO_4^{2-}] = (0.225 + 0.040) = 0.265\ M$$

$$[H_2PO_4^-] = (0.330 - 0.040) = 0.290\ M$$

Now, substitute these new concentrations into the buffer equation:

$$pH = pK_a + \log\left\{\frac{[HPO_4^{2-}]}{[H_2PO_4^-]}\right\} = 7.21 + \log\left\{\frac{(0.265\ M)}{(0.290\ M)}\right\} = 7.17$$

Concentrations after complete reaction with OH^- are new "initial" concentrations.

This result shows that addition of 0.59 g NaOH to the enzyme extract will raise the pH beyond the limits that the enzyme can tolerate. If it is necessary to add this much base to the solution, the biochemist must use a more concentrated buffer solution or a larger volume of buffer solution.

BUFFER PREPARATION

The buffer equation indicates that the pH of a buffer solution is close to the pK_a of the acid used to prepare the buffer:

$$pH = pK_a + \log\left\{\frac{[A^-]_{initial}}{[HA]_{initial}}\right\}$$

Every weak acid has a specific pK_a that determines the pH range over which it can serve as a buffering agent. Remember that a buffer solution must contain a weak acid and its conjugate weak base as *major* species. This condition is met when the ratio of weak base to weak acid is between 0.1 and 10. The buffer equation translates this restriction into a pH *range* over which the acid and its conjugate base can serve as an effective buffer:

$$pH_{low} = pK_a + \log 0.1 = pK_a - 1 \qquad pH_{high} = pK_a + \log 10 = pK_a + 1$$

$$\text{pH range} = pK_a \pm 1$$

With a given weak acid, a buffer solution can be prepared at any pH within about one unit of its pK_a value.

Suppose, for example, that we need a buffer system to maintain the pH of a solution close to 5.0. How do we decide which reagents to use? According to the previous analysis, we must choose a weak acid with a pK_a between 4.0 and 6.0. When the pK_a is far from the desired pH, however, the solution has a reduced buffer capacity. A buffer has maximum capacity, therefore, when its acid has its pK_a as close as possible to the target pH. Table 16-5 lists some acid-base pairs often used as buffer solutions. For a pH = 5.0 buffer, acetic acid ($pK_a = 4.75$) and acetate would be a good choice.

A buffer solution must contain *both* the acid and its conjugate base, so at least *two* reagents in addition to water are required to prepare a buffer solution. An acetate buffer can be prepared, for example, from pure water, concentrated acetic acid, and an acetate salt. The counter ion of the salt must not have acid-base properties of its own, so sodium acetate would be an appropriate choice, but ammonium acetate would not.

The ammonium ion is a weak acid, $pK_a = 9.25$.

Having chosen the acid-base pair for this buffer system, we need to prepare the solution with the correct ratio of base to acid. We use the buffer equation to calculate the molar ratio of acetate to acetic acid that generates a buffer with pH = 5.00:

TABLE 16-5 COMMON BUFFER SYSTEMS

ACID	CONJUGATE BASE	K_a	pK_a	pH RANGE
H_3PO_4	$H_2PO_4^-$	7.5×10^{-3}	2.12	1-3
HCO_2H	HCO_2^-	1.8×10^{-4}	3.74	3-5
CH_3CO_2H	$CH_3CO_2^-$	1.8×10^{-5}	4.75	4-6
$H_2PO_4^-$	HPO_4^{2-}	6.2×10^{-8}	7.21	6-8
NH_4^+	NH_3	5.6×10^{-10}	9.25	8-10
HCO_3^-	CO_3^{2-}	5.6×10^{-11}	10.25	9-11
HPO_4^{2-}	PO_4^{3-}	4.8×10^{-13}	12.31	11-13

$$5.00 = 4.75 + \log \frac{[\text{Acetate}]}{[\text{Acetic acid}]} \quad so \quad \log \frac{[\text{Acetate}]}{[\text{Acetic acid}]} = 0.25$$

$$\frac{[\text{Acetate}]}{[\text{Acetic acid}]} = 10^{0.25} = 1.8$$

To make a buffer solution of pH = 5.00, sodium acetate and acetic acid should be added to pure water in a molar ratio of 1.8 : 1.0. The exact amounts of the reagents depend on the desired volume and concentration of the solution. Sample Problem 16-19 shows an example.

SAMPLE PROBLEM 16-19 BUFFER PREPARATION

What mass of sodium acetate ($NaC_2H_3O_2 \cdot 3\,H_2O$, $MM = 136.08$ g/mol) and what volume of concentrated acetic acid (17.45 M) should be used to prepare 500 mL of a buffer solution at pH = 5.00 that is 0.150 M overall?

METHOD: The buffer equation lets us calculate the ratio of concentrations of conjugate base and acid that will produce a buffer solution of the desired pH. We use mole-mass-volume relationships to translate that ratio into actual quantities.

According to the specifications given in the problem, we require 500 mL of solution with a total molarity of 0.150 mol/L. The total molarity is the combined concentration of the two buffer components:

$$M_{\text{acetate}} + M_{\text{acetic acid}} = 0.150 \text{ M}$$

Use the total volume of the solution, 500 mL, to determine the total number of moles in the system:

$$(0.150 \text{ mol/L})(500 \text{ mL})(10^{-3} \text{ L/mL}) = 7.50 \times 10^{-2} \text{ mol}$$

$$n_{\text{acetate}} + n_{\text{acetic acid}} = 7.50 \times 10^{-2} \text{ mol}$$

We have already determined that a buffer solution with pH = 5.00 requires an acetate–acetic acid molar ratio of 1.8. This ratio can be rewritten as a molar equality:

$$\frac{n_{\text{acetate}}}{n_{\text{acetic acid}}} = 1.8 \qquad n_{\text{acetate}} = 1.8\, n_{\text{acetic acid}}$$

Now substitute to calculate the required moles of acetic acid:

$$1.8\, n_{\text{acetic acid}} + n_{\text{acetic acid}} = 7.50 \times 10^{-2} \text{ mol}$$

$$n_{\text{acetic acid}} = (7.50 \times 10^{-2} \text{ mol})/2.8 = 2.68 \times 10^{-2} \text{ mol}$$

Calculate the required amount of acetate from this amount:

$$n_{\text{acetate}} + 2.68 \times 10^{-2} \text{ mol} = 7.50 \times 10^{-2} \text{ mol}$$

$$n_{\text{acetate}} = 4.82 \times 10^{-2} \text{ mol}$$

Finally, use molarity and molar mass to convert from moles to measurable amounts:

$$\text{Mass sodium acetate} = (4.82 \times 10^{-2} \text{ mol})(136.08 \text{ g/mol}) = 6.6 \text{ g}$$

$$V_{\text{acetic acid}} = \frac{(2.68 \times 10^{-2} \text{ mol})(10^3 \text{ mL/L})}{(17.45 \text{ mol/L})} = 1.5 \text{ mL}$$

The final values are rounded to two significant figures to match the precision of the mole ratio.

There are two other ways to prepare this buffer solution. We could add concentrated acetic acid to pure water and then add enough sodium hydroxide to generate the required 1.8 : 1.0 ratio of acetate to acetic acid:

$$CH_3CO_2H_{(aq)} + OH^-_{(aq)} \rightarrow CH_3CO_2^-_{(aq)} + H_2O_{(l)}$$

Alternatively, we could prepare a solution of sodium acetate and then reach the proper acetate–acetic acid ratio by adding a strong acid:

$$CH_3CO_2^-_{(aq)} + H_3O^+_{(aq)} \rightarrow CH_3CO_2H_{(aq)} + H_2O_{(l)}$$

Buffer preparation requires detailed, step-by-step calculations. Sample Problem 16-20 illustrates the complete procedure.

SAMPLE PROBLEM 16-20 PREPARING A BUFFER

A biochemist asks a technician to prepare a buffer solution at pH = 9.00 with an overall concentration of 0.125 mol/L. The technician has solutions of 1.00 M HCl and NaOH and bottles of all common salts. What reagents should be used, and in what quantities, to prepare 1.00 L of a suitable buffer?

METHOD: The technician must prepare a buffer solution that meets the specifications. This is practical and straightforward, but it requires several separate steps, as follows:

(1) Identify a suitable conjugate acid-base pair.
(2) Determine what reagents to use.
(3) Compute concentrations needed using pH and total concentration.
(4) Determine quantities.

These steps should be taken one at a time.

(1) The technician needs a buffer at pH = 9.00. Of the buffer systems listed in Table 16-5, the combination of NH_3 and NH_4^+ has the proper pH range for the required buffer solution.

(2) The technician has strong acid, strong base, and all common salts. Apparently, no bottles of aqueous ammonia are present in the laboratory, so the reagents for the buffer solution must come from the salts. The technician needs an ammonium salt with a counter anion that has no acid-base properties. Ammonium chloride (NH_4Cl) would be an appropriate choice. This salt contains the conjugate acid, NH_4^+, and the technician can generate NH_3 by adding strong base to the ammonium chloride solution:

$$NH_4^+_{(aq)} + OH^-_{(aq)} \rightarrow NH_{3\,(aq)} + H_2O_{(l)}$$

(3) What concentrations of NH_4^+ and NH_3 are required? First, find the proper ratio of base to acid, then use the total molarity of the solution to determine the concentrations of NH_3 and NH_4^+. Use the buffer equation to compute the ratio of ammonia to ammonium ion that gives a pH of 9.00:

$$\text{pH} = \text{p}K_a + \log \frac{[\text{Base}]}{[\text{Acid}]} \qquad 9.00 = 9.25 + \log \frac{[NH_3]}{[NH_4^+]}$$

$$\log \frac{[NH_3]}{[NH_4^+]} = -0.25 \qquad \frac{[NH_3]}{[NH_4^+]} = 0.56$$

Rearranging gives $[NH_3] = 0.56\,[NH_4^+]$.

Now the desired total molarity of the buffer solution is used to find the actual concentrations.

$$[NH_3] + [NH_4^+] = 0.125\ M \qquad 0.56\ [NH_4^+] + [NH_4^+] = 0.125\ M$$

$$[NH_4^+] = 0.125\ M/1.56 = 0.0801\ M$$

$$[NH_3] = 0.125\ M - 0.0801\ M = 0.045\ M$$

(4) Finally, use stoichiometry to calculate actual amounts. The final buffer solution contains both ammonia and ammonium ions, but both species are derived from ammonium chloride. To make the solution, some of the NH_4^+ ions in an aqueous solution of ammonium chloride can be converted into NH_3 molecules. Thus the total molarity of the system tells us directly how much salt is required:

$$n_{NH_4Cl} = MV = (0.125\ mol/L)(1.00\ L) = 0.125\ mol$$

$$n_{NH_4Cl} = (mol)(MM) = (0.125\ mol)(53.49\ g/mol) = 6.69\ g$$

Ammonia is generated from NH_4^+ by adding sodium hydroxide solution:

$$n_{OH^-} = n_{NH_3} = (0.045\ M)(1.00\ L) = 0.045\ mol$$

$$\text{Volume of 1.00 mol NaOH}_{(aq)} = \frac{0.045\ mol\ OH^-}{1.00\ mol\ OH^-/L} = 0.045\ L$$

To make the buffer, the technician should mix together 6.69 g NH_4Cl, 45 mL 1.00 M NaOH, and enough water to make 1.00 L of solution.

Knowing the characteristics of buffer solutions, we can appreciate how the pH of a person's blood is kept under close control by the chemical equilibria described in Box 16-3.

SECTION EXERCISES

16.5.1 Which of the following sets of chemicals can be used to prepare buffer solutions? For each one that can, specify the pH range over which it behaves as a buffer solution: (a) HCl + KCl; (b) HCl + KNO_2; (c) HCl + NH_4Cl; (d) Na_3PO_4 + Na_2HPO_4; (e) NaOH + H_3PO_4; (f) NaCl + $NaC_2H_3O_2$.

16.5.2 Determine the mass of solid sodium formate and the volume of 0.500 M $HClO_4$ solution required to generate 250 mL of buffer solution with pH = 3.50 and a total concentration (conjugate acid plus base) of 0.225 M.

16.5.3 Calculate the pH of 150 mL of the buffer solution of Problem 16.5.2 to which 0.70 mL of 1.0 M HCl solution has been added.

gradually as hydroxide ions are added to the solution. This buffer region contains the **midpoint** of the titration, the point at which the amount of added OH^- is equal to exactly half the weak acid originally present. In our current example, the solution at the midpoint contains 0.0375 mol each of acetic acid and acetate. Applying the buffer equation reveals the key feature of the midpoint:

$$pH = pK_a + \log \frac{n_{acetate}}{n_{acetic\ acid}} = 4.75 + \log 1 = 4.75$$

We can use moles in place of concentrations in the buffer equation because the volume terms cancel in the ratio of concentrations:

$$\frac{M_{acetate}}{M_{acetic\ acid}} = \frac{\left(\frac{n_{acetate}}{V_T}\right)}{\left(\frac{n_{acetic\ acid}}{V_T}\right)} = \frac{n_{acetate}}{n_{acetic\ acid}}$$

At the midpoint of a titration, the pH of the solution is equal to the pK_a of the weak acid.

Beyond the buffer region, the titration curve rises sharply, passing through an almost vertical region before leveling off again. In this rising region, nearly all of the acetic acid has been consumed, so the pH increases sharply with each added drop of hydroxide solution. Recall from Chapter 4 that the **stoichiometric point** of an acid titration is the point at which the number of moles of added base is exactly equal to the number of moles of acid present in the original solution. At the stoichiometric point of a weak acid titration, the conjugate base is a major species in solution, but the weak acid is not. Sample Problem 16-21 illustrates that the pH at the stoichiometric point in a titration of a weak acid is *not* 7.0.

In some books, the stoichiometric point is called the *equivalence point.*

SAMPLE PROBLEM 16-21 pH AT THE STOICHIOMETRIC POINT

What is the pH at the stoichiometric point of the titration of 150 mL of 0.500 M acetic acid with 2.50 M KOH solution?

METHOD: This is another equilibrium calculation to which the standard procedure applies. Special attention must be given, however, to analyzing the initial conditions *at the stoichiometric point,* bearing in mind that the reaction between hydroxide ions and a weak acid goes essentially to completion.

At the stoichiometric point, the amount of added hydroxide ions is equal to the amount of acetic acid originally present:

$$\text{mol } OH^- = \text{mol } CH_3CO_2H \text{ originally present}$$

$$\text{mol } OH^- = M_{acid} V_{acid} = (0.500 \text{ mol/L})(0.150 \text{ L}) = 0.0750 \text{ mol}$$

This added hydroxide reacts essentially to completion with acetic acid to give the appropriate initial conditions for the equilibrium calculation:

$$CH_3CO_2H_{(aq)} + OH^-_{(aq)} \rightarrow CH_3CO_2^-{}_{(aq)} + H_2O_{(l)}$$

Initial amounts are mol $CH_3CO_2H = 0$, mol $OH^- = 0$, and mol $CH_3CO_2^- = 0.0750$ mol.

Acetic acid is no longer a major species in solution, so the buffer equation cannot be used to calculate pH. Instead, the pH is determined by the proton transfer from water to acetate ions:

$$CH_3CO_2^-{}_{(aq)} + H_2O_{(l)} \rightleftharpoons CH_3CO_2H_{(aq)} + OH^-_{(aq)}$$

$$K_{eq} = K_w/K_a = 5.6 \times 10^{-10} \text{ M}$$

Moles cannot be used in place of concentrations in an equilibrium expression because in most cases the volumes do not cancel in the ratio.

Before constructing a concentration table, convert moles of acetate to molarity. The volume at the stoichiometric point is the original volume *plus* the volume of added titrant:

$$V_{initial} = 0.150 \text{ L}$$

$$V_{titrant} = \frac{\text{Moles}}{\text{Molarity}} = \frac{0.0750 \text{ mol}}{2.50 \text{ mol/L}} = 0.0300 \text{ L}$$

$$V_{total} = 0.150 \text{ L} + 0.0300 \text{ L} = 0.180 \text{ L}$$

$$[CH_3CO_2^-]_{initial} = \frac{(0.0750 \text{ mol})}{(0.180 \text{ L})} = 0.417 \text{ M}$$

Species (reaction)	$H_2O_{(l)}$ +	$CH_3CO_2^-{}_{(aq)}$ $\rightleftarrows$	$CH_3CO_2H_{(aq)}$ +	$OH^-{}_{(aq)}$
Initial concentration, M		0.417	0	0
Change in concentration, M		$-x$	$+x$	$+x$
Equilibrium concentration, M		$0.417 - x$	x	x

We have done this type of calculation many times, so you should be able to show that the pH of the solution at the stoichiometric point is 9.18.

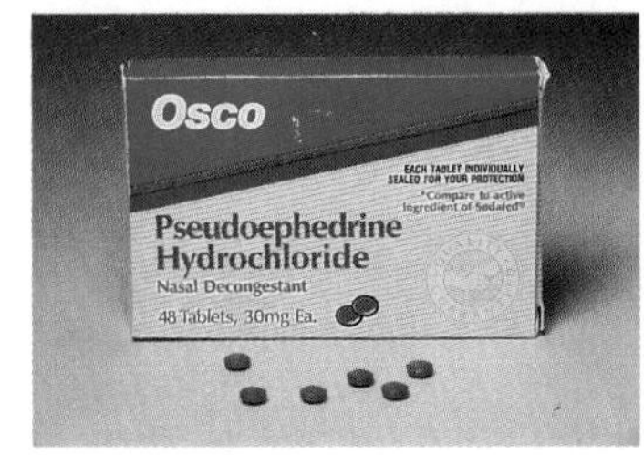

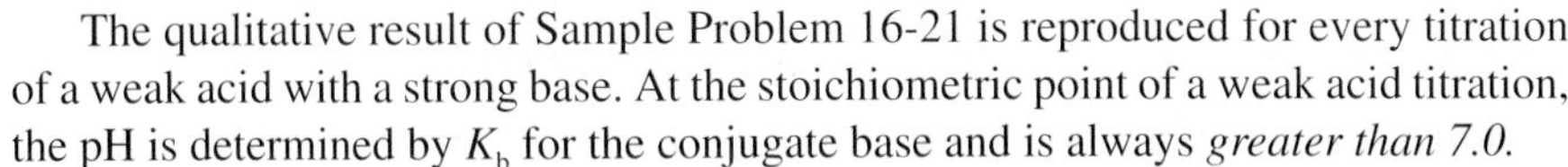

The qualitative result of Sample Problem 16-21 is reproduced for every titration of a weak acid with a strong base. At the stoichiometric point of a weak acid titration, the pH is determined by K_b for the conjugate base and is always *greater than 7.0.*

Beyond the stoichiometric point, in the final region of the titration curve, the concentration of acetic acid is very close to zero. Any further hydroxide ions added from the buret remain in solution as a major species. Beyond the stoichiometric point, the pH of the solution is determined by the amount of excess hydroxide ion.

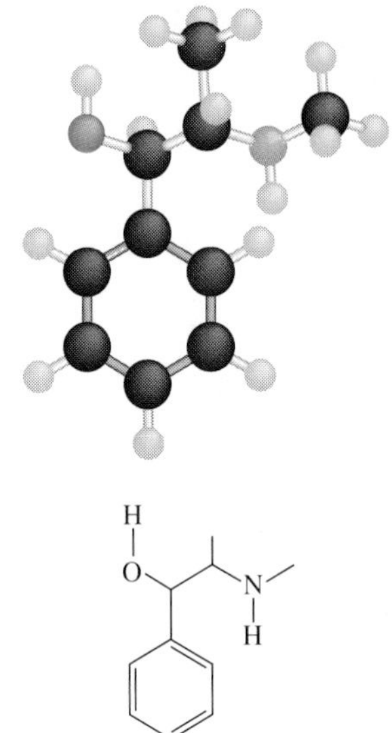

Ephedrine
$C_{10}H_{15}NO$

TITRATION OF A WEAK BASE WITH H_3O^+ IONS

The principles that describe the titration of a weak base with hydronium ions are the same as the ones used to describe the titration of a weak acid with hydroxide ions. For example, the titration curve for ephedrine, a weak base that is the active ingredient in many commercial decongestants, is shown in Figure 16-10.

Notice that the titration curve for ephedrine has the same four regions seen in the titration curve of acetic acid:

1. In a brief region at the beginning of the titration, ephedrine and water are the only major species.
2. In the long, flat buffer region, both ephedrine and its conjugate acid are major species. The midpoint of the titration occurs in the buffer region. At this point, the pH of the solution is equal to the pK_a of the conjugate acid of ephedrine.

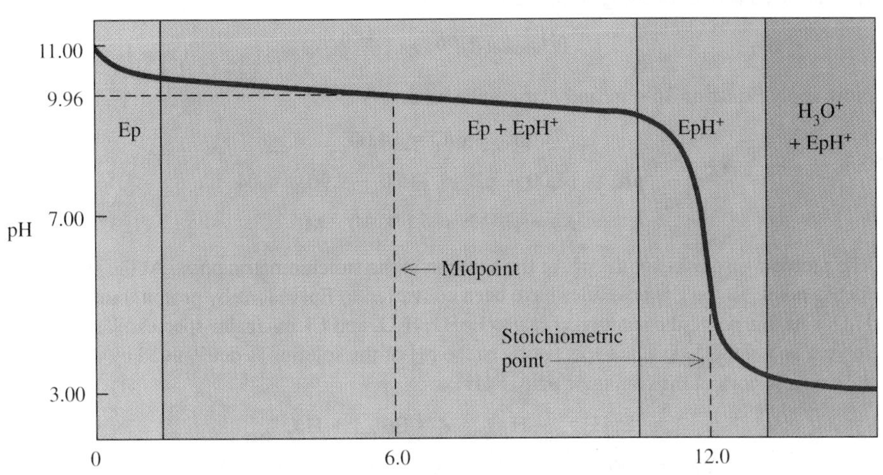

FIGURE 16-10
The titration curve for ephedrine, showing the major species present in each region and the locations of the midpoint and stoichiometric point. Notice that this curve looks similar to the curve shown in Figure 16-9, except that the pH is continually *decreasing* for a titration with a strong acid, whereas it is continually *increasing* for a titration with a strong base.

PROBLEMS

THE COMPOSITION OF AQUEOUS SOLUTIONS

16.1 Identify the major species present in aqueous solutions of each of the following substances: (a) CH_3CO_2H; (b) NH_4Cl; (c) KCl; (d) $NaCH_3CO_2$; and (e) NaOH.

16.2 Identify the major species present in aqueous solutions of each of the following substances: (a) HClO; (b) $CaBr_2$; (c) KClO; (d) HNO_3; and (e) HCN.

16.3 For each solution in Problem 16.1, identify all the equilibria established by the major species. Look up the values of their equilibrium constants, and rank them from largest to smallest.

16.4 For each solution in Problem 16.2, identify all the equilibria established by the major species. Look up the values of their equilibrium constants, and rank them from largest to smallest.

SOLUBILITY EQUILIBRIA

16.5 Write a balanced equation showing the solubility equilibrium of the following salts and then write the solubility product expression for each of them: (a) silver chloride; (b) barium sulfate; (c) iron(II) hydroxide; and (d) calcium phosphate.

16.6 For each of the salts mentioned in Problem 16.5, determine the mass that dissolves in 500 mL of water at 25 °C.

16.7 Only 6.1 mg of calcium oxalate (CaC_2O_4) will dissolve in 1.0 L of water at 25 °C. What is the solubility product of calcium oxalate?

16.8 The solubility of sodium sulfate (Na_2SO_4) in water is 9.5 g/100 mL. What is K_{sp} for sodium sulfate?

16.9 Using the appropriate K_{sp} values from Appendix G, find the concentrations of all ions in the solution at equilibrium after 500 mL of 0.30 M aqueous $Cu(NO_3)_2$ solution has been mixed with 500 mL of 0.40 M aqueous KOH solution.

16.10 Phosphate ions are a major pollutant of water supplies. They can be removed by precipitation using solutions of Ca^{2+} ions because the K_{sp} of calcium phosphate is 2.0×10^{-29} M^5. Suppose that 3000 L of waste water containing phosphate ions at 2.2×10^{-3} M are treated by adding 120 mol of solid $CaCl_2$ (which dissolves completely).

(a) What is the concentration of phosphate ions after treatment?

(b) What mass of calcium phosphate precipitates?

PROTON-TRANSFER EQUILIBRIA

16.11 Convert each of the following hydronium ion concentrations to pH: (a) 4.0 M; (b) 3.75×10^{-6} M; (c) 0.0048 M; and (d) 7.45×10^{-12} M.

16.12 Convert each of the following pH values into a hydronium ion concentration: (a) 0.66; (b) 7.85; (c) 3.68; and (d) 14.33.

16.13 Convert each of the following hydroxide ion concentrations to pH: (a) 2.0 M; (b) 3.75×10^{-6} M; (c) 0.0048 M; and (d) 7.45×10^{-12} M.

16.14 Convert each of the following pH values into a hydroxide ion concentration: (a) 0.66; (b) 7.85; (c) 3.68; and (d) 14.33.

16.15 Identify each of the solutions in Problem 16.1 as a strong or weak acid, strong or weak base, or salt.

16.16 Identify each of the solutions in Problem 16.2 as a strong or weak acid, strong or weak base, or salt.

16.17 Identify each of the following as a strong or weak acid or base: (a) NH_3; (b) $HClO_4$; (c) HClO; and (d) $Ba(OH)_2$.

16.18 Identify the strong and weak acids among the following: (a) $HONO_2$; (b) $HOCH_3$; (c) HOH; (d) HOCl; and (e) NH_2OH.

16.19 For each weak acid in Problems 16.17 and 16.18, identify the conjugate base. For each weak base, identify the conjugate acid.

ACIDS AND BASES

16.20 Calculate the pH of a 2.5×10^{-2} M solution of each of the following compounds: (a) NH_3; (b) $HClO_4$; (c) HClO; and (d) $Ba(OH)_2$.

16.21 Calculate the pH of a 1.5 M solution of each of the following compounds: (a) NaOH; (b) C_5H_5N; (c) NH_2OH; and (d) HCO_2H.

16.22 For a 0.150 M aqueous solution of nitrous acid:

(a) Identify the major and minor species.

(b) Compute concentrations of all species present.

(c) Find the pH.

(d) Draw a molecular picture illustrating the equilibrium that dominates the pH.

16.23 For a 0.350 M aqueous solution of trimethylamine, $N(CH_3)_3$:

(a) Identify major and minor species.

(b) Compute concentrations of all species.

(c) Find the pH.

(d) Draw a molecular picture illustrating the equilibrium that dominates the pH.

16.24 For a 0.45 M solution of Na_2SO_3:
(a) Identify the major species.
(b) Identify the equilibrium that determines the pH.
(c) Compute the pH.

16.25 For a solution that is 0.0100 M in NH_4NO_3:
(a) Identify the major species.
(b) Identify the equilibrium that determines the pH.
(c) Compute the pH.

16.26 Using appropriate K_{eq} values, calculate the value of K_{eq} for the following reaction:

$$HPO_4^{2-}{}_{(aq)} + H_3O^+{}_{(aq)} \rightleftarrows H_2PO_4^-{}_{(aq)} + H_2O_{(l)}$$

16.27 Using appropriate K_{eq} values, calculate the value of K_{eq} for the following reaction:

$$HPO_4^{2-}{}_{(aq)} + OH^-{}_{(aq)} \rightleftarrows PO_4^{3-}{}_{(aq)} + H_2O_{(l)}$$

BUFFER SOLUTIONS

16.28 Which of the following solutions will show buffer properties?
(a) 100 mL of 0.25 M $NaCH_3CO_2$ + 150 mL of 0.25 M HCl
(b) 100 mL of 0.25 M $NaCH_3CO_2$ + 50 mL of 0.25 M HCl
(c) 100 mL of 0.25 M $NaCH_3CO_2$ + 50 mL of 0.25 M NaOH
(d) 100 mL of 0.25 M CH_3CO_2H + 50 mL of 0.25 M NaOH

16.29 Compute the pH of the solutions in Problem 16.28 that are buffered.

16.30 Compute the change in pH resulting from the addition of 5.0 mmol of acid to each solution in Problem 16.28 that is buffered.

16.31 Compute how many moles of base it takes to change the pH of each buffered solution in Problem 16.28 by 0.1 pH unit.

16.32 The pH of a formic acid–formate buffer solution is 4.07. Draw a molecular picture that shows a small region of the buffer solution. (You may omit spectator ions and water molecules.) Use the following symbols:

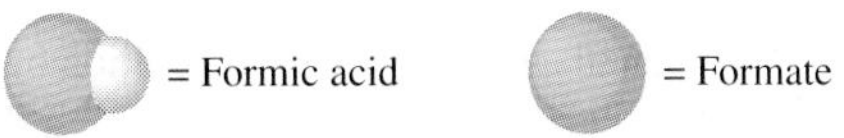

16.33 Calculate the pH of a buffer solution that contains 0.50 M NaH_2PO_4 and 0.20 M Na_2HPO_4.

16.34 Calculate the change in pH if 0.040 g of solid NaOH is added to 150 mL of the solution in Problem 16.33.

16.35 If the acceptable buffer range of the solution in Problem 16.33 is 0.2 pH units, calculate the number of moles of H_3O^+ that can be neutralized by 250 mL of the buffer.

16.36 From Table 16-5, select the best conjugate acid-base pair for buffer solutions at the following pHs: 3.50, 6.85, 11.00, 12.60. If you were going to add HCl solution as part of the buffer preparation, with what other substance should you start in each case?

16.37 If you have 250 mL of 0.200 M $NaHCO_3$ solution, which of the following solutions, and what volume, should be added to make a buffer solution at pH = 10.60: 1.0 M NaOH, 1.0 M HCl, 1.0 M NaCl, H_2O, or 1.0 M CH_3CO_2H?

ACID-BASE TITRATIONS

16.38 For each of the following, decide whether the pH at the stoichiometric point is greater than, less than, or equal to 7. In each case, identify the equilibrium that determines the pH.
(a) $NaClO_{(aq)}$ titrated with $HCl_{(aq)}$
(b) $HNO_{3\,(aq)}$ titrated with $KOH_{(aq)}$
(c) $NaNO_{2\,(aq)}$ titrated with $HClO_{4\,(aq)}$
(d) $NH_4Cl_{(aq)}$ titrated with $NaOH_{(aq)}$

16.39 A laboratory technician wants to determine the aspirin content of a headache pill by acid-base titration. Aspirin has a K_a of 3.0×10^{-4} M. If the pill is dissolved in water to give a solution about 10^{-2} M and is then titrated with KOH solution, find the pH at each of the following points, neglecting dilution effects: (a) before titration begins; (b) at the stoichiometric point; and (c) at the midpoint of the titration.

16.40 Calculate the pH at the first stoichiometric point when a 250-mL 0.025 M solution of H_3PO_4 is titrated with 1.00 M NaOH. What is a suitable indicator for this titration?

16.41 The following figure shows the data obtained in the pH titration of a biochemical substance that is a weak acid. From the information provided, determine the pK_a of this compound.

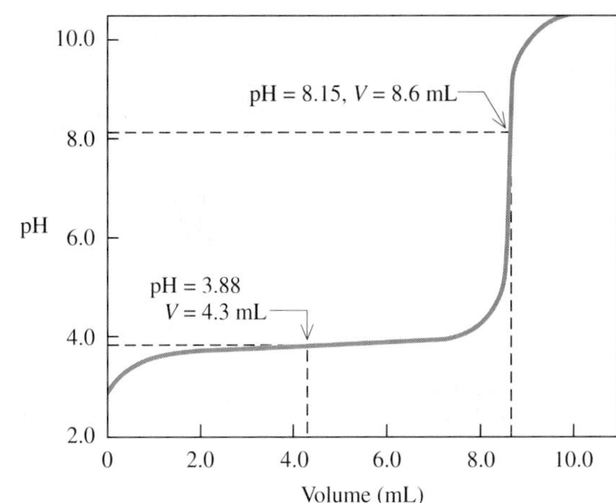

16.75 Calculate the pH of a 1.00×10^{-2} M solution of NaClO.

16.76 Virtually all investigations in cell biology and biochemistry must be carried out in buffered aqueous solutions. Suppose you are studying an enzyme that is active only between pH = 7.1 and 7.4 and that you need to prepare 1.5 L of a phosphate buffer at pH = 7.25 whose total acid concentration is 0.085 M. On the laboratory shelves, you find the following reagents: conc. H_3PO_4, 14.75 M; solid KH_2PO_4; and solid K_2HPO_4.
   (a) Which of these will you use to prepare the buffer solution?
   (b) What quantities of each will you use?

16.77 The enzyme in Problem 16.76 generates H_3O^+ as it functions. If you are running an experiment in 250 mL of the buffer, how many moles of H_3O^+ can the enzyme generate before it loses its activity?

16.78 An unknown acid has a molar mass of 74.1 g/mol. When 8.45 g of the acid is dissolved in 0.750 L of water, the pH of the solution is 2.846. What is the pK_a of the unknown acid?

16.79 A buffer solution is prepared by mixing 0.360 L of 0.300 M NH_3 and 0.640 L of 0.300 M NH_4Cl (pK_b of NH_3 = 4.75).
   (a) Calculate the pH of the buffer solution.
   (b) Write a balanced chemical equation that shows what happens when 1.00 M HNO_3 is added to the buffer solution.
   (c) What is the pH of the solution after 5.00 mL of 1.00 M HNO_3 is added to the buffer? (Neglect the volume change.)
   (d) Write a balanced chemical equation that shows what happens when hydroxide ions are added to the buffer solution described at the beginning of this problem.
   (e) What is the pH of the solution if 14.0 g KOH is added to the original buffer?

16.80 The addictive painkiller morphine, $C_{17}H_{19}NO_3$, is the principal molecule in the milky juice that exudes from unripe poppy seed capsules. (The chemical structure of morphine is shown in Box 16-2.) Calculate the pH of a 0.015 M solution of morphine, given that pK_b = 6.1.

16.81 Water that percolates through dolomite rock is saturated in magnesium carbonate.
   (a) What are the major species present?
   (b) What is the Mg^{2+} concentration?
   (c) What is the pH?
   (d) What is the maximum Ca^{2+} concentration that this solution can have before $CaCO_3$ precipitates?

16.82 One of the most common buffers used in protein chemistry is a weak base called TRIS:

HO, HO, OH, NH_2 = $(HOCH_2)_3CNH_2$ = TRIS

(The nitrogen atom of the amino group is the basic portion of the molecule.)
   (a) Write a balanced equation that shows how TRIS acts as a weak base in water.
   (b) Buffer solutions are prepared from TRIS by adding enough 12 M HCl to give concentrations appropriate for the desired pH. Write a balanced equation that shows what happens when 12 M HCl is added to an aqueous solution of TRIS.
   (c) Write a balanced equation that shows what happens when hydroxide ions are added to a TRIS buffer solution.
   (d) Write a balanced equation that shows what happens when hydronium ions are added to a TRIS buffer solution.

16.83 A biochemist prepares a buffer solution by adding enough TRIS and 12 M HCl to give 1.0 L of a buffer solution whose concentrations are [TRIS] = 0.30 M [$TRISH^+$] = 0.60 M (pK_b of TRIS is 5.7). (See Problem 16.82.)
   (a) Calculate the pH of the buffer solution.
   (b) Suppose 5.0 mL of 12 M HCl is added to 1.0 L of the buffer solution. Calculate the new pH of the solution.

16.84 A technician accidentally pours 35 mL of 12 M HCl into the 1.0 L of buffer solution freshly prepared as described in Problem 16.83. Calculate the new pH to determine whether the buffer has been ruined.

16.85 Is it possible to save the buffer solution described in Problem 16.84? If so, what reagent and how much must be added to restore the buffer?

16.86 Consider a solution that is at pH = 1.00 and contains 0.10 M concentrations of Fe^{2+}, Ca^{2+}, and Mg^{2+} ions. Consult Appendix G for relevant K_{sp} values.
   (a) As NaOH solution is added, which hydroxide precipitates first?
   (b) At what pH does this precipitation begin?
   (c) At what pH does the next ion begin to precipitate?
   (d) What is the concentration of the least soluble cation at the pH in (c)?

16.87 A student was asked to titrate an acetic acid solution that was approximately 0.3 M. What indicator should the student use?

16.88 The solubility of many salts depends on the pH of the solution. Explain the pH effect using $Mg(OH)_2$ as an example. Be sure to consider the solubility of the salt in both acidic and basic solutions. (HINT: Think of the solubility equilibrium in terms of Le Châtelier's principle.)

16.89 Having solved problem 16.88, refer to Appendix G and list four salts that would be more soluble in acidic solution than in pure water. List four salts that would be less soluble in acidic solution than in pure water. List four salts whose solubility does not depend on pH.

16.90 Suppose that you are a technician in a biochemistry laboratory. At your disposal are bottles of sodium carbonate, sodium bicarbonate, and solutions of 6.0 M HCl and 1.0 M NaOH. Your supervisor asks you to prepare 500 mL of a buffer solution that is 0.25 M in acid with pH = 10.00.
(a) Which of the reagents would you use to prepare this solution?
(b) Calculate the quantities of each reagent that you would use.

16.91 Calculate the pH at the stoichiometric point for each of the following titrations:
(a) A 25-mL solution containing 0.375 g of ammonium chloride is titrated with 0.08775 M NaOH.
(b) A 35-mL sample of 0.15 M ammonia is titrated with 0.537 M HCl.
(c) A 50.0-mL solution of 0.175 M HCl is titrated with 0.2546 M NaOH.

16.92 You are doing undergraduate research for a professor in the biology department. Your first assignment is to prepare a pH = 7.50 phosphate buffer solution to be used in the isolation of deoxyribonucleic acid from a cell culture. The buffer must have the capacity to neutralize at least 0.125 mol of either hydronium ions or hydroxide ions. On the shelf you find the following chemicals:

NaOH (MM = 40.0 g/mol)
Concentrated HCl (12.0 M)
Concentrated H_3PO_4 (14.7 M), $pK_{a1} = 2.23$, $pK_{a2} = 7.21$, $pK_{a3} = 12.32$
KH_2PO_4 (MM = 136.1 g/mol)
K_2HPO_4 (MM = 174.2 g/mol)

Write a precise and detailed set of instructions that describe how you would prepare 1.5 L of the buffer solution.

16.93 One of the steps in aluminum refining is the precipitation of aluminum hydroxide from a slightly basic solution. K_{sp} for aluminum hydroxide is 1.8×10^{-33} M^4.
(a) What is the concentration of Al^{3+} in a saturated solution of aluminum hydroxide?
(b) Suppose 1200 L of 0.250 M NaOH is added to a 1300-L solution known to be 0.223 M in Al^{3+}. How much aluminum hydroxide will precipitate, and what will be the residual concentration of Al^{3+} in the solution?

16.94 A buffer solution is prepared by placing approximately 500 mL of distilled water in a 1-L graduated cylinder. Next, 35 mL of concentrated phosphoric acid (14.7 M) and 46.8 g of KOH (MM = 56.1 g/mol) are added to the water. Preparation of the buffer is completed by filling the cylinder to the mark with distilled water.
(a) What is the pH of the buffer solution?
(b) Suppose 8.75 mL of concentrated HCl (12.0 M) is added to the buffer solution. What is the new pH? (You may ignore the volume change.)
(c) While preparing a second batch of the buffer, a technician mistakenly adds 46.8 g NaOH (MM = 40 g/mol) instead of KOH. What is the pH of the resulting solution? Is this a buffer solution? Explain.

16.95 Formic acid is a principal component in the venom of stinging ants. The titration curve for 0.125 L of 0.135 M formic acid is shown here.

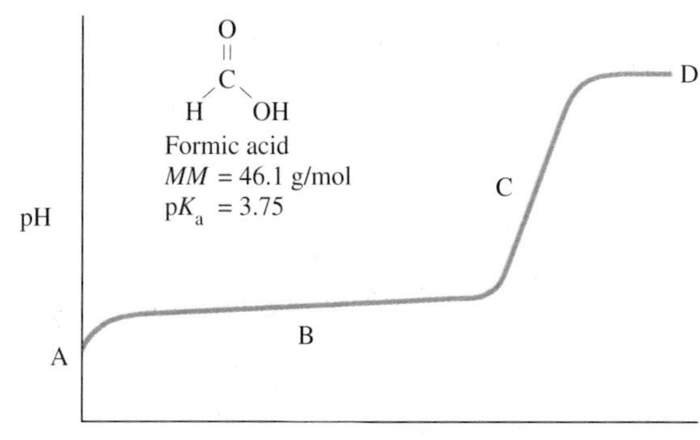

(a) For points A, B, C, and D on the curve, identify the major species in solution at equilibrium.
(b) The titration required 29.8 mL of 0.567 M NaOH to reach the stoichiometric point. What is the pH of the solution at the stoichiometric point?

16.96 Quinine is an alkaloid derived from a tree that grows in tropical rain forests. Quinine is used in the treatment of malaria. Like other alkaloids, quinine is a weak base.

Quinine
$C_{20}H_{24}N_2O_2$
$pK_b = 5.1$
MM = 324 g/mol

(a) One gram of quinine will dissolve in 1.90×10^2 L of water. What is the pH of a saturated solution of quinine?
(b) A 100.0 mL sample of saturated quinine was titrated with 0.0100 M HCl solution. What was the pH at the stoichiometric point of the titration?

16.97 Using the appropriate K_{sp} values from Appendix G, calculate the pH of a saturated solution of $Cd(OH)_2$ in water.

16.98 Explain the difference between the midpoint of a titration and the stoichiometric point.

16.99 For each of the following reactions, write a balanced net ionic equation. Use different-sized arrows to indicate whether the reaction goes nearly to completion or proceeds to only a small extent. (HINT: You may need to compare pK_a values.)

(a) $NaOH_{(aq)} + C_6H_5CO_2H_{(s)} \rightleftarrows ?$
(b) $(CH_3)_3N_{(aq)} + HNO_{3\ (aq)} \rightleftarrows ?$
(c) $Na_2SO_{4\ (aq)} + CH_3CO_2H_{(aq)} \rightleftarrows ?$
(d) $NH_4Cl_{(aq)} + Ca(OH)_{2\ (aq)} \rightleftarrows ?$
(e) $K_2HPO_{4\ (aq)} + NH_{3\ (aq)} \rightleftarrows ?$

16.100 Suppose you titrate 200 mL of a 0.150 M solution of $NaNO_2$ with 6 M HCl (K_a for HNO_2 is 7.1×10^{-4} M).
(a) What is the pH of the solution before beginning the titration?
(b) What is the pH of the solution halfway through the titration?
(c) What is the pH at the stoichiometric point?
(d) What is a suitable indicator for this titration?

16.101 The pH of an acetic acid–acetate buffer solution is 4.26. Draw a molecular picture that shows a small region of the buffer solution. (You may omit spectator ions and water molecules.) Use the following symbols:

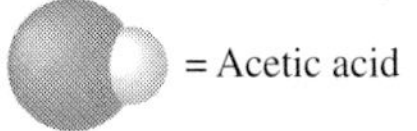

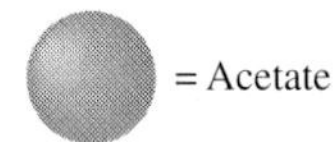

16.102 For each of the following, list the major species in solution and identify the equilibrium that determines the pH. Identify each equilibrium constant in the forward direction as K_a, $1/K_a$, K_b, $1/K_b$, or K_w.
(a) 15 g of ammonium chloride dissolved in 250 mL water
(b) 1.0 M solution of $CaSO_4$
(c) 5.0 g $NaCH_3CO_2$ dissolved in 1.5 M CH_3CO_2H ($K_a = 1.8 \times 10^{-5}$ M)

16.103 In the mid-1930s an alkaloid was isolated from a fungus that is a parasite of ryes and other grasses. This alkaloid, lysergic acid, has been of great interest to chemists because of its strange, dramatic action on the human mind. Many derivatives of lysergic acid are known, some with medicinal applications. Perhaps the best known derivative of lysergic acid is the potent hallucinogen lysergic acid diethylamide (LSD):

LSD
$C_{20}H_{25}N_3O$

Like other alkaloids, LSD is a weak base. The pK_b is 6.12. What is the pH of a 0.55 M solution of LSD?

16.104 In each of the following situations, one reaction goes essentially to completion. In each case, identify the major species in solution under initial conditions, and write a balanced net ionic equation for the reaction that goes essentially to completion.
(a) Gaseous HBr is bubbled through a 0.015 M solution of $Ca(OH)_2$.
(b) 4.0 g of NaOH is added to 0.75 L of 0.055 M $NaHSO_4$.
(c) 25.0 mL of saturated NH_4I is mixed with 50.0 mL of 0.95 M $Pb(NO_3)_2$.

16.105 In aqueous solution, amino acids exist as *zwitterions*, compounds in which internal proton transfer gives a molecule with two charged functional groups. Use Lewis structures to illustrate the proton-transfer equilibrium between the uncharged form of glycine and its zwitterion form. (Glycine = $NH_2CH_2CO_2H$.)

ANSWERS TO SECTION EXERCISES

16.1.1 (a) H_3O^+, ClO_4^-, H_2O; (b) NH_3, H_2O; (c) K^+, HCO_3^-, H_2O; and (d) HClO, H_2O

16.1.2 (a) Ca^{2+}, Cl^-, H_2O; (b) K^+, OH^-, H_2O; and (c) sucrose and water

16.1.3 Precipitate is $Ni(OH)_{2\,(s)}$.
Net reaction is $Ni^{2+}_{(aq)} + 2\,OH^-_{(aq)} \rightarrow Ni(OH)_{2\,(s)}$.
Spectator species are Na^+ and SO_4^{2-}.

16.2.1 1.7×10^{-4} M

16.2.2 79 L

16.2.3 1.5×10^{-9} M. NaCl does not precipitate.

16.3.1 $K_a = 3.0 \times 10^{-8}$ M

16.3.2

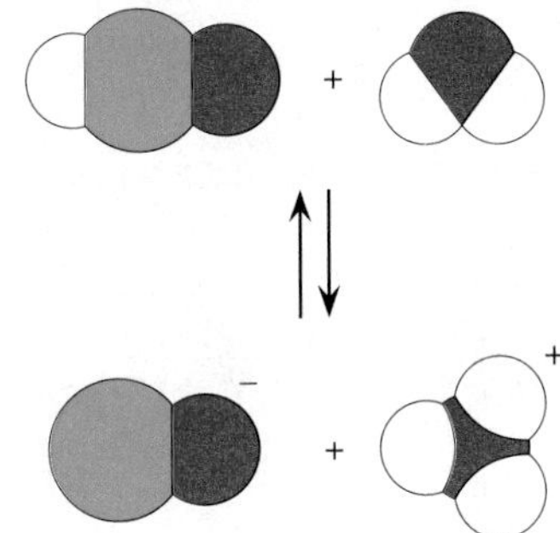

The conjugate base is ClO^-.

16.3.3 $K_b = 3.3 \times 10^{-7}$ M

16.4.1 (a) strong acid; (b) neither; (c) strong base; (d) neither; (e) weak acid; and (f) both

16.4.2 [HCN] = $[OH^-]$ = 2.6×10^{-3} M; $[CN^-]$ = $[K^+]$ = 0.35 M

16.4.3 $NH_4^+{}_{(aq)} + H_2O_{(aq)} \rightleftharpoons NH_{3\,(aq)} + H_3O^+{}_{(aq)}$
$CH_3CO_2^-{}_{(aq)} + H_2O_{(aq)} \rightleftharpoons CH_3CO_2H_{(aq)} + OH^-{}_{(aq)}$
The K_{eq} values for these two equilibria are virtually the same.

16.5.1 (a) Not suitable; (b) pH range between 2.35 and 4.35; (c) not suitable; (d) pH range between 11.32 and 13.32

16.5.2 3.83 g sodium formate and 71.4 mL of 0.500 M $HClO_4$ solution

16.5.3 pH = 3.32

16.6.1

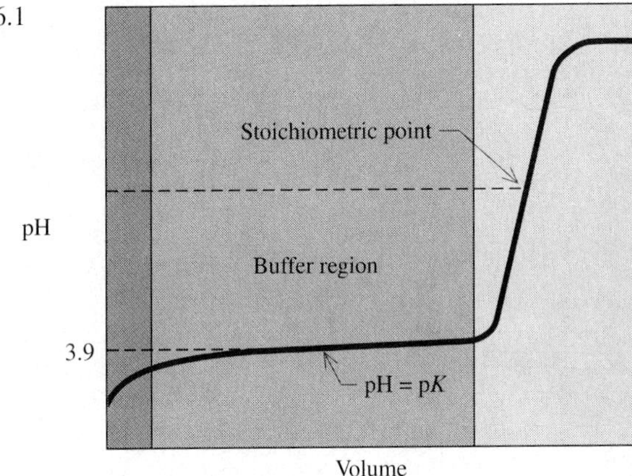

16.6.2 pH = 8.41 at stoichiometric points and 3.4 after 3.0 mL of KOH are added.

16.6.3 Phenol red would be suitable; it would be red at the stoichiometric point.

CHAPTER 17

ELECTRON TRANSFER REACTIONS: REDOX AND ELECTROCHEMISTRY

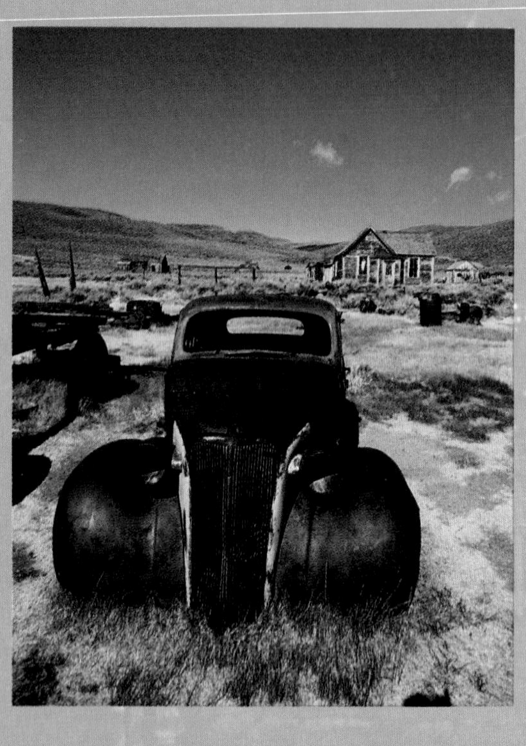

Objects made of iron become coated with rust when they are exposed to moist air. Animals obtain energy by the reaction of carbohydrates with oxygen to form carbon dioxide and water. When you turn on a flashlight, a chemical reaction in the batteries generates a current of electricity. In an aluminum refinery, huge quantities of electricity drive the conversion of aluminum oxide into aluminum metal. These different chemical processes share one common feature: Each involves the *transfer* of electrons from one chemical species to another. As noted in our survey of reaction types in Chapter 4, reactions that involve electron transfer are oxidation-reduction reactions or **redox** reactions.

Many redox reactions proceed by *direct* transfer of electrons between chemical species. Examples are the rusting of iron and the metabolic breakdown of carbohydrates. Many other redox processes proceed by *indirect* electron transfer from one chemical species to another via an electrical circuit. Examples are flashlight batteries and aluminum smelters. When a chemical reaction is coupled with electron flow through a circuit, the process is **electrochemical**.

This chapter begins with a discussion of the principles of redox reactions, including redox stoichiometry. This is followed by an introduction to the principles of electrochemistry. Practical examples of redox chemistry, including corrosion, batteries, and metallurgy, appear throughout the chapter.

17.1 RECOGNIZING REDOX REACTIONS

In a redox reaction, one species loses electrons and another species gains electrons.

Oxidation *is the loss of electrons.*

Reduction *is the gain of electrons.*

A chemical species that loses electrons is oxidized, and a chemical species that gains electrons is reduced.

Electrons are conserved in all chemical processes. That is, electrons can be *transferred* from one species to another, but they are neither created nor destroyed. Thus it is impossible to have just an oxidation or just a reduction because when one species gains electrons, another species must lose electrons.

Oxidation and reduction always occur together.

As a first example of a redox reaction, consider the violent reaction of potassium metal with water to generate hydrogen gas:

$$2\ K_{(s)} + 2\ H_2O_{(l)} \rightarrow 2\ K^+_{(aq)} + H_{2\ (g)} + 2\ OH^-_{(aq)}$$

In potassium metal, each atom is neutral; its electrons exactly counterbalance its nuclear charge. When a potassium atom reacts with a water molecule, it loses its valence electron to produce an aqueous K^+ cation. Potassium atoms are oxidized in this reaction, so another species must be reduced. Water molecules, the only other major species present, accept the electrons lost by the potassium atoms. Each water molecule gains one electron from a potassium atom, which causes the water molecule to fragment into a hydroxide ion and a hydrogen atom. Two hydrogen atoms, in turn, combine to form a molecule of H_2.

The species that loses electrons in a redox process causes the reduction of some other species. Consequently, it is called a **reducing agent.** Potassium metal acts as a reducing agent in the presence of water. Similarly, the species that gains electrons causes the oxidation of some other chemical species and is called an **oxidizing agent.** Water acts as an oxidizing agent in the presence of potassium metal. Every redox reaction has both an oxidizing agent and a reducing agent.

Electron transfer may not be easy to recognize because electrons normally do not appear in chemical formulas and equations. When writing the formula of a molecule or ion, we specify atomic composition and net charge, but we do not list electrons. Instead, we must compute the electron count from the atomic numbers of the atoms contained in the chemical formula. Likewise, electrons never appear in a balanced net chemical equation. The electrons are "hidden" in the formulas of the chemical species involved in the reaction. For example, the chemical formulas of H_2O, OH^-, and H_2 do not immediately suggest that the decomposition of water into hydroxide ions and hydrogen gas is a reduction reaction.

The difficulties in distinguishing redox reactions from nonredox reactions are illustrated by two reactions that occur during the recovery of iron from iron ores:

$$FeO_{(s)} + CO_{(g)} \xrightarrow{\text{Heat}} Fe_{(l)} + CO_{2\,(g)}$$

$$FeCO_{3\,(s)} \xrightarrow{\text{Heat}} FeO_{(s)} + CO_{2\,(g)}$$

The first is a redox reaction, but the second is not. How can we tell? We need some convenient way to assess whether or not electrons have been transferred during a chemical reaction. This can be done by assigning an electron count to each atom in each chemical species.

OXIDATION NUMBERS

The polarity of the O—H bond can be inferred from the electronegativity difference between O and H: O = 3.5 and H = 2.2.

Each atom in a molecule is embedded in an electron cloud that it shares with all the other atoms. Because of electronegativity differences, however, the sharing often is unequal. In H_2O and OH^-, for example, electrons in the O—H bonds are polarized toward the oxygen atom because of the electronegativity difference between hydrogen and oxygen. The bond in H_2, on the other hand, is not polar, so the pair of electrons is shared equally by the two atoms.

When K reacts with H_2O and forms H_2, the electron density around the hydrogen atoms increases. On the other hand, when H_2O loses a proton to become OH^-, the electron density on the oxygen atom increases slightly. Even though actual redox processes often include such fractional changes in electron densities, the total number of electrons transferred is always a whole number. Consequently, we can describe this reduction by assigning the electron removed from the potassium to one of the hydrogen atoms of a water molecule. This assignment is logical because the hydrogen atoms in H_2O do indeed bear a partial positive charge. In a sense, this assignment models the H_2O molecule as if it were a pair of H^+ cations associated with an O^{2-} anion. Thus the reduction of H_2O can be viewed as the addition of an electron to H^+ to form H.

This view is the **oxidation number** model. In this model, each atom in a particular chemical substance is associated with a specific number of electrons.

> ***The oxidation number of an atom is the apparent or real charge that an atom has when all bonds between atoms of different elements are assumed to be ionic.***

Oxidation numbers are useful because in every redox reaction, some atoms change their oxidation numbers. Therefore redox reactions can be identified by noting changes in oxidation numbers.

To assign oxidation numbers, we must examine the net charge on the species and visualize each bond as if it were ionic. As a first example, here are the oxidation numbers of the atoms in the reactants and products of the reaction of potassium with water:

Reactants:	H	O	H	K	Products:	H—H		H—O^-		K^+
	+1	−2	+1	0		0	0	+1	−2	+1

There are no polar bonds in metallic potassium or molecular hydrogen, so their atoms have zero apparent charges and oxidation numbers. The aqueous potassium ion has a real +1 charge and oxidation number of +1. The polar O—H bonds are treated as if they were ionic, yielding apparent charges of +1 on each H atom and −2 on each O atom in H_2O and OH^-. According to the model, two elements change their oxidation numbers in this redox reaction. Potassium atoms change from 0 to +1, whereas some hydrogen atoms change from +1 to 0.

The oxidation numbers of atoms in pure neutral elements are zero, and the oxidation numbers of monatomic ions equal their net charges. Thus each atom in F_2, O_2, and H_2 has an oxidation number of zero. Among aqueous ions, K^+ has an oxidation number of +1, Cl^- has an oxidation number of −1, and Fe^{3+} has an oxidation number of +3.

To determine the oxidation numbers of atoms in ionic compounds, we divide them into their individual ions. Thus NaCl contains Na^+ (oxidation number +1) and Cl^- (oxidation number −1), whereas CaO contains Ca^{2+} (oxidation number +2) and O^{2-} (oxidation number −2).

For polar molecules and polyatomic ions, we need to know about molecular structure and bond polarities to assign oxidation numbers. Bond polarities can be predicted from electronegativity differences. However, three guidelines allow oxidation numbers to be assigned without examining molecular structure in detail:

1. The sum of the oxidation numbers of all atoms equals the net charge on the species.
2. When bonded to a nonmetal, hydrogen has an oxidation number of +1.
3. The most electronegative atom in a polyatomic species has an oxidation number equal to its number of valence electrons minus eight.

Sample Problem 17-1 provides some examples of these guidelines.

These guidelines for assigning oxidation numbers are insufficient for covalent compounds that contain more than two elements other than hydrogen. However, it is unnecessary to assign oxidation numbers to such compounds in introductory chemistry.

SAMPLE PROBLEM 17-1 ASSIGNING OXIDATION NUMBERS

Assign oxidation numbers to all elements in these two reactions involving iron:

$$FeCO_{3\,(s)} \xrightarrow{\text{Heat}} FeO_{(s)} + CO_{2\,(g)}$$

$$FeO_{(s)} + CO_{(g)} \xrightarrow{\text{Heat}} Fe_{(l)} + CO_{2\,(g)}$$

METHOD: Elements have oxidation numbers that match their net charges. Ionic compounds must be divided into their constituent ions. Polyatomic species are treated using the three guidelines.

Fe: This is a neutral element, so its oxidation number is zero.

CO: Oxygen, the more electronegative element, must be assigned an oxidation number of $6 - 8 = -2$. For the sum of the oxidation numbers to be zero, carbon must have an oxidation number of +2.

CO_2: Each oxygen is −2. For the sum of the oxidation numbers to be zero, carbon must be +4.

FeO: This is an ionic substance, in which O is −2 and Fe is +2.

$FeCO_3$: This, too, is ionic, containing carbonate polyatomic anions, CO_3^{2-}, and Fe^{2+} ions. The oxidation number of Fe is +2. For the carbonate ion, the oxidation number of oxygen is −2. The net charge on the ion is −2, and its three oxygen atoms have a total oxidation number of −6, so the carbon atom must have an oxidation number of +4.

Here are the reactions again, with oxidation numbers shown for all elements:

$$\underset{+2\ +4\ -2}{FeCO_{3(s)}} \xrightarrow{\text{Heat}} \underset{+2\ -2}{FeO_{(s)}} + \underset{+4\ -2}{CO_{2(g)}}$$

$$\underset{+2\ -2}{FeO_{(s)}} + \underset{+2\ -2}{CO_{(g)}} \xrightarrow{\text{Heat}} \underset{0}{Fe_{(l)}} + \underset{+4\ -2}{CO_{2(g)}}$$

In the first reaction, none of the elements changes its oxidation number, so this is not a redox process. The second reaction is a redox reaction because carbon's oxidation number increases (oxidation) and iron's oxidation number decreases (reduced):

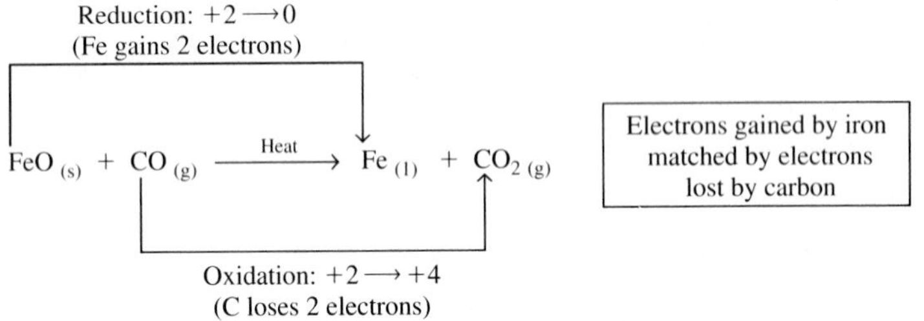

Carbon, which forms an immense variety of compounds, also displays a variety of different oxidation numbers. Sample Problem 17-2 illustrates some of its values.

SAMPLE PROBLEM 17-2 OXIDATION NUMBERS OF CARBON

Determine the oxidation number of carbon in each of the following substances: H_2CO_3, C_3H_8, $C_6H_{12}O_6$, and $[Ni(CN)_4]^{2-}$.

METHOD: Oxidation numbers are assigned using the guidelines. Generally, the oxidation number of carbon is determined by first assigning oxidation numbers to the other elements in the species.

H_2CO_3: Each hydrogen atom has oxidation number +1, and oxygen, the most electronegative atom in this species, has oxidation number −2. Adding the contributions from these atoms, we obtain $2(+1) + 3(-2) = -4$. For the oxidation numbers to add to zero, the carbon atom must have an oxidation number of +4.

C_3H_8: Each hydrogen atom has an oxidation number of +1. This gives a total of +8, so overall neutrality requires that the three carbon atoms contribute a total of −8. The *average* oxidation number for the carbon atoms is −(8/3).

$C_6H_{12}O_6$: As in H_2CO_3, hydrogen is +1 and oxygen is −2. Their total contribution is 12(+1) + 6(−2) = 0. The *average* oxidation number for carbon in this compound is zero.

$[Ni(CN)_4]^{2-}$: We must recognize CN^- as a polyatomic anion that carries a charge of −1. The nitrogen atom is the more electronegative element in this ion, so it has an oxidation number of 5 − 8 = −3. Thus each C atom has an oxidation number of +2. (Nickel must have an oxidation number of +2 to account for the net charge of the complex ion.)

More elaborate guidelines exist for determining the oxidation number of a specific carbon atom in a particular molecule. However, such assignments are not required for our coverage of redox chemistry.

Sample Problem 17-2 illustrates that oxidation numbers can be integers, fractions, or zero. When one type of atom is present in different bonding environments in the same compound, the average oxidation number may be a fraction (as in C_3H_8) or even zero (as in $C_6H_{12}O_6$). Fractional average oxidation numbers are particularly common in carbon compounds. These average oxidation numbers are sufficient to determine whether or not a reaction has redox character.

In some compounds, the guideline that assigns +1 oxidation number to hydrogen conflicts with the guideline for the oxidation number of the most electronegative element. However, hydrogen can never have an oxidation number larger than +1 because it has only one valence electron to lose. Thus the hydrogen guideline takes precedence over the electronegativity guideline. For example, in hydrazine, N_2H_4, each hydrogen atom is assigned an oxidation number of +1, and electrical neutrality requires each nitrogen atom to have an oxidation number of −2.

Hydrazine contains an N—N bond in which electrons are shared equally between the two N atoms:

```
H     H
 \   /
 :N—N:
 /   \
H     H
```

SECTION EXERCISES

17.1.1 Determine the oxidation numbers of all elements in each of the following substances: (a) Fe_3O_4 (magnetite, one of the important iron ores); (b) H_2O_2 (hydrogen peroxide, an antiseptic); (c) $KMnO_4$ (potassium permanganate, a powerful oxidizing agent); and (d) $C_6H_8O_7$ (citric acid, an essential vitamin and an intermediate in metabolic oxidation).

17.1.2 Determine which of the following reactions are redox:
(a) $C_6H_8O_7 \rightarrow C_6H_6O_6 + H_2O$ (one of the steps in metabolism)
(b) $C_6H_6O_7 \rightarrow C_5H_6O_5 + CO_2$ (another step in metabolism)
(c) $3\ Fe_2O_3 + CO \rightarrow 2\ Fe_3O_4 + CO_2$ (one reaction that occurs in iron refining)
(d) $Al_2O_3 + 2\ OH^- + 3\ H_2O \rightarrow 2\ Al(OH)_4^-$ (used in purifying aluminum ores)

17.1.3 Nitrogen can have many different oxidation numbers. Give the formula of a species in which N has the following oxidation numbers: (a) 0; (b) −2; (c) −3; (d) +2; (e) +4; and (f) +5.

17.2 BALANCING REDOX REACTIONS

A redox reaction must be described by a balanced redox equation. Although some redox reactions can be balanced by inspection, others require systematic balancing procedures. Any balanced equation must meet the following requirements:

1. Atoms of each element must be conserved.
2. Electrons must be conserved.

3. Total electrical charge must be conserved.
4. All coefficients must be integers.

Electrons and total charge are conserved automatically when nonredox equations are balanced. However, since redox reactions involve the transfer of electrons from one species to another, we must pay special attention to electrical charges when balancing redox equations. The key to balancing complicated redox equations is to balance electron transfers.

The number of electrons lost in the oxidation must equal the number of electrons gained in the reduction.

Electrons do not appear in formulas or balanced net reactions, however, so we must devise a procedure that reveals the electrons involved in oxidation and reduction.

HALF-REACTIONS

In any redox reaction, some species are oxidized and others are reduced. To reveal the *number* of electrons transferred, it is useful to consider the oxidation and reduction parts of a redox reaction individually. For aqueous solutions, this is most easily accomplished by dividing the redox reaction into two parts called **half-reactions.** One half-reaction describes the oxidation, and the other describes the reduction.

When an aqueous redox process is divided into half-reactions, the electrons appear as reactants or products. This simplifies the balancing of redox equations. In an oxidation, a starting material loses electrons, so electrons must appear among the *products* of the oxidation half-reaction. In a reduction, a starting material gains electrons, so electrons must appear among the *reactants* of the reduction half-reaction.

As we describe in later sections, oxidation and reduction occur at different locations in electrochemistry.

To determine how to divide an aqueous redox reaction into half-reactions, it is usually sufficient to note that each half-reaction eventually must be balanced. Consequently, any element that appears as a reactant in a half-reaction must also appear among the products. Occasionally, however, reactions may not clearly divide into an oxidation and a reduction. In these cases, oxidation number changes tell us how to divide the starting materials up into distinct redox half-reactions. Sample Problem 17-3 illustrates the separation process.

SAMPLE PROBLEM 17-3 IDENTIFYING HALF-REACTIONS

Separate the following unbalanced processes, all of which occur in aqueous solution, into half-reactions:

(a) $Cr_2O_7^{2-} + Fe^{2+} \longrightarrow Cr^{3+} + Fe^{3+}$

(b) $H_2O_2 + SO_3^{2-} \longrightarrow H_2O + SO_4^{2-}$

(c) $HNO_2 \longrightarrow NO + NO_2$

METHOD: A redox equation usually can be separated by placing elements other than hydrogen and oxygen in separate half-reactions. When this is not the case, we use oxidation number changes to determine which species are oxidized and which are reduced.

(a) This reaction can be divided by inspection. Iron must appear in one half-reaction and chromium in the other. Oxygen, which is present only in $Cr_2O_7^{2-}$, will be balanced in a later step.

$$Fe^{2+} \longrightarrow Fe^{3+} \qquad\qquad Cr_2O_7^{2-} \longrightarrow Cr^{3+}$$

(b) In this reaction, sulfur is the only element other than hydrogen and oxygen. Thus sulfur must appear on both sides of one half-reaction. Furthermore, since sulfur appears in only one of the starting materials and in only one of the products, the second half-reaction must contain only hydrogen and oxygen:

$$SO_3^{2-} \rightarrow SO_4^{2-}$$

$$H_2O_2 \rightarrow H_2O$$

The reaction of H_2O_2 to form H_2O is a reduction, as verified by examining the oxidation numbers of each element:

H_2O_2	H_2O
+1 −1	+1 −2

(c) How can a reaction that contains just one reactant be divided into half-reactions? First, examine oxidation numbers:

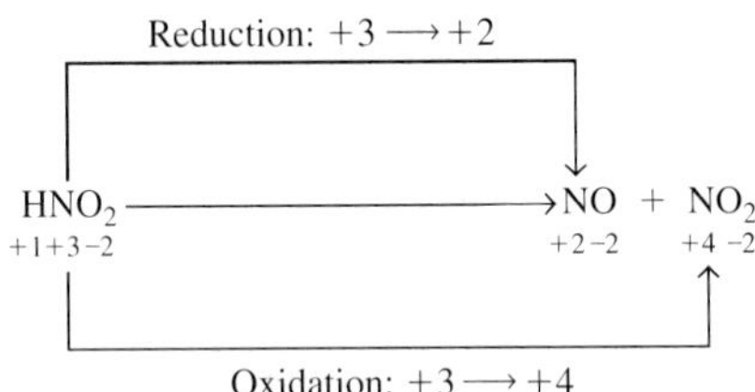

The oxidation numbers reveal that nitrogen monoxide is produced by *reducing* HNO_2, and nitrogen dioxide is produced by *oxidizing* HNO_2. Molecules of HNO_2 react with one other; some are reduced and others are oxidized. Therefore HNO_2 must appear in *both* half-reactions:

$$HNO_2 \rightarrow NO_2 \qquad\qquad HNO_2 \rightarrow NO$$

BALANCING HALF-REACTIONS

After a redox reaction is divided into half-reactions, each half-reaction is balanced independently. This is done in four steps, which *must* be done *in the order listed:*

1. Balance all elements except oxygen and hydrogen by adjusting stoichiometric coefficients.
2. Balance oxygen by adding H_2O to the side that is deficient in oxygen.
3. Balance hydrogen by adding $H^+_{(aq)}$ to the side that is deficient in hydrogen.
   a. If the solution is basic, react $H^+_{(aq)}$ with OH^- to form water.
4. Balance net charge by adding electrons to the side that is deficient in negative charge.

In step 3 of this procedure, we designate the hydronium ion as $H^+_{(aq)}$, even though its covalent structure is best represented as $H_3O^+_{(aq)}$. Redox balancing is easier when the shorter representation is adopted.

Both $H_3O^+_{(aq)}$ and $H^+_{(aq)}$ describe a hydrated proton in water. This species is a proton covalently bonded to a water molecule and encased in a sphere of additional water molecules oriented to maximize coulombic attractions.

These four steps result in a balanced half-reaction, in which elements, electrons, and total charge are all conserved. Sample Problem 17-4 provides an example of the procedure.

SAMPLE PROBLEM 17-4 BALANCING HALF-REACTIONS

Determine the balanced half-reactions for the redox process from Sample Problem 17-3c, which occurs in acid solution:

$$HNO_2 \rightarrow NO + NO_2$$

All species are in aqueous solution, but for convenience we generally omit the phase designation $_{(aq)}$ except for hydronium ions.

METHOD: The half-reactions were identified in Sample Problem 17-3. Balance each using the four-step procedure.

$$HNO_2 \rightarrow NO_2$$

Step 1: Nitrogen is already balanced.

IV. Now recombine the half-reactions and cancel common terms:

$$\cancel{2e^-} + 2\,H_2O + O_2 \rightarrow H_2O_2 + 2\,OH^-$$
$$2\,Au + 4\,CN^- \rightarrow 2\,[Au(CN)_2]^- + \cancel{2e^-}$$
$$2\,H_2O + O_2 + 2\,Au + 4\,CN^- \rightarrow 2\,[Au(CN)_2]^- + 2\,OH^- + H_2O_2$$

Make sure the equation is balanced by taking an inventory of elements and charge:

2 Au		2 Au
4 C		4 C
4 N	⟶	4 N
4 O		4 O
4 H		4 H
Charge = −4		Charge = −4

The equation is balanced.

SECTION EXERCISES

17.2.1 The tarnish that collects on objects made of silver is silver sulfide, a black solid. Tarnish forms from trace amounts of hydrogen sulfide present in the atmosphere. Balance this redox equation:

$$Ag + H_2S + O_2 \rightarrow Ag_2S + H_2O$$

17.2.2 Balance the redox reaction from Sample Problem 17.3(c):

$$HNO_2 \rightarrow NO + NO_2$$

17.2.3 Copper refining traditionally involves "roasting" sulfide ores with oxygen, which produces large quantities of polluting sulfur dioxide. An alternative process uses aqueous nitric acid to convert the CuS into soluble copper(II) hydrogensulfate without generating SO_2. Balance this redox equation:

$$CuS_{(s)} + NO_3^-{}_{(aq)} \rightarrow NO_{(g)} + Cu^{2+}{}_{(aq)} + HSO_4^-{}_{(aq)}$$

17.3 SPONTANEITY OF REDOX REACTIONS

FIGURE 17-1
Potassium and silver are both soft, lustrous, "silvery" metals. Each can be oxidized to the +1 oxidation state, but whereas potassium reacts violently with water, silver does not react at all.

When a piece of silver metal is dropped into water, no reaction occurs. In contrast, potassium metal must be carefully protected from exposure to water. Figure 17-1 shows that when a piece of potassium is dropped into water, the metal oxidizes rapidly, evolving hydrogen gas and heat. The hydrogen ignites and burns. These reactions are spontaneous, rapid, and potentially dangerous.

We can write balanced redox equations for the possible oxidation of each metal by water:

$$2\,K_{(s)} + 2\,H_2O_{(l)} \xrightarrow{\text{Rapid}} 2\,K^+{}_{(aq)} + 2\,OH^-{}_{(aq)} + H_{2\,(g)}$$

$$2\,Ag_{(s)} + 2\,H_2O_{(l)} \xrightarrow{\text{No reaction}} 2\,Ag^+{}_{(aq)} + 2\,OH^-{}_{(aq)} + H_{2\,(g)}$$

Despite their apparent similarities, the potassium reaction is spontaneous, but the silver reaction is not. Thermodynamic calculations verify these observations. Recall from Chapter 13 that spontaneous reactions have negative values for ΔG. Using tabulated free energies of formation, we can calculate standard free energy changes for these reactions. One has a negative value, the other a positive value:

$$2\,K_{(s)} + 2\,H_2O_{(l)} \rightarrow 2\,K^+_{(aq)} + 2\,OH^-_{(aq)} + H_{2\,(g)} \qquad \Delta G^\circ_{rxn} = -407\ \text{kJ}$$

$$2\,Ag_{(s)} + 2\,H_2O_{(l)} \rightarrow 2\,Ag^+_{(aq)} + 2\,OH^-_{(aq)} + H_{2\,(g)} \qquad \Delta G^\circ_{rxn} = +314\ \text{kJ}$$

Both experiments and calculations indicate that electron transfer is facile for potassium, but electron transfer is difficult for silver. Because oxidation involves loss of electrons, these differences in reactivity of silver and potassium can be traced to how easily each metal loses electrons to become an aqueous cation. The main factor is their first ionization energies: 731 kJ/mol for silver compared with 419 kJ/mol for potassium. The stability of the cation in aqueous solution and other properties of the solution play secondary roles.

Only Rb, Cs, and Fr have lower first ionization energies than K. All react violently with water, as does Na, which has a first ionization energy of 495 kJ/mol.

DIRECT AND INDIRECT ELECTRON TRANSFER

The reactivities of potassium and silver with water represent extremes in the spontaneity of electron transfer reactions. Redox reactions between two metals provide convenient illustrations of less drastic differences in reactivity. For instance, when a strip of zinc metal is dipped in a solution of copper(II) sulfate, the zinc slowly dissolves and copper metal precipitates, as shown in Figure 17-2:

$$Cu^{2+}_{(aq)} + Zn_{(s)} \rightarrow Cu_{(s)} + Zn^{2+}_{(aq)}$$

Each zinc atom transfers two electrons to a copper cation. Balanced half-reactions show the electron gains and losses more clearly:

$$\text{Reduction:} \quad Cu^{2+}_{(aq)} + 2\,e^- \rightarrow Cu_{(s)}$$

$$\text{Oxidation:} \quad Zn_{(s)} \rightarrow Zn^{2+}_{(aq)} + 2\,e^-$$

A thermodynamic calculation verifies that the overall reaction is spontaneous: $\Delta G^\circ = -212.55$ kJ.

FIGURE 17-2
When a strip of zinc metal is dipped in a solution of copper(II) sulfate, zinc is oxidized to Zn^{2+} and copper ions are reduced to copper metal. The insoluble metal precipitates from the solution.

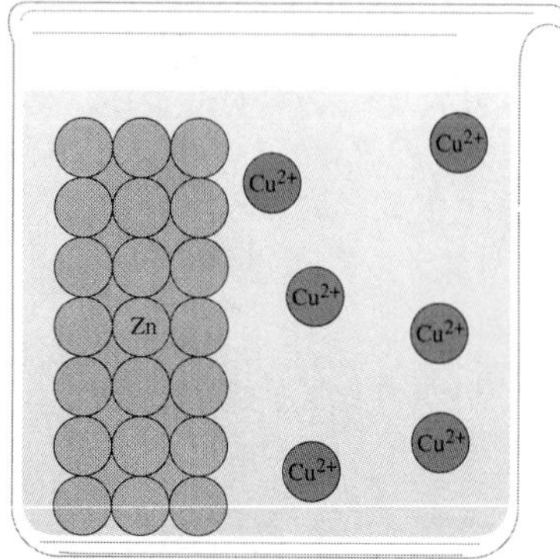

A strip of zinc metal submerged in a solution of Cu^{2+}

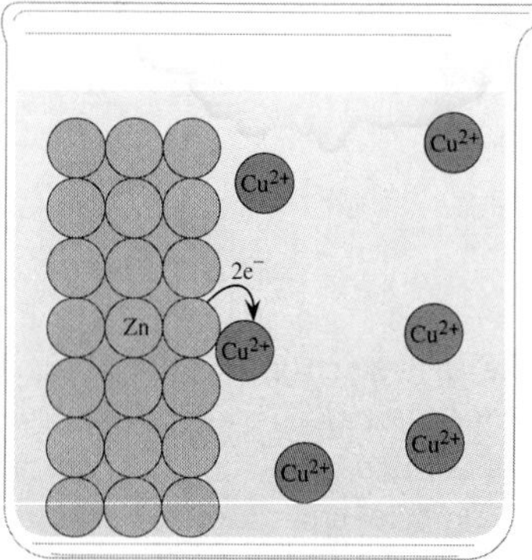

When a Cu^{2+} ion collides with the surface of the Zn metal, the Zn atom gives up two electrons to Cu^{2+}.

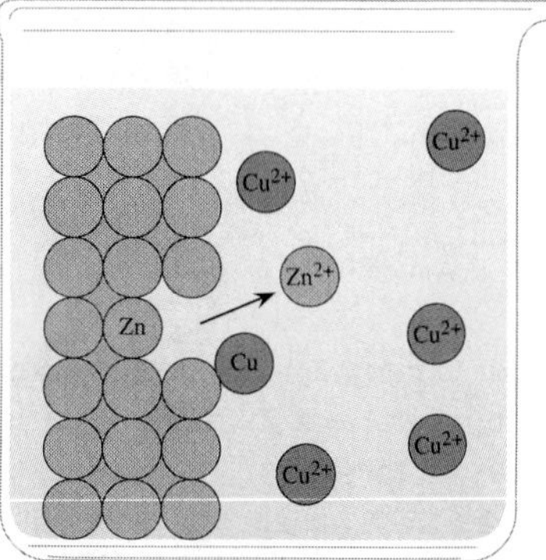

Zn is oxidized to Zn^{2+} while Cu^{2+} is reduced to Cu (elemental copper). Zn^{2+} is soluble in water, but Cu is insoluble, so Zn^{2+} dissolves and Cu sticks to the Zn surface.

FIGURE 17-3

A molecular view of the oxidation of zinc metal by Cu^{2+} ions. Water molecules and spectator anions have been omitted for clarity.

The oxidation of zinc metal by Cu^{2+} ions is an example of **direct electron transfer.** A copper ion accepts two electrons when it collides with the surface of the zinc strip. Direct electron transfer occurs when electrons are transferred during a collision between the species being oxidized and the species being reduced. Figure 17-3 illustrates this process at the molecular level.

Spontaneous redox reactions can also occur by **indirect electron transfer.** In indirect electron transfer, oxidation occurs at one end of a wire, generating free electrons. Reduction occurs at the other end of the wire, consuming free electrons. The wire conducts electrons between the oxidation site and the reduction site. Indirect transfer can be achieved, however, only if direct electron transfer is prevented.

Direct electron transfer from zinc metal to copper cations can be blocked by physically separating the copper and zinc species, as illustrated schematically in Figure 17-4. The beaker on the left contains an aqueous solution of zinc sulfate and a strip of zinc metal. The beaker on the right contains an aqueous solution of copper(II) sulfate and a strip of copper metal. A wire connects the two metal strips to allow indirect electron transfer. The oxidation half-reaction generates free electrons and releases Zn^{2+} ions into the solution containing the zinc electrode:

$$Zn_{(s)} \longrightarrow Zn^{2+}_{(aq)} + 2\ e^-_{(wire)}$$

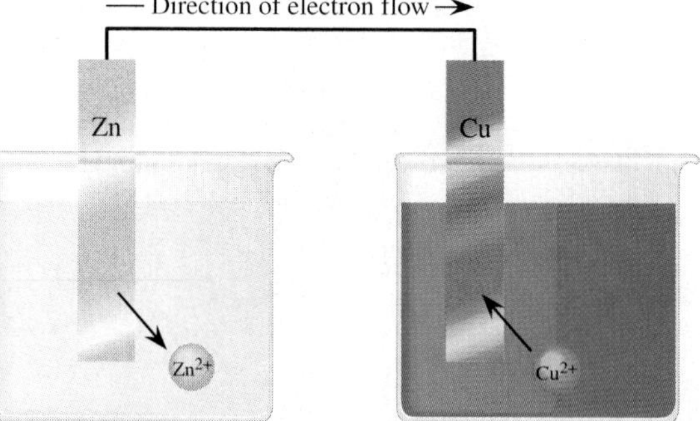

FIGURE 17-4

If the zinc-containing and copper-containing portions of this redox system are physically separated, electron transfer can only occur through an external wire.

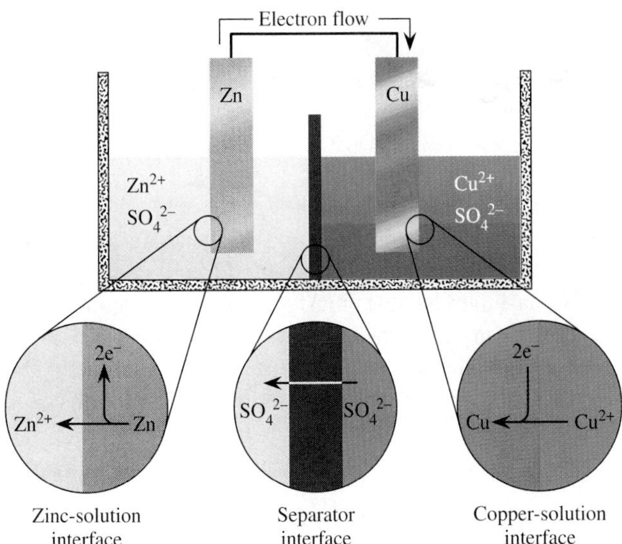

FIGURE 17-5
Schematic view of an arrangement that allows a sustained redox reaction accompanied by an external flow of electrons.

Electrons released in the oxidation flow from left to right through the wire and into the copper strip. Copper cations from the right-hand solution can collect electrons when they collide with the surface of the strip:

$$Cu^{2+}{}_{(aq)} + 2\ e^{-}{}_{(wire)} \rightarrow Cu_{(s)}$$

COMPLETING THE CIRCUIT

The arrangement shown in Figure 17-4 does not generate a sustained flow of electrons. As electrons are transferred, the solutions in both beakers quickly become unbalanced in electrical charge. Oxidation of the zinc strip releases Zn^{2+} ions into solution, generating excess positive charge. On the other side, Cu^{2+} ions are reduced to copper metal, leaving behind a solution with too many sulfate anions. This charge imbalance generates a coulombic force that stops the further flow of electrons.

Before a sustained flow of electrons can be achieved, these excess charges must be removed. As electrons flow through the wire from left to right, sulfate anions must move from right to left to balance the charge. However, this flow of ions must occur in a way that prevents the two solutions from mixing freely. Otherwise, direct electron transfer will replace indirect electron transfer. Figure 17-5 shows an arrangement that meets these needs. The two vessels are connected by a porous glass plate. This plate allows ions to migrate between the two compartments, but the mixing process is too slow to lead to direct electron transfer (Figure 17-6). Electrons flow through the wire, and ions diffuse through the plate. Adding the porous plate completes a circuit that can be used to generate a sustained flow of electrons through the external wire.

In addition to a porous plate that allows charge to pass from one solution to the other, the apparatus shown in Figure 17-5 must also contain solutions that conduct charge. The salts dissolved in the two vessels are essential for the flow of electrons because pure water does not contain enough charged species to support charge flow. Charge can flow only when the solutions contain ions that are provided by an **electrolyte.** An electrolyte is any substance that produces ions when it dissolves in water.

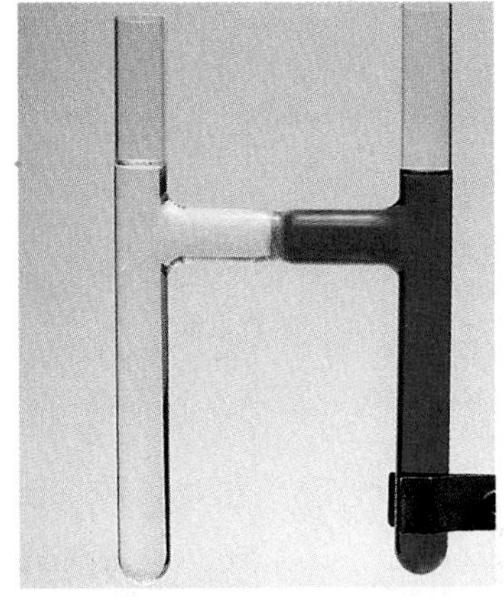

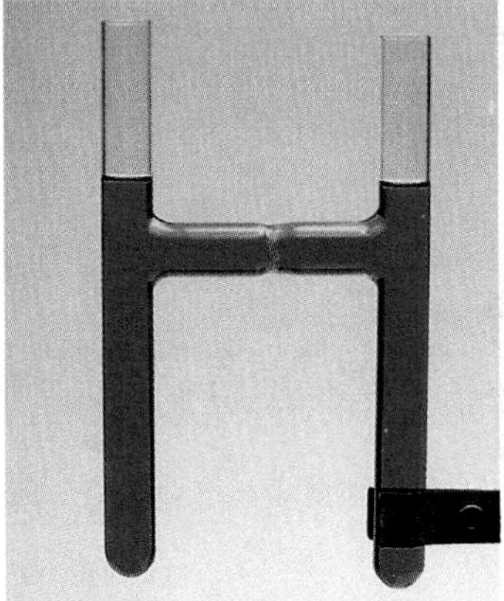

FIGURE 17-6
A porous glass plate prevents rapid mixing of solutions but allows the slow migration of ions. These photos show pure water and a solution of potassium permanganate separated by a porous plate. The second photo was taken several hours after the compartments were filled. Evidence for ion migration is given by the slow development of the characteristic red-violet color of MnO_4^- on the water side.

Recall from Chapter 16 that the concentrations of hydronium and hydroxide ions in pure water are only 10^{-7} M.

GALVANIC CELLS

Electrochemistry is the coupling of a chemical redox process with electron flow through a wire. The process represented in Figure 17-5 is electrochemical because the redox reaction releases chemical energy that is converted into an electrical current through an external wire. On the other hand, Figure 17-2 shows a redox process that is not electrochemical, because direct electron transfer cannot generate an electrical current through a wire.

An arrangement that uses redox reactions to generate an electrical current is called a **galvanic cell.*** Galvanic cells, or batteries, are used widely as sources of electrical current. Flashlight batteries make use of electrochemical reactions. When a flashlight is turned on, chemical redox reactions take place in the battery to generate an electron flow through the light bulb.

The cell sketched in Figure 17-5 illustrates the essential components of a galvanic cell. They follow:

1. *A spontaneous redox reaction.* In Figure 17-5, the spontaneous reaction is $Zn_{(s)} + Cu^{2+}_{(aq)} \longrightarrow Zn^{2+}_{(aq)} + Cu_{(s)}$.
2. *A physical barrier blocking direct reaction.* Here, the barrier is provided by separating the solutions in two compartments.
3. *Physical contact between chemical and electrical parts of the cell.* This is accomplished with devices called **electrodes.** The electrodes in Figure 17-5 are strips of copper and zinc.
4. *An external electrical circuit.* This circuit may simply transfer electrons, as in the Zn/Cu example. In useful applications such as flashlights, the external circuit uses the flow of electrons to perform work.
5. *Some means of completing the circuit.* In Figure 17-5, the porous glass plate completes the circuit.
6. *Electrolytes dissolved in the solutions.* All parts of the circuit must allow the passage of charge. If an aqueous phase is present, it must contain electrolytes.

ELECTRODES

The spontaneous redox reaction that drives a galvanic cell takes place at the surfaces of electrodes. Electrons released in the oxidation half-reaction enter the external circuit through one electrode. A reduction half-reaction withdraws electrons from the external circuit at the other electrode. The electrode where oxidation occurs is the **anode,** and the electrode where the reduction occurs is the **cathode.**

Here is an easy mnemonic for remembering how electrodes are named: Oxidation and anode both begin with vowels; reduction and cathode both begin with consonants.

Electrodes are either active or passive. In addition to conducting electrons to and from the external circuit, an **active electrode** is part of the chemistry of the redox reaction. In the galvanic cell illustrated in Figure 17-5, both metal strips are active electrodes. As the redox reaction progresses, zinc metal dissolves off of the anode, while copper metal deposits on the cathode. The reaction at these active electrodes is conversion between a metal and its aqueous cations. At another type of active electrode, found in many batteries, the reaction is conversion between a metal and an insoluble salt. At the surface of this type of electrode, metal cations combine with anions from the solution to form the salt. One example is the lead anode of an automobile battery, at whose surface lead metal loses electrons and forms lead(II) sulfate:

The oxidation half-reaction produces Pb^{2+} ions, which combine with sulfate ions in solution to make the insoluble salt $PbSO_4$.

* The galvanic cell is named in honor of Luigi Galvani, an Italian physician who discovered electrochemistry in 1791 while studying how nerves work in frogs. Nerves work according to electrochemical principles, but at the time Galvani did his work, scientists' knowledge of cations, anions, and electrons was insufficient to explain his observations.

$$Pb_{(s)} + SO_4{}^{2-}{}_{(aq)} \rightarrow PbSO_{4\,(s)} + 2\,e^-$$

Redox half-reactions may also involve the conversion of one metal salt into another. For example, in rechargeable nickel-cadmium batteries, a nickel(IV) oxide cathode is reduced to nickel(II) hydroxide. The half-reaction reduces Ni(IV) to Ni(II):

$$NiO_{2\,(s)} + 2\,H_2O_{(l)} + 2\,e^- \rightarrow Ni(OH)_{2\,(s)} + 2\,OH^-_{(aq)}$$

Unlike an active electrode, a **passive electrode** conducts electrons to and from the external circuit without participating chemically in the half-reactions. The galvanic cell shown in Figure 17-7 contains passive electrodes. Here, the redox reaction is the reduction of $Fe^{3+}{}_{(aq)}$ to $Fe^{2+}{}_{(aq)}$ and the oxidation of molecular hydrogen to hydronium ions:

$$H_{2\,(g)} + 2\,Fe^{3+}{}_{(aq)} \rightarrow 2\,H^+{}_{(aq)} + 2\,Fe^{2+}{}_{(aq)}$$

Each half-reaction occurs at a metal electrode, but neither electrode takes part in the redox chemistry. In Figure 17-7, the left compartment contains an aqueous solution of iron(III) chloride. Indirect electron transfer at the passive platinum cathode reduces $Fe^{3+}{}_{(aq)}$ to $Fe^{2+}{}_{(aq)}$. To maintain charge balance, ions move through the porous plate into the right-hand container, which contains aqueous hydrochloric acid as the electrolyte. Hydrogen gas is bubbled into the solution and over the surface of the platinum anode. At this surface, hydrogen molecules lose two electrons to become a pair of protons, which bond to water molecules to give hydronium ions. Here are the two half-reactions:

Reduction: $Fe^{3+} + e^- \rightarrow Fe^{2+}$

Oxidation: $H_2 \rightarrow 2\,H^+{}_{(aq)} + 2\,e^-$

Platinum metal is often used as a passive electrode because platinum is one of the least reactive elements. Platinum has a large ionization energy, so it can act as an "electron shuttle" without participating in redox chemistry.

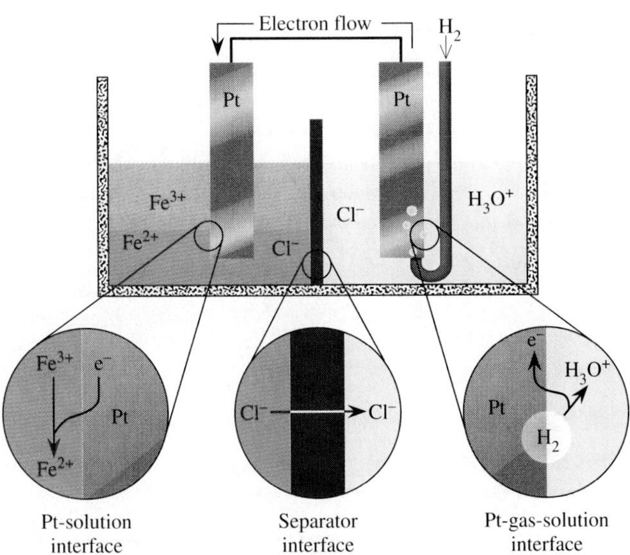

FIGURE 17-7
Diagram of a galvanic cell containing passive electrodes. The two platinum electrodes do not take part in the redox chemistry of this cell. They only conduct electrons to and from the interfaces.

All ionic species in the solutions diffuse through the porous barrier, but we have represented ion flow using only the chloride ions.

The combination of hydrogen gas, aqueous hydronium ions, and a platinum electrode is a hydrogen electrode, as shown in the right-hand portion of Figure 17-7. When this electrode operates under standard conditions, $p(H_2) = 1.00$ atm and $[H^+_{(aq)}] = 1.00$ M, it is a **standard hydrogen electrode (SHE).** The standard hydrogen electrode is particularly important in electrochemistry, as we describe in Section 17.5.

The chemical species involved in the half-reactions dictate what types of electrodes must be used in a particular galvanic cell. If either the reactant or the product is a solid that conducts electrons, an active electrode will be present. When neither the reactant nor the product is a solid conductor, an appropriate passive electrode must be used.

To summarize the features that characterize galvanic cells, Sample Problem 17-8 describes the lead storage battery.

SAMPLE PROBLEM 17-8 DESCRIBING A GALVANIC CELL

The electrical current needed to start an automobile engine is provided by a lead storage battery. These batteries contain aqueous sulfuric acid in contact with two electrodes. One electrode is metallic lead, and the other is solid PbO_2. Both electrodes are coated with solid $PbSO_4$, which is the product of both half-reactions. Determine the balanced half-reactions, the overall redox reaction, and identify the anode and cathode in this galvanic cell.

METHOD: The problem provides a description of the chemical composition of a galvanic cell. To determine what redox reactions take place, we need to identify the elements that change their oxidation numbers.

As with other types of chemical problems, we begin by identifying the major species present in the cell. The aqueous electrolyte contains H_2SO_4, a strong acid. Thus the major species in solution are H_2O, $H^+_{(aq)}$, and $HSO_4^-{}_{(aq)}$. According to the description of the battery, the solid species present are Pb, PbO_2, and $PbSO_4$.

Determine the oxidation numbers using the three guidelines and the fact that the polyatomic sulfate ion has −2 charge:

Pb	PbO_2	$PbSO_4$
0	+4 −2	+2 +6 −2

HSO_4^-	H_2O	$H^+_{(aq)}$
+1 +6 −2	+1 −2	+1

Sulfur, oxygen, and hydrogen have the same oxidation number in all these species, so lead must participate in both redox half-reactions. The description of the battery states that $PbSO_4$ is the product of both half-reactions. Lead metal is oxidized to $PbSO_4$, and lead(IV) oxide is reduced to $PbSO_4$:

$$Pb_{(s)} \longrightarrow PbSO_{4\,(s)} \qquad PbO_{2\,(s)} \longrightarrow PbSO_{4\,(s)}$$

To balance sulfur, we must introduce the other sulfur-containing species, HSO_4^-:

$$Pb_{(s)} + HSO_4^-{}_{(aq)} \longrightarrow PbSO_{4\,(s)} \qquad PbO_{2\,(s)} + HSO_4^-{}_{(aq)} \longrightarrow PbSO_{4\,(s)}$$

Now all elements other than hydrogen and oxygen are balanced, so we proceed with the rest of the balancing procedure.

Here is the procedure for one half-reaction:

$$Pb_{(s)} + HSO_4^-{}_{(aq)} \longrightarrow PbSO_{4\,(s)} + H^+_{(aq)}$$

$$Pb_{(s)} + HSO_4^-{}_{(aq)} \longrightarrow PbSO_{4\,(s)} + H^+_{(aq)} + 2\,e^-$$

Electrons appear on the right, so this is the oxidation that takes place at the anode. The lead electrode is an active anode in a lead storage battery.

Now consider the second half-reaction:

$$PbO_{2\,(s)} + HSO_4^-{}_{(aq)} \rightarrow PbSO_{4\,(s)} + 2\,H_2O_{(l)}$$

$$PbO_{2\,(s)} + HSO_4^-{}_{(aq)} + 3\,H^+{}_{(aq)} \rightarrow PbSO_{4\,(s)} + 2\,H_2O_{(l)}$$

$$PbO_{2\,(s)} + HSO_4^-{}_{(aq)} + 3\,H^+{}_{(aq)} + 2\,e^- \rightarrow PbSO_{4\,(s)} + 2\,H_2O_{(l)}$$

Electrons appear on the left, so this is the reduction that takes place at the cathode. Lead(IV) oxide is an active cathode in a lead storage battery.

Because two electrons are transferred in each half-reaction, the overall redox reaction can be obtained by adding and "cleaning up":

$$PbO_{2\,(s)} + Pb_{(s)} + 2\,HSO_4^-{}_{(aq)} + 2\,H^+{}_{(aq)} \rightarrow 2\,PbSO_{4\,(s)} + 2\,H_2O_{(l)}$$

SECTION EXERCISES

17.3.1 The thermite reaction illustrates that aluminum metal readily loses electrons to iron cations. This suggests that a galvanic cell involving aluminum and iron is highly spontaneous:

$$2\,Al + 6\,OH^- \rightarrow Al_2O_3 + 3\,H_2O + 6\,e^-$$

$$Fe_2O_3 + 3\,H_2O + 6\,e^- \rightarrow 2\,Fe + 6\,OH^-$$

Draw a schematic diagram, similar to Figure 17-5, showing the operation of this galvanic cell. Include the directions of all charge flows.

17.3.2 Use tabulated thermodynamic data to verify that the galvanic cell of Exercise 17.3.1 is spontaneous in the direction written.

17.3.3 Draw a molecular picture similar to the one shown in Figure 17-3 that illustrates the difference between an active electrode and a passive electrode. Use an iron anode in contact with a solution containing Fe^{2+} ions to illustrate an active electrode. Use a platinum cathode immersed in a solution containing Fe^{2+} and Fe^{3+} ions to illustrate a passive electrode.

17.4 REDOX STOICHIOMETRY

Redox reactions are subject to the same stoichiometric principles as other chemical reactions. The quantitative relationship between the oxidizing agent and the reducing agent is provided by the stoichiometric coefficients in the balanced redox equation. Because electrons always cancel in a balanced redox equation, however, we must examine half-reactions to relate the amount of chemical change to the electron flow. A balanced half-reaction provides the stoichiometric coefficients needed to compute the number of moles of electrons transferred for every mole of reagent.

MOLES OF CHARGE

To describe the stoichiometry of an electrochemical process, we need to know the total electrical charge carried by a mole of electrons. The fundamental unit of electrical charge is the **coulomb** (C) and the charge on a single electron (*e*) has been

The experiments that determined the charge of one electron appear in Chapter 2.

measured to a very high degree of accuracy: $e = 1.6021773 \times 10^{-19}$ C. The quantity of charge provided by 1 mol of electrons is obtained by multiplying the charge on a single electron by Avogadro's number (N_A). This quantity is **Faraday's constant (*F*).*** This constant is the link between chemical amounts (moles) and electrical amounts (coulombs):

$$F = e\,N_A = (1.6021773 \times 10^{-19}\ \text{C})(6.022137 \times 10^{23}\ \text{mol}^{-1})$$

$$F = 96{,}485.31\ \text{C mol}^{-1}$$

An electrical current is a flow of electrons through a circuit. The *rate* at which current flows through a circuit is measured in amperes (A):

$$1\ \text{A} = 1\ \text{C s}^{-1}$$

If we multiply current, symbolized I, by time (t), we obtain the *total amount* of charge:

$$\text{Charge} = I\,t$$

The number of moles of electrons transferred in a specific amount of time is this total charge divided by the charge per mole, F. Combining these relationships yields an equation for the moles of electrons provided by an electrical current:

$$\text{Moles of electrons} = n = \frac{I\,t}{F} \qquad \textbf{(17-1)}$$

I = Current (C s^{-1}), t = Time (s), *and* $F = 96{,}485$ C mol^{-1}

Equation 17-1 links the stoichiometry of a redox reaction with the characteristics of an electrochemical cell, and Sample Problem 17-9 shows how to apply this equation.

SAMPLE PROBLEM 17-9 ELECTRON STOICHIOMETRY

An automobile's headlights typically draw 5.9 amperes of current. The galvanic cell of a lead storage battery, described in Sample Problem 17-8, consumes Pb and PbO_2 as it operates. A typical electrode contains about 250 g of PbO_2. Assuming that the battery can supply 5.9 amperes of current until all the PbO_2 has been consumed, how long it will take for a battery to run down if the lights are left on after the engine is turned off.

METHOD: This is an electrochemical stoichiometry problem, in which an amount of a chemical substance is consumed as an electrical current flows. Current will flow as long as there is lead(IV) oxide present to accept electrons. The battery "dies" when all the lead(IV) oxide is consumed. Equation 17-1 links current with moles of electrons, and a balanced half-reaction provides a stoichiometric relationship between moles of electrons and moles of PbO_2.

* Michael Faraday was one of the greatest scientists of all time. Working in the first half of the nineteenth century, he developed many of the fundamental principles of electricity. Faraday discovered the quantitative relationship between electricity and chemical change. Equally at home in chemistry and physics, he discovered benzene, was the first to achieve temperatures low enough to liquefy gases such as H_2S and Cl_2, and invented the electrical generator. He is honored not only by the faraday but also by the unit of electrostatic capacitance, the farad.

The number of moles of electrons consumed by 1 mol of PbO_2 is described by the balanced half-reaction, as was determined in Sample Problem 17-8:

$$PbO_{2\,(s)} + HSO_4^-{}_{(aq)} + 3\,H^+{}_{(aq)} + 2\,e^- \longrightarrow PbSO_{4\,(s)} + 2\,H_2O_{(l)}$$

$$\text{Moles of electrons} = n = \text{mol PbO}_2\left(\frac{2 \text{ mol e}^-}{1 \text{ mol PbO}_2}\right)$$

A standard mole-mass conversion relates mass of PbO_2 to moles of electrons:

$$n = \left(\frac{250 \text{ g PbO}_2}{239.2 \text{ g mol}^{-1} \text{ PbO}_2}\right)\left(\frac{2 \text{ mol e}^-}{1 \text{ mol PbO}_2}\right) = 2.090 \text{ mol electrons}$$

Equation 17-1 provides the link between moles of electrons and time of operation:

$$n = \frac{I\,t}{F} \quad or \quad t = \frac{nF}{I}$$

$$t = \frac{(96{,}485 \text{ C mol}^{-1})(2.090 \text{ mol})}{(5.9 \text{ C s}^{-1})(60 \text{ s min}^{-1})(60 \text{ min hr}^{-1})} = 9.5 \text{ hours}$$

When an automobile engine is running, it drives an electrical generator or alternator that provides current for headlights and other needs. The lead storage battery does not "run down" as long as the generator or alternator is functioning properly.

Redox reactions may involve solids, solutes, gases, or charge flows. Therefore we must be prepared for all the various conversions from molar amounts to measurable variables. As a reminder, here are the four relationships used for mole calculations:

For solids:	$n = m/MM$
For solutes:	$n = MV$
For gases:	$n = PV/RT$
For electrons:	$n = I\,t/F$

Galvanic cells use redox reactions to generate electrical current. We show in Section 17.8 that electrical current can also drive redox reactions and that the same stoichiometric relationships apply to such processes.

REDOX SYNTHESIS

Redox chemistry plays an important role in industrial syntheses. In many large-scale industrial redox reactions, oxygen or hydrogen reacts directly with starting materials in the presence of an appropriate catalyst. The leading example of industrial reduction is the Haber process for reducing N_2 to NH_3. As discussed in Chapter 15, the entire fertilizer industry is based on this reaction.

$$N_2 + 3\,H_2 \xrightarrow{\text{Fe}} 2\,NH_3$$

N = 0	N = −3
H = 0	H = +1

Several oxidation reactions have industrial importance. For example, the leading industrial chemical, sulfuric acid, is produced by oxidizing sulfur, first to SO_2 and then to SO_3.

$$S + O_2 \longrightarrow SO_2 \qquad\qquad 2\,SO_2 + O_2 \xrightarrow{V_2O_5} 2\,SO_3$$

S = 0	S = +4	S = +4	O = 0	S = +6
O = 0	O = −2	O = −2		O = −2

More than 6 billion pounds of formaldehyde, an important monomer in the polymer industry, are produced annually by the oxidation of methanol. In this oxidation, the oxidation number of carbon changes from −2 to zero:

$$\underset{\text{Methanol}}{CH_3OH} + O_2 \longrightarrow \underset{\text{Formaldehyde}}{H_2C{=}O} + H_2O$$

Methanol: O = −2, H = 4(+1), C = −2

Formaldehyde: O = −2, H = 2(+1), C = 0

Another example is the production of terephthalic acid, in which O_2 gas oxidizes xylene. This is an example in which the average oxidation number of carbon changes from one fractional value to another:

Terephthalic acid and ethylene glycol, $HOCH_2CH_2OH$, are copolymerized to make polyester textiles. Polymer chemistry is discussed in Chapter 11.

$$\underset{\substack{\text{Xylene}\\C_6H_4(CH_3)_2}}{\text{xylene}} + 3\ O_2 \xrightarrow{\text{Co, Mn salts}} \underset{\substack{\text{Terephthalic acid}\\C_6H_4(CO_2H)_2}}{\text{terephthalic acid}}$$

Xylene: H = +1, O = 0, C_{avg} = −5/4

Terephthalic acid: H = +1, O = −2, C_{avg} = +1/4

SECTION EXERCISES

17.4.1 In mercury batteries, the spontaneous cell reaction is:

$$HgO + Zn \longrightarrow ZnO + Hg$$

Suppose that a mercury battery contains 250 mg each of HgO and Zn.
(a) Which reagent will be consumed first?
(b) How many coulombs of charge can the battery deliver before this reagent is consumed?
(c) What is the lifetime of the battery (in days) if it powers a digital watch requiring 1.50 microamperes of current?

17.4.2 Draw molecular pictures illustrating the processes that occur at each electrode in a mercury battery.

17.4.3 Potassium chromate, K_2CrO_4, dissolves in acidic solution to generate strongly oxidizing $Cr_2O_7^{2-}$ ions:

$$K_2CrO_{4\ (s)} + H^+_{(aq)} \longrightarrow 2\ K^+_{(aq)} + HCrO^-_{4\ (aq)}$$

$$2\ HCrO^-_{4\ (aq)} \longrightarrow Cr_2O_7^{2-}{}_{(aq)} + H_2O_{(l)}$$

This oxidizing agent is reduced to Cr^{3+} as it oxidizes other substances.
(a) Balance the reduction half-reaction.
(b) What mass of K_2CrO_4 produces 0.250 mol of electrons?

17.5 CELL POTENTIALS

Batteries supply electrical current that consists of electrons flowing from one place to another. In some ways, flowing electrons are like flowing water. Because of gravitational force, water always flows downhill, from higher altitude to lower altitude.

Water at high altitude has gravitational potential energy that can be converted to other forms: kinetic energy in a waterfall, mechanical energy in a waterwheel, or electrical energy in a hydroelectric turbine.

Electrons flow under the influence of coulombic force. Electrons flow from regions of more negative electrical potential energy to regions of more positive electrical potential energy. As electrons flow, their potential energy can be converted to other forms: light energy in a flashlight, mechanical energy in the starter motor of an automobile, or thermal energy in an electrical heater.

The difference in gravitational potential between two points is measured by their difference in altitude. Analogously, a difference in electrical potential is measured as a **voltage.** For electrons, a point at a negative electrical potential is "uphill" from a point at a positive electrical potential. The parallel between gravitational potential and electrical potential is summarized in Figure 17-8.

Gravitational potential results from the attractions between masses, which are always positive. Electrical charges, in contrast, can be positive or negative. Electrical potential results from the force of attraction between opposite charges and the force of repulsion between like charges. Electrons, which are negatively charged, are attracted "downhill" from more negative potentials to more positive potentials.

ELECTRODE EQUILIBRIUM

To visualize how electrochemical cells generate electrical potential differences, consider a zinc electrode dipped into a solution of zinc sulfate. From the *macroscopic* perspective, nothing happens. However, chemical change occurs at the *molecular level*. Some zinc atoms are oxidized to Zn^{2+} ions:

$$Zn_{(s)} \longrightarrow Zn^{2+}_{(aq)} + 2\,e^-_{(metal)}$$

The ions move off into the solution, leaving an excess of electrons in the metal strip. The reverse process also occurs. When a Zn^{2+} ion collides with the surface of the metal, it may capture electrons and become reduced to a neutral zinc atom:

$$Zn^{2+}_{(aq)} + 2\,e^-_{(metal)} \longrightarrow Zn_{(s)}$$

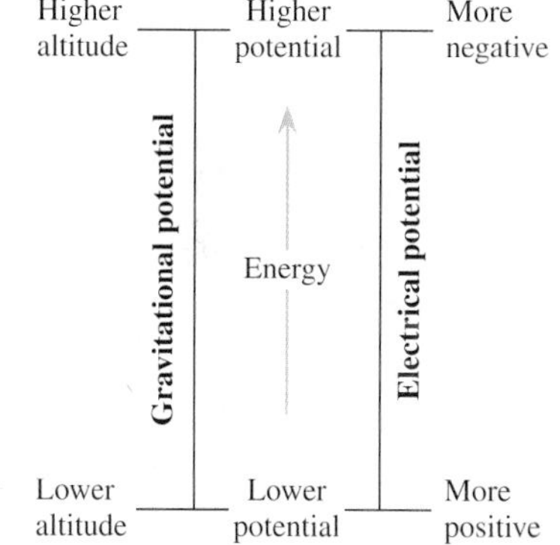

FIGURE 17-8
Gravitational potential and electrical potential have common features.

When a zinc strip is dipped into the solution, the initial rates of these processes are different. The different rates of reaction lead to a charge imbalance across the metal-solution interface. When the concentration of zinc ions in solution is low enough, the initial rate of oxidation is more rapid than the initial rate of reduction. Under these conditions, excess electrons accumulate in the metal, and excess cationic charges accumulate in the solution. As excess charge builds, however, the rates of reaction change until the rate of reduction is balanced by the rate of oxidation. The system is at dynamic equilibrium. Oxidation and reduction continue, but the net rate of exchange is zero:

$$Zn_{(s)} \rightleftharpoons Zn^{2+}_{(aq)} + 2\,e^-_{(metal)}$$

The molecular equilibrium at a zinc electrode is represented in Figure 17-9. At equilibrium, the charge imbalance is about one electron for every 10^{14} atoms, which is negligible from the macroscopic perspective but significant at the molecular level.

An analogous dynamic equilibrium is established when a copper electrode is dipped in a dilute solution of copper sulfate:

$$Cu_{(s)} \rightleftharpoons Cu^{2+}_{(aq)} + 2\,e^-_{(metal)}$$

At the macroscopic level, nothing appears to happen, but at the molecular level, some copper atoms lose electrons and enter the solution as Cu^{2+} ions, and some copper(II) ions capture electrons and deposit on the electrode as Cu atoms. As with zinc, dipping a strip of copper metal in the solution generates a small charge imbalance.

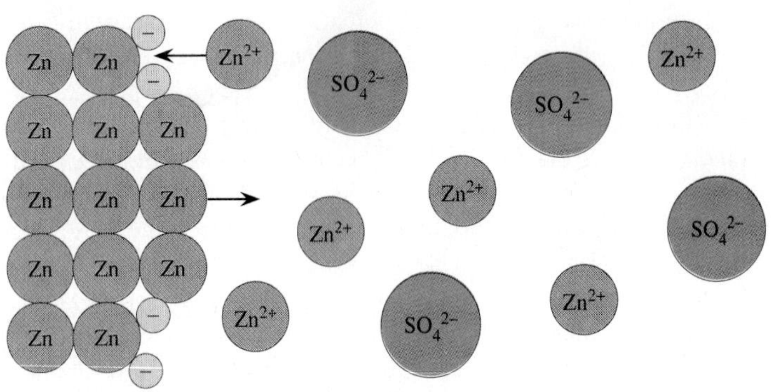

FIGURE 17-9
A zinc electrode immersed in a solution of zinc sulfate comes to a dynamic equilibrium when a few excess charges occur in each phase and the rates of oxidation and reduction balance.

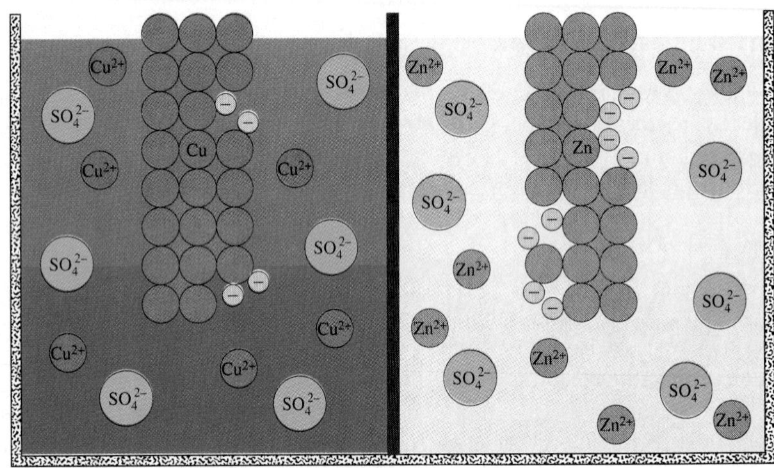

FIGURE 17-10
Copper and zinc generate different equilibrium concentrations of excess charges. Zinc is easier to oxidize than copper, so the zinc electrode contains a higher concentration of electrons. If the electrodes are connected by a wire, electrons will flow from the more negative electrical potential (zinc) toward the more positive electrical potential (copper).

The sums of the first two ionization energies for zinc (2640 kJ/mol) and copper (2700 kJ/mol) are nearly the same, but zinc cations are more effectively stabilized by solvation, so $Zn^{2+}{}_{(aq)}$ forms more readily than $Cu^{2+}{}_{(aq)}$.

Although they are both extremely small, the charge imbalances for copper and zinc have different values. Zinc is easier to oxidize than copper. As a consequence, the concentration of electrons in the zinc electrode is greater than the concentration of electrons in the copper electrode. Because it has a larger number of excess electrons, the zinc electrode is at a *more negative* electrical potential than the copper electrode. Figure 17-10 summarizes the molecular perspective for these two electrodes.

The excess charges present at equilibrium are analogous to water stored behind a dam. Water at the lip of the dam is at equilibrium with water anywhere else on the surface of the lake, but it is at higher gravitational potential than water below the dam. Given the opportunity (for example, if a spillway is opened), water will flow downhill. In the same way, the excess charges within an electrode or within a solution are at equilibrium with other charges in the same phase, but if given the opportunity, they will flow "downhill" to a phase of less negative electrical potential energy (Figure 17-11).

The difference in electrical potential between zinc and copper causes electrons to flow if the circuit is completed, as shown in Figure 17-5. Electrons flow from a region where the concentration of electrons is higher to a region where the concentration of electrons is lower. In this case, electrons flow from the zinc electrode to the copper electrode. The result is a galvanic cell in which an electrical potential difference generates a sustained current.

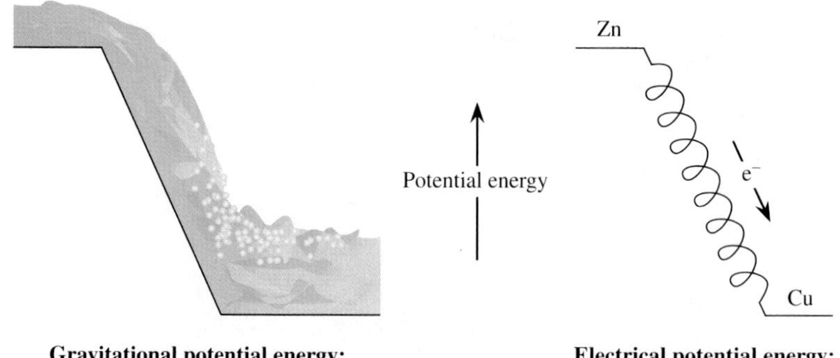

FIGURE 17-11
Water flows downhill from higher to lower gravitational potential energy when a suitable path, such as a spillway, is provided. Analogously, electrons flow "downhill" from higher to lower negative electrical potential energy when a suitable path, such as a conducting wire, is provided.

The difference in potential energy between two electrodes is called the **electromotive force (emf),** symbolized by the italicized letter E. The magnitude of E increases as the amount of charge imbalance between the two electrodes increases. The value of E and the direction of electron flow can be determined experimentally by inserting a voltmeter in the external circuit. The units of electromotive force are volts, and one volt is 1 J of electrical potential energy per coulomb of charge transferred through the circuit.

1 V = 1 J/C.

STANDARD ELECTRICAL POTENTIAL

Electrochemical cells can be constructed using an almost limitless combination of electrodes and solutions, and each combination generates its own cell potential. Moreover, cell potentials vary with chemical concentrations. For example, we have shown that a zinc electrode dipped into a solution containing Zn^{2+} ions establishes an equilibrium in which small quantities of excess charge in the electrode generate an electrical potential. As we described in Chapter 15, the position of any chemical equilibrium shifts in response to changes in concentrations of the species participating in the equilibrium. Consequently, the quantity of excess charge and the electrode potential both change if the concentration of Zn^{2+} in the solution is varied.

Keeping track of the electrical potentials of cells under all possible situations would be extremely tedious without some standard reference conditions. Recall that standard conditions for thermodynamic properties are 1 M for solutes in solution and 1 atm for gases. Chemists use the same standard conditions for electrochemical properties. By definition, the standard electrical potential is the potential developed by a cell in which all chemical species are present under standard thermodynamic conditions. As in thermodynamics, standard conditions are designated with a superscript °. A standard electrical potential is designated $E°$.

The zinc-copper cell is under standard conditions when the concentrations of both ions are 1.00 M. A measurement of the cell potential under these conditions gives $E° = 1.10$ V:

$$Zn_{(s)} + Cu^{2+}_{(aq,\ 1.00\ M)} \rightarrow Zn^{2+}_{(aq,\ 1.00\ M)} + Cu_{(s)} \qquad E° = 1.10\ V$$

Figure 17-12 shows the measurement of the standard electrical potential for this cell.

We have shown that any redox reaction can be broken into two distinct half-reactions, an oxidation and a reduction. It would be convenient if we could assign a

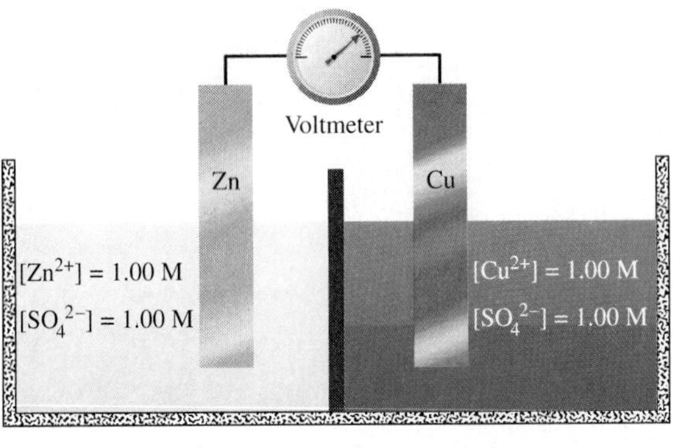

$$E^{o}_{cell} = E^{o}_{Cu^{2+}/Cu} - E^{o}_{Zn^{2+}/Zn} = 1.10 \text{ V}$$

FIGURE 17-12
The measurement of $E°$ for the copper/zinc electrochemical cell. The voltmeter measures the difference in electrical potentials between the two electrodes.

potential to every half-reaction. Then, $E°$ values could be tabulated for all half-reactions, and the standard cell potential for any redox reaction could be obtained by combining the potentials for its two half-reactions. Unfortunately, the potential of a single half-reaction cannot be measured because half-reactions are *always* paired in a redox process. The standard emf of 1.10 V for the Zn/Cu cell, for example, is the difference between the $E°$ values of its two half-reactions, as Figure 17-12 shows.

Although the absolute potential of a single half-reaction cannot be measured, chemists have *defined* one particular half-reaction to have zero potential. All other half-reactions can then be assigned values relative to this reference value of 0 V. This reference half-cell is the reduction of hydronium ions to hydrogen gas:

$$2\,H^{+}_{(aq,\,1.00\,M)} + 2\,e^{-} \rightleftarrows H_{2\,(g,\,1.00\,atm)} \qquad E° = 0 \text{ V by definition}$$

This is the reaction that occurs at the SHE shown in Figure 17-7.

In addition to defining standard conditions and a reference potential, we also need to specify a reference *direction* for half-reactions. As the double arrow in the previous equation indicates, $E°$ values refer to electrode equilibria. Just as the value for an equilibrium constant depends on the direction in which we write the equilibrium, the values of $E°$ depend on whether we write the equilibrium with electrons as reactants or as products. For half-reactions, the conventional reference direction is *reduction*, with electrons always appearing as *reactants*. The conventional $E°$ values for half-reactions are called **standard reduction potentials.**

The convention for electrode potentials can be compared with the convention for acid equilibrium constants, K_a, where the weak acid always appears as a reactant.

Defining a reference value for the SHE makes it possible to determine $E°$ values of all other redox half-reactions. As an example, Figure 17-13 illustrates a cell in which a standard hydrogen electrode is connected to a copper electrode in contact with a 1.00 M solution of Cu^{2+}. In this cell, electrons flow from the SHE to the copper electrode, indicating that reduction of Cu^{2+} and oxidation of H_2 occur spontaneously:

$$Cu^{2+}_{(aq,\,1.00\,M)} + H_{2\,(g,\,1.00\,atm)} \longrightarrow Cu_{(s)} + 2\,H^{+}_{(aq,\,1.00\,M)}$$

Measurements show that this cell has a voltage of 0.34 V, with the copper electrode more positive than the standard hydrogen electrode. Because the potential of the SHE is *defined* to be 0 V, this means that the reduction half-reaction Cu^{2+}/Cu has $E° = +0.34$ V *relative to the SHE:*

$$2\,H^{+}_{(aq,\,1.00\,M)} + 2\,e^{-} \rightleftarrows H_{2\,(g,\,1.00\,atm)} \qquad E° = 0 \text{ V by definition}$$

$$Cu^{2+}_{(aq,\,1.00\,M)} + 2\,e^{-} \rightleftarrows Cu_{(s)} \qquad E° = 0.34 \text{ V (relative to SHE)}$$

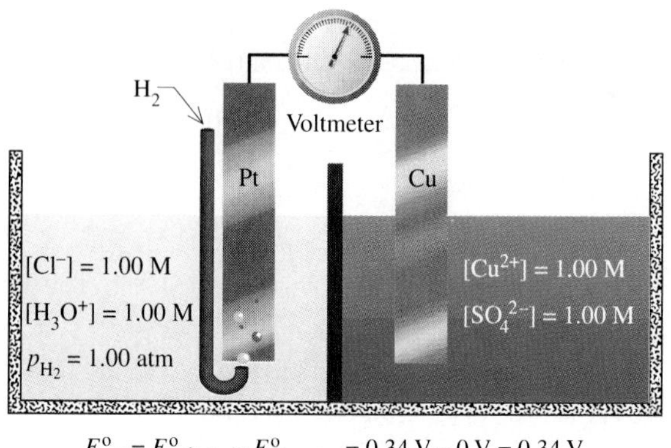

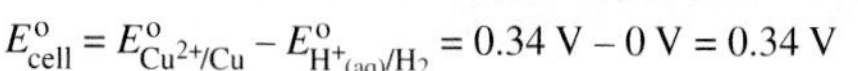

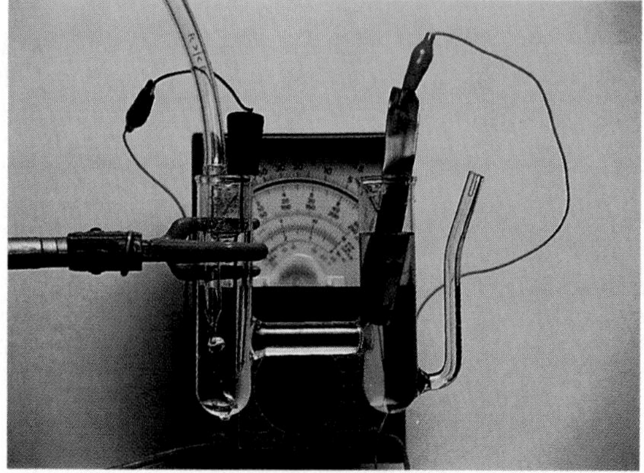

FIGURE 17-13
Photograph and schematic diagram of a cell for measuring the $E°$ of the Cu^{2+}/Cu half-reaction relative to the standard hydrogen electrode (SHE).

Over the years, chemists have carried out many measurements similar to the one in Figure 17-13. As a result, numerous standard reduction potentials are tabulated in reference sources such as the *Handbook of Chemistry and Physics*. Many values appear in Appendix H, and some representative values appear in Table 17-1.

Every standard reduction potential has a specific sign. When a substance is easier to reduce than hydronium ions under standard conditions, its $E°$ is positive. When a substance is more difficult to reduce than hydronium ions under standard conditions, its $E°$ is negative.

STANDARD CELL VOLTAGES

The net reaction that occurs in a galvanic cell under standard conditions can be constructed from standard reduction half-reactions. A redox reaction must include both an oxidation and a reduction, so one of the half-cells must run as an oxidation that supplies electrons for the reduction. An oxidation half-reaction is the *reverse* of the corresponding reduction half-reaction.

Electrons always flow spontaneously from more negative electrical potential to more positive electrical potential. This means that, under standard conditions, electrons are produced by the reaction with the more negative standard potential and consumed by the reaction with the more positive standard potential. Under standard conditions, therefore, the reaction with the more negative $E°$ value occurs as oxidation, and the reaction with the more positive $E°$ value occurs as reduction.

The voltage of any cell under standard conditions can be calculated using tabulated standard reduction potentials. The net cell potential is the *difference* between the individual standard reduction potentials and is obtained by subtracting the more negative standard reduction potential from the more positive standard reduction potential. The cell voltage has a positive value for any spontaneous redox reaction. To summarize:

The reaction with the more negative half-cell reduction potential occurs at the anode as an oxidation.

The reaction with the more positive half-cell reduction potential occurs at the cathode as a reduction.

Combining these features, we can write an equation that summarizes the calculation of the standard potential for a galvanic cell:

$$E°_{cell} = E°_{cathode} - E°_{anode} \qquad \textbf{(17-2)}$$

TABLE 17-1 REPRESENTATIVE STANDARD REDUCTION POTENTIALS

REACTION	$E°$ (V)
Positive Values	
$F_{2\,(g)} + 2\,e^- \rightleftarrows 2\,F^-$	2.866
$PbO_2 + SO_4^{2-} + 4\,H^+_{(aq)} + 2\,e^- \rightleftarrows PbSO_4 + 2\,H_2O$	1.6913
$Au^{3+} + 3\,e^- \rightleftarrows Au$	1.498
$Cl_{2\,(g)} + 2\,e^- \rightleftarrows 2\,Cl^-$	1.35827
$Cr_2O_7^{2-} + 14\,H^+_{(aq)} + 6\,e^- \rightleftarrows 2\,Cr^{3+} + 7\,H_2O$	1.232
$O_{2\,(g)} + 4\,H^+_{(aq)} + 4\,e^- \rightleftarrows 2\,H_2O$	1.229
$Pt^{2+} + 2\,e^- \rightleftarrows Pt$	1.118
$Br_{2\,(l)} + 2\,e^- \rightleftarrows 2\,Br^-$	1.066
$Hg^{2+} + 2\,e^- \rightleftarrows Hg$	0.854
$Ag^+ + e^- \rightleftarrows Ag$	0.7996
$I_2 + 2e^- \rightleftarrows 2\,I^-$	0.5355
$Cu^+ + e^- \rightleftarrows Cu$	0.521
$O_2 + 2\,H_2O + 4\,e^- \rightleftarrows 4\,OH^-$	0.401
$Cu^{2+} + 2\,e^- \rightleftarrows Cu$	0.3419
$AgCl + e^- \rightleftarrows Ag + Cl^-$	0.22233
$Cu^{2+} + e^- \rightleftarrows Cu^+$	0.153
$Sn^{4+} + 2\,e^- \rightleftarrows Sn^{2+}$	0.151
$AgBr + e^- \rightleftarrows Ag + Br^-$	0.07133
$2\,H^+_{(aq)} + 2\,e^- \rightleftarrows H_2$	0 (defined)
Negative Values	
$Fe^{3+} + 3\,e^- \rightleftarrows Fe$	−0.037
$Pb^{2+} + 2\,e^- \rightleftarrows Pb$	−0.1262
$Sn^{2+} + 2\,e^- \rightleftarrows Sn$	−0.137
$PbSO_4 + 2\,e^- \rightleftarrows Pb + SO_4^{2-}$	−0.3588
$Fe^{2+} + 2\,e^- \rightleftarrows Fe$	−0.447
$Ni(OH)_2 + 2\,e^- \rightleftarrows Ni + 2\,OH^-$	−0.72
$Cr^{3+} + 3\,e^- \rightleftarrows Cr$	−0.744
$Zn^{2+} + 2\,e^- \rightleftarrows Zn$	−0.7618
$Cd(OH)_2 + 2\,e^- \rightleftarrows Cd_{(Hg)} + 2\,OH^-$	−0.809
$Al^{3+} + 3\,e^- \rightleftarrows Al$	−1.662
$Mg^{2+} + 2\,e^- \rightleftarrows Mg$	−2.37
$Na^+ + e^- \rightleftarrows Na$	−2.714
$Ca^{2+} + 2\,e^- \rightleftarrows Ca$	−2.868
$Ca(OH)_2 + 2\,e^- \rightleftarrows Ca + 2\,OH^-$	−3.02
$Li^+ + e^- \rightleftarrows Li$	−3.0401

Here is this procedure for the copper-hydrogen cell illustrated in Figure 17-13:

$$Cu^{2+}{}_{(aq,\ 1.00\ atm)} + 2\ e^- \rightleftarrows Cu_{(s)} \qquad E^\circ = +0.34\ V$$

$$H_{2\ (g,\ 1.00\ atm)} \rightleftarrows 2\ H^+{}_{(aq,\ 1.00\ M)} + 2\ e^- \qquad E^\circ = 0\ V$$

$$H_{2\ (g,\ 1.00\ atm)} + Cu^{2+}{}_{(aq,\ 1.00\ M)} \rightleftarrows 2\ H^+{}_{(aq,\ 1.00\ M)} + Cu_{(s)}$$

$$E^\circ{}_{cell} = E^\circ{}_{Cu^{2+}/Cu} - E^\circ{}_{H^+{}_{(aq)}/H_2} = 0.34\ V - 0\ V = 0.34\ V$$

In this spontaneous redox reaction, electrons are generated at the anode through the oxidation of hydrogen. Excess electrons in the platinum electrode create a negative electrical potential. In the other compartment of the cell, Cu^{2+} ions are reduced to copper metal by stripping electrons from the cathode. In the wire connecting the electrodes, electrons flow "downhill" to the region of more positive electrical potential (the cathode, $E^\circ = 0.34$ V) from the region of less positive electrical potential (the anode, $E^\circ = 0$ V).

We could set up another galvanic cell, replacing the Cu^{2+}/Cu half-cell with a standard Zn^{2+}/Zn half-cell. In this cell, electrons would flow from the zinc electrode to the SHE, indicating that the spontaneous reaction is reduction of $H^+{}_{(aq)}$ and oxidation of zinc:

$$Zn_{(s)} + 2\ H^+{}_{(aq,\ 1.00\ M)} \rightarrow Zn^{2+}{}_{(aq,\ 1.00\ M)} + H_{2\ (g,\ 1.00\ atm)}$$

This cell displays a voltage of 0.76 V, with the standard hydrogen electrode being more *positive* than the zinc electrode. Thus the standard cell potential for Zn^{2+}/Zn is *more negative* by 0.76 V than the reference value of 0 V for the SHE: $E^\circ{}_{(Zn^{2+}/Zn)} = -0.76$ V.

$$2\ H^+{}_{(aq,\ 1.00M)} + 2\ e^- \rightleftarrows H_{2\ (g,\ 1.00\ atm)}$$

$$Zn_{(s)} \rightleftarrows Zn^{2+}{}_{(aq,\ 1.00\ M)} + 2\ e^-$$

$$2\ H^+{}_{(aq,\ 1.00\ M)} + Zn_{(s)} \rightleftarrows H_{2\ (g,\ 1.00\ atm)} + Zn^{2+}{}_{(aq,\ 1.00\ M)}$$

$$E^\circ{}_{cell} = E^\circ{}_{H^+{}_{(aq)}/H_2} - E^\circ{}_{Zn^{2+}/Zn} = 0\ V - (-0.76\ V) = 0.76\ V$$

The net voltage generated by a standard galvanic cell is always obtained by *subtracting* one standard reduction potential from the other in the way that gives a positive value for E° cell. Sample Problem 17-10 provides another example, for the zinc-copper galvanic cell.

SAMPLE PROBLEM 17-10 STANDARD CELL POTENTIAL

Figure 17-5 shows a galvanic cell containing a zinc electrode immersed in a solution of zinc sulfate and a copper electrode immersed in a solution of copper(II) sulfate. What is the standard potential of this cell, and what is its spontaneous direction?

METHOD: First, the half-reactions must be determined. Then the standard reduction potentials can be looked up in a table, and the more negative value subtracted from the more positive value.

Write both half-reactions as reductions, and then look up the E° values in Table 17-1:

$$Zn^{2+}_{(aq)} + 2\,e^- \rightleftarrows Zn_{(s)} \qquad E^{\circ}_{Zn^{2+}/Zn} = -0.76\ V$$

$$Cu^{2+}_{(aq)} + 2\,e^- \rightleftarrows Cu_{(s)} \qquad E^{\circ}_{Cu^{2+}/Cu} = +0.34\ V$$

Now, subtract the more negative value (−0.76 V) from the more positive value (+0.34 V) to obtain the standard cell potential:

$$E^{\circ}_{cell} = E^{\circ}_{Cu^{2+}/Cu} - E^{\circ}_{Zn^{2+}/Zn} = 0.34\ V - (-0.76\ V) = 1.10\ V$$

Under standard conditions, the copper-zinc cell operates spontaneously to reduce Cu^{2+} and oxidize Zn.

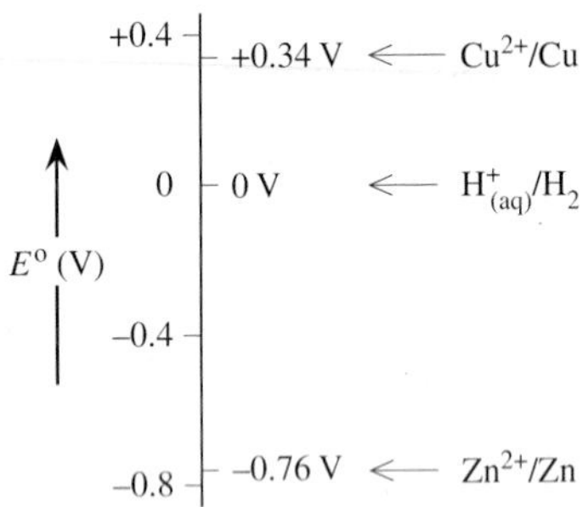

FIGURE 17-14
A voltage diagram illustrating the relationships among the standard potentials for the copper, zinc, and hydrogen half-reactions. The standard potential for any cell constructed using these half-reactions is the difference between two standard reduction potentials.

Figure 17-14 shows a voltage diagram that illustrates the relationships among the three half-cell potentials that we have used in these examples.

CONVENTIONS FOR STANDARD REDUCTION POTENTIALS

Here is a summary of the definitions and conventions for working with electrochemical potentials:

1. Standard conditions for electrochemical half-reactions are the same as those in thermodynamics: 25 °C, 1 M for solutes, and 1 atm for gases.
2. Reduction is the reference direction for electrochemical half-reactions: Electrons are reactants.
3. The standard potential for reducing $H^+_{(aq)}$ to H_2 is defined to be 0 V.
4. The standard potential difference for any cell is the more positive standard reduction potential minus the more negative standard reduction potential. A positive E° indicates spontaneity under standard conditions.
5. In any galvanic cell, the half-reaction with the more positive reduction potential occurs as reduction at the cathode, and the half-reaction with the more negative reduction potential occurs as oxidation at the anode.

Sample Problem 17-11 provides another example of standard cell potentials.

SAMPLE PROBLEM 17-11 HALF-CELL POTENTIALS

The following half-reactions occur in the rechargeable nickel-cadmium battery:

$$Cd(OH)_{2\,(s)} + 2\,e^- \rightleftarrows Cd_{(s)} + 2\,OH^-_{(aq)}$$

$$NiO(OH)_{(s)} + H_2O_{(l)} + e^- \rightleftarrows Ni(OH)_{2\,(s)} + OH^-_{(aq)}$$

This battery has a potential of 1.35 V under standard conditions, with nickel as the cathode. Determine the net reaction, and use the tabulated standard reduction potential for the cadmium half-reaction to find E° for the nickel half-reaction.

METHOD: We can construct the balanced redox equation from the half-reactions. The direction of spontaneity is established with the knowledge that nickel is the cathode. The reduction potential for the Cd half-reaction is determined using Equation 17-2 and the overall cell voltage.

The problem states that the nickel electrode is the cathode. Because reduction takes place at the cathode, the nickel half-reaction is the reduction. In the oxidation half-reaction, cadmium is oxidized at the anode.

To find E° for a half-reaction, use Equation 17-2, the relationship between overall cell potential and standard reduction potentials. The problem states that $E^\circ_{cell} = 1.35$ V. The E° value for the cadmium reaction appears in Table 17-1, but the value for the nickel half-reaction must be determined:

$$E^\circ_{cell} = E^\circ_{cathode} - E^\circ_{anode}$$

$$E^\circ_{cell} = E^\circ_{NiO(OH)/Ni(OH)_2} - E^\circ_{Cd(OH)_2/Cd}$$

$$1.35\text{ V} = E^\circ_{NiO(OH)/Ni(OH)_2} - (-0.809\text{ V})$$

$$E^\circ_{NiO(OH)/Ni(OH)_2} = 1.35\text{ V} + (-0.809\text{ V}) = +0.54\text{ V}$$

To balance the net reaction, multiply the nickel half-reaction by 2 to balance the electrons and combine with the cadmium oxidation. Electrons and hydroxide ions cancel:

$$2\ NiO(OH)_{(s)} + 2\ H_2O_{(l)} + \cancel{2\,e^-} \rightleftarrows 2\ Ni(OH)_{2\,(s)} + \cancel{2\,OH^-}_{(aq)}$$

$$Cd_{(s)} + \cancel{2\,OH^-}_{(aq)} \rightleftarrows Cd(OH)_{2\,(s)} + \cancel{2\,e^-}$$

$$2\ NiO(OH)_{(s)} + 2\ H_2O_{(l)} + Cd_{(s)} \rightleftarrows 2\ Ni(OH)_{2\,(s)} + Cd(OH)_{2\,(s)}$$

The calculation of E° for this cell illustrates an important feature of cell potentials. Cell potentials are simple differences between two standard reduction potentials. This is unchanged by the fact that we must multiply one half-reaction by 2 to cancel electrons in the overall redox reaction.

When a reaction is multiplied by any integer, its cell potential remains unchanged.

To understand why this is so, recall that cell potentials are analogous to altitude differences for water. Whether 1000 or 2000 L of water flow down a spillway, the altitude difference between the top and bottom of the spillway remains unchanged. In the same way, multiplying a reaction by some integer changes the total number of moles of electrons transferred, but it does not change the potential difference through which the electrons are transferred. We return to this point in Section 17.6.

SECTION EXERCISES

17.5.1 Use standard reduction potentials to determine the net reaction and standard cell potential for cells of two compartments, each containing a 1.00 M solution of the indicated cation in contact with an electrode of that neutral metal (that is, cells similar to the one shown in Figure 17-6): (a) Fe^{2+} and Cr^{3+}; (b) Cu^{2+} and Pb^{2+}; and (c) Au^{3+} and Ag^+.

17.5.2 Draw molecular pictures illustrating the charge transfer process taking place in the cell in Exercise 17.5.1(b).

17.5.3 Using the appropriate values from Table 17-1, calculate E° for one cell of a lead storage battery. Refer to Sample Problem 17-9 for the balanced equation. (Six of these cells are connected in series in an automobile storage battery.)

17.6 FREE ENERGY AND ELECTROCHEMISTRY

A spontaneous electrochemical reaction generates a positive E. The spontaneous direction of a redox reaction is given by free energy: a negative ΔG is the thermodynamic signpost for a spontaneous reaction. Thus a reaction that has a *negative* free energy generates a *positive* electromotive force:

$$\Delta G_{\text{reaction}} < 0 \rightarrow \text{Spontaneous redox reaction}$$

$$E_{\text{cell}} > 0 \rightarrow \text{Spontaneous redox reaction}$$

CELL POTENTIAL AND FREE ENERGY

The linkage between free energy and cell potentials can be made quantitative. A redox reaction with a large, negative ΔG° also has a large, positive standard cell potential:

$$Ca_{(s)} + 2\,H_2O_{(l)} \rightarrow Ca(OH)_{2\,(s)} + H_{2\,(g)}$$

$$\Delta G^\circ = -422 \text{ kJ} \qquad E^\circ = +2.868 \text{ V}$$

Similarly, a redox reaction with a smaller standard free energy has a smaller standard cell potential:

$$Cu_2O_{(s)} + H_{2\,(g)} \rightarrow 2\,Cu_{(s)} + H_2O_{(l)}$$

$$\Delta G^\circ = -91 \text{ kJ} \qquad E^\circ = +0.360 \text{ V}$$

These two examples indicate that cell potentials and free energy changes are proportional to each other:

$$\Delta G \propto -E$$

The equality that links these two important parameters is:

$$\Delta G = -nF\,E \qquad \textbf{(17-3)}$$

For a reaction operating under standard conditions, $\Delta G^\circ = -\,nF\,E^\circ$. Faraday's constant *(F)* appears in Equation 17-3 to convert from the electrical units used to measure potentials to the molar units used for thermodynamic quantities. The factor n in Equation 17-3 is the number of electrons transferred in the redox process. It is required because E° is an intensive property independent of the amount of reaction that occurs, but ΔG° is an extensive property whose magnitude depends on the amount of reaction that occurs. The number of electrons transferred is not explicitly stated in the net redox equation, so n must be found from the stoichiometric coefficient for the electrons in the balanced half-reactions. The negative sign in Equation 17-3 is there because a spontaneous reaction has a *negative* value for ΔG° but a *positive* value for E°.

The cell shown in Figure 17-15 can serve as an example for calculations using Equation 17-3. It contains two important electrodes, silver–silver chloride (AgCl/Ag) and mercury–mercury(I) chloride (Hg_2Cl_2/Hg, commonly called the *calomel electrode*). The half-reactions for these electrodes follow:

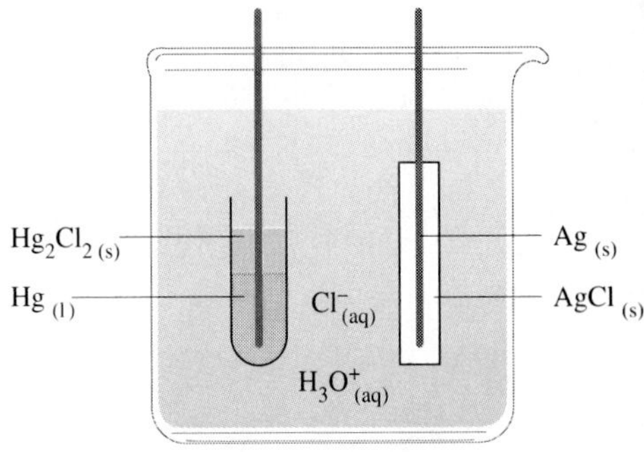

FIGURE 17-15
Two widely used reference electrodes are the silver–silver chloride electrode (*right*) and the mercury–mercury(I) chloride, or calomel, electrode (*left*).

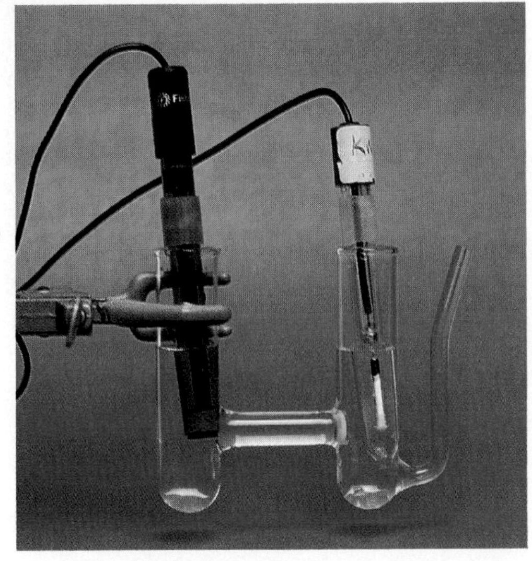

This galvanic cell does not require a physical barrier between the solutions because the species that are oxidized and reduced, Hg, Hg_2Cl_2, AgCl, and Ag, are not free to diffuse through the solution and react by direct electron transfer.

$$AgCl_{(s)} + e^- \rightleftarrows Ag_{(s)} + Cl^-_{(aq)} \qquad E^\circ = 0.2223 \text{ V}$$

$$Hg_2Cl_{2\,(s)} + 2\,e^- \rightleftarrows 2\,Hg_{(s)} + 2\,Cl^-_{(aq)} \qquad E^\circ = 0.2681 \text{ V}$$

In the spontaneous redox reaction, Hg_2Cl_2 is reduced and Ag is oxidized:

$$Hg_2Cl_{2\,(s)} + 2\,Ag_{(s)} \rightleftarrows 2\,Hg_{(s)} + 2\,AgCl_{(s)}$$

$$E^\circ = 0.2681 \text{ V} - 0.2223 \text{ V} = 0.0458 \text{ V}$$

Using Equation 17-3, we can calculate the standard free energy change for this net reaction:

$$\Delta G^\circ = -\,nF\,E^\circ = -\,(2 \text{ mol})(9.6485 \text{ x } 10^4 \text{ C/mol})(0.0458 \text{ V})$$

$$\Delta G^\circ = -8.84 \times 10^3 \text{ V C} = -8.84 \text{ kJ}$$

Recall that 1 J = 1 V C and 10^3 J = 1 kJ.

CELL POTENTIALS AND CHEMICAL EQUILIBRIUM

Equation 17-3 links free energies of reaction with electrochemical cell potentials. According to Equation 16-5, the free energy of a reaction is also related to its equilibrium constant:

$$\Delta G^\circ = -\,nF\,E^\circ \quad \textbf{(17-3)} \qquad \Delta G^\circ = -\,RT\,ln\,K_{eq} \quad \textbf{(16-5)}$$

Combining these two equalities and grouping the constants, we have:

$$-\,RT\,ln\,K_{eq} = -\,nF\,E^\circ$$

$$E^\circ = \frac{RT}{nF}\,ln\,K_{eq} \qquad \textbf{(17-4)}$$

Many calculations using Equation 17-4 refer to standard temperature, 298.15 K. Furthermore, because K_{eq} often has a very large or very small value, calculations using log rather than *ln* are more convenient: log = 2.302585 *ln*. Under these conditions, the multiplier for the *log* term has the following numerical value:

$$\frac{2.302585\ RT}{F} = \frac{(2.302585)(8.31451\ \text{J/ K mol})(298.15\ \text{K})}{(96{,}485.31\ \text{C/mol})} = 5.916 \times 10^{-2}\ \text{J/C}$$

Because 1 J = 1 V C, 1 J/C = 1 V:

$$E^\circ = \left(\frac{5.916 \times 10^{-2}\ \text{V}}{n}\right) \log K_{eq} \qquad \textbf{(17-5)}$$

Equations 17-4 and 17-5 provide a method for calculating equilibrium constants from tables of standard reduction potentials. Sample Problem 17-12 illustrates the technique.

SAMPLE PROBLEM 17-12 CELL POTENTIALS AND EQUILIBRIUM

Use tabulated standard reduction potentials to determine K_{eq} for the following redox reaction:

$$2\ Cu_{(s)} + Br_{2\ (l)} \rightleftharpoons Cu^{2+}_{(aq)} + 2\ Br^-_{(aq)}$$

METHOD: The wording of the problem tells us that we need standard reduction potentials and a link between equilibrium (K_{eq}) and standard reduction potential (E°). The link is Equation 17-5.

Table 17-1 provides the information necessary to determine E°_{cell} and the value of *n:*

$$Br_{2\ (l)} + 2\ e^- \rightleftharpoons 2\ Br^-_{(aq)} \qquad E^\circ = 1.066\ \text{V}$$

$$Cu^{2+}_{(aq)} + 2\ e^- \rightleftharpoons Cu_{(s)} \qquad E^\circ = 0.3419\ \text{V}$$

To obtain the cell potential, we subtract the less positive standard reduction potential from the more positive standard reduction potential. The spontaneous direction of this reaction is reduction of bromine and oxidation of copper.

$$E^\circ = E^\circ_{cathode} - E^\circ_{anode} = 1.066\ \text{V} - (0.3419\ \text{V}) = 0.724\ \text{V}$$

We are now ready to use Equation 17-5 with the appropriate value of *n:*

$$E^\circ = \left(\frac{5.916 \times 10^{-2}\ \text{V}}{n}\right) \log K_{eq}$$

$$\log K_{eq} = \frac{E^\circ\ n}{0.05916\ \text{V}}$$

$$\log K_{eq} = \frac{(0.724\ \text{V})(2)}{0.05916\ \text{V}} = 24.48$$

$$K_{eq} = 10^{24.48} = 3 \times 10^{24}$$

The calculation does not indicate the units that should be associated with this equilibrium constant, but we can deduce them from the equilibrium constant expression:

$K_{eq} = [Cu^{2+}][Br^-]^2$ Units associated with K_{eq}: M^3

The magnitude of this equilibrium constant tells us that the redox reaction goes essentially to completion. This reflects the fact that bromine is a potent oxidizing agent.

THE NERNST EQUATION

In most laboratories, electrochemistry is practiced under nonstandard conditions. That is, concentrations of dissolved solutes often are not 1 M, and gases are not necessarily at 1 atm. In Chapter 13, we showed that ΔG is very sensitive to concentration and pressure. The equation that links ΔG° with free energy changes under nonstandard conditions is Equation 13-12:

$$\Delta G = \Delta G^{\circ} + RT \ln Q \qquad \textbf{(13-12)}$$

Here, Q is the concentration quotient.

The term RT ln Q in Equation 13-12 describes an entropy effect. See Section 13.4 for a review.

Because ΔG and E_{cell} are linked by Equation 17-4, cell potentials must also depend on concentration and pressure. Equation 17-3 lets us substitute a cell potential for each free energy change in Equation 13-12:

$$-nF\,E = -nF\,E^{\circ} + RT \ln Q$$

Dividing both sides by $(-nF)$ gives the **Nernst equation:**

$$E = E^{\circ} - \frac{RT}{nF} \ln Q \qquad \textbf{(17-6)}$$

The Nernst equation is used to convert between standard cell potentials and potentials of electrochemical cells operating under nonstandard concentration conditions.

When measurements are made at standard temperature, 298.15 K, the numerical value calculated earlier can be used in the Nernst equation:

$$E = E^{\circ} - \frac{0.05916 \text{ V}}{n} \log Q \qquad T = 298.15 \text{ K}$$

The numerator of Q contains product concentrations, and the denominator contains reactant concentrations, all raised to powers equal to their stoichiometric coefficients. Solvents and pure substances do not appear in the concentration quotient. Thus only *solutes* and *gases* appearing in the cell reaction affect its cell potential.

The concentration units used in obtaining a numerical value for Q must match standard concentration units. Solute concentrations are expressed as molarities, and gas concentrations are expressed as partial pressures in atmospheres.

Most cell reactions involve solutes, so a typical cell potential differs from E°. Sample Problem 17-13 provides an example.

SAMPLE PROBLEM 17-13 NONSTANDARD CELL POTENTIAL

The permanganate ion is a powerful oxidizing agent that under standard conditions can oxidize water to oxygen:

$$MnO_4^- + 8\,H^+_{(aq)} + 5\,e^- \rightleftarrows Mn^{2+} + 4\,H_2O \qquad E^{\circ} = 1.507 \text{ V}$$

$$O_{2\,(g)} + 4\,H^+_{(aq)} + 4\,e^- \rightleftarrows 2\,H_2O \qquad E^{\circ} = 1.229 \text{ V}$$

What is the potential of a permanganate/oxygen cell operating at pH = 7.000, oxygen at $p = 0.200$ atm, 0.100 M MnO_4^-, and 0.100 M Mn^{2+}?

METHOD: The problem asks about an actual potential under nonstandard conditions. This requires the use of the Nernst equation. We determine E° and n from the balanced half-reactions. The concentration quotient comes from the balanced overall redox equation.

Under standard conditions, permanganate is reduced to Mn^{2+} at the cathode, and water is oxidized at the anode:

$$E°_{cell} = E°_{cathode} - E°_{anode} = 1.507 \text{ V} - 1.229 \text{ V} = 0.278 \text{ V}$$

To obtain the balanced equation, reverse the direction of the oxidation, balance the electrons, and combine the two half-reactions:

$$4\,MnO_4^- + 32\,H^+_{(aq)} + 20\,e^- \rightleftarrows 4\,Mn^{2+} + 16\,H_2O$$

$$10\,H_2O \rightleftarrows 5\,O_2 + 20\,H^+_{(aq)} + 20\,e^-$$

$$4\,MnO_4^- + 12\,H^+_{(aq)} \rightleftarrows 4\,Mn^{2+} + 5\,O_2 + 6\,H_2O$$

The balanced half-reactions show that $n = 20$. Now evaluate Q:

$$Q = \frac{[p(O_2)]^5[Mn^{2+}]^4}{[MnO_4^-]^4[H^+_{(aq)}]^{12}} = \frac{(0.200 \text{ atm})^5(0.100 \text{ M})^4}{(0.100 \text{ M})^4(1.00 \times 10^{-7} \text{ M})^{12}}$$

$(1.00 \times 10^{-7})^{12} = [(1.00)^{12} \times 10^{(-7 \times 12)}] = 1.00 \times 10^{-84}$.

$$Q = \frac{(0.200 \text{ atm})^5}{1.00 \times 10^{-84} \text{ M}^{12}} = 3.20 \times 10^{80} \text{ atm}^5 \text{ M}^{-12}$$

$$\log Q = \log(3.20 \times 10^{80}) = 80.505$$

Now use the Nernst equation in its numerical form:

This result is accurate to three decimal places because the $E°$ value is accurate to three decimal places and the correction is a subtraction.

$$E = E° - \frac{0.05916 \text{ V}}{n} \log Q = 0.278 \text{ V} - \frac{0.05916 \text{ V}}{20}(80.505) = 0.040 \text{ V}$$

The low concentration of hydronium ion in pure water reduces this cell potential nearly to zero, but the reaction is still spontaneous, so permanganate can oxidize water. Solutions of potassium permanganate slowly deteriorate and cannot be stored for long times. The reaction is slow enough, however, that significant oxidation does not occur over days or weeks.

The Nernst equation also applies to half-reactions. That is, an electrode in contact with a solution in which the concentration is not 1.00 M has a half-cell potential different from its $E°$. In evaluating Q for a half-reaction, we treat free electrons as a pure substance. Thus the concentration of electrons does not appear in Q. Sample Problem 17-14 applies the Nernst equation to the $H^+_{(aq)}/H_2$ half-reaction.

SAMPLE PROBLEM 17-14 NONSTANDARD HALF-REACTIONS

Redox reactions in the human body occur under nonstandard concentration conditions. For example, blood is buffered at pH = 7.40. What is E for the hydrogen half-cell at this pH, T = 298 K, and 1.00 atm of H_2?

METHOD: Working with the standard reduction half-reaction and potential, we use the Nernst equation to evaluate E:

$$2\,H^+_{(aq)} + 2\,e^- \rightleftarrows H_2 \qquad E° = 0 \text{ V}$$

$$E = E° - \frac{0.05916 \text{ V}}{n} \log Q = 0 - \frac{0.05916 \text{ V}}{2} \log\left[\frac{p(H_2)}{[H^+_{(aq)}]^2}\right]$$

$$[H^+_{(aq)}] = 10^{-7.40} = 3.98 \times 10^{-8} \text{ M}$$

$$E = 0 - \frac{0.05916 \text{ V}}{2} \log\left[\frac{(1.00 \text{ atm})}{(3.98 \times 10^{-8} \text{ M})^2}\right] = -0.44 \text{ V}$$

This cell potential is substantially less than $E°$ because the hydronium ion concentration in blood is seven orders of magnitude less than standard conditions.

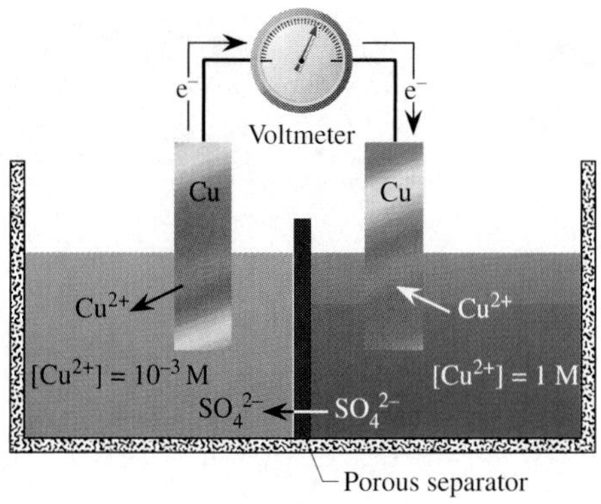

FIGURE 17-16
A copper concentration cell. Copper plates out of the more concentrated solution, copper cations are produced in the less concentrated solution, and electrons move through the external circuit. Sulfate ions migrate through the porous separator to maintain charge balance.

CONCENTRATION CELLS

Because cell potentials change with concentration, it is possible to set up a cell whose potential is determined entirely by concentrations. Two connected half-cells that are identical except for their concentrations form a **concentration cell.** Figure 17-16 shows a concentration cell. Each compartment contains a copper electrode in contact with a solution of $CuSO_4$. One solution is 1.00 M, whereas the other is 0.00100 M. A voltmeter in the external circuit measures the cell potential.

The half-reactions in the two cells are the same, but the concentrations of dissolved copper ions are different:

$$Cu^{2+}_{(aq,\ 1.00\ M)} + 2\ e^- \rightleftharpoons Cu_{(s)}$$

$$Cu^{2+}_{(aq,\ 1.00 \times 10^{-3}\ M)} + 2\ e^- \rightleftharpoons Cu_{(s)}$$

According to the Nernst equation, a concentration cell generates an electrical potential. The spontaneous direction of electron flow can be determined by asking what the ions would do if they were free to diffuse from one solution to the other. Entropy is maximized when the two solutions are thoroughly mixed and the concentrations are uniform throughout. This tells us that Cu^{2+} and $SO_4^{\ 2-}$ would diffuse spontaneously from the side of higher concentration to the side of lower concentration. The porous barrier prohibits the solutions from mixing rapidly. Instead, the concentrations reach chemical equilibrium by the spontaneous half-reactions that take place at the electrodes.

Oxidation of the copper wire immersed in the dilute solution releases Cu^{2+} into solution, so this electrode is the anode. On the other side of the cell, copper ions are reduced to copper atoms and captured by the electrode, so this is the cathode.

Anode:

$[Cu^{2+}] = 0.00100$ M $\qquad Cu_{(s)} \longrightarrow Cu^{2+}_{(aq,\ 0.001\ M)} + 2\ e^-$

Cathode:

$[Cu^{2+}] = 1.00$ M $\qquad Cu^{2+}_{(aq,\ 1.00\ M)} + 2\ e^- \longrightarrow Cu_{(s)}$

There is no net reaction here, but Cu^{2+} ions capture electrons and deposit as Cu atoms in the cell at higher concentration, whereas Cu atoms lose electrons and dissolve as Cu^{2+} ions in the cell at lower concentration. The higher concentration of Cu^{2+} decreases, while the lower concentration of Cu^{2+} increases. We can represent these changes by including the initial Cu^{2+} concentrations:

As current flows in a concentration cell, the concentrations become closer, and the cell potential decreases. Eventually, the two concentrations become equal, and the cell reaches chemical equilibrium, $E = 0$.

$$Cu^{2+}_{(aq,\ 1.00\ M)} \rightarrow Cu^{2+}_{(aq,\ 0.00100\ M)}$$

BOX 17-1

THE pH METER

Chemists who work with aqueous solutions routinely measure acidity with pH meters. A probe is dipped into the sample, and the pH appears on a digital display. The accompanying photos show that pH meters range from simple hand-held units for water testing in the field to high-precision recording instruments for industrial applications. A pH meter measures the electrical potential difference between a reference solution containing acid at known concentration and the sample being tested.

A cell for measuring pH could be a pair of hydrogen electrodes, one immersed in a reference solution at 1.00 M and the other in the solution of unknown concentration. This cell design has experimental difficulties that make it impractical for routine use. In particular, this type of meter would require a continuous flow of explosive hydrogen gas.

Practical pH measurements are carried out with a probe containing two stable reference electrodes separated by a thin glass membrane (see diagram at far right). On one side of the membrane, an electrode is immersed in a buffer solution. The solution whose pH is to be measured is placed in contact with an electrode on the opposite side of the membrane. The difference in H_3O^+ concentration on the two sides of the glass membrane creates a potential difference that is measured by the two electrodes.

Glass pH electrodes are simple to use and maintain. They respond selectively to hydronium ion concentration and provide an accurate measure of pH values between about 0 and 10. In addition, they can be made small enough to be implanted into blood vessels or even inserted into individual living cells.

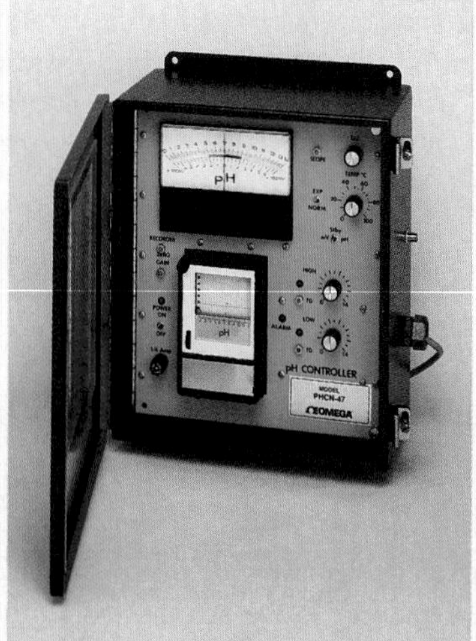

Although glass membranes are versatile, they have some shortcomings. They are fragile, so they must be used with care. They are damaged by strongly basic solutions, so special electrodes must be used to measure pH values greater than about 10. Finally, they must be calibrated before each use because their characteristics change somewhat with time and exposure to solutions. Calibration is easy. The electrode is dipped into a buffer solution of known pH, and the meter reading is electronically adjusted until it reads the correct value. For precision work, two buffer solutions of different pH values are used, and a double calibration is made so that the meter registers both standard values correctly.

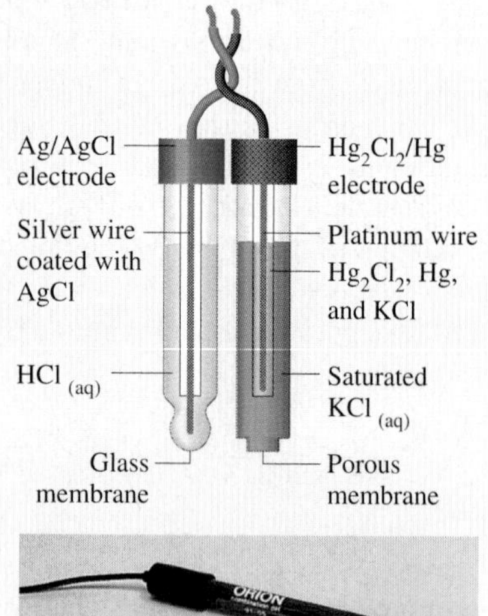

The spontaneous direction of a concentration cell is from the more concentrated solution toward the less concentrated solution.

The voltage developed by this concentration cell can be calculated using the Nernst equation:

$$E = E^{\circ} - \frac{0.05916\ \text{V}}{2}\log\left\{\frac{[\text{Cu}^{2+}{}_{(\text{dilute})}]}{[\text{Cu}^{2+}{}_{(\text{concentrated})}]}\right\}$$

The half-reactions are combined to give E°_{cell}. Because the half-reactions are the same in both half-cells, $E^{\circ}_{\text{cell}} = 0$. This is true for all concentration cells:

$$E^{\circ}_{\text{cell}} = E^{\circ}_{\text{cathode}} - E^{\circ}_{\text{anode}} = E^{\circ}_{\text{Cu}^{2+}/\text{Cu}} - E^{\circ}_{\text{Cu}^{2+}/\text{Cu}} = 0.3419\ \text{V} - 0.3419\ \text{V} = 0\ \text{V}$$

$$E_{\text{cell}} = 0 - \frac{0.05916\ \text{V}}{2}\log\left\{\frac{1.00 \times 10^{-3}\ \text{M}}{1.00\ \text{M}}\right\} = \frac{(0.05916)(3.00)}{2} = 0.0887\ \text{V}$$

Concentration cells have practical applications. Because cell potentials are linked quantitatively to concentrations, potential measurements can be used to determine ionic concentrations in solution. The most common example is the pH meter, described in Box 17-1. A pH meter measures the potential of a concentration cell containing hydronium ions. One compartment contains a standard acid solution, and the other contains the solution whose pH is being measured.

SECTION EXERCISES

17.6.1 Using standard reduction potentials, determine ΔG° and K_{eq} for each of the following reactions:

(a) $2\ \text{Cu}_{(s)} + \text{Hg}^{2+}{}_{(aq)} \rightleftarrows 2\ \text{Cu}^{+}{}_{(aq)} + \text{Hg}_{(l)}$

(b) $4\ \text{Cr}^{3+}{}_{(aq)} + 7\ \text{H}_2\text{O}_{(l)} \rightleftarrows 2\ \text{Cr}_{(s)} + \text{Cr}_2\text{O}_7{}^{2-}{}_{(aq)} + 14\ \text{H}^{+}{}_{(aq)}$

17.6.2 Use the Nernst equation to determine the half-cell potential at 298 K under physiological conditions, pH = 7.35 and $p\ (\text{O}_2) = 0.20$ atm for the following half-reaction:

$$\text{O}_2 + 4\ \text{H}^{+}{}_{(aq)} + 4\ \text{e}^{-} \rightleftarrows 2\ \text{H}_2\text{O}$$

17.6.3 Concentration cells can be used to determine low ionic concentrations. Suppose that a concentration cell is set up with a pair of silver–silver chloride electrodes, one of which dips into a 1.00 M KCl solution while the other dips into a solution containing a small but unknown concentration of chloride ions. If the concentration cell has a potential of 0.0785 V and the electrode dipping into the KCl solution is the anode, what is the unknown concentration of chloride ions?

17.7 REDOX IN ACTION

Oxidation-reduction reactions have many practical applications. Some involve direct reactions, whereas others take place in electrochemical cells. Some are spontaneous, but others are driven "uphill" by applying external electrical potentials. In this section, we present practical examples of spontaneous redox processes. In the following two sections, we describe the principles and applications of externally driven redox reactions.

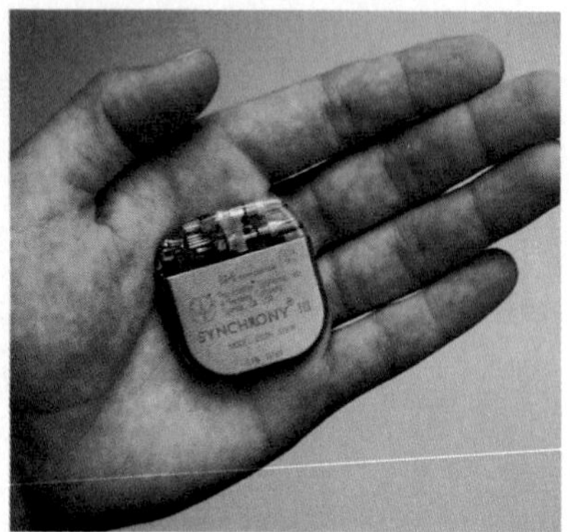

FIGURE 17-17
Batteries range in size from a small pacemaker to the large battery pack of an electric automobile.

BATTERIES

A battery is a galvanic cell that generates enough current to power some practical device. A battery can be as tiny as a heart pacemaker implant or as large as the charge storage banks of an electric automobile (Figure 17-17).

A useful battery must use cell reactions that generate a large electrical potential difference. This requires chemical redox pairs with standard reduction potentials that are substantially different. In addition, a battery that delivers a large current cannot contain porous separators because charge flow through separators is always slow. The ideal battery would be compact, inexpensive, rechargeable, and environmentally safe. This is a stringent set of requirements. No battery meets all of them, and only a few come close.

The **lead storage battery** provides electrical power in automobiles. It is well suited for this use because it supplies the large current needed to drive starter motors and headlights and can be recharged easily. This battery is shown in a schematic view in Figure 17-18. Its half-reactions are:

$$PbO_{2\,(s)} + 3\,H^+_{(aq)} + HSO_4^-{}_{(aq)} + 2\,e^- \rightleftharpoons PbSO_{4\,(s)} + 2\,H_2O_{(l)} \qquad E^\circ = +1.6913\text{ V}$$

$$PbSO_{4\,(s)} + H^+_{(aq)} + 2\,e^- \rightleftharpoons Pb_{(s)} + HSO_4^-{}_{(aq)} \qquad E^\circ = -0.3588\text{ V}$$

Here is the net reaction that occurs in the battery:

$$Pb_{(s)} + 2\,HSO_4^-{}_{(aq)} + PbO_{2\,(s)} + 2\,H^+_{(aq)} \rightleftharpoons 2\,PbSO_{4\,(s)} + 2\,H_2O_{(l)}$$

$$E^\circ = 1.6913 - (-0.3588) = +2.0501\text{ V}$$

The anode is a lead plate that becomes coated with $PbSO_4$ as the battery discharges. The cathode is lead impregnated with PbO_2, which also becomes coated with $PbSO_4$ as the battery discharges. Both electrodes are immersed in a bath of sulfuric acid that is approximately 1 M. Thus, the working potential of the cell is close to its E° value of about 2 V. Automobile batteries use six such cells, connected in series to generate a total electrical potential of 12 V. This battery does not require a porous separator because the starting materials and products for both half-reactions are insoluble in sulfuric acid. The lead-containing materials never come into contact with each other, so there is no possibility of direct electron transfer.

An automobile's battery is needed to supply electrical current when the motor is not running. While the motor is running, it drives an electrical generator that meets

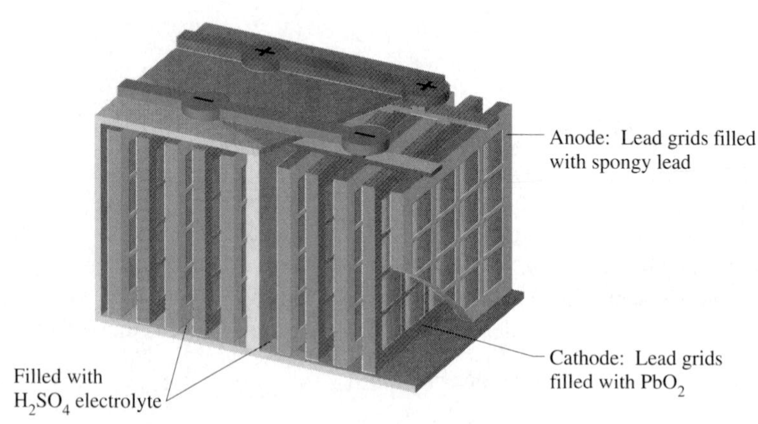

FIGURE 17-18
Schematic view of a lead storage cell. Lead is oxidized and lead(IV) oxide reduced during operation of this battery.

the auto's electrical needs. The generator also recharges the battery by supplying the energy that is required to drive its redox reactions in the reverse direction. When the electrical system is functioning properly, the battery is maintained at its optimum charge level, giving these batteries quite long lifetimes.

Flashlight batteries are usually **alkaline dry cells.** In these batteries, zinc and manganese dioxide are the working materials. The dry cell has a zinc anode in contact with a moist paste of KOH and carbon. The paste contacts a passive graphite cathode around which MnO_2 is packed. Both half-reactions involve multiple steps, but they can be approximated by single reactions:

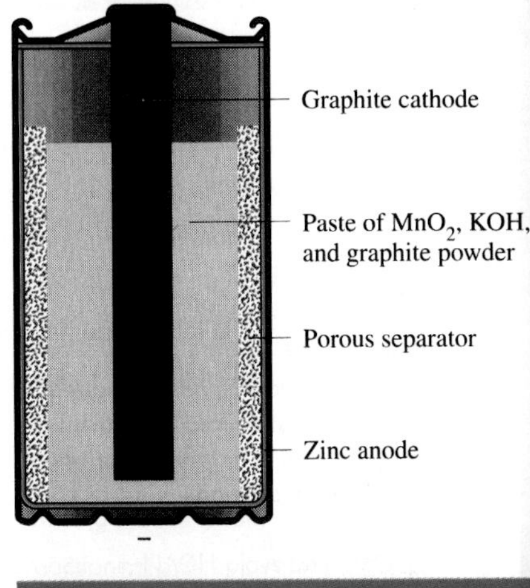

Cathode: $2\ MnO_{2\,(s)} + H_2O_{\,(l)} + 2\ e^- \rightleftarrows Mn_2O_{3\,(s)} + 2\ OH^-_{\,(aq)}$

Anode: $Zn_{\,(s)} + 2\ OH^-_{\,(aq)} \rightleftarrows Zn(OH)_{2\,(s)} + 2\ e^-$

Net: $2\ MnO_{2\,(s)} + H_2O_{\,(l)} + Zn_{\,(s)} \rightleftarrows Mn_2O_{3\,(s)} + Zn(OH)_{2\,(s)}$

A dry cell generates a potential of about 1.5 V. These cells run irreversibly, and their cell potential decreases with use. Nevertheless, they have many uses because they are compact and made of inexpensive materials with low toxicities. Approximately a billion of these batteries are produced annually in the United States.

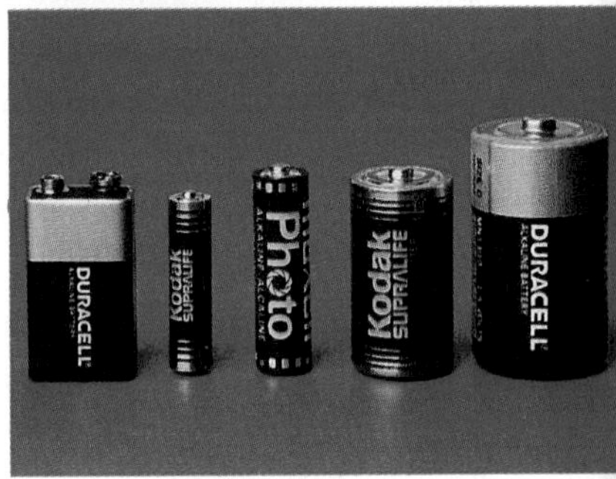

Alkaline batteries such as these are used as sources of electrical current for many portable devices.

Mercury batteries are more expensive than dry cells and contain toxic mercury compounds. These disadvantages are offset by two major advantages: high capacity and a cell potential that does not vary with use. Zinc and mercury are the working chemicals in these batteries, whose cell reactions are:

Cathode: $HgO_{\,(s)} + H_2O_{\,(l)} + 2\ e^- \rightleftarrows Hg_{\,(l)} + 2\ OH^-_{\,(aq)}$

Anode: $Zn_{\,(s)} + 2\ OH^-_{\,(aq)} \rightleftarrows ZnO_{\,(s)} + H_2O_{\,(l)} + 2\ e^-$

Net: $Zn_{\,(s)} + HgO_{\,(s)} \rightleftarrows ZnO_{\,(s)} + Hg_{\,(l)}$

Figure 17-19 shows the molecular processes that occur in a mercury battery.

In this cell, none of the components of the redox reaction changes concentration as the battery operates. The zinc and mercury-containing components are either pure liquids or pure solids, and hydroxide ions consumed at the cathode are regenerated at the anode. Because none of the concentrations changes as the battery functions,

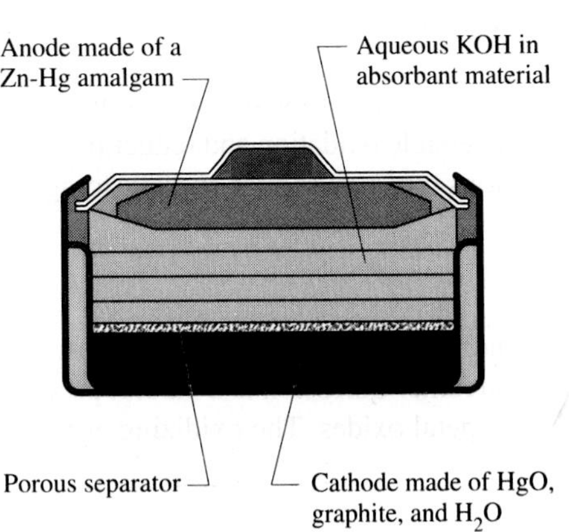

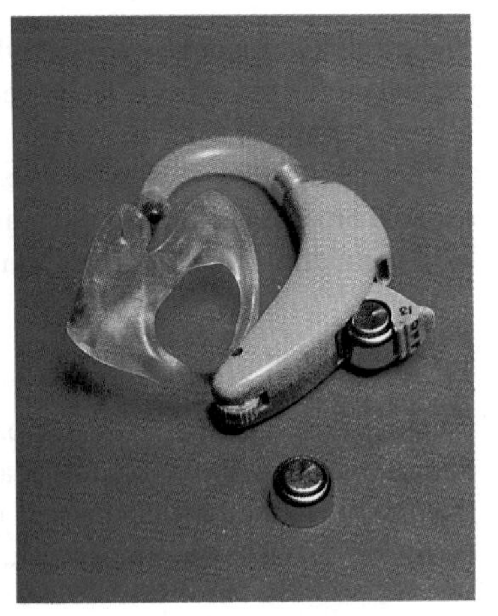

Mercury batteries can be quite compact, because they are designed for applications where the current requirements are low.

Oxygen is a potent oxidizing agent, particularly in the presence of aqueous acids:

$$O_{2\,(g)} + 2\,H_2O + 4\,e^- \rightleftarrows 4\,OH^-_{(aq)} \qquad E^\circ = +\,0.401\ \text{V}$$

$$O_{2\,(g)} + 4\,H^+_{(aq)} + 4\,e^- \rightleftarrows 2\,H_2O_{\,(l)} \qquad E^\circ = +\,1.229\ \text{V}$$

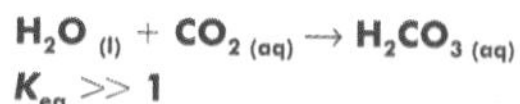

$H_2O_{\,(l)} + CO_{2\,(aq)} \rightarrow H_2CO_{3\,(aq)}$
$K_{eq} >> 1$

$H_2CO_{3\,(aq)} + H_2O_{\,(l)} \rightleftarrows H_3O^+_{\,(aq)} + HCO_3^-{}_{\,(aq)}$

$K_a = 4.5 \times 10^{-7}$ M

Oxygen in the atmosphere has a partial pressure of 0.20 atm, and atmospheric water vapor is saturated with carbon dioxide. This dissolved CO_2 forms carbonic acid, which in turn generates a hydronium ion concentration of about 2.0×10^{-6} M. We can use the Nernst equation to calculate the half-cell potential for the reduction of $O_{2\,(g)}$ under these conditions:

$$E = E^\circ - \frac{0.05916\ \text{V}}{n}\log\left\{\frac{1}{p(O_2)[H^+_{(aq)}]^4}\right\}$$

$$E = 1.229\ \text{V} - \frac{0.05916\ \text{V}}{4}\log\left\{\frac{1}{(0.20)(2.0 \times 10^{-6})^4}\right\} = 0.88\ \text{V}$$

In damp air, materials with standard reduction potentials less than 0.88 V oxidize spontaneously. Iron and aluminum, our most important structural metals, are both oxidized by atmospheric O_2:

Corrosion of iron occurs in two steps. First, an iron atom at the surface of the metal is oxidized to a soluble Fe^{2+} cation. The ion moves off into solution, where it is oxidized further to Fe^{3+}.

$$4\,Fe_{\,(s)} + 3\,O_{2\,(g)} + 12\,H^+_{(aq)} \rightleftarrows 4\,Fe^{3+}_{(aq)} + 6\,H_2O_{\,(l)}$$

$$E = 0.88\ \text{V} - (-0.037\ \text{V}) = +0.92\ \text{V}$$

$$4\,Al_{\,(s)} + 3\,O_{2\,(g)} + 12\,H^+_{(aq)} \rightleftarrows 4\,Al^{3+}_{(aq)} + 12\,OH^-_{(aq)}$$

$$E = 0.88\ \text{V} - (-1.662\ \text{V}) = +2.54\ \text{V}$$

Both Fe^{3+} and Al^{3+} form highly insoluble oxides that precipitate from solution. Overall, then, each metal is oxidized by O_2 to give its metal oxide:

$$4\,Fe_{\,(s)} + 3\,O_{2\,(g)} \rightarrow 2\,Fe_2O_{3\,(s)}$$

$$4\,Al_{\,(s)} + 3\,O_{2\,(g)} \rightarrow 2\,Al_2O_{3\,(s)}$$

The effects of corrosion are readily apparent. The formation of rust on a steel surface is an obvious manifestation of corrosion. Even more damaging effects of corrosion take place beneath the surface, however, where tiny cracks weaken the structural integrity of the metal. Corrosion of iron has a serious economic impact. Approximately 20% of the iron and steel produced in the United States is used to replace rusted metal, and the cost of replacing corroded materials is several billion dollars per year.

Although corrosion of iron and aluminum is highly spontaneous, these metals can withstand exposure to *dry* air for long periods. The direct reaction of iron and aluminum with oxygen gas has a high activation barrier, making oxidation very slow in the absence of moisture. Corrosion is faster, however, when the metals are in contact with water. As illustrated schematically in Figure 17-20, the oxidation of iron and the reduction of water occur at different locations on the metal's surface. In the absence of dissolved ions to act as charge carriers, a complete electrical circuit is missing, and the redox reaction is slow. This is why pure water is not highly corro-

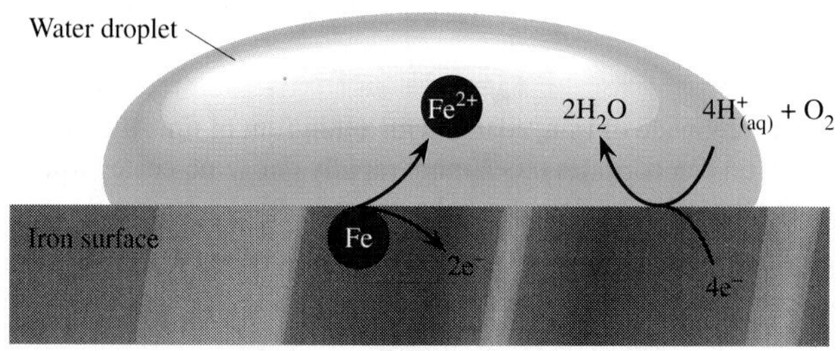

FIGURE 17-20
A water droplet on an iron surface is a miniature electrochemical cell. Oxidation of iron occurs in an interior region of the droplet, whereas reduction of oxygen preferentially occurs near the air-droplet interface. Ionic charge carriers are required to complete the circuit and allow the redox reactions to proceed.

sive. In contrast, the ions present in salt water and acidic water provide an environment in which corrosion can be quite rapid.

Corrosion cannot be made nonspontaneous, but it can be prevented by making the rate of reaction negligible. This can be accomplished by covering the metal surface with a protective coating or by providing an alternative redox pathway. Protective coatings are usually of three types. A paint is a liquid mixture that sets to form a solid film on a surface. Structures such as San Francisco's Golden Gate Bridge are always being painted, ensuring an unbroken layer to protect steel cables and towers from corrosive salt spray.

A metal surface can also be protected by coating it with a thin film of a second metal. When the second metal is easier to oxidize than the first, the process is known as *galvanization.* Objects made of iron, including automobile bodies and steel girders, are dipped in molten zinc to provide a sacrificial coating. If a scratch penetrates the zinc film, the iron is still protected because zinc oxidizes preferentially:

$$Fe^{2+} + 2\,e^- \rightleftarrows Fe \qquad E^\circ = -0.447\ \text{V}$$

$$Zn^{2+} + 2\,e^- \rightleftarrows Zn \qquad E^\circ = -0.7618\ \text{V}$$

Large iron objects, such as the hulls of ships or oil drilling platforms, are too large to dip in a pot of molten zinc. Instead, these objects are protected from corrosion by connecting them to blocks of some more easily oxidized metal. Magnesium and zinc frequently are used for this purpose. As in galvanization, the more active metal is oxidized preferentially over iron. As the sacrificial metal is consumed, it must be replaced. However, the cost of replacing a block of zinc or magnesium is much less than the cost of replacing a sophisticated iron structure.

Another way to protect a metal is by coating it with an impervious metal oxide layer. This process is known as *passivation.* In some cases, passivation is a natural process. You may have seen a thin, white film coating the outer surface of old aluminum window frames. This material is Al_2O_3, built up through atmospheric oxidation of the aluminum surface. Aluminum oxide adheres to the surface of unoxidized aluminum, protecting the metal from further reaction with O_2. Passivation is not effective for iron because iron oxides are porous and do not adhere well to the metal. Rust continually flakes off the surface of the metal, exposing fresh iron to the atmosphere. Alloying with nickel or chromium, whose oxides adhere well to metal surfaces, can be used to prevent corrosion of iron. For example, stainless steel contains small amounts of nickel and chromium.

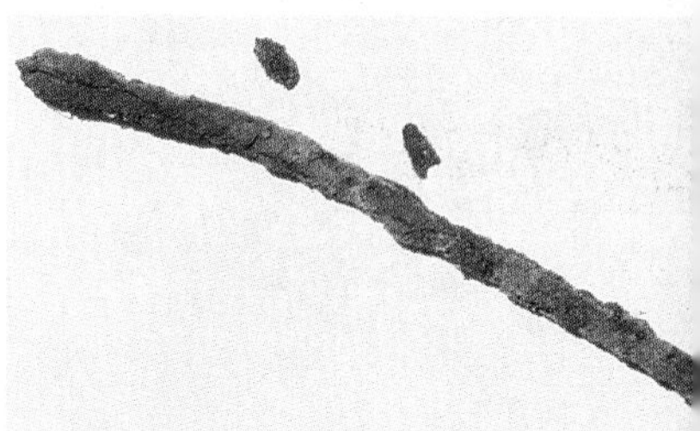

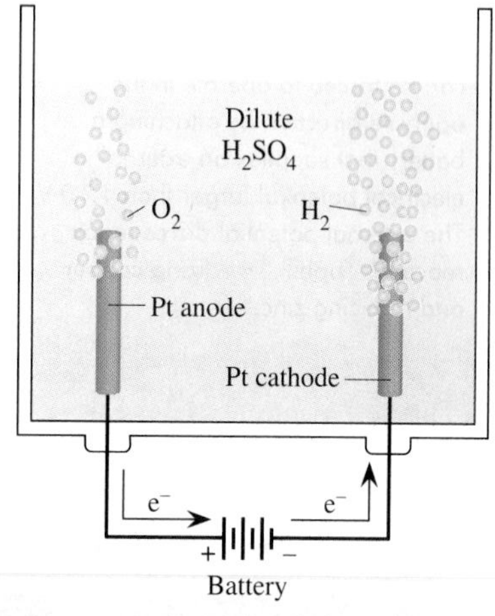

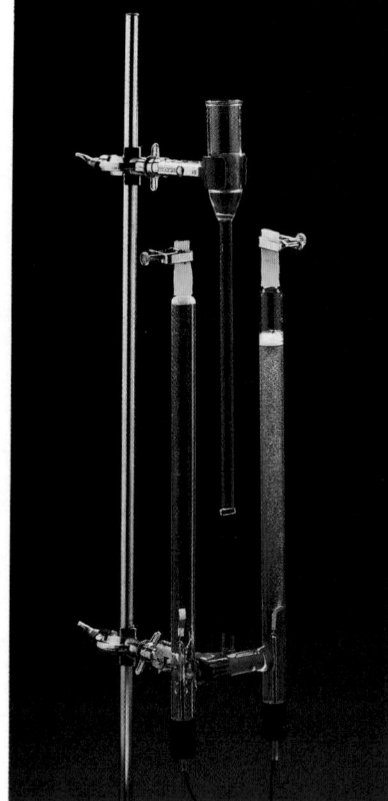

FIGURE 17-22
A photograph and schematic diagram of a cell for electrolysis of water. Hydronium ions capture electrons at the cathode, and electrons are captured by the anode from water molecules. The redox reaction generates hydrogen and oxygen in a 2:1 ratio.

Even though decomposition of water is possible at any potential greater than 1.23 V, the *rate* of electrolysis does not become appreciable until a significant additional potential is applied. This extra potential is called an **overvoltage** or overpotential. A redox reaction that requires an overvoltage is analogous to a poorly lubricated piston. Because of friction, the piston does not move unless the external pressure is significantly greater than the internal pressure.

The potential supplied to an electrolytic cell determines whether or not electrolysis can occur, but the amount of material electrolyzed is determined by the current flow and the time of electrolysis. Recall Equation 17-1 from Section 17.4:

$$\text{Moles of electrons} = n = \frac{It}{F} \tag{17-1}$$

This equation provides the link between electrical measurements and amount of electrons, and the balanced half-reactions for the electrolysis process provide the link between amount of electrons and amounts of chemical substances. Sample Problem 17-15 provides an example of electrolytic stoichiometry.

SAMPLE PROBLEM 17-15 ELECTROLYSIS AND STOICHIOMETRY

The electrolytic cell shown in Figure 17-22 draws a current of 0.775 ampere for 45.0 minutes. Calculate the volumes of H_2 and O_2 produced if these gases are collected at 25 °C and $P = 1.00$ atm.

METHOD: The problem asks about amounts of chemicals produced during electrolysis and provides data about current and time. Equation 17-1 and redox stoichiometry provide the necessary links.

Moles of electrons are calculated from Equation 17-1:

$$n_{\text{electrons}} = \frac{It}{F} = \frac{(0.775 \text{ A})(45.0 \text{ min})(60 \text{ s/min})}{(96{,}485 \text{ C/mol})(1 \text{ A s/C})}$$

$$n_{\text{electrons}} = 2.169 \times 10^{-2} \text{ mol}$$

The balanced half-reactions provide the molar ratios between electrons and chemical species:

$$2\,H_2O_{(l)} \rightarrow O_{2\,(g)} + 4\,H^+_{(aq)} + 4\,e^-$$

$$4\,H^+_{(aq)} + 4\,e^- \rightarrow 2\,H_{2\,(g)}$$

4 mol e^- produces 2 mol H_2 and 1 mol O_2.

$$n_{H_2} = (2.169 \times 10^{-2} \text{ mol e}^-)\frac{(2 \text{ mol H}_2)}{(4 \text{ mol e}^-)} = 1.084 \times 10^{-2} \text{ mol H}_2$$

$$n_{O_2} = (2.169 \times 10^{-2} \text{ mol e}^-)\frac{(1 \text{ mol O}_2)}{(4 \text{ mol e}^-)} = 0.5423 \times 10^{-2} \text{ mol O}_2$$

To complete the calculation, moles of gas must be converted into volumes using the ideal gas equation:

$$V = \frac{nRT}{P}$$

We leave this stoichiometric calculation to you. The volume of H_2 is 0.265 L, and that of O_2 is 0.133 L.

COMPETITIVE ELECTROLYSIS

In designing an electrolytic cell, care must be taken in the selection of the cell components. For example, consider what happens when an aqueous solution of sodium chloride is electrolyzed using platinum electrodes. There are three major species in the solution: H_2O, Na^+, and Cl^-. Platinum is used for passive electrodes because the metal is resistant to oxidation and does not participate in the redox chemistry of the cell. Chloride ions cannot be reduced further, so there are just two candidates for reduction, water molecules and sodium ions:

$$Na^+ + e^- \rightleftarrows Na \qquad E^\circ = -2.714\ V$$

$$2\ H_2O + 2\ e^- \rightleftarrows H_2 + 2\ OH^- \qquad E^\circ = -0.828\ V$$

The standard potentials show that water is much easier to reduce than sodium ions, so the electrolysis will produce hydrogen and hydroxide ions rather than sodium metal. In an electrolysis cell, the most easily oxidized species is oxidized and the most easily reduced species is reduced.

The possibilities for oxidation are more varied. Water and chloride ions can both be oxidized, but sodium ions cannot. The various possibilities for oxidation can be found in the list of reduction potentials given in Appendix H. Because oxidation is the reverse of reduction, we look for half-reactions whose *products* include Cl^- or H_2O. Although several possibilities exist, we need consider only the two with the lowest reduction potentials:

$$O_2 + 4\ H^+_{(aq)} + 4\ e^- \rightleftarrows 2\ H_2O \qquad E^\circ = 1.229\ V$$

$$Cl_2 + 2\ e^- \rightleftarrows 2\ Cl^- \qquad E^\circ = 1.358\ V$$

In general, we should expect the electrolysis cell to drive the reaction with the least negative cell potential. In this case the least negative E° is obtained by combining the reduction of water to hydrogen and hydroxide with the oxidation of water to hydronium ion and oxygen gas:

$$2\ H_2O_{(l)} \longrightarrow 2\ H_{2\ (g)} + O_{2\ (g)} \qquad E^\circ = (-0.828\ V) - (1.229\ V) = -2.057\ V$$

However, chloride ions are almost as easy to oxidize as water, and in fact, electrolysis of aqueous NaCl produces chlorine gas at the anode:

$$\text{Cathode: } 2\ H_2O_{(l)} + 2\ e^- \longrightarrow H_{2\ (g)} + 2\ OH^-_{(aq)} \quad E^\circ = -0.828\ V$$

$$\text{Anode: } 2\ Cl^-_{(aq)} \longrightarrow Cl_{2\ (g)} + 2\ e^- \quad E^\circ = 1.358\ V$$

$$\text{Overall: } 2\ H_2O_{(l)} + 2\ Cl^-_{(aq)} \longrightarrow H_{2\ (g)} + 2\ OH^-_{(aq)} + Cl_{2\ (g)}$$

$$E^\circ_{cell} = E^\circ_{cathode} - E^\circ_{anode} = (-0.828\ V) - (1.358\ V) = -2.186\ V$$

Oxidation of water is favored by thermodynamics, but the oxidation of chloride is a much faster reaction. In other words, the oxidation of H_2O to O_2 requires a substantially higher overvoltage than the oxidation of Cl^- to Cl_2. Among reactions with similar potentials, reactions that require small numbers of electrons often proceed more readily than those that require large numbers of electrons.

17.8.2 If a commercial reactor for electrolysis of HF operates continuously at a current of 1500 amperes and a current efficiency of 92%, how many kilograms of F_2 are produced in 24 hours of operation? What is the volume of the tank required to store the F_2 at 298 K and 60 atm pressure?

17.8.3 Explain why neither aqueous KF nor pure liquid HF can be used for electrolytic production of fluorine, even though both liquids are easier to handle than molten potassium fluoride.

17.9 METALLURGY

Metallurgy is the production and purification of metals from naturally occurring deposits, ores. It has an ancient history and may represent the earliest useful application of chemistry. Metallurgical advances have profoundly changed the course of human civilization, so much so that historians speak of "The Bronze Age" (ca. 3000 to 1000 BC) and "The Iron Age" (ca. 1000 BC to the present).

REDOX IN METALLURGY

Common mineral ores include *(clockwise from top)* cuprite, bauxite, galena, sphalerite, and hematite.

Nearly all metals are readily oxidized, so most metals are found in nature as compounds in which the metals have positive oxidation states. Examples include oxides (Fe_2O_3, hematite; Cu_2O, cuprite; and $Al_2(O)OH{\cdot}xH_2O$, bauxite), sulfides (PbS, galena, and Zn, sphalerite), chlorides (KCl-NaCl, sylvinite), sulfates ($CaSO_4{\cdot}2H_2O$, gypsum) and carbonates ($CaCO_3$, limestone), as well as more complex structures such as kaolinite, $Al_2(OH)_4Si_2O_5$. In all these ores the metals are present in positive oxidation states. To extract and purify the metals, they must be reduced to their elemental forms.

Generally, a metal ore contains a particular compound of some desired metal mixed with various other materials. After mining the ore, the first step in metallurgy is separation of the desired mineral from these other materials. Some compounds must be transformed chemically into a more easily reduced form. After a sufficiently pure compound is obtained, it is reduced to free metal. Finally, the free metal may require further purification. Redox chemistry plays a central role in many of these steps.

SEPARATION AND CONVERSION

Some of the ores can be separated into pure components by physical or chemical processes. Because our focus in this chapter is on redox chemistry, we highlight the separations that require chemical transformations. Frequently, chemical separations involve combinations of solubility/complexation equilibria and redox reactions.

Bauxite, the main aluminum ore, is a mixed oxide-hydroxide, Al(O)OH, contaminated with SiO_2, clays, and iron(III) oxides and hydroxides. To isolate the aluminum-containing material, the ore is treated with a strongly basic solution. At high hydroxide concentration, aluminum forms a soluble complex ion, $[Al(OH)_4]^-$, whereas the impurities in bauxite remain insoluble:

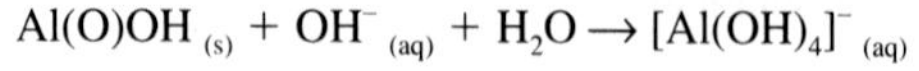

$$Al(O)OH_{(s)} + OH^-_{(aq)} + H_2O \longrightarrow [Al(OH)_4]^-_{(aq)}$$

The liquid is separated from undissolved solids, and then it is diluted to reduce the hydroxide ion concentration. Although $[Al(OH)_4]^-$ is soluble, $Al(OH)_3$ is not. Aluminum hydroxide precipitates as the pH is reduced:

$$[Al(OH)_4]^-_{(aq)} \rightarrow Al(OH)_{3\,(s)} + OH^-_{(aq)}$$

After this separation is complete, $Al(OH)_3$ is heated to drive off water, converting it into pure aluminum oxide. This oxide is the starting material for electrolytic reduction, which we describe later in this section:

$$2\,Al(OH)_3 \xrightarrow{1250\,°C} Al_2O_{3\,(s)} + 3\,H_2O_{(g)}$$

The major titanium ore is rutile, TiO_2. Rutile, which is typically contaminated with iron(III), is converted to titanium(IV) chloride by a redox reaction with chlorine gas and coke, a form of carbon that is obtained by heating coal in the absence of oxygen:

$$TiO_{2\,(s)} + C_{(s)} + 2\,Cl_{2\,(g)} \xrightarrow{500\,°C} TiCl_{4\,(g)} + CO_{2\,(g)}$$

In this reaction, carbon is oxidized and chlorine is reduced. The hot gas is cooled, whereupon titanium tetrachloride condenses to a liquid that is further purified by distillation (boiling point, 140 °C). We describe how $TiCl_4$ is reduced to titanium metal later in this section.

Distillation is described in Section 10.8.

The main source of silicon for semiconductor "chips" is silicon dioxide, or silica. It is purified in a similar fashion:

$$SiO_{2\,(s)} + 2\,C_{(s)} + 2\,Cl_{2\,(g)} \xrightarrow{\text{High temperature}} SiCl_{4\,(g)} + 2\,CO_{(g)}$$

Silicon tetrachloride is condensed and purified by distillation (boiling point, 57 °C). The purification of silicon is especially critical because the semiconductor industry requires silicon of ultrahigh purity.

Several important metals occur naturally as sulfide ores. In general, sulfides are first converted into the corresponding oxide by heating in oxygen. Sulfur is oxidized and oxygen is reduced:

$$2\,ZnS_{(s)} + 3\,O_{2\,(g)} \rightarrow 2\,ZnO_{(g)} + 2\,SO_{2\,(g)}$$

Unfortunately, this treatment produces copious amounts of highly polluting SO_2 gas that has seriously damaged the environment around smelters for sulfide ores.

Vegetation around the nickel smelter in Sudbury, Ontario, Canada, has been devastated by SO_2 emitted during the roasting of NiS ores.

Today, zinc and other metals can be extracted from sulfides by aqueous phase conversion processes that avoid the generation of sulfur dioxide. Aqueous acid reacts with the sulfides to generate free sulfur or sulfate ions rather than sulfur dioxide:

$$2\,ZnS_{(s)} + 4\,H^+_{(aq)} + O_{2\,(g)} \rightarrow 2\,Zn^{2+}_{(aq)} + 2\,S_{(s)} + 2\,H_2O_{(l)}$$

$$3\,CuS_{(s)} + 8\,NO_3^-{}_{(aq)} + 8\,H^+_{(aq)} \rightarrow 8\,NO_{(g)} + 3\,Cu^{2+}_{(aq)} + 3\,SO_4^{2-}{}_{(aq)} + 4\,H_2O_{(l)}$$

Some sulfides can be reduced by making the metal sulfide the anode of an electrolytic cell containing sulfuric acid as the electrolyte:

Anode: $NiS_{(s)} \rightarrow Ni^{2+}_{(aq)} + S_{(s)} + 2\,e^-$

Cathode: $2\,H^+_{(aq)} + 2\,e^- \rightarrow H_{2\,(g)}$

When the cost of preventing SO_2 escape into the atmosphere is taken into account, these more elaborate aqueous separation procedures are economically competitive with oxidation by heating.

REDUCTION

When an ore has been separated, converted into suitably pure form, or both, it is ready to be reduced to free metal. This is accomplished either chemically or electrolytically. Electrolysis is costly because it requires huge amounts of electrical energy. Chemical reduction is used unless the metal is too reactive for chemical reducing agents to be effective.

Mercury and lead, which are relatively easy to reduce, can be purified simply by heating their sulfides in air. Sulfide ion is the reducing agent, and both O_2 and the metal ion gain electrons:

$$HgS_{(s)} + O_{2\,(g)} \rightarrow Hg_{(l)} + SO_{2\,(g)}$$

$$PbS_{(s)} + O_{2\,(g)} \rightarrow Pb_{(l)} + SO_{2\,(g)}$$

These reductions produce undesired SO_2, which must be carefully "scrubbed" from the exhaust gases.

The metals with moderately negative reduction potentials, Co, Ni, Fe, and Zn, can be reduced by carbon in the form of coke. For example, direct oxidative displacement in a high-temperature furnace frees zinc from its oxide:

$$ZnO_{(s)} + C_{(s)} \rightarrow Zn_{(l)} + CO_{(g)}$$

A more active metal can be used as the reducing agent for moderately active metals. Thus magnesium metal is used to reduce $TiCl_4$ to titanium metal, and at high temperature, aluminum reduces chromium(III) oxide to the free metal:

$$TiCl_{4\,(l)} + 2\,Mg_{(s)} \rightarrow Ti_{(s)} + 2\,MgCl_{2\,(s)}$$

$$Cr_2O_{3\,(s)} + 2\,Al_{(s)} \rightarrow Al_2O_{3\,(s)} + 2\,Cr_{(s)}$$

The most active metals, such as Na, Mg, and Al, must be produced by electrolytic reduction. Molten chloride salts are electrolyzed to produce sodium and magnesium:

$$2\,NaCl_{(l)} \xrightarrow{\text{Electrolysis}} 2\,Na_{(l)} + Cl_{2\,(g)}$$

$$MgCl_{2\,(l)} \xrightarrow{\text{Electrolysis}} Mg_{(s)} + Cl_{2\,(g)}$$

PRODUCTION OF ALUMINUM

Aluminum is one of society's most important structural metals. It is light yet very strong, and it resists corrosion by forming a thin, adherent layer of aluminum oxide on the surface of the metal. Alloys of aluminum are used for aircraft bodies, trailers, cooking utensils, highway signs, storage tanks, soda cans, and many other objects. Aluminum is produced by electrolysis of molten aluminum oxide in the Hall-Héroult process. The melting point of Al_2O_3 is too high (2015 °C) and its electrical conduc-

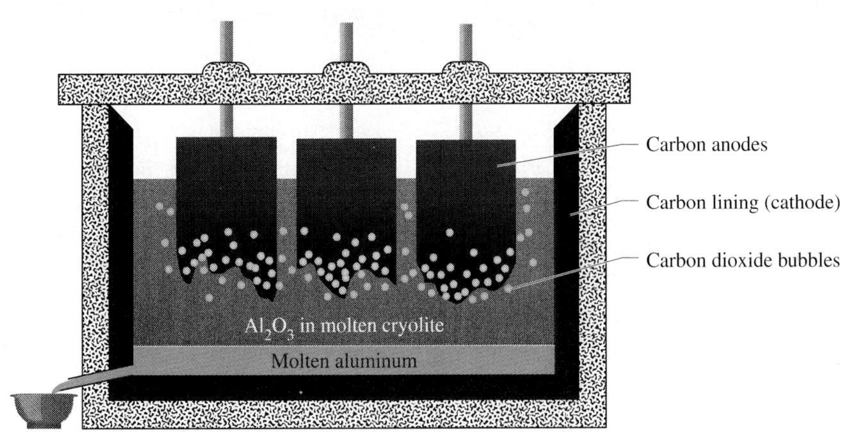

FIGURE 17-24
Aluminum metal is produced by electrolysis of aluminum oxide dissolved in molten cryolite. At the cathode, Al^{3+} is reduced to Al, and at the anode, C is oxidized to CO_2.

tivity too low to make direct electrolysis commercially viable. Instead, Al_2O_3 is dissolved in a molten mixture of cryolite (Na_3AlF_6) containing about 10% CaF_2. This combination has a melting point of 1000 °C, which is high but not prohibitively so. In addition, cryolite is a good electrolyte.

Figure 17-24 shows a schematic representation of an electrolysis cell for aluminum production. An external electrical potential drives electrons into a graphite cathode. Al^{3+} ions are reduced to Al metal at the surface of the cathode:

The reactions that take place at the anode and cathode are more complex than those shown here. In fact, the chemistry of the Hall-Héroult process is still not entirely understood. For our purpose, however, it is sufficient to know that carbon is oxidized at the anode and Al^{3+} reduced at the cathode.

$$\text{Cathode: } Al^{3+} + 3\,e^- \rightarrow Al_{(l)}$$

The anode is also a graphite rod, which is oxidized and combines with oxide ions to form CO_2 gas.

$$\text{Anode: } 2\,O^{2-} + C \rightarrow CO_{2\,(g)} + 4\,e^-$$

BOX 17-3

THE STORY OF THE HALL-HÉROULT PROCESS

Aluminum is the third most abundant element in the Earth's crust and the most abundant metal. However, although the fourth most abundant element, iron, has been used in metallic form for thousands of years, aluminum was not even discovered until 1825 and was still a semiprecious rarity 60 years later. The reason for aluminum's elusiveness is its high stability as Al(III). Reduction of aluminum compounds to the free metal requires stronger reducing power than common chemical reducing agents can provide. Aluminum's discovery had to await the birth of electrochemistry and development of electrolysis.

Twenty-five years after its discovery, aluminum was a precious metal. Then a French chemist developed procedures for reducing aluminum compounds using sodium metal. (Sodium metal, even more reactive than aluminum, was and still is produced by electrolysis.) The price of the metal dropped 100-fold. Still, in the 1880s aluminum remained a semiprecious metal, used for esoteric purposes such as a prince's baby rattle and the cap for the Washington Monument.

Aluminum's conversion from the stuff of princes' toys into recyclable kitchen foil required an inexpensive electrolytic reduction process. Two 22-year-old scientists, the American chemist Charles Hall and the French metallurgist Paul Héroult, independently discovered the same process in 1886. Both became famous, Hall as the founder of what is now the Alcoa Corporation and Héroult as the founder of Europe's aluminum industry.

Charles Hall was inspired by his chemistry professor at Oberlin College, who observed that whoever perfected an inexpensive way of producing aluminum would become rich and famous. After his graduation, Hall set to work in his home laboratory, trying to electrolyze various compounds of aluminum. After only 8 months of work, he had successfully produced globules of the metal. Meanwhile, Héroult was developing the identical process in France.

Hall capitalized on his discovery by founding a company for the manufacture of aluminum. That company was immensely successful, eventually growing into Alcoa. It made Hall a rich man; on his death at age 50, he left $3 million to his alma mater, Oberlin College.

The keys to the Hall-Héroult process are graphite electrodes and the use of molten cryolite, Na_3AlF_6, as a solvent for aluminum oxide. Cryolite melts at an accessible temperature, it dissolves Al_2O_3, and it is available in good purity. Graphite is a better anode than inert electrodes because oxidation of carbon to CO_2 proceeds much more readily than oxidation of O^{2-} to O_2.

It may appear a coincidence that two persons working independently on two different continents came up with an identical process at the same time. Actually, conditions were ripe for someone to discover how to win aluminum from its ores. The metal was known to have advantageous properties, combining strength and ductility with low density. So it was natural for ambitious young scientists to apply their talents to this problem.

The reasoning that led Hall and Héroult to the identical process was probably similar. Electrolysis was an exciting new technique, and electrochemistry was recognized as a powerful reducing method. Because water is electrolyzed before aluminum, the need for a molten salt as the electrolyte must have been clear. Experimenting with various salts, no doubt guided by the principle that "like dissolves like," the two young men eventually tried cryolite, a natural mineral whose constituent elements could not interfere with the reduction of aluminum. Perhaps the choice of graphite electrodes was serendipitous, but carbon electrodes were already in use, so experimenting with them would have been a natural choice.

The ingredients for this invention may have all been in place, but that does not detract from its brilliance. Hall and Héroult had the courage to explore new procedures in homemade laboratories, without the support of research grants. They explored the possibilities systematically to find a process that was a spectacular success. In more than 100 years of growth in the aluminum industry, no other process has replaced the one developed by Hall and Héroult. Moreover, the only significant change over the years is the addition of CaF_2 to the melt to lower the operating temperature.

The entire electrolysis apparatus operates well above aluminum's melting point of 660 °C. Molten aluminum has a higher density than the molten salt mixture, so it settles to the bottom of the reactor. The pure metal is drained through a plug and cast into ingots.

Aluminum refining consumes a tremendous amount of electricity. Approximately 5% of all the electricity consumed in the United States is used to produce aluminum. In Box 17-3, we detail the story of the invention of the Hall-Héroult process.

IRON AND STEEL

Iron has been the dominant structural material of modern times, and despite the growth in importance of aluminum and plastics, iron still ranks first in total use. Whereas aluminum production involves fairly simple chemistry, iron and steel production involve an array of chemical processes.

The most important iron ores are oxides, of which magnetite, Fe_3O_4, is predominant. The ores always contain various amounts of silica (SiO_2), which must be removed chemically during the refining process. This is accomplished by reaction with limestone ($CaCO_3$). Coke is used to reduce iron oxides to the free metal at high temperature. Pellets of ore, coke, and limestone are mixed and fed into a blast furnace. As shown in Figure 17-25, this is an enormous chemical reactor where heating, reduction, and purification all occur together.

Various chemical reactions occur in a blast furnace. Heat is provided by the controlled burning of coke:

$$2\,C_{(s)} + O_{2\,(g)} \rightarrow 2\,CO_{(g)} \qquad \Delta H^{\circ} = -110\text{ kJ}$$

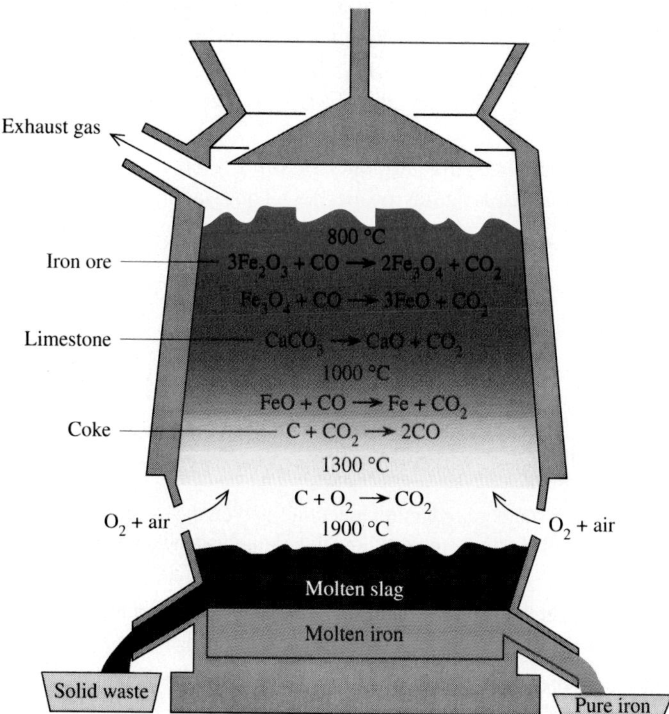

FIGURE 17-25
Diagrammatic view of a blast furnace, showing the reactions occurring at various levels within it.

To control the temperature, water vapor may be injected into the air stream to react with coke in an endothermic reaction:

$$C_{(s)} + H_2O_{(g)} \xrightarrow{\text{Heat}} CO_{(g)} + H_{2\,(g)} \qquad \Delta H^\circ = +131 \text{ kJ}$$

Both CO and H_2 reduce iron oxides to iron metal at elevated temperature:

$$Fe_3O_{4\,(s)} + 4\, CO_{(g)} \xrightarrow{\text{Heat}} 3\, Fe_{(l)} + 4\, CO_{2\,(g)}$$

$$Fe_3O_{4\,(s)} + 4\, H_{2\,(g)} \xrightarrow{\text{Heat}} 3\, Fe_{(l)} + 4\, H_2O_{(g)}$$

At the same time that heating and reduction occur, limestone decomposes into calcium oxide and CO_2. The CaO reacts with silica to generate liquid calcium silicate, commonly called *slag:*

$$CaCO_{3\,(s)} \xrightarrow{\text{Heat}} CaO_{(s)} + CO_{2\,(g)}$$

$$CaO_{(s)} + SiO_{2\,(s)} \xrightarrow{\text{Heat}} CaSiO_{3\,(l)}$$

As the blast furnace operates, liquid iron collects at its base and is covered with less dense liquid calcium silicate.

A blast furnace operates continuously. Solid pellets of ore are fed in at the top, and hot air is blown in near the bottom. Coke burns in the lower portion of the furnace, generating CO at temperatures as high as 1500 °C. The pellets react sequentially as they fall through the hot gases. Liquid products are periodically drained from the bottom of the furnace.

The iron formed in a blast furnace, called *pig iron,* contains impurities that make the metal brittle. Pig iron is purified further in a converter furnace. Here, a stream of O_2 gas blows through molten pig iron. Oxygen reacts with the impurities, primarily Si, P, C, and S, converting them to oxides. As in the blast furnace, CaO is added to convert SiO_2 into a silicate slag, in which the other oxides dissolve. The molten iron is analyzed at intervals until its impurities have been reduced to satisfactory levels. Then the metal, now in the form called *steel,* is poured from the converter and allowed to solidify.

Most steels contain varying amounts of other elements that are deliberately added to give the metal particular properties. These additives may be introduced during the converter process or when the molten metal is poured off. One of the most important additives is manganese, which is added to nearly every form of steel in amounts ranging from less than 1% to higher than 10%. More than 80% of manganese production ends up incorporated into steel.

SECTION EXERCISES

17.9.1 Based on their standard reduction potentials and on the metallurgical methods described in this section, suggest how potassium and nickel metals are reduced from their ores.

17.9.2 Examine Appendix H and explain why zinc oxide can be reduced with coke, but chromium(III) oxide requires a more reactive metal such as magnesium.

17.9.3 Which of the reactions listed in Figure 17-25 are redox reactions? Identify the reducing agent in each case.

CHAPTER SUMMARY

1. Oxidation and reduction, the loss and gain of electrons, always occur together in proportions ensuring that electrons are conserved.
2. Electrons do not appear explicitly in redox reactions. To balance a redox reaction, it is convenient to break down the overall reaction into a reduction half-reaction and an oxidation half-reaction that can be balanced independently.
3. Electrochemical systems couple redox reactions with flows of electrons. The transfer of electrons occurs at electrodes, which can participate actively in the redox chemistry or serve only as passive reservoirs of electrons.
4. In a galvanic cell or battery, a reduction reaction and an oxidation reaction take place at separate electrodes, generating an electrical voltage and a flow of current. Such indirect electron transfer occurs only when direct electron transfer between the reactants is physically blocked.
5. Electron flow is measured in amount of charge but can be related to chemical stoichiometry through the faraday, which is the charge of 1 mol of electrons.
6. The degree of spontaneity of a redox reaction is measured by the voltage, or cell potential. Each half-reaction has a standard reduction potential that reflects the ease with which it accepts electrons.
7. The negative free energy change of a redox reaction is directly proportional to its cell potential. Consequently, equilibrium constants for redox reactions are linked with standard cell potentials.
8. Cell potentials vary logarithmically with chemical concentrations in a manner described by the Nernst equation. As a consequence, a difference in concentration generates an electrical potential.
9. Batteries are galvanic cells that generate useful voltages and currents. Examples include lead storage batteries, alkaline dry cells, and rechargeable batteries.
10. Metals, particularly aluminum and iron, are susceptible to corrosion, which is oxidation by atmospheric oxygen.
11. The application of a sufficiently large external voltage across an electrochemical cell causes electrolysis, which is a redox reaction driven by externally supplied electrons.
12. Metallurgy, the purification of metals from their ores, uses many redox reactions, particularly because the metal must be reduced from a positive oxidation number to zero.

KEY TERMS

electrochemistry
half-reaction
oxidation
oxidation number
oxidizing agent
redox
reducing agent
reduction

active electrode
anode
cathode
direct electron transfer
electrode
electrolyte
galvanic cell
indirect electron transfer
passive electrode
standard hydrogen electrode (SHE)

concentration cell
electromotive force (emf, *E*)
Nernst equation
standard reduction potential
voltage

alkaline dry cell
corrosion
lead storage battery
mercury battery
nickel-cadmium battery

coulomb
electrolysis
electroplating
Faraday's constant *(F)*
overvoltage

SKILLS TO MASTER

- Determining oxidation numbers
- Balancing redox reactions using half-reactions
- Describing galvanic cells
- Doing charge-mole conversions
- Calculating standard cell potentials
- Relating cell potentials and free energies
- Relating cell potentials and equilibrium constants
- Doing Nernst equation calculations
- Describing examples of batteries
- Analyzing electrolytic cells

LEARNING EXERCISES

17.1 Write a chapter summary of two pages or less that outlines the important features of this chapter.

17.2 Describe the steps that must be followed in (a) balancing a redox equation; (b) drawing a molecular diagram of a galvanic cell; (c) calculating the potential of a galvanic cell operating under nonstandard conditions; (d) determining what reactions occur in an electrolytic cell.

17.3 Describe the mechanism for charge movement in each of the following components of an electrochemical cell: (a) the external wire; (b) the electrode-solution interface; (c) the electrolyte solution; and (d) the porous barrier.

17.4 Write a paragraph explaining the linkages between cell potential, free energy, and the equilibrium constant.

17.5 List at least six practical examples of redox chemistry.

17.6 Update your list of memory bank equations. For each new equation, specify the type of calculations for which it is useful.

17.7 List all terms new to you that appear in Chapter 17, and write a one-sentence definition of each in your own words. Consult the glossary if you need help.

PROBLEMS

RECOGNIZING REDOX REACTIONS

17.1 Determine the oxidation numbers of all atoms in the following: (a) $Fe(OH)_3$; (b) NH_3; (c) PCl_5; (d) K_2CO_3; and (e) P_4.

17.2 Determine the oxidation numbers of all atoms in the following: (a) $(CH_3)_2O$; (b) $Al(OH)_4^-$; (c) XeF_4; (d) F_2O; and (e) $K_2Cr_2O_7$.

17.3 Which of the following are redox reactions?
(a) $NH_3 + HCl \rightarrow NH_4Cl$
(b) $2\ Fe^{2+} + H_2O_2 \rightarrow 2\ Fe^{3+} + 2\ OH^-$
(c) $Fe^{2+} + 2\ OH^- \rightarrow Fe(OH)_2$
(d) $3\ O_2 \rightarrow 2\ O_3$

17.4 Which of the following are redox reactions?
(a) $2\ CH_3OH + O_2 \rightarrow 2\ CH_3CO_2H$
(b) $Co(NH_3)_6^{2+} + 2\ Cl^- \rightarrow Co(NH_3)_4Cl_2 + 2\ NH_3$
(c) $CaCO_3 \rightarrow CaO + CO_2$
(d) $2\ Fe(C_2O_4)_3^{3-} \rightarrow 2\ FeC_2O_4 + 2\ CO_2 + 3\ C_2O_4^{2-}$

17.5 Chlorine displays a wide range of oxidation numbers. Give the formulas of species in which Cl has the following oxidation numbers: (a) 0; (b) −1; (c) +1; (d) +3; (e) +5; and (f) +7.

17.6 Sulfur displays a wide range of oxidation numbers. Give the formulas of species in which S has the following oxidation numbers: (a) 0; (b) −1; (c) −2; (d) +2; (e) +4; and (f) +6.

BALANCING REDOX REACTIONS

17.7 Determine the half-reactions for the following redox processes:
(a) Sodium metal reacts with water to give hydrogen gas.
(b) Gold metal dissolves in "aqua regia" (a mixture of hydrochloric acid and nitric acid) to give $AuCl_4^-$ and nitrogen monoxide.
(c) Acidic potassium permanganate reacts with aqueous $K_2C_2O_4$, producing carbon dioxide and Mn^{2+}.

17.8 What are the half-reactions for the following redox processes?
(a) Aqueous hydrogen peroxide acts on Co^{2+}, and the products are hydroxide and Co^{3+}, in basic solution.
(b) An animal consumes glucose and oxygen gas and produces water and carbon dioxide.
(c) To recharge a lead storage battery, lead(II) sulfate is converted to lead metal and to lead(IV) oxide.

17.9 Balance the following half-reactions:
(a) $Cu^+ \rightarrow CuO$ (Acid solution)
(b) $S \rightarrow H_2S$ (Acid solution)
(c) $AgCl \rightarrow Ag$ (Basic solution)
(d) $I^- \rightarrow IO_3^-$ (Basic solution)
(e) $IO_3^- \rightarrow IO^-$ (Basic solution)
(f) $H_2CO \rightarrow CO_2$ (Acid solution)

17.10 Balance the following half-reactions:
(a) $SbH_3 \longrightarrow Sb$ (Acid solution)
(b) $AsO_2^- \longrightarrow As$ (Basic solution)
(c) $BrO_3^- \longrightarrow Br_2$ (Acid solution)
(d) $Cl^- \longrightarrow ClO_2^-$ (Basic solution)
(e) $Sb_2O_5 \longrightarrow Sb_2O_3$ (Acid solution)
(f) $H_2O_2 \longrightarrow O_2$ (Basic solution)

17.11 Balance the net reaction resulting from combining the following half-reactions in Problem 17.9 (the first listed in each case is the oxidation): (a) 9a and 9b; (b) 9d and 9c; (c) 9d and 9e; and (d) 9f and 9b.

17.12 Balance the net reaction resulting from combining the following half-reactions in Problem 17.10 (the first listed in each case is the reduction): (a) 10c and 10a; (b) 10e and 10a; (c) 10b and 10d; and (d) 10b and 10f.

17.13 Balance the following redox equations:
(a) $PbO + Co(NH_3)_6^{3+} \longrightarrow PbO_2 + Co(NH_3)_6^{2+}$ (Basic)
(b) $O_2 + As \longrightarrow HAsO_2 + H_2O$ (Acidic)
(c) $Br^- + MnO_4^- \longrightarrow MnO_2 + BrO_3^-$ (Basic)
(d) $NO_2 \longrightarrow NO_3^- + NO$ (Acidic)
(e) $ClO_4^- + Cl^- \longrightarrow ClO^- + Cl_2$ (Acidic)
(f) $AlH_4^- + H_2CO \longrightarrow Al^{3+} + CH_3OH$ (Basic)

17.14 Balance the following redox equations:
(a) $H_5IO_6 + Cr \longrightarrow IO_3^- + Cr^{3+}$ (Acidic)
(b) $Se + Cr(OH)_3 \longrightarrow Cr + SeO_3^{2-}$ (Basic)
(c) $HClO + Co \longrightarrow Cl_2 + Co^{2+}$ (Acidic)
(d) $CH_3CHO + Cu^{2+} \longrightarrow CH_3CO_2^- + Cu_2O$ (Basic)
(e) $NO_3^- + H_2O_2 \longrightarrow NO + O_2$ (Acidic)
(f) $BrO_3^- + Fe^{2+} \longrightarrow Br^- + Fe^{3+}$ (Acidic)

SPONTANEITY OF REDOX REACTIONS

17.15 Use standard thermodynamic values to determine whether or not each of the following redox reactions is spontaneous under standard conditions:
(a) $O_2 + 2\ Cu \longrightarrow 2\ CuO$
(b) $O_2 + 2\ Hg \longrightarrow 2\ HgO$
(c) $CuS + O_2 \longrightarrow Cu + SO_2$
(d) $FeS + O_2 \longrightarrow Fe + SO_2$

17.16 Use standard thermodynamic values to determine whether or not each of the following redox reactions is spontaneous under standard conditions:
(a) $H_2O + CO \longrightarrow CO_2 + H_2$
(b) $2\ Al + 3\ MgO \longrightarrow 3\ Mg + Al_2O_3$
(c) $PbS + Cu \longrightarrow CuS + Pb$
(d) $N_2 + 2\ O_2 \longrightarrow 2\ NO_2$

17.17 Draw a sketch that shows a molecular view of the charge transfer processes that take place at a silver–silver chloride electrode in contact with aqueous HCl, undergoing reduction:

$$AgCl_{(s)} + e^- \longrightarrow Ag_{(s)} + Cl^-_{(aq)}$$

17.18 Draw a sketch that shows a molecular view of the charge transfer processes that take place at a lead electrode in contact with lead sulfate and aqueous H_2SO_4, undergoing oxidation:

$$Pb_{(s)} + HSO_4^-{}_{(aq)} \longrightarrow PbSO_{4\,(s)} + H^+_{(aq)} + 2\ e^-$$

17.19 Draw a sketch of a cell that could be used to study the following redox reaction:

$$H_{2\,(g)} + Cl_{2\,(g)} \rightleftarrows 2\ H^+_{(aq)} + 2\ Cl^-_{(aq)}$$

17.20 Draw a sketch of a cell that could be used to study the following redox reaction:

$$2\ Cu^+_{(aq)} \rightleftarrows Cu_{(s)} + Cu^{2+}_{(aq)}$$

REDOX STOICHIOMETRY

17.21 If it takes 15 seconds to start your car engine and the battery provides 5.9 amperes of current to the starter motor, what masses of Pb and PbO_2 are used in each battery cell?

17.22 Suppose that automobiles were equipped with "thermite" batteries as described in Section Exercise 17.3.1. What masses of Al and Fe_2O_3 would be consumed in the process described in Problem 17.21?

17.23 A car's alternator recharges the car battery when the engine is running. If the alternator produces 1.750 amperes of current and the operation of the engine requires 1.350 amperes of this current, how long will it take to convert 0.850 g of $PbSO_4$ back into Pb metal?

17.24 A digital watch draws 0.20 milliampere of current provided by a mercury battery, whose net reaction is:

$$HgO_{(s)} + Zn_{(s)} \longrightarrow ZnO_{(s)} + Hg_{(l)}$$

If a partially used battery contains 1.00 g of each of these four substances, for how many more hours will the watch run?

17.25 Dichromate ions, $Cr_2O_7^{2-}$, oxidize acetaldehyde, C_2H_4O, to acetic acid, CH_3CO_2H, and are converted into Cr^{3+}.
(a) Balance the redox equation.
(b) How many moles of electrons are required to oxidize 1.00 g of acetaldehyde?

17.26 Permanganate ions, MnO_4^-, also oxidize acetaldehyde to acetic acid and are reduced to MnO_2 in this process. Balance the redox equation for this oxidation process.

CELL POTENTIALS

17.27 Use standard reduction potentials in Appendix H to calculate E° for the reactions in Problem 17.13, a-c.

17.28 Use standard reduction potentials in Appendix H to calculate E° for the reactions in Problem 17.14, c and e.

17.29 Describe a cell that could be used to measure the E° of the F_2/F^- reduction reaction. Include a sketch similar to that shown in Figure 17-7. Which electrode would be the anode?

17.30 A chemist wanted to determine E° for the Ru^{3+}/Ru reduction reaction. The chemist had all the equipment needed to make potential measurements, but the only chemicals available were $RuCl_3$, a piece of Ru wire, sulfuric acid, water, and a Pb electrode from an old lead storage battery. Describe a cell that the chemist could set up to determine this E°. Show how the measured voltage would be related to E° of the half-reaction.

17.31 The cell of Problem 17.30 has a measured voltage of 0.745 V, with the lead electrode acting as the anode. What is E° for Ru^{3+}/Ru?

17.32 A cell is set up with two Cu wire electrodes, one immersed in a 1.0 M solution of $CuNO_3$, the other in a 1.0 M solution of $Cu(NO_3)_2$. Determine E° of this cell, identify the anode, and draw a picture that shows the direction of electron flow at each electrode and in the external circuit.

FREE ENERGY AND ELECTROCHEMISTRY

17.33 Use standard reduction potentials in Appendix H to calculate ΔG° for the reactions in Problem 17.13, a-e.

17.34 Use standard reduction potentials in Appendix H to calculate ΔG° for the reactions in Problem 17.14, c and e.

17.35 Use standard reduction potentials from Table 17-1 to determine K_{sp} for as many metal hydroxides as the table allows.

17.36 If the cell shown in Figure 17-13 contains 1.00×10^{-3} M concentrations of HCl and $CuSO_4$, what voltage does it produce?

17.37 Sample Problem 17-11 describes the nickel-cadmium battery. What potential does this battery produce if its hydroxide ion concentration is 1.50×10^{-2} M?

17.38 Electrochemical concentration cells can be used to measure ionic concentrations. A cell is set up with a pair of zinc electrodes, each immersed in $ZnSO_4$ solution. One solution is 0.500 M, and its zinc electrode is at 0.040 V higher potential than the other electrode. What is the concentration of the second solution?

REDOX IN ACTION

17.39 Set up the Nernst equation for the standard dry cell. Using this equation, show that the voltage of a dry cell must decrease with use.

17.40 Set up the Nernst equation for the lead storage cell, and use it to show that the voltage of this cell must decrease with use.

17.41 If a chromium-plated steel bicycle handlebar is scratched, exposing steel, will chromium or steel corrode? Use standard potentials to support your prediction.

17.42 Using standard potentials, explain why the steel propeller of an oceangoing yacht has a zinc collar.

17.43 Silver tarnish is Ag_2S. It can be returned to silver metal by placing the tarnished object in an aluminum pan containing water in which baking soda, $NaHCO_3$, has been dissolved. Determine the redox reaction for this "reverse corrosion" process.

17.44 List all the metals that could be used as sacrificial anodes for iron. Which of these could also be sacrificial anodes for aluminum?

ELECTROLYSIS

17.45 In the electrolysis of aqueous NaCl, how many grams of Cl_2 are generated by a current of 4.50 amperes flowing for 200 minutes?

17.46 A "dead" 12-V lead storage battery has 4.80 g of $PbSO_4$ deposited on each of its anodes. It is connected to a "trickle charger" that supplies 0.120 ampere of current at a voltage of 13 V.
(a) To which electrode, Pb or PbO_2, should the anode from the charger be connected? Write the half-reaction occurring at this electrode during charging.
(b) Compute the time needed to convert all 4.80 g of $PbSO_4$ back to SO_4^{2-} ions in solution.

17.47 How long would it take to electrodeposit all the Cu^{2+} in 0.250 L of 0.245 M $CuSO_4$ solution with an applied potential difference of 0.225 V and a current of 2.45 amperes?

17.48 Electrochemistry can be used to measure electrical current in a silver coulometer. The cathode is weighed before and after passage of current. A silver cathode initially has a mass of 10.77 g, and its mass increases to 12.89 g after current has flowed for 15.0 minutes. Compute the quantity of charge in coulombs and the current in amperes.

17.49 When Thomas Edison first sold electricity, he used zinc coulometers to measure charge consumption. If the zinc plate in one of Edison's coulometers increased in mass by 7.55 g, how much charge had passed through it?

17.50 A portable CD player that draws 150 milliamperes of current is powered by Ni–Cd rechargeable batteries. Compute the masses of Cd and NiO_2 consumed when a disk is played whose length is 65 minutes.

METALLURGY

17.51 Write balanced chemical equations for the following metallurgical processes: (a) Roasting $CuFeS_2$; (b) Treatment of bauxite by concentrated sodium hydroxide; (c) Removal of silicon from steel in a converter; (d) Reduction of titanium tetrachloride using sodium metal.

17.52 Write balanced chemical equations for these metallurgical processes:
(a) NiS is heated in air.
(b) Co_3O_4 is chemically reduced by Al metal.
(c) SnO_2 is reduced by coke.

17.53 A copper ore contains 2.37% Cu_2S by mass, and 5.60×10^4 kg of this ore is heated in air. Compute the mass of copper metal obtained and the volume of SO_2 gas produced at ambient conditions, 755 torr and 23.5 °C.

17.54 What mass of limestone, in kilograms, should be added for every kilogram of iron ore processed in a blast furnace if the limestone is 95.5% $CaCO_3$ and the iron ore contains 9.75% SiO_2?

17.55 Calculate the standard free energy change at 25 °C for reduction of ZnO to Zn using carbon and using carbon monoxide.

17.56 Determine ΔG° for the oxidation reactions that occur in a steel-making converter. Compare your values with ΔG° for the reaction of iron with O_2 to give FeO and to give Fe_2O_3.

ADDITIONAL PROBLEMS

17.57 Here are two standard reduction potentials:

$$SO_4^{2-}{}_{(aq)} + 4\,H^+{}_{(aq)} + 2\,e^- \rightarrow SO_{2\,(g)} + 2\,H_2O$$

$$E^\circ = 0.20 \text{ V}$$

$$SO_4^{2-}{}_{(aq)} + 4\,H^+{}_{(aq)} + 2\,e^- \rightarrow H_2SO_{3\,(aq)} + H_2O$$

$$E^\circ = 0.17 \text{ V}$$

Are these data sufficient to allow calculation of the equilibrium vapor pressure of $SO_{2\,(g)}$ over a 1.00 M solution of $H_2SO_{3\,(aq)}$ at 298 K? If so, do the calculation. If not, explain in detail what additional data (thermodynamic or electrochemical) you would need to do the calculation.

17.58 Breathalyzers determine the alcohol content in a person's breath by a redox reaction using dichromate ions:

$$C_2H_5OH + Cr_2O_7^{2-} \rightarrow CH_3CO_2H + Cr^{3+} \quad \text{(Unbalanced)}$$

If analysis of a breath sample generates 4.5×10^{-4} M Cr^{3+} in 50.0 mL of solution, how many milligrams of alcohol did it contain?

17.59 Use data from Appendix H for the reaction,

$$5\,I^-{}_{(aq)} + IO_3^-{}_{(aq)} + 6\,H^+{}_{(aq)} \rightarrow 3\,I_{2\,(s)} + 3\,H_2O_{(l)}$$

(a) Determine the spontaneous direction at pH = 2.00 and $[I^-] = [IO_3^-] = 0.100$ M.
(b) Repeat the calculation at pH = 11.00.
(c) At what pH is this redox reaction at equilibrium at these concentrations of I^- and IO_3^-?

17.60 In cold climates, salt is sprinkled on road surfaces to inhibit icing. Automobile bodies rust more rapidly in these environments. Explain why this is so.

17.61 Consider an electrochemical cell consisting of two vessels connected by a porous separator. One vessel contains 0.500 M HCl solution and an Ag wire electrode coated with AgCl solid. The other vessel contains 1.00 M $MgCl_2$ solution and an Mg wire electrode.
(a) Determine the net reaction.
(b) Calculate the emf of the cell (see Appendix H).
(c) Draw a molecular picture showing the reactions at each electrode.

17.62 A 15.00-mL sample of a solution of $SnCl_2$ is titrated with 0.100 M $K_2Cr_2O_7$ solution, and Cr^{3+} and Sn^{4+} are the products. The endpoint is reached after addition of 22.50 mL. Determine the concentration of the original $SnCl_2$ solution.

17.63 Is iron more likely to rust in contact with water at pH = 10 or in contact with water at pH = 3? Write balanced redox equations and calculate E° values in support of your answer.

17.64 Calcium metal is obtained by the direct electrolysis of molten $CaCl_2$. If a metallurgical electrolysis apparatus operates at 27.6 A, what mass of calcium metal will it produce in 24 hours of operation?

17.65 From the standard reduction potentials in Table 17-1, identify reaction pairs that are candidates for batteries that would produce more than 5 V of electrical potential under standard conditions. Suggest chemical reasons why no such battery has been commercially developed.

17.66 The first battery to find widespread commercial use was the Leclanche cell, in which the cathode reaction is:

$$2\,MnO_{2\,(s)} + Zn^{2+} + 2\,e^- \rightarrow ZnMn_2O_{4\,(s)}$$

In a flashlight, one of these batteries provides 0.0048 A. If the battery contains 4.0 g of MnO_2 and fails after 90% of its MnO_2 is consumed, calculate the operating life of the flashlight.

17.67 For the reaction between strontium and magnesium, $K_{eq} = 2.69 \times 10^{12}$:

$$Sr_{(s)} + Mg^{2+}_{(aq)} \rightleftharpoons Sr^{2+}_{(aq)} + Mg_{(s)}$$

Calculate $E°$ for a strontium-magnesium battery.

17.68 For each of the following pairs of species, select the one that is the better reducing agent under standard conditions (see Appendix H): (a) Cu or Ag; (b) Fe^{2+} or Cr^{2+}; and (c) in acidic solution, H_2 or I^-.

17.69 For each of the following pairs of species, select the one that is the better oxidizing agent under standard conditions (see Appendix H): (a) in acidic solution, $Cr_2O_7^{2-}$ or MnO_4^-; (b) in acidic solution, O_2 or H_2O_2; and (c) Fe^{2+} or Sn^{2+}.

17.70 Predict whether or not, under standard conditions in acidic solution, O_2 is capable of oxidizing each of the substances in Problem 17.68.

17.71 Using standard reduction potentials, determine K_{eq} for the decomposition reaction of hydrogen peroxide:

$$2\ H_2O_2 \rightleftharpoons 2\ H_2O + O_2$$

What does this value tell you about the stability of solutions of hydrogen peroxide?

17.72 Do calculations to show whether sodium or aluminum requires more consumption of electricity per ton of metal produced.

17.73 Balance the redox reactions between MnO_4^- and each of the following sulfur-containing species, if the final products are Mn^{2+} and HSO_4^- and the solution is acidic: H_2SO_3, SO_2, H_2S, and $H_2S_2O_3$.

17.74 A galvanic cell consists of a Pt electrode immersed in a solution containing Fe^{2+} at 1.00 M and Fe^{3+} at unknown concentration, as well as a Cu electrode immersed in a 1.00 M solution of Cu^{2+}. The cell voltage is 0.00 V. What is the concentration of Fe^{3+} ions?

17.75 Give examples of the chemical and electrolytic reduction processes used in the production of metals.

17.76 A galvanic cell is constructed with a silver–silver chloride electrode and a nickel strip immersed in a beaker containing 1.50×10^{-2} M $NiCl_2$.
(a) Determine the balanced cell reaction.
(b) Calculate the potential of the cell.
(c) Draw a sketch showing the electron transfer reactions occurring at each electrode.

17.77 For the reduction of $Cr(OH)_3$ by H_2 in basic solution to give Cr and H_2O, do the following:
(a) Write the balanced net equation.
(b) Compute $E°$.
(c) Compute $\Delta G°$.

17.78 Consider the following redox reaction:

$$MnO_2 \rightarrow MnO_4^- + Mn^{2+} \qquad \text{(Unbalanced)}$$

(a) Balance this reaction in acidic solution.
(b) Write the correct expression for Q.
(c) Determine n, $E°$, $\Delta G°$, and K_{eq} at 298 K.

17.79 A concentration cell is set up using two zinc wires and two solutions, one containing 0.250 M $ZnCl_2$ solution and the other containing 1.25 M $Zn(NO_3)_2$ solution.
(a) Draw a molecular picture showing spontaneous electron transfer processes at the two zinc electrodes.
(b) Compute the potential of this cell.

17.80 Explain why cans made of iron deteriorate rapidly in the environment, but aluminum cans last for many years.

17.81 Given that $E° = -0.34$ V for the reduction of Tl^+ to Tl, find the voltage developed by a cell consisting of Tl metal dipping in an aqueous solution that is 0.050 M in Tl^+, connected by a porous bridge to a 0.50 M aqueous solution of HCl in contact with a Pt electrode over which H_2 gas is bubbling at 0.90-atm pressure.

17.82 Draw a sketch showing the cell described in Problem 17.81. Include molecular views of the processes taking place at the electrodes.

ANSWERS TO SECTION EXERCISES

17.1.1 (a) O = −2, Fe = +8/3; (b) H = +1, O = −1; (c) K = +1, O = −2, Mn = +7; and (d) H = +1, O = −2, C = +1

17.1.2 (a) Not redox; (b) redox (C changes oxidation number); (c) redox (Fe and C change oxidation numbers); and (d) not redox

17.1.3 There are multiple possibilities. Here is one set: (a) N_2; (b) N_2H_4; (c) NH_3; (d) NO; (e) NO_2; and (f) HNO_3.

17.2.1 $4\ Ag + 2\ H_2S + O_2 \rightarrow 2\ Ag_2S + 2\ H_2O$

17.2.2 $2\ HNO_2 \rightarrow NO + NO_2 + H_2O$

17.2.3 $3\ CuS + 11\ H^+_{(aq)} + 8\ NO_3^- \rightarrow 8\ NO + 4\ H_2O + 3\ Cu^{2+} + 3\ HSO_4^-$

17.3.1

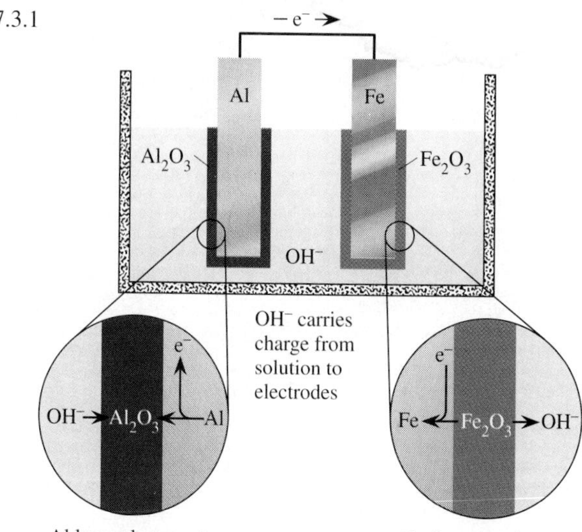

Al loses electrons to become Al_2O_3

Fe_2O_3 gains electrons to become Fe

17.3.2 $\Delta G^\circ = -840.1$ kJ

17.3.3

Active electrode: When an Fe^{2+} ion collides with the surface of the active electrode, Fe^{2+} gains two electrons and sticks to the electrode as an Fe atom.

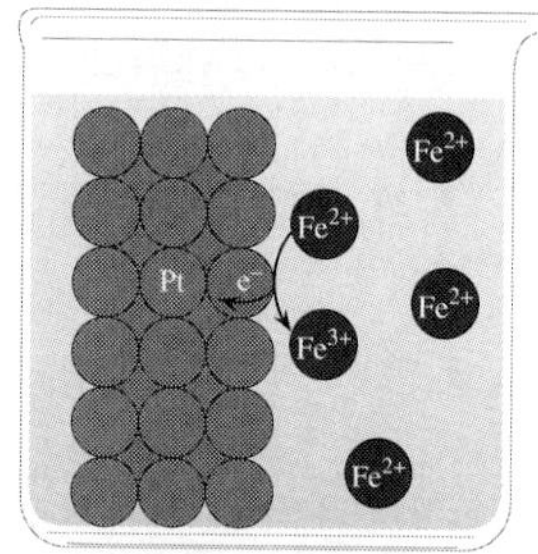

Passive electrode: When an Fe^{2+} ion collides with the surface of the passive electrode, Fe^{2+} loses one electron and becomes an Fe^{3+} ion, which remains dissolved in solution.

17.4.1 (a) HgO; (b) 2.23×10^2 coulombs; and (c) 1720 days

17.4.2

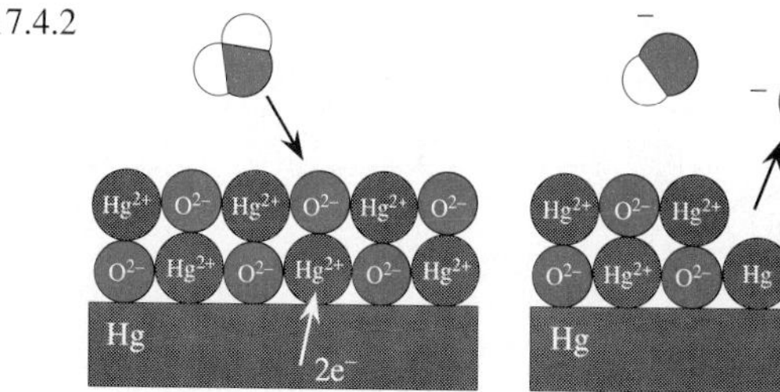

HgO captures 2 electrons to form Hg and O^{2-}

O^{2-} reacts with H_2O to form 2 OH^-

The opposite process occurs at the Zn surface: Zn loses 2 electrons to form Zn^{2+}, which reacts with 2 OH^- to form ZnO and H_2O

17.4.3 (a) $Cr_2O_7^{2-} + 14\ H^+_{(aq)} + 6\ e^- \longrightarrow 2\ Cr^{3+} + 7\ H_2O$; and (b) 16.2 g

17.5.1 (a) $2\ Cr + 3\ Fe^{2+} \longrightarrow 2\ Cr^{3+} + 3\ Fe$, $E^\circ = 0.297$ V
(b) $Pb + Cu^{2+} \longrightarrow Cu + Pb^{2+}$, $E^\circ = 0.4681$ V
(c) $Au^{3+} + 3\ Ag \longrightarrow Au + 3\ Ag^+$, $E^\circ = 0.698$ V

17.5.2

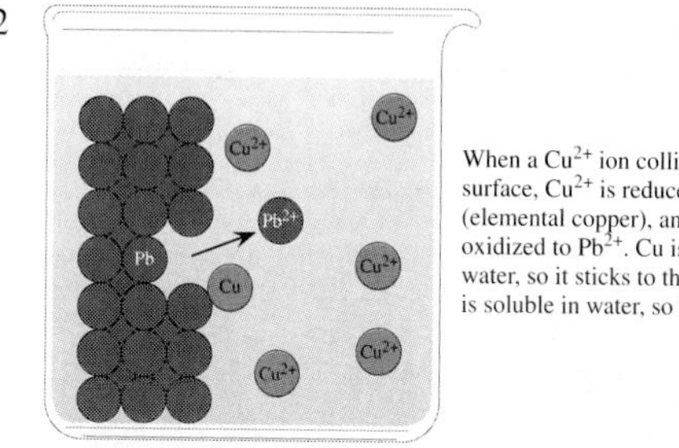

When a Cu^{2+} ion collides with the Pb surface, Cu^{2+} is reduced to Cu (elemental copper), and a Pb atom is oxidized to Pb^{2+}. Cu is insoluble in water, so it sticks to the Pb surface; Pb^{2+} is soluble in water, so it dissolves.

17.5.3 2.0501 V

17.6.1 (a) $\Delta G^\circ = -64.2$ kJ, $K_{eq} = 1.84 \times 10^{11}$ M
(b) $\Delta G^\circ = 1.14 \times 10^3$ kJ, $K_{eq} = 10^{-200}$

17.6.2 0.784 V

17.6.3 4.71×10^{-2} M

17.7.1 E° for tin is less negative than that for iron, whereas E° for zinc is more negative than that for iron. Thus iron oxidizes preferentially to tin, but zinc oxidizes preferentially to iron.

17.7.2 At the aluminum electrode, the deposit of aluminum oxide is impervious to penetration by ions, so it blocks the passage of current.

17.7.3 (a) $H_2C_4O_5^{2-} + 2\ H^+_{(aq)} + 2\ e^- \longrightarrow H_4C_4O_5^{2-}$
Oxaloacetate Malate
(b) $H_2C_4O_5^{2-} + NADH + H^+_{(aq)} \longrightarrow H_4C_4O_5^{2-} + NAD^+$; $E^\circ = 0.15$ V
(c) $8.7 \times 10^4\ M^{-1}$

17.8.1 (a) $2\ HF + 2\ e^- \longrightarrow H_2 + 2\ F^-$ and $2\ F^- \longrightarrow F_2 + 2\ e^-$; and (b) 3.053 V

17.8.2 23.5 kg, requiring a tank whose volume is 252 L

17.8.3 In aqueous KF, water would be electrolyzed rather than KF, generating O_2 instead of F_2; liquid HF does not conduct electricity and support electrolysis.

17.9.1 Potassium, like sodium, has a highly negative standard reduction potential. It is reduced by electrolysis of a molten salt such as KCl. Nickel has a reduction potential similar to iron; its ores can be reduced by heating with coke.

17.9.2 The standard reduction potentials are Cr^{3+}, -0.744 V and Zn^{2+}, -0.7618 V, suggesting that these oxides should be equally easily reduced. However, notice that Cr^{2+} has a potential of -0.913 V. Reduction of chromium(III) oxide using coke stops at Cr^{2+}.

17.9.3 $3\ Fe_2O_3 + CO \longrightarrow 2\ Fe_3O_4 + CO_2$; reducing agent is CO.
$Fe_3O_4 + CO \longrightarrow 3\ FeO + CO_2$; reducing agent is CO.
$FeO + CO \longrightarrow Fe + CO_2$; reducing agent is CO.
$CO_2 + C \longrightarrow 2\ CO$; reducing agent is C.
$C + O_2 \longrightarrow CO_2$; reducing agent is C.

CHAPTER 18

THE CHEMISTRY OF LEWIS ACIDS AND BASES

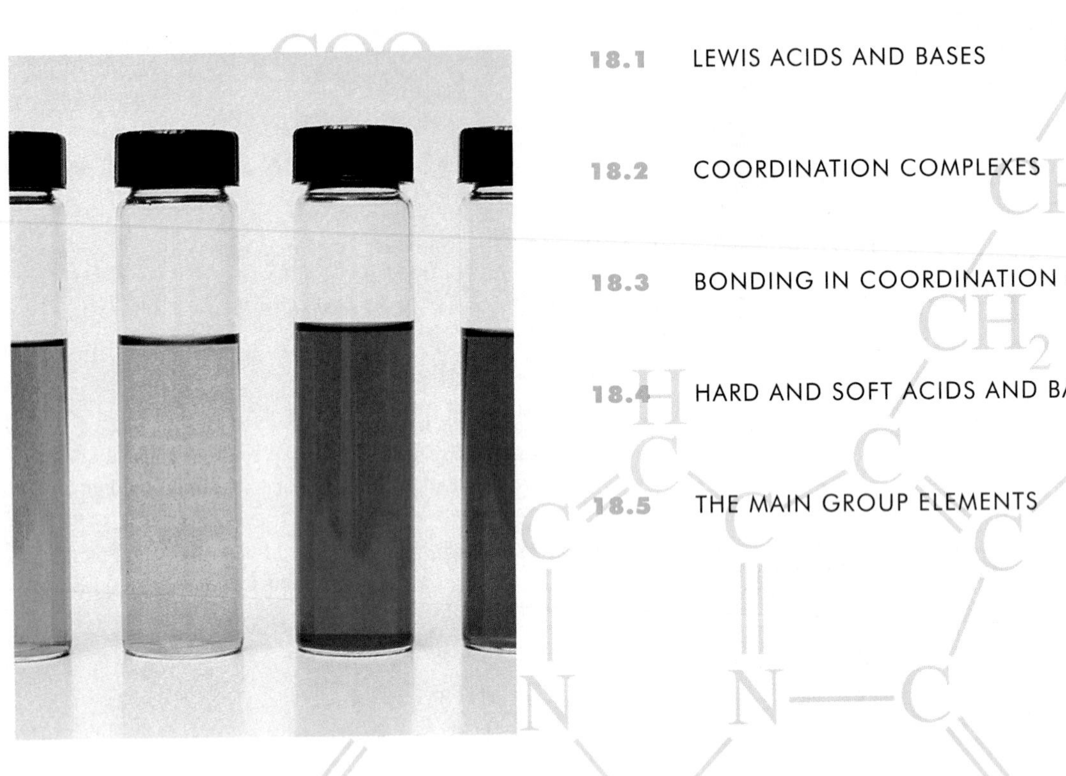

C hemical reactions display a near-infinite variety. Although this provides never-ending opportunities to invent new reactions, the breadth of chemistry can be bewildering in its complexity. Besides searching for new reactions, chemists look for general ways to organize chemical reactivity patterns. We have already described the patterns of proton transfer and oxidation-reduction reactions.

This chapter describes a new pattern of reactivity in which a chemical reaction is viewed as the donation of a pair of electrons to form a new bond. One example is the reaction between aqueous ammonia and silver cations:

$$2\ NH_{3\,(aq)} + Ag^{+}_{(aq)} \longrightarrow Ag(NH_3)_2{}^{+}_{(aq)}$$

Each ammonia molecule uses its nonbonding pair of electrons to form a bond between nitrogen and silver:

$$H_3N: + Ag^{+} + :NH_3 \longrightarrow (H_3N{-}Ag{-}NH_3)^{+}$$

Viewed from the perspective of electrons, there is a similarity between this reaction and the transfer of a proton to an ammonia molecule:

$$H_3N: + H{-}\ddot{O}^{+}(H){-}H \longrightarrow NH_4^{+} + H_2\ddot{O}:$$

In both cases the nitrogen atom uses its pair of nonbonding electrons to make a new covalent bond. This similarity led G.N. Lewis to classify ammonia as a base in its reaction with Ag^+ as well as in its reaction with H_3O^+. The Lewis description of acids and bases is the subject of this chapter.

18.1 LEWIS ACIDS AND BASES

The Brønsted theory of acids and bases focuses on *proton* transfer between two chemical species. The Lewis definition of acids and bases focuses instead on *electron pairs.*

> ***Any chemical species that acts as an electron pair donor is a* Lewis base.**

> ***Any chemical species that acts as an electron pair acceptor is a* Lewis acid.**

Ammonia is a prime example of a Lewis base. The molecule has eight valence electrons, three from the hydrogen atoms and five from the nitrogen atom. Six valence electrons are used to form the N—H bonds. The other two are a lone pair that occupy the remaining hybrid orbital on the nitrogen atom, giving the trigonal pyramidal geometry shown in Figure 18-1. Although all of the valence orbitals of the nitrogen atom in NH_3 are occupied, the molecule can form a fourth covalent bond using its nonbonding pair, provided that the new bonding partner has a vacant valence orbital available to interact with the orbital containing the lone pair.

Nonbonding sp^3 pair

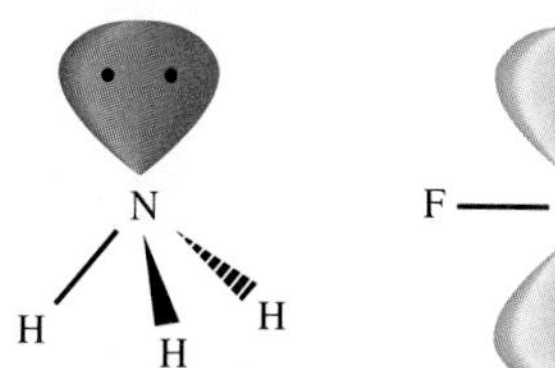

Vacant valence $2p$ orbital

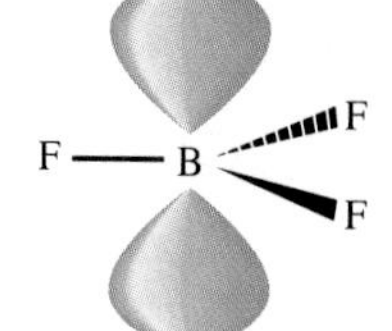

FIGURE 18-1
Ammonia, which has a pair of nonbonding valence electrons, is a typical Lewis base. Boron trifluoride, which has a vacant valence orbital, is a typical Lewis acid.

One important example of a Lewis acid is boron trifluoride, which is described in Chapter 8. This molecule has trigonal planar geometry in which the boron atom is sp^2 hybridized with a $2p$ orbital perpendicular to the plane of the molecule. Boron's unused valence orbital dominates the chemistry of BF_3.

The boron $2p$ orbital in BF_3 is not entirely empty. Later in this chapter, we show that a certain amount of π bonding exists between boron and the filled $2p$ orbitals of the fluorine atoms.

Recall from Chapter 8 that atoms tend to use all their valence s and p orbitals to form covalent bonds. Second-row elements such as boron and nitrogen are most stable when surrounded by eight valence electrons divided among covalent bonds and lone pairs. The boron atom in BF_3 is **electron deficient** because it is associated with only six valence electrons. Boron can use its $2p$ orbital to form a fourth covalent bond, but it has no unused valence electrons to make this fourth bond. To form a fourth bond, boron's new partner must supply *both* electrons. Boron trifluoride is a Lewis acid because it forms an additional bond by accepting a pair of electrons from some other chemical species.

FORMATION OF LEWIS ACID-BASE ADDUCTS

$$NH_{3\,(g)} + BF_{3\,(g)} \longrightarrow H_3N\text{–}BF_{3\,(l)}$$

In the course of this reaction, the geometry about boron changes from trigonal planar to tetrahedral, and the hybrid description of boron's valence orbitals changes from sp^2 to sp^3.

The simplest type of Lewis acid-base reaction is the combination of a Lewis acid and a Lewis base to form an **adduct.** The reaction of ammonia and boron trifluoride is a simple example of adduct formation. A new bond forms between boron and nitrogen, with both electrons supplied by the lone pair of ammonia. In forming an adduct with ammonia, boron is able to use all its valence orbitals to form covalent bonds.

A general equation summarizes the formation of Lewis acid-base adducts:

$$\underset{\text{Lewis acid}}{A} + \underset{\text{Lewis base}}{:B} \longrightarrow \underset{\text{Adduct}}{A\text{—}B}$$

Here are three more examples of adduct formation:

$$\underset{\text{Acid}}{AlCl_3} + \underset{\text{Base}}{:PCl_3} \longrightarrow \underset{\text{Adduct}}{Cl_3Al\text{—}PCl_3}$$

$$\underset{\text{Acid}}{BH_3} + \underset{\text{Base}}{H_3C\ddot{O}CH_3} \longrightarrow \underset{\text{Adduct}}{(H_3C)(CH_3)\dot{O}\text{—}BH_3}$$

$$\underset{\text{Acid}}{SiF_4} + \underset{\text{Base}}{:\ddot{F}:^-} \longrightarrow \underset{\text{Adduct}}{SiF_5^-}$$

RECOGNIZING LEWIS ACIDS AND BASES

A Lewis *base* must have valence electrons available for bond formation. Any molecule whose Lewis structure shows nonbonding electrons may act as a Lewis base. Ammonia, with its sp^3 lone pair, is a Lewis base. Ions can also act as Lewis bases. In the third example of adduct formation just shown, the fluoride ion, with eight electrons in $2s$ and $2p$ orbitals, acts as a Lewis base.

A Lewis *acid* must be able to accept electrons to form a new bond. Because bond formation can occur in several ways, compounds with a wide range of structural characteristics can act as Lewis acids. Nevertheless, we can assign many Lewis acids to one of the following categories:

1. A molecule that has vacant valence orbitals. We have seen that BF_3 uses a vacant p orbital to form an adduct with ammonia. Elements beyond the second row of the periodic table have empty valence *d* orbitals that allow them to act as Lewis acids. The silicon atom in SiF_4 is an example.

2. *Metal cations.* Removing electrons from metal atoms always generates vacant valence orbitals. Many metal cations form complexes with Lewis bases in aqueous solution. In the example that opens this chapter, aqueous Ag^+ acts as a Lewis acid. As another example, $Ni^{2+}_{(aq)}$ forms a Lewis acid-base adduct with six water molecules, each of which donates a pair of electrons:

$$Ni^{2+}_{(aq)} + 6\,H_2O_{(l)} \rightarrow [Ni(H_2O)_6]^{2+}_{(aq)}$$

Each of the six nickel-oxygen bonds forms by the overlap of an empty valence orbital on the metal ion with a lone pair on an oxygen atom. We describe such bonding in greater detail in Section 18.2.

3. *CO_2, SO_2, and SO_3.* These Lewis acids have highly electronegative oxygen atoms π bonded to a less electronegative central atom. Each molecule forms a σ bond between its central atom and a Lewis base. For example, the hydroxide anion, a good Lewis base, attacks the carbon atom of CO_2 to form hydrogencarbonate:

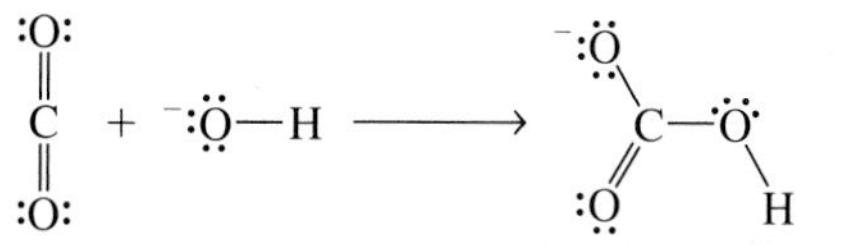

:O:=C=:O: + ⁻:Ö—H ⟶ ⁻:Ö—C(=:O)—Ö—H

Lewis acid Lewis base Hydrogencarbonate adduct

In this reaction the oxygen atom of the hydroxide ion donates a pair of electrons to make a new C—O bond. Because all the valence orbitals of the carbon atom in CO_2 are involved in bonding to oxygen, one of the C—O π bonds must be broken to make an orbital available to overlap with the occupied orbital of the hydroxide anion.

Sample Problem 18-1 provides practice in recognizing Lewis acids and bases.

SAMPLE PROBLEM 18-1 LEWIS ACIDS AND BASES

Identify the Lewis acids and bases in each of the following reactions:

(a) $AlCl_3 + Cl^- \longrightarrow AlCl_4^-$

(b) BF_3 + (Pyridine, C_5H_5N) $\longrightarrow C_6H_5N—BF_3$

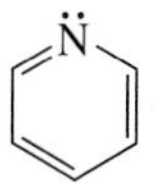

(c) $Co^{3+} + 6\,NH_3 \longrightarrow [Co(NH_3)_6]^{3+}$

(d) $SO_2 + HO^- \longrightarrow HSO_3^-$

METHOD: Every Lewis base has one or more lone pairs of valence electrons. A Lewis acid can have vacancies in its valence shell, or it can sacrifice a π bond to make a valence orbital available for adduct formation. To decide whether a molecule or ion acts as a Lewis acid or base, we must examine its Lewis structure for these features.

See Section 8.3 for a review of Lewis structures.

(a) 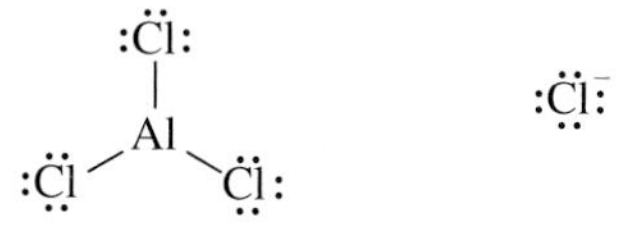 AlCl₃ Lewis structure: Al bonded to three :C̤̈l: atoms; :C̤̈l:⁻

Both species of this pair contain chlorine atoms with lone pairs that might be donated, so either might act as a Lewis base if a suitable Lewis acid is present. The aluminum atom of $AlCl_3$ has a vacant 3*p* orbital perpendicular to the molecular plane. The empty *p* orbital accepts a pair of electrons to form the fourth Al—Cl bond. The Lewis acid is $AlCl_3$, and the Lewis base is Cl^-.

(b)

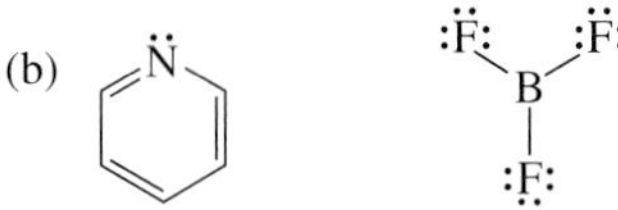

Like the aluminum atom in $AlCl_3$, the boron atom in BF_3 is electron deficient, making this compound a Lewis acid. With a nitrogen lone pair in an sp^2 orbital, pyridine can act as a Lewis base. Pyridine is a common nonaqueous solvent. It is characterized as a *donor solvent* because of its ability to act as a Lewis base.

(c) We have seen that ammonia is a Lewis base because it has a donor pair of electrons on the nitrogen atom. Like other metal cations, Co^{3+} is a Lewis acid. The cation uses vacant 3*d* orbitals to form bonds to NH_3.

(d) O=S=O + :O—H ($^-$)

The Lewis acid-base properties of these species are not immediately evident, but SO_2 appears on our list of Lewis acids. The sulfur atom of SO_2 has a set of 3*d* orbitals that can be used to form an adduct. In this case, the hydroxide ion acts as a Lewis base. The anion uses one lone pair of electrons to form a new bond to sulfur.

SECTION EXERCISES

18.1.1 Identify the Lewis acid and the Lewis base in each of the following reactions:

(a) $SO_3 + OH^- \longrightarrow HSO_4^-$

(b) $SnCl_2 + Cl^- \longrightarrow SnCl_3^-$

(c) $AsF_3 + SbF_5 \longrightarrow [AsF_2]^+[SbF_6]^-$

18.1.2 Draw Lewis structures of each of the species that appear in Section Exercise 18.1(b), and use them to show the donation of electrons that takes place in each reaction.

18.2 COORDINATION COMPLEXES

In earlier chapters, we emphasized the fact that metal salts such as NaCl, $CuSO_4$, and $MgCl_2$ dissolve in water to give solutions of aqueous ions:

$$NaCl_{(s)} \xrightarrow{H_2O} Na^+_{(aq)} + Cl^-_{(aq)}$$

$$CuSO_{4\,(s)} \xrightarrow{H_2O} Cu^{2+}_{(aq)} + SO_4^{2-}{}_{(aq)}$$

$$MgCl_{2\,(s)} \xrightarrow{H_2O} Mg^{2+}_{(aq)} + 2\,Cl^-_{(aq)}$$

FIGURE 18-2
Nickel(II) sulfate *(left solid)* is a yellow solid. When dissolved in water, hydration of the Ni^{2+} cation gives green $[Ni(H_2O)_6]^{2+}$ *(left solution)*. The addition of ammonia causes a ligand substitution reaction to give blue-violet $[Ni(NH_3)_6]^{2+}$ *(right solution)*. This Ni^{2+} species can be isolated as a sulfate salt with the ammonia ligands intact *(right solid)*.

Although these chemical equations show the ions as simple particles in solution, the dissolved ions actually are associated with water molecules of the solvent. The ions are said to be **hydrated** through ion-dipole interactions.

Ion hydration, also known as solvation, is introduced in Chapter 10.

Color changes often provide evidence for the interaction of water molecules and metal cations, particularly for the transition metals. For example, Figure 18-2 shows that nickel(II) sulfate, a yellow crystalline solid, dissolves in water to give a green solution. The green color comes from hydrated Ni^{2+} cations in which each nickel ion is surrounded by six water molecules:

$$\underset{\text{Yellow}}{NiSO_{4\,(s)}} + 6\,H_2O_{\,(l)} \longrightarrow \underset{\text{Green}}{Ni(H_2O)_6{}^{2+}{}_{(aq)}} + SO_4{}^{2-}{}_{(aq)}$$

The water molecules that surround a hydrated cation can be replaced by a variety of other species called **ligands.** Because metal cations are Lewis acids, ligands must be Lewis bases. Ligands include anions such as chloride, cyanide, and hydroxide, as well as neutral molecules such as ammonia, carbon monoxide, and water. When ammonia is added to a solution of hydrated Ni^{2+}, the color changes from green to blue-violet, as shown in Figure 18-2. Ammonia molecules replace water ligands to give the blue-violet species $[Ni(NH_3)_6]^{2+}$:

***Ligand* comes from the Latin verb *ligare*, "to bind."**

$$\underset{\text{Green}}{[Ni(H_2O)_6]^{2+}} + 6\,NH_3 \rightarrow \underset{\text{Blue-violet}}{[Ni(NH_3)_6]^{2+}} + 6\,H_2O$$

The $[Ni(NH_3)_6]^{2+}$ ion is an example of a **coordination complex,** also called a **complex ion.** In a coordination complex, a metal atom or a metal ion is surrounded by a group of ligands in a way that gives a well-defined structural unit. Figure 18-3 shows that the six ammonia ligands in $[Ni(NH_3)_6]^{2+}$ are positioned around the metal in an octahedral arrangement. In forming a coordination complex, the ligands are said to *coordinate* to the metal, or *complex* the metal. Usually, the formula of a coordination complex is enclosed in brackets to show that the metal and all its ligands form a single structural entity. The counterion of an ionic coordination complex is shown outside the brackets. For example the $[Ni(NH_3)_6]^{2+}$ cation can be isolated as its sulfate salt, $[Ni(NH_3)_6]SO_4$.

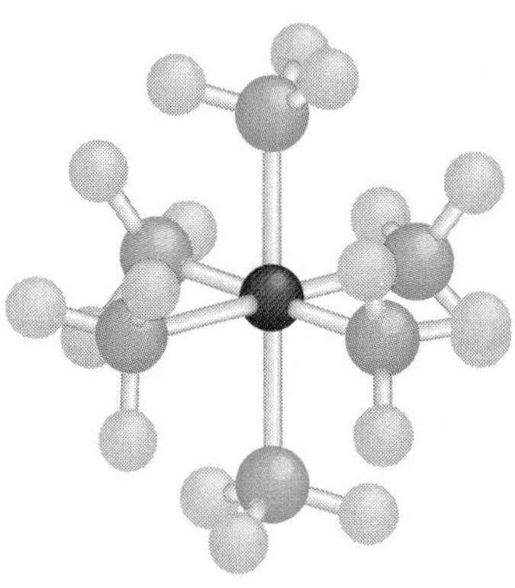

FIGURE 18-3
The Ni^{2+} cation in $[Ni(NH_3)_6]^{2+}$ is surrounded by six ammonia molecules, one at each vertex of an octahedron. Each ammonia molecule bonds to the nickel atom through a Lewis acid-base interaction between the lone pair on the nitrogen and an empty valence orbital on the metal.

NATURE OF METAL-LIGAND BINDING

The ammonia ligands in $[Ni(NH_3)_6]^{2+}$ coordinate to the metal through Lewis acid-base interactions. Ammonia acts as a Lewis base, and the metal cation serves as a

Lewis acid. The bond between them forms by overlap of a valence orbital on the metal cation with the orbital on the nitrogen atom that contains a lone pair of electrons.

$$H_3N: + M^{n+} \longrightarrow H_3N{-}M^{n+}$$

Lewis base Lewis acid Adduct

The word *dentate* is derived from the Latin *dentis,* meaning "tooth." A monodentate ligand has "one tooth" for binding to a metal center, a bidentate ligand has "two teeth," and so on.

Any Lewis base can serve as a ligand in a coordination complex, and hundreds of different ligands are known. The simplest ligands coordinate to the metal through a single Lewis base atom, also known as a **donor atom.** The most common donor atoms in coordination chemistry are nitrogen, oxygen, and the halogens, but other important ligands have carbon or phosphorus donor atoms. Ligands with one donor atom are called *monodentate ligands.* Ammonia is a monodentate ligand with a nitrogen donor atom. Other monodentate ligands include water, halide ions, hydroxide ion, carbon monoxide, and cyanide ion.

$H_2N{-}CH_2CH_2{-}NH_2$

Ligands that have two or more donor atoms are **chelating** ligands, from the Greek work *chele,* meaning "claw." One of the most common chelating ligands is ethylenediamine, $H_2NCH_2CH_2NH_2$. Both nitrogen atoms have lone pairs of electrons, so both can be donor atoms at the same time. Thus ethylenediamine, which is an example of a *bi*dentate ligand, can coordinate to a metal at *two* sites simultaneously. Figure 18-4 shows an example of a coordination complex of ethylenediamine.

Although dozens of chelating ligands are known, we describe just two others. Porphyrins are chelating ligands found in biological organisms. The simplest example of a porphyrin is shown in Figure 18-5. The structure of porphyrin appears complex, but close inspection reveals that it contains a Lewis base portion consisting of four nitrogen donor atoms located in a plane. Each N atom is at the corner of a square. This is a *tetra*dentate ligand that can form *four* bonds to a metal ion positioned at the center of the square.

One of the most important chelating ligands is ethylenediaminetetraacetate, abbreviated $[EDTA]^{4-}$ or simply EDTA. As shown in Figure 18-6, EDTA is a *hexa*dentate ligand because it has *six* donor atoms, all of which can bond to a single metal ion.

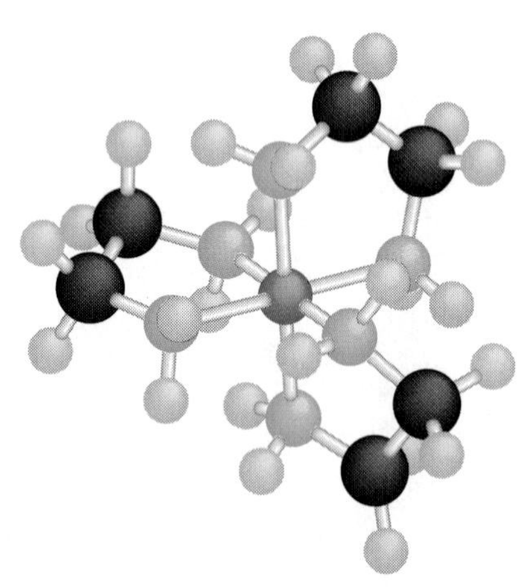

FIGURE 18-4
The orange $[Co(en)_3]^{3+}$ ion has three chelating ethylenediamine ligands wrapped around the metal ion.

THE CHELATE EFFECT

Polydentate ligands form particularly stable coordination complexes. For example, the Ni^{2+} ion forms an octahedral complex with three molecules of ethylenediamine (abbreviated *en*):

$$[Ni(H_2O)_6]^{2+} + 3\ en \rightleftharpoons [Ni(en)_3]^{2+} + 6\ H_2O \qquad K_f = 4 \times 10^{18}\ M^{-3}$$

Compare this value with the formation constant for $[Ni(NH_3)_6]^{2+}$:

$$[Ni(H_2O)_6]^{2+} + 6\ NH_3 \rightleftharpoons [Ni(NH_3)_6]^{2+} + 6\ H_2O \qquad K_f = 6 \times 10^{8}\ M^{-6}$$

The formation constant for the bidentate ligand is almost ten orders of magnitude larger than K_f for the monodentate ligand, which means that $[Ni(en)_3]^{2+}$ forms much more readily than $[Ni(NH_3)_6]^{2+}$. Why does ethylenediamine form such a stable complex with metal ions? Think about complexation at the molecular level. An ammonia molecule that dissociates from $[Ni(NH_3)_6]^{2+}$ immediately floats away into the solution. This gives an opportunity for a water molecule to fill the vacant site on the complex ion, leading to ligand exchange:

$$[Ni(NH_3)_6]^{2+} \rightleftharpoons NH_3 + [Ni(NH_3)_5]^{2+}$$

$$[Ni(NH_3)_5]^{2+} + H_2O \rightleftharpoons [Ni(NH_3)_5H_2O]^{2+}$$

This simple ligand exchange reaction is less likely for $[Ni(en)_3]^{2+}$. As shown in Figure 18-7, when one NH_2 group of an ethylenediamine ligand dissociates from the metal complex, the ligand is *not* free to float away in solution. It is still bound to the metal cation by the second NH_2 group. Consequently, the first NH_2 group quickly snaps back onto the metal. For an en to be replaced, both ends of the ligand must be released at the same time. This stabilization of a metal complex by a polydentate ligand is known as the *chelate effect.*

The chelate effect has important practical applications. As discussed later in this chapter, heavy metal ions such as Pb^{2+} are extremely toxic because they interact with proteins. Lead poisoning is cumulative because the body has no mechanisms for excreting lead. Fortunately, chelating ligands such as EDTA can be used to treat lead poisoning. Because EDTA also complexes with metal ions that are essential in blood, however, it cannot be administered in uncomplexed form. Instead, its calcium disodium salt, $Na_2[Ca(EDTA)]$, is used. Lead preferentially displaces calcium from the complex ion:

$$[Ca(EDTA)]^{2-} + Pb^{2+} \rightleftharpoons [Pb(EDTA)]^{2-} + Ca^{2+} \qquad K_{eq} = 2.5 \times 10^7$$

The kidneys are able to pass chelated lead ions into the urine, so treatment with $[Ca(EDTA)]^{2-}$ cleanses lead from the blood, counteracting its poisoning effects.

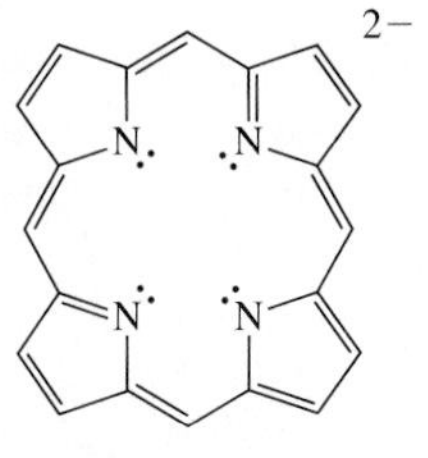

FIGURE 18-5
Porphyrin is a flat molecule with four nitrogen donor atoms arranged in a square, which make its dianion a tetradentate ligand.

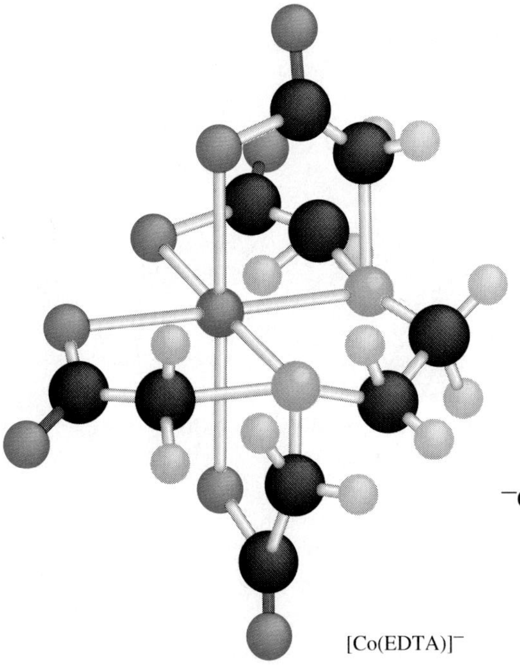

$[Co(EDTA)]^-$ 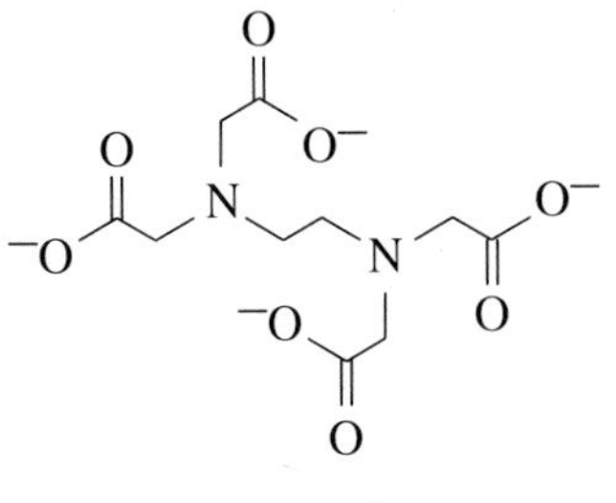 $[EDTA]^{4-}$

FIGURE 18-6
Ethylenediaminetetraacetate, or $[EDTA]^{4-}$, is a hexadentate ligand. Two N atoms and four O atoms act as donors. The ligand completely engulfs a metal cation, as shown here for $[Co(EDTA)]^-$.

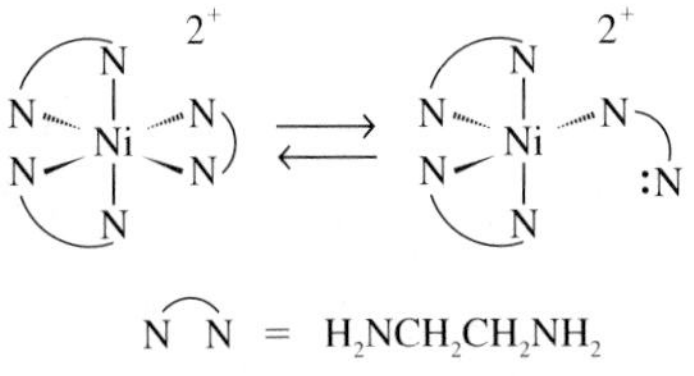

N N = $H_2NCH_2CH_2NH_2$

FIGURE 18-7
Dissociation of one nitrogen leaves the en ligand dangling but "tethered" to the metal by the second nitrogen atom. The chelating ligand quickly snaps back to regenerate the six-coordinate complex.

STRUCTURES OF COORDINATION COMPLEXES

FIGURE 18-8
Vanadium forms coordination complexes in several different oxidation states.

Coordination complexes are a remarkably diverse group of molecules that form from virtually all metals in a variety of oxidation states. They involve an extensive array of ligands, and they adopt several molecular geometries.

The most common oxidation states of the transition metals are +2 and +3, but several of them can form coordination complexes in a very wide range of different oxidation states. Under the appropriate conditions, vanadium forms coordination complexes in every oxidation state from −1 to +5. The colored solutions that are shown in Figure 18-8 all are complexes of vanadium. The metal in a coordination complex can even have zero oxidation state. For example, neutral tungsten atoms coordinate six molecules of carbon monoxide to give the colorless compound $W(CO)_6$.

The number of Lewis base atoms attached to a metal is called the **coordination number** of the metal. The most common coordination number is six. Some metals, such as cobalt(III) and chromium(III), have a coordination number of six in virtually all their coordination complexes. Almost all metal complexes with coordination number six adopt octahedral geometry. This preferred geometry can be traced back to Coulomb's law: The donor atoms take up positions around the metal as far apart as possible to minimize electron-electron repulsion.

The influence of electron-electron repulsion on molecular geometry is discussed in Chapter 8.

Although six is most prevalent, a coordination number of four is also common, and several important complexes have a coordination number of two. A metal complex with a coordination number of two is invariably linear. The silver-ammonia complex described at the beginning of this chapter is one example, and another is the coordination complex used to stabilize gold in plating solutions:

$$2\,CN^-_{(aq)} + Au^+_{(aq)} \rightleftarrows [NC{-}Au{-}CN]^-_{(aq)}$$

Four-coordinate complexes may be either **square planar** or tetrahedral, as shown in Figure 18-9. Tetrahedral geometry is most common among the nontransition elements and first row transition metals. Examples include $[Zn(NH_3)_4]^{2+}$, $[Cd(en)_2]^{2+}$, $[FeCl_4]^-$, and $Ni(CO)_4$. Square planar geometry is characteristic of transition metal ions such as palladium(II), gold(III), and others with eight *d* electrons in

FIGURE 18-9
Four-coordinate complexes adopt either square planar or tetrahedral geometry.

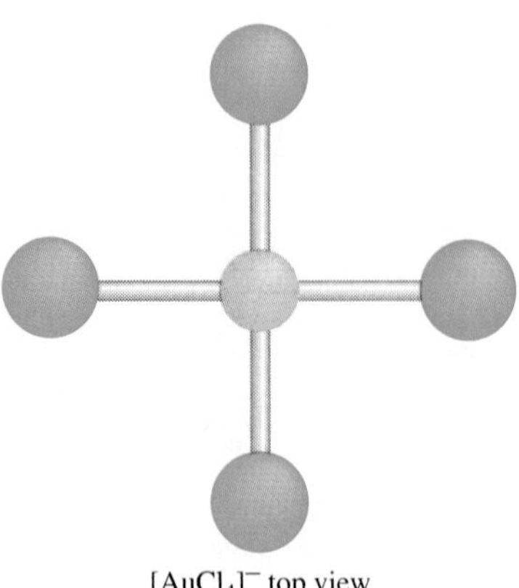

$[AuCl_4]^-$ top view
Square planar geometry

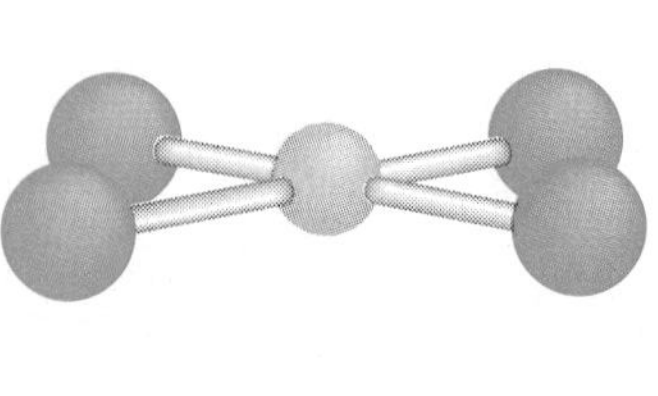

$[AuCl_4]^-$ oblique view
Square planar geometry

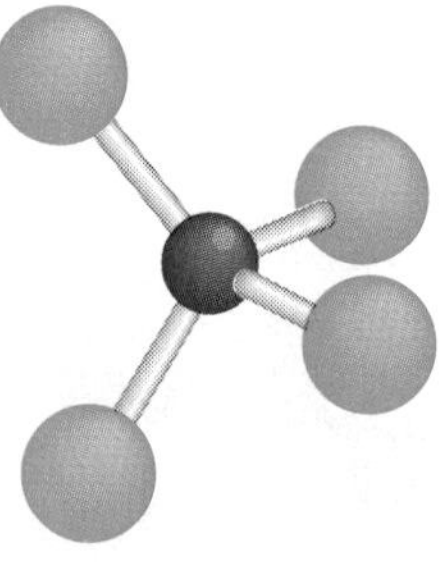

$[NiCl_4]^{2-}$
Tetrahedral geometry

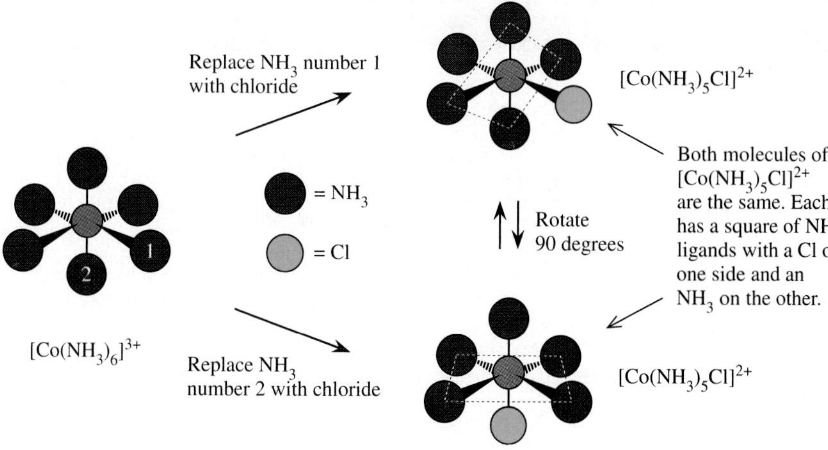

Replace NH_3 number 1 with chloride
$[Co(NH_3)_5Cl]^{2+}$
= NH_3
= Cl
Rotate 90 degrees
Both molecules of $[Co(NH_3)_5Cl]^{2+}$ are the same. Each has a square of NH_3 ligands with a Cl on one side and an NH_3 on the other.
1
2
$[Co(NH_3)_6]^{3+}$
Replace NH_3 number 2 with chloride
$[Co(NH_3)_5Cl]^{2+}$

FIGURE 18-10
There is only one isomer of $[Co(NH_3)_5Cl]^{2+}$. The top structure is identical to the bottom structure because the two can be superimposed on each other after a 90-degree rotation.

the valence shell. We explore the differences between square planar and tetrahedral geometry in more detail in Section 18.3.

ISOMERS

In $[Co(NH_3)_6]^{3+}$, one ammonia ligand occupies each corner of an octahedron. Replacement of one of the six NH_3 ligands with a chloride ion generates $[Co(NH_3)_5Cl]^{2+}$. Regardless of which ligand is replaced, the geometry of the resulting complex is the same because the six positions around an octahedron are equivalent by symmetry. This symmetry is illustrated in Figure 18-10. Any octahedral coordination complex of the general formula ML_5X has just one possible structure.

Now suppose a second ammonia ligand is replaced with a chloride ion. If an ammonia ligand adjacent to the first chloride ion is replaced, the two chloride ions are separated by a bond angle of 90 degrees. This is called the *cis* isomer (Figure 18-11). If the ammonia ligand opposite the chloride ion is replaced, the two chloride ions are separated by a bond angle of 180 degrees. This is called the *trans* isomer. These two isomers of $[Co(NH_3)_4Cl_2]^+$ have different properties. For example, the *cis* isomer is violet and the *trans* isomer is green. Sample Problem 18-2 introduces two more isomers of coordination complexes.

***Cis* means "next to," and *trans* means "across from."**

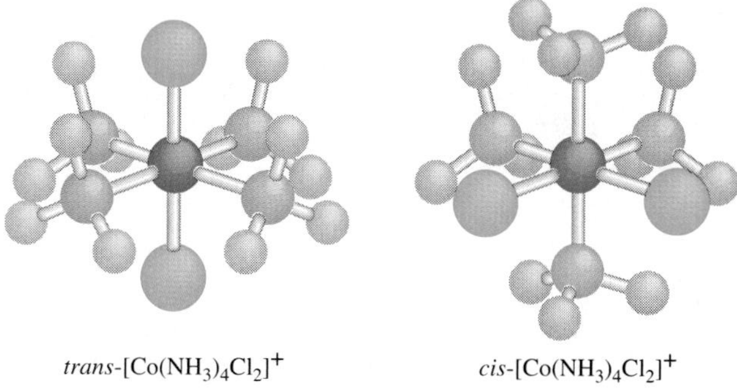

trans-$[Co(NH_3)_4Cl_2]^+$
cis-$[Co(NH_3)_4Cl_2]^+$

FIGURE 18-11
Ball-and-stick models of the two isomers of $[Co(NH_3)_4Cl_2]^+$.

SAMPLE PROBLEM 18-2 ISOMERS OF COORDINATION COMPLEXES

Draw ball-and-stick models of all possible isomers of the octahedral compound $[Cr(NH_3)_3Cl_3]$.

METHOD: It is best to approach this problem starting with $[Cr(NH_3)_6]^{3+}$ and replace one ligand at a time, considering all possible structures. The first substitution gives only one compound. Introducing a second chloride ion creates *cis* and *trans* isomers of $[Cr(NH_3)_4Cl_2]^+$. We choose each of these isomers in turn and consider all possible structures that result from introducing a third chloride ligand. This is best accomplished by drawing pictures.

For the *trans* isomer, replacing any of the four remaining NH_3 ligands gives the same structure, in which the three like ligands are arranged in a T shape about the central cation:

In this isomer the three like ligands lie on an equatorial circle about the complex. Such a circle is called a *meridian,* and this isomer is the *meridional isomer,* abbreviated *mer.*

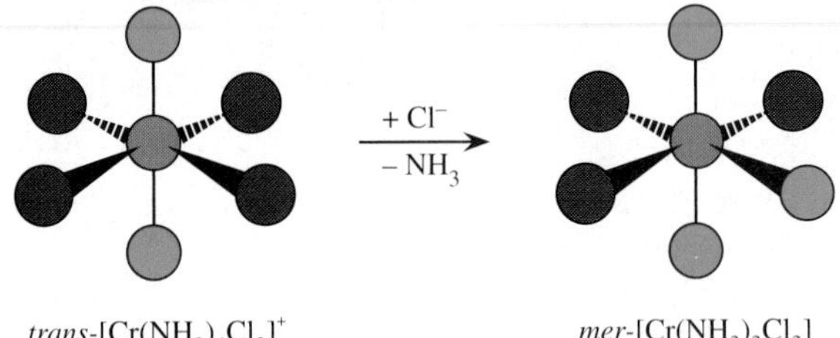

Starting with the *cis*-$[Cr(NH_3)_4Cl_2]^+$, we can make two different isomers of the final product. This can be seen most clearly by labeling the four ammonia ligands. Replacing an NH_3 ligand at site 1 or 2 with Cl^- generates the structure that we have already drawn. However, replacement at position 3 or 4 gives a new isomer in which the three chloride ligands occupy the corners of a triangle:

The three like ligands lie in one of the facial planes of the octahedron, shown in outline in the drawing. This is called the *facial isomer,* abbreviated *fac.*

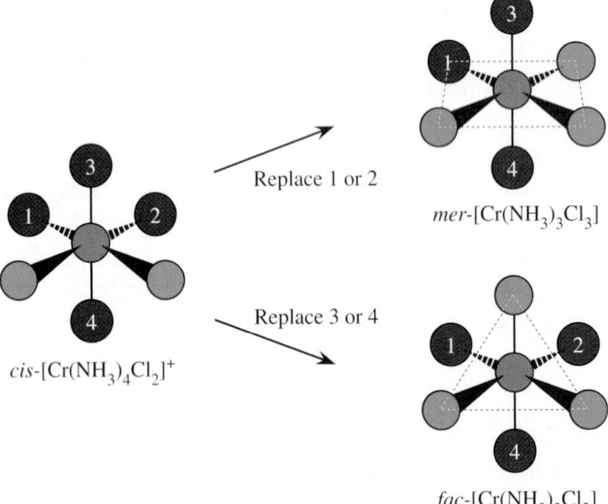

This exhausts all possible structures of $[Cr(NH_3)_3Cl_3]$. Octahedral coordination complexes of general formula ML_3X_3 have two isomers.

Square planar coordination complexes of general formula ML_2X_2 also have *cis* and *trans* isomers, as illustrated for $[Pt(NH_3)_2Cl_2]$ in Figure 18-12. This example highlights the importance of three-dimensional structure in chemical reactivity. The *cis* isomer of $[Pt(NH_3)_2Cl_2]$, known as *cis* platin, is an effective anticancer drug. The

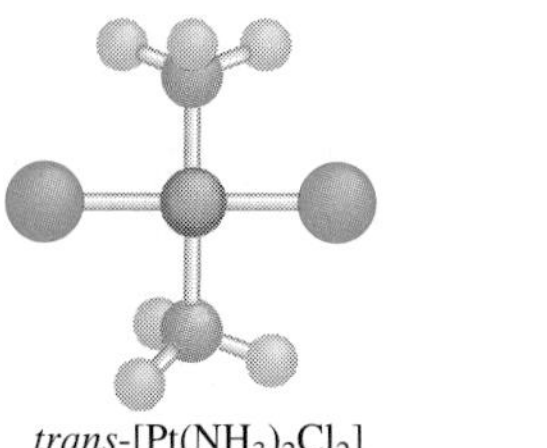

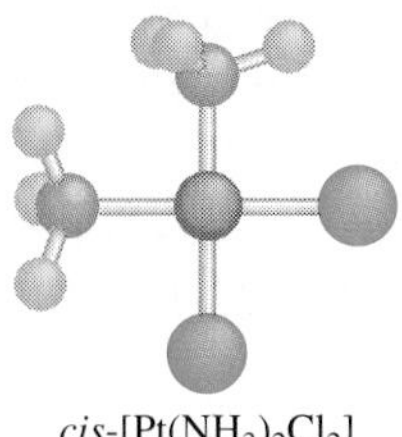

trans-$[Pt(NH_3)_2Cl_2]$ *cis*-$[Pt(NH_3)_2Cl_2]$

FIGURE 18-12
Ball-and-stick models of *cis* and *trans* isomers of $[Pt(NH_3)_2Cl_2]$.

trans isomer shows no anticancer activity at all. The mechanism by which the *cis* isomer destroys cancer cells is not fully understood, but research indicates that *cis* platin disrupts cell duplication by inserting into the DNA double helix. It appears that DNA binds this platinum complex by replacing the two chloride ions. In a sense, the DNA molecule becomes a huge ligand for the platinum atom. Apparently, DNA can bind to the coordination complex only when the chloride ions are adjacent to each other in the *cis* configuration.

The structure of the DNA double helix is discussed in Chapter 11.

NAMING COORDINATION COMPOUNDS

Originally, compounds containing coordination complexes were given common names such as *Prussian blue* ($KFe[Fe(CN)_6]$), which is deep blue, or *Reinecke's salt* ($NH_4[Cr(NH_3)_2(NCS)_4]$), named for its first maker. Eventually, coordination compounds became too numerous for chemists to keep track of all the common names. To solve the nomenclature problem, the International Union of Pure and Applied Chemistry (IUPAC) created a systematic procedure for naming coordination compounds. The following guidelines make it possible to determine the name of a coordination compound from its formula, or vice versa:

1. As with all salts, name the cation before the anion.
2. Within the complex, first name the ligands in alphabetical order, and then name the metal.
3. If the ligand is an anion, add the suffix *-o* to the stem name: *bromo* (Br^-), *cyano* (CN^-), and *hydroxo* (OH^-). The simplest neutral ligands have special names: *aqua* (H_2O), *ammine* (NH_3), and *carbonyl* (CO). Other neutral ligands retain their usual names. Collections of common ligands and their names are given in Table 18-1.

TABLE 18-1 COMMON MONODENTATE LIGANDS

LIGAND	NAME	LIGAND	NAME
Halides		Donor O Atom	
F^-	Fluoro	H_2O	Aqua
Cl^-	Chloro	CO_3^{2-}	Carbonato
Br^-	Bromo	OH^-	Hydroxo
I^-	Iodo		
Donor C Atom		Donor N Atom	
CO	Carbonyl	NH_3	Amine
CN^-	Cyano	NO_2^-	Nitro

4. Use a Greek prefix *(di-, tri-, tetra-, penta-, hexa-)* to indicate the number of ligands. If the name of the ligand already incorporates one of these prefixes (as in ethylenediamine), enclose the ligand name in parentheses and use the alternative prefixes *bis-* (two), *tris-* (three), and *tetrakis-* (four).
5. If the coordination complex is an anion, add the suffix *-ate* to the stem name of the metal.
6. At the very end of the name, give the oxidation state of the metal in parentheses as a Roman numeral or as 0 if the oxidation state of the metal is zero.

The following examples illustrate applications of the IUPAC guidelines:

$[Ni(NH_3)_6]SO_4$	Hexaamminenickel(II) sulfate
$Na_2[FeEDTA]$	Sodium ethylenediaminetetraacetatoferrate(II)
$[Fe(CO)_5]$	Pentacarbonyliron(0)
$[Co(en)_3]Cl_3$	Tris(ethylenediamine)cobalt(III) chloride
$Na[Al(OH)_4]$	Sodium tetrahydroxoaluminate
$K_4[Fe(CN)_6]$	Potassium hexacyanoferrate(II)
$[Rh(NH_3)_5Br]Br_2$	Pentaamminebromorhodium(III) bromide

These examples show that when information is not needed to identify the compound, it is omitted from the name. In the second name, for instance, it is not necessary to tell how many sodium ions are present, since the number can be inferred from the name of the coordination complex. In the fifth name the oxidation state of aluminum is omitted because it is always +3. In the seventh name the single bromo ligand is not preceded by the prefix mono.

The second and seventh examples also illustrate some nuances of the naming rules. Iron in an anionic complex is named by its Latin root *ferr-,* from which the symbol Fe is also derived. Other metals taking their Latin names in anionic coordination complexes are Pb (plumbate), Cu (cuprate), Ag (argentate), Au (aurate), and Sn (stannate). The Greek prefix is ignored when ranking the ligands alphabetically: the seventh name, for example, lists penta*a*mmine before *b*romo. Sample Problem 18-3 provides more practice in working with the names of coordination compounds. Box 18-1 discusses the origins of coordination chemistry.

SAMPLE PROBLEM 18-3 FORMULAS OF COORDINATION COMPOUNDS

Determine the formulas of the following coordination compounds:
(a) *Trans*-tetraamminedichlorocobalt(III) chloride
(b) Tris(ethylenediamine)manganese(II) sulfate
(c) Bromopentacarbonylmanganese(I)

METHOD: To obtain the formula, break the name down, one piece at a time.

(a) First, determine the number of each type of ligand: tetraammine = 4 NH_3; dichloro = 2 Cl^-. Next, identify the metal and its oxidation state: Co^{3+}. Finally, calculate the charge on the complex ion to determine the number of chloride counterions present. Ammonia is neutral, but each chloride ligand contributes a −1 charge to the complex. Overall then, the complex ion has charge $[(+3) + 2(-1)] = +1$. Therefore one chloride anion is required to give a neutral salt: [*trans*-$Co(NH_3)_4Cl_2$]Cl. This example also shows that a particular isomer is indicated by an italicized prefix.

(b) Tris(ethylenediamine) = 3 $H_2NCH_2CH_2NH_2$ ligands. Conventionally, the formula of this ligand is abbreviated "en." The metal is Mn^{2+}. Because the en ligands are neutral, the complex ion has a +2 charge, requiring one sulfate anion for overall electrical neutrality: $[Mn(en)_3]SO_4$.

(c) Bromo = Br^-; pentacarbonyl = 5 CO. The metal ion is Mn^+, so the compound is neutral: $[Mn(CO)_5Br]$.

BOX 18-1

THE BIRTH OF COORDINATION CHEMISTRY

Late in the nineteenth century, just as the principles of chemical bonding were being elucidated, chemists carried out many studies of the interactions of ammonia with cations such as Cr^{3+}, Co^{3+}, Pt^{4+}, and Pd^{2+}. The most intriguing results were obtained for cobalt(III) chloride. By 1890, several different ammonia compounds of $CoCl_3$ had been isolated. These coordination compounds differed in several of their properties, the most striking of which were their beautiful colors. At the time, the formulas of these cobalt complexes were written as follows:

$CoCl_3 \cdot 6NH_3$	Yellow-orange
$CoCl_3 \cdot 5NH_3$	Purple
$CoCl_3 \cdot 4NH_3$	Green
$CoCl_3 \cdot 3NH_3$	Green

Chemists were convinced that all the chlorides had to be bonded to the cobalt in some way, and they could not understand why the ammonia molecules did not evaporate away. One of the first proposed explanations was the *chain theory*, in which the ammine ligands were assumed to form chains between the metal and the chloride. For example, a prominent coordination chemist of the time proposed the following structure for $CoCl_3 \cdot 6NH_3$:

```
  NH3—Cl
 /
Co—NH3—NH3—NH3—NH3—Cl
 \
  NH3—Cl
```

In the 1890s these cobalt complexes attracted the attention of the Swiss chemist Alfred Werner. Only in his early 20s, Werner had just earned his Ph.D. in organic chemistry. He studied the cobalt complexes in detail and developed the basis for our understanding of coordination chemistry.

Werner found that addition of aqueous $AgNO_3$ to solutions of the various cobalt ammine complexes gave different amounts of silver chloride precipitate. For $CoCl_3 \cdot 6NH_3$, all three chloride ions precipitated as AgCl. Only two chloride ions precipitated for $CoCl_3 \cdot 5NH_3$, just one for $CoCl_3 \cdot 4NH_3$, and there was no precipitate for $CoCl_3 \cdot 3NH_3$. Werner explained these results by proposing that the cobalt ion in all four compounds had a coordination number of six. He reformulated the compounds as follows:

$$CoCl_3 \cdot 6NH_3 = [Co(NH_3)_6]Cl_3$$
$$CoCl_3 \cdot 5NH_3 = [Co(NH_3)_5Cl]Cl_2$$
$$CoCl_3 \cdot 4NH_3 = [Co(NH_3)_4Cl_2]Cl$$
$$CoCl_3 \cdot 3NH_3 = [Co(NH_3)_3Cl_3]$$

The chloride ions that appear outside the brackets represent chloride anions that balance the positive charge on the coordination compound. When a coordination compound dissolves in water, the ligands (inside the brackets) remain bound to the metal cation, but the nonligands (outside the brackets) exist as individual ions. These chloride ions precipitate in the presence of silver ions. The chloride ions inside the brackets, which are ligands bonded to the cobalt center, do not precipitate as AgCl.

This elegant insight into chemical structure, based on simple stoichiometric relations, started Werner and his followers down a long path of discovery, along which many remarkable properties of coordination complexes have been discovered and elucidated. Werner was awarded the Nobel Prize in chemistry in 1913 for his work on coordination complexes.

SECTION EXERCISES

18.2.1 For each of the following, determine the charge on the complex ion, the oxidation state of the metal, and the coordination number of the metal: (a) $K_4[Fe(CN)_6]$; (b) $[V(NH_3)_4Cl_2]$; and (c) $[Ni(en)_2]SO_4$.

18.2.2 Draw all of the isomers of $[Cr(en)(NH_3)_2I_2]^+$.

18.2.3 Name the following coordination compounds: (a) $[Cr(NH_3)_5I]SO_4$; (b) $K_4[PtCl_6]$; (c) $[Fe(CO)_4Cl_2]$; and (d) $[Mn(en)_3]Cl_2$.

18.3 BONDING IN COORDINATION COMPLEXES

In the simplest view, a metal-ligand σ bond can be described as the overlap of a filled donor orbital on the ligand with an empty acceptor orbital on the metal. For example, there are six such Lewis acid-base interactions for an octahedral complex of the general formula ML_6^{n+}. This simple view of metal-ligand bonding does not adequately explain the colors and other properties of coordination complexes, however. Molecular orbital theory provides the most complete description of the bonding in coordination complexes, but this approach is beyond the scope of introductory chemistry. Instead, we use a model called **crystal field theory** to explain the colors and magnetic properties of coordination compounds.

The name *crystal field theory* refers to the similarity between this bonding model and an ionic crystal. Crystal field theory assumes that the interaction between the metal and its ligands is entirely ionic. In reality, many metal-ligand bonds are highly covalent, which limits the usefulness of an ionic model. Nevertheless, crystal field theory does a good job of explaining several important properties of transition metal complexes.

CRYSTAL FIELD THEORY OF OCTAHEDRAL COMPLEXES

Crystal field theory focuses on coulombic interactions between the transition metal ion and the electron pairs of the donor ligands. The complex is held together by *attractive* forces between the negatively charged electrons of the lone pairs and the positive charge of the metal ion. However, many interesting properties of coordination complexes result from the *repulsive* interactions between the electrons on the ligands and the valence electrons of the metal ion.

In a free metal ion without any ligands, all five *d* orbitals have exactly the same energy. Now consider what happens when a set of six ligands approaches a metal ion, one from each corner of an octahedron. As the ligands move closer to the metal, coulombic repulsion between the metal electrons and the ligand electrons increases the energy of all the *d* orbitals. However, some orbitals are affected more than others. Figure 18-13 shows the *d* orbitals surrounded by six ligands in an octahedral arrangement. Notice that two orbitals, $d_{x^2-y^2}$ and d_{z^2}, point *directly toward the corners* of the octahedron, whereas the other three, d_{xz}, d_{yz}, and d_{xy}, point *between the corners.* As a consequence, electrons in the d_{xz}, d_{yz}, and d_{xy} orbitals experience less electron-electron repulsion than electrons in the $d_{x^2-y^2}$ and d_{z^2} orbitals. In other words, electrons are more stable when they occupy *d* orbitals that point away from the ligands. Figure 18-14 summarizes the electrostatic interactions between the electrons of the ligands and the *d* orbitals. The set of three lower-energy orbitals are the t_{2g} *orbitals,* whereas the higher-energy pair are the e_g *orbitals.* The difference in energy between the two sets is known as the crystal field **splitting energy,** symbolized by the Greek letter Δ.

The names t_{2g} and e_g are derived from the symmetry properties of the orbitals. The details are not important for general chemistry.

FOUR-COORDINATE COMPLEXES

The octahedral, six-coordinate arrangement is the most common geometry for coordination complexes, but many four-coordinate square planar and tetrahedral

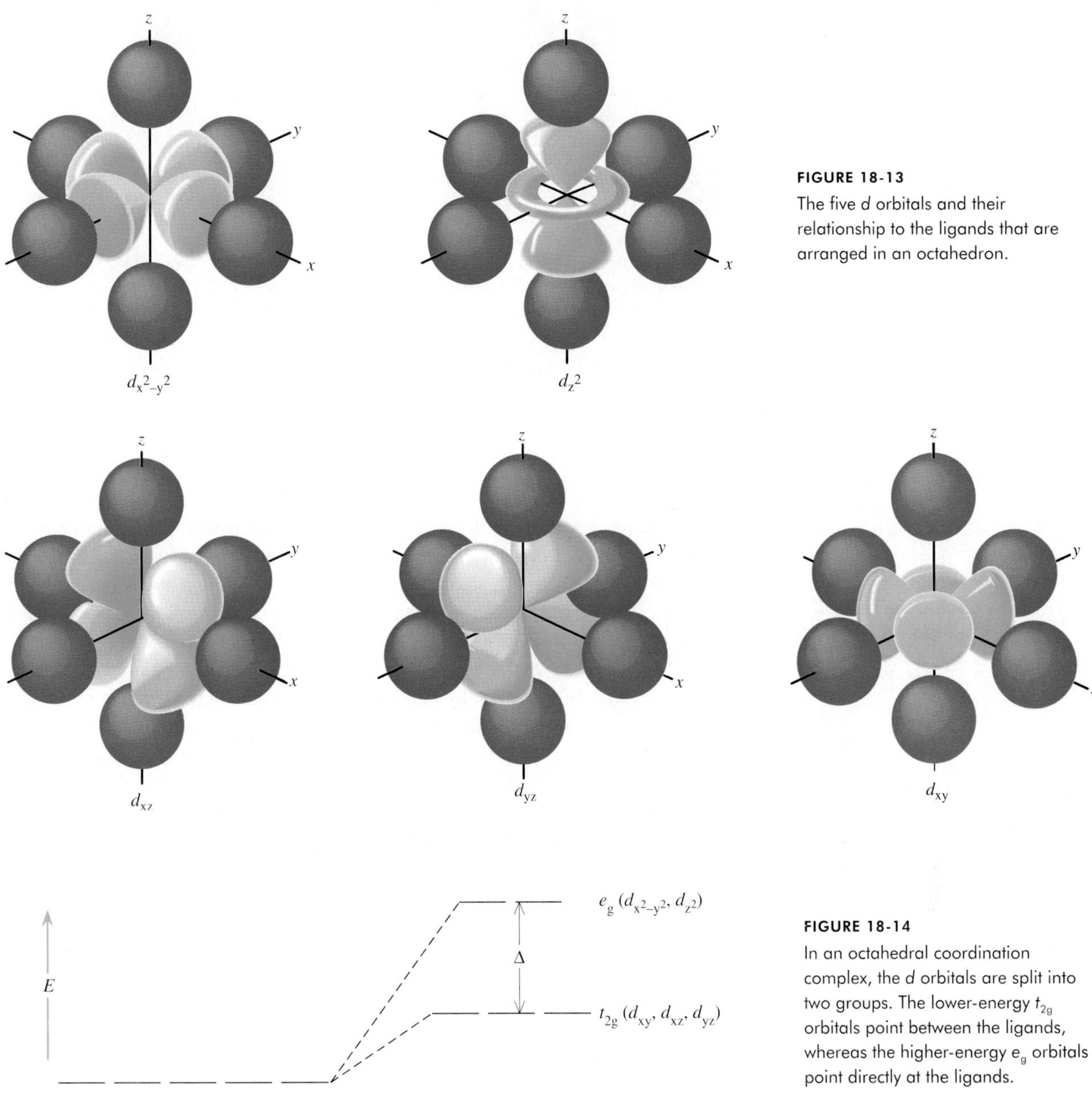

FIGURE 18-13
The five *d* orbitals and their relationship to the ligands that are arranged in an octahedron.

FIGURE 18-14
In an octahedral coordination complex, the *d* orbitals are split into two groups. The lower-energy t_{2g} orbitals point between the ligands, whereas the higher-energy e_g orbitals point directly at the ligands.

complexes also exist. In general, octahedral complexes are favored over four-coordinate structures because of the stability that comes from forming two extra metal-ligand bonds. Nonetheless, some electron arrangements favor four-coordinate geometry. To see how this comes about, we must construct crystal field energy level diagrams for four-coordinate systems.

In square planar geometry, the four ligands lie along the x and y axes. As shown in Figure 18-15, $d_{x^2-y^2}$ is the only *d* orbital that points directly at the four ligands. Thus $d_{x^2-y^2}$ is considerably less stable than the other four orbitals.

The remaining four *d* orbitals are repelled less by the ligands, so they are more stable than $d_{x^2-y^2}$. The d_{xz} and d_{yz} orbitals, which are equivalent in energy, point out of the molecular plane and between the axes (see Figure 18-13). Although the major

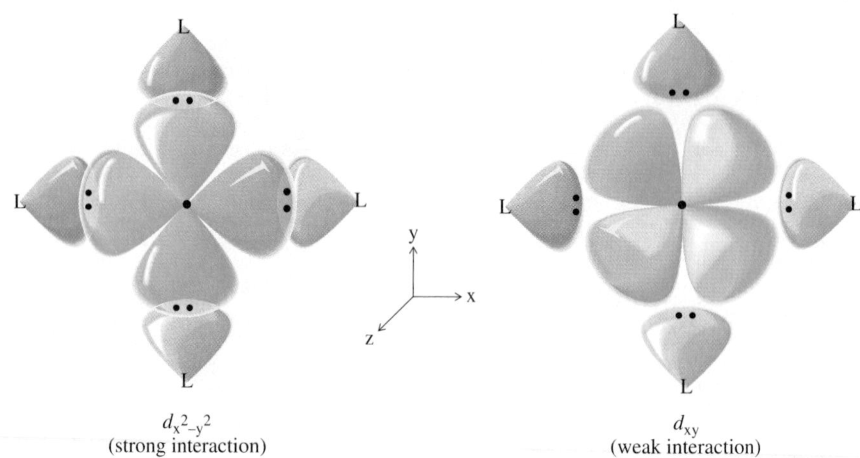

FIGURE 18-15
In square planar geometry, $d_{x^2-y^2}$ is the only orbital strongly destabilized by interactions with ligands. The others, including d_{xy}, point between the ligands.

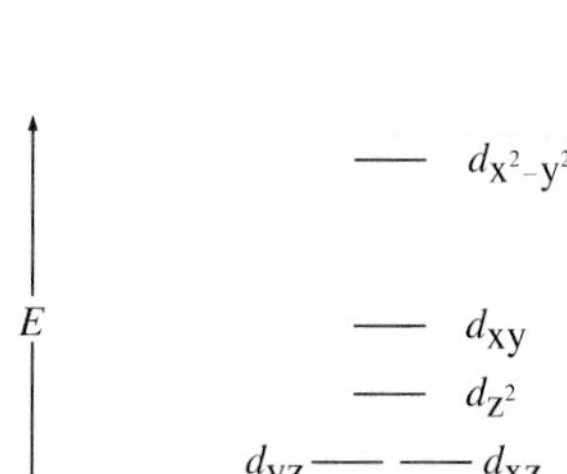

FIGURE 18-16
The crystal field energy level diagram for square planar complexes. The $d_{x^2-y^2}$ orbital is much less stable than the other four orbitals because it is the only one that points directly at the ligands.

lobes of d_{z^2} point out of the molecular plane as well, this orbital has a small band of electron density that circles the metal and lies in the xy plane, giving a small destabilization. Finally, d_{xy} lies in the molecular plane, pointing between the ligands (Figure 18-15). Destabilization of electrons in the d_{xy} orbital is caused by electron-electron repulsion with electrons on nearby ligands. The energy level diagram shown in Figure 18-16 summarizes these energy relationships for a square planar complex.

In tetrahedral complexes the ligands lie at the corners of a tetrahedron rather than at the corner of a square. Figure 18-17 shows the splitting pattern for tetrahedral coordination. Three orbitals are destabilized somewhat more than the other two. The two-three splitting pattern for tetrahedral systems differs from that for octahedral systems in two ways. First, there are three destabilized orbitals rather than two; and second, the magnitude of the splitting is smaller.

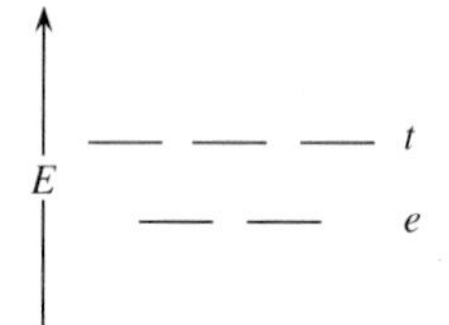

FIGURE 18-17
In a tetrahedral complex, the *d* orbitals are split into two sets, with three orbitals destabilized relative to the two others.

POPULATING THE *d* ORBITALS

Chapter 7 contains descriptions of Hund's rule and the Pauli exclusion principle, which govern the placement of electrons in energy levels. These concepts are used in Chapter 7 for atomic configurations and in Chapters 8 and 9 to describe electron configurations of molecules. The same ideas also apply to transition metal complexes.

The number of electrons in the *d* orbitals depends on the electron configuration of the metal. That configuration can be found from the oxidation state of the metal and its atomic number. As an example, consider $[Cr(NH_3)_6]^{3+}$. Chromium has $Z = 24$, six beyond the rare gas argon, $Z = 18$. Thus a neutral chromium atom has six valence electrons. The charge on the complex is +3, and because ammonia is a neutral ligand, all the charge must arise from the metal ion. In other words, chromium has an oxidation state of +3, which means that three of its valence electrons have been removed. Recall that when transition metals form cations, their *s* electrons are removed before their *d* electrons, so the configuration of Cr^{3+} is $[Ar]3d^3$. The three *d* electrons are placed in the octahedral energy diagram following Hund's rule and the Pauli principle. As shown in Figure 18-18, one electron occupies each of the three t_{2g} orbitals, and all three have the same spin. The crystal field electron configuration of $[Cr(NH_3)_6]^{3+}$ can be summarized as $(t_{2g})^3(e_g)^0$. Sample Problem 18-4 concerns the electron configuration of another coordination complex.

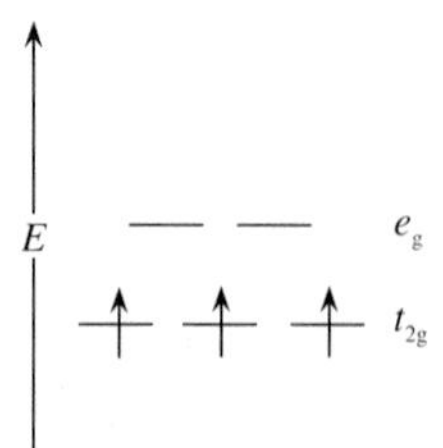

FIGURE 18-18
The crystal field electron configuration of $[Cr(NH_3)_6]^{3+}$.

SAMPLE PROBLEM 18-4 ELECTRON CONFIGURATIONS

Draw an energy level diagram and write the electron configuration of $[Pt(en)_3]Cl_2$.

METHOD: First, identify the ligands and the geometry of the coordination complex. Then construct the crystal field energy level diagram. Finally, count *d* electrons from the metal and place them in the diagram according to the Pauli principle and Hund's rule.

Ethylenediamine is a bidentate ligand, so there are six donor atoms, giving the complex ion octahedral geometry. The two chlorides outside the bracket tell us the complex ion is a +2 cation. Because en is a neutral ligand, Pt is in its +2 oxidation state. Neutral platinum atoms have 10 valence electrons, 2 of which are removed to give the +2 oxidation state, leaving 8 *d* electrons to be placed in the energy level diagram. The Pauli principle and Hund's rule dictate the end result:

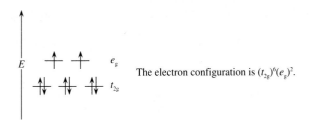

The electron configuration is $(t_{2g})^6(e_g)^2$.

Our previous examples gave an unambiguous electron configuration, but not all configurations are this straightforward. We illustrate using an octahedral complex with four *d* electrons. Following the standard filling procedure, the first three electrons are placed as shown in Figure 18-19. The fourth electron might also be placed in a t_{2g} orbital, but there is a price to pay in energy. Two electrons in a single orbital are destabilized by the placement of like charges in the same region of space (Coulomb's law again). This destabilization is called the **pairing energy, *P*.**

We can avoid this energy price by placing the fourth electron in an e_g orbital. However, these orbitals are higher in energy than the t_{2g} orbitals. This energy difference between the two sets is the crystal field splitting energy, Δ. Whether $(t_{2g})^4(e_g)^0$ or $(t_{2g})^3(e_g)^1$ is lower in energy depends on the relationship between *P* and Δ. If the energy required to pair electrons in a t_{2g} orbital is less than the energy required to populate an e_g orbital ($P < \Delta$), the most stable electron configuration is $(t_{2g})^4(e_g)^0$. On the other hand, if $P > \Delta$, the most stable configuration is $(t_{2g})^3(e_g)^1$. The two possibilities for the four-electron, octahedral case are shown in Figure 18-19.

MAGNETIC PROPERTIES OF COORDINATION COMPLEXES

How do we know whether a complex with four *d* electrons is $(t_{2g})^4(e_g)^0$ or $(t_{2g})^3(e_g)^1$? As we show shortly, there are qualitative guidelines to predict electron configura-

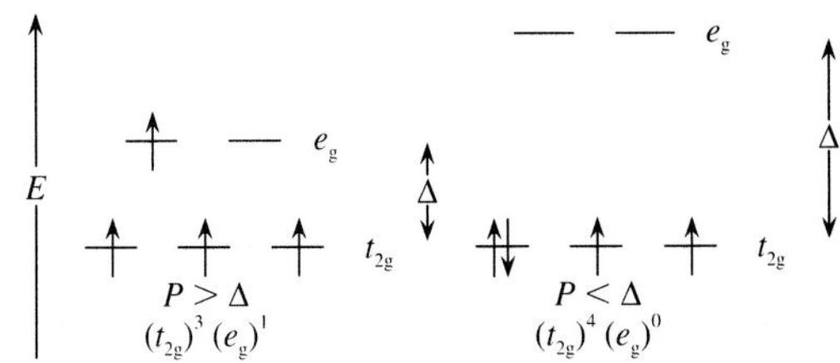

FIGURE 18-19
The two possible electron configurations for a d^4 metal complex. Notice that whereas Δ can be shown on this diagram, *P* cannot, because *P* measures electron-electron repulsion, not a one-electron orbital energy.

tions, but the only way to be certain is to do experiments. One of the most common ways to determine the electron configuration of a coordination complex is to measure its magnetic properties.

Recall from Chapters 6 and 7 that the spin of an electron generates magnetism. When electrons are paired, their spins point in opposite directions and their magnetism cancels. A molecule with all electrons paired has no magnetism from its electron spins and is **diamagnetic,** whereas a molecule that has unpaired electrons is **paramagnetic.** The amount of magnetism in a paramagnetic molecule depends on the number of unpaired electrons: the more unpaired electrons, the greater the magnetism. This provides an experimental method for determining the electron configuration of a coordination complex. The amount of magnetism of a complex tells us how many unpaired electrons are in its *d* orbitals.

A metal complex with the configuration $(t_{2g})^3(e_g)^1$ has four unpaired electrons and is described as **high spin,** meaning it has a configuration that maximizes the number of electrons with unpaired spins. The alternative configuration, $(t_{2g})^4(e_g)^0$, has just two unpaired electrons and is described as **low spin.** Sample Problem 18-5 illustrates high-spin and low-spin complexes.

SAMPLE PROBLEM 18-5 HIGH-SPIN AND LOW-SPIN COMPLEXES

Coordination complexes with the same number of *d* electrons can have different magnetic properties. For example, $[Fe(NH_3)_6]^{2+}$ is high spin, but $[Co(NH_3)_6]^{3+}$ is low spin. Write the electron configuration for each of these metal complexes, and draw energy level diagrams showing which has the higher Δ.

METHOD: We use the formula of a complex to determine its geometry, the form of its energy level diagram, and the number of *d* electrons. The spin information tells us how many of these electrons are paired. Both complexes have six monodentate ligands, so both are octahedral.

Because the ligands are neutral molecules, the charge on the complex is equal to the oxidation state of the metal. Iron loses two of its eight valence electrons to reach the +2 oxidation state, leaving six electrons for the *d* orbitals. Likewise, cobalt in its +3 oxidation state has six *d* electrons.

The iron complex is high spin, so we put one electron in each of the five *d* orbitals before pairing any. This happens only when the crystal field splitting energy is less than the pairing energy. The cobalt complex is low spin, so we fill the lower-energy t_{2g} orbitals before putting electrons in e_g. This happens when Δ is larger than *P*. The energy level diagrams follow:

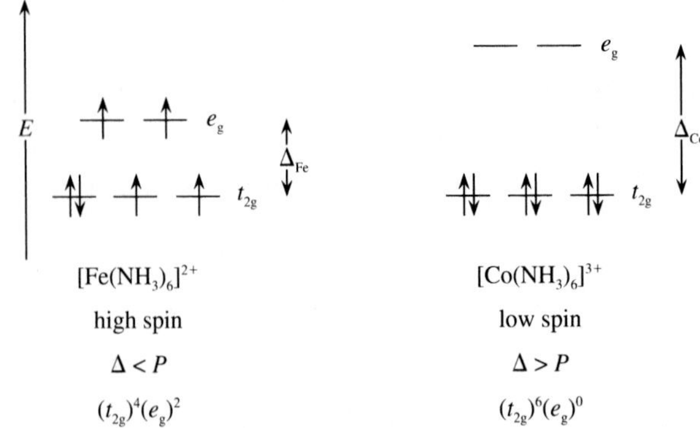

The high-spin configuration is $(t_{2g})^4(e_g)^2$, with four unpaired electrons and measurable magnetism. The low-spin configuration is $(t_{2g})^6(e_g)^0$, with no unpaired electrons and zero magnetism.

THE SPECTROCHEMICAL SERIES

Whether a complex is low spin or high spin depends on the balance between pairing energy and crystal field splitting energy. Pairing energy depends on the shape of the *d* orbitals and changes very little from one coordination complex to the next. Consequently, electron configurations of coordination complexes are governed by the crystal field splitting energy, Δ. Several factors influence the value of Δ, but the most important is the identity of the ligands.

Compare $[Fe(CN)_6]^{4-}$ and $[FeCl_6]^{4-}$, two coordination complexes similar in every respect except for their ligands. Both contain Fe^{2+} ions with six *d* electrons, both have six ligands arranged in an octahedral geometry, and both have the same ionic charge. Despite these similarities, the cyano complex is low spin and diamagnetic, whereas the chloro complex is high spin and paramagnetic. For $[Fe(CN)_6]^{4-}$, the crystal field splitting energy is larger than the pairing energy, so the molecule is low spin. In contrast, $P > \Delta$ for $[FeCl_6]^{4-}$. The chloro ligand generates a small energy gap between the t_{2g} and e_g orbitals, giving a high-spin coordination complex.

Studies of many coordination complexes reveal a common pattern in field strengths of various ligands. This pattern is described by the **spectrochemical series,** in which ligands are listed in order of increasing energy level splitting:

$$I^- < Br^- < Cl^- < F^- < OH^- < H_2O < NH_3 < en < NO_2^- < CN^- < CO$$

Smaller splitting ⟶ Larger splitting

The spectrochemical series reveals the limitations of crystal field theory. Notice that carbon monoxide, a neutral molecule, causes the largest splitting of the *d* orbitals. Furthermore, water, another neutral molecule, is higher in the series than hydroxide ion. If coordination compounds were purely electrostatic, as assumed in crystal field theory, the anionic ligands would be highest in the spectrochemical series. In fact, the spectrochemical series cannot be rationalized using an electrostatic bonding model. Carbon monoxide gives the strongest energy level splitting because of its covalent interactions with a metal. To describe such covalent interactions adequately requires the use of molecular orbital theory and is beyond our scope. Crystal field theory explains the qualitative features of energy level splitting, so it is a useful model despite its inability to account for the quantitative details of the spectrochemical series.

OTHER CONTRIBUTIONS TO THE CRYSTAL FIELD SPLITTING ENERGY

The oxidation state of the metal also contributes to the crystal field splitting energy. We have seen that $[Fe(NH_3)_6]^{2+}$ is a high-spin complex, but $[Co(NH_3)_6]^{3+}$ is low spin. These two complexes have the same ligands and the same molecular geometry, and both are d^6 metal ions. For a given ligand, the energy separation between the t_{2g} and e_g orbitals *increases* as the oxidation state of the metal *increases.* Thus Co^{3+} generates a stronger crystal field than Fe^{2+}. This trend is easy to interpret using Coulomb's law. As the charge on the metal increases, so does the attraction between the metal and its ligands. The ligands approach the metal more closely, resulting in stronger orbital interactions and a larger crystal field splitting.

Another influence on the magnitude of the crystal field splitting is the position of the metal in the periodic table. Within a given row, changes in Δ are rather small, all other factors being the same. However, significant changes occur within a given group. Crystal field splitting energy increases substantially as valence orbitals change from 3*d* to 4*d* to 5*d*. Again, orbital shapes explain this trend. As ***n*** increases, the *d* orbital set becomes more exposed to orbital interactions with approaching

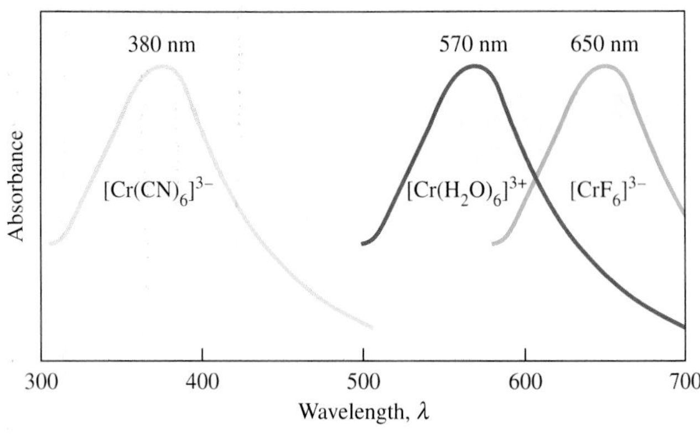

FIGURE 18-22
The colors of Cr^{3+} coordination complexes depend on the position of the ligands in the spectrochemical series.

BOX 18-2

COORDINATION CHEMISTRY IN THE BLOODSTREAM

One of the most important functions of blood is to transport oxygen from the lungs to the tissues. The oxygen carrier in blood is hemoglobin, a molecule that makes oxygen about 70 times more soluble in blood than in water. There are approximately 15 g of hemoglobin in 100 mL of human blood.

Hemoglobin is a protein made up of four nearly identical polypeptide chains, each of which contains a coordination complex of iron(II). The Fe^{2+} ion in hemoglobin is bound to a tetradentate porphyrin ligand. The combination of porphyrin and Fe^{2+} is called *heme*. The d^6 Fe^{2+} ion is most stable in an octahedral environment, so the metal has two axial coordination sites to bind other ligands. One axial site is occupied by a nitrogen donor atom from an amino acid side chain of the protein. This fifth ligand holds the heme in a "pocket" in the protein. The structures of porphyrin, heme, and one of hemoglobin's polypeptide chains are shown below.

The binding and release of oxygen by hemoglobin can be represented as a ligand exchange equilibrium at the sixth coordination site on the Fe^{2+} ion:

$$\text{Heme-}H_2O + O_2 \rightleftarrows \text{Heme-}O_2 + H_2O$$

In the absence of oxygen, the sixth site is occupied by a water molecule. This form of hemoglobin has a bluish color. A ligand substitution reaction takes place when oxygen moves into the

Porphyrin

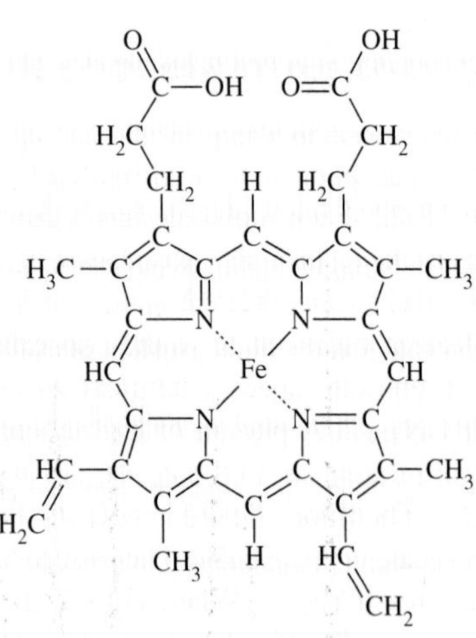

Heme

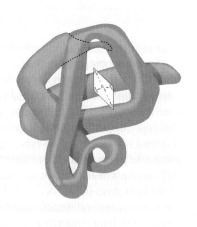

Hemoglobin subunit

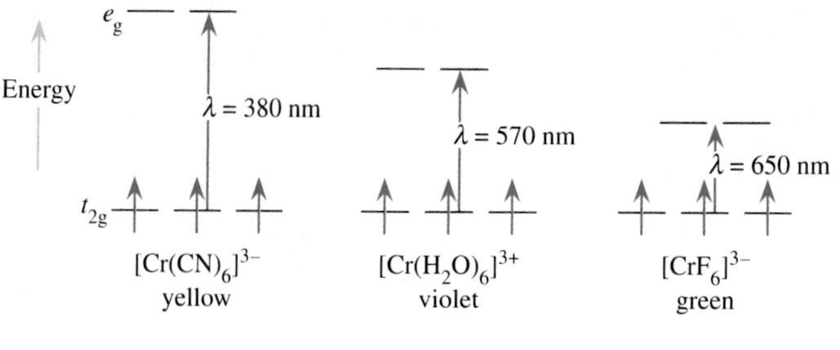

pocket of the protein where the heme is bound. As shown in the following figure, O_2 now becomes the sixth ligand. In this form, hemoglobin is bright red. Because there are four heme groups per hemoglobin, one molecule of the protein transports four molecules of oxygen.

In the lungs, hemoglobin "loads" its four oxygen molecules and then moves through the bloodstream to body tissues, where oxygen is required as an oxidizing agent for metabolism. In the tissues, oxygen concentration is very low, but there is plenty of carbon dioxide, the end product of metabolism. The concentration of CO_2 has an important effect on hemoglobin-oxygen binding. Like oxygen, carbon dioxide can bind to hemoglobin. However, carbon dioxide binds to specific amino acid side chains of the protein, not to the heme group. Binding carbon dioxide to the protein causes small but critical changes in the shape of the hemoglobin molecule. These changes in protein structure reduce the equilibrium constant for O_2 binding, causing hemoglobin to "unload" its O_2 molecules in oxygen-deficient, CO_2-rich tissue. The bloodstream carries this deoxygenated hemoglobin back to the lungs, where it releases carbon dioxide and loads four more molecules of oxygen.

Heme–O_2

Carbon monoxide seriously impedes oxygen transport. The deadly effect of inhaled CO results from its reaction with hemoglobin. The CO molecule is virtually the same size and shape as O_2, so it fits into the binding pocket of the hemoglobin molecule. In addition, the carbon atom of CO forms a stronger bond to Fe^{2+} than does O_2. Under typical conditions in the lungs, hemoglobin binds CO 230 times more strongly than O_2. Hemoglobin complexed to CO cannot transport oxygen, so when a significant fraction of hemoglobin contains CO, oxygen "starvation" occurs at the cellular level, leading to loss of consciousness and then to death.

Many deaths occur through accidental carbon monoxide poisoning. Burning fossil fuels generates some CO, particularly in an oxygen-depleted environment. Automobile engines, gas heaters, and charcoal braziers are all sources of CO. The presence of colorless, odorless CO goes undetected, and in a poorly ventilated room, carbon monoxide may build up to lethal concentrations without the occupants being aware of its presence.

SAMPLE PROBLEM 18-7 DETERMINING THE VALUE OF Δ

Titanium(III) trichloride dissolves in water to give $[Ti(H_2O)_6]^{3+}$. This complex ion has the absorption spectrum shown below. From the wavelength at which maximum absorption occurs, predict the color of the solution and calculate Δ in kJ/mol.

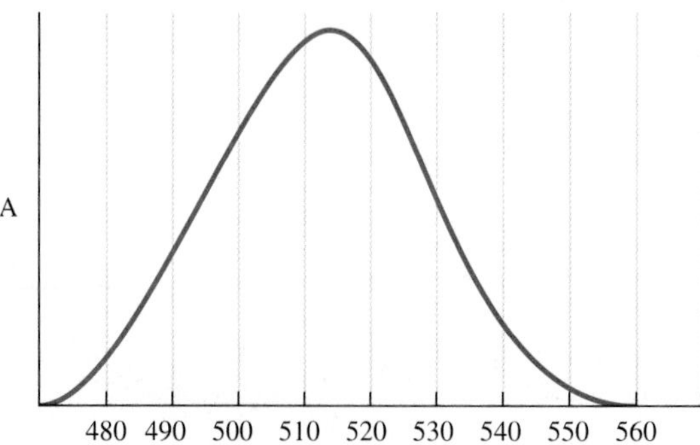

METHOD: The spectrum shows wavelengths of light absorbed by the metal complex. The wavelength absorbed most strongly corresponds to Δ, but we must do appropriate conversions to find the molar energy associated with this wavelength. The color of the solution will be the complementary color of the most strongly absorbed wavelength.

Interpolate on the graph to find that the maximum intensity occurs at 514 nm. Use this wavelength to find the energy of one photon:

$$E_{\text{photon}} = \frac{hc}{\lambda} = \frac{(6.626 \times 10^{-34}\text{ J s})(2.998 \times 10^{8}\text{ m s}^{-1})}{(514\text{ nm})(10^{-9}\text{ m nm}^{-1})} = 3.86 \times 10^{-19}\text{ J/photon}$$

Avogadro's number is used to convert to kJ/mol:

$$(3.86 \times 10^{-19}\text{ J/photon})(10^{-3}\text{ kJ/J})(6.022 \times 10^{23}\text{ photons/mol}) = 232\text{ kJ/mol} = \Delta$$

The $[Ti(H_2O)_6]^{3+}$ ion absorbs at 514 nm, which is in the green to blue-green region of the visible spectrum. According to Table 18-2, the solution should be reddish purple. A photo of a solution of $[Ti(H_2O)_6]^{3+}$ is shown in the margin.

SECTION EXERCISES

18.3.1 Draw crystal field splitting diagrams that show the electron configurations for the following complex ions: (a) $[Cr(H_2O)_6]^{2+}$; (b) $[IrCl_6]^{3-}$; (c) $[V(en)_3]^{3+}$; and (d) $[NiCl_4]^{2-}$ (tetrahedral).

18.3.2 Explain why hexacyano complexes of metals in their +2 oxidation state are usually yellow, whereas the corresponding hexaaqua compounds are often blue or green.

18.3.3 The value of Δ for $[RhCl_6]^{3-}$ is 243 kJ/mol. What wavelength of light will promote an electron from the t_{2g} set to the e_g set? What color is the complex?

18.4 HARD AND SOFT ACIDS AND BASES

Many years ago, chemists recognized that some metallic elements are found in the Earth's crust as sulfides, whereas others are usually encountered as oxides, chlorides, or carbonates. Copper, lead, and mercury are most often found as sulfide ores; Na and K are found as their chloride salts; Mg and Ca exist as carbonates; and Al, Ti, and Fe are all found as oxides. Today we understand why this differentiation among metal compounds exists. The underlying principle is how tightly an atom binds its valence electrons. This notion applies not only to the natural distribution of minerals, but also to most other elements as well.

POLARIZABILITY

Polarizability is discussed in Chapter 10 as a measure of how tightly electrons are bound to an atom or molecule. The polarizability of an atom, ion, or molecule is the ease with which its electron cloud can be distorted by an electrical field. An electron cloud is polarized toward a positive charge and away from a negative charge, as shown in Figure 18-23.

Pushing the electron cloud to one side of an atom causes a polarization of charge. The side with the concentrated electron density builds up a small negative charge, whereas the opposite side bears a small positive charge because of the protons in the nucleus.

Polarizability shows periodic variations that can be understood from Coulomb's law:

1. Polarizability decreases moving across a row of the periodic table. As the effective nuclear charge (Z_{eff}), increases, the nucleus holds the electrons more tightly.
2. Polarizability increases moving down a column of the periodic table. As the principal quantum number, $\boldsymbol{n}$, increases, the valence orbitals become larger. This reduces the net attraction between electrons and the nucleus.

Trends in effective nuclear charge, orbital size, and screening are discussed in Chapter 7.

THE HARD-SOFT CONCEPT

Lewis acids and bases can be organized according to their polarizability. If polarizability is low, the species is categorized as "hard." If polarizability is high, the species is "soft."

A **hard base** has electron pairs of low polarizability. This characteristic correlates with high electronegativity. Fluoride, the anion of the most electronegative element, is the hardest base because it contains a small, dense sphere of negative charge. Molecules and ions that contain oxygen or nitrogen atoms are also hard bases, although not as hard as fluorine. Examples include H_2O, CH_3OH, OH^-, NH_3, and H_2NCH_3.

A **soft base** has a large donor atom of high polarizability and low electronegativity. Iodide ion has its valence electrons in large $\boldsymbol{n} = 5$ orbitals, making this anion highly polarizable and a very soft base. Other molecules and polyatomic anions with donor atoms from rows 3 to 6 are also soft bases. To summarize, the donor atom becomes *softer* as we move *down* a column of the periodic table.

The electron cloud of an atom is attracted by a positive charge

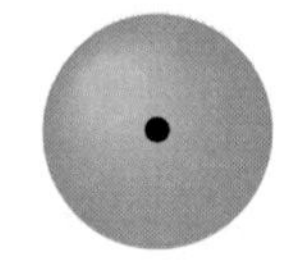

An atom unperturbed by an electrical charge has a spherical electron cloud

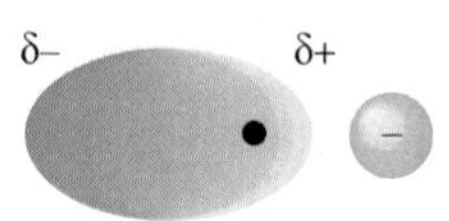

The electron cloud of an atom is repelled by a negative charge

FIGURE 18-23
Polarization is illustrated by the effects of ions on atomic orbitals. An electron cloud is polarized toward an approaching cation, whereas an approaching anion polarizes the electron cloud in the opposite direction.

The only known oxidation states for aluminum are 0 and +3.

A **hard acid** has an acceptor atom with low polarizability. Most metal atoms and ions are hard acids. In general, the smaller the ionic radius and the higher the oxidation state, the harder the acid. The Al^{3+} cation is a prime example of a hard Lewis acid. The Al^{3+} ion has an ionic radius of only 67 pm. The nucleus exerts a strong pull on the compact electron cloud, giving the ion very low polarizability.

The designation of hard acids is not restricted to metal cations. For example, in BF_3 the small boron atom in its +3 oxidation state is bonded to three highly electronegative fluorine atoms. All the B—F bonds are polarized away from a boron center that is already electron deficient. Boron trifluoride is a hard Lewis acid.

A **soft acid** has a relatively high polarizability. Large atoms and low oxidation states often convey softness. Compare Al^{3+} with Hg^{2+}, a typical soft acid. The ionic radius of Hg^{2+} is 116 pm, almost twice the size of Al^{3+}. This is the result of the high value of $\boldsymbol{n} = 6$. Consequently, Hg^{2+} is a highly polarizable, very soft Lewis acid. The relatively few soft metal ions are located around gold in the periodic table.

The terms *hard* and *soft* are relative, so there is no sharp dividing line between the two. In fact, many acids and bases fall into a third category called *borderline*. Sample Problem 18-8 shows how to categorize Lewis acids and bases in order of their hard-soft properties.

SAMPLE PROBLEM 18-8 RANKING HARDNESS AND SOFTNESS

Rank the following groups of Lewis acids and bases from softest to hardest: (a) H_2S, H_2O, and H_2Se; (b) H_2O, NH_3, and PH_3; (c) BCl_3, $GaCl_3$, and $AlCl_3$; and (d) Fe^0, Fe^{3+}, and Fe^{2+}.

METHOD: Our first task is to decide whether the members of a given group are Lewis acids or bases. Then we must evaluate the relative softness and hardness based on polarizability, taking into account correlations with electronegativity, size, and charge.

(a) H–Ö–H   H–S̈–H   H–S̈e–H

These three molecules have lone pairs, so they are Lewis bases. The central atoms are in the same column of the periodic table, so the softness of the molecules increases moving down the column. Thus H_2Se is softer than H_2S, which is softer than H_2O.

(b) H–Ö–H   H—N̈—H (with H below)   H—P̈—H (with H below)

Again, these molecules have lone pairs, so they are Lewis bases. Ammonia and water are both hard bases, but H_2O is the harder of the two because oxygen is more electronegative than nitrogen. Because phosphorus is below nitrogen on the periodic table, we conclude that phosphine, PH_3, is softer than ammonia. Thus PH_3 is softer than NH_3, which is softer than H_2O.

(c) :Cl:–Ga(–:Cl:)–:Cl: :Cl:–Al(–:Cl:)–:Cl: :Cl:–B(–:Cl:)–:Cl:

These three molecules have trigonal planar geometry with sp^2 hybridized central atoms. Each has a valence p orbital perpendicular to the molecular plane, making the molecules Lewis acids. The hardness of the central acceptor atom decreases going down the column. A gallium atom is larger and more polarizable than an aluminum atom. Thus $GaCl_3$ is softer than $AlCl_3$, which is softer than BCl_3. Gallium trichloride is a soft Lewis acid, whereas $AlCl_3$ and BCl_3 are both hard.

(d) Fe^0 Fe^{2+} Fe^{3+}
Metal cations are Lewis acids. As valence electrons are stripped away from a metal atom, the remaining electron cloud undergoes an ever-larger pull from the nuclear charge. This decreases the size of the ion as well as its polarizability. Thus Fe^0 is softer than Fe^{2+}, which is softer than Fe^{3+}.

THE HARD-SOFT ACID-BASE (HSAB) PRINCIPLE

The idea of hard and soft acids and bases can be used to interpret many trends in chemical reactivity. The hard-soft acid-base principle **(HSAB principle)** is an empirical summary of results collected from many thousands of chemical reactions studied through decades of research.

Hard Lewis acids tend to combine with hard Lewis bases.
Soft Lewis acids tend to combine with soft Lewis bases.

The geochemical distribution of metals conforms to the HSAB principle. Metals that form hard acid cations have a strong affinity for hard bases such as oxide, fluoride, and chloride. Most metal ions that are hard acids are found bonded to the oxygen atoms of various silicate anions. These elements, known as *lithophiles,* are concentrated in the Earth's mantle. Hard acid metals are also found with other hard bases, including oxides or, less often, halides, sulfates, or carbonates. Examples include rutile (TiO_2), limestone ($CaCO_3$), gypsum ($CaSO_4$), and sylvite (KCl).

The structure and bonding of silicates are discussed in Chapter 8.

Soft metals such as gold and platinum have a low affinity for hard oxygen atoms, so they are not affected by O_2 in the atmosphere. Consequently, the softest metals are found in the crust of the Earth in their elemental form. These metals, known as *siderophiles,* include Ru, Rh, Pd, Os, Ir, Pt, and Au.

Recall from Chapter 17 that almost all the elements react spontaneously with oxygen.

Elements that occur in nature as sulfides are known as *chalcophiles*. In this category, we find many borderline acids as well as some soft acids. Soft acids may occur either in elemental form or as arsenides or tellurides. Chalcophile minerals include galena (PbS), cinnabar (HgS), chalcopyrite ($CuFeS_2$), argentite (Ag_2S), calaverite ($AuTe_2$), and sperrylite ($PtAs_2$).

In Section 18.5, we show how the HSAB principle can be used to interpret chemical reactions.

SECTION EXERCISES

18.4.1 Rank the following from softest to hardest: (a) NCl_3, NH_3, and NF_3; (b) Pb^{2+}, Pb^{4+}, and Zn^{2+}; (c) ClO_4^-, ClO_2^-, and ClO_3^-; and (d) PCl_3, $SbCl_3$, and PF_3.

18.4.2 Iron is always found in nature in compounds, often with oxygen. Its neighbors in the periodic table, ruthenium and osmium, occur in elemental form. Explain these observations using the HSAB principle.

18.5 THE MAIN GROUP ELEMENTS

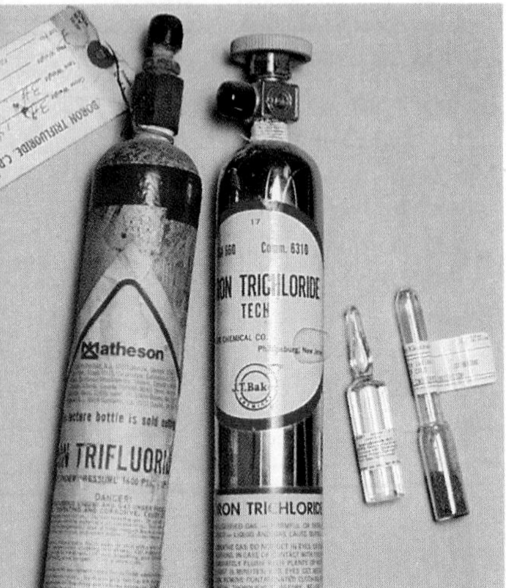

FIGURE 18-24
Boron trifluoride and boron trichloride are gases, boron tribromide is a liquid, and boron triiodide is a solid.

The Lewis acid-base model, augmented by the HSAB principle, provides tools that help organize much of the chemistry characteristic of the main group elements of the periodic table found in Groups III through VII.

GROUP III ELEMENTS

The Group III elements are boron, aluminum, gallium, indium, and thallium. Each has the valence electron configuration s^2p^1, so their most common oxidation state is +3. For thallium, the +1 oxidation state is also common. All elements in this column have fewer valence electrons than valence orbitals and thus typically form molecules that are Lewis acids.

Group III trihalides are the best known Lewis acids. Each boron halide molecule is planar, with a vacant *p* orbital perpendicular to its molecular plane. Because of their low polarizability, BF_3 and BCl_3 are gases. The larger, more polarizable electron clouds on bromine and iodine make BBr_3 a volatile liquid and BI_3 a solid at room temperature, as shown in Figure 18-24. These halides react with a wide collection of Lewis bases. Many adducts form with donor atoms from Group V (N, P, As) or Group VI (O, S). Metal fluorides transfer an F^- ion to BF_3 to give tetrafluoroborate salts:

$$LiF + BF_3 \longrightarrow Li^+\ BF_4^- \quad \text{Lithium tetrafluoroborate}$$

Tetrafluoroborate anion is an important derivative of BF_3 because it is nonreactive. With eight valence electrons around the boron atom, BF_4^- anion has no tendency to coordinate further ligands. Tetrafluoroborate salts are used in synthesis when a bulky inert anion is necessary.

The observed order of reactivity for the boron halides is:

$$BF_3 < BCl_3 < BBr_3 < BI_3$$

From electronegativity considerations, we might expect the opposite trend. The electronegativity difference between boron and fluorine is about 2, whereas boron and iodine differ by only 0.6. Thus fluorine atoms withdraw more electron density from boron than iodine atoms, resulting in a more positive boron atom that should be a stronger Lewis acid. The observed reactivity trend suggests that some mechanism returns electron density to boron in the lighter boron halides. The mechanism is probably π bonding between filled halogen *p* orbitals and the empty *p* orbital on the central boron atom. As shown in Figure 18-25, one filled *p* orbital on each of the three halogens is aligned properly for side-by-side overlap with boron's empty 2*p* orbital. To form an adduct, this B—*X* π bonding must be eliminated to make boron's *p* orbital available for the incoming Lewis base. Fluorine, being the smallest halogen, forms the strongest π bond with boron, since the side-by-side overlap needed for π bonding is greater when $n = 2$ than for larger, more diffuse *p* orbitals. The unusual strength of the B—F bond also indicates the presence of π bonding: 646 kJ/mol is an energy more consistent with double bonds than single bonds.

Average bond energies: C=C is 619 kJ/mol; C=O is 707 kJ/mol; C—F is 485 kJ/mol; and C—O is 335 kJ/mol.

Among Group III halides, only the boron compounds are simple XY_3 molecules. The others form more complex structures because of the Lewis acidity of their central atoms and Lewis *base* character of the halogens. For example, as a gas or a liquid, $AlCl_3$ reacts with itself to form Al_2Cl_6. As shown in Figure 18-26, the compound has two tetrahedral aluminum atoms held together by a pair of chlorine

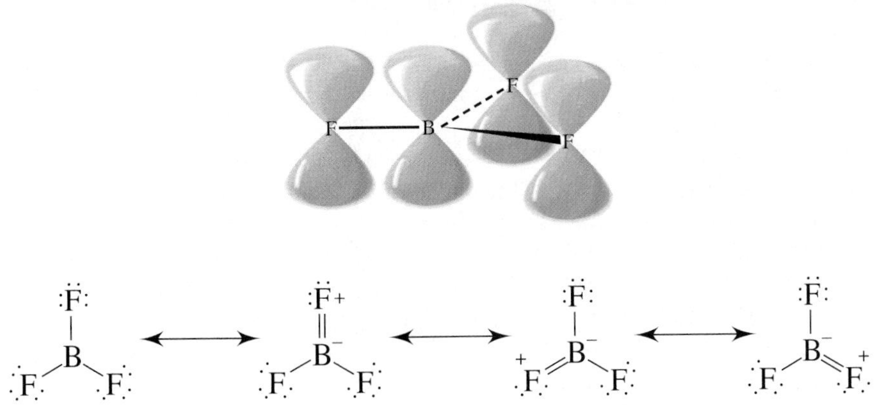

FIGURE 18-25
Side-by-side 2p orbital overlap allows π bonding between boron and fluorine. Because the π-bonded structures have positive formal charges delocalized among highly electronegative fluorine atoms, these structures are not "best" descriptions. Still, the large B—F bond energy (646 kJ/mol) indicates that significant π bonding exists in BF_3.

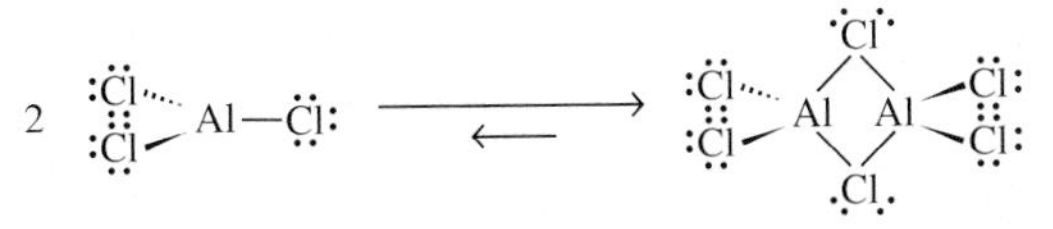

FIGURE 18-26
As a gas and a liquid, $AlCl_3$ is in equilibrium with Al_2Cl_6. One Cl atom from each monomer acts as a Lewis base, forming a pair of bridges between two aluminum atoms.

atoms that bridge the two metal atoms. The 91-degree Al—Cl—Al bond angle suggests the chlorine uses two valence p orbitals to form the bridge. There is an equilibrium between $AlCl_3$ and Al_2Cl_6 molecules, but except in the gas phase above 750 °C, the formation of Al_2Cl_6 goes essentially to completion.

In the solid state, aluminum chloride exists in a crystalline lattice. Each aluminum atom is surrounded by six chlorine atoms arranged around the metal atoms at the corner of an octachedron. In contrast, aluminum bromide and aluminum iodide form Al_2X_6 molecules in all three phases.

The trihalides of boron and aluminum are particularly important Lewis acids in the chemical industry. They promote or catalyze a large variety of reactions. One of the most important applications is a very general, widely used process called the *Friedel-Crafts reaction.* Aluminum chloride or some other Lewis acid is used to promote the reaction between an acid chloride and benzene or one of its derivatives. The simplest example of the Friedel-Crafts reaction is the formation of acetophenone:

An acid chloride is a derivative of a carboxylic acid in which the hydroxyl group is replaced by a chlorine.

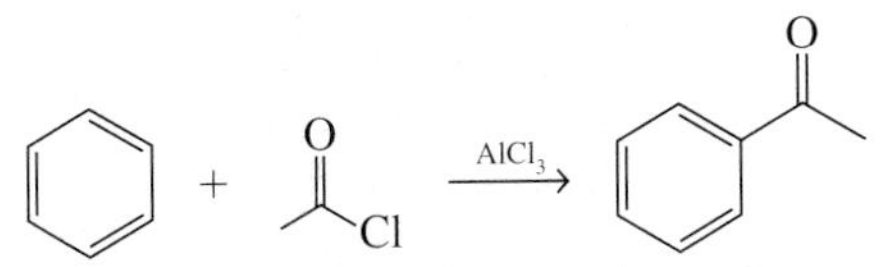

Benzene + Acetyl chloride $\xrightarrow{AlCl_3}$ Acetophenone

The Lewis acid activates the acid chloride by forming an adduct with a chlorine atom bridged between carbon and aluminum. This chlorine bridge is similar to the one found in Al_2Cl_6:

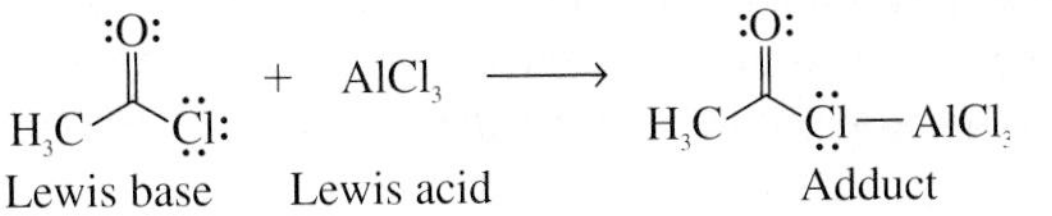

H_3C–C(=O)–Cl (Lewis base) + $AlCl_3$ (Lewis acid) $\longrightarrow$ H_3C–C(=O)–Cl—$AlCl_3$ (Adduct)

$$\text{H}_3\text{C}-\text{C}(=\ddot{\text{O}}\text{:})-\ddot{\text{Cl}}-\text{AlCl}_3 \longrightarrow \text{AlCl}_4^- + \text{H}_3\text{C}-\text{C}\equiv\overset{+}{\text{O}}\text{:} \longleftrightarrow \text{H}_3\text{C}-\overset{+}{\text{C}}=\ddot{\text{O}}$$

Adduct — Acylium ion

The adduct fragments into a stable $AlCl_4^-$ anion and an acylium ion, a very reactive intermediate. The acylium displaces a proton from a benzene molecule.

Friedel-Crafts chemistry is used in the synthesis of dyes, flavorings, fragrances, surfactants, pesticides, and many other types of organic compounds. A variety of Lewis acids are used, including $AlCl_3$, BF_3, $TiCl_4$, $SnCl_4$, SbF_5, and $ZnCl_2$.

Lewis acids such as BF_3 and $AlCl_3$ are also used as catalysts for the polymerization of alkenes. The catalyst reacts with two molecules of water to generate a hydronium ion:

$$BF_3 + H_2\ddot{O}: \longrightarrow F_3B{-}OH_2$$

$$F_3B{-}OH_2 + H_2O \longrightarrow [BF_3(OH)]^- + H_3O^+$$

Protonation of the alkene starts the polymerization. For example, isobutene polymerizes to give a tacky material used in adhesives. Copolymerization with a small amount of isoprene gives butyl rubber, which is used to make inner tubes and tire liners:

$$H_3O^+ + \underset{\text{Isobutene}}{H_2C{=}C(CH_3)_2} \longrightarrow (H_3C)_2\overset{+}{C}{-}CH_3 + H_2O$$

$$(H_3C)_2\overset{+}{C}{-}CH_3 + H_2C{=}C(CH_3)_2 \longrightarrow (H_3C)_3C{-}CH_2{-}\overset{+}{C}(CH_3)_2$$

$$(H_3C)_3C{-}CH_2{-}\overset{+}{C}(CH_3)_2 \xrightarrow{\quad} \xrightarrow[\text{termination}]{\text{Propagation and}} (H_3C)_3C{-}\left(CH_2{-}C(CH_3)_2\right)_n{-}CH_2{-}C(CH_3)_2{-}OH$$

One curious feature of gallium is its low melting point (30 °C). A lump of gallium metal will melt in the palm of your hand (normal body temperature is 37.5 °C).

This cationic polymerization process is analogous to free radical polymerization, as described in Chapter 11.

Unlike boron and aluminum, gallium and indium are *soft* Lewis acids. All four elements have similar patterns of reactivity, but Ga and In show the expected preference for soft bases such as sulfur. The order of reactivity for the trihalides depends on the Lewis base. For a hard base such as ammonia, the trend is $BCl_3 > AlCl_3 > GaCl_3 > InCl_3$. The order is reversed for dimethylsulfide, $(CH_3)_2S$, a soft base.

METATHESIS REACTIONS

Earlier in this chapter, we introduced adduct formation between Lewis acids and bases. Another type of Lewis acid-base reaction is a **metathesis reaction.** A metathesis reaction is an exchange of bonding partners, as exemplified by the following reaction:

$$BI_3 + GaF_3 \rightarrow BF_3 + GaI_3$$

In this case, boron and gallium trade their halogen partners. According to the HSAB principle, metathesis reactions proceed in the direction that couples the harder acid with the harder base. In this case, boron is harder than gallium, and fluoride is harder than iodide.

Metathesis is an important method for making molecules that have boron-carbon and aluminum-carbon bonds. These so-called *organoboron* and *organoaluminum* compounds are valuable reagents in organic chemistry. Their synthesis can be accomplished using a powerful Lewis base called an *alkyllithium* reagent. Alkyllithium reagents are used widely in chemistry as a source of carbon atoms. Although highly reactive (they ignite spontaneously in air), alkyllithium reagents are widely available commercially, and they are easy to prepare in the laboratory by reducing alkyl halides with metallic lithium (Figure 18-27):

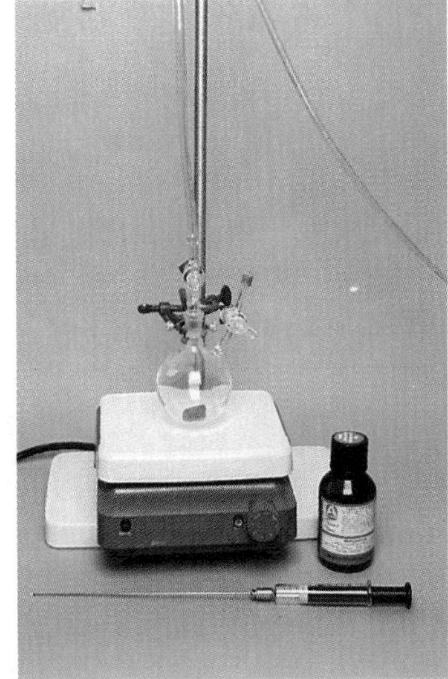

FIGURE 18-27
Alkyllithium reagents can be purchased from chemical manufacturers or prepared in the laboratory. The highly flammable solutions must be transferred with syringes to avoid exposure to oxygen.

$$C_2H_5Cl + 2\,Li \rightarrow LiCH_2CH_3 + LiCl$$

Aluminum and boron halides undergo metathesis reactions with alkyllithium reagents according to the HSAB principle. Both boron and aluminum are softer acids than lithium, and carbon in these compounds is a very soft base. Metathesis generates lithium chloride and an organoaluminum or organoboron compound. To give a specific example, triethylaluminum, a colorless liquid that burns spontaneously in air, can be prepared by treating 1 mol of $AlCl_3$ with 3 mol of ethyllithium, $LiCH_2CH_3$. Many other alkyl groups can be used in place of CH_2CH_3. Organoaluminum compounds, including triethylaluminum, are used to make catalysts for the polymer industry.

$$3\,LiCH_2CH_3 + AlCl_3 \longrightarrow \underset{\text{Triethylaluminum}}{Al(CH_2CH_3)_3} + 3\,LiCl$$

GROUP IV ELEMENTS

In addition to carbon, the Group IV elements include silicon, germanium, tin, and lead. Each has the valence electron configuration s^2p^2. The most common oxidation state is +4, but lead and tin form many compounds in the +2 state. In fact, +2 is the most common oxidation state of lead.

Carbon compounds display oxidation states ranging between −4 (CH_4) and +4 (CO_2). This diversity of oxidation states means that carbon forms a variety of organic Lewis acids and bases. However, because the reactions of carbon compounds are studied in detail in a course on organic chemistry, we do not discuss them further here.

Silicon is also important in the semiconductor (see Chapter 9) and polymer (see Chapter 11) industries.

The most important compounds of silicon are SiO_2 and the related silicate anions. The structure and bonding of Si—O compounds are presented in Chapter 8. As discussed in the previous section, many minerals are combinations of hard silicate anions and hard metal cations.

The tetrahalides of Si, Ge, Sn, and Pb have valence *d* orbitals that can be used for bonding. All these compounds undergo Lewis acid-base reactions to form stable anions of general formula MX_6^{2-}. For example:

$$SiF_4 + 2\ LiF \longrightarrow 2\ Li^+\ [SiF_6]^{2-}$$

The tetrahalides also undergo metathesis reactions. For instance, organotin compounds are prepared on an industrial scale using organoaluminum reagents. These reactions take place because tin is much softer than aluminum, and carbon is much softer than chlorine:

$$3\ SnCl_4 + 4\ AlR_3 \rightarrow 3\ SnR_4 + 4\ AlCl_3$$

As described in Chapter 11, PVC is polyvinylchloride.

Organotin compounds are important industrial chemicals. The greatest use is as stabilizers for PVC plastics (Figure 18-28). These additives, such as dioctyltinmaleate, inhibit degradation of the polymer by heat, light, and oxygen. In the absence of these tin compounds, PVC yellows and becomes brittle. Organotin compounds are also used extensively in agriculture. More than a third of the world's food crops are lost to fungi, bacteria, insects, or weeds. Organotin compounds like tributylhydroxytin, $(CH_3CH_2CH_2CH_2)_3SnOH$, inhibit growth of fungi among crops such as potatoes, peanuts, sugar beets, and rice. Marine paints for wooden boats also contain organotin compounds that inhibit the attachment of barnacles. Organotins are added to cellulose and wool to inhibit attack by moths. The tin compounds used in these applications are specific in their toxicity, so they present little danger to mammalian life.

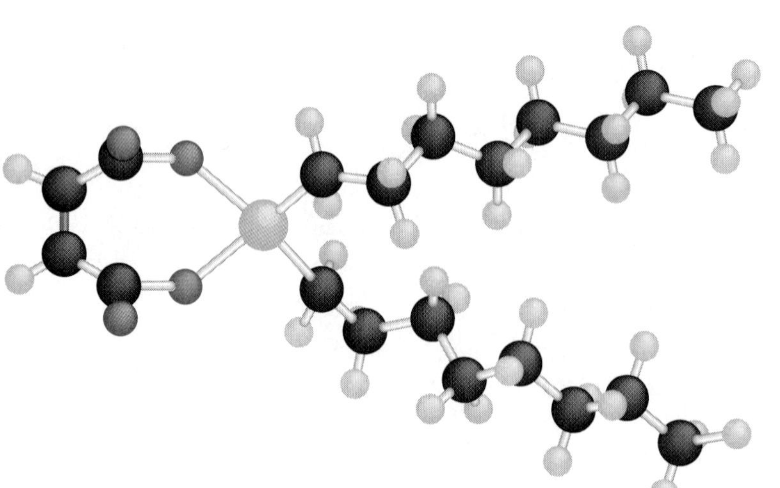

Dioctyltinmaleate

FIGURE 18-28
Organotin compounds such as dioctyltinmaleate are used to stabilize polymers such as PVC.

GROUP V ELEMENTS

Nitrogen and phosphorus are the most familiar members of Group V, which also includes arsenic, antimony, and bismuth. All five have the valence configuration s^2p^3 and have oxidation states ranging from −3 to +5.

Compounds of Group V are familiar Lewis bases. These elements form a wide range of compounds of general formula EL_3. The most common substituents are hydrogen, the halogens, and alkyl groups such as CH_3:

$$\begin{array}{c} L \\ | \\ L-\ddot{E}-L \end{array}$$

$$E = \text{N, P, As, Sb, Bi}$$
$$L = \text{F, Cl, Br, I, H, alkyl}$$

Their basicity comes from the lone pair of electrons on the element. The simplest examples are ammonia, NH_3, and phosphine, PH_3. Organic derivatives of NH_3 and PH_3—the *amines,* NR_3, and the *phosphines,* PR_3—are prepared by metathesis reactions with the corresponding alkyllithium reagents. Amines and phosphines are particularly important for the role they play as ligands in the chemistry of the transition metals. Phosphines, amines, and their various trihalides form adducts with Lewis acids of Groups III and IV.

GROUP VI ELEMENTS

The oxygen family of elements can be divided cleanly into two categories. Oxygen is a hard base whose chemistry is dominated by redox reactions. The other members of the group are relatively soft bases.

Molecular oxygen is a powerful oxidizing agent that reacts spontaneously with carbon-containing compounds and with most metals. Everywhere we look, there are oxides that contain oxygen in its −2 oxidation state: carbon dioxide is CO_2, water is H_2O, limestone is $CaCO_3$, sand is SiO_2, rust is Fe_2O_3, and sulfuric acid is H_2SO_4.

Sulfur displays rich and varied chemical behavior, but from a commercial standpoint, sulfuric acid dominates the chemistry of sulfur. Sulfuric acid is used in every major chemical-related industry: fertilizers, petroleum, chemical manufacture, metallurgy, detergents, fibers, paints and pigments, and paper making. In nearly all these cases, sulfur itself is not of interest and is eventually discarded as sulfate waste. Instead, H_2SO_4 is exploited for its Brønsted acidity, its oxidizing ability, its affinity for water, or its ability to form sulfate precipitates.

Sulfur, selenium, and tellurium form a variety of compounds with the halides. The chemistry of the sulfur fluorides has been developed in particular detail. Sulfur forms seven different binary fluorides, but only SF_4 has any significant Lewis acid-base properties. Sulfur tetrafluoride can act as either an electron pair donor or an electron pair acceptor. With a steric number of five, SF_4 adopts a trigonal bipyramidal arrangement of valence orbitals with the lone pair of electrons in one of the equatorial positions. The molecule acts as a Lewis *base,* but not as a simple sulfur lone-pair donor. Instead, SF_4 is a fluoride donor, as shown in the following reactions. The donor atom in SF_4 is a fluoride ion. After forming an adduct with the Lewis acid, the S—F bond breaks to give the ionic products:

The structure and bonding of the sulfur fluorides are the subject of Problem 8.79 at the end of Chapter 8.

$$SF_4 + BF_3 \rightarrow [SF_3^+][BF_4^-]$$

$$SF_4 + PF_5 \rightarrow [SF_3^+][PF_6^-]$$

Sulfur tetrafluoride is an important industrial fluorinating agent for both organic and inorganic compounds.

With its empty 3*d* orbitals, SF_4 also acts as a Lewis *acid.* For example, the molecule forms adducts with pyridine and with the fluoride ion. Each adduct has square pyramidal geometry with a lone pair of electrons completing the octahedral arrangement of valence orbitals:

$$SF_4 + Pyr \rightarrow SF_4 \cdot Pyr$$

$$SF_4 + CsF \rightarrow [Cs^+][SF_5^-]$$

Sulfur chemistry accounts for the high toxicity of soft Lewis metal cations such as Hg^{2+} and Pb^{2+}. Anything that alters the three-dimensional structure of an enzyme may also change the shape of its active site, thereby destroying its catalytic activity. Recall from Chapter 11 that covalent sulfur-sulfur single bonds are major determinants of protein structure. Because sulfur is a soft Lewis base, it binds preferentially to soft metal ions. Metal ions alter an enzyme's shape by cleaving natural sulfide bridges that link sections of the molecule together and by creating new sulfide bridges that do not belong in the natural molecule. These processes are illustrated schematically in Figure 18-29.

Lead is one of the best known soft metal toxins. Lead ions destroy two enzymes that are essential for biosynthesis of heme. Now that tetraethyllead, $Pb(CH_2CH_3)_4$, has been eliminated as an antiknock ingredient in gasoline, lead contamination of the environment comes from lead-based paints, lead solder in water pipes, and lead-containing glazes on inexpensive pottery. Mercury is another well-known soft metal toxin. Soluble inorganic mercury salts are extremely poisonous.

In the nineteenth century, $Hg(NO_3)_2$ was used to stiffen the felt used in making hats. The phrase "mad as a hatter" refers to long-term effects of ingested mercury.

Another key feature of sulfur chemistry is the Lewis acidity of sulfur dioxide and sulfur trioxide. Sulfur dioxide is a common atmospheric pollutant that results from burning coal to produce electricity. Most coal reserves in North America contain significant amounts of sulfur-containing impurities. When coal is burned, the sulfur is converted to sulfur dioxide, a hard Lewis acid. In the atmosphere, SO_2 reacts with water to give sulfurous acid, a major contributor to acid rain.

Acid rain is discussed in Section 5.7.

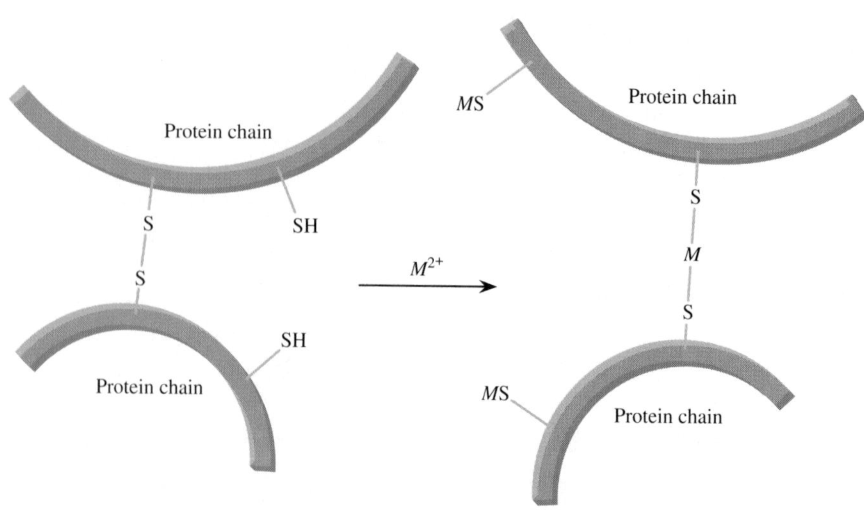

FIGURE 18-29
Soft metal ions destroy enzymes by altering their three-dimensional structure. They create new cross-links by reacting with S—H bonds in cysteine side chains. Soft metal ions also change the shape of an enzyme by destroying disulfide linkages that occur naturally in the active enzyme.

The two S═O double bonds are polarized toward the electronegative oxygens, creating a partial positive charge on the sulfur atom. The sulfur atom can use its empty *d* orbitals to accept a pair of electrons from a water molecule to form an adduct. A second water molecule subsequently acts as a Brønsted base and transfers a proton from one oxygen atom to another to give H_2SO_3.

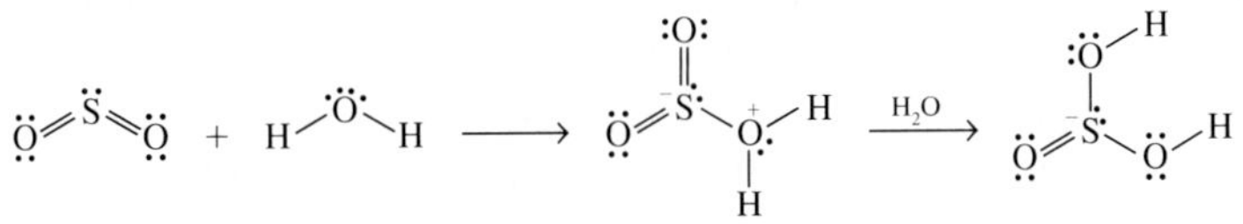

$$SO_2 + H_2O \longrightarrow \text{Lewis acid-base adduct} \xrightarrow{H_2O} \text{Sulfurous acid}$$

Lewis acid-base adduct　　Sulfurous acid

GROUP VII, THE HALOGENS

The halogens, with seven valence electrons, readily gain one electron to form either an anion (F^-, Cl^-, etc.) or a single covalent bond (HBr, H_3CCl, BF_3). In addition, all members of this family except fluorine can use their *d* orbitals to form bonds. Examples include ClO_4^-, ClF_3, BrF_5, and IF_7. As might be expected, halide anions are good Lewis bases, readily donating electron pairs:

$$NiCl_2 + 4\,LiCl \rightarrow 4\,Li^+ + [NiCl_6]^{4-}$$

$$BF_3 + LiF \rightarrow Li^+\,BF_4^-$$

SECTION EXERCISES

18.5.1 The B—F bond energy in boron trifluoride is 646 kJ/mol, which suggests substantial double-bond character. On the other hand, the B—I bond energy in BI_3 is only 267 kJ/mol, consistent with a single bond. Explain why BF_3 appears to have double-bond character but BI_3 has only single bonds.

18.5.2 Complete the following reactions:

(a) $AlCl_3 + LiCH_3 \rightarrow$

(b) $SO_3 + \text{Excess } H_2O \rightarrow$

(c) $SbF_5 + LiF \rightarrow$

(d) 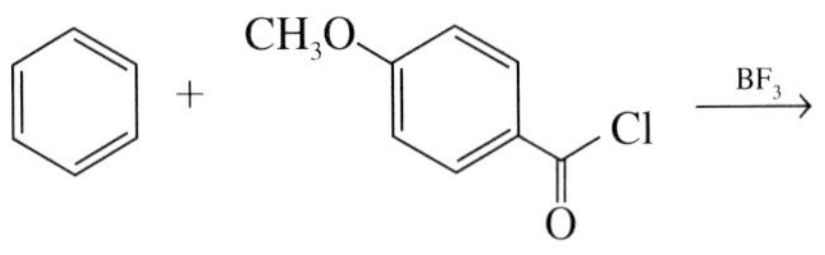 benzene + CH_3O–C_6H_4–C(=O)Cl $\xrightarrow{BF_3}$

(e) $SF_4 + AsCl_5 \rightarrow$

18.5.3 Sulfur tetrafluoride fluorinates boron trichloride according to the following unbalanced equation: $BCl_3 + SF_4 \rightarrow BF_3 + SCl_2 + Cl_2$. This is both a redox reaction and a metathesis reaction.
(a) Balance the equation.
(b) Identify the elements that change oxidation state.
(c) Explain the metathesis portion of the reaction using hard-soft acid-base arguments.

BONDING IN COORDINATION COMPLEXESS

18.15 One method for preparing ultrapure nickel is through its coordination complex with carbon monoxide. Crude nickel metal reacts with carbon monoxide to give tetracarbonylnickel(0):

$$\underset{\text{Crude}}{Ni_{(s)}} + 4\,CO_{(g)} \xrightarrow{60\ ^\circ C} [Ni(CO)_4]_{(g)}$$

The volatile product is easily separated from the impurities present originally in the crude metal sample. Heating to 200 °C causes the nickel carbonyl to decompose to ultrapure nickel and carbon monoxide. This method for purifying nickel is the Mond process, named for the chemist who developed the technique in 1899. What geometry do you predict for $[Ni(CO)_4]$? What color is the compound? Suggest a reason why nickel carbonyl is extremely poisonous.

18.16 For each of the following metal ions, draw a crystal field energy diagram that shows the electron population of the various *d* orbitals in both weak and strong octahedral fields: (a) Ti^{2+}; (b) Cr^{3+}; (c) Mn^{2+}; (d) Fe^{3+}; (e) Zn^{2+}; (f) Cr^{2+}; (g) Co^{2+}; and (h) V^0.

18.17 The absorption spectrum of $[Cr(H_2O)_4Cl_2]^+$ is represented by the diagram:

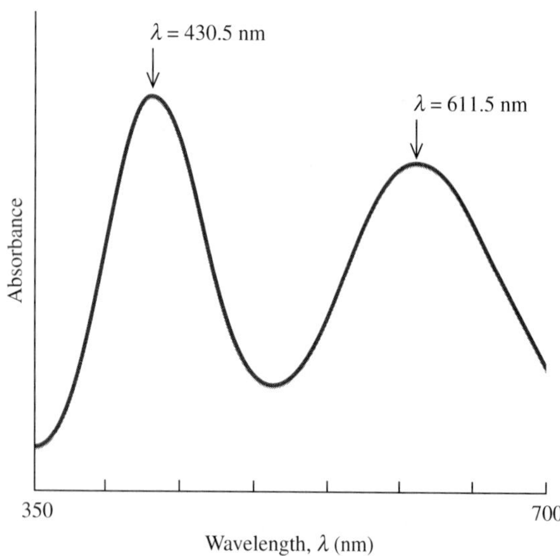

(a) Estimate the crystal field splitting energy, Δ, (in kJ/mol) for this complex.
(b) What color is $[Cr(H_2O)_4Cl_2]^+$?
(c) Name the complex cation.
(d) Draw all possible isomers of $[Cr(H_2O)_4Cl_2]^+$.
(e) Draw the crystal field energy level diagram, and show the electronic transition that gives $[Cr(H_2O)_4Cl_2]^+$ its color.

18.18 Determine whether the following complexes are diamagnetic or paramagnetic. If a complex is paramagnetic, give the number of unpaired electrons: (a) $[Ir(NH_3)_6]^{3+}$; (b) $[Cr(H_2O)_6]^{2+}$; (c) $[CoBr_4]^{2-}$; (d) $[Pd(P(CH_3)_3)_4]$; and (e) $[V(en)_3]^{3+}$.

18.19 Compounds of Zr^{2+} are dark purple, but most Zr^{4+} compounds are colorless. Explain.

18.20 Draw all possible isomers of the following compounds: (a) $[Ir(NH_3)_3Cl_3]$; (b) $[Pd(P(CH_3)_3)_2Cl_2]$; (c) $[Cr(CO)_4Br_2]$; and (d) $[Cr(en)(NH_3)_2I_2]$.

18.21 Of the coordination complexes, $[Cr(H_2O)_6]^{3+}$ and $[Cr(NH_3)_6]^{3+}$, one is violet and the other is orange. Decide which is which and explain your reasoning.

18.22 Predict the number of unpaired electrons in each of the following complexes: (a) $[Mo(CO)_6]$; (b) $[Cr(H_2O)_6]^{2+}$; (c) $[Co(NH_3)_6]^{3+}$; (d) $[CoBr_4]^{2-}$ (tetrahedral); and (e) $[FeCl_4]^-$ (tetrahedral).

HARD AND SOFT ACIDS AND BASES

18.23 Rank the following Lewis acids from hardest to softest, and explain your reasoning: (a) BCl_3, BF_3, and $AlCl_3$; (b) Al^{3+}, Tl^{3+}, and Tl^+; and (c) $AlCl_3$, AlI_3, and $AlBr_3$.

18.24 Rank the following Lewis bases from hardest to softest, and explain your rankings: (a) NH_3, SbH_3, and PH_3; (b) PO_4^{3-}, ClO_4^-, SO_4^{2-}; and (c) O^{2-}, Se^{2-}, and S^{2-}.

18.25 Both sulfur trioxide and sulfur dioxide are Lewis acids, but SO_3 is harder than SO_2. Suggest an explanation.

18.26 Explain why iodide is a soft base but chloride is a hard base.

18.27 The molecule $(CH_3)_2N—PF_2$ is an interesting Lewis base. Both nitrogen and phosphorus have lone pairs of electrons. One of these donor atoms forms a bond to boron in the adduct with BH_3, but the other forms a bond to boron in the BF_3 complex. Draw the Lewis structure of each adduct. Explain your reasoning.

18.28 Give one example of each of the following: (a) a chalcophile; (b) a lithophile; and (c) a siderophile.

THE MAIN GROUP ELEMENTS

18.29 For each of the following, state whether or not a reaction occurs, and write a balanced equation for any reaction:
(a) $NBr_3 + GaCl_3 \rightarrow$
(b) $Al(CH_3)_3 + LiCH_3 \rightarrow$
(c) $SiF_4 + LiF \rightarrow$
(d) $LiCH_2CH_2CH_2CH_3 + SnCl_4 \rightarrow$

18.30 Describe in detail the bonding in Al_2Cl_6. Explain the formation of the molecule in terms of Lewis acid-base chemistry.

18.31 Boron trifluoride is a very strong Lewis acid, but trimethylboron, $B(CH_3)_3$, is a mild Lewis acid. Given the π bonding character that appears to exist in BF_3, does this order of reactivity surprise you? Why or why not? Use bonding arguments to explain the trend in reactivity.

18.32 Arsenic trichloride can act as a Lewis acid and a Lewis base. Explain why this is so, and write a balanced equation for each.

18.33 Propose a mechanism for the following reaction, and explain the chemistry in terms of acids reacting with bases.

$$PCl_3 + (CH_3)_2NH + 3\ H_2O \rightarrow P(N(CH_3)_2)_3 + 3\ H_3O^+ + 3\ Cl^-$$

18.34 For each of the following reactions, determine whether metathesis will occur and identify the products: (a) AlI_3 + NaCl; (b) $TiCl_2$ + TiI_4; (c) CaO + H_2S; (d) CH_3Li + PCl_3; and (e) AgI + $SiCl_4$.

ADDITIONAL PROBLEMS

18.35 The only important ore of mercury is cinnabar, HgS. In contrast, zinc is found in several ores, including sulfides, carbonates, silicates, and oxides. Explain these observations in terms of hard and soft acids and bases.

18.36 Boron trichloride is a gas, boron tribromide is a liquid, and boron triiodide is a solid. Explain this trend in terms of intermolecular forces and polarizability.

18.37 Explain why ligands for transition metals are typically anions or neutral molecules but rarely cations.

18.38 Classify the following metals and minerals as lithophiles, siderophiles, or chalcophiles: (a) ZnS (sphalerite); (b) SnO_2 (cassiterite); (c) Na_3AlF_6 (cryolite); (d) Ir; (e) $CaMg(CO_3)_2$ (dolomite); (f) Li; (g) Ag_3SbS_3 (pyrargyrite); and (h) Pd.

18.39 Consider the following metathesis reaction:

$$BCl_3 + 2\ Al(CH_3)_3 \rightarrow B(CH_3)_2Cl + 2\ Al(CH_3)_2Cl$$

(a) Which starting material is the Lewis acid? Explain your choice.
(b) Why does this reaction not produce $B(CH_3)_3$?

18.40 Name the following coordination compounds:

(a) 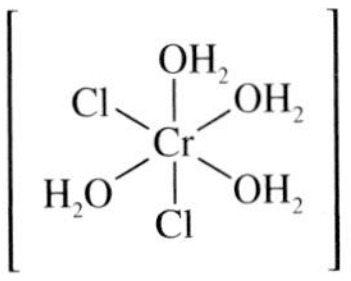 $[Cr(OH_2)_4Cl_2]Cl$ — drawn as: Cr with ligands OH_2 (top), Cl, OH_2, H_2O, OH_2, Cl (bottom); counterion Cl

(b) 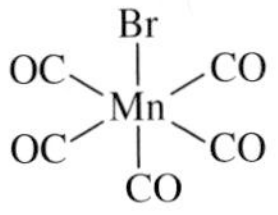 Mn with ligands Br (top), OC, CO, OC, CO, CO (bottom)

(c) 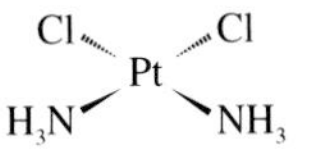 Pt with ligands Cl, Cl, H_3N, NH_3

(d) 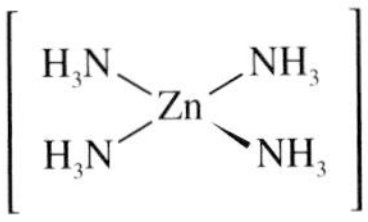 $[Zn(NH_3)_4]SO_4$ — drawn as: Zn with ligands H_3N, NH_3, H_3N, NH_3; counterion SO_4

(e) $K_3[Fe(CN)_6]$ — drawn as: Fe with ligands CN (top), NC, CN, NC, CN, CN (bottom)

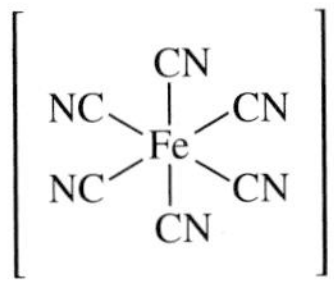

18.41 Metal oxides and sulfide ores are usually contaminated with silica, SiO_2. This impurity must be removed when the ore is reduced to the pure element. Silica can be removed by adding calcium oxide (commonly known as *lime*) to the reactor. Silica reacts with CaO to give $CaSiO_3$, called "slag." Write a balanced equation for the formation of slag, and describe the reaction in terms of Lewis acids and bases.

18.42 Alfred Werner was a pioneer in transition metal chemistry. In the 1890s Werner prepared several platinum complexes that contained both ammonia and chlorine. He determined the formulas of these species by precipitating the chloride ions with Ag^+. The empirical formulas and number of chloride ions that precipitate per formula unit follow:

Empirical formula	Number of Cl^- ions that precipitate per formula unit
$PtCl_4 \cdot 2NH_3$	0
$PtCl_4 \cdot 3NH_3$	1
$PtCl_4 \cdot 4NH_3$	2
$PtCl_4 \cdot 5NH_3$	3
$PtCl_4 \cdot 6NH_3$	4

Determine the molecular formulas, name these compounds, and draw the structures of the platinum complexes.

18.43 Carbon monoxide and tungsten form an octahedral complex of the formula $[W(CO)_6]$. The molecule is colorless even though W(0) is d^6. Sketch the ligand field diagram for hexacarbonyltungsten(0), and suggest why the complex is colorless.

18.44 The black tarnish that forms on pure silver metal is the sulfide Ag_2S, formed by reaction with H_2S in the atmosphere:

$$4\ Ag_{(s)} + 2\ H_2S_{(g)} + O_{2\,(g)} \rightarrow 2\ Ag_2S_{(s)} + 2\ H_2O_{(l)}$$

The sulfide forms in preference to Ag_2O, even though the atmosphere is 20% O_2 with just a slight trace of H_2S. Use Lewis acid-base arguments to explain this behavior.

18.45 Explain why soft metal ions like lead and mercury are so toxic.

18.46 When PCl_5 condenses from a gas to a solid, it changes from trigonal bipyramidal molecules to an ionic crystal of the formula $[PCl_4^+][PCl_6^-]$. Explain the reaction in terms of Lewis acids and bases:

$$2\ PCl_{5\ (g)} \rightarrow [PCl_4^+][PCl_6^-]_{(s)}$$

18.47 One of the factors that controls the interaction of a Lewis base with a Lewis acid is the sizes of the molecules involved. For example, boron trifluoride forms a much stronger adduct with tetrahydrofuran than it does with dimethyltetrahydrofuran. Use this example to explain size effects in adduct formation. (*Hint:* Think about electron-electron repulsion.)

$C_6H_{12}O$
Dimethyltetrahydrofuran

C_4H_8O
Tetrahydrofuran

18.48 Draw the structures of all possible isomers of the following coordination compounds: (a) tetraammine-dibromocobalt(III) bromide; (b) triamminetrichloro-chromium(III); and (c) dicarbonylbis(trimethylphosphine)platinum(0) (trimethylphosphine = $P(CH_3)_3$).

18.49 A solution of $[Fe(H_2O)_6]^{3+}$ has a very pale green color, but a solution of $[Fe(CN)_6]^{3-}$ is deep red. Will $[FeF_6]^{3-}$ be brightly colored? Why or why not?

18.50 Oxyhemoglobin is bright red, but deoxyhemoglobin is blue. In both cases the iron is in the +2 oxidation state. Give a detailed explanation for the difference in color. How would you test your hypothesis? Based on your explanation, what color would you expect for a sample of blood that is saturated with carbon monoxide?

18.51 The complex $[Ni(CN)_4]^{2-}$ is diamagnetic, but $[NiCl_4]^{2-}$ is paramagnetic. Propose structures for the two complexes, and explain why they have different magnetic properties.

18.52 Classify the following complexes as high spin or low spin: (a) $[Fe(CN)_6]^{4-}$; (b) $[MnCl_4]^{2-}$ (tetrahedral); (c) $[Rh(NH_3)_6]^{3+}$; and (d) $[Co(H_2O)_6]^{2+}$.

18.53 Several commercial rust removers contain the bidentate ligand oxalate. Explain how these household products remove rust.

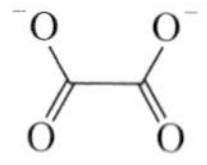

Oxalate
$C_2O_4^{2-}$

ANSWERS TO SECTION EXERCISES

18.1.1 (a) Acid = SO_3, base = OH^-; (b) acid = $SnCl_2$, base = Cl^-; (c) acid = SbF_5, base = AsF_3

18.1.2

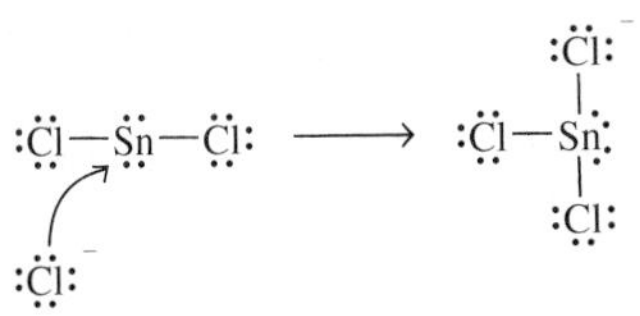

:Cl—Sn—Cl: ⟶ $[SnCl_3]^-$

:Cl:$^-$

18.2.1 (a) +4, Fe(II), six; (b) 0, V(II), six; (c) +2, Ni(II), four

18.2.2

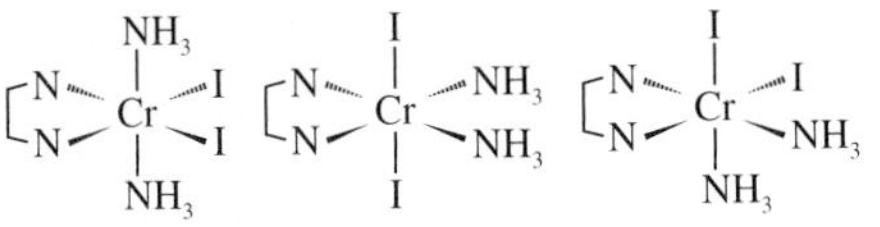

NH$_3$ I I

N Cr I N Cr NH$_3$ N Cr I

N I N NH$_3$ N NH$_3$

NH$_3$ I NH$_3$

18.2.3 (a) Pentaammineiodochromium(III) sulfate; (b) potassium hexachloroplatinate(II); (c) dichlorotetracarbonyliron(II); and (d) tris(ethylenediamine)manganese(II) chloride

18.3.1

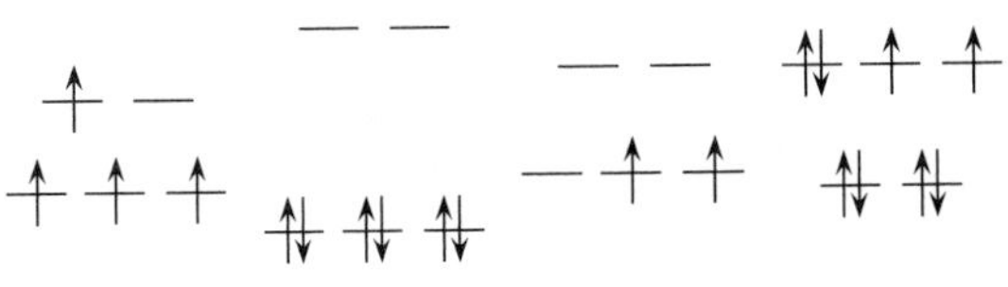

a) $[Cr(H_2O)_6]^{2+}$ **b)** $[IrCl_6]^{3-}$ **c)** $[V(en)_3]^{3+}$ **d)** $[NiCl_4]^{2-}$

18.3.2 Because cyanide is near the top of the spectrochemical series, it generates a relatively large energy gap between the two sets of *d* orbitals. The hexacyano complexes are yellow because they absorb high-energy indigo light. The corresponding aqua complexes have a much smaller crystal field splitting energy. They absorb orange or red light, thus appearing blue or green.

18.3.3 492 nm, orange

18.4.1 (a) NH_3, NCl_3, NF_3; (b) Pb^{2+}, Pb^{4+}, Zn^{2+}; (c) ClO_4^-, ClO_3^-, ClO_2^-; (d) $SbCl_3$, PCl_3, PF_3

18.4.2 Only the softest metals, those clustered around gold in the periodic table, exist in nature in elemental form. Ruthenium and osmium are in this category. Iron forms much harder cations with an affinity for the hard anions that are abundant in the environment, including carbonate, oxide, and the silicates.

18.5.1 Both boron and fluorine are in the second row of the periodic table. Because their valence orbitals are approximately the same size, side-by-side overlap of the 2*p* orbitals in BF_3 is very strong. Thus π bonding is possible despite the high electronegativity of fluorine. Iodine has n = 5 valence orbitals. The size mismatch between the 2*p* and 5*p* orbitals means that there is minimal side-by-side overlap and little or no π bonding.

18.5.2 (a) $AlCl_2(CH_3)$ + LiCl; (b) H_3O^+ + HSO_4^-; (c) Li^+ + SbF_6^-;

(d) 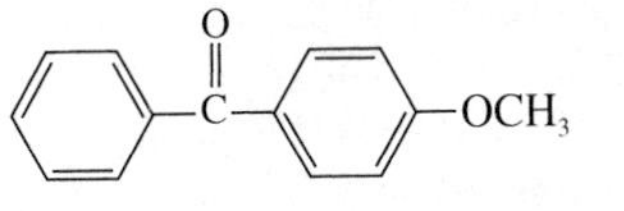 C_6H_5–C(=O)–C_6H_4–OCH_3

and (e) $[SF_3^+][AsCl_5F^-]$

18.5.3 (a) $4\ BCl_3 + 3\ SF_4 \rightarrow 4\ BF_3 + 3\ SCl_2 + 3\ Cl_2$
(b) Chlorine is oxidized, and sulfur is reduced.
(c) Sulfur is softer than boron, and chlorine is softer than fluorine. According to the HSAB principle, sulfur prefers to bond with the softer chlorine, and boron prefers to bond with the harder fluorine.

CHAPTER 19

NUCLEAR CHEMISTRY AND RADIOCHEMISTRY

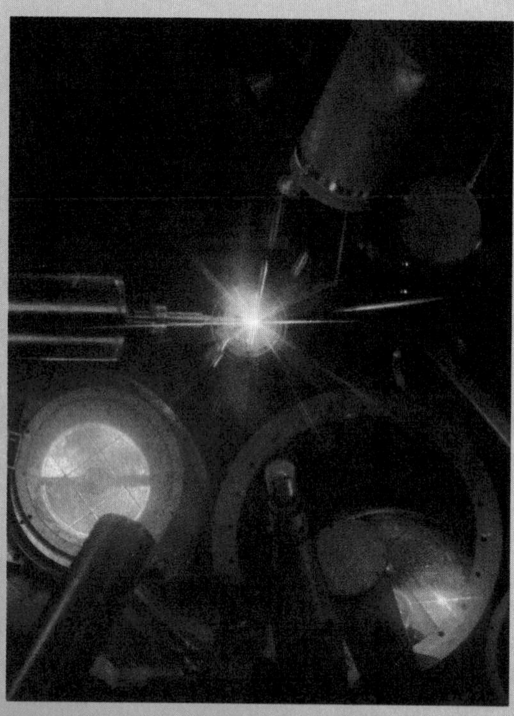

Scientists use combinations of laser beams and magnetic fields to try to duplicate and harness the nuclear fusion reactions that are the sun's source of energy.

For thousands of years, humans have dreamed of converting one element into another. In medieval times, for instance, alchemists tried to make gold from lead. All scientific evidence indicated, however, that chemical elements were immutable—that each element remained forever the same. All the chemistry presented thus far in this text is firmly based on that immutability. Every time a chemical reaction is balanced, we reassert the fact that each element retains its unique identity regardless of the conditions.

Two scientific discoveries made near the beginning of the twentieth century suggested that elements might be converted from one to another after all. In 1896 the Frenchman Antoine-Henri Becquerel observed the emission of powerful high-energy x-rays from a uranium compound, $K_2UO_2(SO_4)_2$. Although their nature was unknown at the time, x-rays had been observed for the first time a year earlier during studies of cathode ray tubes. Then, in 1905, Albert Einstein proposed the theory of relativity, which states that mass and energy are related by the equation, $E = mc^2$. Becquerel's x-rays had enough energy to suggest that this powerful unknown radiation accompanied the decomposition of uranium into some other element.

Marie and Pierre Curie followed Becquerel's observations with pioneering experiments in which they isolated the elements uranium, polonium, and radium. These three naturally occurring elements lose mass spontaneously as they decompose into other elements. In doing so, they emit x-rays and other energetic rays in agreement with Einstein's equation.

The conversion of one element into another is called **transmutation.** We now know that the energy of the sun and all the stars, the energy on which we depend for our very existence, is the result of nuclear transmutations. Nuclear transmutations also provide the energy for the fission and fusion reactions that drive atomic and hydrogen bombs, weapons that could destroy all human life. In this chapter, we explore both the wonderful and the terrifying aspects of this uniquely twentieth-century subject.

19.1 NUCLEAR STRUCTURE

The chemistry we have discussed until now has focused on electrons and has treated the nucleus as a positive point charge. Although the nucleus is tiny compared with the size of an atom, it accounts for nearly all an atom's mass. Moreover, a nucleus has its own internal structure, just as an atom does. Our discussion of nuclear chemistry begins with a description of the structure of the nucleus.

NUCLEAR COMPOSITION

Nuclear radii are about 10^{-14} m, four orders of magnitude smaller than atomic radii. Rutherford's gold foil experiment, which established the size of the nucleus relative to the atom, is described in Chapter 2.

Mass spectrometry experiments reveal that the nuclear *charge* of any element is always an integral multiple of the *charge* of a hydrogen nucleus. In addition, nuclear *mass* is always close to an integral multiple of the *mass* of a hydrogen nucleus.

TABLE 19-1 PROPERTIES OF FUNDAMENTAL PARTICLES

PARTICLE	SYMBOL	CHARGE (10^{-19}C)	MASS (10^{-27} kg)	MOLAR MASS (g/mol)
Proton	p	+1.60218	1.672623	1.007276
Neutron	n	0	1.674929	1.008665
Electron	e	− 1.60218	0.000911	5.486×10^{-4}

Helium, for example, has a nuclear charge of +2 and an atomic mass of 4.00260 g/mol, close to four times the mass of hydrogen, whereas beryllium has a nuclear charge of +4 and an atomic mass of 9.01218 g/mol. Both charge and mass increase stepwise, suggesting that every nucleus is composed of discrete building blocks. These building blocks are the **proton** and the **neutron.** Recall from Chapter 2 that each proton has a charge of $+1.60218 \times 10^{-19}$ C and a mass of 1.672623×10^{-27} kg. The molar mass of protons is 1.007276 g/mol. Neutrons, on the other hand, are electrically neutral with individual mass of 1.674929×10^{-27} kg and a molar mass of 1.008665 g/mol. Table 19-1 summarizes the properties of these nuclear building blocks. The other fundamental atomic particle, the electron, has been included for comparison.

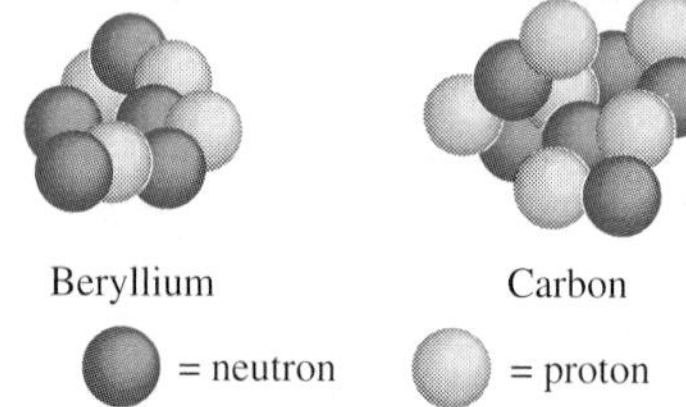

FIGURE 19-1
Each nucleus contains Z protons and N neutrons. Shown here is a beryllium nucleus, composed of five neutrons and four protons, and a carbon nucleus, containing six protons and six neutrons.

Every nucleus except for hydrogen contains both protons and neutrons. Two examples are shown in Figure 19-1. Each of these fundamental particles can also exist by itself. The hydrogen ion, which can be formed by removing the electron from a hydrogen atom, is a single proton. Free neutrons are often generated in the course of nuclear transmutations, but they are easily captured when they collide with nuclei.

Recall from Chapter 2 that many elements are composed of different **isotopes.** The various isotopes of an element have the same nuclear charge but different masses. To have identical nuclear charge, isotopes must have the same number of protons in their nuclei. To have different masses, on the other hand, isotopes must have different numbers of neutrons in their nuclei.

Any particular nucleus is called a **nuclide.** Nuclides are characterized by the number of protons and neutrons they possess. The number of protons in a nuclide is always the same as the atomic number of the element, Z, but the number of neutrons varies from isotope to isotope. The mass number of a nuclide, A, is its total number of protons (Z) and neutrons (N). Because protons and neutrons each have molar mass near 1 g/mol, A is always close to the numerical value of the molar mass of that isotope.

A particular nuclide can be described by its elemental symbol, E, preceded by A as a superscript and Z as a subscript:

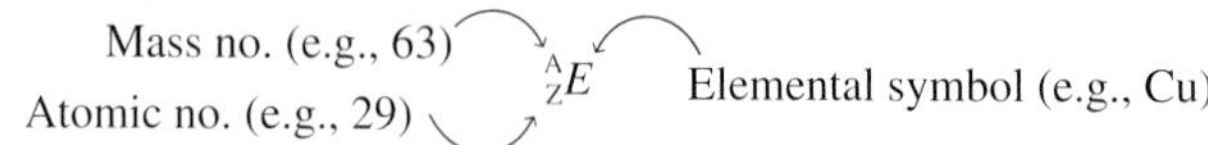

The nuclear building blocks, protons and neutrons, are symbolized formally as $^{1}_{1}$p and $^{1}_{0}$n, but they are often simplified to p and n. These nuclear particles are called *nucleons*. A nucleon is either a proton or a neutron.

Examples include: $^{63}_{29}$Cu, $^{4}_{2}$He, and $^{14}_{6}$C. Nuclides with the same Z value are all the same element, but they are isotopes if they have different values of A. Copper, for example, has two stable isotopes, $^{63}_{29}$Cu and $^{65}_{29}$Cu. Another common method for designating nuclides is to list the name of the element followed by the mass number: copper-63 or copper-65. Sample Problem 19-1 provides some practice in writing the symbols of nuclides.

SAMPLE PROBLEM 19-1 NUCLIDE SYMBOLS

What are the symbols for the nuclide that contains 92 protons and 143 neutrons and the carbon isotope with 8 neutrons?

METHOD: When determining symbols for nuclides, the key is to remember that the atomic number and number of protons are the same and that the mass number is the sum of the number of protons plus the number of neutrons.

The nuclide with 92 protons and 143 neutrons has an atomic number of 92 and a mass number as follows: $A = 92 + 143 = 235$. Atomic number 92 corresponds to uranium, so the symbol for this nuclide is ${}^{235}_{92}U$.

All carbon isotopes have $Z = 6$. From $N = 8$, we deduce: $A = 8 + 6 = 14$. The symbol for this nuclide is ${}^{14}_{6}C$.

STABLE NUCLIDES

In principle, a nuclide can be constructed from any possible combination of Z protons and N neutrons. In practice, however, only a limited number of these combinations are stable. For example, all hydrogen nuclides with $A > 2$ are so unstable that only one of them, tritium, ${}^{3}_{1}H$, exists even briefly. If other nuclides of hydrogen could be made, they would rapidly decompose by expelling neutrons. Fluorine has just one stable nuclide, ${}^{19}_{9}F$, but tin has 10, with mass numbers 112, 114, 115, 116, 117, 118, 119, 120, 122, and 124. All stable nuclides, as well as a few that are unstable, are found in the Earth's crust and atmosphere.

Unstable nuclides occur naturally either because their natural lifetime is longer than the age of the Earth or because they are produced in naturally occurring nuclear reactions. We describe these processes later in this chapter.

Figure 19-2 shows all stable nuclides on a plot of the number of neutrons *(N)* vs. the number of protons *(Z)*. These data show a striking general pattern. Notice that all stable nuclides fall within a "belt of stability." The lighter nuclides lie along the $N = Z$ line, but as the mass of the nuclide increases, the N/Z ratio rises slowly until it reaches 1.54. The trend is illustrated by the following four nuclides: ${}^{19}_{9}F$, 1.11; ${}^{75}_{33}As$, 1.27; ${}^{127}_{53}I$, 1.40; and ${}^{209}_{83}Bi$, 1.52. Any nuclide whose ratio of neutrons to protons falls outside the belt of stability is unstable and decomposes spontaneously.

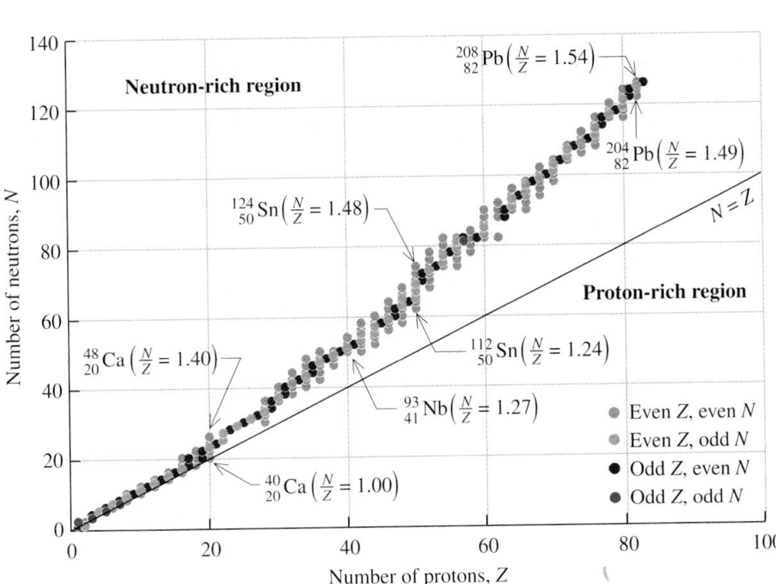

FIGURE 19-2
Plot of the Z and N values of stable nuclides. The stable nuclides fall along a belt that lies between $N = Z$ and $N = 1.54\,Z$.

TABLE 19-2 DISTRIBUTION OF STABLE NUCLIDES

PROTONS	NEUTRONS	STABLE NUCLIDES	%
Even	Even	154	58.8
Even	Odd	53	20.2
Odd	Even	50	19.1
Odd	Odd	5	1.9

The relationships that generate this delicate balance of nuclear stability are quite complex, but they can be summarized qualitatively for our purposes. Compressing more than one positively charged proton into a volume as small as the nucleus leads to strong coulombic forces of repulsion that make the nucleus unstable unless neutrons are also present. Neutrons provide nuclear binding forces that are strong enough to hold the protons within the nuclear volume. When too many neutrons are present, on the other hand, the fundamental instability of neutrons destabilizes the nucleus.

Additional patterns can be observed within the region of nuclear stability. Table 19-2 shows, for example, that nuclides with even numbers of both protons and neutrons are more prevalent than those with odd numbers of either protons or neutrons. Almost 60% of all stable nuclides have even numbers of both protons and neutrons, whereas less than 2% have odd numbers of both. Moreover, of the five stable odd-odd nuclides, four are the lightest odd-*Z* elements: ${}^{2}_{1}H$, ${}^{6}_{3}Li$, ${}^{10}_{5}B$, and ${}^{14}_{7}N$. Above $Z = 7$, there are 152 stable even-even nuclides and just one, ${}^{138}_{57}Ta$, that is odd-odd.

Notice in Figure 19-2 that there are no stable nuclides above bismuth, $Z = 83$. Some elements with higher *Z* are found on Earth, notably polonium ($Z = 84$), radium ($Z = 88$), and uranium ($Z = 92$), but all of them are unstable and eventually disintegrate into nuclei with $Z \leq 83$. As a result, the set of stable nuclides, those that make up the world of "normal" chemistry and provide the material for all terrestrial chemical reactions, is a small subset of all possible nuclides. As we see later, nuclear stability in the superheated interior of a star is quite different than on Earth, and many nuclides that are stable at terrestrial temperature undergo transmutations at extremely high temperature.

SECTION EXERCISES

19.1.1 Write the symbols for the following nuclides: (a) a neon nucleus with the same number of neutrons and protons; (b) element 43 with 55 neutrons; and (c) the unstable nuclide of hydrogen with the lowest mass.

19.1.2 Predict whether each of the following is stable or unstable. If you predict that it is unstable, give your reason: (a) the nuclide with 94 protons and 150 neutrons; (b) the iodine nuclide with 73 neutrons; (c) ${}^{154}_{64}Gd$; and (d) the oxygen nuclide with six neutrons.

19.1.3 Determine *Z*, *N*, and *A* for each nuclide appearing in Section Exercises 19.1.1 and 19.1.2.

19.2 NUCLEAR ENERGETICS

Vast amounts of energy are released when nuclides transmute. The energy output of the sun, for example, is so huge that it warms the entire solar system. On a much smaller scale, the energy released by a nuclear weapon is millions of times larger than the amount of energy released in an exothermic chemical reaction. Energy is always conserved, so nuclear transmutations must release stored energy. How or where is this energy stored? Einstein recognized that mass is a form of stored energy. His famous equation links energy to mass and the speed of light, c:

$$E = mc^2 \quad \textbf{(19-1)}$$

In a typical nuclear transmutation, only a small portion of the nuclear mass is converted into energy. Equation 19-1 gives the amount of mass stored as energy both before and after the transmutation:

$$E_b = m_b c^2 \qquad E_a = m_a c^2$$

The subscript *b* designates before transmutation, whereas the subscript *a* designates after transmutation.

Because energy is conserved, the energy released in the transmutation is the difference between these two amounts:

$$\Delta E = E_a - E_b = m_a c^2 - m_b c^2$$

$$\Delta E = (\Delta m)c^2 \quad \textbf{(19-2)}$$

Equation 19-2 is the fundamental equation of nuclear energetics. The change in energy that accompanies a nuclear transmutation can be calculated from the mass of the nuclide before and after the transmutation. When mass decreases, the energy change is negative. Recall that a negative energy change for a system means an exothermic process, in which energy is released to the surroundings. Thus processes in which mass decreases are exothermic.

Nuclear transmutations, like ordinary chemical reactions, can involve more than one reactant and more than one product. The energy change that accompanies a transmutation is found from the *net change* in mass. To obtain the net change in mass, we must add the masses of all products and subtract the masses of all reactants.

MAGNITUDES OF NUCLEAR ENERGIES

When applying Equation 19-2, we must use consistent units. Recall that energy is expressed in joules, joules per mole, or kilojoules per mole. To compute ΔE in joules, the change in mass is expressed in kilograms and the speed of light in meters per second.

Nuclide masses are ordinarily tabulated as molar masses, with units of grams per mole. It is useful, therefore, to rewrite Equation 19-2 with energy in units of kilojoules per mole and mass change in grams per mole:

$$\Delta E = (\Delta m)c^2 = \Delta m(2.998 \times 10^8 \text{ m/s})^2(10^{-3} \text{ kg/g})(10^{-3} \text{ kJ/J})$$

$c = 2.998 \times 10^8$ m/s

$$\Delta E = (\Delta m)(8.988 \times 10^{10})\left(\frac{\text{kg m}^2 \text{ kJ}}{\text{s}^2 \text{ J g}}\right)$$

1 J = 1 kg m^2/s^2

$$\Delta E = (\Delta m)(8.988 \times 10^{10} \text{ kJ/g}) \quad \textbf{(19-3)}$$

The large positive exponent in Equation 19-3 means that a tiny change in mass gives a huge change in energy. Sample Problems 19-2 and 19-3 illustrate the relationship between mass and energy.

SAMPLE PROBLEM 19-2 NUCLEAR ENERGETICS

A free neutron decays spontaneously into a proton and an electron: n $\rightarrow$ p + e. Compute ΔE for the decay of 1 mol of neutrons and for a single neutron.

METHOD: To compute ΔE, we must find Δm and then use Equation 19-3. Masses of the fundamental particles are given in Table 19-1.

$$m_p = 1.007276 \text{ g/mol} \quad m_n = 1.008665 \text{ g/mol} \quad m_e = 0.0005486 \text{ g/mol}$$

$$\Delta m = (m_p + m_e) - m_n = -0.0008404 \text{ g/mol}$$

This change in mass is used in Equation 19-3:

$$\Delta E = (8.988 \times 10^{10} \text{ kJ/g})(-0.0008404 \text{ g/mol}) = -7.554 \times 10^7 \text{ kJ/mol}$$

This energy change is negative, so the conversion of a neutron into a proton and an electron is exothermic.

To find the energy change for a single neutron, we divide the result for 1 mol of neutrons by Avogadro's number:

$$\Delta E_{\text{per neutron}} = \frac{-7.554 \times 10^7 \text{ kJ mol}^{-1}}{6.022 \times 10^{23} \text{ neutrons mol}^{-1}} = -1.254 \times 10^{-16} \text{ kJ/neutron}$$

Notice that we carry all the significant figures for the masses. It is essential to do this, since a very small change in mass generates an extremely large amount of energy. Even though the mass change in this example is only about one part per thousand, the reaction is exothermic by more than 10^7 kJ/mol.

SAMPLE PROBLEM 19-3 THE MASS OF CHEMICAL ENERGY

Hydrogen is a fuel that releases a large amount of chemical energy for every gram burned. Use standard enthalpies of formation to calculate the change in mass that occurs when 1.00 kg of H_2 is burned.

METHOD: In Sample Problem 19-2, we determined the energy change that accompanies a specific change in mass. In Sample Problem 19-3, we are asked to do the opposite, to calculate the change in mass when a specific amount of energy is released in an exothermic chemical reaction. First, we must determine ΔE for the chemical reaction, then use Equation 19-3.

Standard enthalpies of formation are found in Appendix E. Enthalpy changes and energy changes are nearly the same, so $\Delta E \cong \Delta H$. The combustion reaction per mole of hydrogen is:

$$H_{2\,(g)} + 1/2\ O_{2\,(g)} \rightarrow H_2O_{\,(g)}$$

This is the formation reaction of gaseous H_2O:

$$\Delta H_{\text{molar}} = \Delta H^\circ_f = -242 \text{ kJ/mol}$$

The problem asks for the mass change per kilogram of burned H_2, so we need the energy change for 1 kg:

$$\Delta H = \frac{(-242 \text{ kJ mol}^{-1})(1000 \text{ g})}{2.016 \text{ g mol}^{-1}} = -1.200 \times 10^5 \text{ kJ}$$

$$\Delta E \cong \Delta H = -1.200 \times 10^5 \text{ kJ}$$

Now substitute this value into Equation 19-3:

$$-1.200 \times 10^5 \text{ kJ} = (8.988 \times 10^{10} \text{ kJ g}^{-1})\Delta m$$

$$\Delta m = -1.34 \times 10^{-6} \text{ g}$$

When 1 kg of hydrogen reacts with 8 kg of oxygen, about a microgram, or 0.0000001% of the mass, is converted to energy. This amount, which is typical of the energy released in conventional chemical reactions, is too small to detect.

BINDING ENERGY

Every nucleus contains Z protons and $(A - Z)$ neutrons, so we can visualize a nuclear "formation reaction" in which protons and neutrons combine to form a particular nuclide:

$$(Z)\text{p} + (A - Z)\text{n} \rightarrow {}^{A}_{Z}E$$

Figure 19-3 illustrates this process schematically for fluorine, ${}^{19}_{9}\text{F}$. Ten neutrons and nine protons combine to form a fluorine nuclide of mass m_F. From the mass of this nuclide, we can use mass-energy equivalence to compute the energy of formation of the nuclide. This nuclear formation energy is usually called the **nuclear binding energy.**

The tabulated molar mass of an element divided by Avogadro's number is the *average* mass per atom of that element, but it is not the *exact* mass of an individual nuclide. There are two reasons for this. First, molar masses refer to neutral atoms. The tabulated molar mass of an element includes the mass of its electrons in addition to the mass of its nucleus. Consequently, the mass of Z electrons must be subtracted from the isotopic molar mass when we compute the energy of formation of a nuclide. Second, molar masses of the elements are weighted averages of all naturally occurring isotopes of that element. For example, the most abundant isotope of hydrogen, ${}^{1}\text{H}$, has an *isotopic* molar mass of 1.007825 g/mol, but the presence of small amounts of the isotope ${}^{2}\text{H}$ makes the *elemental* molar mass of naturally occurring hydrogen slightly larger than this, 1.00794 g/mol. In making mass-energy conversions, it is essential to work with isotopic molar masses rather than elemental molar masses. The isotopic molar masses of all stable and many unstable isotopes have been determined using mass spectrometry and can be found in standard data tables. We provide values as needed for these calculations. Sample Problem 19-4 illustrates the calculation of nuclear binding energies from isotopic molar masses.

The use of mass spectrometry to measure isotopic masses with high accuracy is outlined in Section 2.3.

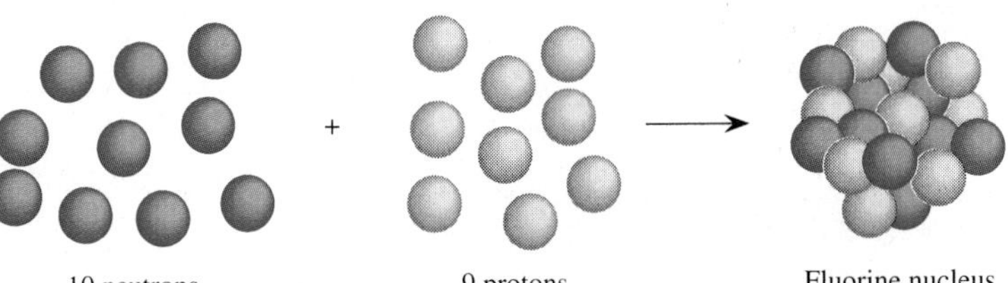

FIGURE 19-3
The nuclear formation reaction for ${}^{19}_{9}\text{F}$.

SAMPLE PROBLEM 19-4 NUCLEAR BINDING ENERGIES

The most abundant isotope of helium has two neutrons and an isotopic molar mass of 4.00260 g/mol. The most abundant isotope of uranium is U-238, with an isotopic molar mass of 238.0508 g/mol. Compute the nuclear binding energies of these nuclides.

METHOD: A particular nuclide is made from the combination of Z protons and $(A - Z)$ neutrons. When these particles are brought together, a small amount of mass is converted to energy. To calculate that energy, we must count protons, neutrons, and electrons, then do a mass-energy calculation using Equation 19-3.

A neutral atom of a specific isotope contains Z protons, Z electrons, and $(A - Z)$ neutrons. The helium isotope has two neutrons, two electrons, and two protons. The theoretical molar mass of this isotope is the sum of the molar masses of the individual particles:

$$\text{Protons: } 2(1.007276 \text{ g mol}^{-1}) = 2.014552 \text{ g mol}^{-1}$$

$$\text{Neutrons: } 2(1.008665 \text{ g mol}^{-1}) = 2.017330 \text{ g mol}^{-1}$$

$$\text{Electrons: } 2(0.0005486 \text{ g mol}^{-1}) = 0.0010972 \text{ g mol}^{-1}$$

$$\text{Theoretical molar mass of } {}^{4}_{2}\text{He} = 4.032979 \text{ g mol}^{-1}$$

The actual mass of the helium isotope is slightly smaller than the theoretical value. The difference represents the amount of mass that is converted to energy when the nuclide forms from the three fundamental particles:

$$\Delta m = \underbrace{(4.00260 \text{ g mol}^{-1})}_{\text{Actual molar mass}} - \underbrace{(4.032979 \text{ g mol}^{-1})}_{\text{Theoretical molar mass}} = -0.03038 \text{ g mol}^{-1}$$

Now use Equation 19-3:

$$\Delta E = (-0.03038 \text{ g/mol})(8.988 \times 10^{10} \text{ kJ/g}) = -2.731 \times 10^{9} \text{ kJ/mol}$$

The uranium nuclide has $A = 238$ and $Z = 92$. You should be able to verify that the theoretical molar mass is 239.98496 g/mol; hence:

$$\Delta m = (238.0508 \text{ g/mol}) - (239.98496 \text{ g/mol}) = -1.9342 \text{ g/mol}$$

$$\Delta E = (8.988 \times 10^{10} \text{ kJ/g})(-1.9342 \text{ g/mol}) = -1.738 \times 10^{11} \text{ kJ/mol}$$

Both energy changes are negative, which is what we expect for stable nuclides.

Notice that the binding energy of uranium is much larger than the binding energy of helium. As the mass number increases, so does the total binding energy of the nuclide. More important for the overall stability of the nucleus, however, is the binding energy *per nucleon.* This quantity is the total binding energy divided by the mass number A. It describes how tightly each individual proton or neutron is bound to the nucleus. As the binding energy per nucleon becomes more negative, nuclei become more stable. Binding energy per nucleon is plotted as a function of mass number in Figure 19-4. Notice the broad minimum around $A = 60$, $Z = 26$, at a binding energy of -8.3×10^{8} kJ/mol of nucleons.

The most stable nuclide of all is ${}^{56}_{26}\text{Fe}$. As a result, there are two classes of energy-releasing nuclear transmutations. When light nuclides combine in a process called **fusion,** energy is released. When heavy nuclides fragment in a process called **fission,** energy is also released.

We describe fission in Section 19.5 and fusion in Section 19.6.

ENERGY BARRIERS

If fission of large nuclides and fusion of small nuclides are both exothermic, why have these processes not occurred over time, converting all elements into the most stable one, iron? The reason is that there are very large energy barriers for nuclear

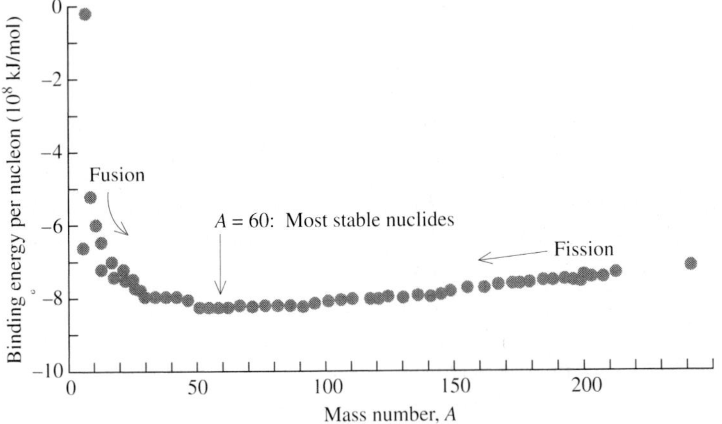

FIGURE 19-4
Plot of the binding energy per nucleon vs. mass number A. The most stable nuclides lie in the region around A = 60. Fusion of lighter nuclides and fission of heavier nuclides are exothermic processes.

transmutations. Lead and other massive nuclides do not fragment into lighter, more stable nuclides because there is a high activation energy barrier for pulling a nucleus apart. Hydrogen and other light nuclides do not fuse to give more massive, more stable nuclides because there is a high activation energy barrier for bringing nuclei together.

The barriers to nuclear transmutation are analogous to those for conventional combustion reactions. The combustion of gasoline, for example, is highly exothermic ($\Delta H \cong -5000$ kJ/mol), but its rate is negligible at room temperature because an activation energy barrier prevents combustion from occurring without an external "boost." The "boost" for the combustion of gasoline can come from a spark plug or from a lighted match. Typical chemical activation energies are about 100 kJ/mol. The following analysis shows the magnitudes of typical activation energies for nuclear reactions.

Nuclei cannot fuse together without first overcoming the coulombic forces between them. Recall that coulombic repulsions prevent the nuclei in molecules from approaching closer than the lengths of chemical bonds, which are about 100 pm. For nuclei to fuse, however, they must be brought within one nuclear radius of each other, which is about 10^{-3} pm. We can use Coulomb's law to calculate the magnitude of this barrier. Because isotopes of hydrogen have the smallest possible nuclear charge (+1), they also have the minimum coulombic barrier to fusion. Consider, for example, the fusion of two deuterium nuclides:

$$^{2}_{1}\text{H} + ^{2}_{1}\text{H} \rightarrow ^{4}_{2}\text{He}$$

Equation 7-1 states Coulomb's law. For a pair of nuclei, the charges q_1 and q_2 are equal to the nuclear charges Z_1 and Z_2:

$$E_{\text{coulomb}} = \frac{(1.389 \times 10^5 \text{ kJ pm/mol})(Z_1)(Z_2)}{d} \qquad \textbf{(7-1)}$$

For fusion of deuterium nuclides, Z_1 and Z_2 are both +1, and d is the sum of the nuclide radii, 2.8×10^{-3} pm. Substituting these values into Equation 7-1 gives $E = 5.0 \times 10^7$ kJ/mol. The graph in Figure 19-5 is a schematic representation of the energy barriers for fusion of deuterium.

Deuterium nuclei cannot fuse unless they first acquire 5×10^7 kJ/mol of energy. At room temperature, the average kinetic energy of deuterium nuclei is only

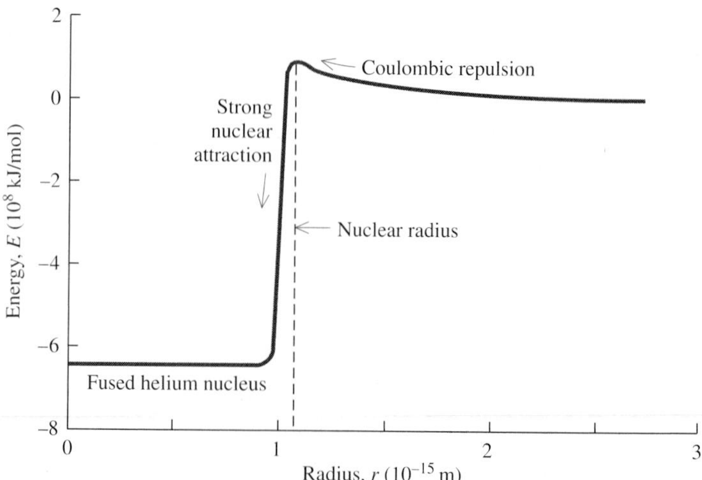

FIGURE 19-5
The energy profile for nuclear fusion between two deuterium nuclides. Separated nuclides must overcome coulombic repulsion to fuse. A nucleon inside a nucleus, on the other hand, must overcome the strong nuclear attraction to escape.

3.7 kJ/mol. To acquire enough kinetic energy to overcome the barrier to fusion, a sample of deuterium would have to be heated to about 5×10^6 K. Because the activation energy barriers for nuclear transmutations of stable nuclides are more than a million times larger than the activation energies of conventional chemical reactions, nuclear processes require immense "boosts" before they can occur.

As the energy profile in Figure 19-5 indicates, nuclei also cannot eject nucleons without overcoming the forces responsible for binding nucleons together. The data in Figure 19-4 show that these forces generate binding energies on the order of 10^8 kJ/mol. For example, the transfer of a neutron from a lead nucleus to an iron nucleus is highly exothermic, as measured by the difference in binding energies for these two nuclides:

$$^{207}_{82}\text{Pb} + ^{56}_{26}\text{Fe} \longrightarrow ^{206}_{82}\text{Pb} + ^{57}_{26}\text{Fe} \qquad \Delta E \cong -0.9 \times 10^8 \text{ kJ/mol}$$

However, the neutron would have to overcome the large binding energy of the lead nucleus before it could be attached to the iron nucleus:

$$^{207}_{82}\text{Pb} \longrightarrow ^{206}_{82}\text{Pb} + ^{1}_{0}\text{n} \qquad \Delta E \cong 7 \times 10^8 \text{ kJ/mol}$$

These strong nuclear binding energies prevent the spontaneous fragmentation of stable heavy nuclides from taking place at a measurable rate.

Neutron-capture reactions, a type of induced nuclear reaction, are described in Section 19.4.

The only nuclear transmutation reaction that has no energy barrier is the capture of a free neutron by a nucleus. Free neutrons, being uncharged, are not repelled by the positive charge of a nucleus. Thus they can penetrate close enough to the nucleus to be captured by the strong nuclear attractive forces.

SECTION EXERCISES

19.2.1 A positron is a subnuclear particle with the same mass as an electron but with a positive charge. Positrons are produced in some nuclear processes, but they do not last long because when a positron encounters an electron, both particles are converted entirely into energy in an annihilation reaction. Compute the energy per event and per mole for the annihilation of a positron and an electron.

19.2.2 Fluorine has only one stable isotope, $^{19}_{9}F$. Compute the total binding energy and binding energy per nucleon for this nuclide.

19.2.3 Compute the coulombic energy barrier in kJ/mol for the fusion reaction of $^{4}_{2}He$ ($r = 2.1 \times 10^{-3}$ pm) with $^{12}_{6}C$ ($r = 3.0 \times 10^{-3}$ pm).

19.3 NUCLEAR DECAY

Unstable nuclides decompose spontaneously into other, more stable nuclides. These decompositions are called **nuclear decay,** and unstable nuclides are said to be **radioactive.** Three features characterize nuclear decay: the products, the energy released, and the rate of decay. Among the products of nuclear decomposition are electrons, helium nuclei, and high-energy photons. Nuclear decay releases energy because the products of decay are more stable than the starting materials. Furthermore, each unstable nuclide decomposes at some particular rate, which can be anywhere from much less than a second to many millions of years.

Like ordinary chemical reactions, nuclear transmutations always obey the fundamental conservation laws. Mass-energy, charge, and mass number all are conserved in nuclear transmutations. Any description of a nuclear transmutation must take these conservation requirements into account.

Mass-energy is conserved, but mass itself is not conserved in nuclear transmutations; instead, some mass is converted into energy, or some energy is converted into mass. In nuclear decay, some mass is always converted into energy. The amount of energy released can be calculated if we know the mass of the decaying nucleus and the masses of its products.

Conservation of charge and mass number restrict the possible products of nuclear transmutations. Consider, for example, the decay of free neutrons, whose energy release we calculated in Sample Problem 19-2. A neutron has $A = 1$, so its decay products must also have $A = 1$. The only other particle with $A = 1$ is a proton, so the decay must be $^{1}_{0}n \rightarrow ^{1}_{1}p$. The neutron has zero charge, so the sum of the charges of its decay products must also be zero. Because the proton carries a +1 charge, another particle with a −1 charge is required. Also, this particle must have $A = 0$ to ensure that mass number is conserved. The only particle with these properties is the electron. Thus the only possible decay process for neutrons is:

$$^{1}_{0}n \rightarrow ^{1}_{1}p + ^{0}_{-1}e$$

The equation for any transmutation is balanced when the total *charge* and total *mass number* of the products equals the total charge and total mass number of the reactants. This conservation requirement is one reason why the symbol for any nuclide includes its charge number as a subscript and its mass number as a superscript. These features provide a convenient way to keep track of charge and mass balances. Notice that in the equation for neutron decay, the sum of the subscripts of reactants equals the sum of the subscripts of products. Likewise, the sum of the superscripts of reactants equals the sum of the superscripts of products. We demonstrate how to balance equations for other transmutations as we introduce various types of nuclear reactions.

Ernest Rutherford observed that the paths taken by energetic particles emitted by radioactive uranium and thorium responded in three ways to magnetic fields: slightly bent, strongly bent, and unaffected. He gave them the designations α, β, and γ. Even though scientists soon identified the particles, they still use these names to emphasize that they are nuclear decay products.

Table 19-3 lists the six nuclear particles observed most often in nuclear decay processes. You are already familiar with neutrons, protons, and electrons. Electrons that originate during nuclear decay are called **β-rays.** Similarly, the photons originating in nuclear decay are called **γ-rays.** The helium nuclei emitted in nuclear decay

TABLE 19-3 PARTICLES THAT APPEAR IN NUCLEAR DECAY

NAME	SYMBOL	CHARGE NO.	MASS NO.	COMMENTS
Neutron	n	0	1	Unstable except in nuclei
Proton	p	1	1	Also symbolized $^{1}_{1}H$
Electron	e or β	−1	0	"β" denotes an energetic electron
Alpha-particle	α	2	4	Energetic $^{4}_{2}He$ nucleus
Gamma-ray	γ	0	0	High-energy photon
Positron	β^{+}	1	0	Annihilates with an electron

processes are called **α-particles.** Finally, a **positron** is a particle that has the same mass as an electron, but the opposite charge, +1. All these decay products typically emerge from the decaying nucleus with large amounts of energy.

DECAY PROCESSES

The particular decay process for an unstable nuclide depends on the reason for its instability. Nuclides with *high* ratios of neutrons to protons decay by converting neutrons into protons. Nuclides with *low* ratios of neutrons to protons, on the other hand, decay by converting protons into neutrons. High-*Z* nuclides stabilize by losing both charge and mass. Unstable odd-odd nuclides that lie within the belt of stability become stable even-even nuclides by proton-neutron conversions.

Nuclides that lie above the belt of stability in Figure 19-2 have high ratios of neutrons to protons. To reach a stable composition, these nuclides need to gain nuclear charge. They accomplish this by ejecting negatively charged β-rays, thus converting neutrons into protons. The following are some examples of **β-emission:**

$$^{3}_{1}H \rightarrow {}^{3}_{2}He + {}^{0}_{-1}\beta$$

$$^{59}_{26}Fe \rightarrow {}^{59}_{27}Co + {}^{0}_{-1}\beta$$

$$^{198}_{79}Au \rightarrow {}^{198}_{80}Hg + {}^{0}_{-1}\beta$$

Notice that β-emission decreases the ratio of neutrons to protons but conserves mass number and charge. The decay converts a neutron to a proton, but the total number of nucleons remains the same. Because the product nucleus has one new proton, its positive charge increases by +1, but the overall charge remains balanced by the −1 charge on the β-ray.

A nuclide that lies below the belt of stability has a low neutron/proton ratio and must reduce its nuclear charge to become stable. For such a nuclide, β-emission is a change in the wrong direction. Instead, it converts a proton into a neutron by emitting a positron (symbolized β^{+}). Each positron carries off a +1 charge, which lowers *Z* of the product nucleus by one unit without changing its mass number. The following are two examples of nuclear decay by **positron emission:**

$$^{18}_{9}F \rightarrow {}^{18}_{8}O + {}^{0}_{+1}\beta^{+}$$

$$^{52}_{26}Fe \rightarrow {}^{52}_{25}Mn + {}^{0}_{+1}\beta^{+}$$

A nuclide with a low neutron/proton ratio can also reduce its nuclear charge by capturing one of its 1*s* orbital electrons in a process called **electron capture.** The

Positron Emission:

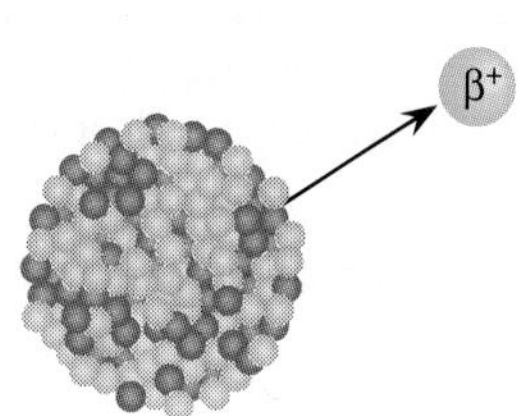

Step 1: Positron emission

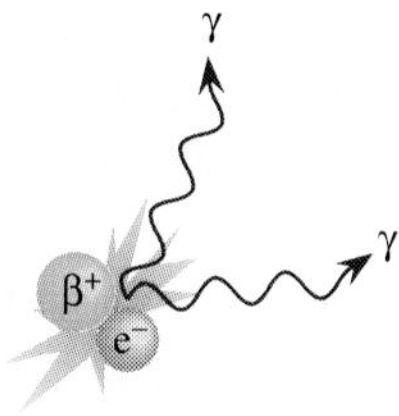

Step 2: Annihilation

Electron Capture:

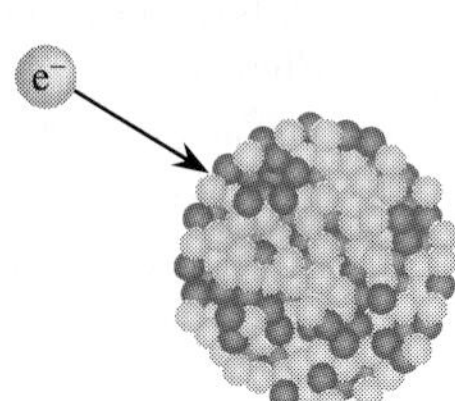

Step 1: Electron capture

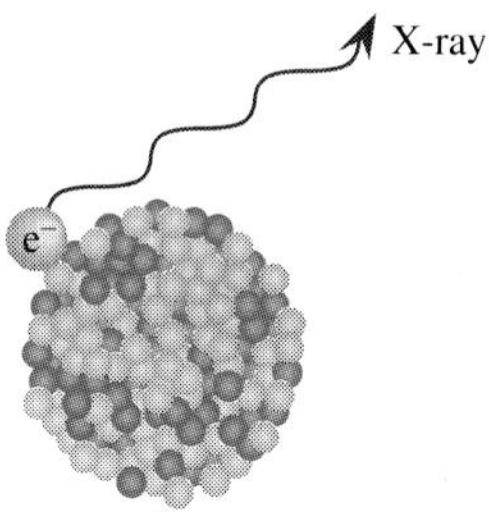

Step 2: Electronic transition

FIGURE 19-6

Positron emission and electron capture can be observed only indirectly. The "signature" of positron emission is two γ-rays generated by the annihilation of a positron and an electron. The "signature" of electron capture is an x-ray emitted when an electron undergoes a transition from an outer to an inner orbital.

captured electron combines with a proton to give a neutron, so Z drops by one unit while A remains fixed. For example:

$$^{26}_{13}\text{Al} + ^{0}_{-1}\text{e} \rightarrow ^{26}_{12}\text{Mg}$$

Neither positron emission nor electron capture is observed directly. Instead, we see their results, which are the product nuclei and high-energy photons. When a positron encounters an electron, the two oppositely charged particles annihilate each another, converting their entire mass into a pair of high-energy photons. Each photon produced in this process has a specific energy, $E_{\text{photon}} = 1.64 \times 10^{-13}$ J, which is in the γ-ray region of the spectrum. On electron capture, the product atom is missing one of its 1*s* electrons. When an electron from an outer orbital occupies this vacancy in the 1*s* orbital, a photon is emitted whose energy falls in the x-ray region of the spectrum ($E \cong 10^{-15}$ J). Figure 19-6 shows these two processes schematically.

The electron captured by a nucleus during electron capture is symbolized e, not β, because β is reserved for electrons that are ejected during nuclear decay.

Every nuclide with $Z > 83$ is unstable, regardless of its neutron/proton ratio. These nuclides must lose both mass and charge to reach stable compositions. Usually, this is accomplished by emitting an α-particle, which is an energetic helium nucleus with $A = 4$ and $Z = 2$. The following are three examples of α-emission:

$$^{226}_{88}\text{Ra} \rightarrow ^{222}_{86}\text{Rn} + ^{4}_{2}\alpha$$

$$^{222}_{86}\text{Rn} \rightarrow ^{218}_{84}\text{Po} + ^{4}_{2}\alpha$$

$$^{218}_{84}\text{Po} \rightarrow ^{214}_{82}\text{Pb} + ^{4}_{2}\alpha$$

Notice that the product of the first transmutation is the starting material for the second, and the product of the second is the starting material for the third. The decay of heavy nuclides often involves sequential transmutations, in which the product of the initial decay is also unstable. The $^{222}_{86}\text{Rn}$ nuclide produced in the initial decay has $Z > 83$, so it is unstable. A second α-emission produces $^{218}_{84}\text{Po}$. Because Z is still greater than 83, this nuclide loses one more α-particle to produce the final stable product, $^{214}_{82}\text{Pb}$. Sample Problem 19-5 traces another example of nuclear decay that occurs through a sequence of transmutations.

SAMPLE PROBLEM 19-5 DECAY SEQUENCES

Radon-222 is an unstable nuclide that has been detected in the air of some homes. Its presence is unhealthy, for reasons that we describe later in this chapter. Radon-222 transmutes to a stable nuclide by emitting α-particles and β-rays in the following sequence: α, α, β, β, α, β, β, α. Write the sequence of nuclear transmutations and identify the final product.

BOX 19-1

COUNTERS FOR NUCLEAR DECAY

Every nuclear decay produces a fragment particle of high energy that can be captured by a counter, such as a film badge, a Geiger counter, or a scintillation counter. The counting device converts the energy of the fragment into some observable property.

Film badges are routinely worn by workers who may be exposed to radioactivity in the course of their duties. A film badge uses decay fragments to "expose" photographic film. This is the same phenomenon that alerted Becquerel to radioactivity in the first place. When a high-energy particle strikes a film badge, its energy reduces molecules of AgBr in the film to metallic Ag. The greater the exposure to radiation, the more metallic Ag is produced. When a film is developed, metallic Ag appears black, just as in a photographic negative. The degree of darkening of a film badge indicates the amount of radiation it and its wearer have absorbed.

Geiger counters contain tubes filled with gas mixtures. Typically, argon is mixed with a small amount of methane. When a high-energy particle passes through the tube, its energy ionizes atoms and molecules of the gas, resulting in an electrical discharge. Two electrodes capture the small burst of electrical current that results, and an electronic circuit counts these current pulses. As shown in the figure, Geiger counters are routinely used by health physics personnel to check for unsafe levels of radiation.

Whereas film badges rely on chemical change and Geiger counters rely on ionization, scintillation counters use the emission of light to detect nuclear decays. The detector substance in a scintillation counter is a molecule that emits visible or near-ultraviolet photons when it gains energy from nuclear radiation. These photons strike a photodetector, which generates a pulse of electrical current. Just as in Geiger counters, an electronic circuit counts and displays the number of pulses.

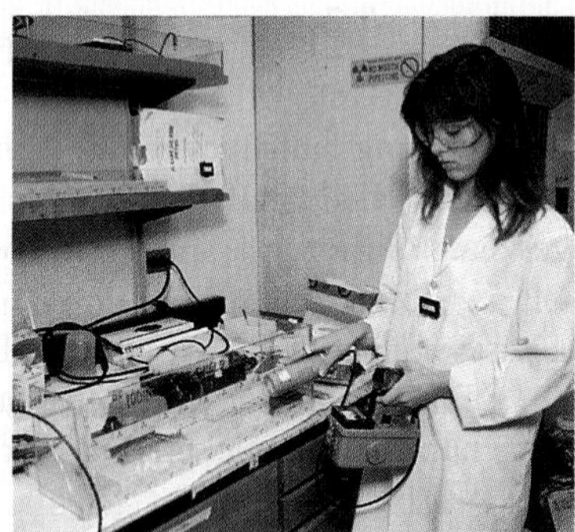

Each of these counters works because of a multiplying effect. The energy of nuclear particles is 10^5 to 10^6 times greater than the energy needed for the atomic and molecular events that are used to detect them. That is, a single energetic nuclear particle can reduce many Ag^+ ions to silver atoms in a film badge, it can ionize many neon atoms in a Geiger counter, or it can generate many photons in a scintillator. The nearly impossible task of detecting single atoms, ions, or photons instead becomes the much easier task of detecting clusters of these species, making individual nuclear decays relatively easy to count.

SAMPLE PROBLEM 19-6 NUCLEAR HALF-LIFE

Plutonium is a synthetic element used in nuclear weapons. A sample of ^{239}Pu whose mass is 1.00 mg emits 2.3×10^6 counts/s. What is the half-life of this isotope?

METHOD: The emission rate is $-\Delta N/\Delta t$, so we can rearrange Equation 19-4 and use it to calculate $t_{1/2}$:

$$\frac{-\Delta N}{\Delta t} = \frac{N \ln 2}{t_{1/2}} \qquad or \qquad t_{1/2} = \frac{N \ln 2}{(-\Delta N/\Delta t)}$$

The number of nuclei can be found from the mass of the sample and the molar mass of the isotope. Because the molar mass of an isotope is nearly equal to its mass number, we can use the mass number without introducing significant error:

$$N = \text{Number of nuclei} = \frac{(\text{Mass})(\text{Avogadro's number})}{(\text{Isotopic molar mass})}$$

$$N = \frac{(1.00 \times 10^{-3}\ \text{g})(6.022 \times 10^{23}\ \text{nuclei/mol})}{(239\ \text{g/mol})} = 2.52 \times 10^{18}\ \text{nuclei}$$

$$t_{1/2} = \frac{(2.52 \times 10^{18}\ \text{nuclei})(0.693)}{(2.3 \times 10^{6}\ \text{nuclei/s})} = 7.6 \times 10^{11}\ \text{s}$$

This half-life is easier to interpret if we convert seconds into years: $t_{1/2} = 2.4 \times 10^4$ years. It takes 24,000 years for half of the plutonium nuclei in any sample of ^{239}Pu to disappear.

SAMPLE PROBLEM 19-7 RADIOACTIVE DECAY

One of the serious problems with radioactive nuclides is that their decay cannot be stopped, so any sample of the nuclide continues to emit potentially lethal amounts of radiation until most of it has decayed. Assume that the radiation level from ^{239}Pu is no longer a hazard when 99% of it has decayed. How long will this take?

METHOD: We are asked to compute the time it takes for 99% of a sample of plutonium to decay. Equation 19-5 relates the ratio N_o/N to time and the half-life for decay. This equation can be solved for t, the time at which the ratio reaches the desired value.

First, Equation 19-5 must be rearranged to give an equation for t:

$$ln\left(\frac{N_0}{N}\right) = \frac{t\ ln\ 2}{t_{1/2}} \qquad or \qquad t = \frac{t_{1/2}\ ln\left(\frac{N_o}{N}\right)}{ln\ 2}$$

When 99% of the Pu has decayed, 1% of it, or 0.01 N_o, remains. This lets us calculate the ratio that will be used to determine the decay time:

$$\frac{N_o}{N} = \frac{N_o}{0.01\ N_o} = 100$$

Recall from Sample Problem 19-6 that for ^{239}Pu, $t_{1/2} = 2.4 \times 10^4$ years:

$$t = \frac{(2.4 \times 10^4\ \text{years})(ln\ 100)}{(ln\ 2)} = 1.6 \times 10^5\ \text{years}$$

Thus it will be a very long time before the plutonium that is stockpiled for use as a nuclear fuel decays sufficiently to be "safe."

SECTION EXERCISES

19.3.1 Write the mode (or modes) of decay that describe the following transmutations: (a) ^{213}Bi to ^{213}Po; (b) ^{213}Bi to ^{209}Tl; (c) ^{213m}Bi to ^{213}Bi; and (d) ^{207}Bi to ^{207}Pb.

19.3.2 Identify the nuclides that decay in the following manner:
(a) It undergoes β- and γ-decay to give $Z = 58$ and $A = 140$.
(b) It undergoes α-decay to give polonium-218.
(c) It captures an orbital electron to give tellurium with 73 neutrons.

19.3.3 Radioisotopes are used in many research applications. Because they decay continuously, radioisotopes have a limited useful "shelf life." An isotope used for bone marrow scanning is ^{111}In, which has $t_{1/2} = 2.8$ days. Within what time must this isotope be used if it is effective down to 5% of its initial activity?

19.4 INDUCED NUCLEAR REACTIONS

Stable nuclides remain the same indefinitely, whereas unstable nuclides disintegrate continuously. In time, therefore, every element should be composed entirely of stable isotopes. On Earth, most elements have no naturally occurring unstable isotopes. With two exceptions, the unstable nuclides that are present either have half-lives longer than the age of the Earth or are products of the decays of these very long-lived nuclides. The two exceptions are ^{3}H ($t_{1/2}$ = 12.3 years) and ^{14}C ($t_{1/2}$ = 5730 years). These half-lives are very short compared with the age of the Earth, so the nuclei of ^{3}H and ^{14}C present during the Earth's formation decayed long ago. Thus the ^{3}H and ^{14}C on Earth today must have formed in nuclear reactions. These nuclides are not formed in any nuclear decay schemes. Instead, each forms through a binuclear reaction in which a nuclear projectile collides with another nucleus, inducing a transmutation. Such reactions, which are **induced nuclear reactions**, are categorized according to the nature of the nuclear projectile that induces the transmutation.

NEUTRON-CAPTURE REACTIONS

One way to create unstable nuclides is by neutron capture. The Earth's atmosphere is constantly exposed to radiation from the sun. Solar radiation contains neutrons in addition to photons of many different energies. Nitrogen-14 in the atmosphere can capture a neutron to form the unstable nuclide ^{15m}N. This nucleus rapidly ejects a proton, producing carbon-14:

$$^{14}_{7}N + ^{1}_{0}n \longrightarrow \left(^{15m}_{7}N\right) \longrightarrow ^{14}_{6}C + ^{1}_{1}H$$

The other short-lived nuclide in the atmosphere, ^{3}H, is also produced by neutron bombardment of ^{14}N. Neutrons with sufficiently high kinetic energy cause this nucleus to fragment into ^{12}C and ^{3}H:

$$^{14}_{7}N + ^{1}_{0}n \longrightarrow ^{12}_{6}C + ^{3}_{1}H$$

Nuclear reactors are described in Section 19.5.

Although carbon-14 decays via β-emission with $t_{1/2}$ = 5730 years, it is replenished continuously by this neutron-capture reaction. We show in Section 19.9 how this isotope is used to estimate the ages of carbon-containing solid matter.

Neutrons are electrically neutral, so there is no coulombic barrier preventing them from penetrating a nucleus. Thus almost every nuclide undergoes neutron capture if a source of neutrons is available. Many unstable nuclides used in radiochemical applications are manufactured by neutron bombardment. A sample containing a suitable target nucleus is exposed to neutrons coming from a nuclear reactor. A target nucleus captures a neutron, increasing its mass number by one:

$$^{A}_{Z}X + ^{1}_{0}n \longrightarrow ^{(A+1)m}_{Z}X$$

Because neutron capture is always accompanied by the release of the binding energy of the neutron, the product nuclide is always in an excited state. These excited nuclei lose energy by emitting either γ-rays or protons:

$$^{(A+1)m}_{Z}X \longrightarrow ^{(A+1)}_{Z}X + \gamma$$

$$^{(A+1)m}_{Z}X \longrightarrow ^{A}_{(Z-1)}Y + ^{1}_{1}p$$

The following are specific examples of each type of decay:

$$^{98}_{42}Mo + ^{1}_{0}n \longrightarrow ^{99}_{42}Mo + \gamma$$

$$^{197}_{79}Au + ^{1}_{0}n \longrightarrow ^{198}_{79}Au + \gamma$$

$$^{14}_{7}N + ^{1}_{0}n \longrightarrow ^{14}_{6}C + ^{1}_{1}p$$

$$^{3}_{2}He + ^{1}_{0}n \longrightarrow ^{3}_{1}H + ^{1}_{1}p$$

One of the most important isotopes in nuclear medicine, ^{99}Tc, is produced by bombarding molybdenum with neutrons. The initial product, ^{99}Mo, has a high neutron/proton ratio, so it decomposes by releasing a β-ray. The product is an excited technetium nuclide that emits a γ-ray:

$$^{98}_{42}\text{Mo} + ^{1}_{0}\text{n} \longrightarrow ^{99}_{42}\text{Mo} + \gamma$$

$$^{99}_{42}\text{Mo} \longrightarrow ^{99m}_{43}\text{Tc} + ^{0}_{-1}\beta$$

$$^{99m}_{43}\text{Tc} \longrightarrow ^{99}_{43}\text{Tc} + \gamma$$

The product of this three-step nuclear process, ^{99}Tc, is also unstable, but it lasts much longer than its predecessor does. It decays by β-emission with $t_{1/2} = 2.12 \times 10^5$ years.

The synthesis of technetium demonstrates how neutron capture can generate a higher-*A* isotope of the same element. The formation of ^{14}C from ^{14}N demonstrates how neutron capture can produce an isotope of one lower atomic number but the same mass number. In either case, the product has a higher neutron/proton ratio than the target nucleus, is likely to be unstable, and will decay by β-emission. Both ^{99}Mo and ^{14}C, for example, are β-emitters.

OTHER BINUCLEAR REACTIONS

Neutrons readily induce nuclear reactions, but they always produce nuclides on the *high* neutron/proton side of the belt of stability. To generate an unstable nuclide with a *low* neutron/proton ratio, the bombarding particle must have a positive charge. Nuclear reactions with positively charged particles require projectile particles that possess enough kinetic energy to overcome the coulombic repulsion between two positive particles.

Ernest Rutherford was the first person to observe a binuclear reaction. In 1919, he exposed a sample of nitrogen to α-particles from a naturally radioactive source. He observed the production of protons and deduced from the requirements of charge and mass balance that the other product was ^{17}O:

$$^{14}_{7}\text{N} + ^{4}_{2}\text{He} \longrightarrow \left(^{18m}_{9}\text{F}\right) \longrightarrow ^{17}_{8}\text{O} + ^{1}_{1}\text{H}$$

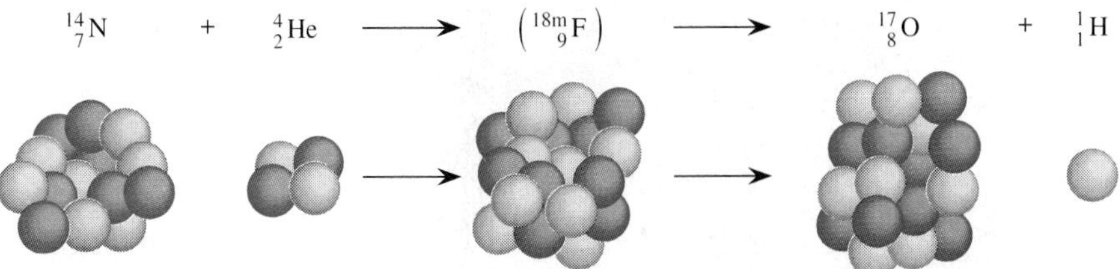

The immediate product of a reaction between two nuclei is called a **compound nucleus.** It has a charge equal to the sum of the charges of the reactants and a mass number equal to the sum of the mass numbers of the reactants. Every compound nucleus has excess energy that is released as the two reactants bind together. Compound nuclei lose this excess energy by emitting one or more neutrons, protons, α-particles, or deuterons (^{2}H nuclei). The sums of charge number and mass number for the products must equal the charge number and mass number of the compound nucleus. As Sample Problem 19-8 shows, conservation of charge and mass number allow us to deduce the participants in binuclear reactions.

SAMPLE PROBLEM 19-8 BALANCING BINUCLEAR REACTIONS

Identify *X* and *Y* in each of the following nuclear reactions:

(a) $^{3}\text{He} + \text{n} \longrightarrow {}^{\text{m}}X \longrightarrow Y + \text{p}$

(b) $^{112}\text{Sn} + X \longrightarrow {}^{113\text{m}}\text{Sn} \longrightarrow {}^{113}\text{Sn} + Y$

(c) $X + \alpha \longrightarrow {}^{113\text{m}}\text{In} \longrightarrow Y + 2\text{ n}$

METHOD: Charge number and mass number are always conserved in nuclear reactions, so the missing components can be identified from the atomic numbers of elements and the charge and mass numbers of elementary particles.

(a) Both reactants are given: $^{3}_{2}\text{He}$ and $^{1}_{0}\text{n}$.

Therefore the compound nucleus must have $A = 4$ and $Z = 2$ (He). It then loses a proton, leaving $A = 3$ and $Z = 1$ (H):

$$^{3}_{2}\text{He} + {}^{1}_{0}\text{n} \longrightarrow ({}^{4\text{m}}_{2}\text{He}) \longrightarrow {}^{3}_{1}\text{H} + {}^{1}_{1}\text{H}$$

(b) Because all the nuclei are isotopes of tin, $Z = 50$ for all of them. Therefore *X* and *Y* both must have charge numbers of zero. The possibilities are a neutron and a γ-ray. To balance mass numbers, *X* must have a mass number of one, and *Y* must have a mass number of zero:

$$^{112}_{50}\text{Sn} + {}^{1}_{0}\text{n} \longrightarrow {}^{113\text{m}}_{50}\text{Sn} \longrightarrow {}^{113}_{50}\text{Sn} + {}^{0}_{0}\gamma$$

(c) The compound nucleus is $^{113\text{m}}_{49}\text{In}$, so *X* must have this configuration minus an α-particle, $^{4}_{2}\alpha$. Thus *X* must have $A = 113 - 4 = 109$ and $Z = 49 - 2 = 47$, and *X* is $^{109}_{47}\text{Ag}$. Similarly, *Y* must have the $^{113\text{m}}_{49}\text{In}$ configuration minus two neutrons. Therefore *Z* does not change, but $A = 113 - 2 = 111$, so *Y* is $^{111}_{49}\text{In}$:

$$^{109}_{47}\text{Ag} + {}^{4}_{2}\alpha \longrightarrow {}^{113\text{m}}_{49}\text{In} \longrightarrow {}^{111}_{49}\text{In} + 2\,{}^{1}_{0}\text{n}$$

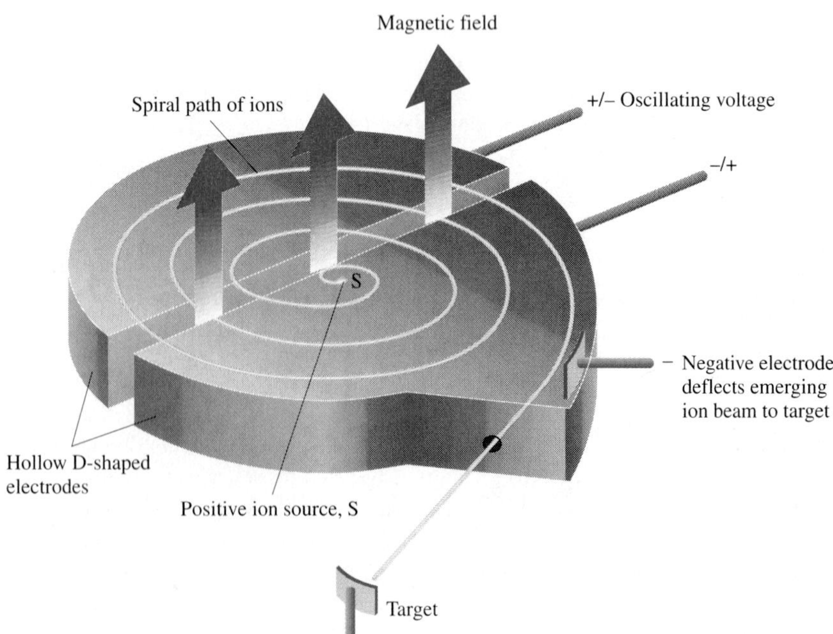

FIGURE 19-7
Diagram of a cyclotron. A beam of charged particles, generated at the center (S), is accelerated by two charged, D-shaped electrodes and is deflected along a spiral path by a strong magnetic field.

Nuclear accelerators generate high-energy beams of positive projectile nuclei. In these machines, appropriate combinations of electrical and magnetic fields accelerate positive ions to high kinetic energies. One such accelerator, called a **cyclotron**, is shown in Figure 19-7. A cyclotron contains two D-shaped electrodes that accelerate the beam to higher energy every time it passes from one electrode to the other. It also contains a strong magnet that causes the ion beam to move along a spiral path, which takes it from one electrode to the other many times. The end result is an ion beam with enough energy to induce nuclear reactions when it strikes a suitable target. Other types of accelerators give higher-energy beams, but cyclotrons are widely used to make useful radioisotopes. Box 19-2 discusses the advances in nuclear accelerators and the resulting costs.

BOX 19-2

BIGGER, BETTER(?) NUCLEAR ACCELERATORS

Accelerators have played a central role in exploring the structure and reactions of nuclides. As the energy and mass of the nuclear projectiles increase, so does the number of possible reactions. Nuclear physicists have constructed several generations of ever-more-powerful nuclear accelerators. Between 1930 and 1945, several versions of cyclotrons were constructed. In the 1950s, more powerful accelerators called *bevatrons* were built. Bevatrons have been complemented by linear accelerators, which can generate high-energy beams of relatively massive nuclei, such as ^{12}C.

Every advance in beam energy comes at a substantial increase in cost. The first cyclotron, which was constructed by the University of California, was relatively inexpensive. Because of substantially higher costs, later accelerators required large subsidies from the U.S. government. The current generation of accelerators includes high-energy linear accelerators at CERN in Switzerland and at Stanford University (shown in the photograph). These accelerators, in which beams of positive ions are accelerated down a mile-long vacuum chamber to bring them to the ultrahigh energies needed to cause exotic nuclear reactions, are supported by large consortia of governments or universities.

The next generation, the Superconducting Supercollider, will cost many billions of dollars and will require worldwide collaboration by all the industrial nations. A current plan calls for constructing one of these colossal accelerators in Texas. The expenditure of huge amounts of public funds on a massive project such as the Supercollider is a subject of intense debate. High-energy physicists expect that such a machine would allow them to probe more deeply into the fundamental structure of matter, which might lead to the formulation of a satisfactory theory describing subatomic matter. Other scientists contend that equal investments in scientific study in other areas, such as alternative energy sources or the genetic code of human beings, would reap larger benefits. Still others believe that resources should be devoted to solving social problems. Establishing such scientific priorities is a highly political issue. In 1993, the U.S. Congress voted to discontinue funding for the Superconducting Supercollider.

SYNTHETIC ELEMENTS

When nuclear reactions were discovered early in the twentieth century, elements 43, 62, 85, and all elements with $Z > 92$ were unknown. Soon after nuclear accelerators were invented in 1930, however, they were used to make samples of these elements. By 1945, the "holes" in the periodic table had been filled.

The trans-uranium elements, those with $Z > 92$, have been the objects of nuclear synthesis experiments for more than 50 years. Elements 93 and 94 form as a result of neutron capture by ^{238}U followed by β-emission to give isotopes with a mass number of 239:

$$^{238}_{92}\text{U} + \text{n} \longrightarrow {}^{239}_{92}\text{U} + \gamma$$

$$^{239}_{92}\text{U} \longrightarrow {}^{239}_{93}\text{Np} + \beta$$

$$^{239}_{93}\text{Np} \longrightarrow {}^{239}_{94}\text{Pu} + \beta$$

Nuclides with still larger Z values can be produced by bathing uranium samples with very high intensities of neutrons, but as Z increases beyond 92, the efficiency of producing elements by neutron bombardment decreases rapidly. Plutonium (element 94), whose production was spurred by its use as a nuclear fuel, has been produced in ton quantities by neutron bombardment of uranium-238. Curium (element 96), however, can be made only in gram amounts, whereas fermium (element 100) has been synthesized in only microgram quantities. Beyond $Z = 100$, synthesis by neutron bombardment of uranium is no longer effective. Instead, nuclides in the $Z = 95$ to 98 range must be bombarded with beams of light nuclei. The elements mendelevium ($Z = 101$), nobelium ($Z = 102$), and lawrencium ($Z = 103$), for example, can be made by the following nuclear reactions:

$$^{253}_{99}\text{Es} + \alpha \longrightarrow {}^{(257-x)}_{101}\text{Md} + x\,\text{n}$$

$$^{246}_{96}\text{Cm} + {}^{12}_{6}\text{C} \longrightarrow {}^{(258-x)}_{102}\text{No} + x\,\text{n}$$

$$^{252}_{98}\text{Cf} + {}^{11}_{5}\text{B} \longrightarrow {}^{(263-x)}_{103}\text{Lw} + x\,\text{n}$$

In these processes the number of emitted neutrons (x) varies from 5 to 10. Only a few atoms of these elements have been made, and these are so unstable that they decay in seconds or minutes. Thus the chemical properties of the elements with $Z > 99$ have not been explored.

SECTION EXERCISES

19.4.1 The only stable isotope of cobalt is ^{59}Co. What induced reaction would generate each of the following nuclides from ^{59}Co? Identify the compound nucleus in each case: (a) ^{59}Fe; (b) ^{60}Co; (c) ^{62}Ni; and (d) ^{58}Ni.

19.4.2 The two best-characterized isotopes of promethium ($Z = 61$) are ^{145}Pm and ^{147}Pm. The two elements next to it in the periodic table have many naturally occurring isotopes. Neodymium ($Z = 60$) has $A = 142, 143, 144, 145, 146, 148$, and 150; and samarium ($Z = 62$) has $A = 144, 147, 148, 149, 150, 152$, and 154. Write nuclear reactions describing the capture of one neutron by naturally occurring isotopes of Nd and Sm, followed by decay to produce ^{145}Pm or ^{147}Pm.

19.4.3 The following partial nuclear reactions show one reactant, the compound nucleus, and one product. Identify the other reactant and any additional products:
(a) $^{112}\text{In} \longrightarrow {}^{113m}\text{In} \longrightarrow {}^{113}\text{In}$
(b) $\alpha \longrightarrow {}^{58m}\text{Ni} \longrightarrow \text{n}$
(c) $^{60}\text{Ni} \longrightarrow {}^{61m}\text{Cu} \longrightarrow {}^{57}\text{Co}$

19.5 NUCLEAR FISSION

The graph of binding energy in Figure 19-4 shows that large amounts of energy are released when heavy nuclei split into lighter ones (fission) and when light nuclei combine into heavier ones (fusion). Thus both fission reactions and fusion reactions can serve as sources of energy. Fission is the subject of this section, and fusion is the subject of Section 19.6.

CHARACTERISTICS OF FISSION

Fission splits a nucleus into two fragments, each with a much lower Z value. Several free neutrons are released during each fission event. Fission is shown in Figure 19-8.

Uranium-235 is one of the most familiar examples of a nuclide that undergoes fission after it captures a neutron:

$$^{235}_{92}\text{U} + {}^{1}_{0}\text{n} \longrightarrow \left({}^{236m}_{92}\text{U}\right) \begin{cases} \longrightarrow {}^{81}_{32}\text{Ge} + {}^{152}_{60}\text{Nd} + 3\,{}^{1}_{0}\text{n} \\ \longrightarrow {}^{103}_{42}\text{Mo} + {}^{131}_{50}\text{Sn} + 2\,{}^{1}_{0}\text{n} \end{cases}$$

The compound nucleus formed on neutron capture, ^{236m}U, is highly unstable, so it quickly splits into fragments. Fission results in a wide range of product nuclides, but we have shown just two of the pairs of products formed. Although there are many modes of decay, charge and mass number are always conserved.

Among naturally occurring nuclides, only ^{235}U undergoes fission, but two other naturally occurring nuclides, ^{238}U and ^{232}Th, are converted by neutron capture and β-decay into ^{239}Pu and ^{233}U, both of which undergo fission.

The characteristics of nuclear fission can be summarized as follows:

1. Fission follows neutron capture by a small group of the heaviest nuclides, notably ^{235}U, ^{239}Pu, and ^{233}U.
2. Fission gives a range of product nuclides. Neutron-induced fission of ^{235}U, for example, yields the distribution shown in Figure 19-9. The distribution includes nuclides from $A = 77$ to $A = 157$. The most likely products are $A = 95$ and 138, but no single nuclide makes up more than 7% of the product fragments.
3. Fission generates free neutrons. Product nuclides have significantly lower neutron/proton ratios than ^{235}U, which means that one to four neutrons are ejected during fission. The average is 2.5 neutrons per ^{235}U nuclide.
4. The process of fission releases large amounts of energy. The energy released for one set of fission fragments is computed in Sample Problem 19-9. Although each set of fragments has a slightly different total mass, the average mass loss is about 0.2 g/mol, and the average energy released in ^{235}U fission is 1.8×10^{10} kJ/mol.

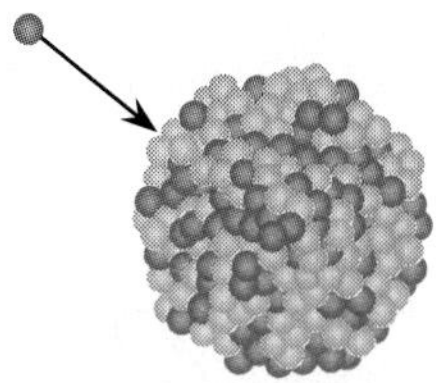

1. Neutron capture destabilizes the nucleus

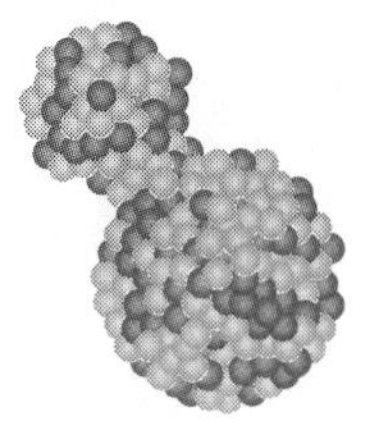

2. The unstable nucleus distorts

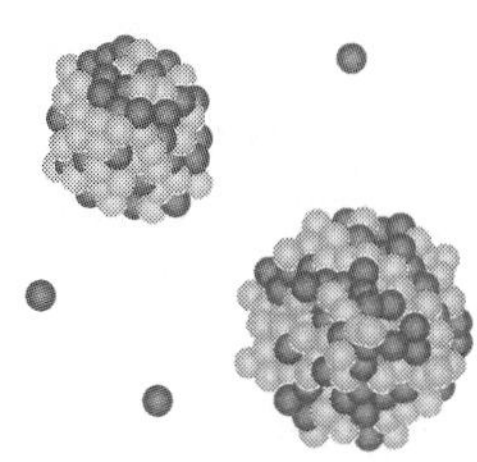

3. The nucleus splits into smaller fragment nuclei and free neutrons

FIGURE 19-8

Schematic view of fission. Neutron capture produces a highly unstable nucleus that distorts and then splits into smaller-fragment nuclei. The sizes of the fragment nuclei and the number of free neutrons vary considerably.

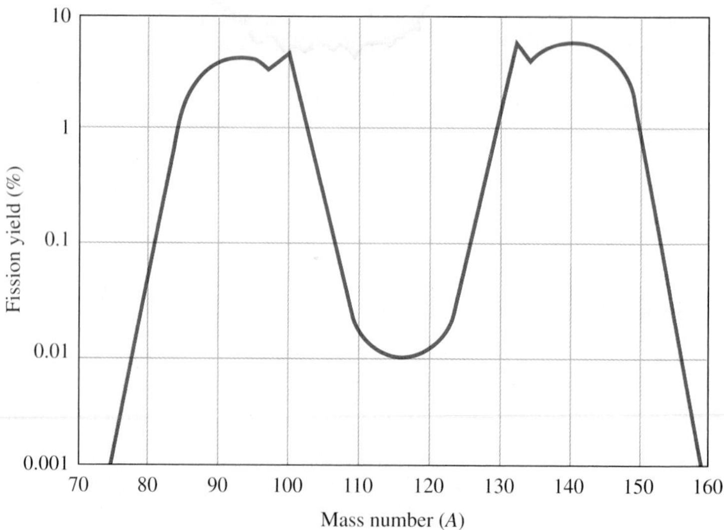

FIGURE 19-9
The isotopic "signature" of the nuclear fission of ^{235}U. Different mass numbers are produced in widely different percentages. (Note that the y-axis is a logarithmic scale.) About 7% of fission events yield products with $A = 95$ and $A = 138$.

SAMPLE PROBLEM 19-9 FISSION ENERGY

From tabulated isotopic molar masses, compute the energy released per mole, per nucleus, and per gram when ^{235}U undergoes fission in the following manner:

$$^{235}U + n \rightarrow {}^{138}Xe + {}^{95}Sr + 3\ n$$

Nuclide	n	^{235}U	^{138}Xe	^{95}Sr
MM, g/mol	1.0087	235.0439	137.908	94.913

METHOD: The first step is to compute the "mass defect," which is the loss of mass per mole of reaction. Next, Equation 19-3 can be used to calculate the amount of energy equivalent to that mass. Finally, use of the usual conversion factors gives energy released per nucleus and per gram.

The mass defect is the difference between the total mass of all products and the total mass of all reactants:

$$\Delta m = [(1\ ^{138}Xe)(137.908\ g/mol) + (1\ ^{95}Sr)(94.913\ g/mol) + (3\ ^{1}n)(1.0087\ g/mol)] - [(1\ ^{235}U)(235.0439\ g/mol) + (1\ ^{1}n)(1.0087\ g/mol)] = -0.2055\ g/mol$$

Next, use Equation 19-3 to find the energy equivalence:

$$\Delta E = (8.988 \times 10^{10}\ kJ/g)(-0.2055\ g/mol) = -1.847 \times 10^{10}\ kJ/mol$$

Finally, use Avogadro's number and the molar mass to convert to energy per nucleus and energy per gram:

$$\Delta E_{\text{per nucleus}} = \frac{-1.847 \times 10^{10}\ kJ\ mol^{-1}}{6.022 \times 10^{23}\ nuclei\ mol^{-1}} = -3.07 \times 10^{-14}\ kJ/nucleus$$

$$\Delta E_{\text{per gram}} = \frac{-1.847 \times 10^{10}\ kJ\ mol^{-1}}{235.0439\ g\ mol^{-1}} = -7.86 \times 10^{7}\ kJ/g$$

Some isotopic molar masses are known to just three decimal places, so the mass defect is precise to three decimal places. Consequently, the results should all be rounded to three significant figures.

Fission of 1 g of ^{235}U releases enough energy to raise the temperature of about 250 million L of water (66 million gallons) from 25 °C to 100 °C. By comparison, about 1.65 million g of octane must be burned to release the same amount of energy.

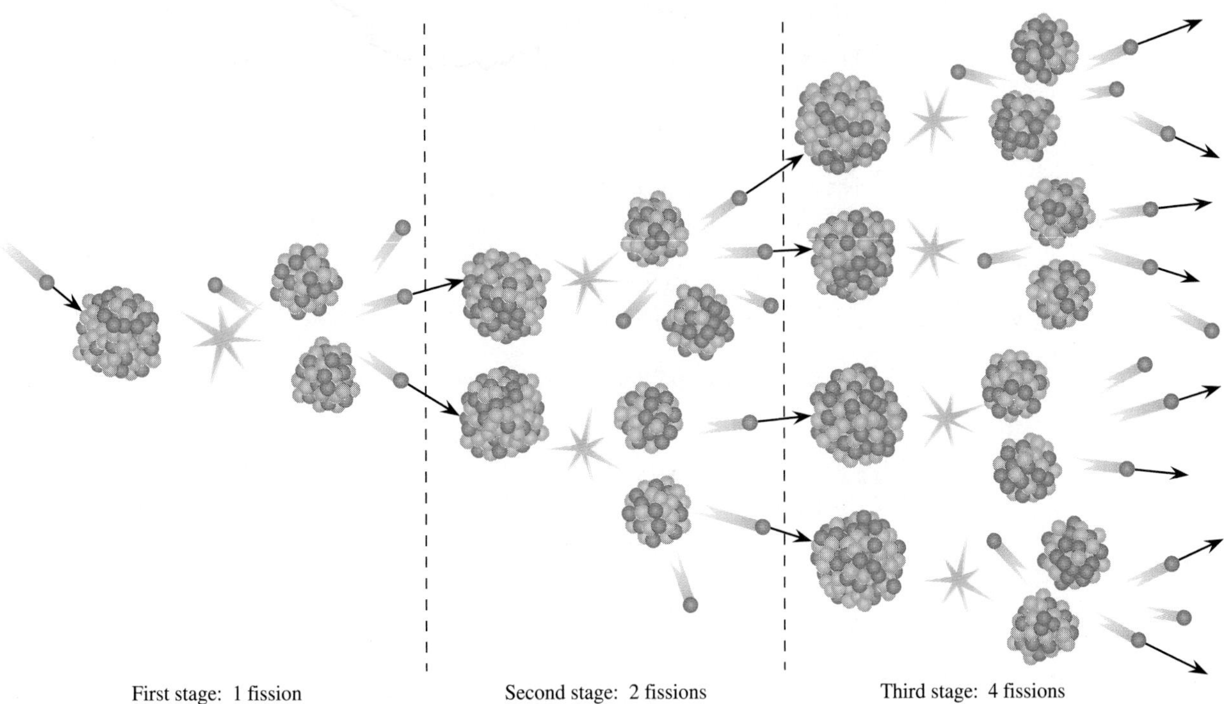

FIGURE 19-10
Schematic view of the start of a fission chain reaction. The first neutron causes fission, which generates additional neutrons. They cause more fission, and the chain continues to grow if more than one neutron, on average, is captured for every fission event.

On average, each fission event releases 2.5 neutrons. Some of these neutrons are recaptured by other fissionable nuclei, causing further fission events. When the amount of fissionable material is small, most neutrons escape from the sample, and only a few neutrons are recaptured. Increasing the amount of fissionable material increases the likelihood that neutrons will be recaptured and cause additional fissions. The **critical mass** is defined to be the amount of fissionable material that is just large enough to recapture one neutron, on average, for every fission event. As long as the amount of fissionable material is less than the critical mass, less than one neutron is recaptured, on average, for every fission that occurs. Under these subcritical conditions, the rate of fission events does not grow, and the *rate* of energy release remains low.

A sample behaves quite differently when the amount of fissionable material is larger than the critical mass. Above the critical mass, more than one neutron, on average, is recaptured for every fission that occurs. Now the number of fission events grows rapidly. For example, consider what happens when two neutrons are recaptured from each fission event. As shown in Figure 19-10, the neutrons produced by the first fission event trigger fragmentation of two additional nuclei. Neutrons from these two fission events are recaptured by four additional nuclei, and this fission cascade goes on, doubling in each successive round. The result is a "chain" reaction that grows quickly to explosive proportions.

The recapture ratio does not have to be two for this multiplying effect to occur. Any recapture value larger than 1.0 results in explosive growth of the fission chain. The critical mass is called "critical" because any mass greater than this value sustains a chain reaction and may explode.

NUCLEAR WEAPONS

The potential of nuclear fission was first realized in the atomic bomb. In 1945, the United States inaugurated the nuclear age by dropping two bombs of unprecedented power on Hiroshima and Nagasaki, Japan. Both were fission weapons. The Hiroshima bomb contained ^{235}U, whereas the Nagasaki bomb contained ^{239}Pu. These tremendously destructive weapons had been developed under total secrecy in a wartime project that involved the best American physicists and chemists.

The central feature of a fission explosion is a growing chain of fission reactions. There are three requirements:

1. The fissionable nuclide must be concentrated enough so that it is capable of becoming critical.
2. Subcritical portions of this fissionable nuclide must be combined into a critical mass.
3. The critical mass must be held together long enough for the chain to multiply to immense size.

The second and third requirements posed engineering problems that were met by a carefully designed detonation of a chemical explosive. This explosion propelled subcritical masses of fissionable material together and confined them while the fission chain multiplied. The first requirement, on the other hand, posed formidable chemical problems. Of the three nuclides that can serve as nuclear fuels, ^{239}Pu, ^{233}U, and ^{235}U, only the latter exists in nature. However, naturally occurring uranium contains only 0.72% ^{235}U, which is much too dilute to use in a bomb. At this concentration, nearly all the neutrons produced by fission of ^{235}U are recaptured by ^{238}U, which does not undergo fission. Thus no mass of natural uranium is enough to be critical. Before a bomb could be constructed from uranium-235, therefore, a way had to be found to increase the percentage of ^{235}U in natural uranium. Neither plutonium-239 nor uranium-233 are naturally occurring nuclides, so a bomb could not be made from these materials without first finding a means of synthesizing these nuclides.

In Chapter 5, we showed that the rate of diffusion of a gas is inversely proportional to the square root of its mass, and two gases diffuse with relative rates given by Equation 5-3:

$$\frac{Rate_A}{Rate_B} = \left(\frac{MM_B}{MM_A}\right)^{1/2}$$

How can ^{235}U be isolated from an isotopic mixture of ^{235}U and ^{238}U? Because isotopes have identical chemical reactivity, they cannot be separated by chemical reactions. Thus it is necessary to use a physical technique based on the small mass difference between the two isotopes. One way to accomplish this is to allow a gas to diffuse through a porous filter. Because light molecules move faster than heavy molecules, the gas that passes through the filter at the beginning of the separation process will be slightly enriched in the component with the lower molar mass.

Uranium hexafluoride can be made by reacting elemental uranium with fluorine to make UF_4 and then treating this product with ClF_3:

$$U + 2\,F_2 \longrightarrow UF_4$$
$$UF_4 + ClF_3 \longrightarrow UF_6 + ClF$$

Like other metals, uranium is not a gas except at very high temperatures. To concentrate ^{235}U by gaseous diffusion, it is necessary to prepare a uranium compound that can be vaporized at a reasonable temperature. One of the few uranium compounds that vaporizes at moderate temperature is UF_6. When UF_6 gas diffuses through porous filters, the first-emerging fraction is slightly enriched in $^{235}UF_6$. The molar mass ratio is only 1.0086 for $^{238}UF_6$ and $^{235}UF_6$, and diffusion rates vary as the square root of this ratio, 1.0043. Thus a sample of UF_6 must pass through thousands of filters before the isotopic composition of the gas is sufficiently enriched in $^{235}UF_6$.

After purification, enriched UF_6 can be reduced to pure uranium metal in a two-step process at temperatures greater than 900 K:

$$UF_{6\,(s)} + H_{2\,(g)} + 2\,H_2O_{\,(g)} \rightarrow UO_{2\,(s)} + 6\,HF_{\,(g)}$$

$$UO_{2\,(s)} + 2\,Mg_{\,(l)} \rightarrow 2\,MgO_{\,(s)} + U_{\,(l)}$$

These reactions look simple, but the materials are highly corrosive at the elevated temperatures required for the process. As a result, special corrosion-resistant materials had to be developed and tested before isotopic enrichment could succeed.

The production of ^{239}Pu presented other challenges because it is a synthetic isotope, produced by the neutron bombardment of ^{238}U. The first nuclear reactor, constructed at the University of Chicago in 1942, was designed and used for this purpose. Significant amounts of plutonium form when natural uranium is placed in a reactor and bombarded with neutrons. The resulting mixture can be treated by appropriate chemical methods to recover the plutonium in pure form.

NUCLEAR REACTORS

A nuclear bomb is a frightening example of the enormous amount of energy released by nuclear fission. A bomb, however, is not the only way to extract the energy produced by nuclear fission. If, instead, the rate of fission is controlled by adjusting the number of emitted neutrons that are recaptured by fissionable nuclei, nuclear fission can be used to generate electrical power. Many countries generate some of their electricity this way, since the fission of just 1 g of ^{235}U releases as much energy as the burning of 430 gallons of gasoline or 6.0 tons of coal.

Nuclear power plants, such as the one diagrammed in Figure 19-11, use the energy released in fission to generate electricity. The fission reaction takes place in a core heated by the released energy. A circulating fluid transfers this thermal energy out of the core to a heat exchanger, where the energy is used to convert water into steam. The steam drives a turbine connected to an electrical generator. Cooling water must be supplied to recondense the steam.

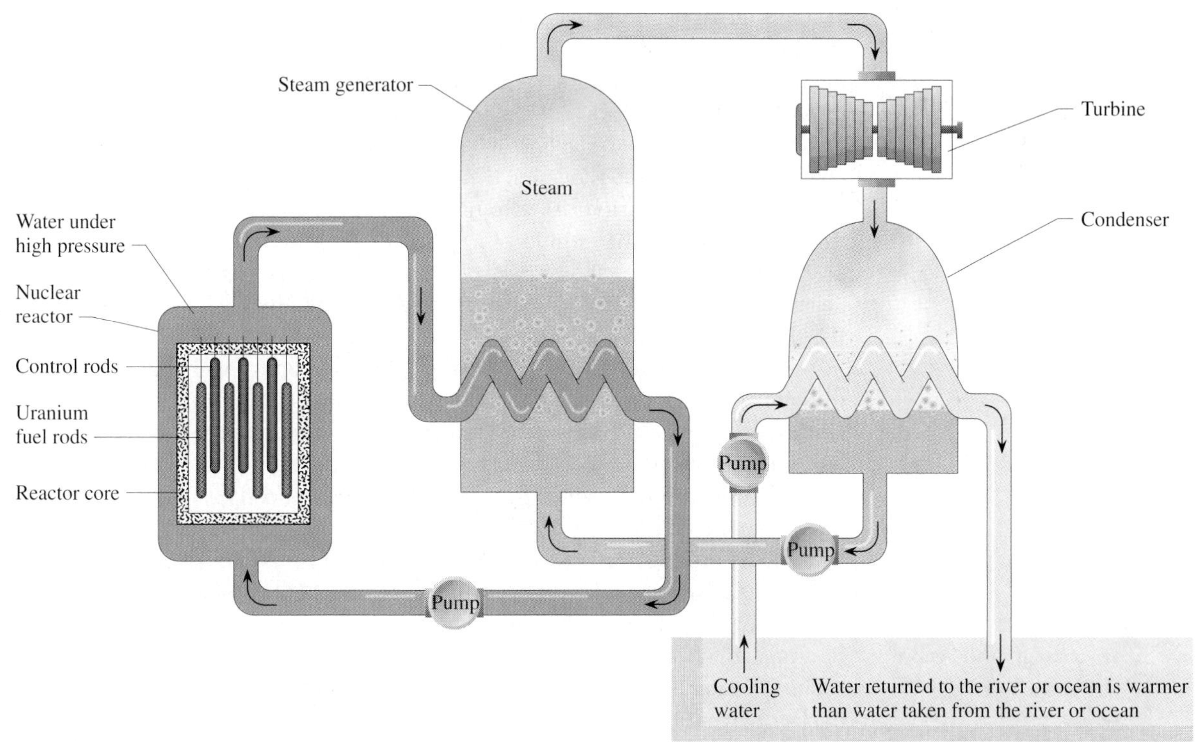

FIGURE 19-11
Schematic view of a nuclear power plant. The energy source is the core, in which a fission reaction occurs. The rest of the plant is designed to transfer the energy released during fission and convert it into electricity.

1. **Nuclear reactor:** Water under high pressure carries heat generated in the nuclear reactor core to the steam generator.
2. **Steam generator:** Heat from the reactor vaporizes water in the steam generator, creating steam.
3. **Turbine and condenser:** Steam from the steam generator powers a turbine, producing useable electricity. The condenser uses cooling water from a river or ocean to re-condense the steam from the turbine.

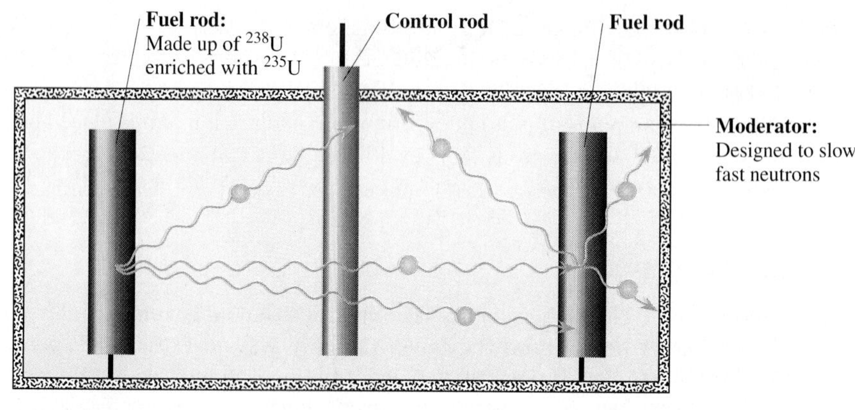
Fuel rod:
Made up of ^{238}U enriched with ^{235}U
Control rod
Fuel rod
Moderator:
Designed to slow fast neutrons
1. Fission of a ^{235}U in the fuel rod emits three fast neutrons
2. The control rod captures one of the neutrons
3. A ^{238}U in the fuel rod captures a second neutron; a ^{235}U captures the third neutron, leading to another fission event

FIGURE 19-12
The neutron processes occurring in the core of a fission reactor. Fission of ^{235}U gives from one to four fast neutrons, which are slowed down by the moderator. Each neutron is captured by another nuclide. In this sketch, three neutrons have been produced. One is captured by the control rod, one by ^{238}U in the fuel rod, and one causes another fission event.

The turbine and generator components of a nuclear power plant have exact counterparts in power plants fueled by fossil fuels. The uniqueness of the nuclear power plant lies in its core. The core is a nuclear reactor where fission takes place under conditions that keep the reactor operating just at the critical level. The core contains three parts: fuel rods, moderators, and control rods. To explain their functions, we must examine the flow of neutrons within the core, which is shown in Figure 19-12.

The fate of neutrons must be controlled carefully so that fission is sustained at a steady rate that produces enough energy to run a generator, but not enough to destroy the reactor. A nuclear reactor runs on its nuclear fuel rods, which contain fissionable material such as uranium that has been enriched in ^{235}U. The fuel rods contain more than the critical mass of fuel, but the rate of fission is kept under control by movable control rods. These rods contain ^{112}Cd, which has a very high affinity for neutrons but does not undergo fission. As a result, the control rods act as a neutron "sponge," capturing neutrons that would otherwise trigger additional fission events. When pushed into the reactor, the control rods capture more neutrons, and the rate of fission decreases. When pulled out, the control rods capture fewer neutrons, and the rate of fission increases.

To start up a reactor, its core is allowed to heat up by withdrawing the control rods until the recapture ratio is slightly greater than 1.0. When the optimum operating temperature is reached, the control rods are inserted until the capture ratio is exactly one, and the reaction proceeds at a steady rate. To shut down a reactor, its control rods are fully inserted, reducing the recapture ratio to nearly zero.

The moderator component of a reactor slows neutrons without capturing them. Moderators are used because the neutrons released in fission have such high kinetic energies that they are difficult to capture. The critical mass of a nuclear fuel is much smaller for slow neutrons than for fast neutrons, so considerably less fuel is needed in a moderated reactor. Graphite (^{12}C) or "heavy" water are good moderators, but ordinary water is a reasonable and inexpensive moderator that is used in many nuclear power plants.

"Heavy" water contains an enhanced amount of the heavier stable isotope of hydrogen, ^2H. Heavy water is a superior moderator to ordinary water because ^2H is much less likely to capture neutrons than ^1H.

In a nuclear power plant, heat must be transferred from the core to the turbines without any transfer of matter. This is because fission and neutron capture generate lethal radioactive products that cannot be allowed to escape from the core. A heat-transfer fluid such as liquid sodium metal flows around the core, absorbing the heat produced by nuclear fission. This hot fluid then flows through a steam generator, where its heat energy is used to vaporize water. After steam has been produced, its energy is used to produce electricity in a conventional steam turbine that has the same design as the steam turbines in fossil fuel power plants.

The radioactive materials that are an inevitable byproduct of nuclear fission are life-threatening. To operate safely, therefore, a nuclear power plant must confine all its radioactive products until they can be disposed of safely. Many people question whether containment and disposal can be guaranteed. Even though radioactivity is fully controlled under normal operating conditions, how to prevent accidents and how to dispose of the radioactive waste remain the subjects of intense debate.

We describe the lethal characteristics of nuclear radiation in Section 19.8.

The main danger in the operation of a nuclear power plant is potential loss of control over the nuclear reaction. If the core overheats, it may either explode or "melt down." In either event, radioactive materials escape from the reactor to contaminate the environment. Designers attempt to make nuclear reactors "fail-safe" by providing mechanisms that automatically shut the core down on overheating. One way this has been done is to design the control rods to fall into the core if their control mechanism fails.

Despite such safeguards, nuclear accidents have occurred. The worst occurred in 1986 at Chernobyl in the Ukraine, shown in Figure 19-13. Engineers who were not well trained in nuclear power turned off many safety systems during a test of the reactor. When the reactor cooled more than anticipated, most of the control rods were removed. In the absence of emergency cooling systems, the reactor surged out of control. The fuel rods melted and mixed with superheated water, which rapidly boiled, building up a high pressure of steam. This blew off the top of the reactor facility, spreading substantial amounts of radioactive material into the atmosphere. In addition, the steam reacted with zirconium and graphite in the reactor, producing hydrogen gas and starting a fire that released more radioactive material. Contamination was most severe within 30 km of the plant, where radioactivity levels became so high that the entire population had to be relocated. However, significant contamination was also detected 1000 km away in Germany, and small amounts of radioactivity attributable to Chernobyl appeared throughout the Northern Hemisphere.

FIGURE 19-13
Aerial view of the Chernobyl nuclear power plant, site of a major nuclear accident in 1986. The graphite core of the disabled reactor burned for more than 3 days. After this accident, all those living near the plant had to be relocated because of dangerous levels of radioactivity.

Nuclear power plants in the United States are supposed to be designed well enough to prevent an accident as serious as the one at Chernobyl. Nevertheless, the Three Mile Island plant in Pennsylvania, an aerial view of which is shown in Figure 19-14, experienced a partial meltdown in 1979. This accident was caused by a malfunctioning coolant system. A small amount of radioactivity was released into the environment, but because there was no explosion, the extent of contamination was minimal.

Even when operated safely, nuclear power plants produce long-lived radioactive wastes that must be sequestered from the biosphere until their radioactivity diminishes to acceptable levels. Plutonium-239, which is formed in nuclear fuel rods when ^{238}U captures neutrons and decays, is a particularly dangerous nuclear waste because it is extremely toxic and has a half-life of nearly 25,000 years. In Europe, nuclear waste is placed far underground in abandoned salt mines. Deep-sea burial and ejection into outer space have also been proposed. Antinuclear activists contend that no current technology is acceptable, since we have no proof that radioactive material can be contained for the thousands of years that are necessary for these dangerous materials to decompose.

Modern nuclear reactors are highly technological, carefully engineered creations of advanced human societies, so it may appear as a surprise that a nuclear reactor could result from natural conditions. Box 19-3 describes evidence indicating that such a natural nuclear reactor did indeed once exist.

FIGURE 19-14
Aerial view of the Three Mile Island power plant, site of a minor nuclear accident in 1979.

BOX 19-3

OKLO, A NATURAL NUCLEAR REACTOR

Naturally occurring uranium mined today contains 99.28% ^{238}U and 0.72% ^{235}U. This is too low a percentage to sustain a fission reaction. In the past, however, the percentage of uranium-235 was higher than it is today because ^{235}U has a shorter half-life than ^{238}U (7.0×10^8 years compared with 4.5×10^9 years). In fact, we can calculate from these half-lives that 1.8 billion years ago, ^{235}U made up 3% of natural uranium. This is comparable to the enrichment levels used in nuclear fuels. Thus long ago the composition of uranium ores was such that a self-sustaining nuclear reaction could have occurred.

But did this ever happen? A sustained reaction requires a neutron recapture ratio of at least one. In addition to enrichment in ^{235}U, there must be a high degree of purity to minimize the fraction of neutrons captured by other nuclides. A sustained reaction also requires a moderator to slow the neutrons before they escape from the uranium mass. These are unique conditions, but at least one deposit of uranium ore has characteristics indicating that, long ago, it operated as a natural nuclear reactor.

At Oklo in the Gabon Republic near the west coast of equatorial Africa, there is a mine with uranium deposits that are about 1.8 billion years old. Thus this uranium originally contained the 3% abundance of ^{235}U needed for a sustained reaction. Currently, the deposits in this mine differ from other uranium deposits in two ways that indicate that Oklo experienced sustained fission at one time. First, the ^{235}U content is slightly depleted, and second, there are unusual amounts of elements with mass numbers between 80 and 150.

The usual percentage of ^{235}U is 0.7207%, but the Oklo deposits contain 0.7071% of this isotope. This difference is small, but significant, because it indicates that, at some time in the past, ^{235}U was consumed faster than its spontaneous decay rate. The question is whether or not that faster rate was caused by sustained fission.

What convinces scientists that sustained fission once occurred at Oklo is the presence of characteristic fission products in the ore. Elements of mass numbers between 75 and 160 occur in the ore in larger amounts than elsewhere. Furthermore, mass analysis of the elements in Oklo ore shows that they are distributed in the characteristic pattern shown in Figure 19-9. This isotopic "signature," which is not found in any other naturally occurring materials, is so characteristic that it has convinced most scientists that the ore deposits at Oklo once formed a huge nuclear reactor.

From the size of the ore deposit and the extent of ^{235}U depletion, scientists estimate that Oklo functioned as a natural nuclear reactor for about 100,000 years, during which time it generated 5×10^{14} kJ of energy. This is an average power output of about 150 kilowatts per year, which is about enough to meet the needs of 10 present-day Americans.

SECTION EXERCISES

19.5.1 Generally, nuclides that are fission products have atomic masses that are 0.09 g/mol less than their mass number. ^{106}Ru, for example, has a molar mass of 105.91 g/mol. Using this general value, calculate the mass loss and energy release for ^{235}U fission that releases one neutron, two neutrons, and three neutrons.

19.5.2 Calculate the isotopic abundances of naturally occurring uranium 10^8 years ago. (*Hint:* Start with a convenient amount of uranium of present-day abundances, and use half-lives to calculate the amounts that were present 10^8 years ago.)

19.6 NUCLEAR FUSION

Fission occurs for only a few rare, extremely heavy nuclides. Fusion, on the other hand, is possible for abundant light nuclides such as ^{1}H. Moreover, some fusion reactions release more energy per unit mass than fission reactions. Fission of ^{235}U releases 7.9×10^{7} kJ/g, for example, whereas the fusion of two isotopes of hydrogen, deuterium and tritium, releases 3.4×10^{8} kJ/g. Another attractive feature of fusion reactions is that the product nuclides are usually stable, so smaller amounts of radioactive byproducts result from fusion than from fission.

The fusion reaction of tritium and deuterium is:
$^{3}_{1}H + ^{2}_{1}H \rightarrow ^{4}_{2}He + ^{1}_{0}n$

THE THRESHOLD FOR FUSION

The major impediment to fusion reactions is that the reacting nuclei must have very high kinetic energies to overcome the coulombic repulsion between positive particles. The fusion of two hydrogen nuclei has the lowest possible coulombic barrier because it involves two $Z = 1$ nuclei. Nevertheless, this reaction requires kinetic energies equivalent to 10^{7} K or greater. As Z increases, so does this energy requirement; the fusion of two ^{12}C nuclei requires kinetic energies equivalent to 10^{9} K.

There are several ways to produce nuclei with enough kinetic energy to fuse. One method uses particle accelerators to generate small quantities of fast-moving nuclei. These are very useful for *studying* fusion reactions, but the scale of fusion events in these experiments is too small to release useful amounts of energy. Another way to induce fusion uses the energy released in gravitational attraction to generate a temperature hot enough to start the reaction. As described in Section 19.7, stars, including the sun, operate in this way. A third way is the fusion bomb, which uses a fission bomb to produce a temperature high enough for fusion. None of these provides a method for harnessing fusion as a practical source of power on Earth. However, scientists have proposed that radiation might be able to initiate a useful fusion reaction by heating a gaseous plasma confined in a magnetic field. If successful, this method may harness fusion as a source of power.

FUSION BOMBS

A "hydrogen bomb," which uses nuclear fusion for its destructive power, is three bombs in one. A conventional explosive charge triggers a fission bomb, which in turn triggers a fusion reaction. Such bombs can be considerably more powerful than fission bombs because they can incorporate larger masses of nuclear fuel. In a fission bomb, no component of fissionable material can exceed the critical mass. In fusion, there is no critical mass because fusion begins at a threshold *temperature* and is independent of the *amount* of nuclear fuel present. Thus there is no theoretical limit on how much nuclear fuel can be squeezed into a fusion bomb.

Hydrogen bombs contain ^{2}H, ^{3}H, and ^{6}Li. The energy released in the fission explosion heats the two hydrogen isotopes hot enough to fuse:

$$^{2}_{1}H + ^{3}_{1}H \rightarrow ^{4}_{2}He + ^{1}_{0}n \qquad \Delta E = -1.7 \times 10^{9} \text{ kJ/mol}$$

Lithium captures neutrons from this reaction in another energy-releasing process:

$$^{6}_{3}Li + ^{1}_{0}n \rightarrow (^{7}_{3}Li) \rightarrow ^{4}_{2}He + ^{3}_{1}H \qquad \Delta E = -4.6 \times 10^{8} \text{ kJ/mol}$$

Tritium nuclei produced in this reaction can fuse with additional deuterons, thus beginning the process again. All these processes occur in an extremely short time to release such an immense amount of energy that the bomb is blown apart.

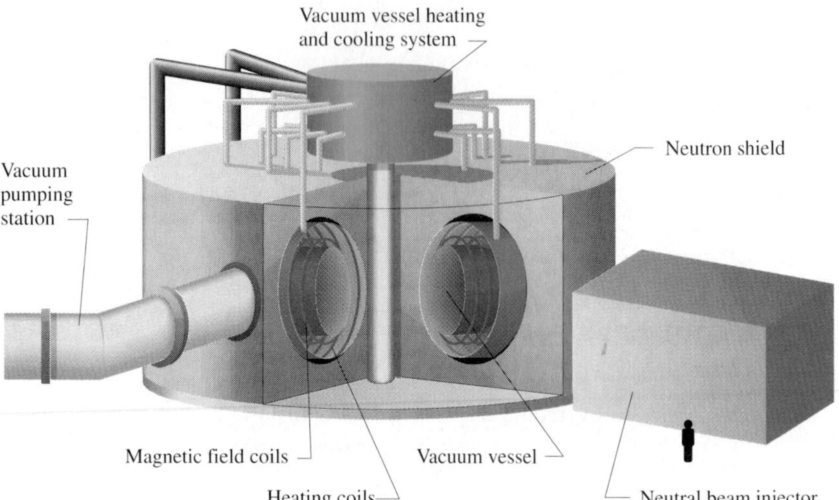

FIGURE 19-15
A version of a fusion reactor that has been the subject of intense development efforts is the Tokomac, an artist's conception of which is shown here.

CONTROLLED FUSION

A long-standing goal of nuclear science has been to harness the energy of nuclear fusion in a sustained process. The technological problems are immense, however, because the fusing material must be confined to a volume small enough to generate high nuclear densities and many nuclear collisions. Unfortunately, all materials vaporize at temperatures well below that required to sustain fusion reactions, so containers that would withstand sustained fusion cannot be built.

The approach most often taken to address these problems is to use a hot, ionized gaseous plasma that contains cations of ^{2}H, ^{3}H, and ^{6}Li, along with enough electrons to maintain charge neutrality. This plasma is heated intensely, usually by powerful laser beams. To keep the plasma from flying apart, it is confined by a toroidal magnetic field. Figure 19-15 shows an artist's drawing of such a plasmoidal fusion machine.

A plasma is a high-temperature ionized gas consisting of free electrons and nuclei.

Fusion cannot become a practical source of energy unless the energy released by fusion exceeds the energy used to heat and confine the plasma. Unfortunately, the energy input requirement is substantial, even in small-scale experimental studies. The best experiments conducted so far have managed to achieve fusion but not sustain it long enough to achieve any net production of energy.

Assuming that a sustained fusion reaction is eventually achieved, some way must be found to harness its energy output. Because the field confining the plasma prevents the escape of charged particles, most of the energy output of the reactor is expected to be photons, ranging in energy from the infrared to γ-rays. These photons will have to be absorbed by a suitable working material that converts their energy, directly or indirectly, into electricity.

PROSPECTS FOR NUCLEAR POWER

At the outset of the nuclear age, scientists had high hopes that nuclear power would be able to supply most of the world's energy needs. Fifty years later, however, those hopes have yet to be realized. In the meantime, society consumes ever-increasing amounts of fossil fuels and hydroelectric power. Solar energy, although unlimited on the time scale of human existence, is difficult to concentrate sufficiently for high-density needs such as aircraft propulsion or aluminum refining. More exotic sources such as geothermal or tidal energy remain problematic.

In France and Japan, fission power from nuclear reactors provides two thirds or more of overall energy needs. In the United States, however, the industry has not grown beyond about 10% of total energy production because of strong public opposition based on the dangers of radioactivity.

There are fewer environmental concerns over fusion power than fission power, but the feasibility of controlled fusion remains uncertain because it can occur only on a gargantuan scale. Fusion occurs only at extreme temperatures that require high-intensity power sources, and confinement of the plasma demands high-intensity fields beyond the reach of current technology. Immense developmental expenditures will be required to overcome these limitations. With such high resource requirements, just one type of design, the Tokomac shown in Figure 19-15, has received the bulk of research funding. Still, it is not clear that this design will be successful.

Controversies over nuclear power have no easy solutions. Proponents point out that oil and coal both contribute to the greenhouse effect, which may have far-reaching and disastrous consequences in coming decades. They also point to an energy shortfall as nonrenewable fossil fuels become depleted. Opponents contend that radioactive wastes are too lethal for too long. They argue that energy conservation coupled with the development of alternate fuels is the only responsible way to prevent an energy crisis. Both points of view have some validity, which makes it risky either to curtail nuclear power or to develop it further.

SECTION EXERCISES

19.6.1 One proposal for controlled fusion involves using an accelerator to propel deuterons into a lithium target, inducing the following reactions:

$$^{7}_{3}\text{Li} + ^{2}_{1}\text{H} \longrightarrow ^{8}_{3}\text{Li} + ^{1}_{1}\text{H}$$

$$^{8}_{3}\text{Li} \longrightarrow ^{0}_{-1}\beta + 2\,^{4}_{2}\text{He}$$

(a) The first reaction can be viewed as the transfer of a neutron. Draw a nuclear picture illustrating this reaction.

(b) The reaction has a barrier that is 50% of the calculated coulombic barrier. What minimum kinetic energy must the deuterons have, if the radius of ^{2}H is 1.4×10^{-3} pm and that of ^{7}Li is 2.4×10^{-3} pm? (Refer to Section 19.2 to calculate the coulombic barrier.)

(c) Use the following isotopic masses, all in grams per mole, to calculate the energy changes for each step of this fusion reaction:

^{7}Li	^{8}Li	^{1}H	^{2}H	^{4}He
7.016005	8.022488	1.007822	2.0141022	4.0026036

19.6.2 Most fusion schemes use ^{2}H as a fuel. Terrestrial hydrogen contains 0.015% of this isotope. Assuming that all the ^{2}H could be extracted from water, what volume of liquid water has to be treated to obtain 5.0 kg of ^{2}H?

19.6.3 If 5.0 kg of ^{2}H is completely consumed in the reaction of Exercise 19.6.1, how much energy can be produced?

19.7 STELLAR NUCLEAR REACTIONS

The sun and all other stars produce energy at a prodigious rate. This sustained energy output is a consequence of nuclear fusion. The stars are fueled by nuclear reactions in which lighter nuclei are fused into heavier ones. Over time, stars evolve through several stages, including stellar explosions. The products of a stellar explosion can form stars of more complex composition. Three distinct generations of stars have been identified.

Nuclear reactions do not occur below a threshold temperature, so a cloud of gas must be heated by some nonnuclear process before it can become a star. This nonnuclear process is gravitational attraction. In outer space, any cloud of material collapses on itself under the force of gravity. The material heats up during collapse, since atoms move faster and faster as their gravitational potential energy is converted into kinetic energy of motion. The temperature attained in the collapsing cloud increases with the total mass of the cloud, and any mass larger than about 0.1 solar mass eventually reaches a temperature sufficient to initiate the fusion of hydrogen nuclei.

One solar mass is the mass of our sun, which is about 2×10^{30} kg. Thus about 2×10^{29} kg of hydrogen is required to form a star. Jupiter, the largest planet in our solar system, has a mass just below the threshold for star formation.

FIRST-GENERATION STARS

Astrophysicists believe that the first stars in the universe formed from collapsing clouds of protons and electrons. Nuclear fusion begins in such a **first-generation star** when the interior temperature reaches 4×10^7 K. Above this temperature, protons combine to yield helium nuclei, releasing about 2.5×10^9 kJ per mole of ^{4}He formed:

$$^{1}_{1}\text{H} + ^{1}_{1}\text{H} \rightarrow \left(^{2}_{2}\text{He}\right) \rightarrow ^{2}_{1}\text{H} + ^{0}_{1}\beta^{+}$$

$$^{2}_{1}\text{H} + ^{1}_{1}\text{H} \rightarrow ^{3}_{2}\text{He} + \gamma$$

$$^{0}_{1}\beta^{+} + ^{0}_{-1}\text{e} \rightarrow 2\,\gamma$$

$$^{3}_{2}\text{He} + ^{3}_{2}\text{He} \rightarrow \left(^{6}_{4}\text{Be}\right) \rightarrow ^{4}_{2}\text{He} + 2\,^{1}_{1}\text{H}$$

The net reaction converts protons and electrons into helium nuclei and radiation:

$$4\,^{1}_{1}\text{H} + 2\,^{0}_{-1}\text{e} \rightarrow ^{4}_{2}\text{He} + 6\,\gamma$$

Stars that are fueled by the fusion of hydrogen are called *main sequence stars.* The appearance of a main sequence star depends on its mass; a higher-mass star attains a higher temperature than a lower-mass star.

As a young star ages, its ratio of helium to hydrogen increases. Eventually, insufficient hydrogen is left to sustain this sequence of nuclear reactions. The time it takes for a star to consume most of its hydrogen depends on its original mass, but it is about 10^{10} years for a star with one solar mass. When the hydrogen is sufficiently depleted, gravitational forces take over once more. The star then collapses until its temperature reaches about 10^8 K. At this temperature, a new fusion reaction begins in which helium nuclei fuse to form beryllium-8:

$$^{4}_{2}\text{He} + ^{4}_{2}\text{He} \rightarrow \left(^{8}_{4}\text{Be}\right)$$

$$\left(^{8}_{4}\text{Be}\right) + ^{4}_{2}\text{He} \rightarrow ^{12}_{6}\text{C} + \gamma$$

In this sequence the ^{8}Be nuclide decomposes back to two helium nuclei unless it collides with a third ^{4}He before it can disintegrate. When it collides with a third helium nucleus, fusion occurs to form carbon-12, a process that is exothermic by about 7.7×10^8 kJ/mol. As ^{12}C builds up, it also reacts with ^{4}He:

A star undergoing helium fusion has a dense, hot core and a large, cooler outer mantle. These stars appear large and red, so they are called *red giants.*

$$^{12}_{6}\text{C} + ^{4}_{2}\text{He} \rightarrow ^{16}_{8}\text{O} + \gamma$$

About 10^8 years after fusion of helium begins, a star also runs out of ^4He fuel. When this happens, the star enters a new stage of gravitational collapse until the temperature increases to about 10^9 K. This triggers an entirely new set of nuclear reactions between nuclides of carbon and oxygen. The following are some examples:

$$^{12}_{6}C + ^{12}_{6}C \rightarrow ^{23}_{11}Na + ^{1}_{1}H$$

$$^{12}_{6}C + ^{12}_{6}C \rightarrow ^{20}_{10}Ne + ^{4}_{2}He$$

$$^{12}_{6}C + ^{16}_{8}O \rightarrow ^{24}_{12}Mg + ^{4}_{2}He$$

$$^{16}_{8}O + ^{16}_{8}O \rightarrow ^{31}_{15}P + ^{1}_{1}H$$

As a result of these and other fusion reactions, the star eventually contains nuclides with Z and A values all the way up to iron-56, which is the most stable of all nuclides.

Some stars become inherently unstable at this stage of their evolution. They generate energy more rapidly than it can be dissipated, so the star explodes like a giant hydrogen bomb. Its inventory of nuclides, ranging from hydrogen to iron, is hurled into space. These explosions, called **supernovae,** have been observed by astronomers over the centuries, and the debris from supernovae explosions have been detected at numerous locations in the heavens. Johannes Kepler and Tycho Brahe, who were two of the most famous astronomers of the late sixteenth century, each observed a supernova, Brahe in 1572 and Kepler in 1604. Supernovae are still being observed. A photograph of a supernova that appeared in 1987 is shown in Figure 19-16.

The larger a star, the more likely it is to become unstable and explode. Stars with masses less than about 1.4 solar mass units do not explode. They shrink and cool instead, becoming white dwarfs that radiate energy relatively slowly and have lifetimes of about 10^{11} years.

The drawing in Figure 19-17 shows the evolutionary stages that we have just described for a first-generation star.

SECOND-GENERATION STARS

Explosions of first-generation stars spew nuclides from $Z = 1$ to $Z = 26$ into interstellar space. There, this matter mixes with interstellar hydrogen, and eventually enough matter clumps together under the force of gravity to collapse and form a **second-generation star.** Young second-generation stars, like young first-generation stars, contain large amounts of hydrogen. Unlike first-generation stars, however, they also contain higher-Z nuclides. One of these, ^{12}C, catalyzes hydrogen-to-helium fusion. Protons add to ^{12}C in a sequence that ultimately produces ^4He.

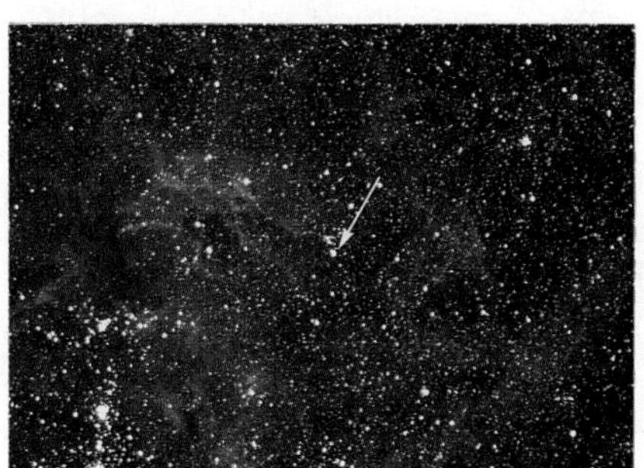
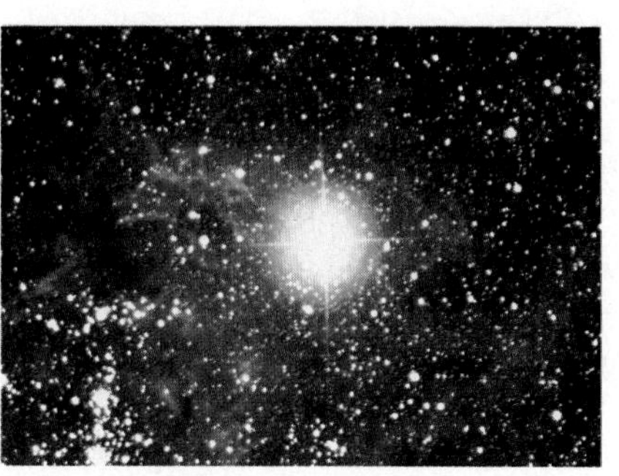

FIGURE 19-16

In 1987 a supernova appeared just 160,000 light years from Earth. The two photographs are the same region of space. On the left, the arrow points to the star that exploded. It had four times the mass of our sun. The picture on the right shows the aftermath of the explosion.

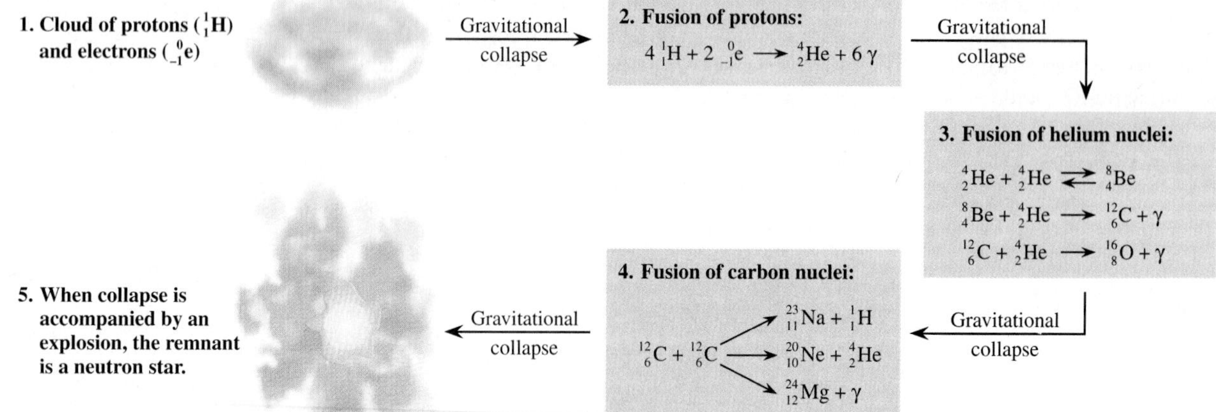

FIGURE 19-17
Schematic depiction of the evolutionary stages of a first-generation star. Gravitational collapse is required to heat stellar material enough for fusion to begin. The energy released during fusion then keeps the star from collapsing further until its nuclear fuel is consumed. There are three different stages of fusion, each of which consumes a different nuclear fuel.

Here are the reactions:

$$^1_1H + {}^{12}_6C \rightarrow {}^{13}_6C + {}^0_1\beta^+$$

$$^0_1\beta^+ + {}^{0}_{-1}e \rightarrow 2\gamma$$

$$^1_1H + {}^{13}_6C \rightarrow {}^{14}_6C + {}^0_1\beta^+$$

$$^0_1\beta^+ + {}^{0}_{-1}e \rightarrow 2\gamma$$

$$^1_1H + {}^{14}_6C \rightarrow {}^{15}_7N$$

$$^1_1H + {}^{15}_7N \rightarrow {}^{12}_6C + {}^4_2He$$

$$\textit{Net: } 4\,^1_1H + 2\,^{0}_{-1}e \rightarrow {}^4_2He + 4\gamma$$

When most of the hydrogen has been consumed, a second-generation star collapses until it is hot enough for helium fusion to occur. Now a larger range of reactions takes place because nuclides such as ^{13}C generate neutrons when they fuse with ^4He. These neutrons, in turn, are captured by other nuclides:

$$^{13}_6C + {}^4_2He \rightarrow {}^{16}_8O + {}^1_0n$$

$$^{56}_{26}Fe + {}^1_0n \rightarrow {}^{57}_{27}Co + {}^{0}_{-1}\beta$$

Sequential capture of neutrons and β-emission results in nuclides heavier than iron. Even though nuclear stability decreases with Z beyond $Z = 26$, neutron capture, with or without β-emission, is always exothermic for nuclides lying within the belt of stability. Thus all possible stable nuclides can form during the lifetime of a second-generation star.

Like first-generation stars, second-generation stars often become unstable when they reach the carbon-burning stage. If they explode in supernovae, their nuclear debris includes their content of heavier nuclides. In addition, supernovae explosions are accompanied by large numbers of neutrons that can be captured by lighter nuclides in the exploding star to form still more heavy nuclides.

Planet Earth contains a significant abundance of elements all the way up to $Z = 92$. This indicates that our solar system resulted from the gravitational collapse of a cloud of matter that included debris from second-generation stellar supernovae. Thus our sun most likely is a **third-generation star.**

The reactions that we have described are just a sample of those that produce heavy nuclides from lighter ones. The production of heavy nuclides in the interior of a star involves many nuclear reactions besides the ones given in this outline because the interiors of stars provide a rich environment for fusion reactions. Additionally, the synthesis of nuclides may occur in space when cosmic radiation encounters the debris from supernovae. Although we know about the composition of various stars and the energetics of nuclear reactions, there is much about the composition of the universe that remains to be discovered.

SECTION EXERCISES

19.7.1 To show how zinc could form in a second-generation star, write a sequence of nuclear reactions that starts at ^{56}Fe and ends at ^{70}Zn and is composed entirely of neutron capture and β-emission. Your sequence should stay within the belt of stability depicted in Figure 19-2.

19.7.2 Describe how the compositions of planets around a second-generation star differ from that of the Earth. Could life as we know it exist on such a planet? Why or why not?

19.8 EFFECTS OF RADIATION

The nuclear explosions that devastated Hiroshima and Nagasaki killed 100,000 to 200,000 people instantaneously. Probably an equal number died later, victims of the radiation released in those explosions. Millions of people were exposed to the radioactivity released by the accident at the Chernobyl nuclear power plant. The full health effects of that accident may never be known, but 31 people died of radiation sickness within a few weeks, and many more will develop cancers caused by their exposure to radiation. In facilities that use radioisotopes, workers monitor their exposure to radiation continually, and they must be rotated to other duties if their total exposure exceeds prescribed levels. Clearly, exposure to nuclear radiation can be highly damaging.

RADIATION DAMAGE

Nuclear radiation causes damage because of its high energy content. As it passes through matter, radiation transfers energy to atoms and molecules in its path. The major result of this energy transfer is ionization. Electrons are torn from molecules, creating positive ions. Free electrons are eventually recaptured, but the positive ions usually undergo chemical changes before recapture occurs.

A single nuclear emission has enough energy to generate many positive ions and free electrons. A typical α-particle, for example, carries an energy of about 10^{-12} J, whereas ionization energies are approximately 2×10^{-18} J. Only about one third of the energy of an α-particle goes into generating ions; the rest is converted into heat. Still, one α-particle generates approximately 150,000 cations. Beta and gamma rays have similar energies, and they also generate ions as they pass through matter.

As a high-energy particle passes through matter, it loses energy, slows, and eventually stops. In this process, it creates an ionization "track." Positive ions produced by nuclear particles are chemically reactive because their bonds are weakened by the loss of bonding electrons. Each cation eventually recaptures an electron to return to electrical neutrality, but many ions first undergo chemical reactions that are the source of the damage done by nuclear radiation.

EFFECTS ON HUMANS

Living cells are delicately balanced chemical machines. The ionization track generated by a nuclear particle upsets this balance, almost always destroying the cell in the process. Although the human body has a remarkable ability to repair and replace damaged cells, exposure to radiation can overload these control mechanisms, causing weakness, illness, and even death.

Because nuclear radiation varies considerably in energy, damage potentials cannot be assessed simply by counting the number of emissions. The energy of emissions must also be taken into account. Furthermore, the three different types of nuclear radiation affect human cells to different extents. When the amount, energy content, and type of radiation are all taken into account, the result is a measure of the effect of radiation on the human body. This is measured using a unit called the **rem.**

Different types of body cells show varying sensitivities to nuclear radiation. Cells that divide most rapidly tend to be most easily damaged. These include bone marrow, white blood cells, blood platelets, linings of the gastrointestinal tract, and cells in the gonads and ovaries. Consequently, the symptoms of radiation sickness include loss of blood functions and gastrointestinal distress.

Individual ability to tolerate radiation damage varies, so a statistical variation exists in the correlation between dose level and health effects. Also, there are effective treatments, such as blood transfusions, for some radiation effects. Thus no specific dose level will inevitably cause death. The statistical patterns of human response to radiation are summarized in Table 19-5.

CUMULATIVE EFFECTS

Exposure to low doses of radiation causes no short-term damage but makes the body more susceptible to cancers. In particular, people who have been exposed to increased radiation levels have a much higher incidence of leukemia than the general population. Medical researchers estimate that about 10% of all cancers are caused by exposure to high-energy radiation.

TABLE 19-5 HEALTH EFFECTS OF RADIATION DOSES

DOSE (rem)	EFFECT
0-25	None that are immediate
25-50	Reduced amounts of white blood cells
50-100	Fatigue and nausea in half of persons exposed
100-200	Nausea and vomiting
200-400	Damage to bone marrow and spleen; death in half of persons exposed
> 600	Usually death, even with treatment

Another cumulative effect of radiation can be the irreversible alteration of deoxyribonucleic acid (DNA) sequences. If part of a DNA molecule is ionized, its molecular chain may be broken. Chain breaks are repaired in the body, but after a serious rupture, the repaired unit may have a different sequence. This type of changed sequence is a genetic mutation. Altered DNA sequences are reproduced and transmitted faithfully, thus passing on the genetic mutations to future generations. Because these effects are cumulative, individuals of childbearing age need to be especially careful about radiation exposure.

All of us are exposed continually to some level of radiation. Naturally occurring radioactivity from nuclides such as ^{14}C, ^{40}K, and ^{222}Rn averages about 100 millirem per year per individual. This exposure may be doubled by radiation from human activities. Medical procedures, notably the use of x-rays for imaging teeth and bones, contribute the largest amount. A typical x-ray film exposes the patient to 0.2 rem. Although this is well below the level at which immediate effects occur, the possibility of cumulative effects makes it prudent to have x-ray films taken no more often than necessary for maintaining good health. Total exposures vary considerably with human activities as well. "Frequent flyers," for example, receive higher doses of radiation because the intensity of cosmic radiation is significantly greater at high altitude than it is at ground level.

RADIATION SHIELDING

Radiation exposure can be reduced by placing a shield that captures the radiation around either the radiation source or the potential target. A lead-lined pad is often worn as a shield during dental x-rays, for example, because x-rays are absorbed more effectively by lead than by any other material. A lead shield a few millimeters thick is sufficient to stop x-rays.

Even though α-particles are the most damaging radiation, they turn out to be the most easily stopped by shielding. In fact, α-particles travel less than 1 mm in solid materials before losing all their excess energy. Beta-rays travel much farther, so a β-ray shield must be 10 to 100 mm thick. Plastic shields several centimeters thick provide excellent shielding from both types of radiation.

The γ-rays that accompany many nuclear decay processes can be more dangerous than α-particles or β-rays because γ-rays travel long distances before losing their energy. The radiation from ^{222}Rn, which is responsible for as much as 40% of the background radiation to which humans are exposed, is a typical example (see Box 19-4). This nuclide decays by α-emission accompanied by γ-rays. When a ^{222}Rn nucleus disintegrates, its α-particle is stopped within 10 cm in air or about 1 mm in a solid. The accompanying γ-ray, on the other hand, may travel many meters and penetrate walls before finally losing its destructive power. Consequently, radioactive materials that emit γ-rays must be shielded using lead blocks that are many centimeters thick. The photo in Figure 19-18 illustrates γ-ray shielding.

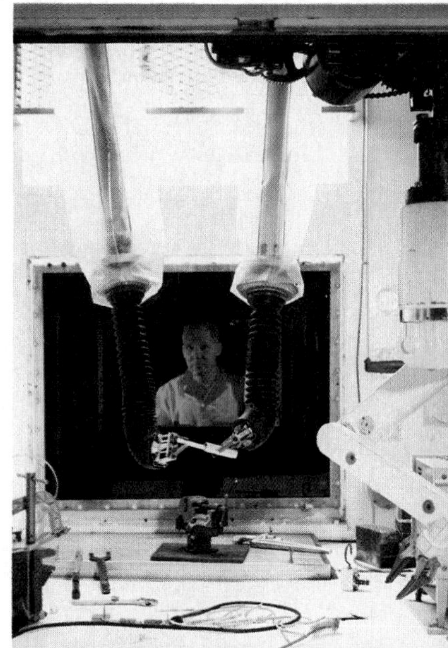

FIGURE 19-18
For radioactive materials that emit γ-rays, thick shields of lead bricks must be used to provide adequate shielding.

SECTION EXERCISES

19.8.1 Potassium-40 is a naturally occurring radioactive nuclide that emits β-rays with energy 1.32×10^8 kJ/mol and $t_{1/2} = 1.28 \times 10^9$ years. It is always present in our bodies because humans require potassium in their body fluids. Our bodies contain about 2.4 mg of potassium per kilogram of body weight, and ^{40}K makes up 0.0118% of the element. How many β-rays is a person weighing 70 kg exposed to daily from this nuclide, and how much energy does this decay deposit in the body?

BOX 19-4

THE INSIDIOUSNESS OF RADON

Radon, Z = 86, has no stable isotopes, but it is found on Earth as a product of the decay sequence of ^{238}U. Although that sequence includes several other radioactive nuclides, radon has properties that make it especially hazardous.

Radon, the heaviest member of the Group VIII rare gases, is the only decay product of uranium that is a gas under normal conditions. As a gas, radon is much more mobile than other decay products of uranium. Thus after forming in soil and rocks, some radon escapes into the atmosphere before decaying. Because of their high mass, radon atoms remain close to the ground, right where humans live and breathe.

The most prevalent isotope of radon is ^{222}Rn, which emits α-particles and γ-rays with a half-life of 3.82 days. When these nuclei decay in air, their α-particles do not penetrate very far. Their γ-rays penetrate much farther, but the amount of radon in most human environments is too low for this radiation to be a serious health hazard.

Much more serious risks develop from the decay of radon inside human lungs. Each α-particle is stopped by lung tissue, creating a track of damage. Moreover, the product nucleus is ^{218}Po, which reacts with an oxygen atom in the lung to give PoO. Polonium oxide binds to the lung and undergoes the following sequence of decays:

$$^{218}Po \rightarrow {}^{214}Pb + \alpha \qquad t_{1/2} = 3.05\ min$$
$$^{214}Pb \rightarrow {}^{214}Bi + \beta + \gamma \qquad t_{1/2} = 26.8\ min$$
$$^{214}Bi \rightarrow {}^{214}Po + \beta + \gamma \qquad t_{1/2} = 19.7\ min$$
$$^{214}Po \rightarrow {}^{210}Pb + \alpha \qquad t_{1/2} = 1.6 \times 10^{-4}\ s$$
$$^{210}Pb \rightarrow {}^{210}Bi + \beta + \gamma \qquad t_{1/2} = 22\ yr$$
$$^{210}Bi \rightarrow {}^{210}Po + \beta \qquad t_{1/2} = 5.0\ days$$
$$^{210}Po \rightarrow {}^{206}Pb + \alpha \qquad t_{1/2} = 46\ s$$

The net result of this chain of events is that the spot where a single ^{222}Rn nucleus decays is exposed to four α-particles, four β-particles, and three γ-rays.

The polonium, bismuth, and lead atoms that form during ^{222}Rn decay are not only radioactive, but also are poisonous heavy metals that irritate the lungs. Consequently, each radon nucleus that decays within a lung does significant cumulative damage. The result is an increased likelihood of lung cancer. About 10,000 of the annual 140,000 lung cancer deaths in the United States can be attributed to radon exposure.

Statistical studies have shown that the damaging effects of radon are multiplied for smokers. That is, radon exposure increases the incidence of lung cancer, and smoking increases the incidence of lung cancer, but smokers who are also exposed to radon develop cancer significantly more often than would be predicted from the sum of these two factors. Apparently, either smoking reduces the lung's ability to repair radiation damage, or radiation damage increases the lung irritation caused by smoking.

As with any statistical correlation, it is impossible to say with certainty what level of exposure to radon is dangerous. The Environmental Protection Agency has set the "action level" at 0.15 decays/L s. Above this level, they recommend that corrective actions be taken. Just how dangerous a little radon can be is illustrated by converting this decay rate into a concentration of radon. This radioactivity level comes from about 7×10^4 atoms/L, out of a total molecular density of 2.5×10^{22} atoms/L. Thus three atoms of Rn for every 10^{18} molecules of N_2 and O_2 is enough to pose a health hazard.

Some regions of the United States have higher radon levels than others. High radon levels are especially prevalent in places where there are uranium deposits, such as Montana and Idaho. Significant radon levels have been detected in some parts of 30 other states, and many areas have not yet been adequately tested for this radioactive nuclide. In addition, some types of houses "trap" radon in their interior atmospheres. In recent years, radon test kits have been marketed to allow people to test their home radon levels. If the radon level is above recommended levels, the condition can usually be corrected by increasing ventilation, particularly in basements, which are where radon is most likely to enter homes.

19.8.2 Although x-ray exposures pose little threat to patients, the technicians administering these exposures must be careful to avoid exposure to the beam. Suppose that an x-ray machine is "leaking" radiation that exposes the technologist to 1% of the dose received by a patient. After how many exposures would the technologist begin to show reduced amounts of white blood cells? If the technologist administers 40 x-ray studies daily and works 250 days per year, would this damage show up?

19.9 APPLICATIONS OF RADIOACTIVITY

Considering the frighteningly destructive potential of nuclear weapons and the health risks posed by exposure to too much nuclear radiation, radioactivity may seem like a curse. Nevertheless, scientists and medical practitioners use radioactivity routinely in many beneficial ways, including dating techniques, tracing techniques, imaging, and therapy. Dating techniques, which rely on the constant half-life of radioactive decay, allow scientists to estimate the ages of human artifacts and of the Earth itself. Tracing techniques exploit the high sensitivity of radiation detectors to elucidate complicated processes such as the mechanisms of chemical reactions and the percolation of water through geological formations. Imaging takes pictures of visually inaccessible objects, exploiting the ability of some radioactive emissions to pass through matter. Even the lethal properties of radioactivity can be used beneficially to treat some forms of cancer.

DATING USING RADIOACTIVITY

Each radioactive nuclide has a characteristic, constant half-life. This means that it acts as a clock, "ticking" (decaying) at a constant rate. Suppose that a nuclear reactor generates 20 mg of ^{32}P, an isotope with a half-life of 14.3 days. After 14.3 days, 10 mg will remain and there will be 10 mg of the decay product, ^{32}S. After 28.6 days, 5 mg of ^{32}P will remain and there will be 15 mg of ^{32}S. A chemist who analyzes a sample of ^{32}P and finds that it contains 15 mg of ^{32}S and only 5 mg of ^{32}P can calculate that it was generated 28.6 days ago from 20 mg of ^{32}P.

Calculating the age of a sample from the amounts of its radioactive nuclides and their decay products forms the basis for radioactive dating techniques. Equation 19-5 is used for such calculations:

$$\ln\left(\frac{N_o}{N}\right) = \frac{t \ln 2}{t_{1/2}}$$

Short-lived isotopes such as ^{32}P are not useful for dating because we almost always have other records that provide the ages of recent materials. Radioactive dating proves to be especially valuable in estimating the age of materials that predate human records, such as the Earth itself.

The Earth's age can be determined qualitatively by examining the half-lives of unstable nuclides that are still present and the half-lives of those that are missing. According to Table 19-5, the shortest-lived naturally occurring nuclide is ^{235}U ($t_{1/2}$ = 7.0×10^8 yr). Nuclides with half-lives shorter than 10^8 years, such as ^{146}Sm ($t_{1/2}$ = 7×10^7 yr), ^{205}Pb ($t_{1/2}$ = 3×10^7 yr), and ^{129}I ($t_{1/2}$ = 1.7×10^7 yr) are missing. If the Earth were less than 10^8 years old, its crust would contain some of these nuclides. If it were older than 10^{10} years, ^{235}U would no longer be present. Thus isotopic abundances indicate that the Earth is older than 10^8 years but younger than 10^{10} years.

More precise estimates are possible using accurate measurements of isotope ratios. Three pairs of radioactive isotopes and their products are abundant enough for such ratios to be measured:

$$^{238}U \longrightarrow \text{(Decay chain)} \longrightarrow {}^{206}Pb \qquad t_{1/2} = 4.5 \times 10^9 \text{ yr}$$

$$^{40}K \longrightarrow {}^{40}Ar + \beta \qquad t_{1/2} = 1.28 \times 10^9 \text{ yr}$$

$$^{87}Rb \longrightarrow {}^{87}Sr + \beta \qquad t_{1/2} = 4.9 \times 10^{11} \text{ yr}$$

If the amount of a radioactive nuclide in a rock sample is N, the sum of this amount plus the amount of its product nuclide is N_o. For argon dating, N_o is the sum of potassium-40 and argon-40 present in a sample of rock. Assuming that argon gas escapes from molten rock but is trapped after the rock cools and solidifies, the lifetime obtained by substituting these values into Equation 19-5 is the time since the rock solidified. Analyses of this type show that the oldest rock samples on Earth are 3.8×10^9 years old. Samples that are 4.55×10^9 years old have been found in meteorites. This is the best present estimate for the age of the solar system. Sample Problem 19-10 illustrates this type of calculation for rock from the Earth's moon.

This analysis is valid only if the product nuclide all comes from radioactive decay. We cannot be certain of this, but when age estimates using different pairs of nuclides give the same age, and when samples from different locations also agree, the age estimate is likely to be accurate. Note also that 3.8×10^9 years agrees with the qualitative limits derived from the naturally occurring radioactive nuclides.

SAMPLE PROBLEM 19-10 ARGON DATING

When a sample of moon rock was analyzed by mass spectroscopy, the ratio of ^{40}K to ^{40}Ar was found to be 0.1295. Based on this ratio, how old is the moon?

METHOD: This is a question about radioactive dating. Convert the isotopic ratio of the radioactive nuclide and its product into an amount ratio, and then use Equation 19-5.

This equation requires a value for N_o/N, which is the ratio of potassium-40 present when the moon was formed to the amount present today. We can derive N_o/N from the isotopic ratio N_K/N_{Ar} given in the problem. The relationship between N_o/N and N_K/N_{Ar} can be found by setting N_o equal to the sum of the amounts currently present:

$$N_o = N_K + N_{Ar}$$

$$\frac{N_o}{N} = \frac{N_K + N_{Ar}}{N_K} = 1 + \frac{N_{Ar}}{N_K}$$

$$\frac{N_K}{N_{Ar}} = 0.1295 \qquad \textit{and} \qquad \frac{N_{Ar}}{N_K} = 7.722$$

$$\frac{N_o}{N} = 1 + 7.722 = 8.722$$

Now rearrange Equation 19-5 to solve for t:

$$t = \frac{t_{1/2}}{ln\ 2}\ ln\left(\frac{N_0}{N}\right)$$

$$ln\left(\frac{N_0}{N}\right) = ln(8.722) = 2.1658$$

Find the half-life of ^{40}K from Table 19-5, $t_{1/2} = 1.28 \times 10^9$ yr:

$$t = \frac{(1.28 \times 10^9 \text{ yr})(2.1658)}{(0.693)} = 4.00 \times 10^9 \text{ yr}$$

According to this analysis, the moon solidified about 4 billion years ago.

Radioactivity serves as a useful clock only for times that are similar to the decay half-life. At times much longer than $t_{1/2}$, the amount of radioactive nuclide becomes too small to measure accurately. At times much shorter than $t_{1/2}$, the amount of the product nuclide is too small to measure. By an accident of nature, one naturally occurring radioisotope, ^{14}C, has a half-life that is close to the age of human civilization. As a result, this isotope has been widely used to determine the age of human artifacts.

The logic underlying carbon-14 dating differs from that for potassium-argon dating. Recall that bombardment of the upper atmosphere by cosmic rays generates small but measurable levels of ^{14}C. This rate of production of ^{14}C by cosmic rays exactly balances its rate of decay by β-emission, so the percentage of ^{14}C in the atmosphere remains nearly constant. Living plants incorporate CO_2 from the atmosphere into carbohydrates, and animals use these carbohydrates as food. As a result, the percentage of carbon-14 in the tissues of *living* organisms is the same as that in the atmosphere. On death, however, the uptake of carbon stops. The carbon-14 in an object that was once alive slowly disappears with $t_{1/2} = 5.73 \times 10^3$ years. This makes it possible to date objects such as bone, wood, and cloth by assaying their level of ^{14}C.

The ratio of ^{14}C to ^{12}C is used for radiocarbon dating. In the atmosphere and in living objects, there is one atom of ^{14}C for every 7.54×10^{11} atoms of ^{12}C. Although this is a tiny amount, it nevertheless results in 15.3 decays of ^{14}C per gram of carbon per minute. After a living organism dies, its ^{14}C content begins decreasing according to the first-order decay law, whereas its ^{12}C content remains fixed. From 15.3 decays/g min, the radioactivity slowly diminishes. After 5.73×10^3 years, for example, it will be 7.65 decays/g min.

The product of ^{14}C decay is ^{14}N, but there is so much ^{14}N already present in the atmosphere that this isotope is not an accurate measure of how much ^{14}C has decayed.

The usual procedure for radiocarbon dating is to burn small samples of the objects to be dated, collect the CO_2 that is produced, and compare its rate of radioactive disintegrations with that of a fresh CO_2 sample. The ratio of counts gives N_o/N, which can then be substituted into Equation 19-5 to calculate *t*. Sample Problem 19-11 illustrates the use of radiocarbon dating techniques.

SAMPLE PROBLEM 19-11 RADIOCARBON DATING

In 1988, the Shroud of Turin, claimed by some to have been used to bury Christ, was age-dated by carbon-14 analysis. A sample from the shroud gave a count rate of 14.1 decays/g min. How old is the shroud? If it were 2000 years old, what count rate would it give?

METHOD: To calculate an age, we need the value of N_o/N. This ratio is equal to the count rate of a fresh carbon sample divided by the count rate of the old sample. This ratio can be inserted into Equation 19-5 to calculate age, *t*.

The data include the count rate of the old sample, 14.1 decays/g min. The text states that the comparable count rate for a fresh sample is 15.3 decays/g min:

$$t = \frac{t_{1/2}}{\ln 2} \ln\left(\frac{N_o}{N}\right)$$

$$\frac{N_o}{N} = \frac{15.3 \text{ decays/g min}}{14.1 \text{ decays/g min}} = 1.085$$

$$t = \frac{5730 \text{ yr}}{0.6931} \ln(1.085) = 674 \text{ years}$$

Thus the cotton or flax from which the shroud was woven was harvested around 1300 AD. The shroud might be younger than this, but it cannot be older.

The Shroud of Turin is imprinted with the image that resembles a male human, thought by some to be a representation of Christ.

We can use the same equation to compute the count rate expected for a 2000-year-old artifact:

$$ln\left(\frac{N_o}{N}\right) = \frac{(2000\text{ yr})(0.6931)}{(5730\text{ yr})} = 0.2419$$

$$\frac{N_o}{N} = e^{0.2419} = 1.274$$

$$N = \frac{N_o}{1.274} = \frac{15.3\text{ decays/g min}}{1.274} = 12.0\text{ decays/g min}$$

This rate is different enough from 14.1 decays/g min to demonstrate conclusively that the shroud does not date from the time of Christ.

Tree-ring dating is more accurate than radiocarbon dating, but radiocarbon dating can be used on objects that do not retain tree rings, such as charcoal and cloth.

Calculations of ages, as illustrated in Sample Problem 19-11, make the assumption that the level of ^{14}C in the atmosphere at the time of death was the same as it is today. To check the validity of ^{14}C dating, its age estimates have been compared with those obtained by other methods, such as tree-ring dating. Wood from a Roman shipwreck, for example, was dated at 40 BC ± 3 years using tree-ring dating and 80 BC ± 200 years using radiocarbon dating. A whole series of such comparisons show small but consistent differences, indicating that the amount of ^{14}C in the atmosphere slowly but steadily changes with time. Archaeologists use a small multiplying factor to correct for this small drift.

RADIOACTIVE TRACERS

Radioactive isotopes are chemically identical to their natural, nonradioactive counterparts, but their high-energy decays allow them to be detected even though they may comprise only a tiny fraction of the overall isotopic composition. For example, radiocarbon dating detects ^{14}C at a concentration of one part in 10^{11} in carbon-containing samples. If an isotopically enriched sample is introduced into some dynamic process, the course of that process can be followed by tracing the whereabouts of the radioactive isotope. Tracer techniques are applied in fields that range from geology to medicine. For example, a holding tank at an industrial plant might be suspected of leaking contaminated water into wells in its vicinity, as shown diagrammatically in Figure 19-19. To trace the path of water draining from the holding tank, water enriched in radioactive tritium could be added to the holding tank. The water from the wells could then be sampled for radioactivity at regular intervals. If, after a few days, water in two wells showed significant radioactivity while the remaining

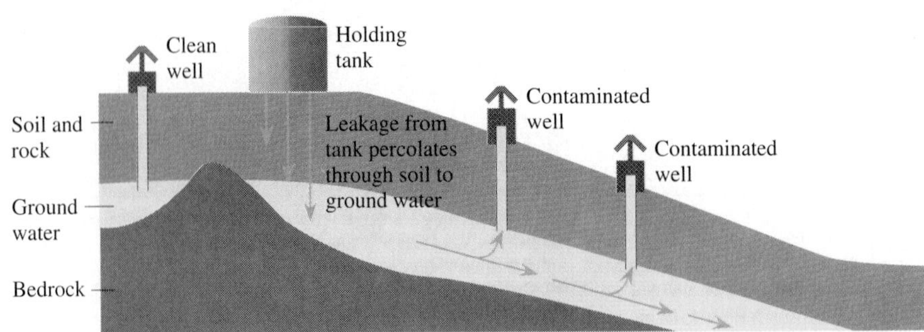

FIGURE 19-19
Radioactive tracers can show flow pathways that are invisible to other methods of detection.

wells were free of contamination even after several months, that would show that two of the wells were receiving water from the holding tank, but that the others were not.

Tracer techniques are used widely in biology. Botanists, for example, work continually to develop new plant hybrids that grow more rapidly. One common way to determine how fast plants grow is to measure how quickly they take up elemental phosphorus from the soil. New hybrids can be planted in a plot that is fertilized with phosphorus enriched in radioactive ^{32}P. When leaves from the plants are assayed for ^{32}P at regular intervals, the rate of increase in radioactivity measures the rate of phosphorus uptake.

One of the first chemical applications of radioactive tracers was the elegant experiments on photosynthesis performed in the 1950s by Melvin Calvin. To determine the complex set of reactions by which plants transform atmospheric CO_2 into carbohydrates, Calvin supplied growing plant cells with CO_2 enriched with carbon-14. By determining which compounds gained enhanced ^{14}C radioactivity and in what sequence, Calvin was able to unravel the elaborate chain of reactions that is now known as the *Calvin cycle.*

Melvin Calvin received the Nobel Prize in chemistry in 1961 for his work using ^{14}C as a tracer.

MEDICAL IMAGING

Physicians need ways to examine internal organs without disturbing those organs. X-ray films work well for teeth, bones, and lungs but do not provide clear images of other vital organs. Radioactive substances that bind to specific organs in the body make it possible to obtain a radioactivity image of one particular organ. Like an x-ray film, this image reveals abnormalities in internal organs, allowing physicians to diagnose ailments.

Because exposure to any radiation carries health risks, the administration of radioactive substances must be carefully monitored and controlled. Only gamma and positron emitters are used because they are not only the easiest to detect, but also minimize tissue damage. Specificity for a single target organ is essential so that the amount of radioactive material can be kept as small as possible. Short half-lives are advantageous, but a half-life shorter than a few hours is impractical because it does not allow enough time to synthesize, isolate, and administer the radioactive compound.

Nuclear medicine most frequently uses a single radioactive nuclide of technetium, ^{99m}Tc. This nuclide has near-perfect properties for medical imaging. It has a half-life of 6 hours, which is long enough to deliver it into the body and generate an image, but short enough to minimize long-term effects. It emits γ-rays of moderate energy (1.35×10^7 kJ/mol) that are easy to detect but are not highly damaging to living tissue. Technetium is not normally found in the body, but the element can be bound to many chemicals that the body recognizes and processes. The radioactive isotope is produced by neutron bombardment of natural molybdenum, from which it can be readily extracted in pure form. The thyroid gland, brain, lungs, heart, liver, stomach, kidney, and bones all can be imaged using compounds containing ^{99m}Tc, making it a very versatile imaging agent.

In addition to Tc, ^{52}Fe is useful for bone marrow scans, ^{133}Xe for studying lung functions, and ^{131}I for the thyroid gland.

To see how imaging can aid medical diagnosis, consider the operation of the heart. In a healthy heart, blood passes from the veins into one chamber of the heart. From there, blood moves into the lungs, where it collects oxygen. Oxygenated blood then moves to the second chamber of the heart, where it is pumped off to other parts of the body. A defective heart may contain a "shunt," where blood leaks between heart chambers instead of following its normal course.

Shunts can be discovered by injecting radioactive substances into the veins and then monitoring their radioactivity as they pass through the heart and lungs. Two

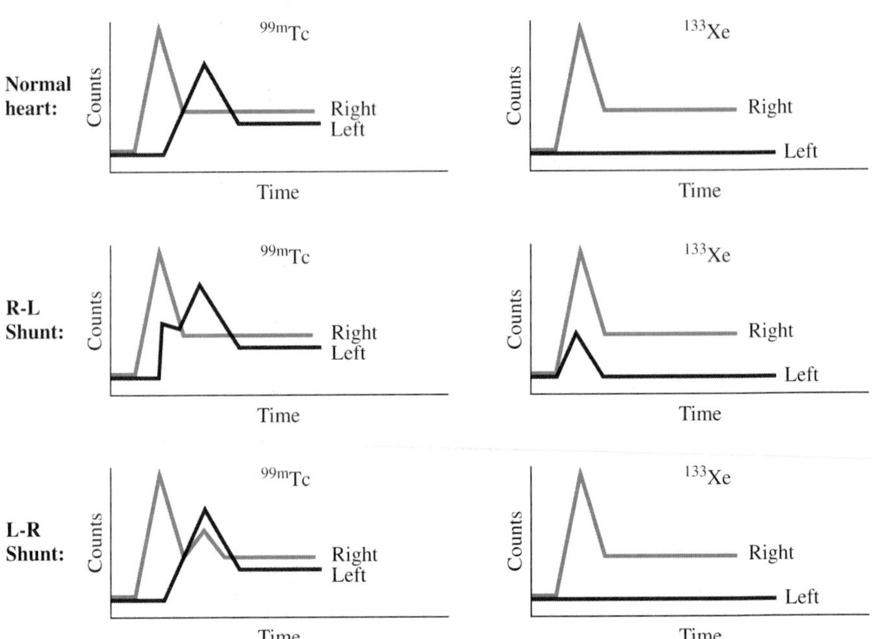

FIGURE 19-20
Time profiles of radioactivity when tracers of technetium and xenon are injected into the veins. The time profiles of hearts in which blood leaks between chambers are characteristically different from those of a normal heart.

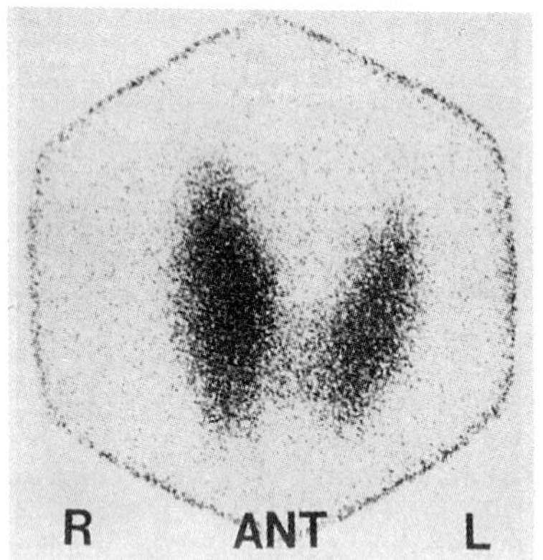

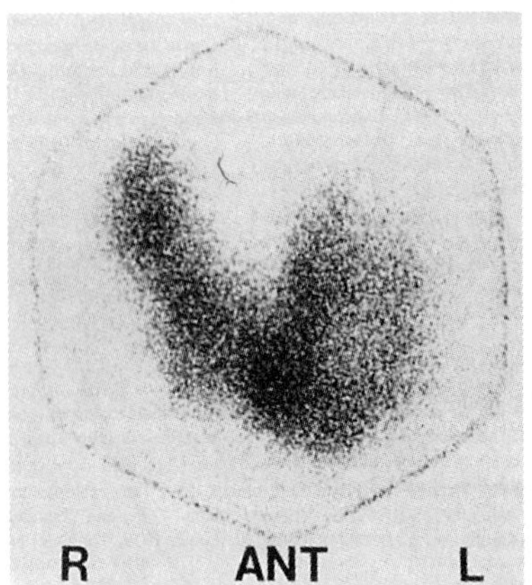

FIGURE 19-21
Radiation images identify abnormalities in organs. **A**, The uniform distribution of ^{99m}Tc in a normal thyroid gland. **B**, The asymmetrical distribution shown in this image indicates a cancerous thyroid gland.

radioisotopes are used in this diagnosis, ^{99m}Tc bound to albumin (a common protein) and ^{133}Xe. Technetium-albumin stays in the bloodstream as it traverses from the first chamber, through the lungs, and into the second chamber. On the other hand, xenon-133 crosses the lung membranes and is exhaled, so in a normal cardiovascular tract, ^{133}Xe never reaches the second heart chamber. Hearts afflicted with shunts have different patterns, as shown in Figure 19-20.

The diagnosis of heart shunts relies on a tracer type of imaging in which the dynamic pattern of radioactivity reveals the abnormality. Static imaging also has many uses. Figure 19-21 shows how static imaging can be used to detect thyroid tumors.

RADIATION THERAPY

Radioactive nuclides can be used to treat and diagnose certain diseases. Some cancers, for example, respond particularly well to a treatment called **radiation therapy.** At first this may seem paradoxical, since we know that exposure to radiation damages cells and eventually causes cancer. Thus we might expect irradiation to worsen rather than retard this disease. The key to radiation therapy is that cancerous cells typically reproduce more rapidly than normal cells, and rapidly reproducing cells are more sensitive to radiation. If concentrated doses of radiation are carefully focused on the malignant cells, a cancer may be destroyed with minimum damage to healthy tissue.

Thyroid cancers are often treated with radioactive iodine, for example, because the thyroid gland preferentially absorbs iodine. Thus if a patient is treated with iodine containing radioactive ^{131}I, its radioactivity is concentrated in that gland. Inside the thyroid gland the radiation destroys cancerous cells more rapidly than normal cells. At the correct dosage, the cancer may be eliminated without destroying the healthy part of the thyroid gland.

The radioactive source need not always be introduced into the body. Inoperable brain tumors can be treated with γ-rays from an external source such as a sample of cobalt-60. The patient is placed in a position where the γ-ray beam passes through the tumor. Then the patient is moved so that the γ-rays travel different paths but always go through the tumor. In this manner the tumor receives a much higher dose than any surrounding tissues.

Box 19-5 discusses another use for radiation, the controversial area of food preservation.

BOX 19-5

FOOD PRESERVATION USING RADIATION

In a society where canned and frozen foods are so prevalent, we tend to take food preservation for granted. We easily forget that prevention of spoilage is a major undertaking when food is harvested at one time and place but eaten at another.

Spoilage is a biological process. Molds, bacteria, and vermin eat foodstuffs, rendering them unfit for human consumption. To stop spoilage, we treat food to kill microorganisms, chill it to slow the metabolism of destruction, and keep it sealed to ward off pests. Even in fully developed societies, these procedures are only partially successful, and in economically developing countries, up to 50% of crops may be lost to spoilage.

Recently, the lethal properties of radiation have been shown to preserve foods. After packaging, the food is exposed to enough gamma radiation to kill microorganisms. Moderate doses retard spoilage, whereas high doses can prevent spoilage completely for as long as the packaging remains intact. The photo demonstrates how effective radiation treatment can be. Both boxes of strawberries were stored in a refrigerator for 15 days. The right-hand box was gamma-irradiated before storage, retarding the growth of mold.

Although gamma irradiation is widely used in Europe, the U.S. Food and Drug Administration has been slow to approve the process because of concern that irradiation may generate unhealthy and perhaps even carcinogenic byproducts. It is important to keep in mind, however, that conventional methods of preservation also carry risks. For example, ethylene dibromide, which has been used for years to kill pests in fruit, has recently been banned because it is implicated as a carcinogen. Nitrites, which are used widely in preserving bacon, bologna, and other processed meats, are now known to be unhealthy at high exposures. European regulators have taken the position that the as-yet uncharted side effects of irradiation are less injurious than those associated with chemical preservatives. Regulators in the United States, on the other hand, believe that irradiation should not be permitted until its side effects are better documented. Unfortunately, no preservative may be completely free of deleterious effects, in which case societies will have to choose high spoilage rates, health hazards of chemical preservatives, or hazards generated by the by-products of irradiation.

SECTION EXERCISES

19.9.1 An archaeologist discovers a new site where small charcoal bits are mixed with human remains. Burning a small sample of this charcoal gives gaseous CO_2 that, when placed in a counter, registers 1.75 decays per second. When an equal mass of CO_2 from fresh charcoal is placed in this counter, the count rate is 3.85 decays per second. How old is the archaeological site?

19.9.2 Classify each of the following radioactive nuclides as a good or a poor choice for medical imaging. State your reason in each case: (a) ^{123}I, a γ-emitter with a 13.2-hour half-life; (b) ^{131}I, a β-emitter with an 8.1-day half-life; (c) ^{60}Co, a γ-emitter with a 5.26-year half-life; and (d) ^{56}Co, a positron-emitter with a 77-day half-life.

19.9.3 A commercial office building is running an excessive heating bill, which is suspected to be caused by the leakage of warm air from its circulation system. Describe how a radioactive tracer might be used to locate the source of the leakage.

CHAPTER SUMMARY

1. Nuclei are made up of protons and neutrons. Stable nuclei fall within a belt of stability in which the ratio of neutrons to protons lies between 1.0 and 1.54. Nuclei that are proton rich, are neutron rich, or have $Z > 83$ are unstable.
2. When protons and neutrons bind together to form a nucleus, there is a loss of mass that appears as energy, $\Delta E = (\Delta m)c^2$. The binding energy per nucleon has a maximum value of about $Z = 26$ and has smaller values for both lighter and heavier nuclides.
3. Unstable nuclides decay by emitting energetic fragments, but mass-energy, charge number, and mass number all must be conserved. The mode of decay is determined by the reason for the instability of the nuclide.
4. All nuclear decay processes obey first-order kinetics and have constant half-lives.
5. Binuclear reactions such as neutron capture, proton capture, and the capture of helium nuclei lead to the formation of many synthetic nuclides that are unstable.
6. Fission of uranium or plutonium produces two smaller nuclides, several neutrons, and large amounts of energy. Fission chain reactions are the energy sources for nuclear bombs and power plants.
7. Fusion of light nuclides also releases large amounts of energy, but fusion cannot take place unless the nuclei possess the immense energy needed to overcome the coulombic barrier to their close approach.
8. Fusion reactions produce the energy that powers the stars, including our sun. Stars first use hydrogen fusion, then helium fusion, and finally carbon fusion as energy sources. Supernovae spew out nuclear debris, including nuclides heavier than iron, which subsequently becomes incorporated into third-generation stars.
9. Nuclear radiation is energetic enough to cause substantial damage to matter through which it passes, and at sufficiently high doses, radiation causes illness and death to living creatures.
10. Objects can be dated, processes can be mapped, organs can be imaged, and cancers can be treated using radioactivity.

KEY TERMS

isotope
neutron
nuclear binding energy
nuclide
proton
transmutation

electron capture
β-emission
half-life ($t_{1/2}$)
nuclear decay
α-particle
positron
positron emission
radioactive
β-ray
γ-ray

compound nucleus
critical mass
cyclotron
fission
fusion
induced nuclear reaction

first-generation star
second-generation star
supernova
third-generation star

radiation therapy
rem

SKILLS TO MASTER

- Writing and interpreting symbols for nuclides
- Predicting whether or not a nuclide is stable
- Calculating energies of nuclear transmutations
- Calculating coulombic barriers for nuclear reactions
- Describing nuclear decay reactions and binuclear reactions
- Working with nuclear half-lives
- Describing the characteristics of fission and fusion
- Tracing the course of stellar nucleosynthesis
- Dating ancient objects

LEARNING EXERCISES

19.1 Prepare a summary of two pages or less that describes the important features in this chapter.

19.2 Write a paragraph summarizing the important features of each of the following topics: (a) nuclear stability; (b) nuclear decay; (c) fission; (d) fusion; and (e) binding energy.

19.3 Outline the requirements for a balanced nuclear equation, and explain how they differ from those for a balanced chemical equation.

19.4 Prepare a list of the beneficial and detrimental effects that have resulted from the discovery of nuclear reactions.

19.5 Make a list of all terms introduced in Chapter 19 that are new to you. Write a one-sentence definition for each, using your own words. If you need help, consult the glossary.

19.6 Update your list of memory bank equations to include those that apply to nuclear chemistry and radiochemistry.

PROBLEMS

NUCLEAR STRUCTURE

19.1 Determine Z, A, and N for each of the following nuclides: (a) ^{6}Li; (b) ^{43}Ca; (c) ^{238}U; (d) ^{130}Te; (e) the nuclide of neon that contains the same number of protons and neutrons; and (f) the nuclide of lead that contains 1.5 times as many neutrons as protons.

19.2 Determine Z, A, and N for each of the following nuclides: (a) ^{22}Ne; (b) ^{202}Pb; (c) ^{41}K; (d) ^{109}Ag; (e) the helium nuclide with one less neutron than proton; and (f) the nuclide of barium whose neutron/proton ratio is 1.25.

19.3 Write the correct elemental symbols for the following nuclides (include the atomic number subscript): (a) helium with the same number of neutrons and protons; (b) tungsten with 110 neutrons; (c) the nuclide with 12 protons and 14 neutrons; and (d) the nuclide with $Z = 28$ and $N = 32$.

19.4 Write the correct elemental symbols for the following nuclides (include the atomic number subscript): (a) the nuclide with $Z = 50$ and $N = 64$; (b) atomic number 86 possessing 133 neutrons; (c) sulfur with two more neutrons than protons; and (d) antimony with 70 neutrons.

19.5 Predict whether each of the following nuclides is stable or unstable, and give reasons for your prediction: (a) carbon-10; (b) neptunium-239; (c) cadmium with 60 neutrons; and (d) element number 43 with 55 neutrons.

NUCLEAR ENERGETICS

19.6 Compute the energy released, in joules per event and in kilojoules per mole, when antiprotons (the antimatter corresponding to protons) annihilate with protons.

19.7 Compute the energy released in kilojoules when the sun converts 1.00 metric ton of matter into energy.

19.8 Use atomic masses to compute the total binding energy and the binding energy per nucleon for elemental cobalt, which has just one stable nuclide.

19.9 Use atomic masses to compute the total binding energy and the binding energy per nucleon for elemental cesium, which has just one stable nuclide.

19.10 Is the coulombic barrier for fusion of two protons larger, smaller, or the same as that for fusion of two deuterium nuclei? Which of the resulting helium nuclei is less stable? Explain.

NUCLEAR DECAY

19.11 Write the correct symbol and give the name for each of the following products of nuclear decay: (a) a photon; (b) a positive particle with mass number 4; and (c) a positron.

19.12 What is the charge number, mass number, and symbol for each of the following: (a) an α-particle; (b) a β-ray; and (c) a neutron?

19.13 Identify the product of each of the following decay processes:
(a) Tellurium with 73 neutrons emits a γ-ray.
(b) Tellurium with 71 neutrons captures an electron.
(c) Tellurium with 75 neutrons undergoes β- and γ-decay.

19.14 A radioactive nuclide of mass number 94 has been prepared by neutron bombardment. If 4.7 μg of this nuclide register 20 counts per minute on a radioactivity counter, what is the half-life of this nuclide?

19.15 Thorium-232 decays by the following sequence of emissions: α, β, β, α, α, α, α, β, α, β, α. Identify the final product and all the unstable intermediates.

19.16 A radioactivity counter gives a reading of 350 min^{-1} for a 12.5-mg sample of cobalt(II) chloride partially enriched with cobalt-60 ($t_{1/2}$ = 5.26 yr). What percentage of the cobalt atoms are cobalt-60?

INDUCED NUCLEAR REACTIONS

19.17 Identify the compound nucleus and final product resulting from each of the following nuclear reactions:
(a) Carbon-12 captures a neutron and then emits a proton.
(b) The nuclide with eight protons and eight neutrons captures an α-particle and emits a γ-ray.
(c) Curium-247 is bombarded with boron-11, and the product loses three neutrons.

19.18 Draw a nuclear picture (see Figures 19-1 and 19-3 for pictures of nuclei) that illustrates the nuclear reaction responsible for the production of carbon-14. Include a picture of the compound nucleus:

$$^{14}N + n \longrightarrow {}^{14}C + p$$

19.19 Draw a nuclear picture that illustrates the capture of an α-particle by ^{14}N, followed by the emission of a positron.

NUCLEAR FISSION

19.20 Compute the energy released in the following fission reaction:

$$^{235}U + n \longrightarrow {}^{100}Mo + {}^{134}Sn + 2\,n$$

The nuclide masses, in grams per mole, are U, 235.0439; Mo, 99.9076; and Sn, 133.9125. Compare your result with the calculation in Exercise 19.5.1.

19.21 From the mass number distribution given in Figure 19-9 and the "belt of stability" shown in Figure 19-2, predict which elements should be found in greatest abundance in the remains of a fission event like that of the Oklo reactor.

19.22 Describe the features of radioactivity that make the consequences of an accident in a nuclear power plant more devastating than those of an accident in a coal-burning power plant.

19.23 A coal-fired generating plant requires just one heat exchanger, in which water is converted to the steam needed to drive the generator. A nuclear power plant requires two. A circulating fluid such as liquid sodium metal absorbs heat from the nuclear core and then transfers this heat to convert water into steam. Describe the features of nuclear reactions that make it necessary to have this second heat exchanger.

NUCLEAR FUSION

19.24 How much energy will be released if 1.50 g of deuterons and 1.50 g of lithium-6 undergo fusion in a hydrogen bomb? (The reactions and energies are given in the text.)

19.25 Compute the velocity of a tritium nucleus with enough kinetic energy to fuse with a deuteron.

19.26 List the advantages and disadvantages of fission power and fusion power. Based on your list, do you think that the United States should continue to develop fission power plants? What about fusion power plants?

19.27 Describe the features of fusion that have prevented fusion power from being commercialized in the way that fission power has been.

STELLAR NUCLEAR REACTIONS

19.28 Tabulate the differences in temperature and composition of a first-generation star at the hydrogen-burning, helium-burning, and carbon-burning stages of its evolution.

19.29 Repeat the tabulation in Problem 19.28 for a second-generation star. List the differences between the two.

19.30 Second- and third-generation stars may contain significant amounts of carbon, but carbon-burning does not begin until the third stage of their evolution. Explain this.

19.31 Using the characteristics of nuclear reactions, explain why no elements with $Z > 26$ form during the evolution and eventual explosion of first-generation stars.

EFFECTS OF RADIATION

19.32 A patient weighing 65 kg is given an intravenous dose of ^{99m}Tc, a radioactive isotope that decays by γ-emission of energy 1.35×10^7 kJ/mol with a 6.0-hour half-life. If 15.0 mL of a 2.50 nanomolar (nano $= 10^{-9}$) solution is administered and the radioactive nuclide decays within the patient's body, what total energy is received?

19.33 How many γ-rays are emitted per second by the dose of ^{99m}Tc described in Problem 19.32?

19.34 Why is it more important to protect the reproductive organs from radiation than other organs?

19.35 Describe how irradiation protects foods against spoilage, and describe how irradiation of foods might also produce undesirable byproducts.

APPLICATIONS OF RADIOACTIVITY

19.36 Uranium deposits are dated by determining the ratio of ^{238}U to its final decay product, ^{206}Pb. The half-life of ^{238}U is 4.5×10^9 years. If the ratio of ^{238}U to ^{206}Pb in an ore sample is 1.21, what is the age of the ore?

19.37 Extremely old rock samples can be dated using the ratio of ^{87}Sr to ^{87}Rb, with the half-life of ^{87}Rb being 4.9×10^{11} years. What is the approximate age of a meteorite that has a ^{87}Sr/^{87}Rb mass ratio of 0.0050?

19.38 A 250-mg sample of CO_2 collected from a small piece of wood at an archaeological site gave 1020 counts over a 24-hour period. In the same counting apparatus, 1.00 g of CO_2 from freshly cut wood gave 18,400 counts in 20 hours. What age does this give for the site?

19.39 List the advantageous properties of ^{99m}Tc as a medical imaging isotope.

ADDITIONAL PROBLEMS

19.40 Complete the following nuclear reactions: (a) Alpha emission from ^{238}U; (b) n + ^{60}Ni $\longrightarrow$? + p; (c) ^{239}Np + ^{12}C $\longrightarrow$? + 3 n; (d) p + ^{35}Cl $\longrightarrow$ α + ?; and (e) Beta emission from ^{60}Co.

19.41 Naturally occurring bismuth contains only one isotope, ^{209}Bi. Compute the total binding energy and binding energy per nucleon of this element.

19.42 Smoke detectors contain small quantities of ^{241}Am, a radioactive nuclide that decays by emitting an α-particle with 5.44×10^8 kJ/mol energy and a 458-year half-life. It also emits γ-rays.
(a) What is the neutron/proton ratio for ^{241}Am?
(b) If a smoke detector operates at five decays per second, what mass of ^{241}Am does it contain?
(c) If malfunction occurs when the decay rate falls below 3.5 decays/s, for how many years could it be used?
d) If your bed was directly under this smoke detector, would you be exposed to nuclear radiation? Explain.

19.43 Free neutrons are unstable. Because they cannot be collected and weighed, it is difficult to measure their half-life accurately. Early estimates gave $t_{1/2} = 1100$ seconds, but more refined experiments give $t_{1/2} = 876 \pm 21$ seconds. Suppose a neutron source generates 10^5 neutrons per second for 30 seconds. Assuming no neutrons are captured by nuclei, how many will be left after 1 hour, according to each of these half-lives?

19.44 A small amount of NaBr containing the radioactive isotope sodium-24 is dissolved in a hot solution of sodium nitrate containing the naturally occurring, nonradioactive isotope sodium-23. The solution is cooled, and sodium nitrate precipitates from the solution. Will the precipitate be radioactive? Explain your answer.

19.45 Neutrons decay into protons. What is the other product of this decay? If all the decay energy is converted into kinetic energy of this other product, how much kinetic energy does it have?

19.46 Neutron bombardment is an elegant way of "doping" silicon with phosphorus to convert it into an n-type semiconductor. Bombardment generates stable ^{31}P from ^{30}Si. Write the nuclear reactions for this transformation.

19.47 A positron has the same mass as an electron. When a positron and an electron annihilate, both masses are converted entirely into the energy of a pair of γ-rays. Calculate the energy per γ-ray and the energy of 1 mol of γ-rays.

19.48 Polonium-210 has a half-life of 138.4 days. If a sample contains 5.0 mg of ^{210}Po, how many milligrams will remain after 365 days? How many emissions per second will this residue emit?

19.49 Polonium-209 has a half-life of 103 years. What fraction of it will remain after 365 days? If a sample of polonium contains equimolar amounts of ^{210}Po and ^{209}Po, what will the isotope ratio be after 10 years? (See Problem 19.48.)

19.50 The radius of a ^{12}C nucleus is 3.0×10^{-15} m. Compute the energy barrier in joules and in kilojoules per mole for the fusion of two ^{12}C nuclei.

19.51 Two isotopes used in positron emission imaging are ^{11}C and ^{15}O. On which side of the "belt of stability" are these nuclides located? Write the nuclear reactions for their disintegrations.

19.52 One isotope of nitrogen and one isotope of fluorine are positron emitters with relatively long half-lives. Identify them and write their decay reactions.

19.53 The amount of radioactive carbon in any once-living sample eventually drops too low for accurate dating. This detection limit is about 0.03/g min, whereas fresh samples have a count rate of 15.3/g min. What is the upper limit for age determinations using carbon dating?

19.54 Strontium-90 is a dangerous fission product because it passes into human bodies and lodges in bones. It decays in two steps to give ^{90}Zr. The atomic masses of these two nuclides are 89.9073 and 89.9043 g/mol.
(a) Write the decay reactions that lead from ^{90}Sr to ^{90}Zr.
(b) Which nuclide has the higher atomic mass?
(c) Calculate the total energy released in the decay scheme. (*Reminder*: Do not forget the masses of the other decay products.)

19.55 Radioactive ^{64}Cu (MM = 63.92976) decays by emission of β-rays with 9.3×10^{-14} J energy or emission of positrons with 1.04×10^{-13} J energy.
(a) Write the two decay reactions.
(b) Calculate the molar masses of the two elemental products, using mass-energy equivalence.

19.56 Complete the following nuclear reactions: (a) Positron emission from ^{26}Si; (b) Electron capture by ^{82}Sr; (c) $^{210}Po \longrightarrow \alpha + ?$; (d) $\alpha + {}^{9}Be \longrightarrow n + ?$; and (e) $^{99m}Tc \longrightarrow \gamma + ?$

19.57 Unlike most other elements, different samples of lead have different atomic masses. This is because lead is the stable end product of two different radioactive decay schemes, one starting from ^{238}U and the other from ^{232}Th. Both decay schemes consist entirely of α-, β-, and γ-emissions. The most abundant stable lead isotopes have mass numbers 206, 207, and 208. Will lead, some of which came from ^{238}U, have a higher or lower atomic mass than lead, some of which came from ^{232}Th? Draw a decay scheme that illustrates your reasoning.

19.58 The Earth captures 3.4×10^{17} J/s of radiant energy, which is one part in 4.5×10^{10} of the sun's total energy output:
(a) By how much does the mass of the sun change every second?
(b) The sun is in the hydrogen-burning stage of its evolution. Calculate how many moles of ^{1}H are converted into ^{4}He per second.

19.59 Nuclear power plants often use boron control rods. Boron-10 absorbs neutrons efficiently, emitting α-particles as a consequence. Write the nuclear reaction. Does this reaction pose any health hazard? Explain your reasoning.

19.60 Phosphorus-30, which has a half-life of 150 seconds, decays by positron emission. How long will it take for (a) 2% and (b) 99.5% of this nuclide to decay?

19.61 The long-lived isotope of radium, ^{226}Ra, decays by α-emission, with a half-life of 1622 years. Calculate how long it will take for 1% of this nuclide to disappear and how long until 1% of it remains.

19.62 State the reason why each of the following nuclides is unstable: (a) tritium (one proton, two neutrons); (b) uranium-238; (c) ^{40}K; and (d) a beryllium nucleus with four neutrons.

19.63 Uranium-238 undergoes eight consecutive α-emissions to give stable lead. In a uranium ore sample, all the α-particles are quickly stopped, becoming trapped ^{4}He atoms. If analysis of a rock sample shows it to contain 6.0×10^{-5} cm^3 of helium (1 atm, 298 K) and 1.3×10^{-7} g ^{238}U per gram of rock, what is the estimated age of the rock?

19.64 What is the "shelf life" of a radioactive nuclide with a half-life of 14.6 days if it loses its usefulness when less than 15% of the radioactivity remains?

19.65 Carbon-14 dating gives 3250 years as the age of a charcoal sample, assuming a constant level of cosmic radiation. If the cosmic ray level in the atmosphere was 20% higher at the time the tree grew, what is the correct age of the sample?

19.66 The heaviest trans-uranium elements are formed by bombardment with relatively heavy nuclides such as ^{58}Fe. What nuclide could be formed by bombarding bismuth with this nuclide?

19.67 Naturally occurring gold contains only one isotope, ^{197}Au. Compute the total binding energy and binding energy per nucleon of this element.

19.68 Iodine-123, $t_{1/2}$ = 13.2 hours, is used in medical imaging of the thyroid gland. If 0.5 mg of this isotope is injected into a patient's bloodstream and 45% of it binds to the thyroid gland, how long will it take for the amount of iodine to fall to less than 0.1 μg?

19.69 In 1934, Irène Curie and Frédéric Joliot produced the first artificial radioisotope by bombarding ^{27}Al with α-particles. The resulting compound nucleus decayed by neutron emission. Write the reaction and predict whether or not the final product is stable. If it is not stable, predict its mode of decay.

19.70 Technetium has no stable isotopes. Which nuclides of this element lie in the belt of stability? Predict modes of decay for each.

19.71 Sodium-24, $t_{1/2}$ = 15.0 hours, can be used to study the sodium balance in animals. If a saline solution containing 25 μg of ^{24}Na is injected into an animal, how long can the study continue before only 1 μg is left?

19.72 Calculate the mass of ^{235}U that reacts in a 20-kiloton bomb, given that one nucleus releases 2.9×10^{-11} J. The designation "20 kiloton" means the same energy as 20×10^3 metric tons of TNT, which releases 2500 kJ of energy per kilogram.

19.73 For how many years could ^{235}U supply the world's energy needs, if the world supply of uranium is 10×10^6 metric tons, uranium contains 0.7% of ^{235}U, world energy consumption is 2×10^{17} kJ/yr, and each ^{235}U nucleus releases 2.9×10^{-11} J?

19.74 Samarium-146 (MM = 145.9129 g/mol) emits an α particle of energy 3.94×10^{-13} J and becomes ^{142}Nd (MM = 141.9075 g/mol). How much energy (in joules per nucleus) is released in this transformation? What fraction of the energy is carried off by the α-particle?

19.75 As discussed in Chapter 11, a condensation reaction between a carboxylic acid and an alcohol provides an ester with the elimination of water:

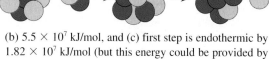

$$R_1C(=O)OH + R_2OH \longrightarrow R_1C(=O)OR_2 + H_2O$$

Explain how the unstable isotope ^{18}O can be used to show whether the oxygen atom in the water molecule comes from the carboxylic acid or from the alcohol.

19.76 Describe the role of the control rods and the moderator in the operation of a nuclear power plant.

19.77 Biochemical studies of DNA can be carried out using the unstable isotope phosphorus-32 ($t_{1/2}$ = 14.3 days). If 125 mg of $K_3{}^{32}PO_4$ is used in one particular study, how many milligrams will remain after 4 days?

ANSWERS TO SECTION EXERCISES

19.1.1 (a) $^{20}_{10}Ne$; (b) $^{98}_{43}Tc$; and (c) $^{3}_{1}H$.

19.1.2 (a) Unstable, $Z > 83$; (b) Unstable, odd-odd; (c) Stable; (d) Unstable, $N < Z$

19.1.3 Each set of numbers is in the order Z, N, A: (1a) 10, 10, 20; (1b) 43, 55, 98; (1c) 1,2,3; (2a) 94, 150, 244; (2b) 53, 73, 126; (2c) 64, 90, 154; and (2d) 8, 6, 14.

19.2.1 1.638×10^{-16} kJ/event and 9.862×10^7 kJ/mol

19.2.2 Total binding energy is 1.39×10^{10} kJ/mol; binding energy per nucleon is 7.29×10^8 kJ/mol.

19.2.3 3.3×10^8 kJ/mol

19.3.1 (a) β-decay; (b) α-decay; (c) γ-emission; and (d) positron emission or electron capture

19.3.2. (a) $^{140}_{57}Lu$; (b) $^{222}_{86}Rn$; and (c) $^{125}_{53}I$

19.3.3 12.1 days

19.4.1 (a) $^{59}_{27}Co + ^{1}_{0}n \longrightarrow (^{60m}_{27}Co) \longrightarrow ^{59}_{26}Fe + ^{1}_{1}p$

(b) $^{59}_{27}Co + ^{1}_{0}n \longrightarrow (^{60m}_{27}Co) \longrightarrow ^{60}_{27}Co + \gamma$

(c) $^{59}_{27}Co + ^{4}_{2}\alpha \longrightarrow (^{63m}_{29}Cu) \longrightarrow ^{62}_{28}Ni + ^{1}_{1}p$

(d) $^{59}_{27}Co + ^{1}_{1}p \longrightarrow (^{60m}_{28}Ni) \longrightarrow ^{58}_{28}Ni + 2\,^{1}_{0}n$

19.4.2 There are several possibilities. Here are two:

(a) $^{144}_{60}Nd + ^{1}_{0}n \longrightarrow (^{145m}_{60}Nd) \longrightarrow ^{145}_{61}Pm + ^{0}_{-1}\beta$

(b) $^{147}_{62}Sm + ^{1}_{0}n \longrightarrow (^{148}_{62}Sm) \longrightarrow ^{147}_{61}Pm + ^{1}_{1}p$

19.4.3 Order of answers is other reactant, other product: (a) neutron, γ-ray; (b) ^{54}Fe, ^{57}Ni; and (c) proton, α-particle.

19.5.1 For one neutron, −0.2152 g/mol and -1.93×10^{10} kJ/mol; for two neutrons, −0.2065 g/mol and -1.86×10^{10} kJ/mol; and for three neutrons, −0.1978 g/mol and -1.78×10^{10} kJ/mol

19.5.2 99.22% ^{238}U and 0.78% ^{235}U

19.6.1 (a)

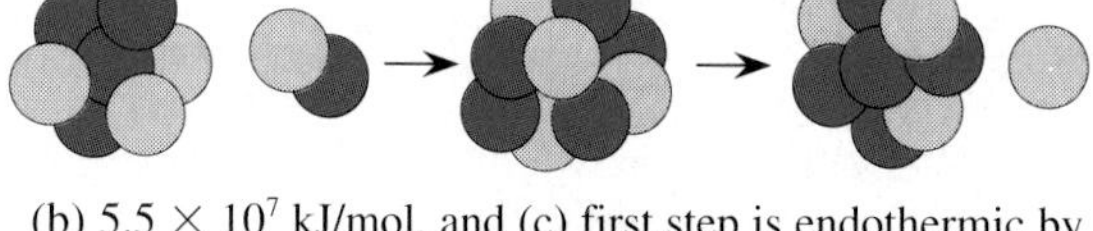

(b) 5.5×10^7 kJ/mol, and (c) first step is endothermic by 1.82×10^7 kJ/mol (but this energy could be provided by the kinetic energy of the deuterons); second step is exothermic by -1.50×10^9 kJ/mol.

19.6.2 1.5×10^5 L

19.6.3 3.7×10^{12} kJ

19.7.1 More than one sequence is possible. Here is one:

$$^{56}_{26}Fe + 3\,n \longrightarrow ^{59}_{26}Fe \longrightarrow ^{59}_{27}Co + \beta$$

$$^{59}_{27}Co + n \longrightarrow ^{60}_{27}Co \longrightarrow ^{60}_{28}Ni + \beta$$

$$^{60}_{28}Ni + 3\,n \longrightarrow ^{63}_{28}Ni \longrightarrow ^{63}_{29}Cu + \beta$$

$$^{63}_{29}Cu + 4\,n \longrightarrow ^{67}_{29}Cu \longrightarrow ^{67}_{30}Zn + \beta$$

$$^{67}_{30}Zn + 3\,n \longrightarrow ^{70}_{30}Zn$$

19.7.2 Planets around a second-generation star contain no elements with $Z > 26$. Simple life as we know it requires no elements with $Z > 26$, but mammalian life depends on enzymes containing copper, zinc, and cobalt.

19.8.1 4.5×10^5 β-rays, which deposit 1.0×10^{-7} J of energy

19.8.2 12,500 x-rays; the damage would not show up in a year.

19.9.1 6.5×10^3 years

19.9.2 (a) Good choice because γ-emitter with a short half-life; (b) poor choice because β-emitter with a relatively long half-life; (c) poor choice because of its long half-life; and (d) good choice, even though its half-life is long, because positron emitters do little damage

19.9.3 Mix the tracer with the warm air leaving the furnace, and monitor the exterior of the circulation system for the tracer. The tracer will appear where leaks are present.

APPENDIX A SCIENTIFIC NOTATION

Special notations are useful for expressing the precisions of very large and very small quantities. The diameter of a helium atom, for instance, is 0.00000000024 m, whereas the average distance from the Earth to the moon is 384,000,000 m. Writing numbers with this many zeros is cumbersome, and it is easy to make a mistake. To shorten the writing of small and large numbers, scientists commonly use **scientific notation.**

Scientific notation is based on the fact that any quantity can be expressed as an integer between 1 and 10 multiplied or divided by 10 an appropriate number of times. For example, 384,000,000 m can be written as:

Although it is not needed for scientific notation, 10^0 means "multiply by 10 zero times." Thus $1 \times 10^0 = 1$.

$$(3.84)(10)(10)(10)(10)(10)(10)\ (10)(10)\text{ m}$$

That looks cumbersome, but we can compress the eight (10)s into 10^8, meaning "multiply by 10 eight times": 3.84×10^8 m. Similarly, 0.00000000024 m is:

$$2.4 \div (10)(10)(10)(10)(10)(10)(10)(10)(10)(10)\text{ m}$$

We can compress the division by ten (10)s into 10^{-10}, meaning "divide by 10 ten times": 2.4×10^{-10} m.

The numeral "8" in 10^8 and the numeral "-10" in 10^{-10} are examples of **exponents** or **powers.** The scientific notation, 3.84×10^8 m, contains an exponent (or power of 10) of 8.

CONVERTING TO SCIENTIFIC NOTATION

When a number is divided by 10, the decimal point moves one place to the left; when a number is multiplied by 10, the decimal point moves one place to the right:

$$\frac{384}{10} = 38.4 \quad \textit{and} \quad (0.0024)(10) = 0.024$$

Multiplying *or* dividing a number by 10 changes its value, but multiplying *and* dividing a number by 10 leaves its value unchanged. Thus to convert a number larger than 10 to scientific notation, first divide by 10 the number of times that give an integer between 1 and 10, then multiply by 10 that same number of times. Here, for example, is the conversion of the number of seconds in a day into scientific notation:

$$\underbrace{\frac{86{,}400\text{ s/day}}{(10)(10)(10)(10)}}_{8.6400} \times \underbrace{(10)(10)(10)(10)}_{10^4} = 8.6400 \times 10^4\text{ s/day}$$

The four divisions by 10 move the decimal point four places to the left, and the four multiplications by 10 are written as 10^4.

A number larger than 10 can be quickly converted into scientific notation by moving the decimal point to the left enough places to give a number between 1 and 10, and multiplying by 10 raised to the positive power that equals the number of places moved. For example:

$$\underbrace{96{,}485}_{\text{4 places}} = 9.6485 \times 10^4$$

To convert a number smaller than 1 into scientific notation, first multiply by 10 as many times as needed to give an integer between 1 and 10 and then divide by 10 that same number of times. Here, for example, is the conversion into scientific notation of the fraction of a day represented by 1 s:

$$\underbrace{0.000011574 \text{ day/s } (10)(10)(10)(10)(10)}_{1.1574} \times \underbrace{\frac{1}{(10)(10)(10)(10)(10)}}_{10^{-5}} = 1.1574 \times 10^{-5} \text{ day/s}$$

To quickly convert a number smaller than 10 into scientific notation, move the decimal point to the right enough places to give an integer between 1 and 10 and multiply by 10 raised to the negative power that equals the number of places moved.

With practice, these conversions can be carried out quite quickly. The key is to count the number of places the decimal point must be moved. Here are some additional examples:

$$\underbrace{5260}_{\text{Move left three places}} \text{ ft/mi} = 5.260 \times 10^3 \text{ ft/mi}$$

$$\underbrace{0.08206}_{\text{Move right two places}} \text{ L atm/mol K} = 8.206 \times 10^{-2} \text{ L atm/mol K}$$

$$\underbrace{384{,}000{,}000}_{\text{Move left eight places}} \text{ mi} = 3.84 \times 10^8 \text{ mi}$$

$$\underbrace{0.00000000024}_{\text{Move right ten places}} \text{ m} = 2.4 \times 10^{-10} \text{ m}$$

WORKING WITH POWERS OF TEN

Chemistry students must be able to add, subtract, multiply, and divide using numbers that are expressed in scientific notation. Multiplication and division are handled in one fashion, whereas addition and subtraction are handled in another fashion.

To *multiply* two numbers expressed in scientific notation, multiply the values and *add* the exponents:

$$\overbrace{(2.450 \times 10^{2})(1.680 \times 10^{3})}^{\text{Add}} = 4.116 \times 10^{5} \quad [2 + 3 = 5]$$

Multiply

When exponents are added, their signs must be retained:

$$(2.450 \times 10^{2})(1.680 \times 10^{-3}) = 4.116 \times 10^{-1} \quad [2 + (-3) = -1]$$

(Add; Multiply)

We can verify that these results are correct by converting to standard notation, then carrying out the multiplications, and then expressing the result in power of 10 notation:

$$(245.0)(1680) = 411600 = 4.116 \times 10^{5}$$

$$(245.0)(0.001680) = 0.4116 = 4.116 \times 10^{-1}$$

To *divide* numbers expressed in power of 10 notation, divide the values and *subtract* the exponent of the divisor from that of the number divided:

$$(2.450 \times 10^{2})/(1.680 \times 10^{3}) = 1.458 \times 10^{-1} \quad [2 - 3 = -1]$$

(Subtract; Divide)

As with multiplication, when two exponents are subtracted, the signs of the exponents must be retained:

$$(2.450 \times 10^{2})/(1.680 \times 10^{-3}) = 1.458 \times 10^{5} \quad [2 - (-3) = 5]$$

(Subtract; Divide)

You should be able to verify that these results are correct by converting to standard notation, carrying out the division, and then converting the results to scientific notation.

Addition and subtraction require a different approach. Consider, for example, the addition of two numbers that we multiplied earlier:

$$2.450 \times 10^{2} + 1.680 \times 10^{3} = ?$$

Using standard notation, this addition is as follows:

$$\begin{array}{r} 1680 \\ +245.0 \\ \hline 1925 \end{array}$$

might be scalloped or fluted, in which case its length would vary by several centimeters, depending on whether it was measured at a protrusion or an indentation. A scientific example of this kind of fluctuation is the distance between the Earth and its moon. Because the moon's orbit is elliptical rather than perfectly circular, this distance fluctuates with time, varying by about 48,000 km in the course of a month.

RELATIVE AND ABSOLUTE PRECISION

The degree of precision in a given experimental value can be expressed either as an **absolute** precision or as a **relative** precision. Absolute precision is the numerical uncertainty in the experimental value, and relative precision is the absolute precision divided by the experimental value. Absolute precisions have units, but relative precisions are always dimensionless ratios. Each of these ways of looking at precision has useful applications.

To illustrate these concepts, return to the example of table length. If a table has been measured to be 1.826 m long, the absolute precision of the measurement is ± 0.001 m. The relative precision is the absolute precision divided by the length, which is 0.001 m/1.826 m, or 5×10^{-4}. This relative precision can be expressed as 1/1826, or 5×10^{-4}, or 0.05%, or 5 parts per 10,000. Each of these expressions is a ratio of two values that have the same units and is therefore dimensionless. Notice that because the absolute precision contains only one significant figure, this relative precision also contains only one significant figure.

When measurements are added or subtracted to compute a result, the absolute precision is more useful. When measurements are multiplied or divided to compute a result, the relative precision is more useful. Consider the volume and perimeter of the table top whose length we measured earlier. Suppose we measure its width (W) to be 3.20×10^{-1} m and its thickness (T) to be 1.5×10^{-2} m. The absolute precision of each of these measurements is 0.001 m. The relative precision of the width measurement is 0.001 m/3.20×10^{-1} m, which is 1/320, or 3×10^{-3}; the relative precision of the thickness measurement is 0.001 m/1.5×10^{-2} m, which is 1/15 or 7×10^{-2}.

Now combine these measurements to determine the perimeter P and the volume V of the table top. Perimeter is $P = L + L + W + W = 2(1.826) + 2(3.20 \times 10^{-1}) = 4.292$ m, and volume is $V = (L)(W)(T) = (1.826)(3.20 \times 10^{-1})(1.5 \times 10^{-2}) = 8.76 \times 10^{-3}$ m. How precisely do we know each of these computed values? We find the precisions of computed results from the precisions of individual measurements by considering the largest possible variation in each measurement.

First, consider the table's perimeter. According to the precision of the length measurement, the length might be as large as 1.827 m or as small as 1.825 m. The width might be 0.321 m or 0.319 m. Thus the perimeter could be as large as $2(1.827) + 2(0.321) = 4.296$ m or as small as $2(1.825) + 2(0.319) = 4.288$ m. The precision in the perimeter is ± 0.004 m. This is the *sum of the absolute precisions* of the individual values: $0.001 + 0.001 + 0.001 + 0.001 = 0.004$.

Applying the same logic to the volume computation, we find that it might be as large as $1.827 \times 0.321 \times 0.016 = 9.38 \times 10^{-3}$ m^3 or as small as $1.825 \times 0.319 \times 0.014 = 8.15 \times 10^{-3}$ m^3. The volume is $8.76 \times 10^{-3} \pm 0.62 \times 10^{-3}$ m^3, or there is an imprecision of $0.62 \times 10^{-3}/8.76 \times 10^{-3} = .071$. This is the *sum of the relative precisions* of length (5×10^{-4}), width (3×10^{-3}), and thickness (7×10^{-2}), totaling 7×10^{-2}.

RULES FOR DETERMINING PRECISION

The precision of a composite result can always be determined by this type of analysis, but the procedure is tedious. Fortunately the outcome is always the same. For *addition and subtraction,* the *absolute* precision of the result is the sum of the *absolute* precisions of the individual values. For *multiplication and division,* the *relative* precision of the result is the sum of the *relative* precisions of the individual values.

Another example illustrates the application of these rules for precision. A student, asked to determine the density of a nonvolatile unknown liquid, filled a 25-mL graduate cylinder until it contained 25.0 mL of liquid. The full cylinder weighed 47.5764 g. Using an eyedropper, the student carefully removed liquid until the cylinder contained 20.0 mL of liquid, whereupon it weighed 43.0464 g. Table B-1 summarizes the measurements, computations, and precisions involved in this example.

The absolute precision of each *measured quantity* is found directly from the measurement. For example, the absolute precision of the initial mass of the cylinder is the precision of the balance, 0.0001 g. Each relative precision is the absolute precision divided by the measured value; thus the relative precision of the initial mass of the cylinder is 1/475,000. The appropriate precision of each *computed quantity* is determined by adding the precisions of quantities used in the calculation. The values in boldface type are the ones that we find directly. The volume transferred (5.0 mL) is obtained by *subtracting* two volumes, so its *absolute* precision is the sum of the *absolute* precisions of the volumes ($0.1 + 0.1 = 0.2$ mL). The mass transferred (4.5300 g) is obtained by *subtracting* two masses, so its *absolute* precision is the sum of the *absolute* precisions of the two masses ($0.0001 + 0.0001 = 0.0002$ g). The density (0.9060 g/mL) is obtained by *dividing* mass by volume, so its *relative* precision is the sum of the *relative* precisions of transferred mass and transferred volume ($1/25 + 1/20{,}000 = 1/25$). After we find the relative precision of the density, we can use it to compute the absolute precision. The absolute precision of the density is $(1/25) \times (0.9060 \text{ g/mL}) = \pm 0.04$ g/mL.

TABLE B-1 MEASURED AND DERIVED QUANTITIES AND PRECISIONS

QUANTITY	VALUE	ABSOLUTE PRECISION	RELATIVE PRECISION
Measured Quantities			
Initial cylinder volume	25.0 mL	0.1 mL	1/250
Initial cylinder mass	47.5764 g	0.0001 g	1/475,000
Final cylinder volume	20.0 mL	0.1 mL	1/200
Final cylinder mass	43.0464 g	0.0001 g	1/430,000
Computed Quantities			
Volume transferred	5.0 mL	**0.2 mL**	2/50 = 1/25
Mass transferred	4.5300 g	**0.0002 g**	1/20,000
Liquid density	0.9060 g/mL	0.04g/mL	**1/25**

We can verify that our procedure gives the correct result by direct calculations of the maximum and minimum possible values for the density:

$$\text{Density}_{\text{calc}} = \frac{4.5300\ \text{g}}{5.0\ \text{mL}} = 0.90600\ \text{g/mL} = 0.91\ \text{g/mL}$$

$$\text{Density}_{\text{max}} = \frac{\text{Maximum mass}}{\text{Minimum volume}} \quad \textit{and} \quad \text{Density}_{\text{min}} = \frac{\text{Minimum mass}}{\text{Maximum volume}}$$

$$\text{Density}_{\text{max}} = \frac{(4.5300 + 0.0002)\ \text{g}}{(5.0 - 0.2)\ \text{mL}} = 0.94379\ \text{g/mL} = 0.94\ \text{g/mL}$$

$$\text{Density}_{\text{min}} = \frac{(4.5300 - 0.0002)\ \text{g}}{(5.0 + 0.2)\ \text{mL}} = 0.87112\ \text{g/mL} = 0.87\ \text{g/mL}$$

$$\text{That is, Density}_{\text{exp}} = 0.91 \pm 0.04\ \text{g/mL}$$

ROUNDING OFF

In the above example, the density might be as large as 0.944 g/mL or as small as 0.871 g/mL. It is incorrect to write it as 0.9060 g/mL because the use of four significant figures implies that the value is known to ±0.0001 g/mL. We must eliminate all nonsignificant figures, a process that is called **rounding off**. Notice that digits are dropped in the density calculations. Because the uncertainty in the density is in the *second* decimal place, this result is rounded off to two decimals: 0.91 g/mL. We have still overstated the precision, because 0.91 g/mL implies a precision of 0.01, whereas we actually know this result only to ±0.04. However, rounding off one more place to give 0.9 g/mL would imply an uncertainty of 0.1, which is larger than the actual uncertainty. The convention is to round off until dropping one more digit would result in an uncertainty larger than the actual uncertainty.

When the digit following the last significant digit is 5 or greater, the remaining digit is increased by 1 unit. For example, 0.9060 becomes 0.91. If the digit after the last significant digit is less than 5, the remaining digit remains unchanged. For example, 0.9045 rounded to 2 significant figures is 0.90.

SHORTCUTS TO PRECISION

As this example indicates, you can spend a lot of time and effort figuring out the appropriate number of significant figures in a result. Every time a chemist makes a measurement, precision and significant figures are a concern, but chemists are more interested in what experiments reveal than they are in significant figures. Chemists do not want to spend time determining precision. The first question, then, is "How important is precision for this particular experiment?" An analytical chemist interested in determining the level of a particular carcinogen in a sample of ground water might measure an amount of the carcinogen that was 1 part per billion. Because the amount of carcinogen may be critical to human health, the precision of this measure ment would have to be carefully stated. On the other hand, a synthetic chemist whose goal is to synthesize new compounds is primarily interested in preparing substances. Here, highly precise values are not important; the chemist wishes to achieve a high yield but is not concerned about whether a yield is 90% or 90.05%.

The following simple guidelines are sufficient to determine the appropriate number of significant figures for quantitative values whose exact values are less important than the qualitative results:

1. To determine the number of significant figures in an individual measurement, count the digits, left to right, beginning with the first one that is not zero:

305	3 significant figures
1.00	3 significant figures
0.020	2 significant figures

2. When adding or subtracting, set the number of *decimal places* in the answer equal to the number of *decimal places* in the number with the fewest places. The number of significant figures is irrelevant:

	0.12	2 significant figures	2 decimal places
	1.6	2 significant figures	**1 decimal place**
	11.490	5 significant figures	3 decimal places
SUM:	13.2	3 significant figures	**1 decimal place**

3. When multiplying or dividing, set the number of *significant figures* in the answer equal to that of the quantity with the fewest **significant figures**. The number of decimal places is irrelevant:

	1.365 ×	2.63 /	3.0 =	1.2
Significant figures:	4	3	**2**	**2**

This example is one in which the simplified procedure gives a different result than the more elaborate one. The divisor (3.0) has a relative precision of 1/30, so the result, 1.19665, could be rounded to 1.20 (1 part in 120) rather than to 1.2 (1 part in 12). If the importance of the result is its *quantitative* value, 1.20 would be the more appropriate number to report; if its importance is in its *qualitative* significance, report 1.2. (But don't spend a lot of time worrying about it: Either way of reporting is legitimate! What is *not* legitimate is to report this result as 1.19665.)

4. Calculators do not necessarily give results with the correct number of significant figures. They automatically drop trailing zeros even when they are significant (try multiplying or adding 3.00 and 5.00 on your calculator) and they carry extra decimal places even when they are insignificant (try dividing 5.00 by 3.00 on your calculator). *Never believe the number of significant figures on your calculator!*

APPENDIX C

SAMPLE CHAPTER SUMMARY

CHAPTER 1

Chemistry focuses on the properties and interactions of matter. It provides insights into many other scientific disciplines, including biology, geology, physics, astronomy, and the health professions. All of chemistry is founded on experimental observations of how things behave.

Matter is made up of atoms and molecules. The chemical description of matter uses elemental symbols for atoms, such as O for oxygen and Fe for iron. Compounds are described by formulas such as Fe_2O_3 that use symbols and subscripts. Elements and compounds can be represented using molecular pictures.

The elements display regular patterns of chemical behavior that can be organized into a periodic table. Within this table, the elements in each column share common chemical behavior. The periodic table also contains several groups of elements, including alkali metals, alkaline earth metals, halogens, and rare gases. Most elements are metals, but there are several nonmetals and a few metalloids that have some properties of both metals and nonmetals.

A substance can be categorized as a chemical element or a compound made up of a combination of elements. We can distinguish between pure samples and mixtures, and mixtures are either uniform in composition (homogeneous) or nonuniform (heterogeneous). A solution is a homogeneous mixture. Another way to categorize matter is by its phase: solids, which have fixed shapes and volumes; liquids, which have fixed volumes but variable shapes; and gases, whose shapes and volumes are easily altered.

Chemists measure physical properties, including mass, volume, time, and temperature. Any measurement must include three aspects: magnitude (how much), precision (how closely measured), and units (what is the standard). Calculators do not specify precision, but precision can be determined using simple rules and is expressed by the number of significant figures in a result. In dealing with small and large quantities, chemists use scientific (power of 10) notation. The sun, for example, is 9.3×10^7 miles from Earth.

Because different units exist for most quantities, chemists must know how to convert between different units. This is done by multiplying by a unit ratio that converts one unit to another without changing the value of the quantity. The ratio is chosen so that the undesired unit cancels:

$$4.5 \times 10^{-5}\,\cancel{m}\,(10^6\,\mu m/1\,\cancel{m}) = 4.5 \times 10^1\,\mu m$$

Temperature conversions are unlike other unit conversions because the zero points differ for the Celsius and kelvin scales. The scales are interconverted by an additive factor:

$$K = °C + 273.15$$

Chemists also compute properties from their measurements. For example, a sample's density can be calculated from its mass and volume:

$$d = m/V$$

Density is an intensive property because it is independent of sample size. Densities can be tabulated and used as needed to calculate volume from mass measurements:

$$V = m/d$$

Following a step-wise procedure makes chemical problem solving easier. After identifying the type of problem, think about what the molecules are doing. Then look for useful equations, organize data into a table, rearrange the equations, substitute, and solve. Finally, check that the result is reasonable, both numerically (is it about the right size and does it have the right units?) and chemically (does it make sense for molecules to behave that way?).

Substance	ΔH_f° (kJ mol^{-1})	ΔG_f° (kJ mol^{-1})	S° (J mol^{-1}K^{-1})	C_p° (J mol^{-1}K^{-1})
Boron				
$B_{(s)}$	0.0	0.0	5.86	11.09
$B_2H_{6\,(g)}$	35.6	86.7	232.11	56.90
$B_2O_{3\,(s)}$	−1272.77	−1193.65	53.97	62.93
$H_3BO_{3\,(s)}$	−1094.33	−968.92	88.83	81.38
$[B(OH)_4]^-_{(aq)}$	−1344.03	−1153.17	102.5	
$BF_{3\,(g)}$	−1137.00	−1120.33	254.12	50.46
$BCl_{3\,(l)}$	−427.2	−387.4	206.3	106.7
$NaBH_{4\,(s)}$	−183.34	−119.54	104.68	86.6
Bromine				
$Br_{2\,(l)}$	0.0	0.0	152.231	75.689
$Br_{2\,(g)}$	30.907	3.110	245.463	36.02
$Br_{(g)}$	111.884	82.396	175.022	20.786
$Br^-_{(aq)}$	−121.55	−103.96	82.4	−141.8
$HBr_{(g)}$	−36.40	−53.45	198.695	29.142
$BrO^-_{(aq)}$	−94.1	−33.4	42	
$BrO^-_{3\,(aq)}$	−67.07	18.60	161.71	
Cadmium				
$Cd_{(s)}$	0.0	0.0	51.76	25.98
$Cd^{2-}_{(aq)}$	−75.90	−77.612	−73.2	
$CdO_{(s)}$	−258.2	−228.4	54.8	43.43
$CdCl_{2\,(s)}$	−391.50	−343.93	115.27	74.68
$CdS_{(s)}$	−161.9	−156.5	64.9	
Calcium				
$Ca_{(s)}$	0.0	0.0	41.42	25.31
$Ca^{2+}_{(aq)}$	−542.83	−553.58	−53.1	
$CaO_{(s)}$	−635.09	−604.03	39.75	42.80
$Ca(OH)_{2\,(s)}$	−986.09	−896.49	83.39	87.49
$CaC_{2\,(s)}$	−59.8	−64.9	69.96	62.72
$CaCO_{3\,(s)}$	−1206.87	−1128.76	92.9	81.88
$CaSO_{4\,(s)}$	−1434.11	−1321.79	106.7	99.66
$CaSO_4{\cdot}6H_2O_{(s)}$	−2022.63	−1797.28	194.1	186.02
$CaF_{2\,(s)}$	−1219.6	−1167.3	68.87	67.03
$CaCl_{2\,(s)}$	−795.8	−748.1	104.6	72.59
$CaBr_{2\,(s)}$	−682.8	−663.6	130	
$Ca(NO_3)_{2\,(s)}$	−938.39	−743.07	193.3	149.37
$Ca_3(PO_4)_{2\,(s)}$	−4120.8	−3884.7	236.0	227.82
Carbon				
$C_{(graphite)}$	0.0	0.0	5.740	8.527
$C_{(diamond)}$	1.895	2.900	2.377	6.113
$CH_{4\,(g)}$	−74.81	−50.72	186.264	35.309
$C_2H_{2\,(g)}$	226.73	209.20	200.94	43.93
$C_2H_{4\,(g)}$	52.26	68.15	219.56	43.56
$C_2H_{6\,(g)}$	−84.68	−32.82	229.60	52.63
$C_3H_{6\,(g)}$	20.41	74.62	226.9	63.89
$C_6H_{6\,(l)}$	49.028	124.50	172.8	
$CO_{(g)}$	−110.525	−137.168	197.674	29.142
$CO_{2\,(g)}$	−393.509	−394.359	213.74	37.11
$CO_{2\,(aq)}$	−412.9	−386.2	121.3	
$HCN_{(g)}$	135.1	124.7	201.78	35.86
$CS_{2\,(l)}$	89.70	65.27	151.34	75.7
$CF_{4\,(g)}$	−925	−879	261.61	61.09
$CCl_{4\,(l)}$	−135.44	−65.21	216.40	131.75
$CH_3Cl_{(g)}$	−80.83	−57.37	234.58	40.75
$CH_2Cl_{2\,(l)}$	−121.46	−67.26	177.8	100.0
$CF_2Cl_{2\,(g)}$	−477	−440	301	72.3
$CHCl_{3\,(l)}$	−134.47	−73.66	201.7	113.8
$CH_3CF_{3\,(l)}$	−737	−668	280	78.2
cis-$CHClCHCl_{(l)}$	−27.6	22.05	198.41	113
trans-$CHClCHCl_{(l)}$	−23.14	27.28	195.85	113

Substance	ΔH_f° (kJ mol^{-1})	ΔG_f° (kJ mol^{-1})	S° (J mol^{-1}K^{-1})	C_p° (J mol^{-1}K^{-1})
$HCHO_{(g)}$	−108.57	−102.53	218.77	35.40
$CH_3CHO_{(g)}$	−166.19	−128.86	250.3	57.3
$HCO_2H_{(l)}$	−424.72	−361.35	128.95	99.04
$CH_3CO_2H_{(l)}$	−484.5	−389.9	159.8	124.3
$CH_3CO_2H_{(aq)}$	−485.76	−396.46	178.7	
$CH_3OH_{(l)}$	−238.66	−166.27	126.8	81.6
$CH_3CH_2OH_{(l)}$	−277.69	−174.78	160.7	111.46
$CH_3NH_{2\,(g)}$	−47.3	35.6	150.21	
$CO(NH_2)_{2\,(s)}$	−334	−198	105	93.2
$CH_3CN_{(l)}$	54	99	150	91.5
$C_3H_3N_{(l)}$	172.9	208.6	188	63.76
$(CH_3)_2SO_{(l)}$	−203	−99	188	147.3
$C_6H_{12}O_{6\,(s)}$ (glucose)	−1274.5	−910.56	212.1	
$C_{12}H_{22}O_{11\,(s)}$ (sucrose)	−2221.7	−1544.3	360.24	
Chlorine				
$Cl_{2\,(g)}$	0.0	0.0	223.066	33.907
$Cl_{(g)}$	121.679	105.680	165.198	21.840
$Cl^-_{(aq)}$	−167.59	−131.228	56.5	−136.4
$HCl_{(g)}$	−92.307	−95.299	186.908	29.12
$ClO^-_{(aq)}$	−107.1	−36.8	42	
$ClO_{2\,(aq)}^-$	−67	17	101	
$ClO_{3\,(aq)}^-$	−104	−3	162	
$ClO_{4\,(aq)}^-$	−129.33	−8.52	182.0	
$ClO_{(g)}$	109	98	227	31.5
$ClO_{2\,(g)}$	102.5	120.5	256.84	41.97
$Cl_2O_{(g)}$	80	98	266	45.4
$ClF_{(g)}$	−54.48	−55.94	217.89	32.05
$ClF_{3\,(g)}$	−163.2	−123.0	281.61	63.85
Chromium				
$Cr_{(s)}$	0.0	0.0	23.77	23.35
$Cr_2O_{3\,(s)}$	−1139.7	−1058.1	81.2	118.74
$Cr_2O_{7\,(aq)}^{2-}$	−1490.3	−1301.1	261.9	
$CrCl_{3\,(s)}$	−556.5	−486.1	123.0	91.80
Cobalt				
$Co_{(s)}$	0.0	0.0	30.04	24.81
$Co^{2+}_{(aq)}$	−58.2	−54.4	−113	
$CoO_{(s)}$	−237.94	−214.20	52.97	55.23
$Co_3O_{4\,(s)}$	−891	−774	102.5	123.4
$CoCl_{2\,(s)}$	−312.5	−269.8	109.16	78.49
$CoSO_{4\,(s)}$	−888.3	782.3	118.0	
Copper				
$Cu_{(s)}$	0.0	0.0	33.150	24.435
$Cu^{2+}_{(aq)}$	64.77	65.49	−99.6	
$CuO_{(s)}$	−157.3	−129.7	42.63	42.30
$Cu_2O_{(s)}$	−168.6	−146.0	93.14	63.64
$CuS_{(s)}$	−53.1	−53.6	66.5	47.82
$Cu_2S_{(s)}$	−79.5	−86.2	120.9	76.32
$CuCl_{2\,(s)}$	−220.1	−175.7	108.07	71.88
$CuCl_{(s)}$	−137.2	−119.86	86.2	48.5
$CuBr_{(s)}$	−104.6	−100.8	96.11	54.73
$CuI_{(s)}$	−67.8	−69.5	96.7	54.06
$CuSO_{4\,(s)}$	−771.36	−661.8	109	100.0
$CuSO_4{\cdot}5H_2O_{(s)}$	−2279.65	−1879.745	300.4	280
Fluorine				
$F_{2\,(g)}$	0.0	0.0	202.78	31.30
$F_{(g)}$	78.99	61.91	158.754	22.744
$F^-_{(aq)}$	−332.63	−278.79	−13.8	−106.7
$HF_{(g)}$	−271.1	−273.2	173.669	29.133
$HF_{(aq)}$	−320.08	−296.82	88.7	

Continued.

Substance	ΔH_f° (kJ mol^{-1})	ΔG_f° (kJ mol^{-1})	S° (J mol^{-1}K^{-1})	C_p° (J mol^{-1}K^{-1})
Germanium				
$Ge_{(s)}$	0	0	3	23.3
$GeCl_{4\,(g)}$	−496	−457	348	
$GeH_{4\,(g)}$	91	113	217	45.0
$GeO_{2\,(s)}$	−551	−497	55	30.9
Gold				
$Au_{(s)}$	0	0	48	25.4
Helium				
$He_{(g)}$	0.0	0.0	126.150	20.786
Hydrogen				
$H_{2\,(g)}$	0.0	0.0	130.684	28.824
$H_{(g)}$	217.965	203.247	114.713	20.784
$H^+_{(aq)}$	0.0	0.0	0.0	0.0
$H_3O^+_{(aq)}$	−285.830	−237.129	69.91	75.291
Iodine				
$I_{2\,(s)}$	0.0	0.0	116.135	54.438
$I_{2\,(g)}$	62.438	19.327	260.69	36.90
$I_{(g)}$	106.838	70.250	180.791	20.786
$I^-_{(aq)}$	−55.19	−51.57	111.3	−142.3
$HI_{(g)}$	26.48	1.70	206.594	29.158
$HIO_{(aq)}$	−138.1	−99.1	95.4	
$IO^-_{(aq)}$	−107.5	−38.5	−5.4	
$IO^-_{3\,(aq)}$	−221.3	−128.0	118.4	
Iron				
$Fe_{(s)}$	0.0	0.0	27.28	25.10
$Fe^{2+}_{(aq)}$	−89.1	−78.90	−137.7	
$Fe^{3+}_{(aq)}$	−48.5	−4.7	−315.9	
$Fe_2O_{3\,(s)}$	−824.2	−742.2	−87.40	103.85
$Fe_3O_{4\,(s)}$	−1118.4	−1015.4	146.4	143.43
$Fe(OH)_{2\,(s)}$	−569.0	−486.5	88	
$Fe(OH)_{3\,(s)}$	−823.0	−696.5	106.7	
$FeCl_{2\,(s)}$	−341.79	−302.30	117.95	76.65
$FeCl_{3\,(s)}$	−399.49	−334.00	142.3	96.65
$FeSO_{4\,(s)}$	−928.4	−820.8	107.5	100.58
$FeSO_4 \cdot 7H_2O_{(s)}$	−3014.57	−2509.87	409.2	394.47
$FeCO_{3\,(s)}$	−741	−667	93	82.1
Lead				
$Pb_{(s)}$	0.0	0.0	64.81	26.44
$Pb^{2+}_{(aq)}$	−1.7	−24.43	10.5	
$PbO_{(s)}$	−217.32	−187.89	68.70	45.77
$PbO_{2\,(s)}$	−277.4	−217.33	68.6	64.64
$PbS_{(s)}$	−100.4	−98.7	91.2	49.50
$PbCl_{2\,(s)}$	−359.41	−314.10	136.0	
$PbSO_{4\,(s)}$	−919.94	−813.14	148.57	103.207
Lithium				
$Li_{(s)}$	0.0	0.0	29.12	24.77
$Li^+_{(aq)}$	−278.49	−293.31	13.4	68.6
$Li_2O_{(s)}$	−597.94	−561.18	37.57	54.10
$LiH_{(s)}$	−90.54	−68.35	20.008	27.87
$LiOH_{(s)}$	−484.93	−438.95	42.80	49.66
$LiF_{(s)}$	−615.97	−587.71	35.65	41.59
$LiCl_{(s)}$	−408.61	−384.37	59.33	47.99
$LiNO_{3\,(s)}$	−483.13	−381.1	90.0	
$LiAlH_{4\,(s)}$	−116.3	−44.7	78.74	83.18
Magnesium				
$Mg_{(s)}$	0.0	0.0	32.68	24.89
$Mg^{2+}_{(aq)}$	−466.85	−454.8	−138.1	
$MgO_{(s)}$	−601.70	−569.43	26.94	37.15
$Mg(OH)_{2\,(s)}$	−924.54	−833.51	63.18	77.03

Substance	ΔH_f° (kJ mol^{-1})	ΔG_f° (kJ mol^{-1})	S° (J mol^{-1}K^{-1})	C_p° (J mol^{-1}K^{-1})
$MgF_{2\,(s)}$	−1123.4	−1070.2	57.24	61.59
$MgCl_{2\,(s)}$	−641.32	−591.79	89.62	71.38
$MgBr_{2\,(s)}$	−524.3	−503.8	117.2	
$MgI_{2\,(s)}$	−364.0	−358.2	129.7	
$MgCO_{3\,(s)}$	−1095.8	−1012.1	65.7	75.52
$Mg(NO_3)_{2\,(s)}$	−790.65	−589.4	164.0	141.92
$Mg_3(PO_4)_{2\,(s)}$	−3780.7	−3538.7	189.20	213.47
$MgSO_{4\,(s)}$	−1284.9	−1170.6	91.6	96.48
Manganese				
$Mn_{(s)}$	0.0	0.0	32.01	26.32
$Mn^{2+}_{(aq)}$	−220.75	−228.1	−73.6	50
$MnO_{(s)}$	−385.22	−362.90	59.71	45.44
$MnO_{2\,(s)}$	−520.03	−465.14	53.05	54.14
$Mn_2O_{3\,(s)}$	−959.0	−881.1	110.5	107.65
$Mn_3O_{4\,(s)}$	−1387.8	−1283.2	155.6	139.66
$MnCl_{2\,(s)}$	−481.29	−440.50	118.24	72.93
$MnSO_{4\,(s)}$	−1065.25	−957.36	112.1	100.50
$MnO^-_{4\,(aq)}$	−541.4	−447.2	191.2	−82.0
$MnO^{2-}_{4\,(aq)}$	−653	−500.7	59	
Mercury				
$Hg_{(l)}$	0.0	0.0	76.02	27.983
$Hg_{(g)}$	61.32	31.82	174.96	20.876
$Hg^{2+}_{(aq)}$	171.1	164.40	−32.2	
$Hg^{2+}_{2\,(aq)}$	172.4	153.52	84.5	
$HgO_{(s)}$	−90.83	−58.539	70.29	44.06
$HgCl_{2\,(s)}$	−224.3	−178.6	146.0	
$Hg_2Cl_{2\,(s)}$	−265.22	−210.745	192.5	
$HgS_{(s)}$	−58.2	−50.6	82.4	48.41
Neon				
$Ne_{(g)}$	0.0	0.0	146.328	20.786
Nickel				
$Ni_{(s)}$	0.0	0.0	29.87	26.07
$Ni^{2+}_{(aq)}$	−54.0	−45.6	−128.9	
$NiO_{(s)}$	−239.7	−211.7	37.99	44.31
$NiS_{(s)}$	−82.0	−79.5	52.97	47.11
$NiCl_{2\,(s)}$	−305.332	−259.032	97.65	71.67
$NiSO_{4\,(s)}$	−872.91	−759.7	92	138
Nitrogen				
$N_{2\,(g)}$	0.0	0.0	191.61	29.125
$NH_{3\,(g)}$	−46.11	−16.45	192.45	35.06
$NH_{3\,(aq)}$	−80.29	−26.50	111.3	
$NH^+_{4\,(aq)}$	−132.51	−79.31	113.4	79.9
$N_2H_{4\,(l)}$	50.63	149.34	121.21	98.87
$NO_{(g)}$	90.25	86.55	210.761	29.844
$NO_{2\,(g)}$	33.18	51.31	240.06	37.20
$N_2O_{(g)}$	82.05	104.20	219.85	38.45
$N_2O_{3\,(g)}$	83.72	139.46	312.28	65.61
$N_2O_{4\,(g)}$	9.16	97.89	304.29	77.28
$N_2O_{5\,(s)}$	−43.1	113.9	178.2	143.1
$HNO_{3\,(l)}$	−174.10	−80.71	155.60	109.87
$HNO_{3\,(g)}$	−135.06	−74.72	266.38	53.35
$NO^-_{3\,(aq)}$	−205.0	−108.74	146.4	−86.6
$NH_4NO_{3\,(s)}$	−365.56	−183.87	151.08	139.3
$NH_4Cl_{(s)}$	−314.43	−202.87	94.6	84.1
$NH_4Br_{(s)}$	−270.83	−175.2	113	96
$NH_4I_{(s)}$	−201.42	−112.5	117	
$(NH_4)_2SO_{4\,(s)}$	−1180.85	−901.67	220.1	187.49
$NH_4HCO_{3\,(s)}$	−847	−666	12.1	

Continued.

Substance	ΔH_f° (kJ mol^{-1})	ΔG_f° (kJ mol^{-1})	S° (J mol^{-1}K^{-1})	C_p° (J mol^{-1}K^{-1})
Oxygen				
$O_{2\,(g)}$	0.0	0.0	205.138	29.355
$O_{(g)}$	249.170	231.731	161.055	21.912
$O_{3\,(g)}$	142.7	163.2	238.93	39.20
$OH^-_{(aq)}$	−229.994	−157.244	−10.75	−148.5
$H_2O_{(l)}$	−285.830	−237.129	69.91	75.291
$H_2O_{(g)}$	−241.818	−228.72	188.825	33.577
$H_2O_{2\,(l)}$	−187.78	−120.35	109.6	89.1
Phosphorus				
$P_{(white)}$	0.0	0.0	41.09	23.840
$P_{(red)}$	−17.6	−12.1	22.80	21.21
$P_{4\,(g)}$	58.91	24.44	279.98	67.15
$PH_{3\,(g)}$	5.4	13.4	210.23	37.11
$P_4O_{10\,(s)}$	−2984.0	−2697.7	228.86	211.71
$H_3PO_{4\,(s)}$	−1279.0	−1119.1	110.50	106.06
$H_3PO_{4\,(aq)}$	−1288.34	−1142.54	158.2	
$H_2PO_4^-{}_{(aq)}$	−1296.29	−1130.28	90.4	
$HPO_4^{2-}{}_{(aq)}$	−1292.14	−1089.15	−33.5	
$PO_4^{3-}{}_{(aq)}$	−1277.4	−1018.7	−222	
$PF_{3\,(g)}$	−918.8	−897.5	273.24	58.70
$PCl_{5\,(g)}$	−374.9	−305.0	364.58	112.80
$PCl_{3\,(l)}$	−319.7	−272.3	217.1	
$PCl_{3\,(g)}$	−287.0	−267.8	311.78	71.84
Potassium				
$K_{(s)}$	0.0	0.0	64.18	29.58
$K^+_{(aq)}$	−252.38	−283.27	102.5	21.8
$KO_{2\,(s)}$	−284.93	−239.4	116.7	77.53
$K_2O_{2\,(s)}$	−494.1	−425.1	102.1	
$KOH_{(s)}$	−424.764	−379.08	78.9	64.9
$KF_{(s)}$	−567.27	−537.75	66.57	49.04
$KCl_{(s)}$	−436.747	−409.14	82.59	51.30
$KBr_{(s)}$	−393.798	−380.66	95.90	52.30
$KI_{(s)}$	−327.900	−324.892	106.32	52.93
$KClO_{4\,(s)}$	−432.75	−303.09	151.0	112.38
$K_2CO_{3\,(s)}$	−1151.02	−1063.5	155.52	114.43
$KNO_{3\,(s)}$	−494.63	−394.86	133.05	96.40
$K_2SO_{4\,(s)}$	−1437.79	−1321.37	175.56	131.46
$KMnO_{4\,(s)}$	−837.2	−737.6	171.71	117.57
$K_2CrO_{4\,(s)}$	−1403.7	−1295.7	200.12	145.98
$K_2Cr_2O_{7\,(s)}$	−2061.5	−1881.8	291.2	219.24
$K_4Fe(CN)_{6\,(s)}$	−594.1	−453.0	418.8	332.21
$K_3Fe(CN)_{6\,(s)}$	−249.8	−129.6	426.06	
Selenium				
$Se_{(s)}$	0.0	0.0	42.442	25.363
$H_2Se_{(g)}$	29.7	15.9	219.02	34.73
Silicon				
$Si_{(s)}$	0.0	0.0	18.83	20.00
$SiH_{4\,(g)}$	34.3	56.9	204.62	42.84
$SiO_{2\,(s)}$	−910.94	−856.64	41.84	44.43
$H_4SiO_{4\,(s)}$	−1481.1	−1332.9	192	
$H_2SiO_{3\,(s)}$	−1188.7	−1092.4	134	
$SiF_{4\,(g)}$	−1614.94	−1572.65	282.49	73.64
$SiCl_{4\,(l)}$	−687.0	−619.84	239.7	145.31
$SiBr_{4\,(l)}$	−457.3	−443.9	277.8	
$SiC_{(s)}$	−65.3	−62.8	16.61	26.86
Silver				
$Ag_{(s)}$	0.0	0.0	42.55	25.351
$Ag^+_{(aq)}$	105.579	77.107	72.68	21.8
$Ag_2O_{(s)}$	−31.05	−11.20	121.3	65.86
$AgS_{(s)}$	−32.59	−40.67	144.01	76.53

Substance	ΔH_f° (kJ mol^{-1})	ΔG_f° (kJ mol^{-1})	S° (J mol^{-1}K^{-1})	C_p° (J mol^{-1}K^{-1})
Silver—cont'd				
$AgCl_{(s)}$	−127.068	−109.789	96.2	50.79
$AgBr_{(s)}$	−100.37	−96.90	107.1	52.38
$AgI_{(s)}$	−61.84	−66.19	115.5	56.82
$AgNO_{3\,(s)}$	−124.39	−33.41	140.92	93.05
$Ag_2SO_{4\,(s)}$	−715.88	−618.41	200.4	131.38
$AgSCN_{(s)}$	87.9	101.39	131.0	63
Sodium				
$Na_{(s)}$	0.0	0.0	51.21	28.24
$Na^+_{(aq)}$	−240.12	−261.905	59.0	46.4
$Na_2O_{(s)}$	−414.22	−375.46	75.06	69.12
$Na_2O_{2\,(s)}$	−510.87	−447.7	95.0	89.24
$NaH_{(s)}$	−56.275	−33.46	40.016	36.401
$NaOH_{(s)}$	−425.609	−379.494	64.455	59.54
$Na_2S_{(s)}$	−364.8	−349.8	83.7	
$NaF_{(s)}$	−573.647	−543.494	51.46	46.86
$NaCl_{(s)}$	−411.153	−384.138	72.13	50.50
$NaBr_{(s)}$	−361.062	−348.983	86.82	51.38
$NaI_{(s)}$	−287.78	−286.06	98.53	52.09
$NaClO_{4\,(s)}$	−383.30	−254.85	142.3	
$Na_2CO_{3\,(s)}$	−1130.68	−1044.44	134.98	112.30
$NaHCO_{3\,(s)}$	−950.81	−851.0	101.7	87.61
$Na_2SO_{4\,(s)}$	−1387.08	−1270.16	149.58	128.20
$NaHSO_{4\,(s)}$	−1125.5	−992.8	113.0	
$Na_2S_2O_{3\,(s)}$	−1123.0	−1028.0	155	146.0
$NaNO_{3\,(s)}$	−467.85	−367.00	116.52	92.88
$Na_3PO_{4\,(s)}$	−1917.40	−1788.80	173.80	153.47
$NaCH_3CO_{2\,(s)}$	−708.80	−607.18	123.0	79.9
$NaCN_{(s)}$	−87.49	−76.43	115.60	70.37
$NaH_2PO_{4\,(s)}$	−1538	−1387	128	116.9
$Na_2HPO_{4\,(s)}$	−1749	−1609	151	135.4
$Na_2B_4O_7\cdot 10H_2O_{(s)}$	−6292	−5519	586	615.3
Strontium				
$Sr_{(s)}$	0.0	0.0	52.3	26.4
$Sr^{2+}_{(aq)}$	−545.80	−559.48	−32.6	
$SrO_{(s)}$	−592.0	−561.9	54.4	45.02
$SrCO_{3\,(s)}$	−1220.1	−1140.1	97.1	81.42
$SrCl_{2\,(s)}$	−828.9	−781.1	114.85	75.60
Sulfur				
$S_{(s)}$	0.0	0.0	31.80	22.64
$S_{8\,(g)}$	102.30	49.63	430.98	156.44
$H_2S_{(g)}$	−20.63	−33.56	205.79	34.23
$SO_{2\,(g)}$	−296.830	−300.194	248.22	39.87
$SO_{3\,(s)}$	−454.51	−374.21	70.7	
$SO_{3\,(g)}$	−395.72	−371.06	256.76	50.67
$H_2SO_{4\,(l)}$	−813.989	−690.003	156.904	138.91
$H_2SO_{4\,(aq)}$	−909.27	−744.53	20.1	−293
$HSO_{4\,(aq)}^-$	−887.34	−755.91	131.8	−84
$SO_{4\,(aq)}^{2-}$	−909.27	−774.53	20.1	−293
$SF_{6\,(g)}$	−1209	−1105.3	291.82	97.28
Tellurium				
$Te_{(s)}$	0.0	0.0	49.71	25.73
$TeO_{2\,(s)}$	−322.6	−270.3	79.5	
Tin				
$Sn_{(white)}$	0.0	0.0	51.55	26.99
$Sn_{(gray)}$	−2.09	0.13	44.14	25.77
$SnO_{(s)}$	−285.8	−256.9	56.5	44.31
$SnO_{2\,(s)}$	−580.7	−519.6	52.3	52.59
$SnCl_{4\,(l)}$	−511.3	−440.1	258.6	165.3

Continued.

Substance	ΔH_f° (kJ mol^{-1})	ΔG_f° (kJ mol^{-1})	S° (J mol^{-1}K^{-1})	C_p° (J mol^{-1}K^{-1})
Uranium				
$U_{(s)}$	0.0	0.0	50.21	27.665
$UO_{2\,(s)}$	−1084.9	−1031.7	77.03	63.60
$UO_{3\,(s)}$	−1223.8	−1145.9	96.11	81.67
$UF_{6\,(g)}$	−2147.4	−2063.7	377.9	129.62
Xenon				
$Xe_{(g)}$	0.0	0.0	169.683	20.786
$XeF_{2\,(g)}$	−130	−96	260	
$XeF_{4\,(g)}$	−215	−138	316	
$XeO_{3\,(g)}$	502	561	287	
Zinc				
$Zn_{(s)}$	0.0	0.0	41.63	25.40
$Zn^{2+}_{(aq)}$	−153.89	−147.06	−112.1	46
$ZnO_{(s)}$	−348.28	−318.30	43.64	40.25
$Zn(OH)_{2\,(s)}$	−643.25	−555.07	81.6	72.4
$ZnS_{(s)}$	−205.98	−201.29	57.7	46.0
$ZnCl_{2\,(s)}$	−415.05	−369.398	111.46	71.34
$ZnSO_{4\,(s)}$	−982.8	−871.5	110.5	99.2
$Zn(NO_3)_2\cdot 6H_2O_{(s)}$	−2306.64	−1772.71	456.9	323.0
$ZnCO_{3\,(s)}$	−812.78	−731.52	82.4	79.71

APPENDIX F

THE MATHEMATICS DESCRIBING CHANGE

CHANGES IN PROPERTIES

Properties undergo changes in many of the processes that chemists describe. For example, volume changes as the gas in a chamber is compressed by a piston, concentrations of chemical substances change as a reaction proceeds, and the total energy content of a substance changes as its temperature is varied. In each of these processes, at least two variables are changing. Volume and pressure change during compression of a gas; concentration and time change during a chemical reaction, and energy and temperature change when a substance is heated.

Usually, we express the change in one variable in terms of the change in the other: Pressure depends on volume, concentration depends on time, and energy depends on temperature. A mathematical equation describes quantitatively how one property depends on another. A convenient way to begin, however, is by drawing a graph of the variation. For example, Figure F-1, a graph of the pressure–volume variation of an ideal gas held at constant temperature, shows how the pressure exerted by a sample of ideal gas changes as the gas volume is allowed to change. The dependent variable (pressure) appears along the y-axis, and the independent variable (volume) along the x-axis. Each point on this graph represents the value of the y-variable associated with one particular value of the x-variable.

From a graph such as this, it is easy to determine the change in variables from one set of conditions to another. For example, as we change the volume from V_1 to V_2, the pressure changes from P_1 to P_2. Changes in variables are conventionally designated by the Greek capital letter Δ (delta). Each such change is defined to be the final value of the variable minus the initial value of the variable. For pressure and volume:

$$\Delta V = V_f - V_i \qquad \textit{and} \qquad \Delta P = P_f - P_i$$

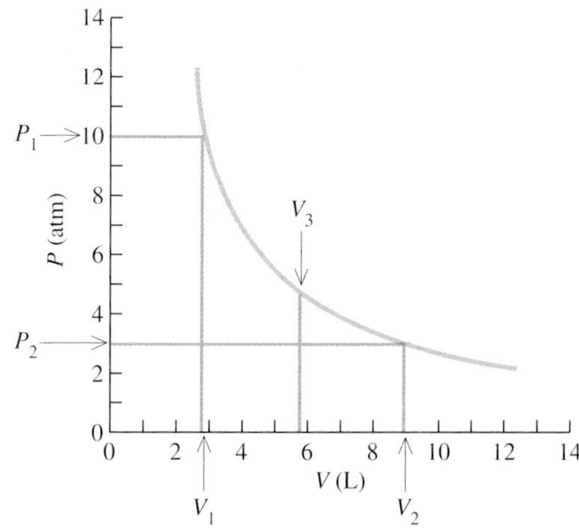

FIGURE F-1
A graph of how pressure varies with volume for an ideal gas. Each point on the graph corresponds to a single volume and pressure. At V_1 = 2.7 L, for example, P_1 = 10.0 atm, and at V_2 = 9.0 L, P_2 = 3.0 atm. What is the pressure at V_3 = 5.8 L?

If the system that is graphed in Figure F-1 undergoes a change of conditions from V_1 to V_2, $\Delta V = 9.0\text{ L} - 2.7\text{ L} = 6.3\text{ L}$ and $\Delta P = 3.0\text{ atm} - 10.0\text{ atm} = -7.0\text{ atm}$.

RATIOS OF CHANGES

The magnitude of the change in a dependent variable is linked to the magnitude of the change in the independent variable. If we change the volume of the system shown in Figure F-1 from V_1 to V_3 rather than to V_2, ΔV is a smaller quantity, and so is ΔP. Suppose, however, that we examine the amount of change in P *per unit change* in V. This quantity is the ratio of the changes, $\Delta P/\Delta V$. It is also the **rate** at which P changes with V.

The usefulness of such ratios is illustrated by an example involving time. Figure F-2 shows the variation in the concentration of a product of a chemical reaction as a function of reaction time. During the time interval $\Delta t = t_1 - t_0$, there is a change in concentration $\Delta c = c_1 - c_0$. The ratio of these two changes, $\Delta c/\Delta t$, describes the average rate at which concentration changes during the time interval Δt. In the example shown in the figure, this average rate is different for different time intervals. For $t_1 = 50$ s, $\Delta c/\Delta t = 0.293\text{ M}/50\text{ s} = 5.86 \times 10^{-3}$ M/s; for $t_1 = 100$ s, on the other hand, $\Delta c/\Delta t = 0.500\text{ M}/100\text{ s} = 5.00 \times 10^{-3}$ M/s. The change in the ratio with time arises because the reaction proceeds at a variable rate rather than at a constant rate.

Even though the rate of this process changes with time, we can identify how fast the process occurs *at any particular time*. This is called the **instantaneous rate.** The instantaneous rate of a chemical reaction is analogous to the speed measured by an automobile speedometer, which describes how fast the automobile is moving at any given instant. Average rates, as defined by $\Delta c/\Delta t$, are different from instantaneous rates in the same way that a speedometer reading is different from average speed. For example, the speedometer may read 60 mi/hr at some time during a trip from one city to another, whereas the average speed for the entire trip, which is obtained by dividing the distance traveled by the total time required, may be only 10 mi/0.25 hr = 40 mi/hr.

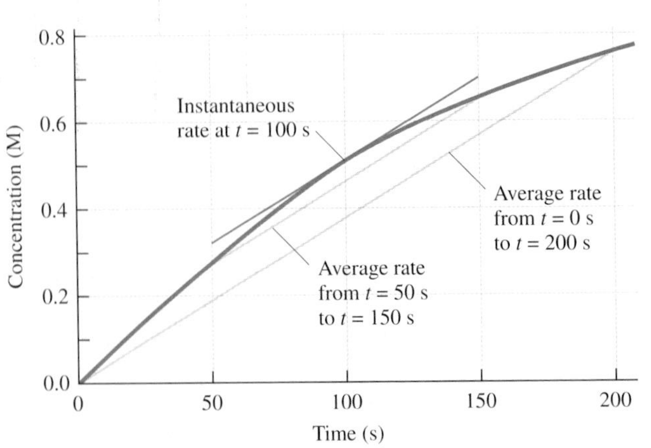

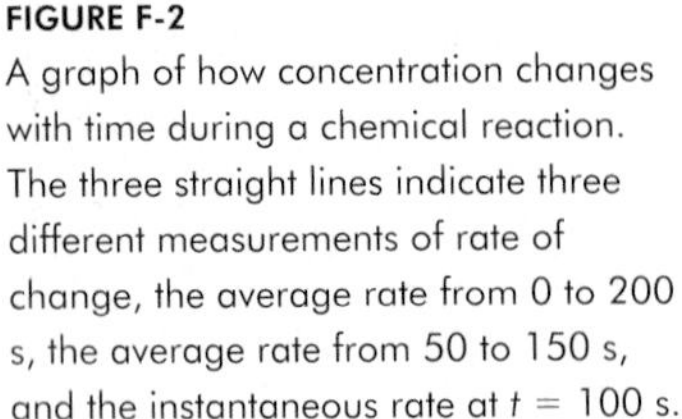

FIGURE F-2
A graph of how concentration changes with time during a chemical reaction. The three straight lines indicate three different measurements of rate of change, the average rate from 0 to 200 s, the average rate from 50 to 150 s, and the instantaneous rate at $t = 100$ s.

TABLE F-1 RATES FOR TIME INTERVALS ABOUT $t = 100$ s

t_1 (s)	t_0 (s)	Δt (s)	c_1 (M)	c_0 (M)	Δc (M)	$\Delta c/\Delta t$ (M/s)
200	0	200	0.750	0	0.750	3.75×10^{-3}
150	50	100	0.646	0.293	0.353	3.53×10^{-3}
110	90	20	0.5334	0.4640	0.0694	3.47×10^{-3}
105	95	10	0.5170	0.4823	0.0347	3.47×10^{-3}

MATHEMATICAL LIMITS

How are instantaneous rates measured? Consider in more detail the chemical reaction whose concentration variations are graphed in Figure F-2. If we determine the average rate for a sequence of smaller and smaller time intervals, all centered around $t = 100$ s, we obtain the data shown in Table F-1.

Whereas the values for $\Delta c/\Delta t$ are different when the time intervals are long, they reach a constant value, 3.47×10^{-3} M/s, for sufficiently short time intervals. This constant value, called the *limiting value* as the time interval approaches zero, is the instantaneous rate at $t = 100$ s. In mathematical terms, we express this instantaneous rate as dc/dt, and it is defined by the equation,

$$\lim_{\Delta t \to 0} (\Delta c/\Delta t) = dc/dt$$

The notion of a limiting rate of change is not restricted to variations with time. For any dependent variable y that varies in some regular way with an independent variable x, we can define an instantaneous rate of change, dy/dx. This quantity is called the *derivative* of y with respect to x, and it is equal to the slope of a graph of y vs. x.

Computing dy/dx by calculations such as those shown in Table F-1 is tedious and uninteresting. Fortunately, the branch of mathematics called *differential calculus* is concerned with finding shortcuts for evaluating derivatives. It does this by deriving mathematical relationships from which a derivative can be calculated. For Figure F-2, the mathematical relationship is $dc/dt = k(1 - c)$, where k is a constant whose value, $3.47 \times 10^{-3}\ s^{-1}$, is independent of time and concentration. From this relationship, dc/dt can be calculated for any value of concentration.

INTEGRATION

The tiny differences dc and dt are differentials, and the expression, $dc/dt = k(1 - c)$, is a differential equation. Although such expressions relate the instantaneous change to the concentration, they do not allow us to determine the concentration at some later time. That is, this expression does not allow us to extend the graph in Figure F-2 to $t = 400$ s. To do this, we need an equation that expresses c as a function of t, rather than dc/dt as a function of c.

INTEGRATION OF RATE LAWS

The integrated rate laws that we introduced in Chapter 14 are derived from differential rate expressions. In calculus notation, as the value of Δt approaches 0, the ratio $\Delta[A]/\Delta t$ can be replaced by the derivative.

$$\text{Rate} = \lim_{\Delta T \to 0}\left[\frac{\Delta[A]}{\Delta t}\right] = -\frac{d[A]}{dt}$$

In a first-order reaction, the rate is proportional to concentration, so rate = k[A]. We can rearrange the differential rate equation so that all concentration terms appear on the left side of the equation and time remains on the right.

$$\frac{d[A]}{[A]} = -k\,dt$$

This procedure is called *separation of variables* because it separates the two variables, [A] and t, so that they appear on different sides of the equation. The expression can now be integrated, giving an equation for concentration as a function of time.

Rearranging gives Equation 14-3, the linear form for the first order integrated rate law:

These are two fundamental integral forms:

$$\int \frac{1}{x}dx = \ln x \quad and \quad c\int dx = cx$$

$$\int_{[A]_o}^{[A]} \frac{d[A]}{[A]} = \int_0^t -k\,dt$$

$$ln[A] - ln[A]_o = -kt$$

$$ln[A] = ln[A]_o - kt \qquad \textbf{(14-3)}$$

For a second-order rate equation, separation of variables also gives an expression that can be integrated.

$$\text{Rate} = -\frac{d[A]}{dt} = k[A]^2$$

$$\int \frac{1}{x^2}dx = \frac{1}{x}$$

$$\frac{d[A]}{[A]^2} = -k\,dt \qquad \int_{[A]_o}^{[A]} \frac{d[A]}{[A]^2} = -k\int_0^t dt$$

Evaluating the integrals and rearranging the result gives the linear form of the second-order rate law.

$$\frac{1}{[A]} - \frac{1}{[A]_0} = kt \qquad and \qquad \frac{1}{[A]} = kt + \frac{1}{[A]_0}$$

APPENDIX G EQUILIBRIUM CONSTANTS

K_a VALUES

Name	Formula	pK_a
Oxyacids		
Arsenic	H_3AsO_4	2.25
Boric	H_3BO_3	9.23
Carbonic	H_2CO_3	6.37
K_{a2}	HCO_3^-	10.32
Chlorous	$HClO_2$	1.96
Chromic	H_2CrO_4	0.82
K_{a2}	$HCrO_4^-$	6.49
Hypobromous	$HBrO$	8.70
Hypochlorous	$HClO$	7.52
Hypoiodous	HIO	10.70
Iodic	HIO_3	0.77
Nitrous	HNO_2	3.35
Paraperiodic	H_5IO_6	1.55
Periodic	HIO_4	8.25
Phosphoric	H_3PO_4	2.16
K_{a2}	$H_2PO_4^-$	7.21
K_{a3}	HPO_4^{2-}	12.32
Phosphorous	H_3PO_3	1.80
K_{a2}	$H_2PO_3^-$	6.15
Sulfuric	H_2SO_4	strong
K_{a2}	HSO_4^-	1.96
Sulfurous	H_2SO_3	1.89
K_{a2}	HSO_3^-	7.20
Carboxylic acids		
Acetic	CH_3CO_2H	4.75
Benzoic	$C_6H_5CO_2H$	4.19
Chloroacetic	$ClCH_2CO_2H$	2.85
Formic	HCO_2H	3.74
Oxalic	$(CO_2H)_2$	1.25
K_{a2}	$HO_2CCO_2^-$	4.29
Propionic	$C_2H_5CO_2H$	4.89
Trichloroacetic	Cl_3CCO_2H	0.70
Other acids		
Cyanic	$HCNO$	3.46
Hydrazoic	HN_3	4.72
Hydrocyanic	HCN	9.31
Hydrofluoric	HF	3.17
Hydrogen peroxide	H_2O_2	11.62
Hydrogen sulfide	H_2S	7.05
K_{a2}	HS^-	12.92
Phenol	C_6H_5OH	9.89

K_b VALUES

Name	Formula	pK_b
Ammonia	NH_3	4.75
Aniline	$C_6H_5NH_2$	9.37
Diethylamine	$(C_2H_5)_2NH$	3.02
Dimethylamine	$(CH_3)_2NH$	3.27
Ethylamine	$C_2H_5NH_2$	3.19
Ethylenediamine	$(CH_2NH_2)_2$	3.28
Hydrazine	H_2NNH_2	5.89
Hydroxylamine	$HONH_2$	7.96
Methylamine	CH_3NH_2	3.36
Pyridine	C_5H_5N	8.72
Triethylamine	$(C_2H_5)_3N$	3.28
Trimethylamine	$(CH_3)_3N$	4.19
Urea	H_2NCONH_2	13.82

pK_{sp} VALUES, SALTS AT 25 °C

Name	Formula	pK_{sp}
Aluminum hydroxide	$Al(OH)_3$	32.34
Barium carbonate	$BaCO_3$	8.29
Barium chromate	$BaCrO_4$	9.92
Barium fluoride	BaF_2	6.00
Barium hydroxide	$Ba(OH)_2$	2.30
Barium oxalate	BaC_2O_4	6.80
Barium phosphate	$Ba_3(PO_4)_2$	22.47
Barium sulfate	$BaSO_4$	9.96
Cadmium carbonate	$CdCO_3$	26.10
Cadmium hydroxide	$Cd(OH)_2$	13.60
Cadmium sulfide	CdS	26.10
Calcium carbonate	$CaCO_3$	8.55
Calcium chromate	$CaCrO_4$	3.15
Calcium fluoride	CaF_2	10.41
Calcium hydroxide	$Ca(OH)_2$	5.26
Calcium phosphate	$Ca_3(PO_4)_2$	28.70
Calcium sulfate	$CaSO_4$	5.04
Chromium(III) hydroxide	$Cr(OH)_3$	30.20
Cobalt(II) carbonate	$CoCO_3$	12.85
Cobalt(II) hydroxide	$Co(OH)_2$	14.80
Cobalt(II) sulfide	CoS	20.40
Cobalt(III) hydroxide	$Co(OH)_3$	43.80
Copper(I) bromide	$CuBr$	8.28
Copper(I) chloride	$CuCl$	5.92
Copper (I) sulfide	Cu_2S	47.60
Copper(II) carbonate	$CuCO_3$	9.85
Copper(II) chromate	$CuCrO_4$	5.44
Copper(II) hydroxide	$Cu(OH)_2$	19.66
Copper(II) phosphate	$Cu_3(PO_4)_2$	36.89
Copper(II) sulfide	CuS	35.20
Iron(II) carbonate	$FeCO_3$	10.49
Iron(II) hydroxide	$Fe(OH)_2$	15.10
Iron(II) sulfide	FeS	17.20
Iron(III) hydroxide	$Fe(OH)_3$	37.4
Lead(II) carbonate	$PbCO_3$	13.13
Lead(II) chloride	$PbCl_2$	4.80
Lead(II) chromate	$PbCrO_4$	12.55

Name	Formula	pK_{sp}
Lead(II) fluoride	PbF_2	7.57
Lead(II) hydroxide	$Pb(OH)_2$	14.92
Lead(II) iodide	PbI_2	8.19
Lead(II) sulfate	$PbSO_4$	7.80
Lead(II) sulfide	PbS	27.10
Magnesium carbonate	$MgCO_3$	5.00
Magnesium hydroxide	$Mg(OH)_2$	10.74
Magnesium oxalate	MgC_2O_4	4.07
Manganese(II) carbonate	$MnCO_3$	10.74
Manganese(II) hydroxide	$Mn(OH)_2$	12.72
Manganese(II) sulfide	MnS	13.00
Mercury(I) chloride	Hg_2Cl_2	17.89
Mercury(I) oxalate	$Hg_2C_2O_4$	12.70
Mercury(I) sulfide	Hg_2S	47.00
Mercury(II) hydroxide	$Hg(OH)_2$	25.52
Mercury(II) sulfide	HgS	52.4
Nickel(II) carbonate	$NiCO_3$	8.18
Nickel(II) hydroxide	$Ni(OH)_2$	13.80
Nickel(II) oxalate	NiC_2O_4	9.4
Nickel(II) sulfide	NiS	18.49
Silver acetate	$AgC_2H_3O_2$	2.70
Silver bromide	$AgBr$	12.30
Silver carbonate	Ag_2CO_3	11.09
Silver chloride	$AgCl$	9.74
Silver chromate	Ag_2CrO_4	11.96
Silver cyanide	$AgCN$	15.92
Silver iodide	AgI	16.08
Silver sulfate	Ag_2SO_4	4.85
Silver sulfide	Ag_2S	49.20
Strontium carbonate	$SrCO_3$	9.96
Tin(II) hydroxide	$Sn(OH)_2$	27.85
Tin(II) sulfide	SnS	25.00
Zinc carbonate	$ZnCO_3$	10.85
Zinc hydroxide	$Zn(OH)_2$	16.92
Zinc oxalate	ZnC_2O_4	7.57
Zinc sulfide	ZnS	20.96

APPENDIX H

STANDARD REDUCTION POTENTIALS ($E°$)

$T = 298.15$ K, $P = 1.00$ atm.
Alphabetical listing is by element; all values are in volts.

Aluminum

$Al^{3+} + 3e^- \rightleftarrows Al$	−1.662
$Al(OH)_4^- + 3e^- \rightleftarrows Al + 4OH^-$	−2.33
$AlF_6^{3-} + 3e^- \rightleftarrows Al + 6F^-$	−2.069

Antimony

$Sb + 3H^+_{(aq)} + 3e^- \rightleftarrows SbH_3$	−0.510
$Sb_2O_5 + 6H^+_{(aq)} + 4e^- \rightleftarrows 2SbO^+ + 3H_2O$	+0.581

Arsenic

$As + 3H^+_{(aq)} + 3e^- \rightleftarrows AsH_3$	−0.608
$As_2O_3 + 6H^+_{(aq)} + 6e^- \rightleftarrows 2As + 3H_2O$	+0.234
$HAsO_2 + 3H^+_{(aq)} + 3e^- \rightleftarrows As + 2H_2O$	+0.248

Barium

$Ba^{2+} + 2e^- \rightleftarrows Ba$	−2.912
$Ba(OH)_2 + 2e^- \rightleftarrows Ba + 2OH^-$	−2.99

Beryllium

$Be^{2+} + 2e^- \rightleftarrows Be$	−1.847

Bismuth

$BiCl_4^- + 3e^- \rightleftarrows Bi + 4Cl^-$	+0.16
$Bi_2O_3 + 3H_2O + 6e^- \rightleftarrows 2Bi + 6OH^-$	−0.46

Boron

$H_3BO_3 + 3H^+_{(aq)} + 3e^- \rightleftarrows B + 3H_2O$	−0.8698

Bromine

$Br_{2\,(aq)} + 2e^- \rightleftarrows 2Br^-$	+1.0873
$Br_{2\,(l)} + 2e^- \rightleftarrows 2Br^-$	+1.066
$HBrO + H^+_{(aq)} + 2e^- \rightleftarrows Br^- + H_2O$	+1.331

Calcium

$Ca^{2+} + 2e^- \rightleftarrows Ca$	−2.868
$Ca(OH)_2 + 2e^- \rightleftarrows Ca + 2OH^-$	−3.02

Carbon

$CO_2 + 2H^+_{(aq)} + 2e^- \rightleftarrows HCO_2H$	−0.199
$2CO_2 + 2H^+_{(aq)} + 2e^- \rightleftarrows H_2C_2O_4$	−0.49
p–Benzoquinone + $H^+_{(aq)} + 2e^- \rightleftarrows$ Hydroquinone	+0.6992

Cesium

$Cs^+ + e^- \rightleftarrows Cs$	−2.92

Chlorine

$Cl_2 + 2e^- \rightleftarrows 2Cl^-$	+1.35827
$HClO + H^+_{(aq)} + 2e^- \rightleftarrows Cl^- + H_2O$	+1.482
$2HClO + 2H^+_{(aq)} + 2e^- \rightleftarrows Cl_2 + 2H_2O$	+1.611
$HClO_2 + 2H^+_{(aq)} + 2e^- \rightleftarrows HClO + H_2O$	+1.645
$HClO_2 + 3H^+_{(aq)} + 4e^- \rightleftarrows Cl^- + 2H_2O$	+1.570
$ClO_3^- + 3H^+_{(aq)} + 2e^- \rightleftarrows HClO_2 + H_2O$	+1.214

Chlorine—cont'd

$ClO_3^- + 6\,H^+_{(aq)} + 6\,e^- \rightleftarrows Cl^- + 3\,H_2O$	+1.451
$ClO_4^- + 2\,H^+_{(aq)} + 2\,e^- \rightleftarrows ClO_3^- + H_2O$	+1.189
$2\,ClO_4^- + 16\,H^+_{(aq)} + 14\,e^- \rightleftarrows Cl_2 + 8\,H_2O$	+1.39
$ClO_4^- + 8\,H^+_{(aq)} + 8\,e^- \rightleftarrows Cl^- + 4\,H_2O$	+1.389

Chromium

$Cr^{3+} + 3\,e^- \rightleftarrows Cr$	−0.744
$Cr^{2+} + 2\,e^- \rightleftarrows Cr$	−0.913
$Cr_2O_7^{2-} + 14\,H^+_{(aq)} + 6\,e^- \rightleftarrows 2\,Cr^{3+} + 7\,H_2O$	+1.232
$Cr(OH)_3 + 3\,e^- \rightleftarrows Cr + 3\,OH^-$	−1.48

Cobalt

$Co^{3+} + e^- \rightleftarrows Co^{2+}$	+1.842
$Co^{2+} + 2\,e^- \rightleftarrows Co$	−0.277
$[Co(NH_3)_6]^{3+} + e^- \rightleftarrows [Co(NH_3)_6]^{2+}$	+0.108
$[Co(CN)_6]^{3-} + e^- \rightleftarrows [Co(CN)_6]^{4-}$	−0.84

Copper

$Cu^{2+} + 2\,e^- \rightleftarrows Cu$	+0.3419
$Cu^{2+} + e^- \rightleftarrows Cu^+$	+0.153
$Cu^+ + e^- \rightleftarrows Cu$	+0.521
$Cu(OH)_2 + 2\,e^- \rightleftarrows Cu + 2\,OH^-$	−0.222
$Cu_2O + H_2O + 2\,e^- \rightleftarrows 2\,Cu + 2\,OH^-$	−0.360

Fluorine

$F_2 + 2\,e^- \rightleftarrows 2\,F^-$	+2.866

Gold

$Au^{3+} + 3\,e^- \rightleftarrows Au$	+1.498
$Au(CN)_2^- + e^- \rightleftarrows Au + 2\,CN^-$	−0.60

Hydrogen

$2\,H^+_{(aq)} + 2\,e^- \rightleftarrows 2\,H_2$	0 (by definition)
$2\,H_2O + 2\,e^- \rightleftarrows H_2 + 2\,OH^-$	−0.828

Iodine

$I_2 + 2\,e^- \rightleftarrows 2\,I^-$	+0.5355
$I_3^- + 2\,e^- \rightleftarrows 3\,I^-$	+0.536
$2\,IO_3^- + 12\,H^+_{(aq)} + 10\,e^- \rightleftarrows I_2 + 6\,H_2O$	+1.195

Iron

$Fe^{3+} + 3\,e^- \rightleftarrows Fe$	−0.037
$Fe^{2+} + 2\,e^- \rightleftarrows Fe$	−0.447
$Fe^{3+} + e^- \rightleftarrows Fe^{2+}$	+0.771
$[Fe(CN)_6]^{3-} + e^- \rightleftarrows [Fe(CN)_6]^{4-}$	+0.358

Lead

$Pb^{2+} + 2\,e^- \rightleftarrows Pb$	−0.1262
$PbO_2 + SO_4^{2-} + 4\,H^+_{(aq)} + 2\,e^- \rightleftarrows PbSO_4 + 2\,H_2O$	+1.6913
$PbO_2 + 4\,H^+_{(aq)} + 2\,e^- \rightleftarrows Pb^{2+} + 2\,H_2O$	+1.455
$PbSO_4 + 2\,e^- \rightleftarrows Pb + SO_4^{2-}$	−0.3588

Lithium

$Li^+ + e^- \rightleftarrows Li$	−3.0401

Magnesium

$Mg^{2+} + 2\,e^- \rightleftarrows Mg$	−2.37
$Mg(OH)_2 + 2\,e^- \rightleftarrows Mg + 2\,OH^-$	−2.69

Manganese

$Mn^{2+} + 2\,e^- \rightleftarrows Mn$	−1.18
$MnO_4^- + 4\,H^+_{(aq)} + 3\,e^- \rightleftarrows MnO_2 + 2\,H_2O$	+1.695
$MnO_4^- + 8\,H^+_{(aq)} + 5\,e^- \rightleftarrows Mn^{2+} + 4\,H_2O$	+1.507
$MnO_2 + 4\,H^+_{(aq)} + 2\,e^- \rightleftarrows Mn^{2+} + 2\,H_2O$	+1.23

Mercury

$Hg^{2+} + 2e^- \rightleftharpoons Hg$	+0.854
$2Hg^{2+} + 2e^- \rightleftharpoons Hg_2^{2+}$	+0.920
$Hg_2^{2+} + 2e^- \rightleftharpoons 2Hg$	+0.789
$Hg_2Cl_2 + 2e^- \rightleftharpoons 2Hg + 2Cl^-$	+0.26808
$Hg_2SO_4 + 2e^- \rightleftharpoons 2Hg + SO_4^{2-}$	+0.6151

Nickel

$Ni^{2+} + 2e^- \rightleftharpoons Ni$	−0.257
$Ni(OH)_2 + 2e^- \rightleftharpoons Ni + 2OH^-$	−0.72
$NiO_2 + 4H^+_{(aq)} + 2e^- \rightleftharpoons Ni^{2+} + 2H_2O$	+1.678

Nitrogen

$N_2 + 8H^+_{(aq)} + 6e^- \rightleftharpoons 2NH_4^+$	+1.275
$N_2O + 2H^+_{(aq)} + 2e^- \rightleftharpoons N_2 + H_2O$	+1.766
$2NO + 2H^+_{(aq)} + 2e^- \rightleftharpoons N_2O + H_2O$	+1.591
$HNO_2 + H^+_{(aq)} + e^- \rightleftharpoons NO + H_2O$	+0.983
$2HNO_2 + 4H^+_{(aq)} + 4e^- \rightleftharpoons N_2O + 3H_2O$	+1.297
$NO_2 + H^+_{(aq)} + e^- \rightleftharpoons HNO_2$	+1.07
$NO_2 + 2H^+_{(aq)} + 2e^- \rightleftharpoons NO + H_2O$	+1.03
$NO_3^- + 3H^+_{(aq)} + 2e^- \rightleftharpoons HNO_2 + H_2O$	+0.934
$NO_3^- + 4H^+_{(aq)} + 3e^- \rightleftharpoons NO + 2H_2O$	+0.957

Oxygen

$O_2 + 2H^+_{(aq)} + 2e^- \rightleftharpoons H_2O_2$	+0.695
$O_2 + 4H^+_{(aq)} + 4e^- \rightleftharpoons 2H_2O$	+1.229
$O_3 + 2H^+_{(aq)} + 2e^- \rightleftharpoons O_2 + H_2O$	+2.076

Phosphorus

$P_{(red)} + 3H^+_{(aq)} + 3e^- \rightleftharpoons PH_3$	−0.111
$P_{(white)} + 3H^+_{(aq)} + 3e^- \rightleftharpoons PH_3$	−0.063
$H_3PO_4 + 2H^+_{(aq)} + 2e^- \rightleftharpoons H_3PO_3 + H_2O$	−0.276

Platinum

$Pt^{2+} + 2e^- \rightleftharpoons Pt$	+1.118
$[PtCl_6]^{2-} + 2e^- \rightleftharpoons [PtCl_4]^{2-} + 2Cl^-$	+0.68

Potassium

$K^+ + e^- \rightleftharpoons K$	−2.925

Silver

$Ag^+ + e^- \rightleftharpoons Ag$	+0.7996
$AgCl + e^- \rightleftharpoons Ag + Cl^-$	+0.22233
$AgBr + e^- \rightleftharpoons Ag + Br^-$	+0.07133
$AgI + e^- \rightleftharpoons Ag + I^-$	−0.15224
$Ag_2O + H_2O + 2e^- \rightleftharpoons 2Ag + 2OH^-$	+0.342

Sodium

$Na^+ + e^- \rightleftharpoons Na$	−2.714

Sulfur

$S + 2H^+_{(aq)} + 2e^- \rightleftharpoons H_2S$	+0.141
$S_4O_6^{2-} + 2e^- \rightleftharpoons 2S_2O_3^{2-}$	+0.08
$H_2SO_3 + 4H^+_{(aq)} + 4e^- \rightleftharpoons S + 3H_2O$	+0.449
$2SO_3^{2-} + 3H_2O + 4e^- \rightleftharpoons S_2O_3^{2-} + 6OH^-$	−0.571
$HSO_4^- + 3H^+_{(aq)} + 2e^- \rightleftharpoons H_2SO_3 + H_2O$	+0.172

Thallium

$Tl^+ + e^- \rightleftharpoons Tl$	−0.336
$Tl^{3+} + 2e^- \rightleftharpoons Tl^+$	+1.25

Tin

$Sn^{2+} + 2e^- \rightleftharpoons Sn$	−0.137

$Sn^{4+} + 2\,e^- \rightleftarrows Sn^{2+}$	+0.151
$HSnO_2^- + H_2O + 2\,e^- \rightleftarrows Sn + 3\,OH^-$	−0.909

Titanium

$Ti^{2+} + 2\,e^- \rightleftarrows Ti$	−1.630
$Ti^{3+} + e^- \rightleftarrows Ti^{2+}$	−0.368
$TiO_2 + 4\,H^+_{(aq)} + 2\,e^- \rightleftarrows Ti^{2+} + 2\,H_2O$	−0.502

Zinc

$Zn^{2+} + 2\,e^- \rightleftarrows Zn$	−0.7618
$[Zn(NH_3)_4]^{2+} + 2\,e^- \rightleftarrows Zn + 4\,NH_3$	−1.04
$[Zn(CN)_4]^{2-} + 2\,e^- \rightleftarrows Zn + 4\,CN^-$	−1.26

APPENDIX I

THE TOP 50 INDUSTRIAL CHEMICALS

Rank	Chemical (formula)	1992 Production (10^9 kg)	Method of manufacture	Major use
1	Sulfuric acid (H_2SO_4)	40.36	Contact process	Multiple uses
2	Nitrogen (N_2)	26.68	Condense air	Fertilizers
3	Oxygen (O_2)	19.26	Condense air	Oxidizer
4	Ethylene (C_2H_4)	18.37	"Crack" oil	Polymers
5	Ammonia (NH_3)	16.34	Haber process	Fertilizers, plastics
6	Lime (CaO)	15.78	Heat limestone	Metallurgy, cement
7	Phosphoric acid (H_3PO_4)	11.53	Acid + phosphate	Fertilizers, detergents
8	Sodium hydroxide (NaOH)	10.92	Brine electrolysis	Various uses
9	Propylene (C_3H_6)	10.27	"Crack" oil	Polymers
10	Chlorine (Cl_2)	10.13	Brine electrolysis	Bleach, purification of water
11	Sodium carbonate (Na_2CO_3)	9.50	Solvay process	Glass, detergents
12	Urea ($(H_2N)_2CO$)	7.65	$NH_3 + CO_2$	Fertilizers, plastics
13	Nitric acid (HNO_3)	7.31	Ostwald process	Fertilizers, explosives
14	Dichloroethylene ($C_2H_2Cl_2$)	7.26	$Cl_2 + C_2H_4$	Polymers
15	Ammonium nitrate (NH_4NO_3)	6.97	$NH_3 + HNO_3$	Fertilizers, explosives
16	Vinyl chloride (C_2H_3Cl)	6.01	From ethylene	Polymers
17	Benzene (C_6H_6)	5.46	From petroleum	Polymers
18	Ethylbenzene (C_8H_{10})	5.00	From benzene	Polymers
19	Methyl t-butyl ether ($C_5H_{12}O$)	4.94	Organic synthesis	Gasoline
20	Carbon dioxide (CO_2)	4.90	Refining byproduct	Various uses
21	Styrene (C_8H_8)	4.06	$C_8H_{10} - H_2$	Polymers
22	Methanol (CH_3OH)	3.97	$CO + H_2$	Chemicals, plastics
23	Formaldehyde (H_2CO)	3.17	From methanol	Polymers
24	Xylene (C_8H_{10})	2.90	From petroleum	Solvent, gasoline
25	Toluene (C_7H_8)	2.74	From petroleum	Gasoline, benzene
26	Hydrochloric acid (HCl)	2.61	Chlorination byproduct	Various uses
27	*p*-Xylene (C_8H_{10})	2.57	From petroleum	Make $C_8H_6O_4$
28	Terephthalic acid ($C_8H_6O_4$)	2.56	Oxidize xylene	Polymers
29	Ethylene oxide (C_2H_4O)	2.53	$O_2 + C_2H_4$	Polymers
30	Ethylene glycol ($C_2H_6O_2$)	2.33	$C_2H_4O + H_2O$	Polymers
31	Ammonium sulfate ($(NH_4)_2SO_4$)	2.16	$NH_3 + H_2SO_4$	Fertilizer
32	Cumene (C_9H_{12})	2.08	From benzene	Other chemicals
33	Potash (K_2O)	1.71	Mined, electrolysis	Fertilizer
34	Phenol (C_6H_5OH)	1.69	Oxidize cumene	Resins
35	Acetic acid (CH_3CO_2H)	1.64	$CO + CH_3OH$	Chemicals, fibers
36	Butadiene (C_4H_8)	1.45	From oil	Tires
37	Carbon black (C)	1.37	Burn oil	Fillers, pigments
38	Acrylonitrile (C_3H_3N)	1.29	$C_3H_6 + NH_3 + O_2$	Fibers
39	Propylene oxide (C_3H_6O)	1.23	O_2 + propylene	Polymers

Data from *Chemical and Engineering News*, April 12, 1993.

Rank	Chemical (formula)	1992 Production (10^9 kg)	Method of manufacture	Major use
40	Vinyl acetate ($C_4H_6O_2$)	1.21	$C_2H_4 + CH_3CO_2H$	Paints, emulsions
41	Titanium dioxide (TiO_2)	1.15	Purify mineral	Paint pigment
42	Acetone ($(CH_3)_2CO$)	1.04	$C_3H_7OH - H_2$	Polymers
43	Cyclohexane (C_6H_{12})	1.00	$C_6H_6 + H_2$	Make caprolactam
44	Aluminum sulfate ($Al_2(SO_4)_3$)	0.99	$Al_2O_3 + H_2SO_4$	Paper manufacture
45	Sodium silicate (Na_2SiO_3)	0.82	Na_2CO_3 + sand	Glass
46	Adipic acid ($C_6H_{10}O_4$)	0.80	Oxidize C_6H_{12}	Fibers
47	Calcium chloride ($CaCl_2$)	0.63	Solvay byproduct	Various uses
48	Caprolactam ($C_6H_{11}NO$)	0.63	From cyclohexane	Fibers
49	Sodium sulfate (Na_2SO_4)	0.61	Mined	Detergents, glass
50	Isobutylene (C_4H_8)	0.59	"Crack" oil	Tires

SOLUTIONS TO SELECTED PROBLEMS

CHAPTER 1

1.9 CCl_4.

1.11 a) Br_2, b) HCl, c) CH_3CH_2I, d) PCl_3, e) SF_4, f) N_2O_4.

1.21 a) pure substance, b) solution, c) heterogeneous mixture, d) solution, e) heterogeneous mixture, f) heterogeneous mixture.

1.23 a) liquid, b) liquid, c) solid, d) solid.

1.25 a) physical change, b) physical change, c) chemical change.

1.27 a) mixture, b) compound, c) mixture, d) element, e) compound, f) mixture.

1.29 a) 1.00000×10^5, b) 1.00×10^4, c) 4.00×10^{-4}, d) 3×10^{-4}, e) 2.753×10^2.

1.31 a) 4.30×10^2 kg, b) 1.35×10^{-6} m, c) 6.24×10^{-10} s, d) 1.024×10^{-9} kg, e) 9.3000×10^7 m, f) 9×10^4 s, g) 1.08×10^{-3} m.

1.33 7.10×10^{-3} kg.

1.35 946 g.

1.37 0.79 g/cm^3.

1.39 5.70 cm^3.

1.43 a) 176 kg, b) 2.54 s, c) 73 mi/hr, d) 924 kg m^2 s^{-2}, e) 34 J.

1.45 9.44×10^{12} km.

1.55 3.1557×10^9 s.

1.63 261.7 K.

1.65 a) 4.52×10^{34}, b) 1×10^{-4}.

1.67 1.94×10^2 m.

1.69 221 s.

1.71 0.19 g.

1.73 2160 ± 6 mm.

1.75 8.3 min.

1.79 1.11×10^9 m^3.

CHAPTER 2

2.5 a) 25 molecules, b) 50 molecules, c) 100 atoms.

2.9 a) increases 3-fold, b) increases 9-fold, c) decreases by factor of 4.

2.13 5.69×10^{-18} kg.

2.15 a) 2 electrons, b) 0.00027411.

2.27 a) H_2O, b) Na^+, c) Cl^-, d) O^{2-}.

2.29 Al_2O_3.

2.35 106 m/s.

2.45 a) 8 protons, 8 neutrons, and 10 electrons; b) 7 protons, 8 neutrons, and 7 electrons; c) 25 protons, 30 neutrons, and 22 electrons; d) 17 protons, 18 neutrons, and 18 electrons; e) 17 protons, 20 neutrons, and 16 electrons.

2.47 a) 27 protons and 33 neutrons, b) 6 protons and 8 neutrons, c) 92 protons and 143 neutrons, d) 92 protons and 146 neutrons.

2.53 3.37×10^5 J.

2.59 a) 30, b) 20, c) 20 N and 60 H.

2.67 3.62×10^4 m/s.

CHAPTER 3

3.1 a) CH_4, c) C_2H_6O, e) PCl_3, g) C_2H_5I.

3.5 a) 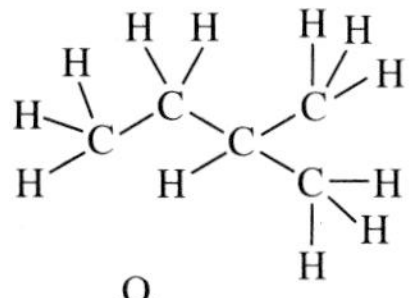 b) 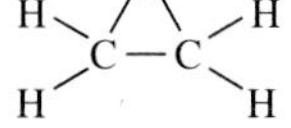 c) 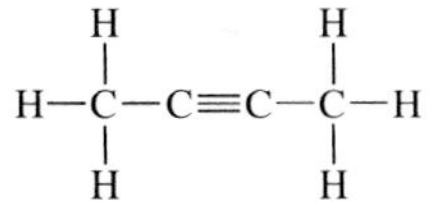 d) 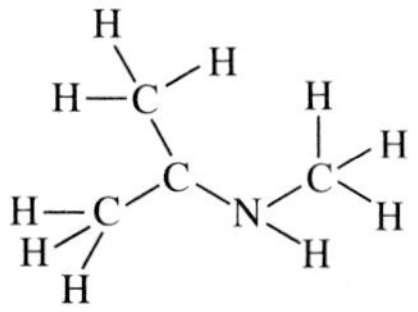 e) 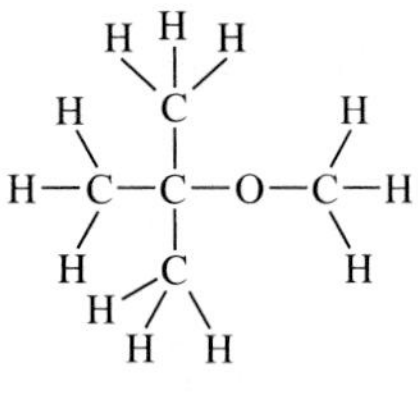 f) 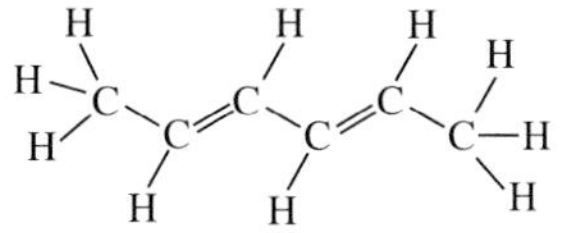 g) 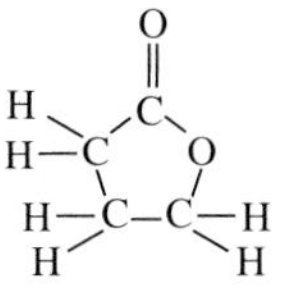 h) 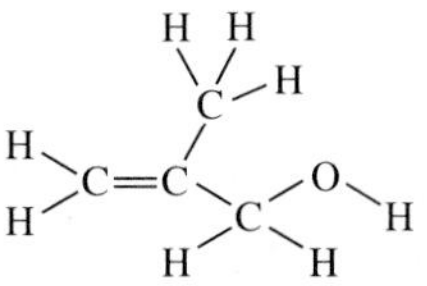 i)

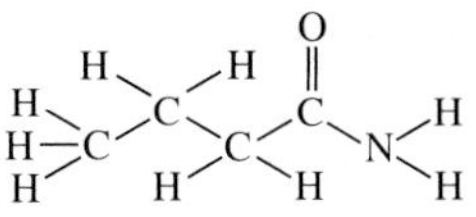

3.11 a) CH_4, c) CaH_2, e) N_2O_5, g) BF_3.

3.13 a) disulfur dichloride, c) hydrogen bromide, e) silicon carbide.

3.15 CaF_2, $Al_2(SO_4)_3$, and ammonium sulfide are ionic.

3.19 a) calcium chloride hexahydrate, c) potassium carbonate, e) sodium hypochlorite, g) copper(II)sulfate, i) sodium nitrite, k) potassium permanganate.

3.21 a) 0.141 mol, b) 1.09×10^{-10} mol, c) 1.67×10^{-7} mol, d) 5.41×10^4 mol.

3.23 39.948 g/mol.

3.25 a) 96.09 g/mol, b) 110.27 g/mol, c) 100.09 g/mol, d) 86.84 g/mol, e) 142.05 g/mol, f) 169.88 g/mol.

3.27 a) 3.92×10^{17} atoms, b) 1.14×10^{17} atoms, c) 3.87×10^{16} atoms, d) 1.48×10^{16} atoms.

3.29 a) 9.99×10^{-18} g, b) 7.6×10^{-13} g, c) 1.484×10^{-21} g.

3.31 1.24×10^7 kg of phosphorus were consumed.

3.33 CaO contains 71.47% Ca, SiO_2 contains 46.75% Si, Al_2O_3 contains 52.92% Al, and Fe_2O_3 contains 69.94% Fe.

3.35 Empirical formula is C_5H_7N, and molecular formula is $C_{10}H_{14}N_2$.

3.39 $[K^+] = [OH^-] = 0.308$ M.
3.45 $C_4H_7Cl_3$.
3.49 a) 454.59 g/mol, b) 2.640×10^{-4} mol, c) 3.180×10^{20} atoms N.
3.51 C_7H_8.
3.55 a) 0.108 mol, c) 0.271 mol, e.) 0.0951 mol.
3.57 a) 57.9 g, c) 30.7 g, e) 26.3 g.
3.59 1.3×10^{15} molecules/L; 5×10^9 L would have to be processed.
3.63 81.72%.
3.65 2.857 kg NH_4NO_3, 2.143 kg $(NH_2)_2CO$.
3.69. 2.6×10^{-4} M.
3.71 a) 334.4 g/mol, b) 1.50×10^{-4} mol, c) 1.45×10^{21} atoms, d) 7.19×10^{-3} g.
3.73 $(C_5H_5)_2Fe$.
3.79 a) 804.0 g/mol, b) 6.2×10^{-6} mol, c) 4.5×10^{19} atoms.
3.81 4.7×10^6 mol.
3.85 1.36×10^3 g/mol.
3.87

3-Methylbutane thiol

Trimethylamine

Cadaverine

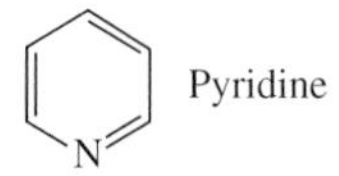

Pyridine

3.89 \$0.0194 per mol, 3.10×10^{25} molecules/dollar.
3.91 $CH_3CH_2CH_2CH_2CH_2CH_2OH$, 1-hexanol; $CH_3CH_2CH_2CH_2CH(OH)CH_3$, 2-hexanol; and $CH_3CH_2CH_2CH(OH)CH_2CH_3$, 3-hexanol.

CHAPTER 4

4.1 a) $5\ H_2 + 2\ NO \rightarrow 2\ NH_3 + 2\ H_2O$, c) $2\ NH_3 + 2\ O_2 \rightarrow N_2O + 3\ H_2O$.
4.3 a) $N_2O_{5\,(g)} + H_2O_{\,(l)} \rightarrow 2\ HNO_{3\,(aq)}$ c) $2\ Fe_{(s)} + O_{2\,(g)} + 2\ H_2O_{(l)} \rightarrow 2\ Fe(OH)_{2\,(s)}$ d) $Au_2S_{3\,(s)} + 3\ H_{2\,(g)} \rightarrow 3\ H_2S_{\,(g)} + 2\ Au_{\,(s)}$
4.9 a) 29.8 g NO, c) 9.40 g O_2, e) 5.55 g NO.
4.11 45.5 kg HF needed, 138 kg CCl_2F_2 and 83.0 kg HCl produced.
4.13 902 kg.
4.15 11.0 g CO_2 and 6.75 g H_2O.
4.17 68.6%.
4.19 23 kg.
4.23 2 "handyman assortments."
4.27 0.60 g of P_4O_{10}, 1.7 g O_2 left over.
4.29 86.1 g.
4.31 a) H_2O, NH_4^+, and Cl^-, c) H_2O, Na^+, and SO_4^{2-}, d) H_2O, K^+, and Br^-.
4.35 a) $Al^{3+}_{(aq)} + 3\ OH^-_{(aq)} \rightarrow Al(OH)_{3\,(s)}$ b) $3\ Mg^{2+}_{(aq)} + 2\ PO_4^{3-}{}_{(aq)} \rightarrow Mg_3(PO_4)_{2\,(s)}$ c) $Ba^{2+}_{(aq)} + SO_4^{2-}{}_{(aq)} \rightarrow BaSO_{4\,(s)}$
4.37 14.9 g of $PbCl_2$ forms; NH_4^+, NO_3^-, and excess Pb^{2+} remains.
4.41 $[Ba^{2+}] = 1.2 \times 10^{-2}$ M, $[Cl^-] = 2.00 \times 10^{-2}$ M, $[OH^-] = 4.00 \times 10^{-3}$ M.
4.43 8.982×10^{-2} M.
4.45 a) $2\ Al_{\,(s)} + 6\ H_3O^+_{\,(aq)} \rightarrow 3\ H_{2\,(g)} + 2\ Al^{3+}_{\,(aq)} + 6\ H_2O_{\,(l)}$ b) $3\ Zn_{\,(s)} + 2\ Au^{3+}_{\,(aq)} \rightarrow 2\ Au_{\,(s)} + 3\ Zn^{2+}_{\,(aq)}$ c) no reaction d) $2\ Na_{\,(s)} + 2\ H_2O_{\,(l)} \rightarrow 2\ Na^+_{\,(aq)} + H_{2\,(g)} + 2\ OH^-_{\,(aq)}$
4.51 390 g superphosphate.
4.53 a) 0.30 mol, b) 1.8×10^{23} molecules, c) 5.4 g.
4.57 2.87×10^2 kg decaborane unreacted.
4.59 45.0 kg Ti.
4.63 30.0 g As and 16.8 g CO.
4.65 $Ca^{2+}_{\,(aq)} + SO_4^{2-}{}_{\,(aq)} \rightarrow CaSO_{4\,(s)}$, mass of precipitate = 20.4 g, $[NH_4^+] = 2.57$ M, $[SO_4^{2-}] = 0.43$ M, $[NO_3^-] = 1.71$ M.
4.67 a) 2.52×10^{11} g, b) 811 million pounds, c) 6.1 million dollars.
4.73 82.3% pure.
4.77 1.33 kg.
4.81 0.138 L.
4.83 0.704 g.
4.85 651 kg.
4.87 $[Ca^{2+}] = 0.050$ M, $[Cl^-] = 0.10$ M.
4.91 c) 14.6 kg.
4.93 12.0% zinc.
4.99 76 kg.
4.101 1.09×10^{-3} g.
4.105 6.20 g O_2 consumed, 2.22 g H_2O produced.

CHAPTER 5

5.5 a) 1.12×10^4 J/mol, b) 3.74×10^3 J/mol, c) 1.12×10^4 J/mol.
5.13 a) 6.07×10^4 Pa, b) 2.48×10^5 Pa, c) 61 Pa, d) 135 Pa.
5.15 n = 4.09 mol, original $V = 1.00 \times 10^2$ L.
5.19 0.225 L.
5.21 317 °C.
5.23 *MM* = 121 g/mol.
5.25 5.9×10^{-4} torr.
5.27 593.4 torr N_2, 159.2 torr O_2, 7.10 torr Ar, and 0.247 torr CO_2.
5.29 2.05 atm CH_4, 0.284 atm C_2H_6, and 9.5×10^{-3} atm C_3H_8.
5.31 3.94 L.
5.33 0.438 atm.
5.35 16 kg.
5.37 about 21 °C.
5.39 about 86%.
5.43 4.81 g, which is 3.46×10^{22} atoms.
5.47 0.693 g C_3H_6 and 2.11 g O_2.
5.49 0.864 L.
5.51 0.14 g O_2.
5.53 69.3%.
5.55 c) 72.70%.
5.57 a) 1.18 g/L, b) 1.16 g/L.
5.61 $C_6H_{15}N$.
5.63 a) B, b) 0.5 atm, c) 4.5 atm, d) 0.38 atm.
5.65 33.6 minutes.
5.67 $p_{Ar} = 1.13$ atm, $p_{Ne} = 0.113$ atm.
5.73 2.9×10^5 L.
5.75 a) 44.0 mol, b) 1.1×10^3 L, c) $p(CO) = 0.60$ atm, $p(H_2) = 0.25$ atm, $p(N_2) = 0.15$ atm.
5.77 2.49×10^{10} molecules.
5.83 10.2 atm.

CHAPTER 6

6.1 Pb is largest; Al is smallest.
6.7 a) 2.44×10^2 kJ/mol, b) 1.80×10^2 kJ/mol, c) 4.69×10^3 kJ/mol, d) 95.7 kJ/mol.
6.9 161 nm.
6.11 a) 231 nm, b) 3.4×10^{-19} J, c) 580 nm.
6.15 745 kJ/mol.
6.17 for $n = 8$, 92.6 nm, and for $n = 9$, 92.3 nm, both in the ultraviolet.
6.23 Insufficient information is provided.
6.25 5.485×10^{-7} kg.
6.27 1.5 nm.
6.33 b) 71.9 nm.
6.35 a) 457.6 nm, b) 764.6 nm.
6.37 a) 1.36×10^{-19} J, b) 486 nm, c) 9×10^{-20} J, d) 1.6 nm.
6.39 1.7×10^{16} photons.
6.41 a) 5.3×10^3 m/s, b) 0.106 pm.
6.45 552.9 nm.
6.49 a) 3.30×10^{-19} J, b) 331 nm, c) 945 pm.
6.51 electron, 48 pm; proton, 2.6×10^{-14} m.
6.55 $\lambda = 11.0$ m, $E = 1.81 \times 10^{-26}$ J.
6.57 487 nm = $6.16 \times 10^{14}\ s^{-1}$; 578 nm = $5.19 \times 10^{14}\ s^{-1}$.

CHAPTER 7

7.1 $n = 6$ and $l = 1$ for all sets;

m_l	1	1	0	0	−1	−1
m_s	½	−½	½	−½	½	−½

7.5 a) nonexistent [m_s cannot be −1], b) actual, c) nonexistent [l cannot equal n], d) actual.

7.13 a) He is more stable, b) 5p is more stable, c) He^+ is more stable, d) 4s is more stable.

7.19 a and b are Pauli-forbidden, c and d are excited states, f and g use nonexistent orbitals, and e is the ground state.

7.23 O and P are paramagnetic.

7.25 There are 7 excited states. Two of them are $1s^2 2s^1 2p^4$ and $1s^0 2s^1 2p^6$.

7.29 [Rn] $7s^2 5f^{14} 6d^9$ or [Rn]$7s^1 5f^{14} 6d^{10}$.

7.31 Ar > Cl > K > Cs.

7.35 $Y^{3+} < Sr^{2+} < Rb^+ < Kr < Br^- < Se^{2-} < As^{3-}$.

7.37 −270 kJ/mol.

7.45 six.

7.47 There are ten possibilities. All have $n = 3$ and $l = 2$.

m_l	2	2	1	1	0	0	−1	−1	−2	−2
m_s	½	−½	½	−½	½	−½	½	−½	½	−½

7.49 8s and 5g.

7.51 S^+ has the most unpaired electrons.

7.57 F^{2+}: $1s^2 2s^2 2p^3$, Ca^{2+}: [Ne]$3s^2 3p^6$, Fe^{2+}: [Ar]$3d^6$, As^{2+}: [Ar]$4s^2 3d^{10} 4p^1$.

7.61 3/2 for P, 0 for Br^-, 0 for Cu^+, 4 for Gd, 0 for Sr.

7.67 Bi, 3 valence p electrons.

7.73 Ce^{3+}: [Xe]$4f^1$, La^{2+}: [Xe] $5d^1$, and Ba^+: [Xe]$6s^1$.

7.77 293.4 kJ/mol.

7.79 a) 9; b) +4, +3, +2, +1, 0, −1, −2, −3, −4; c) $n = 5$, d) 8s, 7d, 6f.

7.81 4g and 2d are nonexistent.

7.83 b) $1s^2 2p^6 2s^2 3d^{10} 3p^6 4f^1$.

7.85 a) element 18, b) element 15, c) element 47.

CHAPTER 8

8.1 Configuration is $1s^2 2s^2$, and 2s electrons are involved in bonding.

8.7 F_2 is nonpolar, NaF is ionic, HF is polar, NaH is ionic, and CaO is ionic.

8.13 HBr, 8; KBr, K^+, 0 and Br^-, 8; NH_4^+, 8, and Br^-, 8; CBr_4, 32; Br_2, 14.

8.17 NH_3, 8; NH_4^+, 8 and NO_3^-, 24; HNO_3, 24; K^+, 0 and NO_2^-, 18; NO_2, 17.

8.21 NH_4^+, 8; HSO_4^-, 32; ClO_3^-, 26; NO_3^-, 24; CO_3^{2-}, 24; PF_6^-, 48; MnO_4^-, 32.

8.23

```
                              Cl
                              |
                          Cl—Cl—Cl              H—P—H
                              |                     |
N—N—O      O—O—O              Cl        H—S—H       H
```

8.25 N_2O :N̈—N—Ö:

$16e^- - 2(2) - 2(6) = 0$ $FC_{N-} = 5 - 7 = -2$

$FC_{-N-} = 5 - 2 = +3$ $FC_O = 6 - 7 = -1$

O_3 :Ö—Ö—Ö:

$18e^- - 2(2) - 2(6) - 2 = 0$

$FC_O = 6 - 7 = -1$ $FC_{-O-} = 6 - 4 = +2$

CCl_4

```
      :C̈l:
        |
:C̈l—Cl—C̈l:
        |
      :C̤l:
```

$32e^- - 4(2) - 4(6) = 0$

$FC_C = 4 - 4 = 0$ $FC_{Cl} = 7 - 7 = 0$

H_2S H—S̈—H

$8e^- - 2(2) - 4 = 0$

$FC_S = 6 - 6 = 0$ $FC_H = 1 - 1 = 0$

PH_3

```
H—P̈—H
  |
  H
```

$8e^- - 3(2) - 2 = 0$

$FC_P = 5 - 5 = 0$ $FC_H = 1 - 1 = 0$

8.27 Structures of CCl_4, H_2O, and PH_3 need no adjustments.

N_2O :N̈—N—Ö:

:N̈=N=Ö: ⟷ :N≡N—Ö:

$FC_{N=} = 5 - 6 = -1$ $FC_{=N=} = 5 - 4 = +1$ $FC_{O=} = 6 - 6 = 0$

$FC_{N\equiv} = 5 - 5 = 0$ $FC_{N-} = 5 - 4 = +1$ $FC_{-O} = 6 - 7 = -1$

N is limited to four available orbitals and, therefore, the formal charges cannot be minimized further.

O_3 :Ö—Ö—Ö: Ö=Ö—Ö: ⟷ :Ö—Ö=Ö:

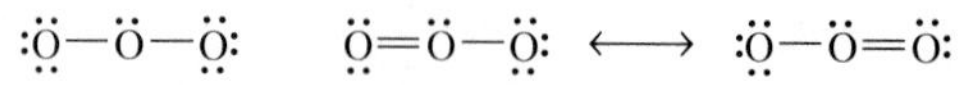

$FC_{O=} = 6 - 6 = 0$ $FC_{=O-} = 6 - 5 = +1$ $FC_{O-} = 6 - 7 = -1$

Oxygen is limited to four available orbitals and the formal charges cannot be minimized further.

8.29 Geometry is a slightly distorted tetrahedron. Carbon sp^3 hybrids overlap with $3p$ orbitals from Cl and $1s$ orbitals from H.

8.31

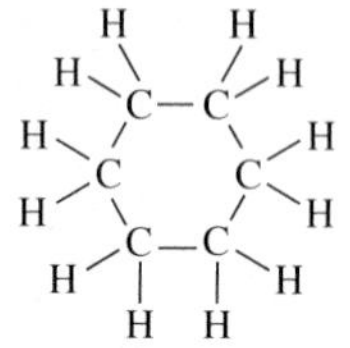

8.37 All inner atoms can be described using sp^3 hybrid orbitals.

8.39 Xe has a steric number of 6, d^2sp^3 hybridization, and the molecular geometry is square pyramidal.

8.41 GeF_4 is tetrahedral, SeF_4 is a seesaw, and XeF_4 is square planar.

8.43 109.5 degrees for GeF_4, <90 and <120 degrees for SeF_4, and 90 degrees for XeF_4.

8.45 H_2S and NF_3 have dipole moments.

8.49

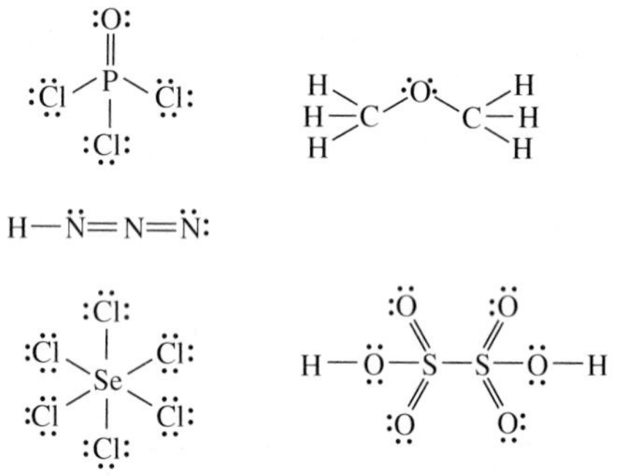

H—N̈=N=N̈:

8.53 There are two structural isomers.

8.57 a) TeF_2, b) TeF_3^-, c) TeF_5^-, d) TeF_5^+, e) TeF_6, f) TeF_4.

8.59 Steric number 2 is not found.

8.61

a) 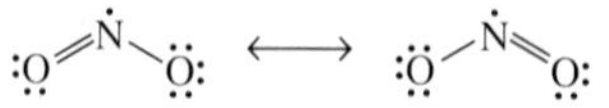 b) 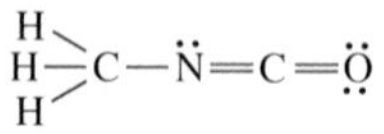 c) 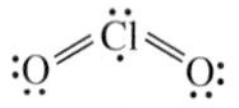 d)

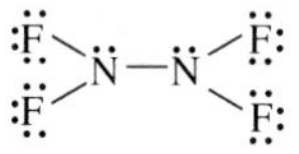

8.63 sulfite, −2; tetrafluoroborate, −1; hypochlorite, −1; and tripolyphosphate, −5.

8.69

a) 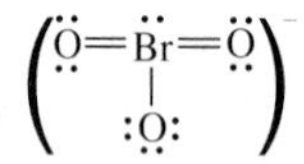 $FC_{Br} = 0$
$FC_{O=} = 0$
$FC_{O-} = 1$
(2 other resonance structures)

b) $(:C{\equiv}N:)^-$
$FC_C = -1$
$FC_N = 0$

c) 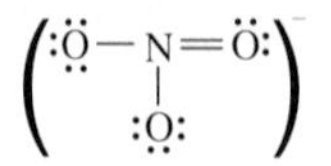 $FC_N = +1$
$FC_{O=} = 0$
$FC_{O-} = -1$
(2 other resonance structure)

d) 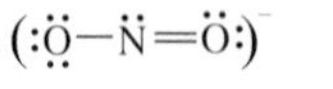 $(:\ddot{O}-\ddot{N}=\ddot{O}:)^-$
$FC_N = 0$
$FC_{O=} = 0$
$FC_{O-} = -1$
(1 other resonance structure)

e) $\left(:\ddot{O}-P(=O)(-\ddot{O}:)-\ddot{O}:\right)^{3-}$

$FC_P = 0$
$FC_{O=} 0$
$FC_{O-}\ -1$
(3 other resonance structures)

f) $\left(\ddot{O}=C(-\ddot{O}:)-\ddot{O}-H\right)^{-}$

$FC_C = 0$
$FC_{O-} = -1$
$FC_{-O-} = 0$
$FC_{O=} = 0$
(1 other resonance structure)

8.71 $SiCl_4$, CI_4, $CdCl_4^{2-}$, and $BeCl_4^{2-}$ are tetrahedral, XeF_4 is a square plane, and SeF_4 is a seesaw.

CHAPTER 9

9.3 All bond angles are approximately 120 degrees.
9.5 H—N < N≡N < C≡N < N—N < Cl—N.
9.7 N—N < Cl—N < H—N < C≡N < N≡N.
9.9 1094 kJ/mol N_2O_4.
9.11 $\Delta E = -989$ kJ.
9.17 NO and NO^- both display magnetism.
9.21 $H-\ddot{N}=N=\ddot{N}: \longleftrightarrow H-\ddot{N}-N\equiv N:$ (atoms numbered 1 2 3)

N_1: has sp^2 hybridization and H—N=N has a bond angle of ~ 120 degrees.
N_2: has sp hybridization N=N=N has a bond angle of 180 degrees.
There is a localized p orbital set for N_2=N_3 and a delocalized π orbital set for all three of the N atoms.
9.25 b) 10 delocalized electrons.
9.29 All six atoms contribute p orbitals to the delocalized π system.
9.31 Four resonance structures of MnO_4^- (each with one Mn—O single bond and three Mn=O double bonds): $\longleftrightarrow$ $\longleftrightarrow$ $\longleftrightarrow$

The MnO_4^- is tetrahedral with the Mn using sp^3 hybrid orbitals to overlap $2p$ orbitals of O to form σ bonds and $3d$ orbitals to overlap other $2p$ orbitals of O to form p orbitals.
9.37 a) 60 π orbitals, b) 60 π bonding electrons.
9.45 $H_2\ddot{N}-C(=O)-\ddot{N}=\ddot{N}-C(=O)-\ddot{N}H_2$

Both C atoms are triangular (bond angles ~ 120 degree) with hybridization of sp^2. The two outer N atoms are tetrahedral with hybridization of sp^3. The two inner Ns are bent with sp^2 hybridization.
9.47 Ethanol is more stable by 30 kJ/mol.
9.59 F—F < Br—Br < Br—Cl < Cl—Cl < Cl—F.
9.63 H—O < H—C < C≡N < C=O.
9.65 −433 kJ/mol Si and −128 kJ/mol C.
9.69 $H_3C-C(=O)-\ddot{O}-\ddot{O}-N(=\ddot{O})-\ddot{O}: \longleftrightarrow H_3C-C(=O)-\ddot{O}-\ddot{O}-N(-\ddot{O}:)=\ddot{O}$

The left carbon has sp^3 hybridization. The other carbon has sp^2 hybridization. The oxygen marked with an asterisk in the question has sp^3 hybridization. The nitrogen has sp^2 hybridization. The bond angles around the left carbon are 109.5 degrees. The O=C—O bond angle is 120 degrees. The O=N—O bond angle is 120 degrees. There is a set of delocalized π orbitals over O=N—O.
9.71 8.14×10^{14} Hz.

CHAPTER 10

10.3 a) less significant, b) more significant, c) more significant.
10.5 a) 8.00%, b) 13%.
10.7 CCl_4 easiest to liquefy, CH_4 hardest to liquefy.
10.9 a) Mg^{2+}, b) Na^+, c) SO_4^{2-}.
10.11 propane < n-pentane < ethanol.
10.13 b and d.
10.15 pentane < gasoline < fuel oil.

10.21 (structure: network of Si and C atoms)

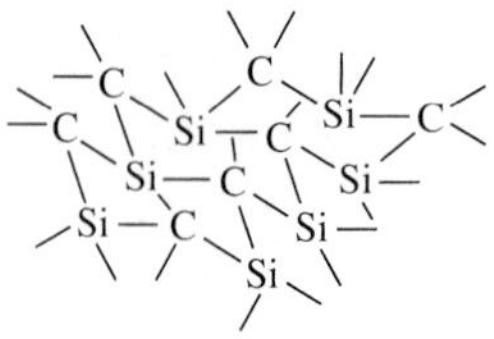

10.29 0.086 g.
10.35 −5.2 °C.
10.37 a) MM = 287 g/mol, b) 132 g/mol.
10.41 625 mL of water is required, and 92% of the $HgCl_2$ will be recovered.
10.45 180 g/mol.
10.47 benzene < pentanol < erythritol.
10.53 pentane < butanol < propane-1,3-diol.
10.55 a) slightly greater than 0.1 M, b) slightly less than 0.4 M, c) 0.2 M, d) 0.3 M.
10.61 b < c < a.
10.67 X = 0.0446 and estimated freezing point is −9.2 °C.
10.69 a) CH_3OH, b) SiO_2, c) HF, d) I_2.
10.77 a) Cl_2, b) SnH_4.
10.79 $CaTiO_3$.
10.81 (structures: ClHC=CHCl, cis and trans isomers)

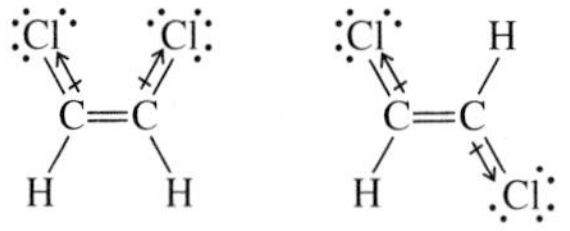

cis	*trans*
dipole moment	no dipole moment
bp = 60 °C	bp = 47 °C

CHAPTER 11

11.1 (structure: $\text{—}(\text{CH}_2\text{—CHCl—CH}_2\text{—CHCl—CH}_2\text{—CHCl—CH}_2\text{—CHCl})_n\text{—}$)

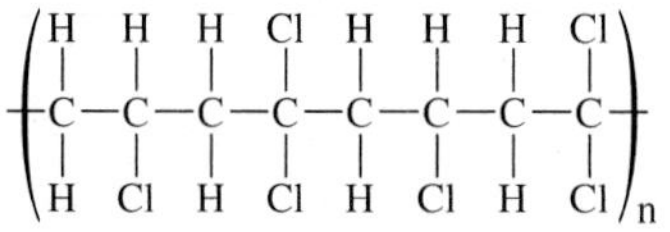

11.3 Initiation: Init.—Init. ⟶ 2 Init.•

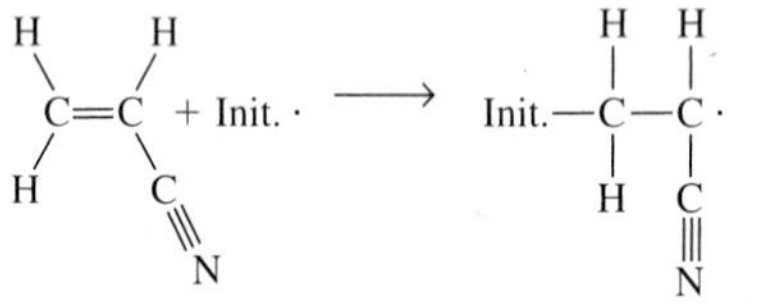

$H_2C{=}CH{-}C{\equiv}N$ + Init.· ⟶ Init.—CH_2—$CH(C{\equiv}N)$·

Propagation: Init.—CH_2—$CH(C{\equiv}N)$· + $H_2C{=}CH{-}C{\equiv}N$ ⟶ Init.—CH_2—$CH(C{\equiv}N)$—CH_2—$CH(C{\equiv}N)$·

Init.—$(CH_2\text{—}CH(C{\equiv}N))_n$—$CH_2$—$CH(C{\equiv}N)$· + $H_2C{=}CH{-}C{\equiv}N$ ⟶ Init.—$(CH_2\text{—}CH(C{\equiv}N))_{n+1}$—$CH_2$—$CH(C{\equiv}N)$·

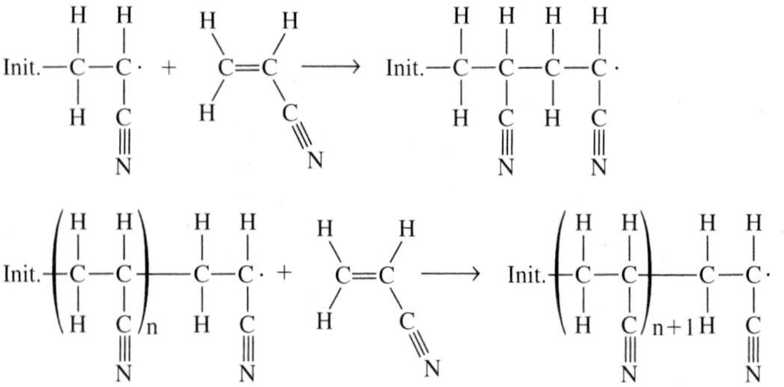

Termination: Init.—$(CH_2\text{—}CH(C{\equiv}N))_n$—$CH_2$—$CH(C{\equiv}N)$· + Init.· ⟶ Init.—$(CH_2\text{—}CH(C{\equiv}N))_n$—$CH_2$—$CH(C{\equiv}N)$—Init.

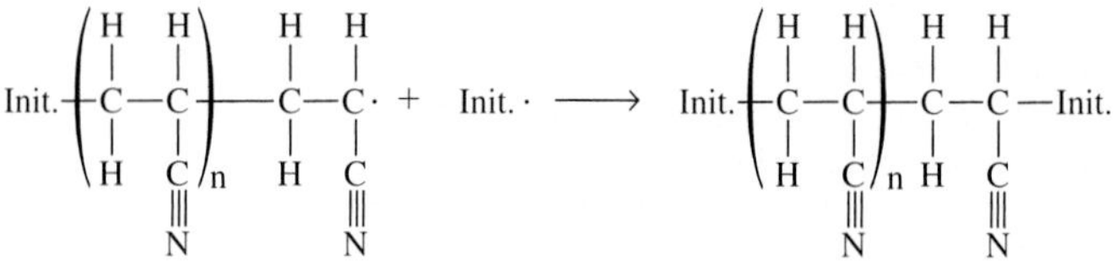

11.5 a) H(H)C=C(H)NO_2 Nitroethene or nitroethylene

b) F(F)C=C(F)Cl Chlorotrifluoroethene or chlorotrifluoroethylene

11.7 ester, amine, aldehyde, alkene and bromide, phenol.

11.9 a) CH_3–CH_2–N(CH_2–CH_3)–CH_2–CH_3 Other isomers are also possible.

b) CH_3–CH_2–CH_2–C(=O)–O–CH_2–CH_2–CH_3 Other isomers are also possible.

c) CH_3–CH_2–CH_2–CH_2–CH=O Others are also possible.

d) C_6H_5–O–CH_3 Others are also possible.

11.11

a) $CH_3CH_2CH_2NH_2$ + HO–C(=O)–C_6H_5 ⟶ $CH_3CH_2CH_2$–NH–C(=O)–C_6H_5 + H_2O

b) CH_3OH + HO–C(=O)–CH_2–C_5H_9 ⟶ CH_3–O–C(=O)–CH_2–C_5H_9 + H_2O

c) 2 $CH_3CH_2CH_2CH_2OH$ ⟶ $CH_3CH_2CH_2CH_2$–O–$CH_2CH_2CH_2CH_3$ + H_2O

11.13

H_2N–$(CH_2)_{10}$–C(=O)OH

11.15 $—CH_2—CH_2—O—CH_2—CH_2—O—CH_2—CH_2—O—$ *or* $\left(CH_2—CH_2—O\right)_n$

11.25

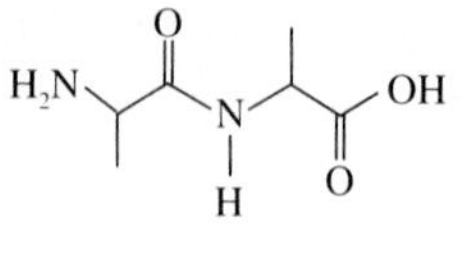

Ala-Ala

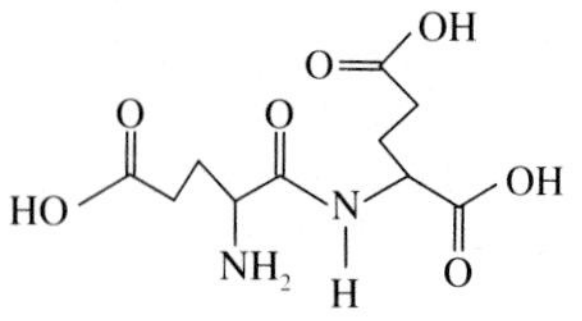

Glu-Glu

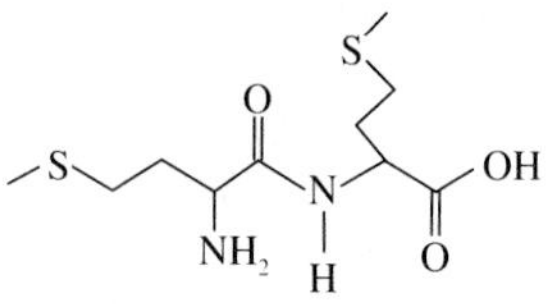

Met-Met

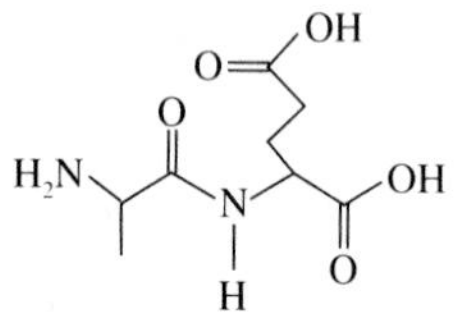

Ala-Glu

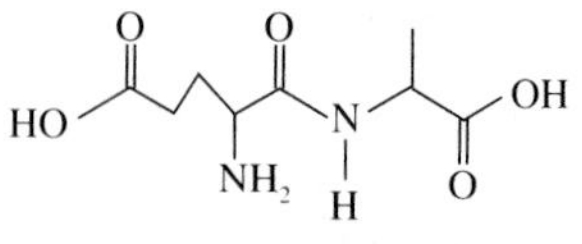

Glu-Ala

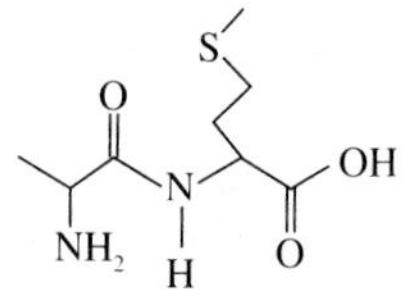

Ala-Met

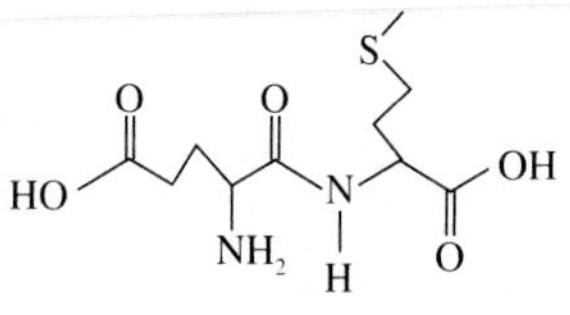

Glu-Met

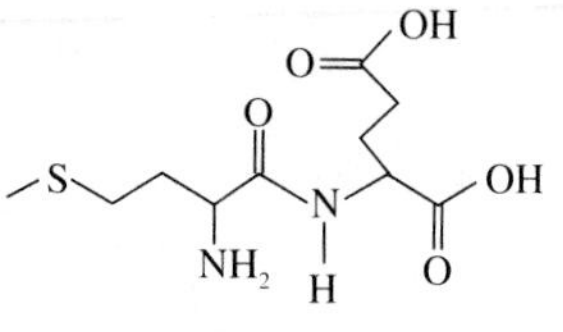

Met-Glu

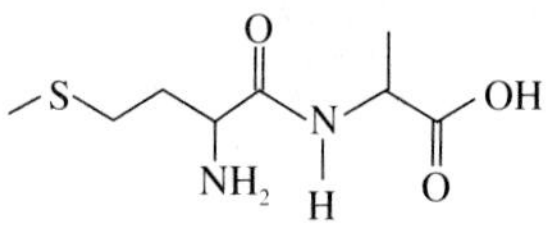

Met-Ala

11.27 Empirical formula is C_3H_5NO; polypeptide contains 17 units.

11.29

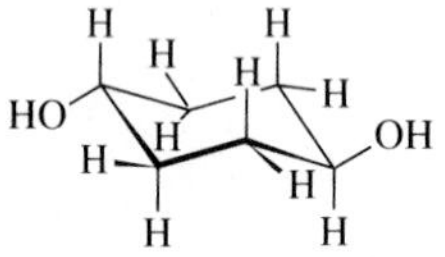

11.31

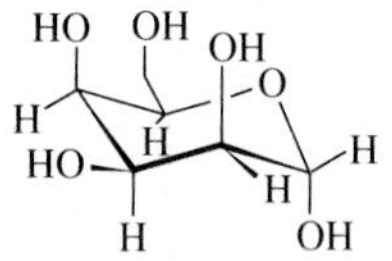

α-Talose

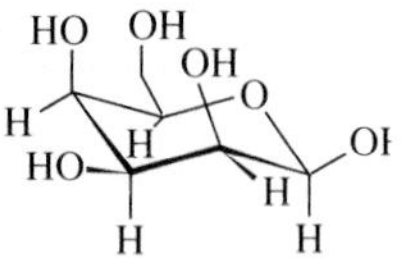

β-Talose

11.35 T—T—A—C—G—T—G—A—C.

11.37

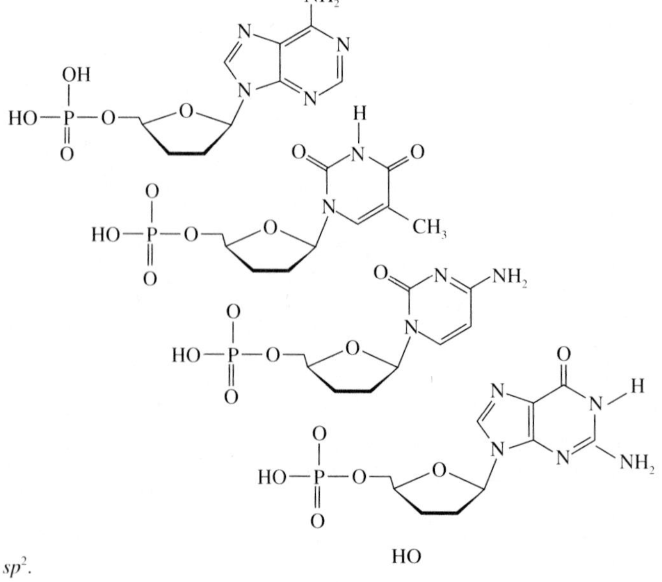

11.41 sp^2.

11.43 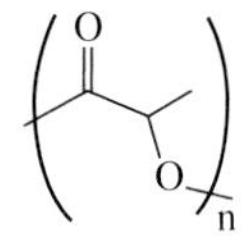 or

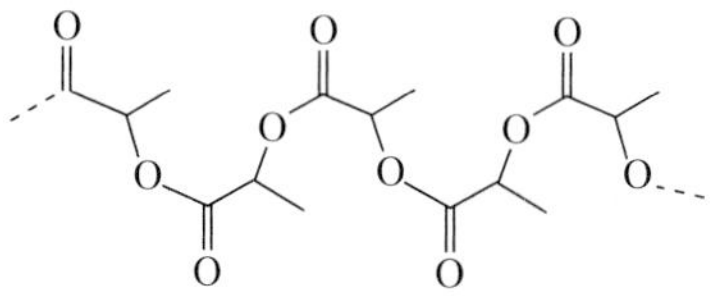

11.45 4.71×10^4 g/mol.

11.51

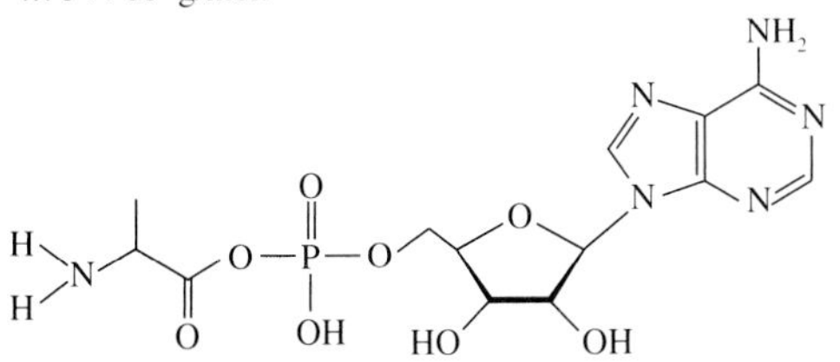

11.53 Four copper atoms.

CHAPTER 12

12.7 a) 17.8 °C, b) 296 K, c) 299 K, d) 22.2 °C.
12.9 23.6 °C.
12.11 -2.5×10^2 J.
12.15 14.4 kJ/K.
12.17 -8.2×10^4 J/mol.
12.19 b) 3221 kJ/mol, c) 429.5 kJ/mol.
12.21 a) 1411 kJ, b) 92.2 kJ, c) −2706.6 kJ, d) −21.5 kJ.
12.23 a) 1416 kJ, b) 87.2 kJ, c) −2706.6 kJ, d) −21.5 kJ.
12.25 a) 0, b) 4.96 kJ, c) −4.96 kJ.
12.27 a) $3\,K_{(s)} + P_{(s)} + 2\,O_{2(g)} \rightarrow K_3PO_{4(s)}$
b) $2\,C_{(s)} + O_{2(g)} + 2\,H_{2(g)} \rightarrow CH_3CO_2H_{(l)}$
c) $3\,C_{(s)} + {}^{9}/_{2}\,H_{2(g)} + {}^{1}/_{2}\,N_{2(g)} \rightarrow (CH_3)_3N_{(g)}$
d) $2\,Al_{(s)} + {}^{3}/_{2}\,O_{2(g)} \rightarrow Al_2O_{3(s)}$.
12.29 a) −1169.4 kJ, b) −1530.4 kJ.
12.31 b) 1.934 kJ, c) 0.926 K.
12.35 a) 653 J, b) 6.31 kJ.
12.37 2.93 g.
12.45 b) −2.83 kJ/mol glucose, c) -1.25×10^3 kJ/mol glucose.
12.47 $\Delta E = -20.1$ J, $\Delta H = -22.4$ J.
12.49 $T = 348.1$ K.
12.51 $q = 0$, $w = 4.05$ kJ, $\Delta E = 4.05$ kJ.
12.53 a) −315.36 kJ, b) −57.20 kJ, c) −851.5 kJ.
12.55 5.4×10^3 kJ.
12.57 a) −1238.0 kJ, b) −2511 kJ, c) −361.2 kJ.
12.59 12.9 g.
12.61 43.9 kJ/mol.
12.63 20.1 J/mol K.
12.65 −197 kJ.
12.71 1.08 kg.

CHAPTER 13

13.1 a) The sand in a sand castle is organized, and waves destroy that organization.
b) The secretary organizes the materials on the desk but must expend energy, which generates disorder elsewhere.
13.3 Initially, the ink is organized in a droplet, but collisions with water molecules generate disorder as the ink molecules become scattered throughout the liquid.
13.7 b) $\Delta S_{overall} = 10.5$ J/K.
13.9 $\Delta S_{water} = -94.0$ J/K.
13.11 a) Negative, b) negative, c) positive.
13.13 a) HgS, b) $MgCl_2$, c) Br_2.
13.15 He, 126.15 J/mol atoms K; H_2, 65.34 J/mol atoms K; CH_4, 37.25 J/mol atoms K, C_3H_6, 25.21 J/mol atoms K.
13.17 a) -198.76 J/K, b) −137.55 J/K, c) 12.5 J/K, d) −267.68 J/K.
13.23 a) −474.26 kJ, b) −50.72 kJ, c) −1325.3 kJ, d) −8401. kJ.
13.25 a) −7.8 kJ, b) 343.9 kJ, c) −211.4 kJ, d) −1217 kJ.
13.27 $\Delta H^o = -559.17$ kJ, $\Delta S^o = -574.19$ J/K, $\Delta G^o = -388.1$ kJ.
13.33 Concentrations are not standard, and temperature is not standard.
13.35 $\Delta G^o = -28$ kJ.
13.39 a) 0, b) positive, c) positive, d) negative, e) positive.
13.41 0.50 mol H_2O (liquid, 298 K) < 1.0 mol H_2O (liquid, 298 K) < 1.0 mol H_2O (liquid, 373 K) 1.0 mol H_2O (gas, 373 K, 1 atm) < 1.0 mol H_2O (gas, 373 K, < 0.1 atm.
13.43 a) −183 J/K, b) 15 J/K, c) yes.
13.45 a) $\Delta G^o = 870.9$ kJ, not spontaneous; b) $\Delta H^o = 818.2$ kJ, absorbs heat; c) $\Delta S^o = -176.58$ J/K, products more ordered.
13.47 40.6%.
13.49 For each *overall* process, $\Delta G < 0$, since each overall process is spontaneous. However, the formation of NO is nonspontaneous unless driven by a highly spontaneous process, in this case the formation of lightning.
13.51 a) −88 J/K, b) 328.6 J/K, c) −358.39 J/K.
13.53 a) −43 kJ, b) 165 kJ, c) −1644 kJ.
13.55 a) 0 because V = constant, b) positive because energy must be supplied to break bonds, c) negative because $q_{surr} < 0$.
13.59 a) Both negative, b) ΔH is positive but $\Delta G = 0$, c) both negative.
13.63 There are stronger ionic forces in CaO because of the larger ionic charges, so the ions are more tightly bound and the crystals are more highly ordered.
13.67 Neither is spontaneous, but the formation of *aqueous* HNO_3 is spontaneous.
13.73 $\Delta G^o = 152.9$ kJ for CCl_4, $\Delta G^o = -1060$ kJ for CS_2; the latter process is highly spontaneous, so special precautions are called for.
13.77. a) $\Delta G^o = -8.995$ kJ, spontaneous; b) $\Delta H^o = 3.443$ kJ, absorbs energy; c) $\Delta S^o = 43.4$ J/K, order decreases.

16.63 a) Yellow, b) red, c) blue, d) blue.
16.65 10.05.
16.67 5.22.
16.69 10.80.
16.71 a) Na^+, SO_3^{2-}, H_2O; CH_3CO_2H, H_2O; b) $CH_3CO_2H_{(aq)} + SO_3^{2-}{}_{(aq)} \rightleftarrows CH_3CO_2^-{}_{(aq)} + HSO_3^-{}_{(aq)}$; c) acid: CH_3CO_2H, base: SO_3^{2-}, conjugate acid: HSO_3^-, conjugate base: $CH_3CO_2^-$.
16.73 1.25 g $ZnCO_3$.
16.75 9.76.
16.77 1.3×10^{-3} mol.
16.79 a) 9.01, b) $NH_{3\,(aq)} + H_3O^+{}_{(aq)} \rightleftarrows NH_4^+{}_{(aq)} + H_2O$, c) 8.98,
d) $NH_4^+{}_{(aq)} + OH^-{}_{(aq)} \rightarrow NH_{3\,(aq)} + H_2O$, e) 10.50.
16.81 a) Mg^{2+}, CO_3^{2-}, H_2O, b) 3.2×10^{-3} M, c) 10.82, d) $[Ca^{2+}]_{max} = 1.1 \times 10^{-6}$ M.
16.83 a) 8.0, b) 7.9.
16.85 Yes, adding 0.42 mol $OH^-{}_{(aq)}$ will restore the buffer.
16.91 a) 11.04, b) 5.09, c) 7.00.
16.93 a) 2.9×10^{-9} M, b) 7.80 kg $Al(OH)_3$ precipitates and $[Al^{3+}]_{residual} = 0.076$ M.
16.95 a) At A, HCO_2H, at B, HCO_2H and HCO_2^-, at C, HCO_2^-, and at D, HCO_2^- and OH^- (H_2O is always a major species); b) 8.39.
16.97 9.57.
16.99 a) $C_6H_5CO_2H_{(s)} + OH^-{}_{(aq)} \rightarrow C_6H_5CO_2^-{}_{(aq)} + H_2O$
b) $(CH_3)_2N_{(aq)} + H_3O^+{}_{(aq)} \rightarrow (CH_3)_2NH^+{}_{(aq)} + H_2O$
c) $CH_3CO_2H_{(aq)} + SO_4^{2-}{}_{(aq)} \rightarrow CH_3CO_2^-{}_{(aq)} + HSO_4^-{}_{(aq)}$
d) $NH_4^+{}_{(aq)} + OH^-{}_{(aq)} \rightarrow NH_{3\,(aq)} + H_2O$
e) $HPO_4^{2-}{}_{(aq)} + NH_{3\,(aq)} \rightarrow PO_4^{3-}{}_{(aq)} + NH_4^+{}_{(aq)}$
16.103 10.81.
16.105

```
       H  :O:                 H   H  :O:                H   H  :Ö:
   ..  |  ||                 +|   |  ||                +|   |  |
 H—N—C—C—Ö—H   ⇄   H—N—C—C—Ö:   ⟷   H—N—C—C=Ö
    |  |       ..              |   |      ..             |   |      ..
    H  H                       H   H                     H   H
```

CHAPTER 17

17.1 a) Fe: +3, O: −2, H: +1; b) N: −3, H: +1; c) P: +3, Cl: −1; d) K: +1, C: +4, O: −2; e) P: 0.
17.3 b and d are redox.
17.7 a) $Na \rightarrow Na^+$ (oxidation), $H_2O \rightarrow H_2$ (reduction)
b) $Au \rightarrow AuCl_4^-$ (oxidation), $HNO_3 \rightarrow NO$ (reduction), c) $C_2O_4^{2-} \rightarrow CO_2$ (oxidation), $MnO_4^- \rightarrow Mn^{2+}$ (reduction)
17.9 a) $H_2O + Cu^+ \rightarrow CuO + 2\,H^+{}_{(aq)} + e^-$
b) $2\,H^+{}_{(aq)} + S + 2\,e^- \rightarrow H_2S$
c) $AgCl + e^- \rightarrow Ag + Cl^-$
d) $I^- + 6\,OH^- \rightarrow IO_3^- + 3\,H_2O + 6\,e^-$
e) $IO_3^- + 2\,H_2O + 4\,e^- \rightarrow IO^- + 4\,OH^-$
f) $H_2CO + H_2O \rightarrow CO_2 + 4\,H^+{}_{(aq)} + 4\,e^-$
17.11 a) $2\,H_2O + 2\,Cu^+ + S \rightarrow 2\,CuO + 2\,H^+{}_{(aq)} + H_2S$
b) $6\,OH^- + I^- + 6\,AgCl \rightarrow IO_3^- + 3\,H_2O + 6\,Ag + 6\,Cl^-$
c) $2\,I^- + IO_3^- \rightarrow 3\,IO^-$
d) $H_2CO + H_2O + 2\,S \rightarrow CO_2 + 2\,H_2S$
17.13 a) $PbO + 2\,[Co(NH_3)_6]^{3+} + 2\,OH^- \rightarrow PbO_2 + H_2O + 2\,[Co(NH_3)_6]^{2+}$
b) $4\,As + 3\,O_2 + 2\,H_2O \rightarrow 4\,HAsO_2$,
c) $Br^- + 2\,MnO_4^- + H_2O \rightarrow BrO_3^- + 2\,MnO_2 + 2\,OH^-$
d) $3\,NO_2 + H_2O - 2\,NO_3 \rightarrow + NO + 2\,H^+{}_{(aq)}$
e) $6\,Cl^- + ClO_4^- + 6\,H^+{}_{(aq)} \rightarrow 3\,Cl_2 + ClO^- + 3\,H_2O$
f) $AlH_4^- + 4\,H_2CO + 4\,H_2O \rightarrow Al^{3+} + CH_3OH + 4\,OH^-$
17.15 a) $\Delta G° = -260$ kJ, spontaneous
b) $\Delta G° = 102.62$ kJ, not spontaneous
c) $\Delta G° = -246.6$ kJ, spontaneous
d) $\Delta G° = -199.8$ kJ, spontaneous
17.21 0.095 g Pb and 0.11 g PbO_2.
17.23 22.5 min.
17.25 a) $3\,C_2H_4O + Cr_2O_7^{2-} + 8\,H^+{}_{(aq)} \rightarrow 3\,HC_2H_3O_2 + 2\,Cr^{3+} + 4\,H_2O$; b) 0.0455 mol.
17.27 a) −0.18 V, b) 0.982 V, c) −0.02 V.
17.31 0.946 V.
17.33 a) 35 kJ, b) -1.14×10^3 kJ, c) 10 kJ.
17.35 a) 8.5×10^{-6} M^3 for $Ca(OH)_2$.

17.37 0.54 V.

17.39 $E = E^\circ - \dfrac{0.05916\ \text{V}}{2} \log \dfrac{[\text{Zn}^{2+}](p_{\text{NH}_3})^2(p_{\text{H}_2})}{[\text{NH}_4^{\ +}]^2}$

17.41 Chromium will corrode preferentially (but in doing so, it forms an impermeable layer of Cr_2O_3 which prevents further corrosion).

17.43 $3\ Ag_2S + 2\ Al \rightarrow 6\ Ag + Al_2S_3$.

17.45 19.8 g Cl_2.

17.47 80.4 min.

17.49 2.23×10^4 C.

17.51 a) $2\ CuFeS_2 + 3\ O_2 \rightarrow 2\ FeO + 2\ CuS + 2\ SO_2$

b) $Al_2O_3 + 2\ OH^- + 3\ H_2O \rightarrow 2\ Al(OH)_4^-$

c) $SiO_2 + 2\ C + 2\ Cl_2 \rightarrow SiCl_4 + 2\ CO$

d) $TiCl_4 + 4\ Na \rightarrow Ti + 4\ NaCl$.

17.53 2.04×10^5 L.

17.55 181.1 kJ using C, 61.1 kJ using CO.

17.57 Equilibrium vapor pressure is about 10 atm.

17.59 c) pH = 8.3.

17.61 b) $E^\circ = 2.594$ V.

17.63 More likely at pH = 3.

17.65 Battery requires F_2 gas and an alkali metal or alkaline earth. Gaseous batteries are not practical.

17.67 $E^\circ = 0.368$ V.

17.69 a) MnO_4^-, b) H_2O_2, c) Sn^{2+}.

17.71 $E^\circ = 1.094$ V, solutions of hydrogen peroxide are unstable.

17.73 $5\ H_2SO_3 + 2\ MnO_4^- + H^+_{(aq)} \rightarrow 5\ HSO_4^- + 2\ Mn^{2+} + 3\ H_2O$,

$5\ SO_2 + 2\ MnO_4^- + 2\ H_2O + H^+_{(aq)} \rightarrow 5\ HSO_4^- + 2\ Mn^{2+}$,

$5\ H_2S + 8\ MnO_4^- + 19\ H^+_{(aq)} \rightarrow 5\ HSO_4^- + 8\ Mn^{2+} + 12\ H_2O$,

$5\ H_2S_2O_3 + 8\ MnO_4^- + 14\ H^+_{(aq)} \rightarrow 10\ HSO_4^- + 8\ Mn^{2+} + 7\ H_2O$

17.77 a) $3\ H_2 + 2\ Cr(OH)_3 \rightarrow 6\ H_2O + 2\ Cr$, b) − 0.47 V, c) 2.7×10^3 kJ.

17.79 b) 0.0207 V.

17.81 0.40 V.

CHAPTER 18

18.1 a) Acid = Ni; base = CO; b) Acid = $SbCl_3$; base = Cl^{-}∀ c) Acid = $AlBr_3$; base = $(CH_3)_3P$

d) Acid = BF_3; base = ClF_3; e) Acid = I_2; base = I^-

18.3 BF_3, etc., have vacant orbitals capable of accepting a pair of electrons; CF_4, etc., do not.

18.5 a) Au = $[Xe]6s^15d^{10}$; Au^+ = $[Xe]5d^{10}$; Au^{3+} = $[Xe]5d^8$

b) Ni = $[Ar]4s^23d^8$; Ni^{2+} = $[Ar]3d^8$; Ni^{3+} = $[Ar]3d^7$

c) Mn^- = $[Ar]4s^23d^6$; Mn = $[Ar]4s^23d^5$; Mn^+ = $[Ar]4s^13d^5$

18.7 a) Hexaammineruthenium(II) chloride

b) Bis(ethylenediamine)diiodochromium(II) iodide

c) *cis*-Dichlorobis(trimethylphosphine)palladium(II)

d) *fac*-Triamminetrichloroiridium(III)

e) Tetracarbonylnickel(0)

18.9 a) Rh(III), d^6; b) Mo(II), d^4; c) Ir(III), d^6; d) Ir(III), d^6; e) Mn(I), d^5

18.11

a) 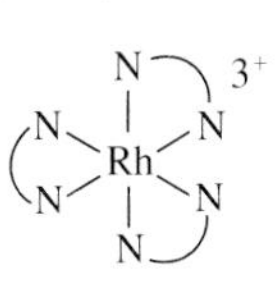 Rh with six N donors (three chelating N–N ligands), charge 3^+

b) 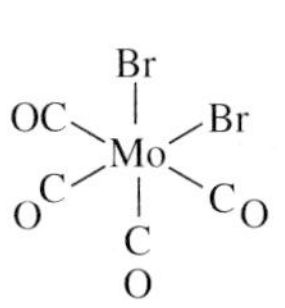 Mo with Br, Br, OC, CO, CO, CO

c) 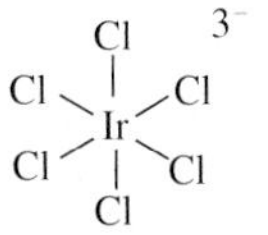 Ir with six Cl, charge 3^-

d) 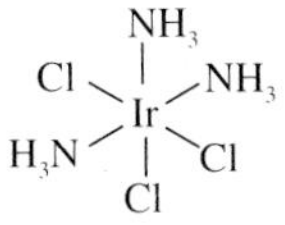 Ir with NH_3, NH_3, H_3N, Cl, Cl, Cl

e) 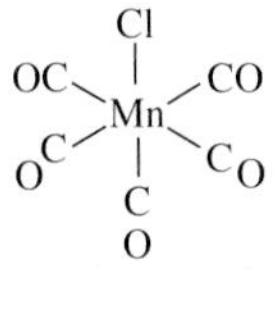 Mn with Cl, OC, CO, CO, CO, CO

18.13 a) *cis*-$[Co(NH_3)_4Cl(NO_2)]^+$; b) $[Pt(NH_3)Cl_3]^-$; c) $[Cu(en)_2(H_2O)_2]^{2+}$; d) $[FeCl_4]^-$

18.15 Geometry = tetrahedral; color = yellow-orange.

18.17 a) $\Delta = 278$ kJ mol^{-1}; b) yellow; c) Tetraaquadichlorochromium(III) ion;

d) 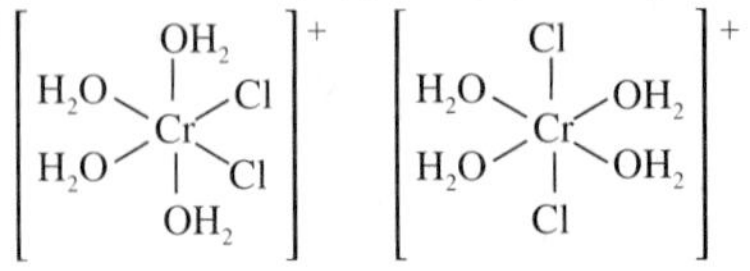 $[\text{Cr}(\text{OH}_2)_2(\text{H}_2\text{O})_2\text{Cl}_2]^+$ (OH$_2$ top and bottom; H$_2$O, H$_2$O, Cl, Cl in plane) and $[\text{Cr}(\text{H}_2\text{O})_2(\text{OH}_2)_2\text{Cl}_2]^+$ (Cl top and bottom; H$_2$O, H$_2$O, OH$_2$, OH$_2$ in plane)

e) 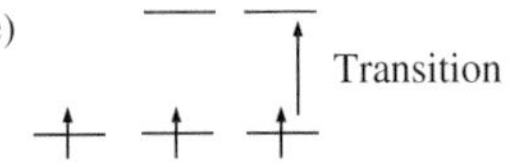 Transition

18.19 a) Zr^{4+} complexes have no *d* electrons.
18.21 $[Cr(NH_3)_6]^{3+}$ is orange; $[Cr(H_2O)_6]^{3+}$ is violet.
18.23 a) $BF_3 > BCl_3 > AlCl_3$; b) $Al^{3+} > Tl^{3+} > Tl^{+}$; C) $AlCl_3 > AlBr_3 > AlI_3$
18.25 The oxidation state of sulfur is +6 in SO_3 but only +4 in SO_2.
18.27 $(CH_3)_2N\text{-}PF_2(BF_3)$ and $(CH_3)_2(BH_3)N\text{-}PF_2$:

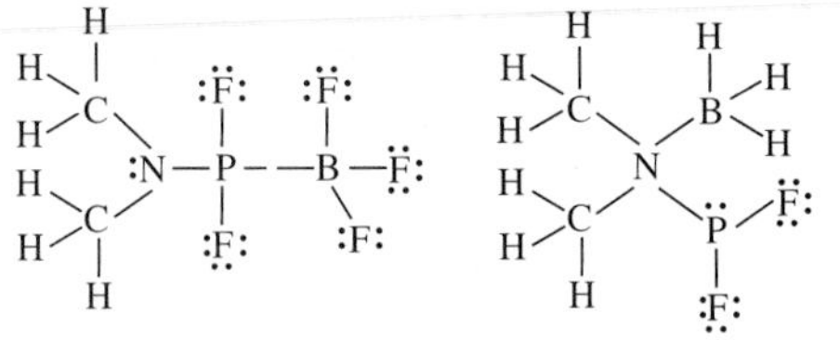

18.29 a) $NBr_3 + GaC_3 \rightarrow Br_3N\text{–}GaCl_3$; b) no reaction; c) no reaction
d) $4\ LiCH_2CH_2CH_2CH_3 + SnCl_4 \rightarrow Sn(CH_2CH_2CH_2CH_3)_4 + 4\ LiCl$
18.31 The bulkiness of the CH_3 groups hinders the ability of approaching Lewis bases to form bonds to the boron atom.
18.35 Because Hg^{2+} is a soft Lewis acid, it does not form complexes with hard Lewis bases. Zinc, a hard Lewis acid, forms complexes with hard Lewis bases such as oxides, carbonates, and silicates.
18.39 a) Acid = $Al(CH_3)_3$.
18.41 $CaO + SiO_2 \rightarrow CaSiO_3$. In this reaction, an O^{2-} anion adds to the SiO_2 structure to form an SiO_3^{2-} anion. Thus O^{2-} acts as a Lewis base, donating a pair of electrons to form an Si—O bond, and SiO_2 acts as a Lewis acid.
18.43 Energy difference corresponds to photon energies in the ultraviolet

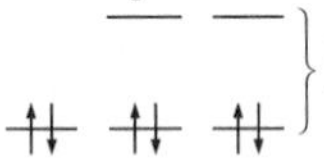

The complex is colorless.
18.45 See Figure 18.29.
18.47 Strong adducts form when the donor and acceptor can approach each other closely. In dimethyl-tetrahydrofuran, the electron clouds around the two methyl groups repel an approaching BF_3 molecule, lengthening the O—B bond and making the adduct weaker.
18.49 Because F^- is at the small splitting end of the spectrochemical series, $[FeF_6]^{3-}$ will absorb light of longer wavelengths than $[Fe(H_2O)_6]^{3+}$. This places its absorption in the infrared, so the complex is colorless.
18.51 The $[Ni(CN)_4]^{2-}$ complex is diamagnetic, meaning that all eight valence electrons of Ni^{2+} are paired. This can only occur if the complex is square planar (see Figure 18-16). The $[NiCl_4]^{2-}$ complex is magnetic because it has unpaired spins. This requires tetrahedral geometry (see Figure 18-17).
18.53 The oxalate ligand forms a Lewis acid-base adduct with Fe^{3+}, giving the soluble complex $[Fe(C_2O_4)_3]^{3-}$.

CHAPTER 19

19.1 a) $Z = 3, A = 6, N = 3$; b) $Z = 20, A = 43, N = 23$; c) $Z = 92, A = 238, N = 146$; d) $Z = 52, A = 130, N = 78$; e) $Z = 10, A = 20, N = 10$; f) $Z = 82, A = 205, N = 123$.
19.3 a) ${}^{4}_{2}He$; b) ${}^{184}_{74}W$; c) ${}^{26}_{12}Mg$; d) ${}^{60}_{28}Ni$.
19.5 a) Unstable (neutron-poor); b) unstable ($Z > 83$); c) stable; d) unstable (Tc has no stable nuclides).
19.7 8.99×10^{16} kJ.
19.9 -1.079×10^{11} kJ/mol, -8.11×10^{8} kJ/mol of nucleons.
19.13 a) ${}^{125}_{52}Te$; b) ${}^{123}_{51}Sb$; c) ${}^{127}_{53}I$.
19.15 Final product is ${}^{208}_{82}Pb$.
19.17 a) ${}^{13}_{6}C$ and ${}^{12}_{5}B$; b) both are ${}^{20}_{10}Ne$; c) ${}^{258}_{101}Md$ and ${}^{255}_{101}Md$.
19.25 5.8×10^{6} m/s.
19.33 7.25×10^{8}/s.
19.37 3.5×10^{9} yr.
19.41 1.583×10^{11} kJ/mol and 7.574×10^{8} kJ/mol of nucleons.
19.43 3.4×10^{2} if half-life is 1100 s, 34 if half–life is 876 s.
19.45 1.25×10^{-13} J.
19.47 8.19×10^{-14} J/γ ray, 4.93×10^{7} kJ/mol of γ rays.
19.47 ${}^{210}Po/{}^{209}Po = 1.2 \times 10^{-8}$.
19.53 52,000 years.
19.55 63.92859 g/mol for one product, 63.92851 g/mol for the other.
19.57 Lead from thorium has a higher molar mass.
19.61 23.5 yr for 1% to decay, 1.08×10^{4} yr until 1% remains.
19.63 2.9×10^{9} yr.
19.65 4760 yr.
19.67 1.504×10^{11} kJ/mol, 7.64×10^{8} kJ/mol of nucleons.
19.69 Final product is not stable, it decays to ${}^{30}_{14}Si$.
19.71 70 hr.
19.73 10 yr.
19.77 103 mg.

GLOSSARY

Absolute entropy. (13.3) The amount of disorder contained in a chemical substance.

Absolute zero. (5.4) The temperature at which the molecular energy of motion is at a minimum.

Absorption spectrum. (6.3) The distribution of wavelengths of light absorbed by a species.

Acid. (Brønsted definition) (4.6) A substance that acts as a proton donor.

Acid ionization constant (K_a). (15.3) The equilibrium constant for proton transfer between an acid and water.

Acid rain. (5.7) Rain whose pH is lower than 5.6, which is the pH of water saturated with carbon dioxide.

Actinide element. (1.3) Any of the elements in the 5*f* block of the periodic table, between Z = 89 and Z = 102.

Activated complex. (14.6) The unstable molecular species through which an elementary reaction proceeds as it evolves from reactant(s) to product(s).

Activation energy (E_a). (14.6) The minimum amount of energy that reactants must possess to react to form products.

Activation energy diagram. (14.6) A graph showing how the energy of a reacting set of molecules varies with the course of the reaction.

Active electrode. (17.2) An electrode whose chemical constituents take part in the redox reaction that occurs at its surface.

Active site. (14.7) The specific location in an enzyme where catalytic activity takes place.

Activity series. (4.7) A list of elements in order of how easily they are oxidized in aqueous solution.

Actual yield. (4.3) The amount of chemical product formed in a chemical reaction.

Adduct. (18.1) A compound formed by bond formation between a Lewis base and a Lewis acid.

Adenosine triphosphate (ATP). (13.6) A biochemical molecule containing adenine and three phosphate groups instrumental in biochemical energetics.

Adhesive force. (10.3) A force of attraction between molecules in one phase and different molecules in another phase.

Adsorption. (14.7) The physical attachment of molecules to a surface.

Alcohol. (11.2) An organic compound that contains the hydroxyl group,—OH.

Aldehyde. (11.2) An organic compound that contains the carbonyl group attached to a hydrogen atom, —CHO.

Alkali metal. (1.3) Any of the Group I elements, all of which are reactive metals with s^1 valence configurations.

Alkaline earth metal. (1.3) Any of the Group II elements, all of which are reactive metals with s^2 valence configurations.

Alkane. (3.2) A compound containing only carbon and hydrogen, with general formula $C_nH_{(2n+2)}$, in which all carbon atoms possess four σ bonds.

Alkene. (3.2) A compound containing only carbon and hydrogen in which there is at least one C = C bond.

Alkyne. (3.2) A compound containing only carbon and hydrogen in which there is at least one C ≡ C bond.

Alloy. (10.5) A metallic solution or mixture of two or more metals.

Alpha helix. (11.5) The protein secondary structure formed like a coil.

Alpha particle (α). (2.2) An energetic helium nucleus emitted by a radioactive nuclide.

Amalgam. (10.5) An alloy containing mercury.

Amide. (11.2) An organic compound that contains the —C—N— linkage.

Amine. (11.2) A compound whose molecules can be viewed as ammonia with one or more N—H bonds replaced by N—C bonds.

Amino acid. (11.5) A compound that contains both an amine (—NH_2) and a carboxylic acid (—CO_2H) functional group.

Amorphous. (10.4) Without any organized regular repeating pattern.

Ampere (A). (1.5) The base unit of electric current in the SI system.

Amplitude. (9.3) The height of a wave.

Analytical balance. (1.5) An accurate mass-measuring instrument.

Anion. (2.4) An ion that possesses negative charge.

Anode. (17.3) The electrode at which oxidation occurs.

Antibonding orbital. (9.3) A molecular orbital that has electron density concentrated outside the bonding region, making it less stable than the atomic orbitals from which it forms.

Aqueous. (3.7) A solution with water as the solvent.

Arrhenius equation. (14.6). The equation describing how rate constants depend on temperature and activation energy.

Atmosphere (atm). (5.3) A unit of pressure based on the normal pressure exerted by the Earth's atmosphere at sea level. 1 atm = 101.325 kPa.

Atom. (1.2) The basic unit of chemical matter, consisting of a nucleus and enough electrons to convey electrical neutrality.

Atomic number (Z). (2.3) The number of protons in an atomic nucleus.

Atomic orbital. (6.5) A description of an atomic electron that provides the distribution of electron density about the nucleus.

Atomic radius. (7.6) The distance from the nucleus of an atom at which electron-electron repulsion prevents closer approach of another atom.

Atomic symbol. (2.3) The letter designation for an element.

Atomic theory. (2.1) The description of matter as composed of atoms that retain their identities during all physical and chemical processes.

Aufbau principle. (7.4) The statement that the most stable arrangement of electrons in an atom results from placing each successive electron in the most stable available atomic orbital.

Avogadro's number (N_A). (3.4) The number of particles in 1 mol, 6.02214×10^{23} particles/mol.

Axial orbital. (8.6) An orbital that lies along the z axis in trigonal bipyramidal geometry.

Azimuthal quantum number (l). (7.1) The quantum number, restricted to integers from 0 to $n - 1$, that indexes the shape of an atomic orbital.

Balanced chemical equation. (4.1) A description of a chemical reaction using chemical formulas in which the coefficients describe the ratios of molecules of each species that react.

Ball-and-stick model. (3.1) A representation of a molecule that shows the atoms as small balls and the chemical bonds as sticks.

Band gap. (9.6) The difference in energy between the highest filled orbital and the lowest vacant orbital in a solid.

Band theory. (9.6) The description of bonding in solids using delocalized orbitals.

Barometer. (5.3) An instrument for measuring atmospheric pressure.

Base (Brønsted definition). (4.6) A substance that acts as a proton acceptor.

Base ionization constant (K_b). (15.3) The equilibrium constant for the proton transfer from water to a base.

Base pairing. (11.7) The formation of hydrogen bonds between strands of DNA or RNA.

Battery. (17.7) One or more galvanic cells that serve as a source of electric current or voltage.

Bent geometry. (8.5) A nonlinear arrangement of three bonded atoms.

Beta particle (β). (19.3) An energetic electron emitted by a radioactive nuclide.

Bilayer. (10.6) A double layer of atoms or molecules.

Bimolecular reaction. (14.1) An elementary step in which two molecules collide and undergo a chemical reaction.

Binary acid. (16.4) An acid containing hydrogen and one other element.

Binary compound. (3.2) A chemical substance that contains only two different elements.

Body centered cubic (BCC). (10.4) The crystal structure whose unit cell is a cube with identical atoms at its corners and at its center.

Boiling point. (10.1) The temperature at which the vapor pressure of a liquid matches the external pressure.

Boiling point elevation. (10.7) The increase in boiling point of a liquid caused by the presence of nonvolatile solutes in solution.

Boltzmann distribution. (14.6) The way that molecular kinetic energies are distributed among a collection of molecules.

Bond. (3.1) A strong coulombic attractive force between atoms in a substance.

Bond angle. (8.4) The angle established when two atoms bond to a third atom.

Bond energy. (9.1) The energy per mole required to break one particular chemical bond in a gaseous substance.

Bond length. (9.1) The average distance between the nuclei of two bonded atoms in a molecule.

Bond order. (9.3) The net number of pairs of bonding electrons in a chemical bond. From Lewis structures, bond order is the average number of electron pairs in the bond. From molecular electron configurations, bond order is half the difference between the number of bonding pairs and the number of antibonding pairs.

Bonding molecular orbital. (9.3) An orbital formed from atomic orbitals that conveys bonding by placing electron density between the bonded atoms.

Brownian motion. (2.1) The random motion of small particles suspended in a liquid or gas.

Buffer capacity. (16.5) The amount of added hydronium or hydroxide ions that can be added to a buffer solution without exceeding a specified pH range.

Buffer equation. (16.5) The equation linking the pH of a buffer solution with the pK_a and concentrations of the acid-base pair.

Buffer solution. (16.5) A solution containing both a weak acid and its conjugate base whose pH changes slowly on addition of small amounts of an acid or base.

Buret. (4.6) A volume-delivering device that is calibrated to allow measurement of the amount of fluid delivered.

Calorimeter. (12.3) An apparatus for measuring the amount of heat absorbed or emitted in the course of a chemical process.

Capillary action. (10.3) The process by which liquids rise in extremely thin tubing.

Carbohydrate. (11.6) A biochemical substance whose empirical formula is $(CH_2O)_n$.

Carbonyl group. (11.2) The $C{=}O$ functional group.

Carboxylic acid. (11.2) An acid that contains the $-CO_2H$ functional group.

Catalyst. (14.7) A substance that increases the rate of a chemical reaction without being consumed or produced in the reaction.

Cathode. (17.3) The electrode at which reduction occurs.

Cation. (2.4) A positively charged ion.

Cell potential. (17.5) The difference in electrical potential (voltage) between the two electrodes in a galvanic cell.

Celsius scale. (1.5) The temperature scale defined by 0 °C as the normal freezing point and 100 °C as the normal boiling point of water.

Change of state. (12.1) Any process in which there is a change in one or more of the variables (P, V, T, n) describing the state of a system.

Chelate. (18.2) A complex formed by polydentate ligands.

Chemical element. (1.2) A substance composed of atoms that have the same number of protons in their nuclei.

Chemical equation. (2.1) An equation using chemical formulas that describes the identities and relative amounts of reactants and products in a chemical reaction.

Chemical equilibrium. (15.0) A chemical reaction that has reacted to the point where no net change occurs, because forward and reverse processes proceed at equal rates.

Chemical formula. (1.2) An expression using chemical symbols that describes the identities and relative amounts of elements in a substance.

Chemical kinetics. (14.2) The study of how fast chemical reactions occur.

Chemical nomenclature. (3.2) The organized pattern for naming chemical substances.

Chemical transformation. (1.4) A process in which new chemical substances are produced.

Chemistry. (1.1) The study of matter and its interactions.

Chromatography. (10.8) A class of separation techniques that make use of differing rates of movement of substances moving with a mobile phase over a stationary phase.

Close packed. (10.4) A most efficient arrangement for packing atoms, molecules, or ions in a regular crystal.

Closed system. (12.1) A system that can exchange energy but not matter with its surroundings.

Cohesive force. (10.3) A force of attraction between like molecules in the same phase.

Colligative property. (10.7) A property of a solution that is proportional to the concentration of solute species.

Combustion. (3.6) A reaction of a substance with oxygen that releases chemical energy.

Common name. (3.2) A nonsystematic name for a chemical substance used in ordinary conversation.

Complementary base pair. (11.7) Two nitrogen-containing organic bases that hydrogen bond in DNA or RNA.

Complementary colors. (18.3) Colors that are related in that if light of one color is absorbed by a substance, the substance displays the complementary color.

Complex ion. (15.3) A species formed by bonding of species containing lone pairs of electrons to a metal ion.

Compound. (1.4) A substance formed of atoms of two or more elements chemically bonded in fixed proportions.

Compound nucleus. (19.4) The transient nucleus that forms from the collision of a nuclear projectile with another nucleus.

Concentration. (3.7) The amount of a solute contained in a standard amount of a solution.

Concentration cell. (17.6) An electrochemical cell in which the oxidation and reduction reactions are the same but operating under different concentrations and in opposite directions.

Concentration quotient (*Q*). (13.4) The ratio of concentrations of products to concentrations of reactants, each raised to its stoichiometric coefficient.

Concentration table. (15.4) A table of amounts for a chemical reaction that reacts to equilibrium.

Condensation reaction. (11.2) A reaction that joins two molecules, accompanied by the elimination of a small molecule such as water.

Conduction band. (9.6) The set of delocalized orbitals in a solid that, when partially occupied, contains mobile electrons and conveys high electrical conductivity.

Conductor. (9.6) A substance that is a good conductor of electrical current.

Conjugate acid-base pair. (16.3) A Brønsted acid and the base that results from removal of one proton.

Conjugated π system. (9.3) A system of alternating single and double bonds delocalized over a number of atoms.

Conservation law. (2.5) A law stating that a quantity is conserved.

Conserved. (2.5) Unchanging in amount.

Conversion ratio. (1.5) A ratio equal to 1 that converts a quantity from one unit to another.

Coordination complex. (18.2) A combination of a metal atom or cation with two or more Lewis bases (ligands) that bind covalently to the metal.

Coordination number. (8.5) The number of atoms bonded to an inner atom in a molecule or metal complex.

Copolymerization. (11.1) The formation of a polymer from two or more different monomers.

Core electrons. (7.5) The inner atomic electrons with principal quantum number less than that of the valence electrons.

Corrosion. (17.7) The oxidation of a metal in contact with its environment.

Coulomb's law. (2.2) The law describing the interaction between two electrically charged objects.

Coupled reactions. (13.5) A pair of reactions, one of which is driven in what is otherwise its nonspontaneous direction by the influence of the second, highly spontaneous reaction.

Covalent bond. (8.1) A bond resulting from the sharing of electrons between atoms.

Covalent solid. (10.4) A solid made up of atoms held together in a crystalline array by covalent bonds.

Critical mass. (19.5) The minimum mass of fissionable material required to generate a self-sustaining nuclear fission reaction.

Cross-linking. (11.1) The formation of additional chemical bonds between the chains of a polymer.

Crystal field theory. (18.3) A model describing the electronic structure of transition metal complexes in terms of the interactions between metal *d* orbitals and the electric field of the ligands.

Crystalline. (10.4) Containing a regular array of atoms, molecules, or ions.

Cubic close packing. (10.4) The close packing arrangement in which hexagonal layers are stacked in an ABCABC . . . pattern.

Cyclotron. (19.5) A particle accelerator used to generate high energy beams of nuclear particles.

Dalton's law of partial pressures. (5.5) The law stating that in a gas mixture, each gas exerts a pressure equal to the pressure that it would exert if present by itself under otherwise identical conditions.

de Broglie equation. (6.5) The equation describing the wave nature of particles, $\lambda = h/mu$.

Heat of solution. (12.5) The enthalpy change accompanying the dissolving of a solute.

Heat of vaporization. (12.5) The enthalpy change accompanying the vaporization process.

Henry's law. (10.4) The statement that the concentration of a gas in solution is directly proportional to the partial pressure of that gas above the solution.

Heterogeneous. (1.4) Containing more than one physically distinct component and therefore not uniform in composition.

Hexagonal close packing. (10.4) The close packing arrangement in which hexagonal layers are stacked in an ABAB . . . pattern.

High-spin complex. (18.3) A complex in which the maximum number of electrons is unpaired.

Homogeneous. (1.4) Uniform in composition.

Hund's rule. (7.4) The observation that the most stable arrangement of electrons among degenerate orbitals is the one that maximizes the number of unpaired electron spins.

Hybrid orbital. (8.4) An atomic orbital obtained by combining two or more valence orbitals on the same atom.

Hybridization. (8.4) The formation of a set of hybrid orbitals with favorable directional characteristics by mixing together two or more valence orbitals of the same atom.

Hydrate. (3.3) A solid compound or complex ion that has water molecules incorporated into its structure.

Hydrocarbon. (8.4) A compound that contains only hydrogen and carbon.

Hydrogen bond. (10.2) A moderately strong intermolecular attraction caused by the partial sharing of electrons between a highly electronegative atom of F, O, or N and the polar hydrogen atom in a F—H, O—H, or N—H bond.

Hydrophilic. (10.6) Compatible with water.

Hydrophobic. (10.6) Incompatible with water.

Hydroxyl group. (11.2) The —OH group.

Ideal gas. (5.2) A gas in which molecular volumes and intermolecular forces both are negligible.

Ideal gas equation. (5.2) The equation describing the behavior of an ideal gas, $PV = nRT$.

Indicator. (16.6) A substance that can be used to identify the equivalence point of an acid-base titration because its color is sensitive to pH changes.

Induced fit. (14.7) The process by which an enzyme and the reactant binding to it accommodate their shapes to each other.

Induced nuclear reaction. (19.4) A reaction that occurs as a result of a nuclear projectile colliding with an atomic nucleus.

Ineffective collision. (14.1) A molecular collision that does not lead to chemical reaction.

Initial concentration. (15.4). The concentration of a reagent immediately after a system is prepared but before any chemical reaction takes place.

Initiator. (11.1) A substance that starts a polymerization chain reaction.

Inner atom. (8.5) Any atom in a molecule that is bonded to more than one other atom.

Insoluble. (16.2) Unable to dissolve in a liquid. Salts with $K_{sp} << 1$ are classified as insoluble in water.

Integrated rate law. (14.4) A rate statement giving the concentration as a function of time.

Intensity. (6.2) The brightness (number of photons) of light.

Intensive property. (1.6) A property whose magnitude is independent of the amount of the substance present.

Intermediate. (14.1) A species that is not part of the overall stoichiometry but is produced in an early step of a reaction mechanism and consumed in a later step.

Intermolecular forces. (10.1) Forces that exist between molecules.

International System of Units (SI). (1.5) The set of metric units that have been chosen by international agreement for expressing scientific quantities.

Intramolecular forces. (10.1) Forces that exist within a molecule.

Ion. (2.4) A charged species resulting from the gain or loss of electrons from a neutral atom or molecule.

Ion exchange. (10.8) A process for exchanging one ionic species in solution for another by passing the solution through a column containing a resin charged with ions.

Ionic compound. (2.4) A neutral compound composed of cations and anions.

Ionization energy. (7.3) The energy required to remove an electron from an isolated species.

Isoelectronic series. (7.6) A group of atoms and ions that have the same number of electrons.

Isolated system. (12.1) A system that can exchange neither energy nor matter with its surroundings.

Isomers. (3.1) Molecules that have the same chemical formulas but different molecular structures.

Isotonic. (10.7) Having identical total molarity of solutes.

Isotopes. (2.3) Atoms of the same element whose nuclei contain different numbers of neutrons.

Joule (J). (2.5) The SI energy unit, defined to be $1\ J = 1\ kg\ m^2\ s^{-2}$.

Kelvin (*K*). (1.5) The SI temperature unit, based on absolute zero with a unit size equal to 1/100 the difference between the normal freezing point and normal boiling point of water.

Ketone. (11.2) An organic compound that contains the carbonyl group (C = O) linked to two carbon atoms.

Kilogram (kg). (1.5) The SI base unit for mass.

Kinetic energy. (2.5) The energy of motion of an object.

Kinetics. (14.2) The study of chemical reaction rates.

Lanthanide element. (1.3) Any of the elements in the 4*f* block of the periodic table, between $Z = 57$ and $Z = 70$.

Law of conservation of energy. (2.5) The statement that energy cannot be created or destroyed.

Law of conservation of mass. (2.5) The statement that mass cannot be created or destroyed.

Lead battery. (17.7) A voltaic cell, widely used for automobile storage batteries, in which both half-reactions involve reactions of lead.

Le Châtelier's principle. (15.6) The observation that when a change of conditions is applied to a system at equilibrium, the system responds in the manner that reduces the amount of change.

Lewis acid. (18.1) An electron-pair acceptor.

Lewis base. (18.1) An electron-pair donor.

Lewis structure. (8.3) A representation of covalent bonding that uses symbols for the elements, dots for nonbonding valence electrons, and lines for pairs of bonding valence electrons.

Ligand. (18.2) A molecule or anion that acts as a Lewis base, forming a bond to a metal atom or cation.

Light. (6.2) Electromagnetic radiation in the visible portion of the spectrum, between $\lambda = 400$ nm and $\lambda = 700$ nm.

Limiting reagent. (4.4) The reactant whose amount falls to zero in a chemical reaction.

Line structure. (3.1) A compact representation of a carbon-containing molecule that shows the molecular structure in a simplified fashion.

Linear geometry. (8.6) The bonding arrangement in which two atoms bond to a third along a straight line, generating a bond angle of 180°.

Liquid. (1.4) The phase of matter in which intermolecular forces are large enough that molecules cannot escape into space but small enough that molecules move freely past one another. A liquid has a distinct volume but no distinct shape.

Liter (L). (1.5) A unit of volume equal to 1000 cm^3 (10^{-3} m^3).

Lone pair (nonbonding pair). (8.3) A pair of valence electrons that is localized on an atom rather than involved in bonding.

Low-spin complex. (18.3) A complex in which the maximum number of electrons is paired.

Macromolecule. (11.1) A molecule that contains a large number of atoms (typically, more than several hundred).

Magnet. (2.2) An object that attracts or repels a moving electrical charge but carries no net electric charge.

Magnetic quantum number (m_l). (7.1) The quantum number, restricted to integers between $+l$ and $-l$, that indexes the orientation in space of an atomic orbital.

Magnitude. (1.5) The size of a number.

Main group element. (1.3) Any of the elements in the *p* block of the periodic table.

Major species. (16.1) The species (ions, molecules) present in relatively high concentration in aqueous solution.

Malleable. (1.3) Able to be formed into various shapes, including thin sheets.

Manometer. (5.3) A tube, containing a liquid and open at both ends, used to measure differences in pressure.

Mass. (1.5) The quantity of matter in a substance.

Mass number (*A*). (2.3) The total number of protons and neutrons in a nucleus.

Mass percent composition. (3.6) The makeup of a chemical substance expressed in parts per hundred by mass of each component.

Mass spectrometer. (2.3) An instrument that separates the atomic/molecular components of a sample according to their masses.

Matter. (1.4) Anything that occupies space and possesses mass.

Mechanism. (14.1) The detailed molecular processes by which a chemical reaction proceeds.

Mesosphere. (6.4) The region of the Earth's atmosphere between 50 and 85 km above its surface.

Metabolism. (13.6) The process of breaking down organic molecules in biochemical cells.

Metal. (1.3) An element that is lustrous, conducts heat and electricity well, and tends to lose electrons to form cations.

Metalloid. (1.3) An element with properties intermediate between those of metals and nonmetals.

Metallurgy. (17.9) The science of extracting, purifying, and forming useful objects from metals.

Metathesis reaction. (18.5) A chemical reaction in which there is an exchange of bonding partners between two atoms or ions.

Meter (m). (1.5) The SI unit of length.

Micelle. (10.6) A cluster of molecules in aqueous solution organized with their hydrophobic ends pointing inward and their hydrophilic ends pointing outward.

Midpoint. (16.6) The point in a titration where the amount of added titrant is exactly half the amount required for complete reaction.

Minor species (16.1) The species (ions, molecules) present in relatively low concentration in aqueous solution.

Miscible. (10.5) Soluble in all proportions.

Mixture. (1.4) A material containing two or more substances that is not homogeneous.

Moderator. (19.5) A substance used to slow down neutrons in a nuclear reactor.

Molar mass (*MM*). (3.4) The mass in grams of 1 mol of atoms or molecules.

Molarity (*M*). (3.7) The amount of moles of solute dissolved in 1 L of solution.

Mole. (3.4) The amount of a substance that contains the same number of units as the number of atoms in exactly 12 g of carbon-12, 6.022×10^{23}.

Mole fraction. (5.5) The ratio of the number of moles of one component to the total number of moles of all components.

Molecular density. (5.2) The number of molecules per unit volume.

Molecular geometry. (8.4) The overall shape of a molecule, arising from the relative positions of its atomic nuclei.

Molecule. (1.2) A group of atoms linked together by chemical bonds.

Monolayer. (10.6) A single two-dimensional layer of atoms or molecules.

Monomer. (11.1) A molecule from which a polymer is synthesized.

Near-degenerate orbitals. (7.4) Those orbitals in a species that have nearly identical energies.

Nernst equation. (17.6) The equation that relates the potential of an electrochemical cell to standard potentials and concentrations.

Net ionic equation. (4.5) A chemical equation showing the actual participants in a reaction of ions in solution.

Neutral atom. (2.3) An atom containing the same number of electrons as it has protons in its nucleus.

Neutralization reaction. (4.6) Proton transfer between an acid and a base to generate a pair of neutral molecules.

Neutron. (2.2) The subatomic constituent of nuclei that is electrically neutral and has a mass of 1.675×10^{-27} kg.

Newton. (5.3) The SI unit for force.

Nitrogen fixation. (4.0) The conversion of molecular nitrogen into nitrogen-containing species such as ammonia or nitrate.

Nomenclature. (3.2) A systematic procedure for naming chemical compounds.

Nonbonding electron. (8.1) A valence electron that does not participate in bond formation.

Nonmetal. (1.3) An element that lacks the properties of metals, in particular the tendency to form cations.

Normal boiling point. (10.1) The boiling point of a substance under one atmosphere pressure.

n-type semiconductor. (9.6) A metalloid that contains a dopant that gives it excess valence electrons.

Nuclear binding energy. (19.2) The amount of energy per nucleon that binds an atomic nucleus together.

Nuclear decay. (19.3) The spontaneous decomposition of an unstable nucleus.

Nucleic acid. (11.7) A biochemical macromolecule containing nucleotide units.

Nucleon. (19.1) One of the protons or neutrons in a nucleus.

Nucleotide. (11.7) The repeating unit in DNA and RNA, containing a base, a five-carbon sugar, and a phosphate group.

Nucleus. (2.2) The central core of an atom, where nearly all the mass is concentrated.

Nuclide. (19.1) One particular nucleus, characterized by its charge number (Z) and mass number (A).

Octahedral geometry. (8.6) The geometry in which a central atom forms six chemical bonds to species located along the cartesian axes.

Open system. (12.1) A system that can exchange both mass and energy with its surroundings.

Orbital. (6.5) A three-dimensional wave describing a bound electron.

Orbital density picture. (7.2) A two-dimensional dot drawing representing the distribution of electron density in an orbital.

Orbital interaction. (7.2) An interaction between electrons in orbitals.

Orbital overlap. (8.1) The extent to which two orbitals on different atoms interact.

Order. (13.1) A regular repeating arrangement.

Order of reaction. (14.3) The exponent to which a concentration is raised in a rate law.

Ore. (17.9) A mineral deposit that serves as a commercial source of a metal.

Organic chemistry. (3.2) The chemistry of carbon and its compounds.

Osmosis. (10.7) The net movement of solvent molecules through a semipermeable membrane.

Osmotic pressure. (10.7) The pressure difference that must be applied to a solution to prevent osmosis from pure solvent.

Outer atom. (8.4) Any atom in a molecule that bonds to only one other atom.

Overall order. (14.3) The sum of the reaction orders of all species in a rate law.

Overvoltage. (17.8) An excess potential that must be applied to force an electrochemical reaction to proceed at an appreciable rate.

Oxidation. (4.7) Loss of electrons by a chemical species.

Oxidation number. (17.1) The charge that an atom would have if all its bonding electrons were assigned to the more electronegative atom involved in the bond.

Oxidizing agent. (4.7) A chemical species that can gain electrons from another substance.

Oxy acid. (16.4) An acid containing an inner atom bonded to OH groups and O atoms.

Oxyanion. (3.3) An anion of general formula XO_m, containing a central atom bonded to two or more oxygen atoms.

Ozone layer. (4.6) The region of the Earth's atmosphere that contains ozone (O_3) and absorbs potentially lethal ultraviolet radiation.

Pairing energy. (18.3) The electron-electron repulsion energy arising from placement of two electrons in the same orbital.

Paramagnetic. (7.4) Attracted by a magnetic field, as a consequence of having unpaired electron spins.

Partial pressure. (5.5) The pressure exerted by one component of a gaseous mixture.

Pascal (Pa). (5.3) The SI unit of pressure, one newton per square meter.

Passive electrode. (17.2) An electrode that serves only to conduct electrons between a wire and a solution; its chemical constituents do not take part in the redox reaction that occurs at its surface.

Path function. (12.1) A quantity whose change depends on the path along which a change takes place.

Pauli exclusion principle. (7.4) The requirement that no two electrons in a chemical species can be described by the same wave function.

Peptide. (11.5) A small polymer of amino acids.

Percent yield. (4.3) The ratio of the actual yield of a reaction divided by its theoretical yield and multiplied by 100%.

Periodic table. (1.3) The table of the chemical elements arranged in rows of increasing atomic number and columns of similar chemical behavior.

pH. (16.3) The negative logarithm of the hydronium ion concentration.

pH meter. (17.6) A device for measuring solution pH.

Phase. (1.4) Any of the three states of matter: gas, liquid, or solid.

Phase change. (1.4) Transformation from one state of matter to another.

Phase diagram. (13.5) A pressure-temperature graph showing the conditions under which a substance exists as solid, liquid, and gas.

Phospholipid. (10.6) A biochemical surfactant molecule that is one component of cell membranes.

Photoelectric effect. (6.2) The ejection of electrons from a metal surface by light.

Photon. (6.2) A particle of light, characterized by energy $E = h\nu$.

Pi (π) bond. (9.1) A chemical bond formed by side-by-side orbital overlap so that electron density is concentrated above and below the bond axis.

Physical transformation. (1.4) A change in properties that is not accompanied by chemical rearrangements.

Physical property. (1.5) A property that can be observed without causing any chemical rearrangements.

Pipet. (3.7) A volumetric device designed to deliver a measured quantity of a liquid.

Planck's constant (*h*). (6.2) The physical constant, 6.63×10^{-34} J s, that relates the energy of a photon to its frequency.

Plastic. (11.4) A polymer that exists as blocks or sheets.

Plasticizer. (11.4) A substance added to a plastic to make it more flexible.

Pleated sheet. (11.5) The protein secondary structure formed like a corrogated plane.

Polar bond. (8.2) A bond that possesses an asymmetric distribution of electrons.

Polarizability. (10.1) The ease with which the electron density about an atom or molecule can be distorted.

Polyamide. (11.3) A polymer containing the amide linkage group.

Polyatomic. (3.2) Containing many bonded atoms.

Polyester. (11.3) A polymer containing the ester linkage group.

Polymer. (11.1) A molecule that contains a large number of identical individual units (monomers) linked together.

Polypeptide. (11.5) A protein molecule.

Polyprotic acid. (16.4) A molecule that contains more than one acidic hydrogen atom.

Positron. (19.3) A subatomic particle with the mass of an electron but a positive unit charge.

Positron emission. (19.3) Nuclear decay by emission of a positron, which decreases the atomic number by one unit without changing the mass number.

Potential energy. (2.5) The energy an object has by virtue of some force (for example, gravitational or coulombic) acting on it.

Precipitate. (3.7) An insoluble solid that separates from a solution.

Precision. (1.5) How reproducible an experimental quantity is.

Pressure. (5.3) Force per unit area.

Primary structure. (11.5) The sequence of amino acids making up a protein.

Principal quantum number (*n*). (7.1) The quantum number, restricted to positive integers, that indexes the energy and size of an atomic orbital.

Product. (2.1) A substance that is formed in a chemical reaction.

Propagation. (11.1) The continuation of a polymerization chain reaction.

Protein. (11.5) A biochemical polymer composed of amino acids.

Proton. (2.2) The subatomic constituent of nuclei that possesses unit positive charge, 1.602×10^{-19} C, and a mass of 1.673×10^{-27} kg.

Proton transfer. (4.6) The transfer of H^+ from one chemical species to another.

p-type semiconductor. (9.6) A metalloid containing a dopant that gives it a deficiency of valence electrons.

Quantized. (6.3) Having discrete allowed values.

Quantum number. (7.1) An integer or half-integer describing the allowed values of some quantized property.

Quantum theory. (6.6) The theory of atomic and molecular structure that includes wave behavior.

Radiant energy. (2.5) The energy possessed by electromagnetic radiation (photons).

Radiation therapy. (19.9) The use of radioactive nuclides to treat cancers.

Radioactivity. (2.3) The spontaneous breakdown of a nucleus by giving off energetic particles.

Rare gas element. (1.3) Any of the elements of Column VIII of the periodic table.

Rate. (14.2) Change per unit time.

Rate constant (*k*). (14.3) The constant of proportionality linking a reaction rate with concentrations of reagents.

Rate law. (14.3) An expression relating the rate of a reaction to the concentrations of reagents.

Rate-determining step. (14.1) The slowest step in a reaction mechanism.

Reactant. (2.1) A species that is consumed in a chemical reaction.

Reaction coordinate. (14.6) The course of a reaction as reactants are converted to products.

Reaction unit. (12.3) A number of moles of a reagent equal to its stoichiometric coefficient in a balanced chemical equation.

Redox reaction. (4.7) A reaction in which electrons are transferred between species.

Reducing agent. (4.7) A substance that lose electrons during a reaction.

Reduction. (4.7) Gain of electrons.

Rem. (19.8) The unit of measure for the effect on humans of the energetic emissions from radioactive elements.

Resonance. (8.3) The use of two or more equivalent Lewis structures to describe a substance that contains delocalized electrons.

Reversibility. (15.2) The ability of any elementary chemical reaction to proceed in either direction.

Ribonucleic acid (RNA). (11.7) A polymer of nucleotide units that transmits genetic information in the cell.

Rounding. (1.6) The procedure for expressing a numerical result with the correct precision (number of significant figures).

Saturated. (10.5) Containing the maximum possible concentration of a solute.

Schrödinger equation. (6.6) The equation describing the behavior of electrons in atoms and molecules.

Screening. (7.3) The reduction in effective nuclear charge caused by electrons in orbitals.

Second (s). (1.5) The SI base unit of time.

Second law of thermodynamics. (13.1) The assertion that entropy (disorder) always increases.

Second-generation star. (19.7) A star formed from the collapse of interstellar matter, including (besides hydrogen and electrons) elements with $Z \leq 26$ that are the debris from supernovae explosions of first-generation stars.

Second-order reaction. (14.4) A reaction whose rate law has an overall order equal to two.

Secondary structure. (11.5) The structural arrangement of a string of amino acids.

Seesaw geometry. (8.6) The geometry derived from a trigonal bipyramid by replacing an atom in an equatorial position with a lone pair.

Semiconductor. (1.3) A substance that is intermediate in electrical conductivity between metals (good conductors) and nonmetals (poor conductors).

Semipermeable membrane. (10.7) A thin sheet that allows the passage of some types of molecules (typically, solvent) but prevents the passage of others (typically, solutes).

SI (Système International). (1.5) The system of units that has been adopted by scientists for general use.

Sigma (σ) bond. (9.1) A bond formed by end-on overlap of atomic orbitals, giving electron density that is concentrated along the bond axis.

Significant figure. (1.5) A digit in a numerical value that is known with certainty or has an uncertainty of one unit.

Silane. (8.5) A binary compound of silicon and hydrogen.

Silicate. (8.5) A compound containing one or more metal cations and a network of Si—O bonds.

Silicone. (11.1) A polymer containing silicon, oxygen, and organic groups.

Single bond. (3.1) A chemical bond formed by one pair of electrons shared between two atoms.

Slightly soluble. (16.2) Able to dissolve to a modest extent. Salts whose K_{sp} lies between 10^{-2} and 10^{-5} are classified as slightly soluble.

Soft acid. (18.4) A Lewis acid whose acceptor atom has a high polarizability.

Soft base. (18.4) A Lewis base whose donor electron pairs are loosely bound, resulting in high polarizability.

Solid. (1.4) The state of matter characterized by a defined volume and shape.

Solubility. (4.5) The amount of a solute that will dissolve in a given amount of solution.

Solubility product (K_{sp}). (15.3) The equilibrium constant for the solubility equilibrium of an ionic compound in water.

Soluble. (16.2) Able to dissolve in a liquid. Salts with $K_{sp} > 10^{-2}$ are classified as soluble in water.

Solute. (3.7) A substance that dissolves in a solvent to form a solution.

Solution. (1.4) A homogeneous mixture of two or more substances.

Solvent. (3.7) The component of a solution that defines its phase. Generally, the solvent is the component present in largest amount.

Space-filling model. (3.1) A representation of a molecule that shows the space occupied by its electron cloud.

Spectator ions. (16.1) Ions that are present in a solution but do not participate in a chemical reaction.

Spectrochemical series. (18.3). The listing of ligands in order of increasing energy-level splitting.

Spectrum. (6.3) A graph of the intensity of light as a function of either frequency or wavelength.

Spin orientation quantum number (m_s). (7.1) The quantum number, restricted to either $+^1/_2$ or $-^1/_2$, that indexes the orientation of electron spin.

Splitting energy. (18.3) The difference in energy between *d* orbitals in the central metal species of a coordination complex.

Spontaneous. (13.1) Able to occur without outside intervention.

Square planar geometry. (8.6) The geometry derived from an octahedron by replacing atoms along one cartesian axis with lone pairs.

Square pyramidal geometry. (8.6) The geometry derived from an octahedron by replacing one atom with a lone pair.

Standard conditions. (12.4) Unit concentrations (1 M for solutes, 1 atm for gases). Unless otherwise specified, standard conditions also means 298 K.

Standard enthalpy of formation (ΔH°_f). (12.4) The enthalpy change accompanying a formation reaction.

Standard hydrogen electrode (SHE). (17.3) The reference standard for standard reduction potentials, with a defined value of exactly 0 V. The electrode is a platinum wire immersed in an acid solution that is 1.00 M in hydronium ion, over which hydrogen gas at a pressure of 1.00 atm bubbles.

Standard reduction potential (E°). (17.5) The electrode potential for reduction under standard conditions.

Standard state. (12.4) The most stable phase of a substance under standard conditions.

Standardization. (4.6) Accurate determination of the concentration of a solution.

Starch. (11.6) The carbohydrate that plants use to store chemical energy.

State function. (12.1) A property that depends only on the present state but not on the previous history of the system.

State of a system. (12.1) A complete description of a system.

Steric number. (8.5) The sum of the coordination number and lone pairs for an inner atom.

Stoichiometric coefficient. (4.1) An integer giving the relative number of molecules of a species that react in a chemical reaction.

Stoichiometric point. (4.6) The point in a titration at which the amount of added titrant is exactly enough to react completely with the species being titrated.

Stoichiometry. (4.2) The amount relationships among chemical substances undergoing reactions.

Stratosphere. (6.4) The region of the Earth's atmosphere between 10 and 50 km above its surface.

Strong acid. (4.6) An acid that generates virtually stoichiometric amounts of hydronium ions in water.

Strong base. (4.6) A base that generates virtually stoichiometric amounts of hydroxide ions in water.

Structural formula. (3.1) A molecular formula that shows how atoms are bonded together.

Structural isomers. (8.4) Compounds that have identical chemical formulas but different molecular structures.

Sublimation. (12.5) The phase change between solid and vapor.

Substance. (1.2) A material that has a definite composition and distinct properties.

Supernova. (19.7) An exploding star, which produces unusually bright emission.

Surface tension. (10.3) The resistance of a liquid to an increase in its surface area.

Surfactant. (10.6) A molecule containing hydrophilic and hydrophobic parts that is used to modify the behavior of aqueous solutions.

Surroundings. (12.1) All of the universe outside of a system.

System. (12.1) Any specific, well-defined part of the universe that is of interest.

Temperature. (1.5) The property of an object that measures the amount of random energy of motion of its molecules and determines the direction of spontaneous heat flow.

Termination. (11.1) The completion of a polymerization chain reaction.

Termolecular reaction. (14.1) An elementary reaction in which three molecular species collide and react.

Tertiary structure. (11.5) The overall shape of a protein molecule.

Tetrahedral geometry. (8.4) The molecular shape in which four atoms occupy the apices of a tetrahedron and bond to a central atom.

Theoretical yield. (4.3) The amount of a product that would formed a reaction proceeded to completion without any losses.

Thermal energy. (2.5) Energy associated with the random motion of atoms and molecules.

Thermal pollution. (13.5) Heating of the environment as a byproduct of industrial operations.

Thermodynamics. (12.1) The scientific study of the relationships among heat and other forms of energy.

Thiol. (11.2) An organic compound that contains the —SH group.

Third law of thermodynamics. (13.3) The statement that the entropy of any pure, perfect crystalline substance is zero at 0 K.

Third-generation star. (19.7) A star formed from the collapse of interstellar matter, including (besides hydrogen and electrons) elements with all *Z* values that are the debris from supernovae explosions of second-generation stars.

Titrant. (4.6) The liquid solution added during a titration.

Titration. (4.6) The gradual addition of measured amounts of one solution to another until a chemical reaction between them is complete.

Transition metal. (1.3) Any of the elements in the *d* block of the periodic table.

Transmutation. (19.1) The conversion of one element into another through a nuclear reaction.

Thermosphere. (6.4) The region of the Earth's atmosphere that lies more than 90 km above its surface.

Trigonal bipyramidal geometry. (8.6) The molecular shape in which a central atom is bonded to five other atoms, three in a plane at 120-degree angles to one another and two along a linear axis perpendicular to that plane.

Trigonal planar geometry. (8.6) The molecular shape in which a central atom is bonded to three other atoms lying in a plane at 120-degree angles to one another.

Trigonal pyramidal geometry. (8.5) The molecular shape derived from a tetrahedron by placing a lone pair of electrons at one of the apices.

Triple bond. (3.1) A bond between two atoms consisting of three pairs of bonding electrons.

Triple point. (13.5) The temperature and pressure at which solid, liquid, and vapor can coexist at equilibrium.

Tritium. (2.3) The atom (an isotope of hydrogen) containing one proton and two neutrons in its nucleus.

Troposphere. (4.6) The region of the Earth's atmosphere between its surface and an altitude of 10 km.

T-shaped geometry. (8.6) The molecular shape derived from a trigonal bipyramid by placing lone pairs at two of the trigonal planar positions.

Uncertainty principle. (6.5) The assertion that position and momentum cannot both be exactly known.

Unimolecular reaction. (14.1) An elementary reaction in which there is only one reactant molecule.

Unit. (1.5) A standard reference value for a quantity.

Unit cell. (10.4) The simplest repeating unit of a regular pattern, such as an atomic or molecular crystal.

Valence electrons. (7.5) The electrons of an atom that occupy orbitals of highest principal quantum number and incompletely filled orbitals.

Vapor pressure. (5.7) The partial pressure of a vapor at equilibrium with a condensed phase.

Vesicle. (10.6) An enclosed bilayer made up of surfactant molecules.

Viscosity. (10.3) The resistance to flow of a fluid.

Visible light. (6.2) Photons in the wavelength range between 400 and 700 nm, to which the human eye is sensitive.

Volt (V). (17.5) The SI unit for electrical potential.

Volumetric flask. (3.7) A vessel calibrated to hold a specified volume of liquid.

Water equilibrium constant (K_w). (15.3). The equilibrium constant for proton transfer between two water molecules.

Wave. (6.2) A periodic variation which can be described by amplitude, wavelength, and frequency.

Wavelength. (6.2) The distance between successive crests in a wave.

Weak acid. (4.6) An acid that undergoes incomplete proton-transfer in water.

Weak base. (4.6) A base that undergoes incomplete proton-transfer in water.

Work (*w*). (12.2) Energy transfer that is described by the product of a force times a displacement.

CHAPTER 14

Chapter opener (inset): NASA; chapter opener (background): Alaska Division of Tourism/June Mackie, FCVB; p. 648: S.C. Delaney/U.S. EPA; 14-8: James A. Leick; p. 659: Kurt Griffin; p. 671: courtesy Maine Department of Conservation; p. 686: AIP Emilio Segrè Visual Archives; p.689: NASA; 14-22: Bassam Z. Shakhashiri; 14-25: courtesy Englehard Corp.; p. 694: AC Rochester Division GMC.

CHAPTER 15

Chapter opener (inset): courtesy M.W. Kellogg Company; chapter opener (background): Nebraska Department of Economic Development; 15-6: John Elk Photography; p. 726: courtesy Johnson Matthey Materials Technology Division; p. 727: Oesper Collection in the History of Chemistry, University of Cincinnati; 15-10: Kurt Griffin.

CHAPTER 16

Chapter opener (inset): courtesy Fisher Scientific; chapter opener (background): Oregon State University/Sea Grant Program; p. 760: Ray Rye/Smithsonian Institution; 16-1: National Parks Service; p. 764 A: courtesy New England Baptist Hospital School of Nursing; p. 804: courtesy Radiometer America, Inc.

CHAPTER 17

Chapter opener (inset): John Elk Photography; chapter opener (background): courtesy Aluminum Company of America; p. 836: AIP Emilio Segrè Visual Archives, E. Scott Barr Collection; p. 839: courtesy Bonneville Power Administration; p. 854 A: courtesy Beckman Instruments, Inc., Fullerton, Calif.; p. 854 B: reproduced with permission of Omega Engineering, Inc., Stamford, Conn.; 17-17 A: courtesy Siemans Pacesetters; 17-17 B: courtesy General Motors Corporation; p. 860: Dick Young/Unicorn Stock Photos; p. 861: Robert E. David; 17-22: courtesy Sargent-Welch Scientific Co.; p. 867 A: courtesy Harley-Davidson; p. 867 B: courtesy Eric C. Svenson, Plating Resources, Inc.; p. 869: Albert Copley/Visuals Unlimited; p. 871 C: courtesy Airstream, Inc.; p. 873: courtesy Bethlehem Steel Corporation.

CHAPTER 18

P. 895: Oesper Collection in the History of Chemistry, University of Cincinnati; p. 914: Betty Sederquist.

CHAPTER 19

Chapter opener (inset): Lawrence Livermore National Laboratory; chapter opener (background): Studio 61; p. 945: Stanford Linear Accelerator Center/US Department of Energy; 19-13: Tass/Sovfoto; 19-14: B. Pierce/Leo de Wys; 19-16: David Malin/Anglo-Australian Observatory; 19-18: Brookhaven National Laboratory; p. 967: Catholic News Service; 19-21: M.A. Quaife and M.V. Nagel, "The Endocrine System." In D.R. Bernier, P.E. Christian, J.K. Langan, and L.D. Wells: *Nuclear Medicine Technology and Techniques,* ed 2, St. Louis, Mosby.

INDEX

O

S

TABLE OF THE ELEMENTS, THEIR ATOMIC SYMBOLS, AND THEIR MOLAR MASSES*

ELEMENT	SYMBOL	ATOMIC NUMBER	MOLAR MASS
Actinium	Ac	89	(227)
Aluminum	Al	13	26.98
Americium	Am	95	(243)
Antimony	Sb	51	121.8
Argon	Ar	18	39.95
Arsenic	As	33	74.92
Astatine	At	85	(210)
Barium	Ba	56	137.3
Berkelium	Bk	97	(247)
Beryllium	Be	4	9.012
Bismuth	Bi	83	209.0
Boron	B	5	10.81
Bromine	Br	35	79.90
Cadmium	Cd	48	112.4
Calcium	Ca	20	40.08
Californium	Cf	98	(249)
Carbon	C	6	12.01
Cerium	Ce	58	140.1
Cesium	Cs	55	132.9
Chlorine	Cl	17	35.45
Chromium	Cr	24	52.00
Cobalt	Co	27	58.93
Copper	Cu	29	63.55
Curium	Cm	96	(247)
Dysprosium	Dy	66	162.5
Einsteinium	Es	99	(254)
Erbium	Er	68	167.3
Europium	Eu	63	152.0
Fermium	Fm	100	(253)
Fluorine	F	9	19.00
Francium	Fr	87	(223)
Gadolinium	Gd	64	157.3
Gallium	Ga	31	69.72
Germanium	Ge	32	72.59
Gold	Au	79	197.0
Hafnium	Hf	72	178.5
Helium	He	2	4.003
Holmium	Ho	67	164.9
Hydrogen	H	1	1.008
Indium	In	49	114.8
Iodine	I	53	126.9
Iridium	Ir	77	192.2
Iron	Fe	26	55.85
Krypton	Kr	36	83.80
Lanthanum	La	57	138.9
Lawrencium	Lr	103	(257)
Lead	Pb	82	207.2
Lithium	Li	3	6.941
Lutetium	Lu	71	175.0
Magnesium	Mg	12	24.31
Manganese	Mn	25	54.94
Mendelevium	Md	101	(256)
Mercury	Hg	80	200.6
Molybdenum	Mo	42	95.94
Neodymium	Nd	60	144.2

ELEMENT	SYMBOL	ATOMIC NUMBER	MOLAR MASS
Neon	Ne	10	20.18
Neptunium	Np	93	(237)
Nickel	Ni	28	58.69
Niobium	Nb	41	92.91
Nitrogen	N	7	14.01
Nobelium	No	102	(253)
Osmium	Os	76	190.2
Oxygen	O	8	16.00
Palladium	Pd	46	106.4
Phosphorus	P	15	30.97
Platinum	Pt	78	195.1
Plutonium	Pu	94	(242)
Polonium	Po	84	(210)
Potassium	K	19	39.10
Praseodymium	Pr	59	140.9
Promethium	Pm	61	(147)
Protactinium	Pa	91	(231)
Radium	Ra	88	(226)
Radon	Rn	86	(222)
Rhenium	Re	75	186.2
Rhodium	Rh	45	102.9
Rubidium	Rb	37	85.47
Ruthenium	Ru	44	101.1
Samarium	Sm	62	150.4
Scandium	Sc	21	44.96
Selenium	Se	34	78.96
Silicon	Si	14	28.09
Silver	Ag	47	107.9
Sodium	Na	11	22.99
Strontium	Sr	38	87.62
Sulfur	S	16	32.07
Tantalum	Ta	73	180.9
Technetium	Tc	43	(99)
Tellurium	Te	52	127.6
Terbium	Tb	65	158.9
Thallium	Tl	81	204.4
Thorium	Th	90	232.0
Thulium	Tm	69	168.9
Tin	Sn	50	118.7
Titanium	Ti	22	47.88
Tungsten	W	74	183.9
Unnilennium	Une	109	(266)
Unnilhexium	Unh	106	(263)
Unniloctium	Uno	108	(265)
Unnilpentium	Unp	105	(260)
Unnilquadium	Unq	104	(257)
Unnilseptium	Uns	107	(262)
Uranium	U	92	238.0
Vanadium	V	23	50.94
Xenon	Xe	54	131.3
Ytterbium	Yb	70	173.0
Yttrium	Y	39	88.91
Zinc	Zn	30	65.39
Zirconium	Zr	40	91.22

*All molar masses have been rounded to four significant figures. Values in parentheses represent the molar mass of the isotope with the longest half-life.